TEACHER'S EDITION

Prentice Hall

ECONOMICS

Arthur O'Sullivan • Steven M. Sheffrin • Grant Wiggins

Upper Saddle River, New Jersey • Boston, Massachusetts • Chandler, Arizona • Glenview, Illinois

The Wall Street Journal Classroom Edition is a supplemental educational program published since 1991 by Dow Jones and Company, publisher of *The Wall Street Journal*. The program is designed to improve the economic and business literacy of America's secondary-school students. The centerpiece of the program is a full-color student newspaper, published monthly from September to May. Regular features focus on business, economics, careers, entrepreneurship, technology, personal finance, and global interdependence. Articles are drawn directly from the pages of the daily *Wall Street Journal*.

Acknowledgments appear on pages R37-R38, which constitute an extension of this copyright page.

PEARSON

ISBN-13: 978-0-13-368018-8
ISBN-10: 0-13-368018-5
4 5 6 7 8 9 10 V011 12 11

About the Authors

Arthur O'Sullivan, Ph.D

Arthur O'Sullivan is a professor of economics at Lewis and Clark College in Portland, Oregon. After receiving his B.S. degree in economics at the University of Oregon, he spent two years in the Peace Corps, working with city planners in the Philippines. He received his Ph.D. degree in economics from Princeton University in 1981 and has taught at the University of California, Davis, and Oregon State University. He recently accepted an endowed professorship at Lewis and Clark College, where he teaches microeconomics and urban economics.

Steven M. Sheffrin, Ph.D

Steven Sheffrin is dean of the division of social sciences and professor of economics at the University of California, Davis. He received his B.A. from Wesleyan University and Ph.D. in economics from the Massachusetts Institute of Technology. He has been a visiting professor at Princeton University, Oxford University, and the London School of Economics and served as a financial economist with the Office of Tax Analysis of the United States Department of the Treasury. Professor Sheffrin is the author of numerous books and articles in the fields of macroeconomics, public finance, and international economics.

iii

Program Reviewers

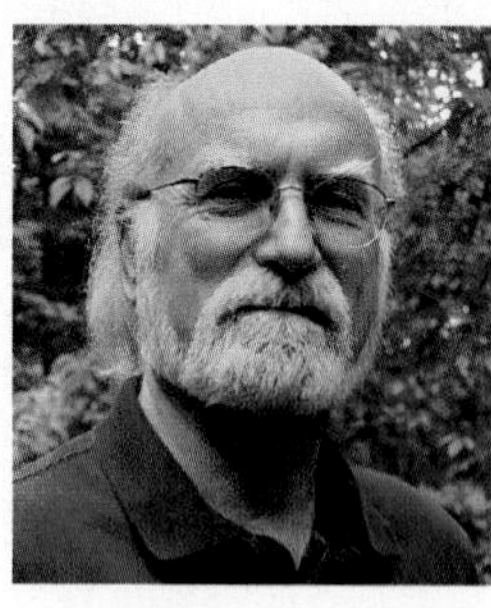

Consulting Author

Grant Wiggins

Grant Wiggins is the President of Authentic Education in Hopewell, New Jersey. He earned his Ed.D. from Harvard University and his B.A. from St. John's College in Annapolis. Wiggins consults with schools, districts, and state education departments on a variety of reform matters; organizes conferences and workshops; and develops print materials and Web resources on curricular change. He is the co-author of award-winning and highly successful materials on curriculum published by ASCD. His work has been supported by the Pew Charitable Trusts, the Geraldine R. Dodge Foundation, and the National Science Foundation.

Over the past twenty years, Wiggins has worked on some of the most influential reform initiatives in the country, including Vermont's portfolio system and Ted Sizer's Coalition of Essential Schools. He has established statewide consortia devoted to assessment reform for the states of North Carolina and New Jersey. Wiggins is the author of *Educative Assessment and Assessing Student Performance,* both published by Jossey-Bass. His many articles have appeared in such journals as *Educational Leadership* and *Phi Delta Kappan.*

iv

Academic Reviewers

Klaus G. Becker
Department of Economics and Geography
Texas Tech University
Lubbock, TX

Bruce Coggins
Economics Department
Truman State University
Kirksville, MO

Antoinette Criss
College of Business
University of South Florida St. Petersburg
St. Petersburg, FL

Cory Koedel
Department of Economics
University of Missouri
Columbia, MO

Daniel E. Saros
Department of Economics
Valparaiso University
Valparaiso, IN

Lesson Plan Reviewer

Diane Van Ausdall
West Hartford, CT

Teacher Advisory Board

Elizabeth Brown
Jackson High School
Jackson, MI

Katherine Case
Parkville High School
Baltimore, MD

Michael J. Collazo
Brentwood High School
Brentwood, NY

Bruce Damasio
Towson University
Towson, MD

Lance Leach
Valparaiso High School
Valparaiso, IN

Len A. Lyberger
Palos Verdes Peninsula High School
Rolling Hills Estates, CA

Kenneth Mengani
Franklin K. Lane High School
Brooklyn, NY

Kurt Stiglbauer
Ridge View High School
Columbia, SC

v

Contents in Brief

UNIT 1 Introduction to Economics

INTRODUCTION

Essential Question, Unit 1

How does economics affect everyone?

Chapter 1
How can we make the best economic choices?

Chapter 2
How does society decide who gets what goods and services?

Chapter 3
What role should government play in a free market economy?

Go online with Unit 1

Find these interactive resources at PearsonSuccessNet.com

Visual Glossary online

- Opportunity Cost
- Incentives
- Free Enterprise

How the Economy Works online

- What does an entrepreneur do?
- How can innovation lead to economic growth?
- How are public goods created?

Video News Update Online
Powered by
The Wall Street Journal Classroom Edition

- Watch video clips of current economic issues in the news.

Economics *on the go*

- Action Graphs
- Content Review Audio
- Economic Dictionary Audio

WebQuest online

- The Economics WebQuest challenges students to use 21st century skills to answer the Essential Question.

UNIT 2 How Markets Work

MICROECONOMICS

Essential Question, Unit 2
Who benefits from the free market economy?
Chapter 4
How do we decide what to buy?
Chapter 5
How do suppliers decide what goods and services to offer?

Chapter 6
What is the right price?

Chapter 7
How does competition affect your choices?

Go online with Unit 2
Find these interactive resources at PearsonSuccessNet.com

Visual Glossary online

- Law of Demand
- Law of Supply
- Equilibrium
- Perfect Competition

How the Economy Works online

- How does elasticity affect demand?
- What are production costs?
- How does a market react to a shortage?
- How is broadcasting regulated?

Video News Update Online
Powered by
The Wall Street Journal Classroom Edition

- Watch video clips of current economic issues in the news.

Economics on the go

- Action Graphs
- Content Review Audio
- Economic Dictionary Audio

WebQuest online

- The Economics WebQuest challenges students to use 21st century skills to answer the Essential Question.

UNIT 3 Business and Labor

MICROECONOMICS

Go online with Unit 3
Find these interactive resources at PearsonSuccessNet.com

Visual Glossary online
- Corporation
- Productivity of Labor

How the Economy Works online
- How can a small business grow?
- How can collective bargaining settle differences?

Video News Update Online
Powered by *The Wall Street Journal* Classroom Edition
- Watch video clips of current economic issues in the news.

Economics on the go
- Action Graphs
- Content Review Audio
- Economic Dictionary Audio

WebQuest online
- The Economics WebQuest challenges students to use 21st century skills to answer the Essential Question.

Essential Question, Unit 3

How can businesses and labor best achieve their goals?

Chapter 8
Why do some businesses succeed and others fail?

Chapter 9
How can workers best meet the challenges of a changing economy?

UNIT 4 Money, Banking, and Finance

MACROECONOMICS

Go online with Unit 4
Find these interactive resources at PearsonSuccessNet.com

Visual Glossary online

- Money
- Capital Gains

How the Economy Works online

- How does the fractional reserve system work?
- What is the function of a municipal bond?

Video News Update Online Powered by *The Wall Street Journal* Classroom Edition

- Watch video clips of current economic issues in the news.

Economics on the go

- Action Graphs
- Content Review Audio
- Economic Dictionary Audio

WebQuest online

- The Economics WebQuest challenges students to use 21st century skills to answer the Essential Question.

Essential Question, Unit 4

How can you make the most of your money?

Chapter 10
How well do financial institutions serve our needs?

Chapter 11
How do your saving and investment choices affect your future?

UNIT 5 # Measuring Economic Performance

MACROECONOMICS

Go online with Unit 5
Find these interactive resources at PearsonSuccessNet.com

Visual Glossary online

- Gross Domestic Product
- Inflation

How the Economy Works online

- What causes a recession?
- How do workers deal with structural unemployment?

Video News Update Online
Powered by *The Wall Street Journal* Classroom Edition

- Watch video clips of current economic issues in the news.

Economics *on the go*

- Action Graphs
- Content Review Audio
- Economic Dictionary Audio

WebQuest online

- The Economics WebQuest challenges students to use 21st century skills to answer the Essential Question.

Essential Question, Unit 5

Why does it matter how the economy is doing?

Chapter 12
How do we know if the economy is healthy?

Chapter 13
How much can we reduce unemployment, inflation, and poverty?

UNIT 6 Government and the Economy

MACROECONOMICS

Essential Question, Unit 6

What is the proper role of government in the economy?

Chapter 14
How can taxation meet the needs of government and the people?

Chapter 15
How effective is fiscal policy as an economic tool?

Chapter 16
How effective is monetary policy as an economic tool?

Go online with Unit 6

Find these interactive resources at PearsonSuccessNet.com

Visual Glossary online

- Progressive Income Taxes
- Fiscal Policy
- Monetary Policy

How the Economy Works online

- Where do your federal taxes go?
- What causes the national debt to spiral?
- How does the Fed make monetary policy?

Video News Update Online
Powered by
The Wall Street Journal Classroom Edition

- Watch video clips of current economic issues in the news.

Economics on the go

- Action Graphs
- Content Review Audio
- Economic Dictionary Audio

WebQuest online

- The Economics WebQuest challenges students to use 21st century skills to answer the Essential Question.

UNIT 7 The Global Economy

MACROECONOMICS

Go online with Unit 7

Find these interactive resources at PearsonSuccessNet.com

Visual Glossary online

- Free Trade
- Globalization

How the Economy Works online

- How do specialization and trade benefit nations?
- What are the stages of economic development?

Video News Update Online
Powered by *The Wall Street Journal* Classroom Edition

- Watch video clips of current economic issues in the news.

Economics on the go

- Action Graphs
- Content Review Audio
- Economic Dictionary Audio

WebQuest online

- The Economics WebQuest challenges students to use 21st century skills to answer the Essential Question.

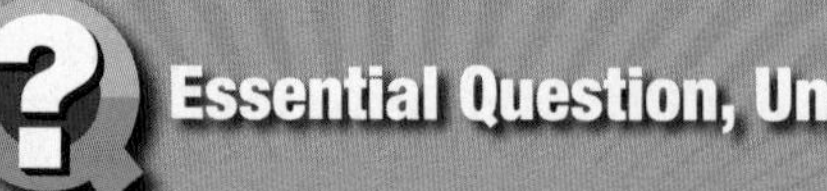

Essential Question, Unit 7

How might scarcity divide our world or bring it together?

Chapter 17
Should free trade be encouraged?

Chapter 18
Do the benefits of economic development outweigh the costs?

Personal Finance Handbook

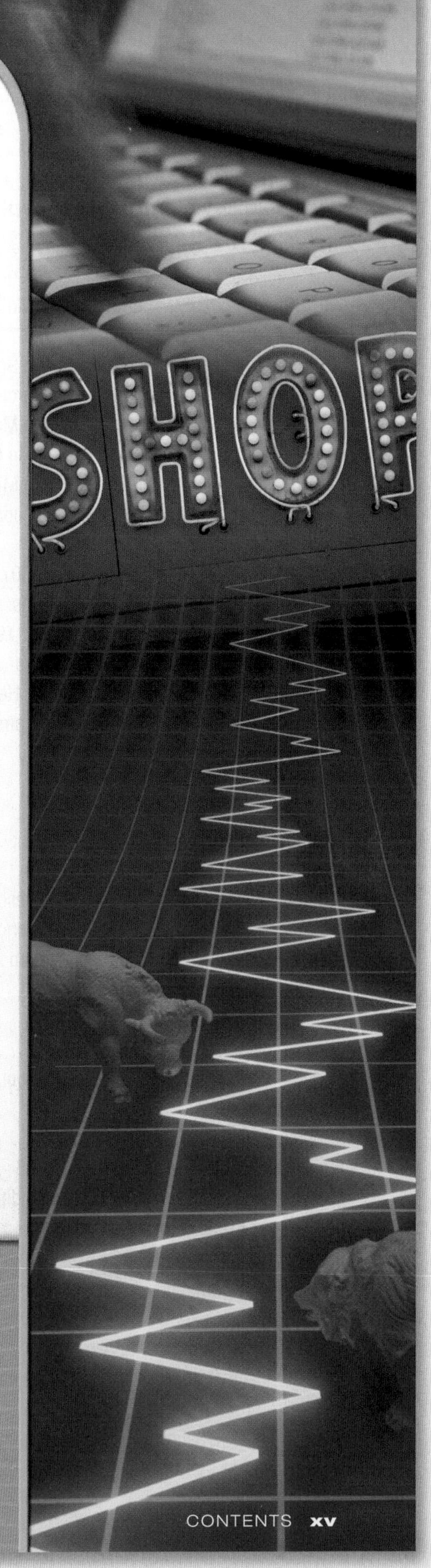

REFERENCE SECTION

Special Features

Action Graph online

Graphs and charts labeled with the **Action Graph** icon have been specially enhanced online. To view these animated charts, visit **PearsonSuccessNet.com** The online label indicates an Action Graph.

Graphs, Charts, and Tables

More than 250 graphs, charts, and tables to help you visualize key economic concepts.

Databank: The World Economy

Graphs, Charts, and Tables (continued)

Economics & YOU

Read and view illustrations to understand how economic principles can affect high school students.

Economics & YOU
The Substitution Effect
Roast Beef sandwich $4.50 $5.25
Chili $1.99
When the price of one good increases, people have an incentive to buy substitutes. Your decision to purchase a less expensive lunch is the substitution effect in action.
REDUCED
The substitution effect also applies when a drop in price creates a cheaper alternative. Your purchase of the reduced car is another example of the substitution effect.

Complex and difficult content is visually displayed to explain how economic principles can affect you.

How the Economy Works

View the illustrated diagrams to understand the processes by which our economy operates.

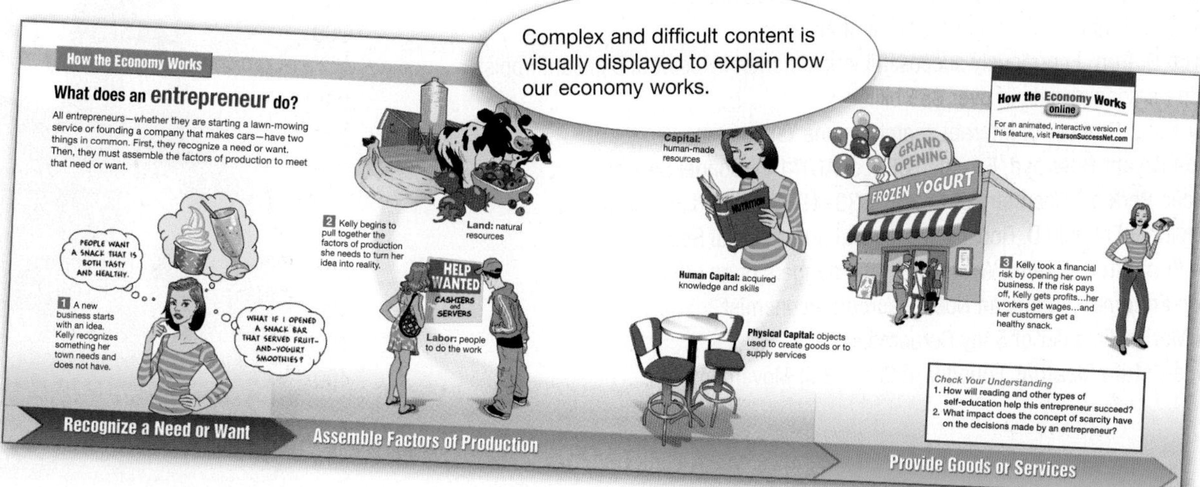

Complex and difficult content is visually displayed to explain how our economy works.
How the Economy Works
What does an entrepreneur do?
All entrepreneurs—whether they are starting a lawn-mowing service or founding a company that makes cars—have two things in common. First, they recognize a need or want. Then, they must assemble the factors of production to meet that need or want.
PEOPLE WANT A SNACK THAT IS BOTH TASTY AND HEALTHY.
1 A new business starts with an idea. Kelly recognizes something her town needs and does not have.
WHAT IF I OPENED A SNACK BAR THAT SERVED FRUIT-AND-YOGURT SMOOTHIES?
2 Kelly begins to pull together the factors of production she needs to turn her idea into reality.
Land: natural resources
HELP WANTED CASHIERS and SERVERS
Labor: people to do the work
Capital: human-made resources
Human Capital: acquired knowledge and skills
Physical Capital: objects used to create goods or to supply services
GRAND OPENING
FROZEN YOGURT
How the Economy Works online
For an animated, interactive version of this feature, visit PearsonSuccessNet.com
3 Kelly took a financial risk by opening her own business. If the risk pays off, Kelly gets profits...her workers get wages...and her customers get a healthy snack.
Check Your Understanding
1. How will reading and other types of self-education help this entrepreneur succeed?
2. What impact does the concept of scarcity have on the decisions made by an entrepreneur?
Recognize a Need or Want
Assemble Factors of Production
Provide Goods or Services

Visual Glossary

Graphs, pictures, and cartoons help deepen your understanding of key economic terms.

VISUAL GLOSSARY
What is Free Trade?
TRADE EMBARGO
OTHER TRADE BARRIERS
TARIFFS
TRADE
FREE TRADE
"Take us to your leader...we've come to negotiate a free trade agreement with earth."
Visual Glossary online
To expand your understanding of this and other key economic terms, visit PearsonSuccessNet.com

Innovators

Wangari Muta Maathai ▶

See how creative entrepreneurs and other individuals have affected our economy and daily life.

▲ Melinda and Bill Gates

Career Center

FUTURE WATCH **Look into the future—explore your different career paths and opportunities.**

Complex and difficult content is visually displayed to explain different career opportunities.

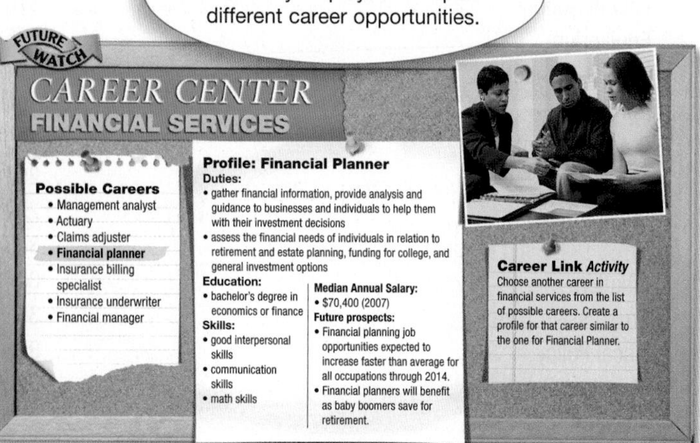

FUTURE WATCH
CAREER CENTER
FINANCIAL SERVICES
Possible Careers
• Management analyst
• Actuary
• Claims adjuster
• Financial planner
• Insurance billing specialist
• Insurance underwriter
• Financial manager
Profile: Financial Planner
Duties:
• gather financial information, provide analysis and guidance to businesses and individuals to help them with their investment decisions
• assess the financial needs of individuals in relation to retirement and estate planning, funding for college, and general investment options
Education:
• bachelor's degree in economics or finance
Skills:
• good interpersonal skills
• communication skills
• math skills
Median Annual Salary:
• $70,400 (2007)
Future prospects:
• Financial planning job opportunities expected to increase faster than average for all occupations through 2014.
• Financial planners will benefit as baby boomers save for retirement.
Career Link Activity
Choose another career in financial services from the list of possible careers. Create a profile for that career similar to the one for Financial Planner.

Case Study

Video News Update Online
Powered by
The Wall Street Journal
Classroom Edition

Read articles by *The Wall Street Journal* to view real-life illustrations of economic principles.

Global Impact

FUTURE WATCH

Explore economic links between the United States and the World.

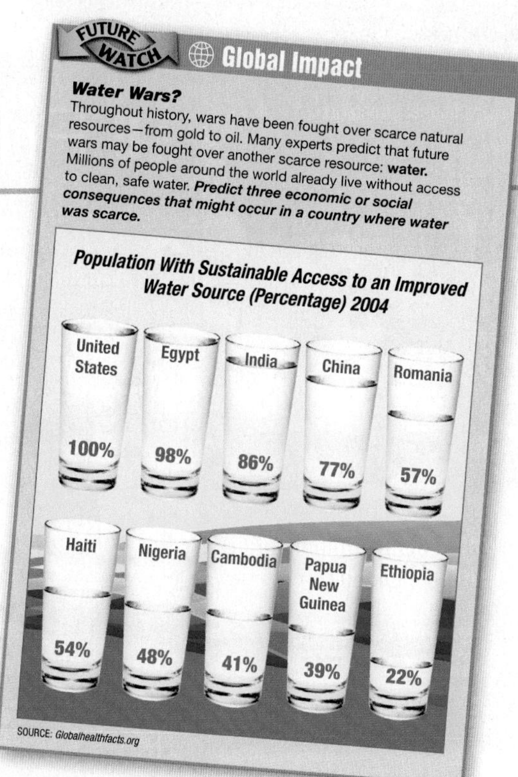

FUTURE WATCH
Global Impact
Water Wars?
Throughout history, wars have been fought over scarce natural resources—from gold to oil. Many experts predict that future wars may be fought over another scarce resource: water. Millions of people around the world already live without access to clean, safe water. Predict three economic or social consequences that might occur in a country where water was scarce.
Population With Sustainable Access to an Improved Water Source (Percentage) 2004
United States 100%
Egypt 98%
India 86%
China 77%
Romania 57%
Haiti 54%
Nigeria 48%
Cambodia 41%
Papua New Guinea 39%
Ethiopia 22%
SOURCE: Globalhealthfacts.org

Economic Simulations

Your teacher may assign these hands-on, role-playing games to help you understand key economic concepts.

How to Use This Program

Economics is all around you. Developing an understanding of the impact of economic principles on your day-to-day life will help you to make better economic choices. It will prepare you to live in a global economy. It is money in your pocket.

To complete the Chapter Essential Question Webquest, visit **PearsonSuccessNet.com**

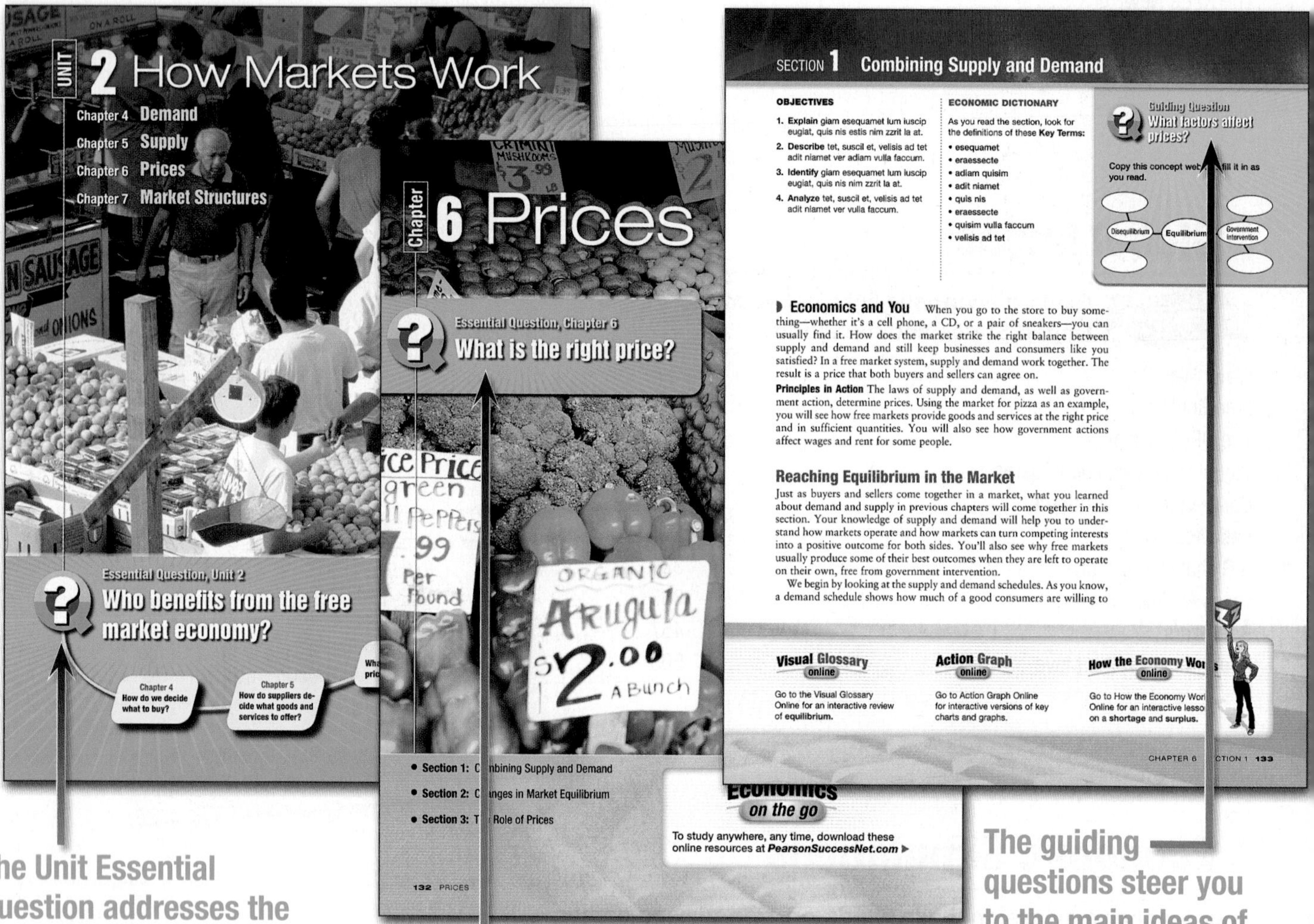

Economics is organized around Essential Questions. An Essential Question is a launching pad for exploring ideas. It doesn't have just one right answer. The answer to an Essential Question changes as you learn more or as circumstances change.

The Unit Essential Question addresses the main idea of the unit.

The Chapter Essential Question addresses the main idea of each chapter. Answering the Chapter Essential Question helps you answer the Unit Essential Question.

The guiding questions steer you to the main ideas of each section of the chapter. Answering the section guiding questions helps you think about the Chapter Essential Question.

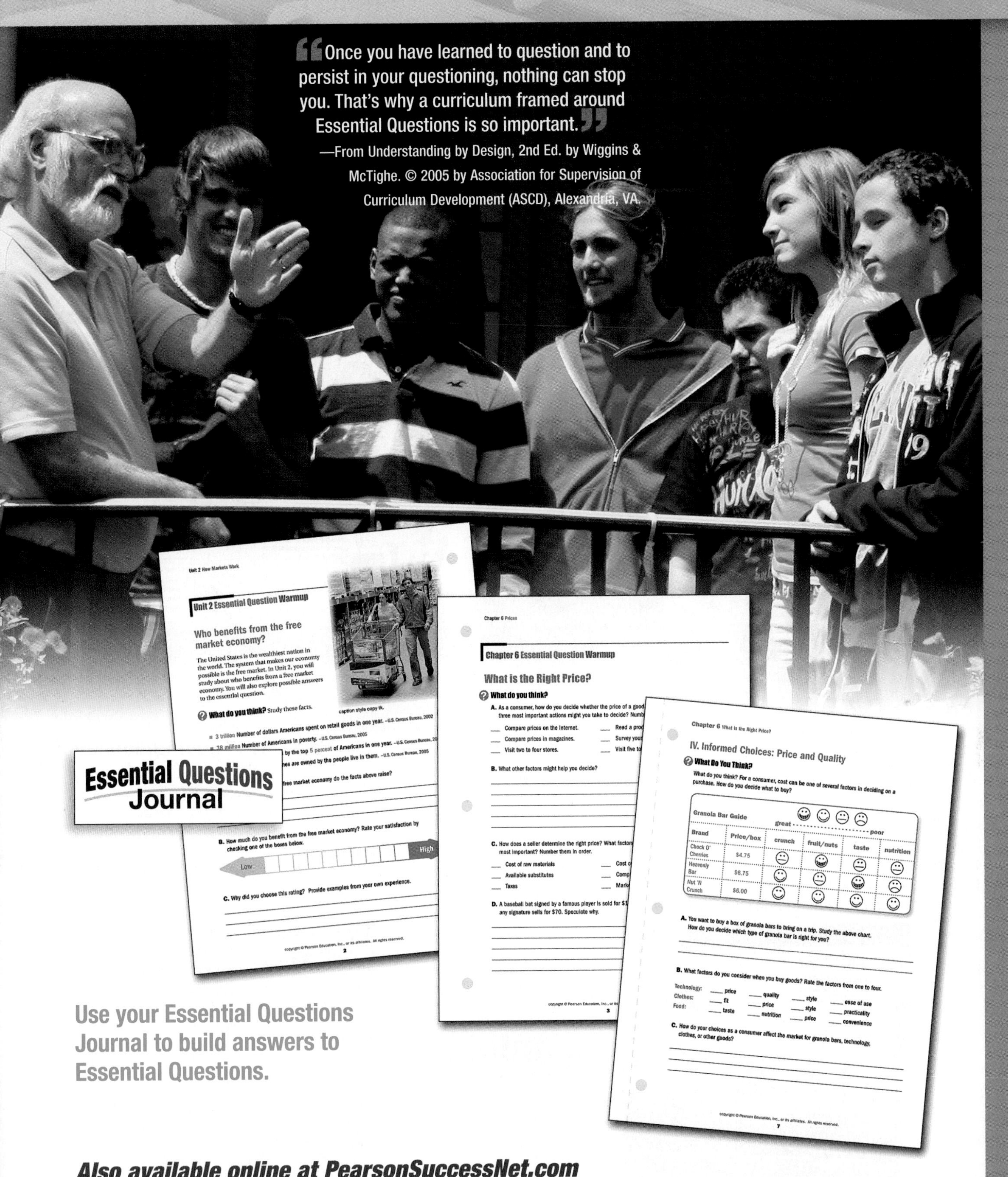
"Once you have learned to question and to persist in your questioning, nothing can stop you. That's why a curriculum framed around Essential Questions is so important."
—From Understanding by Design, 2nd Ed. by Wiggins & McTighe. © 2005 by Association for Supervision of Curriculum Development (ASCD), Alexandria, VA.
Unit 2 Essential Question Warmup
Who benefits from the free market economy?
Chapter 6 Essential Question Warmup
What is the Right Price?
IV. Informed Choices: Price and Quality
Essential Questions Journal

Use your Essential Questions Journal to build answers to Essential Questions.

Also available online at PearsonSuccessNet.com

How the Economy Works

In your textbook

Every chapter has a How the Economy Works feature that helps you visualize economic principles in action.

1 Follow the numbered steps.

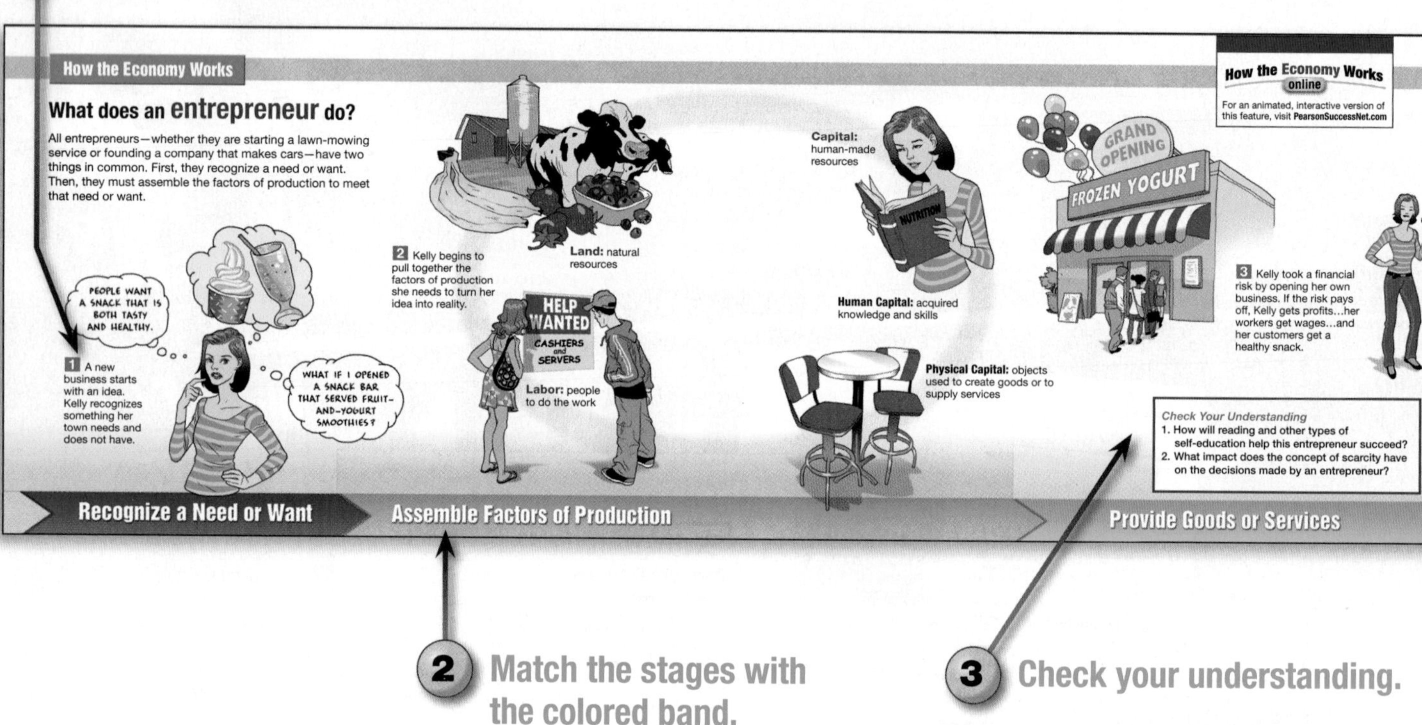

How the Economy Works
What does an entrepreneur do?
All entrepreneurs—whether they are starting a lawn-mowing service or founding a company that makes cars—have two things in common. First, they recognize a need or want. Then, they must assemble the factors of production to meet that need or want.
PEOPLE WANT A SNACK THAT IS BOTH TASTY AND HEALTHY.
1 A new business starts with an idea. Kelly recognizes something her town needs and does not have.
WHAT IF I OPENED A SNACK BAR THAT SERVED FRUIT-AND-YOGURT SMOOTHIES?
2 Kelly begins to pull together the factors of production she needs to turn her idea into reality.
Land: natural resources
HELP WANTED
CASHIERS and SERVERS
Labor: people to do the work
Capital: human-made resources
NUTRITION
Human Capital: acquired knowledge and skills
Physical Capital: objects used to create goods or to supply services
GRAND OPENING
FROZEN YOGURT
3 Kelly took a financial risk by opening her own business. If the risk pays off, Kelly gets profits…her workers get wages…and her customers get a healthy snack.
How the Economy Works online
For an animated, interactive version of this feature, visit PearsonSuccessNet.com
Check Your Understanding
1. How will reading and other types of self-education help this entrepreneur succeed?
2. What impact does the concept of scarcity have on the decisions made by an entrepreneur?
Recognize a Need or Want
Assemble Factors of Production
Provide Goods or Services

2 Match the stages with the colored band.

3 Check your understanding.

Go online at PearsonSuccessNet.com

Use an interactive version of How the Economy Works to help you learn. ▼

◀ Download the Visual Glossary or animated versions of How the Economy Works and Action Graphs to your MP3 player. Study anytime, anywhere.

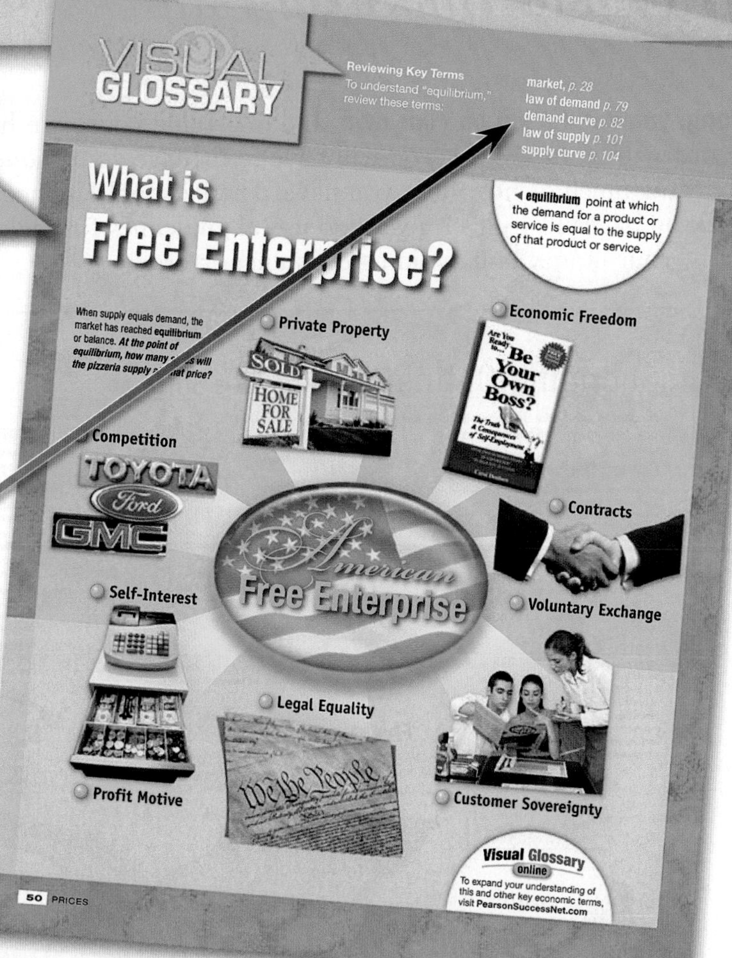

VISUAL GLOSSARY
Reviewing Key Terms
To understand "equilibrium," review these terms:
market, p. 28
law of demand p. 79
demand curve p. 82
law of supply p. 101
supply curve p. 104
What is Free Enterprise?
equilibrium point at which the demand for a product or service is equal to the supply of that product or service.
When supply equals demand, the market has reached equilibrium or balance. At the point of equilibrium, how many slices will the pizzeria supply at what price?
Private Property
Economic Freedom
Competition
Contracts
Self-Interest
American Free Enterprise
Voluntary Exchange
Legal Equality
Profit Motive
Customer Sovereignty
Visual Glossary online
To expand your understanding of this and other key economic terms, visit PearsonSuccessNet.com
50 PRICES

VISUAL GLOSSARY

Use the Visual Glossary in your textbook and online to learn the meaning of key economic terms.

Find these related terms in the Economics Dictionary online, in English and in Spanish.

GDP and the Business Cycle

One measure of a nation's economic well-being is **gross domestic product (GDP),** the total value of all final goods and services produced in a country in a given year. In a period of macroeconomic expansion, or growth, a country produces more than it did before and GDP goes up. (See **Figure 3.2.**) In a period of contraction, or decline, the country produces less and GDP goes down. This pattern of a period of expansion, or growth, followed by a period of contraction, or decline, is called a **business cycle.**

Unlike the day-to-day ups and downs of the stock market, business cycles are major fluctuations. Each phase can last months or

Figure 3.2 Gross Domestic Product, 1990-2004

GDP (billions of dollars 2000): 2,000; 4,000; 6,000; 8,000; 10,000; 12,000; 14,000

Year: 1900 1910 1920 1930 1940 1950 1960 1970 1980 1990 2000

SOURCE: Louis D. Johnston and Samuel H. Williamson, "What Was the U.S. GDP Then?" MeasuringWorth.Com, 2007.

GRAPH SKILLS

This graph shows how an increase in demand affects prices and supply.

1. What was the original equilibrium price?
2. What impact did the change in demand shown here have on the equilibrium price?

Action Graph online

For an animated version of this graph, visit **PearsonSuccessNet.com**

Action Graph online

Follow the references on the text page to the Action Graph. Action Graphs present economic principles in a graphic format.

How to Use This Program

Before long, you will be out on your own and managing your own household. In order to be successful, you will have to manage your money, no matter how much or how little you have. The Personal Finance Handbook on pages PF1–PF49 gives you useful guidelines for making the most of your money and avoiding consumer errors.

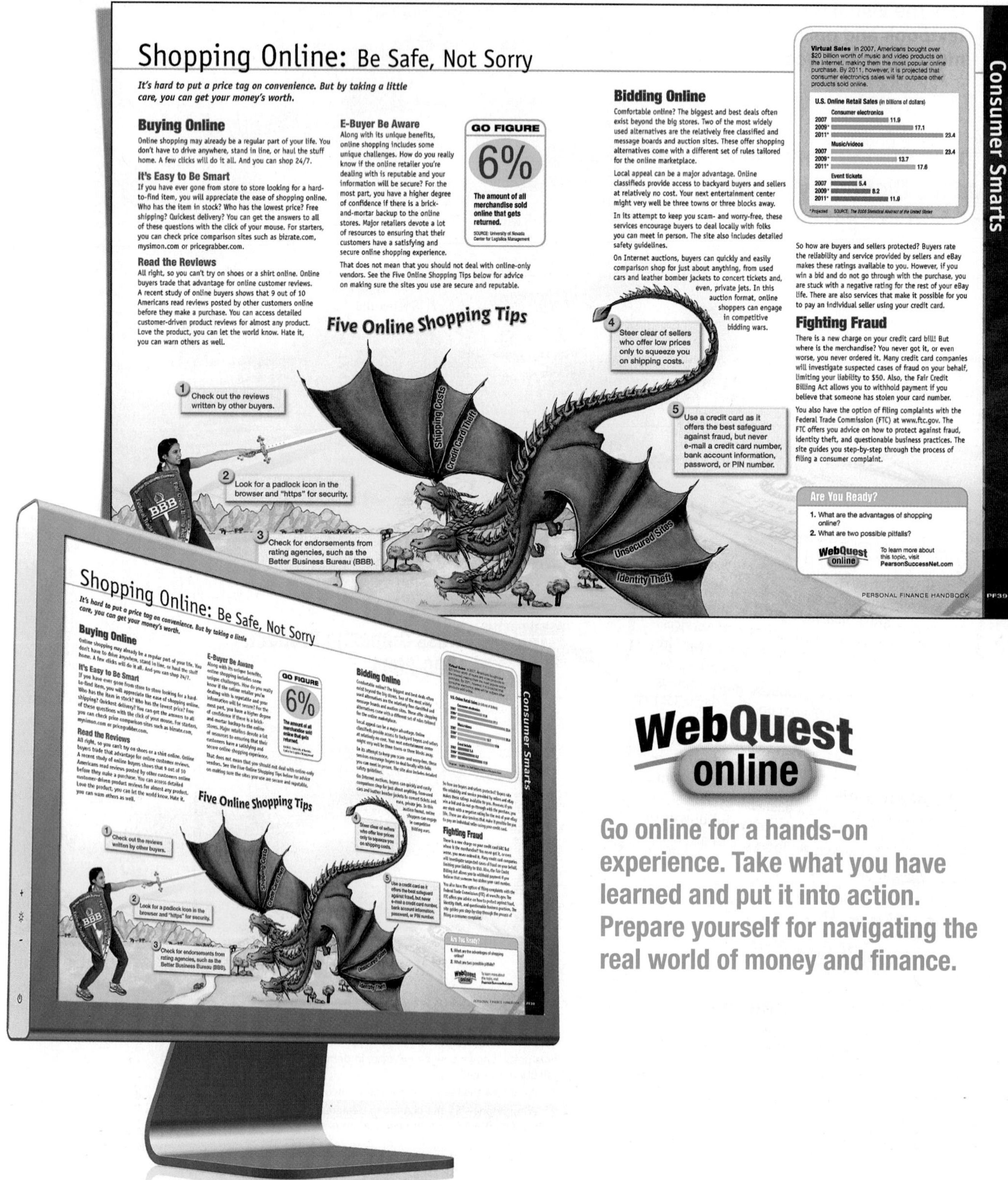

Shopping Online: Be Safe, Not Sorry

It's hard to put a price tag on convenience. But by taking a little care, you can get your money's worth.

Buying Online

Online shopping may already be a regular part of your life. You don't have to drive anywhere, stand in line, or haul the stuff home. A few clicks will do it all. And you can shop 24/7.

It's Easy to Be Smart

If you have ever gone from store to store looking for a hard-to-find item, you will appreciate the ease of shopping online. Who has the item in stock? Who has the lowest price? Free shipping? Quickest delivery? You can get the answers to all of these questions with the click of your mouse. For starters, you can check price comparison sites such as bizrate.com, mysimon.com or pricegrabber.com.

Read the Reviews

All right, so you can't try on shoes or a shirt online. Online buyers trade that advantage for online customer reviews. A recent study of online buyers shows that 9 out of 10 Americans read reviews posted by other customers online before they make a purchase. You can access detailed customer-driven product reviews for almost any product. Love the product, you can let the world know. Hate it, you can warn others as well.

E-Buyer Be Aware

Along with its unique benefits, online shopping includes some unique challenges. How do you really know if the online retailer you're dealing with is reputable and your information will be secure? For the most part, you have a higher degree of confidence if there is a brick-and-mortar backup to the online stores. Major retailers devote a lot of resources to ensuring that their customers have a satisfying and secure online shopping experience.

That does not mean that you should not deal with online-only vendors. See the Five Online Shopping Tips below for advice on making sure the sites you use are secure and reputable.

GO FIGURE

6%

The amount of all merchandise sold online that gets returned.

SOURCE: University of Nevada Center for Logistics Management

Bidding Online

Comfortable online? The biggest and best deals often exist beyond the big stores. Two of the most widely used alternatives are the relatively free classified and message boards and auction sites. These offer shopping alternatives come with a different set of rules tailored for the online marketplace.

Local appeal can be a major advantage. Online classifieds provide access to backyard buyers and sellers at relatively no cost. Your next entertainment center might very well be three towns or three blocks away.

In its attempt to keep you scam- and worry-free, these services encourage buyers to deal locally with folks you can meet in person. The site also includes detailed safety guidelines.

On Internet auctions, buyers can quickly and easily comparison shop for just about anything, from used cars and leather bomber jackets to concert tickets and, even, private jets. In this auction format, online shoppers can engage in competitive bidding wars.

Virtual Sales In 2007, Americans bought over $20 billion worth of music and video products on the Internet, making them the most popular online purchase. By 2011, however, it is projected that consumer electronics sales will far outpace other products sold online.

U.S. Online Retail Sales (in billions of dollars)

Year	Consumer electronics	Music/videos	Event tickets
2007	11.9	23.4	5.4
2009*	17.1	13.7	8.2
2011*	23.4	17.6	11.9

*Projected SOURCE: The 2008 Statistical Abstract of the United States

So how are buyers and sellers protected? Buyers rate the reliability and service provided by sellers and eBay makes these ratings available to you. However, if you win a bid and do not go through with the purchase, you are stuck with a negative rating for the rest of your eBay life. There are also services that make it possible for you to pay an individual seller using your credit card.

Fighting Fraud

There is a new charge on your credit card bill! But where is the merchandise? You never got it, or even worse, you never ordered it. Many credit card companies will investigate suspected cases of fraud on your behalf, limiting your liability to $50. Also, the Fair Credit Billing Act allows you to withhold payment if you believe that someone has stolen your card number.

You also have the option of filing complaints with the Federal Trade Commission (FTC) at www.ftc.gov. The FTC offers you advice on how to protect against fraud, identity theft, and questionable business practices. The site guides you step-by-step through the process of filing a consumer complaint.

Five Online Shopping Tips

1. Check out the reviews written by other buyers.
2. Look for a padlock icon in the browser and "https" for security.
3. Check for endorsements from rating agencies, such as the Better Business Bureau (BBB).
4. Steer clear of sellers who offer low prices only to squeeze you on shipping costs.
5. Use a credit card as it offers the best safeguard against fraud, but never e-mail a credit card number, bank account information, password, or PIN number.

Are You Ready?

1. What are the advantages of shopping online?
2. What are two possible pitfalls?

WebQuest Online — To learn more about this topic, visit PearsonSuccessNet.com

Consumer Smarts

PERSONAL FINANCE HANDBOOK PF39

WebQuest online

Go online for a hands-on experience. Take what you have learned and put it into action. Prepare yourself for navigating the real world of money and finance.

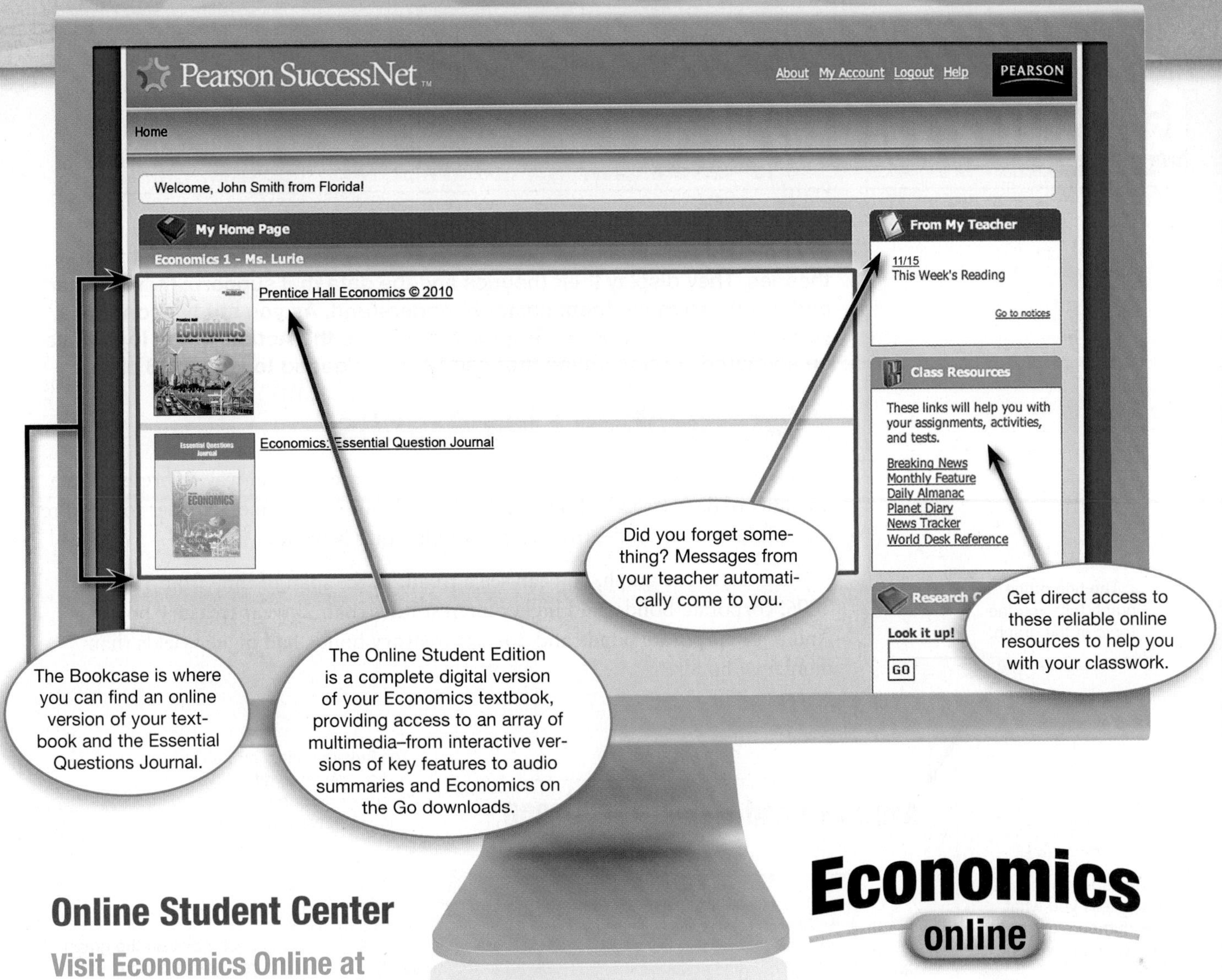

Pearson SuccessNet

About My Account Logout Help PEARSON

Home

Welcome, John Smith from Florida!

My Home Page

Economics 1 - Ms. Lurie

Prentice Hall Economics © 2010

Economics: Essential Question Journal

From My Teacher

11/15
This Week's Reading

Go to notices

Class Resources

These links will help you with your assignments, activities, and tests.

Breaking News
Monthly Feature
Daily Almanac
Planet Diary
News Tracker
World Desk Reference

Research C

Look it up!

GO

The Bookcase is where you can find an online version of your textbook and the Essential Questions Journal.

The Online Student Edition is a complete digital version of your Economics textbook, providing access to an array of multimedia–from interactive versions of key features to audio summaries and Economics on the Go downloads.

Did you forget something? Messages from your teacher automatically come to you.

Get direct access to these reliable online resources to help you with your classwork.

Online Student Center

Visit Economics Online at PearsonSuccessNet.com to access your assignments, review key concepts, and download Economics on the Go.

Economics online

In Partnership

THE WALL STREET JOURNAL. CLASSROOM EDITION

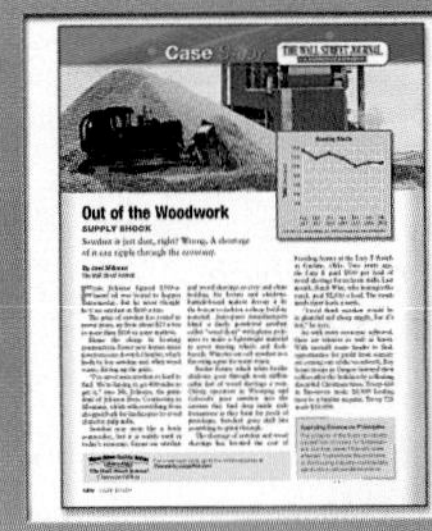

The Wall Street Journal Classroom Edition keeps you up-to-date on what is happening in your world.

Video News Update Online

Powered by

***The Wall Street Journal* Classroom Edition**

Go online for a current video related to the Essential Question topic.

In Partnership

THE WALL STREET JOURNAL. CLASSROOM EDITION

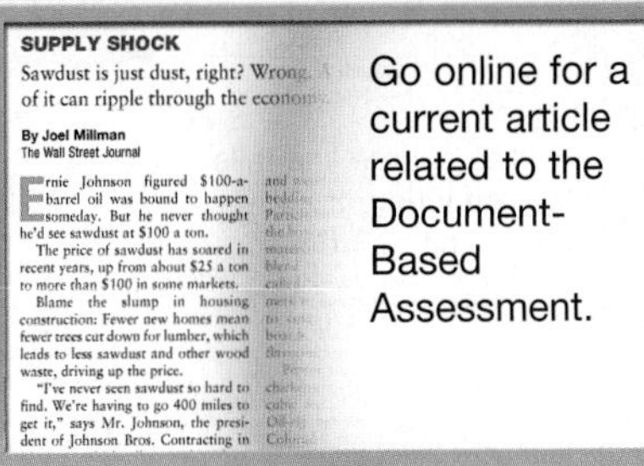

SUPPLY SHOCK

Sawdust is just dust, right? Wrong. ... of it can ripple through the econom...

By Joel Millman
The Wall Street Journal

Ernie Johnson figured $100-a-barrel oil was bound to happen someday. But he never thought he'd see sawdust at $100 a ton.

The price of sawdust has soared in recent years, up from about $25 a ton to more than $100 in some markets.

Blame the slump in housing construction: Fewer new homes mean fewer trees cut down for lumber, which leads to less sawdust and other wood waste, driving up the price.

"I've never seen sawdust so hard to find. We're having to go 400 miles to get it," says Mr. Johnson, the president of Johnson Bros. Contracting in

Go online for a current article related to the Document-Based Assessment.

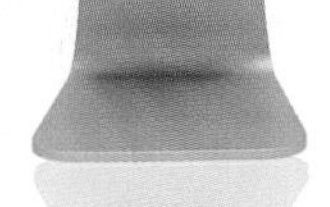

Graph Preview

Economists collect and evaluate data in order to develop and test their theories. They display their theories and the data that supports them in charts and graphs to make them easier to understand. As you study economics, you will see many graphs. Graphs that include the Action Graph logo have an animated version online that can be downloaded to your MP3 player.

Interpreting Line Graphs

Economists track trends in the economy. Graphs are a useful way to present large amounts of data visually. Line graphs show changes over time. In order to interpret a graph, you have to identify the type of data that is being presented.

If you analyze the graph, you can see a trend. In the span of time from 1994 to 2006, corporate bonds paid higher interest rates than 20-year treasury bonds. And both corporate bonds and 20-year treasury bonds had higher yields than municipal bonds.

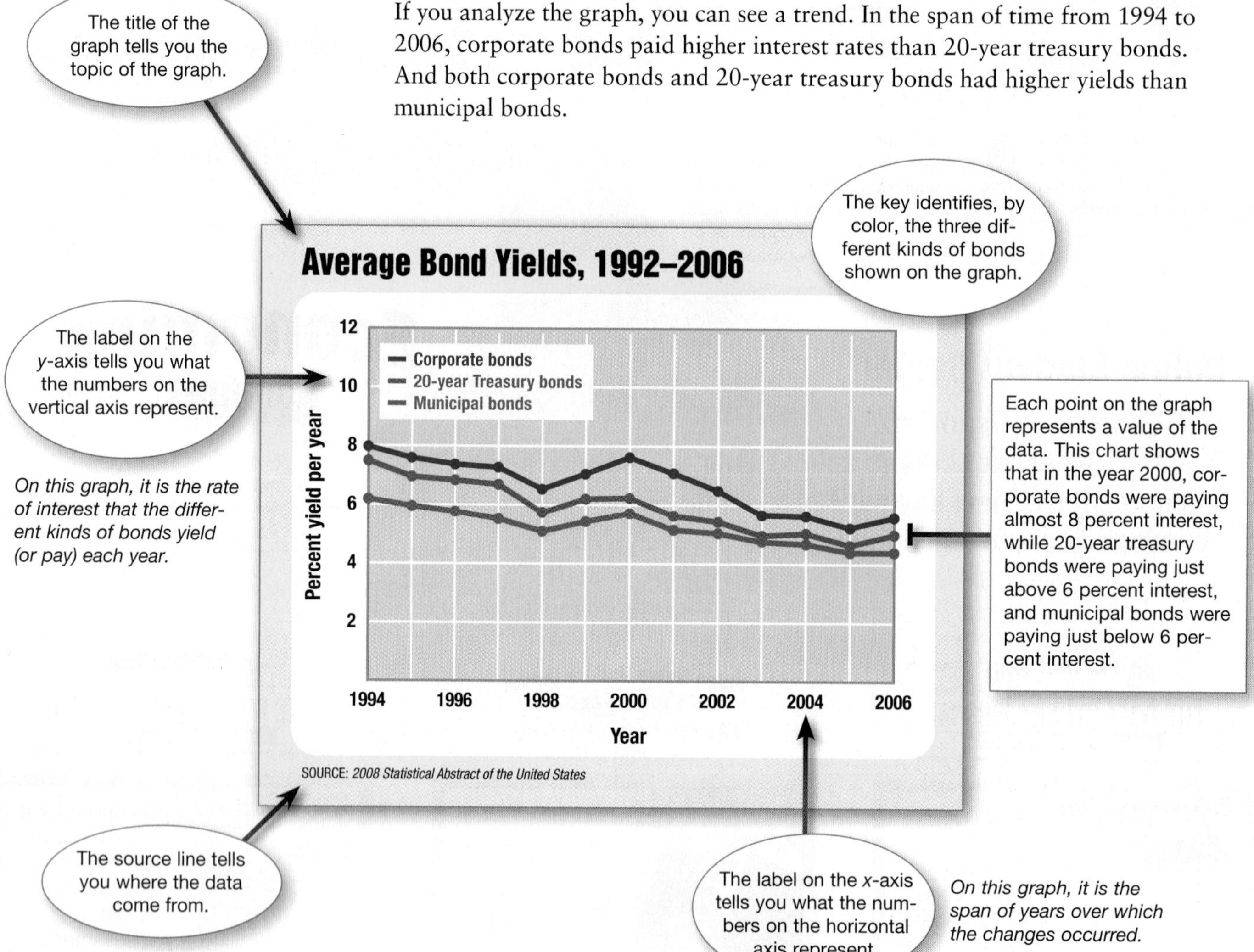

The title of the graph tells you the topic of the graph.
The key identifies, by color, the three different kinds of bonds shown on the graph.
Average Bond Yields, 1992–2006
The label on the y-axis tells you what the numbers on the vertical axis represent.
On this graph, it is the rate of interest that the different kinds of bonds yield (or pay) each year.
Corporate bonds
20-year Treasury bonds
Municipal bonds
Percent yield per year
12
10
8
6
4
2
1994
1996
1998
2000
2002
2004
2006
Year
Each point on the graph represents a value of the data. This chart shows that in the year 2000, corporate bonds were paying almost 8 percent interest, while 20-year treasury bonds were paying just above 6 percent interest, and municipal bonds were paying just below 6 percent interest.
SOURCE: 2008 Statistical Abstract of the United States
The source line tells you where the data come from.
The label on the x-axis tells you what the numbers on the horizontal axis represent.
On this graph, it is the span of years over which the changes occurred.

Interpreting Bar Graphs

Bar graphs are often used to show the relationships between two or more sets of data and to illustrate trends. In the bar graph below, you can see the relationship between level of education and the mean, or average, income for men and women. You can use the data presented on this graph to make two generalizations about levels of income: on average, men make more money than women, and the more education that a person has, the more money they are likely to earn.

Follow the same steps used to interpret a line graph.

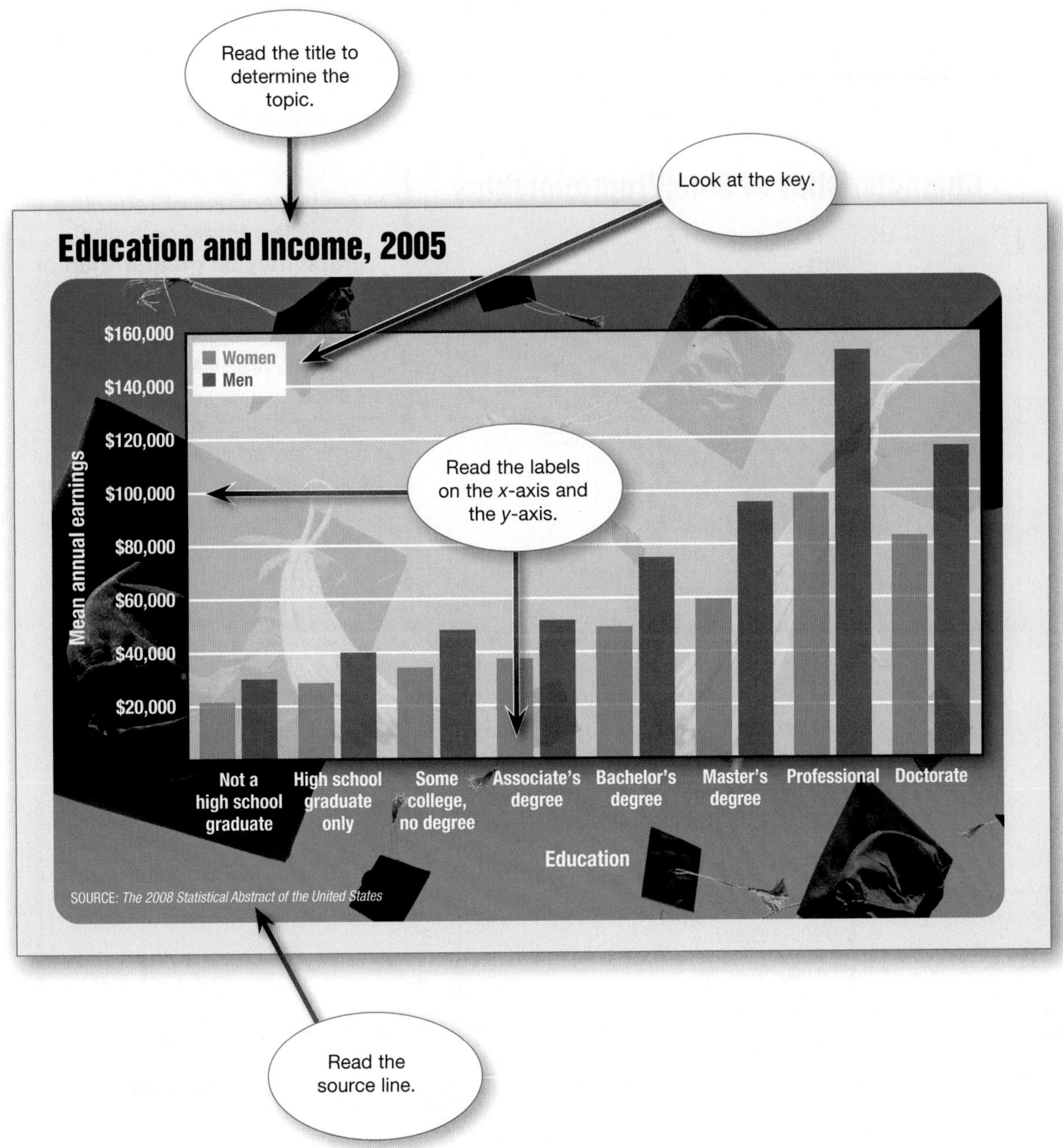

Using Circle Graphs

Circle graphs show how individual parts relate to a whole. Also known as pie charts because they look like a pie cut in wedges, circle graphs represent 100 percent of a given field. The circle graph below shows income information about businesses run by a single proprietor. Use the key to identify what each segment represents.

If you match the blue color which occupies 67 percent of the circle with the information on the key, you see that 67 percent of businesses run by a single owner show income of less than $25,000 per year. Only one percent of businesses with a single owner earn $1,000,000 or more per year.

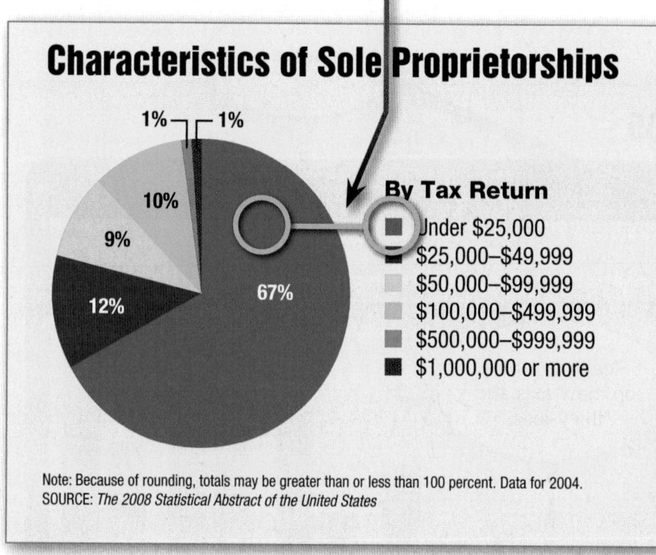

NOTE Because of rounding, the totals on a circle graph may be greater than or less than 100 percent.

For example: 5.8 rounds up to 6 percent, while 4.4 rounds down to 4 percent. When you add 5.8 and 4.4, the total is 10.2 percent. On a circle graph, this would display as 6 percent and 4 percent, adding up to a total of 10 percent.

Data can be transferred from a chart, or table, to a graph. The data in the chart below provide the same information as the circle graph above.

Income	Percentage
Under $25,000	67
$25,000–$49,999	12
$50,000–$99,999	9
$100,000–$499,999	10
$500,000–$999,999	1
$1,000,000 or more	1

Using Circle Graphs

Circle graphs show how individual parts relate to a whole. Also known as pie charts because they look like a pie cut in wedges, circle graphs represent 100 percent of a given field. The circle graph below shows income information about businesses run by a single proprietor. Use the key to identify what each segment represents.

If you match the blue color which occupies 67 percent of the circle with the information on the key, you see that 67 percent of businesses run by a single owner show income of less than $25,000 per year. Only one percent of businesses with a single owner earn $1,000,000 or more per year.

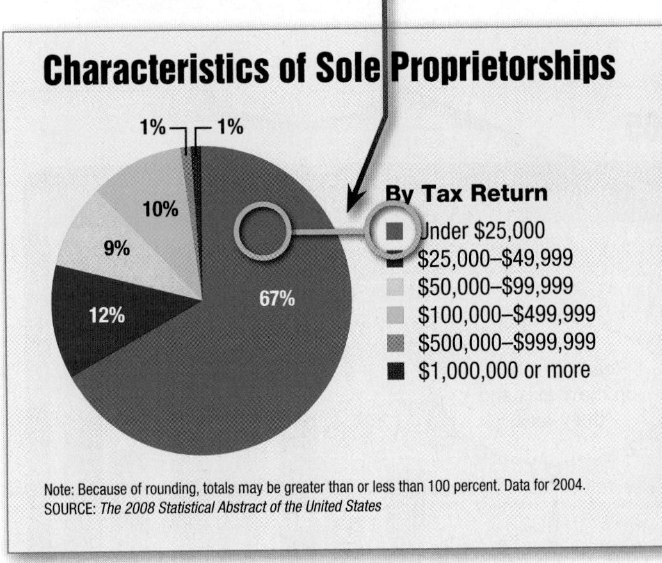

NOTE Because of rounding, the totals on a circle graph may be greater than or less than 100 percent.

For example: 5.8 rounds up to 6 percent, while 4.4 rounds down to 4 percent. When you add 5.8 and 4.4, the total is 10.2 percent. On a circle graph, this would display as 6 percent and 4 percent, adding up to a total of 10 percent.

Data can be transferred from a chart, or table, to a graph. The data in the chart below provide the same information as the circle graph above.

Income	Percentage
Under $25,000	67
$25,000–$49,999	12
$50,000–$99,999	9
$100,000–$499,999	10
$500,000–$999,999	1
$1,000,000 or more	1

Interpreting Bar Graphs

Bar graphs are often used to show the relationships between two or more sets of data and to illustrate trends. In the bar graph below, you can see the relationship between level of education and the mean, or average, income for men and women. You can use the data presented on this graph to make two generalizations about levels of income: on average, men make more money than women, and the more education that a person has, the more money they are likely to earn.

Follow the same steps used to interpret a line graph.

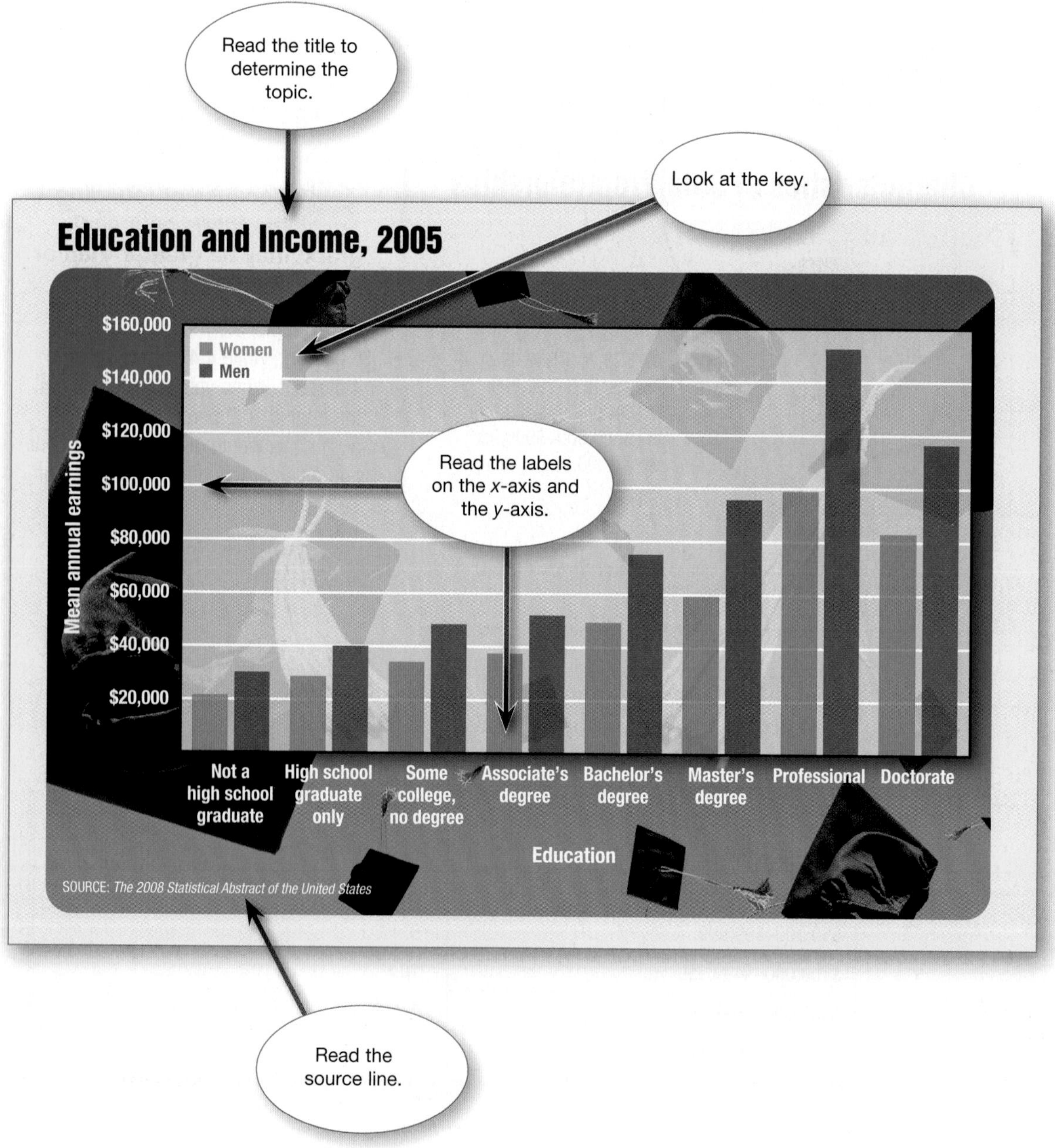

GRAPH PREVIEW

Graph Preview

Economists collect and evaluate data in order to develop and test their theories. They display their theories and the data that supports them in charts and graphs to make them easier to understand. As you study economics, you will see many graphs. Graphs that include the Action Graph logo have an animated version online that can be downloaded to your MP3 player.

Interpreting Line Graphs

Economists track trends in the economy. Graphs are a useful way to present large amounts of data visually. Line graphs show changes over time. In order to interpret a graph, you have to identify the type of data that is being presented.

If you analyze the graph, you can see a trend. In the span of time from 1994 to 2006, corporate bonds paid higher interest rates than 20-year treasury bonds. And both corporate bonds and 20-year treasury bonds had higher yields than municipal bonds.

The title of the graph tells you the topic of the graph.
The key identifies, by color, the three different kinds of bonds shown on the graph.
Average Bond Yields, 1992–2006
The label on the y-axis tells you what the numbers on the vertical axis represent.
On this graph, it is the rate of interest that the different kinds of bonds yield (or pay) each year.
Corporate bonds
20-year Treasury bonds
Municipal bonds
Percent yield per year
12
10
8
6
4
2
1994
1996
1998
2000
2002
2004
2006
Year
Each point on the graph represents a value of the data. This chart shows that in the year 2000, corporate bonds were paying almost 8 percent interest, while 20-year treasury bonds were paying just above 6 percent interest, and municipal bonds were paying just below 6 percent interest.
SOURCE: 2008 Statistical Abstract of the United States
The source line tells you where the data come from.
The label on the x-axis tells you what the numbers on the horizontal axis represent.
On this graph, it is the span of years over which the changes occurred.

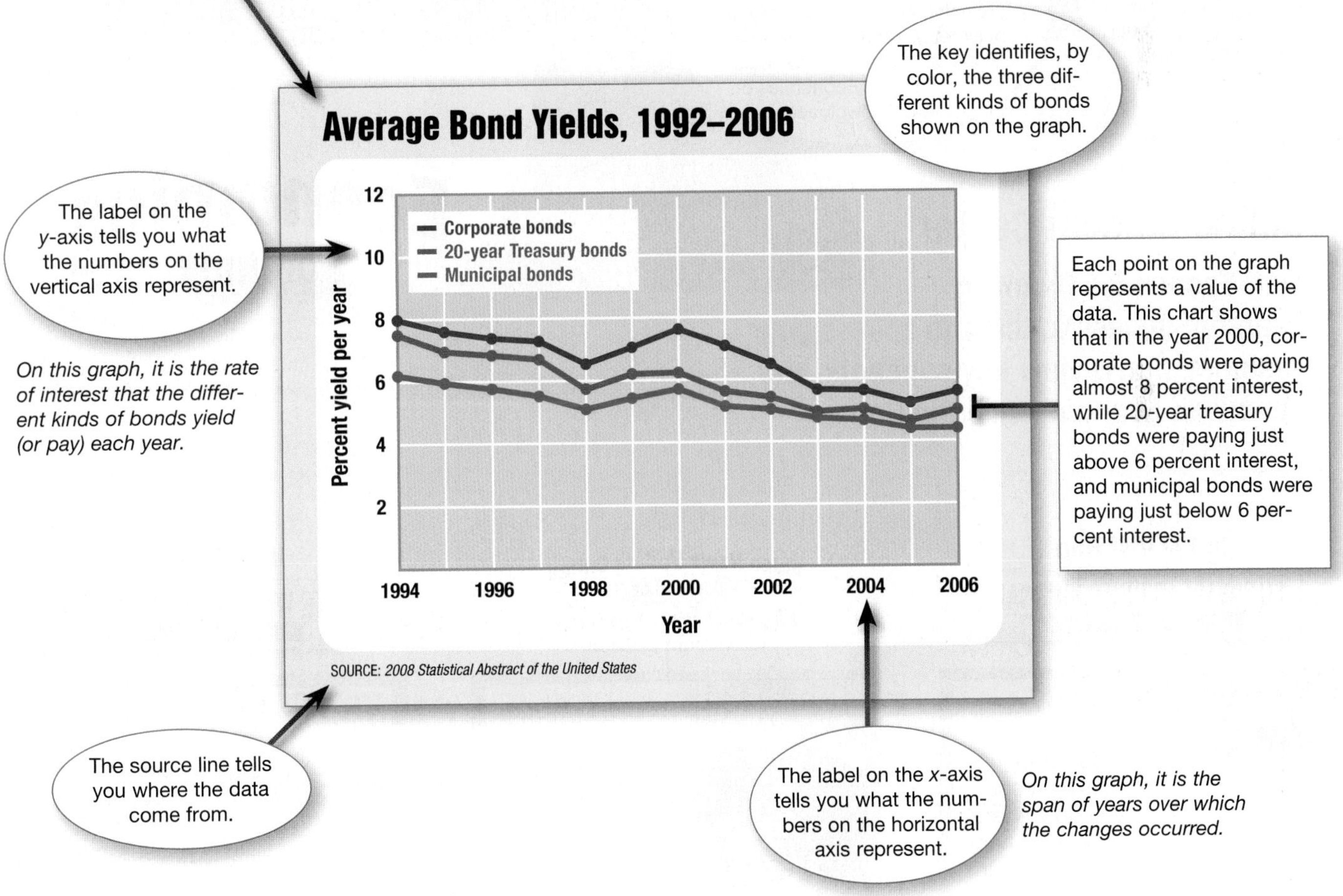

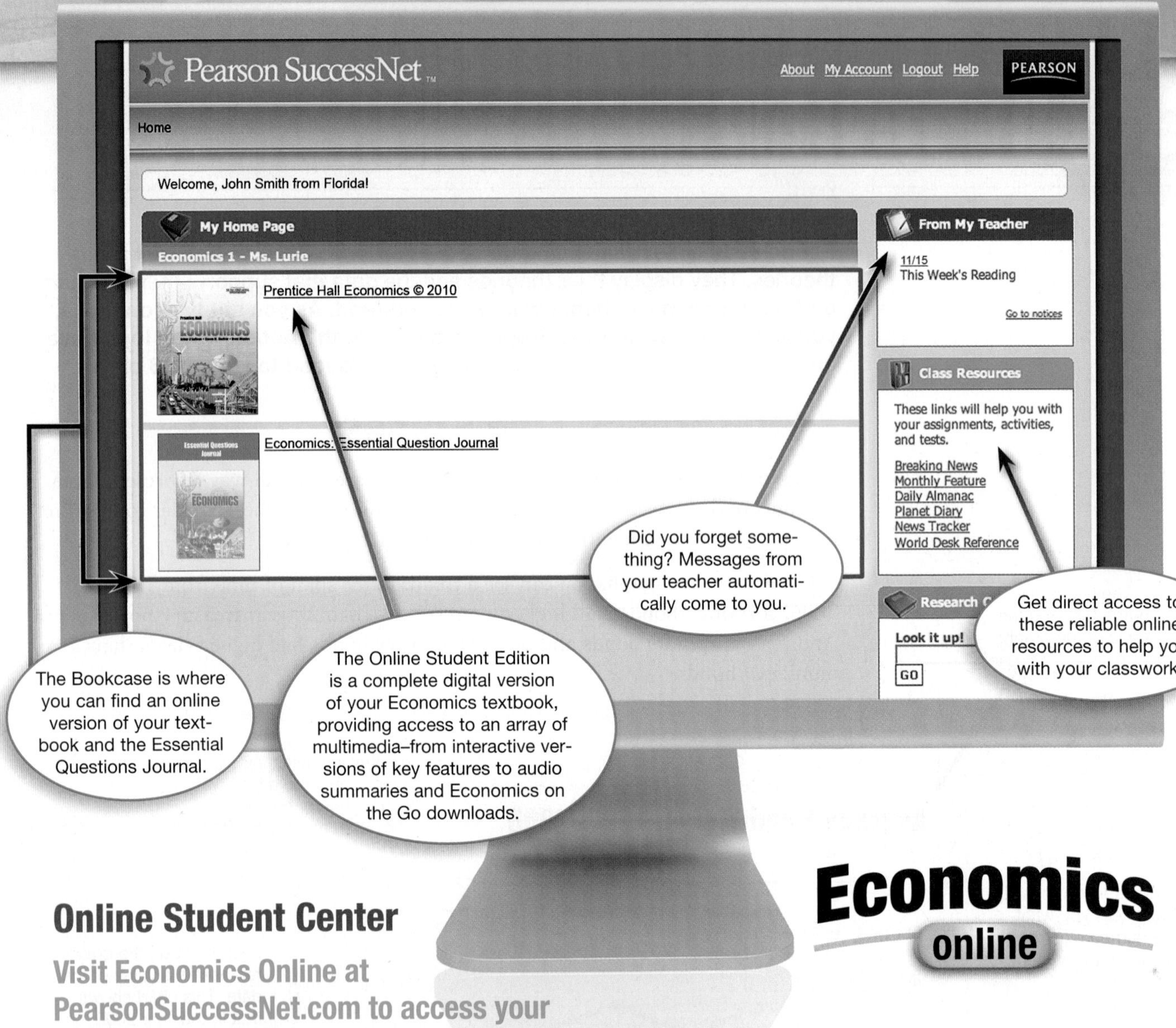

Pearson SuccessNet™

About My Account Logout Help PEARSON

Home

Welcome, John Smith from Florida!

My Home Page

Economics 1 - Ms. Lurie

Prentice Hall Economics © 2010

Economics: Essential Question Journal

From My Teacher

11/15
This Week's Reading

Go to notices

Class Resources

These links will help you with your assignments, activities, and tests.

Breaking News
Monthly Feature
Daily Almanac
Planet Diary
News Tracker
World Desk Reference

Research C...

Look it up!

GO

The Bookcase is where you can find an online version of your textbook and the Essential Questions Journal.

The Online Student Edition is a complete digital version of your Economics textbook, providing access to an array of multimedia–from interactive versions of key features to audio summaries and Economics on the Go downloads.

Did you forget something? Messages from your teacher automatically come to you.

Get direct access to these reliable online resources to help you with your classwork.

Online Student Center

Visit Economics Online at PearsonSuccessNet.com to access your assignments, review key concepts, and download Economics on the Go.

Economics online

In Partnership

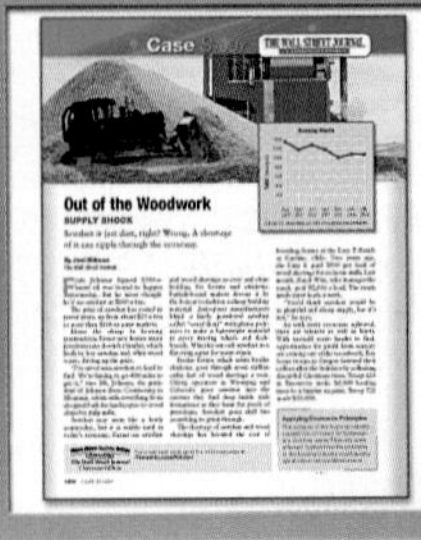

The Wall Street Journal Classroom Edition keeps you up-to-date on what is happening in your world.

Video News Update Online

Powered by

The Wall Street Journal
Classroom Edition

Go online for a current video related to the Essential Question topic.

In Partnership

THE WALL STREET JOURNAL.
CLASSROOM EDITION

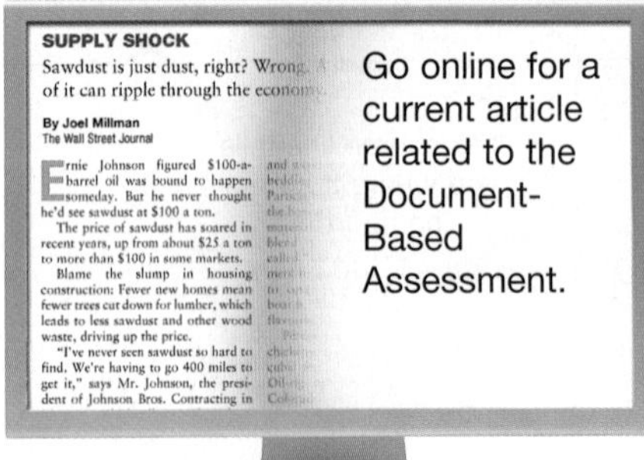

SUPPLY SHOCK

Sawdust is just dust, right? Wrong. ... of it can ripple through the econom...

By Joel Millman
The Wall Street Journal

Ernie Johnson figured $100-a-barrel oil was bound to happen someday. But he never thought he'd see sawdust at $100 a ton.

The price of sawdust has soared in recent years, up from about $25 a ton to more than $100 in some markets.

Blame the slump in housing construction: Fewer new homes mean fewer trees cut down for lumber, which leads to less sawdust and other wood waste, driving up the price.

"I've never seen sawdust so hard to find. We're having to go 400 miles to get it," says Mr. Johnson, the president of Johnson Bros. Contracting in

Go online for a current article related to the Document-Based Assessment.

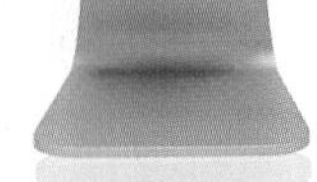

Understanding Population Pyramids

Population pyramids, or age structures, are graphical representations of the distribution of population by age and gender. They are called pyramids because in many instances they are wider at the bottom and narrower at the top.

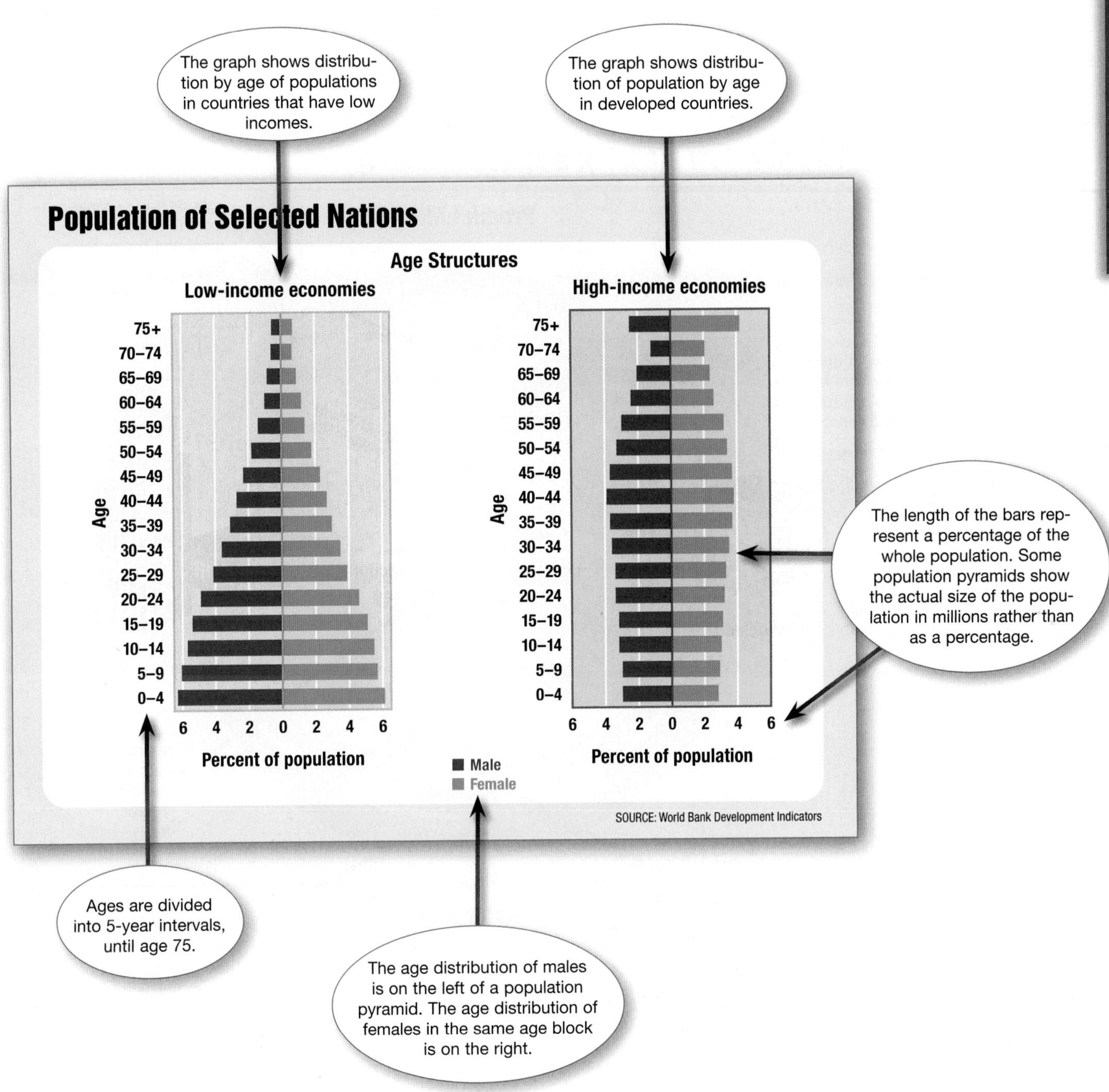
The graph shows distribution by age of populations in countries that have low incomes.
The graph shows distribution of population by age in developed countries.
Population of Selected Nations
Age Structures
Low-income economies
High-income economies
Age
75+
70–74
65–69
60–64
55–59
50–54
45–49
40–44
35–39
30–34
25–29
20–24
15–19
10–14
5–9
0–4
6 4 2 0 2 4 6
Percent of population
Male
Female
SOURCE: World Bank Development Indicators
The length of the bars represent a percentage of the whole population. Some population pyramids show the actual size of the population in millions rather than as a percentage.
Ages are divided into 5-year intervals, until age 75.
The age distribution of males is on the left of a population pyramid. The age distribution of females in the same age block is on the right.

Reading Circular Flow Models

Some charts used in economics do not present data. They are used to illustrate an economic process. The circular flow model shows how three basic parts of the economy work together. In this illustration of the macroeconomy at work, the three elements are households or consumers, firms or businesses, and the government.

Everything on this simplified chart is happening at the same time. The movement of the economy never stops.

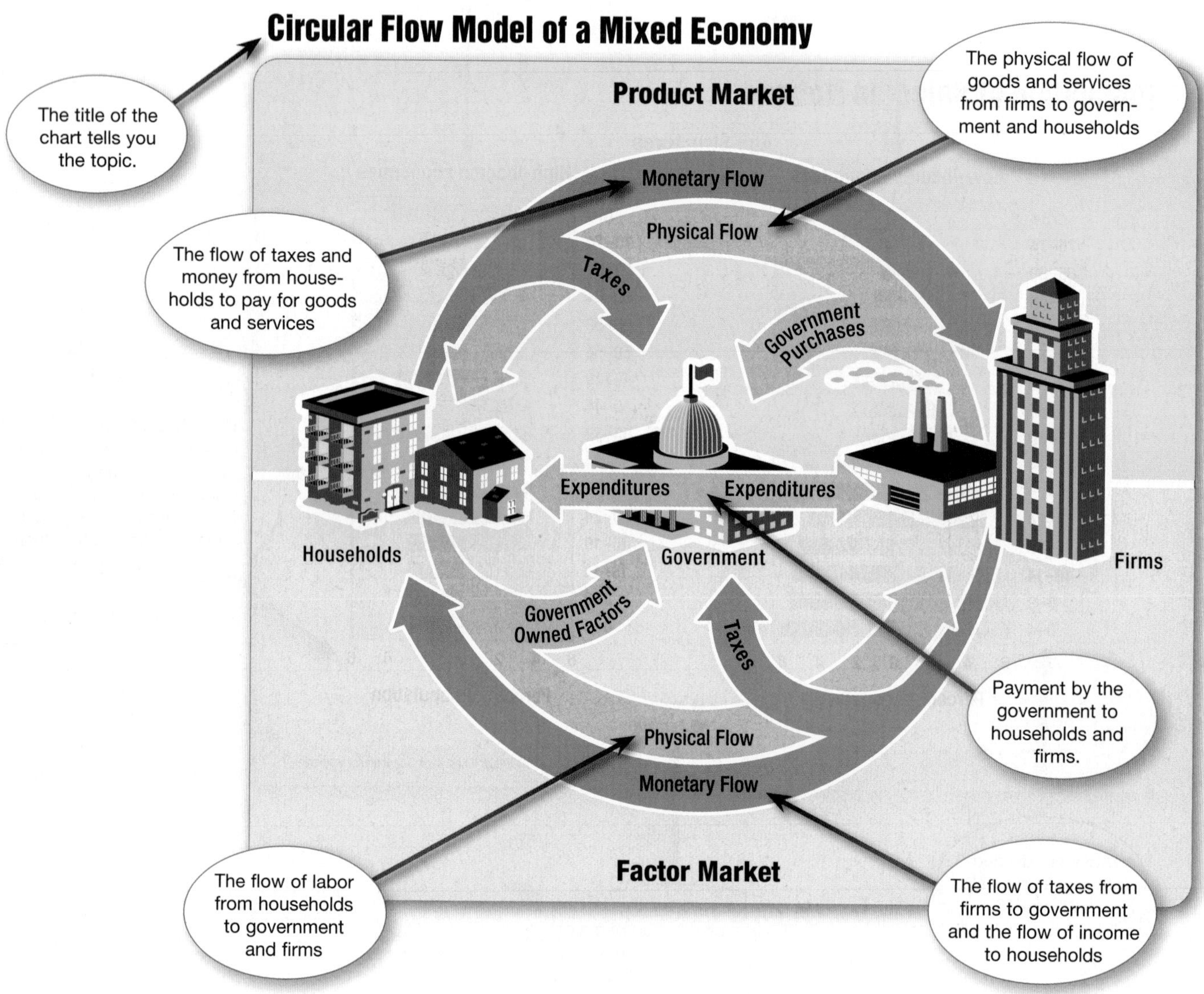

Table of Contents

Raising the achievement level of all students is the number one challenge facing teachers today. To assist in meeting this challenge, we've enlisted a team of respected authors and consultants who specialize in economic education, instructional design, and differentiated instruction. In the following pages, you'll find the key elements woven throughout this program to assure teaching and learning success.

Rising Healthcare Costs Eat Into Family Budgets

CONGRESS DEBATES ECONOMIC RECOVERY

Why Teach Economics?

You don't have to look very far to understand why it's important to teach economics. You see it every day—in the newspapers, on radio and television, and on the Internet.

Economic decisions, whether made on Wall Street or Main Street, affect us all. And it's not just Wall Street or Main Street anymore. Today, the financial markets of Beijing or the factories of Mexico City can be just as close to our lives as the supermarket on the corner.

Acquiring Personal Finance Skills

Now, more than ever, it's vital that students have the knowledge and skills to deal with increasingly complex economic issues. Loans? Credit cards? Careers? Investments? Taxes? Students need to make financial decisions about these and a vast array of other issues on a daily basis. And their decisions have an impact on local, national, and global communities.

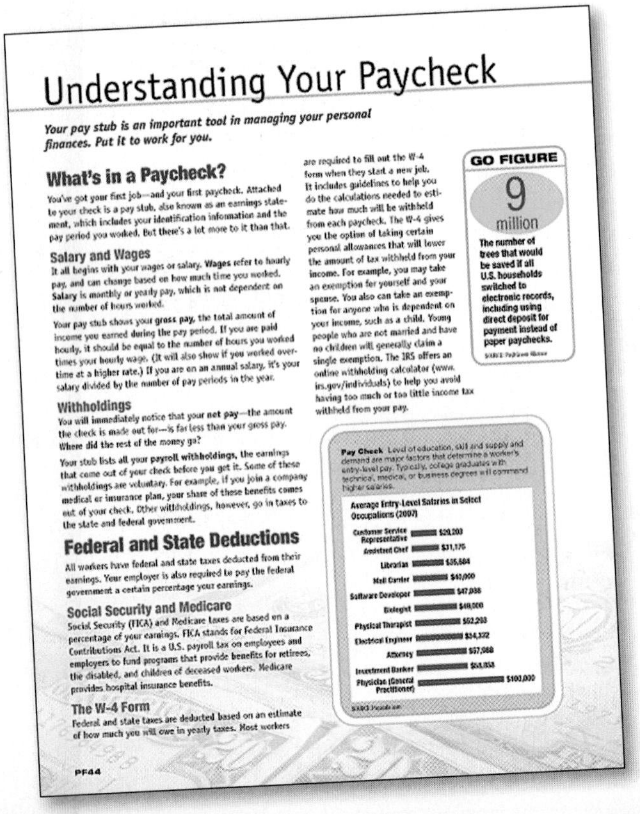

Understanding Your Paycheck

Your pay stub is an important tool in managing your personal finances. Put it to work for you.

What's in a Paycheck?

You've got your first job—and your first paycheck. Attached to your check is a pay stub, also known as an earnings statement, which includes your identification information and the pay period you worked. But there's a lot more to it than that.

Salary and Wages

It all begins with your wages or salary. **Wages** refer to hourly pay, and can change based on how much time you worked. **Salary** is monthly or yearly pay, which is not dependent on the number of hours worked.

Your pay stub shows your **gross pay**, the total amount of income you earned during the pay period. If you are paid hourly, it should be equal to the number of hours you worked times your hourly wage. (It will also show if you worked overtime at a higher rate.) If you are on an annual salary, it's your salary divided by the number of pay periods in the year.

Withholdings

You will immediately notice that your **net pay**—the amount the check is made out for—is far less than your gross pay. Where did the rest of the money go?

Your stub lists all your **payroll withholdings**, the earnings that come out of your check before you get it. Some of these withholdings are voluntary. For example, if you join a company medical or insurance plan, your share of these benefits comes out of your check. Other withholdings, however, go in taxes to the state and federal government.

Federal and State Deductions

All workers have federal and state taxes deducted from their earnings. Your employer is also required to pay the federal government a certain percentage your earnings.

Social Security and Medicare

Social Security (FICA) and Medicare taxes are based on a percentage of your earnings. FICA stands for Federal Insurance Contributions Act. It is a U.S. payroll tax on employees and employers to fund programs that provide benefits for retirees, the disabled, and children of deceased workers. Medicare provides hospital insurance benefits.

The W-4 Form

Federal and state taxes are deducted based on an estimate of how much you will owe in yearly taxes. Most workers are required to fill out the W-4 form when they start a new job. It includes guidelines to help you do the calculations needed to estimate how much will be withheld from each paycheck. The W-4 gives you the option of taking certain personal allowances that will lower the amount of tax withheld from your income. For example, you may take an exemption for yourself and your spouse. You also can take an exemption for anyone who is dependent on your income, such as a child. Young people who are not married and have no children will generally claim a single exemption. The IRS offers an online withholding calculator (www.irs.gov/individuals) to help you avoid having too much or too little income tax withheld from your pay.

GO FIGURE

9 million

The number of trees that would be saved if all U.S. households switched to electronic records, including using direct deposit for payment instead of paper paychecks.

Pay Check Level of education, skill and supply and demand are major factors that determine a worker's entry-level pay. Typically, college graduates with technical, medical, or business degrees will command higher salaries.

Average Entry-Level Salaries in Select Occupations (2007)

Customer Service Representative $29,203
Assistant Chef $31,175
Librarian $35,684
Mail Carrier $40,000
Software Developer $47,038
Biologist $48,000
Physical Therapist $52,203
Electrical Engineer $54,322
Attorney $57,988
Investment Banker
Physician (General Practitioner) $100,000

PF44

Every student should leave high school with a fundamental understanding of economic principles and concepts. National Council of Economics Education (NCEE) President Robert Duvall said, "Financial literacy is not something you're born with. It's learned behavior. And you're either going to learn it from teachers or you're going to learn it the hard way."

The study of economics gives students the tools to analyze their options and make informed decisions. The topics and case studies students encounter this course apply beyond the classroom. There is no better time than now to teach the fundamentals of economic and financial literacy.

Developing Critical Thinking Skills

The goal of economics teachers is to link the principles of economics to the careers and economic decisions individuals make in a free market economy. The National Council of Economics Education has published a list of national content standards. The standards collectively address the central issue of scarcity. The idea that people have unlimited wants and limited resources is emphasized often. Students should realize that scarcity forces us to make choices, and the choices we make have broad consequences.

The National Council of Economics Education also stresses the importance of decision-making skills in economic reasoning. Decision-making skills are critical in all aspects of life. Other critical thinking skills, such as comparing viewpoints, problem solving, and communication are also increasingly important in today's competitive world. Students need to learn these 21st century skills to transfer knowledge and information to various situations, constantly adjusting decisions as circumstances change. The most effective way to practice economic theory is to apply these critical thinking skills to real-life case studies.

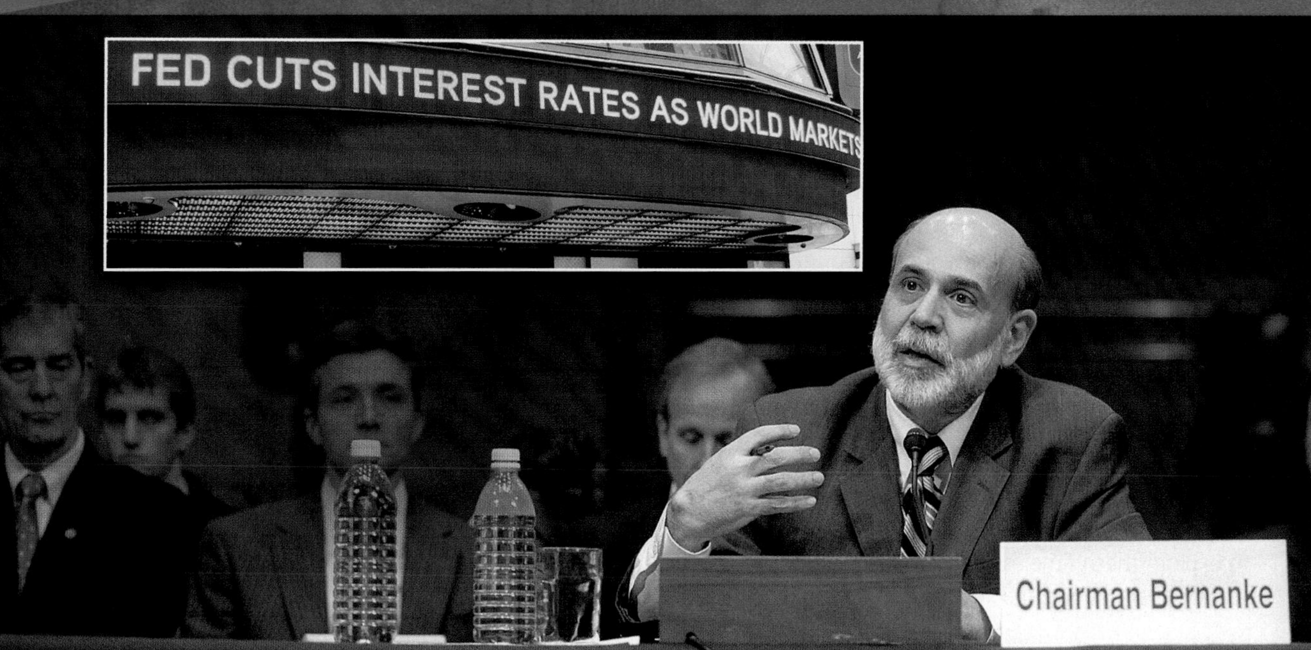

Applying Economic Theory

The charge is often made that economics seems dense and abstract and that students see little relevance in studying it. Some students may perceive economics as a dry, boring subject full of complicated graphs and incomprehensible theory. But economics is more than a long list of concepts. When presented with situations and issues they can relate to, both on an individual level and across a national or global economy, students will learn the essentials of economic theory and the means to apply those principles to their own decisions. As students realize the importance of economics to their everyday lives, and see how economic decisions impact them, they understand that economics is for everyone.

All students are capable of making informed decisions, even students with varying learning abilities and different reading levels. Stories drawn from the news provide a dramatic illustration of the conflicts and dilemmas associated with economics. Access to current data and news stories will provide students with the broadest range of information they need to make informed financial decisions. By providing students with the tools to understand their economic world, we are preparing them to be effective and productive citizens in the twenty-first century.

> **"Economically literate citizens, because they possess an understanding of economic generalizations and concepts, will enjoy a more complete understanding of their world, be better able to make reasoned decisions, and be more fully in control of their economic future."**
>
> —Ronald Banaszak, *The Nature of Economics*, Literacy, 1987

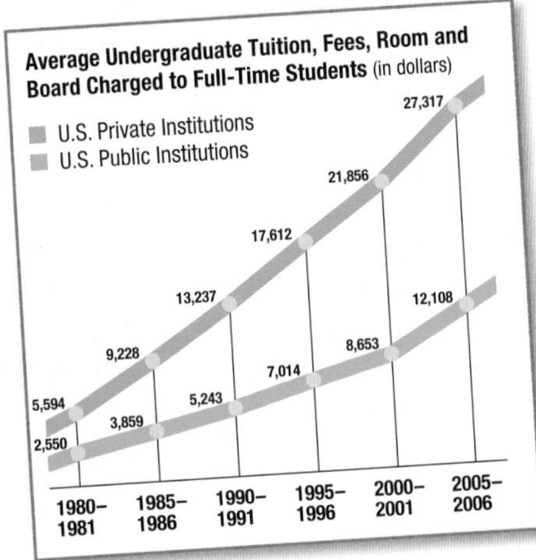

What Makes *Prentice Hall Economics* Unique?

Prentice Hall Economics is a multidimensional program designed around Essential Questions. It helps students of all abilities gain an understanding of key economic principles and see their application in the real-world. The print Student Edition, Teacher Edition, and Essential Questions Journal are supported online by a rich array of resources in the Student Center and Teacher Center.

Unit Essential Questions

1. How does economics affect everyone?
2. Who benefits from the free market?
3. How can businesses and labor best achieve their goals?
4. How can you make the most of your money?
5. Why does it matter how the economy is doing?
6. What is the proper role of government in the economy?
7. How might scarcity divide our world or bring it together?

Based on Essential Questions

Prentice Hall, in partnership with Grant Wiggins, has created an economics program that focuses on Essential Questions. Students have the opportunity to explore these timeless and timely questions in a variety of situations and formats.

1. **Chapter and Unit Essential Question Activities** These activities give students the opportunity to transfer their understanding of the principles of economics to authentic situations. They are challenged to rethink their assumptions and modify their responses based on changing situations and new perspectives.
2. **Essential Questions Journal** Students work through the process of critical thinking in graphic, chart, question, and essay formats. This process helps develop students' abilities to organize and analyze information.
3. **WebQuest** Students develop 21st century skills by using online resources to research topics related to the Essential Questions. These projects foster deeper understandings of key concepts.

WebQuest online

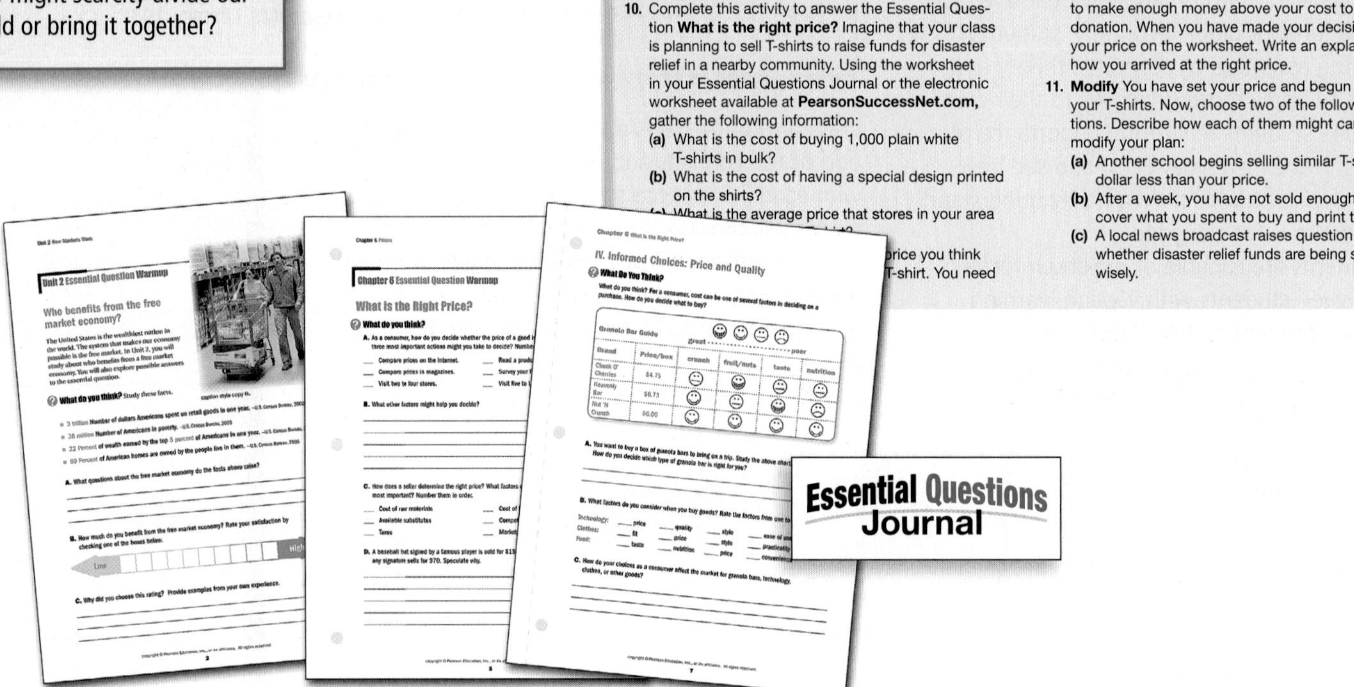

Essential Question Activity

Essential Questions Journal — To respond to the chapter Essential Question, go to your **Essential Questions Journal.**

10. Complete this activity to answer the Essential Question **What is the right price?** Imagine that your class is planning to sell T-shirts to raise funds for disaster relief in a nearby community. Using the worksheet in your Essential Questions Journal or the electronic worksheet available at **PearsonSuccessNet.com,** gather the following information:
    (a) What is the cost of buying 1,000 plain white T-shirts in bulk?
    (b) What is the cost of having a special design printed on the shirts?
    (c) What is the average price that stores in your area ... price you think ... T-shirt. You need to make enough money above your cost to make a donation. When you have made your decision, fill in your price on the worksheet. Write an explanation of how you arrived at the right price.
11. **Modify** You have set your price and begun selling your T-shirts. Now, choose two of the following situations. Describe how each of them might cause you to modify your plan:
    (a) Another school begins selling similar T-shirts for a dollar less than your price.
    (b) After a week, you have not sold enough T-shirts to cover what you spent to buy and print the shirts.
    (c) A local news broadcast raises question about whether disaster relief funds are being spent wisely.

Essential Questions Journal

Accessible

Core content is made accessible through differentiated instruction. Lessons are modified to help students of all abilities and learning styles achieve understanding of key economic principles.

1. **Leveled instruction and worksheets** Lessons provide options for reaching all students, using appropriate pedagogy and activities. Teachers can quickly choose from multiple levels of editable worksheets and assessments found on the Online Teacher Center and on the Resource Library CD-ROM.
2. **Technology to assist learning** Rich digital assets such as audio, video, and animations on the Economics Online Student Center provide multiple ways for learners to access the content. Interactive section and chapter assessments enable students to monitor their own progress.

Personal and Relevant

Economics is all around us. These are among the features and activities that help students connect the real world of economics to their own lives.

1. **Economics and You** stimulates students' interest with real-life situations and motivates learning about economic concepts. Using these models as a starting point, you can encourage students to relate their own examples of how economics affects their lives.
2. **Personal Finance Handbook** enables students to gain the knowledge and skills needed to manage their own money. No time in recent history has been more critical for students to develop the habits of good financial citizenship.

3. **Essential Questions Videos** are developed and created by students to demonstrate their command of key economics standards. Using the style and perspectives of peers, these videos engage students' interest. Based on enduring questions, these videos help make connections to prior learning and provoke lively debate.

4. ***The Wall Street Journal* Classroom Edition** case studies foster economic literacy with enriching and authoritative content that focuses on today's issues both in the Student Edition and online.

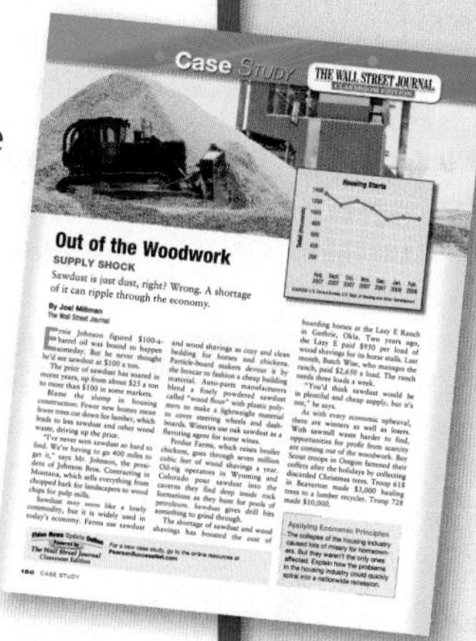

5. ***The Wall Street Journal* Online News Videos** promote student inquiry into ongoing and constantly changing economic issues. How will what is happening now affect students responses to Essential Questions? Updated annually, these videos challenge students to make connections between classroom learning and real-life situations.

Video News Update Online
Powered by
The Wall Street Journal
Classroom Edition

How Can Technology Help?

Visit www.PearsonSuccessNet.com

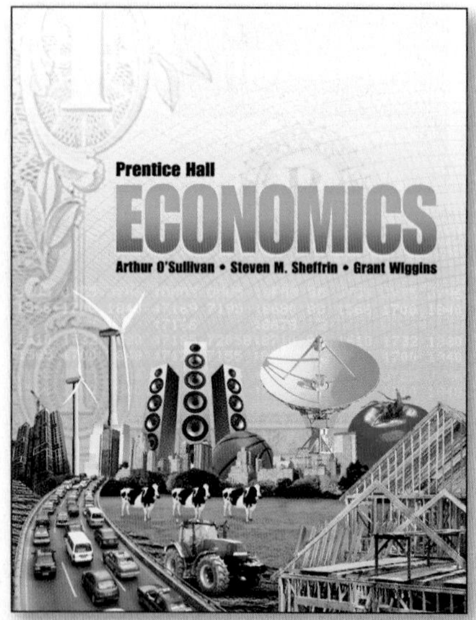

Online Student Center

Students can use a wide array of 21st century learning tools to personalize learning. No matter where they are or what time of day it is, students have access to their work.

Online Student Edition has rich digital assets. Two levels of the Student Edition teach core content, enabling students to use the version that matches their reading level. (Also available on CD-ROM.)

Interactivities help students gain deeper understanding of key concepts.

How the Economy Works puts students in a central role and gives them the chance to see where their decisions take them in a hands-on learning situation.

Visual Glossary provides students the opportunity to take a more in-depth look at key terms and concepts.

Math Online supports math assessment in the Student Edition Section Assessment by providing added math skill development.

WebQuests include research projects that use online resources to explore current economic issues and Personal Finance WebQuests that reinforce real-life personal finance skills.

Essential Questions Videos are developed by students to explore evolving economic issues. Students will be able to produce videos with guidance from an online production manual that provides creative and technical help and advice.

Selected worksheets provide students with the opportunity to reinforce and enrich their learning.

Economics on the Go allows students to access audio and video files, including

Audio Review (English and Spanish) lets students take learning and review offline.

Economic Dictionary (English and Spanish) builds vocabulary support.

Action Graph Animations reinforce economic principles by taking students through each concept using step-by-step animations.

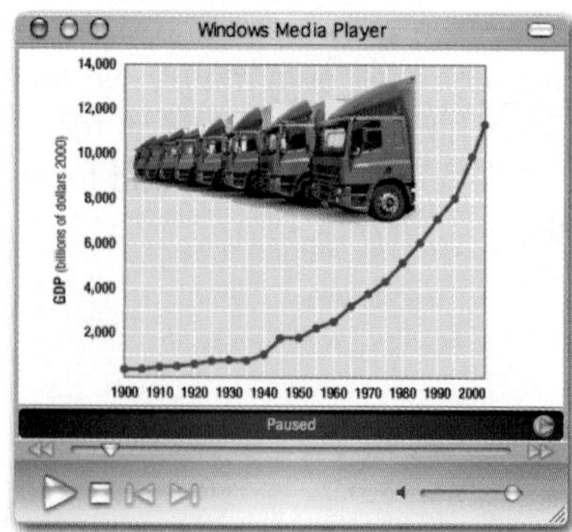

***The Wall Street Journal* Online News Videos** helps students expand their view of economic principles and make connections to the world around them.

Online Teacher Center

The Online Teacher Center is an instructional management tool that saves time by letting teachers plan, teach, assess, remediate, communicate with, and manage your classroom quickly and easily.

This Center provides a single point of access to both student and teacher materials, including two levels of the Teacher's Edition for built-in differentiation. These Teacher's Editions include the Student Editions and lessons in the side columns, as well as access to selected worksheets and other resources.

Teacher's Resource Library provides access to a wide range of teaching support, including

- **Editable lesson plans** give teachers the ability to customize lessons according to their own classroom needs.
- **Editable, leveled worksheets** permit teachers to adjust activities to match learning levels and content.
- **Leveled quizzes and tests** support assessment for differentiated instruction.
- **Color Transparencies** enrich lessons with visuals for teaching and engaging student interest.
- **AYP Monitoring Assessments** provide diagnostic and benchmark tests and remediation.
- **Simulation Activities** allow students to approach the material in an interactive format.
- **Answer Key** speeds the assessment process.
- **Assessment Rubrics** evaluate student understanding and performance.
- **Blank graphic organizers** organize ideas and facilitate learning.

All these resources are also available on disk.

Lecture Notes offer multimedia in-class teaching aids of key concepts.

Success Tracker™ enables teachers to measure each student's progress by assigning tests, tracking progress, assessing learning, and generating reports. **Success Tracker™** makes use of the needs of individual students.

Economic Updates are worksheets provided each year to present students with updated examples of economic principles in action.

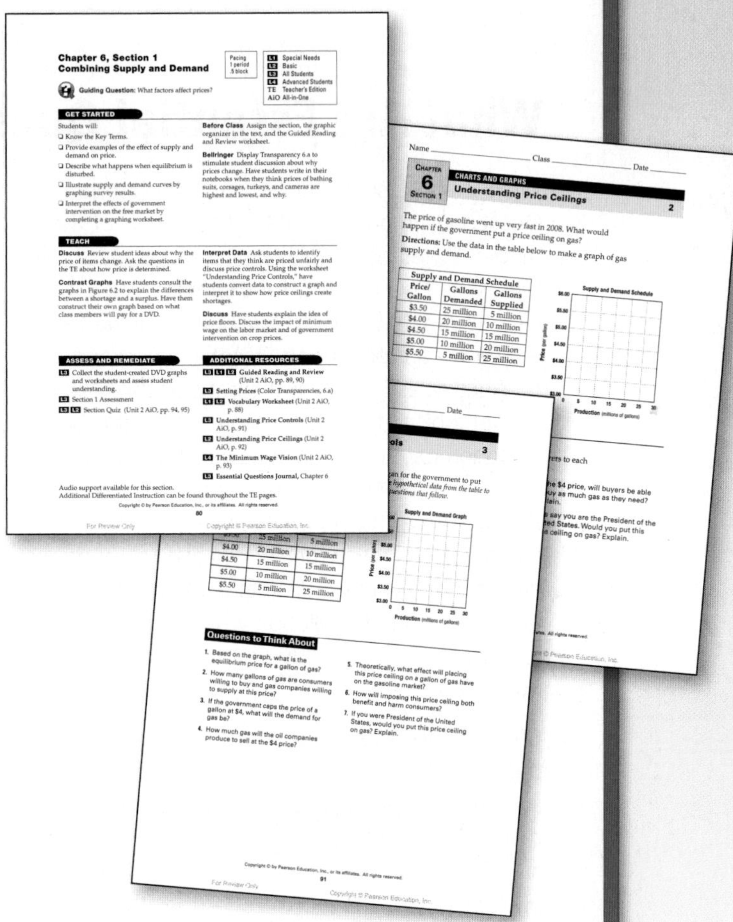

Chapter 6, Section 1
Combining Supply and Demand

Pacing: 1 period, .5 block

L1 Special Needs; L2 Basic; L3 All Students; L4 Advanced Students; TE Teacher's Edition; AiO All-in-One

Guiding Question: What factors affect prices?

GET STARTED

Students will:

- Know the Key Terms.
- Provide examples of the effect of supply and demand on price.
- Describe what happens when equilibrium is disturbed.
- Illustrate supply and demand curves by graphing survey results.
- Interpret the effects of government intervention on the free market by completing a graphing worksheet.

Before Class Assign the section, the graphic organizer in the text, and the Guided Reading and Review worksheet.

Bellringer Display Transparency 6.a to stimulate student discussion about why prices change. Have students write in their notebooks when they think prices of bathing suits, corsages, turkeys, and cameras are highest and lowest, and why.

TEACH

Discuss Review student ideas about why the price of items change. Ask the questions in the TE about how price is determined.

Contrast Graphs Have students consult the graphs in Figure 6.2 to explain the differences between a shortage and a surplus. Have them construct their own graph based on what class members will pay for a DVD.

Interpret Data Ask students to identify items that they think are priced unfairly and discuss price controls. Using the worksheet "Understanding Price Controls," have students convert data to construct a graph and interpret it to show how price ceilings create shortages.

Discuss Have students explain the idea of price floors. Discuss the impact of minimum wage on the labor market and of government intervention on crop prices.

ASSESS AND REMEDIATE

- L3 Collect the student-created DVD graphs and worksheets and assess student understanding.
- L3 Section 1 Assessment
- L3 L2 Section Quiz (Unit 2 AiO, pp. 94, 95)

ADDITIONAL RESOURCES

- L3 L1 L2 **Guided Reading and Review** (Unit 2 AiO, pp. 89, 90)
- L3 **Setting Prices** (Color Transparencies, 6.a)
- L1 L2 **Vocabulary Worksheet** (Unit 2 AiO, p. 88)
- L3 **Understanding Price Controls** (Unit 2 AiO, p. 91)
- L2 **Understanding Price Ceilings** (Unit 2 AiO, p. 92)
- L4 **The Minimum Wage Vision** (Unit 2 AiO, p. 93)
- L3 **Essential Questions Journal,** Chapter 6

Audio support available for this section.
Additional Differentiated Instruction can be found throughout the TE pages.

80

Name ______ Class ______ Date ______

Chapter 6 Section 1

CHARTS AND GRAPHS

Understanding Price Ceilings 2

The price of gasoline went up very fast in 2008. What would happen if the government put a price ceiling on gas?

Directions: Use the data in the table below to make a graph of gas supply and demand.

Supply and Demand Schedule		
Price/ Gallon	Gallons Demanded	Gallons Supplied
$3.50	25 million	5 million
$4.00	20 million	10 million
$4.50	15 million	15 million
$5.00	10 million	20 million
$5.50	5 million	25 million

Date ______

3

Questions to Think About

1. Based on the graph, what is the equilibrium price for a gallon of gas?
2. How many gallons of gas are consumers willing to buy and gas companies willing to supply at this price?
3. If the government caps the price of a gallon at $4, what will the demand for gas be?
4. How much gas will the oil companies produce to sell at the $4 price?
5. Theoretically, what effect will placing this price ceiling on a gallon of gas have on the gasoline market?
6. How will imposing this price ceiling both benefit and harm consumers?
7. If you were President of the United States, would you put this price ceiling on gas? Explain.

In-Service On Demand and Professional Development In addition to our on-site consultant support, Pearson offers online tutorials available 24/7, as well as scheduled instructor-led Webinars for selected products.

VISIT *my*PearsonTraining.com **FOR MORE INFORMATION.**

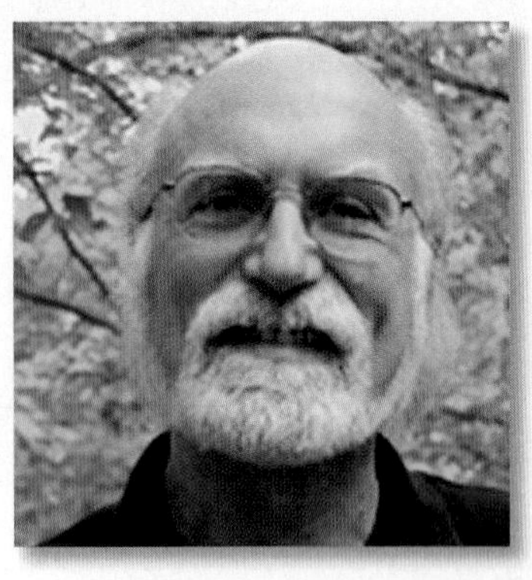

Grant Wiggins, Ed. D.

Grant Wiggins advocates the use of Essential Questions to ensure in-depth and lasting learning. During the development of *Prentice Hall Economics*, Wiggins advised the product team in the creation of the essential questions and pedagogy that supports them.

> **Every textbook has questions for students. *Prentice Hall Economics* is different. It has been deliberately built around a few vital questions – Essential Questions**

What Are Essential Questions?

What is an "Essential Question"? An Essential Question is important, vital, at the heart of the matter. Whether in our teaching or our personal lives, when we wonder, for example: "How do we decide what is true?" "Whom shall we trust?" – then we are pondering Essential Questions.

Such questions form the basis of this textbook. A brief look at the table of contents in this book – economics – raises obvious questions: "How can we make the best economic choices?" "Who benefits from the free market economy?" More general questions follow on their heels: "How do we decide what to buy?" "What is the right price?" "How does a nation decide what and how much to produce?" For a study of economics these questions are key.

Essential *vs.* Basic Questions In what senses are these questions "essential"? An Essential Question is different from many of the questions teachers typically ask students in class. The most commonly asked questions in school are what may be called basic or factual questions—questions that seek or underscore a correct answer. There are definitive responses to basic questions, and they can typically be found in the textbook. There is nothing wrong with this type of question, of course. It just doesn't fit what we mean when we say: Let's consider the Essential Questions.

Essential Questions need to be asked and re-asked as we learn more–because our answers to such are always provisional. It is never clear how "free" the markets are or should be; it is never clear how much we should support or protect industries. These vital issues remain alive over days, months, and years, unlike simple or superficial queries. The key questions in economics are meant to be pondered and discussed as we go. The questions thus provide focus and a way to make sense of all that we learn in a good economics course.

Raising more questions *For what purpose does the government collect taxes?* is a "basic" question. *How can the taxation be fair, meeting the needs of government and the people?* is different. It is more conceptual than technical, and more a matter of judgment than of fact. Indeed, the more we consider the essential questions, the more questions we generate, and that makes learning more fun! *What are the needs of the people? What are the needs of the government? Who decides the needs? Who should be taxed and at what rates?* The questions deepen as well as broaden our inquiry as we read, and they inevitably raise more questions as the inquiry proceeds.

So it is with all essential questions. They don't seek a glib or thought-ending plausible answer. They properly raise *more* questions in our attempts to address them. They beg for inquiry; they rouse our minds to life.

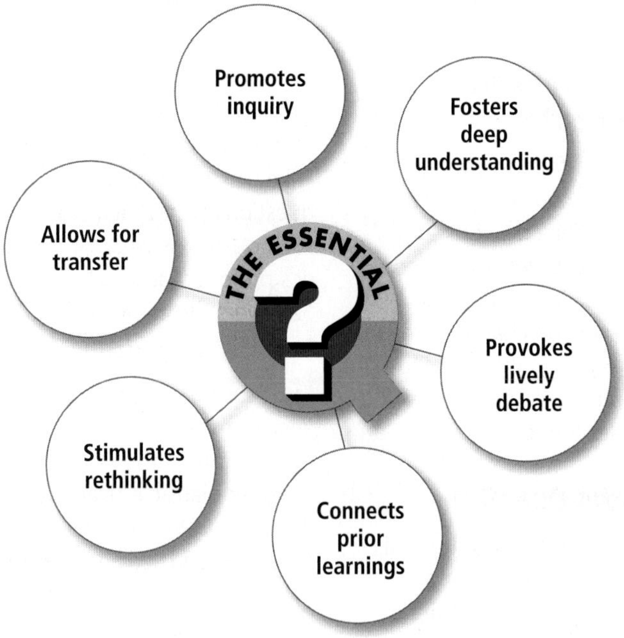

THE ESSENTIAL ?

Promotes inquiry

Fosters deep understanding

Provokes lively debate

Connects prior learnings

Stimulates rethinking

Allows for transfer

Essential Points

In my writing over the years with Jay McTighe for *Understanding by Design*, we remind readers that "essential" has a few different connotations:

- One meaning of "essential" involves **important questions that recur**. Such questions... are perpetually arguable...We may arrive at or be helped to grasp understandings for these questions but we soon learn that answers to them are invariably provisional. In other words, we are liable to change our minds in response to reflection and experience concerning such questions, and that such changes of mind are not only expected but beneficial. A good education is grounded in such life-long questions, even if we sometimes lose sight of them while focusing on content mastery. The big-idea questions signal that education is not just about learning "the answer" but about learning how to learn.
- A second connotation for "essential" refers to **key inquiries within a discipline**. Essential questions in this sense are those that economists and policy-makers are constantly asking. They are historically important, and very much "alive" in the field...
- There is a third important connotation for the term "essential" that refers to what is needed for **learning core content**. In this sense, a question can be considered essential when it helps students make sense of important but complicated and confusing ideas – findings that may be understood by experts, but not yet grasped or seen as valuable by the learner...By actively exploring such questions, the learner is helped to arrive at important understandings as well as greater coherence in their content knowledge and skill.

We summarized by saying a question is essential if it meets the following criteria:

To what extent is the question meant to—

- cause genuine and relevant inquiry into the big ideas and core content?
- provoke deep thought, lively discussion, sustained inquiry, and new understanding as well as more questions?
- require students to consider alternatives, weigh evidence, support their ideas, and justify their answers?
- stimulate vital, ongoing rethinking of big ideas, assumptions, and prior lessons?
- spark meaningful connections with prior learning and personal experiences?
- naturally recur, creating opportunities for transfer to other situations and subjects?

From Understanding by Design, 2nd Ed. by Wiggins & McTighe. © 2005 by Association for Supervision of Curriculum Development (ASCD), Alexandria, VA, p. 110.

How do Essential Questions frame *Prentice Hall Economics*?

Essential Questions provide the *framework* and core content of our economics course. *Prentice Hall Economics* presents Essential Questions at the unit and chapter levels. Questions are scaffolded, with section focus questions acting as building blocks to help students answer the chapter-level essential questions. Taken together, the thinking students do about the chapter-level questions will help them answer the unit-level question.

Working with Essential Questions

For Teachers You will of course be teaching and clarifying content and in so doing, addressing basic questions of fact. But to help student understand the implications of what they are learning and make the subject their own, you will also be constantly posing Essential Questions. An Essential Question is more of a "why?" or "so what?" or "where?" question. We are not looking for a definitive answer; we are inviting inquiry and discussion in ways that make abstract ideas real for students.

An Essential Question sometimes confuses students who are used to a steady diet of factual questions. The Essential Question is supposed to slow students down, make them stop and think! It invites more questions. Students thus learn that they must be active learners. The more we re-ask the Essential Questions and encourage students to do so also, the more it demonstrates that we all learn from reconsidering the same important questions as we read, discuss, experience, and reflect further. That's what keeps Essential Questions alive. That's what this book is designed to help you accomplish.

Your challenge is to make this shift in purpose clear to students – that the goal of the text reading and the activities is to pursue important questions. A key instructional goal in working with essential questions is to coach students in how to address such questions without trying to "guess the teacher's preferred answer" or giving up in despair. The "answers" to the Essential Questions will not be found "in the text" but "in our heads."

For Students Since there is not a single correct answer to complex questions, students need to think carefully and critically. They will have to consider plausible rival answers. They will see the need to become investigators, asking further questions and seeking information that will help them better understand and address an Essential Question. This work has great practical value. Students will be developing the skills commonly tested on high-stakes exams, such as analysis, comparison, making arguments backed up by evidence, and synthesis. By learning to take notes on the questions and their implications, and by being assessed on their growing sophistication in addressing the questions, students will be far better prepared for college.

Long-term Goal A key long-term purpose of the Essential Question is to make the question the student's own. As teachers, you ask Essential Questions repeatedly and build activities and assessments around them to cause transfer. You succeed in the long term, only if and when the Essential Questions are persistently and confidently asked and pursued by students on their own, without your prompts.

What Is Understanding by Design?

This approach to organizing instruction around an essential question is a centerpiece of a more general and comprehensive approach to planning entitled Understanding by Design. As the title suggests, the two big ideas in Understanding by Design are: aim for understanding, not "coverage"; and aim at understanding by design—in other words, by deliberately crafting assessments and activities "backward" from the goal of understanding, not content recall, to make understanding more likely. In short, content mastery is the means, not the long-term goal of education. The point of education is to learn to use content wisely (transfer) and to be able to make sense of new tasks, situations, and texts on one's own. So, you must design backward from such transfer and sense-making, or it will only happen "by good fortune," not "by design."

It's really about common sense, then. If you want students to end up asking the Essential Questions on their own, then your courses have to be designed "backward" from that goal, using this text as a resource. Along the way in *Prentice Hall Economics*, teachers are expected to help students develop skills and strategies for analyzing economics. But those are the *short-term goals. The point of economic literacy is not to learn abstract economic principles, but to have a better understanding of the forces that affect them every day.* The value of economic understanding is in helping people comprehend the modern world and to identify and evaluate the consequences of individual decisions and public policies. That understanding begins with questioning. So, you have to plan to meet this more challenging, *long-term* goal from the start. If you want students to learn from their economic reading, your methods have to foster that inquiry and meaning-making, and make it clear that success in economics requires it. If you aim to have students ponder the Essential Questions and transfer their prior thinking to new texts and discussions, then the course has to be planned to make that happen. So, in Understanding by Design, there is a deliberate process for achieving long-term understanding goals.

Assessment of Essential Questions A key to "backward" design: Make sure your assessments reflect the long-term goal of understanding. So, design your assessments before designing your lessons. This is easily done: Make the Essential Questions central to the assessments. "Is it going to be on the test?" This classic question signals, in no uncertain terms, that you had best practice what you preach, or the Essential Questions will be lost. But it must be done. The mantra in UbD is: If you value it, assess it. If you don't assess it, then you really don't value it. More practically, the kinds of essays, oral presentations, and Socratic seminars with scoring rubrics implied in such a call for higher-order assessment based on Essential Questions is what occurs in every good college in America.

Application in the Classroom

Types of Knowledge	Acquisition of Organized Knowledge	Development of Intellectual Skills	Increased Understanding of Ideas and Values
Teaching Style	Didactic Instruction	Coaching, Exercises, and Supervised Practice	Socratic Questioning and Active Participation

In a Nutshell

1. Understanding by Design is a way of thinking purposefully about curricular planning, a set of helpful design tools, and design standards – not a rigid program or recipe.
2. The end goal of Understanding by Design is student understanding and the ability to transfer learnings – to enable learners to connect, make meaning of, and effectively use discrete knowledge and skills.
3. Evidence of understanding is revealed through performance – when learners transfer knowledge and skills effectively, in varied realistic situations, using one or more "facets"of understanding (explain, interpret, apply, shift perspective, empathize, and self-assess), with minimal scaffolding and prompting.
4. Educators are coaches of understanding, not mere purveyors of content or activity.
5. Planning is best done "backward" from the desired results and the transfer tasks that embody the goals. The 3 Stages (Desired Results, Assessment, Learning Plan) must all align for the unit to be valid and potentially effective.
6. Understanding by Design "unpacks" and transforms content standards into focused learning targets based on "big ideas" and transfer tasks, as well as knowledge and skill.

Backward Planning

As teachers plan their lessons, they are guided by various standards (national, state, etc.) which specify what content students are expected to know and what skills they are to develop. These standards are the framework of the course. Along with the standards, teachers consider the various needs, learning styles, and ability levels of their students. These all figure into class preparation.

Backward design focuses on the desired results first. Then it determines how students will demonstrate their learning. And lastly, it plans instructional activities that will enable students to be successful. "All the methods and materials we use are shaped by a clear conception of the vision of desired results. That means we should be able to state with clarity what the student should understand and be able to do as a result of any plan..." [From *Understanding by Design,* 2nd ed. by Wiggins & McTighe. © 2005 by Association for Supervision of Curriculum Development (ASCD), Alexandria, VA, p.14]. Begin with the end in mind.

Tools to Succeed

Essential Questions are at the core of a model economics course. The challenge is to make this fact clear to students – that a major goal of information gathering is to pursue important questions. The questions are the purpose and rationale for learning. The text and activities are the vehicles to gain insight into these questions.

Prentice Hall Economics has been designed to help you make this aim and framework more transparent. The text and features are organized around the questions. The questions can and do recur, and the assessment requires the student to respond to these questions often and to improve in their response over time. The Understanding by Design template focuses lessons on the Essential Questions. The alignment of assessment, learning activities, and goals is at the core of the organization of this program. The template on the next page shows how you can focus instruction and assessment.

Students are challenged to answer the Essential Questions and are given the tools needed to do so. The Section Guiding questions break down the larger question, providing students with scaffolded support. The Chapter Assessment Activity requires students to transfer learning to authentic tasks. The Essential Question Journal gives students guidelines to explore the Essential Questions, making them more accessible and manageable.

Circumstances always change and students need to prepare to deal with the unexpected and the unfamiliar. This program is designed to have students transfer skills and knowledge beyond the classroom.

Stages of Backward Planning

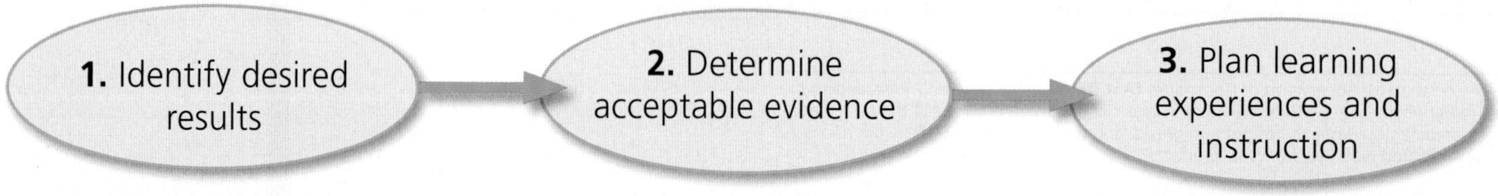

1. Identify desired results → **2.** Determine acceptable evidence → **3.** Plan learning experiences and instruction

Backward Planning Template

STAGE 1

Begin with the end in mind by identifying what students should know, understand and be able to do.

- Long-term transfer goals, content standards, program objectives
- Enduring understandings
- Essential Questions (EQ)
- Enabling knowledge and skills

Identify the "big ideas" you want students to explore. These will be transformed into understandings and Essential Questions on the template.

STAGE 2

Determine needed evidence for the targeted knowledge, skill and understanding in Stage 1, including:

- Performance task(s) involving transfer
- Other assessment evidence
- Rubrics as needed for performance task(s) and other open-ended assessments (e.g., writing prompt)

Strive to make the performance task(s) authentic.

Label each assessment in terms of which Essential Questions it assesses.

Make sure that the rubrics focus on the most important traits related to the unit goals (Stage 1), not only on "surface features" (e.g., word count, neatness).

STAGE 3

Plan learning experiences and instruction that lead toward the desired understandings and transfer performances.

- Pre-assess to find out prior knowledge, skill levels, and misconceptions
- Balance acquisition, meaning-making, and transfer-focused activities.
- Use on-going (formative) assessments to check for understanding and make needed adjustments.

Use diagnostic assessments to check for skill levels and predictable performance errors.

Defining the Stages

STAGE 1 Identify desired results

1. The focus in STAGE 1 is "big ideas" and "transfer"–making sure that our learning goals are framed in terms of the important concepts, issues, themes, strategies, applications, etc. that are at the heart of learning for understanding.
2. A focus on understanding means that we must be mindful of potential student misunderstandings and typical transfer deficits. Establishing clear and explicit goals also means predicting the trouble spots that are likely to arise in teaching and assessing.
3. Resist making a long indiscriminate list of possible goals that are in any way related to the unit topic. Identify only those goals, knowledge, skills, understandings, and questions that you plan to assess in STAGE 2 and teach to in STAGE 3.
4. It is important to make explicit the transfer goal at the heart of the unit. "Transfer" refers to the ultimate desired accomplishment: what, in the end, should students be able to do with all this "content," on their own, if this is successful?

ESSENTIAL QUESTION EXAMPLE

Why does it matter how the economy is doing?

STAGE 2 Determine acceptable evidence

1. The focus in STAGE 2 is "valid evidence"—making sure that what we assess and how we assess follows logically from the STAGE 1 goal.
2. Assessing for understanding requires evidence of the student's ability to explain or interpret their learning—to "show their work" and to "justify" their performance and/or product with commentary.
3. Assessing for understanding also requires evidence of the student's ability to apply their learning in new, varied, and realistic situations.
4. These facets provide a helpful framework for building appropriate assessment tasks:
   - Explain: the student generalizes, makes connections, has a sound theory
   - Interpret: the student offers a plausible and supported account of text, data, experience
   - Apply: the student can transfer, adapt, adjust, address novel problems
   - Perspective: the student can see from different points of view
   - Empathy: the student can walk in the shoes of people
   - Self-understanding: the student can self-assess, see the limits of their understanding

APPLY EXAMPLE

What are the best ideas for reducing unemployment, inflation, and poverty? Do any of these ideas conflict with each other?

STAGE 3 Plan learning experiences and instruction

1. The focus in STAGE 3 is "aligned learning activities"—making sure that *what* we teach and *how* we teach follows logically from and aligns with the STAGE 1 goals.
2. Teaching for understanding requires that students be given many opportunities to draw inferences and make generalizations themselves (via a well-planned design and teacher support.)
3. The acronym WHERETO summarizes the key elements that should be found in the lesson plan:
   - Where: What is expected? Where are you going?
   - Hook: How do you hold student interest?
   - Equip: How do you equip students for expected performances?
   - Rethink: How will you help students rethink and revise?
   - Evaluate: How will students self-assess and self-adjust?
   - Tailor: How do you tailor learning to varied needs, interest, and styles?
   - Organize: How will you organize and sequence the learning?

SELF-ASSESS EXAMPLE

CHECKPOINT How does low unemployment lead to higher inflation?

Table of Contents

The Value of Differentiated Instruction

It's basic, but it's true–not all students learn in the same manner and not all students have the same academic background or abilities. The "one size fits all" approach has not been proven the most successful strategy. As educators, we need to respond to a variety of student learning styles, readiness levels, and interests by developing and using instructional strategies that address the needs of diverse learners.

Under the *No Child Left Behind* mandate, educators are required to work to close the achievement gap. All students are expected to master state academic standards. Our goal as teachers is to enable 100 percent of students to achieve success on the high-stakes assessment tests.

It is critical to properly match the difficulty level of tasks with the ability level of students. Giving students tasks that they perceive as too hard lowers their expectations of success. However, giving students assignments that they think are too easy undermines their feelings of competence. Therefore, it is important for a program to give teachers leveled activities that allow them to match tasks with the abilities of their individual students.

How Is Instruction Differentiated?

It is vital to determine the readiness, interests, and learning styles of all students. Diagnostic tests and assessments will help define the specific needs of students. Then once strengths and weaknesses are determined, you can differentiate curriculum through three facets.

Content

What students learn may be layered to fit their interests and talents. The level of concepts, generalizations, and skills students can acquire will often depend on the complexity of thinking skills required. All students must master the same standards, but depth of learning should be adjusted to meet the needs of diverse learners.

Process

The process of instruction involves differentiating learning activities and strategies. Content can be accessed, or processed, through a combination of methods, such as direct instruction, inquiry-based learning, cooperative learning, and information processing models. It can be done as a class, in groups or pairs, or individually.

Differentiating instruction is also an essential tool for adapting technology into classroom activities. Technology, such as online activities, can provide an ideal opportunity for engaging students. It also can be used to provide additional opportunities to access content. A complete social studies program makes content available in a variety of formats, including text, audio, visuals, and interactivities.

Product

In the end, what students produce demonstrates skills and concepts they have learned. When evaluating student understanding, once again, we cannot assume that "one size fits all." The style, depth, and complexity of the product varies to match ability levels and learning styles. Various methods of assessment–activities, portfolios, performance-based assessment, rubrics, as well as standard tests–can measure students' progress in ways that are fair to multiple styles of learners.

How Does This Improve Learning?

Differentiated instruction provides multiple paths for students to access, use, and transfer understanding of concepts. It integrates instructional strategies to meet the needs of a diverse population of students, and thereby enables all students to achieve success. By using differentiated instruction, we allow students to take more responsibility for learning and create a community of learners who cooperate and respect each other.

How Do We Implement Differentiated Instruction?

The mission of *Prentice Hall Economics* is to provide standards-based instruction in ways that allow all students to participate and to achieve. Our program provides options so that diverse learners meet established goals, using different content, processes, and products to get there. Our effective support helps you close the achievement gap.

Teaching Support Helps You Modify Instruction

The **Teacher's Edition** provides continuous professional development throughout the program, starting with strategies for specific populations at the beginning of this textbook.

The **Teacher's Edition** was designed to make it easy for teachers to modify instruction for diverse learners. Specific activities help you adapt instruction for individual students in five categories: less proficient readers, English language learners, advanced students, special needs, and basic (all) population. Resources are identified as being appropriate for use by each of these categories. All resources are also assigned a level–special needs, basic, all students, and advanced–so you know exactly how to assign tasks of appropriate difficulty.

> **L3** **Differentiate** Call on verbal and kinesthetic learners to team together to write and act out a skit demonstrating an example of elastic or inelastic demand. After they perform the skit, have the class determine which type of elasticity they demonstrated and what factor explains it.
>
> **L4** **Differentiate** Distribute the "Analyzing Elasticity of Demand" worksheet (Unit 2 All-in-One, p. 32) and have students complete the activity, then compare their elasticity of demand for several goods and services.

All-in-One Teaching Resources Everything you need to provide differentiated instruction for each lesson is provided in one convenient location. Leveled worksheets enable students of varying abilities to participate equally in the classroom discussion. Every worksheet for the basic population is paired with a lower-level worksheet; the topic and/or presentation is adapted to the ability of the student. In addition, there are activities to challenge the advanced students requiring more complexity or a higher level of critical thinking.

Varied Resources Address Different Populations

The program also delivers content through a wide variety of formats—including text, transparencies, video, and interactive activities—appealing to all of your students.

- **Guided Reading and Review Worksheets** are leveled to help students understand key concepts.
- **Vocabulary Worksheets** make content accessible to all students.
- **Simulation Activities** allows students of all abilities to transfer understanding.

Using technology as a tool to differentiate content enables students to access content in an engaging method. These include

- **Action Graphs** provide step-by-step animation of economic ideas.
- **Visual Glossary** offers an interactive look at economic concepts.
- **How the Economy Works** enriches economic theory with hands-on experience.
- **WebQuest** uses online research to explore the Essential Question.
- **Virtual Economics** provide NCEE lessons that appeal to different learning styles.

Leveled Assessments Give More Options

The program offers a variety of assessment methods. This allows you to choose the style and level of assessment to meet the needs of your students.

- **AYP Monitoring** provides diagnostic tests to determine student skills and readiness as well as leveled unit assessments to gain feedback on student understanding.
- **Exam*View*® Test Bank CD-ROM,** in English and Spanish, offers leveled tests and helps adapt tests to individual needs.
- **Rubrics** provide both students and teachers clear performance targets and criteria for evaluation.

Strategies for Specific Student Populations

Differentiated instruction can be fostered through modifying instruction to address individual needs. To increase student achievement, teachers can use strategies for specific student populations to offer specialized support. Lesson plans in this **Teacher's Edition** provide differentiated instruction strategies and suggest ancillary support such as the **Guided Reading and Review Worksheets**. The following pages provide general guidelines for modifying instruction for students with special needs, English language learners, less proficient students, and advanced learners.

SPECIAL NEEDS

Students with special education needs are a highly heterogeneous group of learners, presenting unique cognitive, behavioral, social, and physical needs. To help create a classroom culture that supports the participation and achievement of students with such needs, set clear expectations and provide reasonable choices for all students. Lessons should be planned with individual adaptations and modifications. Offer instructional activities that foster the development of relationships among students and between students and teachers.

Preteach

Preteaching helps prepare students for learning.

- Preteach critical social studies terms and high-use academic words using the Vocabulary worksheet and by reviewing the key terms in the side columns.
- Provide preferred seating in the front of the class, face-to-face talk for students who read lips, interpreters, or space for a guide dog as necessary.

Teach

Using a variety of approaches enhances lessons.

- Provide an overview of key ideas and concepts presented in the text using outlines, maps, or study guides.
- Present all ideas orally and visually, and when possible, incorporate tactile and kinesthetic experiences as well.
- Require students to demonstrate that they are listening and following along (e.g., taking notes, running a finger along the text).
- Incorporate active reading strategies (e.g., choral reading, paired reading) to assist in maintaining attention.
- Provide adaptive materials as appropriate (e.g., enlarged print, Braille edition, captions for the video program).
- Incorporate the same comprehension and learning strategies over time to allow for mastery.

Assess

Students need to know what is expected.

- Assess students' understanding by asking them to write questions about what they have learned, identify what they find unclear or confusing, or complete short quick-writes of the key points.
- When having students work in groups or pairs, set up procedures that maintain each student's accountability (e.g., students each having to write, draw, or state a response).
- Make sure that you have adequately scaffolded tasks for special needs students and equipped them with writing instruction and practice that builds the prerequisite skills.
- When appropriate, have students manage and chart their academic performance, homework and assignment completion, and behavior.
- Provide outlines of what is to be done, with suggested dates and timelines for project completion.

ENGLISH LANGUAGE LEARNERS

Students who are learning English are the fastest-growing segment of the school-age population. These students require frontloading, or preteaching, in order to grasp challenging literacy tasks, such as those encountered in a social studies textbook. Since English Language Learners may be approaching an assignment with limited background knowledge and weak English vocabulary, concentrate on activities that build strong conceptual and linguistic foundations, guide them through the text's organization, and model appropriate comprehension strategies. The following practices will support ELL students in making strides in their second-language literacy.

Preteach

English Language Learners require extra preparation.

- Introduce essential words in meaningful contexts, through simple sentences drawing on familiar issues, scenarios, and vocabulary. Ask students to write the definitions in their own words and then identify the words when they occur within the reading.
- Utilize realia and visuals (e.g., photographs, objects, color transparencies) to make the concepts less abstract.
- Lead a quick text prereading, or "text tour," focusing student attention on illustrations, titles and subtopics, and boldfaced words.
- Suggest students use the Economic Dictionary Online, which is presented in both English and Spanish.

Teach

Many of these techniques will benefit all learners.

- Get students physically involved with the page, using sticky notes or small pieces of cardboard to focus and guide their reading.
- Have students engage in repeated readings of the same brief passage to build word recognition, fluency, and reading rate.
- Praise students' efforts to experiment with new language in class, both in writing and in speaking.

Assess

Students will demonstrate learning in different ways.

- Ask students to demonstrate their understanding by drawing upon different language skills: formal and informal writing assignments, posters, small group tasks, and oral presentations.
- Make sure students understand assessment criteria in advance. Distribute rubrics provided in the **Assessment Rubrics**. Whenever possible, provide models of student work to emulate, along with an example of work that fails to meet the specified assessment criteria.

DIFFERENTIATED INSTRUCTION

LESS PROFICIENT READERS

Less proficient readers are individuals who begin the year one or more years below grade level yet do not qualify for special education services. They may or may not be English Language Learners. They may be under-prepared for the academic challenges due to difficulties with attention and memory, learning strategies, or vocabulary and reading fluency. It is especially important to engage these students in challenging lessons while incorporating support or instructional scaffolding to increase their likelihood of success.

Preteach

Preteaching helps build students' confidence.

- *For Difficulties With Attention and Memory:* Gain attention by requesting a simple physical response (e.g., "Everyone, eyes on me please."). Then keep the lesson pace brisk—a "perky not pokey" pace is helpful.
- *For Difficulties With Learning Strategies:* Clarify the rationale for learning a new strategy in terms the students value. Directly teach any requisite skills needed to perform the strategy.
- *For Difficulties With Vocabulary and Fluency:* Directly teach meanings of critical vocabulary required for full understanding of the lesson.

Name ____________ Class ____________ Date ____________

CHAPTER 2 SECTION 2 — GUIDED READING AND REVIEW

The Free Market 3

As You Read

As you read Section 2, supply information missing from the circular flow diagram in the spaces provided. Then apply your knowledge to the Guiding Question:

What are the characteristics of a free market economy?

1. ____________
2. ____________
3. ____________
4. ____________
5. ____________
6. ____________

Households pay firms for goods and services.

1\.
2\.
3\.
4\. ________ Market
5\. ________ Market
6\.

Households

Firms

Physical Flow

Monetary Flow

Firms pay households for land, labor, and capital.

Reviewing Key Terms

Match the terms with the descriptions. Write the letter of the correct answer in the blank provided.

_____ 7. struggle among producers for the dollars of consumers
_____ 8. expectation that encourages people to behave in a certain way
_____ 9. power of consumers to decide what gets produced
_____ 10. economic system whose advantages include economic sufficiency, freedom, and growth
_____ 11. concentration of productive efforts of individuals and firms on a limited number of activities

a. competition
b. free market economy
c. incentive
d. specialization
e. consumer sovereignty

61

Teach

Lessons have to address specific, different needs.

- *For Difficulties With Attention and Memory:* Emphasize connections between new and known information. Engage students in collaborative "read/reflect/discuss/note" cycle, filling out a graphic organizer in the section opener.
- *For Difficulties With Learning Strategies:* Explicitly model the use of the strategy, including a significant focus on thinking aloud during the execution of each step in the strategy. Discuss where else in or out of school students could use the strategy.
- *For Difficulties With Vocabulary and Fluency:* Intentionally revisit newly acquired vocabulary during discussion. Suggest that students use the Visual Glossary Online and the Economic Dictionary Online.

Assess

Assessment must accommodate special needs.

- *For Difficulties With Attention and Memory:* Ask students to reorganize, prioritize, and otherwise reflect on the key aspects of the lesson. Have them explain their graphic organizers to a partner. Monitor and reteach as necessary.
- *For Difficulties With Learning Strategies:* Include explicit use of strategies taught as part of the quiz, report, project, and other formal assessments.
- *For Difficulties With Vocabulary and Fluency:* Randomly call on students to provide examples of the vocabulary word under examination.

ADVANCED LEARNERS

Advanced Learners need modified instruction to achieve their highest potential. They tend to understand complex concepts quickly, learn more rapidly and in greater depth, and may have interests that are different from their peers. Teachers can modify pacing and offer enrichment to allow for exploring topics in-depth, manipulating ideas in novel ways, and making connections to other disciplines.

Preteach

These students may have extensive background.

- Before beginning a new unit, have students write, verbalize, or draw what they know about the topic and present this information to peers.
- Ask students to brainstorm what they'd like to learn, and then work with them to create a plan for advanced study based on their interests.

Teach

Activate students' ability to think creatively and see connections.

- Help students adjust the pace of their learning, speeding through concepts they master quickly or slowing down to study content in depth. The **Teacher's Edition** provides ideas for ways to extend content in the Extend part of the lesson plan.
- Challenge students to tackle more complex topics and offer frequent opportunities to focus on abstract ideas.
- Provide opportunities for in-depth research on student-directed topics. Have students explore topics on the Internet under your direction.
- Encourage students to make connections between content they are learning and other disciplines such as language arts, science, and math. For example, students might want to read about the impact of technology on the economic concept they are studying.

Assess

Assessment can take many forms.

- Give students responsibility for part of the assessment of their learning. Allow them to plan, design, and monitor the project or assignment.
- Encourage students to apply standards-based understanding to new situations. Challenge them to take information and use it in novel ways.

Strategies to Engage All Learners

All students may benefit from strategies that we often consider "differentiation." While these strategies are necessary for success with students with special needs, they also aid many on-level students who are kinesthetic or visual learners, or those who struggle with organization. Here are some tips to keep in mind as you plan.

- **Clarify behavioral expectations** for the lesson. Use rubrics and work with students to create rubrics for class activities and projects. Modeling what students are to do or providing students with examples of finished products are necessary for student success. Explicit instructions do not water down the curriculum; they make it clear so that all students can access it.
- **Use visuals throughout the lesson.** Outlining key ideas, writing key phrases and vocabulary on the overhead projector or board, or putting notes on the overhead projector or board, are critical supports for many students. You may want to provide some students with a copy of your overheads or notes ahead of time so that they can follow along. For other students, make a partial or blank copy of the graphic or outline you will be using and require students to write in key information as it is discussed. It is very helpful if you model this filling-in procedure for students. It also helps them to overcome problems with spelling or capturing complex ideas using only a few words.
- **Explicitly teach skills.** Model note taking as you present information to the classroom. Collect and review the students' notes and provide suggestions for improvement. Teach study skills, listening skills, and reading skills along with the content.
- **Incorporate active reading strategies.** Build vocabulary by teaching the meaning of prefixes and suffixes. Have students make study cards of unfamiliar words. Have students read and summarize the paragraph in their own words. Monitor their work to clarify any misunderstandings.
- **Use a variety of strategies to teach and assess understanding.** Present ideas orally and visually, and when possible, incorporate tactile and kinesthetic experiences. Think beyond the common modes of reading and writing. Students could present information orally, create a poster or visual representation of a work, tape-record their ideas, or act out their understanding. These activities take into consideration multiple intelligences and can provide access for all learners in the classroom.
- **Assist in time management.** When requiring students to complete projects or long-term assignments, provide a calendar that breaks down the requirements by due dates. Go over the checklist with students and monitor their use of the checklist and task completion as the assignment proceeds. Many students will experience significant difficulties in self-managing the time needed to complete complex and long-term assignments.
- **Incorporate students' strengths and interests** to connect them to content and activities.

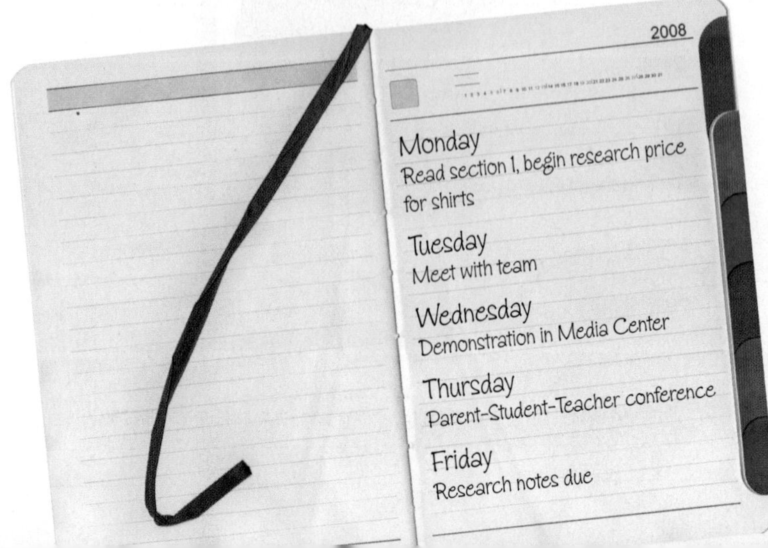

2008
Monday
Read section 1, begin research price for shirts
Tuesday
Meet with team
Wednesday
Demonstration in Media Center
Thursday
Parent-Student-Teacher conference
Friday
Research notes due

CLASSROOM MANAGEMENT

Creating a positive learning environment enables all students reach their full potential. In a supportive, respectful setting, students perform and behave better. Teachers who use effective motivational and management strategies that actively engage students and appeal to individual learning styles and needs create classrooms that enhance students' academic and personal lives.

The following are some tips for classroom management.

- **Make learning relevant.** Help students make connections between their own lives and the classroom content. Ask students to list questions about the topic that they would like to learn about. Allow students to extend the lesson by exploring subtopics of their choice. Use the Essential Questions Journal to enable students to demonstrate understanding in their own words and through their own experiences.
- **Be organized—and help students be organized.** Many students have difficulty organizing their time. Break down assignments into short tasks. Require students to submit a plan for completing a large project. Teach skills such as notebook organization. Hand out assignment sheets ahead of time, allowing students to organize their time for the upcoming week or unit. Keep a master notebook with class notes, handouts, and homework that students may consult if they miss a day of class.
- **Have students begin work in class.** Prior to class dismissal, check to ensure that each student has a good start and understands what is expected.
- **Provide time for students to collect their thoughts.** This gives more reflective learners time to consider the answer. Explain this procedure to the class before using it. Tell students the questions that you will be asking during tomorrow's class in order to give them time overnight to prepare their responses.
- **Use an instructional warmup activity.** Use the bellringers to grab students attention and immediately engage them in a task.
- **Use group activities.** Collaborative work encourages students to be supportive of each other, creating positive interdependence. Explain the task clearly. Teach collaborative skills (such as problem solving, time management, accepting criticism).
- **Use peer tutoring.** This technique helps teachers accommodate academic diversity. All students can be actively involved in tasks they can perform successfully. Students work in pairs to assist each other in learning, which leads to improved self-esteem, personal interaction, and positive attitudes about school. Steps for using this strategy are on the next page.

Chapter 9 • Section 2

BELLRINGER

On the chalkboard, write down the amount paid per year to a current major league baseball player, a brain surgeon, and a day care worker. Ask students to react to the figures and think about what causes the difference and if the difference is fair. Ask them to think of it in terms of what factors affect wages.

DIFFERENTIATED INSTRUCTION

DISCUSSION STRATEGIES

Simple structures for discussion can help students extract and process meaning from reading the text. These strategies guide students to a more productive and inclusive class discussion while enabling students to "take ownership" of the information.

Strategy: Idea Wave Discussion

Purpose: To support all students in actively listening and responding academically to a critical question within a more elaborate unified-class discussion.

How to do it:

1. Pose an open-ended question or task *(e.g., What factors affect price?)*.
2. Provide a model response on the board *(e.g., Price is affected by supply and demand.)*.
3. Give students time to consider what they know about the topic and record a number of responses.

   L2 **Differentiate** Provide two or three sentence starters and ask students to write one or two of their ideas using a sentence starter. These starters should include key academic vocabulary and sentence structures that students wouldn't ordinarily use in casual conversation *(e.g., Price may change when demand increases because...)*.
4. As students jot down ideas, pick volunteers to jumpstart the subsequent class discussion.

   L2 **Differentiate** Get a few answers from students who wouldn't ordinarily respond voluntarily and bolster their confidence by affirming their idea prior to the actual discussion.

   L2 **Differentiate** Read aloud your model response and have students read along with you a second time to build reading fluency.
5. Have students share their responses with a partner to build confidence and accountability to respond, even if all students do not participate in the class discussion.
6. Move around the class in a fast-paced, but structured manner (e.g., down rows, around tables).

   L4 **Differentiate** After this structured debriefing, call on a few volunteers who have additional answers.
7. Provide an active listening and note taking task during the discussion. Ask students to jot down two ideas, such as two perspectives with which you agree, two additional examples, etc.
8. If there tends to be repetition in responses, ask student to point out similarities rather than stating that their idea has already been mentioned. Require that students use language for acknowledging other ideas *(e.g., My idea builds upon _____'s idea. I also believe that...)*.

Strategy: Think-Write-Pair-Share

Purpose: To engage students in responding to instruction.

How to do it:

1. **Think** Students listen while the teacher poses a question or task related to the reading or classroom discussion. The level of questions should vary from lower level literal to higher order inferential or analytical.

   L1 L2 ELL **Differentiate** Write questions on the board or provide them on a piece of paper.
2. **Write** Provide quiet thinking or writing time for students to deal with the question and go back to the text or review notes. Have students record their ideas in their notebooks.

   L1 L2 **Differentiate** Consider providing academic sentence starters for students to complete as a means of encouraging more thoughtful and formal responses.
3. **Pair/Share** Cue students to find a partner and share their written response, noting similarities and differences. Teach students to encourage one another to clarify and justify their responses. To add more accountability for active listening, ask students to share their partner's idea during the structured debriefing and require that they begin their response with a citation expression *(e.g., My partner pointed out / emphasized / predicted that ...)*.
4. Randomly call on students to share during a class discussion after they have rehearsed answers with their partners.

5. Invite volunteers to contribute additional ideas and points of view to the discussion after calling on a reasonable number of students.
6. Direct students to go back to their notes and add any important information garnered during the partner and class discussions.

Strategy: Numbered Heads

Purpose: To engage all students in responding to questions in order to assess reading comprehension and content understanding.

How to do it:

1. Seat students in groups of four and number off one through four.
2. After asking a question or assigning a task, give students a specified amount of time to discuss a response. This time should generally be no longer than ninety seconds to prevent students from wandering off task.
3. Remind students to pay attention to each member of the group because only one member will be chosen to represent the group's ideas.
4. Call a number, one through four, and ask students with that number to raise their hands to respond in a whole-class discussion.
5. Add comments, extend key ideas, ask follow-up questions, and make connections between students' comments. If you have a classroom with native English speakers and English language learners, you may ask an English speaker to take notes on the board as the discussion progresses, using key words and ideas.
6. Finish up by asking students to write a two-to-four sentence summary of the discussion and have a few students read their summaries out loud.

Strategy: Click and Clunk

Purpose: To gauge student understanding of a reading selection or course content.

How to do it:

1. After students have read a selection or finished covering a topic in class, ask students to write down one or two pieces of information or ideas that "clicked," meaning that students feel that they understand well.
2. Then have them write down one or two pieces of information or ideas that "clunked," meaning they did not understand them.
3. Rotate around the room, asking students to list their "clicks" and "clunks." Use the information to guide your follow-up lessons, skipping information that students already understand and spending more time with the information they do not understand. Alternatively, you may collect their lists to read after class.

Strategy: Peer Tutoring and Peer Feedback

Purpose: To pair students of the same or different abilities to help learn or practice educational tasks.

How to do it:

1. Give students directions and model appropriate methods of how to assist each other. List the do's and don'ts of helping someone with the work.
2. Pair students. Match students based on need and personality, or on ability. Students may alternate roles as tutor/tutee or the more advanced student may be assigned the tutor role to a struggling student. As the curriculum progresses, you may want to change the pairing.
3. Clearly define the objectives of peer tutoring. Give a specific assignment or task to work on. These tasks supplement classroom instruction; they do not teach new material or skills.

4. The tutor should give immediate corrective feedback. Students should be reminded that the feedback should be constructive and positive.
5. Monitor the tutoring process to be sure students stay on task and assess student learning. Walk around the room and engage students frequently.
6. Ask students for feedback about the process. Checklists or self-reporting forms can give students opportunities to discuss the experience. Formal assessments can also provide evaluation of achievement.

Strategy: Socratic Discussion

Purpose: To encourage students to come to a consensus about ideas through structured discussion.

How to do it:

1. Pose a question to the class. Emphasize that the class will try to reach a consensus (agreement) about the answer. If they can not come to agreement, they will still try to come to a deeper understanding together. Some questions to start a discussion may be
   - What assumptions does the author make?
   - How does this connect to other things that we have learned?
   - What is the significance of the article?
2. Establish rules for the discussion
   - Students must focus on ideas.
   - Information from readings and class materials must be used to substantiate claims. Every opinion needs proof.
   - Students may not disagree with one another. Instead, they must find something to build on or ask for clarification on a point.
   - Students should take notes so when it is their turn to speak, they can comment accurately on the statements from which they would like to build.
3. Discuss. As much as possible, allow the discussion to be student-directed. Do not act as a participant. You may also consider a system for ensuring that all students participate. For example, you may give each student three paperclips to throw in a bucket when they contribute. A rule may be that everyone must contribute once before anyone may contribute three times.
4. Debrief. Following a Socratic discussion, it is important to have an open discussion afterward in which students may discuss what they found difficult about the exercise and how it made them think differently.

Note: When possible, it is beneficial to use a defined text, such as a primary source, as the basis for a discussion. They must, however, be given ample time to read and make notes about the text. When a text is the basis for a discussion, it is also important that students only discuss what is in that text, rather than bring in information they have learned in other settings.

Modifications: When a class is too large for a single discussion, break the class into two groups, with an inner and outer circle. Partners may then take turns participating in the discussion. The one in the outside circle should take notes about the comments the partner made. For example, "One interesting point was ____ because . . . " or "I'd like to know more about . . ." Alternatively, have two discussions, one following the other.

Strategy: Debate

Purpose: To help students learn to make arguments with strong points and counterpoints.

How to do it:

1. Present a question to students that can be logically answered several different ways. Whenever possible, debates should be based on readings rather than students' opinions alone.
2. Begin by assigning students to one of four groups: A1, A2, B1, or B2. Give each side its argument. Groups A1 and A2 will argue against groups B1 and B2. However, the groups will prepare differently. Hand out Debate Worksheet A.
3. Assign groups A1 and B1 to brainstorm and research the arguments FOR their positions and summarize them in a three-to-four sentence opening statement.
4. Assign groups A2 and B2 to brainstorm and research the arguments AGAINST their positions and come up with counter arguments to support their points.
5. Provide time for students to review sources and make notes on their own, then let each team (A and B) review their case as a group.

Worksheets like those below are available from the Online Teacher Center at **PearsonSuccessNet.com**

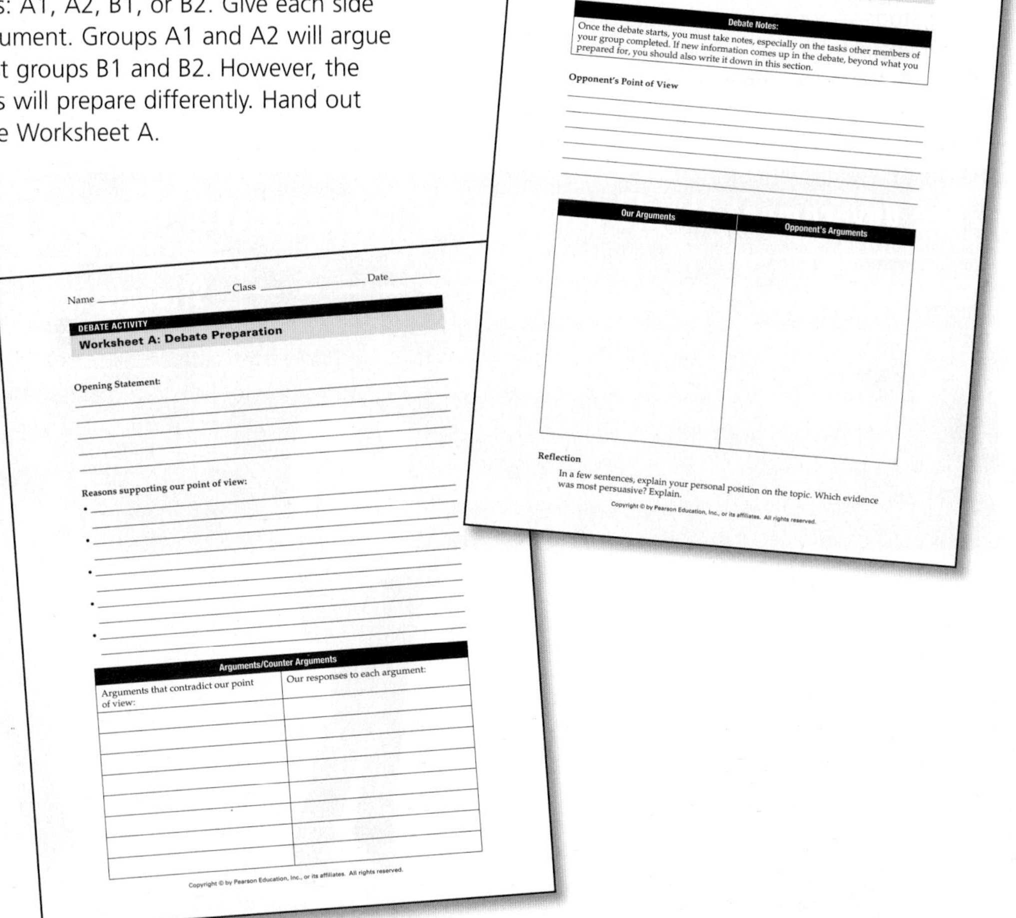

Name ____ Class ____ Date ____

DEBATE ACTIVITY

Worksheet A: Debate Preparation

Opening Statement:

Reasons supporting our point of view:

•
•
•
•
•

Arguments/Counter Arguments	
Arguments that contradict our point of view:	Our responses to each argument:

Name ____ Class ____ Date ____

DEBATE ACTIVITY

Worksheet B: During the Debate

Debate Notes:

Once the debate starts, you must take notes, especially on the tasks other members of your group completed. If new information comes up in the debate, beyond what you prepared for, you should also write it down in this section.

Opponent's Point of View

Our Arguments	Opponent's Arguments

Reflection

In a few sentences, explain your personal position on the topic. Which evidence was most persuasive? Explain.

MAKING CLASS FUN AND MEANINGFUL

Too often, students become bored and listless in the classroom. The chief culprits for this are lessons that are filled with routine, lecture, and/or content that matters little to them. Students who experience classes that are provocative and animated are more engaged with learning and are more motivated.

Here are some tips to manipulate the pace and rhythm of the class.

Strategy: Opinion Line

Purpose: To engage all students by making them active participants and able to defend their position on a given topic.

How to do it:

1. Ask students to write or think about their opinion on a topic that has answers at two extremes *(e.g., The government should use your tax money to help the poor.)*. Meanwhile, post the two extremes *(e.g., "Strongly agree" and "Strongly disagree")* at either end of the wall. If it makes sense, post "I don't know" or "neutral" in the middle.
2. After students write their answers, ask them to stand against the wall at the point where they think they stand in the opinion continuum.
3. Ask several students to explain their positions, either by choosing or asking for volunteers. Tell them that they may move if they are swayed by a classmate's argument.
4. Give students two minutes to revise their original opinion, allowing them to discuss their positions with each other and then repositioning themselves if necessary.
5. You may want to follow up by asking a question that invites students to explain their position or consider arguments made in the course of the activity.

Strategy: Jigsaw

Purpose: To allow students to cover one topic in-depth, becoming the instructors for the rest of the class, while allowing the class to cover large amounts of information.

How to do it:

1. When you have many topics to cover in a short period of time, divide the class into numbered groups *(e.g., 1, 2, 3, 4, . . .)* and assign each group a different topic *(e.g., Principles of Free Enterprise, Economic Growth and Stability, Technology and Productivity, Providing Public Goods)*. These may be referred to as "expert groups," as the members will become "experts" in their topics.
2. Give each group a task *(e.g., make a study guide, prepare a presentation)* that demands that they summarize the key points and significance of the topic. For classes with lower level students, you may consider giving students a worksheet on which they record important information.
3. Divide the class into new, lettered groups *(e.g., A, B, C, D. . .)* that include a member from each of the numbered groups *(e.g., group A has one member from group 1, one from group 2, and so on)*.
4. Assign the new groups a new task that requires them to teach each other the information they learned in their numbered group (*e.g., give a presentation*) or requires collaboration (*e.g., make a plan*).

Strategy: Conversation Wall

Purpose: To give students an opportunity to share ideas and reflect on the work of their classmates.

How to do it:

1. Post stimuli and "conversation boards" around the classroom. The stimuli may be student work (produced individually or in groups) or materials that are new to students, such as images or quotations written on poster board. The conversation boards are blank posters or sheets of paper. Alternatively, students may be given a few sticky notes for comments.
2. Give students a set amount of time to look at the stimuli posted around the room. Each activity should have a defined objective, such as, "comment on the poster that you think is most informative and explain why" or "comment on a quotation that makes you think about the content in a different way." When possible, relate the activity to the Essential Questions for the unit or chapter.
3. Remind students that they may react to another comment as well as a stimulus.
4. Assign several students or groups of students to look at the comments from each stimulus and summarize the "conversation."
5. Use the summaries to launch a class discussion about the content.

easier for me to keep track of what I spend money on.
Debit cards are often more convenient for consumers than paper checks. ...Banks offer debit cards both because consumers have come to expect them, and because debit card transactions can be less costly for banks to process than cash or check transactions.
Banks make more money if we use debit cards.
safer than cash— I can cancel card if lost.
doesn't matter to me; I can't afford much either way.
not true; I know just what I am spending.
The less cash that flows through our hands, the more intangible it becomes and the more we lose our sense of its real value...technology is simply making it easy not to count every dollar...
I agree. I don't realize how much I am spending when I use credit cards.

Developing Reading Skills

Due to the increased emphasis on reading required by the *No Child Left Behind* (NCLB) legislation, social studies teachers may be called on to help improve their students' reading skills. These skills are critical to prepare students for academic success. A teacher using a graph about exports and imports can teach math skills and economic concepts at the same time. The connection between reading and economics is especially important. Many state and local assessments require students to read and interpret informational texts. Therefore, social studies teachers may assist in raising scores by integrating reading instruction into their teaching of economics content.

How does *Prentice Hall Economics* Enhance Reading Skills?

Too often the text is too hard for some students, and far too easy for others. So educators "teach to the middle of the class," trying to keep everyone on board, but always worrying about all the students who are falling off both edges. By providing reading checks and differentiated instruction, *Prentice Hall Economics* helps all students access the material.

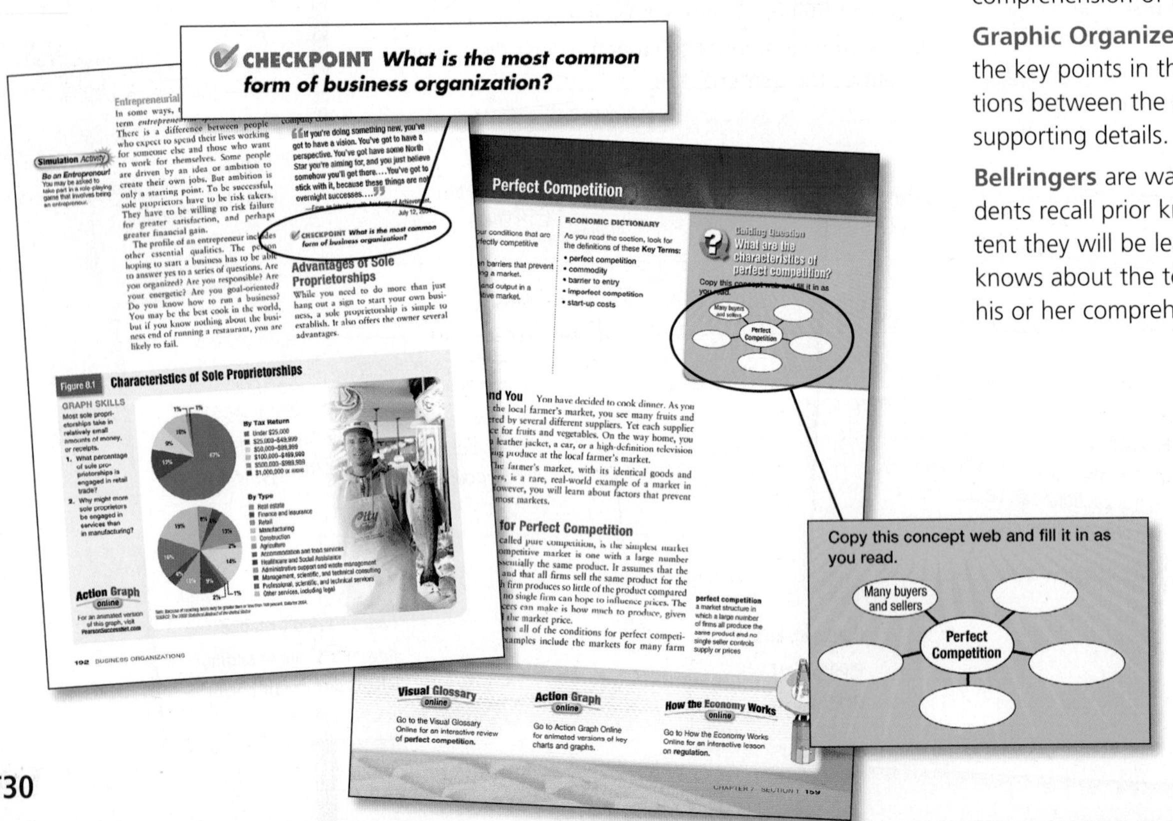

Differentiated Instruction helps meet the needs of students with reading difficulties or disabilities. By using strategies provided in the teacher lesson (such as scaffolding questions and allowing less proficient readers to answer first), students of all levels can access the material and fully participate in class discussions.

Guided Reading and Review worksheets are available for each section. These help both on-level and below-level students take notes on the material and can serve as a study guide to review and reinforce learning.

Visual Glossary provides students with an alternate method to access a key term. Using an interactive format, students explore the definitions of key terms and concepts.

Action Graphs present concepts in a step-by-step animated format, to break down graphs and make them easier to understand.

Vocabulary Worksheets teach students essential content terms they will need to understand and be able to use in reading, discussion, and writing tasks.

Reading Checkpoints help students monitor their comprehension of the text.

Graphic Organizers help struggling readers find the key points in the text and make visual connections between the section focus question and the supporting details.

Bellringers are warmup activities that help students recall prior knowledge or preview the content they will be learning about. The more a reader knows about the topic, context, or issue, the better his or her comprehension will be.

Developing Student Writing Skills

Teachers often assume that if they teach content effectively, their students will be able to communicate what they have learned in writing on state assessments. However, many student falter when asked to write because they don't know how to construct a response that shows what they have learned. Teachers can help students improve their performance by embedding expository writing tasks in class activities, homework assignments, and tests throughout the year.

Take time with students to work through the process of analyzing the task and framing their response. To be successful, students will need to learn how to analyze the prompt, budget their time and answer space, plan and write their response, and then edit their first drafts.

Good writing prompts are key to successful responses. A good prompt will

- test what students have been taught, whether defined by state standards or your own course outline
- communicate what is expected of students in terms of format, length, and level of detail, such as the number of examples or reasons and
- be doable in the time and space allocated for the task

A good prompt provides multiple access points to help students with different learning styles, backgrounds, and abilities engage with the task. This may be done by breaking the task into parts that build from lower- to higher-order thinking skills. This sequencing provides a point of entry for weaker students who may not be capable of completing the entire task and enables them to respond in a limited way.

Assessing the Product

The goal of a writing program should be to empower students to assess and improve their own work. For this to happen, students need to have a clear vision of what good writing looks like and how to bring their own work up to that standard.

An effective way to communicate your expectations is through the consistent use of generic rubrics and/or scoring guides. Generic rubrics describe levels of performance on various aspects of a written task, such as writing mechanics or development of a clear thesis statement. Scoring guides, in contrast, describe levels of performance for each specific task. Teachers can use both of these tools to communicate efficiently with students about their written work.

How Does *Prentice Hall Economics* Address Writing Skills?

Research shows that writing about what you read actually helps you learn new information. Economics provides continuous opportunities for students to prepare and practice writing skills.

Economics Writing Handbook teaches the steps and skills needed to write informative essays. The handbook addresses several categories of writing: Expository and Research Writings, Persuasive Essays, and Writing for Assessment. The Writing Handbook contains a Writing Rubric, for students to assess and improve upon their own work.

Document-Based Questions provided at the end of every chapter and unit give students practice in writing.

Assessment Rubrics found on the Online Teacher Center or the Teacher's Resource Library CD-ROM allow teachers to provide clear expectations and consistent grading.

Essential Questions Journal gives students opportunities to express their own opinions and personal experiences in essays addressing both chapter and unit level Essential Questions.

Lesson Activities often require students to use writing skills as they work on projects such as research papers or writing editorials or letters.

Supporting Media Literacy

> "We are drowning in information but starved for knowledge."
>
> —John Naisbitt, *Megatrends: Ten New Directions Tranforming Our Lives*

Defining Media Literacy

People define *media literacy* in many ways. Some educators understand it to mean teaching students how to use technology. Others see it as meaning teaching them how to evaluate the media. In fact, we need to teach students both the technical and the critical thinking aspects of media literacy in order to equip them with the 21st century skills they need to navigate today's electronic and media-rich era.

Teenagers are spending more time using a wider array of technologies than ever before. What are the challenges for teachers?

- How do we channel this familiarity and time spent with technology toward technology that teaches and informs as well as entertains?
- How do we ensure that we and our students are taking full advantage of the opportunities for learning that technology in the classroom can provide?
- How do we make sure that our students are critical consumers of the media that they are surrounded by on a daily basis?

Teaching With and About Technology

Studies indicate that students in "technology-rich environments" experience increased achievement in all major subject areas (Sivin-Kachela, 1998). By integrating technology into the classroom, teachers not only help students learn the critical tools they need to thrive in a digital age, they also enhance social studies content.

Technology provides easily accessible ways to both present core content and engage students. Audio and video bring dynamic moments to life. Primary sources provide the personal experience. The Internet unlocks a vast array of materials. Together, these materials make economics come alive in the classroom.

Teaching Critical Thinking About Media

Media can be a powerful tool not just to teach through technology, but also to teach critical thinking skills. Studies show that media literacy training increases students' ability to access, analyze, and evaluate media messages (Yates, 2001). Students need to learn to analyze what they see and hear as well as what they read. In a social studies course, sources include primary and secondary documents, quotations, political and economic cartoons, and news reports on television, the Internet, and in newspapers. These are ideal instruments for fostering 21st century skills for critical thinking, including

- comparing viewpoints
- identifying bias
- evaluating evidence
- interpreting cause and effect
- decision making

By embedding these media skills into your course, you not only enhance key concepts, but also teach students key analysis skills, many of which are tested on high-stakes exams and in document-based assessments. In addition, media-literate students will become more effective consumers, decision-makers, and citizens, able to succeed in the classroom and beyond.

Media Literacy Skills include the ability to

Access · *Analyze* · *Evaluate* · *Communicate*

INFORMATION

Media literacy is essential for students in today's classroom as well as in the world at large. *Prentice Hall Economics* supports media literacy in an exciting variety of ways, helping students at all levels become more active and engaged learners. Assets on the Online Teacher Center and Online Student Center and lesson extension ideas provide opportunities to integrate media literacy.

Access Content

Differentiated instruction is designed to help all students access content – no matter their level of ability or learning style. Technology is one method of information delivery that appeals to a variety of students through a variety of learning styles: visual/spatial, auditory/verbal, kinesthetic/body, and logical/mathematical. The program features downloadable multi-media assets for busy on-the-go learners and teachers.

- Student Edition Online (with English and Spanish audio)
- Visual Glossary
- Economic Dictionary (English and Spanish)
- Action Graphs
- How the Economy Works
- Color Transparencies

Enrich and Reinforce Learning

Authentic learning means students will be able to transfer knowledge to new situations. When students use and apply their understandings or further explore concepts, learning becomes more real. Using technology to extend the lesson reinforces learning and improves the retention level of students. These activities make economics more relevant and meaningful.

- WebQuest
- Essential Question Video
- *The Wall Street Journal* videos

Assessment

Monitoring comprehension can take form in multiple ways. For some, using the online format is more engaging and therefore gives more motivation to succeed.

- Know It? Show It Game
- Self-Test
- Academy 1-2-3 Math Skills
- Exam*View* Test Bank

For further information about these features, see the section on Assessment.

> **"Media literacy is...absolutely critical. It's going to make the difference between whether the kids are a tool of the mass media or whether the mass media is a tool for kids to use."**
>
> —Linda Ellerbee, producer/host, *Nick News*

The Need for Assessment

Why Do We Need To Assess Student Learning?

Assessment should be viewed as a process, not an activity, that quickly evaluates instruction or student learning. As such, the goal of assessment is to focus, guide, and support instruction and subsequently learning. When making an assessment, the teacher isn't just "testing," but rather making thoughtful observations about the student's strengths and weaknesses. It is not a value judgment (good/bad), but an analysis of student performance against specific goals and criteria. As a process, the goal of assessment is to assemble information from a variety of sources.

Assessment happens constantly, though you probably don't give a quiz every day. It takes a variety of formats. Traditional assessments focus on written work, such as essays. Performance assessments are geared toward students who prefer to show what they've learned in a less verbal or written format. Alternative assessments range from metacognitive activities, such as journals, to student-generated assessments, such as portfolios.

Formative Assessment

Formative assessment is self-assessment. It provides feedback to modify teaching and learning activities. Formative assessments are conducted throughout the instructional process to monitor students' progress and provide feedback on strengths and weaknesses. The key is feedback. Feedback allows students to correct conceptual errors and encourages instructors to modify their methods. It provides students with an understanding of what they are doing well, links to classroom learning, and gives specific input to adjust the learning process.

Summative Assessment

Summative assessments are used to judge progress. They are meant to gauge student learning at particular points in time. Common summative assessments occur at the end of chapters or units or school terms to determine what students know and do not know. Like formative assessments, they reveal areas that need review before moving on to new topics.

Balancing Assessments

Proper utilization of assessment tools in the classroom will lead to greater learning. Incorporating a variety of assessments (both in format and product), observations, and communications with and between students allows for a more fully developed picture of your students' learning process. The more information you have about your students, the better you can determine teaching effectiveness and the quality of student learning.

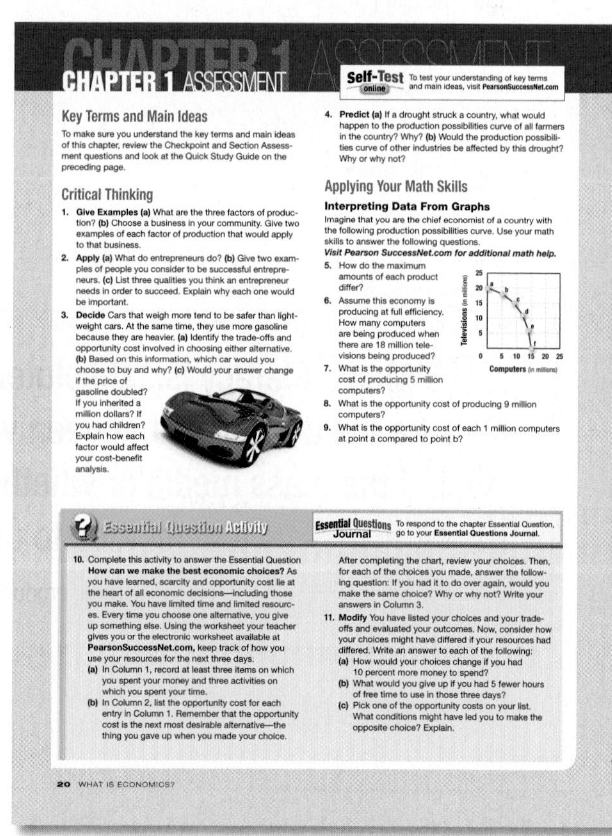

CHAPTER 1 ASSESSMENT

Self-Test online To test your understanding of key terms and main ideas, visit **PearsonSuccessNet.com**

Key Terms and Main Ideas

To make sure you understand the key terms and main ideas of this chapter, review the Checkpoint and Section Assessment questions and look at the Quick Study Guide on the preceding page.

Critical Thinking

1. **Give Examples (a)** What are the three factors of production? **(b)** Choose a business in your community. Give two examples of each factor of production that would apply to that business.
2. **Apply (a)** What do entrepreneurs do? **(b)** Give two examples of people you consider to be successful entrepreneurs. **(c)** List three qualities you think an entrepreneur needs in order to succeed. Explain why each one would be important.
3. **Decide** Cars that weigh more tend to be safer than lightweight cars. At the same time, they use more gasoline because they are heavier. **(a)** Identify the trade-offs and opportunity cost involved in choosing either alternative. **(b)** Based on this information, which car would you choose to buy and why? **(c)** Would your answer change if the price of gasoline doubled? If you inherited a million dollars? If you had children? Explain how each factor would affect your cost-benefit analysis.
4. **Predict (a)** If a drought struck a country, what would happen to the production possibilities curve of all farmers in the country? Why? **(b)** Would the production possibilities curve of other industries be affected by this drought? Why or why not?

Applying Your Math Skills

Interpreting Data From Graphs

Imagine that you are the chief economist of a country with the following production possibilities curve. Use your math skills to answer the following questions.

Visit Pearson SuccessNet.com for additional math help.

5. How do the maximum amounts of each product differ?
6. Assume this economy is producing at full efficiency. How many computers are being produced when there are 18 million televisions being produced?
7. What is the opportunity cost of producing 5 million computers?
8. What is the opportunity cost of producing 9 million computers?
9. What is the opportunity cost of each 1 million computers at point a compared to point b?

Essential Question Activity

Essential Questions Journal To respond to the chapter Essential Question, go to your **Essential Questions Journal.**

10. Complete this activity to answer the Essential Question **How can we make the best economic choices?** As you have learned, scarcity and opportunity cost lie at the heart of all economic decisions—including those you make. You have limited time and limited resources. Every time you choose one alternative, you give up something else. Using the worksheet your teacher gives you or the electronic worksheet available at **PearsonSuccessNet.com,** keep track of how you use your resources for the next three days.
    - **(a)** In Column 1, record at least three items on which you spent your money and three activities on which you spent your time.
    - **(b)** In Column 2, list the opportunity cost for each entry in Column 1. Remember that the opportunity cost is the next most desirable alternative—the thing you gave up when you made your choice.

    After completing the chart, review your choices. Then, for each of the choices you made, answer the following question: If you had it to do over again, would you make the same choice? Why or why not? Write your answers in Column 3.
11. **Modify** You have listed your choices and your trade-offs and evaluated your outcomes. Now, consider how your choices might have differed if your resources had differed. Write an answer to each of the following:
    - **(a)** How would your choices change if you had 10 percent more money to spend?
    - **(b)** What would you give up if you had 5 fewer hours of free time to use in those three days?
    - **(c)** Pick one of the opportunity costs on your list. What conditions might have led you to make the opposite choice? Explain.

20 WHAT IS ECONOMICS?

Assessment Informs Instruction

Assessment is a never-ending cycle. With the spotlight now on improving student performance and providing differentiated instruction, it is essential to use assessment to target goals, identify strategies to achieve results, monitor progress, and assess results to inform lesson planning.

Using AYP Monitoring Assessments

The key to success is using a variety of assessment tools coupled with data analysis and decision making. The Adequate Yearly Progress Monitoring Assessments in this program provide four types of assessments.

Types of Assessment	AYP Monitoring Assessments
Screening assessments are brief procedures used to identify at-risk students who are not ready to work at grade level.	Screening tests identify students who are reading 2–3 years below grade level.
Diagnostic assessments provide a more in-depth analysis of strengths and weaknesses that can help teachers make instructional decisions and plan intervention strategies.	Diagnostic tests focus on social studies skills, including subtests in geographic literacy, visual analysis, critical thinking and reading, as well as vocabulary and writing.
Progress monitoring assessments (sometimes referred to as benchmark tests) provide an ongoing, longitudinal record of student achievement detailing individual student progress toward meeting end-of-year and end-of-schooling, grade level, district, or state standards.	Benchmark tests assess progress toward mastery of the National Council of Economic Education Standards, and offer remediation recommendations tied to specific program content for each question.
Summative assessments judge students' achievement at the end of a course of study. Large-scale assessments, such as state tests and standardized tests, can be used to determine whether individual students have met the expected standards and whether a school system has made adequate progress in improving its performance.	Outcome tests also test standards mastery.

Ongoing Assessment

Assessments may fall in either the formative or the summative category. However, depending on their use, these evaluations may provide information for both categories.

Formative Assessments

AYP Monitoring Assessments as previously described help you to understand where your students are in the learning process and to determine an effective strategy for moving them to the next stage.

Quizzes measure how students are progressing in their skills and understanding of subject matter. These provide snapshot assessments: What have students learned and what do you need to revisit? These quizzes can be found on the Online Teacher Center and the Teacher Resource Library CD-ROM as well as in the Exam*View* Test Bank.

Exam*View* Test Bank questions assess understanding and foster remediation by providing text page numbers for quick references to content.

SuccessTracker Assessment assigns content, tracks student progress to assess learning, and offers remediation.

Teacher's Edition includes remediation suggestions for section assessments to reteach key concepts to struggling students.

Section Wrap-Up Question requires students to apply the information they have learned to answer the section focus question.

Student Self-Assessments give students frequent and varied opportunities to check comprehension and reflect on learning. By taking advantage of these opportunities for personal peer feedback, students become aware of their strengths and weaknesses.

Rubrics enable students to evaluate their own work. *Assessment Rubrics* found on the Online Teacher Center and the Teacher's Resource Library CD-ROM includes reproducible rubrics for students and instructions for teacher rubric use.

Summative Assessment

Exam*View* Test Bank allows teachers to easily create tests from banks of thousands of questions, which can be sorted by difficulty levels to provide leveled quizzes and tests.

Essential Questions Journal provides students with the opportunity to examine and reflect upon what they have learned.

WebQuests encourage students to explore the Essential Questions using technology and the Internet. Students develop products that demonstrate their creativity and critical thinking processes.

Chapter and Unit Activities provide opportunities for students to transfer their learning and demonstrate their application of concepts to different situations.

Document-Based Assessments require students to synthesize information and draw conclusions. As they defend their positions, students demonstrate their critical thinking skills.

Rubrics can also be used as a summative evaluation of understanding.

AYP Monitoring Assessments test how well students have mastered the standards.

Encouraging Student Self-Assessment

As mentioned earlier, formative assessment is self-assessment. An important aspect of the philosophy of Understanding by Design instruction, as explained by Grant Wiggins, is the "need to help students self-monitor, self-assess, and self-adjust their work, individually and collectively, as the work progresses…self-understanding is arguably the most important facet of understanding for lifelong learning." [*Understanding by Design,* 2nd Ed. by Wiggins & McTighe. © 2005 by Association for Supervision of Curriculum Development (ASCD), Alexandria, VA.] Successful people take time to reflect on what they have accomplished and what needs to be adjusted as they work towards their goals. Students need to evaluate their own progress and accept responsibility to manage and adjust their own learning. As part of the educational process, teachers must help students understand the importance of and methods used to achieve such reflection and self-evaluation.

To Develop Self-Assessment General Strategies

- set aside a few minutes at the middle and end of the lesson to ask: What have we learned? What questions do you have about this?
- require that a self-assessment be attached to every formal product or performance.
- include a one-minute essay at the end of a class, in which students summarize the two or three main points and the questions that they still have.
- have students write their questions on an index card as homework. Then, in small groups, have them find the common issues and use these questions to begin class.

Checking Understanding

Students also should use the following checks of their understanding of skills and concepts offered by *Prentice Hall Economics* before moving on to the next topic.

Reading Checkpoints reinforce and confirm students' understanding.

Caption Questions enhance critical thinking skills and maximize the effectiveness of art, graphics, charts, and narrative.

Know It! Show It lets students assess their understanding of content and get instant feedback through an online quiz game.

Scaffolded Section Assessment questions ease students into the review,then challenge them with more advanced questions.

Quick Study Guide and Chapter Assessment enable students to check their understanding and prepare for test-taking success.

Rubrics enable students to judge their own work against desired criteria.

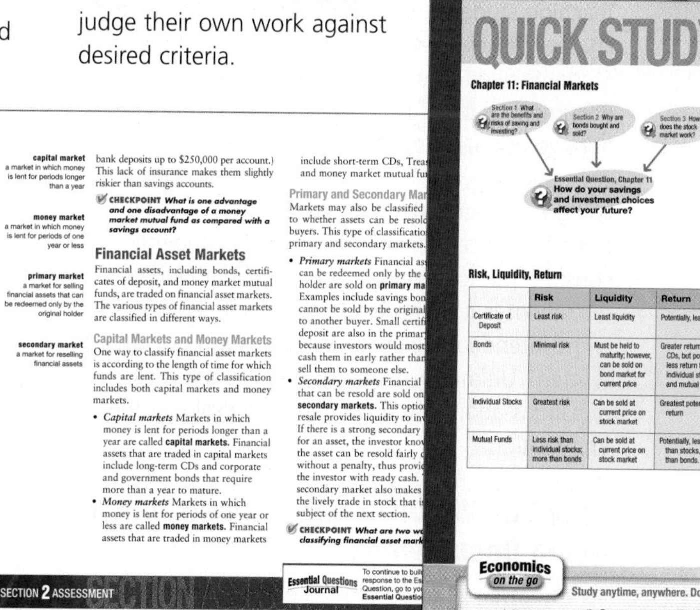

capital market a market in which money is lent for periods longer than a year

money market a market in which money is lent for periods of one year or less

primary market a market for selling financial assets that can be redeemed only by the original holder

secondary market a market for reselling financial assets

bank deposits up to $250,000 per account.) This lack of insurance makes them slightly riskier than savings accounts.

CHECKPOINT ***What is one advantage and one disadvantage of a money market mutual fund as compared with a savings account?***

Financial Asset Markets

Financial assets, including bonds, certificates of deposit, and money market mutual funds, are traded on financial asset markets. The various types of financial asset markets are classified in different ways.

Capital Markets and Money Markets

One way to classify financial asset markets is according to the length of time for which funds are lent. This type of classification includes both capital markets and money markets.

- *Capital markets* Markets in which money is lent for periods longer than a year are called **capital markets.** Financial assets that are traded in capital markets include long-term CDs and corporate and government bonds that require more than a year to mature.
- *Money markets* Markets in which money is lent for periods of one year or less are called **money markets.** Financial assets that are traded in money markets include short-term CDs, Treas and money market mutual fu

Primary and Secondary Mar

Markets may also be classified to whether assets can be resold buyers. This type of classificatio primary and secondary markets.

- *Primary markets* Financial as can be redeemed only by the holder are sold on **primary ma** Examples include savings bon cannot be sold by the original to another buyer. Small certif deposit are also in the primar because investors would most cash them in early rather than sell them to someone else.
- *Secondary markets* Financial that can be resold are sold on **secondary markets.** This optio resale provides liquidity to in If there is a strong secondary for an asset, the investor kno the asset can be resold fairly without a penalty, thus provi the investor with ready cash. secondary market also makes the lively trade in stock that i subject of the next section.

CHECKPOINT ***What are two w classifying financial asset mark***

SECTION 2 ASSESSMENT

Essential Questions Journal To continue to buil response to the Es Question, go to yo Essential Questio

Guiding Question

1. Use your completed chart to answer this question: Why are bonds bought and sold?
2. **Extension** Would you prefer to buy a savings bond or a junk bond? Explain your preference.

Key Terms and Main Ideas

3. Identify the three components of bonds.
4. Why does the United States government issue **savings bonds?**
5. What is the advantage of an **inflation-indexed bond?**
6. Name two advantages of bonds for their issuers.
7. What kinds of financial assets are sold on **secondary markets?**

Critical Thinking

8. **Interpret** When would it be a good investment to sell bonds at a discount from par?
9. **Explain (a)** How are bonds rated? **(b)** How do you think these ratings are helpful to investors?
10. **Contrast (a)** What kinds of financial assets are traded in capital markets? **(b)** How are these different from the financial assets traded in money markets?

Math Skills

11. Suppose that you buy a r bond for $200 with an an of 4 percent. How much you have earned when th reaches maturity in five y *Visit PearsonSuccessN additional math help.*

290 FINANCIAL MARKETS

QUICK STUDY GUIDE

Chapter 11: Financial Markets

Section 1 What are the benefits and risks of saving and investing?

Section 2 Why are bonds bought and sold?

Section 3 How does the stock market work?

Essential Question, Chapter 11
How do your savings and investment choices affect your future?

Risk, Liquidity, Return

	Risk	Liquidity	Return
Certificate of Deposit	Least risk	Least liquidity	Potentially, least return
Bonds	Minimal risk	Must be held to maturity; however, can be sold on bond market for current price	Greater return than CDs, but potentially less return than individual stocks and mutual funds.
Individual Stocks	Greatest risk	Can be sold at current price on stock market	Greatest potential return
Mutual Funds	Less risk than individual stocks; more than bonds	Can be sold at current price on stock market	Potentially, less return than stocks, more than bonds.

Economic Dictionary

investment, *p. 277*
financial system, *p. 278*
financial asset, *p. 278*
financial intermediary, *p. 279*
mutual fund, *p. 279*
hedge fund, *p. 279*
diversification, *p. 280*
portfolio, *p. 282*
prospectus, *p. 282*
return, *p. 282*
coupon rate, *p. 284*
maturity, *p. 284*
par value, *p. 285*
yield, *p. 285*
savings bond, *p. 287*
inflation-indexed bond, *p. 288*
municipal bond, *p. 288*
corporate bond, *p. 288*
junk bond, *p. 289*
capital market, *p. 290*
money market, *p. 290*
primary market, *p. 290*
secondary market, *p. 290*
share, *p. 291*
capital gain, *p. 293*
capital loss, *p. 293*
stock split, *p. 293*
stockbroker, *p. 293*
brokerage firm, *p. 293*
stock exchange, *p. 294*
futures, *p. 295*
options, *p. 295*
call option, *p. 295*
put option, *p. 295*
bull market, *p. 296*
bear market, *p. 296*
speculation, *p. 298*

Economics *on the go*

Study anytime, anywhere. Download these files today.

Economic Dictionary online — Vocabulary Support in English and Spanish
Audio Review online — Audio Study Guide in English and Spanish
Action Graph online — Animated Charts and Graphs
Visual Glossary online — Animated feature
How the Economy Works online — Animated feature

Download to your computer or mobile device at PearsonSuccessNet.com

CHAPTER 11 QUICK STUDY GUIDE 301

The Value of Document-Based Assessment

For years, teachers have understood the value of having students read and analyze primary source documents to acquire knowledge and develop critical thinking skills. Document analysis has become an important assessment tool as well. Both the College Board Advanced Placement examinations and many state-mandated tests use document-based questions. Many of these include a writing task in which students think critically about a variety of sources, form opinions guided by a prompt, and then present their analysis in an essay.

Primary sources are records produced at the time of the event or period that they describe, or soon thereafter. These sources may include written accounts, such as diaries, speeches, government records, law codes, and period cartoons and photographs. They are distinct from secondary sources, which are produced well after the events that they describe and interpret.

How Do We Teach With Primary Sources?

Teaching students to examine primary and secondary sources involves asking the right questions. Students need to understand the purpose of a document in order to analyze it. The first questions to ask are those for which students can find concrete answers. The answers to these questions will give students the information that forms a basis for critical thinking. From there, students can consider the following questions: What kind of document is it? Who wrote this document? Who is the intended audience? Why was this document written? Ultimately, students need to ask their own questions about the document and evaluate the information.

How Can We Differentiate Instruction Using Documents?

As you attempt to differentiate instruction for students' differing abilities and learning styles, you can use document analysis for small group or whole class discussion, individual written reports, in-class presentations, role-playing, or other instructional strategies. Students need direct instruction in using primary sources and conflicting interpretations, as well as repeated opportunities to practice these skills both in class and independently. Regardless of the strategy, teachers must generate one or two well-crafted questions about a document. This may be more difficult than it appears at first glance. The purpose of the questions is to help students find the kernel of information that the document offers. These questions can be used to spark a class discussion or as a focus for independent practice.

The documents can also be used to help students apply the concepts they are learning to new situations and to extend that learning beyond the textbook. The analysis of the documents can be a springboard to a plethora of activities, such as oral presentations in which students take a stand on an issue, writing persuasive letters to an editor, preparing posters to illustrate a point, and more.

What Skills Are Developed?

Working with primary sources will not only increase students' critical thinking skills and their appreciation of economic principles, but will also help to prepare them for the document-based questions on state and College Board examinations and reinforce the 21st century skills needed to become effective citizens. The skills students will develop include the following:

- applying information they have learned in their study of economics
- evaluating the reliability of sources
- identifying the point of view of those sources and determining bias
- identifying problems and considering alternative solutions
- considering issues from multiple perspectives
- building support for a viewpoint by choosing accurate, relevant evidence

CHAPTER 16 ASSESSMENT

DOCUMENT-BASED ASSESSMENT

Do bank mergers benefit or hurt the public?

identify point of view

Today, there are fewer than ha[...]e as there were 30 years ago. W[...] able for bank shareholders, ma[...]t be less beneficial to consumer[...]

Document A

"Since 1988, there have been more than 13,500 applications for the formation, acquisition, or merger of bank holding companies or state-member banks reviewed by the Federal Reserve Board. Over this time, 25 of these applications have been denied, with eight of those failing to obtain Board approval involving unsatisfactory consumer protection and community needs issues. The low incidence of applications that have not received regulatory approval may be due to the fact that institutions seeking to expand their operations are typically in sound financial and manage[...] Maintaining robust and competitive bankin[...] critical objective in the Federal Reserve's [...] applications."

—Sandra Braunstein, Federal Reserve Direc[...] Community Affairs, testimony before Co[...]

comprehension questions

Document B

VIGELAND: "I remember back in the mid-90's there were a whole lot of bank takeovers and I wonder if there was any research done on whether consumers profit when a smaller bank is taken over by a bigger one."

D'ARISTA: "Well, they may profit in terms of convenience. The larger bank may have more branches and more ATMs and things of this sort. My concern at this point is concentration. It makes it a lot easier for a bank to set terms that are really at variance with the needs of a community when they are the only large or dominant institution in an area."

—Tess Vigeland and Jane D'Arista, "What Bank Mergers Mean For You," Marketplace Morning Report, January 18, 2008

Document C

"There's been a big bank merger, sir, so you now have a joint checking account with a Mr. Slavomir Bezparyadok of Zagreb."

SOURCE: www.cartoonstock.com

media literacy

ANALYZING DOCUMENTS

Use your knowledge of opportunity costs and Documents A, B, and C to answer questions 1–3.

1. **Which of the following conclusions does Document A best support?**
   - **A.** The Federal Reserve has significantly limited the number of bank mergers.
   - **B.** Bank mergers generally do not affect the level of service customers receive.
   - **C.** Bank mergers benefit banks but do not benefit local communities.
   - **D.** The Federal Reserve has a definite set of standards for approving bank mergers.

2. **According to Document B, one major concern about bank mergers is the**
   - **A.** increased possibility of fraud.
   - **B.** reduced banking services.
   - **C.** higher bank fees.
   - **D.** possibility of monopoly.

3. **How would you describe the reaction of the bank customer in the cartoon?**
   - **A.** Worried that the bank merger will affect the quality of the service he receives
   - **B.** Confused because he does not know where Zagreb is
   - **C.** Angry because he is opposed to bank mergers
   - **D.** Interested in finding out more about the details of the merger

WRITING ABOUT ECONOMICS

critical thinking and writing skills

People disagree about whether the Federal Reserve has dc[...] enough to control bank mergers. Use the documents on th[...] page and on the Web site below to answer the question: ***Do bank mergers benefit or hurt the public?*** Use the sources to support your opinion.

In Partnership

THE WALL STREET JOURNAL. CLASSROOM EDITION

To read more about issues related to this topic, visit **PearsonSuccessNet.com**

transfer knowledge

Using Rubrics

Assessing a student's understanding and ability can't be a matter of right *vs.* wrong or simple checklists. You have to assess for how sophisticated or effective the work is; you have to consider to what extent a learning task was done well. So you need assessment guides—rubrics.

Scoring rubrics can be **holistic** (to provide a single overall impression of performance), or **analytic** (to permit separate descriptions and sub-scores for varied traits of performance). In either case, rubrics are most effective when they are accompanied by anchors or exemplars—examples or models of responses for each score point.

Rubrics provide teachers with a tool for increasing the validity and consistency of their assessment, and they provide students with clear performance targets, expectations about what is most important, and criteria for evaluating and improving their own work.

Perhaps the greatest advantage of rubrics lies in their capacity to clearly communicate "what quality looks like" to students. Then, learners better understand what they are aiming for and learn to self-assess and self-adjust accordingly. Good rubrics and clear samples completely demystify the goals, tasks, and scoring of work.

What Makes a Rubric Good?

The best rubrics

1. discriminate among performances validly, not arbitrarily – by the *central* features of performance, not by that which is easiest to score.
2. do not combine completely independent criteria in the same descriptors. To combine "very clear" and "very organized" in the same descriptor, for example, often creates a problem since a paper might be clear but not organized and vice versa; why give them the same score when the performance is so different?
3. are based on analysis of many specific work samples, of the widest possible range. In other words, all potential student performances should fit somewhere in the rubric.
4. rely on descriptive language—what quality or its absence looks like—as opposed to relying heavily on mere comparatives or value language (e.g. "not as thorough as," or "excellent product") to make the discrimination.
5. avoid making the lowest score points just sound bad. The lowest score should rather describe what novice performance looks like.
6. highlight the judging of the impact of performance—the effect or bottom-line success of the work, given the purpose—as opposed to over-rewarding just the processes, the content used, or a good-faith effort made. Ultimately, performance is about result—was the paper *persuasive*? the problem *solved*? the speech *informative*? etc. Make sure students understand the purpose of the task as reflected in appropriate criteria.
7. intelligently weight the various criteria relative to one another. Giving 25% equally to four criteria is easy, but rarely valid. Surely "mechanics" is less important than "persuasiveness" in an essay. Give percentages that reflect the relative importance of each criterion to the others.

Misconception Alerts

1. Perhaps the most common misunderstanding about rubrics is that they can only be developed *after* a specific task has been designed. But the rubric is meant as a bridge between any of a variety of unique performance tasks and a more general target. For example, a rubric for judging the effectiveness of an essay should be applicable to *any* essay, and thus can and should be written *before* a particular writing prompt is developed. In other words, the qualities of an effective essay guide the rubric's development. You may add specific indicators to a rubric to make it more unique and helpful to the student, but you should know the general criteria of performance before you go to design a unique task.
2. A common mistake in rubric design is to turn qualitative differences in work quality into arbitrary quotas. For example, many rubrics give a higher score if you have more footnotes or reasons. This is clearly invalid: An essay with one compelling, well-supported argument and a single footnote may be far more persuasive than an essay with three weakly developed and supported reasons and five footnotes. Though more time-consuming, it pays to assess differences in quality at each level by studying samples of work of varying quality.

Sample Rubric: Assessing an Oral Presentation

Grading Criteria	Excellent	Acceptable	Minimal	Unacceptable
Preparation 20%	Gathers information from many reputable sources; prepares thorough and helpful notes (or speaks clearly from memory); creates attractive visual aids to support the presentation.	Gathers information from varied and appropriate sources; prepares notes or visual aids to use during presentation.	Gathers minimal information from one or two sources; the sources may or may not be appropriate or sufficient; does not prepare many notes or visual aids.	Gathers limited information from one easy-to-find source; may not be able to complete task because of lack of preparation.
Content 20%	Abundance of material clearly relates to topic; points are interesting and clear; presentation has coherent thesis.	Has adequate information about the topic; makes good points; has a thesis.	Not enough adequate or total content provided; some information may not be relevant; thesis is simple or unclear.	Information included has little connection to the topic. No explicit or acceptable thesis is provided.
Organization 30%	Information is well organized and logically ordered; argument is easy to follow; conclusion is clear.	Most information is presented in logical order; argument is generally clear and easy to follow.	Ideas loosely connect; organization and flow are choppy and somewhat difficult to follow.	Seemingly random or unconnected information is presented. There is no sense of an organization having been thought through.
Speaking Skills 30%	Is engaging, poised, and confident during the presentation; speaks clearly, naturally, and fluently.	Is mostly engaging during the presentation; speaks clearly and fluently during most of presentation.	Is not very engaging; speech is wooden, enunciation is not always clear; lots of "er" or "um", no eye contact, etc.	Appears uninterested, afraid or unfocused during presentation; is difficult to understand.

(Teacher also posts four video clips to anchor the score points of the rubric and thus "teach" what the expectations are and what the descriptors mean.)

Checklist

When practicing your presentation, ask yourself if you've met these criteria for a top grade:

__ Did I use information from varied and appropriate sources?
__ Are all my sources reliable?
__ Do I have notes about my presentation?
__ Do I use helpful visual aids?
__ Do I have a thesis?
__ Is all the information in my presentation clearly related to my topic?
__ Do my evidence and arguments support my thesis?
__ Is there a logical order to my presentation that is easy to follow?
__ Do I have an introduction, clear position, and conclusion?
__ Do I speak clearly?
__ Is my voice natural and pleasant sounding?
__ Is my voice loud enough?
__ Do I make eye contact or otherwise engage my listeners?

For more information about rubrics and an assortment of rubrics to use in your classroom, visit the Online Teacher Center at PearsonSuccessnet.com.

Simplify Your Planning Using This Program

Where Do I Start?

Right here! These pages will guide you through the program's unique organization and describe the many resources that will enrich your teaching.

How Do I Teach the Unit?

Begin each unit with the Unit Opener, previewing the content to come with the students. At the end of the Unit, use the Unit Activity to help students explore how their ideas about the Essential Question have deepened or changed as a result of their studies.

What Should I Use to Plan and Prepare?

Start your planning with the Pacing Plan to give you a time frame for the year's curriculum. Then use the Lesson Planner before each section to give you a summary of the lesson plan in the Teacher's Edition, with suggestions for incorporating resources into your instruction.

How Do I Differentiate Instruction?

Prentice Hall Economics provides unprecedented opportunities for differentiated instruction:

- **Teacher's Edition** provides a core lesson for the entire class, but within that lesson you will find strategies and modified instruction geared toward different levels of student ability and learning styles.
- **All-in-One** provides leveled resources for each section and chapter to support differentiation.
- **Graphic Organizers** on the section opener give struggling readers additional support.
- **Economics Online** provides students with another format to access the material.
- **Simulation Activities** provide students with opportunities to transfer learning by enacting real-life situations.
- **Virtual Economics** a CD-ROM available through National Council of Economic Education (NCEE), provides alternate lesson plans to differentiate instruction. The CD contains hundreds of economics lesson plans. An appropriate lesson has been selected to support each section.

What Are These Features?

- **Little Red Boxes** Within the core lesson plan, you will notice red boxes labeled **L1**, **L2**, **L3**, or **L4**. These denote differentiation suggestions for different levels of students. In planning your lesson, you should review the lesson plan and resources to determine which differentiation suggestions are appropriate for your class. "**ELL**" or "**LPR**" following the label denotes an activity tailored specifically for English Language Learners or Less Proficient Readers. Many teachers, however, find these strategies helpful for many students.
- **"Bellringer"** You have a lot to do at the beginning of the class: attendance, returning papers, and other housekeeping. These Bellringers are short activities that engage students upon their arrival, allowing you to get organized. They are best used consistently, providing a routine for students to begin working without explicit instructions to do so.
- **Pressed for Time** There is a lot of material to cover in *Prentice Hall Economics*. We know that most of you teach several subjects and may be new to teaching economics. On the chapter level, we suggest an activity that will help you cover a chapter in a short amount of time.
- **Block Scheduling** This format allows for greater depth and flexibility in education. For you, we provide a variety of resources, strategies, and activities to stimulate and engage students.
- **Focus on the Basics** On the section opener, we summarize the most important points to help you focus on the essential facts, concepts, and generalizations that students must grasp. This feature is designed to be a helpful reminder in the three minutes between periods, or when you choose to create your own lesson plan to cover the content.

How Does the Program Help Me Develop as a Teacher?

The Teacher's Edition provides these built-in professional development features:

- **Lesson Plans** Margin notes provide pedagogy, strategies, and activities to teach and extend the content.
- **Differentiated Instruction** Lessons provide leveled instruction, giving support for struggling students, modifications of lessons to address cultural differences, and enrichment for advanced students.
- **Classroom Hints** Tips provided by master teachers to be prepared for common misconceptions, pitfalls, and other ways to present a concept.
- **Background Notes** Notes provide background to the topic, historical development of issues, and connections to students' lives in order to enhance your effectiveness as a teacher.

How Can I Use Technology In My Classroom?

Prentice Hall Economics allows you to teach the entire program without using the print products. It contains all of the components of the program in one central location: all of the print and activity-based materials PLUS integrated videos, animation, interactive practice activities, and audio. You will navigate through the program by the Table of Contents, exactly as you would in the textbook.

In addition to serving as a stand-alone, the digital product can also support a print-based approach, providing material for classroom presentations, assessment, lesson planning, and reporting.

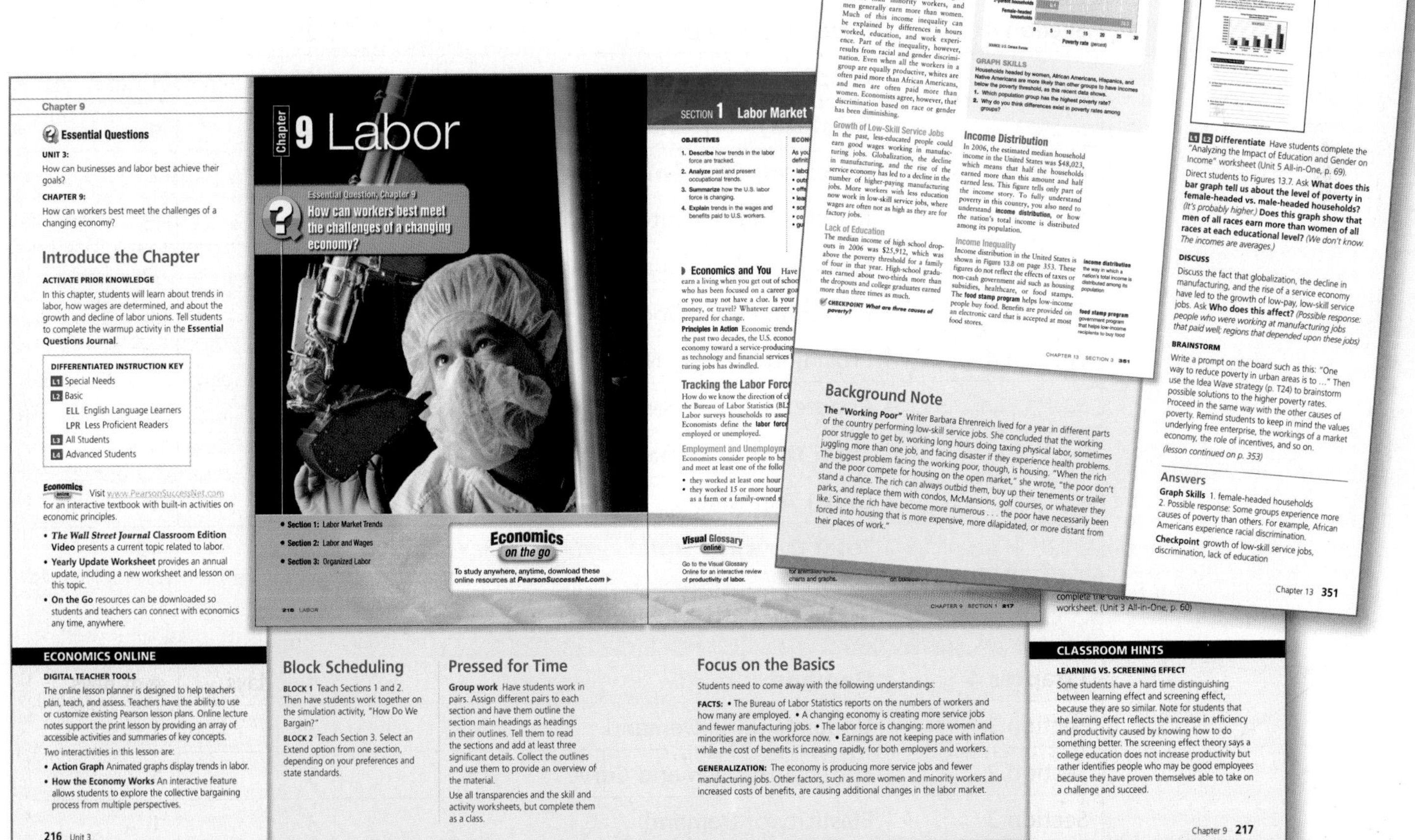

Yearly and Semester Pacing Guides

These pacing guides show how the units and chapters of *Prentice Hall Economics* can be adapted to fit your specific course focus and time constraints. The yearly guide is representative of a course based on 36 weeks or 180 days. The semester guide is representative of a course with 50-minute periods that lasts for 18 weeks or 90 days. Time has been allowed for using the Personal Finance Handbook.

UNIT 1	INTRODUCTION TO ECONOMICS	1-Year Course	1-Semester Course
Chapter 1	**What Is Economics?**	# of days	# of days
Section 1	Scarcity and the Factors of Production	2	1
Section 2	Opportunity Cost	2	1
Section 3	Production Possibilities Curves	2	1
	Chapter 1 Assessment	1	1
	Total Days for Chapter	**7**	**4**
Chapter 2	**Economic Systems**		
Section 1	Answering the Three Economic Questions	2	1
Section 2	The Free Market	2	1
Section 3	Centrally Planned Economies	3	.5
Section 4	Mixed Economies	2	.5
	Chapter 2 Assessment	1	1
	Total Days for Chapter	**10**	**4**
Chapter 3	**American Free Enterprise**		
Section 1	Benefits of Free Enterprise	2	.5
Section 2	Promoting Growth and Stability	2	.5
Section 3	Providing Public Goods	1.5	.5
Section 4	Providing a Safety Net	2	.5
	Chapter 3 Assessment	1	1
	Total Days for Chapter	**9**	**3**
	Unit 1 Assessment	1	1
	Total Days for Unit	**27**	**12**

UNIT 2	HOW MARKETS WORK	1-Year Course	1-Semester Course
Chapter 4	**Demand**	# of days	# of days
Section 1	Understanding Demand	3	1
Section 2	Shifts in the Demand Curve	3	1
Section 3	Elasticity of Demand	3	1
	Chapter 4 Assessment	1	1
	Total Days for Chapter	**10**	**4**

TEACHING ECONOMICS

PROGRAM ORGANIZATION

DIFFERENTIATED INSTRUCTION

ASSESSMENT

PLANNING YOUR INSTRUCTION

Chapter 5	**Supply**		
Section 1	Understanding Supply	3	1
Section 2	Costs of Production	3	1
Section 3	Changes in Supply	3	1
	Chapter 5 Assessment	1	1
	Total Days for Chapter	**10**	**4**
Chapter 6	**Prices**		
Section 1	Combining Supply and Demand	3	1
Section 2	Changes in Market Equilibrium	3	1
Section 3	The Role of Prices	3	1
	Chapter 6 Assessment	1	1
	Total Days for Chapter	**10**	**4**
Chapter 7	**Market Structures**		
Section 1	Perfect Competition	2	.5
Section 2	Monopoly	2	.5
Section 3	Monopolistic Competition and Oligopoly	2	.5
Section 4	Regulation and Deregulation	2	.5
	Chapter 7 Assessment	1	1
	Total Days for Chapter	**9**	**3**
	Unit 2 Assessment	1	1
	Total Days for Unit	**40**	**16**

UNIT 3	**BUSINESS AND LABOR**	1-Year Course	1-Semester Course
Chapter 8	**Business Organizations**	**# of days**	**# of days**
Section 1	Sole Proprietorships	2	1
Section 2	Partnerships and Franchises	2	1
Section 3	Corporations, Mergers, and Multinationals	3	1
Section 4	Nonprofit Organizations	2	1
	Chapter 8 Assessment	1	1
	Total Days for Chapter	**10**	**5**
Chapter 9	**Labor**		
Section 1	Labor Market Trends	2.5	1
Section 2	Labor and Wages	3	1
Section 3	Organized Labor	2.5	1
	Chapter 9 Assessment	1	1
	Total Days for Chapter	**9**	**4**
	Unit 3 Assessment	1	1
	Total Days for Unit	**20**	**10**

PLANNING YOUR INSTRUCTION

UNIT 4	MONEY, BANKING, AND FINANCE	1-Year Course	1-Semester Course
Chapter 10	**Money and Banking**	# of days	# of days
Section 1	Money	2	1
Section 2	The History of American Banking	1.5	1
Section 3	Banking Today	2.5	1
	Chapter 10 Assessment	1	1
	Total Days for Chapter	**7**	**4**
Chapter 11	**Financial Markets**		
Section 1	Saving and Investing	3	1
Section 2	Bonds and Other Financial Assets	3	1
Section 3	The Stock Market	6	1
	Chapter 11 Assessment	1	1
	Total Days for Chapter	**13**	**4**
	Unit 4 Assessment	1	1
	Total Days for Unit	**21**	**9**
UNIT 5	**MEASURING ECONOMIC PERFORMANCE**	1-Year Course	1-Semester Course
Chapter 12	**Gross Domestic Product and Growth**	# of days	# of days
Section 1	Gross Domestic Product	2	2
Section 2	Business Cycles	2	2
Section 3	Economic Growth	2	2
	Chapter 12 Assessment	1	1
	Total Days for Chapter	**7**	**7**
Chapter 13	**Economic Challenges**		
Section 1	Unemployment	2	1
Section 2	Inflation	2	1
Section 3	Poverty	2	1
	Chapter 13 Assessment	1	1
	Total Days for Chapter	**7**	**4**
	Unit 5 Assessment	1	1
	Total Days for Unit	**15**	**12**
UNIT 6	**GOVERNMENT AND THE ECONOMY**	1-Year Course	1-Semester Course
Chapter 14	**Taxes and Government Spending**	# of days	# of days
Section 1	What Are Taxes?	2	1
Section 2	Federal Taxes	10	2

Section 3	Federal Spending	3	2
Section 4	State and Local Taxes and Spending	9	1
	Chapter 14 Assessment	1	1
	Total Days for Chapter	**25**	**7**
Chapter 15	**Fiscal Policy**		
Section 1	Understanding Fiscal Policy	2	2
Section 2	Fiscal Policy Options	2	2
Section 3	Budget Deficits and the National Debt	2	2
	Chapter 15 Assessment	1	1
	Total Days for Chapter	**7**	**7**
Chapter 16	**The Federal Reserve and Monetary Policy**		
Section 1	The Federal Reserve System	1.5	1
Section 2	Federal Reserve Functions	2	1
Section 3	Monetary Policy Tools	2	2
Section 4	Monetary Policy and Macroeconomic Stabilization	1.5	2
	Chapter 16 Assessment	1	1
	Total Days for Chapter	**8**	**7**
	Unit 6 Assessment	1	1
	Total Days for Unit	**41**	**22**
UNIT 7	**THE GLOBAL ECONOMY**	1-Year Course	1-Semester Course
Chapter 17	**International Trade**	**# of days**	**# of days**
Section 1	Absolute and Comparative Advantage	2	1
Section 2	Trade Barriers and Agreements	2	1
Section 3	Measuring Trade	2	1
	Chapter 17 Assessment	1	1
	Total Days for Chapter	**7**	**4**
Chapter 18	**Development and Globalization**		
Section 1	Levels of Development	1.5	.5
Section 2	Issues in Development	2	1
Section 3	Economies in Transition	1.5	.5
Section 4	Challenges of Globalization	2	1
	Chapter 18 Assessment	1	1
	Total Days for Chapter	**8**	**4**
	Unit 7 Assessment	1	1
	Total Days for Unit	**16**	**9**

Block Scheduling Guide

Prentice Hall Economics provides a comprehensive array of resources to meet your block scheduling needs. Flexibility is the key to your success in extended class periods. The variety of materials available with this program provide numerous strategies for you to expand coverage of every topic or to cover essential content in limited time.

This pacing chart is for a nine-week teaching block. Each class day is 90 minutes long. Time has been allowed for using the Personal Finance Handbook. Two days of the 45-day block are set aside for review and for final exams.

UNIT 1	INTRODUCTION TO ECONOMICS	SECTION
Chapter 1	**What Is Economics?**	**# of days**
Day 1	Section 1: Scarcity and the Factors of Production	1
Day 2	Section 2: Opportunity Cost	.5
	Section 3: Production Possibilities Curves	.5
Day 3	Chapter 1 Assessment	1
	Total Days for Chapter 1	**3**
Chapter 2	**Economic Systems**	
Day 4	Section 1: Answering the Three Economic Questions	.5
	Section 2: The Free Market	.5
Day 5	Section 3: Centrally Planned Economies	.5
	Section 4: Mixed Economies	.5
Chapter 3	**American Free Enterprise**	
Day 6	Section 1: Benefits of Free Enterprise	.5
	Section 2: Promoting Growth and Stability	.5
Day 7	Section 3: Providing Public Goods	.5
	Section 4: Providing a Safety Net	.5
Day 8	Chapter 2 and Chapter 3 Assessment	1
	Total Days for Chapters 2 and 3	**5**

UNIT 2	HOW MARKETS WORK	SECTION
Chapter 4	**Demand**	# of days
Day 9	Section 1: Understanding Demand	.75
Day 9, 10	Section 2: Shifts in the Demand Curve	.75
Day 10, 11	Section 3: Elasticity of Demand	.75
Day 11	Chapter 4 Assessment	.75
	Total Days for Chapter 4	**3**
Chapter 5	**Supply**	
Day 12	Section 1: Understanding Supply	.5
	Section 2: Costs of Production	.5
Day 13	Section 3: Changes in Supply	1
Day 14	Chapter 5 Assessment	1
	Total Days for Chapter 5	**3**
Chapter 6	**Prices**	
Day 15	Section 1: Combining Supply and Demand	.5
	Section 2: Changes in Market Equilibrium	.5
Day 16	Section 3: The Role of Prices	1
Day 17	Chapter 6 Assessment	1
	Total Days for Chapter 6	**3**
Chapter 7	**Market Structures**	
Day 18	Section 1: Perfect Competition	.5
	Section 2: Monopoly	.5
Day 19	Section 3: Monopolistic Competition and Oligopoly	.5
	Section 4: Regulation and Deregulation	.5
Day 20	Chapter 7 Assessment	1
	Total Days for Chapter 7	**3**

PLANNING YOUR INSTRUCTION

UNIT 3	BUSINESS AND LABOR	SECTION
Chapter 8	**Business Organizations**	# of days
Day 21	Section 1: Sole Proprietorships	.5
	Section 2: Partnerships and Franchises	.5
Day 22	Section 3: Corporations, Mergers, and Multinationals	.5
	Section 4: Nonprofit Organizations	.5
Day 23	Chapter 8 Assessment	1
	Total Days for Chapter 8	**3**
Chapter 9	**Labor**	
Day 24	Section 1: Labor Market Trends	1
Day 25	Section 2: Labor and Wages	.5
	Section 3: Organized Labor	.5
Day 26	Chapter 9 Assessment	1
	Total Days for Chapter 9	**3**
UNIT 4	**MONEY, BANKING, AND FINANCE**	**SECTION**
Chapter 10	**Money and Banking**	# of days
Day 27	Section 1: Money	.5
	Section 2: The History of American Banking	.5
Day 28	Section 3: Banking Today	.5
Chapter 11	**Financial Markets**	
Day 28	Section 1: Saving and Investing	.5
Day 29	Section 2: Bonds and Other Financial Assets	.5
	Section 3: The Stock Market	.5
Day 30	Chapter 10 and Chapter 11 Assessment	1
	Total Days for Chapters 10 and 11	**4**
UNIT 5	**MEASURING ECONOMIC PERFORMANCE**	**SECTION**
Chapter 12	**Gross Domestic Product and Growth**	# of days
Day 31	Section 1: Gross Domestic Product	.33
	Section 2: Business Cycles	.33
	Section 3: Economic Growth	.33
Chapter 13	**Economic Challenges**	
Day 32	Section 1: Unemployment	.33
	Section 2: Inflation	.33
	Section 3: Poverty	.33
Day 33	Chapter 12 and Chapter 13 Assessment	1
	Total Days for Chapters 12 and 13	**3**

UNIT 6	GOVERNMENT AND THE ECONOMY	SECTION
Chapter 14	**Taxes and Government Spending**	# of days
Day 34	Section 1: What Are Taxes?	.5
	Section 2: Federal Taxes	.5
Day 35	Section 3: Federal Spending	.5
	Section 4: State and Local Taxes and Spending	.5
Chapter 15	**Fiscal Policy**	
Day 36	Section 1: Understanding Fiscal Policy	.5
	Section 2: Fiscal Policy Options	.5
Day 37	Section 3: Budget Deficits and the National Debt	1
Day 38	Chapter 14 and Chapter 15 Assessment	1
	Total Days for Chapters 14 and 15	**5**
Chapter 16	**The Federal Reserve and Monetary Policy**	
Day 39	Section 1: The Federal Reserve System	.33
	Section 2: Federal Reserve Functions	.33
	Section 3: Monetary Policy Tools	.33
Day 40	Section 4: Monetary Policy and Macroeconomic Stabilization	.5
	Chapter 16 Assessment	.5
	Total Days for Chapter 16	**2**
UNIT 7	**THE GLOBAL ECONOMY**	**SECTION**
Chapter 17	**International Trade**	# of days
Day 41	Section 1: Absolute and Comparative Advantage	.33
	Section 2: Trade Barriers and Agreements	.33
	Section 3: Measuring Trade	.33
Chapter 18	**Development and Globalization**	
Day 42	Section 1: Levels of Development	.25
	Section 2: Issues in Development	.25
	Section 3: Economies in Transition	.25
	Section 4: Challenges of Globalization	.25
Day 43	Chapter 17 and Chapter 18 Assessment	1
	Total Days for Chapters 17 and 18	**3**
Day 44	Final Exams/Preparation	1
Day 45	Final Exams	1

Correlation to NCEE Standards

Prentice Hall Economics uses the *Voluntary National Content Standards in Economics* to ensure solid coverage of the fundamentals. The standards were developed by the National Council on Economic Education (NCEE) in partnership with the National Association of Economic Educators and the Foundation for Teaching Economics.

The chart on the following pages lists the standards for grades 4–12 and shows which chapters in *Prentice Hall Economics* focus on each standard.

CONTENT STANDARD	CHAPTER
1. Productive resources are limited. Therefore, people cannot have all the goods and services they want; as a result, they must choose some things and give up others.	Chapter 1
2. Effective decision making requires comparing the additional costs of alternatives with the additional benefits. Most choices involve doing a little more or a little less of something; few choices are "all or nothing" decisions.	Chapter 1
3. Different methods can be used to allocate goods and services. People, acting individually or collectively through government, must choose which methods to use to allocate different kinds of goods and services.	Chapter 2
4. People respond predictably to positive and negative incentives.	Chapters 2, 4, and 5
5. Voluntary exchange occurs only when all participating parties expect to gain. This is true for trade among individuals or organizations within a nation, and among individuals or organizations in different nations.	Chapter 17

CONTENT STANDARD	CHAPTER
6. When individuals, regions, and nations specialize in what they can produce at the lowest cost and then trade with others, both production and consumption increase.	Chapter 17
7. Markets exist when buyers and sellers interact. This interaction determines market prices and thereby allocates scarce goods and services.	Chapters 4 and 17
8. Prices send signals and provide incentives to buyers and sellers. When supply or demand changes, market prices adjust, affecting incentives.	Chapters 5 and 6
9. Competition among sellers lowers costs and prices, and encourages producers to produce more of what consumers are willing and able to buy. Competition among buyers increases prices and allocates goods and services to those people who are willing and able to pay the most for them.	Chapter 7
10. Institutions evolve in market economies to help individuals and groups accomplish their goals. Banks, labor unions, corporations, legal systems, and not-for-profit organizations are examples of important institutions. A different kind of institution, clearly defined and enforced property rights, is essential to a market economy.	Chapters 8, 10, and 11

CONTENT STANDARD	CHAPTER
11. Money makes it easier to trade, borrow, save, invest, and compare the value of goods and services.	Chapter 10
12. Interest rates, adjusted for inflation, rise and fall to balance the amount saved with the amount borrowed, which affects the allocation of scarce resources between present and future uses.	Chapters 11 and 16
13. Income for most people is determined by the market value of the productive resources they sell. What workers earn depends, primarily, on the market value of what they produce and how productive they are.	Chapter 9
14. Entrepreneurs are people who take the risks of organizing productive resources to make goods and services. Profit is an important incentive that leads entrepreneurs to accept the risks of business failure.	Chapter 8
15. Investment in factories, machinery, new technology, and in the health, education, and training of people can raise future standards of living.	Chapters 3, 12, and 18
16. There is an economic role for government in a market economy whenever the benefits of a government policy outweigh its costs. Governments often provide for national defense, address environmental concerns, define and protect property rights, and attempt to make markets more competitive. Most government policies also redistribute income.	Chapters 3 and 14

CONTENT STANDARD	CHAPTER
17. Costs of government policies sometimes exceed benefits. This may occur because of incentives facing voters, government officials, and government employees, because of actions by special interest groups that can impose costs on the general public, or because social goals other than economic efficiency are being pursued.	Chapter 15
18. A nation's overall levels of income, employment, and prices are determined by the interaction of spending and production decisions made by all households, firms, government agencies, and others in the economy.	Chapter 12
19. Unemployment imposes costs on individuals and nations. Unexpected inflation imposes costs on many people and benefits some others because it arbitrarily redistributes purchasing power. Inflation can reduce the rate of growth of national living standards because individuals and organizations use resources to protect themselves against the uncertainty of future prices.	Chapter 13
20. Federal government budgetary policy and the Federal Reserve System's monetary policy influence the overall levels of employment, output, and prices.	Chapters 13, 15, and 16

Chapter 1 What Is Economics?

Essential Questions

UNIT 1 How does economics affect everyone?

CHAPTER 1 How can we make the best economic choices?

Program Resources

Instructional
- Essential Questions Journal
- Video Challenge Online and DVD
- Current Events Update
- Essential Question WebQuest

Assessment
- Test Online
- Chapter Tests, All-in-One
- Assessment Rubrics
- Exam*View* TestBank on CD-ROM
- AYP Monitoring Assessments

SECTION 1

Scarcity and the Factors of Production

Guiding Question: How does scarcity force people to make economic choices?

Student Objectives
- Explain why scarcity and choice are the basis of economics.
- Describe what entrepreneurs do.
- Define the three factors of production and the differences between physical and human capital.
- Explain how scarcity affects the factors of production.

Lesson Overview

Students will discuss what makes something a need or a want. They will provide examples of how scarcity forces people and businesses to make choices. They will describe how entrepreneurs use factors of production by completing a worksheet on the CEO of Facebook. Students will evaluate the impact of capital on other factors of production.

Section Resources in Unit 1 All-in-One

L3 L1 L2 Guided Reading and Review, pp. 13, 14
L1 L2 Vocabulary Worksheet, p. 12
L3 L2 Mark Zuckerberg, CEO of Facebook, pp. 15, 16
L4 Factors of Production in the Global Economy, p. 17
L3 L2 Section Quiz, pp. 18, 19

Virtual Economics on CD-ROM

L3 Teacher's Edition, p. 6

SECTION 2

Opportunity Cost

Guiding Question: How does opportunity cost affect decision making?

Student Objectives
- Explain why every decision involves trade-offs.
- Summarize the concept of opportunity cost.
- Describe how people make decisions by thinking at the margin.

Lesson Overview

Students will analyze a cartoon that addresses the trade-offs involved in decision making. They will read and answer questions about a case that illustrates how changing economic factors can change decisions and opportunity costs. Students will provide examples of decision making at the margin using a role-playing activity.

Section Resources in Unit 1 All-in-One

L3 L1 L2 Guided Reading and Review, pp. 20, 21
L3 L2 Trade-Offs, pp. 22, 23
L4 Price and Opportunity Cost, p. 24
L3 L1 L2 Skill: Decision Making, pp. 25, 26
L3 L2 Section Quiz, pp. 27, 28

Virtual Economics on CD-ROM

L3 Teacher's Edition, p. 11

SECTION 3

Production Possibilities Curves

Guiding Question: How does a nation decide what and how much to produce?

Student Objectives

- Interpret a production possibilities curve.
- Explain how production possibilities curves show efficiency, growth, and cost.
- Explain why a country's production possibilities depend on its resources and technology.

Lesson Overview

Students will analyze production possibilities curves and interpret the information represented on these graphs. They will discuss the law of increasing costs and its relationship to production possibilities curves using a transparency. They will answer questions about outsourcing of car manufacturing. Students will research and debate government policies to promote advances in technology.

Section Resources in Unit 1 All-in-One

L3 L1 L2 Guided Reading and Review, pp. 29, 30

L3 Production Possibilities Curve, Color Transparencies, 1.a

L3 Kitchen Challenge, Simulation Activities, Chapter 1

L3 Promoting Technology, p. 31

L2 Governments Promote Technology, p. 32

L3 L2 Section Quiz, pp. 33, 34

L3 Economic Detective, p. 35

Virtual Economics on CD-ROM

L3 Teacher's Edition, p. 17

DIFFERENTIATED INSTRUCTION KEY

L1 Special Needs

L2 Basic

ELL English Language Learners

LPR Less Proficient Readers

L3 All Students

L4 Advanced Students

Economics online

Online Student Center includes

- **Online Student Editions—Economics and Foundations Series Economics**
  - Action Graph Animations
  - How the Economy Works Interactives
  - Visual Glossary Interactives
  - WebQuests
- **Economics on the Go**
  - Economic Dictionary Audio
  - Audio Review—English and Spanish
  - Action Graph Animations
  - How the Economy Works Animations
  - Visual Glossary Animations
- **Essential Questions Journal**
- **Wall Street Journal Video**
- **Selected Worksheets**

Online Teacher Center includes all Online Student Center material plus

- **Online Teacher's Editions—Economics and Foundations Series Economics**
- **Teacher's Resource Library**
- **Economics Updates**
- **Assessment Rubrics**
- **Blank Graphic Organizers**

PLANNING YOUR INSTRUCTION

Chapter 2 Economic Systems

 Essential Questions

UNIT 1 How does economics affect everyone?

CHAPTER 2 How does a society decide who gets what goods and services?

Program Resources

Instructional
- Essential Questions Journal
- Video Challenge Online and DVD
- Current Events Update
- Essential Question WebQuest

Assessment
- Test Online
- Chapter Tests, All-in-One
- Assessment Rubrics
- Exam*View* TestBank on CD-ROM
- AYP Monitoring Assessments

SECTION 1

Answering the Three Economic Questions

Guiding Question: What goals and values affect how a society answers the key economic questions?

Student Objectives
- Identify the three key economic questions that all societies must answer.
- Analyze the societal values that determine how a country answers the three economic questions.
- Define the characteristics of a traditional economy.

Lesson Overview

Students will give examples of different ways in which the three key economic questions can be answered through class discussion. They will define economic goals and values in the United States economy by completing a worksheet. They will analyze how emphasizing each economic goal or value affects other goals or values. Students will write a persuasive essay advocating the emphasis of particular economic values.

Section Resources in Unit 1 All-in-One

L3 L1 L2 Guided Reading and Review, pp. 53, 54
L1 L2 Vocabulary Worksheet, p. 52
L3 Career Link, p. 134
L3 Evaluating the United States Economy, p. 55
L2 Goals and Values in the United States Economy, p. 56
L3 L1 L2 Skill: Writing a Persuasive Essay, pp. 57, 58
L3 L2 Section Quiz, pp. 59, 60

Virtual Economics on CD-ROM

L3 Teacher's Edition, p. 25

SECTION 2

The Free Market

Guiding Question: What are the characteristics of a free market economy?

Student Objectives
- Explain why markets exist.
- Analyze a circular flow model of a free market economy.
- Describe the self-regulating nature of the marketplace.
- Identify the advantages of a free market economy.

Lesson Overview

Students will demonstrate a market in operation and explain why markets exist through a group activity. They will complete a worksheet that describes the circular flow of goods and services. They will demonstrate the self-regulating nature of the market by completing a worksheet. Students will discuss the advantages of the free market.

Section Resources in Unit 1 All-in-One

L3 L1 L2 Guided Reading and Review, pp. 61, 62
L3 Markets, Color Transparencies, 2.a
L3 L2 Analyzing the Activity of Firms, pp. 63, 64
L3 Competition in Action: Comparing Automobile and Financing Prices, p. 65
L3 L2 Section Quiz, pp. 66, 67

Virtual Economics on CD-ROM

L3 Teacher's Edition, p. 33

CHAPTER LESSON PLANNER

SECTION 3

Centrally Planned Economies

Guiding Question: What are the characteristics of a centrally planned economy?

Student Objectives

- Describe how a centrally planned economy is organized.
- Distinguish between socialism and communism.
- Analyze the use of central planning in the Soviet Union and China.
- Identify the disadvantages of a centrally planned economy.

Lesson Overview

Students will discuss how economic decisions are made in a free market and a centrally planned economy. They will contrast how the three key questions are answered under socialism and communism through class discussion. Students will analyze specific examples to identify problems with centrally planned economies by using a transparency.

Section Resources in Unit 1 All-in-One

L1 L2 Guided Reading and Review, pp. 68, 69
L3 Failures of Centrally Planned Economies, Color Transparencies, 2.b
L4 L2 Comparing Communism and Socialism, pp. 70, 71
L3 Who Decides?, Simulation Activities, Chapter 2
L3 L2 Section Quiz, pp. 72, 73

Virtual Economics on CD-ROM

L3 Teacher's Edition, p. 37

SECTION 4

Mixed Economies

Guiding Question: What are the characteristics of a mixed economy?

Student Objectives

- Explain the rise of mixed economic systems.
- Interpret a circular flow model of a mixed economy.
- Compare the mixed economies of various nations along a continuum between centrally planned and free market systems.
- Describe the role of free enterprise in the United States economy.

Lesson Overview

Students will explore government involvement in the economy through class discussion. They will contrast the circular flow model in a mixed economy to the flow in a free market economy. They will contrast features of national economies by completing a worksheet. Students will evaluate the government's role in the United States economy through class discussion.

Section Resources in Unit 1 All-in-One

L3 L1 L2 Guided Reading and Review, pp. 74, 75
L3 Economic Transition, p. 76
L2 The Food and Drug Administration, p. 77
L4 Comparing Mixed Economies, p. 78
L3 L2 Section Quiz, pp. 79, 80
L3 Economic Detective, p. 81

Virtual Economics on CD-ROM

L3 Teacher's Edition, p. 41

DIFFERENTIATED INSTRUCTION KEY

L1 Special Needs
L2 Basic
ELL English Language Learners
LPR Less Proficient Readers
L3 All Students
L4 Advanced Students

Economics online

Online Student Center includes

- **Online Student Editions—Economics and Foundations Series Economics**
  - Action Graph Animations
  - How the Economy Works Interactives
  - Visual Glossary Interactives
  - WebQuests
- **Economics on the Go**
  - Economic Dictionary Audio
  - Audio Review—English and Spanish
  - Action Graph Animations
  - How the Economy Works Animations
  - Visual Glossary Animations
- **Essential Questions Journal**
- **Wall Street Journal Video**
- **Selected Worksheets**

Online Teacher Center includes all Online Student Center material plus

- **Online Teacher's Editions—Economics and Foundations Series Economics**
- **Teacher's Resource Library**
- **Economics Updates**
- **Assessment Rubrics**
- **Blank Graphic Organizers**

Chapter 3 American Free Enterprise

Essential Questions

UNIT 1 How does economics affect everyone?

CHAPTER 3 What role should government play in a free market economy?

Program Resources

Instructional
- Essential Questions Journal
- Video Challenge Online and DVD
- Current Events Update
- Essential Question WebQuest

Assessment
- Test Online
- Chapter Tests, All-in-One
- Assessment Rubrics
- Exam*View* TestBank on CD-ROM
- AYP Monitoring Assessments

SECTION 1

Benefits of Free Enterprise

Guiding Question: What are the benefits of free enterprise?

Student Objectives
- Define the basic principles of the U.S. free enterprise system.
- Describe the role of the consumer in the American economy.
- Identify the constitutional protections that underlie free enterprise.
- Explain why the government may intervene in the marketplace.

Lesson Overview

Students will evaluate how the principles of free enterprise are applied to a business through class discussion. They will analyze how consumers, through free choice, affect the free enterprise system. They will read and analyze portions of the Constitution that describe the protections that support free enterprise. They will evaluate a Supreme Court case that questioned the government's use of eminent domain.

Section Resources in Unit 1 All-in-One

L3 L1 L2 Guided Reading and Review, pp. 99, 100
L1 L2 Vocabulary Worksheet, p. 98
L3 Entrepreneurs and Free Enterprise, Color Transparencies, 3.a
L4 Constitutional Connections, p. 101
L3 L2 Eminent Domain, pp. 102, 103
L3 Whose Property Is It?, Simulation Activities, Chapter 3
L3 L2 Section Quiz, pp. 104, 105

Virtual Economics on CD-ROM

L3 Teacher's Edition, p. 53

SECTION 2

Promoting Growth and Stability

Guiding Question: How does the U.S. government encourage growth and stability?

Student Objectives
- Explain why the government tracks and seeks to influence business cycles.
- Describe how the government promotes economic strength.
- Analyze the factors that increase productivity.

Lesson Overview

Students will complete a worksheet that asks them to interpret a graph of GDP and its relationship to business cycles. They will predict how the government uses data about the business cycle to promote economic strength. They will provide examples of productivity being influenced by technology, government promotion of innovation and invention, and the American work ethic. Students will identify influences on productivity by reading and analyzing text.

Section Resources in Unit 1 All-in-One

L3 L1 L2 Guided Reading and Review, pp. 106, 107
L3 L2 GDP and Business Cycles, pp. 108, 109
L3 Career Link, p. 134
L3 L2 Section Quiz, pp. 110, 111

Virtual Economics on CD-ROM

L3 Teacher's Edition, p. 59

SECTION 3

Providing Public Goods

Guiding Question: Why does a society provide public goods?

Student Objectives

- Identify examples of public goods.
- Analyze market failures.
- Evaluate how the government allocates some resources by managing externalities.

Lesson Overview

Students will demonstrate understanding of the nature of public goods using public schools as an example. They will make the connection between public goods and the market failures they address by completing a worksheet. Students will analyze a source reading from "The Tragedy of the Commons," and answer questions about the balance between public and private ownership.

Section Resources in Unit 1 All-in-One

L3 L1 L2 Guided Reading and Review, pp. 112, 113
L3 Public School Construction, Color Transparencies, 3.b
L3 Market Failures and Externalities, p. 114
L2 Providing Public Goods, p. 115
L4 The Tragedy of The Commons, p. 116
L3 L2 Section Quiz, pp. 117, 118

Virtual Economics on CD-ROM

L3 Teacher's Edition, p. 64

SECTION 4

Providing A Safety Net

Guiding Question: How does the government help the poor?

Student Objectives

- Explain the U.S. political debate on ways to fight poverty.
- Identify the main programs through which the government redistributes income.
- Describe how the government encourages private efforts to help the needy.

Lesson Overview

Students will discuss government safety net programs and how they are funded. They will conduct a survey about attitudes toward government spending on welfare programs. Students will identify how the government encourages private programs that provide social help by analyzing a political cartoon and participating in a group activity.

Section Resources in Unit 1 All-in-One

L3 L1 L2 Guided Reading and Review, pp. 119, 120
L3 Percent of People in Poverty, Color Transparencies, 3.c
L3 L2 Skill: Analyzing Political Cartoons, pp. 121, 122
L3 Survey on How to Help Those in Need, p. 123
L2 Helping People in Need, p. 124
L3 L2 Section Quiz, pp. 125, 126
L3 Economic Detective, p. 127

Virtual Economics on CD-ROM

L3 Teacher's Edition, p. 71

DIFFERENTIATED INSTRUCTION KEY

L1 Special Needs
L2 Basic
ELL English Language Learners
LPR Less Proficient Readers
L3 All Students
L4 Advanced Students

Economics online

Online Student Center includes

- **Online Student Editions—Economics and Foundations Series Economics**
  - Action Graph Animations
  - How the Economy Works Interactives
  - Visual Glossary Interactives
  - WebQuests
- **Economics on the Go**
  - Economic Dictionary Audio
  - Audio Review—English and Spanish
  - Action Graph Animations
  - How the Economy Works Animations
  - Visual Glossary Animations
- **Essential Questions Journal**
- **Wall Street Journal Video**
- **Selected Worksheets**

Online Teacher Center includes all Online Student Center material plus

- **Online Teacher's Editions—Economics and Foundations Series Economics**
- **Teacher's Resource Library**
- **Economics Updates**
- **Assessment Rubrics**
- **Blank Graphic Organizers**

Chapter 4 Demand

Essential Questions

UNIT 2 Who benefits from the free market economy?

CHAPTER 4 How do we decide what to buy?

Program Resources

Instructional
- Essential Questions Journal
- Video Challenge Online and DVD
- Current Events Update
- Essential Question WebQuest

Assessment
- Test Online
- Chapter Tests, All-in-One
- Assessment Rubrics
- Exam*View* TestBank on CD-ROM
- AYP Monitoring Assessments

SECTION 1

Understanding Demand

Guiding Question: How does the law of demand affect the quantity demanded?

Student Objectives
- Explain the law of demand.
- Describe how the substitution effect and the income effect influence decisions.
- Create a demand schedule for an individual and a market.
- Interpret a demand graph using demand schedules.

Lesson Overview

Students will analyze their own buying decisions to see how the law of demand works. They will interpret a cartoon that will help them understand the substitution and income effects. They will analyze individual and market demand schedules. They will use their knowledge of the relationship between price and demand to create a demand schedule and demand curve.

Section Resources in Unit 2 All-in-One

L3 L1 L2 Guided Reading and Review, pp. 13, 14
L1 L2 Vocabulary Worksheet, p. 12
L3 L2 Food Prices and Demand, pp. 15, 16
L3 L2 Skill: Using Charts and Graphs, pp. 17, 18
L3 L2 Section Quiz, pp. 19, 20

Virtual Economics on CD-ROM

L3 Teacher's Edition, p. 88

SECTION 2

Shifts in the Demand Curve

Guiding Question: Why does the demand curve shift?

Student Objectives
- Explain the difference between change in quantity demanded and a shift in the demand curve.
- Identify the factors that create changes in demand and that can cause a shift in the demand curve.
- Give an example of how a change in demand for one good can affect demand for a related good.

Lesson Overview

Students will interpret graphs to understand the difference between a shift in the demand curve (caused by a change in income) and movement along the demand curve. Using a transparency, they will compare normal goods with inferior goods. They will write a news story to explain the impact of rising demand for a new video game on the demand for a complementary good and a substitute good.

Section Resources in Unit 2 All-in-One

L3 L1 L2 Guided Reading and Review, pp. 21, 22
L3 Normal Goods vs. Inferior Goods, Color Transparencies, 4.a
L3 Creating Demand, Simulation Activities, Chapter 4
L3 L2 Analyzing Shifts in Demand, pp. 23, 24
L4 Explaining Shifts in Demand, p. 25
L3 L2 Section Quiz, pp. 26, 27

Virtual Economics on CD-ROM

L3 Teacher's Edition, p. 95

SECTION 3

Elasticity of Demand

Guiding Question: What factors affect elasticity of demand?

Student Objectives

- Explain how to calculate elasticity of demand.
- Identify factors that affect elasticity.
- Explain how firms use elasticity and revenue to make decisions.

Lesson Overview

Students will describe how elasticity of demand varies from person to person and from price to price. They will identify goods that have elastic or inelastic demand. Students will record the class's demand for a new laptop computer at various prices. They will decide how much they would charge for pizza, considering the product's elasticity of demand.

Section Resources in Unit 2 All-in-One

L3 L1 L2 Guided Reading and Review, pp. 28, 29
L3 Changing Demand, Color Transparencies, 4.b
L3 Calculating Elasticity of Demand, p. 30
L2 Determining Elasticity, p. 31
L4 Analyzing Elasticity of Demand, p. 32
L3 Career Link, p. 164
L3 American Gasoline Use, Color Transparencies, 4.c
L3 L2 Section Quiz, pp. 33, 34
L3 Economic Detective, p. 35

Virtual Economics on CD-ROM

L3 Teacher's Edition, p. 99

DIFFERENTIATED INSTRUCTION KEY

L1 Special Needs
L2 Basic
ELL English Language Learners
LPR Less Proficient Readers
L3 All Students
L4 Advanced Students

Economics online

Online Student Center includes

- **Online Student Editions—Economics and Foundations Series Economics**
  - Action Graph Animations
  - How the Economy Works Interactives
  - Visual Glossary Interactives
  - WebQuests
- **Economics on the Go**
  - Economic Dictionary Audio
  - Audio Review—English and Spanish
  - Action Graph Animations
  - How the Economy Works Animations
  - Visual Glossary Animations
- **Essential Questions Journal**
- **Wall Street Journal Video**
- **Selected Worksheets**

Online Teacher Center includes all Online Student Center material plus

- **Online Teacher's Editions—Economics and Foundations Series Economics**
- **Teacher's Resource Library**
- **Economics Updates**
- **Assessment Rubrics**
- **Blank Graphic Organizers**

PLANNING YOUR INSTRUCTION

Chapter 5 Supply

Essential Questions

UNIT 2 Who benefits from the free market economy?

CHAPTER 5 How do suppliers decide what goods and services to offer?

Program Resources

Instructional
- Essential Questions Journal
- Video Challenge Online and DVD
- Current Events Update
- Essential Question WebQuest

Assessment
- Test Online
- Chapter Tests, All-in-One
- Assessment Rubrics
- Exam*View* TestBank on CD-ROM
- AYP Monitoring Assessments

SECTION 1

Understanding Supply

Guiding Question: How does the law of supply affect the quantity supplied?

Student Objectives
- Explain the law of supply.
- Interpret a supply schedule and a supply graph.
- Examine the relationship between elasticity of supply and time.

Lesson Overview

Students will discuss how the law of supply reflects the profit motive. They will give examples of firms acting according to the law of supply. They will analyze two supply schedules and graph a market supply curve. Students will identify businesses that demonstrate elasticity and inelasticity of supply.

Section Resources in Unit 2 All-in-One

L3 L1 L2 Guided Reading and Review pp. 51, 52
L1 L2 Vocabulary Worksheet, p. 50
L3 L2 Supply Schedules and Supply Curves, pp. 53, 54
L1 L2 Elasticity of Supply, Color Transparencies, 5.a
L3 L2 Section Quiz, pp. 55, 56

Virtual Economics on CD-ROM

L3 Teacher's Edition, p. 113

SECTION 2

Costs of Production

Guiding Question: How can a producer maximize profits?

Student Objectives
- Explain how firms decide how much labor to hire in order to produce a certain level of output.
- Analyze the production costs of a firm.
- Explain how a firm chooses to set output.
- Identify the factors that a firm must consider before shutting down an unprofitable business.

Lesson Overview

Students will experience specialization by taking roles in a production line. They will analyze steps firms can take to improve marginal returns. They will categorize costs as fixed or variable. They will explain how firms make production decisions to maximize profits and how price changes affect those decisions. Students will explain when it makes sense to keep a factory open.

Section Resources in Unit 2 All-in-One

L3 L1 L2 Guided Reading and Review, pp. 57, 58
L3 L2 Skill: Transferring Data, pp. 59, 60
L3 L2 The Cost of Doing Business, pp. 61, 62
L4 Making Production Decisions, p. 63
L3 How Is Output Set?, Simulation Activities, Chapter 5
L3 L2 Section Quiz, pp. 64, 65

Virtual Economics on CD-ROM

L3 Teacher's Edition, p. 118

SECTION 3

Changes in Supply

Guiding Question: Why does the supply curve shift?

Student Objectives

- Explain how factors such as input costs create changes in supply.
- Identify three ways that the government can influence the supply of goods.
- Analyze other factors that affect supply.
- Explain how firms choose a location to produce goods.

Lesson Overview

Students will describe how a good's supply is affected by changes in input costs and give examples of other factors affecting supply. They will analyze how government policies can shift the supply curve. They will analyze how various developments in an economy can affect the supply of goods. Students will describe some of the factors that determine where firms locate.

Section Resources in Unit 2 All-in-One

L3 L1 L2 Guided Reading and Review, pp. 66, 67

L3 When Input Costs Rise, Color Transparencies, 5.b

L4 Evaluating the Ban on Offshore Oil Drilling, p. 68

L3 L2 Analyzing Influences on Supply, pp. 69, 70

L3 L2 Section Quiz, pp. 71, 72

L3 Economic Detective, p. 73

Virtual Economics on CD-ROM

L3 Teacher's Edition, p. 125

DIFFERENTIATED INSTRUCTION KEY

L1 Special Needs
L2 Basic
ELL English Language Learners
LPR Less Proficient Readers
L3 All Students
L4 Advanced Students

Economics online

Online Student Center includes

- **Online Student Editions—Economics and Foundations Series Economics**
  - Action Graph Animations
  - How the Economy Works Interactives
  - Visual Glossary Interactives
  - WebQuests
- **Economics on the Go**
  - Economic Dictionary Audio
  - Audio Review—English and Spanish
  - Action Graph Animations
  - How the Economy Works Animations
  - Visual Glossary Animations
- **Essential Questions Journal**
- **Wall Street Journal Video**
- **Selected Worksheets**

Online Teacher Center includes all Online Student Center material plus

- **Online Teacher's Editions—Economics and Foundations Series Economics**
- **Teacher's Resource Library**
- **Economics Updates**
- **Assessment Rubrics**
- **Blank Graphic Organizers**

PLANNING YOUR INSTRUCTION

Chapter 6 Prices

Essential Questions

UNIT 2 Who benefits from a free market?

CHAPTER 6 What is the right price?

Program Resources

Instructional

- Essential Questions Journal
- Video Challenge Online and DVD
- Current Events Update
- Essential Question WebQuest

Assessment

- Test Online
- Chapter Tests, All-in-One
- Assessment Rubrics
- Exam*View* TestBank on CD-ROM
- AYP Monitoring Assessments

SECTION 1

Combining Supply and Demand

Guiding Question: What factors affect prices?

Student Objectives

- Explain how supply and demand create equilibrium in the marketplace.
- Describe what happens to prices when equilibrium is disturbed.
- Identify two ways that the government steps in to control prices.
- Analyze the impact of price ceilings and price floors on a free market.

Lesson Overview

Students will provide examples to show understanding of how supply and demand affect the market price of a good. They will graph supply and demand curves by taking a survey and representing their results in graphs. Students will interpret the effects of government intervention on the free market by completing a graphing worksheet.

Section Resources in Unit 2 All-in-One

L3 L1 L2 Guided Reading and Review, pp. 89, 90

L3 Setting Prices, Color Transparencies, 6.a

L1 L2 Vocabulary Worksheet, p. 88

L3 Understanding Price Controls, p. 91

L2 Understanding Price Ceilings, p. 92

L4 The Minimum Wage Vision, p. 93

L3 L2 Section Quiz, pp. 94, 95

Virtual Economics on CD-ROM

L3 Teacher's Edition, p. 138

SECTION 2

Changes in Market Equilibrium

Guiding Question: How do changes in supply and demand affect equilibrium?

Student Objectives

- Explain why a free market naturally tends to move toward equilibrium.
- Analyze how a market reacts to an increase or decrease in supply.
- Analyze how a market reacts to an increase or decrease in demand.

Lesson Overview

Students will show an understanding of how changes in technology affect the price of a product over time. Students will interpret a graph to show how a free market tends to move toward equilibrium. They will show understanding of how a market reacts to an increase in supply by deciding on the purchase of a camera. Students will demonstrate understanding of how a market reacts to a decrease in demand by completing a source reading worksheet about the iPhone.

Section Resources in Unit 2 All-in-One

L3 L1 L2 Guided Reading and Review, pp. 96, 97

L3 Changing Market, Color Transparencies, 6.b

L3 Fire Sale Nation, p. 98

L2 Deep Price Cuts, p. 99

L3 L2 Skill: Understanding Cause and Effect, pp. 100, 101

L3 L2 Section Quiz, pp. 102, 103

L3 What Price Water?, Simulation Activities, Chapter 6

Virtual Economics on CD-ROM

L3 Teacher's Edition, p. 143

SECTION 3

The Role of Prices

Guiding Question: What roles do prices play in a free market economy?

Student Objectives

- Identify the many roles that prices play in a free market.
- List the advantages of a price-based system.
- Explain how a price-based system leads to a wider choice of goods and more efficient use of resources.
- Describe the relationship between prices and profit incentive.

Lesson Overview

Students will identify roles that prices play in a free market by selecting items from a menu. They will interpret how a price-based system leads to more efficient allocation of resources by revising prices. Students will demonstrate the relationship between prices and the profit incentive by completing a graphing worksheet.

Section Resources in Unit 2 All-in-One

L3 L1 L2 Guided Reading and Review, pp. 104, 105
L3 Career Link, p. 164
L3 L2 Price of a Slice, pp. 106, 107
L4 The Future of Fortunetelling, p. 108
L3 L2 Section Quiz, pp. 109, 110
L3 Economic Detective, p. 111

Virtual Economics on CD-ROM

L3 Teacher's Edition, p. 151

DIFFERENTIATED INSTRUCTION KEY

L1 Special Needs
L2 Basic
ELL English Language Learners
LPR Less Proficient Readers
L3 All Students
L4 Advanced Students

Economics online

Online Student Center includes

- **Online Student Editions—Economics and Foundations Series Economics**
  - Action Graph Animations
  - How the Economy Works Interactives
  - Visual Glossary Interactives
  - WebQuests
- **Economics on the Go**
  - Economic Dictionary Audio
  - Audio Review—English and Spanish
  - Action Graph Animations
  - How the Economy Works Animations
  - Visual Glossary Animations
- **Essential Questions Journal**
- **Wall Street Journal Video**
- **Selected Worksheets**

Online Teacher Center includes all Online Student Center material plus

- **Online Teacher's Editions—Economics and Foundations Series Economics**
- **Teacher's Resource Library**
- **Economics Updates**
- **Assessment Rubrics**
- **Blank Graphic Organizers**

Chapter 7 Market Structures

 Essential Questions

UNIT 2 Who benefits from a free market?

CHAPTER 7 How does competition affect your choices?

Program Resources

Instructional

- Essential Questions Journal
- Video Challenge Online and DVD
- Current Events Update
- Essential Question WebQuest

Assessment

- Test Online
- Chapter Tests, All-in-One
- Assessment Rubrics
- Exam*View* TestBank on CD-ROM
- AYP Monitoring Assessments

SECTION 1

Perfect Competition

Guiding Question: What are the characteristics of perfect competition?

Student Objectives

- Describe the four conditions that are in place in a perfectly competitive market.
- List two common barriers that prevent firms from entering a market.
- Describe prices and output in a perfectly competitive market.

Lesson Overview

Students will complete a worksheet that asks them to identify examples of perfect competition. They will discuss the two common barriers that make it difficult for firms to enter a market. Students will explain how prices and output are determined in a perfectly competitive market.

Section Resources in Unit 2 All-in-One

L3 L1 L2 Guided Reading and Review, pp. 129, 130
L1 L2 Vocabulary Worksheet, p. 128
L3 Identifying Perfect Competition, p. 131
L2 Perfect Competition, p. 132
L4 Not Enough or Too Many Producers?, p. 133
L3 L2 Section Quiz, pp. 134, 135

Virtual Economics on CD-ROM

L3 Teacher's Edition, p. 162

SECTION 2

Monopoly

Guiding Question: What are the characteristics of monopoly?

Student Objectives

- Describe characteristics and give examples of a monopoly.
- Describe how monopolies, including government monopolies, are formed.
- Explain how a firm with a monopoly makes output decisions.
- Explain why monopolists sometimes practice price discrimination.

Lesson Overview

Students will explain the characteristics of a monopoly and give examples. They will complete worksheets to compare the cost curves of two companies in the same industry, one of which enjoys economies of scale. They will discuss the government's role in regulating and establishing monopolies, and predict the effect of a patent on the market. They will describe how monopolies make output decisions. Students will discuss the market conditions that are necessary for price discrimination to be effective.

Section Resources in Unit 2 All-in-One

L3 L1 L2 Guided Reading and Review, pp. 136, 137
L3 Economies of Scale, p. 138
L2 Understanding Monopoly, p. 139
L4 Determining Price in a Monopoly, p. 140
L3 L2 Section Quiz, pp. 141, 142

Virtual Economics on CD-ROM

L3 Teacher's Edition, p. 171

SECTION 3

Monopolistic Competition and Oligopoly

Guiding Question: What are the characteristics of monopolistic competition and oligopoly?

Student Objectives

- Describe characteristics and give examples of monopolistic competition.
- Explain how firms compete without lowering prices.
- Understand how firms in a monopolistically competitive market set output.
- Describe characteristics and give examples of oligopoly.

Lesson Overview

Students will compare characteristics of pure monopoly and competitive monopoly. They will discuss nonprice competition, and compare prices and output levels under monopolistic competition, monopoly, and perfect competition. They will discuss the characteristics of oligopolies and name barriers to entry for different oligopolies. Students will complete a worksheet that asks them to analyze the market for a good.

Section Resources in Unit 2 All-in-One

L3 L1 L2 Guided Reading and Review, pp. 143, 144
L3 Fresh Vegetables for Sale, Color Transparencies, 7.a
L3 L2 Analyze a Market, pp. 145, 146
L3 L2 Section Quiz, pp. 147, 148

Virtual Economics on CD-ROM

L3 Teacher's Edition, p. 176

DIFFERENTIATED INSTRUCTION KEY

L1 Special Needs
L2 Basic
ELL English Language Learners
LPR Less Proficient Readers
L3 All Students
L4 Advanced Students

SECTION 4

Regulation and Deregulation

Guiding Question: When does the government regulate competition?

Student Objectives

- Explain how firms might try to increase their market power.
- List three market practices that the government regulates or bans to protect competition.
- Define deregulation, and list its effects on several industries.

Lesson Overview

Students will discuss the purpose of antitrust laws, some examples of the government's use of these laws, and ways that firms try to increase their market power. They will analyze arguments for and against monopolies by completing a worksheet. Students will summarize the results of past deregulations using a worksheet.

Section Resources in Unit 2 All-in-One

L3 L1 L2 Guided Reading and Review, pp. 149, 150
L3 The History of Cable Television Regulation, Color Transparencies, 7.b
L3 The Effects of Mergers, Color Transparencies, 7.c
L3 The Monopoly Case, p. 151
L2 Regulation and Deregulation, p. 152
L3 Is the Law Being Broken?, Simulation Activities, Chapter 7
L3 Skill: Note-Taking and Active Listening, p. 153
L1 L2 Skill: Taking Notes and Active Listening, p. 154
L3 L2 Section Quiz, pp. 155, 156
L3 Economic Detective, p. 157

Virtual Economics on CD-ROM

L3 Teacher's Edition, p. 183

Economics online

Online Student Center includes

- **Online Student Editions—Economics and Foundations Series Economics**
  - Action Graph Animations
  - How the Economy Works Interactives
  - Visual Glossary Interactives
  - WebQuests
- **Economics on the Go**
  - Economic Dictionary Audio
  - Audio Review—English and Spanish
  - Action Graph Animations
  - How the Economy Works Animations
  - Visual Glossary Animations
- **Essential Questions Journal**
- **Wall Street Journal Video**
- **Selected Worksheets**

Teacher Center at PearsonSuccessNet.com

Online Teacher Center includes all Online Student Center material plus

- **Online Teacher's Editions—Economics and Foundations Series Economics**
- **Teacher's Resource Library**
- **Economics Updates**
- **Assessment Rubrics**
- **Blank Graphic Organizers**

Chapter 8 Business Organizations

Essential Questions

UNIT 3 **How can businesses and labor best achieve their goals?**

CHAPTER 8 **Why do some businesses succeed and others fail?**

Program Resources

Instructional
- Essential Questions Journal
- Video Challenge Online and DVD
- Current Events Update
- Essential Question WebQuest

Assessment
- Test Online
- Chapter Tests, All-in-One
- Assessment Rubrics
- Exam*View* TestBank on CD-ROM
- AYP Monitoring Assessments

SECTION 1

Sole Proprietorships

Guiding Question: What are the risks and benefits of a sole proprietorship?

Student Objectives
- Explain the characteristics of sole proprietorships.
- Analyze the advantages of a sole proprietorship.
- Analyze the disadvantages of a sole proprietorship.

Lesson Overview

Students will describe the characteristics of sole proprietors by responding to questions on a transparency. They will choose a product or service to sell as a sole proprietor and describe the business. They will evaluate the process of creating and maintaining a sole proprietorship. Students will create a hypothetical sole proprietorship to identify the risks involved.

Section Resources in Unit 3 All-in-One

L3 L1 L2 Guided Reading and Review, pp. 15, 16
L3 What Do You Want to Do?, Color Transparencies, 8.a
L1 L2 Vocabulary Worksheet, p. 14
L4 L2 What Kind of Business?, pp. 17, 18
L3 Career Link, p. 88
L3 Be An Entrepreneur!, Simulation Activities, Chapter 8
L3 L2 Section Quiz, pp. 19, 20

Virtual Economics on CD-ROM

L3 Teacher's Edition, p. 194

SECTION 2

Partnerships and Franchises

Guiding Question: What are the risks and benefits of partnerships and franchises?

Student Objectives
- Compare and contrast different types of partnerships.
- Analyze the advantages of partnerships.
- Analyze the disadvantages of partnerships.
- Explain how a business franchise operates.

Lesson Overview

Students will analyze the skills and assets of potential business partners and recommend a suitable partnership. They will evaluate the advantages and disadvantages of a partnership by completing a worksheet on Procter and Gamble. Students will compare the benefits and risks of various types of partnerships and franchises by forming a hypothetical business.

Section Resources in Unit 3 All-in-One

L3 L1 L2 Guided Reading and Review, pp. 21, 22
L3 Creating a Business, Color Transparencies, 8.b
L3 L2 Procter and Gamble, pp. 23, 24
L3 L2 Skill: Think Creatively and Innovate, pp. 25, 26
L3 L2 Section Quiz, pp. 27, 28

Virtual Economics on CD-ROM

L3 Teacher's Edition, p. 199

SECTION 3

Corporations, Mergers, and Multinationals

Guiding Question: What are the risks and benefits of corporations?

Student Objectives

- Explain the characteristics of corporations.
- Analyze the advantages of incorporation.
- Analyze the disadvantages of incorporation.
- Compare and contrast corporate combinations.
- Describe the role of multinational corporations.

Lesson Overview

Students will create a chart listing the characteristics of a corporation that distinguish it from other types of business organizations. They will compare the advantages and disadvantages of incorporation. They will take the role of a business advisor who evaluates potential mergers and recommend the best type for a given business. Students will assess the impact of consolidation and multinationalism of industries such as telecommunications by analyzing a cartoon.

Section Resources in Unit 3 All-in-One

L3 L1 L2 Guided Reading and Review, pp. 29, 30
L3 L2 Choose to Merge, pp. 31, 32
L3 Final Four, p. 33
L3 L2 Section Quiz, pp. 34, 35

Virtual Economics on CD-ROM

L3 Teacher's Edition, p. 205

SECTION 4

Nonprofit Organizations

Guiding Question: How are some businesses organized to help others?

Student Objectives

- Identify the different types of cooperative organizations.
- Understand the purpose of nonprofit organizations, including professional and business organizations.

Lesson Overview

Students will determine the best type of cooperative or nonprofit organization for specific cases by completing a worksheet. They will give examples of services provided by different nonprofit organizations through class discussion. They will have the opportunity to create a nonprofit organization for a cause.

Section Resources in Unit 3 All-in-One

L3 L1 L2 Guided Reading and Review, pp. 36, 37
L3 L2 What Type of Organization?, pp. 38, 39
L4 Supporting Your Views, p. 40
L3 L2 Section Quiz, pp. 41, 42
L3 Economic Detective, p. 43

Virtual Economics on CD-ROM

L3 Teacher's Edition, p. 211

DIFFERENTIATED INSTRUCTION KEY

L1 Special Needs
L2 Basic
ELL English Language Learners
LPR Less Proficient Readers
L3 All Students
L4 Advanced Students

Economics online

Online Student Center includes

- **Online Student Editions—Economics and Foundations Series Economics**
  - Action Graph Animations
  - How the Economy Works Interactives
  - Visual Glossary Interactives
  - WebQuests
- **Economics on the Go**
  - Economic Dictionary Audio
  - Audio Review—English and Spanish
  - Action Graph Animations
  - How the Economy Works Animations
  - Visual Glossary Animations
- **Essential Questions Journal**
- **Wall Street Journal Video**
- **Selected Worksheets**

Online Teacher Center includes all Online Student Center material plus

- **Online Teacher's Editions—Economics and Foundations Series Economics**
- **Teacher's Resource Library**
- **Economics Updates**
- **Assessment Rubrics**
- **Blank Graphic Organizers**

Chapter 9 Labor

Essential Questions

UNIT 3 How can businesses and labor best achieve their goals?

CHAPTER 9 How can workers best meet the challenges of a changing economy?

Program Resources

Instructional
- Essential Questions Journal
- Video Challenge Online and DVD
- Current Events Update
- Essential Question WebQuest

Assessment
- Test Online
- Chapter Tests, All-in-One
- Assessment Rubrics
- Exam*View* TestBank on CD-ROM
- AYP Monitoring Assessments

SECTION 1

Labor Market Trends

Guiding Question: How do economic trends affect workers?

Student Objectives
- Describe how trends in the labor force are tracked.
- Analyze past and present occupational trends.
- Summarize how the U.S. labor force is changing.
- Explain trends in the wages and benefits paid to U.S. workers.

Lesson Overview

Students will identify local occupational trends. They will assess the current and future impact of outsourcing. They will analyze the relationship between education and wages. They will describe the advantages and disadvantages of temporary work. Students will also interpret a graph of projected changes in the U.S. labor force, and debate the impact of immigration on U.S. employment.

Section Resources in Unit 3 All-in-One

L3 L1 L2 Guided Reading and Review, pp. 59, 60
L1 L2 Vocabulary Worksheet, p. 58
L4 Changes in Unemployment, p. 61
L3 L2 Labor Force Trends, pp. 62, 63
L3 L2 Skill: Give an Effective Presentation, pp. 64, 65
L3 Career Link, p. 88
L3 L2 Section Quiz, pp. 66, 67

Virtual Economics on CD-ROM

L3 Teacher's Edition, p. 219

SECTION 2

Labor and Wages

Guiding Question: Why do some people earn more than others?

Student Objectives
- Analyze how supply and demand in the labor market affect wage levels.
- Describe how skill levels and discrimination affect wage levels.
- Explain how laws against wage discrimination affect wage levels.
- Identify other factors affecting wage levels, such as minimum wage and workplace safety laws.

Lesson Overview

Students will describe the impact of labor supply and labor demand on wage levels and the equilibrium wage by considering the amount paid to people of different professions. Using a political cartoon, they will describe the connection between skill levels and wages. They will assess the progress made with respect to wage discrimination. Students will assess the impact of minimum wage and safety laws, as well as unions, on wage levels.

Section Resources in Unit 3 All-in-One

L3 L1 L2 Guided Reading and Review, pp. 68, 69
L3 L2 Wages and Skill Levels, pp. 70, 71
L4 Minimum Wage and Poverty, p. 72
L3 L2 Section Quiz, pp. 73, 74

Virtual Economics on CD-ROM

L3 Teacher's Edition, p. 229

SECTION 3

Organized Labor

Guiding Question: How do labor unions support the interests of workers?

Student Objectives

- Describe why American workers have formed labor unions.
- Summarize the history of the labor movement in the United States.
- Analyze the reasons for the decline of the labor movement.
- Explain how labor and management negotiate contracts.

Lesson Overview

Students will understand the purposes and goals that spurred establishment of the first unions. Using a transparency, they will summarize the history of the labor movement. They will explain some of the reasons for the decline of unions. Students will describe and then demonstrate the collective bargaining process.

Section Resources in Unit 3 All-in-One

L3 L1 L2 Guided Reading and Review, pp. 75, 76

L3 Taft-Hartley Act Alive and Well, p. 77

L2 Taft-Hartley Act, p. 78

L3 Timeline of 2007 Writers Guild Strike, Color Transparencies, 9.a

L3 How Do We Bargain?, Simulation Activities, Chapter 9

L3 L2 Section Quiz, pp. 79, 80

L3 Economic Detective, p. 81

Virtual Economics on CD-ROM

L3 Teacher's Edition, p. 237

DIFFERENTIATED INSTRUCTION KEY

L1 Special Needs
L2 Basic
ELL English Language Learners
LPR Less Proficient Readers
L3 All Students
L4 Advanced Students

Economics online

Online Student Center includes

- **Online Student Editions—Economics and Foundations Series Economics**
  - Action Graph Animations
  - How the Economy Works Interactives
  - Visual Glossary Interactives
  - WebQuests
- **Economics on the Go**
  - Economic Dictionary Audio
  - Audio Review—English and Spanish
  - Action Graph Animations
  - How the Economy Works Animations
  - Visual Glossary Animations
- **Essential Questions Journal**
- **Wall Street Journal Video**
- **Selected Worksheets**

Online Teacher Center includes all Online Student Center material plus

- **Online Teacher's Editions—Economics and Foundations Series Economics**
- **Teacher's Resource Library**
- **Economics Updates**
- **Assessment Rubrics**
- **Blank Graphic Organizers**

PLANNING YOUR INSTRUCTION

Chapter 10 Money and Banking

Essential Questions

UNIT 4 How can you make the most of your money?

CHAPTER 10 How well do financial institutions serve our needs?

Program Resources

Instructional
- Essential Questions Journal
- Video Challenge Online and DVD
- Current Events Update
- Essential Question WebQuest

Assessment
- Test Online
- Chapter Tests, All-in-One
- Assessment Rubrics
- Exam*View* TestBank on CD-ROM
- AYP Monitoring Assessments

SECTION 1

Money

Guiding Question: How does money serve the needs of our society?

Student Objectives
- Describe the three uses of money.
- List the six characteristics of money.
- Analyze the sources of money's value.

Lesson Overview

Students will demonstrate an understanding of the uses of money by completing a worksheet that compares using money with bartering. They will evaluate how a commodity fits the characteristics of money and describe the source of its value by participating in a group activity.

Section Resources in Unit 4 All-in-One

L3 L1 L2 Guided Reading and Review, pp. 13, 14
L3 Trading Goods or Using Money, Color Transparencies, 10.a
L1 L2 Vocabulary Worksheet, p. 12
L3 L2 Trading Goods or Using Money, pp. 15, 16
L3 Use of Money, Simulation Activities, Chapter 10
L4 Commodity Money, p. 17
L3 L2 Section Quiz, pp. 18, 19

Virtual Economics on CD-ROM

L3 Teacher's Edition, p. 252

SECTION 2

The History of American Banking

Guiding Question: How has the American banking system changed to meet new challenges?

Student Objectives
- Describe the shifts between centralized and decentralized banking before the Civil War.
- Explain how government reforms stabilized the banking system in the later 1800s.
- Describe developments in banking in the early 1900s.
- Explain the causes of two recent banking crises.

Lesson Overview

Students will demonstrate an understanding of the issues of centralization facing the United States in the early years as it established a banking system through class discussion. They will describe the crises and responses to those crises in American banking history. Students will identify the role of central banking, government regulation, and free enterprise in today's banking system by completing a worksheet.

Section Resources in Unit 4 All-in-One

L3 L1 L2 Guided Reading and Review, pp. 20, 21
L3 Crisis and Response in American Banking History, p. 22
L2 Financial Crises, p. 23
L4 Perspectives on American Banking History, p. 24
L3 L2 Section Quiz, pp. 25, 26

Virtual Economics on CD-ROM

L3 Teacher's Edition, p. 260

SECTION 3

Banking Today

Guiding Question: What banking services do financial institutions provide?

Student Objectives

- Explain how the money supply in the United States is measured.
- Describe the functions of financial institutions.
- Identify different types of financial institutions.
- Describe the changes brought about by electronic banking.

Lesson Overview

Students will demonstrate an understanding of how the money supply is measured by analyzing a chart. They will identify the services offered by banks by analyzing a bank statement and researching different types of financial institutions. Students will evaluate aspects of electronic banking using a transparency.

Section Resources in Unit 4 All-in-One

L3 L1 L2 Guided Reading and Review, pp. 27, 28
L3 Career Link, p. 80
L3 Bank Statement, Color Transparencies, 10.b
L3 L2 Make Predictions About Banking, pp. 29, 30
L3 L2 Skill: Digital Age Literacy, pp. 31, 32
L3 L2 Section Quiz, pp. 33, 34
L3 Economic Detective, p. 35

Virtual Economics on CD-ROM

L3 Teacher's Edition, p. 267

DIFFERENTIATED INSTRUCTION KEY

L1 Special Needs
L2 Basic
ELL English Language Learners
LPR Less Proficient Readers
L3 All Students
L4 Advanced Students

Economics online

Online Student Center includes

- **Online Student Editions—Economics and Foundations Series Economics**
  - Action Graph Animations
  - How the Economy Works Interactives
  - Visual Glossary Interactives
  - WebQuests
- **Economics on the Go**
  - Economic Dictionary Audio
  - Audio Review—English and Spanish
  - Action Graph Animations
  - How the Economy Works Animations
  - Visual Glossary Animations
- **Essential Questions Journal**
- **Wall Street Journal Video**
- **Selected Worksheets**

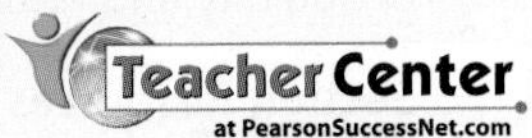

Online Teacher Center includes all Online Student Center material plus

- **Online Teacher's Editions—Economics and Foundations Series Economics**
- **Teacher's Resource Library**
- **Economics Updates**
- **Assessment Rubrics**
- **Blank Graphic Organizers**

Chapter 11 Financial Markets

Essential Questions

UNIT 4 How can you make the most of your money?

CHAPTER 11 How do your saving and investment choices affect your future?

Program Resources

Instructional
- Essential Questions Journal
- Video Challenge Online and DVD
- Current Events Update
- Essential Question WebQuest

Assessment
- Test Online
- Chapter Tests, All-in-One
- Assessment Rubrics
- Exam*View* TestBank on CD-ROM
- AYP Monitoring Assessments

SECTION 1

Saving and Investing

Guiding Question: What are the benefits and risks of saving and investing?

Student Objectives
- Describe how investing contributes to the free enterprise system.
- Explain how the financial system brings together savers and borrowers.
- Explain the role of financial intermediaries in the financial system.
- Identify the trade-offs among liquidity, return, and risk.

Lesson Overview

Students will identify ways that saving and investing benefit the free enterprise system through class discussion. They will use a transparency to compare the functions of various financial intermediaries. They will describe the relationship between financial intermediaries and savers and borrowers by analyzing a diagram of the financial system. Students will identify the types of risk associated with investments that involve different levels of liquidity and return by completing a worksheet.

Section Resources in Unit 4 All-in-One

L3 L1 L2 Guided Reading and Review, pp. 51, 52
L1 L2 Vocabulary Worksheet, p. 50
L3 Career Link, p. 80
L3 The Financial System, Color Transparencies, 11.a
L3 What's the Risk?, p. 53
L2 Investment, Risks, and Return, p. 54
L3 L2 Skill: Writing an E-mail, pp. 55, 56
L3 L2 Section Quiz, pp. 57, 58

Virtual Economics on CD-ROM

L3 Teacher's Edition, p. 279

SECTION 2

Bonds and Other Financial Assets

Guiding Question: Why are bonds bought and sold?

Student Objectives
- Describe the characteristics of bonds as financial assets.
- Identify different types of bonds.
- Describe the characteristics of other types of financial assets.
- List four different types of financial asset markets.

Lesson Overview

Students will be asked to decide under what conditions they would loan money to a friend to start a business. Students will understand the reasons bonds are issued and the information needed in order to decide what bonds to buy through class discussion. They will demonstrate knowledge of the characteristics of bonds and other financial assets by creating an advertisement. Students will evaluate the risk level of various types of financial assets by completing a worksheet.

Section Resources in Unit 4 All-in-One

L3 L1 L2 Guided Reading and Review, pp. 59, 60
L4 Investing for Young People, p. 61
L3 L2 Weighing the Risks, pp. 62, 63
L3 L2 Section Quiz, pp. 64, 65

Virtual Economics on CD-ROM

L3 Teacher's Edition, p. 286

SECTION 3

The Stock Market

Guiding Question: How does the stock market work?

Student Objectives

- Identify the benefits and risks of buying stock.
- Describe how stocks are traded.
- Explain how stock performance is measured.
- Describe the Great Crash of 1929 and more recent stock market events.

Lesson Overview

Students will evaluate stock performance by analyzing and interpreting a newspaper stock report. They will explain the process by which stocks are traded. They will evaluate the benefits and risks of buying stock by comparing them to those of investing in bonds. Students will demonstrate an understanding of the Great Crash of 1929 by presenting a news account of the event.

Section Resources in Unit 4 All-in-One

L3 L1 L2 Guided Reading and Review, pp. 66, 67
L3 Market Pain, Color Transparencies, 11.b
L3 L2 Bulls, Bears, Ants, and Grasshoppers, pp. 68, 69
L3 Becoming a Wizard of Wall Street, Simulation Activities, Chapter 11
L4 Investing in Higher Education, p. 70
L3 L2 Section Quiz, pp. 71, 72
L3 Economic Detective, p. 73

Virtual Economics on CD-ROM

L3 Teacher's Edition, p. 296

DIFFERENTIATED INSTRUCTION KEY

L1 Special Needs
L2 Basic
ELL English Language Learners
LPR Less Proficient Readers
L3 All Students
L4 Advanced Students

Economics online

Online Student Center includes

- **Online Student Editions—Economics and Foundations Series Economics**
  - Action Graph Animations
  - How the Economy Works Interactives
  - Visual Glossary Interactives
  - WebQuests
- **Economics on the Go**
  - Economic Dictionary Audio
  - Audio Review—English and Spanish
  - Action Graph Animations
  - How the Economy Works Animations
  - Visual Glossary Animations
- **Essential Questions Journal**
- **Wall Street Journal Video**
- **Selected Worksheets**

Online Teacher Center includes all Online Student Center material plus

- **Online Teacher's Editions—Economics and Foundations Series Economics**
- **Teacher's Resource Library**
- **Economics Updates**
- **Assessment Rubrics**
- **Blank Graphic Organizers**

Chapter 12 Gross Domestic Product and Growth

 Essential Questions

UNIT 5 Why does it matter how the economy is doing?

CHAPTER 12 How do we know if the economy is healthy?

Program Resources

Instructional
- Essential Questions Journal
- Video Challenge Online and DVD
- Current Events Update
- Essential Question WebQuest

Assessment
- Test Online
- Chapter Tests, All-in-One
- Assessment Rubrics
- Exam*View* TestBank on CD-ROM
- AYP Monitoring Assessments

SECTION 1

Gross Domestic Product

Guiding Question: What does the GDP show about the nation's economy?

Student Objectives
- Explain how gross domestic product (GDP) is calculated.
- Distinguish between nominal and real GDP.
- List the main limitations of GDP.
- Identify factors that influence GDP.
- Describe other output and income measures.

Lesson Overview

Students will identify the goods and services used to calculate gross domestic product and describe two ways to measure GDP by completing a worksheet. They will distinguish between nominal and real GDP by analyzing a chart. They will describe reasons that GDP is an imperfect measure of an economy's performance through class discussion. They will define other measures of economic performance. Students will explain the affect of price level on GDP.

Section Resources in Unit 5 All-in-One

L3 L1 L2 Guided Reading and Review, pp. 13, 14
L1 L2 Vocabulary Worksheet, p. 12
L3 L2 What Counts for GDP?, pp. 15, 16
L4 Calculate GDP, p. 17
L3 L2 Section Quiz, pp. 18, 19

Virtual Economics on CD-ROM

L3 Teacher's Edition, p. 312

SECTION 2

Business Cycles

Guiding Question: What factors affect the phases of a business cycle?

Student Objectives
- Identify the phases of a business cycle.
- Describe the four factors that keep the business cycle going.
- Explain how economists forecast fluctuations in the business cycle.
- Analyze the impact of business cycles in U.S. history.

Lesson Overview

Students will identify the four stages of the business cycle and identify which stage the country is currently in. They will explain how various factors keep the business cycle going through class discussion and using a transparency. They will explain how economists forecast changes in the business cycle. Students will compare a graph of U.S. business cycles and a graph of unemployment.

Section Resources in Unit 5 All-in-One

L3 L1 L2 Guided Reading and Review, pp. 20, 21
L3 Brushback Pitches, Color Transparencies, 12.a
L3 L2 Skill: Analyze Primary and Secondary Sources, pp. 22, 23
L3 Changes in Real GDP and the Unemployment Rate, p. 24
L2 Impact of the Great Depression, p. 25
L3 Ups and Downs, Simulation Activities, Chapter 12
L3 L2 Section Quiz, pp. 26, 27

Virtual Economics on CD-ROM

L3 Teacher's Edition, p. 319

SECTION 3

Economic Growth

Guiding Question: How does the economy grow?

Student Objectives

- Analyze how economic growth is measured.
- Explain what capital deepening is and how it contributes to economic growth.
- Analyze how saving and investment are related to economic growth.
- Summarize the impact of population growth, government, and foreign trade on economic growth.
- Identify the causes and impact of technological progress.

Lesson Overview

Students will explain how capital deepening contributes to GDP growth. They will describe the effects of saving and investment on economic growth. They will explain how population growth, government use of tax revenues, and the types of goods imported affect a nation's economic growth. Students will explain how technological progress impacts economic growth by completing a worksheet.

Section Resources in Unit 5 All-in-One

L3 L1 L2 Guided Reading and Review, pp. 28, 29
L4 Personal Savings, p. 30
L3 Career Link, p. 80
L3 Breakthrough Technology, p. 31
L2 Technology and Business, p. 32
L3 L2 Section Quiz, pp. 33, 34

Virtual Economics on CD-ROM

L3 Teacher's Edition, p. 328

DIFFERENTIATED INSTRUCTION KEY

L1 Special Needs
L2 Basic
ELL English Language Learners
LPR Less Proficient Readers
L3 All Students
L4 Advanced Students

Economics online

Online Student Center includes

- **Online Student Editions—Economics and Foundations Series Economics**
  - Action Graph Animations
  - How the Economy Works Interactives
  - Visual Glossary Interactives
  - WebQuests
- **Economics on the Go**
  - Economic Dictionary Audio
  - Audio Review—English and Spanish
  - Action Graph Animations
  - How the Economy Works Animations
  - Visual Glossary Animations
- **Essential Questions Journal**
- **Wall Street Journal Video**
- **Selected Worksheets**

Online Teacher Center includes all Online Student Center material plus

- **Online Teacher's Editions—Economics and Foundations Series Economics**
- **Teacher's Resource Library**
- **Economics Updates**
- **Assessment Rubrics**
- **Blank Graphic Organizers**

Chapter 13 Economic Challenges

 Essential Questions

UNIT 5 Why does it matter how the economy is doing?

CHAPTER 13 How much can we reduce unemployment, inflation, and poverty?

Program Resources

Instructional
- Essential Questions Journal
- Video Challenge Online and DVD
- Current Events Update
- Essential Question WebQuest

Assessment
- Test Online
- Chapter Tests, All-in-One
- Assessment Rubrics
- Exam*View* TestBank on CD-ROM
- AYP Monitoring Assessments

SECTION 1

Unemployment

Guiding Question: What are the causes of unemployment?

Student Objectives
- Differentiate between frictional, seasonal, structural, and cyclical employment.
- Describe how full employment is measured.
- Explain why full employment does not mean that every worker is employed.

Lesson Overview

Students will describe four causes of unemployment and ways in which each cause may be reduced. They will identify the advantages and disadvantages of outsourcing using a worksheet. They will construct a list of job skills that will be useful for a particular profession. They will compare two viewpoints on extending unemployment benefits. Students will distinguish between full employment and every worker being employed.

Section Resources in Unit 5 All-in-One

L3 L1 L2 Guided Reading and Review, pp. 51, 52
L3 Seasonally Adjusted Unemployment Rate by State, June 2008, Color Transparencies, 13.a
L1 L2 Vocabulary Worksheet, p. 50
L3 Exploring Outsourcing, p. 53
L2 Outsourcing, p. 54
L3 L2 Skill: Compare Viewpoints, pp. 55, 56
L3 L2 Section Quiz, pp. 57, 58

Virtual Economics on CD-ROM

L3 Teacher's Edition, p. 339

SECTION 2

Inflation

Guiding Question: What are the causes and effects of inflation?

Student Objectives
- Explain the effects of rising prices.
- Understand the use of price indexes to compare changes in prices over time.
- Identify the causes and effects of inflation.
- Describe recent trends in the inflation rate.

Lesson Overview

Students will analyze an example of reduced purchasing power due to inflation. They will analyze changes in the Consumer Price Index in recent years and compare with the inflation rate. They will describe how changes in money supply, aggregate demand, or aggregate supply cause inflation. Students will identify the effect of inflation on several consumers in different circumstances.

Section Resources in Unit 5 All-in-One

L3 L1 L2 Guided Reading and Review, pp. 59, 60
L3 Consumer Price Index, 1995–2006, Color Transparencies, 13.b
L4 Analyzing Hyperinflation, p. 61
L3 Analyzing the Impact of Inflation, p. 62
L2 Comparing the Impact of Inflation, p. 64
L3 Creating a Teenage Consumer Price Index, Simulation Activities, Chapter 13
L3 L2 Section Quiz, pp. 64, 65

Virtual Economics on CD-ROM

L3 Teacher's Edition, p. 345

SECTION 3

Poverty

Guiding Question: What factors affect the poverty rate?

Student Objectives

- Define who is poor, according to government standards.
- Describe the causes of poverty.
- Analyze the distribution of income in the United States.
- Summarize government policies intended to combat poverty.

Lesson Overview

Students will analyze a bar graph that shows the levels of poverty for men and women with different levels of education, and discuss other causes of poverty. They will brainstorm solutions to different causes of poverty. They will demonstrate equality and inequality of income distribution using a group activity. They will analyze factors that affect wages and wealth. Students will research and discuss government antipoverty programs.

Section Resources in Unit 5 All-in-One

L3 L1 L2 Guided Reading and Review, pp. 66, 67

L3 L2 Analyzing the Impact of Education and Gender on Income, pp. 68, 69

L4 Studying Income Distribution, p. 70

L3 L2 Section Quiz, pp. 71, 72

L3 Career Link, p. 80

L3 Economic Detective, p. 73

Virtual Economics on CD-ROM

L3 Teacher's Edition, p. 353

DIFFERENTIATED INSTRUCTION KEY

L1 Special Needs

L2 Basic

ELL English Language Learners

LPR Less Proficient Readers

L3 All Students

L4 Advanced Students

Economics online

Online Student Center includes

- **Online Student Editions—Economics and Foundations Series Economics**
  - Action Graph Animations
  - How the Economy Works Interactives
  - Visual Glossary Interactives
  - WebQuests
- **Economics on the Go**
  - Economic Dictionary Audio
  - Audio Review—English and Spanish
  - Action Graph Animations
  - How the Economy Works Animations
  - Visual Glossary Animations
- **Essential Questions Journal**
- **Wall Street Journal Video**
- **Selected Worksheets**

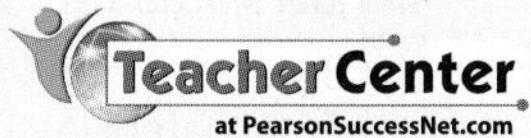

Online Teacher Center includes all Online Student Center material plus

- **Online Teacher's Editions—Economics and Foundations Series Economics**
- **Teacher's Resource Library**
- **Economics Updates**
- **Assessment Rubrics**
- **Blank Graphic Organizers**

Chapter 14 Taxes and Government Spending

 Essential Questions

UNIT 6 What is the proper role of government in the economy?

CHAPTER 14 How can taxation meet the needs of government and the people?

Program Resources

Instructional
- Essential Questions Journal
- Video Challenge Online and DVD
- Current Events Update
- Essential Question WebQuest

Assessment
- Test Online
- Chapter Tests, All-in-One
- Assessment Rubrics
- Exam*View* TestBank on CD-ROM
- AYP Monitoring Assessments

SECTION 1

What Are Taxes?

Guiding Question: What are the features of a tax system?

Student Objectives
- Identify the sources of the government's authority to tax.
- Describe types of tax bases and tax structures.
- Identify who bears the burden of a tax.
- List the characteristics of a good tax.

Lesson Overview

Students will respond to famous quotes on taxation. They will show understanding of the government's power to tax and the purpose of taxation. They will compare and contrast different types of taxes to understand tax structures. Students will use a worksheet to determine whether the individual income tax is a good tax based on four criteria.

Section Resources in Unit 6 All-in-One

L3 L1 L2 Guided Reading and Review, pp. 15, 16
L1 L2 Vocabulary Worksheet, p. 14
L3 Progressive and Regressive Taxes, Color Transparencies, 14.a
L3 L2 A Good Tax?, pp. 17, 18
L4 The Flat Tax, p. 19
L3 L2 Section Quiz, pp. 20, 21

Virtual Economics on CD-ROM

L3 Teacher's Edition, p. 367

SECTION 2

Federal Taxes

Guiding Question: What taxes does the federal government collect?

Student Objectives
- Describe the process of paying individual income taxes.
- Identify the basic characteristics of corporate income taxes.
- Explain the purpose of Social Security, Medicare, and unemployment taxes.
- Identify other types of taxes.

Lesson Overview

Students will use a worksheet to analyze how different deductions and credits affect income tax. They will examine the structure and tax base of different types of federal taxes, and use a worksheet to calculate federal income tax.

Section Resources in Unit 6 All-in-One

L3 L1 L2 Guided Reading and Review, pp. 22, 23
L3 L2 Comparing Tax Situations, pp. 25, 26
L4 Calculating Federal Income Tax, p. 24
L3 L2 Section Quiz, pp. 27, 28

Virtual Economics on CD-ROM

L3 Teacher's Edition, p. 372

CHAPTER LESSON PLANNER

TEACHING ECONOMICS

PROGRAM ORGANIZATION

DIFFERENTIATED INSTRUCTION

ASSESSMENT

PLANNING YOUR INSTRUCTION

SECTION 3

Federal Spending

Guiding Question: How does the federal government spend its income?

Student Objectives

- Distinguish between mandatory and discretionary spending.
- Describe the major entitlement programs.
- Identify categories of discretionary spending.
- Explain the impact of federal aid to state and local governments.

Lesson Overview

Students will distinguish mandatory from discretionary federal spending programs. They will compare and contrast entitlement programs. They will debate possible solutions to the Social Security financing problem. They will assess different options for solving the health insurance problem. Students will discuss the impact of rising mandatory spending on discretionary spending.

Section Resources in Unit 6 All-in-One

L3 L1 L2 Guided Reading and Review, pp. 29, 30
L3 Career Link, p. 134
L3 L2 Skill: Problem Solving, pp. 31, 32
L3 Projected U.S. Population by Age, Color Transparencies, 14.b
L4 Federal Aid to State and Local Governments, p. 33
L2 Medicare and Social Security Funding, p. 34
L3 L2 Section Quiz, pp. 35, 36

Virtual Economics on CD-ROM

L3 Teacher's Edition, p. 378

SECTION 4

State and Local Taxes and Spending

Guiding Question: How do local governments manage their money?

Student Objectives

- Explain how states use a budget to plan their spending.
- Identify where state taxes are spent.
- List the major sources of state tax revenue.
- Describe local government spending and sources of revenue.

Lesson Overview

Students will understand operating and capital budgets and compare levels of state spending in one area. They will analyze different situations to determine who bears the burden of state taxes. They will conduct a debate about state corporate tax rates. Students will discuss the costs and benefits of corporate income taxes.

Section Resources in Unit 6 All-in-One

L3 L1 L2 Guided Reading and Review, pp. 37, 38
L3 Comparing State Spending, p. 39
L2 State and Local Education Spending, p. 40
L3 Taxes and Changing Circumstances, Simulation Activities, Chapter 14
L3 L2 Section Quiz, pp. 41, 42
L3 Economic Detective, p. 43

Virtual Economics on CD-ROM

L3 Teacher's Edition, p. 384

DIFFERENTIATED INSTRUCTION KEY

L1 Special Needs
L2 Basic
ELL English Language Learners
LPR Less Proficient Readers
L3 All Students
L4 Advanced Students

Economics online

Online Student Center includes

- **Online Student Editions—Economics and Foundations Series Economics**
  - Action Graph Animations
  - How the Economy Works Interactives
  - Visual Glossary Interactives
  - WebQuests
- **Economics on the Go**
  - Economic Dictionary Audio
  - Audio Review—English and Spanish
  - Action Graph Animations
  - How the Economy Works Animations
  - Visual Glossary Animations
- **Essential Questions Journal**
- **Wall Street Journal Video**
- **Selected Worksheets**

Online Teacher Center includes all Online Student Center material plus

- **Online Teacher's Editions—Economics and Foundations Series Economics**
- **Teacher's Resource Library**
- **Economics Updates**
- **Assessment Rubrics**
- **Blank Graphic Organizers**

Chapter 15 Fiscal Policy

 Essential Questions

UNIT 6 What is the proper role of government in the economy?

CHAPTER 15 How effective is fiscal policy as an economic tool?

Program Resources

Instructional
- Essential Questions Journal
- Video Challenge Online and DVD
- Current Events Update
- Essential Question WebQuest

Assessment
- Test Online
- Chapter Tests, All-in-One
- Assessment Rubrics
- Exam*View* TestBank on CD-ROM
- AYP Monitoring Assessments

SECTION 1

Understanding Fiscal Policy

Guiding Question: What are the goals and limits of fiscal policy?

Student Objectives
- Describe how the federal budget is created.
- Analyze the impact of expansionary and contractionary fiscal policy on the economy.
- Identify the limits of fiscal policy.

Lesson Overview

Students will describe the process of creating the federal budget by taking on the roles of participants in the process. They will use a worksheet to compare the goals of expansionary and contractionary fiscal policy. Students will describe the limits of fiscal policy.

Section Resources in Unit 6 All-in-One

L3 L1 L2 Guided Reading and Review, pp. 59, 60
L1 L2 Vocabulary Worksheet, p. 58
L3 Career Link, p. 134
L3 L2 Comparing Fiscal Policies, pp. 61, 62
L3 Expand or Contract?, Simulation Activities, Chapter 15
L3 L2 Section Quiz, pp. 63, 64

Virtual Economics on CD-ROM

L3 Teacher's Edition, p. 396

SECTION 2

Fiscal Policy Options

Guiding Question: What economic ideas have shaped fiscal policy?

Student Objectives
- Compare and contrast classical economics and Keynesian economics.
- Explain the basic principles of supply-side economics.
- Describe the role that fiscal policy has played in American history.

Lesson Overview

Students will use a cartoon transparency to stimulate thinking about the use of fiscal policy. They will use a worksheet to describe and compare classical, Keynesian, and supply-side economics. They will describe the impact of the multiplier effect and automatic stabilizers on the economy. Students will analyze the government's use of fiscal policy since the Great Depression.

Section Resources in Unit 6 All-in-One

L3 L1 L2 Guided Reading and Review, pp. 65, 66
L3 The King and His Magician, Color Transparencies, 15.a
L3 L2 Skill: Draw Inferences and Conclusions, pp. 67, 68
L4 The Use of Tax Cuts, p. 69
L3 L2 Economic Dialogue, pp. 70, 71
L3 L2 Section Quiz, pp. 72, 73

Virtual Economics on CD-ROM

L3 Teacher's Edition, p. 403

SECTION 3

Budget Deficits and the National Debt

Guiding Question: What are the effects of budget deficits and national debt?

Student Objectives

- Explain the importance of balancing the budget.
- Analyze how budget deficits add to the national debt.
- Summarize the problems caused by the national debt.
- Identify how political leaders have tried to control the deficit.

Lesson Overview

Students will use a worksheet to identify some of the major categories of federal revenues and expenses. They will describe actions the government can take to balance the budget. They will describe the problems that can arise from a national debt. Students will explain ways in which government leaders have tried to control the deficit since the 1980s.

Section Resources in Unit 6 All-in-One

L3 L1 L2 Guided Reading and Review, pp. 74, 75

L3 L2 The Federal Budget, pp. 76, 77

L4 Taxes and the Budget Deficit, p. 78

L3 Nearly Empty or Almost Full?, Color Transparencies, 15.b

L3 L2 Section Quiz, pp. 79, 80

L3 Economic Detective, p. 81

Virtual Economics on CD-ROM

L3 Teacher's Edition, p. 410

DIFFERENTIATED INSTRUCTION KEY

L1 Special Needs

L2 Basic

ELL English Language Learners

LPR Less Proficient Readers

L3 All Students

L4 Advanced Students

Economics online

Online Student Center includes

- **Online Student Editions—Economics and Foundations Series Economics**
  - Action Graph Animations
  - How the Economy Works Interactives
  - Visual Glossary Interactives
  - WebQuests
- **Economics on the Go**
  - Economic Dictionary Audio
  - Audio Review—English and Spanish
  - Action Graph Animations
  - How the Economy Works Animations
  - Visual Glossary Animations
- **Essential Questions Journal**
- **Wall Street Journal Video**
- **Selected Worksheets**

Online Teacher Center includes all Online Student Center material plus

- **Online Teacher's Editions—Economics and Foundations Series Economics**
- **Teacher's Resource Library**
- **Economics Updates**
- **Assessment Rubrics**
- **Blank Graphic Organizers**

Chapter 16 The Federal Reserve and Monetary Policy

Essential Questions

UNIT 6 What is the proper role of government in the economy?

CHAPTER 16 How effective is monetary policy as an economic tool?

Program Resources

Instructional
- Essential Questions Journal
- Video Challenge Online and DVD
- Current Events Update
- Essential Question WebQuest

Assessment
- Test Online
- Chapter Tests, All-in-One
- Assessment Rubrics
- Exam*View* TestBank on CD-ROM
- AYP Monitoring Assessments

SECTION 1

The Federal Reserve System

Guiding Question: How is the Federal Reserve System organized?

Student Objectives
- Describe banking history in the United States.
- Explain why the Federal Reserve Act of 1913 led to further reform.
- Describe the structure of the Federal Reserve System.

Lesson Overview

Students will use a worksheet to demonstrate understanding of U.S. banking history and the conditions that led to the Federal Reserve Act of 1913. They will interpret a chart to explain the structure of the Federal Reserve System. They will the explore the Federal Reserve System online and identify facts about the Federal Reserve Bank in their district. Students will use a worksheet to distinguish fact from opinion.

Section Resources in Unit 6 All-in-One

L3 L1 L2 Guided Reading and Review, pp. 99, 100
L1 L2 Vocabulary Worksheet, p. 98
L3 L2 The Bad Old Days: Panics and Runs, pp. 101, 102
L3 L2 Skill: Fact and Opinion, pp. 103, 104
L3 L2 Section Quiz, pp. 105, 106

Virtual Economics on CD-ROM

L3 Teacher's Edition, p. 423

SECTION 2

Federal Reserve Functions

Guiding Question: What does the Federal Reserve do?

Student Objectives
- Describe how the Federal Reserve serves the federal government.
- Explain how the Federal Reserve serves banks.
- Describe how the Federal Reserve regulates the banking system.
- Explain the Federal Reserve's role in regulating the nation's money supply.

Lesson Overview

Students will develop and perform in a skit to demonstrate an understanding of one role of the Federal Reserve. They will demonstrate an understanding of the Federal Reserve's other roles.

Section Resources in Unit 6 All-in-One

L3 L1 L2 Guided Reading and Review, pp. 107, 108
L3 Paper Money, Color Transparencies, 16.a
L3 L2 The Fed's Many Roles, pp. 109, 110
L3 L2 Section Quiz, pp. 111, 112

Virtual Economics on CD-ROM

L3 Teacher's Edition, p. 427

SECTION 3

Monetary Policy Tools

Guiding Question: How does the Federal Reserve control the amount of money in use?

Student Objectives

- Describe the process of money creation.
- Explain how the Federal Reserve uses reserve requirements, the discount rate, and open market operations to implement monetary policy.
- Explain why the Fed favors one monetary policy tool over the others.

Lesson Overview

Students will use a worksheet to explain and apply the process of money creation. They will discuss the Federal Reserve's various monetary policy tools. Students will use a worksheet to play the role of an economist and recommend monetary policy tools for two scenarios.

Section Resources in Unit 6 All-in-One

L3 L1 L2 Guided Reading and Review, pp. 113, 114
L3 L2 Making Money, pp. 115, 116
L3 Money and the Federal Reserve, Simulation Activities, Chapter 16
L4 You Be the Fed, p. 117
L3 L2 Section Quiz, pp. 118, 119

Virtual Economics on CD-ROM

L3 Teacher's Edition, p. 431

SECTION 4

Monetary Policy and Macroeconomic Stabilization

Guiding Question: How does monetary policy affect economic stability?

Student Objectives

- Explain how monetary policy works.
- Describe the problem of timing in implementing monetary policy.
- Explain why the Fed's monetary policy can involve predicting business cycles.
- Contrast two general approaches to monetary policy.

Lesson Overview

Students will interpret a transparency to demonstrate an understanding of how monetary policy works. They will use a worksheet to analyze the problem of timing in implementing monetary policy. Students will write a letter or create a cartoon to assess two approaches to monetary policy.

Section Resources in Unit 6 All-in-One

L3 L1 L2 Guided Reading and Review, pp. 120, 121
L3 The Impact of the Federal Reserve on Interest Rates, Color Transparencies, 16.b
L3 L2 Steering the Economy, pp. 122, 123
L4 FOMC Role-Play, p. 124
L3 L2 Section Quiz, pp. 125, 126
L3 Economic Detective, p. 127

Virtual Economics on CD-ROM

L3 Teacher's Edition, p. 437

DIFFERENTIATED INSTRUCTION KEY

L1 Special Needs
L2 Basic
ELL English Language Learners
LPR Less Proficient Readers
L3 All Students
L4 Advanced Students

Economics online

Online Student Center includes

- **Online Student Editions—Economics and Foundations Series Economics**
  - Action Graph Animations
  - How the Economy Works Interactives
  - Visual Glossary Interactives
  - WebQuests
- **Economics on the Go**
  - Economic Dictionary Audio
  - Audio Review—English and Spanish
  - Action Graph Animations
  - How the Economy Works Animations
  - Visual Glossary Animations
- **Essential Questions Journal**
- **Wall Street Journal Video**
- **Selected Worksheets**

Online Teacher Center includes all Online Student Center material plus

- **Online Teacher's Editions—Economics and Foundations Series Economics**
- **Teacher's Resource Library**
- **Economics Updates**
- **Assessment Rubrics**
- **Blank Graphic Organizers**

Chapter 17 International Trade

 Essential Questions

UNIT 7 How might scarcity divide our world or bring it together?

CHAPTER 17 Should free trade be encouraged?

Program Resources

Instructional
- Essential Questions Journal
- Video Challenge Online and DVD
- Current Events Update
- Essential Question WebQuest

Assessment
- Test Online
- Chapter Tests, All-in-One
- Assessment Rubrics
- Exam*View* TestBank on CD-ROM
- AYP Monitoring Assessments

SECTION 1

Absolute and Comparative Advantage

Guiding Question: Why do nations trade?

Student Objectives
- Evaluate the impact of the unequal distribution of resources.
- Apply the concepts of specialization and comparative advantage to explain why countries trade.
- Summarize the position of the United States in world trade.
- Describe the effects of trade on employment.

Lesson Overview

Using a worksheet, students will demonstrate understanding of specialization and comparative advantage. By creating and interpreting a map, they will analyze the impact of the unequal distribution of resources. They will use a transparency and a table to analyze the U.S. position in world trade. Students will show understanding of how trade affects employment by taking a position on this issue in a blog post, poster, or editorial cartoon.

Section Resources in Unit 7 All-in-One

L3 L1 L2 Guided Reading and Review, pp. 13, 14
L3 Where Does It Come From?, Color Transparencies, 17.a
L1 L2 Vocabulary Worksheet, p. 12
L3 L2 Who Should Produce What?, pp. 15, 16
L3 L2 Skill: Analyze Maps, pp. 17, 18
L3 L2 Section Quiz, pp. 19, 20

Virtual Economics on CD-ROM

L3 Teacher's Edition, p. 451

SECTION 2

Trade Barriers and Agreements

Guiding Question: What are the arguments for and against trade barriers and agreements?

Student Objectives
- Define various types of trade barriers.
- Analyze the effects of trade barriers on economic activities.
- Summarize arguments in favor of protectionism.
- Evaluate the benefits and costs of participation in international trade agreements.
- Explain the role of multinationals in the global market.

Lesson Overview

Students will use a graphic organizer to identify the various types of trade barriers. They will assess the effects of trade barriers by completing a table of "winners" and "losers" for various scenarios. They will interpret a political cartoon in order to demonstrate an understanding of protectionism. With the help of a worksheet, students will analyze the arguments for and against international trade agreements and free trade.

Section Resources in Unit 7 All-in-One

L3 L1 L2 Guided Reading and Review, pp. 21, 22
L3 L2 Trade Barriers: Winners and Losers, pp. 23, 24
L3 Benefiting American Business, Color Transparencies, 17.b
L4 NAFTA: Pro and Con, p. 25
L3 L2 Section Quiz, pp. 26, 27

Virtual Economics on CD-ROM

L3 Teacher's Edition, p. 457

SECTION 3

Measuring Trade

Guiding Question: How do exchange rates affect international trade?

Student Objectives

- Explain how exchange rates of world currencies change.
- Describe the effect of various exchange rate systems.
- Define balance of trade and balance of payments.
- Analyze the causes and effects of the U.S. trade deficit.

Lesson Overview

Students will analyze a political cartoon to demonstrate an understanding of foreign exchange, exchange rates, and their effects. With the help of a worksheet, they will show understanding of balance of trade, balance of payments, and trade deficits.

Section Resources in Unit 7 All-in-One

L3 L1 L2 Guided Reading and Review, pp. 28, 29
L3 L2 Making the Most of It, pp. 30, 31
L3 Career Link, p. 88
L4 China and the U.S. Balance of Trade, p. 32
L3 Fair Exchange, Simulation Activities, Chapter 17
L3 L2 Section Quiz, pp. 33, 34
L3 L2 Economic Detective, p. 35

Virtual Economics on CD-ROM

L3 Teacher's Edition, p. 465

DIFFERENTIATED INSTRUCTION KEY

L1 Special Needs
L2 Basic
ELL English Language Learners
LPR Less Proficient Readers
L3 All Students
L4 Advanced Students

Economics online

Online Student Center includes

- **Online Student Editions—Economics and Foundations Series Economics**
  - Action Graph Animations
  - How the Economy Works Interactives
  - Visual Glossary Interactives
  - WebQuests
- **Economics on the Go**
  - Economic Dictionary Audio
  - Audio Review—English and Spanish
  - Action Graph Animations
  - How the Economy Works Animations
  - Visual Glossary Animations
- **Essential Questions Journal**
- **Wall Street Journal Video**
- **Selected Worksheets**

Online Teacher Center includes all Online Student Center material plus

- **Online Teacher's Editions—Economics and Foundations Series Economics**
- **Teacher's Resource Library**
- **Economics Updates**
- **Assessment Rubrics**
- **Blank Graphic Organizers**

PLANNING YOUR INSTRUCTION

Chapter 18 Development and Globalization

 Essential Questions

UNIT 7 How might scarcity divide our world or bring it together?

CHAPTER 18 Do the benefits of economic development outweigh the costs?

Program Resources

Instructional
- Essential Questions Journal
- Video Challenge Online and DVD
- Current Events Update
- Essential Question WebQuest

Assessment
- Test Online
- Chapter Tests, All-in-One
- Assessment Rubrics
- Exam*View* TestBank on CD-ROM
- AYP Monitoring Assessments

SECTION 1

Levels of Development

Guiding Question: How is a nation's level of development defined?

Student Objectives
- Understand what is meant by developed nations and less developed countries.
- Identify the tools used to measure levels of development.
- Describe the characteristics of developed nations and less developed countries.
- Understand how levels of development are ranked.

Lesson Overview

Students will identify characteristics of developed and developing nations. They will use a worksheet to analyze how per capita GDP and income distribution are used to measure development. They will contrast nations by level of development and generalize about the characteristics of developed nations. Students will use data on workforce distribution to make inferences about characteristics of agriculture in LDCs.

Section Resources in Unit 7 All-in-One

L3 L1 L2 Guided Reading and Review, pp. 53, 54
L1 L2 Vocabulary Worksheet, p. 52
L3 L1 L2 Measuring Development, pp. 55, 56
L3 Workforce Distribution and Development, Color Transparencies, 18.a
L3 L2 Section Quiz, pp. 57, 58

Virtual Economics on CD-ROM

L3 Teacher's Edition, p. 483

SECTION 2

Issues in Development

Guiding Question: What factors harm or help development?

Student Objectives
- Identify the causes and effects of rapid population growth.
- Analyze how political factors and debt are obstacles to development.
- Summarize the role investment and foreign aid play in development.
- Describe the functions of various international economic institutions.

Lesson Overview

Students will use a worksheet to demonstrate understanding of the impact of population growth rates. They will compare the likelihood that different factors of production would promote development. They will analyze the possible connection between maternal education and malnutrition in children. Students will debate controversies associated with the issue of promoting development in LDCs.

Section Resources in Unit 7 All-in-One

L3 L1 L2 Guided Reading and Review, pp. 59, 60
L3 L2 Impact of Population Growth, pp. 61, 62
L2 L4 How Will You Help?, Simulation Activities, Chapter 18
L3 L2 Skill: Conducting Research, pp. 63, 64
L3 L2 Section Quiz, pp. 65, 66

Virtual Economics on CD-ROM

L3 Teacher's Edition, p. 489

CHAPTER LESSON PLANNER

SECTION 3

Economies in Transition

Guiding Question: How has economic change affected different countries?

Student Objectives

- Identify the characteristics of economic transition.
- Describe the political and economic changes that have taken place in Russia since the fall of communism.
- Analyze the reasons for rapid economic growth in China and India.
- Summarize the economic challenges facing Africa and Latin America.

Lesson Overview

Students will explore results of economic changes in several countries and make generalizations about them. They will use case studies in a worksheet to compare results of economic changes in several countries. Students will identify how poverty affects a nation's potential.

Section Resources in Unit 7 All-in-One

L3 L1 L2 Guided Reading and Review, pp. 67, 68
L3 L1 L2 Economies in Transition, pp. 69, 71
L4 Analyzing India, p. 72
L3 L2 Section Quiz, pp. 73, 74

Virtual Economics on CD-ROM

L3 Teacher's Edition, p. 497

SECTION 4

Challenges of Globalization

Guiding Question: What are the effects of globalization?

Student Objectives

- Define globalization and identify factors that promoted its spread.
- Explain four problems linked to globalization.
- Describe three challenges that globalization creates.
- Identify the characteristics needed for American workers and companies to succeed in the future.

Lesson Overview

Students will discuss positive and negative aspects of globalization. They will debate the issue of investment in LDCs by multinational corporations. They will show understanding of the effect of job relocation and offshoring on employment in different regions of the United States. Students will discuss the debate over pursuing developmental or environmental goals.

Section Resources in Unit 7 All-in-One

L3 L1 L2 Guided Reading and Review, pp. 75, 76
L3 Job Losses and Relocation, Color Transparencies, 18.b
L3 L1 L2 Land Use, Urbanization, and Development, pp. 77, 78
L3 Career Link worksheet, p. 88
L3 L2 Section Quiz, pp. 79, 80
L3 Economic Detective, p. 81

Virtual Economics on CD-ROM

L3 Teacher's Edition, p. 507

DIFFERENTIATED INSTRUCTION KEY

L1 Special Needs
L2 Basic
ELL English Language Learners
LPR Less Proficient Readers
L3 All Students
L4 Advanced Students

Economics online

Online Student Center includes

- **Online Student Editions—Economics and Foundations Series Economics**
  - Action Graph Animations
  - How the Economy Works Interactives
  - Visual Glossary Interactives
  - WebQuests
- **Economics on the Go**
  - Economic Dictionary Audio
  - Audio Review—English and Spanish
  - Action Graph Animations
  - How the Economy Works Animations
  - Visual Glossary Animations
- **Essential Questions Journal**
- **Wall Street Journal Video**
- **Selected Worksheets**

Teacher Center at PearsonSuccessNet.com

Online Teacher Center includes all Online Student Center material plus

- **Online Teacher's Editions—Economics and Foundations Series Economics**
- **Teacher's Resource Library**
- **Economics Updates**
- **Assessment Rubrics**
- **Blank Graphic Organizers**

Personal Finance Handbook

INTRODUCTION

Your Fiscal Fitness

Lesson Overview

Students will become familiar with basic financial terms by comparing fiscal fitness to physical fitness. They will practice making financial choices by outlining what they might choose to do with $100. Students will contrast the results of various decisions by completing a decision tree.

Personal Finance Handbook All-in-One

- L3 Self-Test, p. 28
- L3 It's Your Choice, pp. 30–31

BUDGETING

Wise Choices for Your Money

Lesson Overview

Students will discuss and understand the reasons for a budget. They will learn how they spend money by keeping a spending journal. Students will use a chart to differentiate between wants and needs.

Personal Finance Handbook All-in-One

- L3 My Spending Journal, pp. 32–33
- L3 Form: My Monthly Budget, p. 34
- L3 The Trouble with Budgets, pp. 35–36
- L3 Wise Choices for Your Money Quiz, p. 37

Additional Resources

- L3 Fixed Income, Color Transparencies, PF.a

CHECKING

Checking Up on Checking Accounts

Lesson Overview

Students will practice writing a check. They will evaluate types of checking accounts and checking services with the help of a worksheet. Students will explain why it's important to balance a checkbook with the help of a worksheet.

Personal Finance Handbook All-in-One

- L3 Checks and Balancing, pp. 38–39
- L3 Debit? Yes. Debt? No., p. 40
- L3 Checking Up on Checking Accounts Quiz, p. 41

Banking Online

Lesson Overview

Students will describe the benefits of online banking. They will assess the risks of online banking. Students will compare traditional and online banking by completing a worksheet.

Personal Finance Handbook All-in-One

- L3 Keeping Track Online, pp. 42–43
- L3 Banking Online Quiz, p. 44

Additional Resources

- L3 Dear Computer User, Color Transparencies, PF.b

INVESTMENTS

Investing with Dollars and $ense

Lesson Overview

Students will understand the rate of return on an investment by calculating the amount of interest earned at various rates. They will analyze a variety of investment vehicles. Students will evaluate different ways to reach a financial objective by completing a worksheet.

Personal Finance Handbook All-in-One

- L3 Informed Investing, pp. 45–46
- L3 Investing with Dollars and Sense Quiz, p. 47

Additional Resources

- L3 Many Happy Returns?, Color Transparencies, PF.c

Building Your Portfolio

Lesson Overview

Students will assess their own attitudes toward risk and investing by completing a survey. They will analyze risks and rewards of six common investment vehicles by completing a worksheet.

Personal Finance Handbook All-in-One

- L3 Assessing Risk and Reward, pp. 48–49
- L3 Form: Attitude Inventory, p. 50
- L3 Good Advice?, p. 51
- L3 Building Your Portfolio Quiz, p. 52

SAVINGS AND RETIREMENT

Saving for the Long Haul

Lesson Overview

Students will identify savings strategies. They will plan to save toward a short- or long-term goal. Students will compare different savings accounts by completing a worksheet.

Personal Finance Handbook All-in-One

- L3 Pay Yourself First, pp. 53–54
- L3 Saving for the Long Haul Quiz, p. 55

Get Personal with Your Savings Plan

Lesson Overview

Students will assess different savings plans by completing a worksheet. They will discuss the benefits and drawbacks of CDs. They will practice saving by collecting spare change for a week.

Personal Finance Handbook All-in-One

- L3 Saving on Your Terms, pp. 56–57
- L3 Form: Automatic Payroll Deduction, p. 58
- L3 Get Personal with Your Savings Plan Quiz, p. 59

Retirement Planning: Me. Now. *Why?*

Lesson Overview

Students will analyze a Social Security benefits statement. They will compare different retirement plans, by completing a worksheet. Students will draw conclusions about income needed in retirement by completing a worksheet.

Personal Finance Handbook All-in-One

- L3 Your Nest Egg, pp. 60–61
- L3 How Much Will You Need to Retire?, p. 62
- L3 Retirement Planning: Me. Now. *Why?* Quiz, p. 63

Additional Resources

- L3 Social Security Statement, Color Transparencies, PF.d

CREDIT AND DEBT

Fundamentals of Good Credit

Lesson Overview

Students will apply criteria to granting credit. They will interpret a chart to analyze household income and debt. They will learn how different factors influence a credit score by completing a worksheet.

Personal Finance Handbook All-in-One

- L3 Keep Track of Your Score, pp. 64–65
- L3 Credit Report Form, p. 66
- L3 Fundamentals of Good Credit Quiz, p. 67

Additional Resources

- L3 Growing Household Debt, Color Transparencies, PF.e

Ready. Set. *Charge?*

Lesson Overview

Students will debate whether teens under age 18 should be allowed to have their own credit cards. They will compare the terms and conditions of different cards by completing a worksheet. They will complete a credit card application form.

Personal Finance Handbook All-in-One

- L3 The Best Card for You, pp. 68–69
- L3 Form: Credit Card Application, p. 70
- L3 Making Peace with Your Plastic, pp. 71–72
- L3 Ready. Set. *Charge?* Quiz, p. 73

Managing Your Debts

Lesson Overview

Students will develop a list of suggestions for using credit wisely. They will explore strategies for getting out of debt by completing a worksheet. They will discuss the implications of bankruptcy.

Personal Finance Handbook All-in-One

- L3 Bills, Bills, Bills, pp. 74–75
- L3 Managing Your Debts Quiz, p. 76

RISK MANAGEMENT

Insurance Basics, Part I

Lesson Overview

Students will compare the cost of car insurance for two different vehicles by completing a worksheet. They will analyze the insurance needs of people in different life situations. They will discuss living wills and power of attorney.

Personal Finance Handbook All-in-One

- L3 Buying Car Insurance, pp. 77–78
- L3 Form: Last Will and Testament, p. 79
- L3 Insurance Basics, Part I Quiz, p. 80

Insurance Basics, Part II

Lesson Overview

Students will compare health plans by completing a worksheet. Students will present ways to slow the growth of healthcare and insurance costs and vote on the best solutions.

Personal Finance Handbook All-in-One

- L3 Choosing a Health Insurance Plan, pp. 81–82
- L3 The Healthcare Debate, p. 83
- L3 Insurance Basics, Part II Quiz, p. 84

Additional Resources

- L3 What About the Uninsured?, Color Transparencies, PF.f

CONSUMER SMARTS

Buying a Car

Lesson Overview

Students will estimate the cost of car ownership by completing a worksheet. They will understand ways to limit risks when buying a car by role-playing. Students will fill out an application for a car loan.

Personal Finance Handbook All-in-One

- L3 Guide to Buying a Car, pp. 85–86
- L3 Form: Application for a Car Loan, p. 87
- L3 Buying a Car Quiz, p. 88

Renting an Apartment

Lesson Overview

Students will evaluate the costs of renting an apartment by completing a worksheet. They will discuss ways to protect themselves when renting by analyzing a cartoon. Students will understand the rights and responsibilities of renting an apartment by filling out a residential lease agreement.

Personal Finance Handbook All-in-One

- L3 Renting an Apartment, pp. 89–90
- L3 Form: Residential Lease Agreement, p. 91
- L3 Renting an Apartment Quiz, p. 88

Additional Resources

- L3 Just Paperwork, Color Transparencies, PF.g

Identity Theft

Lesson Overview

Students will summarize the costs of identity theft by completing a worksheet. They will investigate a variety of types of online scams and other consumer fraud. Students will describe ways to reduce the risk of identity theft and how to restore personal security by completing a worksheet.

Personal Finance Handbook All-in-One

- L3 Avoiding Identity Theft, pp. 93–94
- L3 The Identity Theft Report, p. 95
- L3 Identity Theft Quiz, p. 96

Shopping Online: Be Safe, Not Sorry

Lesson Overview

Students will understand the factors that go into making good online buying choices. They will investigate how online sellers advise customers to conduct online buying. Students will describe their options if they are victims of online shopping fraud by completing a worksheet.

Personal Finance Handbook All-in-One

- L3 Virtual Customer Service, pp. 97–98
- L3 Shopping Online: Be Safe, Not Sorry Quiz, p. 99

LESSON PLANNING

AFTER HIGH SCHOOL

Paying for College

Lesson Overview

Students will understand the real costs of college by completing a worksheet. They will examine options for obtaining financial aid and the characteristics of each. Students will conduct online research on loan repayment.

Personal Finance Handbook All-in-One

L3 How Much Does it Cost?, pp. 100–101
L3 Paying for College Quiz, p. 102

Getting a Job

Lesson Overview

Students will understand what to include in a résumé by completing a résumé worksheet. They will describe how to prepare for and follow up after a job interview. Students will determine appropriate dress for an interview by analyzing a transparency.

Personal Finance Handbook All-in-One

L3 What's in a Résumé?, pp. 103–104
L3 Prepare for the Interview, p. 105
L3 Getting a Job Quiz, p. 106

Additional Resources

L3 Dress for Success, Color Transparencies, PF.h

TAXES AND INCOME

Understanding Your Paycheck

Lesson Overview

Students will practice reading a paycheck to understand terms such as *gross pay, net pay, FICA*, and *Medicare*. They will understand how to assess deductions and estimate their tax obligation by completing a worksheet and filling out a W-4 form. Students will analyze an earnings statement.

Personal Finance Handbook All-in-One

L3 How Much Will You Owe?, pp. 107–108
L3 Form: W-4, p. 109
L3 Understanding Your Paycheck Quiz, p. 110

Paying Your Taxes

Lesson Overview

Students will describe the different kinds of state and federal taxes. They will describe the W-2 form and fill out forms 1040 and 1040EZ with the help of worksheets. Students will learn where to get help filing taxes.

Personal Finance Handbook All-in-One

L3 Tax Time, pp. 111–112
L3 Form: 1040EZ
L3 Taxes and Income, p. 114
L3 Paying Your Taxes Quiz, p. 115

Additional Resources

L3 The Tax Code, Color Transparencies, PF.i

Textbook Cover Lesson

One way to introduce this course is to have students examine the text cover and understand that economics is all around us. Using the book cover as stimuli, have students discuss the impact of economics on their lives.

LESSON GOALS

Students will:
- Understand how economics impacts all aspects of daily life.
- Explain reasons why people often make their choices based on economic factors.
- Create a definition for the term *economics*.

TEACH

Have students spread the book open to look at the full cover and briefly answer the following questions, going from left to right sides. **What are the biggest symbols or pictures? What do you think they represent – what is the connection to economics?** *(The Capitol building represents government and laws; the ATM and coins represent money; ketchup, mustard, salt represent manufactured goods in a supermarket; speakers, home, tractor, cars are manufactured goods; windmills and satellite dish represent technology.)*

Which symbols are smaller? What do you think these represent? *(These represent aspects of daily life: Sneakers and game controller represent leisure; piggy bank represents how much people save; mortarboard and books represent education; cows represent agriculture, etc.)*

DISCUSS

Using the Idea Wave strategy (p. T24), have students explain which symbol they think is the most important. Ask **Why do you think the piggy bank is in the middle of all the symbols?** *(The piggy bank represents how people use their resources – money, means of production, natural resources. This relates to government action (Capitol), recycling laws, control of banks (ATM), production of goods and services, etc.)*

CATEGORIZE

L2 Organize students into groups to list different images according to one or more categories, such as rural or urban, goods or services, and production or consumption. Discuss why they put the item in a particular category, making sure they understand the terms. Do any fall in both categories?

WRAP-UP ACTIVITIES

Have students create a word web around the word economics, using the ideas just mentioned. Then have students look up the term economics in the glossary of the book and compare their word web to the definition.

Have students describe how economics impacts the lives of people in one sentence. Refer to the text cover to help create the sentence. *(Possible answers: Economics affects how people spend or save money; Economics impacts the production, sales, and movement of goods and services; Economics involves the using and saving natural resources; Economics affects all parts of life; Economics is all around us.)*

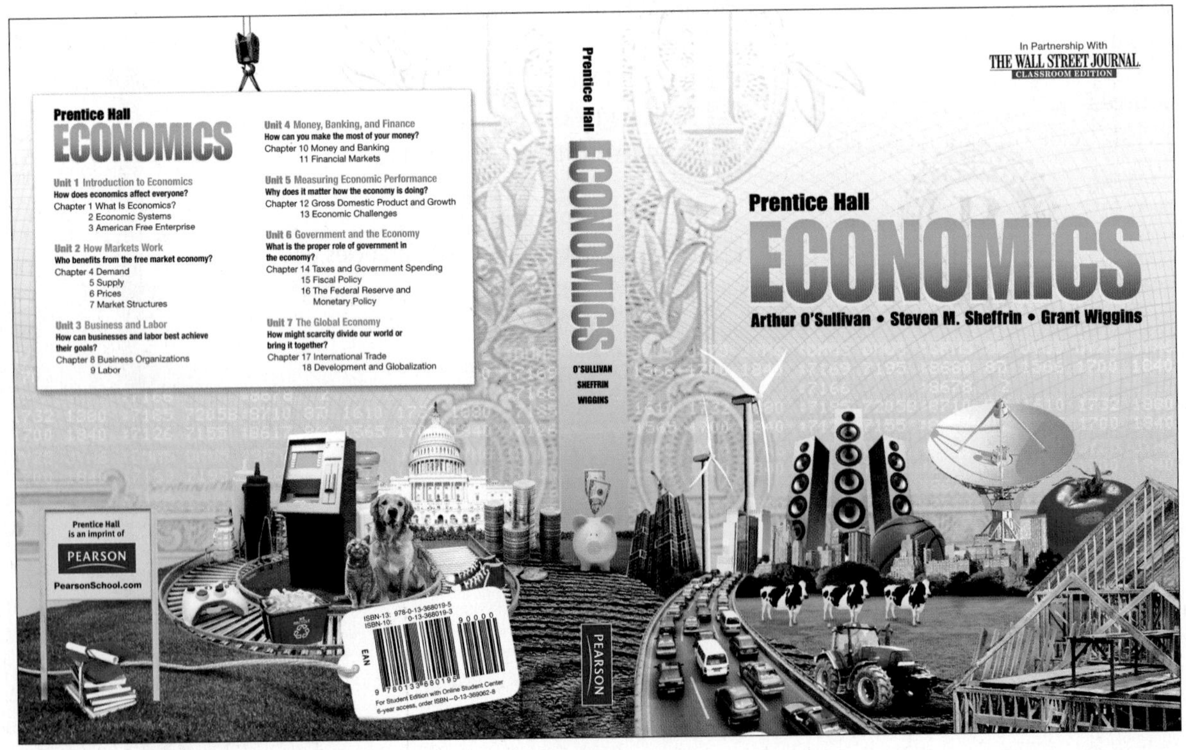

UNIT 1 Introduction to Economics

Chapter 1 What Is Economics?
Chapter 2 Economic Systems
Chapter 3 American Free Enterprise

Essential Question, Unit 1

How does economics affect everyone?

Chapter 1 How can we make the best economic choices?

Chapter 2 How does a society decide who gets what goods and services?

Chapter 3 What role should government play in a free market economy?

UNIT PREVIEW 1

Essential Question

How does economics affect everyone?

Introduce the Unit

ACTIVATE PRIOR KNOWLEDGE

Essential questions frame each unit and chapter of study, asking students to consider big ideas about economics. Write the Unit Essential Question on the board: **How does economics affect everyone?** Using the Idea Wave discussion strategy (p. T24), have students brainstorm answers to the question.

WRITING ACTIVITY

To begin this unit, assign the Unit 1 Warmup Activity in the **Essential Questions Journal**. This will help students start to consider their position on the Unit 1 Essential Question: **How does economics affect everyone?**

Use the **Essential Questions Journal** throughout the program to help students consider these and other big ideas about economics.

BULLETIN BOARD ACTIVITY

Post the Unit Essential Question on a bulletin board. Tell students that they will be learning about the impact of economics on everyone. Ask them to bring in articles about current events to help them answer the question. Students should identify their article and use a sticky note to briefly explain the connection to the Essential Question.

CREATING THE ESSENTIAL QUESTIONS VIDEO

Preview the Unit Challenge on page 82. Consider assigning this activity to your students. Tell them that they will be creating their own video to explore this question, and that they should keep this in mind as they study the effect of economics on everyone. For further information about how to complete this activity, go to PearsonSuccessNet.com.

NATIONAL COUNCIL ON ECONOMIC EDUCATION

The following Voluntary National Content Standards in Economics are addressed in this unit:

★ Standard 1 ★ Standard 3 ★ Standard 15
★ Standard 2 ★ Standard 4 ★ Standard 16

For a complete description of the standards addressed in each chapter, see the Correlations chart on pages T52–T55.

Online Resources

Economics Online Teacher Center at PearsonSuccessNet.com includes

- Online Teacher's Edition with lesson planner
- Online Lecture Notes
- Teacher's Resource Library with All-in-One Resources, Color Transparencies, Simulation Activities, and Adequate Yearly Progress Monitoring
- SuccessTracker Assessment

Economics Online Student Center at PearsonSuccessNet.com includes

- Interactive textbook with audio
- Economics Video
- WebQuests
- Interactivities
- Student Self-Tests

Essential Questions

UNIT 1:
How does economics affect everyone?

CHAPTER 1:
How can we make the best economic choices?

Introduce the Chapter

ACTIVATE PRIOR KNOWLEDGE

In this chapter students will learn how individuals, businesses, and governments make economic choices. Tell students to complete the warmup activity in the **Essential Questions Journal**.

DIFFERENTIATED INSTRUCTION KEY

- **L1** Special Needs
- **L2** Basic
  - **ELL** English Language Learners
  - **LPR** Less Proficient Readers
- **L3** All Students
- **L4** Advanced Students

Economics online Visit www.PearsonSuccessNet.com for an interactive textbook with built-in activities on economic principles.

- ***The Wall Street Journal* Classroom Edition Video** presents a current topic related to making economic decisions.
- **Yearly Update Worksheet** provides an annual update, including a new worksheet and lesson on this topic.
- **On the Go** resources can be downloaded so students and teachers can connect with economics any time, anywhere.

Chapter 1 What Is Economics?

Essential Question, Chapter 1
How can we make the best economic choices?

- **Section 1:** Scarcity and the Factors of Production
- **Section 2:** Opportunity Cost
- **Section 3:** Production Possibilities Curves

Economics on the go

To study anywhere, anytime, download these online resources at ***PearsonSuccessNet.com*** ▶

ECONOMICS ONLINE

DIGITAL TEACHER TOOLS

The online lesson planner is designed to help teachers plan, teach, and assess. Teachers have the ability to use or customize existing Pearson lesson plans. Online lecture notes support the print lesson by providing an array of accessible activities and summaries of key concepts. Two interactivities included in this lesson are:

- **How the Economy Works** allows students to take on the role of an entrepreneur starting a new small business.
- **WebQuest** Students use online resources to complete a guided activity about making the best economic choices for a nation.

Block Scheduling

BLOCK 1 Teach lessons for Sections 1 and 2, briefly introducing the Section 2 material on trade-offs and focusing on opportunity cost.

BLOCK 2 Teach Section 3 lesson, omitting the Extend activity.

Pressed for Time

Visual resources Use How the Economy Works, the Visual Glossary, and the Action Graphs Online to help students master the main concepts from the chapter: factors of production, opportunity cost, and production possibilities curves.

SECTION 1 Scarcity and the Factors of Production

OBJECTIVES

1. **Explain** why scarcity and choice are the basis of economics.
2. **Describe** what entrepreneurs do.
3. **Define** the three factors of production and the differences between physical and human capital.
4. **Explain** how scarcity affects the factors of production.

ECONOMIC DICTIONARY

As you read the section, look for the definitions of these **Key Terms:**

- need
- want
- goods
- services
- scarcity
- economics
- shortage
- entrepreneur
- factors of production
- land
- labor
- capital
- physical capital
- human capital

Guiding Question
How does scarcity force people to make economic choices?

Copy this cause-and-effect chart and fill it in as you read.

Needs and Wants	Resources
A. Definition:	A. Definition:
B. Unlimited	B.
C. Examples:	C. Examples:

Necessity of Making Choices

Economics and You

There are so many ways you could spend your money. You really want that new video game. You also want to attend an upcoming concert. At the same time, you need to pay your car insurance. With limited funds, you can't have it all. How will you choose?

What's true for you is also true for your neighbors, your school, the gas station on the corner, a major television network, and the U.S. Congress. Economics is the study of how individuals, businesses, and governments make choices when faced with a limited supply of resources.

Principles in Action Scarcity forces us all to make choices by making us decide which options are most important to us. In this section, you will examine the problem of scarcity as it relates to such varied resources as water and the ingredients needed to make a plate of French fries.

need something essential for survival

want something that people desire but that is not necessary for survival

Scarcity and Choice

The study of economics begins with the fact that people cannot have everything they need and want. A **need** is something essential for survival such as food or medical care. A **want** is something that we desire but that is not necessary for survival, such as video games or stylish haircuts.

People satisfy their needs and wants with goods and services. **Goods** are physical objects that someone produces, such as food, clothing, or video games. **Services** are actions or activities that one person performs for another. Medical care and haircuts are services.

goods the physical objects that someone produces

services the actions or activities that one person performs for another

Visual Glossary online

Go to the Visual Glossary Online for an interactive review of **opportunity cost.**

Action Graph online

Go to Action Graph Online for animated versions of key charts and graphs.

How the Economy Works online

Go to How the Economy Works Online for an interactive lesson on the role of the **entrepreneur.**

Focus on the Basics

Students need to come away with the following understandings:

FACTS: • Scarcity is the constant condition in which only limited amounts of goods and services are available to meet unlimited needs and wants. • Entrepreneurs combine resources to produce goods or services. • The factors of production are land, labor, and capital.

GENERALIZATION: Economics is the study of how people seek to satisfy their needs and wants by making choices among scarce resources.

Guiding Question

How does scarcity force people to make economic choices?

Get Started

Needs and Wants	Resources
A. A need is something essential for survival; a want is something desired but not essential.	A. Goods are physical objects someone produces; services are actions one person performs for another.
B. Unlimited	B. Limited
C. Example of a need: medical care; examples of a want: video games	C. Examples: land, labor, and capital (physical and human)

Necessity of Making Choices

LESSON GOALS

Students will:

- Know the Key Terms.
- Characterize a good or service as a need, a want, or both.
- Describe the characteristics of a successful entrepreneur.
- Identify the factors of production needed by a business.
- Evaluate the impact of scarce resources.

BEFORE CLASS

Have students complete the graphic organizer as they read. As an alternate activity, have students complete the Guided Reading and Review worksheet (Unit 1 All-in-One, p. 13).

L1 L2 ELL LPR Differentiate Have students complete the Guided Reading and Review worksheet (Unit 1 All-in-One, p. 14).

CLASSROOM HINTS

SCARCITY

One way for students to explore *scarcity* is to have them make choices within a limited time period. For example, set a timer to one minute, and then have students list items they would buy from the supermarket if they were buying enough for one week and money were no object. Another way to explore this concept is to have students list what items they would purchase given a specific amount of money. For example, have students choose what to purchase from the cafeteria with $5. Have them discuss the reasons for their choices.

BELLRINGER

Put a line on the board, with the word *need* on the left end and *want* on the right. Then write the words *car, water,* and *flowers* on the board. Ask students to copy this into their notebook, and place the items on the spectrum. Have them jot down why they placed the item where they did on the line.

Teach

Economics online To present this topic using digital resources, use the lecture notes on www.PearsonSuccessNet.com.

L1 L2 ELL LPR Differentiate To help students who are struggling readers, assign the Vocabulary worksheet (Unit 1 All-in-One, p. 12).

INTERPRET

Have students explain why they decided an item was a need or a want. Did any items show up on both sides of the line? Give students time to discuss how a car could be both a need (transportation to work) and a want (if public transportation were available). Have students consider other goods or services that could be identified in both categories.

Ask students to give examples of scarcity that they have faced. How did they make their choices?

L2 Differentiate To reinforce the difference between shortage and scarcity, explain that musical chairs represents a shortage. To show scarcity, tell students that in 24 hours, they have to accomplish 7 tasks, each requiring 4 hours. Ask **What resource is scarce?** *(time)* **How will scarcity affect what they can do?** *(They will have to choose which task will not be accomplished.)*

HOW THE ECONOMY WORKS

Direct students to the How the Economy Works feature. Ask **What does an entrepreneur need to be successful?** *(an idea, research, factors of production)* **What personality traits do you think an entrepreneur has?** *(risk taker, creative, determined)* Organize students into small groups to brainstorm a new business idea. Ask them to list the factors of production needed to meet the need or want. Then ask **Which factor would be the easiest to obtain? Which would be the most difficult? How did the economic concept of scarcity determine your answers?**

Answer

Checkpoint Economics focuses on how people seek to meet their unlimited needs and wants by making choices among scarce resources.

How the Economy Works

What does an entrepreneur do?

All entrepreneurs—whether they are starting a lawn-mowing service or founding a company that makes cars—have two things in common. First, they recognize a need or want. Then, they must assemble the factors of production to meet that need or want.

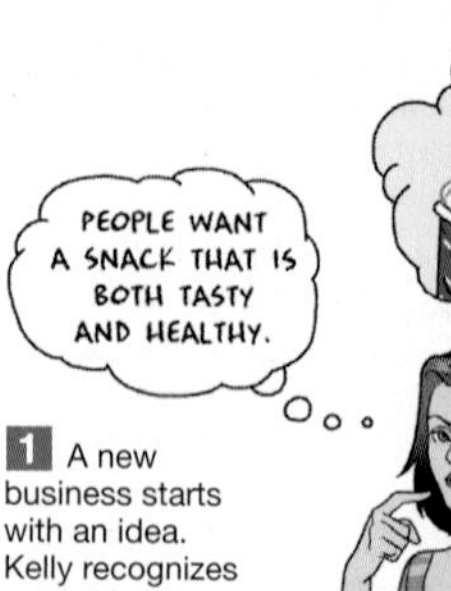

PEOPLE WANT A SNACK THAT IS BOTH TASTY AND HEALTHY.
WHAT IF I OPENED A SNACK BAR THAT SERVED FRUIT-AND-YOGURT SMOOTHIES?
HELP WANTED
CASHIERS and SERVERS

1 A new business starts with an idea. Kelly recognizes something her town needs and does not have.

2 Kelly begins to pull together the factors of production she needs to turn her idea into reality.

Land: natural resources

Labor: people to do the work

Recognize a Need or Want → **Assemble Factors of Production**

The Problem of Limits

People's needs and wants are unlimited. When one want is satisfied, others arise. After eating lunch, you might want to go to a movie or buy some clothes. Goods and services, however, are limited. No one can have an endless supply of anything. Sooner or later, a limit is always reached. The fact that limited amounts of goods and services are available to meet unlimited wants is called **scarcity.**

scarcity the principle that limited amounts of goods and services are available to meet unlimited wants

economics the study of how people seek to satisfy their needs and wants by making choices

shortage a situation in which consumers want more of a good or service than producers are willing to make available at a particular price

At many different levels, scarcity forces people to make choices. You, for example, have to decide how to spend your time. If you decide to study for a test, you cannot go to the mall or do volunteer work at the same time. A store must choose between hiring ten new workers or paying for more advertising to attract new customers. A city council might debate whether to use its money to fix an aging school building or to hire more firefighters.

Economics is the study of how people seek to satisfy their needs and wants by making choices. Because people act individually, in groups (such as businesses), and through governments, economists study all three.

Scarcity Versus Shortage

Scarcity is not the same thing as shortage. A **shortage** occurs when consumers want more of a good or service than producers are willing to make available at a particular price. (You will learn how shortages are related to price in Chapter 6.) Shortages may be temporary or long-term.

Unlike shortages, scarcity always exists. There simply are not enough goods and services to supply all of society's needs and wants. This is because the resources that go into making those goods and services are themselves scarce.

CHECKPOINT ***What is the main focus of economics?***

Differentiated Resources

- **L1 L2 Guided Reading and Review** (Unit 1 All-in-One, p. 14)
- **L1 L2 Vocabulary worksheet** (Unit 1 All-in-One, p. 12)
- **L2 Mark Zuckerberg, CEO of Facebook** (Unit 1 All-in-One, p. 16)
- **L4 Factors of Production in the Global Economy** (Unit 1 All-in-One, p. 17)

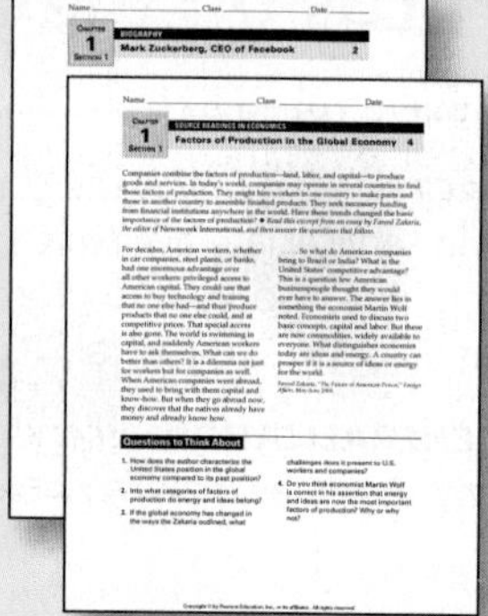

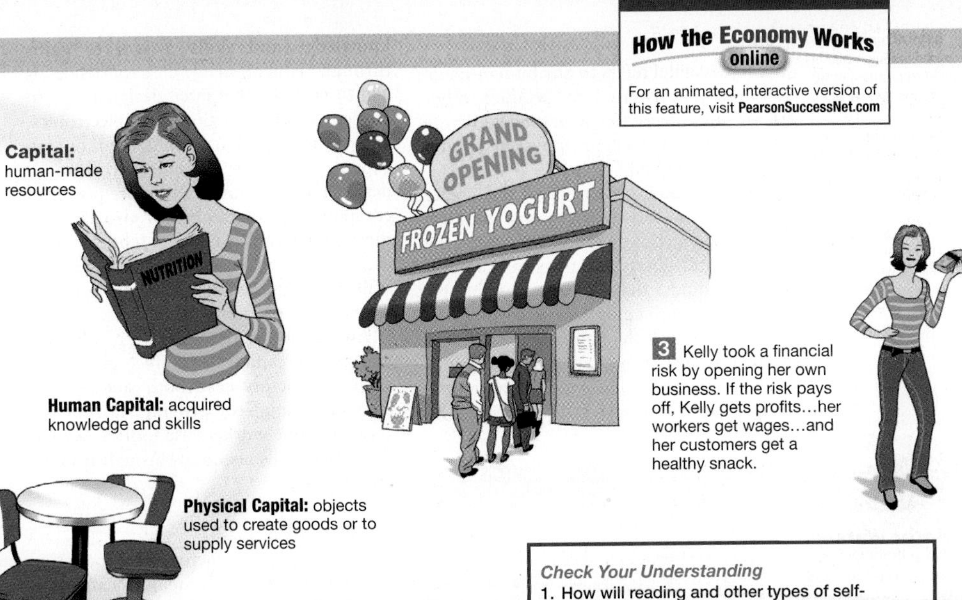
How the Economy Works
online
For an animated, interactive version of this feature, visit PearsonSuccessNet.com
Capital: human-made resources
NUTRITION
Human Capital: acquired knowledge and skills
GRAND OPENING
FROZEN YOGURT
3 Kelly took a financial risk by opening her own business. If the risk pays off, Kelly gets profits…her workers get wages…and her customers get a healthy snack.
Physical Capital: objects used to create goods or to supply services

Check Your Understanding

1. How will reading and other types of self-education help this entrepreneur succeed?
2. What impact does the concept of scarcity have on the decisions made by an entrepreneur?

Provide Goods or Services

Entrepreneurs and the Factors of Production

How are scarce resources turned into goods and services? Entrepreneurs play a key role. **Entrepreneurs** are people who decide how to combine resources to create new goods and services. To make a profit, entrepreneurs are willing to take risks. They develop original ideas, start businesses, create new industries, and fuel economic growth.

You need not be Bill Gates, founder of Microsoft, or Sam Walton, founder of Wal-Mart, to be an entrepreneur. Anyone who opens a business, from a local store to a global Internet company, is an entrepreneur.

The first task facing an entrepreneur is to assemble **factors of production,** or the resources used to make all goods and services. The three main factors of production are land, labor, and capital.

Land

Economists use the term **land** to refer to all natural resources used to produce goods and services. Natural resources are any materials found in nature that people use to make things or to provide services. These resources include fertile land for farming, as well as resources found in or on the land such as oil, iron, coal, water, and forests.

Labor

The second factor of production is labor. **Labor** is the effort people devote to tasks for which they are paid. Labor includes the medical care provided by a doctor, the classroom instruction provided by a teacher, and the tightening of a bolt by an assembly-line worker. Labor is also an artist's creation of a painting or a technician's repair of a television.

entrepreneur a person who decides how to combine resources to create goods and services

factors of production the resources that are used to make goods and services

land all natural resources used to produce goods and services

labor the effort people devote to tasks for which they are paid

DISTRIBUTE ACTIVITY WORKSHEET

Distribute the "Mark Zuckerberg, CEO of Facebook" worksheet (Unit 1 All-in-One, p. 15). Tell students that they will read a biography of a contemporary entrepreneur. After they complete the worksheet, ask **How did scarcity affect Zuckerberg's choices?** *(Possible answers: He developed a product, a social Web site, that students did not have. He did not have time to both go to school and develop a business. He had to decide how to spend money to increase the size of his business.)*

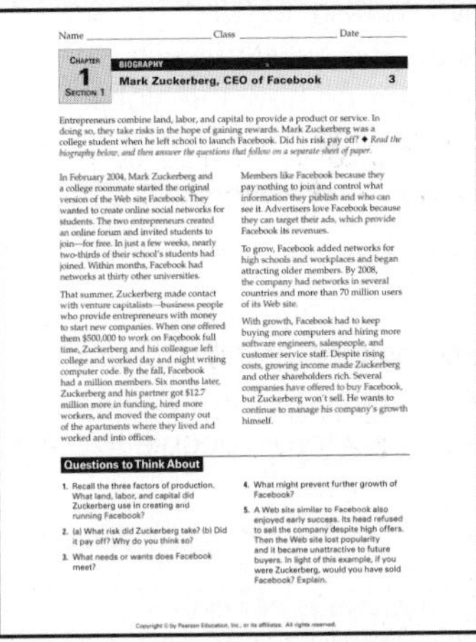
Name ______________ Class ______________ Date ________

CHAPTER 1 SECTION 1

BIOGRAPHY

Mark Zuckerberg, CEO of Facebook 3

Entrepreneurs combine land, labor, and capital to provide a product or service. In doing so, they take risks in the hope of gaining rewards. Mark Zuckerberg was a college student when he left school to launch Facebook. Did his risk pay off? ◆ *Read the biography below, and then answer the questions that follow on a separate sheet of paper.*

In February 2004, Mark Zuckerberg and a college roommate started the original version of the Web site Facebook. They wanted to create online social networks for students. The two entrepreneurs created an online forum and invited students to join—for free. In just a few weeks, nearly two-thirds of their school's students had joined. Within months, Facebook had networks at thirty other universities.

That summer, Zuckerberg made contact with venture capitalists—business people who provide entrepreneurs with money to start new companies. When one offered them $500,000 to work on Facebook full time, Zuckerberg and his colleague left college and worked day and night writing computer code. By the fall, Facebook had a million members. Six months later, Zuckerberg and his partner got $12.7 million more in funding, hired more workers, and moved the company out of the apartments where they lived and worked and into offices.

Members like Facebook because they pay nothing to join and control what information they publish and who can see it. Advertisers love Facebook because they can target their ads, which provide Facebook its revenues.

To grow, Facebook added networks for high schools and workplaces and began attracting older members. By 2008, the company had networks in several countries and more than 70 million users of its Web site.

With growth, Facebook had to keep buying more computers and hiring more software engineers, salespeople, and customer service staff. Despite rising costs, growing income made Zuckerberg and other shareholders rich. Several companies have offered to buy Facebook, but Zuckerberg won't sell. He wants to continue to manage his company's growth himself.

Questions to Think About

1. Recall the three factors of production. What land, labor, and capital did Zuckerberg use in creating and running Facebook?
2. (a) What risk did Zuckerberg take? (b) Did it pay off? Why do you think so?
3. What needs or wants does Facebook meet?
4. What might prevent further growth of Facebook?
5. A Web site similar to Facebook also enjoyed early success. Its head refused to sell the company despite high offers. Then the Web site lost popularity and it became unattractive to future buyers. In light of this example, if you were Zuckerberg, would you have sold Facebook? Explain.

L2 Differentiate Distribute the "Mark Zuckerberg, CEO of Facebook" worksheet (Unit 1 All-in-One, p. 16).

L2 ELL Differentiate Pair English learners with language proficient students to answer the questions on the worksheet.

L4 Differentiate Have students write a paragraph explaining who they think took the bigger risk—Zuckerberg or the venture capitalist who agreed to fund his startup efforts. Tell them to give reasons to support their responses.

Background Note

U.S. Postal Service Point out that government agencies also combine factors of production and provide a good or a service. In this way, they are entrepreneurial. They do not aim to make a profit, however. To underscore the difference, compare the U.S. Postal Service to private delivery companies. Both the Postal Service and companies such as UPS and Federal Express deliver packages. However, while its managers try to control costs and satisfy customers, the U.S. Postal Service is run by the federal government and does not have to make a profit. UPS and Federal Express must make a profit to satisfy their owners—the shareholders.

Answers

Check Your Understanding Possible answers:
1. Kelly will learn more about how to make the smoothies nutritious; she can experiment with recipes to improve the product; she can learn about the best ways to start and run a small business.
2. An entrepreneur has to decide how to best combine limited resources to meet a need or want.

EXTEND

Ask students to imagine that they are planning a new housing development. **What needs and wants would the community have?** *(Needs could be a water source, electricity; wants could be a pool, train access.)* The housing development has been changed to a retirement community. **How would the needs and wants change?** Use this discussion to help students understand that needs, wants, and resources change depending on the situation.

L4 Differentiate Assign the "Factors of Production in the Global Economy" worksheet (Unit 1 All-in-One, p. 17). Discuss the questions with the students, having them focus on how the global economy changes the availability of different factors of production.

GUIDING QUESTION WRAP UP

Have students return to the section Guiding Question. Review the completed graphic organizer and clarify any misunderstandings. Have a wrap up discussion about how scarcity forces people to make choices.

Assess and Remediate

L3 L2 Collect the "Mark Zuckerberg, CEO of Facebook" worksheet and assess student understanding of the role of entrepreneurs.

L4 Collect the "Factors of Production in the Global Economy" worksheet and assess student understanding.

L3 Section 1 Assessment

L3 Give Section Quiz A (Unit 1 All-in-One, p. 18).

L2 Give Section Quiz B (Unit 1 All-in-One, p. 19).

(Assess and Remediate continued on p. 7)

Answer

Global Impact Possible responses: higher rates of disease and death; conflict among those who share water supplies; crops cannot be grown but must be imported

capital any human-made resource that is used to produce other goods and services

physical capital the human-made objects used to create other goods and services

human capital the knowledge and skills a worker gains through education and experience

Capital

The term **capital** refers to any human-made resource that is used to produce other goods and services. Economists divide capital into two types—physical capital and human capital.

Human-made objects used to create other goods and services are **physical capital.** (Sometimes economists use the term capital goods for physical capital.) The buildings that house a computer manufacturing company are physical capital as are all the equipment and tools needed to make those computers.

In addition to producing physical capital, people can also invest in themselves. The knowledge and skills a worker gains through education and experience is **human capital.** Computer designers go to college to study engineering, electronics, and computers. They build their human capital, making it possible for them to design and build faster and more powerful computers. Auto mechanics also increase their human capital through schooling and experience. This knowledge gives them the skills to diagnose and fix an engine that is not running properly.

An economy requires both physical and human capital to produce goods and services. Doctors need both stethoscopes and schooling to provide healthcare. Assembly-line workers use tools as well as their own skills acquired through training and practice.

FUTURE WATCH **Global Impact**

Water Wars?

Throughout history, wars have been fought over scarce natural resources—from gold to oil. Many experts predict that future wars may be fought over another scarce resource: ***water***. Millions of people around the world already live without access to clean, safe water. ***Predict three economic or social consequences that might occur in a country where water was scarce.***

Population With Sustainable Access to an Improved Water Source (Percentage) 2004

United States	100%
Egypt	98%
India	86%
China	77%
Romania	57%
Haiti	54%
Nigeria	48%
Cambodia	41%
Papua New Guinea	39%
Ethiopia	22%

SOURCE: *Globalhealthfacts.org*

Benefits of Capital

Capital is a key factor of production because people and companies can use it to save a great deal of time and money. Physical capital such as machines and tools help workers produce goods and services more easily and at less cost. As a result, they become more productive. Human capital such as technical knowledge has the same result. The more skills a worker gains, the more productive he or she becomes. Many businesses provide training for their employees for this reason.

To understand the benefit of investing in capital, consider the following example. A family of six people washes dishes by hand after every meal—breakfast, lunch, and dinner. That is a total of 21 meals per week. It takes 30 minutes per meal for two family members working together to scrape, stack, wash, rinse, dry, and put away the dishes. As a result, the family spends 21 hours a week cleaning dishes—time that could have been spent on other more productive activities.

Now, suppose that the family saves up and spends $400 on some physical capital—a dishwasher. Using the dishwasher, it takes only one family member 15 minutes after each meal to stack the dishwasher and another family member 15 minutes at the end of the day to put the

Virtual Economics

L3 Differentiate

Exploring Scarcity Use the following lesson from the NCEE **Virtual Economics *CD-ROM*** to define scarcity and determine how it can be an opportunity. Click on Browse Economics Lessons, specify grades 9–12, and use the key words *everyone's problem.*

In this activity, students will analyze the concept of scarcity in goods and services and evaluate the opportunities it presents to entrepreneurs.

LESSON TITLE	SCARCITY: EVERYONE'S PROBLEM IS THE ENTREPRENEUR'S OPPORTUNITY
Type of Activity	Classifying
Complexity	Low
Time	100 minutes
NCEE Standards	1

dishes away. A chore that used to require 21 hours to complete now takes only 7 hours. This example shows the typical benefits of using capital:

1. *Extra time* The family saves 14 hours a week. This is time that can be used for other activities.
2. *More knowledge* By learning how to use the dishwasher, family members learn more about using household appliances in general. They can apply that knowledge to using washing machines, dryers, and other appliances.
3. *More productivity* With extra time and more knowledge, family members can use their resources and labor to do other chores, to learn other skills, or simply to enjoy themselves. Every member of the family benefits.

CHECKPOINT ***What are the factors of production?***

Scarce Resources

All goods and services are scarce because the resources used to produce them are scarce. Consider French fries. A typical portion of French fries might have started as potatoes in a field in Idaho. Ten gallons of water irrigated the half-foot plot where the potatoes grew. Nurtured with fertilizers and protected by pesticides, the potatoes grew until they were harvested, processed, frozen, and then transported to Seattle. There they were fried in corn oil from Nebraska, sprinkled with salt from Louisiana, and eaten in a restaurant.

All of the factors of production used to produce those French fries are scarce. First, the amount of land and water available for growing potatoes is limited. Second, the labor available to grow the crop and to harvest, process, transport, and cook the potatoes is limited by the size, time, age, and energy of the population. Finally, the amount of physical capital available to create the French fries, such as farm machines or cooking equipment, is also limited.

The same principles apply to a pair of blue jeans, an MP3 player, or a space shuttle. No matter what good or service we look at, the supplies of land, labor, and capital used to produce it are scarce. We would also notice another fact about those resources—each one has many alternative uses. Individuals, businesses, and governments have to choose which alternative they most want.

CHECKPOINT ***Why are goods and services scarce?***

Essential Questions Journal To continue to build a response to the Essential Question, go to your **Essential Questions Journal.**

SECTION 1 ASSESSMENT

Guiding Question

1. Use your completed cause-and-effect chart to answer this question: How does scarcity force people to make economic choices?
2. **Extension** Describe how scarcity of time, money, or resources affected a recent economic decision you made.

Key Terms and Main Ideas

3. What is the difference between **goods** and **services?**
4. How does **scarcity** differ from a **shortage?**
5. What does an **entrepreneur** do?
6. What is a benefit of using both **physical capital** and **human capital?**

Critical Thinking

7. **Classify** Identify the factor of production represented by each of the following: **(a)** fishing waters, **(b)** an office building, **(c)** clerks in a store, **(d)** a tractor, **(e)** a student in a cooking school. Explain.
8. **Infer** If companies can become more productive by increasing their physical capital, why would a company not buy up-to-date computers for all employees each year?
9. **Apply** Think of a good or service that you consumed today. List at least five factors of production used to produce that good or service. Include at least one example each of land, labor, and capital.

Quick Write

10. Look at the How the Economy Works feature in this section. Make a list of the risks an entrepreneur takes and the possible rewards he or she might gain. Then, write a brief paragraph explaining why entrepreneurs are important to the economy of a community or nation.

Have students complete the Self-Test Online and continue their work in the **Essential Questions Journal**.

REMEDIATION AND SUGGESTIONS

Use the chart below to help students who are struggling with content.

WEAKNESS	REMEDIATION
Defining key terms (Questions 3, 4, 5, 6)	Have students use the interactive Economic Dictionary Online.
Describing *scarcity* (Questions 1, 2, 4)	Have students summarize the meaning of *scarcity* in their own words.
Explaining factors of production (Questions 5, 6, 7, 8, 9, 10)	Have students review the factors of production used by the entrepreneur to start the frozen yogurt business in How the Economy Works.

Answers

Checkpoint land, labor, and physical and human capital

Checkpoint because resources used to produce them are scarce

Assessment Answers

1. Because resources are scarce, people cannot satisfy all their needs and wants.
2. Possible response: I had enough money to buy an MP3 player or a camera, so I bought the MP3 player.
3. Goods are physical objects someone produces. Services are actions someone does for another.
4. Scarcity is constant; shortages occur when people want more of an item than producers will provide at a particular price.
5. They combine resources to provide goods and services.
6. This can lead to savings in other factors of production.
7. (a) land; (b) physical capital; (c) labor; (d) physical capital; (e) human capital
8. Possible response: It may not have the money to buy new ones every year.
9. Possible response: I took the bus. The trip used land (oil); labor (driver's work); and capital (gasoline, roads, the bus, the bus driver's expertise at driving).
10. Possible response: Entrepreneurs risk losing the money they invest for the possible reward of financial gain.Students' paragraphs should note such contributions as developing original ideas and starting new businesses that create a variety of goods and services, employing people in the process.

Guiding Question

How does opportunity cost affect decision making?

Get Started

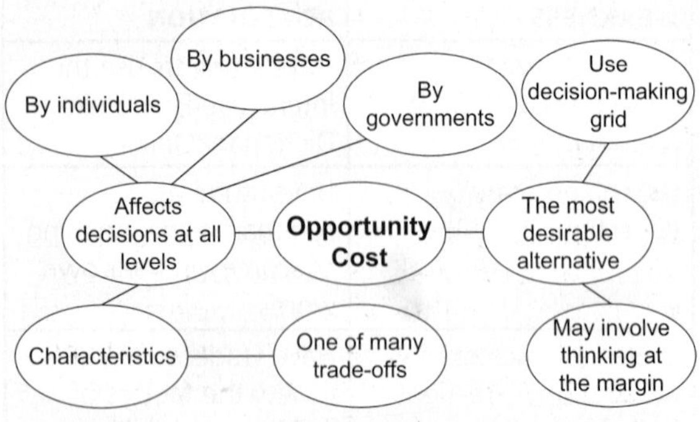

LESSON GOALS

Students will:

- Know the Key Terms.
- Analyze the trade-offs involved in decision making.
- Explain how changing economic factors can change decisions and opportunity costs.
- Provide examples of decision making at the margin.

BEFORE CLASS

Students should read the section for homework before coming to class.

Have students complete the graphic organizer as they read the text. As an alternate activity, have students complete the Guided Reading and Review worksheet (Unit 1 All-in-One, p. 20).

L1 L2 ELL LPR Differentiate Have students complete the Guided Reading and Review worksheet (Unit 1 All-in-One, p. 21).

SECTION 2 Opportunity Cost

OBJECTIVES

1. **Explain** why every decision involves trade-offs.
2. **Summarize** the concept of opportunity cost.
3. **Describe** how people make decisions by thinking at the margin.

ECONOMIC DICTIONARY

As you read the section, look for the definitions of these **Key Terms:**

- trade-off
- "guns or butter"
- opportunity cost
- thinking at the margin
- cost/benefit analysis
- marginal cost
- marginal benefit

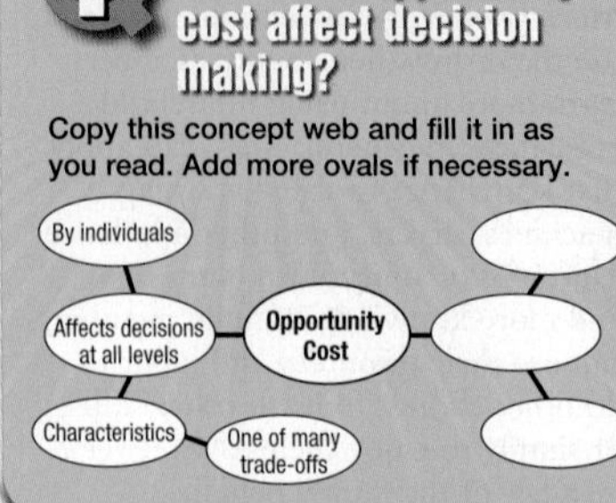

Economics and You You are cleaning your bedroom. Boxes, clothes, and other items cover your bed, the floor, the entire room. Suddenly, your phone rings and a friend invites you to a party. You consider your options and quickly decide that going to the party will be more fun than cleaning your room.

Later, tired but happy, you enter your bedroom and realize that you now have to clear off your bed when all you want to do is sleep. Your decision to go to the party cost you the time you needed to clean up your room. Was the benefit of your choice worth the cost?

Principles in Action Every time we choose to do something, we give up the opportunity to do something else. As you will see, even such a simple decision as how late to sleep in the morning involves weighing costs and benefits. The Economics & You feature shows how scarcity and choice can affect the ways you spend your time and what services your community provides.

Trade-Offs

Economists point out that all individuals, businesses, and large groups of people—even governments—make decisions that involve trade-offs. A **trade-off** is the act of giving up one benefit in order to gain another, greater benefit. Trade-offs often involve things that can be easily measured, such as money, property, or time. But trade-offs may also involve values that are not so easy to measure. Such intangibles include enjoyment, job satisfaction, or the feeling of well-being that comes from helping somebody.

Individuals and Trade-Offs

At every stage of life, you have to make trade-offs. Taking a part in the school play prevents you from playing soccer or getting a part-time job. A few years from now, you might decide to turn down an exciting but low-paying job in favor of a less interesting job that pays better. Still later, you may choose to give up a vacation in order to put more money away for your retirement.

trade-off the act of giving up one benefit in order to gain another, greater benefit

CLASSROOM HINTS

TRADE-OFFS

Have students record ten decisions they made during the day. With a partner, have students identify the trade-offs associated with each decision. For example, a student might have chosen to have cereal for breakfast, instead of having oatmeal, toast and fruit, or pancakes, or getting to school earlier. Then have students identify the most desirable alternative to each decision.

Focus on the Basics

Students need to come away with the following understandings:

FACTS: • Each choice we make involves trade-offs, giving up one benefit for another. • *Opportunity cost* is the single most desirable alternative given up due to a trade-off. • Thinking at the margin involves deciding whether to use one more or one less unit of a resource

GENERALIZATION: Every economic decision we make involves trade-offs; the most desirable choice given up is the opportunity cost.

Businesses and Trade-Offs

The decisions that businesses make about how to use their factor resources—land, labor, and capital—also involve trade-offs. A farmer who plants broccoli cannot at the same time use the same area of land to grow squash. A furniture company that decides to use all of its equipment to make chairs eliminates the possibility of using the same equipment to build tables or desks.

Governments and Trade-Offs

National, state, and local governments also make decisions that involve trade-offs. Economists and politicians use the term **"guns or butter"** to describe one of the common choices facing governments: the choice between spending money on military or domestic needs. A country that decides to produce more military goods ("guns") has fewer resources to devote to consumer goods ("butter") and vice versa. The steel needed to produce a tank cannot then be used to produce a tractor.

In November 2007, as U.S. troops fought in Iraq, one commentator described the tough choice facing American leaders and voters:

> **"Like Santa with a wish list that cannot be satisfied, the country enters the New Year with a needs list that far exceeds our revenue sources. It appears once again that it is time to wage the debate of guns or butter. . . . Citizens are simultaneously confronted with funding a war abroad and dealing with rising health costs, increased fuel costs and declining human services at home."**
>
> —Charles Bogue, "Guns or Butter," *Napa Valley Register*

In the end, the reason for the "guns or butter" trade-off is the same as the reason for any other trade-off: scarcity.

CHECKPOINT ***What are trade-offs?***

Determining Opportunity Cost

In most trade-offs, one of the rejected alternatives is more desirable than the rest. The most desirable alternative somebody gives up as the result of a decision is the **opportunity cost.** Take the farmer in the example above. If squash was the most profitable alternative to broccoli, then the opportunity cost of deciding to plant broccoli was the chance to plant squash.

Even simple decisions carry opportunity costs. Consider the following choices:

- Sleep late or wake up early to study for a test?
- Sleep late or wake up early to eat breakfast?
- Sleep late or wake up early to go on a ski trip?

Most likely, you did not choose "sleep late" for all three decisions. Your decision depended on the specific opportunity cost—the value to you of what you were willing to sacrifice.

"guns or butter" a phrase expressing the idea that a country that decides to produce more military goods ("guns") has fewer resources to produce consumer goods ("butter") and vice versa

opportunity cost the most desirable alternative given up as the result of a decision

Economics & YOU
Trade-offs
You take a part-time job after school in order to save up money to buy a car. *Your trade-off is time for money and wheels.*
Your town can afford to fix local roads or keep the library open on mornings and Saturdays – but not both. *The town council trades off full library service for road improvements.*
CLOSED
Due to staff cuts
Public Library

▲ Every decision we make involves trade-offs. That's why they can be difficult. ***Describe one decision you made this week. Identify the trade-offs involved.***

Differentiated Resources

L1 L2 Guided Reading and Review (Unit 1 All-in-One, p. 21)

L2 Trade-Offs (Unit 1 All-in-One, p. 23)

L4 Price and Opportunity Cost (Unit 1 All-in-One, p. 24)

L2 Decision Making skills worksheet (Unit 1 All-in-One, p. 26)

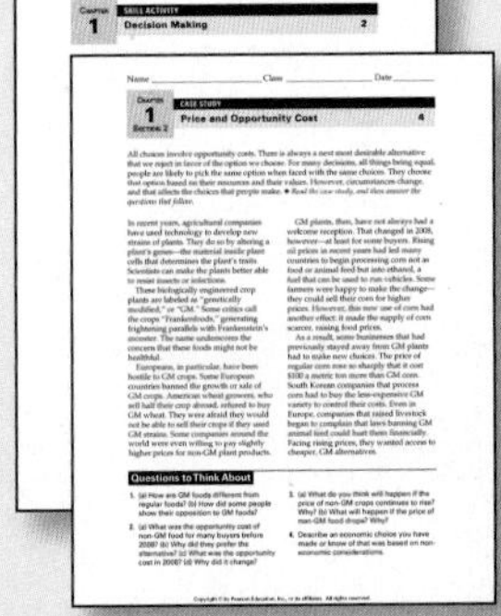

BELLRINGER

Have students think of recent decisions they made and what they had to give up as a result.

Teach

Economics online To present this topic using digital resources, use the lecture notes on www.PearsonSuccessNet.com.

ANALYZE

Create a chart on the board with three columns labeled Decision, Alternatives, and Opportunity Cost. Have volunteers from the class fill in the first two columns with their answer from the Bellringer activity. Ask students **Which of the alternatives you gave up was the most desirable?** Write these answers in the Opportunity Cost column.

DISTRIBUTE ACTIVITY WORKSHEET

Distribute the "Trade-Offs" activity worksheet (Unit 1 All-in-One, p. 22). Review the definitions of *trade-off* and *opportunity cost.* Tell students that they will analyze a political cartoon about choices and the trade-offs involved.

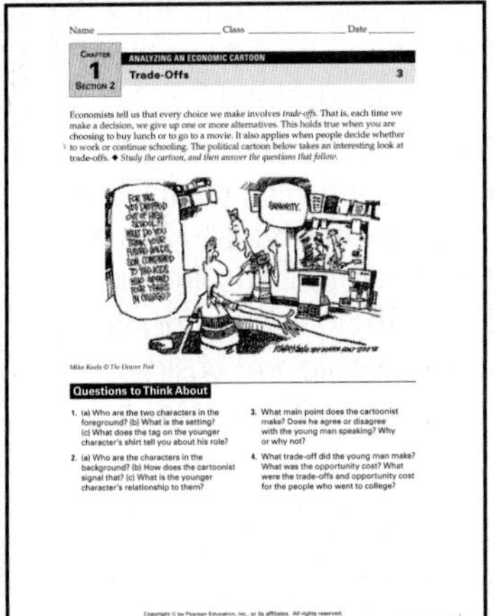

L2 Differentiate Distribute the "Trade-Offs" activity worksheet (Unit 1 All-in-One, p. 23).

After students have completed the worksheet, ask **How do all decisions involve trade-offs?**

(lesson continued on p. 11)

Answers

Checkpoint *Trade-offs* are the decisions we make to give up one benefit to gain another, greater benefit.

Economics & You Possible response: I bought tickets to see a movie. As a result I didn't purchase a CD I want or play basketball.

Teach Visual Glossary

REVIEW KEY TERMS

Pair students and have them write the definitions of the key terms related to the understanding of opportunity cost.

need – *something essential for survival*

want – *something people desire but that is not necessary for survival*

scarcity – *the principle that limited amounts of goods and services are available to meet unlimited needs and wants*

trade-off – *the act of giving up one benefit to gain another, greater benefit*

APPLY

Ask **How does each key term apply to Karen's situation?** *(Need: sleep; Want: better grade; Scarcity: time; Trade-off: gives up sleep or her grade.)*

Ask **What alternatives are Karen and the family in the cartoon choosing between?** *(Karen: sleep, grades; cartoon: money for dinner, ease of driving).* **If Karen decided to sleep late, what is her opportunity cost?** *(study time)*

L1 L2 Differentiate Have students create a decision-making grid for a situation from their own life. Help them use the grid to understand that there is an opportunity cost to each decision.

L4 Differentiate Distribute the "Price and Opportunity Cost" worksheet (Unit 1 All-in-One, p. 24). Tell students that they will read a case study about genetically modified crop plants and how changes in needs and wants changed trade-offs and opportunity costs for people and businesses. Have students read the case study and answer the questions.

Economics online *All print resources are available on the Teacher's Resource Library CD-ROM and online at* www.PearsonSuccessNet.com.

Answers

Decision-Making Grid extra study time

Cartoon The family decided to save money on gas by pushing the car halfway to the restaurant. The opportunity cost is the luxury of riding in the car all the way.

Reviewing Key Terms
To understand *opportunity cost*, review these terms:

need, *p. 3*
want, *p. 3*
scarcity, *p. 4*
trade-off, *p. 8*

What is Opportunity Cost?

◀ **opportunity cost** the most desirable alternative given up as the result of a decision

KAREN'S DECISION-MAKING GRID

	Alternatives	
	Sleep late	**Wake up early to study**
Benefits	• Enjoy more sleep • Have more energy during the day	• Better grade on test • Teacher and parental approval • Personal satisfaction
Benefits forgone	• Better grade on test • Teacher and parental approval • Personal satisfaction	• Enjoy more sleep • Have more energy during the day
Opportunity cost	**Extra study time**	**Extra sleep time**

Opportunity cost is not just money, but *any* benefit you give up. To determine the opportunity cost of any alternative, you must first identify the benefits you will gain and the benefits you will give up. ***What is Karen's opportunity cost if she decides to sleep late?***

"By pushing us halfway, we save money on gas. That way we'll have enough money to eat out."

◀ In this cartoon, scarcity of an important resource—money—has forced the family to make a strange decision. ***What decision has the family made? What is the opportunity cost of this decision?***

Visual Glossary online
To expand your understanding of this and other key economic terms, visit **PearsonSuccessNet.com**

10

Using a Decision-Making Grid

At times, the opportunity cost of a decision may be unclear or complicated. Using a decision-making grid like the one in the Visual Glossary, opposite, can help you determine whether you are willing to accept the opportunity cost of a choice you are about to make.

In this particular example, a high school student named Karen is trying to decide whether to sleep late or get up early to study for a test. Because of the scarcity of time, she cannot do both.

To help her make her decision, Karen lists the benefits of each alternative on the grid. Waking up early to study will probably result in her receiving a better grade. She will also receive teacher and parental approval and experience a sense of personal satisfaction.

On the other hand, Karen enjoys sleeping. In addition, the extra sleep would give her more energy during the day. She would have to give up these benefits if she decided to get up earlier.

Making the Decision

Karen is a practical person. After considering the opportunity cost of each alternative, she decides that waking up early to study offers her the most desirable benefits. She knows that she is giving up the pleasure of more sleep and the extra energy it would provide. But she is willing to accept this opportunity cost.

If Karen faced other decisions with other opportunity costs, she might choose differently. What if the choice was between sleeping late and getting up early to have breakfast? What if her decision to sleep late or study was on a Saturday rather than on a school day? With each different set of alternatives, the possible benefits and opportunity costs change as well.

One thing does not change, though. We always face an opportunity cost. As economists say, "Choosing is refusing." When we select one alternative, we must sacrifice at least one other alternative and its benefits.

CHECKPOINT ***Why does every choice involve an opportunity cost?***

Thinking at the Margin

When economists look at decisions, they point out one more characteristic in addition to opportunity cost. Many decisions involve adding or subtracting one unit, such as one hour or one dollar. From an economist's point of view, when you decide how much more or less to do, you are **thinking at the margin.**

To understand what it means to think at the margin, think about folding a piece of paper with important notes on it to put in your pocket. If you fold the paper in half and then in half again, it can just squeeze into your pocket and will lay fairly flat. If you continued folding it in half two or three more times, it would fit more easily in your pocket. But the paper would also become more bulky with each additional fold. The question is, how many folds is the best number for fitting easily into your pocket and laying flat once inside?

Cost/Benefit Analysis

Deciding by thinking at the margin is just like making any other decision. Decision makers have to compare the opportunity costs and the benefits—what they will sacrifice and what they will gain. This decision-making process is sometimes called **cost/benefit analysis.**

To make rational, or sensible, decisions at the margin, you must weigh marginal costs against marginal benefits. The **marginal cost** is the extra cost of adding one unit, whether it be sleeping an extra hour or building one extra house. The **marginal benefit** is the extra benefit of adding the same unit. As long as the marginal benefits exceed the marginal costs, it pays to add more units.

Decision-Making at the Margin

Look again at the example of Karen's decision on how late to sleep. The decision-making grid in the Visual Glossary used an "all or nothing" approach. Either Karen was going to wake up early to study, or she was going to sleep late and not study at all that morning.

In reality, Karen could have decided from among several options rather than just two. She could have decided to get up

FUTURE WATCH

Personal Finance To see how tradeoffs affect budgeting decisions, see your Personal Finance Handbook in the back of the book or visit **PearsonSuccessNet.com**

thinking at the margin the process of deciding whether to do or use one additional unit of some resource

cost/benefit analysis a decision-making process in which you compare what you will sacrifice and gain by a specific action

marginal cost the extra cost of adding one unit

marginal benefit the extra benefit of adding one unit

APPLY UNDERSTANDING

Review the meaning of thinking at the margin with students. Point out that when they make decisions, it is not usually an all-or-nothing situation. Ask students to look back at their answers to the Bellringer. Ask **If you had a little more time or money, how would your decision have changed?** Discuss how students make their daily decisions based on marginal thinking.

PERSONAL FINANCE ACTIVITY

Tell students that they can learn more about how trade-offs affect spending decisions by reading the Budgeting section, starting on page PF4 in the **Personal Finance Handbook**, and by completing the activity worksheet (Personal Finance All-in-One, p. 32).

DECISION MAKING

Distribute the "Decision Making" skills worksheet (Unit 1 All-in-One, p. 25). Tell students that they will analyze thinking at the margin.

L2 Differentiate Distribute the "Decision Making" skills worksheet (Unit 1 All-in-One, p. 26). Tell students that they will complete a decision-making chart and answer questions about it.

EXTEND

Instruct students to research a recent spending decision in their community or state. Have students analyze the decision using a decision-making grid.

GUIDING QUESTION WRAP UP

Have students return to the section Guiding Question. Review the completed graphic organizer and clarify any misunderstandings. Have a wrap up discussion about how opportunity cost affects decision making.

Assess and Remediate

L3 **L2** Collect the "Trade-Offs" and "Decision Making" worksheets and assess student understanding of opportunity cost and decision making at the margin.

L4 Collect the "Price and Opportunity Cost" worksheets and assess student understanding of trade-offs.

L3 Section 2 Assessment

L3 Give Section Quiz A (Unit 1 All-in-One, p. 27).

L2 Give Section Quiz B (Unit 1 All-in-One, p. 28).

(Assess and Remediate continued on p. 12)

Answer

Checkpoint Every choice has an opportunity cost because every decision includes at least one alternative that is the next most desirable.

Virtual Economics

L3 Differentiate

Comparing Marginal Benefits and Costs Use the following lesson from the NCEE **Virtual Economics *CD-ROM*** to help students understand marginal analysis. Click on Browse Economics Lessons, specify grades 9–12, and use the key words *economic way.*

In this activity, students will take part in a simulation to illustrate how marginal analysis helps people make economic decisions.

LESSON TITLE	**THE ECONOMIC WAY OF THINKING: THREE ACTIVITIES TO DEMONSTRATE MARGINAL ANALYSIS**
Type of Activity	Simulation
Complexity	High
Time	60 minutes
NCEE Standards	1, 3

Have students complete the Self-Test Online and continue their work in the **Essential Questions Journal**.

REMEDIATION AND SUGGESTIONS

Use the chart below to help students who are struggling with content.

WEAKNESS	REMEDIATION
Defining key terms (Questions 3, 4, 5, 6)	Have students use the interactive Economic Dictionary Online.
Understanding opportunity cost (Questions 1, 2, 8, 10)	Draw a decision-making grid on the board similar to the one in the Visual Glossary. With students, complete the grid and lead them to identify the opportunity cost of each alternative.
Explaining thinking at the margin (Questions 5, 6, 9)	Reteach using the Skills worksheet.

Answers

Graph Skills 1. One less hour of study time and a grade of C; 1 hour of sleep 2. third hour of study compared to second hour of study costs Karen a full hour of sleep but increases her grade a partial step from a B to B+

Checkpoint It shows when an added unit of cost no longer provides enough benefit to be worthwhile.

Figure 1.1 Decision Making at the Margin

Options	Benefit	Opportunity Cost
1st hour of extra study time	Grade of C on test	One hour of sleep
2nd hour of extra study time	Grade of B on test	2 hours of sleep
3rd hour of extra study time	Grade of B+ on test	3 hours of sleep

GRAPH SKILLS

Compare this graph to the one in the Visual Glossary. By comparing opportunity costs and benefits of each extra hour, Karen can decide how much sleep is the right amount.

1. **What is the opportunity cost of one extra hour of sleep? What is the benefit?**
2. **At what point is Karen paying an added cost with little added benefit?**

one, two, or three hours earlier. Making a decision about each extra hour would involve thinking at the margin.

To make a decision at the margin, Karen should look at the marginal cost of each extra hour of studying and compare it to the marginal benefit. In **Figure 1.1**, we can see that one hour of studying means an opportunity cost of an hour of sleep, while the probable benefit would be passing the test with a C. Two hours of studying means losing two hours of sleep and perhaps getting a B. When Karen gives up three hours of sleep, however, the probable benefit rises only slightly, to a grade of B+.

Karen concludes that the marginal cost of losing three hours of sleep is no longer worth the marginal benefit because her grade will improve only slightly. Based on her cost-benefit analysis, Karen decides to awaken two hours earlier.

Like opportunity cost, thinking at the margin applies not just to individuals, but to businesses and governments as well. Employers think at the margin when they decide how many extra workers to hire. Legislators think at the margin when deciding how much to increase spending on a government program.

CHECKPOINT ***How can a cost/benefit analysis help people make decisions?***

SECTION 2 ASSESSMENT

Essential Questions Journal To continue to build a response to the Essential Question, go to your **Essential Questions Journal.**

Guiding Question

1. Use your completed concept web to answer this question: How does opportunity cost affect decision making?
2. **Extension** Identify the opportunity cost of the most recent consumer purchase you made. Explain what you gave up and why you chose to purchase the item you did.

Key Terms and Main Ideas

3. Why do all economic decisions involve **trade-offs?**
4. How does the phrase **"guns or butter"** express the principle of trade-offs?
5. Why do many economic decisions involve **thinking at the margin?**
6. Why is it important to compare **marginal costs** to **marginal benefits?**

Critical Thinking

7. **Give Examples** Give two examples of a decision that your school or local government might have to make. Explain how each decision involves trade-offs.
8. **Analyze** Identify a possible opportunity cost for each of the following choices: **(a)** studying for a test on a Saturday afternoon, **(b)** using all the money you received for your birthday to pay for downloading songs, **(c)** spending four hours playing a video game on a Tuesday night, **(d)** having four slices of pizza for lunch.
9. **Make Decisions** What marginal costs and benefits might a business owner have to consider when trying to decide whether to hire one, two, or three additional workers?

Math Skills

10. You have a part-time job where you work 10 hours a week and earn $6 an hour. A friend tells you about another job, at a restaurant, where the pay is only $4 an hour, but in 10 hours of work you can earn as much as $25 in tips. Calculate the probable hourly pay rate for each job. What is the opportunity cost of taking the restaurant job? Would you change jobs? Why or why not? ***Visit PearsonSuccessNet.com for additional math help.***

Assessment Answers

1. Possible response: It clarifies exactly what people give up when choosing one option.
2. Possible response: I chose to buy an expensive pair of designer jeans, but then I had to buy less-expensive sneakers.
3. because resources are limited; using them one way makes them unavailable for other uses
4. Often governments have to choose between military and domestic spending because of limited revenues.
5. Many decisions involve whether to add or subtract one unit of a resource—a weighing of costs versus benefits.
6. to ensure that benefits are proportional to resources used
7. Possible responses: Building a park (trade-offs: hiring more police officers or lowering taxes); providing services to elderly (trade-offs: buying school books or repaving the streets)
8. Possible responses: (a) spending time with friends; (b) seeing a movie; (c) studying for an important test; (d) having a sandwich and a fruit salad
9. how much added output each worker would provide, compared to cost of added wages
10. The opportunity cost of the restaurant job is the potential loss of $20 a week, since tips are not guaranteed. Students may or may not change jobs, depending on how they feel about the risk.

SECTION 3 Production Possibilities Curves

OBJECTIVES

1. **Interpret** a production possibilities curve.
2. **Explain** how production possibilities curves show efficiency, growth, and cost.
3. **Explain** why a country's production possibilities depend on its resources and technology.

ECONOMIC DICTIONARY

As you read the section, look for the definitions of these **Key Terms:**

- production possibilities curve
- production possibilities frontier
- efficiency
- underutilization
- law of increasing costs

Guiding Question

How does a nation decide what and how much to produce?

Copy this concept web and fill it in as you read. Add more ovals if necessary.

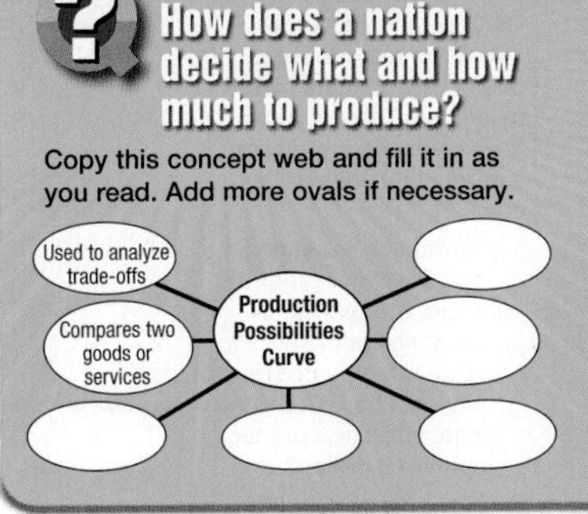

Economics and You Your class decides to sponsor a community breakfast as a fundraiser. Can you make more money by serving eggs or pancakes? Should you offer both? To decide, you'll have to look at the cost of ingredients, the number of workers you have, and the size of the kitchen. Also, does it take more time to scramble eggs or to flip pancakes? What you decide will affect how much money you make.

Nations face similar decisions about what to produce. For nations, however, the consequences of these decisions can be far more serious.

Principles in Action To decide what and how much to produce, economists use a tool known as a production possibilities curve. You will see how an imaginary country uses this tool to decide between producing two very different products: shoes and watermelons.

Production Possibilities

Economists often use graphs to analyze the choices and trade-offs that people make. Why? Because graphs help us see how one value relates to another value. A **production possibilities curve** is a graph that shows alternative ways to use an economy's productive resources. The axes of the graph can show categories of goods and services, such as farm goods and factory goods or capital goods and consumer goods. The axes can also display any pair of specific goods or services, such as hats on one axis and shoes on the other.

Drawing a Production Possibilities Curve

To draw a production possibilities curve, an economist begins by deciding which goods or services to examine. In this example, we will look at a fictional country called Capeland. Government economists in Capeland must decide whether to use the nation's scarce resources to manufacture shoes or to grow watermelons. The economists determine that, if Capeland used all of its resources to produce only shoes, it could produce 15 million pairs of shoes. At the other extreme, if Capeland used all of its resources to produce only watermelons, it could produce 21 million tons of watermelons.

production possibilities curve a graph that shows alternative ways to use an economy's productive resources

Focus on the Basics

Students need to come away with the following understandings:

FACTS: • Production possibilities curves show alternative ways to use resources. • Production possibilities curves show how efficiently an economy uses resources, results of economic growth, and costs of each production choice. • Adopting new technology can improve efficiency and create economic growth.

GENERALIZATION: Production possibilities curves are important tools for decision makers to make the most efficient use of resources.

Guiding Question

How does a nation decide what and how much to produce?

Get Started

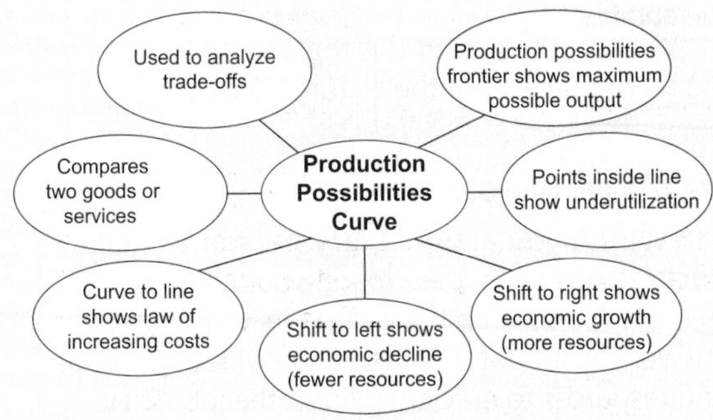

LESSON GOALS

Students will:

- Know the Key Terms.
- Interpret production possibilities curves.
- Analyze a transparency to understand changes in production possibilities curves.
- Discuss the law of increasing costs.
- Research and debate government policies to promote advances in technology.

BEFORE CLASS

Students should read the section for homework before coming to class.

Have students complete the graphic organizer in the Section Opener as they read the text. As an alternative activity, have students complete the Guided Reading and Review worksheet. (Unit 1 All-in-One, p. 29)

L1 L2 ELL LPR Differentiate Have students complete the Guided Reading and Review worksheet. (Unit 1 All-in-One, p. 30)

CLASSROOM HINTS

PRODUCTION POSSIBILITIES CURVES

In this section, students will be asked to draw production possibilities curves. Because these graphs compare one good or service to another, the axes are interchangeable. To help students understand this, have students draw a production possibilities curve of the data from Figure 1.2 on a graph with the horizontal axis labeled *Shoes* and the vertical axis labeled *Watermelons*. Elicit from students the fact that while the graph looks different, it represents the same data as the graph in the book.

BELLRINGER

Tell students to imagine that they and two friends are planning a party for the class. Have them plan who will do what to prepare for the party.

Teach

Economics online To present this topic using digital resources, use the lecture notes on www.PearsonSuccessNet.com.

REVIEW BELLRINGER

Ask **Would you assign every person to make decorations?** *(No; then there would be no one to make food).* Then have students volunteer their answers. Point out that students divided the labor and resources to efficiently finish the job. They used the concept of a production possibilities curve without realizing it.

CHECK UNDERSTANDING

Remind students that all resources are scarce. A production possibilities curve helps determine the best way to allocate these scarce resources.

Direct students' attention to Figure 1.2 in their textbook. Call on volunteers to identify the production possibilities frontier. *(the red line b connecting points a and c)* Ask **What level of production does this line represent?** *(maximum production of both shoes and watermelons, using all the nation's resources)* Make sure that students understand that the values in the table were used to plot the production possibilities frontier.

L1 L2 ELL **Differentiate** Review each label on the graph in Figure 1.2, asking questions to check students' understanding, such as **What does point d mean?** *(underutilization, or a point where the country is not producing as much as it could be)* **How many shoes and watermelons are produced at point a?** *(15 million pairs of shoes, no watermelons)*

Action Graph online Have students review the Action Graph animation for a step-by-step look at a production possibilities curve.

Answers

Graph Skills 1. 18 million tons of watermelons; 4 million fewer tons of watermelons 2. At point d, Capeland does not produce as much of either watermelons or shoes as it could.

Checkpoint Each point on a production possibilities frontier shows how much of two goods can be produced with the same resources.

Figure 1.2 Production Possibilities Curve

GRAPH SKILLS

The table shows six different combinations of watermelons and shoes that Capeland could produce using all of its factor resources. These figures have been used to create a production possibilities curve.

1. How much watermelon can Capeland produce if they are making 9 million pairs of shoes? What will the opportunity cost be if Capeland increases shoe production to 12 million?
2. Why would production at point d in the graph on the right represent an underutilization of resources?

Watermelons (millions of tons)	Shoes (millions of pairs)
0	15
8	14
14	12
18	9
20	5
21	0

KEY

a. No watermelons, all possible shoes
b. A production possibilities frontier
c. No shoes, all possible watermelons
d. A point of underutilization
e. Future production possibilities frontier

Action Graph online

For an animated version of this graph, visit PearsonSuccessNet.com

The Capeland economists use this information to create a production possibilities curve (**Figure 1.2**). The vertical axis of the graph represents how many millions of pairs of shoes Capeland's factories can produce. The horizontal axis shows how many millions of tons of watermelons Capeland's farmers can grow. At Point a, Capeland is producing 15 million pairs of shoes but no watermelons. At Point c, Capeland is producing 21 million tons of watermelons but no shoes.

There is a third, more likely alternative. The citizens of Capeland can use their resources to produce *both* shoes and watermelons. The table shows six different ways that Capelanders could use their resources to produce both shoes and watermelons. Using the made-up data from the table, we can plot points on the graph. This line, is called the **production possibilities frontier,** shows combinations of the production of both shoes and watermelons. Any spot on that line represents a point at which Capeland is using all of its resources to produce a maximum combination of those two products.

production possibilities frontier a line on a production possibilities curve that shows the maximum possible output an economy can produce

Trade-Offs

Each point on the production possibilities frontier reflects a trade-off. Near the top of the curve, factories produce more shoes, but farms grow fewer watermelons. Further down the curve, farms grow more watermelons, but factories make fewer pairs of shoes.

These trade-offs are necessary because factors of production are scarce. Using land, labor, and capital to make one product means that fewer resources are left to make something else.

***CHECKPOINT** How do production possibilities curves show alternative uses of resources?*

Differentiated Resources

L1 L2 **Guided Reading and Review** (Unit 1 All-in-One, p. 30)

L3 **Kitchen Challenge** (Simulation Activities, Chapter 1)

L2 **Governments Promote Technology** (Unit 1 All-in-One, p. 32)

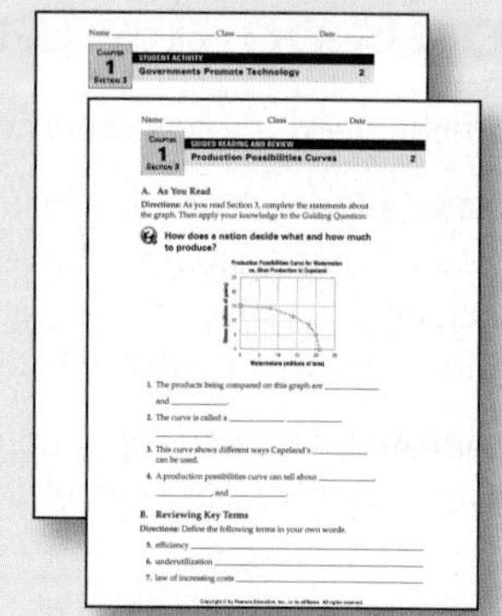

Efficiency, Growth, and Cost

Production possibilities curves give useful information. They can show how efficient an economy is, whether an economy is growing, and the opportunity cost of producing more of one good or service.

Efficiency

A production possibilities frontier represents an economy working at its most efficient level. **Efficiency** is the use of resources in such a way as to maximize the output of goods and services. However, sometimes economies operate inefficiently. For example, suppose some workers were laid off. The farms or factories where they worked would produce fewer goods.

Any point inside the production possibilities frontier indicates **underutilization,** or the use of fewer resources than the economy is capable of using. At Point **d** in **Figure 1.2,** Capeland is growing 5 million tons of watermelons and making 8 million pairs of shoes. This is inefficient because it is less than the maximum possible production.

Growth

A production possibilities curve is a snapshot. It reflects current production possibilities as if a country's resources were frozen in time. In the real world, however, available resources are constantly changing. If the quantity or quality of land, labor, or capital changes, then the curve will move. For example, a wave of immigration may increase a nation's labor supply. This rise in a factor of production increases the maximum amount of goods the nation can produce.

When an economy grows, economists say that the production possibilities curve has "shifted to the right." To see such a shift, look at line e in **Figure 1.2.** Notice that the possible output of both shoes and watermelons has increased at each point along the line.

However, when a country's production capacity decreases, the curve shifts to the left. A decrease could occur, for example, when a country goes to war and loses part of its land as a result.

efficiency the use of resources in such a way as to maximize the output of goods and services

underutilization the use of fewer resources than an economy is capable of using

Innovators

Steven Levitt

"I just wander through life looking for anything that interests me," says economist Steve Levitt. "And every once in a while I stumble onto something that turns into a research idea." This wide curiosity has led him to publish books and articles on topics from illegal drug use to sumo wrestling. Levitt is one of a new generation of economists who are using economic principles such as scarcity and trade-offs to explore all human behavior.

When he was still barely in his early forties, Levitt was already a full professor at a major university. Brilliant but unorthodox, Levitt has shown a rare ability to observe human interactions and create mathematical models that predict future outcomes. He has done ground-breaking work on important "real world" issues, including:

- Does the prison system deter criminal behavior?
- Will adding more police lower the local crime rate?
- What strategies work best to combat drunk driving?

This innovative thinker has an ambition that may seem unusual for an economist. "I'd like to put together a set of tools that lets us catch terrorists," he says. For Levitt, catching terrorists is a matter of finding the right data.

Critical Thinking: ***How can the concept of scarcity help explain a wide range of human behavior?***

Fast Facts

Steven Levitt

Born: May 29, 1967, in Minneapolis, MN

Education: B.A. in Economics from Harvard; Ph.D. in Economics from M.I.T.

Claim to Fame: Co-author of the best selling book *Freakonomics*

ANALYZE

To practice analyzing production possibilities curves, display the transparency "Production Possibilities Curve" (Color Transparencies, 1.a). Ask **What do the red and blue lines represent?** *(production possibilities frontier and future production possibilities frontier)* **How do the values on the blue line compare with those on the red line?** *(The future production values are higher.)* **What does that mean?** *(The nation can produce more jeans or T-shirts.)* **What factors might cause that increased production?** *(immigration, updated technology, or more skilled workers)*

L4 Differentiate Have students research the choices that car manufacturers are making, as customers demand more fuel-efficient cars. Some companies are investing in the design of smaller cars with gas engines. Others are focusing on developing solar-powered or electric cars. Have students write a brief essay explaining how a car company could use quantitative methods, such as production possibilities curves, to help them determine the trade-offs and opportunity costs involved in their choices.

INTERPRET

Review the meaning of the law of increasing costs with students. Then direct students to Figure 1.3 in their textbook. Ask **What happens as more land is used for farming?** *(Less productive land is used.)* **Is this an efficient use of resources?** *(No, the land could be used for something else.)*

L3 Simulation Activities In "Kitchen Challenge" have students determine how to use available resources to plan a fund-raising breakfast.

(lesson continued on p. 17)

Background Note

Steven Levitt Students might be interested to know that Levitt—and *Freakonomics* coauthor Stephen J. Dubner—maintain a Freakonomics blog at the Web site http://freakonomics.blogs.nytimes.com. Postings have addressed such topics as a possible link between the decline of grocery stores and the rise of obesity, the link between a member of the House of Representatives having a daughter and their voting pattern on women's issues, and the use of statistical analysis in professional basketball.

Answer

Critical Thinking Possible answer: People lack many kinds of resources, including time and energy, as well as money and skills, that affect the decisions they make.

Teach Case Study

SUMMARIZE AND EXPLAIN

Have the students explain why companies are looking to outsource operations to developing countries. Ask **Why are auto makers moving high-skilled jobs into low-cost countries?** *(Auto makers are trying to save money. Assembly plants have been in low-cost countries for years, but now auto makers are trying to cut additional costs by moving more jobs into undeveloped areas where they can get cheaper labor).*

Have the students figure out how far the auto makers cited in the article are moving operations from their headquarters. *(General Motors is headquartered in Detroit, Michigan, and is building some cars in China—more than 6,000 miles away),* and have them discuss benefits and drawbacks of having workers in remote locations. Ask **How might production and quality control be compromised if Nissan designs cars in Vietnam?** *(Workers in developing countries are inexperienced; they are often new college graduates from recently started college programs with little experience or exposure to automobiles.)*

L2 Differentiate The article discusses assembly plant jobs and high-skilled jobs, which might be difficult for some students to distinguish. Prepare students by explaining the different types of jobs in the auto industry, and the difference between jobs that have been outsourced in the past *(assembly plant jobs)* and the new trend in the outsourcing of higher-skilled jobs *(engineers).*

Economics online *All print resources are available on the Teacher's Resource Library CD-ROM and online at www.PearsonSuccessNet.com.*

Answer

Applying Economic Principles Possible response: Nissan has been shifting its engineering labor source from industrialized countries such as Germany, Japan, and the United States to Vietnam. By building design centers in the developing world, Nissan has changed its physical capital. Nissan has changed its human capital by hiring engineers who lack experience, while, at the same time, providing them with more advanced design software.

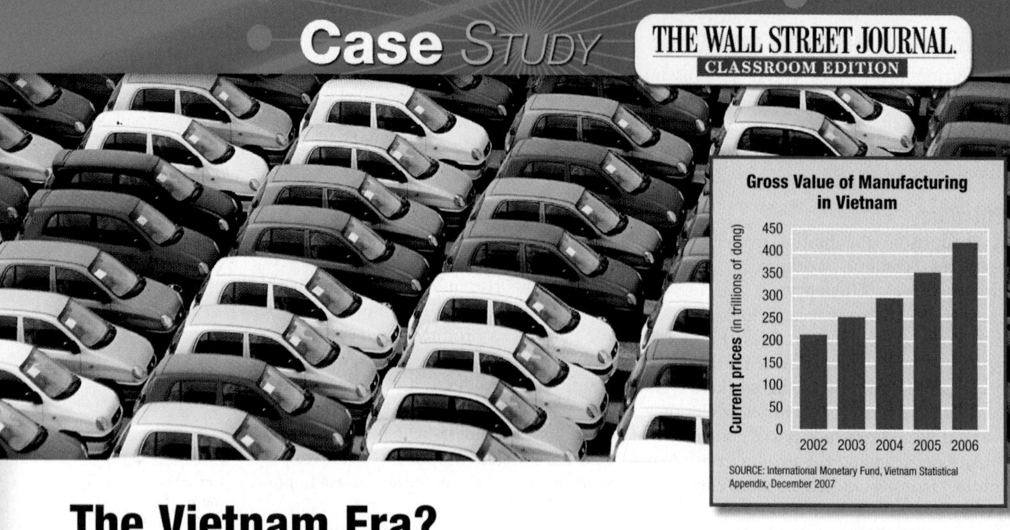

The Vietnam Era?

PRODUCTION POSSIBILITIES

Many low-skill manufacturing jobs have migrated overseas. Now some higher-tech work is beginning to follow them out.

By Norihiko Shirouzu
The Wall Street Journal

Vietnam is barely on the map of the global auto industry, but that is about to change. Nissan Motor sees the southeast Asian nation as a key piece in a strategy to dramatically reduce the cost of developing cars and to compete in the future with rising auto manufacturers from such countries as China and India.

For years, car makers have been slashing expenses by building assembly plants in low-cost countries such as Russia, Turkey and Mexico. Now, high-skill design and engineering operations, which have long remained in industrialized countries like the U.S., Germany and Japan, are starting to follow.

Honda Motor last year announced plans to create a development center in Guangzhou, China with one of its Chinese partners. General Motors has begun designing interiors in China for Buicks it will sell in the U.S.

Nissan has been aggressive among big car makers in moving engineering operations to the developing world. In downtown Hanoi, the capital of Vietnam, Nissan has assembled a team of 700 Vietnamese engineers who are designing basic auto parts such as fuel pipes and nozzles—at a fraction of the cost of doing the work in the auto maker's main engineering center in Japan. The Vietnamese engineers, many of whom have never driven a car before, earn about $200 a month—a 10th of what their counterparts bring home in Japan, according to Nissan.

Over time, Nissan is counting on shifts like these to save hundreds of millions, if not billions, of dollars and sees them as critical to surviving in a world where the cost of cars for consumers in developing markets is falling rapidly.

"If you have an engineer in Hanoi as compared to Japan, there is a lot of savings you can make," says Carlos Ghosn, CEO of Nissan.

But the auto makers like Nissan are still taking a risk. Among the big challenges Nissan faces is a lack of experience among the new college graduates it is recruiting in Vietnam and elsewhere.

Part of what makes it possible for Nissan to allow these engineers to design more of a car are continued advances in computer-aided design tools. But an over-reliance on "virtual engineering" tools at some auto makers' established design centers instead of working with actual components has bred quality problems in recent years.

Video News Update Online Powered by THE WALL STREET JOURNAL. For a new case study, go to the online resources at **PearsonSuccessNet.com**

Applying Economic Principles
Companies, like countries, can increase their productive capacity by shifting factors of production. Based on the above story, what changes did Nissan make in either land, labor, or capital?

Cost

We can also use production possibilities graphs to determine the cost involved in a decision. Remember that cost does not necessarily mean money. To an economist, cost always means opportunity cost.

Looking at the table in **Figure 1.2**, we can see that the opportunity cost of moving from producing no watermelons to producing 8 million tons of watermelons is 1 million pairs of shoes. In other words, in order to produce 8 million tons of watermelons, Capeland had to sacrifice the opportunity to produce 1 million pairs of shoes. In the same way, if Capeland later decides to increase watermelon production from 8 million tons to 14 million tons—an increase of only 6 million tons—it costs 2 million pairs of shoes. In the first step, those 8 million tons of watermelons cost 1 million pairs of shoes. In the second step, an increase of only 6 million tons of watermelons cost an additional 2 million pairs of shoes. This amounts to 3 million pairs of shoes for 14 million tons of watermelons.

The switch from shoes to watermelons has increasing costs. Each time Capeland grows more watermelons, the sacrifice in terms of shoes increases. Eventually, it costs Capeland an additional 5 million pairs of shoes to increase watermelon production by only 1 million tons.

Economists explain these increasingly expensive trade-offs through the **law of increasing costs.** This principle states that as production shifts from making one item to another, more and more resources are necessary to increase production of the second item. Therefore, the opportunity cost increases.

Why does the cost increase? According to **Figure 1.3**, it is because some resources are better suited for use in farming while others are more appropriate for manufacturing. Moving resources from factory to farm production means that farmers must use resources that are not as suitable for farming. For example, when deciding to produce 8 million tons of watermelon, Capeland devoted its most fertile land to this crop. That shift used up the country's best land, so with each additional step, farmers had to use poorer land that produced less per acre than the fertile land could. To increase output on

law of increasing costs an economic principle which states that as production shifts from making one good or service to another, more and more resources are needed to increase production of the second good or service

Simulation *Activity*

Kitchen Challenge
You may be asked to take part in a role-playing game about increasing costs and efficient use of resources.

Figure 1.3 Law of Increasing Costs

STEP 1
Initially, resources are used efficiently to make a balance of watermelons and shoes.

STEP 2
A decision is made to grow more watermelons. Less suitable resources are shifted to farm production. Farm production increases. Shoe production decreases.

STEP 3
A decision is made to grow even more watermelons, and more resources are shifted to farm production. Because the added land is less productive, a greater amount of it must be cultivated. Farm output increases. Shoe output decreases by an even greater amount.

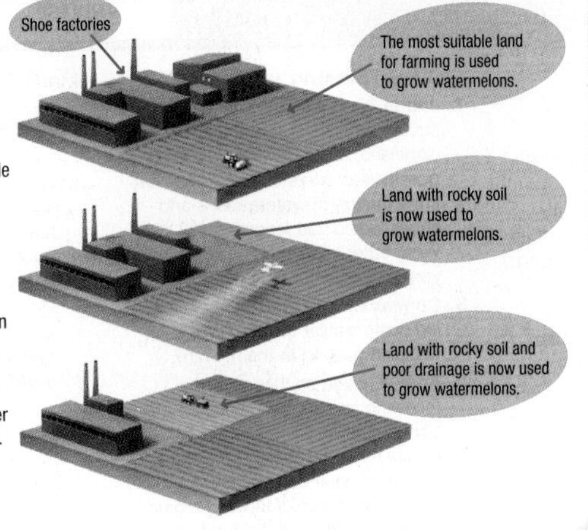

Shoe factories
The most suitable land for farming is used to grow watermelons.
Land with rocky soil is now used to grow watermelons.
Land with rocky soil and poor drainage is now used to grow watermelons.

GRAPH SKILLS

This diagram illustrates the law of increasing costs. As production shifts from shoes to watermelons, more and more resources are needed.

1. Why would moving from Step 1 to Step 2 use up more resources than staying at Step 1?
2. Why do you think Capeland might decide to increase watermelon production in spite of the increasing costs?

RESEARCH AND DEBATE

Have students research the effect of technology on production capacity in the United States. Distribute the "Promoting Technology" worksheet (Unit 1 All-in-One, p. 31). Divide the class into teams and have them debate the question **Should the U.S. government fund technological research that may profit private companies?**

L3 Use the Peer Tutoring and Peer Feedback Strategy (p. T25) to help students of different ability levels work together on debate teams.

L2 Distribute the "Governments Promote Technology" worksheet (Unit 1 All-in-One, p. 32).

EXTEND

Have students create their own data tables and production possibilities curves for two sets of goods for a fictional nation. Have them answer the question: What and how much does your production possibility curve tell this nation to produce?

L2 ELL Differentiate Have students create a poster about one form of technology and how it has increased efficiency in business.

GUIDING QUESTION WRAP UP

Have students return to the section Guiding Question. Review the completed graphic organizer and clarify any misunderstandings. Have a wrap up discussion about how a nation decides what to produce.

Assess and Remediate

L3 L2 Collect the "Promoting Technology," "Governments Promote Technology" worksheets. Assess students' research and debate performance.

L3 Section 3 Assessment

L3 Give Section Quiz A (Unit 1 All-in-One, p. 33).

L2 Give Section Quiz B (Unit 1 All-in-One, p. 34).

(Assess and Remediate continued on p. 18)

Virtual Economics

L2 Differentiate

Constructing a Production Possibilities Curve Use the following lesson from the NCEE **Virtual Economics *CD-ROM*** to evaluate how production decisions are made. Click on Browse Economics Lessons, specify grades 9–12, and use the key words *your mind.*

In this activity, students will use a fictional case study to examine the factors of production and create a possibilities curve.

LESSON TITLE	HAVE YOU EVER HAD TO MAKE UP YOUR MIND?
Type of Activity	Using statistics
Complexity	Low
Time	100 minutes
NCEE Standards	1, 2

Answers

Graph Skills 1. Possible answer: More labor and capital are needed to make poorer land productive. 2. Possible response: increase watermelon production if producing them is more profitable than selling shoes, in spite of increasing costs.

Have students complete the Self-Test Online and continue their work in the **Essential Questions Journal**.

REMEDIATION AND SUGGESTIONS

Use the chart below to help students who are struggling with content.

WEAKNESS	REMEDIATION
Defining key terms (Questions 3, 4, 5, 6)	Have students use the interactive Economic Dictionary Online.
Interpreting production possibilities curves (Questions 1, 3, 7, 9, 10)	Help students construct a table of values from the production possibilities curve in Transparency 1.a.
Describing the law of increasing costs (Questions 2, 8)	Have students review the Action Graphs Online for Figure 1.3.

Answers

Caption *Possible answer:* Milking machines would make milking cows faster.

Checkpoint It can show an economy's efficiency, the results of growth, and the opportunity cost at each level of production.

Checkpoint Technology allows people to work more efficiently, meaning they can produce more.

"Things were done very differently on the farm when I was your age, Kenny."

▲ Technology has changed agriculture—but not quite in the way this cartoon shows. ***What is one example of technology that really could help this dairy farmer increase production?***

the poorer land, farmers had to use more land and other resources. This left even fewer resources for producing shoes.

The law of increasing costs explains why production possibilities curve. As we move along the curve, we trade off more and more for less and less added output.

CHECKPOINT ***What in ormation can a production possibilities curve reveal?***

Technology and Education

When economists collect data to create production possibility curves, they must first determine which goods and services a country can produce with its current resources. A country's resources include its land and natural resources, its workforce, and its physical and human capital.

Both human and physical capital reflect a vital ingredient of economic growth—technology. Technology is the process used to create goods and services. At any time, countries have used different forms of technology to produce shoes or watermelons or any of the thousands of products that are made. So economists must assess each country's level of technological know-how. Do workers in Capeland pick watermelons by hand? Do they use assembly lines to make shoes?

Technology is one of the factors that can increase a nation's efficiency. Therefore, many governments spend money investing in new technology. For the same reason, they may also invest in education and training so that its people can develop and use new technologies. Highly-skilled workers can increase efficiency and lead to economic growth.

CHECKPOINT ***How does technology increase production possibilities?***

SECTION 3 ASSESSMENT

Essential Questions Journal To continue to build a response to the Essential Question, go to your **Essential Questions Journal.**

Guiding Question

1. Use your completed concept web to answer this question: How does a nation decide what and how much to produce?
2. **Extension** Explain why a country might stop growing food and shift its resources to manufacturing clothing.

Key Terms and Main Ideas

3. What is a production **possibilities curve?**
4. What do economists mean by **efficiency?**
5. What do economists mean by growth? What factors can produce economic growth?
6. What is the impact of **underutilization** of resources?

Critical Thinking

7. **Judge** Suppose you were an economic adviser to the leader of Capeland. Based on the production possibilities curve in **Figure 1.2**, what combination of watermelons and shoes would you recommend? Why? What other information might help you make the best decision?
8. **Compare** How is the law of increasing costs similar to the concept of decision making at the margin?
9. **Apply** Explain how each of the following circumstances is likely to affect a nation's production possibilities frontier: the opening of a new college of engineering; an earthquake in the nation's chief farming region; a new type of chemical fertilizer; a shortage of oil.

Math Skills

10. Use the information on the table below to create a production possibilities curve. Then, identify which of the following points on the graph would represent the least efficient use of resources: 3 units of capital goods to 25 units of consumer goods; 9 units of capital goods to 20 units of consumer goods; 12 units of capital goods to 2 units of consumer goods. ***Visit PearsonSuccessNet.com for additional math help.***

Capital Goods (units)	Consumer Goods (units)
0	25
4	24
10	21
18	16
28	9
40	0

Assessment Answers

1. A nation can use a production possibilities curve to find what and how much to produce to use its resources most efficiently.
2. Possible response: if it could produce more clothing than food more profitably
3. graph that shows alternative ways to use an economy's productive resources
4. using resources to maximize production
5. increased production, which can come from improved efficiency or more resources
6. Possible response: higher unemployment and less prosperity
7. Possible response: 14 million tons of watermelons and 12 million pairs of shoes or 18 million tons of watermelons and 9 million pairs of shoes because the trade-offs get increasingly expensive as more resources are shifted from manufacturing one product to another. Other information to be considered: the profits that can be made from shoes vs. watermelons.
8. Both look at marginal costs and benefits of a stepped change in the resources used.
9. Possible responses: new college of engineering and type of fertilizer would increase capital, moving frontier to right; earthquake and oil shortage would reduce resources, cutting production and shifting frontier to left
10. Students graph should show a production possibilities graph that indicates that the least efficient use of resources is 12 units of capital goods to 2 units of consumer goods.

QUICK STUDY GUIDE

QUICK STUDY GUIDE

Chapter 1: What Is Economics?

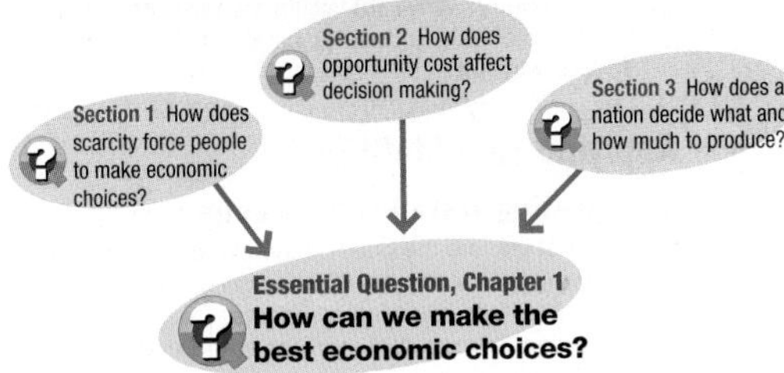
Section 1 How does scarcity force people to make economic choices?
Section 2 How does opportunity cost affect decision making?
Section 3 How does a nation decide what and how much to produce?
Essential Question, Chapter 1
How can we make the best economic choices?

Impact of Scarcity

Needs and wants are unlimited.
Resources, goods, and services are scarce.
Need to make trade-offs and identify opportunity costs.
Impact on Individuals
• Make personal trade-offs (time, money)
• Make decisions at the margin
Impact on Businesses
• Balance factors of production: land, labor, capital
• Identify marginal costs and benefits
Impact on Nations
• Make budgetary trade-offs ("guns or butter")
• Determine production possibilities

Economic Dictionary

- **need,** *p. 3*
- **want,** *p. 3*
- **goods,** *p. 3*
- **services,** *p. 3*
- **scarcity,** *p. 4*
- **economics,** *p. 4*
- **shortage,** *p. 4*
- **entrepreneur,** *p. 5*
- **factors of production,** *p. 5*
- **land,** *p. 5*
- **labor,** *p. 5*
- **capital,** *p. 6*
- **physical capital,** *p. 6*
- **human capital,** *p. 6*
- **trade-off,** *p. 8*
- **"guns or butter",** *p. 9*
- **opportunity cost,** *p. 9*
- **thinking at the margin,** *p. 11*
- **cost/benefit analysis,** *p. 11*
- **marginal cost,** *p. 11*
- **marginal benefit,** *p. 11*
- **production possibilities curve,** *p. 13*
- **production possibilities frontier,** *p. 14*
- **efficiency,** *p. 15*
- **underutilization,** *p. 15*
- **law of increasing costs,** *p. 17*

Economics *on the go*

Study anytime, anywhere. Download these files today.

Economic Dictionary online	Audio Review online	Action Graph online	Visual Glossary online	How the Economy Works online
Vocabulary Support in English and Spanish	Audio Study Guide in English and Spanish	Animated Charts and Graphs	Animated feature	Animated feature

Download to your computer or mobile device at PearsonSuccessNet.com

ASSIGN THE ESSENTIAL QUESTIONS JOURNAL

After students have finished studying the chapter, they should return to the chapter's essential question in the Essential Questions Journal and complete the activity.

Tell students to go back to the chapter opener and look at the image. Using the information they have gained from studying the chapter, ask **How does this illustrate the main ideas of the chapter?** *(Possible answers: even when there is no shortage (such as in this shopping mall), scarcity exists because people have unlimited wants and resources are limited; making decisions involves trade-offs: choosing to go to the mall instead of studying for a test is a trade-off that has certain benefits and opportunity costs.)*

STUDY TIPS

To help students prepare for college, have them practice note taking. For instance, have students record information about key concepts in Chapter 1 in a chart with the headings *Concept* and *Example*. Ask them to trade charts with a partner to check their information and understanding.

Economics *on the go* Have students download the digital resources available on Economics on the Go for review and remediation.

Assessment at a Glance

TESTS AND QUIZZES

Section Assessments

Section Quizzes A and B, **Unit 1 All-in-One**

Self-Test Online

Chapter Assessments

Chapter Tests A and B, **Unit 1 All-in-One**

Economic Detective, **Unit 1 All-in-One**

Document-based Assessment, p. 21

Exam*View*

AYP Monitoring Assessments

PERFORMANCE ASSESSMENT

Teacher's Edition, pp. 5, 6, 9, 10, 11, 17

Simulation Activities, Chapter 1

Virtual Economics on CD-ROM, Teacher's Edition pp. 6, 11, 17

Essential Questions Journal, Chapter 1

Assessment Rubrics

Chapter Assessment

1. (a) land, labor, capital (b) Possible responses: *Land*—natural resources used to generate electricity used at the store; *Labor*—business owner and workers; *Capital*—equipment and special training of workers
2. (a) combine factors of production to produce goods and services (b) examples: owners of Internet companies, movie producers, local store owners (c) Possible responses: imagination, to come up with new business ideas; persuasive speaking, to convince others to invest in the business; and leadership, to guide workers
3. Possible responses: (a) Opportunity cost of lightweight car is greater safety; opportunity cost of heavier car is higher fuel cost. Other trade-offs: heavier car pollutes more; lighter car may carry fewer passengers or less cargo. (b) Students might buy the heavier car due to greater safety. (c) Possible responses: doubling of gasoline price would push them to buy a lighter car to save on fuel costs; having a million dollars might convince them to buy the heavier car because gas cost would be less problematic; having children might push them to buy the heavier, safer car
4. (a) The curve would shift to the left because farmers' productive capacity would go down. (b) Possible response: Yes. The capacity of other industries would decline because the drought would probably result in higher food prices which could cause some people to spend less on other goods and services. This could impact the production possibilities of these other industries.
5. 5 million more televisions than computers (20 million; 15 million)
6. 5 million computers
7. 2 million televisions
8. 5 million televisions
9. At point a, there is no opportunity cost because the maximum number of televisions—20 million—can be produced. At point b, the opportunity cost of 5 million computers is 2 million televisions so the opportunity cost of each 1 million computers is 400,000 televisions.
10. Students' answers will vary. They must list at least three purchases and three activities and have an opportunity cost for each one.
11. (a) Students might opt for a more expensive alternative or, thinking at the margin, more units of a particular item. Some might save the money. (b) Students might give up an option that cost more time. (c) Students should explain which option they would have taken and under what conditions.

CHAPTER 1 ASSESSMENT

Self-Test online To test your understanding of key terms and main ideas, visit **PearsonSuccessNet.com**

Key Terms and Main Ideas

To make sure you understand the key terms and main ideas of this chapter, review the Checkpoint and Section Assessment questions and look at the Quick Study Guide on the preceding page.

Critical Thinking

1. **Give Examples (a)** What are the three factors of production? **(b)** Choose a business in your community. Give two examples of each factor of production that would apply to that business.
2. **Apply (a)** What do entrepreneurs do? **(b)** Give two examples of people you consider to be successful entrepreneurs. **(c)** List three qualities you think an entrepreneur needs in order to succeed. Explain why each one would be important.
3. **Decide** Cars that weigh more tend to be safer than lightweight cars. At the same time, they use more gasoline because they are heavier. **(a)** Identify the trade-offs and opportunity cost involved in choosing either alternative. **(b)** Based on this information, which car would you choose to buy and why? **(c)** Would your answer change if the price of gasoline doubled? If you inherited a million dollars? If you had children? Explain how each factor would affect your cost-benefit analysis.

4. **Predict (a)** If a drought struck a country, what would happen to the production possibilities curve of all farmers in the country? Why? **(b)** Would the production possibilities curve of other industries be affected by this drought? Why or why not?

Applying Your Math Skills

Interpreting Data From Graphs

Imagine that you are the chief economist of a country with the following production possibilities curve. Use your math skills to answer the following questions.

Visit Pearson SuccessNet.com for additional math help.

5. How do the maximum amounts of each product differ?
6. Assume this economy is producing at full efficiency. How many computers are being produced when there are 18 million televisions being produced?
7. What is the opportunity cost of producing 5 million computers?
8. What is the opportunity cost of producing 9 million computers?
9. What is the opportunity cost of each 1 million computers at point a compared to point b?

Televisions (in millions): 0, 5, 10, 15, 20, 25
Computers (in millions): 0, 5, 10, 15, 20, 25
Points: a, b, c, d, e, f

Essential Question Activity

Essential Questions Journal To respond to the chapter Essential Question, go to your **Essential Questions Journal.**

10. Complete this activity to answer the Essential Question **How can we make the best economic choices?** As you have learned, scarcity and opportunity cost lie at the heart of all economic decisions—including those you make. You have limited time and limited resources. Every time you choose one alternative, you give up something else. Using the worksheet in your Essential Questions Journal or the electronic worksheet available at **PearsonSuccessNet.com,** keep track of how you use your resources for the next three days.
    (a) In Column 1, record at least three items on which you spent your money and three activities on which you spent your time.
    (b) In Column 2, list the opportunity cost for each entry in Column 1. Remember that the opportunity cost is the next most desirable alternative—the thing you gave up when you made your choice.

    After completing the chart, review your choices. Then, for each of the choices you made, answer the following question: If you had it to do over again, would you make the same choice? Why or why not? Write your answers in Column 3.
11. **Modify** You have listed your choices and your trade-offs and evaluated your outcomes. Now, consider how your choices might have differed if your resources had differed. Write an answer to each of the following:
    (a) How would your choices change if you had 10 percent more money to spend?
    (b) What would you give up if you had 5 fewer hours of free time to use in those three days?
    (c) Pick one of the opportunity costs on your list. What conditions might have led you to make the opposite choice? Explain.

20 WHAT IS ECONOMICS?

WebQuest online The Economics WebQuest challenges students to use 21st century skills to answer the Essential Question. Students assume the role of political leaders and conduct research on world markets and the situations of the countries they represent to guide them toward making the best economic choices for their people.

THE ESSENTIAL
VIDEO
By Students For Students
For videos on Essential Questions, go to PearsonSuccessNet.com

Remind students to continue to develop an Essential Questions video. Guidelines and a production binder are available at www.PearsonSuccessNet.com.

DOCUMENT-BASED ASSESSMENT

Should the federal government spend money on space exploration?

Since the 1950s, the federal government has spent billions of dollars on its space program. While many have applauded the achievements of astronauts and space scientists, some Americans think the money could have been better spent at home.

Document A

"The fundamental goal of this vision is to advance U.S. scientific, security, and economic interests through a robust space exploration program. In support of this goal, the United States will:

- Implement a sustained and affordable human and robotic program to explore the solar system and beyond;
- Extend human presence across the solar system, starting with a human return to the Moon before the year 2020, in preparation for human exploration of Mars and other destinations;
- Develop the innovative technologies, knowledge, and infrastructures both to explore and to support decisions about the destinations for human exploration; and
- Promote international and commercial participation in exploration to further U.S. scientific, security, and economic interests."

—President George W. Bush, "A Renewed Spirit of Discovery," January 14, 2004

Document B

"Citizens Against Government Waste (CAGW) today cautioned against the proposal by the administration to expand the space program to include a possible manned station on the moon and human flight to Mars. Concerned with NASA's existing obligations and the budget deficit, CAGW believes such a move would be too risky and costly.

'While space exploration may be a noble idea, it is not feasible at this time,' CAGW President Tom Schatz said. 'Cost estimates for the new programs range from $550 billion to $1 trillion. Until the federal government brings the record deficit back down to Earth, it should not launch expensive new space programs of questionable scientific value.'"

—Citizens Against Government Waste, January 13, 2004

Document C

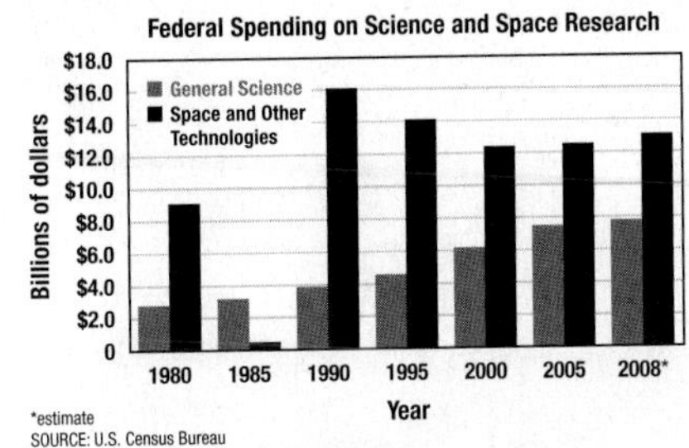

*estimate
SOURCE: U.S. Census Bureau

ANALYZING DOCUMENTS

Use your knowledge of opportunity costs and Documents A, B, and C to answer questions 1–3.

1. **According to Document A, the primary goal of the American space program should be to**
   A. land humans on the moon.
   B. focus on unmanned, or robot, missions.
   C. prepare for human exploration of Mars.
   D. advance the interests of the United States.

2. **According to Document B, the opportunity cost of increased space funding is**
   A. reduced spending on social programs.
   B. the chance to cut the government deficit.
   C. the need to cut defense spending.
   D. abandonment of the Mars mission.

3. **Document C shows that as spending on space and other technology has gone down, spending on general science research**
   A. has gone up.
   B. has gone down.
   C. has stayed the same.
   D. has surpassed it.

WRITING ABOUT ECONOMICS

Spending on programs like NASA's space exploration is an ongoing issue. Use the documents on this page and on the Web site below to answer the question: ***Should the federal government spend money on space exploration?*** Use the sources to support your opinion.

To read more about issues related to this topic, visit **PearsonSuccessNet.com**

Document-Based Assessment

ANALYZING DOCUMENTS

1. D
2. B
3. A

WRITING ABOUT ECONOMICS

Possible responses: Yes, space exploration furthers "U.S. scientific, security, and economic interests." No, space exploration is too costly when the government already has a huge deficit. Use the following as guidelines to assess the essay.

Student essay should demonstrate an understanding of the issues involved in the debate. Use the following as guidelines to assess the essay.

L2 Differentiate Students use all documents on the page to support their thesis.

L3 Differentiate Students use the documents on this page and additional information available online at www.PearsonSuccessNet.com to support their answer.

L4 Differentiate Students incorporate information provided in the textbook and online at www.PearsonSuccessNet.com and include additional research to support their opinion.

Go Online to www.PearsonSuccessNet.com for a student rubric and extra documents.

Economics online *All print resources are available on the Teacher's Resource Library CD-ROM and online at* www.PearsonSuccessNet.com.

Essential Questions

UNIT 1:

How does economics affect everyone?

CHAPTER 2:

How does a society decide who gets what goods and services?

Introduce the Chapter

ACTIVATE PRIOR KNOWLEDGE

In this chapter, students will learn about economic systems. Tell students to complete the activity in the **Essential Questions Journal**.

DIFFERENTIATED INSTRUCTION KEY

- **L1** Special Needs
- **L2** Basic
  - **ELL** English Language Learners
  - **LPR** Less Proficient Readers
- **L3** All Students
- **L4** Advanced Students

Economics online Visit www.PearsonSuccessNet.com for an interactive textbook with built-in activities on economic principles.

- ***The Wall Street Journal* Classroom Edition Video** presents a current topic related to market structures.
- **Yearly Update Worksheet** provides an annual update, including a new worksheet and lesson on this topic.
- **On the Go** resources can be downloaded so students and teachers can connect with economics anytime, anywhere.

Chapter 2 Economic Systems

Essential Question, Chapter 2

How does a society decide who gets what goods and services?

Economics on the go

To study anywhere, anytime, download these online resources at ***PearsonSuccessNet.com*** ▶

ECONOMICS ONLINE

DIGITAL TEACHER TOOLS

The online lesson planner is designed to help teachers plan, teach, and assess. Teachers have the ability to use or customize existing Pearson lesson plans. Online lecture notes support the print lesson by providing an array of accessible activities and summaries of key concepts.

Two interactivities in this lesson are:

- **Visual Glossary** Students learn the difference between positive and negative incentives.
- **Action Graphs** Animated graphs illustrate the different types of economies.

Block Scheduling

BLOCK 1 Teach Sections 1 and 2 lessons, omitting the Career Center and Innovators features.

BLOCK 2 Teach Sections 3 and 4, focusing on the weaknesses of central planning when teaching Section 3.

Pressed for Time

Group work Organize the class into eight groups, assigning each group a subsection of Section 2 or 3. Have the groups outline their assigned subsection and distribute that outline to the rest of the class. As a class, go through the section outlines, focusing on the characteristics, advantages, and disadvantages of the two systems.

SECTION 1 Answering the Three Economic Questions

OBJECTIVES

1. **Identify** the three key economic questions that all societies must answer.
2. **Analyze** the societal values that determine how a country answers the three economic questions.
3. **Define** the characteristics of a traditional economy.

ECONOMIC DICTIONARY

As you read the section, look for the definitions of these **Key Terms:**

- economic system
- factor payment
- profit
- safety net
- standard of living
- innovation
- traditional economy

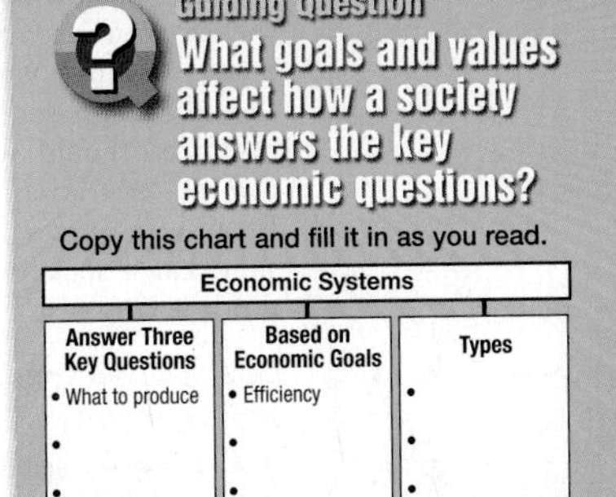
Guiding Question
What goals and values affect how a society answers the key economic questions?
Copy this chart and fill it in as you read.
Economic Systems
Answer Three Key Questions
• What to produce
Based on Economic Goals
• Efficiency
Types

Economics and You When you go to a supermarket, you see rows of shelves stacked with a wide variety of foods and household products. But imagine that the government limited your choice to just one brand of cereal and one brand of soap. Or imagine that the only goods available to you were what you and your neighbors could grow or make yourselves. All of these examples represent ways that different societies have dealt with the challenge of meeting people's needs and wants.

Principles in Action Each society faces three questions about the production and consumption of goods and services. As you'll see, these questions shape our freedom of choice—and also shape what we have to choose from.

Three Key Economic Questions

Resources are scarce everywhere. As a result, every society must answer three key economic questions:

- What goods and services should be produced?
- How should these goods and services be produced?
- Who consumes these goods and services?

The way a society answers these three questions defines its economic system. An **economic system** is the structure of methods and principles a society uses to produce and distribute goods and services.

economic system the structure of methods and principles that a society uses to produce and distribute goods and services

Visual Glossary online

Go to the Visual Glossary Online for an interactive review of **incentives.**

Action Graph online

Go to Action Graph Online for animated versions of key charts and graphs.

How the Economy Works online

Go to How the Economy Works Online for an interactive lesson on **innovation and the economy.**

Guiding Question

What goals and values affect how a society answers the key economic questions?

Get Started

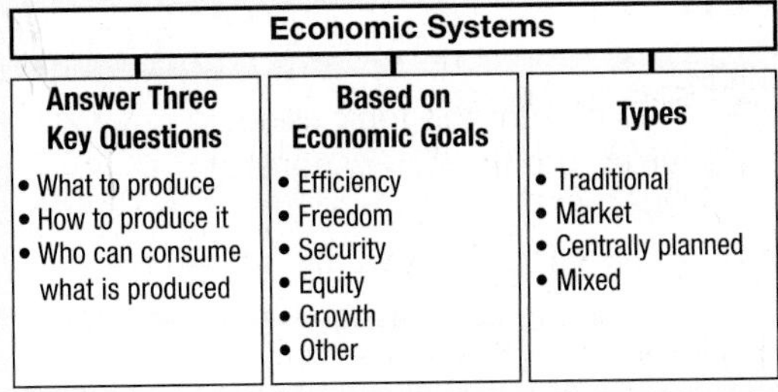

Economic Systems		
Answer Three Key Questions	Based on Economic Goals	Types
• What to produce • How to produce it • Who can consume what is produced	• Efficiency • Freedom • Security • Equity • Growth • Other	• Traditional • Market • Centrally planned • Mixed

LESSON GOALS

Students will:

- Know the Key Terms.
- Give examples of different ways in which the three key economic questions can be answered.
- Define economic goals and values in the United States economy by completing a worksheet.
- Analyze how emphasizing each goal or value affects other goals or values.
- Examine what economic goals are most easily met in a traditional economy.
- Write a persuasive essay advocating the emphasis of particular economic values.

BEFORE CLASS

Have students complete the graphic organizer in the Section Opener as they read the text. As an alternate activity, have students complete the Guided Reading and Review worksheet (Unit 1 All-in-One, p. 53).

L1 L2 ELL LPR Differentiate Have students complete the Guided Reading and Review worksheet (Unit 1 All-in-One, p. 54).

Focus on the Basics

Students need to come away with the following understandings:

FACTS: • All societies must answer three key questions: what is produced, how it is produced, and who consumes what is produced. • Societies answer these questions based on their economic goals and values. • Traditional economies answer these questions based on past practices.

GENERALIZATION: Because societies answer the key economic questions differently, multiple economic systems have developed.

CLASSROOM HINTS

STANDARD OF LIVING IN TRADITIONAL ECONOMIES

Explain to students that households and firms in a traditional economy are often the same. Ask students what their standard of living would be if they needed to raise all of their own food and make their own clothes.

BELLRINGER

Write the following three questions on the blackboard: *What goods should we produce? How should we produce them? Who should consume them?* Tell students they have five minutes to jot down how they would answer each question as it relates to one basic necessity: food.

Teach

Economics online To present this topic using digital resources, use the lecture notes at www.PearsonSuccessNet.com.

L1 L2 ELL LPR Differentiate To help students who are struggling readers, assign the Vocabulary worksheet (Unit 1 All-in-One, p. 52).

DISCUSS

Ask volunteers to read aloud their answers to each of the three questions in the Bellringer. Encourage students to express opposing viewpoints and to challenge one another in an orderly manner. If necessary, prompt discussion by asking leading questions: **Should the government try to influence the types of crops farmers grow or the kinds of animals they raise? Should producers be allowed to produce any kind of food they choose? Should fat content or the use of chemical additives be regulated? Should food be made available to people who can't afford to buy it—and, if so, how?**

After students have discussed various possible answers to the three questions, ask **In our society, how are these three questions actually answered? Who gets to make the decisions regarding what to produce, how to produce it, and who consumes it?** Guide students toward the conclusion that, while many decisions are made freely by producers and consumers, some decisions are made or influenced by government regulation. Ask students to suggest other examples.

Action Graph online Have students review the Action Graph animation for a step-by-step look at combining factor resources.

Answers

Graph Skills 1. Using machinery is more efficient, because it produces more wheat with less labor.
2. Labor would have to increase by a large amount to equal the output achieved by using machinery.

What Goods and Services Should Be Produced?

Each society must decide what to produce in order to satisfy the needs and wants of its people. While all people need food and shelter, societies face additional important considerations. Which consumer goods should we produce? How much of our resources should we devote to national defense, education, or consumer goods? Because resources are limited, each decision that a society makes about what to produce comes at an opportunity cost.

How Should Goods and Services Be Produced?

A society must also decide *how* to produce goods and services. What fuel should we use to generate electricity—oil, solar power, or nuclear power? Is education best delivered through public schools or private schools?

Although there are many ways to produce goods and services, all require land, labor, and capital. These factors of production can be combined in different ways. For example, look at **Figure 2.1.** Before the introduction of modern farming equipment, producing 15 bushels of wheat may have required 56 hours of labor, 1 acre of land, and simple hand tools. Today, mechanical equipment makes farming more efficient. Farmers can use just 2.9 hours of labor to produce 40 bushels of wheat on that same acre of land. While the amount of land used remains the same, labor has gone down, and the amount of capital needed has gone up.

These decisions involve trade-offs, too. What else could the society produce with those 56 hours of work in the time of hand tools? What could today's society make if the capital employed as mechanized farm equipment were used in some other way?

Who Consumes Goods and Services?

Societies also make decisions that determine how goods and services are consumed. How can people meet their

Figure 2.1 Combining Factor Resources

GRAPH SKILLS

Today, capital—not land—dominates the production of many goods, such as wheat.

1. Which method of production shown here is more efficient? Explain.
2. What factor of production would probably need to change in order for farmers using hand tools to produce as many bushels of wheat as farmers using machinery?

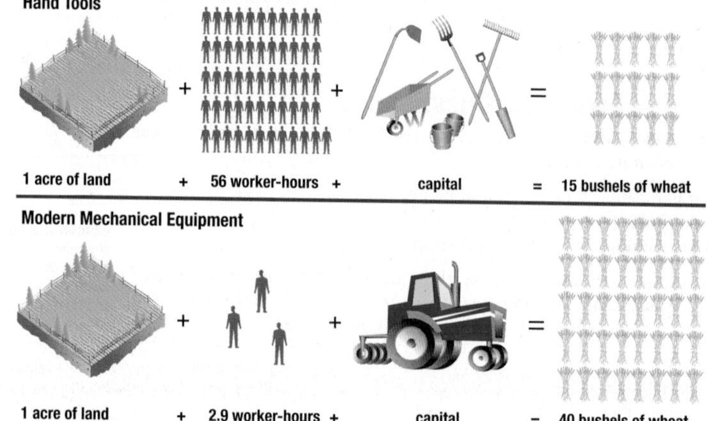

Action Graph online

For an animated version of this graph, visit PearsonSuccessNet.com

Differentiated Resources

- **L1 L2 Guided Reading and Review** (Unit 1 All-in-One, p. 54)
- **L2 Vocabulary worksheet** (Unit 1 All-in-One, p. 52)
- **L1 L2 Writing a Persuasive Essay skills worksheet** (Unit 1 All-in-One, p. 58)
- **L2 Goals and Values in the United States Economy** (Unit 1 All-in-One, p. 56)

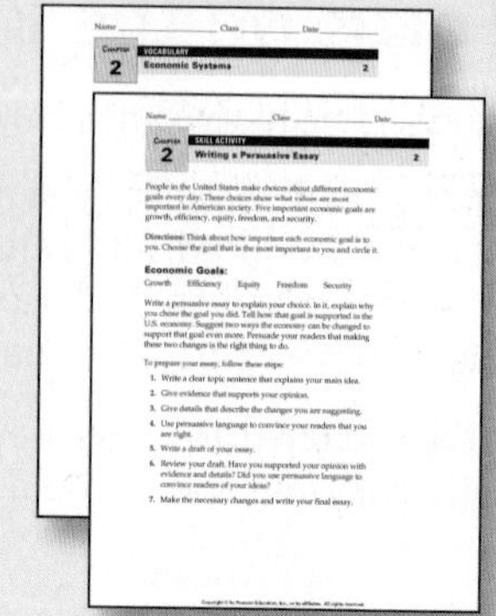

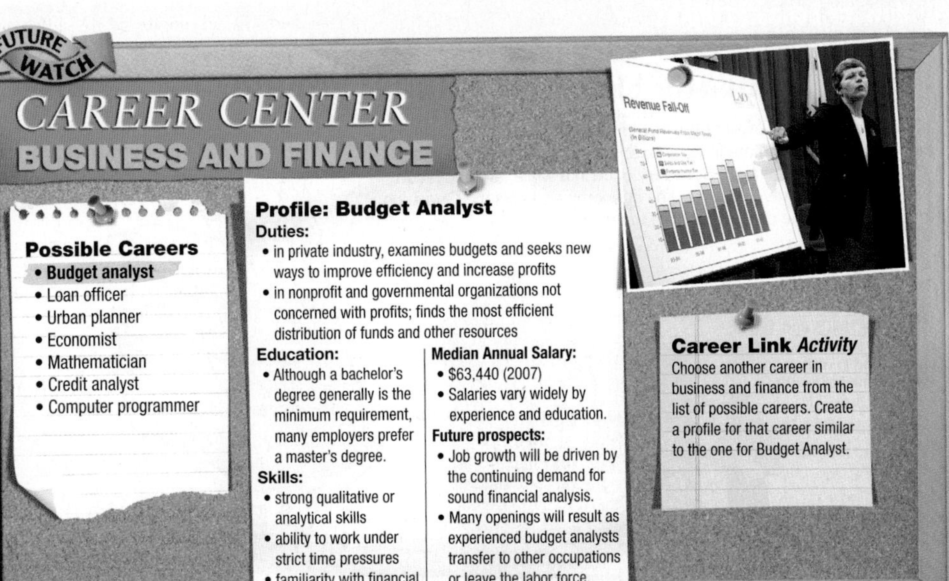

Possible Careers
- **Budget analyst**
- Loan officer
- Urban planner
- Economist
- Mathematician
- Credit analyst
- Computer programmer

Profile: Budget Analyst

Duties:
- in private industry, examines budgets and seeks new ways to improve efficiency and increase profits
- in nonprofit and governmental organizations not concerned with profits; finds the most efficient distribution of funds and other resources

Education:
- Although a bachelor's degree generally is the minimum requirement, many employers prefer a master's degree.

Skills:
- strong qualitative or analytical skills
- ability to work under strict time pressures
- familiarity with financial software packages

Median Annual Salary:
- $63,440 (2007)
- Salaries vary widely by experience and education.

Future prospects:
- Job growth will be driven by the continuing demand for sound financial analysis.
- Many openings will result as experienced budget analysts transfer to other occupations or leave the labor force.

Career Link *Activity*
Choose another career in business and finance from the list of possible careers. Create a profile for that career similar to the one for Budget Analyst.

needs for food and medical care? Who gets to drive a new luxury car and who can only afford bus fare? Who gets access to a college education?

The answer to such questions is largely determined by how societies distribute income. **Factor payments** are the income people receive in return for supplying factors of production—land, labor, or capital. Landowners collect rent, workers earn wages, and those who lend money receive payments called interest. Factor payments also include the profits that entrepreneurs earn if their enterprises succeed. **Profit** is the amount of money a business receives in excess of its expenses. Profits are the rewards entrepreneurs receive for taking the risk of starting a business.

How much should we pay the owners of the factors of production? How do we decide how much teachers should earn versus how much doctors should earn? The answers to such questions tell us a great deal about a society's values.

CHECKPOINT ***What are the three key economic questions?***

Economic Goals and Societal Values

Different societies answer the three economic questions based on the importance they attach to various economic goals. These goals include efficiency, freedom, security, equity, and growth. All societies pursue each of these goals to some degree.

Economic Efficiency

Because resources are always scarce, societies try to maximize what they can produce using the resources they have. If a society can accurately assess what its people need and want, it increases its economic efficiency. A manufacturer would be wasting resources producing desktop computers if people prefer laptops.

The goal of reducing waste also involves the second and third economic questions. Producers seek better ways to create goods and to make them available to consumers. An economy that cannot deliver the right goods in the right quantity to the right people at the right price is not efficient.

factor payment the income people receive in return for supplying factors of production

profit the amount of money a business receives in excess of its expenses

Virtual Economics

L3 Differentiate

Analyze Social Values Use the following lesson from the NCEE **Virtual Economics *CD-ROM*** to evaluate social goals in different societies. Click on Browse Economics Lessons, specify grades 9–12, and use the key words *social goals*. Choose Lesson Two.

In this activity, students will use diary entries to classify six social values in a command and a market economy.

LESSON TITLE	**BROAD SOCIAL GOALS OF AN ECONOMIC SYSTEM**
Type of Activity	Categorizing
Complexity	Moderate
Time	50 minutes
NCEE Standards	1, 3

ACTIVITY

On the board, list the economic goals and values on pages 25–27. Call on students to read aloud the text under each heading defining a goal. Then have volunteers explain each goal.

Next, divide the class into two groups. Tell the first group that they represent a small, primitive farming community that must provide for all its own needs. Tell the second group that they represent a modern industrial society. Have each group work together to describe how their society meets the basic needs of providing food, clothing, and shelter. Have each group share their descriptions with the class. Ask **Which society is best equipped to change and grow?** *(modern industrial)* **In which society is it easiest to achieve economic equity?** *(traditional)* **Which society offers individuals the most freedom to make their own economic decisions?** *(modern industrial)*

CREATE A PROFILE

Have students use the Career Link worksheet to record their research for the activity (Unit 1 All-in-one, p. 134).

DISTRIBUTE ACTIVITY WORKSHEET

Explain that each goal or value affects how each key economic question is answered. Distribute the "Evaluating the United States Economy" worksheet (Unit 1 All-in-One, p. 55).

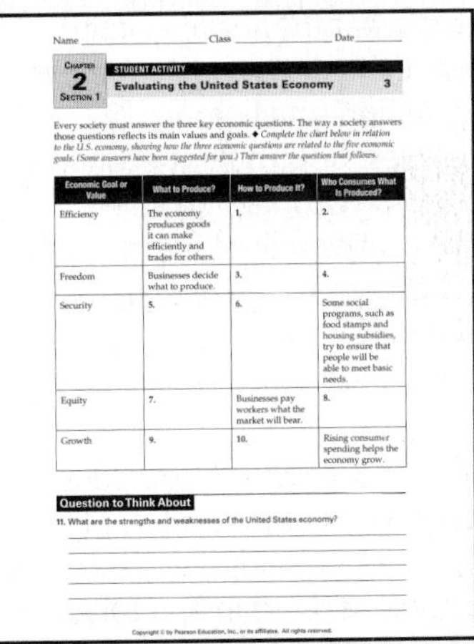
Name ______ Class ______ Date ______

CHAPTER 2 SECTION 1 — STUDENT ACTIVITY — **Evaluating the United States Economy** 3

Every society must answer the three key economic questions. The way a society answers those questions reflects its main values and goals. ◆ *Complete the chart below in relation to the U.S. economy, showing how the three economic questions are related to the five economic goals. (Some answers have been suggested for you.) Then answer the question that follows.*

Economic Goal or Value	What to Produce?	How to Produce It?	Who Consumes What Is Produced?
Efficiency	The economy produces goods it can make efficiently and trades for others.	1.	2.
Freedom	Businesses decide what to produce.	3.	4.
Security	5.	6.	Some social programs, such as food stamps and housing subsidies, try to ensure that people will be able to meet basic needs.
Equity	7.	Businesses pay workers what the market will bear.	8.
Growth	9.	10.	Rising consumer spending helps the economy grow.

Question to Think About

11. What are the strengths and weaknesses of the United States economy?

L2 Differentiate Distribute the "Goals and Values in the United States Economy" worksheet (Unit 1 All-in-One, p. 56).

Discuss students' answers when they have completed the worksheet.

Answer

Checkpoint what to produce, how to produce it, and who consumes what is produced

APPLY

Remind students that technology is closely related to the second economic question, *How should goods and services be produced?* Technology can also determine how well a society meets its economic goals. Direct students' attention to Figure 2.1 on page 24 and to the How the Economy Works feature on pages 26–27. Ask **Which of these two visuals demonstrates the impact of technology on economic efficiency? Explain.** *(Figure 2.1. It shows how the use of machinery allows a society to produce more goods with less labor using the same resources.)* **Which economic goal does the How the Economy Works feature illustrate? How?** *(It shows how the development of new technology led to economic growth by creating new goods, new services, and new markets.)* Make sure students understand the difference between efficiency (meeting current needs) and growth (building for the future).

PERSONAL FINANCE ACTIVITY

To help students make wise economic choices, you may want to use the Personal Finance Handbook section on saving for retirement (pp. PF16–PF21) and the activity worksheets (Personal Finance All-in-One, p. 53).

ROLE-PLAY

Point out that when a society emphasizes one economic goal or value, it places less emphasis on others. Remind students what they have learned about the link between technology and economic growth and efficiency. Assign small groups of students the following roles: government economist; factory owner; skilled factory worker; unskilled factory worker; head of a labor union; president of a technical training school; environmental activist; head of a consumer organization. Have each group brainstorm to write a sentence defining their chief economic goal.

Next, present the following scenario: A company has created a computerized robot that can triple the production of prepackaged foods. Each robot can be operated by a single technician and takes the place of ten workers. Use of the robots reduces the price of each can by 10 percent. The robots are operated by electricity. The increased production and sale of canned foods increases the amount of plastic garbage by 3 percent.

Ask each group to react to the scenario based on their own interests and on their defined economic goals. Discuss the possible benefits and drawbacks of the new technology and how economic goals may conflict. For example, use of the new technology may increase efficiency by allowing greater production, but decrease security as more people are put out of work.

How the Economy Works

How can innovation lead to economic growth?

New resources, new inventions, new processes, new ways of doing business—all of them are innovations. Some innovations are small and limited in their effects. But every once in a while, an innovation comes along that revolutionizes the economy and society. One such innovation was the development of the microchip.

1 In the 1940s and 1950s, computers were huge. Most were found in military installations or university labs.

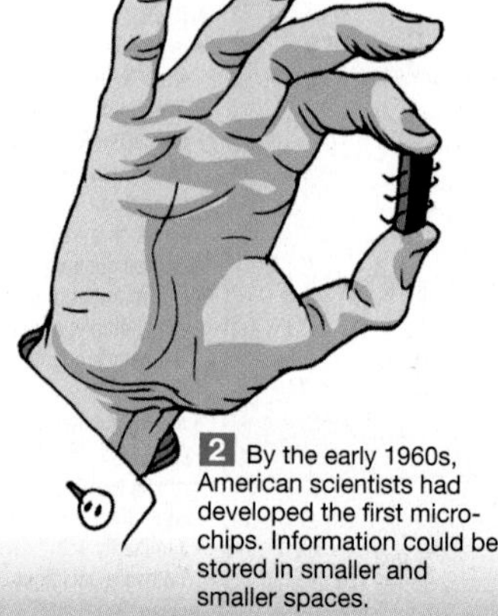

2 By the early 1960s, American scientists had developed the first microchips. Information could be stored in smaller and smaller spaces.

The Way Things Were **The Innovation**

FUTURE WATCH
Personal Finance For tips on achieving economic security through saving and retirement planning, see your Personal Finance Handbook in the back of the book or visit **PearsonSuccessNet.com**

Economic Freedom

Most people value the opportunity to make their own choices. Still, people all over the world face limitations on their economic freedom.

Americans face limitations as well. But in general, individual freedom is a key cultural value for Americans. We prize the freedom to buy what we can pay for, to seek work where we want, to own property, and to become entrepreneurs.

Economic Security

Most people do not like uncertainty. We want to know that we can get milk or bread every time we go to the grocery store. We want the security of knowing that we will get our paychecks every payday. Ideally, economic systems seek to reassure people that goods and services will be available when needed and that they can count on receiving expected payments on time.

safety net a set of government programs that protect people who face unfavorable economic conditions

We also want the security of knowing that help is available if we are in need. Many governments provide a **safety net,** or set of programs to protect people who face unfavorable economic conditions such as layoffs, injuries, or natural disasters. Most modern nations also provide some level of base income for retired persons to ensure that they can support themselves.

Economic Equity

Equity, or fairness, is another economic goal that is defined differently in different societies. Each society must decide how to divide its economic pie. Should everyone get the same share of the goods and services a nation produces? Or should one's consumption depend on how much one produces? How much should society provide for those who are unable or unwilling to produce?

Background Note

Friedman on Freedom Economist Milton Friedman, in a 1991 interview, explained that freedom does not necessarily equal security: "What we have is not a profit system, it's a profit and loss system. The loss part is just as important as the profit part. What distinguishes the private system from a government socialist system is the loss part. If an entrepreneur's project doesn't work, he closes it down. If it had been a government project, it would have been expanded, because there is not the discipline of the profit and loss element."

How the Economy Works online

For an animated, interactive version of this feature, visit **PearsonSuccessNet.com**

3 By the 1980s, computers got smaller and cheaper to manufacture. The home computer had arrived…and ushered in a new period of economic growth.

New Markets: The home computer gave millions of buyers and sellers access to the Internet. Online marketing revolutionized the world economy.

New Goods: Hundreds of products on the market—from MP3 players to GPS systems—make use of microchip technology.

New Services: The home computer gave rise to related businesses, such as computer stores and computer repair services.

Check Your Understanding
1. Why was the microchip a turning point in the development of the Computer Age?
2. Describe another technological innovation that led to the creation of new goods or services.

Economic Growth

Economic Growth

A nation's economy must grow with its population so it can provide jobs for the new people joining the workforce. A nation's economy must grow if people are going to have more income. When that occurs, the nation improves its **standard of living,** or level of economic prosperity.

Innovation plays a huge role in economic growth. **Innovation** is the process of bringing new methods, products, or ideas into use. During the Industrial Revolution of the 1700s and 1800s, innovations in technology increased the efficiency of production and introduced new goods and services. Many problems arose, such as harsh conditions in factories and crowded cities, as well as increased pollution of air and water. Yet, the Industrial Revolution also sparked economic growth and led to an overall rise in standards of living. Today, innovations in computer and networking technology are changing how people work, do business, find information, and communicate.

Goals in Conflict

A society may value other goals than these. Environmental protection, full employment, or protecting national industries may be among a nation's chief economic goals.

Sometimes, economic goals conflict with one another. For example, when a society provides a safety net for all citizens, the added cost may slow economic growth. To protect the environment, a government may impose regulations on manufacturers which curb economic freedom. Thus, all nations must prioritize their economic goals, or arrange them in order of importance. Each choice comes with some kind of trade-off.

✔ **CHECKPOINT** ***What are two examples of economic goals?***

standard of living level of economic prosperity

innovation the process of bringing new methods, products, or ideas into use

DISTRIBUTE SKILL WORKSHEET

To encourage students to explore the different economic goals and values, distribute the "Writing a Persuasive Essay" skill worksheet (Unit 1 All-in-One, p. 57). Have students complete the worksheet and write their persuasive essays. Tell students to review the lesson in the Writing Skills Handbook on page S-5, and use the steps to complete the activity.

L2 Differentiate Distribute the "Writing a Persuasive Essay" skill worksheet (Unit 1 All-in-One, p. 58).

EXTEND

Have students locate a news article in print or online about some aspect of the U.S. economy. Tell them to summarize the article and identify to which economic goals or values the story relates.

L1 L2 Differentiate Have students explain how traditional systems answer each of the key economic questions, and how these answers affect people's lives.

GUIDING QUESTION WRAP UP

Have students return to the section Guiding Question. Review the completed graphic organizer and clarify any misunderstandings. Have a wrap up discussion about how a society answers the key economic questions.

Assess and Remediate

L3 L2 Collect the "Evaluating the United States Economy" worksheet and the "Goals and Values in the United States Economy" worksheet and assess student understanding of the three key economic questions and economic goals and values.

L3 L2 Collect the "Writing a Persuasive Essay" skill worksheets and assess student ability to convey their point of view.

L3 Assign the Section 1 Assessment questions; identify student misconceptions.

L3 Give Section Quiz A (Unit 1 All-in-One, p. 59).

L2 Give Section Quiz B (Unit 1 All-in-One, p. 60).

(Assess and Remediate continued on p. 28)

Answers

Check Your Understanding 1. Microchips made PCs possible and led to new goods, services, and markets. 2. Possible response: cellphones have led to the creation of new goods (accessories, software) and services (repair, push-to-talk).

Checkpoint *(any two)* efficiency, freedom, security, equity, growth

Have students complete the Self-Test Online and continue their work in the **Essential Questions Journal**.

REMEDIATION AND SUGGESTIONS

Use the chart below to help students who are struggling with content.

WEAKNESS	REMEDIATION
Defining key terms (Questions 3, 4, 5, 6, 7, 8)	Have students use the interactive Economic Dictionary Online.
Explain the three key economic questions (Questions 9, 10)	Have students explain how the manufacture and sale of a car answers the three questions.
Explain economic goals and values (Questions 1, 2, 5, 6, 11, 12)	Write the goals and values on the board. Have students give an example of each one as it relates to the U.S. economy.
Describe traditional economies (Questions 8, 12)	Have students contrast traditional economies and the U.S. economy.

Answer

Checkpoint agriculture and hunting, typically

▲ Traditional economies exist in pockets of the modern world. Like earlier generations, this Peruvian woman makes a living producing fine textiles.

Traditional Economies

Societies have developed four different economic systems to address the three key economic questions. Each system reflects a different prioritization of economic goals. It also reflects the values of the societies in which these systems are found.

The oldest and simplest of economic systems is the traditional economy. A **traditional economy** relies on habit, custom, or ritual to answer the three key economic questions. There is little room for innovation or change.

traditional economy an economic system that relies on habit, custom, or ritual to decide the three key economic questions

The traditional economic system revolves around the family unit—often an extended family made up of several generations. Work tends to be divided along gender lines. Boys tend to take up the occupations of their fathers, while girls follow those of their mothers.

Traditional economies are usually found in communities that tend to stay relatively small and close. Often people in these societies work to support the entire community, rather than just themselves or their immediate families. In these societies, agricultural and hunting practices usually lie at the center of people's lives, laws, and religious beliefs.

Societies with traditional economies are economically successful if they meet their own needs. But they have few mechanisms to deal effectively with the effects of environmental disaster, such as a flood or drought. They also tend to be slow to adopt new ideas or technology. They may not have access to a wide range of goods. In most cases, these communities lack modern conveniences and have a relatively low standard of living.

In the next three sections, you will explore three economic systems that have dominated the modern world. They are the free market economy, the centrally planned economy, and the mixed economy.

CHECKPOINT ***What are the chief economic activities in a traditional economy?***

SECTION 1 ASSESSMENT

Essential Questions Journal To continue to build a response to the Essential Question, go to your **Essential Questions Journal.**

Guiding Question

1. Use your completed chart to answer this question: What goals and values affect how a society answers the key economic questions?
2. **Extension** Describe how you think today's American society answers the three key economic questions.

Key Terms and Main Ideas

3. What is an **economic system?**
4. Why aren't all workers paid the same amount in **factor payments** for the resources they provide?
5. How does an entrepreneur make a **profit?**
6. Why does a government provide a **safety net** for its people?
7. What must happen for a nation's **standard of living** to improve?
8. What is likely to be the role of agriculture in a **traditional economy?**

Critical Thinking

9. **Illustrate** A clothing designer releases a new line of jeans. Show how the three economic questions are answered in the process.
10. **Analyze (a)** Why would it be inefficient for a manufacturer to produce audio cassettes instead of CDs today? **(b)** What resources would be wasted?
11. **Explain (a)** What types of investments on the part of manufacturers result in growth? **(b)** How does this help improve a nation's standard of living?
12. **Apply** Which basic economic goals can be achieved easily in a traditional economy? Which cannot? Explain.

Math Skills

13. It takes 14.5 hours to produce 200 bushels of wheat on five acres of land. **(a)** How many bushels could be produced on 23 acres? **(b)** Assuming the number of workers remains the same, how long would it take?

Visit PearsonSuccessNet.com for additional math help.

Assessment Answers

1. efficiency, freedom, security, equity, growth
2. Possible answer: The questions are mainly answered by individuals and businesses making their own decisions.
3. rules society uses to answer the three key economic questions
4. Society values different kinds of labor differently.
5. if income from sales exceeds expenses
6. to give security to retired, injured, or unemployed people
7. The economy must grow so that workers' incomes grow.
8. very important, influencing people's lives, laws, and religious beliefs
9. The designer decides what to produce and how; consumers decide who consumes the jeans.
10. (a) very little demand for cassettes (b) all resources used in producing the cassettes
11. (a) investments in factories and technology (b) Increased output and efficiency make more goods available to consumers at lower prices. Economic growth means an increase in employment and prosperity.
12. Goals that can be met: economic security, economic equity because people often work to support the entire community. Goals not met: economic freedom because people's roles will be determined by tradition; economic growth because the community tends to stay small; economic efficiency because the community may not innovate.
13. (a) 920 bushels (b) 66.7 hours (23 acres is 4.6 times 5 acres; multiply original amounts by 4.6)

OBJECTIVES

1. **Explain** why markets exist.
2. **Analyze** a circular flow model of a free market economy.
3. **Describe** the self-regulating nature of the marketplace.
4. **Identify** the advantages of a free market economy.

ECONOMIC DICTIONARY

As you read the section, look for the definitions of these **Key Terms:**

- market
- specialization
- free market economy
- household
- firm
- factor market
- product market
- self-interest
- incentive
- competition
- invisible hand
- consumer sovereignty

Guiding Question

What are the characteristics of a free market economy?

Copy this concept web and fill it in as you read. Add more ovals if necessary.

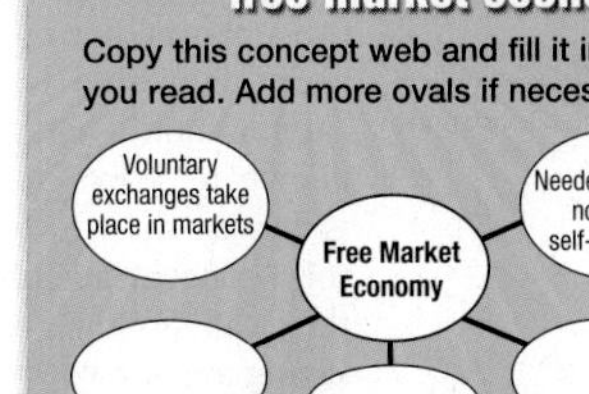

Economics and You

Do you value freedom? If you thought about this question in terms of freedom of speech or freedom of religion, you probably said yes. What about the freedom to own property, get a job, or spend your money the way you want? To Americans, economic freedom is also highly valued. It has shaped the system under which we live.

Principles in Action Economic freedom is the chief characteristic of a free market economy. In this section, you will see how the free market affects every household and community, including yours. You will also see how one entrepreneur used the free market to make a fortune selling something many of us buy and use every day—cosmetics.

market any arrangement that allows buyers and sellers to exchange things

Why Markets Exist

What do a farmer's market, a sporting goods store, the New York Stock Exchange, and a community bulletin board where you posted a sign advertising baby-sitting services have in common? All are examples of markets. A **market** is any arrangement that allows buyers and sellers to exchange things. Markets eliminate the need for any one person to be self-sufficient. None of us produces all we require to satisfy our needs and wants. You probably did not grow cotton plants, process that cotton into cloth, or weave that cloth into the shirt you are wearing. Instead, you purchased your shirt at a store. Markets allow us to exchange the things we have for the things we want.

How do both of these pictures represent markets? ▼

Guiding Question

What are the characteristics of a free market economy?

Get Started

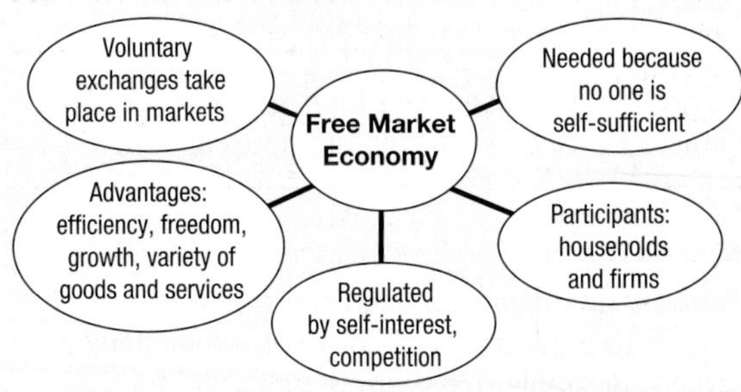

LESSON GOALS

Students will:

- Know the Key Terms.
- Demonstrate a market in operation and explain why markets exist.
- Describe the circular flow of goods and services by completing a worksheet.
- Demonstrate the self-regulating nature of the market by completing a worksheet.
- Discuss the advantages of the free market.

BEFORE CLASS

Students should read the section for homework before coming to class.

Have students complete the graphic organizer in the Section Opener as they read the text. As an alternate activity, have students complete the Guided Reading and Review worksheet (Unit 1 All-in-One, p. 61).

L1 L2 ELL LPR Differentiate Have students complete the Guided Reading and Review worksheet (Unit 1 All-in-One, p. 62).

Focus on the Basics

Students need to come away with the following understandings:

FACTS: • Markets exist so that people can exchange goods and services. • In a free market economy, exchanges are voluntary and take place in two broad kinds of markets to form a circular flow. • According to Adam Smith, the free market works because people act out of their own self-interest.

GENERALIZATION: Because people act out of self-interest, competition develops. Competition helps regulate markets and gives producers incentive to produce what consumers want to consume.

CLASSROOM HINTS

COMPETITION IN THE FACTOR MARKET

Though competition is most easily seen in the product market, it also occurs in the factor market. Help students understand this by explaining that firms compete with each other to hire people (labor) with specialized skills. They may offer incentives, such as signing bonuses or special benefits. Sometimes one firm will outbid another for an employee by offering a higher salary.

BELLRINGER

Display the transparency "Markets" (Color Transparencies, 2.a) and ask students to explain in their notebooks how each of the interactions shown is an example of a market.

Teach

Economics online To present this topic using digital resources, use the lecture notes at www.PearsonSuccessNet.com.

DEMONSTRATE

Distribute five squares of paper to students. Tell students to think of a good or service they think is useful or desirable. Tell them to write the good or service on each piece of paper. Explain that these represent the goods or services that they specialize in making. Call on volunteers to state their good or service aloud. After each student names his or her answer, ask if anyone in the class wants it. When a student says yes, ask what he or she supplies and find out if the first student wants that good or service. If so, have them exchange. If not, have the first students see if they can work out a three- or four-way trade so that they can get the good or service they desire.

Continue with this process until two or three trades have taken place. At that point, ask students whether these trades represented a market and to explain why or why not. *(It was a market because people were exchanging goods or services they provided for those they wanted.)* Then ask why this market came into existence. *(because some people had things that others wanted)*

L1 L2 ELL Differentiate Call on volunteers to define the word *market.* Students might focus on a physical site, thinking of a store or supermarket. Use the examples in Transparency 2.a to emphasize that a market is any exchange of goods or services for money.

L4 Differentiate Have students bring in a newspaper or magazine article about a market. Have them identify the physical and monetary flows in the market, and explain what issue with the market is discussed.

Answers

Checkpoint to allow people to exchange goods and services

Critical Thinking Possible answer: Ash made her own decision to start the business and how to run it. She used incentives to spur her sales reps to work harder.

specialization the concentration of the productive efforts of individuals and businesses on a limited number of activities

free market economy an economic system in which decisions on the three key economic questions are based on voluntary exchange in markets

Specialization

Instead of being self-sufficient, each of us specializes in a few products or services. **Specialization** is the concentration of the productive efforts of individuals and businesses on a limited number of activities. A baker specializes in making breads, cakes, and cookies. A nurse specializes in caring for the sick. An aircraft plant manufactures planes, not refrigerators.

Specialization leads to efficient use of capital, land, and labor. It is easier for people to learn one task or a few tasks very well than to learn them all. Because they concentrate on one or a few tasks, they can do their work more efficiently, saving resources by avoiding waste. For this reason, the top performers in most fields are specialists who have worked hard to sharpen their particular skills.

Specialization also benefits businesses. Focusing on a limited number of related products or services allows them to use capital and labor more efficiently.

Buying and Selling

Without specialization, markets would not be necessary. However, because each of us specializes in producing just a few goods or services, we need a mechanism that allows us to sell what we have produced and buy what we want.

In a modern market-based economy, people typically earn income by specializing in particular jobs. They then use this income to buy the products that they want to consume.

CHECKPOINT ***Why do markets exist?***

Free Market Economy

In a **free market economy,** answers to the three key economic questions are made by voluntary exchange in markets. The choices made by individuals determine what gets made, how it is made, and how much people can consume of the goods and services produced. Individuals and businesses make their own decisions about what to buy or sell. Market economies are also called capitalist economies because the capital that entrepreneurs invest in businesses is a vital part of the system.

In a free market system, individuals and privately owned businesses own the factors of production, make what they want, and

Innovators

Mary Kay Ash

"Pretend that every single person you meet has a sign around his or her neck that says, 'Make me feel important.'"

This philosophy helped Mary Kay Ash become one of the most successful American entrepreneurs.

In 1963, Ash used her life savings of $5000 to launch her "dream" company in Dallas. Her business plan for Mary Kay Cosmetics was simple but powerful. The firm trained women to sell quality cosmetics from their homes. Because sellers brought the product directly to busy homemakers, the firm was able to keep costs down. Ash motivated top achievers with incentives like diamond-studded bumblebee pins and pink luxury cars.

The dream became a hugely successful reality. Today, Mary Kay, Inc., boasts $2.5 billion in retail sales and 1.7 million sales reps in more than 30 countries. It is on *Fortune's* list of most admired companies.

At a time when males dominated the business world, Mary Kay Ash helped create wealth for hundreds of women, annually handing out over $50 million in sales commissions. And she made each of them feel important.

Critical Thinking ***How did free market economics allow Mary Kay Ash to succeed?***

Fast Facts

Mary Kay Ash

Born: May 12, 1918, in Hot Wells, TX

Died: Nov. 22, 2001

Education: One year at the University of Houston

Claim to Fame: Founder of Mary Kay Cosmetics

Differentiated Resources

L1 L2 Guided Reading and Review (Unit 1 All-in-One, p. 62)

L2 Analyzing the Activity of Firms (Unit 1 All-in-One, p. 64)

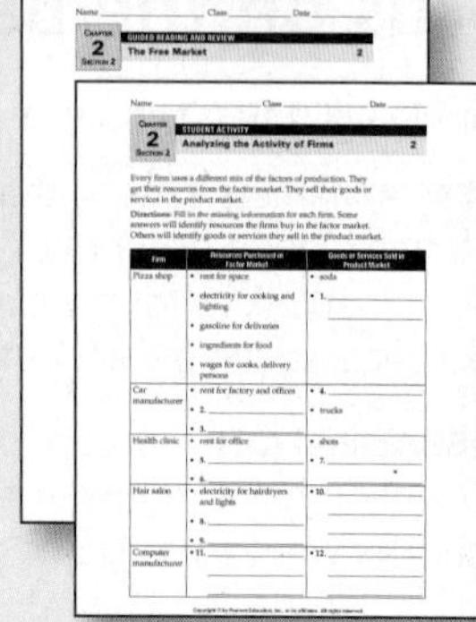

Figure 2.2 **Circular Flow Model of a Market Economy**

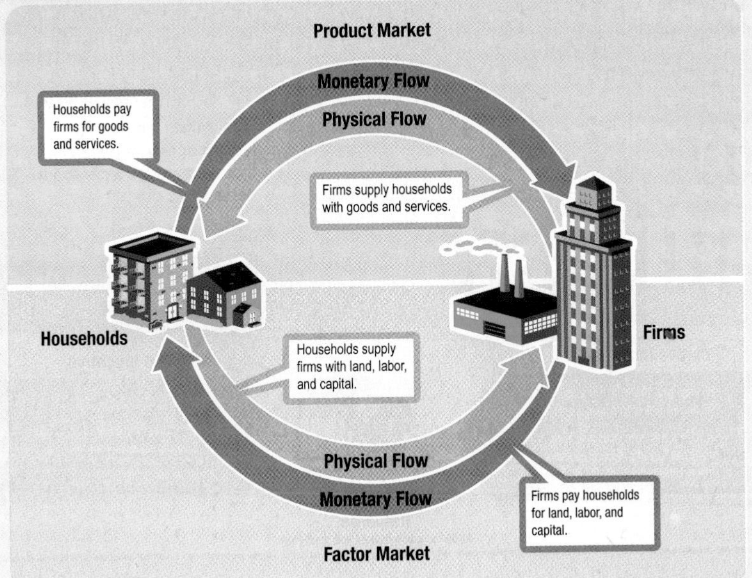

Product Market
Monetary Flow
Physical Flow
Households pay firms for goods and services.
Firms supply households with goods and services.
Households
Firms
Households supply firms with land, labor, and capital.
Physical Flow
Monetary Flow
Firms pay households for land, labor, and capital.
Factor Market

GRAPH SKILLS

A circular flow model shows the interactions between households and firms in the free market.

1. What is the primary item that changes hands in the monetary flow?
2. Give one example from your own life of an exchange that takes place in the factor market.

Action Graph online

For an animated version of this graph, visit **PearsonSuccessNet.com**

buy what they want. In other words, individuals answer the three key economic questions of what to produce, how to produce it, and who consumes what is produced.

Households and Firms

The participants in a free market economy are households and firms. A **household** is a person or group of people living in a single residence. Households own the factors of production—land, labor, and capital. They are also consumers of goods and services.

A business, or **firm**, is an organization that uses resources to produce a product or service, which it then sells. Firms transform inputs, or factors of production, into outputs, or goods and services.

We can represent the exchanges that take place in a free market economy in a diagram called a circular flow model. Look at **Figure 2.2**. The diagram shows how households and firms exchange money, resources, and products in the marketplace. The inner ring of the diagram represents the flow of resources and products. The outer ring represents the flow of money.

Factor and Product Markets

As you can see from the lower half of the circular flow model, firms purchase factors of production from households. This arena of exchange is called the **factor market.** Firms purchase or rent land. They hire workers, paying them wages or salaries for their labor. They also borrow money from households to purchase capital, paying households interest or profits in return.

Now look at the top half of the circular flow model. The arena in which households buy the goods and services that firms produce is the **product market.**

If you follow the rings of the diagram, you will see that households purchase the products made by firms with the money they received from firms in the factor market. The flow between the factor market and the product market is truly circular.

CHECKPOINT ***What is the role of firms in the free market economy?***

household a person or group of people living in a single residence

firm an organization that uses resources to produce a product or service, which it then sells

factor market the arena of exchange in which firms purchase the factors of production from households

product market the arena of exchange in which households purchase goods and services from firms

Background Note

Business-to-Business Transactions Students might point out that firms also buy from other firms, not just from households. An accounting firm buys computers made by a computer manufacturer and paper produced by a paper company. In the market system, those firms are privately owned, however. Ultimately, the business is buying from households. Students might also point out that the government supplies some services—police and fire protection, for example. The role of the government in the circular flow is addressed in Section 4.

ANALYZE

Direct students' attention to Figure 2.2 in their textbook. Ask **Why must firms buy resources from households?** *(Households own resources, including labor.)* Ask **What part of the figure shows these purchases?** *(the bottom; the factor market)* Ask **Why must households buy goods and services from firms?** *(Firms make goods and services.)* Ask **What part of the figure shows these purchases?** *(the top; the product market)*

Action Graph online Tell students to go to the Action Graph online for an animated step-by-step look at the circular flow of goods and services.

DISTRIBUTE ACTIVITY WORKSHEET

Distribute the "Analyzing the Activity of Firms" worksheet (Unit 1 All-in-One, p. 63) to students. Tell them that they will analyze two markets.

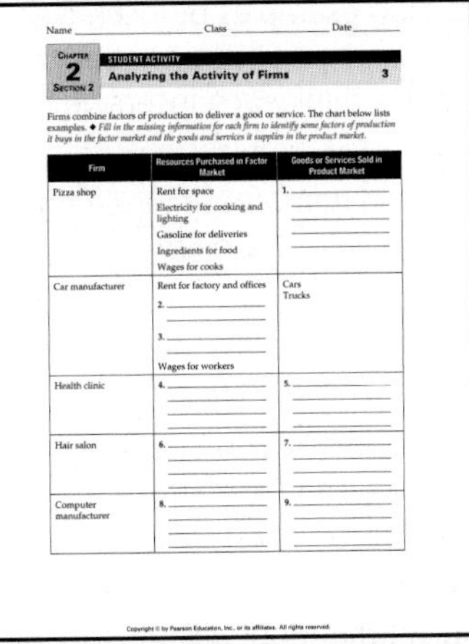

Name ____________ Class ____________ Date ________

Chapter 2 Section 2 — STUDENT ACTIVITY

Analyzing the Activity of Firms 3

Firms combine factors of production to deliver a good or service. The chart below lists examples. ◆ *Fill in the missing information for each firm to identify some factors of production it buys in the factor market and the goods and services it supplies in the product market.*

Firm	Resources Purchased in Factor Market	Goods or Services Sold in Product Market
Pizza shop	Rent for space Electricity for cooking and lighting Gasoline for deliveries Ingredients for food Wages for cooks	1. ________
Car manufacturer	Rent for factory and offices 2. ________ 3. ________ Wages for workers	Cars Trucks
Health clinic	4. ________	5. ________
Hair salon	6. ________	7. ________
Computer manufacturer	8. ________	9. ________

L2 Differentiate Distribute the "Analyzing the Activity of Firms" worksheet (Unit 1 All-in-One, p. 64). Review answers with students.

VISUAL GLOSSARY

Have students look at the chart on the Visual Glossary. Ask them to give examples of positive and negative incentives.

L1 L2 Differentiate Use the lesson on the Visual Glossary page to review this term. As an alternate, direct students to the Visual Glossary Online to reinforce their understanding of incentives.

(continue lesson on p. 33)

Answers

Graph Skills 1. money 2. Students might mention wages they earn from a part-time job.

Checkpoint Firms buy factors of production from households, then use these factors to produce goods and services.

Teach Visual Glossary

REVIEW KEY TERMS

Pair students and have them write the definitions of the key terms related to the understanding of incentive.

entrepreneur—*person who decides how to combine resources to create goods and services*

labor—*the effort people devote to tasks for which they are paid*

profit—*the amount of money a business receives in excess of its expenses*

free market economy—*an economic system in which decisions on the three key economic questions are based on voluntary exchange in markets*

self-interest—*an individual's own personal gain*

ANALYZE

Give students the following examples of incentives. Ask whether each incentive is positive or negative and how effective students think each incentive is.

- A store offers to give consumers a free item when they buy one of the item. *(positive; can be effective because people get a bargain)*
- A legislature passes a law increasing the fine for speeding. *(negative; can be effective because people will not wish to pay the higher fine)*
- Customers pay tips to food servers in restaurants for good service. *(positive; can be effective because servers will want to please customers so they receive bigger tips)*

L2 Differentiate Explain that positive and negative incentives can also be called rewards and punishments. Call on students to identify positive or negative examples from real life.

Economics online *All print resources are available on the Teacher's Resource Library CD-ROM and online at* www.PearsonSuccessNet.com.

Answers

Diagram Caption Possible answer: Since Andre wants to go to the concert and get into a good college, positive incentives move him to study. Since he wants to be able to go out, the negative incentive of being grounded can also push him to study.

Cartoon Possible answer: Since rabbits love carrots, the presence of one near the rabbit's face pushes him to work harder than it pushes the man.

VISUAL GLOSSARY

Reviewing Key Terms
To understand *incentives*, review these terms:

entrepreneur, *p. 5*
labor, *p. 5*
profit, *p. 25*
free market economy, *p. 30*
self-interest, *p. 33*

What are Incentives?

◄ **incentive** the hope of reward or fear of penalty that encourages a person to behave in a certain way

The free market system is based on self-interest. Buyers want affordable goods and services, and entrepreneurs want profits. Employees want good pay, and employers want labor. Incentives influence people to behave in their own self-interest. ***Choose one example from this chart and explain how positive and negative incentives lead to the same behavior.***

Positive Incentive
- Higher grades make it easier for Andre to get into a good college.
- Andre's parents promise him concert tickets if he improves his grades.

Negative Incentive
Andre's parents threaten to ground him if his grades continue to slump.

Response
Andre spends more time studying.

Positive Incentive
State government offers tax credit for commuters who use public transportation.

Negative Incentive
State raises gasoline taxes.

Response
Gas consumption drops as many workers take the bus rather than drive.

"WELL OF COURSE YOU OUTPERFORMED ME. THE INCENTIVES WERE STACKED IN YOUR FAVOR."

◄ The phrase 'carrot-and-stick' refers to the idea that a mule driver can make a donkey move forward either by dangling a carrot in front of him or by hitting him in the back with a stick. ***How is the carrot in this cartoon an incentive?***

Visual Glossary online
To expand your understanding of this and other key economic terms, visit **PearsonSuccessNet.com**

The Self-Regulating Nature of the Marketplace

How is it that firms and households cooperate to give each other what they want—factor resources, in the case of firms, and goods and services, in the case of households? After all, we live in a competitive society. According to Adam Smith, it is, in fact, competition and our own self-interest that keep the marketplace functioning.

Self-Interest

Adam Smith was a Scottish social philosopher who, in 1776, published a book titled *The Wealth of Nations*, in which he described how markets function. Smith observed that an economy is made up of countless individual transactions. In each of these exchanges, the buyer and seller consider only their **self-interest,** or an individual's own personal gain. Smith observed:

> **"Give me that which I want, and you shall have this which you want.... it is in this manner that we obtain from one another the far greater part of those good [services] which we stand in need of. It is not from the benevolence of the butcher, the brewer, or the baker that we expect our dinner, but from their regard to their own interest"**
>
> —Adam Smith, *The Wealth of Nations*

Self-interest, in other words, is the motivating force in t he free market—the push that leads people to act.

Competition

Consumers, pursuing their self-interest, have the incentive to look for lower prices. An **incentive** is the hope of reward or fear of penalty that encourages a person to behave in a certain way. Many incentives are monetary, or based on money, such as the promise of higher wages or profits. Others are non-monetary, such as the prestige and personal satisfaction one gets from running a successful business.

Adam Smith observed that people respond in a predictable way to both positive and negative incentives. Consumers, for instance, will respond to the positive incentive of lower prices by buying more goods, because spending less money on a good lowers the opportunity cost of the purchase.

Firms, meanwhile, seek to make higher profits by increasing sales. Let's take, for example, a shirt manufacturer. The manufacturer finds that striped shirts are far outselling polka-dotted shirts. The manufacturer has the incentive—from more potential sales and profits—to produce more striped shirts. Other manufacturers, seeing consumers' desire for striped shirts, also have the incentive to make those shirts.

Now consumers can get all the striped shirts they want—but what will it cost them? What if all these producers charged high prices for those shirts so they could maximize their profits? The fact that there are so many producers prevents that. Suppose one manufacturer charges $30.00 for a striped shirt while the others sell them for $25.00. Consumers, pursuing their self-interest, will buy the lower-priced shirt. If the first manufacturer wants to sell any shirts, it will have to drop the price.

Economists call this struggle among producers for the dollars of consumers **competition.** While self-interest is the motivating force behind the free market, competition is the regulating force.

The Invisible Hand

Self-interest and competition work together to regulate the marketplace. Self-interest spurs consumers to purchase certain goods and services and firms to produce them. Competition causes firms to produce more and moderates their desire to raise prices. As a result, consumers get the products they want at prices that closely reflect the cost of producing them.

All of this happens without any central planning or direction. No consumer or producer has made decisions based on what's good for the marketplace, yet the end result is a marketplace that operates efficiently. Adam Smith called this self-regulating mechanism "the **invisible hand** of the marketplace."

CHECKPOINT ***Why is competition important in a free market?***

▲ Adam Smith's *The Wealth of Nations* was published the same year that the Continental Congress issued the Declaration of Independence. Both documents helped shape our way of life.

self-interest an individual's own personal gain

incentive the hope of reward or fear of penalty that encourages a person to behave in a certain way

competition the struggle among producers for the dollars of consumers

invisible hand a term coined by Adam Smith to describe the self-regulating nature of the marketplace

APPLY

Ask a volunteer to read the quotation from Adam Smith on this page out loud. Ask another volunteer to restate Adam Smith's main point. Remind students of the buying and selling exercise they took part in at the start of the lesson. Ask **What role did self-interest play in your decisions? If you could change what you offered for sale, would you? Why?** Guide students to recognize that sellers would seek to offer goods and services that buyers wanted to buy. Next, remind students that firms hope to maximize their profits. Ask **What prevents firms from charging as much as they want?** *(Competition. If they charge too much, they will lose business to other firms.)* To help students see price competition in action, distribute the "Competition in Action: Comparing Car Prices" worksheet (Unit 1 All-in-One, p. 65). Have students compare their findings. Ask them how competition makes the car market more efficient.

EXTEND

Tell students to think of a good or service that only one firm supplies. Have them write a paragraph explaining what might lead this firm to raise or lower prices.

GUIDING QUESTION WRAP UP

Have students return to the section Guiding Question. Review the completed graphic organizer and clarify any misunderstandings. Use the Click and Clunk Strategy (p. T25) to have a wrap up discussion about the characteristics of a free market economy.

Assess and Remediate

L2 L3 Collect the "Analyzing the Activity of Firms" worksheets and assess student understanding of the circular flow.

L3 Collect the "Competition in Action" worksheet and assess student understanding of competition.

L3 Assign the Section 2 Assessment questions; identify student misconceptions.

L3 Give Section Quiz A (Unit 1 All-in-One, p. 66).

L2 Give Section Quiz B (Unit 1 All-in-One, p. 67).

Virtual Economics

L2 Differentiate

Creating a Circular Flow Model

Use the following lesson from the NCEE **Virtual Economics *CD-ROM*** to interpret a circular flow model. Click on Browse Economics Lessons, specify grades 9–12, and use the key words *markets in the circular flow.*

In this activity, students will study a circular flow model of resources, goods, services, and money and create one based on their own life.

LESSON TITLE	**MARKETS IN THE CIRCULAR FLOW OF THE ECONOMY**
Type of Activity	Creating a graphic
Complexity	Low
Time	50 minutes
NCEE Standards	3

Answer

Checkpoint It causes firms to produce what consumers want while moderating prices.

Have students complete the Self-Test Online and continue their work in the **Essential Questions Journal**.

REMEDIATION AND SUGGESTIONS

Use the chart below to help students who are struggling with content.

WEAKNESS	REMEDIATION
Defining key terms (Questions 3, 4, 5, 6, 7)	Have students use the interactive Economic Dictionary Online.
Explaining why markets exist (Questions 3, 8)	Have students explain how people who are not farmers get the food they need.
Analyzing the circular flow model (Questions 1, 4, 5, 9)	Have students summarize Figure 2.2 in their own words.
Describing the self-regulating nature of the marketplace (Questions 2, 6, 7, 9)	Have students explain why a store offering items on sale would sell more than a store that did not.
Identifying the advantages of a free market economy (Questions 10, 11)	Have students work in pairs to summarize the list of free market advantages.

Answers

Caption consumer sovereignty

Checkpoint because producers have incentives to meet consumers' desires

▲ A customer is a consumer who does business with a particular firm. ***What free market principle does this cartoon illustrate?***

Advantages of the Free Market

As you saw, each society tries to achieve a variety of economic goals. Under ideal conditions, the free market meets many of these goals on its own.

consumer sovereignty the power of consumers to decide what gets produced

1. *Economic efficiency* Because it is self-regulating, a free market economy responds efficiently to rapidly changing conditions. Producers provide only the goods and services that consumers want, and generally at prices consumers are willing to pay.
2. *Economic freedom* Free market economies have the highest degree of economic freedom of any system. Workers work where they want, firms produce what they want, and individuals consume what they want.
3. *Economic growth* Because competition encourages innovation, free markets encourage growth. Entrepreneurs are always seeking profitable opportunities, contributing new ideas and innovations.
4. *Additional goals* Free markets offer a wider variety of goods and services than any other system, because producers have incentives to meet consumers' desires. Consumers, in essence, have the power to decide what gets produced. This is called **consumer sovereignty.**

Despite the advantages of a free market economy, no country today operates under a pure, unregulated free market system. The same features that make free markets attractive also represent the weaknesses of the free market. The goals of economic equity and security are not always easy to achieve in a pure market system. In Section 4, you will read about how the free market system has been modified in order to better meet the entire array of economic goals.

CHECKPOINT ***Why does a free market economy result in the availability of a wider variety of goods and services?***

SECTION 2 ASSESSMENT

Essential Questions Journal To continue to build a response to the Essential Question, go to your **Essential Questions Journal.**

Guiding Question

1. Use your completed concept web to answer this question: What are the characteristics of a free market economy?
2. **Extension** Give two examples of how an incentive influenced your behavior in your community, in school, or as a consumer.

Key Terms and Main Ideas

3. How does **specialization** make us more efficient?
4. What is the difference between a **household** and a **firm?**
5. How do **self-interest** and **competition** affect the free market?
6. Explain what Adam Smith meant by "the **invisible hand** of the market-place."

Critical Thinking

7. **Infer** How can specialization benefit both buyers and sellers in a free market economy?
8. **Connect** In a free market system, how are incentives related to the principle of consumer sovereignty?
9. **Explain** Why do you think no country has a pure free market economy?

Quick Write

10. Mary Kay Ash (see the Innovators feature) said that for a person to succeed in business they need to have enthusiasm, discipline, a willingness to work, determination, and an appreciation of others. Write a short essay in which you prioritize these qualities from most important to least important in terms of achieving success as an entrepreneur.

Assessment Answers

1. Possible answer: voluntary exchange by people making their own decisions, acting in self-interest
2. Students might mention positive incentives such as the chance to win awards.
3. It is easier for people to learn to do a few tasks well.
4. household: individual workers, consumers; firm: business that produces
5. Self-interest moves consumers and producers to act; competition moderates prices.
6. Producers, acting in self-interest, will regulate the market by competing with each other to produce goods and services that consumers most want.
7. Possible answer: It improves workers' wages and helps producers work efficiently.
8. Possible answer: Producers' desire for profits leads them to try to provide those goods and services that consumers are most willing to pay for.
9. Possible answer: Some government intervention may be necessary to insure fair competition, prevent abuses, or insure goods and services for people who can't afford them.
10. Students' essays should rank the five qualities and state the reasons for the rankings.

OBJECTIVES

1. **Describe** how a centrally planned economy is organized.
2. **Distinguish** between socialism and communism.
3. **Analyze** the use of central planning in the Soviet Union and China.
4. **Identify** the disadvantages of a centrally planned economy.

ECONOMIC DICTIONARY

As you read the section, look for the definitions of these **Key Terms:**

- centrally planned economy
- command economy
- socialism
- communism
- authoritarian

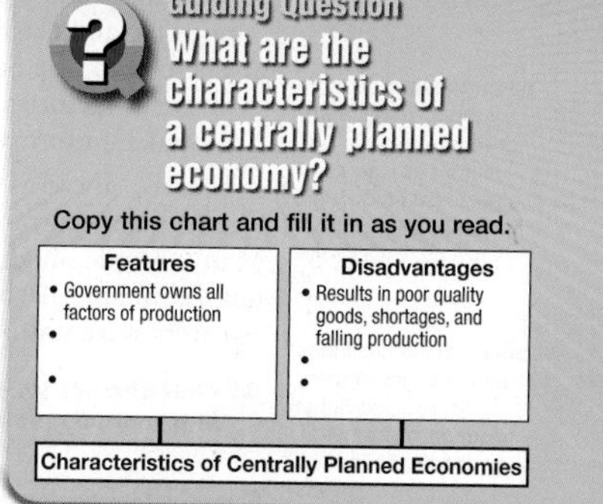
Guiding Question
What are the characteristics of a centrally planned economy?
Copy this chart and fill it in as you read.
Features
• Government owns all factors of production
Disadvantages
• Results in poor quality goods, shortages, and falling production
Characteristics of Centrally Planned Economies

Economics and You Suppose you lived in Cuba. Each month, the government would give you cards entitling you to buy a set amount of food at low prices. However, this amount often will not last the entire month. To buy enough food for the rest of the month, you would need to pay much higher prices. If you are like most Cubans, this is difficult because your salary is low. Even if you had money, you might not be able to buy the food you want because shortages are common.

Why is the situation in Cuba so different from that in the United States? One reason is that the two countries have different economic systems. Cuba does not have a market economy, but a centrally planned one.

Principles in Action The chief characteristic of an economy like Cuba's is the level of government control. In this section, you will see how the ideas of central planning were carried out in two powerful nations.

How Central Planning Works

In a **centrally planned economy,** the government, rather than individual producers and consumers, answers the key economic questions. A central bureaucracy decides what items to produce, how to produce them, and who gets them. The government owns both land and capital. In a sense it owns labor, too, because it controls where people work and what they are paid. The government directs workers to produce a certain number of trucks, so many yards of cotton fabric, and so on. Farmers are told what to plant and where to send their crops.

Centrally planned economies, also known as **command economies,** operate in direct contrast to free market systems. Command economies oppose private property, free market pricing, competition, and consumer choice. Free market forces of self-interest and competition are absent.

To see how such an economy works, we will follow the decision-making process for the production of uniforms for members of the military and the production of sweaters for consumers.

1. The top planners decide that more military uniforms than sweaters will be made. They send this decision to the materials committee.

centrally planned economy an economic system in which the government makes all decisions on the three key economic questions

command economy another name for a centrally planned economy

Guiding Question

What are the characteristics of a centrally planned economy?

Get Started

Features	Disadvantages
• Government owns all factors of production • Government makes all decisions • Bureaucrats make detailed plans • No consumer sovereignty	• Results in poor quality goods, shortages, and falling production • Does not achieve equity • Efficiency suffers • Allows no freedom of choice

Characteristics of Centrally Planned Economies

LESSON GOALS

Students will:

- Know the Key Terms.
- Understand how economic decisions are made in a free market and a centrally planned economy.
- Contrast how the three economic questions are answered under socialism and communism.
- Analyze specific examples to identify problems with centrally planned economies by using a transparency.

BEFORE CLASS

Students should read the section for homework before coming to class.

Have students complete the graphic organizer in the Section Opener as they read the text. As an alternate activity, have students complete the Guided Reading and Review worksheet (Unit 1 All-in-One, p. 68).

L1 L2 ELL LPR Differentiate Have students complete the Guided Reading and Review worksheet (Unit 1 All-in-One, p. 69).

Focus on the Basics

Students need to come away with the following understandings:

FACTS: • In centrally planned economies, governments, rather than individuals, answer the key economic questions. • Centrally planned economies do not depend on competition and the profit incentive. • Russia and China had centrally planned economies that demonstrated the weaknesses of this system.

GENERALIZATION: Because of the lack of competition and profit incentives, people in centrally planned economies have no reason to produce more, making these economies inefficient and less productive than free-market economies.

CLASSROOM HINTS

FOOD COURTS AND FREE MARKETS

Many schools have a "closed lunch," meaning that students may not leave the building to eat. Use the analogy of a school lunch program and a centrally planned economy. The school decides what students can eat and what price they will pay. Then use the analogy of a food court and a free market economy. Ask students which they would rather eat in.

BELLRINGER

Write the following on the board: "The government orders that all video game designers must devote half their time and resources to creating educational games." Tell students to write their first reaction in their notebooks.

Teach

Economics online To present this topic using digital resources, use the lecture notes at www.PearsonSuccessNet.com.

DISCUSS

Discuss students' reactions to the prompt in the Bellringer. Ask **Would a government of a nation with a free market system issue such an order? Why or why not?** *(No; in a free market economy firms make such decisions based on profit incentives.)* Underscore that in a centrally planned economy, government officials answer the three key economic questions. If necessary, review the three key questions. Review the example in the text to demonstrate how central planning works.

CONTRAST

Draw a horizontal line on the board with the words *Free Market* to the right and *Communism* to the left. Ask **How do the two systems answer the three key economic questions differently?** *(Free market: all questions are answered by individuals. Communism: the government decides the answers.)*

Ask **Under socialism, who makes the economic decisions?** *(The government, via central planning, answers the three questions for state-owned enterprises. Individuals answer the questions for private firms.)* Ask students where, on the line, they would place socialism. They should place it between free markets and communism.

DISCUSS

Display the transparency "Problems of Centrally Planned Economies" (Color Transparencies, 2.b). Have volunteers read aloud the two quotations. Ask **What problems did Gorbachev identify in the Soviet economy?** *(failure to meet society's needs for food, transportation, health care, and education)* **What problems did Deng identify in China?** *(He speaks generally of people's suffering and the lack of economic growth.)*

Answers

Checkpoint the government

Checkpoint Marx believed that capitalism led to exploitation of workers and unfair distribution of wealth.

socialism a range of economic and political systems based on the belief that wealth should be distributed evenly throughout a society

communism a political system in which the government owns and controls all resources and means of production and makes all economic decisions

authoritarian describes a form of government that limits individual freedoms and requires strict obedience from its citizens

2. Knowing how much cotton is available, the materials committee decides how many uniforms and sweaters to produce. They send their decision to the makers of cotton, buttons, and elastic.
3. The cotton, the buttons, and the elastic arrive at factories, where they are used to make uniforms and sweaters.

Clearly, there is no consumer sovereignty under centrally planned economies. Many people might need new sweaters but be unable to buy them because the sweaters were not produced.

✔ **CHECKPOINT** ***Who makes key decisions in a centrally planned economy?***

Socialism and Communism

The terms most often linked to central planning are socialism and communism. Though often used interchangeably, the terms actually describe different systems.

Socialism

Socialism is not a single economic system. Rather, the term describes a range of economic and political systems based on the belief that wealth should be evenly distributed throughout society. Economic equity, socialists argue, can exist only if the centers of economic power are controlled by the government or by the public as a whole, rather than by individuals or corporations.

In some nations, such as Sweden, socialism coexists with free market practices. Under this "market socialism," the government uses its powers of taxation to redistribute wealth and provide extensive services. Other socialists stress government ownership of the means of production. They consider socialism to be an intermediate stage between capitalism and communism.

Shortages were a recurring problem in the Soviet Union. Consumers would often wait in long lines at stores, only to discover there was nothing to buy. ▼

Communism

In the 1800s, socialism gave rise to communism. Under **communism,** the central government owns and controls all resources and means of production and makes all economic decisions.

Communism derived largely from the writings of German philosopher Karl Marx. Unlike Adam Smith, who stressed the mutually beneficial relations between producers and consumers, Marx stressed the conflict between labor and capital. He believed that labor was the source of all value. But under capitalism, he said, all the profit created by the labor of workers ended up in the hands of capitalists, such as factory owners:

> **"Capitalist production . . . develops technology and the combining together of various processes . . . only by sapping the original sources of all wealth — the soil and the laborer."**
>
> —Karl Marx, *The Communist Manifesto*

The inevitable result of capitalism, Marx argued, was the exploitation of workers and an unfair distribution of wealth.

Marx and later communists believed that a socialist society could only result from a violent revolution. While countries with socialist economies can be democratic, communist governments have always been authoritarian. **Authoritarian** governments limit individual freedoms and require strict obedience from their citizens. Every communist nation has been dominated by a single dictator or political party.

✔ **CHECKPOINT** ***What beliefs did Karl Marx hold about capitalism?***

Differentiated Resources

- **L1 L2 Guided Reading and Review** (Unit 1 All-in-One, p. 69)
- **L4 L2 Comparing Communism and Socialism** (Unit 1 All-in-One, pp. 70, 71)
- **L3 Who Decides?** (Simulation Activities, Chapter 2)

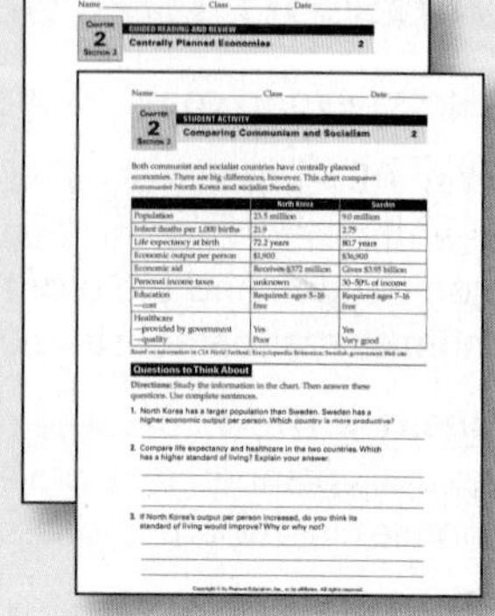

Two Communist Economies

During the twentieth century, communist revolutions occurred in several countries. The histories of two of these nations, the Soviet Union and China, reveal key features of centrally planned economies.

The Soviet Union

In 1917, revolutionaries toppled the Russian government. This marked the beginning of what became the Soviet Union, the world's first communist state. In 1928, Soviet leader Joseph Stalin imposed the first in a series of strict five-year plans to boost industrial and agricultural production. Until it broke up in 1991, the Soviet Union continued to operate as a command economy.

Soviet economic planners sought to build national power and prestige. They allocated the best land, labor, and capital to the armed forces and to heavy industry. Heavy industry requires large capital investment and produces goods, such as chemicals or steel, used in other industries. The decision to favor heavy industry had a harsh effect on factories that made consumer goods. They were stuck with leftover, lower-quality resources. As a result, the goods available to consumers were few in number and poorly made. Severe shortages were common.

Agriculture faced similar problems. Farmers were forced to work on large, state-run farms. The government supplied all materials and set all wages. The results were often disastrous. While Russia had been a major exporter of wheat, the Soviet Union could not always produce enough grain to feed its own people.

Heavy industry and military might helped make the Soviet Union a world superpower, especially after World War II. But in time, economic weaknesses contributed to the fall of communism and the collapse of the state.

China

Like Russia, China adopted central planning as the result of a communist revolution. From 1949 to the late 1970s, government planners controlled every aspect of the Chinese economy.

▲ The communist government of China used posters like these to encourage laborers to work harder and produce more. ***What kind of incentive might a poster like this offer workers?***

At first, the communist government allowed some farmland to remain in private hands while it focused on building industry. The government tried to build small factories to produce goods to be sold in nearby areas. But these goods were expensive to make and of very poor quality.

In the 1950s, the government forced many peasants onto farming communes. Within a few years, farm production dropped sharply. Facing shortages, the government eased its control over decisions made by workers on the communes. They also sent many factory workers to work on farms. The food crisis was solved, but China's economy continued to stumble.

Chinese leaders began to institute new economic policies in the 1970s. They gave farmers the chance to own more land and offered bonuses to factory managers for making better quality products. As a result, China's economy began to grow.

Today, the Chinese government still owns firms in major industries. Government planners control many key economic decisions. Still, China allows entrepreneurs far more economic freedom than in the past. Such changes have given a tremendous boost to China's economy.

✔ **CHECKPOINT** ***What changes led to economic growth in China?***

What do these problems suggest about the weaknesses of central planning? *(Possible answer: Central planning does not meet all of people's needs or promote growth.)* Discuss other disadvantages.

L4 Differentiate Give students the "Comparing Communism and Socialism" worksheet (Unit 1 All-in-One, p. 70). Have them compare two real-world economic systems.

L2 Differentiate Distribute the "Comparing Communism and Socialism" worksheet (Unit 1 All-in-One, p. 71).

EXTEND

Have students write a critique of central planning from the point of view of Adam Smith. Students may want to write it as a Q-and-A interview.

L3 Differentiate Have students compare how decisions are reached under different economic systems using the simulation "Who Decides?" (Simulations Activities, Chapter 2)

GUIDING QUESTION WRAP UP

Have students return to the section Guiding Question. Review the completed graphic organizer and clarify any misunderstandings. Have a wrap up discussion about the characteristics of a centrally planned economy.

Assess and Remediate

L4 L2 Collect the "Comparing Communism and Socialism" worksheets and assess student understanding of the two systems.

L3 Assess student performance in the simulation.

L3 Assign the Section 3 Assessment questions; identify student misconceptions.

L3 Give Section Quiz A (Unit 1 All-in-One, p. 72).

L2 Give Section Quiz B (Unit 1 All-in-One, p. 73).

Virtual Economics

L4 Differentiate

Analyzing the Legacy of the Soviet Command Economy Use the following lesson from the NCEE **Virtual Economics *CD-ROM*** to help students evaluate the command economy of the former Soviet Union. Click on Browse Economics Lessons, specify grades 9–12, and use the key words *Soviet Communism.*

In this activity, students will take part in a simulation to demonstrate the impact of a command economy and research the transition economies in the former Soviet bloc.

LESSON TITLE	THE LEGACY OF SOVIET COMMUNISM
Type of Activity	Simulation, Research
Complexity	Moderate
Time	100 minutes
NCEE Standards	3, 4

Answers

Caption Possible answer: Workers might feel pride by working productively. The poster also appeals to a sense of loyalty to the state.

Checkpoint new policies that gave farmers the chance to own more land and gave factory managers bonuses for improving quality

Have students complete the Self-Test Online and continue their work in the **Essential Questions Journal**.

REMEDIATION AND SUGGESTIONS

Use the chart below to help students who are struggling with content.

WEAKNESS	REMEDIATION
Defining key terms (Questions 3, 4, 5, 6)	Have students use the interactive Economic Dictionary Online.
Stating how central planning works (Questions 1, 2, 6, 9)	Have students describe how decisions are made in this system in a step-by-step process.
Comparing socialism and communism (Question 4)	Reteach the two systems focusing on the three economic questions.
Citing economic problems in the Soviet Union and China (Question 8)	Have students summarize each problem cited in the text and its cause.
Discussing disadvantages of central planning (Questions 8, 9)	Have students explain how central planning fails to meet each goal.

Answer

Checkpoint Workers have no reason to work harder.

Disadvantages of Centrally Planned Economies

Simulation *Activity*

Who Decides?
You may be asked to take part in a role-playing game about decision making in a traditional, free market, and command economy.

Despite the differences between centrally planned and free market economies, the two systems share many of the same basic goals. However, nations with centrally planned economies have often had trouble meeting these goals in practice.

1. *Economic efficiency* In a centrally planned economy, the government owns all production factors. Since the government fixes wages, workers lack the incentive to work faster or produce more. The large, complex bureaucracy needed to make thousands of economic decisions hurts efficiency as well. It is expensive to run and lacks the flexibility to adjust quickly to consumer demands and changing economic conditions.
2. *Economic freedom* Traditionally, command economies sacrifice individual freedoms in order to pursue societal goals. Sometimes, the results have been brutal: millions of peasants were killed in Stalin's drive to reform Soviet agriculture. But even in better circumstances, central planning discourages competition and takes most or all economic choices away from producers and consumers.
3. *Economic growth* Innovation is a key to economic growth. Command economies, however, do not tend to reward innovation—in fact, they discourage change. Managers must follow an approved government plan. There is no profit incentive to encourage entrepreneurship.
4. *Economic equity* In theory, a major goal of communism is to increase equity by distributing goods and services fairly. Such equity has proven rare, though. Government officials and people in favored careers enjoy higher incomes and access to a wider variety of higher quality goods. Ordinary people often suffer shortages and poorly made goods.
5. *Additional goals* Central planning has successfully met some goals. It can guarantee jobs and income. It can also be used to jump-start selected industries. For example, Stalin's five-year plans did increase output in heavy industries.

The disadvantages of central planning have caused leaders in many countries to move away from command economies and toward mixed economies. In the next section, you will read about today's mixed economies.

CHECKPOINT ***Why do centrally planned economies tend not to be efficient?***

SECTION 3 ASSESSMENT

Essential Questions Journal To continue to build a response to the Essential Question, go to your **Essential Questions Journal.**

Guiding Question

1. Use your completed chart to answer this question: What are the characteristics of a centrally planned economy?
2. **Extension** Suppose you were showing around a new arrival from Cuba or China. Where might you go in order to point out the differences between their economic system and ours?

Key Terms and Main Ideas

3. What does a **centrally planned economy** oppose that a market economy encourages?
4. How do **socialism** and **communism** differ?
5. What characterizes an **authoritarian** government?
6. Explain why each of the following goals is difficult to achieve in a centrally planned economy: **(a)** economic freedom, **(b)** economic growth.

Critical Thinking

7. **Infer** Which economic goal do you think was most important to Karl Marx: efficiency, growth, or equity? Explain.
8. **Explain (a)** What was the benefit of the Soviet Union's decision to concentrate on heavy industry? **(b)** What was the opportunity cost of this decision? Who paid it?
9. **Draw Conclusions** Who benefits and who suffers most from a centrally planned economy? How?

Math Skills

10. Look at the chart below. **(a)** What percentage of China's manufacturing employees live in urban units? In town/village units? **(b)** Compare the compensation of the two units. **(c)** What does this chart show you about China's economy?

Visit PearsonSuccessNet.com for additional math help.

Salary of Manufacturing Workers in China, 2002

Worker Category	Average Number of Workers	Annual Salary per Worker (in U.S. dollars)
All	100,610,000	1,252
Urban units	29,980,000	2,071
Town/village units	70,620,000	904

SOURCE: U.S. Bureau of Labor Statistics

Assessment Answers

1. government decision-making, lack of freedom
2. Possible answers: to a supermarket or electronics store to show free exchange of goods for money; to see the stock market in action; to a bank; to a factory to show production of goods.
3. private property, free market pricing, competition, choice
4. *socialism:* government often owns major industries but not all means of production; can be democratic; *communism:* government owns everything; always authoritarian
5. government demands strict obedience; lack of freedom
6. (a) government control of decisions (b) inefficiency of system, lack of incentives
7. Possible answer: equity, because he thought workers were unfairly treated
8. (a) growth of these industries and increase in Soviet military might (b) lack of consumer goods; consumers paid
9. Possible answer: Government officials benefit because they can favor themselves; ordinary people suffer from lack of freedom and choices.
10. (a) 29.8%; 70.2% (b) People in urban units make more than twice as much as those in towns and villages. (c) Possible answer: The system favors city dwellers.

SECTION 4 Mixed Economies

OBJECTIVES

1. **Explain** the rise of mixed economic systems.
2. **Interpret** a circular flow model of a mixed economy.
3. **Compare** the mixed economies of various nations along a continuum between centrally planned and free market systems.
4. **Describe** the role of free enterprise in the United States economy.

ECONOMIC DICTIONARY

As you read the section, look for the definitions of these **Key Terms:**

- laissez faire
- private property
- mixed economy
- economic transition
- privatization
- free enterprise system

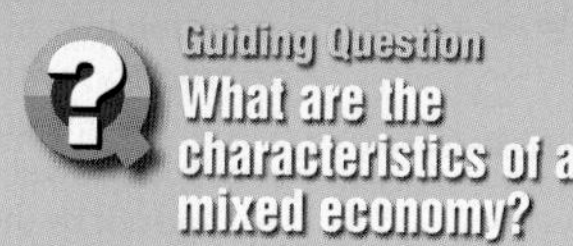
Guiding Question
What are the characteristics of a mixed economy?

Copy this chart and fill it in as you read.

Mixed Economies	
Elements of Market System	Elements of Centrally Planned System
• Private property • • • •	• Government involved in factor market • • •

Economics and You As an American, you expect a high degree of economic freedom. But that does not mean you can walk into a convenience store after school and buy a pack of cigarettes. It doesn't mean that you, as a high school student, can get a part-time job operating a forklift in a factory. And it sure doesn't mean that you get to decide whether or not to pay taxes! Why not?

Principles in Action Most economies today—including ours—blend a market system with elements of central planning. You will see why governments step in to provide for your defense or fulfill other needs. In the Economics & You feature, you will see how government regulations prevent you from freely buying certain items in the marketplace.

laissez faire
the doctrine that government generally should not intervene in the marketplace

The Rise of Mixed Economies

Every economic system has problems. Traditional economies have little potential for growth or change. Centrally planned economies stifle innovation, do not adequately meet consumer needs, and limit freedom. Even free market economies, with all their advantages, have drawbacks.

Reasons for Government Involvement

Early free market thinkers such as Adam Smith believed that, left alone, the free market would provide the greatest benefit for consumers and raise the standard of living. They favored **laissez faire,** the doctrine that government generally should not intervene in the marketplace. Yet even Smith acknowledged the need for a limited degree of government involvement.

Since Smith's time, government intervention has increased for several reasons. First, some needs of modern society would be difficult to meet in the marketplace. How well, for example, could a free market provide for national defense or highway systems? In addition, governments supply some needs in order to ensure that all members of society can benefit. For instance, a society could rely solely on private schools to educate its children. But then some families could not afford to send their children to school. To make sure that all members of society receive a basic education, the government provides public schools.

▲ Defense is one type of service that a government can supply more effectively than the free market can.

Guiding Question

What are the characteristics of a mixed economy?

Get Started

Mixed Economies	
Elements of Market System	Elements of Centrally Planned System
• Private property • Exchanges take place in markets • Balances needs and freedom	• Government involved in factor market • Government involved in product market • Government transfers money • Government regulates markets

LESSON GOALS

Students will:

- Know the Key Terms.
- Explore government involvement in the economy.
- Contrast the circular flow model in a mixed economy to the flow in a free market economy.
- Contrast features of national economies by completing the "Economic Transition" worksheet.
- Evaluate the government's role in the United States economy.

BEFORE CLASS

Students should read the section for homework before coming to class.

Have students complete the graphic organizer in the Section Opener as they read the text. As an alternate activity, have students complete the Guided Reading and Review worksheet (Unit 1 All-in-One, p. 74).

L1 L2 ELL LPR Differentiate Have students complete the Guided Reading and Review worksheet (Unit 1 All-in-One, p. 75).

Focus on the Basics

Students need to come away with the following understandings:

FACTS: • Governments with centrally planned economies have generally failed to meet consumer needs and placed limits on economic freedom. • Modern market economies generally include a degree of government intervention in order to insure fairness and meet certain needs. • The United States is a mixed economy where the free market dominates.

GENERALIZATION: Because pure market and pure centrally planned economies both have drawbacks, nations tend to have mixed economies.

CLASSROOM HINTS

MIXED ECONOMIES, MIXED RESULTS

Help students understand that some mixed economies are more successful than others at meeting their citizens' needs and wants. Less government intervention does not always lead to greater prosperity. On the other hand, neither does more intervention. Governments do not always succeed when they intervene in their nations' economies. Mistakes or poor management are as much a problem for governments as they are for private businesses.

BELLRINGER

Ask each student to list three examples of ways in which the U.S. government or their state government provides goods and services or regulates how goods and services are provided.

Teach

Economics online To present this topic using digital resources, use the lecture notes at www.PearsonSuccessNet.com.

EXPLORE IN-DEPTH

Ask students to read aloud some of their answers to the Bellringer. Direct students' attention to examples of government-provided services such as public schools, national defense, and highways. Ask **What do you think would happen if highways were provided by private firms who tried to charge people for using them?** *(Some people would be unwilling to pay. Firms might not want to provide roads where they were not profitable.)* Next, ask for examples of how the government regulates how goods and services are provided. Ask **Why do you think the government intervenes in the market in these instances?** *(Government may regulate the sale of such items as cigarettes or medicines because public safety is concerned.)*

CONTRAST

Direct students' attention to Figure 2.3, "Circular Flow Model of a Mixed Economy." Ask volunteers to explain the differences between this model and the free market version. *(In this version, money flows to the government from both firms and households when they pay taxes. In addition, the government buys goods from firms and supplies services to households.)* Ask students to give an example of services that firms obtain from the government. *(Possible answers: defense; highways; tax breaks for capital investment or job-creation)*

Action Graph online Have students review the Action Graph animation for a step-by-step look at a mixed economy.

Answers

Checkpoint Possible answer: to meet needs that would not be supplied by markets

Graph Skills 1. by collecting taxes and making purchases 2. Possible answer: Government office workers buy office supplies from a company.

private property property that is owned by individuals or companies, not by the government or the people as a whole

mixed economy a market-based economic system in which the government is involved to some extent

Governments also play a role in the economy by protecting property rights. For instance, the Fifth and Fourteenth amendments to the Constitution declare that no person may be deprived of "Life, liberty, or property, without due process of law." These amendments protect **private property,** or property owned by individuals or companies and not by the government or the people as a whole. As you will see in Chapter 3, private property is a fundamental element of the American economic system.

Finally, governments try to make sure that exchanges in the marketplace are fair. For instance, laws require businesses to give honest information to consumers or block firms from joining together to prevent competition and fix prices.

For all of these reasons, no nation today has a pure free market economy or a pure command economy. Instead, most modern economies are mixed. A **mixed economy** is a market-based economic system in which the government is involved to some extent. The degree of government involvement varies from nation to nation.

Balancing Needs and Freedom

As you have seen, every society must assess its values and prioritize its economic goals. Some goals are better met by the open market, while others may be better achieved through government action. In addition, societies must evaluate the opportunity cost of pursuing each goal.

What are you willing to give up? Are you willing to pay taxes to fund the army? To give money to people who lose their jobs? To give all people an education? In a mixed economy such as ours, questions like these can be the subject of heated debate.

CHECKPOINT ***What is one reason the government plays a role in the economy?***

Circular Flow Model of a Mixed Economy

To illustrate accurately how most modern economies work, we must add government to our circular flow diagram **(Figure 2.3).** Government enters this flow in a variety of ways.

Figure 2.3 Circular Flow Model of a Mixed Economy

GRAPH SKILLS

This circular flow model shows how government typically interacts with households and firms in the marketplace.

1. According to this model, how does government affect the monetary flow in a mixed economy?
2. Give one real-life example of how government can interact with a firm in the product market.

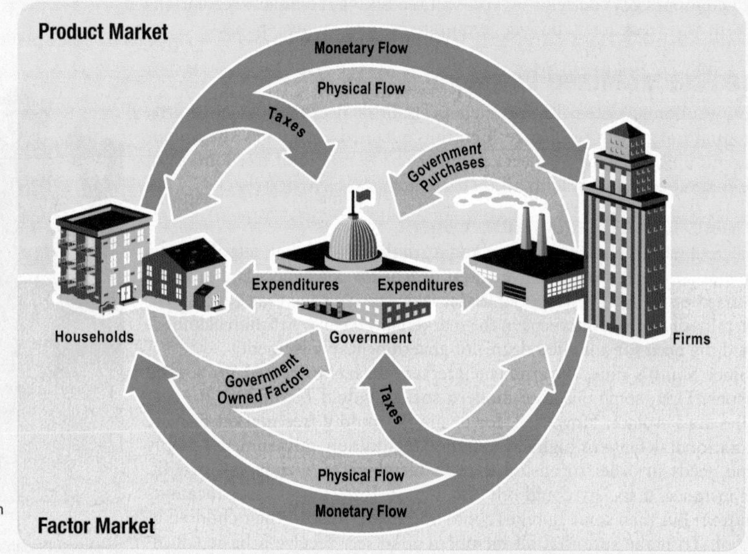

Action Graph online

For an animated version of this graph, visit **PearsonSuccessNet.com**

Differentiated Resources

L1 L2 Guided Reading and Review (Unit 1 All-in-One, p. 75)

L2 The Food and Drug Administration (Unit 1 All-in-One, p. 77)

L4 Comparing Mixed Economies (Unit 1 All-in-One, p. 78)

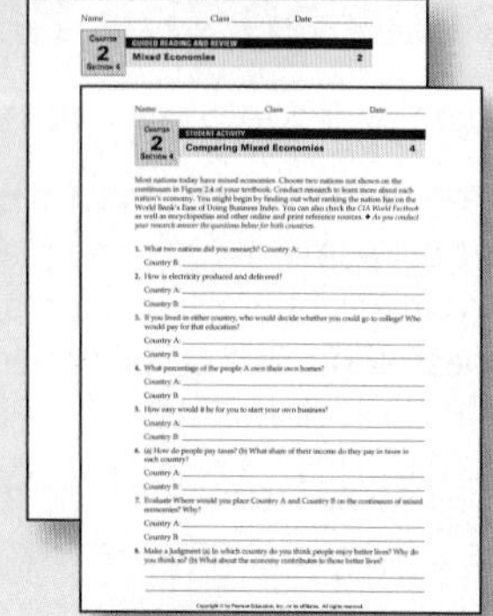

Figure 2.4 **Continuum of Mixed Economies**

GRAPH SKILLS

The degree of government intervention in the marketplace varies among nations.

1. Choose two nations on this continuum. Based on this diagram, write one sentence for each nation describing how its economic system differs from that of the United States.
2. Why is China a little bit farther to the right on this diagram than Cuba?

For an animated version of this graph, visit PearsonSuccessNet.com

Government in the Factor Market

As you saw in **Figure 2.2**, firms purchase land, labor, and capital from households in the factor market. The same is true of governments. For example, the U.S. government pays 2.7 million employees $152.2 billion a year for their labor. State and local governments also employ large numbers of people. Every time a police officer gets a paycheck, a government is buying labor in the factor market.

Government in the Product Market

Like households, governments purchase goods and services from firms in the product market. Government offices need telephones and computers. Printing money requires many tons of paper and gallons of ink. The vast majority of these purchases are made from private firms.

Governments also provide certain goods and services by combining the factor resources they bought. The federal, state, and local governments for example, have used concrete, steel, and other products to build nearly 4 million miles of roads.

Transferring Money

As the outer ring of **Figure 2.3** shows, governments collect taxes from both households and businesses. Governments then transfer some of this money to businesses and individuals for a variety of reasons, such as providing funds to save a failing industry or making payments to disabled workers. The greatest such expenditure of the United States government is Social Security.

CHECKPOINT ***How are governments involved in the product market?***

Comparing Mixed Economies

As you read in Section 1, most modern economies are mixed economies. Governments are involved to some degree, but more in some cases than others. You can see these differences in **Figure 2.4**, which shows a continuum of mixed economies in today's world. A continuum is a range of possibilities with no clear divisions between them.

Mixed Economies Where Government Intervention Dominates

North Korea represents one extreme of the continuum. Like the former Soviet Union, communist North Korea has an

DEMONSTRATE

Repeat the Demonstrate activity from page 30. However, this time allow students providing food to meet in advance to decide what prices they will charge. Discuss with students whether they felt this was fair. Ask **What effect did these agreements have on competition? On consumers?** Explain that in the late 1800s in the United States, large firms in the same industry often joined together to form trusts, which then fixed prices. The government passed laws banning trusts. Ask **How do these events relate to Adam Smith's discussion of the "invisible hand"?** *(Since the firms joined together, competition no longer regulated markets, so the government stepped in.)*

Explain that Congress has passed several laws regulating certain kinds of business activities and created agencies to write detailed rules about those activities.

IDENTIFY

Direct students' attention to Figure 2.4, "Continuum of Mixed Economies." Ask students the following questions. **What economy has the most central planning?** *(North Korea)* **What economies have freer markets than the United States?** *(Hong Kong and Singapore)* **Do you think the government plays a greater role in the economies of France than the United States? Why?** *(yes; because it is farther left, toward central planning)*

L1 Differentiate Compare the continuum to a thermometer, which shows high temperatures at one end and low temperatures at another. In the same way, the continuum shows high or low levels of freedom and planning.

Action Graph online Tell students to go to the Action Graph online for an animated step-by-step look at the continuum of mixed economies.

(lesson continued on p. 43)

Virtual Economics

L3 Differentiate

Relating Economic and Political Freedom Use the following lesson from the NCEE **Virtual Economics *CD-ROM*** to compare points of view about economic freedom. Click on Browse Economics Lessons, specify grades 9–12, and use the key words *necessary condition.*

In this activity, students will work in small groups to compare different viewpoints.

LESSON TITLE	IS ECONOMIC FREEDOM A NECESSARY CONDITION FOR POLITICAL FREEDOM?
Type of Activity	Comparing points of view
Complexity	Low
Time	50 minutes
NCEE Standards	3

Answers

Graph Skills 1. *Sample answers:* North Korea has more central planning and less economic freedom than the United States. Singapore has less central planning and more economic freedom than the United States. 2. because it has taken steps toward a free market economy

Checkpoint They buy goods and services from firms.

Teach Case Study

SUMMARIZE AND EXPLAIN

Have the students explain why the government makes laws regulating personal safety. Ask **Why has the government created laws requiring motorcyclists to wear helmets?** *(It is trying to protect its citizens from injury or death. States that repealed its mandatory helmet law saw an increase in motorcycle deaths.)* Ask **Why should non-motorcyclists care about helmet laws?** *(They may have friends or family members who ride motorcycles.)*

ANALYZE

Have the students list the different parties involved in this helmet-law debate *(helmet makers, doctors, local government, anti-helmet lobbyists)*. Have the students explain the position of each group and discuss them as a class. *(Helmet makers want their product sold so they are for helmet use, doctors want to limit head injuries so they would be for helmet use, anti-helmet lobbyists argue that motorcycle-death statistics are manipulated, and governmental laws vary by state.)*

L4 Differentiate Have students investigate motorcycle helmet laws and motorcycle accident-related deaths in your state. Have them report on the connections they see.

Economics online *All print resources are available on the Teacher's Resource Library CD-ROM and online at* www.PearsonSuccessNet.com.

Answer

Applying Economic Principles The conflict is between concerns for safety and the freedom of motorcycle riders. Possible answers: Bikers should be free to wear helmets or not, as they wish; no one else is harmed if they are hurt in an accident. Just as the government bans some substances as unhealthful, it should require bikers to wear helmets for their own safety.

Case STUDY

THE WALL STREET JOURNAL. CLASSROOM EDITION

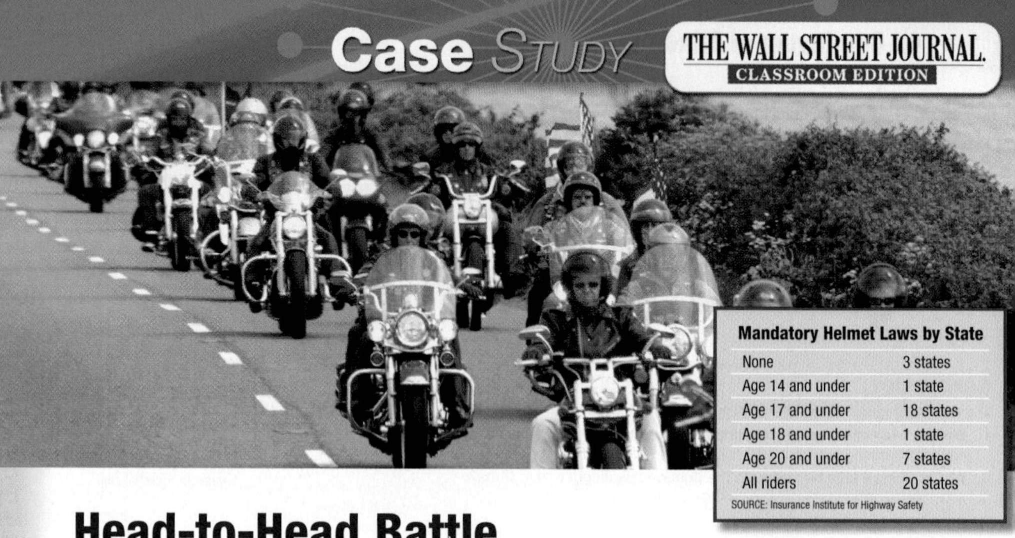

Mandatory Helmet Laws by State

None	3 states
Age 14 and under	1 state
Age 17 and under	18 states
Age 18 and under	1 state
Age 20 and under	7 states
All riders	20 states

SOURCE: Insurance Institute for Highway Safety

Head-to-Head Battle

GOVERNMENT INTERVENTION

Policy makers are often called upon to weigh people's freedom of choice against concerns for their safety. Making such decisions requires a close examination of trade-offs—the basis of all economic analysis.

By Karen Lundegaard
The Wall Street Journal

His name is Sputnik. He wears his hair in a Mohawk. He has five earrings dangling from his left ear. And he's helping to write your state's safety laws.

Sputnik and other biker-lobbyists like him are fighting, state by state, for what they see as freedom on the road—the right to ride a motorcycle without a helmet. Others see it as an assault on safety and common sense.

Over nearly three decades, bikers have pushed successfully to weaken or eliminate helmet laws in 29 states. Since 1997, five states—Texas, Florida, Pennsylvania, Kentucky and Arkansas—have repealed laws requiring all motorcycle riders to wear helmets. Federal statistics show that, on average, in the years after the recent legislative changes, helmet use dropped, and motorcycle deaths increased.

That isn't slowing Sputnik, however. He has traveled to 39 states in recent years to motivate bikers with what he calls his "Five Steps to Freedom," a primer that begins with registering biker voters and aims ultimately at putting them in office.

Many bikers complain that helmets make it harder to see and hear and that they are too hot in the summer. Some motorcyclists also argue that researchers manipulate statistics to show that helmets save lives.

The statistical case for helmet laws seems solid, according to analysis of government figures. In each state that recently repealed its mandatory helmet law, motorcycle deaths have more than doubled, sometimes in as short a span as three years.

Nationally, motorcycle deaths rose 12% in 2003, to 3,661. That is the sixth straight year motorcycle deaths have risen, and the largest annual percentage increase since 1988. The national fatality rate increased 4.4%, to 6.82 deaths per 10,000 motorcycles, the highest such figure since 1990. That rate is four-and-a-half times as high as the auto-fatality rate.

Anti-helmet activists argue that the statistics can be manipulated and that a helmet's weight can actually make injuries worse, by bringing more force to bear on the rider's neck in a crash. Some surgeons and scientists reject that assertion as unsubstantiated.

Even so, Sputnik counters that "the government has no right to protect us from ourselves. They are to protect us from enemies, both domestic and foreign, and we are not our enemies."

Applying Economic Principles
How does the debate over helmet laws represent a conflict between different goals? Which goal do you think should be given a higher priority?

Video News Update Online Powered by *The Wall Street Journal* Classroom Edition

For a new case study, go to the online resources at **PearsonSuccessNet.com** economy almost totally dominated by the government. The government owns all the property and all economic output. State-owned industries produce 95 percent of North Korea's goods. Nearly all imports from other countries are banned, and production of goods and services by foreign companies is forbidden.

In China, the government long dominated the economy. But, as you read in Section 3, China's economy has been changing to allow more private ownership of farms and businesses. As a result, China's place on the continuum is closer to the center than that of North Korea.

Like many nations that have relied heavily on central planning in the past, China is now going through **economic transition,** a period of change in which a nation moves from one economic system to another. In China's case, the transition involves privatizing state-owned firms. **Privatization** is the process of selling businesses or services operated by the government to individual investors, and then allowing them to compete in the marketplace. As you will read in Chapter 18, economic transition is a difficult, and often painful, process.

Mixed Economies Where the Free Market System Dominates

At the other end of the continuum, with one of the world's freest markets, is Hong Kong. Hong Kong, once administered by Great Britain, is now a special administrative region of China. By agreement with the Chinese government, Hong Kong continues to operate largely under the free economic system it had while under British rule.

In Hong Kong, the private sector rules. The government protects private property and rarely interferes in the free market, aside from establishing wage and price controls on rent and some public services. The area is highly receptive to foreign investment and places virtually no barriers on foreign trade. Banks in Hong Kong operate independently of the government, and foreign-owned banks have nearly all the rights of domestic ones.

CHECKPOINT ***Why is China's economy more mixed than North Korea's?***

The United States Economy

While the American economy is a mixed system, the foundation of the United States economy is the free market. An economic system characterized by individual or corporate ownership of capital goods is called a **free enterprise system.** In a free enterprise system, investments in firms are made in a free market by private decision.

Government Intervention

The government of the United States plays a substantial role in the American economy. The American government keeps order, provides vital services, and promotes the general welfare. Federal and state laws protect private property. The marketplace operates with a limited degree of government regulation.

economic transition a period of change in which a nation moves from one economic system to another

privatization the process of selling businesses or services operated by the government to individual investors, and then allowing them to compete in the marketplace

free enterprise system an economic system characterized by private or corporate ownership of capital goods

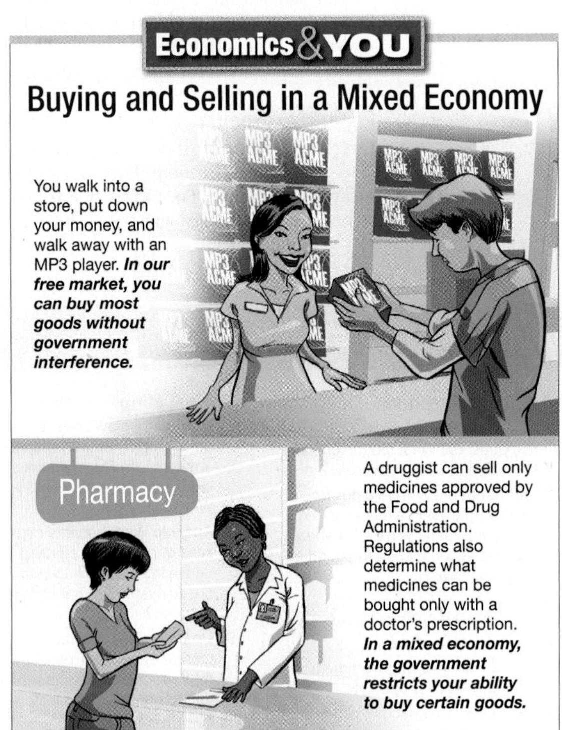

Economics & YOU
Buying and Selling in a Mixed Economy
You walk into a store, put down your money, and walk away with an MP3 player. In our free market, you can buy most goods without government interference.
MP3 ACME
Pharmacy
A druggist can sell only medicines approved by the Food and Drug Administration. Regulations also determine what medicines can be bought only with a doctor's prescription. In a mixed economy, the government restricts your ability to buy certain goods.

▲ Government intervention is part of a mixed economy. ***List two other goods or services that are affected by legal restrictions.***

ANALYZE A CARTOON

Distribute the "Economic Transition" worksheet (Unit 1 All-in-One, p. 76). Have students answer the questions to explore changes in China's economy. Review answers with students.

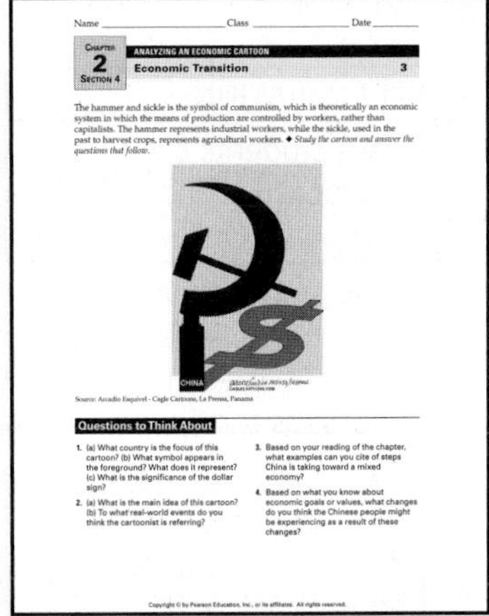
Name ____________ Class ____________ Date ________

CHAPTER 2 SECTION 4 — ANALYZING AN ECONOMIC CARTOON

Economic Transition 3

The hammer and sickle is the symbol of communism, which is theoretically an economic system in which the means of production are controlled by workers, rather than capitalists. The hammer represents industrial workers, while the sickle, used in the past to harvest crops, represents agricultural workers. ◆ *Study the cartoon and answer the questions that follow.*

Source: Arcadio Esquivel - Cagle Cartoons, La Prensa, Panama

Questions to Think About

1. (a) What country is the focus of this cartoon? (b) What symbol appears in the foreground? What does it represent? (c) What is the significance of the dollar sign?
2. (a) What is the main idea of this cartoon? (b) To what real-world events do you think the cartoonist is referring?
3. Based on your reading of the chapter, what examples can you cite of steps China is taking toward a mixed economy?
4. Based on what you know about economic goals or values, what changes do you think the Chinese people might be experiencing as a result of these changes?

L2 Differentiate Distribute the "The Food and Drug Administration" worksheet (Unit 1 All-in-One, p. 77). Have students answer the questions.

L4 Differentiate Distribute the "Comparing Mixed Economies" worksheet (Unit 1 All-in-One, p. 78). Have students answer the questions.

EXTEND

Have students write a paragraph expressing their opinion about whether the United States government is involved enough or too much in the economy.

GUIDING QUESTION WRAP UP

Have students return to the section Guiding Question. Review the completed graphic organizer and clarify any misunderstandings. Have a wrap up discussion about the characteristics of a mixed economy.

Assess and Remediate

L2 L3 Collect the "Economic Transition" and "The Food and Drug Administration" worksheets and assess student understanding.

L4 Collect the "Comparing Mixed Economies" worksheet and assess students' research.

L3 Assign the Section 4 Assessment questions.

L3 Give Section Quiz A (Unit 1 All-in-One, p. 79).

L2 Give Section Quiz B (Unit 1 All-in-One, p. 80).

Answers

Checkpoint China has freer markets.

Economics & You Possible answers: firearms, require licenses; alcohol and cigarettes, which are restricted by age; prescription drugs.

Background Note

The Move to Markets Point out to students that the world had more economies that tended toward central planning in the past. That began to change in the 1980s, when the International Monetary Fund helped promote a greater shift toward market economics in Latin America. The collapse of communism in Eastern Europe in 1989 spurred the development even more. Nearly all the one-time communist countries of that region began market reforms, as did Russia, to a degree, after the collapse of the Soviet Union.

Have students complete the Self-Test Online and continue their work in the **Essential Questions Journal**.

REMEDIATION AND SUGGESTIONS

Use the chart below to help students who are struggling with content.

WEAKNESS	REMEDIATION
Defining key terms (Questions 2, 3, 4, 5, 6)	Have students use the interactive Economic Dictionary Online.
Explaining why governments are involved in economies (Questions 3, 7)	Have students write main ideas for each paragraph under the heading "Reasons for Government Involvement."
Describing the circular flow of a mixed economy (Question 1)	Have students describe the actions of firms, households, and government in this economic model.
Comparing systems (Questions 2, 8, 10, 11)	Have students outline the text under the heading "Comparing Mixed Economies."
Analyzing the government's role in the U.S. economy (Questions 4, 10)	Have students explain how Figure 2.3 describes the U.S. economy.

Answers

Caption Possible answer: "Financial Freedom": highlights major trait of free enterprise

Checkpoint because it has a high level of economic freedom

The freedom to start a business is one of the most important features of the American free enterprise system. Literally thousands of magazines, books, and Web sites are devoted to the needs of entrepreneurs—or people who want to become entrepreneurs. ***Choose one of the headlines shown on these magazines and explain how it relates to the idea of free enterprise.*** ▶

Some Americans argue that there is a need for more government services and stricter regulation of business. Others, however, say that the government already intervenes too much in the economy. They call for relaxation of existing regulations.

Economic Freedom

Overall, the United States enjoys a high level of economic freedom. Foreign investment is encouraged. So, too, is free trade, although the government does protect some domestic industries and does retaliate against trade restrictions imposed by other nations. The banking industry operates under relatively few restrictions. Foreign-owned banks have few additional restrictions.

In the next chapter, you will read in detail about free enterprise and the economic roles of government in the United States.

CHECKPOINT ***Why is the United States said to have a free enterprise system?***

SECTION 4 ASSESSMENT

Essential Questions Journal To continue to build a response to the Essential Question, go to your **Essential Questions Journal**.

Guiding Question

1. Use your completed chart to answer this question: What are the characteristics of a mixed economy?
2. **Extension** If you were a government employee in a mixed economy, would you rather work in a centrally planned economy or a free market economy? Why?

Key Terms and Main Ideas

3. What is **laissez faire?**
4. How does the U.S. government protect **private property?**
5. Why have some nations begun an **economic transition** to a **free enterprise system?**
6. How is China carrying out **privatization?**

Critical Thinking

7. **Explain (a)** How does laissez faire differ from a centrally planned government? **(b)** Do you think a pure laissez faire system could work? Why or why not?
8. **Analyze** What benefits might citizens of a centrally planned economy derive from a move toward a market-based system? What risks might be involved?
9. **Describe (a)** Describe the type of market system in Hong Kong. **(b)** How does the system benefit entrepreneurs and investors?
10. **Contrast** Identify two ways that the American free enterprise system differs from North Korea's centrally planned system.

Quick Write

11. Sweden has a mixed economy that blends a free market with socialism. Around 56 percent of Sweden's gross domestic product is paid in taxes, compared to only 32 percent in the United States. In turn, Swedes pay very little for medical care and employers are required by law to provide a minimum of thirty days of vacation to employees. Write a brief essay comparing and contrasting the Swedish and American systems. Which do you think is more beneficial for workers?

Assessment Answers

1. some elements of both market and centrally planned systems
2. Possible answer: in a free market economy, because you could give people more freedom of choice
3. the doctrine that government should not intervene in the economy
4. Fifth and Fourteenth Amendments and patent laws
5. to keep pace with the global economy
6. by selling government-owned firms to individuals and allowing them to compete
7. (a) absence of government role versus complete government control (b) Possible answer: No, because there needs to be a mechanism to prevent unfair business practices. Otherwise, unscrupulous producers would be free to interfere with free market operations through price fixing or other practices.
8. benefits: more freedom, choice; risk: less job security
9. (a) free market (b) Possible answer: allows them to profit from their own innovations.
10. In the U.S., people make their own choices and own property and economic output; in North Korea, the government controls decisions and owns all property and economic output.
11. Answers will vary, but all responses should recognize the trade-off between higher taxes and increased services.

QUICK STUDY GUIDE

QUICK STUDY GUIDE

Chapter 2: Economic Systems

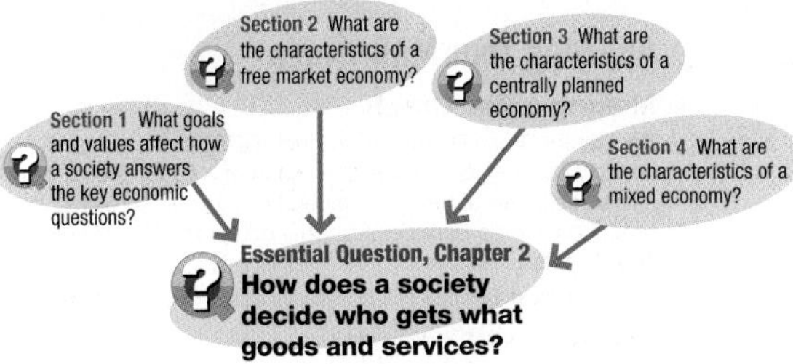

Section 2 What are the characteristics of a free market economy?
Section 3 What are the characteristics of a centrally planned economy?
Section 1 What goals and values affect how a society answers the key economic questions?
Section 4 What are the characteristics of a mixed economy?
Essential Question, Chapter 2
How does a society decide who gets what goods and services?

Answering the Three Economic Questions

The Three Questions
- What goods and services should be produced?
- How should these goods and services be produced?
- Who consumes these goods and services?

Economic System	Three Questions Answered By:
Traditional	Habit, custom, ritual
Free market	Operation of market forces; invisible hand
Centrally planned	Government decision makers; bureaucracy
Mixed	Market forces with some government involvement

Economic Dictionary

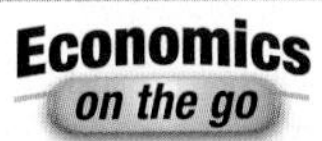

Economics *on the go*

Study anytime, anywhere. Download these files today.

Economic Dictionary online	Audio Review online	Action Graph online	Visual Glossary online	How the Economy Works online
Vocabulary Support in English and Spanish	Audio Study Guide in English and Spanish	Animated Charts and Graphs	Animated feature	Animated feature

Download to your computer or mobile device at PearsonSuccessNet.com

ASSIGN THE ESSENTIAL QUESTIONS JOURNAL

After students have finished studying the chapter, they should return to the chapter's essential question in the Essential Questions Journal and complete the activity.

Tell students to go back to the chapter opener and look at the image. Using the information they have gained from studying the chapter, ask **How does this illustrate the main ideas of the chapter?** *(Possible responses: Schools and playgrounds are examples of services often provided by the government in a mixed economy. The students pulling on the rope may represent competition for scarce resources. These students may also remind students of the competition and self-interest that are characteristic of a free market economy.)*

STUDY TIPS

To help students prepare for college, give them advice on managing their time. In college, professors may inform students of major assignments, such as papers, early in the year, but not remind them of the work later. Creating a semester-long schedule that lists papers and quizzes can help students keep track of these important issues and deliver their work on time.

Economics *on the go* Have students download the digital resources available at Economics on the Go for review and remediation.

Assessment at a Glance

TESTS AND QUIZZES

Section Assessments

Section Quizzes A and B, **Unit 1 All-in-One**

Self-Test Online

Chapter Assessments

Chapter Tests A and B, **Unit 1 All-in-One**

Document-based Assessment, p. 47

Exam*View*

AYP Monitoring Assessments

PERFORMANCE ASSESSMENT

Teacher's Edition, pp. 25, 27, 31, 33, 37, 43

Simulation Activities, Chapter 2

Virtual Economics on CD-ROM, pp. 25, 33, 37, 41

Essential Questions Journal, Chapter 2

Assessment Rubrics

Chapter 2 Assessment

1. (a) Households supply labor and land, for which firms pay them. Firms produce goods and services, which households buy. (b) The store might sell CDs and DVDs and pay wages to workers. (c) Examples are paying taxes and meeting labor laws.
2. (a) Smith thought the government should intervene as little as possible. He believed that competition allowed the market to regulate itself, insuring that producers provided what consumers wanted to consume at a reasonable price. (b) Examples are to provide education, to protect property, and to prevent unfair business practices. (c) Possible answer: Smith would approve of laws against unfair business practices, since such practices stifle competition and prevent the marketplace from operating freely.
3. (a) efficiency, freedom, security, equity, growth (b) Possible answer: The free market system does the best job of providing efficiency, freedom, and growth. Command economies often provide security by insuring jobs.
4. (a) The U.S. economy is a mixed system that tends more toward the free market. (b) Possible answer: If the United States moved more to the right, the government would end or reduce regulations about the environment, workplace safety, and the minimum wage.
5. Answer will be a bar graph with the countries in the order shown on the continuum in Figure 2.4.
6. *Iran:* $12,300; *Hong Kong:* $42,000
7. Singapore has the highest ($48,900); North Korea has the lowest ($1,900).
8. Russia's per capita GDP is 31.8% of that of the U.S.; France's is 73.5% of that of the U.S.; and Singapore's is 106.3% of that of the U.S.
9. The chart does. The seven countries listed as free market economies in Figure 2.4 all have per capita GDP over $30,000 (the highest level), and the five countries with more central planning in Figure 2.4 have lower per capita GDPs.
10. (a) Students arguing for a centrally planned economy might emphasize security and equity as goals and warn against the unfairness that can arise from a laissez faire system. (b) Students arguing for the market system might emphasize the greater potential for growth and efficiency under that system.
11. (a) Caution students to address the arguments used and to give evidence in support of their positions. (b) Guide students to reach a consensus on the system chosen.

CHAPTER 2 ASSESSMENT

Self-Test online To test your understanding of key terms and main ideas, visit **PearsonSuccessNet.com**

Key Terms and Main Ideas

To make sure you understand the key terms and main ideas of this chapter, review the Checkpoint and Section Assessment questions and look at the Quick Study Guide on the preceding page.

Critical Thinking

1. **Illustrate (a)** What are the two ways that households and firms interact in the factor market? In the product market? **(b)** Suppose you were the owner of a music store. Give three specific illustrations of ways that your business might interact with households. **(c)** How might the introduction of government into the circular flow model affect your business?
2. **Explain (a)** Summarize Adam Smith's attitude toward government intervention in the marketplace. **(b)** What are some reasons the government intervenes in a mixed economy? **(c)** Choose one of these reasons and explain whether or not you think Adam Smith would have approved.
3. **Evaluate (a)** List the major economic goals each economic system tries to meet. **(b)** Choose two of the following economic systems—traditional, free market, or centrally planned—and explain which of the two systems you think does the best job of achieving each goal.
4. **Predict (a)** Describe in one sentence the economic system of the United States. **(b)** Look at **Figure 2.4.** Describe three ways your life might change if the United States moved either to the left or to the right on the continuum of mixed economies.

Applying Your Math Skills

Making a Bar Graph

Per Capita Gross Domestic Product (GDP) is one statistic economists use to measure the health of a nation's economy. It is an estimate of the total value of goods and services produced in a country per person. Look at the data below and complete the activity that follows.

Visit Pearson SuccessNet.com for additional math help.

Per Capita GDP in U.S. Dollars, 2007

Country	GDP	Country	GDP
Canada	$38,200	Mexico	$12,500
China	$5,300	North Korea	$1,900
Cuba	$4,500	Poland	$16,200
France	$33,800	Russia	$14,600
Germany	$34,400	Singapore	$48,900
Hong Kong	$42,000	South Africa	$10,600
Iran	$12,300	United Kingdom	$35,300
Japan	$33,800	United States	$46,000

SOURCE: CIA World Factbook

5. Use the figures above to create a bar graph. Arrange the countries in the order shown on the continuum in **Figure 2.4.**
6. What is the per capita gross domestic product of Iran? Of Hong Kong?
7. Which country has the highest per capita gross domestic product? Which has the lowest?
8. How does the per capita gross domestic product of the United States compare to those of Russia, France, and Singapore? Express your answer as a fraction or percentage.
9. Does this graph support the generalization that free-market economies tend to be more efficient than command economies? Explain.

Essential Question Activity

Essential Questions Journal To respond to the chapter Essential Question, go to your **Essential Questions Journal.**

10. Complete the activity to answer the Essential Question. **How does a society decide who gets what goods and services?** Imagine that your class is advising leaders of the newly formed nation, Ervola. Many of the nation's new political leaders favor the use of central planning, but business leaders favor a laissez faire approach. Ervola must determine which economic system will help it to meet the economic goals stated in Section 1 of this chapter. Use the format of a debate, as outlined in the worksheet in your Essential Questions Journal or the electronic worksheet available at **PearsonSuccessNet.com.** Before the debate, participants should identify the economic goals and determine how their team plans to meet each of them.
    - **(a)** For the affirmative, a student team will develop arguments in favor of a strict command economy.
    - **(b)** For the negative, another student team will develop arguments in favor of a totally free market economy.
11. **Modify**
    - **(a)** As a class, discuss and evaluate the arguments given in the debate. Base your evaluation on the logic of the arguments, the analysis the speakers used, the evidence, the organization of the speeches, and the persuasiveness of the arguments.
    - **(b)** Present an agreed-upon economic system to recommend to the nation of Ervola. Include the statements that most strongly support your decision.

WebQuest online The Economics WebQuest challenges students to use 21st century skills to answer the Essential Question.

THE ESSENTIAL
VIDEO
By Students For Students
For videos on Essential Questions, go to PearsonSuccessNet.com

Remind students to continue to develop an Essential Questions video. Guidelines and a production binder are available at www.PearsonSuccessNet.com.

CHAPTER 2 ASSESSMENT

DOCUMENT-BASED ASSESSMENT

Does division of labor benefit or harm workers?

During the Industrial Revolution, factories began to increase the use of machinery and to divide production into many separate, specialized tasks. Free market thinker Adam Smith and communist thinker Karl Marx had very different views on this division of labor.

Document A

"[Take] the trade of the pin-maker. A workman not educated to this business…nor acquainted with the use of the machinery employed in it…could scarce, perhaps, with his utmost industry, make one pin in a day, and certainly could not make twenty. But in the way in which this business is now carried on…it is divided into a number of branches, of which the greater part are likewise peculiar trades. One man draws out the wire, another straights it, a third cuts it, a fourth points it…. Ten persons could make among them upwards of forty-eight thousand pins in a day."

—Adam Smith, *The Wealth of Nations*

Document B

"The greater division of labor enables one laborer to accomplish the work of five, 10, or 20 laborers; it therefore increases competition among the laborers fivefold, tenfold, or twentyfold…. The special skill of the laborer becomes worthless. He becomes transformed into a simple monotonous force of production, with neither physical nor mental elasticity…. The more the division of labor and the application of machinery extend, the more does competition extend among the workers, the more do their wages shrink together."

—Karl Marx, *Wage Labor and Capital*

Document C

▲ These food service workers are using an assembly line to prepare bowls of hot soup.

ANALYZING DOCUMENTS

Use your knowledge of economic systems and Documents A, B, and C to answer questions 1–3.

1. **According to Document A, what does Adam Smith consider an important benefit to the division of labor?**
   A. It produces a more skilled workforce.
   B. It increases daily production.
   C. It improves the quality of products.
   D. It creates more jobs for workers.

2. **What is the main point of Document B?**
   A. Machines produce inferior goods.
   B. Competition is good for workers.
   C. Division of labor contributes to lower wages.
   D. Division of labor and use of machinery are in conflict.

3. **Which of the following views could Document C best be used to support?**
   A. Smith's views on economic efficiency
   B. Marx's views on economic equity
   C. Marx's views on capital
   D. Smith's views on the "invisible hand"

WRITING ABOUT ECONOMICS

Use the documents on this page and on the Web site below to answer the question: ***Does division of labor benefit or harm workers?*** Use the sources to support your opinion.

In Partnership

THE WALL STREET JOURNAL.
CLASSROOM EDITION

To read more about issues related to this topic, visit **PearsonSuccessNet.com**

Document-Based Assessment

ANALYZING DOCUMENTS

1. B
2. C
3. A

WRITING ABOUT ECONOMICS

Possible answers: Benefits workers by enabling them to be more productive; harms workers by increasing competition and leaving them with monotonous tasks.

Student essay should demonstrate an understanding of the issues involved in the debate. Use the following as guidelines to assess the essay.

L2 Differentiate Students use all documents on the page to support their thesis.

L3 Differentiate Students use the documents on this page and additional information available online at www.PearsonSuccessNet.com to support their answer.

L4 Differentiate Students incorporate information provided in the textbook and online at www.PearsonSuccessNet.com and include additional research to support their opinion.

Go Online to www.PearsonSuccessNet.com for a student rubric and extra documents.

Economics online *All print resources are available on the Teacher's Resource Library CD-ROM and online at* www.PearsonSuccessNet.com.

Essential Questions

UNIT 1:

How does economics affect everyone?

CHAPTER 3:

What role should government play in a free market economy?

Introduce the Chapter

ACTIVATE PRIOR KNOWLEDGE

In this chapter, students will learn about the role the government plays in the American free enterprise system. Tell students to complete the activity in their **Essential Questions Journal**.

DIFFERENTIATED INSTRUCTION KEY

- **L1** Special Needs
- **L2** Basic
  - **ELL** English Language Learners
  - **LPR** Less Proficient Readers
- **L3** All Students
- **L4** Advanced Students

Economics online Visit www.PearsonSuccessNet.com for an interactive textbook with built-in activities on economic principles.

- ***The Wall Street Journal* Classroom Edition Video** presents a current topic related to free enterprise.
- **Yearly Update Worksheet** provides an annual update, including a new worksheet and lesson on this topic.
- **On the Go** resources can be downloaded so students and teachers can connect with economics anytime, anywhere.

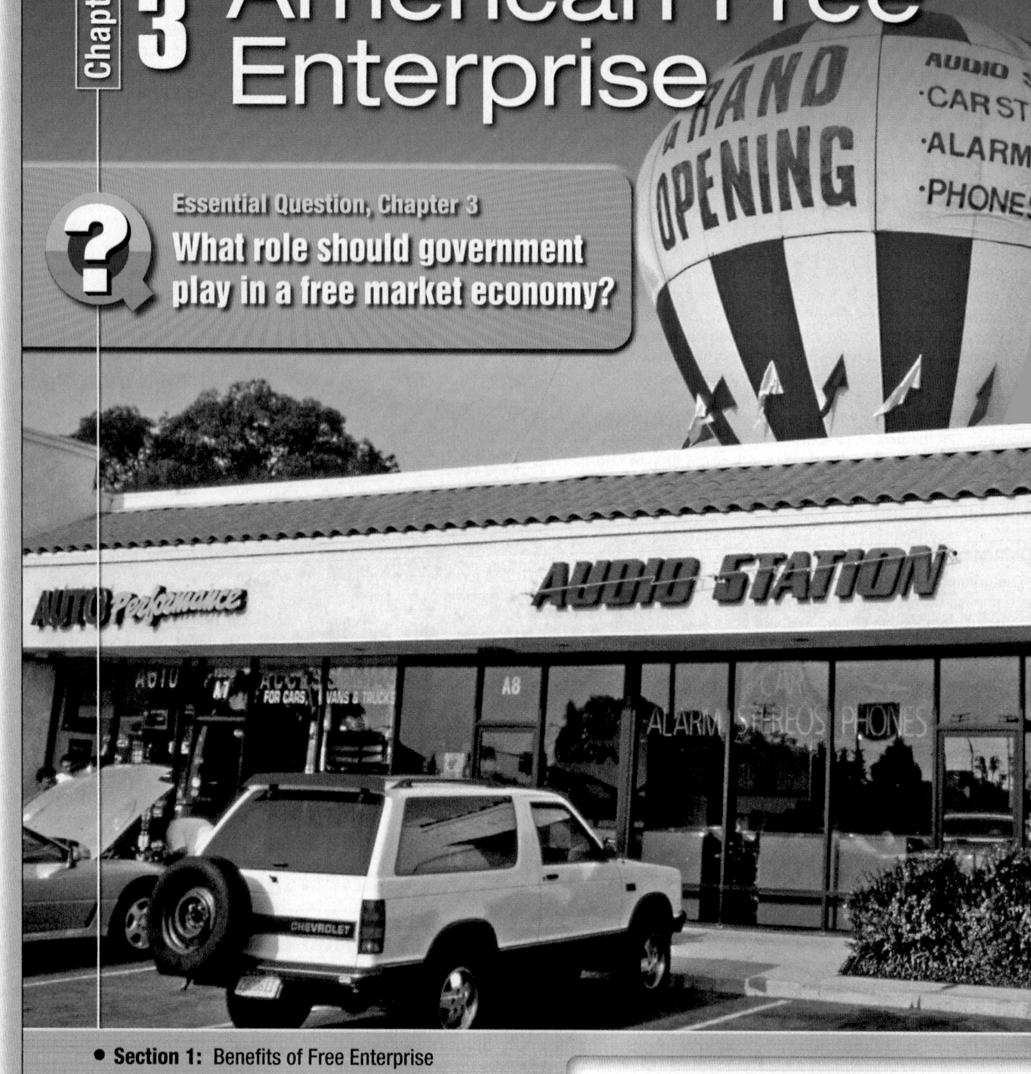

- **Section 1:** Benefits of Free Enterprise
- **Section 2:** Promoting Growth and Stability
- **Section 3:** Providing Public Goods
- **Section 4:** Providing a Safety Net

Economics on the go

To study anywhere, anytime, download these online resources at ***PearsonSuccessNet.com*** ▶

ECONOMICS ONLINE

DIGITAL TEACHER TOOLS

The online lesson planner is designed to help teachers plan, teach, and assess. Teachers have the ability to use or customize existing Pearson lesson plans. Online lecture notes support the print lesson by providing an array of accessible activities and summaries of key concepts.

Two interactivities in this lesson are:

- **Visual Glossary** The elements of the free enterprise system are illustrated.
- **WebQuest** Students use online resources to complete a guided activity further exploring the Essential Questions.

Block Scheduling

BLOCK 1 Teach Sections 1 and 2, but complete the Bellringer activities for both sections at the beginning of the Block. Delete the Extend Activity.

BLOCK 2 Teach Sections 3 and 4 deleting the Extend Activities.

Pressed for Time

Begin with the Visual Glossary for Section 1. For each section, focus on the economic vocabulary and its application in the All-in-One worksheets. Small groups can complete these worksheets and then share information using the section's economic vocabulary.

SECTION 1 Benefits of Free Enterprise

OBJECTIVES

1. **Define** the basic principles of the U.S. free enterprise system.
2. **Describe** the role of the consumer in the American economy.
3. **Identify** the constitutional protections that underlie free enterprise.
4. **Explain** why the government may intervene in the marketplace.

ECONOMIC DICTIONARY

As you read the section, look for the definitions of these **Key Terms:**

- profit motive
- open opportunity
- legal equality
- private property rights
- free contract
- voluntary exchange
- interest group
- patriotism
- eminent domain
- public interest
- public disclosure laws

Guiding Question
What are the benefits of free enterprise?

Copy this chart and fill it in as you read.

Free Enterprise System	
Characteristics	**Benefits**
• Profit motive • • •	• Encourages innovation • •

Economics and You Picture the dozens of services and products you use every week. Somebody had to think of each one and put it into action. Somebody figured out that people would rather rent DVDs from a Web site that offers tens of thousands of choices than go to a store that offers far fewer. Somebody invented a way to send photos as well as messages with cellphones.

Now, suppose *you* had one of these brilliant ideas—or just wanted to start your own neighborhood lawn care or baby-sitting service. Could you try to put your plan into action? Since you live in the United States, you can. Every day, American entrepreneurs begin new businesses that earn profits, create jobs, and offer new goods and services.

Principles in Action The American free enterprise system makes it possible for people who have ideas and persistence to start businesses and make them successful. In this section, you will see how one Dominican immigrant built a successful business in the highly competitive U.S. fashion industry. You will also examine the vital role that you, as a consumer, play in the free enterprise system.

Basic Principles of Free Enterprise

For centuries, people have considered the United States to be a "land of opportunity," where anyone from any background might achieve success. Indeed, this country does offer special opportunities that have allowed business people the freedom to innovate and have contributed to our overall economic prosperity. Today, there are over 22 million unincorporated

Visual Glossary online

Go to the Visual Glossary Online for an interactive review of **free enterprise.**

Action Graph online

Go to Action Graph Online for animated versions of key charts and graphs.

How the Economy Works online

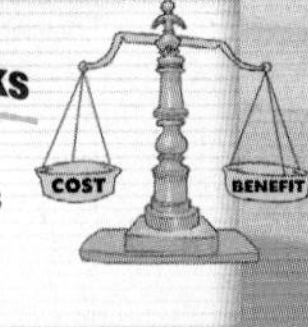

Go to How the Economy Works Online for an interactive lesson on **providing public goods.**

Guiding Question

What are the benefits of free enterprise?

Get Started

Free Enterprise System	
Characteristics	**Benefits**
• Profit motive • Open opportunity • Legal equality • Private property • Free contract • Voluntary exchange	• Encourages innovation • Allows economic mobility • Provides incentive for wise use of property • Encourages competition and market variety

LESSON GOALS

Students will:

- Know the Key Terms.
- Using a transparency, evaluate how the principles of free enterprise are applied to a business.
- Analyze how consumers, through free choice, affect the free enterprise system.
- Describe how the government intervenes in the marketplace and why.

BEFORE CLASS

Students should read the section for homework before coming to class.

Have students complete the graphic organizer in the Section Opener as they read the text. As an alternate activity, have students complete the Guided Reading and Review worksheet (Unit 1 All-in-One, p. 99).

L1 L2 ELL LPR Differentiate Have students complete the Guided Reading and Review worksheet (Unit 1 All-in-One, p. 100).

(lesson continued on p. 51)

Focus on the Basics

Students need to come away with the following understandings:

FACTS: • The American free enterprise system is characterized by the profit motive, open opportunity, legal equality, private property, and the freedom to buy and sell. • Consumers influence free enterprise businesses by making their interests known through voluntary exchange. • The Constitution guarantees certain rights that underlie our economic freedoms. • Conflicts arise when the government exercises its right to take private property for public use. • The government both protects and regulates consumers and businesses.

GENERALIZATION: Under the American free enterprise system, the government aims to protect the public interest by balancing regulation with laws preserving economic freedoms.

CLASSROOM HINTS

THE BENEFITS OF TAXES

Many students have been exposed to the negative aspects of taxation and its effect on businesses. They often do not see how taxes could benefit a community. To broaden students' understanding of how taxes are used in the community, have students construct a political policy where they make key economic decisions about how and when to raise and spend taxes.

Teach Visual Glossary

REVIEW KEY TERMS

Pair students and have them write the definitions of the key terms related to the understanding of free enterprise.

entrepreneur – *a person who decides how to combine resources to create goods and services*

profit – *the amount of money a business receives in excess of its expenses*

free market economy – *an economic system in which decisions on the three key economic questions are based on voluntary exchange in markets*

incentive – *the hope of reward or fear of penalty that encourages a person to behave in a certain way*

competition – *the struggle among producers for the dollars of consumers*

customer sovereignty – *the power of consumers to decide what gets produced*

INTERPRETING THE CONCEPT WEB

Have students explain why the pictures that accompany the terms private property, competition, and customer sovereignty represent these terms. *(The house has just been purchased—it is now someone's private property; Toyota, Ford, and GMC are three competing automobile manufacturers; the boy and girl are customers who can choose what to order.)* Then pair off students to interpret the meaning of the remaining characteristics of free enterprise from the pictures, and report their interpretations to the class.

L2 LPR Differentiate Call on less proficient readers first when having students describe the connection between the words and the visuals.

Economics online *All print resources are available on the Teacher's Resource Library CD-ROM and online at* www.PearsonSuccessNet.com.

Answer

Visual Glossary Possible responses: Consumer sovereignty means consumers choose what gets produced; the profit motive leads businesses to produce what consumers want to buy; private property rights allow people the freedom to make decisions about what they do with their property.

VISUAL GLOSSARY

Reviewing Key Terms
To understand *free enterprise*, review these terms:
entrepreneur, *p. 5*
profit, *p. 25*
free market economy, *p. 30*
incentive, *p. 33*
competition, *p. 33*
consumer sovereignty, *p. 34*

What is
Free Enterprise?

◀ **free enterprise** an economic system in which decisions are made in a free market by private individuals and firms

The characteristics shown here form the foundation of the American free enterprise system. ***Choose two of the characteristics and explain how they protect your freedom of choice.***

Economic Freedom
Private Property
Competition
Contracts
Voluntary Exchange
Self-Interest
Legal Equality
Customer Sovereignty
Profit Motive

American Free Enterprise

Visual Glossary online
To expand your understanding of this and other key economic terms, visit **PearsonSuccessNet.com**

businesses in America, including more than 3.5 million that are owned by members of minority groups. Many of these were started by a single entrepreneur or a small group of friends or family members.

Why has America been such an economic success? Certainly the United States enjoys many advantages in resources: open land, large reserves of natural resources, and a large, talented labor supply fueled by immigrants. But a key factor has also been the American tradition of free enterprise—the social and political commitment to giving people the freedom and flexibility to try out their business ideas and compete in the marketplace. This free enterprise system has several key characteristics.

Profit Motive

The American economy rests on recognition of the profit motive as a key incentive. The **profit motive** drives individuals and businesses to make decisions that improve their material well-being. As you have read, in a centrally planned economic system, the government decides what companies will be formed and how they will be run. In a free enterprise system, business owners and managers make such choices themselves based on what will increase their profits.

Reliance on the profit motive has several benefits. It forces business owners to exercise financial discipline because they are responsible for their own success or failure. It encourages entrepreneurs to take rational risks, and rewards innovation by letting creative companies grow. It also improves productivity by allowing more efficient companies to make more money.

Open Opportunity

The American economy also benefits from a tradition of **open opportunity,** the principle that anyone can compete in the marketplace. We accept that different people and firms will have different degrees of success. At the same time, we believe that anyone who wants to start a business should have a chance. This allows economic mobility up or down: no matter how much money you start out with, you can end up wealthier or poorer depending on how your business performs.

Legal Equality

We also have a commitment to **legal equality**—the principle that everyone has the same legal rights. Legal equality benefits the economy by maximizing a country's use of its human capital. Countries that restrict the legal rights of women or minorities lose the productive potential of a large portion of their society.

Private Property

In many ways, private property is the cornerstone of the free enterprise system. **Private property rights** give people the right to control their possessions and use them as they wish. The free enterprise system allows people to make their own decisions about their own property. Personal ownership provides an incentive for property owners to use their property wisely and conserve their resources.

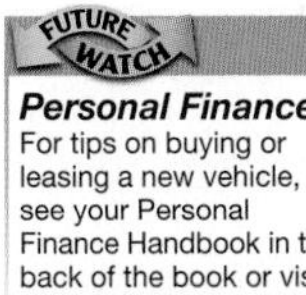

Personal Finance For tips on buying or leasing a new vehicle, see your Personal Finance Handbook in the back of the book or visit **PearsonSuccessNet.com**

Freedom to Buy and Sell

The right of **free contract** allows people to decide what agreements they want to enter into. A singer can sign an agreement with any sponsor or recording company. Consumers can choose to enter a credit card agreement with any of several banks.

The right of **voluntary exchange** allows people to decide what, when, and how they want to buy and sell. They are not forced to buy or sell particular goods at particular times or at specific prices. Voluntary exchange, in turn, encourages competition. As we have seen, competition provides consumers with the choice of a larger variety of goods, most of which are sold at reasonable prices.

CHECKPOINT ***What are three key economic rights that Americans enjoy?***

The Role of the Consumer

A basic principle of the free enterprise system is that consumers have the freedom to make their own economic choices. Through voluntary exchange, consumers send a signal to businesses, telling them what to produce and how much to make. Consumers also send a signal when they do not buy a good or service. They are telling the producer that the good or service is not desirable or is priced too high.

profit motive the incentive that drives individuals and business owners to improve their material well-being

open opportunity the principle that anyone can compete in the marketplace

legal equality the principle that everyone has the same legal rights

private property rights the principle that people have the right to control their possessions and use them as they wish

free contract the principle that people may decide what agreements they want to enter into

voluntary exchange the principle that people may decide what, when, and how they want to buy and sell

Differentiated Resources

- L1 L2 **Guided Reading and Review** (Unit 1 All-in-One, p. 100)
- L2 **Vocabulary worksheet** (Unit 1 All-in-One, p. 98)
- L4 **Constitutional Connections** (Unit 1 All-in-One, p. 101)
- L2 **Eminent Domain** (Unit 1 All-in-One, p. 103)
- L3 **Whose Property Is It?** (Simulation Activities, Chapter 3)

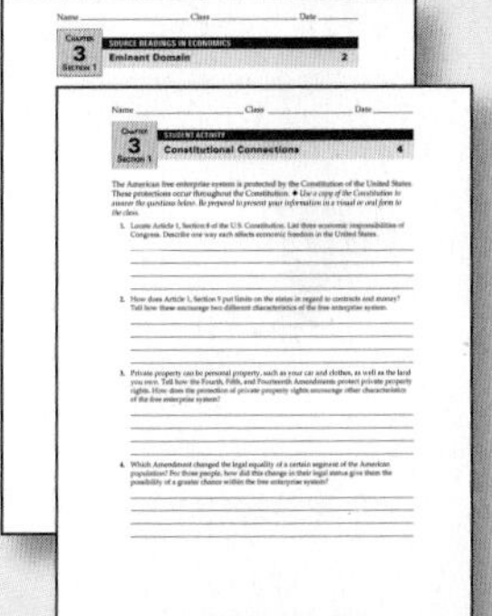

BELLRINGER

Write the following direction on the board: List three ways that government actions affect your economic freedoms. Are they positive or negative effects? Ask students to write their responses in their notebooks.

L2 **Differentiate** Have students work in pairs to brainstorm ideas before writing each answer.

Teach

Economics online To present this topic using digital resources, use the lecture notes at www.PearsonSuccessNet.com.

L1 L2 **ELL LPR Differentiate** To help students who are struggling readers, assign the Vocabulary worksheet (Unit 1 All-in-One, p. 98).

REVIEW BELLRINGER ANSWERS

Using the Think-Write-Pair-Share strategy (p. T24), have students discuss the answers in their notebooks.

DISCUSS

Have students review the basic characteristics of the free enterprise system. Display the transparency "Entrepreneurs and Free Enterprise" (Color Transparencies, 3.a). Ask **How is this entrepreneur benefiting from the free enterprise system?** *(Possible response: The entrepreneur can take advantage of the American tradition of open opportunity, legal equality, the right to own personal property, and the freedom to start a business.)* **What challenges do you think this person faces?** *(Possible responses: meeting customer demands, making enough profit to succeed)*

PERSONAL FINANCE ACTIVITY

To help students make smart purchasing decisions, you may want to use the Personal Finance Handbook lesson on buying or leasing a car (pp. PF 32–33) and the activity worksheet (Personal Finance All-in-One, pp. 85–86).

To help students make wise choices, you may want to use the Personal Finance Handbook section on the basics of insurance (pp. PF 28–29) and the activity worksheet (Personal Finance All-in-One, pp. 77–78).

Answer

Checkpoint private property rights, the right of free contract, and the right of voluntary exchange

EXAMINE

Explain that property rights and the right to make contracts are key pieces of the free enterprise system that enable entrepreneurs to achieve success. These rights are protected in the Constitution. Ask **How does the Constitution protect property rights and the right to make contracts?** *(The Fifth Amendment and the Fourteenth Amendment protect personal property rights; Article 1, Section 10 prohibits states from interfering with contracts made by individuals or businesses.)*

L4 Differentiate Assign the "Constitutional Connections" worksheet (Unit 1 All-in-One, p. 101). Have students analyze the Constitution of the United States to find exactly where the American free enterprise system is protected.

DISTRIBUTE ACTIVITY WORKSHEET

Explain to students that the U.S. government may intervene in the economy. Distribute the "Eminent Domain" worksheet (Unit 1 All-in-One, p. 102).

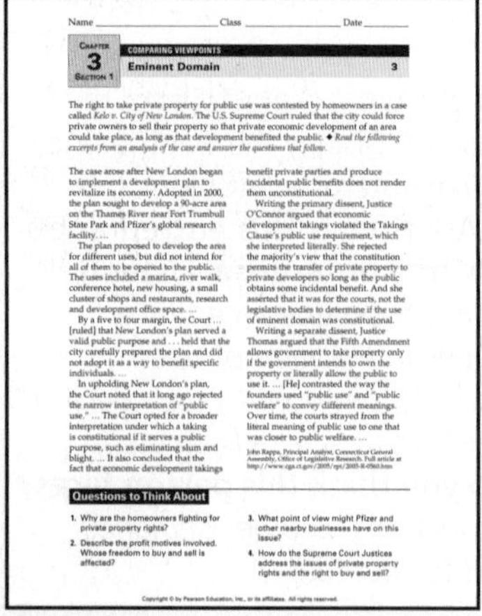

Name ________ Class ________ Date ________

CHAPTER 3 SECTION 1

COMPARING VIEWPOINTS

Eminent Domain 3

The right to take private property for public use was contested by homeowners in a case called *Kelo v. City of New London.* The U.S. Supreme Court ruled that the city could force private owners to sell their property so that private economic development of an area could take place, as long as that development benefited the public. ◆ *Read the following excerpts from an analysis of the case and answer the questions that follow.*

The case arose after New London began to implement a development plan to revitalize its economy. Adopted in 2000, the plan sought to develop a 90-acre area on the Thames River near Fort Trumbull State Park and Pfizer's global research facility. …

The plan proposed to develop the area for different uses, but did not intend for all of them to be opened to the public. The uses included a marina, river walk, conference hotel, new housing, a small cluster of shops and restaurants, research and development office space. …

By a five to four margin, the Court … [ruled] that New London's plan served a valid public purpose and … held that the city carefully prepared the plan and did not adopt it as a way to benefit specific individuals. …

In upholding New London's plan, the Court noted that it long ago rejected the narrow interpretation of "public use." … The Court opted for a broader interpretation under which a taking is constitutional if it serves a public purpose, such as eliminating slum and blight. … It also concluded that the fact that economic development takings benefit private parties and produce incidental public benefits does not render them unconstitutional.

Writing the primary dissent, Justice O'Connor argued that economic development takings violated the Takings Clause's public use requirement, which she interpreted literally. She rejected the majority's view that the constitution permits the transfer of private property to private developers so long as the public obtains some incidental benefit. And she asserted that it was for the courts, not the legislative bodies to determine if the use of eminent domain was constitutional.

Writing a separate dissent, Justice Thomas argued that the Fifth Amendment allows government to take property only if the government intends to own the property or literally allow the public to use it. … [He] contrasted the way the founders used "public use" and "public welfare" to convey different meanings. Over time, the courts strayed from the literal meaning of public use to one that was closer to public welfare. …

John Rappa, Principal Analyst, Connecticut General Assembly, Office of Legislative Research. Full article at http://www.cga.ct.gov/2005/rpt/2005-R-0560.htm

Questions to Think About

1. Why are the homeowners fighting for private property rights?
2. Describe the profit motives involved. Whose freedom to buy and sell is affected?
3. What point of view might Pfizer and other nearby businesses have on this issue?
4. How do the Supreme Court Justices address the issues of private property rights and the right to buy and sell?

L2 Differentiate Distribute the "Eminent Domain" worksheet (Unit 1 All-in-One, p. 103).

interest group a private organization that tries to persuade public officials to act in ways that benefit its members

patriotism love of one's country

eminent domain the right of a government to take private property for public use

Consumers can also make their wishes known by joining an **interest group,** a private organization that tries to persuade public officials to act in ways that benefit its members. One consumer interest group is the Consumers Union, which works to persuade political leaders to pass laws to protect consumers.

Businesses form interest groups as well. For instance, the National Retail Federation represents more than 1.6 million firms, from groceries to department stores. Interest groups have also formed around many economic issues, such as taxation, land use, and aid to farmers.

CHECKPOINT ***What role do consumers play in the free enterprise system?***

FUTURE WATCH **Global Impact**

Free Enterprise in the World

How free is American free enterprise? According to the World Bank, the answer is—very free. The World Bank has ranked 178 nations according to how freely businesses can operate independent of government regulation. On this Ease of Doing Business Index, the U.S. comes in third. ***What are the advantages and disadvantages of allowing businesses to operate with few government limits?***

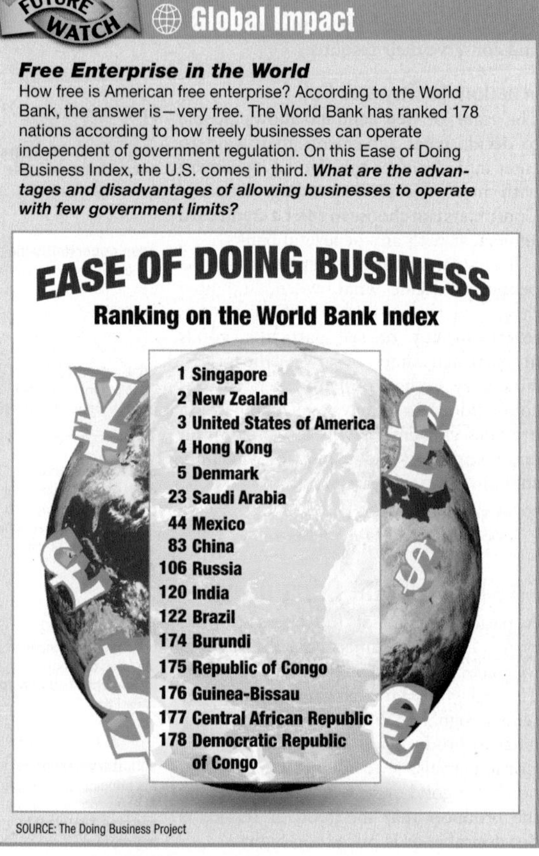

EASE OF DOING BUSINESS
Ranking on the World Bank Index
1 Singapore
2 New Zealand
3 United States of America
4 Hong Kong
5 Denmark
23 Saudi Arabia
44 Mexico
83 China
106 Russia
120 India
122 Brazil
174 Burundi
175 Republic of Congo
176 Guinea-Bissau
177 Central African Republic
178 Democratic Republic of Congo

SOURCE: The Doing Business Project

Economic Freedom and the Constitution

The economic freedoms that Americans enjoy are an important source of **patriotism,** or love of one's country. The rights to own property or to become an entrepreneur are as basic to liberty as freedom of speech or the right to vote. According to a leading economist, these rights cannot be separated:

> **"Economic freedom plays a dual role in the promotion of a free society. On the one hand, freedom in economic arrangements is … an end in itself. In the second place, economic freedom is also an indispensable means toward the achievement of political freedom."**
>
> — Milton Friedman, *Capitalism and Freedom*

Rights that allow people to engage in business activity are written into the framework of our nation: the Constitution. Perhaps the most important of these is the constitutional recognition of property rights.

Property Rights

In many countries, the government has the power to seize property for its own use. To prevent this, early American leaders protected private property under the Bill of Rights. The Fifth Amendment states that "no person shall be … deprived of life, liberty, or property, without due process of law; nor shall private property be taken for public use, without just compensation."

The Fifth Amendment was originally applied only to the federal government. The Fourteenth Amendment, ratified in 1868, extended the same limitations to the state governments.

These due process clauses prevent the government from taking property from its owner except when there is a public reason. For instance, when a state wants to add lanes to a highway, it may take land from people who own property along the route. This right of a government to take private property for public use is called **eminent domain.** Even then, the government must pay the person the fair value of the property that has been taken. This protection applies to businesses as well as to individuals.

Answers

Checkpoint The consumer's role is to signal to producers what to make and how much to make through decisions to purchase—or not to purchase—goods and services.

Global Impact Students' answers will vary, but they should give at least one example of a positive or negative consequence of government regulation.

Innovators

Oscar de la Renta

Like many entrepreneurs, Oscar de la Renta had a vision—and was willing to take risks to pursue it. For this enterprising immigrant, America truly proved to be a land of opportunity.

Born in the Dominican Republic, de la Renta showed a talent for art. His parents sent him to Spain to study painting. But he became fascinated with fashion, and soon found work with a famous Spanish designer. His early career was spent designing for the rich.

In 1963, de la Renta moved to New York to work for another designer. "I came to America," he said, "because I felt the future was not [high fashion]. It was ready-to-wear." Two years later, he struck out on his own. His "off-the-rack" dresses quickly won awards. His clients have included three First Ladies and a long list of celebrities—but also thousands of middle income women.

Oscar de la Renta has never lost his interest in the arts, giving generously of his time as a board member of New York's Metropolitan Opera and Carnegie Hall. Nor has he forgotten his Latin roots. He served as chairman of the Spanish Institute, and helped build a school and day-care center for underprivileged Dominican children.

Critical Thinking: ***How did the American economy provide an environment for Oscar de la Renta's success?***

Fast Facts

Oscar de la Renta
Born: July 22, 1932, in Santo Domingo, Dominican Republic
Education: Academy of San Fernando, Madrid, Spain
Claim to Fame: Successful fashion designer

Taxation

The Constitution also spells out how government can tax individuals and businesses. Congress has the power to tax only in the ways the Constitution allows.

Article I gives Congress the power to levy taxes. However, Section 9 requires that direct taxes be apportioned to states according to population. Thus, taxes collected from each state would be based on the number of people living in the state. This rule initially prevented Congress from passing an income tax, which would be a direct tax.

The Sixteenth Amendment, ratified in 1913, first gave Congress the right to set direct taxes based on income. Under current law, both individuals and corporations must pay federal income tax.

Contracts

Finally, the Constitution guarantees people and businesses the right to make contracts, which are legally binding agreements between people or businesses. Article I, Section 10 prohibits the states from passing any "Law impairing the Obligation of Contracts." This means that individuals or businesses cannot use the political process to get excused from their contracts. No legislature can pass a law changing the terms of someone's business agreement.

CHECKPOINT ***What constitutional protections make it possible for Americans to conduct business?***

The Role of Government in the Marketplace

The government's first role in the American free enterprise system is to carry out its constitutional responsibilities to protect property rights, contracts, and other business activities. Over time, Americans have come to expect the government to take other actions to promote the **public interest,** or the concerns of society as a whole. The government has passed laws to protect us from economic problems that affect us all, such as pollution or unsafe foods and medicines.

Information and Free Enterprise

In a free market system, consumer buying decisions determine what goods get produced. But consumers cannot make informed choices if they do not have

Simulation *Activity*

Whose Property Is It?
You may be asked to take part in a role-playing game about the incentives and responsibilities of owning property.

public interest the concerns of society as a whole

The purpose of this activity is to have students discuss government intervention in the free enterprise system (private property rights, the freedom to buy and sell, legal equality, profit motive) in the context of a contentious issue. After going over the worksheet, ask **Which side do you agree with and why? When should eminent domain be used?** Discuss with the class as a whole or have students work in small groups with a class wrap-up.

L1 L2 Differentiate Remind students to use the Visual Glossary as needed during the discussion.

L3 Differentiate Have students demonstrate how ownership of property creates incentives and responsibilities using the simulation "Whose Property Is It?" (Simulation Activities, Chapter 3).

MAKE CONNECTIONS

Now that students have examined an example of government intervention in the economy, review the Bellringer answers. Discuss the ways that students see the government affecting their economic lives.

Divide the class into three or more groups. Have each group record the main ideas under one of the following sections: Information and Free Enterprise; Protecting Public Health, Safety, and Well-Being; Negative Effects of Regulation. Using the information in their section have each group answer the question **How does government intervention affect the economy?** Discuss each section and have each group share their summary.

Virtual Economics

L3 Differentiate

Understanding Property Rights Use the following lesson from the NCEE **Virtual Economics *CD-ROM*** to analyze characteristics of a market economy. Click on Browse Economics Lessons, specify grades 9–12, and use the key words *property rights.*

In this activity, students will participate in a simulation demonstrating how property rights affect incentives and behavior.

LESSON TITLE	PROPERTY RIGHTS IN A MARKET ECONOMY
Type of Activity	Simulation
Complexity	Moderate
Time	60 minutes
NCEE Standards	4, 9, 10

Answers

Critical Thinking Possible response: The free market provided de la Renta with the freedom to "strike out on his own" in New York.

Checkpoint rules guaranteeing property rights, identifying the government's power of taxation, and protecting contracts

READING A CHART

Using the chart on this page, have students identify the types of business or economic activity each agency would oversee, and why each agency needs to intervene in the marketplace.

L4 Differentiate Have students research and prepare a report on one of the following agencies: the Environmental Protection Agency, the Food and Drug Administration, the Federal Trade Commission, the Federal Communications Commission, and the Federal Aviation Administration. Have them identify why these agencies were created, the ways they have addressed social issues or concerns, and any remaining issues that the agencies are struggling with today.

DRAW CONCLUSIONS

Ask **What benefits and costs does government regulation have on both consumers and businesses?** Call on individuals to share their answers with the class.

EXTEND

Ask students to imagine they are entrepreneurs who are starting their own company. Have them identify which government agencies and regulations they would need to consider.

GUIDING QUESTION WRAP UP

Have students return to the section Guiding Question. Review the completed graphic organizer and clarify any misunderstandings. Have a wrap up discussion about the benefits of free enterprise.

Assess and Remediate

L4 Collect the "Constitutional Connections" worksheet and assess student understanding of government protections of free enterprise.

L3 L2 Collect the "Eminent Domain" worksheets and assess student understanding of conflicts between private property rights, profit motive, and other free enterprise characteristics.

L3 Assign the Section 1 Assessment questions; identify student misconceptions.

L3 Give Section Quiz A (Unit 1 All-in-One, p. 104).

L2 Give Section Quiz B (Unit 1 All-in-One, p. 105).

(Assess and Remediate continued on p. 55)

Answers

Chart Skills 1. Possible responses: (a) FDA, FAA, CPSC; (b) FTC, FDIC; (c) EEOC 2. by making sure broadcast communication conforms to standards so that consumers can receive the signals

Figure 3.1 Major Federal Regulatory Agencies

Agency and Date Created	Role
1906 Food and Drug Administration (FDA)	Sets and provides standards for food, drugs, and cosmetic products
1913 Federal Reserve System (FED)	Regulates banking and manages the money supply
1914 Federal Trade Commission (FTC)	Enacts and enforces antitrust laws to protect consumers
1933 Federal Deposit Insurance Corporation (FDIC)	Insures bank deposits, approves mergers, and audits banking practices
1934 Federal Communication Commission (FCC)	Regulates interstate and international communications by radio, television, wire, satellite, and cable
1934 Securities and Exchange Commission (SEC)	Administers federal laws concerning the buying and selling of securities
1935 National Labor Relations Board (NLRB)	Prevents or corrects unfair labor practices by either employers or unions
1958 Federal Aviation Administration (FAA)	Regulates civil aviation, air-traffic and piloting standards, and air commerce
1964 Equal Employment Opportunity Commission (EEOC)	Promotes equal job opportunity through enforcement of civil rights laws, education, and other programs
1970 Environmental Protection Agency (EPA)	Enacts policies to protect human health and the natural environment
1970 Occupational Safety and Health Administration (OSHA)	Enacts policies to save lives, prevent injuries, and protect the health of workers
1972 Consumer Product Safety Commission (CPSC)	Enacts policies for reducing risks of harm from consumer products
1974 Nuclear Regulatory Commission (NRC)	Regulates civilian use of nuclear products
1995 Surface Transportation Board (STB)	Resolves railroad rate and service disputes and reviews proposed mergers. Oversees certain trucking company, moving van, and shipping company rates

SOURCE: The White House and "Foundations of Business Administration," Professor Bauer-Ramazani

CHART SKILLS

All of these agencies represent ways the federal government intervenes in the marketplace.

1. **Identify one agency meant to protect each of the following: (a) public safety, (b) fair competition, (c) equality.**
2. **How do you think the FCC promotes the public interest?**

basic information about the products they are buying. In other words, educated consumers make the free market system work more efficiently. Because of this, one of the government's important roles in the economy is to make sure that producers provide consumers with information.

public disclosure laws laws requiring companies to provide information about their products or services

Toward this end, Congress has passed **public disclosure laws,** which require companies to give consumers important information about the products or services that they offer. Often this information is attached to the product when it is offered for sale. You may have seen energy efficiency tags on refrigerators, or heard car commercials in which the announcer reads off a long list of terms and conditions. Using this information, consumers can evaluate some important aspects of the products they are thinking about buying.

Other laws require businesses to make the information they supply honest and clear. The Federal Trade Commission Act says that advertisements cannot be deceptive. The Truth-in-Lending Act requires businesses offering loans to disclose certain information to consumers before they sign a loan agreement. Consumers use this information to protect themselves from false claims.

Protecting Public Health, Safety, and Well-Being

Although the government does not get directly involved in running private businesses, it does place some limits on their actions in the public interest. For example, the federal government and many states are actively involved in passing laws aimed at protecting consumers. The government sets manufacturing standards, requires that drugs be safe and effective, and supervises the conditions in which foods are produced to make sure they are sanitary. Labels on consumer packages must include information about safe operation of equipment or expiration dates for perishables.

A variety of federal and state agencies regulate industries whose goods and services affect the public interest. (See **Figure 3.1.**) For example, in response to growing public concern about the environment, the federal government formed the Environmental Protection Agency (EPA) in 1970. Businesses must follow certain rules set by the EPA or by state agencies to protect the environment. Gas stations, for example, must dispose of used motor oil properly and ensure that gas tanks cannot leak into surrounding soil.

Background Note

OSHA (Occupational Safety and Health Administration) is responsible for helping employers establish safe working conditions. It provides guidelines for job safety analysis. OSHA suggests the following set of questions for job hazard analysis: What can go wrong? What are the consequences? How could it happen? What are other contributing factors? How likely is it that the hazard will recur? OSHA will send investigators to review working conditions under extreme conditions. For example, a collapse of construction cranes that results in serious injury or death triggers OSHA investigations.

Both individuals and businesses are subject to local zoning laws. Cities and towns often pass laws designating that certain areas can be used for residential or business purposes only. Zoning laws may forbid homeowners from running certain businesses out of their homes.

Negative Effects of Regulation

During the 1960s and 1970s, popular demand for government protection of consumers and of the environment resulted in the creation of several new governmental agencies and regulations. Government regulation, however, can have negative effects on both businesses and consumers. Businesses pointed out that the rules were costly to implement, cutting into profits and slowing growth. Highly regulated industries, such as the airlines and telephone companies, said that government rules and regulations stifled competition, resulting in prices that were unnecessarily high. The growth in government oversight of industry also raised government spending because the government had to hire workers to do the work.

In the 1980s and 1990s, public pressure for leaner, less costly government resulted in budget cuts that curtailed some government regulation of industry. Today, the government works to balance concerns raised by businesses with the need to protect the public.

ACCOUNTING
DAVE CARPENTER...
" IT LOOKS LIKE THEY'RE BRINGING IN THE NEW REGULATIONS MANUAL. "

▲ Federal regulation requires the creation of complex rules and standards. ***What is this cartoonist's view of federal regulation?***

CHECKPOINT ***Why does the government place some limits on the freedom of businesses?***

SECTION 1 ASSESSMENT

Essential Questions Journal To continue to build a response to the Essential Question, go to your **Essential Questions Journal**.

Guiding Question

1. Use your completed chart to answer this question: What are the benefits of free enterprise?
2. **Extension** Identify which benefits of free enterprise you are enjoying if you **(a)** quit your job in order to take a different job at a higher salary, **(b)** buy a car from your neighbor, **(c)** sign a petition urging your county government to lower property taxes.

Key Terms and Main Ideas

3. How is the **profit motive** the driving force of the American economy?
4. How is the principle of **open opportunity** different from guaranteeing success to everyone in the marketplace?
5. How does the principle of **voluntary exchange** promote competition?
6. What is an **interest group?**
7. What kinds of information are required by **public disclosure laws?**

Critical Thinking

8. **Apply** How can inequality or discrimination hurt an economy's ability to maximize its human capital? Give two examples.
9. **Analyze** How do the decisions you make as a consumer affect the economy?
10. **Predict** What do you think might happen if the government passed a law saying it could overturn the terms of an existing contract between companies?

Quick Write

11. Create a two-column list. On one side, write the basic personal and political rights guaranteed to Americans. On the other side, list basic economic rights under the free enterprise system. Then, write a paragraph explaining in your own words how the two sets of rights are linked.

Have students complete the Self-Test Online and continue their work in the **Essential Questions Journal**.

REMEDIATION AND SUGGESTIONS

Use the chart below to help students who are struggling with content.

WEAKNESS	REMEDIATION
Defining key terms (Questions 3, 4, 5, 6, 7)	Have students use the interactive Economic Dictionary Online.
Characteristics of the free enterprise system (Questions 1, 2)	Have students role-play a scene that relates to each of the characteristics of the free enterprise system
What role consumers play in the American economy (Question 9)	Ask students to consider that each time they spend money they are voting for the product they buy. Ask why their choices affect the economy.
How the Constitution protects economic freedom (Questions 10, 11)	Reteach by having students create a chart summarizing the sections on Property Rights, Taxation, and Contracts. Discuss their summaries to assess comprehension.
Government intervention in the marketplace (Questions 7, 10)	Have students review the regulatory agencies and name one hazard they might face if that agency did not exist.

Answers

Political Cartoon Sample answer: There are too many regulations.

Checkpoint It does so to protect the public.

Assessment Answers

1. Possible responses: a wide variety of goods at reasonable prices, people creating their own businesses
2. (a) open opportunity (b) voluntary exchange; (c) legal equality
3. Possible response: People are motivated to launch or improve businesses by the opportunity to improve their material well-being.
4. Possible response: Open opportunity gives people a chance to try, but other factors determine success.
5. Since consumers can choose to buy from anyone, many businesses will compete to make a sale.
6. an organization that tries to influence the government to help its cause
7. Possible responses: energy efficiency, nutritional information
8. Possible responses: Without equality, people are prevented from pursuing their economic goals. They might remain in low-paying jobs rather than lead corporations. Discrimination allows one group to make all economic decisions.
9. Possible response: Consumer choices determine successful products and services.
10. Possible response: Businesses unhappy with contracts would use the government to get out of their obligations.
11. Answer will include a two-column list describing basic personal and political rights and their corresponding economic rights. The paragraph will link the two sets of rights.

Guiding Question

How does the U.S. government encourage growth and stability?

Get Started

Promoting Economic Strength		
Employment	**Growth**	**Stability and Security**
• Goal: providing jobs for all able workers • Actions: steps to encourage job growth if needed	• Goal: later generations to have a better standard of living • Actions: increase spending or cut taxes	• Goal: stable prices and financial institutions to build confidence • Actions: prevent price fluctuations, monitor and regulate banks

LESSON GOALS

Students will:

- Know the Key Terms.
- Predict how the government uses data about the business cycle to promote economic strength.
- Identify influences on productivity.

BEFORE CLASS

Have students complete the graphic organizer in the Section Opener as they read the text. As an alternate activity, have students complete the Guided Reading and Review worksheet (Unit 1 All-in-One, p. 106).

L1 L2 ELL LPR Differentiate Have students complete the Guided Reading and Review worksheet (Unit 1 All-in-One, p. 107).

Answer

Caption The government building, because macroeconomics concerns a nation's whole economy.

CLASSROOM HINTS

THE EFFECTS OF TECHNOLOGY

Technology provides a competitive edge to many American businesses by allowing manufacturers to increase production and expand their capabilities. There have also been some costs associated with these innovations. To help students organize their thoughts on this subject have them create a chart listing the positive and negative effects of using computers in business. Then ask **What actions can business owners and the government take to encourage positive outcomes with technology?**

SECTION 2 Promoting Growth and Stability

OBJECTIVES

1. **Explain** why the government tracks and seeks to influence business cycles.
2. **Describe** how the government promotes economic strength.
3. **Analyze** the factors that increase productivity.

ECONOMIC DICTIONARY

As you read the section, look for the definitions of these **Key Terms:**

- macroeconomics
- microeconomics
- gross domestic product
- business cycle
- referendum
- obsolescence
- patent
- copyright
- work ethic

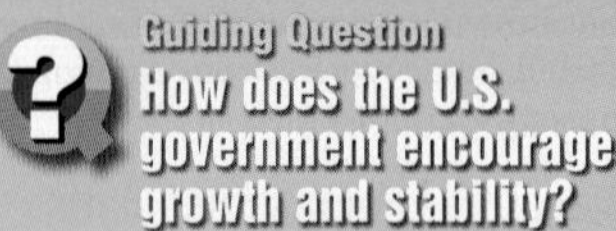
Guiding Question
How does the U.S. government encourage growth and stability?

Copy this flowchart and fill it in as you read. Add more boxes if necessary.

Promoting Economic Strength		
Employment	**Growth**	**Stability and Security**
• Goal: providing jobs for all able workers • Actions: steps to encourage job growth if needed	• Goal: • Actions:	• Goal: • Actions:

macroeconomics the study of economic behavior and decision-making in a nation's whole economy

microeconomics the study of the economic behavior and decision-making in small units, such as households and firms

Economics and You

Yesterday you bought a pack of gum . . . or a new guitar . . . or your first car. Your purchase was just one of millions of exchanges that took place across the country that day. These patterns of buying and selling are tracked by government economists who use the information to assess the state of the American economy.

Principles in Action Tracking economic data is one tool the government uses to promote economic growth and stability. As you will see, supporting education is another economic role taken by the government. You will also see how your participation in the electoral process can help to shape the economy.

Tracking Business Cycles

Even under our free enterprise system, the government intervenes to influence macroeconomic trends. **Macroeconomics** is the study of economic behavior and decision-making in a nation's whole economy. By contrast, **microeconomics** is the study of economic behavior and decision-making in small units, such as households and firms. (The prefix *macro-* means "large," while *micro-* means "small.")

The two major branches of economics are macroeconomics and microeconomics. ***Which of these pictures represents macroeconomics? Explain.*** ▼

Focus on the Basics

Students need to come away with the following understandings:

FACTS: • Microeconomics is the study of small economic units, while macroeconomics is the study of a country's whole economy. • The government collects economic data to predict business cycles. • The government creates public policies to promote employment and economic growth, and to ensure a stable economy. • Technology, innovation, and a strong work ethic produce America's high productivity rates.

GENERALIZATION: The economy is influenced by governmental actions.

GDP and the Business Cycle

One measure of a nation's economic well-being is **gross domestic product** (GDP), the total value of all final goods and services produced in a country in a given year. In a period of macroeconomic expansion, or growth, a country produces more than it did before and GDP goes up. (See **Figure 3.2.**) In a period of contraction, or decline, the country produces less and GDP goes down. This pattern of a period of expansion, or growth, followed by a period of contraction, or decline, is called a **business cycle.**

Unlike the day-to-day ups and downs of the stock market, business cycles are major fluctuations. Each phase can last months or even years. (You will learn more about GDP and the business cycle in Chapter 12.)

Making Predictions

Changes in the business cycles take place because individuals and businesses, acting in their own self-interest, make decisions about factors such as prices, production, and consumption. Business owners who think consumers are going to spend more in the future may increase production and hire more workers. If enough employers take these steps, the economy grows. On the other hand, concern about rising prices might lead consumers to buy fewer goods. If this decrease in consumer spending is widespread and lasts long enough, suppliers might be forced to cut production and lay off workers.

In Washington, armies of government economists track where the country is in the business cycle and try to predict what will happen in the future. They give this information to public officials so they can decide what actions to take—if any.

CHECKPOINT ***Why do government experts track the business cycle?***

Promoting Economic Strength

Because the market is vulnerable to business cycles, the government tries to create public policies that promote economic strength. Policymakers do so by pursuing three main goals: high employment, growth, and stability.

Figure 3.2 **Gross Domestic Product, 1900–2006**

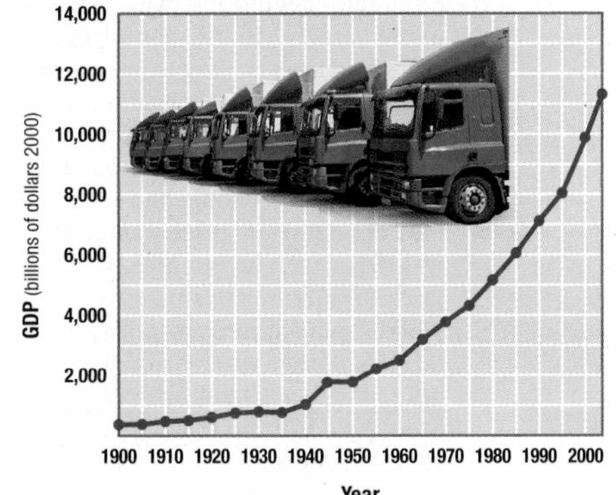

SOURCE: Louis D. Johnston and Samuel H. Williamson, "What Was the U.S. GDP Then?" MeasuringWorth.Com, 2007.

GRAPH SKILLS

A growing GDP is one sign of a healthy economy.

1. How much did the GDP grow between 1990 and 2006?
2. Which periods on this graph may represent downturns in the business cycle?

Action Graph online For an animated version of this graph, visit **PearsonSuccessNet.com**

Employment

One aim of government economic policy is to ensure jobs for everyone who is able to work. In the United States, many economists consider an unemployment rate of between 4 percent and 6 percent to be evidence of a healthy economy. If the unemployment rate rises higher than that, government officials may take steps to encourage job growth.

Economic Growth

Part of the American Dream has always been for each generation to enjoy a higher standard of living than that of previous generations. For that to happen, the economy must grow to provide additional goods and services to succeeding generations. An increasing GDP is a sign of such growth. To help growth, the government may cut taxes or increase spending. Experts often disagree as to which approach stimulates economic growth more effectively.

gross domestic product the total value of all final goods and services produced in a country in a given year

business cycle a period of macroeconomic expansion, or growth, followed by one of contraction, or decline

Differentiated Resources

L1 **L2** **Guided Reading and Review** (Unit 1 All-in-One, p. 107)

L2 **GDP and Business Cycles** (Unit 1 All-in-One, p. 109)

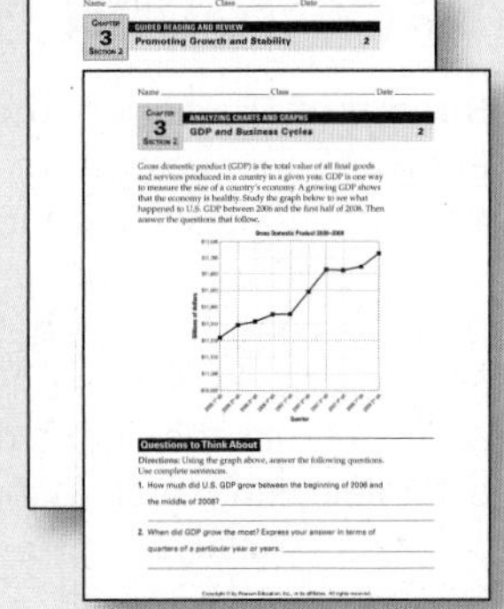

BELLRINGER

Write the following two headlines on the chalkboard:

American Economy Weakening

U.S. Economy Showing Signs of Strength

Have students make a list of things that they might see or hear in the news or in their community that would support either statement.

Teach

Economics online To present this topic using digital resources, use the lecture notes at www.PearsonSuccessNet.com.

REVIEW THE BELLRINGER ANSWERS

Poll students for their answers to the Bellringer. Have students compare their answers. Use this as a springboard to discuss what goals the government should pursue in order to strengthen the national economy. Ask **Why do some people oppose strong government action?** *(Students should recognize that supporters of free enterprise believe the system works best with minimal government intervention.)*

ANALYZE A GRAPH

Review the definition of *gross domestic product.* Ask **What data is on the graph in Figure 3.2?** *(the GDP in five year intervals from 1900 to 2006)* Ask **What trend does the data show?** *(It appears that GDP has generally gone up.)* Ask **What does GDP indicate about an economy's success or failure?** *(The GDP indicates whether the economy as a whole, over a given decade, has grown or shrunk.)* Ask **What has to happen for the economy to grow?** *(Businesses have to produce more goods and services than they did in the previous quarter.)*

L1 **L2** **Differentiate** After reviewing the graph, have students create a word web to describe in their own words the definition of GDP.

Action Graph online Have students review the Action Graph animation for a step-by-step look at Gross Domestic Product.

Answers

Checkpoint They want to see where the country is in the business cycle and try to predict what will happen in the future.

Graph Skills 1. Approximately 4 trillion dollars 2. 1930–1935 and 1945–1950

EXPLAIN

The changes in the GDP allow us to measure how businesses in the country as a whole are doing. Ask **How would you describe a business cycle?** *(a period of expansion, or growth, followed by a period of contraction, or decline)* Ask **What tool do we use to define a business cycle?** *(GDP)*

Distribute the "GDP and Business Cycles" worksheet (Unit 1 All-in-One, p.108).

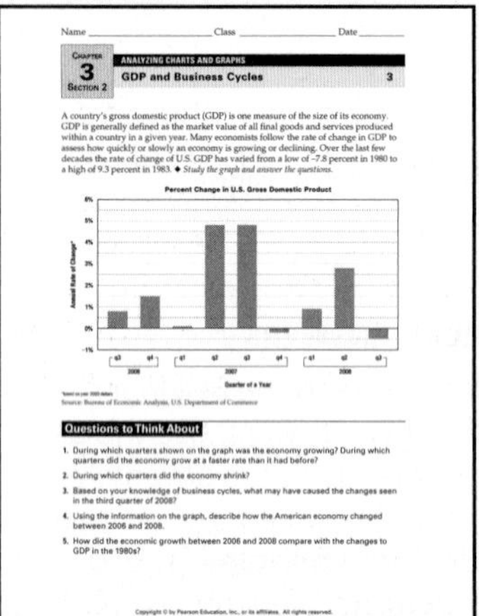

Name ______________ Class ______________ Date ________

Chapter 3 Section 2 — ANALYZING CHARTS AND GRAPHS

GDP and Business Cycles 3

A country's gross domestic product (GDP) is one measure of the size of its economy. GDP is generally defined as the market value of all final goods and services produced within a country in a given year. Many economists follow the rate of change in GDP to assess how quickly or slowly an economy is growing or declining. Over the last few decades the rate of change of U.S. GDP has varied from a low of –7.8 percent in 1980 to a high of 9.3 percent in 1983. ◆ *Study the graph and answer the questions.*

Percent Change in U.S. Gross Domestic Product

Source: Bureau of Economic Analysis, U.S. Department of Commerce

Questions to Think About

1. During which quarters shown on the graph was the economy growing? During which quarters did the economy grow at a faster rate than it had before?
2. During which quarters did the economy shrink?
3. Based on your knowledge of business cycles, what may have caused the changes seen in the third quarter of 2008?
4. Using the information on the graph, describe how the American economy changed between 2006 and 2008.
5. How did the economic growth between 2006 and 2008 compare with the changes to GDP in the 1980s?

L2 Differentiate Distribute the "GDP and Business Cycles" worksheet (Unit 1 All-in-One, p. 109).

Have students work in groups to complete it. Then discuss how the GDP relates to the business cycle. Ask **Why would the government want to influence the business cycle?** *(to keep the economy stable)* **How might the government use the information shown in the worksheet graph to promote economic strength?** *(Possible responses: The government might take action to stimulate higher rates of growth, such as encouraging job growth; adjusting taxes, government spending, or prices; or regulating financial institutions and the interest rate)*

READ AND DISCUSS

Have students read sections aloud about steps the government can take to promote strength and stability. Write the responses on the board.

Ask **Which of these is easiest to implement? Which one do you think is the most effective? Why?**

Answers

Checkpoint high employment, steady growth, and stability through stable prices and secure financial institutions

Future Watch current economic conditions, how existing and potential economic policies affect society in general and themselves personally, and what their personal priorities are

referendum a proposed law submitted directly to the public

Stability and Security

The government also seeks to keep the economy stable. Consumers, producers, and investors need to feel confident that economic conditions will not fluctuate unpredictably. If this confidence wavers, economic growth may slow or even stop.

One indicator of economic stability is the general level of prices. A surge in overall prices puts a strain on consumers, especially poor people and those on fixed incomes. But if prices sink, producers feel the pain. For example, a jump in the price of milk hurts families with children, while a plunge in milk prices hurts dairy farmers. Either way, major fluctuations in price levels can send problems across the economy. The government thus seeks to prevent sudden, drastic shifts in prices.

Another sign of economic stability is the security of our financial institutions, such as banks or the stock market. Imagine going to the bank and finding it boarded up and empty. When we make a bank deposit or a stock purchase, we want to know that our money will be protected from fraud or mismanagement and shielded from the damaging effects of sudden economic downturns.

To provide such protections, the federal government monitors and regulates banks and other financial institutions. Some regulations protect bank deposits and retirees' pensions. Federal regulators also investigate fraud and manage interest rates and the flow of money through the economy. You will learn more about these functions in later chapters.

Economic Citizenship

Economic policy is made by elected officials and the workers they appoint. But it is the voters who put these officials in office. On a state and local level, voters have an even more direct say. Ballots often include **referendums,** proposed laws submitted directly to the public, on spending or other economic issues.

Voters, then, play a vital role in shaping government economic actions. Like others in a market economy, voters make choices based on self-interest. To fully determine what policies best serve their interests, Americans must understand the macroeconomic processes that shape our futures.

✔ **CHECKPOINT** ***What three goals does the government try to meet when promoting economic strength?***

The people you elect will make vital decisions that affect your economic well-being. In addition, you may be asked to vote directly on important economic issues. ***What will you need to know in order to make sensible choices?*** ▼

FUTURE WATCH **Your Vote Counts**

58

Background Note

Bureau of Economic Analysis The Bureau of Economic Analysis (BEA), an agency in the U.S. Department of Commerce, is responsible for compiling and reporting the gross domestic product and other economic statistics. It uses data from many sources, including other governmental agencies. The GDP has four components: personal consumption, businesses' capital investments, government spending, and exports. Personal consumption accounts for 70 percent of the GDP. The BEA also publishes the details of the GDP's components. These show trends in smaller economic units, such as in one industry or region.

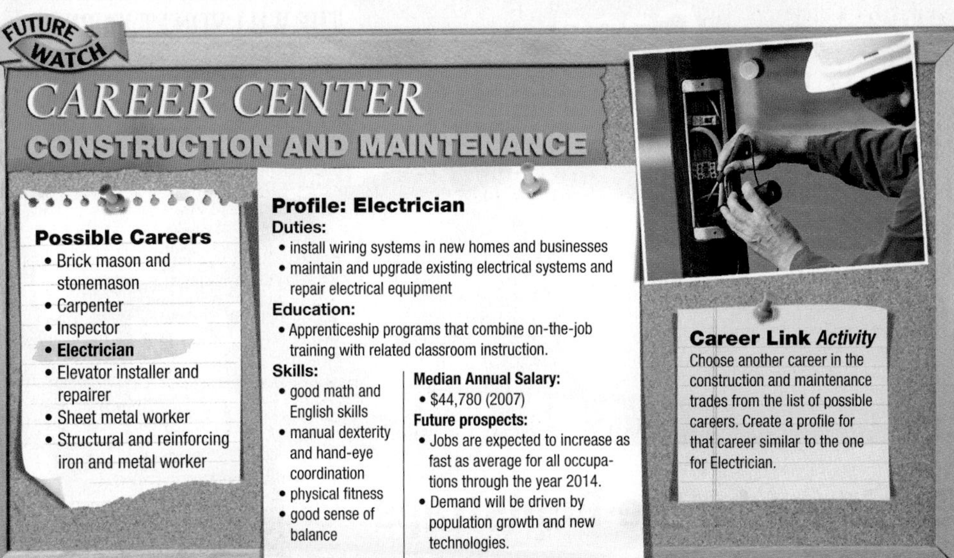
FUTURE WATCH
CAREER CENTER
CONSTRUCTION AND MAINTENANCE
Possible Careers
• Brick mason and stonemason
• Carpenter
• Inspector
• Electrician
• Elevator installer and repairer
• Sheet metal worker
• Structural and reinforcing iron and metal worker
Profile: Electrician
Duties:
• install wiring systems in new homes and businesses
• maintain and upgrade existing electrical systems and repair electrical equipment
Education:
• Apprenticeship programs that combine on-the-job training with related classroom instruction.
Skills:
• good math and English skills
• manual dexterity and hand-eye coordination
• physical fitness
• good sense of balance
Median Annual Salary:
• $44,780 (2007)
Future prospects:
• Jobs are expected to increase as fast as average for all occupations through the year 2014.
• Demand will be driven by population growth and new technologies.
Career Link Activity
Choose another career in the construction and maintenance trades from the list of possible careers. Create a profile for that career similar to the one for Electrician.

Technology and Productivity

The American economy supports a far higher standard of living, in terms of GDP, than most economies of the world. As you read in Chapter 1, one way to preserve that high standard is by increasing productivity—producing more outputs from the same or a smaller quantity of inputs.

Technological Progress

Improved technology is a key factor in boosting productivity. Technological progress has long enabled the economy of the United States to operate more efficiently, increasing GDP and giving American businesses a competitive advantage in the world.

American history is full of innovations that improved productivity. Thomas Edison's invention of the light bulb made a longer workday possible. Henry Ford's use of the assembly line led to mass production of affordable cars. In recent times, computers have allowed workers to do more work in a shorter amount of time.

Innovation often leads to **obsolescence,** as older products and processes become out-of-date. Workers, too, may be subject to obsolescence. One example is telephone operators who lost their jobs due to computerized dialing systems. Still, these physical and human resources can be used in other ways. Old industrial buildings can be converted into stores or apartments. Workers can be retrained to do other jobs.

The Government's Role

To help maintain the country's technological advantage, the government promotes innovation and invention. Federal agencies fund scores of research and development projects at universities. The Morrill Acts of 1862 and 1890 created land-grant colleges that received federal land and money to pursue the study of "agriculture and the mechanical arts." Land-grant schools from the Massachusetts Institute of Technology to Texas A&M University have been powerhouses of innovation.

The government's own research institutions also produce a steady stream of new technologies. Probably the best-known of these federal institutions is the National Aeronautics and Space Administration (NASA). Technologies created by NASA, as part of the effort to send satellites and humans into space, have produced amazing spin-offs, or products with commercial uses. NASA

obsolescence situation in which older products and processes become out-of-date

SUMMARIZE AND LOCATE EXAMPLES

Help students understand the government's interest in constantly improving economic productivity. As the population grows, more people seek a higher standard of living, so productivity must increase.

Divide the class into three groups. Have each group focus on one of the three Technology and Productivity sections. Each group should create and present a poster that includes a summary of their section and two examples beyond those given.

SUMMARY ACTIVITY

Post headlines from local newspapers about actions the government is taking concerning economic growth and stability (such as bank takeovers, tax refunds, housing crisis). Based on the headlines, where do you think we are in the business cycle? Is our economy growing or shrinking? What should the government do about this? Collect responses, and discuss them with the class.

EXTEND

Have students research a period of great technological innovation and improved productivity, the Industrial Revolution. Ask students to write a paper identifying the causes of the Industrial Revolution, and its economic, political, and cultural effects on American society.

GUIDING QUESTION WRAP UP

Have students return to the section Guiding Question. Review the completed graphic organizer and clarify any misunderstandings. Have a wrap up discussion about how the U.S. government encourages growth and sustainability.

CREATE A PROFILE

Have students use the Career Link worksheet to record their research for the activity (Unit 1 All-in-one, p. 134).

Assess and Remediate

L3 L2 Collect the "GDP and Business Cycles" worksheets and assess student understanding of the economic indicators the government uses to assess and promote growth.

L3 Collect the Career Link worksheet.

L3 Assign the Section 2 Assessment questions; identify student misconceptions.

L3 Give Section Quiz A (Unit 1 All-in-One, p. 110).

L2 Give Section Quiz B (Unit 1 All-in-One, p. 111).

(Assess and Remediate continued on p. 61)

Virtual Economics

L2 Differentiate

Determining Gross Domestic Product Use the following lesson from the NCEE **Virtual Economics *CD-ROM*** to understand the components of GDP. Click on Browse Economics Lessons, specify grades 6–8, and use the key word *pizza.*

In this activity, students will categorize the components of GDP and then calculate the GDP for two fictional countries.

LESSON TITLE	GROSS DOMESTIC PIZZA
Type of Activity	Simulation
Complexity	High
Time	50 minutes
NCEE Standards	18

Teach Case Study

SUMMARIZE AND EXPLAIN

Have the students explain how entrepreneurs get a business up and running. Ask **How do would-be entrepreneurs get financial support for their business ideas?** *(They use savings, work extra jobs to bring in extra money, find investors, use credit cards, take out loans).* Ask **What is bootstrapping, and what are the benefits and drawbacks of bootstrapping as means to raise capital for a new business?** *(Bootstrapping is using little or no external money to get a business started. Benefits include: no outside investors to please, more profits for yourself (your employees). Drawbacks include: No outside investors to help during tough economic times; if the business fails, you could lose your savings and/or deal with large credit card bills.)*

GROUP ACTIVITY

Have the students break up into groups of three or four. Tell them to come up with an idea for a new eco-friendly business that would be of interest to young people. Have them write a business plan that uses as little start-up money as possible. Tell the students to make sure their business plan includes growth ideas for when the business turns a profit.

L1 L2 Differentiate This article contains financial terms that might be difficult for some students to understand. In pairs, have students define terms *(such as investors, home-equity lines of credit, capital, profit)* and explain their roles in business.

All print resources are available on the Teacher's Resource Library CD-ROM and online at www.PearsonSuccessNet.com.

Case Study

THE WALL STREET JOURNAL. CLASSROOM EDITION

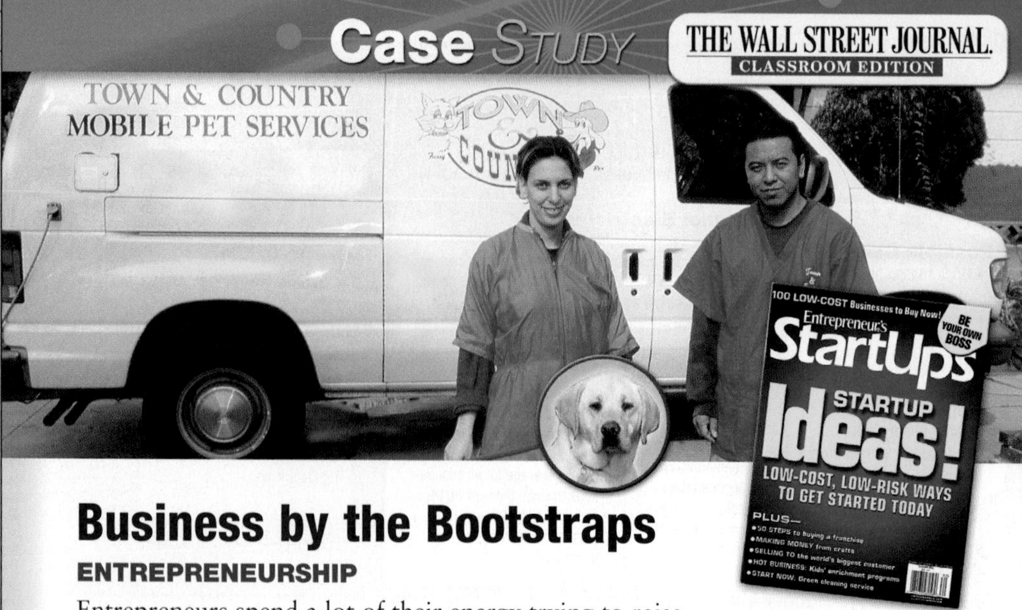

Business by the Bootstraps

ENTREPRENEURSHIP

Entrepreneurs spend a lot of their energy trying to raise capital. But there's another way.

By Kelly K. Spors
The Wall Street Journal

When Seth Riney started a hybrid-auto taxi service in Boston in 2003, he didn't pursue private investors. Instead, he found a more compatible financier: himself.

Mr. Riney traded in his 2002 Dodge Dakota pickup truck for a Toyota Prius. He kept a day job and worked early mornings and evenings ferrying around friends and family willing to pay for a lift. After a few months, he squirreled away enough money to hire his first employee and put a down payment on a second Prius. He kept adding more hybrids and more drivers as his cash stash grew.

Today, Mr. Riney's business, PlanetTran, has grown to a fleet of 35 hybrids and about 75 employees. He recently expanded his taxi service to San Francisco with the help of some investors. The company had $1.5 million in revenue in 2006, and Mr. Riney expects it will reach $4 million this year. "It was the kind of business that could grow organically without spending a lot of money in the early stages," he says.

Would-be entrepreneurs often think starting a successful business requires a large cash infusion to pay for an office, employees and professional marketing to make a cannonball splash in the market. But many are discovering the advantages of "bootstrapping"—or using little or no external capital and conserving as much cash as possible to grow the business.

Among the advantages: The fewer outside investors you take on, the less equity and control you forfeit to people who often have vastly different priorities than yours.

There are many methods that bootstrappers use to self-finance and save on cash. For starters, many tap into their own bank accounts, credit cards, and home-equity lines of credit. Of course, this is risky if the business fails. So one way to make sure you don't go broke early on is to keep a day job until the business is profitable enough to stand on its own.

Other bootstrappers do as much as possible to keep their costs low, whether it's buying used office equipment on eBay, using interns and freelancers instead of hired help or seeking out free advice. Many colleges and universities offer free and low-cost help to local entrepreneurs, such as legal or intellectual-property counseling by law students.

Applying Economic Principles
Why would building a business through "bootstrapping" require a strong work ethic, or commitment to hard work? Give at least one example from this article or from your own knowledge.

Video News Update Online Powered by *The Wall Street Journal* Classroom Edition — For a new case study, go to the online resources at **PearsonSuccessNet.com**

Answer

Applying Economic Principles Possible response: "Bootstrapping" requires entrepreneurs to use their own cash, work extra long hours, and forgo many "wants" to provide human and capital resources. Seth Riney gave up his free time in early mornings and evenings so he could retain his day job and still build his new business.

spin-offs range from a muscle stimulator for people with paralysis to a scanner that allows firefighters to see "invisible flames" given off by alcohol or hydrogen fires.

The government also encourages innovation by granting patents and copyrights. A **patent** gives the inventor of a new product the exclusive right to produce and sell it for 20 years. A **copyright** grants an author exclusive rights to publish and sell his or her creative works. Patents and copyrights are an incentive to innovation because they protect people's right to profit from their creativity in the free market.

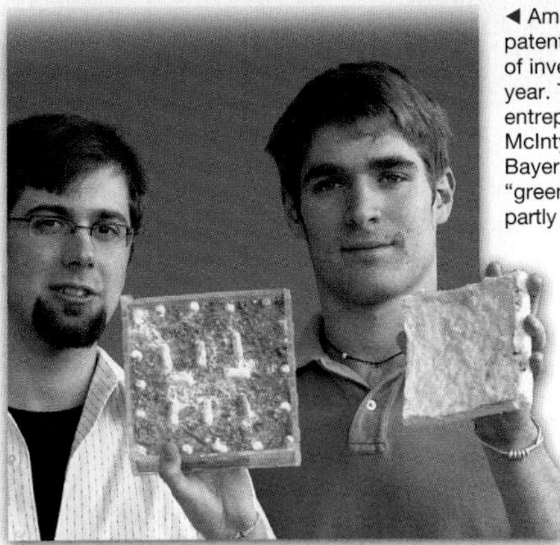

◀ Americans patent thousands of inventions every year. These college entrepreneurs, Gavin McIntyre and Eben Bayer, created a new "green" insulation partly from mushrooms that they grew under their beds.

The American Work Ethic

While government incentives may encourage innovation, economic growth cannot occur without individual effort. When asked to account for his success in the movie and recording industries, Will Smith stated:

> **"I've never really viewed myself as particularly talented. I've viewed myself as slightly above average in talent. And where I excel is ridiculous, sickening work ethic. You know, while the other guy's sleeping? I'm working. While the other guy's eating? I'm working."**
>
> — Will Smith, *60 Minutes* interview

The **work ethic** Smith refers to is a commitment to the value of work. It not only means working hard, but also caring about the quality of one's work. The American work ethic has long been seen as a key ingredient in the nation's productivity and economic success.

✔ **CHECKPOINT** ***How does improved technology help the economy?***

patent a government license that gives the inventor of a new product the exclusive right to produce and sell it

copyright a government license that grants an author exclusive rights to publish and sell creative works

work ethic a commitment to the value of work

Essential Questions Journal To continue to build a response to the Essential Question, go to your **Essential Questions Journal.**

SECTION 2 ASSESSMENT

Guiding Question

1. Use your completed flowchart to answer this question: How does the U.S. government encourage growth and stability?
2. **Extension** You are a member of Congress. Economic conditions in the country are excellent, and the economy is growing. Would you support a new spending plan aimed at providing jobs? Why or why not?

Key Terms and Main Ideas

3. Why is the government decision to increase or decrease spending a matter of **macroeconomic** policy?
4. How does **gross domestic product** provide a means to analyze economic growth?
5. Describe the **business cycle**.
6. How do **patents** act as an incentive to technological innovation?
7. How can technological innovation lead to **obsolescence?**

Critical Thinking

8. **Make Decisions** Suppose you had a job you did not like. If the economy was in the downward part of the business cycle, would you be more or less likely to quit your job to look for a better one? Why or why not?
9. **Predict** Suppose that Congress passed a bill funding research into alternative sources of energy. Which goals of governmental action in the economy would this funding meet?
10. **Analyze** Identify three individual qualities and actions that you think demonstrate a strong work ethic. Explain why you chose each one.

Math Skills

11. The chart below shows the length of periods of expansion and decline in the business cycle. Which expansion and which contraction lasted the longest? Based on this chart, how would you judge the health of the economy over 50 years?
Visit PearsonSuccessNet.com for additional math help.

Periods of Expansion	Periods of Contraction
Apr. 1958–Apr. 1960	Apr. 1960–Feb. 1961
Feb. 1961–Dec. 1969	Dec. 1969–Nov. 1970
Nov. 1970–Nov. 1973	Nov. 1973–Mar. 1975
Mar. 1975–Jan. 1980	Jan. 1980–July 1980
July 1980–July 1981	July 1981–Nov. 1982
Nov. 1982–July 1990	July 1990–Mar. 1991
Mar. 1991–Mar. 2001	Mar. 2001–Nov. 2001

SOURCE: National Bureau of Economic Research

Have students complete the Self-Test Online and continue their work in the **Essential Questions Journal**.

REMEDIATION AND SUGGESTIONS

Use the chart below to help students who are struggling with content.

WEAKNESS	REMEDIATION
Defining key terms (Questions 3–7)	Have students use the interactive Economic Dictionary Online.
How the government tracks the GDP and other economic data to identify expansion and contraction (Questions 1, 11)	Have students write a sentence that describes the connection between the GDP and the business cycle. They can also include visuals.
How the government aims to increase employment, and promote economic growth and stability (Questions 2, 8, 9, 11)	Reteach using a three-column chart. In the first column, list each of the goals; in the second column, list Government Actions to Strengthen these Goals; and, in the third column, list Desired Economic Outcomes.
How technology and the work ethic affect productivity (Questions 6, 7, 10)	Have students compare doing a research paper using the library and writing by hand with using the Internet and a word processing program.

Answer

Checkpoint It allows the economy to operate more efficiently, increasing GDP and giving U.S. firms a competitive advantage.

Assessment Answers

1. Possible response: The government encourages more employment, increases its spending, and regulates banks.
2. Possible response: In a growing economy, there is no need for the government to ensure job growth.
3. Macroeconomics is concerned with the overall performance of the economy, which is affected by government spending.
4. Gross domestic product measures the total value of final goods and services produced by an economy. This is used to determine whether or not the economy is in a period of expansion or contraction.
5. The business cycle is the movement between periods of economic growth (expansion) and decline (contraction).
6. The government protects a patent holder's right to profit from their creativity.
7. Innovations will replace older technology.
8. Possible response: On a downward trend, I would not quit the job without having another job offer first, because I'd fear I could not find another job.
9. employment, long-term growth, innovation
10. Possible response: being on time, working hard, and working well as part of a team.
11. The longest expansion: March 1991 to March 2001. The longest contractions: November 1973 to March 1975 and July 1981 to November 1982. Possible response: very healthy since expansions have lasted longer than contractions

Guiding Question

Why does a society provide public goods?

Get Started

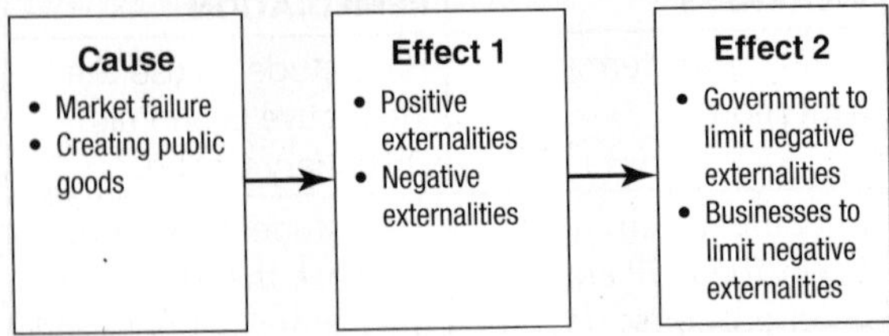

LESSON GOALS

Students will:

- Know the Key Terms.
- Demonstrate understanding of the nature of public goods.
- Make the connection between public goods and the market failures they address.
- Analyze how the government manages externalities in the course of providing public goods.

BEFORE CLASS

Students should read the section for homework before coming to class.

Have students complete the graphic organizer in the Section Opener as they read the text. As an alternate activity, have students complete the Guided Reading and Review worksheet (Unit 1 All-in-One, p. 112).

L1 L2 ELL LPR Differentiate Have students complete the Guided Reading and Review worksheet (Unit 1 All-in-One, p. 113).

SECTION 3 Providing Public Goods

OBJECTIVES

1. **Identify** examples of public goods.
2. **Analyze** market failures.
3. **Evaluate** how the government allocates some resources by managing externalities.

ECONOMIC DICTIONARY

As you read the section, look for the definitions of these **Key Terms:**

- public good
- public sector
- private sector
- infrastructure
- free rider
- market failure
- externality

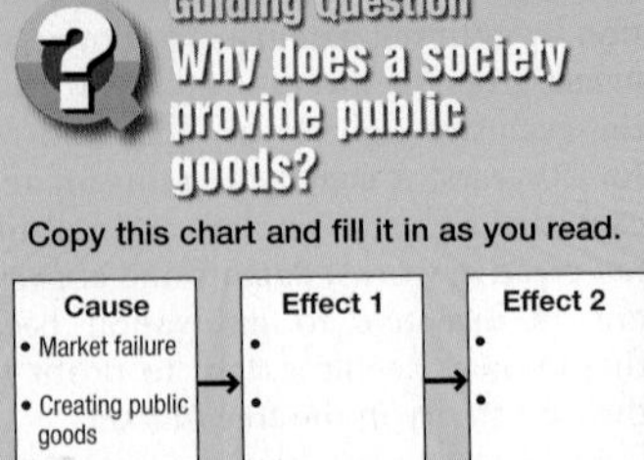

public good a shared good or service for which it would be inefficient or impractical to make consumers pay individually and to exclude those who did not pay

Economics and You You benefit from all kinds of services that federal, state and local governments provide. You go to school, ride on roads, cross bridges, and use public parks. What would your life be like without these services? Or suppose that you could use a specific road or bridge only if your family had helped pay for it. How much would that complicate your life?

Principles in Action Even in a free market economy, the government must provide certain goods and services that the marketplace cannot. For example, you will see how the job of building a bridge would become almost impossible if it had to be done by the joint action of all the people and businesses that would benefit from it. Sometimes, the government has to step in.

Public Goods

Roads and bridges are a few of the many examples in which the government provides a public good. A **public good** is a shared good or service for which it would be inefficient or impractical (1) to make consumers pay individually and (2) to exclude those who did not pay.

Characteristics of Public Goods

Let us look at the first feature of public goods, making each consumer pay individually. How would you like to receive a bill for your share of launching a space shuttle, cleaning Mount Rushmore, or paying the salary of every soldier in the army? To simplify the funding of government projects in the public interest, the government collects taxes.

What about the second feature of a public good, excluding nonpayers? Imagine the arguments and traffic delays that would erupt if drivers who refused to pay to use a street were told they had to turn around and drive away. Also, as a society, we believe that certain facilities or services, such as libraries or protection from fire, should be available to all, rich or poor.

In the case of most public goods, it is simply not practical for a private business to provide the service, charge those who benefit, and exclude nonpayers from using the service. Take, for example, national parks like Yellowstone and Yosemite. If these parks were privately owned, the owner could charge a higher admission fee. Yet some benefits generated by the park, such as the preservation of wildlife, would be enjoyed by nonpayers

▲ Maintaining street signs and traffic lights is one economic role of the government.

62 AMERICAN FREE ENTERPRISE

CLASSROOM HINTS

THE GOVERNMENT AND EDUCATION

This section will teach students how government tries to increase positive outcomes and decrease negative outcomes in the public and private sectors. Have students create a Venn diagram about public and private education. In the center, ask them to include all the benefits that both systems provide. At the ends, have students include benefits or problems that apply to either system individually. Ask **What are the advantages and disadvantages of each system? What can government do to minimize the problems each system faces?**

Focus on the Basics

Students need to come away with the following understandings:

FACTS: • The government balances costs and benefits to determine whether to produce a public good. • When the free market does not distribute resources efficiently, a market failure occurs. • The government tries to increase positive externalities and limit negative externalities in the public and private sectors.

GENERALIZATION: The government provides a public good when the marketplace cannot or will not provide it.

as well as payers. The owner could neither charge people for that benefit nor exclude them from benefiting.

Public goods have another characteristic. Any number of consumers can use them without reducing the benefits to any single consumer. For the most part, increasing the number of consumers does not increase the cost of providing the public good. So if you are driving on a highway and eight other drivers enter it, they do not significantly reduce the road's benefits to you or increase the government's cost of providing the road.

Public goods are financed by the **public sector,** the part of the economy that involves the transactions of the government. The **private sector,** the part of the economy that involves transactions of individuals and businesses, would have little incentive to produce public goods.

Costs and Benefits

As you read in Section 1, governments step in to act in the public interest when they determine that the benefits of a policy outweigh the drawbacks, or the costs. In road construction, the benefits are obvious. Transportation is a vital part of the nation's **infrastructure,** the basic facilities that are necessary for a society to function and grow. American leaders have long regarded investment in infrastructure, not only as a means to provide needed public goods, but as a way to promote economic growth:

> **"Whether we're talking about roads or bridges or mass transit, … sewage and water facilities, whether we're talking about broadband, or we're talking about the grid to transmit electricity, whether we're talking about schools … these infrastructure investments offer our nation job-creating opportunities to reinvigorate the American economy."**
>
> — Nancy Pelosi, Speaker of the House, March 11, 2008

Transportation goes more smoothly when governments build roads. The drawback, though, is the economic freedom we give up. None of us individually gets to decide what roads will be built or where. In this case, the advantages clearly outweigh the drawback. In other cases, weighing benefits against costs is more complex.

Costs and benefits are critical in determining whether something gets produced as a public good. Two cost-benefit criteria must be present.

1. The benefit to each individual is less than the cost that each would have to pay if it were provided privately.
2. The total benefits to society are greater than the total cost.

If just one or a few people got together to fund the project, the cost to each of them would be much higher than the benefits each would gain. In such circumstances, the market would not provide the good.

But if you look at society as a whole, the picture changes. As long as the benefit all people gain exceeds the total cost, it makes sense for government to fund the project. From the individual's point of view, this situation is better too. The government can fund the project by collecting a small amount of money in taxes from a large number of people. That means the share paid by each person is much less than it would be if they had to fund the project alone or even through a small group.

public sector the part of the economy that involves the transactions of the government

private sector the part of the economy that involves the transactions of individuals and businesses

infrastructure the basic facilities that are necessary for a society to function and grow

These California firefighters are using expensive equipment to combat a raging forest fire. ***What do you think might happen if individual consumers, rather than the government, had to pay for fire protection?*** ▼

Differentiated Resources

L1 L2 Guided Reading and Review (Unit 1 All-in-One, p. 113)

L2 Providing Public Goods (Unit 1 All-in-One, p. 115)

L4 The Tragedy of the Commons (Unit 1 All-in-One, p. 116)

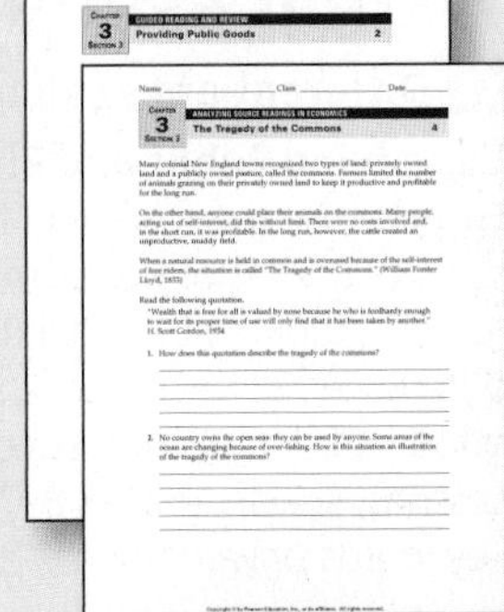

BELLRINGER

Display the transparency "Public School Construction" (Color Transparencies, 3.b). Have students read about the proposal, and imagine it is for their community. Have them identify at least two costs and two benefits.

Teach

Economics online To present this topic using digital resources, use the lecture notes at www.PearsonSuccessNet.com.

COMPARE TERMS

Write on the board the following terms: *private sector, public sector, a public good,* and *the public interest.* Ask students to define and differentiate among the terms, using clear examples. Remind them that the term *good* in the term *a public good* encompasses both goods and services. In this term, *good* is not a value judgment. However, students may sometimes hear the phrase *the public good* used to mean the public interest, or the well-being of society. Make sure students understand this distinction.

L1 L2 ELL LPR Differentiate Have students use a Venn diagram to categorize a wide variety of goods and services provided by the public vs. the private sector. Have them identify the public goods.

DISCUSS

Have volunteers give their responses to the Bellringer. Engage students in a discussion about why there is a need for public goods. Ask **Who benefits from a public school system?** *(individual students, the community at large from improved education)* Ask **Should the community pay for education? Why?**

Create a list on the board of other possible public goods. Identify which of these goods is a public good by discussing why they would be inefficient and impractical to (1) make consumers pay for individually and (2) exclude those who did not pay.

APPLY

Review the costs and benefits criteria of a public good. Have students describe how these criteria can be applied to three items on the class list. Ask **Are there times when something might be provided by both the public and private sectors separately?** *(Yes, but in the private sector the good is more costly and exclusive, e.g., private schools.)*

Answer

Caption Possible response: Many people would not be able or willing to pay for fire protection, which would lead to more destruction due to fires.

APPLY UNDERSTANDING

Have students review the How the Economy Works feature. Ask **Why is this bridge-building scenario a market failure?** *(The criteria for a properly functioning market system do not exist: any private company or individual who built the bridge would be able to charge a high price for tolls because they'd have no competition. Also, there is no profit incentive for the farmers, or any other private company, to build the bridge.)*

PREDICT

Use the following activity to illustrate that public goods are the result of market failures. List the following on the board: police protection, a school, catering, recycling and trash removal, car repair, road maintenance, a restaurant, a gas station, fire protection. Ask **If you wanted to start a business, which of these goods or services would you be willing to provide? Why?** *(catering, car repair, a restaurant, or a gas station—and perhaps a school—because a profit could be made on these businesses)* Discuss why students might not want to start businesses providing the goods or services they did not select, and how this corresponds to the definition of market failure.

L2 Differentiate Have small groups of students use a phone book to identify some of the services provided by their city and by the federal government. Have each group tell the class why one of these services is an example of a market failure.

PROVIDE EXAMPLES

Tell students that providers of each of the above goods or services are considering locating in their neighborhood. Explain that in this situation, externalities are the effects of the goods or services on their community. Brainstorm the externalities each example would have, and classify them as positive or negative. Ask **Are there any ways the government can limit the negative externalities of each provider?** *(enforce building and zoning laws, study traffic pattern changes)*

Answer

Checkpoint The benefit to each individual is less than the cost that each would have to pay if it were provided privately, and the total benefits to society must be greater than the total cost.

How the Economy Works

How are public goods created?

Some public goods are too costly for the free market to satisfy. In these cases, the government may intervene to provide public goods.

1 Farmers in Capp County have to drive an extra hundred miles to get their crops across the river. They want a new bridge built nearby.

2

Cost: $126 million

Benefit: Saves each farmer $5,000 a year

Public Need → **Costs and Benefits**

Free-Rider Problem

A phenomenon associated with public goods is called the "free-rider problem." A **free rider** is someone who would not be willing to pay for a certain good or service, but would get the benefit of it anyway if it were provided as a public good. Unlike consumers in the free marketplace, free riders consume what they do not directly pay for.

You probably would not voluntarily contribute to build roads in a state you did not live in. Yet when the government builds and maintains a system of national roads, you share in the benefit. For example, the national road system makes it easier for trucking companies to bring goods to your state. And if you were traveling through the other state on vacation, you would certainly not refuse to drive on the road yourself. You receive the benefit whether you pay directly or not.

free rider someone who would not be willing to pay for a certain good or service but who would get the benefits of it anyway if it were provided as a public good

Try another example: Everyone on your street wants fire protection except one penny-pinching neighbor, who says it is not worth the money. Don't you want him to have fire protection anyway? If his house catches fire, yours could ignite as well. So local taxes pay for fire-fighting services for all property in an area, because all residents are better off if the government provides this service. Your free rider neighbor benefits from this service as well.

The free-rider problem suggests what would happen if the government stopped collecting taxes to fund public services. If it relied on voluntary contributions instead, many people would refuse to give money. Many public services would then have to be eliminated.

CHECKPOINT ***What two criteria must be present for a public good?***

Virtual Economics

L3 Differentiate

Classifying Public and Private Goods Use the following lesson from the NCEE **Virtual Economics *CD-ROM*** to help students to understand the difference between public and private goods. Click on Browse Economics Lessons, specify grades 9–12, and use the key words *private goods.*

In this activity, students will work in small groups to classify goods and services as either public or private.

LESSON TITLE	PUBLIC VERSUS PRIVATE GOODS
Type of Activity	Classifying
Complexity	Low
Time	45 minutes
NCEE Standards	16

How the Economy Works
online
For an animated, interactive version of this feature, visit PearsonSuccessNet.com
Free Market
3 If the farmers build the bridge themselves, it will cost each farmer $1 million.
BENEFIT
COST
Market Failure: Bridge is not built. ▶
Public Good
3 The state government decides to fund the bridge by setting aside tax money and issuing bonds.
COST
BENEFIT
Bridge is built. ▶
Check Your Understanding
1. How does a cost-benefit analysis influence decision making?
2. How does the creation of public goods affect the economy?
Who Pays?
Market Failure or Public Good?

Market Failures

Public goods are examples of what some economists call a market failure. The term **market failure** does not suggest that the free enterprise system does not work. Rather, it describes a specific situation in which the free market, operating on its own, does not distribute resources efficiently.

To understand market failure, recall how a successful free market operates: Choices made by individuals determine what goods get made, how they get made, and who consumes the goods. Profit incentives attract producers who, because of competition, provide goods and services that consumers need at prices they can afford.

In the road-building scenario, are these features present? No. If a company did build a road, it could charge a high price for tolls because it would have no competition. Also, companies would not choose to build roads in sparsely populated areas because they would see no chance to earn profits—a low population would mean too few drivers to charge.

As a result, the criteria for a properly functioning market system do not exist. For that reason, the road-building scenario is a market failure.

CHECKPOINT ***Why are public goods examples of market failure?***

Externalities

All of the examples above involve what economists call externalities. An **externality** is an economic side effect of a good or service that generates benefits or costs to someone other than the person deciding how much to produce or consume. Externalities may be either positive or negative.

market failure a situation in which the free market, operating on its own, does not distribute resources efficiently

externality an economic side effect of a good or service that generates benefits or costs to someone other than the person deciding how much to produce or consume

DISTRIBUTE ACTIVITY WORKSHEET

Distribute the "Market Failures and Externalities" worksheet (Unit 1 All-in-One, p. 114).

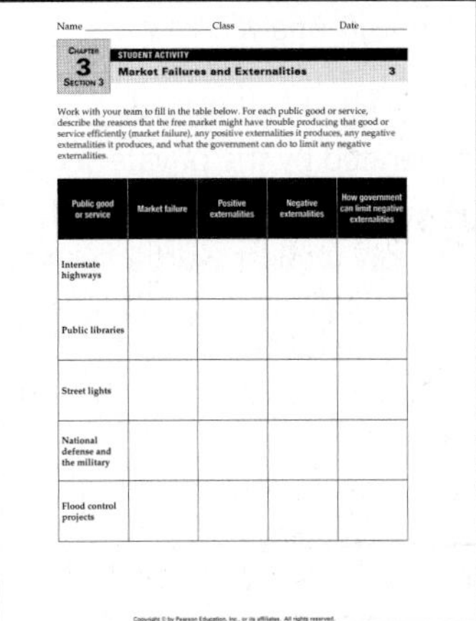
Name Class Date

CHAPTER 3 SECTION 3 STUDENT ACTIVITY
Market Failures and Externalities

Work with your team to fill in the table below. For each public good or service, describe the reasons that the free market might have trouble producing that good or service efficiently (market failure), any positive externalities it produces, any negative externalities it produces, and what the government can do to limit any negative externalities.

Public good or service	Market failure	Positive externalities	Negative externalities	How government can limit negative externalities
Interstate highways				
Public libraries				
Street lights				
National defense and the military				
Flood control projects				

L2 Differentiate Distribute the "Providing Public Goods" worksheet (Unit 1 All-in-One, p. 115).

Discuss the table and the instructions. Have small groups of students work together to complete the worksheet. Collect the worksheets. Ask students if they can think of alternative ways for these services to be provided.

Background Note

Amtrak Some companies, such as Amtrak, provide public goods but are run as profit-making ventures. However, Amtrak does not earn a profit and must have government support. For years, Republicans in Congress wanted Amtrak to become self-sufficient or face cuts. However, changes in Congress and the marketplace, including high gas prices, have led to more funding for Amtrak and support for the growth of other public rail systems.

Answers

Check Your Understanding 1. If the farmers decided to build the bridge on their own (at a cost of $126 million), the cost to each of them would far outweigh the annual savings of $5,000. However, the benefits provided to the public by an improved transportation system outweigh the $126 million cost. 2. The creation of public goods benefits the economy by providing goods and services that cannot be provided efficiently by the free market.

Checkpoint The market cannot distribute public goods efficiently: there is no profit incentive to provide public goods.

EXTEND

Ask **What goods and services are provided by both the public and private sectors?** *(Possible responses: education, transportation, news and entertainment, trash removal)* Analyze with students the resulting externalities and whether the externalities generated by the public sector are different from those generated by the private sector.

L1 **L2** **ELL LPR Differentiate** For students with language issues, discuss how familiar words, such as *failure,* can have different meanings. Have students make visual illustrations of the economic terms in this chapter (such as *free rider* and *public good*) to help them remember definitions.

L4 **Differentiate** Distribute "The Tragedy of the Commons" worksheet (Unit 1 All-in-One, p. 116). Discuss the meaning of the phrase *the tragedy of the commons* and how it applies to the quotation. Then have them answer the questions.

GUIDING QUESTION WRAP UP

Have students return to the section Guiding Question. Review the completed graphic organizer and clarify any misunderstandings. Have a wrap up discussion about why a society provides public goods.

Assess and Remediate

L3 **L2** Collect the "Market Failures and Externalities" worksheets and "Providing Public Goods" worksheets to assess whether students understand market failures, externalities, and the government's role in controlling them.

L4 Collect the "Tragedy of the Commons" worksheet and assess student understanding of limited resources.

L3 Assign the Section 3 Assessment questions; identify student misconceptions

L3 Give Section Quiz A (Unit 1 All-in-One, p. 117).

L2 Give Section Quiz B (Unit 1 All-in-One, p. 118).

(Assess and Remediate continued on p. 67)

Answers

Graph Skills 1. While the main goal of the bridge is to help local farmers, vacationers driving through the area will benefit from the additional route across the river. 2. For some people, increased car traffic will mean more customers for their businesses, while other people will be negatively affected by increased pollution and crowded roads.

Figure 3.3 Positive and Negative Externalities

GRAPH SKILLS

Building a bridge creates dozens of externalities, both positive and negative, depending upon your point of view.

1. Why is use of the bridge by vacationers an externality?
2. Why would increased car traffic be considered a positive externality by some people and a negative externality by others?

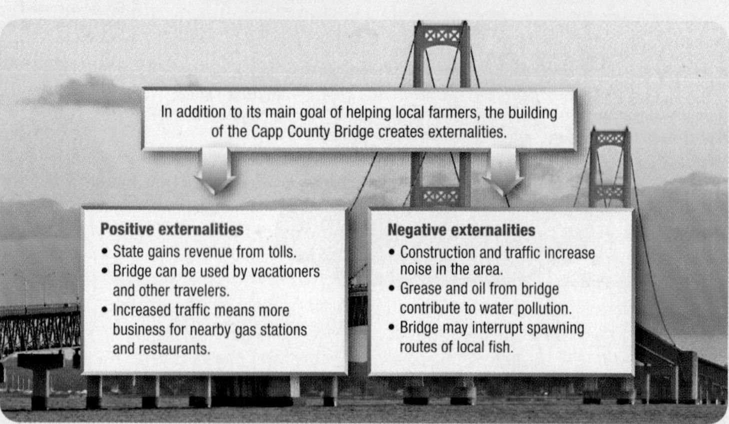

In addition to its main goal of helping local farmers, the building of the Capp County Bridge creates externalities.
Positive externalities
• State gains revenue from tolls.
• Bridge can be used by vacationers and other travelers.
• Increased traffic means more business for nearby gas stations and restaurants.
Negative externalities
• Construction and traffic increase noise in the area.
• Grease and oil from bridge contribute to water pollution.
• Bridge may interrupt spawning routes of local fish.

Positive Externalities

As you read, public goods generate benefits to many people, not just those who pay for the goods. Such beneficial side effects are positive externalities. Consider the example of building a bridge in the How the Economy Works feature on page 64. Some of the positive externalities associated with the bridge are shown in **Figure 3.3**, above.

The private sector—both individuals and businesses—can create positive externalities, too. For instance:

- Walsh Computers hires underprivileged teenagers and trains them to be computer programmers. Walsh set up this training program to serve its own interests. However, the newly trained workers can be hired by other companies, who benefit from the workers' skills without having paid for them.
- Mrs. Ruiz buys an old house that is an eyesore in the neighborhood. She paints the house, cuts the grass, and plants flowers. Her neighbors were not involved in her decision, nor did they share the cost. Yet they receive benefits from it, such as higher property values and a better view.

In fact, many economists believe that the private sector generates positive externalities more efficiently than the public sector can, and at less cost to taxpayers.

Whether private or public, positive externalities allow someone who did not purchase a good to enjoy part of the benefits of that good. In the 1990s, several endangered species, including the bald eagle and the peregrine falcon, were saved from extinction. Protection of species critical to our ecosystem benefits us all.

Negative Externalities

Of course, as **Figure 3.3** shows, producing goods and services can also generate unintended costs, called negative externalities. Negative externalities cause part of the cost of producing a good or service to be paid for by someone other than the producer. For example:

- The Enchanted Forest Paper Mill dumps chemical wastes into a nearby river, making it unhealthy. The city of Tidyville, downstream from the mill, is forced to install special equipment at its water-treatment plant to clean up the chemicals. The community, not the polluter, is paying the cost of cleaning up the river.
- Your next-door neighbor, Mr. Fogler, takes up the accordion and holds Friday night polka parties in his backyard. Unfortunately, you hate polka music.

Government's Goals

Externalities are a sign of market failure because the costs or benefits of a good or service are not assigned properly. Understanding externalities helps us see another role that the government plays in the American economy.

First, the government may take action to create positive externalities. Education, for example, benefits students, yet society as a whole also benefits from an educated population. This is because educated workers are generally more productive.

Second, the government aims to limit negative externalities, such as pollution. Pollutants from coal-burning power plants and auto emissions can drift high into the atmosphere and come down in the form of acid rain, which causes ecological damage. Why is acid rain a negative externality? It is part of the cost of producing power and driving cars, but that cost was imposed upon people other than those who produce the pollution. The cost was damaged trees, lakes, and wildlife.

To address this negative externality, the federal government now requires new cars to have an expensive antipollution device called a catalytic converter. In addition, the Environmental Protection Agency offers incentives to power-plant operators to put "scrubbers" on their smokestacks to cut emissions. These actions transfer the costs of pollution back to its producers.

Government-Driven or Market-Driven Solutions?

As you saw, many economists think that the private sector produces more positive externalities than the government does. This belief has spurred debate over how to stop damage to the environment.

Since the 1970s, the government has often tried to halt pollution by creating strict regulations. Many economists say that this approach is inefficient because it increases costs. It also ties the hands of businesses by requiring specific solutions rather than encouraging innovation.

These economists want the government to allow market-driven solutions to environmental problems. In this approach, the government would still play a role by setting standards that industries would have to meet. Individual firms, though, would have more freedom to find ways to meet those goals.

CHECKPOINT ***What does the government do in response to negative externalities?***

▲ The Environmental Protection Agency tries to limit negative externalities not just by making regulations, but also by encouraging private action. ***How does this poster deal with a negative externality of being a consumer?***

Essential Questions Journal To continue to build a response to the Essential Question, go to your **Essential Questions Journal.**

SECTION 3 ASSESSMENT

Guiding Question

1. Use your completed chart to answer this question: Why does a society provide public goods?
2. **Extension** Suppose people in your neighborhood want to have a community pool. Should the city government build the pool, or should it leave the matter up to the private sector? Explain your answer in economic terms.

Key Terms and Main Ideas

3. What are the two characteristics of **public good?**
4. What is an example of an action taken by the **public sector?** By the **private sector?**
5. Why are public goods examples of **market failure?**
6. Give an example of one positive and one negative **externality.**

Critical Thinking

7. **Analyze** Why is national defense an example of the free-rider problem?
8. **Connect** How do the concepts of limited resources and scarcity explain why the government does not try to meet all demands for providing public goods? What other factors might persuade government leaders to favor taking a more limited role in the economy?
9. **Apply** Because of the interstate highway system, transportation costs are lower. How is this an example of positive externalities?

Quick Write

10. Review the discussion about government-driven versus market-driven solutions for pollution. Write a position paper explaining which approach you favor. Make sure you take into account economic concepts such as property rights, economic freedom, economic growth, equity, efficiency, externalities, and the public good.

Have students complete the Self-Test Online and continue their work in the **Essential Questions Journal**.

REMEDIATION AND SUGGESTIONS

Use the chart below to help students who are struggling with content.

WEAKNESS	REMEDIATION
Defining key terms (Questions 3, 4, 5, 6)	Have students use the interactive Economic Dictionary Online.
Identifying public and private goods (Questions 2, 3, 4)	Collect pictures of goods and services in both sectors. Students should categorize the pictures and defend their choice.
Market failures and externalities (Questions 1, 5, 6, 7, 8, 9)	Give students the following scenario: the community decides that the school district should build an afterschool center for children. Have students explain how it is a market failure and list possible externalities.
Government management of externalities (Question 10)	Bring in newspaper articles that have examples of negative externalities. Have students identify the externality and suggest ways the government might manage them.

Answers

Caption It points out the large amount of waste generated by each consumer.

Checkpoint The government tries to encourage positive externalities and limit negative externalities.

Assessment Answers

1. Possible response: It is too expensive and impractical for consumers to pay for them.
2. Possible response: If the city built the pool, everyone could use it. A private business would have to make a profit, so they would probably charge pool users.
3. The benefit to each person is less than the cost that each would pay if the good were provided privately; the benefit to society is greater than the cost.
4. taxing citizens; a company selling goods
5. The private sector is not willing to provide public goods in the open market since they do not generate enough profit.
6. Possible responses: increased business for a store near an expanding factory; the noise and pollution of additional traffic
7. Some people might not be willing to pay taxes for defense, but receive the benefits.
8. Possible response: Unlimited wants cannot be met because scarce resources force it to make choices; concern that government action would be inefficient compared to the private sector.
9. Possible response: This system was built largely to make it easier to get from one place to another quickly. Lower transportation costs were a side benefit.
10. Students' papers should explain whether they favor a government-driven or a market-driven approach. Students should consider the economic concepts mentioned in the question.

Guiding Question

How does government help the poor?

Get Started

Government Help for the Poor			
Cash Transfers	In-Kind Benefits	Medical Benefits	Education
• TANF • Social Security • Unemployment insurance • Workers' compensation	• Food giveaways • Food stamps • Subsidized housing • Legal aid	• Medicare • Medicaid • State Children's Health Insurance Program	• Funds for students who need aid • Programs for students with learning disabilities

LESSON GOALS

Students will:

- Know the Key Terms.
- Describe the main government safety net programs and how they are funded.
- Survey attitudes toward government spending on welfare programs.
- Identify how the government encourages private programs that provide social help.

BEFORE CLASS

Students should read the section for homework before coming to class.

Have students complete the graphic organizer in the Section Opener as they read the text. As an alternate activity, have students complete the Guided Reading and Review worksheet (Unit 1 All-in-One, p. 119).

L1 L2 ELL LPR Differentiate Have students complete the Guided Reading and Review worksheet (Unit 1 All-in-One, p. 120).

SECTION 4 Providing a Safety Net

OBJECTIVES

1. **Explain** the U.S. political debate on ways to fight poverty.
2. **Identify** the main programs through which the government redistributes income.
3. **Describe** how the government encourages private efforts to help the needy.

ECONOMIC DICTIONARY

As you read the section, look for the definitions of these **Key Terms:**

- poverty threshold
- welfare
- cash transfers
- in-kind benefits
- grant

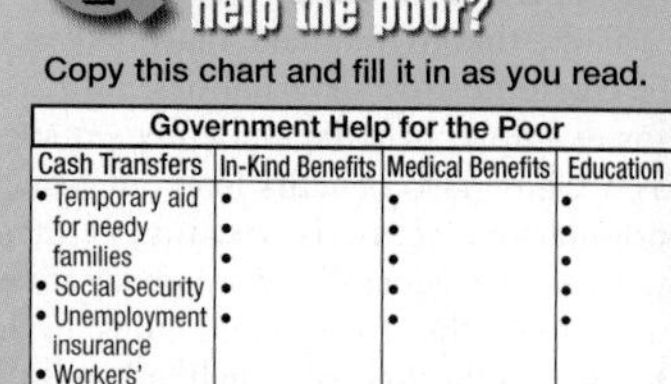
Guiding Question
How does government help the poor?

Copy this chart and fill it in as you read.

Government Help for the Poor			
Cash Transfers	In-Kind Benefits	Medical Benefits	Education
• Temporary aid for needy families • Social Security • Unemployment insurance • Workers' compensation	• • • •	• • • •	• • • •

poverty threshold an income level below that which is needed to support families or households

Economics and You

You've seen it all around you: on TV shows, in the news, maybe even in your community. There are vast differences between people who have a lot of money, enough money, and very little money. On the average, Americans enjoy a high standard of living. Yet about 13 percent of Americans live in poverty. And for people under the age of 18, the number is even higher.

Principles in Action To help the poor, government programs take money from some people and redistribute it to others. Yet critics say such actions violate the economic principle of limited government intervention. The Economics & You feature shows how redistribution programs may both benefit and cost you. You will also see how the government encourages citizens like you to aid the needy.

The Poverty Problem

While the free market has proven better than any other economic system at generating wealth, that wealth is spread unevenly throughout society. This leaves some people below the **poverty threshold,** an income level below that which is needed to support families. The poverty threshold is determined by the federal government and adjusted periodically. In 2006, the poverty threshold for a single parent under age 65, with one child, was $13,896 per year. For a four-person family with two children, it was $20,444 per year.

The U.S. Bureau of the Census, part of the Labor Department, sets the poverty threshold. It sets it at different levels, depending on the number of family members and their ages. Each year, the poverty threshold is adjusted based on the cost of the goods a family needs to buy. As prices rise, so does the poverty threshold.

Poverty conditions can exist anywhere, from city slums, to farming communities, to Indian reservations like this one. ▼

CLASSROOM HINTS

ADDRESSING POVERTY

Students might think that government programs to help those who cannot help themselves are not a proper use of revenues, because such programs may not benefit all citizens directly. This section will teach students how the government has reformed its assistance programs, by varying the provision of services, including more money for education, and encouraging private organizations to provide services to those in need. Ask students to think about the question of poverty in the United States. Ask **What is responsible for causing poverty? What can the government do to eliminate this problem?**

Focus on the Basics

Students need to come away with the following understandings:

FACTS: • People living below the poverty threshold cannot afford basic needs. • The welfare system includes redistribution programs that provide cash transfers, in-kind benefits, medical benefits, and education. • Private agencies provide social services, with and without federal funds. • Americans do not agree how to provide and fund welfare services.

GENERALIZATION: The government has a responsibility to provide a safety net for people in need.

The Government's Role

As a society, we recognize some responsibilities to the very young, the very old, the sick, the poor, and the disabled. The government tries to provide a safety net for people in these groups, with help from various federal, state, and local government programs. These programs aim to raise people's standard of living, or their level of economic well-being as measured by the ability to purchase the goods and services they need and want.

The Welfare System

Since the 1930s, the main government effort to ease poverty has been to collect taxes from individuals and redistribute some of those funds in the form of welfare. **Welfare** is a general term that refers to government aid for the poor. It includes many types of programs that redistribute wealth from some people to others.

The nation's welfare system began under President Franklin Roosevelt during the Great Depression. Welfare spending greatly increased in the 1960s under President Lyndon Johnson's "War on Poverty."

Federal welfare programs came under increasing attack in the 1980s. Critics of welfare voiced increasing concern about people becoming dependent on welfare and being unable or unwilling to get off it. Some critics also claimed that income redistribution discourages productivity, thus actually aggravating poverty. In 1996, Congress responded by making sweeping changes in the welfare system. New reforms limited the amount of time people could receive welfare payments and gave states more freedom to experiment with antipoverty programs.

CHECKPOINT ***What is the goal of government welfare programs?***

Redistribution Programs

In Chapter 13, you will examine in greater detail the many causes of poverty as well as government attempts to solve the problem. Meanwhile, here is a brief overview of the major types of redistribution programs through which the federal government helps the poor, elderly, and disadvantaged.

Cash Transfers

State and federal governments provide **cash transfers,** direct payments of money to poor, disabled, or retired people. The following programs are cash transfers:

- *Temporary Assistance for Needy Families (TANF)* Launched in 1996, TANF does not provide direct federal welfare payments to the poor. Instead, federal money goes to the states, which design and run their own welfare programs. States must adhere to federal rules that create work incentives and establish a lifetime limit for benefits. TANF aims to move people from depending on welfare to joining the workforce.

welfare government aid to the poor

cash transfers direct payments of money by the government to poor, disabled, or retired people

Economics & YOU

Redistribution Programs

Public colleges and universities often have lower tuition than private schools. ***You can pay less to attend a public college, because states have redistributed tax money to support education.***

Social security taxes are taken out of your paycheck. ***The money you pay to social security is redistributed to senior citizens so they can maintain a decent standard of living.***

▲ Redistribution of income is one way government meets people's needs. ***Identify another way that the government may use your money to help somebody else.***

Differentiated Resources

L1 L2 Guided Reading and Review (Unit 1 All-in-One, p. 120)

L2 Analyzing Political Cartoons skill worksheet (Unit 1 All-in-One, p. 122)

L2 Helping People in Need (Unit 1 All-in-One, p. 124)

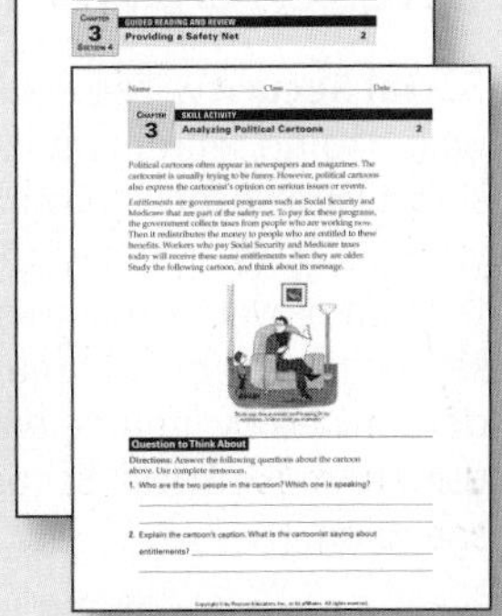

BELLRINGER

Display the transparency "Percent of People in Poverty" (Color Transparencies, 3.c). Write the following questions on the board, and have students answer them in their notebooks: What does the map indicate about poverty in the United States? Which regions have the highest and lowest percentage? What might explain the differences in each region?

Teach

Economics online To present this topic using digital resources, use the lecture notes at www.PearsonSuccessNet.com.

EXPLAIN

Explain that there can be many reasons that people do not have enough resources to meet their needs. Draw a concept web on the board with the words *Inadequate Resources* in the center and have students fill in the web as they discuss factors that contribute to poverty.

DISTRIBUTE SKILL WORKSHEET

Distribute the "Analyzing Political Cartoons" skill worksheet (Unit 1 All-in-One, p. 121).

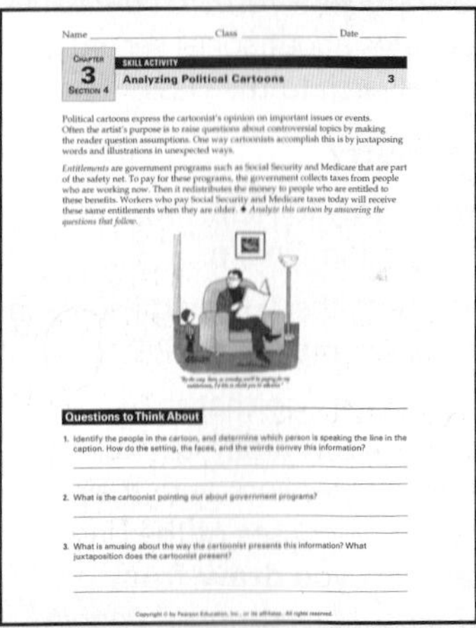

L1 L2 Differentiate Distribute the "Analyzing Political Cartoons" skill worksheet (Unit 1 All-in-One, p. 122). Have pairs of students complete the worksheet. Discuss students' answers.

Tell students to review the lesson in the Skills Handbook on page S-13. Remind them to use the steps of the lesson to complete the activities.

Answers

Checkpoint The government collects money in the form of taxes and redistributes some to the poor.

Economics and You Possible Response: The government can purchase food and other goods for people who have been in a disaster.

DEFINE

Ask **How has the government tried to help those in need?** *(welfare, medical benefits, education)* Explain to students that governments provide programs to assist those in need. Discuss the federal programs described in the text.

L1 L2 Differentiate Assign partners or small groups an agency to investigate. Have each group make a poster to share their information.

DISCUSS

Discuss the programs that are paid for through FICA. Ask **Why are these amounts being taken out of the person's pay?** *(to fund the Social Security and Medicare programs)* Discuss how these amounts are determined and distributed. Ask **Would you save for retirement now if the money were not automatically taken out of your paycheck?** *(Many will say no.)* Ask **To whom is the money taken out of your paycheck redistributed?** *(to people claiming Social Security and Medicare benefits)* **How does that money help you in your retirement?** *(The amount that someone pays into these programs is used to calculate the amount that they can take out of the program at retirement. People who are working when students are retired will be putting the money into these programs.)*

L4 Differentiate Have students research the issues surrounding current debates about social security, and then present their research to the class.

DISTRIBUTE SURVEY ACTIVITY

Distribute the "Survey on How to Help Those in Need" worksheet (Unit 1 All-in-One, p. 123).

L2 Differentiate Distribute the "Helping People in Need" worksheet (Unit 1 All-in-One, p. 124).

Discuss the items with students, so that they understand the questions. Allow a day or two for students to gather responses and write their conclusions. Then tally the responses of the class. Ask **What conclusions can you draw from this limited sample?** *(Possible responses: People supported a safety net, but think it is too expensive. People are split.)* Have students compare and contrast their conclusions.

A Century of Federal Programs to Help Those in Need

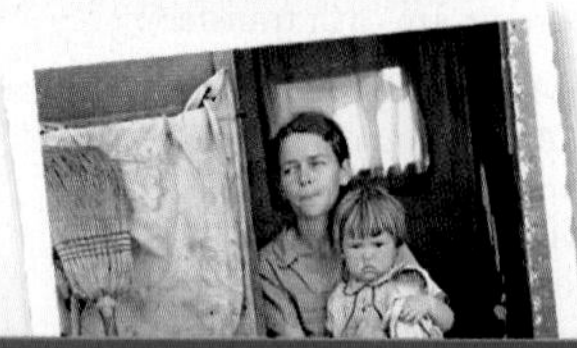

1910 — 1920 — 1930 — 1940 — 1950

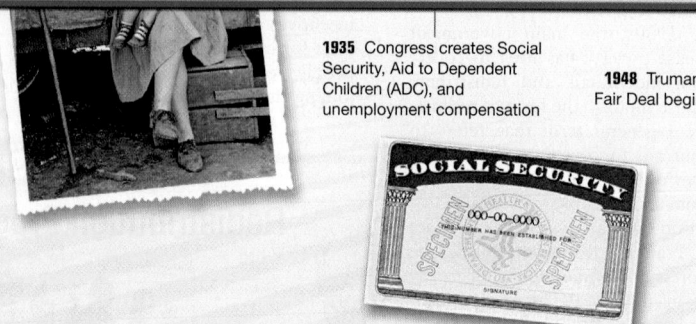

1916 Kern-McGillicuddy Act establishes workers' compensation for federal employees

1932 Franklin Roosevelt is elected President in the midst of the Great Depression

1933 Federal Emergency Relief Administration (FERA) founded

1935 Congress creates Social Security, Aid to Dependent Children (ADC), and unemployment compensation

1948 Truman's Fair Deal begins

1950 Social Security extended to 3.5 million recipients; ADC becomes AFDC (Aid to Families with Dependent Children)

▲ Throughout the 1990s, federal spending on social programs grew to include more and more people in need. ***What are some of the trade-offs involved in spending on social programs?***

in-kind benefits goods and services provided for free or at greatly reduced prices

- ***Social Security*** The Social Security program was created in 1935, during the Great Depression. At the time, many elderly people lost their life savings and had no income. The program collects payroll taxes from current workers and then redistributes that money to current recipients. Those who receive Social Security include retired people, people unable to work because of a disability, and, in some cases, the widowed spouses or orphaned children of such individuals.
- ***Unemployment insurance*** Unemployment insurance is funded by taxes paid by employers. Compensation checks provide money to workers who have lost their jobs. Recipients must offer proof that they have made efforts to get work. As with TANF, states set the rules for this program. The program is supposed to supply only temporary help. As a result, most states pay benefits to workers for only 26 weeks. In periods of high unemployment, however, the government may decide to pay the benefits longer.
- ***Workers' compensation*** This program is an insurance program for workers injured or disabled on the job. It is mandated by state law. Most employers pay workers' compensation insurance to cover future claims by employees.

In-Kind Benefits

The government also provides poor people with **in-kind benefits,** goods and services provided for free or at greatly reduced prices. One example is the food stamp program. People who qualify receive a card with a magnetic memory strip. It contains information about the value of food purchases the person is due that month. He or she can then use the card to help meet food expenses.

Another type of in-kind benefit is subsidized housing. Poor people are allowed to rent housing for less than the regular rent.

Background Note

Social Security The Social Security Act of 1935 was planned to help certain workers who had no retirement income. Over the years, changes to the act have made it the single largest social program of the federal government. It now covers many more workers, their spouses, their children under 18, and disabled workers. Workers and their employers equally share the payroll taxes for Social Security and disability. A self-employed person must pay it all. Social Security and disability payments are determined by lifetime earnings. The money goes into a dedicated fund, which is used to make Social Security and disability payments and is not used for other federal spending.

Answer

Caption Possible responses: less money available for other programs; people will become dependent; possible higher taxes

1996 AFDC changed to Temporary Assistance for Needy Families (TANF)

1965 Congress creates Medicare (for retirees and the disabled) and Medicaid (for the poor)

1974 Food Stamp program extended nationwide

1960 1970 1980 1990 2000

2001 President Bush establishes White House Office of Faith-Based and Community Initiatives

1964 Johnson's Great Society program expands welfare with new programs such as Head Start preschool education

The government pays the difference to the landlord.

Legal aid is legal advice given at no charge. This in-kind benefit covers contracts and other business matters. Poor people charged with a crime may be represented in court by public defenders, who are paid with tax dollars. (The right of an accused person to have legal counsel is guaranteed by the Sixth Amendment.)

Medical Benefits

Another social service that the U.S. government provides is health insurance for the elderly, the disabled, and the poor. Medicare covers Americans over age 65 and disabled people. Medicaid covers some poor people who are unemployed or not covered by their employer's insurance plans. Administered under the Social Security program, Medicare and Medicaid are enormously expensive programs. We will examine them further in Chapter 14.

A program called the State Children's Health Insurance Program (SCHIP) provides health insurance for children who are uninsured. SCHIP is funded by both state and federal governments. States write the rules for the program within federal guidelines. The program covers more than 6.5 million children.

Education

Federal, state, and local governments all provide educational opportunities to those who need aid. The federal government funds programs from preschool to college. State and local programs aid students with learning disabilities.

Education programs add to the nation's human capital and labor productivity. As explained earlier in the chapter, improved education and technology can make an entire economy more productive.

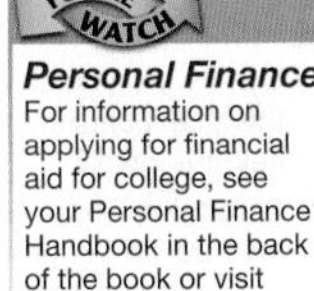

Personal Finance For information on applying for financial aid for college, see your Personal Finance Handbook in the back of the book or visit **PearsonSuccessNet.com**

CHECKPOINT ***Identify four programs that provide cash benefits to the poor.***

Virtual Economics

L3 Differentiate

Understanding Unequal Distribution of Income Use the following lesson from the NCEE **Virtual Economics *CD-ROM*** to explain causes of poverty in the United States. Click on Browse Economics Lessons, specify grades 9–12, and use the key words *income inequality*.

In this activity, students will take part in a simulation of unequal distribution of income in the United States and discuss the measures and causes of poverty.

LESSON TITLE	POVERTY AND INCOME INEQUALITY
Type of Activity	Simulation
Complexity	Moderate
Time	60 minutes
NCEE Standards	13

MAKE DECISIONS

Divide students into groups and assign each group one a type of public assistance. Have each group prepare a two-minute speech on why their program should be funded. The class will then vote on each proposal and decide which programs to fund or discard. Keep track of these results on the board.

L4 Differentiate Have students extend the debate to public vs. private financing of retirement, charities, and medical care. They should research the arguments and actions taken on both sides of the debate and present them to the class.

EXTEND

Have students research one of the following programs: Temporary Assistance for Needy Families (TANF); Medicare; Medicaid; Food Stamp program, State Children's Health Insurance Program (SCHIP); bilingual education; Pell Grants for College Study; or subsidized housing. Have students identify who this program helps, the reason the government provides it, and how effective it is.

PERSONAL FINANCE ACTIVITY

To help students identify sources of financial aid, you may want to use the Personal Finance Handbook lesson on paying for college (pp. PF 40–41) and the activity worksheet (Personal Finance All-in-One, pp. 100–101).

GUIDING QUESTION WRAP UP

Have students return to the section Guiding Question. Review the completed graphic organizer and clarify any misunderstandings. Have a wrap up discussion about how the government helps the poor.

Assess and Remediate

L3 L2 Collect the "Analyzing Political Cartoons" worksheets, the "Survey on How to Help Those in Need" worksheets, and the "Helping People in Need" worksheets to assess students understanding of the government's safety net programs and the debate surrounding their funding.

L3 Assign the Section 4 Assessment questions; identify student misconceptions.

L3 Give Section Quiz A (Unit 1 All-in-One, p. 125).

L2 Give Section Quiz B (Unit 1 All-in-One, p. 126).

Answer

Checkpoint Four programs that provide cash benefits are Temporary Assistance for Needy Families (TANF), Social Security, unemployment insurance, and workers' compensation.

Have students complete the Self-Test Online and continue their work in the **Essential Questions Journal**.

REMEDIATION AND SUGGESTIONS

Use the chart below to help students who are struggling with content.

WEAKNESS	REMEDIATION
Defining key terms (Questions 3, 4, 5, 6)	Have students use the interactive Economic Dictionary Online.
Disagreements over ways to fight poverty (Questions 2, 7)	Have students create a Pro and Con organizer to compare the ideas on both sides of the arguments about funding and delivering welfare services.
Government programs to fight poverty and the purpose of each (Questions 1, 5, 8, 10)	Have students create a summary chart of all the welfare programs and their purposes.
Government support for private solutions (Question 9)	Have students describe the ways they raise funds for school activities or community projects.

▲ Community programs like these help create a safety net by providing meals to senior citizens or children. ***What are two ways that you can support such programs?***

Encouraging Private Action

In addition to providing direct assistance to the needy, federal and state governments also encourage private action. Federal tax law allows both individuals and corporations to take tax deductions for charitable donations. This policy provides an economic incentive to give money and property to relief organizations, as well as to other non-profit groups such as churches, hospitals, colleges, libraries, or museums. In 2006, American individuals and organizations gave $295 billion in deductible charitable contributions. As one tax expert noted:

grant a financial award given by a government agency to a private individual or group in order to carry out a specific task

> **"It's always better to give than receive. The glory of charitable donations is that you give and receive at the same time."**
>
> — Jeff Schnepper, "Give and Grow Rich With Charitable Deductions"

The government may also provide grants and other assistance to organizations that provide social services. A **grant** is a financial award given by a government agency to a private individual or group in order to carry out a specific task. Many people believe that private groups do a more effective job of helping people than the government can.

In 2001, President George W. Bush announced a controversial initiative, or new plan, that allowed religious organizations to compete for federal funds. The President believed that these groups provided a special compassion that made their programs particularly successful. Bush established an Office of Faith-Based and Community Initiatives to help religious groups work more effectively with the federal government. He also encouraged the states to create similar offices. Still, not everyone supported faith-based initiatives. Critics said that giving government money to religious organizations violated the First Amendment.

CHECKPOINT ***How does the tax law provide an incentive to help the needy?***

SECTION 4 ASSESSMENT

Essential Questions Journal To continue to build a response to the Essential Question, go to your **Essential Questions Journal.**

Guiding Question

1. Use your completed chart to answer this question: How does government help the poor?
2. **Extension** Suppose you were a member of Congress during a time of economic contraction. Would you vote in favor of extending unemployment compensation payments beyond 26 weeks? Why or why not?

Key Terms and Main Ideas

3. What is the **poverty threshold?** Why does it vary according to how many people are in a household?
4. What are three examples of **cash transfers?**
5. How are unemployment insurance and workers' compensation alike?
6. What are **in-kind benefits?**

Critical Thinking

7. **Analyze** How does the TANF program seek to answer one of the common objections to the older welfare system?
8. **Make Decisions** Would it make economic sense for the government to spend money giving job training to people who receive TANF payments? Why or why not?
9. **Draw Conclusions** Do you think tax incentives are necessary to encourage charitable giving? Explain.

Math Skills

10. Assume that the poverty threshold is $13,896 per year for a family of one adult and one child. Based on a 40-hour work week, how much salary would a single parent with one child have to take home each week in order to be above the poverty threshold?

Visit PearsonSuccessNet.com for additional math help.

Answers

Caption by volunteering to help these programs; by making a financial donation

Checkpoint Taxpayers are allowed to deduct their donations to charitable organizations from their income taxes.

Assessment Answers

1. Possible responses: cash transfers, such as TANF; in-kind programs, such as food stamps; medical benefits, such as Medicare; and education support, such as college grants
2. Possible response: Extend the payments because in an economic contraction, jobs are scarce.
3. It is the income level below that which is needed to support families. A larger household will need more money to supply their own needs than a smaller family.
4. Possible responses: Temporary Assistance for Needy Families (TANF), Social Security payments, unemployment insurance, and workers' compensation
5. Both are cash transfers made to workers who are not working, but unemployment insurance payments go to people who have lost their jobs and are actively looking for work. Workers who cannot work because they were injured on the job receive workers' compensation payments.
6. goods and services provided for free or at a greatly reduced price
7. Possible response: The TANF program provides work incentives and sets lifetime limits on payments to keep people from staying on welfare.
8. Possible responses: Training programs make it easier for people to find jobs and keep them, so they would not return to welfare. However, it may not make sense to provide training programs unless child care is provided to those who need it.
9. Possible response: Yes; people give more when they receive something in return, such as tax deductions.
10. A single parent would need to earn $6.69 an hour, and work 40 hours a week, 52 weeks a year, to be above the poverty threshold.

QUICK STUDY GUIDE

QUICK STUDY GUIDE

Chapter 3: American Free Enterprise

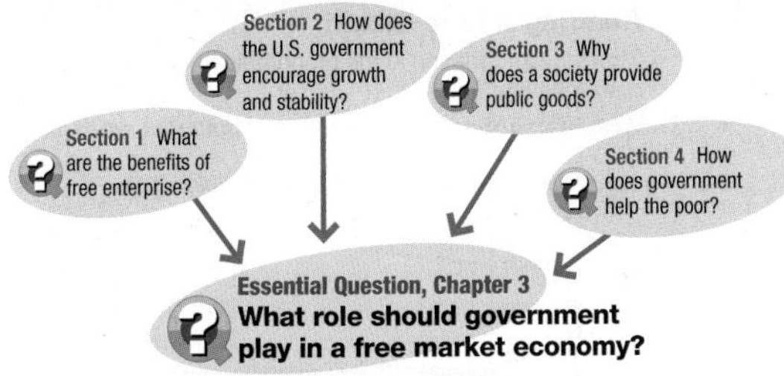

Section 1 What are the benefits of free enterprise?
Section 2 How does the U.S. government encourage growth and stability?
Section 3 Why does a society provide public goods?
Section 4 How does government help the poor?
Essential Question, Chapter 3
What role should government play in a free market economy?

Roles of the Government

Regulating Business	
Examples	• Public disclosure • Environmental rules • Consumer safety

Promoting Growth	
Examples	• Price stability • Regulation of banks • Patents and copyrights

Providing Public Goods	
Examples	• Roads and bridges • Defense • Police and fire protection

Providing a Safety Net	
Examples	• Social Security • Unemployment insurance • Medicare

Economic Dictionary

profit motive, *p. 51*
open opportunity, *p. 51*
legal equality, *p. 51*
private property rights, *p. 51*
free contract, *p. 51*
voluntary exchange, *p. 51*
interest group, *p. 52*
patriotism, *p. 52*
eminent domain, *p. 52*
public interest, *p. 53*
public disclosure laws, *p. 54*
macroeconomics, *p. 56*
microeconomics, *p. 56*
gross domestic product, *p. 57*
business cycle, *p. 57*
referendum, *p. 58*
obsolescence, *p. 59*
patent, *p. 61*
copyright, *p. 61*
work ethic, *p. 61*
public good, *p. 62*
public sector, *p. 63*
private sector, *p. 63*
infrastructure, *p. 63*
free rider, *p. 64*
market failure, *p. 65*
externality, *p. 65*
poverty threshold, *p. 68*
welfare, *p. 69*
cash transfers, *p. 69*
in-kind benefits, *p. 70*
grant, *p. 72*

Economics on the go Study anytime, anywhere. Download these files today.

Economic Dictionary online	Audio Review online	Action Graph online	Visual Glossary online	How the Economy Works online
Vocabulary Support in English and Spanish	Audio Study Guide in English and Spanish	Animated Charts and Graphs	Animated feature	Animated feature

Download to your computer or mobile device at PearsonSuccessNet.com

ASSIGN THE ESSENTIAL QUESTIONS JOURNAL

After students have finished studying the chapter, they should return to the chapter's essential question in the Essential Questions Journal and complete the activity.

Tell students to go back to the chapter opener and look at the image. Using the information they have gained from studying this chapter, ask **How does this illustrate the main ideas of the chapter?** *(Possible response: businesses such as the one shown in the picture benefit from the system of free enterprise. This system is characterized by the profit motive, open opportunity, legal equality, private property, and the freedom to buy and sell.)*

STUDY TIPS

Tell students that they are learning new concepts. To be sure they understand these new concepts, they should tie together ideas that are presented in separate sections of the chapter (or the book). Suggest they integrate concepts from several sections into paragraphs that summarize the chapter. They might reorganize by general concepts, by cause and effect, or by problem and solution.

Economics on the go Have students download the digital resources available at Economics on the Go for review and remediation.

Assessment at a Glance

TESTS AND QUIZZES

Section Assessments

Section Quizzes A and B, **Unit 1 All-in-One**

Self-Test Online

Chapter Assessments

Chapter Tests A and B, **Unit 1 All-in-One**

Economic Detective, **Unit 1 All-in-One**

Document-based Assessment, p. 75

Exam*View*

AYP Monitoring Assessments

PERFORMANCE ASSESSMENT

Teacher's Edition, pp. 52, 58, 65, 66, 69, 70

Simulation Activities, Chapter 3

Virtual Economics on CD-ROM, pp. 53, 59, 64, 71

Essential Questions Journal, Chapter 3

Assessment Rubrics

Chapter Assessment

1. Possible responses: (a) to provide economic stability and security (b) the profit motive, open opportunity, and economic rights (c) Possible answer: Benefits outweigh costs because, if banks fail, many people can lose their savings or businesses.
2. (a) gives authors of copyrighted work exclusive right to sell the work (b) Unauthorized downloading removes the copyright holder's control of access to the work. (c) Answers willl vary, but should reflect awareness that private property rights are involved.
3. (a) benefit to each individual is less than the cost each would have to pay if it were provided privately, and total benefits to society are greater than the total cost; (b) Possible response: new library computers; (c) Possible response: A positive externality is that more patrons will come to the library to use the computers, so more employees might be needed. A negative externality is that the library budget will increase due to increased electricity usage and additional staff.
4. (a) to help the poor, the elderly, and the disadvantaged (b) Possible response: Yes, because resources are not evenly distributed throughout society.
5. Social Security was the most expensive program. It exceeded Medicare, the next most expensive, by just under $300 billion in 2007.
6. Unemployment and TANF both did not increase in cost between 2003 and 2007.
7. Social Security retirement benefits increased by about 20 percent. Medicare increased by about 30 percent. Medicaid increased by between 12 and 20 percent.
8. Unemployment compensation is most likely to change with the business cycle, because an expanding economy is likely to have job growth with fewer unemployment payments, while a contracting economy has more job loss so more unemployment benefit payments.
9. Guide students' search for information by identifying key words and reliable sources. Students must provide in-depth information about their topic in their summary.
10. Answers will vary, but the class should discuss the appropriateness of the government action, alternative actions the government could have taken, the results of the government taking no action, and the appropriate amount of influence the government should have on the economy.

CHAPTER 3 ASSESSMENT

To test your understanding of key terms and main ideas, visit **PearsonSuccessNet.com**

Key Terms and Main Ideas

To make sure you understand the key terms and main ideas of this chapter, review the Checkpoint and Section Assessment questions and look at the Quick Study Guide on the preceding page.

Critical Thinking

1. **Analyze (a)** What goals does the government hope to achieve by regulating banks? **(b)** What principles of free enterprise conflict with this regulation? **(c)** In this case, do you think the benefits of regulation outweigh the costs? Why or why not?
2. **Apply (a)** How do copyright laws protect property rights? **(b)** Some consumers download music or videos from Internet sites not authorized by the copyright holder. Do those actions violate copyright laws? **(c)** Do you think people who do this should be punishable under the law? Why or why not?
3. **Predict (a)** What are the two cost-benefit criteria that a public good must meet? **(b)** Identify which of the following you think meet this test: buying new computers for the library; building a shopping mall; building a cellphone tower. **(c)** Choose one of the above. Identify one positive and one negative externality that might result.
4. **Draw Conclusions (a)** What is the goal of government redistribution programs? **(b)** Do you think redistributing income is an appropriate role for the government to play in a free enterprise economy? Why or why not?

Applying Your Math Skills

Reading a Line Graph

Study the information in the graph below. Then, answer the questions that follow.

Visit PearsonSuccessNet.com for additional math help.

Federal Spending on Social Programs, 2003–2007

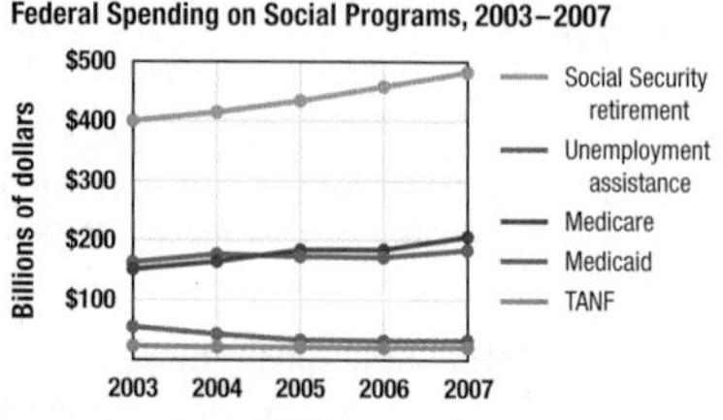

SOURCE: U.S.Census Bureau, *Statistical Abstract of the United States*, 2008

5. Which is the most expensive of these programs? By how much does it exceed the next most expensive program in the final year shown?
6. Which two programs did not increase in cost between 2003 and 2007?
7. To find the percentage increase in spending from 2003 to 2007, you subtract the 2003 figure from the 2007 figure and then divide by the 2003 figure. The result, a decimal answer, is then converted to a percentage by multiplying by 100. Using that formula, what was the percentage increase of the three most expensive programs?
8. Which of these five programs is most likely to change with the business cycle? Why do you think so?

Essential Question Activity

Essential Questions Journal To respond to the chapter Essential Question, go to your **Essential Questions Journal.**

9. As a citizen and a consumer, you will always be affected by the role of government in your economic life. Complete the following activity to answer the Essential Question **What role should government play in a free market economy?** For this activity, the class will be divided into four groups. Each group will look in depth at one of the following topics: government regulation; encouraging economic growth; providing public goods; providing an economic safety net. You will research your topic in print or use online news sources that illustrate the government's role. The worksheet in your Essential Questions Journal or the electronic worksheet available at **PearsonSuccessNet.com** lists some reliable sources and key words you can use in your search. After your group chooses a topic, prepare a brief presentation using the Summary Report form provided in your worksheet. Each group should report its findings and reactions to the whole class.
10. **Modify** After each group has completed the presentation of its findings, the entire class should evaluate the information and discuss the following questions:
    (a) Was the action taken by the government appropriate to the situation?
    (b) What other action might the government have taken?
    (c) What might have happened if the government had taken no action?
    (d) Based on this particular incident, do you think the government should have more or less influence on the economy?
    (e) Under what conditions might you feel differently?

WebQuest online The Economics WebQuest Challenges students to use 21st century skills to answer the Essential Question.

ESSENTIAL
VIDEO
By Students For Students
For videos on Essential Questions, go to PearsonSuccessNet.com

Remind students to continue to develop an Essential Questions video. Guidelines and a production binder are available at www.PearsonSuccessNet.com.

CHAPTER 3 ASSESSMENT

DOCUMENT-BASED ASSESSMENT

When may a government take private property for public use?

According to the Fifth Amendment, a government may appropriate private property for public use (such as road building) as long as "just compensation" is given to the property owner. In a 2005 decision, the Supreme Court ruled that this principle of "eminent domain" also allowed a city to appropriate homes in a poor neighborhood so that developers could improve the area economically.

Document A

"The City has carefully formulated an economic development plan that it believes will provide appreciable benefits to the community, including—but by no means limited to—new jobs and increased tax revenue.... Because that plan unquestionably serves a public purpose, the takings challenged here satisfy the public use requirement of the Fifth Amendment.... Promoting economic development is a traditional and long accepted function of government."

—Justice John Paul Stevens, majority opinion, *Kelo* v. *New London* [source: http://www.law.cornell.edu/supct/html/04-108.ZO.html]

Document B

"Under the banner of economic development, all private property is now vulnerable to being taken and transferred to another private owner, so long as it might be upgraded—i.e., given to an owner who will use it in a way that the legislature deems more beneficial to the public.... The beneficiaries are likely to be those citizens with disproportionate influence and power in the political process, including large corporations and development firms."

—Justice Sandra Day O'Connor, dissenting opinion, *Kelo* v. *New London*

Document C

ANALYZING DOCUMENTS

Use your knowledge of opportunity costs and Documents A, B, and C to answer questions 1–3.

1. **According to Document A, the majority of the Supreme Court in this case believed that**
   - **A.** the principle of eminent domain was unconstitutional.
   - **B.** economic development of a poor area was in the public interest.
   - **C.** a government may take private property without offering compensation.
   - **D.** the Fifth Amendment did not apply to this particular case.
2. **According to Document B, the use of eminent domain in this case was**
   - **A.** justified because it would lead to improvements that were in the public interest.
   - **B.** unjustified because it would not lead to improvements in the neighborhood.
   - **C.** unfair because it would benefit some private citizens at the expense of others.
   - **D.** fair because the people who lost their property would be paid for it.
3. **Which documents express similar viewpoints on the subject of eminent domain and private property?**
   - **A.** A and B
   - **B.** A and C
   - **C.** B and C
   - **D.** A, B, and C

WRITING ABOUT ECONOMICS

The Supreme Court decision in *Kelo* v. *New London* was highly controversial. Use the documents on this page and on the Web site below to answer the question: ***When may a government take private property for public use?*** Use the sources to support your opinion.

In Partnership

To read more about issues related to this topic, visit **PearsonSuccessNet.com**

Document-Based Assessment

ANALYZING DOCUMENTS

1. B
2. C
3. C

WRITING ABOUT ECONOMICS

Possible answer: The government should be able to take private property for public use, such as a road or a reservoir. The government should not be able to take private property so that another private owner can buy it and develop it.

L2 Differentiate Students use all documents on the page to support their thesis.

L3 Differentiate Students use the documents on this page and additional information available online at www.PearsonSuccessNet.com to support their answer.

L4 Differentiate Students incorporate information provided in the textbook and online at www.PearsonSuccessNet.com and include additional research to support their opinion.

Economics online *All print resources are available on the Teacher's Resource Library CD-ROM and online at* www.PearsonSuccessNet.com.

Go Online to www.PearsonSuccessNet.com for a student rubric and extra documents.

Introduce the Databank

This collection of data about the United States economy presents information that can help students as they read, answer questions, and do further research on many chapters. Remind students to use the skills described on the Graph Preview pages at the front of the book (pp. xxviii–xxxii) when they need to interpret or create a graph or chart.

The databank may be used to supplement the information in particular chapters, which are noted in the lesson for each graph. In addition, each graph is accompanied by questions that can be used to stir discussion of the significance of the data.

Economics online Visit www.PearsonSuccessNet.com for updates on the data. Use the updates to have students compare the new data to the data in their books.

Teach

The graphs on this page can supplement or be compared with graphs in Unit 1, as students learn how societies decide how and what they will produce. Students may want to compare these graphs with those in Unit 3, as they work to understand business organizations and labor.

U.S. ECONOMY BY TYPES OF BUSINESS

Explain to students that while corporations account for only 20 percent of U.S. businesses, they account for 80 percent of all sales. Ask **What does this graph show?** *(the value of the business receipts, or sales, made by businesses from 1985 to 2004)* **How did the business receipts of corporations in 1985 differ from those in 2004?** *(In 1985, receipts were about $7.6 trillion; in 2004, they were about $22 trillion.)*

NUMBER OF FARMS

Ask **What type of change does this graph show?** *(the drop in the number of farms between 1930 and 2007)* **Use the graph to explain the concept of urbanization**. *(In 1930, there were more than 6 million farms. As technology changed, many people found work in factories rather than on farms. By 1960 there were fewer than 4 million farms, and by 2007 there were only 2 million.)*

SIZE OF FARMS

Ask **Why do you think there is not much change shown on this graph?** *(The graph starts in 1978, and the size of farms has not changed much during that period.)* Ask **What information would you need to draw conclusions from the two graphs about farms?** *(You would need to know how the acreage changed between 1930 and 1978.)*

Databank The United States Economy

This databank gives you information about the economy of the United States, starting with its resources and producers. You will then take a closer look at American workers and consumers.

U.S. Economy by Types of Business

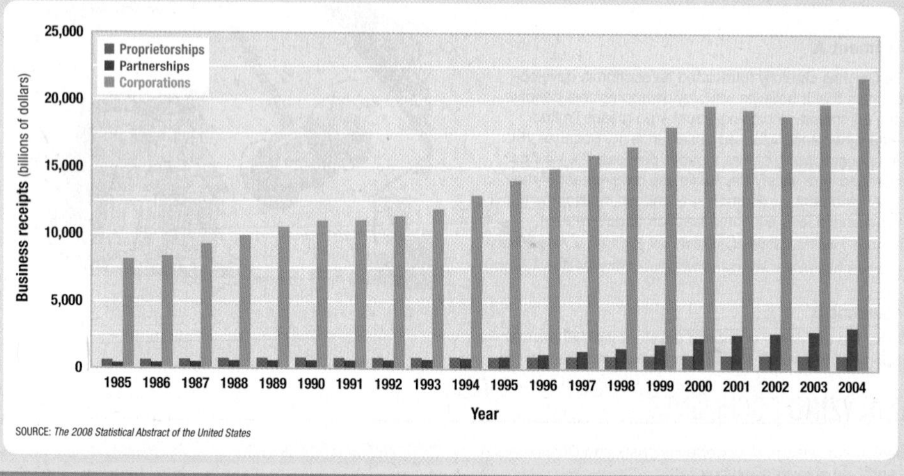

SOURCE: *The 2008 Statistical Abstract of the United States*

Number of Farms

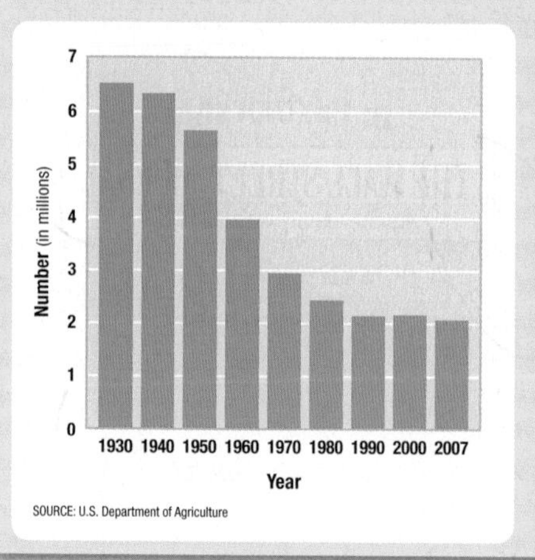

SOURCE: U.S. Department of Agriculture

Size of Farms

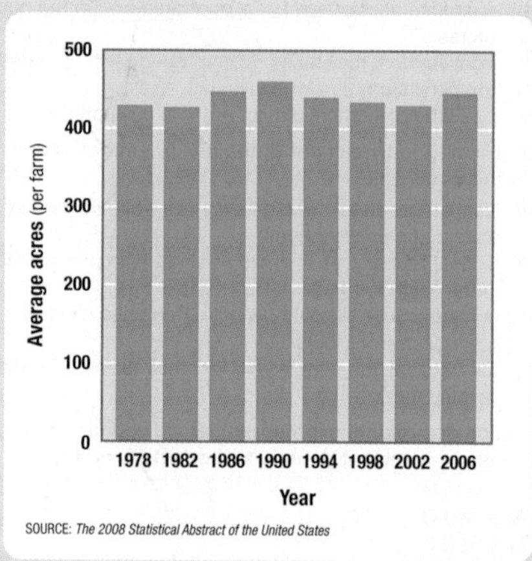

SOURCE: *The 2008 Statistical Abstract of the United States*

Economics online For updated data, visit PearsonSuccessNet.com

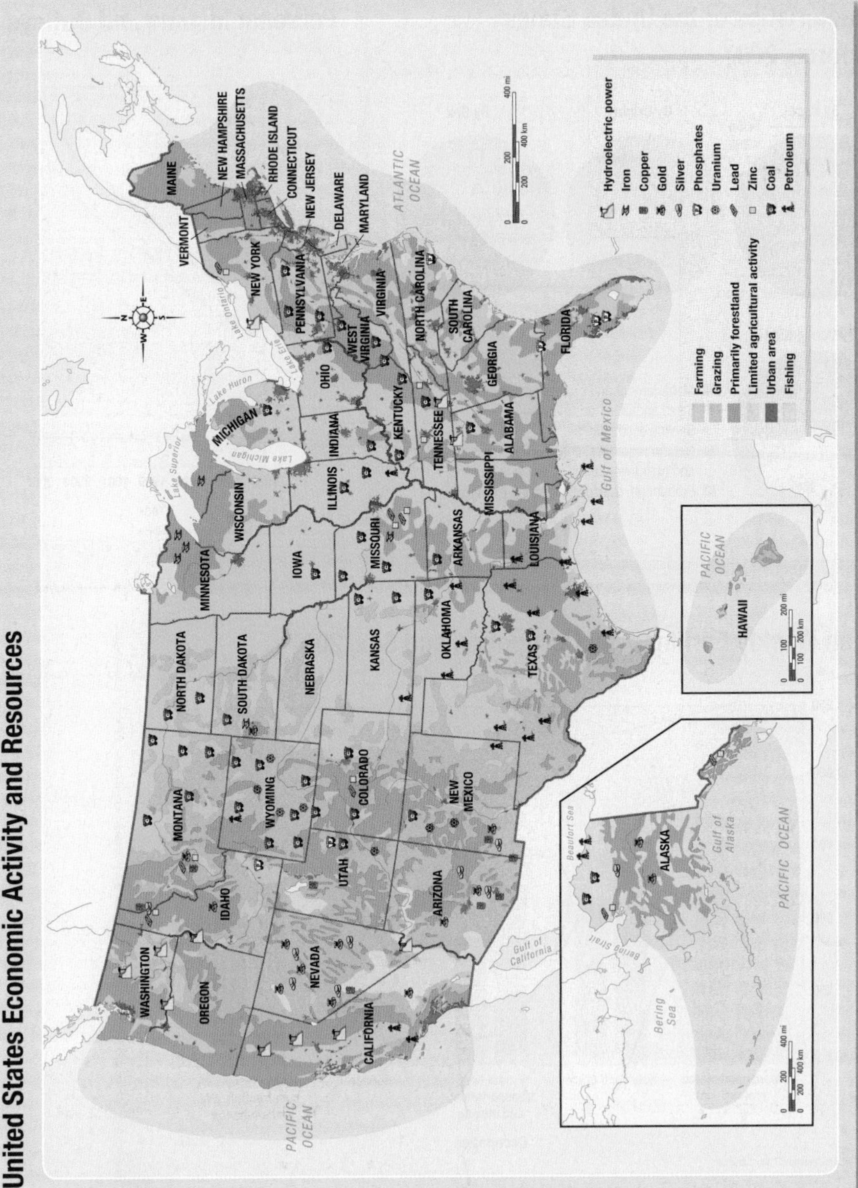

Databank: The United States Economy

Teach

This map can be useful in discussions of the factors of production in Chapter 1 and of gross domestic product in Chapter 12.

UNITED STATES ECONOMIC ACTIVITY AND RESOURCES

Have students look at the map from different perspectives. For example, have them find the various sources of energy shown; the materials that are mined in different locations; and the variety of ways the land is used. Ask **What conclusions about the potential economic activity of different regions can you draw from looking at the map?** *(Possible answers: Most hydroelectric power is produced in the West; coal is shown in north–south lines, usually along mountain ranges; there is very little if any grazing east of the Mississippi River.)* Remind students that land, labor, and capital are the three factors of production that can be combined to produce goods and services. Ask **What specific factors of production are shown on the map, and how could they be combined to produce goods and services?** *(Possible answer: Land that contains coal, laborers who work in the mines, and money to build power plants combine to produce electricity.)*

Have students create a map of economic resources and activity in their own state. Ask them to find three industries in the state that relate to the information on their map.

Teach

When students are learning about business and labor in chapters 8 and 9, they may find it useful to know some statistics about the workforce and incomes in the United States.

CHARACTERISTICS OF THE UNITED STATES WORKFORCE, 2007

Have students look at the first chart on page 78. Ask **How could you use these pie charts to estimate the approximate percentage of Hispanic women in the workforce?** *(You could multiply 46.4 percent of women in the workforce by 14 percent of people of Hispanic origin in the workforce. However, you do not know for sure that the distribution of men and women is the same in each sector of origin.)* **What is that percentage?** *(about 6.5 percent)* Ask **What type of occupation is the largest percentage of the workforce engaged in?** *(management and professional jobs)* **Why?** *(As the United States becomes more of a service-based economy, this sector has grown, while other areas such as production have shrunk.)*

PERSONAL INCOME AND OUTLAYS

This chart tracks how much people earn and how much they spend. It shows totals of both, but does not indicate how any individual's spending compares with income. Ask **With this graph as a starting point, what questions would you ask in order to dig deeper into an understanding of the relationship between income and spending?** *(Possible answers: How does spending relate to income in different income brackets? What percentage of people spend more than they earn? What, exactly, is included in the "outlays" category?)* Assign groups of students one question to research and have them present their findings to the class.

MEDIAN WEEKLY EARNINGS, BY OCCUPATION AND SEX, 2007

Have students compare this bar chart with the pie charts on this page. Ask **What information is clarified here that was not available in the pie charts?** *(the median income for men and women in each occupational category)* Ask **In general, how do women's earnings compare with men's?** *(Women make about 75 percent of what men make.)* Have students research more recent trends to see if this percentage has changed since 2004.

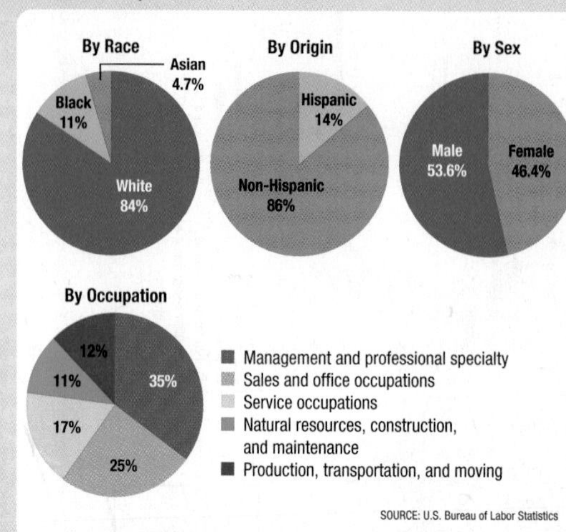

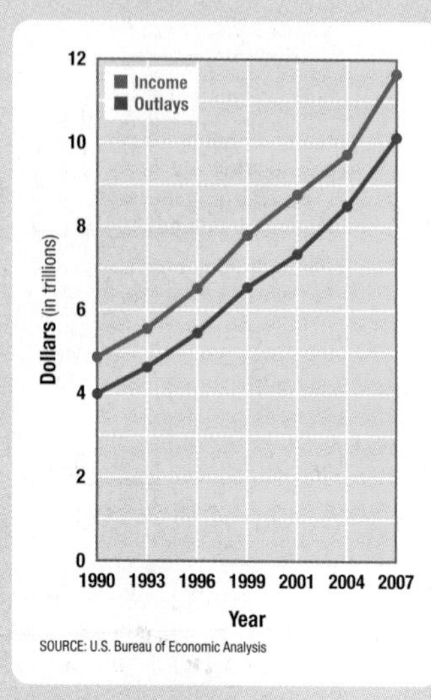

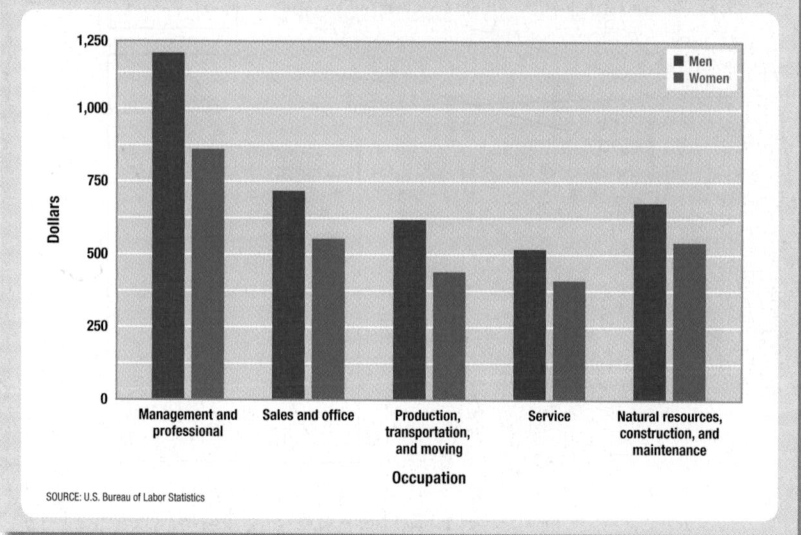

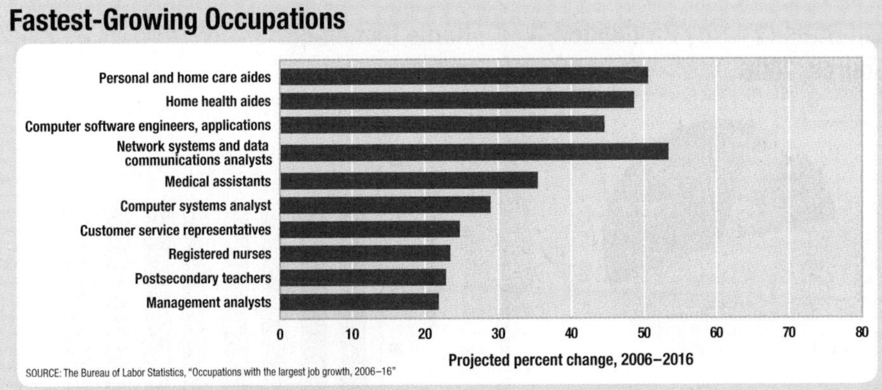

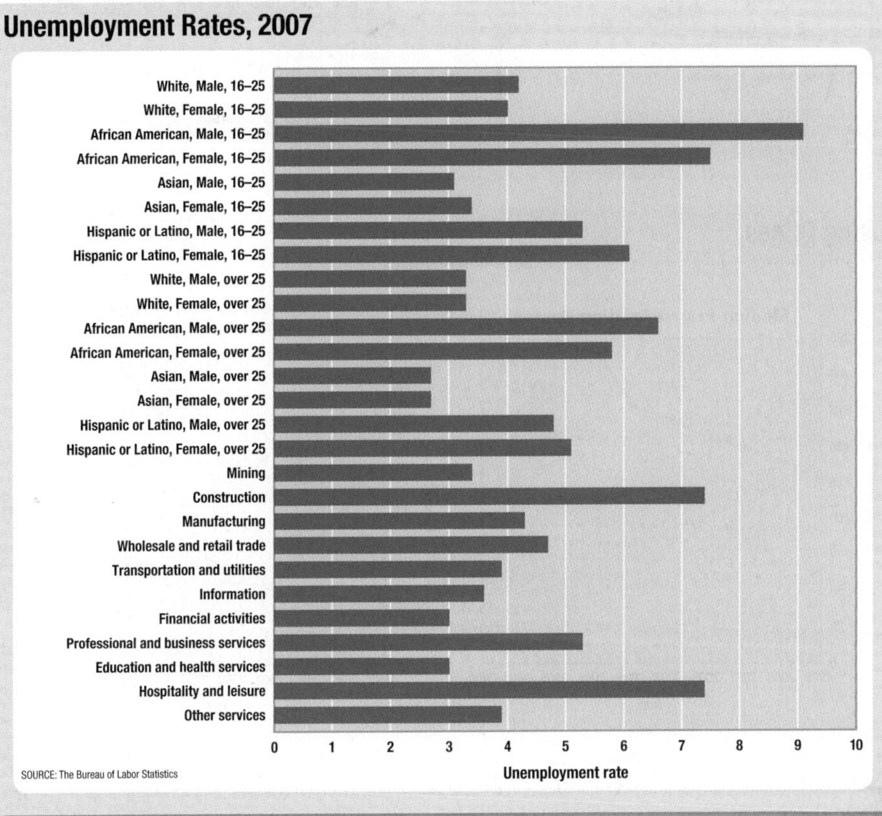

Teach

The graphs on this page can be particularly useful when students are learning about economic challenges in Chapter 13. They can also enhance understanding of the business and labor trends discussed in Unit 3.

FASTEST-GROWING OCCUPATIONS

Tracking occupational trends can help people understand the prospects for employment in various fields. Ask **How would you summarize the information in the chart?** *(Possible answer: Healthcare and computing are both showing strong growth.)* Have students discuss the reasons for these trends. For example, ask them to discuss the impact of the retiring baby boomers on the demand for healthcare professionals.

UNEMPLOYMENT RATES, 2007

Explain to students that this chart breaks down unemployment in two ways: first, by race or ethnicity and age; then by occupation. Ask **What two occupations had the highest levels of unemployment?** *(construction and hospitality and leisure)* Have students research unemployment trends in 2008 and 2009, when unemployment rates were higher than usual. Have them compare the statistics they find with the 2007 figures. Ask **What trends have you found?**

Teach

The graphs on this page can be particularly useful when students are learning about finance in Unit 4, and about government's interaction with the economy in Unit 6. Both the housing market and the energy market have experienced huge swings in recent years, and students should be encouraged to research the changes that have taken place and compare current data with the data in their textbooks. The housing graphs can be used in conjunction with Chapter 10, Money and Banking, to analyze the changes in the mortgage market.

UNITED STATES ENERGY PRODUCTION, BY SOURCE

Explain to students that the two different types of natural gas shown on the chart are "dry," which is the gas that remains after processing; and "plant liquids," which refers to usable liquid material separated out during processing. Ask **What percentage of energy production shown on the graph comes from fossil fuels?** *(82 percent from coal, natural gas, and crude oil)* Ask students **Which sources of energy shown on the chart are considered to be renewable?** *(nuclear, hydroelectric, and biofuels)* Have students research international energy production to understand what percentage of the world's energy is produced by the United States.

HOME OWNERSHIP

Investigating changes in the percentage of home ownership in 2008 and 2009 may provide a useful introduction to the power of the housing market to affect the economy. Have students draw a map of the United States, showing the changes in housing prices in five regions.

HOUSING PRICES

Students should use these graphs to help in the discussion of the subprime mortgage crisis in Chapter 10. Ask students to imagine a homeowner who makes $5,000 per month. Explain that a rule of thumb is that a mortgage should not exceed one week's take-home pay. This owner's gross weekly pay would be $1,153, but after taxes, it would be somewhere around 60 percent of that: $692. Ask **What would the monthly mortgage payment have been in 2002?** *(18 percent of $5,000: $900)* **What would the payment have been in 2006?** *(23.5 percent of $5,000: $1,175)* Ask **How do these numbers help explain what happened during the subprime mortgage crisis?** *(Homeowners were not able to make their mortgage payments, partly because their mortgage was too large relative to their income.)*

United States Energy Production, by Source, 2006

27% · 37% · 15% · 3% · 12% · 4% · 5%

- Coal
- Natural gas (dry)
- Crude oil
- Natural gas (plant liquids)
- Nuclear electric power
- Hydroelectric power
- Biofuels

SOURCE: U.S. Energy Information Administration

Home Ownership

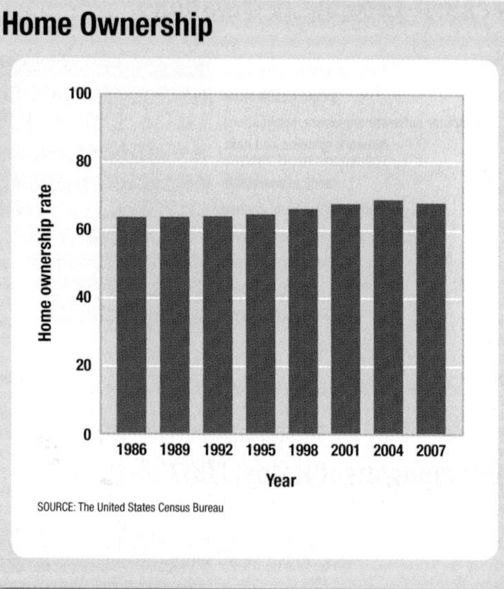

Housing Prices

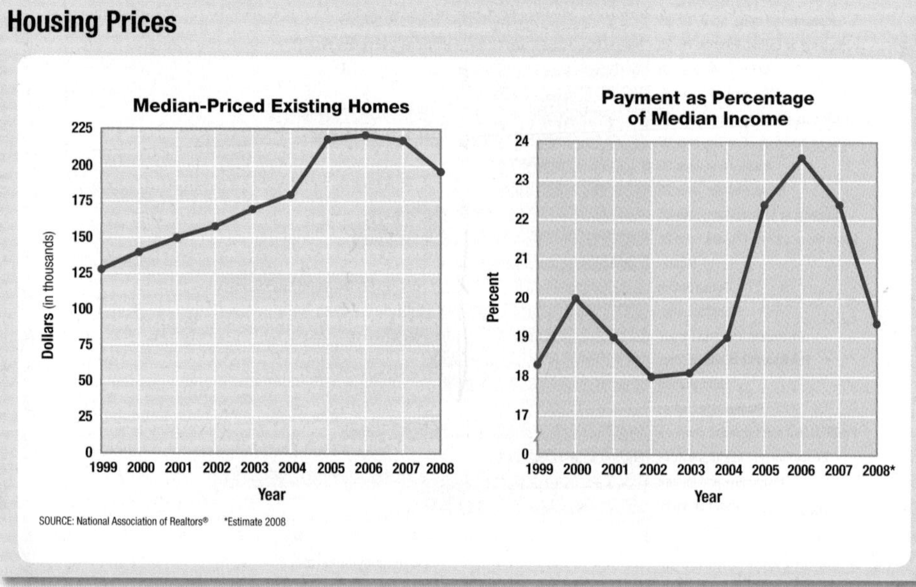

80 DATABANK

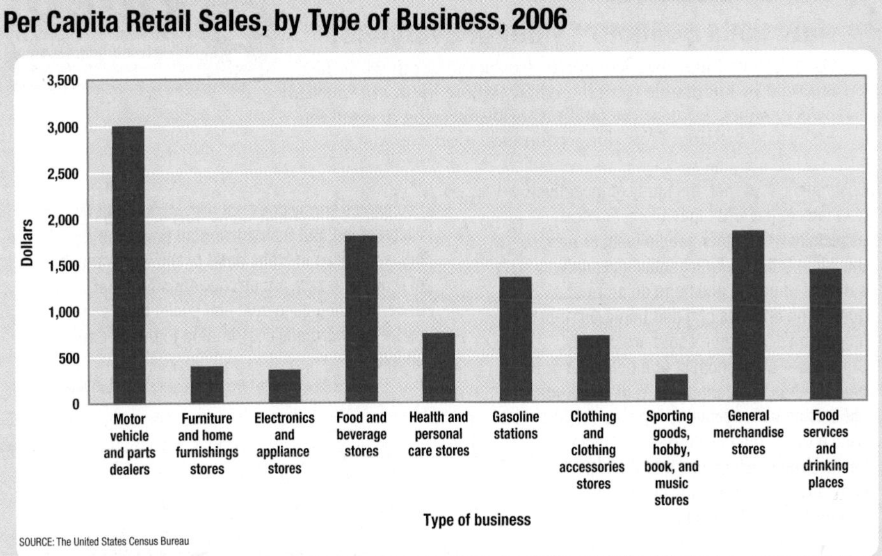

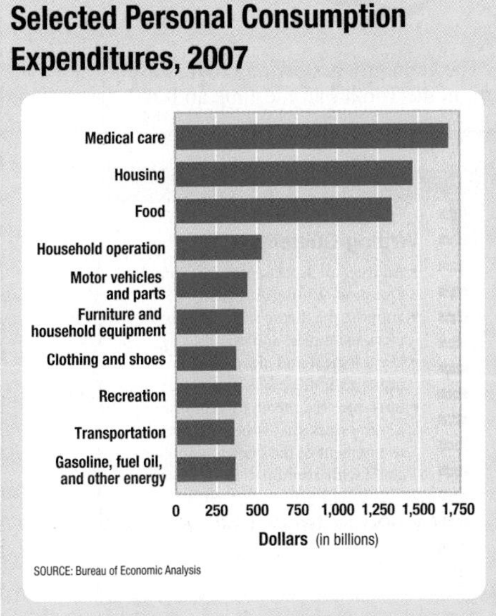

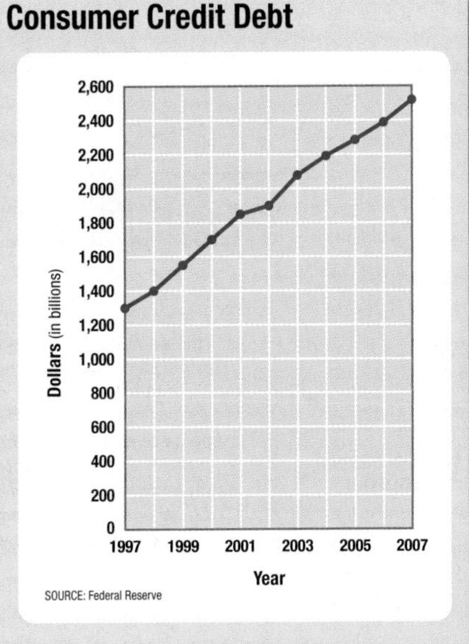

Databank: The United States Economy

Teach

The selling and buying of goods and services is at the heart of economics. The charts on this page can be used throughout the book, but will be particularly useful in understanding how markets work in Unit 2 and how countries measure their economic performance in Unit 5.

PER CAPITA RETAIL SALES, BY TYPE OF BUSINESS, 2006

Ask **What type of business had the largest sales?** *(motor vehicle and parts dealers)* Have students use the graph to write a few sentences describing U.S. buying patterns in 2006.

SELECTED PERSONAL CONSUMPTION EXPENDITURES, 2007

Ask students to look at the expenditures listed in this chart and compare those with the retail sales above. Ask **Which two expenditures do not show up on the retail sales chart?** *(medical care and housing)* Then ask **Why do you think spending on medical care is so high?** Have students look at the graph of health expenditures in other countries in the graph on page 477 and discuss the role that the government plays in healthcare around the world.

CONSUMER CREDIT DEBT

Ask **How much has consumer credit grown in the past ten years? Why?** *(It has almost doubled, from 1.3 trillion to almost 2.6 trillion. Increased credit card use has contributed to this number.)* Ask the class whether anyone has received offers in the mail for credit cards. Ask if their parents receive these offers. Bring a sample credit card offer to class, and evaluate the messages that are in the offer.

Essential Question

How does economics affect everyone?

BELLRINGER

Ask students to read the paragraph under the Essential Question. Then have volunteers suggest examples of how economics affects them personally.

EXPLAIN

Before you read aloud the first excerpt by economists Steven D. Levitt and Stephen J. Dubner, you may want to explain that their book, *Freakonomics,* covers the field of behavioral economics. This field of study combines classical economics with the emotional rules of human behavior.

DISCUSS

Have students review the quotations on the page. Ask students to explain the role of incentives in the economy. **What is the incentive for the steelmaker to avoid polluting the environment?** *(It avoids a large fine.)* **How does this incentive affect you as a consumer?** *(The price of products made from steel, such as cars, goes up.)* **How can understanding economics help the welfare of people?** *(Possible answer: If people can understand how to apply good economic principles throughout the world, fewer people will experience poverty, misery, and crises.)*

L2 Differentiate Pair students to read the articles and summarize the main thesis. Ask them to give any supporting details or arguments to the thesis.

ANALYZE A CARTOON

Have students silently read the cartoon's caption. Have them work in small groups to discuss why a parent might resort to giving an IOU instead of money. Have small groups work together to create their own humorous cartoon about an economic issue. Invite volunteers to share their cartoons with the class.

BULLETIN BOARD ACTIVITY

Have students revisit the Unit Essential Question articles that they have posted as they have studied the chapters. Have them discuss the relevance of the articles to the question and whether their opinions have changed since they first read the article.

EXTEND

Have students complete their work on the Essential Questions Video and present their work to the class.

L4 Differentiate Organize students into small groups to create their own Unit Challenge page. Have them find two articles and a political cartoon that address the Essential Question. Then have them present their work to the class, explaining the relevance of their material to the question.

Unit 1 Challenge

Essential Question, Unit 1

How does economics affect everyone?

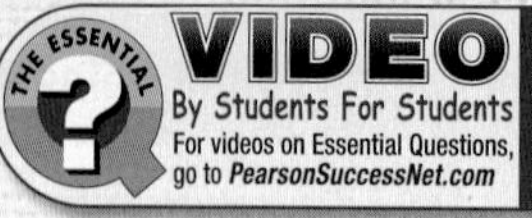
THE ESSENTIAL
VIDEO
By Students For Students
For videos on Essential Questions, go to PearsonSuccessNet.com

Some people think that economics does not affect them. In fact, it would be impossible to find anybody whose life is *not* touched by economics. Look at the opinions below, keeping in mind the Essential Question: How does economics affect everyone?

> "Economics is, at root, the study of incentives: how people get what they want, or need, especially when other people want or need the same thing.... An incentive is simply a means of urging people to do more of a good thing and less of a bad thing. But most incentives don't come about organically. Someone—an economist or a politician or a parent—has to invent them. Your three-year-old eats all her vegetables for a week? She wins a trip to the toy store. A big steelmaker belches too much smoke into the air? The company is fined for each cubic foot of pollutants over the legal limit."
>
> —Steven D. Levitt and Stephen J. Dubner, *Freakonomics*

> "Economics surely does not provide a romantic vision of life. But the widespread poverty, misery, and crises in many parts of the world, much of it unnecessary, are strong reminders that understanding economic and social laws can make an enormous contribution to the welfare of people."
>
> —Gary Becker, Nobel Prize acceptance speech, 1992

"The economy is slowing down. Last night the Tooth Fairy left me an IOU"

Essential Question
Writing Activity

Consider the different views of economics expressed in the sources on this page. Review what you've learned in this unit and your own life experiences about the effects of economics. ***Then write a well-constructed essay expressing your view of how economics affects everyone.***

Writing Guidelines

- Address all aspects of the Essential Question Writing Activity.
- Support the theme with relevant facts, examples, and details.
- Use a logical and clear plan of organization.
- Introduce the theme by establishing a framework that is beyond a simple restatement of the question and conclude with a summation of the theme.

For help with Expository Writing, refer to the *Writer's Handbook* in the Reference section, page S-1.

Essential Questions Journal

To respond to the unit Essential Question, go to your **Essential Questions Journal**.

Essential Question Writing Activity

Before students begin the writing activity, remind them to skim through the unit chapters to read the headings on each page. Have them read through any notes they took and review their chapter assessments and chapter projects.

Students should write a two-paragraph article. Paragraph one should outline how economics affects them personally. Paragraph two should explain why economics affects everyone.

L2 Differentiate Students should write a paragraph that explains how economics affects them personally, providing detailed examples.

L4 Differentiate Students should write a three-paragraph article that provides relevant examples of how economics affects everyone.

Before students begin work, distribute the Writing Assessment rubric, available at the Online Teacher Center at PearsonSuccessNet.com.

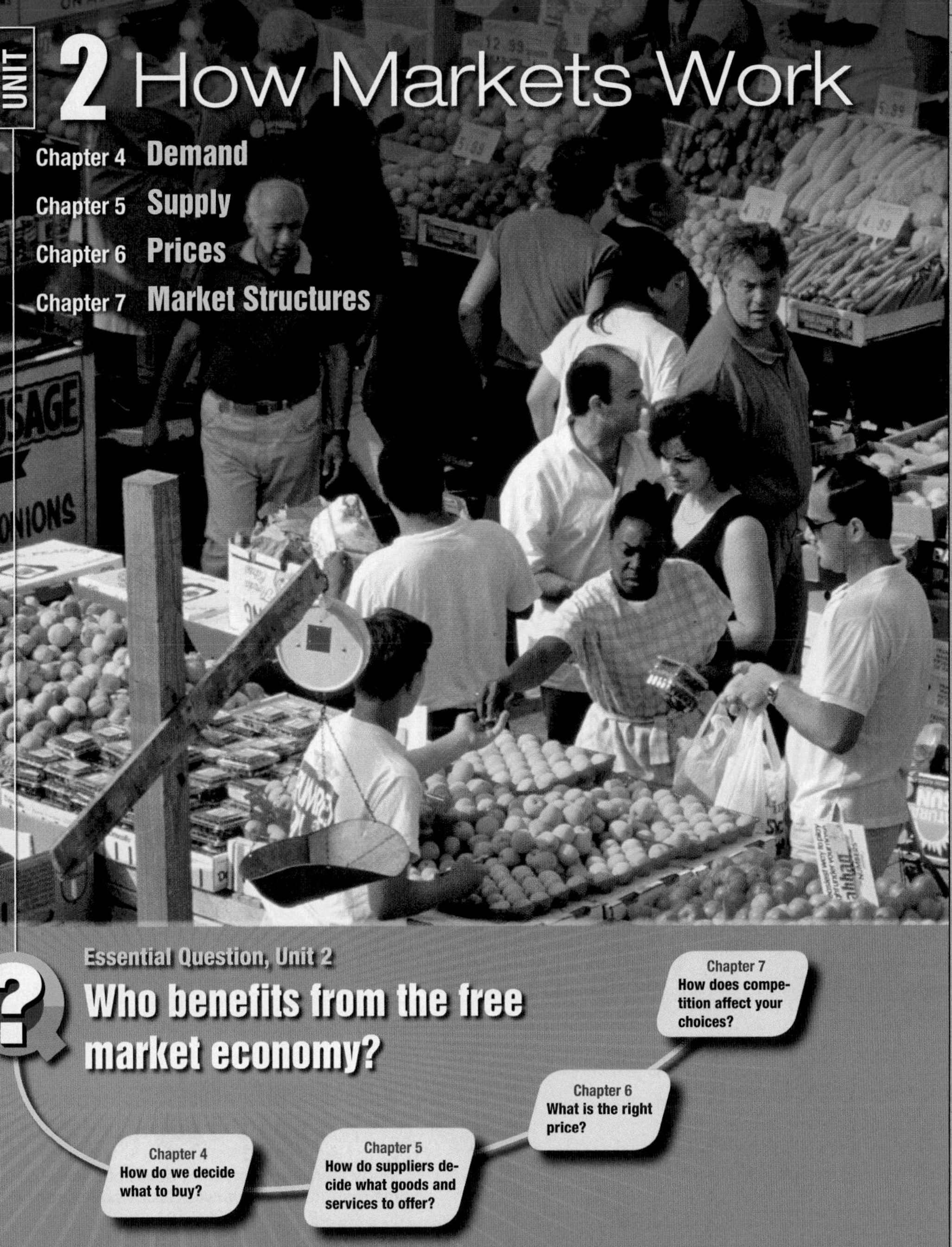

UNIT 2 How Markets Work

Chapter 4 Demand
Chapter 5 Supply
Chapter 6 Prices
Chapter 7 Market Structures

Essential Question, Unit 2

Who benefits from the free market economy?

Chapter 4 How do we decide what to buy?

Chapter 5 How do suppliers decide what goods and services to offer?

Chapter 6 What is the right price?

Chapter 7 How does competition affect your choices?

UNIT PREVIEW 83

Essential Question

Who benefits from the free market economy?

Introduce the Unit

ACTIVATE PRIOR KNOWLEDGE

Essential questions frame each unit and chapter of study, asking students to consider big ideas about economics. Write the Unit Essential Question on the Board: **Who benefits from the free market economy?** Using the Socratic Discussion strategy (p. T26), have students brainstorm answers to the question.

WRITING ACTIVITY

To begin this unit, assign the Unit 2 Warmup Activity in the **Essential Questions Journal**. This will help students start to consider their position on the Unit 2 Essential Question: **Who benefits from the free market economy?**

Use the **Essential Questions Journal** throughout the program to help students consider these and other big ideas about economics.

BULLETIN BOARD ACTIVITY

Post the Unit Essential Question on a bulletin board. Tell students that they will be learning about who benefits from the free market economy. Ask them to bring in articles about current events to help them answer the question. Students should identify their article and use a sticky note to briefly explain the connection to the Essential Question.

CREATING THE ESSENTIAL QUESTIONS VIDEO

Preview the Unit Challenge on page 188. Consider assigning this activity to your students. Tell them that they will be creating their own video to explore this question, and that they should keep this in mind as they study the benefits of the free market economy. For further information about how to complete this activity, go to PearsonSucessNet.com.

NATIONAL COUNCIL ON ECONOMIC EDUCATION

The following Voluntary National Content Standards in Economics are addressed in this unit:

- ★ **Standard 4**
- ★ **Standard 7**
- ★ **Standard 8**
- ★ **Standard 9**

For a complete description of the standards addressed in each chapter, see the Correlations chart on pages T52–T55.

Online Resources

Economics Online Teacher Center at PearsonSuccessNet.com includes

- Online Teacher's Edition with lesson planner
- Online Lecture Notes
- Teacher's Resource Library with All-in-One Resources, Color Transparencies, Simulation Activities, and Adequate Yearly Progress Monitoring
- SuccessTracker Assessment

Economics Online Student Center at PearsonSuccessNet.com includes

- Interactive textbook with audio
- Economics Video
- WebQuests
- Interactivities
- Student Self-Tests

Essential Questions

UNIT 2:

Who benefits from the free market economy?

CHAPTER 4:

How do we decide what to buy?

Introduce the Chapter

ACTIVATE PRIOR KNOWLEDGE

In this chapter, students will learn about factors that affect demand for goods and services. Tell students to complete the warmup activity in the **Essential Questions Journal**.

> **DIFFERENTIATED INSTRUCTION KEY**
>
> **L1** Special Needs
> **L2** Basic
> **ELL** English Language Learners
> **LPR** Less Proficient Readers
> **L3** All Students
> **L4** Advanced Students

Economics online Visit www.PearsonSuccessNet.com for an interactive textbook with built-in activities on economic principles.

- ***The Wall Street Journal* Classroom Edition Video** presents a current topic related to demand.
- **Yearly Update Worksheet** provides an annual update, including a new worksheet and lesson on this topic.
- **On the Go** resources can be downloaded so students and teachers can connect with economics anytime, anywhere.

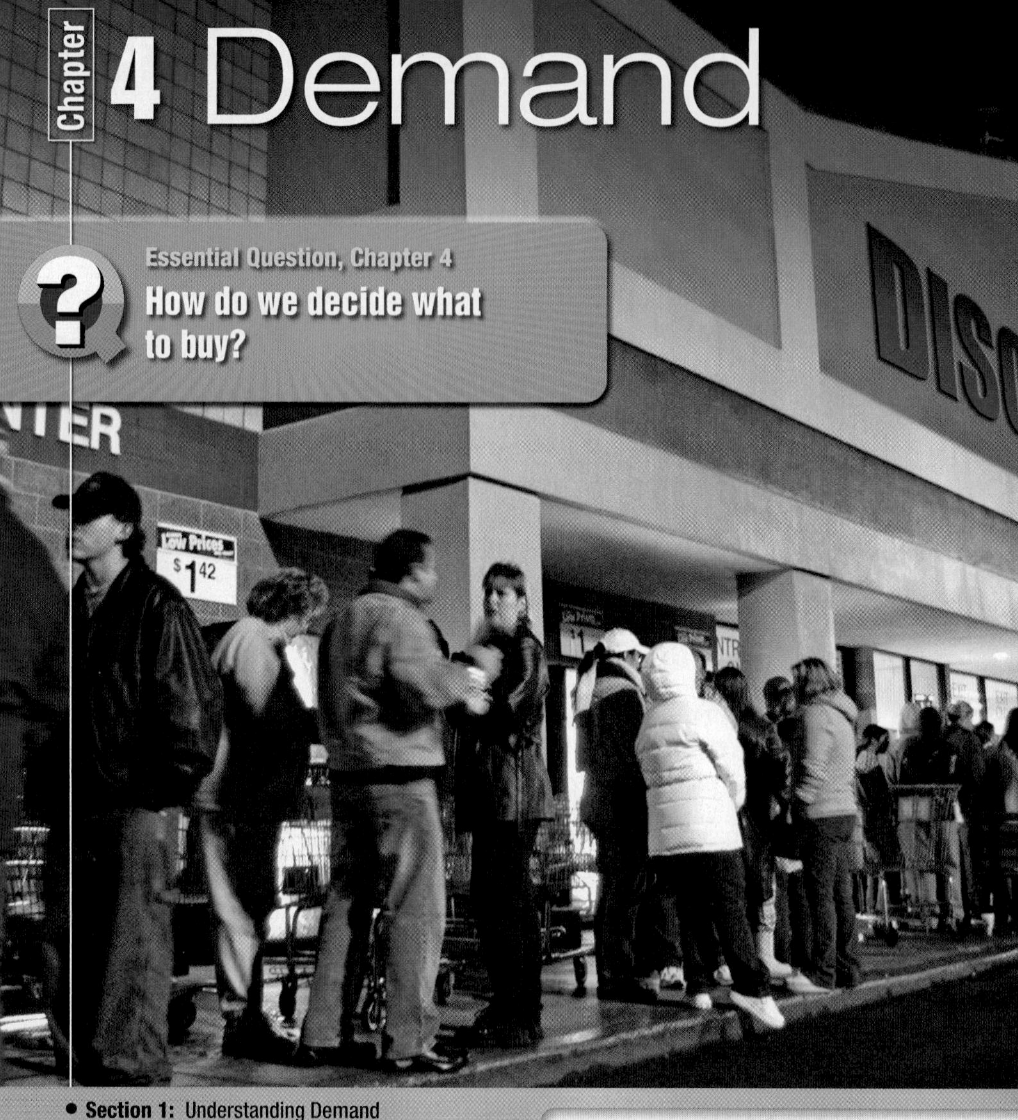

Chapter 4 Demand
Essential Question, Chapter 4
How do we decide what to buy?
Low Prices
$1.42

- **Section 1:** Understanding Demand
- **Section 2:** Shifts in the Demand Curve
- **Section 3:** Elasticity of Demand

Economics on the go

To study anywhere, anytime, download these online resources at ***PearsonSuccessNet.com*** ▶

84 DEMAND

ECONOMICS ONLINE

DIGITAL TEACHER TOOLS

The online lesson planner is designed to help teachers plan, teach, and assess. Teachers have the ability to use or customize existing Pearson lesson plans. Online lecture notes support the print lesson by providing an array of accessible activities and summaries of key concepts. Two interactivities in this lesson are:

- **How the Economy Works** allows students to make decisions on spending based upon the elasticity of everyday purchases.
- **Action Graphs** Animated graphs illustrate the concept of demand.

Block Scheduling

BLOCK 1 Teach Sections 1 and 2 lessons, omitting the Wall Street Journal case study in Section 2.

BLOCK 2 Teach Section 3 lesson, omitting the "Demonstrating Elasticity" activity and the Extend activity.

Pressed for Time

Group Work Organize the class into three groups, assigning each group a section from the chapter. Have each group create a presentation detailing the main points of the assigned section. As groups give their presentations, create a study guide on the board outlining each section's main points.

SECTION 1 Understanding Demand

OBJECTIVES

1. **Explain** the law of demand.
2. **Describe** how the substitution effect and the income effect influence decisions.
3. **Create** a demand schedule for an individual and a market.
4. **Interpret** a demand graph using demand schedules.

ECONOMIC DICTIONARY

As you read the section, look for the definitions of these **Key Terms:**

- demand
- law of demand
- substitution effect
- income effect
- demand schedule
- market demand schedule
- demand curve

Guiding Question
How does the law of demand affect the quantity demanded?

Copy this table and fill it in as you read.

	Demand	
	As the price of a good goes down...	As the price of a good goes up...
Law of Demand		
Substitution Effect		
Income Effect		

Economics and You Anyone who has ever shopped knows the difference between wanting to have something and being able to pay for it. Sometimes you can buy what you want, and other times, the price is just too high.

Principles in Action Price changes always affect the quantity demanded because people buy less of a good when its price goes up. By analyzing how the cost of pizza affects how much people are willing to buy, you will see how consumers react to a change in price. In the Economics & You feature, you will see how changes in price are an incentive.

Demand

Demand is the desire to own something and the ability to pay for it. To have demand for a good or service, *both* of these conditions must be present. We will look at the demand side of markets in this chapter. In the next chapter, we will look at the actions of sellers, which economists call the supply side. In Chapter 6, we will look at supply and demand together and study how they interact to establish the prices that we pay for most goods.

The Law of Demand

Anyone who has ever spent money will easily understand the law of demand. The **law of demand** says that when a good's price is lower, consumers will buy more of it. When the price is higher, consumers will buy less of it. All of us act out this law of demand in our everyday purchasing decisions. Whether your income is $10 or $10 million, the price of a good will strongly influence your decision to buy.

demand the desire to own something and the ability to pay for it

law of demand consumers will buy more of a good when its price is lower and less when its price is higher

Visual Glossary online
Go to the Visual Glossary Online for an interactive review of **the law of demand.**

Action Graph online
Go to Action Graph Online for animated versions of key charts and graphs.

How the Economy Works online
Go to How the Economy Works Online for an interactive lesson on **elasticity of demand.**

Guiding Question

How does the law of demand affect the quantity demanded?

Get Started

	Demand	
	As the price of a good goes down, . . .	As the price of a good goes up, . . .
Law of Demand	demand goes up.	demand goes down.
Substitution Effect	consumers substitute that good for other goods.	consumers substitute other goods for that good.
Income Effect	demand goes up.	demand goes down.

LESSON GOALS

Students will:

- Know the Key Terms.
- Analyze their buying decisions to explain the law of demand.
- Explain how the substitution effect and income effect influence decisions by analyzing a cartoon.
- Create a market demand schedule and demand curve to understand how price affects demand.

BEFORE CLASS

Students should read the section for homework before coming to class.

Have students complete the graphic organizer in the Section Opener as they read the text. As an alternate activity, have students complete the Guided Reading and Review worksheet (Unit 2 All-in-One, p. 13).

L1 L2 ELL LPR Differentiate Have students complete the Guided Reading and Review worksheet (Unit 2 All-in-One, p. 14).

Focus on the Basics

Students need to come away with the following understandings:

FACTS: • Demand is the desire to have a good and the ability to purchase it. • As a good's price rises, people demand less of that good; as a good's price falls, people demand more of that good. • If the price of a good increases, consumers will increase their demand for substitute goods; if the price of a good decreases, consumers will decrease their demand for substitute goods. • Demand schedules show demand for a good across a range of prices. • Demand curves are graphic representations of demand schedules.

GENERALIZATION: If the price of a good increases, the quantity demanded for that good will decrease; if the good's price decreases, quantity demanded for that good by consumers will increase. Demand for a good across a range of prices can be shown in a demand schedule, and graphically represented by a demand curve.

CLASSROOM HINTS

THE INCOME EFFECT

Often students confuse "the income effect" with having more income. Make it clear to them that having more money to spend on something because prices fall is the income effect. You "feel" richer. You can buy a 4 gigabyte flashdrive rather than a 1 gigabyte flashdrive. Having more money to spend because you got a raise means your income actually increased and depending on what happened to prices you may or may not feel richer.

Teach Visual Glossary

REVIEW KEY TERMS

Pair students and have them quiz each other on the definitions of the key terms.

free market economy – *an economic system in which decisions on the three key economic questions are based on voluntary exchange in markets*

consumer sovereignty – *the power of consumers to decide what gets produced*

demand – *the desire to own something and the ability to pay for it*

substitution effect – *when consumers react to an increase in a good's price by consuming less of that good and more of a substitute good*

income effect – *the change in consumption that results when a price increase causes real income to decline.*

CLASS ACTIVITY

Read the definition of the *law of demand.* Ask **According to the law of demand, why has the quantity of goods demanded in the picture on the top increased?** *(Prices have gone down.)* **According to the law of demand, why has the quantity of goods demanded in the picture on the bottom decreased?** *(Prices have gone up.)*

L1 L2 Differentiate Bring a balance scale to class. Slowly place a weight on one side of the balance scale. Ask **What happened to the sides of the scale?** *(When one side went down, the other side went up.)* Ask **How does the scale represent the relationship between price and demand?** *(When price goes up, demand goes down. When price goes down, demand goes up.)*

Economics online *All print resources are available on the Teacher's Resource Library CD-ROM and online at* www.PearsonSuccessNet.com.

Answer

Caption The images show crowds buying goods when the price goes down, thereby increasing quantity demanded, and a customer buying a small amount when prices go up, decreasing quantity demanded.

VISUAL GLOSSARY

Reviewing Key Terms
To understand the *law of demand* review these terms:

free market economy, *p. 30*
consumer sovereignty, *p. 34*
demand, *p. 85*
substitution effect, *p. 87*
income effect, *p. 87*

What is the Law of Demand?

◀ **law of demand** consumers will buy more of a good when its price is lower and less when its price is higher.

LAW OF DEMAND
PRICE
As prices go down...
DEMAND
quantity demanded goes up.
PRICE
As prices go up...
DEMAND
quantity demanded goes down.

People will react to changes in price. ***How do these two images reflect the law of demand in action?***

Visual Glossary online
To expand your understanding of this and other key economic terms, visit **PearsonSuccessNet.com**

David Henderson, an economics professor who served as a senior economist with the President's Council of Economic Advisers, describes the importance of the law of demand:

> "The most famous law in economics, and the one that economists are most sure of, is the law of demand. On this law is built almost the whole edifice of economics."
>
> —David Henderson, "Demand," *The Concise Encyclopedia of Economics*

Now ask yourself a question: Would you buy a slice of pizza for lunch if it cost $2? Many of us would, and some of us might even buy more than one slice. But would you buy the same slice of pizza if it cost $4? Fewer of us would buy it at that price. Even real pizza lovers might reduce their consumption from 3 or 4 slices to just 1 or 2. How many of us would buy a slice for $10? Probably very few would pay that amount. As the price of pizza gets higher and higher, fewer of us are willing to buy it. That is the law of demand in action.

The law of demand is the result of not one pattern of behavior, but two separate patterns that overlap. These two behavior patterns are the substitution effect and the income effect. The substitution effect and the income effect describe two different ways that a consumer can change his or her spending patterns. Together, they explain why an increase in price decreases the amount purchased. As shown in **Figure 4.1**, the substitution effect and the income effect can change a consumer's buying habits.

The Substitution Effect

When the price of pizza rises, pizza becomes more expensive compared with other foods, such as tacos and salads. So, as the price of a slice of pizza rises, consumers have an incentive to buy one of those alternatives as a substitute for pizza. This causes a drop in the amount of pizza demanded. For example, instead of eating pizza for lunch on Mondays and Fridays, a student could eat pizza on Mondays and a bagel on Fridays. This change in consumption is known as the substitution effect. The **substitution effect** takes place when a consumer reacts to a rise in the price of one good by consuming less of that good and more of a substitute good.

The substitution effect can also apply to a drop in prices. If the price of pizza drops, pizza becomes cheaper compared to other alternatives. Consumers will now substitute pizza for tacos, salads, and other lunch choices, causing the quantity of pizza demanded to rise.

The Income Effect

Rising prices have another effect that we have all felt. They make us feel poorer. When the price of movie tickets, shoes, or pizza increases, your limited budget just won't buy as much as it did in the past. It feels as if you have less money. You can no longer afford to buy the same combination of goods, and you must cut back your purchases of some goods. If you buy fewer slices of pizza without increasing your purchases of other foods, that is the **income effect**.

One important fact to remember is that economists measure consumption in the amount of a good that is bought, not the amount of money spent to buy it. Although

substitution effect when consumers react to an increase in a good's price by consuming less of that good and more of a substitute good

income effect the change in consumption that results when a price increase causes real income to decline

Figure 4.1 The Law of Demand in Action

	Price of A Increases		Price of A Decreases	
	Consumption of A	Consumption of other goods	Consumption of A	Consumption of other goods
Income effect	↓	↓	↑	↑
Substitution effect	↓	↑	↑	↓
Combined effect	↓	↕	↑	↕

GRAPH SKILLS

Both the substitution effect and the income effect lead consumers to buy less of good A when it becomes more expensive. However, while the income effect leads consumers to spend less on other goods so they can afford good A, the substitution effect encourages consumers to replace expensive good A with other, less expensive substitutes.

1. How does an increase in the price of good A affect consumption of other goods?
2. How does a decline in the price of good A affect consumption of other goods?

BELLRINGER

Write only the first column of this table on the board. Ask students to write down the maximum they would be willing to pay for each item.

	= to or less than		More than
Cold soda		$2	
Sneakers		$100	
Sandwich		$4	
Cellphone		$70	

Teach

Economics online To present this topic using digital resources, use the lecture notes on www.PearsonSuccessNet.com.

L1 L2 ELL LPR Differentiate To help students who are struggling readers, assign the Vocabulary worksheet (Unit 2 All-in-One, p. 12).

DISCUSS BELLRINGER

Add price thresholds to the list. Call for a show of hands for those students willing to buy the products at each price level. Record the results. Ask **What happens to the number of students willing to buy at higher prices?** *(It drops.)* **Explain.** *(Possible answers: preferences, available money)* Ask **Why might you have been willing to pay less for a sandwich if the other products cost more?** *(less money available)* **If others acted this way too, what would happen to the quantity of sandwiches demanded?** *(It would drop.)* Ask students if they would have responded differently to the Bellringer activity if they had more money to spend than they currently do. Ask **What principle does this demonstrate?** *(income effect)*

VISUAL GLOSSARY

Have students look at the diagram on the Visual Glossary. Ask them why price and demand change.

L1 L2 Differentiate Use the lesson on the Visual Glossary page to review this term. As an alternate, direct students to the Visual Glossary Online to reinforce their understanding of the law of demand.

Answers

Graph Skills 1. The income effect encourages consumers to spend less on other goods; the substitution effect encourages them to increase consumption of cheaper substitutes.
2. The income effect encourages consumers to spend more on other goods (in addition to A); the substitution effect encourages them to decrease consumption of cheaper substitutes.

Differentiated Resources

- **L1 L2 Guided Reading and Review** (Unit 2 All-in-One, p. 14)
- **L1 L2 Vocabulary worksheet** (Unit 2 All-in-One, p. 12)
- **L2 Food Prices and Demand** (Unit 2 All-in-One, p. 16)
- **L2 Using Charts and Graphs skills worksheet** (Unit 2 All-in-One, p. 18)

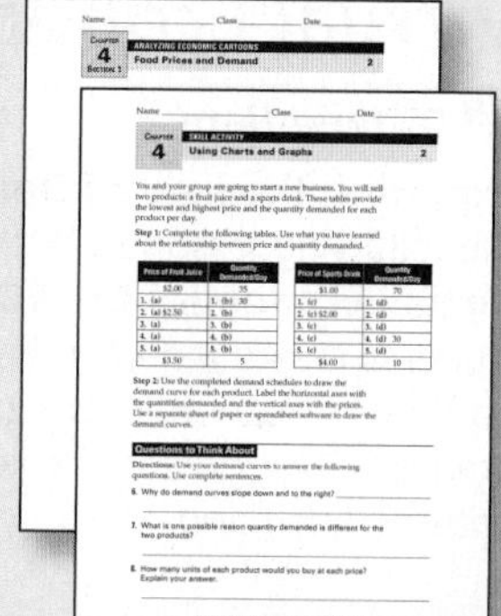

DISTRIBUTE ACTIVITY WORKSHEET

Distribute the "Food Prices and Demand" worksheet (Unit 2 All-in-One, p. 15). Students will analyze the cartoon and describe what it says about the substitution and income effects.

Name ________ Class ________ Date ________

CHAPTER 4 SECTION 1 — ANALYZING AN ECONOMIC CARTOON

Food Prices and Demand 3

In 2007 and 2008, food prices experienced a sharp increase. Many editorial cartoonists tried to depict the impact of this rise in prices upon consumers. ♦ *Study the cartoon, and then answer the questions that follow.*

Questions to Think About

1. (a) What is the man doing? (b) Why is he taking this action? (c) How do the other characters in the cartoon react to this behavior?
2. (a) What is the woman holding? (b) How does this object contribute to the message of the cartoon?
3. Does the man's unusual solution to the rising price of food symbolize the substitution effect or the income effect? Why?
4. Which groups of consumers do rising food prices affect the most? Which groups do rising food prices affect the least? Why?

L2 Differentiate Distribute the "Food Prices and Demand" worksheet (Unit 2 All-in-One, p. 16). Check student answers. Have students give examples of both the substitution and the income effect on their own or their family's purchases.

COMPARE

Direct students' attention to the two demand schedules in Figure 4.2. Ask them to explain what each schedule shows. *(The individual demand schedule shows the quantity demanded by Ashley at different prices. The market demand schedule shows the quantity demanded by all buyers in the market at the same prices.)* Ask **How are they similar and how are they different?** *(In both, demand decreases as price increases. Demand for the entire market is much higher than demand for one individual.)*

L1 L2 Differentiate Direct students' attention to market demand schedule for pizza in Figure 4.2. Ask students to describe what happens to the quantity of pizza slices people want to buy each day as the price goes up *(Quantity demanded goes down.)* and as the price goes down *(Quantity demanded goes up.)* Ask **How many slices could the pizza shop sell if each slice cost less than $1?** *(more than 300)* Have students explain why that response demonstrates the law of demand. *(When the price goes down, quantity demanded goes up.)*

Answers

Checkpoint Quantity demanded for the good goes down.

Economics & You Possible response: When the price of movie tickets rose, I went to afternoon shows instead of evening shows because they cost less.

demand schedule a table that lists the quantity of a good a person will buy at various prices in a market

market demand schedule a table that lists the quantity of a good all consumers in a market will buy at various prices

you are spending more on pizza, you are consuming fewer slices, so your consumption has gone down. If the price rises from $2 a slice to $4 a slice, you may decide to pay extra and order your usual lunch, but you certainly would not choose to buy more slices than before. When the price goes up, consumers spend more of their money on pizza, but they may demand less of it. Thus, the income effect has led to a decrease in the quantity demanded.

Remember, too, that the income effect also operates when the price is lowered. If the price of pizza falls, all of a sudden you feel wealthier. If you buy more pizza as a result of the lower price, that's the income effect.

CHECKPOINT ***What happens to demand for a good when the price increases?***

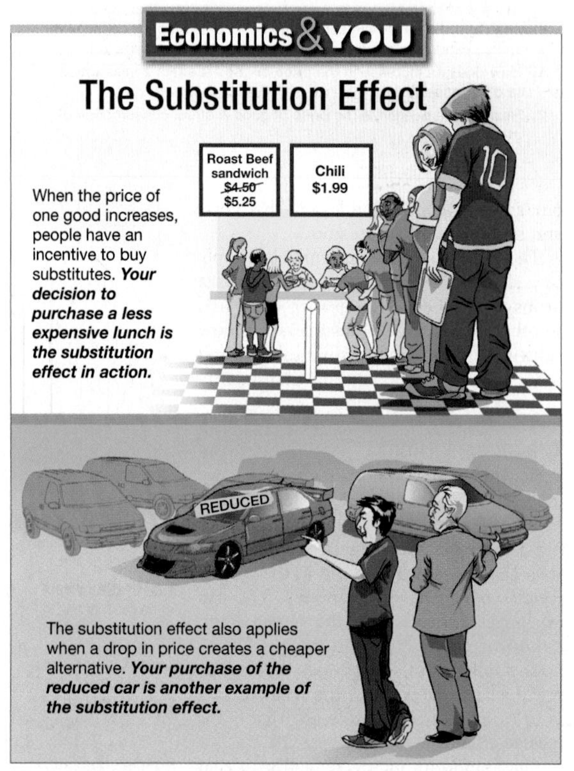

Economics & YOU
The Substitution Effect
Roast Beef sandwich $4.50 $5.25
Chili $1.99
When the price of one good increases, people have an incentive to buy substitutes. ***Your decision to purchase a less expensive lunch is the substitution effect in action.***
REDUCED
The substitution effect also applies when a drop in price creates a cheaper alternative. ***Your purchase of the reduced car is another example of the substitution effect.***
10

▲ A rise in the price of a good will cause consumers to buy more of a substitute good. ***Has the substitution effect been a factor in any of your recent purchases?***

A Demand Schedule

The law of demand explains how the price of any item affects the quantity demanded of that item. Before we look at the relationship between price and the quantity demanded for a specific good, we need to look more closely at how economists use the word *demand*.

Understanding Demand

To have demand for a good, you must be willing and able to buy it at the specified price. Demand means that you want the good and can afford to buy it. You may desperately want a new car, a laptop computer, or a trip to Alaska, but if you can't truly afford any of these goods, then you do not demand them. You might demand digital music downloads, though, if at the current price you have enough money and want to buy some.

A **demand schedule** is a table that lists the quantity of a good that a person will purchase at various prices in a market. For example, the table on the left in **Figure 4.2** illustrates Ashley's individual "demand for pizza." The schedule shows specific quantities of pizza that a student named Ashley is willing and able to purchase at specific prices. For example, at a price of $4, Ashley's "quantity demanded" of pizza is two slices per day.

Market Demand Schedules

If you owned a store, knowing the demand schedule of one customer might not be as helpful as knowing how all of your customers would react to price changes. When you add up the demand schedules of every buyer in the market, you can create a market demand schedule. A **market demand schedule** shows the quantities demanded at various prices by all consumers in the market. A market demand schedule for pizza would allow a restaurant owner to predict the total sales of pizza at several different prices.

The owner of a pizzeria could create a market demand schedule for pizza slices by surveying his or her customers and then adding up the quantities demanded by all individual consumers at each price. The resulting market demand schedule will look

Virtual Economics

L4 Differentiate

Exploring the Law of Demand Use the following lesson from the NCEE **Virtual Economics *CD-ROM*** to help students create a demand curve. Click on Browse Economics Lessons, specify grades 9–12, and use the key words *nature of demand.*

In this activity, students will take part in a simulation to create a demand curve and explain the law of demand.

LESSON TITLE	**THE NATURE OF DEMAND**
Type of Activity	Simulation, Graphing
Complexity	Moderate
Time	80–100 minutes
NCEE Standards	8, 9

Figure 4.2 **Demand Schedules**

Individual Demand Schedule		Market Demand Schedule	
Price of a slice of pizza	Quantity demanded per day	Price of a slice of pizza	Quantity demanded per day
$1.00	5	$1.00	300
$2.00	4	$2.00	250
$3.00	3	$3.00	200
$4.00	2	$4.00	150
$5.00	1	$5.00	100
$6.00	0	$6.00	50

CHART SKILLS

Demand schedules show that the quantity demanded falls as the price rises.

1. How does market demand change when the price falls from $3 to $2 a slice?
2. What behaviors affect individual demand when pizza is $6 per slice?

like Ashley's demand schedule, but the quantities will be larger, as shown in **Figure 4.2**.

Note that the market demand schedule on the right in **Figure 4.2** contains the same prices as Ashley's individual demand schedule, since those are the possible prices that may be charged by the pizzeria. The schedule also exhibits the law of demand. At higher prices the quantity demanded is lower. The only difference between the two demand schedules is that the market schedule lists larger quantities demanded because the market demand schedule reflects the purchase decisions of all potential consumers in the market.

CHECKPOINT ***To have demand for a good, what two conditions must be met?***

The Demand Graph

What if you took the numbers in Ashley's demand schedule in **Figure 4.2** and plotted them on a graph? The result would be a demand curve. A **demand curve** is a graphic representation of a demand schedule.

How do economists create a demand curve? When they transfer numbers from a demand schedule to a graph, they always label the vertical axis with the lowest possible prices at the bottom and the highest price at the top. Likewise, they always label the quantities demanded on the horizontal axis with the lowest possible quantity at the left and the highest possible quantity at the right. All demand graphs show that each pair of price and quantity-demanded numbers on the demand schedule is plotted as a point on the graph. Connecting the points on the graph creates a demand curve.

demand curve a graphic representation of a demand schedule

Reading a Demand Curve

Note two facts about Ashley's demand curve shown in **Figure 4.3** on page 90. First, the graph shows only the relationship between the price of this good and the quantity that Ashley will purchase. It assumes that all other factors that would affect Ashley's demand for pizza—like the price of other goods, her income, and the quality of the pizza—are held constant.

Second, the demand curve on the graph slopes downward to the right. If you follow the curve from the top left to the bottom right, you will notice that as price decreases, the quantity demanded increases. All demand schedules and demand curves reflect the law of demand, which states that higher prices will always lead to lower quantities demanded.

Ashley's demand curve in **Figure 4.3** shows her demand for slices of pizza. The market demand curve in **Figure 4.3** shows the quantities demanded by all consumers at the same prices. Thus, the prices listed on the vertical axis are identical to those in Ashley's demand curve. The quantities listed on the horizontal axis are much larger, corresponding to those in the market demand schedule in **Figure 4.2**.

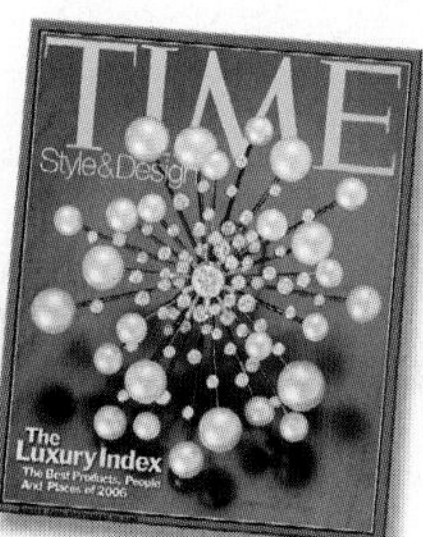

▲ This 2006 magazine cover reflects the increased demand for luxury goods that began in 2003. But an economic downturn in late 2007 led to reduced demand for luxury items. ***What other goods or services might consumers have less demand for during an economic downturn?***

Background Note

The Slope of Demand Curves Students may think that the downward slope of demand curves means that demand decreases as prices drop. Have students review Ashley's demand schedule for pizza (Figure 4.2), and then find each price and corresponding demand on Ashley's demand curve (Figure 4.3). Suggest students read each point on the demand curve in this way: When the price of a slice of pizza is *(have students name the price)*, Ashley wants to buy *(have students fill in the number)* slices.

GRAPHING

Direct students' attention to the demand curves in Figure 4.3. Call on volunteers to explain what each curve shows. Form the class into groups. Distribute the "Using Charts and Graphs" skill worksheet (Unit 2 All-in-One, p. 17). Have students work in their groups to create two demand schedules and two demand curves. Tell students to review the Graph Preview on page xxviii.

L2 Distribute the "Using Charts and Graphs" skill worksheet (Unit 2 All-in-One, p. 18).

Tell students to compare the two demand schedules and demand curves point by point, to see how the curves accurately display the information in the schedules.

EXTEND

Tell students to take the role of the pizza shop owner and decide how much they would charge for each slice of pizza, explaining their reasons based on the demand schedule on this page.

Action Graph online Have students review the Action Graph animation for a step-by-step look at demand curves.

GUIDING QUESTION WRAP UP

Have students return to the section Guiding Question. Review the completed graphic organizer and clarify any misunderstandings. Have a wrap up discussion about the law of demand.

Assess and Remediate

L3 L2 Collect the "Food Prices and Demand" worksheets and assess student understanding of the income and substitution effects.

L3 L2 Collect the "Using Charts and Graphs" skill worksheets and assess student ability.

L3 Assign the Section 1 Assessment questions; identify student misconceptions.

L3 Give Section Quiz A (Unit 2 All-in-One, p. 19).

L2 Give Section Quiz B (Unit 2 All-in-One, p. 20).

(Assess and Remediate continued on p. 90)

Answers

Chart Skills 1. It increases from 200 to 250 slices a day. 2. substitution effect and income effect

Checkpoint the desire to own and ability to pay

Caption new cars, new appliances

Have students complete the Self-Test Online and continue their work in the **Essential Questions Journal**.

REMEDIATION AND SUGGESTIONS

Use the chart below to help students who are struggling with content.

WEAKNESS	REMEDIATION
Defining key terms (Questions 3, 4, 5, 6, 7, 8)	Have students use the interactive Economic Dictionary Online.
Describing the law of demand (Questions 1, 2, 4)	Reteach the concept using the Visual Glossary; then have students summarize the meaning of the *law of demand* in their own words.
Explaining substitution and income effects (Questions 5, 8)	Have students review the relevant sections and write a summary.
Using demand schedules and demand curves (Questions 9, 10, 11)	Reteach using the skill worksheet. Direct students to review the Action Graph online for Figure 4.3.

Answers

Graph Skills 1. 2 slices 2. For both, demand goes down as price goes up.

Checkpoint a curve showing demand for a good by all consumers in a market

Figure 4.3 **Demand Curves**

GRAPH SKILLS

Ashley's demand curve shows the number of slices she is willing and able to buy at each price, while the market demand curve shows demand for pizza in an entire market.

1. How many slices does Ashley demand at is $4.00 per slice?
2. How are the demand curves similar?

Action Graph online

For an animated version of this graph, visit **PearsonSuccessNet.com**

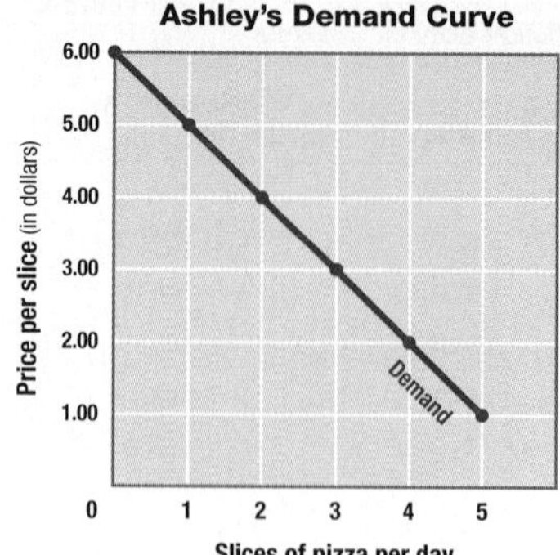

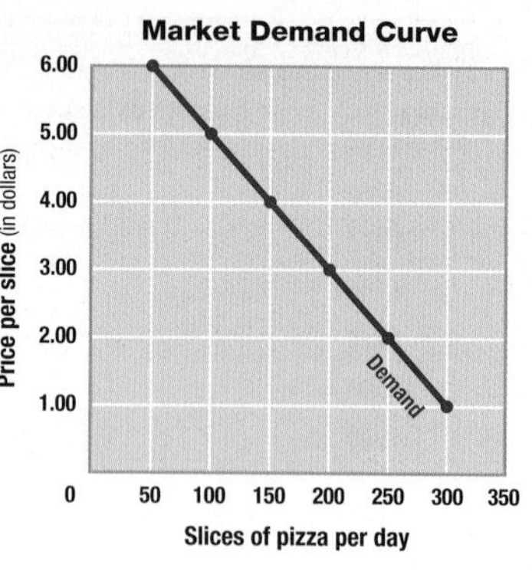

Limits of a Demand Curve

The market demand curve in **Figure 4.3** can predict how people will change their buying habits when the price of a good rises or falls. For example, if the price of pizza is $3 a slice, the pizzeria will sell 200 slices a day.

This market demand curve is only accurate for one very specific set of market conditions. It cannot predict changing market conditions. In the next section, you will learn how demand curves can shift because of changes in factors other than price.

CHECKPOINT ***What is a market demand curve?***

Essential Questions Journal To continue to build a response to the Essential Question, go to your **Essential Questions Journal.**

SECTION 1 ASSESSMENT

Guiding Question

1. Use your completed table to answer this question: How does the law of demand affect the quantity demanded?
2. **Extension** Can you think of a time when the price of something you wanted was raised or dropped? Briefly describe what happened to cause the price change, and how this affected your decision to buy or not buy the product.

Key Terms and Main Ideas

3. What two qualities make up **demand?**
4. According to the **law of demand,** what will happen when the price of a good increases?
5. Under the **substitution effect,** what will happen when the price of a good drops?
6. What does a **market demand schedule** show?
7. What is a **demand schedule** called when it is represented as a graph?

Critical Thinking

8. **Contrast** Describe the difference between the substitution effect and the income effect.
9. **Extend** Suppose you are a small business owner. How would a market demand schedule or a market demand curve be useful to you?
10. **Predict (a)** What can economists predict by creating a demand curve? **(b)** When would a demand curve not be useful?

Math Skills

11. Use the following market demand schedule to draw a demand curve for miniature golf.

Visit PearsonSuccessNet.com for additional math help.

Cost to Play a Game	Games Played per Month
$1.50	350
$2.00	250
$3.00	140
$4.00	80

Assessment Answers

1. Quantity demanded increases when price decreases and quantity demanded decreases when price increases.
2. *Possible response:* A winter jacket that I liked was put on sale at the end of the season, so I bought it.
3. the desire to own something and the ability to pay for it
4. Consumers will buy less of it.
5. Consumers will buy more of the good and less of any substitute goods.
6. the quantities of a good demanded at various prices by all consumers in a market
7. a demand curve
8. *substitution effect:* when people react to an increase in a good's price by buying a substitute good; *income effect:* when people react to an increase in a good's price by buying less of that good because their real income has declined.
9. I can use it to set prices.
10. (a) how demand for a good will change based upon its price (b) when some factor other than price affects demand for the good
11. Students' demand curves will display the data in the market demand schedule.

SECTION 2 Shifts in the Demand Curve

OBJECTIVES

1. **Explain** the difference between a change in quantity demanded and a shift in the demand curve.
2. **Identify** the factors that create changes in demand and that can cause a shift in the demand curve.
3. **Give an example** of how a change in demand for one good can affect demand for a related good.

ECONOMIC DICTIONARY

As you read the section, look for the definitions of these **Key Terms:**

- *ceteris paribus*
- normal good
- inferior good
- demographics
- complements
- substitutes

Guiding Question
Why does the demand curve shift?

Copy this concept web and fill it in as you read.

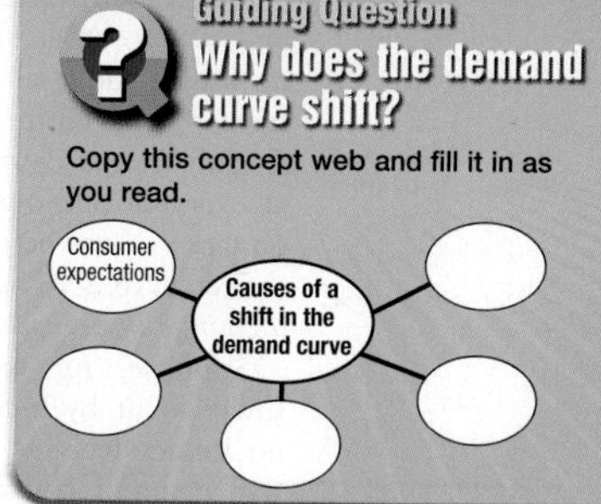

Economics and You The text message says it all: Raining 2 hrd! Your plans to go out to eat with your friends have suddenly been scuttled. No burger is worth the bother. Not only has your demand for burgers at any price dropped, your demand for home-delivered pizza at any price has risen.

ceteris paribus a Latin phrase that means "all other things held constant"

Principles in Action Sometimes increases or decreases in demand are not connected to price. On a stormy night, the Burger Barn may be nearly empty while the phone is ringing off the hook at the Pizza Palace. As you will read, David Ogilvy, the Innovator featured on page 95, based his career on increasing consumers' demand.

Changes in Demand

When we counted the number of pizza slices that would sell as the price went up or down, we assumed that nothing besides the price of pizza would change. Economists refer to this assumption as ***ceteris paribus,*** the Latin phrase for "all other things held constant." The demand schedule took into account only changes in price. It did not consider the effects of news reports or any one of thousands of other factors that change from day to day.

A demand curve is accurate only as long as there are no changes other than price that could affect the consumer's decision. In other words, a demand curve is accurate only as long as the *ceteris paribus* assumption is true. When the price changes, we move along the curve to a different quantity demanded.

For example, in the graph of Ashley's demand for slices of pizza, an increase in the price from $2 per slice to $3 will make Ashley's quantity demanded fall from four slices to three slices per day. This movement along the demand curve

▲ Natural disasters such as hurricanes can create sudden demand for household goods. ***Based on the image, how would the demand curve for plywood change?***

Guiding Question

Why does the demand curve shift?

Get Started

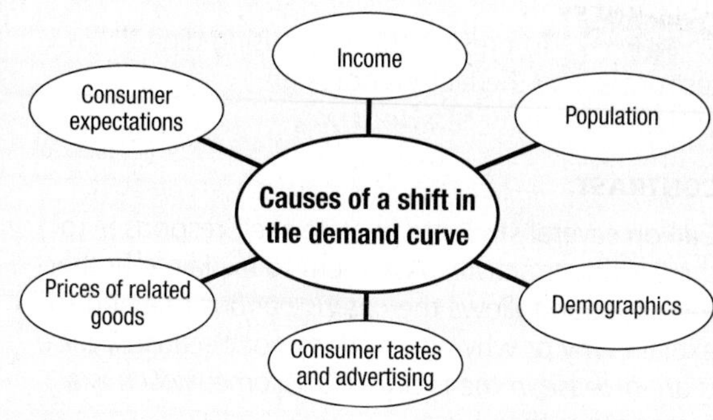

LESSON GOALS

Students will:

- Know the Key Terms.
- Use graphs to distinguish between a change in quantity demanded and a change in demand.
- Describe factors that can cause a shift in the demand curve by completing a worksheet.

BEFORE CLASS

Have students complete the graphic organizer in the Section Opener as they read the text. As an alternate activity, have students complete the Guided Reading and Review worksheet (Unit 2 All-in-One, p. 21).

L1 L2 ELL LPR Differentiate Have students complete the Guided Reading and Review worksheet (Unit 2 All-in-One, p. 22).

Answer

Caption Demand would increase and the demand curve would shift to the right.

Focus on the Basics

Students need to come away with the following understandings:

FACTS: • A demand curve shows how demand varies as price changes. • Changes in factors other than a good's price can cause a good's demand curve to shift to the right or to the left. • Price changes in one good can affect demand for related goods.

GENERALIZATION: Factors other than price can shift the demand curve to the left or to the right. These include income, consumer expectations, demographics, consumer tastes, and advertising.

CLASSROOM HINTS

CHANGE IN QUANTITY DEMANDED VS. CHANGE IN DEMAND

Students may have a hard time differentiating between a change in the quantity demanded and a change in demand. As reinforcement, quiz students by asking them to identify whether each of the following results in a change in the quantity demanded or a change in the demand curve: holiday sale; pay increase, bad publicity for a product, increase in sales tax, rise in price of substitute product, rise in price of complementary good.

BELLRINGER

Tell students to think of something they would be able to buy if they got a raise at a job. Have students write their responses in their notebooks.

Teach

Economics online To present this topic using digital resources, use the lecture notes on www.PearsonSuccessNet.com.

CONTRAST

Call on several students to state their responses to the Bellringer activity. Ask them to explain whether this situation follows the *ceteris paribus* rule and to explain why or why not. *(It does not because a raise is an increase in the recipient's income, which is a factor other than price.)*

Then, direct students' attention to the graphs in Figure 4.4. Have them identify which of the two graphs reflects the situation described in the Bellringer and explain why. *(the right graph: it shows an increase in demand made possible by an increase in income.)*

Have students describe what would happen to the demand curve if they did not receive a raise, but were able to purchase the good because it went on sale. *(The demand curve does not move; price changed to a point on the demand curve where I could now afford it.)*

L1 L2 Differentiate Call on students to restate the two components of demand they learned about in Section 1. Then, have them explain how the raise can change their demand for a good by changing their ability to pay for that good.

Action Graph online Have students review the Action Graph animation for a step-by-step look at changes in demand.

(lesson continued on p. 94)

normal good a good that consumers demand more of when their incomes increase

is referred to as a *decrease in the quantity demanded.* By the same reasoning, a decrease in the price of pizza would lead to an *increase in the quantity demanded.*

When we drop the *ceteris paribus* rule and allow other factors to change, we no longer move along the demand curve. Instead, the entire demand curve shifts. A shift in the demand curve means that at every price, consumers buy a different quantity than before. This shift of the entire curve is what economists refer to as *a change in demand.*

Suppose, for example, that Ashley's town is hit by a heat wave, and Ashley no longer feels as hungry for pizza. She will demand fewer slices at every price. The graph on the left in **Figure 4.4** shows her original demand curve and her new demand curve, adjusted for hot weather.

CHECKPOINT ***What does a shift in the demand curve say about a particular good?***

What Causes a Shift?

As you have read, a change in the price of a good does not cause the demand curve to shift. The effects of changes in price are already built into the demand curve. However, several other factors can cause demand for a good to change. These changes can lead to a change in demand rather than simply a change in the quantity demanded.

Income

A consumer's income affects his or her demand for most goods. Most items that we purchase are **normal goods,** goods that consumers demand more of when their incomes increase. In other words, an increase in Ashley's income from $50 per week to $75 per week will cause her to buy more of a normal good at every price level. If we were to draw a new demand schedule for Ashley, it would show a greater demand for slices of pizza at every price. Plotting the new schedule on a graph would produce a curve to the right of Ashley's original curve. For each of the prices on the vertical axis, the quantity demanded would be greater. This shift to the right of the curve is called *an increase in demand.* A fall in income would cause

Figure 4.4 Graphing Changes in Demand

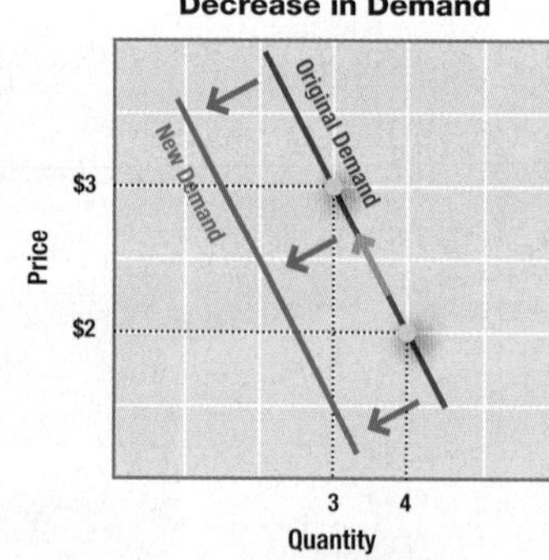

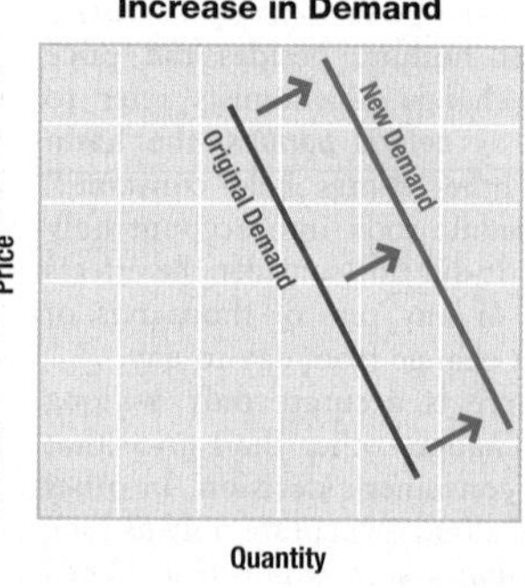

GRAPH SKILLS

When factors other than price cause demand to fall, the demand curve shifts to the left. An increase in demand appears as a shift to the right.

1. If the price of a book rose by one dollar, how would you show the change on one of these graphs?
2. How does a change in the quantity demanded differ from a change in price?

Action Graph online

For an animated version of this graph, visit PearsonSuccessNet.com

Differentiated Resources

L1 L2 Guided Reading and Review (Unit 2 All-in-One, p. 22)

L2 Analyzing Shifts in Demand (Unit 2 All-in-One, p. 24)

L3 Creating Demand (Simulation Activities, Chapter 4)

L4 Explaining Shifts in Demand (Unit 2 All-in-One, p. 25)

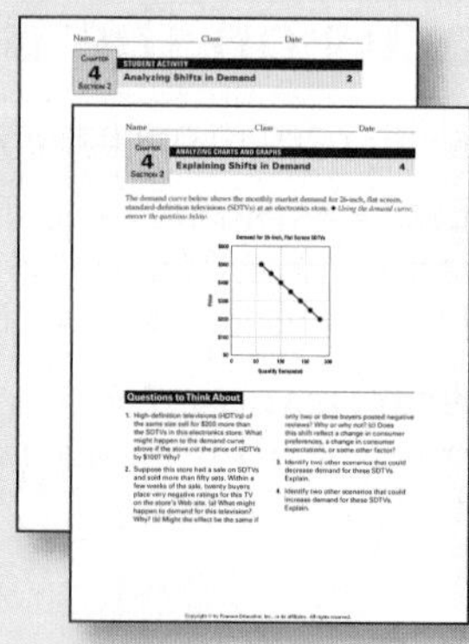

Answers

Checkpoint At every price, consumers will buy a different quantity of the good than before.

Graph Skills 1. as movement up the original demand curve 2. A change in the quantity demanded is a response to a price change only. A change in demand shifts the demand curve left or right, in response to changes that affect the product at every price.

Crop Prices

	Oct. 2007	Nov. 2007	Dec. 2007	Jan. 2008	Feb. 2008	Mar. 2008

Dollars (per bushel): 2, 4, 6, 8, 10, 12, 14. Legend: Soybeans, Wheat, Corn

SOURCE: U.S. Department of Agriculture

Reaping Rewards

A CHANGE IN DEMAND

The rising price of grains has triggered riots in poor countries. But for one farm town in Nebraska, it has brought cheers and prosperity.

By Julie Jargon
The Wall Street Journal

The U.S. economy may be on the brink of recession. But with grain prices surging to historic levels, there's a bountiful harvest down on the farm.

Farm income is running at 51% above the average for the past 10 years, and across much of the Great Plains, unemployment rates are well below national figures and housing markets remain robust.

The new era owes largely to a surge in crop demand from biofuels producers and the growing demand for grains in places like China and India.

While the boom is reversing decades of decline in U.S. rural areas at an otherwise vulnerable time, it's also pushing global food costs higher. Scarce and costly grains have caused riots in poor nations such as Senegal, Haiti and Mexico.

In Albion, Nebraska, a farm town of fewer than 2,000, such problems seem worlds away. People are building new, outsized homes or renovating existing ones. A new ethanol plant has created 55 jobs. A fine-jewelry store moved to town and an upscale coffee shop run by farmers' wives just celebrated its first anniversary.

"There's a buzz in Albion," says Brad Beckwith, a corn and soybean farmer. Although he now faces higher rents for land and higher prices for seed, fertilizer and fuel, he's still turning a profit.

"Farmers have a lot of money to spend," says Jerry Carder, an Albion corn and soybean farmer who recently bought a $40,000 2008 Mercedes-Benz ML350.

Good times haven't sprouted for all farmers. Steep crop prices have made life more difficult for livestock farmers who must buy corn and other grains to fatten their cows and pigs. "Right now, if you're raising hogs, it's hard," says Hank Thieman, chairman of the Boone County Commissioners. "But if all you're raising are corn and soybeans, you're on easy street."

Farmers in Albion and elsewhere know they're not completely immune from a decline in the broader economy. "The biggest concern right now is whether we're in a world recession or not," says Bill Talsma, who farms 9,000 acres in Newton, Iowa. "If the whole economy shuts down, it could clear through the grain and livestock industry."

For that reason he hasn't been rushing out to spend his money. But, he says, "I might update one of my Harleys."

Applying Economic Principles
Growing global demand for grains has had a ripple effect around the world. Increased demand has improved life for some and caused hardships for others. How will increased global demand for grains affect your budget?

Video News Update Online Powered by *The Wall Street Journal* Classroom Edition — For a new case study, go to the online resources at **PearsonSuccessNet.com**

Teach Case Study

SUMMARIZE AND EXPLAIN

Have the students explain why there is an increase in the demand for grains. Ask **What factors have contributed to the rising costs of grains?** *(There is a surge in crop demands due to increased usage in emerging markets and in the creation of biofuels).* Ask students to explain how the demand for grains affects consumers. *(The demand for grains has pushed prices upward making it more expensive to purchase products, such as bread and cereal, made from grains. It also affects the price of some meat because feed is more expensive.)*

ANALYZE

Have the students describe the relationship between the price of grains and the prosperity of the farming industry. *(Grain farmers are thriving and turning large profits, but livestock farmers are struggling because they have to pay more for grain to feed their livestock, therefore limiting their profit margin).*

L2 Differentiate Have the students write a list of products they use that are affected by the increase in the price of grains. Discuss how the price increase could change what they buy and eat.

Economics online *All print resources are available on the Teacher's Resource Library CD-ROM and online at* www.PearsonSuccessNet.com.

Answer

Applying Economic Principles Possible response: If there is a continued increase in the demand, prices might continue to climb. Increased prices will lower real income. I will be able to buy less.

IDENTIFY

Call on volunteers to state the difference between normal and inferior goods in their own words. Have them give examples of each. Then display the transparency "Normal Goods vs. Inferior Goods" (Color Transparencies, 4.a). Point to each good or service and have the class identify the category that each one belongs to. Guide students to see that canned peaches, generic peanut butter, and a used bicycle may be inferior goods because demand for these items is likely to decrease as a person's income increases. To help them see why, contrast each item with another good—for example, fresh blueberries vs. canned peaches—and have them explain which is more desirable.

CONNECT TO STUDENTS' LIVES

Ask students if they have ever put off purchasing something because they knew it would be on sale at a later date. Point out that this behavior demonstrates a shift in demand due to consumer expectations. Ask: **How does Introductory pricing for new products take advantage of this economic behavior?** *(anticipating increase in price)*

Have students give examples of how changing consumer tastes have affected demand for a good. If they have difficulty identifying examples, prompt them to think of clothing styles or gadgets that they have seen grow or decline in popularity.

L3 **Differentiate** For alternative or additional practice with the concept of the effect of advertising on markets have students use the "Creating Demand" activity (Simulation Activities, Chapter 4). Students will create an advertisement that generates demand for a real or imagined product.

L4 Have students research and compare definitions of the words *propaganda* and *marketing*. Have them present their findings, along with examples of propaganda, to the class.

inferior good a good that consumers demand less of when their incomes increase

demographics the statistical characteristics of populations and population segments, especially when used to identify consumer markets

the demand curve to shift left. This shift is called a *decrease in demand.*

There are also other goods called inferior goods. They are called inferior goods because an increase in income causes demand for these goods to fall. **Inferior goods** are goods that you would buy in smaller quantities, or not at all, if your income were to rise and you could afford something better. Possible examples of inferior goods include macaroni and cheese, generic cereals, and used cars.

Consumer Expectations

Our expectations about the future can affect our demand for certain goods today. Suppose that you have had your eye on a new bicycle for several months. One day you walk into the store to look at the bike, and the salesperson mentions that the store will be raising the price in one week. Now that you expect a higher price in the near future, you are more likely to buy the bike today. In other words, the expectation of a higher price in the future has caused your immediate demand to increase.

If, on the other hand, the salesperson were to tell you that the bike will be on sale next week, your immediate demand for the bicycle would fall to zero. You would rather wait until next week to buy the bike at a lower price.

The current demand for a good is positively related to its expected future price. If you expect the price to rise, your current demand will rise, which means you will buy the good sooner. If you expect the price to drop, your current demand will fall, and you will wait for the lower price.

Hispanics, or Latinos, are now the largest minority group in the United States. Firms have responded to this shift by providing products and services for the growing Hispanic population. ▼

Population

Changes in the size of the population will also affect the demand for most products. For example, a growing population needs to be housed and fed. Therefore, a rise in population will increase demand for houses, food, and many other goods and services.

Population trends can have a particularly strong effect on certain goods. For example, when American soldiers returned from World War II in the mid- to late-1940s, record numbers of them married and started families. This trend led to the "baby boom," a jump in the birthrate from 1946 through 1964. Initially, the baby boom led to higher demand for baby clothes, baby food, and books on baby care. In the 1950s and 1960s, towns had to build thousands of new schools. Later, universities opened new classrooms, dormitories, and even whole new campuses to make room for the flood of new students.

The baby boomers have now begun to retire. Over the next few decades the market will face rising demand for the goods and services that are desired by senior citizens, including medical care, recreational vehicles, and homes in the Sunbelt.

Demographics

Demographics are the statistical characteristics of populations, such as age, race, gender, occupation, and income level. Businesses use this data to identify who potential customers are, where they live, and how likely they are to purchase a specific product. Demographics also have a strong influence on the packaging, pricing, and advertising for a product.

Growing ethnic groups like Asians and Latin Americans can create shifts in demand for goods and services. In the United States, Hispanics accounted for about one half of the national population growth between

Background Note

Advertising According to a March 2008 report in TNS Media Intelligence News, companies spent almost $150 billion on advertising in the United States in 2007. While television advertising (including network TV, cable TV, and syndicated TV) accounted for over 43 percent of those ad dollars, the two next largest categories were magazine and newspaper ads at 20.4 and 17.7 percent, respectively. Ads on the Internet (7.6 percent) and radio (7.2 percent) accounted for most of the remaining spending. The auto industry spent the most on ads, $15.17 billion. Financial services were second, at $9.12 billion, with telecommunications ($9.05 billion) a close third.

Innovators

David Ogilvy

"Unless your advertising contains a big idea, it will pass like a ship in the night."

Those words reflect the life experience of their author, David Ogilvy, a legendary ad man who brought a lot of big ideas to the advertising industry.

The son of a Scottish stockbroker, Ogilvy won a scholarship to Oxford. But he left Oxford in 1931, because he was, in his own words, a "dud." After working as a chef at the Hotel Majestic in Paris, he returned to England and sold stoves door-to-door. His brother got him his first advertising job with a London agency. "I loved advertising," Ogilvy later wrote. "I studied and read and took it desperately seriously."

He decided to seek his fortune in America. In 1938, Ogilvy joined the staff of George Gallup's National Research Institute. The experience convinced him that market research was the foundation of good advertising.

In 1948, Ogilvy founded his own ad agency in New York, which became known as Ogilvy & Mather. A series of stylish, successful ads for companies like Hathaway and Rolls Royce attracted blue-chip clients like Shell, General Foods, and American Express. Ogilvy's ads helped to generate demand and led to huge sales increases for his clients.

Ogilvy's lasting legacy is as a pioneer in the development of brand images. He recognized that branding is the key to a company's success: "Every advertisement should be thought of as a contribution to the complex symbol which is the brand image."

Critical Thinking: ***List ways that advertising might affect demand.***

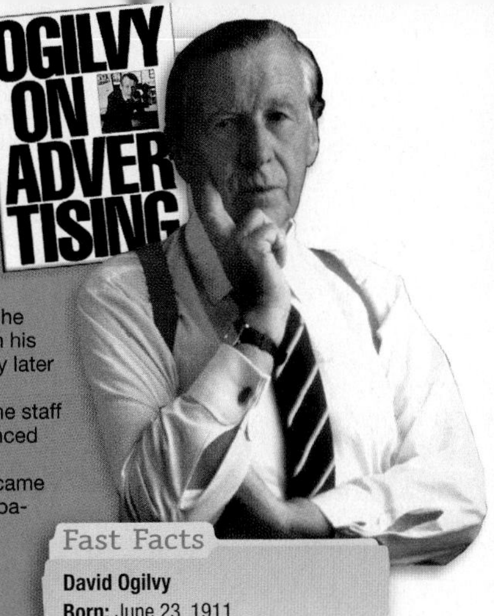

Fast Facts

David Ogilvy
Born: June 23, 1911
Died: July 21, 1999
Education: Oxford University
Claim to Fame: Founded the advertising agency Ogilvy & Mather

03 and 2004. The Census Bureau esti-tes that by 2025, Hispanic Americans ll make up 18.9 percent of the U.S. popu-ion. As their purchasing power grows, ms will devote more of their resources to oducing goods and services demanded by spanic consumers.

nsumer Tastes and Advertising

ho can explain why bell-bottom blue ns were everywhere one year and rarely n the next? Is it the result of clever vertising campaigns, social trends, the luence of television shows, or some mbination of these factors? Although onomists cannot always explain why me fads begin, advertising and publicity ten play an important role.

Changes in tastes and preferences cannot explained by changes in income or pulation or worries about future price creases. Advertising is a factor that shifts mand curves because it plays an impor-nt role in many trends. Meanwhile, new edia and new technology have led to new ends in advertising. Although broadcast evision is still the biggest advertising medium, viewers can now watch television programs on the Internet, cellphones, or DVD players. Digital media makes it easier for consumers to avoid advertisements.

Marketers who want to reach these new media consumers are changing their traditional advertising strategies.

Spending for online ads continues to grow. Video is the fastest growing Internet ad format, topped only by search engine advertising. Ad spending on social network Web sites such as Facebook and MySpace, was estimated at $1.9 billion in 2008.

The popularity of social network Web sites has inspired companies to build their own sites. The goal is to connect with consumers on a personal level while promoting their products and brand names.

Companies spend money on advertising because they hope that it will increase the demand for the goods they sell. Considering the growing sums of money spent on advertising in the United States each year, companies must believe that this investment is paying off.

Simulation *Activity*

Creating Demand
You may be asked to take part in a role-playing game about creating demand.

CHECKPOINT ***How will an anticipated rise in price affect current demand for a good?***

ANALYZE

After reviewing the factors that can shift demand, distribute the "Analyzing Shifts in Demand" worksheet (Unit 2 All-in-One, p. 23). Have students complete the worksheet to identify the factor at work in each scenario.

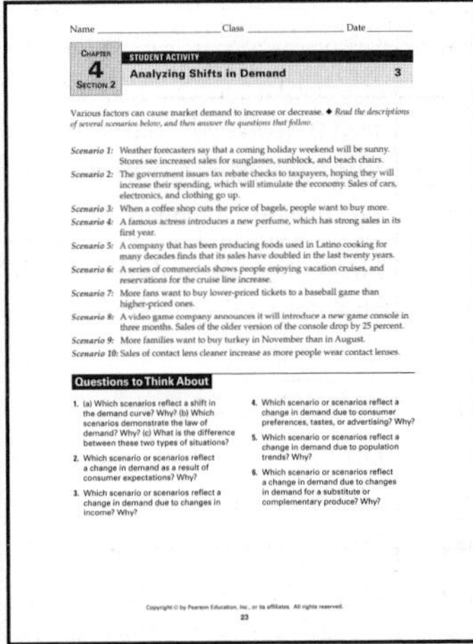
Name ____________ Class ____________ Date ________

Chapter 4 Section 2 — STUDENT ACTIVITY — **Analyzing Shifts in Demand** 3

Various factors can cause market demand to increase or decrease. ◆ *Read the descriptions of several scenarios below, and then answer the questions that follow.*

Scenario 1: Weather forecasters say that a coming holiday weekend will be sunny. Stores see increased sales for sunglasses, sunblock, and beach chairs.
Scenario 2: The government issues tax rebate checks to taxpayers, hoping they will increase their spending, which will stimulate the economy. Sales of cars, electronics, and clothing go up.
Scenario 3: When a coffee shop cuts the price of bagels, people want to buy more.
Scenario 4: A famous actress introduces a new perfume, which has strong sales in its first year.
Scenario 5: A company that has been producing foods used in Latino cooking for many decades finds that its sales have doubled in the last twenty years.
Scenario 6: A series of commercials shows people enjoying vacation cruises, and reservations for the cruise line increase.
Scenario 7: More fans want to buy lower-priced tickets to a baseball game than higher-priced ones.
Scenario 8: A video game company announces it will introduce a new game console in three months. Sales of the older version of the console drop by 25 percent.
Scenario 9: More families want to buy turkey in November than in August.
Scenario 10: Sales of contact lens cleaner increase as more people wear contact lenses.

Questions to Think About

1. (a) Which scenarios reflect a shift in the demand curve? Why? (b) Which scenarios demonstrate the law of demand? Why? (c) What is the difference between these two types of situations?
2. Which scenario or scenarios reflect a change in demand as a result of consumer expectations? Why?
3. Which scenario or scenarios reflect a change in demand due to changes in income? Why?
4. Which scenario or scenarios reflect a change in demand due to consumer preferences, tastes, or advertising? Why?
5. Which scenario or scenarios reflect a change in demand due to population trends? Why?
6. Which scenario or scenarios reflect a change in demand due to changes in demand for a substitute or complementary produce? Why?

23

L2 Differentiate Distribute the "Analyzing Shifts in Demand" worksheet (Unit 2 All-in-One, p. 24)

L4 Differentiate Distribute the "Explaining Shifts in Demand" worksheet (Unit 2 All-in-One, p. 25).

Have students use the worksheets to explore the factors that cause shifts in demand. Check student answers.

EXTEND

Have students write a news story explaining the impact of rising demand for a new video game console on one complementary good.

GUIDING QUESTION WRAP UP

Have students return to the section Guiding Question. Review the completed graphic organizer and clarify any misunderstandings. Have a wrap up discussion about why the demand curve shifts.

Assess and Remediate

L3 L2 L4 Collect the worksheets and assess student understanding of shifts in demand.

L3 Assign the Section 2 Assessment questions; identify student misconceptions.

L3 Give Section Quiz A (Unit 2 All-in-One, p. 26).

L2 Give Section Quiz B (Unit 2 All-in-One, p. 27).

(Assess and Remediate continued on p. 96)

Virtual Economics

L3 Differentiate

Predicting a Demand Shift Use the following lesson from the NCEE **Virtual Economics *CD-ROM*** to analyze shifts in a demand curve. Click on Browse Economics Lessons, specify grades 9–12, and use the key words *picture is worth.*

In this activity, students will conduct an auction to predict consumer behavior and create a demand curve to illustrate it.

LESSON TITLE	A PICTURE IS WORTH A THOUSAND WORDS: DEMAND
Type of Activity	Simulation
Complexity	Moderate
Time	75 minutes
NCEE Standards	4, 8

Answers

Critical Thinking Possible responses: increasing demand by making a product more attractive; changing consumer expectations by announcing a sale

Checkpoint Current demand will increase.

Have students complete the Self-Test Online and continue their work in the **Essential Questions Journal**.

REMEDIATION AND SUGGESTIONS

Use the chart below to help students who are struggling with content.

WEAKNESS	REMEDIATION
Defining key terms (Questions 3, 4, 6, 7)	Have students use the interactive Economic Dictionary Online.
Explaining shifts in demand (Questions 1, 2, 4, 5, 8, 11)	Have students outline the section on changes in demand.
Describing the effect of changes in demand on complements and substitutes (Questions 6, 7, 10)	Reteach the section on complements and substitutes. Show on charts how a change in price for coffee would affect the *quantity* of coffee *demanded* and would cause a *change in demand* for cream, coffee's complement.

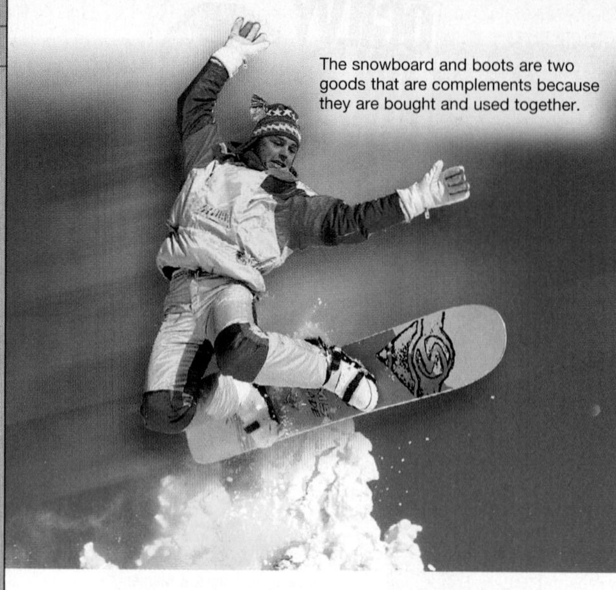

The snowboard and boots are two goods that are complements because they are bought and used together.

complements two goods that are bought and used together

substitutes goods that are used in place of one another

Prices of Related Goods

The demand curve for one good can also shift in response to a change in the demand for another good. There are two types of related goods that interact this way: complements and substitutes.

- **Complements** are two goods that are bought and used together.
- **Substitutes** are goods that are used in place of one another.

When we consider the demand for skis, ski boots are considered a complement. An increase in the price of ski boots will cause people to buy fewer boots. Because skis are useless without boots, the demand for skis will fall at all prices—after all, why buy new skis if you can't afford the ski boots you need?

Now consider the effect on the demand for skis when the price of snowboards rises. Snowboards are a substitute for skis, because consumers will often buy one or the other, but not both. A rise in the price of snowboards will cause people to buy fewer snowboards, and, therefore, people will buy more pairs of new skis at every price. Likewise, a fall in the price of snowboards will lead consumers to buy fewer skis at all price levels.

CHECKPOINT ***If the demand for a good increases, what will happen to the demand for its complement?***

SECTION 2 ASSESSMENT

Essential Questions Journal To continue to build a response to the Essential Question, go to your **Essential Questions Journal.**

Guiding Question

1. Use your completed concept web to answer this question: Why does the demand curve shift?
2. **Extension** Suppose you are about to buy a new pair of shoes. Assume that the price of the shoes will not change. What other factors could affect your demand for the shoes?

Key Terms and Main Ideas

3. How is the ***ceteris paribus*** assumption related to demand curves?
4. How does consumers' income affect the demand for **normal goods?**
5. Name at least three goods that could be bought as **complements** to hamburgers.
6. List at least three goods that could be considered **substitutes** for movie tickets.

Critical Thinking

7. **Summarize (a)** Does a change in the price of a good cause the demand curve to shift? Why or why not? **(b)** What kinds of changes cause shifts in the demand curve?
8. **Contrast** How are normal goods and inferior goods different?
9. **Contrast (a)** If demand for a good increases, what will happen to the demand for its complement? **(b)** What will happen to the demand for its substitute? **(c)** Explain why the changes in demand for the complement and the substitute follow different patterns.

Quick Write

10. Based on what you have read in this section about shifts in the demand curve, write a short essay answering the following questions: How did your demand for a product change based on something other than price? What factors were responsible for this shift in demand? How might these factors have affected other people's demand for the product?

Answers

Checkpoint Demand for its complement will also increase.

Assessment Answers

1. The demand curve shifts when demand changes due to one or more of these factors: income, consumer expectations, population, demographics, consumer tastes and advertising, and the prices of related goods.
2. Possible responses: income; whether I think the price will rise or fall in the future; advertising; whether I can find substitutes that cost less and fit well
3. Demand curves represent demand for a good at different prices only—when all other factors are held constant—*ceteris paribus.*
4. Consumers with increasing incomes demand more normal goods; consumers with decreasing incomes demand fewer normal goods.
5. Possible responses: hamburger buns, ketchup, French fries, pickles, drinks
6. Possible responses: DVD rentals; on-demand movies from cable supplier; tickets for play, concert, or sporting event
7. (a) No; effects of price changes are built into demand curves. (b) changes in consumers' incomes, expectations, or tastes; in population or demographics; in advertising; in prices of related goods
8. Normal goods are goods that consumers demand more of when their incomes increase while inferior goods are goods that consumers demand less of when their incomes increase.
9. (a) will also increase (b) will decrease (c) Since complements are used together, demand for both would move up or down together. Since substitutes are replacements, demand for them moves in the opposite direction.
10. Students should correctly identify a shift in the demand curve and explain it.

SECTION 3 Elasticity of Demand

OBJECTIVES

1. **Explain** how to calculate elasticity of demand.
2. **Identify** factors that affect elasticity.
3. **Explain** how firms use elasticity and revenue to make decisions.

ECONOMIC DICTIONARY

As you read the section, look for the definitions of these **Key Terms:**

- elasticity of demand
- inelastic
- elastic
- unitary elastic
- total revenue

Guiding Question

What factors affect elasticity of demand?

Copy this chart and fill it in as you read.

Effect of a Price Change on Quantity Demanded		
Inelastic Demand	Elastic Demand	Unitary Elastic Demand

Economics and You

Are there some products that you would continue to buy, even if the price were to rise dramatically? Are there other goods that you would cut back on, or stop buying altogether, if there was just a slight increase in price? How much is too much? No matter how you answer these questions, economists have a way to describe your behavior.

Principles in Action Economists have developed a way to calculate just how strongly people react to a change in price. Several factors—including the original price and how much you want or need a particular good—will determine your demand for that product. In this section, you will see how economists measure your behavior. This section's How the Economy Works shows how elasticity of demand affects your daily purchases.

Defining Elasticity

Economists describe the way that consumers respond to price changes as **elasticity of demand.** Elasticity of demand measures how drastically buyers will cut back or increase their demand for a good when the price rises or falls, respectively. If you buy the same amount or just a little less of a good after a large price increase, your demand is **inelastic,** or relatively unresponsive to price changes. If you buy much less of a good after a small price increase, your demand is **elastic.** A consumer with highly elastic demand for a good is very responsive to price changes.

elasticity of demand a measure of how consumers respond to price changes

inelastic describes demand that is not very sensitive to price changes

elastic describes demand that is very sensitive to a change in price

Calculating Elasticity

In order to calculate elasticity of demand, take the percentage change in the quantity of the good demanded, and divide this number by the percentage change in the price of the good. The result is the elasticity of demand for the good.

The law of demand implies that the result will always be negative. That is because an increase in the price of a good will always decrease the quantity demanded, and a decrease in the price of a good will always increase the quantity demanded. For the sake of simplicity, economists drop the negative sign in the result. You can find the equation for elasticity in **Figure 4.5** on page 98.

 **Guiding Question**

What factors affect elasticity of demand?

Get Started

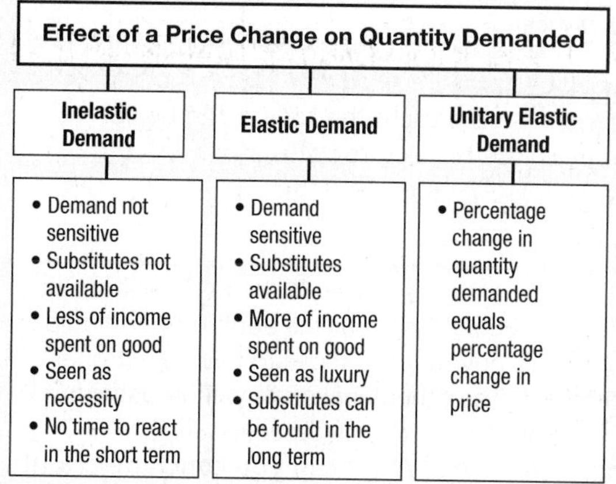

Effect of a Price Change on Quantity Demanded
Inelastic Demand
Elastic Demand
Unitary Elastic Demand
• Demand not sensitive
• Substitutes not available
• Less of income spent on good
• Seen as necessity
• No time to react in the short term
• Demand sensitive
• Substitutes available
• More of income spent on good
• Seen as luxury
• Substitutes can be found in the long term
• Percentage change in quantity demanded equals percentage change in price

LESSON GOALS

Students will:

- Know the Key Terms.
- Explain how elasticity of demand can vary from person to person and from price to price.
- Calculate elasticity of demand and calculate elasticity for a sample product.
- Analyze factors that affect elasticity.
- Explain how businesses can use elasticity of demand to make pricing decisions.

BEFORE CLASS

Have students complete the graphic organizer in the Section Opener as they read the text. As an alternate activity, have students complete the Guided Reading and Review worksheet. (Unit 2 All-in-One, p. 28)

L1 L2 ELL LPR Differentiate Have students complete the Guided Reading and Review worksheet (Unit 2 All-in-One, p. 29)

Focus on the Basics

Students need to come away with the following understandings:

FACTS: • Demand that changes very little in response to a price change is inelastic; demand that changes a great deal in response to a price change is elastic. • A good's elasticity is affected by the availability of substitutes, the relative importance of the good, whether the good is a necessity or a luxury, and the amount of time that has passed since the price change. • Total revenue a firm can make is affected by the elasticity of demand at a given price.

GENERALIZATION: Firms can use information about the elasticity of demand of their goods to make intelligent pricing decisions.

CLASSROOM HINTS

UNITARY ELASTICITY OF DEMAND

Students may be confused about unitary elasticity of demand. Remind students that elasticity of demand is a comparison of two percents: the percentage change in price compared to the resulting percentage change in quantity demanded. Suppose the price of a $50 tire increases by 20 percent to $60. Suppose that increase than causes the quantity demanded to drop by 20 percent. Then the demand for the tire is unitary elastic when its price increases form $50 to $60 because the two percents are the same.

BELLRINGER

Display the "Changing Demand" transparency (Color Transparencies, 4.b). Ask **Which person would be *most* likely to continue purchasing running shoes if their price increased?** (*adult runner*) **Why?**

Teach

Economics online To present this topic using digital resources, use the lecture notes on www.PearsonSuccessNet.com.

EXPLORE

Discuss students' responses to the Bellringer activity. Guide students to see that the adult runner would continue to buy running shoes to have the proper equipment. The other individuals will probably put off such purchases, or buy other less expensive shoes instead. Ask **What can you conclude about a good's elasticity of demand?** *(Elasticity varies from consumer to consumer.)*

Then have a volunteer read aloud the paragraph under the heading "Price Range," which begins on page 98. Have students identify the key point of the paragraph. *(Elasticity of demand for a good can be different at different prices.)* Have them brainstorm their own examples as a class.

Action Graph online Have students review the Action Graph animation for a step-by-step look at elasticity of demand.

unitary elastic describes demand whose elasticity is exactly equal to 1

Price Range

The elasticity of demand for a good varies at every price level. Demand for a good can be highly elastic at one price and inelastic at a different price. For example, demand for a glossy magazine will be inelastic when the price rises 50 percent, from 60 cents to 90 cents. The new price is still very low, and people will buy almost as many copies as they did before. However, when the price of a magazine increases 50 percent, from $4.00 to $6.00, demand will be much more elastic. Many readers will refuse to pay $2.00 more for the magazine. Yet in percentage terms, the change in the magazine's price is exactly the same as when the price rose from 60 cents to 90 cents.

Values of Elasticity

We have been using the terms *inelastic* and *elastic* to describe consumers' responses to price changes. These terms have precise mathematical definitions. If the elasticity of demand for a good at a certain price is *less* than 1, we describe demand as inelastic. If the elasticity is *greater* than one, demand is elastic. If elasticity is *exactly equal* to 1, we describe demand as **unitary elastic.**

When elasticity of demand is unitary, the percentage change in quantity demanded is

Figure 4.5 Elasticity of Demand

GRAPH SKILLS

Elasticity of demand describes how strongly consumers will react to a change in price.

1. What is the formula for computing elasticity of demand?
2. If a good's elasticity of demand is 0.2, how will consumers react to an increase in price?

To determine elasticity of demand, use the following formulas:

$$\text{Percentage change} = \frac{\text{Original number} - \text{New number}}{\text{Original number}} \times 100$$

$$\text{Elasticity} = \frac{\text{Percentage change in quantity demanded}}{\text{Percentage change in price}}$$

Example 1: Elastic Demand

The price decreases from $4 to $3, a decrease of 25 percent. $\frac{\$4-\$3}{\$4} \times 100 = 25$

The quantity demanded increases from 10 to 20. This is an increase of 100 percent. $\frac{10-20}{10} \times 100 = 100$

Elasticity of demand is equal to 4.0. Elasticity is greater than 1 so demand is elastic. In this example, a small decrease in price caused a large increase in the quantity demanded. $\frac{100\%}{25\%} = 4.0$

Example 2: Inelastic Demand

The price decreases from $6 to $2, a decrease of about 67 percent. $\frac{\$6-\$2}{\$6} \times 100 = 67$

The quantity demanded increases from 10 to 15, an increase of 50 percent. $\frac{10-15}{10} \times 100 = 50$

Elasticity of demand is about 0.75. The elasticity is less than 1, so demand for this good is inelastic. The increase in quantity demanded is small compared to the decrease in price. $\frac{50\%}{67\%} = 0.75$

Action Graph online

For an animated version of this graph, visit **PearsonSuccessNet.com**

Differentiated Resources

L1 L2 Guided Reading and Review (Unit 2 All-in-One, p. 29)

L2 Determining Elasticity (Unit 2 All-in-One, p. 31)

L4 Analyzing Elasticity of Demand (Unit 2 All-in-One, p. 32)

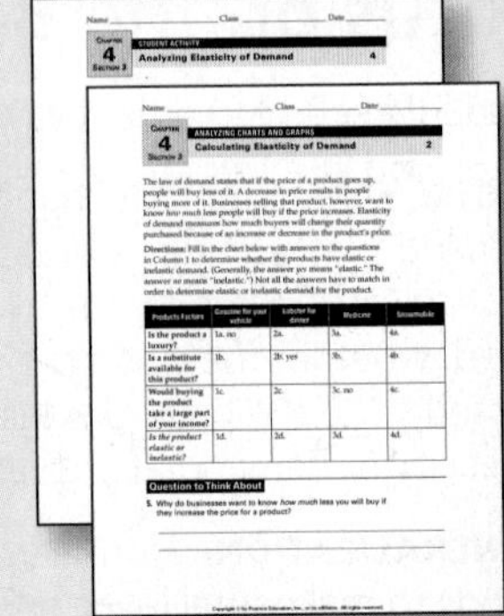

Answers

Graph Skills 1. dividing the percentage change in quantity demanded by percentage change in price 2. Demand will not change much; it is inelastic.

◀ Grazing sheep are this homeowner's solution to the high price of gasoline. ***How does this cartoon illustrate elasticity of demand?***

exactly equal to the percentage change in the price. Suppose the elasticity of demand for a magazine at $2 is unitary. When the price of the magazine rises by 50 percent to $3, the newsstand will sell exactly half as many copies as before.

Think back to Ashley's demand schedule for pizza in Section 1. Ashley's demand schedule shows that if the price per slice were to rise from $2.00 to $3.00, her quantity demanded would fall from 4 slices to 3 slices per day. The change in price from $2.00 to $3.00 is a 50 percent increase. The change in quantity demanded from 4 slices to 3 is a 25 percent decrease. Dividing the 25 percent decrease in quantity demanded by the 50 percent increase in price gives us an elasticity of demand of 0.5.

Since Ashley's elasticity of demand at a price change from $2.00 to $3.00 is less than 1, we say that Ashley's demand for pizza is inelastic. In other words, price increase has a relatively small effect on the number of slices of pizza she buys.

Suppose we survey another customer and find that when the price of pizza rises by 40 percent, this person's quantity demanded falls by 60 percent. The change in the quantity demanded of 60 percent is divided by the change in price of 40 percent, equaling an elasticity of demand of 1.5 (60 percent/40 percent = 1.5). Since this result is greater than 1, this customer's demand is elastic. In other words, this customer is very sensitive to changes in the price of pizza.

CHECKPOINT ***How do economists calculate elasticity?***

Factors Affecting Elasticity

Why is the demand for some goods so much less elastic than for other goods? Rephrase the question and ask yourself, "What is essential to me? What goods must I have, even if the price rises greatly?" The goods you list might have some traits that set them apart from other goods and make your demand for those goods less elastic. Several different factors can affect a person's elasticity of demand for a specific good.

Availability of Substitutes

If there are few substitutes for a good, then even when its price rises greatly, you might still buy it. You believe you have no good alternatives. For example, if your favorite musical group plans to give a concert that you want to attend, there really is no substitute for that ticket. You could go to a concert to hear some other band, but that would not be as good. You've got to have tickets for this concert, and nothing else will do. Under these circumstances, a moderate change in price is not going to change your mind. Your demand for that concert is inelastic.

CALCULATE

Direct students' attention to the two graphs in Figure 4.5. Work through Example 1 with students, and then have them work in pairs to calculate the elasticity of demand in Example 2.

Distribute the "Calculating Elasticity of Demand" worksheet (Unit 2 All-in-One, p. 30). Have students complete the chart by calculating elasticity of demand for a brand of sneakers and then answer the questions that follow.

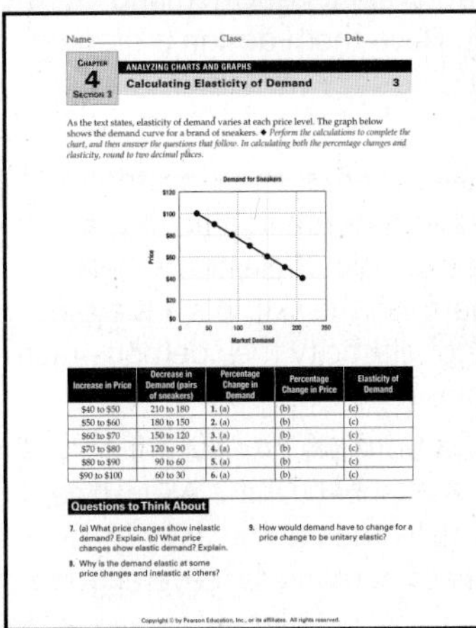
Name ________ Class ________ Date ________

CHAPTER 4 SECTION 3 — ANALYZING CHARTS AND GRAPHS

Calculating Elasticity of Demand 3

As the text states, elasticity of demand varies at each price level. The graph below shows the demand curve for a brand of sneakers. ◆ *Perform the calculations to complete the chart, and then answer the questions that follow. In calculating both the percentage changes and elasticity, round to two decimal places.*

Increase in Price	Decrease in Demand (pairs of sneakers)	Percentage Change in Demand	Percentage Change in Price	Elasticity of Demand
$40 to $50	210 to 180	1. (a)	(b)	(c)
$50 to $60	180 to 150	2. (a)	(b)	(c)
$60 to $70	150 to 120	3. (a)	(b)	(c)
$70 to $80	120 to 90	4. (a)	(b)	(c)
$80 to $90	90 to 60	5. (a)	(b)	(c)
$90 to $100	60 to 30	6. (a)	(b)	(c)

Questions to Think About

7. (a) What price changes show inelastic demand? Explain. (b) What price changes show elastic demand? Explain.

8. Why is the demand elastic at some price changes and inelastic at others?

9. How would demand have to change for a price change to be unitary elastic?

L1 L2 Differentiate Distribute the "Determining Elasticity" worksheet (Unit 2 All-in-One, p. 31)

L4 Differentiate After students complete the worksheet, have them find a price increase for which demand is unitary elastic. *(for an increase in price from $55 to $65, corresponding to a decrease in demand from 165 to 135 pairs, elasticity equals 1)*

Virtual Economics

L3 Differentiate

Applying the Elasticity of Demand
Use the following lesson from the NCEE **Virtual Economics *CD-ROM*** to investigate the impact of price elasticity. Click on Browse Economics Lessons, specify grades 9–12, and use the key words *price changes matter.*

In this activity, students will determine price elasticity and use statistics to analyze its impact.

LESSON TITLE	PRICE CHANGES MATTER
Type of Activity	Using statistics
Complexity	Moderate
Time	150 minutes
NCEE Standards	7, 8

Answers

Cartoon This man has found a substitute for the gasoline in his lawnmower. His demand for gas is elastic.

Checkpoint They divide the percentage change in the demand for a good by the percentage change in the price of the good.

BRAINSTORM

Review the different scenarios described in the "How the Economy Works" feature with the class to clarify how each situation reveals elasticity or inelasticity of demand.

Divide the class into groups. Have each group take one of the three factors illustrated in *How the Economy Works*—availability of substitutes, share of budget, necessity versus luxury—and brainstorm to identify three examples of goods with elastic demand and three that have inelastic demand because of that factor. Have them design a graphic display, computerized slide show, or other visual to show their examples.

L3 Differentiate Call on verbal and kinesthetic learners to team together to write and act out a skit demonstrating an example of elastic or inelastic demand. After they perform the skit, have the class determine which type of elasticity they demonstrated and what factor explains it.

L4 Differentiate Distribute the "Analyzing Elasticity of Demand" worksheet (Unit 2 All-in-One, p. 32) and have students complete the activity, then compare their elasticity of demand for several goods and services.

APPLY UNDERSTANDING

Have students review the feature How the Economy Works. Ask **How do you behave when your demand for a good is elastic?** (*substitute a less expensive good*) **Besides gasoline, what good might you continue to demand even if the price increased?** Have students consider how people's values and incomes might influence the elasticity of their demand for cable television.

How the Economy Works

How does elasticity affect consumer demand?

On any given day, the average consumer faces a series of spending decisions. Elasticity of demand describes how strongly buyers will react to a change in the price of a good. How does elasticity of demand affect your decision to buy or not to buy?

1 The price of your morning latte has increased from $3 to $4. Instead of the latte, you buy a regular coffee for $2. Because a substitute is available, your demand for the latte is **elastic.**

2 You notice that the price of gasoline has increased by twenty cents a gallon. Your car runs on gasoline and there are no substitutes. Despite the increase, your demand for gasoline is **inelastic.**

Availability of Substitutes

Similarly, demand for life-saving medicine is usually inelastic. For many prescription drugs, the only possible substitute is to try an unproven treatment. For this reason, people with an illness will continue to buy as much needed medicine as they can afford, even when the price goes up.

If the lack of substitutes can make demand inelastic, a wide choice of substitute goods can make demand elastic. The demand for a particular brand of apple juice is probably elastic because people can choose from several good substitutes if the price of their preferred brand rises.

Relative Importance

A second factor in determining a good's elasticity of demand is how much of your budget you spend on the good. If you already spend a large share of your income on a good, a price increase will force you to make some tough choices. Unless you want to cut back drastically on the other goods in your budget, you must reduce consumption of that particular good by a significant amount to keep your budget under control. The higher the jump in price, the more you will have to adjust your purchases.

If you currently spend half of your budget on clothes, even a modest increase in the cost of clothing will probably cause a large reduction in the quantity you purchase. In other words, your demand will be elastic.

However, if the price of shoelaces doubled, would you cut back on your shoelace purchases? Probably not. You may not even notice the difference. Even if you spend twice as much on shoelaces, they will still account for only a tiny part of your overall budget. Your demand for shoelaces is inelastic.

Background Note

Budget and the Price Elasticity of Food Economists have found that the price elasticity of food varies from country to country. In nations with higher incomes, such as the United States, Canada, and Western Europe, the price elasticity for food is 0.15. In poorer nations, such as Nigeria and Bolivia, it is 0.34. While both demands are inelastic, elasticity in these poorer nations is closer to 1. The reason for this is that people in poorer nations spend a greater percentage of their income on food. As a result, increases in food prices affect them more.

How the Economy Works online

For an animated, interactive version of this feature, visit PearsonSuccessNet.com

3 You need a new set of tires. The price for the same brand-name tire has increased by 20 percent. That price is too high, so you buy the cheaper tires. Your demand for the brand-name tire is **elastic.**

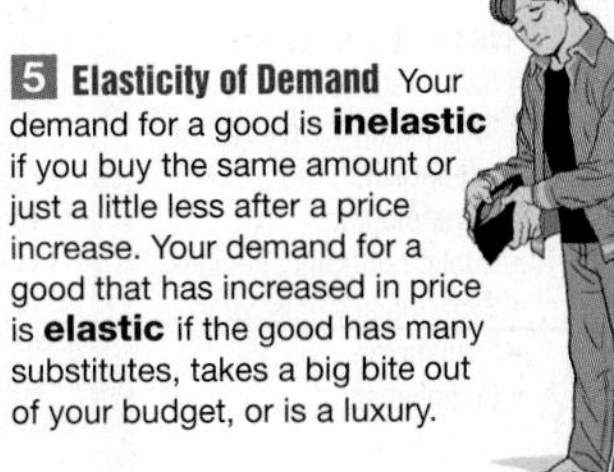

4 That new set of tires put a big dent in your budget. But you have a date, so takeout replaces dining out. Your demand for a restaurant dinner is **elastic.**

5 **Elasticity of Demand** Your demand for a good is **inelastic** if you buy the same amount or just a little less after a price increase. Your demand for a good that has increased in price is **elastic** if the good has many substitutes, takes a big bite out of your budget, or is a luxury.

Check Your Understanding

1. How does knowing the elasticity of demand for a good help entrepreneurs?
2. What changes might make demand for gasoline more elastic over time?

Share of Budget | **Necessity Versus Luxury**

Necessities Versus Luxuries

The third factor in determining a good's elasticity varies a great deal from person to person, but it is nonetheless important. Whether a person considers a good to be a necessity or a luxury has a great impact on a person's elasticity of demand for that good. A necessity is a good people will always buy, even when the price increases. Parents often regard milk as a necessity. They will buy it at any reasonable price. If the price of a gallon of milk rises from $3.49 to $5.49, they will still buy as much milk as their children need to stay healthy. Their demand for milk is inelastic.

The same parents may regard steak as a luxury. When the price of steak increases slightly, say 20 percent, parents may cut their monthly purchases of steak by more than 20 percent, or skip steak altogether. Steak is a luxury, and consumers can easily reduce the quantity they consume. Because it is easy to reduce the quantity of luxury goods demanded, demand is elastic.

Change Over Time

When a price changes, consumers often need time to change their spending habits. Consumers do not always react quickly to a price increase, because it takes time to find substitutes. Because they cannot respond quickly to price changes, their demand is inelastic in the short term. Demand sometimes becomes more elastic over time, however, because people can eventually find substitutes.

Consider the example of gasoline. A person might purchase a large vehicle that requires a greater volume of gasoline per mile to run. This person might work at a job many miles away from home and shop at a supermarket that is not local.

FUTURE WATCH

Personal Finance
For help with establishing a good credit rating, see your Personal Finance Handbook at the back of the book or visit **PearsonSuccessNet.com**

DEMONSTRATE ELASTICITY

Tell students to assume that they are shopping for a computer. They prefer a particular laptop for its features and lengthy warranty. Substitutes include the following:

- A different brand laptop (comparably equipped but with shorter warranty): $850
- A desktop (comparably equipped): $800
- Refurbished laptop (slightly slower speed): $700
- Refurbished desktop (slightly slower speed): $600

Have students raise their hands if they would buy the new laptop for $900, and then at increasingly higher prices: $1,100; $1,300; and $1,500. Record each vote on the board. Have the class determine the elasticity of class demand for each price increase of $200.

Call on volunteers to explain how important the availability of substitutes, the relative importance of the expense, and the luxury of mobility and space saving were in shaping elasticity of demand in this situation.

PERSONAL FINANCE ACTIVITY

Remind students that they can learn more about establishing good credit by reading the Credit and Debt sections starting on page PF22 in the **Personal Finance Handbook**. You may want to assign the activity worksheets (Personal Finance All-in-One, pp. 64–76).

Background Note

New Products and Time The passage of time increases demand for innovative products. Marketing experts identify five groups of consumers in terms of their willingness to purchase innovative products: *innovators* purchase such products soon after introduction; *early adopters* follow closely after; *early majority adopters* come next and signal the spread of the innovation into a larger market; *later majority* adopters buy products after they have become established; and *laggards* are very slow to adopt new products.

Answers

Check Your Understanding 1. Possible response: Entrepreneurs need to know how much they can vary the price of the good or service they plan to sell, and how price change will affect revenue. 2. Possible responses: consumers buying more fuel-efficient cars or engineers developing different kinds of car engines or fuels

CREATE A PROFILE

Have students use the Career Link worksheet to record their research for the activity (Unit 2 All-in-One, p. 164).

PREDICT

Show the "American Gasoline Use" transparency (Color Transparencies, 4.c), which roughly tracks changes in U.S. gasoline prices and consumer behavior over several recent decades. Review with students the changes in consumer behavior regarding gasoline use and vehicle purchases. Ask **What factors other than gasoline price affect people's gasoline use?** *(Possible responses: age of vehicle driven; vehicle's gas mileage (mpg); distance needed to travel to and from jobs and other frequently visited locations; use of cars for leisure travel; degree to which trips to run errands are consolidated; practice of sharing rides; using public transportation)*

Using the Idea Wave strategy (p. T24), ask students to write down their responses to the following question: **What impact do you think the price of gas will have on consumer behavior?** Provide an example answer on the board: *People will buy smaller cars and drive them for shorter distances.* After they write down their responses, pair students and have them share their answers. Then pick volunteers to start the class discussion. As students give their answers, have everyone write down two answers with which they agree. If a student has the same answer as another student, have that student acknowledge that as they give their answer.

L4 Differentiate Instruct students to use the Internet or other resources to develop a list of steps consumers can take to reduce gasoline usage. Tell them to divide their list into short-term and long-term steps and to assess the impact that each would have on fuel consumption.

Answer

Checkpoint availability of substitutes, relative importance of the good, whether the good is a necessity or luxury, length of time since price changed

FUTURE WATCH

CAREER CENTER

MARKET RESEARCH

Possible Careers

- Sales representative
- **Market and survey researcher**
- Psychologist
- Public relations specialist
- Systems administrator
- Statistician
- Sociologist

Profile: Market and Survey Researcher

Duties:

- gather statistical data and examine prices, sales, and methods of marketing and distribution
- design telephone, mail, or Internet surveys to assess consumer preferences
- conduct personal interviews with the public and lead focus group discussions

Education:

- bachelor's degree essential, master's degree helpful

Skills:

- background in mathematics and statistics
- attention to detail
- communication skills
- ability to work well in a team

Median Annual Salary:

- $58,820 (2006)

Future prospects:

- Employment of market researchers is expected to grow faster than average through 2014.

Career Link *Activity*

Choose another career in market research from the list of possible careers. Create a profile for that career similar to the one for Market and Survey Researcher.

These factors determine how much gasoline this person demands, and none can be changed easily.

In the early 1970s, several oil-rich countries cut their oil exports to the United States. Gasoline prices rose quickly. In the short term, people could do little to reduce their consumption of gasoline. They still needed to drive to school and work. At first, drivers were more likely to pay the higher price for gasoline than they were to buy fuel-efficient cars or move closer to their workplaces.

However, because gas prices stayed high for a considerable period of time, some people eventually switched to more fuel-efficient cars, formed car pools, or used public transportation. In the long run, people reduced their consumption of gasoline by finding substitutes. Demand for gasoline, inelastic in the short term, is more elastic in the long term.

The story did not end there. In the early 1980s, the price of a gallon of gas began to fall. Gasoline prices, adjusted for inflation, stayed low for the next two decades. At first, people continued to buy fuel-efficient cars. But over time, many Americans switched to larger vehicles that got fewer miles to the gallon. Because the price of gas remained low, people gradually adjusted their habits and consumed more gasoline. Just as demand for gasoline responded slowly to an increase in price, it also responded slowly to a decrease in price.

In the early 2000s, gasoline prices shot up again. Once more, consumers were slow to change their car-buying habits and their demand for gasoline. If prices remain high over the long term, however, economists expect that demand for gasoline will again be more elastic.

CHECKPOINT ***What factors affect elasticity of demand?***

Elasticity and Revenue

Elasticity is important to the study of economics because elasticity helps us measure how consumers respond to price changes for different products. Elasticity is also an important tool for business planners like the pizzeria owner described in Sections 1 and 2. The elasticity of demand determines how a change in prices will affect a firm's total revenue, or income.

Computing a Firm's Total Revenue

A company's **total revenue** is defined as the amount of money the company receives by selling its goods. This is determined by two factors: the price of the goods and the quantity sold. If a pizzeria sells 150 slices of pizza per day at $4.00 per slice, total revenue would be $600 per day.

Total Revenue and Elastic Demand

The law of demand tells us that an increase in price will decrease the quantity demanded. When a good has an elastic demand, raising the price of each unit sold by 20 percent will decrease the quantity sold by a larger percentage, say 50 percent. The quantity sold will drop enough to actually *reduce* the firm's total revenue. The revenue table in **Figure 4.6**—drawn from the pizzeria's demand curve—shows how this can happen. An increase in price from $5 to $6, or 20 percent, decreases the quantity sold from 100 to 50, or 50 percent. As a result, total revenue drops from $500 to $300.

The same process can also work in reverse. If the firm were to reduce the price by a certain percentage, the quantity demanded could rise by an even greater percentage. In this case, total revenues could rise.

It may surprise you that a firm could lose revenue by raising the price of its goods. But if the pizzeria started selling pizza at $10 a slice, it would not stay in business very long. Remember that elastic demand comes from one or more of these factors:

- The availability of substitute goods
- A limited budget that does not allow for price changes
- The perception of the good as a luxury item

If these conditions are present, then the demand for the good is elastic, and a firm may find that a price increase reduces its total revenue.

Total Revenue and Inelastic Demand

Remember that if demand is inelastic, consumers' demand is not very responsive to price changes. When demand is inelastic, price and total revenue move in the same direction: An increase in price raises total revenue, and a decrease in price reduces total revenue. Thus, if a firm raises its price by 25 percent, the quantity demanded will fall, but not by enough to lower total revenue. As a result, the firm will have greater total revenues, because the higher price will make up for the lower quantity of sales. The firm brings in more money.

On the other hand, a decrease in price will lead to an increase in the quantity demanded even if demand is inelastic. However, the percentage of increase in the quantity demanded will be less than the percentage of increase in price, and the firm's total revenue will decrease. For example, if you lower the price of socks by 50 percent, you may sell only 20 percent more socks. The increase in the quantity sold does not compensate for the lost revenue.

CHECKPOINT ***How does elasticity affect revenue?***

total revenue the total amount of money a company receives by selling goods or services

Figure 4.6 **Revenue Table**

Price of a Slice of Pizza	Quantity Demanded (per day)	Total Revenue
$1.00	300	$300
$2.00	250	$500
$3.00	200	$600
$4.00	150	$600
$5.00	100	$500
$6.00	50	$300

CHART SKILLS

Setting prices too high or too low can hurt revenue.

1. What two factors determine total revenue?
2. When the price doubles from $2.00 to $4.00, is demand elastic, unitary elastic, or inelastic?

Background Note

Why Luxury Goods Have Inelastic Demand *Forbes* magazine calculates an index of luxury spending it calls the Cost of Living Extremely Well Index. The index charts the cost of such luxury goods as catered meals at top restaurants, private jets, and fur coats. In a recent year, *Forbes* reported, the cost of these luxury goods rose twice as fast as the cost of ordinary consumer goods. A comment by a *Forbes* spokesperson reveals why luxury goods show inelastic demand: "The bottom line is, if you have money and you want to spend it, you're going to spend it."

MAKE A DECISION

Direct students' attention to the revenue table in Figure 4.6. Tell them to assume that they own the pizza shop. Instruct them to determine how much they would charge for a slice of pizza and to explain their choice.

Then tell students to look at Figure 4.7 on page 104. Have them review their decision in light of the information in that figure. Would they change their mind about the best price? Why or why not? Discuss students' responses as a class.

L1 L2 Differentiate Make sure that students understand that a firm's total revenue is not the same as its profits. Total revenue is simply the income received from all sales. Expenses—the cost of making and selling goods and services—must be subtracted from that number to determine a firm's profits.

EXTEND

Have students choose one business in their community that they think could raise its prices and raise revenue, and one business that they think would lose revenue if it raised its prices. Have them describe why they think this would be the outcome.

L1 L2 LPR Differentiate Have students write a paragraph explaining how they can apply what they learned about demand elasticity to their own purchasing decisions.

GUIDING QUESTION WRAP UP

Have students return to the section Guiding Question. Review the completed graphic organizer and clarify any misunderstandings. Have a wrap up discussion about elasticity of demand.

Assess and Remediate

L3 L2 L4 Collect the worksheets on elasticity of demand and assess student understanding of factors affecting demand elasticity.

L3 Assign the Section 3 Assessment questions; identify student misconceptions.

L3 Give Section Quiz A (Unit 2 All-in-One, p. 33).

L2 Give Section Quiz B (Unit 2 All-in-One, p. 34).

(Assess and Remediate continued on p. 104)

Answers

Checkpoint If demand for a good is elastic raising price could reduce revenue.

Chart Skills 1. price and quantity sold 2. Demand is inelastic (0.4): the percent that quantity demanded decreases (40%) is less than the percent that price increases (100%), so elasticity is less than 1.

Have students complete the Self-Test Online and continue their work in the **Essential Questions Journal**.

REMEDIATION AND SUGGESTIONS

Use the chart below to help students who are struggling with content.

WEAKNESS	REMEDIATION
Defining key terms (Questions 3, 4, 5, 7)	Have students use the interactive Economic Dictionary Online.
Evaluating impact of demand elasticity (Questions 1, 2, 4, 5, 8, 9, 11)	Have students quiz a partner on the factors affecting demand in "How the Economy Works."
Using elasticity to make pricing decisions (Questions 10, 11)	Have students review using the Action Graph for Figure 4.7.

Answers

Chart Skills 1. Demand decreases by a larger percentage than price increases, so sales and revenue decrease. 2. It decreases.

Checkpoint to make wise pricing decisions, and to estimate revenues.

Figure 4.7 Elasticity and Revenue

Elastic Demand

As the price is lowered... Total revenue rises

As the price is raised... Total revenue falls

Inelastic Demand

As the price is lowered... Total revenue falls

As the price is raised... Total revenue rises

CHART SKILLS

Elasticity of demand determines the effect of a price change on total revenues.

1. Why will revenue fall if a firm raises the price of a good whose demand is elastic?
2. What happens to total revenue when price decreases, but demand is inelastic?

Elasticity and Pricing Policies

Because of these relationships, a firm needs to know whether the demand for its product is elastic or inelastic at a given price. The ways that elasticity of demand can affect a firm's total revenues are shown in **Figure 4.7**. This knowledge helps the firm make pricing decisions that lead to the greatest revenue. If a firm knows that the demand for its product is elastic at the current price, it knows that an increase in price would reduce total revenues. When the price of gasoline rose in 2008, demand for SUVs proved to be elastic. As a result, car manufacturers could not raise prices to compensate for lower sales.

On the other hand, if a firm knows that the demand for its product is inelastic at its current price, it knows that an increase in price will increase total revenue. In the next chapter, you will read more about the choices producers make to reach an ideal level of revenue.

***CHECKPOINT* Why does a firm need to know whether demand for its product is elastic or inelastic?**

SECTION 3 ASSESSMENT

Essential Questions Journal To continue to build a response to the Essential Question, go to your **Essential Questions Journal.**

Guiding Question

1. Use your completed chart to answer this question: What factors affect elasticity of demand?
2. **Extension** Think about goods you buy regularly. Suppose the price of everything doubled. Which items would you continue to buy?

Key Terms and Main Ideas

3. What is **elasticity of demand?**
4. If demand for a good is **elastic,** what will happen when the price increases?
5. If demand for a good is **inelastic,** how will a drop in price affect demand for the good?
6. Name three factors that determine a good's elasticity.
7. Suppose demand for a product is elastic at a given price. What will happen to the company's **total revenue** if it raises the price of that product? Why?

Critical Thinking

8. **Analyze (a)** How does the percentage of your budget you spend on a good affect its elasticity? **(b)** Why is this the case?
9. **Summarize** Why does demand become more elastic over time?
10. **Interpret (a)** What factors determine a company's total revenue? **(b)** Do higher prices lead to increased revenues for a company? Explain your answer.

Math Skills

11. To find the elasticity of a good, divide the percentage change in the quantity demanded by the percentage change in price. Review this formula and the formula for finding the percentage changes for prices and for quantity demanded in Figure 4.5 on page 98. Use the formulas to calculate the elasticity of demand in the following cases. Identify whether demand is elastic, inelastic, or unitary elastic. **(a)** When the price of a car wash rises from \$10.00 to \$11.00, the number of daily customers drops from 60 to 48. **(b)** A dentist with 80 patients cuts his fee for a cleaning from \$60.00 to \$54.00 and attracts two new patients.

Visit PearsonSuccessNet.com for additional math help.

Assessment Answers

1. availability of substitutes, relative importance, necessity or luxury, amount of time since price change
2. Possible responses: food, medications, clothing
3. measurement of consumer response to price changes
4. Demand will drop.
5. Demand will not change much.
6. Three of the four factors: availability of substitutes, relative importance, necessity or luxury, amount of time since price change
7. Total revenue will fall. While the product's price is higher, the firm will sell much less of the product.
8. (a) The more of your budget you spend on a good, the more elastic your demand is. (b) When you spend a large share of your budget on a good, price changes have a big impact. For example, an increase in a good's price could cause you to spend your entire budget on that good unless you reduce your demand for that item.
9. People have time to find substitutes and change behaviors.
10. (a) price of their goods and demand for their goods (b) Not necessarily: if demand is elastic, increased prices lead to lower revenues.
11. (a) 2; elastic (b) 0.25, inelastic

QUICK STUDY GUIDE

Chapter 4: Demand

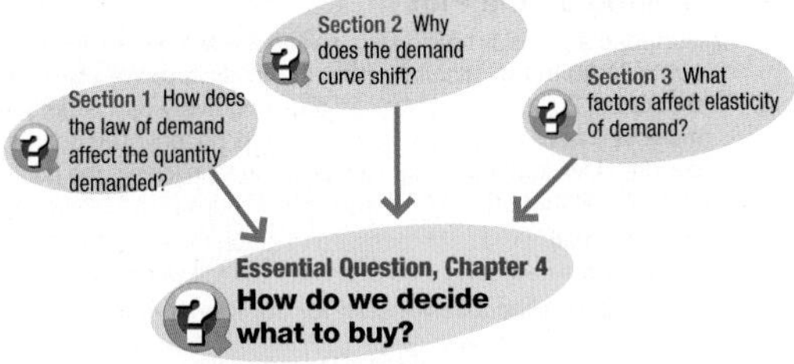

Section 2 Why does the demand curve shift?
Section 1 How does the law of demand affect the quantity demanded?
Section 3 What factors affect elasticity of demand?

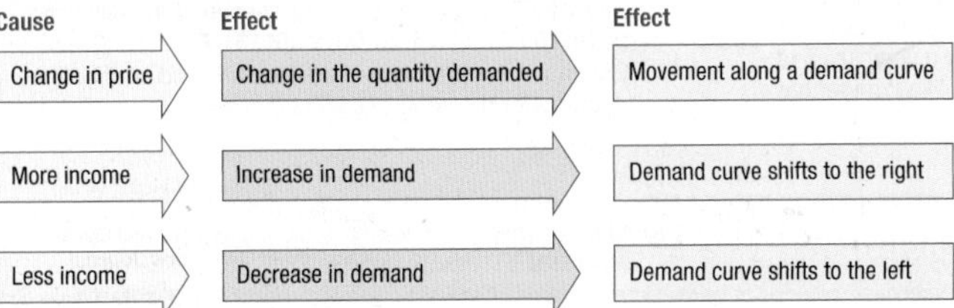

Essential Question, Chapter 4
How do we decide what to buy?

Elasticity of Demand

Inelastic	Elastic	Unitary Elastic
• Not sensitive to price change • Price increase: demand is the same • Elasticity less than 1	• Very sensitive to price change • Price increase: demand is less • Elasticity is greater than 1	• Percentage change in demand equals percentage change in price • Elasticity equals 1

Changes in Demand

Cause	Effect	Effect
Change in price	Change in the quantity demanded	Movement along a demand curve
More income	Increase in demand	Demand curve shifts to the right
Less income	Decrease in demand	Demand curve shifts to the left

Economic Dictionary

demand, *p. 85*
law of demand, *p. 85*
substitution effect, *p. 87*
income effect, *p. 87*
demand schedule, *p. 88*
market demand schedule, *p. 88*
demand curve, *p. 89*
ceteris paribus, *p. 91*
normal good, *p. 92*
inferior good, *p. 94*
demographics, *p. 94*
complements, *p. 96*
substitutes, *p. 96*
elasticity of demand, *p. 97*
inelastic, *p. 97*
elastic, *p. 97*
unitary elastic, *p. 98*
total revenue, *p. 103*

Economics on the go

Study anytime, anywhere. Download these files today.

Economic Dictionary online	Audio Review online	Action Graph online	Visual Glossary online	How the Economy Works online
Vocabulary Support in English and Spanish	Audio Study Guide in English and Spanish	Animated Charts and Graphs	Animated feature	Animated feature

Download to your computer or mobile device at PearsonSuccessNet.com

ASSIGN THE ESSENTIAL QUESTIONS JOURNAL

After students have finished studying the chapter, they should return to the chapter's essential question in the Essential Questions Journal and complete the activity.

Tell students to go back to the chapter opener and look at the image. Using the information they have gained from studying the chapter, ask **How does this illustrate the main ideas of the chapter?** *(Possible answers: A sale on some goods at this store may be the reason for the increased quantity demanded.)*

STUDY TIPS

To help students study effectively, teach them to do the following:

Set aside a place just for studying. That place should have good lighting, a comfortable chair, a table on which you can spread out your work, good ventilation, and no distractions such as a television, friends who want to talk, or other forms of entertainment.

Divide your work into small, short-range, reasonable goals before you begin to work. For example, set a goal of reading one section in a chapter and filling in the Guided Reading and Review for that section as you read.

Economics on the go Have students download the digital resources available on Economics on the Go for review and remediation.

Assessment at a Glance

TESTS AND QUIZZES

Section Assessments

Section Quizzes A and B, **Unit 2 All-in-One**
Self-Test Online

Chapter Assessments

Chapter Tests A and B, **Unit 2 All-in-One**
Economic Detective, **Unit 2 All-in-One**
Document-based Assessment, p. 107
Exam*View*

AYP Monitoring Assessments

PERFORMANCE ASSESSMENT

Teacher's Edition, pp. 87, 89, 95, 99, 100
Simulation Activities, Chapter 4
Virtual Economics on CD-ROM, pp. 88, 95, 99
Essential Questions Journal, Chapter 4
Assessment Rubrics

Chapter 4 Assessment

1. (a) Quantity demanded increases. (b) This change is shown as movement along the demand curve from upper left (higher price and lower demand) to lower right (lower price and higher demand). (c) Bad publicity might cause the demand curve to shift to the left.
2. (a) an increase in demand (b) a decrease in demand (c) It would cause the demand curve to shift to the right.
3. (a) $60.00 (b) Her total revenue will stay the same: $60.00. (c) inelastic (33% change in demand divided by 50% change in price equals 0.66 elasticity of demand)
4. (a) inelastic (5% divided by 50% equals 0.1 elasticity of demand) (b) Few substitutes are available, and the medicine is a necessity for customers. (c) Possible responses: People had time to find new substitutes; other companies started making similar products.
5. Demand for the song is unitary elastic for a price increase of $1.00 to $1.50.
6. (a) about 550 people (b) about 75 people
7. The graph should show the following intersections:
   at $0.50, 300 people;
   at $0.75, 250 people;
   at $1.00, 200 people;
   at $1.50, 100 people;
   at $1.75, 50 people;
8. The slope of the demand curve would become less steep, because small price changes on the vertical axis would have a relatively large impact on the quantity demanded.
9. Help students define their budgets. Given the many variables in their sources of income—jobs, allowances, gifts—they may have difficulty determining their monthly average. Be sure to check their worksheets before they move on to modify the activity.
10. Answers will vary but factors that affect students' decisions to buy items that are not needs may include the availability of substitutes, how much of their budget they must spend, their expectations about the future, and the impact of advertising.

CHAPTER 4 ASSESSMENT

Self-Test online To test your understanding of key terms and main ideas, visit **PearsonSuccessNet.com**

Key Terms and Main Ideas

To make sure you understand the key terms and main ideas of this chapter, review the Checkpoint and Section Assessment questions and look at the Quick Study Guide on the preceding page.

Critical Thinking

1. **Infer (a)** According to the law of demand, what happens when the price of a good drops? **(b)** How is this change shown in a demand curve? **(c)** If a product gets bad publicity, how might that affect the demand curve?
2. **Draw Conclusions (a)** What is a right shift of the demand curve called? **(b)** What is a left shift of the demand curve called? **(c)** How would an increase in income affect the demand curve for a normal good?
3. **Calculate** Suppose that Susan mows lawns for six customers a week and charges $10.00 per lawn. **(a)** What is her total revenue? **(b)** Imagine that Susan raises her prices to $15.00 per lawn and loses two customers. What will happen to her total revenue? **(c)** Is the demand for Susan's lawn-mowing service at this price elastic or inelastic?
4. **Apply (a)** Suppose the price of a certain medicine rises by 50 percent. In the month following the change, sales decrease by 5 percent. Is the demand elastic or inelastic? **(b)** What factors might be responsible for the elasticity or inelasticity of this product? **(c)** After a year, sales of the medicine decrease by 50 percent. What might have happened?

Applying Your Math Skills

Making a Line Plot

Suppose a popular musician is selling a new song online. It costs $1.00 to buy the song from the musician's Web site. At that price, 200 people download the song every day. After the musician raises the price of the song to $1.50, only 100 people per day download the song. The musician then lowers the price to $0.75. At that price, 300 people per day download the song. Use your math skills to determine and graph the elasticity of demand for the new song, and to answer the following questions: ***Visit PearsonSuccessNet.com for additional math help.***

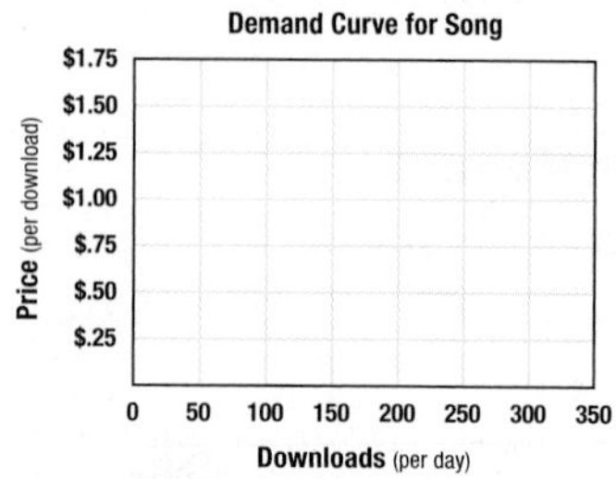

5. Based on the original price of $1.00, would you describe demand for the song as inelastic, elastic, or unitary elastic?
6. **(a)** How many people would download the song per day if it cost $0.50? **(b)** How many people would download the song per day if it cost $1.75?
7. On the grid, create a demand curve for the new song. Show the demand for the song at each of the following prices: $0.50, $0.75, $1.00, $1.50, $1.75.
8. Describe how the slope of the graph would change if demand for the song became more elastic.

Essential Question Activity

Essential Questions Journal To respond to the chapter Essential Question, go to your **Essential Questions Journal.**

9. We all make buying decisions on a daily basis. Complete this activity to answer the Essential Question **How do we decide what to buy?** Use the worksheet in your Essential Questions Journal or the electronic worksheet available at **PearsonSuccessNet.com** to record information about your recent purchases. Include items such as clothing, electronics, food, and entertainment. List the item, its cost, the quantity you purchased, the percentage of your budget that you spent on the item, and whether a substitute was available. You will be asked to share your list.

   After you have finished the worksheet, discuss demand as a class. Review the factors that affect demand and create a class list of all the factors that contributed to your decisions. For example, did you need the item, or did you just want it? Was it on sale? Did an advertisement influence you? Did you buy a substitute item?
10. **Modify** Students will use the list to analyze their buying decisions. Circle all of the items on the class list that were needs. Eliminate those items from the analysis. Now look at the remaining items. For each item, identify at least one factor that affected your demand. Go back to the Essential Question and write your own answers to these questions: How do I decide what to buy? Could I make better choices?

WebQuest online The Economics WebQuest challenges students to use 21st century skills to answer the Essential Question.

Remind students to continue to develop an Essential Questions video. Guidelines and a production binder are available at www.PearsonSuccessNet.com.

Document-Based Assessment

ANALYZING DOCUMENTS

1. D
2. B
3. C

WRITING ABOUT ECONOMICS

Possible answers: The government should regulate advertising aimed at children, since it can have negative impacts including obesity and aggression. Government regulation of advertising would violate First Amendments rights; the industry should regulate itself.

Student essay should demonstrate an understanding of the issues involved in the debate. Use the following as guidelines to assess the essay.

L2 Differentiate Students use all documents on the page to support their thesis.

L3 Differentiate Students use the documents on this page and additional information available online at www.PearsonSuccessNet.com to support their answer.

L4 Differentiate Students incorporate information provided in the textbook and online at www.PearsonSuccessNet.com and include additional research to support their opinion.

Go Online to www.PearsonSuccessNet.com for a student rubric and extra documents.

Economics online *All print resources are available on the Teacher's Resource Library CD-ROM and online at* www.PearsonSuccessNet.com.

CHAPTER 4 ASSESSMENT

DOCUMENT-BASED ASSESSMENT

Should the government regulate advertising aimed at children?

Children in the United States are exposed to an onslaught of advertising—on television, in video games, and over the Internet. Critics say that the ads aimed at children are deceptive and create demand for unhealthy products. They want the government to regulate this advertising. Others believe that a self-regulating private sector is the answer.

Document A

"Children are bombarded by advertisements for junk food and for violent movies across the media they use—television, the Internet and video games. These aggressive marketing practices have negative effects on children's health and well-being by contributing to childhood obesity and aggressive behavior. As these media converge, we need rules to protect kids. We have been fighting to protect children from the harmful effects of advertising for many years...."

—childrennow.org, June 11, 2008

Document B

"Some in industry may criticize us for using our bully pulpit to encourage companies to do a better job of marketing healthier products to youth. Such criticism would be misguided. In many ways, industry self-regulation with encouragement from government is really a middle ground approach—somewhere between the government-mandated advertising restrictions adopted in some foreign nations (which might be subject to First Amendment challenge in this country) and the *laissez-faire* approach once urged by many in the business community. Indeed, especially here, a little government involvement—combined with a lot of private sector commitment—can go a long way toward the healthier future for our children that all of us want to see."

—Commissioner Jon Leibowitz, on the FTC Report: *Marketing Food to Children and Adolescents: A Review of Industry Expenditures, Activities, and Self-Regulation* July 29, 2008

Document C

"... No, he can't really fly... No, the bad guys don't really have a ray gun... No, this cereal really isn't the best food in the whole world... No, it won't make you as strong as a giant..."

ANALYZING DOCUMENTS

Use your knowledge of advertising and Documents A, B, and C to answer questions 1–3.

1. According to Document A, certain advertisements aimed at children can lead to

A. aggressive marketing practices.
B. increased health and wellbeing.
C. new multimedia rules.
D. childhood obesity and aggressive behavior.

2. Document B suggests that the best way to get companies to do a better job of marketing healthier products to children is

A. government-mandated advertising restrictions.
B. a little government involvement and a lot of industry self-regulation.
C. a First Amendment challenge to offending companies.
D. a *laissez-faire* approach.

3. In Document C, the father is teaching his young son

A. which products are the best ones to buy.
B. that television is an interactive medium.
C. the difference between advertising and reality.
D. how to activate the closed caption feature.

WRITING ABOUT ECONOMICS

The influence of advertising on children is an ongoing issue. Use the documents on this page and resources on the Web site below to answer the question: ***Should the government regulate advertising aimed at children?*** Use the sources to support your opinion.

In Partnership

THE WALL STREET JOURNAL. CLASSROOM EDITION

To read more about issues related to this topic, visit **PearsonSuccessNet.com**

Essential Questions

UNIT 2:

Who benefits from the free market economy?

CHAPTER 5:

How do suppliers decide what goods and services to offer?

Introduce the Chapter

ACTIVATE PRIOR KNOWLEDGE

In this chapter, students will learn about supply. Tell students to complete the warmup activity in their **Essential Questions Journal**.

DIFFERENTIATED INSTRUCTION KEY

- **L1** Special Needs
- **L2** Basic
  - **ELL** English Language Learners
  - **LPR** Less Proficient Readers
- **L3** All Students
- **L4** Advanced Students

Economics online Visit www.PearsonSuccessNet.com for an interactive textbook with built-in activities on economic principles.

- ***The Wall Street Journal* Classroom Edition Video** presents a current topic related to supply.
- **Yearly Update Worksheet** provides an annual update, including a new worksheet and lesson on this topic.
- **On the Go** resources can be downloaded so students and teachers can connect with economics anytime, anywhere.

Chapter 5 Supply

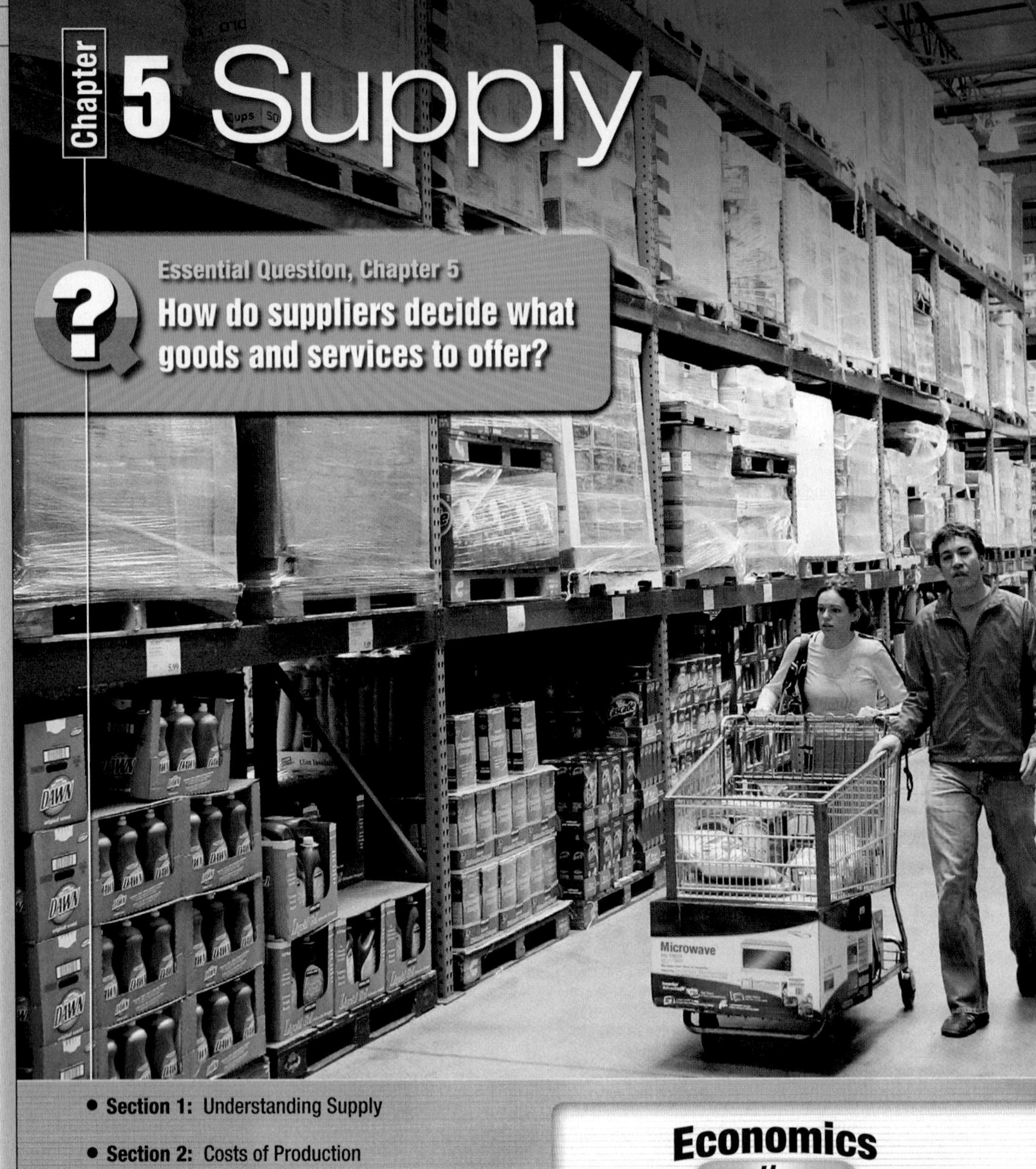

Essential Question, Chapter 5

How do suppliers decide what goods and services to offer?

- **Section 1:** Understanding Supply
- **Section 2:** Costs of Production
- **Section 3:** Changes in Supply

Economics on the go

To study anywhere, anytime, download these online resources at ***PearsonSuccessNet.com*** ▶

ECONOMICS ONLINE

DIGITAL TEACHER TOOLS

The online lesson planner is designed to help teachers plan, teach, and assess. Teachers have the ability to use or customize existing Pearson lesson plans. Online lecture notes support the print lesson by providing an array of accessible activities and summaries of key concepts.

Two interactivities included in this lesson are:

- **Visual Glossary** An online activity that illustrates the Law of Supply.
- **WebQuest** Students use online resources to complete a guided activity further exploring the Essential Questions.

Block Scheduling

BLOCK 1 Teach Sections 1 and 2 and have students use the Action Graph online feature to help their understanding of supply curves.

BLOCK 2 Teach Section 3, and then have students do the simulation activity, in which they act as producers reacting to a change in supply.

Pressed for Time

Group work Use the Jigsaw strategy (p. T29), dividing the class into groups and assigning each group half a section of the chapter. Have members of each group confer with each other about which topics they will cover.

OBJECTIVES

1. **Explain** the law of supply.
2. **Interpret** a supply schedule and a supply graph.
3. **Examine** the relationship between elasticity of supply and time.

ECONOMIC DICTIONARY

As you read the section, look for the definitions of these **Key Terms:**

- supply
- law of supply
- quantity supplied
- supply schedule
- variable
- market supply schedule
- supply curve
- market supply curve
- elasticity of supply

Guiding Question

How does the law of supply affect the quantity supplied?

Copy this concept web and fill it in as you read.

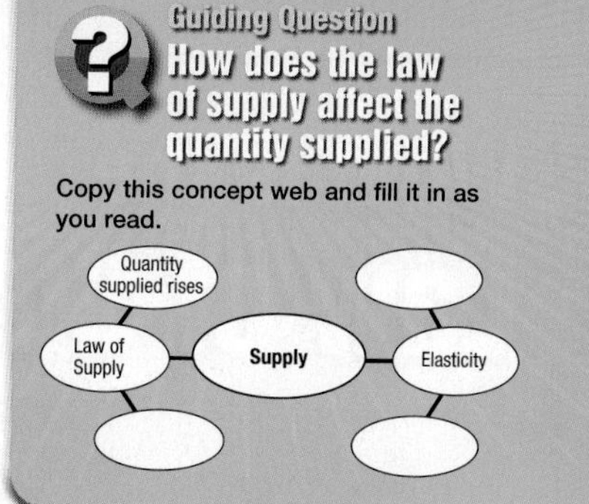

Economics and You Suppose you were running a business. What would you do if you discovered that customers were still willing to buy your product if you raised the price 20 percent? Why not take an extra day off each week? You would still earn the same income with 20 percent less work. Or, like most entrepreneurs, would you react by producing more and increasing your revenue?

Principles in Action As prices rise, producers will offer more of a good, while new suppliers will enter the market to earn their share of the profits. The markets for music and pizza show how higher prices increase the quantity supplied, while the example of an orange grove helps to explain elasticity of supply over time.

The Law of Supply

Supply is the amount of goods available. How do producers decide how much to supply? According to the **law of supply,** producers offer more of a good as its price increases and less as its price falls. Economists use the term **quantity supplied** to describe how much of a good a producer is willing and able to sell at a specific price. A producer may also be called a supplier, a company, or an owner—whoever supplies a product to the market.

The law of supply develops from the choices of both current and new producers of a good. As the price of a good rises, existing firms will produce more in order to earn additional revenue. A price increase is

supply the amount of goods available

law of supply producers offer more of a good as its price increases and less as its price falls

quantity supplied the amount that a supplier is willing and able to supply at a specific price

Visual Glossary online

Go to the Visual Glossary Online for an interactive review of the **law of supply.**

Action Graph online

Go to Action Graph Online for animated versions of key charts and graphs.

How the Economy Works online

Go to How the Economy Works Online for an interactive lesson on **production costs.**

Guiding Question

How does the law of supply affect the quantity supplied?

Get Started

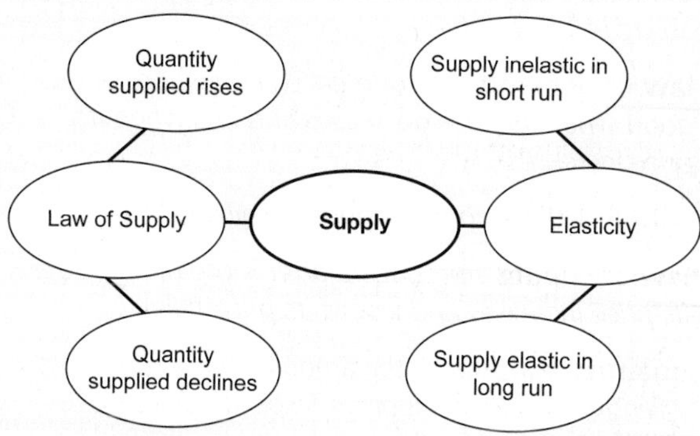

LESSON GOALS

Students will:

- Know the Key Terms.
- Demonstrate how the law of supply reflects the profit motive.
- Give examples of firms acting according to the law of supply.
- Graph a market supply curve given two supply schedules.
- Identify businesses that demonstrate elasticity of supply and inelasticity of supply.

BEFORE CLASS

Students should read the section for homework before coming to class.

Have students complete the graphic organizer in the Section Opener as they read the text. As an alternate activity, have students complete the Guided Reading and Review worksheet (Unit 2 All-in-One, p. 51).

L1 L2 ELL LPR Differentiate Have students complete the Guided Reading and Review worksheet (Unit 2 All-in-One, p. 52).

Focus on the Basics

Students need to come away with the following understandings:

FACTS: • Producers offer more of a good as price increases and less as it decreases. • Supply schedules and curves can show individual and market supply. • Suppliers find it easier to change quantity supplied the more time passes.

GENERALIZATION: Producers are willing to supply more of a product or service when prices are higher.

CLASSROOM HINTS

INTERPRET DEMAND CURVES AND SUPPLY CURVES

Demonstrate supply curves graphically whenever possible. Remind students that graphs showing supply or demand typically show price on the *y*-axis and quantity on the *x*-axis. The demand curve is visually challenging, because as price goes up, demand goes down. The curve slopes downward, from upper left to lower right. Yet this downward line shows *increasing* demand. Since supply and price go up together, the supply curve slopes up from lower left to upper right, and that upward slope makes more sense visually as an *increase* in supply. Draw a grid on the board that volunteers can fill in.

Teach Visual Glossary

REVIEW KEY TERMS

Pair students and have them write the definitions of the key terms related to the understanding of the law of supply.

demand – *the desire to own something and the ability to pay for it*

law of demand – *consumers will buy more of a good when its price decreases and less when its price increases*

supply – *the amount of goods available*

law of supply – *producers offer more of a good as its price increases and less as its price falls*

quantity supplied – *the amount that a supplier is willing and able to supply at a specific price*

ANALYZE

Ask **What motivates entrepreneurs in a market economy?** *(the desire for profit)* **How can they best meet that goal?** *(Possible responses: by entering markets that are flourishing; by raising prices or cutting costs; or by selling more and more units of whatever they produce)* Then direct students' attention to the graphic illustrating the law of supply. Ask **How does the desire for profit increase supply?** *(Firms are willing to make more of an item if they can profit more from making it; new firms decide to enter the market when they are attracted by the possibility of making a profit.)*

L1 L2 Differentiate Suggest that students use graphic organizers to summarize and contrast the effect of price changes on both demand and supply. They might use a three-column chart with columns headed *Price, Demand,* and *Supply*. In the two rows below the heading *Price*, they should draw an arrow pointing up, to show price increases, and one pointing down, to show price decreases. Under the headings *Demand* and *Supply,* they should draw arrows pointing in the correct direction.

Economics online *All print resources are available on the Teacher's Resource Library CD-ROM and online at www.PearsonSuccessNet.com.*

Answer

Photo Caption The law of demand describes how consumers respond to price changes while the law of supply describes how producers respond to price changes.

VISUAL GLOSSARY

Reviewing Key Terms
To understand the *law of supply,* review these terms:

demand, *p. 85*
law of demand, *p. 85*
supply, *p. 109*
law of supply, *p. 109*
quantity supplied, *p. 109*

What is the Law of Supply?

◀ **law of supply** producers offer more of a good as its price increases and less as its price falls

LAW OF SUPPLY
PRICE
As price increases...
SUPPLY
quantity supplied increases.
PRICE
As price falls...
SUPPLY
quantity supplied falls.

The price of a good determines how much of that good a supplier will provide. ***How is the law of supply different from the law of demand?***

Visual Glossary online
To expand your understanding of this and other key economic terms, visit **PearsonSuccessNet.com**

110

also an incentive for new firms to enter the market to earn their own profits. If the price of a good falls, some firms will produce less, and others might drop out of the market. These two movements—individual firms changing their level of production and firms entering or exiting the market—combine to create the law of supply.

Higher Production

If a firm is already earning a profit by selling a good, then an increase in the price—*ceteris paribus*—will increase the firm's profits. The promise of higher revenues for each sale encourages the firm to produce more. The pizzeria you read about in Chapter 4 probably makes a reasonable profit by selling a certain number of slices a day at the market price. If the pizzeria wasn't making a profit, the owner would raise the price or switch from pizzas to something more profitable.

If the price of pizza rises, but the firm's cost of making pizza stays the same, the pizzeria will earn a higher profit on each slice. A sensible entrepreneur would produce and sell more pizza to take advantage of the higher prices.

Similarly, if the price of pizza goes down, the pizzeria will earn less profit per slice or even lose money. The owner will choose to sell less pizza and produce something else, such as calzones, which will yield more profit.

In both cases, the search for profit drives the supplier's decision. When the price goes up, the supplier recognizes the chance to make more money and works harder to produce more pizza. When the price falls, the same entrepreneur is discouraged from producing as much as before.

Market Entry

Profits appeal both to producers already in the market and people who may decide to join the market. As you have seen, when the price of pizza rises, a pizzeria provides a good opportunity to make money. If you were to open your own restaurant, a pizzeria would look like a safe bet. This is how rising prices draw new firms into a market and add to the quantity supplied of the good.

◀ Appliance makers try to profit from a trend. ***Which trend are appliance makers trying to cash in on in this cartoon?***

Consider the market for music. In the late 1970s, disco music became popular. The music industry quickly recognized the popularity of disco, and soon, more and more groups released disco recordings. Groups that once recorded soul and rhythm and blues music chose to record disco albums. New entrants crowded the market to take advantage of the potential for profit. Disco, however, was a short-lived fad. By the early 1980s, stores couldn't sell disco albums.

This pattern of sharp increases and decreases in supply occurs again and again in the music industry. In the early 1990s, grunge music emerged from Seattle to become widely popular among high school and college students across the country. How did the market react? Record labels hired more grunge groups. Music stores devoted more space to grunge music. However, grunge soon lost its appeal, and many groups disbanded or moved on to new styles. Other styles of music, such as hip-hop and independent rock, achieved new popularity.

In each of these examples, many musicians joined the market to profit from a trend. Their actions reflected the law of supply, which says that the quantity supplied increases as the price of the good increases.

✔ **CHECKPOINT** ***Why do firms increase production when the price of a good goes up?***

Differentiated Resources

L1 L2 Guided Reading and Review (Unit 2 All-in-One, p. 52)

L1 L2 Vocabulary worksheet (Unit 2 All-in-One, p. 50)

L2 Supply Schedules and Supply Curves (Unit 2 All-in-One, p. 54)

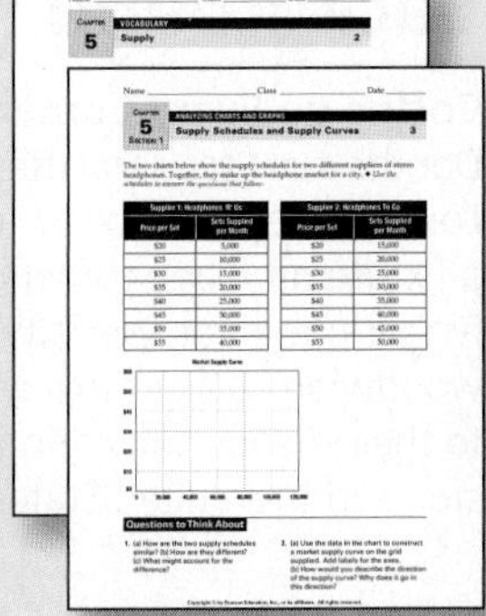

BELLRINGER

Divide the class into groups of four. Have each group list the names of as many bottled beverages as they can within three to five minutes. Then have each group decide how to divide their lists into categories. For example, they might categorize by type of beverage, price, type of container, whether the drink is marketed for sports or health. Ask each group **How many names did you list? How did you categorize the beverages?**

Teach

Economics online To present this topic using digital resources, use the lecture notes on www.PearsonSuccessNet.com.

L1 L2 ELL LPR Differentiate To help students who are struggling readers, assign the Vocabulary worksheet (Unit 2 All-in-One, p. 50).

DISCUSS BELLRINGER

Discuss the variety of products that are available. Ask **Why were there so many varieties in each category? Why is there more than one type of bottled water?** *(People are willing to pay for water to be bottled, so more producers are willing to supply bottled water.)*

PROVIDE EXAMPLES

Review with students the two actions suppliers take in response to higher prices—increasing production and choosing to enter the market. Ask **What are some examples of firms increasing production when prices rise?** *(Possible responses: farmers growing more of a crop when its price is high; clothing manufacturers producing greater quantities of a trendy jacket when the price goes up)* Then ask **What are examples of new firms entering a market when prices are high?** *(Possible responses: toy companies producing their own version of a competitor's best-selling action figure; more banks offering loans when interest rates are high; movie studios producing more Westerns after a competitor's Western does well at the box office)*

Answers

Cartoon the trend toward flat-panel televisions and computers

Checkpoint They hope to increase revenues and profit.

CONNECT TO PRIOR LEARNING

Remind students that they learned about demand schedules in Chapter 4. Call on a volunteer to explain what a demand schedule shows. Then ask **What do you expect a supply schedule to show?** *(quantity supplied by a particular supplier at each price)* Direct students' attention to Figure 5.1. Discuss how the quantity supplied changes in each supply schedule and how those changes relate to the law of supply.

L1 L2 Differentiate Call on students to restate the difference between an individual demand schedule and a market demand schedule. Then have them compare the two supply schedules in Figure 5.1. Make sure that they recognize that the market supply schedule is the total quantity supplied by all firms in the market.

Ask **What is the relationship between price and quantity demanded?** *(As price goes up, demand goes down.)* **What is the relationship between price and quantity supplied?** *(As price goes up, supply goes up.)*

supply schedule a chart that lists how much of a good a supplier will offer at various prices

variable a factor that can change

market supply schedule a chart that lists how much of a good all suppliers will offer at various prices

The Supply Schedule

Similar to a demand schedule, a **supply schedule** shows the relationship between price and quantity supplied for a specific good, or how much of a good a supplier will offer at various prices. The pizzeria discussed earlier might have a supply schedule that looks like the one in **Figure 5.1**. This table compares two **variables**, or factors that can change. These variables are the price of a slice and the number of slices supplied by a pizzeria. We could collect this information by asking the pizzeria owner how many slices she is willing and able to make at different prices, or we could look at records to see how the quantity supplied has varied as the price has changed. We will almost certainly find that at higher prices, the pizzeria owner is willing to make more pizza. At a lower price, she prefers to make less pizza and devote her limited resources to other, more profitable, items.

Like a demand schedule, a supply schedule lists supply for a very specific set of conditions. The schedule shows how the price of pizza, and only the price of pizza, affects the pizzeria's output. The other factors that could change the restaurant's output decisions, such as the costs of tomato sauce, labor, and rent, are assumed to remain constant.

Figure 5.1 Supply Schedule

Individual Supply Schedule

Price Per Slice of Pizza	Slices Supplied Per Day
$1.00	100
$2.00	150
$3.00	200
$4.00	250
$5.00	300
$6.00	350

Market Supply Schedule

Price Per Slice of Pizza	Slices Supplied Per Day
$1.00	1,000
$2.00	1,500
$3.00	2,000
$4.00	2,500
$5.00	3,000
$6.00	3,500

CHART SKILLS

The individual supply schedule lists how many slices of pizza one pizzeria will offer at different prices. The market supply schedule represents all suppliers in a market.

1. What does the individual supply schedule tell you about the pizzeria owner's decisions?
2. How does the market supply schedule compare to the individual supply schedule?

A Change in the Quantity Supplied

Economists use the word *supply* to refer to the relationship between price and quantity supplied, as shown in the supply schedule. The pizzeria's supply of pizza includes all possible combinations of price and output. According to this supply schedule, the pizzeria's supply is 100 slices at $1.00 a slice, 150 slices at $2.00 a slice, 200 slices at $3.00 a slice, and so on. The number of slices that the pizzeria offers at a specific price is called the quantity supplied at that price. At $5.00 per slice, the pizzeria's quantity supplied is 300 slices per day.

A rise or fall in the price of pizza will cause the quantity supplied to change, but not the supply schedule. In other words, a change in a good's price moves the seller from one row to another in the same supply schedule, but does not change the supply schedule itself. When a factor other than the price of pizza affects output, we have to build a whole new supply schedule for the new market conditions.

Market Supply Schedule

All of the supply schedules of individual firms in a market can be added up to create a **market supply schedule.** A market supply schedule shows the relationship between prices and the total quantity supplied by *all* firms in a particular market. This information becomes important when we want to determine the total supply of pizza at a certain price in a large area, like a city.

Background Note

Coffee on Every Corner Why did McDonald's open McCafes? Why did Dunkin' Donuts start serving lattes? The answer is the law of supply—and Starbucks, of course. The enormously successful chain of specialty coffee franchises has become a fixture on many corners all over the world. So many people proved willing to pay higher prices for specialty coffee that the firm has opened more than 15,000 stores worldwide. Other firms saw a profitable market and decided to add coffee drinks to their menus, increasing the supply even more. Starbucks has closed some of its stores in the United States, but is still opening new stores in Japan.

Answers

Chart Skills 1. The pizzeria owner is willing to supply more slices of pizza as the price goes up. 2. The market supply schedule shows much larger quantities of pizza slices because it takes into account all pizzerias.

Figure 5.2 Supply Curves

Individual Supply Curve

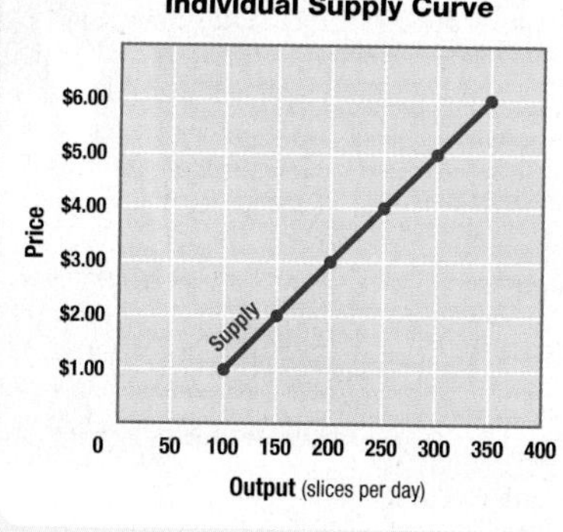

Market Supply Curve

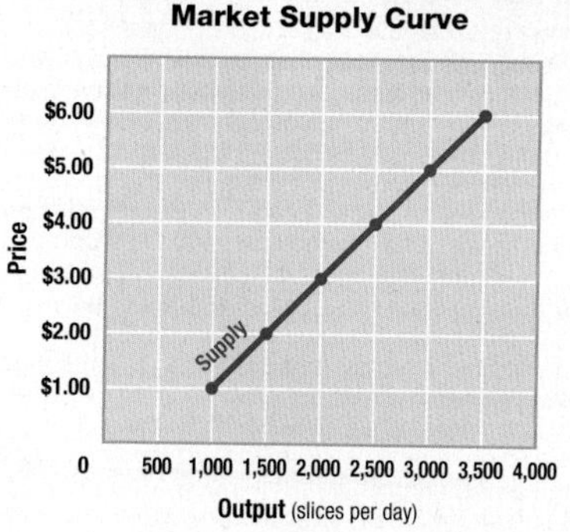

GRAPH SKILLS

Supply curves always rise from left to right. As price increases, so does the quantity supplied, as predicted by the law of supply.

1. How many slices will one pizzeria produce at $3.00 a slice?
2. How does a producer create a market supply schedule or curve?

Action Graph online

For an animated version of this graph, visit PearsonSuccessNet.com

The market supply schedule for pizza in **Figure 5.1** shows the supply of pizza for a hypothetical city. It resembles the supply schedule for a single pizzeria, but the quantities are much larger.

This market supply schedule lists the same prices as those in the supply schedule for the single pizzeria, since all restaurants will charge prices within the same range. The quantities supplied are much larger because there are many pizzerias in the community. Like the individual supply schedule, this market supply schedule reflects the law of supply. Pizzerias supply more pizza at higher prices.

The Supply Graph

When the data points in the supply schedule are graphed, they create a **supply curve.** A supply curve is a graphic representation of a supply schedule. A supply curve is very similar to a demand curve, except that the horizontal axis now measures the quantity of the good supplied, not the quantity demanded. The supply graph on the left in **Figure 5.2** shows a supply curve for one pizzeria. The graph on the right shows a **market supply curve** for all the pizzerias in the city. The data used to draw the two curves are from the supply schedules in **Figure 5.1**. The prices shown along the vertical axes are the same in both graphs. However, the quantities of pizza supplied at each price are much larger in the market supply curve.

The key feature of the supply curve is that it always rises from left to right. As your finger traces the curve from left to right, it moves toward higher and higher output levels (on the horizontal axis) and higher and higher prices (on the vertical axis). This illustrates the law of supply, which says that a higher price leads to higher output.

CHECKPOINT ***What are the two variables represented in a supply schedule or a supply curve?***

Supply and Elasticity

In Chapter 4, you learned that elasticity of demand measures how consumers will react to price changes. Elasticity of supply is based on the same concept.

Elasticity of supply measures how firms will respond to changes in the price of a good. The labels *elastic, inelastic,* and

supply curve a graph of the quantity supplied of a good at various prices

market supply curve a graph of the quantity supplied of a good by all suppliers at various prices

elasticity of supply a measure of the way quantity supplied reacts to a change in price

DISTRIBUTE ACTIVITY WORKSHEET

Direct students' attention to Figure 5.2. Explain that these two graphs visually display the information in the two supply schedules.

Action Graph online Have students review the Action Graph animation for a step-by-step look at Supply Curves.

Next, distribute the "Supply Schedules and Supply Curves" worksheet (Unit 2 All-in-One, p. 53). Have students answer the worksheet questions to analyze the two supply schedules provided and use the information in those schedules to draw a market supply curve.

L2 Differentiate Before assigning the worksheet, have students work in pairs to compare, point by point, the data in the two supply schedules in Figure 5.1 and the two supply curves in Figure 5.2. Once they see how the schedules and curves are connected, distribute the "Supply Schedules and Supply Curves" (Unit 2 All-in-One, p. 54) and have them complete the activity on it.

After students have completed the worksheets, ask **How does the slope of a supply curve differ from the slope of a demand curve?** *(A supply curve slopes up; a demand curve slopes down.)* Ask **Why are they different?** *(They differ because, for suppliers, quantity supplied increases as price increases, whereas for consumers, quantity demanded decreases as price increases.)*

Virtual Economics

L3 Differentiate

Applying the Law of Supply Use the following lesson from the NCEE **Virtual Economics *CD-ROM*** to help students to understand the law of supply. Click on Browse Economics Lessons, specify grades 9–12, and use the key words *picture is worth.*

In this activity, students will gather data and use it to create a supply graph and analyze shifts.

LESSON TITLE	A PICTURE IS WORTH A THOUSAND WORDS: SUPPLY
Type of Activity	Graphing
Complexity	Moderate
Time	75 minutes
NCEE Standards	4, 8

Answers

Graph Skills 1. 200 slices 2. The producer can create a market supply schedule by adding up all of the supply schedules of producers in the same market. Using this market supply schedule, the producer can draw a market supply curve.

Checkpoint price and quantity supplied

EXPLORE

Display the transparency "Elasticity of Supply" (Color Transparencies, 5.a). Use the graphics to contrast the effect of price changes on goods with elastic and inelastic supply. Discuss with students the example of the orange grower vs. barbershops and hair salons. Then have them work in groups to brainstorm types of businesses whose supply would be inelastic in the short run and elastic in the long run.

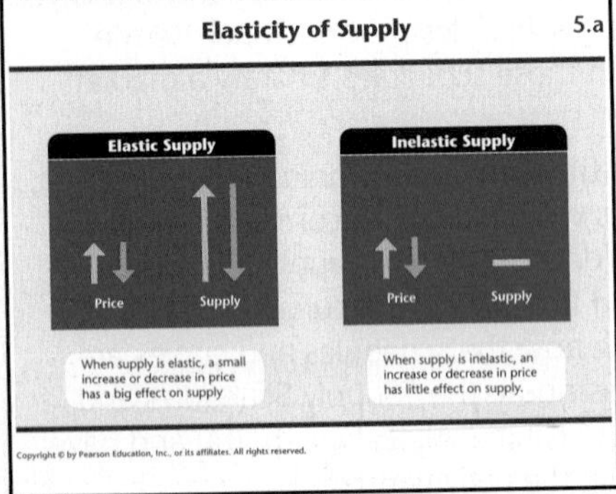

Elasticity of Supply
5.a
Elastic Supply
Price
Supply
Inelastic Supply
Price
Supply
When supply is elastic, a small increase or decrease in price has a big effect on supply
When supply is inelastic, an increase or decrease in price has little effect on supply.

EXTEND

Have students review how to calculate the elasticity of demand, in Chapter 4. Give students the formula for calculating elasticity of supply: the percentage change in quantity supplied divided by the percentage change in price. Then have them look at the supply schedule in Figure 5.1. Tell them that the market supply is unitary elastic when the price changes from $1 to $2, but that any price changes beyond that result in an inelastic supply. Have students calculate elasticity of supply. Ask **What do these calculations tell you about the elasticity of supply in this pizza market?** *(Pizza suppliers will increase the supply of pizza most readily from 1,000 to 1,500 slices if the price goes from $1 to $2. At least in the short term, the supply at higher prices is inelastic, because pizza suppliers cannot reach those levels of production quickly.)*

Assess and Remediate

L3 **L2** Collect the "Supply Schedules and Supply Curves" worksheets and assess student understanding of the relationship between price and supply.

L3 Assign the Section 1 Assessment questions; identify student misconceptions.

L3 Give Section Quiz A (Unit 2 All-in-One, p. 55).

L2 Give Section Quiz B (Unit 2 All-in-One, p. 56).

(Assess and Remediate continued on p. 115)

Answer

Critical Thinking They might put similar magazines on the market in order to compete for the profits.

Innovators

John H. Johnson

"To succeed, one must be creative and persistent."

It was those very qualities that helped John H. Johnson, the founder and publisher of *Ebony* and *Jet* magazines, to build his business empire and create the world's largest African American publishing company.

Johnson grew up in rural Arkansas. Seeking better opportunities, the family moved to Chicago in 1933. At DuSable High School, Johnson served as class president and editor of the school newspaper and yearbook.

A speech he gave at an Urban League dinner impressed the president of an insurance company, who offered him a job. Johnson edited the company newsletter, gathering articles on African Americans from other publications.

Realizing that there were few positive images of blacks in the white-owned media, Johnson decided to start his own magazine. He borrowed $500, using his mother's furniture as collateral. The first edition of the *Negro Digest* appeared in 1942.

The photo essay magazines *Look* and *Life* inspired Johnson to create *Ebony* in 1945. *Ebony* magazine emphasized the achievements of successful African Americans. It is still widely read today.

In 1951, Johnson had another success with *Jet*, a pocket-sized magazine that became the largest African American news weekly. Johnson later said that to succeed, you must have "an idea for a business that meets a need that cannot be satisfied elsewhere."

Johnson was awarded the Presidential Medal of Freedom in 1996 for his many contributions to the black community.

Critical Thinking: ***How do you think other publishers might respond to Johnson's success?***

Fast Facts

John H. Johnson
Born: Jan. 19, 1918, in Arkansas City, AR
Died: August 8, 2005, in Chicago, IL
Education: University of Chicago, Northwestern University
Claim to Fame: Founder, publisher, and CEO of the Johnson Publishing Co.

unitary elastic represent the same values of elasticity of supply as those of elasticity of demand. When elasticity is greater than one, supply is very sensitive to changes in price and is considered elastic. If supply is not very responsive to changes in price, and elasticity is less than one, supply is considered inelastic. When a percentage change in price is perfectly matched by an equal percentage change in quantity supplied, elasticity is exactly one, and supply is unitary elastic.

Elasticity of Supply and Time

What determines whether the supply of a good will be elastic or inelastic? The key factor is time. In the short run, a firm cannot easily change its output level, so supply is inelastic. In the long run, firms are more flexible, so supply is more elastic.

Elasticity of Supply in the Short Run

An orange grove is one example of a business that has difficulty adjusting to a change in price in the short term. Orange trees take several years to mature and grow fruit. If the price of oranges goes up, an orange grower can buy and plant more trees, but he will have to wait several years for his investment to pay off. In the short term, the grower could take smaller steps to increase output. For example, he could use a more effective pesticide. While this step might increase his output somewhat, it would probably not increase the number of oranges by very much. Economists would say that his supply is inelastic, because he cannot easily change his output. The same factors that prevent the owner of the orange grove from expanding his supply will also prevent new growers from entering the market and supplying oranges in the short term.

In the short run, supply is inelastic whether the price increases or decreases. If the price of oranges falls, the grove owner has few ways to cut his supply. Years ago, he invested in land and trees, and his grove will provide oranges no matter what the price is. Even if the price drops drastically, the grove owner will probably pick and sell nearly as many oranges as before. His competitors have also invested heavily in land and trees and won't drop out of the market if they

Background Note

Land and Elasticity Theoretically, the supply of land is perfectly inelastic. Suppliers cannot generate more land, so the quantity supplied can show no change at all prices. However, land is not perfectly inelastic, as rising prices can convince some landowners to change unproductive land—draining a swamp, for instance—to make it usable.

can survive. In this case, supply is inelastic whether prices rise or fall.

While orange groves illustrate a business in which supply is inelastic, other businesses have a more elastic supply. For example, a business that provides a service, such as a haircut, is highly elastic. Unlike oranges, the supply of haircuts is easily expanded or reduced. If the price rises, barbershops and salons can hire workers fairly quickly or extend their business hours.

In addition, new barbershops and salons will open. This means that a small increase in price will cause a large increase in quantity supplied, even in the short term.

If the price of a haircut drops, some shop owners will lay off workers or close earlier in the day. Others will leave the market. Quantity supplied will fall quickly. Because haircut suppliers can quickly change their operations, the supply of haircuts is elastic.

Elasticity in the Long Run

Like demand, supply can become more elastic over time. The orange grower could not increase his output much when the price of oranges rose, but he can plant more trees to increase his supply. This response becomes more effective over time, as the trees grow and bear fruit. After several years, he will be able to sell more oranges at the higher market price.

If the price drops and stays low for several years, orange growers who survived the first two or three years of losses might decide to grow something else. Given five years to respond instead of six weeks, the supply of oranges will be far more elastic. Just like demand, supply becomes more elastic if the supplier has a longer time to respond to a price change.

CHECKPOINT ***How does a business that is highly elastic respond to a fall in prices?***

▲ Because the vines take three or four years to produce fruit, cranberries are another product for which supply is inelastic in the short term.

SECTION 1 ASSESSMENT

Essential Questions Journal To continue to build a response to the Essential Question, go to your **Essential Questions Journal**.

Guiding Question

1. Use your completed concept web to answer this question: How does the law of supply affect the quantity supplied?
2. **Extension** Describe how a recent change in supply has affected a product that you regularly purchase.

Key Terms and Main Ideas

3. What is the difference between **supply** and **quantity supplied?**
4. What does a **supply schedule** show?
5. What does a **market supply curve** show?

Critical Thinking

6. **Apply** Give an example of a variable other than price for each of these markets: **(a)** a rock band's concert tour, **(b)** an electronic equipment maker, **(c)** a bakery.
7. **Predict** When the price of gold rises, what will happen to the market for second-hand jewelry? Explain your answer.
8. **Analyze** State whether you think the supply of the following services is elastic or inelastic, and explain why: **(a)** a lawn-care service, **(b)** making movies, **(c)** professional baseball.

Math Skills

9. Use the following supply schedule for corn to create a supply curve. ***Visit PearsonSuccessNet.com for additional math help.***

Corn Supply Schedule

Price Per Ton	Quantity Supplied
100	50
150	75
200	100
250	125
300	150
350	175
400	200

Have students complete the Self-Test Online and continue their work in the **Essential Questions Journal**.

REMEDIATION AND SUGGESTIONS

Use the chart below to help students who are struggling with content.

WEAKNESS	REMEDIATION
Defining key terms (Questions 3, 4, 5)	Have students use the interactive Economic Dictionary Online.
Understanding the law of supply (Questions 1, 2, 7)	Reteach using the Visual Glossary and students' answers to the Bellringer.
Using supply schedules and supply curves (Questions 4, 5, 6, 9)	Use the Action Graph Online to walk students through the creation of a supply curve.
Distinguishing elasticity and inelasticity (Question 8)	Pair students to identify two products they think demonstrate elasticity and two that demonstrate inelasticity. Have them explain why they put each item in a particular category.

Answer

Checkpoint It acts quickly to reduce the quantity supplied by cutting production, laying off workers, or reducing hours.

Assessment Answers

1. Supply increases as price rises, and decreases as price falls.
2. Possible response: changes in supply of clothing as styles change or seasons end; decreasing oil supplies make gasoline more expensive to buy
3. supply—amount of goods available; quantity supplied—how much of a good is supplied at specific prices
4. how much of a good or service a firm will supply at various prices
5. quantity of good or service supplied by all firms at different prices
6. Possible responses: (a) number of dates band plays or seats in arenas where it plays; (b) the supply of computer chips that go into the equipment; (c) seasonal demand
7. Firms that supply second-hand jewelry will supply more (at higher prices) to profit from higher gold prices.
8. Possible answers: (a) elastic because entry costs are small; (b) inelastic because movies are expensive and time-consuming to make; (c) inelastic because entry costs are high and players cannot be manufactured
9. Students' supply curves should correctly graph the points shown in the supply schedule.

Guiding Question

How can a producer maximize profits?

Get Started

To Maximize Profit...	
Managing Labor	**Setting Output**
• Marginal return: change in output from hiring one additional worker • Look for highest marginal return • Buy capital to increase marginal return	• Marginal revenue: additional income from selling one more unit • Marginal cost: additional cost from producing one more unit • Set output where marginal revenue equals marginal cost

LESSON GOALS

Students will:

- Know the Key Terms.
- Demonstrate and explain changes in marginal returns by doing a class activity.
- Analyze how firms can improve marginal returns.
- Categorize costs as fixed or variable.
- Determine production decisions to maximize profits and the effect of price changes.
- Explain decisions to shut down a business facility.

BEFORE CLASS

Students should read the section for homework.

Have students complete the graphic organizer in the Section Opener as they read the text. As an alternate activity, have students complete the Guided Reading and Review worksheet (Unit 2 All-in-One, p. 57).

L1 L2 ELL LPR Differentiate Have students complete the Guided Reading and Review worksheet (Unit 2 All-in-One, p. 58).

SECTION 2 Costs of Production

OBJECTIVES

1. **Explain** how firms decide how much labor to hire in order to produce a certain level of output.
2. **Analyze** the production costs of a firm.
3. **Explain** how a firm chooses to set output.
4. **Identify** the factors that a firm must consider before shutting down an unprofitable business.

ECONOMIC DICTIONARY

As you read the section, look for the definitions of these **Key Terms**:

- marginal product of labor
- increasing marginal returns
- diminishing marginal returns
- fixed cost
- variable cost
- total cost
- marginal cost
- marginal revenue
- average cost
- operating cost

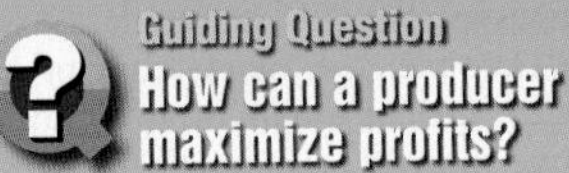

Guiding Question

How can a producer maximize profits?

Copy this table and fill it in as you read.

To Maximize Profit...	
Managing Labor	**Setting Output**
• Increase marginal returns •	• •

marginal product of labor the change in output from hiring one additional unit of labor

Economics and You

You are making egg salad sandwiches for a picnic. The knife is the physical capital. Your labor, the bread, and the egg salad are the inputs. In a beanbag factory, the physical capital is one sewing machine and one pair of scissors. Its inputs are workers and materials, including cloth, thread, and beans. Each beanbag requires the same amount of materials. How does the company decide how many beanbags to produce? How many sandwiches should you make?

Principles in Action Producers think about the cost of making one more unit of a good when deciding how to maximize profits. You'll also see what happens when a factory's operating costs are greater than its revenue.

▲ When workers specialize in specific tasks, output per worker increases and the firm enjoys increasing marginal returns.

Labor and Output

One basic question that any business owner has to answer is how many workers to hire. Owners have to consider how the number of workers they hire will affect their total production. For example, at the beanbag factory, one worker can produce four beanbags per hour. Two workers can make a total of ten bags per hour, and three can make a total of seventeen beanbags per hour. As each new worker joins the company, total output increases. After the seventh worker is hired, production peaks at 32 beanbags per hour. When the firm hires the eighth worker, however, total output drops to 31 bags per hour. The relationship between labor, measured by the number of workers in the factory and the number of beanbags produced, is shown in **Figure 5.3**.

Marginal Product of Labor

The third column of **Figure 5.3** shows the **marginal product of labor,** or the change in output from hiring one more worker. This is called the marginal product because it measures the change in output at the margin, where the last worker has been hired or fired.

The first worker to be hired produces four bags an hour, so her marginal product is four bags. The second worker raises total output from four bags per hour to ten, so her marginal product of labor is six. Looking at this column, we see that the marginal product of labor increases for the first three workers, rising from four to seven.

CLASSROOM HINTS

RESOURCES ON THE WEB

You may find the video or DVD called "Wages and Production" (18 minutes) useful in explaining how wage rates affect types of labor services that are offered and demanded. On the Web site http://www.stlouisfed.org/education/video_library.html, you will find instructions for borrowing this and other materials from the Federal Reserve Bank of St. Louis.

Focus on the Basics

Students need to come away with the following understandings:

FACTS: • Firms look for highest marginal return product of labor; they avoid diminishing or negative marginal return. • Firms set output where marginal revenue equals marginal cost. • Firms continue to operate as long as total revenues exceed variable cost.

GENERALIZATION: Firms make business decisions by weighing various types of cost against various types of revenue.

Increasing Marginal Returns

The marginal product of labor increases for the first three workers because there are three tasks involved in making a beanbag. Workers cut cloth into the correct shape, stuff it with beans, and sew the bag closed. A single worker performing all these tasks can produce only four bags per hour. Adding a second worker allows each worker to specialize in one or two tasks. If each worker focuses on only one part of the process, she wastes less time switching between tasks and becomes more skillful at her assigned tasks. Because specialization increases output per worker, the second worker adds more to output than the first. The firm enjoys **increasing marginal returns.**

In our example, there are benefits from specialization, and the firm enjoys a rising marginal product of labor for the first three workers.

Diminishing Marginal Returns

When workers four through seven are hired, the marginal product of labor is still positive. Each new worker still adds to total output. However, the marginal product of labor shrinks as each worker joins the company. The fourth worker increases output by six bags, while the seventh increases output by only one bag. Why?

After the beanbag firm hires its first three workers, one for each task, the benefits of specialization end. At that point, adding more workers increases total output but at a decreasing rate. This situation is known as **diminishing marginal returns.** A firm with diminishing marginal returns of labor will produce less and less output from each additional unit of labor.

The firm suffers from diminishing marginal returns from labor because its workers have a limited amount of capital. Capital—any human-made resource used to produce other goods—is represented by the factory's single sewing machine and its pair of scissors. With three workers, only one needs to use the sewing machine, so this worker never has to wait to get to work. When there are more than three workers, the factory may assign more than one to work at the sewing machine.

Figure 5.3 Marginal Product of Labor

Marginal Product of Labor

Labor (number of workers)	Output (beanbags per hour)	Marginal Product of Labor
0	0	—
1	4	4
2	10	6
3	17	7
4	23	6
5	28	5
6	31	3
7	32	1
8	31	–1

CHART SKILLS

The marginal product of labor is the increase in output added by the last unit of labor.

1. In this example, why does the marginal product of labor increase with the first three workers?
2. Why does the marginal product of labor decrease with more than four workers in this example?

So while one works, the other worker waits. She may cut fabric or stuff bags, but every bag must be sewn at some point, so she cannot greatly increase the speed of production.

The problem gets worse as more workers are hired and the amount of capital remains constant. Time wasted waiting for the sewing machine or scissors means that additional workers will add less and less to total output as shown in **Figure 5.4.**

increasing marginal returns a level of production in which the marginal product of labor increases as the number of workers increases

diminishing marginal returns a level of production at which the marginal product of labor decreases as the number of workers increases

Figure 5.4 Marginal Returns

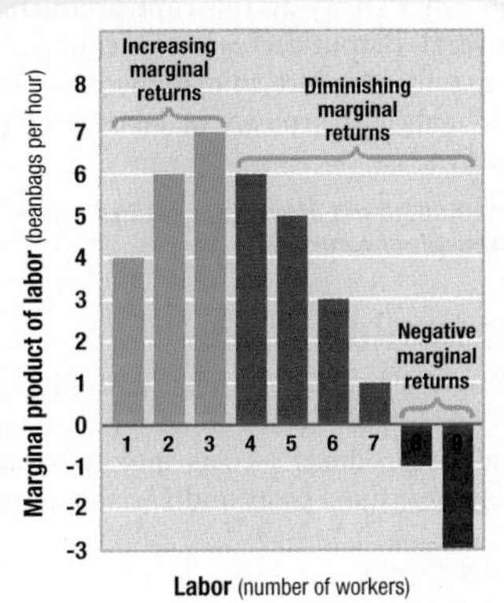

GRAPH SKILLS

Labor has increasing and then diminishing marginal returns.

1. What is the marginal product of labor when the factory employs five workers?
2. Why does the factory experience diminishing marginal returns with more than three workers?

BELLRINGER

Write the following on the board: *According to some reports, supermarkets make a profit of three to six cents for every dollar of revenue. Where does the rest of the money go?*

Have students write their answers in their notebooks. Tell them to list specific costs the supermarket has to pay to operate. Elicit the fact from students that the money goes toward the cost of the products they sell, as well as rent, utilities, and salaries.

Teach

Economics online To present this topic using digital resources, use the lecture notes at www.PearsonSuccessNet.com.

DEMONSTRATE

Review the discussion in the text of how specialization can lead to increasing marginal returns but lack of capital can lead to diminishing returns. Then select six students, and tell them that their task is to write a number on a piece of paper and then fold the paper in half to cover the number. One student will do both tasks alone. Two will work together, with one writing numbers and the other folding. The remaining three will also work together, with two students taking turns using the same pen to write numbers and providing the papers to the third student, who folds. Give the three groups a minute to do as many papers as they can. When they are done, have them count the completed papers. The demonstration should reveal that the pair can produce more papers than either the individual or the team of three. Ask **How do you explain these results?** *(The pair specialized, enabling it to produce more than the lone individual. The team of three lacked capital—another pen—which slowed production.)*

Differentiated Resources

- **L1 L2 Guided Reading and Review** (Unit 2 All-in-One, p. 58)
- **L2 Transferring Data skills worksheet** (Unit 2 All-in-One, p. 60)
- **L2 The Cost of Doing Business** (Unit 2 All-in-One, p. 62)
- **L4 Making Production Decisions** (Unit 2 All-in-One, p. 63)
- **L3 How Is Output Set?** (Simulation Activities, Chapter 5)

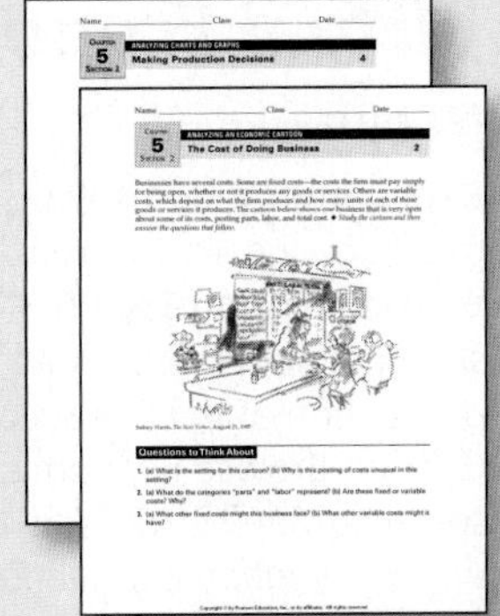

Answers

Chart Skills 1. because the workers can specialize in performing the three tasks in making beanbags, improving efficiency 2. It decreases because the workers are working with a limited amount of capital and the benefits of specialization ends.

Graph Skills 1. five beanbags per hour 2. It can no longer benefit from specialization because there is limited physical capital. There may not be enough equipment for more than three workers.

ANALYZE

Review the example of the beanbag company in the text. Ask students **How many workers should the beanbag firm hire? Why?** *(It should only hire three; after that, it experiences diminishing returns.)* Ask **What could the firm do to experience increasing returns with more than three workers?** *(It could invest in more capital equipment, such as more scissors and sewing machines.)* Ask **If the company bought one more pair of scissors and one more sewing machine, when would it see diminishing returns again? Why?** *(It would probably see diminishing returns if it hired a seventh worker because producing the bags can be divided into three specialized tasks. The seventh worker would still experience waiting and nonproductive time.)*

L1 L2 Differentiate Have students work in pairs to write their own explanations of *increasing marginal returns, diminishing marginal returns,* and *negative marginal returns.* Tell them to include suggestions on how firms can use these concepts as tools for making decisions.

DISTRIBUTE THE ACTIVITY

Have students examine the graph in Figure 5.4. Distribute the "Transferring Data" skill worksheet (Unit 2 All-in-One, p. 59) and have students practice presenting data on a line graph.

Tell students to review the lesson in the Graph Preview on page xxviii. Remind them to use the steps of the lesson to complete the activity.

L2 Differentiate Distribute the "Transferring Data" skill worksheet (Unit 2 All-in-One, p. 60) and have student pairs complete the activity.

After students have completed the activity, have a volunteer draw their line graph on the board. (You can draw the grid from the worksheet on the board while students are completing the worksheet.) Have volunteers give their answers to worksheet questions 1 and 2. Have students discuss the impact of the use of color in the bar graph.

How the Economy Works

What are production costs?

Production costs are the costs an entrepreneur must pay to run a business. Production costs are divided into two categories: fixed costs and variable costs.

1 Fixed Cost
Rent: Fixed costs are costs that do not change, no matter how much of a good is produced. The rent for the storefront is a fixed cost.

2 Fixed Cost
Manager: The new manager is essential to the operation of the store. The manager's salary is a fixed cost.

3 Variable Costs
Goods and electricity: Variable costs are costs that change as the level of production changes. The cost of all the merchandise the store sells is a variable cost. The cost of the electricity that the store uses during business hours is also a variable cost.

Fixed Cost

Negative Marginal Returns

As the table in **Figure 5.3** shows, adding an eighth worker actually decreases output by one bag. At this stage, workers get in each other's way and disrupt production, so overall output decreases. Of course, few companies ever hire so many workers that their marginal product of labor becomes negative.

CHECKPOINT ***How does capital affect marginal returns?***

Production Costs

fixed cost a cost that does not change, no matter how much of a good is produced

variable cost a cost that rises or falls depending on the quantity produced

Paying workers and purchasing capital are all costs of producing goods. Economists divide a producer's costs into two main categories: fixed costs and variable costs.

Fixed Costs

A **fixed cost** is a cost that does not change, no matter how much of a good is produced. Most fixed costs involve the production facility—the cost of building and equipping a factory, office, store, or restaurant. Examples of fixed costs include rent, machinery repairs, property taxes, and the salaries of workers who run the business even when production temporarily stops.

Variable Costs

Variable costs are costs that rise or fall depending on the quantity produced. They include the costs of raw materials and some labor. For example, to produce more beanbags, the firm must purchase more beans and hire more workers. If the company wants to produce less and cut costs, it can buy fewer beans or reduce weekly hours for some workers. The cost of labor is a variable cost because it changes with the number of workers, which changes with the quantity produced. Electricity and heating bills are also variable costs,

Virtual Economics

L3 Differentiate

Exploring Costs of Production Use the following lesson from the NCEE **Virtual Economics *CD-ROM*** to help students understand how costs of production affect the success of a firm. Click on Browse Economics Lessons, specify grades 9–12, and use the key words *invention connection.*

In this activity, students will conduct a simulation of a business, determining what to produce, costs of production, and profit or loss.

LESSON TITLE	THE INVENTION CONNECTION
Type of Activity	Simulation
Complexity	High
Time	60 minutes
NCEE Standards	1, 14

Answer

Checkpoint More capital means more workers can work more efficiently, increasing output. Less capital means added workers must wait to use equipment, reducing marginal output.

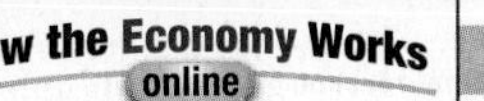

For an animated, interactive version of this feature, visit **PearsonSuccessNet.com**

4 Variable Cost
Part-time workers: Some companies hire part-time workers, whose hours are reduced when business is slow. The salaries for part-time workers are a variable cost.

5 Total Cost
When fixed costs and variable costs are added together, the result is a firm's total cost—the amount of money needed to operate a business.

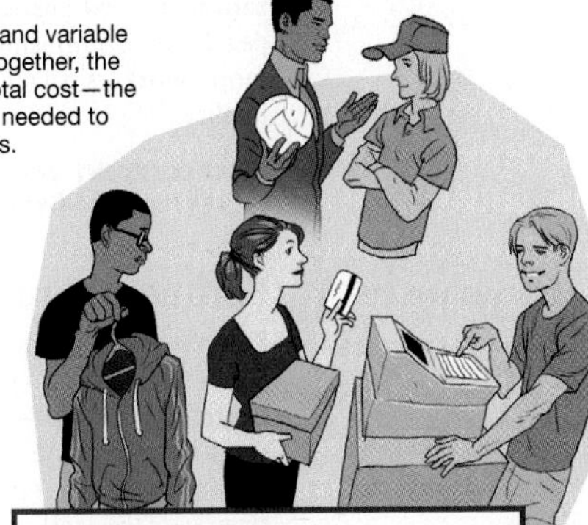

Check Your Understanding
1. Would an advertisement for the store that runs every week in a local newspaper be a fixed cost or a variable cost?
2. Is the separate storage space the owner rents for two months a fixed cost or a variable cost?

Variable Cost

Total Cost

because the company only uses heat and electricity during business hours.

Total Cost

Costs for the firm that produces beanbags are shown in **Figure 5.5** on the next page. The firm's factory is fully equipped to produce beanbags. How does the cost of producing beanbags change as the output increases?

In our example, the fixed costs are the costs of the factory building and all the machinery and equipment. As shown in the second column in **Figure 5.5**, the fixed costs are $36.00 per hour.

Variable costs include the cost of beans, fabric, and most of the workers. As shown in the third column, variable costs rise with the number of beanbags produced. Fixed costs and variable costs are added together to find **total cost.** Total cost is shown in the fourth column.

Marginal Cost

If we know the total cost of production at several levels of output, we can determine the marginal cost of production at each level. **Marginal cost** is the additional cost of producing one more unit.

As shown in **Figure 5.5**, even if the firm is not producing a single beanbag, it still must pay $36.00 per hour for fixed costs. If the firm decides to produce just one beanbag per hour, its total cost rises by $8.00, from $36.00 to $44.00 per hour. The marginal cost of the first beanbag is $8.00.

For the first three beanbags, marginal cost falls as output increases. The marginal cost of the second beanbag is $4.00, and the marginal cost of the third beanbag is $3.00. Each additional beanbag is cheaper to make because of increasing marginal returns resulting from specialization.

At four beanbags per hour, the marginal cost starts to rise. The marginal cost of the

FUTURE WATCH
Personal Finance
For help with setting your own budget, see your Personal Finance Handbook in the back of the book or visit **PearsonSuccessNet.com**

total cost the sum of fixed costs plus variable costs

marginal cost the cost of producing one more unit of a good

Background Note

Fixed Costs Fixed costs are not necessarily fixed over time, of course. A company renting office space will sign a lease for that space covering a certain period of months or years. When the lease ends, it must sign a new agreement with the company owning the property. That company might raise the rent, creating a new and higher fixed cost for the firm renting the space. Of course, it also has the option of looking for space at lower rent.

CATEGORIZE

Review the definitions of fixed and variable costs and the examples in the text. Then distribute the "The Cost of Doing Business" worksheet (Unit 2 All-in-One, p. 61), which includes a political cartoon that refers to the costs of a diner restaurant. Have students study the cartoon and then answer the questions on the worksheet.

L2 Review the definitions of fixed and variable costs by turning to the How the Economy Works feature. Have students identify the fixed costs *(rent and manager's salary)* and variable costs *(goods, electricity, part-time workers' salaries)* that, together, equal Jack's Sporting Goods total cost. Then distribute the "The Cost of Doing Business" worksheet (Unit 2 All-in-One, p. 62).

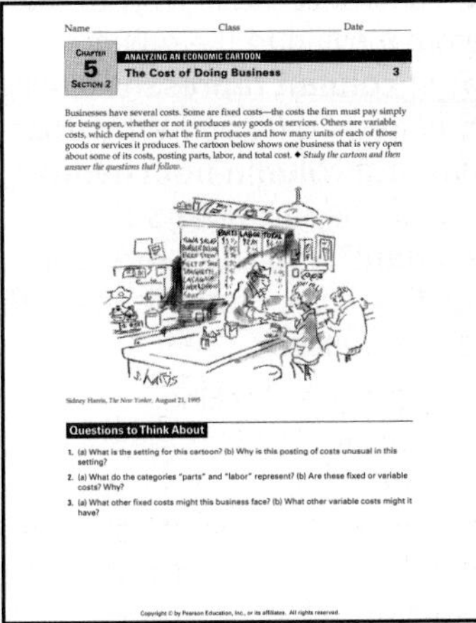
Name ____________ Class ____________ Date ________

CHAPTER 5 SECTION 2 — ANALYZING AN ECONOMIC CARTOON — **The Cost of Doing Business** 3

Businesses have several costs. Some are fixed costs—the costs the firm must pay simply for being open, whether or not it produces any goods or services. Others are variable costs, which depend on what the firm produces and how many units of each of those goods or services it produces. The cartoon below shows one business that is very open about some of its costs, posting parts, labor, and total cost. ◆ *Study the cartoon and then answer the questions that follow.*

Sidney Harris, *The New Yorker*, August 21, 1995

Questions to Think About

1. (a) What is the setting for this cartoon? (b) Why is this posting of costs unusual in this setting?
2. (a) What do the categories "parts" and "labor" represent? (b) Are these fixed or variable costs? Why?
3. (a) What other fixed costs might this business face? (b) What other variable costs might it have?

After students have completed the worksheet, have students discuss their answers to questions 2 and 3 on the worksheet. Then have them return to the list of production costs for the supermarket in the Bellringer activity. Have students categorize each cost as fixed or variable. Encourage them to add to the list of costs to gain more practice identifying the two types.

PERSONAL FINANCE ACTIVITY

Guide students to read "Wise Choices for Your Money" in the Personal Finance Handbook (pp. PF4–5) to learn about making a budget. Assign the activity worksheet (Personal Finance All-in-One, pp. 32–33).

Answers

Check Your Understanding 1. a fixed cost, because the cost is the same no matter how much the store sells 2. a fixed cost for those two months

EXPLAIN

Direct students' attention to the chart on page 120. Walk students through the derivation of each entry in the table. Use the example of output of two beanbags per hour. Explain the addition of fixed plus variable costs to find total costs. Ask **Why is the marginal cost for producing two beanbags per hour $4?** *($48 total cost for two beanbags minus $44 total cost for 1 beanbag equals $4 marginal cost).* Then ask for volunteers to demonstrate the derivation of the total revenue and profits for this same production level.

Ask **How many beanbags should the firm produce each hour? Why?** *(9 or 10 beanbags per hour; because the profit of $98 is the most the company can earn)*

L1 L2 Differentiate Familiarize students with the first three columns before moving to the others. Ask **What does the first column represent?** *(how many beanbags are produced each hour)* **Why does the quantity in the second column not change?** *(Since these costs are fixed, they are always the same.)* **Why does the quantity in the "variable costs" column change?** *(Variable costs change with the number of beanbags produced.)*

L4 Differentiate Distribute the "Making Production Decisions" worksheet (Unit 2 All-in-One, p. 63), which gives students a scenario involving marginal costs and revenue. Have students complete the worksheet to determine the optimum level of output for the imaginary firm.

L3 Differentiate For alternative or additional practice with the concept of determining output, have students use the "How Is Output Set?" activity in the **Simulation Activities.** Students will role-play producers reacting to conditions that might affect their decisions on how much of their product to supply.

Answers

Checkpoint The owner must still pay fixed costs, such as rent.

Chart Skills 1. That is the market price for each unit, and the price of each unit does not change. 2. $12 ($84 total cost divided by 7)

marginal revenue the additional income from selling one more unit of a good; sometimes equal to price

fifth beanbag per hour is $7.00, the sixth costs $9.00, and the seventh, $12.00. The rising marginal cost reflects diminishing returns of labor. The benefits of specialization are exhausted at three beanbags per hour. Diminishing returns set in as more workers share a fixed production facility.

CHECKPOINT ***Why does a closed factory still have production costs?***

Simulation Activity

How Is Output Set? You may be asked to take part in a role-playing game about setting output.

Setting Output

Behind all of the hiring decisions is the firm's basic goal: to maximize profits. Profit is defined as total revenue minus total cost. As you read in Chapter 4, a firm's total revenue is the money the firm gets by selling its product. Total revenue is equal to the price of each good multiplied by the number of goods sold. Total revenue when the price of a beanbag is $24.00 is shown in **Figure 5.5.** To find the level of output with the highest profit, we look for the biggest gap between total revenue and total cost. The gap is greatest and profit is highest when the firm makes 9 or 10 beanbags per hour. At this rate, the firm can expect to make a profit of $98.00 per hour.

Marginal Revenue and Marginal Cost

Another way to find the best level of output is to find the output level where marginal revenue is equal to marginal cost. **Marginal revenue** is the additional income from selling one more unit of a good. If the firm has no control over the market price, marginal revenue equals the market price. Each beanbag sold at $24.00 increases the firm's total revenue by $24.00, so marginal revenue is $24.00. According to the table, price equals marginal cost with ten beanbags, so that's the quantity that maximizes profit at $98 per hour.

To understand how an output of ten beanbags maximizes the firm's profits, suppose that the firm made only four beanbags per hour. Is it making as much money as it can?

From **Figure 5.5,** we know that the marginal cost of the fifth beanbag is $7.00. The market price for a beanbag is $24.00, so the marginal revenue from that beanbag is $24.00. The $17.00 difference between the marginal revenue and marginal cost represents pure profit for the company from the fifth beanbag. The company should increase production to five beanbags an hour to capture that profit on the fifth beanbag.

Figure 5.5 **Production Costs**

CHART SKILLS

Firms consider a variety of costs when deciding how much to produce.

1. Why is the marginal revenue always equal to $24?
2. What is the average cost when output is seven beanbags per hour?

Beanbags (per hour)	Fixed Cost	Variable Cost	Total Cost (fixed cost + variable cost)	Marginal Cost	Marginal Revenue (market price)	Total Revenue	Profit (total revenue – total cost)
0	$36	$0	$36	—	$24	$0	$–36
1	36	8	44	$8	24	24	–20
2	36	12	48	4	24	48	0
3	36	15	51	3	24	72	21
4	36	20	56	5	24	96	40
5	36	27	63	7	24	120	57
6	36	36	72	9	24	144	72
7	36	48	84	12	24	168	84
8	36	63	99	15	24	192	93
9	36	82	118	19	24	216	98
10	36	106	142	24	24	240	98
11	36	136	172	30	24	264	92
12	36	173	209	37	24	288	79

Background Note

Marginal Savings and High Volume Large businesses constantly look for ways to cut costs. Even small savings can substantially increase profits when many units are produced. Suppose a manufacturer of MP3 players cut its cost for a memory chip from $1 to 80 cents. The 20-cent difference might not seem like much, but if the firm makes and sells a million MP3 players, that makes an additional $200,000 in profit.

The same calculations show that the company can capture a profit of $15.00 by producing a sixth beanbag per hour. The price of the seventh beanbag is $12.00 higher than its marginal cost, so that beanbag earns an additional $12.00 in profit for the company. The profit is available any time the company receives more for the last beanbag than the cost to produce it. Any rational entrepreneur would take this opportunity to increase profit.

Now suppose that the firm is producing so many beanbags per hour that marginal cost is *higher* than price. If the firm produces eleven beanbags per hour, it receives $24.00 for that eleventh beanbag, but the $30.00 cost of producing that beanbag wipes out the profit. The firm actually loses $6.00 on the sale of the eleventh beanbag. Because marginal cost is increasing, and price is constant in this example, the losses get worse at higher levels of output. The company would be better off producing less and keeping costs down.

The ideal level of output is where marginal revenue (price) is equal to marginal cost. Any other quantity of output would generate less profit. As **Figure 5.5** shows, profit per hour can be determined by subtracting total cost from total revenue. We can also determine profit by comparing price and average cost. **Average cost** is total cost divided by the quantity produced. At an output of 10 beanbags per hour, the average cost is $14.20 ($142—total cost—divided by 10). Profit is the difference between market price and average cost ($24 − 14.20 = $9.80) multiplied by the quantity ($9.80 × 10 = $98).

Responding to Price Changes

What happens if the price of a beanbag rises from $24.00 to $37.00? Thinking at the margin, the firm would probably increase production to twelve beanbags per hour. At that quantity, marginal cost is equal to the new, higher price. At the original price of $24.00, the firm would not produce more than ten beanbags, according to **Figure 5.6.** When the price rises to $37.00, marginal revenue soars above marginal cost at that output level. By raising production to 12 beanbags per hour, the firm earns profits on the eleventh and twelfth beanbags.

This example shows the law of supply in action. An increase in price from $24.00 to $37.00 causes the firm to increase the quantity supplied from ten to twelve beanbags per hour.

Figure 5.6 Output and a Change in Price

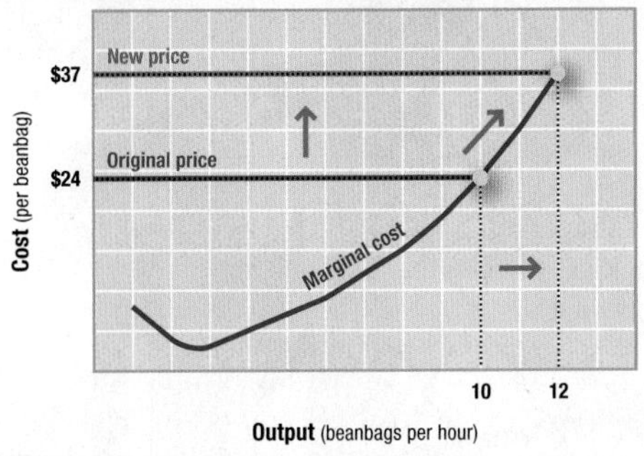

GRAPH SKILLS

The most profitable level of output is where price (or marginal revenue) is equal to marginal cost.

1. What would happen to output if the market price fell to $20?
2. Why would the firm increase output if the price of a beanbag rose to $37?

Action Graph online
For an animated version of this graph, visit PearsonSuccessNet.com

CHECKPOINT ***What is a firm's basic goal when it sets its level of output?***

The Shutdown Decision

Consider the problems faced by a factory that is losing money. The factory is producing at the most profitable level of output, where marginal revenue is equal to marginal cost. However, the market price is so low that the factory's total revenue is still less than its total cost, and the firm is losing money. Should this factory continue to produce goods and lose money, or should its owners shut the factory down?

In fact, there are times when keeping a money-losing factory open is the best choice. The firm should keep the factory open if the total revenue from the goods the factory produces is greater than the cost of keeping it open.

average cost the total cost divided by the quantity produced

INTERPRET

Direct students' attention to Figure 5.6. Call out different new prices and have volunteers identify the firm's desired output at each price.

Action Graph online Have students review the Action Graph animation for a step-by-step look at Output and a Change in Price.

DISCUSS

Have students define *operating cost.* Ask **Is operating cost a variable cost or a fixed cost?** *(variable cost)* Ask **When does it make sense to keep a factory operating?** *(when the total revenue is greater than the operating cost)* Have students explain why they are not considering the fixed costs. Ask **When does it make more sense to shutdown a factory?** *(when the total revenue is less than the operating cost)*

L1 L2 Differentiate Work through the example with students to help them understand why it costs less to continue producing beanbags at a price of $7 than to shut the factory down.

EXTEND

Have students find an example in the news about a company shutting down a facility or moving a facility from one location to another. Have them explain why the firm made that decision in light of the discussion in this section. Examples of companies include automotive plants, airlines, or retail outlets like Starbuck.

L1 L2 Differentiate Give students this scenario: The price of beanbags drops to $20 for three months, but the beanbag company owner expects it to return to $24. Have them write a paragraph explaining whether the firm would stay in business and why.

Assess and Remediate

L2 L3 Collect "The Cost of Doing Business" worksheets and assess student understanding.

L3 Assign the Section Assessment questions; identify student misconceptions.

L3 Give Section Quiz A (Unit 2 All-in-One, p. 64).

L2 Give Section Quiz B (Unit 2 All-in-One, p. 65).

(Assess and Remediate continued on p. 122)

Answers

Graph Skills 1. Output would decrease to about 9 beanbags per hour. 2. because marginal revenue would increase

Checkpoint to maximize profit; firms earn their highest profits when the cost of making one more unit is the same as the market price of that good

Background Note

Development Costs Unlike beanbags—which are relatively close in average costs—some goods have high initial development costs and low reproduction costs. A computer game, for example, might cost $1 million to develop but only $1 to copy onto CDs. Just two copies, then, average $500,000.50 in cost. The average cost of a hundred drops to $10,001, and 1,000 copies cost, on average, only $1,001. If the company produces a million copies, each costs just $2. With information goods such as books, CDs, software, and movies, producers need high volume to recover high development costs.

Have students complete the Self-Test Online and continue their work in the **Essential Questions Journal**.

REMEDIATION AND SUGGESTIONS

Use the chart below to help students who are struggling with content.

WEAKNESS	REMEDIATION
Defining key terms (Questions 3, 4, 5, 6)	Have students use the interactive Economic Dictionary Online.
Explaining marginal returns (Questions 2, 7, 8)	Draw a table on the board like Figure 5.3. With students, complete the table and lead them to identify the marginal returns. Have them compare their results with Figure 5.4.
Identifying costs and revenues (Questions 1, 9, 10)	Use the Action Graph Online to walk students through the creation of a supply curve.

Answer

Checkpoint when the total revenue from the goods produced is greater than the cost of operating the facility

▲ When a factory is losing money, operating cost and revenue are the factors that determine whether or not the factory remains open.

For example, if the price of beanbags drops to $7 and the factory produces at the profit-maximizing level of five beanbags per hour, the total revenue drops from $120 per hour to $35 per hour. Weigh this against the factory's **operating cost,** the cost of operating the facility. Operating cost includes the variable costs the owners must pay to keep the factory running, but not fixed costs, which the owners must pay whether the factory is open or closed.

operating cost the cost of operating a facility, such as a factory or a store

According to **Figure 5.5**, if the factory produces five beanbags, the variable cost is $27 per hour. Therefore, the benefit of operating the facility (total revenue of $35) is greater than the variable cost ($27), so it makes sense to keep the facility running.

Consider the effects of the other choice. If the firm shuts down the factory, it would still have to pay all of its fixed costs. The factory's total revenue would be zero because it produces nothing for sale. Therefore, the firm would lose an amount of money equal to its fixed costs.

For this beanbag factory, the fixed costs equal $36 per hour, so the factory would lose $36 for each hour it is closed. If the factory produced five beanbags per hour, its total cost would be $63 ($36 in fixed costs plus $27 in variable costs) per hour, but it would lose only $28 ($63 in total cost minus $35 in revenue) for each hour it is open. The factory would lose less money while producing because the total revenue ($35) would exceed the variable costs ($27), leaving $8 to cover some of the fixed costs. Although the factory would lose money either way, it loses less money by continuing to produce and sell beanbags.

When will a business replace a factory that is operating at a loss? The firm will build a new factory and stay in the market only if the market price of beanbags is high enough to cover all the costs of production, including the cost of building a new factory.

CHECKPOINT ***When should a firm keep a money-losing factory open?***

Essential Questions Journal To continue to build a response to the Essential Question, go to your **Essential Questions Journal.**

SECTION 2 ASSESSMENT

Guiding Question

1. Use your completed table to answer this question: How can a producer maximize profits?
2. **Extension** How would it help the company where you worked to maximize profits if you received advanced training?

Key Terms and Main Ideas

3. What does **marginal cost** refer to?
4. What are examples of **fixed costs** and **variable costs** for a farm?
5. What is **marginal revenue?**
6. Is **operating cost** a **fixed cost** or a **variable cost?** Why?

Critical Thinking

7. **Solve** Suppose you are advising a company that is seeing diminishing marginal returns. Other than reducing staff, what steps would you recommend to its managers to improve its performance?
8. **Decide** Suppose your company has two office spaces, one twice as large as the other. Would you add the same number of employees to each facility? Why or why not?
9. **Analyze (a)** Why would a company produce more units of a good if its marginal cost is less than its marginal revenue? **(b)** Why would the company not simply produce more and more units?

Math Skills

10. Use the table below to answer the following questions. **(a)** What is the total cost when output is 2? **(b)** What is the marginal cost of the third unit? **(c)** How much should this firm produce if the market price is $24? Why?

Visit PearsonSuccessNet.com for additional math help.

Output	Fixed Cost	Variable Cost
1	$5	$10
2	$5	$27
3	$5	$55
4	$5	$91
5	$5	$145

Assessment Answers

1. by setting output at the point where marginal revenue equals marginal cost
2. Possible response: The skills gained would increase marginal output.
3. additional cost of producing one more unit of a good
4. Possible responses: Fixed costs—cost of land, barn, and equipment; variable costs—cost of seeds, fertilizer, energy
5. additional income from selling one more unit of a good
6. It is a variable cost, because the firm pays the cost of operating only if the firm remains open.
7. Possible responses: raising prices, obtaining capital to upgrade facilities and equipment, encouraging specialization to increase productivity
8. Possible response: Workers should be added to the larger facility at a faster rate because it has greater capacity to handle more workers.
9. Possible responses: (a) doing so increases profits (b) because at some point marginal return from added units will diminish, reducing profits
10. (a) $32 (b) $28 (c) 2 units, because marginal revenue ($24) exceeds marginal cost ($17)

SECTION 3 Changes in Supply

OBJECTIVES

1. **Explain** how factors such as input costs create changes in supply.
2. **Identify** three ways that the government can influence the supply of goods.
3. **Analyze** other factors that affect supply.
4. **Explain** how firms choose a location to produce goods.

ECONOMIC DICTIONARY

As you read the section, look for the definitions of these **Key Terms:**

- subsidy
- excise tax
- regulation

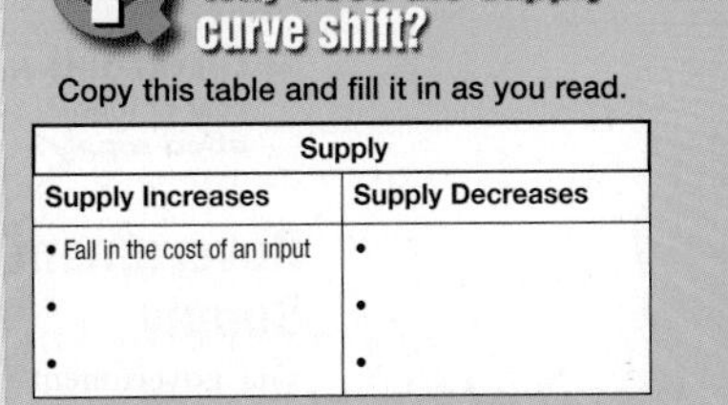

Guiding Question
Why does the supply curve shift?

Copy this table and fill it in as you read.

Supply	
Supply Increases	**Supply Decreases**
• Fall in the cost of an input • •	• • •

Economics and You

You own a collection of original action figures from a popular movie. You notice that the price of these figures is increasing rapidly on Web auction sites. Should you sell the figures now, or wait? How would your decision affect the supply of these action figures?

Principles in Action Several factors, including the number of suppliers in a market, can lead to a shift in the supply curve. Government actions and global events also have an impact on supply. Input costs are the subject of the Economics & You feature.

Input Costs

Any change in the cost of an input used to produce a good—such as raw materials, machinery, or labor—will affect supply. A rise in the cost of an input will cause a fall in supply at all price levels because the good has become more expensive to produce. On the other hand, a fall in the cost of an input will cause an increase in supply at all price levels.

Effect of Rising Costs

Think of the effects of input costs on the relationship between marginal revenue (price) and marginal cost. A supplier sets output at the most profitable level, where price is equal to marginal cost. Marginal cost includes the cost of the inputs that go into production, so a rise in the cost of labor or raw materials will result in a higher marginal cost. If the cost of inputs increases enough, the marginal cost may become higher than the price, and the firm may not be as profitable.

If a firm has no control over the price, the only solution is to cut production and lower marginal cost until marginal cost equals the lower price. Supply falls at each price, and the supply curve shifts to the left, as illustrated in **Figure 5.7.**

Technology

Input costs can drop as well. Advances in technology can lower production costs in many industries. Automation, including the use of robotic tools, has spread throughout the manufacturing sector, saving on labor costs. Computers have simplified tasks and cut costs in many fields. Inexpensive e-mail allows

The higher input costs that dairy farmers pay for feed, labor, and fuel result in higher prices for milk and other dairy products. ▼

Guiding Question

Why does the supply curve shift?

Get Started

Supply	
Supply Increases	**Supply Decreases**
• Fall in the cost of an input • If government pays subsidies for good • If government ends regulation of good • If production increases in another country • If producers expect price to rise in future • If more suppliers enter market	• Rise in an input cost • If government places excise tax on good • If government regulates good • If production costs increase in another country • If producers expect price to fall in future • If some suppliers leave market

LESSON GOALS

Students will:

- Know the Key Terms.
- Analyze how businesses are affected by and can respond to changes in input costs.
- Analyze how government policies can shift the supply curve.
- Evaluate arguments on a question of changing government policy to increase supply.
- Give examples of factors affecting supply.

BEFORE CLASS

Have students complete the graphic organizer in the Section Opener as they read the text. As an alternate activity, have students complete the Guided Reading and Review worksheet. (Unit 2 All-in-One, p. 66)

L1 L2 ELL LPR Differentiate Have students complete the Guided Reading and Review worksheet. (Unit 2 All-in-One, p. 67)

Focus on the Basics

Students need to come away with the following understandings:

FACTS: • Changes in input costs affect supply. • Government affects supply through subsidies, taxes, and regulations. • Changes in the global economy, future expectations about prices, the number of suppliers, and decisions about where to locate facilities all affect supply.

GENERALIZATION: Firms must base their decisions about supply not only on their own operations but also in response to several external factors.

CLASSROOM HINTS

INPUT COSTS AND CONSUMER PRICES

Help students relate to the content of this section by discussing the effect of rising input costs on consumer prices. Have students give their opinions on how a rise in input costs could affect the supply of cars. How will the supply of cars change?

BELLRINGER

Display the transparency "When Input Costs Rise" (Color Transparencies, 5.b). Have students read the article excerpt, and then write the answers to the following questions in their notebooks:

- Why is Hershey's increasing the price of their candy?
- How do you think an increase in the cost of candy ingredients will affect the cost of producing Hershey's candy?

Teach

Economics online To present this topic using digital resources, use the lecture notes at www.PearsonSuccessNet.com.

DISCUSS

Read the questions from the Bellringer activity and have students present their answers. Ask **If Hershey's cannot raise the prices of their candy bars, what could they do?** *(produce smaller candy bars but charge the same price)*

Tell students to take the role of the owner of a Thai restaurant, which serves rice with many of its meals. Tell them that the price of rice has increased by 30 percent, but the owner does not want to raise the price of meals. Ask **What options does the owner have?** *(Possible responses: look for another supplier who charges less; give smaller portions; substitute another food for the rice; cut costs in other ways)* Point out that reducing portion size in response to the rising cost of rice is an example of reducing supply due to increased input costs.

REVIEW

Review the difference discussed in Chapter 4 between an increase (or decrease) in the quantity demanded for a good, and an increase (or decrease) in demand for a good. One is represented by movement along the demand curve, the other by a shift in the demand curve. Tell students that a similar situation exists with supply and the supply curve.

Answers

Checkpoint Supply would go down because of increased marginal cost.

Economics & You Possible answers: candy and soft drinks

subsidy a government payment that supports a business or market

excise tax a tax on the production or sale of a good

businesses to communicate in an instant. Future advances promise to decrease production costs even further.

Technology lowers costs and increases supply at all price levels. This effect is seen in a rightward shift in the supply curve in **Figure 5.7.**

CHECKPOINT ***How would a rise in the cost of inputs, such as raw materials, affect supply?***

Government's Influence on Supply

The government has the power to affect the supplies of many types of goods. By raising or lowering the cost of producing goods, the government can encourage or discourage an entrepreneur or an industry within the country or abroad.

Subsidies

One method used by governments to affect supply is to give subsidies to the producers of a good, particularly for food. A **subsidy** is a government payment that supports a business or market. The government often pays a producer a set subsidy for each unit of a good produced. Subsidies generally lower costs, allowing a firm to produce more goods.

Governments have several reasons for subsidizing producers. During and after World War II, European countries faced food shortages. Today, European governments protect farms so that some will be available to grow food in case cheaper imports are ever restricted. In France, the government subsidizes small farms to protect the lifestyle and character of the French countryside.

Governments in developing countries often subsidize manufacturers to protect young, growing industries from strong foreign competition. Countries such as Indonesia and Malaysia have subsidized a national car company as a source of pride, even though imported cars were less expensive. In Western Europe, banks and national airlines were allowed to suffer huge losses with the assurance that the government would cover their debts. In many countries, governments have stopped providing industrial subsidies in the interest of free trade and fair competition.

In the United States, the federal government subsidizes producers in many industries. Farm subsidies are particularly controversial, especially when farmers are paid to take land out of cultivation to keep prices high. In these cases, more efficient farmers are penalized, and farmers use more herbicides and pesticides on lands they do cultivate to compensate for production lost on the acres the government pays them not to plant.

Taxes

A government can reduce the supply of some goods by placing an excise tax on them. An **excise tax** is a tax on the production or sale of a good. An excise tax increases production costs by adding an extra cost for each unit sold.

Economics & YOU
Input Costs
Rising costs for wheat, fertilizer, and fuel make this box of cereal more expensive to produce. *As a result of higher input costs, you pay more for your morning bowl of cereal.*
WONDER WHEATS
MILK
You receive special offers and discount coupons by e-mail. *Technology helps companies to reduce costs for advertising and postage.*
Special Offer

▲ Input costs affect the price you pay for a good or service. ***Name two items that would become more expensive if sugar rose in price.***

Differentiated Resources

L1 L2 Guided Reading and Review (Unit 2 All-in-One, p. 67)

L4 Evaluating the Ban on Offshore Oil Drilling (Unit 2 All-in-One, p. 68)

L1 L2 Analyzing Influences on Supply (Unit 2 All-in-One, p. 70)

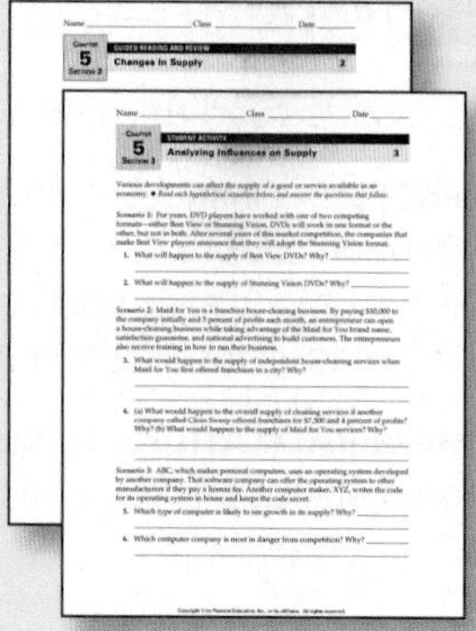

Excise taxes are sometimes used to discourage the sale of goods that the government thinks are harmful to the public good, like cigarettes, alcohol, and high-pollutant gasoline. Excise taxes are indirect—they are built into the prices of these and other goods—so consumers may not realize that they are paying them. Like any increase in cost, an excise tax causes the supply of a good to decrease at all price levels. The supply curve shifts to the left.

Regulation

Subsidies and excise taxes represent ways that government directly affects supply by changing revenue or production costs. Government can also raise or lower supply through indirect means. Government regulation often has the effect of raising costs. **Regulation** is government intervention in a market that affects the price, quantity, or quality of a good.

Even members of government recognize the burden that regulation can place on business. In a 2006 speech to the Economic Club of New York, Treasury Secretary Henry M. Paulson Jr. described how over-regulation of business can affect economic progress:

> **"Excessive regulation slows innovation, imposes needless costs on investors, and stifles competitiveness and job creation."**
>
> —Henry M. Paulson Jr., Secretary of the Treasury, washingtonpost.com, Nov. 11, 2006

For many years, pollution from automobiles harmed the environment. Starting in 1970, the federal government required car manufacturers to install technology to reduce pollution from auto exhaust. For example, new cars had to use lead-free fuel because scientists linked health problems to lead in gasoline. Regulations such as these increased the cost of manufacturing cars and reduced the supply. The supply curve shifted to the left.

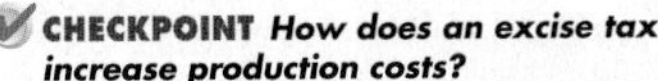

CHECKPOINT ***How does an excise tax increase production costs?***

Other Influences on Supply

While government can have an important influence on the supply of goods, there are other important factors that influence supply.

Figure 5.7 Shifts in the Supply Curve

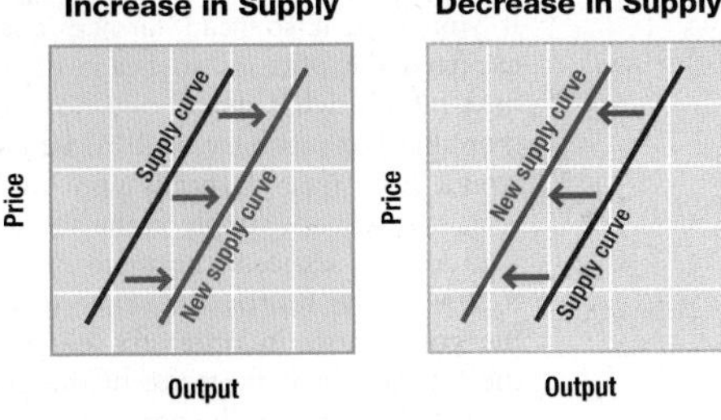

GRAPH SKILLS

Factors that reduce supply shift the supply curve to the left, while factors that increase supply move the supply curve to the right.

1. Which graph best represents the effects of higher costs?
2. Which graph best represents advances in technology?

Action Graph online

For an animated version of this graph, visit **PearsonSuccessNet.com**

Changes in the Global Economy

As you read in earlier chapters, a large and rising share of goods and services are imported. The supplies of imported goods are affected by changes in other countries. Here are two examples of possible changes in the supply of products imported by the United States.

- The U.S. imports carpets from India. An increase in the wages of Indian workers would decrease the supply of carpets to the U.S. market, shifting the supply curve to the left.
- The United States imports oil from Russia. A new oil discovery in Russia could increase the supply of oil to the U.S. market and shift the supply curve to the right.

Import restrictions also affect supply. The total supply of a product equals the sum of imports and domestically produced products. An import ban on sugar would eliminate foreign sugar suppliers from the market, shifting the market supply curve to the left. At any price, a smaller quantity of sugar would be supplied. If the government restricted imports by establishing an import quota, the supply curve would shift to the

regulation government intervention in a market that affects the production of a good

DEMONSTRATE

When the costs of producing a good increase or decrease, the whole supply curve shifts, representing how supply falls (or rises) at each price, respectively. Demonstrate this by drawing Figure 5.7 on the board. Have the graph on the right represent a supply curve for milk, and the other represent a supply curve for computers. Place numbers on the axes and work through each example.

Action Graph online Have students review the Action Graph animation for a step-by-step look at Shifts in the Supply Curve.

ANALYZE

Have students analyze how government policies affect the supply curve. Ask **In which direction would the supply curve for solar power shift if the government gave subsidies to companies making solar power?** *(shift to the right)* **What would happen to the supply of private jets if the government put an excise tax on them?** *(The supply curve would shift to the left.)*

L4 Differentiate Distribute and have students complete the "Evaluating the Ban on Offshore Oil Drilling" worksheet (Unit 2 All-in-One, p. 68), which reprints parts of two editorials commenting on a proposal to allow offshore oil drilling.

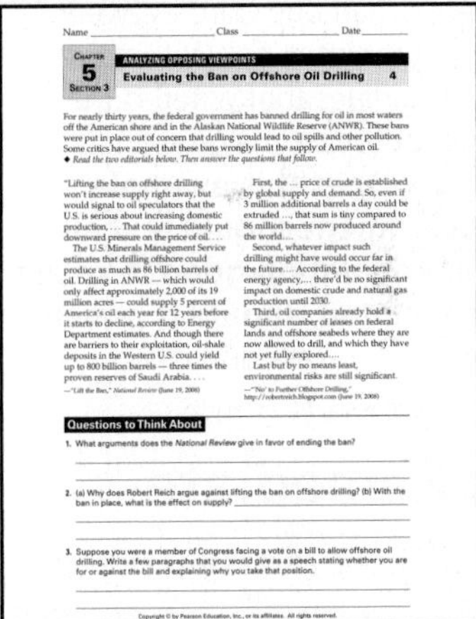

Name ________ Class ________ Date ________

CHAPTER 5 SECTION 3 — ANALYZING OPPOSING VIEWPOINTS

Evaluating the Ban on Offshore Oil Drilling 4

For nearly thirty years, the federal government has banned drilling for oil in most waters off the American shore and in the Alaskan National Wildlife Reserve (ANWR). These bans were put in place out of concern that drilling would lead to oil spills and other pollution. Some critics have argued that these bans wrongly limit the supply of American oil.

◆ *Read the two editorials below. Then answer the questions that follow.*

"Lifting the ban on offshore drilling won't increase supply right away, but would signal to oil speculators that the U.S. is serious about increasing domestic production, . . . That could immediately put downward pressure on the price of oil. . . .

The U.S. Minerals Management Service estimates that drilling offshore could produce as much as 86 billion barrels of oil. Drilling in ANWR — which would only affect approximately 2,000 of its 19 million acres — could supply 5 percent of America's oil each year for 12 years before it starts to decline, according to Energy Department estimates. And though there are barriers to their exploitation, oil-shale deposits in the Western U.S. could yield up to 800 billion barrels — three times the proven reserves of Saudi Arabia. . . .

—"Lift the Ban," *National Review* (June 19, 2008)

First, the ... price of crude is established by global supply and demand. So, even if 3 million additional barrels a day could be extruded ..., that sum is tiny compared to 86 million barrels now produced around the world....

Second, whatever impact such drilling might have would occur far in the future.... According to the federal energy agency,... there'd be no significant impact on domestic crude and natural gas production until 2030.

Third, oil companies already hold a significant number of leases on federal lands and offshore seabeds where they are now allowed to drill, and which they have not yet fully explored....

Last but by no means least, environmental risks are still significant.

—"'No' to Further Offshore Drilling," http://robertreich.blogspot.com (June 19, 2008)

Questions to Think About

1. What arguments does the *National Review* give in favor of ending the ban?
2. (a) Why does Robert Reich argue against lifting the ban on offshore drilling? (b) With the ban in place, what is the effect on supply?
3. Suppose you were a member of Congress facing a vote on a bill to allow offshore oil drilling. Write a few paragraphs that you would give as a speech stating whether you are for or against the bill and explaining why you take that position.

Ask **What effect has this ban on drilling had on the supply of oil?** *(held down the supply of American oil)* **Why was the ban instituted?** *(to protect the environment)* **What economic impact could drilling have?** *(Possible response: Environmental damage could have a negative impact on the tourism and fishing industries.)*

Virtual Economics

L2 Differentiate

Evaluating Nonprice Determinants of Supply Use the following lesson from the NCEE **Virtual Economics *CD-ROM*** to help students to understand factors that affect supply. Click on Browse Economics Lessons, specify grades 6–8, and use the key words *should we sell.*

In this activity, students will participate in a simulation to predict the impact of nonprice determinant on supply.

LESSON TITLE	HOW MANY SHOULD WE SELL?
Type of Activity	Simulation
Complexity	High
Time	150 minutes
NCEE Standards	4, 8

Answers

Checkpoint by adding extra cost for each unit sold

Graph Skills 1. "Decrease in Supply" graph
2. "Increase in Supply" graph

BRAINSTORM

State each of the factors affecting supply mentioned in the text: changes in foreign supply, import restrictions, future expectation of prices, and changes in competition. Form students into groups and challenge each group to brainstorm examples. Discuss as a class the examples offered by the groups.

DISTRIBUTE ACTIVITY WORKSHEET

Distribute and have students complete the "Analyzing Influences on Supply" worksheet (Unit 2 All-in-One, p. 69).

L1 L2 **Differentiate** Distribute the "Analyzing Influences on Supply" worksheet (Unit 2 All-in-One, p. 70). Have students work in pairs to complete the worksheets, then have them discuss their answers.

DISCUSS

Ask **Why does it matter to firms where they are located?** *(because they want to keep costs down)* Ask **What do you think a software company would consider when establishing an office?** *(Possible response: the availability of specialized workers)*

EXTEND

Give students the following example: In 1978, Congress passed the Airline Deregulation Act. After it did so, many small airlines entered the market, and airfares dropped by more than one third between 1977 and 1992, adjusted for inflation. Within the same time period, many airlines that entered the market, as well as three of the six major airlines, went out of business. Ask **Does this example indicate that the government should end all regulation or is some regulation good? Explain. If an industry is deregulated, should it remain deregulated?** Allow time for class discussion.

Assess and Remediate

L2 L3 Collect the worksheets and assess student understanding.

L3 Assign the Section Assessment questions; identify student misconceptions.

L3 Give Section Quiz A (Unit 2 All-in-One, p. 71).

L2 Give Section Quiz B (Unit 2 All-in-One, p. 72).

(Assess and Remediate continued on p. 128)

left, but the shift would be smaller than it would be for a total ban on sugar imports.

Future Expectations of Prices

If you were a soybean farmer, and you expected the price of soybeans to double next month, what would you do with the crop that you just harvested? Most farmers would store their soybeans until the price rose, cutting back supply in the short term.

If a seller expects the price of a good to rise in the future, the seller will store the goods now in order to sell more in the future. But if the price of the good is expected to drop in the near future, sellers will earn more money by placing goods on the market immediately, before the price falls. Expectations of higher prices will reduce supply now and increase supply later. Expectations of lower prices will have the opposite effect.

Inflation is a condition of rising prices. During periods of inflation, the value of cash in a person's pocket decreases from day to day as prices rise. Over many years, inflation has reduced the value of the dollar. However, a good will continue to hold its value, provided that it can be stored for a long period of time.

When faced with inflation, suppliers prefer to hold on to goods that will maintain their value rather than sell them for cash that loses its value rapidly. Inflation can affect supply by encouraging suppliers to hold on to goods as long as possible. In the short term, supply can fall dramatically.

During the Civil War, the South faced terrible inflation. There were shortages of food, and shopkeepers knew that prices on basic food items like flour, butter, and salt would rise each month. A few decided to hoard their food and wait for higher prices. They succeeded too well; the supply of food fell so much that prices rose out of the reach of many families. Riots broke out in Virginia and elsewhere when hungry people decided they weren't going to wait for the food to be released from the warehouses, and the shopkeepers lost their goods and their profits.

Number of Suppliers

Another factor to consider when looking at changes in supply is the number of suppliers in the market. If more suppliers enter a market to produce a certain good, the market supply of the good will rise and the supply curve will shift to the right. However, if suppliers stop producing the good and leave the market, the supply will decline. There is a positive relationship between the number of suppliers in a market and the market supply of the good.

CHECKPOINT ***What happens to supply if the price of a good is expected to rise in the future?***

Declining oil supplies have led to higher energy prices and the need to develop alternative energy sources. ***Select three images and describe their connection to higher energy costs.*** ▼

FUTURE WATCH
Impact of Rising Energy Costs
ELECTRIC

126

Background Note

Competition and Price Economists have found a clear connection between competition and price. One study looked at the price of automobile tires. It found that the price dropped as competition rose. When only two stores in a market sold tires, the average price for tires was $55. With three stores, the price fell to $53. With four, the average tire cost $51, and with five stores, the price was $50. More competition led to increased supply and lower prices.

Answer

Checkpoint Sellers store or otherwise hold on to their goods and supply falls.

Ballooning Problem

A SHIFT IN THE SUPPLY CURVE

Dwindling supplies and surging demand combine to inflate the price of helium.

By Ana Campoy
The Wall Street Journal

Syracuse University physicist Gianfranco Vidali spends most of his time studying how molecules are made in outer space, but he has had to drop his interstellar research to address an earthly issue: the global shortage of helium.

The airy element best known for floating party balloons is also the lifeblood of a widening world of scientific research. Mr. Vidali uses the gas to re-create conditions similar to the cold of outer space. Without it, he can't work. So when his helium supplier informed him it was cutting deliveries to his lab, Mr. Vidali said, "it sent us into a panic mode."

Helium is found in varying concentrations in the world's natural-gas deposits, and is separated out in a special refining process. As with oil and natural gas, the easiest-to-get helium supplies have been tapped and are declining. Meanwhile, scientific research has rapidly multiplied the uses of helium in the past 50 years. It is needed to make computer microchips, flat-panel displays, fiber optics and to operate MRI scans and welding machines.

The technology explosion is sucking up helium supplies at dizzying rates. U.S. helium demand is up more than 80% in the past two decades, and is growing at more than 20% annually in developing regions such as Asia.

Meanwhile, supplies in the world's largest helium reserve near Amarillo, Texas, are expected to run out in eight years. Finding and developing new helium sources will take years and millions of dollars in investment.

"We're running on the edge of the supply-demand curve," says Jane Hoffman, global helium director for Praxair Inc.

Experts predict this situation will eventually price out many helium users, who will have to find substitutes or modify their technology. Some party balloon businesses are filling balloons with mixtures that contain less helium. Some welders are using argon.

Physicists are particularly affected by the helium shortage because their equipment requires more frequent helium refills. Myriam Sarachik, a physicist at City University of New York, might have to shut down her research, because helium now absorbs most of her lab's budget, leaving little extra for everything else.

"I'm going to retire. That's the handwriting on the wall," says Ms. Sarachik.

Applying Economic Principles
Advances in technology usually increase supply. But increased demand for helium used in new technologies has led to a helium shortage. Describe an event that might cause the supply curve for helium to shift to the right.

Video News Update Online Powered by *The Wall Street Journal* Classroom Edition

For a new case study, go to the online resources at **PearsonSuccessNet.com**

Teach *Wall Street Journal* Case Study

SUMMARIZE AND EXPLAIN

Have the students explain how a supply chain is affected by a dwindling supply of one of its components. Ask **Why is the supply of helium decreasing?** *(It is used in more research and more products than ever before and the easiest to tap supplies are dwindling.)* Ask **How will the diminishing supply of helium affect consumers?** *(Consumer products might increase in price; for example, the price of popular flat-panel televisions).* Have volunteers use Web sites to research products that need helium in the manufacturing process or in order to function. Have other volunteers research substitute helium sources and examine the price and supply of those substitutes.

ANALYZE

Have the students compare the diminishing supply of helium to another shortage of a vital natural resource today. *(oil, for example)*

DIFFERENTIATE

Have the students role-play as operators of a party balloon store. Have them discuss how limited or no supply of helium would affect their business. *(They would have to raise prices, offer fewer products, or find substitutes.)*

Answer

Applying Economic Principles Possible answers: The price of helium could continue to increase, limiting or stopping important scientific research, especially if there are no suitable alternative sources, or if new sources are expensive to tap. It could also affect the price of goods and services in which helium is used in production or operation.

Have students complete the Self-Test Online and continue their work in the **Essential Questions Journal**.

REMEDIATION AND SUGGESTIONS

Use the chart below to help students who are struggling with content.

WEAKNESS	REMEDIATION
Defining key terms (Questions 3, 4, 5)	Have students use the interactive Economic Dictionary Online.
Understanding the effect of changing input costs on supply curves (Questions 1, 2, 6, 7)	Have students outline the discussion under the heading Input Costs.
Identify government actions that affect the supply curve (Questions 1, 3, 4, 5, 7, 8)	Have students work in pairs to quiz each other on the topic.
Understanding why production facilities are located in certain regions (Question 9)	Reteach the section on Where Do Firms Produce, emphasizing the importance for both the firm that produces tomato sauce and the firm that bottles soft drinks to reduce costs.

Answer

Checkpoint when transportation costs are high

Where Do Firms Produce?

So far, we have ignored the issue of where firms locate their production facilities. For many firms, the key factor is the cost of transportation—the cost of transporting inputs to a production facility and the cost of transporting the finished product to consumers. One firm will locate close to input suppliers when inputs, such as raw materials, are expensive to transport. Another firm will locate close to its consumers when output is more costly to transport.

Consider the example of a firm that processes tomatoes into tomato sauce. Suppose that the firm uses seven tons of tomatoes to produce one ton of sauce. The firm locates its plant close to the tomato fields—and far from its consumers—because it is much cheaper to ship one ton of sauce to consumers than to ship seven tons of tomatoes to a faraway plant. Tomato sauce producers cluster in places like California's Central Valley, where weather and soil conditions are favorable for the growing of tomatoes.

Now consider the example of a firm that bottles soft drinks. The firm combines concentrated syrup with local water, so the firm's output (bottled drinks) weighs more than its transportable input (syrup). As a result, the firm locates close to its consumers—and far from its syrup supplier—because the firm saves more on transporting soft drinks than it pays to transport its syrup. In general, if a firm's output is bulky or perishable, the firm will locate close to its consumers.

Other firms locate close to inputs that cannot be transported at all. Some firms are pulled toward concentrations of specialized workers such as artists, engineers, and computer programmers. Other firms are pulled toward locations with low energy costs. Many firms locate in cities because of the rich variety of workers and business services available in urban areas.

CHECKPOINT ***When is a firm likely to locate close to its consumers?***

SECTION 3 ASSESSMENT

Essential Questions Journal To continue to build a response to the Essential Question, go to your **Essential Questions Journal.**

Guiding Question

1. Use your completed table to answer this question: Why does the supply curve shift?
2. **Extension** Give an example of how a change in the number of suppliers has changed the supply of a good or service.

Key Terms and Main Ideas

3. What is a **subsidy,** and how do subsidies affect the supply curve?
4. What is an **excise tax,** and how do excise taxes affect the supply curve?
5. What effect do **regulations** have on the supply curve? Why?

Critical Thinking

6. **Apply (a)** Suppose the United States buys most of its bananas from a particular country. If that country suffered a drought, what would happen to the supply curve for bananas? **(b)** What response by American companies would shift the curve in the opposite direction?
7. **Apply** Analyze and explain the impact on the supply curve for American-made computers from each of the following events: **(a)** The government places an excise tax on laptops, **(b)** An engineer invents a way to produce desktop cases more cheaply, **(c)** European countries end an import quota on American-made computers.
8. **Judge** If regulation increases price and decreases supply, why does the government issue regulations?
9. **Analyze (a)** Why would an automaker want to have manufacturing plants in several different regions? **(b)** Why would a software company not necessarily want facilities in several different regions?

Quick Write

10. In the past, animated movies were created by teams of artists drawing and coloring illustrations by hand. Now, many animation companies use computers to create these movies. Write a brief paragraph explaining what effect that change will have on the supply curve of animated movies.

Assessment Answers

1. Possible responses: due to rising or falling production costs, government action, changes in the global economy, expectations about future prices, number of suppliers
2. Possible response: falling prices of cellular phone plans or electronic gadgets as more suppliers enter market
3. government payments that support firms producing a good; subsidies usually increase supply by encouraging production
4. tax on production or sale of good; reduces supply
5. reduce supply because they increase marginal costs
6. (a) Supply curve would shift to the left, reflecting lower supply. (b) buying bananas from other countries
7. (a) Manufacturers would make fewer laptops and the curve would shift to the left, reducing supply. (b) New technology reduces costs and the curve would shift to the right, increasing supply. (c) New markets cause the curve to shift to the right, increasing supply.
8. Possible responses: Government wants to ensure that businesses do not take actions that can harm public health or safety or endanger workers.
9. (a) because it would be close to consumers and so reduce transportation costs (b) because transportation costs would be low, and centralized operating would probably cost less
10. Essays will vary, but students might say that computer animation would cut costs and increase supply, shifting the supply curve to the right.

QUICK STUDY GUIDE

QUICK STUDY GUIDE

Chapter 5: Supply

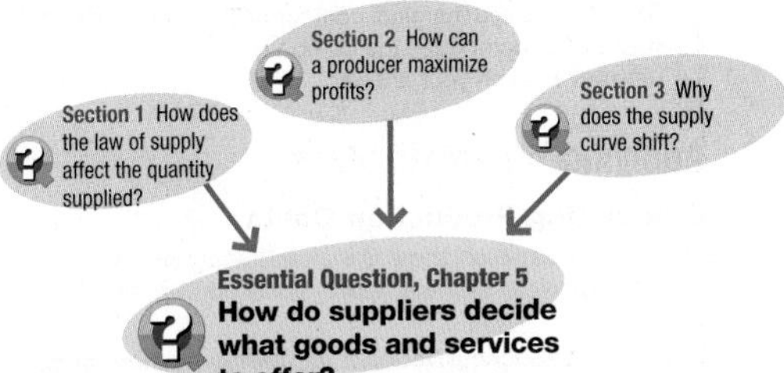

Section 1 How does the law of supply affect the quantity supplied?
Section 2 How can a producer maximize profits?
Section 3 Why does the supply curve shift?

Essential Question, Chapter 5
How do suppliers decide what goods and services to offer?

Costs of Production

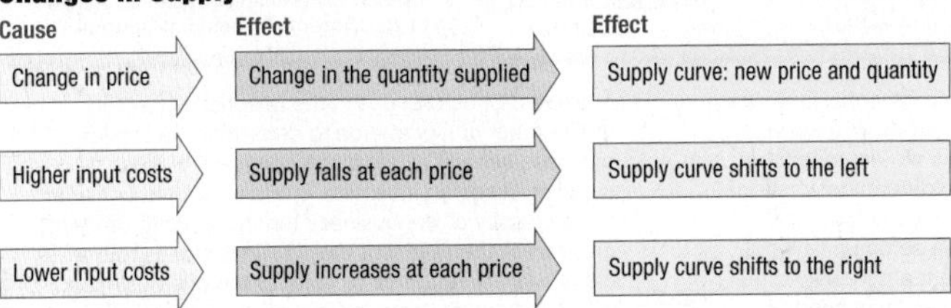

Marginal Product of Labor	Production Costs	Marginal Cost and Marginal Revenue
• Marginal product of labor: the change in output from hiring one more worker. • Increasing marginal returns: increased output per worker. • Diminishing marginal returns: additional workers produce less output.	• Fixed costs do not change, no matter how much of a good is produced. • Variable costs rise or fall depending on the quantity produced. • Fixed costs plus variable costs equal total cost.	• Marginal cost: the additional cost of producing one more unit. • Marginal revenue: the additional income from selling one more unit. • Most profitable level of output: marginal revenue equals marginal cost.

Economic Dictionary

supply, *p. 109*
law of supply, *p. 109*
quantity supplied, *p. 109*
supply schedule, *p. 112*
variable, *p. 112*
market supply schedule, *p. 112*
supply curve, *p. 113*
market supply curve, *p. 113*
elasticity of supply, *p. 113*
marginal product of labor, *p. 116*
increasing marginal returns, *p. 117*
diminishing marginal returns, *p. 117*
fixed cost, *p. 118*
variable cost, *p. 118*
total cost, *p. 119*
marginal cost, *p. 119*
marginal revenue, *p. 120*
average cost, *p. 121*
operating cost, *p. 122*
subsidy, *p. 124*
excise tax, *p. 124*
regulation, *p. 125*

Changes in Supply

Cause	Effect	Effect
Change in price	Change in the quantity supplied	Supply curve: new price and quantity
Higher input costs	Supply falls at each price	Supply curve shifts to the left
Lower input costs	Supply increases at each price	Supply curve shifts to the right

Economics on the go

Study anytime, anywhere. Download these files today.

Economic Dictionary online	Audio Review online	Action Graph online	Visual Glossary online	How the Economy Works online
Vocabulary Support in English and Spanish	Audio Study Guide in English and Spanish	Animated Charts and Graphs	Animated feature	Animated feature

Download to your computer or mobile device at PearsonSuccessNet.com

ASSIGN THE ESSENTIAL QUESTIONS JOURNAL

After students have finished studying the chapter, they should return to the chapter's essential question in the Essential Questions Journal and complete the activity.

Tell students to go back to the chapter opener and look at the image. Using the information they have gained from studying the chapter, ask **How does this illustrate the main ideas of the chapter?** *(Possible answers: It reflects the law of supply, higher production, market entry; or the quantity supplied: how much of a good a producer is willing and able to sell at a specific price.)*

STUDY TIPS

Remind students that they will grasp and retain material better if they study it actively—asking questions and looking for answers and finding ways to apply the principles discussed—than if they simply memorize concepts. In addition, they will master the material more fully if they study and review over several days than if they try to cram all their study time into the night before an exam.

Economics on the go Have students download the digital resources available on Economics on the Go for review and remediation.

Assessment at a Glance

TESTS AND QUIZZES

Section Assessments

Section Quizzes A and B, **Unit 2 All-in-One**
Self-Test Online

Chapter Assessments

Chapter Tests A and B, **Unit 2 All-in-One**
Economic Detective, **Unit 2 All-in-One**
Document-based Assessment, p. 131
Exam*View*

AYP Monitoring Assessments

PERFORMANCE ASSESSMENT

Teacher's Edition, pp. 113, 119, 120, 125, 126
Simulation Activities, Chapter 5
Virtual Economics on CD-ROM, pp. 113, 118, 125
Essential Questions Journal, Chapter 5
Assessment Rubrics

Chapter 5 Assessment

1. Possible answers: (a) easy-entry industries, such as hair salons, restaurants, or landscaping services (b) industries with high barriers to entry, such as oil refining and auto manufacturing
2. (a) The individual supply schedule lists how much of a good a *single* supplier will offer at various prices, whereas the market supply schedule will list the same data for *all* suppliers. (b) supply curve is the supply schedule data plotted on a graph (c) supply curve shows how price increases are accompanied by increase in supply, which is predicted by the law of supply.
3. (a) The supply of cable shows would decrease. (b) Higher fees are a change in supply: an increase in the fees paid by cable companies for network television will cause a decrease in the supply of cable television programs at all price levels because cable television shows will become more expensive to produce.
4. Possible answers: (a) fixed costs: rent for the shop and equipment; variable costs: electricity, salaries, and supplies (b) by adding up the money the shop makes from repairing shoes
5. (a) The marginal costs are $5 for 1 unit; $4 for 2 units; $3 for 3 units; $2 for 4 units; and $3 for 5 units. (b) Diminishing returns set in at 5 units, when the marginal cost begins to rise.
6. (a) $4,000 a month (b) Variable costs in April and May are $5,000; they go up $1,000 in each of the next two-month periods. (c) Total costs go from $9,000 to $10,000, then to $11,000.
7. In both April and May, Sal's revenues are less than total costs, but revenues are greater than his operating costs. Since he can cover his operating costs, he should stay open.
8. In July and August, he makes $1,000 profit.
9. Possible answer: Sal's total revenues are $60,000, as are his total costs. He needs to cut costs, raise prices, or take some other steps to make his business profitable.
10. You may choose to give students an example of the two types of articles they are to read a few days before they are to complete this activity, and then have students find and read two articles.
11. (a) Students will calculate the elasticity of supply for their good or service. (b) Students will identify the fixed and variable costs for their good or service. (c) Possible response: If my product were a new cell phone, the government might require me to provide a hands-free headset with the phone because of concern over safety while driving.

CHAPTER 5 ASSESSMENT

Self-Test online To test your understanding of key terms and main ideas, visit **PearsonSuccessNet.com**

Key Terms and Main Ideas

To make sure you understand the key terms and main ideas of this chapter, review the Checkpoint and Section Assessment questions and look at the Quick Study Guide on the preceding page.

Critical Thinking

1. **Give Examples (a)** Give two examples of industries that would draw new firms into the market if profits of existing businesses rose. **(b)** Give two examples of industries that would see fewer new firms enter the market, even if profits rose.
2. **Recognize (a)** What is the difference between an individual supply schedule and a market supply schedule? **(b)** How does a supply curve relate to a supply schedule? **(c)** How does a supply curve reflect the law of supply?
3. **Predict (a)** Suppose television networks raise the fees that cable television systems must pay to show their programs. How would that affect the supply of programs for cable television? **(b)** Are higher fees a change in the quantity supplied or a change in supply? Explain.
4. **Apply (a)** Suppose you open a shoe repair shop. What fixed and variable costs would you have? **(b)** How would you calculate total revenue?

5. **Determine (a)** A company has the following total costs: 1 unit: $5, 2 units: $9, 3 units: $12, 4 units: $14, 5 units: $17. What is the marginal cost for each number of units? **(b)** At what point does the company see diminishing returns? Explain your answer.

Applying Your Math Skills

Calculating Production Costs

Study the information about Sal's Ice Cream Shop in the chart below. Note: Monthly supply costs apply to each month.

Visit PearsonSuccessNet.com for additional math help.

Monthly Costs
Rent: $2,000
Manager's salary: $2,000
Workers' wages: $3,000
Supplies (April and May): $2,000
Supplies (June and September): $3,000
Supplies (July and August): $4,000

Expected Revenues
April: $8,000
May: $8,000
June: $10,000
July: $12,000
August: $12,000
September: $10,000

6. The manager has a contract that requires Sal to pay his salary. **(a)** How much does Sal pay in fixed costs? **(b)** How much does he pay in variable costs? **(c)** What are Sal's total costs?
7. Should Sal close the ice cream shop in April or May? Why or why not?
8. In what months does Sal earn a profit? How much does he make?
9. Should Sal take steps to change the way he does business? Explain your answer.

Essential Question Activity

Essential Questions Journal To respond to the chapter Essential Question, go to your **Essential Questions Journal.**

10. Complete the activity to answer the Essential Question **How do suppliers decide what goods and services to offer?** For this activity, students will act as market researchers and conduct a poll to determine what one good or service their community needs most. Each student will poll three people in the community (family, friends, or other students) to have them identify the one good or service that best serves local needs. When the poll is completed, the class will separate poll results into five different categories: entertainment, food establishments, medical services, recreational facilities, and other. Use the worksheet in your Essential Questions Journal or the electronic worksheet available at **PearsonSuccessNet.com,** for instructions on how to conduct the poll.
11. **Modify** Students will form five marketing groups based on the poll categories. Each group will use poll results from one category to create a description of a business that supplies a good or service that satisfies the need of the *greater number* of people in the community. Note that two ideas could be combined to create one business. Check listings in the telephone directory or Chamber of Commerce to determine if a similar business already exists in the community. Since a supplier needs an incentive, students should consider the necessity of the business turning a profit. Student groups will then present their business ideas to the class and ask students to vote for the one business plan from the five categories that is most likely to be successful. After students have made their selections, have them answer the following questions:
    (a) Why do you think the business you chose would have a greater chance of success?
    (b) Can you identify some fixed or variable costs for this business?
    (c) How might the government regulate this good or service?
    As a final exercise, present the choices from the original poll to a different class. Ask those students to vote on the product or service they think would benefit the majority of people in the community.

WebQuest online The Economics WebQuest challenges students to use 21st century skills to answer the essential question.

Remind students to continue to develop an Essential Questions video. Guidelines and a production binder are available at www.PearsonSuccessNet.com.

DOCUMENT-BASED ASSESSMENT

Should the government subsidize ethanol production?

The government pays subsidies to companies that produce ethanol, a fuel made from corn. In recent years, ethanol production has increased rapidly. Critics say that the subsidies are a waste of money, that corn-based ethanol cannot supply enough energy to reduce oil imports, and that using food crops for fuel causes other problems.

Document A

Uses of U.S. Corn Crop, 2006 and 2017

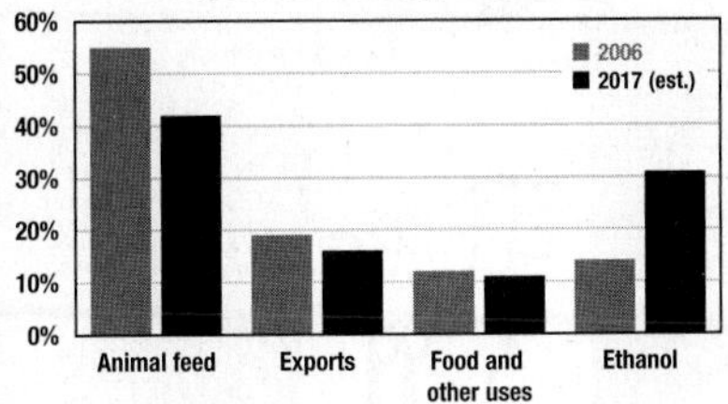

SOURCE: USDA Agricultural Projections

Document B

With crude oil soaring to nearly $78 a barrel last year, the price of alternatives to gasoline soared as well. . . . The federal incentive for ethanol is a tax break of 51 cents a gallon. Last year, more than 5.3 billion gallons were produced. . . . President Bush is urging Congress and the nation's biofuels industry to accelerate the use of ethanol to curb gasoline consumption by 20 percent by 2017. . . . A big difference won't come about until refiners start turning corn stalks, wheat straw, wood chips and grasses into ethanol.

—*The Dallas Morning News*, January 30, 2007

Document C

In the United States, the explosive growth of the biofuels sector and its demand for raw stocks of plants has triggered run-ups in the prices not only of corn, other grains, and oilseeds, but also of [other] crops and products. . . . In Minnesota, land diverted to corn to feed the ethanol maw is reducing the acreage planted to a wide range of other crops, especially soybeans. Food processors with contracts with farmers to grow crops such as peas and sweet corn have been forced to pay higher prices to keep their supplies secure. Eventually, these costs will appear in the prices of frozen and canned vegetables. Rising feed prices are also hitting the livestock and poultry industries.

—*Issues in Science and Technology*, September 22, 2007

ANALYZING DOCUMENTS

Use your knowledge of subsidies and Documents A, B, and C to answer questions 1–3.

1. **Document A shows that as more corn is used for ethanol,**
   - **A.** more will also be used for animal feed.
   - **B.** exports of corn will increase.
   - **C.** corn for food and other uses will drop slightly.
   - **D.** the price of corn will rise.

2. **Document B explains that the subsidy for ethanol production**
   - **A.** is $78 a barrel.
   - **B.** is 51 cents a gallon.
   - **C.** is going up by 20 percent.
   - **D.** plays little role in ethanol production.

3. **Document C shows that the ethanol boom**
   - **A.** results in higher food prices.
   - **B.** drives farmers to grow soybeans.
   - **C.** forces corn prices down.
   - **D.** is likely to end by 2017.

WRITING ABOUT ECONOMICS

Whether to support ethanol production or not is an ongoing issue. Use the documents on this page and resources on the Web site below to answer the question: ***Should the government subsidize ethanol production?*** Use the sources to support your opinion.

In Partnership

THE WALL STREET JOURNAL.
CLASSROOM EDITION

To read more about issues related to this topic, visit **PearsonSuccessNet.com**

Document-Based Assessment

ANALYZING DOCUMENTS

1. C
2. B
3. A

WRITING ABOUT ECONOMICS

Possible answer: Advantages of ethanol subsidies: cuts reliance on foreign oil. Disadvantages of ethanol subsidies: contributes to rising food prices.

Student essay should demonstrate an understanding of the issues involved in the debate. Use the following as guidelines to assess the essay.

L2 Differentiate Students use all documents on the page to support their thesis.

L3 Differentiate Students use the documents on this page and additional information available online at www.PearsonSuccessNet.com to support their answer.

L4 Differentiate Students incorporate information provided in the textbook and online at www.PearsonSuccessNet.com and include additional research to support their opinion.

Go Online to www.PearsonSuccessNet.com for a student rubric and extra documents.

Economics online *All print resources are available on the Teacher's Resource Library CD-ROM and online at* www.PearsonSuccessNet.com.

 **Essential Questions**

UNIT 2:

Who benefits from the free market economy?

CHAPTER 6:

What is the right price?

Introduce the Chapter

ACTIVATE PRIOR KNOWLEDGE

In this chapter, students will learn how the price of a good or service is determined. Tell students to complete the warmup activity in the **Essential Questions Journal**.

DIFFERENTIATED INSTRUCTION KEY

- **L1** Special Needs
- **L2** Basic
  - **ELL** English Language Learners
  - **LPR** Less Proficient Readers
- **L3** All Students
- **L4** Advanced Students

Economics online Visit www.PearsonSuccessNet.com for an interactive textbook with built-in activities on economic principles.

- ***The Wall Street Journal* Classroom Edition Video** presents a current topic related to prices.
- **Yearly Update Worksheet** provides an annual update, including a new worksheet and lesson on this topic.
- **On the Go** resources can be downloaded so students and teachers can connect with economics anytime, anywhere.

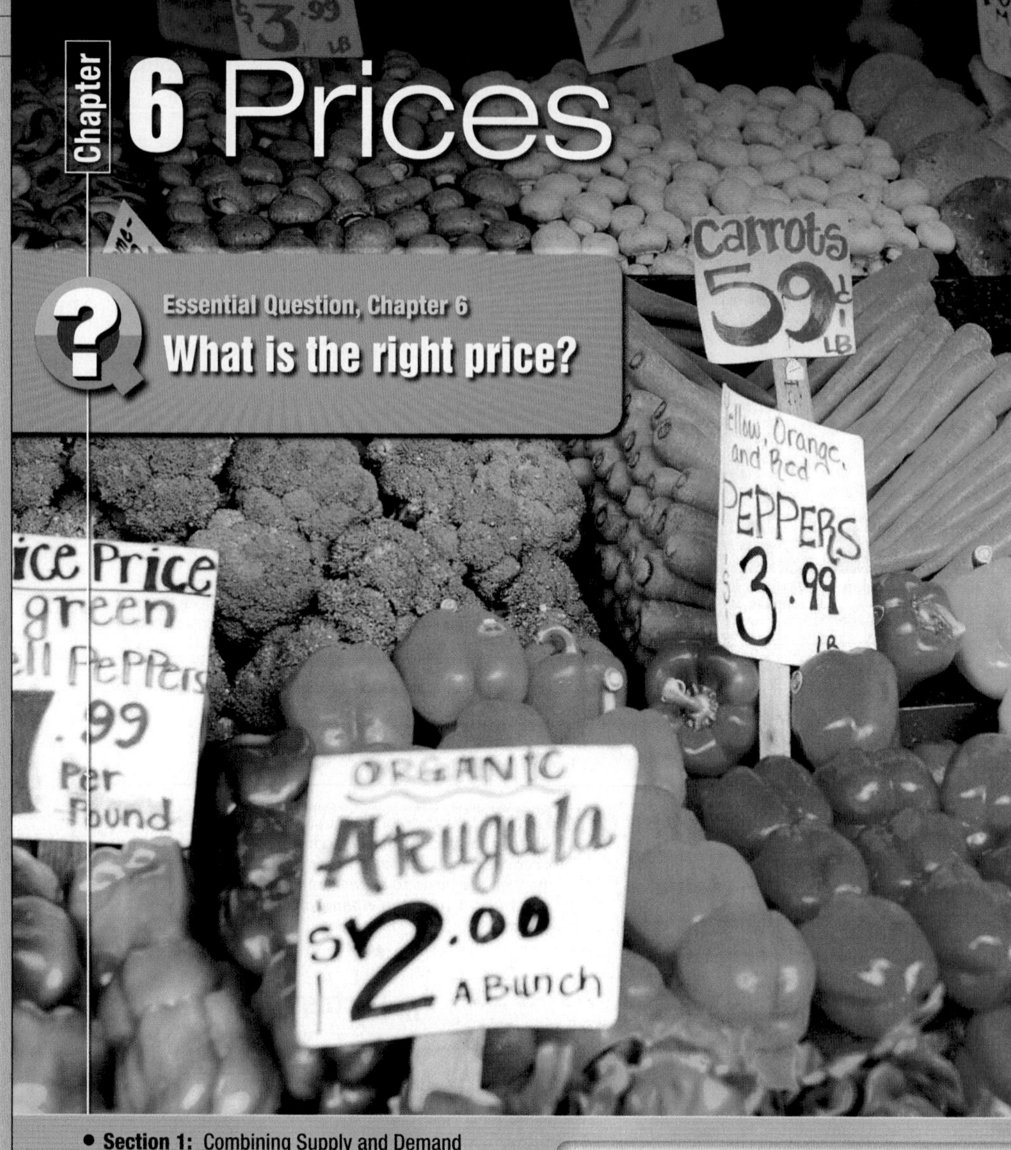

Chapter 6 Prices

Essential Question, Chapter 6

What is the right price?

- **Section 1:** Combining Supply and Demand
- **Section 2:** Changes in Market Equilibrium
- **Section 3:** The Role of Prices

Economics on the go

To study anywhere, anytime, download these online resources at ***PearsonSuccessNet.com*** ▶

ECONOMICS ONLINE

DIGITAL TEACHER TOOLS

The online lesson planner is designed to help teachers plan, teach, and assess. Teachers have the ability to use or customize existing Pearson lesson plans. Online lecture notes support the print lesson by providing an array of accessible activities and summaries of key concepts.

Two interactivities in this lesson are:

- **How the Economy Works** An interactive feature that allows students to explore the effects of shortages and surpluses on a market.
- **Action Graphs** Animated graphs illustrate the relationship between supply and demand.

Block Scheduling

BLOCK 1 Teach Sections 1 and 2 lessons, omitting the Bellringer activities, their follow-up discussion, and the Extend options.

BLOCK 2 Teach Section 3 lesson, including the extend options.

Pressed for Time

Group work Organize the class into three groups, assigning each group a section from the chapter. Have each group create a presentation detailing the main points of the assigned section. As groups give their presentations, create a study guide on the board outlining each section's main points.

SECTION 1 Combining Supply and Demand

OBJECTIVES

1. **Explain** how supply and demand create equilibrium in the marketplace.
2. **Describe** what happens to prices when equilibrium is disturbed.
3. **Identify** two ways that the government intervenes in markets to control prices.
4. **Analyze** the impact of price ceilings and price floors on a free market.

ECONOMIC DICTIONARY

As you read the section, look for the definitions of these **Key Terms:**

- equilibrium
- disequilibrium
- shortage
- surplus
- price ceiling
- rent control
- price floor
- minimum wage

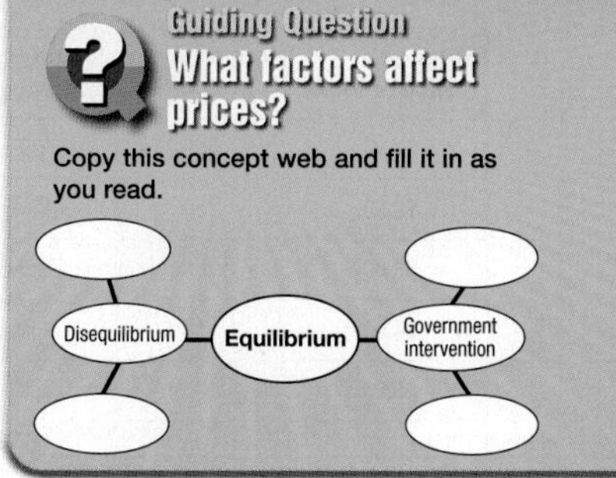

Guiding Question
What factors affect prices?
Copy this concept web and fill it in as you read.
Disequilibrium
Equilibrium
Government intervention

Economics and You When you go to the store to buy something—whether it's a cellphone, a CD, or a pair of sneakers—you can usually find it. You are benefiting from the free market system at work. Businesses are making enough profit to produce and sell the goods you want at a price you are willing to pay.

Principles in Action Prices are affected by the laws of supply and demand and by government action. Using the market for pizza as an example, you will see how free markets provide goods and services at the right price and in sufficient quantities. You will also see examples of how government intervention affects the wages of some workers and the rent that some people pay.

Reaching Equilibrium

Just as buyers and sellers come together in a market, what you have learned about demand and supply in previous chapters will come together in this section. Your knowledge of supply and demand will help you to understand how markets operate and how markets can turn competing interests into a positive outcome for both sides. You'll also see why free markets usually produce some of their best outcomes when they are left to operate on their own, free from government intervention.

We begin by looking at a supply and demand schedule. As you know, a demand schedule shows how much of a good consumers are willing to buy at various prices. A supply schedule shows how much firms are willing to sell at various prices. Comparing these schedules will help us to find common ground for the two sides of the market.

Visual Glossary online
Go to the Visual Glossary Online for an interactive review of **equilibrium.**

Action Graph online
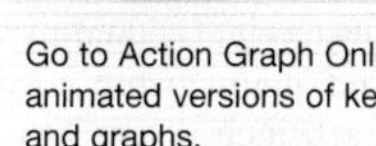
Go to Action Graph Online for animated versions of key charts and graphs.

How the Economy Works online
Go to How the Economy Works Online for an interactive lesson on **shortage** and **surplus.**

Guiding Question

What factors affect prices?

Get Started

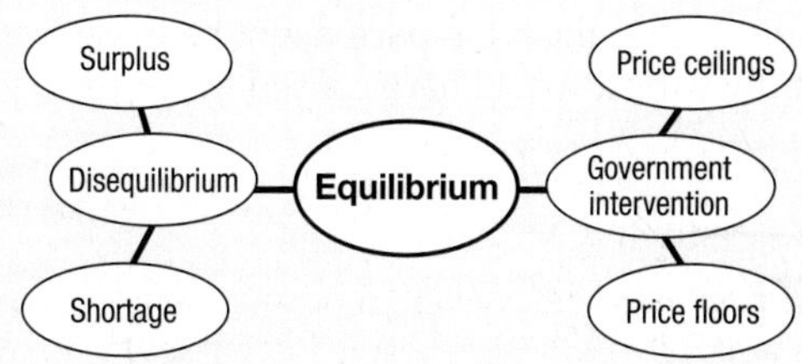

LESSON GOALS

Students will:

- Know the Key Terms.
- Provide examples to show understanding of how supply and demand affect the market price of a good (equilibrium).
- Describe what happens when equilibrium is disturbed.
- Graph supply and demand curves by taking a survey and transferring information gathered to graphs.
- Interpret the effects of government intervention on the free market by completing the "Understanding Price Controls" worksheet.

BEFORE CLASS

Students should read the section for homework before coming to class.

Have students complete the graphic organizer in the Section Opener as they read the text. As an alternate activity, have students complete the Guided Reading and Review worksheet (Unit 2 All-in-One, p. 89).

L1 L2 ELL LPR Differentiate Have students complete the Guided Reading and Review worksheet (Unit 2 All-in-One, p. 90).

Focus on the Basics

Students need to come away with the following understandings:

FACTS: • Equilibrium is the point of balance at which the quantity demanded equals the quantity supplied. • Price is determined by supply and demand. • Prices change when supply and/or demand changes. • The government may establish price ceilings or price floors to control prices. • Government intervention may cause market disequilibrium.

GENERALIZATION: Supply and demand create an equilibrium in the market. This equilibrium can be disturbed by changes in either supply, demand, or by government intervention.

CLASSROOM HINTS

COMBINING SUPPLY AND DEMAND

Some students may struggle with the combination of the supply and demand curves on one graph. On an overhead transparency, draw the *y*-axis (vertical) and label it "Price," and then the *x*-axis (horizontal) with the label "Quantity." Use the data from the supply and demand schedule on page 134 to add the scale to each axis. Using two more transparencies, draw the supply line on one and the demand line on the other. Overlay the three transparencies on an overhead projector and move the lines around to demonstrate changes in supply, demand, and price. You can also use the overlays to demonstrate elasticity.

BELLRINGER

Display the "Setting Prices" transparency (Color Transparencies, 6.a) to prompt a discussion of price changes.

Ask students to jot down in their notebooks for each of these items when they think its price might be the highest, when they think the price might be lowest, and what they think would have caused the price change.

Teach

Economics online To present this topic using digital resources, use the lecture notes at www.PearsonSuccessNet.com.

L1 L2 ELL LPR Differentiate To help students who are struggling readers, assign the Vocabulary worksheet (Unit 2 All-in-One, p. 88).

DISCUSS

Have students share their ideas from the Bellringer activity. Using the Idea Wave strategy (p. T24), have students offer their ideas about why prices differ at different points in time. Ask students to review the determinants of price. *(supply and demand)* Ask students to recall items that go on sale after the season in which they are used. *(sweaters, beach towels)* What happens to the prices when the demand drops?

Bring into the discussion what the students have learned about elasticity and shifts in demand and supply from previous chapters.

Ask **How is price determined?** *(Price is determined when supply equals demand.)* **What is the result of change in demand or supply?** *(The price changes.)*

Be sure that students understand how the factors work together and influence one another.

VISUAL GLOSSARY

Have students look at the political cartoon on the Visual Glossary. Ask them for other ways they would illustrate the concept of equilibrium.

L1 L2 Differentiate Use the lesson on the Visual Glossary page to review this term. As an alternate activity, direct students to the Visual Glossary Online to reinforce understanding of equilibrium.

(lesson continued on p. 136)

Answers

Graph Skills 1. 150 slices 2. 200 slices

Checkpoint at the point where the demand curve and the supply curve intersect

Figure 6.1 Finding Equilibrium

Combined Supply and Demand Schedule

Price of a Slice of Pizza	Quantity Demanded	Quantity Supplied	Result
$1.00	300	100	Shortage from excess demand
$2.00	250	150	
$3.00	200	200	Equilibrium
$4.00	150	250	Surplus from excess supply
$5.00	100	300	
$6.00	50	350	

GRAPH SKILLS

Market equilibrium will be found at the price at which the quantity demanded is equal to the quantity supplied.

1. How many slices are sold at $2.00 a slice?
2. How many slices are sold at equilibrium?

Supply and Demand Meet

The point where demand and supply come together is called the equilibrium. **Equilibrium** is the point of balance at which the quantity demanded equals the quantity supplied. At equilibrium, the market for a good is stable.

To find the equilibrium price and quantity, simply look for the price at which the quantity supplied equals the quantity demanded. In the combined supply and demand schedule for a pizza market in **Figure 6.1**, this occurs at a price of $3.00 per slice.

As you know, supply and demand schedules can be graphed. Look at the three graphs in the Visual Glossary on the next page. The first two graphs are the supply curve and the demand curve for pizza slices from the last two chapters. The third graph, Finding Equilibrium, combines the first two graphs. This graph shows both the number of slices that consumers in a market will buy at various prices and the number of slices that pizzerias will supply.

To find the equilibrium price and quantity on the graph, locate the point at which the supply curve and the demand curve intersect. At that point, quantity supplied equals quantity demanded. As you can see, the supply and demand curves intersect at $3.00 per slice. At that price and only at that price, the quantity demanded and the quantity supplied are equal, at 200 slices per day. At that price, the market is in a state of equilibrium.

equilibrium the point at which the demand for a product or service is equal to the supply of that product or service

disequilibrium any price or quantity not at equilibrium; when quantity supplied is not equal to quantity demanded in a market

shortage when quantity demanded is more than quantity supplied

Market Benefits

In any market, supply and demand will be equal at only one price and one quantity. At this equilibrium price, buyers will purchase exactly as much of a good as firms are willing to sell.

Buyers who are willing to purchase goods at the equilibrium price will find ample supplies on store shelves. Firms that sell at the equilibrium price will find enough buyers for their goods. When a market is at equilibrium, both buyers and sellers benefit.

CHECKPOINT ***At what point on a combined supply and demand graph is the market at equilibrium?***

Disequilibrium

If the market price or quantity supplied is anywhere but at the equilibrium, the market is in a state of disequilibrium. **Disequilibrium** occurs when quantity supplied is not equal to quantity demanded in a market. In **Figure 6.1**, or in the Finding Equilibrium graph in the Visual Glossary, disequilibrium occurs at any price other than $3.00 per slice, or any quantity other than 200 slices. Disequilibrium can produce one of two outcomes: shortage or surplus.

Shortage

The problem of **shortage**—also known as excess demand—exists when the quantity demanded in a market is more than the quantity supplied. When the actual price in a market is below the equilibrium price, you have a shortage, because the low price encourages buyers and discourages sellers. For example, in **Figure 6.1**, a price of $2.00 per slice of pizza will lead to a quantity demanded of 250 slices per day but a quantity supplied of only 150 slices per day. At this price, there is a shortage of 100 slices per day.

134 PRICES

Differentiated Resources

- **L1 L2 Guided Reading and Review** (Unit 2 All-in-One, p. 90)
- **L1 L2 Vocabulary worksheet** (Unit 2 All-in-One, p. 88)
- **L2 Understanding Price Ceilings** (Unit 2 All-in-One, p. 92)
- **L4 The Minimum Wage Vision** (Unit 2 All-in-One, p. 93)

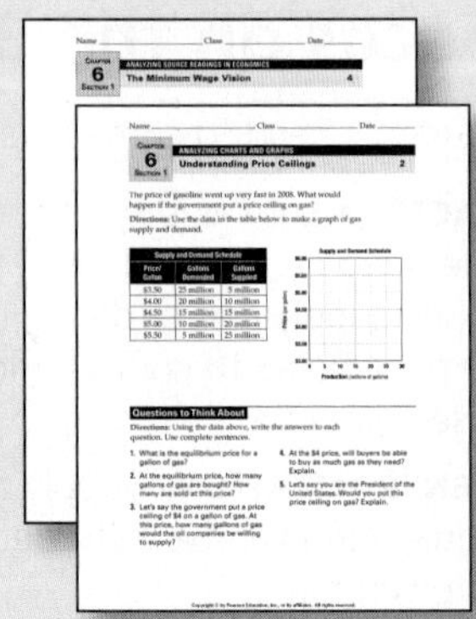

VISUAL GLOSSARY

Reviewing Key Terms
To understand *equilibrium*, review these terms:

market, *p. 29*
law of demand, *p. 85*
demand curve, *p. 89*
law of supply, *p. 109*
supply curve, *p. 113*

What is Equilibrium?

◀ **equilibrium** the point at which the demand for a product or service is equal to the supply of that product or service

DEMAND CURVE

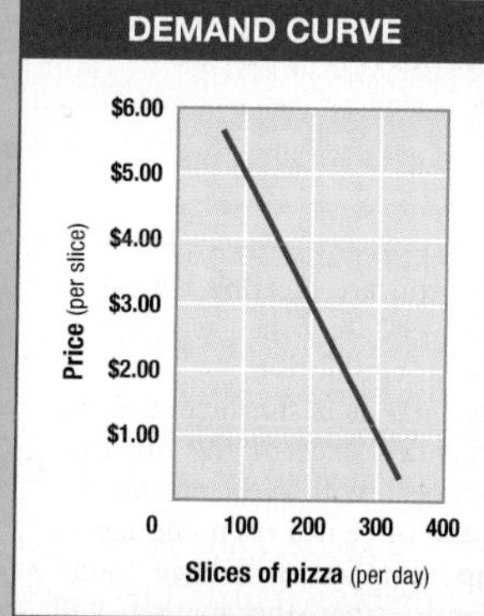

The **law of demand** says that buyers will purchase more of a certain product if the price is lower.

SUPPLY CURVE

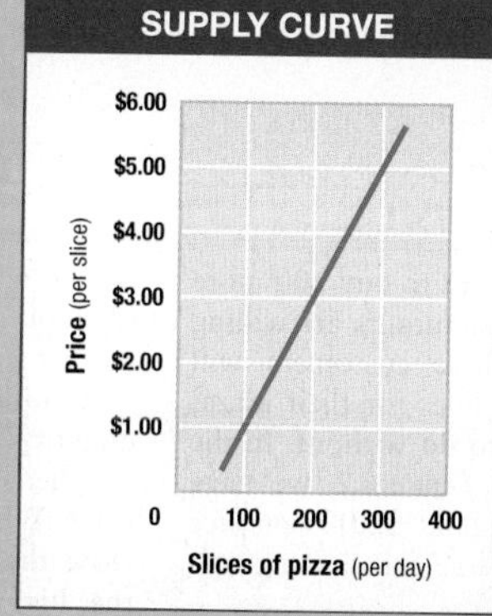

The **law of supply** says that suppliers will offer more of a certain product if the price is higher.

FINDING EQUILIBRIUM

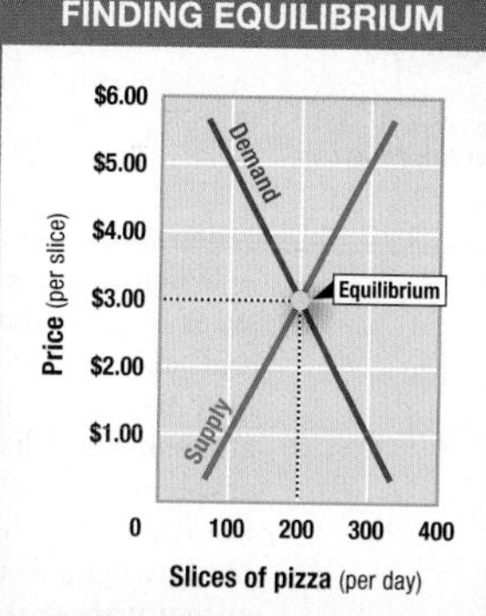

When supply equals demand, the market has reached **equilibrium**, or balance. ***At the point of equilibrium, how many slices will the pizzeria supply at what price?***

◀ This cartoon shows the concept of equilibrium as it applies to the real estate market. ***How does this cartoon show the relationship of supply and demand? What will happen to the market if supply becomes stronger than demand?***

Visual Glossary online
To expand your understanding of this and other key economic terms, visit **PearsonSuccessNet.com**

Teach Visual Glossary

REVIEW KEY TERMS

Pair students and have them write the definitions of the key terms related to the understanding of equilibrium.

market – *an arrangement that allows buyers and sellers to exchange things*

law of demand – *economic law that states that consumers buy more of a good when its price decreases and less when its price increases*

demand curve – *a graphic representation of a demand schedule*

law of supply – *tendency of suppliers to offer more of a good at a higher price*

supply curve – *a graph of the quantity of a good supplied at different prices*

CREATE A CONCEPT WEB

Students should understand the relationship between each of these key terms and *equilibrium*. Draw a concept web on the board, with the word *equilibrium* in the center circle. Draw five circles around the center circle and write one of these related terms in each of the surrounding circles. Ask students to explain the relationships between these terms and *equilibrium*.

L2 LPR Differentiate Remember to call on less proficient readers first when having students describe the connection between the words.

Have students use the Visual Glossary Online to reinforce their understanding of the term *equilibrium*.

L2 ELL Differentiate Have students explain the images in the cartoon. What is the man holding above his head? *(a level, which is a tool that shows whether something is straight or balanced by the position of an air bubble in a tube of liquid)* How does the tool illustrate the term *equilibrium*? *(It shows that when supply and demand are equally balanced, the tool is straight and balanced.)*

Economics online *All print resources are available on the Teacher's Resource Library CD-ROM and online at* www.PearsonSuccessNet.com.

Answers

Visual Glossary Graph 200 slices at $3.00 per slice

Political Cartoon The cartoon shows supply and demand struggling to reach equilibrium. If supply is stronger than demand, the price will go down.

CONTRAST GRAPHS

Have students look at the graphs in Figure 6.2 showing the effects of shortage and surplus on sales. Have them use the graphs to contrast and explain the differences between a shortage and a surplus. Explain that both of these graphs illustrate the term *disequilibrium. (Quantity supplied is not equal to quantity demanded.)* Ask **Why is it important that the market move back to equilibrium?** *(so that there is not an excess of supply or demand)*

Have students give their own examples of what causes a market to move to a state of disequilibrium.

L1 L2 Differentiate Have students recall that price is determined by the balance of supply and demand. Review with them what each line in the graphs represents. Ask **At what price of a slice of pizza is there a shortage of pizza?** *(any price less than $3)* **At what price is there a surplus?** *(any price over $3)* Point out that the surplus or shortage occurs at any price not at equilibrium.

CREATE SUPPLY AND DEMAND CURVES

Tell students that many producers do marketing surveys to see what consumers want and how much they will pay for it. Poll the class to create a combined supply and demand schedule on how much students will pay for a new DVD of a feature film. Use Figure 6.1 on page 134 as an example of a way to record the data. Then have half the students create a supply curve, and the other half create a demand curve. Then pair students to create a combined supply and demand curve.

Action Graph online Have students review the Action Graph animation for a step-by-step look at Shortage and Surplus.

Figure 6.2 Shortage and Surplus

GRAPH SKILLS

Shortage and surplus both lead to a market with fewer sales than at equilibrium.

1. How much is the shortage when pizza is sold at $2.00 per slice?
2. Based on the second graph, how might the pizzeria solve the problem of excess supply?

Action Graph online

For an animated version of this graph, visit **PearsonSuccessNet.com**

Shortage

Price (per slice): $6.00, $5.00, $4.00, $3.00, $2.00, $1.00, 0

Demand; Supply; Excess demand; Quantity supplied; Quantity demanded

Slices of pizza (per day): 50, 100, 150, 200, 250, 300, 350

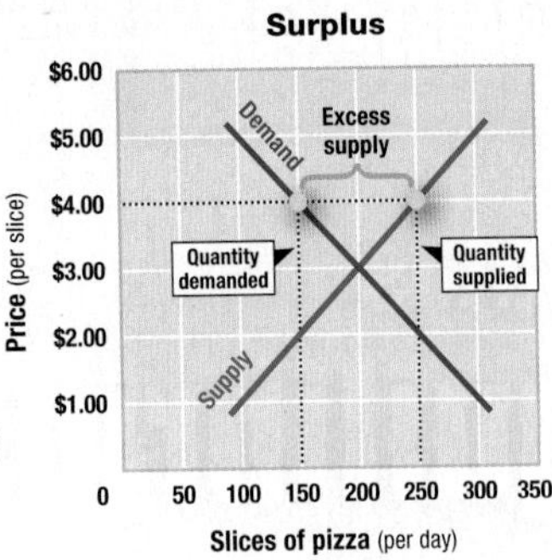

When customers want to buy 100 more slices of pizza than restaurants are willing and able to sell, these customers will have to wait in long lines for their pizza, and some will have to do without. In the graph on the left in **Figure 6.2**, we have illustrated the shortage at $2.00 per slice by drawing a dotted line across the graph at that price.

If you were running the pizzeria, and you noticed long lines of customers waiting to buy your pizza at $2.00 per slice, what would you do? Assuming that you like to earn profits, you would probably raise the price. As the price increased, you would be willing to work harder and bake more pizzas, because you would know you could earn more money for each slice you sell.

From Shortage to Equilibrium

Of course, as the price rises, customers will buy less pizza, since it is becoming relatively more expensive. When the price reaches $3.00 per slice, you will find that you are earning more profit and can keep up with demand, but the lines are much shorter. Some days you may throw out a few leftover slices, and other days you may have to throw an extra pizza or two in the oven to keep up with customers, but on the whole, you are meeting the needs of your customers. In other words, the market is now at equilibrium.

surplus when quantity supplied is more than quantity demanded

As long as there is a shortage and the quantity demanded exceeds the quantity supplied, suppliers will keep raising the price. When the price has risen enough to close the gap, suppliers will have found the highest price that the market will bear. They will continue to sell at that price until one of the factors described in Chapter 4 or Chapter 5 changes either the demand or the supply curve, and creates new pressures to raise or lower prices and, eventually, a new equilibrium.

Surplus

If the price is too high, the market will face the problem of surplus, also known as excess supply. A **surplus** exists when quantity supplied exceeds quantity demanded and the actual price of a good is higher than the equilibrium price. For example, at a price of $4.00 per slice of pizza, the quantity supplied of 250 slices per day is much greater than the quantity demanded of 150 slices per day. This means that pizzeria owners will be making 100 more slices of pizza each day than they can sell at that price.

Background Note

Supply and Demand An everyday example of how supply and demand affect price can be found at your neighborhood movie theater. Theaters typically charge full price for tickets to evening movies and offer lower-priced tickets for daytime screenings of the same movies. The supply of seats remains the same, but the number of potential moviegoers is far fewer since many people are at work or school. By discounting tickets to matinees, theaters are trying to increase demand among those remaining persons who are available to go to a daytime movie.

Answers

Graph Skills 1. 100 slices 2. lower the price and produce fewer slices

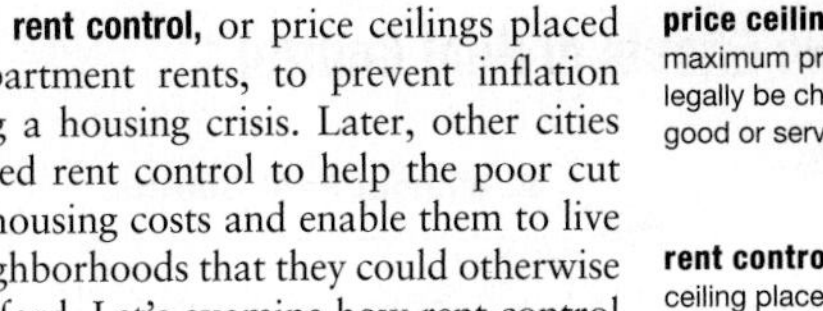

The relatively high price encourages zeria owners to make more pizza, but it courages customers from buying pizza, ce it is relatively more expensive than er menu items. Some customers will buy e slice instead of two, while others will eat ewhere. At the end of the day, it is likely t 100 slices will have to be thrown out.

om Surplus to Equilibrium

fore long, pizzeria owners will get tired throwing out unsold pizza and will cut ir prices. As the price falls, the quantity manded will rise, and more customers ll buy more pizza. At the same time, zeria owners will supply fewer pizzas. is process will continue until the price ches the equilibrium price of $3.00 per ce. At that price, the amount of pizza t pizzeria owners are willing and able to is exactly equal to the amount that their stomers are willing and able to buy.

Whenever the market is in disequilibrium d prices are flexible, market forces will sh the market toward the equilibrium. lers do not like to waste their resources a surplus, particularly when the goods nnot be stored for long, like pizza. And en there is a shortage, profit-seeking lers realize that they can raise prices to rn more profits. For these reasons, market ices move toward the equilibrium level.

CHECKPOINT *What market condition might cause a pizzeria owner to throw out many slices of pizza at the end of the day?*

rice Ceiling

arkets tend toward equilibrium, but some cases the government intervenes control prices. The government can pose a **price ceiling,** or a maximum price at can be legally charged for a good or rvice. The price ceiling is set below the uilibrium price.

nt Control

price ceiling is a maximum price, set law, that sellers can charge for a good service. The government places price ilings on some goods that are considered ssential" and might become too expen- ve for some consumers. For example, the early 1940s, New York City introduced **rent control,** or price ceilings placed on apartment rents, to prevent inflation during a housing crisis. Later, other cities imposed rent control to help the poor cut their housing costs and enable them to live in neighborhoods that they could otherwise not afford. Let's examine how rent control affects the quantity and quality of housing available to consumers.

The housing market data for a hypothetical city is shown in **Figure 6.3** on the next page. Look at Graph A. The supply and demand curves for two-bedroom apartments meet at point *a*, where the rental price is $900 a month. At this equilibrium rent, consumers will demand 30,000 apartments and suppliers will offer 30,000 apartments for rent.

Suppose that the city government passes a law that limits the rent on two-bedroom apartments to $600 per month. This price ceiling is below the equilibrium price. The effect on the market is shown in Graph B in **Figure 6.3.** At a price of $600, the quantity of apartments demanded is 45,000 (point *c*), and the quantity supplied is 15,000 (point *b*). At such a low price, apartments seem inexpensive. Many people will try to rent apartments instead of living with their families or investing in their own houses.

However, some landlords will have difficulty earning profits or breaking even at these low rents. Fewer new apartment buildings will be built,

price ceiling a maximum price that can legally be charged for a good or service

rent control a price ceiling placed on apartment rent

Restaurants and other businesses often donate surplus food to charities. In New York City, an organization called City Harvest collects and distributes food to community programs throughout the city. ***What other kinds of businesses might donate surplus food to charities?*** ▼

BRAINSTORM

Have students list products that they think might have an unfair price. On the board, list the items that students consider too high in price. *(music downloads, gasoline, car insurance, concert tickets, hair cuts)* or too low *(minimum wage, pay for certain kinds of jobs; in farming communities students may say certain food crops)*

DISCUSS

Ask **Should the government do something about these prices that some of you think are unfair?** Allow the class to discuss which items listed might warrant government regulations.

Ask students to identify examples of actual price ceilings and floors and provide some additional examples. *(Rent controls and "usury" law setting maximum interest rates on loans are examples of price ceilings; minimum wage and agricultural price supports are examples of price floors.)*

Remind students that cab fares in most cities are set by the local government. The fares establish both a ceiling—the maximum that taxis can charge per mile—and a floor—the minimum cost of the cab ride, before the taxi's meter begins to run. When the price of gasoline goes up, a cab driver may not be able to raise fares.

L1 L2 Differentiate Have students explain the meaning of the words *ceiling* and *floor* by pointing to each of these in the classroom. Discuss the meanings of *price floor* and *price ceiling*. Point out the figurative language in these terms. Ask students to explain why the terms are appropriate for the economic concepts they represent.

Answers

Checkpoint when the market demand is down, causing a surplus

Photo grocery stores, hotels, company cafeterias, wholesalers

EXPLAIN

Have students explain the difference between a price ceiling and a price floor. *(maximum price; minimum price)* Ask them for an example of each and why government sometimes sets price ceilings or price floors on goods or services. *(rent controls, minimum wage laws; to regulate prices when free market prices might be harmful to society)*

Discuss the impact of rent controls on the housing market. Ask students to explain why rent controls are sometimes imposed, and to summarize their benefits and drawbacks.

Distribute the "Understanding Price Controls" worksheet (Unit 2 All-in-One, p. 91). Tell students they will convert tabular data to construct a graph and interpret it to show how price ceilings create shortages. Review student answers.

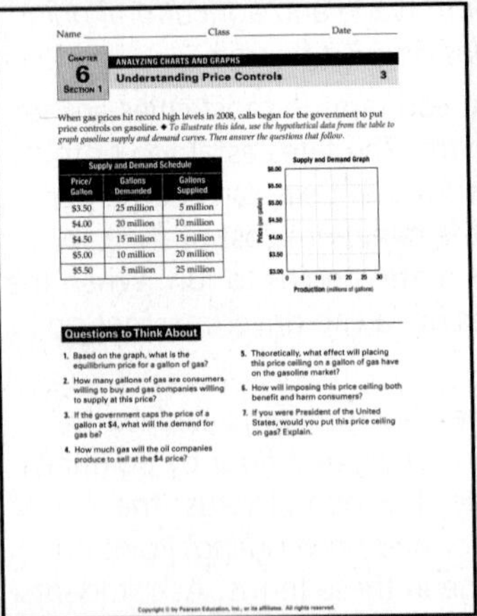

Name ____________ Class ____________ Date ________

CHAPTER 6 SECTION 1

ANALYZING CHARTS AND GRAPHS

Understanding Price Controls 3

When gas prices hit record high levels in 2008, calls began for the government to put price controls on gasoline. ◆ *To illustrate this idea, use the hypothetical data from the table to graph gasoline supply and demand curves. Then answer the questions that follow.*

Supply and Demand Schedule		
Price/Gallon	Gallons Demanded	Gallons Supplied
$3.50	25 million	5 million
$4.00	20 million	10 million
$4.50	15 million	15 million
$5.00	10 million	20 million
$5.50	5 million	25 million

Supply and Demand Graph

Questions to Think About

1. Based on the graph, what is the equilibrium price for a gallon of gas?
2. How many gallons of gas are consumers willing to buy and gas companies willing to supply at this price?
3. If the government caps the price of a gallon at $4, what will the demand for gas be?
4. How much gas will the oil companies produce to sell at the $4 price?
5. Theoretically, what effect will placing this price ceiling on a gallon of gas have on the gasoline market?
6. How will imposing this price ceiling both benefit and harm consumers?
7. If you were President of the United States, would you put this price ceiling on gas? Explain.

L2 Differentiate Distribute the "Understanding Price Ceilings" worksheet (Unit 2 All-in-One, p. 92). Work with students in a group to create the graph.

L4 Differentiate Assign the "The Minimum Wage Vision" worksheet (Unit 2 All-in-One, p. 93). Have students read the passage and answer the questions.

Action Graph online Have students review the Action Graph animations for a step-by-step look at The Effects of Rent Control and The Effects of Minimum Wage.

Answers

Graph Skills 1. $900 per month 2. Landlords are less likely to increase the supply of rentals when their profits are lower.

Figure 6.3 The Effects of Rent Control

GRAPH SKILLS

While rent control helps many tenants, it also creates disequilibrium in the housing market.

1. At what price is the market for apartments at equilibrium without rent control?
2. How does rent control lead to a shortage of desirable apartments?

Action Graph online

For an animated version of this graph, visit **PearsonSuccessNet.com**

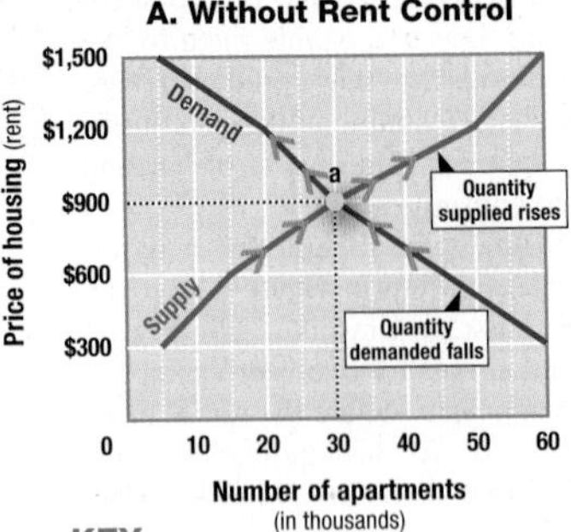

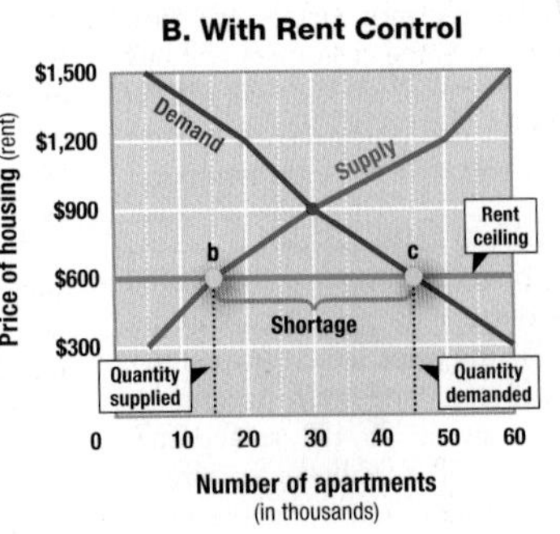

KEY

a. The supply and demand curves for two-bedroom apartments meet at the equilibrium rent of $900 per month.

b. With rent control keeping rents at $600 per month, landlords are willing to supply 15,000 two-bedroom apartments.

c. With rent control keeping rents at $600 per month, potential tenants are seeking 45,000 two-bedroom apartments.

and older ones might be converted into offices, stores, or condominiums. The result is a shortage of 30,000 apartments. The price ceiling increases the quantity demanded but decreases the quantity supplied. Since rents are not allowed to rise, this shortage will last as long as the price ceiling holds.

The Cost of Rent Control

When the price cannot rise to the equilibrium level, the market must determine which 15,000 of the 45,000 households will get an apartment, and which 30,000 will do without. Although governments usually pass rent control laws to help renters with the greatest need, few of these renters benefit from rent control. Methods besides prices—including long waiting lists, discrimination by landlords, a lottery system, and even bribery—may be used to allocate the scarce supply of apartments. Luck becomes an important factor, and sometimes the only way to get a rent-controlled apartment is to inherit it from a parent or grandparent.

In addition, since the rent controls limit landlords' profits, landlords may try to increase their income by cutting costs. Why should a landlord give a building a fresh coat of paint and a new garden if he or she can't earn the money back through higher rent? Besides, if there's a waiting list to get an apartment, the landlord has no incentive to work hard and attract renters. As a result, many rent-controlled apartment buildings become run-down, and renters may have to wait months to have routine problems fixed.

The Impact of Ending Rent Control

If rents were allowed to rise to the market equilibrium level, which is $900 per month, the quantity of apartments in the market would actually rise to 30,000 apartments. The market would be in equilibrium, and people who could afford $900 a month would have an easier time finding vacant apartments. Instead of spending time and money searching for apartments, and then having to accept an apartment in a poorly maintained building, many renters would be able to find a wider selection of apartments. Landlords would also have a greater incentive to properly maintain their buildings and invest in new construction.

Virtual Economics

L3 Differentiate

Evaluating Price Controls Use the following lesson from the NCEE **Virtual Economics *CD-ROM*** to help students evaluate price controls. Click on Browse Economics Lessons, specify grades 9–12, and use the key words *price controls*.

In this activity, students will use supply-and-demand graphs to illustrate the effects of legal price controls in competitive markets.

LESSON TITLE	PRICE CONTROLS —TOO HIGH OR TOO LOW
Type of Activity	Using Statistics
Complexity	Moderate
Time	50 minutes
NCEE Standards	7, 8

)n the other hand, once rent control nded, people living in formerly rent-trolled apartments may no longer be e to afford the higher rents. As soon as neighborhood improves, these renters y be priced out of their apartments, replaced by people willing to pay the ilibrium price.

Certainly, the end of rent control bene- some people and hurts others. Nearly economists agree that the benefits of ing rent control exceed the costs, and gest that there are better ways to help)r households find affordable housing.

CHECKPOINT How does a price ceiling affect the quantity demanded and the quantity supplied?

'ice Floors

rice floor is a minimum price, set by the ernment, that must be paid for a good service. Governments set price floors to ure that certain sellers receive at least a imum reward for their efforts. Sellers include workers, who sell their labor.

e Minimum Wage

e price floor that is well-known is the imum wage, which sets a minimum price t an employer can pay a worker for one ır of labor. The federal government s a base level for the minimum wage, t states can make their own minimum ges even higher. A full-time worker ng paid the federal minimum wage will n less than the federal government says necessary to support a couple with one ld. Still, the minimum wage does ensure ower limit for workers' earnings. But the benefits to minimum-wage workers tweigh the loss of some jobs?

The supply curve of labor and the nand curve for labor are combined in ure 6.4. This supply curve shows the mber of workers available at various ge rates, and the demand curve shows number of workers that employers will e at various wages. (In this example, worker is the supplier of labor that is ught by an employer.) If the minimum ge is set above the market equilibrium ge rate, the demand for workers will down.

If the market equilibrium wage for low-skilled labor is $6.60 per hour, and the minimum wage is set at $7.25, the result is a surplus of labor. Firms will employ 2 million fewer low-skilled workers—including teenagers—than they would at the equilibrium wage rate, because the price floor on labor keeps the wage rate artificially high. If the minimum wage is below the equilibrium rate, it will have no effect, because employers would have to pay at least the equilibrium rate anyway to find workers in a free market.

We should note here that **Figure 6.4** is a theoretical model of the effects of a minimum wage. The real world is more complex, and some economists believe that the actual effect of the minimum wage on employment rates is not as severe as in this example.

Price Supports in Agriculture

Agricultural price supports are another example of price floors that are used for many farm products around the world. Like the minimum wage, price supports have both supporters and opponents.

During the Great Depression of the 1930s, the federal government began setting minimum prices for many commodities.

price floor a minimum price for a good or service

minimum wage a minimum price that an employer can pay a worker for one hour of labor

Figure 6.4 Effects of Minimum Wage

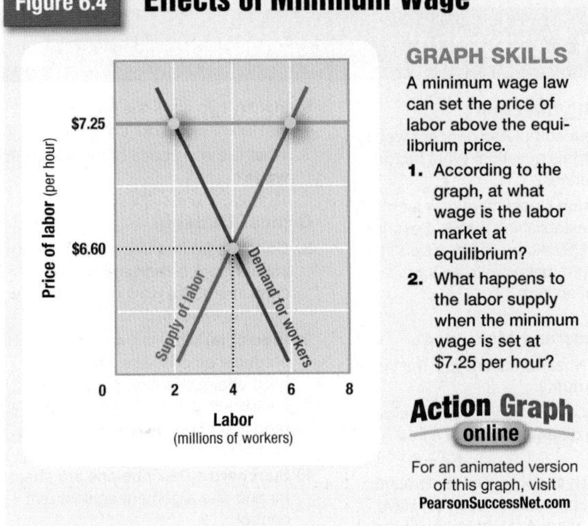

GRAPH SKILLS

A minimum wage law can set the price of labor above the equilibrium price.

1. According to the graph, at what wage is the labor market at equilibrium?
2. What happens to the labor supply when the minimum wage is set at $7.25 per hour?

DISCUSS

Discuss the impact of minimum wage on employment. Ask **What effect does a minimum wage have on wages?** *(sets a price floor per hour worked)* **What effect does it have on supply and demand?** *(lowers demand, creates a supply surplus)* **How do price supports in agriculture differ from a price floor such as the minimum wage?** *(Instead of setting a minimum price for produce, the government bought excess crops to lower the supply and increase demand.)*

EXTEND

Have students reread the information on price ceilings and rent control. Have students consider the following: **If economists have determined that rent control disadvantages outweigh the advantages, why do we still have it?** Allow time for class discussion.

L4 Differentiate Have students research the terms of rent control laws for various cities. Ask them to report their findings to the class. Then have the class compare and contrast the laws.

GUIDING QUESTION WRAP UP

Have students return to the section Guiding Question. Review the completed graphic organizer and clarify any misunderstandings. Have a wrap up discussion about the factors that affect prices.

Assess and Remediate

L3 Collect student-created graphs and assess student understanding of market equilibrium.

L3 L2 Collect the "Understanding Price Controls" and "Understanding Price Ceilings" worksheets and assess student understanding of price controls.

L4 Collect the "The Minimum Wage Vision" worksheet and assess student understanding of the effects of the minimum wage on the labor supply.

L3 Assign the Section 1 Assessment questions; identify student misconceptions.

L3 Give Section Quiz A (Unit 2 All-in-One, p. 94).

L2 Give Section Quiz B (Unit 2 All-in-One, p. 95).

(Assess and Remediate continued on p. 140)

Answers

Checkpoint A price ceiling leads to an increase in demand and a decrease in supply.

Graph Skills 1. $6.60 per hour 2. A surplus of 4 million workers will exist because employers will employ only two million workers at that wage.

Have students complete the Self-Test Online and continue their work in the **Essential Questions Journal**.

REMEDIATION AND SUGGESTIONS

Use the chart below to help students who are struggling with content.

WEAKNESS	REMEDIATION
Defining key terms (Questions 3, 4, 7)	Have students use the interactive Economic Dictionary Online.
How to read a supply and demand chart (Questions 8, 9, 11)	Reteach using the interactive graph on supply and demand, available online.
How a market in disequilibrium reaches equilibrium (Questions 3, 4, 5)	Have students imagine that the world oil supply has been interrupted. How would they be affected? Discuss how the market would regain equilibrium.
The pros and cons of price ceilings (Questions 6, 7, 10)	Have students role-play the landlord and tenant at a hearing before a rent control board.

Answers

Cartoon Possible answer: The cartoonist opposed price supports. The giant appears to be throwing away money.

Checkpoint The market condition would be excess supply.

▲ This cartoon comments on federal programs that give financial aid to farmers. ***Do you think this cartoonist probably favored or opposed price supports for farm products? Explain.***

Unlike the minimum wage, these price floors were not legal minimums set for buyers. Instead, whenever prices fell below a certain level, the government created demand by buying excess crops.

Supporters of price floors believed that they were necessary because American farms would not easily survive in a freely competitive agricultural market. If many American farms were to go out of business, the United States would have to depend on other nations for its vital food supply. Opponents of price supports argued that the regulations were a burden to farmers. The government dictated what farmers should produce and in what quantities. Congress voted to phase out most of these programs in 1996, because they seemed to conflict with free market principles.

Some people worried that, without the government stepping in to buy up excess crops, farmers would begin to overproduce. One Minnesota farmer commented:

> **"When you have bumper crops, if it truly is a supply-and-demand market, and you're supplying more than what the demand is, it's financial suicide."**
>
> —Brian Romsdahl, Minnesota Public Radio, 1998

Despite the effort to end price supports, many commodities, such as dairy products, remain relatively untouched by the new laws. For example, the Department of Agriculture has continued to buy tons of powdered milk in order to keep the price from dropping below the set minimum. This milk is stored in warehouses and even in caves across the country. In addition, the federal government often responds to low prices by providing emergency financial aid to farmers.

CHECKPOINT ***How does a minimum wage above the equilibrium rate affect the supply of labor?***

SECTION 1 ASSESSMENT

Essential Questions Journal To continue to build a response to the Essential Question, go to your **Essential Questions Journal.**

Guiding Question

1. Use your completed concept web to answer this question: What factors affect prices?
2. **Extension** Consumers play a critical role in establishing prices. Describe how a specific buying decision that you might make could affect the price of an item.

Key Terms and Main Ideas

3. Under what conditions is a market at **equilibrium?**
4. Identify the two conditions that can lead to **disequilibrium** in a free market.
5. **(a)** When supply exceeds demand, what happens to prices? **(b)** How will the market return to equilibrium?
6. Identify two ways the government can intervene to control prices.
7. What is the purpose of the **minimum wage?**

Critical Thinking

8. **Contrast (a)** In a free market, what impact does a shortage have on consumers? **(b)** How does this differ from the effect on producers?
9. **Predict (a)** What action will a producer usually take when the price charged is higher than the equilibrium price? **(b)** Why might the producer choose to keep the price as it is?
10. **Summarize** Describe one argument for and one argument against rent control.

Math Skills

11. Look at the supply and demand schedule for cans of soda pop, below. **(a)** Use the information on the schedule to create a supply-and-demand curve. **(b)** Identify and label the equilibrium price. **(c)** What is the shortage when the price is $1.00 per can?

Visit PearsonSuccessNet.com for additional math help.

Combined Supply and Demand Schedule

Price of a can of soda pop	Quantity demanded	Quantity supplied
$.50	600	50
$1.00	500	200
$1.50	300	300
$2.00	200	500
$2.50	50	600

Assessment Answers

1. The basic factors that affect prices are supply, demand, and government intervention.
2. Possible response: My decision alone would probably not affect the price, but when I buy notebooks when school begins, so do a lot of other people. If notebooks are too expensive, people may buy fewer, and there would be a surplus.
3. when the quantity supplied and the quantity demanded are equal
4. when the market price is too high or too low; when the quantity supplied is too high or too low
5. (a) prices go down (b) As the price goes down, the demand will increase, pushing the market toward equilibrium.
6. The government can impose price ceilings or price floors.
7. to set a lower limit or price floor for workers' earnings
8. (a) Consumers may have to wait to purchase an item or may not be able to find the item in stores. (b) Producers have the opportunity to raise prices or increase production or both to earn more profits.
9. (a) Producers will lower prices to increase demand. (b) The producer might keep the price as it is if the product can be stored easily until seasonal demand rises.
10. Possible response: Rent control helps poor people afford housing. Rent control causes housing shortages.
11. (a) Graph shows a combined supply and demand schedule, with quantity of cans on the *x*-axis (in increments of 100) and price per can on the *y*-axis (in $.50 increments). (b) $1.50 (c) 300 cans

SECTION 2 Changes in Market Equilibrium

OBJECTIVES

1. **Explain** why a free market naturally tends to move toward equilibrium.
2. **Analyze** how a market reacts to an increase or decrease in supply.
3. **Analyze** how a market reacts to an increase or decrease in demand.

ECONOMIC DICTIONARY

As you read the section, look for the definitions of these **Key Terms:**

- inventory
- fad
- search costs

Guiding Question

How do changes in supply and demand affect equilibrium?

Copy this flowchart and fill it in as you read.

Restoring Equilibrium			
Increase in supply	Decrease in supply	Increase in demand	Decrease in demand

▶ Economics and You Have you ever stood in a long line to buy concert tickets or the latest video game? Do you anxiously scan the signs at the pump to see if the price of gas is up or down? Have you ever seen ads trumpeting the words *"Great Bargains . . . Everything Must Go!"* These are all elements of the market system at work. And often, the one who gets the benefit—or pays the price—is you.

Principles in Action Changes in supply and demand upset market equilibrium and cause prices to change. Sometimes prices go up, sometimes prices go down. But either way, the principle of market equilibrium is at work. This section's How the Economy Works describes the events surrounding a market shortage. You will also see how changes in supply and demand affect a variety of products, from digital cameras to toys.

The "sneaker blow-out" sign suggests that this store may be experiencing a surplus. ▼

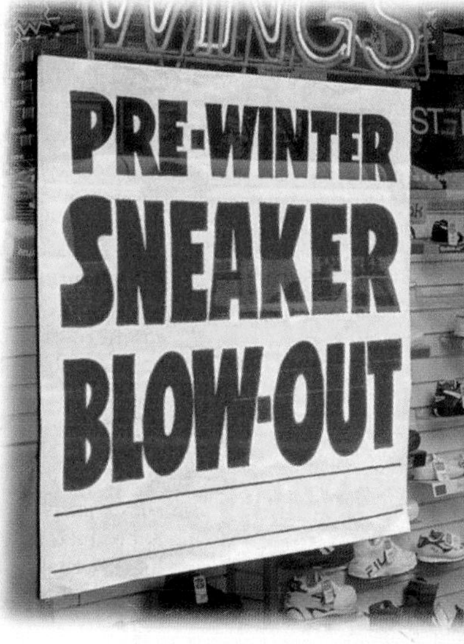

Moving Toward Equilibrium

Economists say that a market will tend toward equilibrium, which means that the price and quantity will gradually move toward their equilibrium levels. Why does this happen? Remember that a shortage will cause firms to raise prices. Higher prices cause the quantity supplied to rise and the quantity demanded to fall until the two values are equal. On the other hand, a surplus will force firms to cut prices. Falling prices cause quantity demanded to rise and quantity supplied to fall until, once again, they are equal. Through these relationships, the market price of a good and the quantity supplied will move toward their equilibrium values.

As you learned in Chapter 4 and Chapter 5, the changes in demand and supply described above are changes along a demand or supply curve. Assuming that a market starts at equilibrium, there are two factors that can push it into disequilibrium: a shift in the entire demand curve or a shift in the entire supply curve.

✔ **CHECKPOINT** ***What changes can push a market into disequilibrium?***

Guiding Question

How do changes in supply and demand affect equilibrium?

Get Started

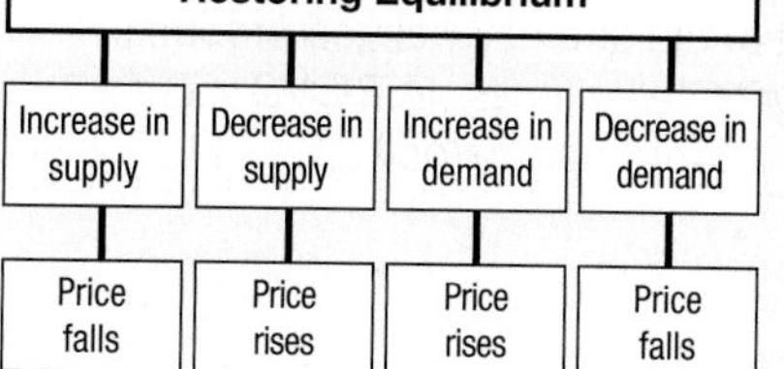

LESSON GOALS

Students will:

- Know the Key Terms.
- Interpret a graph to show how a free market tends to move toward equilibrium.
- Work in groups to determine how changing camera technology has an impact on the supply of related products.
- Demonstrate understanding of how a market reacts to a decrease in demand by completing a worksheet.

BEFORE CLASS

Have students complete the graphic organizer as they read; or have students complete the Guided Reading and Review worksheet (Unit 2 All-in-One, p. 96).

L1 L2 ELL LPR Differentiate Have students complete the Guided Reading and Review worksheet (Unit 2 All-in-One, p. 97).

Answer

Checkpoint a shift in the entire demand curve or a shift in the entire supply curve

Focus on the Basics

Students need to come away with the following understandings:

FACTS: • Markets that are in disequilibrium naturally move toward equilibrium.
• An increase in supply lowers price; a decrease in supply causes price to rise.
• Increased demand causes price to rise; a decrease in demand lowers price.

GENERALIZATION: Changes in supply and demand upset market equilibrium and cause prices to change. But over time, supply, demand, and prices will gradually move to their equilibrium levels.

CLASSROOM HINTS

PATENTS AND COMPETITION

Students may have read about the high price of some medicines and may wonder why they are so expensive. Explain that developing and testing a new drug takes several years and is very expensive. When pharmaceutical companies want to develop a new drug, they apply for a patent, which gives them the exclusive right to make, use, sell, or import the new drug for twenty years. The patent restricts competition, allowing the drug manufacturer to dictate the drug's price until the patent expires. However, when the patent expires, new suppliers come into the market, causing the equilibrium to change and the prices to drop.

BELLRINGER

Display the "Changing Market" transparency (Color Transparencies, 6.b). Discuss the evolution of these cameras. How have the products been improved? *(faster, smaller, easier, more features)* Have students consider other products that have gone through similar changes. If they were creating a series of transparencies with this idea, what other products would they show? Have students work in pairs to sketch samples of old and new related products. *(Possible products: telephones, VCR/DVD, CDs/portable audio players, calculators)*

Teach

Economics online To present this topic using digital resources, use the lecture notes at www.PearsonSuccessNet.com.

DISCUSS

Using the Idea Wave strategy (p. T24), have students discuss how changing technology affects the original product. Ask **How did the advent of the camera on p. 142 affect the demand for conventional 35-mm cameras, like the one on the transparency? How did the 7.1 megapixel camera affect the 1.3 megapixel camera?** *(The demand for the newer cameras caused a decrease in demand for the older ones.)* **What happens to supply as demand increases?** *(Supply increases to keep up with demand.)* **What does this do to the supply curve? Why?** *(The curve shifts to the right. As the new cameras become cheaper and easier to produce, supply increases.)*

Ask students to consider how many products they have in their homes that can take pictures. *(camcorder, digital camera, cellphone, Web camera)* **Why do you think there are so many ways to take pictures?** *(It became easy, fast, and inexpensive to take pictures, which led to increased demand. In response to growing demand, competitors developed new products to take photos.)*

Answers

Graph Skills 1. Advances in the technology for producing digital cameras caused the supply curve to shift to the right. 2. continue shifting right; decreased demand for such cameras

Figure 6.5 Falling Prices and the Supply Curve

GRAPH SKILLS

As digital cameras became cheaper and easier to produce, the supply increased.

1. What accounts for the trend in digital camera prices?
2. Based on these graphs, what is likely to happen to the supply curve for digital cameras in the future? What might change this trend?

Falling Prices*

Price of a digital camera: $500, $400, $300, $200, $100

Year: 2000, 2002, 2004, 2006

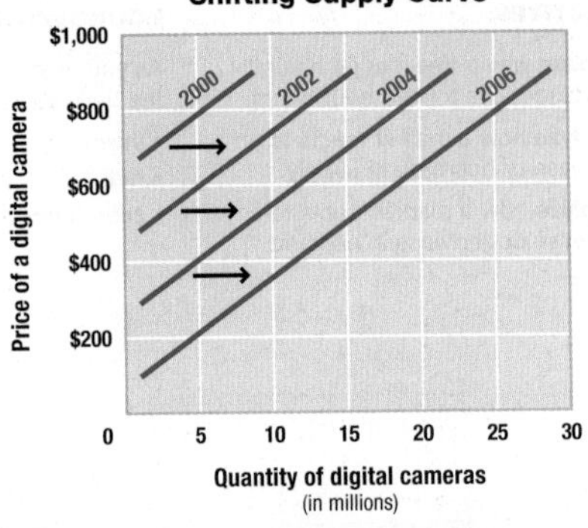

*Estimated data for a mid-priced digital camera

Action Graph online

For an animated version of this graph, visit PearsonSuccessNet.com

A 1.3 megapixel digital camera sold for $650 in 1998. ▶

Simulation Activity

What Price Water?
You may be asked to take part in a role-playing game about the price of water.

An Increase in Supply

In Chapter 5, you read about the different factors that can shift a supply curve to the left or to the right. These factors include advances in technology, new government taxes and subsidies, and changes in the prices of the raw materials and labor used to produce the good.

Since market equilibrium occurs at the intersection of a demand curve and a supply curve, a shift of the entire supply curve will change the equilibrium price and quantity. A shift in the supply curve to the left or the right creates a new equilibrium. Markets tend toward equilibrium, so a change in supply will set into motion market forces that lead the market to a new equilibrium price and quantity sold.

To see what happens when the supply curve shifts to the right, we will look at a product that has undergone a radical market change in a relatively short period of time: the digital camera.

A Changing Market

Digital cameras were first introduced into the consumer market in 1994. These early digital cameras were far less sophisticated than the ones that people use today. They produced grainy pictures of lower quality than cameras that used film. The first digital cameras were also expensive, at a cost of $749 each.

Gradually, improved technology for producing digital cameras caused prices to fall. By 2000, a consumer could purchase a mid-priced digital camera for $500; just two years later, a similar camera cost about $350. Today, the same camera that cost $749 in 1994 sells for less than $100.

At the same time, the quality of digital cameras has improved. For the same price you paid in 2000, you can now get a digital camera that has more features and produces better quality photographs than the original $749 device.

Why has this happened? Advances in technology have lowered the cost of manu-

Differentiated Resources

- **L1 L2 Guided Reading and Review** (Unit 2 All-in-One, p. 97)
- **L2 Deep Price Cuts** (Unit 2 All-in-One, p. 99)
- **L2 Understanding Cause and Effect skills worksheet** (Unit 2 All-in-One, p. 101)
- **L3 What Price Water?** (Simulation Activities, Chapter 6)

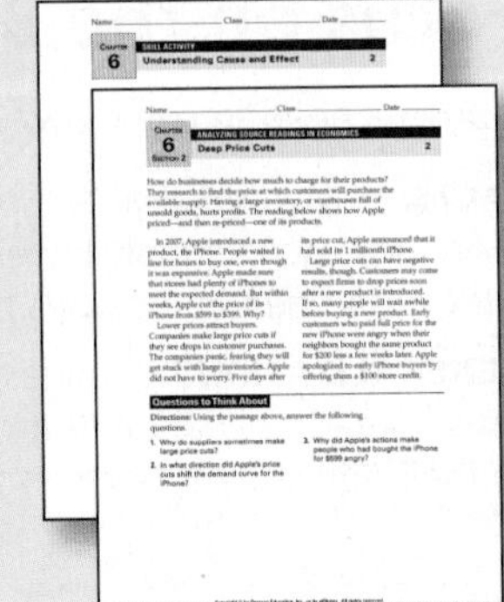

facturing digital cameras by reducing some of the input costs, such as computer chips. Advances in production have allowed manufacturers to produce digital cameras at lower costs. These lower costs have been passed on to consumers in the form of lower prices.

We can use the tools developed in Chapter 5 to graph the effect of these changes on the digital camera market's supply curve. As shown in **Figure 6.5**, the supply curve shifted to the right as manufacturers continued to offer a greater supply of digital cameras at lower prices. In 2000, no digital cameras were offered for $100. They were simply too expensive to develop and manufacture. Today, manufacturers can offer millions of cameras at this price and still make a profit.

Finding a New Equilibrium

Digital cameras evolved from an expensive luxury good to a mid-priced good when a new generation of computer chips reduced the cost of production. These lower costs shifted the supply curve to the right, where, at each price, producers are willing to supply a larger quantity.

This shift, shown in **Figure 6.6** using fictional quantities, has thrown the market into disequilibrium. At the old equilibrium price, suppliers are now willing to offer 4,000,000 digital cameras per year, up from 2,000,000.

In **Figure 6.6**, the increase in quantity supplied at the old equilibrium price is shown as the change from point *a* to point *b*. However, the quantity demanded at this price has not changed, and consumers will only buy 2,000,000 digital cameras. At this market price, unsold digital cameras—or **inventory,** the quantity of goods that a firm has on hand—will begin to pile up in the warehouse. When quantity supplied is greater than quantity demanded at a given price, there is a surplus. Something will have to change to bring the market to equilibrium.

As you know, suppliers will respond to a surplus by reducing prices. As the price falls from $900 to $450, more consumers buy digital cameras, and the quantity demanded rises. The combined movement of falling prices and increasing quantity demanded can be seen in **Figure 6.6** as a change from point *a* to point *c*. Notice that this change is a movement along the demand curve, not a shift of the entire demand curve.

At point *c*, the price has fallen to a level where quantity supplied and quantity demanded is equal. Surplus is no longer a problem. This new equilibrium point marks a lower equilibrium price and a higher equilibrium quantity supplied than before the supply curve shifted. This is how equilibrium changes when supply increases, and the entire supply curve shifts to the right.

inventory the quantity of goods that a firm has on hand

Changing Equilibrium

As improved technology caused the price of digital cameras to fall, sales increased. Market equilibrium then started moving gradually downward and to the right, where the quantities demanded and supplied are higher and prices are lower.

The supply curve for digital cameras has been moving to the right ever since the first cameras were sold. The curve continues to shift today as new technology drives down the production cost and market price of the most basic cameras.

Figure 6.6 A Change in Supply

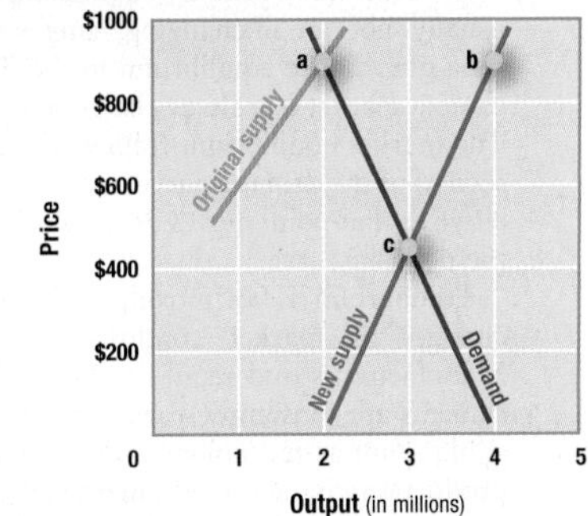

GRAPH SKILLS

This graph shows how an increase in supply affects prices and demand.

1. What was the original equilibrium price?
2. What impact did the change in supply shown here have on the equilibrium price? Why?

Action Graph online

For an animated version of this graph, visit PearsonSuccessNet.com

EXPLAIN

Tell students that many companies, such as Kodak, struggled with the technology revolution that changed from film-based products to digital imagery. Other companies created products in order to support these new items. Color printers and computer software for online photo sharing and organization are examples of related products that have been developed to support digital cameras. Ask **What other products might have been affected by the advancement in camera technology?** *(film; film development, including laboratories, chemicals, paper, and labor)*

ASSIGN GROUPS

Organize the class into four or five groups to consider how a market change impacts related fields. Tell students to choose one product from the examples they sketched for the Bellringer and discuss it with their group. How did the supply curves change for each of the paired items? What happened to the price of unsold items? Why? What related fields were affected and how? Ask one student from each group to summarize its discussion. Have the class suggest other products that may also experience rapid change in the near future.

L1 L2 Differentiate To help students understand the ripple effect of a changing market, have students work in pairs to draw a concept web. With one product in a center oval, have students add ovals with the names of jobs or products related to the main item. *(materials, labor, advertising, transportation, warehouse, and so on)* Tell them that they can continue to see the spread of this effect by repeating the process with any one of the other ovals.

L3 Differentiate For alternative or additional practice with the concept of equilibrium, have students use the "What Price Water?" activity (Simulation Activities, Chapter 6). Students will enact roles as buyers and sellers to see how prices affect their decisions.

Virtual Economics

L3 Differentiate

Finding Equilibrium Use the following lesson from the NCEE **Virtual Economics *CD-ROM*** to evaluate student understanding of equilibrium. Click on Browse Economics Lessons, specify grades 9–12, and use the key word *equilibrium.*

In this activity, students will create a supply and demand curve in order to identify the equilibrium price and quantities of Frisbees.

LESSON TITLE	EQUILIBRIUM PRICES AND EQUILIBRIUM QUANTITIES
Type of Activity	Creating Graphs
Complexity	Low
Time	45 minutes
NCEE Standards	7, 8

Answers

Graph Skills 1. $900 2. lowered it to $450; producers are willing to make enough cameras to meet the demand at that price.

ANALYZE

Have students look at the graph on page 143 (Figure 6.6) in their textbooks. Explain that this graph illustrates how changes in demand, supply, and price are related. Tell students that a manufacturer has been able to reduce the cost of making a good, such as a digital camera, by $450 per unit, and that the manufacturer has passed that savings on to the consumer by lowering the good's price. Point out that this development is illustrated on the graph by a price drop from $900 to $450.

Note that the manufacturer increased the supply of this good when it lowered the price. Ask students how this is shown on the graph. *(by the new supply curve which has shifted to the right of the old supply curve)* Ask **Why did the manufacturer increase the supply of this good when it lowered the price?** *(to meet the higher demand for the good at the lower price)* Ask students what the immediate effect on the market would be if the manufacturer lowered the price and did *not* increase the supply. *(a shortage of 2 million units)*

L1 L2 Differentiate For students who have difficulty recognizing this relationship, ask the following questions: **How many units was the manufacturer producing when it sold the good for $900?** *(2 million units)* **According to the demand curve on the graph, what is the demand for this good at the new, lower price of $450?** *(3 million units)* **By how many units will the manufacturer need to increase the supply in order to meet the demand for the good?** *(1 million units more)*

Action Graph online Have students review the Action Graph animation for a step-by-step look at how changes in supply affect prices.

APPLY UNDERSTANDING

Have students review the feature How the Economy Works. Ask **When does the market experience a shortage?** *(when there is an increase in demand or a shortage of supply)* **How does a shortage affect price?** *(Price increases.)* Have students consider whether producers always increase the supply to meet demand. For example, works of art are limited. What would be the equilibrium price for da Vinci's *Mona Lisa?* Have students consider other products or services that cannot be increased to meet demand.

How the Economy Works

How does a market react to a shortage?

When supply and demand are balanced, a market is at equilibrium. But a sudden change in supply or demand can result in a shortage. How does the market react?

1 Disequilibrium The market can be thrown out of balance.
Demand increases Wants or needs may increase demand. For example:
- More people need warm coats during a cold winter.
- Advertising creates a new fad.

Supply decreases An interruption in production can affect supply. For example:
- A natural disaster disrupts the flow of raw materials.
- Problems at the factory slow down production.

2 Whether the cause is an increase in demand or a decrease in supply, the result is the same: **shortage!**

Z-CUBE GET ONE NOW! OR GET LEFT OUT

Shift in Supply or Demand

In real-life markets, equilibrium is usually not an unchanging, single point on a graph. The equilibrium in the digital camera market has always been in motion. The market equilibrium follows the intersection of the demand curve and the supply curve as that point moves downward along the demand curve.

Equilibrium is a "moving target" that changes as market conditions change. Manufacturers and retail sellers of digital cameras are constantly searching for a new equilibrium as technology and methods of production change. Consumers can easily recognize the impact of this search by the frequent price changes, sales, and rebates for digital cameras. Each of these tactics is designed to keep older cameras moving out of stores as fast as new cameras come in.

CHECKPOINT ***What happens to the equilibrium price when the supply curve shifts to the right?***

A Decrease in Supply

New technology or lower costs can shift the supply curve to the right. However, other factors that reduce supply can shift the supply curve to the left.

Consider the market for cars. If the price of steel or rubber rises, automobile manufacturers will produce fewer cars at all price levels, and the supply curve will shift to the left. If auto workers win higher wages, and the company must pay more for labor to build the same number of cars, supply will decrease. If the government imposes a new tax on car manufacturers, supply will decrease. In all of these cases, the supply curve will move to the left, because the quantity supplied is lower at all price levels.

When the supply curve shifts to the left, the equilibrium price and quantity sold will change as well. This process is the

144 PRICES

Background Note

Shifts in Demand A sustained increase in gas prices shifts the demand curve for large cars to the left and the demand curve for smaller, more fuel-efficient cars to the right. Because it takes time for auto manufacturers to shift production to fuel-efficient cars, the supply curve lags behind. Car makers must use other techniques to boost demand for the gas guzzlers that sit on the lot. Companies offer discounts, rebates, and low interest rates on car loans. Some have also offered customers a guaranteed $3 per gallon price for gasoline for three years, at a time when gasoline is $4 per gallon.

Answer

Checkpoint It falls.

How the Economy Works online

For an animated, interactive version of this feature, visit **PearsonSuccessNet.com**

3 The immediate effects of a shortage are obvious. People line up at stores or storm the Internet to buy the hard-to-find item . . . and the price goes up.

4 If the shortage continues, other suppliers will seek to enter the market. Demand is up, prices are up . . . and everybody wants a piece of the profit.

5 A New Equilibrium In time, supply and demand will balance out again. This may happen in two ways:

Quantity demanded decreases
- Fads end
- Higher prices drive buyers out of the market

Quantity supplied increases
- Problems in production are solved
- New suppliers fill in the gap

Whatever the cause, the hard-to-get item is no longer so hard to get . . . and the shortage ends.

Check Your Understanding
1. Why would a shortage of a product lead to a price increase?
2. What circumstances might lead to a shortage of bananas? Gasoline? Solar-powered cellphones?

The Market Reacts | **A New Equilibrium**

exact opposite of the change that results from an increase in supply. As the supply curve shifts to the left, suppliers raise their prices and the quantity demanded falls. The new equilibrium point will be at a spot along the demand curve above and to the left of the original equilibrium point. The market price is higher than before, and the quantity sold is lower.

CHECKPOINT ***What happens to price and quantity demanded when the supply curve shifts to the left?***

An Increase in Demand

Almost every year, we experience a new **fad**—a product that enjoys enormous popularity for a fairly short time. Around November, a new doll, toy, or video game emerges as the "must-buy" item of the season. Holiday shoppers across the country stand in long lines, waiting for stores to open, just to obtain that year's version of Tickle Me Elmo or Webkinz®.

As you read in Chapter 4, fads reflect the impact of consumer tastes and advertising on consumer behavior. Fads like these, in which demand rises quickly, are real-life examples of a rapid, rightward shift in a market demand curve. Let's see how a swift, unexpected increase in market demand can affect the equilibrium in a market for a hypothetical, trendy new toy.

The Shortage Problem

As **Figure 6.7** on page 147 shows, the fad causes a sudden increase in market demand, and the demand curve shifts to the right. This shift reflects a shortage at the original price of $24 (point *b*). Before the fad began, quantity demanded and quantity supplied were equal at 300,000 toys (point *a*). On the graph, the shortage appears as a gap at the $24 price level between the quantity

fad a product that is popular for a short period of time

CHECK UNDERSTANDING

Call students' attention to the graph on page 147. Tell them to imagine this is a graph of the supply and demand for a video game that is selling for $25. Ask **How many games is the manufacturer willing to sell at that price?** *(300,000)* Tell students to imagine that the game becomes very popular and demand increases. Point out that 500,000 people are now willing to pay $25 to own this game (point b on the graph). Ask **How many games is the manufacturer willing to sell at that price?** *(300,000)* **How has the relationship between the supply of this $25 game and the demand for it changed?** *(A 200,000-game shortage has developed.)* **According to the graph, how will the manufacturer react to this shortage?** *(produce 100,000 more games and sell them for $30)*

PERSONAL FINANCE ACTIVITY

To help students make wise choices as consumers when purchasing an item online, you may want to read "Shopping Online" (PF 38) and assign the related activity worksheet (Personal Finance All-in-One, p. 97).

DISTRIBUTE ACTIVITY WORKSHEET

Distribute the "Fire Sale Nation" worksheet (Unit 2 All-in-One, p. 98). This worksheet analyzes Apple's response when demand for its new iPhone was lower than expected, and the consequences of such responses for Apple and for markets in general.

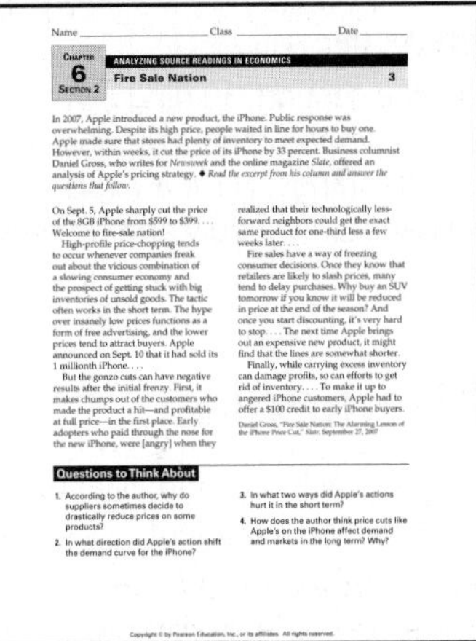

Name ____________ Class ____________ Date ________

CHAPTER 6 SECTION 2 — ANALYZING SOURCE READINGS IN ECONOMICS

Fire Sale Nation 3

In 2007, Apple introduced a new product, the iPhone. Public response was overwhelming. Despite its high price, people waited in line for hours to buy one. Apple made sure that stores had plenty of inventory to meet expected demand. However, within weeks, it cut the price of its iPhone by 33 percent. Business columnist Daniel Gross, who writes for *Newsweek* and the online magazine *Slate*, offered an analysis of Apple's pricing strategy. ◆ *Read the excerpt from his column and answer the questions that follow.*

On Sept. 5, Apple sharply cut the price of the 8GB iPhone from $599 to $399. . . . Welcome to fire-sale nation!

High-profile price-chopping tends to occur whenever companies freak out about the vicious combination of a slowing consumer economy and the prospect of getting stuck with big inventories of unsold goods. The tactic often works in the short term. The hype over insanely low prices functions as a form of free advertising, and the lower prices tend to attract buyers. Apple announced on Sept. 10 that it had sold its 1 millionth iPhone. . . .

But the gonzo cuts can have negative results after the initial frenzy. First, it makes chumps out of the customers who made the product a hit—and profitable at full price—in the first place. Early adopters who paid through the nose for the new iPhone, were [angry] when they realized that their technologically less-forward neighbors could get the exact same product for one-third less a few weeks later. . . .

Fire sales have a way of freezing consumer decisions. Once they know that retailers are likely to slash prices, many tend to delay purchases. Why buy an SUV tomorrow if you know it will be reduced in price at the end of the season? And once you start discounting, it's very hard to stop. . . . The next time Apple brings out an expensive new product, it might find that the lines are somewhat shorter.

Finally, while carrying excess inventory can damage profits, so can efforts to get rid of inventory. . . . To make it up to angered iPhone customers, Apple had to offer a $100 credit to early iPhone buyers.

Daniel Gross, "Fire Sale Nation: The Alarming Lesson of the iPhone Price Cut," Slate, September 27, 2007

Questions to Think About

1. According to the author, why do suppliers sometimes decide to drastically reduce prices on some products?
2. In what direction did Apple's action shift the demand curve for the iPhone?
3. In what two ways did Apple's actions hurt it in the short term?
4. How does the author think price cuts like Apple's on the iPhone affect demand and markets in the long term? Why?

L2 Distribute the "Deep Price Cuts" worksheet (Unit 2 All-in-One, p. 99). Have students read and answer questions about Apple's strategy for increasing demand for its iPhone.

Answers

Check Your Understanding 1. The equilibrium price goes up when there is a shortage. 2. Answers will vary but could include any set of circumstances (poor crop, new technology, higher inputs) that decreases supply and/or increases demand.

Checkpoint price rises; demand falls

EXPLAIN

Ask students why demand for some goods falls. *(They are replaced by new trends or technology.)* Ask **What direction will the demand curve for these goods move?** *(to the left)*

L1 L2 Differentiate Create two columns on the board. In the left column, write each of the following goods, as you ask students to identify the product that caused demand for this item to fall: film camera *(digital camera)*; VCR *(DVD player)*; cassette tape player *(CD player)*; CD player *(iPod/MP3 player)*. Write student responses in the right column.

L3 Distribute the "Understanding Cause and Effect" skill worksheet (Unit 2 All-in-One, p. 100).

L2 Distribute the "Understanding Cause and Effect" skill worksheet (Unit 2 All-in-One, p. 101).

Have students complete the worksheet to learn about factors that can affect markets.

Tell students to review the lesson on understanding cause and effect in the Skill Handbook (p. S-14). Remind them to use the steps of the lesson to complete the activities.

EXTEND

Tell students to research the Polaroid camera. Have them write a one-page report that summarizes Polaroid's market history and that explains what happened to it, using what they have learned about shifts in supply and demand.

GUIDING QUESTION WRAP UP

Have students return to the section Guiding Question. Review the completed graphic organizer and clarify any misunderstandings. Have a wrap up discussion about how changes in supply and demand affect equilibrium.

Assess and Remediate

L3 L2 Collect the "Fire Sale Nation" and "Deep Price Cuts" worksheets and assess student understanding of how changes in supply and demand affect markets, prices, and equilibrium.

L3 Assign the Section 2 Assessment questions; identify student misconceptions.

L3 Give Section Quiz A (Unit 2 All-in-One, p. 102).

L2 Give Section Quiz B (Unit 2 All-in-One, p. 103).

(Assess and Remediate continued on p. 147)

Answers

Critical Thinking Such sites make it easier to comparison shop, which increases competition; less time and effort needed to compare prices reduces search costs.

Checkpoint by increasing supply and/or raising price

Innovators

Pierre Omidyar

"I want people to be entrepreneurs," said Pierre Omidyar, "...because they think they can change the world...not because they think they can make a lot of money." As the founder of the online auction site eBay, Omidyar has done both.

Born in France to Iranian parents, Omidyar moved to Maryland with his family as a child. He graduated from college in 1988 with a degree in computer science. Omidyar then worked as a software engineer for several companies and became interested in the technical challenges of online commerce.

Inspired by his fiancée's desire to buy and sell Pez dispensers online, Omidyar founded the Web site that would become eBay in 1995. He thought of eBay as an experiment, a way to "give the individual the power to be a producer as well as a consumer."

Omidyar's experiment succeeded beyond his wildest dreams. Within just two years, his site was hosting 80,000 auctions a day. In 2007, total sales of goods at eBay.com reached $59.35 billion. The value of many things is now determined by what they sell for on eBay.

The success of eBay has made Pierre Omidyar a billionaire. But Omidyar's goal is to give away 99 percent of his fortune within 20 years. In 2004, he started the Omidyar Network, a philanthropic investment firm that gives financial support to organizations that help people to improve their lives and communities.

Critical Thinking: ***How can online sites such as eBay affect pricing and reduce search costs?***

Fast Facts

Pierre Omidyar
Born: June 21, 1967, in Paris, France
Education: B.S., Tufts University, computer science
Claim to Fame: Founder of eBay

Personal Finance For more help in making wise online shopping decisions, see your Personal Finance Handbook in the back of the book.

supplied of 300,000 toys and the new quantity demanded of 500,000 toys, shown at point *b*. The fad has caused the quantity demanded to increase by 200,000.

In the stores that carry the toy, the shortage appears as empty shelves or long lines. Shortage also appears in the form of **search costs**—the financial and opportunity costs that consumers pay in searching for a product or service. Driving to or calling different stores to find an available toy are examples of search costs. Today, the Internet has dramatically reduced search costs for many items, but finding the exact product you want can still be a costly and time-consuming process.

In the meantime, the available toys must be distributed in some other manner. In this case, long lines, limits on the quantities each customer may buy, and "first come, first serve" policies are used to distribute a limited number of toys among customers.

search costs the financial and opportunity costs that consumers pay when searching for a good or service

Return to Equilibrium

As time passes, firms will react to the signs of shortage by increasing supply and raising their prices. Customers may actually push prices up on their own if there is "bidding" in the market, as there is for real estate, antiques, fine art, and rare items. For example, if parents cannot find the toy they want at the store, they might offer the storekeeper an extra $10 to guarantee getting a toy from the next shipment. Through methods like this, the market price will rise until the quantity supplied equals the quantity demanded at 400,000 toys. All of these toys are sold at the new equilibrium price of $30, shown at point *c* in **Figure 6.7**.

When demand increases, both the equilibrium price and the equilibrium quantity also increase. The demand curve has shifted, and the equilibrium point has moved, setting in motion market forces that push the price and quantity toward their new equilibrium values.

CHECKPOINT ***How is equilibrium restored after a shortage?***

A Decrease in Demand

When a fad passes its peak, demand can fall as quickly as it rose. The shortage turns into a surplus for the once-popular toy, as parents look for new, trendier gifts for their children. Overflowing store shelves and silent cash registers, the symptoms of a surplus, replace long lines and policies that limit purchases.

As demand falls, the demand curve shifts to the left. Suppliers will respond to decreased demand for the once-fashionable toy by cutting prices on their inventory. Price and quantity supplied slide down to the equilibrium point shown at point *a* in **Figure 6.7.** The end of the fad has restored the original price and quantity supplied.

New technology can also lead to a decrease in consumer demand. Digital camera sales captured just 18 percent of the market in 2000. But in 2006, digital camera sales accounted for 92 percent of the market. Digital technology has led to a steep decline in film camera sales. Some firms have switched to digital camera production while others have left the market.

Digital technology has also changed the music industry. While sales of music CDs dropped by 20 percent in early 2007, digital sales of individual songs increased by 54 percent during the same period. New technology has caused the supply curve for CDs to shift to the left. However, in the future, new technology may lead to a change in demand for both digital cameras and digital music.

Figure 6.7 A Change in Demand

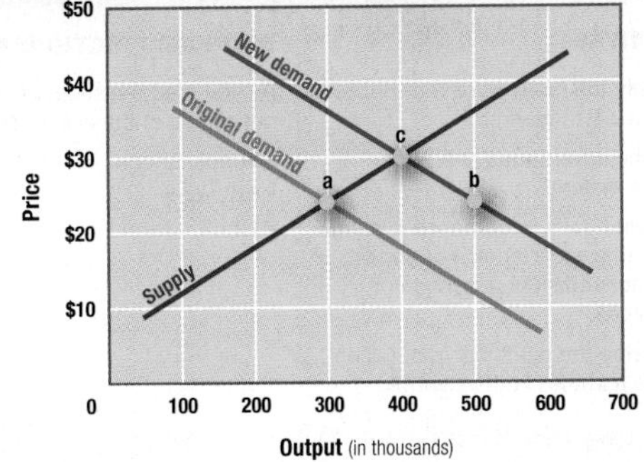

GRAPH SKILLS

This graph shows how an increase in demand affects prices and supply.

1. What was the original equilibrium price?
2. What impact did the change in demand shown here have on the equilibrium price?

Action Graph online

For an animated version of this graph, visit PearsonSuccessNet.com

✔ **CHECKPOINT** ***How does a demand curve reflect decreased demand?***

Essential Questions Journal To continue to build a response to the Essential Question, go to your **Essential Questions Journal.**

SECTION 2 ASSESSMENT

Guiding Question

1. Use your completed flowchart to answer this question: How do changes in supply and demand affect equilibrium?
2. **Extension** Shifts in either supply or demand can create a new equilibrium. Describe how increased supply of a good might benefit you as a consumer.

Key Terms and Main Ideas

3. What do **fads** reflect?
4. What kinds of goods require **search costs?**
5. What does a large **inventory** mean to a supplier?

Critical Thinking

6. **Explain** Why is equilibrium described as a "moving target"?
7. **Describe** What does a rapid increase in demand for a good mean for a consumer?
8. **Compare (a)** What are the signs of a shortage in a market? **(b)** What signs indicate that a market has a surplus?
9. **Review** The changing market for digital cameras was discussed in this section. **(a)** What factors caused the price of digital cameras to fall? **(b)** How did this affect the supply curve?

Math Skills

10. The graph shows the market for microwaves where an improvement in technology has shifted the supply curve. **(a)** Use the letters to identify the following elements: original supply curve, new supply curve, demand curve, original equilibrium point, and new equilibrium point. **(b)** Has supply increased or decreased? Explain.

Visit PearsonSuccessNet.com for additional math help.

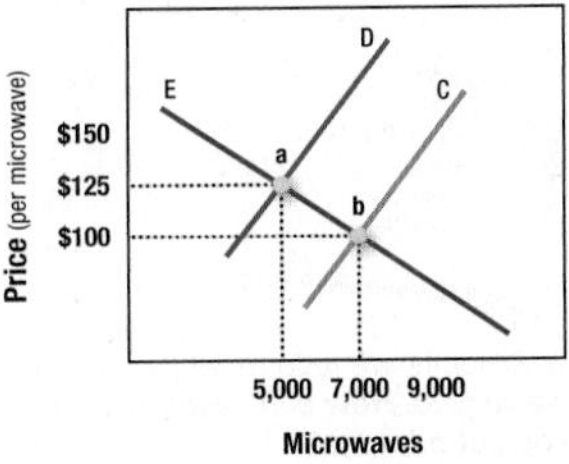

Have students complete the Self-Test Online and continue their work in the **Essential Questions Journal**.

REMEDIATION AND SUGGESTIONS

Use the chart below to help students who are struggling with content.

WEAKNESS	REMEDIATION
Defining key terms (Questions 3, 4, 5)	Have students use the interactive Economic Dictionary Online.
How a free market naturally tends to move toward equilibrium (Questions 6, 10)	Reteach using the seesaw image to explain the interaction of supply and demand.
How a market reacts to increases or decreases in supply (Questions 1, 2, 8, 9)	Reteach using the interactive graph on changes in supply, available online.
How a market reacts to increases or decreases in demand (Questions 1, 7)	Reteach using the interactive graph on changes in demand, available online.

Answers

Graph Skills 1. $25 2. caused it to increase

Checkpoint shifts to left

Assessment Answers

1. Changes in supply and demand create a new equilibrium at a higher or lower price.
2. Possible response: An increased supply of a popular video game would benefit me because I would be able to buy it at a lower price.
3. a large but temporary increase in the demand for something; also reflects impact of consumer tastes and advertising on consumer behavior
4. goods that are in short supply
5. The supplier has a large quantity of the good on hand.
6. It is constantly changing as market conditions that affect demand, supply, and price change.
7. A shortage may develop and its price may increase and a consumer might incur search costs.
8. (a) An item is hard to find and is offered at a high price. (b) The item is widely available and it is discounted or on sale.
9. (a) new technologies and lower manufacturing input costs (b) shifted it to the right
10. (a) D, C, E, a, b (b) increased; the supply curve has shifted to the right

Guiding Question

What roles do prices play in a free market economy?

Get Started

LESSON GOALS

Students will:

- Know the Key Terms.
- Identify roles that prices play in a free market by selecting food items from a menu.
- Interpret how a price-based system leads to more efficient allocation of resources by revising prices on a menu.
- Demonstrate the relationship between prices and the profit incentive by completing a worksheet.

BEFORE CLASS

Have students complete the graphic organizer as they read; or have students complete the Guided Reading and Review worksheet (Unit 2 All-in-One, p. 104).

L1 L2 ELL LPR Differentiate Have students complete the Guided Reading and Review worksheet (Unit 2 All-in-One, p. 105).

Answers

Illustration by helping to keep track of spending

CLASSROOM HINTS

THE ROLE OF PRICES

Extremely high prices, or price gouging, after a natural disaster seems unfair to most students. Students need to understand that a sudden increase in price after such an event plays a role in distributing scarce resources. For example, after a hurricane, drinking water may be scarce. If the price of bottled water did not rise dramatically, people would buy up and hoard the existing supply of bottled water before the government and relief agencies could set up a rationing system. If prices are allowed to rise to high levels, people will only buy what they need. Thus the high price reduces the quantity demanded and rations a scarce resource.

SECTION 3 The Role of Prices

OBJECTIVES

1. **Identify** the many roles that prices play in a free market.
2. **List** the advantages of a price-based system.
3. **Explain** how a price-based system leads to a wider choice of goods and more efficient allocation of resources.
4. **Describe** the relationship between prices and the profit incentive.

ECONOMIC DICTIONARY

As you read the section, look for the definitions of these **Key Terms:**

- supply shock
- rationing
- black market

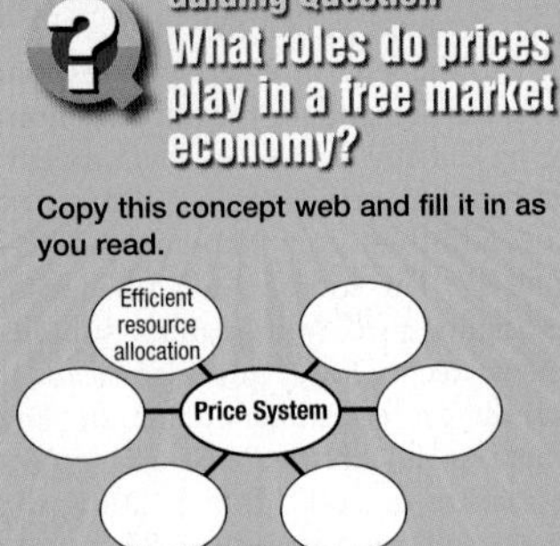

Guiding Question
What roles do prices play in a free market economy?
Copy this concept web and fill it in as you read.
Efficient resource allocation
Price System

Economics and You The price system is a delicate balance of supply and demand in which consumers, producers, and sellers all play a role. How does the price system affect you as a consumer? Consider the following example.

You want to buy a pair of athletic shoes, so you go to a local mall to compare prices. A discount shoe store offers low-end sneakers for $20. At other stores, you find that you can spend as little as $50 for brand-name sneakers, or more than $200 for a pair of designer basketball shoes. Basing your decision on the available supply, the price, and your demand, you buy the $50 sneakers.

Later, through online research, you find a pair of sneakers similar to the pair you bought, on sale for $5 less, including shipping. You buy the online sneakers with your credit card and return the sneakers you bought at the mall.

Principles in Action In a free market economy, prices offer a number of advantages to both consumers and producers. Simple purchases would be much more complicated and inefficient without the price system to help us make informed decisions. In this section, you will see how prices affect consumer behavior and how producers respond. Economics & You shows how profits act as an incentive.

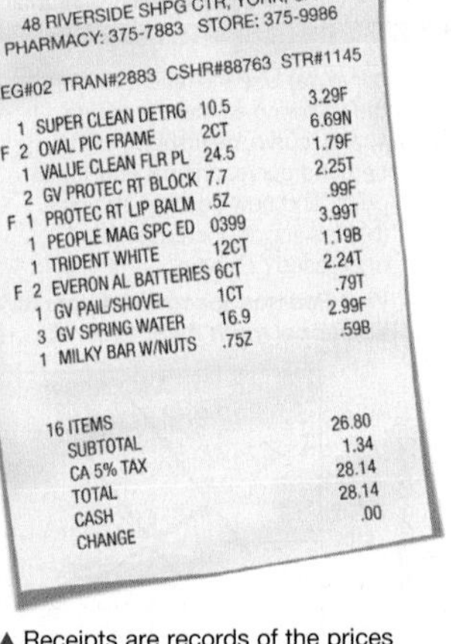

▲ Receipts are records of the prices we've paid. ***How can receipts help you set a budget?***

Prices in a Free Market

In Section 1, you read how supply and demand interact to determine the equilibrium price and quantity sold in a market. You also read about how prices change over time, based on shifts in the demand curve or supply curve. Prices are a key element of equilibrium. Price changes can move markets toward equilibrium and solve problems of shortage and surplus.

In a free market, prices are a tool for distributing goods and resources throughout the economy. Prices are nearly always the most efficient way to allocate, or distribute, resources. Prices help move land, labor, and capital into the hands of producers and finished goods into the hands of buyers. The alternative method for distributing goods and resources,

Focus on the Basics

Students need to come away with the following understandings:

FACTS: • Prices act as incentives for buyers and sellers. • Prices are signals that tell buyers and sellers what to do or not to do. • Prices provide a common language and standard measure of value. • Prices allow producers to allocate their resources efficiently.

GENERALIZATION: Prices make markets more efficient and help buyers and sellers make informed choices.

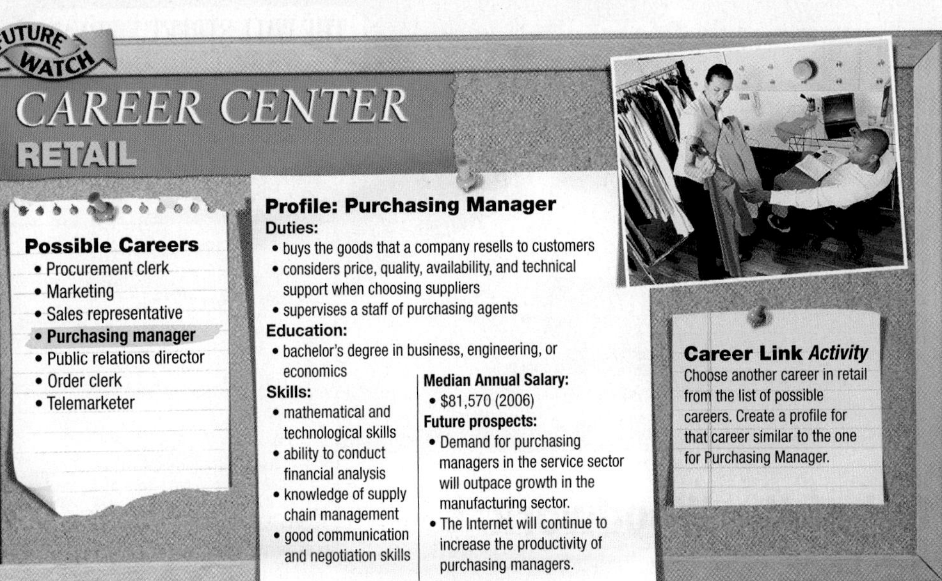

namely a centrally planned economy, is not nearly as efficient as a market system based on prices.

FUTURE WATCH
CAREER CENTER
RETAIL
Possible Careers
• Procurement clerk
• Marketing
• Sales representative
• Purchasing manager
• Public relations director
• Order clerk
• Telemarketer
Profile: Purchasing Manager
Duties:
• buys the goods that a company resells to customers
• considers price, quality, availability, and technical support when choosing suppliers
• supervises a staff of purchasing agents
Education:
• bachelor's degree in business, engineering, or economics
Skills:
• mathematical and technological skills
• ability to conduct financial analysis
• knowledge of supply chain management
• good communication and negotiation skills
Median Annual Salary:
• $81,570 (2006)
Future prospects:
• Demand for purchasing managers in the service sector will outpace growth in the manufacturing sector.
• The Internet will continue to increase the productivity of purchasing managers.
Career Link Activity
Choose another career in retail from the list of possible careers. Create a profile for that career similar to the one for Purchasing Manager.

As you will see, prices play other vital roles in a free market economy. Prices serve as a language, as an incentive, and as a signal of economic conditions. The price system is flexible and free, and it allows for a wide diversity of goods and services.

CHECKPOINT ***List three roles that prices play in a free market system.***

The Advantages of Prices

Prices provide a common language for buyers and sellers. Could you conceive of a marketplace without prices? Without prices as a standard measure of value, a seller would have to barter for goods by trading shoes or apples for a sweater. A sweater might be worth two pairs of shoes to one customer, but another customer might be willing to trade three pairs of shoes for the same sweater. The supplier would have no consistent and accurate way to measure demand for a product. Such a system would be inconvenient, impractical, and inefficient.

Price as an Incentive

Buyers and sellers alike look at prices to find information on a good's demand and supply. The law of supply and the law of demand describe how people and firms respond to a change in prices. In these cases, prices are signals that tell producers or consumers how to adjust. Prices communicate to buyers and to sellers whether goods are in short supply or readily available.

In the example of the "fad" toy discussed in Section 2, the sudden increase in demand for the toy told suppliers that people wanted more of those toys, and soon! However, the signal that producers respond to is not simply the demand but also the high price consumers are willing to pay for the toy, well above the usual retail price. This higher price tells firms that people want more of the toys, but also that the firms can earn more profit by producing more toys, because they are in demand. Therefore, rising prices in a market will provide an incentive for existing firms to produce more of the goods that are in demand and will encourage new firms to enter a market.

Differentiated Resources

L1 L2 Guided Reading and Review (Unit 2 All-in-One, p. 105)

L2 Price of a Slice (Unit 2 All-in-One, p. 107)

L4 The Future of Fortunetelling (Unit 2 All-in-One, p. 108)

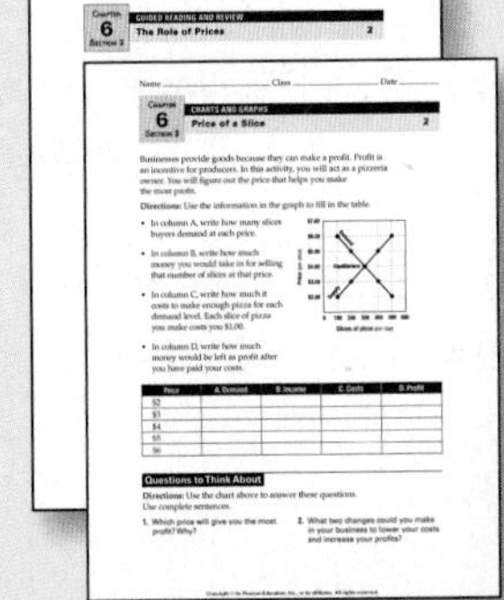

BELLRINGER

Write the following information on the board:

GOURMET CAFÉ LUNCH MENU	
Hamburger	$2.50
Bologna Sandwich	$1.50
French Fries	$1.50
Chili	$3.50
Garden Salad	$3.00
Milkshake	$4.00
Soft Drink	$1.00
Cookie	$ .25

Your lunch budget is $5.00.

Tell students to select the items they would buy for lunch and to write down how many of each they would buy. Remind them that they have only $5.

Teach

Economics online To present this topic using digital resources, use the lecture notes at www.PearsonSuccessNet.com.

DISCUSS

Poll the class to determine how many students purchased each item on the menu. Record the results for each next to the item's name. Use these results to begin a discussion of the role prices play in a free market. Call on students to describe how price served as an incentive in choosing which items to eat for lunch. Ask them to explain how the prices helped them determine the value of items in making their purchase decisions.

Pick an item on the menu that relatively few students chose—probably "chili" or "milkshake." Ask why so few of them purchased that item. *(Price is too high.)* Ask students to explain how price functioned as a signal in this situation. Note the number of students who bought cookies. Have them explain how price acted as a signal for that item. Ask how many bought more than one cookie and why. *(Possible response: The low price signaled that they were a "good deal," so I bought more than one.)*

CREATE A PROFILE

Have students use the Career Link worksheet to record their research for the activity (Unit 2 All-in-One, p. 164).

(lesson continued on p. 151)

Answers

Checkpoint (any three) move markets toward equilibrium; solve problems of shortage and surplus; efficiently distribute goods and resources; serve as a language, an incentive, or a signal

Teach Case Study

ANALYZE

Have students explain why sawdust has value. *(uses cited in article)* Ask **What signals does the price of this good send to consumers about trends in the sawdust market?** *(that supply is limited and that prices could continue to rise)* Ask students what signal sawdust prices send to people who eat chicken, drink wine, buy gasoline, or who are planning to buy a car. *(that the prices of those goods may rise)*

Have students cite an example from the case study of how price has served as an incentive in this situation. *(shaped how Oregon Boy Scouts raise money)* Ask what incentives sawdust prices have provided to producers who use sawdust. *(Possible answers: find a substitute resource, pass increased costs through to consumers of their products by raising prices)*

L1 **L2** **Differentiate** Ask students to explain the relationship between the chart of housing starts and the rising price of sawdust. *(Less construction leads to less lumber being sawed and less sawdust. Price rises when there is a shortage.)*

SUMMARIZE

Have students work in pairs to write a short paragraph summarizing the roles that sawdust prices play in the economy.

Economics online *All print resources are available on the Teacher's Resource Library CD-ROM and online at* www.PearsonSuccessNet.com.

Answer

Applying Economic Principles Possible response: Construction workers may lose their jobs. Sales of housing-related goods, such as lumber and furniture, may decline. As people spend less, shrinking demand may lower companies' earnings and production and cause even more workers to lose their jobs.

Case Study — THE WALL STREET JOURNAL. CLASSROOM EDITION

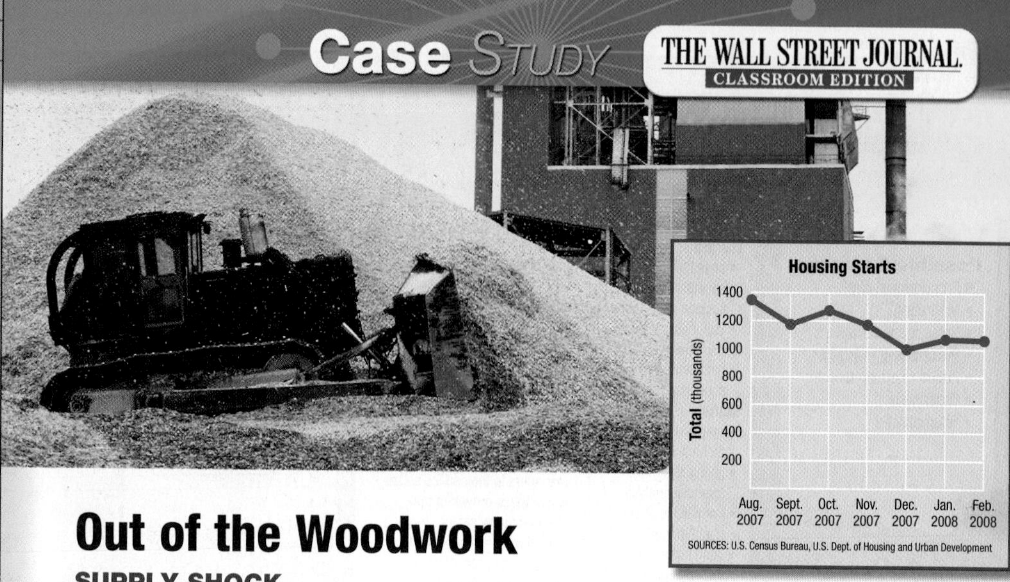

Out of the Woodwork

SUPPLY SHOCK

Sawdust is just dust, right? Wrong. A shortage of it can ripple through the economy.

By Joel Millman
The Wall Street Journal

Ernie Johnson figured $100-a-barrel oil was bound to happen someday. But he never thought he'd see sawdust at $100 a ton.

The price of sawdust has soared in recent years, up from about $25 a ton to more than $100 in some markets.

Blame the slump in housing construction: Fewer new homes mean fewer trees cut down for lumber, which leads to less sawdust and other wood waste, driving up the price.

"I've never seen sawdust so hard to find. We're having to go 400 miles to get it," says Mr. Johnson, the president of Johnson Bros. Contracting in Montana, which sells everything from chopped bark for landscapers to wood chips for pulp mills.

Sawdust may seem like a lowly commodity, but it is widely used in today's economy. Farms use sawdust and wood shavings as cozy and clean bedding for horses and chickens. Particle-board makers devour it by the boxcar to fashion a cheap building material. Auto-parts manufacturers blend a finely powdered sawdust called "wood flour" with plastic polymers to make a lightweight material to cover steering wheels and dashboards. Wineries use oak sawdust as a flavoring agent for some wines.

Perdue Farms, which raises broiler chickens, goes through seven million cubic feet of wood shavings a year. Oil-rig operators in Wyoming and Colorado pour sawdust into the caverns they find deep inside rock formations as they hunt for pools of petroleum. Sawdust gives drill bits something to grind through.

The shortage of sawdust and wood shavings has boosted the cost of boarding horses at the Lazy E Ranch in Guthrie, Okla. Two years ago, the Lazy E paid $950 per load of wood shavings for its horse stalls. Last month, Butch Wise, who manages the ranch, paid $2,650 a load. The ranch needs three loads a week.

"You'd think sawdust would be in plentiful and cheap supply, but it's not," he says.

As with every economic upheaval, there are winners as well as losers. With sawmill waste harder to find, opportunities for profit from scarcity are coming out of the woodwork. Boy Scout troops in Oregon fattened their coffers after the holidays by collecting discarded Christmas trees. Troop 618 in Beaverton made $3,000 hauling trees to a lumber recycler. Troop 728 made $10,000.

Video News Update Online Powered by *The Wall Street Journal* Classroom Edition — For a new case study, go to the online resources at **PearsonSuccessNet.com**

Applying Economic Principles
Bad loans and tight credit have led to a slowdown in housing construction. But home buyers aren't the only ones affected. Identify other ways that housing industry problems can ripple through the economy.

Prices as Signals

Think of prices as a traffic light. A relatively high price is a green light that tells producers that a specific product is in demand and that they should use their resources to produce more. New suppliers will also join the market. But a low price is a red light to producers that a good is being overproduced. In this case, low prices tell a supplier that he or she might earn higher profits by using existing resources to produce a different product.

For consumers, a low price is a green light to buy more of a product. A low price indicates that the product carries a low opportunity cost for the consumer and offers a chance to get a good deal. By the same token, a high price is a red light that tells consumers to stop and think carefully before buying.

Flexibility

Another important aspect of prices is that they are flexible. When a supply shift or a demand shift changes the equilibrium in a market, price and quantity supplied need to change to solve problems of too much or too little demand. In many markets, prices are much more flexible than output levels. Prices can easily be increased to solve a problem of shortage, and they can just as easily be decreased to eliminate a problem of surplus.

For example, a **supply shock** is a sudden shortage of a good, such as gasoline or wheat. A supply shock creates a shortage because suppliers can no longer meet consumer demand. The immediate problem is how to divide up the available supply among consumers.

What are the options? Increasing supply can be a time-consuming and difficult process. For example, wheat takes time to plant, grow, and harvest. **Rationing,** a system of allocating goods and services using criteria other than price, is expensive and can take a long time to organize. Rationing is the basis of the economic system known as central planning, which you read about in Chapter 2.

Raising prices is the quickest way to resolve a shortage. A quick increase in prices can reduce quantity demanded to the same level as quantity supplied and avoid the problem of distribution. The people who have enough money and value the product most highly will pay the most for it. These consumers will be the only consumers still in the market at the higher price, and the market will settle at a new equilibrium.

Price System Is "Free"

A free market distribution system, based on prices, costs nothing to administer. Central planning, however, requires many administrators to collect information on production and decide how resources are to be distributed. In the former Soviet Union, the government employed thousands of bureaucrats in an enormous agency called GOSPLAN to organize the economy. During World War II, the United States government set up a similar agency, called the Office of Price Administration to prevent inflation and coordinate the rationing of important goods.

Unlike central planning, free market pricing distributes goods through millions of decisions made daily by consumers and suppliers. At the beginning of the section, looking at the prices of sneakers helped you decide what product to buy and which supplier to buy it from. A farmer looks at prices listed in crop reports and decides whether to grow corn instead of soybeans next year. Everyone is familiar with how prices work and knows how to use them. In short, prices help goods flow through the economy without a central plan.

CHECKPOINT ***How does the price system provide incentives for both producers and consumers?***

Choice and Efficiency

One benefit of a market-based economy is the diversity of goods and services that consumers can buy. Prices help consumers choose among similar products. You could have bought footwear along a wide range of prices, from the cheap $20 pair to the $200 designer basketball shoes. Based on your income, you decided on a pair of sneakers at the lower end of the price range. The prices provided an easy way for you to narrow your choices to

supply shock a sudden shortage of a good

rationing a system of allocating scarce goods and services using criteria other than price

CHECK COMPREHENSION

L1 L2 Differentiate Make sure students understand that an *incentive* is something that encourages someone to act in some way. Next, review the lunch choices they made in the Bellringer activity. Ask each student which items he or she was encouraged to buy because of the item's price. Ask which menu items he or she *didn't* buy because of the price was too high. Then tell students to think of these menu prices as traffic signals—a green light meaning go ahead and buy the item, and a red light meaning now is not the time to buy. Point to each item on the menu and have students tell you whether its price was a green light or a red light for them.

ANALYZE

Tell students to imagine that they are the owner of the Gourmet Café. Have them analyze the class's lunch selections and decide whether they should use ground beef to make hamburgers or chili. Would they allocate the most buns to making hamburgers or bologna sandwiches? *(Choices should depend on how many of these items students purchased.)* Have them explain how price has helped them allocate these resources efficiently. *(to the items that would make the most money)*

ASSIGN GROUPS

Organize students into small groups to revise the prices on the Gourmet Café's lunch menu. Tell the groups that all items must remain on the menu and that the cost of providing each item, from least costly to most costly, is: soft drink, cookie, garden salad, bologna sandwich, French fries, milkshake, chili, and hamburger. Groups should decide which menu items are most valuable to the café and how to adjust prices to make the café a more successful business. Have each group write its revised menu on the board and explain the reasons for its decisions. The new prices and rationale should show recognition of ways that prices serve as signals and provide production and consumption incentives.

Virtual Economics

L2 Differentiate

Identifying Price Changes Use the following lesson from the NCEE **Virtual Economics *CD-ROM*** to evaluate student understanding of how prices ration scarce resources. Click on Browse Economics Lessons, specify grades 9–12, and use the key word *rationing*.

In this activity, students will examine how in a market economy the price mechanism allocates scarce goods.

LESSON TITLE	PRICE AS A RATIONING METHOD: HOW DOES A MARKET WORK?
Type of Activity	Simulation
Complexity	Moderate
Time	100 minutes
NCEE Standards	1, 8

Answer

Checkpoint helps producers decide what and how much to supply; helps consumers decide what and how much to buy

DISTRIBUTE ACTIVITY WORKSHEET

Tell students that they will act as the owner of a pizzeria and calculate their profits at different prices. Distribute the "Price of a Slice" worksheet (Unit 2 All-in-One, p. 106) for students to complete.

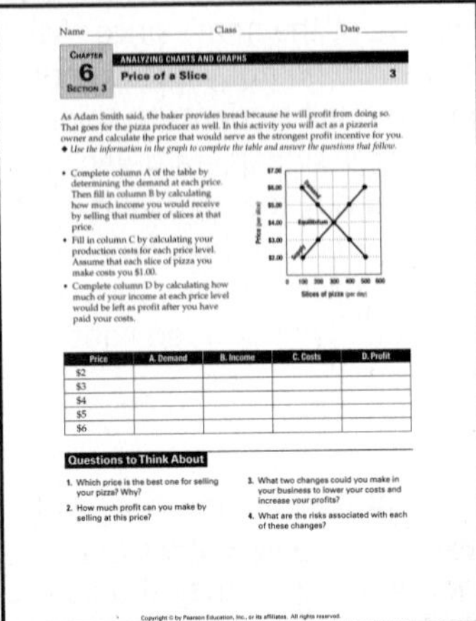

Name ____________ Class ____________ Date ________

CHAPTER 6 SECTION 3 — ANALYZING CHARTS AND GRAPHS

Price of a Slice 3

As Adam Smith said, the baker provides bread because he will profit from doing so. That goes for the pizza producer as well. In this activity you will act as a pizzeria owner and calculate the price that would serve as the strongest profit incentive for you.

◆ *Use the information in the graph to complete the table and answer the questions that follow.*

- Complete column A of the table by determining the demand at each price. Then fill in column B by calculating how much income you would receive by selling that number of slices at that price.
- Fill in column C by calculating your production costs for each price level. Assume that each slice of pizza you make costs you $1.00.
- Complete column D by calculating how much of your income at each price level would be left as profit after you have paid your costs.

Price	A. Demand	B. Income	C. Costs	D. Profit
$2				
$3				
$4				
$5				
$6				

Questions to Think About

1. Which price is the best one for selling your pizza? Why?
2. How much profit can you make by selling at this price?
3. What two changes could you make in your business to lower your costs and increase your profits?
4. What are the risks associated with each of these changes?

After students have completed the worksheet, discuss how the profit incentive affects business decisions. Ask **How do the owner and customer benefit from the profit incentive?** *(The owner benefits because he allocates resources efficiently and makes money; the customer gets what he wants.)*

L1 L2 LPR Differentiate Distribute the "Price of a Slice" worksheet (Unit 2 All-in-One, p. 107) to students. Have them work in pairs, following the instructions on the worksheet. Have students explain how the graph illustrates the principles of demand and supply.

During World War II, the federal government used rationing to control shortages. Each family was given tickets for such items as butter, sugar, or shoes. If you used up your allotment, you could not legally buy these items again until new tickets were issued. ***How would you react if tomorrow the government passed a rationing law for gasoline, chocolate, or bottled water?*** ▶

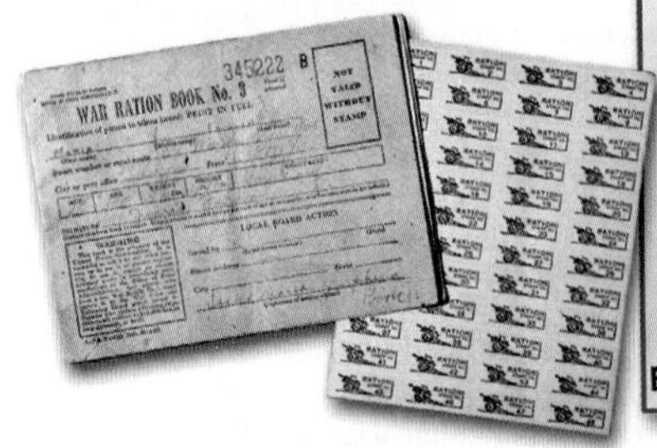

a certain price range. Prices also allow producers to target the audience they want with the products that will sell best to that audience.

In a command economy, however, one organization decides what goods are produced and how much stores will charge for those goods. To limit their costs, central planners restrict production to a few varieties of each product. As a result, consumers in the former Communist states of Eastern Europe and the Soviet Union had far fewer choices of goods than consumers in Western Europe and the United States. The government of the Soviet Union even built whole neighborhoods of identical apartment blocks and supermarkets with names such as "Supermarket No. 3."

Rationing and Shortages

Although goods in the Soviet Union were inexpensive, consumers could not always find them. When they did, they often had to wait hours for eggs or soap, and years for apartments or telephones. The United States experienced similar problems, although far less severe, when the federal government instituted temporary price controls during World War II.

The needs of the U.S. armed forces for food, metal, and rubber during World War II created tremendous shortages at home. In order to ensure that enough resources were available for military use, the government controlled the distribution of food and consumer goods.

Rationing in the United States was only a short-term hardship. Still, like rationing in the Soviet Union, it was expensive and inconvenient and left many consumers unhappy. Choices were limited, and consumers felt, rightly or wrongly, that some people fared better than others. However, rationing was chosen because a price-based system might have put food and housing out of the reach of some Americans, and the government wanted to guarantee every civilian a minimum standard of living during wartime.

The Black Market

Despite the World War II ration system, the federal government was unable to control the supply of all goods passing through the economy. A butcher could sell a steak without asking for ration points, or a landlord might be willing to rent an apartment at the rate fixed by the government only if the renter threw in a cash "bonus" or an extra two months' rent as a "deposit."

When people conduct business without regard for government controls on price

Background Note

Price Signals Apple introduced a black version of its popular iPod in the fall of 2005. It was technically identical to the traditional white version and sold for the same price. Inventories of the black version were quickly depleted, while the white iPod remained in stock. Apple continued to sell both versions at the same price. The company reacted to this price signal in a different way, however. When it introduced its new laptop computer, MacBook, in the spring of 2006, the white machines sold for $1349. The identical black MacBook cost $1499.

Answer

Illustration Possible responses: I would respect the government's actions; I would try to buy as many of these goods as possible before rationing began; I would not like it and might try to buy these goods on the black market.

or quantity, they are said to do business on the **black market.** Black markets allow consumers to pay more so they can buy a product when rationing makes it otherwise unavailable. Although black markets are a nearly inevitable consequence of rationing, such trade is illegal and strongly discouraged by governments.

black market a market in which goods are sold illegally, without regard for government controls on price or quantity

Efficient Resource Allocation

All of the advantages of a free market allow prices to allocate, or distribute, resources efficiently. Efficient resource allocation means that economic resources—land, labor, and capital—will be used for their most valuable purposes. A market system, with its freely changing prices, ensures that resources go to the uses that consumers value most highly. A price-based system also ensures that resource use will adjust relatively quickly to the changing demands of consumers.

These changes take place without any central control, because the people who own resources—landowners, workers who sell their labor, and people who provide capital to firms—seek the largest possible returns. How do people earn the largest returns? They sell their resources to the highest bidder. The highest bidder will be that firm that produces goods that are in the highest demand. Therefore, the resources will flow to the uses that are most highly valued by consumers. This flow is the most efficient way to use our society's scarce resources in a way that benefits both producers and consumers.

✔ **CHECKPOINT** ***What impact does rationing have on the availability of goods?***

Prices and the Profit Incentive

In a free market, efficient resource allocation goes hand in hand with the profit incentive. Suppose that scientists predicted extremely hot weather for the coming summer. In most parts of the country, consumers would buy up air conditioners and fans to prepare for the heat. Power companies would buy reserves of oil and natural gas to supply these appliances with enough power. Since demand would exceed supply, consumers would bid up the price of fans, and power plants would bid up the price of fuel.

Suppliers would recognize the possibility for profit in the higher prices charged for these goods, and they would produce more fans and air conditioners. Oil and natural gas fields would hire workers to pump more fuel for power plants. Eventually, more fans, air conditioners, and fuel would move into the market. The potential heat wave would have created a need among consumers for certain goods, and the rise in prices would have given producers an incentive to meet this need.

As we previously noted, efficient resource allocation occurs naturally in a market system as long as the system

Movie producers are quick to create sequels of highly profitable films. ***Your ticket purchase provides an incentive for the producer to make a sequel.***

As a high school athlete, you make an extra effort when you know a college scout is watching. ***You profit by winning an athletic scholarship.***

▲ Financial rewards motivate people. ***How have you provided or benefited from the profit incentive?***

EXTEND

Tell students that the government has rationed gasoline to control rising prices and demand. Have them write a blog post opposing this action and explaining why retaining a price-based system is a better solution to this market problem than central planning is.

L4 Differentiate Have students complete the "Future of Fortunetelling" worksheet (Unit 2 All-in-One, p. 108). Have students discuss an industry that has been changed by increased competition, such as the auto industry or Internet businesses.

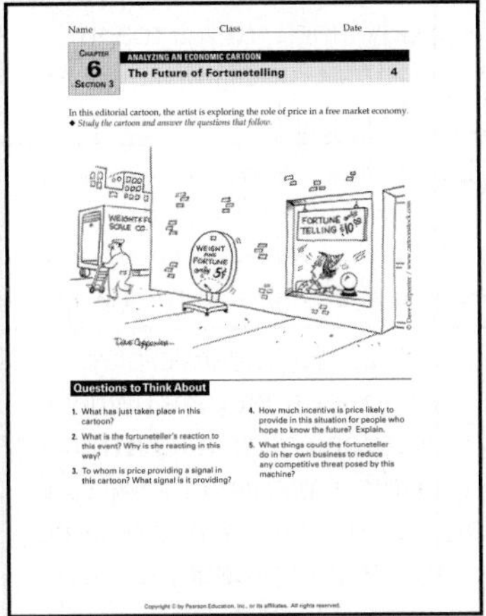
Name ______ Class ______ Date ______

CHAPTER 6 SECTION 3 — ANALYZING AN ECONOMIC CARTOON

The Future of Fortunetelling 4

In this editorial cartoon, the artist is exploring the role of price in a free market economy.

◆ *Study the cartoon and answer the questions that follow.*

Questions to Think About

1. What has just taken place in this cartoon?
2. What is the fortuneteller's reaction to this event? Why is she reacting in this way?
3. To whom is price providing a signal in this cartoon? What signal is it providing?
4. How much incentive is price likely to provide in this situation for people who hope to know the future? Explain.
5. What things could the fortuneteller do in her own business to reduce any competitive threat posed by this machine?

GUIDING QUESTION WRAP UP

Have students return to the section Guiding Question. Review the completed graphic organizer and clarify any misunderstandings. Have a wrap up discussion about the roles prices play in a free-market economy.

Assess and Remediate

L3 **L2** Collect the "Price of a Slice" worksheets and assess students' understanding of the relationship between price and profit.

L4 Collect the "Future of Fortunetelling" worksheet and assess student understanding of the role of prices in the face of competition.

L3 Assign the Section 3 Assessment questions; identify student misconceptions.

L3 Give Section Quiz A (Unit 2 All-in-One, p. 109).

L2 Give Section Quiz B (Unit 2 All-in-One, p. 110).

(Assess and Remediate continued on p. 154)

Answers

Checkpoint limits the supply

Economics & You Sample answer: When I was younger I had a lemonade stand in the summer. The money I made the first week encouraged me to keep selling lemonade until I got enough money to buy the things I wanted.

Have students complete the Self-Test Online and continue their work in the **Essential Questions Journal**.

REMEDIATION AND SUGGESTIONS

Use the chart below to help students who are struggling with content.

WEAKNESS	REMEDIATION
Defining key terms (Questions 3, 4, 5)	Have students use the interactive Economic Dictionary Online.
The roles prices play in a free market (Questions 1, 2, 6)	Ask students if they would buy lunch from a menu with no prices on it. Have them explain their answers.
The advantages of a price-based system (Questions 7, 8)	Have students review how the Gourmet Café's menu helped them make the best use of their lunch money.
How a price-based system leads to a wider choice of goods and more efficient allocation of resources (Questions 6, 8, 9)	Have students role-play the Gourmet Café owner responding to a government official who wants the café to sell all items at the same price and produce identical amounts of each.
The relationship between prices and the profit incentive (Question 10)	Review the Charts and Graphs worksheet with students.

Answer

Checkpoint when imperfect competition, negative externalities, or imperfect information prevents efficient allocation of resources

works reasonably well. Landowners tend to use their scarce property in the most profitable manner. Workers usually move toward higher-paying jobs, and capital will be invested in the firms that pay the highest returns.

The Wealth of Nations

Adam Smith wrote about the profit incentive in his famous book *The Wealth of Nations*, published in 1776. Smith explained that it was not because of charity that the baker and the butcher provided people with their food. Rather, they provide people with bread and meat because prices are such that they will profit from doing so. In other words, businesses prosper by finding out what people want, and then providing it. This has proved to be a more efficient system than any other that has been tried in the modern era.

Market Problems

There are some exceptions to the general idea that markets lead to an efficient allocation of resources. The first problem, imperfect competition, can affect prices, and higher prices can affect consumer decisions. If only a few firms are selling a product, there might not be enough competition among sellers to lower the market price down to the cost of production. When only one producer sells a good, this producer will usually charge a higher price than we would see in a market with several competitive businesses. In the following chapter, you will read more about how markets behave under conditions of imperfect competition.

A second problem can involve negative externalities, which you learned about in Chapter 3. Negative externalities are side effects of production that can include unintended costs such as air and water pollution. They affect people who have no control over how much of a product is produced or consumed. Since producers do not have to pay these unintended costs, their total costs seem artificially low, and they will produce more than the equilibrium quantity of the good. The extra costs will be paid by consumers or, in some cases, by society at large.

Imperfect information is a third problem that can prevent a market from operating smoothly. If buyers and sellers do not have enough information to make informed choices about a product, they may not make the choice that is best for them.

CHECKPOINT ***Under what circumstances may the free market system fail to allocate resources efficiently?***

Essential Questions Journal To continue to build a response to the Essential Question, go to your **Essential Questions Journal.**

SECTION 3 ASSESSMENT

Guiding Question

1. Use your completed concept web to answer this question: What roles do prices play in a free market economy?
2. **Extension** Prices often act as signals. Describe how prices acted as a signal or an incentive in the last two major purchases that you made.

Key Terms and Main Ideas

3. How does a **supply shock** affect equilibrium price?
4. How is **rationing** different from a price-based market system?
5. Why do buyers and sellers conduct business on the **black market?**

Critical Thinking

6. **Review (a)** What does a higher price for a good tell a producer? **(b)** What does a higher price for a good tell producers of other goods?
7. **Summarize (a)** What is the quickest way to solve a shortage? **(b)** What is the quickest way to eliminate a surplus?
8. **Explain (a)** What does efficient resource allocation mean? **(b)** Why is the price system an efficient way to allocate resources?
9. **Identify** Describe three market problems that prevent efficient allocation of resources.

Quick Write

10. Look at the illustrated Economics & You feature on the profit incentive in this section. List additional examples of how the desire for profit motivates people. Then write a short essay answering the following questions: Do you agree or disagree that incentives motivate people's actions? How do incentives affect your daily life?

Assessment Answers

1. Prices provide incentives, signals, and a basis for decisions; they guide efficient allocation of resources.
2. Possible responses: A pair of shoes that I liked went on sale. The lower sale price convinced me to buy the shoes then rather than to wait.
3. raises it
4. A central authority (such as government) controls supply instead of price determining supply.
5. to avoid government controls on price and quantity
6. (a) to allocate resources to produce more of the good to earn more profits (b) to enter the market to earn their own profits
7. (a) raise the price of the good (b) reduce the price of the good
8. (a) that economic resources—land, labor, and capital—are used for their most valuable purposes (b) It ensures that resources will go to uses that consumers value most—that resources are "sold" to the "highest bidder."
9. imperfect competition, negative externalities, imperfect information
10. Possible response: popular reality show on television leads to spin offs of other similar shows; gourmet coffee cafés are profitable, so fast food places begin to offer gourmet coffee; I agree that incentives motivate people's actions. I work hard in school in hopes of earning the grades I need to get into the college I want to attend.

QUICK STUDY GUIDE
QUICK STUDY GUIDE

Chapter 6: Prices

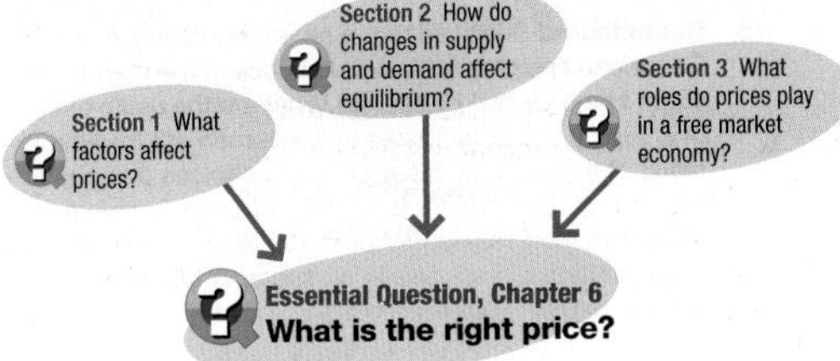

Section 2 How do changes in supply and demand affect equilibrium?
Section 3 What roles do prices play in a free market economy?
Section 1 What factors affect prices?

Essential Question, Chapter 6
What is the right price?

Economic Dictionary

equilibrium, *p. 134*
disequilibrium, *p. 134*
shortage, *p. 134*
surplus, *p. 136*
price ceiling, *p. 137*
rent control, *p. 137*
price floor, *p. 139*
minimum wage, *p. 139*
inventory, *p. 143*
fad, *p. 145*
search costs, *p. 146*
supply shock, *p. 151*
rationing, *p. 151*
black market, *p. 153*

Advantages of Price-Based System

	Free Market (price based)	Command Economy
Prices determined by	Supply and demand	Government bureaucracy
Use of rationing	Under emergency conditions	Normal
Response to changing conditions	Flexible	Rigid
Variety of goods available	Wide	Limited
Allocation of resources	Efficient (under ideal competitive conditions)	Less efficient

Shortage and Surplus

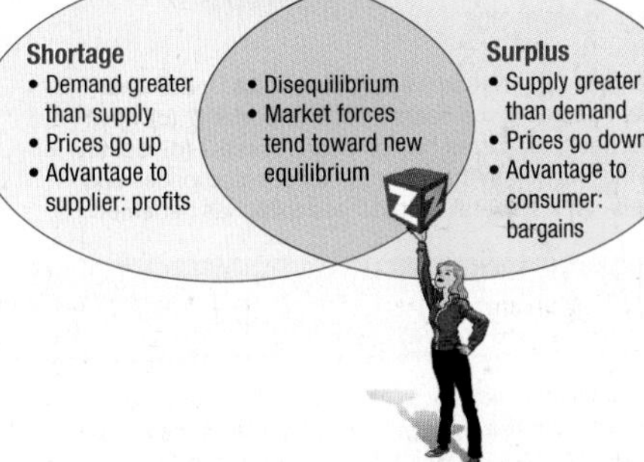

• Demand greater than supply

• Advantage to supplier: profits

• Market forces tend toward new equilibrium

• Supply greater than demand

• Advantage to consumer: bargains

Economics on the go

Study anytime, anywhere. Download these files today.

Economic Dictionary online	Audio Review online	Action Graph online	Visual Glossary online	How the Economy Works online
Vocabulary Support in English and Spanish	Audio Study Guide in English and Spanish	Animated Charts and Graphs	Animated feature	Animated feature

Download to your computer or mobile device at PearsonSuccessNet.com

ASSIGN THE ESSENTIAL QUESTIONS JOURNAL

After students have finished studying the chapter, they should return to the chapter's essential question in the Essential Questions Journal and complete the activity.

Tell students to go back to the chapter opener and look at the image. Using the information they have gained from studying the chapter, ask **How does this illustrate the main ideas of the chapter?** *(Possible answers: prices vary by season; prices vary by supply and demand; prices determine distribution; price is an incentive to buy or sell)*

STUDY TIPS

Explain to students that analyzing the work they have done on worksheets and quizzes can help them prepare for tests. Have students look back at the mistakes they made on previous work and take notes about areas they found confusing. Have each student write a question on a notecard, and weave answers to these questions into review sessions.

Economics on the go Have students download the digital resources available at Economics on the Go for review and remediation.

Assessment at a Glance

TESTS AND QUIZZES

Section Assessments

Section Quizzes A and B, **Unit 2 All-in-One**
Self-Test Online

Chapter Assessments

Chapter Tests A and B, **Unit 2 All-in-One**
Economic Detective, **Unit 2 All-in-One**
Document-based Assessment, p. 157
Exam*View*

AYP Monitoring Assessments

PERFORMANCE ASSESSMENT

Teacher's Edition, pp. 138, 145, 146, 152, 153
Simulation Activities, Chapter 6
Virtual Economics on CD-ROM, pp. 138, 143, 151
Essential Questions Journal, Chapter 6
Assessment Rubrics

Chapter Assessment

1. (a) the amount available (supply) and demand for it (b) Shortages cause prices to rise; surpluses cause prices to fall. (c) Sales would fall.
2. (a) to prevent rent increases during a housing shortage; to allow poor people a place to live at a price they can afford (b) Landlords would raise prices, increase the supply, and better maintain their properties; renters would have more choices but fewer at prices they could afford.
3. (a) increases in supply, decreases in supply, increases in demand, decreases in demand (b) The supply curve would shift right (increased supply) and the equilibrium price would fall; the demand curve would shift left (decreased demand) and the equilibrium price would fall; the demand curve would shift right (increased demand) and the equilibrium price would rise.
4. (a) the financial and opportunity costs a consumer pays in searching for a product or service (b) when a product or service is in short supply (shortage) (c) lowered them (d) Possible responses: lowered prices and increased market competition (e) Possible response: Buyers have benefited because it is easier to shop for the lowest price. Sellers have benefited because production costs are lower.
5. (a) rapid increases (b) consumers: pay more and/or use less; producers: supply more and/or raise prices (c) Possible response: I would recommend rationing because even though it might lead to a black market, it will more fairly distribute a limited supply. A price ceiling will prolong the shortage by discouraging production increases, and doing nothing is unfair to consumers who cannot afford sugar at free-market prices.
6. 400
7. $1200
8. 900
9. 600
10. Organize students into pairs or small groups to complete the activity. Discuss where students might find information (on the Internet, by visiting stores, in advertisements). Be sure to check their worksheets before they move on to modify the activity.
11. Possible responses: (a) I'd compete with the other school's shirts by lowering my price and settling for a smaller profit and donation from each shirt I sell. (b) I'd lower the price of the shirts, stop making donations, and apply the profits toward covering the costs of my remaining inventory. (c) I'd stop making donations and perhaps lower the price until the issue is resolved, since the bad publicity might negatively affect demand and leave me with an unsold inventory.

CHAPTER 6 ASSESSMENT

Self-Test online To test your understanding of key terms and main ideas, visit **PearsonSuccessNet.com**

Key Terms and Main Ideas

To make sure you understand the key terms and main ideas of this chapter, review the Checkpoint and Section Assessment questions and look at the Quick Study Guide on the preceding page.

Critical Thinking

1. **Predict (a)** What determines the equilibrium price of a product? **(b)** How do shortages and surpluses affect the equilibrium price? **(c)** Predict what would happen if a seller raised the price of an item at a time when there was a market surplus.
2. **Predict (a)** Why have some cities passed rent control laws? **(b)** Suppose that a city repealed its rent control laws. What effect do you think the repeal would have on landlords? On renters?
3. **Recognize Cause and Effect (a)** Identify the four basic causes for a shift in market equilibrium. **(b)** Describe how each of the following would affect equilibrium in the egg market: scientists breed a new chicken that lays twice as many eggs a week; an outbreak of food poisoning is traced to eggs; a popular talk show host convinces her viewers to eat an egg a day.

4. **Generalize (a)** What are search costs? **(b)** Under what market conditions are search costs important? **(c)** What impact has the Internet had on search costs? **(d)** Identify two other ways that the Internet has affected prices and markets. **(e)** In general, who do you think has benefited the most from the Internet: buyers or sellers? Explain your reasoning.
5. **Recommend** Suppose that a recent hurricane in the Caribbean has caused a supply shock in the market for sugar in the United States. **(a)** What are the usual effects of a supply shock on prices in a free market? **(b)** As a result of this change in supply, what choices do consumers and food producers face? **(c)** Suppose you were an adviser to the President. Would you recommend rationing sugar, setting a price ceiling on sugar, or taking no action? Explain your reasoning.

Applying Your Math Skills

Interpreting Data From Graphs

Imagine you own a bakery. The graph below shows supply and demand curves for whole-grain bagels. You now charge $3.00 for a bagel. Use your math skills to answer the following questions:

Visit PearsonSuccessNet.com for additional math help.

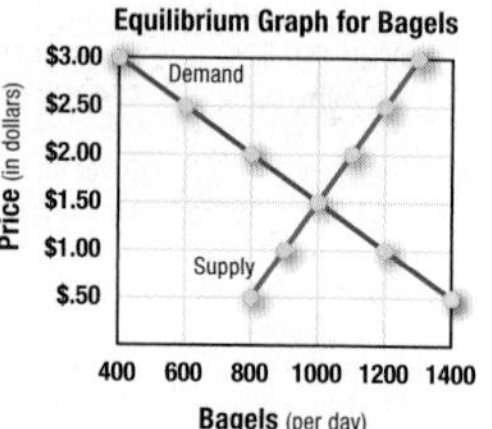

6. At $3.00 per bagel, how many bagels do you sell on an average day?
7. How much money per day are you taking in from bagels?
8. How many bagels per day are you throwing away?
9. To reach the equilibrium price, how many more bagels could you expect to sell each day?

Essential Question Activity

Essential Questions Journal To respond to the chapter Essential Question, go to your **Essential Questions Journal.**

10. Complete this activity to answer the Essential Question **What is the right price?** Imagine that your class is planning to sell T-shirts to raise funds for disaster relief in a nearby community. Using the worksheet in your Essential Questions Journal or the electronic worksheet available at **PearsonSuccessNet.com,** gather the following information:
    - **(a)** What is the cost of buying 1,000 plain white T-shirts in bulk?
    - **(b)** What is the cost of having a special design printed on the shirts?
    - **(c)** What is the average price that stores in your area charge for a printed T-shirt?

    Using this information, decide what price you think people would be willing to pay for a T-shirt. You need to make enough money above your cost to make a donation. When you have made your decision, fill in your price on the worksheet. Write an explanation of how you arrived at the right price.
11. **Modify** You have set your price and begun selling your T-shirts. Now, choose two of the following situations. Describe how each of them might cause you to modify your plan:
    - **(a)** Another school begins selling similar T-shirts for a dollar less than your price.
    - **(b)** After a week, you have not sold enough T-shirts to cover what you spent to buy and print the shirts.
    - **(c)** A local news broadcast raises questions about whether disaster relief funds are being spent wisely.

WebQuest online The Economics WebQuest challenges students to use 21st Century Skills to answer the Essential Question.

Remind students to continue to develop an Essential Questions video. Guidelines and a production binder are available at www.PearsonSuccessNet.com.

CHAPTER 6 ASSESSMENT

DOCUMENT-BASED ASSESSMENT

Does the minimum wage help or hurt the economy?

In the United States, the federal minimum wage sparks debate. Critics claim that the minimum wage creates unemployment through an unnatural price floor. Supporters say that a minimum wage is needed to help low-wage workers.

Document A

Document B

"In the House debate last week, opponents again claimed that the small business community is vehemently opposed to an increase. They think small businesses will suffer or collapse even with our modest increase. That's preposterous. A recent Gallup poll found that 86% of small business owners don't think that the minimum wage affects their business—at all. In fact, small businesses have historically prospered after past increases. More than half the states have already acted to increase minimum wages above the federal level today, and these states are generating more small businesses than states with a minimum wage of $5.15 an hour."

—Sen. Edward M. Kennedy, TheHuffingtonPost.com, January 23, 2007

Document C

"Economic research has shown time and again that increasing the minimum wage destroys jobs for low-skilled workers while doing little to address poverty. . . . for every 10 percent increase in the minimum wage, employment for high school dropouts and young black adults and teenagers falls by 8.5 percent. . . . Most of the work still gets done, but customers may get stuck standing in longer lines, and teens suffer because they've been priced out of work. . . . increasing the minimum wage causes four times more job loss for employees without a high school diploma than it does for the general population."

—Kristen Lopez Eastlick, "Dude, where's my summer job?", examiner.com, June 9, 2008

ANALYZING DOCUMENTS

Use your knowledge of the minimum wage and Documents A, B, and C to answer questions 1–3.

1. **Document A shows that the minimum wage**
   - A. is greeted enthusiastically by both workers and business.
   - B. forces people to beg on the streets.
   - C. is too low for workers, and too high for business.
   - D. brings workers and businesses together.
2. **According to Document B, how does raising the minimum wage affect small businesses?**
   - A. It forces small businesses to lay off workers.
   - B. Small businesses prospered after previous minimum wage increases.
   - C. Small businesses strongly oppose an increase.
   - D. Without a minimum wage increase, small businesses will collapse.
3. **What is the main point of Document C?**
   - A. Most minimum wage work gets done.
   - B. Adults are not affected by an increase in the minimum wage.
   - C. An increase in the minimum wage hurts low-skilled workers by causing many to lose their jobs.
   - D. Increasing the minimum wage will not hurt the general population.

WRITING ABOUT ECONOMICS

Debate over the minimum wage is an ongoing issue. Use the documents on this page and resources on the Web site below to answer the question: ***Does the minimum wage help or hurt the economy?*** Use the sources to support your opinion.

In Partnership

To read more about issues related to this topic, visit **PearsonSuccessNet.com**

Document-Based Assessment

ANALYZING DOCUMENTS

1. C
2. B
3. C

WRITING ABOUT ECONOMICS

Possible answer: Advantages of minimum wage: protects low-income workers; Disadvantages of minimum wage: prices for goods and services may be raised to pay for the minimum wage.

Student essay should demonstrate an understanding of the issues involved in the debate. Use the following as guidelines to assess the essay.

L2 Differentiate Students use all documents on the page to support their thesis.

L3 Differentiate Students use the documents on this page and additional information available online at www.PearsonSuccessNet.com to support their answer.

L4 Differentiate Students incorporate information provided in the textbook and online at www.PearsonSuccessNet.com and include additional research to support their opinion.

Go Online to www.PearsonSuccessNet.com for a student rubric and extra documents.

Economics online *All print resources are available on the Teacher's Resource Library CD-ROM and online at www.PearsonSuccessNet.com.*

Essential Questions

UNIT 2:

Who benefits from the free market economy?

CHAPTER 7:

How does competition affect your choices?

Introduce the Chapter

ACTIVATE PRIOR KNOWLEDGE

In this chapter, students will learn about different types of market structures. Tell students to complete the warmup activity in their **Essential Questions Journal.**

DIFFERENTIATED INSTRUCTION KEY

- **L1** Special Needs
- **L2** Basic
  - **ELL** English Language Learners
  - **LPR** Less Proficient Readers
- **L3** All Students
- **L4** Advanced Students

Economics online Visit www.PearsonSuccessNet.com for an interactive textbook with built-in activities on economic principles.

- ***The Wall Street Journal* Classroom Edition Video** presents a current topic related to market structures.
- **Yearly Update Worksheet** provides an annual update, including a new worksheet and lesson on this topic.
- **On the Go** resources can be downloaded so students and teachers can connect with economics anytime, anywhere.

Chapter 7 Market Structures

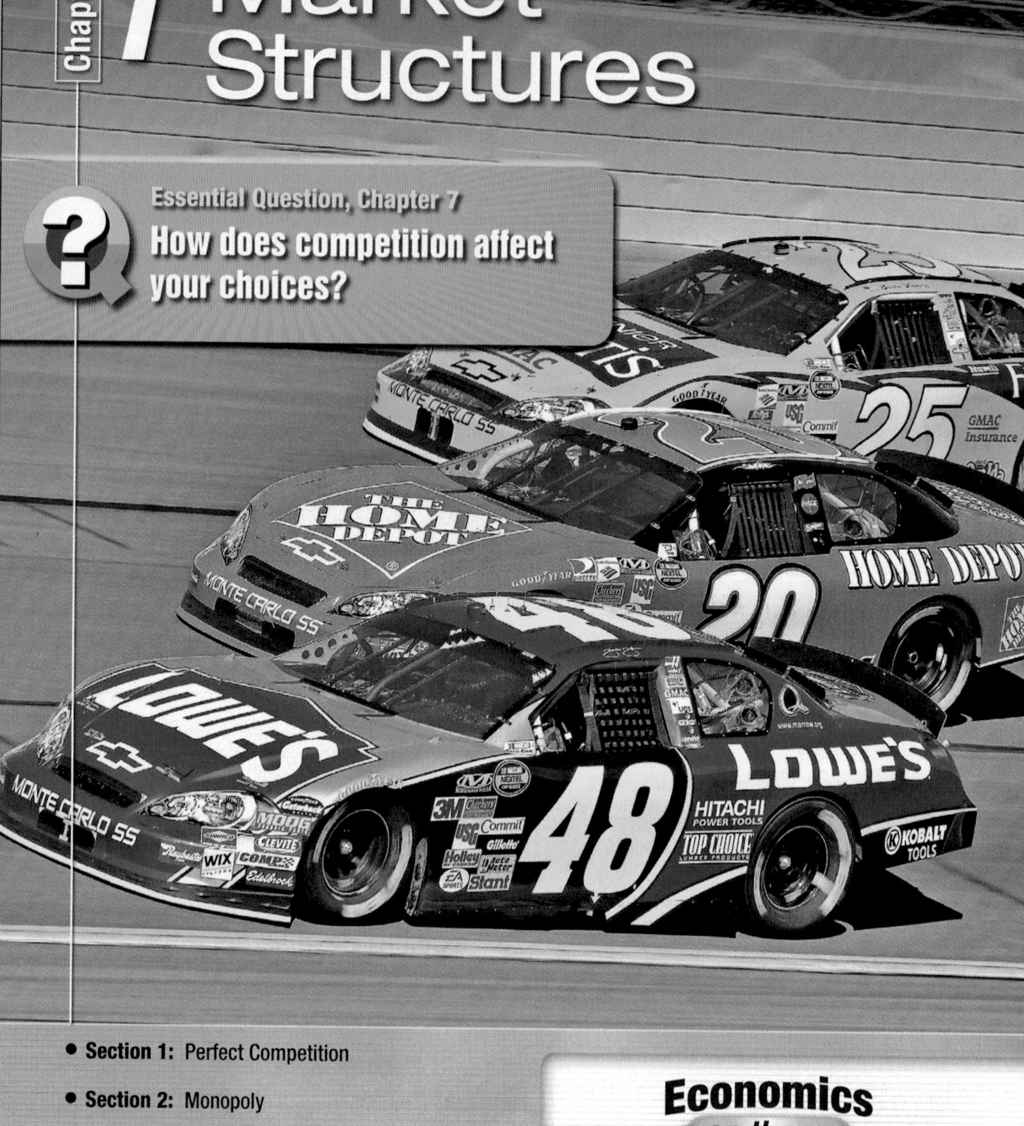

Economics on the go

To study anywhere, anytime, download these online resources at ***PearsonSuccessNet.com*** ▶

ECONOMICS ONLINE

DIGITAL TEACHER TOOLS

The online lesson planner is designed to help teachers plan, teach, and assess. Teachers have the ability to use or customize existing Pearson lesson plans. Online lecture notes support the print lesson by providing an array of accessible activities and summaries of key concepts.

Two interactivities included in this lesson are:

- **Visual Glossary** Students participate in an activity that illustrates the concept of perfect competition.
- **WebQuest** Students use online resources to complete a guided activity further exploring the essential questions.

Block Scheduling

BLOCK 1 Teach Sections 1 and 2. Teach the Extend option from Section 1.

BLOCK 2 Teach Sections 3 and 4. Then have students work together to decide whether to take legal action under antitrust laws against a firm using the Simulation Activity, "Is the Law Being Broken?"

Pressed for Time

Group work Divide students into four groups and assign a section to each. Have groups study their section carefully, taking notes, and discussing it as a group until they know the material. Then have each group present a panel discussion based on the guiding question that reviews their section. Encourage other students to ask questions. Complete the transparencies, skill, and activity worksheets as a class.

SECTION 1 Perfect Competition

OBJECTIVES

1. **Describe** the four conditions that are in place in a perfectly competitive market.
2. **List** two common barriers that prevent firms from entering a market.
3. **Describe** prices and output in a perfectly competitive market.

ECONOMIC DICTIONARY

As you read the section, look for the definitions of these **Key Terms:**

- perfect competition
- commodity
- barrier to entry
- imperfect competition
- start-up costs

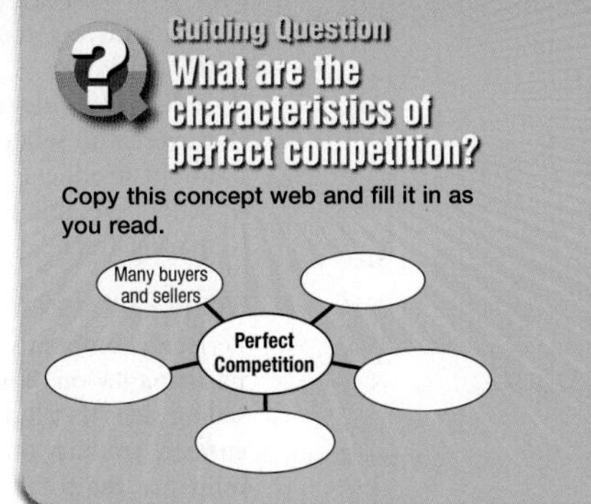

Economics and You You have decided to cook dinner. As you shop for produce at the local farmer's market, you see many fruits and vegetables being offered by several different suppliers. Yet each supplier charges the same price for fruits and vegetables. On the way home, you wonder why buying a leather jacket, a car, or a high-definition television isn't as simple as buying produce at the local farmer's market.

Principles in Action The farmer's market, with its identical goods and many buyers and sellers, is a rare, real-world example of a market in perfect competition. However, you will learn about factors that prevent perfect competition in most markets.

Four Conditions for Perfect Competition

Perfect competition, also called pure competition, is the simplest market structure. A perfectly competitive market is one with a large number of firms all producing essentially the same product. It assumes that the market is in equilibrium and that all firms sell the same product for the same price. However, each firm produces so little of the product compared with the total supply that no single firm can hope to influence prices. The only decision such producers can make is how much to produce, given their production costs and the market price.

While few industries meet all of the conditions for perfect competition, some come close. Examples include the markets for many farm

perfect competition a market structure in which a large number of firms all produce the same product and no single seller controls supply or prices

Visual Glossary online
Go to the Visual Glossary Online for an interactive review of **perfect competition.**

Action Graph online
Go to Action Graph Online for animated versions of key charts and graphs.

How the Economy Works online
Go to How the Economy Works Online for an interactive lesson on **regulation.**

Focus on the Basics

Students need to come away with the following understandings:

FACTS: • Perfectly competitive markets are characterized by many well-informed buyers and sellers, identical products being sold, and easy access into and out of the market for sellers. • Start-up costs and a need for technological training can present barriers to entry into some markets. • Competition in perfectly competitive markets promotes efficient use of resources and the lowest possible prices.

GENERALIZATION: Perfect competition exists when a market has many buyers and sellers of the same good so that no one buyer or seller can affect the price.

 **Guiding Question**

What are the characteristics of perfect competition?

Get Started

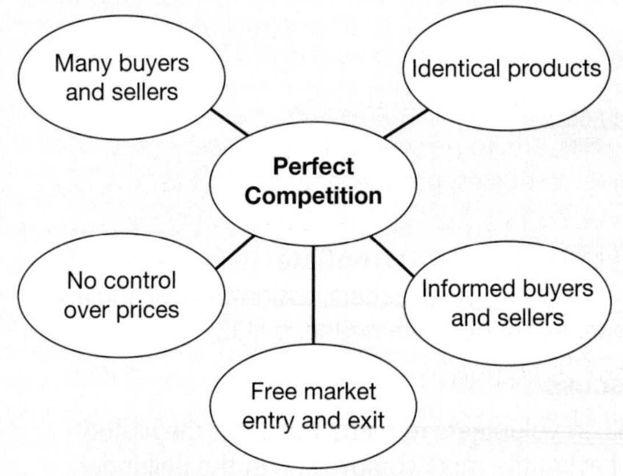

LESSON GOALS

Students will:

- Know the Key Terms.
- Identify examples of perfect competition by completing a worksheet.
- Describe the two common barriers that make it difficult for firms to enter a market.
- Explain how prices and output are determined in a perfectly competitive market.

BEFORE CLASS

Students should read the section for homework before coming to class.

Have students complete the graphic organizer in the Section Opener as they read the text. As an alternate activity, have students complete the Guided Reading and Review worksheet (Unit 2 All-in-One, p. 129).

L1 L2 ELL LPR Differentiate Have students complete the Guided Reading and Review worksheet (Unit 2 All-in-One, p. 130).

CLASSROOM HINTS

To help students understand perfect competition, have them role play buying and selling at a farmer's market. Make a list of a few products, such as apples, and their prices. One group should act as sellers, and the other as buyers. Sellers must come up with ideas to increase efficiency if they want to lower prices. Buyers must seek out the lowest price and keep themselves well informed.

BELLRINGER

Write the following list of items on the chalkboard: tomatoes, cars, electricity, notepaper, water, dairy farms, baseball teams, kitchen appliances, fast food. Have students arrange the items on a continuum from those that have the greatest to those that have the least competition.

Teach

Economics online To present this topic using digital resources, use the lecture notes at www.PearsonSuccessNet.com.

L1 L2 ELL LPR Differentiate To help students who are struggling readers, assign the Vocabulary worksheet (Unit 2 All-in-One, p. 128).

DISCUSS

Call on volunteers to name the items they listed as having the most competition in the Bellringer activity. List these items and the four conditions of perfect competition on the board. Have students explain why the markets they have volunteered do or do not fit the conditions of perfect competition.

DISTRIBUTE ACTIVITY WORKSHEET

Distribute the "Identifying Perfect Competition" worksheet (Unit 2 All-in-One, p. 131). Have students determine whether or not various markets are perfectly competitive. When they finish, guide a class discussion of the answers.

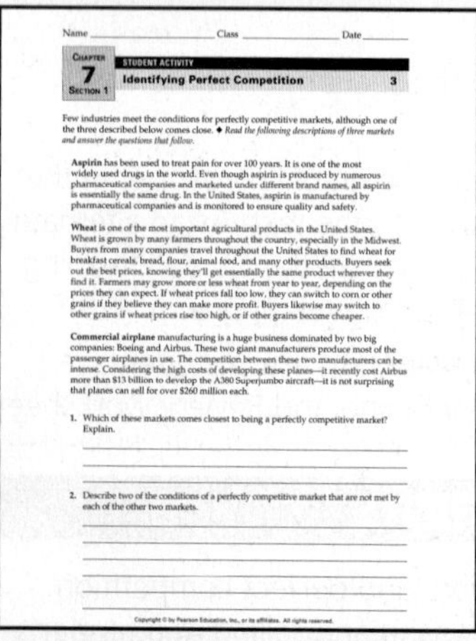

Name ________ Class ________ Date ________

Chapter 7 Section 1 — STUDENT ACTIVITY — **Identifying Perfect Competition** 3

Few industries meet the conditions for perfectly competitive markets, although one of the three described below comes close. ◆ *Read the following descriptions of three markets and answer the questions that follow.*

Aspirin has been used to treat pain for over 100 years. It is one of the most widely used drugs in the world. Even though aspirin is produced by numerous pharmaceutical companies and marketed under different brand names, all aspirin is essentially the same drug. In the United States, aspirin is manufactured by pharmaceutical companies and is monitored to ensure quality and safety.

Wheat is one of the most important agricultural products in the United States. Wheat is grown by many farmers throughout the country, especially in the Midwest. Buyers from many companies travel throughout the United States to find wheat for breakfast cereals, bread, flour, animal food, and many other products. Buyers seek out the best prices, knowing they'll get essentially the same product wherever they find it. Farmers may grow more or less wheat from year to year, depending on the prices they can expect. If wheat prices fall too low, they can switch to corn or other grains if they believe they can make more profit. Buyers likewise may switch to other grains if wheat prices rise too high, or if other grains become cheaper.

Commercial airplane manufacturing is a huge business dominated by two big companies: Boeing and Airbus. These two giant manufacturers produce most of the passenger airplanes in use. The competition between these two manufacturers can be intense. Considering the high costs of developing these planes—it recently cost Airbus more than $13 billion to develop the A380 Superjumbo aircraft—it is not surprising that planes can sell for over $260 million each.

1. Which of these markets comes closest to being a perfectly competitive market? Explain.

2. Describe two of the conditions of a perfectly competitive market that are not met by each of the other two markets.

L2 Differentiate Distribute the "Perfect Competition" worksheet (Unit 2 All-in-One, p. 132).

(lesson continued on p. 162)

Answer

Checkpoint If a market has many buyers and sellers it is not very likely that large enough groups of either buyers or sellers will work together to bargain for better prices.

products and the stocks traded on the New York Stock Exchange. These examples fulfill the four strict conditions for a perfectly competitive market:

1. Many buyers and sellers participate in the market.
2. Sellers offer identical products.
3. Buyers and sellers are well informed about products.
4. Sellers are able to enter and exit the market freely.

Many Buyers and Sellers

Perfectly competitive markets require many participants on both the buying and the selling sides. No individual can be powerful enough to buy or sell enough goods to influence the total market quantity or the market price. Everyone in the market must accept the market price as given.

As we saw in Chapter 6, supply and demand interact to determine both price and output. If a market has many independent buyers and sellers, it is not very likely that large enough groups of either buyers or sellers will work together to bargain for better prices. Instead, the market determines price without any influence from individual suppliers or consumers.

Identical Products

In a perfectly competitive market, there are no differences between the products sold by different suppliers. This is the second condition for perfect competition. If a rancher needs to buy corn to feed his cattle, he will not care which farmer grew the corn, as long as every farm is willing to deliver the corn he needs for the same price. If an investor buys a share of a company's stock, she will not care which particular share she is buying.

A product that is considered the same regardless of who makes or sells it is called a **commodity.** Examples of commodities include low-grade gasoline, notebook paper, sugar, and silicon chips. Identical products are a key to perfect competition for one reason: the buyer will not pay extra for one particular company's goods. The buyer will always choose the supplier with the lowest price.

commodity a product, such as petroleum or milk, that is considered the same no matter who produces or sells it

barrier to entry any factor that makes it difficult for a new firm to enter a market

imperfect competition a market structure that fails to meet the conditions of perfect competition

Informed Buyers and Sellers

The third condition for a perfectly competitive market is that buyers and sellers know enough about the market to find the best deal. Under conditions of perfect competition, the market provides the buyer with full information about the features of the product and its price. For the market to work effectively, both buyers and sellers have clear incentives to gather as much information as possible.

In most markets, a buyer's willingness to find information about prices and availability represents a trade-off. The time spent gathering information must be worth the amount of money that will be saved. For example, most buyers would not search the Internet or visit a dozen convenience stores to save five cents on a pack of chewing gum.

Free Market Entry and Exit

The final condition of perfectly competitive markets is that firms must be able to enter them when they can make money and leave them when they can't earn enough to stay in business. For example, when the first companies began earning a lot of money by selling frozen dinners, several competitors jumped into the market to seek profits with their own products. Later, when consumers didn't buy those dinners, the firms withdrew their products from the market.

Studies show that markets with more firms, and thus more competition, have lower prices. When one firm can keep others out of the market, it can sell its product at a higher price.

CHECKPOINT ***How does perfect competition ensure that prices aren't determined by individual suppliers or consumers?***

Barriers to Entry

Factors that make it difficult for new firms to enter a market are called **barriers to entry.** Barriers to entry can lead to **imperfect competition,** a market structure that fails to meet the conditions of perfect competition. Common barriers to entry include start-up costs and technology.

Differentiated Resources

- **L1 L2 Guided Reading and Review** (Unit 2 All-in-One, p. 130)
- **L2 Vocabulary worksheet** (Unit 2 All-in-One, p. 128)
- **L2 Perfect Competition** (Unit 2 All-in-One, p. 132)
- **L4 Not Enough or Too Many Producers?** (Unit 2 All-in-One, p. 133)

VISUAL GLOSSARY

Reviewing Key Terms
To understand *perfect competition*, review these terms:

market, *p. 29*
competition, *p. 33*
profit motive, *p. 51*
commodity, *p. 160*

What is Perfect Competition?

◀ **perfect competition** a market structure in which a large number of firms all produce the same product and no single seller controls supply or prices

A perfectly competitive market includes a large number of suppliers selling identical products called commodities. ***Why isn't the market for automobiles a perfectly competitive market?***

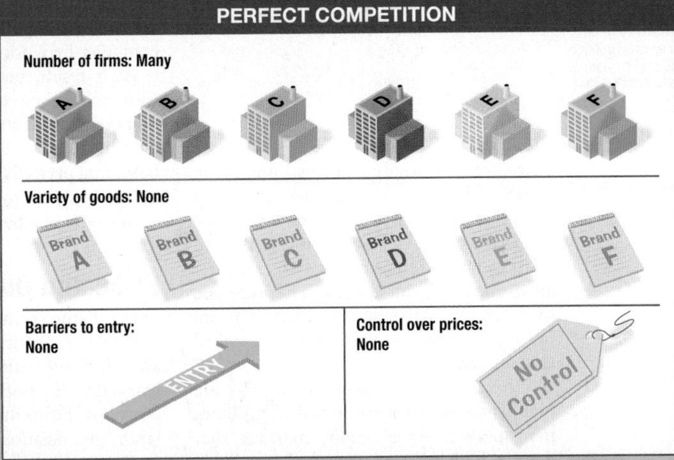

◀ In a perfectly competitive market, both buyers and sellers are well informed about products. ***What other condition of a perfectly competitive market does this cartoon represent?***

Visual Glossary online
To expand your understanding of this and other key economic terms, visit **PearsonSuccessNet.com**

161

Teach Visual Glossary

REVIEW KEY TERMS

Call on students to define each key term. Have students describe the relationship between each term and *perfect competition.*

market – *any arrangement that allows buyers and sellers to exchange things*

competition – *the struggle among producers for the dollars of consumers*

profit motive – *the incentive that drives individuals and business owners to improve their material well-being*

commodity – *a product, such as petroleum or milk, that is considered the same no matter who produces or sells it*

DISCUSS

Discuss the diagram with students. Remind students that, in addition to a large number of sellers shown in the diagram, there must be a large number of buyers. Ask **Why doesn't any one seller have control over price?** *(No one seller or buyer is large enough to affect prices.)* Ask **Why can conditions of perfect competition exist only if all products are considered to be the same?** *(The buyer must not prefer one company's products over another's; price must be the only factor.)* Have them give examples of such commodity products.

Have students explain how the cartoon illustrates the idea of perfect competition.

L1 L2 Differentiate Be sure students understand the meaning and significance of the terms *Thingymajigs* and *Watchamacallits* in the cartoon.

Economics online *All print resources are available on the Teacher's Resource Library CD-ROM and online at* www.PearsonSuccessNet.com.

Answers

Visual Glossary Diagram There are many types of cars and barriers to entry are high.

Cartoon It's easy for a new business to enter a perfectly competitive market

DISTRIBUTE ACTIVITY WORKSHEET

L4 Differentiate Distribute the "Not Enough or Too Many Producers?" worksheet (Unit 2 All-in-One, p. 133). Use the worksheet to discuss which scenario best serves the consumer. Discuss how, in a perfectly competitive market, prices and output are determined by the market, forcing each firm to be as efficient as possible. Ask why sellers in a perfectly competitive market do not set price.

Action Graph online Have students review the Action Graph animation for a step-by-step look at Market Equilibrium in Perfect Competition.

EXTEND

The Chicago Commodity Exchange is a global commodity market dealing in futures (a contract to deliver a product at a certain price at a future date). Have students work individually or in pairs to research the workings of this world-famous commodity exchange. Ask students to evaluate the role of a commodity exchange in setting prices.

L4 Differentiate Have students do research on real-world perfect competition. Some possible areas are non-unionized unskilled labor, dairy farms, and online auctions. Have students describe how these fill the definition of a perfectly competitive market.

GUIDING QUESTION WRAP UP

Have students return to the section Guiding Question. Review the completed graphic organizer and clarify any misunderstandings. Have a wrap up discussion about perfect competition.

Assess and Remediate

L3 L2 Collect the "Identifying Perfect Competition" and the "Perfect Competition" worksheets and assess students understanding of the conditions required for perfect competition.

L4 Collect the "Not Enough or Too Many Producers?" worksheet and assess student understanding.

L3 Assign the Section 1 Assessment questions.

L3 Give Section Quiz A (Unit 2 All-in-One, p. 134)

L2 Give Section Quiz B (Unit 2 All-in-One, p. 135)

(Assess and Remediate continued on p. 163)

Answers

Graph Skills 1. Large numbers of individual buyers and sellers lead to intense competition, forcing prices and output down to the point where prices just cover the most efficient producers' costs.
2. Consumers would buy products from other firms.

Checkpoint technological know-how

Figure 7.1 Market Equilibrium in Perfect Competition

GRAPH SKILLS

In a perfectly competitive market, price and output reach their equilibrium levels.

1. What factors allow a perfectly competitive market to reach equilibrium?
2. What prevents any one firm from raising its prices?

Action Graph online

For an animated version of this graph, visit PearsonSuccessNet.com

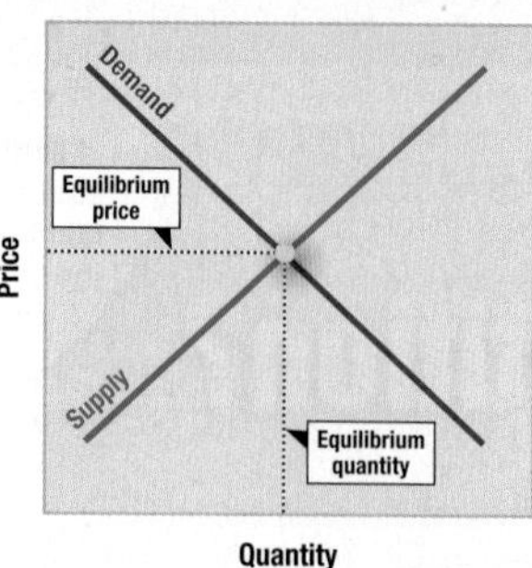

Start-Up Costs

Entrepreneurs need to invest money in a new firm long before they can start earning income. Before a new sandwich shop can open, the owner needs to rent a store, buy a refrigerator, a freezer, and an oven, and print menus. The expenses that a new business must pay before it can begin to produce and sell goods are called **start-up costs.**

When the start-up costs in a market are high, entrepreneurs are less likely to enter that market. As a result, markets that involve high start-up costs are less likely to be perfectly competitive markets. For example, the start-up costs for a sandwich shop are much lower than the start-up costs for a lumber mill or a supermarket. An entrepreneur with a small income is much more likely to try her luck with a sandwich shop.

Use of the Internet reduced start-up costs in many markets, including books and music. However, many entrepreneurs discovered that a Web page did not attract and hold customers as easily as a shop window. The high costs of advertising, shipping, and discounting goods pushed many out of business. With a few exceptions, the Internet-based companies that have succeeded paid substantial start-up costs.

start-up costs the expenses a new business must pay before it can begin to produce and sell goods

Technology

When a school group needs to raise money, its members can sell goods like flowers, cookies, or candy. Some technically skilled students might offer to fix cars or bicycles. But very few student groups would be able to raise money by creating and selling a new computer word-processing program.

Some markets require a high degree of technological know-how—the knowledge and skills needed to create or repair something. A carpenter, pharmacist, or electrician can spend years in training before he or she has learned all the necessary skills. Computer software engineers need extensive training to develop, create, and customize computer software and manage computer network systems.

As a result, new entrepreneurs cannot easily enter these markets without a lot of preparation and study. These technological barriers to entry can keep a market from becoming perfectly competitive.

CHECKPOINT ***Which barrier to entry can be overcome by education or vocational training?***

Price and Output

One of the primary characteristics of perfectly competitive markets is that they are efficient. Competition within these markets keeps both prices and production costs low. Firms must use all inputs—land, labor, organizational skills, machinery and equipment—to their best advantage. As a result, the prices that consumers pay and the revenue that suppliers receive accurately reflect how much the market values the resources that have gone into the product. In a perfectly competitive market, prices correctly represent the opportunity costs of each product.

Prices in a perfectly competitive market are the lowest sustainable prices possible. Because many sellers compete to offer their commodities to buyers, intense competition forces prices down to the point where the prices just cover the most-efficient sellers' costs of doing business. As you read in Chapter 6, this equilibrium is usually the most efficient state a market can achieve. Equilibrium in a perfectly competitive market is shown in **Figure 7.1**.

Virtual Economics on CD-Rom

L2 Differentiate

Comparing Perfect and Imperfect Competition Use the following lesson from the NCEE **Virtual Economics *CD-ROM*** to help students to understand competitive markets. Click on Browse Economics Lessons, specify grades 9–12, and use the key words *entrepreneur* and *market structure*.

In this activity, students will analyze the characteristics of competitive markets and evaluate the costs and benefits.

LESSON TITLE	THE ENTREPRENEUR AND MARKET STRUCTURE
Type of Activity	Small groups
Complexity	Moderate
Time	100 minutes
NCEE Standards	9, 14

▲ Landscaping presents no technical challenges and start-up costs are low. However, an auto-repair shop requires advanced technical skills. The equipment needed to run the shop makes start-up costs another significant barrier to entry.

We saw in Chapter 5 that producers earn their highest profits when they produce enough that their cost to produce one more unit exactly equals the market price of the unit. Since no supplier can influence prices in perfectly competitive markets, producers will make their output decisions based on their most efficient use of available land, labor, capital, and management skills.

In the long run, output in a perfectly competitive market will reach the point where each supplying firm just covers all of its costs, including paying the firm's owners enough to make the business worthwhile.

CHECKPOINT ***How are output decisions made in a perfectly competitive market?***

SECTION 1 ASSESSMENT

Essential Questions Journal To continue to build a response to the Essential Question, go to your **Essential Questions Journal.**

Guiding Question

1. Use your completed concept web to answer this question: What are the characteristics of perfect competition?
2. **Extension** Imagine that you are baking a cake for a friend's birthday. You need flour, milk, and eggs. Three nearby stores sell the items you need. How will you decide where to buy your groceries?

Key Terms and Main Ideas

3. List the four conditions for **perfect competition.**
4. When does **imperfect competition** occur?
5. What are two examples of **barriers to entry** in the magazine market?
6. How do **start-up costs** discourage entrepreneurs from entering a market?
7. Why must firms use land, labor, and other resources efficiently in perfectly competitive markets?

Critical Thinking

8. **Apply** How many of these markets come close to perfect competition: **(a)** televisions, **(b)** bottled water, **(c)** pizza, **(d)** cars, **(e)** white socks, **(f)** baseballs, **(g)** paper clips? Explain your choices.
9. **Predict (a)** What are commodities? **(b)** Why must perfectly competitive markets always deal in commodities? **(c)** What would happen to a perfectly competitive market if it stopped dealing in commodities? Explain your answer.
10. **Recognize (a)** What are barriers to entry? **(b)** Other than technology and start-up costs, what are two specific examples of barriers that could prevent a company or individual from entering a market?

Quick Write

11. Reread Four Conditions for Perfect Competition in this section. Write a short essay answering the following questions: Why is perfect competition the simplest market structure? How well does the model of perfect competition fit the real world? Why do you think economists use this model?

Have students complete the Self-Test Online and continue their work in the **Essential Questions Journal.**

REMEDIATION AND SUGGESTIONS

Use the chart below to help students who are struggling with content.

WEAKNESS	REMEDIATION
Identifying key terms (Questions 3, 4, 5, 6, 9)	Have students use the interactive Economic Dictionary Online.
The four conditions for perfect competition (Questions 1, 3, 4, 8, 9, 11)	Use a cluster diagram with "four conditions" in the center. Add four surrounding circles. Have students copy the diagram and write each condition. Have them add two more circles to each of the four surrounding circles and add details.
What are barriers to competition (Questions 5, 6, 10)	Have students work in pairs and outline the section under "Barriers to Entry."
What determines price and output (Questions 2, 7)	Review Figure 7.1. Draw the graph on the board. Have students review and explain what happens if demand and supply change.

Answer

Checkpoint on the basis of the most efficient use of available land, labor, capital, and management skills

Assessment Answers

1. many buyers and sellers, identical products, informed buyers and sellers, free market entry and exit, no control over prices
2. wherever the price is lowest
3. many buyers and sellers, identical products, informed buyers and sellers, free market entry and exit
4. Possible response: when barriers to competition make it difficult for new firms to enter the market
5. Possible response: cost of computers, skill in writing and photography
6. Entrepreneurs may not have enough money.
7. Producers cannot control price, so they must use resources as efficiently as possible.
8. Paper clips and white socks; they are nearly identical and there are many buyers.
9. (a) products considered the same regardless of who makes or sells them (b) If products are considered identical, buyers will not pay more for one company's goods. (c) Buyers would make decisions based on differences between products.
10. (a) factors that make it difficult for new firms to enter a market (b) Possible response: difficulty in obtaining raw materials, difficulty in finding workers
11. It is the simplest market structure because all firms are producing the same product and selling it for the same price. Markets usually fail to meet all conditions of perfect competition. Economists use it to explain how markets work.

Guiding Question

What are the characteristics of monopoly?

Get Started

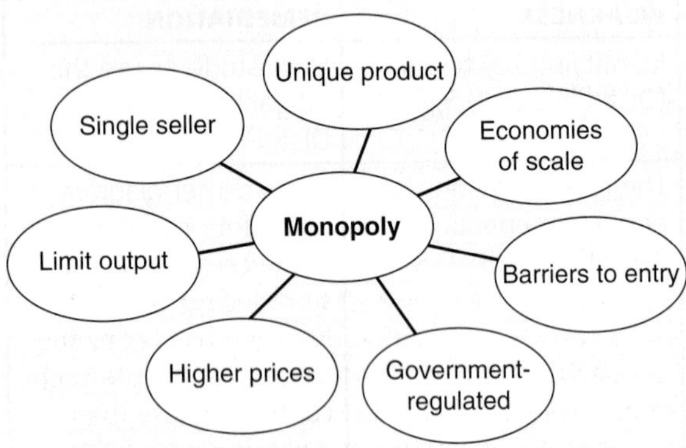

LESSON GOALS

Students will:

- Know the Key Terms.
- Explain the characteristics of a monopoly.
- Understand economies of scale by completing a worksheet.
- Discuss the government's role in regulating and establishing monopolies.
- Analyze graphs to determine how monopolies make output decisions.
- Describe price discrimination.

BEFORE CLASS

Students should read the section for homework.

Have students complete the graphic organizer in the Section Opener as they read the text. As an alternate activity, have students complete the Guided Reading and Review worksheet (Unit 2 All-in-One, p. 136).

L1 L2 ELL LPR Differentiate Have students complete the Guided Reading and Review worksheet (Unit 2 All-in-One, p. 137).

OBJECTIVES

1. **Describe** characteristics and give examples of a monopoly.
2. **Describe** how monopolies, including government monopolies, are formed.
3. **Explain** how a firm with a monopoly makes output decisions.
4. **Explain** why monopolists sometimes practice price discrimination.

ECONOMIC DICTIONARY

As you read the section, look for the definitions of these **Key Terms:**

- monopoly
- economies of scale
- natural monopoly
- government monopoly
- patent
- franchise
- license
- price discrimination
- market power

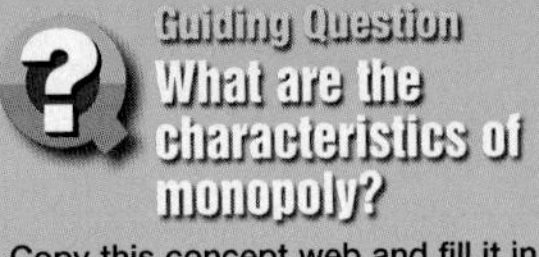

Copy this concept web and fill it in as you read.

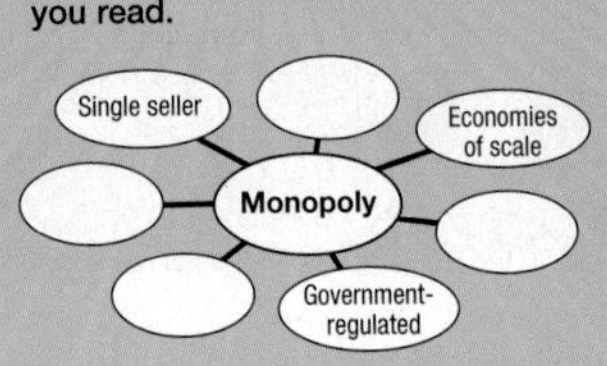

monopoly a market in which a single seller dominates

Economics and You Unfortunately, you have been diagnosed with a rare and serious infection. The doctor prescribes a ten day supply of a new medication. At the pharmacy, you discover that the medicine costs $97.35—nearly ten dollars a pill! There are no substitutes, so you buy the medicine. Later, you learn that only one company has the right to produce that drug. The company says that revenue from the medicine pays for the research and development costs of producing it.

Principles in Action While there are different types of monopolies, all are characterized by a single seller that controls an entire market. This arrangement allows monopolies to control output and charge higher prices. This section's Innovators describes Andrew Carnegie's journey from ambitious monopolist to generous philanthropist.

Describing Monopoly

A **monopoly** forms when barriers prevent firms from entering a market that has a single supplier. While a perfectly competitive market has many buyers and sellers, monopoly markets have only one seller, but any number of buyers. In fact, barriers to entry are the principal condition that allows monopolies to exist.

Economists use a strict set of requirements to characterize a monopoly. Besides having a single seller and barriers to entry, a monopoly is also characterized by supplying a unique product. But suppliers may only appear to have a unique product, because if we take a broader view, we may uncover alternatives. For example, you might think that a convenience store on a highway in the middle of the desert has a monopoly. However, travelers can carry their own supplies in their car instead of paying high prices for items at the store. Or, if they have enough money, they can fly across the desert and bypass the store altogether. In other words, there are options. In a monopoly, the good or service provided has no close substitute.

▲ To prevent resources from being wasted, public water is a natural monopoly.

CLASSROOM HINTS

Students may have read about the high price of diamonds and may wonder why they are always expensive. Diamonds are relatively rare, but normally changes in supply and demand would make prices go up and down. Students may not know that a single seller, DeBeers, has controlled the diamond supply for most of the last century. The company's market power has allowed it to match supply with demand, and keep diamond prices high.

Focus on the Basics

Students need to come away with the following understandings:

FACTS: • A monopoly is a market in which a single supplier provides a unique product to any number of buyers. • Monopolies form when barriers prevent competitors from entering the market. • Different market factors create different types of monopolies. • The government is involved in creating and regulating monopolies. • Monopolies may use price discrimination to increase sales.

GENERALIZATION: Monopolies exist when one seller controls a market, allowing the seller to control output and set prices. Monopolies are so powerful that the government strictly regulates them.

The problem with monopolies is that they can take advantage of their market power and charge high prices. Given the law of demand, this means that the quantity of goods sold is lower than in a market with more than one seller. For this reason, the United States has outlawed some monopolistic practices, as you will read in Section 4.

CHECKPOINT ***What are three characteristics of a monopoly?***

Forming a Monopoly

All monopolies have one trait in common: a single seller in a market. However, different market conditions can create different types of monopolies.

Economies of Scale

If a firm's start-up costs are high, and its average costs fall for each additional unit it produces, then it enjoys what economists call economies of scale. **Economies of scale** are characteristics that cause a producer's average cost to drop as production rises.

The graph on the left in **Figure 7.2** shows an average total cost curve for a firm without economies of scale. Follow the curve from left to right. As output increases from zero, the average cost of each good drops, and the curve initially slopes downward. This is because large, initial, fixed costs, like the cost of the factory and machinery, can be spread out among more and more goods as production rises. If the factory cost $1,000 to build and each unit of output costs $10 to make, producing one unit will cost $1,010, but producing two units will cost $1,020, or only $510 each. However, if the industry has limited economies of scale, output will eventually rise to a level at which the limited scale economies are exhausted, and the cost of making each unit will rise. The average cost of producing each good increases as output increases, and the curve slopes upward to match the rising cost per unit.

A factory in an industry with economies of scale never reaches this second stage of rising costs per unit. As production increases, the firm becomes more efficient, even at a level of output high enough to supply the entire market. The graph on the right in **Figure 7.2** shows how cost and output are related in economies of scale. Follow the curve from left to right. As output increases, the cost per unit falls, and continues to fall.

A good example is a hydroelectric plant, which generates electricity from a dam on a river. A large dam is expensive to build. However, once the dam is built, the plant can produce energy at a very low additional cost simply by letting water flow through the dam. The average cost of the first unit of electricity produced is very high because the cost of the dam is so high. As output

economies of scale factors that cause a producer's average cost per unit to fall as output rises

Figure 7.2 Effect of Economies of Scale

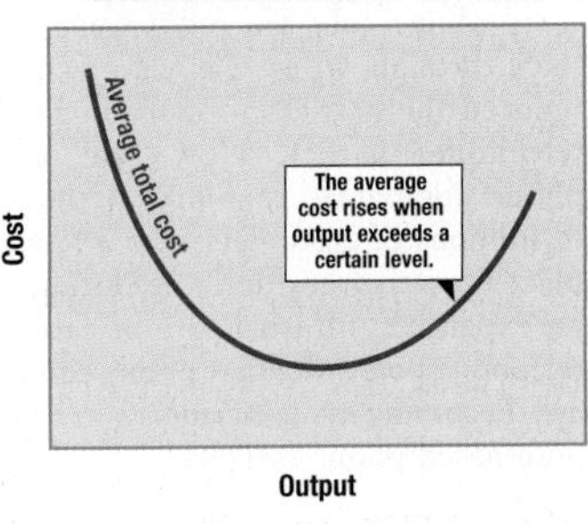

Average Total Cost Curve
Without Economies of Scale
Average total cost
The average cost rises when output exceeds a certain level.
Cost
Output

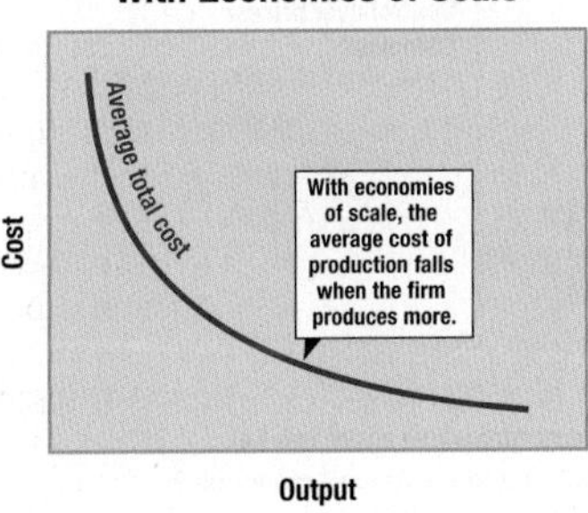

Average Total Cost Curve
With Economies of Scale
Average total cost
With economies of scale, the average cost of production falls when the firm produces more.
Cost
Output

GRAPH SKILLS

With economies of scale, production costs continue to fall as output increases.

1. Why do production costs fall as output increases?
2. Describe the cost curve for a firm without economies of scale.

BELLRINGER

Have students return to the list of products and services that they categorized in Section 1. List cars, kitchen appliances, and fast food on the chalkboard. Have students work together in pairs to brainstorm brand names in each category.

Teach

Economics online To present this topic using digital resources, use the lecture notes at www.PearsonSuccessNet.com.

DISCUSS

Have student volunteers write the names of all the brands that they have brainstormed. Ask **Is there competition? Why?** Then erase all but one brand for each category. Ask **If all the other brands disappeared, what would happen to price? Quality? Consumer choice?**

DEFINE

Have students identify the three characteristics of a monopoly—having a single seller and any number of buyers, having barriers to entry, and providing a unique product.

L1 L2 ELL Differentiate Create a concept web for the word *monopoly*. Ask volunteers to describe what it is and what it is not. Ask **How is the post office a monopoly?** Ask students to give an example of something that is not a monopoly.

Differentiated Resources

- **L1 L2 Guided Reading and Review** (Unit 2 All-in-One, p. 137)
- **L2 Understanding Monopoly** (Unit 2 All-in-One, p. 139)
- **L4 Determining Price in a Monopoly** (Unit 2 All-in-One, p. 140)

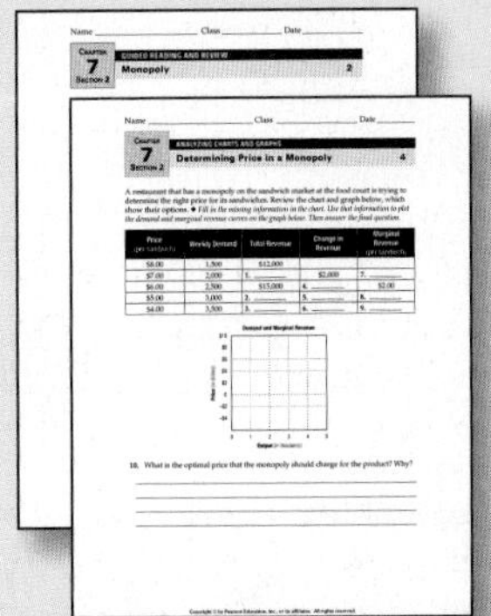

Answers

Checkpoint single seller, barriers to entry, unique product

Graph Skills 1. As output increases, cost per unit falls. 2. When economies of scale do not exist, increasing production beyond a certain point becomes costly. Other firms may enter the industry and produce additional units profitably.

GIVE EXAMPLES

Ask students to list four monopolies found in every school. *(cafeteria, vending machines, student store, school ring, yearbook, team outfits)* Then ask students to name monopolies that come into their homes. *(cable TV, U.S. mail, gas, electric, water)* Divide the class into four groups. Have each group list the benefits and liabilities of monopolies. *(Some benefits are: economies of scale, efficiency, waste reduction, and controlled access to scarce resources. Some liabilities are: lack of consumer choice, limits on other entrepreneurs, power to control price, unfair competition. Student answers could also be specific based on their previous answers.)*

DISTRIBUTE STUDENT ACTIVITY

Use Figure 7.2, and the paragraph in the text that refers to Figure 7.2, to introduce economies of scale. Have students trace each curve from left to right. Note that each curve shows the average cost of making *one* unit at different output levels.

Distribute the "Economies of Scale" worksheet (Unit 2 All-in-One, p. 138). Have students study the cost curves for two different companies and answer the questions about economies of scale.

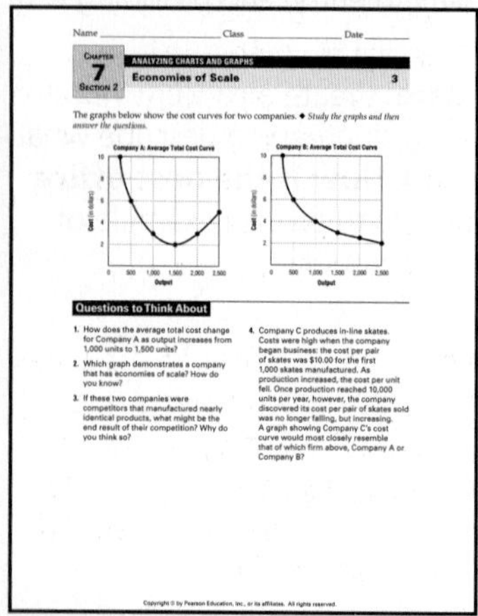

Name ____________ Class ____________ Date ________

CHAPTER 7 SECTION 2

ANALYZING CHARTS AND GRAPHS

Economies of Scale 3

The graphs below show the cost curves for two companies. ◆ *Study the graphs and then answer the questions.*

Questions to Think About

1. How does the average total cost change for Company A as output increases from 1,000 units to 1,500 units?
2. Which graph demonstrates a company that has economies of scale? How do you know?
3. If these two companies were competitors that manufactured nearly identical products, what might be the end result of their competition? Why do you think so?
4. Company C produces in-line skates. Costs were high when the company began business: the cost per pair of skates was $10.00 for the first 1,000 skates manufactured. As production increased, the cost per unit fell. Once production reached 10,000 units per year, however, the company discovered its cost per pair of skates sold was no longer falling, but increasing. A graph showing Company C's cost curve would most closely resemble that of which firm above, Company A or Company B?

L2 Differentiate Distribute the "Understanding Monopoly" worksheet (Unit 2 All-in-One, p. 139). Check students' answers.

Answers

Chart Skills 1. Government controls the prices it can charge and what services it must provide. 2. Possible response: public utilities, such as electricity, gas, sewer.

Checkpoint Technology can destroy a natural monopoly and make small companies as efficient as a large firm.

---

natural monopoly a market that runs most efficiently when one large firm supplies all of the output

increases, the fixed costs of the dam can be spread over more units of electricity, so the average cost drops. In a market with economies of scale, bigger is better. An industry that enjoys economies of scale can easily become a natural monopoly.

However, new strategies are emerging. Some business leaders now favor sidestepping economies of scale:

> "Many business leaders are re-examining their assumptions about the benefits of scale. Scaling down, not up, and building "disposable factories" and even "disposable strategies" are becoming new keys to lowering costs and boosting performance."
>
> —George Stalk, *5 Future Strategies You Need Right Now*, Harvard Business School Press, 2008

Natural Monopolies

A **natural monopoly** is a market that runs most efficiently when one large firm provides all of the output. If a second firm enters the market, competition will drive down the market price charged to customers and decrease the quantity each firm can sell. One or both of the firms will not be able to cover their costs and will go out of business.

Public water provides a good example of a natural monopoly. In a competitive market, different water companies would invest huge amounts of money to dig reservoirs and set up overlapping networks of pipes and pumping stations to deliver water to the same town. Companies would use more land and water than necessary. Each company would have to pay for all of the unneeded pipes and would serve customers no better than a single network.

In cases like this, the government often steps in to allow just one firm in each geographic area to provide these necessary services. The government action ensures that resources are not wasted by building additional plants when only one is needed. In return for monopoly status, a firm with a natural monopoly agrees to let government control the prices it can charge and what services it must provide.

Figure 7.3 Monopoly

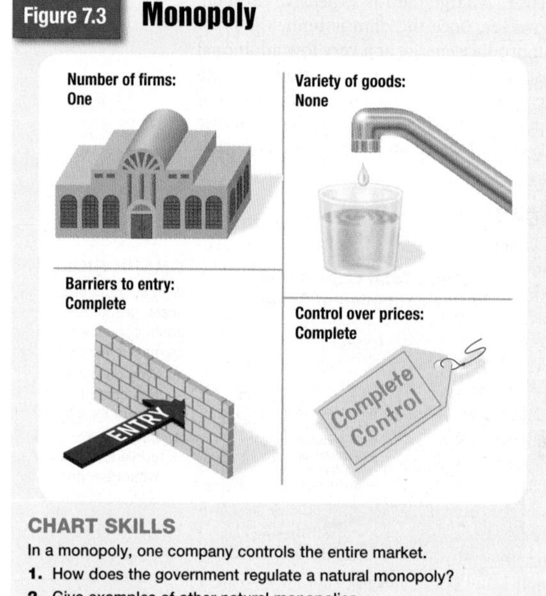

CHART SKILLS

In a monopoly, one company controls the entire market.

1. How does the government regulate a natural monopoly?
2. Give examples of other natural monopolies.

Technology and Change

Sometimes the development of a new technology can destroy a natural monopoly. A new innovation can cut fixed costs and make small companies as efficient as one large firm.

When telephone calls were carried by thick copper wires, local telephone service was considered a natural monopoly. No one wanted to build more than one network of wires to connect thousands of homes and businesses. In the 1980s and 1990s, consumers began using cellular phones, which were portable and could carry phone calls via radio waves rather than through wires. Cellular technology reduced the barriers to entry in the local telephone market. Now that cellular phone companies can link to thousands or millions of customers with a few, well-placed towers, they don't need to invest in an expensive infrastructure of cables and telephone poles. Cellular phone companies are becoming as efficient as traditional wire-based phone services.

CHECKPOINT ***How can technology affect a monopoly?***

Innovators

Andrew Carnegie

"I believe the true road to preeminent success in any line is to make yourself master in that line."

Andrew Carnegie certainly traveled that "true road" to success. He arrived in Pittsburgh in 1848, the son of poor Scottish immigrants. In 1901, J. P. Morgan called him "the richest man in the world."

Carnegie's career began in 1853, when he got a job as a telegraph operator for the Pennsylvania Railroad (PRR). Carnegie soon became the personal assistant to Thomas Scott, superintendent of the PRR's western division. He was paid a monthly salary of $35.

Railroads were a growth industry. Scott taught Carnegie how to control costs and profit from related businesses. By 1865, Carnegie was earning $40,000 a year from his investments.

After the Civil War, Carnegie realized that there would be increased demand for steel. He built a modern steel plant near Pittsburgh, which used the new Bessemer process to convert large batches of iron into steel. Carnegie supplied steel for railroads, bridges, and naval ships.

Carnegie had a simple motto: "Watch the costs and the profits will take care of themselves." In 1901, when he sold the Carnegie Steel Company to J.P. Morgan for $480 million, it was producing more steel than all of Great Britain.

Carnegie believed that "the man who dies rich dies disgraced." Before he died, he donated $350 million to establish 2,500 public libraries, support higher education, and promote world peace.

Critical Thinking: ***How did Carnegie benefit from technology?***

Fast Facts

Andrew Carnegie

Born: November 25, 1835, in Dunfermline, Scotland

Died: August 11, 1919, in Lenox, MA

Education: 5 years of grade school

Claim to Fame: Founder, Carnegie Steel Company; Philanthropist

Government Monopolies

In the case of a natural monopoly, the government allows the monopoly to form and then regulates it. In other cases, however, government actions themselves can create barriers to entry in markets and thereby create monopolies. A **government monopoly** is a monopoly created by the government.

Technological Monopolies

One way that the government can give a company monopoly power is by issuing a patent. A **patent** gives a company exclusive rights to sell a new good or service for a specific period of time. Suppose that Leland Pharmaceuticals developed a new asthma medication called BreatheDeep that helped people with asthma to breathe more easily. If Leland's researchers could prove to the government that they had invented BreatheDeep, the Food and Drug Administration would grant Leland a patent. This patent would give Leland the exclusive right to sell BreatheDeep for 20 years.

Why would the government want to give a company monopoly power? Patents guarantee that companies can profit from their own research without competition. For this reason, patents encourage firms to research and develop new products that benefit society as a whole, even though the research and development costs may be very high. The patent allows firms to set prices that maximize their opportunity to make a profit.

Franchises and Licenses

A **franchise** is a contract issued by a local authority that gives a single firm the right to sell its goods within an exclusive market. National companies often grant franchises to entrepreneurs, who then sell that company's product in a local market.

A government entity can also grant a franchise. For example, the National Park Service picks a single firm to sell food and other goods at national parks, such as Yellowstone, Yosemite, and the Everglades. Your school may have contracted with one bottled-water company to install and stock vending machines. The franchise may include a condition that no other brand of water will be sold in the building. Governments,

government monopoly a monopoly created by the government

patent a license that gives the inventor of a new product the exclusive right to sell it for a specific period of time

franchise a contract that gives a single firm the right to sell its goods within an exclusive market

Background Note

U.S. Postal Service The U.S. Postal Service is one of the best known government monopolies. The core rationale for this monopoly is the USO, or universal service obligation. It was summarized in the Postal Reorganization Act of 1970, which defines the fundamental purpose of the Postal Service as ensuring postal service to all areas and populations of the United States at a uniform cost. The postal service is also obligated to consider the educational, cultural, and informational value of mail when setting rates. For example, book and magazine rates are low relative to the weight of the materials. Interestingly, despite its monopoly status, U.S. postal rates are actually lower than those in most other developed countries.

DISCUSS

Have students divide the list of monopolies that they generated into natural monopolies and government monopolies. Have students explain the criteria they used to categorize the monopolies. **What are the characteristics of the natural monopolies?** *(more efficient for there to be one producer)* Discuss why it is often reasonable in certain industries for the government to permit natural monopolies. *(It would be very expensive, and less efficient, for more than one company to set up the business, and would serve customers no better than a single producer.)* Ask **Why is government involvement in price-setting essential in a natural monopoly?** *(With no other supplier, price gouging could occur.)* Ask **How does a natural monopoly differ from a government monopoly?** *(Government creates the monopoly by granting a patent, franchise, or license.)* Using the list students generated as a starting point, ask **How do government monopolies touch your life?** *(Answers will vary; provide prompts if necessary to cover the three ways government creates monopolies: patents, franchises, licenses)* Ask **Do you think the results are always beneficial?** *(Answers will vary.)*

L1 L2 Differentiate Reinforce student understanding of monopolies by asking how the local water company meets the requirements for a monopoly. *(single seller of the product with multiple buyers; difficult for competitors to enter the market; a good that has no obvious substitute)*

L4 Differentiate Tell students that AT&T and the airline industry were once treated as natural monopolies by the government. Later both industries were deregulated and competition allowed. Have students do research to learn the history of one of these industries. Then assign students a position for or against the statement: "The public benefited/did not benefit from the deregulation of the _______ industry." Have students present their reasoned opinions to the class.

Answer

Critical Thinking The Bessemer process allowed Carnegie to mass produce steel at lower costs.

ROLE-PLAY

Discuss how industrial organizations are a special kind of monopoly allowed by the government. Explain Major League Baseball's exemption from antitrust laws. Then assign students roles to play in a discussion about changing Major League Baseball's exemption from antitrust laws: a major league owner, a first-class baseball player, mayor of a city with a team, mayor of a city without a team, minor league baseball player, baseball player not chosen for a team, building contractor, environmentalist, national sports supply chain, representative of cable networks. Summarize the arguments for and against the baseball exemption. Ask **Why would there be a variety of viewpoints?** *(Some people would benefit from and some would be hurt by the baseball monopoly.)*

DISCUSS

Ask **Can monopolists charge any price they want?** *(No, they face the limited choice between output and price.)* Examine with students how the monopolist's dilemma over price versus output affects consumers who may need more output than the monopolist decides to produce.

(lesson continued on p. 170)

Answer

Checkpoint Government can issue patents, franchises, and licenses, and it can also allow companies in an industry to become a monopoly.

license a government-issued right to operate a business

parks, and schools use franchises to keep small markets under control.

On a larger scale, governments can issue a **license** granting firms the right to operate a business, especially where scarce resources are involved. Examples of scarce resources that require licensing include land and radio and television broadcast frequencies. The Federal Communications Commission issues licenses for individual radio and television stations. Local governments might license a single firm to manage all of their public parking lots.

Industrial Organizations

In rare cases, the government allows the companies in an industry to restrict the number of firms in a market. For example, the United States government lets Major League Baseball and other sports leagues restrict the number and location of their teams. The government allows team owners of the major professional sports leagues to choose new cities for their teams and does not charge them with violating the laws that prevent competitors from working together.

Major League Baseball has an exemption from these laws, which are known as antitrust laws, because they were originally passed to break up an illegal form of monopoly known as a trust. Other sports leagues do not have an official exemption, but the government treats them as it treats baseball. The restrictions that the leagues impose help keep team play orderly and stable by preventing other cities from starting their own major league teams and crowding the schedule.

The problem with this type of monopoly is that team owners may charge high prices for tickets. In addition, if you're a sports fan in a city without a major league team, you're out of luck.

CHECKPOINT ***What government actions can lead to the creation of monopolies?***

Output Decisions

If you had severe asthma, which can be fatal, what would BreatheDeep be worth to you? You would probably want the medicine no matter how much it cost. So Leland, the company that invented and patented the drug, could charge a very high price for its new medication. In fact, they could charge enough to earn well above what it cost to research and manufacture the drug. The resulting profits would give the company a reason, or incentive, for inventing the new medication in the first place. But could Leland sell as much medication as it wanted to at whatever price it chose?

Even a monopolist faces a limited choice—it can choose either output or price, but not both. The monopolist looks at the big picture and tries to maximize profits. This usually means that, compared to a perfectly competitive market for the same good, the monopolist produces fewer goods at a higher price.

The Monopolist's Dilemma

The law of demand states that buyers will demand more of a good at lower prices and less at higher prices. A possible demand curve for BreatheDeep is shown in **Figure 7.4**, on page 170 with prices in dollars on the vertical axis and doses on the horizontal axis. Many people with life-threatening asthma will pay whatever the medicine costs. But some people with milder asthma will choose a cheaper, weaker medicine if the price rises too high.

Trace the demand curve from left to right. At $12 per dose, consumers might demand 8,000 doses of BreatheDeep each week. But at $9 per dose, as many as 11,000 doses will sell. The law of demand means that when the monopolist increases the price, it will sell less, and when it lowers the price, it will sell more. Another way to interpret this graph is that if a monopolist produces more, the price of the good will fall, and if it produces less, the price will rise.

Falling Marginal Revenue

Remember from Chapter 5 that to maximize profits, a seller should set its marginal revenue, or the amount it earns from the last unit sold, equal to its marginal cost, or the extra cost from producing that unit. This same rule applies to a firm with a monopoly. The key difference is that in a perfectly competitive market, marginal revenue is always the same as price, and

Background Note

Baseball's Antitrust Exemption Baseball's exemption from antitrust laws commenced in 1922 when the Supreme Court declared that baseball was a local business, not an interstate business subject to antitrust. In 1953, the Court acknowledged that baseball had become interstate commerce, but it said the Sherman Antitrust Act was never intended to apply to baseball, but only to commercial trusts like Standard Oil. The court added that only Congress could change baseball's exemption. In 1998 Congress passed the Curt Flood Act that partly removed the exemption by allowing players the right to sue under antitrust laws, but it otherwise reinforced baseball's exemption. Today, the exemption applies mostly to the ability of teams to relocate without league approval.

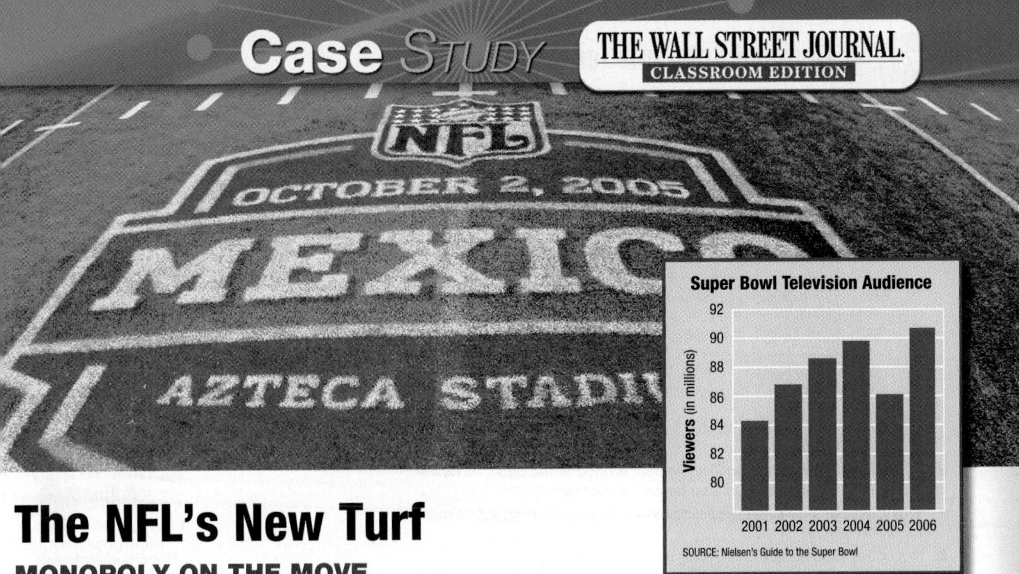

The NFL's New Turf

MONOPOLY ON THE MOVE

A monopoly may be the sole player in its market. But it still has to compete.

By John Lyons
The Wall Street Journal

The National Football League is making a big marketing push to make soccer-mad Mexico a football haven, too.

In Mexico City, the NFL teamed with the Cinemex theater chains to show Monday night games live on big screens. The league sponsors youth flag-football tournaments to win young fans. By the time the Super Bowl rolls around, Mexicans will be drinking from cans emblazoned with team logos, and finding NFL team stickers in loaves of bread and bags of potato chips.

The NFL's efforts in Mexico have become a cornerstone in the league's strategy to win additional overseas fans, from Germany to China. Millions of Mexicans have spent some time in the U.S., making Mexico a natural expansion market. In 2005, the NFL chose Mexico City's giant Azteca soccer stadium for the first of its regular-season games ever to be played outside the U.S. More than 103,000 people showed up. The success of that game prompted the NFL to schedule up to two regular-season games a year in foreign sites such as Mexico City, Toronto, London, Frankfurt and Cologne, Germany.

The plan represents a big investment—and risk—for NFL team owners who forgo a home game, and all ticket sales that go with it, to send their players abroad. Owners are betting that the overseas games will produce more fans, who will buy team-licensed clothing and souvenirs. The NFL believes it can grab a bigger share of the $43 billion international sports market, where the football league is a relatively small player today.

Overseas marketing isn't new for the NFL: The league has played overseas exhibition games since 1986, and NFL Europa, a league of lesser pros that plays in the spring, has teams in five German cities and Amsterdam. But the league now believes its best marketing tool is exporting regular-season NFL games, with all the excitement of having the stars on the field and playing for keeps. The buzz created by these games should lead to increased merchandise sales and TV viewership—two sources of revenue that have long since outstripped ticket sales in financial importance.

"We're convinced we have the best game," says Mark Waller, who was hired last year to head an overseas push. "If we can be successful in the U.S., the world's most competitive market, there's no reason why we can't compete elsewhere."

Applying Economic Principles
The National Football League wants to expand its audience. Their goal is to increase revenues from broadcasting and merchandising. Describe the advantages the NFL has when it comes to pricing.

Video News Update Online Powered by *The Wall Street Journal* Classroom Edition

For a new case study, go to the online resources at **PearsonSuccessNet.com**

Teach Case Study

SUMMARIZE AND EXPLAIN

Have students explain why the National Football League is trying to market itself internationally. Ask **What does the NFL have to gain by expanding its brand into Mexico?** *(The NFL wants to make money. It equates an increase in fans to an increase in the sales of team-licensed merchandise. It also wants revenue from TV viewership.)* Ask **What challenges does the NFL face as it tries to market internationally?** *(Soccer is more popular, there is a language barrier, interest might fade.)*

ANALYZE

Ask **What other U.S. professional sports have tried to gain market share outside of the U.S.?** *(Major League Baseball in Japan and Mexico, the National Basketball Association in China, NASCAR in Mexico.)* Have the students discuss whether the globalization of these sports would diminish their value or appeal in the United States.

L2 ELL Differentiate Football is extremely popular in the United States but is a small player globally, where most countries know football as soccer. Ask students to discuss what spectator sports are most popular in their home country. How popular were U.S. sports in their country?

Economics online *All print resources are available on the Teacher's Resource Library CD-ROM and online at* www.PearsonSuccessNet.com.

Answer

Applying Economic Principles Because the NFL provides a unique product (professional football), and there are often many fans for a team, the NFL can set prices on tickets, merchandise, and other NFL related products at the point where they will make the most profit.

ANALYZE

Review the production costs chart presented in Figure 5.5 on page 120 in Chapter 5. Point out the relationship between marginal cost, marginal revenue, and maximized profits. Then discuss the information presented in Figure 7.4 on p. 170. Have students summarize the relationship between price and output in a monopoly.

Ask students what happens to marginal revenue when the price is lowered to $9 per dose. *(Marginal revenue becomes negative.)* Explain that this demonstrates a characteristic of monopolies that occurs because there is only one seller. In a perfectly competitive market marginal revenue is equal to price since the price does not drop as more of the product is sold.

L1 L2 Differentiate Review the definitions of marginal revenue *(the amount a seller earns from the last unit sold)* and marginal cost *(the cost for producing one more unit of a good).*

Elicit the fact from students that the graph in Figure 7.4 is a demand graph, derived from the first two columns of the chart for price and weekly demand.

Help students understand why marginal revenue does not equal price in this case by calculating the marginal revenue in Figure 7.4 with students.

Action Graph online Have students review the Action Graph animation for a step-by-step look at Demand Schedule for BreatheDeep.

Answers

Graph Skills 1. because marginal revenue is –$1 when 11,000 doses are produced. 2. A monopolist can keep production at a level that gives the company the greatest revenue.

Figure 7.4 **Demand Schedule for BreatheDeep**

Price	Weekly Demand	Total Revenue	Change in Revenue	Marginal Revenue (per dose)
$12	8,000	$96,000	—	—
$11	9,000	$99,000	$3,000	$3
$10	10,000	$100,000	$1,000	$1
$9	11,000	$99,000	–$1,000	–$1
$8	12,000	$96,000	–$3,000	–$3

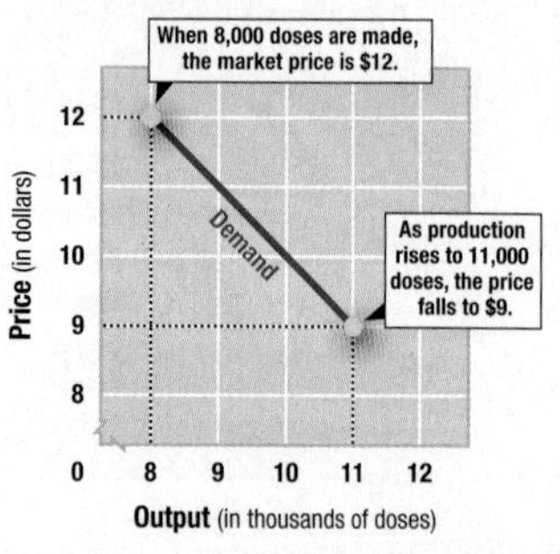

When 8,000 doses are made, the market price is $12.
As production rises to 11,000 doses, the price falls to $9.
Demand
Price (in dollars)
Output (in thousands of doses)
0
8
9
10
11
12

GRAPH SKILLS

By increasing output, a monopolist lowers the price of the good. Above a certain level of output, revenue also begins to decrease.

1. **Why does revenue fall when production increases from 10,000 doses to 11,000 doses?**
2. **How does producing fewer goods benefit a monopolist?**

Action Graph online

For an animated version of this graph, visit **PearsonSuccessNet.com**

each firm receives the same price no matter how much it produces. Neither assumption is true in a monopoly.

To understand how this happens, consider the demand schedule for BreatheDeep in **Figure 7.4**. When BreatheDeep is sold at $12 per dose, consumers buy 8,000 doses per week, providing $96,000 in revenue. If Leland lowers the price of BreatheDeep to $11 per dose, 9,000 doses will be bought for a total revenue of $99,000. The sale of 1,000 more doses brought Leland $3,000 in new revenue.

In Chapter 5, you read that marginal revenue in most markets is equal to price. In this monopoly, the marginal revenue at a market price of $11 is roughly $3 per dose, far below the market price. This is because the lower market price affects both the 1,000 new doses sold and the 8,000 doses people buy for $11 each instead of $12.

Now suppose that Leland lowers the price of BreatheDeep from $11 to $10 per dose. Consumers will buy 10,000 doses, for a total revenue of $100,000. This time, the sale of 1,000 more doses brought only $1,000 in additional revenue. The $10,000 in revenue from 1,000 new sales barely exceeds the $9,000 fall in revenue from selling the 9,000 doses for $10 each, not $11. The market price is $10 per dose, but the marginal revenue has fallen to a mere $1 for each dose of BreatheDeep sold.

As you've seen, when a firm has some control over price—and can cut the price to sell more—marginal revenue is less than price. In contrast, in a perfectly competitive market, the price would not drop at all as output increased, so marginal revenue would remain the same as price. The firm's total revenue would increase at a steady rate with production.

The table in **Figure 7.4** lists marginal revenues for several different prices. Note that marginal revenue actually becomes negative when the quantity demanded is greater than 10,000 doses per week.

Setting a Price

Leland will choose a level of output that yields the highest profits. As you read in Chapter 5, this is the point at which marginal revenue is equal to marginal cost.

In **Figure 7.4**, we have plotted the demand for BreatheDeep at market prices of $8, $9, $10, $11, and $12 per dose. According to **Figure 7.4**, output per week at these prices will be 12,000, 11,000, 10,000, 9,000, and 8,000 doses, respectively. These points form the market demand curve for BreatheDeep shown in red in **Figure 7.4.**

Then, based on this data, we plotted Leland's marginal revenue at these levels of output. These points form the marginal revenue curve shown in blue in **Figure 7.5.** The marginal revenue curve is at the bottom of the graph because a monopolist's marginal revenue is lower than the market price.

Marginal cost equals marginal revenue at point *a* in **Figure 7.5.** This is the most profitable level of output. The monopolist produces 9,000 units, the quantity at which marginal revenue and marginal cost are both $3. According to the market demand curve, the market price is $11 when 9,000 units are sold (point *b*). Therefore, the monopolist will set the price of each dose at $11 or set production at 9,000 units.

If dozens of firms sold BreatheDeep and the market were perfectly competitive, price and output would be different, as shown in **Figure 7.5.** In a perfectly competitive market, marginal revenue is always equal to market price, so the marginal revenue curve would be the same as the demand curve. Firms will set output where marginal revenue is equal to marginal cost, shown at point *c*. As you can see, a perfectly competitive market for BreatheDeep would have more units sold *and* a lower market price than a monopoly.

Profits

How much profit does the monopolist earn? As you recall from Chapter 5, profit can be determined by comparing price and average cost. For Leland, the company that makes BreatheDeep, the profit per dose is the difference between the market price and the average cost at that level of production. Suppose the average cost of producing 9,000 doses is $5, or slightly higher than the marginal cost. Each dose is sold for $11. The monopolist will earn a profit of $6 per dose ($11−$5), so the total profit is $54,000, or $6 per dose for 9,000 doses.

CHECKPOINT ***Where does a monopolist usually set output and price compared with a seller in a perfectly competitive market?***

Price Discrimination

The previous example assumed that the monopolist must charge the same price to all consumers. But in some cases, the monopolist may be able to divide consumers into two or more groups and charge a different price to each group. This practice is known as **price discrimination.**

Price discrimination is based on the idea that each customer has a maximum price that he or she will pay for a good. If a monopolist sets the good's price at the highest maximum price of all the buyers in the market, the monopolist will sell only to the one customer willing to pay that much. If the monopolist sets a low price, the monopolist will gain a lot of customers, but the monopolist will lose the profits it could have made from the customers who bought at the low price but were willing to pay more.

Although price discrimination is a feature of monopoly, it can be practiced by any company with market power. **Market power** is the ability to control prices and total market output. As you will read in the next section, many companies have some market power without having a true monopoly. Market power and price discrimination may be found in any market structure except for perfect competition.

price discrimination the division of consumers into groups based on how much they will pay for a good

market power the ability of a company to control prices and total market output

Personal Finance For help with evaluating insurance needs, see your Personal Finance Handbook in the back of the book or visit **PearsonSuccessNet.com**

Figure 7.5 **Setting a Price in a Monopoly**

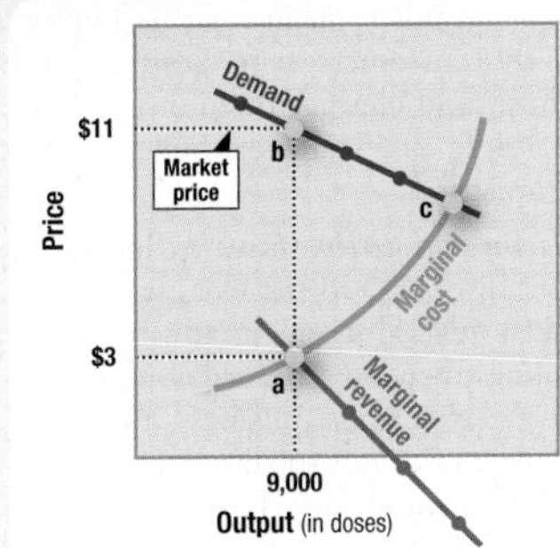

GRAPH SKILLS

A monopolist sets output at a point (a) where marginal revenue is equal to marginal cost.

1. How does point c show the benefits to consumers in a perfectly competitive market?
2. Why is the marginal revenue curve at the bottom of the graph?

Action Graph online

For an animated version of this graph, visit **PearsonSuccessNet.com**

ANALYZE A GRAPH

Discuss Figure 7.5. Help students read the graph by explaining that this is the demand curve shown in Figure 7.4. The marginal revenue curve is the graph of marginal revenue at each price using data from Figure 7.4. The marginal cost curve is given.

Ask **What information is provided by point a?** *(This is the point where marginal revenue equals marginal cost.)* **What information is provided by point b?** *(the price the company should charge to maximize profits)* **What information is provided by point c?** *(This is the point where price/marginal revenue in a perfectly competitive market equals marginal cost; if the market were perfectly competitive, the companies that sell BreatheDeep would maximize profits if they produced the number of doses indicated for the lower price indicated at this point.)*

Action Graph online Have students review the Action Graph animation for a step-by-step look at Setting a Price in a Monopoly.

L4 Differentiate Distribute the "Determining Price in a Monopoly" worksheet (Unit 2 All-in-One, p. 140). Have students complete the chart and plot the demand and marginal revenue curves.

PERSONAL FINANCE ACTIVITY

To help students make wise choices, you may want to use the Personal Finance Handbook lesson on the basics of insurance on page PF-28 and the activity worksheet (Personal Finance All-in-One, p. 77).

EXPLAIN

Call on a student to define *price discrimination*. Ask **How might price discrimination help monopolists solve their price/output dilemma?** *(Price discrimination allows a monopolist, or any company with market power, to charge groups of people the maximum they will pay.)*

L1 L2 Differentiate Help students understand the difference between a company with *market power* and a company that is a monopoly by giving an example, such as General Motors, which can control industry prices and output for cars to some extent.

Virtual Economics on CD-Rom

L3 Differentiate

Distinguishing Between Monopoly and Competition. Use the following lesson from the NCEE **Virtual Economics *CD-ROM*** to review the effects of monopoly in the nineteenth century. Click on Browse Economics Lessons, specify grades 9–12, and use the key words *19th century monopoly.*

In this activity, students will use evidence to analyze the impact of business consolidation on consumers and workers in the late 1800s

LESSON TITLE	**THE ECONOMIC EFFECTS OF 19TH CENTURY MONOPOLY**
Type of Activity	Case study
Complexity	Low
Time	100 minutes
NCEE Standards	9

Answers

Checkpoint The monopolist sets output lower and price higher than a seller in a perfectly competitive market.

Graph Skills 1. Price is lower and output is greater than in a monopoly. 2. For monopolies, marginal revenue is lower than market price.

DISCUSS

Ask **How have any of you ever benefited from price discrimination? Did the price discrimination influence your decision about what or when you made a purchase?**

Ask **What are some other examples of these targeted discounts?** *(discounted airline fares, rebate offers, senior discounts, discounts for children)* Call on students to explain why companies might consider these a win-win situation. *(It maximizes profits; more people can afford the good or service.)*

Talk about the limits of price discrimination. Ask **When would price discrimination be a losing strategy for a company?** *(If a company has no market power, competitors will take advantage of the higher prices charged to some customers by lowering their own prices. If a monopoly cannot divide customers into distinct groups, it cannot identify a price structure that will capture a broad range of buyers.)*

EXTEND

Write the following headline on the chalkboard:

Expiring Drug Patents Open Possibilities for Producers of Generics

Ask students to discuss what this headline means and who might be the winners and losers.

L1 **L2** **Differentiate** Draw a comparison and contrast chart on the board with two columns, labeling one column "Perfect Competition" and one column "Monopoly." Have students work in pairs to list details comparing the two market structures.

GUIDING QUESTION WRAP UP

Have students return to the section Guiding Question. Review the completed graphic organizer and clarify any misunderstandings. Have a wrap up discussion about the characteristics of monopoly.

Assess and Remediate

L3 **L2** Collect the "Economies of Scale" and "Understanding Monopoly" worksheets and assess students' understanding of how economies of scale affect cost curves.

L4 Collect the "Determing Price in a Monopoly" worksheets and assess students' understanding.

L3 Assign the Section 2 Assessment questions; identify student misconceptions.

L3 Give Section Quiz A (Unit 2 All-in-One, p. 141).

L2 Give Section Quiz B (Unit 2 All-in-One, p. 142).

(Assess and Remediate continued on p. 173)

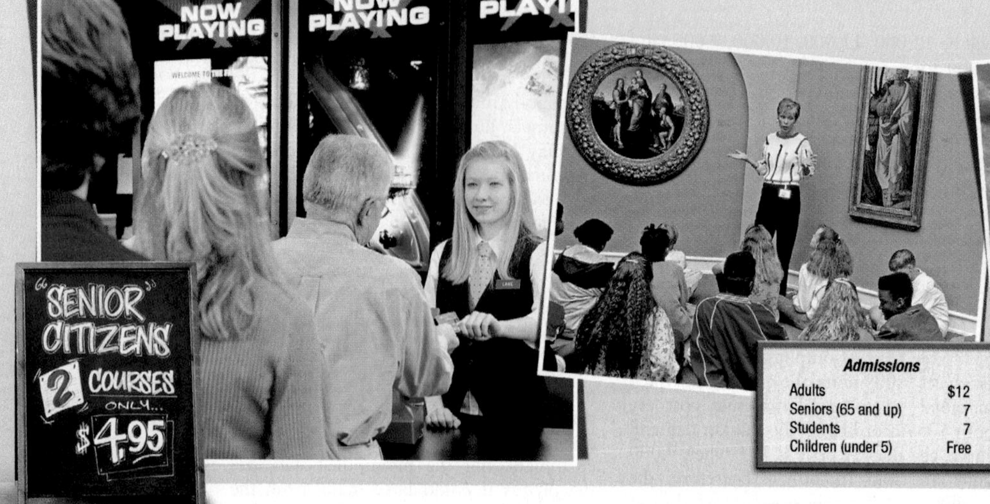

▲ Discounts for senior citizens, children, and students are a popular form of price discrimination.

Targeted Discounts

In the monopolist's ideal world, the firm could charge each customer the maximum that he or she is willing to pay, and no less. However, this is impractical, so companies divide consumers into large groups and design pricing policies for each group. The different prices that firms charge each group for the same good or service are not related to production costs.

One common form of price discrimination identifies some customers who are not willing to pay the regular price and offers those customers a discount. Price discrimination can also mean that a company finds the customers who need the good the most, and charges them more for that good. Here are some examples of price discrimination.

- ***Discounted airline fares*** Airlines offer discounts to travelers who buy tickets several weeks in advance or are willing to spend a Saturday night at their destinations. Business travelers would prefer not to stay over on a Saturday night, but these tickets are appealing to vacationers who wouldn't otherwise pay to fly and don't mind the restrictions.
- ***Manufacturers' rebate offers*** At times, manufacturers of refrigerators, cars, televisions, and other items will refund a small part of the purchase price to buyers who fill out a rebate form and mail it back. People who take the time to fulfill the rebate requirements are likely more price-conscious than those who don't and may be unwilling to pay full price.
- ***Senior citizen or student discounts*** Many retirees and students have lower incomes than people who work full time. Zoos, theaters, museums and restaurants often offer discounts to people in these groups, because they are unlikely to be able to pay full price for what some consider luxuries.
- ***Children fly or stay free promotions*** Families with young children spend more of their income on food, clothing, and school expenses. As a result, they have less money to spend on vacations. Once again, firms would rather have their business and earn lower profits than earn no profits at all, so they offer discounts for families with children.

Limits of Price Discrimination

For price discrimination to work, a market must meet three conditions. Firms that use price discrimination must have some market power, customers must be divided into distinct groups, and buyers must not be in a position in which they can easily resell the good or service.

1. *Some market power* For price discrimination to work, firms must have some control over prices. For this reason, price discrimination doesn't happen in perfectly competitive markets.
2. *Distinct customer groups* The price-discriminating firm must be able to divide customers into distinct groups based on their sensitivity to price. In other words, monopolists must be able to guess the demand curves of different groups, one of which is more elastic, or price-sensitive, than the others. By grouping customers, firms can increase profits by charging each group a different price.
3. *Difficult resale* If one set of customers could buy the product at the lower price and then resell the product for a profit, the firm could not enforce its price discrimination. Because consumer goods like shoes, groceries, and clothes are easily resold, price discrimination works best in marketing services that are consumed on the spot. Examples include theme-park admissions and restaurant meals. Airlines can offer senior discounts because the company can ask for identification and proof of age before letting the customer board the plane.

Although most forms of price discrimination are perfectly legal, sometimes firms use price discrimination to drive other firms out of business. This illegal form of the practice is called predatory pricing, and you will read more about it in Section 4.

CHECKPOINT ***What three conditions must a market meet in order for price discrimination to work?***

SECTION 2 ASSESSMENT

Essential Questions Journal To continue to build a response to the Essential Question, go to your **Essential Questions Journal.**

Guiding Question

1. Use your completed concept web to answer this question: What are the characteristics of monopoly?
2. **Extension** Suppose your family wants to install a high-speed Internet connection at home. However, only one company offers the service in your area. How do you think this will affect the service? Do you think your family should still order the high-speed connection?

Key Terms and Main Ideas

3. Why must a **monopoly** supply a unique product?
4. What is the problem with monopolies?
5. Explain the rights that a **patent** gives a company.
6. What is **market power?**
7. Why must firms be able to divide customers into distinct groups in order for **price discrimination** to work?

Critical Thinking

8. **Compare (a)** What is a natural monopoly? **(b)** How are natural monopolies and government monopolies different? **(c)** How are they similar?
9. **Interpret (a)** List three different forms of price discrimination. **(b)** How does price discrimination benefit producers and consumers? **(c)** Do you think price discrimination is fair? Why or why not?
10. **Apply (a)** In your own words, define the term "economies of scale." **(b)** This section used the example of a hydroelectric power plant as an industry with economies of scale. Give two of your own examples of economies of scale.

Math Skills

11. Suppose that Abra Cadabra, Inc. sells 1,000 magic tricks per month for $5 each. Last month, Abra Cadabra launched a special promotion—magic tricks for only $4 each. Sales increased to 1,500 magic tricks for the month. **(a)** What is the company's marginal revenue for each extra magic trick? **(b)** Compare the marginal revenue with the price of the magic tricks. What does the difference tell you about competition in the magic trick market?

Visit PearsonSuccessNet.com for additional math help.

CHAPTER 7 SECTION 2 **173**

Have students complete the Self-Test Online and continue their work in the **Essential Questions Journal**.

REMEDIATION AND SUGGESTIONS

Use the chart below to help students who are struggling with content.

WEAKNESS	REMEDIATION
Identifying key terms (Questions 3, 5, 6, 7)	Have students use the interactive Economic Dictionary Online.
The characteristics of a monopoly (Questions 1, 3, 4, 8, 10)	Draw a cluster diagram on the board with "Monopoly" in the center. Have students help complete the organizer by listing characteristics of monopolies.
How government impacts monopolies (Questions 5, 8)	Have students choose one monopoly and describe what market conditions would be like without government intervention.
How prices are set in a monopoly (Questions 2, 6, 7, 9, 11)	Have able students act out the roles of demand, marginal revenue, and marginal cost in setting prices. Let other students ask them questions.

Answer

Checkpoint The firm must have some market power; there are distinct customer groups; the product is difficult to resell.

Assessment Answers

1. single seller, unique product, barriers to entry, economies of scale, higher prices, limited output, government-regulated
2. Possible response: The price will be high and the service may not be as good as it would be if the company had a competitor. If you want it, you have no choice.
3. If it's not unique, customers will buy alternative products at lower prices.
4. Some people cannot afford products they want or need.
5. It gives a company a monopoly on the sale of a product for 20 years.
6. the ability to control prices and market output
7. because firms maximize profits by charging higher prices to groups with greater demand
8. (a) a market that runs best when one firm provides all output (b) The government allows a natural monopoly, then regulates it; a government monopoly is formed by the government. (c) both require government regulation
9. (a) Possible response: discounts for seniors; rebate offers; free services for children (b) Producers earn more profit; some consumers get products at lower prices. (c) Possible response: Yes, because both monopolists and consumers win.
10. (a) the average cost of an item drops as the quantity produced increases (b) Possible response: cable television company; a city public transportation system.
11. (a) $2.00 (b) It's a monopoly.

Guiding Question

What are the characteristics of monopolistic competition and oligopoly?

Get Started

Monopolistic Competition	Both	Oligopoly
• Many firms • Few barriers to entry • Little price control	• Similar but differentiated products	• A few firms • Significant barriers to entry • Some price control

LESSON GOALS

Students will:

- Know the Key Terms.
- Identify the similarities and differences between pure monopoly and competitive monopoly.
- Assess how monopolistic competition compares with monopoly and perfect competition.
- Describe oligopolies and name their barriers to entry.
- Analyze the market for a good.

BEFORE CLASS

Students should read the section for homework.

Have students complete the graphic organizer in the Section Opener as they read the text. As an alternate activity, have students complete the Guided Reading and Review worksheet (Unit 2 All-in-One, p. 143).

L1 L2 ELL LPR Differentiate Assign the Guided Reading and Review (Unit 2 All-in-One, p. 144).

Answer

Checkpoint Monopolistic competition: similar but not identical products; perfect competition: identical products.

SECTION 3 Monopolistic Competition and Oligopoly

OBJECTIVES

1. **Describe** characteristics and give examples of monopolistic competition.
2. **Explain** how firms compete without lowering prices.
3. **Understand** how firms in a monopolistically competitive market set output.
4. **Describe** characteristics and give examples of oligopoly.

ECONOMIC DICTIONARY

As you read the section, look for the definitions of these **Key Terms:**

- monopolistic competition
- differentiation
- nonprice competition
- oligopoly
- price war
- collusion
- price fixing
- cartel

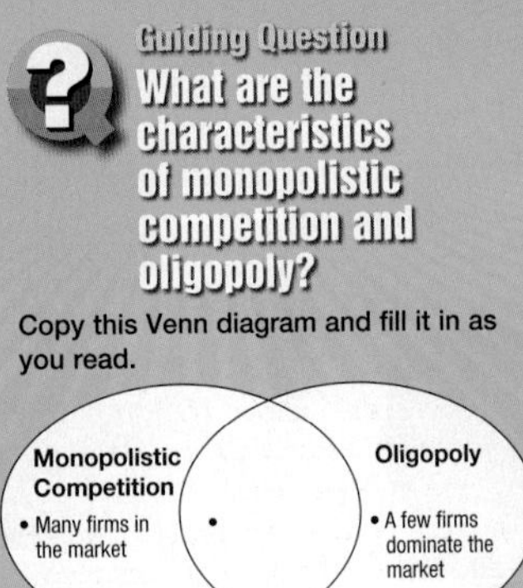
Guiding Question
What are the characteristics of monopolistic competition and oligopoly?
Copy this Venn diagram and fill it in as you read.
Monopolistic Competition
• Many firms in the market
•
Oligopoly
• A few firms dominate the market

monopolistic competition a market structure in which many companies sell products that are similar but not identical

Economics and You At the supermarket, you roam through aisles filled with various brands of soap, toothpaste, and paper towels. Although they are produced by different companies, these everyday products are very similar. To compete, producers find ways to make their products unique to attract customers like you.

Principles in Action While monopolistic competition is similar to perfect competition, oligopoly describes a market with only a few large producers. These are the market structures most familiar to consumers. This section's Economics & You highlights competition outside of the price arena.

Monopolistic Competition

In **monopolistic competition,** many companies compete in an open market to sell products that are similar but not identical. Each firm is monopolistic—it holds a monopoly over its own particular product design. You can think of monopolistic competition as a modified version of perfect competition with minor differences in products.

The differences between perfect competition and monopolistic competition arise because monopolistically competitive firms sell goods that are similar enough to be substituted for one another but are not identical. Monopolistic competition does not involve identical commodities. An example of a monopolistically competitive market is the market for jeans. All jeans can be described as denim pants, but in stores, buyers can choose from a variety of brand names, styles, colors, and sizes.

Unlike perfect competition, monopolistic competition is a fact of everyday life. You and your friends probably buy from monopolistically competitive firms several times a week. Common examples include bagel shops, ice cream stands, gas stations, and retail stores.

▲ The market for jeans is monopolistically competitive because jeans can vary by size, color, style, and designer.

CHECKPOINT ***How does monopolistic competition differ from perfect competition?***

174 MARKET STRUCTURES

CLASSROOM HINTS

To give students a concrete example of monopolistic competition, have them look at their pens and think about them as products. Pens are similar, but not identical. There are many kinds of pens, which means they are differentiated. Companies that make pens have some control over prices, but not very much. If you think a pen is too expensive, you can always buy a different pen that will write just as well. Pen makers engage in nonprice competition by adding features, such as different grips and changing colors and styles.

Focus on the Basics

Students need to come away with the following understandings:

FACTS: • Monopolistic competition is a market characterized by many firms, few barriers to entry, little control over price, and differentiated products. • Because distinctions can be made among goods sold in a monopolistic competition, firms engage in nonprice competition in addition to competing on price. • An oligopoly is a market dominated by a few large, profitable firms that sell differentiated products and have some control over price.

GENERALIZATION: Monopolistic competition is similar to perfect competition, except that the goods sold are not considered identical and firms have a small amount of control over prices. An oligopoly is a market made up of only a few large producers who have more control over the pricing of the goods they sell.

Four Conditions of Monopolistic Competition

Monopolistic competition develops from four conditions. As you read about the types of markets that favor monopolistic competition, note how similar they are to the rules that define perfect competition.

1. *Many firms* As a rule, monopolistically competitive markets are not marked by economies of scale. They do not have high start-up costs. Because firms can begin selling goods and earning money after a small initial investment, new firms spring up quickly to join the market.
2. *Few artificial barriers to entry* Firms in a monopolistically competitive market do not face the high barriers to entry discussed in Section 1. Patents do not protect anyone from competition, either because they have expired or because each firm sells a product that is distinct enough to fall outside the zone of patent protection. Just like a perfectly competitive market, a monopolistically competitive market includes so many competing firms that producers cannot work together to keep out new competitors.
3. *Little control over price* In a monopolistically competitive market structure, each firm's goods are a little different from everyone else's, and some people are willing to pay more for the difference. For this reason, firms have a bit of freedom to raise or lower their prices. However, unlike a monopoly, a monopolistically competitive firm has only limited control over price. If the price rises too high, consumers will buy a rival's product, because close substitutes are readily available. For example, many customers will choose a carton of brand-name orange juice over the store brand even if it costs $.50 more per carton. If the difference in price rose to $2 more per carton, however, most people would think seriously about buying the store brand of orange juice or some other drink altogether.
4. *Differentiated products* Firms have some control over their selling price because they can differentiate, or distinguish their goods from the other products in the market. The ability to differentiate goods is the main way that monopolistic competition differs from perfect competition. **Differentiation** enables a monopolistically competitive seller to profit from the differences between his or her products and competitors' products.

Figure 7.6 Monopolistic Competition

Number of firms: Many

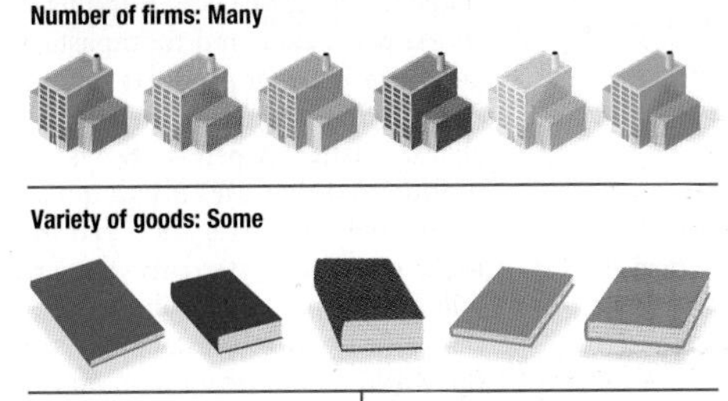

Variety of goods: Some

Barriers to entry: Low

Control over prices: Little

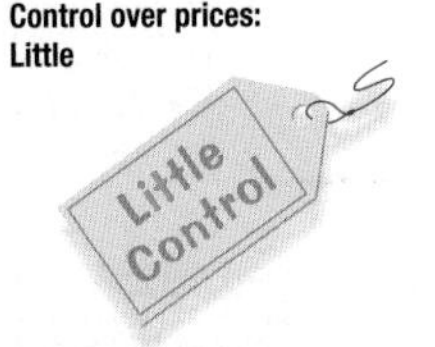

CHART SKILLS

Many firms provide a variety of goods in a monopolistically competitive market.

1. Why do firms in monopolistic competition have limited control over prices?
2. What features of a monopolistically competitive market are similar to a perfectly competitive market?

✔ **CHECKPOINT** ***Why is it easy for firms to enter and leave a monopolistically competitive market?***

Nonprice Competition

The ability to differentiate products means that firms do not have to compete on price alone. The alternative is **nonprice competition,** or competition through ways other than lower prices. Nonprice competition takes several different forms.

differentiation making a product different from other, similar products

nonprice competition a way to attract customers through style, service, or location, but not a lower price

BELLRINGER

Write the definition of monopolistic competition on the chalkboard: *A market structure in which many companies sell products that are similar but not identical.* Direct students to think of a product they buy that is similar but not the same as others, for example, jeans, toothpaste, or bread. Tell them to pick one and jot down the ways they are the same and all the ways they are different.

Teach

Economics online To present this topic using digital resources, use the lecture notes at www.PearsonSuccessNet.com.

COMPARE

Have students compare Figure 7.6 with the diagram on page 161. Discuss the similarities and differences between these two diagrams. Draw a 2-column chart on the board. Write *Perfect Competition* as the heading of one column and *Monopolistic Competition* as the heading of the other. Ask two volunteers to quickly list the characteristics of each. Ask students how the product they analyzed in the Bellringer meets the characteristics of monopolistic competition.

PERFECT COMPETITION	MONOPOLISTIC COMPETITION
• many buyers and sellers • free market entry and exit • informed buyers and sellers • identical products	• many firms • few artificial barriers to entry • little control over price • differentiated products

L1 L2 Differentiate Direct students to the Visual Glossary Online to reinforce understanding of *perfect competition.*

Differentiated Resources

L1 L2 Guided Reading and Review (Unit 2 All-in-One, p. 144)

L2 Analyze a Market (Unit 2 All-in-One, p. 146)

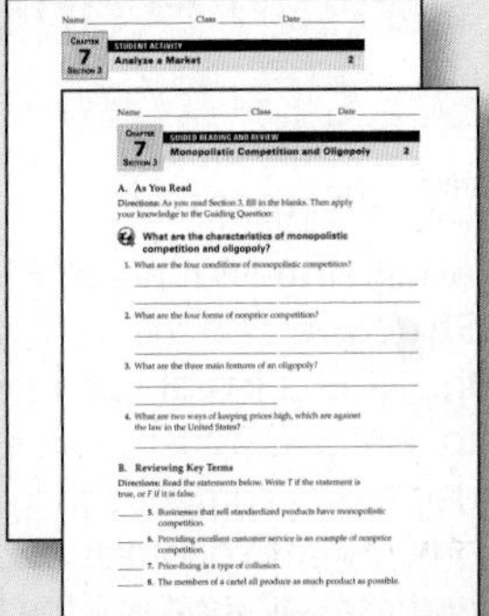

Answers

Graph Skills 1. There are many firms selling similar products that can be substituted for each other if prices vary by much. 2. many firms, few barriers to entry

Checkpoint There are few barriers to entry, patents do not protect anyone from competition, and there are so many competing firms that they cannot work together to keep out new competitors.

ANALYZE

Display the "Fresh Vegetables for Sale" transparency (Color Transparencies, 7.a). Ask

- What does the cartoon show?
- Are the goods essentially the same? Explain.
- How do the farmers differentiate their products?
- What must a producer do to get people to pay more for nearly identical products or services?

Remind students that in the real world agriculture is basically a commodity market in perfect competition.

L1 L2 ELL Differentiate Address the first two or three questions to these groups first before opening the discussion to the class as a whole.

- *Physical characteristics* The simplest way for a firm to distinguish its products is to offer a new size, color, shape, texture, or taste. Running shoes, pens, cars, and toothpaste are good examples of products that can be easily differentiated by their physical characteristics. A pen is always a writing tool that uses ink, but many people will pay extra for a pen that looks or writes differently. Similarly, you can probably describe a "car" in only a few words, but factories around the world manufacture thousands of car models to fit a range of personalities, jobs, families, and incomes.
- *Location* Real estate agents say that the three most important factors when buying property are "location, location, location." Some goods can be differentiated by where they are sold. Gas stations, movie theaters, and grocery stores succeed or fail based on their locations. A convenience store in the middle of a desert differentiates its product simply by selling it hundreds of miles away from the nearest competitor. Such a location allows the seller to charge a lot more for a quart of water.
- *Service level* Some sellers can charge higher prices because they offer their customers a high level of service. Conventional restaurants and fast-food restaurants both offer meals to customers. However, conventional restaurants provide servers who bring the food to your table, whereas fast-food restaurants offer a more barebones, do-it-yourself atmosphere. Conventional restaurants and fast-food chains sell many of the same food items, but fast-food chains sell their meals for less. Customers at conventional restaurants pay more for the service and the relaxing atmosphere.
- *Advertising, image, or status* Firms often use advertising to point out differences between their own offerings and other products in the marketplace. These product differences are often more a matter of perception than reality. For example, a designer can apply his or her name to a plain white T-shirt and charge a higher price, even if the quality of fabric and stitching is no different than what generic T-shirts offer. Customers will pay extra for a designer or a brand-name T-shirt because the image and status that go with the name are worth the extra money to them.

CHECKPOINT ***What role does advertising play in monopolistically competitive firms?***

Economics & YOU
Nonprice Competition
The designer athletic shoes are way more expensive than the sensible sneakers, but you buy them anyway. ***The image and status associated with the designer shoe is a form of nonprice competition.***
Quick N Ez
The snacks would have cost less at the supermarket, but the Quick N Ez is so much closer to home. ***The location of the convenience store is another example of nonprice competition.***

▲ Firms find ways other than price to distinguish their products. ***Which recent purchase that you made was based on nonprice competition?***

Prices, Output, and Profits

Economists study prices, output, and profits when comparing market structures. They find that under monopolistic competition, the market looks very much as it would under perfect competition.

Answers

Economics & You Answers will vary. Students should cite examples of products purchased on the basis of nonprice competition.

Checkpoint Monopolistically competitive firms use advertising to differentiate their products so they can sell their products at a higher price than similar products sold by their competitors.

Virtual Economics on CD-Rom

L2 Differentiate

Analyzing Models of Market Structure Use the following lesson from the NCEE **Virtual Economics *CD-ROM*** to reinforce student understanding of the degrees of competition in a market. Click on Browse Economics Lessons, specify grades 9–12, and use the key words *how competitive.*

In this activity, students will work in small groups to classify markets based on their level of competition.

LESSON TITLE	HOW COMPETITIVE IS THE INDUSTRY?
Type of Activity	Classifying
Complexity	Low
Time	50 minutes
NCEE Standards	9

Prices

Prices under monopolistic competition will be higher than they would be in perfect competition, because firms have some power to raise prices. However, the number of firms and ease of entry prevent companies from raising prices as high as they would if they were a true monopoly. As you have read, if a monopolistically competitive firm raised prices too high, most customers would buy the cheaper product. Because customers can choose among many substitutes, monopolistically competitive firms face more elastic demand curves than true monopolists do.

Output

The law of demand says that output and price are negatively related. As one rises, the other falls. Monopolistically competitive firms sell their products at higher prices than do perfectly competitive firms, but at lower prices than a monopoly. As a result, total output under monopolistic competition falls somewhere between that of monopoly and that of perfect competition.

Profits

Like perfectly competitive firms, monopolistically competitive firms earn just enough to cover all of their costs, including salaries for the workers. If a monopolistically competitive firm started to earn profits well above its costs, two market trends would work to take those profits away.

First, fierce competition would encourage rivals to find new ways to differentiate their products and lure customers back. If one company hires a basketball star to promote its soft drink, a rival might hire a popular singer. The rivalries among firms prevent any one firm from earning excessive profits for long.

Second, new firms will enter the market with slightly different products that cost less than the market leaders. If the original good costs too much, consumers will switch to these substitutes. You've seen this happen when a brand-name line of clothing or a video game becomes popular. Competitors quickly flood the market with cheap imitations to appeal to people who can't afford the original or don't care about the difference in quality.

Figure 7.7 Oligopoly

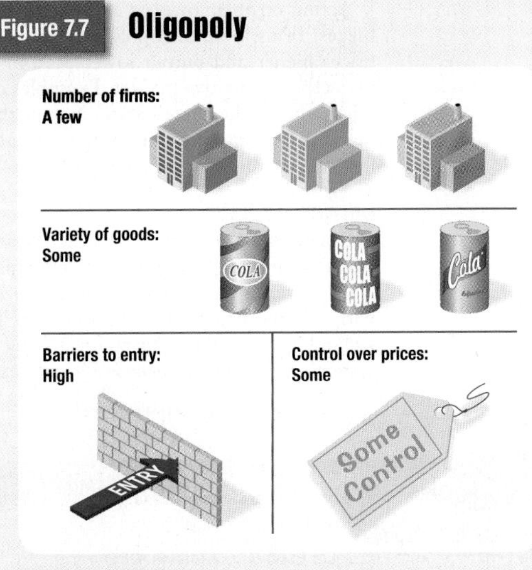

CHART SKILLS

In an oligopoly, a few large firms dominate a market.

1. Why are high barriers to entry an important part of oligopoly?
2. Why are there only a few firms in an oligopoly?

Although monopolistically competitive firms can earn profits in the short run, they have to work hard to keep their product distinct to stay ahead of their rivals. Often, they don't succeed.

Production Costs and Variety

Firms in monopolistic competition may not be able to produce their goods at the lowest possible average cost. Monopolistically competitive markets have many firms, each producing too little output to minimize costs and use resources efficiently. But consumers in these markets benefit from having a wide variety of goods to choose from.

CHECKPOINT ***What keeps monopolistically competitive firms from making high profits?***

Oligopoly

Oligopoly describes a market dominated by a few large, profitable firms. Oligopoly looks like an imperfect form of monopoly. Economists usually call an industry an oligopoly if the four largest firms produce at least 70 to 80 percent of the output.

oligopoly a market structure in which a few large firms dominate a market

DISCUSS

Emphasize that monopolistic competition is very similar to perfect competition. Ask students why a clever producer in a market with monopolistic competition might be able to charge more for his or her product. Ask **How does this situation differ from a market in perfect competition?**

Discuss output. Ask them to explain why output in a competitive monopoly is greater than in a monopoly but not as great as in perfect competition.

L1 L2 LPR Differentiate Review the negative relationship between price and output with students. Draw a graph on the board to illustrate.

Ask **What would happen if a competitive monopoly began to earn profits that were much higher than its cost?** *(Competitors would find ways to differentiate their products and lure away consumers; new firms would enter the market with lower priced products.)*

Discuss how students benefit when goods or services they want to buy are sold by many different producers.

EXAMINE

Review the definition of an oligopoly. Point out that some of the markets dominated by a few producers include airlines, breakfast cereals, and the appliance markets. Have students imagine that they have created their own granola mix and want to market it. Ask **What are some barriers to your entering the breakfast cereal market?** *(Possible responses: name recognition, sales networks, manufacturing plants, economies of scale, getting shelf space in a supermarket)*

Ask **How could you, as a consumer of breakfast cereal, be hurt by an oligopoly?** *(It can prevent competitors from entering the market, thus limiting choices and affecting prices)* Ask **How do illegal actions of oligopolies affect your choices?** *(They can keep other businesses out of the market, limit supply, raise prices.)*

Background Note

Market Efficiency Perfectly competitive markets are efficient because as much product is produced as can be sold at a price that matches cost. One characteristic of monopolies and monopolistic competition is that there is no guarantee of market efficiency. In both a monopoly and monopolistic competition, price can be greater than marginal cost, so consumers will pay more for an item than they would in a perfectly competitive market. As a result, there may be less output than there is demand. However, in monopolistic competition, there may be too many firms with moderately differentiated products. In that case, there is no mechanism to prevent overproduction, as there is with a monopoly.

Answers

Chart Skills 1. They keep new competitors from entering the market and competing with existing companies. 2. They can act on their own or as a team to set prices and output. Too many firms would undermine the ability of the group to dominate the market.

Checkpoint The number of competing firms and the ease of entry create competition that keeps profits low.

DISTRIBUTE ACTIVITY WORKSHEET

Distribute the "Analyze a Market" worksheet (Unit 2 All-in-One, p. 145). You may want to have a local phone book, such as a Yellow Pages, and newspapers with advertisements available for students to refer to in order to spark some ideas. When students finish, discuss their results and compile a list on the board of the market structures represented. Ask students how their results reflect the market structures prevalent in the United States.

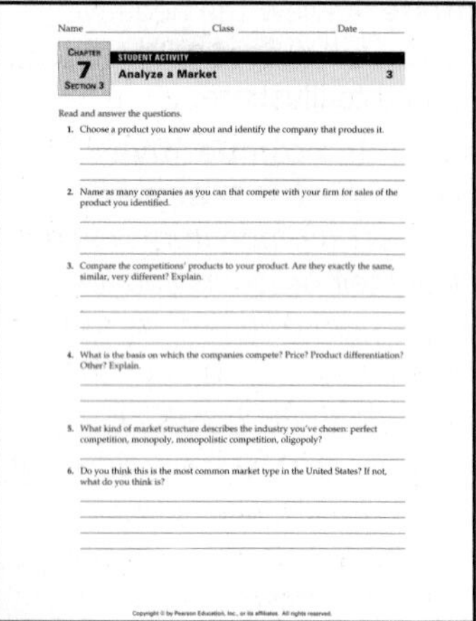

Name ______ Class ______ Date ______

CHAPTER 7 SECTION 3 — STUDENT ACTIVITY

Analyze a Market 3

Read and answer the questions.

1. Choose a product you know about and identify the company that produces it.
2. Name as many companies as you can that compete with your firm for sales of the product you identified.
3. Compare the competitions' products to your product. Are they exactly the same, similar, very different? Explain.
4. What is the basis on which the companies compete? Price? Product differentiation? Other? Explain.
5. What kind of market structure describes the industry you've chosen: perfect competition, monopoly, monopolistic competition, oligopoly?
6. Do you think this is the most common market type in the United States? If not, what do you think is?

L2 Distribute the "Analyze a Market" worksheet (Unit 2 All-in-One, p. 146).

EXTEND

Tell students that OPEC is an organization that comprises the world's most important oil-producing nations. Have students research OPEC and explain how it fulfills the characteristics of a cartel.

L4 Differentiate Have students research and share their findings about why OPEC is not prosecuted as a cartel in the United States.

GUIDING QUESTION WRAP UP

Have students return to the section Guiding Question. Review the completed graphic organizer and clarify any misunderstandings. Have a wrap up discussion about the characteristics of monopolistic competition and oligopoly.

Assess and Remediate

L3 **L2** Collect the "Analyze a Market" worksheets and assess students' understanding of market structures.

L3 Assign the Section 3 Assessment questions; identify student misconceptions.

L3 Give Section Quiz A (Unit 2 All-in-One, p. 147).

L2 Give Section Quiz B (Unit 2 All-in-One, p. 148).

(Assess and Remediate continued on p. 179)

Acting on their own or as a team, the biggest firms in an oligopoly may well set prices higher and output lower than in a perfectly competitive market. Examples of oligopolies in the United States include the markets for air travel, automobiles, breakfast cereals, and household appliances.

Barriers to Entry

An oligopoly can form when significant barriers to entry keep new companies from entering the market to compete with existing firms. These barriers can be technological or they can be created by a system of government licenses or patents.

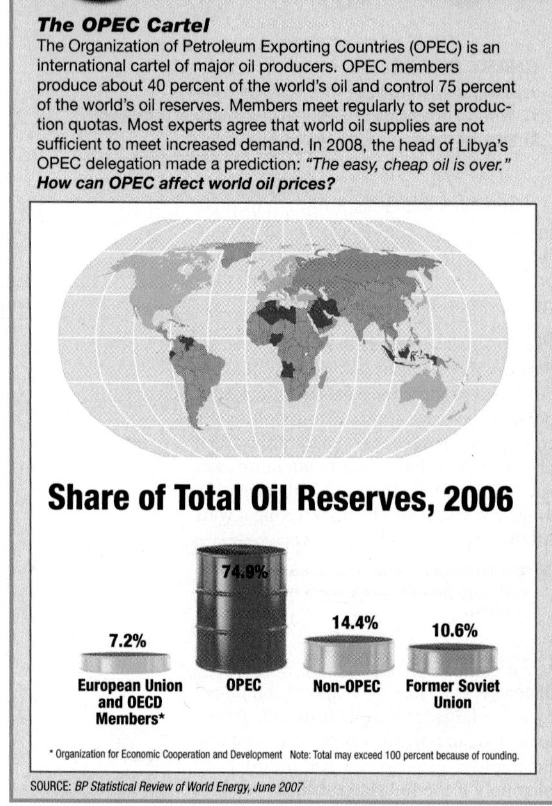

FUTURE WATCH
Global Impact
The OPEC Cartel
The Organization of Petroleum Exporting Countries (OPEC) is an international cartel of major oil producers. OPEC members produce about 40 percent of the world's oil and control 75 percent of the world's oil reserves. Members meet regularly to set production quotas. Most experts agree that world oil supplies are not sufficient to meet increased demand. In 2008, the head of Libya's OPEC delegation made a prediction: "The easy, cheap oil is over." How can OPEC affect world oil prices?
Share of Total Oil Reserves, 2006
7.2%
European Union and OECD Members*
74.9%
OPEC
14.4%
Non-OPEC
10.6%
Former Soviet Union
* Organization for Economic Cooperation and Development Note: Total may exceed 100 percent because of rounding.
SOURCE: BP Statistical Review of World Energy, June 2007

In other cases, the economic realities of the market lead to an oligopoly. Take the soft-drink market, for example. The two big cola manufacturers have invested so much money to develop their brand names and sales networks over the last century that few companies think they can successfully challenge their grip on the market.

High start-up costs, such as expensive machinery, and large production facilities present additional barriers to entry. Many small airlines have had trouble competing with larger, better-financed rivals because airplanes are very expensive to buy and maintain. The biggest airlines compound the problem because they often own the most desirable gates at the airport, and already enjoy name recognition and the trust of the consumer.

Some oligopolies occur because of economies of scale. As you have read, when a firm experiences economies of scale, the average cost of production decreases as output increases. Greater economies of scale mean that there will be fewer firms in an industry. In a monopoly market, only one company can produce enough goods to earn a profit. In an oligopoly, perhaps three or four companies can reach a profitable level of output before the market becomes too crowded and revenue falls below costs.

Cooperation and Collusion

Oligopoly presents a big challenge to government, because oligopolistic firms often *seem* to work together as a monopoly, even when they are not actually doing so. Many government regulations try to make oligopolistic firms act more like competitive firms. When determined oligopolists work together illegally to set prices and bar competing firms from the market, they can become as damaging to the consumer as a monopoly.

The three practices that concern government the most are price leadership, collusion, and cartels. While these three practices represent ways that firms in an oligopoly can try to control a market, they don't always work. Each tactic includes an incentive for the firms to cheat and thereby undo any benefits.

Sometimes the market leader in an oligopoly can start a round of price increases or price cuts by making its plans clear to other sellers. This firm becomes a price leader. Price leaders can set prices and output for entire industries as long as other member firms go along with the leader's policy. But disagreements among those companies can spark a **price war,** when competitors cut their prices very low to win business. A price war is harmful to producers but good for consumers because they will pay less for a good or service.

Collusion refers to an agreement among members of an oligopoly to illegally set prices and production levels. One outcome of collusion is called **price fixing,** an agreement among firms to sell at the same or very similar prices. Collusive agreements set prices and output at the levels that would be chosen by a monopolist. Collusion is illegal in the United States, but the lure of monopolistic profits can tempt businesses to make such agreements despite the illegality and risks.

Collusion is not, however, the only reason for nearly identical pricing in oligopolistic industries. Such pricing may actually result from intense competition, especially if advertising is vigorous and new lines of products are being introduced.

Cartels

Stronger than a collusive agreement, a **cartel** is an agreement by a formal organization of producers to coordinate prices and production. Although other countries and international organizations permit them, cartels are illegal in the United States. OPEC is perhaps the most familiar international cartel.

Cartels can survive only if every member keeps to its agreed output levels and no more. Otherwise, prices will fall, and firms will lose profits. However, each member has a strong incentive to cheat and produce more than its quota. If every cartel member cheats, too much product reaches the market, and prices fall. Cartels can also collapse if some producers are left out of the group and decide to lower their prices below the cartel's levels. Therefore, cartels usually do not last very long.

CHECKPOINT ***What role can market leaders play in an oligopoly?***

price war a series of competitive price cuts that lowers the market price below the cost of production

collusion an illegal agreement among firms to divide the market, set prices, or limit production

price fixing an agreement among firms to charge one price for the same good

cartel a formal organization of producers that agree to coordinate prices and production

SECTION 3 ASSESSMENT

Essential Questions Journal To continue to build a response to the Essential Question, go to your **Essential Questions Journal.**

Guiding Question

1. Use your completed Venn diagram to answer this question: What are the characteristics of monopolistic competition and oligopoly?
2. **Extension** You want to buy a new pair of jeans. The store offers several brands and styles. Each one looks different. Prices and colors vary. How will you decide which jeans to buy?

Key Terms and Main Ideas

3. What four conditions define **monopolistic competition?**
4. How does **differentiation** help monopolistically competitive firms sell their products?
5. Explain what happens during a **price war.**
6. How do economists determine whether or not a market is an **oligopoly?**
7. How would **price fixing** and **collusion** help producers?

Critical Thinking

8. **Apply (a)** Name four kinds of nonprice competition. **(b)** Which example would you use to promote the following products: a new brand of bottled water, in-home computer repair, and protein bars? Explain your reasoning.
9. **Extend (a)** What are the advantages of a monopolistically competitive market for consumers? **(b)** What are some of the disadvantages?
10. **Interpret (a)** In what ways does the government regulate oligopolies? **(b)** Why do you think the government has imposed these regulations?

Quick Write

11. Choose a product in a monopolistically competitive industry. Write an ad for your product. Your ad can be for television, radio, newspapers, or the Internet. Remember, there are many similar products on the market. How can you persuade consumers to buy your product? Then write a paragraph answering the following questions: Would you see an ad like this in a purely competitive market? Would you see this ad in a market with a monopoly? Why or why not?

Have students complete the Self-Test Online and continue their work in the **Essential Questions Journal.**

REMEDIATION AND SUGGESTIONS

Use the chart below to help students who are struggling with content.

WEAKNESS	REMEDIATION
Identifying key terms (Questions 3, 4, 5, 6, 7)	Have students use the interactive Economic Dictionary Online.
The conditions and characteristics of monopolistic competition (Questions 1, 3, 4, 9)	Have students identify a firm that is in monopolistic competition and tell how it meets the definition of this market structure.
How firms conduct nonprice competition (Questions 2, 4, 8, 11)	Reteach by listing the forms of nonprice competition. Have students give an example of each.
The conditions and characteristics of oligopolies (Questions 1, 7, 11)	Have students list the characteristics of oligopolies and explain why the government tries to regulate them.

Answer

Checkpoint Market leaders can raise or reduce prices for the entire industry if other firms go along.

Assessment Answers

1. Monopolistic competition: many firms, few barriers to entry, little price control, differentiated products; oligopoly: a few firms dominate market, significant barriers to entry, considerable price control, similar but differentiated products **2.** Student answers should recognize that product differentiation affects buying decisions. **3.** many firms, few artificial barriers to entry, little control over price, differentiated products **4.** Differentiation enables these firms to profit from the differences among products. **5.** Firms compete by lowering prices. **6.** if the four largest firms produce 70 to 80 percent of the output **7.** They allow producers to work together to set prices and output levels so that they earn more profit than they would otherwise be able to. **8.** (a) physical characteristics; location; service level; advertising, image, or status (b) advertising, image, or status because differences between bottled waters are negligible; service level because computer buyers will pay more for service; physical characteristics because buyers may prefer one bar to another based on taste. **9.** (a) Competition keeps prices low and production high while providing a wide variety of goods. (b) Prices will be higher than in perfect competition; prices will vary among similar goods **10.** (a) through laws to make them act more like competitive firms (b) to protect consumers **11.** Ads will vary, but students should recognize that the ads would not appear in a purely competitive market because products are not differentiated. They would not appear in a monopoly because there is no competition.

Guiding Question

When does the government regulate competition?

Get Started

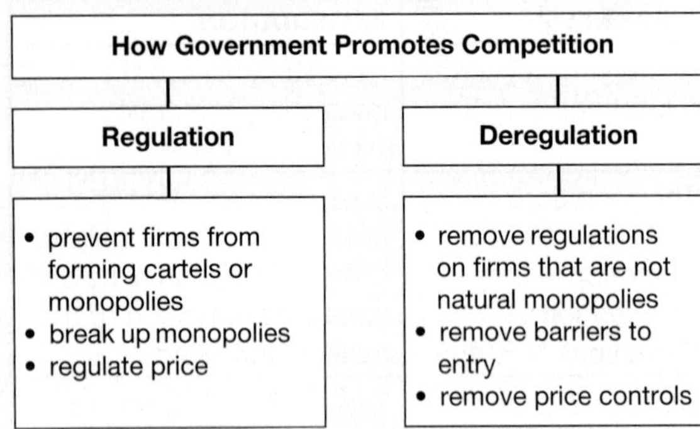

How Government Promotes Competition
Regulation
Deregulation
• prevent firms from forming cartels or monopolies
• break up monopolies
• regulate price
• remove regulations on firms that are not natural monopolies
• remove barriers to entry
• remove price controls

LESSON GOALS

Students will:

- Know the Key Terms.
- Describe the purpose of antitrust laws, how the government uses them, and how monopolies try to work around them.
- Summarize the results of past deregulations.

BEFORE CLASS

Students should read the section for homework.

Have students complete the graphic organizer in the Section Opener as they read the text. As an alternate activity, have students complete the Guided Reading and Review worksheet (Unit 2 All-in-One, p. 149).

L1 L2 ELL LPR Differentiate Have students complete the Guided Reading and Review worksheet (Unit 2 All-in-One, p. 150).

Answer

Checkpoint They tend to have higher prices and lower output. Competition is reduced.

CLASSROOM HINTS

Have students discuss the cartoon about Standard Oil on this page. Explain that Standard Oil was a monopoly and abused its market power. Have students use a search engine to find information about the Standard Oil trust.

SECTION 4 Regulation and Deregulation

OBJECTIVES

1. **Explain** how firms might try to increase their market power.
2. **List** three market practices that the government regulates or bans to protect competition.
3. **Define** deregulation, and list its effects on several industries.

ECONOMIC DICTIONARY

As you read the section, look for the definitions of these **Key Terms:**

- predatory pricing
- antitrust laws
- trust
- merger
- deregulation

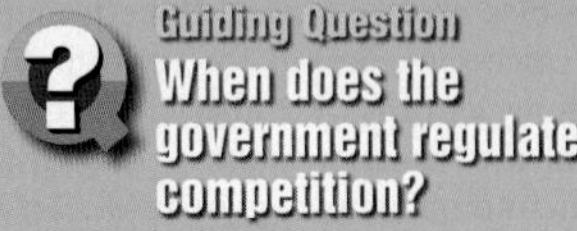

Copy this chart and fill it in as you read.

How Government Promotes Competition	
Regulation	Deregulation
• • •	• • •

predatory pricing selling a product below cost for a short period of time to drive competitors out of the market

Economics and You As a consumer, you have choices. You can choose from a variety of cellphone plans or Internet service providers. But until recently, you had no choice when it came to cable television service. Critics said the cable television industry was a monopoly. The Federal Communications Commission agreed. In 2007, the FCC approved a rule that says no one company can control more than 30 percent of the cable television market.

Principles in Action Sometimes the government takes steps to promote competition because markets with more competition have lower prices. In this section, you will read about the tools the government uses to stop anticompetitive practices.

▲ Public outrage with powerful trusts in the late 1800s led Congress to pass antitrust legislation.

Market Power

Recall that market power is the ability of a firm to control prices and total market output. As you have read, monopoly and oligopoly can be bad for the consumer and for the economy as a whole. Markets dominated by one firm or a few large ones tend to have higher prices and lower output than markets with many sellers. Competition is reduced. Before we look at antitrust policies, let's look at ways in which a firm might try to increase its market power.

To control prices and output like a monopoly, the leading firms in a market can merge with one another, form a cartel, or set the market price below their costs for the short term to drive competitors out of business. The last practice is known as **predatory pricing.** Economists are skeptical about most claims of predatory pricing because the predator loses money each time it drives an endless series of rivals out of business.

CHECKPOINT ***How does a market with a few large firms act like a monopoly?***

Government and Competition

The federal government has a number of policies that keep firms from controlling the price and supply of important goods. If a firm controls

Focus on the Basics

Students need to come away with the following understandings:

FACTS: • The government uses antitrust laws to regulate markets dominated by one or a few firms, to breakup monopolies, and to block mergers that can hurt competition. • The government tries to promote competition and the greater choice that may accompany it. • The government sometimes deregulates industries to promote competition.

GENERALIZATION: Markets dominated by one or a few firms tend to have higher prices and lower output than markets with multiple firms. The government can use regulatory laws and deregulation to promote competition, often resulting in more choices, lower prices, and better products for consumers.

a large share of a market, the Federal Trade Commission and the Department of Justice's Antitrust Division will watch the firm closely to ensure that it does not unfairly force out its competitors. These government policies are known as **antitrust laws,** because a **trust** is a business combination similar to a cartel.

In 1890, Congress passed the Sherman Antitrust Act, which outlawed mergers and monopolies that limit trade between states. This and other laws gave the government the power to regulate industry, to stop firms from forming cartels or monopolies, and to break up existing monopolies. Over the years, Congress passed new laws to outlaw other anticompetitive practices.

Despite the antitrust laws, companies have used many strategies to gain control over their markets. Some firms require a customer who buys one product to buy other products from the same company, whether or not the customer wants them. For example, a tennis shoe manufacturer can demand that a chain also buy and resell its brand-name shirts, windbreakers, and watches if it wants to sell its shoes. Buying out competitors is another strategy used by many large firms.

Regulating Business Practices

The government has the power to regulate all of these practices if they give too much power to a company that already has few competitors. Microsoft is such a company. It sells operating systems, software that tells a computer how to run. In 1997, the Department of Justice accused Microsoft of using its near-monopoly over the operating-system market to try to take control of the browser market. A browser is a program that allows people to access Web sites.

Microsoft insisted that computer manufacturers selling its operating system must also include its browser. The government accused Microsoft of predatory pricing, because the company gave away its browser for free, a policy that could ruin the other browser company, Netscape. Microsoft's power in one market gave it a big—and possibly unfair—advantage in a related market.

Microsoft argued that the browser was part of its operating system and could not be sold separately. Microsoft's defenders said that companies do compete with Microsoft, and people buy Microsoft software because they like it. In November 1999, a federal judge ruled against Microsoft. The company appealed, and in 2001, the Justice Department and Microsoft reached an agreement to settle the case. According to the settlement, Microsoft could link its browser to its operating system but could not force computer manufacturers to provide only Microsoft software on new computers.

Key Events in Federal Antitrust Policy

Date	Event
1901	Theodore Roosevelt becomes President and begins enforcing the 1890 Sherman Antitrust Act, which outlaws mergers and monopolies that restrain trade between states
1911	Supreme Court breaks up John D. Rockefeller's Standard Oil Trust
1950	Celler-Kefauver Act allows government to stop mergers that could hurt competition
1982	AT&T agrees to break up its local phone service into several companies
2001	Department of Justice settles its lawsuit with Microsoft

▲ Over the past century, the federal government has acted to promote competition in American industry.

Breaking Up Monopolies

In 1911, the government used the Sherman Antitrust Act to break up two monopolies, John D. Rockefeller's Standard Oil Trust and the American Tobacco Company. The Supreme Court ordered these powerful monopolies to split apart into competing firms. Antitrust laws have been put to use many times since then.

In 1982, the government broke American Telephone and Telegraph (AT&T) into seven regional phone companies, including BellSouth, USWest, and PacificBell. Because the government treated local telephone service as a natural monopoly, AT&T had legally controlled all the cables and networks that linked telephones in homes and businesses. The government stepped in only when AT&T used its legal monopoly in local phone

Simulation *Activity*

Is the Law Being Broken?
You may be asked to take part in a role-playing game about government regulation.

antitrust laws laws that encourage competition in the marketplace

trust an illegal grouping of companies that discourages competition, similar to a cartel

BELLRINGER

Display "The History of Cable Television Regulation" transparency (Color Transparencies, 7.b). Have students study the transparency and jot down ways that the government has tried to maintain competition.

Teach

Economics online To present this topic using digital resources, use the lecture notes at www.PearsonSuccessNet.com.

ANALYZE

Ask **Why do you think the government regulates the cable television industry?** *(The industry has market power and can control prices and output.)* Discuss with students the possible consequences if cable TV providers were not limited by government action.

Have students explain the purpose of antitrust laws. Then discuss ways that companies may try to get around these laws and gain market control.

L1 L2 ELL Differentiate Have students read the Key Events in Federal Antitrust Policy graphic. Provide background on the 1890 Sherman Antitrust Act and Standard Oil Trust.

DISCUSS

Display "The Effects of Mergers" transparency (Color Transparencies, 7.c). Have students list the characteristics of the cellphone company that are presented in the comic strip. Ask **How might more competition improve the situation?** *(It would force the cellphone company to provide better phones and service in order to stay in business.)* Ask **What does the character mean by asking "Where's Congress when you need them?"** *(Congress has the power to break up monopolies; why doesn't it do that in this case?)*

L1 Differentiate Call on a student to describe what is happening in the comic strip. Guide a discussion of why the cartoon is humorous.

Differentiated Resources

L1 L2 Guided Reading and Review (Unit 2 All-in-One, p. 150)

L2 Regulation and Deregulation (Unit 2 All-in-One, p. 152)

L3 Is the Law Being Broken? (Simulation Activities, Chapter 7)

L2 Taking Notes and Active Listening Skill Worksheet (Unit 2 All-in-One, p. 154)

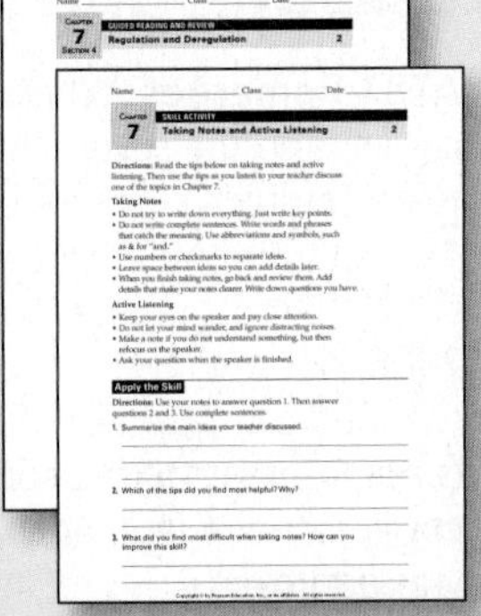

ANALYZE

Tell students that there are different views on the role government should have in regulating businesses. Distribute "The Monopoly Case" worksheet (Unit 2 All-in-One, p. 151). Have students read the opposing perspectives of Microsoft and the government. Use students' answers to initiate a discussion about the implications of monopolies.

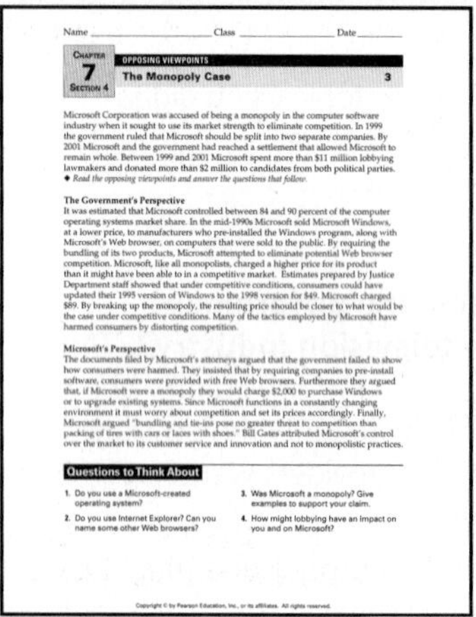

Name ____________ Class ____________ Date ________

Chapter 7 Section 4 — OPPOSING VIEWPOINTS

The Monopoly Case 3

Microsoft Corporation was accused of being a monopoly in the computer software industry when it sought to use its market strength to eliminate competition. In 1999 the government ruled that Microsoft should be split into two separate companies. By 2001 Microsoft and the government had reached a settlement that allowed Microsoft to remain whole. Between 1999 and 2001 Microsoft spent more than $11 million lobbying lawmakers and donated more than $2 million to candidates from both political parties.

◆ *Read the opposing viewpoints and answer the questions that follow.*

The Government's Perspective

It was estimated that Microsoft controlled between 84 and 90 percent of the computer operating systems market share. In the mid-1990s Microsoft sold Microsoft Windows, at a lower price, to manufacturers who pre-installed the Windows program, along with Microsoft's Web browser, on computers that were sold to the public. By requiring the bundling of its two products, Microsoft attempted to eliminate potential Web browser competition. Microsoft, like all monopolists, charged a higher price for its product than it might have been able to in a competitive market. Estimates prepared by Justice Department staff showed that under competitive conditions, consumers could have updated their 1995 version of Windows to the 1998 version for $49. Microsoft charged $89. By breaking up the monopoly, the resulting price should be closer to what would be the case under competitive conditions. Many of the tactics employed by Microsoft have harmed consumers by distorting competition.

Microsoft's Perspective

The documents filed by Microsoft's attorneys argued that the government failed to show how consumers were harmed. They insisted that by requiring companies to pre-install software, consumers were provided with free Web browsers. Furthermore they argued that, if Microsoft were a monopoly they would charge $2,000 to purchase Windows or to upgrade existing systems. Since Microsoft functions in a constantly changing environment it must worry about competition and set its prices accordingly. Finally, Microsoft argued "bundling and tie-ins pose no greater threat to competition than packing of tires with cars or laces with shoes." Bill Gates attributed Microsoft's control over the market to its customer service and innovation and not to monopolistic practices.

Questions to Think About

1. Do you use a Microsoft-created operating system?
2. Do you use Internet Explorer? Can you name some other Web browsers?
3. Was Microsoft a monopoly? Give examples to support your claim.
4. How might lobbying have an impact on you and on Microsoft?

L3 Use the How the Economy Works feature to show how one industry, in this case broadcasting, is regulated.

L2 **LPR Differentiate** Distribute the "Regulation and Deregulation" worksheet (Unit 2 All-in-One, p. 152).

Call on students to explain how and why the government blocks some mergers. Emphasize that although the merger of large corporations is assessed by the FTC, only those deemed to restrict competition may be regulated.

L3 **Differentiate** For alternative or additional practice with the concepts of monopolies and government use of antitrust laws, have students use the "Is the Law Being Broken?" activity (Simulation Activities, Chapter 7). Working in groups, students will decide whether to take legal action under antitrust laws against a firm.

DISTRIBUTE ACTIVITY WORKSHEET

Distribute the "Note-Taking and Active Listening" skill worksheet (Unit 2 All-in-One, p. 153). Tell students to review the lesson in the Skills Handbook on page S-17. Remind them to use the steps of the lesson to complete the activities.

L2 **Differentiate** Distribute the "Taking Notes and Active Listening" skill worksheet (Unit 2 All-in-One, p. 154). Have students read the suggestions for improving their note-taking and active listening skills and apply the ideas while you present the section on deregulation.

How the Economy Works

How is broadcasting regulated?

The Federal Communications Commission (FCC) is a government agency that regulates the broadcasting industry. The FCC issues licenses to radio and television stations. Creating a new television station requires FCC approval.

1 A broadcaster who wants to start a new television station begins with a search for an unused frequency. If a frequency can be found, the broadcaster files a petition to add a new station with the FCC. An attorney can help with the complex process.

2 The FCC grants (or denies) the broadcaster permission to apply for the station. Applications are filed online. The broadcaster must announce his application in a Public Notice. The FCC will conduct an electronic auction of licenses for broadcast stations.

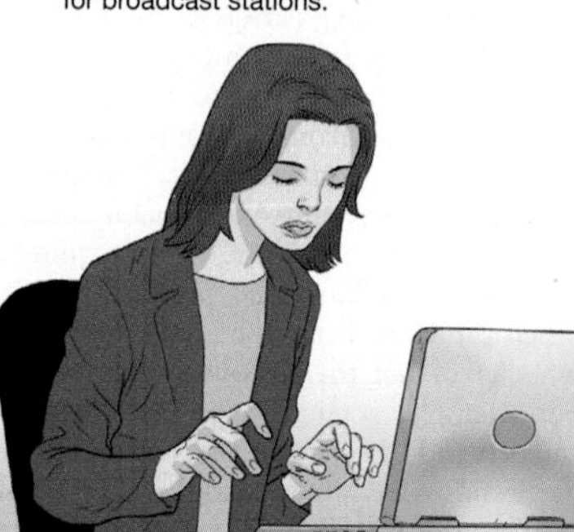

Applying for a New Television Station

service to take control of other markets for long-distance phone calls and communications equipment.

Today, the market for long-distance service has many firms and is more competitive. Although the break-up of AT&T cost thousands of workers their jobs, consumers have benefited from lower prices and improved technology.

Blocking Mergers

In addition to breaking up existing monopolies, the government has the power to prevent the rise of monopolies. The government does this by blocking mergers that might reduce competition and lead to higher prices. A **merger** occurs when a company joins with another company or companies to form a single firm. Government regulators also follow the effects of past mergers to check that they did not lead to unfair market control. You read in Section 1 that prices often fall when the number of firms in a market increases. The reverse is also true. Prices often rise when the number of firms in a market falls.

merger when two or more companies join to form a single firm

When the government considers whether or not to approve a merger, it tries to predict the effects of the merger on prices and service. Sometimes it determines that the effects will be minimal. In 2000, the Federal Trade Commission (FTC) and the Federal Communications Commission both approved the merger of media giants America Online (AOL) and Time Warner. Approval came with several conditions designed to ensure consumer choice. Two years later, the government drew a different conclusion when the FTC blocked the merger of the glassware makers Libbey and Anchor Hocking. The FTC argued that the merger would create a monopoly. A federal court agreed, and the deal fell apart.

Background Note

AT&T Remerges When AT&T was broken up, AT&T survived as a long-distance carrier, and the seven "Baby Bells" provided local phone service. Since then the telecommunications industry has changed with the emergence of cellphones, cable TV, VoIP, and other technology. Simultaneously, the Baby Bells gradually merged. SBC, the most prosperous of the Baby Bells, acquired AT&T in 2005 and BellSouth in 2006, bringing the company full circle. (SBC changed its name to AT&T.) The merger required the approval of 20 regulatory agencies. The FCC ruled that the new AT&T is not a threat to free competition and might produce efficiencies that would reduce costs. Nonetheless, AT&T had to agree to 19 pages of conditions before the merger was approved.

How the Economy Works online

For an animated, interactive version of this feature, visit **PearsonSuccessNet.com**

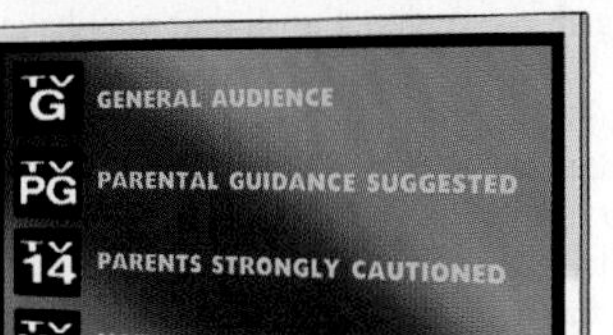

3 The FCC also sets broadcasting standards and monitors programs for indecent content. Stations that violate rules are subject to fines and penalties.

4 Broadcasting without a license is illegal. The FCC shuts down illegal broadcasters and takes their equipment. Illegal operation of an unlicensed station may result in criminal prosecution.

5 The FCC grants a construction permit for the new station to the highest bidder. The permit allows the station to broadcast before the FCC license has been issued.

Check Your Understanding
1. Who can apply for a license to broadcast?
2. What would happen if the FCC didn't limit the number of broadcasters?

Broadcasting Rules | **FCC Approval**

Preserving Incentives

While some mergers hurt consumers by reducing competition, others can actually benefit consumers. In these cases, corporate mergers will lower overall average costs and lead to lower prices, more reliable products or service, and a more efficient industry. The government must act carefully to make the right decision.

In 1997, the Justice Department and the FTC released new guidelines for proposed mergers. Companies now have the chance to prove that the merger would lower costs and prices or lead to a better product.

CHECKPOINT ***How does the government break up monopolies?***

Deregulation

In the late 1970s and 1980s, Congress decided that some government regulation was reducing competition. It passed laws to deregulate several industries. **Deregulation** means that the government no longer decides what role each company can play in a market and how much it can charge its customers.

Over several years, the government deregulated the airline, trucking, banking, railroad, natural gas, and television broadcasting industries. Depending on the degree of deregulation, the government's action allowed—or forced—firms in these industries to compete by eliminating many price controls and barriers to entry.

While deregulation weakens government control, antitrust laws strengthen it. Yet the government uses both deregulation and antitrust laws for the same purpose: to promote competition.

Many critics say that government efforts to regulate industries have created inefficiencies. In some cases, the economic facts that created the need for regulation in the

deregulation the removal of some government controls over a market

EVALUATE

Ask **Why did Congress decide to deregulate some industries?** *(Regulation was reducing competition.)* Have students identify industries that were affected. Then discuss with students the actions the government took.

Call on students to summarize the results of different deregulations. Select one instance of deregulation and use the Opinion Line strategy (p. T-28) to discuss this question: **Was deregulation a good decision?** Have students support their opinions using information from the text. Students who completed the L4 extension for Section 2 could contribute their findings at this time.

EXTEND

Have students find an article on monopolies such as DeBeers or Microsoft and identify the issues and actions taken by the government. Then have students analyze the ethics policy of the business they selected or of another monopoly, cartel, or trust that has recently been in the news. Have students assess and give their opinions on the fairness of the company's pricing or other policies.

GUIDING QUESTION WRAP UP

Have students return to the section Guiding Question. Review the completed graphic organizer and clarify any misunderstandings. Have a wrap up discussion about government regulation and competition.

Assess and Remediate

L3 **L2** Collect "The Monopoly Case" and "Regulation and Deregulation" worksheets and assess students' understanding of government regulation of business.

L3 **L2** Collect the skill worksheets on active listening and taking notes and assess student understanding.

L3 Assign the Section 4 Assessment questions.

L3 Give Section Quiz A (Unit 2 All-in-One, p. 155).

L2 Give Section Quiz B (Unit 2 All-in-One, p. 156).

(Assess and Remediate continued on p. 184)

Virtual Economics on CD-Rom

L4 **Differentiate**

Analyzing the Role of Government
Use the following lesson from the NCEE **Virtual Economics *CD-ROM*** to explore how government tries to preserve competition. Click on Browse Economics Lessons, specify grades 9–12, and use the key words *maintaining competition.*

In this activity, students will role-play a team of Justice Department economists as they decide whether to approve a merger.

LESSON TITLE	MAINTAINING COMPETITION
Type of Activity	Simulation
Complexity	High
Time	100 minutes
NCEE Standards	9

Answers

Checkpoint It uses antitrust laws.

Check Your Understanding 1. A broadcaster that has permission from the FCC. 2. Frequencies would be overcrowded.

Have students complete the Self-Test Online and continue their work in the **Essential Questions Journal.**

REMEDIATION AND SUGGESTIONS

Use the chart below to help students who are struggling with content.

WEAKNESS	REMEDIATION
Identifying key terms (Questions 3, 4, 6, 7)	Have students use the interactive Economic Dictionary Online.
How companies use market power (Questions 2, 3, 8)	Have students write a paragraph telling how a fictitious company might use market power to control an industry.
How the government controls competition (Questions 1, 4, 5, 6, 9, 10, 11)	Reteach using the graphic organizer from this section.
Deregulating markets (Question 7)	Form two teams and have them debate the merits of deregulating the television broadcasting industry.

Answer

Checkpoint It allows new firms to enter an industry and compete through lower prices and improved efficiency.

first place have changed. In Section 2 you read how cellular phones challenged the natural monopoly of local phone service and opened the market to new companies. The trucking industry was also regulated as a natural monopoly from the early 1900s until 1978. By then, many had decided that the government was regulating industries that were not natural monopolies at all.

Judging Deregulation

Deregulation has met with mixed success. In most cases, many new firms entered the deregulated industries right away. Competition certainly increased in the airline, trucking, and banking industries. Typically, years of wild growth were followed by the disappearance of some firms. This weeding out of weaker players is considered healthy for the economy, but it can be hard on workers in the short term.

In the 1990s, several states deregulated their electricity markets to allow private, competing companies to produce and sell energy to homeowners. In some markets, energy prices fell, but elsewhere, customers paid more. California experienced a massive energy crisis in 2000 that forced the state to pay extraordinarily high rates for electricity. Many attributed this crisis to companies like Enron that may have used deregulation rules to create an electricity shortage.

Airlines: A Complicated Deregulation

Many new airlines started operating after President Carter deregulated the industry in 1978, but some eventually failed or were acquired. Freed from regulatory restriction, many of the large airlines competed aggressively for the busiest routes. For most travelers, increased competition created lower prices. However, many busy airports now have one dominant airline. In some cases, fares are actually higher than before deregulation.

In the early 2000s, changing conditions transformed the airlines. Over-expansion and sharply rising labor costs squeezed profits. The terrorist hijackings of four commercial passenger jets on September 11, 2001, caused many people to stop flying. Revenues plunged while costs for security, insurance, and fuel rose. Several major airlines filed for bankruptcy. Due to market forces the future of the airline industry is still uncertain.

CHECKPOINT ***How does deregulation encourage competition in a market?***

SECTION 4 ASSESSMENT

Essential Questions Journal To continue to build a response to the Essential Question, go to your **Essential Questions Journal.**

Guiding Question

1. Use your completed chart to answer this question: When does the government regulate competition?
2. **Extension** Name a company that has a lot of market power today. Why do you think it has so much market power? Do you think this is fair? Why or why not?

Key Terms and Main Ideas

3. How does **predatory pricing** hurt competition?
4. What is the purpose of **antitrust laws?**
5. How did the Sherman Antitrust Act affect the monopolies of Standard Oil Trust and the American Tobacco Company?
6. Under what conditions will the government approve a **merger?**
7. How did **deregulation** change the air travel industry?

Critical Thinking

8. **Predict (a)** How does predatory pricing affect a company's market power? **(b)** Why might a firm not want to practice predatory pricing, even if it was legal? **(c)** When might a firm try to practice predatory pricing?
9. **Summarize (a)** Why did the government try to prevent Microsoft from including its browser when it sold its operating system? **(b)** What was the government's final decision? **(c)** Do you think the government achieved its goals? Why or why not?
10. **Examine (a)** Why does the government intervene in markets? **(b)** Is this consistent with the idea of laissez faire and free markets? Why or why not?

Quick Write

11. Reread Blocking Mergers in Section 4. Then write a short essay answering the following questions: Why does the government block mergers? What happens to prices when there are fewer firms in a market? Do you think the government should block the merger of the two largest American automobile manufacturers? Why or why not?

Assessment Answers

1. when firms try to form cartels or monopolies or to control prices
2. Answers will vary, but students should demonstrate knowledge of market power and how companies acquire it.
3. By setting prices below cost, they force competitors out of business.
4. to break up monopolies
5. It gave the government the power to break up these monopolies.
6. when the merger does not restrict competition or lead to higher prices
7. reduced prices initially; later led to higher prices, reduced profits, and bankruptcies
8. (a) It increases a company's market power by eliminating competition. (b) It loses money by selling products below cost. (c) Possible answer: when it is a member of a cartel
9. (a) predatory pricing—the browser was free. (b) It compromised with Microsoft, prohibiting it from forcing manufacturers to provide only Microsoft software. (c) Possible response: No, because Microsoft remains dominant.
10. (a) to promote competition and keep prices low for consumers (b) Possible response: No, because laissez faire and free markets would be free from all government intervention.
11. Possible responses: The government blocks mergers because having too few firms in a market reduces competition and makes prices increase. Yes, because the competition between firms will encourage each firm to innovate more.

QUICK STUDY GUIDE

Chapter 7: Market Structures

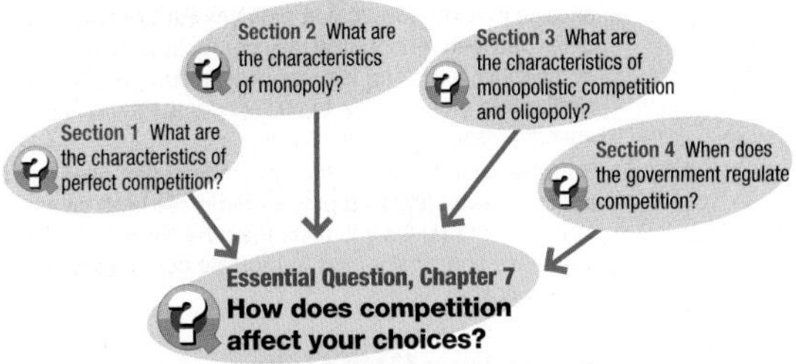
Section 2 What are the characteristics of monopoly?
Section 3 What are the characteristics of monopolistic competition and oligopoly?
Section 1 What are the characteristics of perfect competition?
Section 4 When does the government regulate competition?
Essential Question, Chapter 7
How does competition affect your choices?

Comparison of Market Structures

	Perfect Competition	Monopolistic Competition	Oligopoly	Monopoly
Number of firms	Many	Many	A few dominate	One
Variety of goods	None	Some	Some	None
Control over prices	None	Little	Some	Complete
Barriers to entry	None	Low	High	Complete
Examples	Wheat, shares of stock	Jeans, books	Cars, movie studios	Public water

Regulation and Deregulation

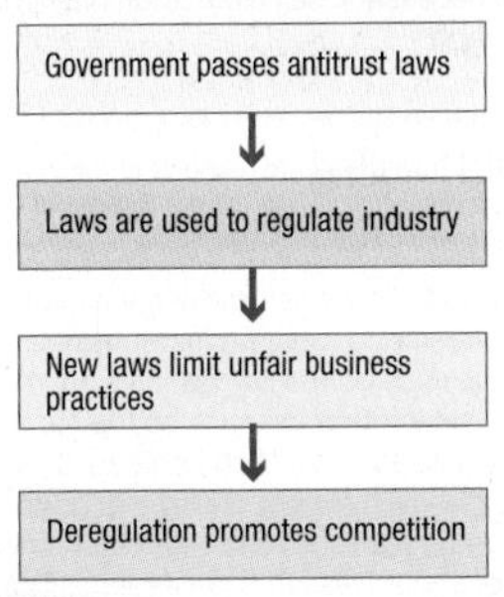
Government passes antitrust laws
Laws are used to regulate industry
New laws limit unfair business practices
Deregulation promotes competition

Economic Dictionary

perfect competition, *p. 159*
commodity, *p. 160*
barrier to entry, *p. 160*
imperfect competition, *p. 160*
start-up costs, *p. 162*
monopoly, *p. 164*
economies of scale, *p. 165*
natural monopoly, *p. 166*
government monopoly, *p. 167*
patent, *p. 167*
franchise, *p. 167*
license, *p. 168*
price discrimination, *p. 171*
market power, *p. 171*
monopolistic competition, *p. 174*
differentiation, *p. 175*
nonprice competition, *p. 175*
oligopoly, *p. 177*
price war, *p. 179*
collusion, *p. 179*
price fixing, *p. 179*
cartel, *p. 179*
predatory pricing, *p. 180*
antitrust laws, *p. 181*
trust, *p. 181*
merger, *p. 182*
deregulation, *p. 183*

Economics on the go

Study anytime, anywhere. Download these files today.

Economic Dictionary online	Audio Review online	Action Graph online	Visual Glossary online	How the Economy Works online
Vocabulary Support in English and Spanish	Audio Study Guide in English and Spanish	Animated Charts and Graphs	Animated feature	Animated feature

Download to your computer or mobile device at PearsonSuccessNet.com

ASSIGN THE ESSENTIAL QUESTIONS JOURNAL

After students have finished studying the chapter, they should return to the chapter's essential question in the Essential Questions Journal and complete the activity.

Tell students to go back to the chapter opener and look at the image. Using the information they have gained from studying the chapter, ask **How does this illustrate the main ideas of the chapter?** *(Possible response: The cars are competing to win the race, just as firms in an industry compete for customers; the cars each advertise different businesses that are competing for consumer dollars; in some markets, consumers choose products based on price as well as how well the producer has been able to differentiate the product to make it more appealing.)*

STUDY TIPS

Explain to students that they can take better lecture notes if they pay attention to how the ideas are organized. Teachers may divide their lecture into an introduction, a thesis statement, the body of the lecture, and a summary. The material in the body of the lecture may be organized chronologically, by cause and effect, or sequentially. Looking for the structure of a lecture can help students recognize the most important ideas and organize their notes.

Economics on the go Have students download the digital resources available at Economics on the Go for review and remediation.

Assessment at a Glance

TESTS AND QUIZZES

Section Assessments

Section Quizzes A and B, **Unit 2 All-in-One**
Self-Test Online

Chapter Assessments

Chapter Tests A and B, **Unit 2 All-in-One**
Economic Detective, **Unit 2 All-in-One**
Document-based Assessment, p. 187
Exam*View*

AYP Monitoring Assessments

PERFORMANCE ASSESSMENT

Teacher's Edition, pp. 160, 162, 165, 171, 178, 182, 183
Simulation Activities, Chapter 7
Virtual Economics on CD-ROM, pp. 162, 171, 176, 183
Essential Questions Journal, Chapter 7
Assessment Rubrics

Chapter Assessment

1. (a) Possible response: lemons, sugar, cups; about $15.00 (b) Possible response: Yes, because it will help them learn about business and sales. (c) Possible response: set up in a busy location; charge a lower price.
2. (a) These occur in markets that operate most efficiently with one large firm. (b) because there is no competition (c) No, because there are alternatives: private schools offer a similar service and parents can home-school their children.
3. (a) It allows the city to control a small market. (b) high prices (c) No, because competition will result in lower prices, more choices, and higher quality.
4. (a) Firms in monopolistic competition have lower prices, higher output, and lower profits than monopolies. (b) Perfectly competitive firms have lower prices, higher output, and even lower profit than monopolistically competitive firms. (c) It is closer to perfect competition because there are many firms, limited barriers to entry and limited control over price. Monopolies do not engage in competition.
5. (a) to outlaw mergers and monopolies that limited trade between states (b) to regulate industry, to stop firms from forming cartels or monopolies, to break up monopolies (c) Possible responses: Yes, otherwise monopolies would take advantage of consumers. No, government should not interfere with private business.
6. $20,008
7. $10,008
8. ten meals: $2,008; fifty meals: $408; one hundred meals: $208; one thousand meals: $28
9. The line graph should resemble the Average Total Cost Curve with Economies of Scale graph in Figure 7.2 on p. 165. The downward sloping average total cost curve should reflect the lower costs of producing each additional meal.
10. You may choose to divide the class into groups of 6 or 7 first, give each group a different category of high-tech product—for example, televisions, cellphones, computers, or handheld games—then have each group decide on three features that their product will have.
11. Answers will vary, but students should identify some strategies to differentiate their product that will make it more appealing to consumers. For example, one group may offer ways for the customer to customize the product, or provide additional services for free or at a reduced price.

CHAPTER 7 ASSESSMENT

Self-Test online To test your understanding of key terms and main ideas, visit **PearsonSuccessNet.com**

Key Terms and Main Ideas

To make sure you understand the key terms and main ideas of this chapter, review the Checkpoint and Section Assessment questions and look at the Quick Study Guide on the preceding page.

Critical Thinking

1. **Apply** You are babysitting for children who want to start a lemonade stand. **(a)** List at least three items they will have to buy before they can start selling lemonade. How much do you think these start-up expenses will cost? **(b)** Would you recommend that the children set up a lemonade stand? Why or why not? **(c)** Suppose that another family down the street already has a lemonade stand. How would you recommend that the children compete?
2. **Draw Conclusions (a)** Why does government usually approve of natural monopolies? **(b)** Why does it regulate them? **(c)** Do you believe that public education is a natural monopoly? Why or why not?
3. **Make Judgments** Suppose that you are the mayor of your town. A local candy maker asks you to franchise his shop as the only approved chocolate shop in town. **(a)** What might be one benefit to the town in granting his request? **(b)** What would be a disadvantage? **(c)** Considering the benefit and disadvantage, would you agree to the candy maker's request?
4. **Compare and Contrast (a)** How do prices, output, and profits differ between monopolies and firms that engage in monopolistic competition? **(b)** How do they differ between monopolistically competitive and perfectly competitive firms? **(c)** Is monopolistic competition more similar to a monopoly or to perfect competition? Give specific reasons for your choice.
5. **Summarize (a)** Why did the government first pass antitrust laws? **(b)** What powers did these laws give the government? **(c)** Do you think the government should use these and similar laws to regulate companies? Why or why not?

Applying Your Math Skills

Making a Line Graph Create a line graph for an industry with economies of scale to show how much it costs to produce each given amount of a product. Suppose it costs $20,000 to set up and furnish a new restaurant. The cost for each meal the restaurant serves is $8. Use your math skills and the information above to answer the following questions:

Visit PearsonSuccessNet.com for additional math help.

6. How much does it cost to produce the first meal the restaurant serves?
7. How much does it cost per meal to produce two meals?
8. What is the cost per meal to produce ten meals? Fifty meals? One hundred meals? One thousand meals?
9. Based on your answers to questions 6, 7, and 8, create a line graph titled: Costs per Meal at the New Restaurant. If necessary, calculate additional points to put on your graph.

Essential Question Activity

Essential Questions Journal To respond to the chapter Essential Question, go to your **Essential Questions Journal.**

10. Complete this activity to answer the Essential Question **How does competition affect your choices?** To welcome a new student and inform them about the goods and services available in the community, the class will create a newcomer's kit. To create this kit, the class will generate a list of businesses that provide goods and services that would be helpful to a new student. The list will identify categories of goods and services such as fast food, clothing, sporting goods, entertainment, and automobile services. Use the worksheet in your Essential Questions Journal or the electronic worksheet available at **PearsonSuccessNet.com,** to gather information about the products or services. Then use the worksheet to answer the following questions:
   (a) Which categories have the greatest number of choices? Is there a wide range of prices?
   (b) Give one example of nonprice differentiation between products in a category.
   (c) Identify the market structure for each business.
11. **Modify** The class will use the information they have gathered to create a mini-business directory. Each business on the list will have an entry that provides basic information such as the name of the business, and its street or Web address. Entries for each business will highlight the type of goods or services that the business provides and their price range. Each entry should also include a rating. The rating could be in the form of a one to two sentence review. Or, students can create a rating system with a key that explains what the rating symbols mean. Students will also create a map for the directory that shows the locations of all the businesses. When the directory is finished, give it to the school guidance office so that it can be distributed to students who are new to the area.

186 MARKET STRUCTURES

WebQuest online The Economics WebQuest challenges students to use twenty-first century skills to answer the Essential Question.

THE ESSENTIAL
VIDEO
By Students For Students
For videos on Essential Questions, go to PearsonSuccessNet.com

Remind students to continue to develop an Essential Questions video. Guidelines and a production binder are available at www.PearsonSuccessNet.com.

When is government regulation necessary?

In 2007, some members of Congress introduced a bill that would ensure "net neutrality." The bill would prevent Internet service providers from charging fees to Web sites in order to run at higher speeds. Industry members and consumer interest groups clashed over the bill.

Document A

"Left free to create new business opportunities and services, broadband providers (including cable, DSL, satellite and wireless operators) have invested billions of dollars to bring high-speed Internet access to consumers nationwide. With bandwidth usage growing at a rapid pace, continued investment will be needed to keep broadband services robust.

If broadband providers are to continue to make these investments, and if consumers are going to be given the levels of services and innovative new products and features they desire, all at prices they can afford, broadband providers need to have continuing flexibility to develop new business models and pricing plans."

—National Cable & Telecommunications Association, January 2007

Document B

"[Without a net neutrality law,] Internet service providers would be free to block or impede any online content or services, for any reason. They could also charge websites or applications for 'priority service,' practically assuring that any site that couldn't or wouldn't pay their fees would no longer work as well or be as easy to find. That could spell the end of innovation, as small businesses, entrepreneurs, local governments, nonprofits and others would be locked out of a system controlled by the big telephone and cable companies. If network providers are allowed to control the flow of information, the open and freewheeling nature of the Internet could be lost."

—Common Cause, "Some Straight Talk on Net Neutrality"

Document C

ANALYZING DOCUMENTS

Use your knowledge of government regulation and Documents A, B, and C to answer questions 1–3.

1. **According to Document A, Internet service providers need the flexibility to charge additional fees so they can**
   A. increase corporate profits.
   B. expand broadband services.
   C. remain competitive with foreign companies.
   D. raise prices to consumers.

2. **According to Document B, a "net neutrality" bill is necessary to ensure**
   A. unlimited access to Web sites.
   B. low prices.
   C. expanded broadband service.
   D. consumer safety.

3. **The cartoon in Document C suggests that government regulation**
   A. is good for business.
   B. traps consumers.
   C. holds down innovation.
   D. raises prices.

WRITING ABOUT ECONOMICS

Whether to regulate Internet businesses is an ongoing issue. Use the documents on this page and resources on the Web site below to answer the question: ***When is government regulation necessary?*** Use the sources to support your opinion.

In Partnership

THE WALL STREET JOURNAL. CLASSROOM EDITION

To read more about issues related to this topic, visit **PearsonSuccessNet.com**

Document-Based Assessment

ANALYZE DOCUMENTS

1. B
2. A
3. C

WRITING ABOUT ECONOMICS

Possible answer: Regulations are too restrictive because they remove incentives for businesses to innovate; regulations are not too restrictive, because without them, access to the Internet would become too expensive.

Student essay should demonstrate an understanding of the issues involved. Use the following as guidelines to assess the essay.

L2 Differentiate Students use all documents on the page to support their thesis.

L3 Differentiate Students use the documents on this page and additional information available online at www.PearsonSuccessNet.com to support their answer.

L4 Differentiate Students incorporate information provided in the textbook and online at www.PearsonSuccessNet.com and include additional research to support their opinion.

Go Online to PearsonSuccessNet.com for a student rubric and extra documents.

Economics online *All print resources are available on the Teacher's Resource Library CD-ROM and online at* www.PearsonSuccessNet.com.

Essential Question

Who benefits from the free market economy?

BELLRINGER

Ask students to read the paragraph under the Essential Question. Then have volunteers suggest examples of who may benefit from the free market economy.

DISCUSS

Have students review the quotations on the page. Ask students to explain the role of government in the economy. **What kind of rules is Gatsby 999 referring to?** *(Possible answer: antitrust laws)* **How would the enforcement of certain rules benefit you as a consumer?** *(Possible answer: Breaking up monopolies allows competition, which gives consumers many choices and keeps prices low.)* **What happens when the free market does not operate efficiently?** *(Possible answer: The government may need to intervene by imposing a price ceiling, such as rent control.)*

L2 Differentiate Remind students to review their Guided Reading and Review worksheets to recall information that will help them complete the activity.

ANALYZE A CARTOON

Have students silently read the cartoon's text. Have them work in small groups to discuss how the economy might "run us down." Have small groups work together to create their own humorous cartoon about an economic issue. Invite volunteers to share their cartoons with the class.

BULLETIN BOARD ACTIVITY

Have students revisit the Unit Essential Question articles that they have posted as they have studied the chapters. Have them discuss the relevance of the articles to the question and whether their opinions have changed since they first read the article. Remind students to review their work in their **Essential Questions Journal**.

EXTEND

Have students complete their work on the Essential Questions Video and present their work to the class.

L4 Differentiate Organize students into small groups to research the commerce clause of the Constitution. Have them summarize the basic meaning of the clause and find examples of the clause being used in court cases during the last 20 years. Have students present their findings to the class.

Unit 2 Challenge

Essential Question, Unit 2

Who benefits from the free market economy?

People have different opinions about who benefits in the free marketplace. Look at the opinions below, keeping in mind the Essential Question: Who benefits from the free market economy?

"I'm all for a free economy, but competitors need to play by some rules. Congress has the power to regulate this trade through the commerce clause of the Constitution and needs to begin to do so."

—Gatsby 999, msnbc.com

"I suspect ignorance about economics leads many to believe that when two people exchange goods and money, one wins and the other loses. If rich capitalists profit, the poor and the weak suffer. That's a myth. How many times have you paid $1 for a cup of coffee and after the clerk said, "thank you," you responded, "thank you"? There's a wealth of economics wisdom in the weird double thank-you moment. Why does it happen? Because you want the coffee more than the buck, and the store wants the buck more than the coffee. Both of you win."

—John Stossel, Real Clear Politics.com, "The Double Thank-You Moment," May 30, 2007

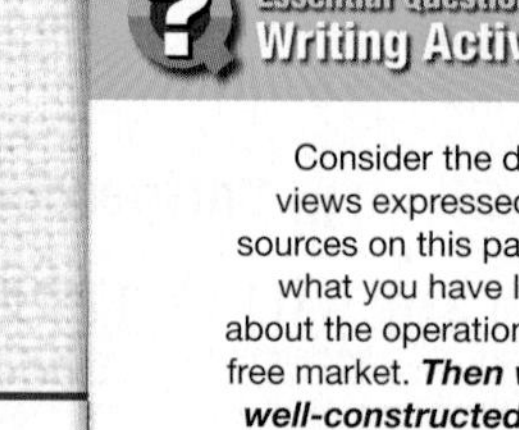

Essential Question Writing Activity

Consider the different views expressed in the sources on this page and what you have learned about the operation of the free market. ***Then write a well-constructed essay expressing your view of who benefits in a free market economy.***

Essential Questions Journal

To respond to the unit Essential Question, go to your **Essential Questions Journal**.

Writing Guidelines

- Address all aspects of the Essential Question Writing Activity.
- Support the theme with relevant facts, examples, and details.
- Use a logical and clear plan of organization.
- Introduce the theme by establishing a framework that is beyond a simple restatement of the question and conclude with a summation of the theme.

For help in writing a Persuasive Essay, refer to the *Writer's Handbook* in the Reference section, page S-5.

Essential Question Writing Activity

Before students begin the writing activity, remind them to skim through the unit chapters to read the headings on each page. Have them read through any notes they took and to review their chapter assessments and chapter projects.

Students should write a two-paragraph article. Paragraph one should outline how they personally might benefit from a free market economy. Paragraph two should explain who benefits from the free market economy.

L2 Differentiate Students should write a paragraph that explains how they personally might benefit from a free market economy, providing detailed examples.

L4 Differentiate Students should write a three-paragraph article that provides relevant examples of who benefits from the free market economy.

Before students begin work, distribute the Writing Assessment rubric, available at the Online Teacher Center at PearsonSuccessNet.com.

UNIT 3 Business and Labor

Chapter 8 Business Organizations

Chapter 9 Labor

Essential Question, Unit 3

How can businesses and labor best achieve their goals?

Chapter 8
Why do some businesses succeed and others fail?

Chapter 9
How can workers best meet the challenges of a changing economy?

Online Resources

Economics Online Teacher Center at PearsonSuccessNet.com includes

- Online Teacher's Edition with lesson planner
- Online Lecture Notes
- Teacher's Resource Library with All-in-One Resources, Color Transparencies, Simulation Activities, and Adequate Yearly Progress Monitoring
- SuccessTracker Assessment

Economics Online Student Center at PearsonSuccessNet.com includes

- Interactive textbook with audio
- Economics Video
- WebQuests
- Interactivities
- Student Self-Tests

Essential Question

How can businesses and labor best achieve their goals?

Introduce the Unit

ACTIVATE PRIOR KNOWLEDGE

Essential questions frame each unit and chapter of study, asking students to consider big ideas about economics. Write the Unit Essential Question on the Board: **How can businesses and labor best achieve their goals?** Using the Think-Write-Pair-Share strategy (p. T24), have students brainstorm answers to the question.

WRITING ACTIVITY

To begin this unit, assign the Unit 3 Warmup Activity in the **Essential Questions Journal**. This will help students start to consider their position on the Unit 3 Essential Question: **How can businesses and labor best achieve their goals?**

Use the **Essential Questions Journal** throughout the program to help students consider these and other big ideas about economics.

BULLETIN BOARD ACTIVITY

Post the Unit Essential Question on a bulletin board. Tell students that they will be learning about how businesses and labor achieve their goals. Ask them to bring in articles about current events to help them answer the question. Students should identify their article and use a sticky note to briefly explain the connection to the Essential Question.

CREATING THE ESSENTIAL QUESTIONS VIDEO

Preview the Unit Challenge on page 246. Consider assigning this activity to your students. Tell them that they will be creating their own video to explore this question, and that they should keep this in mind as they study the goals of businesses and labor. For further information about how to complete this activity, go to PearsonSucessNet.com.

NATIONAL COUNCIL ON ECONOMIC EDUCATION

The following Voluntary National Content Standards in Economics are addressed in this unit:

- ★ Standard 10
- ★ Standard 14
- ★ Standard 13

For a complete description of the standards addressed in each chapter, see the Correlations chart on pages T52–T55.

Essential Questions

UNIT 3:

How can businesses and labor best achieve their goals?

CHAPTER 8:

Why do some businesses succeed and others fail?

Introduce the Chapter

ACTIVATE PRIOR KNOWLEDGE

In this chapter, students will learn about the different ways businesses are organized, as well as the advantages and disadvantages of each type. Tell students to complete the warmup activity in their **Essential Questions Journal.**

DIFFERENTIATED INSTRUCTION KEY

- **L1** Special Needs
- **L2** Basic
  - **ELL** English Language Learners
  - **LPR** Less Proficient Readers
- **L3** All Students
- **L4** Advanced Students

Economics online Visit www.PearsonSuccessNet.com for an interactive textbook with built-in activities on economic principles.

- ***The Wall Street Journal* Classroom Edition Video** presents a current topic related to business organizations.
- **Yearly Update Worksheet** provides an annual update, including a new worksheet and lesson on this topic.
- **On the Go** resources can be downloaded so students and teachers can connect with economics anytime, anywhere.

Chapter 8 Business Organizations

Essential Question, Chapter 8

Why do some businesses succeed and others fail?

- **Section 1:** Sole Proprietorships
- **Section 2:** Partnerships and Franchises
- **Section 3:** Corporations, Mergers, and Multinationals
- **Section 4:** Nonprofit Organizations

Economics on the go

To study anywhere, anytime, download these online resources at ***PearsonSuccessNet.com*** ▶

ECONOMICS ONLINE

DIGITAL TEACHER TOOLS

The online lesson is designed to help teachers plan, teach, and assess. Teachers have the ability to use or customize existing Pearson lesson plans. Online lecture notes support the print lesson by providing an array of accessible activities and summaries of key concepts. Two interactivities in this lesson are:

- **How the Economy Works** An interactive feature that allows the user to explore the issues involved when a small business expands.
- **Visual Glossary** An online activity that breaks down the structure of corporations for ease of understanding.

Block Scheduling

BLOCK 1 Teach Sections 1 and 2. Then have students work together to write a business plan using the Simulation Activity, "Be an Entrepreneur!"

BLOCK 2 Teach Sections 3 and 4 lessons. Select an Extend option from one section, depending on your preferences and state standards.

Pressed for Time

Group work Divide the class into four groups and assign each group one section. Use the Jigsaw strategy to have groups become "experts" on one type of business or organization. Each group sharing a section collaborates on a presentation for the class. Complete the worksheets and transparencies as a class.

OBJECTIVES

1. **Explain** the characteristics of sole proprietorships.
2. **Analyze** the advantages of a sole proprietorship.
3. **Analyze** the disadvantages of a sole proprietorship.

ECONOMIC DICTIONARY

As you read the section, look for the definitions of these **Key Terms:**

- sole proprietorship
- business organization
- business license
- zoning laws
- liability
- fringe benefits

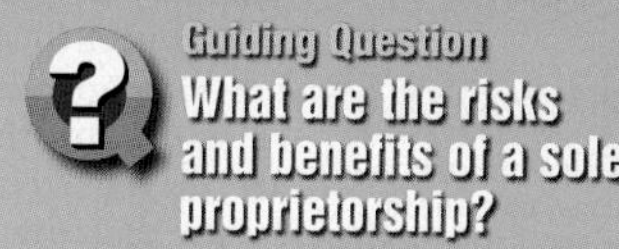

Guiding Question
What are the risks and benefits of a sole proprietorship?

Copy this comparison chart and fill it in as you read.

Sole Proprietorships	
Advantages	**Disadvantages**
• Ease of start-up • • • •	• Unlimited personal liability • • • •

Economics and You You may be one of the lucky people who is able to turn something you really like to do into a business. Imagine launching a web site that reviews video games or opening a baseball camp or a car detailing business. One of the many challenges you will face is finding the best way to organize your business.

Principles in Action The easiest business to set up is the one in which you are the only owner. In this section you will learn that being your own boss has its advantages as well as its disadvantages. In the Economics & You feature, you will see how doing business with a sole proprietorship might affect you.

The Role of Sole Proprietorships

A **sole proprietorship** is a business owned and managed by a single individual. In this type of **business organization,** which is the ownership structure of a company or firm, the lone entrepreneur earns all of the firm's profits and is responsible for all its debts. This type of company is by far the most popular in the United States. According to the Internal Revenue Service, more than 70 percent of all businesses are organized as sole proprietorships. Most sole proprietorships are small, however. All together they generate only about 4 percent of all United States sales.

Many types of businesses can flourish as sole proprietorships. Look around your neighborhood or town. It is more likely than not that your local bakery, your barber shop or hair salon, your bike-repair shop, and the corner grocery store are all sole proprietorships.

sole proprietorship a business owned and managed by a single individual

business organization the ownership structure of a company or firm

Visual Glossary online

Go to the Visual Glossary Online for an interactive review of **corporation.**

Action Graph online

Go to Action Graph Online for animated versions of key charts and graphs.

How the Economy Works online

Go to How the Economy Works Online for an interactive lesson on how a small business grows.

Guiding Question

What are the risks and benefits of a sole proprietorship?

Get Started

Sole Proprietorships	
Advantages	**Disadvantages**
• Ease of start-up • Few regulations • Sole receiver of profit • Full control	• Unlimited personal liability • Limited access to resources • Lack of permanence

LESSON GOALS

Students will:

- Know the Key Terms.
- Describe the characteristics of sole proprietorships.
- Choose a product or service to sell as a sole proprietor and describe the business.
- Understand the process of creating and maintaining a sole proprietorship.
- Create a hypothetical sole proprietorship to identify the risks involved.

BEFORE CLASS

Students should read the section for homework before coming to class.

Have students complete the graphic organizer in the Section Opener as they read the text. As an alternate activity, have students complete the Guided Reading and Review worksheet (Unit 3 All-in-One, p. 15).

L1 L2 ELL LPR Differentiate Have students complete the Guided Reading and Review worksheet (Unit 3 All-in-One, p. 16).

Focus on the Basics

Students need to come away with the following understandings:

FACTS: • Sole proprietorships are owned by one person who makes all the profit and bears all the responsibility for the business. • Sole proprietorships are easy to set up and face few regulations. • The sole proprietor has full control of the business, with great flexibility in how it is run, and can terminate it easily. • Sole proprietors have unlimited personal liability and limited access to resources.

GENERALIZATION: Sole proprietorship is one way to organize a business. An owner makes all the decisions and profits while accepting all the responsibilities and debts.

CLASSROOM HINTS

TEEN ENTREPRENEURS

The term "entrepreneur" may be easier for students to understand, if they can imagine themselves starting a business. There are many examples of businesses owned by teenagers that are listed on the Web in response to a search on the keywords *teen entrepreneurs.* Have each student research one teen entrepreneur and describe the business to the class. How many of these businesses used the Internet to sell products or services?

BELLRINGER

Use the transparency, "What Do You Want to Do?" (Color Transparencies, 8.a). Have students write their answers–*Never, Sometimes,* or *Always*–in their notebooks.

Teach

Economics online To present this topic using digital resources, use the lecture notes on www.PearsonSuccessNet.com.

L1 L2 ELL LPR Differentiate To help students who are struggling readers, assign the Vocabulary worksheet (Unit 3 All-in-One, p. 14).

DISCUSS

Talk about the risks of owning and running a business, emphasizing the cost and the responsibility that fall on the sole proprietor to make it succeed. Tell students that their answers to the questions on the transparency can help them identify their ability to be a successful sole proprietor. Ask **What are important qualities of a successful sole proprietor?** *(willingness to take risks, sense of responsibility, desire to work hard, energy, business sense, dedication to a vision)* Discuss whether or not they think they have the necessary qualities to be a sole proprietor.

Ask **Would some qualities be more important than others?**

Action Graph online Have students review the Action Graph animation for a step-by-step look at Characteristics of Proprietorships.

L3 Differentiate For alternative or additional practice with the concept of entrepreneurship, have students use the "Be an Entrepreneur!" activity (Simulation Activities, Chapter 8). Students work in groups to create a detailed business plan for a small business.

Answers

Graph Skills 1. 13 percent 2. Manufacturing usually requires a larger investment in equipment than a service does, and sole proprietorships have less access to money and financing.

Checkpoint sole proprietorship

Entrepreneurial Spirit

Simulation Activity

Be an Entrepreneur! You may be asked to take part in a role-playing game that involves being an entrepreneur.

In some ways, the word *spirit* in the term *entrepreneurial spirit* says it all. There is a difference between people who expect to spend their lives working for someone else and those who want to work for themselves. Some people are driven by an idea or ambition to create their own jobs. But ambition is only a starting point. To be successful, sole proprietors have to be risk takers. They have to be willing to risk failure for greater satisfaction, and perhaps greater financial gain.

The profile of an entrepreneur includes other essential qualities. The person hoping to start a business has to be able to answer yes to a series of questions. Are you organized? Are you responsible? Are your energetic? Are you goal-oriented? Do you know how to run a business? You may be the best cook in the world, but if you know nothing about the business end of running a restaurant, you are likely to fail.

Steve Case, co-founder of America Online, is a model of the successful entrepreneur who believed in himself and had the vision that a company could thrive on the Internet.

> **"If you're doing something new, you've got to have a vision. You've got to have a perspective. You've got have some North Star you're aiming for, and you just believe somehow you'll get there. . . . You've got to stick with it, because these things are not overnight successes. . . ."**
>
> —From an interview with Academy of Achievement, July 12, 2004

CHECKPOINT ***What is the most common form of business organization?***

Advantages of Sole Proprietorships

While you need to do more than just hang out a sign to start your own business, a sole proprietorship is simple to establish. It also offers the owner several advantages.

Figure 8.1 Characteristics of Sole Proprietorships

GRAPH SKILLS

Most sole proprietorships take in relatively small amounts of money, or receipts.

1. What percentage of sole proprietorships is engaged in retail trade?
2. Why might more sole proprietors be engaged in services than in manufacturing?

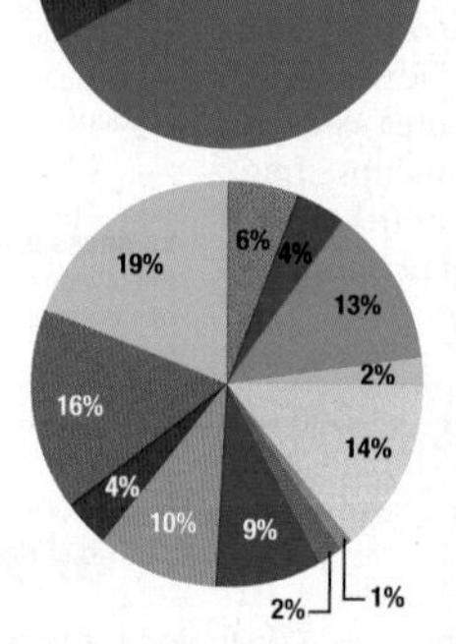

Action Graph online For an animated version of this graph, visit **PearsonSuccessNet.com**

Note: Because of rounding, totals may be greater than or less than 100 percent. Data for 2004.
SOURCE: *The 2008 Statistical Abstract of the United States*

Differentiated Resources

- **L1 L2 Guided Reading and Review** (Unit 3 All-in-One, p. 16)
- **L1 L2 Vocabulary worksheet** (Unit 3 All-in-One, p. 14)
- **L4 L2 What Kind of Business?** (Unit 3 All-in-One, pp. 17, 18)
- **L3 Be an Entrepreneur!** (Simulation Activities, Chapter 8)

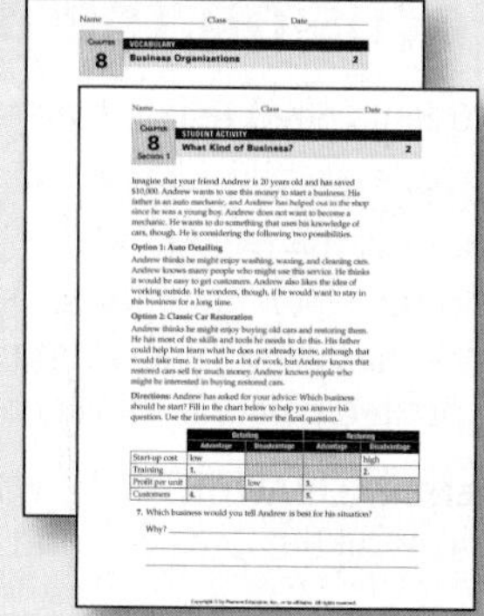

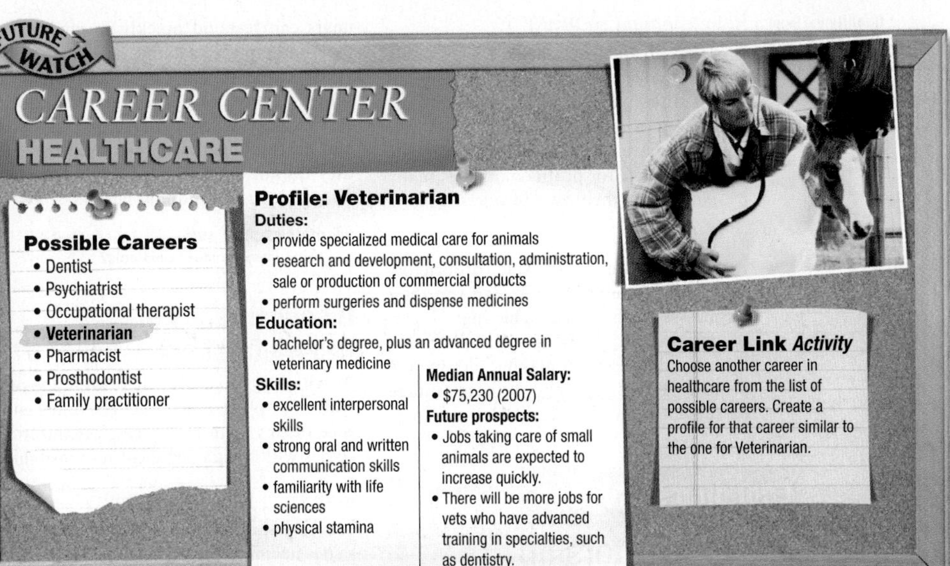

FUTURE WATCH
CAREER CENTER
HEALTHCARE
Possible Careers
• Dentist
• Psychiatrist
• Occupational therapist
• Veterinarian
• Pharmacist
• Prosthodontist
• Family practitioner
Profile: Veterinarian
Duties:
• provide specialized medical care for animals
• research and development, consultation, administration, sale or production of commercial products
• perform surgeries and dispense medicines
Education:
• bachelor's degree, plus an advanced degree in veterinary medicine
Skills:
• excellent interpersonal skills
• strong oral and written communication skills
• familiarity with life sciences
• physical stamina
Median Annual Salary:
• $75,230 (2007)
Future prospects:
• Jobs taking care of small animals are expected to increase quickly.
• There will be more jobs for vets who have advanced training in specialties, such as dentistry.
Career Link Activity
Choose another career in healthcare from the list of possible careers. Create a profile for that career similar to the one for Veterinarian.

Easy to Start and End

Easy start-up is the main advantage of the sole proprietorship. With just a small amount of paperwork and legal expense, just about anyone can start such a business. The exact requirements vary from city to city and state to state. Typically, though, sole proprietors must meet the following minimum requirements:

1. *Authorization* Many sole proprietors must obtain a **business license,** which is an authorization from the local government to operate a business. Certain professionals, such as doctors and day-care providers, may also need a special license from the state.
2. *Site permit* If not operating the business out of his or her home, a sole proprietor must obtain a certificate of occupancy to use another building for business. Some zoning laws prohibit doing business in a residential area.
3. *Name* If not using his or her own name as the name of the business, a sole proprietor must register a business name.

This paperwork often takes only a day or two to complete. Because they require little legal paperwork, sole proprietorships are usually the least expensive form of ownership to establish.

The federal government offers aid to entrepreneurs to help their businesses grow. Once a business has been started, the federal government's Small Business Administration provides a variety of loan programs and other support.

Relatively Few Regulations

A proprietorship is the least-regulated form of business organization. Even the smallest business, however, is subject to some regulation, especially industry-specific rules. For example, a soft pretzel stand would be subject to health codes, and a furniture refinishing business would have to follow laws about disposing of dangerous chemicals.

Sole proprietorships may also be subject to local **zoning laws.** Cities and towns often designate certain areas, or zones, for residential use and for business. Zoning laws may prohibit sole proprietors from operating businesses out of their homes.

business license authorization to operate a business issued by a local government

zoning laws laws in a city or town that designate certain areas, or zones, for residential and business use

EXPLORE

Have students explore the rationale behind requirements for starting up a business. Ask **Why would a local government require a sole proprietor to have a business license?** *(Possible answers: to keep track of businesses operating in a city; to protect consumers; to maintain standards)* **Why would a city require a site permit?** *(to ensure the business is right for the building and location)*

Discuss the advantage of a sole proprietor's flexibility in making decisions. Ask **When might a sole proprietor need to make a quick decision?** *(Possible answers: when a supplier goes out of business; when prices need to be adjusted)*

L2 Differentiate Distribute the "What Kind of Business?" worksheet (Unit 3 All-in-One, p. 18).

L4 Differentiate Distribute the "What Kind of Business?" worksheet (Unit 3 All-in-One, p. 17), which asks students to imagine themselves as business advisors and to make their recommendations. Emphasize that successful entrepreneurs must objectively assess their skills and resources and choose the most suitable kind of business to enter. When students have completed the worksheet, have them present their answers using the Idea Wave strategy (p. T24).

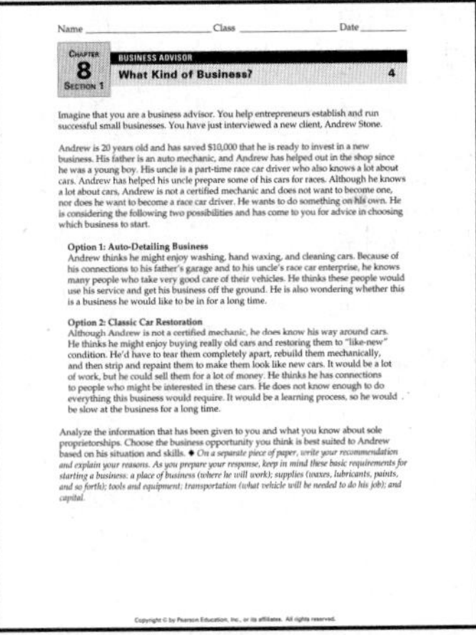

Name ____________ Class ____________ Date ________

CHAPTER 8 SECTION 1 — BUSINESS ADVISOR

What Kind of Business? 4

Imagine that you are a business advisor. You help entrepreneurs establish and run successful small businesses. You have just interviewed a new client, Andrew Stone.

Andrew is 20 years old and has saved $10,000 that he is ready to invest in a new business. His father is an auto mechanic, and Andrew has helped out in the shop since he was a young boy. His uncle is a part-time race car driver who also knows a lot about cars. Andrew has helped his uncle prepare some of his cars for races. Although he knows a lot about cars, Andrew is not a certified mechanic and does not want to become one, nor does he want to become a race car driver. He wants to do something on his own. He is considering the following two possibilities and has come to you for advice in choosing which business to start.

Option 1: Auto-Detailing Business
Andrew thinks he might enjoy washing, hand waxing, and cleaning cars. Because of his connections to his father's garage and to his uncle's race car enterprise, he knows many people who take very good care of their vehicles. He thinks these people would use his service and get his business off the ground. He is also wondering whether this is a business he would like to be in for a long time.

Option 2: Classic Car Restoration
Although Andrew is not a certified mechanic, he does know his way around cars. He thinks he might enjoy buying really old cars and restoring them to "like-new" condition. He'd have to tear them completely apart, rebuild them mechanically, and then strip and repaint them to make them look like new cars. It would be a lot of work, but he could sell them for a lot of money. He thinks he has connections to people who might be interested in these cars. He does not know enough to do everything this business would require. It would be a learning process, so he would be slow at the business for a long time.

Analyze the information that has been given to you and what you know about sole proprietorships. Choose the business opportunity you think is best suited to Andrew based on his situation and skills. ◆ *On a separate piece of paper, write your recommendation and explain your reasons. As you prepare your response, keep in mind these basic requirements for starting a business: a place of business (where he will work); supplies (waxes, lubricants, paints, and so forth); tools and equipment; transportation (what vehicle will be needed to do his job); and capital.*

CREATE A PROFILE

Have students use the Career Link worksheet to record their research for the activity (Unit 3 All-in-One, p. 88).

BRAINSTORM

Guide students in creating a hypothetical landscaping business as a sole proprietorship. Ask **How do you plan to attract clients to your business?** Have students discuss how they would market it. Ask **What must you buy to start the business? How much will the items cost?** *(Examples include lawn mower at $1,500; trimmer at $250; leaf blower at $200; hand tools, such as rakes and gloves, at $300; fertilizer and mulch, at $300; and used truck and trailer at $7,000, for a total of $9,550.)* List the items and prices on the board.

EXTEND

Tell students to suppose a bank has made them a loan at 9 percent interest for one year. Then have students work in small groups to estimate the cost of the interest and the monthly payment, that is, principal plus interest. *(0.09 × $9,550 = $859.50 per year); ($9,550 + $859.50 = $10,409.50 ÷ 12 months = $867.46 per month)*

L4 Differentiate Engage students in speculating how much they would have to earn each month to make a reasonable profit and to pay off the loan. Ask **What would happen if you could not repay the loan?** Present the possibility that even by selling the equipment they could not pay back the loan, in which case they would be responsible for the debt.

GUIDING QUESTION WRAP UP

Have students return to the section Guiding Question. Review the completed graphic organizer and clarify any misunderstandings. Have a wrap up discussion about sole proprietorships, reviewing their advantages and disadvantages.

Assess and Remediate

L4 L3 L2 Collect the "What Kind of Business?" worksheets and assess students' understanding.

L3 Assign the Section 1 Assessment questions; identify student misconceptions.

L3 Give Section Quiz A (Unit 3 All-in-One, p. 19).

L2 Give Section Quiz B (Unit 3 All-in-One, p. 20).

(Assess and Remediate continued on p. 195)

Answers

Economics & You Sole proprietors can adjust business hours to meet personal needs.

Checkpoint They are easy to start because they face few regulations and require little paperwork or legal expense. They are easy to end because sole proprietors have few obligations, such as to pay debts.

liability the legal obligation to pay debts

Sole Receiver of Profit

A major advantage of the sole proprietorship is that the owner gets to keep all profits after paying income taxes. If the business succeeds, the owner does not have to share the success with anyone else. The desire for profits motivates many people to start their own businesses.

Full Control

Another advantage of sole proprietorship is that sole proprietors can run their businesses as they wish. This high degree of freedom appeals to entrepreneurs. Fast, flexible decision-making allows sole proprietorships to take full advantage of sudden opportunities. These entrepreneurs can respond quickly to changes in the marketplace. Finally, if sole proprietors decide to stop operations and do something else for a living, they can do so easily. They must, of course, pay all debts and other obligations, such as taxes, but they do not have to meet any other legal obligations to stop doing business.

CHECKPOINT ***Why are sole proprietorships easy to start and end?***

Economics & YOU
Sole Proprietorship
A clothing store owner takes pride in the quality of her customer service, wanting to make sure you get what you need. You appreciate the personalized attention.
Sorry we're CLOSED
On Vacation
Back August 1
The store owner is on vacation. You are inconvenienced.

▲ Every business has advantages and disadvantages. One advantage a sole proprietor has is the ability to set flexible business hours. ***Why is this an advantage a sole proprietorship has over other types of businesses?***

Disadvantages of Sole Proprietorships

As with everything else, there are trade-offs with sole proprietorships. The independence of this form of business organization comes with a high degree of responsibility.

Unlimited Personal Liability

The biggest disadvantage of sole proprietorship is unlimited personal liability. **Liability** is the legal obligation to pay debts. Sole proprietors are fully and personally responsible for all their business debts. If the business fails, the owner may have to sell personal property—such as a car or home—to cover any outstanding obligations. Business debts can ruin a sole proprietor's personal finances.

Limited Access to Resources

Suppose you start a landscaping business that grows quickly. You might need to expand your business by buying more equipment. But as a sole proprietor, you may have to pay for that equipment out of your own pocket. Banks are sometimes unwilling to offer loans to a business that has not been operating for very long. This makes it difficult or impossible for many sole proprietorships to expand quickly.

Physical capital may not be the only factor resource in short supply. Human capital may be lacking, too. A sole proprietor, no matter how ambitious, may lack some of the skills necessary to run a business successfully. For example, you may be great at sales, but not at accounting. You may love working outdoors landscaping, but hate to call on people to drum up business. Some aspects of the business suffer if the owner's skills do not match the needs of the business.

Virtual Economics

L2 Differentiate

Evaluating Entrepreneurship Use the following lesson from the NCEE **Virtual Economics *CD-ROM*** to help students understand the pros and cons of being an entrepreneur. Click on Browse Economics Lessons, specify grades 9–12, and use the key words *making your own.*

In this activity, students will investigate potential business opportunities as entrepreneurs.

LESSON TITLE	MAKING YOUR OWN JOB
Type of Activity	Classifying
Complexity	Low
Time	50 minutes
NCEE Standards	14

Finally, as a sole proprietor, you may have to turn down work because you simply do not have enough hours in the day or enough workers to keep up with demand. A small business often presents its owner with too many demands, and that can be exhausting both personally and financially.

Lack of Permanence

A sole proprietorship has a limited life. If a sole proprietor dies or retires, the business simply ceases to exist if there is no one willing to buy it or run it. The same can happen if the owner suffers an extended illness or loses interest in the business.

Sole proprietorships often have trouble finding and keeping good employees. Small businesses generally cannot offer the security and advancement opportunities that many employees look for in a job. In addition, a sole proprietorship usually has limited access to capital, which means that most small business owners lack the resources to offer workers fringe benefits. **Fringe benefits** are payments to employees other than wages or salaries, such as paid vacation, retirement pay, and health insurance. Lack of experienced employees can hurt a business. Once again, the other side of total control is total responsibility: a sole proprietor cannot count on anyone else to maintain the business.

▲ The sole proprietor enjoys full control, and this includes a flexible work schedule. ***How does this cartoon show a major disadvantage of a sole proprietorship?***

fringe benefits
payments to employees other than wages or salary

✔ **CHECKPOINT** ***What are the disadvantages of sole proprietorships?***

SECTION 1 ASSESSMENT

Essential Questions Journal To continue to build a response to the Essential Question, go to your **Essential Questions Journal.**

Guiding Question

1. Use your completed comparison chart to answer this question: What are the risks and benefits of a sole proprietorship?
2. **Extension** Choose a business you are familiar with. Identify what resources you would need to start up a similar business.

Key Terms and Main Ideas

3. What is a **sole proprietorship?**
4. (a) What is **liability?** (b) Why is it the biggest disadvantage of a sole proprietorship?
5. What role do **business licenses** and **zoning laws** play in sole proprietorships?
6. How does the lack of fringe benefits affect the sole proprietor's ability to run a business?

Critical Thinking

7. **Analyze** Since sole proprietors cannot usually offer benefits to workers, why do some people work for sole proprietors rather than large companies?
8. **Identify (a)** In addition to a soft pretzel stand, name another sole proprietorship that would be subject to health codes. Explain. **(b)** Name a business other than furniture refinishing that would be subject to laws that regulate the disposal of dangerous chemicals. Explain.
9. **Infer** Why are some of the benefits of a sole proprietorship also its greatest disadvantages?

Math Skills

10. The table below shows data for the average homebased sole proprietorship (HBSP) and nonhomebased sole proprietorship. **(a)** Which type of business has the greatest expenditures and receipts? **(b)** Based on the total business **expenses,** which type has the most profitable ratio between receipts and expenses? **(c)** Why do you think that is so? ***Visit PearsonSuccessNet.com for additional math help.***

	HBSP	Non-HBSP
Receipts	$62,523	$178,194
Net income	$22,569	$38,243
Total business expenses	$39,958	$139,955
Cost of sales	$14,228	$64,334
Salaries and wages	$2,010	$17,315
Travel costs	$4,797	$4,948

SOURCE: Small Business Administration, Office of Advocacy

Have students complete the Self-Test Online and continue their work in the **Essential Questions Journal.**

REMEDIATION AND SUGGESTIONS

Use the chart below to help students who are struggling with content.

WEAKNESS	REMEDIATION
Defining key terms (Questions 3, 4, 5)	Have students use the interactive Economic Dictionary Online.
Risks of a sole proprietorship (Questions 1, 4, 5, 6, 8, 9)	Reteach using a comparison-and-contrast chart showing risks and benefits of the sole proprietorship.
Benefits of sole proprietorship (Questions 1, 2, 7)	Have students role-play a sole proprietor trying to sell a business to a potential buyer.

Answers

Checkpoint Disadvantages include unlimited personal liability, limited access to resources, and a limited business lifetime.

Cartoon Sole responsibility for a business means that the owner might have to forgo taking personal time, such as a vacation from running the business.

Assessment Answers

1. The risks include unlimited liability, difficulty getting financing, and limited lifetime. Benefits include ease of start up and shut down, few regulations, the owner's receipt of all profits, and the owner's full control.
2. Students should identify a business and list the equipment and workers they would need to start up this type of business.
3. a business owned by an individual
4. (a) legal obligation to pay debts (b) The owner could lose all personal property if the business fails.
5. Sole proprietors may need a business license from the local government. Zoning laws may prevent sole proprietors from operating from certain locations.
6. Lack of fringe benefits may make it difficult to attract good employees.
7. Possible answers: to gain experience; to be able to work directly with the top person in the organization
8. (a) Possible answer: health facility. Medical doctors come in contact with patients and must maintain clean facilities and control infectious materials. (b) Sample answer: gas station. Automotive lubricants, cleaning fluids, and batteries contain chemicals that must be disposed of properly.
9. Possible answer: Complete control gives the owner both flexibility and all the risk.
10. (a) the Non-HBSP (b) the HBSP (c) The HBSP's expenses are low, because it does not have rent or as many salaries to pay.

 **Guiding Question**

What are the risks and benefits of partnerships and franchises?

Get Started

Advantages and Disadvantages	
Partnership	**Franchise**
• Easy, inexpensive to start up • Owners willing to share control and profits • Few government regulations • Owners each contribute assets • Owners must provide all expertise • Owners must market product or service	• Owner sacrifices some freedom • Owner wants control but not complete control • Franchiser provides training • Franchiser standardizes quality • Franchiser advertises • Franchiser provides financial assistance • Centralized buying reduces costs

LESSON GOALS

Students will:

- Know the Key Terms.
- Analyze the skills and assets of partners and recommend a suitable partnership.
- Evaluate the advantages and disadvantages of a partnership by examining a company biography.
- Use the "Think Creatively and Innovate" skill worksheet in order to evaluate the benefits and risks of partnerships and franchises.

BEFORE CLASS

Have students complete the graphic organizer in the Section Opener as they read the text. As an alternate activity, have students complete the Guided Reading and Review worksheet (Unit 3 All-in-One, p. 21).

L1 L2 ELL LPR Differentiate Have students complete the Guided Reading and Review worksheet (Unit 3 All-in-One, p. 22).

SECTION 2 Partnerships and Franchises

OBJECTIVES

1. **Compare and contrast** different types of partnerships.
2. **Analyze** the advantages of partnerships.
3. **Analyze** the disadvantages of partnerships.
4. **Explain** how a business franchise operates.

ECONOMIC DICTIONARY

As you read the section, look for the definitions of these **Key Terms:**

- partnership
- general partnership
- limited partnership
- limited liability partnership
- articles of partnership
- assets
- business franchise
- royalties

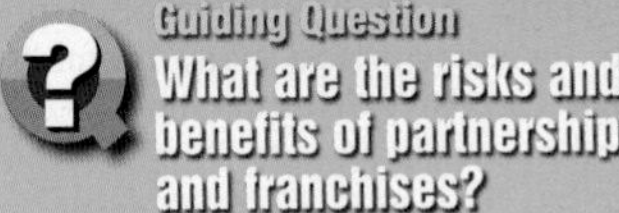

Guiding Question

What are the risks and benefits of partnerships and franchises?

Copy this chart and fill it in as you read. Add more boxes if necessary.

Advantages and Disadvantages	
Partnership	**Franchise**
• Easy, inexpensive to start up • •	• Owner sacrifices some freedom • •

Economics and You Would you ever consider setting up your own business? Suppose the idea is very appealing, but you aren't sure that you want to take on all the responsibilities needed to be successful. You may be great at doing the job, like repairing computers, but you may dread all the paperwork that goes along with being in business. Do you have to give up your dream?

Principles in Action Some business owners overcome their problems, whether it is a shortage of money or talent, by taking on a partner.

Types of Partnerships

A **partnership** is a business organization owned by two or more persons who agree on a specific division of responsibilities and profits. In the United States, partnerships account for nearly 9 percent of all businesses. They generate about 12 percent of all receipts and nearly a quarter of all the income earned by all businesses.

Partnerships are a good choice if owners are willing to share both the responsibility of running the business and the profits it earns. They can also be a good choice if the partners get along well and have skills that complement each other.

Partnerships fall into three categories: general partnerships, limited partnerships, and limited liability partnerships. Each divides responsibility and liability differently.

partnership a business organization owned by two or more persons who agree on a specific division of responsibilities and profits

General Partnership

The most common type of partnership is the **general partnership.** In this type, all partners share equally in both responsibility and liability. Many of the same kinds of businesses that operate as sole proprietorships can operate as general partnerships. Doctors, lawyers, accountants, and other professionals often form partnerships. Small retail stores, farms, construction firms, and family businesses often form partnerships as well.

general partnership a type of partnership in which all partners share equally in both responsibility and liability

CLASSROOM HINTS

PARTNERSHIPS

Help students understand that partnerships involve bringing together people with diverse skills. Have students form pairs or groups of three or four. Groups make a list of the five top skills of each group member by interviewing each other. They make a list of skills that they might need to seek outside their group. This activity can be extended into interviewing members of other groups to see if they might have the missing skills. Students will probably notice that they need to come up with rules for decision-making.

Focus on the Basics

Students need to come away with the following understandings:

FACTS: • Partnerships are owned by two or more people who share responsibilities and profits. • There are three types of partnerships: general partnerships, limited partnerships, and limited liability partnerships. • Partnerships are easy to set up and face few regulations. • Except for limited liability partnerships, people in partnerships can have unlimited personal liability. • Business franchises overcome many of the disadvantages of partnerships but also face disadvantages of their own.

GENERALIZATION: In a partnership, two or more owners share control, profits, and risk. With franchises, owners lose some control and profit but have support and less risk.

Limited Partnership

In a **limited partnership,** only one partner is required to be a general partner. That is, only one partner has unlimited personal liability for the firm's actions. The remaining partner or partners contribute only money. If the business fails, they can lose only the amount of their initial investment. If the business succeeds, though, limited partners share in the profits. A limited partnership must have at least one general partner, but may have any number of limited partners.

Limited partners play no role in managing the business. The general partner runs the company. That control is the main advantage of being a general partner. The main drawback, of course, is the unlimited liability that the general partner has.

Limited Liability Partnerships

The **limited liability partnership** (LLP) is a newer type of partnership recognized by many states. In this type of partnership, all partners are limited partners. An LLP functions like a general partnership, except that all partners have limited personal liability in certain situations, such as another partner's mistakes. Not all types of businesses are allowed to register as limited liability partnerships. Most states allow professionals such as attorneys, physicians, dentists, and accountants to register as LLPs.

CHECKPOINT ***What is a partnership?***

limited partnership a type of partnership in which only one partner is required to be a general partner

limited liability partnership a type of partnership in which all partners are limited partners

articles of partnership a partnership agreement that spells out each partner's rights and responsibilities

Advantages of Partnerships

Partnerships are easy to establish and are subject to few government regulations. They provide entrepreneurs with a number of advantages.

Ease of Start-Up

Like proprietorships, partnerships are easy and inexpensive to establish. The law does not require a written partnership agreement. Most experts, however, advise partners to work with an attorney to develop **articles of partnership,** or a partnership

Figure 8.2 Characteristics of Partnerships

GRAPH SKILLS

Partnerships can range in size from a pair of house painters to an accounting firm with thousands of partners.

1. Using the data in these charts, describe partnerships in terms of industry and income.
2. Why do you think real estate businesses form the largest percentage of partnerships?

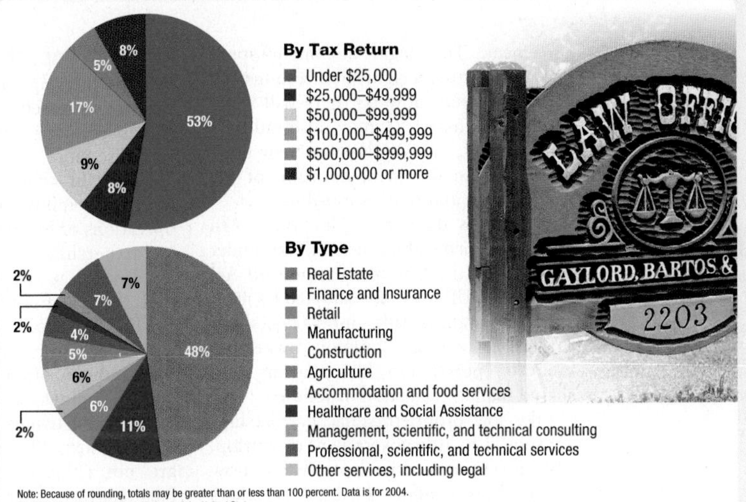

Note: Because of rounding, totals may be greater than or less than 100 percent. Data is for 2004.
SOURCE: *The 2008 Statistical Abstract of the United States*

Action Graph online

For an animated version of this graph, visit **PearsonSuccessNet.com**

Differentiated Resources

- **L1 L2 Guided Reading and Review** (Unit 3 All-in-One, p. 22)
- **L2 Procter and Gamble** (Unit 3 All-in-One, p. 24)
- **L2 Think Creatively and Innovate skills worksheet** (Unit 3 All-in-One, p. 26)

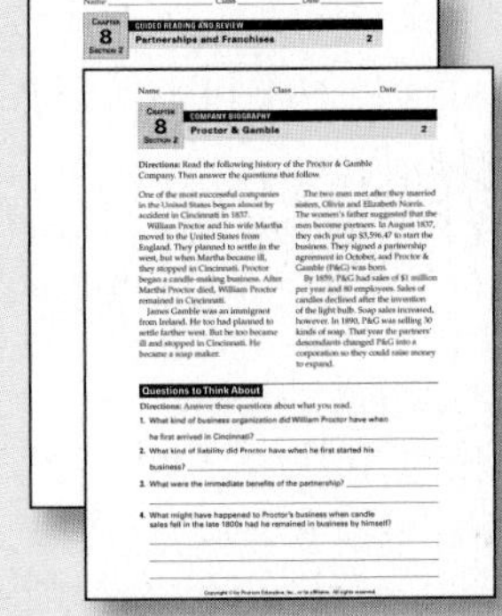

BELLRINGER

Tell students that a partnership is a type of business organization. It is like a sole proprietorship, except two or more people work together to finance and run the business. Tell them to think about their experiences working in partnership with others, such as working on a group project, and how this experience would work in a business. Have them write answers to these questions in their journal:

- What are the advantages of a partnership?
- What are the disadvantages of a partnership?
- What kind of business might work well as a partnership?

Teach

Economics online To present this topic using digital resources, use the lecture notes on www.PearsonSuccessNet.com.

EVALUATE

Ask **What advantage might doctors, lawyers, or other professionals have in joining together in a general partnership?** *(shared office space and staff)* Have students give examples of how this might work for other professionals.

Ask **How might a doctor benefit more from a limited liability partnership than from a general partnership?** *(A limited liability partnership would shield them from liability for their partner's actions and free them from management tasks.)* Ask **Why might people enter a limited partnership?** *(They have money to invest and want to share in profits but don't have expertise in the business, do not have time to work in the business, or do not want the liability.)*

L1 L2 Differentiate Have students review the Action Graph animation for a step-by-step look at Characteristics of Partnerships.

L4 Differentiate Ask students why states might not allow some types of business to organize as limited liability partnerships. *(Added liability protection might make businesses less responsive to customers.)*

Answers

Checkpoint a type of business organization owned by two or more persons who share responsibilities and profits

Graph Skills 1. Most earn less than $25,000 per year; the highest percentage is in real estate. 2. Possible answers: Property transactions are often complex. Partnerships allow expertise to be shared.

DISPLAY TRANSPARENCY

Display the "Creating a Business" transparency (Color Transparencies, 8.b), and tell students that these three people are planning to go into business together. Read aloud each character description, and ask students to speculate on the type of business they might form. *(Possible answer: catering, restaurant)* Have them suggest the type of partnership they might form and the roles that each partner might have in the business. *(Possible answer: The chef and bookkeeper become general partners. The chef manages food and the bookkeeper manages payroll, vendors, and marketing. The trucker is a limited partner who invests money.)*

DISCUSS

Have student volunteers read aloud the How the Economy Works feature. Ask **What is the advantage to Calvin in having Diego be an equal partner in the business?** *(Calvin can keep up with orders; he can focus on one aspect of the business; the business can be expanded)*

Point out the conflict that occurs between Calvin and Diego after a few months of partnership. Guide a discussion of why partners might come into conflict over business issues. Include a discussion of different styles of management, personal conflicts, different business goals. Ask **What qualities do people in a partnership need to have if the business is to be successful?** *(Possible answer: willingness to compromise, awareness of each person's weaknesses and strengths, desire to work hard, high energy, optimism)* Ask **Why is it a good idea for partners to have their own partnership agreement even though the Uniform Partnership Act establishes rules?** *(It spells out responsibilities and roles in the partnership particular to that business and those partners. It can reduce misunderstandings later on.)*

APPLY UNDERSTANDING

Have students review the feature How the Economy Works. Ask **Why might a sole proprietor hesitate to take on a partner?** *(loss of control, sharing of profits)* Ask **What might have happened to Calvin's business if he had decided to remain a sole proprietor?** *(Possible response: a competitor might grow larger and offer better service; Calvin may have become overworked and made decisions that were bad for business.)*

PERSONAL FINANCE ACTIVITY

To help students make wise choices, you may want to use the Personal Finance Handbook lesson on understanding a paycheck on pp. PF44–45, and the activity worksheet (Personal Finance All-in-One, pp. 107–108).

How the Economy Works

How can a small business grow?

All businesses begin with an idea to sell a product or service. Sole proprietors, working on their own, sometimes find that adding a partner will help them be more successful.

1 Calvin, an enterprising college student, has launched an online business, Hiyerminds.com. He creates and sells college survival kits to incoming freshmen. He keeps his costs down and makes a tidy profit. He is keeping up with a steady stream of orders and with his schoolwork.

2 Calvin finds that as his product becomes more popular, he can't manage the ordering and accounting part of the business. He decides to ask his friend Diego to join Hiyerminds.com as an equal partner. The partnership allows the business to expand.

Expansion

agreement. This legal document spells out each partner's rights and responsibilities. It outlines how partners will share profits or losses. It may also address other details, such as the ways new partners can join the firm, duration of the partnership, and tax responsibilities.

If partners do not develop their own articles of partnership, they will fall under the rules of the Uniform Partnership Act (UPA). The UPA is a law adopted by most states to establish rules for partnerships. The UPA requires common ownership interests, profit and loss sharing, and shared management responsibilities.

Like sole proprietorships, partnerships are subject to little government regulation. The government does not dictate how partnerships conduct business. Partners can distribute profits in whatever way they wish, as long as they abide by the partnership agreement or by the UPA.

FUTURE WATCH

Personal Finance
For information about wages and the benefits businesses offer, see your Personal Finance Handbook in the back of the book or visit **PearsonSuccessNet.com**

assets the money and other valuables belonging to an individual or business

Financial Impact

In a partnership, more than one person contributes **assets,** or money and other valuables. As a result, these businesses can raise more capital than a sole proprietorship. In addition, partnerships have improved ability to borrow funds for operations or expansion.

Partnerships offer advantages to employees as well. They can attract and keep talented employees more easily than sole proprietorships can. Graduates from top accounting schools, for example, often seek jobs with large and prestigious accounting LLPs, hoping to become partners themselves someday. Partnerships, like sole proprietorships, are not subject to any special taxes. Partners pay taxes on their share of the income that the partnership generates. The business itself does not have to pay taxes.

How the Economy Works **online**

For an animated, interactive version of this feature, visit **PearsonSuccessNet.com**

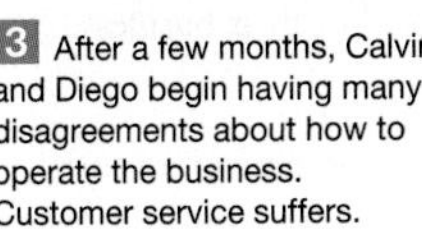

3 After a few months, Calvin and Diego begin having many disagreements about how to operate the business. Customer service suffers.

4 Calvin and Diego realize that their differences are bad for business and threaten their income. They revise the articles of partnership to set new rules about individual responsibilities and their business goals.

5 As a result, Calvin and Diego hire employees to assemble the kits. Calvin focuses on finding new customers and Diego manages the business.

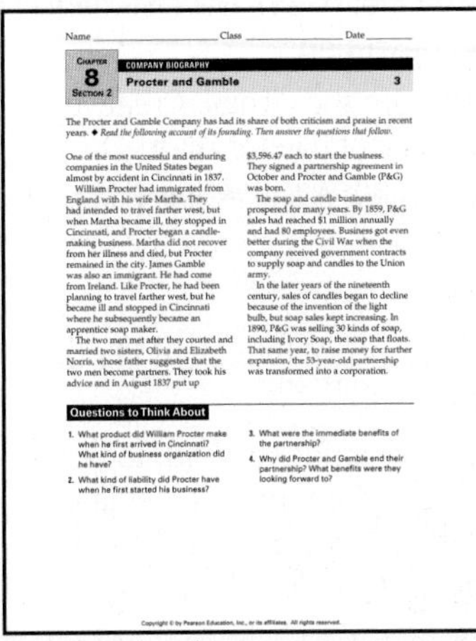

Check Your Understanding

1. **What basic change did Calvin make in his small business to enable it to grow?**
2. **How did his solution create both advantages and disadvantages?**

Conflict and Resolution | **Further Expansion**

Shared Decision Making

In a sole proprietorship, the owner has the burden of making all business decisions. In a partnership, the responsibility for the business may be shared. A sole proprietorship requires the owner to wear many hats, some of which might not fit very well. For example, the sole proprietor may have good managerial abilities but lack marketing skills and experience. In a successful partnership, however, each partner brings different strengths and skills to the business.

CHECKPOINT ***What are the advantages of partnerships?***

Disadvantages of Partnerships

Partnerships also present some disadvantages. Many of the disadvantages of sole proprietorships are present in partnerships. Limited liability partnerships have fewer disadvantages than partnerships with general partners. All partnerships, however, have the potential for conflict.

Unlimited Liability

Unless the partnership is an LLP, at least one partner has unlimited liability. As in a sole proprietorship, any general partner could lose everything, including personal property, in paying the firm's debts. Since limited partners can lose only their investment, they avoid this threat.

In a partnership, each general partner is bound by the acts of all other general partners. If one partner's actions cause the firm losses, then all of the general partners suffer. If one doctor in a partnership is sued for malpractice, all of the doctors in the partnership stand to lose. This problem is not present, of course, in limited liability partnerships.

COMPARE

To help students see the differences among types of partnerships, draw a three-column chart on the board, and label the columns *General Partnership, Limited Partnership,* and *Limited Liability Partnership.* Have students guide you in listing points of comparison and contrast.

EXAMINE A CASE HISTORY

Distribute the "Procter and Gamble" activity worksheet (Unit 3 All-in-One, p. 23). Tell students that the company has had its share of both criticism and praise, but its founding is a classic tale of partnership.

Name ______ Class ______ Date ______

CHAPTER 8 SECTION 2 — COMPANY BIOGRAPHY

Procter and Gamble 3

The Procter and Gamble Company has had its share of both criticism and praise in recent years. ◆ *Read the following account of its founding. Then answer the questions that follow.*

One of the most successful and enduring companies in the United States began almost by accident in Cincinnati in 1837.

William Procter had immigrated from England with his wife Martha. They had intended to travel farther west, but when Martha became ill, they stopped in Cincinnati, and Procter began a candle-making business. Martha did not recover from her illness and died, but Procter remained in the city. James Gamble was also an immigrant. He had come from Ireland. Like Procter, he had been planning to travel farther west, but he became ill and stopped in Cincinnati where he subsequently became an apprentice soap maker.

The two men met after they courted and married two sisters, Olivia and Elizabeth Norris, whose father suggested that the two men become partners. They took his advice and in August 1837 put up $3,596.47 each to start the business. They signed a partnership agreement in October and Procter and Gamble (P&G) was born.

The soap and candle business prospered for many years. By 1859, P&G sales had reached $1 million annually and had 80 employees. Business got even better during the Civil War when the company received government contracts to supply soap and candles to the Union army.

In the later years of the nineteenth century, sales of candles began to decline because of the invention of the light bulb, but soap sales kept increasing. In 1890, P&G was selling 30 kinds of soap, including Ivory Soap, the soap that floats. That same year, to raise money for further expansion, the 53-year-old partnership was transformed into a corporation.

Questions to Think About

1. What product did William Procter make when he first arrived in Cincinnati? What kind of business organization did he have?
2. What kind of liability did Procter have when he first started his business?
3. What were the immediate benefits of the partnership?
4. Why did Procter and Gamble end their partnership? What benefits were they looking forward to?

L1 **L2** **ELL LPR Differentiate** Distribute the "Procter and Gamble" worksheet (Unit 3 All-in-One, p. 24). Pair students to complete the worksheet. Encourage students to ask the meanings of unfamiliar words.

Ask **What were the benefits of the partnership for each man? What were the disadvantages of the partnership for each man?**

Virtual Economics

L3 **Differentiate**

Exploring a Partnership Use the following lesson from the NCEE **Virtual Economics *CD-ROM*** to examine the advantages and disadvantages of a partnership. Click on Browse Economics Lessons, specify grades 9–12, and use the key words *financial institutions.*

In this activity, students will analyze a case study of a partnership that grew into a major corporation.

LESSON TITLE	**HOW FINANCIAL INSTITUTIONS HELP BUSINESSES GROW**
Type of Activity	Case studies
Complexity	Low
Time	50 minutes
NCEE Standards	10

Answers

Checkpoint ease of start-up, little government regulation, potential for raising capital, ability to attract and keep skilled employees, no special taxes

Check Your Understanding 1. Calvin asked Diego to join him as an equal partner. 2. The business expanded, but the partners disagreed on how to run it. The arguments forced the partners to create new rules; then the company grew more.

PROVIDE EXAMPLES

Ask **What are some familiar franchises?** *(Possible answers: McDonald's, 7-Eleven, Gold's Gym)* Ask **Do you know of any global franchises?** *(Possible answers: Dairy Queen, Starbucks, Subway)* Have students name reasons for owning a franchise.

L2 ELL Differentiate Have students name businesses they know in other countries that they see in the United States. Identify the franchises. Have students talk about how the products are similar wherever the businesses operate.

DISTRIBUTE STUDENT ACTIVITY

Distribute the "Think Creatively and Innovate" skills worksheet (Unit 3 All-in-One, p. 25). Have students talk about the scenario described.

L2 Differentiate Distribute the "Think Creatively and Innovate" skills worksheet (Unit 3 All-in-One, p. 26). Then have students answer the questions on their own.

EXTEND

Have students do Internet research to learn about franchise opportunities.

L1 L2 Differentiate Have students work together to list local franchises. Have them research at least two. How did they start and why did they become franchises? What made them well-suited to become franchises?

GUIDING QUESTION WRAP UP

Have students return to the section Guiding Question. Review the completed graphic organizer and clarify and misunderstandings. Have a wrap up discussion about partnerships and franchises.

Assess and Remediate

L3 L2 Collect the "Procter and Gamble" and the "Think Creatively and Innovate" worksheets and assess student understanding of the risks and benefits of starting a partnership and franchise.

L3 Assign the Section 2 Assessment questions; identify student misconceptions.

L3 Give Section Quiz A (Unit 3 All-in-One, p. 27).

L2 Give Section Quiz B (Unit 3 All-in-One, p. 28).

(Assess and Remediate continued on p. 201)

Answer

Global Impact Possible responses: identifying and satisfying local tastes; meeting different requirements for doing business

Checkpoint A general partnership is controlled by at least two people, so no one person has the complete control that a sole proprietor does.

business franchise a semi-independent business that pays fees to a parent company in return for the exclusive right to sell a certain product or service in a given area

Potential for Conflict

As in any close relationship, partnerships have the potential for conflict. If a business has more than one general partner, each one has only partial control over the firm. None of them enjoys as much freedom as sole proprietors do. Partnership agreements address technical aspects of the business, such as profit and loss. Many issues vital to the success of the business exist outside these guidelines, however. Partners need to ensure that they agree on matters such as work habits, management styles, ethics, and general business philosophies.

Still, friction between partners often arises and can be difficult to resolve. Many partnerships dissolve because of interpersonal conflicts. Partners must learn to communicate openly and find ways to resolve conflicts to ensure the survival of their business.

Lack of Permanence

Like a sole proprietorship, a partnership may not outlast the life of one of the general partners. If a partner dies or decides to leave, the partnership might cease to exist unless the articles of partnership state that the business can continue and the remaining partner, or partners, have the needed resources.

CHECKPOINT ***How do general partnerships differ from sole proprietorships in terms of control?***

FUTURE WATCH **Global Impact**

Global Business, Local Tastes

If you're like most Americans, you've probably visited a Subway or a McDonald's. But have you ever biggie-sized your chinese take-out? Or seen Subway's Halal menu? Americans traveling abroad will find the familiar face of U.S. business customized to meet local tastes. The graph below shows the global presence of three major U.S. companies. ***What are some of the difficulties that businesses might encounter in their efforts to expand in other countries?***

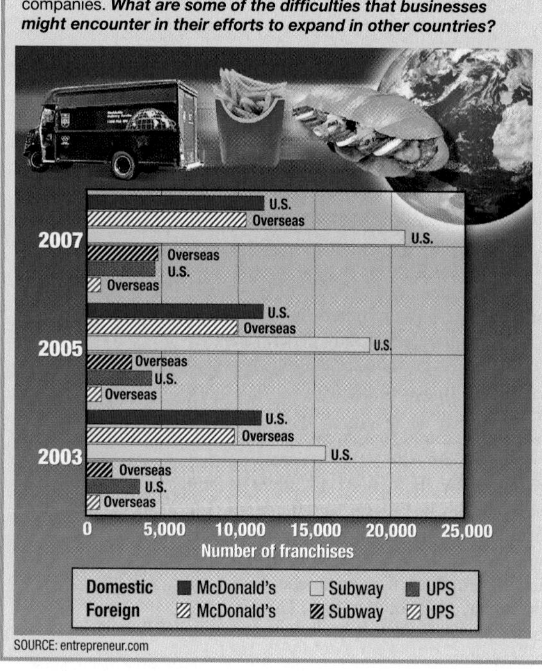

SOURCE: entrepreneur.com

Business Franchises

As you read in Section 1, sole proprietorships can suffer from a lack of resources or the lack of skills on the part of the owner. Some people solve these problems by forming partnerships. Others choose another form of business—a franchise.

What Is a Franchise?

In Chapter 7, you learned about franchises issued by government authorities. These franchises give one firm the sole right to sell its goods within a limited market, such as within a national park. In business, too, a franchise signals exclusive rights. A **business franchise** is a semi-independent business that pays fees to a parent company. In return, the business is granted the exclusive right to sell a certain product or service in a given area. Franchises offer a wide array of goods and services, from fast-food restaurants to stores that sell diamonds.

In this arrangement, the parent company is called a franchiser. The franchiser develops the products and systems to produce it efficiently and reliably. Franchisers then work with local franchise owners to help them produce and sell their products. Each owner is called a franchisee.

Franchising has become popular in recent years. This is because franchises allow each owner a degree of control. At the same time, the owners benefit from the support of the parent company. Of course, franchises offer both advantages and disadvantages.

Background Note

Protections for Potential Franchisees Franchises are a popular business organization. As of 2005, there were more than 909,000 franchises that operated in all 50 states. Because of their popularity, the Federal Trade Commission (FTC) has acted to protect buyers of franchises. Franchisers must follow rules when offering franchises for sale. They must give a history of the franchise, information about any legal problems, financial statements, a list of current franchise owners with their names and phone numbers, and information about persons running the franchising company. The intent is to ensure that would-be owners of franchises are fully informed before they invest.

Advantages of Franchises

A franchise provides advantages a completely independent business cannot. First, a franchise comes with a built-in reputation. Consumers may already be familiar with the product and brand. Other benefits make running the business easier:

1. *Management training and support* Franchisers help owners gain the experience they need to succeed, with training and support programs.
2. *Standardized quality* Most parent companies require franchise owners to follow certain rules and processes to guarantee product quality. High-quality products attract customers.
3. *National advertising programs* Parent companies pay for advertising campaigns to establish their brand names. These ads can increase sales.
4. *Financial assistance* Some franchisers provide financing to help franchise owners start their businesses. This aid can help people with fewer resources become business owners.
5. *Centralized buying power* Franchisers buy materials in bulk for all of their franchise locations. They pass on the savings to their franchisees.

Disadvantages of Franchises

The biggest disadvantage of a franchise is that the owner must sacrifice some freedom in return for the parent company's guidance. Other disadvantages include:

1. *High franchising fees and royalties* Buying into a franchise is not cheap. Franchisers often charge high fees for the right to use the company name. They also charge franchise owners a share of the earnings, or **royalties.**
2. *Strict operating standards* Franchise owners must follow all of the rules laid out in the franchising agreement for such matters as hours of operation, employee dress codes, and operating procedures. If they do not, the owners may lose the franchise.
3. *Purchasing restrictions* Franchise owners must often buy their supplies from the parent company or from approved suppliers.
4. *Limited product line* Franchise agreements allow stores to offer only approved products. Franchisees usually cannot launch new product lines that might appeal more to local customers.

CHECKPOINT ***What are the advantages and disadvantages of franchises?***

royalties the share of earnings given by a franchisee as payment to the franchiser

SECTION 2 ASSESSMENT

Essential Questions Journal To continue to build a response to the Essential Question, go to your **Essential Questions Journal.**

Guiding Question

1. Use your completed chart to answer this question: What are the risks and benefits of partnerships and franchises?
2. **Extension** Your uncle is sole proprietor of a camera shop. You know much more about digital cameras than he does. He is looking for a partner. What questions would you ask him before you would consider going into business with him?

Key Terms and Main Ideas

3. List four reasons that make a **partnership** a good business choice.
4. How do **general partnerships, limited partnerships,** and **limited liability partnerships** differ?
5. What is the difference between the role of a franchiser and the role of a franchisee?

Critical Thinking

6. **Interpret** Why might physicians and lawyers find limited liability partnerships attractive?
7. **Compare** Think about the advantages and disadvantages of partnerships and franchises. From your point of view, which do you think would be a better way to be in business?
8. **Contrast (a)** Give an example of the technical aspect of a business that partnership agreements address. **(b)** What is an example of issues outside legal guidelines that partners need to resolve themselves?

Quick Write

9. All articles of partnership spell out the rights and responsibilities of each partner. Some of the common sections found in articles of partnership include:
   Leadership This addresses the granting of one partner the rights to manage and administer the business.
   Misconduct expulsion This allows for the expelling of partners who commit gross misconduct that harms a business, such as leading to bankruptcy.
   Resolution of dispute This details how disagreements will be resolved.
   With a partner, draw up articles of partnership for a business.

Have students complete the Self-Test Online and continue their work in the **Essential Questions Journal.**

REMEDIATION AND SUGGESTIONS

Use the chart below to help students who are struggling with content.

WEAKNESS	REMEDIATION
Defining key terms (Questions 3, 4)	Have students use the interactive Economic Dictionary Online
Characteristics of partnerships (Questions 3, 4)	Reteach using a comparison-and-contrast chart to compare types of partnership organizations
Characteristics of franchises (Questions 5, 7)	Review the terms *franchiser* and *franchisee*.
Advantages and disadvantages of partnerships (Questions 7, 8, 9)	Pair students and assign a business to each. Have them discuss the type of partnership they might form.

Answer

Checkpoint Advantages include management and training support, standardized quality, national advertising, financial aid, and centralized buying power. Disadvantages include high fees and royalties, strict operating standards, purchasing restrictions, and a limited product line.

Assessment Answers

1. The risks include liability for losses and debt, shared control, and potential for conflict. Benefits include easy start-up, little regulation, shared liability, and access to more skills and capital.
2. Possible answers: What would be my responsibility? What debt does the company owe? How would profits be divided?
3. ease of start-up; little government regulation; better access to financing; attractive to skilled employees
4. All partners in a general partnership share the liabilities and profits equally; in limited partnerships, only general partners share the personal liability; in LLPs, all partners have only limited personal liability.
5. The franchiser develops the products and systems; the franchisee sells the product or service.
6. They can operate independently, sharing a building and staff, but do not have to share liability for another partner's mistakes.
7. Possible answers: a franchise, because the owner gets support; a partnership, because it allows more independent decision-making
8. (a) Possible answer: how the company's profits will be divided and distributed (b) which decisions must be made by all partners
9. Students should prepare articles of partnership that include a specific division of responsibility.

 Guiding Question

What are the risks and benefits of corporations?

Get Started

Corporations	ALL	Sole Proprietorships and Partnerships
• Benefits: Limited liability for owners • Risks: Double taxation	• Benefits: Owners receive profits • Risks: Can go out of business	• Benefits: Owners have more control • Risks: Owners have full liability

LESSON GOALS

Students will:

- Know the Key Terms.
- Create a chart to list the characteristics of a corporation that distinguish it from other types of business organizations.
- Compare the advantages and disadvantages of incorporation.
- Evaluate potential mergers and recommend the best type for a given business in a worksheet.
- Analyze the effects of corporate mergers by interpreting an illustration.
- Assess the impact of consolidation and multinationalism.

BEFORE CLASS

Students should read the section for homework before coming to class.

Have students complete the graphic organizer in the Section Opener as they read the text. As an alternate activity, have students complete the Guided Reading and Review worksheet (Unit 3 All-in-One, p. 29).

L1 L2 ELL LPR **Differentiate** Have students complete the Guided Reading and Review worksheet (Unit 3 All-in-One, p. 30).

SECTION 3 Corporations, Mergers, and Multinationals

OBJECTIVES

1. **Explain** the characteristics of corporations.
2. **Analyze** the advantages of incorporation.
3. **Analyze** the disadvantages of incorporation.
4. **Compare and contrast** corporate combinations.
5. **Describe** the role of multinational corporations.

ECONOMIC DICTIONARY

As you read the section, look for the definitions of these **Key Terms:**

- corporation
- stock
- closely held corporation
- publicly held corporation
- bond
- certificate of incorporation
- dividend
- limited liability corporation
- horizontal merger
- vertical merger
- conglomerate
- multinational corporation

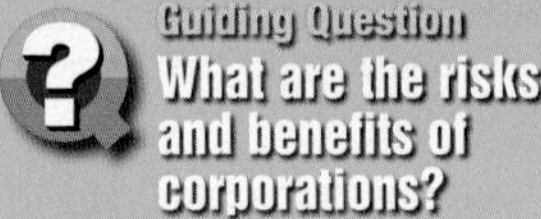

Guiding Question

What are the risks and benefits of corporations?

Copy this Comparison Chart and fill it in as you read. Add more bullets if necessary.

Corporations	Sole Proprietorships/ Partnerships
Benefits: • limited liability for owners •	**Benefits:** • owners have more control •
Risks: • •	**Risks:** • •

Economics and You

Every day you use goods and services provided by a variety of businesses, both large and small. Did the bread you ate today come from a local bakery or a huge multinational food producer? Some goods can be provided by either. But what about the car or bus you took to school? Some products can be produced only by big businesses.

Principles in Action Goods and services that require huge amounts of capital to produce require a special kind of business organization, or ownership structure. Sole proprietorships and partnerships lack the resources to carry out expensive processes, such as making cars or developing software, or having operations that reach across the country or around the world. What form of business do these companies have? Most of these businesses are corporations.

Corporations

The most complex form of business organization is the corporation. A **corporation** is a legal entity, or being, owned by individual stockholders, each of whom has limited liability for the firm's debts. Stockholders own **stock,** a certificate of ownership in a corporation. Each person who owns stock is a part-owner of the corporation issuing it. If a corporation issues 1,000 shares of stock, and you purchase 1 share, you own 1/1000th of the corporation.

Sole proprietorships have no identity beyond that of the owners. A corporation, on the other hand, does have a legal identity separate from the identities of its owners. Legally, it is regarded much like an individual. A corporation may engage in business, make contracts, sue other parties or be sued by others, and pay taxes.

corporation a legal entity, or being, owned by individual stockholders, each of whom has limited liability for the firm's debts

In the United States, corporations account for about 20 percent of all businesses but more than 80 percent of all sales. They generate nearly 60 percent of the net income earned in the nation. Because of the advantages of corporations, most large business firms do incorporate.

Types of Corporations

stock a certificate of ownership in a corporation

Some corporations issue stock to only a few people, often family members. These stockholders rarely trade their stock, but pass it on, typically within

CLASSROOM HINTS

RESEARCH A CORPORATION

Have students choose a corporation that sells a product or service they use and enjoy. Have students do some basic research on the corporation, and as they read the section, keep notes about their corporation's board of directors, price of a share of stock, or any mergers the corporation has considered or made. Finally, have students research an ethical policy of the corporation. Examples may include equal opportunity employment practices, environmental policies, or another issue. Have students evaluate the company's policy and report back to the class.

Focus on the Basics

Students need to come away with the following understandings:

FACTS: • A corporation is a legal entity owned by stockholders who have limited liability for the firm's debts. • Corporations sell shares to raise capital. • Corporations are run by a board of governors, corporate officers, and other managers. • Corporations are difficult to start up and are subject to double taxation. • Corporations can grow very large and merge with other companies.

GENERALIZATION: A corporation is a business owned by its stockholders and run by professional managers. Corporations can amass large amounts of capital, making it possible for them to efficiently carry out expensive processes.

the family. Such corporations are called **closely held corporations.** They are also known as privately held corporations.

A **publicly held corporation,** however, has many shareholders who can buy or sell stock on the open market. Stocks are bought and sold in financial markets called stock exchanges, such as the New York Stock Exchange or the Tokyo Stock Exchange.

Corporate Structure

While the exact organization varies from firm to firm, all corporations have the same basic structure. The owners—the stockholders—elect a board of directors. The board of directors makes all the major decisions of the corporation. It appoints corporate officers, such as the chief executive officer or president. These officers run the corporation and oversee its operations. Corporate officers, in turn, hire managers and employees, who work in various departments such as finance, sales, research, marketing, and production.

CHECKPOINT ***What is the role of corporate officers?***

Advantages of Incorporation

Incorporation, or forming a corporation, offers advantages to both stockholders and the corporation itself. These advantages include limited liability for owners, transferable ownership, ability to attract capital, and long life.

Advantages for Stockholders

The primary reason that entrepreneurs choose to form a corporation is to gain the benefit of limited liability. Individual stockholders do not carry personal responsibility for the corporation's actions. They can lose only the amount of money they have invested in the business. If a corporation is sued and loses the case, it must pay the money award but the assets of individual stockholders cannot be touched.

Corporations usually also provide owners with more flexibility than other forms of ownership. Shares of stock are easily transferable. That is, stockholders can easily sell their stock to others and get money in return. That is not the case with other forms of business organization.

closely held corporation a type of corporation that issues stock to only a few people, who are often family members

publicly held corporation a type of corporation that sells stock on the open market

Figure 8.3 **Characteristics of Corporations**

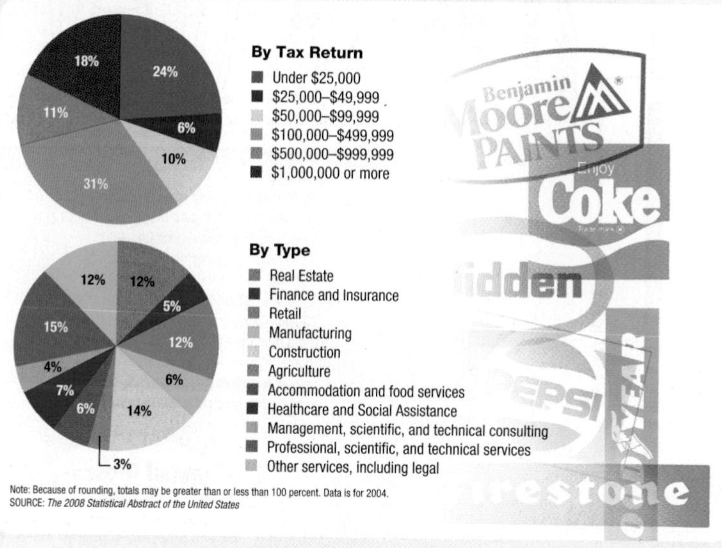

Note: Because of rounding, totals may be greater than or less than 100 percent. Data is for 2004.
SOURCE: *The 2008 Statistical Abstract of the United States*

GRAPH SKILLS

Approximately 38 percent of corporations are engaged in construction, manufacturing, real estate and retail business.

1. What incentives to incorporate do businesses have in these industries?
2. Firms that sell services make up a large fraction of corporations. Given this fact, what can you conclude about the U.S. economy?

Action Graph online

For an animated version of this graph, visit PearsonSuccessNet.com

BELLRINGER

Write the word *corporation* on the board. Write these questions on the board:

- What are some words that describe your idea of a corporation?
- What corporations do you know?
- What do you think makes these corporations similar or different from the sole proprietorships, partnerships, and franchises you have studied?

Tell students to write their answers in their journals.

Teach

Economics online To present this topic using digital resources, use the lecture notes on www.PearsonSuccessNet.com.

COMPARE

Draw a three-column chart on the board, and label the columns *Sole Proprietorship, Partnership,* and *Corporation.* As you discuss the section, use the chart to compare and contrast corresponding elements of the three organizations. These could include identity of the business, ease of organization, taxation, distribution of profits and losses, liability, and permanence. Instruct students to make copies in their notebooks.

Use Figure 8.3 to discuss some characteristics of corporations. Ask **What conclusions can you draw from the data on tax returns?** *(Most corporations are very large, with receipts of at least $100,000; 18 percent have receipts over $1 million.)*

Action Graph online Have students review the Action Graph animation for a step-by-step look at Characteristics of Corporations.

Differentiated Resources

L1 L2 Guided Reading and Review (Unit 3 All-in-One, p. 30)

L2 Choose to Merge (Unit 3 All-in-One, p. 32)

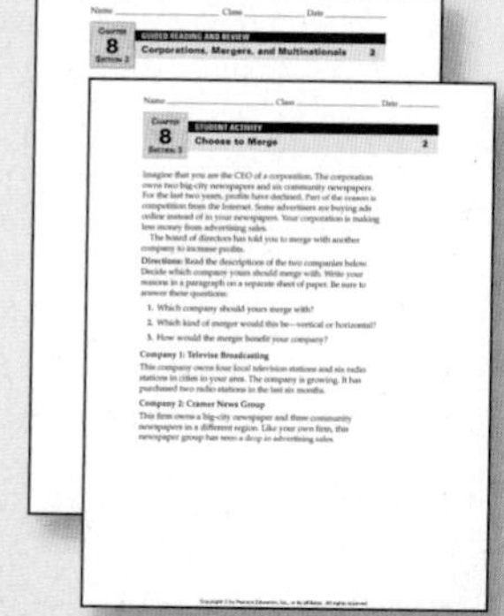

Answers

Checkpoint Corporate officers run the business and oversee its operations. They hire managers and employees.

Graph Skills 1. They can raise money easily and the owners have limited liability for the businesses' debts. 2. The U.S. economy depends more upon providing services than on manufacturing or other industries that produce products.

(lesson continued on p. 205)

Teach Visual Glossary

REVIEW KEY TERMS

Have students write definitions of the key terms related to the understanding of corporations.

business organization—*the ownership structure of a company or firm*

liability—*the legal obligation to pay debts*

assets—*the money and other valuables belonging to an individual or business*

business franchise—*a semi-independent business that pays fees to a parent company in return for the exclusive right to sell a certain product or service in a given area*

stock—*a certificate of ownership in a corporation*

publicly held corporation—*a corporation that sells stock on the open market*

ANALYZE

Students should understand the differences between the structure of a corporation and that of other types of business organizations. Discuss how the corporation is treated as an individual in the legal code. That "individual" is responsible for its own actions. Have students explain why, if stockholders are the owners of the corporation, they are not personally responsible for the company's debts. *(As a legal entity apart from the individual stockholders, the corporation is responsible for its debts.)*

L2 LPR ELL Have students discuss their understanding of the words *legal* and *entity. (according to the law; a separate being or individual)* Ask students to explain how these words relate to corporations.

Have students describe how the diagram reflects the structure of a corporation.

Answers

Visual Glossary Diagram No individual is personally liable for the debts of corporations. Stockholders risk no more than the amount of their investment. The board of directors, corporate officers, managers, and employees of the corporation are not personally liable either, but their performance is judged by the stockholders.

Cartoon when their stock goes down in value

VISUAL GLOSSARY

Reviewing Key Terms
To understand *corporation*, review these terms:

business organization, *p. 191*
liability, *p. 194*
assets, *p. 198*
business franchise, *p. 200*
stock, *p. 202*
publicly held corporation, *p. 203*

What is a Corporation?

◄ **corporation** a legal entity, or being, owned by individual stockholders, each of whom faces limited liability for the firm's debts

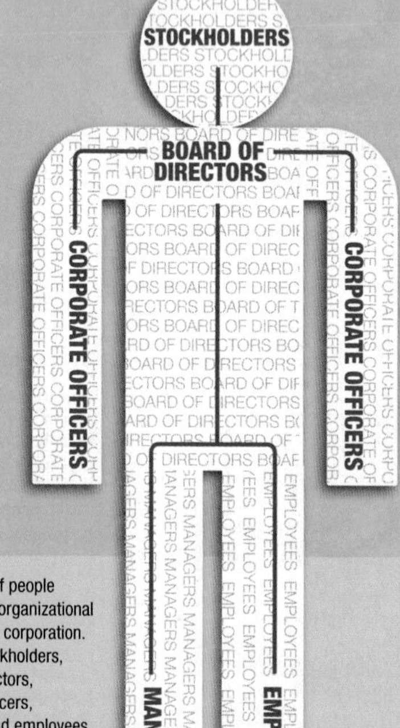

Five groups of people make up the organizational structure of a corporation. They are stockholders, board of directors, corporate officers, managers, and employees. ***How does limited liability benefit each group?***

"Whoever said 'The only thing we have to fear is fear itself' never had to face a room full of angry shareholders."

▲ The management of a corporation includes its officers and the board of directors. They make decisions that have a major impact on a corporation's earnings, which may result in profits or losses. In either case, the corporation's stockholders, or shareholders, will hold management accountable for the company's performance. ***Under what circumstances might stockholders not be pleased with management?***

Visual Glossary online
To expand your understanding of this and other key economic terms, visit **PearsonSuccessNet.com**

▲ Corporations have a self interest in developing profitable products and services. Consumer concerns about global warming have spurred new companies—like SolarCity—to produce eco-friendly products and are driving other companies like 3M to respond with eco-conscious business lines.

Advantages for the Corporation

The corporate structure also presents advantages for the firm itself. Corporations have more potential for growth than other business forms. By selling shares on the stock market, corporations can raise large amounts of capital.

Corporations can also raise money by borrowing it. They do this by selling bonds. A **bond** is a formal contract issued by a corporation or other entity that includes the promise to repay borrowed money with interest at fixed intervals.

Because ownership is separate from the running of the firm, corporate owners—that is, stockholders—do not need any special managerial skills. Instead, the corporation can hire various experts—the best financial analysts, the best engineers, and so forth.

Corporations also have the advantage of long life. Because stock is transferable, corporations are able to exist longer than simple proprietorships or even partnerships. Unless it has stated in advance a specific termination date, the corporation can do business indefinitely.

CHECKPOINT ***What are the four advantages of incorporating?***

Disadvantages of Incorporation

Corporations do have some disadvantages, including expense and difficulty of start-up, double taxation, potential loss of control by the founders, and more legal requirements and regulations.

Difficulty and Expense of Start-Up

Businesses that wish to incorporate must first file for a state license known as a **certificate of incorporation,** or corporate charter. The application includes crucial information, such as corporate name, statement of purpose, length of time that the business will run (usually "for perpetuity," or without limit), founders' names and addresses, where business is based, method of fundraising, and rules for management.

Once state officials review and approve the application, they grant the corporation its charter. Then the corporation organizes itself to produce and sell a good or service. Corporate charters can be difficult, expensive, and time consuming to create. Though most states allow people to form corporations without legal help, few experts would recommend this shortcut.

Double Taxation

The law considers corporations legal entities separate from their owners. Corporations, therefore, must pay taxes on their income.

Corporate earnings are taxed a second time as well. When corporations determine their profits, they often choose to pay a share of those profits to stockholders in payments called **dividends.** These dividends count as income for the stockholder, and the stockholder must pay personal income tax on them. This double taxation keeps many firms from incorporating.

When stockholders sell shares, they must compare the selling price to how much they paid for them. If the selling price is higher, they earned what is called a capital gain. That gain is also taxed.

Some owners form **limited liability corporations** (LLCs). These businesses have the advantage of limited liability for owners, which all corporations enjoy. They also have tax advantages because the firm does not pay corporate income tax.

Loss of Control

The original owners of a corporation often lose control of the company. Corporate officers and boards of directors, not owners, manage corporations. These managers do not always act in the owners' best interests. They might be more interested in protecting their own jobs or salaries today than in making difficult decisions that would benefit the firm tomorrow.

bond a formal contract issued by a corporation or other entity that includes a promise to repay borrowed money with interest at fixed intervals

certificate of incorporation a license to form a corporation issued by a state government

dividend the portion of corporate profits paid out to stockholders

limited liability corporation a type of business with limited liability for the owners, with the advantage of not paying corporate income tax

CHAPTER 8 SECTION 3 **205**

USE VISUAL GLOSSARY

Have students look at the diagram on the Visual Glossary. According to the image, who controls a corporation? *(stockholders)* Who do you think actually runs the corporation and why? *(Board of Governors)*

L1 L2 Differentiate Use the lesson on the Visual Glossary page or direct students to the Visual Glossary Online to reinforce understanding of the term *corporation.*

DISCUSS

Have students list and explain the advantages of incorporation for stockholders. Be sure students understand that stockholders can sell their shares, although those who own shares in a publicly traded corporation can sell shares more easily than those who own shares in a privately held corporation.

Have students summarize the disadvantages of incorporation. Make sure students understand the two forms of taxation by working through an example.

Ask **Given the disadvantages, what are some situations that might impel a business to incorporate?** Have students give examples.

DISTRIBUTE ACTIVITY WORKSHEET

Discuss the reasons one corporation might decide to merge with another. Then distribute the "Choose to Merge" worksheet (Unit 3 All-in-One, p. 31). Have students read and complete the worksheet.

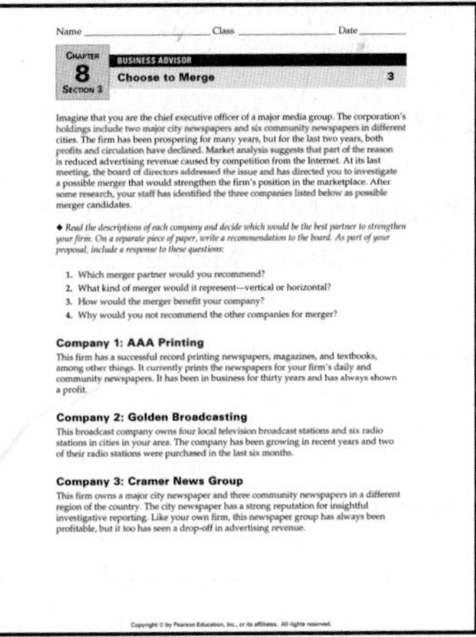

Name ____________ Class ____________ Date ________

Chapter 8 Section 3 — BUSINESS ADVISOR

Choose to Merge 3

Imagine that you are the chief executive officer of a major media group. The corporation's holdings include two major city newspapers and six community newspapers in different cities. The firm has been prospering for many years, but for the last two years, both profits and circulation have declined. Market analysis suggests that part of the reason is reduced advertising revenue caused by competition from the Internet. At its last meeting, the board of directors addressed the issue and has directed you to investigate a possible merger that would strengthen the firm's position in the marketplace. After some research, your staff has identified the three companies listed below as possible merger candidates.

◆ *Read the descriptions of each company and decide which would be the best partner to strengthen your firm. On a separate piece of paper, write a recommendation to the board. As part of your proposal, include a response to these questions:*

1. Which merger partner would you recommend?
2. What kind of merger would it represent—vertical or horizontal?
3. How would the merger benefit your company?
4. Why would you not recommend the other companies for merger?

Company 1: AAA Printing

This firm has a successful record printing newspapers, magazines, and textbooks, among other things. It currently prints the newspapers for your firm's daily and community newspapers. It has been in business for thirty years and has always shown a profit.

Company 2: Golden Broadcasting

This broadcast company owns four local television broadcast stations and six radio stations in cities in your area. The company has been growing in recent years and two of their radio stations were purchased in the last six months.

Company 3: Cramer News Group

This firm owns a major city newspaper and three community newspapers in a different region of the country. The city newspaper has a strong reputation for insightful investigative reporting. Like your own firm, this newspaper group has always been profitable, but it too has seen a drop-off in advertising revenue.

L2 Differentiate Distribute the "Choose to Merge" worksheet (Unit 3 All-in-One, p. 32). Guide a discussion. Pair students to complete the worksheet.

After students have completed the worksheet, have them defend their choice.

Answer

Checkpoint Potential for growth; resources to hire experts; corporations can raise large amounts of capital; they have a long life.

Virtual Economics

L2 Differentiate

Comparing Business Organizations

Use the following lesson from the NCEE **Virtual Economics *CD-ROM*** to evaluate student understanding of the pros and cons of different business organization. Click on Browse Economics Lessons, specify grades 9–12, and use the key words *business organization.*

In this activity, students will work in small groups to decide the best business organization for a fictional company.

LESSON TITLE	BUSINESS ORGANIZATIONS
Type of Activity	Role play
Complexity	Low
Time	50 minutes
NCEE Standards	10

EVALUATE

Have students describe what the diagrams in Figure 8.4 illustrate. Discuss how these mergers benefit a corporation. Have students explain why the government oversees these mergers. Ask **Who are antitrust regulators trying to protect when they oversee mergers?** *(customers)*

L1 L2 Differentiate Remind students that *economies of scale* refers to the lower cost of products or services that result when larger quantities are purchased, as by a larger corporation.

ANALYZE

Distribute the "Final Four" worksheet (Unit 3 All-in-One, p. 33). Explain that the Final Four refers to national college basketball playoffs where many teams compete. Have students complete the worksheet. Have them explain the chart and the effects of mergers on the businesses involved and consumers.

EXTEND

Tell students that in recent years there have been many mergers in certain industries, sometimes resulting in huge multinational corporations. Have students write an editorial expressing their views on a merger such as the merger of Chrysler and Daimler-Benz.

GUIDING QUESTION WRAP UP

Have students return to the section Guiding Question. Review the completed graphic organizer and clarify any misunderstandings. Have a wrap up discussion about corporations, mergers, and multinationals.

Assess and Remediate

L3 L2 Collect the "Choose to Merge" and "Final Four" worksheets and assess student understanding of setting corporations.

L3 Assign the Section 3 Assessment questions; identify student misconceptions.

L3 Give Section Quiz A (Unit 3 All-in-One, p. 34).

L2 Give Section Quiz B (Unit 3 All-in-One, p. 35).

Answers

Mergers 1. Horizontal mergers: Exxon and Mobil (petroleum corporations); Ford and Volvo (car manufacturers); SBC and AT&T (telephone and communications corporations). Vertical mergers: Disney (movies and entertainment) and ABC (network TV); News Corporation (newspapers) and Direct TV (cable TV). 2. A horizontal merger joins firms that are in the same market; a vertical merger joins firms involved in different stages of producing the same good.

Checkpoint difficulty of start-up, double taxation, loss of control by original owners, greater regulation

Figure 8.4 Horizontal Merger and Vertical Merger

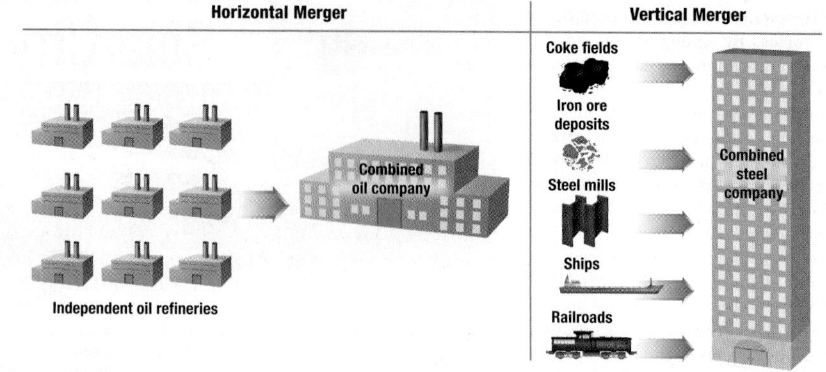

Beginning in the 1880s, John D. Rockefeller's Standard Oil Company (left) combined horizontally with 40 other oil refineries. The power gained by Standard Oil and similar monopolies prompted passage of the Sherman Antitrust Act in 1890.

In 1899, Andrew Carnegie established the Carnegie Steel Company (right). He used the vertical merger to purchase companies that produced the raw materials needed to make steel, as well as companies that would move his products to market. Within a short time, Carnegie controlled the steel industry. Most vertical mergers, however, do not result in monopolies.

1. What are some modern examples of horizontal mergers and vertical mergers?
2. Explain the difference between horizontal mergers and vertical mergers.

More Regulation

Corporations face more regulations than other types of businesses. They must hold annual meetings for stockholders and keep records of all business transactions. Publicly held corporations are required to file quarterly and annual reports with the Securities and Exchange Commission (SEC). The SEC is a federal agency that regulates the stock market.

CHECKPOINT ***What are the disadvantages of incorporation?***

Corporate Combinations

horizontal merger the combination of two or more firms competing in the same market with the same good or service

vertical merger two or more firms involved in different stages of producing the same good or service

Corporations can grow very large. One way to grow is to raise money by selling stocks or bonds. Corporations may also grow by merging, or combining, with another corporation. The three kinds of mergers are horizontal mergers, vertical mergers, and conglomerates.

Horizontal Mergers

Horizontal mergers join two or more firms competing in the same market with the same good or service. In 2004, Cingular—a wireless telephone company—bought the wireless business of AT&T. This was a horizontal merger. Two firms might choose to merge if the newly established firm would result in economies of scale or would otherwise improve efficiency.

As you read in Chapter 7, the federal government watches horizontal mergers carefully. The resulting single firm might gain monopoly power in its market. If that is the case, the government might try to block the merger in court. Judges then listen to arguments and read evidence to decide whether to allow the merger.

Vertical Mergers

Vertical mergers join two or more firms involved in different stages of producing the same good or service. A vertical merger can allow a firm to operate more efficiently. A vertically combined firm can control all phases of production, rather than rely on the goods or services of outside suppliers. Sometimes firms take this step out of fear that they may otherwise lose crucial

Background Note

Multinational Corporations Multinational corporations can trigger strong responses in the countries where they operate. Objections may stem from political concerns that override free market forces. Five years after the September 11, 2001, attacks on the World Trade Center and the Pentagon, a Dubai multinational corporation called Dubai Ports World tried to buy a British firm that operates cargo terminals in New York City, Philadelphia, New Orleans, and several other U.S. port cities. There was harsh criticism of the deal and congressional debate about whether to allow the deal to go through because of concern about allowing a foreign company, in this case one of the United Arab Emirates, to control major U.S. ports. Because of political pressure, Dubai Ports withdrew from the deal and sold its interests in the United States.

supplies. Antitrust regulators become concerned when firms in the same industry merge vertically, especially if supplying firms suffer. Most vertical mergers do not substantially lessen competition, however.

Conglomerates

Sometimes firms buy other companies that produce totally unrelated goods or services. When three or more unrelated businesses are involved, these combinations are called **conglomerates.** In a conglomerate, no one business earns the majority of the firm's profits. The government usually allows this kind of merger, because it does not result in decreased competition.

CHECKPOINT ***Why might the government block a horizontal merger?***

Multinational Corporations

The world's largest corporations produce and sell their goods and services in more than one country. They are called **multinational corporations** (MNCs). MNCs usually have headquarters in one country and branches in other countries. Multinationals must obey laws and pay taxes in each country where they operate.

In the early 2000s, an estimated 64,000 multinational firms operated about 866,000 foreign branches. These foreign affiliates provided jobs for more than 53 million people. The United States, France, Germany, Britain, Japan, and China are home countries with the largest number of multinational corporations.

Advantages of Multinationals

Multinationals benefit consumers and workers by providing jobs and products around the world. Often the jobs they provide help people in poorer nations enjoy better living standards. MNCs also spread new technologies and production methods across the globe.

Disadvantages of Multinationals

On the downside, many people feel that multinational firms unduly influence the culture and politics in the countries in which they operate. While MNCs do provide jobs, critics say that in poorer countries those jobs are marked by low wages and poor working conditions.

CHECKPOINT ***How would you describe a multinational corporation?***

conglomerate a business combination merging more than three businesses that produce unrelated products or services

multinational corporation a large corporation that produces and sells its goods and services in more than one country

SECTION 3 ASSESSMENT

Essential Questions Journal To continue to build a response to the Essential Question, go to your **Essential Questions Journal.**

Guiding Question

1. Use your completed Venn diagram to answer this question: What are the risks and benefits of corporations?
2. **Extension** As a stockholder, would you be more interested in the benefits or the risks of the corporation in which you held stock? Explain.

Key Terms and Main Ideas

3. **(a)** What is another name for a **closely held corporation? (b)** How does it differ from a **publicly held corporation?**
4. What is the financial impact on owners when a corporation is sued and loses its case?
5. **(a)** What is a **dividend? (b)** What kind of tax must be paid on dividends received by stockholders?
6. How do **horizontal mergers, vertical mergers**, and **conglomerates** differ?

Critical Thinking

7. **Explain (a)** Which business in a conglomerate earns the most profits? **(b)** Why is it that conglomerates do not tend to decrease competition?
8. **Analyze** Choose one corporation that does business in your community. What benefits do you think the community gains from this business being incorporated?
9. **Compare (a)** How does a multinational benefit consumers and workers? **(b)** How might a corporation benefit from becoming multinational?

Math Skills

10. The bar graph (right) shows the percentage of business types organized as partnerships and as corporations. **(a)** For which types of business is the partnership form of organization most popular? **(b)** For which types of business is the corporation form of organization most popular? **(c)** Explain why you think this is so.

Visit PearsonSuccessNet.com for additional math help.

Percentage of Partnerships and Corporations by Type

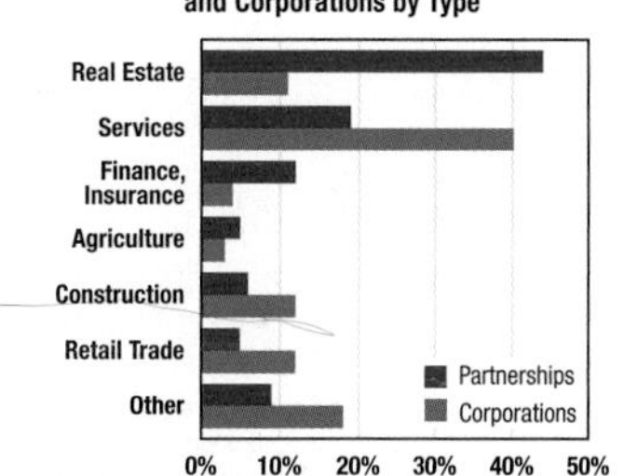

SOURCE: *The 2008 Statistical Abstract of the United States*

Have students complete the Self-Test Online and continue their work in the **Essential Questions Journal.**

REMEDIATION AND SUGGESTIONS

Use the chart below to help students who are struggling with content.

WEAKNESS	REMEDIATION
Defining key terms (Questions 3, 5, 6)	Have students use the interactive Economic Dictionary Online
The risks and benefits of corporations (Questions 3, 4, 5, 8, 10)	Have students role-play a discussion between two business partners considering incorporation. Would we lose control? Why would people invest? How would the corporation benefit the community?
The characteristics of corporate combinations (6, 7)	Pair students to create a chart comparing horizontal mergers, vertical mergers, and conglomerates.
The advantages and benefits of multinational corporations (9)	Have students outline the discussion under the heading Multinational Corporations.

Answers

Checkpoint A horizontal merger might result in one corporation dominating a particular market and becoming a monopoly.

Checkpoint a firm that produces and sells its goods in more than one country.

Assessment Answers

1. Risks: difficulty of start-up, owners' loss of control, double taxation, more regulation. Benefits: limited liability, ease of selling, professional management, ability to raise large sums of money, permanence.
2. Some students may say loss of control and double taxation are big risks. Others may prefer the benefit of increased money flow and ease of selling.
3. (a) privately held corporation (b) It has a limited number of owners.
4. Owners can lose only the money they have invested.
5. (a) a share of profits paid to stockholders (b) personal income tax
6. Horizontal mergers: firms competing in the same market join. vertical mergers: firms involved in different stages of production join. conglomerates: firms buy companies producing unrelated products.
7. (a) no one business (b) The combining does not reduce the total number of businesses in an industry.
8. The community gains a large employer and increased tax revenue.
9. (a) Multinationals provide jobs in many places and lower-priced goods for consumers. (b) A corporation could move production where costs are lower.
10. (a) real estate (b) services (c) Real estate can be started up with few start-up expenses; some services require large amounts of capital and training

 **Guiding Question**

How are some businesses organized to help others?

Get Started

Cooperatives		
Consumer Cooperatives	**Service Cooperatives**	**Producer Cooperatives**
• Buy in large quantities to be able to sell at low prices • Members contribute work or membership fees	• Provide services at discounted prices • Financial services provided by credit unions	• Agricultural marketing cooperatives, e.g., helps members market products • Members focus on growing crops and raising livestock

LESSON GOALS

Students will:

- Know the Key Terms.
- Determine the best type of cooperative organization for specific cases by completing a worksheet.
- Give examples of services provided by different nonprofit organizations.

BEFORE CLASS

Students should read the section for homework before coming to class.

Have students complete the graphic organizer in the Section Opener as they read the text. As an alternate activity, have students complete the Guided Reading and Review worksheet (Unit 3 All-in-One, p. 36).

L1 L2 ELL LPR Differentiate Have students complete the Guided Reading and Review worksheet (Unit 3 All-in-One, p. 37).

SECTION 4 Nonprofit Organizations

OBJECTIVES

1. **Identify** the different types of cooperative organizations.
2. **Understand** the purpose of nonprofit organizations, including professional and business organizations.

ECONOMIC DICTIONARY

As you read the section, look for the definitions of these **Key Terms:**

- cooperative
- consumer cooperative
- service cooperative
- producer cooperative
- nonprofit organization
- professional organization
- business association
- trade association

Guiding Question

How are some businesses organize to help others?

Copy this chart and fill it in as you rea
Add more bullets if necessary.

Cooperatives		
Consumer Cooperatives	Service Cooperatives	Producer Cooperativ
• Buy in large quantities to be able to sell at low prices • Members contribute work or membership fees	• •	• •

Economics and You Any time you go to a museum, the z or a hospital, you are benefiting from a business organization wh main goal is to provide a service to you rather than to make a profit itself. If you meet certain criteria, you may join a credit union whose m purpose is to benefit its members. Although these various institutions m appear like other businesses, they are not quite the same.

Principles in Action Success in business is not measured only in dol and cents. Some businesses are not organized to maximize profits. Inst their goals are to work for the good of all their members or to work the good of society in general. In this section, you will learn about th other kinds of business organizations.

Cooperative Organizations

Ben Franklin, one of our nation's founders, was a remarkable innova In 1752, he organized a company that collected money from its memb in order to make payments to any one of them who suffered losses fr a fire. This group was America's first cooperative. Franklin explained nature of this group in a letter to a Boston newspaper.

> **"I would leave this to the Consideration of all who are concern'd for thei own or their Neighbour's Temporal Happiness; and I am humbly of Opinion, that the Country is ripe for many such *Friendly Societies*, whereby every Ma might help another, without any Disservice to himself."**
>
> —*The New-England Courant*, August 13, 172

A **cooperative** is a business organization owned and operated b group of individuals for their shared benefit. In other words, work together, the individuals help one another. Cooperatives are based several principles, which include

- voluntary and open membership
- control of the organization by its members
- sharing of contributions and benefits by members

cooperative a business organization owned and operated by a group of individuals for their shared benefit

CLASSROOM HINTS

NONPROFIT ORGANIZATIONS

Students need to understand the fact that nonprofit organizations are not volunteer groups. Many nonprofits employ large numbers of people. A recent survey by Nonprofit Technology Network (NTEN) showed that salaries in nonprofits were about 25 to 30 percent lower than in equivalent positions in for-profit organizations. However, the survey did not take into account the size of the organizations. Large companies, whether non- or for-profit, on average pay higher salaries than small organizations do.

Focus on the Basics

Students need to come away with the following understandings:

FACTS: • Cooperatives are businesses owned and operated for the benefit of members. • Types of cooperatives are consumer cooperatives, service cooperatives, and producer cooperatives. • Nonprofit organizations operate like businesses except that their goal is to help people rather than to make a profit. • Professional organizations, business associations, trade associations, and labor unions promote the interests of their members.

GENERALIZATION: Many businesses are organized to help different groups of people rather than to make profits for owners.

Cooperatives enjoy some tax benefits. Since they are not corporations, they do not pay income tax on their earnings as long as they handle those earnings in certain ways. At least 20 percent must be paid out to members. Members, of course, must then pay personal income taxes on that money. The cooperative invests as much as 80 percent of its earnings to expand its operations.

Cooperatives, or co-ops, are found in many industries, from farming and energy to healthcare and childcare. They fall into three main categories: consumer, or purchasing cooperatives; service cooperatives; and producer cooperatives. Any group of consumers or producers with common social or economic goals can band together to form a cooperative.

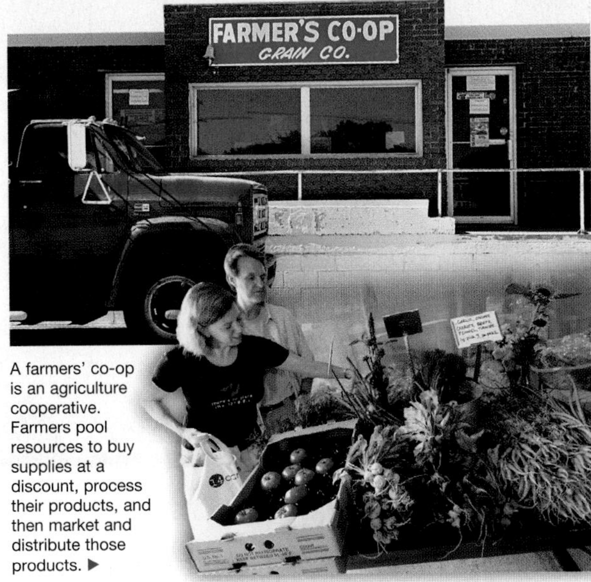

A farmers' co-op is an agriculture cooperative. Farmers pool resources to buy supplies at a discount, process their products, and then market and distribute those products. ▶

Consumer Cooperatives

Retail outlets owned and operated by consumers are called consumer cooperatives, or purchasing cooperatives. **Consumer cooperatives** sell merchandise to their members at reduced prices. By purchasing goods in large quantities, these cooperatives can obtain goods at a lower cost. They then pass the savings on to members by setting prices low. Examples of consumer cooperatives include discount price clubs, compact disc or book clubs, some health food stores, and housing cooperatives.

Some co-ops require members to work a small number of hours to maintain membership. For example, your health food store may require you to work 20 hours per month to remain in the cooperative. Consumer co-ops range in size from small buying clubs to Fortune 500 businesses.

Service Cooperatives

Cooperatives that provide a service, rather than goods, are called **service cooperatives.** Some service co-ops offer discounted insurance, banking services, healthcare, legal help, or baby-sitting services.

Credit unions, or financial cooperatives, are a special kind of service cooperative. People deposit money in these institutions. The credit unions then use those funds to lend money to members at reduced rates.

Producer Cooperatives

Producer cooperatives are agricultural marketing cooperatives that help members sell their products. These co-ops allow members to focus their attention on growing their crops or raising their livestock. The co-ops, meanwhile, market these goods for the highest prices possible. In a recent year, producer cooperatives sold more than $70 billion worth of crops and livestock. These groups are involved in marketing dairy products, grain, beef and chicken, and many other products. Some co-ops have more than a million members.

CHECKPOINT ***How do members benefit from cooperatives?***

Nonprofits

Some institutions function much like business organizations, but do not operate for the purpose of generating profit. For that reason, they are called **nonprofit organizations.** Nonprofit organizations are usually in the business of benefiting the public. Examples include museums, public schools, the American Red Cross, hospitals, adoption agencies, churches, synagogues, YMCAs, and many other

consumer cooperative a retail outlet owned and operated by consumers that sells merchandise to members at reduced prices

service cooperative a type of cooperative that provides a service rather than a good

producer cooperative an agricultural marketing cooperative that helps members sell their products

nonprofit organization an institution that functions much like a business, but does not operate for the purpose of generating profit

BELLRINGER

Remind students that some organizations exist not to make a profit but to help the public. Tell students to brainstorm a list of organizations whose goal is primarily to help the public in some social, cultural, or economic way. As students list organizations, write them on the board. Then write these questions on the board:

- How does the organization help people?
- How does the organization raise money to operate?
- Do you think such an organization could make a profit? Why or why not?

Have students answer the questions about each organization. As students study the section, point out examples of each type of organization from the list.

Teach

Economics online To present this topic using digital resources, use the lecture notes on www.PearsonSuccessNet.com.

MAKE CONNECTIONS TO STUDENTS' LIVES

Ask students to name cooperatives their families or people they know belong to. Have them identify the type of cooperative, explain how the cooperative works, and tell how it benefits the members. If cooperatives are uncommon locally, have students suggest a type of cooperative they would like to join.

DISCUSS

Discuss the functions and goals of nonprofit organizations. Draw on the list compiled by students during the Bellringer activity to help explain their purpose.

Differentiated Resources

- **L1 L2 Guided Reading and Review** (Unit 3 All-in-One, p. 37)
- **L2 What Type of Organization?** (Unit 3 All-in-One, p. 39)
- **L4 Supporting Your Views** (Unit 3 All-in-One, p. 40)

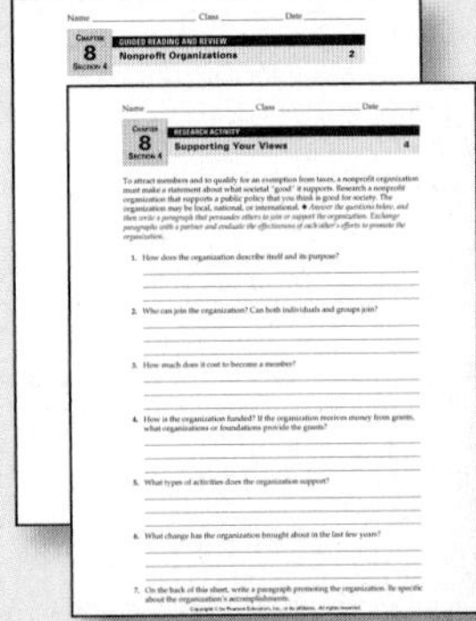

Answer

Checkpoint From consumer cooperatives, reduced prices; from service cooperatives, reduced prices on services; from producer cooperatives, assistance in marketing goods

(lesson continued on p. 211)

Teach Case Study

SUMMARIZE AND DISCUSS

Call on students to summarize the case study. Ask **What is the main idea of the study?** *(Nonprofits are turning more and more toward the social-networking sites on the Internet to raise awareness and funds for their causes.)* Have students find details in the study that support this summary.

Ask **Why might young donors ignore traditional methods of raising funds, such as direct mail and phone calls?** *(Possible response: Young people are familiar and comfortable with the Internet. They may be more trusting of social-networking sites than they are of strangers on the phone who ask for money.)*

Have volunteers locate the Web sites and projects mentioned in the case study and report back to the class on the sites and the information they contain. Have them bring sample pages as examples to discuss.

L1 L2 ELL LPR Differentiate This case study contains vocabulary words that may cause problems for students with limited reading and language skills. Prepare students for the reading by reviewing difficult words and passages. Have them read it in pairs.

Economics online *All print resources are available on the Teacher's Resource Library CD-ROM and online at* www.PearsonSuccessNet.com.

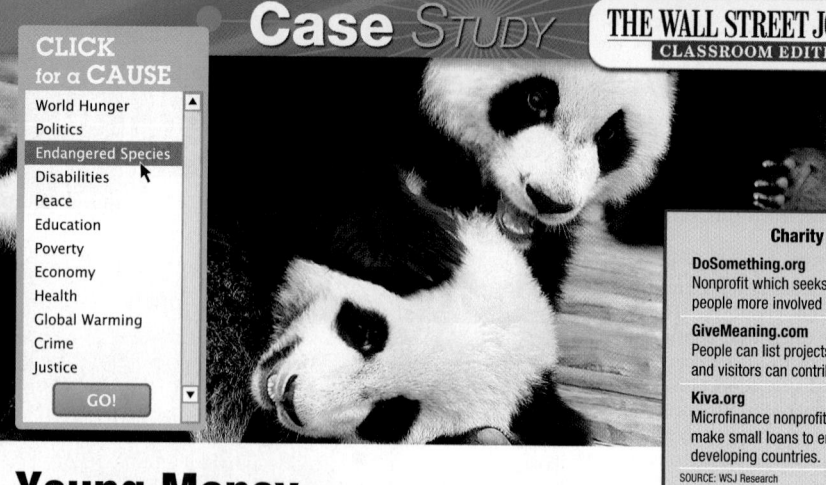

Answer

Applying Economic Principles Possible responses: Social networking is very popular on the Internet, so linking to those sites gives nonprofits access to vast numbers of people. Many of the people using social Web sites are young people who have had little previous experience with nonprofits or charities, so it is a good method for introducing them. Nonprofits might raise money for their causes by selling advertising on their sites.

Charity 2.0

DoSomething.org
Nonprofit which seeks to get young people more involved in social action.

GiveMeaning.com
People can list projects to raise money, and visitors can contribute funds.

Kiva.org
Microfinance nonprofit allows visitors to make small loans to entrepreneurs in developing countries.

SOURCE: WSJ Research

Young Money

BUSINESS ORGANIZATIONS

Charitable giving used to be dominated by wealthy, middle-aged donors. Now, a new generation is using online tools to reinvent philanthropy.

By Rachel Emma Silverman
The Wall Street Journal

Joe Alamo didn't set out to become a do-gooder. But one day, while surfing on MySpace, he chanced onto the profile of Kiva.org, a nonprofit that allows people to make zero-interest "microfinance" loans over the Internet to needy entrepreneurs in developing countries.

Soon after, Mr. Alamo not only became a lender through Kiva, but also started a new Web site devoted to Kiva enthusiasts. "This is the first time I've ever gotten so involved with a charity," says Mr. Alamo, a 30-year-old Web designer.

He's among a rising tide of young donors and volunteers who are satisfying their philanthropic urges on the Internet. They're increasingly turning to blogs and social-networking Web sites, such as MySpace and Facebook, to spread the word about—and raise funds for—their favorite nonprofits and causes. Some are turning to "viral fund-raising": sending appeals to their network of contacts that are forwarded on to others, to maximize the power of small donations.

Visitors to Change.org can join "virtual foundations" of peers dedicated to specific causes, such as fighting AIDS in Africa, and raise money for the charities or political candidates that support those issues. So far, its 30,000 members have raised nearly $50,000, says founder Ben Rattray, 27. Before launching the site, Mr. Rattray had never made a charitable donation, finding charities' traditional pitches to be "unengaging."

Established charities, to be sure, have long had programs targeted to young donors, and many of them have used peer-to-peer fund-raising to help raise money. But many of these charities either tend to target wealthier donors or are focused on occasional events, rather than on ongoing operations.

Some of the newer Web-based nonprofits, such as DonorsChoose and Kiva, are attractive because contributors say they allow them to connect directly with their recipients. Donors or lenders can hand over money directly to, respectively, teachers and students in urban public schools or individual entrepreneurs in developing countries, rather than sending a check that ends up with an abstract recipient.

"You can donate money to a charity, but it seems like it just goes into a pile and you never know what really goes on there," says Mr. Alamo. "With Kiva, you just pick someone out and lend to them directly and watch what they do and how they succeed."

Video News Update Online Powered by *The Wall Street Journal* Classroom Edition — For a new case study, go to the online resources at **PearsonSuccessNet.com**

Applying Economic Principles
Why do you think social networking Web sites have proven to be so useful for nonprofit organizations? What might be other ways a nonprofit can make use of the Internet to further its goals?

groups and charities. Almost all of them provide services rather than goods.

The government exempts nonprofit organizations from income taxes. The nonprofit must meet certain requirements to qualify for this tax-exempt status. Nonprofits cannot issue stock, so profits cannot be distributed to stockholders. The group must devote its activities exclusively to those that the Internal Revenue Service says will qualify. For instance, a charity must act only to help people, such as the poor or those disabled by illness or injury. An educational nonprofit must devote itself to the advancement of learning.

Nonprofits have some limits on their political activity. Charities and religious groups, for instance, can meet with members of Congress to try to influence laws being considered. They cannot devote too much of their resources to this lobbying activity, however.

Some nonprofit organizations provide support to particular occupations or geographical areas. These include professional organizations, business associations, trade associations, and labor unions.

Professional Organizations

Professional organizations work to improve the image, working conditions, and skill levels of people in particular occupations. The National Education Association for public school, college, and university workers, the American Veterinary Medical Association for veterinary professionals, the American Bar Association for lawyers, and the American Management Association for business professionals are examples.

Professional organizations keep their members up-to-date on industry trends. Many of these organizations provide members with employment-related services such as job boards, training workshops, and networking opportunities. They also set codes of conduct that members are expected to follow. For example, the American Medical Association opposes advertising. It believes that doctors present a less professional, authoritative, and caring image if they seek new patients through advertisements. Likewise, the American Bar Association frowns upon law firms that advertise their services for personal injury complaints.

professional organization a nonprofit organization that works to improve the image, working conditions, and skill levels of people in particular occupations

Innovators

Bill and Melinda Gates

"We believe that lives have equal value, no matter where they are being lived."

The well-known success story behind Bill and Melinda Gates begins with the Microsoft Corporation. As founder of the phenomenally successful high-tech firm, Gates built upon his vision that computer software could revolutionize business practices. In 1987, the software architect met his future wife, Melinda. Bill hired the then-recent Duke University graduate, who had earned degrees in computer science, economics, and business, to help him develop Microsoft into one of the world's premier technology companies.

Today Bill and Melinda Gates are investing much of their considerable wealth and resources to help the less fortunate. The couple has donated more than $24 billion to endow the Bill and Melinda Gates Foundation, the world's largest nonprofit corporation. Their foundation is fulfilling a unique mission to use financial and technological resources to improve the quality of life for people everywhere through extensive health, education, and agricultural programs. Some of these efforts include the funding of technology resources in U.S. public libraries, rice agricultural development in the Philippines, and global vaccination programs.

The Gateses are recognized for taking philanthropy to a new level, using their fortune to plant the seeds for a better life for all people.

Critical Thinking ***How can a nonprofit organization such as the Bill and Melinda Gates Foundation help to create economic wealth worldwide?***

Fast Facts

Melinda French Gates (1965 -)
Education: B.A. and M.B.A. at Duke University

Fast Facts

William (Bill) H. Gates, III (1955 -)
Education: 2+ years at Harvard Univ.
Family Life: Married in 1994, three children
Claim to Fame: Founder of Microsoft Corporation, Co-founder of the Bill and Melinda Gates Foundation

ANALYZE

Have students identify the main constituencies of professional, business, trade, and labor organizations. Ask **Which provides the greatest service to the public?** Have students include details from the text to support their responses.

Assign the "What Type of Organization?" worksheet (Unit 3 All-in-One, p. 38).

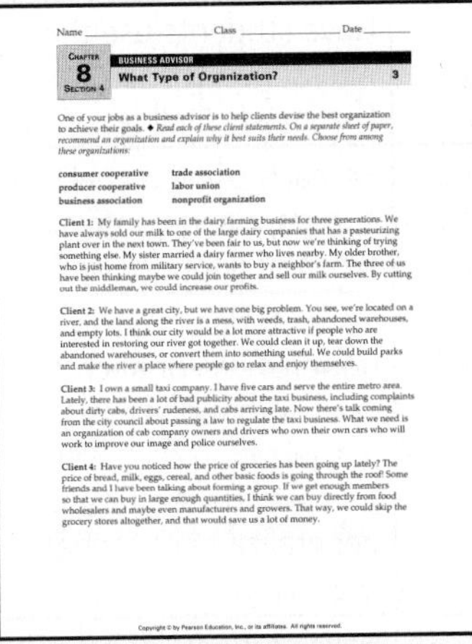

Name ______ Class ______ Date ______

CHAPTER 8 SECTION 4 — BUSINESS ADVISOR

What Type of Organization? 3

One of your jobs as a business advisor is to help clients devise the best organization to achieve their goals. ◆ *Read each of these client statements. On a separate sheet of paper, recommend an organization and explain why it best suits their needs. Choose from among these organizations:*

consumer cooperative **trade association**
producer cooperative **labor union**
business association **nonprofit organization**

Client 1: My family has been in the dairy farming business for three generations. We have always sold our milk to one of the large dairy companies that has a pasteurizing plant over in the next town. They've been fair to us, but now we're thinking of trying something else. My sister married a dairy farmer who lives nearby. My older brother, who is just home from military service, wants to buy a neighbor's farm. The three of us have been thinking maybe we could join together and sell our milk ourselves. By cutting out the middleman, we could increase our profits.

Client 2: We have a great city, but we have one big problem. You see, we're located on a river, and the land along the river is a mess, with weeds, trash, abandoned warehouses, and empty lots. I think our city would be a lot more attractive if people who are interested in restoring our river got together. We could clean it up, tear down the abandoned warehouses, or convert them into something useful. We could build parks and make the river a place where people go to relax and enjoy themselves.

Client 3: I own a small taxi company. I have five cars and serve the entire metro area. Lately, there has been a lot of bad publicity about the taxi business, including complaints about dirty cabs, drivers' rudeness, and cabs arriving late. Now there's talk coming from the city council about passing a law to regulate the taxi business. What we need is an organization of cab company owners and drivers who own their own cars who will work to improve our image and police ourselves.

Client 4: Have you noticed how the price of groceries has been going up lately? The price of bread, milk, eggs, cereal, and other basic foods is going through the roof! Some friends and I have been talking about forming a group. If we get enough members so that we can buy in large enough quantities, I think we can buy directly from food wholesalers and maybe even manufacturers and growers. That way, we could skip the grocery stores altogether, and that would save us a lot of money.

L2 Differentiate Distribute the "What Type of Organization?" worksheet (Unit 3 All-in-One, p. 39) and have students complete the activity.

EXTEND

Ask students to identify a cause suitable for a nonprofit organization and to devise a plan to promote the cause. What will be their goal for the organization and how can they accomplish that goal? Have students write a plan of action.

L4 Differentiate Assign the "Supporting Your Views" worksheet (Unit 3 All-in-One, p. 40). Have students promote the organization and partners evaluate the effectiveness of the presentation.

GUIDING QUESTION WRAP UP

Have students return to the section Guiding Question. Review the completed graphic organizer and clarify any misunderstandings. Have a wrap up discussion.

Assess and Remediate

L4 L3 L2 Collect the worksheets and assess student understanding.

L3 Assign the Section 4 Assessment questions; identify student misconceptions.

L3 Give Section Quiz A (Unit 3 All-in-One, p. 41).

L2 Give Section Quiz B (Unit 3 All-in-One, p. 42).

(Assess and Remediate continued on p. 212)

Answer

Critical Thinking by providing seed money to help entrepreneurs develop businesses

Virtual Economics

L3 Differentiate

Deciding on a Business Organization Use the following lesson from the NCEE **Virtual Economics *CD-ROM*** to review student understanding of different business organizations. Click on Browse Economics Lessons, specify grades 9–12, and use the key words *business organization.*

In this activity, students will evaluate several fictional case studies to decide the best business organization for each.

LESSON TITLE	ENTREPRENEURS CHOOSE DIFFERENT TYPES OF BUSINESS ORGANIZATION
Type of Activity	Case studies
Complexity	Moderate
Time	100 minutes
NCEE Standards	10, 14

Have students complete the Self-Test Online and continue their work in the **Essential Questions Journal.**

REMEDIATION AND SUGGESTIONS

Use the chart below to help students who are struggling with content.

WEAKNESS	REMEDIATION
Identifying key terms (Questions 3, 4, 5, 6)	Have students use the interactive Economic Dictionary Online.
The differences among cooperatives (Questions 3, 4, 7, 8)	Reteach using a chart to compare and contrast types of cooperatives.
The role and purpose of nonprofits (Questions 1, 2, 5, 8)	Have students list some nonprofits. For each, ask: "What does this organization do?" When finished, have students generalize about what they all do.
How professional, business, and trade associations serve the public (Questions 6, 8, 9)	Have students debate this statement: "Professional and trade associations have outlived their usefulness."

Answers

Checkpoint Similar: they are organized like businesses and are subject to government regulation. Different: they are exempt from income taxes.

Cartoon One that is fair, has clear rules.

An ethical and successful business will be clear about its return policies, because it is in its best interest to keep a good relationship with its customers. Much of its success depends on repeat business. ***What would you consider to be a good return policy?*** ▶

I NEVER PROMISED YOU HE COULD TALK... I SAID HE "CHATS."
RETURN POLICY
offthemark.com

Business Associations

business association a group organized to promote the collective business interests of an area or group of similar businesses

trade association nonprofit organizations that promote the interests of particular industries

Business associations promote the collective business interests of a city, state, or other geographical area, or of a group of similar businesses. A city or state chamber of commerce, for instance, works with government officials to try to promote policies that will help businesses grow and thrive. Business associations may also address codes of conduct, just as professional associations do. Your local Better Business Bureau (BBB), sponsored by local businesses, is a nonprofit group. It aims to protect consumers by promoting an ethical and fair marketplace. Consumers who have complaints about the actions of a local business can take them to the BBB. Workers there will contact the business and try to work out a solution that satisfies both parties.

Trade Associations

Nonprofit organizations that promote the interests of particular industries are called **trade associations.** The American Marketing Association, for example, aims to improve the image of companies that sell goods and services. All kinds of industries, from publishing to food processing, enjoy the support of trade associations. Many of these groups hire people, called lobbyists, to work with state legislatures and the U.S. Congress. They try to influence laws that affect an industry. These groups hold meetings that members can attend to improve their skills or learn about industry trends.

Labor Unions

A labor union is an organized group of workers whose aim is to improve working conditions, hours, wages, and fringe benefits for members. In the next chapter, you will read about their history and role.

CHECKPOINT ***How are nonprofit organizations similar to and different from corporations?***

SECTION 4 ASSESSMENT

Essential Questions Journal To continue to build a response to the Essential Question, go to your **Essential Questions Journal.**

Guiding Question

1. Use your completed chart to answer this question: How are some businesses organized to help others?
2. **Extension** There are many nonprofit organizations that offer services in your community. Select one and explain how you would use your talents to help this organization help others.

Key Terms and Main Ideas

3. What is a **cooperative?**
4. How do **consumer cooperatives, service cooperatives,** and **producer cooperatives** differ?
5. **(a)** What is a **nonprofit organization? (b)** Give an example of one.
6. What is the purpose of **professional organizations, business associations,** and **trade associations?**

Critical Thinking

7. **Generalize** If cooperatives offer benefits to their members, why do you think everyone doesn't belong to them?
8. **Analyze (a)** Do you think professional organizations and business associations benefit consumers? **(b)** Explain your reasoning.
9. **Synthesize** What are the advantages and disadvantages of trade associations trying to influence legislation?

Quick Write

10. Think about a need, such as transportation, child care, or tutoring, that might be met through a cooperative. Write a brief proposal explaining how the cooperative would work to meet the need, including who could join, what would be the terms of membership, and what would be the benefits.

Assessment Answers

1. They may do this by sharing contributions and benefits with members or promoting the welfare of members.
2. Possible response: I might volunteer at a hospital where I could work at the information desk helping visitors.
3. a business organization owned and operated by a group of individuals for their shared benefit
4. Consumer cooperatives sell goods to their members at reduced prices. Service cooperatives provide discounted services to members. Producer cooperatives help members sell their products.
5. (a) Usually its purpose is to benefit society. (b) The American Red Cross helps people during disasters, providing clothing and medical care as well as filling other needs.
6. to improve the image, working conditions, and skill levels of people in particular occupations
7. Possible response: They wouldn't benefit enough to contribute time or money.
8. Possible responses: (a) yes (b) Their efforts to improve the skills and knowledge of members and business practices result in better products for consumers.
9. Possible response: Advantages—associations might support licensing, which might result in better quality products and services. Disadvantages—associations might support efforts to manipulate price controls or reduce government oversight.
10. Essays will vary, but students should identify a need and write a proposal spelling out specific ways in which a cooperative could meet that need.

QUICK STUDY GUIDE

QUICK STUDY GUIDE

Chapter 8: Business Organizations

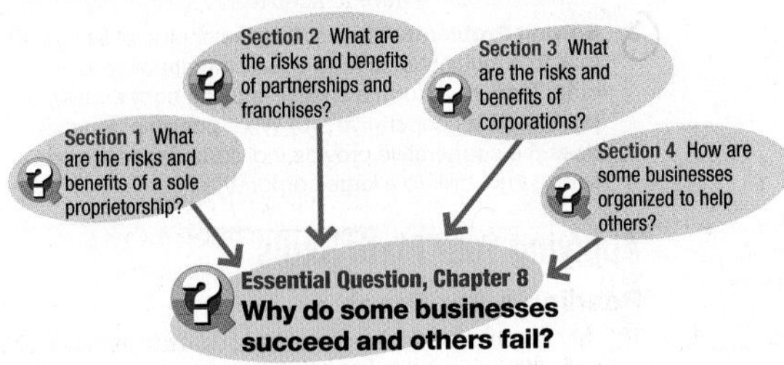

Section 2 What are the risks and benefits of partnerships and franchises?
Section 3 What are the risks and benefits of corporations?
Section 1 What are the risks and benefits of a sole proprietorship?
Section 4 How are some businesses organized to help others?
Essential Question, Chapter 8
Why do some businesses succeed and others fail?

Advantages and Disadvantages of Business Organizations

	Advantages	Disadvantages
Sole Proprietorship	• Ease of start-up • Fewer regulations • Sole receiver of profit • Full control • Easy to discontinue	• Unlimited personal liability • Limited access to resources • Lack of permanence
Partnership	• Ease of start-up • Shared decision making • More capital • Attractive to employees	• Unlimited liability • Lack of control • Potential for conflict • Lack of permanence
Business Franchise	• Built-in reputation • Management training/support • Paid national advertising • Financial assistance • Centralized buying power	• High fees/royalties • Strict operating standards • Purchasing restrictions • Limited product line
Corporation	• Potential for growth • Ability to raise capital/money • Long lifespan • Ability to hire specialists	• Difficult/expensive to start up • Double taxation • Loss of control • More regulation

Economic Dictionary

Economics *on the go*

Study anytime, anywhere. Download these files today.

Economic Dictionary online	Audio Review online	Action Graph online	Visual Glossary online	How the Economy Works online
Vocabulary Support in English and Spanish	Audio Study Guide in English and Spanish	Animated Charts and Graphs	Animated feature	Animated feature

Download to your computer or mobile device at PearsonSuccessNet.com

ASSIGN THE ESSENTIAL QUESTIONS JOURNAL

After students have finished studying the chapter, they should return to the chapter's essential question in the Essential Questions Journal and complete the activity.

Tell students to go back to the chapter opener and look at the image. Using the information they have gained from studying the chapter, ask **How does this illustrate the main ideas of the chapter?** *(Possible answers: Many different types of businesses exist; choosing the right type of business for a given product or service is important to success; entrepreneurs bring together the factors of production.)*

STUDY TIPS

Tell students that class notes will be more useful if they use a large notebook so that they can clearly indicate indents and use an accurate outline form. Encourage them to allow extra space between important points so they can add related ideas or information later.

Economics *on the go* Have students download the digital resources available on Economics on the Go for review and remediation.

Assessment at a Glance

TESTS AND QUIZZES

Section Assessments

Section Quizzes A and B, **Unit 3 All-in-One**

Self-Test Online

Chapter Assessments

Chapter Tests A and B, **Unit 3 All-in-One**

Economic Detective, **Unit 3 All-in-One**

Document-based Assessment, p. 215

Exam*View*

AYP Monitoring Assessments

PERFORMANCE ASSESSMENT

Teacher's Edition, pp. 193, 199, 200, 205, 206, 211

Simulation Activities, Chapter 8

Virtual Economics on CD-ROM, pp. 194, 199, 205, 211

Essential Questions Journal, Chapter 8

Assessment Rubrics

Chapter Assessment

1. (a) Possible answers: unlimited personal liability, lack of capital (b) The sole proprietor could lose his or her personal savings, home, and other personal property. (c) The owner might not be able to raise capital.
2. The rules determine who is liable in different types of partnerships and establish ownership interests, profit and loss sharing, and management responsibilities.
3. (a) only for the amount of their investment (b) by electing the board of directors
4. (a) through the merger of firms involved in different stages of producing the same good or service (b) Sample answer: farms, food processing plant, canning plant
5. Possible answers: (a) owners and customers (b) The owners can borrow more money to expand and hire people. Customers might benefit from more professional services. Prices might or might not be reduced.
6. (a) The government exercises few restraints on sole proprietors and partnerships, but oversees both mergers and the incorporation of businesses. (b) Corporations are often very large and can dominate an entire industry.
7. Possible answer: (a) willing to take risks, very commited, able to work hard, focused, highly energetic, optimistic (b) Answers will vary, but should include an explanation of the value of each quality.
8. (a) by merging with businesses at all stages of the process from farmers to distributors (b) farms, slaughterhouses, distributors, stores
9. (a) a business owned and operated by a group of individuals for their shared benefit (b) Possible answer: They market their own products, potentially getting better prices for it.
10. 43 percent
11. 38 percent
12. 38 percent
13. business and restaurant franchises
14. To prepare students for interviews, have them brainstorm a list of questions to ask. Have students designate the person they plan to interview so that students will not all approach the same local businesses.
15. Answers will vary, but should include the contribution to success made by choosing the right type of business for a product or service.

CHAPTER 8 ASSESSMENT

Self-Test online To test your understanding of key terms and main ideas, visit **PearsonSuccessNet.com**

Key Terms and Main Ideas

To make sure you understand the key terms and main ideas of this chapter, review the Checkpoint and Section Assessment questions and look at the Quick Study Guide on the preceding page.

Critical Thinking

1. **Predict (a)** What is the greatest disadvantage of sole proprietorships? **(b)** What personal financial problems could result? **(c)** How might that negatively affect future business ventures for that owner?
2. **Describe** How do rules and laws help determine the way partnerships are organized?
3. **Analyze (a)** What liability are stockholders subject to? **(b)** How can stockholders influence the actions of the corporation in which they have ownership?
4. **Explain (a)** How is a vertical merger formed? **(b)** Give examples of types of businesses that might be part of a vertical merger involving the canned food industry.
5. **Analyze (a)** Who benefits from the incorporation of a business? **(b)** Analyze the consequences of incorporating a landscaping business that is expanding.
6. **Drawing Conclusions (a)** What is the difference in government involvement in a sole proprietorship, partnership, and corporation? **(b)** Why do you think that the government is more involved in corporations?

7. **Evaluate (a)** Identify the qualities of a successful entrepreneur. **(b)** Choose the three that you think are most important and explain why.
8. **Analyze** A major meat producer decides to create a vertical merger that will advertise, "From the stable to your table." **(a)** How could it achieve this goal? **(b)** What other business would it have to acquire?
9. **Solving Problems** A farmer has the choice of selling his milk to a multinational food conglomerate or to join with other farmers to form a cheese-making cooperative. **(a)** What is a cooperative? **(b)** What possible benefits does the cooperative provide individual farmers over selling their milk to a large corporation?

Applying Your Math Skills

Reading a Bar Graph

This bar graph shows the percentage of growth in franchises between 2000 and 2006. Look at the chart and answer the questions that follow.

Visit PearsonSuccessNet.com for additional math help.

Increase in Franchises, 2000–2006

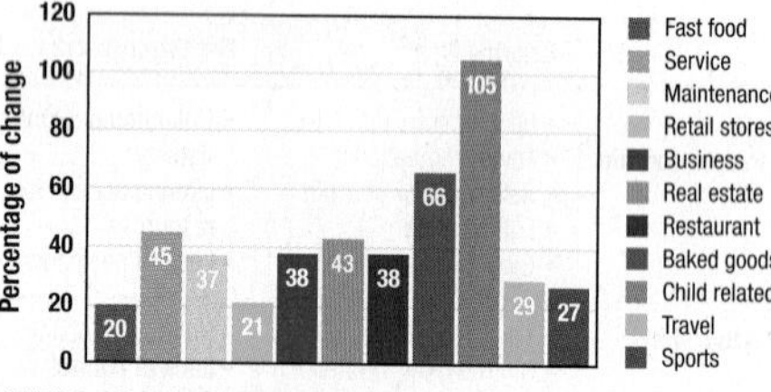

SOURCE: *Franchising World*, November 2007

10. Using the franchise graph, what would be the mean of those having positive growth? Give your answer to the nearest percent.
11. What would be the median percent of those having positive growth?
12. What would be the mode of the of those having positive growth?
13. Is any percent change actually equal to the group median? If so, which franchises grew median percentage?

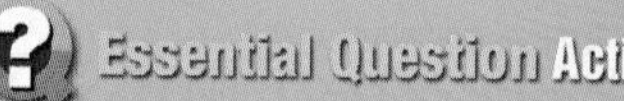

Essential Questions Journal To respond to the chapter Essential Question, go to your **Essential Questions Journal.**

14. Complete either of the following activities to answer the Essential Question **Why do some businesses succeed and others fail?** Using the worksheet in your Essential Questions Journal or the electronic worksheet available at **PearsonSuccessNet.com,** gather the following information:
    - Conduct an interview with either a current or former sole proprietor, partner in a partnership, manager of a corporation, or a franchisee to uncover their personal view of the pros and cons of doing business. Focus on why he or she thought the business succeeded or failed.
    - Using information on the Internet or in a business magazine or newspaper, such as *The Wall Street Journal*, research why a specific entrepreneur or business succeeded or failed.
15. **Modify** In groups of three or four students, share the specific information that you gathered. Then, as a group, formulate a response to the Essential Question. Share your answer with the class. Together create a list of guidelines for business success.

WebQuest online The Economics WebQuest challenges students to use 21st Century skills to answer the Essential Question.

Remind students to continue to develop an Essential Questions video. Guidelines and a production binder are available at www.PearsonSuccessNet.com.

DOCUMENT-BASED ASSESSMENT

Are corporate executives paid too much?

Some financial analysts think CEOs should be compensated for the risks they take. Others see unfair disparity between the amount of pay Chief Executive Officers (CEOs) and average workers receive.

Document A

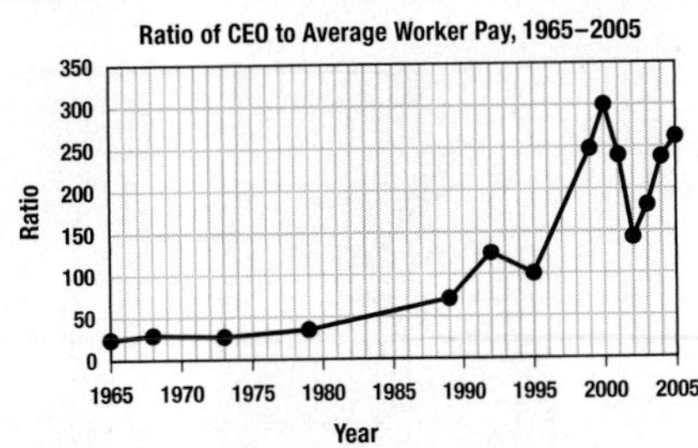

SOURCE: *Economic Policy Institute*

Document B

I don't think the government should be telling people what to pay. I think the shareholders should.... With regard to CEOs in particular, I do not think the boards of directors work as effective independent checks.... I think the time has come to say we need the shareholders to do this.

—*From an interview with Representative Barney Frank, National Public Radio, December 1, 2006*

Document C

Nau, a retailer of outdoor clothing, has written new corporate ethics into its corporate bylaws. They stipulate that Nau will cap corporate officer salaries at 12 times the lowest salary paid at the company. Nau has generated tremendous buzz—and business—by making corporate social responsibility (CSR) integral to its business strategy. It clearly passes *The Economist's* test for generating long-term profits while serving the public good.

—*From "The New Corporate Ethics," by Mark Bain,* Direct Selling News, *January 2008*

ANALYZING DOCUMENTS

Use your knowledge of Documents A, B, and C to answer questions 1–3.

1. **Document A shows that the ratio of CEO salaries to average worker pay**
   A. was greater in 1965 than in 2005.
   B. in 2000 meant that CEOs earned 300 times as much as workers.
   C. has not varied much since 1965.
   D. in 1965 meant that workers earned just as much CEOs.

2. **What is the main point of Document B?**
   A. Government determines CEOs' pay.
   B. Shareholders should be deciding CEOs' pay.
   C. Shareholders should just sell stock if they are unhappy.
   D. Boards of directors are good independent checks on CEOs' pay.

3. **According to Document C, what is Nau's goal?**
   A. to make news.
   B. to pay both CEOs and workers less.
   C. to ignore long-term profit issues.
   D. to integrate corporate and social responsibility.

WRITING ABOUT ECONOMICS

The disparity between CEO and average worker pay is both an economic and a social issue. Use the documents on this page and resources on the Web site below to answer this question: ***Are corporate executives paid too much?*** Use the sources to support your opinion.

In Partnership

THE WALL STREET JOURNAL.
CLASSROOM EDITION

To read more about issues related to this topic, visit **PearsonSuccessNet.com**

Document-Based Assessment

ANALYZING DOCUMENTS

1. B
2. B
3. D

WRITING ABOUT ECONOMICS

Possible answer: Yes, they are paid too much. In 2005, CEOs earned more than 250 times what the average worker was paid. Even The Economist *recognizes that CEOs are paid too much. No, these types of salaries are reasonable compensation for the responsibility of running a corporation. They are also necessary for attracting the kind of talent needed to run a business, when many corporations are paying similarly high salaries.*

Student essay should demonstrate an understanding of the issues involved in the debate. Use the following as guidelines to assess the essay.

L2 Differentiate Students use all documents on the page to support their thesis.

L3 Differentiate Students use the documents on this page and additional information available online at www.PearsonSuccessNet.com to support their answer.

L4 Differentiate Students incorporate information provided in the textbook and online at www.PearsonSuccessNet.com and include additional research to support their opinion.

Go Online to www.PearsonSuccessNet.com for a student rubric and extra documents.

Economics online *All print resources are available on the Teacher's Resource Library CD-ROM and online at* www.PearsonSuccessNet.com.

 **Essential Questions**

UNIT 3:

How can businesses and labor best achieve their goals?

CHAPTER 9:

How can workers best meet the challenges of a changing economy?

Introduce the Chapter

ACTIVATE PRIOR KNOWLEDGE

In this chapter, students will learn about trends in labor, how wages are determined, and about the growth and decline of labor unions. Tell students to complete the warmup activity in the **Essential Questions Journal**.

DIFFERENTIATED INSTRUCTION KEY

- **L1** Special Needs
- **L2** Basic
  - **ELL** English Language Learners
  - **LPR** Less Proficient Readers
- **L3** All Students
- **L4** Advanced Students

Economics online Visit www.PearsonSuccessNet.com for an interactive textbook with built-in activities on economic principles.

- ***The Wall Street Journal* Classroom Edition Video** presents a current topic related to labor.
- **Yearly Update Worksheet** provides an annual update, including a new worksheet and lesson on this topic.
- **On the Go** resources can be downloaded so students and teachers can connect with economics any time, anywhere.

Chapter 9 Labor

Essential Question, Chapter 9

How can workers best meet the challenges of a changing economy?

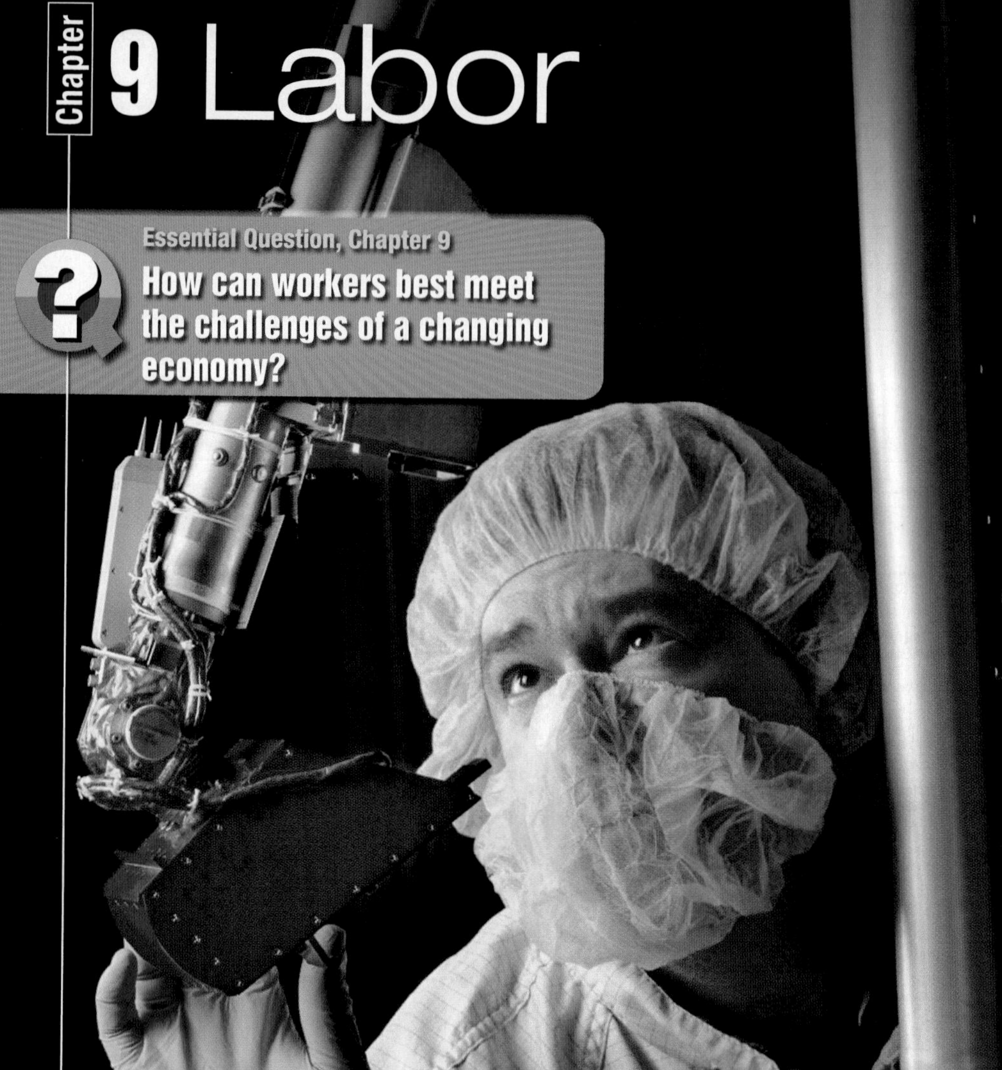

- **Section 1:** Labor Market Trends
- **Section 2:** Labor and Wages
- **Section 3:** Organized Labor

Economics on the go

To study anywhere, anytime, download these online resources at ***PearsonSuccessNet.com*** ▶

ECONOMICS ONLINE

DIGITAL TEACHER TOOLS

The online lesson planner is designed to help teachers plan, teach, and assess. Teachers have the ability to use or customize existing Pearson lesson plans. Online lecture notes support the print lesson by providing an array of accessible activities and summaries of key concepts.

Two interactivities in this lesson are:

- **Action Graph** Animated graphs display trends in labor.
- **How the Economy Works** An interactive feature allows students to explore the collective bargaining process from multiple perspectives.

Block Scheduling

BLOCK 1 Teach Sections 1 and 2. Then have students work together on the simulation activity, "How Do We Bargain?"

BLOCK 2 Teach Section 3. Select an Extend option from one section, depending on your preferences and state standards.

Pressed for Time

Group work Have students work in pairs. Assign different pairs to each section and have them outline the section main headings as headings in their outlines. Tell them to read the sections and add at least three significant details. Collect the outlines and use them to provide an overview of the material.

Use all transparencies and the skill and activity worksheets, but complete them as a class.

SECTION 1 Labor Market Trends

OBJECTIVES

1. **Describe** how trends in the labor force are tracked.
2. **Analyze** past and present occupational trends.
3. **Summarize** how the U.S. labor force is changing.
4. **Explain** trends in the wages and benefits paid to U.S. workers.

ECONOMIC DICTIONARY

As you read the section, look for the definitions of these **Key Terms:**

- labor force
- outsourcing
- offshoring
- learning effect
- screening effect
- contingent employment
- guest workers

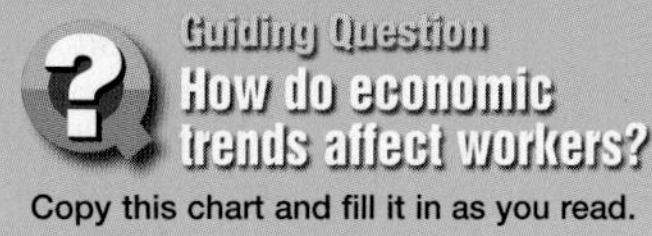

Guiding Question
How do economic trends affect workers?

Copy this chart and fill it in as you read.

How Economic Trends Affect Workers		
Workforce Trends	Changing Labor Force	Trends in Wages and Benefits
• Growing importance of computers • More service workers, fewer goods workers •	• Demand for workers with more education • •	• • •

Economics and You Have you considered how you want to earn a living when you get out of school? You may be one of those people who has been focused on a career goal for as long as you can remember or you may not have a clue. Is your goal to help others, make a lot of money, or travel? Whatever career you decide on, you will have to be prepared for change.

Principles in Action Economic trends affect workers in many ways. Over the past two decades, the U.S. economy has shifted from a manufacturing economy toward a service-producing economy. As jobs in industries such as technology and financial services have soared, the number of manufacturing jobs has dwindled.

Tracking the Labor Force

How do we know the direction of changes in the job market? Each month, the Bureau of Labor Statistics (BLS) of the United States Department of Labor surveys households to assemble information on the labor force. Economists define the **labor force** as all nonmilitary people who are employed or unemployed.

Employment and Unemployment

Economists consider people to be employed if they are 16 years or older and meet at least one of the following requirements:

- they worked at least one hour for pay in the past week;
- they worked 15 or more hours without pay in a family business, such as a farm or a family-owned store; and

labor force all nonmilitary people who are employed or unemployed

Visual Glossary online
Go to the Visual Glossary Online for an interactive review of **productivity of labor.**

Action Graph online
Go to Action Graph Online for animated versions of key charts and graphs.

How the Economy Works online
Go to How the Economy Works Online for an interactive lesson on **collective bargaining.**

STRIKE!

Guiding Question

How do economic trends affect workers?

Get Started

How Economic Trends Affect Workers		
Workforce Trends	Changing Labor Force	Trends in Wages and Benefits
• Growing importance of computers • More service workers, fewer goods workers • Impact of foreign competition	• Demand for workers with more education • More women in the workforce • More temporary workers • Many foreign-born workers	• Real wages down • Cost of benefits up significantly

LESSON GOALS

Students will:

- Know the Key Terms.
- Identify local occupational trends.
- Assess the current and future impact of outsourcing.
- Analyze the relationship between education and wages.
- Interpret a graph of projected changes in the U.S. labor force by completing a worksheet.
- Debate the impact of immigration on U.S. employment.

BEFORE CLASS

Have students complete the graphic organizer in the Section Opener as they read the text. As an alternate activity, have students complete the Guided Reading and Review worksheet. (Unit 3 All-in-One, p. 59)

L1 L2 ELL LPR Differentiate Have students complete the Guided Reading and Review worksheet. (Unit 3 All-in-One, p. 60)

Focus on the Basics

Students need to come away with the following understandings:

FACTS: • The Bureau of Labor Statistics reports on the numbers of workers and how many are employed. • A changing economy is creating more service jobs and fewer manufacturing jobs. • The labor force is changing: more women and minorities are in the workforce now. • Earnings are not keeping pace with inflation while the cost of benefits is increasing rapidly, for both employers and workers.

GENERALIZATION: The economy is producing more service jobs and fewer manufacturing jobs. Other factors, such as more women and minority workers and increased costs of benefits, are causing additional changes in the labor market.

CLASSROOM HINTS

LEARNING VS. SCREENING EFFECT

Some students have a hard time distinguishing between learning effect and screening effect, because they are so similar. Note for students that the learning effect reflects the increase in efficiency and productivity caused by knowing how to do something better. The screening effect theory says a college education does not increase productivity but rather identifies people who may be good employees because they have proven themselves able to take on a challenge and succeed.

BELLRINGER

List 10 adults you know who have jobs in the vicinity or in the state and what jobs they have. Identify whether each job is in manufacturing or service.

Based on their list, have students make a generalization about the economy of your region of (name your state). Tell students that they will come back to their lists later in the lesson.

Teach

Economics online To present this topic using online digital resources, use the lecture notes at www.PearsonSuccessNet.com.

L1 L2 ELL LPR Differentiate To help students who are struggling readers, assign the Vocabulary worksheet (Unit 3 All-in-One, p. 58).

DISCUSS

Tell students to stand up if they are employed or looking for a job. Of those standing, ask students to sit down if they are not at least 16 years old. Those students who remain standing are considered a part of the labor force. Clearly define labor force. *(16 or older with a job or seeking employment, someone who works 15 hours in a family business; someone who works but has taken time off because of illness, vacation, labor dispute, or bad weather)* Ask the other students who are not in the labor force **Why are you not in the labor force?** *(not at least 16, not looking for a job)* Ask **Who else in the population is not considered in the labor force?** *(military, people who have given up looking for a job, retired people, those who are institutionalized)*

L4 Differentiate Students may better understand employment trends by looking at *un*employment rates. Assign the "Changes in Unemployment" worksheet (Unit 3 All-in-One, p. 61). When students finish, have them report their findings to the class and discuss their conclusions.

- they held jobs but did not work due to illnesses, vacations, labor disputes, or bad weather.

People who have more than one job are counted only once. In 2005, more than 7.5 million people had more than one job.

People who do not meet these criteria are counted as unemployed if they are either temporarily without work or are not working but have looked for jobs within the last four weeks. To be counted as unemployed, then, a person either must have work lined up for the future, or must be actively searching for a new job.

Some groups of people are considered to be outside the labor force. The BLS uses the term "discouraged workers" to describe people who once sought work but have given up looking for a job. They are not counted in employment statistics. In addition, full-time students, parents who stay at home to raise children, and retirees are not considered unemployed, and thus are not counted in employment statistics. **Figure 9.1** summarizes the groups that make up the U.S. labor force.

Figure 9.1 Composition of U.S. Labor Force

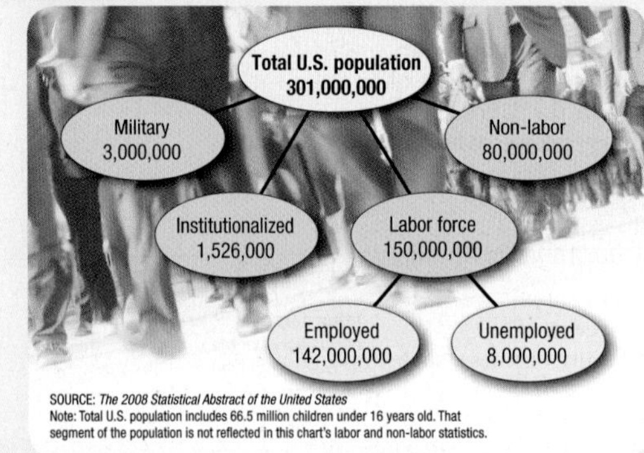

SOURCE: *The 2008 Statistical Abstract of the United States*
Note: Total U.S. population includes 66.5 million children under 16 years old. That segment of the population is not reflected in this chart's labor and non-labor statistics.

GRAPH SKILLS

This chart shows how the Bureau of Labor Statistics defines who is in the labor force and who is employed or unemployed.

1. What are the parts that form the total U.S. population?
2. How does being unemployed differ from not being part of the labor force?

The Labor Market Today

The Bureau of Labor Statistics provides answers to two important economic questions. First, it says how many people are in the labor force. Second, it tells us how many are employed and unemployed at any given time. You can find BLS data in the Census Bureau's *Statistical Abstract of the United States,* available in print and on the Internet.

The BLS provides information about historical trends. For example, the percentage of the U.S. population in the labor force has increased from 59.2 percent in 1950 to 66.0 percent in 2005. The number of employed civilians in the U.S. in 2005 was about 141.7 million. Nearly 76 million of these workers were men. Almost 66 million were women.

The BLS also reports the unemployment rate each month. Economists studying the health of the economy monitor these monthly unemployment figures. In July 2007, the unemployment rate was 4.6 percent. The highest unemployment rate from 1997 to 2007 was 6.3 percent in June of 2003.

CHECKPOINT ***What important information can we learn from the Bureau of Labor Statistics?***

Occupational Trends

The job market does not stay the same all the time. It grows as the nation's economy and population grows. The jobs that make up the job market also change. New technologies or new industries bring new jobs to life—and cause others to fade. Shifts in the job market reflect major shifts in what our economy produces. You can better understand these changes by looking at them in a historical context.

A Changing Economy

At its founding, the United States was a nation of farmers. Most people had few job opportunities beyond the corn, wheat, cotton, and tobacco fields. In the 1800s in the North, however, this focus on agriculture gradually yielded to the Industrial Revolution. The coming of the machine age energized the economy and created

Answers

Graph Skills 1. military, institutionalized, labor force, and non-labor 2. Unemployed people are not working, but they are looking for work. Persons who are not part of the labor force are not looking for work.

Checkpoint how many persons are in the labor force and how many are employed and unemployed

Differentiated Resources

L1 L2 Guided Reading and Review (Unit 3 All-in-One, p. 60)

L1 L2 Vocabulary worksheet (Unit 3 All-in-One, p. 58)

L4 Changes in Unemployment (Unit 3 All-in-One, p. 61)

L2 Labor Force Trends (Unit 3 All-in-One, p. 63)

L2 Give an Effective Presentation skills worksheet (Unit 3 All-in-One, p. 65)

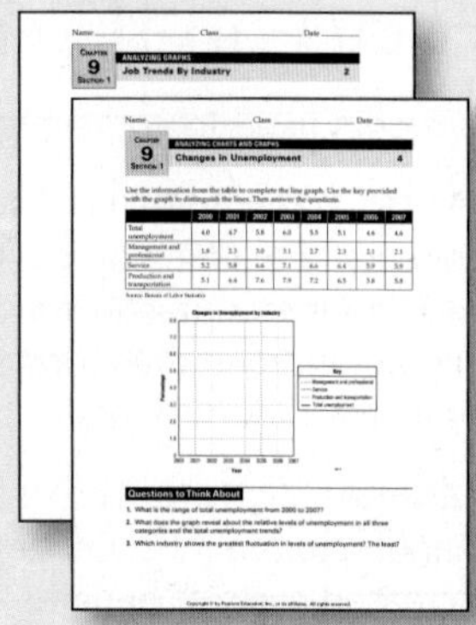

new jobs in textile mills, shoe factories, and other new manufacturing enterprises.

By the early decades of the 1900s, heavy manufacturing had become the powerhouse of the U.S. economy. New corporate empires were born: John D. Rockefeller's Standard Oil in 1863; Andrew Carnegie's steelworks in the 1870s; Henry Ford's automobile company in 1903. These huge firms employed thousands of workers.

The mid-twentieth-century boom in electronics—led by radio and television—produced a new surge of factory jobs. Employment growth centered in the Northeast and Midwest, in companies such as General Electric, Westinghouse, Carrier, and Goodyear.

In the 1970s, the revolution in personal computers opened another new horizon for employment. As computer use continues to rise, the demand for computer-related occupations continues to grow. In this "Information Age," even some traditional jobs, from trucking to farming to car sales, now require some computer skills. By the early 2000s, over half of American workers reported using computers on the job. More than a quarter of all workers in the agriculture, forestry, fishing and construction industries used computers.

Fewer Goods, More Services

The spread of computers is not the only change that has transformed the American economy. In the past one hundred or so years, the United States has shifted from a manufacturing economy to a service economy. Our production of services is increasing faster than our production of goods. (See **Figure 9.2.**) In 2005, five workers produced services for every one who produced goods. The service sector includes financial services, banking, education, and online services.

Effects of International Competition

While the number of service jobs has increased, the United States has lost manufacturing jobs. In 1990, almost 17.7 million Americans worked in manufacturing industries. Fifteen years later, the number had fallen to 14.2 million. Many workers have been laid off due to plant closings or moves, too little work, or the replacement of jobs by new technology. These conditions can be the result of **outsourcing,** in which companies contract with another company to do a specific job that would otherwise be done by a company's own workers. Most companies will outsource work in some way.

In the past, limits on the mobility of capital and labor meant that most goods sold in the United States were made by American workers in American factories. Today, capital and labor can be easily moved from place to place—and even from country to country. The movement of some of a company's operations, or resources of production, to another country is known as **offshoring.** American firms can build factories and hire workers in countries where wages and other costs are lower. American stores can buy a wide range of goods made in foreign countries to sell in the United States.

As less-skilled manufacturing jobs moved overseas, the Americans who had filled these jobs had to find new work. Many went back to school or entered job-training programs to gain new skills.

Figure 9.2 **Changes in Employment, by Industry**

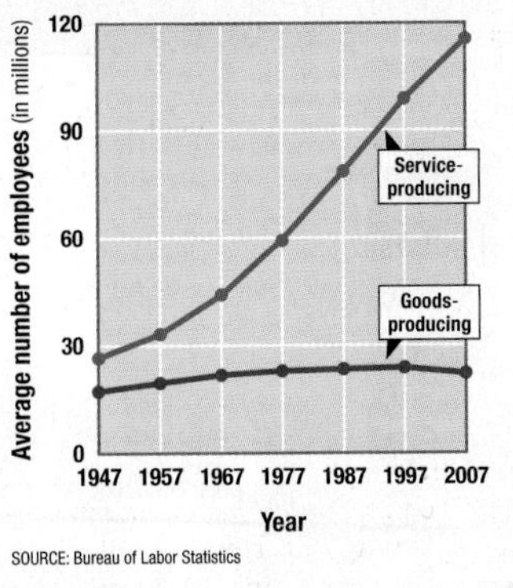

SOURCE: Bureau of Labor Statistics

GRAPH SKILLS

This chart shows the shift toward a service economy in the United States.

1. How many service-producing employees were added in the period shown?
2. Describe the changes in the U.S. economy since 1947.

Action Graph online

For an animated version of this graph, visit **PearsonSuccessNet.com**

outsourcing the practice of contracting with another company to do a specific job that would otherwise be done by a company's own workers

offshoring the movement of some of a company's operations to another country

DISCUSS

Using the Think-Write-Pair-Share strategy (p. T24), tell pairs of students to brainstorm for 3 minutes how jobs have changed in the past 150 years. On the board, list student responses. Then have students contribute from their Bellringer lists the jobs that would or would not have existed 50 years ago. Categorize these as service or manufacturing in columns. Ask **What changes have occurred in the local or state labor market in the last 150 years?** Note trends and jobs that show the shift from agriculture and farming to industry and manufacturing, and the shift to a service industry and developments in information technology.

L1 L2 Differentiate Have 14 students each take one of the Career Centers and label a placard with the major category. Point out that these categories were chosen from among the faster growing job categories as defined by the Department of Labor. Have students with placards representing service industries stand on one side of the room and those with placards representing manufacturing stand on the other side. (Note that construction/maintenance could be either.) Have students look at the results and make a generalization about labor trends.

MAKE A DECISION

Have students give examples of how computers are used in different industries. Using the Opinion Line strategy, (p. T28), have them speculate on how this might change in the future. Post two extremes, "Great Deal" and "Not Much," on either end of the board. Have students stand against the board at the point where they stand in the continuum, and then explain their opinion. Allow students to move if they are swayed by another's opinion. Emphasize the importance of computer skills in preparing for employment.

Discuss the impact of the service and technology industries on manufacturing. Ask **Why has the U.S. lost manufacturing jobs?** *(plants have closed, outsourcing increasing, technology has replaced jobs)*

Action Graph online Have students review the Action Graph animation for a step-by-step look at Changes in Employment, by Industry.

Virtual Economics

L3 Differentiate

Measuring Unemployment Use the following lesson from the NCEE **Virtual Economics *CD-ROM*** to help students understand how unemployment is measured. Click on Browse Economics Lessons, specify grades 9–12, and use the key words *measuring unemployment.*

In this activity, students will study statistics to determine how employment and unemployment can increase at the same time.

LESSON TITLE	MEASURING UNEMPLOYMENT: A LABOR MARKET MYSTERY
Type of Activity	Using statistics
Complexity	Low
Time	50 minutes
NCEE Standards	18

Answers

Graph Skills 1. about 90 million jobs 2. The number of goods-producing jobs has remained about the same but the number of service jobs has increased steadily.

CONNECT TO STUDENTS' LIVES

Have students identify where the items they have with them or are wearing were manufactured. List the countries on the board. Have students offer their own ideas about why so many products are produced in other countries. Ask **Does any nation dominate the list? Why or why not? What changes have made it possible to manufacture products in other countries and import them into the United States?** Guide a discussion of services provided by workers in other countries. *(Call centers, reading and interpreting x-rays, computer support services)*

Tell students to speculate on what happens when workers' jobs are outsourced. **What options do workers have when this happens?** Ask students to consider the effects outsourcing has on the local economy. Ask **How might you prepare for more than one career?**

L2 ELL Differentiate Have students discuss service and manufacturing industries in their first countries. Ask them if jobs in those industries are growing or declining and what markets they are serving.

INTERPRET A GRAPH

Discuss levels of education. Have students study Figure 9.3. Explain that professionals are persons who get degrees in a particular field, such as law or medicine. People cannot get jobs in these fields without the degree. Have students summarize their conclusion about the data in their own words.

Action Graph online Have students review the Action Graph animation for a step-by-step look at Education and Income, 2005.

Figure 9.3 Education and Income, 2005

GRAPH SKILLS

This bar chart shows that higher levels of education correspond to higher income.

1. When are men and women likely to see the greatest potential increase in income?
2. What can be concluded about the opportunity costs for men and women of moving up to that higher-paying level?

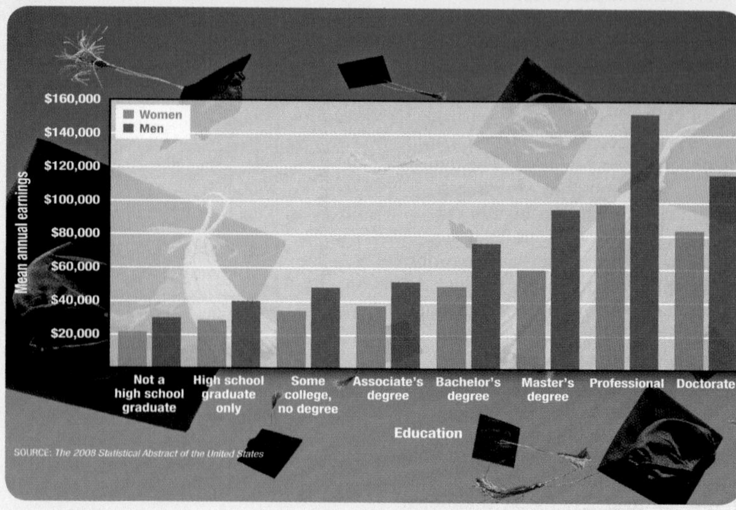

Action Graph online

For an animated version of this graph, visit **PearsonSuccessNet.com**

These shifts in demand for workers are another example of supply and demand in operation. Demand for skilled service workers is rising, so wages for skilled workers go up. These higher wages persuade more people to train for these jobs to meet the demand. Meanwhile, as demand for manufacturing workers drops off, there is a surplus of these workers who find that they must become more skilled in order to compete in the job market.

In recent years, businesses have looked abroad not just for factory workers but also for the labor of highly skilled workers. By the early 2000s, companies increasingly looked offshore for computer engineers, software programmers, and other high-skilled jobs. This trend has affected other fields, such as auto design and some medical services as well.

CHECKPOINT ***Why do companies engage in offshoring?***

The Changing Labor Force

learning effect the theory that education increases efficiency of production and thus results in higher wages

Not only have jobs changed; workers have also changed. In the 1950s, a typical American worker was a white man who had graduated from high school and had found a secure 40-hour-a-week job where he probably hoped to stay until retiring at age 65. Not anymore. Today, more women and members of minority groups are in the workforce. In addition, someone entering the workforce can expect to have four or five different jobs during his or her working life.

College Graduates

To get jobs, people must have human capital—the education, training, and experience that make them useful in the workplace. More and more, a high-school diploma alone is not enough to prepare a person for financial success. To get—and succeed in—a job, people need more education. Getting a good education, however, requires money, time, and effort. Higher earnings compensate these workers for their advanced-training costs.

Economists offer two explanations for the connection between educational advancement and higher wages. The theory that education increases efficiency of production and thus results in higher wages is called the **learning effect.** The statistics in **Figure 9.3** support this theory. They show that college-educated workers have

Answers

Graph Skills 1. when they achieve a professional degree 2. Students should consider the high cost of education as well as the tradeoff of putting off entering the working world in order to be able to make more money later. Although the opportunity cost might be substantial, the payoff in terms of increased income would bring maximum return if the worker gets a degree as a professional.

Checkpoint Companies engage in offshoring because labor and costs of building factories are lower in some other countries than in the United States.

Background Note

The Effects of Technology Point out to students that while globalization and offshoring are costing some Americans their jobs, the major culprit in loss of jobs is caused by increases in worker productivity due to technology. In fact, manufacturing output in the United States has grown during recent decades even though employment has declined. Moreover, the United States is not alone in experiencing the effects of technology. From 1994 to 2004, China lost 25 million manufacturing jobs, which is ten times more than the United States lost during the same period. Other countries, such as Germany, Japan, and South Korea, are undergoing the same job losses.

higher median income than high-school dropouts. Income continues to increase as people gain even more education. People with doctorates and professional degrees, such as doctors and lawyers, earn more than people with bachelor's degrees.

Another theory about the relationship of education to wages is called the **screening effect.** This theory suggests that the completion of college signals to employers that a job applicant is intelligent and hard-working. The skills and determination necessary to complete college may also be useful qualities for employees to have. According to this theory, a college degree does not increase productivity, but simply identifies people who may be good employees because of their perseverance and innate skills.

Women at Work

The changing face of the labor force can be seen at your local bank. A few decades ago, men greeted customers at the tellers' windows and served as loan officers. Today, most bank tellers and many loan officers are women. Women have also taken a greater role in national defense and in police and fire departments across the country.

Figure 9.4 shows that in 1960, almost 38 percent of women belonged to the labor force. By 2010, that rate was projected to be over 62 percent.

The increase may be due to several factors. One is that women were encouraged to pursue a higher education and add to their human capital. By increasing their human capital, they increased their potential earnings. With the expectation of earning more, more women entered the workforce. In addition, as more and more jobs become available in the service sector of the economy, fewer jobs call for physical strength. Instead, jobs require brainpower and personal skills, placing men and women on equal footing.

For women in their prime working years (**Figure 9.4** shows data for *all* women.), however, there appears to be a slight drop in employment. In 2008, the Bureau of Labor Statistics reported that 72.7 percent of women ages 25 to 54 were employed. This was down from 74.9 percent in 2000. Economists believe that women are being affected by the same economic problems as men, including layoffs and offshoring.

Temporary Workers

In another important trend, more and more businesses are replacing permanent, full-time workers with part-time and temporary workers. These temporary and part-time jobs are known as **contingent employment.**

Some temporary workers come from "temp" agencies. These are companies that have a pool of experienced workers who can be hired out to organizations on a short-term basis. The organization that needs the workers pays the temp agency. The agency, in turn, pays the worker a share of that fee, keeping the rest to cover expenses and profit.

Other temporary workers are hired directly by firms as contract workers, people hired for a specified time period or to complete a certain task.

Contingent employment is becoming more common even in occupations that had been very secure jobs. For example, some software engineers and attorneys are now hired as contract workers. When the workers complete their part of the project they were hired for, they are released. These highly skilled workers are generally well paid, with some earning as much as permanent workers.

screening effect the theory that the completion of college indicates to employers that a job applicant is intelligent and hard-working

contingent employment a temporary and part-time job

Figure 9.4 **Women in U.S. Labor Force, 1960–2010**

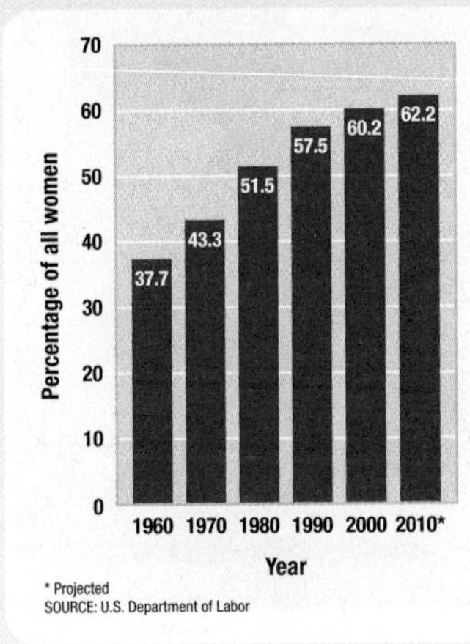

* Projected
SOURCE: U.S. Department of Labor

GRAPH SKILLS

There has been a steady rise of women in the working world.

1. Which decade shows the largest increase in the percentage of women entering the labor force?
2. What might be the reasons why the increases are smaller in recent decades?

Action Graph online

For an animated version of this graph, visit **PearsonSuccessNet.com**

SPECULATE

Ask **How do you think the change in jobs may be influencing the changes in the labor force?** *(Students may speculate that as jobs become more sophisticated, workers are compelled to seek more training and education in order to get better jobs.)*

Ask **What are two ways economists explain the connection between education and wages?** *(efficiency of production; screening effect)* **Which explanation seems most reasonable to you?** Have them give reasons, and list their responses on the board.

Point out that level of education also reflects unemployment figures. These 2007 figures show the correlation between education and unemployment. Write them on the board:

- high school graduate—4.4 percent
- associate degree—3.0 percent
- bachelor's degree—2.2 percent
- master's degree—1.8 percent
- professional degree—1.3 percent
- doctoral degree—1.4 percent

Have students offer reasons to explain the differences. Ask **How does this affect your view of what you will need for your future job?**

Action Graph online Have students review the Action Graph animation for a step-by-step look at Women in U.S. Labor Force, 1960–2010.

Answers

Graph Skills 1. 1970–1980 (8.2 percent increase) 2. Possible answers: Students should recognize that, as the percentage of women already in the labor force increases, there is less room for statistical growth.

LIST

Discuss the trend toward use of temporary workers. Have students list the reasons why businesses and workers may prefer temporary work. Then ask **What disadvantages are there for both employers and workers?** *(Possible answers: Workers will have lower wages, fewer benefits, less job predictability. Employers will have workers who are less familiar with the company, not trained as well in the company's business, and less loyal.)*

L1 L2 Differentiate Give these students a chance to respond to the questions above first. Prompt them by asking **Why would you or would you not like to be a temporary worker?**

INTERPRET TRENDS

Distribute the "Labor Force Trends" worksheet (Unit 3 All-in-One, p. 62) Have students study the graph and answer the questions.

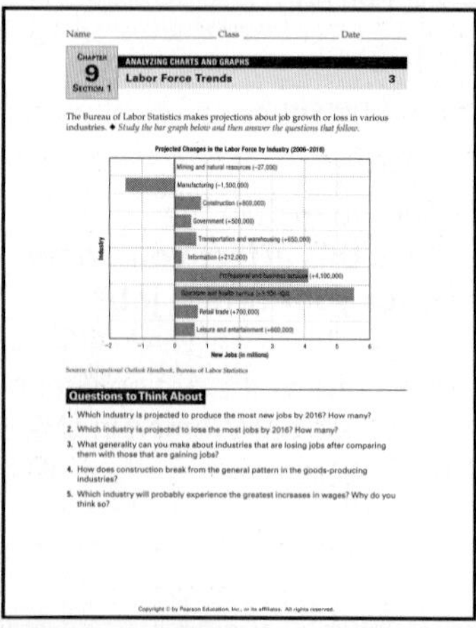

L2 LPR ELL Differentiate Distribute the "Labor Force Trends" worksheet (Unit 3 All-in-One, p. 63). Have students work in pairs or small groups to collaborate in completing the worksheet.

When students have completed the worksheets, ask **What careers may have the most opportunities five and ten years from now? In which careers do you think workers might experience the most difficulty in finding employment and high wages?**

(lesson continued on p. 224)

Answer

Global Impact Students' responses should focus on what age children are allowed to work full time and what legal restrictions are placed on the kinds of jobs children are allowed to do, the hours they may work, and whether any special educational or safety considerations are required for child workers.

guest workers members of the labor force from another country who are allowed to live and work in the United States only temporarily

Experts have identified several reasons for the increased use of temporary employees.

1. Flexible work arrangements allow firms to easily adjust their workforce to changing demand for their output. At times of reduced demand, they can easily lay off temporary workers or reduce workers' hours instead of paying employees who are idle. When business picks up, companies can rehire whatever workers they need.
2. Temporary workers in many industries are paid less and given fewer benefits (if any) than permanent, full-time workers. Thus, hiring more temporary workers cuts costs.
3. Discharging temporary workers is easier and less costly than discharging regular, permanent employees. Many employers give full-time employees severance pay of several weeks worth of wages or salary when they lay off workers. They do not have to make these payments to temporary workers.
4. Some workers actually prefer these flexible arrangements to traditional, permanent jobs. The market, then, reflects their preferences. On the other hand, BLS studies show that a majority of temporary workers would prefer permanent jobs.

The Impact of Foreign-Born Workers

One topic that has received much attention in recent years is the impact of foreign-born workers on the labor force. In 2005, foreign-born workers numbered about 22 million people, nearly 15 percent of all workers in the United States.

Many immigrant workers come to this country as permanent residents. Some foreign-born workers are **guest workers.** They are allowed to live and work in the United States only temporarily. Companies that want to hire guest workers must show that they cannot meet their labor needs from native-born workers and that using guest workers will not lower the wages of native-born workers. If companies can prove this, the government gives them permission to bring in guest workers. Guest workers hold jobs in high-tech industries that demand highly skilled workers, and in lower-skilled work also, such as agricultural labor.

The impact of immigrants on the labor force is hotly debated. Some analysts say that immigrant workers hold down the wages of Americans. This effect shows supply and demand at work. As more immigrants enter the country, they increase the supply of workers. The demand of employers for workers does not necessarily increase, though. With greater quantity supplied than quantity demanded, employers can pay less for their workers as the market reaches a new equilibrium. The result, say critics of immigration, is that American-born workers see their wages drop. They also face stiffer competition for jobs.

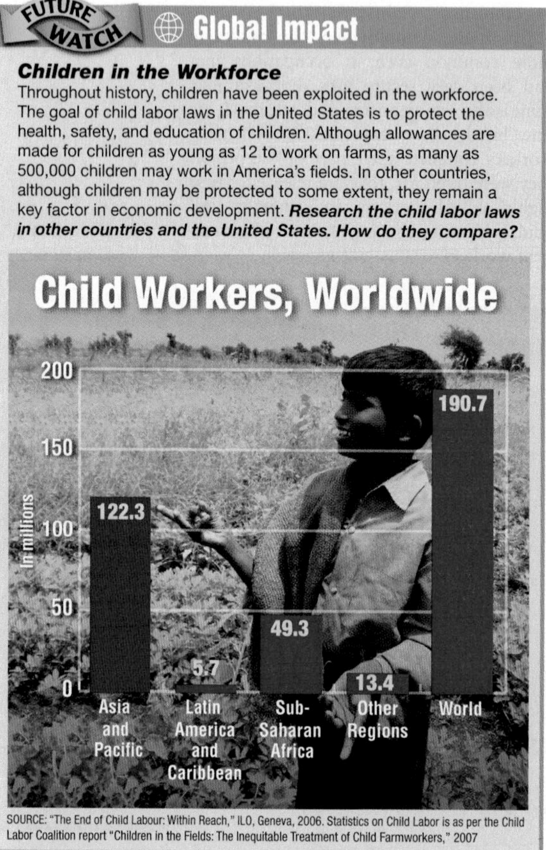

Future Watch
Global Impact
Children in the Workforce
Throughout history, children have been exploited in the workforce. The goal of child labor laws in the United States is to protect the health, safety, and education of children. Although allowances are made for children as young as 12 to work on farms, as many as 500,000 children may work in America's fields. In other countries, although children may be protected to some extent, they remain a key factor in economic development. Research the child labor laws in other countries and the United States. How do they compare?
Child Workers, Worldwide
In millions
200
150
100
50
0
122.3
5.7
49.3
13.4
190.7
Asia and Pacific
Latin America and Caribbean
Sub-Saharan Africa
Other Regions
World

SOURCE: "The End of Child Labour: Within Reach," ILO, Geneva, 2006. Statistics on Child Labor is as per the Child Labor Coalition report "Children in the Fields: The Inequitable Treatment of Child Farmworkers," 2007

Case Study THE WALL STREET JOURNAL. CLASSROOM EDITION

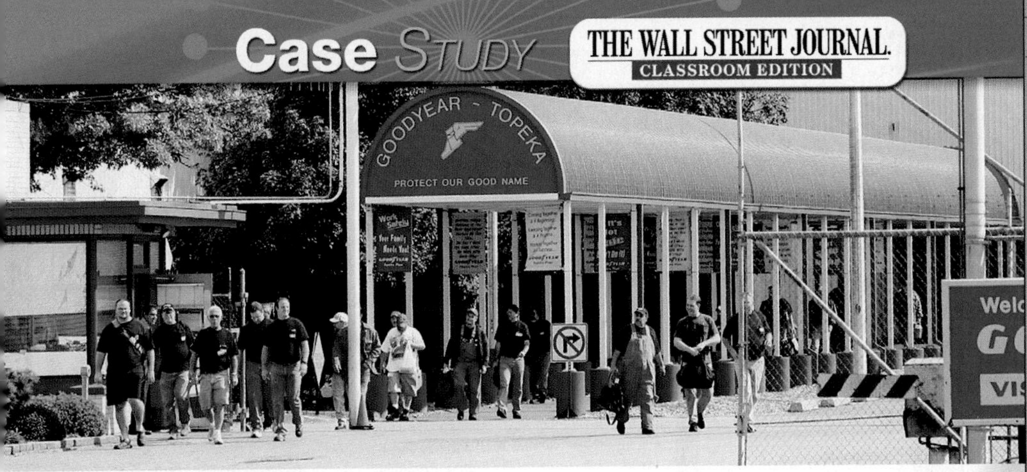

Unlucky 13

LABOR FORCE

Goodyear's two-tier wage system is a sign of changing fortunes for American factory workers.

By Timothy Aeppel
The Wall Street Journal

Few things better illustrate the diminished fortunes of the American factory worker than the emergence of "$13 workers" at Goodyear Tire & Rubber.

Jobs at Goodyear used to be coveted mainly because everyone from janitors to skilled machine operators could expect to eventually earn more than $20 an hour, with lush benefits.

That rich compensation is now slipping away. New workers hired under Goodyear's latest labor agreement earn just $13 an hour, with fewer benefits, and many will likely never achieve the lofty pay levels of the past.

A growing number of manufacturers have decided such two-tier pay systems are the only way to keep domestic factories viable. But the move also can sow seeds of conflict between employees with different wages.

"You can't help thinking about it," says Ronald Guffey, who signed on for a $13 job at Goodyear's Gadsden, Ala., plant in 2007. Scott Bruton, a fellow tire builder who does the same job as Mr. Guffey, has been at the plant since 1984 and earns $23 an hour. "I feel sorry for these guys," Mr. Guffey says of the $13 hires.

Goodyear's labor contract sought to undo a problem known as wage compression. Over the years, Goodyear found that workers migrated toward a narrow band of relatively high wages, regardless of their job. Skilled tire builders and janitors got roughly the same wage, even though their jobs and the skills required for doing them were drastically different.

Goodyear is counting on a stream of new $13 workers coming in the door as well as turnover among the $13 newcomers, who also would be replaced by lower-paid workers. Newcomers must wait six months to get company-supported health insurance, and even then, they pay more out-of-pocket costs than long-term employees. After three years, the workers move into a new pay-grading system that is designed to avoid the compression problem of the past—locking lower-skilled workers such as janitors into lower pay brackets, for instance.

In all, the company figures the advent of $13 workers will save $140 million a year by 2009. By then, the company estimates about 20 percent of workers at its unionized U.S. plants will be $13 workers.

"Call it a sign of the times, or the movement of traditional to more modern industry, but we had to change how we compensate people," says James Davis, Gadsden's plant manager.

Applying Economic Principles
Goodyear's efforts to end wage compression resulted in lower pay and benefits for new hires. Give reasons why a new worker is willing to be paid less than another worker, when both have the same jobs and skills.

Video News Update Online Powered by *The Wall Street Journal* Classroom Edition
For a new case study, go to the online resources at **PearsonSuccessNet.com**

Teach Case Study

SUMMARIZE AND EXPLAIN

Have the students explain the relationship between wages and cost-cutting. Ask **What is the main idea behind Goodyear's decision to change its wage system?** *(It needs to save money by replacing highly paid veteran workers with new workers paid $13 an hour. Goodyear is trying to end wage compression where workers went for high-paying jobs regardless of skill.)* Ask **How does this wage system preserve employment opportunities for U.S. workers?** *(The wage system keeps domestic factories viable. Many companies outsource operations because they can pay workers less. By offering all new workers $13 an hour and forcing them to pay more for healthcare, Goodyear can cut costs and still run operations in the United States.)*

ANALYZE

Ask **How is today's aging population changing the labor force?** *(People are living longer and working longer. Some retirees run out of savings and need to return to the workforce. Older workers, who have been with a company for a long time, tend to have the highest wages, while entry-level workers save companies money.)*

L1 L2 Differentiate Have the students research the history (*provide a timetable*) of factory work and workers. Have them compare and contrast their findings with the work and wages cited in the article.

Economics online *All print resources are available on the Teacher's Resource Library CD-ROM and online at www.PearsonSuccessNet.com.*

Answer

Applying Economic Principles Possible responses: Outsourcing of jobs, machines doing work people used to do, recession fears leading to downsizing, rising costs of health insurance

DEBATE

Distribute the "Give an Effective Presentation" skill worksheet (Unit 3 All-in-One, p. 64). Divide the class into teams to debate this idea: *Immigration is costing Americans jobs and increasing unemployment.* Assign teams the pro or con position. Have students use the worksheet to prepare for a debate.

Tell students to review the lesson in the Social Studies Skills Handbook on page S-19. Remind them to use the lesson steps to complete the activities.

L1 L2 **LPR Differentiate** Distribute the "Give an Effective Presentation" skill worksheet (Unit 3 All-in-One, p. 65). As moderator, ensure opportunities for each student to speak.

L2 **ELL Differentiate** Instruct students to practice speaking their part of the debate and remind them to speak slowly. Suggest they write words they have difficulty pronouncing on the board beforehand and point to them as they speak.

CREATE A PROFILE

Have students use the Career Link worksheet to record their research for the activity (Unit 3 All-in-One, p. 88).

EXTEND

Have students work independently to review some of the topics reported on by the *Monthly Labor Review Online* over the past twelve months. Ask students to write a summary of the information they find including who benefits from the trends and who pays the costs.

GUIDING QUESTION WRAP UP

Have students return to the section Guiding Question. Review the completed graphic organizer and clarify any misunderstandings. Have a wrap up discussion about how economic trends affect workers.

Assess and Remediate

L3 L2 L4 Collect the "Labor Force Trends" worksheets and the "Changes in Unemployment" worksheets and assess student understanding.

L3 Assign the Section 1 Assessment questions; identify student misconceptions.

L3 Give Section Quiz A (Unit 3 All in-One, p. 66).

L2 Give Section Quiz B (Unit 3 All in-One, p. 67).

(Assess and Remediate continued on p. 225)

Answer

Checkpoint Generally, the higher the education, the greater the income.

FUTURE WATCH

CAREER CENTER
COMPUTER SCIENCE

Possible Careers
- Computer applications engineer
- **Internet Web designer**
- Computer programmer
- Database administrator
- Systems administrator
- Computer scientist
- Computer hardware engineer

Profile: Internet Web Designer

Duties:
- connect people, businesses, and organizations to the Internet by designing Web sites
- design, construct, test, and maintain Web sites based on analysis of user needs
- create databases of content and corresponding Internet addresses in a format that is easy to search

Education:
- bachelor's degree in computer science

Skills:
- strong problem-solving skills
- ability to communicate well with team members and customers
- ability to concentrate and pay close attention to detail

Median Annual Salary:
- $48,849 (2007)

Future prospects:
- Expected to experience 37 percent growth
- 40 percent of employment will be concentrated in California, Texas, Florida, Virginia, and New York

Career Link *Activity*
Choose another career in computer science from the list of possible careers. Create a profile for that career similar to the one for Internet Web Designer.

Other analysts say that immigrant workers fill an important role in the economy. First, they say, lower-skilled immigrant workers do jobs that Americans are unwilling to do because the wages are low. As a result, important work gets done that would not be done otherwise. Second, because immigrants take those jobs, the companies that hire them can charge less for their goods or services, which benefits everyone.

CHECKPOINT ***How are education and income connected?***

Wages and Benefits Trends

Labor economists study not only who is in and out of the workforce, but how they are doing in terms of earnings and benefits. Today, the picture is mixed.

Real Wages Down

American workers enjoy higher wages than those in many other countries. In recent decades, though, the paychecks of American workers actually have been shrinking. The Bureau of Labor Statistics reports that average weekly earnings rose from $241 in 1980 to almost $590 in 2007. In reality, however, there has been no actual increase. To make a better comparison, economists make calculations to hold the value of the dollar constant. This takes away the effect of inflation—the rise of prices over time. In constant dollars, average wages actually declined to just about $222. In other words, real weekly wages have fallen about $19 in 27 years.

Why have average real wages decreased in the last couple of decades? One reason, as you have read, is that greater competition from foreign companies has decreased the demand for workers. Deregulation of many domestic industries, such as trucking, air travel, and telecommunications, may have forced firms to cut employees' wages as competition has intensified. The increased use of temporary work has also held down wages.

Cost of Benefits

For many workers, benefits such as pensions and health insurance are a significant share of total compensation. This share rose fairly steadily during the 1900s and early

2000s. By 2005, employer-provided benefits added $7.87 an hour to the cost of workers. Benefits now make up nearly 30 percent of workers' compensation. This adds up to a large cost for employers—especially since benefits like health insurance are becoming more expensive.

Social Security and Medicare taxes are included in these benefits, since they are used to pay benefits to retired and disabled workers. Most workers know that Social Security taxes are deducted from their paychecks each month. Did you know that employers pay a matching amount? Thus, workers and employers share this cost. In addition, Social Security and Medicare tax rates have risen substantially in recent decades, causing further increases in employers' benefits costs.

Employers are finding that these rising benefits costs increase the cost of doing business and thus cut into their profits. As a result some types of contingent employees, such as independent contractors, become an attractive labor resource for companies because these workers do not have to be paid benefits. Offshoring and outsourcing also help firms to cut their expenses. If benefits costs continue to rise, companies will be pressured to pursue these steps to a greater extent. Those responses may prove unpopular with workers.

CHECKPOINT ***Why have real wages dropped in recent years?***

Figure 9.5 Earnings for U.S. Workers, 2005

Industry
Retail Trade $385.20
Services $476.98
All Production Workers $589.78
Manufacturing $711.61
Construction $815.94
$0 $200 $400 $600 $800
Average weekly earnings

SOURCE: Bureau of Labor Statistics

GRAPH SKILLS

This graph shows the differences in average weekly earnings among workers.

1. What is the average salary of a worker who is employed in a retail trade or services job?
2. Why might wages for workers in retail be lower than those for service workers?

Action Graph online

For an animated version of this graph, visit PearsonSuccessNet.com

SECTION 1 ASSESSMENT

Essential Questions Journal To continue to build a response to the Essential Question, go to your **Essential Questions Journal.**

Guiding Question

1. Use your completed chart to answer this question: How do economic trends affect workers?
2. **Extension** What kinds of jobs are available to high school students in your region? Which of these jobs might not exist 20 years from now? Why?

Key Terms and Main Ideas

3. Who does the **labor force** include?
4. (a) What is **offshoring? (b)** What economic changes have brought it about?
5. Historically, the United States economy changed from an economy based on agriculture, to manufacturing, and then to service. What brought about these changes?

Critical Thinking

6. **Conclude (a)** Who are "discouraged workers"? **(b)** Why do you think the government does not consider them unemployed?
7. **Predict** What do you think would happen in the U.S. economy, if the pool of immigrant labor was cut drastically?
8. **Identify** Provide an example of a time of high demand for temporary workers.
9. **Analyze Effects** What effect does increased benefits paid by employers have on workers' wages?

Math Skills

10. **Estimating Rates of Change** The graph at the right shows recent unemployment rates for women. Figure 9.4, on page 221 shows the percentage of all women in the workforce over a selected period of time. Given that Figure 9.4 projects data into 2010, what can be estimated about the unemployment rate for women in 2010? Why? ***Visit PearsonSuccessNet.com for additional math help.***

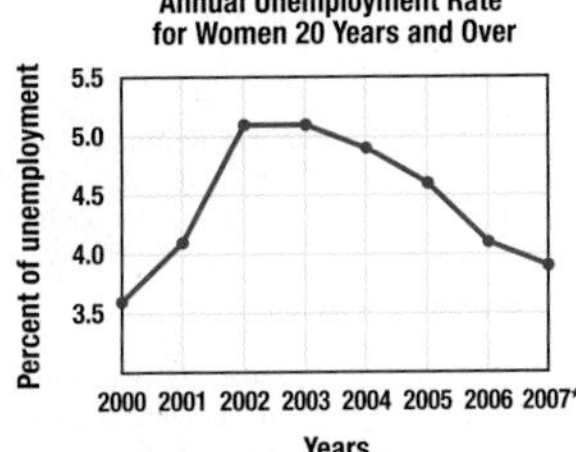

*based on 10 months
SOURCE: Bureau of Labor Statistics

Have students complete the Self-Test Online and continue their work in the **Essential Questions Journal**.

REMEDIATION AND SUGGESTIONS

Use the chart below to help students who are struggling with content.

WEAKNESS	REMEDIATION
Defining key terms (Questions 3, 4)	Have students use the interactive Economic Dictionary Online.
How the labor market reacts to events (Questions 1, 3, 5, 6, 7, 9)	Reteach by listing events in the labor market on the board. Have students search the section to find the effect of each event.
Trends that characterize the labor market (Questions 2, 4, 8)	Have students work in pairs to review the section, listing employment and job trends.

Answers

Graph Skills 1. $385.20 in retail and $476.98 in services 2. Possible answer: The services category encompasses highly skilled labor whose wages would be higher.

Checkpoint greater competition from foreign companies, deregulation of domestic industries, increased use of temporary workers

Assessment Answers

1. Economic trends create shortages or surpluses of jobs, which cause demand and wages for workers to increase or decrease.
2. Possible answer: Jobs include landscaping, office jobs, retail clerk, childcare. Some retail and office jobs may disappear as technology improves efficiency.
3. all nonmilitary people who are employed or unemployed
4. (a) the hiring of overseas workers to do jobs previously done by American workers (b) greater mobility of capital and labor plus lower costs of labor and production costs in other countries
5. increases in technology, outsourcing
6. (a) workers who have given up trying to find jobs (b) They have made themselves unavailable to work.
7. Possible answer: There will be a labor shortage in some businesses.
8. Possible answer: During the December holiday season, consumers do more shopping, which causes an increased demand for retail clerks.
9. Because employers must pay more for benefits, they cannot pay more for wages.
10. The unemployment rate will probably drop at a slower pace. This is because the percentage of women in the labor force has grown. Therefore there are fewer women entering the job market.

Guiding Question

Why do some people earn more than others?

Get Started

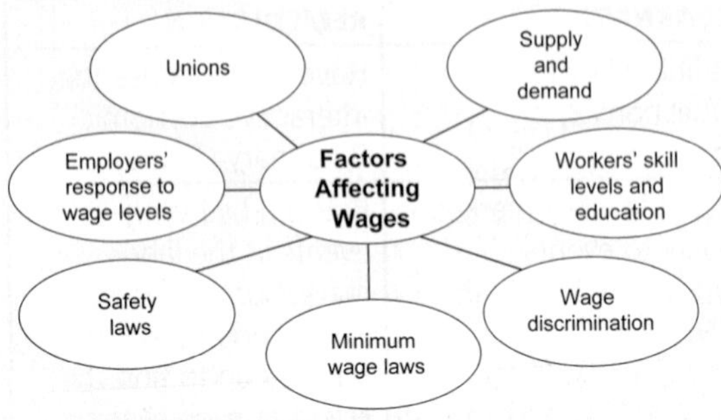

LESSON GOALS

Students will:

- Know the Key Terms.
- Describe the impact of labor supply and labor demand on wage levels and the equilibrium wage.
- Describe the connection between skill levels and wages by completing a worksheet.
- Assess the progress made with respect to wage discrimination.
- Assess the impact of minimum wage and safety laws, as well as unions, on wage levels.

BEFORE CLASS

Students should read the section for homework before coming to class.

Have students complete the graphic organizer in the Section Opener as they read the text. As an alternate activity, have students complete the Guided Reading and Review worksheet (Unit 3 All-in-One, p. 68).

L1 L2 ELL LPR Differentiate Have students complete the Guided Reading and Review worksheet (Unit 3 All-in-One, p. 69).

CLASSROOM HINTS

LAW OF DEMAND AND LAW OF SUPPLY

Review the law of demand, the law of supply, and market equilibrium in Chapters 4, 5, and 6. Refer to demand and supply curves in these chapters. This may help students understand the relationship between labor demand, labor supply, and wage level.

SECTION 2 Labor and Wages

OBJECTIVES

1. **Analyze** how supply and demand in the labor market affects wage levels.
2. **Describe** how skill levels and education affect wage levels.
3. **Explain** how laws against wage discrimination affect wage levels.
4. **Identify** other factors affecting wage levels, such as minimum wage and workplace safety laws.

ECONOMIC DICTIONARY

As you read the section, look for the definitions of these **Key Terms:**

- derived demand
- productivity of labor
- equilibrium wage
- unskilled labor
- semi-skilled labor
- skilled labor
- professional labor
- glass ceiling
- labor union
- featherbedding

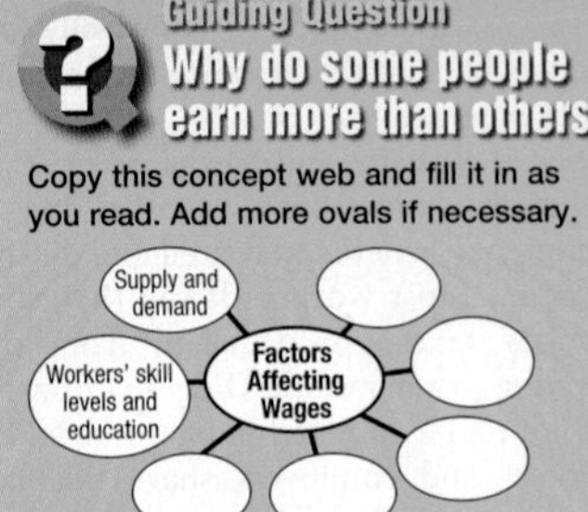

Guiding Question
Why do some people earn more than others?
Copy this concept web and fill it in as you read. Add more ovals if necessary.
Supply and demand
Factors Affecting Wages
Workers' skill levels and education

Economics and You How important is it to you to make a lot of money? If it is very important, then you had better think carefully about what you want to do for a living. Some jobs and professions are very well paid. A top-notch surgeon can charge $150,000 for one operation. A lawyer might make $600 for an hour consultation, while the clerk at the local convenience store might make $8.00 an hour. What will determine the size of your paycheck?

Principles in Action The law of supply and demand applies to the world of labor and wages. What people earn for what they do is largely a matter of how many people are willing and able to do the job and how much that job is in demand. Like eggs or airplanes or pet iguanas, labor is a commodity that is bought and sold. In a free market economy, the market finds its own equilibrium price for labor. In a mixed economy, the government also plays a role. In the Economics & You feature, you will see how government action affects the labor market for teen workers.

Supply and Demand for Labor

Employment or unemployment in a labor market depends on how closely the demand for workers—the number of available jobs—meets the supply of workers seeking jobs. Let's examine how supply and demand operate in labor markets.

Labor Demand

The demand for labor comes from private firms and government agencies that hire workers to produce goods and services. In most labor markets, dozens, or even hundreds, of firms compete with one another for workers.

Demand for labor is called a **derived demand** because it is derived, or set, by the demand for another good or service. In this case, that other demand is the demand for what a worker produces. For example, the demand for cooks in a market depends on the demand for restaurant meals.

In a competitive labor market, workers are usually paid according to the value of what they produce. For example, competition among restaurants results in a wage for cooks that reflects the cook's productivity. **Productivity of labor** is the quantity of output produced by a unit of labor.

derived demand a type of demand that is set by the demand for another good or service

productivity of labor the quantity of output produced by a unit of labor

Focus on the Basics

Students need to come away with the following understandings:

FACTS: • Wages are partly determined by supply and demand. • Workers' skill level and education influence wages. • Discrimination affects the wages of some workers. • Other factors affecting wages include minimum wage laws, safety, the costs of benefits, the availability of technology, and labor unions.

GENERALIZATION: Wages are determined by the supply and demand for labor and also by workers' education and training, technology, unions, and discrimination.

The productivity of a cook's labor, for example, can be measured as the cost of a meal. Suppose that most of the restaurants in a city pay $12 an hour for cooks and that each cook generates $20 an hour in revenue for the restaurants. The possibility of profit will attract other entrepreneurs to open restaurants. Competition will push up the wage for cooks. As a result, cooks will be paid close to the value of their productivity of labor. The flowchart in **Figure 9.6** shows the ripple effect that occurs when a new restaurant hires cooks at a higher wage.

Now look at the demand curve for labor, shown in the right-hand graph of **Figure 9.7** on page 229. Notice that it is negatively sloped, reflecting the law of demand. The higher the price of labor, the smaller the quantity of labor demanded by employers. Restaurants are more likely to hire more cooks at $12 an hour than at $16 an hour because the lower cost means they can earn more profits on each cook's labor.

Labor Supply

The supply of labor comes from people willing to work for wages. As the graph on the left in **Figure 9.7** shows, the supply curve is positively sloped, reflecting the law of supply. In other words, the higher the wage, the larger the quantity of labor supplied.

This is logical. It simply means that the higher the wage for a job, the greater the number of people who will be attracted to that job. A higher wage for cooks encourages people who would choose other occupations to acquire the training required to become a cook.

Equilibrium Wage

We know that at market equilibrium, the quantity of a good supplied will equal the quantity demanded. Economic factors—the supply of labor and the demand for it—combine to determine an equilibrium price. Because the equilibrium price makes the quantity that suppliers want to sell equal to the quantity that demanders want to buy, there is a tendency for the price or quantity not to change. That stability applies to the equilibrium price in one market, though. These factors may be different in different parts of the country, or at different times.

The **equilibrium wage** is the wage rate, or price of labor services, that is set when the supply of workers meets the demand for workers in the labor market. On a graph, the equilibrium wage is shown by the intersection of the supply and demand curves. (See **Figure 9.8** on page 230.) At equilibrium, there is no pressure to raise or lower wages.

How do these theories affect how much you should expect to earn working in a pet store or a grocery store next summer? It depends on supply and demand in your area. If stores do not hire many additional workers during the summer and a lot of teenagers wanted to work, the wage will be relatively low. On the other hand, if stores want to hire a lot of teenagers and few teens want to work, the wage will be higher.

CHECKPOINT ***What determines the equilibrium wage of labor?***

equilibrium wage the wage rate, or price of labor services, that is set when the supply of workers meets the demand for workers in the labor market

Figure 9.6 Effects of Competition

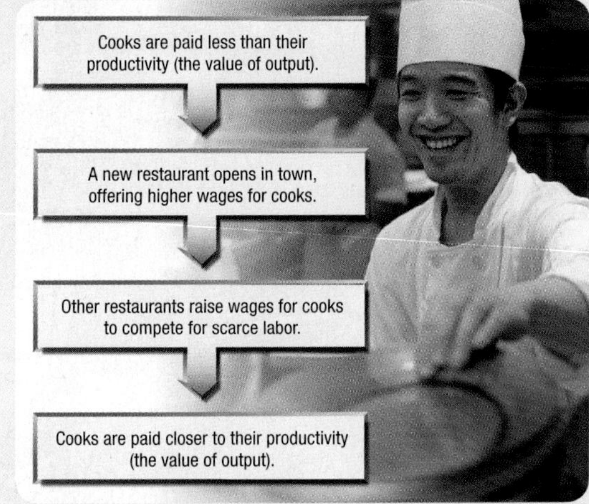

Cooks are paid less than their productivity (the value of output).
A new restaurant opens in town, offering higher wages for cooks.
Other restaurants raise wages for cooks to compete for scarce labor.
Cooks are paid closer to their productivity (the value of output).

GRAPH SKILLS

This flowchart shows how competition causes workers to be paid a wage close to their productivity.

1. Explain how the outcome of this scenario affects **(a)** the cooks, **(b)** the restaurants.
2. Describe the conditions in which a restaurant might not be motivated to raise its wages to compete for scarce labor.

BELLRINGER

On the chalkboard, write down the amount paid per year to a current major league baseball player, a brain surgeon, and a day care worker. Ask students to react to the figures and think about what causes the difference and if the difference is fair. Ask them to think of it in terms of what factors affect wages.

Teach

Economics online To present this topic using online digital resources, use the lecture notes at www.PearsonSuccessNet.com.

DISCUSS

Discuss the Bellringer activity with students. Ask volunteers **Do the numbers surprise you? How would you account for the difference? Do you think that they are fair?** Review the relationship between supply and demand and prices. *(When the demand for a particular good is greater than the supply, prices increase. When the demand for a good is less than the supply, the prices go down.)* Have students compare the prices of goods in a competitive market and wages paid to workers. Ask **How might the laws of supply and demand contribute to the difference in earnings of the ball player, the surgeon and the day care worker?**

Have students analyze Figure 9.6. Explain that the first box is the status quo. There are more cooks than jobs, so wages are low. Ask **Why might the new restaurant offer higher wages?** *(to lure the best cooks away from existing restaurants)* **How do the existing restaurants keep their cooks?** *(Raise their wages.)* **What other than higher wages might they offer to attract employees?** *(flexible schedules, better working conditions, advancement opportunities)*

(lesson continued on p. 229)

Differentiated Resources

- L1 L2 **Guided Reading and Review** (Unit 3 All-in-One, p. 69)
- L2 **Wages and Skill Levels** (Unit 3 All-in-One, p. 71)
- L4 **Minimum Wage and Poverty** (Unit 3 All-in-One, p. 72)

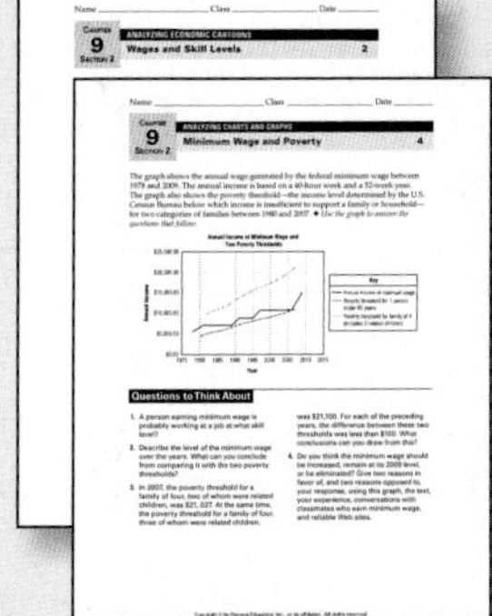

Answers

Checkpoint This wage is reached when the supply of workers in a field meets the demand for workers.

Graph Skills 1. (a) Cooks get higher wages, and (b) restaurants pay higher salaries, compete for scarce labor, and may have to raise prices. 2. Possible responses: A restaurant might already pay higher wages than its competitors; a restaurant might be doing poorly and unable to raise wages.

Teach Visual Glossary

REVIEW KEY TERMS

Have students define each term and give an example.

production possibilities curve – *a graph that shows alternative ways to use an economy's productive resources*

productions possibilities frontier – *a line on a production possibilities curve that shows the maximum possible output an economy can produce*

efficiency – *the use of resources in such a way as to maximize the output of goods and services*

law of increasing costs – *an economic principle which states that as production shifts from making one good or service to another, more and more resources are needed to increase production of the second good or service*

diminishing marginal returns – *a level of production at which the marginal product of labor decreases as the number of workers increases*

labor force – *all nonmilitary people who are employed or unemployed*

derived demand – *a type of demand that is set by the demand for another good or service*

learning effect – *the theory that education increases efficiency of production and thus results in higher wages*

DISCUSS

Ask **What inputs help increase productivity of labor?** *(Possible responses: wages, training, energy resources, technology, land)* Write answers on the board and have students give examples of each. Discuss how adding these inputs increases productivity, which in turn increases company profits.

L1 L2 Differentiate Use the lesson on the Visual Glossary page to review this term. Direct students to the Visual Glossary Online to reinforce understanding of *productivity of labor.*

Economics online *All print resources are available on the Teacher's Resource Library CD-ROM and online at www.PearsonSuccessNet.com.*

Answer

Caption They increase worker efficiency, which increases productivity. This will occur when workers and technology have reached their maximum efficiency or when supply saturates the market.

VISUAL GLOSSARY

Reviewing Key Terms
To understand *productivity of labor,* review these terms:
production possibilities curve, *p. 13*
production possibilities frontier, *p. 14*
efficiency, *p. 15*
law of increasing costs, *p. 17*
diminishing marginal returns, *p. 11*
labor force, *p. 217*
derived demand, *p. 251*
learning effect, *p. 253*

What is Productivity of Labor?

◄ **productivity of labor** is the quantity of output produced by a unit of labor

The worker above is able to make 10 toys in an hour. The one on the right, however, has been trained to use new toy-making techniques. She is able to make 15 toys in an hour.

This worker uses a machine to make 300 toys in an hour.

Why are investments in training and technology important for a business? At what point would increased investment not result in increased productivity?

Visual Glossary online
To expand your understanding of this and other key economic terms, visit **PearsonSuccessNet.com**

Figure 9.7 Labor Supply and Demand

GRAPH SKILLS

This graph shows (a) how the quantity of labor demanded varies depending on the price of labor, and (b) how the labor supply varies depending on the wage rate.

1. According to the demand curve, if each cook works a 40-hour work week, how many cooks will be hired at $12 an hour and $16 an hour?
2. Why is the supply curve positively sloped?

Action Graph online
For an animated version of this graph, visit PearsonSuccessNet.com

Wages and Skill Levels

Why do lawyers earn more money than carpenters, and carpenters more than cashiers? Wages vary according to workers' skill levels and education, as well as according to supply and demand. Jobs are often categorized into four skill levels:

1. **Unskilled labor** requires no specialized skills, education, or training. Workers in these jobs usually earn an hourly wage. They include dishwashers, messengers, janitors, and many farm workers.
2. **Semi-skilled labor** requires minimal specialized skills and education, such as the operation of certain types of equipment. Semi-skilled workers usually earn an hourly wage. They include lifeguards, word processors, short-order cooks, and many construction and factory workers.
3. **Skilled labor** requires specialized abilities and training to do tasks such as operating complicated equipment. Skilled workers need little supervision, yet usually earn an hourly wage. They include auto mechanics, bank tellers, plumbers, firefighters, chefs, and carpenters.
4. **Professional labor** demands advanced skills and education. Professionals are usually white-collar workers who receive a salary. Professionals include managers, teachers, bankers, doctors, actors, professional athletes, and computer programmers.

Labor supply and demand can create a significant difference in pay scales for workers with various skills. For example, the labor market for medical doctors is relatively high compared to construction workers. Because the supply of doctors is relatively low and the demand is relatively high, there is a high equilibrium wage.

By comparison, the supply of construction workers is high relative to the demand for them. Hence, the equilibrium wage for construction workers would be much lower than that for doctors.

Doctors and other highly educated workers—and those with extensive training and experience—enjoy demand for their services that is high relative to

unskilled labor work that requires no specialized skills, education, or training

semi-skilled labor work that requires minimal specialized skills and education

skilled labor work that requires specialized skills and training

professional labor work that requires advanced skills and education

Virtual Economics

L2 Differentiate

Determining Effect of Specialization Use the following lesson from the NCEE **Virtual Economics *CD-ROM*** to help students to understand how specialization affects productivity. Click on Browse Economics Lessons, specify grades 9–12, and use the key word *productivity.*

In this activity, students will take part in a production simulation to demonstrate the effect of specialization.

LESSON TITLE	PRODUCTIVITY
Type of Activity	Simulation
Complexity	Moderate
Time	60 minutes
NCEE Standards	6, 13, 15

EXPLAIN GRAPHS

Discuss Figure 9.7. Point to the Labor Supply graph and ask **If cooks are paid $12 an hour for working a 40-hour week, how many will be in the labor market?** *(6 cooks)* Have volunteers explain how to calculate this answer.

L1 L2 Differentiate Make sure that students understand what the graphs show. Draw them on the board and demonstrate how they explain Figure 9.6.

Action Graph online Have students review the Action Graph animation for a step-by-step look at Labor Supply and Demand.

DISCUSS

Have students state the skill and training expected in each labor category and explain why employers might pay more for one type of worker than another. Ask **Why don't all workers strive to increase their training and education? What is the lure to take a job right out of school rather than to continue your education?** *(immediate gratification, pay bills)* **Is money the only job satisfaction?**

ANALYZE A CARTOON

Distribute the "Wages and Skill Levels" worksheet (Unit 3 All-in-One, p. 70). Have students read the cartoon and answer the questions. When they finish, call on students to share their answers.

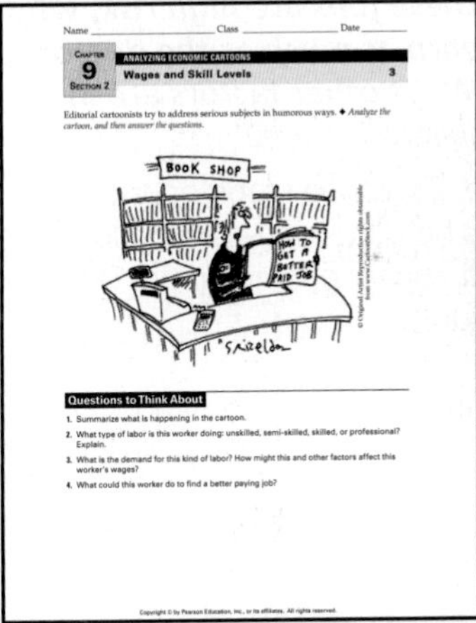
Name ______ Class ______ Date ______

Chapter 9 Section 2 — ANALYZING ECONOMIC CARTOONS — Wages and Skill Levels 3

Editorial cartoonists try to address serious subjects in humorous ways. ◆ *Analyze the cartoon, and then answer the questions.*

Questions to Think About

1. Summarize what is happening in the cartoon.
2. What type of labor is this worker doing: unskilled, semi-skilled, skilled, or professional? Explain.
3. What is the demand for this kind of labor? How might this and other factors affect this worker's wages?
4. What could this worker do to find a better paying job?

L1 L2 ELL LPR Differentiate Distribute the "Wages and Skill Levels" worksheet (Unit 3 All-in-One, p. 71). Ensure that students understand that the person is a cashier in a bookstore. Have students work in pairs to answer the questions.

Answers

Graph Skills 1. $12: 6 cooks; $16: 4 cooks 2. The higher the wage, the larger the supply of available labor.

INTERPRET GRAPHS

Direct students to Figure 9.8 and discuss factors that determine wage equilibrium. Ask **Is the supply curve positive or negative? What does that mean?** *(Positive; as wages go up, supply increases.)* **Why is the demand curve negative?** *(As the cost of labor increases, employers will hire fewer workers.)*

Action Graph online Have students review the Action Graph animation for a step-by-step look at Equilibrium Wage.

Ask students how supply and demand curves are affected by training and education. Make sure that students understand that both increase the value of the worker, increasing demand and reducing supply. Draw a graph on the board to illustrate the hypothetical equilibrium wage for a high school graduate who works in a retail store. Add lines to show how the equilibrium wage increases when the worker earns a bachelor's degree.

Follow up with a discussion on how working conditions affect the equilibrium wage. Demonstrate by referring students to Figure 9.9 on p. 231. Have volunteers explain what the two graphs show. Ask them to tell how the demand and supply curves would shift to reflect even more dangerous jobs. Ask **What are some examples of these high-risk jobs?** *(Possible responses: fire fighter, coal miner, police officer)* Ask ***If these jobs are high risk, why don't any of them earn as much as the doctor or the ball player? What other factors are in play?*** *(education, required skill level)*

L1 L2 Differentiate Draw one graph on the board. Demonstrate where the high-risk and low-risk demand curves would appear on one graph. Do the same for the supply curve.

Action Graph online Have students review the Action Graph animation for a step-by-step look at Comparison: Wages for High-Risk, Low-Risk Jobs.

Figure 9.8 Equilibrium Wage

GRAPH SKILLS

This graph shows the wage at which the quantity demanded equals the quantity supplied.

1. Explain why a stable wage means stable restaurant prices.
2. Under what circumstances would the equilibrium wage be $8 an hour?

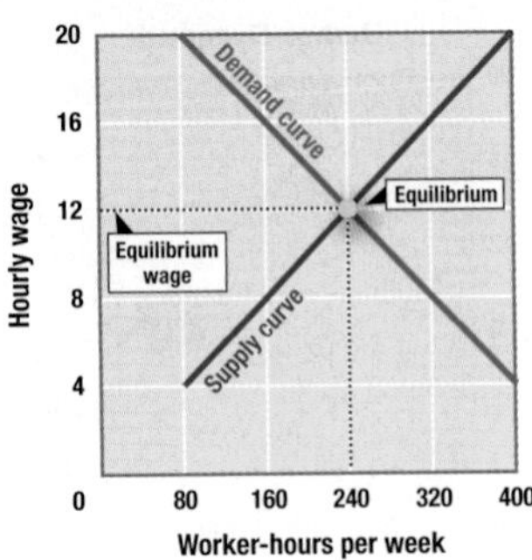

Action Graph online

For an animated version of this graph, visit PearsonSuccessNet.com

the supply, leading to higher earnings. The demand for workers with less education and training tends to be lower relative to the supply, so their earnings are lower. Experienced workers are desirable because they tend to be more productive than those newer to that job.

Another reason that earnings vary is differences in working conditions. The level of danger in doing a job, the physical or emotional stress involved, and the location of the work can all change the equilibrium wage.

Economic studies have shown that jobs with high accident and fatality rates pay relatively high wages. Workers who do dangerous jobs require compensation for the risks they take. Thus, there is a higher equilibrium wage rate for dangerous jobs, as shown in **Figure 9.9.**

CHECKPOINT ***How do education, training, and experience affect wages?***

Wage Discrimination

As we have seen, wages for a particular job should end up at the equilibrium price of labor for that job. However, some people are paid less because of the social group they belong to. For instance, in the past, women and members of minority groups often received lower wages than white male workers for the same work. This practice is wage discrimination.

Some employers defended wage discrimination against women by claiming that men needed the money to support families, while women were simply working to earn extra cash. Discrimination against minority workers reflected racial and ethnic prejudice in society. In recent decades, national or state legislators have tried to end these practices by passing laws prohibiting wage discrimination.

Laws Against Wage Discrimination

In the 1960s, the United States Congress passed several anti-discrimination laws that prevent companies from paying lower wages to some employees based on factors like gender or race that are not related to skill or productivity. The Equal Pay Act of 1963 required that male and female employees in the same workplace performing the same job receive the same pay. Title VII of the Civil Rights Act of 1964 prohibited job discrimination on the basis of race, sex, color, religion, or nationality. (Religious institutions and small businesses are exempt from the law.)

The Civil Rights Act also established the Equal Employment Opportunity Commission (EEOC) to enforce the provisions of the law. Workers who feel they have been discriminated against can complain to the EEOC, which will investigate the matter. If necessary, the commission can take companies to court to force them to comply with the law.

Pay Levels for Women

Despite protections, women still earn less than men. This earnings gap has closed somewhat, but not completely. Historically, this gap has been the result of three factors:

1. *"Women's work."* Women have historically been discouraged from entering certain high-paying occupations, such as doctors, lawyers, and corporate managers. Instead, they have been encouraged to pursue careers such as teaching, nursing, and clerical work. With so many women seeking work in these occupations,

Background Notes

The Wage Gap While wage discrimination remains a problem, the gap between the earnings of men and women has steadily but slowly narrowed over time. In 1979, women earned about 61 percent of what men earned. By 1989, it was 71 percent, and by 1999, it was 77 percent. In 2006, women earned about 81 percent of what men earned. Earnings by race generally parallel overall gains. In 2006, white women earned about 80 percent of what white men earned. Black women earned almost 88 percent, Asian women earned 79 percent, and Hispanic women earned about 87 percent of what males of the same race earned.

Answers

Graph Skills 1. Labor costs are one cost of production. If wages remain stable, there is less impetus to increase prices. 2. if demand lessened to 160 worker-hours per week

Checkpoint They increase demand for the workers, which results in higher wages.

Figure 9.9

Comparison: Wages for High-Risk, Low-Risk Jobs

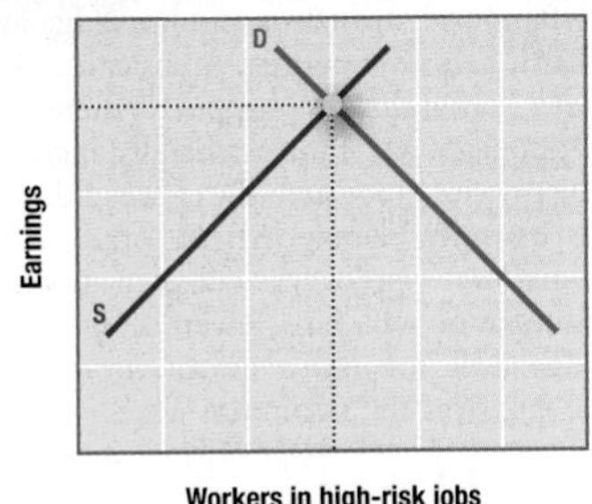

Workers in high-risk jobs

Earnings

Workers in low-risk jobs

GRAPH SKILLS

These graphs show how wages compare for similar jobs with different degrees of risk.

1. Write a sentence that compares the demand curves on the two graphs.
2. Write a sentence that compares the two supply curves.

Action Graph online

For an animated version of this graph, visit PearsonSuccessNet.com

the labor supply has been generally high. As you know, a large supply of labor tends to produce a relatively low equilibrium wage.

2. *Human capital.* Overall, women have had less education, training, and experience than men. This lack of human capital makes women's labor, in economic terms, less productive. As a result, fewer women are eligible for the higher-paying, traditionally male-dominated jobs in fields such as engineering.
3. *Women's career paths.* Even today, some employers assume that female employees are not interested in career advancement. This perception can be a roadblock for women in the workplace. The challenges many women face in trying to balance child-rearing and a career adds to this perception.

Much progress has been made in creating job opportunities for women. Yet some qualified women still find that they cannot receive promotions to top-level jobs. This unofficial barrier that sometimes prevents women and minorities from advancing to the top ranks of organizations that are dominated by white men is called a **glass ceiling.**

Pay Levels Across Society

On average, members of minority groups tend to receive lower pay than whites do. Part of the wage gap has been caused by a history of racial discrimination. On average, whites have had access to more education and work experience, enabling them to develop skills that are in demand. Non-discrimination laws, in part, are designed to give minority workers improved access to education and job opportunities so they can develop

glass ceiling an unofficial barrier that sometimes prevents women and minorities from advancing to the top ranks of organizations dominated by white men

◀ The term "corporate ladder" refers to the series of rungs, or steps, an employee climbs on the way to corporate leadership. Workers at the upper rungs of the corporate ladder have more responsibility, decision-making power, and income. ***How does this cartoon symbolize a glass ceiling for women?***

EXAMINE DATA

Write the following facts on the board:

In the 1930s

- the test to become a math teacher in New York City was administered only to men.
- many pregnant teachers, as well as female teachers who married or had young children, had to give up their jobs.
- it was virtually impossible for a black teacher to get a job in a school with white students.

Ask **How far have we come?** Have students discuss where we have and have not made progress. Have students examine issues of wage discrimination against women and minorities. Ask them to list the rationales employers give for paying women less than men for the same work.

L2 ELL Differentiate Explain *discrimination* to students. If necessary, provide a brief review of the civil rights and women's liberation movements. Encourage volunteers to describe similar struggles in their first countries.

DISCUSS

When Hillary Clinton conceded defeat to Barack Obama in the 2008 election primaries she said in reference to her 18 million primary votes:

"Although we weren't able to shatter that highest, hardest glass ceiling this time, thanks to you, it has about 18 million cracks in it and the light is shining through like never before." What did she mean?

L2 ELL Differentiate Explain the meaning of the idiom *glass ceiling* by saying that women were prevented from advancing by a barrier to their upward movement in companies. The barrier was like glass—difficult to see, but completely solid.

Discuss the cartoon on this page. Ask students if they think the glass ceiling still exists.

Answers

Graph Skills 1. The demand curve for high-risk jobs is shifted to the right of the low-risk curve, indicating higher demand. 2. The supply curve for high-risk jobs is shifted to the left of the low-risk curve, indicating there are fewer workers willing to do the job.

Cartoon women's opportunity to advance in business is limited compared to men's; women can often only advance so far and not as far as men can

CHECK COMPREHENSION

Point to Figure 9.10. Have a volunteer describe what the bar graph shows.

L1 L2 Differentiate Explain that median income is the middle term of a series that contains all incomes arranged from smallest to largest.

Action Graph online Have students review the Action Graph animation for a step-by-step look at Income for Full-Time Workers, by Gender and Ethnicity, 2005.

DEBATE

Using the Opinion Line strategy (p. T28), have students discuss the importance of minimum wage laws. Tell them to reread the information on the issue on page 139. Allow students a few minutes to prepare arguments. Then have students give their arguments and counterarguments.

L1 Differentiate Call on these students to give the first arguments and the first counterarguments.

L4 Differentiate Distribute the "Minimum Wage and Poverty" worksheet (Unit 3 All-in-One, p. 72). Have students complete the worksheet and then share their findings and conclusions in small groups.

DISCUSS

Tell students that federal and state laws regulate workplace safety. The federal Occupational Safety and Health Administration (OSHA) was established in 1970 to protect all workers from job-related risks of injury, illness, or death. It also works closely with states to establish an additional layer of worker protection. Ask **How did this agency influence equilibrium wages?** *(By making jobs safer, more workers would be willing to work at jobs. The greater supply of workers could lead to lower equilibrium wages.)*

Figure 9.10 Income for Full-Time Workers, by Gender and Ethnicity, 2005

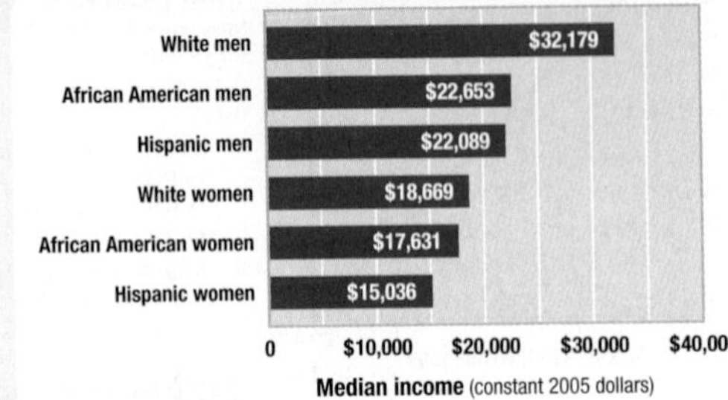

SOURCE: *The 2008 Statistical Abstract of the United States*

GRAPH SKILLS

Despite the progress in efforts to end wage discrimination, significant differences exist between men and women and among workers of various minority groups.

1. According to the bar chart, which group has the lowest median income?
2. What factors might help explain why African American women earn more than Hispanic women?

For an animated version of this graph, visit **PearsonSuccessNet.com**

more human capital and lessen the wage gap. (See **Figure 9.10.**) The entire economy benefits when all workers have a higher level of skill and can be more productive.

✔ **CHECKPOINT** ***What groups have been hurt by wage discrimination?***

Other Factors Affecting Wages

In addition to laws forbidding discrimination, several other factors can affect wages. These include minimum wage laws, workplace safety laws, employer actions, and labor unions.

Minimum Wage Laws

In 1938, Congress passed the Fair Labor Standards Act. This law created a minimum wage—the lowest amount employers could lawfully pay for most types of work—and required employers to pay overtime for work beyond 40 hours a week. Many states also have their own minimum wage laws. Because of these laws, employers may be forced to pay more than the equilibrium wage for unskilled labor.

Supporters of the minimum wage argue that it helps the poorest American workers earn enough to support themselves. Opponents say that artificially increasing the price of labor actually causes a decrease in quantity demanded. In other words, individual employees will earn more, but companies will hire fewer of them. (See page 139 for more information on the debate over the minimum wage.)

Safety Laws

As you read in Chapter 3, the federal government created the Occupational Safety and Health Administration (OSHA) in 1970 to establish standards for safer working conditions. OSHA policies were issued in an effort to save lives, prevent injuries, and protect the health of workers in the private sector. All laws requiring certain minimum levels of safety also could have an impact on wages.

If a law or policy increases safety at work, it may also decrease wages because workers are willing to work for lower wages when jobs are safer. By holding down wages, the law lowers an employer's costs. Of course, the employer will usually have to spend money to comply with safety regulations, which may more than offset the employer's savings from any wage reduction.

Employers Respond to Wage Levels

Employers may also take actions to try to affect wage levels. For example, a company might try to cut labor costs by substituting machines for people. In other words, employers can replace human capital with physical capital.

Take furniture making, for example. In countries where labor is relatively cheap, furniture may be handmade by workers. In the United States, where labor is relatively expensive, manufacturers have substituted sophisticated machinery for more expensive human labor. Another increasingly common substitution involves customer service call centers, where automated answering services have replaced live telephone operators to direct incoming calls.

Background Notes

Robots and Productivity One of the ways employers are reducing labor costs is by substituting machines for human workers. The auto industry, in particular, is increasingly using robots to make cars. General Motors installed the first one in 1961, and the investment in robots throughout the industry has grown steadily and rapidly since then. During the first nine months of 2007, the auto industry invested over one-half billion dollars in robots. The reason why they are turning to robots is for increased productivity. In 2006, plants using robots assembled vehicles in an average of fewer than 16 hours with fewer employees than ever.

Answers

Graph Skills 1. Hispanic women. 2. Possible answer: greater educational opportunities, more marketable job skills, lack of language barrier

Checkpoint all women, African American men, Hispanic men

Other examples of substituting physical for human capital include automated teller machines (ATMs), which take the place of bank tellers, and mechanized assembly lines, which can eliminate the need for some manufacturing workers. These technological advances have greatly reduced the number of employees that banks and manufacturing companies hire.

Even if firms cannot use technology to replace labor, they may be able to reduce their labor costs in other ways. As you learned in Section 1, companies may outsource jobs to other parts of the world where labor is more plentiful, and therefore cheaper. They may also choose to hire temporary workers.

Unions

Workers who are unhappy with their wages also have several choices. In a competitive labor market, they might get higher-paying jobs from another employer. Some people change careers, either by choice or out of necessity. Although labor unions are becoming less of a force in the American economy, workers might decide to join a union and press for higher pay.

A **labor union** is an organization of workers that tries to improve working conditions, wages, and benefits for its members. One of the key goals of unions is to get wage increases for their members. As you will see in Section 3, unions allow workers to negotiate wage levels as a group rather than having to deal individually with employers. Their combined bargaining power is sometimes more effective at persuading employers to raise wages.

Nationally, union members do tend to earn higher wages than nonunion workers in similar jobs. In 2005, the average union wage was nearly $5 an hour higher than the average wage for nonunion wage earners. That amounts to a $200 difference in a 40-hour workweek.

Some economists argue that unions depress the wages of nonunion workers. They offer this reasoning:

1. Unions press employers to raise their members' wages.
2. When wages go up, the quantity of labor demanded goes down. Thus, the number of union jobs decreases.
3. As union jobs are cut, more workers are forced to seek nonunion jobs.
4. An increase in the supply of nonunion workers causes the wage rate for nonunion jobs to fall.

In addition, some unions have engaged in **featherbedding,** negotiating labor contracts that keep unnecessary workers on the company payroll. A notable example of this practice occurred in the railroad industry. In the early days of railroads, a "cabooseman" had to ride at the back of the train to operate a rear brake that stopped the train. Yet even after design

labor union an organization of workers that tries to improve working conditions, wages, and benefits for its members

featherbedding the practice of negotiating labor contracts that keep unnecessary workers on a company's payroll

Economics & YOU

Safety and Minimum Wage Laws

Many jobs teenagers hold are closely regulated by the federal government, which restricts hours and sets safety standards for workers under 18. ***It is against the law for teens to operate a forklift because of the dangers.***

Some jobs, like stocking produce, are well-suited for young workers and pay the minimum wage.

▲ Explain the relationship between safety and wage levels. ***Under what conditions might the teenager in the second picture not be allowed to work?***

EVALUATE

Guide a discussion of unions. Ask **Why do workers join unions?** *(to collectively work for higher wages, more benefits)* **What other options do workers have if they are not satisfied with their jobs?** *(change employers or careers)*

Have students restate the reasons some economists give to support the concept that unions depress the wages of nonunion workers. Draw an equilibrium graph to illustrate the arguments. Demonstrate how the wages demanded by unions reduce demand for workers and result in lower equilibrium wages.

Have students talk about their work experiences. Ask **Did you work for minimum wage? How many hours did you work weekly? Did you join a union?**

EXTEND

Have students research the issues of mandatory retirement and age discrimination. Then have them write a summary of their findings.

L2 Differentiate Explain that the Fair Labor Standards Act (FLSA) is a federal labor law passed to protect children and young people. Have students visit http://www.dol.gov/dol/topic/youthlabor/ and report on the purpose of this law and the extent of its protection for young people.

GUIDING QUESTION WRAP UP

Have students return to the section Guiding Question. Review the completed graphic organizer and clarify any misunderstandings. Have a wrap up discussion about why some people earn more than others.

Assess and Remediate

L3 L2 L4 Collect the "Wages and Skill Levels" worksheets and the "Minimum Wage and Poverty" worksheets and assess student understanding of the factors that affect wages.

L3 Assign the Section 2 Assessment questions; identify student misconceptions.

L3 Give Section Quiz A (Unit 3 All in-One, p. 73).

L2 Give Section Quiz B (Unit 3 All in-One, p. 74).

(Assess and Remediate continued on p. 234)

Answer

Economics & You Possible responses: if she was under a set age limit; if she was expected to do work that could cause injury, such as lifting crates; if there was a union and she was not a member.

Have students complete the Self-Test Online and continue their work in the **Essential Questions Journal**.

REMEDIATION AND SUGGESTIONS

Use the chart below to help students who are struggling with content.

WEAKNESS	REMEDIATION
Defining key terms (Questions 3, 4, 5, 6)	Have students use the interactive Economic Dictionary Online.
How supply and demand for labor affect wages (Questions 1, 3, 5, 7)	Reteach by having students skim the section, and then explain what is shown in Figures 9.6 and 9.7 in their own words.
How skill levels and education affect wages (Questions 1, 2, 6, 7)	Have students look at want ads and note salary and qualifications for two high-wage and two low-wage jobs. Have them identify the level of skill, experience, or education needed.
How laws against wage discrimination affect wages (Questions 1, 7)	Have students create a profile of two equally qualified people and identify the person most likely to get a job and why.
Other factors that affect wages (Questions 8, 9)	Have students work in pairs to review this section.

Answers

Caption: Possible answers: wages, benefits, payroll personnel, human resources personnel

Checkpoint substitute machines for people, outsource jobs, hire temporary workers

▲ Sometimes when companies invest in technology, the work performed by human labor becomes automated, such as a welder's job in an auto factory. ***What are some of the costs that are eliminated when a company replaces workers with machines?***

changes allowed the engineer at the front of the train to operate rear brakes, unions managed to keep caboosemen on the payroll. These workers received full wages and benefits for doing nothing.

People who support unions counter that without the ability to organize, workers have little power compared to that of employers. Unless workers join together, they say, employers can dictate wage levels and working conditions. Since they can usually find replacement workers, their employees might have little real choice. The next section will trace the history of unions in the United States and further describe their advantages and disadvantages.

CHECKPOINT ***What three actions can employers take to reduce the cost of wages?***

SECTION 2 ASSESSMENT

Essential Questions Journal To continue to build a response to the Essential Question, go to your **Essential Questions Journal.**

Guiding Question

1. Use your completed concept web to answer this question: Why do some people earn more than others?
2. **Extension** Consider one of four job skill levels: unskilled, semi-skilled, skilled, or professional. Identify one job in that category. Describe the education or training you would need for that skill level. Would it be in the higher or lower wage earning range?

Key Terms and Main Ideas

3. Why is the demand for labor called a **derived demand?**
4. If an advertising business buys new computers for its employees, how might its **productivity of labor** be affected?
5. What generally happens to the **equilibrium wage** when **(a)** demand for workers is low and supply is high, and **(b)** demand for workers is high and supply is low?
6. How does **skilled labor** differ from **professional labor?** Give an example of each.

Critical Thinking

7. **Compare** Choose two occupations, one that pays high wages and one that pays low wages. **(a)** Explain the reasons for the difference in wages in terms of supply and demand. **(b)** Are there any additional factors that could help explain the difference?
8. **Explain (a)** How do employers benefit from workplace safety laws? **(b)** How might such laws affect an employer with respect to employee lawsuits regarding safety?

Quick Write

9. Assume that a labor organizer is trying to get a union started in a local business and the local business is waging a campaign against unionization. Write a letter in support of the union or the business, in which you defend a pro- or anti-union position based on the principles of a free enterprise economy.

234 LABOR

Assessment Answers

1. supply and demand for labor, differences in skill levels and education, wage discrimination, minimum wage laws, safety laws, how employers respond to wage levels, unions
2. Possible answer: Skilled job: a heavy equipment operator requires training in how to operate heavy equipment. The skill would ensure a higher earning range.
3. The demand for labor is based on, or derived from, a demand for the service or product that the labor produces.
4. The computers would make it easier and faster for employees to do their work, thereby making them more productive.
5. (a) It gets lower. (b) It gets higher.
6. Skilled labor, such as auto mechanics, requires special training, needs little supervision, and usually earns an hourly wage. Professional labor, such as teachers, requires advanced skills and education, is usually white-collar, and is paid a salary.
7. (a) Possible answer: Retail clerks receive low wages and plumbers receive high wages. The supply of people able to work as clerks is high, reducing demand and wages. The supply of plumbers is limited, increasing demand and wages. Plumbing is also more of a necessity to modern life than are retail services. (b) Possible answer: Clerks require limited training and education; plumbers require much specialized training.
8. (a) More workers will do the work, increasing supply, which results in lower wages. (b) Possible answer: It might reduce lawsuits if the employer is complying with safety laws.
9. Answers will vary, but students should cite reasons from the text to support their position and follow the correct format for a business letter.

SECTION 3 Organized Labor

OBJECTIVES

1. **Describe** why American workers have formed labor unions.
2. **Summarize** the history of the labor movement in the United States.
3. **Analyze** reasons for the decline of the labor movement.
4. **Explain** how labor and management negotiate contracts.

ECONOMIC DICTIONARY

As you read the section, look for the definitions of these **Key Terms:**

- strike
- right-to-work law
- blue-collar worker
- white-collar worker
- collective bargaining
- mediation
- arbitration

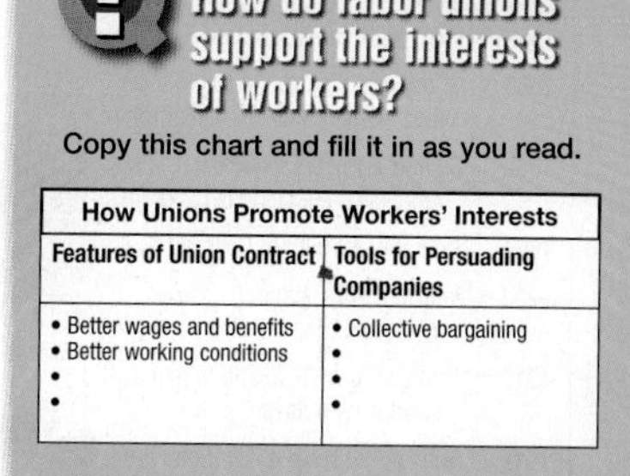
Guiding Question
How do labor unions support the interests of workers?

Copy this chart and fill it in as you read.

How Unions Promote Workers' Interests	
Features of Union Contract	Tools for Persuading Companies
• Better wages and benefits • Better working conditions • •	• Collective bargaining • • •

Economics and You What comes to mind when you think of Labor Day? Do you think of the holiday as summer's last hurrah—a final weekend spent frolicking at the beach or enjoying a summer picnic at the park before school gets underway? The origins of the holiday can be traced to 1882, when labor leader Peter J. McGuire suggested a day celebrating the American worker. On September 5, 1882, some 10,000 workers marched in New York City in a parade sponsored by a labor group called the Knights of Labor. Twelve years later, Congress made Labor Day a federal holiday to be spent any way workers wished, including going to the beach or a picnic at the park.

Principles in Action Labor unions support the interests of workers with respect to wages, benefits, and working conditions. They provide workers with the power of collective bargaining, which has proven to be an effective tool to extract concessions from employers. Shifts in the U.S. economy, however, have had a major impact on unions. The loss of manufacturing-sector jobs and the increased number of women in the workplace have been major factors contributing to the steep decline in union membership over the past 50 years.

Labor and Labor Unions

As you read in Section 2, wages are determined by the forces of supply and demand. Competition among firms keeps a worker's wages close to his or her level of productivity. In general, workers who command the highest wages are those with specialized skills and who are in short supply.

What about employees who feel that they are paid too little, work too many hours, or labor in unsafe conditions? What can these employees do? One option is to seek better wages and working conditions with a different employer. Many economists, in fact, argue that a competitive labor market helps prevent low pay and dangerous working conditions because workers will leave companies with these characteristics to work elsewhere.

Guiding Question

How do labor unions support the interests of workers?

Get Started

How Unions Promote Workers' Interests	
Features of Union Contract	Tools for Persuading Companies
• Better wages and benefits • Better working conditions • Job security	• Collective bargaining • Strikes

LESSON GOALS

Students will:

- Know the Key Terms.
- Understand the purposes and goals that spurred establishment of the first unions.
- Summarize the history of the labor movement.
- Describe one of the reasons for the decline of unions by completing a worksheet.
- Describe and then demonstrate the collective bargaining process.

BEFORE CLASS

Students should read the section for homework before coming to class.

Have students complete the graphic organizer in the Section Opener as they read the text. As an alternate activity, have students complete the Guided Reading and Review worksheet (Unit 3 All-in-One, p. 75).

L1 L2 ELL LPR Differentiate Have students complete the Guided Reading and Review worksheet (Unit 3 All-in-One, p. 76).

Focus on the Basics

Students need to come away with the following understandings:

FACTS: • Unions arose to help workers who were subject to poor working conditions and low wages. • Arguments used to discredit unions were that they supported outdated business practices and were linked with crime. • Unions use collective bargaining and strikes to win higher wages and better benefits for workers.

GENERALIZATION: Unions arose during the early days of the Industrial Revolution and fought to improve working conditions, wages, and benefits.

CLASSROOM HINTS

CONNECT TO THE NINETEENTH CENTURY

Show students pictures of nineteenth-century factory workers. Have students imagine that they are workers from that time. Ask them how they might regard the idea of organized labor. Would they support unionization? Would they participate in organizing a union? Would they participate in a strike? Call on volunteers to generalize on the early need for, and the dangers of, unionization.

BELLRINGER

Write the following list on the chalkboard (leave room to tally results) and instruct students to divide the list into those who, in their opinion, should have the right to strike and those who should not: bus drivers, store clerks, doctors, nurses, actors, teachers, factory workers, librarians, police officers, fire fighters, truck drivers, cafeteria workers. Tell them to be prepared to explain the general criteria they used to divide the list.

Teach

Economics online To present this topic using digital resources, use the lecture notes on www.PearsonSuccessNet.com.

DISCUSS THE BELLRINGER

Poll the results, having students raise their hands to indicate which category they think each should fall in. Choose the two jobs with the greatest agreement for and against being allowed to strike and discuss with students their general reasons for their views. Segue into a discussion of how and why workers have struggled for the right to strike.

REVIEW KEY EVENTS

Call on a student to explain what a *labor union* is. Then use Figure 9.11 to review the history of the U.S. labor movement. Ask **How would you summarize the main events of the first fifty years of unions?** *(Those years were characterized by the founding of different unions, legal conflicts, and strikes.)* **What was the significance of the Triangle Shirtwaist fire?** *(It spurred action to improve workplace safety.)* **How did the Wagner Act promote unions?** *(It made it legal to organize unions.)*

Answers

Checkpoint to seek higher wages, better working conditions, and more benefits

Chart Skills 1. Workers were feeling desperate and angry and also felt a new power to assert themselves. 2. As union membership grew, more laws were passed to support them.

Figure 9.11 Key Events in the U.S. Labor Movement

Year	Event
1869	Knights of Labor founded
1886	11 dead, 50 injured in Haymarket Riot, fueling anti-union sentiment
1886	Samuel Gompers founds the American Federation of Labor (AFL)
1894	Courts halt Pullman Railroad Strike
1900	International Ladies' Garment Workers Union (ILGWU) founded
1910	Strike by ILGWU wins pay gains, shorter workdays
1911	Triangle Shirtwaist Company fire spurs action on workplace safety
1919	Strikes raise fear of revolution
1919	John L. Lewis becomes president of United Mine Workers by leading a successful strike
1932	Norris-La Guardia Act outlaws "yellow-dog" contracts, gives other protection to unions
1935	Wagner Act gives workers right to organize
1938	Congress of Industrial Organizations (CIO), headed by John L. Lewis, splits from AFL
1938	Fair Labor Standards Act creates minimum wage and bans child labor
1940s	Union membership peaks at 35 percent
1947	Taft-Hartley Act allows states to pass right-to-work laws
1955	AFL and CIO merge to create AFL-CIO
1960s	Government employees begin to organize
1962	César Chávez begins organizing the first farmworkers' union, which eventually establishes the first labor agreement with growers
1970s	Rise in anti-union measures by employers
2000s	Increase in public-sector unions; decline in overall union membership

CHART SKILLS

The American labor movement had its roots in the 1800s, when the rise of factories led to difficult and dangerous working conditions.

1. Why do you think the early years of the labor movement were marked by violence?
2. Describe the relationship shown here between labor laws and union membership in the 1900s.

Many American workers have tried to gain some control over their wages and working conditions by forming labor unions. They reason that an individual worker does not have the power to change how an employer acts but that by banding together, workers can win gains from employers. Today, only about one out of eight workers in the United States belongs to a labor union. In the past, though, unions had a strong influence on the nation's economy. In order to understand the role of labor unions today, we will look at how labor unions rose to power.

CHECKPOINT ***Why do workers join labor unions?***

The Labor Movement

The union movement took shape over the course of more than a century. It faced many obstacles along the way, including violence and legal challenges from companies. **Figure 9.11** highlights some of the key events in the U.S. labor movement.

Workers in the 1800s

Labor unions arose largely in response to changes in working conditions brought by the Industrial Revolution in the early and mid-1800s. The spread of manufacturing in this period introduced factory work to the United States.

By today's standards, this work was not enviable. In garment factories, iron plants, and gunpowder mills, laborers worked 12- to 16-hour days, 7 days a week, for meager wages. Working conditions were poor. Men, women, and children as young as five years old operated machines so dangerous that many people lost fingers and limbs. Injured workers often lost their jobs.

Today, many firms try to retain their most skilled workers by treating them well. In 1855, however, that was hardly the case. One factory boss bluntly summarized his attitude toward workers:

> **"I regard people just as I regard my machinery. So long as they can do my work for what I choose to pay them, I keep them, getting out of them all I can."**
>
> —Manager of a textile mill in Fall River, Massachusetts, 1855

Differentiated Resources

L1 L2 Guided Reading and Review (Unit 3 All-in-One, p. 76)

L2 Taft-Hartley Act (Unit 3 All-in-One, p. 78)

L3 How Do We Bargain? (Simulation Activities, Chapter 9)

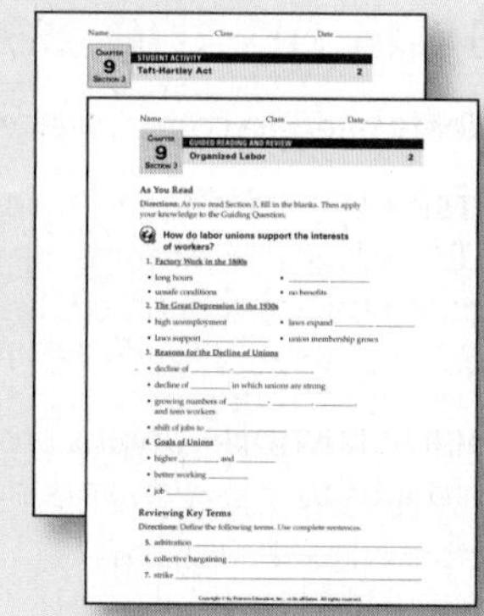

Innovators

Walter Reuther

"There is no greater calling than to serve your fellow men. There is no greater contribution than to help the weak."

Measured by his own words, Walter Reuther was a natural leader. Born to poor immigrant parents, Reuther had little formal education. But his upbringing fostered in him a sense of courage and conviction, which helped him fight for worker rights and become one of the greatest leaders in the American labor movement.

As a local union boss in the United Auto Workers, Reuther used sit-down strikes to help organize manufacturing plants. On May 26, 1937, Reuther and three colleagues clashed with Ford Motor Company security forces outside a plant in Detroit, Michigan. News reporters witnessed a bloodbath as Reuther and his friends were badly beaten. The incident caused public outrage against Ford and was a key factor in helping the UAW gain public sympathy and support for worker rights. It was a strategic victory.

Reuther went on to make the UAW a major labor force, eventually becoming its president in 1947. He was a pioneer. He was one of the first American labor organizers to successfully negotiate for benefits that American workers take for granted today: decent hourly wages, paid vacations, health insurance, and employer-paid pensions.

Critical Thinking: ***What impact did Reuther have on the costs of production (and the supply curve) of major American producers?***

Fast Facts

Walter Reuther
Born: September 1, 1907, in Wheeling, WV
Died: May 9, 1970
Education: Received H.S. diploma from Detroit City College at age 22
Claim to Fame: Early leader of the United Auto Workers union

Unions Take Hold

As early as the 1790s, whispers of worker discontent grew into organized protests. Skilled workers began to form unions to protect their interests. The chief tool of these early unions was the **strike,** an organized work stoppage intended to force an employer to address union demands. Employers responded by firing and replacing workers who tried to organize. Workers could not find help in the courts because the courts treated unions as illegal.

The man who started the United States labor movement was Samuel Gompers. The young cigarmaker rose within union ranks in New York City, focusing on three goals: higher wages, shorter hours, and safer work environments. In 1886, he founded the American Federation of Labor (AFL).

Employer Resistance

Attempts to unionize brought swift responses from employers. Viewing strikers as threats to free enterprise and social order, companies identified and fired union organizers. They forced workers to sign so-called yellow-dog contracts, in which workers promised not to join a union. (Yellow was slang for "coward.") Companies also used court orders called injunctions to force striking employees back to work. Some companies hired their own militias to harass union organizers or fight striking workers.

Congressional Protections

As the nation struggled through the Great Depression in the 1930s, Congress passed a number of measures that favored unions. The expansion of workers' rights in the 1930s contributed to a new rise in union strength. Membership grew, peaking in the 1940s at about 35 percent of the nation's non-farm workforce.

Unions became a dominant force in many industries. They controlled the day-to-day operations of activities from shipbuilding to garbage collection to steel production. Unions amassed billions of dollars in union dues to cover the costs of union activities including organizing, making political donations, and providing aid to striking workers.

✔ **CHECKPOINT** ***Why did union membership rise in the 1930s?***

strike an organized work stoppage intended to force an employer to address union demands

DISCUSS

Have students summarize the early years of labor movement. Ask **What was labor unions' chief tool in forcing employers to give workers what they wanted?** *(strikes)*

Be sure students understand that there were two sides to the labor struggles. Draw a T-chart on the board. Write *Union Views* at the top of the left column and *Employers' View* at the top of the right column. Have students give arguments each side might present.

L4 Differentiate Ask **Why do you think the courts regarded unions as illegal?** *(They interfered with business owners' right to run their business as they saw fit. They fostered civil unrest.)*

Have students describe the role Congress played in union organizing.

L1 L2 ELL Differentiate Review the history, causes, and effects of the Great Depression with students. Make sure that they understand the effect it had on the lives of working people. Help students understand why events of this period favored the growth of unions.

Virtual Economics

L4 Differentiate

Negotiating a Contract Use the following lesson from the NCEE **Virtual Economics *CD-ROM*** to enforce student understanding of the relationship of labor and management. Click on Browse Economics Lessons, specify grades 9–12, and use the key words *collective bargaining.*

In this activity, students will form labor and management teams to negotiate a contract.

LESSON TITLE	COLLECTIVE BARGAINING: A NEGOTIATION SIMULATION
Type of Activity	Simulation
Complexity	High
Time	250 minutes
NCEE Standards	13

Answers

Critical Thinking Reuther increased the power of organized labor, which in turn made demands that increased the costs of production. Employers had to pay higher wages and provide health insurance, vacations, and other benefits, which made the cost of production higher.

Checkpoint Congress passed laws benefiting unions.

DISCUSS

Discuss reasons for the decline of labor unions. Ask students how unions were able to preserve outdated and inefficient production methods. Ask **Do you think this policy was good for workers in the long term?**

Ask students if they think there is anything wrong with allowing workers to choose to join a union. Have students debate the issue based on their own ideas, textbook information, and their prior knowledge.

Point to Figure 9.12. Have volunteers describe what the graphs show. Discuss the questions.

Action Graph online Have students review the Action Graph animation for a step-by-step look at U.S. Economic Changes That Have Affected Unions.

DISTRIBUTE ACTIVITY WORKSHEET

Distribute the "Taft-Hartley Act Alive and Well" worksheet (Unit 3 All-in-One, p. 77). Explain terms and concepts such as injunction, 80-day cooling-off period, longshoremen, and job slowdown. Have students read the excerpt and answer the questions. Then, discuss students' answers as a class.

Name ______________ Class ______________ Date ________

Chapter 9 Section 3 — ANALYZING SOURCE READINGS IN ECONOMICS

Taft-Hartley Act Alive and Well 3

After World War II, the United States experienced a wave of labor union strikes, some of which involved industries that produced critical goods. In 1947, Congress passed the Taft-Hartley Act, giving the President the authority to prohibit for 80 days strikes in industries that affect public health or safety. In October 2002, President Bush used the act to end a 10-day shutdown of West Coast ports. ◆ *Read the excerpt and answer the questions that follow.*

The Bush administration took preliminary steps today toward seeking an injunction to reopen 29 West Coast ports, just hours after negotiations broke off between port operators and the longshoremen's union. . . .

Peter Hurtgen, the federal government's top mediator, said . . . that there was a good chance that Mr. Bush would reopen the ports by ordering an 80-day cooling-off period under the Taft-Hartley Act. . . .

"The country has been patient," [said Secretary of Labor Elaine Chao.] "But now ordinary Americans are being seriously harmed by this dispute. Factory workers are being laid off because they can't get vital parts delivered. These layoffs will only increase if the ports do not re-open. . . ."

. . . On Sunday, Sept. 29, the port operators announced an indefinitely long shutdown of the ports and locked out the West Coast's 10,500 longshoremen. The operators said the move was a response to a job slowdown by the workers. . . .

Officials with the International Longshore and Warehouse Union have urged the employers to end the shutdown and said the longshoremen were working more slowly because of safety concerns stemming from the deaths of five longshoremen this year.

Leaders of the longshoremen and other unions have denounced the idea of a cooling-off period, saying it would represent improper governmental meddling in the collective bargaining process. . . .

But business leaders warn that unless the president orders a cooling-off period, the economic damage could snowball. . . .

Robert Parry, president of the Federal Reserve Board of San Francisco, estimated that the port shutdown has cost the nation's economy about $2 billion each day.

The main issue in the dispute is management's demand to introduce new technology to speed cargo-handling. [This] plan would mean the loss of 400 positions, but [management] promised job security for all the longshoremen.

The union said it would not accept the new technology unless all the new jobs resulting from the new technology were within union jurisdiction.

Steven Greenhouse, "White House Moves to Intervene as Port Talks Break Off," *The New York Times*, October 7, 2002.

Questions to Think About

1. What issue was being negotiated between port owners and the union prior to the shutdown?
2. Why did the port operators shut down the ports? What reason did the union give for the longshoremen's actions before the shutdown?
3. What action was President Bush about to take? What did the union think about this?

L1 L2 ELL PLR Differentiate Distribute the "Taft-Hartley Act" worksheet (Unit 3 All-in-One, p. 78). Have pairs of students complete the worksheet.

right-to-work law a measure that bans mandatory union membership

blue-collar worker someone who performs manual labor, often in a manufacturing job, and who earns an hourly wage

Decline of the Labor Movement

As they grew, some unions began to abuse their power. Some sought to preserve outdated and inefficient production methods in order to protect jobs. As you read in Section 2, some unions managed to preserve job positions that were unnecessary—called "featherbedding"—in order to keep more members employed. As a result, companies that badly needed to improve efficiency to stay competitive found that unions could be an obstacle.

The reputation of unions suffered further because of their links to organized crime. Corrupt crime bosses gained a foothold in many local unions and used union funds to finance illegal operations.

"Right-to-Work" Laws

In an effort to curb union power, Congress passed the Taft-Hartley Act in 1947. This act allowed states to pass **right-to-work laws,** measures that ban mandatory union membership. Today, most right-to-work states are in the South, which has a lower level of union membership than other regions.

Right-to-work laws may be one of several reasons for a decline in union membership in recent decades. By 2005, union membership had dropped to about 8 percent of the labor force. Today, unionism in the United States is far more limited than in many other countries.

Loss of Traditional Strongholds

One theory suggests that structural changes in the U.S. economy have caused union membership to decline. The charts in **Figure 9.12** illustrate these influential economic trends. For example:

1. Unions have traditionally been strongest among **blue-collar workers.**

Figure 9.12 U.S. Economic Changes That Have Affected Unions

CHART SKILLS

These charts show changes in industry and in the labor force.

1. What is the change indicated by each of these charts?
2. How have each of these changes affected union membership?

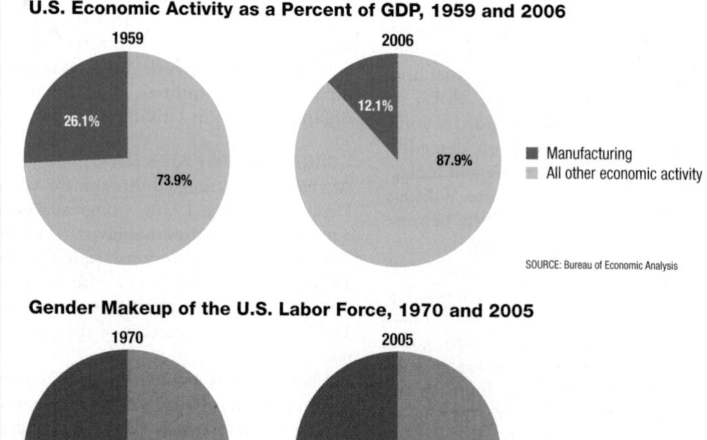

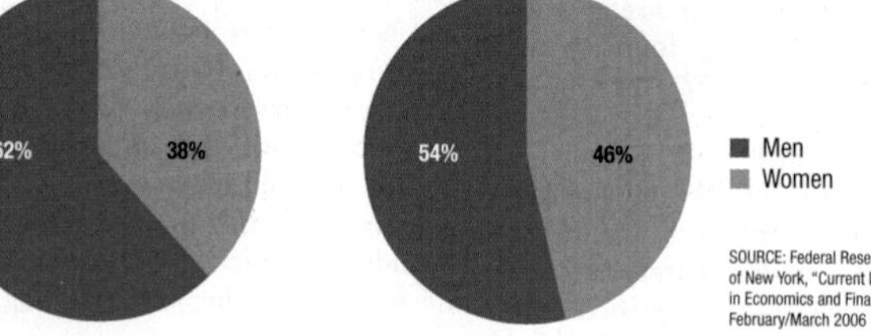

Action Graph online

For an animated version of this graph, visit **PearsonSuccessNet.com**

238 LABOR

Background Notes

The Decline of Unions Unions have been very strong in some industries that are now struggling, such as airlines and auto manufacturers. Past contracts created high salaries and huge pension programs. Today, many firms cannot afford to maintain these programs and remain competitive. The airline industry was deregulated in 1979, and new airlines with little overhead started up. The older airlines often have union contracts that add to their costs and make them less competitive. The auto industry faces similar problems.

Answers

Chart Skills 1. Top charts: manufacturing declined as a percentage of GDP by 14 percent between 1959 and 2006; bottom charts: the number of women in the labor market has increased by 10 percent. 2. Unions were strong in manufacturing, so with fewer of these jobs, union membership dropped. Women are less likely to join unions, and since they make up a larger portion of the labor force, union membership dropped.

These workers perform manual labor, often in a manufacturing job, and earn an hourly wage. The decline of manufacturing activity, shown in the top chart in **Figure 9.12**, has caused union jobs to disappear.

Unions are weakest among white-collar employees. A **white-collar worker** is someone in a professional or clerical job who usually earns a weekly salary.

While white-collar workers generally do not belong to unions, workers in the public sector are an exception. Unionization among government workers has increased in recent decades. This growth of union membership has partially made up for losses in the private sector. Some people object when public sector workers like teachers go on strike. Members of these unions argue that, just as in the private sector, these unions are needed to promote the interests of their workers.

2. Certain manufacturing industries, such as automobiles, steel, and textiles, have traditionally employed large numbers of union workers. These industries have been hurt by foreign competition in recent years. As a result, many industries have laid off union workers, which has cut into union strength. The graphs in **Figure 9.13** show that despite the fact that there has been only a relatively modest decline in the number of production workers (also a traditional source of union membership), the percentage of workers belonging to unions has continued to fall sharply.
3. The rising proportion of women in the labor force (see bottom chart in **Figure 9.12**) also has affected union membership, since women have been less likely to join unions.
4. Seeking to reduce their production costs, some industries have relocated from the Northeast and Midwest to the South, which has historically been less friendly to unions.

Lessened Need for Unions

Another theory for union decline is that other institutions now provide many of the services that had been won in the past through union activity. For example, the government has passed laws setting workplace safety standards and a shorter workweek. It provides unemployment insurance and Social Security. More non-unionized employers offer benefits such as medical insurance.

CHECKPOINT ***What are three explanations for the decline in union membership?***

white-collar worker someone who works in a professional or clerical job and who usually earns a weekly salary

Figure 9.13 Labor and Union Membership

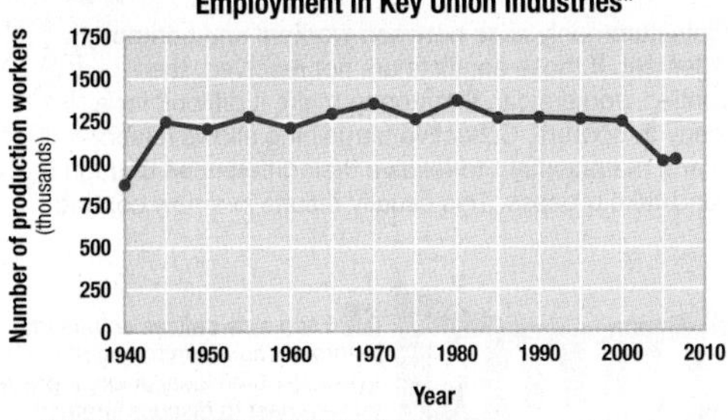

*companies producing manufacturing-related goods and services
SOURCE: Bureau of Labor Statistics

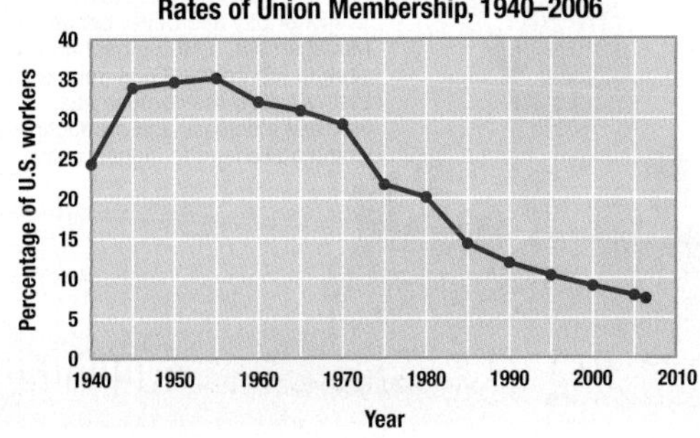

SOURCE: "Sluggish Institutions in a Dynamic World: Can Unions and Industrial Competition Coexist?," by Barry Hirsch and David MacPherson, *Journal of Economic Perspectives*, Fall 2007.

GRAPH SKILLS

These graphs show the rise and fall of union membership and the employment of production workers.

1. What was the peak of union membership?
2. What reasons might help explain why the rate of decline in union membership is greater than the rate of decline in production workers?

Action Graph online

For an animated version of this graph, visit **PearsonSuccessNet.com**

EXPLAIN GRAPHIC DATA

Refer students to Figure 9.13. Ask students what the graphs show. Have them read points on the graph and describe the trends indicated.

L1 L2 Differentiate Call on a student to read the title of the first graph and to explain what it shows. Explain that the first chart shows numbers of workers in thousands. Ask **How many production workers were there in 1945?** *(1,250,000)* **What does the second graph show?** *(percentage of U.S. workers who belong to unions)*

Action Graph online Have students review the Action Graph animation for a step-by-step look at Labor and Union Membership.

ASK

Display "Timeline of 2007 Writers Guild Strike" transparency (Color Transparencies, 9.a) and tell students that in November 2007, television and movie writers went on strike for higher wages and for a share of the profits from Internet and other media broadcasts of their work. They were represented by their union, the Writers Guild of America. The strike lasted 100 days and shut down the production of more than 60 television shows. Ask **How did this strike follow a common pattern of labor-management disputes? What leverage did the writers have over the studios? How did the studios show their strength? Why were there winners and losers on both sides?**

Answers

Graph Skills 1. The largest percentage of workers in unions occurred in 1955. The largest number of production workers in unions occurred in 1980.
2. Production workers have traditionally been unionized. However, production workers form a smaller segment of the total workforce now than they did in the past.

Checkpoint right-to-work laws, loss of traditional strongholds, lessened need for unions

DISCUSS

Have students use the How the Economy Works feature to review the collective bargaining process. Ask students to give examples of the goals a union might have in particular industries or businesses, such as the coal industry, a department store, or a construction company and how that might lead to a conflict with management. Ask students why a strike or a lockout is undesirable on all sides.

PERSONAL FINANCE ACTIVITY

Remind students that they can increase their understanding of wages and benefits by reading the lesson "Understanding your Paycheck" on pages PF44–45 in the Personal Finance Handbook and completing the worksheet (Personal Finance All-in-One, pp. 107–108).

L3 Differentiate For alternative or additional practice with the process of collective bargaining, have students use the "How Do We Bargain?" activity (Simulation Activities, Chapter 9). Students will take part in a role-playing game about compromise and negotiation in collective bargaining.

How the Economy Works

How can collective bargaining settle differences?

Conflicts commonly arise between workers and company management. If those conflicts are not resolved, then disgruntled workers can threaten to make it difficult for a company to operate. Collective bargaining allows a labor union and management to resolve their differences through a give-and-take process. This usually results in a new contract.

1 Each side defines an agenda before sitting down to negotiate. In the case of the local union, representatives meet to discuss strategy and concessions they wish to get from management. These contract disputes usually involve issues such as higher pay and better benefits. Management, on the other hand, will seek to win concessions from labor that will allow the company to increase efficiency and production, which could lead to higher profits.

2 Union leaders hold a series of negotiating sessions with management. Both sides list and explain their needs. To agree on a new contract, discussions revolve around strategies to satisfy those needs in ways that are beneficial for all.

Negotiations

Simulation Activity

How Do We Bargain?
You may be asked to take part in a role-playing game about compromise and negotiation in collective bargaining.

FUTURE WATCH

Personal Finance
For more information on wages and benefits, see your Personal Finance Handbook in the back of the book or visit **PearsonSuccessNet.com**

collective bargaining the process in which union and company management meet to negotiate a new labor contract

Labor and Management

A union gains the right to represent workers at a company when a majority of workers in a particular work unit, such as a factory, vote to accept the union. After that, the company is required by law to bargain with the union in good faith to negotiate an employment contract.

Collective Bargaining

Picture a room and, on each side of a table, a team of lawyers and trained negotiators determined to get what they want—or at least part of it. This is **collective bargaining,** the process in which union and company management meet to negotiate a new labor contract.

Union contracts generally last two to five years and can cover hundreds of issues. The resulting contract spells out each side's rights and responsibilities for the length of the agreement.

Generally the union comes to the bargaining table with certain goals that set the agenda for collective bargaining talks. Let's examine those goals.

- ***Wages and Benefits.*** The union negotiates on behalf of all members for wage rates, overtime rates, planned raises, and benefits. In seeking higher wages, the union is aware that if wages go too high, the company may lay off workers to reduce costs.
- ***Working Conditions.*** Safety, comfort, worker responsibilities, and many other workplace issues are negotiated and written into the final contract.
- ***Job Security.*** One of the union's primary goals is to secure its members' jobs, so the contract spells out the conditions under which a worker may be fired. If a union member is discharged for reasons that the

How the Economy Works online

For an animated, interactive version of this feature, visit **PearsonSuccessNet.com**

3 Sometimes one side will decide it can't budge on one or more of its goals. For example, a union might believe that workers' pay is too low. Management decides it will compromise on job security and working conditions but will not yield on pay, because profits are down.

4 If neither side concedes, negotiations break off. This can lead to one of several possible scenarios:

1. Both sides can agree to enter into mediation, where a neutral third party can help them settle their differences.
2. Workers can vote to go on strike.
3. Management can lock out workers.

5 Labor and management generally don't benefit from a prolonged work stoppage. Both sides often come back to the collective bargaining process to reach a new contract.

Check Your Understanding

1. Identify two actions that can lead to a work stoppage.
2. Why do you think both labor and management reach a point where they are willing to compromise?

Conflict Arises — **Deal or No Deal**

union believes to be in violation of the contract, the union might file a grievance, or formal complaint. The union contract specifies how such grievances are handled. The procedure usually involves hearings by a committee of union and company representatives.

Strikes

When a contract is about to expire, or when the union is negotiating its first agreement with a company, the negotiators can wind up in tough late-night bargaining sessions. Most of the time, the parties manage to reach an agreement. But when a deadlock occurs, tensions escalate.

The union may ask its members to vote to approve a strike. A strike is the union's ultimate weapon. A strike, particularly a lengthy one, can cripple a company. Some firms can continue to function by using managers to perform key tasks. They may hire workers who do not belong to the union, called "strikebreakers." If a company can withstand a strike, it is in a good bargaining position. Most firms, however, cannot produce goods and services without their union workers.

A long strike can also be devastating to workers, since they do not get paid while they are not working. Many unions do make some payments to their members during a strike, funded by the dues the union has collected. These payments can help workers, but they are generally much smaller than what the members would have earned while working.

It may seem as though workers strike frequently since strikes are often front-page news when they do occur. In fact, the collective bargaining process usually goes

EXTEND

Ask students to research labor unions and find out how they are organized. Ask them to identify five jobs that people in a labor union might have, including a leadership position. Ask them to write a description of the qualities that a union leader would need to have. You may wish students to begin by visiting the Web site of one or more unions to read their statements of purpose.

L1 ELL Differentiate Have visual learners create an editorial cartoon expressing their point of view about the need for unions today.

GUIDING QUESTION WRAP UP

Have students return to the section Guiding Question. Review the completed graphic organizer and clarify any misunderstandings. Have a wrap-up discussion about how labor unions support the interests of workers.

Assess and Remediate

L3 L2 Collect the "Taft-Hartley Act Alive and Well" worksheets and the "Taft-Hartley Act" worksheets and assess student understanding of organized labor.

L3 Assign the Section 3 Assessment questions; identify student misconceptions.

L3 Give Section Quiz A (Unit 3 All-in-One, p. 79).

L2 Give Section Quiz B (Unit 3 All-in-One, p. 80).

(Assess and Remediate continued on p. 242)

Background Note

Labor Strikes Strikes are not always successful. One of the most costly strikes in U.S. history occurred in 1934 when 400,000 members of the United Textile Workers of America (UTWA) went on strike for better wages and working conditions. Most of the workers were in the South where unions were especially weak. Local governments and other unions did not provide support. Gradually, many workers went back to work and the union achieved none of its goals. Many workers were blacklisted and never returned to the mills. Union power was broken in the South and union organizing took 40 years to recover.

Answers

How the Economy Works 1. Workers can go on strike; managers can lock out workers. 2. Both suffer losses: workers don't get paid during a strike and business loses profits.

Have students complete the Self-Test Online and continue their work in the **Essential Questions Journal**.

REMEDIATION AND SUGGESTIONS

Use the chart below to help students who are struggling with content.

WEAKNESS	REMEDIATION
Defining key terms (Questions 3, 4, 5, 6, 7)	Have students use the interactive Economic Dictionary Online.
The purpose and goals of unions (Questions 1, 2, 3, 4, 6, 7)	Reteach by having students skim the section and name the purposes and goals discussed.
History of labor unions (Questions 2, 8, 11)	Have students create a timeline and insert key events in labor history.
Controversies with labor unions (Questions 4, 8, 9, 10)	Have students review the reasons for and against labor unions. Put a plus sign on one side of the room and a minus sign on the other. Have students find one argument for or against labor unions and stand under the appropriate sign. Call on students to explain the reason they represent.

Answers

Caption Union members have always seen management as unprincipled and greedy.

Checkpoint wages and benefits, working conditions, job security

For many striking workers, the rat is a symbol used to protest unfair work conditions and publicize that a business is using nonunion labor. ***Why might this symbol be seen as an example of the historical relationship between unions and management?*** ▶

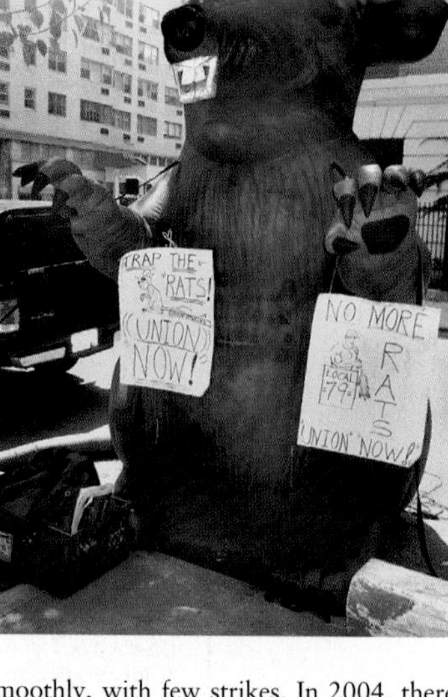

mediation a settlement technique in which a neutral person, the mediator, meets with each side to try to find a solution that both sides will accept

arbitration a settlement technique in which a neutral third party listens to both sides and then imposes a decision that is legally binding for both the company and the union

smoothly, with few strikes. In 2004, there were only 22 major strikes across the entire nation, involving about 100,000 workers. This number represents only a small fraction of the nation's workforce, however.

Outside Help Reaching Settlements

If a strike continues for a long time, the two sides sometimes call in a third party to help settle the dispute. They might agree to **mediation,** a settlement technique in which a neutral person, the mediator, meets with each side to try to find a solution that both sides will accept. A mediator often can help each side understand the other's concerns, leading to an agreement.

However, the decision reached by the mediator is nonbinding—that is, neither side is required to accept it. If either side rejects the mediator's decision, the dispute could continue indefinitely. Sometimes, the talks will end up in **arbitration.** In this settlement technique, a neutral third party listens to both sides and then imposes a decision. Since the company's management and the union had agreed to enter the arbitration stage, the decision is legally binding for both sides. It can be a risky step because the decision might be seen as more favorable to one side than the other.

CHECKPOINT ***What issues are addressed in collective bargaining?***

SECTION 3 ASSESSMENT

Essential Questions Journal To continue to build a response to the Essential Question, go to your **Essential Questions Journal.**

Guiding Question

1. Use your completed chart to answer this question: How do labor unions support the interests of workers?
2. **Extension** Name two benefits workers take for granted now that did not exist before labor organized.

Key Terms and Main Ideas

3. What is the purpose of a **strike?**
4. How do **right-to-work laws** diminish union power?
5. How do **blue-collar workers** and **white-collar workers** differ in the types of work they perform? Give examples of each.
6. What is **collective bargaining?** Who usually sets the agenda for it?
7. In working toward a strike settlement, the two sides seek **mediation** and sometimes **arbitration.** How do the two techniques differ?

Critical Thinking

8. **Compare** What is the difference between the need for labor unions now and in the 1800s?
9. **Decide** Some manufacturing companies have been moving their factories to countries where nonunion labor is cheap. They say they do this to reduce costs and compete with foreign companies. United States unions have opposed the cuts in U.S. jobs, insisting that companies must care for their workers. Which side would you support if you were **(a)** a union worker, **(b)** a consumer, **(c)** an investor in the company? Explain your reasoning for each response.
10. **Reflect** Today, some white-collar professionals such as teachers and doctors belong to labor unions. **(a)** Do you think this is a good idea? Why or why not? **(b)** If you were to become a white-collar professional, would you want the support of a union? Explain.

Math Skills

11. **Drawing a Line Graph** The table below details the number of members in the United Auto Workers Union (UAW) in different years. **(a)** Construct a line graph from the data. Then, compare the graph to **Figure 9.13** on page 239. **(b)** What conclusions about the U.S. labor movement can you make from this comparison?

Visit PearsonSuccessNet.com for additional math help.

United Auto Workers

Years	Members
1979	1,527,858
1983	1,100,000
1987	1,000,000
1991	810,000
1995	780,000
1999	760,000
2003	638,722
2007	464,910

SOURCE: Department of Labor, Office of Labor Management Standards, LM Filings and "UAW membership hits post-WWII low" by David Shepardson, *Detroit News*, March 28, 2008.

Assessment Answers

1. They use collective bargaining and strikes to try to improve wages, benefits, working conditions, and job security for workers.
2. Possible answer: 8-hour day, pensions
3. to force management to accept union conditions
4. If workers don't join a union, unions are less able to influence management.
5. Blue-collar workers do manual labor and earn an hourly wage; white-collar workers do professional work and earn a salary.
6. the process by which management and the union negotiate a new labor contract; the union's goals
7. Mediation uses a neutral person to meet with each side to seek a solution. Arbitration uses a neutral person to hear each party and then to make a binding decision.
8. In the 1800s, workers had lower wages, fewer benefits, worked in more dangerous conditions for much longer hours. Now they have higher wages, many benefits, work fewer hours in safer conditions.
9. Possible answers: (a) keep jobs at home so I keep my job (b) move jobs overseas so goods will be cheaper (c) move jobs overseas so I make more profit.
10. Possible answers: (a) No; they already have good working conditions, wages, benefits, and job security. Yes; unions make sure that management honors the terms of their contract. (b) No because I have special skills that make me valuable.
11. (a) Students' graphs should show the years on the horizontal axis and membership on the vertical axis. The line graph should decline. (b) The union membership in 2007 was less than one third of its 1979 membership. This union's decline in membership was steeper than the decline of production workers in general, whose 2006 membership increased.

QUICK STUDY GUIDE

Chapter 9: Labor

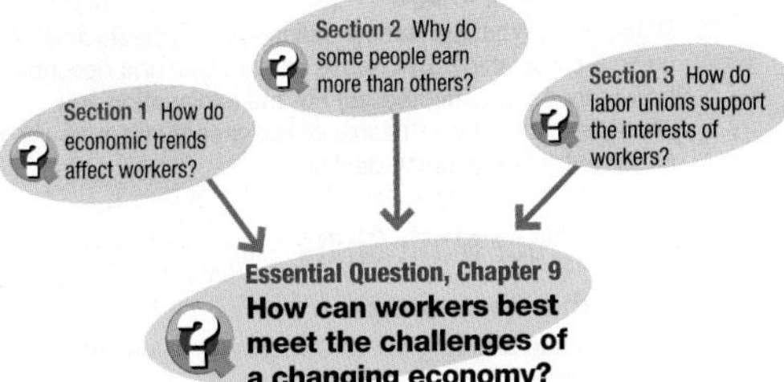
Section 1 How do economic trends affect workers?
Section 2 Why do some people earn more than others?
Section 3 How do labor unions support the interests of workers?
Essential Question, Chapter 9
How can workers best meet the challenges of a changing economy?

Trends in U.S. Labor

Occupational
• Overall shift from manufacturing to service sector jobs • More women in the workplace • More reliance on part-time and temporary workers • Unskilled workers face competition from foreign workers • Increased demand for educated workforce
Wages and Benefits
• General decline in wage levels • Rise in benefits • Minorities earning lower pay • Increased regulation of wages • Increase in safety laws
Decline of Unions
• Taft-Hartley Act spurs decline of labor unions • Loss of manufacturing jobs erodes membership • Public sector unions on the rise • Government provides traditional union services • More white-collar workers

Economic Dictionary

Economics on the go

Study anytime, anywhere. Download these files today.

Economic Dictionary online	Audio Review online	Action Graph online	Visual Glossary online	How the Economy Works online
Vocabulary Support in English and Spanish	Audio Study Guide in English and Spanish	Animated Charts and Graphs	Animated feature	Animated feature

Download to your computer or mobile device at PearsonSuccessNet.com

ASSIGN THE ESSENTIAL QUESTIONS JOURNAL

After students have finished studying the chapter, they should return to the chapter's essential question in the Essential Questions Journal and complete the activity.

Tell students to go back to the chapter opener and look at the image. Using information they have gained from studying the chapter, ask **How does this illustrate the main ideas of the chapter?** *(Possible answer: increasing the value of their human capital through education and learning new skills; learning about technology)*

STUDY TIPS

Tell students that studying in groups can be more effective than studying alone. They should aim for groups of three to five people, with one person serving as leader to keep the group focused on studying. Plan on short study sessions—thirty minutes to an hour—instead of long "cram" sessions—and emphasize discussing ideas, connections between ideas, and "why?" questions rather than specific facts, although some drill is okay.

Economics on the go Have students download the digital resources available at Economics on the Go for review and remediation.

Assessment at a Glance

TESTS AND QUIZZES

Section Assessments

Section Quizzes A and B, **Unit 3 All-in-One**

Self-Test Online

Chapter Assessments

Chapter Tests A and B, **Unit 3 All-in-One**

Economic Detective, **Unit 3 All-in-One**

Document-based Assessment, p. 245

Exam*View*

AYP Monitoring Assessments

PERFORMANCE ASSESSMENT

Teacher's Edition, pp. 218, 222, 224, 229, 232, 238

Simulation Activities, Chapter 9

Virtual Economics on CD-ROM, pp. 219, 229, 237

Essential Questions Journal, Chapter 9

Assessment Rubrics

Chapter 9 Assessment

1. (a) to save money: wages and overall costs are less in some other countries (b) U.S. companies are also hiring offshore skilled workers, such as engineers and programmers. (c) get training in jobs that are still being done in the United States
2. (a) lower wages and greater competition (b) They do work Americans won't do, and companies can charge less for these goods and services. (c) Possible answer: Congress wants to protect U.S. workers but also wants to protect businesses and consumers.
3. (a) They replace workers with machines. (b) Welders in factories are replaced by robot welders. (c) Workers will find fewer of these jobs; they will have to train for new jobs that still exist.
4. (a) when negotiations have been long and union members are suffering; when management is likely not to accept a compromise unless it is binding (b) when the company is losing a lot of money because of the strike; when the union is powerful and will not accept a compromise unless it is binding (c) when all other possibilities have been exhausted; when the differences are not extreme
5. White-collar workers often have higher wages and better benefits than blue-collar workers. White-collar workers include a lot of managers.
6. (a) right to work laws, loss of traditional union strongholds, lessened need for unions (b) Lessened need for unions: other institutions provide services unions once did. For example, the government sets workplace safety standards and ensures shorter workweek. (c) Possible answer: Unions would be duplicating these efforts, so workers have less interest in joining.
7. management and professional; about 1 percent
8. service: 37%; sales and office: 18%; construction, maintenance, natural resources: 35%; production, transportation: 30%
9. construction, maintenance, natural resources
10. Possible response: The supply is high and skill requirements are low, so nonunion workers have little bargaining power.
11. Organize students into pairs or small groups in which students can brainstorm about their interests and potential careers. Check students' worksheets before they move on to modify the activity.
12. Answers will vary. Students should analyze their career choices and evaluate how these choices can prepare them to meet the global challenges listed.

CHAPTER 9 ASSESSMENT

Self-Test online To test your understanding of key terms and main ideas, visit **PearsonSuccessNet.com**

Key Terms and Main Ideas

To make sure you understand the key terms and main ideas of this chapter, review the Checkpoint and Section Assessment questions and look at the Quick Study Guide on the preceding page.

Critical Thinking

1. **Decide (a)** Why do companies engage in offshoring? **(b)** How has offshoring led to the loss of factory jobs and jobs for highly skilled workers? **(c)** Suppose you are a worker and your job has been cut due to offshoring. What options would you have?
2. **Generalize (a)** Identify the negative impact some analysts say foreign-born workers have on the domestic workforce. **(b)** Identify the positive impact foreign-born workers have on the domestic workforce as noted by other analysts. **(c)** Why do you think that the U.S. Congress struggles with immigration reform?
3. **Predicting Consequences (a)** What does it mean for employers to replace human capital with physical capital? **(b)** Give examples of this trend. **(c)** How might this trend affect the workforce in the future?
4. **Describe (a)** Under what circumstances might it be in the best interest of workers to seek arbitration in order to settle contract negotiations? **(b)** Under what circumstances might management prefer that a contract dispute be settled in arbitration? **(c)** Under what circumstances might arbitration be favorable to both labor and management?
5. **Interpret** Why do think that white-collar workers generally do not belong to unions?
6. **Discuss (a)** What are three explanations for the decline in union membership? **(b)** Choose one of these and describe how workers are affected. **(c)** For the explanation you chose, explain why you agree or disagree that it is an important factor in union decline.

Applying Your Math Skills

Finding the Percentage

Look at the chart showing full-time wages for union and nonunion members.

Visit PearsonSuccessNet.com for additional math help.

Weekly Wage for Full-Time Workers 16 Years and Older, 2006

Occupations	Union	Nonunion
Management, Professional	966	968
Service	638	404
Sales and Office	706	578
Construction, Maintenance, Natural Resources	934	608
Production, Transportation	741	519

SOURCE: Bureau of Labor Statistics

7. For which occupation do nonunion members have higher weekly wages? What percentage of change in wages is there for nonunion workers?
8. Express as a percentage the increase in wages for the remaining union members over those of nonunion members.
9. Which industry shows the greatest increase in wages for union members?
10. Why do you think that is so?

Essential Question Activity

Essential Questions Journal To respond to the chapter Essential Question, go to your **Essential Questions Journal.**

11. People who have successful careers know that their success depends on being able to plan ahead. Preparation helps to overcome setbacks, such as a job layoff, or if new technology makes skills obsolete. It also helps to be ready in case you start a family and need to have a job that helps meet your financial needs. Complete the activity to answer the Essential Question **How can workers best meet the challenges of a changing economy?** Think about the kind of careers that interest you the most. Identify your interests and potential careers using the worksheet in the Essential Questions Journal or the electronic worksheet available at **PearsonSuccessNet.com.**
12. **Modify** Review your completed career worksheet. Then research trends in the U.S. and global economy that will have an impact on your future career.
    The trends listed below are seen by many economists as posing some of the greatest challenges for workers in the future.
    - Climate Change
    - Global Trade
    - Speed of Technological Change
    - Rise of Megacities
    - Shifts in World Populations
    - Genetic Engineering

    Explain how your career choices will prepare you to meet those challenges.

244 LABOR

WebQuest online The Economics WebQuest challenges students to use 21st century skills to answer the Essential Question.

THE ESSENTIAL
VIDEO
By Students For Students
For videos on Essential Questions, go to PearsonSuccessNet.com

Remind students to continue to develop an Essentials Questions video. Guidelines and a production binder are available at www.PearsonSuccessNet.com.

DOCUMENT-BASED ASSESSMENT

Should public sector employees have the right to strike?

Public sector workers in many nations have the right to form unions, engage in collective bargaining, and go on strike. The story, however, is much different in the United States. State and federal laws often place restrictions on the ability of public employees to form unions, negotiate contracts, and walk off the job. Government officials cite the need to protect the public interest. In turn, supporters of public workers cite the need to receive fair wages and benefits, and establish safe working conditions, just like workers in the private sector.

Document A

In 1990 the Louisiana Supreme Court ruled that "public sector employees are covered by the state's 'Little Norris LaGuardia Act' which protects 'all employees in the exercise of their right to engage in concerted activities.' The court rejected the ... argument that public employee strikes are illegal under common law (since Louisiana is not a common law state) and found that the state constitution gives public employees 'the same right to engage in collective bargaining as held by their counterparts in the private sector. Except for police strikes which by their nature endanger the public, public employee strikes are legal as long as they don't pose danger to public health and safety.'"

From "Public Employment in a Time of Transition"
By John Lund & Cheryl L. Maranto

Document B

"New York City Mayor Michael Bloomberg lashed out at union leaders for 'thuggishly' turning their backs on the city, vowing there would be no further contract negotiations until the strike (by the Metropolitan Transit Workers) ends. 'You can't break the law and use that as a negotiating tactic,' he said at an afternoon news conference. "This is unconscionable, he added.... The strike brought to a grinding halt all Metropolitan Transportation Authority buses and subways throughout the city.... City officials have said a transit strike could cost the city $440 million to $660 million a day.... Bloomberg said the strike affects everything from the restaurant and hotel industries to working-class New Yorkers who could lose their jobs as a result of the strike.... 'The economic consequences of the strike range from severe to devastating, depending on the business,' he said."

From CNN.com, December 20, 2005

Document C

Number of States with Strike Policies

	Police & Firefighters	State workers	Education workers	Municipal workers
Allowed without restriction	2	3	3	3
Allowed with minor restrictions	1	8	9	9
Prohibited, no penalty specified	10	6	4	7
Prohibited, penalties specified	22	14	19	14
Total states with strike policy	35	31	35	33

SOURCE: "Public Employment in a Time of Transition" by John Lund & Cheryl L. Maranto

ANALYZING DOCUMENTS

Use your knowledge of labor unions and Documents A, B, and C to answer questions 1–3.

1. **According to Document A, why did the Louisiana Supreme Court support public workers' right to strike?**
   - **A.** Public workers, like police officers, are not essential to public safety.
   - **B.** Public workers are covered under the state's "Little Norris LaGuardia Act."
   - **C.** Public workers cannot engage in collective bargaining.
   - **D.** The state's common laws allow it.
2. **What is the main point of Document B?**
   - **A.** The transit workers' strike is illegal because union leaders are thugs.
   - **B.** Mayor Bloomberg isn't going to negotiate with union leaders even if many New Yorkers end up losing their jobs.
   - **C.** Mayor Bloomberg will not negotiate with workers because their strike is illegal.
   - **D.** Transit workers are not suffering like other New Yorkers.
3. **Document C shows that**
   - **A.** Only a few states allow strikes by public workers.
   - **B.** Thirty-five states allow education employees to strike.
   - **C.** Fourteen states allow municipal workers to strike without penalty.
   - **D.** Most states do not allow strikes without some restrictions.

WRITING ABOUT ECONOMICS

The right of public employees to strike is of serious concern because of the necessity of their work. Use the documents on this page and resources on the Web site below to answer the question: ***Should public sector employees have the right to strike?*** Use the sources to support your opinion.

In Partnership

To read more about issues related to this topic, visit **PearsonSuccessNet.com**

Document-Based Assessment

ANALYZING DOCUMENTS

1. B
2. C
3. D

WRITING ABOUT ECONOMICS

Possible answers: Reason public sector employees should have the right to strike: these employees have the same need as private sector employees for fair wages and safe working conditions; they should not have the right to strike: the needs of the public must be protected, strikes by public sector workers can have serious economic consequences.

Student essay should demonstrate an understanding of the issues involved in the debate over whether public sector employees have the right to strike. Use the following as guidelines to assess the essay.

L2 Differentiate Students use all documents on the page to support their thesis.

L3 Differentiate Students use the documents on this page and additional information available online at www.PearsonSuccessNet.com to support their answer.

L4 Differentiate Students incorporate information provided in the textbook and online at www.PearsonSuccessNet.com and include additional research to support their opinion.

Go Online to www.PearsonSuccessNet.com for a student rubric and extra documents.

Economics online *All print resources are available on the Teacher's Resource Library CD-ROM and online at* www.PearsonSuccessNet.com.

Essential Question

How can businesses and labor best achieve their goals?

BELLRINGER

Ask students to read the paragraph under the Essential Question. Then have volunteers suggest examples of how businesses and labor might best achieve their goals.

DISCUSS

Have students review the quotations on the page. Ask students to explain the goals of businesses and labor. **Why are jobs requiring non-routine thinking skills growing?** *(Possible answer: Less-skilled jobs are frequently sent overseas.)* **What costs might a community suffer from the self-protecting decisions of a company?** *(Possible answer: Multinational corporations might exploit local workers.)* **What costs might someone suffer from the self-protecting decisions of a labor union?** *(Possible answer: An increase in union wages could result in lower wages for nonunion workers.)*

L2 Differentiate Have students go through the documents and list unfamiliar words to look up in a dictionary. Then pair students with more proficient readers to summarize the main points of each reading.

ANALYZE A CARTOON

Have students silently read the cartoon's caption. Have them work in small groups to discuss how a business's goals might conflict with a labor union's goals. Ask each group to brainstorm solutions to these issues. Invite volunteers to share their ideas with the class.

BULLETIN BOARD ACTIVITY

Have students revisit the Unit Essential Question articles that they have posted as they have studied the chapters. Have them discuss the relevance of the articles to the question and whether their opinions have changed since they first read the article. Remind students to review their work in their **Essential Questions Journal**.

EXTEND

Have students complete their work on the Essential Questions Video and present their work to the class.

L4 Differentiate Organize students into two groups. Have them debate the following statement: Labor unions are the most effective way for workers to achieve their goals. Review the Debate strategy (p. T27) with students and distribute the debate worksheets at Online Teacher Center at PearsonSuccessNet.com.

Unit 3 Challenge

Essential Question, Unit 3

How can businesses and labor best achieve their goals?

VIDEO — The Essential Question — By Students For Students. For videos on Essential Questions, go to *PearsonSuccessNet.com*

There are differing views on how business and labor can achieve their goals. Look at the opinions below, keeping in mind the Essential Question: How can businesses and labor best achieve their goals?

"Slower labor force growth will encourage employers to [encourage] greater labor force participation among women, the elderly, and people with disabilities.... Rapid technological change and increased international competition spotlight the need for the workforce to be able to adapt to changing technologies and shifting product demand. Shifts in the nature of business organizations and the growing importance of knowledge-based work also favor strong non-routine [thinking] skills, such as abstract reasoning, problem-solving, communication, and collaboration."

—Lynn Karoly and Constantijn Panis, Rand Corporation

"I think the low road is where somebody thinks of only their immediate self-interest in solving their particular problem no matter what it costs to somebody else. Which means you'll have an owner of a company that'll make money...by destroying the community. I think you can have a labor union that...has a problem of protecting wages, jobs of its own members even at the expense of a regional development strategy."

—Dan Swinney, Center for Labor and Community Research, Interview, 2005

"Gentlemen, nothing stands in the way of a final accord except that management wants profit maximization and the union wants moola."

Essential Question Writing Activity

Consider the different views of economics expressed in the sources on this page and what you have learned about the needs of business and labor. ***Then write a well-constructed essay expressing your view of how business and labor can meet their goals.***

Writing Guidelines

- Address all aspects of the Essential Question Writing Activity.
- Support the theme with relevant facts, examples, and details.
- Use a logical and clear plan of organization.
- Introduce the theme by establishing a framework that is beyond a simple restatement of the question and conclude with a summation of the theme.

For help in writing a Persuasive Essay, refer to the *Writer's Handbook* in the Reference section, page S-5.

Essential Questions Journal

To respond to the unit Essential Question, go to your **Essential Questions Journal**.

Essential Question Writing Activity

Before students begin the writing activity, remind them to skim through the unit chapters to read the headings on each page. Have them read through any notes they took and to review their chapter assessments and chapter projects.

Students should write a two-paragraph article. Paragraph one should outline how businesses can best achieve their goals. Paragraph two should explain how workers can best achieve their goals.

L2 Differentiate Students should write a paragraph that explains how *either* business *or* labor can best achieve its goals, providing detailed examples.

L4 Differentiate Students should write a three-paragraph article using relevant examples of how businesses and labor can meet their goals.

Before students begin work, distribute the Writing Assessment rubric, available at the Online Teacher Center at PearsonSuccessNet.com.

UNIT 4 Money, Banking, and Finance

Chapter 10 **Money and Banking**

Chapter 11 **Financial Markets**

Essential Question, Unit 4

How can you make the most of your money?

Chapter 10 How well do financial institutions serve our needs?

Chapter 11 How do your saving and investment choices affect your future?

Online Resources

Economics Online Teacher Center at PearsonSuccessNet.com includes

- Online Teacher's Edition with lesson planner
- Online Lecture Notes
- Teacher's Resource Library with All-in-One Resources, Color Transparencies, Simulation Activities, and Adequate Yearly Progress Monitoring
- SuccessTracker Assessment

Economics Online Student Center at PearsonSuccessNet.com includes

- Interactive textbook with audio
- Economics Video
- WebQuests
- Interactivities
- Student Self-Tests

 **Essential Question**

How can you make the most of your money?

Introduce the Unit

ACTIVATE PRIOR KNOWLEDGE

Essential questions frame each unit and chapter of study, asking students to consider big ideas about economics. Write the Unit Essential Question on the Board: **How can you make the most of your money?** Using the Think-Write-Pair-Share strategy (p. T24), have students brainstorm answers.

WRITING ACTIVITY

To begin this unit, assign the Unit 4 Warmup Activity in the **Essential Questions Journal**. This will help students start to consider their position on the Unit 4 Essential Question: **How can you make the most of your money?**

Use the **Essential Questions Journal** throughout the program to help students consider these and other big ideas about economics.

BULLETIN BOARD ACTIVITY

Post the Unit Essential Question on a bulletin board. Tell students that they will be learning about how they can make the most of their money. Ask them to bring in articles about current events to help them answer the question. Students should identify their article and use a sticky note to briefly explain the connection to the Essential Question.

CREATING THE ESSENTIAL QUESTIONS VIDEO

Preview the Unit Challenge on page 304. Consider assigning this activity to your students. Tell them that they will be creating their own video to explore this question, and that they should keep this in mind as they study the ways they can handle their money. For further information about how to complete this activity, go to PearsonSucessNet.com.

NATIONAL COUNCIL ON ECONOMIC EDUCATION

The following Voluntary National Content Standards in Economics are addressed in this unit:

★ **Standard 10** ★ **Standard 12**

★ **Standard 11**

For a complete description of the standards addressed in each chapter, see the Correlations chart on pages T52–T55.

 **Essential Questions**

UNIT 4:

How can you make the most of your money?

CHAPTER 10:

How well do financial institutions serve our needs?

Introduce the Chapter

ACTIVATE PRIOR KNOWLEDGE

In this chapter, students will learn about money and banking. Tell students to complete the warmup activity in the **Essential Questions Journal**.

DIFFERENTIATED INSTRUCTION KEY

- **L1** Special Needs
- **L2** Basic
  - **ELL** English Language Learners
  - **LPR** Less Proficient Readers
- **L3** All Students
- **L4** Advanced Students

Economics online Visit www.PearsonSuccessNet.com for an interactive textbook with built-in activities on economic principles.

- ***The Wall Street Journal* Classroom Edition Video** presents a current topic related to financial institutions.
- **Yearly Update Worksheet** provides an annual update, including a new worksheet and lesson on this topic.
- **On the Go** resources can be downloaded so students and teachers can connect with economics anytime, anywhere.

Chapter 10 Money and Banking

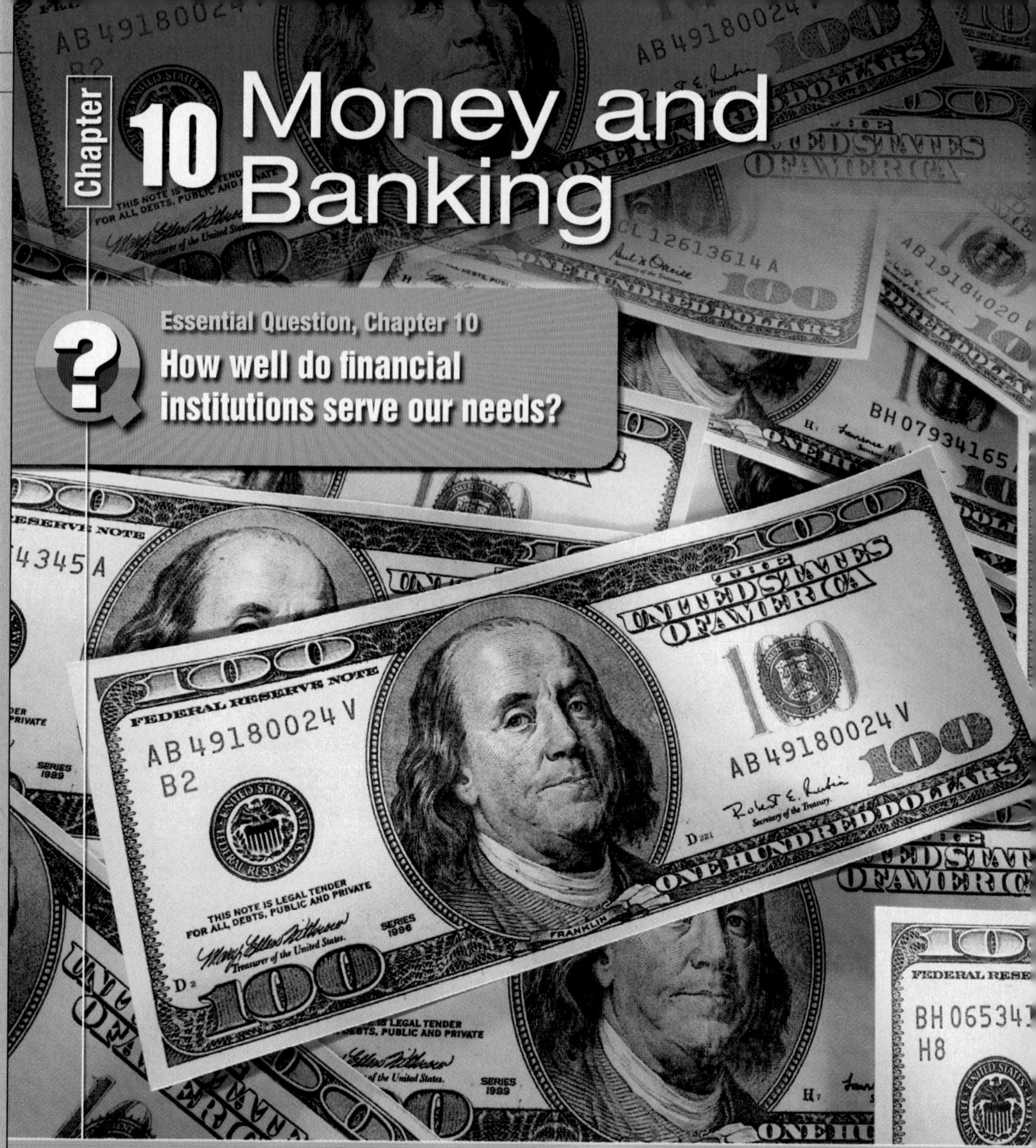

Essential Question, Chapter 10

How well do financial institutions serve our needs?

- **Section 1:** Money
- **Section 2:** The History of American Banking
- **Section 3:** Banking Today

Economics on the go

To study anywhere, anytime, download these online resources at ***PearsonSuccessNet.com*** ▶

ECONOMICS ONLINE

DIGITAL TEACHER TOOLS

The online lesson planner is designed to help teachers plan, teach, and assess. Teachers have the ability to use or customize existing Pearson lesson plans. Online lecture notes support the print lesson by providing an array of accessible activities and summaries of key concepts.

Two interactivities in this lesson are:

- **Visual Glossary** An online tool that helps define the functions of money.
- **WebQuest** Students use the tools of the Internet to explore the question, "How well do financial institutions serve our needs?"

Block Scheduling

BLOCK 1 Teach Section 1. Have students participate in the "Use of Money" simulation activity. End with students working on the group research projects.

BLOCK 2 Begin with the Bellringer for Section 2. Complete Section 2, eliminating the Extend option, and then complete Section 3.

Pressed for Time

Outline Have students create an outline of Section 1. Discuss the terms. For Section 2, have students refer to the text to explain the timeline in Figure 10.1. For Section 3, have students analyze and explain the components of the money supply shown in Figure 10.2 and how banking works, as shown in Figure 10.4. Have students include the banking functions.

SECTION 1 Money

OBJECTIVES

1. **Describe** the three uses of money.
2. **List** the six characteristics of money.
3. **Analyze** the sources of money's value.

ECONOMIC DICTIONARY

As you read the section, look for the definitions of these **Key Terms:**

- money
- medium of exchange
- barter
- unit of account
- store of value
- currency
- commodity money
- representative money
- specie
- fiat money

Guiding Question
How does money serve the needs of our society?

Copy this concept web and fill it in as you read.

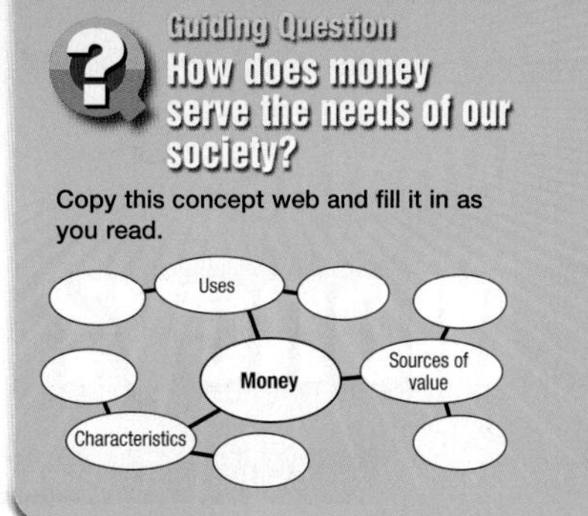

Economics and You It's been a hot day, and you have just arrived at your neighborhood store after playing basketball. You grab a soda and search the pockets of your jeans for some money. You find a pen, keys, and a chewing gum wrapper, but, unfortunately, no money. Then you reach into your jacket pocket. Finally!—a crumpled dollar bill. You hand the money to the clerk and take a long, cold drink.

Principles in Action Money, like the dollar you used to buy the soda, serves the needs of individuals and society in many ways. It provides a means for comparing values of goods and services, and it serves as a store of value. Without it, we can't get the things we need and want. That's not the whole story of money, as you will see. In fact, money has functions and characteristics that you might never have thought about.

money anything that serves as a medium of exchange, a unit of account, and a store of value

The Three Uses of Money

If you were asked to define money, you would probably think of the coins and bills in your wallet. Economists define money in terms of its three uses. To an economist, **money** is anything that serves as a medium of exchange, a unit of account, and a store of value.

medium of exchange anything that is used to determine value during the exchange of goods and services

Money as a Medium of Exchange

A **medium of exchange** is anything that is used to determine value during the exchange of goods and services. Without money, people acquire goods and services through **barter,** or the direct exchange of one set of

barter the direct exchange of one set of goods or services for another

Visual Glossary online
Go to the Visual Glossary Online for an interactive review of **money.**

Action Graph online
Go to Action Graph Online for animated versions of key charts and graphs.

How the Economy Works online
Go to How the Economy Works Online for an interactive lesson on **what happens when you put money in the bank.**

Guiding Question

How does money serve the needs of our society?

Get Started

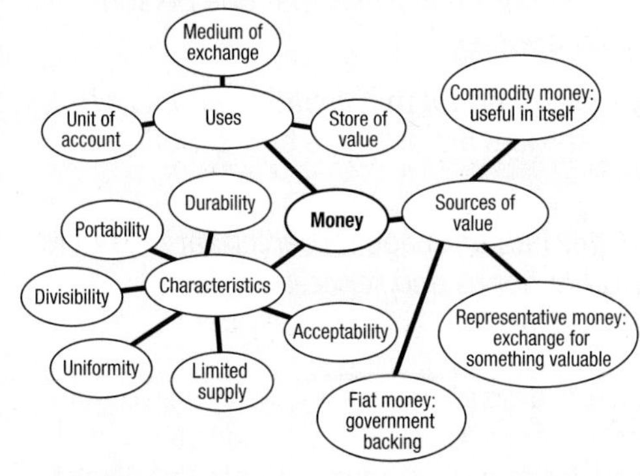

LESSON GOALS

Students will:

- Know the Key Terms.
- Demonstrate an understanding of the uses of money by comparing using money with barter.
- Evaluate how a commodity fits the characteristics of money and describe the source of its value.

BEFORE CLASS

Students should read the section for homework before coming to class.

Have students complete the graphic organizer in the Section Opener as they read the text. As an alternate activity, have students complete the Guided Reading and Review worksheet (Unit 4 All-in-One, p. 13).

L1 L2 ELL LPR Differentiate Have students complete the Guided Reading and Review worksheet (Unit 4 All-in-One, p. 14).

Focus on the Basics

Students need to come away with the following understandings:

FACTS: • Money is anything that serves as a medium of exchange, a unit of account, and a store of value. • Money has six characteristics: durability, portability, divisibility, uniformity, limited supply, and acceptability. • Money's value is determined by commodities, real or represented, or is backed by the government. • The three types of money are commodity money, representative money, and fiat money.

GENERALIZATION: Money provides a means for comparing the value of goods and services and facilitates the exchange of goods and services.

CLASSROOM HINTS

FIAT MONEY—FEDERAL RESERVE NOTES

While students have used money, they may not have paid much attention to what's written on it. Have students look at a Federal Reserve note. Ask **What information on the note tells you that this is fiat money?** *(the text which reads "This note is legal tender for all debts, public and private")* Explain the meaning of *tender.* Students can learn more about the other information and symbols that appear on currency by using the U.S. Department of the Treasury Web site.

Teach Visual Glossary

REVIEW KEY TERMS

Pair students and have them write two sentences about how each key term relates to money.

goods – *physical objects that someone produces*

services – *actions or activities that one person performs for another*

scarcity – *the principal that limited amounts of goods and services are available to meet unlimited wants*

capital – *any human-made resource that is used to produce other goods and services*

DISCUSS

Have students describe what they see in the pictures using the key terms. Help students understand the three functions of money using prompts. Ask **What does it mean to exchange something?** Tell students to make a list of words related to exchange. Ask **What does the word *account* in "unit of account" mean?** Think of the phrase "to account for." It means to keep track of. Think about ways you use numbers to keep track of things you own. Ask **What can be used to store or hold value?** Think about the word *storage*, to put something away for a long time. You can't store something that doesn't last. In the same way, things that are not durable are not good stores of value.

L1 L2 Differentiate Use the lesson on the Visual Glossary page to review this term. As an alternate activity, direct students to the Visual Glossary Online to reinforce their understanding of money.

Economics online *All print resources are available on the Teacher's Resource Library CD-ROM and online at* www.PearsonSuccessNet.com.

Answers

Chart Possible responses: Money can be used to buy goods such as groceries. Having a unit, such as a dollar, allows us to compare the prices of similar goods. Money can be saved and exchanged for goods at a later time.

Photo Possible response: The feather coil is a way to store money. It can be made and kept until it is needed for a marriage ceremony.

VISUAL GLOSSARY

Reviewing Key Terms
To understand *money*, review these terms:

goods, *p. 3*
services, *p. 3*
scarcity, *p. 4*
capital, *p. 6*

What is Money?

◄ **money** anything that serves as a medium of exchange, a unit of account, and a store of value

THE THREE FUNCTIONS OF MONEY

Medium of Exchange	Unit of Account	Store of Value

Money serves as a medium of exchange, a unit of account, and a store of value. ***How does each illustration represent functions of money?***

◄ Money is essential to easy exchanges of property. This coil of feathers was used by people on the Santa Cruz Islands in the Pacific Ocean as payment at marriage ceremonies. ***How does it represent one of the three functions of money?***

Visual Glossary online
To expand your understanding of this and other key economic terms, visit **PearsonSuccessNet.com**

goods or services for another. Barter is still used in many parts of the world, especially in traditional economies in Asia, Africa, and Latin America. It is also sometimes used informally in the United States. For example, a person might agree to mow a neighbor's lawn in exchange for vegetables from the neighbor's garden. In general, however, as an economy becomes more specialized, it becomes too difficult to establish the relative value of items to be bartered.

To appreciate how much easier money makes exchanges, suppose that money did not exist, and that you wanted to trade your portable DVD player for a spanking new mountain bike. You probably would have a great deal of trouble making the exchange. First, you would need to find a person who wanted to both sell the model of mountain bike you want and buy your particular DVD player. Second, this person would need to agree that your DVD player is worth the same as his or her bike. As you might guess, people in barter economies spend a great deal of time and effort exchanging the goods they have for the goods they need and want. That's why barter generally works well only in small, traditional economies. In those small economies, people can devote much of their time to exchanging goods.

Now consider how much easier your transaction would be if you used money as a medium of exchange. All you would have to do is find someone who is willing to pay you $100 for your DVD player. Then you could use that money to buy a mountain bike from someone else. The person selling you the bike could use the $100 however he or she wished. By the same token, the person who pays $100 for your DVD player could raise that money however he or she wished. Because money makes exchanges so much easier, people have been using it for thousands of years.

Money as a Unit of Account

In addition to serving as a medium of exchange, money serves as a **unit of account.** That is, money provides a means for comparing the values of goods and services. For example, suppose you see a jacket on sale for $30. You know this is a good price because you have checked the price of the same or similar jackets in other stores. You can compare the cost of the jacket in this store with the cost in other stores because the price is expressed in the same way in every store in the United States—in terms of dollars and cents. Similarly, you would expect seeing a movie in a theater to cost about $8.00, a new DVD rental about $3.50, and so forth.

Other countries have their own forms of money that serve as units of account. The Japanese quote prices in terms of yen, the Russians in terms of rubles, Mexicans in terms of pesos, and so forth.

Money as a Store of Value

Money also serves as a **store of value.** This means that money keeps its value if you decide to hold on to—or store—it instead of spending it. For example, when you sell your DVD player to purchase a mountain bike, you may not have a chance to purchase a bike right away. In the meantime, you can keep the money in your wallet or in a bank. The money will still be valuable and will be recognized as a medium of exchange weeks or months from now when you go to buy the bike.

Money serves as a good store of value with one important exception. Sometimes economies experience a period of rapid inflation, or a general increase in prices. For example, suppose the United States experienced 10-percent inflation during a particular year. If you sold your DVD player at the beginning of that year for $100, the money you received would have 10 percent less value, or buying power, at the end of the year. Inflation would have caused the price of the mountain bike to increase by 10 percent during the year, to $110. The $100 you received at the beginning of the year would no longer be enough to buy the bike.

In short, when an economy experiences inflation, money does not function as well as a store of value. You will read more about the causes and effects of inflation in Chapter 13.

✔ ***CHECKPOINT** Under what circumstance does money not serve as a good store of value?*

Simulation *Activity*

Use of Money
You may be asked to take part in a role-playing game about alternatives to printed money.

unit of account a means for comparing the values of goods and services

store of value something that keeps its value if it is stored rather than spent

BELLRINGER

Write the following "advertisement" on the board:

> **FOR SALE OR BARTER**
> Kittens! Adorable 6-week-olds.
> Make your best offer!

Have students write down how much cash they would be willing to pay for a kitten. Then, have them write down one or more goods or services they would be willing to trade for a kitten.

Teach

Economics online To present this topic using digital resources, use the lecture notes on www.PearsonSuccessNet.com.

L1 L2 ELL LPR Differentiate To help students who are struggling readers, assign the Vocabulary worksheet (Unit 4 All-in-One, p. 12).

DISTRIBUTE ACTIVITY WORKSHEET

Call on volunteers to read their cash and barter offers out loud. Ask students how they measured the value of the kitten against the value of what they offered. Have students describe any difficulties they may have had in deciding what to offer.

Next, display the "Trading Goods or Using Money" transparency (Color Transparencies, 10.a). Distribute the "Trading Goods or Using Money" worksheet (Unit 4 All-in-One, p. 15). Tell students to describe the transactions on the transparency and fill in the Venn diagram on the worksheet, indicating what the transactions have in common and what is unique to each transaction.

L1 L2 Differentiate Distribute the "Trading Goods or Using Money" worksheet (Unit 4 All-in-One, p. 16), and have students answer the questions. Check students' answers.

L3 Differentiate For alternative or additional practice with the concept of using money, have students use the "Use of Money" activity (Simulation Activities, Chapter 10). Students will perform transactions and then evaluate the effectiveness of the medium of exchange.

Differentiated Resources

- **L1 L2 Guided Reading and Review** (Unit 4 All-in-One, p. 14)
- **L1 L2 Vocabulary worksheet** (Unit 4 All-in-One, p. 12)
- **L2 Trading Goods or Using Money** (Unit 4 All-in-One, p. 16)
- **L3 Use of Money** (Simulation Activities, Chapter 10)

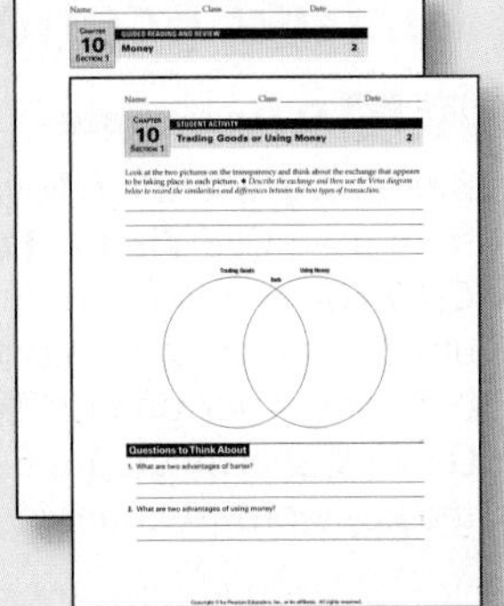

Answer

Checkpoint Money is not a good store of value during a time of high inflation.

APPLY

Discuss the characteristics of money.

Draw a chart on the board with 7 columns and 8 rows. Label the columns as follows: *Currency, Durability, Portability, Divisibility, Uniformity, Limited Supply, Acceptability.* In the first column list the following currencies: cattle, wampum (shell beads), gold coins, olive oil, salt, dried fish, precious stones, grains.

Have students rate each characteristic of each currency on a scale of 0–5, with 5 being the highest. Ask **Which currency do you think would work best as a medium of exchange?** *(wampum or coins, because they are portable and divisible)* Have students explain their choices based on the chart and their ratings. Ask **Which currency is best as a store of value?** *(coins or precious stones, because they are very durable and have very limited supply)*

L4 Differentiate Choose one of the currencies in the chart and research how people have used it as money in the past.

Answer

Caption durability, limited supply, acceptability

▲ Without the portability, divisibility, and uniformity of our currency, sharing a restaurant bill would be very complicated. ***What other characteristics are essential to a sound currency?***

The Six Characteristics of Money

The coins and paper bills used as money are called **currency.** In the past, societies have also used an astoundingly wide range of other objects as currency. Cattle, salt, dried fish, furs, precious stones, gold, and silver have all served as currency at various times in various places. So have porpoise teeth, rice, wheat, seashells, tulip bulbs, and olive oil.

These items all worked well in the societies in which they were used. None of them, however, would function very well in our economy today. Each lacks at least one of the six characteristics that economists use to judge how well an item serves as currency. These six characteristics are durability, portability, divisibility, uniformity, limited supply, and acceptability.

currency coins and paper bills used as money

Durability

Objects used as money must withstand the physical wear and tear that comes with being used over and over again. If money wears out or is easily destroyed, it cannot be trusted to serve as a store of value.

Unlike wheat or olive oil, coins last for many years. In fact, some collectors have ancient Roman coins that are more than 2,000 years old. Although our paper money may not seem very durable, its rag (cloth) content helps $1 bills typically last at least a year in circulation. When paper bills wear out, the United States government can easily replace them.

Portability

People need to be able to take money with them as they go about their daily business. They also must be able to transfer money easily from one person to another when they use money for purchases. Paper money and coins are very portable, or easy to carry, because they are small and light.

Divisibility

To be useful, money must be easily divided into smaller denominations, or units of value. When money is divisible, people can use only as much of it as necessary for any exchange. In the sixteenth and seventeenth centuries, people actually used parts of coins to pay exact amounts for their purchases. Spanish dollars, widely circulated in the American colonies, were often cut into as many as eight "bits," or pieces. For this reason these coins came to be called "pieces of eight."

Today, of course, if you use a $20 bill to pay for a $5 lunch, the cashier will not rip your bill into four pieces in order to make change. That's because American currency, like currencies around the world, consists of various denominations—$5 bills, $10 bills, and so on.

Uniformity

Any two units of money must be uniform—that is, the same—in terms of what they will buy. In other words, people must be able to count and measure money accurately.

Suppose everything were priced in terms of dried fish. One small dried fish might buy an apple. One large dried fish might buy a sandwich. This method of pricing is not a very accurate way of establishing the standard value of products, because the size of a dried fish can vary. Picture the arguments people would have when trying to agree whether a fish was small or large. A dollar bill, however, always buys $1 worth of goods.

Virtual Economics

L1 L2 Differentiate

Bartering Use the following lesson from the NCEE **Virtual Economics *CD-ROM*** to reinforce student understanding of the concept of bartering. Click on Browse Economics Lessons, specify grades 6–8, and use the key words *exchanging goods.*

In this activity, students will take part in a simple simulation to demonstrate bartering as a market tool.

LESSON TITLE	**EXCHANGING GOODS AND SERVICES**
Type of Activity	Simulation
Complexity	Low
Time	50 minutes
NCEE Standards	11

Limited Supply

Suppose a society uses certain pebbles as money. These rare pebbles have been found only on one beach. One day, however, someone finds an enormous supply of similar pebbles on a different beach. Now anyone can scoop up these pebbles by the handful. Since these pebbles are no longer in limited supply, they are no longer useful as currency.

In the United States, the Federal Reserve System controls the supply of money in circulation. By its actions, the Federal Reserve is able to keep just the right amount of money available. You'll read more about how the Federal Reserve monitors and adjusts the money supply in Chapter 16.

Acceptability

Finally, everyone in an economy must be able to take the objects that serve as money and exchange them for goods and services. When you go to the store, why does the person behind the counter accept your money in exchange for a carton of milk or a box of pencils? After all, money is just pieces of metal or paper. Your money is accepted because the owner of the store can spend it elsewhere to buy something he or she needs or wants.

In the United States, we expect that other people in the country will continue to accept paper money and coins in exchange for our purchases. If people suddenly lost confidence in our currency's value, they would no longer be willing to sell goods and services in return for dollars.

CHECKPOINT ***Why would gold cease to be a good form of currency if scientists could create gold out of sand?***

Sources of Money's Value

Think about the bills and coins in your pocket. They are durable and portable. They are also easily divisible, uniform, in limited supply, and accepted throughout the country. As convenient and practical as they may be, however, bills and coins have very little value in and of themselves. What, then, makes money valuable? The answer is that there are actually several possible sources of money's value, depending on whether it is commodity money, representative money, or fiat money.

Americans used both commodity and representative money during the colonial period. Representative money was used until 1913, when the first Federal Reserve notes were issued. ***What are some advantages of fiat money over commodity and representative money?*** ▼

Sources of Money's Value

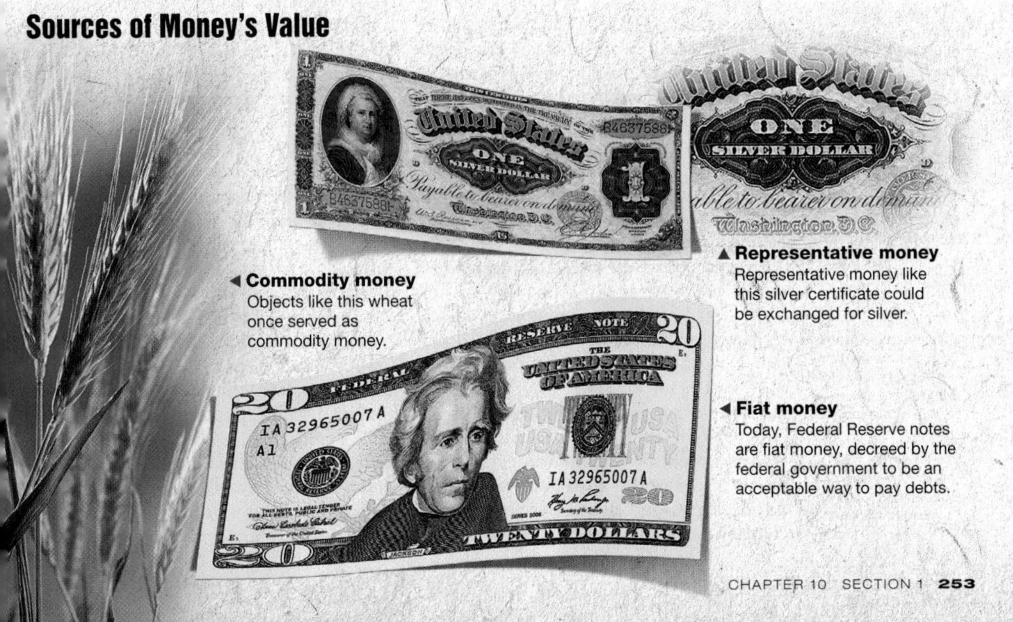

◀ **Commodity money**
Objects like this wheat once served as commodity money.

▲ **Representative money**
Representative money like this silver certificate could be exchanged for silver.

◀ **Fiat money**
Today, Federal Reserve notes are fiat money, decreed by the federal government to be an acceptable way to pay debts.

INTRODUCE THE ACTIVITY

Write the following list on the board: cattle, dried corn, diamonds, shells, beaver pelts, iron nails, cacao beans, tobacco leaves, cigarettes, gold, silver, olive oil, salt, wheat, wampum, wine, copper, ivory, ochre, barrels of meat. Distribute the "Commodity Money" worksheet (Unit 4 All-in-One, p. 17). Tell students that each of these commodities has been used as money in the past. Assign a different commodity to each pair of students and have them complete the worksheet for that commodity. Have students do research on their commodity as needed. Their findings can be shared with the class as a poster or as a written or oral report.

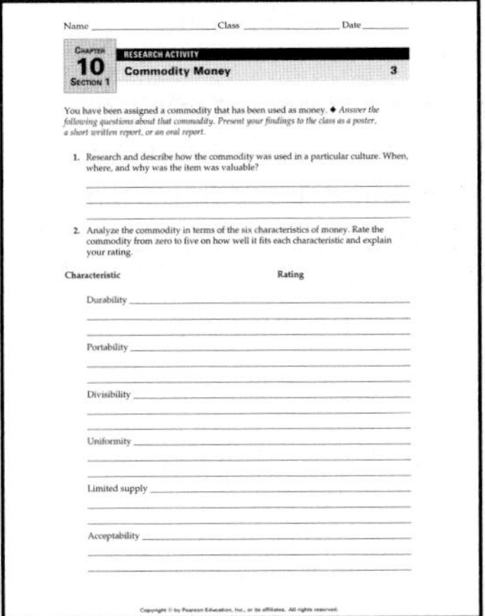

Name ________ Class ________ Date ________

CHAPTER 10 SECTION 1 — RESEARCH ACTIVITY
Commodity Money 3

You have been assigned a commodity that has been used as money. ◆ *Answer the following questions about that commodity. Present your findings to the class as a poster, a short written report, or an oral report.*

1. Research and describe how the commodity was used in a particular culture. When, where, and why was the item was valuable?

2. Analyze the commodity in terms of the six characteristics of money. Rate the commodity from zero to five on how well it fits each characteristic and explain your rating.

Characteristic **Rating**

Durability ________
Portability ________
Divisibility ________
Uniformity ________
Limited supply ________
Acceptability ________

COMPARE

Call students attention to the illustration "Sources of Money's Value" on this page. Ask students, **Why is commodity money valuable?** *(It is an item that has value in itself.)* **Why is representative money valuable?** *(It can be exchanged for something that has value in itself.)* **Why is fiat money valuable?** *(Because the government says it has value.)* Discuss the advantages and disadvantages of each type.

Answers

Checkpoint Gold would no longer be in limited supply.

Caption Possible response: With fiat money, goods do not need to be moved constantly, as with commodity money. With fiat money, the government does not need to keep a large supply of whatever is represented by the representative money, such as silver or gold.

ANALYZE

Ask students to look at the cartoon on this page. Have students describe the action and the commodity being used. Ask **Why does the frog fail to fit into any of the three acceptable sources of value?** *(It is not valuable in itself, it can't be exchanged for something valuable, and the government has not declared that it can be used as money.)* Ask **Under what circumstances might a frog be an acceptable form of money?** *(Possible answers: if frogs served an economic function in a society, such as a main source of food; if the government declared that frogs were acceptable as payment for all debts.)* Have them compare this transaction to a barter transaction.

RETURN TO WORKSHEET

Ask students to review their "Trading Goods or Using Money" worksheet and to add information that they have learned so far. Ask them to then write a paragraph in which they choose one of the transactions on Transparency 10.a, and explain how people have used that type of transaction.

EXTEND

Divide the class into small groups. Assign each group a different reason for buying items, such as preparing a meal or getting reading for school. Then have each group create a role play to show how people would get the necessary items using barter, commodity money, and representative or fiat money.

L4 Differentiate Have students create a monetary system using a commodity good of their choice. They can create a visual or role play to show the class.

GUIDING QUESTION WRAP UP

Have students return to the section Guiding Question. Review the completed graphic organizer and clarify any misunderstandings. Have a wrap up discussion about how money serves society's needs.

Assess and Remediate

L3 L2 Collect the "Trading Goods or Using Money" worksheets and the "Commodity Money" worksheet and assess student understanding.

L3 Assign the Section 1 Assessment questions; identify student misconceptions.

L3 Give Section Quiz A (Unit 4 All-in-One, p. 18).

L2 Give Section Quiz B (Unit 4 All-in-One, p. 19).

(Assess and Remediate continued on p. 255)

Answer

Caption Possible response: Cattle live longer, have more useful parts, more people would want them.

© 2004, Mike Twohy.
M2Ecomics@aol.com
cartoonistgroup.com
"Sorry. Cash only."

▲ To be useful as commodity money, the commodity has to have some value. ***Why are cattle more useful as commodity money than the frog?***

Commodity Money

A commodity is an object. **Commodity money** consists of objects that have value in and of themselves and that are also used as money. For example, various societies have used salt, cattle, and precious stones as commodity money. The usefulness of objects is what gives them value. If not used as money, salt can preserve food and make it tastier. Cattle can be slaughtered for their meat, hides, and horns. Gems can be made into beautiful jewelry. Tobacco, corn, and cotton all served as commodity money in the American colonies.

commodity money objects that have value in and of themselves and that are also used as money

representative money objects that have value because the holder can exchange them for something else of value

specie coined money, usually gold or silver, used to back paper money

As you can guess, commodity money tends to lack several of the characteristics that make objects good to use as money. Take cattle, for example. Cows and bulls are not all that portable, or even durable. A cow is not divisible, at least not if you want to keep it alive. That's why commodity money only works in simple economies. As the American colonies developed more complex economic systems, tobacco and other objects were no longer universally accepted as money. The colonies needed a more convenient payment system. They turned to representative money to meet their needs.

Representative Money

Representative money makes use of objects that have value solely because the holder can exchange them for something else of value. For example, if your brother gives you an IOU for $20, the piece of paper itself is worth nothing. The promise that he will do all of your chores for a month may be worth quite a lot, however. The piece of paper simply represents his promise to you.

Early representative money took the form of paper receipts for gold and silver. Gold or silver money was heavy and thus inconvenient for customers and merchants to carry around. Each time someone made a transaction, the coins would have to be weighed and tested for purity. People therefore started to leave their gold in goldsmiths' safes. Customers would carry paper ownership receipts from the goldsmith to show how much gold they owned. After a while, merchants began to accept goldsmiths' receipts instead of the gold itself. In this way, the paper receipts became an early form of paper money.

Colonists in the Massachusetts Bay Colony first used representative money in the late 1600s when the colony's treasurer issued bills of credit to lenders to help finance King William's War. The bills of credit showed the exact amount that colonists had loaned to the Massachusetts government. Holders of these bills could redeem the paper for **specie,** or coins made of gold or silver.

Representative money was not without its problems. During the American Revolution, the Second Continental Congress issued representative money called Continentals to finance the war against England. Unfortunately, few people were able to redeem these early paper currencies for specie because the federal government had no power to collect taxes. Until the Constitution replaced the Articles of Confederation in 1789, the federal

Background Note

The Gold Standard On the gold standard, a government backs its currency with gold. It can only print as much money as it has gold. For years, the United States kept a lot of gold because, at any time, people could exchange all the money they had for gold at the fixed rate of $20.67 for every ounce. The gold standard provides long-term price stability. However, the government has less control over the economy because it cannot tighten or loosen money (by printing more money) to help control the business cycle. Today, no countries use the gold standard.

government depended on the states' voluntary contributions to fill the treasury. As a result, the federal treasury held very little gold or silver to back the Continentals. People even began to use the phrase "not worth a Continental" to refer to something of no value.

> "During the summer of 1780, this wretched "Continental" currency fell into contempt. As Washington said, it took a wagon-load of money to buy a wagon-load of provisions. At the end of the year 1778, the paper dollar was worth 16 cents in the northern states and twelve cents in the south. Early in 1789 its value had fallen to two cents and before the end of the year it took ten paper dollars to make a cent. A barber in Philadelphia papered his shop with bills."
>
> —John Fiske, *The American Revolution*, 1896

Later, the United States government issued representative money in the form of silver and gold certificates. These certificates were "backed" by gold or silver. In other words, holders of such certificates could redeem them for gold or silver at a local bank. The United States government thus had to keep vast supplies of gold and silver on hand to be able to convert all paper dollars to gold if the demand arose. Some silver certificates circulated until 1968, but for the most part, the government stopped converting paper money into silver or gold in the 1930s.

fiat money objects that have value because a government has decreed that they are an acceptable means to pay debts

Fiat Money

If you examine a dollar bill, you will see George Washington's picture on one side. To the left of the portrait are the words "This note is legal tender for all debts, public and private." In essence, these words mean that this Federal Reserve Note is valuable because our government says it is.

United States money today is fiat money. A fiat is an order or decree. **Fiat money,** also called "legal tender," has value because a government has decreed that it is an acceptable means to pay debts. Furthermore, citizens have confidence that the money will be accepted. It remains in limited supply, and therefore valuable, because the Federal Reserve controls its supply. This control of the money supply is essential for a fiat system to work. If the money supply grows too large, the currency may become worthless due to inflation.

CHECKPOINT ***Why is commodity money impractical for use in our modern society?***

Essential Questions Journal To continue to build a response to the Essential Question, go to your **Essential Questions Journal.**

SECTION 1 ASSESSMENT

Guiding Question

1. Use your completed concept web to answer this question: How does money serve the needs of our society?
2. **Extension** Money helps people and groups in a society meet their needs. Individuals, governments, and other groups use money to buy things they want and need. Describe a time when you used money to meet one of your needs.

Key Terms and Main Ideas

3. Identify the three uses of **money.**
4. Would a pair of sneakers be a good **store of value?** Explain why or why not.
5. Economists use six characteristics to judge how well an item serves as currency. List these six characteristics.
6. Describe how American dollars are divisible.
7. Salt has been used as money in some societies in the past. Is salt an example of **commodity money** or **representative money?** Explain.

Critical Thinking

8. **Contrast (a)** How does barter work? **(b)** How does this differ from the way money is used?
9. **Predict** What might happen if currency were not portable, or easy to carry?
10. **Summarize (a)** What was the problem with the Continentals issued during the American Revolution? **(b)** Describe a challenge facing governments that issue representative money in the form of silver and gold certificates.

Quick Write

11. Reread Sources of Money's Value in this section. Write a short essay answering the following questions: What are the advantages and disadvantages of each? Which kind of money do you think is the most practical? Consider how well each kind of money—commodity money, representative money, and fiat money—meets the six characteristics of currency.

Have students complete the Self-Test Online and continue their work in the **Essential Questions Journal**.

REMEDIATION AND SUGGESTIONS

Use the chart below to help students who are struggling with content.

WEAKNESS	REMEDIATION
Defining key terms (Questions 3, 4, 7)	Have students use the interactive Economic Dictionary Online.
Uses of money (Questions 2, 3, 7)	Have students write one example of each of the uses of money.
Characteristics of money (Questions 5, 6, 9)	Have pairs of students list a visual image that will help them remember the characteristics, e.g., a backpack for portability.
Sources of value (Questions 7, 10, 11)	Create a chart with students to compare the three sources of value of money.

Answer

Checkpoint Possible response: Commodity money is impractical to carry around and one commodity would not be acceptable to everyone.

Assessment Answers

1. We use money to purchase goods and services, to compare the values of goods, and to save. It lasts; is easy to carry, count, and to make change; is in limited supply; and is accepted by everyone.
2. Possible answer: bought lunch at school
3. medium of exchange, unit of account, store of value
4. No; sneakers become worn or out of style and lose value.
5. durability, portability, divisibility, uniformity, limited supply, acceptability
6. Possible response: Currency is issued in various denominations from one cent to bills of $100 or more.
7. Salt is commodity money because it is useful in itself, not just as money.
8. (a) Barter is the direct exchange of one good or service for another. (b) Money can be exchanged for any goods and services.
9. Possible response: People would go shopping less often, and when they did, they would need help in order to transport whatever currency they had with them.
10. (a) The government was unable to collect taxes, so it could not redeem the Continentals. (b) They must keep enough gold or silver at hand to redeem the certificates.
11. Students should write an essay that discusses how each kind of money fits the six characteristics, compares the advantages and disadvantages of each, and expresses a viewpoint on which is the most practical. You may wish to refer students to the Writer's Handbook.

Guiding Question

How has the American banking system changed to meet new challenges?

Get Started

American Banking			
Pre-Civil War	**Later 1800s**	**Early 1900s**	**Modern Times**
• Federalists: national bank; antifederalists: state control. • The first and second national banks provided a safe, stable banking system. • Free Banking Era: bank runs, panics, fraud, multiple currencies.	• The Union printed greenbacks. • Federal government gained power to charter banks, require banks to hold adequate reserves, and issue a single national currency. • Gold standard allowed for a stable currency.	• Federal Reserve System • The Fed helped prevent bank failures. • Failure of many banks during the Great Depression led to needed reforms.	• Close federal regulation of banks from 1933-the 1960s included restrictions on interest rates, lending. • Deregulation of the banking industry contributed to a crisis among Savings and Loans. • Sub-prime mortgages led to a crisis.

LESSON GOALS

Students will:

- Know the Key Terms.
- Demonstrate an understanding of the issues of centralization facing the United States in the early years as it established a banking system.
- Describe the crises and responses to those crises in American banking history.
- Identify the role of central banking, regulation, and free enterprise in today's banking system.

BEFORE CLASS

Have students complete the graphic organizer in the Section Opener as they read the text. As an alternate activity, have students complete the Guided Reading and Review worksheet (Unit 4 All-in-One, p. 20).

L1 L2 ELL LPR Differentiate Have students complete the Guided Reading and Review worksheet (Unit 4 All-in-One, p. 21).

OBJECTIVES

1. **Describe** the shifts between centralized and decentralized banking before the Civil War.
2. **Explain** how government reforms stabilized the banking system in the later 1800s.
3. **Describe** developments in banking in the early 1900s.
4. **Explain** the causes of two recent banking crises.

ECONOMIC DICTIONARY

As you read the section, look for the definitions of these **Key Terms:**

- bank
- national bank
- bank run
- greenback
- gold standard
- central bank
- member bank
- foreclosure

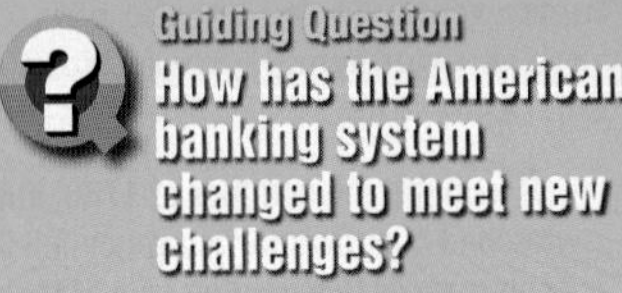

Guiding Question

How has the American banking system changed to meet new challenges?

Copy this chart and fill it in as you read.

American Banking			
Pre-Civil War	Later 1800s	Early 1900s	Modern Times
• • •	• • •	• • •	• • •

bank an institution for receiving, keeping, and lending money

Economics and You

If you need a large sum of cash to make a purchase, do you get it from under your mattress, under a floorboard, or from a cookie jar? These options are unlikely in today's world. In the past, many Americans used to keep their savings hidden in similar places. However, times have changed. Today, almost all Americans prefer to entrust their savings to a **bank**—an institution for receiving, keeping, and lending money.

Principles in Action Over time, the American banking system has changed in order to meet new challenges. In earlier days, people distrusted banks because they sometimes distributed worthless money and caused financial panics. In this section, you will see how government regulations and the efforts of bankers such as the Innovator in this chapter, Amadeo Giannini, helped increase confidence in American banks. You will also see how American banking has developed over the years to meet the needs of a growing and changing population.

▲ Alexander Hamilton, top, and Thomas Jefferson held very different views of how the new nation should satisfy its banking needs.

American Banking Before the Civil War

During the first part of our nation's history, local banks were informal businesses that merchants managed in addition to their regular trade. For example, a merchant who sold cloth, grain, or other goods might allow customers to deposit money. The merchant would then charge a small fee to keep the money safe. These informal banks were not completely safe, however. If a merchant went out of business or invested deposits in risky schemes, customers could lose all of their savings.

Two Views of Banking

After the American Revolution, the leaders of the new nation agreed on the need to establish a safe, stable banking system. Such a system was important for ensuring the economic growth of the new United States. The nation's leaders did not, however, agree on how that goal should be accomplished. The debate on banking between followers of Alexander Hamilton

CLASSROOM HINTS

BANKING HISTORY TIMELINE

While learning about the history of the U.S. banking system, students may benefit from seeing a timeline on the board of the events discussed in this section. Alternatively, you can assign pairs of students a particular event, have them identify when the event occurred, and then have them make a timeline.

Focus on the Basics

Students need to come away with the following understandings:

FACTS: • The lack of a strong central bank in the 1800s caused an unstable banking system. • National regulations and the Federal Reserve System created a more stable American banking system. • The FDIC insures deposits up to $250,000 on basic accounts to prevent panics and bank runs. • Risky loans and lax regulation can cause banking crises.

GENERALIZATION: Financial institutions and government regulations have changed over the history of the United States due to political and economic factors.

and followers of Thomas Jefferson was part of a larger political debate about the role of government in the young country.

As you may remember from your study of American history, the Federalists believed that the country needed a strong central government to establish order. The Antifederalists favored leaving most powers in the hands of the states. These two groups viewed the country's banking needs quite differently.

The Federalists, led by Alexander Hamilton, believed that a centralized banking system was a key to promoting industry and trade. After President Washington appointed Hamilton secretary of the treasury in 1789, Hamilton proposed a **national bank**—a bank chartered, or licensed, by the federal government. The bank would have the power to issue a national currency, manage the federal government's funds, and monitor other banks throughout the country.

The Antifederalists, led by Thomas Jefferson, opposed this plan. They feared that the wealthy would gain control of the bank and use its resources to increase their power. They supported a decentralized banking system. In this system, the states would establish and regulate all banks within their borders.

The First Bank of the United States

At first, the Federalists were successful in creating a strong central bank. In 1791, Congress set up the Bank of the United States, granting it a 20-year charter to operate. The United States Treasury used the Bank to hold the money that the government collected in taxes and to issue representative money in the form of bank notes, which were backed by gold and silver. The Bank also supervised state-chartered banks, making sure they held sufficient gold and silver to exchange for bank notes should the demand arise.

The Bank succeeded in bringing stability to American banking. However, opponents of the Bank charged that ordinary people who needed to borrow money to maintain or expand their farms and small businesses were being refused loans. In addition, the Antifederalists pointed out that the Constitution does not explicitly give Congress the power to create a national bank. Therefore, they argued, the Bank was unconstitutional. When Alexander Hamilton died in a famous duel with Vice President Aaron Burr in 1804, the Bank lost its main backer. The Bank functioned only until 1811, when its charter ran out.

Chaos in American Banking

Once the Bank's charter expired, state banks (banks chartered by state governments) began issuing bank notes that they could not back with specie—gold or silver coins. The states also chartered many banks without considering whether these banks would be stable and creditworthy.

Without any kind of regulation, financial confusion resulted. Prices rose rapidly. Neither merchants nor customers had confidence in the value of the paper money in circulation. Different banks issued different currencies, and bankers always faced the temptation to print more money than they had gold and silver to back.

The Second Bank of the United States

To eliminate this financial chaos, Congress chartered the Second Bank of the United States in 1816. Like the first Bank, the Second Bank was limited to a 20-year charter. The Second Bank slowly managed to rebuild the public's confidence in a national banking system.

GENERAL JACKSON SLAYING THE MANY HEADED MONSTER.

▲ Andrew Jackson's opposition insured the downfall of the Second Bank of the United States, shown here as a many-headed monster. ***Why did Jackson oppose the bank?***

national bank a bank chartered by the federal government

Differentiated Resources

L1 **L2** **Guided Reading and Review** (Unit 4 All-in-One, p. 21)

L2 **Financial Crises** (Unit 4 All-in-One, p. 23)

L4 **Perspectives on American Banking History** (Unit 4 All-in-One, p. 24)

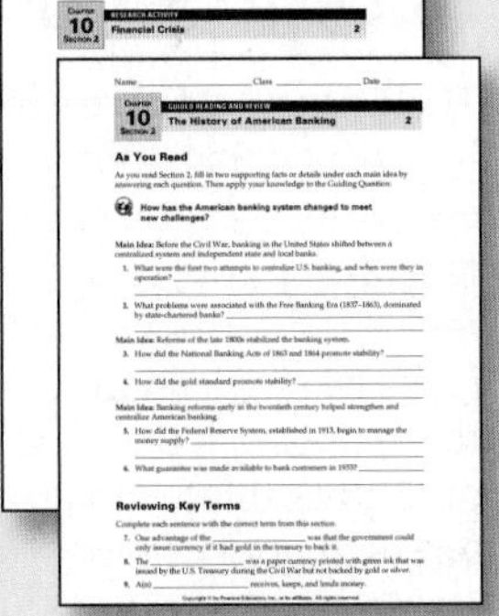

BELLRINGER

Ask students to imagine that your school was going to set up its own system of banking, but that there was a choice of two ways to do it. One was to allow each classroom to create its own bank with its own rules. The other would be to create a single bank for the entire school under the direction of the principal, along with a small committee of teachers and students. Ask students, working in groups of two or three, to list the possible advantages and disadvantages of each system.

Teach

Economics online To present this topic using digital resources, use the lecture notes on www.PearsonSuccessNet.com.

DISCUSS THE BELLRINGER

Ask volunteers to state their conclusion about the question in the Bellringer. Write the advantages and disadvantages of each system on the chalkboard. If the following points do not come up on their own, encourage students to think about them: **How would a centralized school bank offer more stability than individual banks? Which would make it easier to interact with other classrooms? Which system would respond most quickly to the needs of your individual classroom? What would be the risk of placing decisions in the hands of a small number of people?**

Then, tell students that many of the same issues faced the United States in its earlier years. Ask **Why did Hamilton favor a strong central banking system? Why might people have distrusted a central bank after the Revolution?** Encourage students to see the connection between the concerns they expressed in the Bellringer activity and the issues facing the young republic.

ANALYZE

Refer students to the cartoon on this page. Ask **What does the many-headed monster represent?** *(the Second Bank of the United States)* **What is President Jackson doing?** *(slaying the monster)* **Is the cartoonist supporting a central bank or a decentralized banking system? How do you know?** *(decentralized system, because the central bank is pictured as a monster)*

Answer

Caption He believed the central bank was a tool for the wealthy.

DISTRIBUTE ACTIVITY WORKSHEET

Explain to students that there have been a series of major crises in the history of the U.S. banking system. Each crisis required a response from the government to restore stability. Looking at these past events can help us understand how the banking system works today. Then, distribute the "Crisis and Response in American Banking History" worksheet (Unit 4 All-in-One, p. 22). Tell students they can form groups by topic, or work on their own.

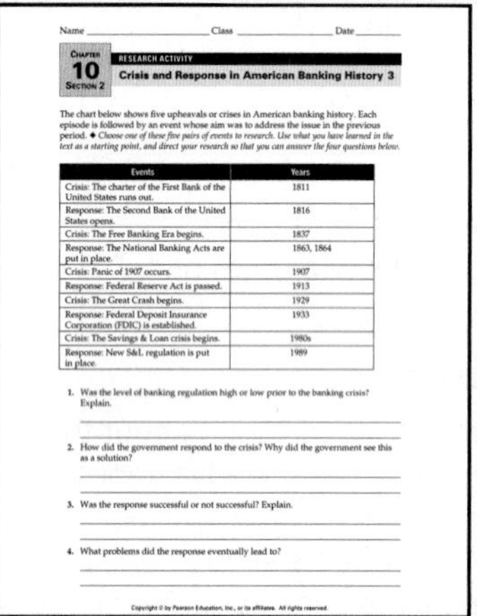

Name ______ Class ______ Date ______

Chapter 10 Section 2

RESEARCH ACTIVITY

Crisis and Response in American Banking History 3

The chart below shows five upheavals or crises in American banking history. Each episode is followed by an event whose aim was to address the issue in the previous period. ◆ *Choose one of these five pairs of events to research. Use what you have learned in the text as a starting point, and direct your research so that you can answer the four questions below.*

Events	Years
Crisis: The charter of the First Bank of the United States runs out.	1811
Response: The Second Bank of the United States opens.	1816
Crisis: The Free Banking Era begins.	1837
Response: The National Banking Acts are put in place.	1863, 1864
Crisis: Panic of 1907 occurs.	1907
Response: Federal Reserve Act is passed.	1913
Crisis: The Great Crash begins.	1929
Response: Federal Deposit Insurance Corporation (FDIC) is established.	1933
Crisis: The Savings & Loan crisis begins.	1980s
Response: New S&L regulation is put in place.	1989

1. Was the level of banking regulation high or low prior to the banking crisis? Explain.
2. How did the government respond to the crisis? Why did the government see this as a solution?
3. Was the response successful or not successful? Explain.
4. What problems did the response eventually lead to?

L1 L2 Differentiate Distribute the "Financial Crises" worksheet (Unit 4 All-in-One, p. 23) to help students understand recent banking crises.

Action Graph online Have students review the Action Graph animation for a step-by-step look at Developments in American Banking.

Figure 10.1 Developments in American Banking

CHART SKILLS

The history of American banking shows a series of shifts between stability and instability.

1. What event reinforced the need for the creation of a central banking system in the United States?
2. What does the chart suggest about the role of government in banking during the twentieth century?

Action Graph online

For an animated version of this graph, visit PearsonSuccessNet.com

Date	Development
1780s	The Nation has no reliable medium of exchange. Federalists and Antifederalists disagree about a banking system.
1791	First Bank of the United States is established.
1811–1816	Period of instability follows expiration of First Bank's charter.
1816	Second Bank of the United States reestablishes stability.
1830s–1860s	President Jackson vetoes recharter of Second Bank in 1832, giving rise to the Free Banking Era.
1861–1863	Civil War makes clear the need for a better monetary and banking system.
1863–1864	National Banking Acts of 1863 and 1864 establish national banking system and uniform national currency.
1913	President Wilson signs the Federal Reserve Act.
1929	The Great Depression begins.
1933	President Roosevelt helps restore confidence in the nation's banks by establishing the FDIC.
1940s–1960s	Period of government regulation and long-term stability.
1980s	Period of deregulation; savings and loans face bankruptcies.
2000s	In 2007, a result of the subprime mortgage crisis is a sharp increase in the number of people who lose their homes because they can't pay their mortgage. This leads to the worst economic crisis since World War II.

Nicholas Biddle, who became president of the Second Bank in 1823, was responsible for restoring stability. If Biddle thought that a particular state bank was issuing bank notes without enough gold and silver reserves, he would surprise the bank with a great number of its notes all at once, asking for gold or silver in return. Some state banks, caught without the necessary reserves, went out of business. Others quickly learned to limit how many notes they issued.

Still, many Americans continued to be wary of the federal government's banking powers. They believed that the bank was a tool for the wealthy to further increase their wealth. Although the Supreme Court had ruled a national bank constitutional in 1819, President Andrew Jackson agreed with the bank's opponents. In 1832, Jackson vetoed its renewal.

bank run a widespread panic in which many people try to redeem their paper money at the same time

The Free Banking Era

The fall of the Second Bank once again allowed state-chartered banks to flourish. For this reason, the period between 1837 and 1863 is known as the Free Banking, or "Wildcat," Era. Between 1830 and 1837 alone, the number of state-chartered banks nearly tripled. As you might expect, the sheer number of banks gave rise to a variety of problems.

1. ***Bank runs and panics*** State-chartered banks often did not keep enough gold and silver to back the paper money that they issued. This sometimes led to **bank runs**—widespread panics in which great numbers of people try to redeem their paper money at the same time. Many banks failed as a result, and public confidence plummeted.
2. ***Wildcat banks*** Some banks were located on the frontier. They were called wildcat banks because people joked that only wildcats lived in such remote places. Wildcat banks were inadequately financed and had a high rate of failure.
3. ***Fraud*** A few banks engaged in out-and-out fraud. They issued bank notes, collected gold and silver money from

Background Note

The Second Bank of the United States When President Andrew Jackson attacked the Second Bank of the United States, the issue brought on a political and economic war. After he vetoed the renewal of the bank's charter, he demanded that all federal deposits be withdrawn from the bank and placed in chosen state banks. In retaliation, Nicholas Biddle, who had worked against Jackson's reelection, created a panic by restricting the bank's loans. Since other banks needed that money for loans to expanding industries, they printed more money than they could redeem. Because of this worthless money, President Jackson decreed that buyers of public land had to pay with gold or silver.

Answers

Chart Skills 1. the Civil War 2. When the government regulated banks, they were more stable.

people who bought the notes, and then disappeared. Customers who were left holding the notes lost their money.

4. *Many different currencies* State-chartered banks—as well as cities, private banks, railroads, stores, churches, and individuals—were allowed to issue currency. Notes of the same denomination often had different values, so that a dollar issued by the "City of Atlanta" was not necessarily worth the same as a dollar issued by the "City of New York." The profusion of currencies made it easier to create counterfeits, or worthless imitations of real notes.

CHECKPOINT ***Why was a safe, stable banking system important to the young United States?***

Stability in the Later 1800s

By 1860, an estimated 8,000 different banks were circulating currency. To add to the confusion, the federal government played no role in providing paper currency or regulating reserves of gold or silver. The Civil War, which erupted in 1861, made existing problems worse.

Currency in the North and South

During the Civil War, both the Union and Confederacy needed to raise money to finance their military efforts. In 1861, the United States Treasury issued its first paper currency since the Continental. The official name of the currency was "demand notes," but people called them **greenbacks** because they were printed with green ink.

In the South, the Confederacy issued currency backed by cotton, hoping that a Confederate victory would ensure the currency's value. As the war weakened the Confederate economy, however, Confederate notes became worthless.

Unifying American Banks

With war raging, the federal government enacted reforms aimed at restoring confidence in paper currency. These reforms resulted in the National Banking Acts of 1863 and 1864. Together, these Acts gave the federal government the power to charter banks, the power to require that banks hold adequate gold and silver reserves to cover their bank notes, and the power to issue a single national currency. The new national currency led to the elimination of the many different state currencies in use and helped stabilize the country's money supply.

The Gold Standard

Despite the reforms made during the Civil War, money and banking problems still plagued the country. In the 1870s, the nation adopted a **gold standard**—a monetary system in which paper money and coins had the value of certain amounts of gold. The gold standard set a definite value for the dollar, so that one ounce of gold equaled about $20. Since the value was set, people knew that they could redeem the full value of their paper money at any time.

Now, the government could issue currency only if it had enough gold in the treasury to back the notes. Because of the limited supply of gold, the government was prevented from printing an unlimited number of notes. The gold standard thus fulfilled an essential requirement of a banking system: a stable currency that inspires the confidence of the public.

CHECKPOINT ***What powers did the National Banking Acts give to the federal government?***

Banking in the Early 1900s

Reforms such as creating a single national currency and adopting the gold standard helped stabilize American banking. They did not, however, provide for a central decision-making authority. Such an authority could help banks provide funds for growth and manage the money supply based on what the economy needed.

Continuing problems in the nation's banking system resulted in the Panic of 1907. Lacking adequate reserves, many banks had to stop exchanging gold for paper money. Several long-established New York banks failed, and many people lost their jobs because businesses could not borrow money to invest in future projects.

The Federal Reserve System

The Federal Reserve Act of 1913 established the Federal Reserve System. The Federal Reserve System, or Fed, served

greenback a paper currency issued during the Civil War

gold standard a monetary system in which paper money and coins had the value of certain amounts of gold

CIRCULATE TO MONITOR PROGRESS

As students fill in their worksheets, circulate to facilitate their work. Suggest they review the Section 2 Key Terms.

L4 Differentiate Distribute the "Perspectives on American Banking History" worksheet (Unit 4 All-in-One, p. 24) to individuals or pairs of students. Students will do research on debates about banking in U.S. history.

Name ______ Class ______ Date ______

CHAPTER 10 SECTION 2 — COMPARING PRIMARY AND SECONDARY SOURCES

Perspectives on American Banking History 4

Choose a conflict in American banking history. For example, you might choose the Hamilton-Jefferson debate over a national bank, the Jackson-Biddle debate over the Second Bank of the United States, the debate over a gold or silver standard, the debate over creating the Federal Reserve, or the debate over Roosevelt's banking reforms. ◆ *Describe the conflict. From primary sources, locate a quotation that represents the perspective of each side. Analyze each to show how it represents the ideas of that side. Finally, locate a secondary source that identifies the importance of the conflict, the effect it had on the economy of that period, and its relevance to today's economy.*

Conflict: ______

Quotation 1 and analysis: ______

Quotation 2 and analysis: ______

Secondary Source Quotation: ______

Answers

Checkpoint to ensure economic growth

Checkpoint It gave the federal government the power to charter banks, to require banks to hold adequate gold or silver reserves, and to issue a national currency.

COMPARE AND CONTRAST

Have students discuss the similarities and differences between the events they chose. Discuss or clarify students' answers if necessary.

DRAW CONCLUSIONS

After the discussion, ask students to draw conclusions about American banking history. Discuss how central banking, government regulation, and the free enterprise system have played a part in the development of today's banking system.

DISCUSS

Using the Innovators feature, discuss the differences between Giannini and other bankers of his day. Include a discussion of his goals, how he responded after the San Francisco earthquake, and his relationship to entrepreneurs.

CREATE DIAGRAM

Read the Economics and You feature with students. Create a cause-and-effect diagram to show the connection between economic events (the stock market crash) and government regulations. Ask **What other events were the reason for changes by the government?** *(Possible responses: panics, savings and loan crisis, sub-prime mortgage crisis)* **Are there any modern banking practices you would like to see regulated by the government? Why?** *(Possible response: I would like to see more regulation of the fees banks charge, because they are too high.)*

Innovators

Bank of America

Amadeo P. Giannini

"Money itch is a bad thing. I never had that trouble."

Amadeo Giannini was determined to be a different kind of banker. Unlike other bankers of his time who catered to the rich, Giannini built his bank by providing services to everyday people.

Like many of his customers, Giannini was the son of Italian immigrants. At the age of 12, he went to work on the San Francisco docks. As a young man, he built a thriving business buying produce from local farmers. Although he had no previous training in banking, he opened a small bank in 1904. When a devastating earthquake hit the city in 1905, Giannini's bank was destroyed. However, he put a plank across two barrels in front of the ruined building and set up office. Here, he offered loans to people who had been devastated by the earthquake.

By the 1930s, he had merged with other banks and controlled the Bank of America, the world's largest commercial bank. Giannini provided banking services, such as home mortgages and small-business loans, to the average citizen. His generous lending helped local entrepreneurs, including those in the California wine and motion picture industries. He even loaned money to help the Walt Disney studio make *Snow White*, the first full length animated feature.

Giannini himself had little interest in personal wealth and he left a small estate at his death. He feared that great wealth would make him lose touch with the ordinary people he served.

Critical Thinking: ***Why is a bank with a nationwide reach able to withstand regional economic downturns?***

Fast Facts

Amadeo P. Giannini
Born: May 6, 1870
Died: June 3, 1949
Education: No formal education beyond 8th grade
Claim to Fame: Founded the Bank of America, now the largest U.S.-owned bank

as the nation's first true **central bank,** or bank that can lend to other banks in time of need. It reorganized the federal banking system as follows:

- *Federal Reserve Banks* The system created as many as 12 regional Federal Reserve Banks throughout the country. All banks chartered by the national government were required to become members of the Fed. The Federal Reserve Banks are the central banks for their districts. **Member banks**—banks that belong to the Fed—store some of their cash reserves at the Federal Reserve Bank in their district.
- *Federal Reserve Board* All of the Federal Reserve Banks were supervised by a Federal Reserve Board appointed by the President of the United States.
- *Short-Term Loans* Each of the regional Federal Reserve Banks allowed member banks to borrow money to meet short-term demands. This helped prevent bank failures that occurred when large numbers of depositors withdrew funds during a panic.
- *Federal Reserve Notes* The system also created the national currency we use today in the United States—Federal Reserve notes. This allowed the Federal Reserve to increase or decrease the amount of money in circulation according to business needs.

central bank a bank that can lend to other banks in time of need

member bank a bank that belongs to the Federal Reserve System

You will read more about the role of the Federal Reserve and how the system works today in Chapter 16.

Banking and the Great Depression

The Fed helped restore confidence in the nation's banking system. It was unable, however, to prevent the terrifying Great Depression—the severe economic decline that began in 1929 and lasted more than a decade.

During the 1920s, banks loaned large sums of money to many high-risk businesses. Many of these businesses were unable to pay back their loans. Because of hard times on the nation's farms, many farmers also failed to repay bank loans. Then, the 1929 stock market crash led to widespread bank runs as depositors in all

Virtual Economics

L3 Differentiate

Exploring Early Banking in the United States Use the following lesson from the NCEE **Virtual Economics *CD-ROM*** to help students understand how banking developed in the United States. Click on Browse Economics Lessons, specify grades 9–12, and use the key word *boom.*

In this activity, students will complete activities about U.S. banking in the 1830s.

LESSON TITLE	**BOOM AND BUST IN THE 1830s**
Type of Activity	Using statistics
Complexity	Moderate
Time	50 minutes
NCEE Standards	10

Answer

Critical Thinking Because other regions are probably on an upswing and balance the bank's problems in the downswing region.

parts of the country rushed to withdraw their money. The combination of unpaid loans and bank runs resulted in the failure of thousands of banks across the country.

Banking Reforms

After becoming President in 1933, Franklin D. Roosevelt acted to restore public confidence in the nation's banking system. Only days after his inauguration, Roosevelt closed the nation's banks. This "bank holiday" was a desperate last resort to restore trust in the nation's financial system. Within a matter of days, sound banks began to reopen.

Later in 1933, Congress passed the act that established the Federal Deposit Insurance Corporation (FDIC). The FDIC insures customer deposits if a bank fails. By 2008, each depositor's basic accounts in one bank were insured up to $250,000.

In addition, federal legislation severely restricted individuals' ability to redeem dollars for gold. Eventually, currency became fiat money backed only by the government's decree that established its value. In this way, the Federal Reserve could maintain a money supply at adequate levels to support a growing economy.

CHECKPOINT ***How did the Federal Deposit Insurance Corporation (FDIC) help restore confidence in the banking industry?***

Two Crises for Banking

As a result of the many bank failures of the Great Depression, banks were closely regulated from 1933 through the 1960s. The government restricted the interest rates banks could pay depositors and the rates that banks could charge consumers for loans. By the 1970s, bankers were eager for relief from federal regulation.

The Savings and Loan Crisis

In the late 1970s and 1980s, Congress passed laws to deregulate, or remove some restrictions on, several industries. Unfortunately, this deregulation contributed to a crisis in a class of banks known as Savings and Loans (S&Ls). Government regulation had protected S&Ls from some of the stresses of the marketplace. Thus they were unprepared for the intense competition they faced after deregulation.

There were other reasons for the crisis. During the 1970s, S&Ls had made long-term loans at low rates of interest. By the 1980s, interest rates had skyrocketed. This meant that S&Ls had to pay large amounts of interest to their depositors.

The S&L industry made many risky loans in the early 1980s. Losses on bad loans forced many banks out of business. A few S&L managers also used S&L funds for their own personal gain.

In 1989, Congress passed legislation that essentially abolished the independence of the savings and loan industry. This legislation also transferred insurance responsibilities to the FDIC.

Economics & YOU

How Your Deposit Is Protected

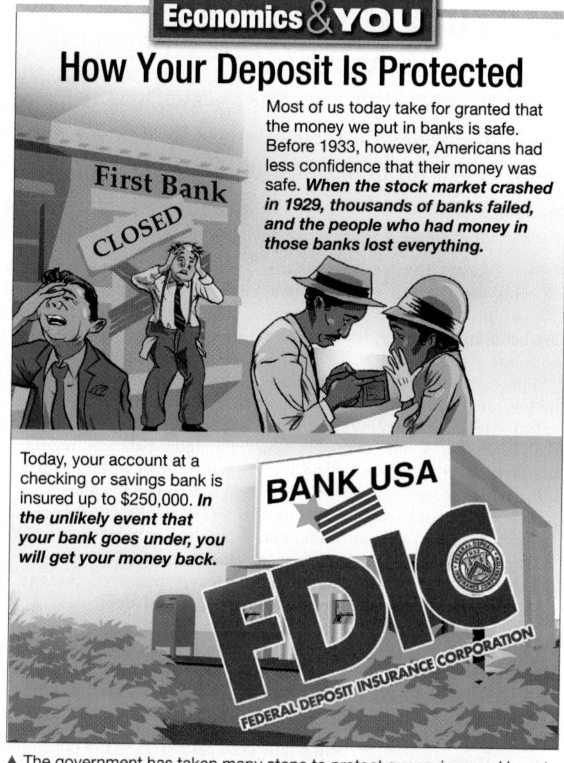

Most of us today take for granted that the money we put in banks is safe. Before 1933, however, Americans had less confidence that their money was safe. ***When the stock market crashed in 1929, thousands of banks failed, and the people who had money in those banks lost everything.***
First Bank
CLOSED
Today, your account at a checking or savings bank is insured up to $250,000. ***In the unlikely event that your bank goes under, you will get your money back.***
BANK USA
FDIC
FEDERAL DEPOSIT INSURANCE CORPORATION

▲ The government has taken many steps to protect our savings and investments. ***What other protections does the U.S. government provide?***

EXTEND

Have students scan newspapers and national news magazines for articles on banking, the Federal Reserve, and mortgages. Have students choose one article and write a paragraph summarizing the information and how it relates to what they learned in this section.

L2 ELL Differentiate Have students create picture flashcards for the most important changes in banking history. On one side students draw or paste on a picture representing the event, and on the back they should write one two or three key words that describe the event.

GUIDING QUESTION WRAP UP

Have students return to the section Guiding Question. Review the completed graphic organizer and clarify any misunderstandings. Have a wrap up discussion about how the American banking system has changed to meet challenges.

Assess and Remediate

L3 **L2** Collect the "Crisis and Response in American Banking History" worksheets and the "Financial Crisis" worksheets and assess students' understanding of how the banking industry grew and was regulated.

L4 Collect the "Perspectives on American Banking History" worksheets and assess students' understanding.

L3 Assign the Section 2 Assessment questions; identify student misconceptions.

L3 Give Section Quiz A (Unit 4 All-in-One, p. 25).

L2 Give Section Quiz B (Unit 4 All-in-One, p. 26).

(Assess and Remediate continued on p. 263)

Answers

Checkpoint People were no longer afraid to put money into a bank because with the FDIC insuring their money, they would not lose it.

Caption regulates financial institutions including banks and investment houses

Teach Case Study

SUMMARIZE AND EXPLAIN

Call on the students to explain the relationship between interest-rate cuts and banking. Ask **What is the main idea behind community banks and credit unions offering "reward checking accounts"?** *(Banks are trying to help consumers earn a higher rate on their money because interest-rate cuts have decreased the yield of some savings accounts. If consumers follow a certain set of account rules, they earn a higher yield.)*

Have the students bring in information about the account types and fees at their bank or their parents' bank. Compare and contrast these account types with the ones cited in the article. Ask the students which account they would open and why.

L4 Differentiate This case study cites the Federal Reserve's interest-rate cuts prompting banks to offer new services. What is the Federal Reserve and what does it do? Have the students work in pairs and explore the Fed's Web site (www.federalreserve.gov). Tell them to write a list of three functions of the Fed.

Economics online *All print resources are available on the Teacher's Resource Library CD-ROM and online at* www.PearsonSuccessNet.com.

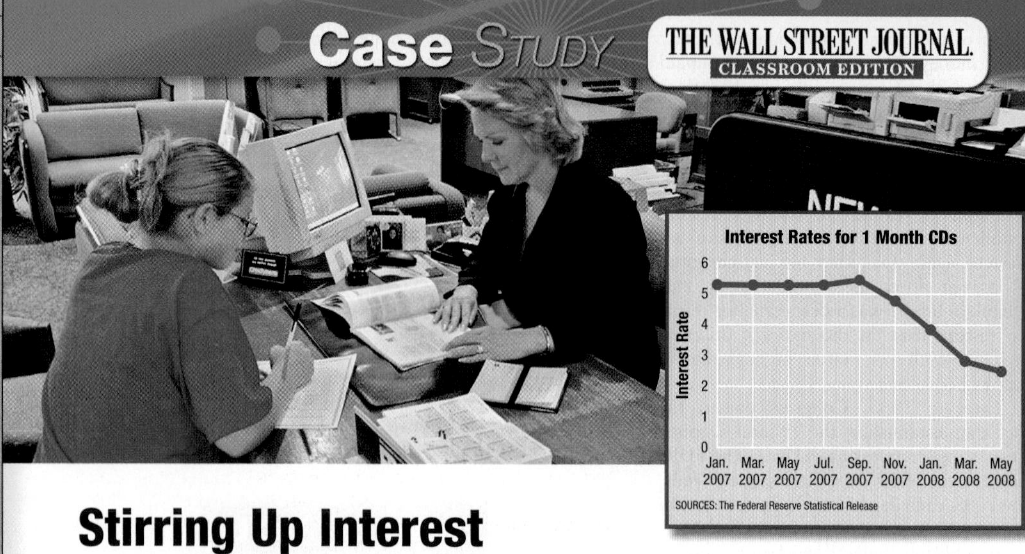

Stirring Up Interest

BANKING SERVICES

At a time when interest rates are low, how can customers get higher yields on their savings? By being among the bank's most profitable customers.

By Jane J. Kim
The Wall Street Journal

The Federal Reserve's interest-rate cuts are sending yields on bank certificates of deposit and money-market accounts lower, leaving savers with few places to park their cash.

But community banks and credit unions are pushing a new product called "reward checking accounts" with higher yields for customers who use their debit cards heavily and meet other requirements.

While some banks require customers to visit a branch to open an account or, in the case of credit unions, meet certain membership requirements, a handful of banks are offering the reward on checking accounts nationwide.

The accounts, which are insured by the Federal Deposit Insurance Corp. or its credit-union equivalent, come with a few strings. In order to earn the high yields, customers must get their bank statements delivered to them electronically, have at least one direct deposit or automatic debit in the account each month and use their debit cards at least 10 times a month. There are usually no monthly fees or minimum-balances requirements and many banks will also offer refunds of ATM fees charged by other banks.

The banks say they're able to pay the higher rates because they don't have to mail paper statements or process paper checks and also earn fees from debit-card transactions. BancVue, a company that provides reward checking accounts for roughly 400 banks and credit unions, says the accounts are on average twice as profitable to those financial institutions as a free checking account.

"It's sort of a game that banks are playing with their customers, but it's a pretty fair game overall," says Jim Bruene, publisher of Online Banking Report. "Most of what customers are being asked to do is relatively reasonable and can be good for tracking their finances."

So are these accounts right for you? If you're a frequent debit-card user, pay most of your bills online and rarely visit a bank branch, they are worth investigating.

There are catches. If you fail to meet one of the requirements, then you earn a paltry interest rate, typically less than 1%, on your entire balance (you'll get another chance to earn the higher yield the following month). Some banks also cap the amount of deposits that savers can earn the higher rates on, often at $25,000.

Applying Economic Principles
Low interest rates benefit people who want to borrow money. At the same time, they lower the return for bank depositors. Explain how depositors are getting higher yields on their savings.

Video News Update Online Powered by *The Wall Street Journal* Classroom Edition — For a new case study, go to the online resources at **PearsonSuccessNet.com**

262 MONEY AND BANKING

Answer

Applying Economic Principles Depositors are getting higher yields by depositing their money into "reward checking accounts," which offer higher interest rates. These accounts require customers to have bank statements delivered electronically, have at least one direct deposit or automatic debit in the account each month, and use their debit cards at least 10 times per month.

Financial "Meltdown" and Bailout

In late 2006, problems in the U.S. banking industry began to threaten the housing market. The episode quickly spiraled into a full-fledged crisis, the most serious threat to the U.S. economy since the Great Depression.

Beginning in the 1990s, U.S. banks decided to issue "subprime" loans to people seeking to purchase homes. The term "subprime" refers to loans that are made to borrowers with an unfavorable credit history. The higher interest rate banks charge because of the greater risk makes these loans more profitable.

Banks began to market these loans aggressively among people who did not qualify for standard loans. By 2005, subprime loans made up more than a quarter of all U.S. mortgages. Bankers also devised ways of packaging these mortgages in ways that they could be sold off to investors. The value of these bundled mortgages, of course, depended on the ability of individual homeowners to repay their loans.

The situation reached a crisis point when many homeowners had trouble repaying their loan. This led to a sharp rise in **foreclosures,** the seizure of property from borrowers who are unable to repay their loans. This hurt the lenders, as well as investors who had bought the mortgage bundles. A number of the nation's largest financial institutions that had invested heavily in subprime mortgages were forced into bankruptcy. The ripple effect was great, as hundreds of thousands of U.S. workers lost their jobs. Businesses and individuals found it difficult to get credit.

By late 2008, the U.S. economy was on the edge of a financial catastrophe. It was officially in a recession. Treasury Secretary Henry M. Paulson, President George Bush, and U.S. lawmakers organized a $700 billion bailout of banks, automakers, and Wall Street financial firms. The money was used to help them avoid bankruptcy and restart the flow of credit to businesses and individuals. The then-President-elect Barack Obama announced that, when in office, he would push for a massive public works program that would create millions of new jobs and jumpstart the nation's economy. Many economists believed that without government intervention the nation might sink into a severe depression.

CHECKPOINT ***How did the rash of subprime loans endanger the U.S. economy?***

foreclosure the seizure of property from borrowers who are unable to repay their loans

SECTION 2 ASSESSMENT

Essential Questions Journal To continue to build a response to the Essential Question, go to your **Essential Questions Journal.**

Guiding Question

1. Use your completed chart to answer this question: How has the American banking system changed to meet new challenges?
2. **Extension** When would you feel safest keeping money in a bank: today, during the "Wildcat" Era, or during the early 1900s? Explain why.

Key Terms and Main Ideas

3. Identify the three functions of a **bank.**
4. List four banking problems that arose during the Free Banking, or "Wildcat," Era.
5. Under the **gold standard,** paper money and coins were equivalent to what?
6. As a **central bank,** what can the Federal Reserve System do for other banks?
7. Name one advantage of Federal Reserve notes, the national currency we use today.

Critical Thinking

8. **Contrast (a)** Explain the views of Alexander Hamilton and the Federalists about establishing a centralized banking system. **(b)** How did the Federalists' views differ from the views of Thomas Jefferson and the Antifederalists?
9. **Interpret (a)** When did the United States start issuing greenbacks? **(b)** What significant event happened at this time in history? **(c)** How are these two events related?
10. **Discuss** How did laws passed during the Great Depression change the type of money used in the United States?

Quick Write

11. Based on what you have read in this section about the history of the American banking system, write a short essay answering the following questions: What powers do you think the federal government should have to regulate banks? Why are these powers necessary?

Have students complete the Self-Test Online and continue their work in the **Essential Questions Journal**.

REMEDIATION AND SUGGESTIONS

Use the chart below to help students who are struggling with content.

WEAKNESS	REMEDIATION
Defining key terms (Questions 3, 5, 6)	Have students use the interactive Economic Dictionary Online.
Development of American banking (Questions 1, 2, 4, 8)	Reteach using Figure 10.1 on page 258. Have students make a timeline that shows two important events in each century.
Currency (Questions 5, 9)	Have students make a graphic organizer showing changes in the types of money used in the United States.
Banking crises (Questions 10, 11)	Have students compare two crises and note one difference and one similarity between the two.

Answer

Checkpoint It caused some large mortgage companies to go into bankruptcy, which hurt banks that held their loans. This affected the stock market and caused major layoffs from banks.

Assessment Answers

1. Central banking system regulates banks, controls currency flow, and helps banks. Government also provides other protections, such as FDIC.
2. Possible response: Today is safest because of government regulation and insurance like the FDIC.
3. receiving, keeping, and lending money
4. bank runs, high bank failure rate, fraud, and many different currencies
5. a specified amount of gold
6. store their cash reserves, loan them money, increase amount of money in circulation
7. The Federal Reserve can change the amount of notes in circulation to help control the business cycle.
8. (a) Hamilton wanted a strong central bank. This would help industry and trade develop. (b) Jefferson didn't want a central bank because he feared the rich would use it to get richer and control the government.
9. (a) 1861 (b) the Civil War (c) The Union needed to raise money to fight the war.
10. The government moved from the gold standard with representative money to fiat money, which allowed the government to better help the growing economy.
11. Students should write an essay that identifies powers the federal government should have to regulate banks and why these powers are necessary. You may wish to refer students to the Writer's Handbook.

Guiding Question

What banking services do financial institutions provide?

Get Started

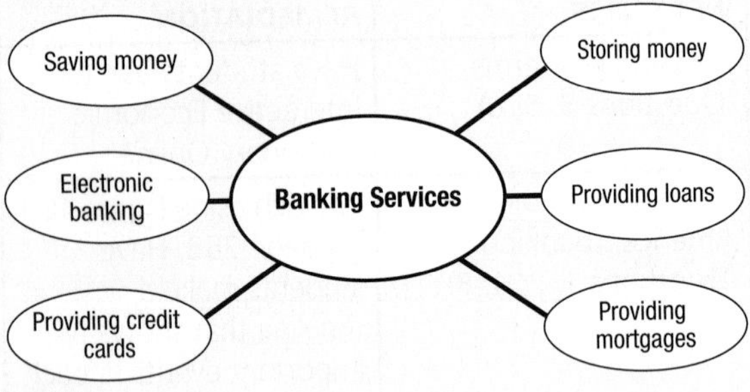

LESSON GOALS

Students will:

- Know the Key Terms.
- Demonstrate understanding of how the money supply is measured.
- Identify the services offered by banks by analyzing a bank statement and researching different types of financial institutions.
- Evaluate aspects of electronic banking.

BEFORE CLASS

Students should read the section for homework before coming to class.

Have students complete the graphic organizer in the Section Opener as they read the text. As an alternate activity, have students complete the Guided Reading and Review worksheet (Unit 4 All-in-One, p. 27).

L1 L2 ELL LPR Differentiate Have students complete the Guided Reading and Review worksheet (Unit 4 All-in-One, p. 28).

SECTION 3 Banking Today

OBJECTIVES

1. **Explain** how the money supply in the United States is measured.
2. **Describe** the functions of financial institutions.
3. **Identify** different types of financial institutions.
4. **Describe** the changes brought about by electronic banking.

ECONOMIC DICTIONARY

As you read the section, look for the definitions of these **Key Terms:**

- money supply
- liquidity
- demand deposit
- money market mutual fund
- fractional reserve banking
- default
- mortgage
- credit card
- interest
- principal
- debit card
- creditor

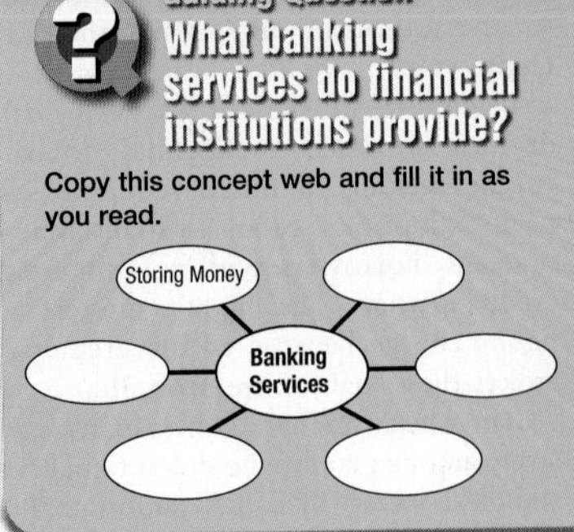

Guiding Question
What banking services do financial institutions provide?
Copy this concept web and fill it in as you read.
Storing Money
Banking Services

Economics and You It's Friday. You just got your paycheck for the week. You take it to the bank, where you fill out a deposit slip and then stand in line and wait... and wait... and wait for the next available teller. Hold on a minute. That scenario is out-of-date! You don't have time for standing in line. You deposit your check quickly at an ATM. Or better yet, you have arranged to have your week's pay electronically deposited directly into your bank account.

Principles in Action Financial institutions provide these electronic services—and many others suited to the computer age. They issue credit cards, make loans to businesses, and provide mortgages to prospective home buyers. They also manage automated teller machines that enable a person to deposit or withdraw money in almost any place on the globe. In this section you'll learn more about electronic transactions, the fractional reserve system, and other aspects of banking today.

Measuring the Money Supply

You are familiar with paying for the items you need with currency—the bills and coins in your pocket. Currency is money. So are traveler's checks, checking account deposits, and a variety of other components. All of these components make up the United States **money supply**—all the money available in the United States economy. To more easily keep track of these different kinds of money, economists divide the money supply into several categories. The main categories are called M1 and M2.

money supply all the money available in the United States economy

M1

M1 represents money that people can gain access to easily and immediately to pay for goods and services. In other words, M1 consists of assets that have **liquidity,** or the ability to be used as, or directly converted into, cash.

liquidity the ability to be used as, or directly converted into, cash

As you can see from **Figure 10.2**, about 55 percent of M1 is made up of currency held by the public, that is, all currency held outside of bank vaults. Another large component of M1 is deposits in checking accounts. Funds in checking accounts are also called **demand deposits,** because checks can be paid "on demand," that is, at any time.

demand deposit money in a checking account that can be paid out "on demand," or at any time

CLASSROOM HINTS

THE MONEY SUPPLY

Prior to discussing Figure 10.2, students may gain a better understanding of M1 and M2 by seeing a diagram. Draw a large oval on the board with a smaller oval inside of it. Within the smaller oval, write "M1," as well as major components of the money supply that are part of M1: currency held by the public, demand deposits, other checkable deposits, traveler's checks. Outside of this oval, but within the large oval, write "M2" as well as components of the money supply that do not belong to M1: savings deposits, retail money market funds, small denomination time deposits. Label the whole diagram "The U.S. Money Supply."

Focus on the Basics

Students need to come away with the following understandings:

FACTS: • The money supply is determined by calculating the money available in the economy. • Financial institutions store, loan, and invest money. • Today, different types of financial institutions provide overlapping services. • Electronic banking has changed how banking is conducted.

GENERALIZATION: Society depends on financial institutions to carry out many functions.

Until the 1980s, checking accounts did not pay interest. When they began paying interest, the Fed introduced a new component to measure M1, called *other checkable deposits*, to describe those accounts. Today this category is not as meaningful as it once was, since many checking accounts pay interest if the balance is sufficiently high.

Traveler's checks make up a very small part of M1. Unlike personal checks, traveler's checks can be easily turned into cash.

M2

M2 consists of all the assets in M1 plus several additional assets. These additional M2 funds cannot be used as cash directly, but can be converted to cash fairly easily. M2 assets are also called *near money*.

For example, deposits in savings accounts are included in M2. They are not included in M1 because they cannot be used directly in financial exchanges. You cannot hand a sales clerk your savings account passbook to pay for a new backpack. You can, however, withdraw money from your savings account and then use that money to buy a backpack.

Deposits in **money market mutual funds** are also included as part of M2. These are funds that pool money from a large number of small savers to purchase short-term government and corporate securities. They earn interest and can be used to cover checks written over a certain minimum amount, such as $250. You will read more about money market mutual funds in Chapter 11.

money market mutual fund a fund that pools money from small savers to purchase short-term government and corporate securities

CHECKPOINT ***Which category of the money supply includes deposits in money market mutual funds?***

Functions of Financial Institutions

Banks and other financial institutions are essential to managing the money supply. They also perform many functions and offer a wide range of services to consumers.

Storing Money

Banks provide a safe, convenient place for people to store money. Banks keep cash in fireproof vaults and are insured against the loss of money in the event of a robbery.

Personal Finance
For more help in finding the right bank, see your Personal Finance Handbook in the back of the book or visit **PearsonSuccessNet.com**

Figure 10.2 Major Components of the Money Supply

M1 Components	Billions
Currency	$749.6
Demand deposits	$305.9
Other checkable deposits	$304.0
Traveler's checks	$6.7
Total M1	$1,366.2

M2 Components	Billions
Savings deposits	$2,902.1
Retail money market funds	$805.0
Small denomination time deposits	$398.7
Total M1	$1,366.2
Total M2	$5,472.0

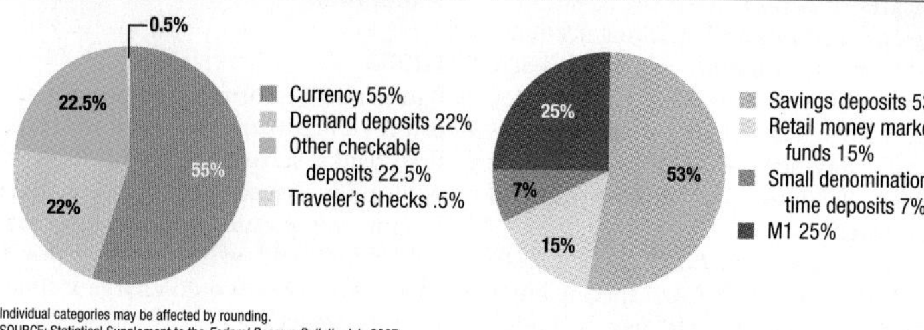

Individual categories may be affected by rounding.
SOURCE: Statistical Supplement to the *Federal Reserve Bulletin*, July 2007

GRAPH SKILLS

To keep track of the money supply in the United States, economists divide the money supply into two main categories, M1 and M2.

1. What is the largest component of M1? What is the largest component of M2?
2. What is the difference between M1 and M2?

Action Graph online

For an animated version of this graph, visit **PearsonSuccessNet.com**

BELLRINGER

Bring in a pile of bank advertisements or brochures describing the different services they offer. Distribute these to students, asking them to look at them quickly and then pass them around. Then, ask students to write two lists in their notebooks. On the first list, have them write down all the services they might use a bank for today. On the second list, have them write down all the services they might go to a bank for ten years from now.

Teach

Economics online To present this topic using digital resources, use the lecture notes on www.PearsonSuccessNet.com.

PERSONAL FINANCE ACTIVITY

Remind students that by reading "Checking Up on Checking Accounts" in the Personal Finance Handbook (pp. PF6–7), they can get help in evaluating banks to choose the one that is right for them. You may want to assign the activity worksheet (Personal Finance All-in-One, pp. 38–39).

DISCUSS FIGURE 10.2

Have students list with you on the board each component of the M1 and M2 as shown in Figure 10.2. Discuss each one. Ask **How can your actions affect these components?** *(more deposits, more spending, move money around)* **Why do you think the economist's interest in these numbers is like a doctor's interest in someone's blood pressure?** *(It is a view of how much money is in circulation. It is a clue to the health of the economy.)*

Action Graph online Have students review the Action Graph animation for a step-by-step look at major components of the money supply.

Differentiated Resources

L1 L2 Guided Reading and Review (Unit 4 All-in-One, p. 28)

L2 Make Predictions About Banking (Unit 4 All-in-One, p. 30)

L2 Digital Age Literacy (Unit 4 All-in-One, p. 32)

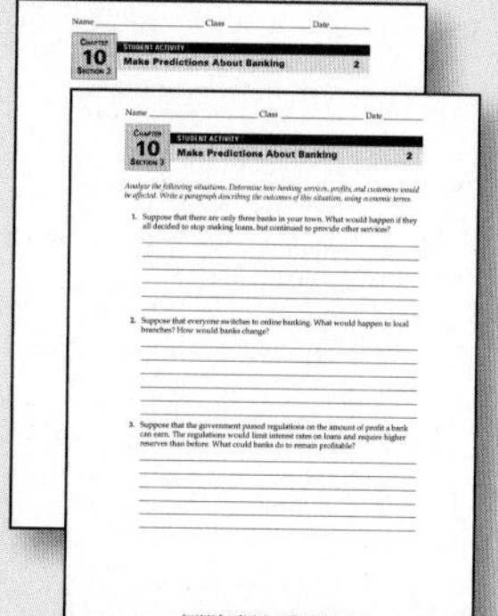

Answers

Checkpoint M2

Graph Skills 1. currency; savings deposits
2. M1 includes only liquid assets, while M2 includes those that are less liquid, too.

REVIEW THE BELLRINGER

Ask students to share the services they listed in their Bellringer entries. Create a class list. Ask **Why would some of these services be useful to you in the future, but not now?** *(Students may note that today they need to get access to cash, to save for college, and to get a car. They would not be looking to buy a house or start a retirement fund yet, but might do so once they have jobs and families.)* **What do you think the bank gets out of it when you use these services?** *(The bank gets to use your money to loan to others.)*

ANALYZE

Display the "Bank Statement" transparency (Color Transparencies, 10.b) and tell students this is a monthly bank statement for a customer of Clear Fast Bank. Ask **What services is this customer using?** *(checking account, debit card, savings account, online bill payment)* Add these to the class list of banking services. Ask **What does the statement tell the customer about the account?** *(account balance, amounts paid out, amounts deposited, bank charges, transaction dates)* **Is saving money the purpose for any of these transactions? How do you know?** *(The statement shows a transfer to a savings account.)* **How has the bank made money from this customer?** *(check fees, debit card fees, monthly checking account fee)*

Refer students to the How the Economy Works feature. Note that Friendly Bank is required to keep 20 percent of its deposits on hand. Ask **If Clear Fast Bank is required to keep 10 percent of deposits in reserve, how much of the money deposited into this checking account can the bank lend to customers?** *(90% x $995.56 = $896.00)*

L2 ELL Differentiate Have students talk through what is happening in each transaction, so that they can see the movement of money. Emphasize what the statement tells the customer.

How the Economy Works

How does the fractional reserve system work?

In fractional reserve banking, banks keep a fraction of their funds on hand and lend the remainder to customers.

1 It's been a good week at Acme Products, so owner Don Hennessey is able to deposit **$10,000** in his account at the Friendly Bank.

2 Marco Gonzalez wants to buy a car. Friendly Bank can lend him 80 percent of the money Don deposited, or **$8,000.** The bank holds 20 percent, or **$2,000,** in reserve.

Original Deposit | **Loans**

As you read in Section 2, FDIC insurance protects people from losing their money if the bank is unable to repay funds.

Saving Money

Banks offer a variety of ways for people to save money. Four of the most common ways are savings accounts, checking accounts, money market accounts, and certificates of deposit (CDs).

Savings accounts and checking accounts are the most common types of bank accounts. They are especially useful for people who need to make frequent withdrawals. Savings accounts and most checking accounts pay interest at an annual rate.

Money market accounts and certificates of deposits (CDs) are special kinds of savings accounts that pay a higher rate of interest than savings and checking accounts. Money market accounts allow you to save and to write a limited number of checks. Interest rates are not fixed, but can move up or down. CDs, on the other hand, offer a guaranteed rate of interest. Funds placed in a CD, however, cannot be removed until the end of a certain time period, such as one or two years. Customers who remove their money before that time pay a penalty for early withdrawal.

Loans

Banks also perform the important service of providing loans. As you have read, the first banks started doing business when goldsmiths issued paper receipts. These receipts represented gold coins that the goldsmiths held in safe storage for their customers. They would charge a small fee for this service.

In early banks, those receipts were fully backed by gold—every customer who held

For an animated, interactive version of this feature, visit **PearsonSuccessNet.com**

3 The car dealer who sold Marco the car puts the $8,000 in his bank account at the Even Friendlier Bank. The bank lends 80 percent, or **$6,400,** to Jack and Ginny Li, who are redecorating their living room. The bank holds the remaining **$1,600** in reserve.

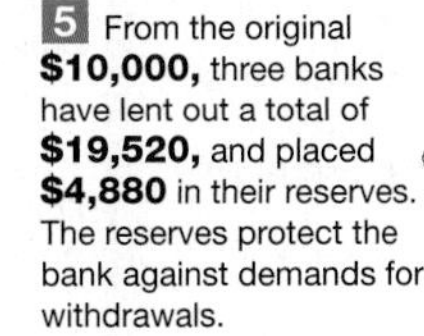

4 The owner of the furniture store deposits the $6,400 in the Friendliest of All Bank. The bank then lends 80 percent of $6,400, or **$5,120,** to C.S. Perkins, to help him pay for college. The bank puts the remaining **$1,280** in reserve.

5 From the original **$10,000,** three banks have lent out a total of **$19,520,** and placed **$4,880** in their reserves. The reserves protect the bank against demands for withdrawals.

Check Your Understanding

1. By Step 3, how much of the original $10,000 is still being held in bank reserves?
2. What would happen if banks were required to keep all deposits in reserve?

Final Result

a receipt could be sure that the goldsmith kept the equivalent amount of gold in his safe. Gradually, however, goldsmiths realized that their customers seldom, if ever, asked for all of their gold on one day. Goldsmiths could thus lend out half or even three quarters of their gold at any one time and still have enough gold to handle customer demand. Why did goldsmiths want to lend gold? The answer is that they charged interest on their loans. By keeping just enough gold reserves to cover demand, goldsmiths could run a profitable business lending deposits to borrowers and earning interest.

A banking system that keeps only a fraction of its funds on hand and lends out the remainder is called **fractional reserve banking.** Like the early banks, today's banks also operate on this principle. They lend money to homeowners for home improvements, to families to pay for college tuition, and to businesses. The more money a bank lends out, and the higher the interest rate it charges borrowers, the more profit the bank is able to make.

By making loans, banks help new businesses get started, and they help established businesses grow. When a business gets a loan, that business can create new jobs by hiring new workers or investing in physical capital in order to increase production.

A business that gets a loan may also help other businesses grow. For example, suppose you and a friend want to start a window-washing business. Your business will need supplies like window cleaner and ladders, so the companies that make your supplies will also benefit. They may even hire workers to expand their businesses.

Bankers must, however, consider the security of the loans they make. Suppose

fractional reserve banking a banking system that keeps only a fraction of its funds on hand and lends out the remainder

DISTRIBUTE ACTIVITY WORKSHEET

Distribute the "Make Predictions About Banking" Worksheet (Unit 4 All-in-One, p. 29) to students. Tell them that they will make predictions about the results of three banking scenarios. Their predictions should be based on reasonable economic business decisions. Tell students to use appropriate economic terms. Students can share their predictions with the class.

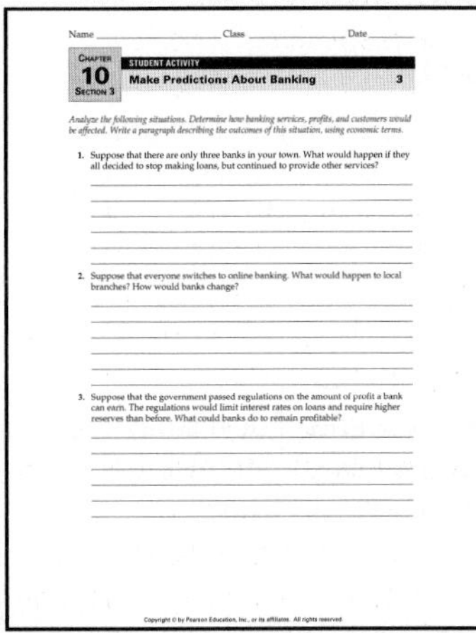

Name ________ Class ________ Date ________

CHAPTER 10 SECTION 3 — STUDENT ACTIVITY

Make Predictions About Banking 3

Analyze the following situations. Determine how banking services, profits, and customers would be affected. Write a paragraph describing the outcomes of this situation, using economic terms.

1. Suppose that there are only three banks in your town. What would happen if they all decided to stop making loans, but continued to provide other services?
2. Suppose that everyone switches to online banking. What would happen to local branches? How would banks change?
3. Suppose that the government passed regulations on the amount of profit a bank can earn. The regulations would limit interest rates on loans and require higher reserves than before. What could banks do to remain profitable?

L1 L2 Differentiate Distribute the "Make Predictions About Banking" worksheet (Unit 4 All-in-One, p. 30) to help students understand the topic.

Virtual Economics

L3 Differentiate

Compare Mainstream and Alternative Financial Institutions Use the following lesson from the NCEE **Virtual Economics *CD-ROM*** to help students evaluate alternative financial institutions. Click on Browse Economics Lessons, specify grades 9–12, and use the key words *financial institutions.*

In this activity, students will use case studies to compare the advantages and disadvantages of mainstream and alternative financial institutions.

LESSON TITLE	FINANCIAL INSTITUTIONS
Type of Activity	Case studies
Complexity	Moderate
Time	50 minutes
NCEE Standards	10

Answers

Check Your Understanding 1. 3,600.00, or 20%
2. They would be unable to make loans.

EXPLAIN

Have students explain what is happening at each line of Figure 10.3, "Compound Interest." They should be able to explain why the principal amount changes, why the interest amount changes, and why compound interest is better than simple interest.

Action Graph online Have students review the Action Graph animation for a step-by-step look at Compound Interest.

PERSONAL FINANCE ACTIVITY

To help students make wise saving and investment decisions, you may want to use the Personal Finance Handbook lesson "Get Personal with Your Savings Plan" (pp. PF18–19) and the activity worksheet (Personal Finance All-in-One, pp. 56–57).

CALCULATE

Discuss mortgages with students. Form small groups of students and have them investigate mortgages using the Internet and local banks as resources. Have each group find a house that they like to use as a model purchase, and then investigate mortgage rates, and determine what their payments would be with at least three different down payments. Have students determine the total amount they would pay as well as the interest and the principal. There are mortgage calculators available on the Internet to help determine these amounts.

L4 Differentiate Have students determine the amount of income that would be needed to maintain the mortgage on a specific house. They will need to determine normal expenses, including utilities and mortgage payments, at the prevailing rates.

CREATE A PROFILE

Have students use the Career Link worksheet to record their research for the activity (Unit 4 All-in-One, p. 80).

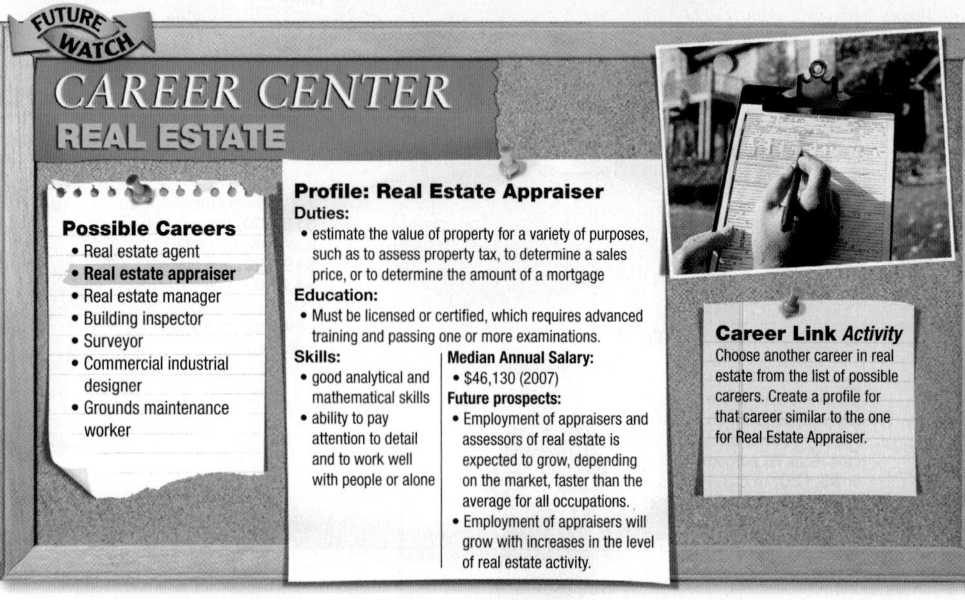
FUTURE WATCH
CAREER CENTER
REAL ESTATE
Possible Careers
• Real estate agent
• Real estate appraiser
• Real estate manager
• Building inspector
• Surveyor
• Commercial industrial designer
• Grounds maintenance worker
Profile: Real Estate Appraiser
Duties:
• estimate the value of property for a variety of purposes, such as to assess property tax, to determine a sales price, or to determine the amount of a mortgage
Education:
• Must be licensed or certified, which requires advanced training and passing one or more examinations.
Skills:
• good analytical and mathematical skills
• ability to pay attention to detail and to work well with people or alone
Median Annual Salary:
• $46,130 (2007)
Future prospects:
• Employment of appraisers and assessors of real estate is expected to grow, depending on the market, faster than the average for all occupations.
• Employment of appraisers will grow with increases in the level of real estate activity.
Career Link Activity
Choose another career in real estate from the list of possible careers. Create a profile for that career similar to the one for Real Estate Appraiser.

default failing to pay back a loan

mortgage a specific type of loan that is used to buy real estate

credit card a card entitling its owner to buy goods and services based on the owner's promise to pay for those goods and services

interest the price paid for the use of borrowed money

principal the amount of money borrowed

borrowers **default,** or fail to pay back their loans. Then the bank may lose a large part, or even the entire amount, of the money it has loaned. Bankers therefore always face a trade-off between profits and safety. If they make too many bad loans—loans that are not repaid—they may go out of business altogether. (See your Personal Finance Handbook to learn more about banks and the services they offer.)

Mortgages

A **mortgage** is a specific type of loan that is used to buy real estate. Suppose the Lee family wants to buy a house for $250,000. They are unlikely to have the cash on hand to be able to pay for the house. Like almost all home buyers, they will need to take out a mortgage.

The Lees can afford to make a down payment of 20 percent of the price of the house, or $50,000. After investigating the Lees' creditworthiness, their bank agrees to lend them the remaining $200,000 so that they can purchase their new house. Mortgages usually last for 15, 25, or 30 years. According to the terms of their loan, the Lees are responsible for paying back the loan, plus whatever interest the bank charges, in regular monthly payments over a period of 25 years.

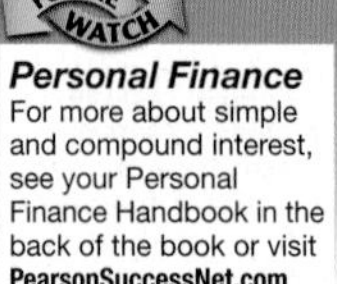
FUTURE WATCH

Personal Finance
For more about simple and compound interest, see your Personal Finance Handbook in the back of the book or visit **PearsonSuccessNet.com**

Credit Cards

Another service that banks provide is issuing **credit cards**—cards entitling their owners to buy goods and services based on the owners' promise to pay. How do credit cards work? Suppose you buy a sleeping bag and tent for $100 on May 3. Your credit-card bill may not arrive until June. You do not actually pay for the gear until you pay that bill. In the meantime, however, the credit-card issuer (often a bank) will have paid the sporting-goods store. Your payment repays the bank for the "loan" of $100. If you do not pay your credit-card bill in full when you receive it, you will end up paying a high rate of interest on that loan.

Simple and Compound Interest

As you have read, **interest** is the price paid for the use of borrowed money. The amount borrowed is called the **principal.** Simple interest is interest paid only on principal. For example, if you deposit

$100 in a savings account at 5 percent simple interest, you will make $5 in a year (assuming that interest is paid annually).

Suppose that you leave the $5 in interest in the bank, so that at the end of the year you have $105 in your account—$100 in principal and $5 in interest. Compound interest is interest paid on both principal and accumulated interest. That means that in the second year, as long as you leave both the principal and the interest in your account, interest will be paid on $105. In **Figure 10.3** you can see how an account paying compound interest grows over time.

Banks and Profit

The largest source of income for banks is the interest they receive from customers who have taken loans. Banks, of course, also pay out interest on customers' savings and most checking accounts. The amount of interest they pay out, however, is less than the amount of interest they charge on loans. The difference in the amounts is how banks cover their costs and make a profit.

CHECKPOINT ***Why are checking accounts more useful than CDs for people who must make frequent withdrawals?***

Types of Financial Institutions

Several kinds of financial institutions operate in the United States. These include commercial banks, savings and loan associations, mutual savings banks, and credit unions. During the 1990s, these financial institutions became more similar than dissimilar, although differences still remain.

Commercial Banks

Commercial banks, which traditionally served businesses, offer a wide range of services today. Commercial banks offer checking accounts, accept deposits, and make loans to businesses and to individuals. Some commercial banks are chartered by states and are regulated by state authorities and by the Federal Deposit Insurance Corporation (FDIC). About one third of all commercial banks are national banks and are part of the Federal Reserve System. Commercial banks provide the most services and play the largest role in the economy of any type of bank.

Figure 10.3 Compound Interest

End of Year	Principal Amount	Interest Earned at 5%	Principal at End of Year
—	$100.00	$5.00	$105.00
1	$105.00	$5.25	$110.25
2	$110.25	$5.51	$115.76
5	$127.63	$6.38	$134.01
10	$162.90	$8.14	$171.04
15	$207.90	$10.39	$218.29

CHART SKILLS

The chart at left shows the money earned on a $100 deposit when interest is compounded yearly at 5 percent.

1. How many years does it take for the original deposit to double?
2. After five years, what is the total interest that the deposit-holder will have earned?

Action Graph online

For an animated version of this graph, visit **PearsonSuccessNet.com**

CREATE A CHART

Form a small group for each type of financial institution mentioned on pages 269–271. Have each group contribute to a class chart identifying the common services offered by each type of institution. Have them use a telephone book or the Internet to locate examples of each. Once the chart is complete, have students identify how many of the services are offered by more than one type of institution. Ask **Which type of institution would you prefer to use for each service? Why? What questions would you have to ask to make an informed decision?**

Background Note

Adjustable-Rate Mortgages With an adjustable-rate mortgage (ARM), the interest rate changes. An ARM usually starts with low monthly payments because of a low interest rate. After an initial period, the interest may change every year or five years. It is recalculated, based on a chosen index, like Treasury securities. The interest, and so the payment, can go up or down. Some ARMs limit the amount the interest or payment can increase; many do not. Sometimes ARM payments rise so high that people cannot afford their revised mortgage payments. Many try to refinance their mortgage with a lower interest rate or decide to sell. Sometimes a house will go into foreclosure because of these revised payments.

Answers

Checkpoint You must pay a penalty for withdrawing funds from a CD early. Early withdrawals would probably be necessary during the term of a CD for someone who makes frequent withdrawals.

Chart Skills 1. about 15 years 2. $34.01

ACT OUT A PROCESS

Have students walk through the process shown in Figure 10.4 and in the How the Economy Works feature on pp. 266–267. Distribute paper 'money' to students and have them play the roles of bankers, savers, and borrowers. At each stage, ask students to describe what is occurring and what has happened to the money. Discuss the decisions bankers must make about the money deposited or paid to them and what benefits each party receives.

L2 Differentiate Have students draw a flowchart to show the path that $100 might take from their pocket to the various outcomes.

Action Graph online Have students review the Action Graph animation for a step-by-step look at How Banks Make a Profit.

CHECK COMPREHENSION

Display the "Bank Statement" transparency (Color Transparency 10.b) again. Ask **What electronic banking services are shown on this statement?** *(automatic payroll deposit, debit card, online bill payment)* Discuss aspects of electronic banking. For each of the services listed in this section, ask students to explain what is actually happening, how information is being transmitted, and offer benefits and drawbacks in using this type of banking.

PERSONAL FINANCE ACTIVITY

Remind students they can learn how to use online banking by reading the "Banking Online" section in the Personal Finance Handbook (pp. PF8–9). You may want to assign the activity worksheet (Personal Finance All-in-One, pp. 41–42).

Answers

Chart Skills 1. deposits from customers, interest from borrowers, and fees for services 2. to cover its costs and make a profit

Figure 10.4 How Banks Make a Profit

CHART SKILLS

A bank uses the money customers have deposited to lend to businesses and other borrowers. The bank uses this income to cover its costs and make a profit.

1. What are the sources of a bank's income?
2. Why is the interest banks pay to depositors at a lower rate than the interest banks charge to lenders?

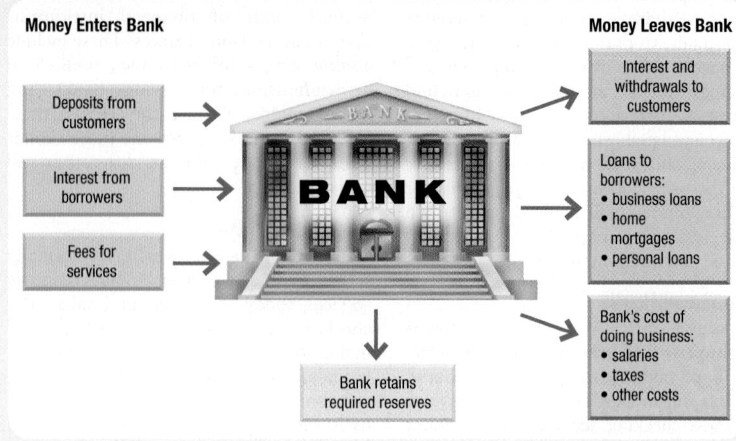

Action Graph online

For an animated version of this graph, visit PearsonSuccessNet.com

Savings and Loan Associations

Savings and Loan Associations (S&Ls), which you read about in Section 2, were originally chartered to lend money for building homes during the mid-1800s. Members of S&Ls deposited funds into a large general fund and then borrowed enough money to build their own houses. Savings and Loans are also called thrifts because they originally enabled "thrifty" working-class people—that is, people who were careful with their money—to save up and borrow enough to build or buy their own homes. Over time, S&Ls have taken on many of the same functions as commercial banks.

Savings Banks

Mutual savings banks (MSBs) originated in the early 1800s to serve people who made smaller deposits and transactions than commercial banks wished to handle. Mutual savings banks were owned by the depositors themselves, who shared in any profits. Later, many MSBs began to sell stock to raise additional capital. These institutions became simply savings banks because depositors no longer owned them.

Although savings banks were traditionally concentrated in the Northeast, they had an important influence on the national economy. In 1972, the Consumer's Savings Bank of Worcester, Massachusetts, introduced a Negotiable Order of Withdrawal (NOW) account, a type of checking account that pays interest. NOW accounts became available nationwide in 1980.

Credit Unions

Credit unions are cooperative lending associations usually established by and for particular groups, usually employees of a specific firm or government agency. Some are open to an entire community. Credit unions are commonly fairly small and specialize in consumer loans, usually at interest rates favorable to members. Some credit unions also provide checking account services.

Finance Companies

Finance companies make installment loans to consumers. These loans spread the cost of major purchases such as computers, cars, and large appliances over a number of months. Because people who borrow from finance companies more frequently fail to repay the loans, finance companies generally charge higher interest rates than banks do.

CHECKPOINT ***Which type of financial institution plays the largest role in the economy?***

Electronic Banking

Banks began to use computers in the early 1970s to keep track of transactions. As computers have become more common in the United States, their role in banking has also increased dramatically. In fact, computerized banking may revolutionize banking in much the same way that paper currency changed banking long ago.

Automated Teller Machines

If you use an Automated Teller Machine (ATM), you are already familiar with one of the most common types of electronic banking. ATMs are computers that customers can use to deposit money, withdraw cash, and obtain account information at their convenience. Instead of having to conduct banking business face-to-face with a teller during the bank's hours of operation, you can take care of your finances at an ATM.

ATMs are convenient for both banks and for customers, since they are available 24 hours a day and reduce banks' labor costs. Their popularity has made them a standard feature of modern banking.

Debit Cards

At an ATM, bank customers can use a **debit card** to withdraw money from an account. They can also use a debit card in stores equipped with special machines. When you "swipe" your debit card through one of those machines, the card sends a message to your bank to debit, or subtract money from, your checking account. The money goes directly into the store's bank account. For security, debit cards require customers to use personal identification numbers, or PINs, to authorize financial transactions.

debit card a card used to withdraw money from a bank account

Home Banking

More and more people are using the Internet to conduct their financial business. Many banks, credit unions, and other financial institutions allow people to check account balances, transfer money to different accounts, automatically deposit their paychecks, and pay their bills via computer. Many Americans have also opened accounts with private online bill-paying services and money-transfer services that allow them to send money instantly over the Internet.

Personal Finance For more help in beginning online banking, see your Personal Finance Handbook in the back of the book or visit **PearsonSuccessNet.com**

Global Impact

Easy Access

The first electronic Automated Teller Machine network was unveiled in Dallas, Texas, in 1968. Today, there are more than 1.5 million ATMs throughout the world, in banks, stores, shopping centers, cruise ships, even on ships in the U.S. Navy. Every eight minutes a new ATM is installed somewhere in the world. ***Review the chart tracking the number of ATMs per 100,000 people in a number of countries. Do you think the wide gap in ATM access among nations will lessen over time? Why or Why not?***

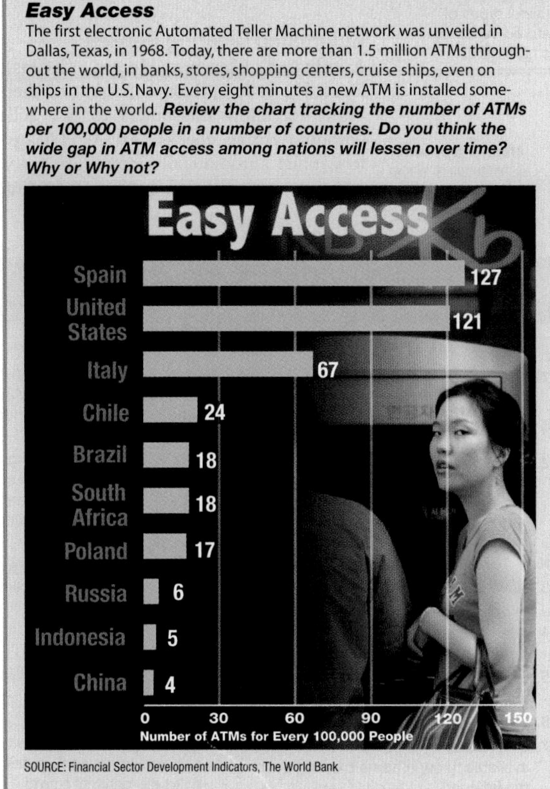

SOURCE: Financial Sector Development Indicators, The World Bank

DISTRIBUTE SKILL WORKSHEET

Ask students if they have heard warnings about banking and making purchases over the Internet. Distribute the "Digital Age Literacy" skill worksheet (Unit 4 All-in-One, p. 31).

Have students review the lesson in the Social Studies Skills Handbook on page S-20. Remind them to use the lesson steps to complete the activities.

L2 Differentiate Distribute the "Digital Age Literacy" worksheet (Unit 4 All-in-One, p. 32) to students. Ask students to complete the worksheet keeping in mind the class discussion on electronic banking. Make a class list of "warnings."

EXTEND

Have students find information from two local banks and determine the services each offers to businesses. Have students create a comparative brochure of business services.

L4 Differentiate Have students research the terms of one major credit card and identify annual fees, interest rates, and other fees. Have students investigate how long the customer has to pay the bill and what happens if they do not pay it on time. Students should then use newspaper ads to create a monthly bill with at least five purchases. Have students write a paragraph explaining how the bill will be paid and the costs for immediate full payment and for paying over six months.

GUIDING QUESTION WRAP UP

Have students return to the section Guiding Question. Review the completed graphic organizer and clarify any misunderstandings. Have a wrap up discussion about financial institutions.

Assess and Remediate

L3 L2 Collect the "Make Predictions About Banking" worksheets and the "Digital Age Literacy" worksheets and assess students understanding of banking services.

L3 Assign the Section 3 Assessment questions; identify student misconceptions.

L3 Give Section Quiz A (Unit 4 All-in-One, p. 33).

L2 Give Section Quiz B (Unit 4 All-in-One, p. 34).

(Assess and Remediate continued on p. 272)

Answers

Checkpoint commercial banks

Global Impact Possible responses: Yes. Nations with less ATM access will further develop their electronic banking systems.

Have students complete the Self-Test Online and continue their work in the **Essential Questions Journal**.

REMEDIATION AND SUGGESTIONS

Use the chart below to help students who are struggling with content.

WEAKNESS	REMEDIATION
Defining key terms (Questions 3, 4, 5, 6)	Have students use the interactive Economic Dictionary Online.
The money supply (Question 8)	Reteach by having students create cards with each component and then accurately categorize each card under M1 or M2 and tell why they put it there. Be sure that students understand that M2 includes all components of M1.
Functions and types of financial institutions (Questions 2, 9, 11)	Have students work in pairs to quiz each other on the functions of financial institutions.
Electronic banking (Questions 7, 10)	Have students clearly describe how each type of electronic banking works.

Answer

Checkpoint When a debit card is used, it automatically draws money from the checking account and that is transferred to the store's account.

▲ Phone cards, gift cards, and mass transit cards are among the many useful types of stored-value, or smart, cards.

Automated Clearing Houses

Automated Clearing Houses (ACHs), located at Federal Reserve Banks and their branches, allow consumers to pay bills without writing checks. An ACH transfers funds automatically from customers' accounts to creditors' accounts. (A **creditor** is a person or institution to whom money is owed.) People can use ACHs to pay regular monthly bills such as mortgage payments, rent, utility bills, and insurance premiums. They save time and postage costs, and end any worries about forgetting to make a payment.

creditor a person or institution to whom money is owed

Stored-Value Cards

Stored-value cards, or smart cards, are similar to debit cards. These cards carry embedded magnetic strips or computer chips with account balance information. College students may be issued a smart card to pay for cafeteria food, computer time, or photocopying. Phone cards, with which customers prepay for a specified amount of long-distance calling, are also smart cards, as are gift cards. Some people even use a special kind of smart card in place of a bank account. They can make deposits, withdraw cash, or pay bills with the card.

Will stored-value smart cards someday replace cash altogether? No one can know for sure, but private companies and public facilities continue to explore new uses for smart card technology.

CHECKPOINT ***How does a debit card work?***

SECTION 3 ASSESSMENT

Essential Questions Journal To continue to build a response to the Essential Question, go to your **Essential Questions Journal.**

Guiding Question

1. Use your completed concept web to answer this question: What banking services do financial institutions provide?
2. **Extension** If you were opening a checking account at a local bank, what services would you expect your bank to provide?

Key Terms and Main Ideas

3. How does **fractional reserve banking** help banks earn a profit?
4. What happens when borrowers **default** on their loans?
5. Describe a situation in which a person would need a **mortgage** from a bank.
6. When would you pay **interest?**
7. List at least three services that are available through home banking over the Internet.

Critical Thinking

8. **Summarize (a)** What kinds of money are included in M1 and M2? **(b)** Why do economists use these different categories?
9. **Extend** If you are planning to leave money in a savings account for 10 years, would it be better to receive simple interest or compound interest? Explain.
10. **Contrast (a)** In what ways are debit cards and stored-value cards similar? **(b)** How are they different?

Math Skills

11. There is a simple formula for finding simple interest:

$$I = prt.$$

To find the interest (I), multiply your principal (p) times the interest rate (r) times the length of time (t). The interest rate must be expressed in the form of a decimal. For example, 1% interest would equal 0.01, and 10% interest would equal 0.10. The time is the number of years your deposit draws interest. Use this formula to answer the following questions:

(a) Suppose your bank pays an interest rate of 6% per year. What is the interest rate in decimal form? **(b)** Suppose you keep $500 in the bank for ten years, receiving 6% simple interest. Write the numbers into the formula to calculate simple interest. **(c)** How much interest will you receive at the end of the ten years?

Visit PearsonSuccessNet.com for additional math help.

Assessment Answers

1. Possible response: Financial institutions provide checking services, savings accounts, investment opportunities, and loans.
2. Possible answers: checking account that pays interest, direct deposit, ATM access
3. Banks must keep only a fraction of their reserves on hand and can lend the rest, which earns interest. The interest can be taken as profit.
4. They fail to pay back their loans.
5. People need a mortgage when purchasing a house that costs more than they can pay in cash.
6. When you take a loan, you pay interest on it.
7. check account balances, make transfers, pay bills
8. (a) M1 includes currency, demand deposits in banks, and traveler's checks. M2 includes everything in M1 plus savings deposits, money market funds, and small time deposits. (b) to get an accurate picture of the size and nature of the current money supply
9. For a ten-year deposit, compound interest is better, because you would receive interest on the accumulated interest as well as on the principal.
10. (a) Both access account balance information and change the balance when used. (b) Debit cards can be used in many places, while smart cards are used only in specified places.
11. (a) .06 (b) I = 500 × .06 × 10 (c) $300

QUICK STUDY GUIDE

QUICK STUDY GUIDE

Chapter 10: Money and Banking

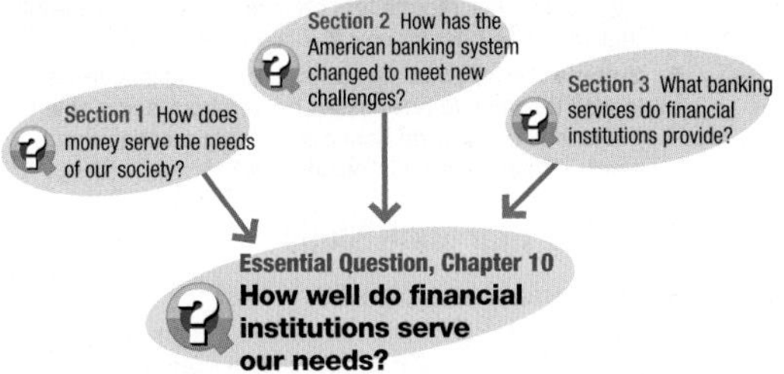

Section 2 How has the American banking system changed to meet new challenges?
Section 1 How does money serve the needs of our society?
Section 3 What banking services do financial institutions provide?
Essential Question, Chapter 10
How well do financial institutions serve our needs?

Developments in U.S. Banking

Problem	Problem Resolved by	Date
Many different currencies in the U.S.	National Banking Acts	1863, 1864
Gold did not support U.S. currency	U.S. adopts gold standard	1870s
No central decision-making authority to regulate banks	Federal Reserve System	1913
No central bank to monitor reserves	Federal Reserve System	1913
No insurance on savings deposits	FDIC	1933
No convenient way of getting bank credit for small purchases	First bank-issued credit card	1946
Difficult for people to get consumer credit	Development of credit unions	1909
Making deposits and withdrawals outside business hours	Automated teller machines	1968

Economic Dictionary

money, *p. 249*
medium of exchange, *p. 249*
barter, *p. 249*
unit of account, *p. 251*
store of value, *p. 251*
currency, *p. 252*
commodity money, *p. 254*
representative money, *p. 254*
specie, *p. 254*
fiat money, *p. 255*
bank, *p. 256*
national bank, *p. 257*
bank run, *p. 258*
greenback, *p. 259*
gold standard, *p. 259*
central bank, *p. 260*
member bank, *p. 260*
foreclosure, *p. 263*
money supply, *p. 264*
liquidity, *p. 264*
demand deposit, *p. 264*
money market mutual fund, *p. 265*
fractional reserve banking, *p. 267*
default, *p. 268*
mortgage, *p. 268*
credit card, *p. 268*
interest, *p. 268*
principal, *p. 268*
debit card, *p. 271*
creditor, *p. 272*

Economics *on the go*

Study anytime, anywhere. Download these files today.

Economic Dictionary online	Audio Review online	Action Graph online	Visual Glossary online	How the Economy Works online
Vocabulary Support in English and Spanish	Audio Study Guide in English and Spanish	Animated Charts and Graphs	Animated feature	Animated feature

Download to your computer or mobile device at PearsonSuccessNet.com

ASSIGN THE ESSENTIAL QUESTIONS JOURNAL

After students have finished studying the chapter, they should return to the chapter's essential question in the Essential Questions Journal and complete the activity.

Tell students to go back to the chapter opener and look at the image. Using the information they have gained from studying the chapter, ask **How does this illustrate the main ideas of the chapter?** *(Possible responses: Financial institutions meet our needs by keeping money in circulation, by making money available through loans, and by regulating banking and other financial functions.)*

STUDY TIPS

Tell students that when reading they need to understand how details fit into the main idea. Suggest that they turn headings into main idea statements and determine then how the details from the paragraph support that statement.

Economics *on the go* Have students download the digital resources available at Economics on the Go for review and remediation.

Assessment at a Glance

TESTS AND QUIZZES

Section Assessments

Section Quizzes A and B, **Unit 4 All-in-One**

Self-Test Online

Chapter Assessments

Chapter Tests A and B, **Unit 4 All-in-One**

Economic Detective, **Unit 4 All-in-One**

Document-based Assessment, p. 275

Exam*View*

AYP Monitoring Assessments

PERFORMANCE ASSESSMENT

Teacher's Edition, pp. 251, 253, 258, 259, 267, 271

Simulation Activities, Chapter 10

Virtual Economics on CD-ROM, pp. 252, 260, 267

Essential Questions Journal, Chapter 10

Assessment Rubrics

Chapter Assessment

1. (a) Possible answers: because the person receiving the money can spend it; because people have confidence in its value (b) if the federal government stopped supporting it (c) Possible answers: through barter; using money from other countries
2. (a) power to charter banks, to require banks to hold adequate gold and silver reserves to cover bank notes, and to issue national currency (b) Since banks were chartered and required to have adequate reserves, wildcat banks and fraud were better controlled. A national currency meant all money was worth the same amount. (c) Possible answer: Requiring adequate reserves forced banks everywhere to meet their obligations and stopped panics.
3. (a) Regulations included the amount of interest the banks paid customers and customers paid for loans. (b) deregulation, which allowed intense competition; long-term loans at low interest; high interest paid to depositors; losses on bad loans; individual bank managers acting for their own gain (c) Possible answers: federal laws regulating interest rates; protection by the FDIC.
4. (a) checking account, savings account, CD, money market account (b) A CD would be the best choice because you do not need access to the money for two years and it will earn the most interest.
5. (a) to buy houses and cars and to open businesses (b) They can expand operations, purchase more goods, hire more employees, or open new markets. (c) Every loan banks make generates interest, which is their profit; loans contribute to the growth of businesses, which may bring more customers into the bank.
6. $250
7. $1,250
8. $1,276.28
9. $26.28
10. (a) Students should list activities that include holding, saving, and loaning money for various purposes. (b) There should be a direct relationship between the bank activities and the benefit to the community.
11. Possible answers: (a) My bank would offer free debit cards and electronic banking, too, but might add live support 24 hours a day. (b) My bank might rely on its knowledge of the community to offer low-interest loans to people whose history of paying back loans is not perfect but has improved over time. (c) My bank will not match this offer.

CHAPTER 10 ASSESSMENT

Self-Test online To test your understanding of key terms and main ideas, visit **PearsonSuccessNet.com**

Key Terms and Main Ideas

To make sure you understand the key terms and main ideas of this chapter, review the Checkpoint and Section Assessment questions and look at the Quick Study Guide on the preceding page.

Critical Thinking

1. **Predict (a)** Why is money acceptable to people in the United States? **(b)** What could cause people to stop accepting money? **(c)** Suppose American merchants stopped accepting dollars. Predict how people might get the goods and services they need.
2. **Evaluate (a)** Identify the powers the National Banking Acts of 1863 and 1864 gave to the federal government. **(b)** How did each of these powers help stabilize the American banking system? **(c)** Which of these reforms do you think contributed most to the stability of American money and banks? Why?
3. **Extend (a)** In what ways did the government regulate banks from the 1930s until the 1960s? **(b)** What factors contributed to the S&L crisis in the 1980s? **(c)** What regulations could help prevent another S&L crisis in the future?

CLOSED

4. **Select** Suppose you have $2,000 that you want to save for college. You plan to leave the money in the bank for at least two years. **(a)** List four types of accounts where you could keep your money. **(b)** Suppose interest rates today are very high. Using this information, choose the type of account that would be best for you. Explain your choice.
5. **Summarize (a)** What are some reasons individuals need loans? **(b)** How do businesses benefit from being able to get loans? **(c)** How do banks profit from meeting these needs of individuals and businesses?

Applying Your Math Skills

Simple and Compound Interest

You have already learned how to calculate simple interest: $I = prt$. To find a final balance with simple interest, add the interest and the principal. Your new formula will look like this:

$$B = prt + p$$

The formula to find a final balance using compound interest uses the same original values as the formula for simple interest: principal, interest rate expressed as a decimal, and time. Here is the formula for finding a balance using compound interest:

$$B = p(1 + r)^t$$

Suppose you have $1,000 in a bank account that pays 5% interest per year. Use your math skills and the formulas above to answer the following questions:

Visit PearsonSuccessNet.com for additional math help.

6. How much interest would you receive after five years if the bank paid simple interest?
7. How much would be in your bank account after five years if the bank paid simple interest?
8. How much would you have if the bank paid compound interest?
9. How much more money would you have if you received compound interest rather than simple interest?

Essential Question Activity

Essential Questions Journal To respond to the chapter Essential Question, go to your **Essential Questions Journal.**

10. Complete this activity to answer the Essential Question **How well do financial institutions serve our needs?** Imagine that after many years of service, you become the manager of the bank that serves the neighborhood in which you grew up. Your responsibility to the bank is to increase its profits. However, you also want to do good works in your community. Using the worksheet in your Essential Questions Journal or the electronic worksheet available at **PearsonSuccessNet.com,** gather the following information:
    (a) In the first column, write the services you will offer your customers.
    (b) In the second column, write how these services will benefit your neighborhood. For example, how might giving people mortgages be good for the neighborhood?

    Think about which services and benefits are most likely to attract customers to your bank. Based on your ideas, write one or more advertising slogans for your bank in the third column.
11. **Modify** Now suppose another bank opens down the block from your bank. Choose two of the following situations. Describe how each of them might cause you to modify the services you offer and how you choose to advertise.
    (a) The new bank offers free debit cards and electronic banking through the Internet.
    (b) The new bank offers low-interest mortgages—but only to borrowers who have an excellent history of paying back loans.
    (c) The new bank offers low interest mortgages to poor people who want to live in their own house but who may not be able to pay back their debt.

WebQuest online The Economics WebQuest challenges students to use 21st century skills to answer the Essential Question by providing details as to how well financial institutions serve our needs.

THE ESSENTIAL
VIDEO
By Students For Students
For videos on Essential Questions, go to PearsonSuccessNet.com

Remind students to continue to develop an Essential Questions video. Guidelines and a production binder are available at www.PearsonSuccessNet.com.

CHAPTER 10 ASSESSMENT

DOCUMENT-BASED ASSESSMENT

Is the move toward a "cashless" economy good or bad?

In the United States, people are replacing cash and paper checks with credit cards, debit cards, and electronic banking in many situations. Some people argue that this development has negative consequences for individuals and the economy. Others believe that going "cashless" can benefit the economy.

Document A

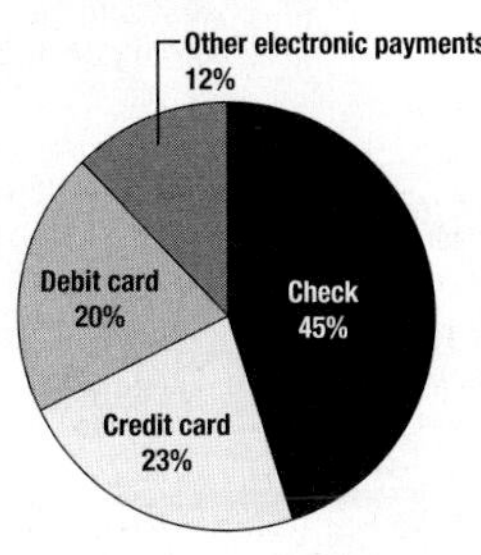

Document B

"The less cash that flows through our hands, the more intangible it becomes and the more we lose our sense of its real value.... Technology is simply making it easy not to count every dollar....

"Before you apply for a new "smart card," consider the tradeoff for convenience. The next time you're making a major purchase, say for a new washing machine, go to the bank, take out $450 and count out that fistful of bills for the sales clerk. You'll have a fuller appreciation of the cost, the satisfaction of exchanging tangible earnings for your betterment — and a sense of just what we're losing."

—From "Cash: An Endangered Species," by Chris Plummer, CBS Marketwatch, June 8, 2004

Document C

"Debit cards are often more convenient for consumers than paper checks.... Banks offer debit cards both because consumers have come to expect them, and because debit card transactions can be less costly for banks to process than cash or check transactions. Finally, ... merchants find debit cards attractive because it is often faster and less costly to accept payments by debit card than by cash or check. Card payments have become increasingly important in situations where transaction speed is a priority for merchants, such as in check-out lines and at fast food restaurants."

—From "A Summary of the Atlanta Forum on Transforming U.S. Retail Payments," The Federal Reserve Board, February 6, 2007

ANALYZING DOCUMENTS

Use your knowledge of the "cashless" economy and Documents A, B, and C to answer questions 1–3.

1. **Document A shows that, of payments that were not made in cash, the largest number were made by**
   - A. checks.
   - B. credit cards.
   - C. debit and credit cards combined.
   - D. debit cards and other electronic payments.

2. **According to Document B, what is the problem with having fewer cash transactions?**
   - A. Electronic transactions have serious security risks.
   - B. People who do not use cash have a harder time keeping track of their money.
   - C. There is no problem with having fewer cash transactions.
   - D. People who use electronic transactions are often charged additional fees.

3. **The authors of Document B and Document C would probably agree that debit cards**
   - A. are convenient for consumers.
   - B. should be used in more places.
   - C. benefit banks more than consumers.
   - D. help consumers borrow money easily.

WRITING ABOUT ECONOMICS

Whether increasing electronic payments will help or harm the U.S. economy is an ongoing issue. Use the documents on this page and resources on the Web site below to answer the question: ***Is the move toward a "cashless" economy good or bad?*** Use the sources to support your opinion.

In Partnership

To read more about issues related to this topic, visit **PearsonSuccessNet.com**

Document-Based Assessment

ANALYZING DOCUMENTS

1. A
2. B
3. A

WRITING ABOUT ECONOMICS

Possible answers: The move is good because electronic transactions are fast and convenient for both buyers and sellers. The move is bad because money transferred electronically does not seem real to people and they can lose a sense of real value.

Student essay should demonstrate an understanding of the issues involved in increasing electronic payments and a cashless economy. Use the following as guidelines to assess the essay.

L2 Differentiate Students use all documents on the page to support their thesis.

L3 Differentiate Students use the documents on this page and additional information available online at www.PearsonSuccessNet.com to support their answer.

L4 Differentiate Students incorporate information provided in the textbook and online at www.PearsonSuccessNet.com[end and include additional research to support their opinion.

Go Online to www.PearsonSuccessNet.com for a student rubric and extra documents.

Economics online *All print resources are available on the Teacher's Resource Library CD-ROM and online at* www.PearsonSuccessNet.com.

Essential Questions

UNIT 4:

How can you make the most of your money?

CHAPTER 11:

How do your saving and investment choices affect your future?

Introduce the Chapter

ACTIVATE PRIOR KNOWLEDGE

In this chapter, students will learn how to invest money and about the risks and benefits associated with various financial assets. Tell students to complete the warmup activity in the **Essential Questions Journal**.

DIFFERENTIATED INSTRUCTION KEY

- **L1** Special Needs
- **L2** Basic
  - **ELL** English Language Learners
  - **LPR** Less Proficient Readers
- **L3** All Students
- **L4** Advanced Students

Economics online Visit www.PearsonSuccessNet.com for an interactive textbook with built-in activities on economic principles.

- ***The Wall Street Journal*** **Classroom Edition Video** enhances the lesson on financial markets.
- **Yearly Update Worksheet** provides an annual update, including a new worksheet and lesson on this topic.
- **On the Go** resources can be downloaded so students and teachers can connect with economics anytime, anywhere.

Chapter 11 Financial Markets

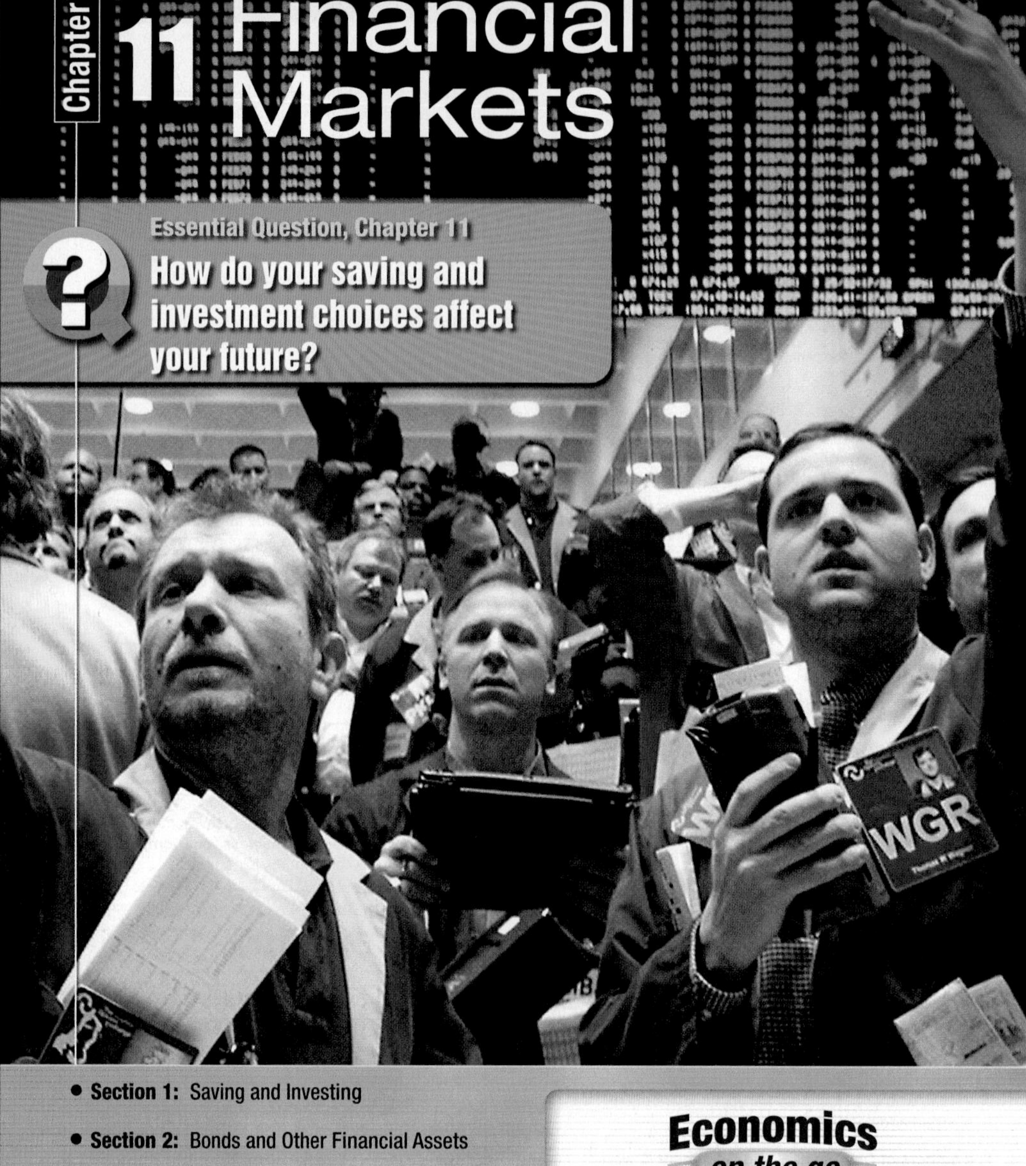

Essential Question, Chapter 11

How do your saving and investment choices affect your future?

- **Section 1:** Saving and Investing
- **Section 2:** Bonds and Other Financial Assets
- **Section 3:** The Stock Market

Economics on the go

To study anywhere, anytime, download these online resources at ***PearsonSuccessNet.com*** ▶

276 FINANCIAL MARKETS

ECONOMICS ONLINE

DIGITAL TEACHER TOOLS

The online lesson planner is designed to help teachers plan, teach, and assess. Teachers have the ability to use or customize existing Pearson lesson plans. Online lecture notes support the print lesson by providing an array of accessible activities and summaries of key concepts.

Two interactivities in this lesson are:

- **Visual Glossary** makes it easy to understand what capital gains are.
- **How the Economy Works** demonstrates a step-by-step look at the bond process.

Block Scheduling

BLOCK 1 Teach Section 1 and 2, omitting the Bellringer activities, and the Create an Advertisement option in Section 2.

BLOCK 2 Teach all of Section 3, including the Reenact and Role-Play activity.

Pressed for Time

Group work Organize the class into three groups. Assign each group one of the sections. Have each group create a presentation of the main points of its assigned material. As groups give their presentations, create a study guide on the board outlining each section's main points.

OBJECTIVES

1. **Describe** how investing contributes to the free enterprise system.
2. **Explain** how the financial system brings together savers and borrowers.
3. **Explain** the role of financial intermediaries in the financial system.
4. **Identify** the trade-offs among liquidity, return, and risk.

ECONOMIC DICTIONARY

As you read the section, look for the definitions of these **Key Terms:**

- investment
- financial system
- financial asset
- financial intermediary
- mutual fund
- hedge fund
- diversification
- portfolio
- prospectus
- return

Guiding Question

What are the benefits and risks of saving and investing?

Copy this concept web and fill it in as you read.

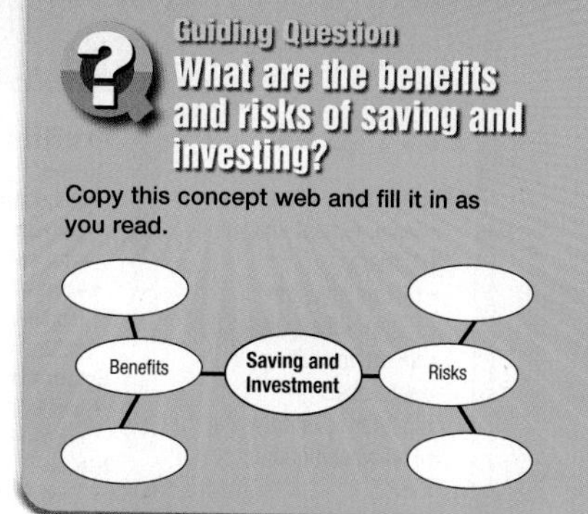

Economics and You

Right now, you are making a huge investment. You are investing your time and energy in your education. This investment is likely to pay off later, in the form of a satisfying career. In the same way, businesses and governments look to the future. If a firm builds a new plant, it invests money today for the sake of earning more money later. If the government builds a new dam, it invests money today to ensure that people will have hydroelectric power in the future.

Principles in Action There are both benefits and risks to savings and investment. The savings you put in the bank will grow with almost no risk to the principle. However, as this section points out, a properly timed investment can bring a much greater reward than the same money put away in savings. On the other hand, if your investment is wrongly placed or ill-timed, you may wish you had never taken the money out of the bank.

FUTURE WATCH

Personal Finance
For more help in making wise investment decisions, see your Personal Finance Handbook in the back of the book or visit **PearsonSuccessNet.com**

Investing and Free Enterprise

In its most general sense, **investment** is the act of redirecting resources from being consumed today so that they may create benefits in the future. In more narrow, economic terms, investment is the use of assets to earn income or profit.

Investing, in fact, is an essential part of the free enterprise system. It promotes economic growth and contributes to a nation's wealth. When people deposit money in a savings account in a bank, for example, the bank may then lend the funds to businesses. The businesses, in turn,

investment the act of redirecting resources from being consumed today so that they may create benefits in the future; the use of assets to earn income or profit

Visual Glossary online

Go to the Visual Glossary Online for an interactive review of **capital gains.**

Action Graph online

Go to Action Graph Online for animated versions of key charts and graphs.

How the Economy Works online

Go to How the Economy Works Online for an interactive lesson on **the bond market.**

Focus on the Basics

Students need to come away with the following understandings:

FACTS: • Investing contributes to the free enterprise system by promoting economic growth. • The financial system promotes investment by facilitating the transfer of money between savers and borrowers. • Financial intermediaries provide information about borrowers, help savers reduce risk through diversification, and provide investors with liquidity. • The trade-offs for greater returns are greater financial risk and loss of liquidity. The trade-off for lower financial risk and greater liquidity is lower returns.

GENERALIZATION: Economic growth and capital growth are the two main benefits of saving and investing. Loss of liquidity and loss of capital are the two main risks.

Guiding Question

What are the benefits and risks of saving and investing?

Get Started

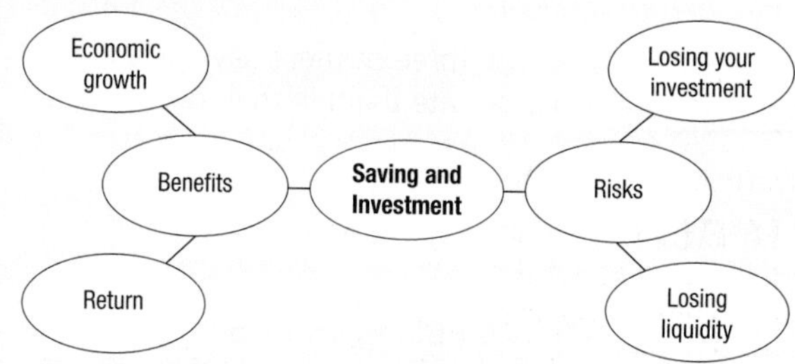

LESSON GOALS

Students will:

- Know the Key Terms.
- Identify ways that saving and investing benefit the free enterprise system.
- Describe and compare the functions of various financial intermediaries.
- Describe the relationship between financial intermediaries and savers and borrowers by analyzing a diagram of the financial system.
- Identify the types of risk associated with investments that involve different levels of liquidity and return.

BEFORE CLASS

Students should read the section for homework before coming to class.

Have students complete the graphic organizer in the Section Opener as they read the text. As an alternate activity, have students complete the Guided Reading and Review worksheet (Unit 4 All-in-One, p. 51).

L1 L2 ELL LPR Differentiate Have students complete the Guided Reading and Review worksheet (Unit 4 All-in-One, p. 52).

CLASSROOM HINTS

WHO INVESTS?

Some students might think that investing is something that only corporations or people who work on Wall Street do. Explain that many ordinary Americans are investors, too. They invest in mutual funds or stocks and bonds in retirement accounts such as 401ks. They have savings accounts or own CDs. Some people invest in real estate, or in their own business. Many people are investors, in one way or another.

BELLRINGER

Write the following sentences on the board:
"Better safe than sorry."
Nothing ventured, nothing gained.
"Don't put all your eggs in one basket."
"The riskier the road, the greater the reward."
"A penny saved is a penny earned."
Look before you leap.

Have students choose three of these sayings and, in their notebooks, restate them in their own words.

Teach

Economics online To present this topic using digital resources, use the lecture notes on www.PearsonSuccessNet.com.

L1 L2 ELL LPR Differentiate To help students who are struggling readers, assign the Vocabulary worksheet (Unit 4 All-in-One, p. 50).

MAKE CONNECTIONS

Write the following definition on the board: An *investment* is the act of redirecting the use of a resource today to create benefits in the future. Ask **Why is studying for a test a type of investment?** *(I invest a resource—my time now in order to get a better grade in the future.)* Then, have students replace "a resource" in the above definition with "an asset." Tell students that this is the definition of investment in the financial world. Ask **What "benefits" are created?** *(profits, income).* Ask students to give examples of financial investments that they or their families have made or that have been made for them.

Finally, ask students to read aloud their responses to the bellringer activity. Encourage them to relate each of these sayings to an aspect of investment or saving—for example, return; risk and reward; diversification; the importance of research. Ask them to think of illustrations for each saying that relate to saving and investment.

CREATE A PROFILE

Have students use the Career Link worksheet to record their research for the activity (Unit 4 All-in-One, p. 80).

Answers

Checkpoint provides money for businesses to expand and promotes economic growth

Checkpoint Savers deposit their money in the bank, which it then lends to borrowers.

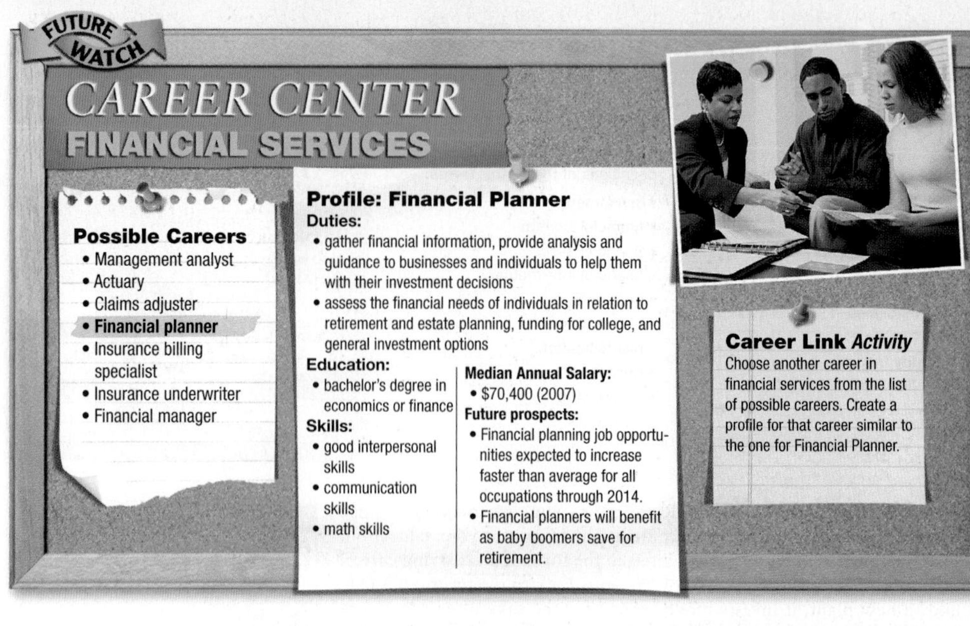

may invest that money in new plants and equipment to give them the resources to increase production. As these businesses use their investments to purchase new capital equipment for expansion and growth, they create new and better products and provide new jobs.

FUTURE WATCH
CAREER CENTER
FINANCIAL SERVICES
Possible Careers
• Management analyst
• Actuary
• Claims adjuster
• Financial planner
• Insurance billing specialist
• Insurance underwriter
• Financial manager
Profile: Financial Planner
Duties:
• gather financial information, provide analysis and guidance to businesses and individuals to help them with their investment decisions
• assess the financial needs of individuals in relation to retirement and estate planning, funding for college, and general investment options
Education:
• bachelor's degree in economics or finance
Skills:
• good interpersonal skills
• communication skills
• math skills
Median Annual Salary:
• $70,400 (2007)
Future prospects:
• Financial planning job opportunities expected to increase faster than average for all occupations through 2014.
• Financial planners will benefit as baby boomers save for retirement.
Career Link Activity
Choose another career in financial services from the list of possible careers. Create a profile for that career similar to the one for Financial Planner.

CHECKPOINT ***What role does investment play in the free enterprise system?***

The Financial System

In order for investment to take place, an economy must have a financial system. A **financial system** is the network of structures and mechanisms that allows the transfer of money between savers and borrowers.

financial system the network of structures and mechanisms that allows the transfer of money between savers and borrowers

Financial Assets

When people save, they are, in essence, lending funds to others. Whether they put cash in a savings account, purchase a certificate of deposit, or buy a government or corporate bond, savers obtain a document that confirms their purchase or deposit. These documents may be passbooks, monthly statements, bond certificates, or other records.

financial asset a claim on the property or income of a borrower

Such documents represent claims on the property or income of the borrower. These claims are called **financial assets,** or securities. If the borrower fails to pay back the loan, these documents can serve as proof in court that money was borrowed and that commitments were made that were not fulfilled.

The Flow of Savings and Investments

Figure 11.1 on the next page shows how the financial system brings together savers and borrowers, fueling investment and economic growth. On one side are savers—households, individuals, and businesses that lend out their savings in return for financial assets—for example, the promise of regular interest payments. On the other side are investors—governments and businesses—who invest the money they borrow to build roads, factories, and homes. Investors may also use these funds to develop new products, create new markets, or provide new services.

CHECKPOINT ***How does a bank serve as a way for savers and borrowers to transfer money between them?***

Differentiated Resources

- **L1 L2 Guided Reading and Review** (Unit 4 All-in-One, p. 52)
- **L1 L2 Vocabulary worksheet** (Unit 4 All-in-One, p. 50)
- **L2 Investment, Risks, and Return** (Unit 4 All-in-One, p. 54)
- **L2 Writing an E-mail skill worksheet** (Unit 4 All-in-One, p. 56)

Financial Intermediaries

Savers and borrowers may be linked directly. As you examine **Figure 11.1**, you will notice that borrowers and savers may also be linked through a variety of institutions pictured as "in between" the two. These **financial intermediaries** are institutions that help channel funds from savers to borrowers. They include the following:

- *Banks, savings and loan associations, credit unions, and finance companies* As you read in Chapter 10, banks, S&Ls, and credit unions take in deposits from savers and then lend out some of these funds to businesses and individuals. Finance companies make loans to consumers and small businesses.
- *Mutual funds* A **mutual fund** pools the savings of many individuals and invests this money in a variety of stocks, bonds, and other financial assets. Mutual funds allow people to invest in a broad range of companies in the stock market. Investing in this way is less risky than purchasing the stock of only one or two companies that might do poorly.
- *Hedge funds* A **hedge fund** is a private investment organization that employs risky strategies that often made huge profits for investors. These investors are generally wealthy and often are knowledgeable about investing. Because hedge funds are private, they have not been regulated by the SEC and have not had to reveal information about themselves to the public.
- *Life insurance companies* The main function of life insurance is to provide financial protection for the family or other people named as beneficiaries of the insured. Working members of a family, for example, may buy life insurance policies so that, if they die, money will be paid to survivors to make up for lost income. Insurance companies collect payments called premiums from the people who buy insurance. They lend out to investors part of the premiums that they collect.
- *Pension funds* A pension is income that some retirees receive after working

financial intermediary an institution that helps channel funds from savers to borrowers

mutual fund an organization that pools the savings of many individuals and invests this money in a variety of stocks, bonds, and other financial assets

hedge fund a private investment organization that employs risky strategies that often made huge profits for investors

Figure 11.1 **Financial Intermediaries**

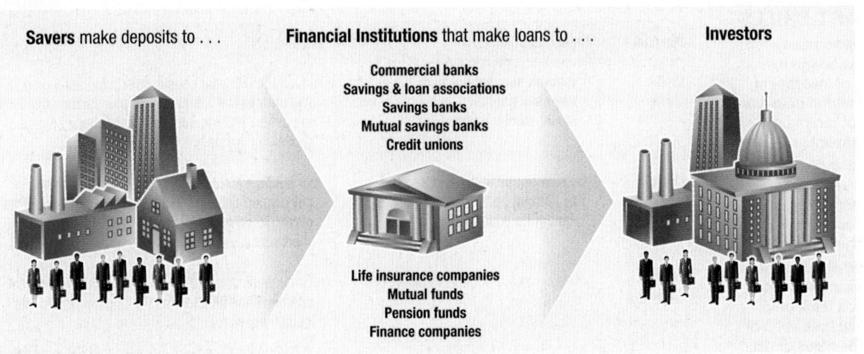

CHART SKILLS

Financial intermediaries, including banks and other financial institutions, accept funds from savers and make loans to investors. Investors include entrepreneurs, businesses, and other borrowers.

1. What advantages do financial intermediaries provide for savers?
2. What advantages do financial intermediaries provide for investors?

CHECK COMPREHENSION

Direct students' attention to Figure 11.1 which diagrams the financial system. Students may be unfamiliar with most of the financial intermediaries. Display the transparency, "The Financial System" (Color Transparencies, 11.a). Have students define and compare the functions of each financial intermediary in the transparency.

Point out the savers and borrowers on the chart. Tell students that both savers and borrowers are investors: they are both redirecting resources that could be used today so that they may create benefits in the future. Ask **Is a person who purchases a CD a saver or a borrower?** *(saver)* **Is a business that gets a business loan a saver or a borrower?** *(a borrower)* **What are some other examples of savers who are investors?** *(a person who places money in a savings account, CDs, or mutual funds; a business that contributes to a pension fund or a 401K, or invests company funds in a money market account)* **What are some other examples of borrowers who are investors?** *(a person who takes out a mortgage or a loan; a business that sells stock to raise money for the business; the local or federal government borrowing money to finance building roads or buildings)* Tell students that they will be learning more about how companies and the government raise money through bonds and stocks.

Use the transparency to clarify any student misconceptions about purposes and methods of saving and borrowing.

Virtual Economics

L2 Differentiate

Distinguishing Between Savings and Investment Use the following lesson from the NCEE **Virtual Economics *CD-ROM*** to help students to decide when it is best to save. Click on Browse Economics Lessons, specify grades 9–12, and use the key words *making choices.*

In this activity, students will take part in a brief simulation and use statistics to evaluate whether to save or invest.

LESSON TITLE	MAKING CHOICES ABOUT SAVING AND INVESTING
Type of Activity	Using statistics
Complexity	Low
Time	90 minutes
NCEE Standards	2, 12

Answers

Chart Skills 1. provide liquidity, diversification, and information 2. provide loans and information

DISTRIBUTE ACTIVITY WORKSHEET

Ask students to describe the various types of risk identified in the section. Discuss how diversification reduces risk. Tell students that they will assess risks associated with various kinds of financial assets by completing the "What's the Risk?" worksheet (Unit 4 All-in-One, p. 53).

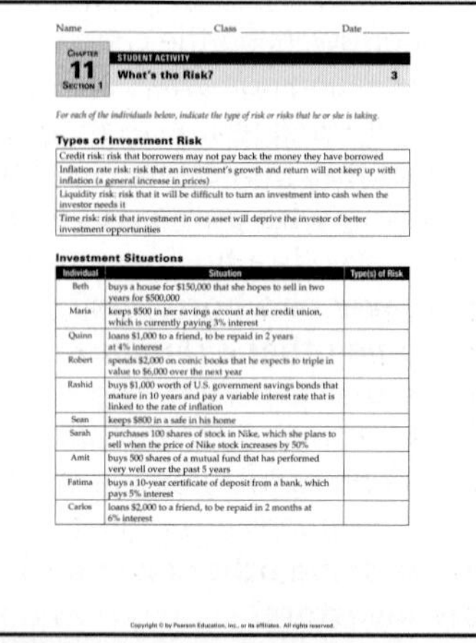

Name ______ Class ______ Date ______

CHAPTER 11 SECTION 1 — STUDENT ACTIVITY — **What's the Risk?** 3

For each of the individuals below, indicate the type of risk or risks that he or she is taking.

Types of Investment Risk

Types of Investment Risk
Credit risk: risk that borrowers may not pay back the money they have borrowed
Inflation rate risk: risk that an investment's growth and return will not keep up with inflation (a general increase in prices)
Liquidity risk: risk that it will be difficult to turn an investment into cash when the investor needs it
Time risk: risk that investment in one asset will deprive the investor of better investment opportunities

Investment Situations

Individual	Situation	Type(s) of Risk
Beth	buys a house for $150,000 that she hopes to sell in two years for $500,000	
Maria	keeps $500 in her savings account at her credit union, which is currently paying 3% interest	
Quinn	loans $1,000 to a friend, to be repaid in 2 years at 4% interest	
Robert	spends $2,000 on comic books that he expects to triple in value to $6,000 over the next year	
Rashid	buys $1,000 worth of U.S. government savings bonds that mature in 10 years and pay a variable interest rate that is linked to the rate of inflation	
Sean	keeps $800 in a safe in his home	
Sarah	purchases 100 shares of stock in Nike, which she plans to sell when the price of Nike stock increases by 50%	
Amit	buys 500 shares of a mutual fund that has performed very well over the past 5 years	
Fatima	buys a 10-year certificate of deposit from a bank, which pays 5% interest	
Carlos	loans $2,000 to a friend, to be repaid in 2 months at 6% interest	

L2 Differentiate Distribute the "Investments, Risks, and Return" worksheet (Unit 4 All-in-One, p. 54). Students may find it useful to review the examples of each type of risk described in Figure 11.2 as they identify types of risk in the activity.

After completing the worksheet, ask **Do the situations in this worksheet demonstrate the expression *"The riskier the road, the greater the reward"*?** Have students explain their answers. *(Possible response: Yes. The investments that held the potential for the highest returns, such as Beth's and Robert's, were the most risky; situations that carried less risk, such as Fatima's, provided smaller returns.)*

PERSONAL FINANCE ACTIVITY

Tell students that they can learn more about risk related to financial assets by reading the Investments sections starting on PF10 in the Personal Finance Handbook and completing the worksheets (Personal Finance All-in-One, pp. 45–52).

(lesson continued on p. 282)

Answers

Chart Skills 1. spreads the risk over varied investments 2. Answers will vary but should demonstrate an understanding of the type of risk represented.

diversification the strategy of spreading out investments to reduce risk

a certain number of years or reaching a certain age. In certain cases, injuries may qualify a working person for pension benefits. Employers may set up pension funds in a number of ways. They may contribute to the pension fund on behalf of their employees, they may withhold a percentage of workers' salaries to deposit in a pension fund, or they may do both. Employers set up pension funds to collect deposits and distribute payments. Pension fund managers invest those deposits in stocks, bonds, and other financial assets.

Now that you know something about the types of financial intermediaries, you may wonder why savers don't deal directly with investors. The answer is that, in general, dealing with financial intermediaries offers three advantages. Intermediaries share risks, provide information, and provide liquidity.

Sharing Risk

As a saver, you may not want to invest your entire life savings in a single company or enterprise. For example, if you had $500 to invest and your neighbor was opening a new restaurant, would you give her the entire $500? Since it is estimated that more than half of all new businesses fail, you would be wise not to risk all of your money in one investment. Instead, you would want to spread the money around to various businesses. This will reduce the chances of losing your entire investment.

This strategy of spreading out investments to reduce risk is called **diversification.** If you deposited $500 in the bank or bought shares of a mutual fund, those institutions could pool your money with other people's savings and put your money to work by making a variety of investments. In other words, financial intermediaries can diversify your investments and thus reduce the risk that you will lose all of your funds if a single investment fails.

Providing Information

Financial intermediaries are also good sources of information. Your local bank collects information about borrowers by monitoring their income and spending.

Figure 11.2 Types of Risk

CHART SKILLS

Investors must always weigh the risks of investment against the potential rate of return on their investment.

1. **How does diversification lessen the risks described in the chart?**
2. **What additional examples can you think of to illustrate each of the types of risk explained in this chart?**

Name	Description	Example
Credit risk	Borrowers may not pay back the money they have borrowed, or they may be late in making payments.	You lend $20 to your cousin, who promises to pay you back in two weeks. When your cousin fails to pay you on time, you don't have money for the basketball tickets you had planned to buy.
Liquidity risk	You may not be able to convert the investment back into cash quickly enough for your needs.	Your MP3 player is worth $100. You need cash to buy concert tickets, so you decide to sell your MP3 player. To convert your MP3 player into cash on short notice, you have to discount the price to $75.
Inflation rate risk	Inflation rates erode the value of your assets.	Ricardo lends Jeff $1,000 for one year at 10 percent interest. If the inflation rate is 12 percent, Ricardo loses money.
Time risk	You may have to pass up better opportunities for investment.	Lili invests $100 in May's cleaning business, to be repaid at 5 percent interest one year later. Six months later, Lili is unable to invest in Sonia's pet-sitting business, which pays 10 percent interest, because she has already invested her savings.

Background Note

American Savers The rate at which Americans save is among the lowest of the industrialized nations. More than 90 percent of American families own some kind of financial asset, according to a Federal Reserve study. Savings accounts are by far the most common asset, but some 55 percent of Americans also own stocks, bonds, or mutual funds. However, the rate of investment in most financial assets has fallen since the late 1990s. In 2006, Americans' savings rate fell to –0.5 percent—meaning Americans spent more than they earned. This is the first negative annual savings rate since the Great Depression.

Case STUDY THE WALL STREET JOURNAL. CLASSROOM EDITION

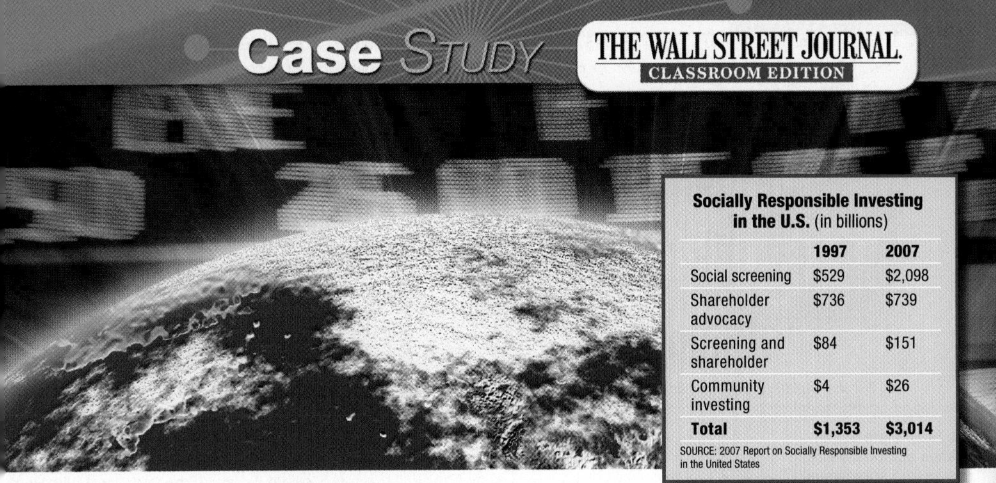

Socially Responsible Investing in the U.S. (in billions)	1997	2007
Social screening	$529	$2,098
Shareholder advocacy	$736	$739
Screening and shareholder	$84	$151
Community investing	$4	$26
Total	**$1,353**	**$3,014**

SOURCE: 2007 Report on Socially Responsible Investing in the United States

Principles and Principal

INVESTMENT

Socially responsible investing used to be about sacrificing choice and profits. Not anymore.

By Jilian Mincer
The Wall Street Journal

Socially responsible investing is growing up.

For many years, individuals who wanted to invest with their consciences had limited options, and many resigned themselves to making smaller returns in exchange for putting their money where their values were.

But in recent years, building a well-balanced, profitable portfolio using a socially responsible investing, or SRI, strategy has gotten easier. Greater awareness about the environment and growing demand for these kinds of investments have fueled the growth of high-quality options, meaning you can now build diversified SRI portfolios, including different types of mutual funds, bonds, exchange-traded funds and individual stocks.

Bruce M. Kahn, a vice president at Smith Barney, says that while socially responsible investing traditionally was based on negative criteria—screening out investments connected to tobacco or guns, for example—the latest trend is to screen in companies with strong environmental and management records.

The theory behind this "sustainable" investing approach is that those are the types of companies that will be more profitable in the long term, he says.

There are now 173 different socially and environmentally screened mutual funds in 358 different share classes, the Social Investment Forum says. And a study last year by the consulting firm Mercer and the United Nations Environment Programme Finance Initiative found that SRI investments perform as well as or better than non-SRI investments over time.

Paul Hilton, a research director at Calvert Group, a top provider of SRI funds, says there are three basic approaches to socially responsible investing: One of the most common is the use of screens to include or exclude certain securities, depending on social or environmental criteria such as strong records on community involvement or safe products, he says. A second part involves shareholder activism, whereby investors use their ownership to influence a company's behavior. The third is community investing, in which individuals invest in certificates of deposit and other vehicles that are federally insured but then lent to individuals in low-income communities.

Casey Neistat, New York filmmaker decided two years ago to move his assets into socially responsible investments. He favors funds that invest in companies with good environmental records and avoids funds with investments in China because of that nation's ties to the government in Sudan.

Still, Mr. Neistat says he can't afford to not make a profit. "I don't see this as charity," he says. "My gains have not dipped."

Applying Economic Principles
People who want to participate in socially responsible investing now have hundreds of mutual funds to choose from. Which of the three basic approaches to SRI cited by Paul Hilton do you think is the most effective? Explain your choice.

Video News Update Online Powered by *The Wall Street Journal* Classroom Edition — For a new case study, go to the online resources at **PearsonSuccessNet.com**

Teach Case Study

SUMMARIZE AND DISCUSS

Have students explain the appeal of socially responsible investing. Ask **What is socially responsible investing?** *(investing in mutual funds, stocks, bonds that use environmental, social and management criteria as means of selection)* Have students discuss the benefits and drawbacks of a socially responsible portfolio. Ask **Why would someone want a socially responsible portfolio?** *(Investors believe that a socially responsible portfolio is more sustainable—the types of companies in a socially responsible portfolio will be more profitable in the long run. It's also investing with a conscious; investors can select funds that coincide with personal beliefs.)*

ANALYZE

Ask students to explain the relationship between money and social responsibility.

L3 Differentiate Have the students use the Internet to look at the types of companies in a socially responsible mutual fund, print out information about those companies and discuss what those companies make or do and what makes them socially responsible.

Economics online *All print resources are available on the Teacher's Resource Library CD-ROM and online at* www.PearsonSuccessNet.com.

Answer

Applying Economic Principles Possible answer: Using screens with social or environmental criteria to exclude certain securities. This approach makes it possible to invest responsibly while still maintaining a diversified portfolio.

EXTEND

Distribute the "Writing an E-mail" skills worksheet (Unit 4 All-in-One, p. 55). In this worksheet students will compose an e-mail inviting a college economics professor to speak to their class about saving and investing. Students should include background information about what the class has learned so far, and any specific questions they have about saving and investing.

Tell students to review the lesson in the Social Studies Skills Handbook on page S-20. Remind them to use the steps of the lesson to complete the activity.

L2 **Differentiate** Distribute the "Writing an E-mail" skills worksheet (Unit 4 All-in-One, p. 56). List the section topics on the board and help students come up with a list of questions for the professor.

GUIDING QUESTION WRAP UP

Have students return to the section Guiding Question. Review the completed graphic organizer and clarify any misunderstandings. Have a wrap up discussion about the benefits and risks of saving and investing.

Assess and Remediate

L3 Review student responses to the transparency to assess their understanding of investing and the financial system.

L3 L2 Collect the "What's the Risk?" and "Investment, Risks, and Return" worksheets and assess students' understanding of risk.

L3 L2 Collect the "Writing an E-mail" skill worksheet and asses students' ability.

L3 Assign the Section 1 Assessment questions; identify student misconceptions.

L3 Give Section Quiz A (Unit 4 All-in-One, p. 57).

L2 Give Section Quiz B (Unit 4 All-in-One, p. 58).

(Assess and Remediate continued on p. 283)

Answers

Caption Warren is pessimistic: he thinks that he will lose money if he keeps it in stocks since he will get no return on cash.

Checkpoint Dealing with intermediaries can reduce risk because intermediaries provide investors with greater opportunity for diversification, access to information, and liquidity.

"Forgive the mess. Warren just put everything into cash."

▲ Stocks are sometimes a good investment and sometimes they are not. ***Is "Warren" optimistic or pessimistic about the prospects for stocks? How do you know?***

Finance companies collect information when borrowers fill out credit applications. Mutual fund managers know how the stocks in their **portfolios,** or collections of financial assets, are performing. As required by law, all intermediaries provide this and other information to potential investors in an investment report called a **prospectus.** The typical prospectus also warns potential investors that "past performance does not necessarily predict future results." An investment that looks great today may fizzle tomorrow. As economic conditions change, an investment once considered safe may look very risky.

By providing vital data about investment opportunities, financial intermediaries reduce the costs in time and money that lenders and borrowers would pay if they had to search out such information on their own. The information, however, is sometimes provided in lengthy documents with small type. So the careful investor must be knowledgeable and must study whatever information has been provided.

portfolio a collection of financial assets

prospectus an investment report that provides information to potential investors

return the money an investor receives above and beyond the sum of money initially invested

Providing Liquidity

Financial intermediaries also provide investors with liquidity. (Recall that liquidity is the ability to convert an asset into cash.) Suppose, for example, that you decide to invest in a mutual fund. Two years later, you need cash to pay your college tuition. You can get cash quickly by selling your shares in the mutual fund. Other investments are not so liquid. If you had purchased an investment-quality painting instead, you would need to find another investor who would buy the art from you. As you can see, financial intermediaries and the liquidity they provide are crucial to meeting borrowers' and lenders' needs in our increasingly complex financial system.

CHECKPOINT ***Why do savers and investors generally work through financial intermediaries?***

Liquidity, Return, and Risk

As you have read, most decisions involve trade-offs. For example, the trade-off for not going to a movie may be two additional hours of sleep. Saving and investing involve trade-offs as well.

Liquidity and Return

Suppose you save money in a savings account. Savings accounts are good ways to save when you need to be able to get to your cash for immediate use. On the other hand, savings accounts pay relatively low interest rates, about 2 to 3 percentage points below a certificate of deposit (CD). In other words, savings accounts are liquid, but they have a low return. **Return** is the money an investor receives above and beyond the sum of money that has been invested.

What if, however, you unexpectedly inherit $5,000? You do not need ready access to those funds, since your part-time job pays your day-to-day expenses. If you are willing to give up some degree of ready access to your money, you can earn a higher interest rate than you would earn if you put the money into a savings account. For example, you can invest your money in a CD that pays 4 percent interest. You would not be allowed to withdraw your money for, say, two years without paying a penalty. Therefore, before buying the CD, you would want to weigh the greater return on your investment against the loss of liquidity.

Return and Risk

Certificates of deposit (up to $250,000) are considered very safe investments because they are insured by the federal government. When you buy a CD valued at less than $250,000, you are giving up liquidity for a certain period of time, but you are not risking the loss of your money. What if, however, you decided to invest the money in a new company that your friends are starting? You must consider the risk you are now incurring. If the company succeeds, you could double your investment. However, it may take years before it is clear that the company is successful. If it fails, however, you could lose all or part of the money you invested. The government does not insure you against the risk of an investment gone bad. You may benefit from the rewards of a good investment, but you face the risks of a bad one.

To take another example, suppose your savings account is earning 2 percent interest. Would you be willing to lend money to your friend Emily for that same 2 percent interest rate, knowing that she rarely pays back loans on time? Probably not. For you to lend Emily the money, she would have to offer you a higher return than the bank could offer. This higher return would help offset the greater risk that Emily will not repay the loan on time—or that she does not repay the loan at all. Likewise, investors and lenders must consider the degree of risk involved in an investment they are considering and decide what return they would require to make up for the extra risk they may be taking on.

In general, the higher the potential return on an investment, the riskier the investment. Whenever individuals evaluate an investment, they must balance the risks involved with the rewards they expect to gain from the investment. Balancing this risk may be exceedingly tricky. As *Forbes* magazine has commented:

> **"The risk/return tradeoff could easily be called the 'ability-to-sleep-at-night test.' While some people can handle the equivalent of financial skydiving without batting an eye, others are terrified to climb the financial ladder without a secure harness. Deciding what amount of risk you can take while remaining comfortable with your investments is very important. . . ."**
>
> *Forbes,* "The Risk-Return Tradeoff"

CHECKPOINT ***Which investment has greater liquidity, a savings account or a certificate of deposit?***

SECTION 1 ASSESSMENT

Essential Questions Journal To continue to build a response to the Essential Question, go to your **Essential Questions Journal.**

Guiding Question

1. Use your completed concept web to answer this question: What are the benefits and risks of saving and investing?
2. **Extension** Suppose you have $500 to invest. What questions and concerns would you have as you decide how to invest your money?

Key Terms and Main Ideas

3. What is **investment?**
4. Identify the three parts of the **financial system.**
5. Describe the main benefit of **diversification.**
6. What is the purpose of a **prospectus?**
7. List three examples of **returns** on an investment.

Critical Thinking

8. **Contrast (a)** How are mutual funds and hedge funds similar? **(b)** How are they different?
9. **Extend** What kinds of financial assets might you find in a portfolio?
10. **Infer (a)** Rank the following investments from the least risky to the most risky: a certificate of deposit, stock in one company, and a mutual fund. **(b)** Which has the greatest potential to have the highest possible return? Explain your answer.

Quick Write

11. Reread Investing and Free Enterprise and Liquidity, Return, and Risk in this section. Give two examples of a liquid investment and two examples of an investment that is not liquid. Then write a short essay answering the following question. Why would people invest money in an investment that is not liquid?

Have students complete the Self-Test Online and continue their work in the **Essential Questions Journal**.

REMEDIATION AND SUGGESTIONS

Use the chart below to help students who are struggling with content.

WEAKNESS	REMEDIATION
Defining key terms (Questions 3, 4, 5, 6, 7)	Have students use the interactive Economic Dictionary Online.
How investing contributes to the free enterprise system (Question 11)	Have students reread and identify the links between savers and borrowers in Financial Intermediaries.
How the financial system brings together savers and borrowers (Questions 4, 11)	Reteach using Transparency 11.a.
The role of financial intermediaries in the financial system (Questions 5, 6, 8, 9)	Have students reread and outline Financial Intermediaries.
Understanding liquidity, return, and risk (Questions 7, 10)	Review the answers to the What's the Risk? worksheet with students.

Answer

Checkpoint a savings account

Assessment Answers

1. earning returns, growth of the economy; low return or loss of investment, lack of liquidity, loss of other opportunities
2. Possible responses: What are my goals? How much risk am I willing to take? Am I guaranteed to get my investment back or not? How liquid is my investment? What opportunities would I be passing up?
3. redirecting resources to create future benefits
4. savers, borrowers, financial intermediaries
5. to reduce the risk of losing money invested
6. to provide information about an investment to potential investors
7. interest on a bank account; interest on a CD; money received from the investment in a startup company that succeeds
8. (a) Both combine the savings of individual investors. (b) Hedge funds employ risky strategies to make very large profits for their investors, while mutual funds invest in a broad range of companies.
9. Possible response: stocks, bonds, CDs, mutual funds, hedge funds
10. (a) certificate of deposit, mutual fund, stock in one company; (b) stock in one company because the company might be very successful; CDs have fixed returns and not all the stocks in a mutual fund may do well.
11. Possible response: Savings accounts and mutual funds are liquid; CDs and pension funds are not liquid. People might invest in an investment that is not liquid if they do not need the money right away and the rate of return is higher than for a more liquid investment.

Guiding Question

Why are bonds bought and sold?

Get Started

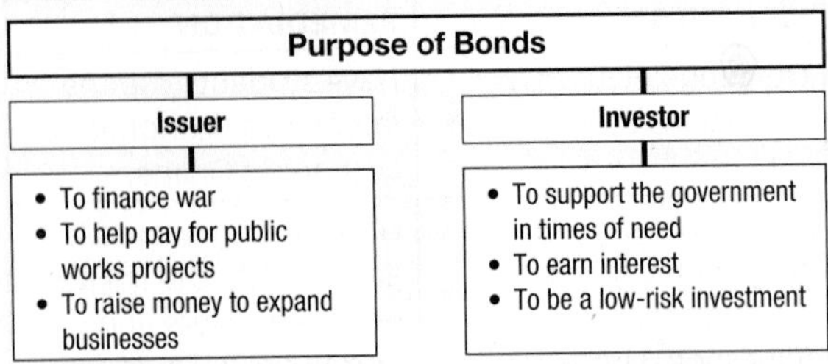

Purpose of Bonds	
Issuer	**Investor**
• To finance war • To help pay for public works projects • To raise money to expand businesses	• To support the government in times of need • To earn interest • To be a low-risk investment

LESSON GOALS

Students will:

- Know the Key Terms.
- Understand the reasons bonds are issued and the information needed to decide what bonds to buy.
- Demonstrate knowledge of the characteristics of bonds and other financial assets by creating an advertisement.
- Evaluate the risk level of various assets by completing a worksheet.
- Describe four different financial asset markets.

BEFORE CLASS

Have students complete the graphic organizer in the Section Opener as they read the text. As an alternate activity, have students complete the Guided Reading and Review worksheet (Unit 4 All-in-One, p. 59).

L1 L2 ELL LPR Differentiate Have students complete the Guided Reading and Review worksheet (Unit 4 All-in-One, p. 60).

Answer

Caption usually lower risk investments

CLASSROOM HINTS

THE RELATIONSHIP BETWEEN BOND PRICES AND BOND YIELDS

When bond prices go up, bond yields go down. When prices go down, yields go up. This can be hard to understand. But remember that the yield, or what the issuer pays to investors in return for borrowing their money, is a combination of the coupon and the price. The coupon stays the same, but the price can change. For example, when demand for Treasury bonds is high, prices go up, sometimes well above 100% of the original price. Since the coupon remains the same, but the price has gone up, the overall yield that buyers get from Treasury bonds goes down.

SECTION 2 Bonds and Other Financial Assets

OBJECTIVES

1. **Describe** the characteristics of bonds as financial assets.
2. **Identify** different types of bonds.
3. **Describe** the characteristics of other types of financial assets.
4. **List** four different types of financial asset markets.

ECONOMIC DICTIONARY

As you read the section, look for the definitions of these **Key Terms:**

- coupon rate
- maturity
- par value
- yield
- savings bond
- inflation-indexed bond
- municipal bond
- corporate bond
- junk bond
- capital market
- money market
- primary market
- secondary market

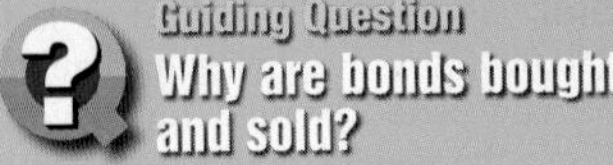

Guiding Question

Why are bonds bought and sold?

Copy this chart and fill it in as you read.

Purpose of Bonds	
Issuer	**Investor**
• To finance war • •	• To support the government in times of need • •

coupon rate the interest rate that a bond issuer will pay to the bondholder

maturity the time at which payment to a bondholder is due

Economics and You It is 1942, and the world is at war. The United States has thrown all of its resources into the Allied effort to defeat the Axis powers. To keep the armed forces equipped, the government needs money. To raise that money, the Treasury Department begins selling savings bonds.

Americans from every walk of life support the war effort by buying these "war bonds." Even though money is tight, you manage to do your part by bringing a few nickels and dimes to school to buy war stamps. Added to the money that other students bring, the class collects enough stamps to buy a bond.

Principles in Action Why are bonds bought and sold? Like the war bonds that helped finance our effort in World War II, bonds are sold by governments or corporations to finance projects. Using the example of a community that needs to construct a major road, you will see how municipal bonds offer the best method of financing expensive community projects. You will also learn another advantage of bonds. They usually offer a higher return than savings accounts, although they generally are riskier than savings accounts.

▲ Bonds generally pay a fixed amount of interest at regular intervals. ***Are bonds usually lower or higher risk investments?***

Bonds as Financial Assets

Bonds are basically loans, or IOUs, that represent debt that the seller, or issuer, must repay to an investor. Bonds typically pay the investor a fixed amount of interest at regular intervals for a specific amount of time. Bonds are generally lower-risk investments. As you might expect from your reading about the relationship between risk and return, the rate of return on bonds is usually also lower than for many other investments.

The Three Components of Bonds

Bonds have three basic components:

- *Coupon rate* The **coupon rate** is the interest rate that a bond issuer will pay to a bondholder.
- *Maturity* The time at which payment to a bondholder is due is called the bond's **maturity.** The length of time to maturity varies with different bonds. Bonds usually mature in 10, 20, or 30 years.

Focus on the Basics

Students need to come away with the following understandings:

FACTS: • Bonds are loans that the bond seller or issuer must repay to the bond buyer or holder. Bonds typically pay a fixed amount of interest and have a set repayment date. • Both the government and corporations sell bonds to finance projects. • Bonds and other financial assets are traded on financial asset markets, classified as capital or money markets, and as primary or secondary markets.

GENERALIZATION: Bonds carry greater risk but greater potential returns than savings accounts, CDs, or money market funds. At the same time, they are generally safer and have lower returns than stocks.

- *Par value* A bond's **par value,** assigned by the issuer, is the amount to be paid to the bondholder at maturity. Par value is also called face value or principal.

Suppose that you buy a $1,000 bond from the corporation Jeans, Etc. The investor who buys the bond is called the holder. The seller of a bond is the issuer. You are, therefore, the holder of the bond, and Jeans, Etc. is the issuer. The components of this bond are as follows:

- *Coupon rate:* 5 percent, paid to the bondholder annually
- *Maturity:* 10 years
- *Par value:* $1,000

How much money will you earn from this bond, and over what period of time? The coupon rate is 5 percent of $1,000 per year. This means that you will receive a payment of $50 (0.05 × $1,000) each year for 10 years, or a total of $500 in interest. In 10 years, the bond will have reached maturity, and the company's debt to you will have ended. Jeans, Etc. will now pay you the par value of the bond, or $1,000. Thus, for your $1,000 investment, you will have received $1,500 over a period of 10 years.

Not all bonds are held to maturity. Over their lifetime they might be bought or sold, and their price may change. Because of these shifts in price, buyers and sellers are interested in a bond's yield, or yield to maturity. **Yield** is the annual rate of return on a bond if the bond is held to maturity (5 percent in the earlier example involving Jeans, Etc.).

Buying Bonds at a Discount

Investors earn money from interest on the bonds they buy. They can also earn money by buying bonds at a discount, called a discount from par. In other words, if Nate were buying a bond with a par value of $1,000, he may have to pay only $960 for it. When the bond matures, Nate will redeem the bond at par, or $1,000. He will thus have earned $40 on his investment, in addition to interest payments from the bond issuer.

Why would someone sell a bond for less than its par value? The answer lies in the fact that interest rates continually change. For example, suppose that Sharon buys a $1,000 bond at 5 percent interest, the current market rate. A year later, she needs to sell the bond to help pay for a new car. By that time, however, interest rates have risen to 6 percent. No one will pay $1,000 for Sharon's bond at 5 percent interest when they could go elsewhere and buy a $1,000 bond at 6 percent interest. For Sharon to sell her bond at 5 percent, she will have to sell it at a discount. (See **Figure 11.3.**)

Figure 11.3 Discounts From Par

1. Sharon buys a bond with a par value of $1,000 at 5 percent interest.

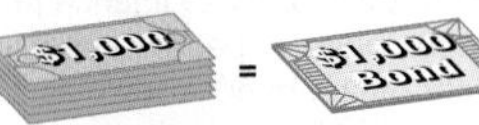

Bond purchase without discount from par

2. Interest rates go up to 6 percent.
3. Sharon needs to sell her bond. Nate wants to buy it, but is unwilling to buy a bond at 5 percent interest when the current rate is 6 percent.
4. Sharon offers to discount the bond, taking $40 off the price and selling it for $960.
5. Nate accepts the offer. He now owns a $1,000 bond paying 5 percent interest, which he purchased at a discount from par.

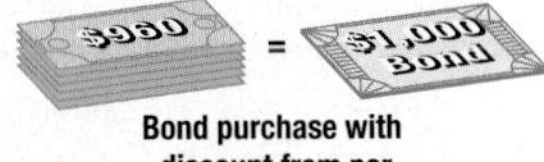

Bond purchase with discount from par

CHART SKILLS

Investors can earn money by buying bonds at a discount, called a discount from par.

1. How do interest rates affect bond prices?
2. If Sharon buys the bond at $1,000 and sells it five years later at $960, would she necessarily have lost money on the purchase?

Personal Finance For more help in making wise investment decisions, see your Personal Finance Handbook in the back of the book or visit **PearsonSuccessNet.com**

Bond Ratings

How does an investor decide which bonds to buy? Investors can check bond quality through independent firms that publish bond issuers' credit ratings. These firms include Standard & Poor's and Moody's. They rate bonds on a number of factors, focusing on the issuer's financial strength—its ability to make future interest payments and its ability to repay the principal when the bond matures.

Their rating systems rank bonds from the highest investment grade (AAA in Standard & Poor's system and Aaa in

par value a bond's stated value, to be paid to the bondholder at maturity

yield the annual rate of return on a bond if the bond is held to maturity

Differentiated Resources

L1 L2 Guided Reading and Review (Unit 4 All-in-One, p. 60)

L2 Weighing the Risks (Unit 4 All-in-One, p. 63)

L4 Investing for Young People (Unit 4 All-in-One, p. 61)

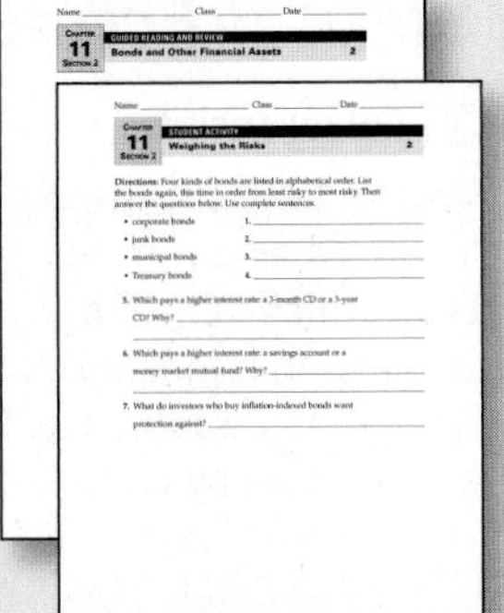

BELLRINGER

Tell students: You have $200 to save or invest. A friend wants to borrow from you to start a business. In your notebook describe how much you would be willing to loan, what conditions you would set, and all the factors you should consider in deciding whether to make the loan.

Teach

Economics online To present this topic using digital resources, use the lecture notes on www.PearsonSuccessNet.com.

MAKE DECISIONS

Draw a 4-column table on the board. Label the columns *Amount of Loan, Interest, Due Dates, Other Factors.* As students report their answers to the Bellringer, fill in the table. Guide students by asking questions such as **How much can you rely on your friend to repay the loan? What else might you do with the money? How much would you make if you kept it in the bank instead?** Remind students that, when they buy a bond, they are lending money to the issuer. Ask **Who sells or issues bonds?** *(the government and corporations)* **Why are bonds issued?** *(Possible response: to finance projects)* **Why would you choose to loan money to the issuer of the bond?** *(to make money; to help pay for a needed service).*

DEFINE

Have students define in their own words some of the components of bonds: *coupon rate, maturity, par value,* and *yield* (also known as *yield to maturity*).

L1 L2 ELL LPR Differentiate Some of the terms—coupon, maturity, par, yield—have more than one meaning. Have pairs of students make a list of, and compare, each term's multiple meanings. Have them make flash cards and drill each other.

PERSONAL FINANCE ACTIVITY

To help students make sensible investment decisions, you may want to use the Personal Finance Handbook lessons on investing on page PF10 and the activity worksheet (Personal Finance All-in-One, p. 45)

Answers

Chart Skills 1. If interest rates increase, bonds with lower coupon rates may be sold at a discount from par. Falling interest rates may cause buyers to pay some amount over par for the same bond. 2. not unless the bond paid less than $40 in interest

DISCUSS

Discuss Figure 11.3, *Discounts From Par,* on page 286 with the class. Tell students that investors can purchase new bonds directly from issuers, as well as buy existing bonds from current bondholders. Ask **When would an investor want to buy an existing bond instead of a new bond at par value?** *(when the interest rate on the existing bond is higher than what is available on new bonds)* Discuss how changing interest rates affect existing bonds. Ask **Could you sell a $1,000 bond you hold at 6% for $1,000 if interest rates rise to 8%?** *(No)* **Why?** *(For the same money, potential buyers can buy a bond that pays a better return.)* **What would you have to do to be able to sell your bond in such a market?** *(Discount its price below par value.)*

L4 Differentiate Challenge students to think of other situations in which a bond would have to be discounted in order to be sold. *(Possible responses: close to maturity, a rating change or other change to the issuer that increases the bond's risk)*

Review the meaning of yield *(the annual rate of return on a bond if it is held to maturity).* Note that when a bond is purchased with a discount from par, the bond's yield will be greater than its coupon rate. For example, by paying $960 for a $1,000 bond, Nate will receive a yield higher than the coupon rate of 5% because he will also earn $40 at the bond's maturity. Have students guess the relationship between a bond's yield and its coupon rate if it is sold for a value greater than its par value.

How the Economy Works

What is the function of a municipal bond?

Companies or governments sell bonds in order to finance projects. Most bonds are bought because the buyer expects to earn interest on the investment. Here's the story of one bond, known as a municipal bond: why it was issued and why it was bought.

1 The main state road connecting Mudville and Saltville is in terrible shape. People don't want to use it. The economies of both cities are suffering.

2 Mudville and Saltville and all the towns in between need a new road. But how can the citizens pay for it? The state steps in and proposes to repair the road and make it into a toll road. State voters approve the bond issue narrowly.

The Problem

Financing the Solution

Moody's) through the lower grades. An investment-grade bond is considered safe enough for banks to invest in. The lowest grade generally means that the bond is in default—that is, the issuer has not kept up with interest payments or has defaulted on paying principal.

The higher the bond rating, the lower the interest rate the company usually has to pay to get people to buy its bonds. For example, an AAA (or "triple A") bond may be issued at a 5 percent interest rate. A BBB bond, however, may be issued at a 7.5 percent interest rate. The buyer of the AAA bond trades off a lower interest rate for lower risk. The buyer of the BBB bond trades greater risk for a higher interest rate.

Similarly, the higher the bond rating, the higher the price at which the bond will sell. For example, a $1,000 bond with an AAA rating may sell at $1,100. A $1,000 bond with a BBB rating may sell for only $950 because of the increased risk that the seller could default.

Holders of bonds with high ratings who keep their bonds until maturity face relatively little risk of losing their investment. Holders of bonds with lower ratings, however, take on more risk in return for potentially higher interest payments.

Advantages and Disadvantages to the Issuer

From the point of view of the investor, bonds are good investments because they are relatively safe. Bonds are desirable from the issuer's point of view as well, for two main reasons:

1. Once the bond is sold, the coupon rate for that bond will not go up or down. For example, when Jeans, Etc. sells bonds, it knows in advance that it will be making fixed payments for a specific length of time.

Virtual Economics

L4 Differentiate

Understanding Bonds Use the following lesson from the NCEE **Virtual Economics *CD-ROM*** to introduce students to bonds. Click on Browse Economics Lessons, specify grades 9–12, and use the key words *what is a bond.*

In this activity, students will participate in a simulation to explore what bonds are and how they work.

LESSON TITLE	WHAT IS A BOND?
Type of Activity	Simulation
Complexity	High
Time	90 minutes
NCEE Standards	10

How the Economy Works online

For an animated, interactive version of this feature, visit PearsonSuccessNet.com

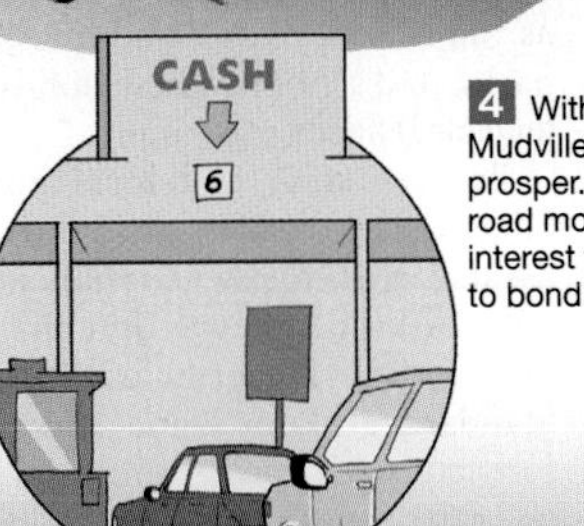

3 The bonds go on sale and sell well. The state's credit is good, and interest on the bond is tax exempt. There's enough money to begin construction on a new road.

4 With a new road, Mudville and Saltville prosper. Tolls from the road more than cover the interest that must be paid to bond holders.

5 Investors are happy because they receive a nice check every three months. The citizens of Mudville and Saltville are happy because the repaired road makes travel between the two cities easier.

Check Your Understanding

1. What is the cost and benefit of buying a municipal bond?
2. Why do you think bond issues like this one must be approved by voters?

Problem Solved

2. Unlike stockholders, bondholders do not own a part of the company. Therefore, the company does not have to share profits with its bondholders if the company does particularly well.

On the other hand, bonds also pose two main disadvantages to the issuer:

1. The company must make fixed interest payments, even in bad years when it does not make money. In addition, it cannot change its interest payments even when interest rates have gone down.
2. If the firm does not maintain financial health, its bonds may be downgraded to a lower bond rating and, thus, may be harder to sell unless they are offered at a discount.

CHECKPOINT ***Why do some people invest in bonds with a low interest rate?***

Types of Bonds

Despite these risks to the issuer, when corporations or governments need to borrow funds for long periods, they often issue bonds. There are several different types of bonds.

Savings Bonds

You may already be familiar with savings bonds, which are sometimes given to young people as gifts. **Savings bonds** are low-denomination ($50 to $10,000) bonds issued by the United States government. The government uses funds from the sale of savings bonds to help pay for public works projects such as buildings, roads, and dams. Like other government bonds, savings bonds have virtually no risk of default, or failure to repay the loan.

The federal government pays interest on savings bonds. However, unlike most

savings bond a low-denomination bond issued by the United States government

CHECK COMPREHENSION

Have students identify the advantages of buying bonds. Ask **What does a bond rating tell you?** *(the financial strength of the issuer; the amount of risk to the investor who buys the bond)* **What kinds of information would you consider before buying a bond?** *(Possible responses: bond rating/risk, current interest rate, liquidity)*

Ask **What are the advantages to the bond issuer?** *(The interest rates—payments to bond holders—are known in advance; bondholders do not own part of the company.)* **What are the disadvantages to the issuer?** *(Payments to bond holders cannot decrease if interest rates go down or if the company does not do well; bonds can be downgraded.)*

CREATE AN ADVERTISEMENT

L2 L3 Differentiate After students have discussed the financial assets presented on the next few pages of the text, have them work in pairs or triads to create an advertisement for one of the financial assets discussed in the section. The ad should be from the asset's issuer, such as a bank, municipality, business, or the U.S. government. Remind students that their ad should include the asset's terms (cost, yield, maturity, etc.) as well as other information to encourage investors to buy it. Tell students to decide on a location for their ad—a newspaper, highway billboard, poster on a bus or train, or similar—and to design their ad accordingly.

Economics online *All print resources are available on the Teacher's Resource Library CD-ROM and online at www.PearsonSuccessNet.com.*

Answers

Check Your Understanding 1. Possible response: the cost: the money used to buy the bond cannot be invested in other financial assets until the bond matures; the benefit: these bonds are fairly safe and will pay a fixed rate of (tax exempt) interest at regular intervals until the bond matures. 2. There may be a financial impact on residents in the form of increased taxes or fees.

Checkpoint The bonds may be available at a discount from par; the investor may want a low-risk investment.

COMPARE

Have students identify the four main kinds of bonds and their issuers *(savings bonds and Treasury bonds: U.S. government; municipal bonds: state and local governments and municipalities; corporate bonds: corporations)* Ask **Which types of bonds are the safest investments? Why?** *(U.S. government bonds, because they are backed by the "full faith and credit" of the U.S. government)* **Why are corporate bonds riskier investments than government bonds?** *(Corporations have no tax base to guarantee revenue and depend on the corporation's success for repayment.)*

Refer to the feature How the Economy Works. Ask **Why would you purchase this municipal bond rather than a Treasury bond?** *(municipal bond interest is tax exempt)*

Ask **What is a "junk bond"?** *(a bond with a high risk of default)* **Why might an investor buy a junk bond?** *(high rate of return)* **Could a municipal bond ever be classified as a junk bond?** *(yes, if the issuer's credit rating were low enough)* Have students discuss if they would ever buy a junk bond.

L4 **Differentiate** Distribute the "Investing for Young People" worksheet (Unit 4 All-in-One, p. 61). By completing this worksheet, students learn more about investing in bonds.

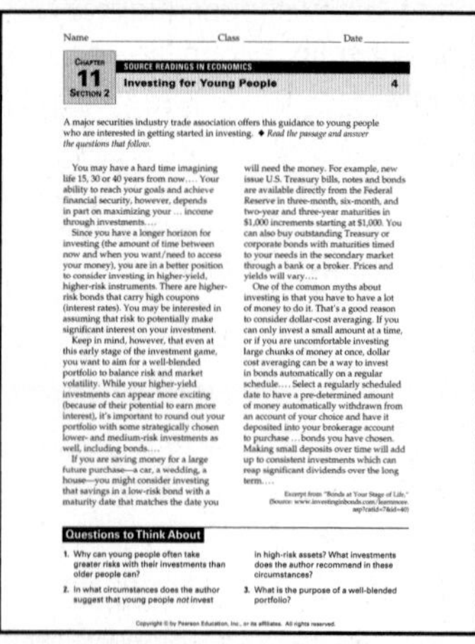

Name ______________ Class ______________ Date ________

Chapter 11 Section 2 — SOURCE READINGS IN ECONOMICS

Investing for Young People 4

A major securities industry trade association offers this guidance to young people who are interested in getting started in investing. ◆ *Read the passage and answer the questions that follow.*

You may have a hard time imagining life 15, 30 or 40 years from now.... Your ability to reach your goals and achieve financial security, however, depends in part on maximizing your ... income through investments....

Since you have a longer horizon for investing (the amount of time between now and when you want/need to access your money), you are in a better position to consider investing in higher-yield, higher-risk instruments. There are higher-risk bonds that carry high coupons (interest rates). You may be interested in assuming that risk to potentially make significant interest on your investment.

Keep in mind, however, that even at this early stage of the investment game, you want to aim for a well-blended portfolio to balance risk and market volatility. While your higher-yield investments can appear more exciting (because of their potential to earn more interest), it's important to round out your portfolio with some strategically chosen lower- and medium-risk investments as well, including bonds....

If you are saving money for a large future purchase—a car, a wedding, a house—you might consider investing that savings in a low-risk bond with a maturity date that matches the date you will need the money. For example, new issue U.S. Treasury bills, notes and bonds are available directly from the Federal Reserve in three-month, six-month, and two-year and three-year maturities in $1,000 increments starting at $1,000. You can also buy outstanding Treasury or corporate bonds with maturities timed to your needs in the secondary market through a bank or a broker. Prices and yields will vary....

One of the common myths about investing is that you have to have a lot of money to do it. That's a good reason to consider dollar-cost averaging. If you can only invest a small amount at a time, or if you are uncomfortable investing large chunks of money at once, dollar cost averaging can be a way to invest in bonds automatically on a regular schedule.... Select a regularly scheduled date to have a pre-determined amount of money automatically withdrawn from an account of your choice and have it deposited into your brokerage account to purchase ... bonds you have chosen. Making small deposits over time will add up to consistent investments which can reap significant dividends over the long term....

Excerpt from "Bonds at Your Stage of Life." (Source: www.investinginbonds.com/learnmore.asp?catid=7&id=40)

Questions to Think About

1. Why can young people often take greater risks with their investments than older people can?
2. In what circumstances does the author suggest that young people *not* invest in high-risk assets? What investments does the author recommend in these circumstances?
3. What is the purpose of a well-blended portfolio?

After completing the worksheet, have students research dollar-cost averaging and report their findings to the class.

inflation-indexed bond a bond that protects the investor against inflation by its linkage to an index of inflation

municipal bond a bond issued by a state or local government or a municipality to finance a public project

corporate bond a bond issued by a corporation to help raise money for expansion

other bond issuers, it does not send interest payments to bondholders on a regular schedule. Instead, the purchaser buys a savings bond for less than par value. For example, you can purchase a $50 savings bond for only $25. When the bond matures, you receive the $25 you paid for the bond plus $25 in interest.

Treasury Bonds, Bills, and Notes

The United States Treasury Department issues Treasury bonds, as well as Treasury bills and notes (T-bills and T-notes). These investments offer different lengths of maturity, as shown in **Figure 11.4**. Backed by the "full faith and credit" of the United States government, these securities are among the safest investments in terms of default risk.

One possible problem with bonds (and investments in general) is inflation. The purchase price and return on Treasury securities are governed by changing interest rates and market conditions. As a result, the value of Treasury securities as an investment must be carefully understood.

If a Treasury bond pays you 5 percent interest per year but the inflation rate is 3 percent, you are really getting just 2 percent interest on the bond. One type of bond issued mainly by the government seeks to protect against inflation—a general rise in prices. The **inflation-indexed bond** links the principal and interest to an inflation index—a measure of how fast prices are rising. If the index rises by 3 percent, this bond's par value will also rise by 3 percent. As a result, you will receive the return on the bond that you expected when you bought it.

Figure 11.4 **Treasury Bonds, Notes, and Bills**

	Treasury Bond	Treasury Note	Treasury Bill
Term	long-term	intermediate-term	short-term
Maturity	30 years	2, 5, or 10 years	4, 13, 26, or 52 weeks
Liquidity and safety	safe	safe	liquid and safe
Minimum purchase	$100	$100	$100
Denomination	$100	$100	$100

CHART SKILLS

Treasury bonds, notes, and bills represent debt that the government must repay the investor.

1. Which of these three types of government securities is the most liquid?
2. How do these three types of government securities differ?

Municipal Bonds

State and local governments and municipalities (government units with corporate status) issue bonds to finance such projects as highways, state buildings, libraries, parks, and schools. These bonds are called **municipal bonds,** or "munis."

Because state and local governments have the power to tax, investors can assume that these governments will be able to keep up with interest payments and repay the principal at maturity. Standard & Poor's and Moody's therefore consider most municipal bonds to be safe investments. In addition, the interest paid on municipal bonds is not subject to income taxes at the federal level or in the issuing state. Because they are relatively safe and are tax-exempt, "munis" are very attractive to investors as a long-term investment. A high-quality municipal bond can pay a good return for quite a long time.

Corporate Bonds

As you read in Chapter 8, corporations issue bonds to help raise money to expand their businesses. These **corporate bonds** are generally issued in denominations of $1,000 or $5,000. The interest on corporate bonds is taxed as ordinary income.

Unlike governments, corporations have no tax base to help guarantee their ability to repay their loans. Thus, these bonds have moderate levels of risk. Investors in corporate bonds must depend on the success of the corporation's sales of goods and services to generate enough income to pay interest and principal.

Corporations that issue bonds are watched closely not only by the independent ratings firms, but also by the Securities and Exchange Commission (SEC). The SEC is

Background Note

Municipal Bond Safety Although municipal bonds are traditionally considered to be second only to U.S. Treasury bonds as safe bond investments, the rate of default on municipal bonds since the late 1970s has raised concern about their credit risk. Of about 250,000 municipal bonds issued between 1977 and 1998, more than 1,700—with a face value of nearly $25 billion—were defaulted. The most infamous example took place in 1994, when Orange County, California, declared bankruptcy and defaulted on some $600 million in bonds it had issued. However, the largest municipal bond default in U.S. history occurred in 1982 when the Washington Public Power Supply System defaulted on municipal bonds worth $2.25 billion.

Answers

Chart Skills 1. Treasury bills 2. in term, maturity, and liquidity an independent government agency that regulates financial markets and investment companies. It enforces laws prohibiting fraud and other dishonest investment practices.

Each bond is issued with an indenture agreement. It sets forth all the features associated with the bond. The interest rate is specified on the indenture agreement.

Junk Bonds

Bonds with a fairly high risk of default but a potentially high yield are known as **junk bonds.** These non-investment-grade securities became especially popular investments during the 1980s and 1990s, when large numbers of aggressive investors made—but also sometimes lost—large sums of money buying and selling them.

Junk bonds have been known to pay more than 12 percent interest at a time when government bonds were yielding only about 8 percent. On the other hand, the speculative nature of most junk bonds makes them very risky. Investors in junk bonds face a strong possibility that some of the issuing firms will default on their debt. Nevertheless, issuing junk bonds has enabled many companies to undertake activities that would otherwise have been impossible to complete. Junk bond funds, which pool large numbers of individual high-risk bonds, may reduce the risk somewhat for the average investor. Still, investment in junk bond funds can be hazardous.

CHECKPOINT ***Which type of bond might have been used to fund the construction of your school?***

Figure 11.5 Average Bond Yields, 1992–2006

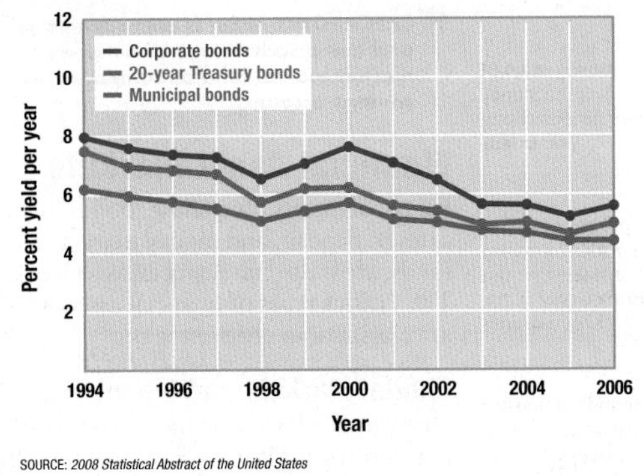

SOURCE: *2008 Statistical Abstract of the United States*

GRAPH SKILLS

From the early 1990s to the early 2000s, bond yields dipped slightly for all three types of bonds shown.

1. **Which type of bond had the highest yield?**
2. **Which of the three types of bonds would you expect to carry the least risk? Explain your answer.**

For an animated version of this graph, visit **PearsonSuccessNet.com**

Other Types of Financial Assets

In addition to bonds, investors may choose other financial assets. These include certificates of deposit and money market mutual funds, as well as stock. You will read more about stock in Section 3.

Certificates of Deposit

Certificates of deposit (CDs) are one of the most common forms of investment. As you read in Chapter 10, CDs are available through banks, which lend out the funds deposited in CDs for a fixed amount of time, such as six months or two years.

CDs are attractive to small investors because they can deposit as little as $100. Investors can also choose among several terms of maturity. This means that if an investor foresees a future expenditure, he or she can buy a CD that matures just before the expenditure is due.

Money Market Mutual Funds

Money market mutual funds are special types of mutual funds. As you read in Section 1, financial intermediaries collect money from individual investors and then buy stocks, bonds, or other financial assets to form a mutual fund.

In the case of money market mutual funds, intermediaries buy short-term financial assets. Investors receive higher interest on a money market mutual fund than they would receive from a savings account. On the other hand, money market mutual funds are not covered by FDIC insurance. (As you read in Chapter 10, FDIC insurance protects

junk bond a bond with high risk and potentially high yield

DISTRIBUTE ACTIVITY WORKSHEET

Distribute the "Weighing the Risks" worksheet (Unit 4 All-in-One, p. 62). Have students compare the risk attached to different financial assets.

L2 Distribute the "Weighing the Risks" section activity worksheet (Unit 4 All-in-One, p. 63).

After students have completed the worksheets, have a few volunteers with different rankings present their rankings to the class. Use the Opinion Line strategy (p. T28) with a few of the assets that students have ranked differently so that all students can defend their positions.

Action Graph online Have students review the Action Graph animation for a step-by-step look at the average bond yields of three types of bonds between 1992 and 2006.

EXTEND

Have students research financial intermediaries or visit the Securities Industry and Financial Markets Association (www.investinginbonds.com), and find two corporate bonds, one municipal bond, and one Treasury bond or T-bill available for sale. Have them record the following information for each asset: the issuer, rating (if applicable), maturity date, coupon, yield to maturity, and price. Students should explain which of these assets they would invest in and why.

GUIDING QUESTION WRAP UP

Have students return to the section Guiding Question. Review the completed graphic organizer and clarify any misgivings. Have a wrap up discussion about bonds.

Assess and Remediate

L3 L2 Collect the "Weighing the Risks" worksheet to assess students' understanding of bonds and other financial assets.

L4 Collect the "Investing for Young People" worksheet and assess student understanding of investment plans.

L3 Assign the Section 2 Assessment questions; identify student misconceptions.

L3 Give Section Quiz A (Unit 4 All-in-One, p. 64).

L2 Give Section Quiz B (Unit 4 All-in-One, p. 65).

Answers

Checkpoint municipal bond

Graph Skills 1. corporate bond 2. municipal bond because it has the lowest yield per year

Have students complete the Self-Test Online and continue their work in the **Essential Questions Journal**.

REMEDIATION AND SUGGESTIONS

Use the chart below to help students who are struggling with content.

WEAKNESS	REMEDIATION
Defining key terms (Questions 4, 5, 7)	Have students use the interactive Economic Dictionary Online.
Characteristics of bonds (Questions 1, 3, 6, 8, 9, 11)	Have students reread and outline Bonds as Financial Assets
Types of bonds (Questions 2, 4, 5)	Pair students to create flashcards describing each type of bond and drill each other.
Characteristics of other types of financial assets (Question 10)	Work with students to create a graphic organizer from the material in Other Types of Financial Assets

Answers

Checkpoint advantage: higher interest; disadvantage: more risk (not insured by FDIC)

Checkpoint by length of time for which funds are lent and whether assets can be resold to other buyers

capital market a market in which money is lent for periods longer than a year

money market a market in which money is lent for periods of one year or less

primary market a market for selling financial assets that can be redeemed only by the original holder

secondary market a market for reselling financial assets

bank deposits up to $250,000 per account.) This lack of insurance makes them slightly riskier than savings accounts.

CHECKPOINT ***What is one advantage and one disadvantage of a money market mutual fund as compared with a savings account?***

Financial Asset Markets

Financial assets, including bonds, certificates of deposit, and money market mutual funds, are traded on financial asset markets. The various types of financial asset markets are classified in different ways.

Capital Markets and Money Markets

One way to classify financial asset markets is according to the length of time for which funds are lent. This type of classification includes both capital markets and money markets.

- *Capital markets* Markets in which money is lent for periods longer than a year are called **capital markets.** Financial assets that are traded in capital markets include long-term CDs and corporate and government bonds that require more than a year to mature.
- *Money markets* Markets in which money is lent for periods of one year or less are called **money markets.** Financial assets that are traded in money markets include short-term CDs, Treasury bills, and money market mutual funds.

Primary and Secondary Markets

Markets may also be classified according to whether assets can be resold to other buyers. This type of classification includes primary and secondary markets.

- *Primary markets* Financial assets that can be redeemed only by the original holder are sold on **primary markets.** Examples include savings bonds, which cannot be sold by the original buyer to another buyer. Small certificates of deposit are also in the primary market because investors would most likely cash them in early rather than try to sell them to someone else.
- *Secondary markets* Financial assets that can be resold are sold on **secondary markets.** This option for resale provides liquidity to investors. If there is a strong secondary market for an asset, the investor knows that the asset can be resold fairly quickly without a penalty, thus providing the investor with ready cash. The secondary market also makes possible the lively trade in stock that is the subject of the next section.

CHECKPOINT ***What are two ways of classifying financial asset markets?***

SECTION 2 ASSESSMENT

Essential Questions Journal To continue to build a response to the Essential Question, go to your **Essential Questions Journal.**

Guiding Question

1. Use your completed chart to answer this question: Why are bonds bought and sold?
2. **Extension** Would you prefer to buy a savings bond or a junk bond? Explain your preference.

Key Terms and Main Ideas

3. Identify the three components of bonds.
4. Why does the United States government issue **savings bonds?**
5. What is the advantage of an **inflation-indexed bond?**
6. Name two advantages of bonds for their issuers.
7. What kinds of financial assets are sold on **secondary markets?**

Critical Thinking

8. **Interpret** When would it be a good investment to sell bonds at a discount from par?
9. **Explain (a)** How are bonds rated? **(b)** How do you think these ratings are helpful to investors?
10. **Contrast (a)** What kinds of financial assets are traded in capital markets? **(b)** How are these different from the financial assets traded in money markets?

Math Skills

11. Suppose that you buy a municipal bond for $200 with an annual yield of 4 percent. How much money will you have earned when the bond reaches maturity in five years?

Visit PearsonSuccessNet.com for additional math help.

Assessment Answers

1. bought: to support the government in times of need, to invest in a fairly safe financial vehicle, to earn interest; sold: to finance war, to help pay for a public works project, to raise money to expand businesses
2. Student responses should respect their financial goals and their awareness of the risk/return issues. Possible responses: a savings bond because I'm guaranteed to receive the par value of the bond when the bond matures; a junk bond because I can potentially get a higher return
3. coupon rate, maturity, par value
4. to pay for public works projects
5. The interest rate is linked to inflation so that the buyer receives the return he or she expected at the time of purchase.
6. Size of payments and repayment schedule are known in advance; bondholders have no ownership of the company so they don't share its profits.
7. stocks and bonds
8. when interest rates are rising or when principal might be at risk
9. (a) by independent firms that rate the issuer's ability to repay the loan (b) They help investors judge potential risk.
10. (a) long-term CDs and long-term government and corporate bonds; (b) Money markets are markets in which assets that have maturities of a year or less are traded; in capital markets, assets with maturities of more than a year are traded.
11. $200 × 0.04 × 5 = $40

SECTION 3 The Stock Market

OBJECTIVES

1. **Identify** the benefits and risks of buying stock.
2. **Describe** how stocks are traded.
3. **Explain** how stock performance is measured.
4. **Describe** the Great Crash of 1929 and more recent stock market events.

ECONOMIC DICTIONARY

As you read the section, look for the definitions of these **Key Terms:**

- share
- capital gain
- capital loss
- stock split
- stockbroker
- brokerage firm
- stock exchange
- futures
- options
- call option
- put option
- bull market
- bear market
- speculation

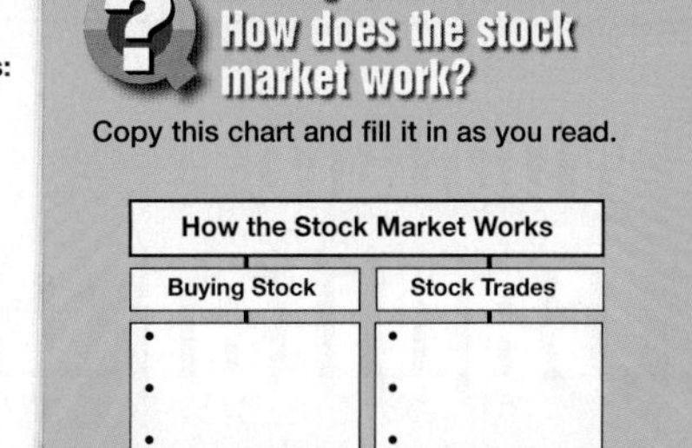

Economics and You You hear it on the news every day. "Stock prices fell today in heavy trading" or "The bulls controlled Wall Street today as the Dow surged." Lots of long faces follow a drop in the stock market. A substantial rise prompts smiles and general enthusiasm. Lots of people—maybe even you—are interested in the stock market. But is the stock market a place where you should invest your precious resources?

Principles in Action If you want to know how the stock market works, you will not lack sources of information and advice. A section of your daily newspaper provides a list of stocks with the changes in price per share. Every television news broadcast highlights the latest price changes. You may even see stock prices crawling across the bottom of your TV screen. But just what is stock, exactly how is it traded, and when is it a good investment?

share a portion of stock

Buying Stock

Besides bonds, corporations can raise funds by issuing stock, which represents ownership in the corporation. Stock is issued in portions known as **shares.** By selling shares of stock, corporations raise money to start, run, and expand their businesses.

Benefits of Buying Stock

There are two ways for stockholders to make a profit:

- *Dividends* As you read in Chapter 8, many corporations pay out part of their profits as dividends to their stockholders. Dividends are usually paid four times per year (quarterly). The size of the dividend depends on the corporation's profit. The higher the profit, the larger the dividend per share of stock.
- *Capital gains* A second way an investor can earn a profit is to sell the stock for more than he or she paid for it. The

Stock certificates show the number of shares the holder owns. ***What is the difference between a stock and a bond?*** ▼

Guiding Question

How does the stock market work?

Get Started

How the Stock Market Works	
Buying Stock	**Stock Trades**
• Benefits: dividend and capital gains • Types of stock: income, growth, common, preferred • Stock splits • Risks: lower profits than expected or lose money • Measuring performance	• Stockbroker, brokerage firms • Stock exchanges: New York Stock Exchange & Nasdaq • Internet sites • Futures and options (call and put options) • Day trading

LESSON GOALS

Students will:

- Know the Key Terms.
- Evaluate the benefits and risks of buying stock by comparing them to those of investing in bonds.
- Demonstrate an understanding of the Great Crash of 1929 by presenting a news account.

BEFORE CLASS

Have students complete the graphic organizer in the Section Opener as they read the text. As an alternate activity, have students complete the Guided Reading and Review worksheet (Unit 4 All-in-One, p. 66).

L1 L2 ELL LPR Differentiate Have students complete the Guided Reading and Review worksheet (Unit 4 All-in-One, p. 67).

Answer

Caption Possible response: Stocks generally have a higher rate of return, and are riskier, than bonds.

Focus on the Basics

Students need to come away with the following understandings:

FACTS: • Shares of stock represent ownership in a corporation. Corporations issue stock to raise money to start, run, or expand their businesses. • Stock owners can earn profits from stocks through dividends and capital gains. • Stocks are traded on stock markets such as the New York Stock Exchange and the NASDAQ, and on Internet sites. The performance of the stock market is measured by the Dow Jones Industrial Average and the Standard & Poor's 500. • The crash of the stock market in 1929 led to the Great Depression.

GENERALIZATION: While a risky investment, stocks offer liquidity and great potential for returns.

CLASSROOM HINTS

WHAT MAKES STOCK TRADING POSSIBLE?

All trades have at least two sides. Stock trading is no different. Traders who believe that a stock's value will go down sell it, and traders who believe that it will go up buy it. The balance of this trading determines the price of a stock at the end of a trading day. If there are more buyers than sellers, a stock's price will rise, and if there are more sellers than buyers, it will go down. Stock exchanges are designed to make this trading, or exchange, possible.

Teach Visual Glossary

REVIEW KEY TERMS

Pair students and have them write the definitions of the key terms related to the understanding of capital gains.

capital – *any human-made resource that is used to produce other goods and services*

profit – *the amount of money a business receives in excess of its expenses*

stock – *a certificate of ownership in a corporation*

share – *a portion of stock*

DISCUSS

Read the definition of *capital gain*. Tell students that the capital referred to in *capital gains* includes stocks and bonds, as well as property. Ask **How does the term *profit* apply to the term *capital gain*?** *(A capital gain is a profit made from selling stocks, bonds, or property.)*

Have students read through the cartoon about "Splendid Widgets." Ask **How does the purchase price compare to the selling price?** *(The selling price is higher than the purchase price.)* Have volunteers explain how the selling and purchase prices, as well as the capital gains, were calculated.

Point to the cartoon "Bought low, sold even lower." Ask **Did the man experience a capital gain? Explain.** *(No. The price of what he sold was lower than the price of what he bought.)* **What did he experience?** *(a capital loss)*

L1 L2 Differentiate After pointing out the "Bought low, sold even lower" cartoon, ask **What seems to be true about the man's financial situation? Why?** *(He appears to have little money. For example, his pants are torn and he hasn't shaved.)* Ask **How does the price of what the man sold compare to the price of what he bought?** *(it was "even lower" than what he bought)* Tell students that this is called a *capital loss*.

Economics online *All print resources are available on the Teacher's Resource Library CD-ROM and online at* www.PearsonSuccessNet.com.

VISUAL GLOSSARY

Reviewing Key Terms
To understand *capital gains*, review these terms.

capital *p. 6*
profit *p. 25*
stock *p. 202*
share *p. 291*

What are Capital Gains?

◀ **capital gain** the difference between the higher selling price and the lower purchase price of an investment

▲ Carey Williams seems to have a knack for the stock market. Two years ago, she bought 300 shares of Splendid Widgets at $25 a share. Since then, she has followed the market closely and happily watched the stock go up. Yesterday, when she checked the stock pages, she saw that it had reached $32.50 a share. Although she has done well with Widget, she will have to pay a capital gains tax on the profit, $2,250.

◀ Of course, not everyone does well in the stock market. If you sell a stock for less than you bought it, you incur a "capital loss." You do not have to pay a tax on a capital loss. In fact, you can usually deduct the loss from other capital gains that you may have.

Visual Glossary online
To expand your understanding of this and other key economic terms, visit **PearsonSuccessNet.com**

292

difference between the higher selling price and the lower purchase price is called a **capital gain.** An investor who sells a stock at a price lower than the purchase price, however, suffers a **capital loss.**

Types of Stock

Stock may be classified in several ways, such as whether or not it pays dividends.

- *Income stock* By paying dividends, this stock provides investors with income.
- *Growth stock* This stock pays few or no dividends. Instead, the issuing company reinvests its earnings in its business. The business (and its stock) thus grows in value over time.

Stock may also be classified as to whether or not the stockholders have a vote in company policy.

- *Common stock* Investors who buy common stock are usually voting owners of the company. They usually receive one vote for each share of stock owned. They may use this vote, for example, to help elect the company's board of directors. In some cases, a relatively small group of people may own enough shares to give them control over the company.
- *Preferred stock* Investors who buy preferred stock are usually nonvoting owners of the company. Owners of preferred stock, however, receive dividends before the owners of common stock. If the company goes out of business, preferred stockholders get their investments back before common stockholders.

Stock Splits

Owners of common stock may sometimes vote on whether to initiate a stock split. A **stock split** means that each single share of stock splits into more than one share. A company may seek to split a stock when the price of stock becomes so high that it discourages potential investors from buying it.

For example, suppose you own 200 shares in a sporting goods company called Ultimate Sports. Each share is worth $100. After a 2-for-1 split, you own 400 shares of Ultimate Sports, or two shares of stock for every single share you owned before. Because the price is divided along with the stock, however, each share is now worth only $50. Thus a stock split does not immediately result in any financial gain. Shareholders like splits, however, because splits usually demonstrate that the company is doing well, and the lower stock price tends to attract more investors.

Risks of Buying Stock

Purchasing stock is risky because the firm selling the stock may earn lower profits than expected, or it may lose money. If so, the dividends will be smaller than expected or nothing at all, and the market price of the stock will probably decrease. If the price of the stock decreases, investors who choose to sell their stock will get less than they paid for it, experiencing a capital loss.

How do the risk and rate of return on stocks compare with the risk and rate of return on bonds? As you have read, investors expect higher rates of return when they take on greater risk. Because of the laws governing bankruptcy, stocks are more risky than bonds. When a firm goes bankrupt, it sells its assets (such as land and equipment) and then pays its creditors, including bondholders, first. Stockholders receive a share of the assets only if there is money left over after bondholders are paid. As you might expect, because stocks are riskier than bonds, the return on stocks is generally higher.

CHECKPOINT ***What are two ways that an investor can make a profit from buying stocks?***

How Stocks Are Traded

Suppose you decide that you want to buy stock. Do you call up the company and place an order? Probably not, because very few companies sell stock directly. Instead, you would contact a **stockbroker,** a person who links buyers and sellers of stock. Stockbrokers usually work with individual investors, advising them to buy or sell particular stocks.

Stockbrokers work for **brokerage firms,** or businesses that specialize in trading

capital gain the difference between the selling price and purchase price that results in a financial gain for the seller

capital loss the difference between the selling price and purchase price that results in a financial loss for the seller

stock split the division of each single share of a company's stock into more than one share

stockbroker a person who links buyers and sellers of stock

brokerage firm a business that specializes in trading stocks

BELLRINGER

Display transparency "Market Pain" (Color Transparencies, 11.b), a cartoon of a stockbroker hitting an investor with a mallet. Ask students to explain in a paragraph what is going on in the cartoon and its message about investing in stocks.

Teach

Economics online To present this topic using digital resources, use the lecture notes on www.PearsonSuccessNet.com.

CHECK COMPREHENSION

Ask students to identify the figure holding the mallet *(a stockbroker),* the figure being hit on the head *(an investor).* Ask **Why has the stockbroker hit the investor?** *(He wants to test the investor's tolerance for pain.)* **What point is the cartoonist making?** *(investing in stock can be painful: the investor can lose a lot of money).* Conclude with this open-ended question: **If the risk is so high, why do you think people would choose to invest in the stock market?** Tell students they will learn in more detail about the risks and rewards of the stock market.

COMPARE

Have students consider their future financial goals, such as buying a car, going to college, or purchasing a house. With these in mind, tell students to imagine that they have $1,000 to invest in stocks, bonds, or both. Poll the class to see how many students would choose to buy each type of asset. Use students' responses to launch a discussion of the benefits and risks of buying stock. Ask **What are the benefits of investing in stocks over investing in bonds?** *(greater liquidity and potential for greater returns; stocks can be split)* Ask **Why is the potential for profit greater for stocks?** *(Share values can increase and dividends are not set or limited like bond yields.)* Have students compare the risks of investing in stock to the risks of investing in bonds. *(Possibility for little or no return, perhaps even capital loss, is greater.)* Make sure students understand how diversification can minimize risks.

Differentiated Resources

L1 L2 Guided Reading and Review (Unit 4 All-in-One, p. 67)

L2 Bulls, Bears, Ants, and Grasshoppers (Unit 4 All-in-One, p. 69)

L4 Investing in Higher Education (Unit 4 All-in-One, p. 70)

L3 Becoming a Wizard of Wall Street (Simulation Activities, Chapter 11)

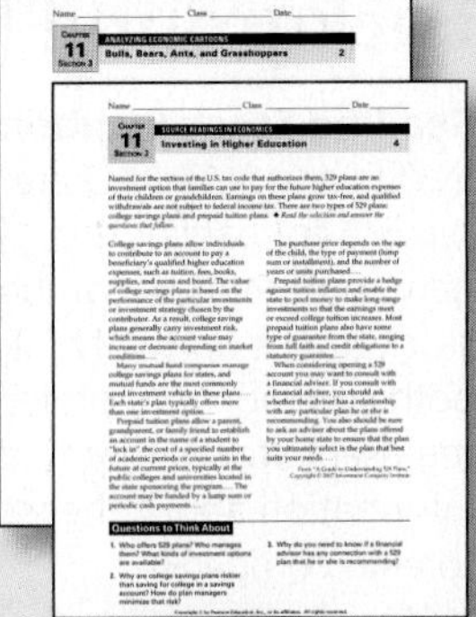

Answer

Checkpoint from dividends paid on each share and by making a capital gain from reselling shares

INTERPRET

Refer students to Figure 11.6. Have them read the report and answer the following questions: **What does DIS mean?** *(the symbol for Disney)* **What is the symbol for Dole Food?** *(DOL)* **How many shares of Dole stock were traded on this day?** *(2,927,000 shares)* **How did Dole Food's shares do on this day compared to the previous day's close?** (up 44 cents per share) **Which company's stock performed the worst on this trading day?** *(Disney lost 25 cents a share.)* **Which performed best?** *(Dow Chemical's stock went up $3.38 per share)*

L4 Differentiate Have students research the meaning of the PE ratio, and then explain its meaning to the class.

L2 Differentiate Have students use the section narrative, the Visual Glossary, and the Electronic Glossary to write definitions of *capital gain, capital loss, dividend, share,* and *stock split.* Have them identify which terms are related to the benefits of buying stock and which to the risks.

Figure 11.6 **Reading a Newspaper Stock Report**

CHART SKILLS

Many newspapers publish daily reports of stock market transactions. The explanations of the abbreviations in this sample report will help you read stock market reports in your own daily paper.

1. Which of the companies listed pays the highest dividend?
2. How many of the companies listed reached their high price for the year on the day the chart was published? Which companies are they?

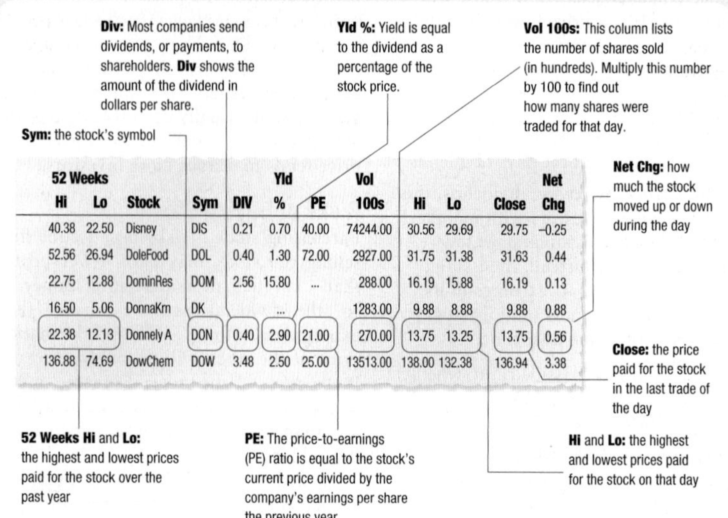

52 Weeks Hi	52 Weeks Lo	Stock	Sym	DIV	Yld %	PE	Vol 100s	Hi	Lo	Close	Net Chg
40.38	22.50	Disney	DIS	0.21	0.70	40.00	74244.00	30.56	29.69	29.75	−0.25
52.56	26.94	DoleFood	DOL	0.40	1.30	72.00	2927.00	31.75	31.38	31.63	0.44
22.75	12.88	DominRes	DOM	2.56	15.80	...	288.00	16.19	15.88	16.19	0.13
16.50	5.06	DonnaKrn	DK		...		1283.00	9.88	8.88	9.88	0.88
22.38	12.13	Donnely A	DON	0.40	2.90	21.00	270.00	13.75	13.25	13.75	0.56
136.88	74.69	DowChem	DOW	3.48	2.50	25.00	13513.00	138.00	132.38	136.94	3.38

Div: Most companies send dividends, or payments, to shareholders. Div shows the amount of the dividend in dollars per share.
Yld %: Yield is equal to the dividend as a percentage of the stock price.
Vol 100s: This column lists the number of shares sold (in hundreds). Multiply this number by 100 to find out how many shares were traded for that day.
Sym: the stock's symbol
Net Chg: how much the stock moved up or down during the day
Close: the price paid for the stock in the last trade of the day
52 Weeks Hi and Lo: the highest and lowest prices paid for the stock over the past year
PE: The price-to-earnings (PE) ratio is equal to the stock's current price divided by the company's earnings per share the previous year.
Hi and Lo: the highest and lowest prices paid for the stock on that day

stocks. Stockbrokers and brokerage firms cover their costs and earn a profit by charging a commission, or fee, on each stock transaction. Sometimes, they also act as dealers of stock, meaning that they buy shares at a lower price and sell them to investors at a slightly higher price, profiting from the difference, or "spread."

Simulation Activity

Wall Street Wizard
You may be asked to take part in a role-playing game about the stock market.

Stock Exchanges

A market for buying and selling stock is known as a **stock exchange.** Stock exchanges act as secondary markets for stocks and bonds. Most newspapers publish data on transactions in major stock exchanges. (See **Figure 11.6** to learn how to read a newspaper stock market report.)

stock exchange a market for buying and selling stock

Major United States stock markets include the New York Stock Exchange (NYSE) and Nasdaq. In addition, a large number of people trade stocks on the Internet, using online brokerage firms or special trading software. The ease of this approach also makes it very risky because snap judgments can often be wrong—and very costly.

The New York Stock Exchange

The New York Stock Exchange (NYSE) is the country's largest and most powerful exchange. The NYSE began in 1792 as an informal, outdoor exchange in New York's financial district. Over time, as the financial market developed and the demand to buy and sell financial assets grew, the exchange moved indoors and became restricted to a limited number of members, who bought "seats" allowing them to trade on the exchange.

The NYSE handles stock and bond transactions for the top companies in the United States and in the world. The largest, most financially sound, and best-known firms listed on the NYSE are referred to as blue chip companies. Blue chip stocks are often in high demand, because investors expect the companies to continue to do business profitably for a long time.

Nasdaq

Despite the importance of organized markets like the New York Stock Exchange, many stocks, as well as bonds, are not

Background Note

Reading Stock Symbols All securities listed on the New York Stock Exchange (NYSE) and NASDAQ are identified by a unique stock symbol or ticker symbol. This symbol appears on the "ticker tape" that scrolls across the bottom of most financial news programs. A symbol of one, two, or three letters represents companies whose stock trades on the NYSE. An A or B will appear as a fourth letter if a company has both common and preferred shares. In general, however, four-letter stock symbols represent stocks that trade on NASDAQ. A fifth letter in a NASDAQ symbol provides information about the stock. For example, an F as a fifth letter means that it's a foreign company.

Answers

Chart Skills 1. DowChem 2. one; DowChem

traded on the floor of stock exchanges. Instead, they are traded directly, on the over-the-counter (OTC) market. Using a telephone or the Internet, investors may buy directly from a dealer or broker who will search other dealers or brokers on the OTC market for the best price.

The Nasdaq (National Association of Securities Dealers Automated Quotation) system was created in 1971 to help organize the OTC market through the use of automation. It grew rapidly in the 1990s in part by focusing on new-technology stocks. Today, the Nasdaq Stock Market (as it became known) is the second largest securities market in the country and the largest electronic market for stocks. It handles more trades on average than any other American market. True to its OTC roots, Nasdaq has no physical trading floor. Instead it has a telecommunications network through which it broadcasts trading information to computer terminals throughout the world.

Futures and Options

Futures are contracts to buy or sell commodities at a particular date in the future at a price specified today. For example, a buyer and seller might agree today on a price of $4.50 per bushel for soybeans that would not reach the market until six or nine months from now. The buyer would pay some portion of the money today, and the seller would deliver the goods in the future. Many of the markets in which futures are bought and sold are associated with grain and livestock exchanges. These markets include the New York Mercantile Exchange and the Chicago Board of Trade.

Similarly, **options** are contracts that give investors the choice to buy or sell stock and other financial assets. Investors may buy or sell a particular stock at a particular price up until a certain time in the future—usually three to six months.

The option to buy shares of stock until a specified time in the future is known as a **call option.** For example, you may pay $10 per share today for a call option. The call option gives you the right, but not the obligation, to purchase a certain stock at a price of, say, $100 per share. If at the end of six months, the price has gone up to $115 per share, your option still allows you to purchase the stock for the agreed-upon $100 per share. You thus earn $5 per share ($15 minus the $10 you paid for the call option). If, on the other hand, the price has dropped to $80, you can throw away the option and buy the stock at the going rate.

The option to sell shares of stock at a specified time in the future is called a **put option.** Suppose that you, as the seller, pay $5 per share for the right to sell a particular stock that you do not yet own at $50 per share. If the price per share falls to $40, you can buy the share at that price and require the contracted buyer to pay the

futures contracts to buy or sell commodities at a particular date in the future at a price specified today

options contracts that give investors the right to buy or sell stock and other financial assets at a particular price until a specified future date

call option a contract for buying stock at a particular price until a specified future date

put option a contract for selling stock at a particular price until a specified future date

Risk *vs.* Return: Stocks and Bonds

Your grandmother, who does not like risk, gave you a savings bond when you were in grade school. ***The rate of return is fixed, so you know exactly what the bond will be worth when you cash it in.***

You decide to take some money from your pay and buy a few shares of stock. ***You can't predict how your stock will perform, so the possible risk and return are both greater than if you bought bonds.***

▲ Generally with investing in stocks and bonds, the greater the potential risk, the greater the potential return. ***How do age and family circumstance affect the makeup of your investment choices?***

ROLE-PLAY

To help students understand the process by which stocks are bought and sold, divide the class into small groups. In each group, some students will be corporations issuing stock, some will be stockbrokers, and some will be investors. Ask each group to walk through each of the following situations: a new corporation issues stock for the first time; a company votes to split its stock; an investor seeks to buy futures; an investor seeks to buy a call option; an investor seeks to buy a put option. In each situation, the students representing corporations, brokers, and investors should define their roles, actions, and goals. Bring the class together as a whole and ask volunteers to describe their actions in each situation. Encourage students from different groups to correct any misunderstandings. Ask **How do corporations, brokers, and investors benefit from trading?** *(Corporations get capital; brokers earn commissions; investors have the potential to earn capital gains.)* **How has the Internet affected the way stock is bought and sold?** *(growth of online trading)*

L2 ELL LPR Differentiate Call on students to use one of the following Key Terms in a sentence: *stockbroker, brokerage firm, stock exchange, call option, put option, speculation.*

Help students understand *put options* and *call options* by working through the examples in the text on the board. Use a single share. For example:

You pay	Actual share value
$10 call option	
+ $100 price per share	
$110 total paid	$115

Earned: $115 – $110 = $5

L4 Differentiate Tell students to research another nation's stock exchange on the Internet. Suggest that they begin their search using such key words as "Argentina's stock exchange" or "Denmark's stock exchange." Have students identify the location of the country's stock exchange and the major companies traded on that exchange, and compare that exchange's daily volume with the volume of trades on the NYSE or Nasdaq. Have students present their findings to the class.

Answer

Economics and You Possible response: The younger you are, and the fewer people you have to take care of, the more risks you can take.

ASK

Ask **What are two measures of stock performance?** *(the Dow Jones Industrial Average and the S&P 500)* Have students explain how each measures stock market performance.

Ask **What is a bull market?** *(a steady rise in the stock market over a period of time)* **What is a bear market?** *(a steady drop in the stock market over a period of time)*

DISTRIBUTE ACTIVITY WORKSHEET

Have students complete the "Bulls, Bears, Ants, and Grasshoppers" worksheet (Unit 4 All-in-One, p. 68). In this activity, students compare different attitudes toward investment represented in a cartoon.

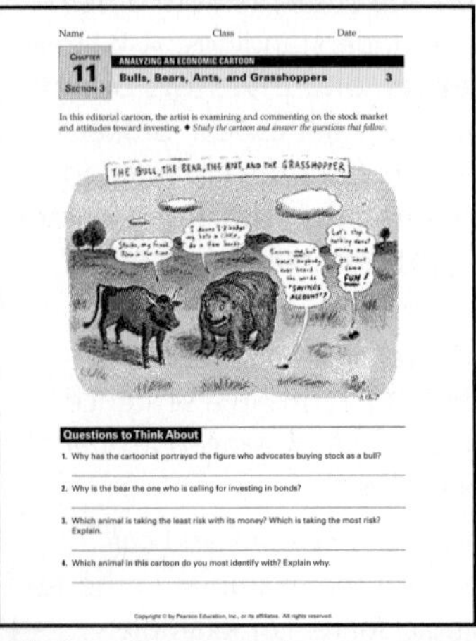
Name ______ Class ______ Date ______

Chapter 11 Section 3 — ANALYZING AN ECONOMIC CARTOON

Bulls, Bears, Ants, and Grasshoppers 3

In this editorial cartoon, the artist is examining and commenting on the stock market and attitudes toward investing. ◆ *Study the cartoon and answer the questions that follow.*

Questions to Think About

1. Why has the cartoonist portrayed the figure who advocates buying stock as a bull?
2. Why is the bear the one who is calling for investing in bonds?
3. Which animal is taking the least risk with its money? Which is taking the most risk? Explain.
4. Which animal in this cartoon do you most identify with? Explain why.

L2 Differentiate Distribute the "Bulls, Bears, Ants, and Grasshoppers" worksheet (Unit 4 All-in-One, p. 69).

After students have completed the activity, have students describe situations when the best strategy to follow is (1) the bull's; (2) the bear's; (3) the ant's; or (4) the grasshopper's.

L3 Differentiate Becoming a Wizard of Wall Street (Simulation Activities, Chapter 11) lets students get hands-on experience researching, selecting, and purchasing stocks and mutual funds.

L4 Differentiate In the "Investing in Higher Education" worksheet (All-in-One, Unit 4, p. 70), students learn about 529 investment plans. After completing the worksheet, tell students to research their state's 529 plans.

Answers

Checkpoint futures and options

Checkpoint buy stock

agreed-upon $50. You would then make $5 per share on the sale ($10 minus the $5 you paid for the put option). If the price rises to $60, however, you can throw away the option and sell the stock for $60.

Day Trading

Most people who buy stock hold their investment for a significant period of time—sometimes many years—with the expectation that it will grow in value. Day traders use a different strategy. They might make dozens of trades per day, sometimes holding a stock for just minutes or even seconds. The typical day trader, sitting in front of a computer, hopes to ride a rising stock's momentum for a short time and then sell the stock for a quick profit. Day trading is a bit like gambling—it is a very risky business in which traders can lose a great deal of money. As the United States Security and Exchange Commission has warned:

> **"While day trading is neither illegal nor is it unethical, it can be highly risky. Most individual investors do not have the wealth, the time, or the temperament to make money and to sustain the devastating losses that day trading can bring."**
>
> —"Day Trading, Your Dollars at Risk," U.S. Securities and Exchange Commission

CHECKPOINT ***What two kinds of contracts allow investors to buy and sell commodities or financial assets at some later date?***

Measuring Stock Performance

You may have heard newscasters speak of a "bull" or "bear" market or of the market rising or falling. What do these terms mean and how are increases and decreases in the sale of stocks measured?

Bull and Bear Markets

bull market a steady rise in the stock market over a period of time

bear market a steady drop or stagnation in the stock market over a period of time

When the stock market rises steadily over a period of time, a **bull market** exists. On the other hand, when the stock market falls or stagnates for a period of time, people call it a **bear market**. In a bull market, investors expect an increase in profits and, therefore, buy stock. During a bear market, investors sell stock in expectation of lower profits. The 1980s and 1990s brought the longest sustained bull market in the nation's history. Between 2000 and 2006, the market went through brief cycles of bear and bull markets. Then, the sub-prime mortgage crisis of 2008 gave the stock market a nasty jolt, and by the fall of the year, the nation entered a severe, and seemingly lengthy, bear market.

The Dow Jones Industrial Average

When people say "the stock market rose today," they are often referring to the Dow Jones Industrial Average, a measure of stock performance known simply as "the Dow." The Dow is the average value of a particular set of stocks, and it is reported as a certain number of points. For example, on a good day the Dow might rise 60 points.

The group of stocks listed on the Dow is intended to represent the market as a whole. To make sure it does, some of the stocks are periodically dropped and others added. Today, those stocks represent 30 large companies in various industries, such as food, entertainment, and technology.

S&P 500

The S&P 500 (Standard & Poor's 500) gives a broader picture of stock performance than the Dow. It tracks the price changes of 500 different stocks as a measure of overall stock market performance. The S&P 500 reports mainly on stocks listed on the NYSE, but some of its stocks are traded on the Nasdaq market.

CHECKPOINT ***What do investors tend to do during a bull market?***

The Great Crash and Beyond

Like the 1980s and 1990s, the 1920s saw a long-term bull market. Unfortunately, this period ended in a horrifying collapse of the stock market known as the Great Crash of 1929. The causes of this collapse contain important lessons for investors in the twenty-first century.

Investing During the 1920s

When President Herbert Hoover took office in 1929, the United States economy seemed to be in excellent shape. The booming economy had dramatically changed the lives of Americans. Factories produced a steady

Virtual Economics

L3 Differentiate

Comparing Stocks and Mutual Funds Use the following lesson from the NCEE **Virtual Economics *CD-ROM*** to evaluate students' understanding of stocks and savings plans. Click on Browse Economics Lessons, specify grades 6–8, and use the key words *stocks and mutual.*

In this activity, students will take part in a role play and complete an analogy activity.

LESSON TITLE	STOCKS AND MUTUAL FUNDS
Type of Activity	Role play
Complexity	Moderate
Time	45 minutes
NCEE Standards	10, 15

stream of consumer products, including refrigerators, washing machines, toasters, and automobiles. The stock market was soaring. In 1925, the market value of all stocks had been $27 billion. By early October 1929, combined stock values had hit $87 billion.

Despite widespread optimism about continuing prosperity, there were signs of trouble. A relatively small number of companies and families held much of the nation's wealth, while many farmers and workers were suffering financially. In addition, many ordinary people went into debt buying consumer goods such as refrigerators and radios—new and exciting inventions at the time—on credit. Finally, industries were producing more goods than consumers could buy. As a result, some industries, including the important automobile industry, developed large surpluses of goods, and prices began to slump.

Figure 11.7 **The Dow, 1896–2009**

January 20, 2009
After climbing to over **14,000** points in October 2007, the Dow begins a slide caused by the global financial crisis. On January 20, 2009, the Dow slumps to **7,949**.

October 9, 2002
DJIA closes at a five-year low, **7,286.27,** on worries of recession and war in Iraq.

September 17, 2001
The NYSE reopens after the September 11 terrorist attacks force a four-day closure. Biggest point loss to date, **684.81** or **7.13%**

March 16, 2000
New record point gain, **499.19** or **4.93%** as technology boom peaks

May 3, 1999
DJIA reaches **11,014.69,** breaking the **11,000** points mark. It will attain a new high of **11, 722.98** on January 14, 2000.

November 21, 1995
DJIA first-ever close above **5,000** just nine months after **4,000**

October 19, 1987
Black Monday crash of record **22.61%,** or **508** points

August 12, 1982
Birth of long-term bull market, in some analysts' view

November 14, 1972
First close above **1,000,** called Wall Street's equivalent of breaking the sound barrier

February 8, 1971
NASDAQ Stock Market is born.

October 28–29, 1929
Stock market crashes of **12.82%** and **11.73%** back-to-back (**38.33** and **30.57** points) usher in Great Depression.

May 26,1896
Index's launch by Charles Dow, at **40.94** points. Index then had only 12 stocks, not 30.

13,000 12,000 11,000 10,000 9,000 8,000 7,000 6,000 5,000 4,000 3,000 2,000 1,000 0

1900 1910 1920 1930 1940 1950 1960 1970 1980 1990 2000 2009

SOURCE: Dow Jones Indexes

CHART SKILLS

The Dow Jones Industrial Average (DJIA) has had some down years, but many more up years since it began measuring stock performance in 1896.

1. In which decade did the Dow first top 1,000? In which decade did it top 2,000? 3,000? 6,000? 8,000?
2. Which was the best decade for the Dow? Which was the lowest decade for the Dow?

Action Graph online
For an animated version of this graph, visit **PearsonSuccessNet.com**

REENACT AND ROLE-PLAY

L3 LPR Differentiate Organize the class into groups to create a "breaking news" radio report on Black Tuesday, October 29, 1929. Roles should include: (1) a news "anchor" to coordinate the story, provide context, and transition the coverage to the on-site reporters; (2) on-site reporters to interview each of the following persons: (3) a trader observing the scene from the floor of the New York Stock Exchange; (4) a stockbroker whose clients have margin accounts with the brokerage; (5) two or more stockholders, at least one of whom had purchased his or her stock on margin; (6) an economist to provide background and analysis for the crisis.

Tell the groups to outline a script for their report, and tell each reporter and interviewee to prepare their interview. Then call on each group to present a 5-minute "broadcast" of the breaking event. To better simulate the radio news format, you may wish to have the groups present their broadcasts from behind a screen or some other means by which they can be heard but not seen.

Action Graph online Have students review the Action Graph animation for a step-by-step look at the Dow between 1896 and 2009.

Answers

Chart Skills 1. 1970s; 1980s; 1990s; 1990s; 1990s
2. 1990s; 1930s

ANALYZE A CURRENT EVENT

A day or two before teaching this lesson, tell students to look in newspapers and magazines or on the Internet for a news story that involves stocks or the stock market. Tell them to write a summary of the story and bring both the story and their summary to class. Call on students to present their story to the class and discuss how it relates to what they have learned about stocks and the stock market.

Innovators

Warren Buffett

BERKSHIRE HATHAWAY

"Why should I buy real estate when the stock market is so easy?"

Warren Buffett believed he would be very rich someday, and he was right. In 2008, shares in his investment company, Berkshire Hathaway, traded at more than $125,000 for a single share. To many people, he is the ultimate stock market expert, nicknamed "the Oracle of Omaha."

Buffett learned how to invest at Columbia University, where a professor taught him to pick his investments by doing his own research. "You're not right or wrong because 1,000 people agree with you or disagree with you," the professor said. "You're right because your facts and reasons are right."

In 1965 Buffett purchased Berkshire Hathaway, a large manufacturer in the declining textile industry. Where others saw an aging dinosaur that was practically worthless, Buffett saw a business that could still produce large amounts of capital. Although the stock market valued Berkshire at $14.86 per share, Buffett knew the company had working capital (current assets minus liabilities) of more than $19 a share. Using the excess capital from Berkshire he went on to invest in a wide range of businesses, including insurance, utilities, and home furnishings. Like Berkshire Hathaway, the companies Buffett has bought are exceptional values.

Today Buffett focuses on a new venture—giving his money away. In 2006, he donated 80 percent of his fortune to charities.

Critical Thinking: ***What do you think Warren Buffett meant when he said, "It's far better to buy a wonderful company at a fair price than a fair company at a wonderful price."***

Fast Facts

Warren Buffett

Born: August 30, 1930, in Omaha, NE

Education: B.A./B.S. University of Nebraska; M.S. Columbia University

Claim to Fame: Enormously successful stock market investor and philanthropist, with personal assets of more than $55 billion

Another economic danger sign was the debt that investors were piling up by playing the stock market. The dizzying climb of stock prices encouraged widespread **speculation,** the practice of making high-risk investments with borrowed money in hopes of getting a big return. Before World War I, only the wealthy had bought and sold shares in the stock market. Now, however, the press was reporting stories of ordinary people making fortunes in the stock market. Small investors thus began speculating in stocks, often with their life savings.

The *Saturday Evening Post* printed a poem that captured the fever of the times:

> **"Oh, hush thee, my babe, granny's bought some shares**
> **Daddy's gone out to play with the bulls and the bears**
> **Mother's buying on tips, and she simply can't lose,**
> **And Baby shall have some expensive shoes"**
>
> —Appeared in the *Saturday Evening Post,* 1929

speculation the practice of making high-risk investments with borrowed money in hopes of getting a big return

To attract less-wealthy investors, stockbrokers encouraged a practice called buying on margin. Buying on margin allowed investors to purchase a stock for only a fraction of its price and borrow the rest from the brokerage firm. The Hoover administration did little to discourage such risky loans.

The Crash

By September 3, 1929, the Dow had reached an all-time high of 381 points. The rising stock prices dominated the news. Prices for many stocks soared far above their real values in terms of the company's earnings and assets.

After their peak in September, stock prices began to fall. Some brokers demanded repayment of loans. When the stock market closed on Wednesday, October 23, 1929, the Dow had dropped 21 points in an hour. The next day, worried investors began to sell, and stock prices fell further. Although business and political leaders told the public not to worry about their losses, widespread panic began.

By Monday, October 28, 1929, shares of stock were dropping in value to a fraction of what people had paid for them. Investors all over the country were racing

Background Note

The Impact of the Great Depression Around the World

Almost every country in the world was affected by the Depression, although the timing differed from country to country. For example, in Germany the depression began in early 1928, while in South Africa, the depression began early in 1930. The severity of the Depression varied as well. For example, annual industrial production in Argentina declined by 17.0 percent, in France it declined by 31.3 percent, and in Poland it declined by 46.6 percent. (Industrial production in the United States declined by 46.8 percent.)

Answer

Innovators that paying a higher price for stock in a highly successful company is less risky than buying stock at a bargain price in a company that has less chance of being very successful.

to get what was left of their money out of the stock market. On October 29, 1929, forever known as Black Tuesday, a record 16.4 million shares were sold, compared with the average 4 to 8 million shares per day earlier in the year. The Great Crash had begun.

The Aftermath of the Crash

During the bull market that led up to the Crash, about 4 million people had invested in the stock market. Although they were the first to feel the effects of the Crash, eventually the whole country was affected. The Crash was one cause of the Great Depression, in which millions of Americans lost their jobs, homes, and farms.

Massive unemployment became the most obvious sign of the deepening depression. By 1933, more than one quarter of the labor force was out of work.

Many Americans lost their homes as well as their jobs during the Great Depression. Desperate for shelter, they erected shacks of scrap wood, old tin, and other materials that they could scavenge. As more and more shacks sprang up, they formed shabby little villages. The residents, who blamed their troubles on the policies of President Hoover, called these shanties "Hoovervilles."

Mistakes in monetary policy slowed the nation's recovery. In 1929, the Federal Reserve had begun limiting the money supply in order to discourage speculation. With too little money in circulation, individuals and businesses could not spend enough to help the economy improve.

Changing Attitudes Toward Stocks

After the Depression, many people saw stocks as risky investments to be avoided. As late as 1980, a relatively small percentage of American households held stock. Gradually, however, attitudes began to change. For one thing, the development of mutual funds made it easy to own a wide range of stocks. Americans became more comfortable with stock ownership.

After a period of very strong growth, stocks crashed again on "Black Monday," October 18, 1987. The Dow lost 22.6 percent of its value that day—nearly twice the one-day loss that began the Great Crash of 1929. However, this time the market rebounded on

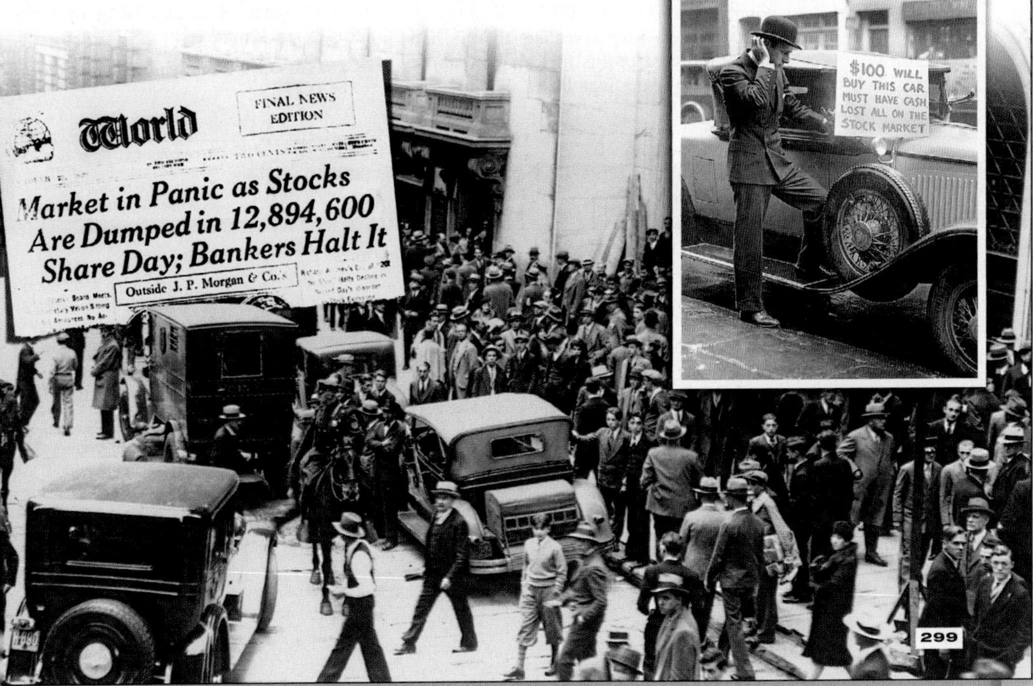

Worried investors gather outside the New York Stock Exchange in October 1929. ***Why was the man in the inset willing to sell his auto cheaply?*** ▼

EXTEND

Have students research the 1987 stock market crash, the mortgage crisis of 2007–2008, or a famous stock market scandal such as the Enron collapse. Have them write a report on their findings. Select students to present their reports to the class.

GUIDING QUESTION WRAP UP

Have students return to the section Guiding Question. Review the completed graphic organizer and clarify any misunderstandings. Have a wrap up discussion about how the stock market works.

Assess and Remediate

L3 L2 Review the "Bulls, Bears, Ants and Grasshoppers" worksheets and assess students' understanding of the benefits and risks of buying stock.

L4 Review the "Investing in Higher Education" worksheet and assess student understanding of college savings plans.

L3 Evaluate students' performances in the radio report to assess their understanding of the Great Crash of 1929.

L3 Assign the Section 3 Assessment questions; identify student misconceptions.

L3 Give Section Quiz A (Unit 4 All-in-One, p. 71).

L2 Give Section Quiz B (Unit 4 All-in-One, p. 72).

(Assess and Remediate continued on p. 300)

Answer

Caption He lost all of his money in the stock market crash and needs cash.

Have students complete the Self-Test Online and continue their work in the **Essential Questions Journal**.

REMEDIATION AND SUGGESTIONS

Use the chart below to help students who are struggling with content.

WEAKNESS	REMEDIATION
Defining key terms (Questions 3, 4, 5, 6)	Have students use the interactive Economic Dictionary Online.
The benefits and risks of buying stock (Questions 5, 9)	Have students reread the Economics & You feature and answer the question.
How stocks are traded (Questions 1, 2, 3, 4, 8)	Have pairs of students role-play being a stockbroker and an investor making a trade.
How stock performance is measured (Questions 7, 9)	Review Figures 11.6 and 11.7 with students.
The causes of the Great Crash of 1929 (Questions 10, 11)	Have students write a one-sentence summary for each of the first three subheads under "The Great Crash and Beyond."

Answer

Checkpoint a stock market crash that began in October of 1929 when stock values plunged to a fraction of their previous prices due to a huge sell-off

each of the next two days, and the impact on the economy was much less severe. The Fed moved quickly to add liquidity and reduce interest rates to stimulate economic growth. Within two years, the Dow had returned to pre-crash levels.

Starting in 1990, stock prices began to soar on the strength of a growing economy and a technology boom. Many people bought stock for the first time, investing heavily in Internet-based companies and other new, high-tech enterprises. A so-called dot.com boom raised stock prices of Internet-based securities to wildly unrealistic levels. At the end of the 1990s, almost half of American households owned mutual funds.

Scandals Rock the Stock Market

By that time, however, investors had begun worrying that many companies—especially the new ones—could not make enough money to justify their high stock prices. Those prices began dropping, and a lot of investors lost most or all of their prior gains. In 2001, an economic downturn and the September 11 terrorist attacks further battered the stock market.

That same year, the stock market took yet another hit. An enormous energy-trading company named Enron filed for bankruptcy in December after revealing that it had falsely reported profits for several years in order to cover up huge losses. The price of its once high-flying stock fell from $90 per share to less than $1. Soon, several other large firms faced similar financial scandals.

In 2002, Congress responded to the scandals with the Sarbanes-Oxley Act. This legislation was aimed at reforming lax accounting practices. As a result of Sarbanes Oxley, top corporate leaders now have to verify that financial reports are accurate or face criminal charges.

A Market in Turmoil

In time, the stock market recovered and reached new heights, boosted by a red-hot real estate market. In October 2006, the Dow passed the 11,700-point mark. It reached 14,000 in 2007. Then, as investors realized the full extent of the subprime mortgage crisis, the stock market again nosedived.

By the end of 2008, it had plunged back to the 8,000 range. Trillions of dollars worth of investments were lost and people saw their retirement savings lose much of their value. Safe investments, such as corporate and municipal bonds, also were badly hit. The financial crisis even caused the collapse of Lehman Brothers, one of Wall Street's most renowned investment firms. A sense of unease hung over the nation's stock markets.

CHECKPOINT ***What was the Great Crash of 1929?***

SECTION 3 ASSESSMENT

Essential Questions Journal To continue to build a response to the Essential Question, go to your **Essential Questions Journal.**

Guiding Question

1. Use your completed flowchart to answer this question: How does the stock market work?
2. **Extension** Suppose you had $1,000 to invest in the stock market. How would you go about investing your money?

Key Terms and Main Ideas

3. Describe the job of a **stockbroker.**
4. Identify two major United States **stock exchanges.**
5. What is a **capital gain?** A **capital loss?**
6. How did **speculation** contribute to the Great Crash of 1929?
7. What factors caused stock prices to rise in the 1990s and 2000s?

Critical Thinking

8. **Contrast (a)** In what ways are futures and options similar? **(b)** How are they different?
9. **Extend** Would you buy stock during a bear market? Why or why not?
10. **Infer (a)** Name the main causes of the Great Crash of 1929. **(b)** What lessons can investors learn from the Crash?

Quick Write

11. Reread The Great Crash and Beyond in this section. Suppose you were a newspaper reporter at the time of the Crash. Write a short article answering the following questions. What caused the Crash? What are the effects of the Crash on individuals? What are the effects on businesses? How do you think the stock market will perform in the future? Remember, you are writing from the point of view of someone in 1929!

Assessment Answers

1. Possible response: The stock market is a secondary market for trading stocks and bonds. Two major U.S. stock exchanges are the New York Stock Exchange and the Nasdaq. An individual investor can trade stocks through a stockbroker or directly on the Nasdaq or on the Internet.
2. Possible response: I would buy income stock for immediate income from dividends and growth stock for long-term investment.
3. buys and sells stock for, and provides advice about stocks to, investors
4. New York Stock Exchange and Nasdaq
5. the difference between the purchase price of stock and a higher selling price; the difference between the purchase price of stock and a lower selling price
6. People bought stock with borrowed money. But after prices began to fall, many people had to sell their stocks to repay their loans. As the prices fell, the resulting number of sales created a panic and drove stock prices down further.
7. a growing economy, a technology boom, a large number of people buying stock
8. (a) Both are contracts to buy or sell at a future time. (b) Futures apply to commodities; options apply to stocks and other financial assets.
9. Possible response: Yes, values will be lower and I can resell in a bull market.
10. (a) speculation and buying on margin (b) Possible responses: Don't buy stock with borrowed money; don't buy based on the expectation of quick profits (speculation).
11. Answers will vary, but the tone of students' articles should reflect the 1929 time frame and should accurately address all questions.

QUICK STUDY GUIDE

QUICK STUDY GUIDE

Chapter 11: Financial Markets

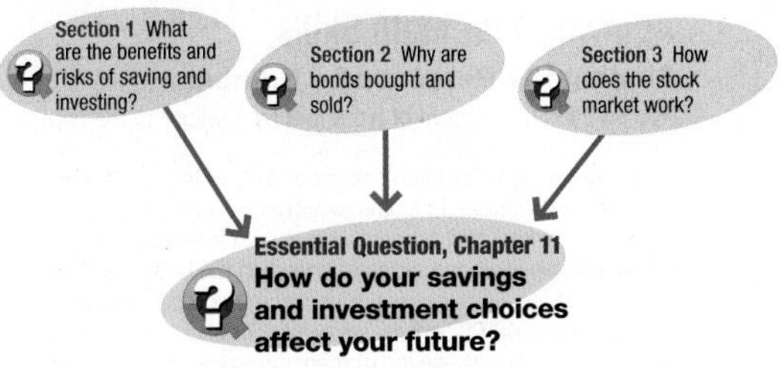

Section 1 What are the benefits and risks of saving and investing?
Section 2 Why are bonds bought and sold?
Section 3 How does the stock market work?
Essential Question, Chapter 11
How do your savings and investment choices affect your future?

Risk, Liquidity, Return

	Risk	Liquidity	Return
Certificate of Deposit	Least risk	Least liquidity	Potentially, least return
Bonds	Minimal risk	Must be held to maturity; however, can be sold on bond market for current price	Greater return than CDs, but potentially less return than individual stocks and mutual funds.
Individual Stocks	Greatest risk	Can be sold at current price on stock market	Greatest potential return
Mutual Funds	Less risk than individual stocks; more than bonds	Can be sold at current price on stock market	Potentially, less return than stocks, more than bonds.

Economic Dictionary

- **investment,** *p. 277*
- **financial system,** *p. 278*
- **financial asset,** *p. 278*
- **financial intermediary,** *p. 279*
- **mutual fund,** *p. 279*
- **hedge fund,** *p. 279*
- **diversification,** *p. 280*
- **portfolio,** *p. 282*
- **prospectus,** *p. 282*
- **return,** *p. 282*
- **coupon rate,** *p. 284*
- **maturity,** *p. 284*
- **par value,** *p. 285*
- **yield,** *p. 285*
- **savings bond,** *p. 287*
- **inflation-indexed bond,** *p. 288*
- **municipal bond,** *p. 288*
- **corporate bond,** *p. 288*
- **junk bond,** *p. 289*
- **capital market,** *p. 290*
- **money market,** *p. 290*
- **primary market,** *p. 290*
- **secondary market,** *p. 290*
- **share,** *p. 291*
- **capital gain,** *p. 293*
- **capital loss,** *p. 293*
- **stock split,** *p. 293*
- **stockbroker,** *p. 293*
- **brokerage firm,** *p. 293*
- **stock exchange,** *p. 294*
- **futures,** *p. 295*
- **options,** *p. 295*
- **call option,** *p. 295*
- **put option,** *p. 295*
- **bull market,** *p. 296*
- **bear market,** *p. 296*
- **speculation,** *p. 298*

Economics *on the go*

Study anytime, anywhere. Download these files today.

Economic Dictionary online	Audio Review online	Action Graph online	Visual Glossary online	How the Economy Works online
Vocabulary Support in English and Spanish	Audio Study Guide in English and Spanish	Animated Charts and Graphs	Animated feature	Animated feature

Download to your computer or mobile device at PearsonSuccessNet.com

ASSIGN THE ESSENTIAL QUESTIONS JOURNAL

After students have finished studying the chapter, they should return to the chapter's essential question in the Essential Questions Journal and complete the activity.

Tell students to go back to the chapter opener and look at the image. Using the information they have gained from studying the chapter, ask **How does this illustrate the main ideas of the chapter?** *(Possible responses: You can invest your money in a variety of financial assets including stocks, bonds, mutual funds, and money markets; the type of market (bull or bear) has an impact on the value of your investments; different types of investments carry different levels of risk and vary in liquidity; diversifying your investments is a way to reduce risk; investments with potentially higher returns are generally riskier than investments offering lower returns.)*

STUDY TIPS

Explain to students that analyzing the work they have done on worksheets and quizzes can help them prepare for tests. Have students look back at the mistakes they made on previous work and work in pairs to correct their mistakes.

Have students download the digital resources available on Economics on the Go for review and remediation.

Assessment at a Glance

TESTS AND QUIZZES

Section Assessments

Section Quizzes A and B, **Unit 4 All-in-One**

Self-Test Online

Chapter Assessments

Chapter Tests A and B, **Unit 4 All-in-One**

Economic Detective, **Unit 4 All-in-One**

Document-based Assessment, p. 303

Exam*View*

AYP Monitoring Assessments

PERFORMANCE ASSESSMENT

Teacher's Edition, pp. 280, 282, 288, 289, 293, 296

Simulation Activities, Chapter 11

Virtual Economics on CD-ROM, Teacher's Edition pp. 279, 286, 296

Essential Questions Journal, Chapter 11

Assessment Rubrics

Chapter Assessment

1. (a) a bond, because it would be easier to sell than a business; (b) inflation-rate risk, time risk, liquidity risk; (c) loss of interest and loss of principal if they must sell at a discount
2. (a) reduced risk through diversification (b) allows people to invest in a broad range of stocks (c) People who buy a stock should be in a financial position to tolerate more risk and possible capital losses.
3. (a) provide modest but steady long-term income at relatively low risk (b) mainly inflation-rate risk if the bond's yield doesn't keep up with inflation; liquidity risk, especially if they have to discount their bond to sell it before maturity; and time risk if holding the bond deprives them of the opportunity to use the money for a better investment (c) Advantages: bonds are more stable and generally less risky than stock, especially as regards loss of principal; disadvantages; inflation-rate risk is similar, although stock can produce capital gains as well as dividends, and bonds have more liquidity risk and time risk than stock.
4. (a) People lost money when they invested in Enron and several other large companies that falsely reported their profits or engaged in other illegal behaviors. (b) passed the Sarbanes-Oxley Act to reform corporate accounting practices and criminally punish those who file false financial reports (c) Possible response: I don't have much faith in individual stocks but I would spread the risk by buying mutual funds.
5. (a) $48 (b) $448
6. $22.40
7. $425.60
8. $383.04
9. (a) Possible response: I plan to be a critical care nurse and on earning about $60,000 per year. (b) Possible response: I will have loans to pay for nursing school. I also will own a house and hope to have two children. I don't see any expensive travel or other interests in my future. (c) Possible response: I don't think I will need to rely heavily on the income from the $5,000, so I could probably take some risks with it.
10. (a) Possible response: I would want to invest at least some of the money in Treasury bonds and money market mutual funds. (b) Possible response: I would invest a lot of the money in stocks. (c) Possible response: I would purchase both stocks and bonds. (d) Possible response: I would be looking for more liquidity in case of emergency and investing some of the money for the long term.

CHAPTER 11 ASSESSMENT

Self-Test online To test your understanding of key terms and main ideas, visit **PearsonSuccessNet.com**

Key Terms and Main Ideas

To make sure you understand the key terms and main ideas of this chapter, review the Checkpoint and Section Assessment questions and look at the Quick Study Guide on the preceding page.

Critical Thinking

1. **Discuss (a)** Which is a more liquid investment, a business or a bond? Explain your answer. **(b)** What risk do investors face if they keep their bonds until they reach maturity? **(c)** What risks do they face if they sell them before maturity?
2. **Infer (a)** What is the main advantage of mutual funds? **(b)** How did the development of mutual funds change the stock market? **(c)** How does the choice of whether to buy a particular stock or a mutual fund relate to the life situation of the purchaser?

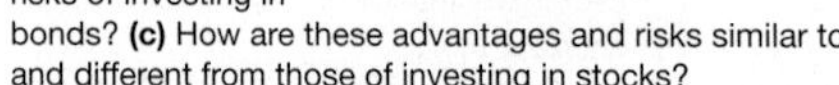

3. **Compare and Contrast (a)** What are the advantages of bonds for investors? **(b)** What are the risks of investing in bonds? **(c)** How are these advantages and risks similar to and different from those of investing in stocks?
4. **Evaluate (a)** Describe the scandals that rocked the stock market in the early 2000s. **(b)** How did the United States government respond to these scandals? **(c)** Do you have faith in the stock market? Why or why not?

Applying Your Math Skills

Finding the Percent of a Number

You can find the percent of a number by multiplying the original number by the percent in decimal or fraction form. Remember, percentages represent hundredths of a quantity. As a fraction, percents are expressed as the percent over one hundred. As a decimal, single-digit percents are shown in the hundredths place. Double-digit percents are shown in the tenths and hundredths places. For example, four percent could be expressed as the fraction 4/100 (which can be reduced to 1/25), or as the decimal 0.04. Twenty-seven percent could be expressed either as the fraction 27/100 or as the decimal 0.27.

Suppose you bought $400 worth of stock two years ago. Since then, the stock's value has risen by 12 percent. You decide to sell your shares. Use your math skills, and the tips above, to answer the following questions.

Visit PearsonSuccessNet.com for additional math help.

5. **(a)** How much profit will you make on the sale? **(b)** Add the profit to the original price to find the total value of the stock you want to sell.
6. You are planning to sell the stock through a stockbroker, who charges a commission of 5 percent on the entire value of the sale. How much will you have to pay the stockbroker?
7. How much money will you receive from the sale after you pay this fee?
8. After you sell the stock and pay the stockbroker, you decide to reinvest your principal and profits in a different stock. After another year, the new stock's value has declined by 10 percent. How much is your stock worth now?

Essential Question Activity

Essential Questions Journal To respond to the chapter Essential Question, go to your **Essential Questions Journal.**

9. Complete this activity to answer the Essential Question: **How do your saving and investment choices affect your future?** Imagine that you have just turned 21 when you learn that a relative you have never met has died—and left you $5,000. According to the will, you must provide a plan for investing the money in the stock, mutual fund, and bond markets that will meet the financial needs you expect to have when you are 30 years old. Using the worksheet in your Essential Questions Journal or the electronic worksheet available at **PearsonSuccessNet.com,** gather the following information:
   (a) What career path do you expect to be following when you are 30? How much money do you expect to be making?
   (b) What financial responsibilities will you have when you are 30? Will you have student loans to pay? Will you have a family to support? Will you own a house? Will you have expensive interests such as travel or collecting?
   (c) Based on your income and your responsibilities, how much money will you need from your investments? Will you depend on that income, or can you risk losing some of it?

Use your answers to these questions about your financial needs to help you make your investment plan. Remember to diversify between relatively safe and relatively high-return investments, depending on your predicted needs.

10. **Modify** When you are 30, you decide to review your investment. Look at the situations below. Briefly describe how each of them might cause you to change your investment plan.
    (a) Interest rates are very high.
    (b) There is a bull market with low interest rates.
    (c) The stock market is doing well, but many economists are predicting a bleak future in the next year for stocks.
    (d) You are about to buy a house—and become the parent of twins!

WebQuest online The Economics WebQuest challenges students to use 21st century skills to answer the essential question.

Remind students to continue to develop an Essential Questions video. Guidelines and a production binder are available at www.PearsonSuccessNet.com.

DOCUMENT-BASED ASSESSMENT

Should financial markets be more strictly regulated?

In the early 2000s, investor confidence in the stock market was shaken by a series of scandals, such as the bankruptcy of Enron. To restore the faith of investors, Congress passed legislation to regulate corporate accounting. Today, some people support increased government regulation of financial markets. Others believe that government regulation is harmful to the financial markets.

Document A

"In an unregulated market, investors will not have enough information to guide their investments, which should not be based on rumor. Companies have incentives not to share information, such as bad news about themselves or information about others that is not commonly known. That's why regulators require companies to fully disclose information. That way, the entire market is better informed. This results in a greater willingness of firms or individuals to invest."

—Randall Dodd, director of the Financial Policy Forum, in *The Wall Street Journal Classroom Edition*

Document B

"The long-term impact of increasing strict rules and regulations can be just as damaging as the fraud and manipulation that occurs in an open system—probably more so. The increase of rules and regulation adds costs and administrative effort. In effect, companies face disincentives to engage in fair and honest activity. Thus, overregulation is also a destructive activity."

—U.S. Congressman Jeff Flake (Republican, Arizona), in *The Wall Street Journal Classroom Edition*

Document C

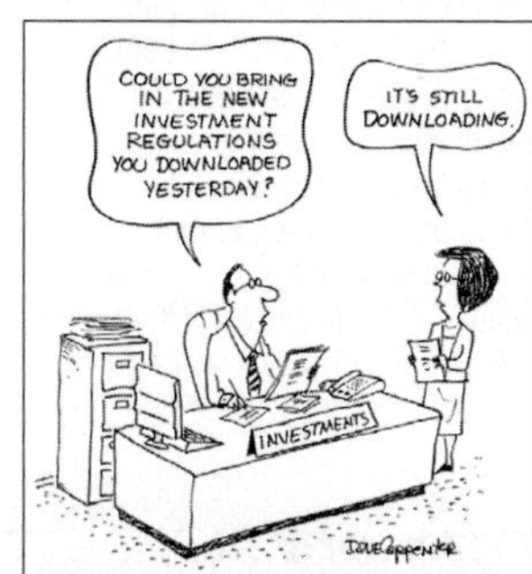

ANALYZING DOCUMENTS

Use your knowledge of the regulation of U.S. financial markets and Documents A, B, and C to answer Questions 1–3.

1. **Which document's author would be most likely to agree with the following idea: "In order to limit harm to others, better regulations are needed"?**
   A. Document A
   B. Document B
   C. Document C
   D. Documents A and C

2. **What does the cartoonist who drew Document C think of new government regulations on financial markets?**
   A. They are necessary to prevent widespread financial problems.
   B. They may cause problems, but they will give investors the information they need.
   C. They are unconstitutional.
   D. They are lengthy and overly complex.

3. **The authors of Document A and Document B disagree that**
   A. regulation makes companies behave honestly.
   B. company leaders who commit fraud should be punished.
   C. the government has the ability to regulate companies.
   D. investors need information.

WRITING ABOUT ECONOMICS

Whether regulation helps or hurts U.S. financial markets is an ongoing issue. Use the documents on this page and resources on the Web site below to answer the question: ***Should financial markets be more strictly regulated?***

In Partnership

To read more about issues related to this topic, visit **PearsonSuccessNet.com**

Document-Based Assessment

ANALYZING DOCUMENTS

1. A
2. D
3. A

WRITING ABOUT ECONOMICS

Possible responses: Yes, financial markets should be more strictly regulated because well-informed investors can make investment decisions that are more likely to keep them financially secure. No, financial markets should not be more strictly regulated because the resulting costs will discourage companies from engaging in fair and honest activities.

Student essay should demonstrate an understanding of the issues involved in the debate. Use the following as guidelines to assess the essay.

L2 Differentiate Students use all documents on the page to support their thesis.

L3 Differentiate Students use the documents on this page and additional information available online at www.PearsonSuccessNet.com to support their answer.

L4 Differentiate Students incorporate information provided in the textbook and online at www.PearsonSuccessNet.com and include additional research to support their opinion.

Go Online to www.PearsonSuccessNet.com for a student rubric and extra documents.

Economics online *All print resources are available on the Teacher's Resource Library CD-ROM and online at* www.PearsonSuccessNet.com.

Essential Question

How can you make the most of your money?

BELLRINGER

Ask students to read the paragraph under the Essential Question. Then have volunteers suggest examples of how to make the most of their money.

EXPLAIN

Before you read aloud the quotation from Mary Dalrymple, you may want to explain that a "nest egg" is money that has been saved or invested to provide for a specific future purpose. Explain that a nest egg is typically used for long-term goals such as retirement and education.

DISCUSS

Have students review the quotations on the page. Ask students to explain ways they can make the most of their money. **What kind of debt is likely to make your money "go up in smoke"?** *(Possible answer: credit card debt)* **What does Caspar mean when he says that stocks are long-term investments?** *(that the overall value of good stock will pay off, even if the price drops in the short term)*

L2 Differentiate Pair students to read the document aloud, breaking it into short segments. Then have them work to paraphrase each quotation.

ANALYZE A CARTOON

Have students silently read the cartoon's caption. Have them work individually to create a list of long-term goals they want to save for. Invite volunteers to share their ideas with the class.

BULLETIN BOARD ACTIVITY

Have students revisit the Unit Essential Question articles that they have posted as they have studied the chapters. Have them discuss the relevance of the articles to the question and whether their opinions have changed since they first read the article. Remind students to review their work in their **Essential Questions Journal**.

EXTEND

Have students complete their work on the Essential Questions Video and present their work to the class.

L4 Differentiate Read aloud the following quote. Owen Young said, "We are not to judge thrift solely by the test of saving or spending. If one spends what he should prudently save, that certainly is to be deplored. But if one saves what he should prudently spend, that is not necessarily to be commended. A wise balance between the two is the desired end." Ask students if they agree with this quote, and if it reflects their own spending habits.

Unit 4 Challenge

Essential Question, Unit 4

How can you make the most of your money?

There are many differing opinions about how individuals can make the most of their money. Look at the opinions below, keeping in mind the Essential Question: How can you make the most of your money?

"Legend has it that Albert Einstein once called compound interest the most powerful force in the universe. Compound interest is the engine that can turn even meager savings into a nice nest egg over time. Inattention to debt puts you on the wrong side of that equation. You spend dollars that could be put to work making you wealthy. You want to be on the right side—the side that uses debt to make money but avoids debt when it hurts.... Stop watching your money go up in smoke."

—Mary Dalrymple, "Habits for Wealth: Dump Your Debt Habit"

"I don't know what the stock market will do tomorrow. (And, let me be equally clear, neither does anyone else.) Bad things may happen tomorrow. Certainly, bad things will happen on some days.... You get a great return [from stocks] by noticing that the day-to-day price of the market doesn't have much to do with the real long-term value of the best companies within that market. You get an even better return than the market averages by never mixing up three very important facts: Extreme stock market pessimism is great for buyers, extreme exuberance is great for sellers... and stocks are long-term investments."

—John Casper, "Lessons Learned"

Essential Question Writing Activity

Consider the different views of economics expressed in the sources on this page and what you have learned about banking and financial institutions. ***Then write a well-constructed essay expressing your view of how you can make the most of your money.***

Writing Guidelines

- Address all aspects of the Essential Question Writing Activity.
- Support the theme with relevant facts, examples, and details.
- Use a logical and clear plan of organization.
- Introduce the theme by establishing a framework that is beyond a simple restatement of the question and conclude with a summation of the theme.

For help in writing a Persuasive Essay, refer to the *Writer's Handbook* in the Reference section, page S-5.

Essential Questions Journal

To respond to the unit Essential Question, go to your **Essential Questions Journal**.

Essential Question Writing Activity

Before students begin the writing activity, remind them to skim through the unit chapters to read the headings on each page. Have them read through any notes they took and to review their chapter assessments and chapter projects.

Students should write a two-paragraph article. Paragraph one should outline how they personally would like to manage their money. Paragraph two should explain other ways that people in general might manage their money.

L2 Differentiate Students should write a paragraph that explains how they personally plan to make the most of their money, providing detailed examples.

L4 Differentiate Students should write a three-paragraph article that provides relevant examples of how they could make the most of their money.

Before students begin work, distribute the Writing Assessment rubric, available at the Online Teacher Center at PearsonSuccessNet.com.

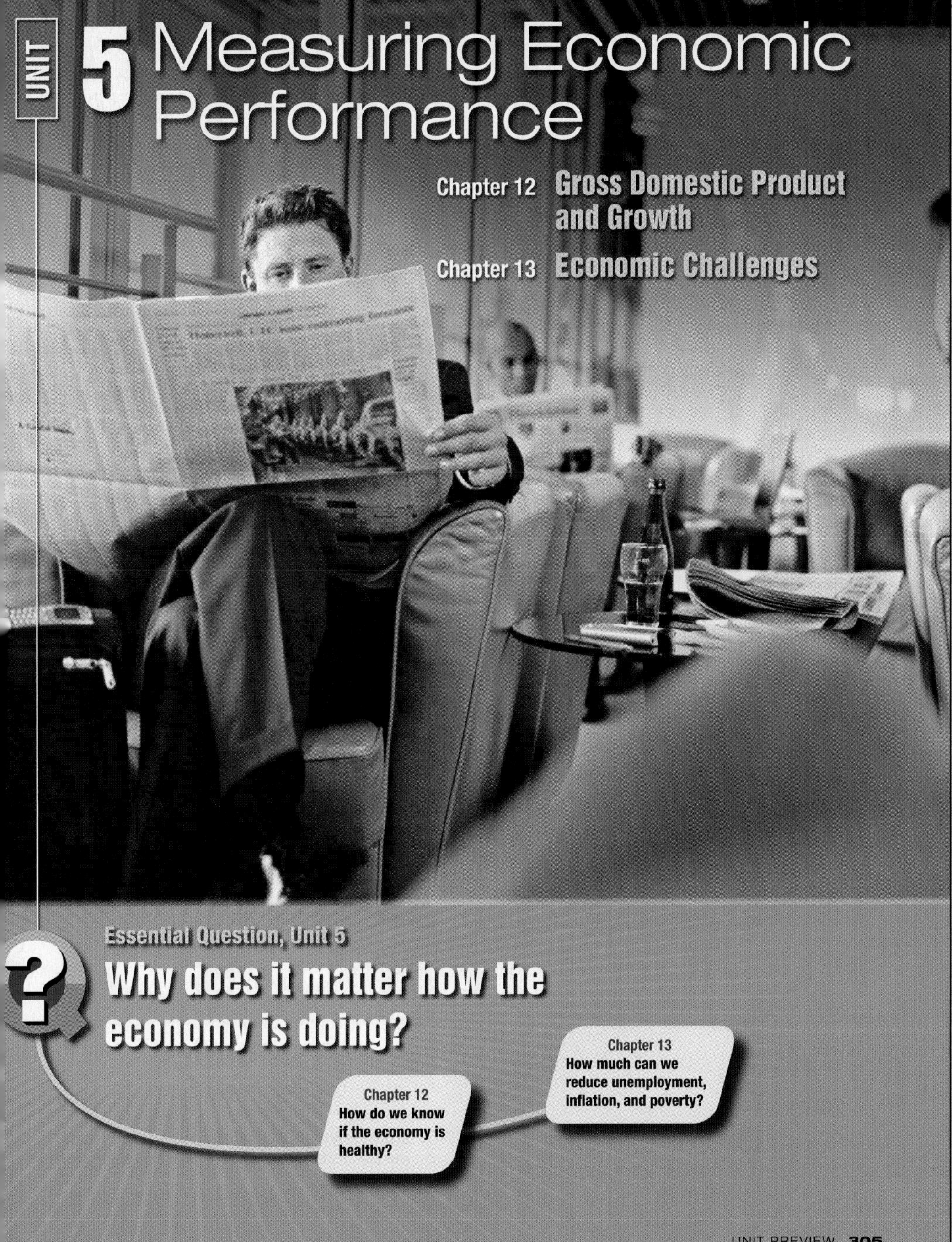

UNIT 5 Measuring Economic Performance
Chapter 12 Gross Domestic Product and Growth
Chapter 13 Economic Challenges

Essential Question, Unit 5

Why does it matter how the economy is doing?

Chapter 12
How do we know if the economy is healthy?

Chapter 13
How much can we reduce unemployment, inflation, and poverty?

Essential Question

Why does it matter how the economy is doing?

Introduce the Unit

ACTIVATE PRIOR KNOWLEDGE

Essential questions frame each unit and chapter of study, asking students to consider big ideas about economics. Write the Unit Essential Question on the Board: **Why does it matter how the economy is doing?** Using the Think-Write-Pair-Share strategy (p. T24), have students brainstorm answers.

WRITING ACTIVITY

To begin this unit, assign the Unit 5 Warmup Activity in the **Essential Questions Journal**. This will help students start to consider their position on the Unit 5 Essential Question: **Why does it matter how the economy is doing?**

Use the **Essential Questions Journal** throughout the program to help students consider these and other big ideas about economics.

BULLETIN BOARD ACTIVITY

Post the Unit Essential Question on a bulletin board. Tell students that they will be learning about why it matters whether the economy is doing well or doing poorly. Ask them to bring in articles about current events to help them answer the question. Students should identify their article and use a sticky note to briefly explain the connection to the Essential Question.

CREATING THE ESSENTIAL QUESTIONS VIDEO

Preview the Unit Challenge on page 360. Consider assigning this activity to your students. Tell them that they will be creating their own video to explore this question, and that they should keep this in mind as they study economic performance. For further information about how to complete this activity, go to PearsonSucessNet.com.

NATIONAL COUNCIL ON ECONOMIC EDUCATION

The following Voluntary National Content Standards in Economics are addressed in this unit:

- ★ **Standard 15**
- ★ **Standard 19**
- ★ **Standard 18**
- ★ **Standard 20**

For a complete description of the standards addressed in each chapter, see the Correlations chart on pages T52–T55.

Online Resources

Economics Online Teacher Center at PearsonSuccessNet.com includes

- Online Teacher's Edition with lesson planner
- Online Lecture Notes
- Teacher's Resource Library with All-in-One Resources, Color Transparencies, Simulation Activities, and Adequate Yearly Progress Monitoring
- SuccessTracker Assessment

Economics Online Student Center at PearsonSuccessNet.com includes

- Interactive textbook with audio
- Economics Video
- WebQuests
- Interactivities
- Student Self-Tests

Essential Questions

UNIT 5:

Why does it matter how the economy is doing?

CHAPTER 12:

How do we know if the economy is healthy?

Introduce the Chapter

ACTIVATE PRIOR KNOWLEDGE

In this chapter, students will learn about GDP and the factors that influence it. Tell students to complete the warmup activity in their **Essential Questions Journal**.

DIFFERENTIATED INSTRUCTION KEY

- **L1** Special Needs
- **L2** Basic
  - **ELL** English Language Learners
  - **LPR** Less Proficient Readers
- **L3** All Students
- **L4** Advanced Students

Economics online Visit www.PearsonSuccessNet.com for an interactive textbook with built in activities on economic principles.

- ***The Wall Street Journal* Classroom Edition Video** presents a current topic related to economic expansion or contraction.
- **Yearly Update Worksheet** provides an annual update, including a new worksheet and lesson on this topic.
- **On the Go** resources can be downloaded so students and teachers can connect with economics anytime, anywhere.

Chapter 12 Gross Domestic Product and Growth

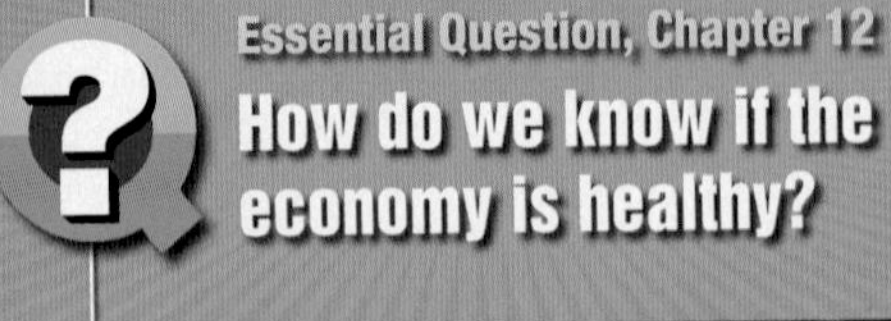

Essential Question, Chapter 12

How do we know if the economy is healthy?

- **Section 1:** Gross Domestic Product
- **Section 2:** Business Cycles
- **Section 3:** Economic Growth

Economics on the go

To study anywhere, anytime, download these online resources at ***PearsonSuccessNet.com*** ▶

ECONOMICS ONLINE

DIGITAL TEACHER TOOLS

The online lesson planner is designed to help teachers plan, teach, and assess. Teachers have the ability to use or customize existing Pearson lesson plans. Online lecture notes support the print lesson.

Two interactivities included in this lesson are:

- **WebQuest** Students complete a guided activity further exploring the essential questions.
- **Action Graph** Animated graphs show the measurements of the macroeconomy and business cycles.

Block Scheduling

BLOCK 1 Teach the complete Section 1.

BLOCK 2 Teach Sections 2 and 3, omitting the Bellringer activities and extend options.

Pressed for Time

Group work Use the Jigsaw strategy (p. T29) to cover the chapter content. Organize students into study groups, and divide the sections equally among them. Have groups read their section and take notes of details under each heading. Have the groups assigned to each section then collaborate to "teach" the section to the rest of the class. Complete the transparencies and skill and activity worksheets as a class.

OBJECTIVES

1. **Explain** how gross domestic product (GDP) is calculated.
2. **Distinguish** between nominal and real GDP.
3. **List** the main limitations of GDP.
4. **Identify** factors that influence GDP.
5. **Describe** other output and income measures.

ECONOMIC DICTIONARY

As you read the section, look for the definitions of these **Key Terms:**

- national income accounting
- gross domestic product
- intermediate goods
- durable goods
- nondurable goods
- nominal GDP
- real GDP
- gross national product
- depreciation
- price level
- aggregate supply
- aggregate demand

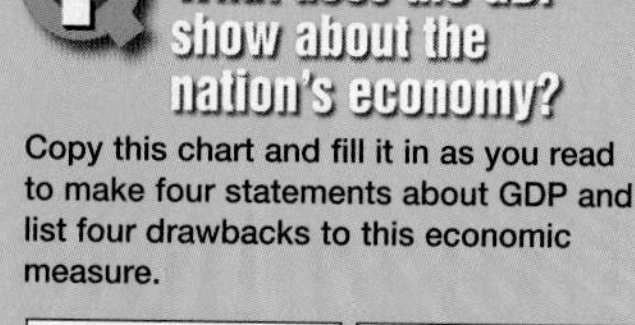

Copy this chart and fill it in as you read to make four statements about GDP and list four drawbacks to this economic measure.

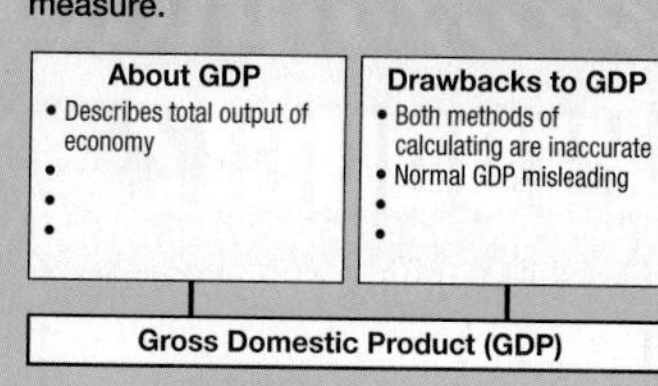

About GDP
• Describes total output of economy
Drawbacks to GDP
• Both methods of calculating are inaccurate
• Normal GDP misleading
Gross Domestic Product (GDP)

Economics and You

How much attention do you pay to the economic news? If you're like most people your age—or most Americans in general—your answer is probably, "Not much." After all, you'd have to be some kind of genius to keep track of the GDP, the GNP, the NNP, the NI, the DPI, and the rest of the economic alphabet soup. Who has the time? And who cares anyway?

But, whether you care or not, the GDP, the NI, and the rest do affect you. What's more, you affect them. Every time you buy a shirt or rent a movie or get a paycheck, you toss your bit into the alphabet soup.

Principles in Action Economists have developed many tools to monitor the nation's economic performance. They even have a way to measure how much money families like yours have to spend. You will learn what these measures tell us—and don't tell us—about the economy.

Gross Domestic Product

Economists use a system called **national income accounting** to monitor the U.S. economy. They collect and organize macroeconomic statistics on production, income, investment, and savings. The Department of Commerce then presents this data in the form of National Income and Product Accounts (NIPA). The government uses NIPA data to determine economic policies, as you will read about in Chapters 15 and 16.

national income accounting a system economists use to collect and organize macroeconomic statistics on production, income, investment, and savings

Visual Glossary online

Go to the Visual Glossary Online for an interactive review of **Gross Domestic Product.**

Action Graph online

Go to Action Graph Online for animated versions of key charts and graphs.

How the Economy Works online

Go to How the Economy Works Online for an interactive lesson on what causes a **recession.**

 **Guiding Question**

What does the GDP show about a nation's economy?

Get Started

About GDP	Drawbacks to GDP
• Describes total output of economy • Can be calculated using the expenditure approach or the income approach • Nominal GDP is measured in current prices. • Real GDP is measured in a constant, or unchanging, prices.	• Both methods of calculating are inaccurate. • Nominal GDP is misleading when comparing one year to the next. • GDP does not include certain economic activities or negative externalities. • GDP does not measure quality of life.

Gross Domestic Product (GDP)

LESSON GOALS

Students will:

- Know the Key Terms.
- Identify the goods and services used to calculate gross domestic product and describe two ways to measure GDP by completing a worksheet.
- Distinguish between nominal and real GDP.
- Describe reasons that GDP is an imperfect measure of an economy's performance.
- Define other measures of economic performance.
- Explain the effect of price level on GDP.

BEFORE CLASS

Students should read the section for homework.

Have students complete the graphic organizer in the Section Opener as they read the text. As an alternate activity, have students complete the Guided Reading and Review worksheet (Unit 5 All-in-One, p. 13).

L1 L2 ELL LPR Differentiate Have students complete the Guided Reading and Review worksheet (Unit 5 All-in-One, p. 14).

Focus on the Basics

Students need to come away with the following understandings:

FACTS: • GDP is the annual dollar value of all final goods and services produced within a country. • GDP is a measure of the performance of the economy. • GDP can be calculated using the expenditure or the income approach. • Economists distinguish between nominal and real GDP. • GDP is not a perfect measure of economic performance. • Specific factors influence activity measured by GDP. • GNP, depreciation, and other measures are also used to analyze the economy.

GENERALIZATION: Although it is not perfect, GDP is the most important and useful yardstick economists have to analyze the performance of the economy.

CLASSROOM HINTS

CALCULATING GDP

Some students may have difficulty understanding the difference between the expenditure approach and the income approach to calculating GDP. Explain that expenditures are money spent, and income is money earned. When people or companies spend, or expend, money on U.S. final goods and services, the producers of the goods and services earn income. Economists look at expenditures and income in the whole U.S. economy to calculate GDP. The income approach is considered more accurate, but economists use both.

Teach Visual Glossary

REVIEW KEY TERMS

Read each key term aloud. Then call on volunteers to define the term and give an example.

goods – *physical objects that someone produces*

services – *actions or activities that one person performs for another*

DISCUSS

Ask **Where must goods and services be produced?** *(within the country)* Define and compare the terms *final goods and services* and *intermediate goods and services.* Have students give examples of these two types of goods and services. Ask **Why do you think intermediate goods and services are not measured by GDP, although final goods and services are?** *(so goods and services aren't counted twice)* Discuss the implications of the fact that GDP is measured in dollar value. For example, work that is done for oneself or that is donated is not counted as GDP. Ask **Can a good or service be either an intermediate good or a final good? Explain.** *(Yes. For example, a memory board is an intermediate good if sold to a computer manufacturer, but a final good if purchased by a consumer.)*

Economics online *All print resources are available on the Teacher's Resource Library CD-ROM and online at* www.PearsonSuccessNet.com.

Answers

Visual Glossary 1. U.S. shoppers paid for the product, which was grown in the United States. 2. The cars were made and bought within U.S. borders. 3. The dental service was offered to and paid by consumers in the United States. 4. The computer chips are intermediate goods. 5. The goods and services involved in processing wood pulp were used to produce another good. 6. The jeans were produced outside the United States.

VISUAL GLOSSARY

Reviewing Key Terms
To understand *gross domestic product,* review these terms:

goods, *p. 3*
services, *p. 3*

What is Gross Domestic Product?

◀ **gross domestic product** the dollar value of all final goods and services produced within a country's borders in a given year

Dollar Value	Final Goods & Services	Within a Country's Borders
 YES Cash value of all goods and services sold	 YES Goods and services offered to consumers	 YES American or foreign companies producing in the United States
NO Cost of producing goods and services	NO Intermediate goods used to produce other goods and services	NO American companies producing overseas

Money paid by shoppers in New York for corn grown in Iowa — YES

Money paid by buyers in Indiana for cars made by a Japanese company at a factory in Kentucky — YES

Fees charged to patients by a dentist in Texas — YES

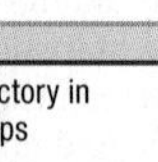
Money paid by a computer factory in New Mexico for computer chips produced in California — NO

Cost of processing wood pulp into paper at a factory in Maine — NO

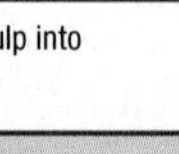
Money paid by shoppers in Florida for jeans manufactured in Mexico by a company headquartered in North Carolina — NO

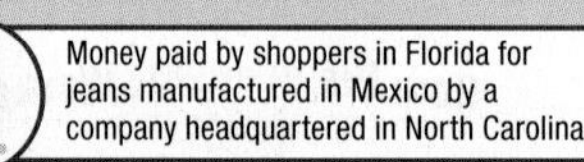

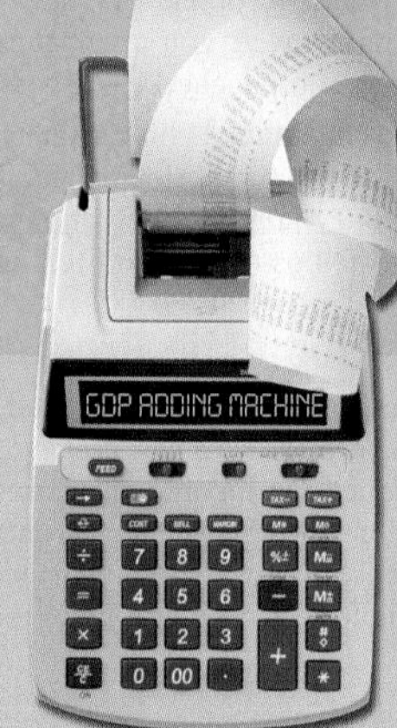

▲ Basically, gross domestic product tracks exchanges of money. To understand GDP, you need to understand which exchanges are included in the final calculation—and which ones are not. ***Look at the six examples shown here. Compare each one to the definition of gross domestic product and explain why it is or is not included in the GDP.***

Visual Glossary online
To expand your understanding of this and other key economic terms, visit **PearsonSuccessNet.com**

Defining GDP

The most important measure in NIPA is **gross domestic product** (GDP), which is the dollar value of all final goods and services produced within a country's borders in a given year. To help you understand GDP, let us examine each part of this definition:

- *Dollar value* refers to the total cash value of the sales of all goods and services produced in a country's households, firms, and government in a calendar year. Since different quantities of goods such as oranges, computers, and movie tickets are sold at different prices, economists figure out the average prices of these items and the total number sold during the year. These cash figures are then used to calculate GDP.
- *Final goods and services* are products in the form sold to consumers. They differ from **intermediate goods,** which are products used in the production of final goods. The memory chips that a computer maker buys to put into its machines are intermediate goods; the computer is a final good.
- *Produced within a country's borders* is especially important to remember. Because we are trying to find the country's gross *domestic* product, we can look only at the goods and services produced within that country. For example, the GDP of the U.S. economy includes cars made in Ohio by a Japanese car company but not cars made in Brazil by an American automaker.
- *In a given year* takes into account when a good was produced. Suppose your neighbor sells you his used car. When the car was originally made, it was counted in the GDP of that year. Thus, it would be inaccurate to count it toward GDP again this year when it was resold.

Expenditure Approach

Government economists calculate GDP two ways. In one method, they use the expenditure approach, sometimes called the output-expenditure approach. First, economists estimate the annual expenditures, or amounts spent, on four categories of final goods and services:

1. consumer goods and services
2. business goods and services
3. government goods and services
4. net exports

Two of these categories need explanation. First, bear in mind that consumer goods include two kinds of goods. They are **durable goods**—those that last for a relatively long time, such as refrigerators and DVD players—and **nondurable goods**—those that last a short period of time, such as food, light bulbs, and sneakers.

Net exports are found by adding up exports—goods produced in the country but purchased in other countries—and then subtracting imports. Imports, of course, were produced in another country.

After finding the value of those four categories, economists add them together to arrive at the total expenditures on goods and services produced during the year. This total equals GDP. **Figure 12.1** provides a simplified example of calculating GDP with the expenditure approach.

Income Approach

The second method to calculate GDP, known as the income approach, calculates GDP by adding up all the incomes in the economy. The rationale for this approach is that when a firm sells a product or service, the selling price minus the dollar value of goods and services purchased

gross domestic product the dollar value of all final goods and services produced within a country's borders in a given year

intermediate goods products used in the production of final goods

durable goods those goods that last for a relatively long time, such as refrigerators, cars, and DVD players

nondurable goods those goods that last a short period of time, such as food, light bulbs, and sneakers

Figure 12.1 Expenditure Approach

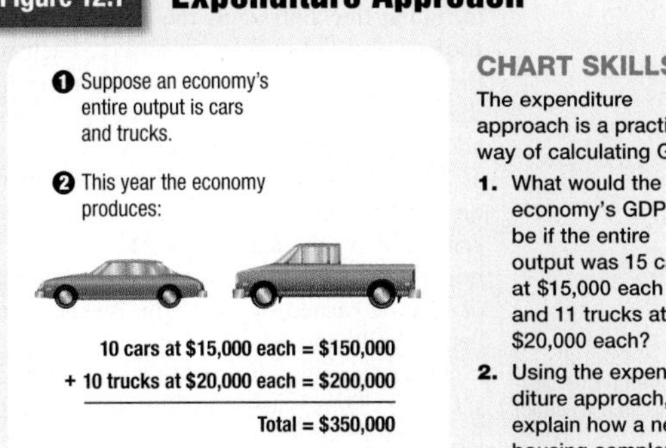

1 Suppose an economy's entire output is cars and trucks.
2 This year the economy produces:
10 cars at $15,000 each = $150,000
+ 10 trucks at $20,000 each = $200,000
Total = $350,000
3 The economy's GDP for this year is $350,000.

CHART SKILLS

The expenditure approach is a practical way of calculating GDP.

1. What would the economy's GDP be if the entire output was 15 cars at $15,000 each and 11 trucks at $20,000 each?
2. Using the expenditure approach, explain how a new housing complex would add to the GDP.

BELLRINGER

Write the following on the board:

Gross domestic product (GDP) is defined as the dollar value of all final goods and services produced within a country's borders in a given year.

Have students list at least 10 services or items that they have bought or used this year that are counted as part of the GDP. Remind them that they must be produced in the United States this year and that most clothes and electronics are not.

Teach

Economics online To present this topic using digital resources, use the lecture notes on www.PearsonSuccessNet.com.

L1 L2 ELL LPR Differentiate To help students who are struggling readers, assign the Vocabulary worksheet (Unit 5 All-in-One, p. 12).

DISCUSS

Have students volunteer their answers. Review them and discuss the meaning of intermediate vs. final goods and services. This would be a good time to reinforce the idea that the United States is shifting toward a service economy. Students may have had more difficulty identifying products produced in the United States than they had identifying services.

As part of the discussion, ask students to identify which of the following is or is not part of GDP and why.

- a restaurant meal – *yes; final good*
- a chair manufactured this year in Mexico by an American company – *no; made elsewhere*
- childcare provided by a parent – *no; not compensated*
- a bicycle manufactured this year in the United States by a British company – *yes; made in U.S.*
- childcare provided by a daycare center – *yes; compensated*
- a 3-year-old used truck – *no; counted 3 years ago*
- an item made this year, but not yet sold – *yes; considered part of business investment*

Differentiated Resources

L1 L2 Guided Reading and Review (Unit 5 All-in-One, p. 14)

L2 Vocabulary worksheet (Unit 5 All-in-One, p. 12)

L2 What Counts for GDP? (Unit 5 All-in-One, p. 16)

L4 Calculate GDP (Unit 5 All-in-One, p. 17)

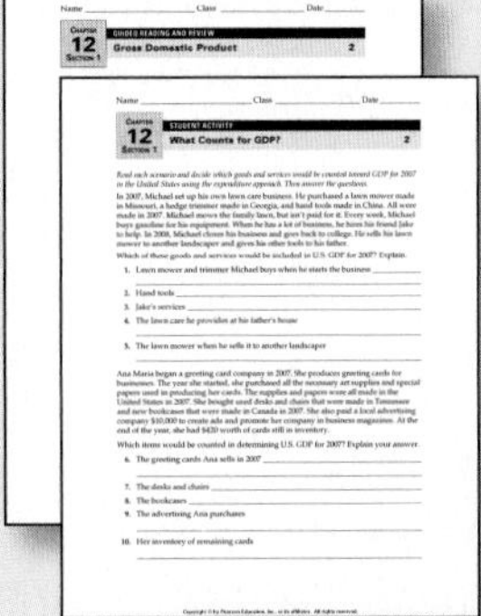

Answers

Chart Skills 1. $445,000 2. The selling price of the houses would add to the GDP when they were sold, but not the price paid for the goods and services used to build the house, such as plumbing, nails, siding, or labor.

DISTRIBUTE ACTIVITY WORKSHEET

Tell students one way economists calculate GDP is the Expenditure Approach. Have students identify and explain the four categories of final goods and services. Clarify that, to be counted as part of a country's current GDP, the final goods and services must be made in this country and produced, though not necessarily sold, this year. Work through the example in Figure 12.1. Distribute the "What Counts for GDP?" worksheet (Unit 5 All-in-One, p. 15)

L2 Differentiate Distribute the "What Counts for GDP?" worksheet (Unit 5 All-in-One, p. 16). Read through the worksheet with students and answer any questions they may have. When they finish, guide a class discussion of the answers.

COMPARE

Use Figure 12.2 to examine the income approach. Point out that income includes wages, profits, rent, and interest on investments. Ask **Why does rent count toward GDP?** *(because it is income for the owner of the building)* Ask **Why does the government use both expenditure and income approaches in calculating GDP?** *(Neither method is perfect. They examine the figures from each and make adjustments to get a more accurate GDP.)*

COMPARE

Tell students that the GDP that they have been examining is called the *nominal GDP*. Nominal GDP is based on the current price of goods and services.

Remind students that GDP is used to measure an economy's production. Have students define *real GDP*. Work through Figure 12.3, comparing real and nominal GDP. Ask **What does the real GDP show about this economy for Years 1 and 2?** *(The economy's output was the same for Year 2 as it was for Year 1.)*

Visual Glossary Use the lesson on the Visual Glossary page to review this term. Direct students to the Visual Glossary Online to reinforce understanding of *gross domestic product*.

Answers

Chart Skills 1. GDP would increase to $365,000 2. Income earned by everyone working on the housing complex would count toward GDP.

Checkpoint Imports are produced outside the country.

Checkpoint distortions caused by changes in prices over time

Figure 12.2 Income Approach

❶ Suppose an economy's entire output is cars and trucks.

❷ All employed citizens, therefore, would work in the car and truck industry, or for its suppliers.

❸ The combined selling price of all the cars and trucks reflects the money paid to all the people who helped build the vehicles.

❹ The economy's GDP for this year, then, is the sum of the income of all its working citizens, or $350,000.

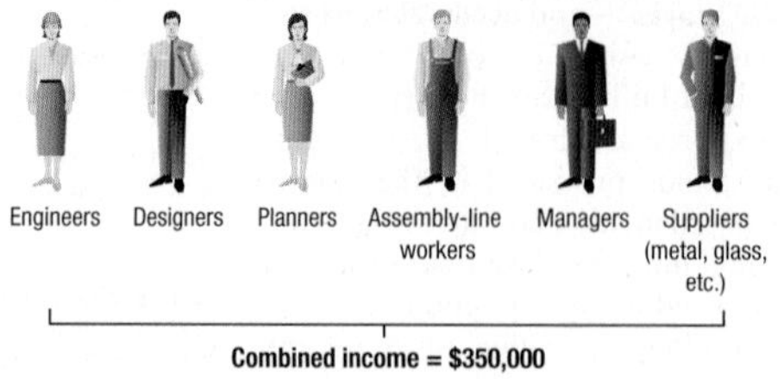

CHART SKILLS

The income approach is generally a more accurate way of calculating GDP than the expenditure approach.

1. What would the economy's GDP be if the auto company in the example also had to pay the $15,000 in fees to an advertising agency?
2. Using the income approach, explain how a new housing complex would add to the GDP.

from other firms represents income for the firm's owners and employees.

Suppose your neighbor bought a newly built house for $200,000. That $200,000 (minus what the builder spent on lumber, plaster, etc.) is income shared by all of the people who helped build and sell the house—including the contractor, the bricklayer, the roofers, and the real estate broker. Each of these people may get only a small share of the house's selling price. However, if we added up all those shares, we would arrive at $200,000 (minus what the builder spent on lumber, plaster, etc.) worth of income generated by the sale. In other words, the house's selling price is equal to the amount of income earned by all of the people who helped build and sell it.

nominal GDP GDP measured in current prices

real GDP GDP expressed in constant, or unchanging, prices

This same logic holds for all goods and services. Thus, we may calculate GDP by adding up all income earned in the economy, as shown in **Figure 12.2.**

In theory, calculating GDP with the income approach and the expenditure approach should give us the same total. In fact, there are usually differences because of errors in the underlying data. Economists who work in the federal government take those differences into account. They first determine GDP using both approaches. Then they compare the two totals and make adjustments to offset the differences. This gives them a more accurate result.

CHECKPOINT ***Why are imports not included in gross domestic product?***

Nominal Versus Real GDP

Government officials use gross domestic product to find out how well the economy is performing. To help them understand what is really going on in the economy, economists distinguish between two measures of GDP, nominal and real.

Nominal GDP

In **Figures 12.1** and **12.2,** we calculated **nominal GDP**—that is, GDP measured in current prices. Because it is based on current prices, this type of GDP is also called "current GDP." To calculate nominal GDP, we simply use the current year's prices to calculate the value of the current year's output. **Figure 12.3** shows how the definition of nominal GDP applies to the small economy that produces only cars and trucks.

Real GDP

The data in **Figure 12.3** reveal a problem with nominal GDP. The GDP of Year 2 is higher than that of Year 1 even though the output of cars and trucks in the two years is the same. The difference is due to an increase in prices. As a result of these price increases, the higher GDP figure in the second year is misleading. To correct for this distortion, economists determine **real GDP,** which is GDP expressed in constant, or unchanging, prices.

Look at the third section of **Figure 12.3.** Notice that GDP in Year 2 is based on the prices from Year 1. By using real GDP, economists can discover whether an economy is actually producing more goods and services, regardless of changes in the prices of those items. In **Figure 12.3,** we can quickly see that output did not increase in Year 2.

CHECKPOINT ***What problem is solved by using real GDP?***

Limitations of GDP

Even though GDP is a valuable tool, it is still not a perfect yardstick. For instance, GDP does not take into account certain economic activities or aspects of life. These include nonmarket activities, the underground economy, negative externalities, and quality of life.

Nonmarket Activities

GDP does not measure goods and services that people make or do themselves, such as caring for children, mowing the lawn, cooking dinner, or washing the car. GDP does rise, however, when people pay someone else to do these things for them. When these nonmarket activities are shifted to the market, GDP goes up, even though production has not really increased.

The Underground Economy

A large amount of production and income is never recorded or reported to the government. For instance, transactions on the black market—the market for illegal goods—are not counted. Income from illegal gambling goes unreported. So do "under the table" wages that some companies pay workers to avoid paying business and income taxes.

Many legal, informal transactions are also not reported, for example, selling your bike to a friend or trading that bike for a stereo. If you earned money baby-sitting, mowing lawns, or shoveling snow, those payments are not included in the GDP either, even though goods and services were produced and income was earned.

Negative Externalities

Unintended economic side effects, or externalities, have a monetary value that often is not reflected in GDP. (See Chapter 3, Section 3, for a discussion of externalities.) For example, a power plant that emits smoke and dust is polluting the air. That negative result is not subtracted from GDP.

Quality of Life

Although some economists and politicians interpret rising GDP as a sign of rising well-being, we should remember that additional goods and services do not necessarily make people any happier. In fact, some things that are not counted in GDP contribute greatly to most people's quality

Figure 12.3 Nominal and Real GDP

Year 1: Nominal GDP	Year 2: Nominal GDP	Year 2: Real GDP
❶ Suppose an economy's entire output is cars and trucks. ❷ This year the economy produces: **10 cars at $15,000 each = $150,000** **+ 10 trucks at $20,000 each = $200,000** **Total = $350,000** ❸ Since we have used the current year's prices to express the current year's output, the result is a nominal GDP of $350,000.	❶ In the second year, the economy's output does not increase, but the prices of the cars and trucks do: **10 cars at $16,000 each = $160,000** **+ 10 trucks at $21,000 each = $210,000** **Total = $370,000** ❷ This new GDP figure of $370,000 is misleading. GDP rises because of an increase in prices. Economists prefer to have a measure of GDP that is not affected by changes in prices. So they calculate real GDP.	❶ To correct for an increase in prices, economists establish a set of constant prices by choosing one year as a base year. When they calculate real GDP for other years, they use the prices from the base year. So we calculate the real GDP for Year 2 using the prices from Year 1: **10 cars at $15,000 each = $150,000** **+ 10 trucks at $20,000 each = $200,000** **Total = $350,000** ❷ Real GDP for Year 2, therefore, is $350,000.

CHART SKILLS

Real GDP reflects actual increases in output without the misleading effects of price increases.

1. **How much did the real GDP increase by in the second year if output stayed the same but prices increased by $1,000 for each car and $1,500 for each truck?**
2. **Using the figures from Year 1 as your base, calculate the real GDP for Year 3 in which 15 cars and 14 trucks were sold.**

Background Note

Underground Economy The underground economy represents a larger portion of the economic activities of some other countries than it does in the United States. Still, the output of this economy is enormous and growing faster than GDP. It is nearly impossible to determine the exact size of the output of the underground economy, but a 2005 report places it close to $970 billion—about 9 percent of the output of the legitimate economy. In that same report, it was estimated that the underground economy had been growing at about 5.6 percent each year since the early 1990s. The underground economy is significant for two reasons. First, it makes it difficult to accurately measure true economic activity. Secondly, it represents lost tax revenue. The IRS has estimated that it loses at least $311 billion every year to the underground economy.

DISTRIBUTE ACTIVITY WORKSHEET

L4 Differentiate Distribute the "Calculate GDP" worksheet (Unit 5 All-in-One, p. 17), where students calculate the nominal and real GDP of a small country.

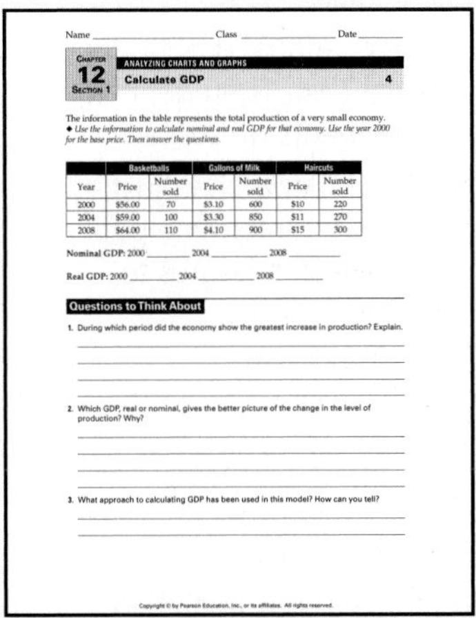

Name ____________ Class ____________ Date ________

Chapter 12 Section 1 — ANALYZING CHARTS AND GRAPHS

Calculate GDP 4

The information in the table represents the total production of a very small economy.

◆ *Use the information to calculate nominal and real GDP for that economy. Use the year 2000 for the base price. Then answer the questions.*

	Basketballs		Gallons of Milk		Haircuts	
Year	Price	Number sold	Price	Number sold	Price	Number sold
2000	$56.00	70	$3.10	600	$10	220
2004	$59.00	100	$3.30	850	$11	270
2008	$64.00	110	$4.10	900	$15	300

Nominal GDP: 2000 ________ 2004 ________ 2008 ________

Real GDP: 2000 ________ 2004 ________ 2008 ________

Questions to Think About

1. During which period did the economy show the greatest increase in production? Explain.
2. Which GDP, real or nominal, gives the better picture of the change in the level of production? Why?
3. What approach to calculating GDP has been used in this model? How can you tell?

When students have completed the worksheets, ask **Could the real GDP go down between 2008 and 2012 (using 2000 for the base year), while the nominal GDP for 2012 is greater than for 2008? Justify your response.** *(Yes. For example, in 2012, if 105 basketballs were purchased for $68 each, 875 gallons of milk were sold for $4.22 each, and 280 light bulbs were sold for $0.65, the real GDP will drop between 2008 and 2012 while the nominal GDP will be greater than in 2008.)*

CHECK COMPREHENSION

Ask **What are four limitations of GDP?** *(It does not count nonmarket activities, exchanges in the underground economy, negative externalities, or quality of life.)* Call on students to define each limitation and give examples.

Discuss how nonmarket activities can skew the GDP when the economy worsens. For example, point out that when the economy is performing well, people might hire others to do certain jobs, such as cutting their grass or installing a new faucet. When the economy is performing more poorly, people might do more things for themselves. In the former situation, the GDP would be better (assuming the people who were hired reported their income) than in the latter situation, even though the same work is being done and production has not really decreased.

Answers

Chart Skills 1. Real GDP stays the same because Year 2 prices will be adjusted to equal Year 1 prices. 2. $505,000

COMPARE

Emphasize that no measure of economic activity can give a complete picture of the economy. As a result, economists use various measures to look at economic activity. By combining what they learn, they get a more complete look.

With the class, define *gross national product* and answer question 1 in Figure 12.4. Then define and compare the other measurements presented.

L1 L2 Differentiate Tell students that, just as doctors use a variety of tests to determine patients' health, economists use different measures to determine the health of the economy.

Action Graph online Have students review the Action Graph animation for a step-by-step look at Measurements of the Macroeconomy.

EXPLAIN

Help students develop the concepts: aggregate supply, aggregate demand, and price level. Begin by having students volunteer synonyms for the word aggregate *(whole, mass, total, combined).* Ask them to explain what aggregate supply and aggregate demand mean in their own words. Tell students that price level is an average of all prices in the economy. Ask them to explain how they think this number would be arrived at.

L1 L2 Differentiate Demonstrate on the board how price level is calculated using this example:

CARS	NUMBER AVAILABLE	PRICE PER CAR	TOTAL PRICE
CAR 1	20	$15,000	$300,000
CAR 2	10	$20,000	$200,000
CAR 3	5	$30,000	$150,000
TOTAL	35	$18,571	$650,000

Explain how the total price for each car is obtained by multiplying the number of cars available by the price of each car. Then add to find the total number of cars available (35) and the total price of all the cars ($650,000). Calculate the price level by dividing the total price of all the cars by the total number of cars available ($18,571).

Answers

Chart Skills 1. income of U.S.-owned firms and U.S. citizens within and outside the U.S. minus income earned by foreign citizens and firms in U.S. 2. to get a more accurate picture of U.S. economic health

Checkpoint nonmarket activities, underground economy

Figure 12.4 Measurements of the Macroeconomy

CHART SKILLS

These equations summarize the formulas for calculating some of the key macroeconomic measurements.

1. Using the information on the chart, define gross national product.
2. Why might economists track so many different indicators of the nation's economic health?

Action Graph online

For an animated version of this graph, visit **PearsonSuccessNet.com**

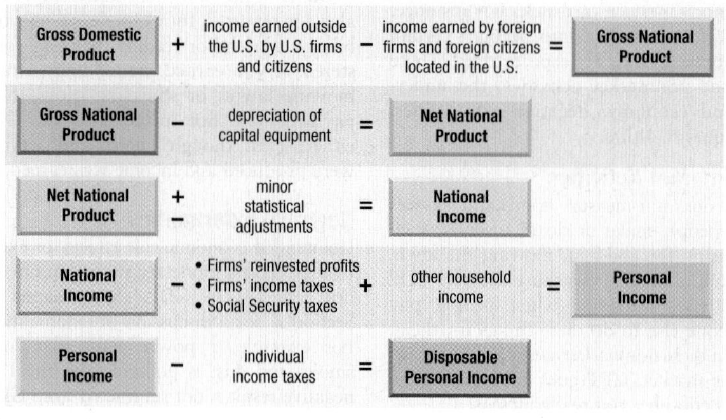

of life, such as pleasant surroundings, ample leisure time, and personal safety.

All of these limitations suggest that GDP is a somewhat flawed measure of output and income and a poor measure of people's well-being. Nevertheless, while the measure may be imperfect, when calculated consistently over a period of time, GDP helps reveal economic growth rates. For this reason, economists and policymakers closely watch the nation's GDP.

CHECKPOINT ***What are two economic activities that GDP does not include?***

Other Output and Income Measures

As you have read, our system of National Income and Product Accounts provides numerous measurements of the performance of the nation's economy. While gross domestic product is the primary measure of income and output, economists also look at other measures to focus on specific parts of the economy. Many of these other yardsticks are derived from GDP. **Figure 12.4** shows how GDP is used to determine five other economic measures.

gross national product the annual income earned by a nation's firms and citizens

depreciation the loss of the value of capital equipment that results from normal wear and tear

The first is **gross national product** (GNP), the annual income earned by a nation's firms and citizens. GNP is a measure of the market value of all goods and services produced by Americans in one year. Study the chart above to see how GNP is related to GDP.

GNP does not account for **depreciation,** or the loss of the value of capital equipment that results from normal wear and tear. The cost of replacing this physical capital slightly reduces the value of what we produce. GNP minus the cost of depreciation of capital equipment is called net national product (NNP). NNP measures the net output for one year, or the output made after the adjustment for depreciation.

Once they have calculated NNP, government economists adjust their figures to account for minor discrepancies between different sources of data. After making these minor adjustments to NNP, they get another measure, called national income (NI).

From NI, we can find out how much pretax income businesses actually pay to U.S. households. This is found by subtracting profits that firms reinvest in the business and the income taxes and Social Security taxes they pay out. What remains is called personal income (PI).

Finally, we want to know how much money people actually have to spend after

Virtual Economics

L2 Differentiate

Understanding Gross Domestic Product Use the following lesson from the NCEE **Virtual Economics *CD-ROM*** to evaluate student understanding of GDP. Click on Browse Economics Lessons, specify grades 6–8, and use the key words *nation consume.*

In this activity, students will examine components of GDP by classifying products and services.

LESSON TITLE	WHAT DOES THE NATION CONSUME?
Type of Activity	Classifying
Complexity	Low
Time	90 minutes
NCEE Standards	18

they pay *their* taxes, a figure called disposable personal income (DPI). To find DPI, we take personal income and subtract individual income and Social Security taxes.

See how far we have come. Beginning with GDP, the value of all goods and services produced in a year, we wind up knowing how much cash Americans have to spend or put in the bank.

CHECKPOINT ***What does disposable personal income show?***

Influences on GDP

So far, we have defined GDP, calculated it, and learned about its limitations. One important issue remains, however: What influences GDP? That is, in a real economy, what factors can make GDP go up or down? These questions go to the heart of macroeconomics.

Aggregate Supply

As you read earlier, market supply is the amount of a particular good or service available for purchase at all possible prices in an individual market. But how do we look at supply and prices on a macroeconomic level? Think of aggregate supply as a supply curve for the whole economy.

First, economists add up the total supply of goods and services produced for sale in the economy—in other words, GDP. Then they calculate the **price level,** the average of all prices in the economy. Now they can determine **aggregate supply,** the total amount of goods and services in the economy available at all possible price levels.

In a nation's economy, as the prices of most goods and services change, the price level changes. Firms respond by changing their output. For example, if the price level rises, which means that the prices of most goods and services are rising, firms have an incentive to increase their output. Similarly, as prices throughout the economy fall, companies' profits shrink. In response, they reduce output. You can see this effect in the aggregate supply (AS) curve in **Figure 12.5.** As the price level rises, real GDP, or aggregate supply, rises. As the price level falls, real GDP falls.

price level the average of all prices in the economy

aggregate supply the total amount of goods and services in the economy available at all possible price levels

Figure 12.5 **Aggregate Supply and Demand**

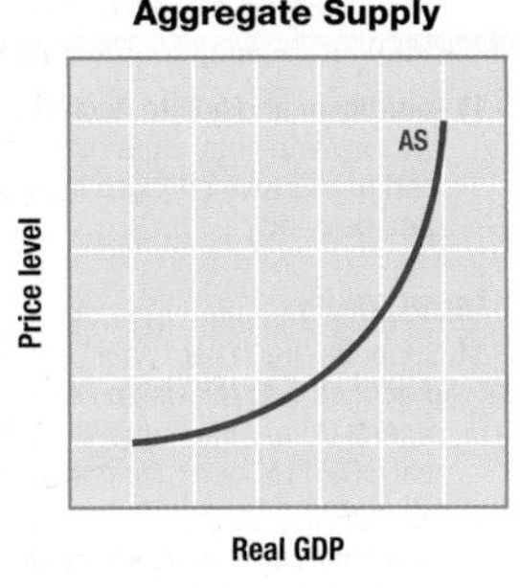

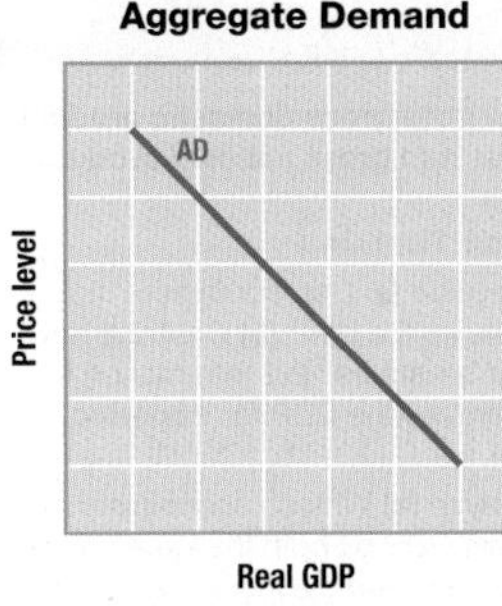

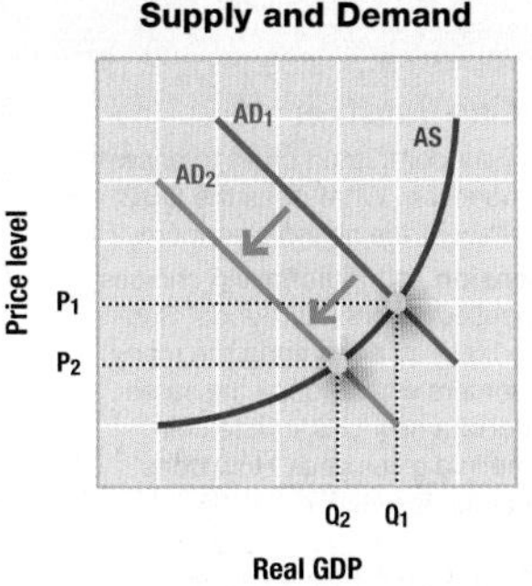

GRAPH SKILLS

Aggregate supply and demand represent supply and demand on a nationwide scale. The far right-hand chart shows what happens to GDP and price levels when aggregate demand shifts from AD_1 to AD_2.

1. What do the positive (upward to the right) and negative (downward to the right) slopes of these curves mean?
2. If a country goes to war, causing an increase in government demand for all kinds of goods, how might real GDP and price levels be affected?

For an animated version of this graph, visit **PearsonSuccessNet.com**

ANALYZE GRAPHS

Refer students to Figure 12.5. Discuss the meaning of the aggregate supply and the aggregate demand curves. Elicit the definition of GDP from students. Refer to the Aggregate Supply Curve. Ask **What happens to the GDP if the price level rises? Explain.** *(If the price level rises, the prices of most goods and services rises. Therefore, the GDP—the supply of final goods and services—rises because producers have an incentive to increase production.)* Have students describe what happens to GDP when the price level falls. Have students answer similar questions about Aggregate Demand.

Review the meaning of equilibrium points from Chapter 6. Have students describe what points Q1 and Q2 represent. Tell them that they will learn more about factors that cause the AS or AD curves to shift.

Action Graph online Have students review the Action Graph animation for a step-by-step look at Aggregate Supply and Demand.

EXTEND

Have students use the DK World Atlas online at phschool.com to look up the World Ranking of six countries including the United States, at least two other developed countries, and three less developed countries. Have them create a bar graph comparing their GNP, literacy, infant mortality, and human development index. Have students make and justify a generalization about GNP and quality of life.

GUIDING QUESTION WRAP UP

Have students return to the section Guiding Question. Review the completed graphic organizer. Have a wrap up discussion about GDP.

Assess and Remediate

L3 **L2** **L4** Collect the "What Counts for GDP?" and "Calculate GDP" worksheets and assess student understanding of GDP.

L3 Assign the Section Assessment questions; identify student misconceptions.

L3 Give Section Quiz A (Unit 5 All in-One, p. 18).

L2 Give Section Quiz B (Unit 5 All in-One, p. 19).

(Assess and Remediate continued on p. 314)

Answers

Checkpoint how much people have to spend after paying their taxes

Graph Skills 1. positive slope: as price increases, real GDP increases; negative slope: as prices drop, GDP falls 2. Prices would increase due to greater demand, and real GDP might decline because of reduced consumer spending and decreased investment in production of capital goods.

Have students complete the Self-Test Online and continue their work in the **Essential Questions Journal**.

REMEDIATION AND SUGGESTIONS

Use the chart to help struggling students.

WEAKNESS	REMEDIATION
Defining key terms (Questions 3, 4, 5, 6)	Have students use the interactive Economic Dictionary Online.
What is GDP (Questions 1, 3, 4, 5, 7)	Draw a cluster diagram with GDP in the center. Have students find details in the section to link to GDP.
What influences GDP (Questions 2, 6, 7, 9, 10)	Assign the roles of suppliers, consumers, business owners considering capital investments. Assign one student to each category when prices go up and when they go down. Put prices-go-up students on one side of the room and prices-go-down students on the other side. Have them explain their actions and how it affects GDP.
Calculating GDP (Questions 7, 8, 11)	Review figures 12.1, 12.2, and 12.3. Provide hypothetical data and have students calculate nominal and real GDP.

Answer

Checkpoint consumer spending, business spending on capital investment, government spending, and foreigners' demand for export goods

aggregate demand the amount of goods and services in the economy that will be purchased at all possible price levels

Aggregate Demand

Aggregate demand is the amount of goods and services in the economy that will be purchased at all possible price levels. As price levels in the economy move up and down, individuals and businesses change how much they buy—in the opposite direction that aggregate supply changes.

For example, a lower price level translates into greater purchasing power for households, because the real value of money rises as price levels drop. The dollars that we hold are worth more at lower price levels than they are at higher price levels. Therefore, falling prices increase wealth and demand. This scenario is called the wealth effect.

On the other hand, as the price level rises, purchasing power declines, causing a reduction in the quantity of goods and services demanded. The aggregate demand (AD) curve shows this relationship between price and real GDP demanded. As you can see from **Figure 12.5**, this curve is negatively sloped; that is, it moves downward to the right. Consumers account for most of aggregate demand, but business spending on capital investment, government spending, and foreigners' demand for export goods all play roles, too.

Aggregate Supply/Aggregate Demand Equilibrium

When we put together the aggregate supply (AS) and aggregate demand (AD) curves, we can find the AS/AD equilibrium in the economy as a whole. Look at **Figure 12.5.** The intersection of the AS and AD_1 curves indicates an equilibrium price level of P_1 and an equilibrium real GDP of Q_1.

Now consider how GDP might change. Any shift in either the AS or AD curve will cause real GDP to change. For example, the graph shows aggregate demand falling from line AD_1 to line AD_2. As a result, the equilibrium GDP (Q_2) falls, and so does the equilibrium price level (P_2).

Any shift in aggregate supply or aggregate demand will have an impact on real GDP and on the price level. In the next section, we will discuss some factors that may cause such shifts.

✔ **CHECKPOINT** ***What four types of demand are included in aggregate demand?***

SECTION 1 ASSESSMENT

Essential Questions Journal To continue to build a response to the Essential Question, go to your **Essential Questions Journal.**

Guiding Question

1. Use your completed chart to answer this question: What does the GDP show about the nation's economy?
2. **Extension** Your purchasing choices help reflect economic trends. Suppose that you are among the many consumers who choose the same model of a new U.S.-made cellphone in a given year. How does that affect the GDP?

Key Terms and Main Ideas

3. **(a)** What is the difference between **intermediate goods** and final goods? **(b)** Why are intermediate goods not included in GDP?
4. How does **nominal GDP** differ from **real GDP?**
5. **(a)** If **aggregate demand** rises, what happens to real GDP? **(b)** What happens to the **price level?**
6. How does **gross domestic product** differ from **gross national product?**

Critical Thinking

7. **Describe (a)** List four factors that make up the GDP. **(b)** Describe how economists use this information to determine the GDP for a specific year.
8. **Analyze (a)** Why do economists calculate GDP by both the expenditure approach and the income approach? **(b)** Why is the expenditure approach sometimes called the "output expenditure approach"?
9. **Interpret (a)** What incentive do rising prices give to firms? **(b)** What might prevent firms from earning increased profits during a time of rising prices?
10. **Identify** In addition to declining business investments, what other factors lead to negative changes in aggregate demand?

Math Skills

11. Suppose that a very small economy produces only televisions and computers. Determine nominal GDP and real GDP in Year 4, using the following chart:

Visit PearsonSuccessNet.com for additional math help.

Production	Year 1 (base)	Year 4
Computers	10 sold at $2,000 each	17 sold at $2,500 each
Televisions	15 sold at 500 each	20 sold at $550 each

Assessment Answers

1. GDP has drawbacks, but gives an overall picture of the health of the economy and well-being of the population.
2. The sales of all final products, such as the cellphone, would boost GDP.
3. (a) Intermediate goods are products used to produce final goods, whereas final goods are products that are purchased by consumers. (b) to avoid double counting
4. Nominal GDP is based on current prices; real GDP is based on constant prices.
5. (a) Real GDP also rises. (b) The price level rises.
6. GDP is the dollar value of all final goods and services produced within the country in a year. GNP is the annual income earned by a nation's firms and citizens.
7. (a) dollar value, final goods, produced within a country, in a given year (b) Add the dollar value for final goods produced in a country in a given year.
8. (a) to arrive at a more accurate measure (b) Economists estimate expenditures on the output of final goods and services.
9. (a) Rising prices are incentives for firms to increase production. (b) Possible responses: Increased costs might offset gains from higher prices. Demand might go down.
10. decreased consumer spending, decreased government spending, or decreased foreign demand for export goods
11. Nominal: $53,500; Real: $44,000.

OBJECTIVES

1. **Identify** the phases of a business cycle.
2. **Describe** four key factors that keep the business cycle going.
3. **Explain** how economists forecast fluctuations in the business cycle.
4. **Analyze** the impact of business cycles in U.S. history.

ECONOMIC DICTIONARY

As you read the section, look for the definitions of these **Key Terms:**

- business cycle
- expansion
- economic growth
- peak
- contraction
- trough
- recession
- depression
- stagflation
- leading indicators

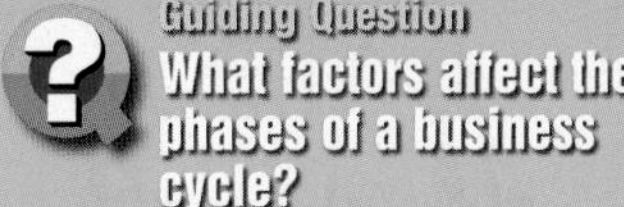
Guiding Question
What factors affect the phases of a business cycle?

Copy this table and fill it in as you read to explain what economic factors influence the phases of a business cycle.

Business Investment	Interest Rates and Credit	Consumer Expectations	External Shocks
• Increased investment boosts aggregate demand, gross GDP • Decreased investment cuts AD, causing GDP decline	• •	• •	• •

Economics and You Sometimes, you don't have to read the newspaper to tell how the economy is doing. You can see the signs all around you. They may be *Help Wanted* signs in front of local stores and factories—when the economy is doing well, businesses hire and it's easier for you to find a part-time job. Or they may be *Closed* or *Going Out of Business* signs in the windows of those same businesses. You might even get an idea by counting the number of *For Sale* or *Foreclosure* signs where you live. The ups and downs of the economy affect us all.

Principles in Action The national economy undergoes periodic cycles of good times, then bad times, and then good times again. Recognizing this pattern, economists try to predict what the economy will do in the future—what can be done to make the good times last longer and keep the bad times brief. In this section, you will learn what factors affect these ups and downs and how they have shaped the country's economy. You will also see how the actions of ordinary consumers and borrowers can affect the phases of the economy and how long these phases last.

Phases of a Business Cycle

As you read in Chapter 3, a **business cycle** is a period of macroeconomic expansion followed by a period of macroeconomic contraction. Economists also call these periods of change "economic fluctuations."

Business cycles are not minor, day-to-day ups and downs. They are major changes in real gross domestic product above or below normal levels. The typical business cycle consists of four phases: expansion, peak, contraction, and trough.

1. *Expansion* An **expansion** is a period of economic growth as measured by a rise in real GDP. To economists, **economic growth** is a steady, long-term increase in real GDP. In the expansion phase, jobs are plentiful, the unemployment rate falls, and businesses prosper.
2. *Peak* When real GDP stops rising, the economy has reached its **peak,** the height of an economic expansion.

business cycle a period of macroeconomic expansion followed by one of macroeconomic contraction

expansion a period of economic growth as measured by a rise in real GDP

economic growth a steady, long-term increase in real GDP

peak the height of an economic expansion, when real GDP stops rising

Guiding Question

What factors affect the phases of a business cycle?

Get Started

Business Investment	Interest Rates and Credit	Consumer Expectations	External Shocks
• Increased investment boosts aggregate demand (AD), gross GDP • Decreased investments cuts AD, causing GDP decline	• Low interest rates encourage consumers and businesses to purchase goods, borrow money • High interest rates discourage consumers and businesses from purchasing goods, borrowing money	• If consumers expect the economy to contract, they reduce spending. • If consumers expect the economy to grow, they increase spending.	• Negative external shocks can result in decreased production and higher prices. • Positive external shocks can cause increases in production and lower prices.

LESSON GOALS

Students will:

- Know the Key Terms.
- Identify the four stages of the business cycle.
- Explain how various factors keep the business cycle going.
- Explain how economists forecast changes in the business cycle.
- Compare a graph of U.S. business cycles and a graph of unemployment.

BEFORE CLASS

Students should read the section for homework before coming to class.

Have students complete the graphic organizer in the Section Opener as they read the text. As an alternate activity, have students complete the Guided Reading and Review worksheet (Unit 5 All-in-One, p. 20).

L1 L2 ELL Differentiate Have students complete the Guided Reading and Review worksheet (Unit 5 All-in-One, p. 21).

CLASSROOM HINTS

RECESSIONS

Tell students that the word *recession* comes from the word *recede*, which means to go or move back. In a recession, economic growth has moved backward significantly from the peak.

Focus on the Basics

Students need to come away with the following understandings:

FACTS: • The business cycle has four phases: expansion, peak, contraction, and trough. • Business cycles are influenced by business investment, interest rates and credit, consumer expectations, and external shocks. • Economists watch leading indicators, including the stock market and interest rates, to predict changes in GDP. • The American economy has experienced some major business cycles, including the Great Depression.

GENERALIZATION:

Many factors affect economic growth and contraction. Economists try to predict this business cycle to manage the economy and maintain growth of the GDP.

BELLRINGER

Write the definitions of *expansion* and *contraction* on the board: *A period of economic growth as measured by a rise in real GDP; a period of economic decline marked by falling real GDP.* Pair students to identify whether we are in a period of expansion or contraction. Have them jot down their justification for their view of the economy including their own personal experiences.

Teach

Economics online To present this topic using digital resources, use the lecture notes on www.PearsonSuccessNet.com.

USE A GRAPH

Have volunteers give their answers. Point out Figure 12.6, then ask students to name and describe each phase of the business cycle. Have them give examples of how the economy performs during each stage. Ask **What does the shape of the graph tell you about economic growth?** (*Sometimes the economy grows and other times it declines.*) **What would you expect the shape of the graph of real GDP to be?** (*It would go up and down.*)

USE GRAPHIC ORGANIZER

Draw a blank chart on the board. Have students name the three types of contractions. Ask **What do they have in common?** (*falling real GDP*) Complete the chart as a class.

RECESSION	DEPRESSION	STAGFLATION
• real GDP falls for at least 2 consecutive quarters	• longer and more severe than recession	• decline in real GDP
• prolonged economic contraction	• high unemployment	• rise in the price level (inflation)
• 6% to 10% unemployment	• low economic output	

Action Graph online Have students review the Action Graph animation for a step-by-step look at Tracking a Business Cycle.

Answers

Graph Skills 1. trough; expansion 2. Possible response: Contraction; unemployment is rising, reduced consumer spending, falling output.

Checkpoint expansion, peak, contraction, trough

Figure 12.6 Tracking a Business Cycle

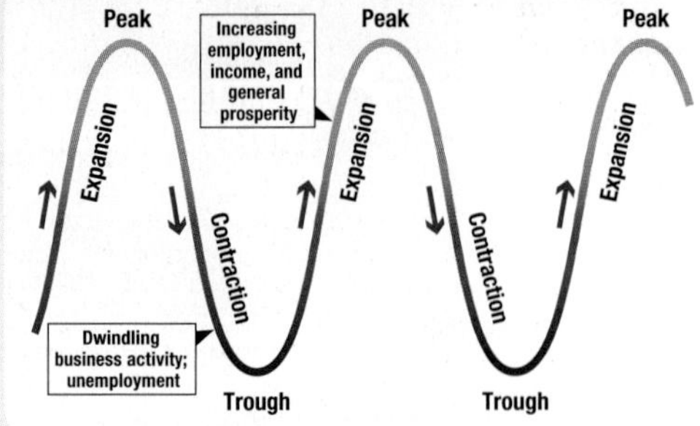

GRAPH SKILLS

A business cycle reaches a peak, then falls into a contraction. When the contraction reaches the low point, a new expansion begins.

1. What is the low point of the cycle called? What is the period of increasing business activity called?
2. In which part of a business cycle do you think the United States is right now? Give evidence to support your conclusion.

For an animated version of this graph, visit PearsonSuccessNet.com

3. *Contraction* After reaching its peak, the economy enters a period of **contraction,** an economic decline marked by falling real GDP. Falling output generally causes unemployment to rise.
4. *Trough* When the economy has "bottomed out," it has reached the **trough** (trawf), the lowest point in an economic contraction. At that point, real GDP stops falling and a new period of expansion begins.

contraction a period of economic decline marked by falling real GDP

trough the lowest point of an economic contraction, when real GDP stops falling

recession a prolonged economic contraction

depression a recession that is especially long and severe

stagflation a decline in real GDP combined with a rise in the price level

During a contraction, GDP is always falling. But other economic conditions, such as price levels and the unemployment rate, may vary. Economists created terms to describe contractions with different characteristics and levels of severity. They include:

- *Recession* If real GDP falls for two consecutive quarters (at least six straight months), the economy is said to be in a recession. A **recession** is a prolonged economic contraction. Generally lasting from 6 to 18 months, recessions are typically marked by unemployment reaching the range of 6 percent to 10 percent.
- *Depression* If a recession is especially long and severe, it may be called a **depression.** The term has no precise definition but usually refers to a deep recession with features such as high unemployment and low economic output.
- *Stagflation* This term combines parts of *stagnant*—a word meaning unmoving or decayed—and *inflation*. **Stagflation** is a decline in real GDP (output) combined with a rise in the price level (inflation).

Although economists know much about business cycles, they cannot predict how long the phases in a particular cycle will last. The only certainty is that a growing economy will eventually experience a downturn, and that a contracting economy will eventually bounce back.

CHECKPOINT ***What are the four phases of a business cycle?***

What Keeps a Business Cycle Going?

The shifts that occur during a business cycle have many causes, some more predictable than others. Often, two or more factors will combine to push the economy into the next phase of a business cycle. Typically, a sharp rise or drop in some important economic variable will set off a series of events that bring about the next phase. Business cycles are affected by four main economic variables:

1. business investment
2. interest rates and credit
3. consumer expectations
4. external shocks

Business Investment

When the economy is expanding, businesses expect their sales and profits to keep rising. Therefore, they may invest heavily in building new plants and buying new equipment. Or they may invest in the expansion of old plants in order to increase the plants' productive capacity. All of this investment spending creates additional output and jobs, helping to increase GDP and maintain the expansion.

Differentiated Resources

- **L1 L2 Guided Reading and Review** (Unit 5 All-in-One, p. 21)
- **L2 Analyze Primary and Secondary Sources skill worksheet** (Unit 5 All-in-One, p. 23)
- **L2 Impact of the Great Depression** (Unit 5 All-in-One, p. 25)
- **L3 Ups and Downs** (Simulation Activities, Chapter 12)

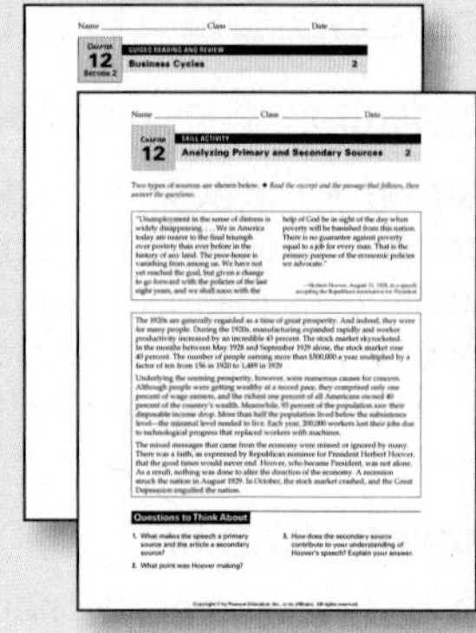

At some point, however, firms may decide that they have expanded enough or that demand for their products is dropping. They cut back on investment spending; as a result, aggregate demand falls. The result is a decline in GDP and also in the price level. The drop in business spending reduces output and income in other sectors of the economy.

When that occurs, industries that produce capital goods slow their own production and begin to lay off workers. Other industries might follow, causing overall unemployment to rise. Jobless workers cannot buy new cars, eat at restaurants, or perhaps even pay their rent. If the downward spiral picks up speed, a recession results.

Interest Rates and Credit

In the United States economy, consumers often use credit to purchase "big ticket" items—from new cars and houses to home electronics and vacations. The cost of credit is the interest rate that financial institutions charge their customers. If the interest rate rises, consumers are less likely to buy those new cars and appliances.

Businesses, too, look to interest rates in deciding whether or not to purchase new equipment, expand their facilities, or make many other large investments. When interest rates are low, companies are more willing to borrow money. When interest rates climb, business borrowing falls. One result of rising interest rates, then, is less output. Such a result may lead to a contraction phase.

Consider one example of the impact of interest rates on the business cycle. In the early 1980s, high consumer interest rates helped bring on the worst economic slump in the United States since the Great Depression. Some credit-card interest rates reached 21 percent. As a result, the cost of expensive items usually purchased using credit was too high for many Americans. With reduced consumer spending, the economy entered a recession that pushed unemployment rates over 9 percent—the highest since the Depression.

Consumer Expectations

Consumer spending is determined partly by consumers' expectations. If people expect the economy to begin contracting, they may reduce their spending because they expect layoffs and lower incomes.

This reduced spending can actually help bring on a contraction, as firms respond to reduced demand for their products. Thus consumer expectations often become self-fulfilling prophecies, creating the very outcome that consumers fear. In the summer of 2007, consumer confidence fell. By September, consumer confidence was the lowest it had been in two years. This low level of consumer confidence affected the holiday shopping season at the end of the year.

High consumer confidence has the opposite effect on the economy. If people expect a rapidly growing economy, they will also expect abundant job opportunities and rising incomes. Thus, they will buy more goods and services, pushing up gross domestic product.

External Shocks

Of all the factors that affect the business cycle, perhaps most difficult to predict are external shocks, which you read about in Chapter 6. External shocks can dramatically affect an economy's

Simulation *Activity*

Ups and Downs
You may be asked to take part in a role-playing game about the ups and downs of the business cycle.

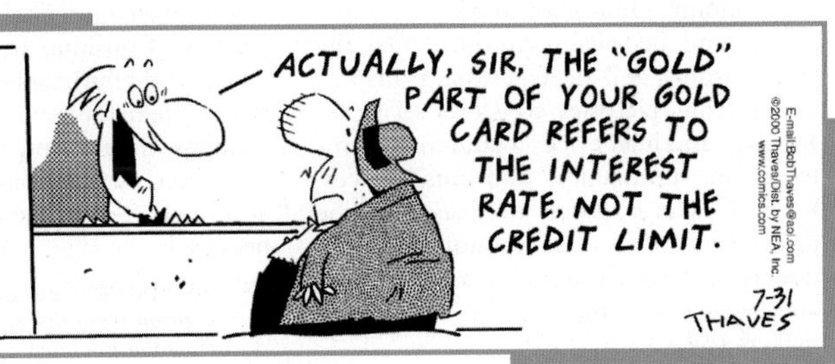

CREDIT CARD SERVICE DESK
ACTUALLY, SIR, THE "GOLD" PART OF YOUR GOLD CARD REFERS TO THE INTEREST RATE, NOT THE CREDIT LIMIT.
E-mail: BobThaves@aol.com
©2000 Thaves/Dist. by NEA, Inc.
www.comics.com
7-31
THAVES

◀ High interest rates are one of the pitfalls of easy access to credit. ***How do high interest rates affect businesses as well as individuals?***

DISCUSS

Ask **What main economic variables affect business cycles?** *(business investment, interest rates and credit, consumer expectations, and external shocks)* **How is an increase in business investment in capital both a cause and a result of economic expansion?** (*When economy is expanding, businesses expect their sales and profits to rise so they invest in capital, which in turn causes the economy to expand.*) **How is a decrease in business investment in capital both a cause and result of economic contraction?** *(When an economy is contracting, businesses may cut back on investment spending, causing GDP to decline. This in turn may cause suppliers of capital equipment to cut back on production, causing further decline in GDP.)*

Discuss how interest rates and credit affect the business cycle. Point out the cartoon and discuss the caption. Draw a seesaw on the chalkboard. Label the low end "low interest rates" and the high end "business cycle peak." Ask **How can low interest rates affect the business cycle?** *(They can contribute to expansion: lower interest rates may encourage consumers to spend and businesses to invest.)* Relabel the seesaw with "business cycle trough" at the low end and "high interest rates" at the high end. Ask **How can high interest rates affect the business cycle?** *(It can contribute to contraction: consumers and businesses are discouraged from spending, or investing in capital.)*

Answer

Caption High interest rates discourage businesses and individuals from borrowing money to make purchases.

HOW THE ECONOMY WORKS

After students review How the Economy Works, have them give other examples of external shocks. Have students explain why external shocks are the most difficult factors to predict. Ask students the meaning of the phrase *self-fulfilling prophecy.* Ask how this concept applies to consumer expectations of economic growth or decline.

L3 Simulation Activities For alternative or additional practice with the concept of a business cycle, have students use the "Ups and Downs" activity (Simulation Activities, Chapter 12). Students will take the roles of producers, bankers, and consumers to see what decisions they make under different economics conditions and the effects of those decisions on the business cycle.

EXAMINE A CARTOON

Display the "Brushback Pitches" transparency (Color Transparencies, 12.a). Have a volunteer explain that a *brushback pitch* is a throw, generally a fastball, made by a baseball pitcher that is meant to scare the hitter and get him to back away from the plate. Ask students to describe the meaning of the cartoon. Talk about some of the elements in the cartoon and how the different "pitches" can "scare" the economy. Explain those that may be unfamiliar to students. Have students categorize these "pitches" where possible as one of the factors just discussed.

How the Economy Works

What causes a recession?

Recessions are an inevitable part of the business cycle. A number of conditions and events may trigger a recession–or deepen a recession that has already begun.

1 The economy has enjoyed an extended period of growth. Businesses are expanding, spending is up, and unemployment and inflation are largely under control.

2 Despite the best efforts of government and business, recessions occur. Here are four possible reasons:

External shock War breaks out in a nation where U.S. banks and businesses have invested heavily. This nation is also an important supplier of goods to the U.S.

Business investment The war cuts into the assets of many U.S. firms. They lay off workers and cut back on plans to expand.

MALL

Peak

Contraction

aggregate supply. Examples of negative external shocks include disruptions of the oil supply, wars that interrupt trade, and droughts that severely reduce crop harvests.

Let's consider what might happen if a shock occurred. Suppose that the nation's supply of imported oil was suddenly cut off. Immediately, the price of any remaining oil would skyrocket. This rapid increase would have a powerful ripple effect on the economy. Oil is used to produce many goods, and petroleum products fuel the trucks, trains, and airplanes that transport goods from factories to stores. The oil shortage and high prices would force firms to reduce production and raise prices. In other words, GDP declines and the price level rises. This economic condition is particularly harmful to businesses and households and difficult for policymakers to fix.

Of course, an economy may also enjoy positive external shocks. The discovery of a large deposit of oil or minerals will contribute to a nation's wealth. A growing season with a perfect mix of sun and rain may create bountiful harvests that drive food prices down. Positive shocks tend to shift the AS curve to the right, lowering the price level and increasing real GDP.

External shocks usually come without much warning. The other key factors capable of pushing an economy from one phase of the business cycle to another are more predictable. So economists track business investment, interest rates, and consumer expectations in order to more accurately forecast new stages of the business cycle.

CHECKPOINT ***How are external shocks different from the other factors that affect the business cycle?***

Answer

Checkpoint The other factors that affect the business cycle can be predicted to some extent. External shocks occur suddenly and unexpectedly.

For an animated, interactive version of this feature, visit **PearsonSuccessNet.com**

Interest rates and credit
As the war and threat of recession continue, banks are slower to extend credit. Interest rates creep up.

Consumer expectations
Predictions about a long recession discourage people from spending.

3 As these factors feed into one another, unemployment rises and business activity dwindles. In time, though, the cycle will move into a new phase of expansion.

Check Your Understanding
1. How can interest rates help bring on a recession?
2. Look at the four headings under #2. For each one, identify a condition that might lead to an economic expansion.

Trough

Business Cycle Forecasting

Predicting changes in a business cycle is difficult. For example, in the summer of 1929, John J. Raskob, Senior financial officer of General Motors, declared his firm belief that the United States was on the verge of the greatest industrial expansion in its history.

> "In my opinion the wealth of the country is bound to increase at a very rapid rate… Anyone who believes that opportunities are now closed and that from now on the country will get worse instead of better is welcome to the opinion—and whatever increment it will bring. I think that we have scarcely started… I am firm in my belief that anyone not only can be rich but ought to be rich."
>
> —John Jakob Raskob, Interview in the *Ladies Home Journal*, August 1929

Less than two months later, the stock market crashed, setting off the worst depression in American history.

Economists today know a lot more about the workings of our economy than Raskob did in 1929. However, economic predictions are still tricky. To predict the next phase of a business cycle, forecasters must anticipate movements in real GDP before they occur. This is no easy task, given the large number of factors that influence the level of output in a modern economy.

Government and business decision makers need economic predictions to be accurate, however, so they can respond properly to changes in a business cycle. If businesses expect a contraction, they may postpone building new factories. If government policymakers expect a contraction, they may take steps to try to prevent a recession.

CHECK COMPREHENSION

Identify who John Raskob was and have a volunteer read his statement on this page aloud. Have students discuss the significance of this statement, given the date on which it was quoted in the *Ladies Home Journal.*

Ask **Why do government and business decision makers try to predict what the economy is going to do?** *(possible response: so businesses can postpone making new investments; so the government can take steps to try to limit the economic contraction and prevent a recession)*

Ask **What information do business and government decision makers use to make predictions?** *(They use leading indicators. These include stock prices, interest rates, and manufacturers' orders for capital goods)*

DISTRIBUTE SKILL WORKSHEET

Distribute the "Analyze Primary and Secondary Sources" skill worksheet (Unit 5 All-in-One, p. 22). Have a volunteer read aloud the quotation from Herbert Hoover. Have students discuss the quotation and explain the significance of the date of the speech. Have students read the rest of the text and complete the worksheet.

Tell students to review the lesson in the Skills Handbook on page S10. Remind them to use the steps of the lesson to complete the activities.

L2 Differentiate Distribute the "Analyze Primary and Secondary Sources" skill worksheet (Unit 5 All-in-One, p. 23). Have students complete it in pairs.

After students have completed the worksheet, review their answers. Ask **What type of source is the quote from John Raskob?** *(a primary source)*

Virtual Economics

L3 Differentiate

Comparing Stock Market Crashes
Use the following lesson from the NCEE **Virtual Economics *CD-ROM*** to compare stock market crashes in 1929 and 1987. Click on Browse Economics Lessons, specify grades 9–12, and use the key words *stock market crashes.*

In this activity, students will work in small groups to make posters comparing two stock market crashes.

LESSON TITLE	LESSONS FROM HISTORY: STOCK MARKET CRASHES
Type of Activity	Small group
Complexity	Moderate
Time	60 minutes
NCEE Standards	18, 20

Answers

Check Your Understanding 1. Higher interest rates discourage borrowing, which limits business investment. 2. Possible answers: A nation that buys goods from the United States has a bumper crop and has more money to spend; peace comes to a war-torn country and American businesses are tapped to rebuild; interest rates drop and businesses expand; consumers gain confidence and begin spending more.

ANALYZE GRAPH

Have students look at the graph on this page. Ask **In what year did the stock market crash?** *(1929)* Have students describe the trend in the GDP before and after that date. Ask **When did the economy begin to recover?** *(1933)* **What effect did World War II have on the GDP?** *(It caused it to increase.)*

L1 **L2** **ELL Differentiate** Ask students what is happening in the picture. Refer to the graph and help them identify the period when this picture might have been taken.

DISTRIBUTE ACTIVITY WORKSHEET

Distribute the "Changes in Real GDP and the Unemployment Rate" worksheet (Unit 5 All-in-One, p. 24). Have a volunteer read the text aloud. Ask students to explain how each of these graphs shows that the economy goes through cycles. Then have students complete the worksheet on their own.

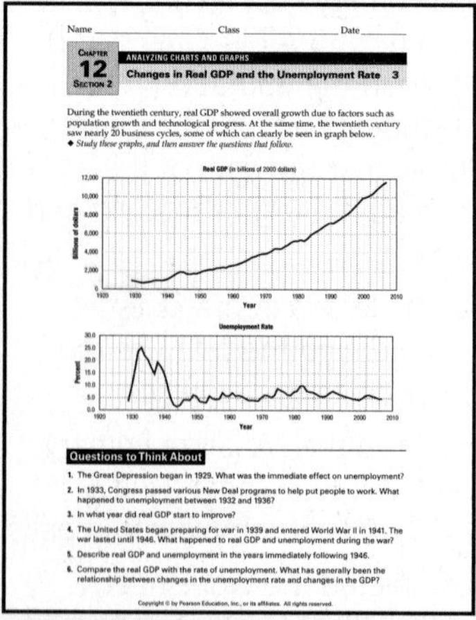

Name ______________ Class ______________ Date ________

CHAPTER 12 SECTION 2 — ANALYZING CHARTS AND GRAPHS

Changes in Real GDP and the Unemployment Rate 3

During the twentieth century, real GDP showed overall growth due to factors such as population growth and technological progress. At the same time, the twentieth century saw nearly 20 business cycles, some of which can clearly be seen in graph below.

◆ *Study these graphs, and then answer the questions that follow.*

Questions to Think About

1. The Great Depression began in 1929. What was the immediate effect on unemployment?
2. In 1933, Congress passed various New Deal programs to help put people to work. What happened to unemployment between 1932 and 1936?
3. In what year did real GDP start to improve?
4. The United States began preparing for war in 1939 and entered World War II in 1941. The war lasted until 1946. What happened to real GDP and unemployment during the war?
5. Describe real GDP and unemployment in the years immediately following 1946.
6. Compare the real GDP with the rate of unemployment. What has generally been the relationship between changes in the unemployment rate and changes in the GDP?

L2 **Differentiate** Distribute the "Impact of the Great Depression" worksheet (Unit 5 All-in-One, p. 25).

After students have completed the worksheet, have them identify two factors that contributed to rising GDP. *(New Deal programs and increased production due to World War II)*

▲ Declining GDP and high unemployment were two major signs of the Great Depression, the longest recession in U.S. history. ***In what year did the Great Depression hit its trough? How long did it take for GDP to return to its pre-Depression peak?***

Economists have many tools available for making these predictions. The **leading indicators** are a set of key economic variables that economists use to predict future trends in a business cycle.

The stock market is one leading indicator. Typically, the stock market turns sharply downward before a recession begins. For example, the crash of the Nasdaq exchange in 2000 preceded the recession of 2001. Interest rates are another indicator. As you have seen, interest rates have a strong effect on consumer and business spending.

The Conference Board, a private business research organization, maintains an index of ten leading economic indicators, including stock prices, interest rates, and manufacturers' new orders of capital goods. Economists and policymakers closely watch this index, which is updated monthly. However, like the other important tools used to forecast changes in the business cycle, it is not altogether reliable.

leading indicators a set of key economic variables that economists use to predict future trends in a business cycle

✔ **CHECKPOINT** ***Why is it difficult to predict the future of a business cycle?***

Business Cycles in American History

Economic activity in the United States has indeed followed a cyclical pattern. Periods of GDP growth alternate with periods of GDP decline.

The Great Depression

As you read earlier, before the 1930s many economists believed that when an economy declined, it would quickly recover on its own. This explains why, when the U.S. stock market crashed in 1929, and the economy took a nosedive, President Herbert Hoover felt little need to change his economic policies.

However, the Great Depression did not rapidly cure itself. Rather, it was the most severe economic downturn in the history of industrial capitalism. Between 1929 and 1933, GDP fell by about a quarter, and unemployment rose sharply. In fact, one out of every four workers was jobless, and those who could find work often earned very low wages.

As the effects of the Great Depression spread throughout the world, it affected

Background Note

Controlling Business Cycles Economists not only want to predict business cycles, but they want to control them as well. Economists have sought to extend the period of expansion by advocating the use of particular fiscal and monetary policies. To some extent, they are succeeding. Since the end of World War II, the length of expansions has steadily increased and the length of recessions has steadily decreased.

PERIOD	EXPANSION (MONTHS)	RECESSION (MONTHS)
Before World War II	26.5	21.2
Since World War II	54.1	10.4

Answers

Caption 1933; 4+ years

Checkpoint Many factors influence business cycles.

economists' beliefs about the macroeconomy. The depression, along with the publication of John Maynard Keynes's *The General Theory of Employment, Interest, and Money*, pushed economists to consider the idea that modern market economies could fall into long-lasting contractions. In addition, many economists accepted Keynes's idea that government intervention might be needed to pull an economy out of a depression. You will read more about Keynes and his ideas in Chapter 15.

The depression also affected American politics. Rejecting Hoover, voters in 1932 elected the Democratic governor of New York, Franklin Delano Roosevelt, to the presidency. Roosevelt soon began a series of government programs, known as the New Deal, designed to get people back to work.

Programs such as the Works Progress Administration and the Civilian Conservation Corps got able-bodied workers back on the job and earning income, which they then spent supporting their families. In this way, spending increased throughout the economy.

Still, although the New Deal relieved some of the effects of hard times, it did not end the Great Depression. Not until the United States entered into World War II did the economy achieve full recovery. The sudden surge in government defense spending boosted real GDP well above pre-depression levels.

Some Later Recessions

Thankfully, no economic downturns since the 1930s have been nearly as severe as the Great Depression. We have had recessions, though.

In the 1970s, an international cartel, the Organization of Petroleum Exporting Countries (OPEC), placed an embargo on oil shipped to the United States and quadrupled the price of its oil. These actions caused external shocks in the American oil market. As oil prices skyrocketed, raw material costs rose, and the economy quickly contracted into a period of stagflation.

Reeling from higher-than-ever prices for gasoline and heating fuel prices, Americans began looking for ways to conserve energy. They turned down their heat; bought smaller, more fuel-efficient cars; and began researching energy alternatives to petroleum. When the United States and other nations developed more of their own energy resources, OPEC finally lowered its oil prices.

As you read earlier, there was another recession in the early 1980s. High interest rates and other factors caused real GDP to fall and the unemployment rate to rise to over 9 percent in the early 1980s.

Following a brief recession in 1991, the U.S. economy grew steadily, with real GDP rising each year during the 1990s.

FUTURE WATCH **Global Impact**

A Global Depression

The impact of the Great Depression spread far beyond the United States. American banks stopped making loans abroad and demanded repayment of foreign loans. And when the U.S. raised taxes on imported goods, a trade war resulted that had a disastrous impact on the world economy. ***How might banking problems and reduced trade lead to higher unemployment?***

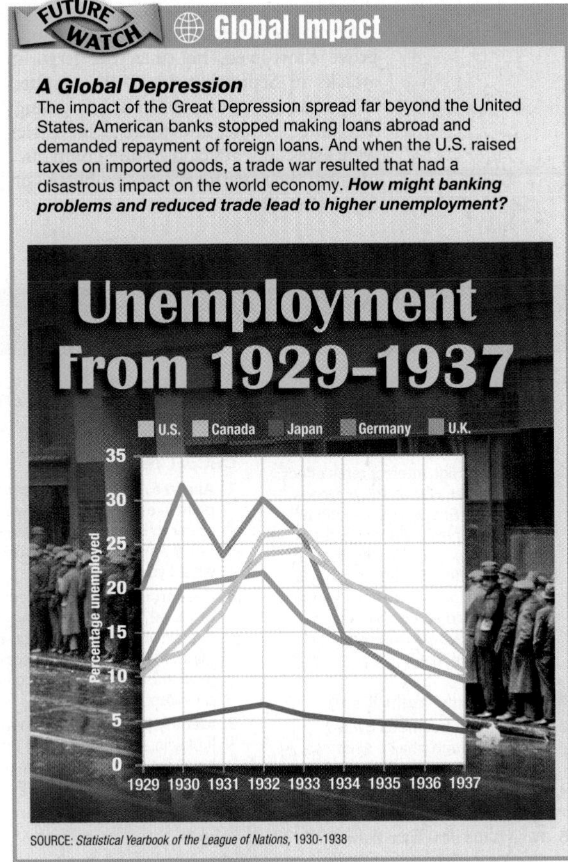

SOURCE: *Statistical Yearbook of the League of Nations*, 1930-1938

SUMMARIZE

Have students summarize later recessions, describe what factors led to them, and explain how these later economic events correspond to what they have already learned about the business cycle.

EXTEND

Ask students to investigate and write a brief report or presentation on the current phase of the business cycle. They can do research using their local paper, *The Wall Street Journal*, or other library or Internet resources. Tell students to identify the phase and report on details about unemployment, interest rates and credit, and other major factors driving current conditions.

L2 ELL **Differentiate** Have students work in pairs to research the current phase of the business cycle and then create an editorial cartoon or poster showing how current economic conditions are affecting average people.

GUIDING QUESTION WRAP UP

Have students return to the section Guiding Question. Review the completed graphic organizer and clarify any misunderstandings. Have a wrap up discussion about the factors that affect the business cycle.

Assess and Remediate

L3 L2 Collect the "Changes in Real GDP and the Unemployment Rate" and "Impact of the Great Depression" worksheets and assess student understanding of how economic events affect people.

L3 L2 Collect the "Analyze Primary and Secondary Sources" worksheets and assess student understanding of the readings.

L3 Evaluate student understanding of the business cycle in the "Ups and Downs" simulation.

L3 Assign the Section Assessment questions; identify student misconceptions.

L3 Give Section Quiz A (Unit 5 All-in-One, p. 26).

L2 Give Section Quiz B (Unit 5 All-in-One, p. 27).

(Assess and Remediate continued on p. 322)

Answer

Global Impact If banks stop making loans, business growth might slow, leading to layoffs and fewer new jobs, which in turn would increase unemployment.

Have students complete the Self-Test Online and continue their work in the **Essential Questions Journal**.

REMEDIATION AND SUGGESTIONS

Use the chart below to help students who are struggling with content.

WEAKNESS	REMEDIATION
Defining key terms (Questions 3, 4, 5, 6)	Have students use the interactive Economic Dictionary Online.
What are the phases of the business cycle (Questions 3, 4, 5, 7, 8, 11)	Have students review the section, list the phases of the business cycle, and provide a definition of each in their own words.
Factors affecting the business cycle (Questions 1, 2, 6, 9, 10)	Have students bring in articles from the newspaper or printed out from the Web that show factors affecting the business cycle. Have students explain the relationship between what is happening in the news and the factors affecting the business cycle.

Answer

Checkpoint Possible response: The government now tries to intervene in the economy to promote ongoing expansion.

The country enjoyed record growth, low unemployment, and low inflation. Some economists began to suggest that the nature of the business cycle had changed. Perhaps we had learned how to control recessions and promote long-term growth.

Much of this growth was fueled by the rise of Internet companies, called dot.coms, after part of their Internet address. As the dot.com boom of the 1990s ended, however, the U.S. growth slowed. Businesses and individuals invested billions of dollars in new technology that proved to be unprofitable and, in some cases, worthless. The negative effects of the technology crash spread throughout the economy to other industries. In March 2001, the country slipped into a recession.

Economists hoped this decline would prove short-lived, but then the terrorist attacks of September 11, 2001, resulted in a sharp drop in consumer spending. The hotel, airline, and tourism industries were especially affected. Many companies blamed their performance problems on September 11.

The Business Cycle Today

The recession ended in November 2001 when the economy began to grow slowly. Historically low interest rates prevented the economy from slipping back into a recession. However, unemployment continued to rise steadily over the following years as companies laid off more workers and kept spending low. Growth was not strong enough to dispel the feeling of bad times even though the recession had ended.

The economy did recover, though. By late 2003, it was surging, with GDP growing at a rate of 7.5 percent over three months. After that, growth slowed, though it did continue. High gasoline prices in 2006 caused the economy's growth to slow even further. Difficulties in the home mortgage market in 2007 raised fears about the short-term future of the economy, though. By 2008, those difficulties had cast a pall of gloom over the banking industry and given a number of severe shocks to the stock and bond markets.

CHECKPOINT ***What was a lasting effect of the Great Depression?***

Essential Questions Journal To continue to build a response to the Essential Question, go to your **Essential Questions Journal**.

SECTION 2 ASSESSMENT

Guiding Question

1. Use your completed table to answer this question: What factors affect the phases of a business cycle?
2. **Extension** High interest rates affect individuals as well as the business cycle itself. Suppose you wanted to purchase a new cellphone but did not have the money to pay for it. If someone offered you the money at 15 percent interest over a six-month period, would you be interested? What might you do instead of borrowing the money?

Key Terms and Main Ideas

3. **(a)** What is a **business cycle?** **(b)** In its **trough** phase, what has happened to the economy?
4. How can interest rates push a business cycle into a **contraction?**
5. What is the difference between a **recession, depression,** and **stagflation?**
6. Why is the stock market considered to be a **leading indicator** of economic change?

Critical Thinking

7. **Analyze** As a consumer, at which point in a business cycle would you prefer to be, the peak or the trough? Why? As a producer, at which point would you prefer to be?
8. **Research (a)** Select the recession of the 1970s, 1980s, or early 1990s. Explain what economic activity triggered it. **(b)** How did the economy recover? **(c)** Can such recessions be prevented?
9. **Identify (a)** What role did World War II play in ending the Great Depression? **(b)** Were the New Deal programs of Franklin Delano Roosevelt effective? Explain.
10. **Differentiate (a)** What factors other than declining business investments lead to changes in aggregate demand? **(b)** Is the price level a cause or an effect?

Math Skills

11. **(a)** Draw a line graph plotting four quarters of a year showing the real GDP. The first quarter reports 4.6 trillion, the second 4.3 trillion, the third 4.5 trillion, and the fourth 4.9 trillion. **(b)** On the graph, label the expansion, peak, contraction, and trough.

Visit PearsonSuccessNet.com for additional math help.

Assessment Answers

1. business investment, interest rates and credit, consumer expectations, and external shocks
2. Possible response: No. I might wait until I saved enough money to buy the phone.
3. (a) a cycle that includes expansion, a peak, contraction, and a trough (b) has reached its lowest point in an economic contraction
4. High interest rates discourage businesses from investing in capital, resulting in less output.
5. recession: real GDP falls for two consecutive quarters; depression: long and severe recession; stagflation: decline in real GDP coupled with inflation.
6. The stock market typically turns sharply downward before a recession begins.
7. Both would prefer being at a peak because jobs are plentiful, unemployment falls, and businesses prosper.
8. (a) Possible response: 1970; was triggered by an oil embargo by OPEC. (b) The United States developed more of its own energy resources, and OPEC lowered its prices. (c) Recessions caused by an external shock can be hard to prevent.
9. (a) The surge in war spending created jobs and boosted real GDP. (b) Yes; they put people back to work.
10. (a) interest rates and credit, consumer expectations, external shocks (b) both: higher prices cause a reduction; lower prices are an effect of reduced demand.
11. (a) Graphs should show Q1 GDP of 4.6 trillion, Q2 4.3 trillion, Q3 4.5 trillion, Q4 4.9 trillion. (b) Contraction between Q1 and Q2; Q2 is trough; Q3 and Q4 show expansion; Q4 marks a peak if GDP for the next quarter is less than 4.9 trillion.

OBJECTIVES

1. **Analyze** how economic growth is measured.
2. **Explain** what capital deepening is and how it contributes to economic growth.
3. **Analyze** how saving and investment are related to economic growth.
4. **Summarize** the impact of population growth, government, and foreign trade on economic growth.
5. **Identify** the causes and impact of technological progress.

ECONOMIC DICTIONARY

As you read the section, look for the definitions of these **Key Terms:**

- real GDP per capita
- capital deepening
- saving
- savings rate
- technological progress

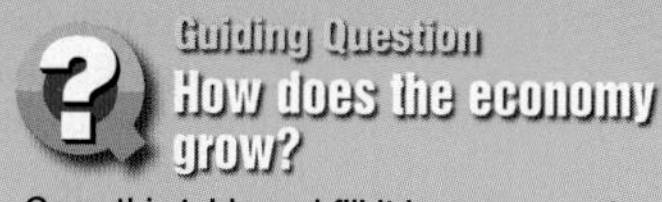

Copy this table and fill it in as you read to explain how an economy grows.

Changes in Real GDP	
Causes of Growth	**Causes of Decline**
• Capital deepening (more business investment) • Higher saving rate • Population growth with capital growth • •	• Less business investment • Lower saving rate • • •

Economics and You If you had lived in a typical American home 125 years ago, you would have owned a box filled with ice to preserve food, a wood-burning stove, and a horse or bicycle for transportation. For most of us today, those necessities of life have turned into a refrigerator-freezer; a furnace powered by gas, oil, or electricity; and a car. Clearly, as far as material possessions go, Americans of your generation are generally much better off today than they were 100 years ago. The biggest reason is economic growth.

real GDP per capita real GDP divided by the total population of a country

Principles in Action Economic growth, allows successive generations to have more and better goods and services than their parents had. In this section, we will describe how economic growth enables an entire society to make major improvements in its quality of life. Economics & You shows how you both benefit from and contribute to economic growth.

Measuring Economic Growth

The basic measure of a nation's economic growth rate is the percentage of change in real GDP over a period of time. For example, real GDP in 1996 was \$8.3 trillion, and in 2006, it was \$11.3 trillion. The economic growth rate for this decade was about 36 percent (\$11.3 trillion − \$8.3 trillion) ÷ \$8.3 trillion × 100).

GDP and Population Growth

To satisfy the needs of a growing population, real GDP must grow at least as fast as the population does. This is one reason that economists prefer a measure that takes population growth into account. For this, they rely on **real GDP per capita,** which is real GDP divided by the total population of a country (*per capita* means "for each person"). **Figure 12.7** shows growth in real GDP per capita.

Figure 12.7 Real GDP per Capita, 1970–2005

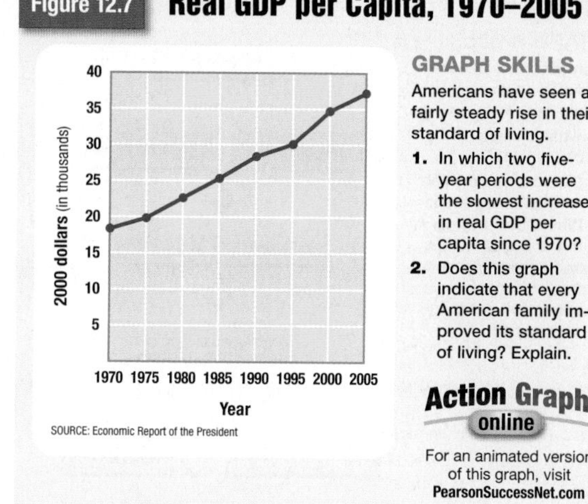

SOURCE: Economic Report of the President

GRAPH SKILLS

Americans have seen a fairly steady rise in their standard of living.

1. In which two five-year periods were the slowest increases in real GDP per capita since 1970?
2. Does this graph indicate that every American family improved its standard of living? Explain.

Action Graph online

For an animated version of this graph, visit PearsonSuccessNet.com

Guiding Question

How does the economy grow?

Get Started

Changes in Real GDP	
Causes of Growth	**Causes of Decline**
• Capital deepening • Higher saving rate • Population growth with capital growth • Government investment • Technological progress	• Decreased business investment • Lower saving rate • Use of tax revenue for additional services or war • Importing goods to be used for short-term consumption

LESSON GOALS

Students will:

- Know the Key Terms.
- Explain how capital deepening contributes to GDP growth.
- Describe the effects of saving and investment.
- Explain how population growth, use of tax revenues, and imported goods affect growth.
- Explain how technological progress impacts economic growth by completing a worksheet.

BEFORE CLASS

Students should read the section for homework.

Have students complete the graphic organizer in the Section Opener or the Guided Reading and Review worksheet (Unit 5 All-in-One, p. 28).

L1 L2 ELL LPR Differentiate Have students complete the Guided Reading and Review worksheet (Unit 5 All-in-One, p. 29).

Answers

Graph Skills 1. 1970–1975, 1990–1995 2. No, it represents an average increase.

Focus on the Basics

Students need to come away with the following understandings:

FACTS: • A nation's economic growth rate is the percentage of change in real GDP over a period of time. • Real GDP per capita is a good measure of the standard of living. • Capital deepening and technological growth are important sources of economic growth. • A higher savings rate leads to more investment funds for businesses, resulting in capital deepening. • A nation's population growth, the ways tax revenues are spent, and the types of goods imported affect economic growth.

GENERALIZATION: Economic growth can be measured by calculating real GDP per capita. Economic growth is affected by a variety of related factors, including capital deepening, savings rate, and technological growth.

CLASSROOM HINTS

REAL GDP PER CAPITA

Real GDP per capita measures standard of living, but if the wealth of a nation is unevenly distributed, the numbers can be misleading. For example, consider a hypothetical country of 100 citizens. Its real GDP per capita is \$1,000, so its real GDP is \$100,000. But 10% of the population control 90% of the goods and services produced in the country. So 10 people share \$90,000 of real GDP, and the remaining 90 share \$10,000. The real GDP per capita of \$1,000 is misleading, because the actual share of real GDP for 90% of the population is about \$111 per person, which provides a much lower standard of living than \$1,000.

BELLRINGER

Have students consider the following "headlines":

- Occupancy Up in Commercial Buildings
- Improved Battery Increases Demand for Hybrid Cars
- Consumer Saving Continues to Drop
- R&D Spending Down 7%
- Government Funds More Bridge Repair

Have them prepare to explain which of these headlines show economic growth or decline and why.

Teach

Economics online To present this topic using digital resources, use the lecture notes on www.PearsonSuccessNet.com.

DISCUSS BELLRINGER

Have volunteers explain their answers. Recall the definition of *economic growth*: a steady, long-term increase in real GDP. Explain that they will learn more about the causes of economic growth in this section.

CLARIFY

Tell students to imagine a family of two and a family of five, both living on $40,000 per year. Ask **Which family has a higher standard of living?** *(the family of two)* **Why?** *(This family has more money per person.)* Have students define real GDP per capita and describe how it is calculated. Ask **Why is real GDP per capita a better measure of standard of living than real GDP?** *(It measures the average income per person.)* Have students identify what is being shown in the graph in Figure 12.7, describe any trend they see, and answer the two questions.

L1 L2 Differentiate Clarify that real GDP per capita is the average income per person: some people will have higher incomes and some people will have lower incomes.

Action Graph online Have students review the Action Graph animation for a step-by-step look at Real GDP per Capita, 1970–2005.

Answers

Graph Skills 1. the process of increasing the amount of capital per worker 2. special training increases human capital, new clothing line increases physical capital.

Checkpoint High GDP per capita usually indicates better nutrition, housing, education, and job opportunities.

capital deepening the process of increasing the amount of capital per worker

Real GDP per capita is considered the most accurate measure of a nation's standard of living. As long as real GDP is rising faster than the population, real GDP per capita will rise, and so will the standard of living. Economists can see how the standard of living has changed over time by comparing real GDP per capita from two different time periods. They can also examine the growth rates of real GDP per capita to compare the economic strength of two different nations.

GDP and Quality of Life

GDP measures standard of living, which relates to material goods. We cannot use it, however, to measure people's quality of life. As you read in Section 1, GDP excludes many factors that affect the quality of life, such as the state of the environment or the level of stress people feel in their daily lives.

In addition, while real GDP per capita represents the average output per person in an economy, it tells us nothing about how that output is distributed across the population. There are a number of ways that economists measure how income is distributed in the United States, such as "personal income distribution" and "functional income distribution." These measures, while complicated, are important. If most of the income in a nation goes to relatively few people while the majority earn next to nothing, the typical person will not enjoy a very high standard of living even if the real GDP per capita figure is high.

Despite these facts, real GDP per capita is a good starting point for measuring a nation's quality of life. Nations with greater availability of goods and services usually enjoy better nutrition, safer and more comfortable housing, lower infant mortality, longer life spans, better education, greater job opportunities, and other indicators of a favorable quality of life.

Since economic growth has an enormous impact on quality of life, economists devote significant resources to figuring out what causes a nation's real GDP to rise. They focus on the roles of capital goods, technology, and a few related factors.

CHECKPOINT ***How is high GDP per capita linked to quality of life?***

Capital Deepening

Physical capital, the equipment used to produce goods and services, makes an important contribution to the output of an economy. With more physical capital, each worker can be more productive, producing more output per hour of work. Economists use the term *labor productivity* to describe the amount of output produced per worker.

Even if the size of the labor force does not change, more physical capital will lead to more output—in other words, to economic growth. This process of increasing the amount of capital per worker, called **capital deepening,** is one of the most important sources of growth in modern economies. (See **Figure 12.8.**)

Human capital, the productive knowledge and skills acquired by a worker through education and experience, also contributes to output. Firms, and employees themselves, can deepen human capital through training programs and on-the-job experience. Better-trained and more-experienced workers can produce more output per hour of work.

Figure 12.8 Capital Deepening

GRAPH SKILLS

There are many benefits of capital deepening, as shown here.

1. What is capital deepening?
2. Suppose you own a small clothing shop. Why should buying a new line of clothes and providing special training for sales staff result in capital deepening?

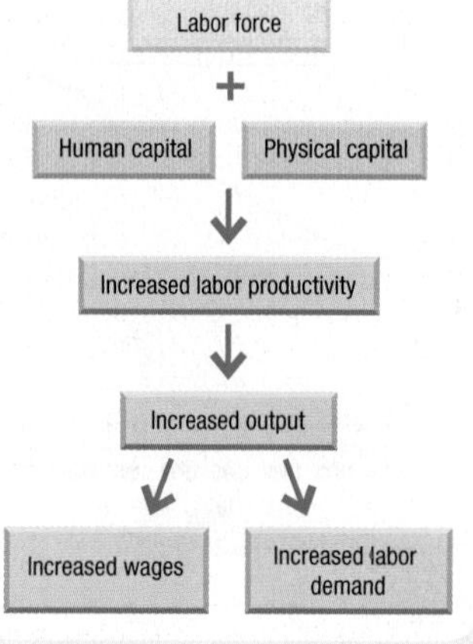

Differentiated Resources

- **L1 L2 Guided Reading and Review** (Unit 5 All-in-One, p. 29)
- **L4 Personal Savings** (Unit 5 All-in-One, p. 30)
- **L2 Breakthrough Technology** (Unit 5 All-in-One, p. 32)

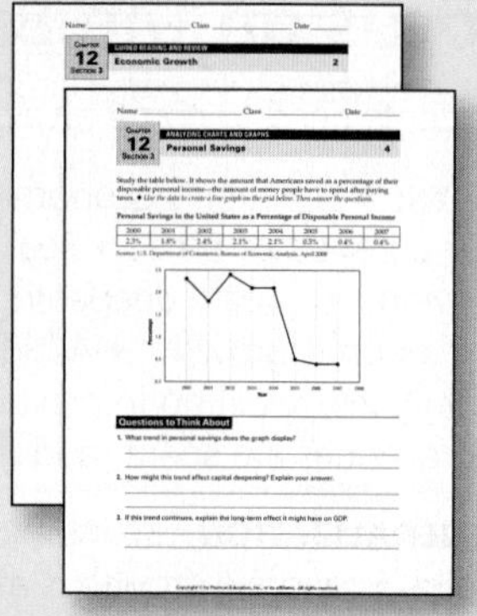

Along with increasing output per worker, capital deepening tends to increase job opportunities and workers' earnings. To understand why this happens, consider the effect of greater worker productivity on the demand for workers. As you read in Chapter 9, if workers can produce more output per hour, they become more valuable to their employers. As a result, employers will demand more workers. This increase in demand will increase the equilibrium wage rate in the labor market.

Therefore, with a labor force of a given size, capital deepening will increase output and workers' wages. How, then, does an economy increase its stock of capital per worker? It does so through saving and investment.

CHECKPOINT ***Why does capital deepening work with human capital?***

Saving and Investment

To see how saving and investment are related, consider an economy with no government sector and no foreign trade. In this simplified economy, consumers and business firms purchase all output. In other words, output can be used for consumption (by consumers) or investment (by firms). Income that is not used for consumption is called **saving.**

Since output can only be consumed or invested, whatever is not consumed must be invested. Therefore, in this simplified economy, saving is equal to investment. The proportion of disposable income that is saved is called the **savings rate.**

To see this another way, look at an individual's decision, as shown in **Figure 12.9.** Shawna had an after-tax income of $30,000 last year, but she spent only $25,000. That left her with $5,000 available for saving. She used some of her leftover income to purchase shares in a mutual fund, giving her ownership of some stocks and bonds. She put the rest of the money into a savings account at her bank.

Through her mutual-fund firm, her bank, and other intermediaries, Shawna's $5,000 was made available to businesses. The firms used the money to invest in new plants and equipment. So, when Shawna chose not to spend her entire income but

Figure 12.9 How Saving Leads to Capital Deepening

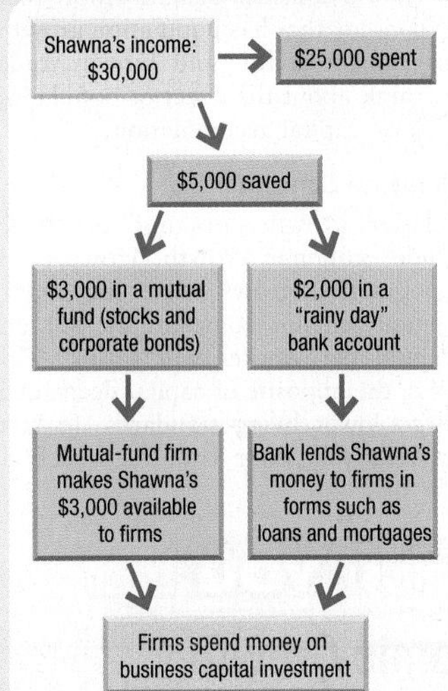

GRAPH SKILLS

Saving leads to capital deepening by providing funds for financial institutions to invest.

1. How much money has Shawna made available for investment in this example?
2. If people saved a high proportion of their incomes, how might the economy be affected?

to save a share, the amount that she saved became available for business investment.

If we consider the economy as a whole, the process works the same way. If total saving rises, more investment funds become available to businesses. Those firms will use most of these funds for capital investment. That is, they will expand the stock of capital in the business sector.

Higher saving, then, leads to higher investment, and thus to higher amounts of capital per worker. In other words, higher saving leads to capital deepening. Now we can understand why most nations promote saving. In the long run, more saving will lead to higher output and income for the population, raising GDP and the standard of living.

The United States has a low savings rate. To obtain the investment funds they need, businesses and the government borrow from other countries with higher savings rates.

CHECKPOINT ***How is saving linked to capital deepening?***

Personal Finance
For tips on savings and investment, see your Personal Finance Handbook in the back of the book or visit **PearsonSuccessNet.com**

saving income not used for consumption

savings rate the proportion of disposable income that is saved

MAKE CONNECTIONS

Point out Figure 12.8 to students. Have a volunteer define *capital deepening.* Ask **What are some examples of capital deepening?** *(Possible responses: worker training and education, new equipment, new buildings, new technology)* Ask **Which "headline" from the Bellringer shows capital deepening?** *("Improved Battery...")* Ask **What types of capital deepening have helped you do your schoolwork or job more efficiently than students 50 years ago? Explain.** *(possible response: school improvements: I have access to computers which help me to work more quickly and do research on the Internet)* Challenge students to explain why capital deepening leads to greater output, higher wages, and economic growth.

DISCUSS

Point out Figure 12.9, and then have students discuss how the savings rate affects capital deepening. Tell students that the U.S. savings rate, which was as high as 11.2% in 1982, has dropped to 0.4% in 2007 (see the chart in the Personal Finance Handbook on page PF 19). Ask **How much of the money that you earn do you save (after any taxes)?** *(Responses will vary.)* Ask **How would you want your savings to be invested?** *(Responses will vary.)*

L4 Differentiate Distribute the "Personal Savings" worksheet (Unit 5 All-in-One, p. 30).

Have students find recent savings rates and report what has happened to the rate since 2007.

PERSONAL FINANCE ACTIVITY

You may want to use the Personal Finance Handbook lesson "Investing with Dollars and $ense" on pp. PF10–PF13 and the activity worksheet (Personal Finance All-in-One, pp. 45–46).

Answers

Checkpoint Greater skill increases workers' output.

Graph Skills 1. $5,000 2. It would provide more money for businesses to invest, increasing output.

Checkpoint Saving provides money for investment in human and physical capital.

EXAMINE CONNECTIONS

Have students explain the connection between population growth and capital deepening.

L1 L2 **Differentiate** Help students understand the connection between population growth and capital deepening by presenting the following hypothetical situation: You have an assignment to complete on the computer. Working alone, it takes about one hour. Ask **Will your class of 20 complete the task more quickly with 5 computers or 20 computers? Why?** *(20 computers: everyone can work at the same time.)*

EXPLAIN

Have students define *infrastructure. (public goods such as roads and telecommunications)* Have students identify examples from their own community. Explain that if your taxes are increased, you have less money to save. However, if the government invests these additional revenues in infrastructure, this spending increases investment and contributes to economic growth.

L4 **Differentiate** Have students research the concept that raising taxes to pay for additional services or war reduces investment. Then have students present their findings.

Have students explain how foreign trade may or may not contribute to investment. Ask **If a country imports road-building equipment, does this contribute to capital deepening?** *(Yes, because the equipment allows the government to invest in infrastructure.)* **If a country imports televisions, does this contribute?** *(No, this does not increase the amount of capital per worker.)* Have students identify ways that they could spend their own money that would or would not lead to capital deepening. *(would: education, a laptop, equipment to provide a service; would not: eating out, movies, gas)*

Have a volunteer read "Economics and You." Have the class discuss the answer to the question: How would you be affected if the economy stopped growing?

CREATE A PROFILE

Have students use the Career Link worksheet to record their research for the activity (Unit 5 All-in-One, p. 80).

Answer

Economics & You Possible answer: I might not be able to get loans for college. This could affect my quality of life for years.

Population, Government, and Foreign Trade

Now we will consider a slightly more realistic economy that has population growth, a government sector, and foreign trade. First, think about the effect of population growth on capital accumulation.

Population Growth

Population growth does not necessarily preclude economic growth. However, if the population grows while the supply of capital remains constant, the amount of capital per worker will shrink. This process, the opposite of capital deepening, leads to lower living standards. In fact, some relatively poor countries, such as Bangladesh, have large labor forces but small capital stocks.

The result is that output per worker—and earnings per worker—are relatively low. Conversely, a nation with low population growth and expanding capital stock will enjoy significant capital deepening.

Economics & YOU
Economic Growth
When the economy is on the upswing, financial institutions are more likely to lend money. ***A strong economy means you have greater access to loans that help pay for education.***
Student Loans!!
APPLY HERE
Many economists see teen spending as a huge source of future economic growth. ***When you spend money responsibly, you help the economy expand.***

▲ Economic growth has enabled our high standard of living. ***How would you be affected if the economy stopped growing?***

Government

Government can affect capital deepening in several ways. If government raises tax rates to pay for additional services or to finance a war, households will have less money. People will reduce saving, thus reducing the money available to businesses for investment. In these cases, the government is taxing households in order to pay for its own consumption spending. The net effect is reduced investment.

On the other hand, a different result occurs if government invests the extra tax revenues in public goods, such as roads and telecommunications. These public goods are called infrastructure, the underlying necessities of modern life. Spending on infrastructure increases investment. To see why, consider what share of income the average household saves.

Suppose that, on average, households save 10 percent of their income. In this case, for every extra dollar in tax revenue the government collects, household saving (and investment) drops by 10 cents. However, government investment in infrastructure rises by $1. The net result is an increase in total investment of 90 cents. This kind of spending, then, is capital deepening, since the government is taxing its citizens to provide investment goods.

Foreign Trade

Foreign trade can result in a trade deficit, a situation in which the value of goods a country imports is higher than the value of goods it exports. (You will read more about trade deficits in Chapter 17.) Running a trade deficit may not seem like a wise practice, but if the imports consist of investment goods, the practice can foster capital deepening. Investment goods are the structures and equipment purchased by businesses.

Capital deepening can offset the negative effects of a trade deficit by helping generate economic growth, helping a

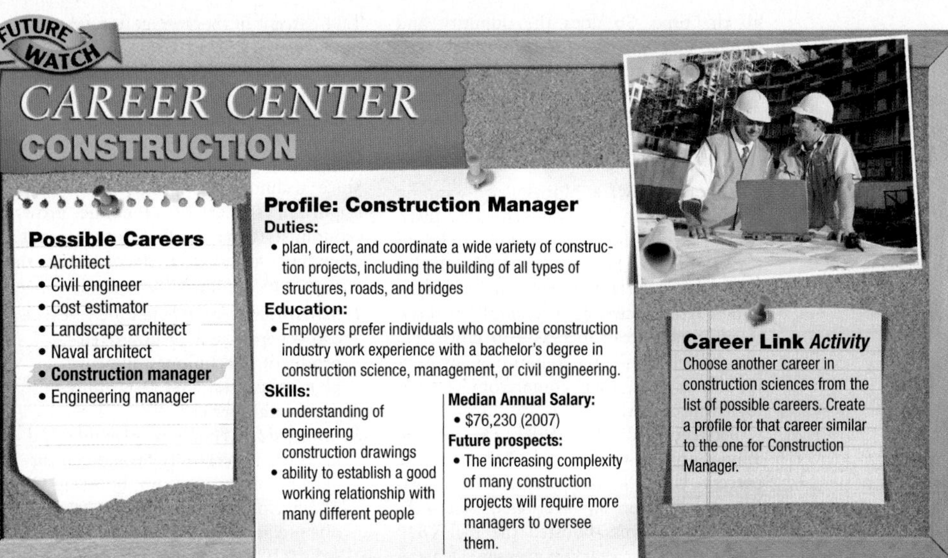
FUTURE WATCH
CAREER CENTER
CONSTRUCTION
Possible Careers
• Architect
• Civil engineer
• Cost estimator
• Landscape architect
• Naval architect
• Construction manager
• Engineering manager
Profile: Construction Manager
Duties:
• plan, direct, and coordinate a wide variety of construction projects, including the building of all types of structures, roads, and bridges
Education:
• Employers prefer individuals who combine construction industry work experience with a bachelor's degree in construction science, management, or civil engineering.
Skills:
• understanding of engineering construction drawings
• ability to establish a good working relationship with many different people
Median Annual Salary:
• $76,230 (2007)
Future prospects:
• The increasing complexity of many construction projects will require more managers to oversee them.
Career Link Activity
Choose another career in construction sciences from the list of possible careers. Create a profile for that career similar to the one for Construction Manager.

country pay back the money it borrowed in the first place. In the mid-1800s, for example, the United States financed the building of the transcontinental railroad in part by borrowing funds from investors in other countries. The borrowing created a trade deficit, but it also helped create a much higher rate of economic growth than would have occurred otherwise. The railroad promoted new industries and opened up vast areas to farming, leading to a huge increase in the nation's farm output.

Of course, not all trade deficits promote capital deepening. In this regard, trade deficits are similar to government taxation. Whether they encourage capital deepening and economic growth depends on how the funds are used. If they are used for short-term consumption, the economy will not grow any faster, and it will not have any additional GDP to pay back the debts. If the funds are used for long-term investment, however, they will foster capital deepening. The resulting economic growth will bring the country prosperity in the future.

✔ **CHECKPOINT** ***Do higher tax rates increase or reduce investment?***

Technological Progress

Another key source of economic growth is technological progress. This term usually brings to mind new inventions or new ways of performing a task, but in economics, it has a more precise definition. **Technological progress** is an increase in efficiency gained by producing more output without using more inputs.

Technological progress occurs in many ways. It can result from new scientific knowledge—for example, nano-technology, making computer chips smaller and smaller—that has practical uses. It can be a new invention that allows workers to produce goods more efficiently. It could even be a new method for organizing production. All of these advances raise a nation's productivity. Increased productivity means producing more output with the same amounts of land, labor, and capital. With technological progress, a society enjoys higher real GDP per capita, which leads to a higher standard of living.

technological progress an increase in efficiency gained by producing more output without using more inputs

Measuring Technological Progress

In most modern economies, the amount of physical and human capital changes

DISCUSS

Ask students to guess what the top recent technological innovations are. Jot down their answers. Then put the following list of the top innovations on the chalkboard: 1. The Internet; 2. Cellphone; 3. Personal computers; 4. Fiber optics; 5. E-mail; 6. Commercialized GPS; 7. Portable computers; 8. Memory storage discs; 9. Consumer-level digital camera; 10. Radio frequency ID tags. Ask students how they think these innovations have increased efficiency. Discuss how technology increases the amount that can be produced from a given amount of land, labor, and capital.

Have a volunteer define *technological progress. (an increase in efficiency gained by producing more output without using more inputs)* Ensure that students understand how technological progress results in higher real GDP per capita.

L1 **L2** **Differentiate** Give an example of technological progress: Roads were once built by many workers using shovels and other hand tools. Now road-building equipment does the work. One worker does as much as many in the past. Have students give more examples.

DISTRIBUTE ACTIVITY WORKSHEET

Distribute the "Breakthrough Technology" worksheet (Unit 5 All-in-One, p. 31). Have students complete the worksheet.

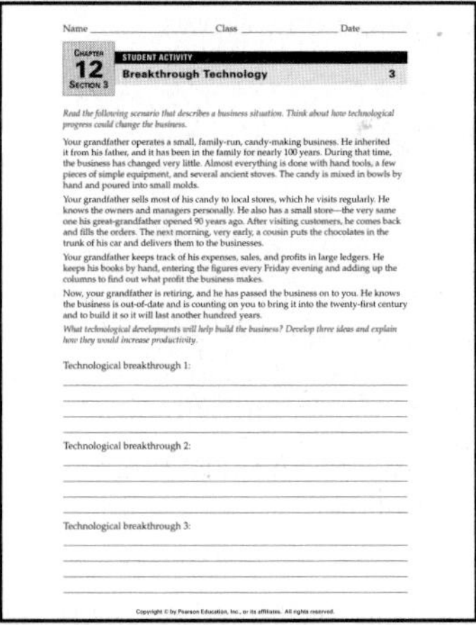
Name ____________ Class ____________ Date ________

Chapter 12 Section 3 — STUDENT ACTIVITY — **Breakthrough Technology** 3

Read the following scenario that describes a business situation. Think about how technological progress could change the business.

Your grandfather operates a small, family-run, candy-making business. He inherited it from his father, and it has been in the family for nearly 100 years. During that time, the business has changed very little. Almost everything is done with hand tools, a few pieces of simple equipment, and several ancient stoves. The candy is mixed in bowls by hand and poured into small molds.

Your grandfather sells most of his candy to local stores, which he visits regularly. He knows the owners and managers personally. He also has a small store—the very same one his great-grandfather opened 90 years ago. After visiting customers, he comes back and fills the orders. The next morning, very early, a cousin puts the chocolates in the trunk of his car and delivers them to the businesses.

Your grandfather keeps track of his expenses, sales, and profits in large ledgers. He keeps his books by hand, entering the figures every Friday evening and adding up the columns to find out what profit the business makes.

Now, your grandfather is retiring, and he has passed the business on to you. He knows the business is out-of-date and is counting on you to bring it into the twenty-first century and to build it so it will last another hundred years.

What technological developments will help build the business? Develop three ideas and explain how they would increase productivity.

Technological breakthrough 1:

Technological breakthrough 2:

Technological breakthrough 3:

L2 **Differentiate** Distribute the "Breakthrough Technology" worksheet (Unit 5 All-in-One, p. 32).

Have students report their answers using the Idea Wave strategy.

Answer

Checkpoint Higher tax rates reduce investment if the tax revenues are used for additional services or war; they increase investment if they are used to improve the infrastructure.

DISCUSS

Remind students that modern economies are very complex and that physical and human capital and the factors affecting them are changing all the time. Discuss Solow's method of measuring the effects of technological progress. Ask **What are the most important factors that increase GDP?** *(increases in labor, technological progress, capital)*

Ask **Why has the United States advanced technologically while less developed nations have not?** *(Government has contributed to scientific research, innovation, has scale of market, population is educated and experienced, abundant natural resources)*

EXTEND

Have students write a persuasive essay on the topic "What role should government play in promoting research and development?" Tell them to support their ideas with research and examples.

L4 **Differentiate** Have students choose a specific area of technology that they feel needs further development, such as alternative energy or transportation. Have them research it, and then write an essay on ways to develop the technology.

GUIDING QUESTION WRAP UP

Have students return to the section Guiding Question. Review the completed graphic organizer and clarify any misunderstandings. Have a wrap up discussion about how the economy grows.

Assess and Remediate

L4 Collect the "Personal Savings" worksheet and assess student understanding of trends in savings.

L3 **L2** Collect the "Breakthrough Technology" worksheets and assess student understanding of the role technology plays in economic growth.

L3 Assign the Section Assessment questions; identify student misconceptions.

L3 Give Section Quiz A (Unit 5 All-in-One, p. 33).

L2 Give Section Quiz B (Unit 5 All-in-One, p. 34).

(Assess and Remediate continued on p. 330)

Answer

Critical Thinking Technological progress increases GDP by increasing the efficiency of workers.

all the time. So does the quantity and quality of labor and the technology used to produce goods and services. These interconnected variables work together to produce economic growth. How then can we isolate and measure the effects of technological progress?

Robert Solow, a Nobel Prize-winning economist from the Massachusetts Institute of Technology, developed a method for doing so. Solow's method was to determine how much growth in output comes from increases in capital and how much comes from increases in labor. He concluded that any remaining growth in output must then come from technological progress.

Between 1929 and 1982, the average annual growth rate of real GDP was 2.92 percent. Using Solow's method, economist Edward Denison has estimated that technological progress boosted the real GDP 1.02 percent per year, on average. Denison determined that increases in capital and labor were responsible for 0.56 percent and 1.34 percent of the average annual growth, respectively $(2.92 - 0.56 - 1.34 = 1.02)$. Technological progress, then, was the second most important factor in promoting economic growth in that period.

Causes of Technological Progress

Since technological progress is such an important source of economic growth, economists have looked for its causes. They have found a variety of factors that influence technological progress.

1. ***Scientific research*** Scientific research can generate new or improved production techniques, improve physical capital, and result in better goods and services.
2. ***Innovation*** When new products and ideas are successfully brought to the market, output goes up, boosting GDP and business profits. Yet innovation often requires costly research. Companies willing to carry out that research need assurance that they will profit from the products they develop.

Innovators

YAHOO!

Jerry Yang

"On the outside, Yahoo is a fun and irreverent place, but on the inside we are extremely competitive."

It has become a familiar story. Two engineering students meet in college and turn their personal hobby into a technology-based start-up company. The company grows beyond all expectations and alters the lives of its founders, employees, users, and shareholders. And in this case the company, Yahoo! Inc., changes the face of business on a global scale.

Jerry Yang was born in Taiwan in 1968 and moved to the U.S. with his mother and brother at the age of 10. He co-founded Yahoo! with another Stanford student, David Filo, while studying for a doctoral degree at Stanford University in 1994. By 2008, Microsoft, the giant software company, had offered more than $45 billion to take it over.

Yang and Filo created Yahoo! to organize their own Internet searches. When they showed their new program to friends, Yang and Filo realized its huge business potential. Today Yahoo! is an Internet giant with more than 500 million users worldwide and a well-respected brand name. It is a starting point for many consumers as they search the Web. Yahoo! offers personalized home pages, e-mail, music, news, and more. In a global economy that requires many office workers to access, organize, and manage information on a daily basis, Yahoo! has proved its great value to society.

Critical Thinking: ***How does technological progress, such as the development of Internet search engines like Yahoo!, affect the nation's GDP and overall economic growth?***

Fast Facts

Jerry Yang

Born: 1968, in Taipei, Taiwan

Education: Stanford University, B.S. and M.S. in Electrical Engineering

Claim to Fame: Founder of Internet search engine Yahoo.com

Virtual Economics

L4 **Differentiate**

Comparing Economic Growth Use the following lesson from the NCEE **Virtual Economics *CD-ROM*** to compare economic growth in different countries. Click on Browse Economics Lessons, specify grades 9–12, and use the key words *growth and development.*

In this activity, students will participate in a simulation to identify the major factors that promote or hinder economic growth.

LESSON TITLE	ECONOMIC GROWTH AND DEVELOPMENT
Type of Activity	Simulation
Complexity	High
Time	100 minutes
NCEE Standards	15, 18

Case Study — THE WALL STREET JOURNAL. CLASSROOM EDITION

7 Most Networked Economies in 2007–2008
(ranked by Internet use and innovation)

Ranking	Country
1	Denmark
2	Sweden
3	Switzerland
4	United States
5	Singapore
6	Finland
7	Netherlands

SOURCE: World Economic Forum, *Global Information Technology Report, 2007–2008*

Off the Beaten Superhighway

TECHNOLOGICAL PROGRESS

Some small cities, tired of waiting for faster Internet service, are beginning to build their own.

By Christopher Rhoads
The Wall Street Journal

Internet traffic is growing faster than at any time since the boom of the late-1990s. Places like Chattanooga, Tenn., are trying hard not to get stuck in the slow lane.

Some 60 towns and small cities, including Bristol, Va., Barnsville, Minn., and Sallisaw, Okla., have built state-of-the-art fiber networks, capable of speeds many times faster than most existing connections from cable and telecom companies. Many others, including Chattanooga, have launched or are considering similar initiatives.

The efforts highlight a battle over Internet policy in the U.S. Once the undisputed leader in the technological revolution, the U.S. now lags a growing number of countries in the speed, cost and availability of high-speed Internet. While cable and telecom companies are spending billions to upgrade their service, they're focusing their efforts mostly on larger U.S. cities for now.

Smaller ones such as Chattanooga say they need to fill the vacuum themselves or risk falling further behind and losing better-paying jobs. Chattanooga's city-owned electric utility began offering ultrafast Internet service to downtown business customers five years ago. Now it plans to roll out a fiber network to deliver TV, high-speed Internet and phone service to some 170,000 residential customers. The city has no choice but to foot the bill itself for a high-speed network—expected to cost $230 million—if it wants to remain competitive in today's global economy, says Harold DePriest, the utility's CEO.

Mr. DePriest compares his agency's plan for high-speed Internet to the rollout of electricity, which came to many parts of Tennessee only in the 1930s as a result of the federal government's Tennessee Valley Authority project. That was three decades after many businesses and homes in major urban areas were first electrified.

It's a risky bet. Some municipal Internet efforts, including wireless projects known as Wi-Fi, have failed in recent months. And some private-sector Internet providers, like phone and cable companies, are raising opposition, saying the initiatives are a poor use of taxpayer money and create unfair competition.

Mr. DePriest remains undeterred. He expects to have most of the network completed within three years, serving 80% of the city. "The issue is, does our community control our own fate," says Mr. DePriest. "Or does someone else control it?"

Video News Update Online Powered by *The Wall Street Journal* Classroom Edition — For a new case study, go to the online resources at **PearsonSuccessNet.com**

Applying Economic Principles
What are the potential benefits and drawbacks of a small city investing in high-speed Internet? Would such an investment promote capital deepening?

Teach Case Study

SUMMARIZE AND EXPLAIN

Have the students explain the importance of connectivity in small cities. Ask **Why are towns and small cities building their own fiber networks?** *(In a competitive global economy, small cities do not want to be irrelevant by lagging in technology. The cities want to be wired and the United States has focused its efforts on large cities, forcing smaller ones to do the work themselves.)*

ANALYZE

Have students work in pairs and write a short paragraph describing the relationship between technology and economic growth. Ask **How has technology helped companies compete in the global marketplace?** *(makes communication easier and quicker, erases distances—when business can be conducted via phone or Internet).*

L1 L2 Differentiate Have students compare the information in this case study with their own town. Have them find out what type of connectivity is available *(through cable or telecom; is wireless available)* and who paid to have the fiber or other network built *(national government, local government, cable or telecom companies).* Have a volunteer call your local government offices and share his or her findings with the class.

Economics online *All print resources are available on the Teacher's Resource Library CD-ROM and online at* www.PearsonSuccessNet.com.

Answer

Applying Economic Principles Possible response: benefits: control, competitiveness; drawbacks: time, cost, networks might be underutilized, money could be used for other things. Yes, would increase human capital.

Have students complete the Self-Test Online and continue their work in the **Essential Questions Journal**.

REMEDIATION AND SUGGESTIONS

Use the chart below to help students who are struggling with content.

WEAKNESS	REMEDIATION
Defining key terms (Questions 3, 4, 5, 6, 7)	Have students use the interactive Economic Dictionary Online.
How economic growth is measured (Questions 3, 8)	Have students outline the text under the heading Measuring Economic Growth.
Causes of GDP growth (Questions 1, 2, 4, 5, 6, 9, 10)	Draw the section graphic organizer on the board and complete with input from students. Explain each cause of growth or decline.
Causes and effects of technological progress (Questions 7, 11, 12)	Pair students and have them explain each of these terms in their own words and how they relate to technological progress: scientific research, innovation, scale of market, education and experience, natural resource use.

Answer

Checkpoint Technological progress is an increase in efficiency, raising a nation's productivity and resulting in a higher GDP.

The government issues patents to provide that assurance. A patent is a set of exclusive rights to produce and sell a product for a particular period of time. It is given to people who can show that they have discovered or invented a new product or process. Currently, patents last 20 years. A patent helps companies recover the cost of research by earning profits before its competitors can copy its new products.

Government aids innovation in several other ways as well. Through organizations such as the National Science Foundation and the National Institutes of Health, the United States government sponsors *basic research*. This term describes theoretical research that is often expensive and might not bring a new product to market in a timely way.

3. ***Scale of the market*** Larger markets provide more incentives for innovation, since the potential profits are greater. For this reason, larger economies will come up with more technological advances.
4. ***Education and experience*** As you read earlier, firms increase their human capital by providing education and on-the-job experience for their employees. Human capital makes workers more productive, which accelerates economic growth. It can also stimulate growth in another way. A more educated and experienced workforce can more easily handle technological advances and may well create some new advances, too.
5. ***Natural resource use*** Increased use of natural resources can create a need for new technology. For example, new technology can turn previously useless raw materials into usable resources. It can also allow us to obtain and use resources more efficiently, develop substitute resources, and discover new resource reserves. Because price is based on the cost of obtaining a resource (and not necessarily on its scarcity), new technology can also lead to lower prices.

✔ CHECKPOINT ***How is technological progress related to the economic growth of a nation?***

SECTION 3 ASSESSMENT

Essential Questions Journal To continue to build a response to the Essential Question, go to your **Essential Questions Journal.**

Guiding Question

1. Use your completed table to answer this question: How does the economy grow?
2. **Extension** Suppose an uncle left you $500 and you had three choices to use the money. You could (1) save the $500 in a bank, (2) buy computer equipment, or (3) keep it in your closet. How would each of these actions affect the growth of the economy?

Key Terms and Main Ideas

3. **(a)** What is **real GDP per capita?** **(b)** Why do economists measure it?
4. **(a)** What is **capital deepening?** **(b)** How does it contribute to economic growth?
5. What role does **saving** play in the process of economic growth?
6. What is the effect of the United States having a low **savings rate?**
7. How do patents encourage **technological progress?**

Critical Thinking

8. **Examine (a)** What is real GDP per capita unable to measure? **(b)** How does that limit economists' knowledge of individuals' standard of living? **(c)** Why do economists use it anyway?
9. **Connect (a)** What is the connection between saving and capital deepening? **(b)** Is it possible for capital deepening to occur without saving? Explain.
10. **Explain (a)** How can foreign trade lead to a trade deficit? **(b)** Explain why a trade deficit caused by foreign trade may not necessarily be bad for the economy.
11. **Describe (a)** Identify five factors that influence technological progress. **(b)** Which of these factors is the most important? Explain your answer.

Quick Write

12. In the mid-1800s, railroad companies borrowed money from foreign investors to create a transcontinental rail line. The completed railroad made enough money to pay off the loans and return a profit. Identify a possible transportation or communications project that might benefit the country or your community. Write an outline for a proposal relating to this project. Explain what benefits the project would provide and whether you favor borrowing money in order to accomplish the project.

Assessment Answers

1. from capital deepening, higher savings rate, population growth, government investment, trade that fosters capital deepening, technological progress
2. Saving it would make it available to businesses to invest to deepen capital. Buying computer would add to GDP. Keeping it in closet would not increase economic growth.
3. (a) real GDP divided by total population (b) to measure standard of living
4. (a) increasing the amount of capital per worker (b) increases output and wages.
5. Higher saving leads to greater business investment and to capital deepening.
6. Businesses, government must borrow from countries with higher savings rates.
7. Patents encourage research.
8. (a) quality of life (b) Standard of living is linked to quality of life. (c) It is a starting point.
9. (a) makes money available for investment in capital deepening (b) Yes, with government spending, money borrowed from other countries, technological progress.
10. (a) when the value of goods imported exceeds the value of goods exported (b) when the goods imported are used as investment in physical or human capital
11. (a) scientific research, innovation, scale of market, education, natural resource use (b) Possible response: Innovation, because it boosts output, GDP, and profit.
12. Possible response: A town bus service. The benefits would include reducing dependence on cars and addressing the problem of parking. Money should be borrowed if necessary.

QUICK STUDY GUIDE

Chapter 12: Gross Domestic Product and Growth

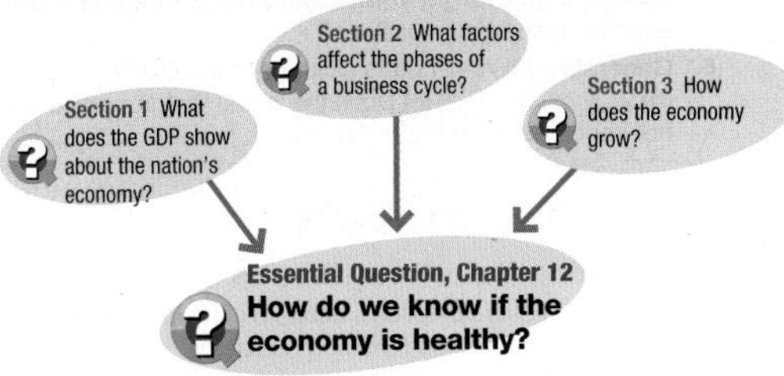
Section 1 What does the GDP show about the nation's economy?
Section 2 What factors affect the phases of a business cycle?
Section 3 How does the economy grow?
Essential Question, Chapter 12
How do we know if the economy is healthy?

Important Measures of Economic Growth

	Definition	Does Not Include	How Compiled?
Gross Domestic Product (GDP)	Dollar value of all final goods and services produced within a country's borders in a year	Products made in another country by an American manufacturer	Expenditure Approach Income Approach **Variations:** Nominal GDP Real GDP
Gross National Product (GNP)	Annual income earned by U.S.-owned firms and U.S. citizens	Depreciation	GDP plus income earned outside U.S. by U.S. firms and citizens minus income earned by foreign firms and foreign citizens located in the U.S.
Net National Product (NNP)	GNP with the cost of replacing the physical capital	Taxes	GNP minus cost of depreciation
National Income (NI)	How much pretax income businesses actually pay to U.S. households		NNP minus taxes

Economic Dictionary

national income accounting, *p. 307*
gross domestic product, *p. 309*
intermediate goods, *p. 309*
durable goods, *p. 309*
nondurable goods, *p. 309*
nominal GDP, *p. 310*
real GDP, *p. 310*
gross national product, *p. 312*
depreciation, *p. 312*
price level, *p. 313*
aggregate supply, *p. 313*
aggregate demand, *p. 314*
business cycle, *p. 315*
expansion, *p. 315*
economic growth, *p. 315*
peak, *p. 315*
contraction, *p. 316*
trough, *p. 316*
recession, *p. 316*
depression, *p. 316*
stagflation, *p. 316*
leading indicators, *p. 320*
real GDP per capita, *p. 323*
capital deepening, *p. 324*
saving, *p. 325*
savings rate, *p. 325*
technological progress, *p. 327*

Economics on the go Study anytime, anywhere. Download these files today.

Economic Dictionary online	Audio Review online	Action Graph online	Visual Glossary online	How the Economy Works online
Vocabulary Support in English and Spanish	Audio Study Guide in English and Spanish	Animated Charts and Graphs	Animated feature	Animated feature

Download to your computer or mobile device at PearsonSuccessNet.com

ASSIGN THE ESSENTIAL QUESTIONS JOURNAL

After students have finished studying the chapter, they should return to the chapter's essential question in the Essential Questions Journal and complete the activity.

Tell students to go back to the chapter opener and look at the image. Using the information they have gained from studying the chapter, ask **How does this illustrate the main ideas of the chapter?** *(Possible responses: The building under construction shows an economy that is healthy and growing. The construction services provided are part of GDP.)*

STUDY TIPS

Tell students that highlighting information in their notes, handouts, or books they own can help them find and recall information. Suggest that they write a question in the margin about the information they highlight. The question does two things: It helps them remember the information and it creates a bridge so they can relate the highlighted information to broader ideas in what they are studying.

Economics on the go Have students download the digital resources available at Economics on the Go for review and remediation.

Assessment at a Glance

TESTS AND QUIZZES

Section Assessments

Section Quizzes A and B, **Unit 5 All-in-One**
Self-Test Online

Chapter Assessments

Chapter Tests A and B, **Unit 5 All-in-One**
Economic Detective, **Unit 5 All-in-One**
Document-based Assessment, p. 333
Exam*View*

AYP Monitoring Assessments

PERFORMANCE ASSESSMENT

Teacher's Edition, pp. 310, 311, 319, 320, 325, 327
Simulation Activities, Chapter 12
Virtual Economics on CD-ROM, pp. 312, 319, 328
Essential Questions Journal, Chapter 12
Assessment Rubrics

Chapter 12 Assessment

1. (a) Only by knowing about the influences on real GDP can economists attempt to extend periods of expansion and reduce periods of contraction. (b) Possible response: capital deepening and technological progress (c) Possible response: When a business increases its investment in human capital by providing employees with additional training and on-the-job experience, those employees can produce more output per hour of work.
2. (a) During a peak in a business cycle, business investment and consumer expectations are high, while interest rates are low. Any external shocks would have a positive effect. (b) external shocks (c) by watching leading economic indicators such as the stock market and interest rates
3. (a) World War II (b) the government sector; defense spending surged (c) Possible response: guns, ammunition, planes, ships
4. (a) High interest rates discouraged spending and caused, along with other factors, real GDP to drop. (b) The unemployment rate increased. (c) Lower interest rates make inflation worse.
5. (a) To satisfy the needs of a growing population, real GDP must grow at least as fast as the population. Real GDP per capita gives this information. (b) It most accurately reflects changes in standard of living over time, or provides a good comparison of two countries' standards of living.
6. (a) no (b) GDP only measures goods produced within the country. (c) No, because imports that add to capital deepening increase GDP.
7. Lowest: United States; Highest: Germany
8. a nation's total population
9. The economic health of the United States is higher: highest GDP per capita, lowest unemployment rate.
10. Discuss where students might find this information (on the Internet, at the library). Stress the importance of using government sources for the data. Check their worksheets before they move on to the Modify activity.
11. Students should use one of the economic indicators to determine the current phase of the business cycle and to predict any change over the upcoming quarter.

CHAPTER 12 ASSESSMENT

Self-Test online To test your understanding of key terms and main ideas, visit **PearsonSuccessNet.com**

Key Terms and Main Ideas

To make sure you understand the key terms and main ideas of this chapter, review the Checkpoint and Section Assessment questions and look at the Quick Study Guide on the preceding page.

Critical Thinking

1. **Connect (a)** Why is it important for economists to determine the influences on a nation's real GDP? **(b)** Identify two of the factors on which they focus. **(c)** Select one and give an example of how it affects the nation's GDP.
2. **Compare (a)** Compare the factors that affect the phases of a business cycle in peak periods. **(b)** Which factor is the most difficult to predict? **(c)** How do economists attempt to understand the timing of a business cycle?
3. **Interpret (a)** What major event allowed the U.S. to recover from the Great Depression? **(b)** With regard to this event, what sector, government or private, saw the greatest spending increase? How? **(c)** Name goods and services that would have been a part of this increased spending.

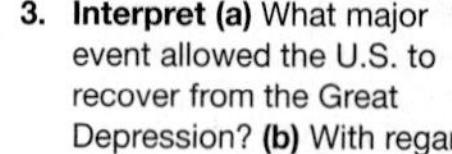

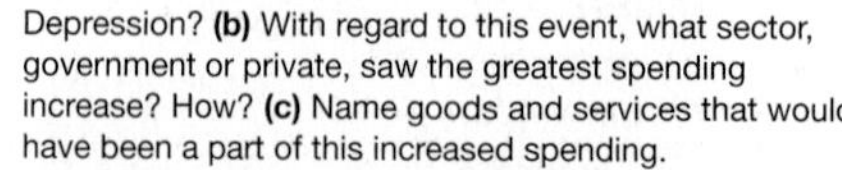

4. **Infer (a)** Why did a 21 percent credit card interest rate in the 1980s create a problem within the business cycle? **(b)** What happened to the unemployment rate during this period? **(c)** Why can't the government lower interest rates to spur the economy when inflation is high?
5. **Infer (a)** Why is real GDP per capita used to measure economic growth? **(b)** In what ways is this measure more effective than other measures?
6. **Generalize (a)** Are imports included in the GDP? **(b)** Why or why not? **(c)** Does this mean that imports are not important in promoting economic growth?

Applying Your Math Skills

Interpreting Data From Graphs

How do you measure a nation's economic health? Use the chart below to answer the following questions.

Visit PearsonSuccessNet.com for additional math help.

Economic Health of Selected Countries

Country	GDP Per Capita (2007, in thousands)	Unemployment Rate (% of labor force, 2007)
Czech Rep.	$24.2	6.6
Germany	$34.2	9.1
U. K.	$35.1	5.4
U. S.	$45.8	4.6

SOURCE: World Bank

7. Which country has the lowest unemployment rate? Which country has the highest unemployment rate?
8. What information would you need to know in order to find out which country had the highest total GDP?
9. How does the economic health of the United States compare with that of the other countries shown? On what evidence do you base your answer?

Essential Question Activity

Essential Questions Journal To respond to the chapter Essential Question, go to your **Essential Questions Journal**.

10. Complete the activity to answer the Essential Question **How do we know if the economy is healthy?** Work in groups to gather information to take the current pulse of the American economy. Track your data over a three-year period. Using the worksheet in your Essential Questions Journal or the electronic worksheet available at **PearsonSuccessNet.com,** gather the following information:
    (a) What trend does the real Gross Domestic Product of the United States reveal?
    (b) Was there an unemployment rate contraction phase? If so, how long did it last?
    (c) At what point during these three years did the rate of inflation peak?
11. **Modify** Once you have collected your information, provide a forecast for the next three months (quarter).
    (a) Select one of the economic indicators used.
    (b) In which phase of the business cycle does the graph end? Do you anticipate a change? If so, to which phase?
    (c) Determine the pattern that this indicator has followed over the past three years. Indicate what you think it might do within the next quarter.

332 GROSS DOMESTIC PRODUCT AND GROWTH

WebQuest online The Economics WebQuest challenges students to use twenty-first century skills to answer the Essential Question.

THE ESSENTIAL
VIDEO
By Students For Students
For videos on Essential Questions, go to PearsonSuccessNet.com

Remind students to continue to develop an Essential Questions video. Guidelines and a production binder are available at www.PearsonSuccessNet.com.

CHAPTER 12 ASSESSMENT

DOCUMENT-BASED ASSESSMENT

How can economic growth be balanced with environmental concerns?

The economy of the United States depends heavily on foreign oil. Some American leaders want to limit this economic dependence by allowing greater domestic oil drilling, especially in the protected Arctic National Wildlife Refuge (ANWR) in Alaska.

Document A

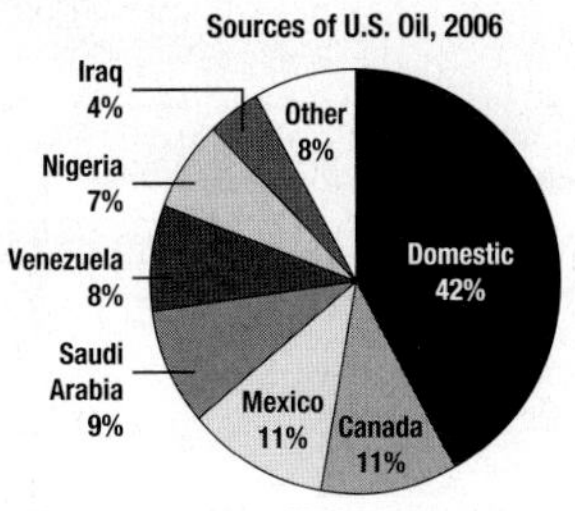

SOURCE: U.S. Department of Energy

Document B

"REASONS TO SUPPORT DEVELOPMENT IN ANWR

- Only 8% of ANWR would be considered for exploration….
- Federal revenues would be enhanced by billions of dollars from bonus bids, lease rentals, royalties and taxes….
- Between 250,000 and 735,000 ANWR jobs are estimated to be created by development of the Coastal Plain….
- Between 1977 and 2004, North Slope oil field development and production activity contributed over $50 billion to the nation's economy, directly impacting each state in the union….
- In 2007, the US imported an average of 60% of its oil and during certain months up to 64%. That equates to over $330 billion in oil imports. That's $37.75 million per hour gone out of our economy."

—"Top Ten Reasons to Support Development in ANWR," anwr.org

Document C

"What would America gain by allowing heavy industry into the refuge? Very little. Oil from the refuge would hardly make a dent in our dependence on foreign oil…. Oil produced from the Arctic Refuge would come at enormous, and irreversible, cost. The refuge is among the world's last true wildernesses, and it is one of the largest sanctuaries for Arctic animals…. Only by reducing American reliance on oil—foreign and domestic—and investing in cleaner, renewable forms of power will our country achieve true energy security…. If America made the transition to more efficient vehicles, far more oil would be saved than the Arctic Refuge is likely to produce."

—Natural Resources Defense Council, 2005

ANALYZING DOCUMENTS

Use your knowledge of economic concerns, the environmental effects of oil drilling, and Documents A, B, and C to answer questions 1–3.

1. **Document A best supports the conclusion that the United States**
   - **A.** has limited reserves of oil.
   - **B.** depends on foreign sources for most of its oil supply.
   - **C.** has sufficient oil available for its immediate needs.
   - **D.** should not use foreign sources of oil.

2. **According to Document B, oil drilling would support economic growth by**
   - **A.** enabling the United States to sell oil to foreign countries.
   - **B.** creating government and private revenue.
   - **C.** leading to tax cuts.
   - **D.** increasing U.S. oil imports.

3. **What is the main point of Document C?**
   - **A.** Drilling in ANWR would increase dependence on foreign oil.
   - **B.** Drilling in ANWR would be too expensive to be profitable.
   - **C.** The environmental costs of drilling in ANWR would outweigh the benefits.
   - **D.** U.S. dependence on foreign oil is not a major economic problem.

WRITING ABOUT ECONOMICS

Maintaining our energy supplies and natural resources is at the forefront of the news today. Use the documents on this page and other resources on the Web site below to answer the question: ***How can economic growth be balanced with environmental concerns?***

In Partnership

THE WALL STREET JOURNAL. CLASSROOM EDITION

To read more about issues related to this topic, visit **PearsonSuccessNet.com**

Document-Based Assessment

ANALYZING DOCUMENTS

1. B
2. B
3. C

WRITING ABOUT ECONOMICS

Possible answer: One way to balance economic growth and environmental concerns is to invest in renewable energy technology. This could result in an increase of jobs in this sector; reduce our dependence on oil, the price of which we may have little control over; and reduce the pollution caused by oil and other traditional fuels.

Student essays should demonstrate an understanding of the issues involved with economic growth and environmentalism. Use the following as guidelines to assess the essay.

L2 Differentiate Students use all documents on the page to support their thesis.

L3 Differentiate Students use the documents on this page and additional information available online at www.PearsonSuccessNet.com to support their answer.

L4 Differentiate Students incorporate information provided in the textbook and online at www.PearsonSuccessNet.com and include additional research to support their opinion.

Go Online to www.PearsonSuccessNet.com for a student rubric and extra documents.

Economics online *All print resources are available on the Teacher's Resource Library CD-ROM and online at* www.PearsonSuccessNet.com.

Essential Questions

UNIT 5:

Why does it matter how the economy is doing?

CHAPTER 13:

How much can we reduce unemployment, inflation, and poverty?

Introduce the Chapter

ACTIVATE PRIOR KNOWLEDGE

In this chapter, students will learn about different economic challenges. Tell students to complete the warmup activity in the **Essential Questions Journal**.

DIFFERENTIATED INSTRUCTION KEY

- **L1** Special Needs
- **L2** Basic
  - **ELL** English Language Learners
  - **LPR** Less Proficient Readers
- **L3** All Students
- **L4** Advanced Students

Economics online Visit www.PearsonSuccessNet.com for an interactive textbook with built-in activities on economic principles.

- ***The Wall Street Journal* Classroom Edition Video** presents a current topic related to unemployment, inflation, and poverty.
- **Yearly Update Worksheet** provides an annual update, including a new worksheet and lesson on this topic.
- **On the Go** resources can be downloaded so students and teachers can connect with economics anytime, anywhere.

ECONOMICS ONLINE

DIGITAL TEACHER TOOLS

The online lesson planner is designed to help teachers plan, teach, and assess. Teachers have the ability to use or customize existing Pearson lesson plans. Online lecture notes support the print lesson by providing an array of accessible activities and summaries of key concepts.

Two interactivities included in this lesson are:

- **How the Economy Works** Students predict and observe the effects of unemployment on an economy in this interactive feature.
- **WebQuest** Students use online resources to complete a guided activity further exploring the essential questions.

Chapter 13 Economic Challenges

Essential Question, Chapter 13

How much can we reduce unemployment, inflation, and poverty?

Job Opportunities

- **Section 1:** Unemployment
- **Section 2:** Inflation
- **Section 3:** Poverty

Economics on the go

To study anywhere, anytime, download these online resources at ***PearsonSuccessNet.com*** ▶

Block Scheduling

BLOCK 1 Teach Section 1, using the How the Economy Works interactive to give students an opportunity to explore unemployment.

BLOCK 2 Teach Sections 2 and 3, omitting the Bellringer activity and focusing on the Visual Glossary to teach Section 2.

Pressed for Time

Group work Use the Jigsaw strategy (p. T29) to have students read and prepare a study guide for the sections. Number students 1 through 6 and assign one student with each number to the same group. Assign each student half of one section to study and summarize in a study guide. Then call on the students to present their study guides to the rest of their group.

OBJECTIVES

1. **Differentiate** between frictional, seasonal, structural, and cyclical unemployment.
2. **Describe** how full employment is measured.
3. **Explain** why full employment does not mean that every worker is employed.

ECONOMIC DICTIONARY

As you read the section, look for the definitions of these **Key Terms:**

- frictional unemployment
- structural unemployment
- globalization
- seasonal unemployment
- cyclical unemployment
- unemployment rate
- full employment
- underemployed
- discouraged worker

Guiding Question
What are the causes of unemployment?

Copy this concept web and fill it in as you read to identify the causes of unemployment.

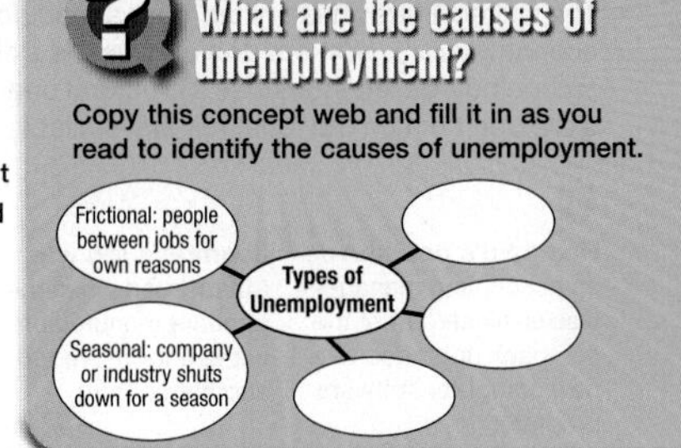

Economics and You Many people face unemployment at some point in their lives. For the jobless worker it is a very personal issue. For the government, it is a national economic issue. Economists measure the health of the economy by tracking the number of people who are out of work. The government pays close attention to these statistics so that it can take actions that will spur economic recovery.

Principles in Action General economic conditions, lengthy job searches, and seasonal production schedules are some of the factors that cause unemployment. A woman who believes in "keeping the humanity in human resources" is profiled in this section's Innovators.

Types of Unemployment

Economists look at four categories of unemployment: frictional, seasonal, structural, and cyclical. Sometimes, factors outside the economy can cause unemployment. The various kinds of unemployment have different effects on the economy as well as on the people who are unemployed.

Frictional Unemployment

Unemployment always exists, even in a booming economy. **Frictional unemployment** occurs when people take time to find a job. For example, people might change jobs, be laid off from their current jobs, or need some time to find the right position after they finish their schooling. They might be returning to the workforce after a long period of time. In the following examples, all three people are considered frictionally unemployed.

frictional unemployment type of unemployment that occurs when people take time to find a job

Visual Glossary online
Go to the Visual Glossary Online for an interactive review of **inflation.**

Action Graph online
Go to Action Graph Online for animated versions of key charts and graphs.

How the Economy Works online
Go to How the Economy Works Online for an interactive lesson on **structural unemployment.**

Guiding Question

What are the causes of unemployment?

Get Started

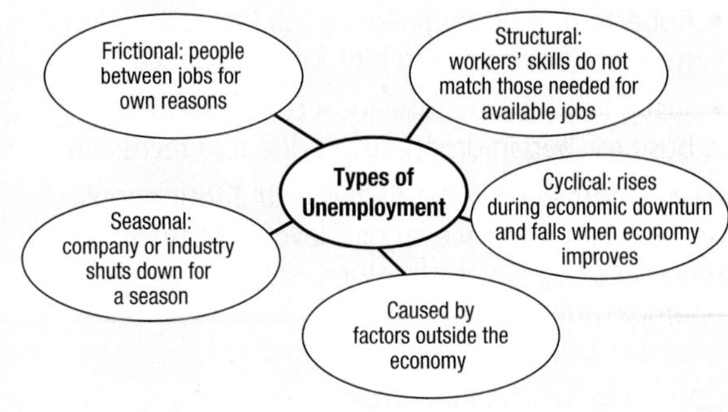

LESSON GOALS

Students will:

- Know the Key Terms.
- Describe four causes of unemployment and ways in which each cause may be reduced.
- Identify the advantages and disadvantages of outsourcing using the activity worksheet.
- Construct a list of job skills that will be useful for a particular profession.
- Distinguish between full employment and every worker being employed.

BEFORE CLASS

Students should read the section for homework.

Have students complete the graphic organizer in the Section Opener as they read the text. As an alternate activity, have students complete the Guided Reading and Review worksheet (Unit 5 All-in-One, p. 51).

L1 L2 ELL LPR Differentiate Have students complete the Guided Reading and Review worksheet (Unit 5 All-in-One, p. 52).

Focus on the Basics

Students need to come away with the following understandings:

FACTS: • There are four types of unemployment: frictional, structural, seasonal, and cyclical. Unemployment can also be caused by factors outside of the economy. • The government measures the rate of unemployment each month by surveying a representative sample of the population. • Full employment is defined as the level of employment that exists when there is no cyclical unemployment.

GENERALIZATION: Economists track unemployment to help them judge the health of the economy. The rate of unemployment will never be zero percent because frictional, structural, and seasonal unemployment will always exist.

CLASSROOM HINTS

TYPES OF UNEMPLOYMENT

Students may have trouble understanding the differences between types of unemployment (particularly cyclical and structural). Make sure that examples are clear and different. Students may also have problems understanding that full employment does not mean an unemployment rate of zero. Take time to explain this concept.

BELLRINGER

Write the following scenarios on the board:

- Marie lost her job as an accountant when her company hired an outside company to do her job.
- Vinita was laid off during the winter because the landscaping business for which she works only operates between March and October.
- Roberto quit his engineering job last year to look for a position teaching high school science.
- Justin lost his job at the local coffee shop when business began dropping off due to a recession.

Have students copy the names of the four people described in these scenarios. Have them match each name with frictional, structural, seasonal, or cyclical unemployment.

Teach

Economics online To present this topic using digital resources, use the lecture notes at www.PearsonSuccessNet.com.

L1 L2 ELL LPR Differentiate To help students who are struggling with comprehension, assign the Vocabulary worksheet (Unit 5 All-in-One, p. 50).

DISCUSS

Have a volunteer give the definition of *frictional unemployment.* Ask **Which person from the Bellringer activity is frictionally unemployed? Explain.** *(Roberto: he is in the process of looking for another job.)* **Can frictional unemployment be eliminated? Explain.** *(No. There will always be people looking for work.)* **How might a computerized national job bank or more affordable daycare reduce frictional unemployment?** *(Possible answer: by providing people with much more information about the jobs that are available or by providing parents with greater flexibility in accepting jobs)*

L1 L2 Differentiate As the class discusses the different types of unemployment, have students organize this information in a three-column chart. Label the columns *Type of Unemployment, Definition or Example,* and *Type of Intervention.*

L4 Differentiate Have students research and report on some other ways that have been proposed to reduce frictional unemployment.

How the Economy Works

How do workers deal with structural unemployment?

The United States has shifted from a manufacturing economy to a service economy. Many workers do not have the skills needed for jobs in the new technology-based industries. Structural unemployment occurs when workers' skills don't match the jobs that are available.

1

Reginald's position as an accounting manager was eliminated after the company upgraded to a new computer software program.

Jennifer's job was outsourced when the furniture manufacturer she worked for moved to another country.

Matthew's job as a landscaper was eliminated when the Parks Department's budget was cut.

2 **Reginald** contacts former associates and gets a couple of interviews.

Jennifer realizes that she needs to get training in another field.

Matthew searches online for a new job, but discovers that his high school education leaves him unqualified for many positions.

Structural Unemployment

- Hannah was not satisfied working as a nurse in a large hospital. Last month she left her job to look for a position at a small health clinic.
- Since Jorge graduated from law school three months ago, he has interviewed with various law firms to find the one that best suits his needs and interests.
- Liz left her sales job two years ago to care for an aging parent. Now she is trying to return to the workforce.

None of these three people found work immediately. While they look for work, they are frictionally unemployed. In the large, diverse U.S. economy, economists expect to find many people in this category.

structural unemployment type of unemployment that occurs when workers' skills do not match those needed for the jobs available

Unemployment insurance, which provides income to laid-off workers seeking new jobs, may contribute slightly to frictional unemployment. A worker receiving unemployment insurance faces somewhat less financial pressure to find a new job immediately.

Structural Unemployment

As you read in Chapter 9, the structure of the American economy has changed over time. Two centuries ago, people needed basic farming skills to survive. As the country developed an industrial economy, farm workers moved to urban areas to work in factories. Today, service industries are rapidly replacing manufacturing industries, and information services are expanding at breakneck speed.

All these shifts lead to upheavals in the labor market. When the structure of the economy changes, the skills that workers need to succeed also change. Workers who lack the necessary skills lose their jobs. **Structural unemployment** occurs when workers' skills do not match those needed for the jobs that are now available.

Differentiated Resources

- **L1 L2 Guided Reading and Review** (Unit 5 All-in-One, p. 52)
- **L1 L2 Vocabulary worksheet** (Unit 5 All-in-One, p. 50)
- **L2 Outsourcing** (Unit 5 All-in-One, p. 54)
- **L2 Compare Viewpoints skills worksheet** (Unit 5 All-in-One, p. 56)

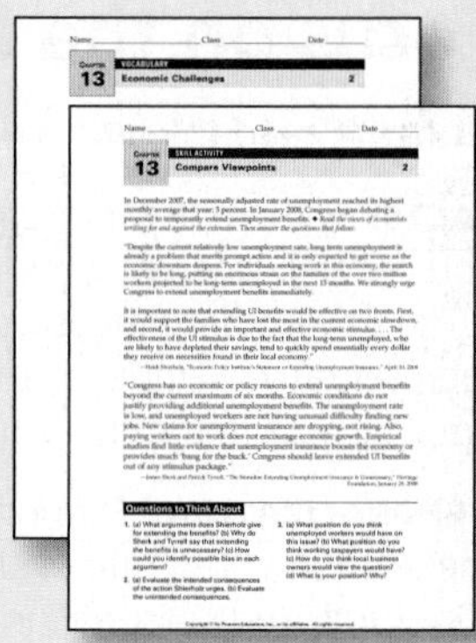

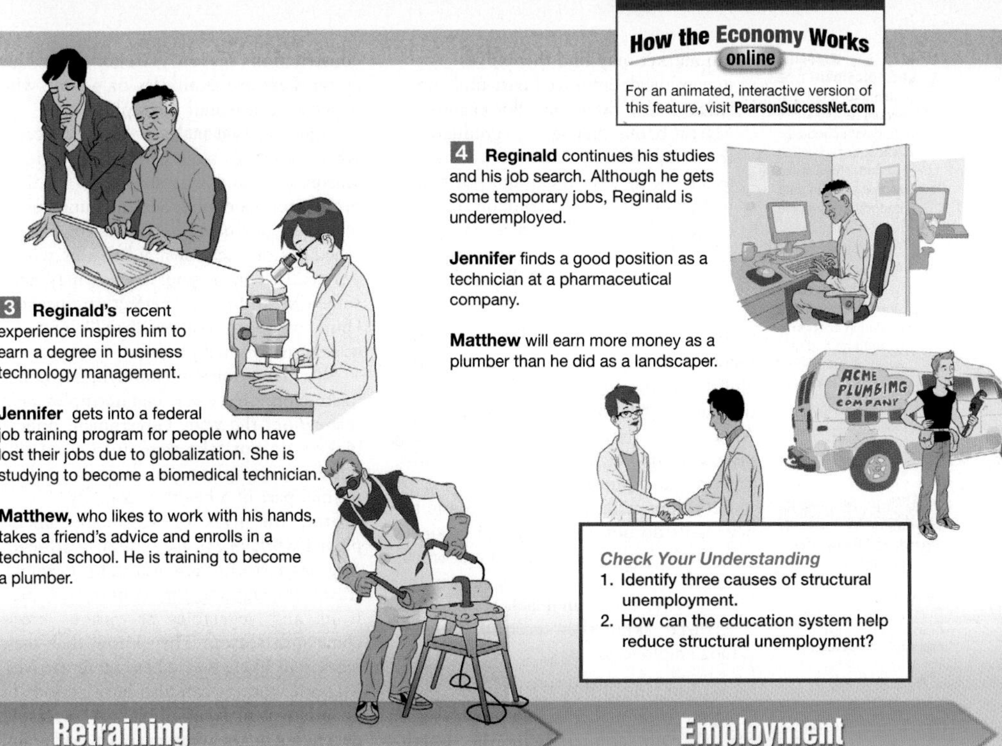

How the Economy Works
online
For an animated, interactive version of this feature, visit PearsonSuccessNet.com
3 Reginald's recent experience inspires him to earn a degree in business technology management.
Jennifer gets into a federal job training program for people who have lost their jobs due to globalization. She is studying to become a biomedical technician.
Matthew, who likes to work with his hands, takes a friend's advice and enrolls in a technical school. He is training to become a plumber.
4 Reginald continues his studies and his job search. Although he gets some temporary jobs, Reginald is underemployed.
Jennifer finds a good position as a technician at a pharmaceutical company.
Matthew will earn more money as a plumber than he did as a landscaper.
ACME PLUMBING COMPANY
Check Your Understanding
1. Identify three causes of structural unemployment.
2. How can the education system help reduce structural unemployment?
Retraining
Employment

There are five major causes of structural unemployment.

- *The development of new technology* New inventions and ideas often push out older ways of doing things. For example, downloading music has hurt the sales of compact discs. Firms making CDs have let workers go, and those workers must find jobs in another field.
- *The discovery of new resources* New resources replace old resources. The discovery of petroleum in Pennsylvania in 1859 severely hurt the whale-oil industry. Whaling ship crews lost their jobs and did not have the skills needed for the petroleum industry.
- *Changes in consumer demand* Consumers often stop buying one product in favor of another. Many people now favor athletic shoes over more traditional kinds of shoes. As a result, traditional shoemaking jobs have declined.
- *Globalization* The mobility of capital and labor has fueled a shift from local to international markets. Countries have become more open to foreign trade and investment in a trend called **globalization.** As a result, companies often relocate jobs or entire facilities to other countries where costs are lower. Celia, for example, spent many years working on an automobile assembly line in Michigan. When her company moved much of its auto assembly work to Mexico where labor is less expensive, Celia lost her job. Unfortunately, there were no local jobs that matched Celia's skills.
- *Lack of education* People who drop out of school or fail to acquire the minimum skills needed for today's

globalization the shift from local to global markets as countries seek foreign trade and investment

Background Note

Technology and Jobs Economists have long debated the net effect of new technology on jobs. In the 1820s, David Ricardo saw labor-saving technology as a threat to workers. He constructed an analytical model, with which he hoped to prove that "the discovery and use of machinery may be attended with a diminution of gross produce: and whenever that is the case, it will be injurious to the laboring class, as some of their number will be thrown out of employment." In the 1750s, though, economist Josiah Tucker had taken a different view of the results of adopting new technology: "What is the Consequence of this Abridgment of Labor, both regarding the Price of the Goods, and the Number of Persons employed? The Answer is very short and full, viz. That the Price of Goods is thereby prodigiously lowered from what otherwise it must have been; and that a much greater Number of Hands are employed."

DISTRIBUTE ACTIVITY WORKSHEET

Have a volunteer give the definition of *structural unemployment*. Discuss its causes. Ask **Which person in the Bellringer scenarios is structurally unemployed? Explain.** *(Marie: her work has been given to an outside company.)* Direct students' attention to the paragraph about globalization. Explain that the situation facing Celia is an example of *outsourcing*, the practice of obtaining goods or services from an outside supplier. Then distribute the "Exploring Outsourcing" worksheet (Unit 5 All-in-One, p. 53). Have students complete the worksheet, identifying the benefits and drawbacks of outsourcing.

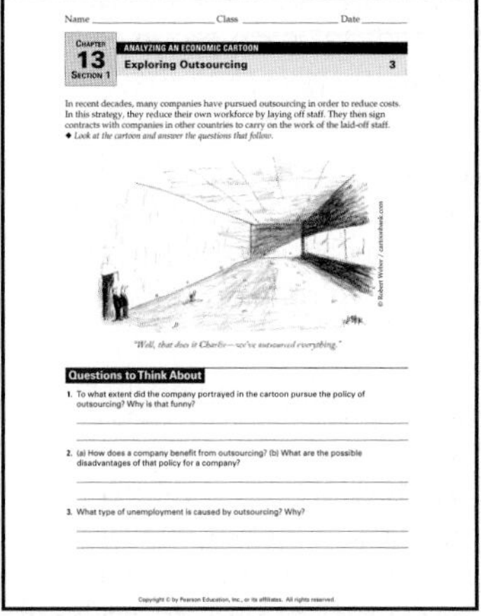
Name ______ Class ______ Date ______

CHAPTER 13 SECTION 1 — ANALYZING AN ECONOMIC CARTOON

Exploring Outsourcing 3

In recent decades, many companies have pursued outsourcing in order to reduce costs. In this strategy, they reduce their own workforce by laying off staff. They then sign contracts with companies in other countries to carry on the work of the laid-off staff.

◆ *Look at the cartoon and answer the questions that follow.*

© Robert Weber / cartoonbank.com

"Well, that does it Charlie—we've outsourced everything."

Questions to Think About

1. To what extent did the company portrayed in the cartoon pursue the policy of outsourcing? Why is that funny?
2. (a) How does a company benefit from outsourcing? (b) What are the possible disadvantages of that policy for a company?
3. What type of unemployment is caused by outsourcing? Why?

L2 Differentiate Distribute the "Outsourcing" worksheet (Unit 5 All-in-One, p. 54) Have students complete the worksheet.

After students have completed the worksheet, have volunteers read the How the Economy Works feature aloud. Ask **Who's job was outsourced?** *(Jennifer's)* After students answer the Check Your Understanding questions, ask **Why is it impossible to eliminate structural unemployment?** *(Its causes, such as changes in consumer demand and the development of new technology, are normal parts of the economy and cannot be stopped.)* **How might the government and businesses reduce structural unemployment? Explain.** *(Possible responses: government—provide incentives to businesses that help employees update skills or job training for the structurally unemployed; businesses—provide training to displaced workers)*

Answers

Check Your Understanding 1. Possible response: development of new technology; changes in consumer demand; globalization 2. help provide students with the skills they will need to compete

CONNECT

Direct students' attention to the discussion of Martin's employment situation, found on pp. 337-338 of the text under the heading *Lack of education.* Call on students with work experience to give examples of on-the-job training that they received. Ask **What training did you receive for this job?** *(Answers will vary.)* **What skills did you bring to the job?** *(Possible responses: computer skills; being responsible)* **What skills did you learn that you can use elsewhere?** *(Possible responses: how to use a cash register; how to work with groups of children)*

Form the class into small groups of four or five. Have one person in the group identify a profession in which they are interested. Tell each group to brainstorm a list of skills that a person in that profession would need. Challenge the groups to identify ways they might best gain those skills: through formal schooling, technical training, or on-the-job training. Remind students to consider transferable skills, ones that would apply to other careers in case of job loss.

Have the groups present their ideas and discuss them as a class.

L4 Differentiate Give students this statement: "The most important job skill in the future will be the ability to ..." Have them research which jobs the U.S. Bureau of Labor Statistics predicts will be in demand and explain their answers to the class.

DESCRIBE

Have volunteers define and give examples of *seasonal unemployment.* Ask **Which person in the Bellringer scenarios is seasonally unemployed? Explain.** *(Vinita: Landscaping businesses in colder climates shut down during the winter.)* Point out that high school and college students seeking summer jobs are considered seasonally unemployed until they find work. Have volunteers describe strategies they have used to find summer work.

PERSONAL FINANCE ACTIVITY

To teach students about getting a job, you may want to use the Personal Finance Handbook lesson on page PF42, and assign the activity worksheet (Personal Finance All-in-One, p. 103).

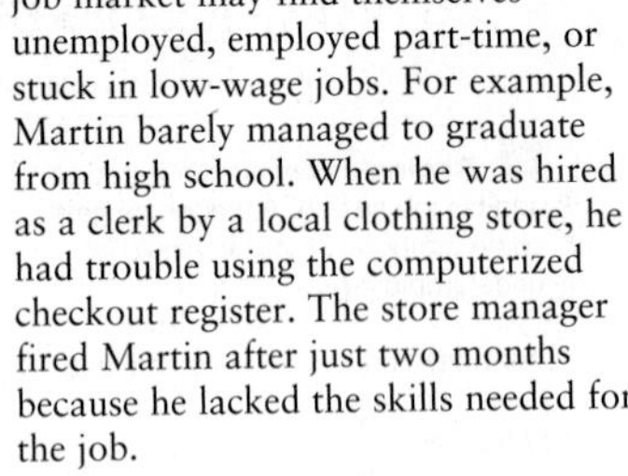

seasonal unemployment type of unemployment that occurs as a result of harvest schedules, vacations, or when industries make seasonal shifts in their production schedule

cyclical unemployment unemployment that rises during economic downturns and falls when the economy improves

job market may find themselves unemployed, employed part-time, or stuck in low-wage jobs. For example, Martin barely managed to graduate from high school. When he was hired as a clerk by a local clothing store, he had trouble using the computerized checkout register. The store manager fired Martin after just two months because he lacked the skills needed for the job.

Policymakers in the 1990s and 2000s recognized that computer technology, globalization, and other structural changes threatened the futures of many workers. As a result, they developed job-training programs to help workers gain new skills, especially computer skills.

Retraining takes time, however, and the new skills do not ensure that the trainees will obtain high-wage jobs. Some companies offer their own training programs. In this way, they can teach trainees the specialized skills they need to become valued employees.

FUTURE WATCH
Personal Finance
For more about how to find a job, see your Personal Finance Handbook in the back of the book or visit **PearsonSuccessNet.com**

Seasonal Unemployment

Gregory is a brick mason for a small construction company in the northeastern United States. Every winter Gregory's employer lays off all seven of his employees when cold weather forces an end to outdoor work. In the spring, he hires them back again for the new construction season. Gregory and his co-workers are examples of people who experience seasonal unemployment.

In general, **seasonal unemployment** occurs when industries slow or shut down for a season or make seasonal shifts in their production schedules. Seasonal unemployment can also occur as a result of harvest schedules or vacations. When this school year ends, you or your friends may need some time to find the perfect summer job. Until you do so, economists will count you as seasonally unemployed.

As with frictional unemployment, economists expect to see seasonal unemployment throughout the year. Government policymakers do not take steps to prevent this kind of unemployment, because it is a normal part of a healthy economy.

Still, the lives of seasonally unemployed workers can be extremely difficult. Migrant agricultural workers, for example, travel throughout the country to pick fruits and vegetables as various crops come into season. They know that their work will likely end when winter arrives. Migrant workers can also have periods of unemployment even during harvest season, depending on the weather. Heat, cold, rain, and drought can ruin harvest schedules by causing fruits and vegetables to ripen sooner or later than expected. Instead of moving smoothly from crop to crop, migrant workers might lose work time waiting for a crop to be ready for picking.

Migrant farm workers face seasonal unemployment once the harvest season is over. ▼

Cyclical Unemployment

Unemployment that rises during economic downturns and falls when the economy improves is called **cyclical unemployment.** During recessions, or downturns in the business cycle, the demand for goods and services drops. The resulting slowdown in production causes the demand for labor to drop as well, and companies begin to lay off employees. Many of these laid-off employees will be rehired when the recession ends and the business cycle resumes an upward trend. Although economists expect cyclical unemployment, it can severely strain the economy and greatly distress the unemployed.

The most damaging example of cyclical unemployment in the twentieth century was

Background Note

Future Prospects The *Occupational Outlook Handbook*, published by the Bureau of Labor Statistics every two years, gives detailed information about hundreds of careers. Among the useful data included is a projection of each career's expected growth in the future. Students can use this resource to identify careers that both interest them and are likely to need more workers in the future.

the Great Depression. During the Great Depression, one out of every four workers was unemployed. Many remained jobless for years. In 1935, President Franklin D. Roosevelt proposed, and Congress passed, the Social Security Act. In addition to providing monthly payments for retirees and people who could not support themselves, the Social Security Act established a program of unemployment insurance.

Today, unemployment insurance still provides weekly payments to workers who have lost their jobs. The payments usually provide about half of a worker's lost wages each week for a limited amount of time.

Factors Outside the Economy

Sometimes events outside the economy can cause unemployment. The September 11, 2001, terrorist attacks on the World Trade Center and the Pentagon cost the country an estimated 1.5 to 2 million jobs. Many of the lost jobs were in the travel and tourism industries. About 20 percent of the lost jobs were in the airline industry. In Manhattan, the area around the World Trade Center site was especially hard-hit, and New York City lost some 150,000 jobs.

Natural disasters also affect employment. In October 2005, Hurricane Katrina slammed into the Gulf Coast region. The powerful storm caused widespread destruction and thousands of people lost their jobs. Many families were relocated to other areas while their communities were being rebuilt. Months later, unemployment among people affected by Hurricane Katrina was still higher than the national average.

CHECKPOINT ***Why are policymakers less concerned about frictional and seasonal unemployment?***

Figure 13.1 Calculating the Unemployment Rate

To calculate the unemployment rate, use the following formula:

Number of people unemployed divided by number of people in the civilian labor force multiplied by 100

For example,

if the number of people unemployed = 7 million and the number of people in the civilian labor force = 151.4 million

then,

7 ÷ 151.4 = .046

.046 x 100 = 4.6

Therefore,

the unemployment rate is 4.6%

SOURCE: Bureau of Labor Statistics

CHART SKILLS

To calculate the unemployment rate, follow the steps in the chart.

1. In May 2008, the civilian labor force was 154.5 million and 8.5 million were unemployed. What was the unemployment rate?
2. Does the unemployment rate accurately reflect the number of people who are unemployed? Why or why not?

Measuring Employment

The amount of unemployment in the nation is an important clue to the health of the economy. For this reason, the government keeps careful track of how many people are unemployed, and why.

To measure employment, the United States Bureau of the Census conducts a monthly household survey for the Bureau of Labor Statistics (BLS). For this survey, called the Current Population Survey, interviewers poll 60,000 families about employment during that month. This sample is designed to represent the entire population of the United States. The BLS, a branch of the U.S. Department of Labor, analyzes the data from the survey to identify how many people are employed and how many are unemployed. Using these numbers, the BLS computes the **unemployment rate,** or the percentage of the nation's labor force that is unemployed.

Determining the Unemployment Rate

As you read in Chapter 9, the labor force is composed of civilians age 16 and older who have a job or are actively looking for a job. To determine the unemployment rate, BLS officials add up the number of employed and unemployed people. That figure equals the total labor force. Then they divide the number of unemployed people by the total labor force and multiply by 100. As Figure 13.1 shows, the result is the percentage of people who are unemployed.

For example, in September 2007, the Current Population Survey showed that 146.3 million people were employed, and 7.2 million were unemployed. The total labor force, therefore, was 153.5 million. Dividing 7.2 million by 153.5 million, and then multiplying the result by 100, yields

unemployment rate the percentage of the nation's labor force that is unemployed

DISCUSS

Have a volunteer define *cyclical unemployment.* Ask **Which person in the Bellringer scenarios is cyclically unemployed? Explain.** *(Justin: job lost due to a recession-related drop in business)* **What causes this type of unemployment?** *(changes in the business cycle: unemployment goes up during contractions and down during expansions)* **What factors can reduce cyclical unemployment?** *(capital deepening; increased saving and investing; government spending on public goods; importing capital goods)*

COMPARE VIEWPOINTS

The federal and state governments together provide unemployment insurance for up to 26 weeks for unemployed workers. During some economic downturns, Congress temporarily extends benefits. Economists disagree over the wisdom of that action. Have students complete the "Compare Viewpoints" skill worksheet (Unit 5 All-in-One, p. 55). Tell students to review the lesson in the Social Studies Skills Handbook on page S-11. Remind them to use the steps of the lesson to complete the activity.

L2 Differentiate Distribute the "Compare Viewpoints" skills worksheet (Unit 5 All-in-One, p. 56) Read the two viewpoints and have students work in pairs to answer the questions.

Use the Opinion Line strategy (p. T28) to invite all students to give and explain their position on the question of extending unemployment benefits in 2008.

L4 Differentiate Have students research the organizations whose viewpoints were presented in the worksheet and the outcome of the debate. Have them present this information to the class.

CALCULATE

Refer to Figure 13.1. Have volunteers explain how to calculate the rate of unemployment.

L1 L2 Differentiate Work through the calculation in Figure 13.1 with students. Then help students work through the first question.

Virtual Economics

L1 L2 Differentiate

Exploring the Role of Government

Use the following lesson from the NCEE **Virtual Economics *CD-ROM*** to examine how government can affect unemployment. Click on Browse Economics Lessons, specify grades 9–12, and use the key words *what can the government.*

In this activity, students will classify types of unemployment and investigate various government policies.

LESSON TITLE	WHAT CAN THE GOVERNMENT DO ABOUT UNEMPLOYMENT?
Type of Activity	Classifying
Complexity	Low
Time	50 minutes
NCEE Standards	18, 19, 20

Answers

Checkpoint They are expected to exist in a healthy economy.

Chart Skills 1. 5.5 percent 2. No. It does not include people who have stopped looking for work.

DISPLAY TRANSPARENCY

Display the "Seasonally Adjusted Unemployment Rate by State, June 2008" transparency (Color Transparencies, 13.a). Ask **What was the national unemployment rate in June 2008?** *(5.5 percent)* Have students consider what economic conditions may be causing the state unemployment rate to differ.

CHECK COMPREHENSION

Write the following on the board: **UNEMPLOYMENT IS OVER! EVERYONE HAS A JOB!** Ask **Is this situation what economists mean by *full employment*?** *(No,* full employment *refers to the situation when the economy is expanding and cyclical unemployment does not exist.)* **What is the difference between full employment and everybody having a job?** *(At full employment, unemployment is at a normal level of 4 to 6 percent. Frictional, structural, and seasonal unemployment still exist.)* Have students describe the two categories of workers not represented in the unemployment rate.

EXTEND

Have students compare the latest monthly unemployment rate for their city or town to the state and national average for the same time period. If it is lower or higher, have students analyze why.

GUIDING QUESTION WRAP UP

Have students return to the section Guiding Question. Review the completed graphic organizer and clarify any misunderstandings. Have a wrap up discussion about the causes of unemployment.

Assess and Remediate

L3 **L2** Collect the "Exploring Outsourcing" worksheets and the "Outsourcing" worksheets and assess student understanding of the impact of outsourcing.

L3 Assign the Section 1 Assessment questions; identify student misconceptions.

L3 Give Section Quiz A (Unit 5 All-in-One, p. 57).

L2 Give Section Quiz B (Unit 5 All-in-One, p. 58).

(Assess and Remediate continued on p. 341)

Answers

Critical Thinking To remain profitable, companies must always prepare employees to adapt to new economic conditions and use new technology.

Checkpoint Divide the number of unemployed people by the total labor force and multiply by 100.

Innovators

Janice Bryant Howroyd

ACT•1 GROUP

"Never compromise who you are personally to become who you wish to be professionally."

Careers are all about making a commitment. In 1978, Janice Bryant Howroyd rented a small office in Beverly Hills and launched ACT•1 Personnel Services, an employment services agency. From the outset, her focus was on providing employers with qualified employees and developing long-term business relationships.

Howroyd did not advertise. Instead, she relied on the WOMB method. WOMB means "Word of Mouth, Brother!" Her strategy was successful: today, the company is approaching $1 billion in annual revenue.

Initially, Howroyd focused on the entertainment field. But soon her business expanded to include the technical, clerical, engineering, and accounting industries. Loyal clients include General Mills, DuPont, and Wachovia.

Howroyd's once small company has grown. The ACT•1 Group of companies includes Agile•1, which uses talent procurement software and workforce planning to help businesses meet their staffing needs.

Equally important is her emphasis on skills. Howroyd owns a continuing-education school. She wants to supply clients with employees who have basic academic skills, as well as higher-order thinking skills such as problem solving and decision making.

It's no surprise that ACT•1's motto is "pride in performance."

Critical Thinking: ***Employers want to hire lifelong learners. Why is there an emphasis on continuing education for employees?***

Fast Facts

Janice Bryant Howroyd
Born: Sept. 1, 1952, in Tarboro, NC
Education: University of Maryland, North Carolina State University
Claim to Fame: Founder, CEO, of ACT•1 Personnel Services

an unemployment rate of 4.7 percent for that month.

Adjusting the Unemployment Rate

When you see the unemployment rate for a particular month, it has usually been "seasonally adjusted." This means that the rate has been increased or decreased to take into account the level of seasonal unemployment. Taking this step allows economists to more accurately compare unemployment rates from month to month. This comparison helps them better detect changing economic conditions.

The unemployment rate is only an average for the nation. It does not reflect regional differences. Some areas, such as the coal-mining region of Appalachia in the southeastern United States, have long had a higher-than-average unemployment rate. The BLS and individual state agencies therefore establish unemployment rates for states and other geographic areas. These rates help pinpoint trouble areas on which policymakers can focus attention.

full employment the level of employment reached when there is no cyclical unemployment

underemployed working at a job for which one is over-qualified or working part-time when full-time work is desired

CHECKPOINT ***How is the unemployment rate calculated?***

Full Employment

Look at **Figure 13.2.** Notice the low levels of unemployment in the late 1960s and late 1990s. As you read earlier, zero unemployment is not an achievable goal in a market economy, even under the best of circumstances. Economists generally agree that in an economy that is working properly, an unemployment rate of around 4 to 6 percent is normal. Such an economy would still experience frictional, seasonal, and structural unemployment. In other words, **full employment** is the level of employment reached when no cyclical unemployment exists.

Underemployment

Full employment means that nearly everyone who wants a job has a job. But are all those people satisfied with their jobs? Not necessarily. Some people working at low-skill, low-wage jobs may be highly skilled or educated in a field with few opportunities. They are **underemployed,** that is, working at a job for which they are over-qualified, or working part-time when they desire full-time work.

For example, Jim, a philosophy major, earned a graduate degree in philosophy. When he left school, Jim found that although the economy was booming, he could not find jobs in which he could apply his knowledge of philosophy. Jim found a part-time job that did not pay well and did not challenge his mind. He was underemployed.

So was Celia, the auto worker described earlier. After her company sent her auto-assembly job to Mexico, she could not find a similar job locally. She was forced to take a low-skill, low-wage job.

Underemployment also describes the situation of people who want a permanent, full-time job but have not been able to find one. Many part-time workers and seasonal workers fit into this category.

Discouraged Workers

Some people, especially during a long recession, give up hope of finding work. These **discouraged workers** have stopped searching for employment and may rely on other family members or savings to support them. Although they are without jobs, discouraged workers do not appear in the unemployment rate determined by the Bureau of Labor Statistics because they are not actively looking for work.

discouraged worker someone who wants a job but has given up looking

CHECKPOINT ***What kinds of unemployment are present even in a healthy economy?***

Figure 13.2 Unemployment Rate, 1968–2006

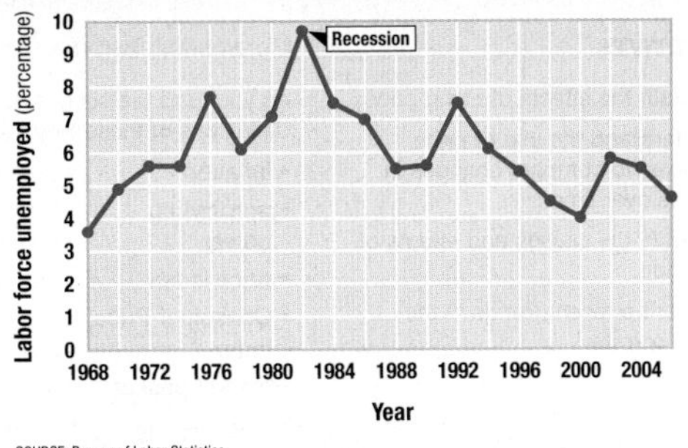

SOURCE: Bureau of Labor Statistics

GRAPH SKILLS

The unemployment rate reached a 40-year peak in 1982.

1. In what years was the unemployment rate between 4 and 6 percent, the rate considered normal for a healthy economy?
2. Why does a high unemployment rate correspond with a recession?

Essential Questions Journal To continue to build a response to the Essential Question, go to your **Essential Questions Journal**.

SECTION 1 ASSESSMENT

Guiding Question

1. Use your completed concept web to answer this question: What are the causes of unemployment?
2. **Extension** Suppose that you are unemployed and looking for work. You are a good worker, but it is taking you longer than expected to find a job. What might be making your search so difficult?

Key Terms and Main Ideas

3. What are some factors that affect **seasonal unemployment?**
4. When does **cyclical unemployment** take place?
5. What is **globalization?**
6. How does the Bureau of Labor Statistics determine the **unemployment rate?**
7. Why isn't **full employment** the same as zero unemployment?

Critical Thinking

8. **Contrast (a)** What are frictional unemployment and structural unemployment? **(b)** Give an example of each. **(c)** In what ways are frictional unemployment and structural unemployment different?
9. **Apply** After a car accident, Santo needed six months to recover. Since his recovery, he has spent the last year trying to find work in his former occupation, medical technology. So far, he has not found a position, even though the economy is booming. Which of the four kinds of unemployment best describes Santo's situation? Explain.
10. **Calculate (a)** What is the formula for calculating the unemployment rate? **(b)** Determine the unemployment rate for a month in which 125.4 million people were employed and 7.3 million people were unemployed.

Quick Write

11. A recent magazine article listed the jobs of the future along with the jobs that won't exist in twenty years. One promising career is computer software engineer. However, there will be little need for film processors in the future. Write a paragraph on each occupation. Suggest reasons why there will be a greater need for computer software engineers and less need for film processors.

Have students complete the Self-Test Online and continue their work in the **Essential Questions Journal**.

REMEDIATION AND SUGGESTIONS

Use the chart below to help students who are struggling with content.

WEAKNESS	REMEDIATION
Identifying key terms (Questions 3, 4, 5, 6, 7)	Have students use the interactive Economic Dictionary Online.
Understanding types of unemployment (Questions 3, 4, 8, 9)	Reteach using How the Economy Works.
Calculating unemployment rates (Question 6 and 10)	Reteach using Figure 13.1 and easier numbers, e.g., 200 people in labor force with 20 unemployed.
Considering full employment (Questions 7, 11)	Have students review types of unemployment that exist during full unemployment, and describe underemployed and discouraged workers.

Answers

Graph Skills 1. 1970–1974, 1988–1990, 1996–2006 2. During recessions, demand for goods and services drops. The resulting slowdown in production causes the demand for labor to drop.

Checkpoint frictional, seasonal, and structural unemployment

Assessment Answers

1. Frictional: people change jobs; cyclical: problems with economy; seasonal: dropping seasonal demand; structural: skills don't match jobs; factors outside economy **2.** If the economy is not doing well, it will take longer to find work. **3.** weather, harvest schedules, vacations **4.** during a recession **5.** companies more open to trade, investment around world **6.** surveys a sample of the population every month, calculates the percentage of the total labor force unemployed **7.** Zero unemployment means a job for every person. **8.** (a) frictional—when people take time to find new jobs; structural—when workers' skills don't match those needed (b) Possible examples: frictional—person who turns down job that would require move; structural—steelworkers who do not have skills for computer operator jobs (c) Frictional: individual decisions; structural: changing technology or conditions **9.** frictional, because Santo is taking longer than expected to find a new job **10.** (a) number of unemployed people divided by total labor force and convert the decimal to a percent (b) 5.5% **11.** Demand for software engineers will grow as we use computers more. Demand for film processors will drop as more and more people use digital cameras.

Guiding Question

What are the causes and effects of inflation?

Get Started

Inflation	
Causes	**Effects**
• Growth of the money supply • Changes in aggregate demand, as during wartime • Changes in aggregate supply, as firms respond to higher costs by increasing prices	• Decreases purchasing power • Does not erode income if wages rise at same rate; hurts individuals on fixed income • Lowers purchasing power of interest on savings

LESSON GOALS

Students will:

- Know the Key Terms.
- Analyze an example of reduced purchasing power.
- Analyze changes in the Consumer Price Index in recent years and compare with the inflation rate.
- Describe how changes in money supply, aggregate demand, or aggregate supply cause inflation.

BEFORE CLASS

Students should read the section for homework.

Have students complete the graphic organizer in the Section Opener as they read the text. As an alternate activity, have students complete the Guided Reading and Review worksheet (Unit 5 All-in-One, p. 59).

L1 L2 ELL LPR Differentiate Have students complete the Guided Reading and Review worksheet (Unit 5 All-in-One, p. 60).

Answer

Checkpoint because prices in general increase

SECTION 2 Inflation

OBJECTIVES

1. **Explain** the effects of rising prices.
2. **Understand** the use of price indexes to compare changes in prices over time.
3. **Identify** the causes and effects of inflation.
4. **Describe** recent trends in the inflation rate.

ECONOMIC DICTIONARY

As you read the section, look for the definitions of these **Key Terms:**

- inflation
- purchasing power
- price index
- Consumer Price Index
- market basket
- inflation rate
- core inflation rate
- hyperinflation
- quantity theory
- wage-price spiral
- fixed income
- deflation

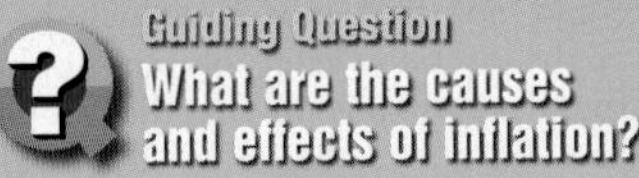

Guiding Question
What are the causes and effects of inflation?

Copy this chart and fill it in as you read to explain the causes and effects of inflation.

Inflation	
Causes	**Effects**
• Growth of the money supply • Changes in aggregate demand, as during wartime •	• Decreases purchasing power • •

inflation a general increase in prices across an economy

purchasing power the ability to purchase goods and services

Economics and You

At first, the changes are hardly noticeable. You pay more for lunch at your favorite eatery. Your personal grooming products are more expensive. Clothing prices are higher. A ticket for the movies costs two dollars more. You realize that as a result of these steady price increases, your money doesn't buy as much as it did just a few months ago.

Principles in Action As you will see, you cannot escape rising prices. Economists believe that the money supply, changes in demand, and increased production costs all contribute to a rise in prices throughout the economy. This section's Economics & You shows how higher prices can affect your life.

The Effects of Rising Prices

Josephine and Jack Barrow have owned the same house for 50 years. Recently, they had a real estate agent estimate their home's present market value. The Barrows were astounded. The house that they had bought for $12,000 was now worth nearly $150,000—a rise in value of more than 1,100 percent.

How could the value of a house, or anything else, increase so much? The main reason is inflation. **Inflation** is a general increase in prices across an economy. Over the years, prices generally go up. Since World War II, real estate prices have risen greatly.

The Barrows were pleased that they could get so much money for their house. Then they realized that inflation had raised the prices of all houses, just as it had also raised wages and the prices of most other goods and services. As a result, they could not buy a similar house in their area for $12,000 or even $120,000.

Another way to look at the Barrows' situation is that inflation had shrunk the value, or purchasing power, of the Barrows' money. **Purchasing power** is the ability to purchase goods and services. As prices rise, the purchasing power of money declines. That is why $12,000 buys much less now than it did 50 years ago.

CHECKPOINT ***Why does purchasing power decrease over time?***

Food Prices*

	March 1996	March 2008
Bread, white (per lb.)	0.85	1.35
Eggs, large (per dozen)	1.14	2.20
Milk, whole (per gallon)	2.54	3.78

* U.S. City average
Source: Bureau of Labor Statistics

▲ The effects of inflation over the years can be seen in this comparison of prices for basic food items.

CLASSROOM HINTS

A GENERAL INCREASE IN PRICES

As students consider specific examples (in the Bellringer and the Visual Glossary, for example) of the loss of purchasing power due to inflation, students may begin to think of inflation as an increase in the price of a particular good or category of good. Remind them that inflation is a *general* increase in prices, which is reflected in higher prices for specific goods and services.

Focus on the Basics

Students need to come away with the following understandings:

FACTS: • Over the years, the prices of goods and services have generally gone up.
• The government uses price indexes to measure changes in prices from year to year.
• Economists have several theories about the causes of inflation relating to growth of the money supply, changes in aggregate demand, and changes in aggregate supply.
• Inflation affects purchasing power, income, and personal savings.

GENERALIZATION: Inflation, a general increase in prices across the economy, affects purchasing power, income, and saving. Economists have several theories about the causes of inflation. The government uses price indexes to measure inflation.

Price Indexes

Housing costs are just one element that economists consider when they study inflation. The economy has thousands of goods and services, with millions of individual prices. How do economists compare the changes in all these prices in order to measure inflation? The answer is that they do not compare individual prices; instead, they compare price levels. As you read in Chapter 12, price level is the cost of goods and services in the entire economy at a given point in time.

To help them calculate price level, economists use a price index. A **price index** is a measurement that shows how the average price of a standard group of goods changes over time. A price index produces an average that economists compare to earlier averages to see how much prices have changed over time.

Using Price Indexes

Price indexes help consumers and businesspeople make economic decisions. For example, after Marina read in the newspaper that prices for consumer goods had been rising, she increased the amount of money she was saving for a new car. She wanted to be sure that when the time came to buy the car, she had saved enough money to pay for it.

The government also uses indexes in making policy decisions. A member of Congress, for example, might push for an increase in the minimum wage if she thinks inflation has reduced purchasing power.

The Consumer Price Index

Although there are several price indexes, the best-known index focuses on consumers. The **Consumer Price Index** (CPI) is computed each month by the Bureau of Labor Statistics (BLS). The CPI is determined by measuring the price of a standard group of goods meant to represent the "market basket" of a typical urban consumer. This **market basket** is a representative collection of goods and services. By looking at the CPI, consumers, businesses, and the government can compare the cost of a group of goods this month with what the same or a similar group cost months or even years ago.

Figure 13.3 CPI Market Basket Items

Category	Examples
Food and Drinks	cereals, coffee, chicken, milk, restaurant meals
Housing	rent, homeowners' costs, fuel oil
Apparel and upkeep	men's shirts, women's dresses, jewelry
Transportation	airfares, new and used cars, gasoline, auto insurance
Medical care	prescription medicines, eye care, physician's services
Entertainment	newspapers, toys, musical instruments
Education and communication	tuition, postage, telephone services, computers
Other goods and services	haircuts, cosmetics, bank fees

SOURCE: Bureau of Labor Statistics

CHART SKILLS

The CPI market basket helps economists calculate the average inflation rate for the country.

1. Why might an individual family experience an inflation rate that is higher or lower than the national average?
2. Which categories of market basket items are currently experiencing sharp price increases?

As you can see from **Figure 13.3**, the CPI market basket is divided into eight categories of goods and services. These categories and a few examples of the many items in each group are shown above.

About every 10 years, the items in the market basket are updated to account for shifting consumer buying habits. The BLS determines how the market basket should change by conducting a Consumer Expenditure Survey. The BLS conducted one such survey from 2000 to 2001, collecting spending information from 10,000 families. Another 7,500 families kept diaries, noting everything they purchased during a two-week period for both years. This process resulted in the list of market basket items used today.

Price Indexes and the Inflation Rate

Economists also find it useful to calculate the **inflation rate**—the percentage rate of change in price level over time. (To learn how to calculate the inflation rate, go to page 358.) Since the CPI is the most familiar price index, we will focus on it. How does the BLS determine the CPI and use it to calculate the inflation rate?

price index a measurement that shows how the average price of a standard group of goods changes over time

Consumer Price Index a price index determined by measuring the price of a standard group of goods meant to represent the "market basket" of a typical urban consumer

market basket a representative collection of goods and services

inflation rate the percentage rate of change in price level over time

BELLRINGER

Write the following on the board.

LAST YEAR:

TACO SPECIAL: Six four-ounce tacos for $4.00

THIS YEAR:

A. TACO SPECIAL: Six four-ounce tacos for $5.00

B. TACO SPECIAL: Four four-ounce tacos for $4.00

C. TACO SPECIAL: Six three-ounce tacos for $4.00

Answer these questions in your notebooks: **Why are A, B, and C all examples of reduced purchasing power? Why might the restaurant have increased its prices? How will this price increase affect you?**

Teach

Economics online To present this topic using digital resources, use the lecture notes at www.PearsonSuccessNet.com.

DEFINE

Define *purchasing power.* Elicit from students the fact that their purchasing power has been reduced in A, by an increase in price; in B, by a decrease in quantity; in C, by a decrease in size or quality. Ask **How much of a taco could you buy with $1 last year?** *(1.5)* **How much of a taco can you buy with $1 now under A?** *(1.2)* **Under B?** *(1.0)* Note that, even though the price rises under A and stays the same under B, B represents a larger decline in purchasing power. If the economy is currently experiencing inflation, ask **What examples of rising prices have you seen?** *(Possible responses: gas prices, prices for their favorite meals)*

VISUAL GLOSSARY

Have students look at the chart on the Visual Glossary. Have students explain what happened to purchasing power between 1985 and 2005.

L1 L2 Differentiate Use the lesson on the Visual Glossary page to review this term. As an alternate, direct students to the Visual Glossary Online to reinforce their understanding of inflation.

(lesson continued on p. 345)

Differentiated Resources

- **L1 L2 Guided Reading and Review** (Unit 5 All-in-One, p. 60)
- **L4 Analyzing Hyperinflation** (Unit 5 All-in-One, p. 61)
- **L2 Comparing the Impact of Inflation** (Unit 5 All-in-One, p. 63)
- **L3 Creating a Teenage Consumer Price Index** (Simulation Activities, Chapter 13)

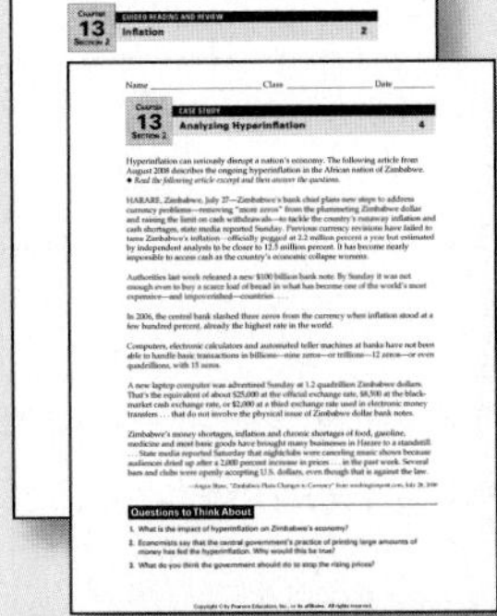

Answers

Chart Skills 1. Possible answer: They spend a large amount of money on items whose prices are rising respectively faster or slower than the rate of inflation. 2. Possible answers: food, transportation, medicine

Teach Visual Glossary

REVIEW KEY TERMS

Read each key term and call on students to define the term. Have students describe the relationship between each of the other terms and *inflation*.

business cycle – *a period of macroeconomic expansion, or growth, followed by one of contraction, or decline*

inflation – *a general increase in prices across the economy*

purchasing power – *the ability to purchase goods and services*

price index – *a measurement that shows how the average price of a standard group of goods changes over time*

inflation rate – *the percentage rate of change in price level over time*

COMPARE

Point out that the chart provides three examples of how inflation has affected prices in general. Ask **What has happened to the purchasing power of the dollar between 1985 and 2005? Explain.** *(It has gone down; it buys less in 2005 than it did in 1985.)*

L4 Differentiate Have students research information needed to complete the chart for this year. Have them present this information to the class.

Economics online *All print resources are available on the Teacher's Resource Library CD-ROM and online at* www.PearsonSuccessNet.com.

Answers

Caption Increased costs for operating stadium or theater (lease, taxes, utilities); increased costs for leasing a movie, producing a concert, or hosting a game; higher wages for performers and athletes

Cartoon Possible responses: Consumers may spend less; an increase in wages might cause prices to rise, since companies will face higher costs.

VISUAL GLOSSARY

Reviewing Key Terms
To understand *inflation*, review these terms:

business cycle, *p. 57*
inflation, *p. 342*
purchasing power, *p. 342*
price index, *p. 343*
inflation rate, *p. 343*

What is Inflation?

◀ **inflation** a general rise in prices across an economy

The Effects of Inflation on Entertainment

	1985	1995	2005
Average Price of a Ticket for a Major League Baseball Game	$10.14	$10.65	$21.17
Average Price of a Movie Theater Ticket	$3.55	$4.35	$6.41
Average Price for a Top 25 Concert Ticket	$15.31	$25.40	$56.88

SOURCE: EH. Net Encyclopedia; www.teammarketing.com; National Association of Theatre Owners; www.msnbc.msn.com

Inflation has driven up the price you pay for admission to different kinds of entertainment. ***What inputs may have contributed to higher ticket prices for these events?***

◀ In this cartoon, inflation has caused the cost of living to skyrocket while wages remain the same. ***How will consumers react to an increase in the cost of goods and services? How might an increase in wages affect prices?***

Visual Glossary online
To expand your understanding of this and other key economic terms, visit **PearsonSuccessNet.com**

Determining the CPI

To determine the CPI, the BLS establishes a base period to which it can compare current prices. Currently, the base period is 1982–1984. The cost of the market basket for that period is assigned the index number 100. Every month, BLS representatives update the cost of the same market basket of goods and services by rechecking all the prices. Each updated cost is compared with the base-period cost to determine the index for that month. As costs rise, the index rises.

The BLS determines the CPI for a given year using the following formula.

$$\text{CPI} = \frac{\text{updated cost}}{\text{base period cost}} \times 100$$

For example, suppose the market basket cost $200 during the base period and costs $360 today. The CPI for today would be:

$$\frac{\$360}{\$200} \times 100 = 180$$

In this example, the CPI rose from 100 in the base period to 180 today.

Types of Inflation

Inflation rates in the United States have changed greatly over time. When the inflation rate stays low—between 1 and 3 percent—it does not typically cause problems for the economy. In this environment, businesses and governments can make plans. When the inflation rate exceeds 5 percent, however, the inflation rate itself becomes unstable and unpredictable. This makes planning very difficult.

As you can see in **Figure 13.4**, the inflation rate sometimes spikes sharply, as in 1974 and 1980. These sharp increases in the inflation rate were due in part to increases in prices in world food and oil markets. In order to study long-term trends in the inflation rate, analysts need to set aside temporary spikes in food and fuel prices. To do this, economists have developed the concept of a core inflation rate. The **core inflation rate** is the rate of inflation excluding the effects of food and energy prices.

By far the worst kind of inflation is **hyperinflation,** or inflation that is out of control. During periods of hyperinflation, inflation rates can go as high as 100 or even 500 percent per month, and money loses much of its value. This level of inflation is rare, but when it occurs it often leads to a total economic collapse.

CHECKPOINT ***How do economists calculate the CPI?***

Figure 13.4 Inflation Rate, 1970–2006

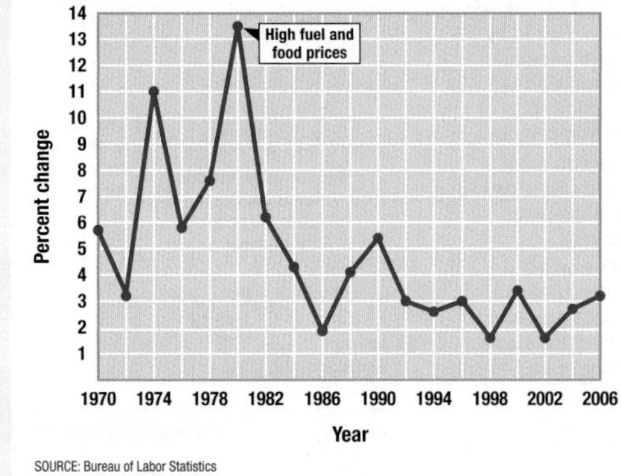

SOURCE: Bureau of Labor Statistics

GRAPH SKILLS

Sharp inflation rate increases in 1974 and 1980 were due in part to increases in food and oil prices. An inflation rate of 1 to 3 percent does not typically cause economic problems.

1. In what years was the inflation rate so high that it made economic planning difficult?
2. Why are lower and fixed-income families hardest hit by inflation?

Simulation *Activity*

Creating a Teenage Consumer Price Index

You may be asked to create a Teenage Consumer Price Index as part of a role-playing game.

Causes of Inflation

Where does inflation come from? Price levels can rise steeply when demand for goods and services exceeds the supply available at current prices, such as during wartime. They can also rise steeply when productivity is restricted, for example, when a long drought leads to poor harvests.

Nobody can explain every instance of rising price levels. However, economists have several theories about the causes of inflation. These include the growth of the money supply, changes in aggregate demand, and changes in aggregate supply. Economists look at all these elements when they try to understand the inflation process.

core inflation rate the rate of inflation excluding the effects of food and energy prices

hyperinflation inflation that is out of control

DISPLAY TRANSPARENCY

Define the Consumer Price Index (CPI) and discuss how it is calculated. Then display the "Consumer Price Index, 1995–2006" transparency (Color Transparencies, 13.b). Explain that this shows, for the years from 1995 through 2006, the overall CPI and the index for seven different groups of goods and services in the CPI market basket. Ask **How did the overall CPI change in that period?** *(rose from about 150 to about 200)* **How big a role did clothing costs play in the increase in the overall CPI? Why?** *(not much because clothing costs went down)* **In which years might energy costs have contributed most to the CPI increase? Why?** *(Energy costs rose more than the CPI during 1998–2000 and 2002–2006, so they probably contributed most to increases.)*

L3 Differentiate For alternate or additional practice with the concept of price indexes, have students engage in the "Creating a Teenage Consumer Price Index" activity (Simulation Activities, Chapter 13).

COMPARE

Compare the transparency and the inflation rate graph (Figure 13.4). Discuss the relationship between CPI and inflation. Note that larger increases in CPI, particularly for energy and transportation, correspond to greater rates of inflation.

DISCUSS

Ask a volunteer to define *hyperinflation.* Demonstrate its impact by drawing a chart with three columns, labeled *Month, Inflation Rate,* and *Price,* which shows how a 50 percent inflation rate every month causes the price of a $1.00 good to increase to $7.60 after six months. Explain that hyperinflation often leads to total economic collapse. Ask **Why would that be the case?** *(Possible response: Since prices rise so high so fast, money loses much of its value. Consumers would be unable to afford essential goods.)*

L4 Differentiate Distribute the "Analyzing Hyperinflation" worksheet (Unit 5 All-in-One, p. 61). Students can use this worksheet to explore the causes and effects of hyperinflation in Zimbabwe.

Virtual Economics

L4 Differentiate

Exploring Inflation Use the following lesson from the NCEE **Virtual Economics *CD-ROM*** to help students understand the effects of inflation. Click on Browse Economics Lessons, specify grades 9–12, and use the key words *price indexes.*

In this activity, students will create price indexes and play a simulation game to illustrate the effects of inflation.

LESSON TITLE	PRICE INDEXES AND INFLATION
Type of Activity	Role play
Complexity	High
Time	90 minutes
NCEE Standards	19, 20

Answers

Graph Skills 1. 1974 and 1980 2. Loss of purchasing power means losing the ability to buy essential goods.

Checkpoint They divide the updated cost by the base period cost, and then convert the decimal to a percent.

DISCUSS

Using the Numbered Heads strategy (p. T25), divide the class into three groups. Assign each group one of the three theories about the causes of inflation discussed in this section: quantity theory, change in aggregate demand, or change in aggregate supply. Students should work together until they understand the theory and how it works. Then, have students explain or demonstrate what they have learned to the rest of the class. Conclude by asking the class as a whole **According to the quantity theory, why would a faster rate of growth cause inflation?** *(Possible answer: If there is more money available for the same amount of goods and services, the value of the money will go down. Producers will raise prices in order to receive the value they want for their goods.)* **How might an increase in aggregate demand cause inflation?** *(Heavily demanded goods and services increase in value, pushing prices up. Wages also increase as demand for these services increases.)* **How might increased costs for raw materials and labor cause inflation?** *(Producers cover increased costs by increasing prices, leading workers to demand higher wages.)*

Answers

Chart Skills 1. because workers demand higher wages to pay for food, which causes companies to raise the price of their products, which will lead workers to demand higher wages 2. Possible response: These trends could reduce prices (at least initially) because firms use these strategies to reduce costs.

Figure 13.5 The Wage-Price Spiral

CHART SKILLS

Inflation caused by the push of higher costs can lead to a wage-price spiral of increasing prices.

1. Why do rising food prices fuel a wage-price spiral?
2. How might globalization and outsourcing affect the wage-price spiral?

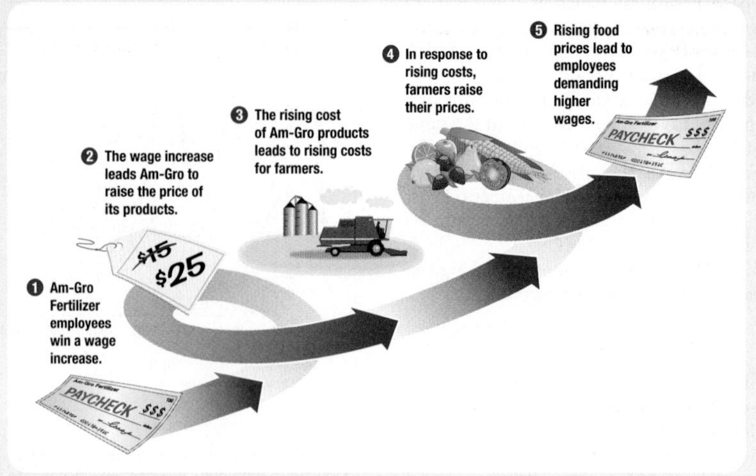

1 Am-Gro Fertilizer employees win a wage increase.
2 The wage increase leads Am-Gro to raise the price of its products.
3 The rising cost of Am-Gro products leads to rising costs for farmers.
4 In response to rising costs, farmers raise their prices.
5 Rising food prices lead to employees demanding higher wages.
$15
$25
PAYCHECK $$$
PAYCHECK $$$

Growth of the Money Supply

The **quantity theory** of inflation states that too much money in the economy causes inflation. Therefore, the money supply should be carefully monitored to keep it in line with the nation's productivity as measured by real GDP.

Economists at the University of Chicago developed a popular version of this theory in the 1950s and 1960s. They maintained that the money supply could be used to control price levels in the long term. The key to stable prices, they said, was to increase the supply of money at the same rate as the economy was growing.

Changes in Aggregate Demand

As you learned in Chapter 12, aggregate demand is the amount of goods and services in the economy that will be purchased at all possible price levels. Inflation can occur when demand for goods and services exceeds existing supplies. During wartime, for example, the government's need for military supplies puts pressure on producers. The heavy demand for new equipment, supplies, and services increases the value of those items, pushing prices up. Wages also rise as the demand for labor increases along with the demand for goods.

quantity theory the theory that too much money in the economy causes inflation

Changes in Aggregate Supply

Finally, inflation occurs when producers raise prices in order to meet increased costs. Higher prices for raw materials can cause costs to increase. Wage increases, however, are most often the biggest reason, because wages are the largest single production cost for most companies.

One cause of wage increases is low unemployment. Employers must then offer higher wages to attract workers. Wage increases can also occur as a result of collective bargaining.

For example, Jen is a union laborer at Am-Gro Fertilizer. The union she belongs to recently won a large wage increase from the company. The increased cost for labor led Am-Gro to raise its prices in order to maintain its profits.

Such a situation can lead to a spiral of ever-higher prices, because one increase in costs leads to an increase in prices, which leads to another increase in costs, and on and on. The process by which rising wages cause higher prices, and higher prices cause higher wages, is known as the **wage-price spiral.** The effect of a wage-price spiral on Am-Gro Fertilizer is shown in **Figure 13.5.**

CHECKPOINT ***What are the three causes of inflation?***

Effects of Inflation

High inflation is a major economic problem, especially when inflation rates change greatly from year to year. Buyers and sellers find planning for the future difficult, if not impossible. The effects of inflation can be seen mainly in purchasing power, income, and interest rates.

Effects on Purchasing Power

You have seen, in the example of Jack and Josephine Barrow's house, how inflation can erode purchasing power. In an inflationary economy, a dollar will not buy the same number of goods that it did in years past. When there is no inflation, $1.00 buys the same amount of goods it did in the previous year. If the inflation rate is 10 percent this year, however, $1.00 will buy the equivalent of only $.90 worth of goods today. In this case, the purchasing power of a dollar has fallen.

Effects on Income

Inflation sometimes, but not always, erodes income. If wage increases match the inflation rate, a worker's real income stays the same. People who do not receive their income as wages, such as doctors, lawyers, and businesspeople, can often increase their incomes by raising the prices they charge in order to keep up with inflation.

Not all people are so fortunate. If workers' wages do not increase as much as inflation does, they are in a worse economic position than before. Since prices are higher, their income has less purchasing power.

People living on a fixed income are especially hard hit by inflation. A **fixed income** is income that does not increase even when prices go up. The Barrows, for example, who are retired, are hurt by high inflation. The portion of their income from Social Security payments rises with the price level, because the government raises Social Security benefits to keep up with inflation. Much of their income, however, comes from a pension fund that pays them a fixed amount of money each month. Inflation steadily eats away at the real value of that pension check.

Effects on Interest Rates

People receive a given amount of interest on money in their savings accounts, but their true return depends on the rate of inflation. For example, Sonia had her savings in an account that paid 7 percent interest. At the same time, the annual inflation rate was 5 percent. As a result, the purchasing power of Sonia's savings increased that year by only 2 percent, because 5 percent of her interest was needed to keep up with inflation.

wage-price spiral the process by which rising wages cause higher prices, and higher prices cause higher wages

fixed income income that does not increase even when prices go up

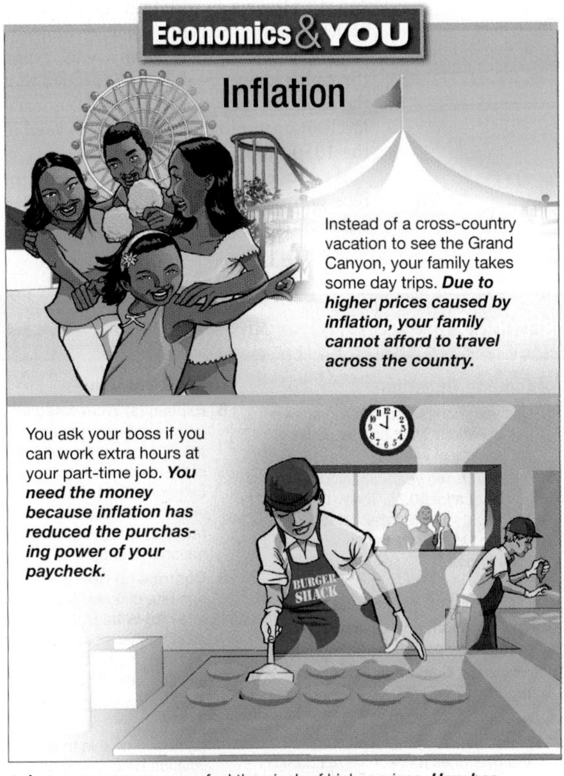

Economics & YOU
Inflation
Instead of a cross-country vacation to see the Grand Canyon, your family takes some day trips. ***Due to higher prices caused by inflation, your family cannot afford to travel across the country.***
You ask your boss if you can work extra hours at your part-time job. ***You need the money because inflation has reduced the purchasing power of your paycheck.***
BURGER SHACK

▲ As a consumer, you can feel the pinch of higher prices. ***How has inflation changed your spending habits?***

APPLY

Discuss inflation. Assign the "Analyzing the Impact of Inflation" worksheet (Unit 5 All-in-One, p. 62).

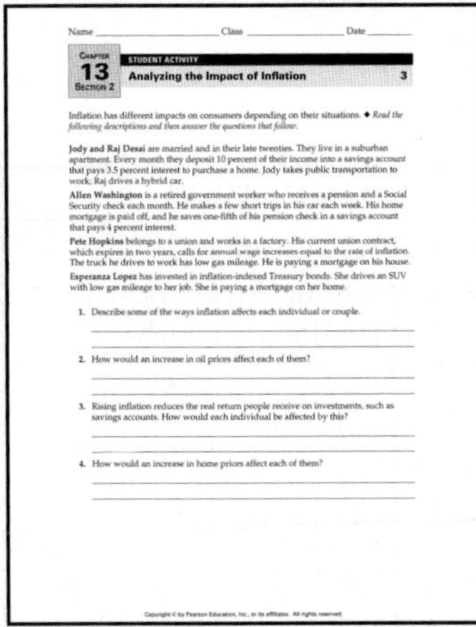

Name ____________ Class ____________ Date ________

CHAPTER 13 SECTION 2 — STUDENT ACTIVITY

Analyzing the Impact of Inflation 3

Inflation has different impacts on consumers depending on their situations. ◆ *Read the following descriptions and then answer the questions that follow.*

Jody and Raj Desai are married and in their late twenties. They live in a suburban apartment. Every month they deposit 10 percent of their income into a savings account that pays 3.5 percent interest to purchase a home. Jody takes public transportation to work; Raj drives a hybrid car.

Allen Washington is a retired government worker who receives a pension and a Social Security check each month. He makes a few short trips in his car each week. His home mortgage is paid off, and he saves one-fifth of his pension check in a savings account that pays 4 percent interest.

Pete Hopkins belongs to a union and works in a factory. His current union contract, which expires in two years, calls for annual wage increases equal to the rate of inflation. The truck he drives to work has low gas mileage. He is paying a mortgage on his house.

Esperanza Lopez has invested in inflation-indexed Treasury bonds. She drives an SUV with low gas mileage to her job. She is paying a mortgage on her home.

1. Describe some of the ways inflation affects each individual or couple.
2. How would an increase in oil prices affect each of them?
3. Rising inflation reduces the real return people receive on investments, such as savings accounts. How would each individual be affected by this?
4. How would an increase in home prices affect each of them?

L2 Differentiate Have students complete the "Comparing the Impact of Inflation" worksheet (Unit 5 All-in-One, p. 63).

Ask **Is it possible to remain unaffected by inflation? Explain.** *(No. It affects everyone.)*

EXTEND

Have students take the role of the owner of a neighborhood restaurant whose customers are low-wage workers. Ask **How would you respond to a 25 percent increase in the cost of ingredients?**

GUIDING QUESTION WRAP UP

Have students return to the section Guiding Question. Review the completed graphic organizer and clarify any misunderstandings. Have a wrap up discussion.

Assess and Remediate

L3 **L2** Collect the "Analyzing the Impact of Inflation" worksheet and the "Comparing the Impact of Inflation" worksheets and assess student understanding of inflation.

L4 Collect the "Analyzing Hyperinflation" worksheet and assess student understanding of hyperinflation.

L3 Assign the Section 2 Assessment questions.

L3 Give Section Quiz A (Unit 5 All-in-One, p. 64).

L2 Give Section Quiz B (Unit 5 All-in-One, p. 65).

(Assess and Remediate continued on p. 348)

Answers

Checkpoint an increase in the money supply and changes in aggregate demand and aggregate supply

Economics & You Possible response: Rising prices have caused me to spend less on movies and music.

Have students complete the Self-Test Online and continue their work in the **Essential Questions Journal**.

REMEDIATION AND SUGGESTIONS

Use the chart below to help students who are struggling with content.

WEAKNESS	REMEDIATION
Identifying key terms (Questions 3, 4, 5, 6)	Have students use the interactive Economic Dictionary Online.
Using indexes (Questions 4, 8, 9, 11)	Reteach how to calculate the CPI and the contents of the market basket.
Describing the causes of inflation (Questions 1, 2, 6, 10)	Have students work in pairs and outline the section under "Causes of Inflation."
Analyzing the effects of inflation (Questions 1, 8)	Use the graphic organizer to reteach the material.

Answers

Checkpoint People have less purchasing power; they are in a worse economic position than before.

Checkpoint Companies must raise wages to compete for scarce workers.

deflation a sustained drop in the price level

When a bank's interest rate matches the inflation rate, savers break even. The amount they gain from interest is taken away by inflation. However, if the inflation rate is higher than the bank's interest rate, savers lose money.

CHECKPOINT ***What happens when income doesn't keep pace with inflation?***

Recent Trends in Inflation

Americans over age 30 have experienced fairly low inflation rates for most of their lifetimes. In the late 1990s, unemployment levels were low. Typically, low unemployment leads to higher inflation because companies compete for scarce workers by offering higher wages. Rising wages can push the inflation rate up, as you know from the discussion of the wage-price spiral. However, inflation crept along at less than 3 percent. Some economists suggested that the economy was going through a lucky streak. Others argued that the economy was returning to the normal levels of unemployment that had existed in the 1950s and 1960s.

As the economy entered a period of recession and slow growth in the 2000s, inflation fell to less than 2 percent. Rising unemployment and falling capital investment removed two factors that might have led to inflation due to increases in aggregate supply. Prices at times seemed to be falling. Some experts even predicted a period of **deflation,** or a sustained drop in the price level. However, the economy recovered.

Although inflation remained relatively low through 2007, by mid-2008, soaring energy costs had pushed the inflation rate past 4 percent. The CPI recorded its biggest monthly gain since 1982. Consumers, pressured by sharp price increases for food and gasoline, had less demand for big-ticket items such as household appliances and automobiles.

By the end of 2008, the economy was in crisis. A severe recession led to a slowdown in economic activity. Global demand for oil dropped and the price of gasoline plunged by 30 percent in one month. The CPI was 3 percent lower than it had been just three months earlier. The record decline in retail prices and sales put added pressure on the federal government to solve the economic crisis and avoid a deflationary spiral in prices.

CHECKPOINT ***How does low unemployment lead to higher inflation?***

SECTION 2 ASSESSMENT

Essential Questions Journal To continue to build a response to the Essential Question, go to your **Essential Questions Journal.**

Guiding Question

1. Use your completed chart to answer this question: What are the causes and effects of inflation?
2. **Extension** Ten years ago you could buy a soda for $0.75. Today the same soda costs $1.25. What factors might have caused the price of the soda to rise?

Key Terms and Main Ideas

3. How does **inflation** influence **purchasing power?**
4. Why is the **Consumer Price Index** important?
5. What is **hyperinflation?**
6. What causes a **wage-price spiral,** and how does it affect the economy?
7. What are three possible effects of inflation? Explain or give an example of each.

Critical Thinking

8. **Explain (a)** What categories of goods and services are included in the CPI market basket? **(b)** What is the purpose of including these categories? **(c)** Why might an individual family experience an inflation rate that is higher or lower than the national average?
9. **Contrast (a)** How is the core inflation rate different from the inflation rate? **(b)** What is the purpose of calculating these two separate rates? **(c)** In what situation might the core inflation rate *not* be useful?
10. **Apply (a)** According to the quantity theory, what causes inflation? **(b)** Based on this theory, how can inflation be prevented? **(c)** What tools can the government use to achieve this goal? Give at least two examples.

Math Skills

11. Suppose the market basket cost $800 during the base period and $1,800 today. What is the CPI for today? (Remember, to calculate CPI, divide today's cost by the base period cost and multiply by 100.)

Visit PearsonSuccessNet.com for additional math help.

Assessment Answers

1. Causes—growth in money supply, changes in aggregate demand or supply; Effects—reduced purchasing power **2.** higher costs, demand **3.** reduces purchasing power **4.** Consumers, businesses, and the government can use it to make economic decisions. **5.** inflation that is out of control **6.** increase in wages causes firms to increase prices, which leads to a demand for higher wages; causes inflation **7.** lower purchasing power, consumers spend more money for same quantity of goods; reduced income, consumers cannot live as comfortably on their income, reduced savings, interest earned is reduced by inflation **8.** (a) food and drinks, housing, apparel and upkeep, transportation, medical care, entertainment, education and communication, other (b) representative consumer goods, services (c) Possible answer: If a family spends on goods whose prices rise faster or slower than inflation. **9.** (a) excludes food and energy prices (b) to better see long-term changes in inflation (c) steady increase in food prices or energy prices **10.** (a) too much money in the economy (b) by increasing the supply of money at the same rate that the economy is growing (c) monitoring growth rate of the economy and the CPI **11.** 225

SECTION 3 Poverty

OBJECTIVES

1. **Define** who is poor, according to government standards.
2. **Describe** the causes of poverty.
3. **Analyze** the distribution of income in the United States.
4. **Summarize** government policies intended to combat poverty.

ECONOMIC DICTIONARY

As you read the section, look for the definitions of these **Key Terms:**

- poverty threshold
- poverty rate
- income distribution
- food stamp program
- Lorenz Curve
- enterprise zone
- block grant
- workfare

Guiding Question

What factors affect the poverty rate?

Copy this table and fill it in as you read to explain the causes of poverty.

Causes of Poverty	
Lack of education	Less education equals lower wages
Location	

▶ Economics and You The United States has millions of people living in poverty. It also has one of the highest per capita GDPs in the world. How can that be? Looking at poverty rates among different groups of Americans reveals some important reasons.

Principles in Action Statistically, you are at greater risk for living in poverty if you come from a single-parent home, live in the inner city, or do not have at least a high school education. Other factors, including the way that income is distributed, also affect the poverty rate.

poverty threshold the income level below which income is insufficient to support a family or household

The Poor

As you have read, the United States Bureau of the Census conducts extensive surveys to gather data about the American people. Its economists then analyze the data and organize it to reveal important characteristics. One key feature they look at is how many families and households live in poverty. The Census Bureau defines a *family* as a group of two or more people related by birth, marriage, or adoption who live in the same housing unit. A *household* is all people who live in the same housing unit, regardless of how they are related.

The Poverty Threshold

According to the government, a poor family is one whose total income is less than the amount required to satisfy the family's minimum needs. The Census Bureau determines the income level, known as the poverty threshold, required to meet those minimum needs. The **poverty threshold** is the income level below which income is insufficient to support a family or household.

The poverty threshold, or poverty line, varies with the size of the family. For example, in 2006, the poverty threshold for a single parent under age 65 with one child was $13,896. For a family of four with two children, it was $20,444. If a family's total income is below the poverty threshold, everyone in the family is counted as poor.

Limited job opportunities and lower levels of education are some of the factors that contribute to rural poverty. ▼

Guiding Question

What factors affect the poverty rate?

Get Started

Causes of Poverty	
Lack of education	Less education equals lower wages.
Location	People living far from higher-wage jobs.
Racial and gender discrimination	Unfair practices result in lower pay for minority and women workers.
Growth of low-skill service jobs	With a decline in higher-paying manufacturing jobs, a growing number of less-educated workers work in low-skill, lower-paying service jobs.
Family structure	Families headed by a single parent, particularly a mother, are more likely to be poor.

LESSON GOALS

Students will:

- Know the Key Terms.
- Analyze a bar graph that shows the levels of poverty for men and women with different levels of education, and discuss other causes of poverty.
- Brainstorm solutions to different causes of poverty.
- Demonstrate equality and inequality of income distribution.
- Analyze factors that affect wages and wealth.
- Research government antipoverty programs.

BEFORE CLASS

Students should read the section for homework.

Have students complete the graphic organizer in the Section Opener as they read the text. As an alternate activity, have students complete the Guided Reading and Review worksheet (Unit 5 All-in-One, p. 66).

L1 L2 ELL LPR Differentiate Have students complete the Guided Reading and Review worksheet (Unit 5 All-in-One, p. 67).

CLASSROOM HINTS

VIEWS ON POVERTY

Beware the value judgments associated with terms like poverty and poor. Students often have personal and charged opinions about poverty, and what to do for the poor. If you can establish from the outset that the nature of the discussion is morally neutral, then these opinions can be harnessed as an engine for learning.

Focus on the Basics

Students need to come away with the following understandings:

FACTS: • The government tracks the number of people living in poverty. • Poverty is caused by many different factors, including level of education, gender, race and ethnic origin, age, family structure, and location. • Over time, the richest one percent of the population has gained an increasingly larger share of wealth. • The government tries to reduce the number of poor people through a variety of policies.

GENERALIZATION: Since there are several causes of poverty, attempts to lower poverty would have to take several different approaches.

BELLRINGER

Have students work in pairs to write down words and ideas they associate with the word *poverty.* Ask each pair to write a description of what poverty means to them.

Teach

Economics online To present this topic using digital resources, use the lecture notes on www.PearsonSuccessNet.com.

DEFINE

Ask students for their responses to the Bellringer activity. List these on the board. Then, remind students that when the government defines poverty, they use a much more specific and measurable set of criteria. Write the definition of *poverty threshold* on the board. Have students compare this definition to the definitions they suggested in their responses to the Bellringer activity. Ask **Why do you think the government has to use a very precise definition of poverty?** *(First, defining poverty helps government economists determine how many poor people live in the nation, which gives clues about how the economy as a whole is performing. Second, people who live below the poverty threshold are eligible to receive certain kinds of government aid or to participate in particular programs. Having a definition of poverty makes it possible to determine who is eligible and who is not.)* **Why would the government want to provide aid to poor people?** *(Possible answers: to help them escape poverty; to provide care for children)*

Answers

Graph Skills 1. It decreased. 2. Possible responses: to measure the health of the economy; to measure the impact of antipoverty programs

Checkpoint Job prospects are limited.

Figure 13.6 Poverty Rate, 1986–2006

GRAPH SKILLS

In 2006, 12% of the population equaled 36.5 million people.

1. What happened to the poverty rate from 1994 to 2000?
2. Why do you think the government tracks the poverty rate?

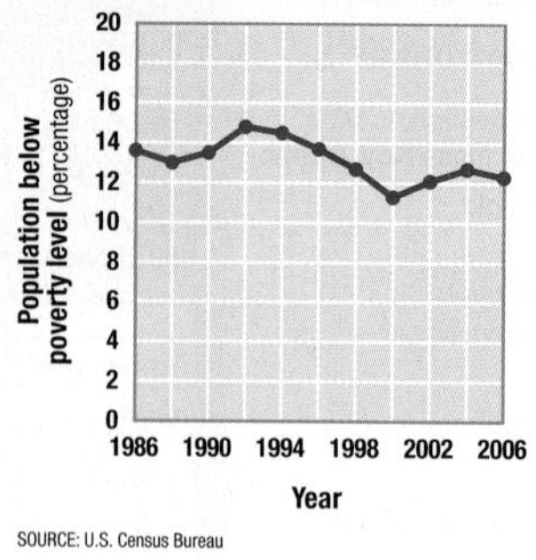

SOURCE: U.S. Census Bureau

The Poverty Rate

Trends in the national poverty rate are shown in **Figure 13.6.** The **poverty rate** is the percentage of people who live in households with income below the official poverty threshold.

Poverty rates for various groups are shown in **Figure 13.7.** We can use poverty rates to discover whom the government considers to be poor and what factors seem to contribute to poverty. Poverty rates differ sharply by groups, according to several different indicators:

- *Race and ethnic origin* The poverty rate among African Americans, Hispanics, and Native Americans is more than twice the rate for white Americans.
- *Type of family* Families with a single mother have a poverty rate almost six times greater than that of two-parent families.
- *Age* The percentage of children living in poverty is significantly larger than that for any other age group. Young adults make up the next largest group.
- *Residence* Inner city residents have double the poverty rate of those who live outside the inner city. People who live in rural areas also have a higher poverty rate, especially in regions where job prospects are limited.

poverty rate the percentage of people who live in households with income below the official poverty threshold

CHECKPOINT ***What is one reason for the higher poverty rate in rural areas?***

Causes of Poverty

Put simply, a family is poor when the adults in the family fail to earn enough income to provide for its members' basic needs. This failure to earn adequate income is often the result of unemployment.

As you read in Section 1, millions of Americans are unemployed for a variety of reasons. While they are out of a job, their families might well fall below the poverty threshold. Many other poor adults are not even considered a part of the labor force. Some suffer from chronic health problems or disabilities that prevent them from working. Others are discouraged workers who are no longer looking for work.

Many poor adults do have jobs, however. In fact, more than half of poor households have someone who works at least part-time, and one in five have a full-time, year-round worker. For these "working poor," the problem is usually low wages or a limited work schedule, rather than the lack of a job. For example, Ray makes $9.00 an hour as a full-time clerk in a clothing store. While he is at work, his wife stays at home with their two young children. Although Ray works 40 hours per week, and his salary is well above the minimum wage, his annual earnings amount to just $18,720, which is below the poverty threshold for a family of four.

Economists agree that poverty and lack of income go hand in hand, but they have different ideas about the causes of poverty. Here are some of the most important explanations for why some people are poor.

Shifts in Family Structure

Single-parent families are more likely to live in poverty than two-parent families. That is especially the case when the lone parent is a single mother. The divorce rate has risen significantly since the 1960s, as has the number of children born to unmarried parents. These demographic shifts tend to result in more single-parent families and more children living in poverty.

Differentiated Resources

- L1 L2 **Guided Reading and Review** (Unit 5 All-in-One, p. 67)
- L2 **Analyzing the Impact of Education and Gender on Income** (Unit 5 All-in-One, p. 69)
- L4 **Studying Income Distribution** (Unit 5 All-in-One, p. 70)

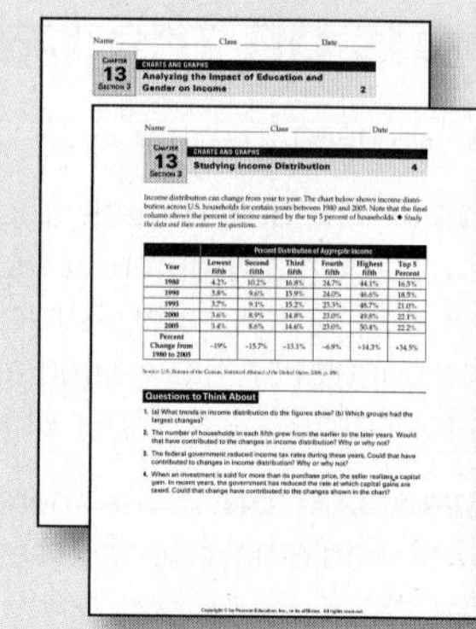

Location

In most American cities, racial minorities are concentrated in the inner cities, far from the higher-wage jobs in suburban areas. Many of these inner-city residents do not own cars, and mass-transit systems are often not an efficient means of commuting from the inner city to the suburbs. As a result, people who live in the inner city earn less than people living outside the inner city. Similar obstacles exist for many people living in rural areas, where there is little business or industry.

Racial and Gender Discrimination

White workers generally earn higher salaries than minority workers, and men generally earn more than women. Much of this income inequality can be explained by differences in hours worked, education, and work experience. Part of the inequality, however, results from racial and gender discrimination. Even when all the workers in a group are equally productive, whites are often paid more than African Americans, and men are often paid more than women. Economists agree, however, that discrimination based on race or gender has been diminishing.

Growth of Low-Skill Service Jobs

In the past, less-educated people could earn good wages working in manufacturing jobs. Globalization, the decline in manufacturing, and the rise of the service economy has led to a decline in the number of higher-paying manufacturing jobs. More workers with less education now work in low-skill service jobs, where wages are often not as high as they are for factory jobs.

Lack of Education

The median income of high school dropouts in 2006 was $25,912, which was above the poverty threshold for a family of four in that year. High-school graduates earned about two-thirds more than the dropouts and college graduates earned more than three times as much.

CHECKPOINT ***What are three causes of poverty?***

Figure 13.7 Poverty Rates by Group, 2006

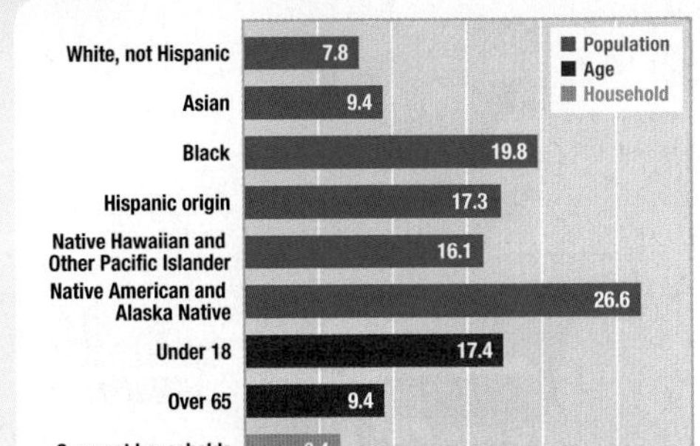

SOURCE: U.S. Census Bureau

GRAPH SKILLS

Households headed by women, African Americans, Hispanics, and Native Americans are more likely than other groups to have incomes below the poverty threshold, as this recent data shows.

1. Which population group has the highest poverty rate?
2. Why do you think differences exist in poverty rates among groups?

Income Distribution

In 2006, the estimated median household income in the United States was $48,023, which means that half the households earned more than this amount and half earned less. This figure tells only part of the income story. To fully understand poverty in this country, you also need to understand **income distribution,** or how the nation's total income is distributed among its population.

Income Inequality

Income distribution in the United States is shown in **Figure 13.8** on page 353. These figures do not reflect the effects of taxes or non-cash government aid such as housing subsidies, healthcare, or food stamps. The **food stamp program** helps low-income people buy food. Benefits are provided on an electronic card that is accepted at most food stores.

income distribution the way in which a nation's total income is distributed among its population

food stamp program government program that helps low-income recipients to buy food

CHAPTER 13 SECTION 3 **351**

Background Note

The "Working Poor" Writer Barbara Ehrenreich lived for a year in different parts of the country performing low-skill service jobs. She concluded that the working poor struggle to get by, working long hours doing taxing physical labor, sometimes juggling more than one job, and facing disaster if they experience health problems. The biggest problem facing the working poor, though, is housing. "When the rich and the poor compete for housing on the open market," she wrote, "the poor don't stand a chance. The rich can always outbid them, buy up their tenements or trailer parks, and replace them with condos, McMansions, golf courses, or whatever they like. Since the rich have become more numerous . . . the poor have necessarily been forced into housing that is more expensive, more dilapidated, or more distant from their places of work."

DISTRIBUTE ACTIVITY WORKSHEET

Have students complete the "Analyzing the Impact of Education and Gender on Income" worksheet (Unit 5 All-in-One, p. 68).

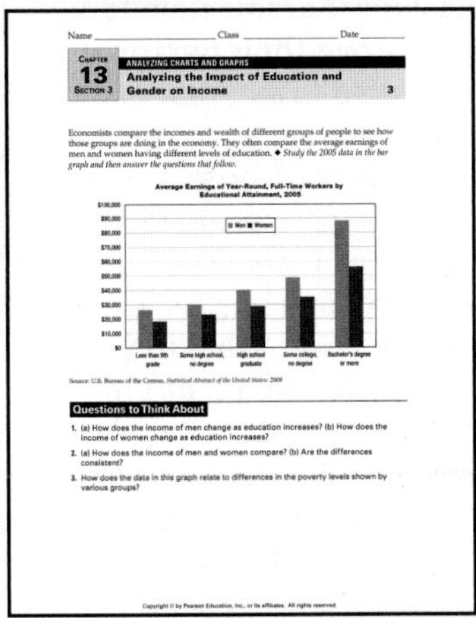

L1 L2 Differentiate Have students complete the "Analyzing the Impact of Education and Gender on Income" worksheet (Unit 5 All-in-One, p. 69).

Direct students to Figures 13.7. Ask **What does this bar graph tell us about the level of poverty in female-headed vs. male-headed households?** *(It's probably higher.)* **Does this graph show that men of all races earn more than women of all races at each educational level?** *(We don't know. The incomes are averages.)*

DISCUSS

Discuss the fact that globalization, the decline in manufacturing, and the rise of a service economy have led to the growth of low-pay, low-skill service jobs. Ask **Who does this affect?** *(Possible response: people who were working at manufacturing jobs that paid well; regions that depended upon these jobs)*

BRAINSTORM

Write a prompt on the board such as this: "One way to reduce poverty in urban areas is to ..." Then use the Idea Wave strategy (p. T24) to brainstorm possible solutions to the higher poverty rates. Proceed in the same way with the other causes of poverty. Remind students to keep in mind the values underlying free enterprise, the workings of a market economy, the role of incentives, and so on.

(lesson continued on p. 353)

Answers

Graph Skills 1. female-headed households
2. Possible response: Some groups experience more causes of poverty than others. For example, African Americans experience racial discrimination.

Checkpoint growth of low-skill service jobs, discrimination, lack of education

Teach Case Study

SUMMARIZE AND DISCUSS

Call on students to summarize the case study. Ask **How do incentive-based programs help low-income participants improve their personal finances?** *(Incentives are used to meet specific goals—for example, find a job, get a TV. That helps a family's finances. If enough goals are met, and rewards are met, it could promote long-term financial changes for a family.)* The article cites the relationship between program success and an already motivated participant. Ask **Why do you think this program works for some, but might not work for others?** *(Desire, or lack of desire, to change personal financial situation is a factor; someone might not be motivated by material things.)*

DEBATE

Divide the class into two groups and call on them to debate whether incentive-based programs should be paying people to do things they ought to be doing anyway *(for example: paying rent, going to school, looking for employment)*

L1 L2 Differentiate To help your students better understand the case study, it is important to learn how Pathways to Rewards differs from traditional government-assistance programs. In pairs, have your students use the Internet to research your state's assistance programs (usually located within the Department of Human Services). Discuss the findings as a class.

Economics online *All print resources are available on the Teacher's Resource Library CD-ROM and online at* www.PearsonSuccessNet.com.

Answer

Applying Economic Principles Possible answers: *food banks, food stamps, child care assistance, transportation assistance, public housing, cash assistance, financial planning/budgeting, Medicaid*

Case Study — THE WALL STREET JOURNAL. CLASSROOM EDITION

Extra Credit

ANTIPOVERTY PROGRAMS

Incentive programs for the poor offer an alternative to traditional welfare.

By Jonathan Eig
The Wall Street Journal

Consumers earn rewards for flying, for using credit cards and for staying at hotels. In one low-income Chicago neighborhood, residents are earning rewards for paying their rent, getting their children to school every day and seeking work.

The "Pathways to Rewards" program has awarded about $19,000 in prizes to about 130 people since its inception. It is one of several small, local programs around the country attempting to use incentives to help the poor improve their lives.

At a recent rewards banquet, more than 150 people gathered in a church basement to celebrate and cash in points for prizes. Devant-e and Ireyonna Brown, 10 and 7, rode off on new bicycles with points earned for school attendance and volunteer work. Their mother, Marilyn, walked away with a DVD player, thanks to points earned mostly for attending PTA meetings.

In the Pathways program, participants tell a counselor what they want to buy and how much it costs. Then the required number of points is set. Each point is worth one dollar. When the participant accumulates enough points, the counselor arranges either a gift certificate or a check made out to the store. Cash is never exchanged.

Incentive-based programs have sprung up in recent years because they are more politically palatable than traditional welfare benefits, and because advocates say such programs offer a better chance of changing the behaviors tied up with poverty. But incentives aren't safety nets. And it's not clear whether they are enough to prompt meaningful long-term changes for those entrenched in poverty.

No one is saying this small experiment will be enough to transform a poor neighborhood. "It's a piece of the puzzle," says Crystal Palmer, a social worker with the nonprofit Near West Side Community Development Corp., a partner in the Pathways to Rewards program.

"The clients who are doing well [in Pathways] are the clients who are already motivated," says Vorricia Harvey, program director for the Near West Side CDC. "It's an incentive to say, 'You're doing well, keep it up.'"

Some social workers and area residents complain that Pathways is paying people to do things they ought to be doing anyway. Even some of the program's participants say there's truth to that. "But why not use it to my advantage?" asks Willie Wright. She used her points to help buy a computer.

Applying Economic Principles
Rewards programs are one approach to changing behaviors linked to poverty. But rewards programs do not provide basic necessities as traditional welfare programs do. Use the information in this section to give examples of other ways that people might be able to pull themselves out of poverty.

Video News Update Online Powered by *The Wall Street Journal* Classroom Edition — For a new case study, go to the online resources at **PearsonSuccessNet.com**

Look at the table on the left side of **Figure 13.8.** To compute the numbers in the table, economists take four steps.

1. First, they rank the nation's households according to income.
2. Then, they divide the list into fifths, or quintiles, with equal numbers of households in each fifth. The lowest fifth, which appears at the top of the list, includes the poorest 20 percent of households. The highest fifth, shown at the bottom of the list, includes the richest 20 percent of households. The first column in **Figure 13.8** shows this division into quintiles.
3. Next, they compute each group's average income by adding up the incomes of all the households in the group, and then dividing by the number of households.
4. Finally, they compute each group's share, or percentage, of total income by dividing the group's total income by the total income of all the groups. The second column shows each group's share. The third column shows the cumulative total. (For example, the lowest two fifths of households earned 12 percent of total income.)

Compare the share of the poorest fifth with that of the richest fifth. If you divide richest by poorest, you will see that the richest fifth receives nearly 15 times the income of the poorest fifth.

Now look at the graph on the right side of **Figure 13.8.** It shows that the numbers for shares of total income, when they are plotted on a graph, form a curve. This graph, called the **Lorenz Curve,** illustrates the distribution of income in the economy.

Let's see what this Lorenz Curve tells you. First, read the label on each axis. Then look at the straight line running diagonally across the graph. This reference line represents complete equality. Under conditions of complete equality, each quintile would receive one fifth of total income. That means the lowest 20 percent of households would receive 20 percent of total income, as shown by the point (lowest, 20). Similarly, the lowest 40 percent (the first two quintiles) would receive 40 percent of total income, as shown by the point (second, 40), and so on.

Lorenz Curve the curve that illustrates income distribution

Figure 13.8 **Income Distribution**

Percent of Total Income, 2006

Quintile	Percent of income for quintile	Cumulative: Percent of income for this and lower quintiles
Lowest fifth	3.4%	3.4%
Second fifth	8.6%	12.0%
Third fifth	14.5%	26.5%
Fourth fifth	22.9%	49.4%
Highest fifth	50.5%	100.0%

Note: Because of rounding, totals may be greater than or less than 100 percent.
SOURCE: U.S. Census Bureau

Lorenz Curve

GRAPH SKILLS

The table (left) shows family income ranked by category. When plotted on a Lorenz Curve (right), these data show the distribution of income in the United States.

1. What percent of total income did the lowest three fifths of households make in 2006?
2. How would taxes and government programs affect the Lorenz Curve?

Action Graph online

For an animated version of this graph, visit **PearsonSuccessNet.com**

DEMONSTRATE AND DRAW GRAPH

Have students review the Action Graph animation for a step-by-step look at income distribution. To help them see how income distribution is calculated, demonstrate the process. Mark twenty pieces of paper with the notation *$100*. Divide the class into five groups, each with an equal number of students, and call them Groups A through E. Assign any extra students to the task of recording results. Then give each group their total income: four *$100s*.

Draw a five-column, six-row chart on the board. Label the columns *Group, Round One Income, Round One Percent of Income, Round Two Income,* and *Round Two Percent of Income*. In the *Group* column, label the rows *A, B, C, D,* and *E*.

In Round One, have the students in each group report their income. (Each group should report an income of $400.) Then have students calculate the percent of income for their group by dividing the group's income by the total amount of "money" handed out. (For each group in Round One, that will be $400 ÷ $2,000 which equals 20%.) Have students draw a Lorenz Curve for these results, following the models in Figure 13.8. This result illustrates an equal distribution of income.

Next, in Round Two, have students distribute income in a way that more closely reflects current statistics: Group E should be given three $100s from Group A, two $100s from Group B, and one $100 from Group C. Tally the income for each group after this exchange and fill in the chart. (For example, income for Group A is now $100 and their percent of income is $100 ÷ $2,000 which equals 5%.) Then draw a second Lorenz Curve.

Discuss the data and the second Lorenz curve. Ask students to speculate about what factors might lead to unequal distribution of income. Record the suggestions and compare them to the discussion on the next page of text.

Virtual Economics

L3 Differentiate

Evaluating Income Distribution Use the following lesson from the NCEE **Virtual Economics *CD-ROM*** to help students evaluate income distribution in the United States. Click on Browse Economics Lessons, specify grades 9–12, and use the key words *income distributed*.

In this activity, students will use statistics to explore the unequal distribution of income in the United States.

LESSON TITLE	WHY ISN'T INCOME DISTRIBUTED MORE EQUALLY?
Type of Activity	Using statistics
Complexity	Moderate
Time	90 minutes
NCEE Standards	13, 19

Answers

Graph Skills 1. 26.5 percent 2. Both could either increase or decrease incomes at any level.

ANALYZE

Write the following estimated average national annual wages from 2007 on the board:

Chief executive: $151,370

Air traffic controller: $107,780

Computer programmer: $72,010

Registered nurse: $62,480

Secondary school teachers: $52,450

Firefighter: $44,130

Farmer: $42,480

Substance abuse counselor: $37,830

Dental assistant: $32,280

School bus driver: $26,190

Restaurant cook: $21,960

Home health aide: $20,850

Child-care worker: $19,670

Cashier: $18,380

Dishwasher: $17,060

Tell students to identify what factors—education, skill, or field of work—they think explain why each occupation's pay is positioned higher or lower than the others in the list. Ask **Do these wages seem reasonable for these jobs? Explain.** *(Possible response: Some do: air traffic controllers have a lot of responsibility. Some don't: child-care workers also have a lot of responsibility.)*

Ask **What is another factor of the income gap? Why?** *(Inheritances: some people inherit money or businesses from which they can earn money.)*

L4 Differentiate Point out that income distribution has become more unequal in the United States over the last few decades. Distribute the "Studying Income Distribution" worksheet (Unit 5 All-in-One, p. 70) to give students the opportunity to analyze changes in income distribution between 1980 and 2005.

In 2006, the distribution of income was not equal, as the Lorenz Curve indicates. For example, the point (lowest, 3.4) shows that the lowest 20 percent, or one fifth, of households received just 3.4 percent of the nation's total income. The point (second, 12) shows that the lowest 40 percent, or two fifths, of households received only 12 percent of the income. The area on the graph between the line of equality and the Lorenz Curve represents the amount of inequality in income distribution. The larger the area between the curves, the greater the income inequality.

Income Gap

As you can see from Figure 13.8, the wealthiest fifth of American households earned more income (50.5 percent) than the bottom four fifths combined. A study published in 1999 showed that after taxes are deducted, the richest 2.7 million Americans receive as much income as the poorest 100 million Americans. Why are there such differences in income among Americans? Here are some factors.

- *Differences in skills and education* Some people are more highly skilled than others, so they earn higher wages. Labor skills are determined by education, training, and by a worker's natural ability.
- *Inheritances* Some people inherit large sums of money and earn income by investing it. Others inherit businesses that produce income from profits.
- *Field of work* Wages are determined by the demand for labor. As you read in Chapter 9, labor demand is a "derived demand" because it is set by demand for what people produce. People who produce goods with a low market value usually earn lower wages.

James Webb, a former Secretary of the Navy who won election to the United States Senate in 2006, commented on the growing income gap:

> **"America's top tier has grown infinitely richer and more removed over the past 25 years.... The top 1 percent now takes in an astounding 16 percent of national income, up from 8 percent in 1980."**
>
> —James Webb, Democratic Senator-elect from Virginia, *The Wall Street Journal*, Nov. 15, 2006

In fact, in the last two decades, the distribution of income has become less equal. Since 1977, the share of income earned by the lowest three fifths has decreased by 12 percent, while the share earned by the top 1 percent has more than doubled.

CHECKPOINT ***What does income distribution tell economists?***

The electronic benefits transfer card authorizes the transfer of government benefits, such as food stamps, for payment to retailers. Private charities run soup kitchens and food pantries to help the poor. ▶

354

Background Note

State Differences The income figures in the activity on this page are national averages from 2007. Workers' earnings can vary considerably from state to state, as the following figures for computer programmers show.

States with the Five Highest Annual Average Wage

New Jersey: $83,000

Washington: $82,800

Connecticut: $81,980

Virginia: $79,380

California: $79,300

States with the Five Lowest Annual Average Wage

Mississippi: $51,940

West Virginia: $46,820

North Dakota: $45,760

South Dakota: $45,690

Wyoming: $43,520

Answer

Checkpoint what share of national income is going to different groups of people

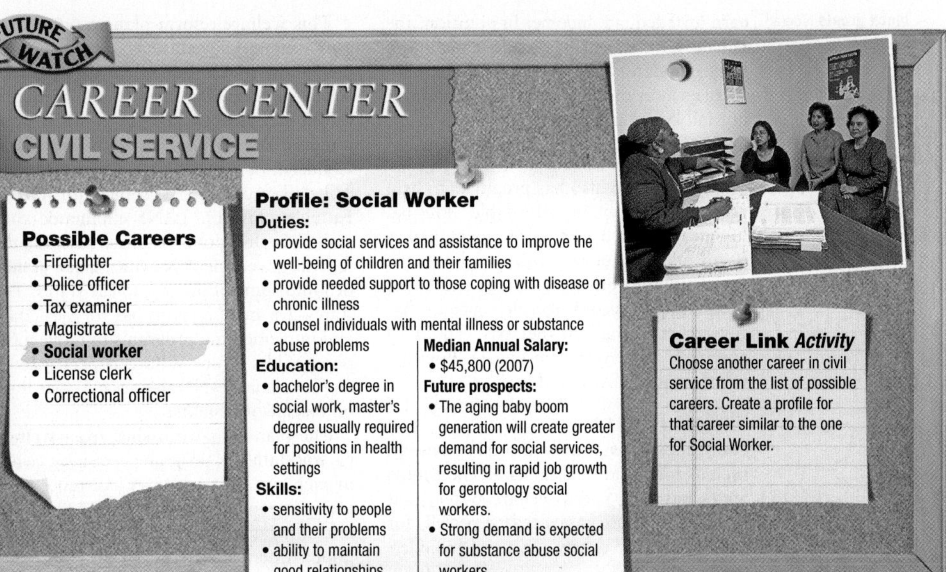

FUTURE WATCH
CAREER CENTER
CIVIL SERVICE
Possible Careers
• Firefighter
• Police officer
• Tax examiner
• Magistrate
• Social worker
• License clerk
• Correctional officer
Profile: Social Worker
Duties:
• provide social services and assistance to improve the well-being of children and their families
• provide needed support to those coping with disease or chronic illness
• counsel individuals with mental illness or substance abuse problems
Education:
• bachelor's degree in social work, master's degree usually required for positions in health settings
Skills:
• sensitivity to people and their problems
• ability to maintain good relationships
Median Annual Salary:
• $45,800 (2007)
Future prospects:
• The aging baby boom generation will create greater demand for social services, resulting in rapid job growth for gerontology social workers.
• Strong demand is expected for substance abuse social workers.
Career Link *Activity*
Choose another career in civil service from the list of possible careers. Create a profile for that career similar to the one for Social Worker.

Antipoverty Policies

As you read in Chapter 3, the government spends billions of dollars on programs designed to reduce poverty. This money is spent mainly on cash assistance, education, medical benefits, and non-cash benefits such as food stamps and subsidized housing.

Critics of antipoverty programs say that much of the money is wasted. Many argue that the programs themselves harm the very people they are intended to help. The criticisms have led to new policies. These include the Earned Income Tax Credit, the establishment of enterprise zones, job training and other employment assistance, housing assistance, and welfare reform.

The Earned Income Tax Credit

One of the government's most successful antipoverty programs is the Earned Income Tax Credit (EITC). The EITC is a refundable tax credit that low-income families with children receive when they file their federal income tax return. Eligibility is based on the taxpayer's earned income and the number of qualifying children. In 2008 for example, a married couple with an earned income of $38,646 and two or more qualifying children would receive the maximum credit of $4,824.

Established in 1975 to offset the impact of the Social Security payroll tax on low-income families, the EITC has been expanded over the years. A report by the Center on Budget and Policy Priorities said that in 2005, the EITC lifted more than four million people above the official poverty line and was "the nation's most effective antipoverty program for working families."

Enterprise Zones

Enterprise zones, which became popular in the 1980s, are areas where companies can locate and be free of certain state, local, and federal taxes and restrictions on business operations. Zones benefit businesses by lowering their costs. They help local people by making it easier for them to find work. By providing jobs, these zones can help revitalize rundown areas such as inner cities.

Employment Assistance

In recent decades, federal and state governments have designed job-training programs to help workers who lack the skills to

enterprise zone area where businesses can locate free of certain state, local, and federal taxes and restrictions

MAKE A POSTER

Have groups of four or five students research one of the antipoverty policies in the text. Students should design a poster that provides a description of the program; its history; an analysis of the support for, and criticism of, the program; and an analysis of the program's effectiveness. Encourage students to use a chart or graph to convey information if appropriate.

Display posters around the class for students to read. During a class discussion, have each group answer other students' questions about their poster. Ask **What causes of poverty does this program address? What support and/or criticism has this program received and why? How effective has this program been at reducing poverty? How was this measured? Based on this information, would you change or discontinue support for the program? Explain.**

CREATE A PROFILE

Have students use the Career Link worksheet to record their research for the activity (Unit 5 All-in-One, p. 80).

EXTEND

Have student pairs research the antipoverty policies in different countries, and then report on them to the class.

GUIDING QUESTION WRAP UP

Have students return to the section Guiding Question. Review the completed graphic organizer and clarify any misunderstandings. Have a wrap up discussion about what affects the poverty rate.

Assess and Remediate

L3 **L2** Collect the "Analyzing the Impact of Education and Gender on Income" worksheets and assess student understanding of two causes of poverty.

L4 Collect the "Studying Income Distribution" worksheets and assess student understanding of changes in income distribution.

L3 Assign the Section 3 Assessment questions; identify student misconceptions.

L3 Give Section Quiz A (Unit 5 All-in-One, p. 71).

L2 Give Section Quiz B (Unit 5 All-in-One, p. 72).

(Assess and Remediate continued on p. 356)

Have students complete the Self-Test Online and continue their work in the **Essential Questions Journal**.

REMEDIATION AND SUGGESTIONS

Use the chart below to help students who are struggling with content.

WEAKNESS	REMEDIATION
Identifying key terms (Questions 3, 4, 6)	Have students use the interactive Economic Dictionary Online.
Understanding causes of poverty (Questions 1, 4, 5, 8, 11)	Review the lesson graphic organizers with students.
Explaining income distribution (Questions 6, 9)	Reteach using Figure 13.8 and the data from the in-class activity.
Analyzing antipoverty measures (Questions 7, 10, 11)	Have students review and take notes on the posters.

Answer

Checkpoint to replace welfare with workfare and encourage people to get jobs

block grants federal funds given to the states in lump sums

workfare a program requiring work in exchange for temporary government assistance

earn an adequate income. In addition, the federal government has made a minimum wage mandatory since 1938. The minimum wage ensures that workers' hourly pay will not fall below a certain point.

Housing Assistance

The government also has programs to help poor people obtain affordable housing. In one approach, the government makes payments to landlords who then lower the rent they would otherwise charge. In another program, poor people receive vouchers that cover part of the rent they pay. The third approach is government-owned housing, which charges low rental fees.

Welfare Reform

Poor people often cannot afford basic needs, such as food and medical care. The United States has long had a welfare system that provides for those basic needs, especially for children and the elderly. That system underwent major reform when President Clinton signed the Personal Responsibility and Work Opportunity Reconciliation Act of 1996.

This welfare-reform plan responded to criticisms that welfare encouraged poor people to remain unemployed in order to keep receiving aid. It replaced the traditional antipoverty program for poor families (Aid to Families with Dependent Children, or AFDC) with a new program called Temporary Assistance for Needy Families (TANF). TANF eliminated cash assistance for poor families. Instead, the federal government provides **block grants,** or lump sums of money, to the states. The states are now responsible for designing and implementing programs to move most poor adults from welfare dependence to employment. TANF also set a 5-year limit on receipt of benefits.

The plan calls for a shift from welfare to **workfare**—a program requiring work in exchange for temporary assistance from the government. It was hoped that this reform would reduce poverty by providing poor Americans with labor skills and access to a steady, adequate income.

CHECKPOINT ***What was the goal of TANF?***

SECTION 3 ASSESSMENT

Essential Questions Journal To continue to build a response to the Essential Question, go to your **Essential Questions Journal.**

Guiding Question

1. Use your completed table to answer this question: What factors affect the poverty rate?
2. **Extension** Two candidates for your state legislature have outlined their plans to reduce poverty in the state. The candidates will debate next week, and the public is invited to submit suggestions. What one suggestion would you offer to reduce poverty?

Key Terms and Main Ideas

3. How is the **poverty threshold** related to the **poverty rate?**
4. Explain how a family can include working adults but still have an income below the poverty threshold.
5. How does lack of education contribute to poverty?
6. What is the **Lorenz Curve** and what does a current Lorenz Curve show about the distribution of income in the United States?
7. Describe at least three ways in which the government combats poverty.

Critical Thinking

8. **Extend (a)** What kinds of families are likely to live in poverty? **(b)** Why do you think these families have a greater risk of being poor?
9. **Predict (a)** What are three reasons for differences in income among Americans? **(b)** Do you think these differences are a problem? Why or why not? **(c)** In what ways might the government help make these differences smaller?
10. **Explain (a)** How did the Personal Responsibility and Work Opportunity Reconciliation Act of 1996 change the assistance the government provides to poor families? **(b)** What are some benefits of these new programs? **(c)** What are some drawbacks? Explain your answers.

Quick Write

11. Reread the text under the Income Gap heading in this section. Then write two paragraphs on the income gap. In the first paragraph, describe how the income gap affects society, including economic growth and standard of living. In the second paragraph, predict what the long-term effects would be if the income gap increased, or what the long-term effects would be if the income gap decreased.

Assessment Answers

1. race and ethnicity, gender, type of family, education, age, and place of residence
2. Possible responses: help people gain skills needed for higher-wage jobs; give more direct financial assistance
3. The poverty rate is the percentage of people in the population with incomes below the poverty threshold.
4. The working adults have low-wage jobs.
5. People with less education tend to earn lower wages.
6. A graph that illustrates the distribution of income in a country; income is unequally distributed.
7. Any three: earned income tax credit, enterprise zones, employment assistance, housing assistance, TANF
8. (a) single-parent families (b) Possible responses: because women earn less than men; because it is difficult for one person to earn as much as two can
9. (a) differences in skills and education, inheritances, and type of work they do (b) Possible response: Some degree of difference is inevitable, but efforts are needed to make sure that all people have an equal chance to gain skills and education. (c) Possible response: by funding job-training programs
10. (a) It put a time limit on aid to encourage people to find work. (b) Possible response: It encouraged people to get off welfare because they had to find work. (c) Possible response: If people live in an area where there are no jobs, they have little opportunity.
11. Students' answers should indicate an understanding of the income gap, economic growth, society, and the standard of living.

QUICK STUDY GUIDE

QUICK STUDY GUIDE

Chapter 13: Economic Challenges

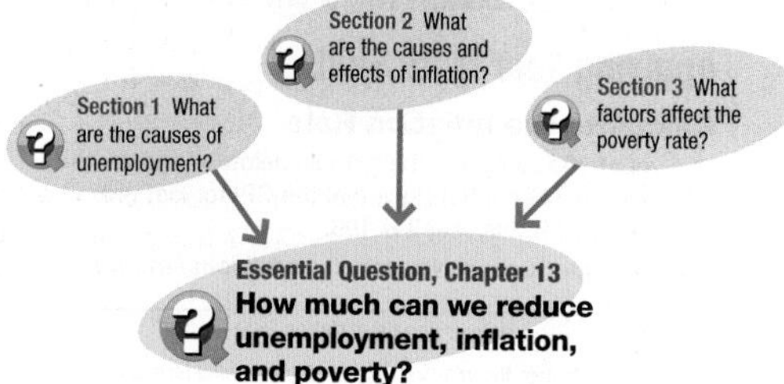
Section 1 What are the causes of unemployment?
Section 2 What are the causes and effects of inflation?
Section 3 What factors affect the poverty rate?
Essential Question, Chapter 13
How much can we reduce unemployment, inflation, and poverty?

Economic Indicators

Unemployment rate	The percentage of the nation's labor force that is unemployed	To find the unemployment rate, divide the number of unemployed people by the total labor force and multiply by 100.
Inflation rate	The percentage rate of change in price level over time as measured by the Consumer Price Index	To calculate the inflation rate, subtract the base year CPI from the current CPI. Then divide the result by the base year CPI and multiply that result by 100.
Poverty rate	The percentage of people who live in households with income below the official poverty threshold	The government establishes a poverty threshold, an income level below which total income is insufficient to support a family or household.

Economic Dictionary

frictional unemployment, *p. 335*
structural unemployment, *p. 336*
globalization, *p. 337*
seasonal unemployment, *p. 338*
cyclical unemployment, *p. 338*
unemployment rate, *p. 339*
full employment, *p. 340*
underemployed, *p. 340*
discouraged worker, *p. 341*
inflation, *p. 342*
purchasing power, *p. 342*
price index, *p. 343*
Consumer Price Index, *p. 343*
market basket, *p. 343*
inflation rate, *p. 343*
core inflation rate, *p. 345*
hyperinflation, *p. 345*
quantity theory, *p. 346*
wage-price spiral, *p. 347*
fixed income, *p. 347*
deflation, *p. 348*
poverty threshold, *p. 349*
poverty rate, *p. 350*
income distribution, *p. 351*
food stamp program, *p. 351*
Lorenz Curve, *p. 353*
enterprise zone, *p. 355*
block grant, *p. 356*
workfare, *p. 356*

Economics on the go

Study anytime, anywhere. Download these files today.

Economic Dictionary online	Audio Review online	Action Graph online	Visual Glossary online	How the Economy Works online
Vocabulary Support in English and Spanish	Audio Study Guide in English and Spanish	Animated Charts and Graphs	Animated feature	Animated feature

Download to your computer or mobile device at PearsonSuccessNet.com

ASSIGN THE ESSENTIAL QUESTIONS JOURNAL

After students have finished studying the chapter, they should return to the chapter's essential question in the Essential Questions Journal and complete the activity.

Tell students to go back to the chapter opener and look at the image. Using the information they have gained from studying the chapter, ask **How does this illustrate the main ideas of the chapter?** *(Possible response: The person may be at an employment center looking over job opportunities because she is out of work.)*

STUDY TIPS

Point out that procrastination is a common reason that students do not get needed work done, and that many students procrastinate when faced with tasks they perceive as large and complex. One way of avoiding this problem is to break tasks into several small steps. By doing a little bit every day, what seemed overwhelming becomes manageable.

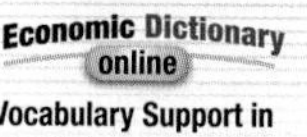 Have students download the digital resources available at Economics on the Go for review and remediation.

Assessment at a Glance

TESTS AND QUIZZES

Section Assessments

Section Quizzes A and B, **Unit 5 All-in-One**
Self-Test Online

Chapter Assessments

Chapter Tests A and B, **Unit 5 All-in-One**
Economic Detective, **Unit 5 All-in-One**
Document-Based Assessment, p. 359
Exam*View*

AYP Monitoring Assessments

PERFORMANCE ASSESSMENT

Teacher's Edition, pp. 337, 339, 345, 347, 351, 354
Simulation Activities, Chapter 13
Virtual Economics on CD-ROM, pp. 339, 345, 353
Essential Questions Journal, Chapter 13
Assessment Rubrics

Chapter Assessment

1. (a) A higher-than-normal unemployment rate is one possible sign that the economy is unhealthy. (b) Full employment exists at an unemployment rate of about 4 to 6 percent, due to frictional, seasonal, and structural unemployment. (c) inflation **2.** Possible responses: (a) rising production costs; weather conditions; rising demand for food (b) Possible answers: buy less expensive food items; cut back on other purchases (c) As prices go up, purchasing power goes down, making it difficult for people to make ends meet. Higher prices could cause drops in demand, leading to layoffs. **3.** (a) by making sure the supply of money grows at the same rate as the economy as a whole (b) Possible responses: fixing prices; forcing employers to hold down wages (c) Possible responses: to protect purchasing power; to prevent inflation from leading to a recession **4.** (a) shifts in family structure, location, racial and gender discrimination, growth of low-skill service jobs, lack of education (b) the earned income tax credit, expanded job opportunities for those who live in enterprise zones, help with finding a job and paying for housing, temporary help through TANF (c) Possible response: Someone who works hard to gain more education and skills would be more likely to get a higher wage job and thus escape poverty. **5.** Possible responses: (a) might help people to escape poverty; might contribute to wage-price spiral (b) to make it easier for businesses to plan ways to accommodate the change (c) Possible response: This strategy does not make sense, because prices will probably rise faster than those small wage increases. To escape poverty for good, people need better skills that allow them to get higher wage jobs. **6.** 2.4 percent **7.** 2.5 percent **8.** 168 **9.** 184.8 **10.** Give the groups time to brainstorm their ideas. Be sure to check their worksheets before they move on to modify the activity. **11.** (a) Possible responses: encouraging businesses to provide computer training to their employees in exchange for the employees' commitment to stay; careful monitoring of the money supply; providing early childhood education programs for poorer families (b)–(d) Discuss the various groups' suggestions as a class. As students discuss each proposal, challenge them to examine the advantages and disadvantages, with each group offering constructive comments on other groups' suggestions. Guide the class to develop a consensus solution.

CHAPTER 13 ASSESSMENT

Self-Test online To test your understanding of key terms and main ideas, visit **PearsonSuccessNet.com**

Key Terms and Main Ideas

To make sure you understand the key terms and main ideas of this chapter, review the Checkpoint and Section Assessment questions and look at the Quick Study Guide on the preceding page.

Critical Thinking

1. **Predict (a)** What does the unemployment rate tell about a country's economy? **(b)** How is full employment related to the unemployment rate? **(c)** What issues might arise if the economy reached full employment?
2. **Apply (a)** What might cause inflation in food prices? **(b)** How would you react to higher food prices? **(c)** How could this type of inflation contribute to unemployment and poverty? Explain your answers.
3. **Draw Conclusions (a)** According to the quantity theory, how can the government limit inflation? **(b)** What other tools can the government use to control inflation? **(c)** Why would the government want to reduce inflation?
4. **Extend (a)** What are the most recognized causes of poverty? **(b)** What kinds of assistance might a poor family be able to get from the government? **(c)** What combination of personal action and good fortune could help a person rise out of poverty?
5. **Make Judgments (a)** On May 25, 2007, President George W. Bush signed a bill to increase the federal minimum wage in three steps: to $5.85 per hour starting in July 2007; to $6.55 per hour starting in July 2008; and to $7.25 per hour starting in July 2009. What are some possible results of raising the minimum wage? **(b)** Why do you think the government chose to raise the minimum wage in stages, rather than all at once? **(c)** Do you think this is a good strategy? Why or why not?

Applying Your Math Skills

Calculate the Inflation Rate

Use your math skills and the formula below to answer the following questions. Suppose that the CPI for last year was 164 and that for this year it is 168.

Visit PearsonSuccessNet.com for additional math help.

Calculating the Inflation Rate

To calculate the inflation rate, use the following formula:

CPI for Year A **minus** CPI for Year B **divided by** CPI for Year B **multiplied by** 100

For example,
If the CPI for 2004 (Year A) = 188.9
and the CPI for 2003 (Year B) = 184.0

then,
188.9 – 184.0 = 4.9
4.9 ÷ 184.0 = .027
.027 x 100 = 2.7

Therefore,
the inflation rate for 2004 was 2.7%.

6. Calculate the inflation rate from last year to this year.
7. Suppose the CPI for the year before last year was 160. What was the inflation rate from the previous year to last year?
8. If the inflation rate were 0%, what would the CPI be for next year?
9. If the inflation rate were 10%, what would the CPI be for next year?

Essential Question Activity

Essential Questions Journal To respond to the chapter Essential Question, go to your **Essential Questions Journal**.

10. Complete this activity to answer the Essential Question **How much can we reduce unemployment, inflation, and poverty?** Your class should be divided into three groups. Each group is advising the President of the United States on ways that the federal government can help reduce unemployment, inflation, and poverty. Using the worksheet in your Essential Questions Journal or the electronic worksheet available at **PearsonSuccessNet.com,** gather the following information:
    - **(a)** With globalization accelerating, and the loss of America's manufacturing base, what can we do to reduce unemployment? What is one benefit and one drawback of your plan?
    - **(b)** What strategy or strategies would you recommend to reduce inflation? What is one benefit and one drawback of your plan?
    - **(c)** What strategy or strategies would you recommend to reduce poverty? What is one benefit and one drawback of your plan?
11. **Modify** Present your group's ideas to the class. As a class, discuss the suggestions from all the groups.
    - **(a)** What are the best ideas for reducing unemployment? What are the best ideas for controlling inflation? What are the best ideas for reducing poverty?
    - **(b)** Do any of these ideas and goals conflict with each other? (For example, cutting taxes without reducing government spending could trigger inflation. Cutting taxes and cutting spending on entitlement programs could put more children below the poverty level.) How?
    - **(c)** How can these conflicts best be resolved?
    - **(d)** At the conclusion of your discussion, identify which steps you think would be most effective and most acceptable to the majority of the population.

WebQuest online The Economics WebQuest challenges students to use 21st century skills to answer the Essential Question.

THE ESSENTIAL
VIDEO
By Students For Students
For videos on Essential Questions, go to PearsonSuccessNet.com

Remind students to continue to develop an Essential Questions video. Guidelines and a production binder are available at www.PearsonSuccessNet.com.

DOCUMENT-BASED ASSESSMENT

Should the government help the poor?

In the United States, the federal government and local governments provide many kinds of welfare assistance to the poor. Some people argue that this aid is necessary to help reduce poverty. Others believe that providing welfare is not an appropriate role for government, and that private organizations can do a better job of helping the poor. Some also feel that government aid makes people less able and willing to earn a living independently.

Document A

"Voluntary charities and organizations, such as friendly societies that devoted themselves to helping those in need, flourished in the days before the welfare state turned charity into a government function.... Today, government welfare programs have supplemented the old-style private programs.... Releasing the charitable impulses of the American people by freeing them from the excessive tax burden so they can devote more of their resources to charity, is a moral and constitutional means of helping the needy."

—Representative Ron Paul (R-TX) in the U.S. House of Representatives, February 13, 2003

Document B

"What's most overwhelming about urban poverty is that it's so difficult to escape—it's isolating and it's everywhere....When you're in these neighborhoods, you can see what a difference it makes to have a government that cares. You can see what a free lunch program does for a hungry child. You can see what a little extra money from an earned income tax credit does for a family that's struggling. You can see what prenatal care does for the health of a mother and a newborn. So don't tell me there's no role for government in lifting up our cities."

—Senator Barack Obama (D-IL) speech in Washington, DC, July 18, 2007
www.barackobama.com

Document C

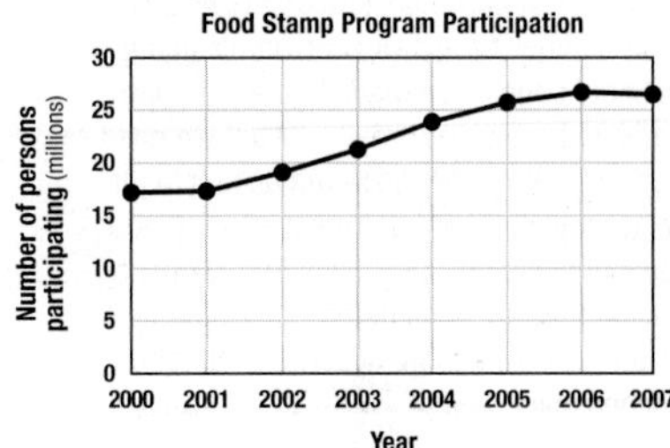

SOURCE: United States Department of Agriculture, Food and Nutrition Service

ANALYZING DOCUMENTS

Use your knowledge of government aid to the poor and Documents A, B, and C to answer questions 1–3.

1. **According to Document A, what does Representative Ron Paul believe would be a better alternative to federal welfare payments to the poor?**
   A. local government welfare programs
   B. private charities
   C. state government welfare programs
   D. ignoring poverty

2. **The author of Document B believes**
   A. that ending poverty is too costly.
   B. that Americans hear too much about poverty.
   C. that fighting poverty is a job for government.
   D. that government is not accountable for poverty.

3. **What does Document C suggest?**
   A. Food stamps are preventing poverty.
   B. The food stamp program is unsuccessful.
   C. Poverty is increasing, so more people need food stamps.
   D. The food stamp program should be privatized.

WRITING ABOUT ECONOMICS

Whether government aid is the best way to reduce poverty is an ongoing question. Use the documents on this page and resources on the Web site below to answer the question: ***Should the government help the poor?***

In Partnership

THE WALL STREET JOURNAL.
CLASSROOM EDITION

To read more about issues related to this topic, visit **PearsonSuccessNet.com**

Document-Based Assessment

ANALYZING DOCUMENTS

1. B
2. C
3. C

WRITING ABOUT ECONOMICS

Possible answers: Advantages of helping the poor: Doing so prevents people from starving or being homeless; the purchases that poor people are able to make with the government's assistance help the economy. Disadvantages of helping the poor: Giving aid to poor people does not encourage them to improve their lives; government aid to the poor means higher taxes for working people.

Student essay should demonstrate an understanding of the issues involved in poverty. Use the following as guidelines to assess the essay.

L2 Differentiate Students use all documents on the page to support their thesis.

L3 Differentiate Students use the documents on this page and additional information available online at www.PearsonSuccessNet.com to support their answer.

L4 Differentiate Students incorporate information provided in the textbook and online at www.PearsonSuccessNet.com and include additional research to support their opinion.

Go Online to www.PearsonSuccessNet.com for a student rubric and extra documents.

Economics online *All print resources are available on the Teacher's Resource Library CD-ROM and online at* www.PearsonSuccessNet.com.

Essential Question

Why does it matter how the economy is doing?

BELLRINGER

Ask students to read the paragraph under the Essential Question. Then have volunteers suggest examples of why it might matter to ordinary people if the economy is doing well or doing poorly.

EXPLAIN

Before you read aloud the quotation from the *Christian Science Monitor* article, you may want to explain that although the *Monitor* is published by the First Church of Christ, Scientist, it is not a religious newspaper. The *Monitor* is a highly respected international news source and has won seven Pulitzer Prizes.

DISCUSS

Have students review the quotations on the page. Ask students to explain how the economy's health may or may not matter to ordinary people. **Why is GDP an imperfect measure of the economy's health?** *(It does not measure quality of life, so it does not reflect the wealth of an average person.)* **Why is housing so vital to the nation's economic well-being?** *(There is a ripple effect: houses foreclose, people lose their homes, building trades decline, and the effect is felt by most people.)* **Why might it be a good idea to keep an eye on the economy's health?** *(Possible answer: Considering the possible consequences of changes in the economy will aid you in making wise investment decisions.)*

ANALYZE A CARTOON

Have students silently read the cartoon's caption. Have them work in small groups to brainstorm a list of ways an everyday person might suffer from high inflation rates or high interest rates. Invite volunteers to share their work with the class.

BULLETIN BOARD ACTIVITY

Have students revisit the Unit Essential Question articles that they have posted as they have studied the chapters. Have them discuss the relevance of the articles to the question and whether their opinions have changed since they first read the article. Remind students to review their work in their **Essential Questions Journal**.

EXTEND

Have students complete their work on the Essential Questions Video and present their work to the class.

Unit 5 Challenge

Essential Question, Unit 5
Why does it matter how the economy is doing?

THE ESSENTIAL
VIDEO
By Students For Students
For videos on Essential Questions, go to PearsonSuccessNet.com

Does economic news about GDP or inflation really matter to ordinary people? Plenty of people think that it does. Look at the opinions below, keeping in mind the Essential Question: Why does it matter how the economy is doing?

"Economists readily concede that GDP is not a one-number-fits-all view of what's going on. Some suggest changes to make it more useful and more accurate…. 'What we need to end up with is two separate accounts [of the economy]—a market price account and a quality of life account,' says Rob Atkinson, an economist in Washington…. 'It is an opportunity to think more accurately about our economic well-being.'"

—Mark Trumbull, "Does GDP Really Capture Economic Health?" Christian Science Monitor, March 12, 2008

"The U.S. economy is taking hits from all directions, or that's how it seems to many Americans…. Home foreclosures are multiplying. People with houses can't sell them. Home prices and sales dropped dramatically in January, and there's no sign of improvement soon. Banks no longer provide easy credit. Stock-market investments are on a roller-coaster ride. Pay checks don't buy as much today as yesterday…. Americans want to know what will turn the economy around. They want help and answers—from Congress and the president."

—*Miami Herald*, February 29, 2008

edgar argo

"I DON'T UNDERSTAND HOW HIGH INTEREST RATES AND THE NATIONAL DEFICIT AFFECT MY ALLOWANCE."

Essential Question Writing Activity

Consider the different views of economics expressed in the sources on this page and what you have learned about measuring economic performance. ***Then write a well-constructed essay expressing your view of why it is important to keep track of the economy.***

Writing Guidelines

- Address all aspects of the Essential Question Writing Activity.
- Support the theme with relevant facts, examples, and details.
- Use a logical and clear plan of organization.
- Introduce the theme by establishing a framework that is beyond a simple restatement of the question and conclude with a summation of the theme.

For help in writing a Persuasive Essay, refer to the *Writer's Handbook* in the Reference section, page S-5.

Essential Questions Journal

To respond to the unit Essential Question, go to your **Essential Questions Journal.**

360 UNIT REVIEW

Essential Question Writing Activity

Before students begin the writing activity, remind them to skim through the unit chapters to read the headings on each page. Have them read through any notes they took and to review their chapter assessments and chapter projects.

Students should write a two-paragraph article. Paragraph one should outline how the economy's performance could affect them personally. Paragraph two should explain how the economy's performance affects people in general.

L2 Differentiate Students should write a paragraph that explains how the economy's performance affects them personally, providing detailed examples.

L4 Differentiate Students should write a three-paragraph article that provides relevant examples of why it matters how the economy is doing.

Before students begin work, distribute the Writing Assessment rubric, available at the Online Teacher Center at PearsonSuccessNet.com.

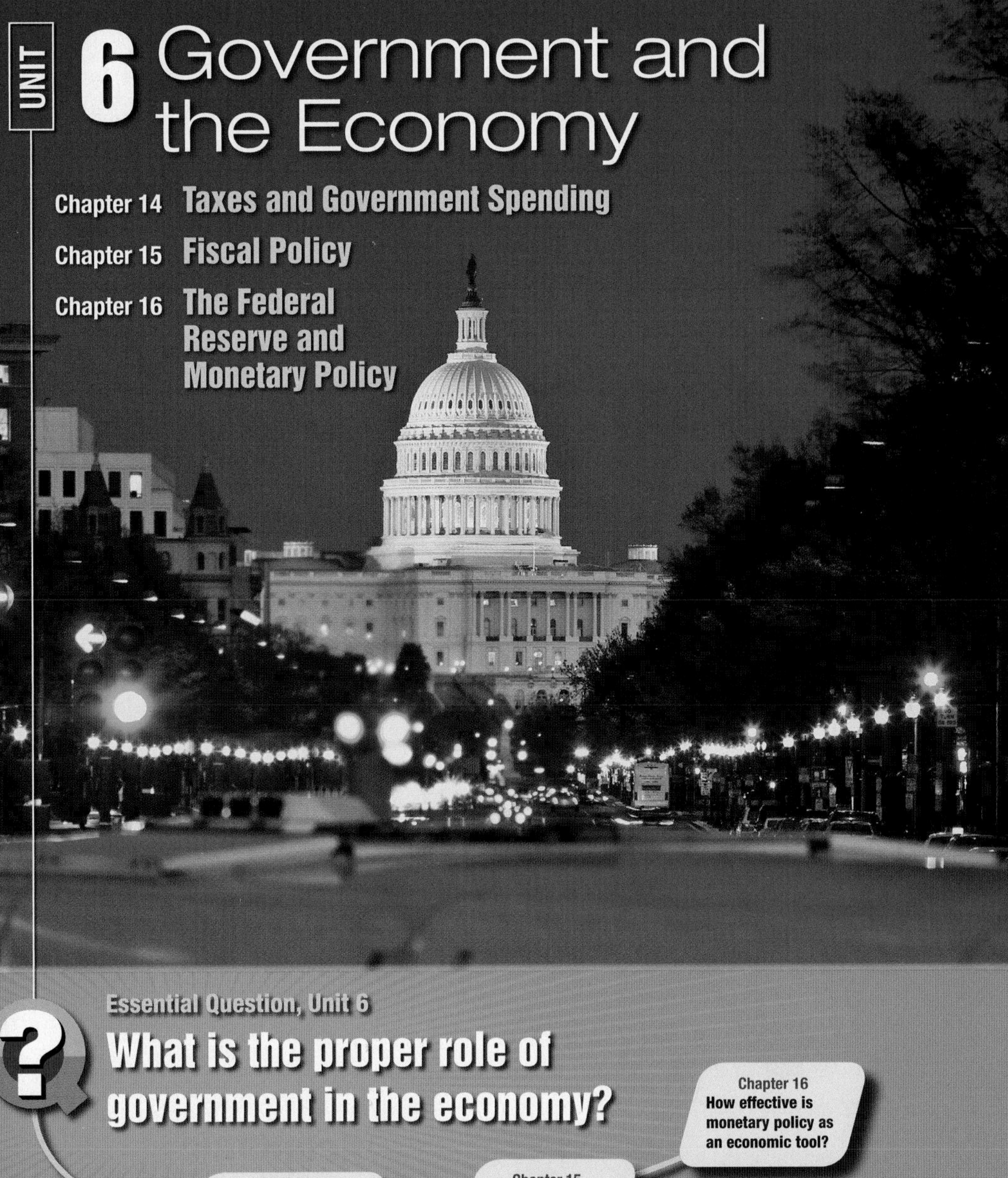

UNIT 6 Government and the Economy
Chapter 14 Taxes and Government Spending
Chapter 15 Fiscal Policy
Chapter 16 The Federal Reserve and Monetary Policy

Essential Question, Unit 6

What is the proper role of government in the economy?

Chapter 14
How can taxation meet the needs of government and the people?

Chapter 15
How effective is fiscal policy as an economic tool?

Chapter 16
How effective is monetary policy as an economic tool?

Online Resources

Economics Online Teacher Center at PearsonSuccessNet.com includes

- Online Teacher's Edition with lesson planner
- Online Lecture Notes
- Teacher's Resource Library with All-in-One Resources, Color Transparencies, Simulation Activities, and Adequate Yearly Progress Monitoring
- SuccessTracker Assessment

Economics Online Student Center at PearsonSuccessNet.com includes

- Interactive textbook with audio
- Economics Video
- WebQuests
- Interactivities
- Student Self-Tests

Essential Question

What is the proper role of government in the economy?

Introduce the Unit

ACTIVATE PRIOR KNOWLEDGE

Essential questions frame each unit and chapter of study, asking students to consider big ideas about economics. Write the Unit Essential Question on the Board: **What is the proper role of government in the economy?** Using the Idea Wave Discussion strategy (p. T24), have students brainstorm answers to the question.

WRITING ACTIVITY

To begin this unit, assign the Unit 6 Warmup Activity in the **Essential Questions Journal**. This will help students start to consider their position on the Unit 6 Essential Question: **What is the proper role of government in the economy?**

Use the **Essential Questions Journal** throughout the program to help students consider these and other big ideas about economics.

BULLETIN BOARD ACTIVITY

Post the Unit Essential Question on a bulletin board. Tell students that they will be learning about the government's role in the economy. Ask them to bring in articles about current events to help them answer the question. Students should identify their article and use a sticky note to briefly explain the connection to the Essential Question.

CREATING THE ESSENTIAL QUESTIONS VIDEO

Preview the Unit Challenge on page 444. Consider assigning this activity to your students. Tell them that they will be creating their own video to explore this question, and that they should keep this in mind as they study the government's role in the economy. For further information about how to complete this activity, go to PearsonSuccessNet.com.

NATIONAL COUNCIL ON ECONOMIC EDUCATION

The following Voluntary National Content Standards in Economics are addressed in this unit:

- ★ **Standard 12**
- ★ **Standard 16**
- ★ **Standard 17**
- ★ **Standard 20**

For a complete description of the standards addressed in each chapter, see the Correlations chart on pages T52–T55.

Essential Questions

UNIT 6:

What is the proper role of government in the economy?

CHAPTER 14:

How can taxation meet the needs of government and the people?

Introduce the Chapter

ACTIVATE PRIOR KNOWLEDGE

In this chapter, students will learn about taxes and government spending policies. Tell students to complete the warmup activity in their **Essential Questions Journal**.

DIFFERENTIATED INSTRUCTION KEY

- **L1** Special Needs
- **L2** Basic to Average includes
  - **ELL** English Language Learners
  - **LPR** Less Proficient Readers
- **L3** All Students
- **L4** Advanced Students

Economics online Visit www.PearsonSuccessNet.com for an interactive textbook with built-in activities on economic principles.

- ***The Wall Street Journal*** **Classroom Edition Video** presents a current topic related to federal taxes.
- **Yearly Update Worksheet** provides an annual update, including a new worksheet and lesson on this topic.
- **On the Go** resources can be downloaded so students and teachers can connect with economics anytime, anywhere.

ECONOMICS ONLINE

DIGITAL TEACHER TOOLS

The online lesson planner is designed to help teachers plan, teach, and assess. Teachers have the ability to use or customize existing Pearson lesson plans. Online lecture notes support the print lesson.

Two interactivities in this lesson are:

- **Action Graphs** Animated graphs break down a print graph on the Elasticities of Demand and Tax Effects.
- **How the Economy Works** provides an interactive look at how the government uses taxes to fund different programs and what those programs can do.

Chapter 14 Taxes and Government Spending

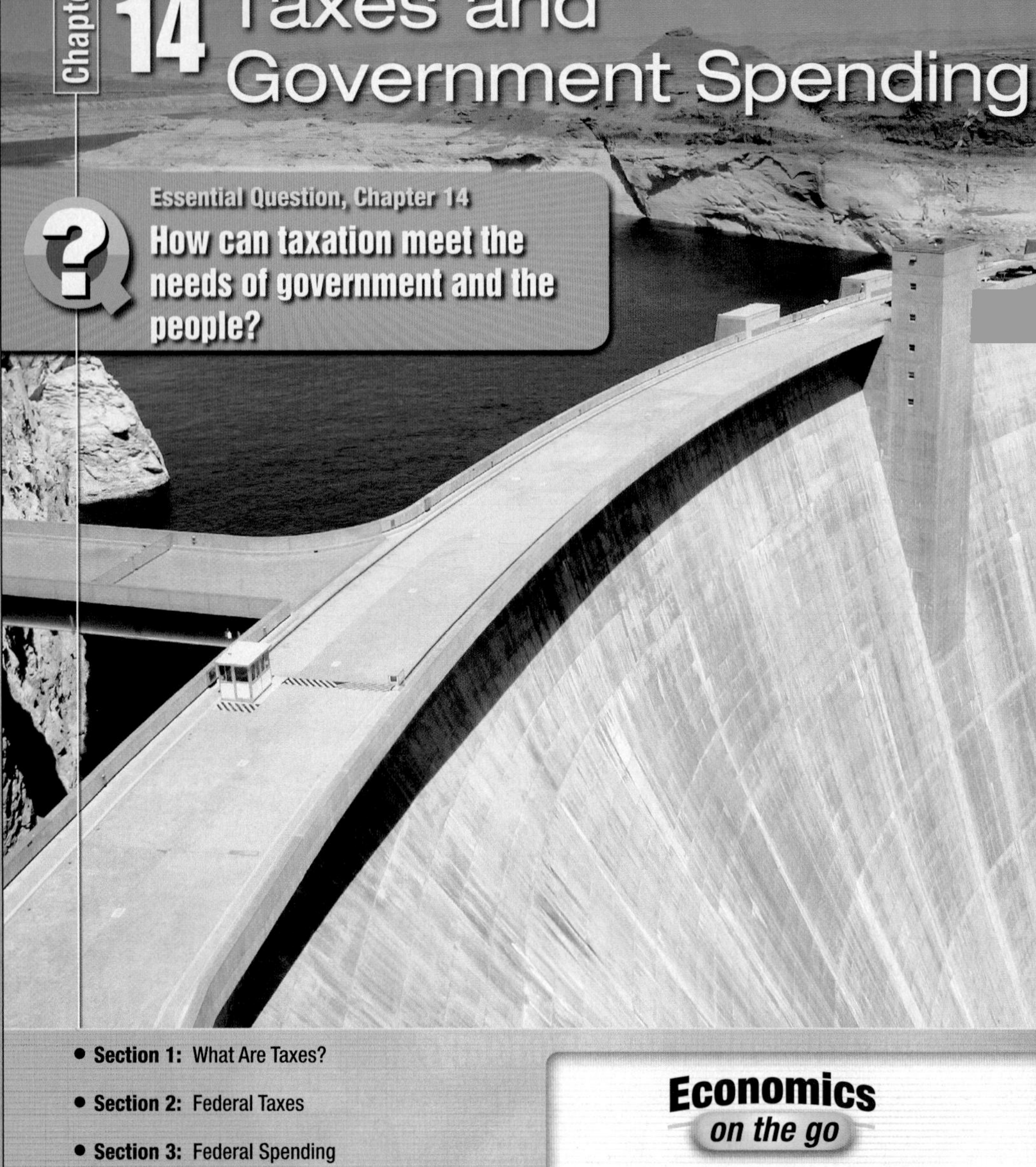

Essential Question, Chapter 14

How can taxation meet the needs of government and the people?

Economics on the go

To study anywhere, anytime, download these online resources at ***PearsonSuccessNet.com*** ▶

Block Scheduling

BLOCK 1 Teach Sections 1 and 2 lessons, omitting the Bellringer activity and Extend options.

BLOCK 2 Use the Section 3 Bellringer and How the Economy Works feature to teach Section 3 and teach the Section 4 lesson.

Pressed for Time

Summarizing Organize the class into four groups, assigning each group one of the sections. Use the Jigsaw strategy to have one student from each group learn about and brief three other students—one from each of the other groups—on his or her section.

Have students complete the Self-Test Online and continue their work in the **Essential Questions Journal**.

REMEDIATION AND SUGGESTIONS

Use the chart below to help students who are struggling with content.

WEAKNESS	REMEDIATION
Identifying key terms (Questions 3, 4, 5, 6, 7)	Have students use the interactive Economic Dictionary Online.
Describing tax bases and structures (Questions 6, 7, 9, 10)	Have students identify every tax that they are aware of that they or members of their families pay. Have them discuss and identify the tax base and tax structure for each.
Identifying who bears the burden of a tax (Question 10)	Reteach the concept using the Action Graph online.

Answers

Caption only those who use gas pay the tax

Checkpoint simplicity, efficiency, certainty, equity

▲ The gasoline tax is an example of the benefits-received principle. ***How does it fit that principle?***

- ***Certainty*** Certainty is also a characteristic of a good tax. It should be clear to the taxpayer when a tax is due, how much money is due, and how the tax should be paid.
- ***Equity*** The tax system should be fair, so that no one bears too much or too little of the tax burden.

Determining Fairness

Although everyone agrees that a tax system should be fair to taxpayers, people often disagree on what "fair" really means. Over time, economists have proposed two different ideas about how to measure the fairness of a tax.

The first idea is called the benefits-received principle. According to this principle, a person should pay taxes based on the level of benefits he or she expects to receive from the government. People who drive, for example, pay gasoline taxes that are used to build and maintain highways. In this way, the people who receive the most benefit from the roads also contribute the most to their upkeep.

The second idea about fairness is called the ability-to-pay principle. According to this principle, people should pay taxes according to their ability to pay. The ability-to-pay principle is the idea behind a progressive income tax: people who earn more income pay more taxes.

Balancing Tax Revenues and Tax Rates

How much revenue does a good tax generate? The answer is "enough, but not too much." That is, enough so that citizens' needs are met, but not so much that the tax discourages production. For example, if a company has to pay $100,000 in taxes, it will not be able to use that $100,000 to expand production. If tax rates are lower, however, the company can use more of its income to stimulate production rather than to pay taxes. Ultimately, many people argue, the economy benefits from lower, rather than higher, tax rates.

CHECKPOINT *What are the four characteristics of a good tax?*

Essential Questions Journal To continue to build a response to the Essential Question, go to your **Essential Questions Journal**.

SECTION 1 ASSESSMENT

Guiding Question

1. Use your completed concept web to answer this question: What are the features of a tax system?
2. **Extension** Tax revenue helps governments provide citizens with goods and services. What kind of taxes do you pay to get these services?

Key Terms and Main Ideas

3. Where does the U.S. government get the power to impose **taxes** today?
4. What is a government's **revenue?**
5. Name two limits the Constitution places on the government's power to tax.
6. What is the tax base for the **sales tax?**
7. Suppose Michelle earns $40,000 per year and Rosa earns $100,000 per year. Under a **proportional tax,** who would pay a greater percentage of her income in taxes?

Critical Thinking

8. **Extend (a)** What does it mean if a tax system is efficient? **(b)** Why is it important that taxes be efficient?
9. **Contrast** How do progressive taxes work? How are they different from regressive taxes?
10. **Predict** Suppose the government imposed a new tax on toothpaste. **(a)** Who would probably end up bearing the incidence of the tax? **(b)** Give a reason for your answer.

Math Skills

11. **Finding Sales Tax** To find sales tax, start by converting the percent of the tax into a decimal. Multiply the decimal by the price of the item that is taxed. Your result is the amount of the sales tax. To find the total cost of the product, add the original price to the sales tax. Suppose Victor buys a pair of pants that cost $38. He has to pay 8 percent sales tax on the pants. What is the total amount Victor has to pay?

Visit PearsonSuccessNet.com for additional math help.

Assessment Answers

1. Possible response: They have regressive, progressive, proportional structures; taxes evaluated for simplicity, equity, efficiency, and certainty.
2. Possible responses: income tax, sales tax
3. from the people and the Constitution
4. money collected from taxes and other sources
5. Federal taxes must be for the common good and the same in every state.
6. goods and services that are sold
7. They would both pay the same percentage.
8. (a) Taxes are collected in short time at low cost. (b) Efficiency reduces waste, allowing more revenue to be spent on goods and services rather than on collecting the tax itself.
9. With a progressive tax, people with a higher income pay a higher percentage of their income in tax. By contrast, with a regressive tax, the percentage of income paid in taxes goes down as income increases.
10. Possible responses: (a) consumers (b) because demand is inelastic—people need toothpaste.
11. $41.04 ($38 + $3.04)

different set of answers. Graph A represents the effect of a gasoline tax when demand is inelastic. Graph B reflects elastic demand.

Both graphs show two supply curves: an original supply line and a line showing the supply after the $.50 tax is imposed. When a tax is imposed on a good, the cost of supplying the good increases. The supply of the good then decreases at every price level.

Before the tax, the market was in equilibrium, and consumers bought gas at $1.00 per gallon. This is shown as point *i* on both graphs. If demand for gas is relatively inelastic (that is, if consumers buy about the same amount no matter what the price), the tax will increase the price of each gallon by a relatively large amount. Consumers will bear a large share of the tax. This is shown in Graph A. Demand is inelastic, so the demand curve is relatively steep, and a $.50 tax increases the equilibrium price by $.40 (from $1.00 to $1.40 from point *i* to point *f*). In other words, consumers pay about four fifths of the tax.

In contrast, if demand is relatively elastic, the demand curve will be relatively flat, as in Graph B. Consumers will pay a relatively small part of the tax. As Graph B shows, a $.50 tax increases the equilibrium price by only $.10 (from $1.00 to $1.10 from point *i* to point *g*). In this case, consumers pay only one fifth of the tax. The service stations pay the other four fifths.

This example shows the **incidence of a tax**—that is, the final burden of a tax. When policymakers consider a new tax, they examine who will actually bear the burden. As in the example above, producers can "pass on" a portion of the burden to consumers. Generally, the more inelastic the demand, the more easily the seller can shift the tax to consumers. The more elastic the demand, the more the seller bears the burden.

CHECKPOINT ***Who bears the greater burden of a tax when demand is inelastic?***

Characteristics of a Good Tax

Although it is sometimes difficult to decide whether a specific tax is proportional, progressive, or regressive, economists do generally agree on what makes a good tax. A good tax should have four characteristics: simplicity, efficiency, certainty, and equity, or fairness.

- *Simplicity* Tax laws should be simple and easily understood. Taxpayers and businesses should be able to keep the necessary records and pay the taxes on a predictable schedule.
- *Efficiency* Government administrators should be able to assess and collect taxes without spending too much time or money. Similarly, taxpayers should be able to pay taxes without giving up too much time or paying too much money in fees.

incidence of a tax the final burden of a tax

FUTURE WATCH **Global Impact**

Taxes Around the World

Not every nation levies an income tax on people who work within its borders. Oil rich Saudi Arabia, for example, abolished the income tax in 1975. However, the vast majority of nations depend to some extent on income taxes to pay for government programs. American taxpayers have neither the heaviest, nor the lightest of tax burdens. ***Suggest two reasons why countries might have vastly different tax burdens.***

Tax Rates in Different Countries

Percent of Earnings Paid in Income and Social Security Taxes

Mexico	5%
Korea	10.6%
Ireland	14.8%
Japan	19.5%
United States	23.4%
Canada	24.2%
United Kingdom	26.8%
Sweden	31.1%
Denmark	40.9%
Germany	42.7%

Taxes paid by single taxpayers with no children

SOURCE: OECD, Economic Outlook No.79, June 2006

ANALYZE

Distribute the worksheet "A Good Tax?" (Unit 6 All-in-One, p. 17). Review with students the four criteria described in the text for determining if a tax is a good tax. Encourage students to describe each of the four criteria in their own words. Then have students study and analyze the cartoon and answer the questions.

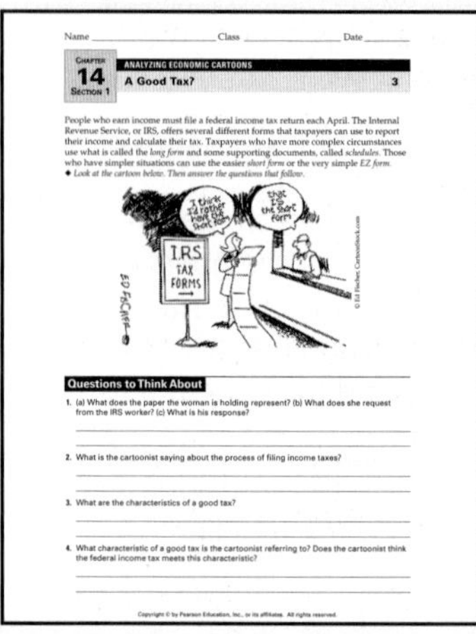
Name ______ Class ______ Date ______

CHAPTER 14 SECTION 1 — ANALYZING ECONOMIC CARTOONS — A Good Tax? — 3

People who earn income must file a federal income tax return each April. The Internal Revenue Service, or IRS, offers several different forms that taxpayers can use to report their income and calculate their tax. Taxpayers who have more complex circumstances use what is called the *long form* and some supporting documents, called *schedules*. Those who have simpler situations can use the easier *short form* or the very simple *EZ form*.

◆ *Look at the cartoon below. Then answer the questions that follow.*

Questions to Think About

1. (a) What does the paper the woman is holding represent? (b) What does she request from the IRS worker? (c) What is his response?
2. What is the cartoonist saying about the process of filing income taxes?
3. What are the characteristics of a good tax?
4. What characteristic of a good tax is the cartoonist referring to? Does the cartoonist think the federal income tax meets this characteristic?

L2 Differentiate Distribute the "A Good Tax?" worksheet (Unit 6 All-in-One, p. 18).

EXTEND

Have students return to the three quotes in the Bellringer. Have them chose one and write a paragraph in which they agree or disagree with the view and explain why.

L4 Differentiate Distribute the worksheet "The Flat Tax" (Unit 6 All-in-One, p. 19). Have students read the pros and cons of a proportional or flat tax, answer the questions, and state their own views.

GUIDING QUESTION WRAP UP

Have students return to the section Guiding Question. Review the completed graphic organizer. Have a discussion about the features of a tax system.

Assess and Remediate

L3 L2 L4 Collect the "A Good Tax?" and "The Flat Tax" worksheets and assess student understanding of tax systems.

L3 Assign the Section 1 Assessment questions.

L3 Give Section Quiz A (Unit 6 All-in-One, p. 20).

L2 Give Section Quiz B (Unit 6 All-in-One, p. 21).

(Assess and Remediate continued on p. 368)

Answers

Checkpoint consumers

Global Impact different tax bases, different government services

Virtual Economics

L3 Differentiate

Predicting How Taxes Affect People Use the following lesson from the NCEE **Virtual Economics *CD-ROM*** to explore how taxes can be incentives. Click on Browse Economics Lessons, specify grades 9–12, and use the key words *taxes be incentives.*

In this activity, students will work in small groups to predict the outcome of various situations.

LESSON TITLE	CAN TAXES BE INCENTIVES?
Type of Activity	Small group
Complexity	Low
Time	60 minutes
NCEE Standards	4, 16

COMPARE AND CONTRAST

Display the "Progressive and Regressive Taxes" transparency (Color Transparencies, 14.a). Explain to students that the graph estimates the proportion of income that households at three income levels would pay in taxes in the state of Indiana. Make sure students understand that the percentages show a proportion of income, not tax rates. Ask **How does the proportion of income paid for state income tax differ for these three households?** *(3 percent for the lowest-income household, just under 4 percent for the middle-level household, just over 4 percent for the highest-income household)* **What is the structure of this income tax? Why?** *(It is progressive because the percentage of income paid goes up as income goes up.)*

Ask **What percentage of income goes to the state sales tax?** *(The percentage falls from a high of about 3.3 percent for the lowest-income household to a low of about 1.4 percent for the highest-income household.)* **What structure does that tax have?** *(It is regressive because the percentage of income paid for this tax decreases as income increases.)*

Ask **What is the structure of the gasoline tax? Why?** *(It is also regressive because the proportion declines as income increases.)* Ask **Why does the incidence of a tax on gasoline fall most heavily on the consumer?** *(Demand for gasoline is relatively inelastic in the short run.)*

Action Graph online Have students review the Action Graph animation for a step-by-step look at Elasticities of Demand and Tax Effects.

L4 Differentiate Explain to students that some states institute tax holidays, during which no sales tax is charged for certain goods, at particular times of the year. Ask students to research the sales tax rates in their community, county, and state, and show which items are or are not subject to sales tax, and the existence of any sales tax holidays. Students should prepare a chart for distribution. Note that some states do not have a sales tax.

Figure 14.1 Elasticities of Demand and Tax Effects

Graph A

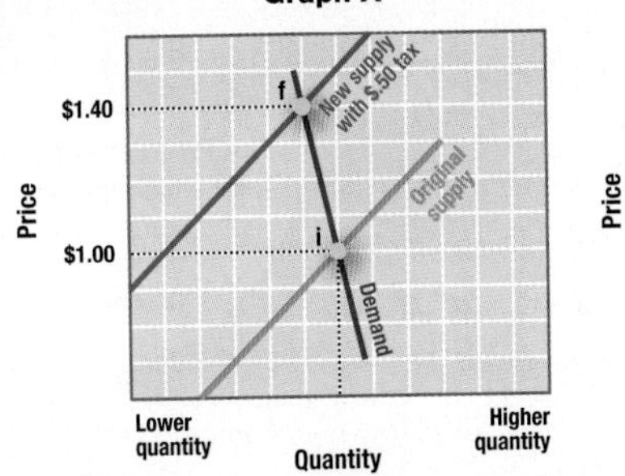

Graph B

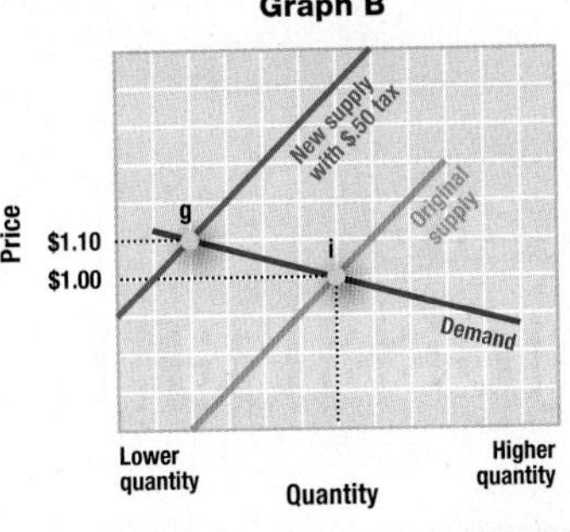

GRAPH SKILLS

If demand for a good is relatively inelastic (Graph A), a new tax will increase the price by a relatively large amount, and consumers will pay a large share of the tax.

1. Under what conditions, elastic or inelastic demand, would price of the good increase from $1.00 to $1.10?
2. Who bears the burden of a tax if demand is relatively elastic?

Action Graph online

For an animated version of this graph, visit PearsonSuccessNet.com

year. Tony Owens, a nurse, earns $50,000 per year. If a 6 percent proportional tax were levied on their incomes, Leslie would pay 6 percent of $350,000, or $21,000, in taxes. Tony would pay 6 percent of $50,000, or $3,000, in taxes. With a proportional income tax, whether income goes up or down, the percentage of income paid in taxes stays the same.

regressive tax a tax for which the percentage of income paid in taxes decreases as income increases

tax base the income, property, good, or service that is subject to a tax

individual income tax a tax based on a person's earnings

corporate income tax a tax based on a company's profits

property tax a tax based on real estate and other property

sales tax a tax based on goods or services that are sold

Regressive Taxes

A **regressive tax** is a tax for which the percentage of income paid in taxes decreases as income increases. For example, although the sales tax rate remains constant, a sales tax is regressive. This is because higher-income households spend a lower proportion of their incomes on taxable goods and services. As a result, although they may pay more actual dollars in sales taxes, the proportion of their income spent on sales taxes is lower than that of lower-income households.

Tax Bases

A **tax base** is the income, property, good, or service that is subject to a tax. Different taxes have different bases. The **individual income tax** is based on a person's earnings. The **corporate income tax** uses a company's profits as its base. The **property tax** is based on real estate and other property. The tax base for the **sales tax** is goods or services that are sold. When government policymakers create a new tax, they first decide what the base will be for the tax: income, profits, property, sales, or some other category.

CHECKPOINT ***Is the federal income tax proportional, progressive, or regressive?***

Who Bears the Tax Burden?

Government tax policies affect individuals, businesses, and even whole regions. They may benefit some regions more than others. Thus, it is important to think about who actually bears the burden of the tax. Taxes affect more than just the people who send in the checks to pay them. Why? The answer lies in supply and demand analysis.

Suppose that the government imposes a gasoline tax of $.50 per gallon and collects the tax from service stations. You may think that the burden of the tax falls only on the service stations, because they mail the checks to the government. Graphs A and B in **Figure 14.1**, however, provide a

Background Note

Sales Tax Exemptions Several state governments have tried to lessen the regressive nature of sales taxes by exempting goods that are judged to be essential from the general sales tax. Eleven states and the District of Columbia do not levy sales tax on food or medicines, either prescription or over the counter. More than twenty others exempt food and prescription drugs, though not over-the-counter medications. Some states retain the sales tax on such goods but at a lower rate. In Illinois, the 6.25% sales tax is cut to only 1% on food and medicines.

Answers

Graph Skills 1. elastic demand 2. producers

Checkpoint progressive

VISUAL GLOSSARY

Reviewing Key Terms
To understand *progressive income tax*, review these terms:

economic growth, *p. 315*
tax, *p. 364*
revenue, *p. 364*

What are Progressive Taxes?

◄ **Progressive Taxes** a tax for which the percentage of income paid in taxes increases as income increases.

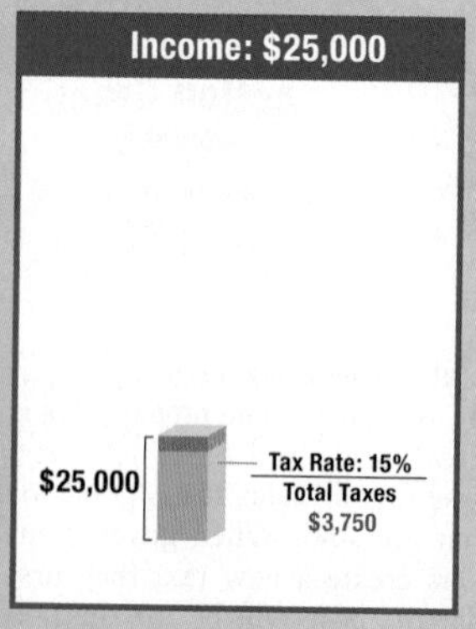

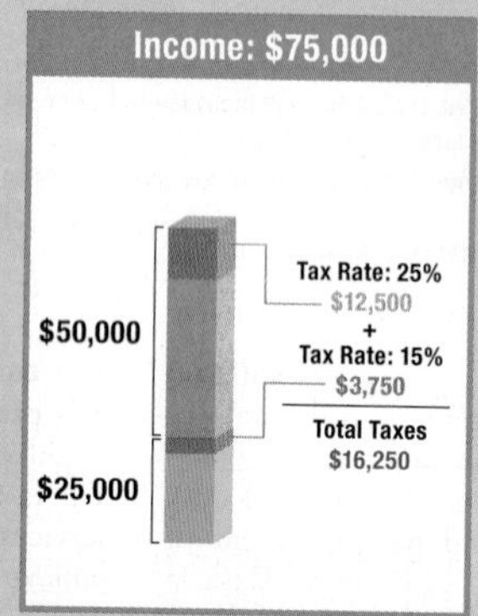

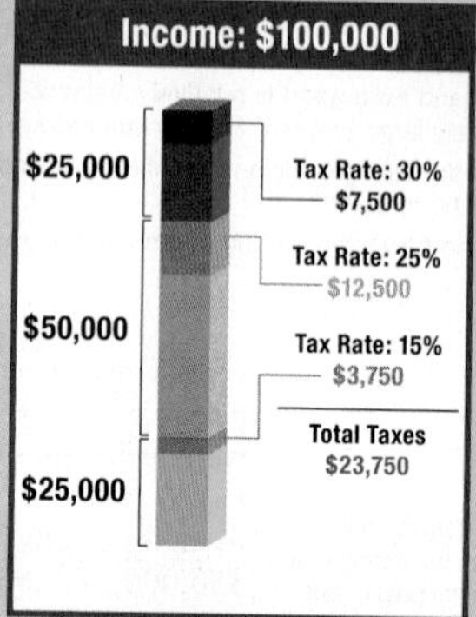

In a progressive tax structure, the higher a taxpayer's income, the greater percentage he or she must pay in taxes. Above are three examples of how progressive taxes have an impact on people with different incomes. **What would be the total tax on taxable income of $65,000?**

▲ With a progressive tax system, some people pay a higher rate of taxes than others. ***What is the complaint that the "millionaire" expresses?***

Visual Glossary online
To expand your understanding of this and other key economic terms, visit **PearsonSuccessNet.com**

Teach Visual Glossary

REVIEW KEY TERMS

Pair students and have them write the definitions of the key terms related to the understanding of progressive taxes.

economic growth – *a steady, long-term increase in real GDP*

tax – *a required payment to a local, state, or national government*

revenue – *income received by a government from taxes and other sources*

COMPARE GRAPHS

Direct students' attention to the three bar graphs. Ask **How are the three graphs similar?** *(At each income level, the first $25,000 in earnings is taxed at the same rate, 15 percent.)* **How are they different?** *(The two higher incomes have the remainder of their incomes taxed at higher rates.)* Have students connect these similarities and differences to the definition of a progressive tax.

L1 Differentiate Suggest that students draw a series of three steps in their notebooks, labeling the bottom step *15%*, the second step *25%*, and the third step *30%*. Have them use the steps as a reminder of the idea that *progressive* taxes increase as income increases.

L3 Differentiate Ask mathematical learners **What is the *overall* tax rate for each of the three income levels?** *(found by dividing total amount of taxes by total income: $25,000—15 percent; $75,000—21.7 percent; $100,000—23.75 percent)*

Economics online *All print resources are available on the Teacher's Resource Library CD-ROM and online at* www.PearsonSuccessNet.com.

Answers

Graph Caption $13,750 ($3,750 on first $25,000 and $10,000 on next $40,000)

Cartoon Possible response: The millionaire is complaining about being taxed at a higher rate than the worker.

BELLRINGER

Write the following quotes on the board. Ask students to choose one and write what they think it means.

Taxes are what we pay for civilized society. (Oliver Wendell Holmes, Jr., U.S. Supreme Court Justice)
The power to tax is the power to destroy. (John Marshall, U.S. Supreme Court Chief Justice)
The power of taxing people and their property is essential to the very essence of government. (James Madison, U.S. President)

Teach

Economics online To present this topic using digital resources, use the lecture notes on www.PearsonSuccessNet.com.

L1 L2 ELL LPR Differentiate For students struggling with comprehension, assign the Vocabulary worksheet (Unit 6 All-in-One, p. 14).

DISCUSS

Call on students to offer their answers to the Bellringer activity. Discuss why taxation is a topic on which everyone has an opinion. Remind students of the rallying cry of the American Revolution, *No taxation without representation.* Ask **Why were the colonists protesting against taxes imposed on them by the British Parliament?** *(They had no representation in Parliament.)* Ask **Why do you think the British felt that the colonists should pay taxes?** *(The British felt they were providing services, like defense, that the colonists would not have had otherwise.)*

Ask **Who determines what taxes Americans will pay?** *(the U.S. Congress, state legislatures, and local governing bodies)* **Who elects congressional, state, and local representatives?** *(voters)* **How is this different from the situation of the American colonists?** *(Americans today elect their representatives, who enact taxes. The colonists did not have representation in the British Parliament.)*

Finally, ask students **Where does the federal government get the power to tax?** *(from the people and the Constitution)*

(lesson continued on p. 366)

The Purpose of Taxation

A **tax** is a required payment to a local, state, or national government. Taxation is the primary way that the government collects money. Taxes give the government the money it needs to operate.

The income received by a government from taxes and other nontax sources is called **revenue.** Without revenue from taxes, the government would not be able to provide the goods and services that we not only benefit from, but that we expect the government to provide. For example, we authorize the government to provide national defense, highways, education, and law enforcement. We also ask the government to provide help to people in need. All of these goods and services cost money—in workers' salaries, in materials, in land and labor. All members of our society share these costs through the payment of taxes.

The Power to Tax

Taxation is a powerful tool. The founders of the United States thought long and hard before giving this tool to their new national government. The Constitution they created assigned each branch of the government certain powers and responsibilities. The first power granted to the legislative branch—Congress—is the power to tax. This clause is the basis for all federal tax laws.

tax a required payment to a local, state, or national government

revenue the income received by a government from taxes and other nontax sources

progressive tax a tax for which the percentage of income paid in taxes increases as income increases

proportional tax a tax for which the percentage of income paid in taxes remains the same at all income levels

Limits on the Power to Tax

The Constitution also spells out specific limits on the government's power to tax. Two of those limits are in the taxation clause. First, the purpose of a tax must be "for the common defense and general welfare." A tax cannot bring in money that goes to individual interests. Second, federal taxes must be the same in every state. The federal gas tax, for example, cannot be 4 cents per gallon in Maryland and 10 cents per gallon in South Dakota.

Other provisions of the Constitution also limit the kinds of taxes Congress can levy, or impose. For example, Congress cannot tax church services, because that would violate the freedom of religion promised by the First Amendment. Another clause of the Constitution prohibits taxing exports. The government can collect taxes only on imports—goods brought into the United States. (Congress can restrict or prohibit the export of certain goods, however, such as technology or weapons.)

Yet another clause of the Constitution (Article 1, Section 9, Clause 4) prohibited Congress from levying direct taxes unless they were divided among the states according to population. The Sixteenth Amendment overturned this clause when it legalized a direct tax on citizens' personal income. This income-tax amendment was ratified in 1913.

CHECKPOINT ***For what purpose does the government collect taxes?***

Tax Structures and Tax Bases

Despite the constitutional limits on its power, the government actually collects a wide variety of taxes. Economists describe these taxes in different ways. First, they describe how the tax is structured. Economists describe three different tax structures: progressive, proportional, and regressive. Second, they describe a tax according to the object taxed—the tax base.

Progressive Taxes

A **progressive tax** is a tax for which the percentage of income paid in taxes increases as income increases. People with higher incomes pay a higher percentage of their income in taxes. People with very small incomes might pay no tax at all.

The federal income tax is the clearest example of a progressive tax in the United States. A sample progressive income tax system is shown in the Visual Glossary. Notice that the tax rate in this example rises from 15, to 25, and then to 30 percent as income rises. This is a progressive tax rate structure because as income rises, the percentage of income paid in taxes also rises.

Proportional Taxes

A **proportional tax** is a tax for which the percentage of income paid in taxes remains the same at all income levels. Leslie Wilson, a corporate executive, earns $350,000 per

Differentiated Resources

- **L1 L2 Guided Reading and Review** (Unit 6 All-in-One, p. 16)
- **L2 Vocabulary worksheet** (Unit 6 All-in-One, p. 14)
- **L2 A Good Tax?** (Unit 6 All-in-One, p. 18)
- **L4 The Flat Tax** (Unit 6 All-in-One, p. 19)

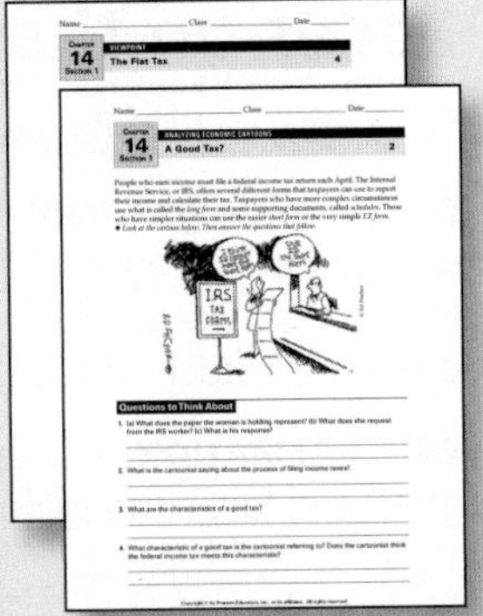

Answer

Checkpoint to have money so it can provide goods and services

SECTION 1 What Are Taxes?

OBJECTIVES

1. **Identify** the sources of the government's authority to tax.
2. **Describe** types of tax bases and tax structures.
3. **Identify** who bears the burden of a tax.
4. **List** the characteristics of a good tax.

ECONOMIC DICTIONARY

As you read the section, look for the definitions of these **Key Terms:**

- tax
- revenue
- progressive tax
- proportional tax
- regressive tax
- tax base
- individual income tax
- corporate income tax
- property tax
- sales tax
- incidence of a tax

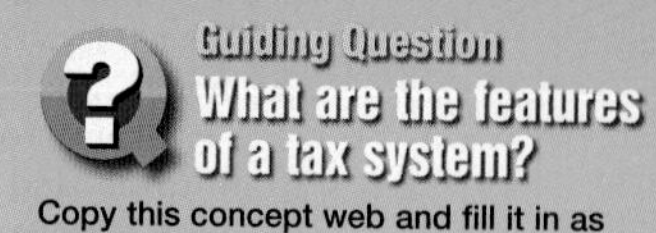

Copy this concept web and fill it in as you read.

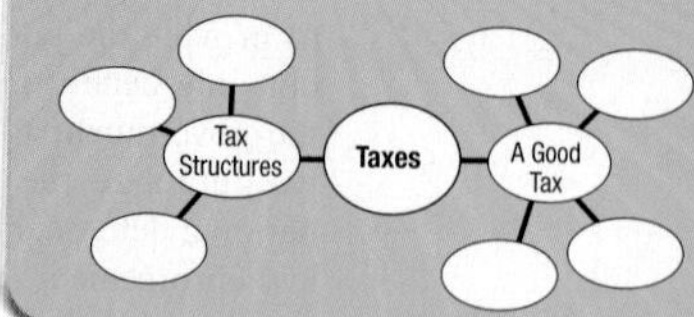

Economics and You You're looking forward to getting your first paycheck. You figure that at $7 per hour, you should be getting $140 for the 20 hours you worked. When you open the envelope, you find that the check is for much less than $140. Where did the money go? The answer is ... taxes! The federal government and most state governments levy taxes on personal income. Is this fair?

Principles in Action Fairness is one of the main features of a tax system. But what is fair to one person may not be fair to another. For example, at first glance, it may seem fair that all Americans are taxed at the same rate. However, in this section, you will learn why most Americans believe that the person who earns more money should pay a higher percentage of income in taxes. This concept, known as progressive taxation, lies at the base of our income tax system.

The Government's Authority to Tax

Looking at all of the taxes taken from your paycheck can be discouraging. You worked hard for that money, and now it is being taken away. Similar feelings of frustration over taxes helped persuade American colonists to declare their independence from Britain. Unlike those colonists, however, an overwhelming majority of citizens today consent to having a portion of their earnings taken by the government. We authorize the federal government, through the Constitution and our elected representatives in Congress, to raise money in the form of taxes.

Visual Glossary online

Go to the Visual Glossary Online for an interactive review of **progressive taxes.**

Action Graph online

Go to Action Graph Online for animated versions of key charts and graphs.

How the Economy Works online

Go to How the Economy Works Online for an interactive lesson on your **federal taxes.**

Guiding Question

What are the features of a tax system?

Get Started

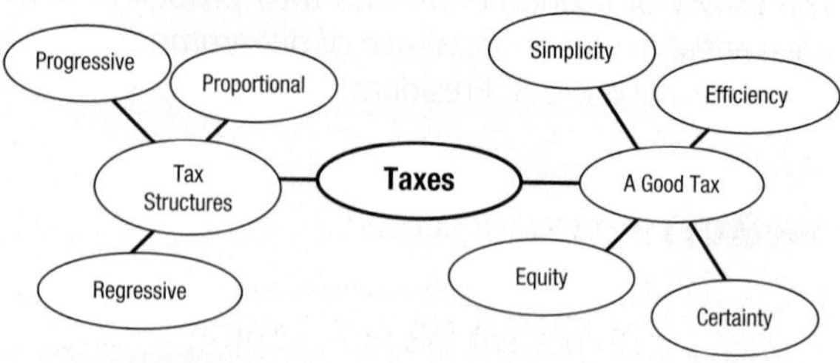

LESSON GOALS

Students will:

- Know the Key Terms.
- Show understanding of the government's power to tax and the purpose of taxation.
- Compare and contrast different types of taxes to understand tax structures.
- Determine whether the individual income tax is a good tax based on four criteria by completing a worksheet.

BEFORE CLASS

Students should read the section for homework before coming to class.

Have students complete the graphic organizer in the Section Opener as they read the text. As an alternate activity, have students complete the Guided Reading and Review worksheet (Unit 6 All-in-One, p. 15).

L1 L2 ELL LPR Differentiate Have students complete the Guided Reading and Review worksheet (Unit 6 All-in-One, p. 16).

Focus on the Basics

Students should come away with the following understandings:

FACTS: • The government has the need, authority, and power to levy taxes. • Taxes are categorized on the basis of their structure and the tax base. • Taxes are evaluated as good or bad based on their simplicity, efficiency, certainty, and equity and on who bears the burden of the tax.

GENERALIZATION: Governments try to devise tax systems that can be considered good and fair, although people disagree about what those terms mean.

CLASSROOM HINTS

HOW TAX REVENUES ARE USED

One issue related to this section is the view that many students have about income taxes. Since they have been exposed many times to negative opinions about taxation, they may not see how taxes could benefit them, their families, or their communities. Have students brainstorm a list of services provided by federal, state, and local governments. Write these on the board. Lead a class discussion on whether they would be willing to do without any or all these services.

SECTION 2 Federal Taxes

OBJECTIVES

1. **Describe** the process of paying individual income taxes.
2. **Identify** the basic characteristics of corporate income taxes.
3. **Explain** the purpose of Social Security, Medicare, and unemployment taxes.
4. **Identify** other types of taxes.

ECONOMIC DICTIONARY

As you read the section, look for the definitions of these **Key Terms:**

- withholding
- tax return
- taxable income
- personal exemption
- tax deduction
- tax credit
- estate tax
- gift tax
- tariff
- tax incentive

Guiding Question
What taxes does the federal government collect?

Copy this table and fill it in as you read.

Type of Tax	Description
Individual income	Taxes paid throughout year. Employers withhold taxes from pay. Individuals file taxes. Tax is progressive.
Corporate income	
Social insurance	
Excise	
Estate	
Gift	
Import	

Economics and You The United States has a government "of the people, by the people, and for the people." For that government to function, it needs the economic backing of the American people. If you work and pay income taxes, you are helping to support the work the government does.

Principles in Action The income tax is just one of the wide variety of taxes collected by the federal government. As you will read in this section, individual taxpayers like you are not the only source of federal revenues. Federal revenues come from corporate income taxes, social insurance taxes, excise taxes, estate and gift taxes, and taxes on imports.

Individual Income Taxes

The government's main source of revenues comes from the federal tax on individuals' taxable income. As **Figure 14.2** shows, about 43 percent of the federal government's revenues come from the payment of individual income taxes.

"Pay-As-You-Earn" Taxation

The amount of federal income tax a person owes is determined on an annual basis. In theory, the federal government could wait until the end of the tax year to collect individual income taxes. In reality, that would be a problem for both taxpayers and the government. Like other employers, the government has to pay regularly for rent, supplies, services, and employees' salaries. A single annual payment from all the nation's taxpayers at once would make meeting these expenses difficult.

Figure 14.2 Federal Revenue

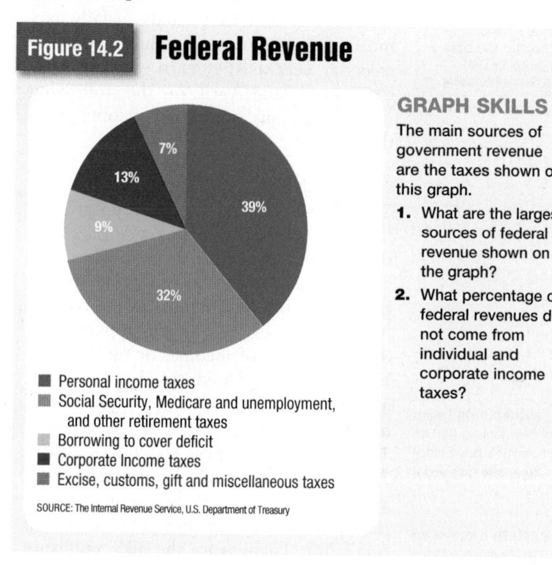

SOURCE: The Internal Revenue Service, U.S. Department of Treasury

GRAPH SKILLS

The main sources of government revenue are the taxes shown on this graph.

1. What are the largest sources of federal revenue shown on the graph?
2. What percentage of federal revenues do not come from individual and corporate income taxes?

Focus on the Basics

Students should come away with the following understandings:

FACTS: • The largest source of federal revenue is individual income taxes. • Corporations also pay income tax, but those taxes contribute a small share of federal revenue. • Social insurance taxes that fund Social Security and Medicare are another major source of federal revenue.

GENERALIZATION: Changes in income and social taxes would greatly affect federal revenues.

Guiding Question

What taxes does the federal government collect?

Get Started

Type of Tax	Description
Individual income	Paid throughout year. Employers withhold, individuals file. Progressive.
Corporate income	On business earnings. Difficult to calculate due to deductions. Progressive.
Social insurance	Social Security, Medicare, unemployment. Ceiling on income for Social Security tax.
Excise	On goods such as gas, cigarettes, cable TV
Estate	On estates above $2 million. Progressive.
Gift	On gifts. Protects estate tax. Progressive.
Import	Tariffs on imported goods.

LESSON GOALS

Students will:

- Know the Key Terms.
- Analyze how different deductions and credits affect income tax by completing a worksheet.
- Examine the structure and tax base of different types of federal taxes.

BEFORE CLASS

Have students complete the graphic organizer in the Section Opener as they read the text. As an alternate activity, have students complete the Guided Reading and Review worksheet (Unit 6 All-in-One, p. 22).

L1 L2 ELL LPR Differentiate Have students complete the Guided Reading and Review worksheet (Unit 6 All-in-One, p. 23).

Answers

Graph Skills 1. personal income taxes, Social Security, Medicare, unemployment, other retirement taxes 2. 48%

CLASSROOM HINTS

SHARING THE BURDEN OF FICA TAXES

Students may have trouble understanding the way FICA taxes are split between employees and employers. FICA taxes, which pay for Social Security and Medicare, are proportional. Employees pay 6.2% of income (up to a $97,500 limit in 2008) for Social Security and 1.45% (no limit) for Medicare. Employers pay matching amounts of tax, 6.2% and 1.45%. Because self-employed people are their own employers, they pay both halves of each tax. In both cases, the total percentage paid to the government for FICA taxes is 15.3%: 12.4% for Social Security and 2.9% for Medicare.

BELLRINGER

Have students review the sample earnings statement on page PF 45 and identify three taxes collected by the federal government. Calculate what percentage of the gross pay is withheld for taxes that go to the federal government.

Teach

Economics online To present this topic using digital resources, use the lecture notes on www.PearsonSuccessNet.com.

DISCUSS BELLRINGER

Call on volunteers to give their Bellringer responses. Ask students to determine what percentage of their pay they see in their paycheck. *(average for teens is between 50 and 75 percent)* Discuss how mandatory withholding (established by law in 1943) makes it easier for the federal government to collect taxes and reduce taxpayer resistance.

L1 L2 Differentiate Assign each of several students a wage rate of $100 a week. Tell them they will be paid their weekly wage minus the amount withheld to pay taxes. Have them subtract each of the following percentages from their $100 wage: Federal income tax, 10%, Social Security tax, 6.2%, and Medicare tax, 1.45%. Call on the students to state how much will be withheld from their pay ($17.65) and how much take-home pay they will receive ($82.35).

PERSONAL FINANCE ACTIVITY

This would be a good time to use the Personal Finance Handbook lesson on paying taxes (pp. PF46–47) and complete the worksheet (Personal Finance All-in-One, pp. 111–112). Students will have a hands-on opportunity to complete a W-4 form and complete a 1040EZ based on a W-2 form.

(lesson continued on p. 372)

Answers

Table Skills 1. $4,481.25 plus 25 percent of the amount over $32,550 2. $11,865 ($8,962.50 plus $2,475 [25 percent of $9,900, the amount of income over $65,100])

Figure 14.3 Federal Income Tax Rates, 2008

TABLE SKILLS

According to these sample individual income tax tables, a single individual with $5,000 of taxable income would pay $5,000 × .10, or $500 in taxes.

1. If you are single, at what rate would you pay taxes on income over $32,550 and less than $78,850?
2. What would be the tax for a married couple filing jointly with $75,000 in taxable income?

Schedule	If your taxable income is over –	but not over –	the tax is	of the amount over –
Schedule X – use if your filing status is single	$0	$8,025	10%	$0
	$8,025	$32,550	$802.50 plus 15%	$8,025
	$32,550	$78,850	$4,481.25 plus 25%	$32,550
	$78,850	$164,550	$16,056.25 plus 28%	$78,850
	$164,550	$357,700	$40,052.25 plus 33%	$164,550
	$357,700	no limit	$103,791.00 plus 35%	$357,700
Schedule Y – use if your filing status is married filing jointly	$0	$16,050	10%	$0
	$16,050	$65,100	$1,605.00 plus 15%	$16,050
	$65,100	$131,450	$8,962.50 plus 25%	$65,100
	$131,450	$200,300	$25,550.00 plus 28%	$131,450
	$200,300	$357,700	$44,828.00 plus 33%	$200,300
	$357,700	no limit	$96,770.00 plus 35%	$357,700

SOURCE: Internal Revenue Service, Revenue Procedure 2007-66.

Personal Finance For more help in understanding tax liabilities, see your Personal Finance Handbook in the back of the book or visit **PearsonSuccessNet.com**

Similarly, many people might have trouble paying their taxes in one large sum. For these reasons, federal income tax is collected in a "pay-as-you-earn" system. This means that individuals usually pay most of their income tax throughout the calendar year as they earn income. They have until mid-April of the following year to pay any additional income taxes they owe.

Tax Brackets

The federal income tax is a progressive tax. In other words, the tax rate rises with the amount of taxable income. The 2008 tax rate schedules shown in **Figure 14.3** both have six rates, defined in the column headed "the tax is." Each applies to a different range of income, or tax bracket. For example, married couples who filed a return together (a joint return) and had a taxable income of $16,050 or less paid 10 percent income tax. The highest rate—35 percent—was paid by high-income single people or married couples on the portion of their taxable incomes that exceeded $357,700. Each year, the IRS publishes new tax rate schedules that reflect any changes in the federal tax code.

withholding taking tax payments out of an employee's pay before he or she receives it

tax return a form used to file income taxes

Tax Withholding

Employers are responsible in part for carrying out the system of collecting federal income taxes. They do so by **withholding,** or taking payments out of your pay before you receive it. The amount they withhold is based on an estimate of how much you will owe in federal income taxes for the entire year. After withholding the money, the employer forwards it to the federal government as an "installment payment" on your upcoming annual income tax bill.

Filing a Tax Return

After the calendar year ends, employers give their employees a report stating how much income tax has already been withheld and sent to the government. The employee uses that information to complete a tax return. A **tax return** is a form used to file income taxes. On it, you declare your income to the government and figure out how much of that income is taxable.

Differentiated Resources

- **L1 L2 Guided Reading and Review** (Unit 6 All-in-One, p. 23)
- **L2 Comparing Tax Situations** (Unit 6 All-in-One, p. 26)
- **L4 Calculating Federal Income Tax** (Unit 6 All-in-One, p. 24)

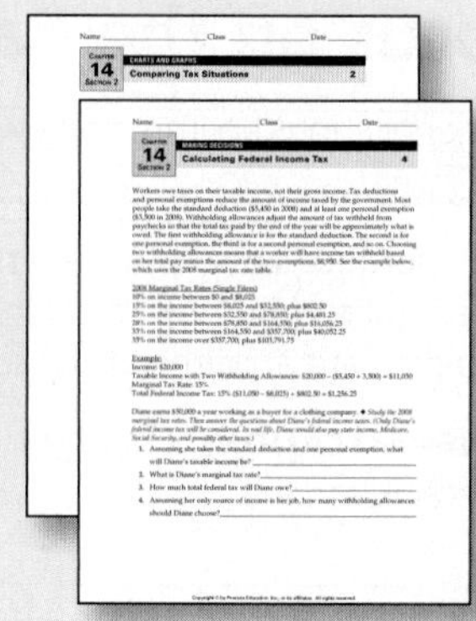

Case Study

THE WALL STREET JOURNAL. CLASSROOM EDITION

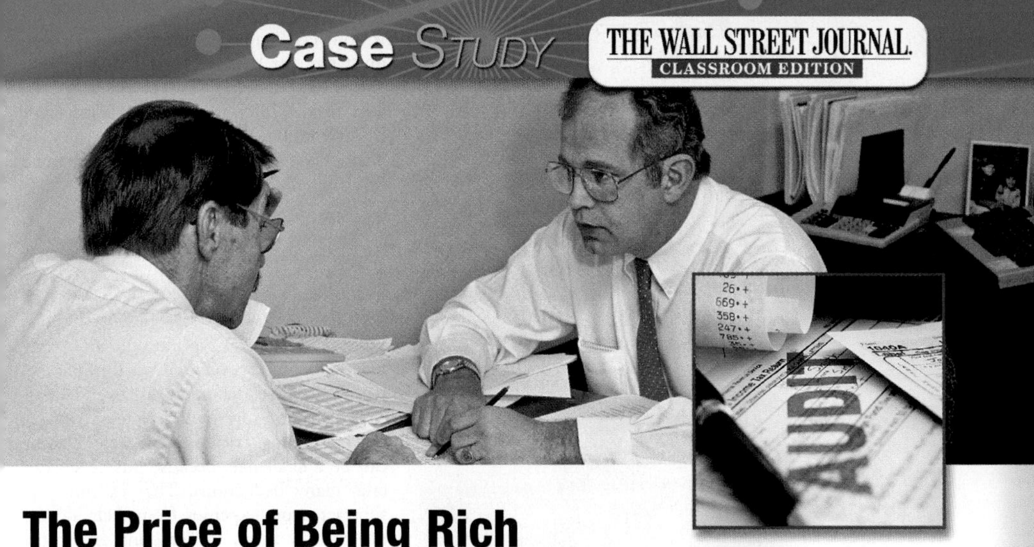

The Price of Being Rich

TAXATION

The IRS uses audits to crack down on people who may not be paying all the taxes they're supposed to. Now, a lot of high-income earners are feeling the heat.

By Tom Herman
The Wall Street Journal

The Internal Revenue Service is turning up the heat on high-income taxpayers, especially those who work for themselves.

Internal Revenue Service officials say audits of taxpayers making $100,000 or more rose 14% in 2007 from 2006. Recent IRS data also show a 29% increase in audits of people making $200,000 or more—and an 84% surge in audits of those with incomes of $1 million or more.

The push comes as the agency faces heavy pressure from Congress to raise additional revenue and shrink the nation's $290 billion "tax gap," or the difference between what's collected and what should be collected each year.

IRS research indicates much of the tax-noncompliance is committed by self-employed workers, such as consultants and small-business owners, whose taxes aren't withheld from their paychecks and whose income isn't reported separately to the government. By contrast, compliance is much higher among people whose pay is reported by their employers and whose taxes are withheld from their pay.

It's not just Americans who face the IRS's intensified crackdown. IRS officials say they have uncovered "significant noncompliance" among foreign athletes, such as golf and tennis stars, and foreign musicians who perform in the U.S., says Barry Shott, an IRS deputy commissioner.

IRS officials won't divulge any names of foreign athletes or entertainers under scrutiny. But Mr. Shott says the cases involve not only taxation of prize money won by athletes competing in U.S. events but also product-endorsement money.

The IRS relies on numerous techniques to choose which returns are audited. Many returns are selected on the basis of a secret computerized-scoring system. Computer programs assign each tax return a score that evaluates the potential for inaccuracies, based on the IRS's experience with similar returns.

Many returns are picked because of "mismatches"— something a taxpayer reported doesn't match what was reported separately to the IRS by employers, banks or other financial institutions. Some returns get selected because of a tip from confidential informants, such as former business partners, ex-spouses or an angry neighbor.

Applying Economic Principles
From the viewpoint of the federal government, describe two costs and two possible benefits of conducting tax audits.

Video News Update Online Powered by *The Wall Street Journal* Classroom Edition

For a new case study, go to the online resources at **PearsonSuccessNet.com**

Teach Case Study

SUMMARIZE AND EXPLAIN

Call on the students to explain why the IRS is increasing the number of audits it conducts. Ask **Why does the IRS audit taxpayers?** *(There is a lot of noncompliance; people make mistakes in their reporting of earnings and deductions.)* Have the students explain the relationship between personal responsibility and taxation. Ask **Why doesn't everyone pay what they are supposed to?** *(Taxpayers, especially those who do not have taxes taken out of their paychecks, can make honest mistakes in the preparation process because they do not understand their tax liability; others make deliberate errors in order to pay less tax.)*

L1 L2 Differentiate This case study examines federal taxation process, which is something not all students will understand, especially if they have never filed a tax return. Prepare students for this case study with an explanation of the process. Distribute examples of tax return forms and explain key terms such as deductions, exemptions, and adjusted gross income.

Economics online *All print resources are available on the Teacher's Resource Library CD-ROM and online at* www.PearsonSuccessNet.com.

Answer

Applying Economic Principles costs: auditor salaries, cost of collecting debts; benefits: increased revenue, increased tax compliance

COMPARE AND CONTRAST

Distribute the "Comparing Tax Situations" worksheet (Unit 6 All-in-One, p. 25). Explain to students that people with identical incomes often pay different amounts of federal income tax based on their circumstances. The worksheet presents four people with the same income and the federal income tax they pay after adjustments.

Have students complete the worksheet to see the different impact of these adjustments to taxes.

Name ______________ Class ______________ Date ________

Chapter 11 Section 2 — SOURCE READINGS IN ECONOMICS

Investing for Young People 4

A major securities industry trade association offers this guidance to young people who are interested in getting started in investing. ◆ *Read the passage and answer the questions that follow.*

You may have a hard time imagining life 15, 30 or 40 years from now.... Your ability to reach your goals and achieve financial security, however, depends in part on maximizing your ... income through investments....

Since you have a longer horizon for investing (the amount of time between now and when you want/need to access your money), you are in a better position to consider investing in higher-yield, higher-risk instruments. There are higher-risk bonds that carry high coupons (interest rates). You may be interested in assuming that risk to potentially make significant interest on your investment.

Keep in mind, however, that even at this early stage of the investment game, you want to aim for a well-blended portfolio to balance risk and market volatility. While your higher-yield investments can appear more exciting (because of their potential to earn more interest), it's important to round out your portfolio with some strategically chosen lower- and medium-risk investments as well, including bonds....

If you are saving money for a large future purchase—a car, a wedding, a house—you might consider investing that savings in a low-risk bond with a maturity date that matches the date you will need the money. For example, new issue U.S. Treasury bills, notes and bonds are available directly from the Federal Reserve in three-month, six-month, and two-year and three-year maturities in $1,000 increments starting at $1,000. You can also buy outstanding Treasury or corporate bonds with maturities timed to your needs in the secondary market through a bank or a broker. Prices and yields will vary....

One of the common myths about investing is that you have to have a lot of money to do it. That's a good reason to consider dollar-cost averaging. If you can only invest a small amount at a time, or if you are uncomfortable investing large chunks of money at once, dollar cost averaging can be a way to invest in bonds automatically on a regular schedule.... Select a regularly scheduled date to have a pre-determined amount of money automatically withdrawn from an account of your choice and have it deposited into your brokerage account to purchase ... bonds you have chosen. Making small deposits over time will add up to consistent investments which can reap significant dividends over the long term....

Excerpt from "Bonds at Your Stage of Life" (Source: www.investinginbonds.com/learnmore.asp?catid=7&id40)

Questions to Think About

1. Why can young people often take greater risks with their investments than older people can?
2. In what circumstances does the author suggest that young people *not* invest in high-risk assets? What investments does the author recommend in these circumstances?
3. What do you need to consider to create a well-blended portfolio? Give three factors to consider in your decision.

L2 Differentiate Distribute the "Comparing Tax Situations" worksheet (Unit 6 All-in-One, p. 26). Have students answer the questions.

L4 Differentiate Distribute the "Calculating Federal Income Tax" worksheet (Unit 6 All-in-One, p. 24). Have students calculate federal income tax and answer questions about withholding allowances.

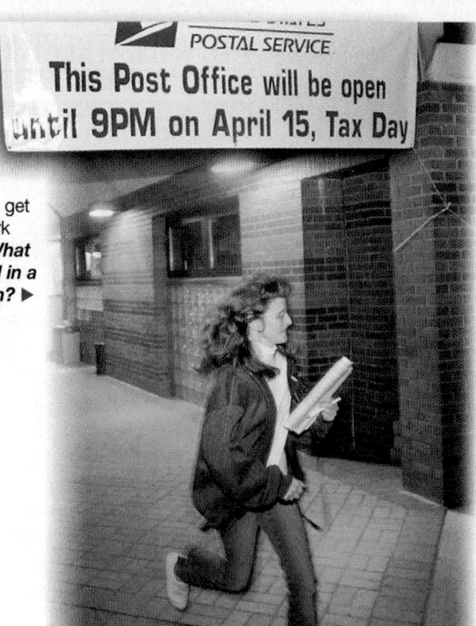

A taxpayer races to get an April 15 postmark on her tax return. ***What items are included in a person's tax return?*** ▶

Taxable income is a person's gross (or total) income minus exemptions and deductions. Gross income includes earned income—salaries, wages, tips, and commissions. It also includes income from investments such as interest on savings accounts and dividends from stock. **Personal exemptions** are set amounts that you subtract from your gross income for yourself, your spouse, and any dependents. **Tax deductions** are variable amounts that you can subtract, or deduct, from your gross income. Deductions include such items as interest on a mortgage, donations to charity, significant medical expenses, and state and local tax payments.

taxable income the earnings on which tax must be paid; total income minus exemptions and deductions

personal exemption a set amount that taxpayers may subtract from their gross income for themselves, their spouse, and any dependents

Once you determine how much tax you owe, you can apply any tax credits that you may be allowed. A **tax credit** is an amount that you can subtract from the total amount of your income tax. You can claim a credit for such things as a portion of the cost of child-care and higher education.

tax deduction a variable amount that taxpayers may subtract from their gross income

Completing a tax return allows you to determine whether the amount of income taxes you have already paid was higher or lower than the actual amount of tax you owe. If you have paid more than you owe, the government sends you a refund.

tax credit a variable amount that taxpayers may subtract from the total amount of their income tax

If you have paid less than you owe, you must pay the balance to the government. All federal income tax returns must be sent to the Internal Revenue Service, or IRS, by midnight on April 15 (or the next business day if April 15 falls on a weekend or holiday).

✔ **CHECKPOINT** ***What is the difference between a personal exemption and a tax deduction?***

Corporate Income Taxes

Like individuals, corporations must pay federal income tax on their taxable income. Corporate taxes made up just over 10 percent of federal revenues in recent years.

Determining corporate taxable income can be a challenge, because businesses can take many deductions. That is, they can subtract many expenses from their income before they reach the amount of income that is subject to taxation. For example, companies deduct the cost of employees' health insurance. Many other costs of doing business can also be deducted.

Like individual income tax rates, corporate income tax rates are progressive. In 2007, rates began at 15 percent on the first $50,000 of taxable income. On the highest corporate income, above $18,333,333, the tax rate was 35 percent.

✔ **CHECKPOINT** ***Why is it difficult to determine a corporation's taxable income?***

Social Security, Medicare, and Unemployment Taxes

In addition to withholding money for income taxes, employers withhold money for taxes authorized under the Federal Insurance Contributions Act, or FICA. FICA taxes fund two large government social-insurance programs, Social Security and Medicare. Employees and employers share FICA payments.

Social Security Taxes

Most of the FICA taxes you pay go to the Social Security Administration to fund Old-Age, Survivors, and Disability Insurance (OASDI), or Social Security. Social Security was established in 1935 to ease the hardships of the Great Depression.

Answers

Caption Gross income, personal exemptions, tax exemptions, taxable income, any tax credits, amount withheld, and whether there is a tax due or a refund to be received.

Checkpoint Personal exemptions are available to all taxpayers for each taxpayer and any dependents he or she supports. Tax deductions are available only to those taxpayers who have the expenses that can be deducted.

Checkpoint Businesses can take many deductions, which affects their taxable income.

Virtual Economics

L2 Differentiate

Estimating Tax Revenue Use the following lesson from the NCEE **Virtual Economics *CD-ROM*** to examine the categories of federal taxes. Click on Browse Economics Lessons, specify grades 6–8, and use the key words *federal taxes.*

In this activity, students will estimate the level of taxes in various situations and analyze the sources of government revenue.

LESSON TITLE	**WHERE DOES THE MONEY COME FROM?**
Type of Activity	Using statistics
Complexity	Moderate
Time	100 minutes
NCEE Standards	16

From the start, Social Security provided old-age pensions and unemployment insurance to workers. Today, it also provides benefits to surviving family members of wage earners and to people whose disabilities keep them from working.

Each year the government establishes an income cap for Social Security taxes. In 2008, the cap was $102,000. No Social Security taxes could be withheld from a taxpayer's wages and salaries above that amount.

Medicare Taxes

FICA taxes also fund Medicare. The Medicare program is a national health insurance program that helps pay for healthcare for people over age 65. It also covers people with certain disabilities.

Both employees and self-employed people pay the Medicare tax on all their earnings. There is no ceiling as there is for Social Security payments.

Unemployment Taxes

The federal government also collects an unemployment tax, which is paid by employers. In effect, the tax pays for an insurance policy for workers. If workers are laid off from their jobs through no fault of their own, they can file an "unemployment compensation" claim and collect benefits for a fixed number of weeks. In order to collect unemployment benefits, an unemployed person usually must show that he or she is actively looking for another job. The unemployment program is financed by both state and federal unemployment taxes.

***CHECKPOINT** What is the Medicare program?*

Other Types of Taxes

What are the taxes on gasoline and cable television service called? If you inherit money from your great aunt, will you have to pay a tax? Why are some imported products so expensive? To answer these questions, you need to look at excise, estate, gift, and import taxes.

Excise Taxes

As you read in Chapter 5, an excise tax is a general revenue tax on the sale or manufacture of a good. Federal excise taxes apply to gasoline, cigarettes, alcoholic beverages, telephone services, cable television, and other items.

Estate Taxes

An **estate tax** is a tax on the estate, or total value of the money and property, of a person who has died. It is paid out of the person's estate before the heirs receive their share. A person's estate includes not only money, but also real estate, cars, furniture, investments, jewelry, paintings, and insurance.

As of 2008, if the total value of an estate is $2 million or less, there is no federal estate tax. Because an estate tax is a progressive tax, the rate rises with increasing value. That is, a $5 million estate will be taxed by the federal government at a higher rate than a $3 million estate.

Gift Taxes

The **gift tax** is a tax on the money or property that one living person gives to another. The goal of the gift tax, established in 1924, was to keep people from avoiding estate taxes by giving away their money before they died. The tax law sets limits on gifts, but still allows the tax-free transfer of fairly large amounts each year. Under current law, a person can give up to $12,000 a year tax-free to each of several different people.

Import Taxes

Taxes on imported goods (foreign goods brought into the country) are called

estate tax a tax on the total value of the money and property of a person who has died

gift tax a tax on the money or property that one living person gives to another

After Christmas, even Santas need the support of unemployment insurance. ***How is the unemployment program financed?*** ▼

CHECK UNDERSTANDING

Remind students that income taxes are not the government's only source of revenue. Ask **Who pays Social Security and Medicare taxes?** *(all employees, employers, self-employed individuals)* Ask **How do excise, estate, gift, and import taxes differ from these two taxes?** *(excise, import taxes: paid only by consumers who purchase certain goods; estate, gift taxes: paid only by people who dispose of wealth in certain ways and above certain amounts.)*

L1 L2 Differentiate Suggest that students use a two-column graphic organizer to take notes on the different types of taxes. They should put the name of the tax in the first column and the definition in the second.

EXTEND

Explain that some critics say estate taxes are unfair because they punish people who have had success. Others favor an estate tax as a limit on the accumulation of wealth in the hands of a few families. Have students research the topic and write an essay in which they express their views.

L1 L2 Differentiate Have students explain how the federal government uses taxes and tax credits to try to encourage or discourage certain kinds of behavior.

GUIDING QUESTION WRAP UP

Have students return to the section Guiding Question. Review the completed graphic organizer and clarify any misunderstandings. Have a wrap up discussion about taxes.

Assess and Remediate

L3 L2 Collect the "Comparing Tax Situations" worksheets and assess student understanding of the U.S. tax structure.

L4 Collect the "Calculating Federal Income Tax" worksheet and assess student understanding of tax rates.

L3 Assign the Section 2 Assessment questions.

L3 Give Section Quiz A (Unit 6 All-in-One, p. 27).

L2 Give Section Quiz B (Unit 6 All-in-One, p. 28).

(Assess and Remediate continued on p. 374)

Background Note

Social Insurance Tax Contributions Individuals pay taxes into the Social Security and Medicare funds. Those payments are matched by employers, which pay at the same rate. Thus, every dollar collected in taxes from a worker is equaled by a dollar collected from that worker's employer. Self-employed workers—those who work for themselves—pay twice the tax rate of employees, but that rate is equal to the combined employee-employer rate. These individuals can take some tax credits on their Social Security tax to lessen the overall tax burden.

Answers

Checkpoint a national health insurance program that pays for healthcare for people over age 65

Cartoon through taxes collected from employers

Have students complete the Self-Test Online and continue their work in the **Essential Questions Journal**.

REMEDIATION AND SUGGESTIONS

Use the chart below to help students who are struggling with content.

WEAKNESS	REMEDIATION
Identifying key terms (Questions 5, 6)	Have students use the interactive Economic Dictionary Online.
Describing income taxes (Questions 3, 4, 7, 9)	Have pairs of students quiz each other on the individual income tax.
Explaining Social Security (Question 8)	Have students draw flow chart diagrams showing how Social Security works.

Answers

Checkpoint excise taxes

Caption tax credits for energy conservation

In sunny climates, solar panels can help reduce energy consumption. ***How does the government provide tax incentives to encourage solar panels?*** ▶

tariff a tax on imported goods

tax incentive the use of taxation to discourage or encourage certain types of behavior

tariffs. Today, most tariffs are intended to protect American farmers and industries from foreign competitors rather than to generate revenue. Tariffs raise the price of foreign items, which helps keep the price of American products competitive. You will read more about tariffs in Chapter 17.

Taxes That Affect Behavior

The basic goal of taxation is to create revenue. However, governments sometimes use tax policy to discourage the public from buying harmful products. They also use taxes to encourage constructive or helpful behavior. The use of taxation to discourage or encourage certain types of behavior is called a **tax incentive.**

Federal taxes on tobacco products and alcoholic beverages are examples of so-called sin taxes. Their main purpose is to discourage people from buying and using these products.

Incentives also come in the form of tax credits. Congress has tried to encourage energy conservation by offering a variety of credits to consumers and industry. To persuade people to purchase more fuel-efficient cars, buyers of hybrid vehicles received an income tax credit. Owners of homes and commercial buildings can also claim credits for improvements that decrease the use of oil and other fossil fuels, including insulation and replacement windows.

CHECKPOINT ***What are the taxes on gasoline and cable television service called?***

Essential Questions Journal To continue to build a response to the Essential Question, go to your **Essential Questions Journal.**

SECTION 2 ASSESSMENT

Guiding Question

1. Use your completed table to answer this question: What taxes does the federal government collect?
2. **Extension** How do federal taxes affect your life? For example, suppose the federal government announced a new tax credit for income from savings accounts. What if the government imposed a high tax on chocolate? How would you respond?

Key Terms and Main Ideas

3. What kind of form do taxpayers use to file income taxes?
4. Would a person earning $15,000 per year and a person earning $300,000 per year be in the same federal income tax bracket? Why or why not?
5. When would you have to pay a **gift tax?**
6. What is a **tax incentive?**

Critical Thinking

7. **Predict (a)** Explain how "pay-as-you-earn" taxation works. **(b)** Why is this system important? **(c)** What might happen if the government did not use this system to collect income taxes?
8. **Contrast (a)** How are the systems for collecting Social Security and Medicare taxes similar? **(b)** List one way they are different. **(c)** Which system of collecting do you think makes more sense?
9. **Extend** Contributions to charitable organizations such as the American Cancer Society are tax deductible. **(a)** What does this mean? **(b)** Explain the reason for this tax policy. **(c)** What is your opinion of this tax deduction?

Quick Write

10. Based on what you have read in this section about tax incentives, write a short essay answering the following question. What kind of behavior do you think the government should encourage or discourage in its tax policy? How can the government do this through its tax policy?

Assessment Answers

1. individual and corporate income taxes; social insurance, excise, estate, gift, and import taxes
2. Possible responses: Tax credit would convince me to save more; tax on chocolate would force me to buy less chocolate.
3. tax return
4. no; because federal income tax is progressive
5. if you give someone more than $12,000
6. use of tax laws to encourage or discourage certain behaviors
7. (a) Tax payments are withheld from wages. (b) It keeps money flowing into the federal treasury on a regular basis. (c) Government would have to borrow more money to operate.
8. (a) Both are based on and withheld from earnings. (b) Social Security tax has an income cap; Medicare does not. (c) Possible response: Having a cap is a bad idea; all people should pay the same rate.
9. (a) They are taken off gross income, which lowers taxable income. (b) Possible response: It encourages donations to charity. (c) Possible response: It is wise because many charities effectively do needed work.
10. Possible response: The government should encourage people to use less energy by giving tax incentives for conserving fuel.

SECTION 3 Federal Spending

OBJECTIVES

1. **Distinguish** between mandatory and discretionary spending.
2. **Describe** the major entitlement programs.
3. **Identify** categories of discretionary spending.
4. **Explain** the impact of federal aid to state and local governments.

ECONOMIC DICTIONARY

As you read the section, look for the definitions of these **Key Terms:**

- mandatory spending
- discretionary spending
- entitlement

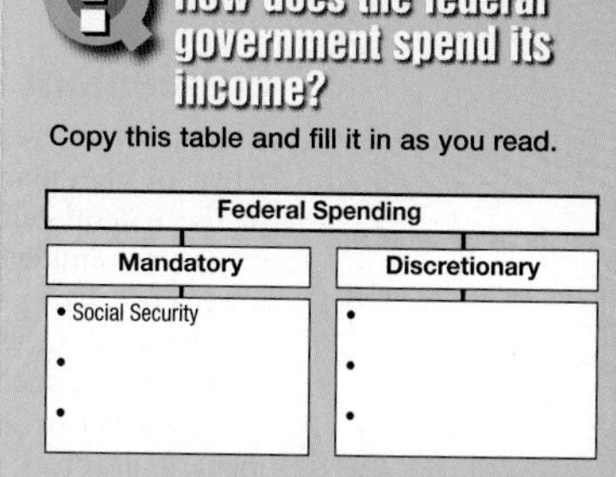

Copy this table and fill it in as you read.

Federal Spending	
Mandatory	Discretionary
• Social Security • •	• • •

Economics and You Suppose that each year you were given a million dollars to spend on serious expenses. So much money! So many choices! Where would you begin? In the same way, the federal government, with a budget of around $2.8 trillion, faces a similar "dilemma" every year.

Principles in Action Through the democratic process, the American public provides government officials with clear guidelines on how the federal government should spend its income. As you will read, government spending meets numerous needs. However, the American people have decided that much of the money should provide for our health and welfare.

mandatory spending spending that Congress is required by existing law to do

discretionary spending spending about which Congress is free to make choices

Mandatory and Discretionary Spending

In reality, when the government receives the $2.8 trillion in the form of taxes, most of it is already accounted for. After the government fulfills all its legal obligations, only about a third of the money remains to be spent.

The graph in Figure 14.4 shows the major categories of federal spending. Some of these categories, such as Social Security and Medicare, are mandatory. **Mandatory spending** refers to money that Congress is mandated, or required, by existing law to spend on certain programs or to use for interest payments on the national debt. Other categories, such as defense and education, are discretionary. **Discretionary spending** is spending about which lawmakers are free to make choices.

Figure 14.4 Federal Spending, 2006

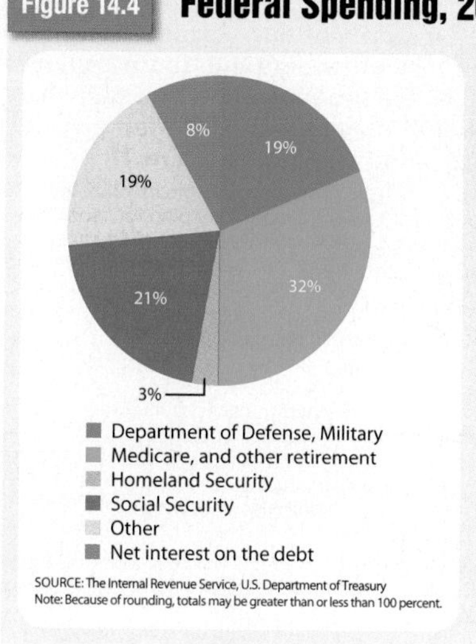

SOURCE: The Internal Revenue Service, U.S. Department of Treasury
Note: Because of rounding, totals may be greater than or less than 100 percent.

GRAPH SKILLS

The federal government spends the funds it collects from taxes and other sources on a variety of programs.

1. Which are the three largest categories of expenditures in the federal budget?
2. On which area(s) does the federal government spend more: military and homeland security or dealing with the needs of elderly and retired citizens?

Focus on the Basics

Students should come away with the following understandings:

FACTS: • Congress cannot control all the money spent by the federal government; some expenditures are required by law. • The percentage of mandatory spending has increased over the years while the share of discretionary spending—which Congress can control—has dropped.

GENERALIZATION: Since mandatory spending takes so much of the federal budget, it is difficult for Congress to cut spending or to devote large amounts of money to new programs.

Guiding Question

How does the federal government spend its income?

Get Started

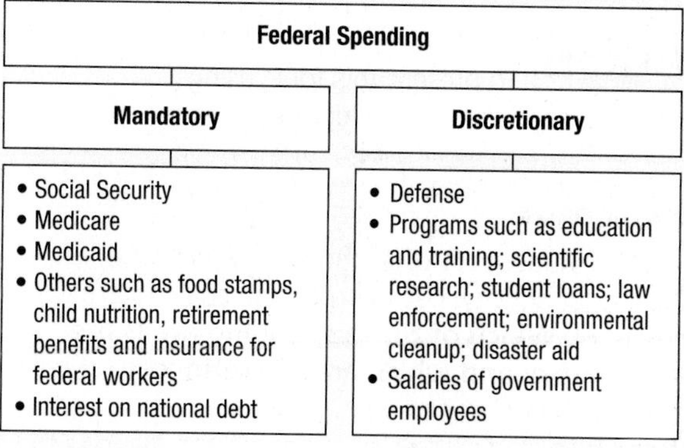

Federal Spending	
Mandatory	Discretionary
• Social Security • Medicare • Medicaid • Others such as food stamps, child nutrition, retirement benefits and insurance for federal workers • Interest on national debt	• Defense • Programs such as education and training; scientific research; student loans; law enforcement; environmental cleanup; disaster aid • Salaries of government employees

LESSON GOALS

Students will:

- Know the Key Terms.
- Distinguish mandatory from discretionary spending.
- Compare and contrast entitlement programs.
- Debate possible solutions to the Social Security financing problem.
- Discuss the impact of rising mandatory spending on discretionary spending.

BEFORE CLASS

Have students complete the graphic organizer in the Section Opener or the Guided Reading and Review worksheet (Unit 6 All-in-One, p. 29).

L1 L2 ELL LPR Differentiate Have students complete the Guided Reading and Review worksheet (Unit 6 All-in-One, p. 30).

Answers

Graph Skills 1. military, Social Security, Medicare 2. military and homeland security (35%)

CLASSROOM HINTS

PAYING INTEREST ON THE NATIONAL DEBT

Students may not understand what interest on the national debt is. The national debt is money the government has borrowed and not yet paid back. As the national debt grows, the government must pay larger and larger amounts of interest to finance it. Look at Figure 14.4. As you can see, eight percent of federal spending in 2006 was for interest on the national debt.

BELLRINGER

Have students write a list of every way that they or someone they know benefits from federal spending. Students could review the federal spending chart on page 375 for help.

Teach

Economics online To present this topic using digital resources, use the lecture notes on www.PearsonSuccessNet.com.

CATEGORIZE

Call on students to offer their answers to the Bellringer activity. List them on the chalkboard. Then ask **Which of these spending areas are mandatory and which are discretionary?** *(Circle the mandatory spending.)*

COMPARE

Direct students' attention to Figure 14.4 on page 375. Ask **What is the total percentage of federal spending that goes to entitlement programs?** *(53%)* Then ask **What do Social Security, Medicare, and military and federal employee retirement programs have in common?** *(All are entitlement programs; all are mandatory spending.)* **How do they differ?** *(Medicare is means-tested; Social Security and military and employee retirement programs are not.)* Have students review the How The Economy Works feature on pp. 378–379 to understand more about these programs.

L1 L2 Differentiate Encourage students to create a concept web for each entitlement program. The center shape should have the name of the program, such as Social Security. The outer shapes should contain basic information, such as purpose, covered individuals, whether the program is means-tested or not, and special issues.

entitlement social welfare program that people are "entitled to" benefit from if they meet certain eligibility requirements

In general, the percentage of federal spending that is mandatory has grown in recent years. The percentage of discretionary spending has decreased.

CHECKPOINT ***Is spending for Medicare mandatory or discretionary?***

Entitlement Programs

Except for interest on the national debt, most of the mandatory spending items in the federal budget are for entitlement programs. **Entitlements** are social welfare programs that people are "entitled to" benefit from if they meet certain eligibility requirements, such as being at a particular income level or age. The federal government guarantees assistance for all those who qualify. As the number of people who qualify rises, mandatory spending rises as well. As a result, managing costs has become a major concern.

Some, but not all, entitlements are "means-tested." In other words, people with higher incomes may receive lower benefits or no benefits at all. Medicaid, for instance, is means-tested. Social Security is not. A retired person who has worked and paid Social Security taxes is entitled to certain benefits. Similarly, military veterans and retired federal employees are entitled to receive pensions from the government.

Entitlements are a largely unchanging part of government spending. Once Congress has set the requirements, it cannot control how many people become eligible for each kind of benefit. Congress can change the eligibility requirements or reduce the amount of the benefit in order to try to keep costs down. Such actions, however, require a change in the law.

Social Security

Social Security makes up a huge portion of all federal spending. About 50 million Americans receive monthly benefits from the Social Security Administration. Of those beneficiaries, some are disabled workers, but the great majority are retired workers. Many of those retirees rely solely on their Social Security checks to support themselves.

The Social Security system faces an uncertain future today. To understand the

Innovators

Frances Perkins

"The large majority of our citizens need protection against the loss of income due to unemployment, old age, death of the breadwinners and disabling accident and illness, not only on humanitarian grounds, but in the interest of our national welfare."

With these words, delivered on national radio in 1935, Labor Secretary Frances Perkins unveiled an extraordinary plan for "social insurance"—the plan that became our Social Security program. Perkins helped write the Social Security Act, and later developed and administered the Social Security System and other key entitlement programs.

Frances Perkins fought for the rights of workers throughout her long career. In 1929, as Industrial Commissioner of New York State, she reduced the number of hours a woman was allowed to work in a factory to 48. Later, as the first female Cabinet member, she helped win workers the right to unionize and to earn a guaranteed minimum wage.

Her greatest achievement was the Social Security Act. "The real roots of the Social Security Act were in the Great Depression of 1929. Nothing else would have bumped the American people into a social security system except something so shocking, so terrifying, as that depression."

Critical Thinking: ***Why did Perkins believe that Social Security was "in the interest of our national welfare"? Why is social security controversial today?***

Fast Facts

Frances Perkins

Born: April 10, 1880, in Boston, MA

Died: May 14, 1965, in New York, NY

Education: Columbia University, M.A. in economics and social history

Claim to Fame: Secretary of Labor, 1933–1945; drafted and promoted President Franklin D. Roosevelt's legislation for Social Security

Differentiated Resources

- **L1 L2 Guided Reading and Review** (Unit 6 All-in-One, p. 30)
- **L1 L2 Problem Solving skills worksheet** (Unit 6 All-in-One, p. 32)
- **L4 Federal Aid to State and Local Governments** (Unit 6 All-in-One, p. 33)
- **L2 Medicare and Social Security Funding** (Unit 6 All-in-One, p. 34)

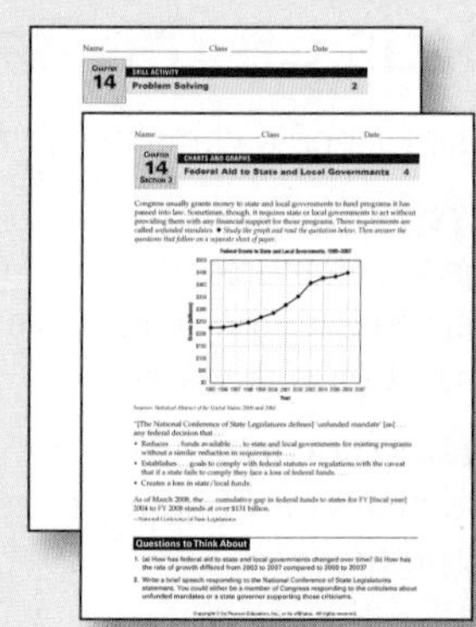

Answers

Checkpoint mandatory

Critical Thinking Possible response: By providing payments to the unemployed, elderly, or disabled, the government gives them resources they can use to buy goods, which helps fuel the economy; It is very expensive.

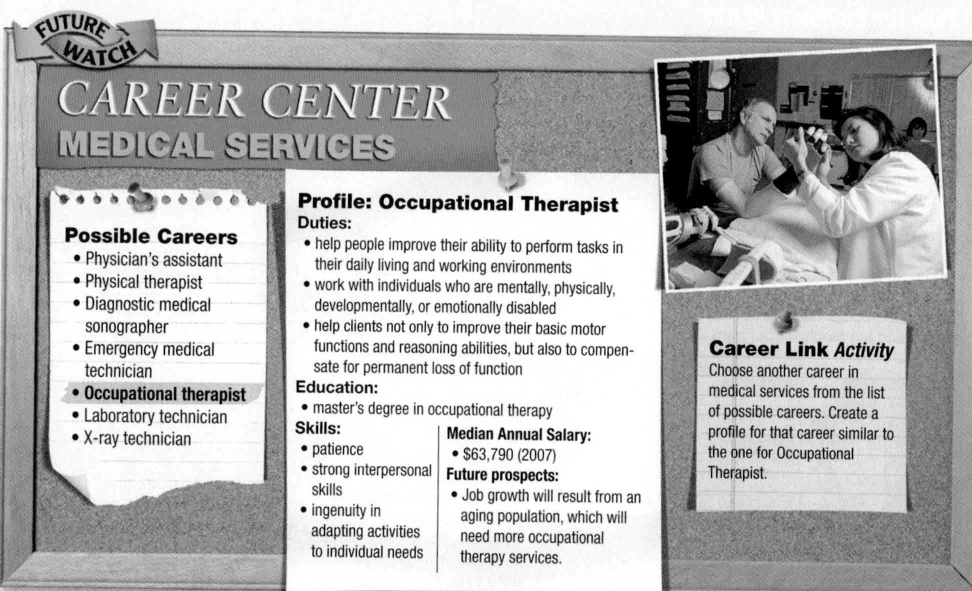

uncertainty, you must understand how the Social Security system is set up. American workers pay into the system through taxes. Those taxes go toward benefits for people who are no longer working. That is, the money that you pay into Social Security today does not go into a fund for your own future retirement. It goes toward supporting people who have already retired.

FUTURE WATCH
CAREER CENTER
MEDICAL SERVICES
Possible Careers
• Physician's assistant
• Physical therapist
• Diagnostic medical sonographer
• Emergency medical technician
• Occupational therapist
• Laboratory technician
• X-ray technician
Profile: Occupational Therapist
Duties:
• help people improve their ability to perform tasks in their daily living and working environments
• work with individuals who are mentally, physically, developmentally, or emotionally disabled
• help clients not only to improve their basic motor functions and reasoning abilities, but also to compensate for permanent loss of function
Education:
• master's degree in occupational therapy
Skills:
• patience
• strong interpersonal skills
• ingenuity in adapting activities to individual needs
Median Annual Salary:
• $63,790 (2007)
Future prospects:
• Job growth will result from an aging population, which will need more occupational therapy services.
Career Link Activity
Choose another career in medical services from the list of possible careers. Create a profile for that career similar to the one for Occupational Therapist.

For the system to function properly, there must be enough workers paying in to support all the retired workers receiving benefits. Although the system has worked well until now, the population increase known as the baby boom threatens to undermine it. As the millions of baby boomers—the generation born after World War II—start to retire, the ratio of existing workers to retirees will fall.

The system may not reach crisis levels for several decades. But unless something is done, today's high school students might receive only limited benefits from Social Security when they retire.

Medicare

Medicare serves about 42 million people, most of them over 65 years old. The program pays for hospital care and for the costs of physicians and medical services. It also pays healthcare bills for people who suffer from certain disabilities and diseases.

Like Social Security, Medicare is funded by taxes withheld from people's paychecks. Monthly payments paid by people who make certain levels of taxable income and receive Medicare benefits also help pay for the program.

Medicare costs have been growing rapidly, partly as a result of expensive technology, but also because people are living longer. The basic problem facing Medicare is the same as that facing Social Security. In 1995, there were four people paying Medicare taxes for every Medicare recipient. By 2050, there will only be two people paying taxes for every recipient.

Medicaid

Medicaid benefits low-income families, some people with disabilities, and elderly people in nursing homes. It is the largest source of funds for medical and health-related services for America's poorest people. The federal government shares the costs of Medicaid with state governments.

CREATE A PROFILE

Have students use the Career Link worksheet to record their research for the activity (Unit 6 All-in-One, p. 134).

DEBATE

After discussing the financial problems of the Social Security system, distribute the "Problem Solving" skill worksheet (Unit 6 All-in-One, p. 31). Have students read the introductory material and the various possible solutions described in the chart. Then debate the proposals as a class, calling on volunteers to comment on the significance of the benefits and drawbacks of each option. For each student who speaks in favor of, or against, a particular option, ask for volunteers who hold the opposite view to speak. After students have debated all the options, hold a class vote on each idea to determine what solution—or solutions—most students favor.

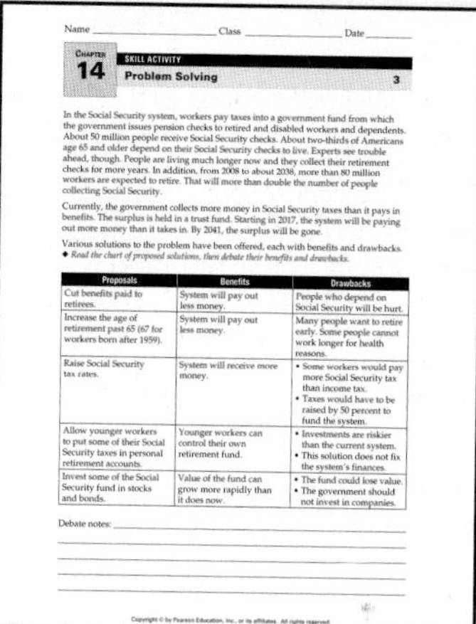

Name ____________ Class ____________ Date ________

CHAPTER 14 SKILL ACTIVITY

Problem Solving 3

In the Social Security system, workers pay taxes into a government fund from which the government issues pension checks to retired and disabled workers and dependents. About 50 million people receive Social Security checks. About two-thirds of Americans age 65 and older depend on their Social Security checks to live. Experts see trouble ahead, though. People are living much longer now and they collect their retirement checks for more years. In addition, from 2008 to about 2038, more than 80 million workers are expected to retire. That will more than double the number of people collecting Social Security.

Currently, the government collects more money in Social Security taxes than it pays in benefits. The surplus is held in a trust fund. Starting in 2017, the system will be paying out more money than it takes in. By 2041, the surplus will be gone.

Various solutions to the problem have been offered, each with benefits and drawbacks.
◆ *Read the chart of proposed solutions, then debate their benefits and drawbacks.*

Proposals	Benefits	Drawbacks
Cut benefits paid to retirees.	System will pay out less money.	People who depend on Social Security will be hurt.
Increase the age of retirement past 65 (67 for workers born after 1959).	System will pay out less money.	Many people want to retire early. Some people cannot work longer for health reasons.
Raise Social Security tax rates.	System will receive more money.	• Some workers would pay more Social Security tax than income tax. • Taxes would have to be raised by 50 percent to fund the system.
Allow younger workers to put some of their Social Security taxes in personal retirement accounts.	Younger workers can control their own retirement fund.	• Investments are riskier than the current system. • This solution does not fix the system's finances.
Invest some of the Social Security fund in stocks and bonds.	Value of the fund can grow more rapidly than it does now.	• The fund could lose value. • The government should not invest in companies.

Debate notes: ____________

Tell students to review the lesson in the Social Studies Skills Handbook on page S-15. Remind them to use the steps of the lesson to complete the activity.

L1 L2 Differentiate Distribute the "Problem Solving" skill worksheet (Unit 6 All-in-One, p. 32). Have students complete the activity.

L3 Differentiate Call on students with spatial skills to prepare a line graph showing the increase in life expectancy for Americans from 1935, when Social Security began, to the present.

L4 Differentiate Have students research the Social Security program to find out what changes were made in the past to address financial problems.

DISCUSS

Tell students that even though a large part of federal mandatory spending is for healthcare, millions of Americans still do not have health insurance coverage. Remind students about the three options for addressing the health insurance problem outlined on this page: (1) adopting a single-payer system run by a federal agency, (2) tax credits for private health insurance, or (3) leaving the issue to market forces. Ask **What are the proposed healthcare solutions meant to do?** *(provide coverage for the uninsured, reduce healthcare costs)* **What is a major financial obstacle to any new federal health care spending?** *(it would increase mandatory spending, which is already a large share of the federal budget)* Invite students to suggest other solutions and describe their advantages and disadvantages. Use the Opinion Line strategy (p. T28) to have students show their support for each option before and after the entire discussion.

Answer

Checkpoint Social Security

How the Economy Works

Where do your federal taxes go?

Not everybody is happy about all the taxes taken from their paychecks. However, taxes give the government the money it needs to operate.

1 Federal Spending: Deductions from your paycheck finance many federal programs, but among the largest of the expenses are defense spending, the Social Security program, and the Medicare program.

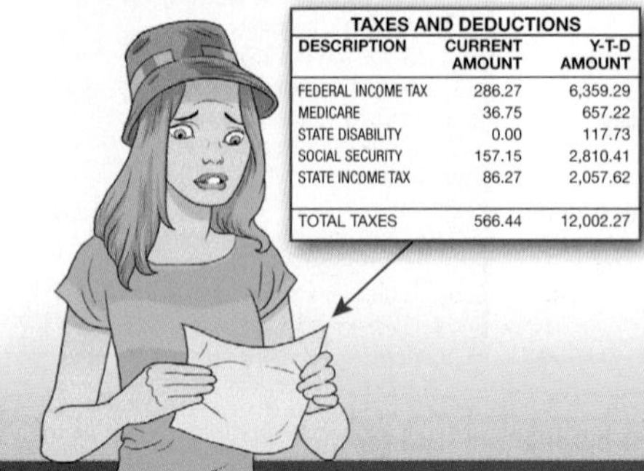

TAXES AND DEDUCTIONS		
DESCRIPTION	CURRENT AMOUNT	Y-T-D AMOUNT
FEDERAL INCOME TAX	286.27	6,359.29
MEDICARE	36.75	657.22
STATE DISABILITY	0.00	117.73
SOCIAL SECURITY	157.15	2,810.41
STATE INCOME TAX	86.27	2,057.62
TOTAL TAXES	566.44	12,002.27

2 Defense spending makes up about one fifth of the federal budget. It is a discretionary item and can be changed each year by government planners. However, since it pays for the salaries of everyone in the armed forces as well as weapons, planes, and ships, it has generally gone up each year.

The Deductions **Defense**

Other Mandatory Spending Programs

Other means-tested entitlements benefit people and families whose incomes fall below a certain level. Requirements vary from program to program. Federal programs include food stamps and child nutrition. The federal government also pays retirement benefits and insurance for federal workers, as well as veterans' pensions and unemployment insurance.

Some members of Congress have pushed for additional government programs related to healthcare. One reason is that healthcare costs have increased at more than twice the rate of inflation over the last few decades. The average expenditure for healthcare rose from \$891 per person in 1960 to \$5,670 in 2003. To keep pace, health insurance costs have also skyrocketed. As a result, some 47 million Americans had no health insurance coverage in 2006.

To resolve this problem, some leaders call for a single-payer system, in which a government organization would take over the role now played by private insurance companies. This organization would provide health coverage for all Americans. Others prefer a system of federal tax credits to help individuals pay for private health insurance. Still others insist that we should rely on free market forces, not the government, to rein in healthcare costs.

CHECKPOINT ***What entitlement program costs the federal government the most money?***

Discretionary Spending

Spending on defense accounts for about half of the federal government's discretionary spending. The remaining funds available for

Virtual Economics

L4 Differentiate

Comparing Federal Spending Use the following lesson from the NCEE **Virtual Economics *CD-ROM*** to help students analyze government spending and the relationship between taxes and political freedom. Click on Browse Economics Lessons, specify grades 9–12, and use the key words *scope and size.*

In this activity, students will use statistics to compare government spending in two periods of U.S. history and compare to other countries.

LESSON TITLE	THE SCOPE AND SIZE OF GOVERNMENT
Type of Activity	Using statistics
Complexity	High
Time	100 minutes
NCEE Standards	16, 18

How the Economy Works online

For an animated, interactive version of this feature, visit **PearsonSuccessNet.com**

3 Social Security is the largest category of federal spending. It is one of the government's most important and successful programs, providing more than $500 billion in benefits to Americans each year.

4 Medicare provides benefits to people who are 65 years or older or who suffer from certain disabilities. Total Medicare spending reached $440 billion in 2007.

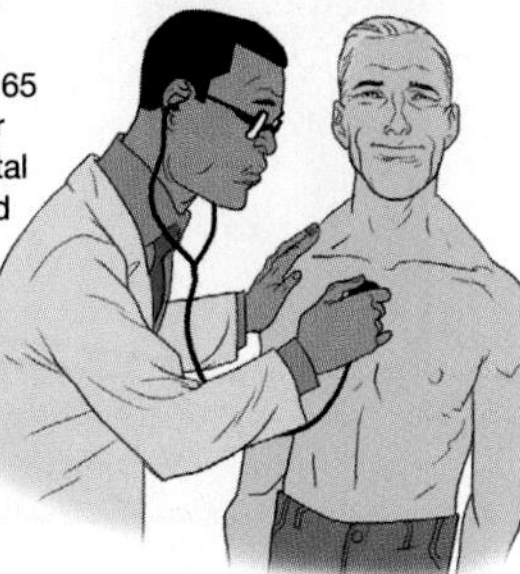

These deductions from paychecks can be unwelcome, but the programs they pay for are essential to the well-being of the United States.

Check Your Understanding

1. Why does the federal government take money from the paychecks of American workers?
2. List two areas where the money aids the safety and security of Americans. List two areas where the deductions improve the quality of life of Americans.

Social Security **Medicare**

discretionary spending are divided among a wide variety of programs.

Defense Spending

Defense spending has dropped somewhat since the end of the Cold War as a percentage of the total federal budget. As you can see from the graph in **Figure 14.4**, defense spending consumes about 19 percent of the federal budget.

The Department of Defense spends most of the defense budget. It pays the salaries of all the men and women in the army, navy, air force, and marines, as well as the department's civilian employees. Defense spending, of course, also buys weapons, missiles, battleships, tanks, airplanes, and ammunition equipment.

Other Discretionary Spending

You may be surprised at how small a portion of federal spending goes into the category that could be labeled "everything else." Here are some of the many programs that this category of federal spending pays for:

- education and training
- scientific research
- student loans
- law enforcement
- environmental cleanup
- disaster aid

This part of the federal budget also pays the salaries of the millions of people who work for the civilian branches of the federal government. They include park rangers, FBI agents, file clerks, senators and members of Congress, geologists, CIA agents, Cabinet secretaries, meat inspectors, and many others.

CHECKPOINT ***Approximately how much of the federal government's discretionary spending goes toward defense?***

Background Note

Federal Government Employment More than 2.7 million civilians work for the federal government. This total does not include military personnel. Only a small share—about 63,000 people—work for Congress and in federal courts. The vast majority work in the executive branch. Just over 1,700 people work in the Executive Office of the President, which includes the White House staff. Nearly 1.7 million work in the various cabinet departments. More than 945,000 work in the various independent agencies. The U.S. Postal Service, with 760,000, supplies the great majority of these workers, about four of every five.

ANALYZE

Display the "U.S. Projected Population by Age" transparency (Color Transparencies, 14.b). Ask **What does the chart show about the age distribution of the U.S. population in the future?** *(a larger proportion will be older).* Ask **What implications does the aging of the population have for Medicare and Social Security costs?** *(higher costs in the future)* Remind students that Medicare and Social Security are forms of mandatory spending. Ask **How are these rising costs likely to affect discretionary spending in the future?** *(There is likely to be less money for such spending.)*

L1 L2 Differentiate Have students make two circle graphs of mandatory spending. Have them color in 61 percent for 2006, and 67 percent for a future year. Point out the shrinking share available for discretionary spending.

EXTEND

Have students write an essay on federal aid to states:

• Should aid be proportioned according to each state's population? • Should the federal government give more to poorer states and less to wealthier ones?

L4 Differentiate Distribute the "Federal Aid to State and Local Governments" worksheet (Unit 6 All-in-One, p. 33). Have students answer the questions.

L2 LPR Differentiate Distribute the **"Medicare and Social Security Funding"** worksheet (Unit 6 All-in-One, p. 34).

GUIDING QUESTION WRAP UP

Have students return to the section Guiding Question. Review the completed graphic organizer and clarify any misunderstandings. Have a discussion about how the federal government spends its income.

Assess and Remediate

L3 L2 Collect the "Problem Solving" skill worksheets and assess student understanding.

L2 L4 Collect the "Federal Aid to State and Local Governments" worksheet and the "Medicare and Social Security Funding" worksheet and assess student understanding of government aid.

L3 Assign the Section 3 Assessment questions.

L3 Give Section Quiz A (Unit 6 All-in-One, p. 35).

L2 Give Section Quiz B (Unit 6 All-in-One, p. 36).

(Assess and Remediate continued on p. 380)

Answers

Check Your Understanding 1. to fund its operations 2. Defense, Social Security; Social Security, Medicare

Checkpoint about half

Have students complete the Self-Test Online and continue their work in the **Essential Questions Journal**.

REMEDIATION AND SUGGESTIONS

Use the chart below to help students who are struggling with content.

WEAKNESS	REMEDIATION
Identifying key terms (Questions 3, 4)	Have students use the interactive Economic Dictionary Online.
Mandatory and discretionary spending (Questions 1, 4, 8)	Have students create flash cards with a category of spending on one side and type of spending on the other. Have them test one another.
Entitlements (Questions 5, 6, 8, 9, 11)	Have students review related content in pairs.

Answers

Cartoon The cartoonist suggests that the states have few resources to cover these increased expenses.

Checkpoint They did not have the resources to deal with the widespread destruction.

▲ In recent years, responsibility for more social programs has been passed from the Federal government to the states. ***What point is the cartoonist making about financing for these programs?***

Federal Aid to State and Local Governments

Some federal tax dollars find their way to state and local governments. In total, about $404 billion a year in federal monies is divided among the states. This is an average of about $1,400 per person.

As you have read, state and federal governments share the costs of Medicaid and unemployment compensation. They also share in funding other social programs. Additional federal money goes to the states for education, lower-income housing, highway construction, mass-transit, healthcare, employment training, and dozens of other programs.

Federal grants-in-aid are grants of federal money for certain closely defined purposes. States must use the federal funds only for the purpose specified and obey the federal guidelines for which aid is given.

State and local governments rely on federal aid for a variety of needs. But nothing reveals that reliance as vividly as a disaster. For example, after Hurricane Katrina slammed into coastal Louisiana, Mississippi, and Alabama in 2005, those states did not have the resources to deal with the widespread destruction and human misery that the storm left behind. They looked to the federal government for help. Although critics denounced the federal relief agencies for their slow response, Congress appropriated $116 billion to help the states recover from the disaster.

CHECKPOINT ***Why did states call on the federal government for help after Hurricane Katrina?***

SECTION 3 ASSESSMENT

Essential Questions Journal To continue to build a response to the Essential Question, go to your **Essential Questions Journal.**

Guiding Question

1. Use your completed table to answer this question: How does the federal government spend its income?
2. **Extension** What federal government services do you use in your life? What services do you think you might use in the future?

Key Terms and Main Ideas

3. What are means-tested **entitlements?**
4. Name at least three examples of federal **discretionary spending.**
5. Whose retirements are funded by the money today's wage earners are now paying into Social Security?
6. What services does Medicaid provide, and who benefits from these services?
7. List at least three programs in which state governments and the federal government share funding.

Critical Thinking

8. **Extend (a)** How are mandatory spending and discretionary spending different? **(b)** How can a mandatory spending program be changed into a discretionary spending program?
9. **Discuss** What problems do entitlement programs cause? Why might it be difficult for lawmakers to make changes to entitlement programs?
10. **Select (a)** Why have some members of Congress pushed for additional government programs related to healthcare? **(b)** Describe their suggestions to help solve this problem.

Quick Write

11. Reread the part of this section titled Entitlement Programs. Then suppose you are running for federal office. Write a short essay answering the following questions. What public needs should government move to fill immediately? Would you propose any new entitlement programs? If so, what would they be? Would you propose eliminating or modifying any existing entitlement programs? Explain your answers.

Assessment Answers

1. mainly on mandatory programs but also on discretionary programs
2. Possible response: We all depend on the government for defense and security. School students benefit from government aid to schools. In the future, I may need Social Security.
3. benefits programs in which people with higher income may receive lower benefits or none at all
4. Possible responses: spending on defense, homeland security, education, research
5. people now retired
6. healthcare; lower-income people who have no health insurance
7. Any three: Medicaid, unemployment compensation, other social programs, education, lower-income housing, highway building, mass-transit, healthcare, employment training
8. (a) Amounts spent on mandatory spending are fixed by law; discretionary spending can change from year to year. (b) by changing the law
9. Possible responses: Since benefits are fixed, Congress cannot cut them to control costs; members of Congress might fear that cutting benefits will cost them reelection.
10. (a) because nearly 50 million Americans lack health insurance (b) three options: single-payer system, with government taking the lead; using federal tax credits to help individuals afford insurance; rely on free market
11. Possible response: Some students might suggest benefits ensuring college tuition or healthcare for all people; others might suggest changing Social Security. Students should offer explanations for the proposals.

SECTION 4 State and Local Taxes and Spending

OBJECTIVES

1. **Explain** how states use a budget to plan their spending.
2. **Identify** where state taxes are spent.
3. **List** the major sources of state tax revenue.
4. **Describe** local government spending and sources of revenue.

ECONOMIC DICTIONARY

As you read the section, look for the definitions of these **Key Terms:**

- budget
- operating budget
- capital budget
- balanced budget
- tax exempt
- real property
- personal property
- tax assessor

Guiding Question
How do local governments manage their money?

Copy this table and fill it in as you read.

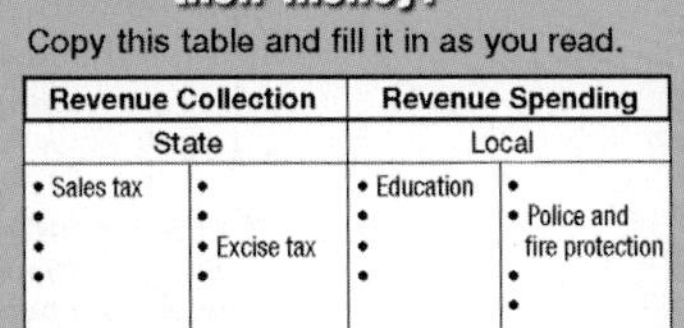

Revenue Collection		Revenue Spending	
State		Local	
• Sales tax • • •	• • • Excise tax •	• Education • • •	• • Police and fire protection • •

Economics and You You and your family are thinking about colleges. Which one offers the courses you want? How much does it cost? During your research, you find that colleges within your state's university system are far less expensive than private schools. The reason is that your state government pays part of the cost of running the state colleges. In fact, higher education is one of the largest areas of state government spending.

Principles in Action Because they are democracies, local governments manage their money in accordance with priorities set by elected local government officials. In this section, you will examine these priorities. For example, in the Economics & You feature, you will see that while school tax increases can be painful to the taxpayer, the programs they fund are sometimes essential to quality education and necessary to enriching the school experience.

State Budgets

Like families and individuals, governments must plan their spending ahead of time. That planning involves drawing up a budget. A **budget** is an estimate of future revenues and expenses. While the federal government has just one budget for planned revenue and expenses, states have two budgets: operating budgets and capital budgets.

Operating Budgets

A state puts together an **operating budget** to plan for its day-to-day spending needs. Those expenses include salaries of state employees, supplies such as computers and paper, and maintenance of state facilities, such as recreation areas and roadside parks.

Capital Budgets

A state also draws up a **capital budget** to plan for major capital, or investment, spending. If the state builds a new bridge, the money comes from this budget. Most of these expenses are met by long-term borrowing or the sale of bonds.

budget an estimate of future revenue and expenses

operating budget a budget for day-to-day spending needs

capital budget a budget for spending on major investments

Guiding Question

How do local governments manage their money?

Get Started

Revenue Collection		Revenue Spending	
State		Local	
• Sales tax • Individual income tax • Corporate income tax • Licensing fees	• Transfer tax • Inheritance tax • Excise tax • Property taxes	• Education • Parks and recreational facilities • Public health • Public transportation	• Elections • Police and fire protection • Record keeping • Social services

LESSON GOALS

Students will:

- Know the Key Terms.
- Understand operating and capital budgets and compare levels of state spending in one area.
- Analyze different situations to determine who bears the burden of state taxes.
- Discuss the costs and benefits of corporate income taxes.

BEFORE CLASS

Students should read the section for homework before coming to class.

Have students complete the graphic organizer in the Section Opener as they read the text. As an alternate activity, have students complete the Guided Reading and Review worksheet (Unit 6 All-in-One, p. 37).

L1 L2 ELL Differentiate Have students complete the Guided Reading and Review worksheet (Unit 6 All-in-One, p. 38).

Focus on the Basics

Students should come away with the following understandings:

FACTS: • State governments have operating budgets for ongoing expenses and capital budgets for major investments. • States rely mainly on sales taxes and income taxes. • Local governments use property taxes, income taxes, and other taxes to fund a variety of activities.

GENERALIZATION: State and local governments must make careful decisions to balance spending and revenues.

CLASSROOM HINTS

STATE SPENDING

Have pairs of students allocate a hypothetical state's $500 million budget between the six spending categories mentioned in Section 4: education, public safety, highways and transportation, general welfare, arts and recreation, and administration. Once pairs have decided on an amount to spend in each category, have them compute the percentage of the total budget each category represents.

BELLRINGER

Write the definition of operating budget and capital budget on the chalkboard. Have students list which items in the school budget are in the operating budget and which are capital expenditures.

Teach

Economics online To present this topic using digital resources, use the lecture notes on www.PearsonSuccessNet.com.

DISCUSS

Call on students to discuss the differences between operating and capital budgets. Then have them review their lists and volunteer their answers.

L1 L2 Differentiate Have students use a two-column graphic organizer to define and compare operating budget and capital budget. Remind them to include whether the budget type must be balanced.

ANALYZE CHARTS

The states vary greatly in size, making it difficult to compare state budgets. Point out that using charts is one way of determining how states compare. Distribute the "Comparing State Spending" worksheet (Unit 6 All-in-One, p. 39). Have students answer the questions.

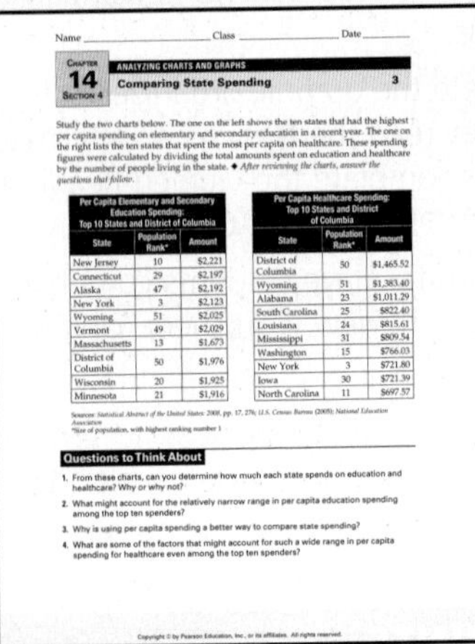

Name ____________ Class ____________ Date ______

CHAPTER 14 SECTION 4 — ANALYZING CHARTS AND GRAPHS

Comparing State Spending 3

Study the two charts below. The one on the left shows the ten states that had the highest per capita spending on elementary and secondary education in a recent year. The one on the right lists the ten states that spent the most per capita on healthcare. These spending figures were calculated by dividing the total amounts spent on education and healthcare by the number of people living in the state. ◆ *After reviewing the charts, answer the questions that follow.*

Per Capita Elementary and Secondary Education Spending: Top 10 States and District of Columbia

State	Population Rank*	Amount
New Jersey	10	$2,221
Connecticut	29	$2,197
Alaska	47	$2,192
New York	3	$2,123
Wyoming	51	$2,025
Vermont	49	$2,029
Massachusetts	13	$1,673
District of Columbia	50	$1,976
Wisconsin	20	$1,925
Minnesota	21	$1,916

Per Capita Healthcare Spending: Top 10 States and District of Columbia

State	Population Rank*	Amount
District of Columbia	50	$1,465.52
Wyoming	51	$1,383.40
Alabama	23	$1,011.29
South Carolina	25	$822.40
Louisiana	24	$815.61
Mississippi	31	$809.54
Washington	15	$766.03
New York	3	$721.80
Iowa	30	$721.39
North Carolina	11	$697.57

Sources: Statistical Abstract of the United States: 2008, pp. 17, 276; U.S. Census Bureau (2005); National Education Association

*Size of population, with highest ranking number 1

Questions to Think About

1. From these charts, can you determine how much each state spends on education and healthcare? Why or why not?
2. What might account for the relatively narrow range in per capita education spending among the top ten spenders?
3. Why is using per capita spending a better way to compare state spending?
4. What are some of the factors that might account for such a wide range in per capita spending for healthcare even among the top ten spenders?

L2 Differentiate Distribute the "State and Local Education Spending" worksheet (Unit 6 All-in-One, p. 40).

L3 Differentiate Have students use the Statistical Abstract of the United States to create a profile of revenue sources and expenditures for their state. Have them compare their state with another state with a similar population.

Answers

Checkpoint capital budget

Checkpoint from state tax revenues

Simulation Activity

Taxes and Changing Circumstances
You may be asked to take part in a role-playing game about taxes.

Balancing State Budgets

In most states, the governor prepares the budget with the help of a budget agency. The legislature then discusses and eventually approves the budget. Unlike the federal government, 49 states require **balanced budgets**—budgets in which revenues are equal to spending. These laws, however, apply only to the operating budget, not the capital budget. That makes it easier to balance a state budget than to balance the federal budget.

CHECKPOINT ***Would the construction of a new courthouse come out of a state's operating budget or capital budget?***

Where Are State Taxes Spent?

Spending policies differ among the 50 states. You are probably most familiar with state spending on education, highways, police protection, and state recreation areas. You can see other significant spending categories in **Figure 14.5.**

Education

Every state spends taxpayer money to support at least one public state university. Some, such as California, have large systems with many campuses throughout the state. In many states, tax dollars also support agricultural and technical colleges, teacher's colleges, and two-year community colleges.

State governments also provide financial help to their local governments, which run public elementary, middle, and high schools. The total amount of money spent per student varies among the states. The national average is $8,701 per student per year.

Public Safety

State police are a familiar sight along the nation's highways. The state police enforce traffic laws and help motorists in emergencies. State police also maintain crime labs that can assist local law-enforcement agencies. State governments build and run corrections systems. These institutions house people convicted of state crimes.

balanced budget a budget in which revenue and spending are equal

Highways and Transportation

Building and maintaining highway systems is another major state expense. State crews resurface roads and repair bridges. Some money for roads comes from the federal government. In turn, states contribute money to federal and interstate highway systems.

States pay at least some of the costs of other kinds of transportation facilities, such as waterways and airports. Money for such projects may also come from federal and local government budgets.

Public Welfare

States look after the health and welfare of the public in various ways. State funds support some public hospitals and clinics. State regulators inspect water supplies and test for pollution.

As you have read, states also help pay for many of the federal programs that assist individuals, such as unemployment compensation benefits. Because states determine their own benefits, they can meet local needs better than the federal government can. For example, during a local recession, they may decide to extend the number of weeks that people can claim benefits.

Arts and Recreation

If you've hiked in a state forest or picnicked in a state park, you've enjoyed another benefit of state tax dollars. Nature reserves and parks preserve scenic and historic places for people to visit and enjoy. States also run museums and help fund music and art programs.

Administration

Besides providing services, state governments need to spend money just to keep running. Like the federal government, state governments have an executive branch (the governor's office), a legislative branch, and a court system. State tax revenues pay the salaries of all these and other state workers, including judges, maintenance crews in state parks, the governor, and professors in state universities.

CHECKPOINT ***Where does a state get the money to fund public schools, prisons, and highway construction?***

Differentiated Resources

L1 L2 Guided Reading and Review (Unit 6 All-in-One, p. 38)

L2 State and Local Education Spending (Unit 6 All-in-One, p. 40)

L3 Taxes and Changing Circumstances (Simulation Activities, Chapter14)

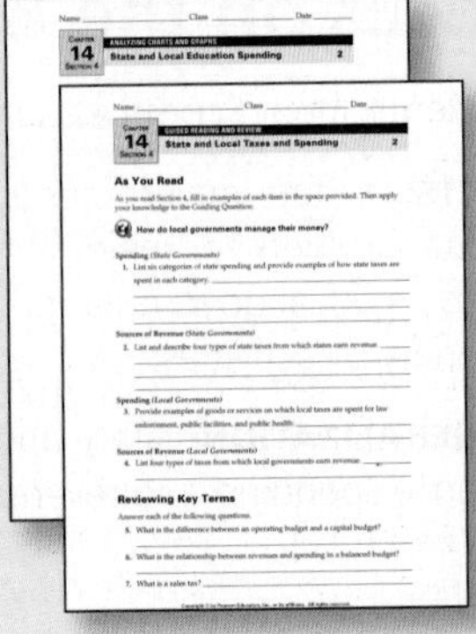

Figure 14.5 **State Revenue and Spending, 2004–2005**

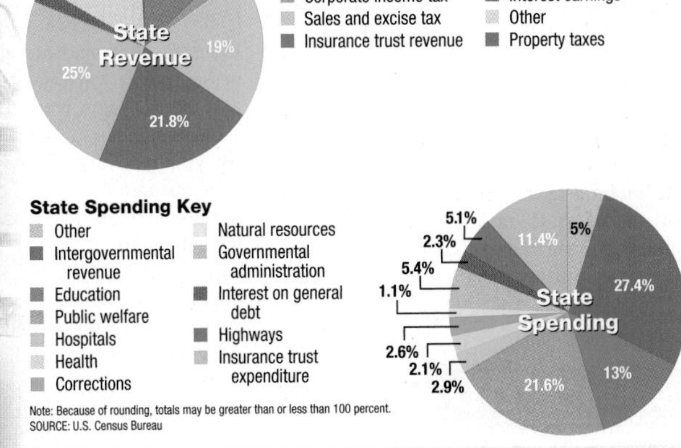

Note: Because of rounding, totals may be greater than or less than 100 percent.
SOURCE: U.S. Census Bureau

GRAPH SKILLS

Individual income taxes, sales, and other taxes, insurance premiums, and local and federal funds are major sources of state revenue.

1. **What are the three largest categories of state government spending?**
2. **What percentage of state government spending goes towards education and public welfare?**

State Tax Revenue

For every dollar a state spends, it must take in a dollar in revenue. Otherwise, it cannot maintain a balanced budget. The 50 states now take in more than $500 billion a year from taxes. Where does this money come from? The pie chart on the left in **Figure 14.5** shows you the major sources of state revenue.

Just as the United States Constitution limits the federal government's power to tax, it also puts limits on the states. Because trade and commerce are considered national enterprises, states cannot tax imports or exports. They also cannot tax goods sent between states. Nonprofit organizations, religious groups, and charities are usually **tax exempt;** that is, they are not subject to taxes.

Sales Tax

Sales taxes are a main source of revenue for state governments. A sales tax is a tax on goods and services. The tax—a percentage of the purchase price—is added on at the cash register and paid by the purchaser.

All but a few of the 50 states collect sales taxes. Their sales tax rates range from 2.9 to 7.25 percent. Some local governments have their own, additional sales tax. In every state, some categories of products are exempt from sales tax. For example, many states do not charge sales tax on basic needs such as food and clothing.

Even states without a sales tax impose excise taxes that apply to specific products and activities. Some are sin taxes—taxes that are intended to discourage harmful behavior—on products like alcoholic beverages and tobacco. Other taxes apply to hotel and motel rooms, automobiles, rental cars, and insurance policies. Many states also tax gasoline. This state gasoline tax is in addition to the federal tax.

Individual Income Tax

Individual income taxes are another large contributor to many states' budgets. People pay this state income tax in addition to the federal income tax. **Figure 14.5** shows that state individual income taxes contribute about 13 percent of state revenue.

Some states tax incomes at a flat rate (that is, as a proportional tax). Others use a progressive tax—either by creating their own progressive rate structure, or by

tax exempt not subject to taxes

DETERMINE BURDEN

Remind students of the discussion of the burden of taxes in Section 1. Ask **Who bears the burden of the following state taxes?**

- A state sales tax of 5 percent added to the total of every qualifying purchase. *(any consumer who buys any goods or services in the state)*
- A state gasoline tax of 20 percent included in the displayed price of gasoline; there is no requirement for gas stations to provide notice of the tax. *(Unclear; gas stations might pass the entire tax onto consumers but might absorb some of it themselves.)*
- A county hotel and entertainment tax of 10 percent added to the cost of each hotel room and ticket to a major amusement park that attracts many out-of-county visitors. *(all people who take hotel rooms and buy amusement park tickets, including many people from outside the county)*
- The state charges tolls to all drivers who use certain state-run highways. *(All drivers who use the toll highways pay the burden. In addition, consumers in general might if companies whose trucks must use the highway pass on the cost of the toll.)*

L1 L2 Differentiate Use the Visual Glossary page to review the term *progressive taxes.* As an alternate, direct students to the Visual Glossary Online to reinforce their understanding of *progressive taxes.*

L1 L2 Differentiate Guide students to answer the questions in these hypothetical situations by having them use these questions: What group of consumers might use the good or service? Can the seller of a good or service pass the tax onto consumers or not?

L4 Differentiate Give students the following situation: State A has a sales tax of 5 percent on all items, including food and medicines. State B—a neighboring state—has a sales tax of 6 percent, but exempts food and medicines from that tax. Have them write a paragraph explaining whether they think these tax differences would have any effect on the purchasing decisions of residents of the two states and to explain why or why not.

Background Note

State Income Tax Rates Seven states—Alaska, Florida, Nevada, South Dakota, Texas, Washington, and Wyoming—have no state income taxes. New Hampshire does not tax wage income but only the income from dividends and interest. Seven more states—Colorado, Illinois, Indiana, Maryland, Massachusetts, Pennsylvania, and Utah—have a flat state income tax rate: one rate applies to all levels of income. Some of these states, though not all, reduce the burden on some taxpayers by giving personal exemptions. The remaining states have variable income tax rates, with as few as two brackets (in Connecticut) to as many as ten (Missouri). The lowest tax rate is 0.36 percent in Iowa. The highest is California's 9.3 percent (which becomes 10.3 percent on income over $1 million).

Answers

Graph Skills 1. intergovernmental revenue, public welfare, education 2. 34.6 percent

ROLE-PLAY

Review the discussion of corporate income taxes. Ask **Why would the heads of corporations prefer lower corporate tax rates?** *(Lower taxes mean higher profits.)* **Why might individual residents of the state prefer higher corporate tax rates?** *(Higher corporate income taxes might mean lower individual income tax rates.)* **What might small business owners think about this issue?** *(Possible response: They might prefer higher corporate tax rates, feeling that it would reduce their own tax burden and help them better compete with bigger companies.)*

Divide the class into five groups. One group of seven students will take the role of members of the state legislature holding a hearing on whether to increase corporate tax rates from 3 percent to 5 percent. Assign the others to one of these groups: (1) representatives of a major corporation in the state or of a business association, such as bankers, minority-owned businesses, or farmers; (2) owners of small businesses; (3) people who work for groups that represent consumers, low-income individuals, community activists, or labor unions; (4) ordinary citizens. Have the members of each of these groups meet and prepare a five-minute presentation to the legislators. They should choose one or two speakers to deliver their views. Have the four groups take turns.

After the groups have made their presentations, have the seven legislators state their views on the issue and the reasons for them. They should refer to the arguments they have heard. Then have the legislators vote for or against the change in corporate tax.

When the role-playing exercise is complete, have the class discuss the implications of the decision for the state as a whole and for each of the groups.

L3 Differentiate For additional practice with the concept of raising or lowering taxes, have students use the simulation "Taxes and Changing Circumstances" (Simulation Activities, Chapter 14). Students will participate in a role-playing game about taxes.

Answers

Economics & You Students should check with the local school board or other government authority to answer the question.

Checkpoint intergovernmental revenue and insurance trust revenue (based on Figure 14.5)

real property land and any permanent structures on the land to which a person has legal title

personal property movable possessions or assets

charging taxpayers a given percentage of their federal income tax. A few states tax only interest and dividends from investments, not wages and salaries.

Corporate Income Tax

Most states collect income taxes from corporations that do business in the state. Some states levy taxes at a fixed, flat rate on business profits. A few charge progressive rates—that is, higher tax rates for businesses with higher profits.

As you can see from **Figure 14.5**, corporate income taxes make up only a small portion of state tax revenues—about 2 percent. Nevertheless, corporate income taxes can influence a state's economy. Low corporate taxes, along with a well-educated workforce and efficient public services, can make it easier to attract entrepreneurs and new businesses to a state. Politicians keep this fact in mind when they determine their state's taxing policies.

Economics & YOU

Paying for Our Schools

School taxes make up the largest part of the local taxes Americans pay. Across the country, increases in school taxes have far outpaced the national rate of inflation. ***No one enjoys paying taxes, but schools will have to cut services if they are not funded.***

School taxes pay for a wide range of curricular and extracurricular activities. ***You have more choices when funding is sufficient.***

▲ In many communities, school taxes are subject to community vote. ***In your community, do taxpayers vote on school tax proposals?***

Other State Taxes

Besides the corporate income tax, businesses pay a variety of other state taxes and fees. Do you want to be a hairdresser, a carpenter, or a building contractor? If so, you will have to pay a licensing fee. A licensing fee is a kind of tax that people pay to carry on different kinds of business within a state.

Some states charge a transfer tax when documents such as stock certificates are transferred and recorded. Other states tax the value of the stock shares that corporations issue.

As you read in Section 2, the federal government taxes the estate of a person who has died. Some states, in turn, charge an inheritance tax on the value of the property that goes to each heir.

Some states also tax property. That includes real estate, or **real property**—land and any permanent structures on the land to which a person has legal title. It also includes **personal property**—movable possessions or assets—such as jewelry, furniture, and boats. Some states even tax property that is intangible ("not able to be touched"), such as bank accounts, stocks, and bonds. Today, however, most property taxes, especially on real estate, are levied by local governments.

✔ **CHECKPOINT** ***What two categories of taxes provide the largest contribution to state revenues?***

Local Government Spending and Revenue

Your local government plays a part in many aspects of everyday life, including public elementary, middle, and high schools. Local governments hire police and firefighters. They build roads, libraries, hospitals, and jails. They pay teachers. Even though this is the level of government closest to you, it may be the one you know the least about.

Virtual Economics

L3 Differentiate

Exploring Local Government Spending Use the following lesson from the NCEE **Virtual Economics *CD-ROM*** to evaluate how taxes are used on the local or state level. Click on Browse Economics Lessons, specify grades 6–8, and use the key words *what taxes.*

In this activity, students will investigate what services are provided by different levels of government and how they are funded.

LESSON TITLE	WHAT TAXES AFFECT YOU?
Type of Activity	Brainstorming
Complexity	Low
Time	50 minutes
NCEE Standards	16

Figure 14.6 **Local Revenue and Spending, 2004–2005**

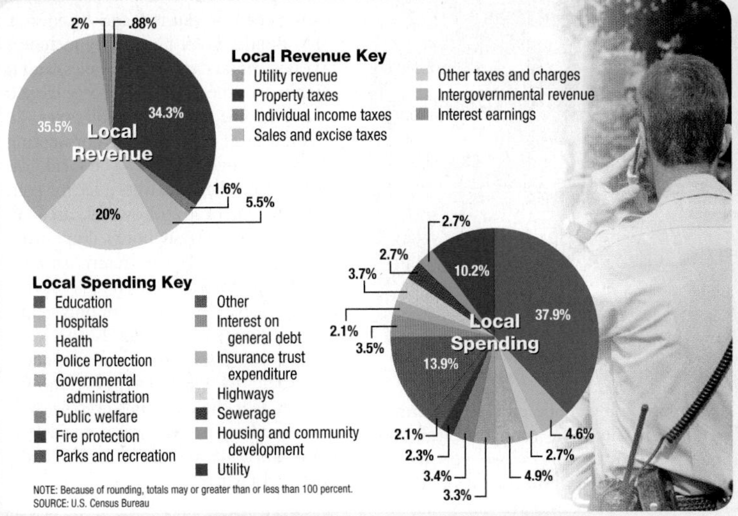

CHART SKILLS

Property taxes and state and federal funds (intergovernmental revenue) are the major sources of local revenue.

1. What are the three largest categories of local government spending?
2. How do the sources of local revenue compare with state revenue sources shown on page 383?

Forms of Local Government

You probably think of "local government" as a town or city. There are other types as well, including townships, counties, and special districts, such as school districts. Today, there are more than 87,000 local government units in the United States. Together they collect about $484 billion in tax revenues.

The Jobs of Local Government

Local governments carry major responsibilities in many areas, such as public school systems, law enforcement (local police, county sheriff's departments, park police), and fire protection. They manage public facilities (libraries, airports, public hospitals) and parks and recreational facilities (beaches, swimming pools, zoos). They monitor public health (restaurant inspection, water treatment, sewer systems), public transportation, elections (voter registration, ballot preparation, election supervision, vote counting), record keeping (birth/death certificates, wills, marriage licenses) and social services (food stamps, child-care and welfare).

Many of these responsibilities are reflected in the Local Revenue and Spending pie charts in **Figure 14.6.** In some towns and cities, separate commissions or private corporations carry out some of these jobs. You can see, though, that local governments touch our lives every day.

Property Tax

Property taxes are levied on property owners in local communities to offset the expense of services such as street construction and maintenance. An official called a **tax assessor** determines the value of the property. Property taxes are usually figured as a fixed dollar amount per $1,000 of the assessed value. They are a main source of funding for public schools.

Other Local Taxes

Local taxes are similar to the types of taxes imposed by the states. Besides property taxes, local governments levy sales, excise, and income taxes. These taxes affect not only residents of a community but also visitors. In fact, many are designed specifically to raise revenue from nonresidents.

tax assessor an official who determines the value of property

Background Note

Assessments and Taxes While property taxes are based on the assessed value of a property, the assessed value is not necessarily equal to the market value. Considering the value of the home, then, the effective tax rate may actually be much lower than the nominal tax rate. In Philadelphia, for instance, the nominal tax rate in a recent year was $8.26 per $100 of assessed value. The assessed value was assumed to be only 32 percent of the home's market value, however. As a result, the effective tax rate was only $2.64 per $100 of market value. That was still enough to rank Philadelphia seventh highest in effective tax rates. The highest was Indianapolis, Indiana, with a tax rate of $3.21 per $100 and an assumed assessment at 100 percent of market value.

GIVE EXAMPLES

Direct students' attention to the local spending pie graph in Figure 14.6. Say each category of local government spending and call on volunteers to give examples of local government spending in that area.

L1 L2 Differentiate Encourage students to use a two-column chart to track each area of spending and related examples.

L4 Differentiate Have students use Figures 14.2 (federal), 14.5 (state), and 14.6 (local) to compare the variety and types of sources of revenue for these three areas of government. Have them write at least three conclusions about why the proportions and the numbers of different types of revenue sources differ.

EXTEND

Explain that one controversial area of local spending is government funding for professional sports stadiums. Supporters say these facilities promote business and generate revenue through lease payments and taxes. Critics say that taxpayers foot the bill while teams realize vast profits. Tell students to take the role of the mayor of a city facing pressure to accept a large share of the cost of a new stadium. Tell them to write a brief speech on the issue.

GUIDING QUESTION WRAP UP

Have students return to the section Guiding Question. Review the completed graphic organizer and clarify any misunderstandings. Have a wrap up discussion about how local governments manage their money.

Assess and Remediate

L3 L2 Collect the "Comparing State Spending" worksheet and the "State and Local Education Spending" worksheet and assess student understanding of state spending on education and healthcare.

L3 Assign the Section 4 Assessment questions; identify student misconceptions.

L3 Give Section Quiz A (Unit 6 All-in-One, p. 41).

L2 Give Section Quiz B (Unit 6 All-in-One, p. 42).

(Assess and Remediate continued on p. 386)

Answers

Chart Skills 1. education, utilities, and other 2. Both get a significant sum of money from taxes and intergovernmental revenue.

Have students complete the Self-Test Online and continue their work in the **Essential Questions Journal**.

REMEDIATION AND SUGGESTIONS

Use the chart below to help students who are struggling with content.

WEAKNESS	REMEDIATION
Identifying key terms (Questions 3, 5, 7)	Have students use the interactive Economic Dictionary Online.
State revenue and spending (Questions 3, 4, 5, 6, 8, 9)	Have students outline the subsection on state government.
Local revenue and spending (Questions 2, 7, 10)	Reteach using Figure 14.6.

Answers

Caption Supporters say the tax would decrease congestion and cut greenhouse gas emissions. Critics say city businesses would be hurt.

Checkpoint property tax

▲ Wall-to-wall traffic jams are prompting a few large cities to consider a congestion tax. ***What are the main arguments for or against such a tax?***

Suppose you've gone on a school trip to New York City. The room rate for your hotel is $200 a night. When you see the bill in the morning, however, it's $230.25! Three different taxes have been added—an 8.375 percent sales tax, a hotel room occupancy tax of $2 per room plus 5 percent of the room rate, and an additional fee of $1.50 per room. Many other cities have taxes aimed at tourists and business travelers. Besides hotel taxes, they include sales taxes on rental cars, airport taxes, and taxes on movie or theater tickets. Some large cities collect income taxes as payroll taxes.

A few large cities are also considering the idea of a congestion tax. The local government would charge drivers a fee for entering a congested, or overcrowded, area of the city between certain hours. Supporters of a congestion tax say many commuters would opt to use mass transit instead of automobiles. This would not only help clear clogged streets but would also decrease the emission of gases into the atmosphere that contribute to local air pollution. Critics counter that the city's businesses would be hurt, as many people would decide to stay out of the downtown area—and spend their money elsewhere.

✔ **CHECKPOINT *What type of tax is a main source of funding for public schools?***

Essential Questions Journal To continue to build a response to the Essential Question, go to your **Essential Questions Journal.**

SECTION 4 ASSESSMENT

Guiding Question

1. Use your completed table to answer this question: How do local governments manage their money?
2. **Extension** What local government services do you use in your everyday life?

Key Terms and Main Ideas

3. What is a **balanced budget?**
4. List at least four programs and services on which states spend their money.
5. What kinds of organizations are **tax exempt?** What does this mean?
6. Identify at least three kinds of state taxes and fees that businesses pay.
7. What is the job of a **tax assessor?**

Critical Thinking

8. **Predict** Suppose a state operating budget included more spending than revenue. **(a)** What action might lawmakers take to balance the budget? **(b)** Now suppose the operating budget includes more revenue than spending. How might lawmakers react?
9. **Contrast (a)** What are the main tax sources of state revenue? **(b)** How do they differ from the main tax sources of local revenue?
10. **Make Inferences (a)** Describe the differences between real property and personal property. **(b)** Which type of property is taxed more frequently?

Math Skills

11. **Reading a Bar Graph** Look at the double bar graph below. Use it to answer the following questions: **(a)** What do the blue bars represent? **(b)** Which source or sources of local government revenue increased as a percentage of total revenue between 1995 and 2005?

For added practice in reading a bar graph, see the Math Home Video Tutor.

Taxes and State Aid

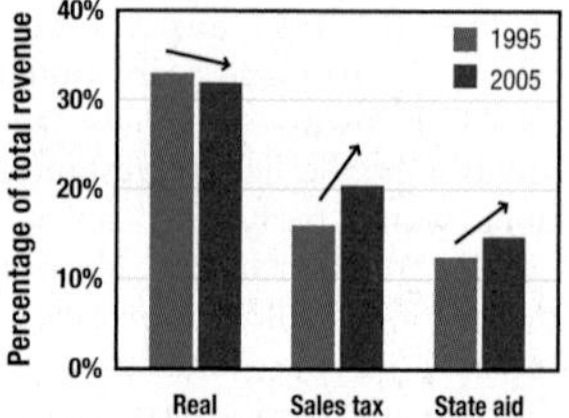

SOURCE: 2007 Annual Report on Local Governments, Office of the New York State Controller, page 10

Assessment Answers

1. Possible response: They try to balance the revenues they take in with the spending they incur.
2. Possible responses: school, bus transportation, water and power
3. a budget in which spending equals revenues
4. any four categories from the bottom circle graph in Figure 14.5
5. nonprofit organizations, religious groups, charities; They do not have to pay taxes.
6. any three: corporate income taxes, licensing fees, corporate stock taxes, property taxes
7. determines the value of property subject to property tax
8. (a) raise taxes or cut spending (b) cut taxes or raise spending
9. (a) money transferred from other parts of the government; money earned from insurance trusts, sales and excise taxes, individual income taxes (b) Local governments rely much more on property taxes.
10. (a) Real property is permanent, such as land and buildings; personal property is movable, such as jewelry. (b) real property
11. (a) percentage of total revenue in 1995 (b) sales tax and state aid

QUICK STUDY GUIDE

Chapter 14: Taxes and Government Spending

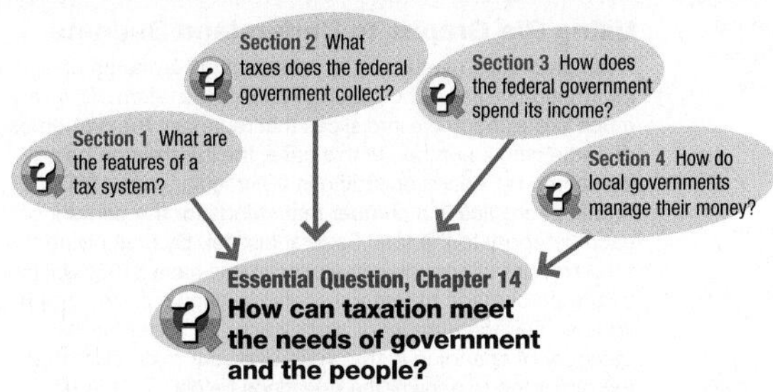
Section 1 What are the features of a tax system?
Section 2 What taxes does the federal government collect?
Section 3 How does the federal government spend its income?
Section 4 How do local governments manage their money?
Essential Question, Chapter 14
How can taxation meet the needs of government and the people?

Three Types of Tax Structures

Type of Tax	Description	Example	Ron's Taxes on a $50,000 Income	Mary's Taxes on a $150,000 Income
Proportional	A constant percentage of income is taken in taxes as income increases	Some state taxes	$7,500, or 15 percent of income	$22,500, or 15 percent of income
Progressive	A larger percentage of income is taken in taxes as income increases	Income tax	$5,000, or 10 percent of income	$45,000, or 30 percent of income
Regressive	A smaller percentage of income is taken in taxes as income increases	Sales tax	$2,000, or 5 percent of total purchases of $40,000; tax bill is 4 percent of income	$3,000, or 5 percent of total purchases of $60,000; tax bill is 2 percent of income

Two Types of Government Spending

Mandatory	Discretionary
• Interest on national debt • Medicare • Medicaid • Social Security	• Defense • Education • Law enforcement • Environmental cleanup

Economic Dictionary

Economics on the go

Study anytime, anywhere. Download these files today.

Economic Dictionary online	Audio Review online	Action Graph online	Visual Glossary online	How the Economy Works online
Vocabulary Support in English and Spanish	Audio Study Guide in English and Spanish	Animated Charts and Graphs	Animated feature	Animated feature

Download to your computer or mobile device at PearsonSuccessNet.com

ASSIGN THE ESSENTIAL QUESTIONS JOURNAL

After students have finished studying the chapter, they should return to the chapter's essential question in the Essential Questions Journal and complete the activity.

Tell students to go back to the chapter opener and look at the image. Using the information they have gained from studying the chapter, ask **How does this illustrate the main ideas of the chapter?** *(Possible response: A dam is an example of the kind of project a government would fund because no private company could make money building and running it.)*

STUDY TIPS

Suggest that students work with partners, or even in groups, to review the section content and to practice applying the concepts to real-life situations.

Have students download the digital resources available on Economics on the Go for review and remediation.

Assessment at a Glance

TESTS AND QUIZZES

Section Assessments

Section Quizzes A and B, **Unit 6 All-in-One**
Self-Test Online

Chapter Assessments

Chapter Tests A and B, **Unit 6 All-in-One**
Economic Detective, **Unit 6 All-in-One**
Document-Based Assessment, p. 389
Exam*View*

AYP Monitoring Assessments

PERFORMANCE ASSESSMENT

Teacher's Edition, pp. 367, 370, 372, 377, 379, 382
Simulation Activities, Chapter 14
Virtual Economics on CD-ROM, pp. 367, 372, 378, 384
Essential Questions Journal, Chapter 14
Assessment Rubrics

Chapter Assessment

1. (a) the benefits-received principle and the ability-to-pay principle (b) Possible response: If a tax is used to supplement the income of poor people, they are clearly in the worst position to pay that tax even though they receive the benefits. (c) Possible response: The ability-to-pay principle is most important because only those who have money have the means to pay a tax.
2. (a) It would increase the store owner's costs. (b) It would not affect wealthy consumers much because, unless they consumed huge quantities of milk, milk purchases would represent only a small percentage of their total spending. (c) No, because milk would take a larger share of their budget—unless they bought none.
3. (a) federal and any state or local income tax; Social Security and Medicare taxes (b) They will be collected on a "pay-as-you-go" basis from each paycheck. (c) Possible response: Yes, because all wage earners should pay some taxes to help provide the services we all use.
4. Any response is acceptable as long as students give three forms and valid reasons that support the choices.
5. (a) the cost of rent and utilities, taxes, prices, and wage rates in both locations (b) Possible response: That might make the city less attractive, but other factors, such as market size and income levels, would be very important too.
6. defense
7. Social Security—$37.2 billion; defense—$93.9 billion
8. Social Security—$615.51 billion; defense—$556.89 billion
9. (a) Responses should show understanding of the difference between spending and revenue, and use the correct numbers. (b) Responses should show understanding of the pros and cons of each alternative, including voter opposition to tax hikes and consequences of service cuts. (c) In budget and tax proposal, revenue and spending should be balanced. Budget should cover all anticipated needs.
10. (a) The removal will reduce the amount of money available for discretionary spending. (b) A new truck may benefit the community, but the cost will impact other safety needs. (c) Money will have to be taken from other parts of the budget.

CHAPTER 14 ASSESSMENT

Self-Test online To test your understanding of key terms and main ideas, visit **PearsonSuccessNet.com**

Key Terms and Main Ideas

To make sure you understand the key terms and main ideas of this chapter, review the Checkpoint and Section Assessment questions and look at the Quick Study Guide on the preceding page.

Critical Thinking

1. **Select (a)** What are two principles that help determine the fairness of a tax? **(b)** How might these principles conflict with each other? **(c)** Which of these principles do you think is more important? Why?
2. **Compare and Contrast**
   (a) Suppose your state imposed a new tax on milk. How would this decision affect the owner of an ice cream store? **(b)** How would it affect wealthy consumers? **(c)** Would it affect poor consumers the same way? Why or why not?
3. **Evaluate (a)** If you get a part-time job, what taxes will you probably pay on your earnings? **(b)** Briefly explain how the government will collect these taxes. **(c)** Do you think it is fair that you must pay these taxes? Why or why not?
4. **Rank (a)** Imagine that you are a member of Congress. What are the three most important forms of discretionary spending that you support? **(b)** Why did you select these categories?
5. **Extend (a)** You have the chance to open a restaurant in a suburban area or in the center of the city. What financial considerations would help you make your decision? **(b)** Suppose the city announces that it will adopt congestion taxes. How will this affect your decision?

Applying Your Math Skills

Using Pie Graphs to Understand Budgets

A pie graph is a useful way to present large amounts of information visually. The pie chart divides the information very much like a cherry pie into slices that represent the proportion of some whole number. In this case, the information being presented is Federal spending in a particular year, 1970. Within each slice is a number that stands for the percent of each category to the total Federal budget. By multiplying the total amount of spending in a year, in this case $195.6 billion, by the percentage of Federal spending shown on the graph, you can find the amount of money actually spent for that category of spending in that year. Use your math skills and the pie graph to answer the questions below.

Visit PearsonSuccessNet.com for additional math help.

6. Which is greater: the amount spent on social security, health, and education in 1970 or the amount spent on defense?
7. About how much money was spent on social security in 1970? How much was spent on defense in 1970?
8. Compare this chart with the one on page 375. If Federal spending in 2006 was estimated at $2,931 billion, how much was spent on social security in 2006? On defense?

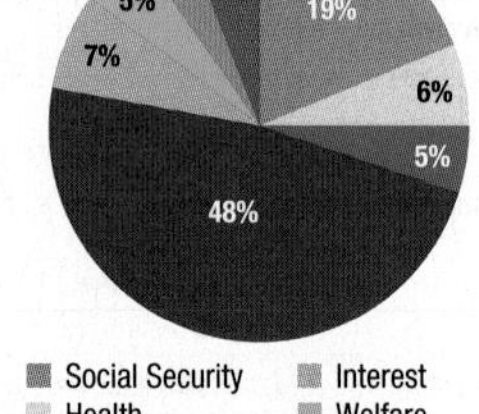

SOURCE: usgovernmentspending.com

Essential Question Activity

Essential Questions Journal To respond to the chapter Essential Question, go to your **Essential Questions Journal.**

9. Complete this activity to answer the Essential Question **How can taxation meet the needs of government and the people?** Suppose you are on the council of your local community. At current tax rates, the community will have $59 million in revenue in the coming year. You have collected the estimated spending needs for all budget categories—education, fire and police protection, maintenance, etc. Using the worksheet in your Essential Questions Journal or the electronic worksheet available at **PearsonSuccessNet.com,** gather the following information:
   (a) What is the difference between your spending needs and your revenue?
   (b) Can you best meet this shortage by raising taxes, cutting services, or some combination of the two? What are the advantages and disadvantages of each alternative?
   (c) Create a budget and tax proposal.
10. **Modify** Evaluate the impact of each of the following on your proposed budget.
    (a) Asbestos must be removed from two school buildings in your community. The cost of the cleanup is $3 million.
    (b) Your fire department wants to replace its outmoded pumper truck with a more up-to-date model. The cost is $500,000.
    (c) You are having trouble hiring road maintenance workers because neighboring communities pay higher wages. In order to compete, you have to raise wages and benefits a total of $750,000.

WebQuest online The Economics WebQuest challenges students to use 21st century skills to answer the Essential Question.

Remind students to continue to develop an Essential Questions video. Guidelines and a production binder are available at www.PearsonSuccessNet.com.

DOCUMENT-BASED ASSESSMENT

Should the United States have a national health insurance plan?

In the United States, more than 40 million people lack health insurance. Some people argue that a national health insurance program can help solve this problem. Others believe that private insurance companies can deal with Americans' healthcare better than a national health insurance program.

Document A

To achieve universal coverage would require either having the government provide it to everyone or forcing everyone to buy it. The first option, national health insurance in some form or other, would either bust the budget or cripple medical innovation, and possibly have both effects. Mandatory health insurance, meanwhile, would entail a governmental definition of a minimum package of benefits that insurance has to cover. Over time, that minimum package would grow more and more expensive as provider groups lobbied the government to include their services in the mandate.

— "Against Universal Coverage," by the Editors, *National Review*, June 21, 2007

Document B

"In the future, everybody will have fifteen minutes of health-care coverage."

Document C

Under a single-payer system, all Americans would be covered for all medically necessary services, including: doctor, hospital, long-term care, mental health, dental, vision, prescription drug and medical supply costs. Patients would regain free choice of doctor and hospital, and doctors would regain autonomy over patient care....

A single-payer system would be financed by eliminating private insurers and recapturing their administrative waste. Modest new taxes would replace premiums and out-of-pocket payments currently paid by individuals and business. Costs would be controlled through negotiated fees, global budgeting and bulk purchasing.

—"Single-Payer National Health Insurance," www.pnhp.org Physicians for a National Health Program

ANALYZING DOCUMENTS

Use your knowledge about national health insurance and Documents A, B, and C to answer questions 1–3.

1. **What is one reason the authors of Document A oppose national health insurance?**
   - **A.** It would be very expensive.
   - **B.** It would not cover important medical treatments.
   - **C.** Doctors' pay would decrease.
   - **D.** It would give people too many confusing choices.
2. **What problem does Document B address?**
   - **A.** Health insurance companies waste too much time and money on administration.
   - **B.** Americans would have to pay much higher taxes to fund a national health insurance program.
   - **C.** Health insurance is so expensive that many Americans cannot afford it.
   - **D.** Roosevelt prevented many Americans from getting adequate health insurance.
3. **According to Document C, a single-payer health insurance system would**
   - **A.** cover medical care for all Americans.
   - **B.** allow patients to choose where to get medical care.
   - **C.** reduce wasteful administrative costs.
   - **D.** All of the above

WRITING ABOUT ECONOMICS

Whether a national health insurance program will benefit Americans is an ongoing issue. Use the documents on this page and resources on the Web site below to answer the question: ***Should the United States have a national health insurance plan?***

In Partnership

THE WALL STREET JOURNAL. CLASSROOM EDITION

To read more about issues related to this topic, visit **PearsonSuccessNet.com**

Document-Based Assessment

ANALYZING DOCUMENTS

1. A
2. C
3. D

WRITING ABOUT ECONOMICS

Possible answer: Advantages of national health insurance: universal coverage; more consumer choice; less waste. Disadvantages of national health insurance: too great a governmental role; higher government costs; deterrent to medical innovation.

Student essay should demonstrate an understanding of the issues involved in providing national health insurance. Use the following as guidelines to assess the essay.

L2 Differentiate Students use all documents on the page to support their thesis.

L3 Differentiate Students use the documents on this page and additional information available online at www.PearsonSuccessNet.com to support their answer.

L4 Differentiate Students incorporate information provided in the textbook and online at www.PearsonSuccessNet.com and include additional research to support their opinion.

Go Online to www.PearsonSuccessNet.com for a student rubric and extra documents.

Economics online *All print resources are available on the Teacher's Resource Library CD-ROM and online at* www.PearsonSuccessNet.com.

Essential Questions

UNIT 6:

What is the proper role of government in the economy?

CHAPTER 15:

How effective is fiscal policy as an economic tool?

Introduce the Chapter

ACTIVATE PRIOR KNOWLEDGE

In this chapter, students will learn about the federal government's fiscal policy. Tell students to complete the warmup activity in the **Essential Questions Journal**.

DIFFERENTIATED INSTRUCTION KEY

- **L1** Special Needs
- **L2** Basic to Average includes
  - **ELL** English Language Learners
  - **LPR** Less Proficient Readers
- **L3** All Students
- **L4** Advanced Students

Economics online Visit www.PearsonSuccessNet.com for an interactive textbook with built-in activities on economic principles.

- ***The Wall Street Journal*** **Classroom Edition Video** presents a current topic related to market structure.
- **Yearly Update Worksheet** provides an annual update, including a new worksheet and lesson on this topic.
- **On the Go** resources can be downloaded so students and teachers can connect with economics anytime, anywhere.

ECONOMICS ONLINE

DIGITAL TEACHER TOOLS

The online lesson planner is designed to help teachers plan, teach, and assess. Teachers have the ability to use or customize existing Pearson lesson plans. Online lecture notes support the print lesson by providing an array of accessible activities and summaries of key concepts.

Two interactivities in this lesson are:

- **Visual Glossary** An online tool helps students learn what fiscal policy is and what it consists of.
- **How the Economy Works** breaks down information on how the national debt is created and why it is a problem.

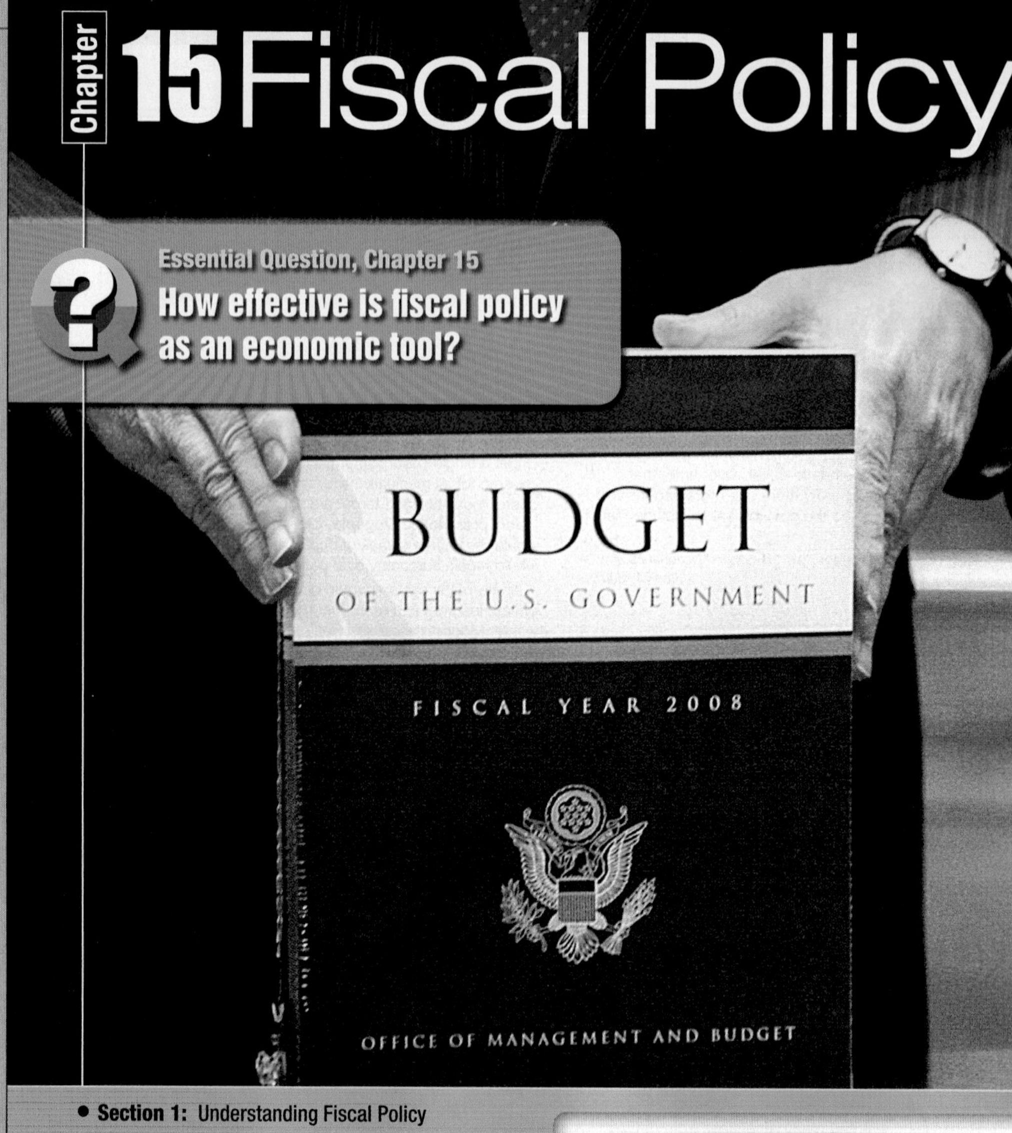

Chapter
15 Fiscal Policy
Essential Question, Chapter 15
How effective is fiscal policy as an economic tool?
BUDGET
OF THE U.S. GOVERNMENT
FISCAL YEAR 2008
OFFICE OF MANAGEMENT AND BUDGET

- **Section 1:** Understanding Fiscal Policy
- **Section 2:** Fiscal Policy Options
- **Section 3:** Budget Deficits and the National Debt

Economics on the go

To study anywhere, anytime, download these online resources at ***PearsonSuccessNet.com*** ▶

Block Scheduling

BLOCK 1 Teach the complete Section 1.

BLOCK 2 Teach Sections 2 and 3. Omit the Bellringer activities and extend options.

Pressed for Time

Group work Divide students into three groups and use the Jigsaw Strategy (p. T29) to have students teach each other the material in the three sections. Complete the transparencies and worksheets as a class.

SECTION 1 Understanding Fiscal Policy

OBJECTIVES

1. **Describe** how the federal budget is created.
2. **Analyze** the impact of expansionary and contractionary fiscal policy on the economy.
3. **Identify** the limits of fiscal policy.

ECONOMIC DICTIONARY

As you read the section, look for the definitions of these **Key Terms:**

- fiscal policy
- federal budget
- fiscal year
- appropriations bill
- expansionary policy
- contractionary policy

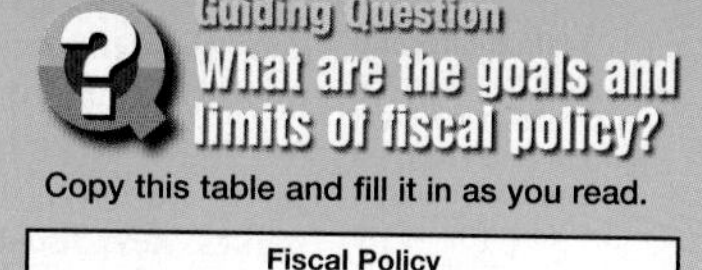
Guiding Question
What are the goals and limits of fiscal policy?

Copy this table and fill it in as you read.

Fiscal Policy	
Goals	**Limits**
• increase economic growth • • •	• difficulty of changing spending levels • • •

Economics and You Does your family have a household budget? Or have you ever tried to budget your own money? Either way, you know that you have to take a close look at how much money you have coming in and how much you have to spend. Your goal is to get those two figures in line. But it's not easy. Sometimes it requires giving something up. Sometimes—although you try to avoid it—it may even require borrowing money. No matter what, making the plan takes time. Somebody has to sit down with a calculator and a stack of bills and a checkbook and a calendar and figure it all out.

Now, imagine how much more effort it would take if your expenses totaled $3.1 *trillion* a year. Suppose everyone in the house had to agree on every single item in the budget, and you had to send it to somebody else for a final okay. Now you have an idea what the U.S. federal government must do before it can spend your tax money.

Principles in Action Unlike a family, the federal government is not just interested in making income meet expenses. As you will see, the government may also use its taxing and spending policies to speed up economic growth—or even to slow it down.

FUTURE WATCH

Personal Finance For tips on creating your own budget, see your Personal Finance Handbook in the back of the book or visit **PearsonSuccessNet.com**

Setting Fiscal Policy: The Federal Budget

As you saw in Chapter 14, the federal government takes in and spends huge amounts of money. In fact, it spends an average of $7.7 billion every day. This tremendous flow of cash into and out of the economy has a large impact on aggregate supply and aggregate demand.

Visual Glossary online

Go to the Visual Glossary Online for an interactive review of **fiscal policy.**

Action Graph online

Go to Action Graph Online for animated versions of key charts and graphs.

How the Economy Works online

Go to How the Economy Works Online for an interactive lesson on the **national debt.**

Guiding Question

What are the goals and limits of fiscal policy?

Get Started

Fiscal Policy	
Goals	**Limits**
• To increase or decrease the output of the economy, as needed • Achieve full employment • Maintain price stability	• Difficult to change spending levels • Difficult to identify the current state of the economy or to predict the future • Results are delayed • Political considerations may outweigh doing what is best for the economy • Coordinating fiscal policy among branches of government is difficult

LESSON GOALS

Students will:

- Know the Key Terms.
- Describe the process of creating the federal budget by taking the roles of the participants.
- Compare the goals of expansionary and contractionary fiscal policy by completing a worksheet.
- Describe the limits of fiscal policy.

BEFORE CLASS

Have students complete the graphic organizer in the Section Opener as they read the text. As an alternate activity, have students complete the Guided Reading and Review worksheet (Unit 6 All-in-One, p. 59).

L1 L2 ELL LPR Differentiate Have students complete the Guided Reading and Review worksheet (Unit 6 All-in-One, p. 60).

Focus on the Basics

Students need to come away with the following understandings:

FACTS: • Fiscal policy is the use of government spending and revenue collection to influence the economy. • The President and Congress follow a series of steps in the process of creating a budget. • Expansionary fiscal policy is used to increase the level of output in the economy through tax cuts or increased government spending. • Contractionary fiscal policy is used to decrease the level of output in the economy through tax increases or decreased government spending. • Several factors limit the effectiveness of fiscal policy, including the difficulty of predicting the future and the time it takes for policies to have an impact.

GENERALIZATION: The government uses fiscal policy to manage the growth of the economy, promote full employment, and maintain stable prices.

CLASSROOM HINTS

THE FEDERAL BUDGET

Students with an intrapersonal or linguistic learning style may gain a greater understanding of the federal budget and the budgeting process by imagining that they are voters writing to their representatives in Congress. Each student is the spokesperson for an existing or invented local group that seeks to receive federal money for a specific purpose. Instruct students to give logical arguments for their requests. Have volunteers read their letters. Note that these letters illustrate the kinds of pressure legislators face as they work on the budget.

BELLRINGER

Write this list on the board:

- More teachers
- New books
- New computers
- Reduced lunch prices
- Sports
- Art and music programs

Tell students to imagine that the school has received a federal grant of $100,000, and they must decide how to distribute the grant money among these categories. Tell students to write their budget and an explanation for their choices in their notebooks.

Teach

Economics online To present this topic using digital resources, use the lecture notes on www.PearsonSuccessNet.com.

L1 L2 ELL LPR Differentiate For students struggling with comprehension, assign the Vocabulary worksheet (Unit 6 All-in-One, p. 58).

DEFINE

Call on volunteers to present their budgets for the Bellringer activity. Ask all students **What percentage of the money would you budget for each category? Why?** Point out that Congress and the President decide how the government will spend trillions of dollars each year. Have students define *fiscal policy.* Elicit from students the fact that decisions about the federal budget are shaped by two factors: budgetary needs and fiscal policy. Ask **What is the goal of fiscal policy?** *(to expand or slow economic growth as needed, achieve full employment, and maintain price stability)*

L1 L2 Differentiate Use the lesson on the Visual Glossary page to review this term. As an alternate activity, direct students to the Visual Glossary Online to reinforce understanding of fiscal policy.

(lesson continued on p. 394)

fiscal policy the use of government spending and revenue collection to influence the economy

federal budget a written document estimating the federal government's revenue and authorizing its spending for the coming year

fiscal year any 12-month period used for budgeting purposes

The government's taxing and spending decisions are shaped both by budgetary needs and by fiscal policy.

Fiscal policy is the use of government spending and revenue collection to influence the economy. Fiscal policy is a tool used to expand or slow economic growth, achieve full employment, and maintain price stability. The federal government makes key fiscal policy decisions—how much to spend and how much to tax—each year when it establishes the federal budget.

Federal Budget Basics

The **federal budget** is a written document estimating the federal government's revenue and authorizing its spending for the coming year. Like any organization's budget, it lists expected income and shows exactly how the money will be spent.

The federal government prepares a new budget for each fiscal year. A **fiscal year** is a 12-month period used for budgeting purposes. It is not necessarily the same as the January-to-December calendar year. The federal government uses a fiscal year that runs from October 1 through September 30.

The federal budget takes about 18 months to prepare. During this time, citizens, Congress, and the President debate the government's spending priorities. There are four basic steps in the federal budget process.

Agencies Write Spending Proposals

The federal budget must fund many offices and agencies in the federal government, and Congress cannot know all of their needs. So, before the budget is put together, each federal agency writes a detailed estimate of how much it expects to spend in the coming fiscal year.

These spending proposals are sent to a special unit of the executive branch, the Office of Management and Budget (OMB). The OMB is part of the Executive Office of the President. As its name suggests, the OMB is responsible for managing the federal government's budget. Its most important job is to prepare that budget.

The Executive Branch Creates a Budget

The OMB reviews the federal agencies' spending proposals. Representatives from the agencies explain their spending proposals to the OMB and try to persuade the OMB to give them as much money as they have requested. Usually, the OMB gives each agency less than it requests.

The OMB then works with the President's staff to combine all of the individual agency budgets into a single budget document. This document reveals the President's overall spending plan for the coming fiscal year. The President presents the budget to Congress in January or February.

Congress Debates and Compromises

The President's budget is only a starting point. The number of changes Congress makes to the President's budget depends on the relationship between the President and Congress. Congress carefully considers, debates, and modifies the President's proposed budget. For help, members of Congress rely on the assistance of the Congressional Budget

Figure 15.1 Creating the Federal Budget

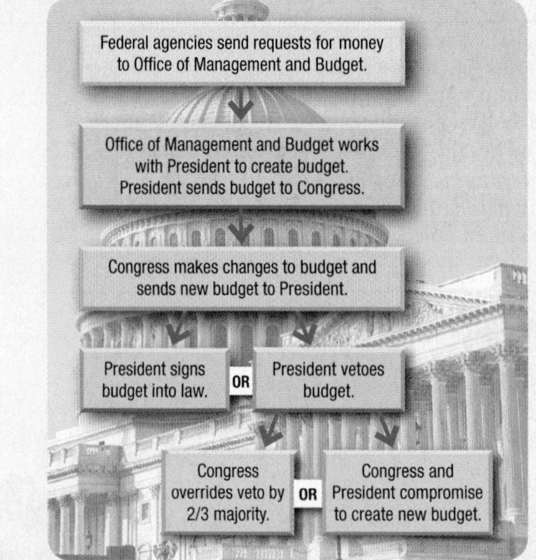
Federal agencies send requests for money to Office of Management and Budget.
Office of Management and Budget works with President to create budget. President sends budget to Congress.
Congress makes changes to budget and sends new budget to President.
President signs budget into law.
OR
President vetoes budget.
Congress overrides veto by 2/3 majority.
OR
Congress and President compromise to create new budget.

CHART SKILLS

Congress and the White House work together over the course of the year to put together a federal budget.

1. Who takes the first step in the budget process?
2. What happens to the proposed budget if it is vetoed by the President?

Differentiated Resources

- **L1 L2 Guided Reading and Review** (Unit 6 All-in-One, p. 60)
- **L1 L2 Vocabulary worksheet** (Unit 6 All-in-One, p. 58)
- **L2 Comparing Fiscal Policies** (Unit 6 All-in-One, p. 62)
- **L3 Expand or Contract?** (Simulation Activities, Chapter 15)

Answers

Chart Skills 1. Federal agencies write spending proposals and submit them to the OMB. 2. Congress can either override the veto with a two-thirds majority vote, or Congress and the President must reach a compromise.

Reviewing Key Terms
To understand *fiscal policy*, review these terms.

gross domestic product, *p. 309*
aggregate demand, *p. 314*
depression, *p. 316*
revenue, *p. 364*
balanced budget, *p. 382*

What is Fiscal Policy?

◀ **fiscal policy** the use of government spending and revenue collection to influence the economy

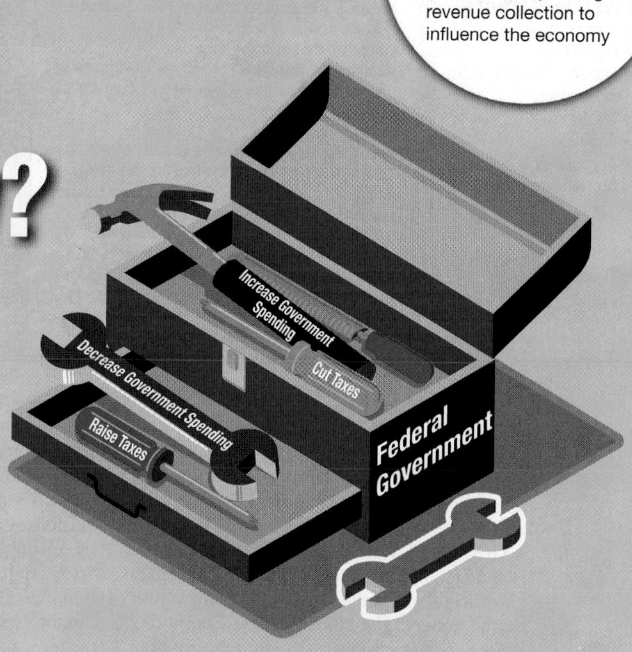

Fiscal policy has been described as the economic toolbox of the federal government. ***Choose one of the tools shown in the toolbox here and explain how it might be used to influence the nation's economy.***

HERE WE GO.. HOLD ON..ANY MINUTE NOW.. GET READY.
TAX CUT
ECONOMY

◀ This cartoon appeared at a time when the national economy was in a downturn. The man in the balloon is then-President George W. Bush, who believed that tax cuts would lead to economic growth by giving people more money to spend. ***How is Bush's action an example of using fiscal policy? Does the cartoonist believe the plan will work?***

Visual Glossary online
To expand your understanding of this and other key economic terms, visit **PearsonSuccessNet.com**

393

Teach Visual Glossary

REVIEW KEY TERMS

Read each key term and call on students to define the term and describe how it relates to *fiscal policy.*

gross domestic product – *the dollar value of all final goods and services produced within a country's borders in a given year*

depression – *a recession that is especially long and severe*

aggregate demand – *the amount of goods and services in the economy that will be purchased at all possible price levels*

revenue – *income received by a government from taxes and other nontax sources*

balanced budget – *budget in which revenue and spending are equal*

DISCUSS

Have students speculate about how each tool in the diagram might be used to influence the economy. Write their answers on the board to reference later.

L1 L2 Differentiate Assign groups one of the four fiscal policy tools. Have each group explain to the class the effect their tool could have on the economy.

CHECK COMPREHENSION

Call on students to explain what is happening in the cartoon. Ask **How did then-President Bush expect tax cuts to help the economy?** *(By taking less money from consumers and business, he expected more money to be spent, thereby stimulating more production, employment, and economic growth.)*

Economics online *All print resources are available on the Teacher's Resource Library CD-ROM and online at* www.PearsonSuccessNet.com.

Answers

Diagram Tax cuts or an increase in government spending would put more money into the economy, increase production, and create jobs, stimulating the overall economy. Raising taxes or decreasing government spending would take money out of the economy, slowing production, reducing employment, and slowing the overall economy.

Cartoon Bush is using tax cuts to stimulate the economy; no, because the balloon is already deflated.

ASSIGN ROLES

Refer to Figure 15.1 to review the process of creating the federal budget. As an alternative, assign the following roles to students: representatives of federal agencies, members of corresponding Congressional committees, OMB officials, the President, CBO officials, members of both the Senate and House Budget Committees, and members of both the Senate and House Appropriations Committees. Have the participants stand in front of the class, holding signs identifying their role in the budget process. The back of the signs should have a description of each role. Have the rest of the class physically arrange these students in the order of their participation in the creation of the federal budget. Do this two or three times until the students are arranged in the proper order. After each attempt, have the participating students read the description of their character to the class.

Ask **What is the difference between the Office of Management and Budget and the Congressional Budget Office?** *(The OMB is part of the Executive Office and helps prepare the budget for the President. The CBO is part of Congress and provides Congress with independent economic data to help with its decisions.)* **Why do you think Congress established the Congressional Budget Office?** *(so it would have professional advice from a source independent of the executive branch)*

DESCRIBE

Describe the work of different Congressional committees in the budget-creation process. Emphasize that this process gives those legislators with responsibilities for different functions, such as agriculture, education, and justice, the chance to review how the budget will affect these areas. Ask **What impact does the work of the Congressional committees have on the budget?** *(It's an opportunity for legislators to hold hearings and get more input from different agencies and individuals.)*

CREATE A PROFILE

Have students use the Career Link worksheet (Unit 6 All-in-One, p. 134) to record their research for the activity.

PERSONAL FINANCE ACTIVITY

To help students make their own budgets, you may want to use the Personal Finance Handbook section on budgeting (pp. PF4–5) and the activity worksheets (Personal Finance All-in-One, pp. 32, 34, 35).

Answer

Checkpoint The Office of Management and Budget helps the President and the Congressional Budget Office helps Congress with budget decisions.

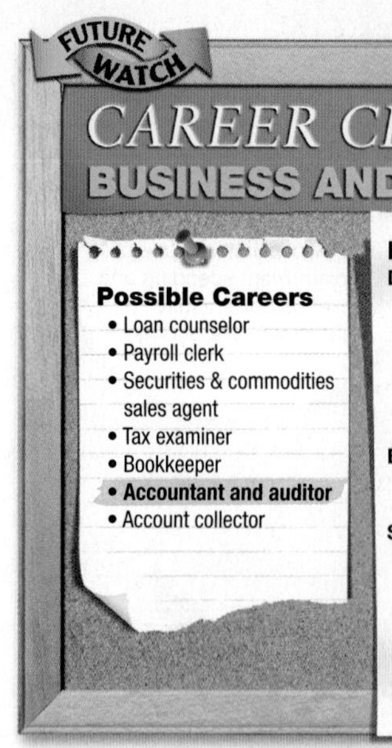

Possible Careers
- Loan counselor
- Payroll clerk
- Securities & commodities sales agent
- Tax examiner
- Bookkeeper
- **Accountant and auditor**
- Account collector

Profile: Accountant and Auditor

Duties:
- advise clients about tax advantages and disadvantages of certain business decisions
- prepare individual income tax returns
- audit clients' financial statements and inform investors and authorities that the statements have been correctly prepared and reported

Education:
- bachelor's degree in accounting or a related field. Some employers prefer applicants with a master's degree.

Skills:
- aptitude for mathematics and ability to analyze facts and figures quickly
- ability to work with people
- familiarity with basic accounting software
- high standards of integrity

Median Annual Salary:
- $57,060 (2007)

Future prospects:
- An increase in the number of businesses as well as changing financial laws will drive growth.

Career Link *Activity*
Choose another career in business and finance from the list of possible careers. Create a profile for that career similar to the one for Accountant and Auditor.

Office (CBO). Created in 1974, the CBO gives Congress independent economic data to help with its decisions.

Much of the work done by Congress is done in small committees. Working at the same time, committees in the House of Representatives and the Senate analyze the budget and hold hearings at which agency officials and others can speak out about the budget. The House Budget Committee and Senate Budget Committee combine their work to propose one initial budget resolution, which must be adopted by May 15, before the beginning of the fiscal year. This resolution is not intended to be final. It gives initial estimates for revenue and spending to guide the legislators as they continue working on the budget.

Then, in early September, the budget committees propose a second budget resolution that sets binding spending limits. Congress must pass this resolution by September 15, after which Congress cannot pass any new bills that would spend more money than the budget resolution allows.

appropriations bill a bill that authorizes a specific amount of spending by the government

Finally, the Appropriations Committee of each house submits bills to authorize specific spending, based on the decisions Congress has made. By this time, the new fiscal year is about to start and Congress faces pressure to get these **appropriations bills** adopted and submitted to the President quickly before the previous year's funding ends on September 30. If Congress cannot finish in time, it must pass short-term emergency spending legislation known as "stopgap funding" to keep the government running. If Congress and the President cannot even agree on temporary funding, the government "shuts down" and all but the most essential federal offices close.

In the White House

Once Congress approves the appropriations bills, they are sent to the President, who can sign the bills into law. If the President vetoes any of the bills, Congress has two options. It can vote to override the President's veto—a difficult task, because an override requires a 2/3 majority vote. More often, Congress works with the President to write an appropriations bill on which both sides can agree. Once that is completed, the President signs the new budget into law.

CHECKPOINT ***What two offices help the President and the Congress make budget decisions?***

Background Note

Continuing Resolutions Congress and the President do not always reach agreement on all parts of the federal budget by October 1, the beginning of the next fiscal year. In fact, in the 30 years prior to 2007, Congress and the President met that deadline only three times. In most cases, temporary continuing appropriations acts, known as continuing resolutions, keep the affected agencies and departments funded until a new deadline passes or the appropriations bill is enacted. However, government shutdowns do happen. One of the longest lasted from December 12, 1995, to January 6, 1996. When a shutdown occurs, it affects "nonessential" government services, not critical functions such as national security or public safety.

Fiscal Policy and the Economy

Government officials who take part in the budget process debate how much should be spent on specific programs such as defense or education. They also consider how much should be spent in all. The total government spending can be raised or lowered to help increase or decrease the output of the economy. Similarly, taxes can be raised or lowered to help reduce or boost output.

Fiscal policy that tries to increase output is known as **expansionary policy.** Fiscal policy intended to decrease output is called **contractionary policy.** By carefully choosing to follow expansionary or contractionary fiscal policy, the federal government tries to make the economy run as smoothly as possible.

Expansionary Fiscal Policy

Governments use an expansionary fiscal policy to raise the level of output in the economy. That is, they use expansionary policy to encourage growth, either to try to prevent a recession or to move the economy out of a recession. Recall from Chapter 12 that a recession is the part of the business cycle that occurs when output declines for two quarters, or three-month periods, in a row. Expansionary fiscal policy involves either increasing government spending or cutting taxes, or both.

If the federal government increases its spending, or buys more goods and services, it triggers a chain of events that raises output and creates jobs. Government spending increases aggregate demand, which causes prices to rise, as shown in **Figure 15.2.** According to the law of supply, higher prices encourage suppliers of goods and services to produce more. To do this, firms will hire more workers. In short, an increase in demand will lead to lower unemployment and to an increase in output. The economy will expand.

Tax cuts work much like higher government spending to encourage economic expansion. If the federal government cuts taxes, individuals have more money to spend, and businesses keep more of their profits. Consumers have more money to spend on goods and services, and firms have more money to spend on land, labor, and capital. This spending will increase demand, prices, and output.

Contractionary Fiscal Policy

At some stages in the business cycle, the government may follow contractionary fiscal policy. Contractionary fiscal policy

expansionary policy a fiscal policy used to encourage economic growth, often through increased spending or tax cuts

contractionary policy a fiscal policy used to reduce economic growth, often through decreased spending or higher taxes

Figure 15.2 Effects of Expansionary Fiscal Policy

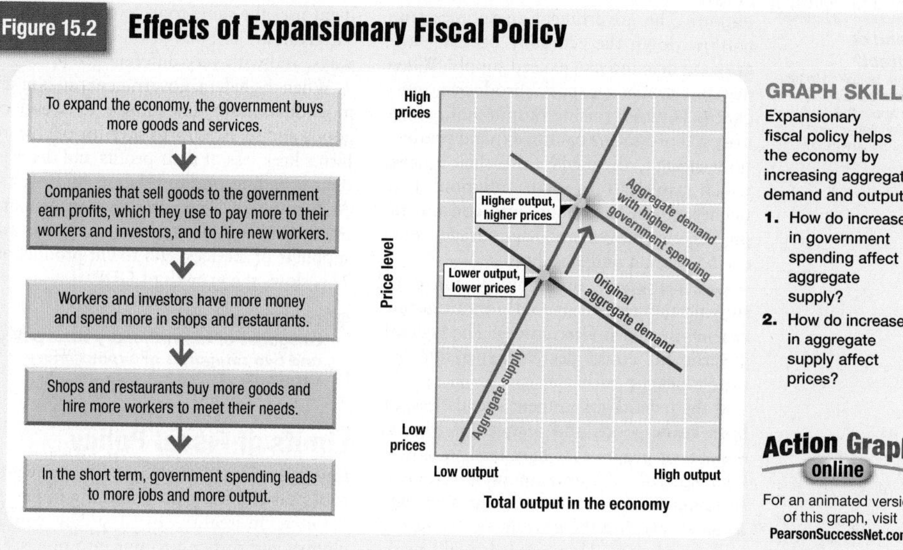

To expand the economy, the government buys more goods and services.
Companies that sell goods to the government earn profits, which they use to pay more to their workers and investors, and to hire new workers.
Workers and investors have more money and spend more in shops and restaurants.
Shops and restaurants buy more goods and hire more workers to meet their needs.
In the short term, government spending leads to more jobs and more output.
High prices
Low prices
Price level
Higher output, higher prices
Lower output, lower prices
Aggregate demand with higher government spending
Original aggregate demand
Aggregate supply
Low output
High output
Total output in the economy

GRAPH SKILLS

Expansionary fiscal policy helps the economy by increasing aggregate demand and output.

1. How do increases in government spending affect aggregate supply?
2. How do increases in aggregate supply affect prices?

Action Graph online

For an animated version of this graph, visit PearsonSuccessNet.com

COMPARE

Ask **What is expansionary policy?** *(a fiscal policy used to encourage economic growth through lower taxes and increased government spending)* Stress that the goal of this policy is to encourage economic growth. Ask **How is this achieved?** *(by increasing government spending, reducing taxes or both)* Have students describe the kinds of economic situations that might trigger an expansionary policy.

Using Figure 15.2, discuss the effect of an expansionary policy. Have students analyze the graph. Ask **What increases when aggregate demand increases?** *(Prices and output increase.)*

L1 L2 Differentiate Examine the flow chart in Figure 15.2. Call on students to explain what happens at each step. Ensure they understand the cause-and-effect relationship that exists between the stages of the process. Students also may benefit from a quick review of aggregate demand curves and aggregate supply curves in Chapter 12.

Ask **How is contractionary policy different from expansionary policy?** *(Contractionary fiscal policy is used to reduce economic growth to prevent inflation.)* Stress that the goal of contractionary policy is to reduce economic growth. **How is this achieved?** *(by decreasing government spending, increasing taxes, or both)* Have students describe the kinds of economic situations that might trigger a contractionary policy.

Refer students to Figure 15.3 on page 396. Have students describe what happens to price and output when the government implements a contractionary policy. Ask them to compare the change in equilibrium between this chart and the chart in Figure 15.2.

Action Graph online Have students review the Action Graph animations for a step-by-step look at the Effects of Expansionary Fiscal Policy and the Effects of Contractionary Fiscal Policy.

Answers

Graph Skills 1. There is an increase in the amount of goods and services supplied. 2. Increases in aggregate supply cause prices to rise.

DISTRIBUTE ACTIVITY WORKSHEET

Have students review expansionary and contractionary fiscal policy by completing the "Comparing Fiscal Policies" worksheet (Unit 6 All-in-One, p. 61).

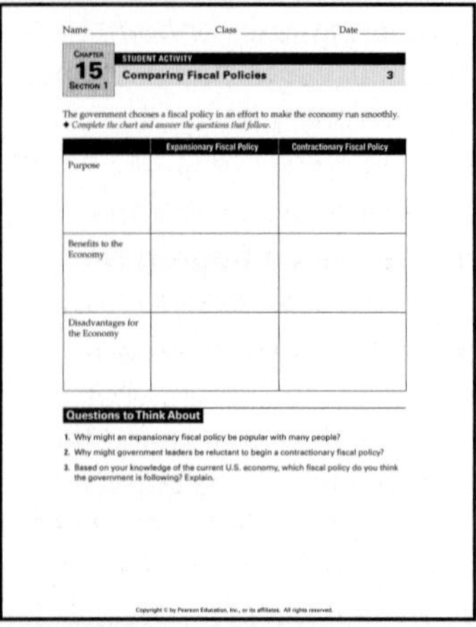
Name ____________ Class ____________ Date ________

CHAPTER 15 SECTION 1

STUDENT ACTIVITY

Comparing Fiscal Policies 3

The government chooses a fiscal policy in an effort to make the economy run smoothly.
◆ *Complete the chart and answer the questions that follow.*

	Expansionary Fiscal Policy	Contractionary Fiscal Policy
Purpose		
Benefits to the Economy		
Disadvantages for the Economy		

Questions to Think About

1. Why might an expansionary fiscal policy be popular with many people?
2. Why might government leaders be reluctant to begin a contractionary fiscal policy?
3. Based on your knowledge of the current U.S. economy, which fiscal policy do you think the government is following? Explain.

L2 Distribute the "Comparing Fiscal Policies" worksheet (Unit 6 All-in-One, p. 62). Work with students to complete the chart.

Have volunteers give their answers to questions 2 and 3 on the worksheet. Ask **What fiscal policy do you think the government should currently follow?** Have students justify their responses.

L3 Differentiate For alternative or additional practice with the concepts of expansionary policy and contractionary policy, have students use the "Expand or Contract?" activity (Simulation Activities, Chapter 15). Students will take part in a role-playing game about the use of these policies.

Figure 15.3 Effects of Contractionary Fiscal Policy

GRAPH SKILLS

By cutting spending, the government can slow economic growth.

1. Why would the government want to slow economic growth?
2. How does lower government spending affect equilibrium?

Action Graph online

For an animated version of this graph, visit **PearsonSuccessNet.com**

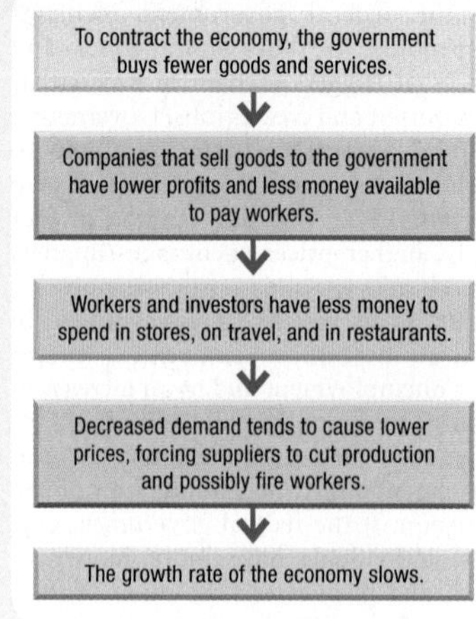
To contract the economy, the government buys fewer goods and services.
Companies that sell goods to the government have lower profits and less money available to pay workers.
Workers and investors have less money to spend in stores, on travel, and in restaurants.
Decreased demand tends to cause lower prices, forcing suppliers to cut production and possibly fire workers.
The growth rate of the economy slows.

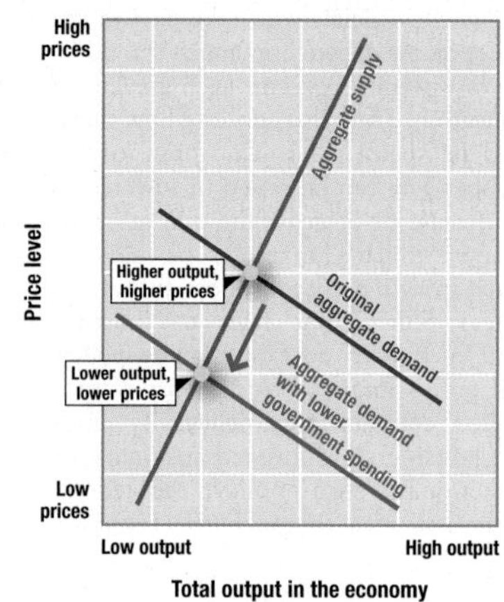
High prices
Low prices
Price level
Aggregate supply
Higher output, higher prices
Original aggregate demand
Lower output, lower prices
Aggregate demand with lower government spending
Low output
High output
Total output in the economy

tries to decrease aggregate demand, and by decreasing demand, reduce the growth of economic output. If contractionary fiscal policy is strong enough, it may slow the growth of output to zero, or even lead to a fall in gross domestic product (GDP).

Simulation Activity

Expand or Contract?
You may be asked to take part in a role-playing game about the use of expansionary and contractionary fiscal policy.

Why would the government institute policies intended to decrease economic output? The government sometimes tries to slow down the economy because fast-growing demand can exceed supply. When demand exceeds supply, producers must choose between raising output and raising prices. If producers cannot expand production enough, they will raise their prices, which can lead to high inflation. Left unchecked, inflation cuts into consumers' purchasing power and discourages economic growth and stability.

Contractionary fiscal policy aimed at slowing the growth of total output generally involves two alternatives. The Federal government could decrease spending, or raise taxes, or both.

If the federal government spends less, or buys fewer goods and services, it triggers a chain of events that may lead to slower GDP growth. A decrease in government spending leads to a decrease in aggregate demand, because the government is buying less than before. Decreased demand tends to lower prices. According to the law of supply, lower prices encourage suppliers to cut their production and possibly lay off workers. Lower production lowers the growth rate of the economy and may even reduce GDP. This chain of events is the exact opposite of what happens when the government increases spending. The government uses the same tools to try to influence the economy in both cases, but in different ways, and with very different goals.

When the federal government raises taxes, individuals have less money to spend on goods and services or to save for the future. Firms keep less of their profits and decrease their spending on land, labor, and capital. As a result of these decreases in demand, prices tend to fall. Producers of goods and suppliers of services tend to cut production. This slows the growth of GDP.

CHECKPOINT ***What are the two categories of contractionary fiscal policy and two categories of expansionary fiscal policy?***

Limits of Fiscal Policy

On paper, fiscal policy looks like a powerful tool that can keep the economy in perfect balance. In reality, fiscal policy can be clumsy and difficult to put into practice.

Virtual Economics

L3 Differentiate

Analyzing Fiscal Policies Use the following lesson from the NCEE **Virtual Economics *CD-ROM*** to introduce students to expansionary and contractionary fiscal policies. Click on Browse Economics Lessons, specify grades 9–12, and use the key words *two-act play.*

In this activity, students will write lines and enact a play that explores fiscal policy concepts.

LESSON TITLE	FISCAL POLICY: A TWO-ACT PLAY
Type of Activity	Role play
Complexity	Moderate
Time	75 minutes
NCEE Standards	20

Answers

Graph Skills 1. to prevent demand from exceeding supply and avoid inflation 2. Equilibrium occurs at a lower output and lower price.

Checkpoint contractionary fiscal policy: tax increases and reductions in government spending; expansionary fiscal policy: tax decreases and increases in government spending

Difficulty of Changing Spending Levels

Increasing or decreasing the amount of federal spending is not an easy task. As you read in Chapter 14, many of the spending categories in the federal budget are entitlements that are fixed by law. More than half of the federal budget is set aside for programs such as Medicaid, Social Security, and veterans benefits before Congress even begins the budget process. The government cannot change spending for entitlements under current law. Also, it must continue to pay the interest on the national debt. As a result, significant changes in federal spending generally must come from the smaller, discretionary spending part of the federal budget. This gives the government less leeway for raising or lowering spending.

Predicting the Future

Governments use fiscal policy to prevent big changes in the level of GDP. Despite the statistics, however, it is difficult to know the current state of the economy. As you read in Chapter 12, no one can predict how quickly the business cycle will move from one stage to the next, nor can anyone identify exactly where in the cycle the economy is at any particular time.

Predicting future economic performance is even more difficult.

> **"If economists forecast well, then the lag would not matter. They could tell Congress in advance what the appropriate fiscal policy is. But economists do not forecast well. Most economists, for example, badly under predicted both the rise in unemployment in 1981 and the strength of the recovery that began in late 1982. Absent accurate forecasts, attempts to use discretionary fiscal policy to counteract business cycle fluctuations are as likely to do harm as good."**
>
> —David N. Weil, professor of economics at Brown University

Delayed Results

Although changes in fiscal policy affect the economy, changes take time. Once government officials decide when and how to change fiscal policy, they have to put these changes into effect within the federal budget, which itself takes more than a year to develop. Finally, they have to wait for the change in spending or taxing to affect the economy.

By the time the policy takes effect, the economy might be moving in the opposite direction. The government could propose massive public spending on highways in the middle of a recession, only to have the economy recover before construction begins. In cases like this, fiscal policy would only strengthen the new trend, instead of correcting the original problem. If the government continued to spend money freely on highways in the middle of a recovery, it could lead to high inflation and a labor shortage.

Political Pressures

The President and members of Congress, who develop the federal budget and the federal government's fiscal policy, are elected officials. If they wish to be reelected, they must make decisions that please the people who elect them, not necessarily decisions that are good for the overall economy.

For example, government officials have an incentive to practice expansionary fiscal policy by boosting government spending and lowering taxes. These actions are usually popular with voters. Government spending benefits the firms that receive government contracts and the individuals who receive direct payments from the government. Lower taxes leave more disposable income in people's pockets.

On the other hand, contractionary fiscal policy, which decreases government spending or raises taxes, is often unpopular. Firms and individuals who expect income from the government are not happy when the income is reduced or cut off. No one likes to pay higher taxes, unless the tax revenue is spent on a specific, highly valued good or service.

Coordinating Fiscal Policy

For fiscal policy to be effective, various branches and levels of government must plan and work together. This is very difficult to do. For example, if the federal government is pursuing contractionary policy, state and local governments should, ideally, pursue a similar fiscal policy. Yet, state and local

DISCUSS

Ask **What factors can interfere with the effectiveness of fiscal policy as a tool for keeping the economy in balance?** *(the difficulty of changing spending levels because of entitlements; the difficulty of knowing current and future economic conditions; the delay between the decision to change fiscal policy and its impact on the economy; pressure to make decisions for political reasons; the difficulty in getting various branches of government to work together)*

Ask **Why is it difficult to reduce federal spending?** *(Many entitlement programs such as Medicaid, Social Security, and veterans' benefits are fixed by law and cannot be reduced.)* Discuss the delayed results of implementing any fiscal policy. Illustrate the difficulty by calling on students to recall the budgetary process and the time involved in implementing it. Discuss ways in which political pressure may influence fiscal policy. Ask students why contractionary fiscal policy is not popular with most voters.

EXTEND

Have students research public reaction to current fiscal policy by reading one or more editorials in newspapers or news magazines. Have students present the points of view and discuss how these views may limit or encourage the government to implement fiscal policy.

L1 L2 Differentiate Have students interview their parents and other adults to learn their views regarding how well the government is managing the economy. Have them share their findings with the class.

GUIDING QUESTION WRAP UP

Have students return to the section Guiding Question. Review the completed graphic organizer and clarify any misunderstandings. Have a wrap up discussion about the goals and limits of fiscal policy.

Assess and Remediate

L3 L2 Collect the "Comparing Fiscal Policies" worksheet and assess students' understanding of fiscal policy.

L3 Assign the Section 1 Assessment questions; identify student misconceptions.

L3 Give Section Quiz A (Unit 6 All-in-One, p. 63).

L2 Give Section Quiz B (Unit 6 All-in-One, p. 64).

(Assess and Remediate continued on p. 398)

Have students complete the Self-Test Online and continue their work in the **Essential Questions Journal**.

REMEDIATION AND SUGGESTIONS

Use the chart below to help students who are struggling with content.

WEAKNESS	REMEDIATION
Identifying key terms (Questions 3, 4, 5, 6)	Have students use the interactive Economic Dictionary Online.
How the federal budget is created (Questions 2, 3, 4, 5, 7, 8)	Tell students to imagine they have been asked to explain to fifth graders how the federal budget is created. Have students present their explanation to a partner.
The impact and limits of fiscal policy (Questions 1, 6, 9, 10)	Review the graphic organizer for this section with students. Then draw two circles on the board, and write "Expansionary" in one and "Contractionary" in the other. Draw four other circles around each and have students help fill them in with the goals and tools of each type of policy.

Answer

Checkpoint More than half of the federal budget is set aside for entitlement spending and servicing the national debt. Current law prohibits changes to these spending categories.

governments may be pursuing different fiscal policies than the federal government.

For example, after the federal government cut income taxes in 2001 and 2003, many state and local governments raised income and property taxes to close budget deficits and avoid deep spending cuts. The federal government was willing to cut taxes and run a deficit in poor economic times, but most state and local governments were legally forbidden to do so.

Businesspeople, politicians, and economists often disagree about how well the economy is performing and what the goals of fiscal policy should be. Also, different regions of the economy can experience very different conditions. California and Hawaii may have high unemployment while Nebraska and Massachusetts face rising prices and a labor shortage.

In addition, in order for the federal government's fiscal policy to be effective, it must also be coordinated with the monetary policy of the Federal Reserve. You'll read more about monetary policy in the next chapter.

Even when all of these obstacles are overcome, governments must recognize that the short-term effects of fiscal policy will differ from the long-term effects. For example, a tax cut or increased government spending will give a temporary boost to economic production and to employment. However, as the economy returns to full employment, high levels of government spending combined with increased market spending will lead to increased inflation and higher interest rates.

Similarly, an increase in taxes or fees or a decrease in government spending may "cool" the economy and lead to a recession. However, in the long run, reduced government spending will allow other types of spending to increase without risking higher inflation. If there is more private investment spending, this could lead to higher economic growth in the long run. In this way, slow growth or even recession in the short term can lead to prosperity and more jobs in the future.

CHECKPOINT ***Why is it so difficult for government to change spending levels?***

SECTION 1 ASSESSMENT

Essential Questions Journal To continue to build a response to the Essential Question, go to your **Essential Questions Journal.**

Guiding Question

1. Use your completed table to answer this question: What are the goals and limits of fiscal policy?
2. **Extension** Like the government, individuals benefit from budgets. Plan your coming month's expenditures. Start with your current income. List your necessary expenditures. What, if anything, is left for discretionary spending?

Key Terms and Main Ideas

3. Explain **fiscal policy** and how it relates to the **federal budget.**
4. When does the federal government's **fiscal year** begin?
5. What is an **appropriations bill**?
6. What is **expansionary policy**?

Critical Thinking

7. **Analyze (a)** What are the four basic steps in the federal budget process? **(b)** What is the advantage of having both the President and Congress involved in the budget process?
8. **Identify Effects (a)** Identify entitlement programs. **(b)** How do they affect creation of the federal budget?
9. **Solve Problems** Which fiscal policy strategy do you think policymakers would use in each of these scenarios and why? **(a)** Inflation is rising, and real GDP is up by 4 percent. **(b)** GDP is down, and the unemployment rate has increased to 10 percent.

Math Skills

10. **Creating a Graph** Use the information from the chart below to create a line graph showing consumer confidence in January of each of the years shown. **(a)** In which two-year period did consumer confidence rise the most? **(b)** What was the percent of decline in consumer confidence over the period from 2000 through 2003?

Visit PearsonSuccessNet.com for additional math help.

Consumer Confidence Index
Annual Average (1985 = 100)

2000	2001	2002	2003	2004	2005	2006	2007	2008
144.7	115.7	97.8	78.8	97.7	105.1	106.8	110.2	87.9

SOURCE: *www.pollingreport.com*

Assessment Answers

1. Goals: to increase (or decrease) economic growth, achieve full employment, maintain price stability; Limits: there is a long delay between policy proposal and impact; it is difficult to change spending levels, predict the future, and avoid political pressures.
2. Budgets will vary, but students should understand discretionary spending.
3. Fiscal policy is the use of government spending and revenue to influence the economy. The federal budget is the plan for how to spend revenue over a year. The budget can be used to effect fiscal policy.
4. October 1
5. Congressional bill to authorize spending
6. a policy to increase government spending and/or cut taxes to stimulate economic growth
7. (a) Federal agencies propose spending; executive branch creates budget; Congress debates and compromises on budget; President signs or vetoes budget. (b) Possible answer: The budget is assessed from different points of view: the President, who is elected by the nation, and members of Congress, who represent districts.
8. (a) social welfare programs such as Social Security, Medicaid, and veterans benefits (b) Entitlement programs make up much of the budget and, by law, cannot be changed. Spending changes must come from the discretionary part of the budget.
9. (a) Contractionary policy because, by cutting federal spending or increasing taxes, the economy can be cooled down. (b) Expansionary policy because increased federal spending will stimulate production and increase employment.
10. (a) 2004 and 2005 (b) 46 percent

SECTION 2 Fiscal Policy Options

OBJECTIVES

1. **Compare and contrast** classical economics and Keynesian economics.
2. **Explain** the basic principles of supply-side economics.
3. **Describe** the role that fiscal policy has played in American history.

ECONOMIC DICTIONARY

As you read the section, look for the definitions of these **Key Terms:**

- classical economics
- productive capacity
- demand-side economics
- Keynesian economics
- multiplier effect
- automatic stabilizer
- supply-side economics

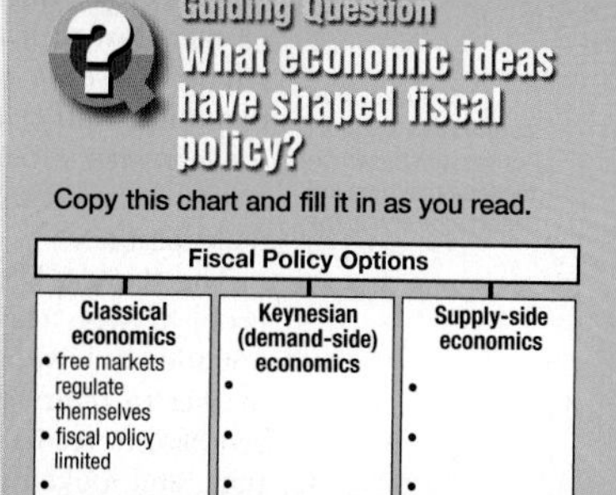

Guiding Question

What economic ideas have shaped fiscal policy?

Copy this chart and fill it in as you read.

Fiscal Policy Options		
Classical economics	Keynesian (demand-side) economics	Supply-side economics
• free markets regulate themselves • fiscal policy limited •	• • •	• • •

Economics and You Look at the picture of the two children on this page. They are poor and hungry, and the family breadwinner is out of work. Even if you have never been in a situation like this, it's probably not hard to imagine how these children feel. And the time is the Great Depression, so there are millions of families facing the same problem.

"WHY CAN'T YOU GIVE MY DAD A JOB?" But who is the boy asking? A factory owner? The local supermarket? Or is he asking the government itself? Would *you* expect the government to spend large amounts of money to give your father or mother—as well as thousands of other people—a job?

Principles in Action Nowadays, many of us are used to the idea that the government might use its spending power to stimulate the economy. But at the time of the Depression, this was a radical new idea. And today, there are plenty of people who think that there are better ways the government can stimulate the economy than by spending. In this section, you will look at two very different fiscal policy options that the government can pursue. In the Economics & You feature, you will see how tax policy can affect your income and the services you use.

classical economics a school of thought based on the idea that free markets regulate themselves

Classical Economics

Throughout this book, you have read about the workings of a free-market economy. In a free market, people act in their own self interest, causing prices to rise or fall so that supply and demand will always return to equilibrium. This idea that free markets regulate themselves is central to the school of thought known as **classical economics.** Adam Smith, David Ricardo, and Thomas Malthus all contributed basic ideas to this school. For well over a century, classical economics dominated economic theory and government policies. Some aspects of classical economic thought are still widely followed today.

The Great Depression, which began in 1929, challenged the classical theory. Prices fell over several years, so demand should have increased enough to stimulate production as consumers took advantage of low prices. Instead, demand also fell as people lost their jobs and bank failures

▲ These children are taking part in a protest march of the unemployed during the Great Depression.

Guiding Question

What economic ideas have shaped fiscal policy?

Get Started

Fiscal Policy Options		
Classical economics	Keynesian (demand-side) economics	Supply-side economics
• Free markets regulate themselves. • very limited use of fiscal policy	• Demand for goods drives the economy. • Increase government spending to avoid recession. • Decrease government spending to control inflation.	• Supply of goods drives the economy. • Tax cuts increase employment and total output. • Less government intervention is better for the economy.

LESSON GOALS

Students will:

- Know the Key Terms.
- Describe and compare classical, Keynesian, and supply-side economics.
- Describe the impact of the multiplier effect and automatic stabilizers on the economy.
- Analyze the government's use of fiscal policy since the Great Depression.

BEFORE CLASS

Students should read the section for homework before coming to class.

Have students complete the graphic organizer in the Section Opener as they read the text. As an alternate activity, have students complete the Guided Reading and Review worksheet (Unit 6 All-in-One, p. 65).

L1 L2 ELL LPR Differentiate Have students complete the Guided Reading and Review worksheet (Unit 6 All-in-One, p. 66).

Focus on the Basics

Students need to come away with the following understandings:

FACTS: • Classical economics is a school of thought based on the idea that free markets regulate themselves. • Keynesian economics uses demand-side theory as the basis for encouraging the government to use fiscal policy to fight periods of inflation and recession. • Supply-side economics supports the use of tax cuts to increase aggregate supply, favoring less government intervention in the economy.

GENERALIZATION: The Great Depression spurred economist John Maynard Keynes to develop his idea that, in the absence of consumer and business spending, the government needed to support the economy. Supply-side economics gained prominence beginning in 1981 when Ronald Reagan became President.

CLASSROOM HINTS

THREE ECONOMIC THEORIES

Arrange students into small groups. Write the names of the three economic theories discussed in this section on the board and then have volunteers note the basic features of each theory under its heading. Include historic examples in which each theory influenced fiscal policy and the apparent results. Then have each group list the strengths and weaknesses of one of these theories. Have each group create a political cartoon illustrating some of these traits. Have groups share their cartoons, explaining which traits are illustrated. This activity may help students with a visual or logical learning style.

BELLRINGER

Display the "The King and His Magician" transparency (Color Transparencies, 15.a). Then write the following on the board:

- Describe what is happening in the cartoon.
- What type of fiscal policy is the king advocating?
- What is the cartoonist saying about the king's job?
- Who do you think has the harder job: the king or his magician? Explain.

Tell students to write their answers in their notebooks.

Teach

Economics online To present this topic using digital resources, use the lecture notes on www.PearsonSuccessNet.com.

DEFINE KEY TERMS

Discuss the Bellringer activity. Call on students to give their responses. Recall that the government, like the king in the cartoon, manages the economy through fiscal policy, and that there are several models that the government has used for this purpose. One of these is classical economics. Ask **What is classical economics?** *(the theory that free markets regulate themselves)* Ask students to explain the ideas behind this theory. Emphasize that classical economics came under attack as the Great Depression worsened, and the government did little to pull the economy out of its decline.

Ask **What is demand-side economics?** *(a school of thought based on the idea that demand for goods drives the economy)* **Explain the theory.** *(Possible answer: Buying more of goods and services would encourage production and increase employment. John Maynard Keynes believed that the government should buy these goods and services.)*

Answers

Checkpoint The Great Depression

Graph Skills 1. The government should monitor the whole economy and spend money on goods and services to encourage production and increase employment. 2. It could shorten periods of recession and inflation.

productive capacity the maximum output that an economy can sustain over a period of time without increasing inflation

demand-side economics a school of thought based on the idea that demand for goods drives the economy

wiped out their savings. According to classical economics, the market should have reached equilibrium, with full employment. But it didn't, and millions suffered from unemployment and other hardships. Farmers lost their farms because corn was selling for seven cents a bushel, beef for two and a half cents a pound, and apples for less than a penny. Still, many people were too poor to buy enough food for their families.

The Great Depression highlighted a problem with classical economics: it did not address how long it would take for the market to return to equilibrium. Classical economists recognized it could take some time, and looked to the long run for equilibrium to reestablish itself. One economist, who was not satisfied with the idea of simply waiting for the economy to recover on its own, commented, "In the long run we are all dead." That economist was John Maynard Keynes (pronounced CANES).

CHECKPOINT ***What event challenged the dominance of the classical economics school of thought?***

Figure 15.4 Keynesian Economics

High output
Productive capacity
Output
Consumer spending | Business spending
Government | Consumer spending | Business spending
Low output

In a recession or depression, businesses and consumers do not demand as much as the economy can produce. Keynes argued that government spending can bring the economy up to its productive capacity.

GRAPH SKILLS

John Maynard Keynes added government spending to the classical model of demand.

1. What role did Keynes envision for government in the economy?
2. How might this government intervention affect the business cycle?

Keynesian Economics

British economist John Maynard Keynes developed a new theory of economics to explain the Depression. Keynes presented his ideas in 1936 in a book called *The General Theory of Employment, Interest, and Money*. He wanted to develop a comprehensive explanation of macroeconomic forces. Such an explanation, he argued, should tell economists and politicians how to get out of economic crises like the Great Depression. In sharp contrast to classical economics, Keynes wanted to give government a tool it could use immediately to boost the economy in the short run.

A Broader View

Classical economists had always looked at how the equilibrium of supply and demand applied to *individual products*. In contrast, Keynes focused on the workings of the economy *as a whole*.

Keynes looked at the productive capacity of the entire economy. **Productive capacity,** often called full-employment output, is the maximum output that an economy can sustain over a period of time without increasing inflation. Keynes attempted to answer the difficult question posed by the Great Depression: Why does actual production in an economy sometimes fall far short of its productive capacity?

Keynes argued that the Depression was continuing because neither consumers nor businesses had an incentive to spend enough to cause an increase in production. After all, why would a company spend money to increase production when demand for its products was falling? How could consumers significantly increase demand when they had barely enough money to survive?

The only way to end the Depression, Keynes thought, would be to find a way to boost demand. Economists who agreed with the idea that demand drives the economy developed a school of thought known as **demand-side economics.** They asked themselves this question: Who could spend enough to spur demand and revitalize production?

Differentiated Resources

- **L1 L2 Guided Reading and Review** (Unit 6 All-in-One, p. 66)
- **L2 Draw Inferences and Conclusions skills worksheet** (Unit 6 All-in-One, p. 68)
- **L4 The Use of Tax Cuts** (Unit 6 All-in-One, p. 69)
- **L2 Economic Dialogue** (Unit 6 All-in-One, p. 71)

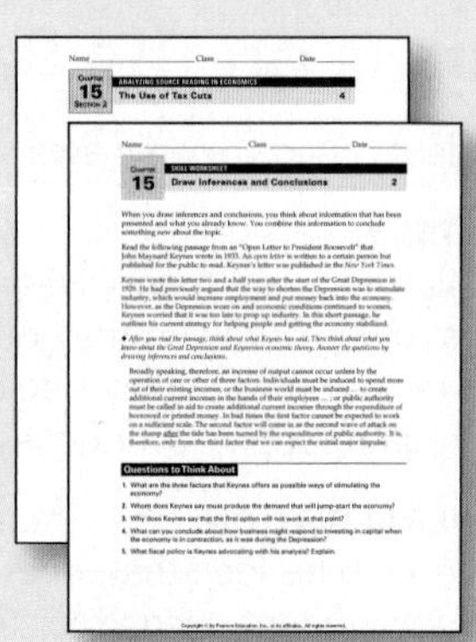

A New Role for Government

Keynes thought that the spender should be the federal government. In the early 1930s, only the government still had the resources to spend enough to affect the whole economy. The government could, in effect, make up for the drop in private spending by buying goods and services on its own. This, Keynes argued, would encourage production and increase employment. Then, as people went back to work, they would spend their wages on more goods and services, leading to even higher levels of production. This ever-expanding cycle would carry the economy out of the Depression. Once the crisis was over, the government could then step back and reduce its spending.

These ideas form the core of Keynes's approach to resolving problems with the economy. **Keynesian economics** uses demand-side theory as the basis for encouraging government action to help the economy. Keynesian economics proposes that the government can, and should, use fiscal policy to help the economy.

Avoiding Recession

Keynes argued that fiscal policy can be used to fight the two fundamental macroeconomic problems. These two opposing problems are periods of recession and periods of inflation.

The federal government, Keynes argued, should keep track of the total level of spending by consumers, businesses, and government. If total spending begins to fall far below the level required to keep the economy running at full capacity, the government should watch out for the possibility of recession.

The government can respond by increasing its own spending until spending by the private sector returns to a higher level. Or it can cut taxes so that spending and investment by consumers and businesses increases. As you read in the previous section, raising government spending and cutting taxes are expansionary fiscal policies.

After he was elected President in 1932, Franklin D. Roosevelt carried out expansionary fiscal policies. His New Deal put people to work—whether planting forests, building dams and schools, or painting murals. The federal budget paid for all these programs.

Many people argue that instead of creating new jobs, such public works projects only shift employment from the private to the public sector. The dispute over Keynes' ideas is reflected today generally in the philosophies of the two political parties. Republicans generally have been associated with using tax cuts to stimulate the economy. Democrats, generally, have favored more expansive government programs to stimulate the economy.

Controlling Inflation

Keynes also argued that the government could use a contractionary fiscal policy to prevent inflation or reduce its severity. The government can reduce inflation either by increasing taxes or by reducing its own spending. Both of these actions decrease overall demand.

The Multiplier Effect

Fiscal policy, although difficult to control, is an extremely powerful tool. The key to its power is the multiplier effect. The **multiplier effect** in fiscal policy is the idea that every one dollar change in fiscal policy—whether an increase in spending or a decrease in taxes—creates a change

▲ During the Great Depression, the Civilian Conservation Corps (CCC) employed more than 2 million young men in jobs such as planting forests and digging irrigation ditches. ***How did the CCC meet the goals of Keynesian economics?***

Keynesian economics a school of thought that uses demand-side theory as the basis for encouraging government action to help the economy

multiplier effect the idea that every one dollar change in fiscal policy creates a change greater than one dollar in the national income

EXPLAIN

Ask **What prompted John Maynard Keynes to develop a new economic theory?** *(The economy was not recovering from the Great Depression on its own.)* **Describe his economic solution to the Great Depression in your own words.** *(He believed that only the government had the financial resources to increase demand by buying goods and services. This would encourage private sector production, increase employment, and lead to an economic recovery.)*

Ask **According to Keynes, what steps could the government take to prevent a recession?** *(Increase spending until private sector spending returns to normal; cut taxes so consumer or business spending increases.)* **What type of fiscal policy is this?** *(expansionary)* **What steps could the government take to control inflation?** *(Increase taxes and/or reduce its spending in order to decrease overall demand.)* **What type of fiscal policy is this?** *(contractionary)*

DRAW INFERENCES AND CONCLUSIONS

Have students complete the "Draw Inferences and Conclusions" skill worksheet (Unit 6 All-in-One, p. 67).

Tell students to review the lesson in the Social Studies Skills Handbook on page S-12. Remind them to use the steps of the lesson to complete the activity.

L2 Differentiate Distribute the Draw Inferences and Conclusions skill worksheet (Unit 2 All-in-One, p. 68).

Discuss the ways Roosevelt promoted expansionary policy. Ask **How effective does Keynesian economics appear to have been? Explain.** *(apparently successful since the economy recovered)*

Encourage students to speculate about the effects of demand-side economics in today's world. Ask **What problems might demand-side economics cause or solve in our country today?**

(lesson continued on p. 403)

Answer

Caption The CCC was a government program that created a demand for labor.

Teach Case Study

SUMMARIZE AND EXPLAIN

Call on students to summarize how the federal budget is allocated. Ask **What are entitlement programs, and why are they the biggest source of spending in the federal budget?** *(Entitlement programs are programs such as Medicare, Medicaid, and Social Security; the formulas for funding these programs are set by law and spending on these programs is growing by about 8 percent per year.)* **Why has neither political party been willing to reduce entitlement spending?** *(This could lead to reduced benefits or higher taxes, which would be very unpopular with voters.)* **How would you revise Social Security or other entitlement programs so that you will have benefits when you need them?** *(Possible responses: increase the retirement age; limit benefits for wealthy people; increase the amount of income subject to social security taxes)*

ANALYZE

Have the students examine why, if both political parties think entitlement spending is a problem, will no one do anything about it?

L2 Differentiate This case study contains vocabulary words, such as *surplus*, *deficit*, and *discretionary spending*, that students with limited language and reading skills might not understand. Prepare students for the reading by reviewing these terms and how they affect the federal budget.

Economics online *All print resources are available on the Teacher's Resource Library CD-ROM and online at www.PearsonSuccessNet.com.*

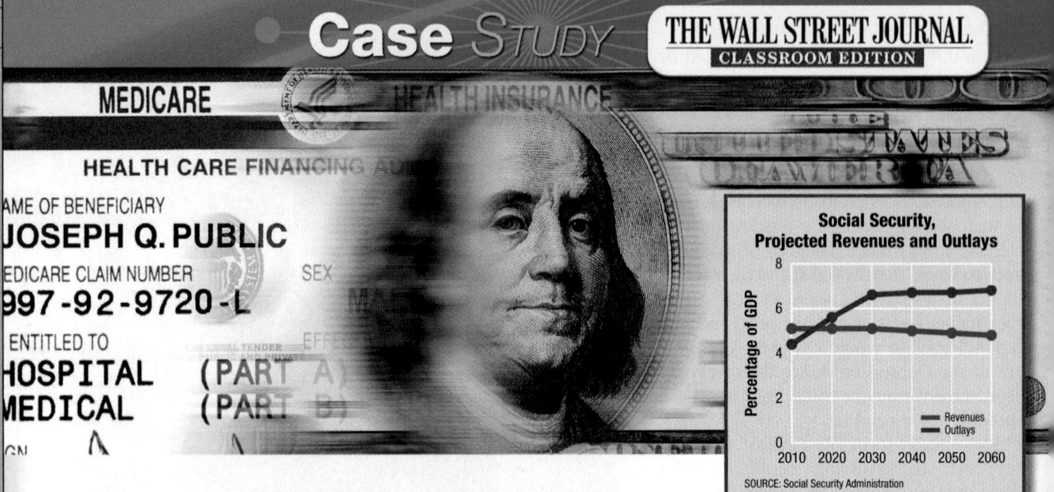

The $1.1 Trillion Question

FEDERAL SPENDING

Entitlement spending is exploding. When will Washington do something?

By Jackie Calmes
The Wall Street Journal

Here's a statistic that will put the budget negotiations in Washington in perspective: Roughly 84 cents of every dollar the federal government spends was essentially spoken for before President Bush and Congress even began their discussions.

That is the amount that goes to three all-but-untouchable elements of federal spending: interest on the federal debt; defense and homeland security; and, above all, "entitlement" programs such as Medicare, Medicaid and Social Security. That leaves just one-sixth of the total available for nearly everything else the government does domestically, from secretaries' salaries to research—what is known in budget jargon as "discretionary" spending.

Entitlements are the biggest source of trouble in the federal budget—not post-Katrina rebuilding or the Iraq war. Formulas for spending on these programs are set by law. And the programs are growing faster than inflation and the economy, about 8% a year.

Medicare itself, at $391 billion this year, is close to equaling the entire domestic discretionary slice of the budget. Add in Social Security and the federal share of the state-run Medicaid program for the poor, and the big-three entitlements total $1.1 trillion for this year—$3 billion a day—with a $93 billion increase expected in the coming fiscal year.

The president has called for a bipartisan commission to offer solutions to the entitlement crush. But skeptics abound in both parties. What is missing, they say, is political will and trust. Even some supporters predict Mr. Bush will end up doing what he has repeatedly vowed not to: Leave these problems to a future president and Congress.

Cost-saving options on Social Security could be simple and straightforward. They include slightly increasing retirement ages; reducing annual cost-of-living increases and revising the formula for computing retirees' initial benefit; and expanding the amount of income subject to Social Security payroll taxes so the biggest earners pay more. Neither party will do any of this without political cover.

The budget surplus Mr. Bush inherited from Mr. Clinton could have eased the pain of transforming the program. But Mr. Bush pursued a different priority: cutting taxes. The rise of deficits, along with the partisan bad blood built up in Mr. Bush's first term, helped doom his 2005 Social Security effort.

"That was the opportunity for the big fix," says Douglas Holtz-Eakin, a former White House economist. "I don't see that opportunity coming again in the near term."

Video News Update Online Powered by *The Wall Street Journal* Classroom Edition

For a new case study, go to the online resources at **PearsonSuccessNet.com**

Applying Economic Principles
According to this article, discretionary spending makes up only 16 percent of the federal budget. How might this limit the effectiveness of fiscal policy?

Answer

Applying Economic Principles Although the federal budget is massive, the fact that most of it is already "spoken for" means federal spending has less of an impact on the overall economy than it would if more of the budget were discretionary.

much greater than one dollar in the national income. In other words, the effects of changes in fiscal policy are multiplied.

Suppose the federal government finds that business investment is dropping. To prevent a recession, in the next budget the government decides to spend an extra $10 billion to stimulate the economy. How will this affect the economy?

With this government spending, demand, income, and GDP will increase by $10 billion. After all, if the government buys an extra $10 billion of goods and services, then an extra $10 billion of goods and services have been produced. However, the GDP will increase by more than $10 billion. Here's why:

The businesses that sold the $10 billion in goods and services to the government have earned an additional $10 billion. These businesses will spend their additional earnings on wages, raw materials, and investment, sending money to workers, other suppliers, and stockholders. What will the recipients do with this money? They will spend part of it, perhaps 80 percent, or $8 billion. The businesses that benefit from this second round of spending will then pass it back to households and other businesses, who will again spend 80 percent of it, or $6.4 billion. The next round will add an additional $5.1 billion to the economy, and so on.

When all of these rounds of spending are added up, the initial government spending of $10 billion leads to an increase of about $50 billion in GDP. The multiplier effect gives fiscal policy initiatives a much bigger kick than the initial amount spent.

Automatic Stabilizers

Fiscal policy is used to achieve many economic goals. One of the most important things that fiscal policy can achieve is a more stable economy. A stable economy is one in which there are no rapid changes in the economic indicators you read about in Chapter 12. What's more, set up properly, fiscal policy can come close to stabilizing the economy *automatically*.

Figure 15.5 shows how real GDP in the United States changed each year from 1928 to 2006. Prior to World War II, there were much larger changes in GDP from year to year than after World War II. Although GDP still fluctuates, these fluctuations have been smaller than they were before the war. Economic growth has been much more stable in the United States in the last 60 or so years.

Why did this happen? After the war, federal taxes and spending on transfer payments—two key tools of fiscal policy—increased sharply. Taxes and transfer payments, or transfers of cash from the government to consumers, stabilize economic growth. When national income is high, the government collects more in taxes and pays out less in transfer payments. Both of these actions take money away from consumers, and therefore reduce spending. This decrease in spending balances out the increase in spending that results from rising income in a healthy economy.

The opposite is also true. When income in the country is low, the government collects less in taxes and pays out more in transfer payments. Both actions increase the amount of money held by consumers, and thus increase spending. This increase in spending balances out the decrease in spending resulting from decreased income.

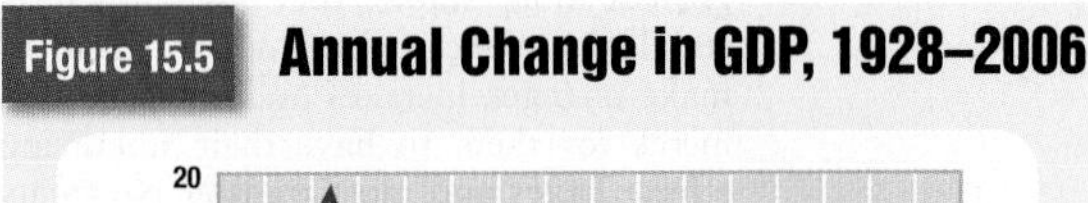

Figure 15.5
Annual Change in GDP, 1928–2006

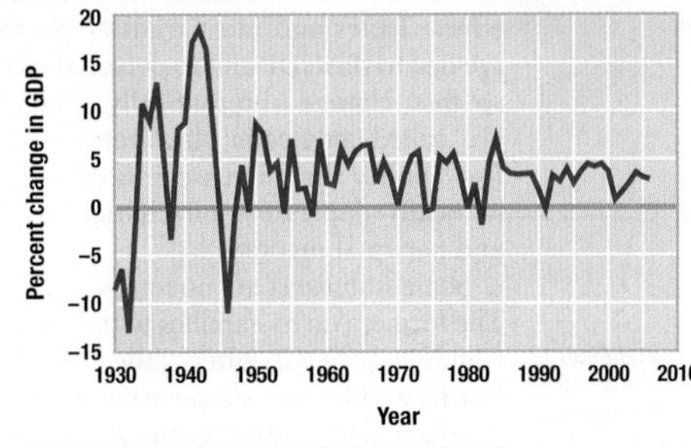

SOURCE: Bureau of Economic Analysis, *Historical Statistics of the United States*

GRAPH SKILLS

The United States experienced strong economic swings before World War II.

1. How do the years after the war show the effect of automatic stabilizers on the economy?
2. Why did the 1930s see the largest percent losses in GDP?

DISCUSS

Have a few volunteers explain or act out the multiplier effect, using the text example of how the multiplier effect works as a guide. Ask **How did money spent on the Civilian Conservation Corps have a multiplier effect?** *(The CCC paid salaries to its workers. Those workers then spent their wages on goods and services, leading businesses to increase production and spend their additional earnings on wages, raw materials, and investments. As these rounds of spending continued, the multiplier effect pumped even more money into the economy than the government's original spending on CCC wages.)* Then ask **How does the multiplier effect act as a key tool of fiscal policy?** *(Any changes in fiscal policy the government makes have an impact on GDP that is much greater than the initial investment.)*

ANALYZE

Have students describe what the graph in Figure 15.5 shows. Ask **How does the annual change in GDP from 1930 to 1945 compare with the annual changes in the 60 years that followed?** *(There are much smaller changes in GDP after 1945.)* **Why?** *(Federal taxes and spending on transfer payments increased dramatically after World War II.)* **How do these two factors—known as automatic stabilizers—act as key tools of fiscal policy?** *(When national income is high, the government pays out less in transfer payments and collects more in taxes. These actions take money away from the consumer, reducing spending. That balances out the increased spending that results from rising income. When national income is low, the opposite happens. In both cases, economic growth is stabilized.)*

L1 L2 Differentiate Write *taxes* and *transfer payments* on the board. Call on students to define the terms, and then write their definitions on the board. During the discussion of automatic stabilizers, call attention to the use of this terminology.

Virtual Economics

L4 Differentiate

Using Fiscal Policy Tools Use the following lesson from the NCEE **Virtual Economics *CD-ROM*** to evaluate student understanding of fiscal policy, its tools, and analysis. Click on Browse Economics Lessons, specify grades 9–12, and use the key words *Macroeconomics: Unit 3 Lesson 8.*

In this activity, students will complete a number of activities using fiscal policy tools to analyze its impact.

LESSON TITLE	FISCAL POLICY
Type of Activity	Using graphics
Complexity	Moderate
Time	180 minutes
NCEE Standards	16, 20

Answers

Graph Skills 1. While there are constant changes in GDP, the changes are within a narrower range than seen in the years prior to World War II. 2. The 1930s were the years of the Great Depression.

COMPARE

Ask **What is supply-side economics?** *(a school of thought based on the idea that the supply of goods drives the economy)* Stress that, just like Keynesian economists, supply-side economists also favor government intervention in the economy to maintain growth and high employment. Ask **What type of government intervention do supply-side economists favor? Why?** *(They favor tax cuts because they believe that taxes have a strong negative impact on economic output.)* Ask **How does supply-side economics differ from Keynesian economics?** *(Possible response: Keynesian economics focuses on increasing aggregate demand whereas supply-side economics focuses on increasing aggregate supply, mainly through tax cuts.)*

ANALYZE

Help students understand the argument for using taxes to regulate the economy. Call attention to Figure 15.6, the Laffer Curve, and ask **What do you notice about the relationship between tax revenues and tax rates?** *(As tax rates increase, tax revenues increase up to a fifty percent tax rate. Then revenues decrease.)* **Why would less money go to the government if taxes are higher?** *(As more people have to pay higher taxes, fewer people are willing to work.)* Explain that supply-side economics says that if taxes are cut, more workers will be willing to work because they could keep more of their money. More workers would be employed and government revenues would increase. Ask **What does actual experience show?** *(Some workers work more hours but, in general, taxpayers do not react strongly enough to tax cuts to increase tax revenue.)*

L4 Differentiate Have students complete the "The Use of Tax Cuts" worksheet (Unit 6 All-in-One, p. 69).

Action Graph online Have students review the Action Graph animation for a step-by-step look at the Laffer Curve. Have students analyze the goals of tax cuts aimed at different segments of society.

Answers

Graph Skills 1. low revenues 2. Workers have little motivation to work or produce goods because they are paying such a high percentage of it in taxes.

Checkpoint Keynes favored more spending by the federal government to increase demand and generate higher spending and production by the private sector.

Figure 15.6 Laffer Curve

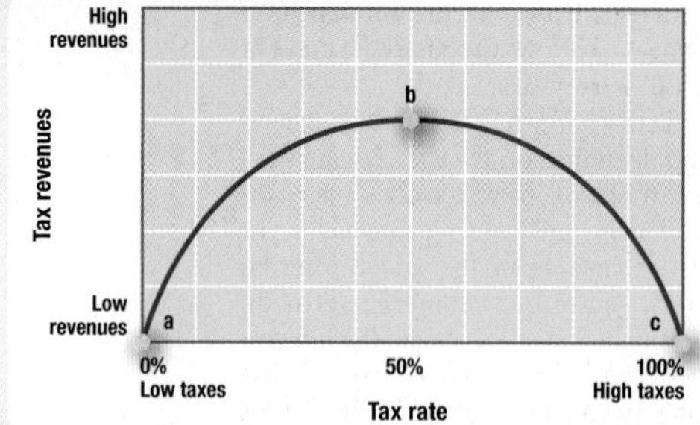

GRAPH SKILLS

The Laffer Curve illustrates the effects of high taxes on revenues.

1. According to the Laffer curve, what do both a high tax rate and a low tax rate produce?
2. Why do higher tax rates sometimes cause revenues to fall?

For an animated version of this graph, visit PearsonSuccessNet.com

Taxes and transfer payments do not eliminate changes in the rate of growth of GDP, but they do make these changes smaller. Because they help make economic growth more stable, they are known as stabilizers. Policymakers do not have to make changes in taxes and transfer payments for them to have their stabilizing effect. Taxes and most transfer payments are tied to the GDP and to personal income, so they change automatically. Thus they are called **automatic stabilizers**—tools of fiscal policy that increase or decrease automatically depending on changes in GDP and personal income.

Some stabilizers are no longer automatic. The former Aid to Families with Dependent Children (AFDC), often called "welfare," lost its entitlement status in 1996 and was renamed Temporary Assistance for Needy Families (TANF). Now the federal government gives the states a set amount of money each year to spend as they wish. However, the stabilizer effect was not completely lost. When the economy boomed in the late 1990s, state spending on TANF fell.

automatic stabilizer a tool of fiscal policy that increases or decreases automatically depending on changes in GDP and personal income

supply-side economics a school of thought based on the idea that the supply of goods drives the economy

CHECKPOINT ***How did Keynes favor ending the Great Depression?***

Supply-Side Economics

Another school of economic thought promotes a different direction for fiscal policy. **Supply-side economics** is based on the idea that the supply of goods drives the economy. While Keynesian economics tries to encourage economic growth by increasing aggregate demand, supply-side economics relies on increasing aggregate supply. It does this by focusing on taxes.

The Laffer Curve

Supply-side economists believe that taxes have a strong negative impact on economic output. They often use the Laffer curve, named after the economist Arthur Laffer, to illustrate the effects of taxes. The Laffer curve shows the relationship between the tax rate and the total tax revenue that the government collects. The total revenue depends on both the tax rate and the health of the economy. The Laffer curve suggests that high tax rates may not bring in much revenue if they cause economic activity to decrease.

Figure 15.6 depicts the Laffer curve. Suppose the government imposes a tax on the wages of workers. If the tax rate is zero, as at point *a* on the graph, the government will collect no revenue, although the economy will benefit from the lack of taxes. As the government raises the tax rate, it starts to collect some revenue. Follow this change in **Figure 15.6** by tracing the curve from no taxes at point *a* to 50 percent taxation at point *b*.

From point *a* to point *b* on the curve, rising tax rates discourage some people from working as many hours and hinder companies from investing and increasing production. The net effect of a higher tax rate and a slightly lower tax base is an increase in revenue.

To the right of point *b*, the decrease in workers' effort is so large that the higher tax rate actually decreases total tax revenue. In other words, high rates of taxation will eventually discourage so many people from working that tax revenues will fall. In the extreme case of a 100 percent tax rate, no one would want to work! In this case, shown at point *c* on the curve, the government would collect no revenue.

Taxes and Output

The heart of the supply-side argument is that a tax cut increases total employment so much that the government actually collects more in taxes at the new, lower tax rate. Suppose the initial tax on labor is $3 an hour, and the typical worker works 30 hours per week, paying a total of $90 in taxes each week. If the government cuts the tax on labor to $2 an hour, and the worker responds by working 50 hours per week, the worker will pay $100 in taxes a week, an increase of $10.

Actual experience has proven that while a tax cut encourages some workers to work more hours, the end result is a relatively small increase in the number of hours worked. In the example above, if the tax cut increased the hours worked from 30 hours to 35 hours, the worker would pay only $70 in taxes ($2 per hour times 35 hours), down from $90 ($3 per hour times 30 hours). In general, taxpayers do not react strongly enough to tax cuts to increase tax revenue.

CHECKPOINT ***How does the theory of supply-side economics link taxation to employment levels?***

Fiscal Policy in American History

As you recall, Keynes presented his ideas at a same time when the world economy was engulfed in the Great Depression. President Herbert Hoover, a strong believer in classical economics, thought that the economy was basically sound and would return to equilibrium on its own, without government interference. His successor, President Franklin D. Roosevelt, was much more willing to increase government spending to help lift the economy out of the Depression.

World War II

Keynes's theory was fully tested in the United States during World War II. As the country geared up for war, government spending increased dramatically. The government spent large sums of money to feed soldiers and equip them with everything from warplanes to rifles to medical supplies. This money was given to the private sector in exchange for goods. Just as Keynesian economics predicted, the additional demand for goods and services moved the country sharply out of the Great Depression and toward full productive capacity.

After World War II ended, Congress created the Council of Economic Advisers (CEA). Made up of three respected economists, the CEA advised the President on economic policy.

Postwar Keynesian Policy

Between 1945 and 1960, the U.S. economy was generally healthy and growing, despite a few minor recessions. The last recession continued into the term of President John F. Kennedy, with unemployment reaching a level of 6.7 percent.

Economics & YOU
The Impact of Taxes
Paycheck $539.15
Sometimes, when the economy is overheated, the government resorts to increasing taxes on individuals. *Tax increases can be very painful because they leave you with less money to spend on goods and services or to save for the future.*
These tax increases do more than help stabilize the economy and move it on to the next phase of the business cycle. *They also provide the government with more resources to pay for a wide variety of public services.*

▲ Sometimes the government lowers taxes to stimulate the economy. ***If you had a few more dollars each week from a tax cut, would you save it or spend it?***

DISCUSS ECONOMICS & YOU

After discussing tax cuts with students, refer to the Economics & You feature. Ask **Do you think that the benefits of tax increases are worth the pain of tax increases?** Encourage students to make connections between their own views on taxes and the economic goals of tax increases and cuts described in this section.

DISTRIBUTE ACTIVITY WORKSHEET

Distribute the "Economic Dialogue" worksheet (Unit 6 All-in-One, p. 70). Have students read a dialogue among three economists to check their comprehension of the differences between classical, Keynesian, and supply-side fiscal policies.

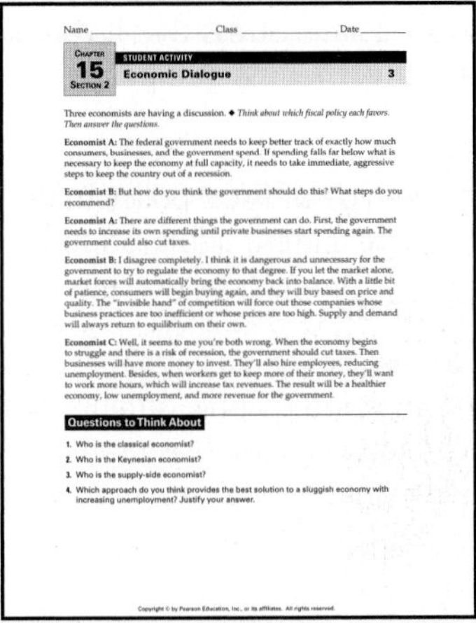

L2 Differentiate Distribute the "Economic Dialogue" worksheet (Unit 2 All-in-One, p. 71).

Review student responses to the worksheet. Use the Idea Wave strategy (p. T24) to get all students participating in a class discussion of their answers to question 4.

Background Note

Becoming a Business Economist According to a publication of the National Association for Business Economics, "to work in the field of business economics, an individual should obtain a sound undergraduate education that includes training in economics and a number of related subjects [including] finance, cost and financial accounting, business administration, statistics, mathematics, and English." In addition, "because business economists are most often generalists rather than specialists, they should have a broad, rather than narrow, education in economics and business administration." It is also recommended that they take courses in history, political science, psychology, and sociology. A graduate degree in economics or related subject is a plus.

Answers

Checkpoint Reducing taxes increases employment because workers take home more income and are willing to work more hours. As a result, the government collects more in taxes

Economics & You Answers will vary, but students should give a reason for their choice.

ANALYZE

Have students identify the fiscal policy used by different administrations, starting with Herbert Hoover, and the reasons that these policies were applied. Analyze the apparent impact of these policies on the economy.

DRAW CONCLUSIONS

Review the meaning of marginal tax rates. Have students explain what Figure 15.7 is showing. Ask **During which years does it appear that the biggest tax cuts occurred?** *(1960–1965; 1980–1990)* Have students describe how the economy fared during these periods. Ask **What conclusions, if any, can you draw about the effectiveness of supply-side and demand-side economics?** Encourage students to speculate. Stress that it can be difficult to prove the effectiveness of a policy.

EXTEND

Have students identify the type of fiscal policy that appears to be favored by the current administration.

GUIDING QUESTION WRAP UP

Have students return to the section Guiding Question. Review the completed graphic organizer and clarify any misunderstandings. Have a wrap up discussion about the ideas that have shaped fiscal policy.

Assess and Remediate

L3 **L2** Collect the "Draw Inferences and Conclusions" skills worksheet and check students' understanding.

L4 Collect "The Use of Tax Cuts" worksheet and assess students' understanding of supply-side and demand-side economics.

L3 **L2** Collect the "Economic Dialogue" worksheet and assess students' understanding of classical, Keynesian, and supply-side fiscal policies.

L3 Assign the Section 2 Assessment questions; identify student misconceptions.

L3 Give Section Quiz A (Unit 6 All-in-One, p. 72).

L2 Give Section Quiz B (Unit 6 All-in-One, p. 73).

(Assess and Remediate continued on p. 407)

Answer

Critical Thinking Economic forecasting is not reliable. Possible response: Reliable data and sound economic reasoning can give insights into the future.

Innovators

John Kenneth Galbraith

"The conventional view serves to protect us from the painful job of thinking."

John Kenneth Galbraith was the world's most famous economist for the last half of the twentieth century. He was also a witty commentator on politics and social life and the author of a number of bestselling books.

During World War II, Galbraith was selected by President Roosevelt to lead the Office of Price Administration, which meant he had total control over the prices charged by U.S. companies.

After the war, Galbraith wrote a number of widely read books about the government's role in society. He favored an active government, using funds provided by a progressive income tax and high sales taxes. He warned against "the affluent society," an economy that produced a glut of frivolous goods for the affluent while the public sector—education, roads and bridges, parks and concert halls—suffered neglect.

Galbraith advised President John F. Kennedy, who appointed him Ambassador to India in 1960. Later, he was the inspiration for President Lyndon B. Johnson's Head Start program, an early childhood education program for poor children.

Galbraith's long service to America did not go unnoticed. He received the Presidential Medal of Freedom, the nation's highest civilian honor, twice.

Critical Thinking: *Galbraith once said "The only function of economic forecasting is to make astrology look respectable." What did he mean by that? Do you agree with him?*

Fast Facts

John Kenneth Galbraith
Born: 1908 in Ontario, Canada
Died: 2006 in Cambridge, MA
Education: Ph.D., University of California at Berkeley
Claim to Fame: Wrote about the dangers of an affluent society

Kennedy's chief financial policy advisor, Walter Heller, thought that the economy was below its productive capacity. He convinced Kennedy that tax cuts would stimulate demand, bring the economy closer to full productive capacity, and lower unemployment.

As **Figure 15.7** shows, tax rates were extremely high in the early 1960s. The highest individual income tax rate was about 90 percent, compared with about 40 percent in 2007. Kennedy proposed tax cuts, both because he agreed with Heller and because tax cuts are popular.

A version of Kennedy's tax cuts was enacted in 1964, under President Lyndon Johnson. At the same time, the Vietnam War raised government spending. Over two years, consumption and GDP increased by more than 4 percent a year. There is no way to prove that the tax cut caused this growth, but the result was generally what Keynesian economics predicted.

Keynesian economics was used often in the 1960s and 1970s. One Keynesian economist, John Kenneth Galbraith, greatly influenced national policies. Galbraith, a strong supporter of public spending, helped develop the social welfare programs that lay at the heart of President Johnson's vision of a Great Society.

Supply-Side Policy in the 1980s

During the late 1970s, with Keynesian fiscal policy in place, unemployment and inflation rates soared. When Ronald Reagan became President in 1981, he vowed to cut taxes and spending. An "anti-Keynesian," Reagan did not believe that government should spend its way out of a recession:

> **"Government spending has become so extensive that it contributes to the economic problems it was designed to cure. More government intervention in the economy cannot possibly be a solution to our economic problems."**
>
> —Ronald Reagan, White House Report on the Program for Economic Recovery, 1981

As President, Reagan instituted new policies based on supply-side economics. Among his economic advisers was

Milton Friedman, a former professor of economics. Friedman supported individual freedom and pushed for more laissez-faire policies—hallmarks of classical and supply-side economics. (You will read a profile of Friedman in the next chapter.)

In 1981, Reagan proposed a tax cut that reduced taxes by 25 percent over three years. In a short time, the economy recovered and flourished. Still, tax cuts plus an increased defense budget led to deficit spending; just as Keynesian policy would.

Under the next few Presidents, the federal government spent much more money than it took in. As you will read in the next section, this gap caused increasing concern among economists and policymakers.

Return to Keynesian Policy?

In late 2008, the United States was hit with what many economists believed was the worst financial crisis since the Great Depression. A number of major financial institutions failed. Credit became harder to get, consumer spending dropped, and unemployment rose.

That year, voters elected a new President, Barack Obama. He promised to take firm action to stimulate the economy. Like Roosevelt during the 1930s, Obama proposed to increase government spending on major public works programs, such as repairing the nation's infrastructure. To many observers, such proposals seemed to signal a shift back to a Keynesian fiscal policy, as in the New Deal.

CHECKPOINT ***What Keynesian fiscal policy tool did President Kennedy use?***

Figure 15.7 Top Marginal Tax Rate, 1925–2007

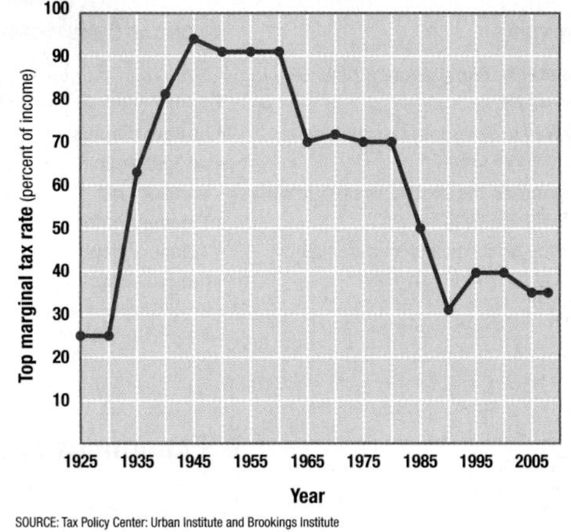

SOURCE: Tax Policy Center: Urban Institute and Brookings Institute

GRAPH SKILLS

Tax rates varied widely throughout the last century.

1. When were top marginal income tax rates at their highest?
2. What has been the trend in tax rates since 1985?

SECTION 2 ASSESSMENT

Essential Questions Journal To continue to build a response to the Essential Question, go to your **Essential Questions Journal.**

Guiding Question

1. Use your completed chart to answer this question: What economic ideas have shaped fiscal policy?
2. **Extension** You're a struggling worker during a recession. Leading economists urge you to be patient because the economy will right itself. How do you reply?

Key Terms and Main Ideas

3. What is **classical economics**?
4. How is full employment related to **productive capacity**?
5. What is the **multiplier effect**?
6. Compare and contrast **Keynesian economics** and **supply-side economics.**

Critical Thinking

7. **Analyze (a)** What might be the costs and benefits of Keynesian economic policies? **(b)** How did Keynes's policies work during the Great Depression?
8. **Analyze Causes and Effects** Why can low tax rates encourage investment and increase jobs and wages?
9. **Contrast** Choose two Presidents and explain how their fiscal policies reflected differing economic beliefs.

Quick Write

10. Write a brief position paper supporting or opposing the use of tax funds to put people to work today. Include at least two arguments to support your position, indicating which argument you feel is most important. Make sure your final sentence strongly restates your position.

Have students complete the Self-Test Online and continue their work in the **Essential Questions Journal**.

REMEDIATION AND SUGGESTIONS

Use the chart below to help students who are struggling with content.

WEAKNESS	REMEDIATION
Identifying key terms (Questions 3, 4, 5, 6)	Have students use the interactive Economic Dictionary Online.
Three theories of economics (Questions 1, 2, 3, 4, 5, 6, 7, 8, 9)	Form groups of three students. Have each group draw three graphic organizers, one for each theory, that list as many characteristics of the theory as possible.
Fiscal policy in history (Questions 2, 4, 8, 11)	Have pairs of students draw a timeline for the years 1930–2008, labeling the administrations. Have students describe the economic conditions that existed during, and the economic policies followed by, each administration.

Answers

Checkpoint He wanted to reduce taxes to stimulate demand and bring the economy closer to full productive capacity.

Graph Skills 1. 1945 2. Keep them somewhere between 30 and 40 percent.

Assessment Answers

1. Free markets regulate themselves; the economy is stimulated by increasing demand; it is the government's role to achieve full productive capacity; the economy is helped by influencing supply.
2. Sample answer: waiting will take too long
3. The theory that free markets can regulate themselves.
4. Productive capacity is the maximum output that an economy can sustain over a period of time without increasing inflation.
5. The idea that every one dollar change in fiscal policy creates a change greater than one dollar in the national income.
6. Keynesian: demand drives the market, focuses on government spending; supply-side: focuses on cutting taxes
7. (a) Possible response: Costs include increasing national debt; benefits include higher employment. (b) They helped.
8. More money to spend leads to greater demand, which leads to higher employment and wages.
9. Sample response: Roosevelt believed government should increase spending while Reagan supported tax cuts.
10. Positions will vary, but should display an understanding of fiscal policy.

Guiding Question

What are the effects of budget deficits and national debt?

Get Started

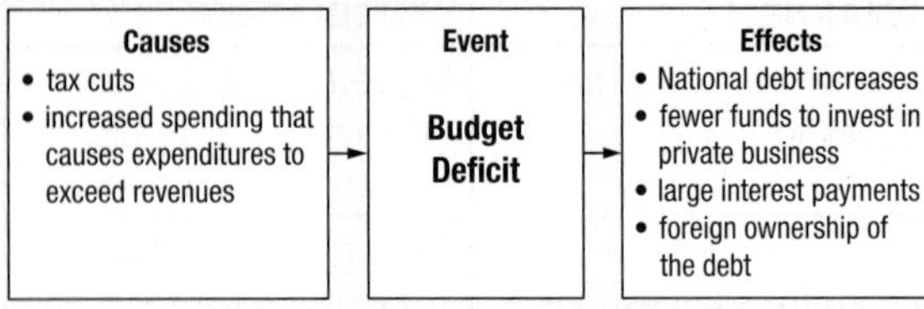

LESSON GOALS

Students will:

- Know the Key Terms.
- Identify some of the major categories of federal revenues and expenses by using a worksheet.
- Describe actions the government can take to balance the budget.
- Describe the problems that can arise from a national debt.
- Explain ways in which government leaders have tried to control the deficit since the 1980s.

BEFORE CLASS

Students should read the section for homework before coming to class.

Have students complete the graphic organizer in the Section Opener as they read the text. As an alternate activity, have students complete the Guided Reading and Review worksheet (Unit 6 All-in-One, p. 74).

L1 L2 ELL LPR Differentiate Have students complete the Guided Reading and Review worksheet (Unit 6 All-in-One, p. 75).

SECTION 3 Budget Deficits and the National Debt

OBJECTIVES

1. **Explain** the importance of balancing the budget.
2. **Analyze** how budget deficits add to the national debt.
3. **Summarize** the problems caused by the national debt.
4. **Identify** how political leaders have tried to control the deficit.

ECONOMIC DICTIONARY

As you read the section, look for the definitions of these **Key Terms:**

- budget surplus
- budget deficit
- Treasury bill
- Treasury note
- Treasury bond
- national debt
- crowding-out effect

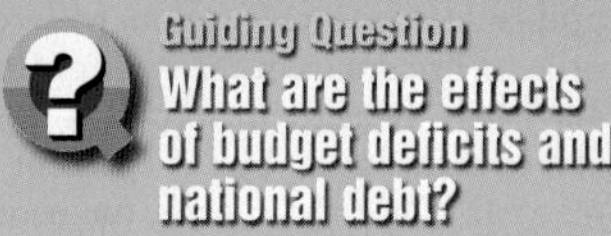

Copy this cause-and-effect chart and fill it in as you read.

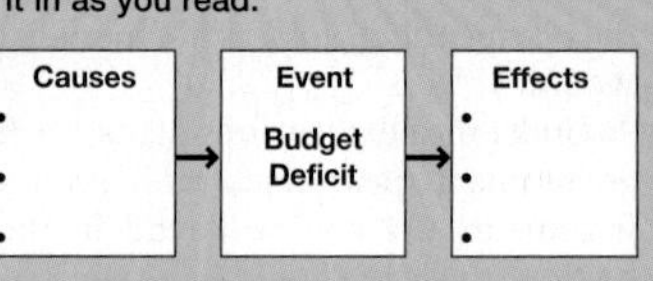

Economics and You If you have used a credit card, you might have some idea about how easy it is to spend money that you don't have. If you fail to pay the credit-card bill in full each month, the high interest rate may mean that the amount you owe just keeps increasing. Soon you may face a mountain of debt.

The federal government is no stranger to spending more than it has. You have been reading about how the government uses spending as a fiscal policy tool to improve the economy.

Principles in Action As you will see in this section, unchecked spending can lead to a soaring national debt. The How the Economy Works feature shows how that debt resulted from numerous budget decisions. The costs of this debt must be measured against the benefits of government spending.

Balancing the Budget

The basic tool of fiscal policy is the federal budget. It is made up of two fundamental parts: revenue (taxes) and expenditures (spending programs). When the federal government's revenues equal its expenditures in any particular fiscal year, the federal government has a balanced budget.

In reality, as **Figure 15.8** shows, the federal budget is almost never balanced. Usually, it is either running a surplus or a deficit. A **budget surplus** occurs in any year when revenues exceed expenditures. In other words, there is more money going into the Treasury than coming out of it. A **budget deficit** occurs in any year when expenditures exceed revenues. In other words, there is more money coming out of the Treasury than going into it.

Assume the federal government starts with a balanced budget. If the government decreases expenditures without changing anything else, it will run a budget surplus. Similarly, if it increases taxes—revenues—without changing anything else, it will run a surplus.

This analysis also explains budget deficits. If the government increases expenditures without changing anything else, it will run a deficit. Similarly, if it decreases taxes without changing anything else, it will run a deficit. The deficit can grow or shrink because of forces beyond the government's control. Surpluses and deficits can be very large figures. The largest deficit, in 2004, was nearly $413 billion.

budget surplus a situation in which budget revenues exceed expenditures

budget deficit a situation in which budget expenditures exceed revenues

CLASSROOM HINTS

DEFICITS AND THE NATIONAL DEBT

To clarify the difference between a deficit and the national debt, explain that the federal budget for each year is made up of two parts: revenues and expenditures. When these are equal, the budget is balanced; when revenues are less than expenditures, a deficit occurs; when revenues are greater than expenditures, a surplus occurs. A deficit is the amount the government borrows for one year to cover the difference between revenues and expenditures. The national debt is the sum of all the borrowing from previous years minus repaid borrowings.

Focus on the Basics

Students need to come away with the following understandings:

FACTS: • In each fiscal year, the federal budget is either balanced, running a surplus, or a deficit. • Each fiscal year's budget deficit adds to the national debt. • The national debt causes less money to be available for businesses to invest, burdens the government with interest payments, and may make the country more vulnerable to foreign holders of the debt. • Since the 1980s, several attempts have been made to control the national debt.

GENERALIZATION: Deficits and the national debt can cause problems, but whether they are so serious that laws should be passed to force a balanced budget remains undecided.

Responding to Budget Deficits

When the government runs a deficit, it is because it did not take in enough revenue to cover its expenses for the year. When this happens, the government must find a way to pay for the extra expenditures. There are two basic actions the government can take to do so.

Creating Money

The government can create new money to pay salaries for its workers and benefits for citizens. Traditionally, governments simply printed the bills they needed. Today, the government can create money electronically by actions that effectively deposit money in people's bank accounts. The effect is the same. This approach works for relatively small deficits but can cause severe problems when there are large deficits. What are these problems?

When the government creates more money, it increases the amount of money in circulation. This increases the demand for goods and services and can increase output. But once the economy reaches full employment, output cannot increase. The increase in money will mean that there are more dollars but the same amount of goods and services. Prices will rise so that a greater amount of money will be needed to purchase the same amount of goods and services. In other words, prices go up, and the result is inflation.

Covering very large deficits by printing more money can cause hyperinflation. This happened in Germany and Russia after World War I, in Brazil and Argentina in the 1980s, and in Ukraine in the 1990s. If the United States experienced hyperinflation, a shirt that cost $30 in June might cost $50 in July, $80 in August, and $400 in December!

Borrowing Money

The federal government usually does not resort to creating money to cover a budget deficit. Instead, it borrows money. The government commonly borrows money by selling bonds. As you read in Chapter 11, a bond is a type of loan: a promise to repay money in the future, with interest. Consumers and businesses buy bonds from the government. The government thus has the money to cover its budget deficit. In return, the purchasers of the bonds earn interest on their investment over time.

Figure 15.8 **Budget Surpluses and Deficits, 1940–2007**

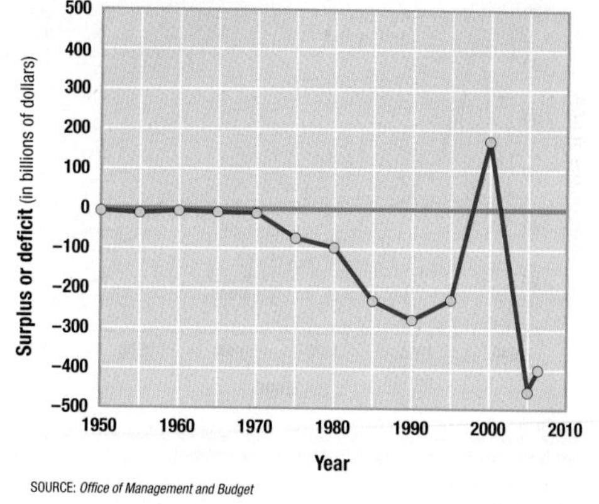

GRAPH SKILLS

Budget deficits swelled in the early 2000s due to recession, tax cuts, and defense spending.

1. In which of the years shown on the graph did the budget have a surplus?
2. What was the dominant trend in deficits in the late 1990s?

United States Savings Bonds ("EE Bonds") allow millions of Americans to lend small amounts of money to the federal government. In return, they earn interest on the bonds for up to 30 years. Other common forms of government borrowing are Treasury bills, notes, and bonds. **Treasury bills** are short-term bonds that have maturity dates of 26 weeks or less. **Treasury notes** have terms of from 2 to 10 years. **Treasury bonds** mature 30 years after issue.

Federal borrowing lets the government undertake more projects than it could otherwise afford. Wise borrowing allows the government to create more public goods and services. Federal borrowing, however, also has serious disadvantages.

CHECKPOINT ***What is the most common way that the federal government pays for expenditures that exceed revenues?***

Treasury bill a government bond with a maturity date of 26 weeks or less

Treasury note a government bond with a term of from 2 to 10 years

Treasury bond a government bond that is issued with a term of 30 years

Differentiated Resources

- **L1 L2 Guided Reading and Review** (Unit 6 All-in-One, p. 75)
- **L2 The Federal Budget** (Unit 6 All-in-One, p. 77)
- **L4 Taxes and the Budget Deficit** (Unit 6 All-in-One, p. 78)

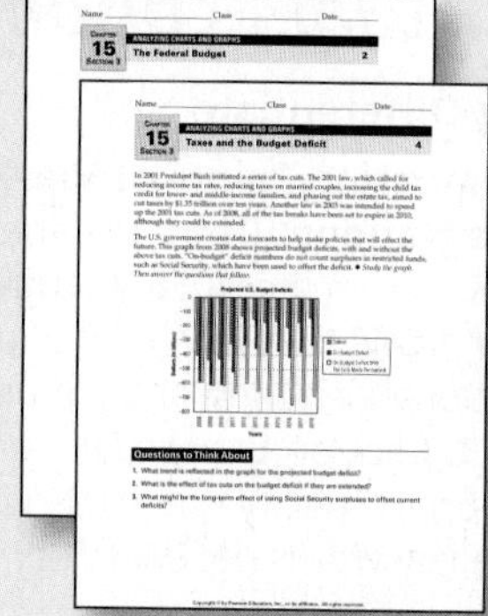

BELLRINGER

Write these questions on the board:

- Have you ever tried to live on a budget? Were you successful?
- Have you ever spent more money than you had? Why or why not?
- Have you ever borrowed money from a friend? What did you need it for?

Tell students to write their answers in their notebooks.

Teach

Economics online To present this topic using digital resources, use the lecture notes on www.PearsonSuccessNet.com.

DISCUSS

Review answers to the Bellringer. Discuss the difficulties of staying within a budget. Then ask **How does the federal government try to balance the budget?** *(It aims for revenue to equal expenditures.)* **What happens when the budget is not balanced?** *(If revenue exceeds expenditures there is a budget surplus; the opposite leads to a budget deficit.)*

DISTRIBUTE ACTIVITY WORKSHEET

Distribute "The Federal Budget" worksheet (Unit 6 All-in-One, p. 76), in which students analyze pie charts of the nation's revenues and expenses for fiscal year 2006 to understand how budget deficit can occur.

L2 LPR Differentiate Distribute "The Federal Budget" worksheet (Unit 6 All-in-One, p. 77). Have students work in pairs.

CHECK COMPREHENSION

Ask **What options do you have if you want to spend more money than you have?** *(don't spend it or borrow money)* **What options does the government have when it runs a deficit?** *(creating money or borrowing money)* Ask **What is one possible effect of creating money? Why?** *(Inflation; more money in circulation increases the demand for goods and services and can increase output until the economy reaches full employment. At that point, output cannot increase, and prices will rise because there are more dollars, which will be needed to purchase the same amount of goods and services.)* Ask **How does the government borrow money?** *(by selling bonds)*

Answers

Graph Skills 1. 2000 2. They were decreasing.

Checkpoint borrowing

APPLY UNDERSTANDING

Have students define *national debt* in their own words. Ask **To whom it the debt owed?** *(to individuals and businesses who hold Treasury bonds, bills, and notes)* **Why do businesses and individuals loan money to the government?** *(The bonds, bills, and notes are considered to be a safe investment.)*

Refer students to Figure 15.9. Have them describe what the graph shows. Review the definition of GDP—the dollar value of all final goods and services produced within a country's borders in a given year. Ask **Why is the national debt shown as a percentage of GDP?** *(The national debt is so large that it makes sense to compare it to the size of the economy as a whole.)*

DISCUSS

Refer students to "The Federal Budget" worksheet. Explain that "net interest" represents payments the government makes on federal debt to bondholders. Then ask **How does debt affect the federal budget?** *(Servicing the debt—paying interest on the debt—leaves less money to be spent on other government programs.)* Elicit the fact from students there is an opportunity cost—dollars spent servicing the debt cannot be spent on other government programs. Point out that this is one of the problems of the national debt.

PERSONAL FINANCE ACTIVITY

To help students make wise economic choices, you may want to use the Personal Finance Handbook section on managing debt (pp. PF26–27) and the activity worksheet (Personal Finance All-in-One, p. 74).

Figure 15.9 National Debt as a Percentage of GDP

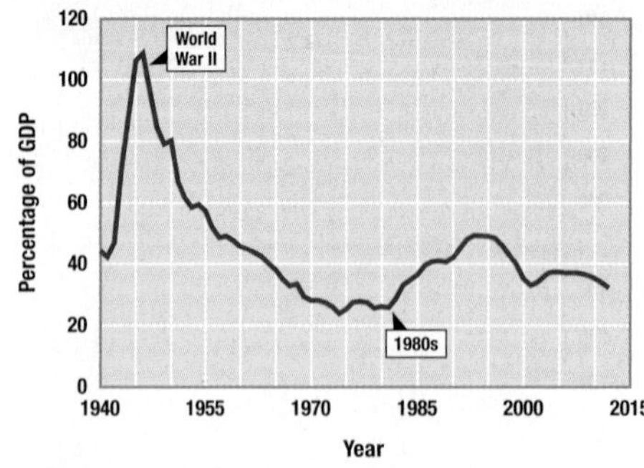

Note: Figures for the years 2007–2012 are projected.
SOURCE: *The Executive Office of the President of the United States, The Office of Management and Budget. The Budget of the United States Government, Fiscal Year 2008. Historical Tables.*

GRAPH SKILLS

1. Do you think budgets are in surplus, balanced, or in debt during times of war?
2. Why does the national debt as a percentage of GDP soar during times of war?

The National Debt

FUTURE WATCH

Personal Finance For tips on managing your own debt, see your Personal Finance Handbook in the back of the book or visit **PearsonSuccessNet.com**

Like people, when the government borrows money, it goes into debt. The **national debt** is the total amount of money the federal government owes to bondholders. Every year that there is a budget deficit and the federal government borrows money to cover it, the national debt will grow.

The national debt is owed to investors who hold Treasury bonds, bills, and notes. These bonds are considered to be among the safest investments in the world. As such, they offer a secure investment for individuals and businesses. Because the United States is widely viewed as stable and trustworthy, the federal government can borrow money at a lower rate of interest than private citizens or corporations can. Lower interest rates benefit taxpayers by reducing the cost of government borrowing.

national debt the total amount of money the federal government owes to bondholders

The Difference Between Deficit and Debt

Many people are confused about the difference between the deficit and the debt. The deficit is the amount of money the government borrows for one budget, representing one fiscal year. The debt, on the other hand, is the sum of all the government borrowing before that time, minus the borrowings that have been repaid. Each deficit adds to the debt. Each surplus subtracts from it.

Measuring the National Debt

In dollar terms, the size of the national debt is extremely large. In 2008, it exceeded $10.6 trillion! Such a large number can best be analyzed in relation to the size of the economy as a whole. Therefore, let's look at the size of the debt as a percentage of gross domestic product (GDP) over time. This can be seen in **Figure 15.9.** Historically, debt as a percentage of GDP rises during wartime, when government spending increases faster than taxation, and it falls during peacetime.

Notice how the pattern changed in the 1980s, when the United States began to run a large debt, even though the country wasn't at war. The debt was in part a result of increases in spending during President Ronald Reagan's terms. As you read in the previous section, the Reagan administration also cut taxes. The combined effect of higher spending and lower tax rates was several years of increased budget deficits. The government borrowed billions of dollars to cover these deficits, adding to the national debt. As a result, the ratio of debt to GDP grew very large for peacetime.

CHECKPOINT ***To whom does the government owe the national debt?***

Is the Debt a Problem?

The growth of the national debt during the Reagan administration led many to focus on the problems caused by a national debt. In general, three problems can arise from a national debt.

Problems of a National Debt

The first problem with a national debt is that it reduces the funds available for businesses to invest. This is because in order to sell its bonds, the government must offer a higher interest rate. Individuals and

Virtual Economics

L2 Differentiate

Comparing Points of View About the National Debt Use the following lesson from the NCEE **Virtual Economics *CD-ROM*** to review causes of the national debt and analyze issues related to it. Click on Browse Economics Lessons, specify grades 9–12, and use the key words *national debt.*

In this activity, students will review the causes of the national debt and will compare points of view related to it.

LESSON TITLE	SHOULD WE WORRY ABOUT THE NATIONAL DEBT
Type of Activity	Comparing Points of view
Complexity	Low
Time	60 minutes
NCEE Standards	17, 20

Answers

Graph Skills 1. in debt because the government spends large amounts of money to support the war effort 2. Possible response: While spending has increased, GDP is reduced because there is less money in the private sector to finance business investment.

Checkpoint investors who hold United States Savings Bonds, Treasury bonds, Treasury bills, and Treasury notes businesses, attracted by the higher interest rates and the security of investing in the government, use their savings or profits to purchase government bonds.

However, every dollar spent on a government bond is one dollar less that can be invested in private business. Less money is available for companies to expand their factories, conduct research, and develop new products, and so interest rates rise. This loss of funds for private investment caused by government borrowing is called the **crowding-out effect.** Federal borrowing "crowds out" private borrowing by making it harder for private businesses to borrow. A national debt, then, can hurt investment and slow economic growth over the long run.

The second problem with a high national debt is that the government must pay interest to bondholders. The more the government borrows, the more interest it has to pay. Paying the interest on the debt is sometimes called servicing the debt. Over time, the interest payments have become very large. About the year 2000, the federal government spent about $250 billion a year servicing the debt. Moreover, there is an opportunity cost—dollars spent servicing the debt cannot be spent on something else, such as defense, healthcare, or infrastructure.

A possible third problem involves foreign ownership of the national debt. The biggest holder of that debt is the United States government itself. The government uses bonds as a secure savings account for holding Social Security, Medicare, and other funds. But about a quarter of the debt is owned by foreign governments, including Japan, China, and the United Kingdom. Some critics of the debt fear that a country like China could use its large bond holdings as a tool to extract favors from the United States. Others disagree, arguing that foreign states own too little of the debt to cause any concern.

crowding-out effect the loss of funds for private investment caused by government borrowing

Other Views of a National Debt

Some people insist that the national debt is not a big problem. Traditional Keynesian economists believe that fiscal policy is an important tool that can be used to help achieve full productive capacity. To these analysts, the benefits of a productive economy outweigh the costs of interest on national debt.

In the short term, deficit spending may help create jobs and encourage economic growth. However, a budget deficit can be an effective tool only if it is temporary. Most people agree that if the government runs large budget deficits year after year, the costs of the growing debt will eventually outweigh the benefits.

CHECKPOINT ***What are the problems of having a huge national debt?***

Figure 15.10 Effects of the Budget Deficit on Investment

UNITED STATES SAVINGS BOND

The federal government spends more than it takes in, and has to borrow money to cover the deficit. → Investors trust the U.S. government and loan money to the government by buying bonds. → Banks and investors have less money to lend private businesses. Private businesses must pay a higher interest rate to borrow scarce money.

CHART SKILLS

Government borrowing tends to reduce private investment by taking away some funds that could have been invested in private business. Economists describe this phenomenon as the crowding-out effect.

1. Why do lenders put their money in government bonds rather then use it for private investment?
2. What are some ways that private investors and banks deal with the crowding-out effect?

DISCUSS

Ask **What are the effects of the national debt on the U.S. economy?** *(the crowding-out effect, foreign ownership in the economy)* Refer to Figure 15.10 and have students explain how debt reduces funds available for businesses to invest. For example, during wars, the government's borrowing makes loans too expensive for many businesses.

L1 L2 Differentiate Help students with the concept of crowding out by comparing money with goods. When goods are scarce and demand is high, the price of goods increases. Similarly, when demand for money is high and supply is limited, interest rates increase, making loans unaffordable for many.

L4 Differentiate Distribute the "Taxes and the Budget Deficit" worksheet (Unit 6 All-in-One, p. 78). Have students study the graph and answer the questions.

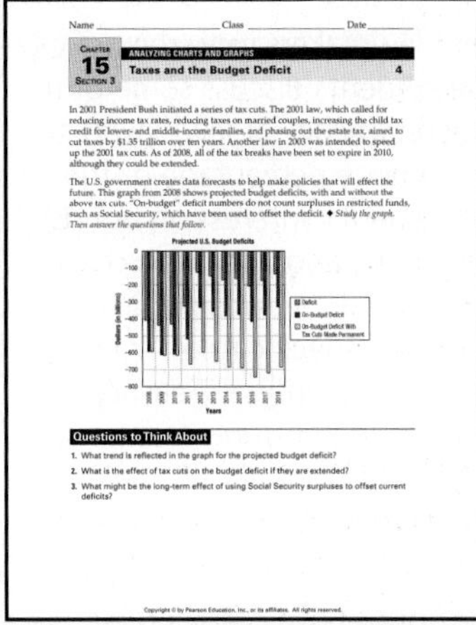

Name ______________ Class ______________ Date ________

CHAPTER 15 SECTION 3 — ANALYZING CHARTS AND GRAPHS

Taxes and the Budget Deficit 4

In 2001 President Bush initiated a series of tax cuts. The 2001 law, which called for reducing income tax rates, reducing taxes on married couples, increasing the child tax credit for lower- and middle-income families, and phasing out the estate tax, aimed to cut taxes by $1.35 trillion over ten years. Another law in 2003 was intended to speed up the 2001 tax cuts. As of 2008, all of the tax breaks have been set to expire in 2010, although they could be extended.

The U.S. government creates data forecasts to help make policies that will effect the future. This graph from 2008 shows projected budget deficits, with and without the above tax cuts. "On-budget" deficit numbers do not count surpluses in restricted funds, such as Social Security, which have been used to offset the deficit. ◆ *Study the graph. Then answer the questions that follow.*

Questions to Think About

1. What trend is reflected in the graph for the projected budget deficit?
2. What is the effect of tax cuts on the budget deficit if they are extended?
3. What might be the long-term effect of using Social Security surpluses to offset current deficits?

After students have completed the worksheet hold a class discussion about tax policy and its effects on yearly deficits and the national debt.

Background Note

Foreign Debt As of May 2007, the three largest foreign holders of U.S. Treasury securities were Japan, China, and the United Kingdom. Between them, they owned almost $1.2 trillion of debt. Perhaps even more importantly, foreign investors owned about 80 percent of the Treasury notes, which mature in 3 to 10 years. These nations, as well as other countries, have invested heavily in the United States, in part because U.S. bonds, notes, and bills have had a higher yield than similar notes offered by Japan and European Union members, making them a more desirable investment.

Answers

Checkpoint Fewer funds are available for businesses; government pays interest to bondholders; foreign debt holders may have undue influence on government.

Chart Skills 1. Investors trust that investing in government bonds is safer than in business, and the interest rate is higher. 2. Both have less money to lend, so they charge higher interest rates.

HOW THE ECONOMY WORKS

Have students look back at Figure 15.8. Ask **What can you conclude about the national debt?** *(It has grown.)* Have volunteers read How the Economy Works aloud. Then have students summarize in their own words why the national debt has grown over the past 30 years.

ANALYZE CARTOON

Display the "Nearly Empty or Almost Full?" transparency (Color Transparencies, 15.b). Discuss these questions: • Whom do the elephant and the donkey represent? • According to the cartoonist, who views a deficit as a problem? Why? • Who does not view a deficit as a problem? Why? • With which view might a Keynesian economist agree? Explain.

L1 Differentiate Explain the meaning of the expression "Is the glass half empty or half full?"

DISCUSS

In the cartoon, different lawmakers view the deficit in different ways. Have students discuss some of the other reasons it has been difficult for lawmakers to control budget deficits: a large percentage of the budget consists of entitlements; interest on bonds must be paid to bondholders; and interest groups work to oppose some spending reductions. You may want to assign students specific roles, such as a person receiving Social Security, a Treasury bondholder, a person receiving housing assistance, and a person receiving money for scientific research. Have students justify why they should continue to receive money.

Point out that interest groups have considerable influence because of their political affiliations, financial support of certain legislators, and other factors. Discuss how this influence affects efforts to control the deficit.

L4 Differentiate Have students research the answer to the question **What do lobbyists do?**

CHECK COMPREHENSION

Ask students to define and explain the purpose of the Gramm-Rudman-Hollings Act. Have them identify its advantages and disadvantages. Ask **Why did Congress give up on the Gramm-Rudman-Hollings Act?** *(The budget deficit was much larger than expected, and because the act exempted so many programs from cuts, remaining programs would have had to be drastically cut.)*

Ask **How did the PAYGO system seek to limit the deficit?** *(It required Congress to raise revenue to cover any additional increases in direct spending.)*

How the Economy Works

What causes the national debt to spiral?

The National Debt is the amount of money the United States government owes to the people and institutions who hold its bonds, bills, and notes. In the past 30 years, the national debt has grown enormously. Here is why the debt has grown.

1 Each year, the federal government has to pay for hundreds of essential services, from military protection to healthcare. Tax revenues pay for most of these expenses. But in most years, there is a gap between revenue and expenditures.

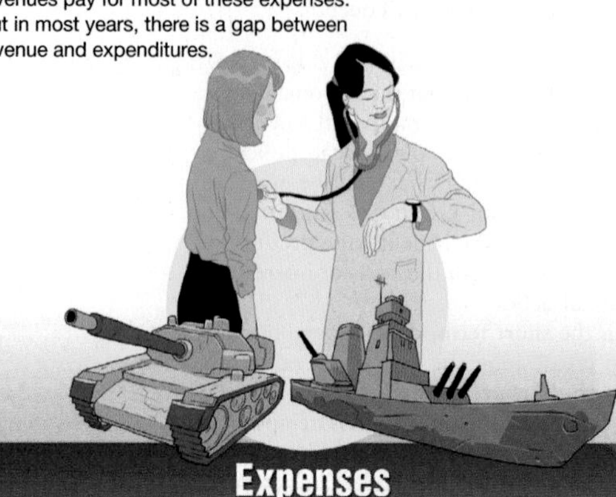

2 To make up the gap, the government borrows money. It issues Treasury bonds, bills, and notes. The interest paid on this money becomes part of the federal budget.

Expenses

Borrowing

Controlling the Deficit

During the 1980s and the early 1990s, annual budget deficits added substantially to the national debt. Several factors frustrated lawmakers in their attempts to control the deficit. As we have seen, much of the budget consists of entitlement spending that is politically difficult to change. Another large part of the budget consists of interest that must be paid to bondholders. Finally, specific budget cuts are often opposed by interest groups.

Efforts to Reduce Deficits

Concerns about the budget deficits of the mid-1980s caused Congress to pass the Gramm-Rudman-Hollings Act. This law created automatic across-the-board cuts in federal expenditures if the deficit exceeded a certain amount. The automatic nature of the cuts saved lawmakers from having to make difficult decisions about individual funding cuts. However, the act exempted significant portions of the budget (such as interest payments and many entitlement programs such as Social Security) from the cuts.

The Supreme Court found that some parts of the Gramm-Rudman-Hollings Act were unconstitutional. Congress attempted to correct the flaws. In 1990, however, lawmakers realized that the deficit was going to be much larger than expected. Because Congress had exempted so many programs from automatic cuts, funding for nonexempt programs would be dramatically slashed.

To resolve the crisis, President George H. W. Bush and congressional leaders negotiated a new budget system that replaced Gramm-Rudman-Hollings. The 1990 Budget Enforcement Act created a

For an animated, interactive version of this feature, visit **PearsonSuccessNet.com**

3 Economic downturns or external shocks such as natural disasters may add unplanned costs to the federal budget. This leads to even more borrowing.

4 As the government borrows more, the slice of the federal budget taken up by interest payments grows. The more interest, the greater the gap between revenue and expenses...and the greater the gap, the more the government borrows.

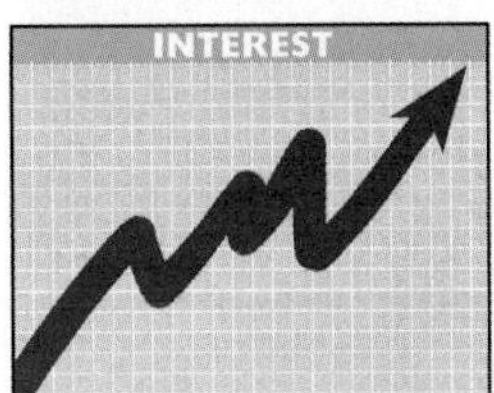

5 Large deficits over a period of years have caused the national debt to spiral to enormous proportions. However, economists differ on whether this large debt is a serious problem to the U.S. economy.

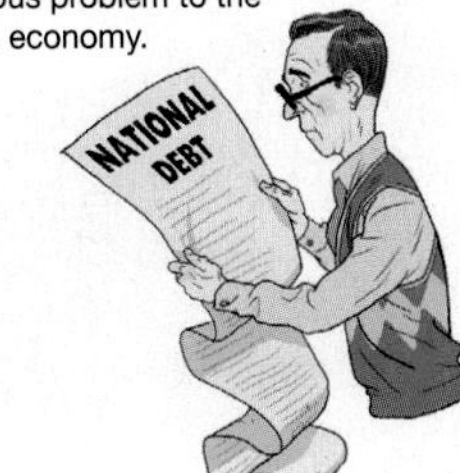

Check Your Understanding

1. How does borrowing lead to greater interest payments and greater debt?
2. How important do you think it is to immediately reduce the national debt?

More Expenses → **More Borrowing**

"pay-as-you-go" system (also known as PAYGO). PAYGO required Congress to raise enough revenue to cover increases in direct spending that would otherwise contribute to the budget deficit. This law expired in 2002, but in 2007 the House and Senate restored PAYGO in the form of special budget rules.

At various times, citizens and politicians have suggested amending the Constitution to require a balanced budget. In 1995, a balanced budget amendment gained the two-thirds majority it needed to pass the House, but the next year it failed by a single vote in the Senate. Supporters argued that the amendment would force the federal government to be more disciplined about its spending. Opponents said that a constitutional amendment requiring a balanced budget would not give the government the flexibility it needed to deal with rapid changes in the economy.

End-of-Century Surpluses

The late 1990s brought a welcome reversal of fortune. For the first time in thirty years, the President and the Office of Management and Budget were able to announce that the federal government was running a surplus.

How did this happen? First, the new budget procedures begun under President Bush and extended under President Clinton did help Congress control the growth of government spending. Second, tax increases by President Clinton in 1993 resulted in more federal revenue. Finally, the strong economy and low unemployment meant that more individuals and corporations were earning more money—and thus paying more to the government in taxes.

Return to Deficits

The changeover from deficits to surplus brought with it a different set of political

DEBATE

Discuss the idea of a balanced budget amendment. Then use the Debate Strategy (p. T27) to debate whether or not a balanced budget amendment should be passed.

DISCUSS

Discuss how the surpluses of the 1990s developed. Then ask **What caused deficits to return?** *(An economic slowdown and a new federal income tax cut lowered tax revenues while new defense spending increased costs to the government.)* Discuss new challenges: more spending on Social Security and Medicare, as new retirees begin to outnumber new workers.

EXTEND

Have students write letters to the editor of their local newspaper addressing some aspect of the federal budget or the national debt that is having an impact on their city or town. Have them give facts and details to support their position. Then have them report the results and evaluate the effectiveness of their letters.

GUIDING QUESTION WRAP UP

Have students return to the section Guiding Question. Review the completed graphic organizer and clarify any misunderstandings. Have a wrap up discussion about the effects of budget deficits and national debt.

Assess and Remediate

L3 **L2** Collect "The Federal Budget" worksheets and assess students' understanding of budget surplus and deficit.

L4 Collect the "Taxes and the Budget Deficit" worksheet and assess students' understanding.

L3 Assign the Section 3 Assessment questions; identify student misconceptions.

L3 Give Section Quiz A (Unit 6 All-in-One, p. 79).

L2 Give Section Quiz B (Unit 6 All-in-One, p. 80).

(Assess and Remediate continued on p. 414)

Answers

Check Your Understanding 1. The more the government borrows, the more interest it has to pay, and the portion of the budget taken up by interest payments grows. As the gap between revenues and expenses grows, the government borrows even more money. 2. Possible response: In the short term, deficit spending may help create jobs and encourage growth. In the long term, the costs of growing debt will outweigh the benefits.

Have students complete the Self-Test Online and continue their work in the **Essential Questions Journal**.

REMEDIATION AND SUGGESTIONS

Use the chart below to help students who are struggling with content.

WEAKNESS	REMEDIATION
Identifying key terms (Questions 3, 4, 5, 6)	Have students use the interactive Economic Dictionary Online.
Balancing the budget (Questions 1, 3, 4)	Ask students to write five questions about balancing the budget. Have them exchange questions and write answers.
The national debt (Questions 1, 2, 5, 6, 8)	Reteach using the graphic organizer from this section, but replacing the event "Budget Deficit" with "National Debt."
Controlling the deficit (Questions 5, 7, 9)	Have students work in pairs and outline the section under "Controlling the Deficit."

Answers

Caption to bring the size of the debt to people's attention

Checkpoint New budget procedures helped Congress control the growth of government spending; President Clinton increased taxes in 1993; a strong economy and high employment resulted in greater tax revenues.

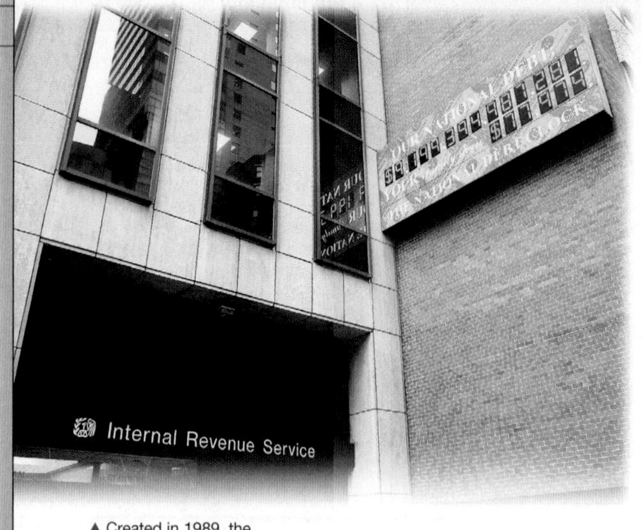

▲ Created in 1989, the National Debt Clock in New York continually ticks off the growing national debt plus each family's share. There are similar clocks in other cities and on the Internet. ***Why do you think someone decided to build the National Debt Clock?***

concerns. Investors who had come to rely heavily upon Treasury bonds as the basic "safe" investment worried that the federal government would remove all bonds from the market as it repaid its debt.

Americans debated how to make best use of the budget surplus. As a presidential candidate in 2000, George W. Bush pledged to use the surplus to guarantee Social Security into the new century, provide additional medical benefits to seniors, and reduce income taxes.

However, the surplus was short-lived. The end of the stock market boom, an economic slowdown, and a new federal income tax cut reduced federal revenues. The terrorist attacks of September 11, 2001, dealt a double blow to the federal budget by disrupting the economy and imposing a new set of defense costs.

In response, the federal government returned to deficit spending. The federal budget continued to show a large deficit for the next several years, due in part to counterterrorism efforts and the very costly wars in Afghanistan and Iraq. In fiscal year 2008 alone, the President's funding requests for the war on terrorism approached $200 billion.

The long-term outlook for the federal budget is uncertain. Federal spending on Social Security and Medicare is projected to rise sharply in the next 30 years as large numbers of baby boomers leave the job market and retire. With new retirees outnumbering new workers, balancing the budget is expected to become even more difficult.

CHECKPOINT ***What factors contributed to the budget surpluses in the 1990s?***

SECTION 3 ASSESSMENT

Essential Questions Journal To continue to build a response to the Essential Question, go to your **Essential Questions Journal.**

Guiding Question

1. Use your completed cause-and-effect chart to answer this question: What are the effects of budget deficits and national debt?
2. **Extension** Look at a credit card statement. Notice how finance charges add to the original purchase expenses. If one does not pay the full amount owed, there are additional interest charges. There are also transaction, over-limit, and late fees. Even without additional purchases, the amount owed continues to grow—until the debt is paid in full. How does this compare to the way increased federal deficits add to the national debt?

Key Terms and Main Ideas

3. What causes a **budget surplus**?
4. How does a **Treasury note** differ from a **Treasury bill**?
5. How might a **budget deficit** be related to the **national debt**?
6. Explain the **crowding-out effect** that results from national debt.

Critical Thinking

7. **Evaluate (a)** Why does the federal government usually not create new money to cover a budget deficit? **(b)** Do you think this is sound reasoning? Explain why or why not.
8. **Rank (a)** What are three possible problems with having a national debt? **(b)** Which problem do you see as most serious? Explain.
9. **Predict (a)** Why did the federal budget show a large deficit for several years following 2001? **(b)** What federal spending is projected to increase greatly during the coming years, and why?

Math Skills

10. **Relating Graphs to Events** Use the data in Figure 15.8 to determine the approximate size of the largest budget deficits in each of the following decades: **(a)** 1950s, **(b)** 1970s, **(c)** 1990s, **(d)** 2000s.

Visit PearsonSuccessNet.com for additional math help.

Assessment Answers

1. Budget deficits increase the national debt. The debt reduces the funds that are available to invest in private business; the government must pay interest to bondholders; there is an opportunity cost associated with those payments; and there are concerns over foreign ownership.
2. As long as the debt is not paid off, deficits are added to it; the debt must be serviced.
3. Revenues exceed expenditures in a year.
4. Treasury notes have terms of from 2 to 10 years whereas Treasury bills have maturity dates of 26 weeks or less.
5. A budget deficit is a shortfall in funds for one year's budget. That deficit adds to the debt, which is the total of all budget deficits before that time, plus interest, minus any repaid borrowings.
6. Federal borrowing makes it harder for private businesses to borrow. Less money is available for businesses to grow as interest rates rise.
7. (a) This can cause inflation. (b) Possible response: Yes. The government should avoid causing inflation because it will hurt consumers and businesses.
8. (a) the "crowding out" of private borrowing; interest payments on debt; foreign ownership of debt (b) Possible response: the crowding out effect, because it limits the ability of the economy to grow
9. (a) The economy slowed down; income taxes were cut; the "war on terrorism" and costly wars in Afghanistan and Iraq increased defense costs. (b) Social Security and Medicare because a large part of the population is reaching retirement age.
10. (a) almost $0 (b) $75 billion (c) $230 billion (d) $470 billion

QUICK STUDY GUIDE

Chapter 15: Fiscal Policy

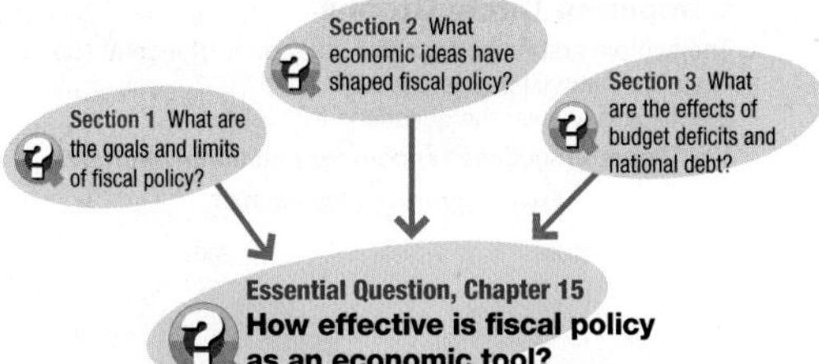

Section 1 What are the goals and limits of fiscal policy?
Section 2 What economic ideas have shaped fiscal policy?
Section 3 What are the effects of budget deficits and national debt?

Essential Question, Chapter 15
How effective is fiscal policy as an economic tool?

Effects of Expansionary Fiscal Policy

To expand the economy, the government buys more goods and services.

↓

Companies that sell goods to the government earn profits, which they use to pay their workers and investors more and to hire new workers.

↓

Workers and investors have more money and spend more in shops and restaurants.

↓

Shops and restaurants buy more goods and hire more workers to meet their needs.

↓

In the short term, government spending leads to more jobs and more output.

Economic Dictionary

- **fiscal policy,** *p. 392*
- **federal budget,** *p. 392*
- **fiscal year,** *p. 392*
- **appropriations bill,** *p. 394*
- **expansionary policy,** *p. 395*
- **contractionary policy,** *p. 395*
- **classical economics,** *p. 399*
- **productive capacity,** *p. 400*
- **demand-side economics,** *p. 400*
- **Keynesian economics,** *p. 401*
- **multiplier effect,** *p. 401*
- **automatic stabilizer,** *p. 404*
- **supply-side economics,** *p. 404*
- **budget surplus,** *p. 408*
- **budget deficit,** *p. 408*
- **Treasury bill,** *p. 409*
- **Treasury note,** *p. 409*
- **Treasury bond,** *p. 409*
- **national debt,** *p. 410*
- **crowding-out effect,** *p. 411*

Economics on the go

Study anytime, anywhere. Download these files today.

Economic Dictionary online	Audio Review online	Action Graph online	Visual Glossary online	How the Economy Works online
Vocabulary Support in English and Spanish	Audio Study Guide in English and Spanish	Animated Charts and Graphs	Animated feature	Animated feature

Download to your computer or mobile device at PearsonSuccessNet.com

ASSIGN THE ESSENTIAL QUESTIONS JOURNAL

After students have finished studying the chapter, they should return to the chapter's essential question in the Essential Questions Journal and complete the activity.

Tell students to go back to the chapter opener and look at the image. Using the information they have gained from studying the chapter, ask **How does this illustrate the main ideas of the chapter?** *(Possible responses: The federal budget contains estimates of the government's revenue and authorizes its spending for the following fiscal year; the budget is used to set fiscal policy; budget deficits occur when expenditures exceed revenues; these deficits contribute to the national debt.)*

STUDY TIPS

Tell students to use active reading techniques when reading a textbook.

1. Preview the material before reading in depth. Read headings and subheadings, look at illustrations and graphs, read captions.
2. Read the material carefully, looking for main ideas.
3. Pause occasionally and ask questions: What are the main ideas? What details support the main ideas?
4. After finishing reading, summarize the material. Go back and check any ideas that are unclear.

Economics on the go Have students download the digital resources available on Economics on the Go for review and remediation.

Assessment at a Glance

TESTS AND QUIZZES

Section Assessments

Section Quizzes A and B, **Unit 6 All-in-One**
Self-Test Online

Chapter Assessments

Chapter Tests A and B, **Unit 6 All-in-One**
Economic Detective, **Unit 6 All-in-One**
Document-based Assessment, p. 417
Exam*View*

AYP Monitoring Assessments

PERFORMANCE ASSESSMENT

Teacher's Edition, pp. 396, 401, 404, 405, 409, 411
Simulation Activities, Chapter 15
Virtual Economics on CD-ROM, pp. 396, 403, 410
Essential Questions Journal, Chapter 15
Assessment Rubrics

Chapter Assessment

1. (a) According to classical economics, free markets regulate themselves. Keynesian economics encourages government action to resolve economic problems through the use of fiscal policy. (b) By building pyramids, the government put people to work, thereby reducing unemployment and increasing output. (c) Possible response: The Civilian Conservation Corps put over 2 million young men to work, fighting soil erosion and planting trees.
2. (a) Possible response: It provides funding for school lunches and educational programs; it affects general economic conditions and prices. (b) Possible response: Fiscal policy affects the amount of money the government spends on financial aid programs for college.
3. (a) Taxes and transfer payments are tied to the GDP and personal income and stabilize economic growth. When the economy slows, automatic stabilizers help stimulate it. When the economy is growing too fast, stabilizers slow it down. (b) The economy would be more volatile with larger changes in GDP.
4. (a) When the government borrows money, it means less money is available to invest in private business, making it harder for businesses to borrow and invest. (b) It can hurt investment, slow growth, and reduce capital deepening.
5. (a) Benefits: less debt so more money is available for businesses to borrow, elimination of interest payments and associated opportunity costs; drawbacks: government would not have the flexibility to deal with rapid changes in the economy. (b) Possible response: No, because the government needs the ability to use fiscal policy.
6. (a) It is used to increase or decrease taxes and spending. (b) It has had mixed success. During the Great Depression, spending on federal programs moved the economy toward full productive capacity. However, in the 1970s, with Keynesian fiscal policy in place, unemployment and inflation rates soared.
7. It decreased from 12 percent to 9 percent.
8. Medicare/Medicaid and Defense: 4 percent
9. (a) decreased from 23 percent to 21 percent (b) No, because the number of people receiving money from Social Security will increase as baby boomers retire.
10. After dividing the class into small groups, assign each President to at least one group. Invite a resource librarian into the classroom to identify good sources of information.
11. Answers will vary, but students should be able to justify the order and make a reasoned generalization about the use of fiscal policy.

CHAPTER 15 ASSESSMENT

Self-Test online To test your understanding of key terms and main ideas, visit **PearsonSuccessNet.com**

Key Terms and Main Ideas

To make sure you understand the key terms and main ideas of this chapter, review the Checkpoint and Section Assessment questions and look at the Quick Study Guide on the preceding page.

Critical Thinking

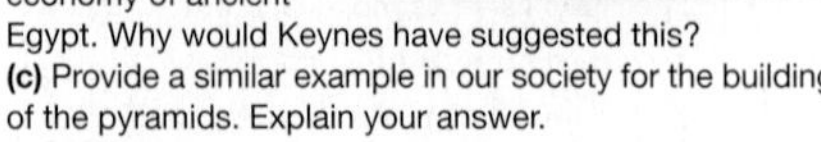

1. **Compare (a)** Describe the fundamental differences between classical economics and Keynesian economics. **(b)** Keynes suggested that building pyramids was good for the economy of ancient Egypt. Why would Keynes have suggested this? **(c)** Provide a similar example in our society for the building of the pyramids. Explain your answer.
2. **Main Ideas (a)** Make a list of ways in which governmental fiscal policy affects your daily life. **(b)** Which aspects of fiscal policy have the greatest effect on you? Explain.
3. **Infer (a)** How do automatic stabilizers affect our economy? **(b)** What would our economy be like without them?
4. **Analyze (a)** In your own words, describe the crowding-out effect. **(b)** Explain how it can influence economic growth over the long term.
5. **Evaluate (a)** What are the benefits and drawbacks of a balanced budget amendment? **(b)** Would you support such an amendment? Explain why or why not?
6. **Main Ideas (a)** How is the federal budget a tool of fiscal policy? **(b)** How effective has this tool been in promoting full employment and economic growth?

Applying Your Math Skills

Comparing Circle Graphs

The two pie graphs below show categories of federal spending in the national budgets for 2000 and 2007. Look at the graphs and answer the questions that follow.

Visit PearsonSuccessNet.com for additional math help.

Federal Spending, 2000 and 2007

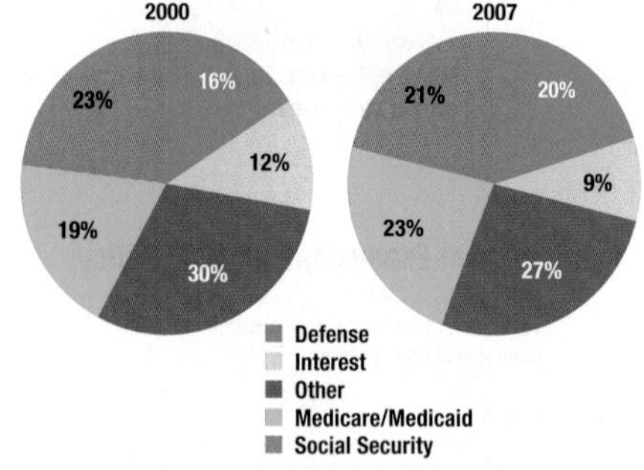

SOURCE: U.S. Senate and U.S. House Budget Offices

7. How did the percentage of federal spending on interest payments change between 2000 and 2007?
8. Which categories of federal spending have seen the same percentage increase since 2000?
9. **(a)** How have Social Security outlays changed as a percentage of the federal budget? **(b)** Do you think this pattern will continue? Explain why or why not.

Essential Question Activity

Essential Questions Journal To respond to the chapter Essential Question, go to your **Essential Questions Journal**.

10. Complete this activity to answer the Essential Question **How effective is fiscal policy as an economic tool?** Work in small groups, with each group researching the administrations of John F. Kennedy to the current President. Using the worksheet in your Essential Questions Journal or the electronic worksheet available at **PearsonSuccessNet.com,** gather the following information:
    (a) Identify the President by political party and years in office.
    (b) Identify the main economic goals and challenges under that administration.
    (c) Describe any tax and spending changes that grew out of the administration's fiscal policy.
    (d) Evaluate how successful that administration was at meeting its goals.
11. **Modify** After your group has filled out its worksheet, make enough copies to distribute to the other groups in the class.
    (a) Each group will take the worksheets and evaluate which President they think had the most successful fiscal policy. Place the sheets in order from most effective to least effective.
    (b) The class will share and compare their conclusions.
    (c) As a class, make a generalization about the use of fiscal policy by Presidents since 1960 to stabilize economic conditions, stimulate growth, or cool down an overheated economy.

WebQuest online The Economics WebQuest challenges students to use 21st century skills to answer the Essential Question.

Remind students to continue to develop an Essentials Questions video. Guidelines and a production binder are available at www.PearsonSuccessNet.com.

CHAPTER 15 ASSESSMENT

DOCUMENT-BASED ASSESSMENT

Is the national debt a threat to the country?

Many economists blame the huge U.S. national debt for many economic problems, including high interest rates, unemployment, and trade deficits. However, some economists believe that the problems of the national debt are exaggerated.

Document A

Interest on the National Debt, 1990–2008

Fiscal Year	Percentage of Federal Outlays for Interest on Debt	Fiscal Year	Percentage of Federal Outlays for Interest on Debt
1990	14.7	2000	12.5
1992	14.4	2002	8.5
1994	13.9	2004	7.0
1996	15.4	2006	8.5
1998	14.6	2008*	9.0

*Estimated

Document B

"The national debt places a drag on the economy and hinders economic growth. It also affects every American in very real ways every day. For example, last year [2007] 18 percent of all federal taxes collected were spent just paying interest on the debt. Almost one dollar you paid out of every five was not used to educate our children, pave our roads, or defend our nation. The interest we all must pay on the national debt represents a "debt tax" that can never be repealed as long as the debt remains at its current levels. The debt tax will consume larger portions of our money as government spending continues to increase at alarming levels."

—"The National Debt: How Does It Affect Me?" Representative Dennis Cardoza, D-California

Document C

The National Debt: Myths and Reality

"Myth: We have to pay back all of the $5.6 trillion in debt.

Reality: The U.S. can simply "roll over" its debt year after year. That is, the Treasury Department issues new bonds to pay off the old ones. This is not a problem as long as investors are willing to hold U.S. Treasury bonds. U.S. Treasury bonds are very popular due to their liquidity (they are easily converted to cash), their low risk (they have zero default risk because they are backed by "the full faith and credit" of the U.S. government), and certain tax advantages.

Myth: The interest payments on the national debt are a burden to future generations.

Reality: U.S. citizens or even agencies of the U.S. government own most of the debt. Thus we are just paying interest to ourselves."

—Elizabeth Dunne Smith, Asst. Professor of Economics, SUNY, Oswego

ANALYZING DOCUMENTS

Use your knowledge of the national debt and Documents A, B, and C to answer Questions 1–3.

1. **According to Document A, the percentage of the federal budget devoted to paying interest on the national debt**
   - A. has risen steadily since 1990.
   - B. has fallen steadily since 1990.
   - C. has fluctuated wildly from year to year.
   - D. began to rise again after reduction.

2. **According to Representative Cardoza, money spent on the national debt**
   - A. is taken from money that would otherwise be spent on education or national defense.
   - B. does not go toward paying the interest on the debt.
   - C. is separate from government spending.
   - D. remains at current levels.

3. **In Document C, Professor Dunne Smith argues that the national debt**
   - A. does not affect national defense spending.
   - B. will not be a burden to future generations.
   - C. will damage the liquidity of U.S. Treasury bonds.
   - D. injures the "full faith and credit" of the U.S. government.

WRITING ABOUT ECONOMICS

The ever-growing national debt causes much debate during budget preparation each fiscal year. Use the documents on this page and resources on the Web site below to answer this question: **Is the national debt a threat to the country?** Use the sources to support your opinion.

In Partnership

THE WALL STREET JOURNAL. CLASSROOM EDITION

To read more about issues related to this topic, visit **PearsonSuccessNet.com**

Document-Based Assessment

ANALYZING DOCUMENTS

1. D
2. A
3. B

WRITING ABOUT ECONOMICS

Possible answers: The national debt is not a threat to the country because the Treasury can continue to issue new bonds, which are very popular with investors; the national debt is a threat to the country because money that goes to pay off the debt, and interest on the debt, cannot be used to pay for education or national defense.

Student essay should demonstrate an understanding of the issues involved in the debate over the growing national debt. Use the following as guidelines to assess the essay.

L2 Differentiate Students use all documents on the page to support their thesis.

L3 Differentiate Students use the documents on this page and additional information available online at www.PearsonSuccessNet.com to support their answer.

L4 Differentiate Students incorporate information provided in the textbook and online at www.PearsonSuccessNet.com and include additional research to support their opinion.

Go Online to www.PearsonSuccessNet.com for a student rubric and extra documents.

Economics online *All print resources are available on the Teacher's Resource Library CD-ROM and online at* www.PearsonSuccessNet.com.

Essential Questions

UNIT 6:

What is the proper role of government in the economy?

CHAPTER 16:

How effective is monetary policy as an economic tool?

Introduce the Chapter

ACTIVATE PRIOR KNOWLEDGE

In this chapter, students will learn about the Federal Reserve System and its role in setting and managing the nation's monetary policy. Tell students to complete the warmup activity in their **Essential Questions Journal**.

DIFFERENTIATED INSTRUCTION KEY

- **L1** Special Needs
- **L2** Basic to Average includes
  - **ELL** English Language Learners
  - **LPR** Less Proficient Readers
- **L3** All Students
- **L4** Advanced Students

Economics online Visit www.PearsonSuccessNet.com for an interactive textbook with built-in activities on economic principles.

- ***The Wall Street Journal* Classroom Edition Video** presents a current topic related to the Federal Reserve and monetary policy.
- **Yearly Update Worksheet** provides an annual update, including a new worksheet and lesson on this topic.
- **On the Go** resources can be downloaded so students and teachers can connect with economics any time, anywhere.

Chapter 16 The Federal Reserve and Monetary Policy

Essential Question, Chapter 16

How effective is monetary policy as an economic tool?

Economics *on the go*

To study anywhere, anytime, download these online resources at ***PearsonSuccessNet.com*** ▶

ECONOMICS ONLINE

DIGITAL TEACHER TOOLS

The online lesson planner is designed to help teachers plan, teach, and assess. Teachers have the ability to use or customize existing Pearson lesson plans. Online lecture notes support the print lesson by providing an array of accessible activities and summaries of key concepts.

Two interactivities in this lesson are:

- **Visual Glossary** An online tool gives students a way to learn what monetary policy is and what it consists of.
- **WebQuest** Students use online resources to complete a guided activity further exploring the essential questions.

Block Scheduling

BLOCK 1 Teach Sections 1 and 2 without the worksheets or the Extend activities.

BLOCK 2 Teach Sections 3 and 4 without the worksheets or Extend activities.

Pressed for Time

Group work Organize the class into four groups, assigning each group a section from the chapter. Have each group present a summary of the main points of its section. Then complete the chapter's transparencies and worksheets as a class.

SECTION 1 The Federal Reserve System

OBJECTIVES

1. **Describe** banking history in the United States.
2. **Explain** why the Federal Reserve Act of 1913 led to further reform.
3. **Describe** the structure of the Federal Reserve System.

ECONOMIC DICTIONARY

As you read the section, look for the definitions of these **Key Terms:**

- monetary policy
- reserves
- reserve requirements

Guiding Question
How is the Federal Reserve System organized?

Copy this concept web and fill it in as you read.

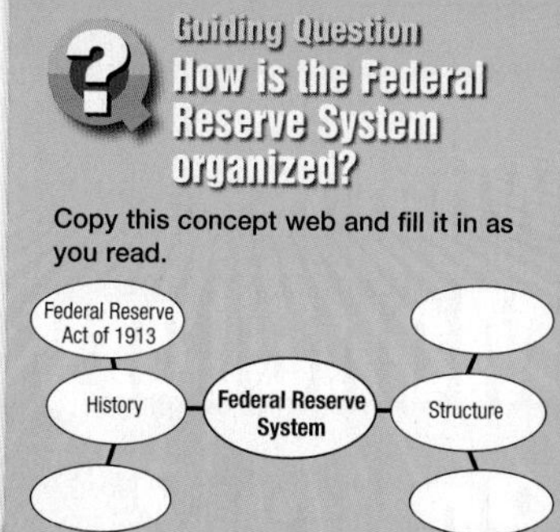

Economics and You It's Saturday night, and you've gone out to a movie with friends. Now everyone wants to eat, but you realize that you have only a dollar and some change left. What can you do? If you have access to an ATM, you could get cash out of your bank account. Here's a crazy thought—what if your bank runs out of money? What can *it* do?

Principles in Action As you'll see in this section, when American banks need emergency cash, they turn to the Federal Reserve System for a loan. The Federal Reserve System is organized to provide this and a host of essential services to banks, to the federal government, and, most importantly, to the national economy.

Banking History

The Federal Reserve in American History

The Federal Reserve System, as you read in Chapter 10, is the central bank of the United States. It has many important tasks, but the most prominent one is to act as the main spokesperson for the country's monetary policy. **Monetary policy** refers to the actions that the Fed takes to influence the level of real GDP and the rate of inflation in the economy.

The role of a central bank in the U.S. economy has been hotly debated since 1790, when Federalists lined up in favor of establishing a central bank. The first Bank of the United States issued a single currency. It also reviewed banking practices and helped the federal government carry out

monetary policy the actions that the Federal Reserve System takes to influence the level of real GDP and the rate of inflation in the economy

Visual Glossary online

Go to the Visual Glossary Online for an interactive review of **monetary policy.**

Action Graph online

Go to Action Graph Online for animated versions of key charts and graphs.

How the Economy Works online

Go to How the Economy Works Online for an interactive lesson on **making monetary policy.**

Guiding Question

How is the Federal Reserve System organized?

Get Started

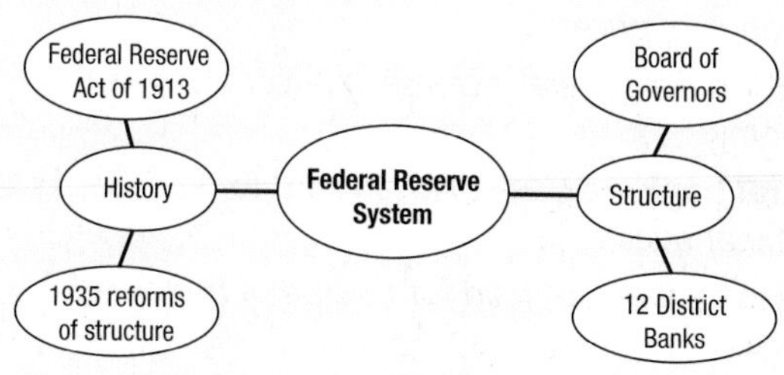

LESSON GOALS

Students will:

- Know the Key Terms.
- Demonstrate understanding of U.S. banking history and the conditions that led to the Federal Reserve Act of 1913 by completing a worksheet.
- Explain the structure of the Federal Reserve System by interpreting a chart.

BEFORE CLASS

Students should read the section for homework before coming to class.

Have students complete the graphic organizer in the Section Opener as they read the text. As an alternate activity, have students complete the Guided Reading and Review worksheet (Unit 6 All-in-One, p. 99).

L1 L2 ELL LPR Differentiate Have students complete the Guided Reading and Review worksheet (Unit 6 All-in-One, p. 100).

(lesson continued on p. 421)

Focus on the Basics

Students need to come away with the following understandings:

FACTS: • Chaos in the nation's banking system caused Congress to create the Federal Reserve System in 1913. • In 1935, Congress adjusted the structure of the Federal Reserve System. • The Federal Reserve System, or "Fed," is a network of 12 Federal Reserve Banks, one in each of the 12 Federal Reserve districts into which the United States is divided. • The Federal Reserve System is privately owned by the member banks, but publicly controlled by the federal government.

GENERALIZATION: The Federal Reserve System is a network of twelve banks that act as one bank controlled by a seven-member Board of Governors. The Federal Reserve System oversees, regulates, and provides services to the nation's banks.

CLASSROOM HINTS

HAVE A PRESS CONFERENCE

Divide the class into four groups. Assign each group one of the following topics: First Bank of the United States, Second Bank of the United States, Federal Reserve Act of 1913, and Federal Reserve reforms of 1935. Have each group select two members to act as advocates—from government or other leadership—for the group's topic. Remaining members will be reporters who interview the spokespersons at a press conference. They will ask questions such as why the bank is needed, what problems it will correct, and how it will be structured and will function. Have them address both supporting and opposing points of view.

TEACH VISUAL GLOSSARY

REVIEW KEY TERMS

Pair students and have them write the definitions of these key terms related to an understanding of monetary policy.

real GDP – *GDP expressed in constant, or unchanging, prices*

inflation – *a general increase in prices across an economy*

central bank – *a bank that can lend to other banks in time of need*

interest – *the price paid for the use of borrowed money*

fiscal policy – *the use of government spending and revenue collection to influence the economy*

CHECK COMPREHENSION

Have students make connections between the labeled tools in the toolbox and the bulleted descriptions. Elicit the fact from students that money creation is a function of all banks, while reserve requirements, open market operations, and discount rates are tools for adjusting the amount of money in the economy.

Call students' attention to the cartoon. Point out that the Fed has no direct control over what interest rates banks charge to their borrowers. Discuss how the Fed uses the tools it does have to indirectly cause an increase or a cut in consumer interest rates.

L1 L2 ELL LPR Differentiate Have students use the Visual Glossary Online to reinforce their understanding of these tools and the following additional terms (introduced in later sections) associated with monetary policy: *prime rate, discount rate, easy money policy,* and *tight money policy.*

Economics online *All print resources are available on the Teacher's Resource Library CD-ROM and online at www.PearsonSuccessNet.com.*

Answer

Cartoon make even larger cuts in interest rates

VISUAL GLOSSARY

Reviewing Key Terms
To understand *monetary policy,* review these terms.

central bank, *p. 260*
interest, *p. 268*
real GDP, *p. 310*
inflation, *p. 342*
fiscal policy, *p. 392*

What is Monetary Policy?

◀ **monetary policy** the actions that the Fed takes to influence the level of real GDP and the rate of inflation in the economy

To achieve its mission of stabilizing the U.S. economy, the Federal Reserve board uses a variety of tools.

- The Fed can encourage money creation by making it cheaper for banks to borrow.
- The Fed can raise and lower reserve requirements and raise and lower the discount rate.
- Open market operations, the buying and selling of government securities, is the most used monetary policy tool.

◀ Fed chair Ben Bernanke uses one of his important tools to stabilize the economy. ***What action does the cartoonist suggest Bernanke is about to take?***

Visual Glossary online
To expand your understanding of this and other key economic terms, visit **PearsonSuccessNet.com**

its duties and powers. Partly because of the impassioned debate over state versus federal powers, however, the first Bank lasted only until 1811. At that time, Congress refused to extend its charter.

Congress established the Second Bank of the United States in 1816 to restore order to the monetary system. However, many people still feared that a central bank placed too much power in the hands of the federal government. Political opposition toppled the Second Bank in 1836 when its charter expired.

A period of confusion followed. States chartered some banks, while the federal government chartered and regulated others. Banks had to keep a certain amount of reserves on hand. **Reserves** are deposits that a bank keeps readily available as opposed to lending them out. **Reserve requirements**—the amount of reserves that banks are required to keep on hand—were difficult to enforce, and the nation experienced several serious bank runs. The Panic of 1907 finally convinced Congress to act.

The nation's banking system needed to address two issues. First, consumers and businesses needed greater access to funds to encourage business expansion. Second, banks needed a source of emergency cash to prevent depositor panics that resulted in bank runs.

CHECKPOINT ***Why did some Americans oppose establishing a central bank?***

Federal Reserve Act of 1913

Attempting to solve these problems, Congress passed the Federal Reserve Act in 1913. The resulting Federal Reserve System, now often referred to simply as "the Fed," consisted of a group of 12 independent regional banks. These banks could lend to other banks in times of need.

Continued Need for Reform

The Great Depression was exactly the situation Congress had hoped to avoid by creating the Federal Reserve System. The system did not work well, however, because the regional banks each acted independently. Their separate actions often canceled one another out.

For example, in 1929 and 1930, the Governors of the Federal Reserve Banks of New York and Chicago wanted the Fed to lower interest rates. Many of the assets used to make business loans had lost value as a result of the stock market crash. Lower interest rates would make more money available to banks. However, the Federal Reserve Board of Governors was against lowering interest rates. Concerned about the growth of the stock market, the board favored a contractionary monetary policy. They also restrained the New York board from taking strong action. Many economists believe that the failure of the Fed to act contributed to the deepening of the financial crisis.

A Stronger Fed

In 1935, Congress adjusted the Federal Reserve's structure so that the system could respond more effectively to future crises. These reforms created the Federal Reserve System as we know it today. The new Fed enjoyed more centralized power so that the regional banks were able to act consistently with one another while still representing their own districts' banking concerns. One example shows how the new Fed helped fight a Depression-era crisis in a small Minnesota town. Picture this scene:

Outside the bank, a large crowd was growing frantic. A large number of withdrawals had badly depleted the bank's supply of cash. Inside the bank, a worried banker phoned the Federal Reserve Bank in Minneapolis—200 miles away—and begged the Fed to send him money. Fed officers snapped into action. They hired an airplane and packed a half million dollars into satchels.

> "Upon approaching the town the pilot guided the plane low over the main street to dramatize its arrival and then landed in a nearby field. From there the Fed officials were ceremoniously escorted into town by the police and the money was stacked along the bank's teller windows. The sight of all that money piled up inside the bank quelled the customers' fears and saved the bank from failing."
>
> —"Born of a Panic: Forming the Federal Reserve System" Federal Reserve Board, Minneapolis

CHECKPOINT ***Why did the Fed fail to prevent the financial crises that led to the Great Depression?***

reserves deposits that a bank keeps readily available as opposed to lending them out

reserve requirements the amount of reserves that banks are required to keep on hand

Differentiated Resources

- **L1 L2 Guided Reading and Review** (Unit 6 All-in-One, p. 100)
- **L1 L2 Vocabulary worksheet** (Unit 6 All-in-One, p. 98)
- **L2 The Bad Old Days: Panics and Runs** (Unit 6 All-in-One, p. 102)
- **L2 Fact and Opinion skills worksheet** (Unit 6 All-in-One, p. 104)

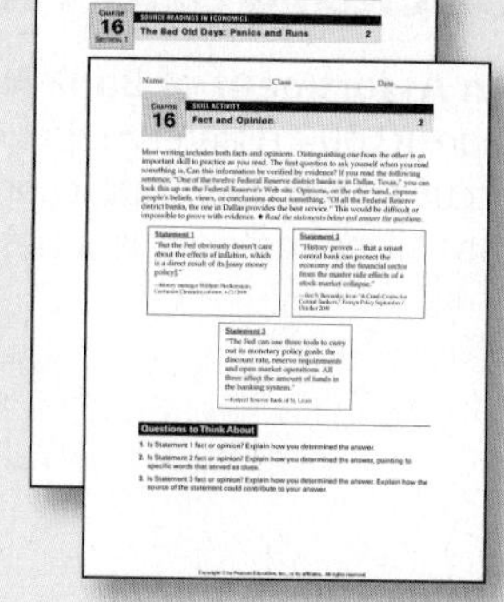

BELLRINGER

Write the following on the board: You go to the bank to withdraw the $300 that you earned from a summer job. The teller informs you that the bank cannot give you your $300 because it does not have the funds on hand. This happens to other people you know. Write a letter to your local newspaper about this.

Teach

Economics online To present this topic using digital resources, use the lecture notes on www.PearsonSuccessNet.com.

L1 L2 ELL LPR Differentiate To help students who are struggling readers, assign the Vocabulary worksheet (Unit 6 All-in-One, p. 98).

DISTRIBUTE ACTIVITY WORKSHEET

Review students' responses to the Bellringer question. Discuss how they think the nation and the U.S. economy would be affected if this happened on a widespread basis. Distribute "The Bad Old Days: Panics and Runs" worksheet (Unit 6 All-in-One, p. 101) which discusses the conditions that motivated the creation of the Federal Reserve System.

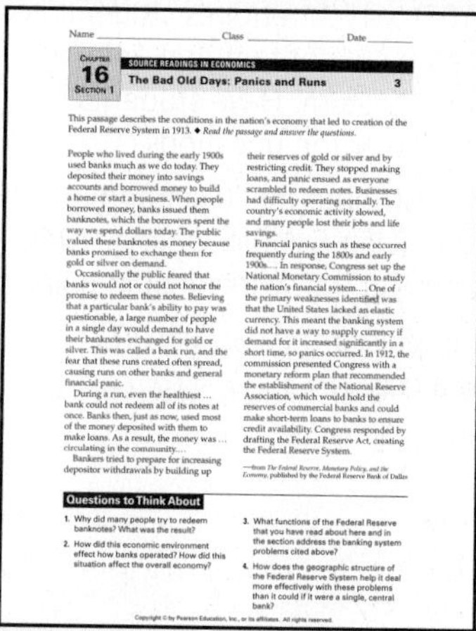

Name ______ Class ______ Date ______

CHAPTER 16 SECTION 1 — SOURCE READINGS IN ECONOMICS

The Bad Old Days: Panics and Runs 3

This passage describes the conditions in the nation's economy that led to creation of the Federal Reserve System in 1913. ◆ *Read the passage and answer the questions.*

People who lived during the early 1900s used banks much as we do today. They deposited their money into savings accounts and borrowed money to build a home or start a business. When people borrowed money, banks issued them banknotes, which the borrowers spent the way we spend dollars today. The public valued these banknotes as money because banks promised to exchange them for gold or silver on demand.

Occasionally the public feared that banks would not or could not honor the promise to redeem these notes. Believing that a particular bank's ability to pay was questionable, a large number of people in a single day would demand to have their banknotes exchanged for gold or silver. This was called a bank run, and the fear that these runs created often spread, causing runs on other banks and general financial panic.

During a run, even the healthiest ... bank could not redeem all of its notes at once. Banks then, just as now, used most of the money deposited with them to make loans. As a result, the money was ... circulating in the community....

Bankers tried to prepare for increasing depositor withdrawals by building up their reserves of gold or silver and by restricting credit. They stopped making loans, and panic ensued as everyone scrambled to redeem notes. Businesses had difficulty operating normally. The country's economic activity slowed, and many people lost their jobs and life savings.

Financial panics such as these occurred frequently during the 1800s and early 1900s.... In response, Congress set up the National Monetary Commission to study the nation's financial system.... One of the primary weaknesses identified was that the United States lacked an elastic currency. This meant the banking system did not have a way to supply currency if demand for it increased significantly in a short time, so panics occurred. In 1912, the commission presented Congress with a monetary reform plan that recommended the establishment of the National Reserve Association, which would hold the reserves of commercial banks and could make short-term loans to banks to ensure credit availability. Congress responded by drafting the Federal Reserve Act, creating the Federal Reserve System.

—from *The Federal Reserve, Monetary Policy, and the Economy*, published by the Federal Reserve Bank of Dallas

Questions to Think About

1. Why did many people try to redeem banknotes? What was the result?
2. How did this economic environment effect how banks operated? How did this situation affect the overall economy?
3. What functions of the Federal Reserve that you have read about here and in the section address the banking system problems cited above?
4. How does the geographic structure of the Federal Reserve System help it deal more effectively with these problems than it could if it were a single, central bank?

L2 Differentiate Distribute "The Bad Old Days: Panics and Runs" worksheet (Unit 6 All-in-One, p. 102). Have students read the passage aloud, taking turns reading one paragraph at a time.

Have students discuss their answers to worksheet questions 3 and 4.

Answers

Checkpoint They feared that it gave the federal government too much power.

Checkpoint Some regional banks did not follow a course of action that would have helped the economy.

CHECK COMPREHENSION

Lead the class in interpreting Figure 16.1. Ask **Why is the illustration shaped like a pyramid?** *(It illustrates the Federal Reserve System, a hierarchy in which the 7-member Board of Governors oversees the 12 district banks. Each of these banks oversees the hundreds of member banks in its district.)* Ask **Why does the label Federal Open Market Committee span the top two levels of the chart?** *(The FOMC consists of all members of the Board of Governors, plus the presidents of 5 of the 12 District Reserve Banks.)* Ask **Why are the banks on the bottom level shown using two different colors? How many individual banks does each bank in the diagram represent?** *(A minority—about 2,600—are national banks, which must be members, while 25,000 other institutions—such as state-chartered banks—join voluntarily. Each bank represents 1,000 banks.)*

L4 Differentiate Working in groups, have students create a news video about the Federal Reserve. They may conduct interviews or act out roles themselves. They should incorporate at least one current issue related to the Fed in their reporting.

ANALYZE AND EVALUATE

Distribute the "Fact and Opinion" skills worksheet (Unit 6 All-in-One, p. 103), which requires students to distinguish between statements of fact and opinion about the Federal Reserve System. Have students read the passages and answer the questions.

L1 L2 Differentiate Distribute the "Fact and Opinion" skills worksheet (Unit 6 All-in-One, p. 104). Then have students complete the worksheet in pairs.

When everyone has completed the worksheet, discuss the answers as a class.

Structure of the Federal Reserve

The Federal Reserve System is privately owned by the member banks themselves. But it is publicly controlled by the federal government. Like so many American institutions, the structure of the Federal Reserve System represents compromises between centralized power and regional powers. **Figure 16.1** illustrates that structure.

The Board of Governors

The Federal Reserve System is overseen by the Board of Governors of the Federal Reserve. The Board of Governors is headquartered in Washington, D.C. Its seven governors, or members, are appointed for staggered 14-year terms by the President of the United States with the advice and consent of the Senate. The terms are staggered to prevent any one President from appointing a full Board of Governors and to protect board members from day-to-day political pressures. Members cannot be reappointed after serving a full term. Geographical restrictions on these appointments ensure that no one district is overrepresented.

The President also appoints the chair of the Board of Governors from among these seven members. The Senate confirms the appointment. Chairs serve four-year terms, which can be renewed.

Recent chairs of the Fed have been economists from the business world, the academic world, or government. They have a keen sensitivity toward public opinion and an ability to use the media to affect public opinion. Alan Greenspan, a former head of an economics consulting firm and chair of the President's Council of Economic Advisers (CEA), has been the most notable chair of the Fed in modern times. He took office in 1987 and served both Republican and Democratic administrations. After Greenspan resigned in 2006, President George W. Bush replaced him with Ben Bernanke, the head of the Council of Economic Advisers and a former professor of economics. Bernanke learned about monetary policy and Milton Friedman as a graduate student. He spent much of his career as an economist researching the Great Depression. His own writings on the topic focused on how to keep financial crises from getting out of control.

Figure 16.1 Structure of the Federal Reserve System

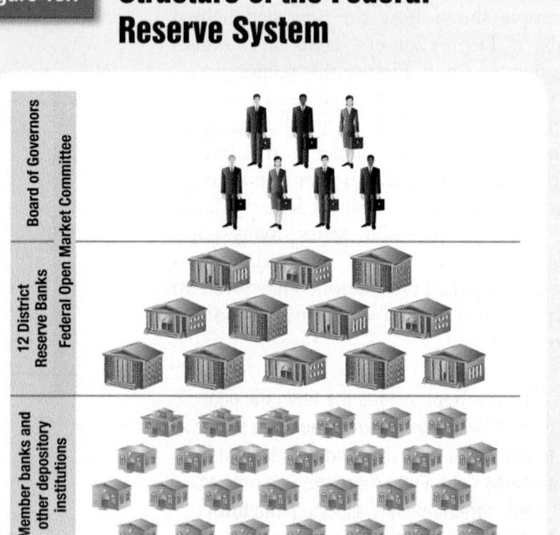

CHART SKILLS

More than 30 percent of all United States banks belong to the Federal Reserve System.

1. At which of the three levels of this Fed structure would a nationally chartered bank in your community fit?
2. How does the structure of the Fed reflect a compromise between centralized power and regional powers?

Twelve Federal Reserve Banks

The Federal Reserve Act divided the United States into 12 Federal Reserve Districts, as shown in **Figure 16.2.** One Federal Reserve Bank is located in each district. Each of these Banks monitors and reports on economic and banking conditions in its district.

Each Federal Reserve District is made up of more than one state. The Federal Reserve Act aimed to establish a system in which no one region could exploit the central bank's power at another region's expense.

Congress regulates the makeup of each Reserve Bank's board of nine directors to make sure that it represents many interests. The nine directors consist of three sets of three persons each. The first set of three represents commercial banks, and they are elected by the district's member banks.

Background Note

An Assortment of Bank Notes At one point in the nineteenth century, more than 10,000 different types of bank notes were circulating in the United States. This occurred because state-chartered banks printed their own bank notes, backed by their silver and gold reserves.

Answers

Chart Skills 1. on the bottom level as a member bank 2. The system is overseen by a central Board of Governors but the District Reserve Banks also have their own governance. Also, both the central Board of Governors and the District Reserve Banks are represented on the FOMC.

Figure 16.2 Federal Reserve Districts

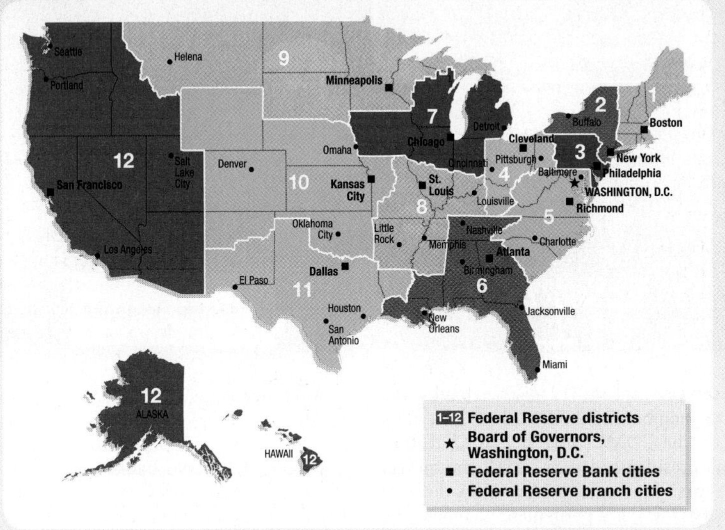

MAP SKILLS

Most Federal Reserve Districts contain a variety of agricultural, manufacturing, and service industries, as well as rural and urban areas.

1. Which are the largest and smallest of the Federal Reserve Districts? Name the Federal Reserve Bank cities in each of these districts.
2. How does the makeup of the Federal Reserve Districts help ensure that no single region is dominant?

The member banks also elect the second set—three people who represent the interests of groups such as industry, commerce, labor, services, and consumers. The third set of directors is appointed by the Board of Governors of the Federal Reserve. These three represent the same broad public interests as the second group. The Board of Governors then selects one of the nine directors to serve as chair of the Reserve Bank's board. Each board of directors appoints a president of the Reserve Bank, subject to approval by the Board of Governors.

Member Banks

All nationally chartered banks are required to join the Federal Reserve System. The remaining members are state-chartered banks that join voluntarily. Since 1980, all banks have equal access to Fed services, whether or not they are Fed members. These services include reserve loans to banks in need of short-term cash.

Each of the approximately 2,400 Fed member banks contributes a small amount of money to join the system. In return, it receives stock in the system. This stock earns the bank dividends from the Fed at a rate of up to 6 percent.

The fact that the banks themselves, rather than a government agency, own the Federal Reserve gives the system a high degree of political independence. This independence helps the Fed to make decisions that best suit the interests of the country as a whole.

The Federal Open Market Committee

The Federal Open Market Committee (FOMC) makes key monetary policy decisions about interest rates and the growth of the United States money supply. The committee meets about eight times a year in private to discuss the cost and availability of credit, for business and consumers, across the country. Announcements of the FOMC's decisions can affect financial markets and rates for home mortgages, as well as many economic institutions around the world. You will read more about the effects of monetary policy later in this chapter.

Members of the Federal Open Market Committee are drawn from the Board of

RESEARCH

Either as a class or in small groups, have students visit the Federal Reserve System Online (http://www.federalreserveonline.org/). Tell them to identify the Federal Reserve Bank in their own district and then click on the link for that bank. Explore the site with students and ask them to identify at least three facts about the Federal Reserve in their district that they did not know.

EXTEND

Invite students to create single or multipanel cartoons that illustrate how various parts of the Federal Reserve (including the chairman) work in relation to one another.

GUIDING QUESTION WRAP UP

Have students return to the section Guiding Question. Review the completed graphic organizer and clarify any misunderstandings. Have a wrap-up discussion about how the Federal Reserve System is organized.

Assess and Remediate

L3 L2 Collect "The Bad Old Days: Panics and Runs" worksheets and assess students' understanding of banking history and the Federal Reserve's reforms.

L3 L2 Collect the "Fact and Opinion" skill worksheets and assess student ability to distinguish between fact and opinion.

L3 Collect students' graphic organizers and assess their understanding of the structure of the Federal Reserve System.

L3 Assign the Section 1 Assessment questions; identify student misconceptions.

L3 Give Section Quiz A (Unit 6 All-in-One, p. 105).

L2 Give Section Quiz B (Unit 6 All-in-One, p. 106).

(Assess and Remediate continued on p 424)

Virtual Economics

L3 Differentiate

Reviewing the Need for the Federal Reserve System Use the following lesson from the NCEE **Virtual Economics *CD-ROM*** to help students understand the importance of a fractional reserve banking system. Click on Browse Economics Lessons, specify grades 9–12, and use the key words *system is established.*

In this activity, students will work in small groups to examine the causes of money panics and how the Federal Reserve was created to address them.

LESSON TITLE	THE FEDERAL RESERVE SYSTEM IS ESTABLISHED
Type of Activity	Case studies
Complexity	Low
Time	50 minutes
NCEE Standards	10, 20

Answers

Map Skills 1. largest: District 12, with the bank located in San Francisco; smallest: District 3, with the bank located in Philadelphia 2. Each district is made up of more than one state; the makeup of each Reserve Bank's board of directors is regulated by the Congress to make sure it represents many interests.

Have students complete the Self-Test Online and continue their work in the **Essential Questions Journal**.

REMEDIATION AND SUGGESTIONS

Use the chart below to help students who are struggling with content.

WEAKNESS	REMEDIATION
Defining key terms (Questions 3, 4, 5)	Have students use the interactive Economic Dictionary Online.
U.S. banking history (Question 6)	Have students make a timeline of events in banking history from 1790 to 1913. As an alternative, have them review Chapter 10 Section 2, including the timeline in Figure 10.1.
The Federal Reserve Act and further reforms (Questions 2, 8)	Have students outline the material under "Federal Reserve Act of 1913."
The structure of the Federal Reserve System (Questions 1, 7, 9, 10)	Reteach Figure 16.1 and review selected student-created graphic organizers with students

Answers

Caption because the Fed's actions and decisions have a major impact on the U.S. economy and thus on world markets

Checkpoint to monitor and report on economic and banking conditions in its district; each is also represented at different times on the FOMC

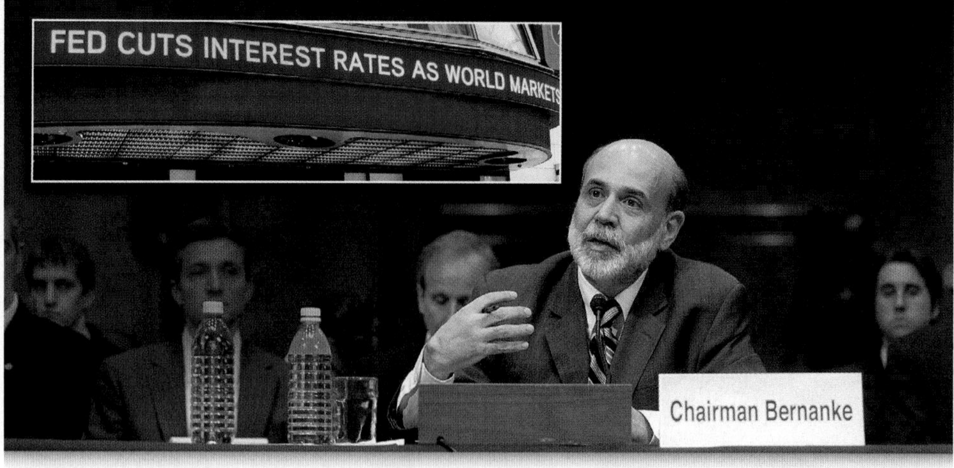

▲ Ben Bernanke testifies on the economy before a committee of Congress. ***Why are both Congress and world markets interested in what he has to say?***

Governors and the 12 district banks. All seven members of the Board of Governors sit on the FOMC. Five of the 12 district bank presidents also sit on the committee. The president of the New York Federal Reserve Bank is a permanent member. The four other district presidents serve one-year terms on a rotating basis. The Board of Governors holds a majority of the seats on the FOMC, giving it effective control over the committee's actions.

After meeting with the FOMC, the chair of the Board of Governors announces the committee's decisions to the public. The Federal Reserve Banks and financial markets spring into action as they react to Fed decisions. In the next section, you will read about how the Fed's decisions are carried out and what functions the Federal Reserve serves.

CHECKPOINT ***What is the role of each of the 12 Federal Reserve banks?***

Essential Questions Journal To continue to build a response to the Essential Question, go to your **Essential Questions Journal.**

SECTION 1 ASSESSMENT

Guiding Question

1. Use your completed concept web to answer this question: How is the Federal Reserve System organized?
2. **Extension** Since you do not deal directly with the Federal Reserve, why should you care how it operates?

Key Terms and Main Ideas

3. What are **reserves** held by banks?
4. What **reserve requirements** do banks have?
5. What is **monetary policy**?

Critical Thinking

6. **Summarize (a)** What three responsibilities did the first Bank of the United States have? **(b)** Why did the bank not last?
7. **Infer (a)** Which type of bank is required to belong to the Federal Reserve System? Which can join voluntarily? **(b)** Why do you think that the Federal Reserve has both a public and a private character?
8. **Evaluate (a)** Describe the two issues that the Panic of 1907 forced the nation's banking system to address. **(b)** Why do you think it took so long for the nation to establish a central banking authority?
9. **Conclude (a)** What is the role of the Federal Open Market Committee (FOMC)? **(b)** Why do you think the FOMC is drawn from so many different sectors of the Federal Reserve Board?
10. **Compare (a)** Who replaced Alan Greenspan as chair of the Federal Reserve Bank in 2006? **(b)** What did the two men have in common?

Quick Write

11. Locate a newspaper editorial on a topic relating to economics, and look for the author's point of view. First, identify the author or news service. Then, provide words that indicate the point of view. Finally, describe the point the author is trying to make in the article and what conclusion you reach as to whether you agree with it.

Assessment Answers

1. It consists of 12 district banks that are overseen by a 7-member Board of Governors. Each bank has a board of nine directors. All nationally chartered banks must join the Federal Reserve System.
2. Possible response: Their decisions affect my ability to borrow money and the interest rate on that money.
3. readily available sums of money that a bank keeps in its vaults
4. to keep on hand a percent of funds
5. the actions the Fed takes to influence the level of real GDP and the rate of inflation
6. (a) issue currency, review banking practices, help the federal government carry out its duties and powers (b) Congress refused to extend its charter due to a disagreement over state vs. federal powers.
7. (a) all nationally chartered banks; state-chartered banks (b) The structure represents a compromise between centralized power and regional powers that characterizes many American institutions.
8. (a) the need to ensure adequate reserves in order to prevent runs on banks, and the need for greater consumer and business access to funds which would encourage expansion (b) People feared that it would put too much power in the hands of the federal government.
9. (a) to make monetary policy decisions about interest rates and the money supply (b) so that monetary policies will consider the needs or interests of all regions
10. (a) Ben Bernanke (b) Both were economics professors and heads of the President's Council of Economic Advisors.
11. Answers will vary but should summarize the author's point and draw a conclusion in agreement with or opposition to it.

SECTION 2 Federal Reserve Functions

OBJECTIVES

1. **Describe** how the Federal Reserve serves the federal government.
2. **Explain** how the Federal Reserve serves banks.
3. **Describe** how the Federal Reserve regulates the banking system.
4. **Explain** the Federal Reserve's role in regulating the nation's money supply.

ECONOMIC DICTIONARY

As you read the section, look for the definitions of these **Key Terms:**

- check clearing
- bank holding company
- federal funds rate
- discount rate

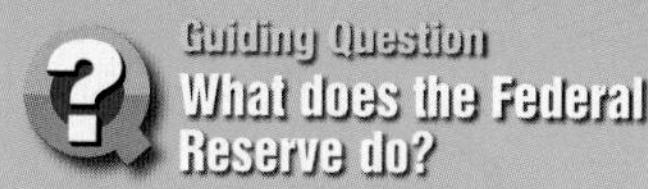

Copy this flowchart and fill it in as you read.

Functions of the Fed			
Serve Government	Serve Banks	Regulate Banks	Regulate Money Supply
•	•	•	•
•	•	•	•
•	•	•	•

Economics and You Your summer job is going great—you like the work and it pays well. The trouble is, the paychecks are handed out just once a month and you desperately need that first paycheck. Finally the end of the month arrives and you rush to your bank to cash your paycheck. But the bank teller has an unpleasant surprise for you. The bank will not credit the amount to your account until the paycheck clears. It will take at least two days, the teller says, for the check-clearing process to be completed.

Principles in Action The teller doesn't explain—probably because he or she doesn't know—that most check-clearing functions in the United States are handled through the Federal Reserve. In addition to your check, the Fed will process another 18 billion checks this year. What else does the Fed do? One function, as you will read in the Economics & You feature, is to issue money. In fact, you may have a bill now that says "Federal Reserve Note." This and the many other responsibilities of the Fed are the subject of this section.

Serving Government

As the central bank of the United States, the 12 district banks that make up the core of the Federal Reserve System carry out several important functions. Among the most important of these functions is to provide banking and fiscal services to the federal government.

The United States government pays out about $1.2 trillion each year to support such social insurance programs as Medicare, Social Security, and veterans benefits. To handle its banking needs when dealing with such enormous sums, the federal government turns to the Federal Reserve.

Banker and Agent

The Federal Reserve serves as banker for the United States government. It maintains a checking account for the Treasury Department that it uses to process Social Security checks, income tax refunds, and other government payments. For example, if you receive a check from the federal government and cash it at your local bank, it is the Federal Reserve that deducts the amount from the Treasury's account.

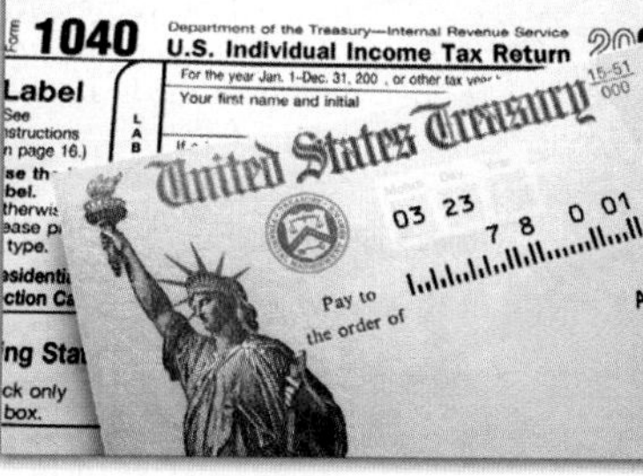

▲ The Federal Reserve is the banker for the U.S. government. Among its many functions, it processes social security checks and income tax refunds. ***What are some of its other responsibilities?***

 **Guiding Question**

What does the Federal Reserve do?

Get Started

Functions of the Fed			
Serve Government	Serve Banks	Regulate Banks	Regulate Money Supply
• Maintain Treasury Department checking account • Sell, transfer, and redeem government securities • Issue currency	• Check clearing • Lender of last resort	• Approve charters and proposed mergers • Enforce truth-in-lending laws • Set reserve requirements • Conduct bank examinations	• Monitor indicators of money supply • Adjust money supply to stabilize economy

LESSON GOALS

Students will:

- Know the Key Terms.
- Demonstrate an understanding of one role of the Federal Reserve by performing a skit.
- Demonstrate an understanding of the Federal Reserve's other roles.

BEFORE CLASS

Students should read the section for homework before coming to class.

Have students complete the graphic organizer in the Section Opener as they read the text. As an alternate activity, have students complete the Guided Reading and Review worksheet (Unit 6 All-in-One, p. 107).

L1 L2 ELL LPR Differentiate Have students complete the Guided Reading and Review worksheet (Unit 6 All-in-One, p. 108).

Answer

Caption Possible response: It makes loans to banks and provides banking and fiscal services to the government.

Focus on the Basics

Students need to come away with the following understandings:

FACTS: • The Federal Reserve serves the U.S government by acting as its banker and by issuing its currency. • The Federal Reserve serves banks through the check clearing process and by lending them money. • The Federal Reserve regulates banks by setting their reserve requirement and by supervising their lending practices. • The Federal Reserve regulates the nation's money supply.

GENERALIZATION: The Federal Reserve serves the government as its personal bank, helps other banks across the country meet their responsibilities to their customers, and regulates the banking system. Through its regulation of the money supply, the Federal Reserve also plays a key role in stabilizing the economy.

CLASSROOM HINTS

VIDEO AND DVD RESOURCES

For a $2 shipping fee, the Federal Reserve Bank of St. Louis lends videos and DVDs, several of which examine the role of the Federal Reserve. To select and request these resources for your classroom, visit the Federal Reserve System DVD and Video Lending Library (http://www.stlouisfed.org/education/) and click on the link for the Video/DVD Lending Library.

BELLRINGER

Display the transparency "Paper Money" (Color Transparencies 16.a). Write these two questions on the board: What major differences exist between these two notes? What function of the Federal Reserve do these bills illustrate?

Tell students to write their answers in their notebooks.

Teach

Economics online To present this topic using digital resources, use the lecture notes on www.PearsonSuccessNet.com.

DISCUSS THE TRANSPARENCY

Discuss the answers to the first question. Students should have observed that the first note is a "gold certificate" and its value is payable to the bearer on demand in gold. The second bill is a "federal reserve note" that is redeemable in "lawful money." Students' answers to Question 2 should have observed that the second bill demonstrates the Fed's function of issuing currency.

ROLE-PLAY

Divide the class into three groups. Assign each group one of these functions: serving the government, serving banks, and regulating banks. Distribute the "The Fed's Many Roles" worksheet (Unit 6 All-in-One, p. 109), which guides students in organizing skits.

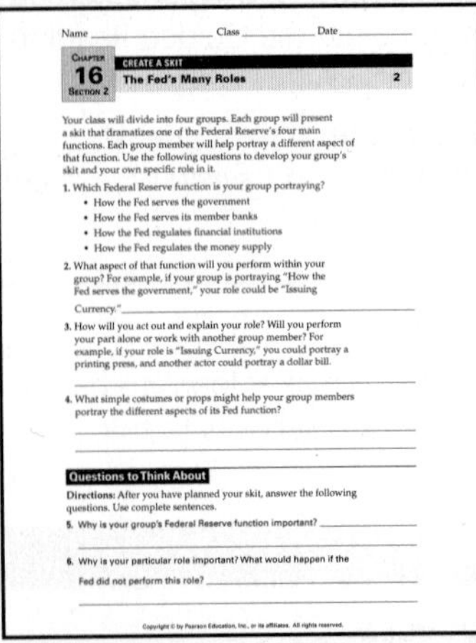

Name ______________ Class __________ Date __________

Chapter 16 Section 2 — CREATE A SKIT — **The Fed's Many Roles** 2

Your class will divide into four groups. Each group will present a skit that dramatizes one of the Federal Reserve's four main functions. Each group member will help portray a different aspect of that function. Use the following questions to develop your group's skit and your own specific role in it.

1. Which Federal Reserve function is your group portraying?
   - How the Fed serves the government
   - How the Fed serves its member banks
   - How the Fed regulates financial institutions
   - How the Fed regulates the money supply
2. What aspect of that function will you perform within your group? For example, if your group is portraying "How the Fed serves the government," your role could be "Issuing Currency." ______________
3. How will you act out and explain your role? Will you perform your part alone or work with another group member? For example, if your role is "Issuing Currency," you could portray a printing press, and another actor could portray a dollar bill. ______________
4. What simple costumes or props might help your group members portray the different aspects of its Fed function? ______________

Questions to Think About

Directions: After you have planned your skit, answer the following questions. Use complete sentences.

5. Why is your group's Federal Reserve function important? ______________
6. Why is your particular role important? What would happen if the Fed did not perform this role? ______________

L2 Differentiate Distribute "The Fed's Many Roles" worksheet (Unit 6 All-in-One, p. 110).

Answers

Graph Skills 1. two days 2. supervises lending practices and serves as the lender of last resort

Checkpoint maintains the Treasury Department's checking account; serves as financial agent for the Treasury and other government agencies; auctions off bonds, bills, and notes; and issues currency

Figure 16.3 The Path of a Check

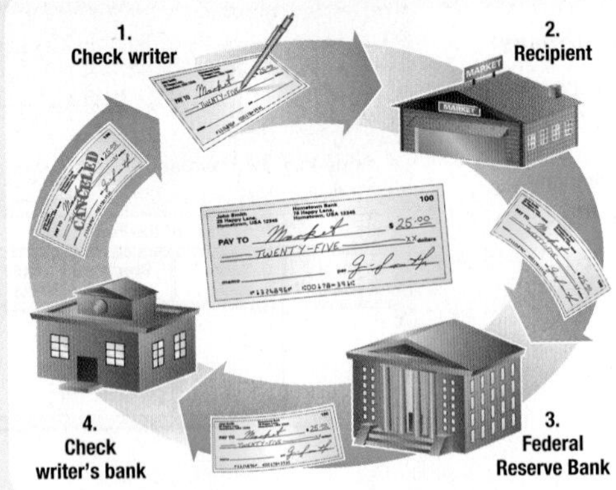

GRAPH SKILLS

When you receive a check, you present it at a bank. The check is then sent to a Federal Reserve Bank, which collects the necessary funds from the bank of the person who wrote the check.

1. How long does it generally take for checks to clear?
2. In what other ways does the Fed serve banks?

The Federal Reserve also serves as a financial agent for the Treasury Department and other government agencies. The Fed sells, transfers, and redeems securities such as government bonds, bills, and notes. It also makes interest payments on these securities.

The Treasury Department auctions off government bills, bonds, and notes to finance the many programs of the U.S. government. Funds raised from these auctions are automatically deposited into the Federal Reserve Bank of New York.

Issuing Currency

Only the federal government can issue currency. The Treasury Department issues coins minted at the United States Mint. The district Federal Reserve Banks issue paper currency (Federal Reserve Notes). As bills become worn out or torn, the Fed takes them out of circulation and replaces them with fresh ones.

check clearing the process by which banks record whose account gives up money and whose account receives money when a customer writes a check

bank holding company a company that owns more than one bank

CHECKPOINT ***How does the Fed serve as the government's banker?***

Serving Banks

The Federal Reserve also provides services to banks throughout the nation. It clears checks, safeguards bank resources, and lends funds to help banks that need to borrow in order to maintain their legally required reserves.

Check Clearing

Figure 16.3 shows how checks "clear" within the Fed system. **Check clearing** is the process by which banks record whose account gives up money and whose account receives money when a customer writes a check. The Fed can clear millions of checks at any one time using high-speed equipment. Most checks clear within two days—a remarkable achievement when you consider that the Fed processes about 18 billion checks per year.

Supervising Lending Practices

To ensure stability, the Federal Reserve monitors bank reserves throughout the banking system. Each of the 12 Federal Reserve Banks sends out bank examiners to check up on lending and other financial activities of member banks. The Board of Governors also approves or disapproves proposed bank mergers.

The Board studies proposed bank mergers and bank holding company charters to ensure competition in the banking and financial industries. A **bank holding company** is a company that owns more than one bank. The Board of Governors approves or disapproves mergers and charters based on the findings and recommendations of the Reserve Banks.

The Federal Reserve also protects consumers by enforcing truth-in-lending laws, which require sellers to provide full and accurate information about loan terms. Under a provision called Regulation Z, consumers receive useful information about retail credit terms, automobile loans, and home mortgages.

Lender of Last Resort

Under normal circumstances, banks lend each other money on a day-to-day basis, using money from their reserve balances.

Differentiated Resources

L1 L2 Guided Reading and Review (Unit 6 All-in-One, p. 108)

L2 The Fed's Many Roles (Unit 6 All-in-One, p. 110)

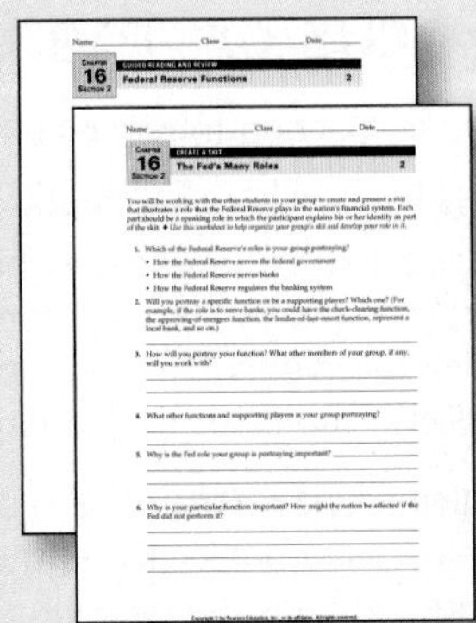

These funds are called federal funds. The interest rate that banks charge each other for these loans is the **federal funds rate.**

Banks also borrow from the Federal Reserve, especially in financial emergencies such as recessions. The Fed acts as a lender of last resort, making emergency loans to commercial banks so that they can maintain required reserves. The rate the Federal Reserve charges for these loans is called the **discount rate.** You will read more about the discount rate in Section 3.

An Expanded Role

As you read in Chapter 10, a serious financial crisis erupted in 2008. It began because many banks had made home loans that borrowers were unable to repay. As the crisis deepened, corporations and other borrowers could not obtain loans from banks, and the financial system ceased to function effectively.

The Federal Reserve responded to the crisis by expanding its function as lender of last resort. It began auctioning large amounts of reserves to banks and providing funds to financial institutions. It also announced that it would purchase short-term debt of corporations and began a program to extend loans to money market funds which had come under financial pressure. All these programs were designed to restore confidence in the financial system so that lenders would resume full participation in the market.

CHECKPOINT ***How does the Fed protect consumers who take out bank loans?***

Regulating the Banking System

Banks, savings and other financial institutions are supervised by a number of state and federal authorities. The Fed coordinates all these regulatory activities.

Reserves

As you read in Chapter 10, United States banks operate under a fractional reserve system. Banks hold in reserve only a fraction of their funds—just enough to meet customers' daily needs. Banks then lend their remaining funds, charging interest to earn returns.

Each financial institution that holds deposits for customers must report daily to the Fed about its reserves and activities. The Fed uses these reserves to control how much money is in circulation.

Bank Examinations

The Federal Reserve and other regulatory agencies also examine banks periodically to insure that each institution is obeying laws and regulations. Examiners may make unexpected bank visits to ensure that banks are following sound lending practices.

Bank examiners can force banks to sell risky investments or to declare loans that will not be repaid as losses. If examiners find that a bank has taken excessive

federal funds rate the interest rate that banks charge each other for loans

discount rate the interest rate that the Federal Reserve charges commercial banks for loans

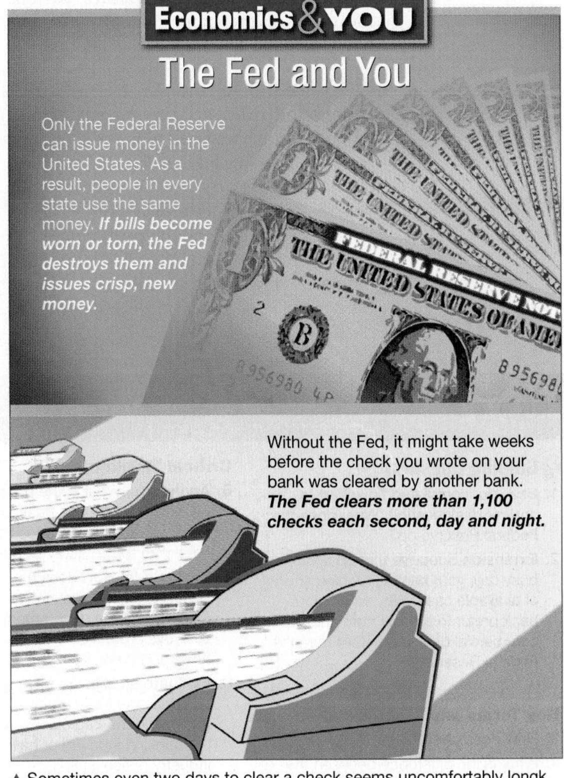

Economics & YOU
The Fed and You
Only the Federal Reserve can issue money in the United States. As a result, people in every state use the same money. *If bills become worn or torn, the Fed destroys them and issues crisp, new money.*
Without the Fed, it might take weeks before the check you wrote on your bank was cleared by another bank. *The Fed clears more than 1,100 checks each second, day and night.*

▲ Sometimes even two days to clear a check seems uncomfortably longk ***What would happen to commerce and industry if it took all checks a month to clear?***

DISCUSS THE ROLE PLAY

After each group has presented its skit, have each student explain why his or her function is important, and have the group answer any questions students have. When all groups have presented their skits, ask **What functions overlapped between groups?** *(the role of bank examiners who check up on the financial practices of banks)* Ask **Are some functions more important than others?** Have students justify their responses.

Ask **What other important role does the Fed have?** *(regulating the money supply)* Tell students that they will learn more in the next section about how the Fed does this.

EXTEND

Have students write a paragraph explaining how one of the functions or activities of the Federal Reserve affects their own life.

GUIDING QUESTION WRAP UP

Have students return to the section Guiding Question. Review the completed graphic organizer and clarify any misunderstandings. Have a wrap-up discussion about the functions of the Federal Reserve.

Assess and Remediate

L3 L2 Collect "The Fed's Many Roles" worksheets and assess students' understanding of the Fed's various roles.

L3 Assign the Section 2 Assessment questions; identify student misconceptions.

L3 Give Section Quiz A (Unit 6 All-in-One, p. 111).

L2 Give Section Quiz B (Unit 6 All-in-One, p. 112).

(Assess and Remediate continued on p. 428)

Virtual Economics

L2 Differentiate

Exploring How Banks Create Money
Use the following lesson from the NCEE **Virtual Economics *CD-ROM*** to help students understand how banks affect the money supply. Click on Browse Economics Lessons, specify grades 9–12, and use the key words *money and.*

In this activity, students will take part in a simulation that illustrates how banks create money and affect the money supply.

LESSON TITLE	MONEY AND MONETARY POLICY
Type of Activity	Simulation
Complexity	Moderate
Time	60 minutes
NCEE Standards	10, 20

Answers

Checkpoint It sends examiners to monitor banks' lending and other financial practices.

Economics and You Possible response: Some businesses would close because they could not wait the additional month to meet their expenses.

Have students complete the Self-Test Online and continue their work in the **Essential Questions Journal**.

REMEDIATION AND SUGGESTIONS

Use the chart below to help students who are struggling with content.

WEAKNESS	REMEDIATION
Defining key terms (Questions 3, 4, 5)	Have students use the interactive Economic Dictionary Online.
How the Federal Reserve serves the federal government (Questions 1, 4, 6)	Have students work in pairs, outlining the material under Serving Government.
How the Federal Reserve serves banks (Questions 1, 2, 3, 7)	Reteach the concepts of check clearing (using Figure 16.3), truth-in-lending laws, and lender of last resort.
How the Federal Reserve regulates the banking system (Questions 1, 7, 8)	Use the graphic organizer to review this Fed role.
The Federal Reserve's role in regulating the money supply (Questions 1, 4, 9, 10)	Have students write five questions about how the Fed regulates the money supply. Have them exchange questions and write answers.

Answer

Checkpoint to make sure banks are following sound lending practices

Checkpoint Too much money in circulation leads to inflation.

risks, they may classify that institution as a problem bank and force it to undergo more frequent examinations.

CHECKPOINT ***Why does the Federal Reserve examine banks?***

Regulating the Money Supply

The Federal Reserve is best known for its role in regulating the nation's money supply. You will recall from Chapter 10 that economists and the Fed watch several indicators of the money supply. M1 is simply a measure of the funds that are easily accessible or in circulation. M2 includes the funds counted in M1 as well as money market accounts and savings instruments. The Fed compares various measures of the money supply with the likely demand for money.

The Demand for Money

People and firms need to have a certain amount of cash on hand to make economic transactions—to buy groceries, supplies, clothing, and so forth. The more of your wealth you hold as money, the easier it will be to make economic transactions.

Of course, we can't earn interest on money that we hold as cash. As interest rates rise, it becomes more expensive to hold money as cash rather than placing it in assets that pay returns. So, as interest rates rise, people and firms will generally keep their wealth in assets such as bonds, stocks, or savings accounts.

The final factor that influences money demand is the general level of income. As GDP or real income rises, families and firms keep more of their wealth or income in cash.

Stabilizing the Economy

The laws of supply and demand affect money, just as they affect everything else in the economy. Too much money in the economy leads to inflation. In inflationary times, it takes more money to purchase the same goods and services. It is the Fed's job to keep the money supply stable.

Ideally, if real GDP grew smoothly and the economy stayed at full employment, the Fed would increase the money supply just to match the growth in the demand for money, thus keeping inflation low. As you read in Chapter 15, however, it is hard to predict economic effects. In the next section, you will read about the tools that the Fed can use to help the economy function at full employment without contributing to inflation.

CHECKPOINT ***What is the effect of too much money in circulation?***

SECTION 2 ASSESSMENT

Essential Questions Journal To continue to build a response to the Essential Question, go to your **Essential Questions Journal.**

Guiding Question

1. Use your completed flowchart to answer this question: What does the Federal Reserve do?
2. **Extension** Suppose that on a very busy day, your bank is running short of available cash. Why would your bank prefer to borrow from another commercial bank instead of from the Federal Reserve?

Key Terms and Main Ideas

3. How does **check clearing** work?
4. What is the difference between the **federal funds rate** and the **discount rate**?
5. How is net worth calculated?

Critical Thinking

6. **Analyze (a)** What is the purpose of auctions held by the Treasury? **(b)** What relationship does the Fed have with the Treasury Department?
7. **Evaluate (a)** How does the Federal Reserve protect consumers? **(b)** Should state governments take over this protection instead of the Federal Reserve?
8. **Evaluate (a)** What regulatory activities does the Fed coordinate? **(b)** Should the Fed closely oversee the banking industry or have the industry police itself?
9. **Infer (a)** How do the laws of supply and demand affect money? **(b)** Why can't the Fed automatically maintain full employment and low inflation?

Math Skills

10. **Calculating Incentives for Saving** How do interest rates determine the rate at which people keep their savings in bank deposits? **(a)** Which of the following interest rates would encourage savings rather than spending: 2 percent or 4 percent? Explain your answer. **(b)** How do savings of $500 at a 4 percent interest rate compare with savings of $1,000 at 2 percent? Explain how you calculated your answer.

Visit PearsonSuccessNet.com for additional math help.

Assessment Answers

1. serves government as its banker and financial agent and issues currency; serves banks by clearing checks and acting as a lender of last resort; regulates banks; and regulates the money supply
2. It is probably faster and easier to borrow from a local bank. The Fed is generally used for more serious long-term needs.
3. The bank of the person to whom the check was written sends the check to the Federal Reserve, which collects the funds from the bank of the person who wrote the check.
4. federal funds rate—rate banks charge each other for loans; discount rate—rate the Fed charges banks for loans
5. subtracting liabilities from total assets
6. (a) to sell government securities in order to raise money to finance government programs (b) It maintains the Treasury's checking account and serves as its financial agent.
7. (a) by making sure that banks follow laws (b) Possible response: No: many transactions occur between banks in different states.
8. (a) monitoring bank reserves and bank activities (b) Possible response: Yes: no such oversight resulted in bank failures.
9. (a) When there is a lot of a good, the price is lower; when there is a little, the price is higher. (b) Because real GDP does not grow smoothly, the economy does not stay at full employment, and it is hard to predict economic effects; the Fed cannot just automatically increase the money supply to match the demand.
10. (a) 4 percent because a higher return would provide a greater incentive to save (b) If compounded annually, the interest earned after one year is the same: $20. However, starting at the end of the second year, the amount of interest earned at 4 percent interest is higher than at 2 percent interest.

Monetary Policy Tools

OBJECTIVES

1. **Describe** the process of money creation.
2. **Explain** how the Federal Reserve uses reserve requirements, the discount rate, and open market operations to implement monetary policy.
3. **Explain** why the Fed favors one monetary policy tool over the others.

ECONOMIC DICTIONARY

As you read the section, look for the definitions of these **Key Terms:**

- money creation
- required reserve ratio
- money multiplier formula
- excess reserves
- prime rate
- open market operations

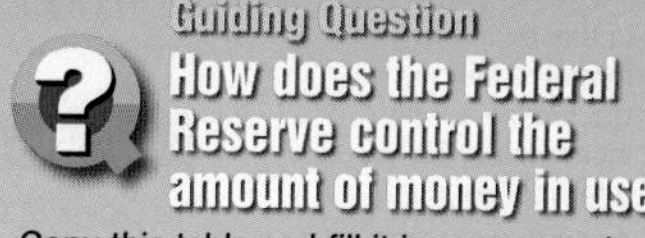

Guiding Question

How does the Federal Reserve control the amount of money in use?

Copy this table and fill it in as you read.

Controlling the Money Supply		
Tools	To increase it	To decrease it
Reserve requirements		
Discount rate		
Open market operations		

Economics and You Suppose you have a checkbook that allows you to write as many checks as you wish for any amount you desire. You don't need to worry about the balance in your account, and the checks will always be cashed, no matter how much you spend. Of course, no person has an account like that. However, the Federal Reserve, through its monetary policy tools, comes close.

money creation the process by which money enters into circulation

Principles in Action The Federal Reserve has the power to create money. It also has the power to decrease the amount of money in the United States. The Fed controls the amount of money in use in order to stabilize the American economy. How does the Federal Reserve control the amount of money in use? You will read how in this section.

Money Creation

The U.S. Department of the Treasury is responsible for manufacturing money in the form of currency. The Federal Reserve is responsible for putting money into circulation. How does this money get into the economy? The process is called **money creation,** and it is carried out by the Fed and by banks all around the country. Recall from Chapter 15 the multiplier effect of government spending. The multiplier effect in fiscal policy holds that every one dollar change in fiscal policy creates a change greater than one dollar in the economy. The process of money creation works in much the same way.

How Banks Create Money

Money creation does not mean the printing of new bills. Banks create money not by printing it, but by simply going about their business.

For example, suppose you take out a loan of $1,000. You decide to deposit the money in a checking account. Once you have deposited the money, you now have a balance of $1,000. Since demand deposit account balances, such as your checking account, are included in

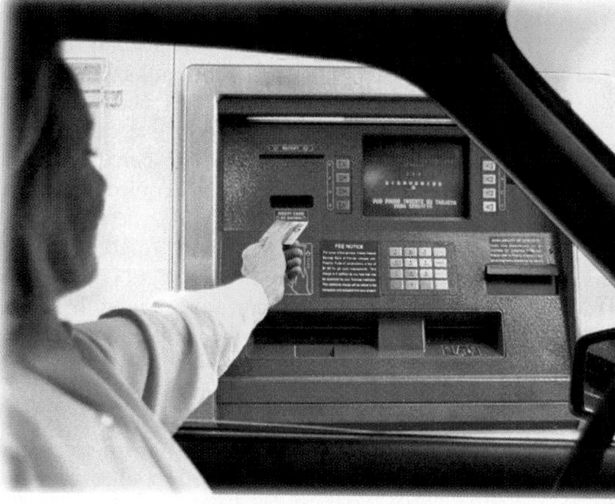

▲ When you deposit money in the bank, you are not only increasing your net worth, you are also increasing the money supply of the United States. ***Explain how your deposit begins the process of money creation.***

Guiding Question

How does the Federal Reserve control the amount of money in use?

Get Started

Controlling the Money Supply		
Tools	To increase it	To decrease it
Reserve requirements	Lower reserve requirements	Raise reserve requirements
Discount rate	Lower discount rate	Raise discount rate
Open market operations	Buy government securities	Sell government securities

LESSON GOALS

Students will:

- Know the Key Terms.
- Explain and apply the process of money creation by completing a worksheet.
- Demonstrate an understanding of the Federal Reserve's various monetary policy tools through participation in class discussion.

BEFORE CLASS

Students should read the section for homework before coming to class.

Have students complete the graphic organizer in the Section Opener as they read the text. As an alternate activity, have students complete the Guided Reading and Review worksheet (Unit 6 All-in-One, p. 113).

L1 L2 ELL LPR Differentiate Have students complete the Guided Reading and Review worksheet (Unit 6 All-in-One, p. 114).

Answer

Caption Possible response: The bank will hold a percentage of my deposit in reserve and loan out the remainder.

CLASSROOM HINTS

UNDERSTAND OPEN MARKET OPERATIONS

Some students may have trouble understanding open market operations. To help them visualize this concept conduct an activity. Use pieces of green paper to represent dollars, and colored paper to represent Treasury bills, Treasury notes, and Treasury bonds. Act out with the class what happens when the Federal Reseve conducts open market operations.

Focus on the Basics

Students need to come away with the following understandings:

FACTS: • Banks create money by making loans. • The amount of money created is limited by the money multiplier formula, which is determined by banks' reserve requirements. • The reserve requirement is the percentage of a bank's deposits that it must keep in reserve. • The discount rate and the federal funds rate affect the interest rate that banks charge for making loans. • Open market operations, in which the Fed buys or sells government securities, is the Fed's most important and most used monetary policy tool.

GENERALIZATION: The Federal Reserve uses reserve requirements, the discount rate, and open market operations as monetary policy tools to regulate the nation's money supply.

BELLRINGER

Write the following on the board: Reread *How the Economy Works* on pages 266–267. Has the money supply increased as a result of Don's $10,000 deposit into his bank account? If so, explain why and by how much. Write your answer in your notebook.

Teach

Economics online To present this topic using digital resources, use the lecture notes on www.PearsonSuccessNet.com.

DISCUSS THE BELLRINGER

Have students discuss their answers. **What is this process called?** *(money creation)* **Who creates money?** *(banks, including the Federal Reserve)* **How does the Federal Reserve influence this process?** *(Possible answer: It sets the required reserve ratio.)*

L2 Differentiate Work through the example of money creation in Figure 16.4.

DISTRIBUTE ACTIVITY WORKSHEET

Define and illustrate how the money multiplier formula is used. Then distribute the "Making Money" activity worksheet (Unit 6 All-in-One, p. 115).

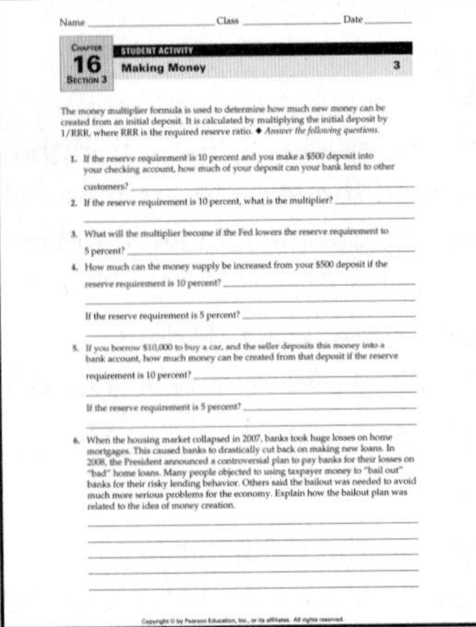

Name ______ Class ______ Date ______

Chapter 16 Section 3 — STUDENT ACTIVITY — **Making Money** 3

The money multiplier formula is used to determine how much new money can be created from an initial deposit. It is calculated by multiplying the initial deposit by 1/RRR, where RRR is the required reserve ratio. ◆ *Answer the following questions.*

1. If the reserve requirement is 10 percent and you make a $500 deposit into your checking account, how much of your deposit can your bank lend to other customers? ______
2. If the reserve requirement is 10 percent, what is the multiplier? ______
3. What will the multiplier become if the Fed lowers the reserve requirement to 5 percent? ______
4. How much can the money supply be increased from your $500 deposit if the reserve requirement is 10 percent? ______

   If the reserve requirement is 5 percent? ______
5. If you borrow $10,000 to buy a car, and the seller deposits this money into a bank account, how much money can be created from that deposit if the reserve requirement is 10 percent? ______

   If the reserve requirement is 5 percent? ______
6. When the housing market collapsed in 2007, banks took huge losses on home mortgages. This caused banks to drastically cut back on making new loans. In 2008, the President announced a controversial plan to pay banks for their losses on "bad" home loans. Many people objected to using taxpayer money to "bail out" banks for their risky lending behavior. Others said the bailout was needed to avoid much more serious problems for the economy. Explain how the bailout plan was related to the idea of money creation.

L2 Differentiate Distribute "Making Money" worksheet (Unit 6 All-in-One, p. 116). Have students work together on the calculations.

When students have completed the activity, ask **Why do you think the Fed prefers to use other methods besides changing the reserve requirement to manage the nation's money supply?** *(A small change to the multiplier leads to a substantial expansion—or contraction—of the money supply.)*

Answers

Chart Skills 1. 10 percent 2. $1,000 + $900 + $450 = $2,350

Figure 16.4 Money Creation

CHART SKILLS

In this example of money creation, the money supply increases to $2,710 after four rounds.

1. In this example, what is the RRR?
2. Suppose Joshua deposited only $500 of Elaine's payment into his account. How much would the money supply increase then?

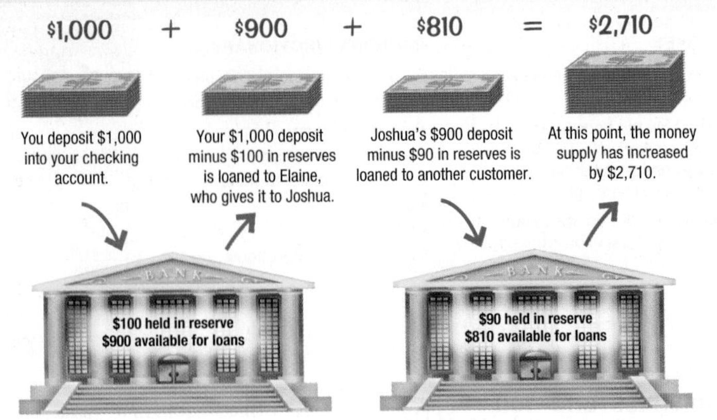

$1,000 + $900 + $810 = $2,710
You deposit $1,000 into your checking account.
Your $1,000 deposit minus $100 in reserves is loaned to Elaine, who gives it to Joshua.
Joshua's $900 deposit minus $90 in reserves is loaned to another customer.
At this point, the money supply has increased by $2,710.
BANK
$100 held in reserve
$900 available for loans
BANK
$90 held in reserve
$810 available for loans

Simulation Activity

Money and the Federal Reserve
You may be asked to participate in a role-playing game about Money and the Federal Reserve.

M1, the money supply has now increased by $1,000. The process of money creation begins here.

Banks make money by charging interest on loans. Your bank will lend part of the $1,000 that you deposited. The maximum amount that a bank can lend is determined by the **required reserve ratio** (RRR)—the fraction of deposits that banks are required to keep in reserve. This is calculated as the ratio of reserves to deposits. The RRR, which is established by the Federal Reserve, ensures that banks will have enough funds to supply customers' withdrawal needs.

Suppose in our example that the RRR is 0.1, or 10 percent. This means that the bank is required to keep 10 percent of your $1,000 demand deposit balance, or $100, in reserve. It is allowed to lend $900.

required reserve ratio the fraction of deposits that banks are required to keep in reserve

Let's say the bank lends that $900 to Elaine, and she deposits it in her checking account. Elaine now has $900 she didn't have before. Elaine's $900 is now included in M1. You still have your $1,000 in your account, on which you can write a check at any time. Thus, your initial deposit to the bank, and the subsequent loan, have caused the money supply to increase by $1,000 + $900 for a total of $1,900.

money multiplier formula a formula (initial cash deposit × 1 ÷ RRR) used to determine how much new money can be created with each demand deposit and added to the money supply

Now suppose that Elaine uses the $900 to buy Joshua's old car. Joshua deposits the $900 from Elaine into his checking account. His bank keeps 10 percent of the deposit, or $90, as required reserves. It will lend the other $810 to its customers. So, Joshua has a demand deposit balance of $900, which is included in the money supply, and the new borrowers get $810, which is also added to the money supply. This means that the money supply has now increased by $1,000 + $900 + $810 = $2,710—all because of your initial $1,000 deposit. **Figure 16.4** shows how this increase came about.

The Money Multiplier

This money creation process will continue until the loan amount, and hence the amount of new money that can be created, becomes very small. To determine the total amount of new money that can be created and added to the money supply, economists use the **money multiplier formula,** which is calculated as 1 ÷ RRR. To apply the formula, they multiply the initial deposit by the money multiplier:

Increase in money supply = initial cash deposit × 1/RRR

In our example the RRR is 0.1, so the money multiplier is 1 ÷ 0.1 = 10. This means

Differentiated Resources

- **L1 L2 Guided Reading and Review** (Unit 6 All-in-One, p. 114)
- **L2 Making Money** (Unit 6 All-in-One, p. 116)
- **L4 You Be the Fed** (Unit 6 All-in-One, p. 117)
- **L3 Money and the Federal Reserve** (Simulation Activities, Chapter 16)

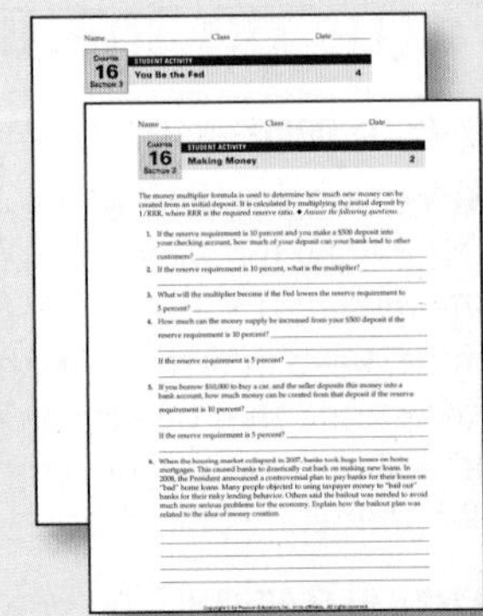

that the deposit of $1,000 can lead to a $10,000 increase in the money supply.

As of 2008 in the United States, banks had no reserve requirement on the first $9.3 million of demand deposit assets. They were required to hold 3 percent reserves on demand deposit assets between $9.3 million and $43.9 million, and 10 percent on all demand deposit assets exceeding $43.9 million.

In the real world, however, people hold some cash outside of the banking system, meaning that some funds leak out of the money multiplier process. Also, banks sometimes hold **excess reserves,** which are reserves greater than the required amounts. These excess reserves ensure that banks will always be able to meet their customers' demands and the Fed's reserve requirements. The actual money multiplier effect in the United States is estimated to be between 2 and 3.

The Federal Reserve has three tools for adjusting the amount of money in the economy. These tools for creating money (or destroying it, if need be) are reserve requirements, the discount rate, and open market operations.

CHECKPOINT ***How do banks create money simply by going about their business making loans?***

Reserve Requirements

The simplest way for the Fed to adjust the amount of reserves in the banking system is to change the required reserve ratio. (See **Figure 16.5.**) The Fed's Board of Governors has sole responsibility over changes in reserve requirements. However, changing the reserve requirement is not the Fed's preferred tool.

A reduction of the RRR frees up reserves for banks, allowing them to make more loans. It also increases the money multiplier. Both effects will lead to a substantial expansion of the money supply.

The process also works in reverse. Even a slight increase in the RRR forces banks to hold more money in reserves. This causes a contraction in the money supply.

Although changing reserve requirements can be an effective means of changing the money supply, the Fed does not use this tool often because it is disruptive to the banking system. Even a small increase in the RRR would force banks to call in significant numbers of loans, that is, to require the borrower to pay the entire outstanding balance of the loan. This may be difficult for the borrower. For this reason, the Fed rarely changes reserve requirements.

CHECKPOINT ***What effect would a reduction in the required reserve rate (RRR) have on banks?***

The Discount Rate

In the past, the Fed lowered or raised the discount rate to increase or decrease the money supply. Recall that the discount rate is the interest rate that the Federal Reserve charges on loans to financial institutions. Today, the discount rate is primarily used to ensure that sufficient funds are available in the economy. For example, during a financial crisis, there may not be enough funds available in the banking system to

excess reserves bank reserves greater than the amount required by the Federal Reserve

Figure 16.5 **Reserve Requirements**

Reserve Requirement
An increase in reserve requirements causes banks to increase reserves.

Money Supply
Banks reduce lending, causing the money supply to contract.

Reserve Requirement
A reduction in reserve requirements causes banks to decrease reserves.

Money Supply
Banks increase lending, causing the money supply to expand.

CHART SKILLS

Reducing and increasing reserve requirements directly affects the money supply.

1. What is the effect of reducing reserve requirements?
2. What action of the Fed with respect to reserve requirements causes the money supply to decrease?

APPLY

Divide the class into groups of two or three. Assign each group one of the following: (a) The Fed lowers the reserve requirement. (b) The Fed raises the reserve requirement. (c) The Fed lowers the discount rate. (d) The Fed raises the discount rate. (e) The Fed lowers the federal funds rate. (f) The Fed raises the federal funds rate. (g) The FOMC sells government securities. (h) The FOMC buys government securities. Ask each group to consult and answer the question: **What would the effects be if the Fed took this action?** Have each group explain its answer. If more than one group has been assigned to the same action, have them compare answers and discuss if their answers disagree. After all groups have shared their answers, ask **What is the difference between the discount rate and the federal funds rate?** *(discount rate: interest rate that Fed charges on loans it makes to banks; fed funds rate: interest rate that banks charge each other for loans)* **What do the discount rate, federal funds rate, and prime rate have in common?** *(They are short-term rates, which have limited impact on the long-term growth of the economy.)* **What are the advantages of the Fed using open market operations to control the amount of money in the economy?** *(Open market operations allow for making finer adjustments and do not cause banks to drastically change their lending plans.*

L1 L2 ELL LPR Differentiate Have pairs of students make flash cards, and drill each other on the meaning of reserve requirements, discount rate, federal funds rate, and open market operations. Have them order their cards from most-often used to least-often used tools utilized to adjust the money supply. Have each pair explain their ranking.

L1 L2 Differentiate Use the lesson on the Visual Glossary page to review the tools of fiscal policy.

(lesson continued on p. 433)

Virtual Economics

L4 Differentiate

Using Balance Sheets Use the following lesson from the NCEE **Virtual Economics *CD-ROM*** to use balance sheets to analyze actions of the Federal Reserve. Click on Browse Economics Lessons, specify grades 9–12, and use the key words *its tools.*

In this activity, students will complete balance sheets to evaluate the impact of actions by the Federal Reserve.

LESSON TITLE	**THE FEDERAL RESERVE SYSTEM AND ITS TOOLS**
Type of Activity	Using statistics
Complexity	Low
Time	45 minutes
NCEE Standards	20

Answers

Checkpoint Once a loan is used to pay for a good or service, and the seller of the good or service deposits this money into a bank account, the money that is not required to be held by that bank can be loaned out.

Checkpoint They could lend and create more money.

Chart Skills 1. an increase in the money supply 2. an increase in the reserve requirement

Teach Case Study

SUMMARIZE AND EXPLAIN

Call on the students to summarize the case study. Ask **What is the main idea of the study?** *(Because of the credit crunch, auto loan terms have gotten tougher, particularly for subprime borrowers and consumers who live in areas where home prices are dropping. This has made it more difficult, if not impossible, for some consumers to buy cars.)* Have students find details in the case study to support this summary. **What interest rates can the Federal Reserve change?** *(the discount rate; while it doesn't set the federal funds rate, it can take steps to reach a target level for that rate)* **Why might the Fed have cut interest rates?** *(According to the article, fewer loans have been available to consumers.)* Have students speculate about why consumers are having a harder time finding attractive terms on auto loans, in spite of interest-rate cuts by the Federal Reserve.

L2 Differentiate This case study contains terms, such as *credit crunch, subprime, bear the brunt,* and *collateral,* that students with limited language and reading skills might not understand. Prepare students for the reading by defining these terms.

L4 Differentiate Have each student find and summarize a current newspaper or magazine article about the credit markets. Use the articles to have a class discussion about the current availability of credit for businesses, car shoppers and home owners.

Economics online *All print resources are available on the Teacher's Resource Library CD-ROM and online at* www.PearsonSuccessNet.com.

Answer

Applying Economic Principles Possible response: larger down payments; smaller loans

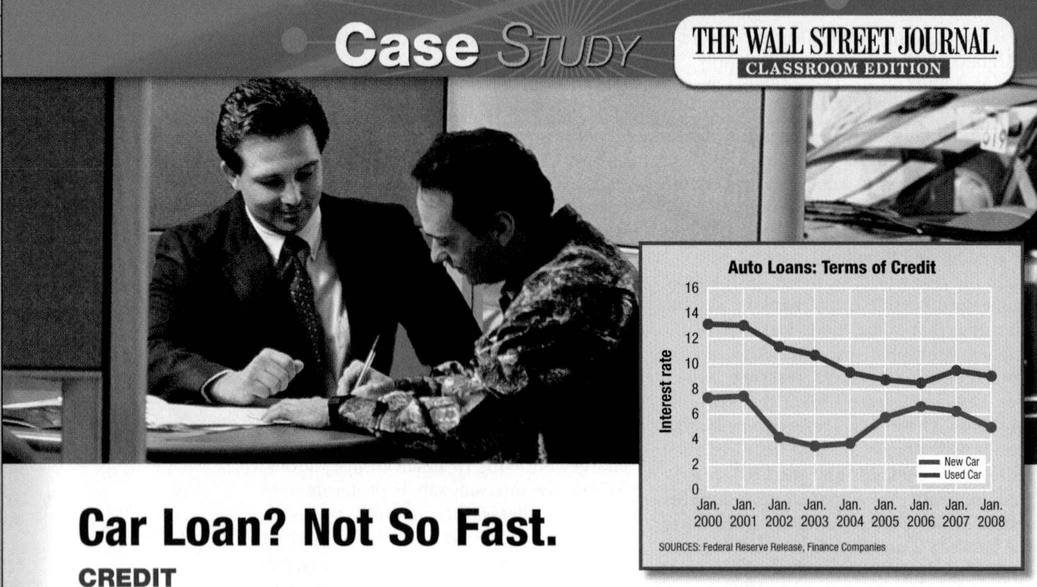

Car Loan? Not So Fast.

CREDIT

Lenders' stricter standards are making it tougher to drive off the lot.

By Eleanor Laise
The Wall Street Journal

The credit crunch, having knocked around the American home, is now rolling into the garage.

Despite interest-rate cuts by the Federal Reserve, it's getting tough for many consumers to find attractive terms on auto loans. Many lenders are making fewer loans and instituting stricter standards on loans they do approve, often requiring higher credit scores, making smaller loans and demanding bigger down payments.

While "subprime" borrowers with poor credit will bear the brunt of the shifting lending standards, even "prime" borrowers with good credit may be affected by some changes. And some consumers may not be able to get a car loan at all.

When Michael Staggs, 36, of Spring Hill, Fla., set out to buy a Dodge truck recently, he was looking for an auto loan with an interest rate below 10% and monthly payments between $250 and $300. But Mr. Staggs, an engineer who says his credit isn't bad, but not great, didn't get the terms he was banking on. He put down $1,500, and his $14,000, 72-month loan came with $298 monthly payments and a 13.5% rate. "That's a lot higher than I wanted," he says.

Not all borrowers will see tougher terms; lenders still want to gain business from prime borrowers. But some borrowers may find they can't get as large a loan as they'd like. Whereas lenders in recent years have made loans substantially exceeding the car's worth, some are now keeping loan amounts closer to the vehicle's value. Jon Garcia, finance manager at a Toyota dealership in Janesville, Wis., says he's seeing subprime lenders supply only 85% to 90% of the car's book value, down from as much as 140% previously.

And these borrowers with good credit may find tougher loan terms if they live in areas where home prices are dropping. Chase Auto Finance is requiring more collateral on longer-term loans in "high risk" states like Arizona, California and Nevada, which have been hit hard by the housing crisis.

But terms are getting especially tough for subprime borrowers. Chase Auto Finance recently boosted by 10 points the credit score required of subprime customers borrowing more than 110% of the car's value. "We're trying to lend to people who will be able to pay us back," says Thomas Kelly, a Chase spokesman.

Video News Update Online Powered by *The Wall Street Journal* Classroom Edition — For a new case study, go to the online resources at **PearsonSuccessNet.com**

Applying Economic Principles
The credit crunch of 2008 made it tough for many consumers to get a car loan. What are some of the terms that car and truck buyers whose credit rating was not prime were forced to accept in order to get loans?

provide the necessary loans to businesses and individuals. In that case, the ability of banks to borrow at the discount rate from the Federal Reserve provides an important safety net.

Today, to enact monetary policy, the Federal Reserve primarily adjusts the federal funds rate, which is the interest rate that banks charge one another for loans. It does not actually *set* a new federal funds rate, however. Instead, it decides on a "target" level for the rate and then takes steps to reach that target. These steps are part of the Fed's open market operations, which you will read about shortly.

The Fed does set the discount rate, and it keeps this rate above the federal funds rate. Banks usually choose to borrow from one another at the funds rate. Only if they need additional reserves will they turn to the Federal Reserve and borrow at the higher discount rate.

Changes in the federal funds rate and the discount rate affect the cost of borrowing to banks or other financial institutions. In turn, these changes in interest rates affect the prime rate. The **prime rate** is the rate of interest that banks charge on short-term loans to their best customers—usually large companies with good credit ratings. Ultimately, other interest rates follow, including the rates that banks pay on savings accounts and the rates that they charge for personal loans. The discount rate, federal funds rate, and prime rate are short-term rates. They determine the cost of borrowing money for a few hours, days, or months. Short-term rates have a limited impact on the long-term growth of the economy. To influence long-term interest rates, the Federal Reserve uses other tools.

CHECKPOINT ***What is the main tool that the Federal Reserve uses in order to adjust the money supply?***

Open Market Operations

Open market operations are the buying and selling of government securities in order to alter the supply of money. (See **Figure 16.6.**) Open market operations are by far the most important—and most often used—monetary policy tool.

Figure 16.6 Open Market Operations

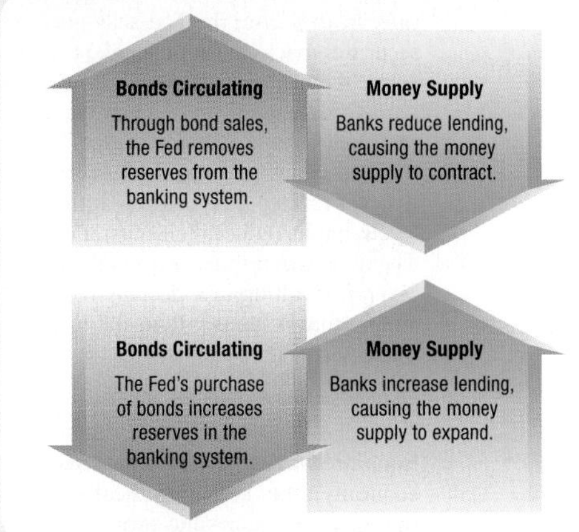

Bonds Circulating
Through bond sales, the Fed removes reserves from the banking system.
Money Supply
Banks reduce lending, causing the money supply to contract.
Bonds Circulating
The Fed's purchase of bonds increases reserves in the banking system.
Money Supply
Banks increase lending, causing the money supply to expand.

CHART SKILLS

Open market operations are the most often used monetary policy tool.

1. When the Fed sells government securities to bond dealers, does that increase or decrease the amount of money in circulation?
2. How do open market operations differ from reserve requirements?

Bond Purchases

When the Federal Open Market Committee (FOMC) chooses to increase the money supply, it orders the trading desk at the Federal Reserve Bank of New York to purchase a certain quantity of government securities on the open market. The Federal Reserve Bank buys these securities with checks drawn on Federal Reserve funds. The bond sellers then deposit the money from the bond sales into their banks. As the Federal Reserve Board explains:

> "[Now], the bank now has more reserves than it wants. So the bank can lend these unwanted reserves to another bank in the federal funds market. Thus, the Fed's open market purchase increases the supply of reserves to the banking system, and the federal funds rate falls."
>
> —"What Are Open Market Operations?" Federal Reserve Bank of San Francisco

In this way, funds enter the banking system, setting in motion the money creation process described earlier.

Personal Finance For more about the prime rate, see your Personal Finance Handbook in the back of the book or visit **PearsonSuccessNet.com**

prime rate the rate of interest that banks charge on short-term loans to their best customers

open market operations the buying and selling of government securities in order to alter the supply of money

PERSONAL FINANCE ACTIVITY

Remind students that they can get help in understanding the prime rate by reading the lesson "Building Your Portfolio" on pages PF14–15 in the Personal Finance Handbook and completing the worksheet (Personal Finance All-in-One, pp. 48–49).

CHECK COMPREHENSION

For additional practice with the role of the Federal Reserve in managing the supply of money, have students use the "Money and the Federal Reserve" activity (Simulation Activities, Chapter 16).

L4 Differentiate Have students complete the "You Be the Fed" worksheet (Unit 6 All-in-One, p. 117), in which students analyze two economic situations and decide what the Fed needs to do.

EXTEND

Have students find examples of the Federal Reserve using one of the monetary policy tools discussed in the chapter. Have them write a paragraph summarizing the Fed's action, what prompted it, and their prediction about the action's effect.

GUIDING QUESTION WRAP UP

Have students return to the section Guiding Question. Review the completed graphic organizer and clarify any misunderstandings. Have a wrap-up discussion about how the Federal Reserve controls the amount of money in use.

Assess and Remediate

L2 L3 Collect the "Making Money" worksheets and assess students' understanding of the reserve requirement and how money is created.

L4 Collect the "You Be the Fed" worksheet and assess students' understanding of different monetary policy tools.

L3 Assign the Section 3 Assessment questions; identify student misconceptions.

L3 Give Section Quiz A (Unit 6 All-in-One, p. 118).

L2 Give Section Quiz B (Unit 6 All-in-One, p. 119).

(Assess and Remediate continued on p. 434)

Background Note

The Value of Money Money serves several functions in an economy. It's a commonly accepted medium of exchange, and it provides a standard for measuring value. Money is also a store of value that can be used for later purchases. Since the 1970s, when the United States went off the gold standard, the value of money has been set solely by the amount of it in the economy. When the money supply grows faster than the rate at which goods and services are produced, the result is inflation. When the supply is scarce, the purchasing power of each dollar increases.

Answers

Checkpoint adjusting the federal funds rate through open market operations

Chart Skills 1. decrease 2. Open market operations involve the buying or selling of government securities by the Fed; if the Fed changes reserve requirements, banks must change the amount of money they hold.

Have students complete the Self-Test Online and continue their work in the **Essential Questions Journal**.

REMEDIATION AND SUGGESTIONS

Use the chart below to help students who are struggling with content.

WEAKNESS	REMEDIATION
Defining key terms (Questions 3, 4, 5, 6, 7, 8)	Have students use the interactive Economic Dictionary Online.
The process of money creation (Questions 3, 9)	Reteach Figure 16.4 using different numbers.
How the Fed uses reserve requirements, the discount rate, and open market operations in making monetary policy (Questions 1, 8, 9, 10, 11, 12)	Have students role-play the Fed, the FOMC, banks, consumers, and other players when reserve requirements and then open market operations are used to increase, then decrease, the money supply.
Why the Fed favors one monetary policy tool over the others (Question 12)	Have students outline the Reserve Requirements, Discount Rate, and Open Market Operations sections, and then explain why the Fed uses each tool as it does.

Answers

Checkpoint sells government securities to bond dealers

Checkpoint These operations can be conducted smoothly and on an ongoing basis and do not disrupt financial institutions.

Bond Sales

If the FOMC chooses to decrease the money supply, it must make an open market bond sale. In this case, the Fed sells government securities back to bond dealers, receiving from them checks drawn on their own banks. After the Fed processes these checks, the money is out of circulation. This operation reduces reserves in the banking system. In order to keep their reserves at the required levels, banks reduce their outstanding loans. The money multiplier process then works in reverse, resulting in a decline in the money supply that is greater than the value of the initial securities purchase.

Targets

To judge whether its open market operations are having the desired effect on the economy, the Fed periodically evaluates one or more economic targets. You have read about how the federal funds rate serves as the main target for interest rates. The Fed also keeps an eye on various money measures such as M1 and M2. Close analysis of these targets helps the Fed meet its goal of promoting a stable and prosperous economy.

CHECKPOINT ***What action does the Federal Open Market Committee take if it wants to decrease the money supply?***

Using Monetary Policy Tools

Open market operations are the most often used of the Federal Reserve's monetary policy tools. They can be conducted smoothly and on an ongoing basis to meet the Fed's goals. The Fed changes the discount rate less frequently. It usually follows a policy of keeping the discount rate in line with other interest rates in the economy in order to prevent excess borrowing by member banks from the Fed that might threaten economic stability.

Today, the Fed does not change reserve requirements to conduct monetary policy. Changing reserve requirements would force banks to make drastic changes in their plans. Open market operations or changes in the discount rate do not disrupt financial institutions.

In setting its monetary policy goals, the Federal Reserve keeps close touch on market forces, studying inflation and business cycles to determine its policy. As you just read, changes in the money supply affect interest rates. You will find out more about how this process works in the next section.

CHECKPOINT ***Why are open market operations the Fed's preferred monetary policy tool?***

Essential Questions Journal To continue to build a response to the Essential Question, go to your **Essential Questions Journal.**

SECTION 3 ASSESSMENT

Guiding Question

1. Use your completed table to answer this question: How does the Federal Reserve control the amount of money in use?
2. **Extension** What method do you use to be sure you have cash for necessary expenditures such as transportation and lunch? Prepare a budget for the coming month. List your expected expenses and revenue. Be sure to allow reserves for unexpected expenses.

Key Terms and Main Ideas

3. What is **money creation**?
4. What is the **required reserve ratio**?
5. Describe the **money multiplier formula.**
6. Why do banks sometimes hold **excess reserves**?
7. If the discount rate rose, would you expect the **prime rate** to rise or fall? Why?
8. What are **open market operations**?

Critical Thinking

9. **Explain (a)** How do commercial banks make money? **(b)** How does the required reserve ratio affect the amount of money they can lend?
10. **Infer (a)** When the Fed cuts interest rates, what effect does it expect to have on business and consumers? **(b)** How is the Fed influenced by market forces in making rate decisions?
11. **Describe (a)** What are three tools the Fed has for adjusting the amount of money in the economy? **(b)** Choose one of the tools and describe it.
12. **Analyze** Why do the discount rate, federal funds rate, and prime rate have a limited impact on the long-term growth of the economy?

Math Skills

13. **Calculating Money Supply** Suppose the RRR is 0.15. **(a)** Use the money multiplier formula to determine by how much a $2,000 checking account deposit will increase the money supply. **(b)** Will the money supply actually increase by the amount you calculated? Why or why not?

Visit PearsonSuccessNet.com for additional math help.

Assessment Answers

1. by changing reserve requirements, changing the discount rate, and buying or selling government securities on the open market
2. Possible response: by saving money from a part-time job; budgets will vary.
3. the way money enters into circulation
4. the percent of their deposits that the Fed requires banks to keep on hand
5. a formula to determine how much money can be created with each demand deposit
6. so they have enough cash to meet customers' demands and Fed requirements
7. to rise; When banks have to pay higher interest on money they borrow, they pass that cost on to customers.
8. the buying and selling of government securities on the open market by the Fed to change the money supply
9. (a) through interest charged on loans (b) If the ratio increases, banks have to keep more in reserve and will have less to lend. If the RRR goes down, the reverse is true.
10. (a) more borrowing since it is less expensive (b) Increasing inflation may cause the Fed to raise interest rates, reducing the amount of money, thus fighting inflation. A slowdown may cause the Fed to lower rates in order to promote economic growth.
11. (a) changing reserve requirements, changing the discount rate, buying or selling government securities on the open market (b) Possible response: Open market operations are the Fed's most used tool. These involve buying or selling government securities on the bond market. The money supply is increased when the Fed buys and contracted when the Fed sells.
12. They are interest rates on short-term loans.
13. (a) (1 ÷ 0.15) × $2,000 = $13,333 (b) Probably not, because people keep some money out of the banking system.

SECTION 4 Monetary Policy and Macroeconomic Stabilization

OBJECTIVES

1. **Explain** how monetary policy works.
2. **Describe** the problem of timing in implementing monetary policy.
3. **Explain** why the Fed's monetary policy can involve predicting business cycles.
4. **Contrast** two general approaches to monetary policy.

ECONOMIC DICTIONARY

As you read the section, look for the definitions of these **Key Terms:**

- monetarism
- easy money policy
- tight money policy
- inside lag
- outside lag

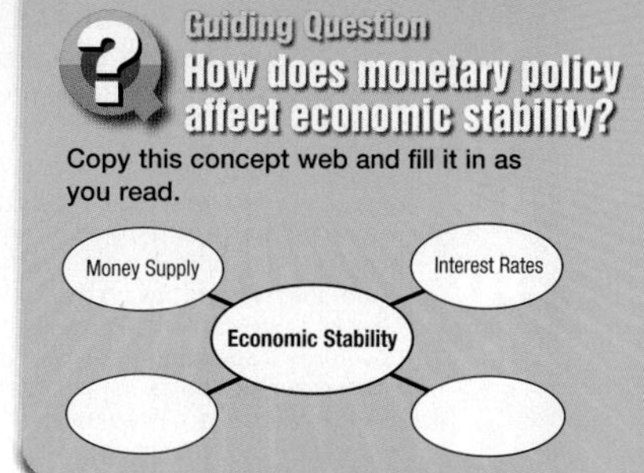

Economics and You

Have you ever asked a parent for money—a raise in your allowance, perhaps, or cash to buy concert tickets? If so, you know that timing is everything. If, for example, your parent has just paid a huge bill for home or car repairs, you know that's the wrong time to be asking for spending money.

Principles in Action As you'll see in this section, timing is also critical to the Fed. Proper timing can support the Fed's efforts to bring economic stability. Bad timing can destroy it. In the How the Economy Works feature, you will see how the Fed copes with the many factors that can make its monetary policy succeed or fail.

monetarism the belief that the money supply is the most important factor in macroeconomic performance

How Monetary Policy Works

Some economists have great faith in monetary policy. These believers in **monetarism** believe that the money supply is the most important factor in macroeconomic performance—which as you have read is the functioning of the entire economy. How, then, does monetary policy influence macroeconomic performance?

Monetary policy alters the supply of money. The supply of money, in turn, affects interest rates. As you read earlier, interest rates affect the level of investment and spending in the economy.

The Money Supply and Interest Rates

It is easy to see the cost of money if you are borrowing it. The cost—the price that you as a borrower pay—is the interest rate. Even if you spend your own money, the interest rate still affects you because you are giving up interest by not saving or investing.

The market for money is like any other market. If the supply is higher, the price—the interest rate—is lower. If the supply is lower, the price—the interest rate—is higher. In other words, when the money supply is high, interest rates are low. When the money supply is low, interest rates are high.

Interest Rates and Spending

Recall from Chapter 12 that interest rates are important factors of spending in the economy. Lower interest rates encourage greater investment spending by business firms. This is because a firm's cost of borrowing—or of using

This bank advertises the cost of borrowing for mortgages. ***How is the market for money like any other market?*** ▼

Guiding Question

How does monetary policy affect economic stability?

Get Started

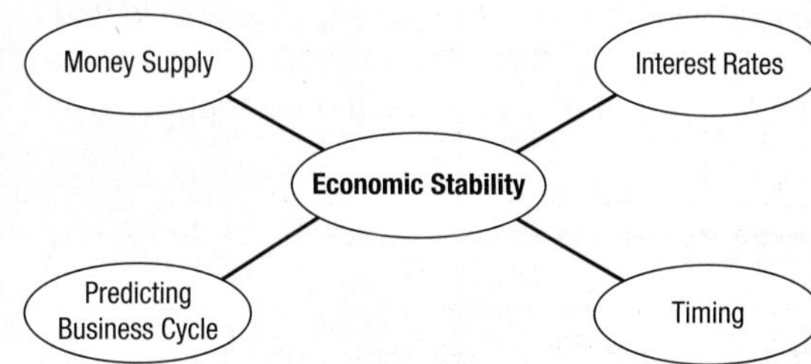

LESSON GOALS

Students will:

- Know the Key Terms.
- Demonstrate an understanding of how monetary policy works by interpreting a transparency.
- Analyze the problem of timing in implementing monetary policy by completing a worksheet.
- Assess the two approaches to monetary policy through a writing activity or by creating a cartoon.

BEFORE CLASS

Students should read the section for homework before coming to class.

Have students complete the graphic organizer in the Section Opener as they read the text. As an alternate activity, have students complete the Guided Reading and Review worksheet (Unit 6 All-in-One, p. 120).

L1 L2 ELL LPR **Differentiate** Have students complete the Guided Reading and Review worksheet (Unit 6 All-in-One, p. 121).

Focus on the Basics

Students need to come away with the following understandings:

FACTS: • Monetary policy alters the supply of money, which affects interests rates. • Lower interest rates cause investment spending and aggregate demand to rise; higher interest rates cause investment spending and aggregate demand to decline. • An easy money policy increases the amount of money in circulation; a tight money policy reduces the amount of money in circulation. • Inside lags, outside lags, and the difficulty of predicting the business cycle make the proper timing of monetary policy difficult to achieve.

GENERALIZATION: Monetary policy must be carefully timed if it is to help the macroeconomy. If implemented correctly and at the right time, monetary policy can lessen the frequency and amplitude of the fluctuations in the economy.

CLASSROOM HINTS

USE FEDERAL RESERVE CASE STUDIES

The EconEdLink (http://www.econedlink.org/) is an Internet-based source of economic lesson materials. These lessons include case studies that focus on recent announcements of the FOMC on Federal Reserve monetary policy actions and goals. Such lessons provide students with the opportunity to apply what they are learning and gain a greater understanding of what's happening in today's economy.

BELLRINGER

Write the following on the board: Read *How the Economy Works* on page 438–439, and then answer these questions:

- What would happen to the money supply if the Fed lowered the discount rate during a period of growth? What problem might this lead to?
- If you were the chair of the Fed, what would you want to know before acting to reduce or increase the amount of money in the money supply?

Teach

Economics online To present this topic using digital resources, use the lecture notes on www.PearsonSuccessNet.com.

DISCUSS BELLRINGER ANSWERS

Discuss students' responses to the Bellringer questions. Ask how students' responses to the second question might change if they knew it could take up to two years for their policies to be fully effective.

Innovators

Milton Friedman

"Mr. Friedman...never held elected office but he has had more influence on economic policy as it is practiced around the world today than any other modern figure." —*Lawrence H. Summers, former Treasury Secretary*

As economic advisor to Presidents Nixon and Reagan, Milton Friedman argued that less government is better government. The policies he recommended have lowered income tax rates, helped control inflation, and decreased unemployment. His ideas are taught in most economics textbooks today.

But that was not always the case. For the first half of the twentieth century, the ideas of John Maynard Keynes dominated economic thought. Keynes believed government spending was the key to economic health, and government should emphasize fiscal policy in managing the economy.

In sharp contrast, Friedman argued that market forces must operate freely. In the view of Friedman and other monetarists, the government, through the Federal Reserve Board, must control the supply of money available to banks. Friedman argued that the most important power of the Fed is to grow or shrink the money supply by buying or selling government securities. The differences between supply siders such as Friedman and demand siders such as Keynes are one of the most important economic issues of our times.

Critical Thinking: ***In what ways were the ideas of John Maynard Keynes at odds with those of Milton Friedman? Which economist do you think is right?***

Fast Facts

Milton Friedman
Born: 1912 in Brooklyn, NY
Died: 2006 in San Francisco, CA
Education: Ph.D., Columbia University, economics
Claim to Fame: Nobel Prize, Economic Science; Presidential Medal of Freedom

its own funds—decreases as the interest rate decreases. Higher interest rates discourage business spending.

Firms find that lower interest rates give them more opportunities for profitable investment. If a firm has to pay 15 percent interest on its loans, it may find few profitable opportunities. If interest rates fall to 6 percent, however, the firm may find that some opportunities are now profitable.

If the macroeconomy is experiencing a contraction—declining income—the Federal Reserve may want to stimulate, or expand, it. The Fed will follow an **easy money policy.** That is, it will increase the money supply. An increased money supply will lower interest rates, thus encouraging investment spending. Such a policy may, however, encourage overborrowing and overinvestment, followed by layoffs and cutbacks.

If the economy is experiencing a rapid expansion that may cause high inflation, the Fed may introduce a **tight money policy.** That is, it will reduce the money supply. The Fed reduces the money supply to push interest rates upward. By raising interest rates, the Fed causes investment spending to decline. This brings real GDP down, too.

easy money policy a monetary policy that increases the money supply

tight money policy a monetary policy that reduces the money supply

Even though it can only alter the money supply, the Fed has a great impact on the economy. The money supply determines the interest rate, and the interest rate determines the level of aggregate demand. Recall from Chapter 12 that aggregate demand represents the relationship between price levels and quantity demanded in the overall economy. Thus, the level of aggregate demand helps determine the level of real GDP.

CHECKPOINT ***How are monetary policy, money supply, and interest rates connected?***

The Problem of Timing

Monetary policy, like fiscal policy, must be carefully timed if it is to help the macroeconomy. If policies are enacted at the wrong time, they could actually intensify the business cycle, rather than stabilize it. To see why, consider **Figure 16.7**.

Good Timing

Figure 16.7A shows the business cycle with a properly timed stabilization policy. The green curve, which shows greater

Answers

Innovators Keynes argued that government spending was the key to economic health, and government should emphasize fiscal policy in managing the economy. Friedman argued for less government rather than more government, that market forces must operate freely, and that the government, through the Fed, must control the supply of money through open market operations. Student opinions on who was right will vary.

Checkpoint An easy money policy increases the money supply and lowers interest rates. A tight money policy shrinks the money supply and raises interest rates.

Differentiated Resources

- L1 L2 **Guided Reading and Review** (Unit 6 All-in-One, p. 121)
- L2 **Steering the Economy** (Unit 6 All-in-One, p. 123)
- L4 **FOMC Role-Play** (Unit 6 All-in-One, p. 124)

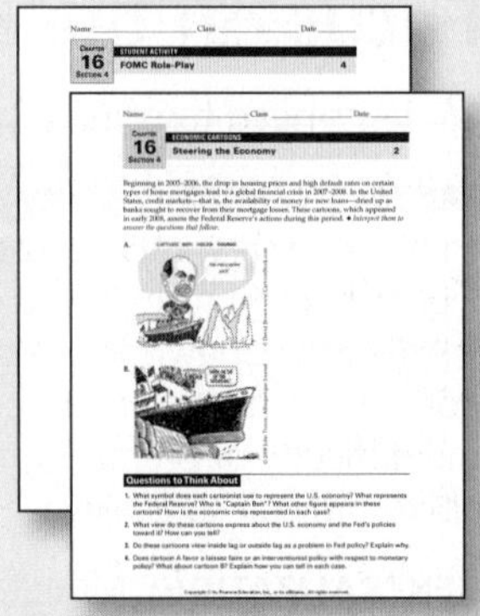

fluctuations, is the business cycle as explained in Chapter 12. The goal of stabilization policy is to smooth out those fluctuations—in other words, to make the peaks a little bit lower and the troughs not quite so deep. This will minimize inflation in the peaks and the effects of recessions in the troughs. Properly timed stabilization policy smoothes out the business cycle, as shown by the red curve in **Figure 16.7A.**

Bad Timing

If stabilization policy is not timed properly, however, it can actually make the business cycle worse, not better. For example, suppose that policymakers are slow to recognize the contraction shown as the green line in **Figure 16.7B.** Perhaps because their data are inaccurate, government economists simply do not realize that a contraction is occurring until the economy is deeply into it. Some period of time may pass before they respond to the contraction.

Likewise, it takes time to enact expansionary policies and have those policies take effect. By the time this takes place, the economy may already be coming out of the recession on its own. If the expansionary effects of an easy money policy boost the economy while it is already expanding, the result could be an even larger expansion that causes high inflation. If expansionary policies are enacted too late, the economy may have slowed down so much that businesses are reluctant to borrow at *any* rate for new investment.

As you can see, there are a couple of problems in the timing of macroeconomic policy. These are called policy lags.

Inside Lags

The **inside lag** is the time it takes to implement monetary policy. Such lags, or delays, occur for two reasons. First, it takes time to identify a problem. Although economists have developed sophisticated computer models for predicting economic trends, they still cannot know for sure that the economy is headed into a new phase of the business cycle until it is already there. Statistics may conflict, and it can take up to a year to recognize a serious economic downturn.

A second reason for inside lags is that once a problem has been recognized, it can take additional time to enact policies. This problem is more severe for fiscal policy than for monetary policy. Fiscal policy,

inside lag the time it takes to implement monetary policy

Figure 16.7 Business Cycles and Stabilization Policy

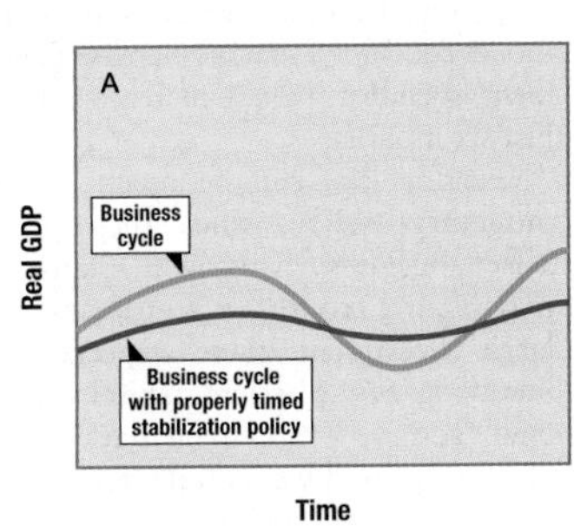

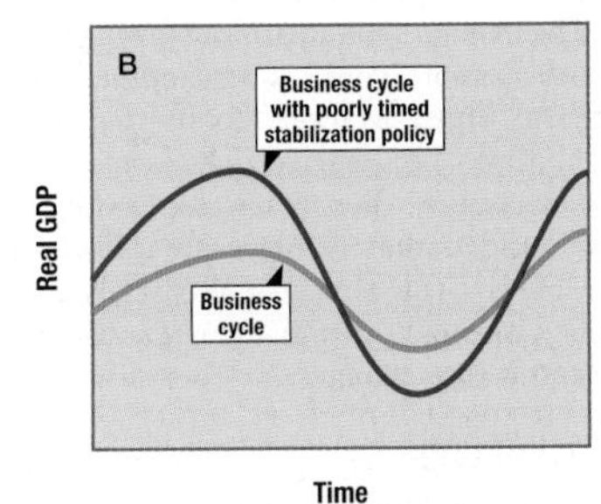

GRAPH SKILLS

The timing of monetary policy measures can intensify the business cycle.

1. Which troughs are lower, business cycles with proper timing or ones with improper timing?
2. What are the effects of proper timing and improper timing?

Action Graph online

For an animated version of this graph, visit PearsonSuccessNet.com

ANALYZE A TRANSPARENCY

Display transparency, "The Impact of the Federal Reserve on Interest Rates," (Color Transparencies, 16.b). Have students use this transparency to review the connection between the level of reserves and short-term interest rates.

Connect the terms *easy money policy* and *tight money policy* with what students have already learned about how the Fed applies monetary policy by regulating the money supply, thereby raising or lowering interest rates. Discuss the fact that interest rates have an impact on real GDP. Ask **Which row of the transparency illustrates an easy money policy and which a tight money policy?** *(top; bottom).* Have students speculate at what point in the business cycle the Fed might use each of these policies.

CHECK COMPREHENSION

Refer students to Figure 16.7, graph A. Have students explain the meaning of graph A, and then guide you in drawing the graph on the board. Ask **Which curve shows less change in the real GDP?** *(red curve representing business cycle with properly timed stabilization policy)* Elicit the fact from students that, as with fiscal policy, monetary policy will stabilize the economy if it is properly timed. Perform the same steps with graph B. Elicit the fact from students that poorly timed fiscal policy will actually intensify the peaks and troughs of the business cycle.

L2 Differentiate When asking students which curve shows less change in either graph, point to the vertical distance between the two curves.

Action Graph online Have students review the Action Graph animations for a step-by-step look at Business Cycles and Stabilization Policy.

Virtual Economics

L3 Differentiate

Exploring Monetary Policy Use the following lesson from the NCEE **Virtual Economics *CD-ROM*** to help students understand the impact of monetary policies. Click on Browse Economics Lessons, specify grades 9–12, and use the key words *money interest.*

In this activity, students will participate in two simulations to discover the effects of money creation on prices and the different tools the Federal Reserve uses to adjust the money supply.

LESSON TITLE	**MONEY, INTEREST, AND MONETARY POLICY**
Type of Activity	Simulation
Complexity	High
Time	100 minutes
NCEE Standards	20

Answers

Graph Skills 1. those with improper timing
2. Improper timing causes greater fluctuations in the level of real GDP over a business cycle. Proper timing minimizes fluctuations in real GDP over a business cycle.

DISTRIBUTE ACTIVITY WORKSHEET

Distribute the "Steering the Economy" activity worksheet (Unit 6 All-in-One, p. 122). This worksheet asks students to compare and interpret two political cartoons from early 2008 about the Fed's timing in managing the nation's financial crisis.

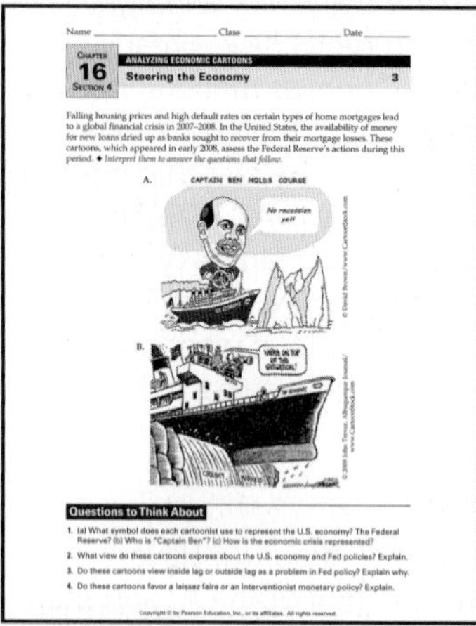
Name ______________ Class ______________ Date ________

CHAPTER 16 SECTION 4

ANALYZING ECONOMIC CARTOONS

Steering the Economy 3

Falling housing prices and high default rates on certain types of home mortgages lead to a global financial crisis in 2007–2008. In the United States, the availability of money for new loans dried up as banks sought to recover from their mortgage losses. These cartoons, which appeared in early 2008, assess the Federal Reserve's actions during this period. ◆ *Interpret them to answer the questions that follow.*

A. CAPTAIN BEN HOLDS COURSE

No recession yet!

B.

WE'RE ON TOP OF THE SITUATION!

Questions to Think About

1. (a) What symbol does each cartoonist use to represent the U.S. economy? The Federal Reserve? (b) Who is "Captain Ben"? (c) How is the economic crisis represented?
2. What view do these cartoons express about the U.S. economy and Fed policies? Explain.
3. Do these cartoons view inside lag or outside lag as a problem in Fed policy? Explain why.
4. Do these cartoons favor a laissez faire or an interventionist monetary policy? Explain.

Copyright © by Pearson Education, Inc., or its affiliates. All rights reserved.

L2 Differentiate Distribute "Steering the Economy" worksheet (Unit 6 All-in-One, p. 123). Help students interpret the cartoons as needed.

After students have completed the worksheet, discuss the answers to its questions as a class. Use these answers and the cartoons themselves to launch a discussion of what the Fed could, and eventually did, do in the situation depicted and of the general challenges it faces in properly timing its policies so that they achieve the goal of stabilizing the economy. Make sure that students understand the difference between *inside lag* and *outside lag,* and between laissez-faire and interventionist approaches.

EXPRESS A POINT OF VIEW

Poll the class to see how many students subscribe to a laissez-faire approach to monetary policy and how many support an interventionist position. Then have students write a newspaper editorial stating their position and the reasons they hold it.

L2 L3 ELL Differentiate Offer students the option of expressing their position on the laissez-faire vs. interventionist monetary policy debate by creating a bumper sticker, or drawing a panel or editorial cartoon.

How the Economy Works

How does the Fed make monetary policy?

Monetary policy may be explained simply as the steps the Federal Reserve Board takes to control the business cycle and make sure that the economy remains prosperous and stable.

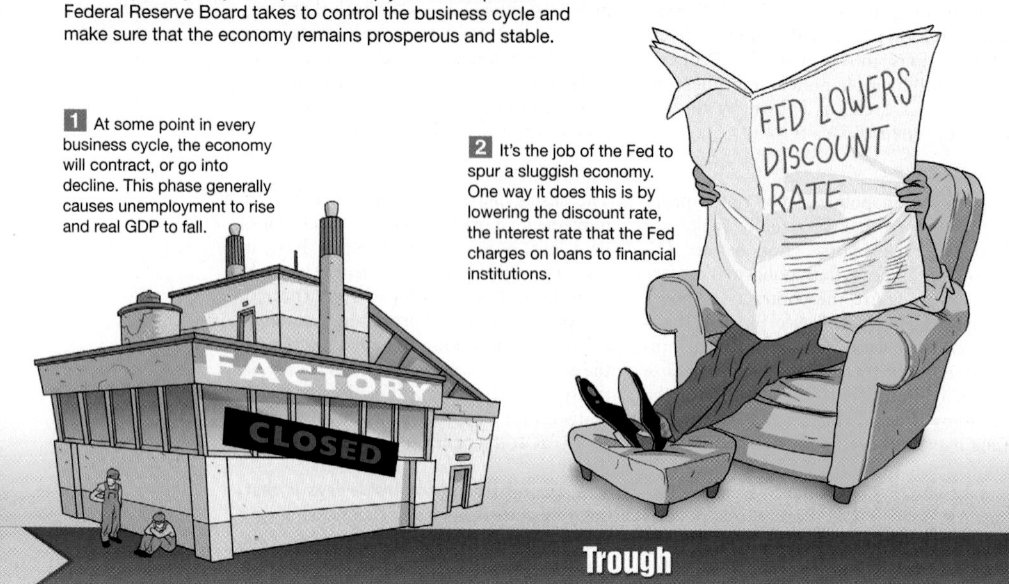

1 At some point in every business cycle, the economy will contract, or go into decline. This phase generally causes unemployment to rise and real GDP to fall.
2 It's the job of the Fed to spur a sluggish economy. One way it does this is by lowering the discount rate, the interest rate that the Fed charges on loans to financial institutions.
FED LOWERS DISCOUNT RATE
FACTORY
CLOSED
Trough

which includes changes in government spending and taxation, requires actions by Congress and the President. Since Congress must debate new plans and get the approval of the President, it takes time to get a new policy enacted.

The enactment of monetary policy, on the other hand, is streamlined. The Federal Open Market Committee meets eight times per year to discuss monetary policy—more often if necessary. Once it has decided that changes are called for, the FOMC can almost immediately enact policy through open market operations or discount rate changes.

Outside Lags

outside lag the time it takes for monetary policy to have an effect

Once a new policy is determined, it takes time to become effective. This time period, known as the **outside lag,** also differs for monetary and fiscal policy. For fiscal policy, the outside lag lasts as long as is required for new government spending or tax policies to take effect and begin to affect real GDP and the inflation rate. This time period can be relatively short, as with a tax rebate that returns government revenues to households eager for spending money. One statistical model concluded that an increase in government spending would increase GDP after just six months.

Outside lags can be much longer for monetary policy, since they primarily affect business investment plans. Firms may require months or even years to make large investment plans, especially those involving new physical capital, such as a new factory. Thus, a change in interest rates may not have its full effect on investment spending for several years. This conclusion is supported by several studies that suggest that more than two years may pass before the maximum impact of monetary policy is felt.

Background Note

Laissez-Faire Economists and the Federal Reserve System Laissez-faire economists criticize the Fed for trying to micromanage employment, interest rates, and economic growth. They claim that the Fed cannot permanently increase economic growth or permanently lower the unemployment rate or interest rates by increasing money growth, but that it can throw the economy off track by policy errors. They note that the only instrument the Fed has control over is the money supply, and that it should adjust the supply only to keep the inflation rate close to zero over the long term. They maintain that Congress should restrict the Fed to achieving only that goal—and not allow it to intervene in the economy by responding to money supply shocks that would lead to one-time increases or decreases in the price levels.

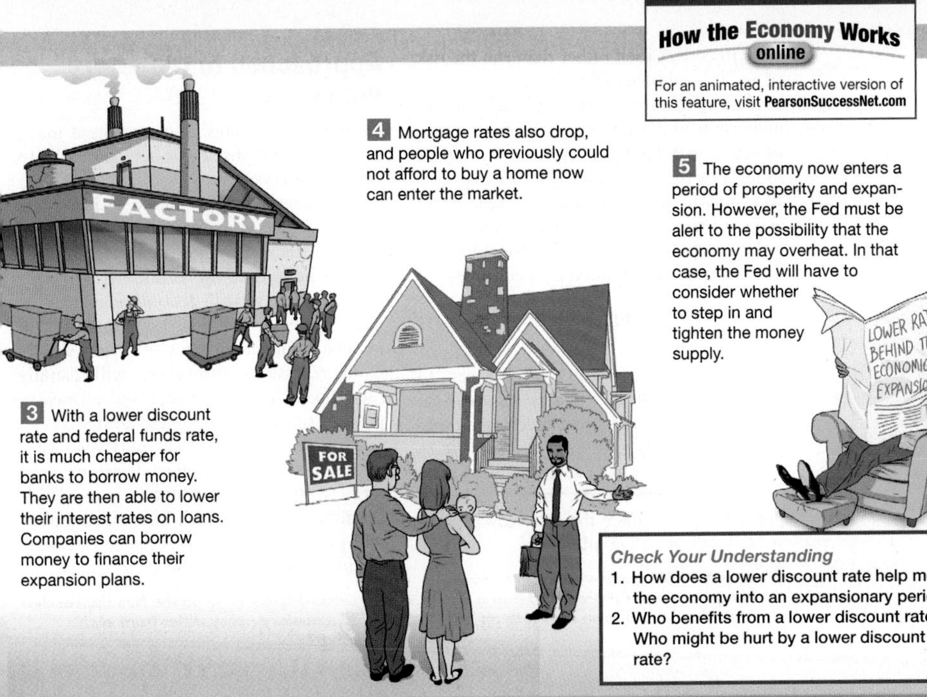

How the Economy Works
online
For an animated, interactive version of this feature, visit PearsonSuccessNet.com
FACTORY
3 With a lower discount rate and federal funds rate, it is much cheaper for banks to borrow money. They are then able to lower their interest rates on loans. Companies can borrow money to finance their expansion plans.
4 Mortgage rates also drop, and people who previously could not afford to buy a home now can enter the market.
5 The economy now enters a period of prosperity and expansion. However, the Fed must be alert to the possibility that the economy may overheat. In that case, the Fed will have to consider whether to step in and tighten the money supply.
FOR SALE
LOWER RATES BEHIND THE ECONOMIC EXPANSION
Check Your Understanding
1. How does a lower discount rate help move the economy into an expansionary period?
2. Who benefits from a lower discount rate? Who might be hurt by a lower discount rate?

Expansion → **Peak**

Given the longer inside lag for fiscal policy and the longer outside lag for monetary policy, it is difficult to know which policy has the shorter total lag. In practice, partisan politics and budgetary pressures often prevent the President and Congress from agreeing on fiscal policy. Because of the political difficulties of implementing fiscal policy, we rely to a greater extent on the Fed to use monetary policy to soften the business cycle.

***CHECKPOINT** What problem can result from expansionary monetary policy that takes effect after the economy has already emerged from recession?*

Predicting Business Cycles

The Federal Reserve must not only react to current trends. It must also anticipate changes in the economy. How should policymakers decide when to intervene in the economy?

Monetary Policy and Inflation

You have already read that expansionary policy, if enacted at the wrong time, may push an economy into high inflation, thus reducing any beneficial impact. This is the chief danger of using an easy money policy to get the economy out of a recession.

An inflationary economy can be tamed by a tight money policy, but the timing is again crucial. If the policy takes effect as the economy is already cooling off on its own, the tight money could turn a mild contraction into a full-blown recession.

The decision of whether to use monetary policy, then, must be based partly on our expectations of the business cycle. Some recessions are short-run phenomena that will, in the long run, disappear. Some inflationary peaks may also be expected to last for the short run and end in the long run. Given the timing problems of monetary policy, in some cases it may be wiser to allow the business

EXTEND

L4 Differentiate Organize students into small groups to act as the Federal Open Market Committee by researching current economic information and making a decision about future monetary policy. Then distribute the "FOMC Role-Play" worksheet (Unit 6 All-in-One, p. 124). Have students use the worksheet as a guide in completing the activity.

GUIDING QUESTION WRAP UP

Have students return to the section Guiding Question. Review the completed graphic organizer and clarify any misunderstandings. Have a wrap-up discussion about how monetary policy affects economic stability.

Assess and Remediate

L2 L3 Collect the "Steering the Economy" worksheets and assess students' understanding of timing, approaches, and the business cycle in setting monetary policy.

L4 Collect the "FOMC Role-Play" worksheets and assess students' understanding the duties of the FOMC.

L3 Assign the Section 4 Assessment questions; identify student misconceptions.

L3 Give Section Quiz A (Unit 6 All-in-One, p. 125).

L2 Give Section Quiz B (Unit 6 All-in-One, p. 126).

(Assess and Remediate continued on p. 440)

Answers

Checkpoint high inflation

Check Your Understanding 1. A lower discount rate means it is cheaper for banks to borrow money, and, therefore, to lend money. Lower interest rates on loans to businesses and consumers will lead to greater investment spending by businesses and increased home-buying by consumers, assuming interest rates on mortgages have also fallen. An increase in aggregate demand will positively influence the level of real GDP. 2. Consumers and businesses benefit; banks—because they will not make as much money on loans—do not benefit.

Have students complete the Self-Test Online and continue their work in the **Essential Questions Journal**.

REMEDIATION AND SUGGESTIONS

Use the chart below to help students who are struggling with content.

WEAKNESS	REMEDIATION
Defining key terms (Questions 3, 4, 5, 6, 7)	Have students use the interactive Economic Dictionary Online.
How monetary policy works (Questions 1, 4, 5, 6, 7)	Reteach using the transparency.
The business cycle, timing, and monetary policy (Questions 2, 4, 5, 6, 7, 9, 10)	Refer students to the Action Graph Online and How the Economy Works Online.
Approaches to monetary policy (Question 11)	Have pairs of students role-play a laissez faire economist and an economist who favors interventionist policy.

Answers

Checkpoint It may take little or no action to change monetary policy and let the economy correct itself.

Checkpoint Economists who believe that economies emerge slowly from recession may favor using fiscal and monetary policies to help the business cycle adjust, while laissez-faire economists (who believe that the economy will self-adjust quickly) will recommend against enacting new policies.

cycle to correct itself rather than run the risk of an ill-timed policy change.

If a recession is expected to turn into an expansion in a short time, the best course of action may be to let the economy correct itself. On the other hand, if we expect a recession to last several years, then most economists would recommend an active policy. So the question is this: How long will a recessionary or inflationary period last?

How Quickly Does the Economy Self-Correct?

Economists disagree on the answer to this question. Their estimates for the U.S. economy range from two to six years. Since the economy may take quite a long time to recover on its own from an inflationary peak or a recessionary trough, there is time for policymakers to guide the economy back to stable levels of output and prices.

CHECKPOINT ***How would the Fed most likely respond if it predicted that a recession would soon turn into an expansion?***

Approaches to Monetary Policy

In practice, the lags discussed here make monetary and fiscal policy difficult to apply. Interventionist policy, a policy encouraging action, is likely to make the business cycle worse if the economy self-adjusts quickly. Laissez-faire economists who believe that the economy will self-adjust quickly will recommend against enacting new policies. Economists who believe that economies emerge slowly from recessions, however, will usually recommend enacting fiscal and monetary policies to move the process along.

The rate of adjustment may also vary over time, making policy decisions even more difficult. This debate over which approach to take with monetary policy will probably never be settled to the satisfaction of all economists.

CHECKPOINT ***How do the two approaches to monetary policy differ from each other?***

SECTION 4 ASSESSMENT

Essential Questions Journal To continue to build a response to the Essential Question, go to your **Essential Questions Journal.**

Guiding Question

1. Use your completed concept web to answer this question: How does monetary policy affect economic stability?
2. **Extension** Suppose you asked for an advance on your salary or allowance and were told that you would have to pay interest on it. Would you still want the advance? Would you want the interest to come out of future paychecks or be deducted up front from your advance? This kind of example is a part of your personal monetary policy.

Key Terms and Main Ideas

3. What is **monetarism**?
4. Why would the Federal Reserve enact an **easy money policy**?
5. Why would it enact a **tight money policy**?
6. What are **inside lags,** and why do they occur?
7. Why does monetary policy have such long **outside lags**?

Critical Thinking

8. **Explain** What is the relationship between aggregate demand and GDP?
9. **Evaluate (a)** Why do business cycles make monetary policy difficult to time? **(b)** What could happen if monetary policy is enacted at the wrong time?
10. **Compare and Contrast (a)** How are inside and outside lags similar? **(b)** How are they different?

Quick Write

11. With a partner, prepare a debate on monetary policy. One of you should write an argument for an interventionist approach, encouraging action. The other should write an argument for a laissez-faire approach, discouraging action. Use information from your textbook to help develop your argument.

Assessment Answers

1. The use of the right monetary tools at the right time can be an effective way to even out the business cycle.
2. Possible response: That would depend on the interest rate. If it is too high, I would just reduce my spending to match the funds I had. Otherwise, I might want the advance. How I have it taken out would depend upon the interest rate I could get on a bank account.
3. the belief that the money supply is the most important factor in the functioning of the economy
4. to stimulate the economy by increasing the money supply
5. to slow down expansion and the rate of inflation by reducing the money supply
6. the time it takes to implement monetary policy; a problem must first be identified and then policies chosen to deal with it
7. because they mainly affect business investment plans, which can take months or years for businesses to change
8. Aggregate demand represents the relationship between price levels and quantity demanded in an economy. It helps determine the level of GDP.
9. (a) Monetary policies are slow to have an effect and business cycles are hard to predict. (b) Policies enacted too late could intensify the peaks or troughs of the cycle.
10. (a) Both involve the passage of time. (b) Inside lag is the time it takes to execute a policy, while outside lag is the time it takes for that policy to have an effect.
11. Possible response: An interventionist may argue that waiting to find out if a recession will last very long hurts people, while a laissez-faire economist may argue that it hurts people if cycles are overcorrected.

QUICK STUDY GUIDE

Chapter 16: The Federal Reserve and Monetary Policy

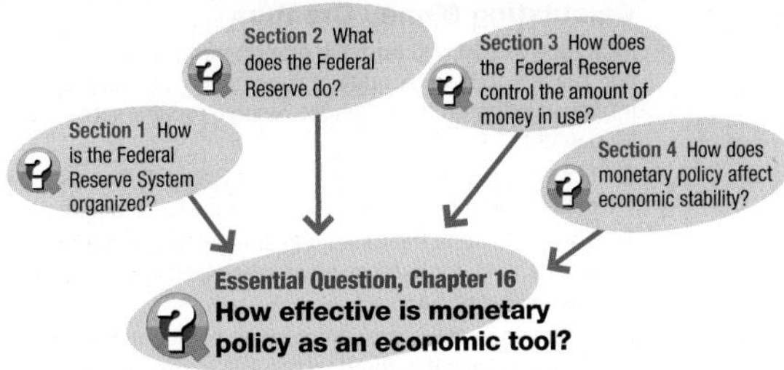
Section 1 How is the Federal Reserve System organized?
Section 2 What does the Federal Reserve do?
Section 3 How does the Federal Reserve control the amount of money in use?
Section 4 How does monetary policy affect economic stability?
Essential Question, Chapter 16
How effective is monetary policy as an economic tool?

Responsibilities of the Federal Reserve Board

Responsibilities That Serve Government	Maintain checking account for the Treasury Department
	Serve as financial agent for the Treasury Department
	Issue currency
Responsibilities That Serve the Banking System	Maintain check clearing system
	Monitor bank reserves
	Approve or disapprove proposed bank mergers
	Lend money to banks
Regulating Banks	Regulate the banking system
Regulating the Money Supply	Regulate the money supply to stabilize the economy
	Alter the discount rate
	Alter the federal funds rate
	Buy or sell government securities on the open market

Economic Dictionary

- **monetary policy,** *p. 419*
- **reserves,** *p. 421*
- **reserve requirements,** *p. 421*
- **check clearing,** *p. 426*
- **bank holding company,** *p. 426*
- **federal funds rate,** *p. 427*
- **discount rate,** *p. 427*
- **money creation,** *p. 429*
- **required reserve ratio,** *p. 430*
- **money multiplier formula,** *p. 430*
- **excess reserves,** *p. 431*
- **prime rate,** *p. 433*
- **open market operations,** *p. 433*
- **monetarism,** *p. 435*
- **easy money policy,** *p. 436*
- **tight money policy,** *p. 436*
- **inside lag,** *p. 437*
- **outside lag,** *p. 438*

Economics *on the go*

Study anytime, anywhere. Download these files today.

Economic Dictionary online	Audio Review online	Action Graph online	Visual Glossary online	How the Economy Works online
Vocabulary Support in English and Spanish	Audio Study Guide in English and Spanish	Animated Charts and Graphs	Animated feature	Animated feature

Download to your computer or mobile device at PearsonSuccessNet.com

ASSIGN THE ESSENTIAL QUESTIONS JOURNAL

After students have finished studying the chapter, they should return to the chapter's essential question in the Essential Questions Journal and complete the activity.

Tell students to go back to the chapter opener and look at the image. Using the information they have gained from studying the chapter, ask **How does this illustrate the main ideas of the chapter?** *(Possible response: The imposing nature of the building symbolizes the importance of the role played by the Federal Reserve in the nation's monetary policy.)*

STUDY TIPS

Explain to students that analyzing the work they have done on worksheets and quizzes can help them prepare for tests. Have students look back at the mistakes they made on previous work and take notes about areas they found confusing. Have each student write a question on a notecard, and weave answers to these questions into review sessions.

Economics *on the go* Have students download the digital resources available on Economics on the Go for review and remediation.

Assessment at a Glance

TESTS AND QUIZZES

Section Assessments

Section Quizzes A and B, **Unit 6 All-in-One**

Self-Test Online

Chapter Assessments

Chapter Tests A and B, **Unit 6 All-in-One**

Economic Detective, **Unit 6 All-in-One**

Document-based Assessment, p. 443

Exam*View*

AYP Monitoring Assessments

PERFORMANCE ASSESSMENT

Teacher's Edition, pp. 421, 422, 426, 430, 433, 438, 439

Simulation Activities, Chapter 16

Virtual Economics on CD-ROM, pp. 423, 427, 431, 437

Essential Questions Journal, Chapter 16

Assessment Rubrics

Chapter Assessment

1. (a) services: check clearing, lender of last resort, approves or disapproves bank mergers; regulations: reserve requirements, supervision of lending practices, bank examinations (b) Possible response: the check clearing function because of its importance to the everyday functioning of the nations' economy
2. (a) They allow the Fed to alter the amount of money in the economy without disrupting financial institutions and can be done on an ongoing basis. (b) Changes in the reserve requirement can force banks to take actions that are disruptive, such as calling in loans. Changes in the short-term interest rates, such as the discount rate or fed funds rate, have limited impact on achieving long-term changes in the economy.
3. (a) It would expand the money supply due to the multiplier effect as banks used reserves to make more loans. (b) an increase in the reserve requirement, discount rate, or fed funds rate, or the selling of bonds and other government securities in open market operations
4. (a) The Fed either buys government bonds on the open market, which puts more money into circulation and thereby increases the money supply, or sells securities, which decreases the money supply by taking money out of circulation. (b) Open market operations are long-term, ongoing operations that produce smooth changes in the money supply, whereas changes in the reserve requirement or in interest rates produce sharp or short-term effects.
5. (a) most likely buy government bonds on the open market (b) It would put more money into the economy, which would make loans less costly and easier to get, thereby encouraging spending and growth. (c) when the economy is in a long-term recession or depression
6. 15% of $3,000 = $450
7. 85% of $3,000 = $2,550
8. 15% of $2,550 = $382.50; 85% of $2,550 = $2,167.50
9. $3,000 + $2,550 + $2,167.50 = $7,717.50
10. Organize students into pairs or small groups to complete this activity. Discuss where students might find reliable information, including government or educational Web sites. Check students' worksheets before they move on to modify the activity.
11. Answers will vary. Students should be able to justify their assessment of the economy, the political pressures on the Fed, and their plan for the next four quarters.

CHAPTER 16 ASSESSMENT

Self-Test online To test your understanding of key terms and main ideas, visit **PearsonSuccessNet.com**

Key Terms and Main Ideas

To make sure you understand the key terms and main ideas of this chapter, review the Checkpoint and Section Assessment questions and look at the Quick Study Guide on the preceding page.

Critical Thinking

1. **Conclude (a)** List three services the Federal Reserve offers banks and three regulations it places on banks. **(b)** Which service or regulation do you think is most important to the American banking system?
2. **Analyze (a)** Why are open market operations the most commonly used actions taken by the Fed? **(b)** What advantages do open market operations have over other monetary policy tools?
3. **Infer (a)** What effect would a reduction in the required reserve rate (RRR) have on banks? **(b)** What action of the Fed would cause a contraction of the money supply?
4. **Compare (a)** Describe the action of open market operations. **(b)** How do open market operations differ from other monetary policy tools?
5. **Analyze (a)** If the Federal Reserve Board were to implement an easy money policy, what actions would it take? **(b)** What would be the expected results of this policy? **(c)** What conditions could lead the Fed to take such actions?

Applying Your Math Skills

Calculating Money Creation

Pete received $3,000 from his grandparents as a graduation present to help him pay college tuition. He placed the money in Brighton Bank, whose reserve requirement ratio is 15 percent.

6. How much of Pete's deposit must Brighton Bank keep in reserve before it is able to lend money to someone else?
7. The bank loans the remaining amount to Sandra so that she can pay for extensive car repairs. How much does the bank lend Sandra?
8. Upon receiving Sandra's car repair payment, the repair shop deposits it in the Brighton Bank. How much of this money must the bank hold in reserve? How much can it lend to Roy?
9. What would be the total increase in the money supply based upon the initial cash deposit of $3,000 and the two loans?

Visit PearsonSuccessNet.com for additional math help.

Essential Question Activity

Essential Questions Journal To respond to the chapter Essential Question, go to your **Essential Questions Journal.**

10. Complete this activity to answer the Essential Question **How effective is monetary policy as an economic tool?** Work in groups to gather information about the use of monetary policy to stimulate, downsize, or otherwise stabilize economies. Using the worksheet in your Essential Questions Journal or the electronic worksheet available at **PearsonSuccessNet.com,** gather the following information:
    (a) What steps did the United States take in order to prevent a recurrence of the Panic of 1907?
    (b) How did the Federal Reserve Board attempt to deal with the Great Depression? How successful was it?
    (c) How effective was the Federal Reserve Board in controlling the double-digit inflation of the late 1970s?
    (d) How did the Fed under Alan Greenspan attempt to steer the U.S. economy between recession and inflation? How effective was it?
    (e) What would happen to monetary policy if the United States abolished the Fed and returned to the gold standard?
11. **Modify** You are members of the Federal Reserve Board who have just heard the above reports prepared by your research committees. Based on this history of government attempts to use monetary policy to control the economy, what advice would you give the Chairman of the Board for his testimony next week before the Senate Finance Committee?
    (a) Decide which is more likely today, inflation or recession.
    (b) Describe the political pressures on the Fed in determining monetary policy.
    (c) Come up with a plan for Fed action in the next four quarters.
    (d) Describe the pitfalls the Fed faces in creating monetary policy.

WebQuest online The Economics WebQuest challenges students to use 21st century skills to answer the Essential Question.

THE ESSENTIAL
VIDEO
By Students For Students
For videos on Essential Questions, go to PearsonSuccessNet.com

Remind students to continue to develop an Essentials Questions video. Guidelines and a production binder are available at www.PearsonSuccessNet.com.

DOCUMENT-BASED ASSESSMENT

Do bank mergers benefit or hurt the public?

Today, there are fewer than half as many banks in existence as there were 30 years ago. While bank mergers are profitable for bank shareholders, many worry that the trend might be less beneficial to consumers.

Document A

"Since 1988, there have been more than 13,500 applications for the formation, acquisition, or merger of bank holding companies or state-member banks reviewed by the Federal Reserve Board. Over this time, 25 of these applications have been denied, with eight of those failing to obtain Board approval involving unsatisfactory consumer protection and community needs issues. The low incidence of applications that have not received regulatory approval may be due to the fact that institutions seeking to expand their operations are typically in sound financial and managerial condition.... Maintaining robust and competitive banking markets is a critical objective in the Federal Reserve's review of banking applications."

—Sandra Braunstein, Federal Reserve Director of Consumer and Community Affairs, testimony before Congress, May 21, 2007

Document B

VIGELAND: "I remember back in the mid-90's there were a whole lot of bank takeovers and I wonder if there was any research done on whether consumers profit when a smaller bank is taken over by a bigger one."

D'ARISTA: "Well, they may profit in terms of convenience. The larger bank may have more branches and more ATMs and things of this sort. My concern at this point is concentration. It makes it a lot easier for a bank to set terms that are really at variance with the needs of a community when they are the only large or dominant institution in an area."

—Tess Vigeland and Jane D'Arista, "What Bank Mergers Mean For You," Marketplace Morning Report, January 18, 2008

Document C

"There's been a big bank merger, sir, so you now have a joint checking account with a Mr. Slavomir Bezparyadok of Zagreb."

SOURCE: www.cartoonstock.com

ANALYZING DOCUMENTS

Use your knowledge of opportunity costs and Documents A, B, and C to answer questions 1–3.

1. **Which of the following conclusions does Document A best support?**
   A. The Federal Reserve has significantly limited the number of bank mergers.
   B. Bank mergers generally do not affect the level of service customers receive.
   C. Bank mergers benefit banks but do not benefit local communities.
   D. The Federal Reserve has a definite set of standards for approving bank mergers.

2. **According to Document B, one major concern about bank mergers is the**
   A. increased possibility of fraud.
   B. reduced banking services.
   C. higher bank fees.
   D. possibility of monopoly.

3. **How would you describe the reaction of the bank customer in the cartoon?**
   A. Worried that the bank merger will affect the quality of the service he receives
   B. Confused because he does not know where Zagreb is
   C. Angry because he is opposed to bank mergers
   D. Interested in finding out more about the details of the merger

WRITING ABOUT ECONOMICS

People disagree about whether the Federal Reserve has done enough to control bank mergers. Use the documents on this page and on the Web site below to answer the question: ***Do bank mergers benefit or hurt the public?*** Use the sources to support your opinion.

In Partnership

THE WALL STREET JOURNAL. CLASSROOM EDITION

To read more about issues related to this topic, visit **PearsonSuccessNet.com**

Document-Based Assessment

ANALYZING DOCUMENTS

1. D
2. D
3. A

WRITING ABOUT ECONOMICS

Possible answers: Bank mergers benefit the public because the larger number of branches and ATMs make banking more convenient; bank mergers hurt the public because the larger banks are less likely to be concerned with meeting the needs of the communities in which they are located.

Student essay should demonstrate an understanding of the issues involved in the debate over bank mergers. Use the following as guidelines to assess the essay.

L2 Differentiate Students use all documents on the page to support their thesis.

L3 Differentiate Students use the documents on this page and additional information available online at www.PearsonSuccessNet.com to support their answer.

L4 Differentiate Students incorporate information provided in the textbook and online at www.PearsonSuccessNet.com and include additional research to support their opinion.

Go Online to www.PearsonSuccessNet.com for a student rubric and extra documents.

Economics online *All print resources are available on the Teacher's Resource Library CD-ROM and online at* www.PearsonSuccessNet.com.

Essential Question

What is the proper role of government in the economy?

BELLRINGER

Ask students to read the paragraph under the Essential Question. Then have volunteers suggest examples of how the government intervenes in the economy.

EXPLAIN

Before students read the quotations, explain that Daniel J. Mitchell is an economist at the Heritage Foundation, a conservative think tank. Vice President Joe Biden chose Jared Bernstein to serve as his chief economic advisor.

DISCUSS

Have students review the quotations on the page. Ask students to explain the role of the government in the economy. **What else might the government spend money on besides security and defense?** *(Possible answers: student loans; disaster aid)* **How can government help build a better society?** *(Possible answers: stabilize the economy; provide for people with disabilities)*

L2 Differentiate Pair students to read the articles and summarize the main thesis. Ask them to give any supporting details or arguments to the thesis.

ANALYZE A CARTOON

Have students silently read the cartoon's caption. Have them work in small groups to discuss reasons the man might be angry with the IRS worker. Have small groups work together to create a possible response that the IRS worker could give the angry man. Invite volunteers to share their work with the class.

BULLETIN BOARD ACTIVITY

Have students revisit the Unit Essential Question articles that they have posted as they have studied the chapters. Have them discuss the relevance of the articles to the question and whether their opinions have changed since they first read the article. Remind students to review their work in their **Essential Questions Journal**.

EXTEND

Have students complete their work on the Essential Questions Video and present their work to the class.

L4 Differentiate Have students choose a recent influential politician and explain his or her view about the role of government in the economy. Ask **Do you agree or disagree with that point of view? Why?**

Unit 6 Challenge

Essential Question, Unit 6

What is the proper role of government in the economy?

THE ESSENTIAL
VIDEO
By Students For Students
For videos on Essential Questions, go to PearsonSuccessNet.com

People have different opinions about what the government's role in the economy should be. Look at the opinions below, keeping in mind the Essential Question: What is the proper role of government in the economy?

"Government spending should be significantly reduced. It has grown far too quickly in recent years, and most of the new spending is for purposes other than homeland security and national defense. Combined with rising entitlement costs associated with the looming retirement of the baby-boom generation, America is heading in the wrong direction. To avoid becoming an uncompetitive European-style welfare state like France or Germany, the United States must adopt a responsible fiscal policy based on smaller government."

—Daniel J. Mitchell, "The Impact of Government Spending on Economic Growth"

"Global competition, rising health costs, longer life spans with weaker pensions, less secure employment, and unprecedented inequalities of opportunity and wealth are calling for a much broader, more inclusive approach to helping all of us meet these challenges, one that taps government as well as market solutions.... We can wield the tools of government to build a more just society, one that preserves individualist values while ensuring that the prosperity we generate is equitably shared."

—Jared Bernstein, *All Together Now: Common Sense for a Fair Economy*

WHAT DID YOU DO WITH ALL THE MONEY I GAVE YOU LAST YEAR?
INTERNAL REVENUE SERVICE

Essential Question Writing Activity

Consider the different views of economics expressed in the sources on this page and what you have learned about government and the economy. ***Then write a well-constructed essay expressing your view of the economic role of the government.***

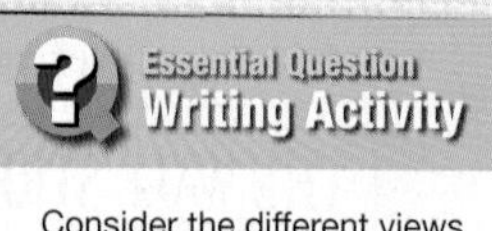
Essential Questions Journal

To respond to the unit Essential Question, go to your **Essential Questions Journal**.

Writing Guidelines

- Address all aspects of the Essential Question Writing Activity.
- Support the theme with relevant facts, examples, and details.
- Use a logical and clear plan of organization.
- Introduce the theme by establishing a framework that is beyond a simple restatement of the question and conclude with a summation of the theme.

For help in writing a Persuasive Essay, refer to the *Writer's Handbook* in the Reference section, page S-5.

444 UNIT REVIEW

Essential Question Writing Activity

Before students begin the writing activity, remind them to skim through the unit chapters to read the headings on each page. Have them read through any notes they took and review their chapter assessments and chapter projects.

Students should write a two-paragraph article. Paragraph one should outline ways in which the government is involved in the economy. Paragraph two should explain why some government involvement in the economy is controversial.

L2 Differentiate Students should write a paragraph that explains how the government is involved in the economy, providing detailed examples.

L4 Differentiate Students should write a three-paragraph article that provides relevant examples of how the government is involved in the economy.

Before students begin work, distribute the Writing Assessment rubric, available at the Online Teacher Center at PearsonSuccessNet.com.

UNIT 7 The Global Economy
Chapter 17 International Trade
Chapter 18 Development and Globalization
Essential Question, Unit 7
How might scarcity divide our world or bring it together?
Chapter 18
Do the benefits of economic development outweigh the costs?
Chapter 17
Should free trade be encouraged?

Essential Question

How might scarcity divide our world or bring it together?

Introduce the Unit

ACTIVATE PRIOR KNOWLEDGE

Essential questions frame each unit and chapter of study, asking students to consider big ideas about economics. Write the Unit Essential Question on the Board: **How might scarcity divide our world or bring it together?** Using the Idea Wave Discussion strategy (p. T24), have students brainstorm answers to the question.

WRITING ACTIVITY

To begin this unit, assign the Unit 7 Warmup Activity in the **Essential Questions Journal**. This will help students start to consider their position on the Unit 7 Essential Question: **How might scarcity divide our world or bring it together?**

Use the **Essential Questions Journal** throughout the program to help students consider these and other big ideas about economics.

BULLETIN BOARD ACTIVITY

Post the Unit Essential Question on a bulletin board. Tell students that they will be learning about the potential for scarcity to divide or unite the world. Ask them to bring in articles about current events to help them answer the question. Students should identify their article and use a sticky note to briefly explain the connection to the Essential Question.

CREATING THE ESSENTIAL QUESTIONS VIDEO

Preview the Unit Challenge on page 512. Consider assigning this activity to your students. Tell them that they will be creating their own video to explore this question, and that they should keep this in mind as they study the impact of scarcity on the world. For further information about how to complete this activity, go to PearsonSuccessNet.com.

NATIONAL COUNCIL ON ECONOMIC EDUCATION

The following Voluntary National Content Standards in Economics are addressed in this unit:

- ★ Standard 5
- ★ Standard 6
- ★ Standard 7
- ★ Standard 15

For a complete description of the standards addressed in each chapter, see the Correlations chart on pages T52–T55.

Online Resources

Economics Online Teacher Center at PearsonSuccessNet.com includes

- Online Teacher's Edition with lesson planner
- Online Lecture Notes
- Teacher's Resource Library with All-in-One Resources, Color Transparencies, Simulation Activities, and Adequate Yearly Progress Monitoring
- SuccessTracker Assessment

Economics Online Student Center at PearsonSuccessNet.com includes

- Interactive textbook with audio
- Economics Video
- WebQuests
- Interactivities
- Student Self-Tests

 **Essential Questions**

UNIT 7:

How might scarcity divide our world or bring it together?

CHAPTER 17:

Should free trade be encouraged?

Introduce the Chapter

ACTIVATE PRIOR KNOWLEDGE

In this chapter, students will learn how and why nations trade, and about the effects on exchange rates and trade balances on nations' economies. Tell students to complete the warmup activity in their **Essential Questions Journal.**

DIFFERENTIATED INSTRUCTION KEY

- **L1** Special Needs
- **L2** Basic to Average includes
  - **ELL** English Language Learners
  - **LPR** Less Proficient Readers
- **L3** All Students
- **L4** Advanced Students

Economics online Visit www.PearsonSuccessNet.com for an interactive textbook with built-in activities on economic principles.

- ***The Wall Street Journal* Classroom Edition Video** presents a current topic related to international trade.
- **Yearly Update Worksheet** provides an annual update, including a new worksheet and lesson on this topic.
- **On the Go** resources can be downloaded so students and teachers can connect with economics anytime, anywhere.

Chapter 17 International Trade

Essential Question, Chapter 17

Should free trade be encouraged?

- **Section 1:** Absolute and Comparative Advantage
- **Section 2:** Trade Barriers and Agreements
- **Section 3:** Measuring Trade

Economics on the go

To study anywhere, anytime, download these online resources at ***PearsonSuccessNet.com*** ▶

ECONOMICS ONLINE

DIGITAL TEACHER TOOLS

The online lesson planner is designed to help teachers plan, teach, and assess. Teachers have the ability to use or customize existing Pearson lesson plans. Online lecture notes support the print lesson by providing an array of accessible activities and summaries of key concepts. Two interactivities in this lesson are:

- **Visual Glossary** allows students to explore the concept of free trade.
- **Action Graphs** Animated graphs illustrate various aspects of world trade.

Block Scheduling

BLOCK 1 Teach Sections 1 and 2 without the worksheets or the Extend activities.

BLOCK 2 Teach Section 3, adding those Extend activities and worksheets from Sections 1 and 2 that address your state standards and learning objectives.

Pressed for Time

Group work Organize the class into three groups, assigning each group a section from the chapter. Have each group create a presentation detailing the main points of the assigned section. As groups give their presentations, create a study guide on the board outlining each section's main points. After each section is outlined, complete its worksheets and transparencies as a class.

SECTION 1 Absolute and Comparative Advantage

OBJECTIVES

1. **Evaluate** the impact of the unequal distribution of resources.
2. **Apply** the concepts of specialization and comparative advantage to explain why countries trade.
3. **Summarize** the position of the United States in world trade.
4. **Describe** the effects of trade on employment.

ECONOMIC DICTIONARY

As you read the section, look for the definitions of these **Key Terms:**

- export
- import
- absolute advantage
- comparative advantage
- law of comparative advantage
- interdependence

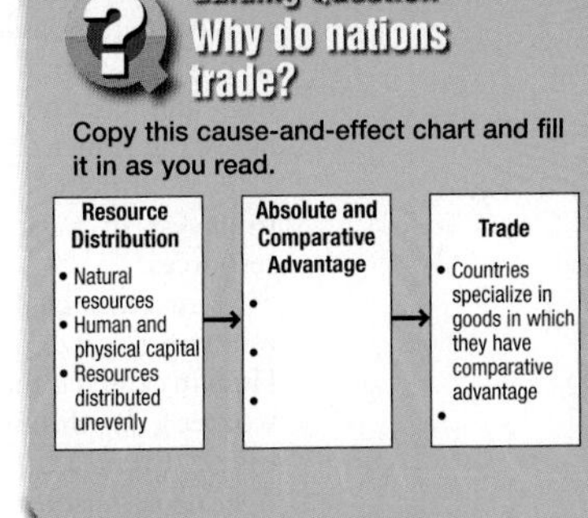

Economics and You Have you used a computer or bought a pair of jeans lately? The chances are good that the computer and the jeans were made outside the United States. But why do Americans buy so many goods from overseas? Wouldn't it make a lot more sense for us to produce everything we need ourselves?

Principles in Action The answer to these questions lies in an economic idea you already know about: factors of production. By looking at two odd products—birdhouses and T-shirts—you can better understand why nations trade. You will also learn how one Japanese entrepreneur built a business empire by selling electronics in a worldwide market.

Resource Distribution and Specialization

As you read in Chapter 1, the resources that are used to make goods and services are called the factors of production. They include land (natural resources), labor, and capital (both physical and human).

Natural Resources

Natural resources, along with climate and geographic location, help determine what goods and services an economy produces. Fertile soil and a good growing climate allowed the central United States to develop an economy based on agriculture. Much of Southwest Asia—with scarce farmland and water, but large reserves of oil and natural gas—has an economy based on the extraction and sale of these resources.

Visual Glossary online

Go to the Visual Glossary Online for an interactive review of **free trade.**

Action Graph online

Go to Action Graph Online for animated versions of key charts and graphs.

How the Economy Works online

Go to How the Economy Works Online for an interactive lesson on the **benefits of trade.**

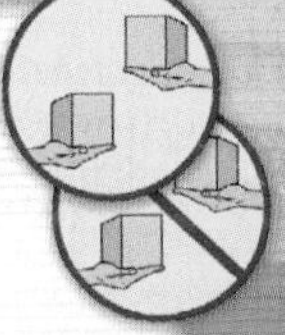

Focus on the Basics

Students need to come away with the following understandings:

FACTS: • The distribution of natural resources, capital, and labor help determine what goods and services nations export and import. • Absolute advantage and comparative advantage cause countries to specialize in making some products and to trade for others. • The United States is the world's second-largest exporter of goods, the largest exporter of services, and the world's top importer. • Trade can change a nation's employment patterns by creating new job opportunities while causing other jobs to be lost.

GENERALIZATION: Nations trade in order to benefit themselves by exporting things they produce efficiently and importing other things that they need.

Guiding Question

Why do nations trade?

Get Started

Resource Distribution	Absolute and Comparative Advantage	Trade
• Natural resources • Human and physical capital • Resources distributed unevenly	• Best for countries to specialize and trade • Absolute: greater production with given amount of resources • Comparative: country that can produce with lowest opportunity cost	• Countries specialize in goods in which they have comparative advantage • Comparative advantage and world trade result in interdependence

LESSON GOALS

Students will:

- Know the Key Terms.
- Demonstrate understanding of specialization and comparative advantage by completing a worksheet.
- Analyze the impact of the unequal distribution of resources through participation in discussion and by creating and interpreting a map.
- Analyze the U.S. position in world trade by interpreting and discussing a transparency and a table.
- Show understanding of how trade affects employment by taking a position on this issue in a blog post, poster, or editorial cartoon.

BEFORE CLASS

Students should read the section for homework before coming to class.

Have students complete the graphic organizer in the Section Opener as they read the text. As an alternate activity, have students complete the Guided Reading and Review worksheet (Unit 7 All-in-One, p. 13).

L1 L2 ELL LPR Differentiate Have students complete the Guided Reading and Review worksheet (Unit 7 All-in-One, p. 14).

CLASSROOM HINTS

WHY PEOPLE TRADE

Some students may think of trade as a zero-sum game where there is always a winner and a loser. Explain that trade usually benefits both sides, and this is the reason trade exists. Illustrate by using a simple example such as buying a tank of gas. A driver exchanges, or trades, an amount of money with a gas station owner for a tank of gas. She benefits by getting the gas she needs. The gas station owner benefits by making a profit.

BELLRINGER

Display the "Where Does It Come From?" transparency (Color Transparencies, 17.a). Keep the two right columns of the transparency covered. Tell students to follow the directions on the transparency and identify the products on the list that are imported into the United States or that are produced in the United States by foreign-owned companies.

Teach

Economics online To present this topic using digital resources, use the lecture notes on www.PearsonSuccessNet.com.

L1 L2 ELL LPR Differentiate To help students who are struggling readers, assign the Vocabulary worksheet (Unit 7 All-in-One, p. 12).

REVIEW BELLRINGER ANSWERS

Call on students to provide their responses to the Bellringer activity. Then remove the covering from the right two columns of the transparency to reveal to the class that all the items on the list are either foreign-produced or are produced in the United States by foreign-owned companies. (Note: Some students may identify Dr. Pepper as a Coca Cola or Pepsi product. However, Coca Cola and Pepsi only *distribute* Dr. Pepper for Cadbury in different parts of the United States. Neither company owns or manufactures Dr. Pepper.) Ask students whether they are surprised by these results, and have them explain. Ask how the results illustrate the global nature of the U.S. economy.

Capital and Labor

Capital and labor also shape a region's economy. Physical capital includes the things that people make in order to produce final goods and services. Machinery, tractors, computers, and factories are examples of physical capital, as are the transportation and communication networks that allow the flow of goods and information. Capital also includes the money needed to invest in businesses and use natural resources.

Human capital differs from labor. Labor refers to the size of a nation's workforce. Human capital is the knowledge and skills a worker gains through education and experience. Every job requires human capital. A surgeon must learn anatomy and how to use a scalpel. A taxi driver must memorize the layout of a city's streets.

One way to measure a nation's human capital is to look at the general educational level of the populace. A country whose citizens have more schooling than those of another country has more human capital.

Unequal Resource Distribution

As **Figure 17.1** shows, the availability of resources differs greatly from one country to another. For example, the United Kingdom has less than one fifth the land area of Peru but nearly twice as many airports. This suggests that the United Kingdom has more available physical capital than Peru does.

A nation's ability to exploit, or use, its physical resources is affected by culture and history. For example, prolonged warfare may severely damage a nation's farms, forests, and transportation systems. History and culture affect human resources as well. In colonial America, a labor shortage led to the establishment of slavery. Today, a culture that bans education of women wastes much of its potential human capital.

Specialization and Trade

Unequal distribution of resources creates a need for specialization. (As you read in Chapter 2, specialization occurs when individuals, businesses, or nations produce only certain goods and services.) In the United

Figure 17.1 Resource Distribution

	India	Peru	United Kingdom	United States
Total area (sq km)	3,287,590	1,285,220	244,820	9,826,630
Arable land (%)	48.83	2.88	23.23	18.01
Natural resources	Coal, iron ore, manganese, mica, bauxite, titanium ore, chromite, natural gas, diamonds, petroleum, limestone, arable land	Copper, silver, gold, petroleum, timber, fish, iron ore, coal, phosphate, potash, hydropower, natural gas	Coal, petroleum, natural gas, iron ore, lead, zinc, gold, tin, limestone, salt, clay, chalk, gypsum, potash, silica sand, slate, arable land	Coal, copper, lead, molybdenum, phosphates, uranium, bauxite, gold, iron, mercury, nickel, potash, silver, tungsten, zinc, petroleum, natural gas, timber
Population	1.1 billion	28,674,757	60,776,238	301,139,947
Labor force	509.3 million	9.21 million	31.1 million	151.4 million
Literacy rate	61%	87.7%	99%	99%
Telephones	215.85 million	10.83 million	103.26 million	405 million
Airports	341	268	471	14,858

SOURCE: *CIA World Factbook*

CHART SKILLS

Like all countries, the countries shown on this table possess different natural, human, and physical resources.

1. Which resource on this list is most closely related to human capital?
2. Which nation has the most potential farmland? Which has the largest percentage of potential farmland?

Differentiated Resources

- **L1 L2 Guided Reading and Review** (Unit 7 All-in-One, p. 14)
- **L2 Vocabulary worksheet** (Unit 7 All-in-One, p. 12)
- **L2 Who Should Produce What?** (Unit 7 All-in-One, p. 16)
- **L2 Analyze Maps skills worksheet** (Unit 7 All-in-One, p. 18)

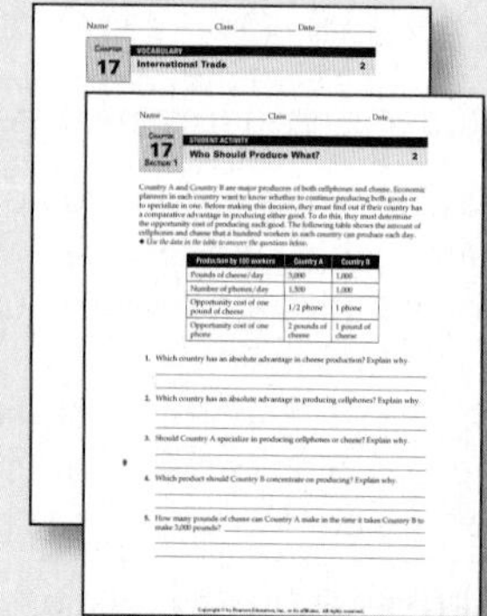

Answers

Chart Skills 1. literacy rate 2. United States; India

States, we grow wheat, corn, and other crops for which we have suitable soil and climate conditions. However, we cannot grow large quantities of coffee or bananas.

When nations specialize in certain goods, they obtain the goods they do not or cannot produce through importing and exporting. An **export** is a good or service sent to another country for sale. An **import** is a good or service brought in from another country for sale. For example, Costa Rica specializes in growing and exporting coffee. The nation uses the money to import goods that it does not produce.

In some cases, more than 70 percent of a nation's export trade depends upon a single resource. Examples include Kuwait (petroleum and natural gas), Guinea-Bissau (cashews), and the Marshall Islands (fish).

CHECKPOINT ***How does specialization create a need for trade?***

Absolute and Comparative Advantage

Suppose a nation enjoys an abundance of resources, including a rich natural environment, an educated workforce, and the latest technologies. In theory, such a nation could be self-sufficient, producing almost all that it needs by itself. Why, then, would it choose to engage in foreign trade?

Although self-sufficiency may sound appealing, it is actually better for countries to specialize in some products and trade for others. To see why, you need to look at two related concepts—absolute advantage and comparative advantage. A person or nation has an **absolute advantage** when it can produce more of a given product than another person or nation using a given amount of resources.

Absolute Advantage

A simple example can illustrate the idea of absolute advantage. Suppose that two people, Jenny and Carlos, work at making both birdhouses and printed T-shirts. In one hour, Carlos can either print six T-shirts or make two birdhouses. (See **Figure 17.2.**) Jenny can print one T-shirt or make one birdhouse per hour. In other words, Carlos is more productive than Jenny in making both T-shirts and birdhouses. In economic terms, Carlos has an absolute advantage over Jenny in producing both goods.

Figure 17.2 Productivity and Opportunity Cost

	Carlos	Jenny
T-shirts per hour	6	1
Birdhouses per hour	2	1
Opportunity cost of one T-shirt	1/3 birdhouse	1 birdhouse
Opportunity cost of one birdhouse	3 T-shirts	1 T-shirt

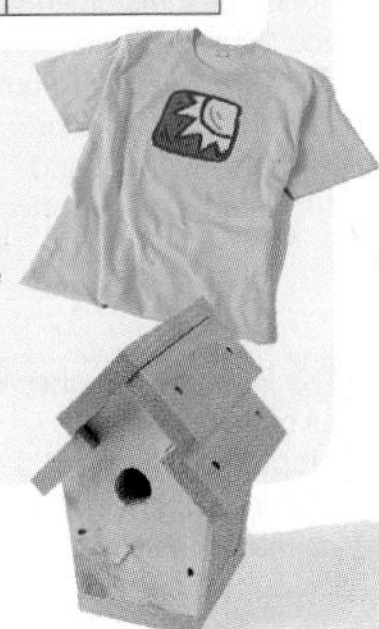

CHART SKILLS

Carlos has an absolute advantage over Jenny in producing both T-shirts and birdhouses. However, their opportunity costs are different.

1. **How many T-shirts can Carlos make in the time it takes Jenny to make five T-shirts?**
2. **Based on this table, why would Carlos be more productive making T-shirts than making birdhouses?**

Because Carlos enjoys an absolute advantage in both goods, should he remain self-sufficient? Or would he be better off specializing in either T-shirts or birdhouses? What about Jenny? Should she make T-shirts, birdhouses, or both?

Countries have to face the same sorts of questions. Should a wealthy country with many resources be self-sufficient, or should it specialize in producing a few products and trade for the others? How does a poorer nation decide what to produce? The answer to these questions lies with the concept of comparative advantage.

Comparative Advantage

Early in the nineteenth century, British economist David Ricardo argued that the key to determining which country should produce which goods is opportunity cost. Remember that opportunity cost is what you give up in order to produce a certain product.

A country has a **comparative advantage** in the product that it can produce most efficiently given all the products it could choose to produce. It is the nation with the comparative advantage—not necessarily the one with the absolute advantage—that should specialize in producing that good.

export a good or service sent to another country for sale

import a good or service brought in from another country for sale

absolute advantage the ability to produce more of a given product using a given amount of resources

comparative advantage the ability to produce a product most efficiently given all the other products that could be produced

DISCUSS

Note that many of the products on the transparency are produced in the United States, and that their manufacturers—such as Breyers Ice Cream and Gerber baby foods—are former U.S. companies that were purchased by companies located in other countries. Ask students to speculate about why these foreign owners have decided to keep production in the United States. *(proximity to markets, available labor and other resources)*

Then note that Sony, by comparison, exports TVs from Japan for sale in the United States. Have the class speculate why Sony doesn't manufacture TVs in the United States instead. *(Responses should include the labor and human capital advantages of manufacturing in Japan.)*

Ask students to explain how these two examples illustrate absolute and comparative advantage. *(Responses will vary but should recognize the concept that the products can be produced more efficiently in their current location than elsewhere.)* Ask **What would happen to American workers if Honda decided to move production of all Honda vehicles to Japan and export them back to the United States?** *(loss of jobs in the United States)*

L1 L2 Differentiate Review the meanings of *import, export, absolute advantage,* and *comparative advantage* with students. Ask students if Sony televisions are U.S. imports or U.S. exports. *(imports)* Ask **Are Honda Accords U.S. imports?** *(no)* **Why not?** *(They are produced in the United States.)* Ask students to give examples of goods that the United States imports and exports. Refer students who still have trouble to the interactive Economic Dictionary Online.

L4 Differentiate Have students research a major international company, such as Unilever or Kraft. They should discover which brands the company owns, and which countries they do business in. Ask students, **Are any of the items you use created by this company? How many?** Discuss the complicated nature of modern international business with students.

Background Note

For many years, science and engineering knowledge have given the United States a comparative advantage in many industries. Now, that advantage may be shifting to Asia. The National Science Board (NSB) collects data on science and technology education. According to author Thomas Friedman, a 2004 NSB report found that the United States has fallen from third to seventeenth in the number of science degrees awarded each year. Since the mid-1980s, the number of engineering degrees alone has fallen by more than 10 percent. Asian universities now graduate eight times as many engineers as U.S. universities. Science and engineering degrees represent 60 percent of the degrees awarded in China, 41 percent in Taiwan, 33 percent in South Korea, and 31 percent in the United States. In addition, many of the U.S. degrees are awarded to foreign students, a number of whom return home to work.

Answers

Checkpoint Nations must export goods they specialize in and use the money to import goods they do not produce.

Chart Skills 1. 30 2. He can produce more T-shirts per hour than birdhouses.

DETERMINE COMPARATIVE ADVANTAGE

Distribute the "Who Should Produce What?" worksheet (Unit 7 All-in-One, p. 15). This activity asks students to calculate opportunity costs in order to determine comparative advantage and to decide which of two products each of two countries should specialize in.

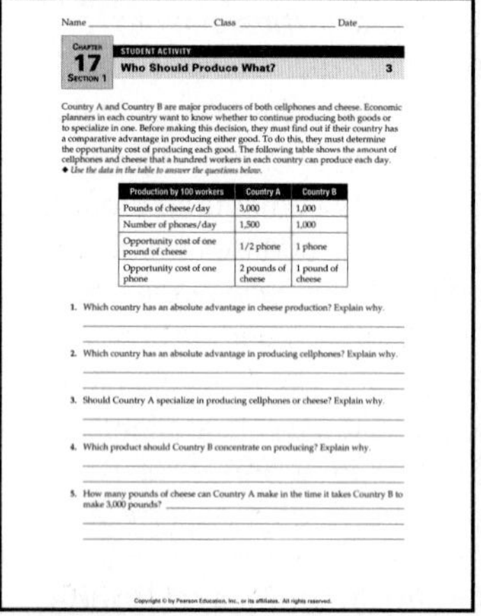

Name ____________ Class ____________ Date ________

Chapter 17 Section 1

STUDENT ACTIVITY

Who Should Produce What? 3

Country A and Country B are major producers of both cellphones and cheese. Economic planners in each country want to know whether to continue producing both goods or to specialize in one. Before making this decision, they must find out if their country has a comparative advantage in producing either good. To do this, they must determine the opportunity cost of producing each good. The following table shows the amount of cellphones and cheese that a hundred workers in each country can produce each day.

◆ *Use the data in the table to answer the questions below.*

Production by 100 workers	Country A	Country B
Pounds of cheese/day	3,000	1,000
Number of phones/day	1,500	1,000
Opportunity cost of one pound of cheese	1/2 phone	1 phone
Opportunity cost of one phone	2 pounds of cheese	1 pound of cheese

1. Which country has an absolute advantage in cheese production? Explain why.
2. Which country has an absolute advantage in producing cellphones? Explain why.
3. Should Country A specialize in producing cellphones or cheese? Explain why.
4. Which product should Country B concentrate on producing? Explain why.
5. How many pounds of cheese can Country A make in the time it takes Country B to make 3,000 pounds?

When all class members have completed their worksheets, call on students to give their answers to the questions. Then discuss how the results from this comparison could affect trade between these two nations.

L2 Differentiate Distribute the "Who Should Produce What?" worksheet (Unit 7 All-in-One, p. 16). Have students use the table to answer the questions.

How the Economy Works

How do specialization and trade benefit nations?

Every nation in the world engages in trade–even nations that have the ability to be self-sufficient. One reason is that specialization increases the number of products available to all.

1 Left on its own, Bartonia can produce 6 million bushels of wheat and 2 millions bales of cotton in a year. Alisium can produce 1 million bushels of wheat and 1 million bales of cotton.

BARTONIA
ALISIUM
6M
COTTON 2M
1M
COTTON 1M

2 The two countries do not trade.

1 Bartonia switches all of its cotton production to wheat. Alisium switches all of its resources to producing cotton.

BARTONIA
ALISIUM
9M
COTTON 4M

2 Bartonia trades 2 million bushels of wheat to Alisium in return for 2 million bales of cotton.

Production

Trade

According to the **law of comparative advantage,** a nation is better off when it produces goods and services for which it has a comparative advantage. Each nation can then use the money it earns selling those goods and services to buy those that it cannot produce as efficiently.

law of comparative advantage the principle that a nation is better off when it produces goods and services for which it has a comparative advantage

Importance of Opportunity Cost

To see how comparative advantage works, look again at **Figure 17.2.** It shows the opportunity costs of producing T-shirts and birdhouses for both Carlos and Jenny.

- *Carlos's opportunity costs* In an hour, Carlos can make either six T-shirts or two birdhouses. He therefore sacrifices three T-shirts for every birdhouse he produces. In terms of opportunity cost, the opportunity cost of a birdhouse is the three T-shirts he could have produced instead. The opportunity cost of a T-shirt is one third of a birdhouse.
- *Jenny's opportunity costs* In an hour, Jenny can make either one T-shirt or one birdhouse. Therefore, her opportunity cost for one birdhouse is one T-shirt, and her opportunity cost for one T-shirt is one birdhouse.

According to the law of comparative advantage, each person should produce the good for which he or she has a lower opportunity cost. Carlos's opportunity cost for producing a T-shirt (one third of a birdhouse) is lower than Jenny's (one birdhouse), so it is sensible for Carlos to produce T-shirts. Jenny's opportunity cost for producing a birdhouse (one T-shirt) is lower than Carlos's (three T-shirts), so Jenny should produce birdhouses.

Mutual Benefits

If Carlos wants a birdhouse, he can either make it himself or make T-shirts and trade

How the Economy Works online

For an animated, interactive version of this feature, visit **PearsonSuccessNet.com**

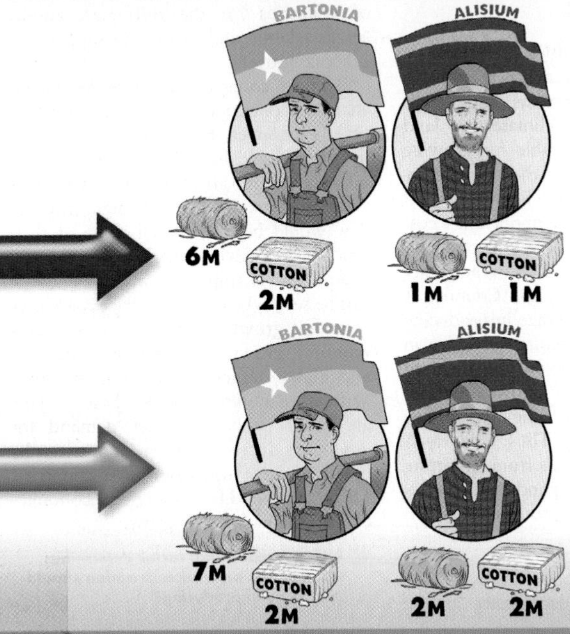

3 The two countries end up only with what each of them can produce.

3 Both countries end up with more than they would have if they had not specialized and traded.

Check Your Understanding

1. Which nation has a comparative advantage in producing wheat? Cotton?
2. What impact might trade between Bartonia and Alisium have on **(a)** production efficiency, **(b)** consumer choice, and **(c)** standard of living?

Net Result

some of them to Jenny for a birdhouse. Suppose Carlos and Jenny agree to trade two T-shirts for one birdhouse. In this case, Carlos is clearly better off producing T-shirts and trading for a birdhouse. After all, in the time he would have used to make his own birdhouse, he can make three T-shirts. Since he pays Jenny only two T-shirts for a birdhouse, he has a T-shirt left over. Trade makes Carlos better off by one T-shirt.

Jenny is also better off as the result of trade. She can make two birdhouses in the time she would need to produce two T-shirts for herself. Since she only pays one birdhouse to Carlos for the two T-shirts, she will still have one birdhouse left over. Trade makes her better off by one birdhouse.

Carlos and Jenny both benefit from trade. Each person specializes in producing the good for which he or she has a comparative advantage. Since both producers are operating at greater efficiency, more total goods are produced overall. After the trade, each of them is left with an extra unit of the good originally produced, which can be used to trade for other goods.

CHECKPOINT ***How is trade affected by opportunity cost?***

Comparative Advantage and World Trade

The lessons from the example of Carlos and Jenny also apply to trade between nations. As you saw, David Ricardo argued that the nation which has the lower opportunity cost in producing a good has a comparative advantage in producing that good. Remember, comparative advantage is the ability of one nation to produce a good at a lower opportunity cost than that of another nation. It is the nation with the comparative advantage—not necessarily the

ANALYZE AND COMPARE

Explain to students that the key ingredients in comparative advantage are specialization and trade. Nations specialize in the goods or services they produce most efficiently (with the lowest opportunity cost). Trade allows nations to export these goods and services, and import those that other nations produce most efficiently. Trading partners benefit because each nation can get more of the goods and services it needs at lower cost. The How the Economy Works feature on page 450 shows an example of this.

Divide students into two groups: one for the nation of Landia, and the other for the nation of Seanium. Tell students that Landia can produce 12,000 bushels of corn and 4,000 pounds of fish, and Seanium can produce 1,000 bushels of corn and 2,000 pounds of fish. Then have each group discuss what happens if Landia switches half of its fish production to producing corn, and Seanium switches all of its production to producing fish. Ask each group **How much corn and fish is Landia producing?** *(18,000 bushels corn, 2,000 pounds fish)* **How much corn and fish is Seanium producing?** *(no corn, 4,000 pounds fish)* **Which product does your nation have a comparative advantage in producing?** *(Landia: corn; Seanium: fish)* **Why?** *(Landia: produces corn more efficiently than Seanium.; Seanium: produces fish more efficiently than Landia.)* **Which product should you export, and which should you import?** *(Landia: export corn, import fish; Seanium: export fish, import corn.)* Tell students that Landia trades 4,000 bushels of corn for 2,000 pounds of fish from Seanium. **How does comparative advantage benefit both nations when they trade with each other?** *(Both countries end up with more corn that they would have had if they had not traded.)*

L2 ELL LPR Differentiate Make sure that students understand the difference between *human capital* and *labor.* Then ask **How are labor and human capital related?** *(Possible answer: Knowledge and skills are needed do jobs.)* Ask students how their presence in school is affecting the nation's human capital. *(increasing it by getting an education)*

Virtual Economics

L1 L2 Differentiate

Understanding the Uneven Distribution of Resources Use the following lesson from the NCEE **Virtual Economics *CD-ROM*** to help students understand why trade develops between nations. Click on Browse Economics Lessons, specify grades 6–8, and use the key words *international trade.*

In this activity, students will take part in a simulation that illustrates how uneven distribution of resources leads to trading relationships.

LESSON TITLE	INTERNATIONAL TRADE
Type of Activity	Simulation
Complexity	High
Time	50 minutes
NCEE Standards	5, 6

Answers

Check Your Understanding 1. Bartonia; Alisium 2. (a) increased efficiency (b) greater choice (c) higher standards of living

Checkpoint Nations concentrate on goods that have low opportunity costs to produce and trade for goods that have high opportunity costs to produce.

ANALYZE RESOURCE DISTRIBUTION

Distribute the "Analyze Maps" skill worksheet (Unit 7 All-in-One, p. 17). This activity asks students to create a map of world oil resources and then answer questions about the relationship of oil resources, oil consumption, and world trade. Have students create their maps and answer the questions on their own. When everyone has completed the worksheet, discuss the answers as a class.

L1 L2 Differentiate Distribute the "Analyze Maps" skills worksheet (Unit 7 All-in-One, p. 18), and have students answer the questions.

COMPARE AND CONTRAST

Remind students that the United States is the world's leading importer and second-largest exporter and copy the following table on the chalkboard:

TOP U.S. TRADE PARTNERS, 2008

RANK	IMPORTS	PERCENT OF TOTAL IMPORTS	EXPORTS	PERCENT OF TOTAL EXPORTS
1	Canada	17%	Canada	21%
2	China	15%	Mexico	11%
3	Mexico	11%	China	6%
4	Japan	7%	Japan	5%
5	Germany	5%	Britain	4%

Source: U.S. Department of Commerce

Discuss the table with the class. Call on students to compare and contrast the U.S. position as an importer with its position as an exporter. Students should note that about half of all U.S. trade (50% of imports and 43% of exports) takes place with the same four nations, and that Canada is the nation's leading trade partner. Call attention to the positions of Mexico and China as destinations for U.S. exports and as sources of imports to the United States. Ask students to give examples of imports from each of the countries on the import list.

L2 ELL Differentiate Ask students to identify products from their first countries that are available in the United States. Also ask them to name U.S. products that are sold in their first countries. *(Possible responses: Coca Cola, McDonalds, Microsoft)*

Answers

Checkpoint comparative advantage

Critical Thinking He was able to succeed by tapping an overseas demand for his products when none existed at home.

interdependence the shared need of countries for resources, goods, services, labor, and knowledge supplied by other countries

absolute advantage–that should specialize in producing that good.

Comparative Advantage in Action

Suppose two countries, A and B, are capable of producing both bananas and sugar. However, Country A's climate and land are somewhat more suitable for growing bananas. For Country A, the opportunity cost of a ton of bananas is two tons of sugar. For Country B, the opportunity cost of a ton of bananas is three tons of sugar. Since Country A has a lower opportunity cost than does Country B, Country A has a comparative advantage in producing bananas. It should therefore specialize in growing bananas and exporting them to the world market. Trade allows countries to obtain goods for which they might have a high opportunity cost. Thus, Country A can use the money it earns from exporting bananas to import other goods and services that it cannot efficiently produce for itself.

Growing Interdependence

The growth of international trade has led to greater economic interdependence among nations. **Interdependence** is the shared need of countries for the resources, goods, services, labor, and knowledge supplied by other countries.

Because countries are interdependent, changes in one country's economy influence other economies. For example, a drought in Brazil would hurt that country's coffee growers. Coffee growers in Costa Rica or Colombia may benefit, though, because they would be able to sell more of their product on the world market.

Another example of interdependence can be seen when one country experiences economic growth. Suppose that Mexico's economy grows, resulting in more jobs and higher wages for Mexican workers. With more money available, these workers are likely to have greater demand for goods produced in other countries. By buying those goods from other countries, Mexicans would be helping the economies of its trade partners to grow.

CHECKPOINT ***What factor determines what goods or services a nation should specialize in producing?***

Innovators

Akio Morita

"I knew we needed a weapon to break through to the US market," recalled Akio Morita. The Japanese entrepreneur had co-founded a telecommunications company in 1946. But the firm found few buyers in a country still recovering from war. After visiting America, Morita dreamed of creating a blockbuster product for the booming economy. "It had to be something different," he realized.

The solution came quickly. Company engineers devised a transistorized radio to fit in one's pocket. Morita returned to America in 1957 to market it. At first, there was little interest. Then Bulova Watch offered to purchase 100,000 radios. There was a catch, though. The radios had to bear Bulova's name. Morita refused—the best decision of his career, he later said. Why? Early on, he recognized that the radio could help establish a global brand name. To that end, he also changed the corporate name to something easy to say and remember: Sony.

The Sony Corporation went on to create other innovative products, like the Walkman, for the world market. Morita also formed multinational partnerships that led Sony into new areas such as entertainment and finance. By the time he died in 1999, he had built a global business empire.

Critical Thinking ***How was Morita's success related to global supply and demand?***

SONY

Fast Facts

Akio Morita
Born: January 26, 1921, in Nagoya, Japan
Died: October 3, 1999, in Tokyo, Japan
Education: Osaka Imperial University, 1944
Claim to Fame: Founder of Sony Corporation

The United States and Trade

The United States enjoys a comparative advantage in producing many goods and services. What, then, is its position as an importer and exporter?

The United States as Exporter

The United States is the world's third largest exporter, close behind Germany and China. One reason is its wide range of export products, from soybeans to telecommunications equipment. Another reason is that the United States excels in technologically sophisticated goods such as software, chemicals, and medical testing supplies. In 2007, a journalist explained the reasons for a surge in U.S. exports:

> "An expanding foreign appetite for capital goods such as tractors, medical equipment and electrical machinery is driving much of the boom. . . . There also is increased international demand for complex . . . products for which 'made in the U.S.A.' remains shorthand for reliability."
>
> —Michael A. Fletcher, *Washington Post*

Goods make up the bulk of international trade, but the United States is also the world's leading exporter of services. These include education, computer and data processing, financial services, and medical care. Exports of services have grown rapidly over the last decade.

The United States as Importer

The United States is also the world's top importer—by a significant amount. U.S. imports total nearly $1.9 trillion, or 15.5 percent of the world's total. That amount exceeds the combined totals for Germany and China, the next two largest importers.

The World Economy Databank on pages 474–476 gives additional information about American foreign trade—whom we trade with, how much we trade, and what we trade. As you might expect, we export more to neighboring Canada and Mexico than to any other nations. However, you might be surprised to see how high China ranks in terms of imports. In Chapter 18, you will learn more about the growing role of China in the world economy.

✔ **CHECKPOINT** ***How does the United States rank in world exports and imports?***

▲ In recent decades, many American jobs have gone overseas or become obsolete due to technological changes. Many companies offer programs to help workers gain new skills. ***How might a company benefit from retraining workers rather than hiring new ones?***

The Effects of Trade on Employment

Trade allows nations to specialize in producing a limited number of goods while consuming a greater variety of goods. However, specialization can also dramatically change a nation's employment patterns. The impact may be negative (loss of jobs) or positive (creation of new job opportunities)—or both.

Specialization and Job Loss

To help you better understand the effects of international trade on employment, think back to the example of Carlos and Jenny. Remember that Carlos can make six T-shirts or two birdhouses by himself in an hour. Suppose he hires Amy to help him build birdhouses. He later realizes that he should specialize only in T-shirts since that is where his comparative advantage lies. Since he no longer needs Amy to help him make birdhouses, he fires her.

Up to this point, Amy has specialized in the skills needed to make birdhouses. These skills are no longer in demand where she lives. She now has several options:

- Amy can gain new job skills that are more in demand. She might find a job retraining program and learn to make T-shirts or some other product. With her new skills, Amy might even find herself better off than when she was making birdhouses.

PERSONAL FINANCE ACTIVITY

Remind students that they can increase their understanding of how to find a job by reading the lesson "Getting a Job" in the Personal Finance Handbook on pages PF42–43 and completing the worksheet (Personal Finance All-in-One, pp. 103–104).

EXTEND

Have students reread the information under The Effects of Trade on Employment on pages 453 and 454 of their textbook. Then have them write a blog post that takes a position on the following issue: Should the United States limit trade in order to prevent possible job loss or become more self-sufficient? Call on students to present their work to the class.

L1 L2 ELL LPR Differentiate Have students create a poster or draw an editorial cartoon expressing a position on the effect of trade on employment in the United States.

GUIDING QUESTION WRAP UP

Have students return to the section Guiding Question. Review the completed graphic organizer and clarify any misunderstandings. Have a wrap-up discussion about why nations trade.

Assess and Remediate

L3 L2 Collect the "Who Should Produce What?" worksheets and assess students' understanding of comparative advantage and specialization.

L3 L2 Collect the "Analyze Maps" skill worksheet and assess student understanding of world oil production.

L3 Assign the Section 1 Assessment questions; identify student misconceptions.

L3 Give Section Quiz A (Unit 7 All-in-One, p. 19).

L2 Give Section Quiz B (Unit 7 All-in-One, p. 20).

(Assess and Remediate continued on p. 454)

Answers

Checkpoint world's third-largest exporter and top importer

Photo Possible answer: Current workers have known abilities, a work record, and company loyalty. The hiring of new workers introduces unknown factors.

Have students complete the Self-Test Online and continue their work in the **Essential Questions Journal**.

REMEDIATION AND SUGGESTIONS

Use the chart below to help students who are struggling with content.

WEAKNESS	REMEDIATION
Defining key terms (Questions 4, 5, 7)	Have students use the interactive Economic Dictionary Online.
The impact of unequal distribution of resources (Questions 1, 8, 9)	Review the section's graphic organizer with students
Specialization and comparative advantage (Questions 4, 5, 6, 8, 9, 11)	Reteach the "Who Should Do What?" worksheet by working through each question.
The U.S. position in world trade (Questions 2, 8, 11)	Review the Bellringer transparency and the table on p. 452 with students.
The effects of trade on employment (Question 10)	Have students role-play a manager explaining options to a worker who has lost his or her job as a result of trade.

Answer

Checkpoint Retrain for a different job or relocate to a place where his or her old type of job is available.

- Amy can move to another location where her existing skills are still in demand. If she chooses to relocate, she may or may not be better off. How well she does depends on the wages she earns from her new job, housing prices in her new location, the impact on her family, and a variety of other factors.
- Amy can stay where she is and take a job that calls for lesser skills. In this case, she might well earn less money than she did making birdhouses. As a result, she may have to cut back on the goods and services she consumes, or take a second job to maintain her standard of living.
- If Amy takes none of these three options, she will be unemployed.

FUTURE WATCH **Personal Finance** For information on finding a job, see your Personal Finance Handbook in the back of the book or visit **PearsonSuccessNet.com**

Trade and Employment in the United States

Carlos's decision to focus on his comparative advantage and specialize in making T-shirts had an impact on Amy's economic well-being. In the same way, the comparative advantage of nations affects the economic well-being of workers living in those nations.

In the past two decades, international trade has led to significant changes in U.S. employment patterns. During the 1970s, for example, high worker productivity and new technologies like robotics helped give Japan a comparative advantage in making automobiles. As a result, Japanese cars became less expensive than many comparable American-made cars. As more consumers bought Japanese cars, American car companies lost business. Falling sales led them to reduce their workforce, costing many American auto workers their jobs.

Businesses and government often provide help to retrain laid-off workers or assist them in relocating. However, these two options are not easy, especially in the case of older workers or workers with families. In some cases, retraining or relocation are not possible at all. Some workers may be forced to take lower-paying jobs or face prolonged unemployment.

Of course, job loss is not the only possible result of trade. If American exports grow, there will be more demand for workers to make those products. Workers who lost jobs because they were on the negative end of comparative advantage can try to find work in those growing industries. To do so, they might have to retrain so they can gain the needed skills.

CHECKPOINT ***What options might a worker have who loses a job due to trade?***

SECTION 1 ASSESSMENT

Essential Questions Journal To continue to build a response to the Essential Question, go to your **Essential Questions Journal.**

Guiding Question

1. Use your completed cause-and-effect chart to answer this question: Why do nations trade?
2. **Extension** What are three products or services that you enjoy having or using that depend on trade?

Key Terms and Main Ideas

3. What impact does the distribution of resources have on trade?
4. How do **absolute advantage** and **comparative advantage** differ?
5. According to the **law of comparative advantage,** what goods should a nation choose to produce?
6. What is the role of opportunity cost in determining comparative advantage?
7. What role do **exports** and **imports** play in the United States economy?

Critical Thinking

8. **Apply** Susan, who lives in North Dakota, grows coffee in a greenhouse under sunlamps. This effort requires high energy costs for heating. She also grows sunflowers, which do not require such high energy costs. Which product should she specialize in growing, and why?
9. **Cause and Effect** What effect might the invention of an inexpensive sugar substitute have on the trade of other countries? Why?
10. **Analyze** Review the four possible outcomes for a worker who loses his or her job as a result of trade. What are the advantages and disadvantages of each outcome?

Math Skills

11. The chart below shows the total value of U.S. exports and U.S. imports in 2007 and the percentage of both exports and imports that came from agricultural products. Calculate the dollar value of farm products, exports and imports. Explain whether you think the data supports the conclusion that the United States has a comparative advantage in farming. ***Visit PearsonSuccessNet.com for additional math help.***

	Exports	Imports
Total Value	$1.14 trillion	$1.987 trillion
Agricultural products as percent of total	9.2%	4.9%

SOURCE: *CIA World Factbook, 2008*

Assessment Answers

1. to sell goods they make and to buy goods they need but do not make efficiently
2. Possible answer: my jeans, which were made in Mexico; my Chinese-made cellphone; the family car, which was imported from Germany
3. Nations produce goods that they have the resources to produce and trade for those that they do not.
4. Absolute advantage is the ability to produce more of something, given the same amount of resources. Comparative advantage is the ability to produce something at a lower opportunity cost.
5. those that it can produce at the lowest opportunity cost
6. Nations that can produce goods at a lower opportunity cost than other nations have a comparative advantage.
7. Both play an important role. The U.S. is the world's second-largest exporter and the largest importer.
8. Sunflowers, for which her costs are not so high. Warmer places such as Costa Rica have the comparative advantage over her in growing coffee.
9. It would reduce U.S. sugar imports because of lower demand for sugar. Also, more sugar produced in the United States would be available for export.
10. gain new skills: advantages–new job might pay better than old one; disadvantages–new job might not pay as well as old one; relocate: advantages–same kind of work; disadvantages–inconvenience; take a lesser job: advantages–gets to stay where she is; disadvantages–lower income and standard of living; unemployment: advantages–time to get new training; disadvantages–no income
11. Exports: $104,880,000,000; Imports: $97,363,000,000; Yes, because the U.S. exports more agricultural products than it imports.

SECTION **2** Trade Barriers and Agreements

OBJECTIVES

1. **Define** various types of trade barriers.
2. **Analyze** the effects of trade barriers on economic activities.
3. **Summarize** arguments in favor of protectionism.
4. **Evaluate** the benefits and costs of participation in international trade agreements.
5. **Explain** the role of multinationals in the global market.

ECONOMIC DICTIONARY

As you read the section, look for the definitions of these **Key Terms:**

- trade barrier
- tariff
- import quota
- sanctions
- embargo
- trade war
- protectionism
- infant industry
- free trade
- free-trade zone

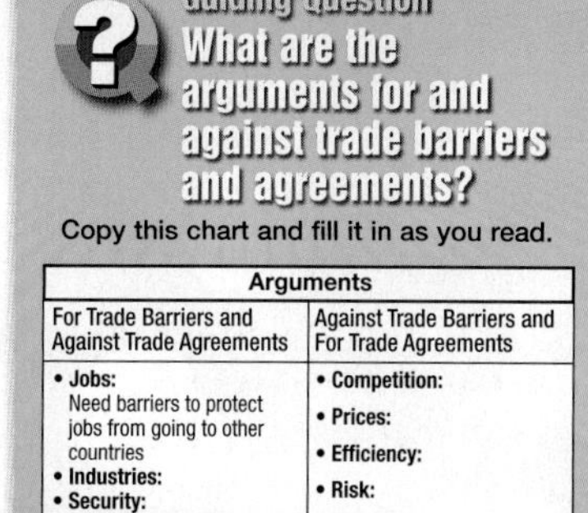
Guiding Question
What are the arguments for and against trade barriers and agreements?

Copy this chart and fill it in as you read.

Arguments	
For Trade Barriers and Against Trade Agreements	Against Trade Barriers and For Trade Agreements
• Jobs: Need barriers to protect jobs from going to other countries • Industries: • Security: • Multinationals:	• Competition: • Prices: • Efficiency: • Risk:

Economics and You Would you take part in a march to protest against a trade policy? That's what more than 100,000 citizens of Costa Rica did in September 2007. Chanting slogans like "Costa Rica is not for sale," the marchers voiced opposition to a trade agreement that their government was about to sign with the United States. To these protesters, trade policy was not just an economic idea, it had a major impact on their lives. And the same is true of you—whether you know it or not.

trade barrier a means of preventing a foreign product or service from freely entering a nation's territory

tariff a tax on imported goods

Principles in Action Today, many people favor increased foreign trade, while others fear its effects. To understand why, you need to understand the kinds of barriers that nations sometimes erect to trade. In this section, you will also see how trade policies may affect what you pay for dozens of products, from chocolate to cars.

Figure 17.3 **Average Tariff Rates, 1900–2005**

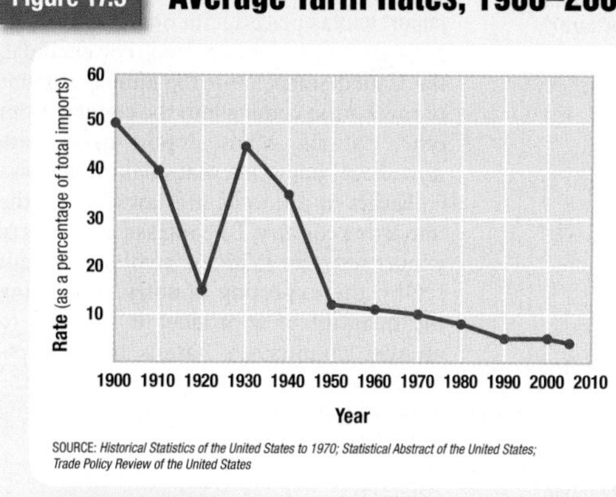

SOURCE: *Historical Statistics of the United States to 1970; Statistical Abstract of the United States; Trade Policy Review of the United States*

GRAPH SKILLS

One purpose of a high tariff is to shield American producers from foreign competition.

1. Describe the overall trend in tariff rates since 1930.
2. Why was it less risky for American manufacturers to charge high prices in 1900 than in 2000?

Trade Barriers

A **trade barrier,** or trade restriction, is a means of preventing a foreign product or service from freely entering a nation's territory. Trade barriers take several forms and may be used for various purposes.

Tariffs

One common trade barrier is a **tariff,** or a tax on imported goods. Until the early 1900s, tariffs were a major tool of fiscal policy and the main source of revenue for the federal government. As you can see from **Figure 17.3,** however, tariffs today are much

Guiding Question

What are the arguments for and against trade barriers and agreements?

Get Started

Arguments	
For Trade Barriers and Against Trade Agreements	Against Trade Barriers and For Trade Agreements
• **Jobs:** Need barriers to protect jobs from going to other countries • **Industries:** Need trade barriers to protect domestic industries • **Security:** Need trade barriers to protect national security • **Multinationals:** To limit power of multinationals	• **Competition:** Trade agreements allow and enhance competition • **Prices:** Trade barriers increase prices for foreign goods • **Efficiency:** Free trade increases efficiency • **Risk:** Trade barriers increase risk of trade wars

LESSON GOALS

Students will:

- Know the Key Terms.
- Identify the various types of trade barriers.
- Assess the effects of trade barriers by completing a table of winners and losers.
- Analyze the arguments for and against international trade agreements and free trade.

BEFORE CLASS

Have students complete the graphic organizer in the Section Opener or the Guided Reading and Review worksheet (Unit 7 All-in-One, p. 21).

L1 **L2** **ELL LPR Differentiate** Have students complete the Guided Reading and Review worksheet (Unit 7 All-in-One, p. 22).

Answers

Graph Skills 1. Rates have fallen. 2. High tariffs on imports protected high domestic prices in 1900.

Focus on the Basics

Students need to come away with the following understandings:

FACTS: • Trade barriers prevent foreign products from freely entering a nation's territory. They include tariffs, import quotas, sanctions, and embargoes. • Trade barriers protect domestic industries and jobs by increasing the prices of foreign goods. • International trade agreements lower or eliminate trade barriers and encourage trade among participating nations. • Multinational corporations avoid some barriers by locating production in other countries.

GENERALIZATION: Trade barriers protect domestic industries and jobs by discouraging trade, while trade agreements encourage trade and benefit consumers at the cost of some domestic jobs.

CLASSROOM HINTS

BEEF WARS

To show students an example of a trade war, have them look at the "Beef Wars" Future Watch feature on page 457. Have them discuss why the trade war was probably a bad thing for consumers and producers in both the EU and the United States. To facilitate discussion, remind students of the effects tariffs have on prices. Clarify the sequence of events in the trade war if necessary.

BELLRINGER

Before class begins, draw a cluster diagram on the board. Put the words *Trade Barriers* in the center oval and five empty ovals around it. Tell students to copy it into their notebooks and complete it.

Teach

Economics online To present this topic using digital resources, use the lecture notes on www.PearsonSuccessNet.com.

REVIEW BELLRINGER ANSWERS

Remind students of their responses to the Extend activity at the end of Section 1 and the reasons they gave for limiting trade. Ask **Can you think of other reasons for limiting trade with particular countries?** *(political disagreements; need to encourage domestic industries; environmental concerns)* Then, review answers to the Bellringer with the class. Students should have listed the following examples of trade barriers: *tariffs, import quotas, voluntary export restraints [VERs], sanctions, embargoes.* Call on students to explain what each of these barriers is and how it meets one of the goals of restricting trade.

▲ Travelers returning from overseas must declare what purchases they are bringing back and pay any required customs duties on these items. Customs agents like these try to prevent people from smuggling undeclared items into the country. ***What makes customs duties a form of tariff?***

lower. Still, the United States continues to collect tariffs on steel, foreign-made cars, and many other products.

If you have traveled abroad, you may have had to pay a tax on foreign goods you brought back to the United States. These customs duties are another form of tariff.

Quotas and VERS

Another kind of barrier is an import quota. **Import quotas** place a limit on the amount of a good that can be imported. For example, the United States limits the annual amount of raw cotton coming into the country from other nations. Many import quotas are now illegal under international trade laws.

Tariffs and quotas are laws set by the importing country. By contrast, a voluntary export restraint (VER) is a voluntary limit set by the exporting country, restricting the quantity of a product it will sell to another country. A nation that adopts a VER seeks to reduce the risk that the importing country will impose damaging trade barriers itself.

import quota a set limit on the amount of a good that can be imported

Other Barriers to Trade

Other government actions may also create trade barriers. For example, a government may require foreign companies to obtain a license to sell goods in that country. High licensing fees or slow licensing processes act as informal trade barriers.

sanctions actions a nation or group of nations takes in order to punish or put pressure on another nation

embargo a ban on trade with a particular country

Health, safety, or environmental regulations can also act as trade barriers. Suppose a nation treats the fruit it grows with a particular insecticide. Another nation might ban any fruit treated with that insecticide in order to discourage imports of foreign fruit. The U.S. anti-pollution standards that require cars to be equipped with catalytic converters is another example. Cars that do not meet this requirement cannot be exported to the United States.

Finally, a nation may impose trade barriers and other economic sanctions for political reasons. **Sanctions** are actions a nation or group of nations takes in order to punish or put pressure on another nation. For example, in the 1960s, the United States banned all trade with Cuba. The purpose of this trade **embargo** was to cause economic strain that might weaken Cuba's communist dictatorship.

CHECKPOINT ***How do voluntary export restraints differ from import quotas?***

Effects of Trade Barriers

By limiting supply, trade barriers can have very different effects on domestic producers and consumers. Trade barriers may also create tense relations between importing and exporting countries.

Increased Prices for Foreign Goods

Trade barriers can help domestic producers compete with foreign firms. By limiting imports from those firms, or by making the prices of those imports higher, trade barriers help domestic companies.

Although domestic producers may benefit, consumers can lose out. Restrictions on imports result in higher prices. For example, suppose the market price of an imported car is $20,000. If the government places a 10 percent tariff on all imported foreign cars, the price of the average imported car would increase from $20,000 to $22,000. Consumers who bought such a vehicle would be paying a higher price than if there had been no tariff. Also, with foreign competition limited, domestic carmakers would have no incentive to keep prices low.

Differentiated Resources

- **L1 L2 Guided Reading and Review** (Unit 7 All-in-One, p. 22)
- **L2 Trade Barriers: Winners and Losers** (Unit 7 All-in-One, p. 24)
- **L4 NAFTA: Pro and Con** (Unit 7 All-in-One, p. 25)

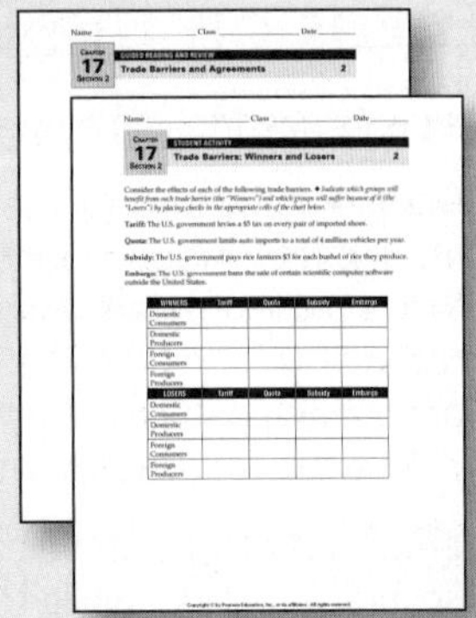

Answers

Photo They are taxes on goods coming into the country.

Checkpoint A VER is a voluntary limit on how much of a good a country exports to another country. An import quota applies to how much of the good a country allows to be imported, and it is mandatory.

Trade Wars

Trade barriers may also fuel international conflict. When one country restricts imports, its trading partner may retaliate by placing its own restrictions on imports. If the first country responds with further trade limits, the result is a **trade war,** a cycle of escalating trade barriers. Trade wars often cause economic hardship for both sides.

Probably the most damaging trade war in American history began during the Great Depression. In 1930, Congress passed the Smoot-Hawley Act, raising average tariff rates on all imports to 50 percent. Congress hoped the tariff would protect American workers and businesses from foreign competition and help the economy rebound.

The reverse effect took place, though. Other countries responded by raising tariffs on American-made goods. The resulting trade war decreased international trade and deepened the worldwide depression. Most economists blame the Smoot-Hawley tariff for increasing American unemployment.

Trade wars still occur, but they usually involve a few products rather than all imports. In 2002, the United States placed temporary tariffs on imported steel to help American steelmakers recover from bankruptcy. European nations threatened to retaliate. This "steel war" ended when an international panel ruled that the tariffs were illegal.

CHECKPOINT ***Why are trade wars harmful?***

Arguments for Protectionism

Why does a nation impose trade barriers? One reason is **protectionism,** the use of trade barriers to shield domestic industries from foreign competition. Protectionists have generally used three main arguments to support their view: saving jobs, protecting infant industries, and safeguarding national security.

Protecting Jobs

One argument for protectionism is that it shelters workers in industries that may be hurt by foreign competition. Suppose that certain East Asian nations had a comparative advantage in producing textiles. If the United States cut tariffs on textile imports, domestic manufacturers might find it hard to compete with imports from East Asia. They would have to close their factories and lay off workers.

Ideally, the laid-off workers would take new jobs in other industries. In practice, however, many of these workers would find retraining or relocation difficult. In addition, few industry or political leaders want to see existing industries shut down or large numbers of people lose their jobs. For this reason, public officials might favor protectionism to keep companies alive and people working.

trade war a cycle of escalating trade barriers

protectionism the use of trade barriers to shield domestic industries from foreign competition

FUTURE WATCH **Global Impact**

Beef Wars

In 1985, the European Union banned imports of meat derived from animals treated with growth hormones. The EU said the ban was motivated by health concerns. However, the U.S. beef industry saw it as protectionism, an unfair attempt to shield European producers from American competition. What followed became known as the Beef War. ***How else might health and environmental concerns affect trade?***

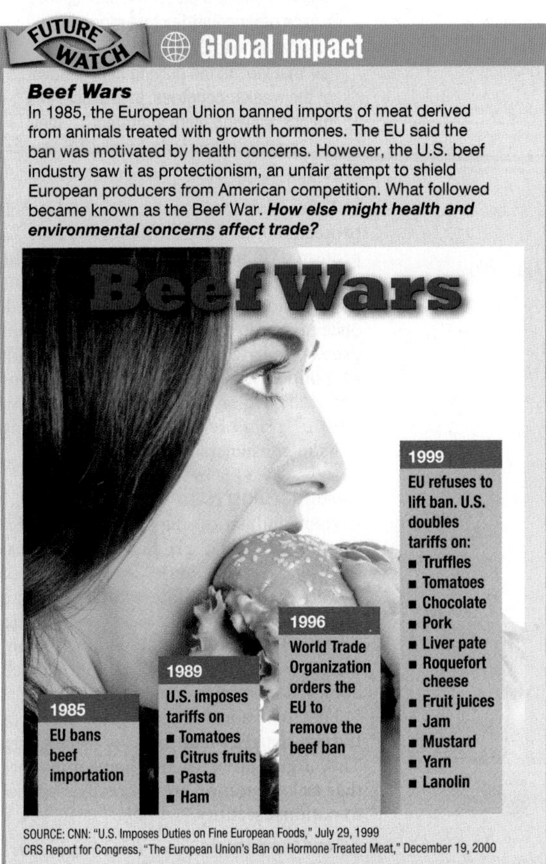

Beef Wars
1985
EU bans beef importation
1989
U.S. imposes tariffs on
■ Tomatoes
■ Citrus fruits
■ Pasta
■ Ham
1996
World Trade Organization orders the EU to remove the beef ban
1999
EU refuses to lift ban. U.S. doubles tariffs on:
■ Truffles
■ Tomatoes
■ Chocolate
■ Pork
■ Liver pate
■ Roquefort cheese
■ Fruit juices
■ Jam
■ Mustard
■ Yarn
■ Lanolin

SOURCE: CNN: "U.S. Imposes Duties on Fine European Foods," July 29, 1999
CRS Report for Congress, "The European Union's Ban on Hormone Treated Meat," December 19, 2000

DISTRIBUTE STUDENT ACTIVITY

Distribute the "Trade Barriers: Winners and Losers" worksheet (Unit 7 All-in-One, p. 23). This activity asks students to determine how various types of trade barriers affect domestic and foreign producers and consumers.

L1 L2 Differentiate Distribute the "Trade Barriers: Winners and Losers" worksheet (Unit 7 All-in-One, p. 24).

DISCUSS

Review the answers to the worksheet with the class. Ask students why tariffs benefit domestic producers and hurt domestic consumers. *(protect industries, raise prices)* Ask **How do tariffs benefit foreign consumers?** *(By discouraging the export of a product, they increase its supply on the home market.)* Discuss why quotas have the same effects on producers and consumers that tariffs do. *(Both have the effect of limiting imports.)*

Ask students to explain how subsidies function as trade barriers. *(They make it harder for foreign producers to compete.)* Discuss why both foreign and domestic consumers benefit from subsidies. *(They encourage production for both domestic markets and for export.)* Discuss how embargoes help domestic consumers and hurt foreign ones. *(increase domestic supply; good unavailable to foreign consumers)* Ask **Why does an embargo hurt domestic producers of the embargoed good?** *(deprives them of markets)* **How would it benefit foreign producers?** *(encourages the growth of industries in other countries to produce the embargoed product)*

Virtual Economics

L3 Differentiate

Analyzing Barriers to Trade Use the following lesson from the NCEE **Virtual Economics *CD-ROM*** to help students to understand the pros and cons of various barriers to trade. Click on Browse Economics Lessons, specify grades 9–12, and use the key words *international trade.*

In this activity, students will use data on U.S. trade and analyze various ways governments erect barriers to trade.

LESSON TITLE	WHY WOULD GOVERNMENTS LIMIT INTERNATIONAL TRADE?
Type of Activity	Using statistics
Complexity	Moderate
Time	100 minutes
NCEE Standards	5, 6

Answers

Checkpoint They cause economic hardship in the countries involved.

Global Impact Possible answer: The EU was concerned about health issues, but may also have been trying to protect European farmers from competition. The U.S. was trying to pressure the EU to lift the ban.

DISPLAY TRANSPARENCY

Display the "Benefiting American Business" transparency (Color Transparencies, 17.b). Guide students through the interpretation of this editorial cartoon. Ask **Where is the setting of this cartoon and what is taking place?** *(a company conference or boardroom; a meeting of company executives, officers, or board members)* **What is the man who has his hand raised doing?** *(saying "I move that we go on record for fewer imports here and more imports there.")* Ask students if this man is a protectionist, and to explain why or why not. *(Yes, because he wants fewer imports ["fewer imports here"].)* Ask what the man's desire for "more imports there" means. *(calling for more exports to other places ["there"])* Ask **If the man in the cartoon got his way, under what circumstances could it lead to a trade war?** *(If this country took steps to bar imports from 'there,' foreign countries might retaliate by banning imports from 'here.' This could escalate into a trade war.)*

Ask students whether they agree with the sentiments expressed in this cartoon. Discuss who benefits from protectionism and whether consumers are among the beneficiaries. Consider the impact of protectionism on domestic employment, international relations, and world trade.

L2 ELL LPR Differentiate Review the meaning of protectionism with students. Point out that the root word of *protectionism* is *protect,* and ask what clues that connection provides to the term's meaning. Ask students what a barrier is. Note that building a barrier is one way of protecting something. Ask students how trade barriers, including tariffs and import quotas, are related to protectionism.

(lesson continued on p. 460)

infant industry an industry in the early stages of development

free trade the lowering or elimination of protective tariffs and other trade barriers between two or more nations

Protecting Infant Industries

Another argument for protectionism is that industries in the early stages of development need time and experience to become efficient producers. Tariffs that raise the price of imported goods provide a period of time for these **infant industries** to become more competitive. Once that happens, the tariff can be eliminated.

In the early years of the United States, Alexander Hamilton favored using tariffs to protect young American industries from European competition. Today, many developing nations adopt protectionist policies for similar reasons:

> "Global economic competition is a game of unequal players. It pits against each other countries that range from Switzerland to Swaziland.... It is only fair that we 'tilt the playing field' in favor of the weaker countries. In practice, this means allowing them to protect ... their producers more vigorously."
>
> —Ha-Joon Chang, "Protecting the Global Poor"

Three problems may arise with such protective tariffs, however. First, a protected infant industry may lack the incentive to "grow up," that is, to become more efficient and competitive. Second, once an industry has been given tariff protection, lawmakers may find it difficult for political reasons to take the protections away. Third, a protected industry can keep its prices relatively high, increasing costs to consumers.

Safeguarding National Security

Certain industries may require protection because their products are essential to defending the country. In the event of a war, the United States would need an uninterrupted supply of steel, energy, and advanced technologies. For this reason, the government wants to ensure that such domestic industries remain active.

Foes of trade barriers agree that protecting defense industries is important. They argue, however, that some industries that seek protection are not really essential to national security.

CHECKPOINT ***What are three arguments given for protectionism?***

Trade Agreements

In opposition to protectionism is the principle of free trade. **Free trade** involves the lowering or elimination of protective tariffs and other trade barriers between two or more nations. Supporters argue that free trade is the best way to pursue comparative advantage, raise living standards, and further cooperative relationships among nations.

To encourage free trade, a number of countries in recent decades have signed international free trade agreements. Some of these pacts involve dozens of nations.

Roots of Free Trade

Today's free trade movement began in the 1930s. As you read, the Smoot-Hawley Act caused a rapid decline in international trade. To encourage trade, Congress passed the Reciprocal Trade Agreements Act of 1934. It gave the President the power to reduce tariffs by as much as 50 percent.

That law also allowed Congress to grant most-favored-nation (MFN) status to U.S. trading partners. Today, MFN status is called normal trade relations status, or NTR. All countries with NTR status pay the same tariffs, though imports from non-NTR nations may be taxed at a higher rate.

In 1948, after World War II had disrupted world trade, many nations reached an agreement called the General Agreement on Tariffs and Trade (GATT). Its goal was to reduce tariffs and stabilize world trade.

World Trade Organization

In 1995, the World Trade Organization (WTO) was founded with the goal of making global trade more free. The WTO works to ensure that countries comply with GATT, to negotiate new trade agreements, and to resolve trade disputes. Various conferences, or rounds, of tariff negotiations have advanced the goals of GATT and the WTO. For example, the Uruguay round of negotiations, completed in 1994, decreased average global tariffs by about a third.

Today, the World Trade Organization also acts as a referee, enforcing the rules agreed upon by the member countries. WTO decisions resolved the beef war and the steel tariff disputes between the United States and the European Union.

Background Note

Dumping One issue that has accompanied the lowering of trade barriers is a practice known as "dumping." In international trade law, dumping occurs when a manufacturer exports a product to another country at a price lower than the price in its home market, or at a price below the cost of production. GATT allows nations to protect their domestic industries against dumping. For example, U.S. law empowers the Department of Commerce to impose import duties on nations that dump goods on American markets. However, a nation penalized for dumping can fight back by complaining to the WTO. To continue its anti-dumping penalties, the accusing nation must then prove to the WTO that the dumping is hurting one of its domestic industries.

Answer

Checkpoint protects jobs, protects industries, protects national security

VISUAL GLOSSARY

Reviewing Key Terms
To understand *free trade*, review these terms:

free market economy, *p. 30*
competition, *p. 33*
regulation, *p. 125*
trade barrier, *p. 455*
tariff, *p. 455*
embargo, *p. 456*

What is Free Trade?

◀ **free trade** the lowering or elimination of protective tariffs and other trade barriers between two or more nations

Usually, normal trade relations between countries involve a certain number of restrictions, including tariffs. In free trade, these restrictions are greatly reduced or eliminated. ***Do you think all trade barriers can be eliminated even under free trade?***

"Take us to your leader...we've come to negotiate a free trade agreement with earth."

◀ Free trade agreements require a great deal of negotiation between the parties involved. ***What sorts of issues might the two sides shown in this cartoon need to discuss in order to reach a free trade agreement?***

Visual Glossary online
To expand your understanding of this and other key economic terms, visit **PearsonSuccessNet.com**

Teach Visual Glossary

REVIEW KEY TERMS

Pair students and have them write the definitions of these key terms related to an understanding of international trade.

free market economy – *an economic system in which decisions on the three key economic questions are based on voluntary exchange in markets*

competition – *the struggle among producers for the dollars of consumers*

regulation – *government intervention in a market that affects the production of a good*

trade barrier – *a means of preventing a foreign product or service from freely entering a nation's territory*

tariff – *a tax on imported goods*

embargo – *a ban on trade with a particular country*

CREATE A CONCEPT WEB

Draw a concept web on the board, with the term *free trade* in the center circle. Draw six circles around the center circle and write one of these terms in each of the surrounding circles. Ask students to explain the relationships between these terms and free trade.

L2 LPR Differentiate Remember to call on less proficient readers first when having students describe the connections between the terms.

Have students use the Visual Glossary Online to reinforce their understanding of the term *free trade.*

L2 ELL Differentiate Have students identify the images in the cartoon. Ask students to explain how a free trade agreement might affect trade between Earth and the other planet.

Economics online *All print resources are available on the Teacher's Resource Library CD-ROM and online at* www.PearsonSuccessNet.com.

Answers

Visual Glossary Diagram Possible answer: No, because countries will always have some national security interests they want to protect.

Cartoon Possible answer: products and services the aliens want and those they are willing to supply to Earth without trade restrictions

COMPARE AND ANALYZE VIEWPOINTS

Explore the arguments surrounding international trade agreements and free trade. Use NAFTA to ground this discussion in concrete examples. First, have students work in groups of two or three to find quotations for and against NAFTA. Have volunteers read these aloud. Using these quotations as a jumping-off point, discuss who might benefit from trade agreements such as NAFTA and what those benefits might be. Have students analyze and explain to what extent each of the following groups might benefit or be harmed: (1) domestic consumers; (2) domestic producers; (3) foreign producers; (4) foreign consumers. Explore the potential consequences trade agreements can have on employment in the nations that are part of them. Ask **Why do you think NAFTA stirred such strong feelings in the United States?** *(concern for jobs; worries about being left behind in the world economy; concerns about national independence and too much foreign influence on U.S. economy)*

L1 L2 ELL LPR Differentiate Pair students to create flash cards with the name of a free-trade group on one side and its description or membership on the other. Have pairs use their cards to drill each other on the main international trade organizations.

L4 Differentiate Distribute the "NAFTA: Pro and Con" worksheet (Unit 7 All-in-One, p. 25). Emphasize that the readings represent just two of many viewpoints, foreign and domestic, on the benefits and drawbacks of this trade agreement.

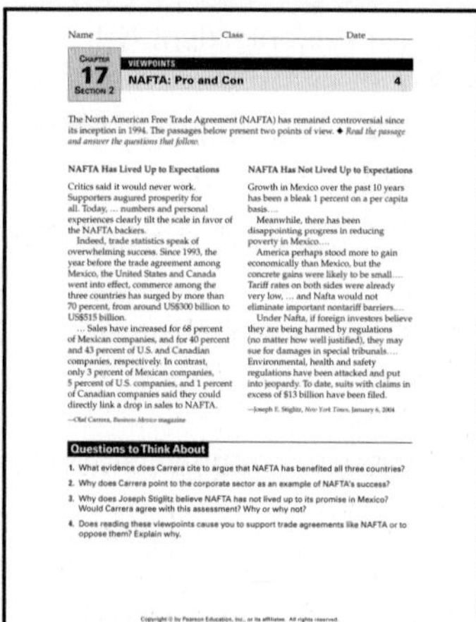

Name ________ Class ________ Date ________

Chapter 17 Section 2 — VIEWPOINTS

NAFTA: Pro and Con 4

The North American Free Trade Agreement (NAFTA) has remained controversial since its inception in 1994. The passages below present two points of view. ◆ *Read the passage and answer the questions that follow.*

NAFTA Has Lived Up to Expectations

Critics said it would never work. Supporters augured prosperity for all. Today, ... numbers and personal experiences clearly tilt the scale in favor of the NAFTA backers.

Indeed, trade statistics speak of overwhelming success. Since 1993, the year before the trade agreement among Mexico, the United States and Canada went into effect, commerce among the three countries has surged by more than 70 percent, from around US$300 billion to US$515 billion.

... Sales have increased for 68 percent of Mexican companies, and for 40 percent and 43 percent of U.S. and Canadian companies, respectively. In contrast, only 3 percent of Mexican companies, 5 percent of U.S. companies, and 1 percent of Canadian companies said they could directly link a drop in sales to NAFTA.

—[illegible] Carrera, *Business Mexico* magazine

NAFTA Has Not Lived Up to Expectations

Growth in Mexico over the past 10 years has been a bleak 1 percent on a per capita basis....

Meanwhile, there has been disappointing progress in reducing poverty in Mexico....

America perhaps stood more to gain economically than Mexico, but the concrete gains were likely to be small.... Tariff rates on both sides were already very low, ... and Nafta would not eliminate important nontariff barriers....

Under Nafta, if foreign investors believe they are being harmed by regulations (no matter how well justified), they may sue for damages in special tribunals.... Environmental, health and safety regulations have been attacked and put into jeopardy. To date, suits with claims in excess of $13 billion have been filed.

—Joseph E. Stiglitz, *New York Times*, January 6, 2004

Questions to Think About

1. What evidence does Carrera cite to argue that NAFTA has benefited all three countries?
2. Why does Carrera point to the corporate sector as an example of NAFTA's success?
3. Why does Joseph Stiglitz believe NAFTA has not lived up to its promise in Mexico? Would Carrera agree with this assessment? Why or why not?
4. Does reading these viewpoints cause you to support trade agreements like NAFTA or to oppose them? Explain why.

free-trade zone region where a group of countries agrees to reduce or eliminate trade barriers

The European Union

In recent years, many countries have signed agreements to abolish tariffs and trade restrictions among member nations and adopt uniform tariffs for all countries that are not members. The most successful example is the European Union (EU).

The European Union developed slowly over several decades. In 1957, six western European nations set up the Common Market to coordinate economic and trade policies. In the years that followed, more countries joined the Common Market. In 1986, the member nations agreed to eliminate tariffs on one another's exports. They created a single market, called the European Economic Community (EEC).

In 1993, the EEC nations formed the European Union. This new organization became the largest trading bloc in the world. By 2008, the EU included 27 countries—almost all of Europe. This includes Poland, Hungary, Romania, and other former Soviet bloc nations that had once been forbidden to trade with the rest of Europe.

The EU adopted various policies to strengthen member economies, such as using agricultural subsidies and tariffs to keep farm prices high. Some member nations signed the European Monetary Union, agreeing to adopt a single currency and monetary system. In 2002, twelve member nations replaced their individual currencies with a single currency called the euro. The EU also adopted political ties, forming a parliament and council that make laws all member nations must follow. Still, many Europeans feared such measures threatened each nation's right to make decisions in its own interest.

▲ This NAFTA symbol suggests how the United States, Canada, and Mexico became more interdependent as a result of the free trade agreement.

NAFTA

Other nations have created **free-trade zones,** where a group of countries agrees to reduce or eliminate trade barriers. One such pact, the North American Free Trade Agreement (NAFTA), created a free-trade zone linking the United States, Canada, and Mexico.

NAFTA aroused controversy in the United States. Opponents worried that American companies would move factories to Mexico, where wages were lower and environmental regulations were less strict. As a result, they said, American workers would lose jobs. Supporters of NAFTA claimed that the measure would instead create more jobs in the United States because it would increase exports to Mexico and Canada.

After a spirited debate, the Senate ratified NAFTA in 1993. Major provisions include:

1. Tariffs on all farm products and on some 10,000 other goods were to be eliminated over 15 years.
2. Automobile tariffs were to be phased out over 10 years.
3. Trucks were to have free access across borders and throughout the three member countries.
4. Special judges were given authority to resolve trade disputes.
5. The agreement could not be used to override national and state environmental, health, or safety laws.

More than a decade after it went into effect, the agreement has remained controversial. Critics continue to charge that NAFTA has resulted in a loss of American jobs and damage to the environment. In 2004, the Congressional Research Service reviewed the effects of NAFTA after ten years. It found that trade between Mexico and the United States had increased substantially in that period, but some of that increase resulted from trends at work before NAFTA. The report also concluded that the agreement had relatively little effect on jobs and wages in the United States.

DR-CAFTA and FTAA

In 2003, the United States government reached a free trade agreement with five nations of Central America. At the time, the deal was called the Central American Free Trade Agreement (CAFTA). The next year, when the Dominican Republic joined the pact, the name was changed to DR-CAFTA. Congress approved the agreement in July 2005, and the other nations formally approved it as well. Costa Rica—despite the protests described at the beginning of the chapter—formally accepted DR-CAFTA in late 2007.

Free trade hit a roadblock with the failure of the Free Trade Area of the Americas (FTAA). This trade deal would have opened trade among 34 nations of

Figure 17.4 **Major Trade Organization Members**

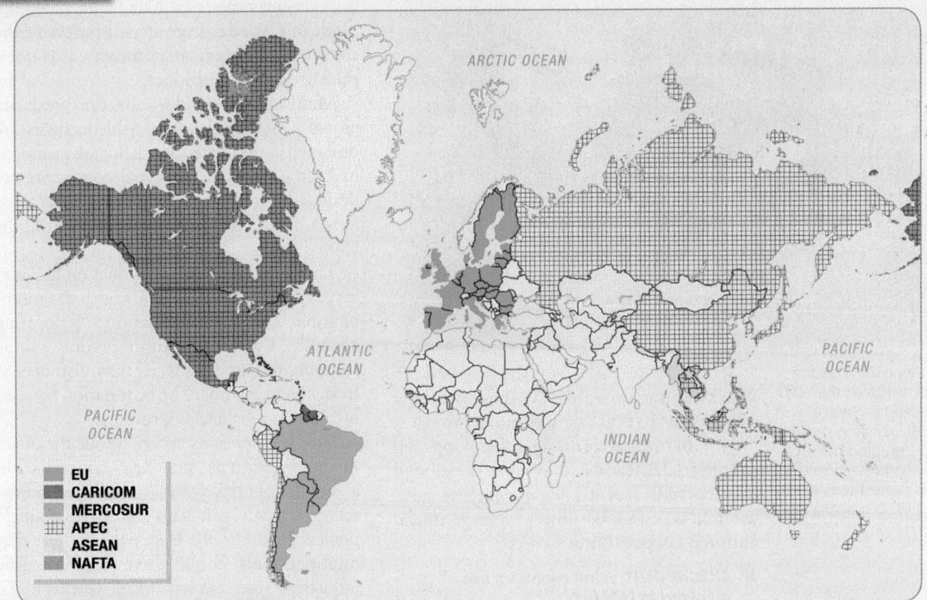

MAP SKILLS

Many countries are members of regional trade organizations.

1. To what trade organizations does the United States belong?
2. What do the nations belonging to APEC have in common? Why do you think they would be interested in signing a trade agreement?

Action Graph online

For an animated version of this map, visit PearsonSuccessNet.com

North and South America. However, after more than a decade of negotiations, the proposal was rejected by several key South American nations in 2005.

Other Regional Trade Agreements

About 100 regional trading organizations operate in the world today. They include the following, shown in **Figure 17.4**:

- *APEC* The Asia-Pacific Economic Cooperation includes 21 countries along the Pacific Rim, including the United States. They have signed a nonbinding agreement to reduce trade barriers.
- *MERCOSUR* The Southern Common Market is similar to the EU in its goals. Its members are the South American nations of Brazil, Paraguay, Uruguay, Argentina, and Venezuela.
- *CARICOM* The Caribbean Community and Common Market includes countries from South America and the Caribbean.
- *ASEAN* The ten-member Association of Southeast Asian Nations has taken steps to establish a free trade zone similar to the EU.

The Debate Over Free Trade

While the world's economies have moved toward free trade, controversy on trade continues. Debates over the impact of NAFTA became a campaign issue in the American presidential election of 2008. As you saw, protests across the Americas slowed negotiations on the FTAA.

Meetings of the World Trade Organization have also spurred large protests. A 1999

Action Graph online Have students review the Action Graph animation for a step-by-step look at various international trade organizations and their membership.

EXTEND

Have students provide a small item—such as a sticker, pencil, toy, piece of gum—in order to make a trade. Have them rate the value of their item to them on a scale of 1 to 10 and record the rating on a slip of paper. Collect the ratings and tally their total on the board. Then allow students to exchange their item for a classmate's if they wish to trade. Tell students to rate the value of the item they now possess. (Again, remind them that they are to rate the value of the item *to themselves.*) Collect, total, and post these new ratings. Repeat this process a third time, again placing the ratings total on the board. Note that values totals increased with each round of trading. Explain that this occurred because people (and nations) don't trade unless they benefit. Stress that free trade creates wealth and that both parties involved in free trade expect to gain from the trade.

GUIDING QUESTION WRAP UP

Have students return to the section Guiding Question. Review the completed graphic organizer and clarify any misunderstandings. Have a wrap-up discussion about the arguments for and against trade barriers and trade agreements.

Assess and Remediate

L3 **L2** Collect the "Trade Barriers: Winners and Losers" worksheets and assess students' understanding of how various types of trade barriers affect economic activities.

L4 Collect the "NAFTA: Pro and Con" worksheet and assess student understanding of this trade agreement.

L3 Assign the Section 2 Assessment questions; identify student misconceptions.

L3 Give Section Quiz A (Unit 7 All-in-One, p. 26).

L2 Give Section Quiz B (Unit 7 All-in-One, p. 27).

(Assess and Remediate continued on p. 462)

Answers

Map Skills 1. NAFTA, APEC 2. They all border the Pacific Ocean, which would facilitate trade among them by sea.

Have students complete the Self-Test Online and continue their work in the **Essential Questions Journal**.

REMEDIATION AND SUGGESTIONS

Use the chart below to help students who are struggling with content.

WEAKNESS	REMEDIATION
Defining key terms (Questions 3, 4, 5)	Have students use the interactive Economic Dictionary Online.
Effects of trade barriers on economic activities (Questions 1, 2, 4, 6, 8)	Reteach by reviewing the "Trade Barriers: Winners and Losers" worksheet.
Arguments in favor of protectionism (Questions 4, 6)	Pair students to role-play a discussion between a proponent and an opponent of protectionism
Participating in international trade agreements (Questions 1, 2, 5, 6, 7, 8)	Reteach using a chart showing the benefits and costs of participation in trade agreements.

Answers

Checkpoint Canada, Mexico, and the United States

Checkpoint They might drive domestic companies out of business, exploit local workers, and gain too much political power.

▲ Since the violence that disrupted the WTO meeting in Seattle in 1999, similar protests have erupted at WTO meetings elsewhere. This protest took place at a WTO meeting in Hong Kong in 2005.

WTO meeting in Seattle, Washington, drew as many as 50,000 angry demonstrators.

Not all of these protesters were opposed to free trade. Rather, they were concerned that current free trade agreements gave too much economic power to large multinational corporations.

CHECKPOINT ***What countries are involved in NAFTA?***

The Role of Multinationals

As you read in Chapter 8, a multinational is a large corporation that sells goods and services throughout the world. For example, an automobile company might design its cars in the United States and import parts made in Asia to an assembly plant in Canada. Even if you purchase the car from an American company, it is not a purely domestic product.

Many goods besides cars are produced globally. Some brands of athletic shoes are designed in the United States but are produced in East Asia. Some personal computers are designed in the United States and assembled abroad with parts and components from the United States.

The decision to build production facilities in a foreign country benefits both the multinational and the host nation. By locating abroad, the corporation avoids some shipping fees and tariffs. It may also benefit from cheaper labor. The host nation benefits by gaining jobs and tax revenue.

Still, host nations worry about the effect of multinationals on their countries. In a small country with a fragile economy, multinationals can gain excessive political power. In addition, host nations fear that multinationals could drive out domestic industries and exploit local workers. To protect domestic industries, some host nations have created rules requiring multinationals to export a certain percentage of their products.

CHECKPOINT ***Why are some nations concerned about multinationals?***

Essential Questions Journal To continue to build a response to the Essential Question, go to your **Essential Questions Journal.**

SECTION 2 ASSESSMENT

Guiding Question

1. Use your completed chart to answer this question: What are the arguments for and against trade barriers and agreements?
2. **Extension** Describe two ways that trade barriers or free trade can affect you as a consumer.

Key Terms and Main Ideas

3. What is the difference between an **import quota** and a **tariff?**
4. What are three arguments in favor of **protectionism?**
5. What happens when two countries sign a **free trade** agreement?

Critical Thinking

6. **Take a Position** Some people argue that trade barriers are needed to protect jobs. According to the idea of comparative advantage, consumers benefit from trade by having a wider variety of less expensive goods. Which benefit—securing jobs or increasing consumer choices—do you think is more important? Why?
7. **Analyze** What are the advantages of international trade agreements? What might be some disadvantages?
8. **Illustrate** Give three examples from this section to show how trading partnerships and relationships change over time.

Quick Write

9. Suppose you were a member of Congress considering a bill that would place higher tariffs on imported video game systems. Write a brief speech that you would deliver for or against the bill. Base your argument on economic principles.

Assessment Answers

1. Trade barriers protect jobs and industries from foreign competition and strengthen national security, but they keep prices high. Trade agreements promote competition and efficiency and keep prices down, but weaken U.S. industries and cost jobs.
2. Possible answer: Trade barriers would raise the price of the video games that I buy, which are made in China. Free trade keeps down the price of the jeans I wear, which are made in Mexico.
3. An import quota limits how much of a good can be imported, while a tariff is merely a tax on that good.
4. Protectionism saves jobs and infant industries and helps national security.
5. They import and export goods between them with low or no trade barriers.
6. Possible answers: Securing jobs is more important because high employment is more important to a strong economy than increasing consumer choices. Increasing consumer choice is more important because a free market works best when consumers can make decisions based on self-interest with limited interference.
7. Trade agreements increase the exchange of goods between nations, which increases consumer choice and helps keep prices low. However, they also can cost jobs in domestic industries that cannot compete with tariff-free imports.
8. Possible answer: NAFTA changed trade relationships between the U.S., Mexico, and Canada; the European Union adopted a uniform currency and eliminated trade barriers between most of the countries of Europe; the WTO acts as a referee between member nations involved in trade disputes.
9. Responses should deal with the issues raised by protectionism and consumer choice.

SECTION 3 Measuring Trade

OBJECTIVES

1. **Explain** how exchange rates of world currencies change.
2. **Describe** the effect of various exchange rate systems.
3. **Define** balance of trade and balance of payments.
4. **Analyze** the causes and effects of the U.S. trade deficit.

ECONOMIC DICTIONARY

As you read the section, look for the definitions of these **Key Terms:**

- exchange rate
- appreciation
- depreciation
- foreign exchange market
- fixed exchange-rate system
- flexible exchange-rate system
- balance of trade
- trade surplus
- trade deficit
- balance of payments

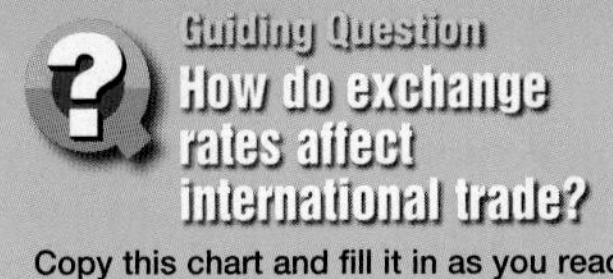
Guiding Question
How do exchange rates affect international trade?

Copy this chart and fill it in as you read.

Effect of Exchange Rates on Trade	
Effect of Appreciating Currency	**Effect of Depreciating Currency**
• Value of currency rises, making goods produced in country more expensive • Exports: •	• • •

Economics and You It's happened to everyone. You buy something in a store. You hand over a couple of bills. The clerk hands you your change. When you get outside, you notice something funny about one of the quarters. Instead of the familiar profile of George Washington, you see a caribou with a large pair of antlers. You've been given a Canadian quarter.

Maybe you feel cheated. But should you? Is this Canadian quarter worth less than a U.S. quarter—or more? How would you find out? These questions may seem unimportant when you're dealing with just a single quarter. But if you were dealing with hundreds or thousands of dollars, the questions might be very important indeed!

Principles in Action The difference in value between an American dollar and a Canadian dollar—or a British pound or a Japanese yen or a Saudi Arabian riyal—does not stay the same from day to day. In this section, you will see how these fluctuations have a huge impact on imports and exports. In Economics & You, you will also see how changes in the value of the dollar can directly affect what many American consumers spend and where they can afford to travel.

Foreign Exchange

International trade is more complex than buying and selling within one country because of the world's many currencies and their changing values. If you want to buy a newspaper in Beijing, you will need to change your American dollars for Chinese yuan. If a Mexican family visiting New York wants to buy lunch, they must change their pesos to dollars.

Understanding Exchange Rates

Changing money from one nation's currency to another's is never a simple matter of exchanging, say, one yuan or one peso for one American dollar. A dollar might be worth 8 yuan or 11 pesos. The value of a nation's currency in relation to a foreign currency is called the **exchange rate.** Understanding how exchange rates work enables you to convert prices in one currency to prices in another currency.

exchange rate the value of a nation's currency in relation to a foreign currency

Guiding Question

How do exchange rates affect international trade?

Get Started

Effects of Exchange Rates on Trade	
Effect of Appreciating Currency	**Effect of Depreciating Currency**
• Value of currency rises, making goods produced in country more expensive • Exports: Cost of exports rises for foreign buyers, causing sales of exports to fall • Imports: Cost of imports falls, making sales of imports rise	• Value of currency falls, making goods produced in country less expensive • Exports: Cost of exports falls for foreign buyers, causing sales of exports to rise • Imports: Cost of imports rises, making sales of imports fall

LESSON GOALS

Students will:

- Know the Key Terms.
- Demonstrate an understanding of foreign exchange, exchange rates, and their effects.
- Show understanding of balance of trade, balance of payments, and trade deficits.

BEFORE CLASS

Students should read the section for homework before coming to class.

Have students complete the graphic organizer in the Section Opener as they read the text. As an alternate activity, have students complete the Guided Reading and Review worksheet (Unit 7 All-in-One, p. 28).

L1 L2 ELL LPR Differentiate Have students complete the Guided Reading and Review worksheet (Unit 7 All-in-One, p. 29).

Focus on the Basics

Students need to come away with the following understandings:

FACTS: • Changing exchange rates among the world's currencies affect the cost of trade goods. • A rise in a currency's value makes a nation's exports more costly to buyers and its imports cheaper to consumers. A fall in a currency's value has the opposite effect. • When the value of a nation's exports exceeds the value of what it imports, a trade surplus exists. If the value of imports exceeds the value of exports, a trade deficit exists. • A large trade deficit and a weak dollar have caused large foreign investment in the U.S. economy.

GENERALIZATION: Exchange rates and the value of a nation's currency affect that nation's balance of payments and balance of trade.

CLASSROOM HINTS

EXCHANGE RATES

Divide the class into two groups, Japanese buyers and American buyers. Give the groups pieces of paper representing Japanese yen and U.S. dollars. The American group wants to buy manga comic books that cost 2,500 yen. The Japanese group wants to buy jeans that cost 40 dollars. Give students a dollar/yen exchange rate of \$1/¥105. Tell each group to exchange as much currency with the other group as they need to buy the item their group wants. Have students repeat with an exchange rate of \$1/¥112 and discuss what might have caused the rate to change.

BELLRINGER

Write the following in the board:

If someone offered you one of six envelopes with the following amounts of money in them, which envelope would you choose and why?

- *$100*
- *100 £ (pounds)*
- *100 pesos*
- *100 yen*
- *100 yuan*
- *100 euros*

Tell students to use the exchange rates in Figure 17.5 to help them rank these envelopes from most to least valuable and to record this in their notebooks.

Teach

Economics online To present this topic using digital resources, use the lecture notes on www.PearsonSuccessNet.com.

REVIEW BELLRINGER ANSWERS

Call on students to explain which currency gift they would choose and why. Point out that at the exchange rates noted in Figure 17.5 on page 464 of their textbook, the British pounds would be the most valuable gift, 100 £ being worth more than 200 U.S. dollars ($204.00). Have students calculate what each of the other gifts of foreign currency would be worth in dollars. *(100 Mexican pesos = $9.00; 100 Japanese yen = 80¢; 100 Chinese yuan = $13.00; 100 euros = $142.00)*

BRAINSTORM

Have students brainstorm reasons why each country's currency doesn't have equal value. For example, ask why a Mexican peso, a U.S. dollar, and a Japanese yen aren't all worth the same amount. As students suggest reasons, list them on the board. *(Possible responses might include differences in each country's economy, differences in economies' strength, differing systems of value and coinage)* When ideas have been exhausted, review the list and lead a class discussion of how each item on the list might relate to differing values of world currencies.

Answers

Chart Skills 1. 7.449 yuan; 99 cents Canadian 2. 15.54 pesos

Figure 17.5 Foreign Exchange Rates

	U.S. $	Aust. $	U.K. £	Canadian $	Japanese ¥en	€uro	Mexican peso	Chinese yuan
U.S. $	1	.88	2.04	1.00	.008	1.42	.09	.13
Australian $	1.12	1	2.30	1.13	.009	1.60	.10	.15
U.K. £	.49	.43	1	.49	.004	.69	.04	.07
Canadian $	.99	.88	2.03	1	.008	1.42	.09	.13
Japanese ¥en	114.97	101.81	234.41	115.44	1	163.47	10.52	15.34
€uro	.70	.62	1.43	.71	.006	1	.06	.09
Mexican peso	10.93	9.68	22.29	10.98	.095	15.54	1	1.46
Chinese yuan	7.449	6.63	15.28	7.52	.065	10.65	.69	1

SOURCE: *X-rates.com* accessed on Friday, September 28, 2007. Note: These data are highly time sensitive and can change hourly.

CHART SKILLS

This table shows exchange rates on a single day. Read down the first column of the chart to find out what one U.S. dollar was worth in various foreign currencies. Read across the top row to find out how much a selected foreign currency was worth in U.S. dollars.

1. On this day, how much was one U.S. dollar worth in Chinese yuan? In Canadian dollars?
2. How much was a euro worth in pesos?

Daily exchange rates are listed in major newspapers and on the Internet. **Figure 17.5** shows a sample table of exchange rates. If you read down the first column, you will see that one U.S. dollar can be exchanged for more than one (1.12) Australian dollar, for less than one euro (0.70), and so forth.

An exchange rate table shows what one U.S. dollar is worth on one particular day. Remember, the rates change daily, so it is important to keep checking, especially if you are visiting a foreign country or doing business overseas.

Simulation Activity

Fair Exchange
You may be asked to take part in a role-playing game about foreign exchange rates.

Calculating Prices

A simple formula allows you to convert the price of an item from foreign currency to American dollars. Just divide the price by the value of the currency per one dollar according to the exchange rate.

Look at the following example. Suppose your family is planning a trip to Mexico and that the exchange rate is as shown in **Figure 17.5.** If a hotel room in Mexico costs 500 pesos per night, the price in U.S. dollars is $45.75:

appreciation an increase in the value of a currency

$$\frac{500 \text{ pesos}}{10.93 \text{ pesos/dollar}} = \$45.75$$

Now suppose your family decides to go to Mexico next year instead, and the exchange rate has risen to 12.5 pesos per dollar. Assuming that the room rate is still 500 pesos, the hotel room will cost only about $40.00 a night:

$$\frac{500 \text{ pesos}}{12.5 \text{ pesos/dollar}} = \$40.00$$

Appreciating Currency

You have probably heard newscasters talk about a "strong" or "weak" dollar or a currency like the Japanese yen "rising" or "falling." What do these terms mean? Do they indicate good news or bad news for the United States economy?

An increase in the value of a currency is called **appreciation.** When a currency appreciates, it becomes "stronger." If the exchange rate between the dollar and the yen increases from 100 yen per dollar to 120 yen per dollar, each dollar can buy more yen. Since the dollar has increased in value, we say that the dollar has appreciated against the yen. This appreciation means that people in Japan will have to spend more yen to purchase a dollar's worth of goods from the United States. On the other hand, Americans who travel

464 INTERNATIONAL TRADE

Differentiated Resources

- **L1 L2 Guided Reading and Review** (Unit 7 All-in-One, p. 29)
- **L2 Making the Most of It** (Unit 7 All-in-One, p. 31)
- **L4 China and the U.S. Balance of Trade** (Unit 7 All-in-One, p. 32)
- **L3 Fair Exchange** (Simulation Activities, Chapter 17)

to Japan can buy more goods and services for the same amount of money than they could before the dollar appreciated.

When a nation's currency appreciates, its products become more expensive in other countries. For example, a strong dollar makes American goods and services more expensive for Japanese consumers. Japan will therefore probably import fewer products from the United States. As a result, total United States exports to Japan will likely decline. On the other hand, a strong dollar makes foreign products less expensive for consumers in the United States. A strong dollar is therefore likely to lead consumers in the United States to purchase more imported goods.

Depreciating Currency

A decrease in the value of a currency is called **depreciation.** You might also hear depreciation referred to as "weakening." If the dollar exchange rate fell to 80 yen per dollar, you would get fewer yen for each dollar. In other words, the dollar has depreciated against the yen.

When a nation's currency depreciates, its products become cheaper to other nations. A depreciated, or weak, dollar means that foreign consumers will be able to better afford products made in the United States. A weakened dollar probably results in increased exports. At the same time, other nations' products become more expensive for consumers in the United States, so they will buy fewer imports.

The Foreign Exchange Market

Suppose that a company in the United States sells computers in Japan. That company is paid in yen. It must, however, pay its workers and suppliers back in the United States in dollars. The company must therefore exchange its yen for U.S. dollars. This exchange takes place on the foreign exchange market. International trade would not be possible without this market.

The **foreign exchange market** consists of about 2,000 banks and other financial institutions that facilitate the buying and selling of foreign currencies. These banks are located in various financial centers around the world, including such cities as New York, London, Paris, Singapore, and Tokyo. These banks maintain close links to one another through telephones and computers. This technology allows for the instantaneous transmission of market information and rapid financial transactions.

CHECKPOINT ***What are the likely effects of the dollar becoming stronger?***

depreciation a decrease in the value of a currency

foreign exchange market system of financial institutions that facilitate the buying and selling of foreign currencies

Exchange Rate Systems

As you read in Chapter 10, currencies varied in value from state to state in early America. In the United States today, of course, it doesn't matter what state you live in. All prices are in dollars, and all dollars have the same value.

Economics & YOU

The Value of the Dollar

A weak dollar makes it more expensive to visit another country whose currency is stronger. ***Your family may decide to postpone its vacation until the dollar is stronger.***
A weak dollar means that goods produced in foreign countries and sold in the United States become more expensive. ***Even if you do not travel, the exchange rate has an impact on your purchasing power.***

▲ The strength of the dollar directly affects the prices we pay. ***Identify one item you buy that might be affected by exchange rates.***

DEMONSTRATE

Call on students to explain what each of the following terms means, and how it is related to international trade: *exchange rate, appreciation,* and *depreciation.* Demonstrate by asking two volunteers to represent the United States and Canada. Give one student ten pieces of paper representing U.S. dollars, and the other student ten pieces of paper representing Canadian dollars. First, ask them to imagine a state where one U.S. dollar is equal in value to one Canadian dollar. Then, have the student representing the U.S. depreciate the value of the dollar in relation to the Canadian dollar. Make sure they correctly indicate that it now takes more U.S. dollars to buy one Canadian dollar. Repeat the demonstration to illustrate appreciation. Discuss how shifting exchange rates affect the prices they pay for foreign-made goods that they buy. Ask **If the Chinese yuan becomes stronger against the dollar, how will that affect the price of Chinese-made sneakers at the mall?** *(higher price)* **If the dollar appreciates against the Japanese yen, how will that likely affect the sales of Toyota cars in the United States? Why?** *(Sales may increase because the price will probably fall.)*

Ask students whether as consumers they would prefer a strong dollar or a weak dollar, and why. *(A strong dollar makes imported consumer goods less expensive.)* Ask students which they think American manufacturers who export their products would prefer. *(a weak dollar because it makes their goods cheaper overseas, increasing sales)*

L1 L2 ELL LPR Differentiate Make sure students understand the meanings of the key terms associated with this topic. Have pairs of students make flashcards with each term on one side and its explanation or definition on the other. Have pairs use the cards to quiz each other. Refer students who still are having difficulty to the Visual Glossary Online.

(lesson continued on p. 467)

Virtual Economics

L3 Differentiate

Measuring International Trade Use the following lesson from the NCEE **Virtual Economics *CD-ROM*** to construct a balance of payments account. Click on Browse Economics Lessons, specify grades 9–12, and use the key words *international trade.*

In this activity, students will create a balance of payments account to help them draw conclusions about the economy.

LESSON TITLE	INTERNATIONAL TRADE: HOW DO WE MEASURE TRADES ACROSS POLITICAL BORDERS?
Type of Activity	Using statistics
Complexity	Moderate
Time	90 minutes
NCEE Standards	5, 6

Answers

Checkpoint decreased exports and higher prices for them; increased imports and lower prices for them

Economics & You Possible answer: shoes

Teach the Case Study

SUMMARIZE AND DISCUSS

Call on students to summarize the case study. Ask **What is the main idea of this article?** *(The weak dollar is causing more foreign investment in the United States, especially in real estate.)* Have students find details in the study that support this summary. Ask **Why are some U.S. real estate brokers aggressively seeking foreign buyers?** *(The slow U.S. real estate market and tight credit for U.S. buyers make foreign buyers attractive with their tendency for high down payments or cash.)* **Why is U.S. real estate attractive to foreign buyers?** *(The weak dollar and depressed real estate values mean buyers get more value than homes for sale elsewhere.)* **Why might some foreign buyers look at homes in the U.S. more as investment property than as places to live?** *(Depressed home prices and the weak dollar could bring big profits at resale, when the dollar and market appreciate and rebound.)*

Call students' attention to the Case Study table. Ask them why American real estate would be an especially attractive investment for people in the United Kingdom (Great Britain). *(the value of the dollar against the British pound)* If students have trouble making this connection refer them to Figure 17.5 on page 464. Ask students why investors from the OPEC nations would have such a large amount of money to invest in the United States. *(High imports of foreign oil by the U.S. gives them dollars to spend.)*

L1 L2 ELL LPR Differentiate This case study contains financial terms such as *down payment, foreclosure,* and *overvalued* that may cause problems for students with limited reading and language skills. Prepare students for the reading by reviewing these and other terms with which they might have trouble.

Economics online *All print resources are available on the Teacher's Resource Library CD-ROM and online at* www.PearsonSuccessNet.com.

Answer

Applying Economic Principles Even if the price stayed the same, the dollar's appreciation would make the property worth more in the foreign buyer's currency than when the buyer bought the property.

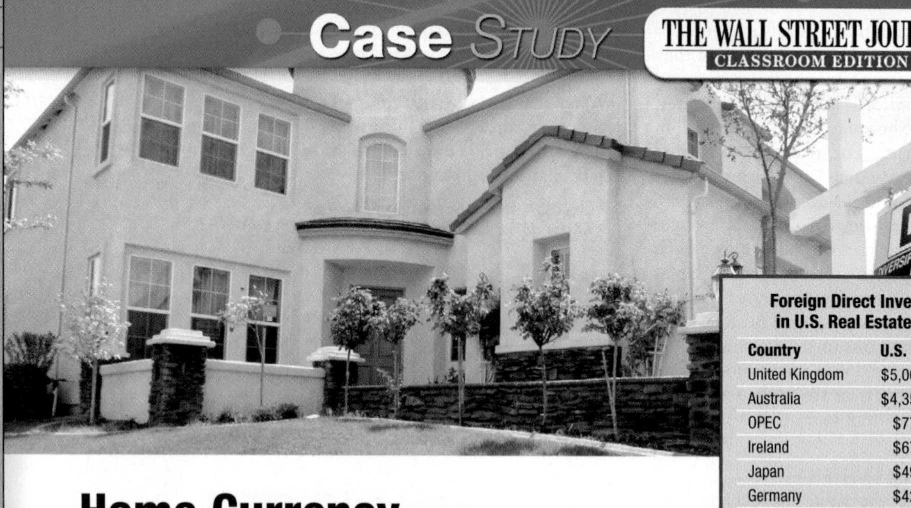

Foreign Direct Investment in U.S. Real Estate, 2006

Country	U.S. Dollars
United Kingdom	$5,068,000,000
Australia	$4,356,000,000
OPEC	$775,000,000
Ireland	$678,000,000
Japan	$496,000,000
Germany	$422,000,000
Spain	$100,000,000

Note: Data reflect preliminary findings
SOURCE: "Foreign Direct Investment in the United States" by Lawrence McNeil, Bureau of Economic Analysis June 2007

Home Currency

EXCHANGE RATES

Foreign buyers are taking advantage of a weak dollar to pick up real-estate bargains.

By Ben Casselman
The Wall Street Journal

One group hasn't soured on the U.S. real-estate market: foreign buyers.

With the dollar at historic lows against the euro and other currencies, real-estate agents, appraisers and developers say overseas buyers are stepping up their purchases in the U.S. Some are buying vacation homes in Florida, California and Colorado that would previously have been considered out of reach. Others are gambling that properties purchased now will translate into savvy investments down the road, when both the dollar and the U.S. housing market eventually rebound.

Some brokers are aggressively marketing to such potential customers, translating brochures into Russian, buying ads in Irish newspapers and hitting the road—pitching new condos to prospects in Dubai and Seoul. Developers are getting into the act, too, opening foreign offices and trumpeting amenities they hope will appeal to foreign tastes.

Moutaz Kaissi, an executive in Abu Dhabi, and his wife, Fawzia, see opportunity in the troubled Las Vegas market. Recently, the Kaissis closed on a bank-owned two-bedroom house on a golf course in North Las Vegas. The Kaissis paid $295,000 for the home, a price more than $100,000 lower than the original owner paid for it new.

Foreign buyers are particularly attractive because they tend to put more money down, and are therefore less likely to walk away from deals. Garrett Kenney, a developer and real-estate agent in Florida, says most of his overseas buyers put down 25%, compared with the usual 10% down payment by many Americans. And because they tend to be wealthy, foreign buyers are also more likely to pay entirely in cash, which is significant at a time when tight credit is derailing many deals.

Christopher Mayer, director of the Paul Milstein Center for Real Estate, warns bargain-hunting foreign investors to think twice about comparing U.S. prices to those in their home countries. For example, despite recent discounts, residential properties in Miami may still be overvalued—even if they are far cheaper than equivalent homes in the south of France. "One of the mistakes foreign buyers make is to put things in the context of their [local] market," Mr. Mayer says. "When you see foreign buyers in a market where locals are not buying, that's a troubling sign."

Video News Update Online Powered by *The Wall Street Journal* Classroom Edition — For a new case study, go to the online resources at **PearsonSuccessNet.com**

Applying Economic Principles
According to the article, foreign investors in U.S. real estate expect to make a profit when the dollar eventually appreciates. Explain why this would be the case.

Think how much more complicated it would be to do business if each state still had different currencies. To buy goods from a mail-order company in Indiana, for instance, someone in Texas would have to find out the exchange rate between a Texas dollar and an Indiana dollar. The economy would become less efficient as individuals and businesses spent time keeping track of exchange rates.

Such complications do not exist within the United States. They do, however, apply to international trade.

Fixed Exchange-Rate Systems

Of course, it would be simpler if all countries either used the same currency or kept their exchange rates constant. Then no one would have to worry about rate shifts. A system in which governments try to keep the values of their currencies constant against one another is called a **fixed exchange-rate system.**

In a typical fixed exchange-rate system, one country with a stable currency is at the center. Other countries fix, or "peg," their exchange rates to this currency. Normally, the fixed exchange-rate is not a single value, but is kept within a certain specified range (for example, plus or minus 2 percent). If the exchange rate moves outside of this range, governments usually intervene to maintain the rate.

How do governments intervene to maintain an exchange rate? The exchange rate is essentially the price of a currency. Like the price of any product or service, the exchange rate relies on supply and demand. To preserve its exchange rate, a government may buy or sell foreign currency in order to affect a currency's supply and demand. It will follow this course of action until the exchange rate is back within the specified limits.

The Bretton Woods Conference

In 1944, as World War II was drawing to a close, representatives from 44 countries met in Bretton Woods, New Hampshire. Their purpose was to make financial arrangements for the postwar world.

The Bretton Woods conference resulted in the creation of a fixed exchange-rate system for the United States and much of western Europe. Because the United States had the strongest economy and most stable currency, conference participants agreed to peg their currencies to the United States dollar.

To make the new system work, the Bretton Woods conference established the International Monetary Fund (IMF). Today, the IMF promotes international monetary cooperation, currency stabilization, and trade. You will read more about the International Monetary Fund in Chapter 18.

Flexible Exchange-Rate Systems

Although fixed exchange-rate systems make trade easier, they depend on countries maintaining similar economic policies, as well as similar inflation and interest rates. By the late 1960s, worldwide trade was growing and changing rapidly. At the same time, the war in Vietnam was causing inflation in the United States. These factors made it increasingly difficult for many countries to rely on a fixed exchange rate.

In 1971, the Netherlands and West Germany abandoned the fixed exchange-rate system. Other countries followed. By 1973, even the United States had adopted a system based on flexible exchange rates. Under a **flexible exchange-rate system,** the exchange rate is determined by supply and demand rather than according to any preset range.

Today, the countries of the world use a mixture of fixed and flexible exchange rates. Most major currencies—including the U.S. dollar and the Japanese yen—use the flexible exchange-rate system. This system accounts for the day-to-day changes in currency values that you read about earlier in this section.

When the current flexible exchange-rate system was first adopted, some economists worried that changes in the exchange

fixed exchange-rate system a system in which governments try to keep the values of their currencies constant against one another

flexible exchange-rate system a system in which the exchange rate is determined by supply and demand

Anyone traveling in a foreign country keeps a close eye on changing daily exchange rates as they are posted in hotels, banks, and other locations. ▼

DISTRIBUTE ACTIVITY WORKSHEET

Distribute the "Making the Most of It" worksheet (Unit 7 All-in-One, p. 30). This activity asks students to interpret a cartoon about foreign exchange and to apply the principles and concepts of exchange rates to an everyday situation.

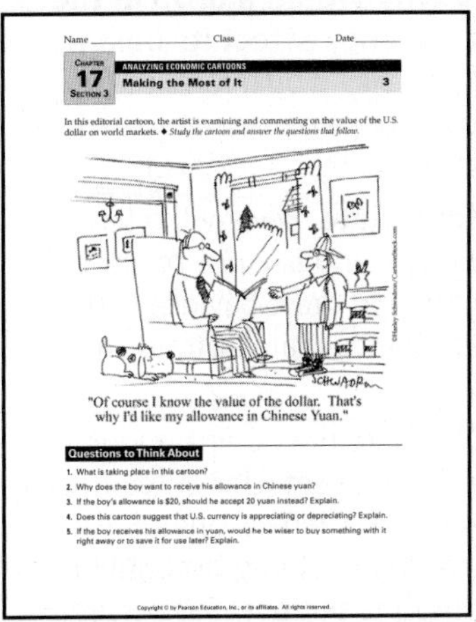
Name ____________ Class ____________ Date ________

Chapter 17 Section 3 — ANALYZING ECONOMIC CARTOONS — **Making the Most of It** 3

In this editorial cartoon, the artist is examining and commenting on the value of the U.S. dollar on world markets. ◆ *Study the cartoon and answer the questions that follow.*

"Of course I know the value of the dollar. That's why I'd like my allowance in Chinese Yuan."

Questions to Think About

1. What is taking place in this cartoon?
2. Why does the boy want to receive his allowance in Chinese yuan?
3. If the boy's allowance is $20, should he accept 20 yuan instead? Explain.
4. Does this cartoon suggest that U.S. currency is appreciating or depreciating? Explain.
5. If the boy receives his allowance in yuan, would he be wiser to buy something with it right away or to save it for use later? Explain.

L1 L2 Differentiate Distribute the "Making the Most of It" worksheet (Unit 7 All-in-One, p. 31).

DISCUSS AND COMPARE

Discuss the difference between a fixed exchange-rate system and a flexible exchange-rate system. Ask why much of the world has moved from a fixed-rate to a flexible-rate system. *(problems with the U.S. dollar to which many currencies were pegged in the fixed-rate system)* Have students discuss whether a fixed-rate system or a flexible-rate system would make international trade easier to conduct, and why.

L3 Differentiate For alternative or additional practice with the role of exchange rates in international trade, have students use the "Fair Exchange" activity (Simulation Activities, Chapter 17). Students will enact roles as foreign exchange bankers, importers, and exporters in three fictitious countries to see how exchange rates affect trade.

Background Note

The Foreign Exchange Market On a typical day, currency trades valued at over $3 trillion take place on the foreign exchange market. Because each transaction involves two currencies, the total for all transactions adds up to 200 percent. More than 86 percent of these transactions involve the buying or selling of U.S. dollars. The other currencies that are usually heavily traded are the euro (about 37 percent of all transactions), the Japanese yen and British pound (16.5 percent and 15 percent respectively), and the Swiss franc (about 7 percent).

sources: *Triennial Central Bank Survey* (December 2007), Bank for International Settlements.

EXAMINE CAUSE AND EFFECT

Discuss how changes in the value of a nation's currency would affect its balance of trade. Ask **Why would a negative balance of trade cause the value of a nation's currency to fall?** *(The resulting glut in the currency's supply on world markets would devalue it.)* **How and why would a drop in the value of a nation's currency affect its balance of trade?** *(Depreciated currency would raise the price of imports and lower the price of exports, which would shrink surpluses or increase deficits.)*

L1 L2 ELL LPR Differentiate Review the terms *trade surplus, trade deficit,* and *balance of trade* with students. Invite them to draw balance scales, teeter totters, or other figures that illustrate each of these terms.

L4 Differentiate Distribute the "China and the U.S. Balance of Trade" worksheet (Unit 7 All-in-One, p. 32). Remind students that China is one of the top trading partners of the United States, accounting for 16.5 percent of U.S. imports but only 5.6 percent of U.S. exports (in 2007). Point out that many people blame this situation as a major cause for the large U.S. trade deficit and the nation's negative balance of trade. After students have completed the reading, discuss the views that it presents. Then have students take the role of presidential advisors and write a memo to the President recommending a U.S. position on the revaluation of the yuan.

CREATE A PROFILE

Have students use the Career Link worksheet (Unit 7 All-in-One, p. 88) to record their research for the activity.

Answer

Checkpoint Nations peg the value of their currency to the currency of a country whose currency is stable.

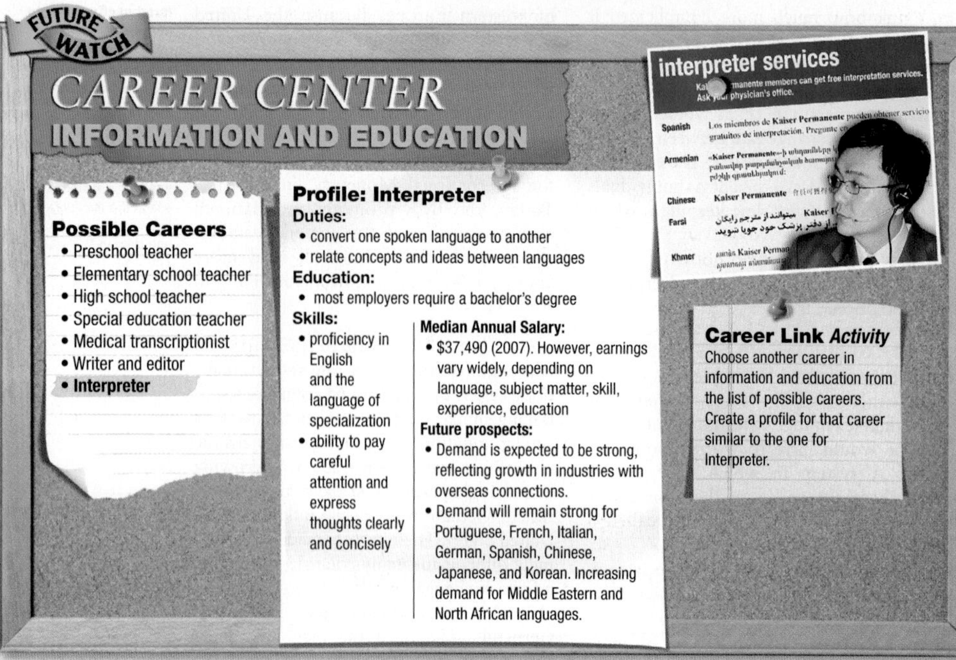

rate might interrupt the flow of world trade. In actual fact, trade has grown rapidly since the flexible exchange-rate system was adopted. Today, more nations trade than ever before.

The Euro

Although the flexible exchange-rate system works well, some countries whose economies are closely tied together want the advantages of fixed rates. One way to enjoy the advantages but avoid some of the difficulties of fixed exchange rates is to abolish individual currencies and establish a single currency.

As you read, this is what 12 members of the European Union did by adopting the euro. Use of this common currency requires countries to coordinate their economic policies, but it also simplifies trade. People traveling from, say, Germany to France do not need to exchange marks for francs at the border. They simply use their euros.

CHECKPOINT ***How are exchange rates set in a fixed exchange-rate system?***

balance of trade the relationship between the value of a country's exports and the value of its imports

trade surplus situation in which a nation exports more goods and services than it imports

trade deficit situation in which a nation imports more goods and services than it exports

Balance of Trade

The value of a nation's currency is affected by the overall flow of goods and services into and out of the country. In turn, exchange rates can affect a nation's **balance of trade,** the relationship between the value of its exports and the value of its imports.

Surpluses and Deficits

When a large difference between a nation's imports and exports arises, it is said to have a trade imbalance. A nation that exports more goods and services than it imports has a positive trade balance, or **trade surplus.** A nation that imports more goods and services than it exports has a negative trade balance, or **trade deficit.**

Nations seek to maintain a balance of trade. That is, they hope the value of imports is roughly equal to the value of exports. By balancing trade, a nation can protect the value of its currency on the international market. When a country has a continuing negative balance of trade, importing more than it is exporting over an extended period of time, the value of its currency falls.

For example, in the 1980s, the United States imported considerably more than it exported. As a result of this trade imbalance, the foreign exchange market was glutted with U.S. dollars. Because the supply of dollars was so high, the value of the dollar fell. The prices of imports increased and American consumers had to pay more for imported goods.

A negative balance of trade can be corrected either by limiting imports or by increasing the number or value of exports. Both of these actions affect trading partners, of course, who may then retaliate by raising tariffs. Maintaining a balance of trade thus requires international cooperation and fair trade practices.

Balance of Payments

Balance of trade measures the flow of goods and services among nations. Economists get a more complex picture of international trade by looking at balance of payments. **Balance of payments** is the value of all monetary transactions between all sectors of a country's economy—households, firms, and government—and the rest of the world.

Look again at the circular flow model of a mixed economy (**Figure 2.3**) in Chapter 2. It shows the movement of money and goods within a single economy. Now suppose you had to add in the international sector as well. Foreign transactions would enter into every stage. For example, if an American invested in a foreign company, the capital he or she invested would be part of the monetary flow going overseas. Any returns from the investment would be part of the monetary flow coming into the country. Income from foreign companies, government aid to foreign countries, borrowing from foreign banks, exchange rates—all of these must be factored into the balance of payments.

CHECKPOINT ***What causes a trade surplus?***

The United States Trade Deficit

Although the United States sells many goods abroad, it generally imports more than it exports. As a result, the United States currently runs a trade deficit. (See **Figure 17.6**, below.)

balance of payments the value of all monetary transactions between a country's economy and the rest of the world

Causes of the Deficit

The U.S. trade deficit began to take shape in the 1970s, when the Organization of Petroleum Exporting Countries (OPEC) dramatically raised the price of oil. The United States, which depends heavily on foreign oil, thus had to increase the money spent on this vital resource. As a result, the total cost of imports to the United States began to exceed the income from its exports.

The United States suffered record trade deficits in 1986 and 1987. In the early 1990s, the trade deficit began to fall. By the late 1990s, however, the deficit had skyrocketed to record levels, largely as a result of a new increase in oil prices and an economic boom that fueled consumer buying of imported goods.

In 2005, the trade deficit totaled over $717 billion, with the largest amounts owed to China, Japan, Germany, Canada, Mexico, and oil exporting nations such as Venezuela. Petroleum imports accounted for more than a third of the deficit.

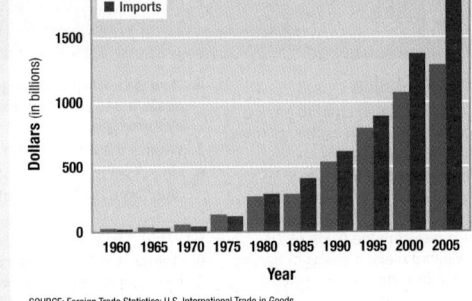

Figure 17.6 U.S. Balance of Trade, 1960–2005

SOURCE: Foreign Trade Statistics: U.S. International Trade in Goods

GRAPH SKILLS

Although the United States has a large trade deficit today, that was not always true.

1. What was the difference between imports and exports in 1960? In 1980? In 2005?
2. During what year shown here did the United States begin to show a trade deficit?

Action Graph online For an animated version of this graph, visit **PearsonSuccessNet.com**

EXTEND

Hold an informal classroom debate on the following proposition: *Resolved that the U.S. government should impose high tariffs and strict import quotas in order to eliminate the trade deficit and restore a favorable balance of trade.* Assign students to each position. Remind them to consider which Americans would be most likely to favor each side in the debate, and why.

Action Graph online Have students review the Action Graph animation for a step-by-step look at changes in the U.S. balance of trade.

GUIDING QUESTION WRAP UP

Have students return to the section Guiding Question. Review the completed graphic organizer and clarify any misunderstandings. Have a wrap-up discussion about how exchange rates affect international trade.

Assess and Remediate

L3 **L2** Collect the "Making the Most of It" worksheets and assess student understanding of exchange rates and their effects.

L4 Collect the "China and the U.S. Balance of Trade" worksheet and assess student understanding.

L3 Assign the Section 3 Assessment questions; identify student misconceptions.

L3 Give Section Quiz A (Unit 7 All-in-One, p. 33).

L2 Give Section Quiz B (Unit 7 All-in-One, p. 34).

(Assess and Remediate continued on p. 470)

Answers

Checkpoint The value of a country's exports is greater than the value of what it imports.

Graph Skills 1. about equal in 1960 and 1980; in 2005 imports were about $750 billion greater than exports. 2. 1980

Have students complete the Self-Test Online and continue their work in the **Essential Questions Journal**.

REMEDIATION AND SUGGESTIONS

Use the chart below to help students who are struggling with content.

WEAKNESS	REMEDIATION
Defining key terms (Questions 3, 5, 6, 7, 8)	Have students use the interactive Economic Dictionary Online.
World currencies, exchange rates, and their effects (Questions 1, 2, 3, 4, 9, 12)	Reteach and review Figure 17.5. Work with students to calculate how changes in exchange rates affect the costs of things.
Balance of trade, balance of payments, and the U.S. trade deficit (Questions 7, 8, 19, 11)	Have students write a summary of each side's positions in the Extend debate. Reteach Figure 17.6

Answer

Checkpoint increasingly large trade deficits

Effects of the Deficit

When Americans import more than they export, more dollars end up in the hands of foreigners. They can then use these extra dollars to purchase American land, stocks, bonds, and other assets. As a result of America's trade deficits, people from other countries now own a large piece of the U.S. economy. Many people fear this trend threatens national independence and even national security.

Some economists worry that foreign financial investment might not always support the trade deficit. They worry that, with U.S. imports on the rise and American foreign debt growing, overseas investors might become reluctant to purchase American assets. As a result, that monetary flow into the United States would slow down. In 2000, a federal commission formed to study the deficit concluded that "maintaining large and growing trade deficits is neither desirable nor likely to be sustainable for the extended future."

Can Balance Be Restored?

To reduce the trade deficit, the government could depreciate the exchange rate. As you saw, when the dollar is weak, American products become cheaper to buy on the world market and other countries' goods become correspondingly more expensive. As a result, exports rise and imports fall. The head of the nation's largest steelmaker noted this process at work in 2008:

> **"The opportunities for exporting are infinitely greater than they were a year or two years ago. We have folks who were bringing in steel for decades coming to us and saying we'd like to talk to you about exporting. That is a huge change. It's because of the dollar."**
>
> —Dan DiMicco, interview

The federal government could also cut back spending by adjusting its monetary or fiscal policy, as you have seen in Chapters 15 and 16. Individuals could voluntarily purchase fewer foreign goods, despite the higher price of certain domestic items. Or American companies could try to sell more domestic products overseas. All of these approaches involve sacrifices or risk, but they would result in fewer surplus dollars ending up in foreign hands.

CHECKPOINT ***What has been the trend in the United States balance of trade in recent decades?***

SECTION 3 ASSESSMENT

Essential Questions Journal To continue to build a response to the Essential Question, go to your **Essential Questions Journal.**

Guiding Question

1. Use your completed chart to answer this question: How do exchange rates affect international trade?
2. **Extension** You are saving money to buy a video game system made in Japan. Suddenly, Japan announces that it is reducing the value of the yen. Will that make it easier or harder for you to buy your game system? Why?

Key Terms and Main Ideas

3. What is an **exchange rate?**
4. What is the effect of **appreciation** and **depreciation** on the price of goods?
5. What happens in the **foreign exchange market?**
6. How do a **fixed exchange-rate system** and a **flexible exchange-rate system** differ?
7. What is the **balance of trade?**
8. How does the **balance of payments** differ from the **balance of trade?**

Critical Thinking

9. **Categorize** Explain how each of the following Americans might react to a rise in the value of the U.S. dollar and why: **(a)** a farmer who exports crops, **(b)** a consumer shopping for a new car, **(c)** the owner of a store selling imported food.
10. **Predict** How do you think a nation's balance of trade might be affected if its government instituted policies to support science education and give tax breaks to high-tech industries?
11. **Understand Cause and Effect** Explain how each of the following has contributed to the growth of the United States trade deficit: **(a)** consumer demand, **(b)** dependence on foreign oil, **(c)** exchange rates.

Math Skills

12. Assume that the numbers in Figure 17.5 represent today's exchange rates. Using the formula shown in this section, calculate the price of a car that costs $18,000 in the United States in: **(a)** Australian dollars, **(b)** euros, **(c)** yen.

Visit Pearson SuccessNet.com for additional math help.

Assessment Answers

1. Appreciating currency encourages imports by making them cheaper to buy and discourages exports by making them more expensive overseas. Depreciating currency has the opposite effects.
2. easier, because the devalued yen will make the game cost less in U.S. dollars
3. the value of one nation's currency in relation to another nation's currency
4. Appreciation raises the price of a country's exports and makes imports cost less. Depreciation lowers the cost of a country's exports and raises prices on imports.
5. Currencies are bought and sold.
6. In a fixed-rate system, governments try to keep exchange rates constant. In a flexible-rate system, exchange rates are determined by supply and demand.
7. the relationship between the value of a country's exports and imports
8. Balance of payments includes all monetary transactions between a country's economy and the rest of the world.
9. (a) mixed feelings because the change would raise prices on exported crops, but might reduce demand for those exports (b) might benefit because the price of imported cars would fall (c) pleased because prices on what he or she sells would fall, increasing sales
10. This would shrink trade deficits or increase trade surpluses by making the nation's high-tech products more competitive.
11. (a) Increased demand for imported goods contributed to a negative balance of trade. (b) Dependence on costly foreign oil increased imports and drove the growing trade deficit. (c) A weakening dollar increased the value of imported goods.
12. (a) 20,160 Australian dollars (b) 12,600 euros (c) 2,069,460 yen

QUICK STUDY GUIDE

QUICK STUDY GUIDE

Chapter 17: International Trade

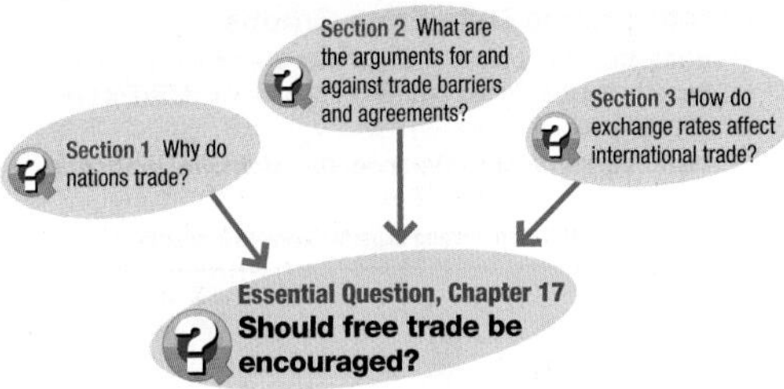
Section 1 Why do nations trade?
Section 2 What are the arguments for and against trade barriers and agreements?
Section 3 How do exchange rates affect international trade?
Essential Question, Chapter 17
Should free trade be encouraged?

Strong Dollar

As the dollar becomes stronger... American exports decline

Weak Dollar

As the dollar becomes weaker... American exports rise

Two International Trade Organizations

EU	Both	NAFTA
• 27 nations of Europe • 12 members use common currency • Parliament and council • Uniform tariffs for non-members	• Reduction or elimination of trade barriers • Increased trade • Controversy within countries	• 3 nations of North America • No common currency • No common legislative body • Independent tariff policies

Economic Dictionary

export, *p. 449*
import, *p. 449*
absolute advantage, *p. 449*
comparative advantage, *p. 449*
law of comparative advantage, *p. 450*
interdependence, *p. 452*
trade barrier, *p. 455*
tariff, *p. 455*
import quota, *p. 456*
sanctions, *p. 456*
embargo, *p. 456*
trade war, *p. 457*
protectionism, *p. 457*
infant industry, *p. 458*
free trade, *p. 458*
free-trade zone, *p. 460*
exchange rate, *p. 463*
appreciation, *p. 464*
depreciation, *p. 465*
foreign exchange market, *p. 465*
fixed exchange-rate system, *p. 467*
flexible exchange-rate system, *p. 467*
balance of trade, *p. 468*
trade surplus, *p. 468*
trade deficit, *p. 468*
balance of payments, *p. 469*

Economics on the go

Study anytime, anywhere. Download these files today.

Economic Dictionary online	Audio Review online	Action Graph online	Visual Glossary online	How the Economy Works online
Vocabulary Support in English and Spanish	Audio Study Guide in English and Spanish	Animated Charts and Graphs	Animated feature	Animated feature

Download to your computer or mobile device at PearsonSuccessNet.com

ASSIGN THE ESSENTIAL QUESTIONS JOURNAL

After students have finished studying the chapter, they should return to the chapter's essential question in the Essential Questions Journal and complete the activity.

Tell students to go back to the chapter opener and look at the image. Using the information they have gained from studying the chapter, ask **How does this illustrate the main ideas of the chapter?** *(Countries can import goods that they need and export goods that they have an absolute or comparative advantage in producing.)*

STUDY TIPS

Explain to students that analyzing the work they have done on worksheets and quizzes can help them prepare for tests. Have students look back at the mistakes they made on previous work and take notes about areas they found confusing. Have each student write a question on a notecard, and weave answers to these questions into review sessions.

Economics on the go Have students download the digital resources available on Economics on the Go for review and remediation.

Assessment at a Glance

TESTS AND QUIZZES

Section Assessments

Section Quizzes A and B, **Unit 7 All-in-One**
Self-Test Online

Chapter Assessments

Chapter Tests A and B, **Unit 7 All-in-One**
Economic Detective, **Unit 7 All-in-One**
Document-based Assessment, p. 473
Exam*View*

AYP Monitoring Assessments

PERFORMANCE ASSESSMENT

Teacher's Edition, pp. 450, 452, 457, 460, 467, 468, 469
Simulation Activities, Chapter 17
Virtual Economics on CD-ROM, pp. 451, 457, 465
Essential Questions Journal, Chapter 17
Assessment Rubrics

Chapter Assessment

1. (a) Natural, capital, and labor resources influence the goods and services that a country can efficiently produce, and also shape what it cannot produce. (b) Advantages include being able to export that natural resource at high prices to pay for imported needs and still have a favorable balance of trade. Disadvantages include a lack of economic diversity and too heavy a dependence on that resource. (c) goods and services that require skill and training to produce
2. (a) natural and other resources, absolute or comparative advantage, dependence on outside sources for other needs (b) What countries are good markets? Do I have a comparative advantage? Are there any trade barriers? Are the currency exchange rates favorable? Would the profits make up for the cost of shipping? Are there any political considerations?
3. (a) it is worth less in relation to other currencies (b) makes overseas travel more expensive; makes their products cheaper overseas (c) Possible answer: Yes, because it benefits U.S. exporters and protects U.S. jobs.
4. (a) weak dollar, dependence on oil imports, U.S. consumerism, excess of imports over exports (b) raises concerns about national independence and national security. (c) Possible answers: Yes, so that the U.S. can be truly independent. No, because American consumers would suffer.
5. (a) oil and gas (b) about $200 billion
6. (a) agricultural products (b) about $15 billion
7. (a) would reduce oil imports and shrink the trade deficit (b) Increased cost of oil imports would increase the trade deficit. (c) would reduce oil imports and shrink the trade deficit
8. (a) Consumer group should favor the agreement and manufacturer, labor, and environmental groups should oppose it. The WTO should be pro free trade but against China's allegedly unfair trade practices. (b) Positions should be similar to (a). Labor, manufacturer groups should be concerned with the impact on industry and jobs. (c) Positions should be consistent with (a) and (b). Environmental group should express concern about Chinese pollution. Consumer groups should push the benefits of cheap imports.
9. (a) Responses should recognize the positions presented in 8. (b) Added provisions might include environmental requirements for Chinese industries and protections against predatory practices.

CHAPTER 17 ASSESSMENT

Self-Test online To test your understanding of key terms and main ideas, visit **PearsonSuccessNet.com**

Key Terms and Main Ideas

To make sure you understand the key terms and main ideas of this chapter, review the Checkpoint and Section Assessment questions and look at the Quick Study Guide on the preceding page.

Critical Thinking

1. **Infer (a)** How does resource distribution affect trade? **(b)** What might be the advantages and disadvantages of having an economy based on one or two natural resources that are in high demand? **(c)** If a nation has few natural resources but abundant human capital, what kinds of goods and services might it specialize in?
2. **Ask Questions (a)** What factors affect the decision to trade? **(b)** Choose a particular product. Suppose you were the owner of a small American company that made that product. List four questions you would ask before deciding whether to sell that product overseas.
3. **Analyze (a)** What does it mean when economists say the dollar is "weak"? **(b)** What impact would a weakening dollar have on Americans traveling overseas? On an American company selling products overseas? **(c)** Do you think the benefits of depreciation outweigh the costs? Explain.

4. **Decide (a)** What are the causes of the United States trade deficit? **(b)** What are some of the dangers of running a trade deficit? **(c)** Would you be in favor of aggressive federal action to reduce the trade deficit if it meant paying higher prices for many goods? Why or why not?

Applying Your Math Skills

Interpreting Data From Graphs

Study the chart below, which shows the total exports and imports for the United States in 2006 for six different types of products.

Visit PearsonSuccessNet.com for additional math help.

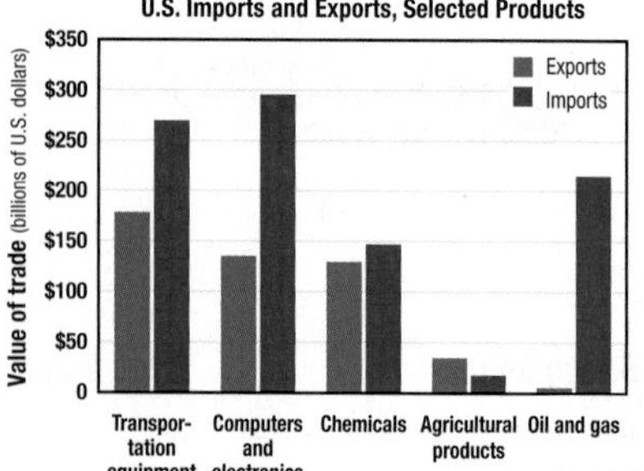

SOURCE: U.S. Census Bureau, *Statistical Abstract of the United States: 2008*

5. **(a)** Which category of products had the largest trade deficit? **(b)** How large was that deficit?
6. **(a)** Which category of products had the only surplus? **(b)** How large was that surplus?
7. Explain what would be likely to happen to the trade deficit under each of the following circumstances, and why: **(a)** engineers invent a new car engine that runs on hydrogen, **(b)** oil exporters raise prices by 10 percent, **(c)** new oil fields are discovered within the United States.

Essential Question Activity

Essential Questions Journal To respond to the chapter Essential Question, go to your **Essential Questions Journal.**

8. Complete the activity to answer the Essential Question **Should free trade be encouraged?** For this activity, the class will be divided into six groups. One group will represent members of a Senate committee holding a hearing on a free-trade agreement with China being debated in Congress. Each of the other groups will represent one of the following: economists at the World Trade Organization; an American consumer interest group; an American automobile manufacturer; the American Federation of Labor; an organization of environmentalists. The senators should prepare their questions; the others should develop positions for or against the agreement. Using the worksheet in your Essential Questions Journal or the electronic worksheet available at **PearsonSuccessNet.com,** gather the following information:
   (a) What effects do the speakers think the agreement will have on the people or businesses they represent?
   (b) What effects do the groups think the agreement will have on the people of each senator's state?
   (c) What effects do the groups think the agreement will have on the country as a whole?
9. **Modify** Congress sometimes insists on additions to agreements with other nations. Senators should explore these issues with each group. Then, they should announce:
   (a) whether they will vote for or against the agreement.
   (b) what added provisions, if any, they would support and why.

WebQuest online The Economics WebQuest challenges students to use 21st century skills to answer the Essential Question.

Remind students to continue to develop an Essentials Questions video. Guidelines and a production binder are available at www.PearsonSuccessNet.com.

CHAPTER 17 ASSESSMENT

DOCUMENT-BASED ASSESSMENT

Should foreign ownership of U.S. assets be restricted?

High trade deficits have resulted in foreign businesses and countries holding large sums of U.S. dollars. Some have used that money to purchase U.S. companies or property, or to make loans to the federal government. Some critics are concerned that this trend could harm the U.S. economy.

Document A

	2001	2002	2003	2004	2005	2006
U.S. investment abroad (billions of dollars)	$6,309	$6,652	$7,643	$9,257	$11,576	$13,755
Percent change from prior year	+1.1%	+5.4%	+14.9%	+21.1%	+25.1%	+18.8%
Foreign investment in U.S. (billions of dollars)	$8,228	$8,740	$9,784	$11,551	$13,815	$16,295
Percent change from prior year	+8.0%	+6.2%	+11.9%	+18.1%	+19.6%	+18.0%

SOURCE: U.S. Census Bureau, *Statistical Abstract of the United States: 2008*

Document B

"Our trade deficit makes us increasingly vulnerable. That's because our trade deficit makes us dependent on foreign ownership of U.S. assets to finance our debt. [In the last five years] the United States has accumulated more foreign debt than in the entire first 220 years of our country's history.

"Unfair trade practices place American workers and businesses at a competitive disadvantage. We can compete with any country in the world—as long as the rules of trade are fair and equitable.

"We need an aggressive U.S. trade policy that stands up for American workers and businesses. To accomplish that goal, we need to use all the tools at our disposal to pry open foreign markets, enforce our intellectual property rights and make sure China, Japan, the European Union and other countries are not given an artificial trading advantage."

—Rep. Benjamin L. Cardin (Dem.-MD), 2006

Document C

"About 20 percent of all U.S. exports originate from U.S. affiliates of foreign-owned companies. [Foreign direct investment (FDI)] supports about 5.3 million U.S. jobs.... U.S. subsidiaries support an annual payroll of $317.9 billion with average compensation per employee worth almost $60,000—more than one-third more than the average American salary. Moreover, the benefits of FDI extend into the American economy as a whole. Increased investment and competition generate higher productivity and more efficient resource use. Ultimately, this culminates in greater economic growth, job creation and higher living standards for all. Any new rules that restrict, delay, or politicize foreign investment, will result in the loss of FDI.... Consequently, America will pay for higher investment barriers with lower growth and fewer jobs. FDI restrictions would undermine America's chances of remaining an economic superpower in an increasingly competitive global economy."

—Daniella Markheim, testimony to House Homeland Security committee, 2006

ANALYZING DOCUMENTS

Use your knowledge of foreign trade and Documents A, B, and C to answer questions 1–3.

1. Document A shows that, since 2000,

A. foreign investment in the U.S. has grown while U.S. investment abroad has fallen.
B. both foreign investment in the U.S. and U.S. investment abroad have risen.
C. foreign investment in the U.S. has fallen while U.S. investment abroad has grown.
D. both foreign investment in the U.S. and U.S. investment abroad have fallen.

2. Document B argues that

A. the trade deficit is a threat to the U.S. economy.
B. American workers benefit from foreign investment.
C. foreign investment will fall on its own.
D. there is no way to reverse the trade deficit.

3. Document C argues that foreign investment in the U.S.

A. promotes competition but costs jobs.
B. results in higher prices.
C. generates jobs and innovation.
D. is not matched by U.S. investment abroad.

WRITING ABOUT ECONOMICS

Whether to put limits on foreign investment in the United States is a controversial issue. Use the documents on this page and resources on the Web site below to answer the question: ***Should foreign ownership of U.S. assets be restricted?*** Use the sources to support your opinion.

In Partnership

THE WALL STREET JOURNAL.
CLASSROOM EDITION

To read more about issues related to this topic, visit **PearsonSuccessNet.com**

Document-Based Assessment

ANALYZING DOCUMENTS

1. B
2. A
3. C

WRITING ABOUT ECONOMICS

Possible answers: Foreign ownership of U.S. assets puts American workers and businesses at a disadvantage, and should be restricted. Foreign investment creates jobs in the United States and improves living standards.

Student essay should demonstrate an understanding of the issues involved in the debate. Use the following as guidelines to assess the essay.

L2 Differentiate Students use all documents on the page to support their thesis.

L3 Differentiate Students use the documents on this page and additional information available online at www.PearsonSuccessNet.com to support their answer.

L4 Differentiate Students incorporate information provided in the textbook and online at www.PearsonSuccessNet.com and include additional research to support their opinion.

Go Online to www.PearsonSuccessNet.com for a student rubric and extra documents.

Economics online *All print resources are available on the Teacher's Resource Library CD-ROM and online at* www.PearsonSuccessNet.com.

Introduce the Databank

This collection of data about the world economy presents information that can help students as they read, answer questions, and do further research on many chapters. Remind students to use the skills described on the Graph Preview pages at the front of the book (pp. xxviii–xxxii) when they need to interpret or create a graph or chart.

The databank may be used to supplement the information in particular chapters, which are noted in the lesson for each graph. In addition, each graph is accompanied by questions that can be used to stir discussion of the significance of the data.

Economics online Visit www.PearsonSuccessNet.com for updates on the data. Use the updates to have students compare the new data to the data in their books.

Teach

The graphs on this page can supplement or be compared with graphs in chapters 17 and 18, as students learn about international trade.

U.S. EXPORTS AND IMPORTS, BY MAJOR TRADING PARTNERS, AUGUST 2006–AUGUST 2007

Have students examine the chart. Ask **Does the United States export more than it imports with any country shown?** *(only with the Netherlands)* Have students add the value of the three largest imports. Ask **What is the total?** *(about $203 billion each from Canada and China plus about $135 billion from Mexico, for a total of $541 billion)* Have students compare that with the total U.S. exports to those countries. *(about $160 billion to Canada, $40 billion to China, and $90 billion to Mexico, for a total of $290 billion)* Have students discuss the reasons for the disparity in these numbers. Have students research current import and export data.

MAJOR U.S. EXPORTS AND IMPORTS, 2004

Have students note that imports are shown in red in this graph (they were blue in the previous graph). Have students research the changes in manufacturing that have taken place from 1950 to the present. Have them chart the changes in the ratio of imports to exports of manufactured goods.

Databank The World Economy

In this databank, you will look at the major role that the United States plays in world trade. You will also compare the United States economy to the economies of other nations.

U.S. Exports and Imports, by Major Trading Partners, August 2006–August 2007

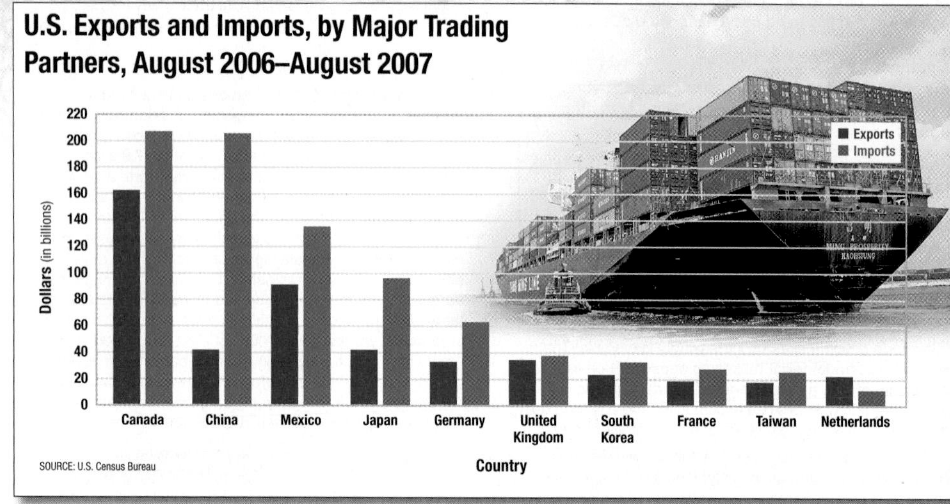

Major U.S. Exports and Imports, 2004

Exports
Imports
Dollars (in thousands)
1,600,000
1,400,000
1,200,000
1,000,000
800,000
600,000
400,000
200,000
0
Agricultural products
Manufactured goods
Mineral fuels
Commodity group
SOURCE: U.S. International Trade Administration

Exchange Rates of the Dollar

Country	1998	2001	2004	2007
Canada $	1.4836	1.5487	1.3017	1.0734
China Yuan	8.3008	8.2770	8.2768	7.6058
European Union €uro	N/A	0.8952	1.2438	1.3711
Japan ¥en	130.99	121.57	108.15	117.76
Mexico Peso	9.152	9.337	11.290	10.928
United Kingdom £	1.6573	1.4396	1.8330	2.0020

SOURCE: U.S. Federal Reserve

Economics online For updated data, visit PearsonSuccessNet.com

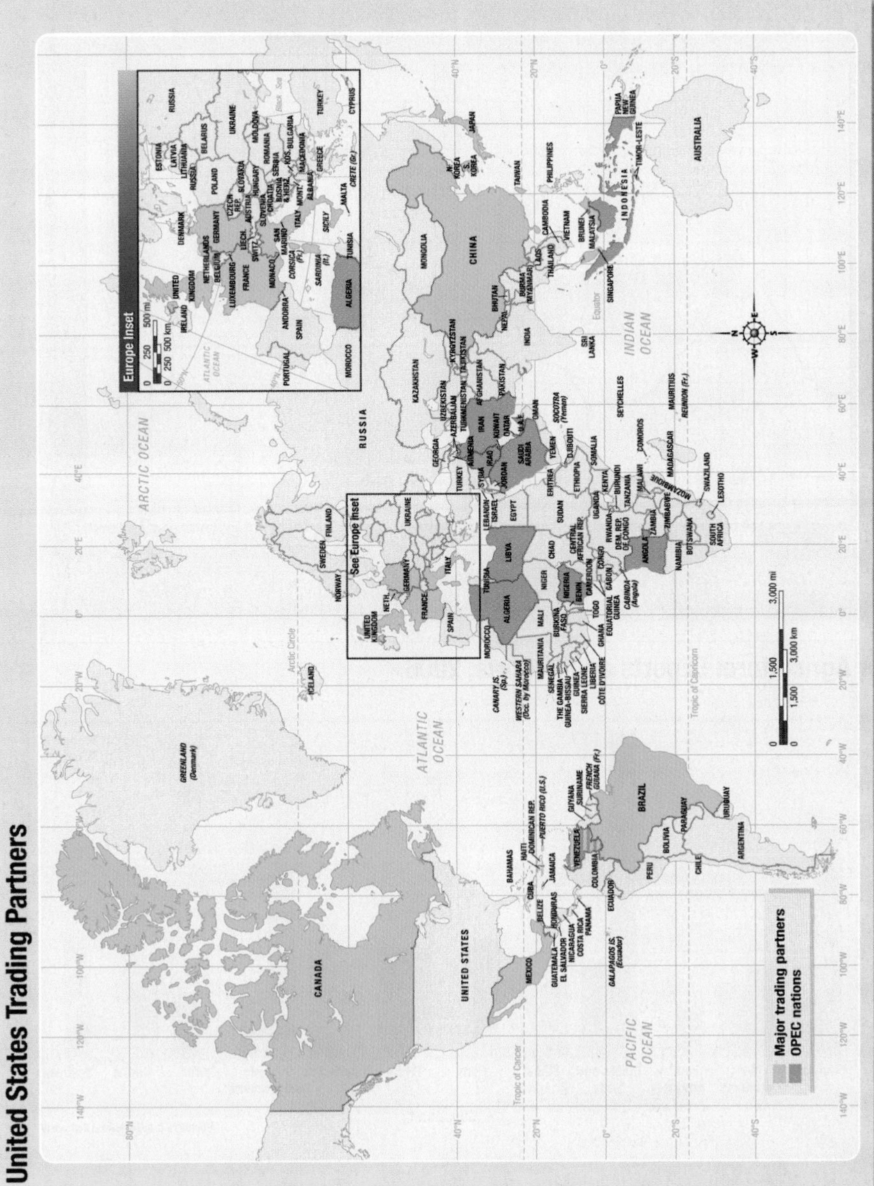

Databank: The World Economy

Teach

EXCHANGE RATES OF THE DOLLAR

Explain that exchange rates are stated as the value of one currency against another. However, the rate can be stated in different ways, depending on which currency you are converting to and from. The rates in the table on page 474 show how many U.S. dollars it would take to buy one of the listed currencies. So, for example, in 2007, £1 would cost just over $2. However, if you stated instead how many pounds you could buy for a dollar, you would be able to buy just under .5 pounds. Ask **What has the trend been in the exchange rate for the Chinese yuan in the years shown? Has the value of the dollar gone up or down relative to the yuan?** *(When the exchange rate goes down, as it has for the yuan, it means that the value of the dollar goes up, which was the trend from 1998 to 2007. In 1998, one yuan cost $8.31. In 2007, it cost $7.61.)*

This map can be useful in discussions of the economic systems in Chapter 2 and of international trade in chapters 17 and 18.

UNITED STATES TRADING PARTNERS

Have students use the map to identify the major trading partners of the United States. Have students choose one country and research to find out what products account for the largest percentage of imports to and exports from that country.

Point out the OPEC nations in orange on the map. Ask **What is the main export of the OPEC nations?** *(oil)* Have students research to find out which countries are the largest importers of oil.

Teach

When students are learning about measuring economic performance in Unit 5, it can be helpful for them to consider the relationship between imports and exports. In addition, these graphs are particularly helpful in Unit 7, The Global Economy.

U.S. OIL IMPORTS, 1973–2007

Ask **How many barrels of oil did the United States import at the peak shown on this chart?** *(about 3.8 billion barrels in 2004)* Ask **What can you infer about the price of oil between 2004 and 2007?** *(Demand went down, which could indicate that price went up.)*

Explain that the price of a barrel of crude oil in 2004 was around $30 per barrel. After 2004, the price fluctuated, but generally went up, skyrocketing in 2008 to more than $130 dollars a barrel, then dropping precipitously back toward $40.

MAJOR AGRICULTURAL EXPORTS AND IMPORTS, 2006

Have students examine the graph. Ask students to find the agricultural products that the United States exports but does not import. *(poultry products, wheat products, corn, cotton, and soybeans)* Have students compare this graph with "Major U.S. Exports and Imports, 2004" on page 474. Ask **How does the U.S. balance of imports to exports in agricultural products differ from its balance in other products?** *(Exports are much higher than imports of agricultural products, whereas for manufactured goods, imports are much higher than exports.)*

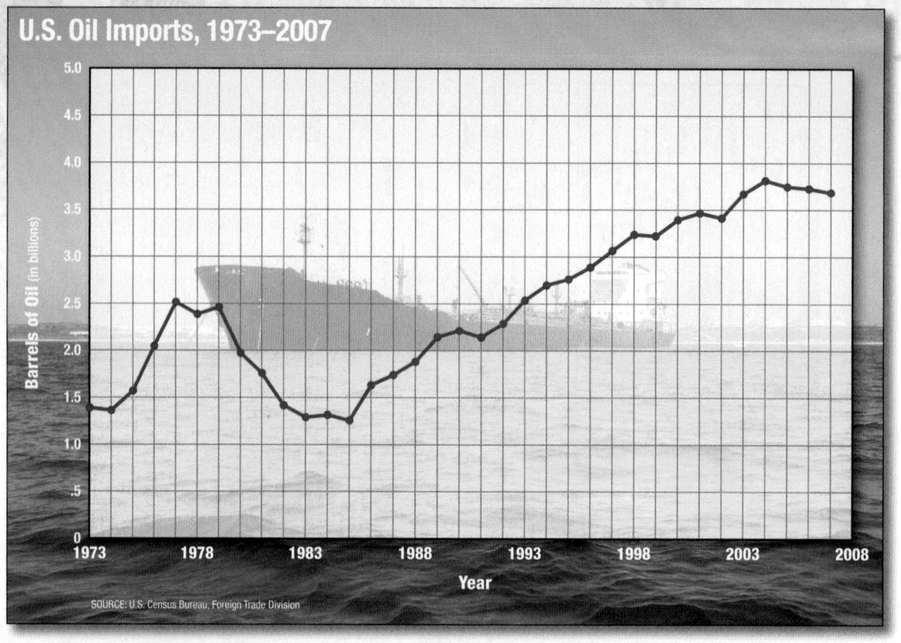

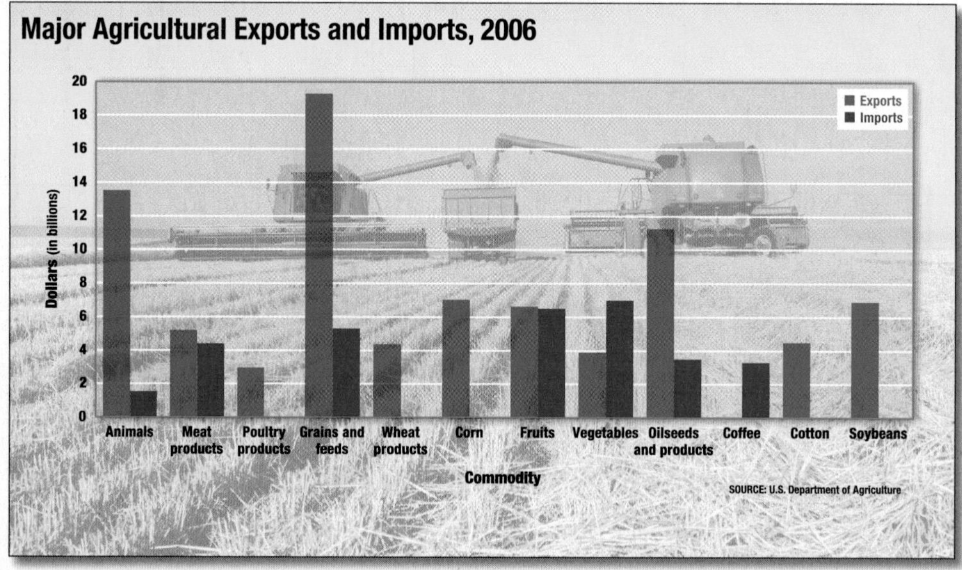

Economics online For updated data, visit PearsonSuccessNet.com

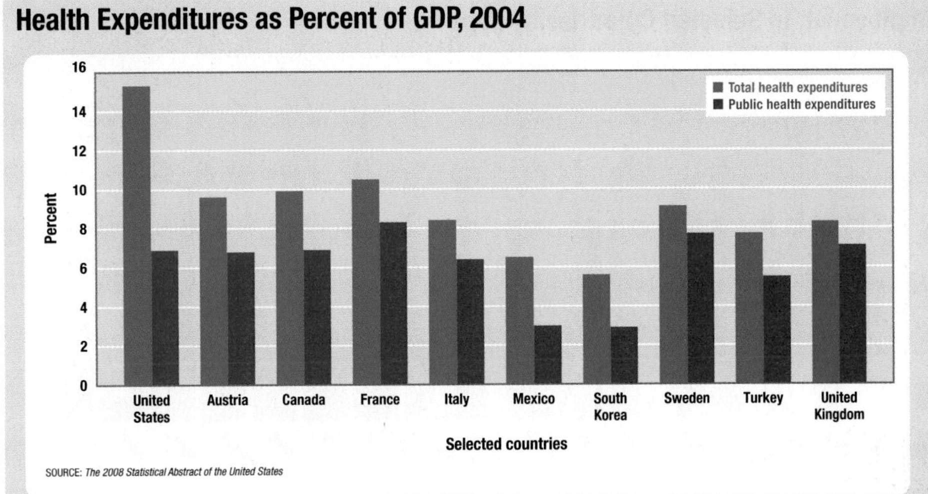

Taxes as Percent of GDP 2004

Selected countries: United States, Austria, Canada, France, Germany, Italy, Mexico, South Korea, Sweden, Turkey, United Kingdom

0 10 20 30 40 50 60

Percent

SOURCE: OECD

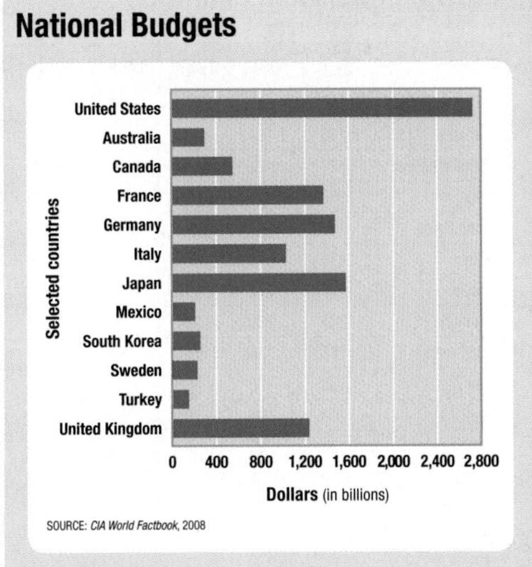

Databank: The World Economy

Teach

As students study GDP in Chapter 12, taxes and government spending in Chapter 14, and the global economy in Unit 7, have them use these graphs to deepen their understanding of the role the United States government plays in the economy. Have them compare U.S. data with data from other governments around the world.

HEALTH EXPENDITURES AS PERCENT OF GDP, 2004

Remind students that the gross domestic product, or GDP, is the dollar value of all final goods and services produced within a country's borders in a given year. Have students compare the highest and lowest percentages of total health expenditures shown. Ask **What is the difference between the two countries?** *(The highest total expenditure is in the United States, at just over 15 percent of GDP; the lowest is in South Korea, at about 5.7 percent of GDP; the difference is 9.3 percent.)* **In which three countries are the public expenditures half or less than half of the total expenditures?** *(the United States, Mexico, and South Korea)*

TAXES AS PERCENT OF GDP 2004

Have students compare the chart showing percent of GDP represented by taxes with the percent of public expenditure on health. Ask **What is the relationship between these two sets of data?** *(Countries that pay more of their citizens' healthcare costs generally tax citizens to pay for that care.)*

NATIONAL BUDGETS

Ask **How many times greater is the United States' budget than that of Turkey?** *(The U.S. national budget, at about \$2.7 trillion is about 14 times that of Turkey, at about 200 billion)* Have students look at the following population chart and make the same comparison. *(The U.S. population is about 4.25 times that of Turkey.)* Have students compare populations with national budgets to get a sense of the differences among nations.

COUNTRY	POPULATION (IN MILLIONS)
United States	301.1
Australia	20.4
Canada	33.3
France	60.1
Germany	82.4
Italy	58.1
Japan	127.4
Mexico	108.7
South Korea	49.0
Sweden	9.0
Turkey	71.1
United Kingdom	58.1

Teach

The graphs on this page and the next can be particularly useful when students are learning about growth and economic challenges in Unit 5 as well as the global economy in Unit 7. Have students look at and discuss the four charts together. Students should be encouraged to research changes that have taken place and compare current data with the data in their textbooks.

EMPLOYMENT IN SELECTED COUNTRIES BY TYPE

Have students discuss the categories in the chart. Ask for examples of the types of jobs that would fit into each category. Then have students compare the GDPs shown in the chart below with the types of employment in these countries.

GDP GROWTH OF SELECTED COUNTRIES

Note that the GDP shown is not per capita GDP, so the relative amounts may be less telling than the changes from year to year. The difference in the size of populations has a large effect on GDP. Assign each student a country, and have them calculate the growth rate of GDP from 1997 to 2007 for that country. Then compare those rates with the types of employment in each country.

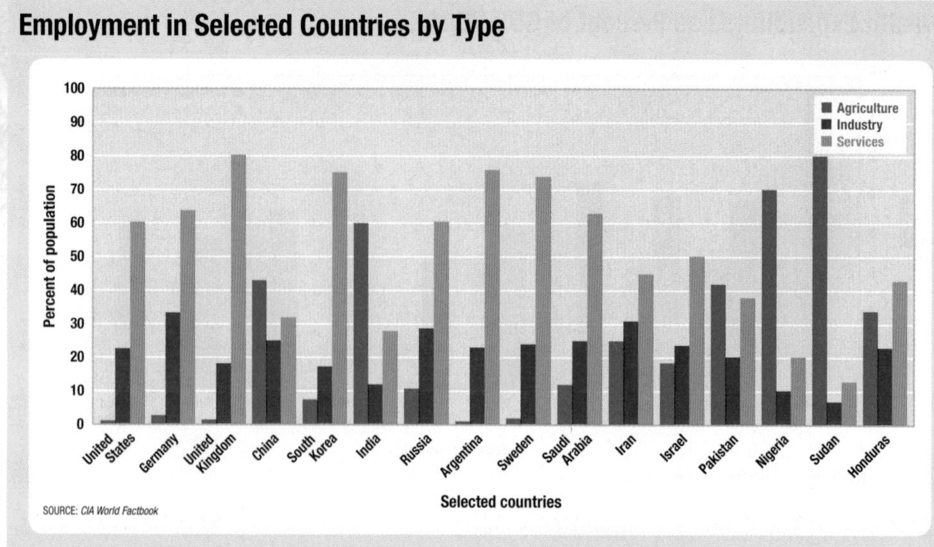

GDP Growth of Selected Countries

Country	1997	1998	1999	2000	2001	2002	2003	2004	2005	2006	2007*
United States	8,250	8,695	9,216	9,765	10,076	10,418	10,919	11,679	12,417	13,202	13,860
Germany	2,160	2,184	2,144	1,900	1,891	2,019	2,442	2,751	2,795	2,907	2,833
United Kingdom	1,327	1,425	1,465	1,443	1,435	1,571	1,806	2,132	2,199	2,345	2,147
China	953	1,019	1,083	1,198	1,325	1,454	1,641	1,932	2,234	2,668	7,043
South Korea	516	345	445	512	482	547	608	680	788	888	1,206
India	410	414	450	460	478	508	602	696	806	906	2,965
Russia	405	271	196	260	307	345	431	589	764	987	2,076
Argentina	293	299	284	284	269	102	130	153	183	214	524
Saudi Arabia	165	146	161	188	183	189	215	250	310	310	572
Iran	105	103	105	101	115	116	136	163	190	223	853
Israel	104	104	104	115	114	104	110	117	123	123	185
Nigeria	36	32	35	46	48	47	58	72	99	115	295
Sudan	12	11	11	12	13	15	18	21	28	38	108
Honduras	5	5	5	6	6	7	7	7	8	9	25

Note: Amounts in billions of dollars.
*Estimates for 2007
SOURCE: *CIA World Factbook*, World Bank

Economics online For updated data, visit PearsonSuccessNet.com

Labor Productivity by Country

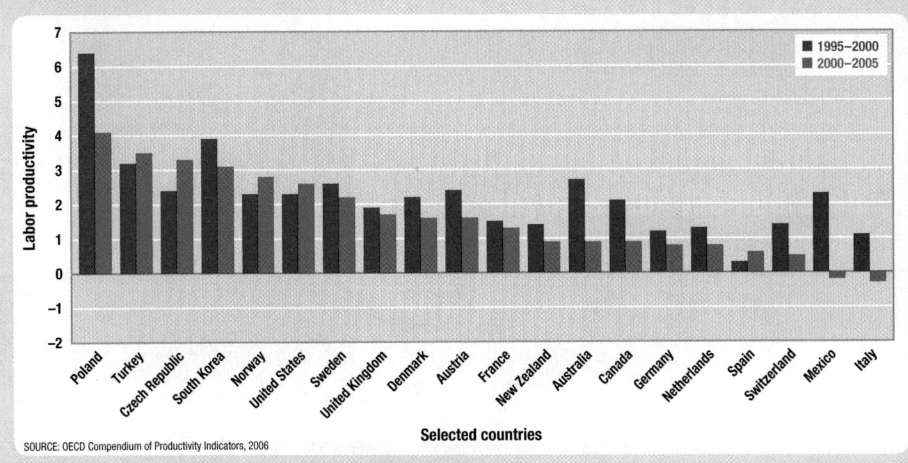

SOURCE: OECD Compendium of Productivity Indicators, 2006

Economic Health of Selected Countries

Country	Infant Mortality (per 1,000 live births)	Life Expectancy	Median Age	Literacy (by percent)	Unemployment (by percent)	Internet Users	Cellular Telephone Users
United States	6.37	78	36.6	99	4.6	208 million	233 million
Germany	4.08	78.95	43	99	9.1	38.6 million	84.3 million
United Kingdom	5.01	78.7	39.6	99	5.4	33.534 million	69.657 million
China	22.12	72.88	33.2	90.9	4	162 million	461.1 million
South Korea	6.05	77.23	35.8	97.9	3.2	34.12 million	40.197 million
India	34.61	68.59	24.8	73.4	7.2	60 million	166.1 million
Russia	11.06	65.87	38.2	99.4	5.9	25.689 million	150 million
Argentina	14.29	76.32	29.9	97.2	8.9	8.184 million	31.51 million
Saudi Arabia	12.41	75.88	21.4	78.8	13	4.7 million	19.663 million
Iran	38.12	70.56	25.8	77	11	18 million	13.659 million
Israel	6.75	79.59	29.9	97.1	7.6	1.899 million	8.404 million
Nigeria	95.52	47.44	18.7	68	5.8	8 million	32.322 million
Sudan	91.78	49.11	18.7	61.1	18.7	3.5 million	4.683 million
Honduras	25.21	69.35	19.7	80	27.8	337,300	2.241 million

SOURCE: *CIA World Factbook*, 2008

Databank: The World Economy

LABOR PRODUCTIVITY BY COUNTRY

Have students list the countries whose productivity was higher in the 2000–2005 period than it was in the 1995–2000 period. *(Turkey, Czech Republic, Norway, United States, and Spain)* Have students look at the productivity chart and the GDP growth chart on page 478. Have students choose a country to analyze, and ask them to write a sentence that describes the relationship between changes in productivity and changes in GDP in that country.

ECONOMIC HEALTH OF SELECTED COUNTRIES

Explain to students that each column heading in this chart contributes to a picture of the economic health of the country. Ask **How is infant mortality related to economic health?** *(The lower the number of deaths per 1,000 live births, the more likely it is that the country has a healthy, productive population that is receiving adequate medical care.)* Ask volunteers to explain how each of the indicators that are rated in this chart contributes to economic health. Ask **What are some other indicators that could be added to the chart?** *(Possible answers: per capita income, highest level of education, percent school attendance)* Have students fill in a world map that shows the outline of land masses using different colors to represent each bracket of infant mortality. Brackets should be 0–10, 11–20, and so on. Have them research this statistic for five other countries and add these to the map.

Essential Questions

UNIT 7:

How might scarcity divide our world or bring it together?

CHAPTER 18:

Do the benefits of economic development outweigh the costs?

Introduce the Chapter

ACTIVATE PRIOR KNOWLEDGE

In this chapter, students will learn about economic development and globalization. Tell students to complete the warmup activity in the **Essential Questions Journal**.

DIFFERENTIATED INSTRUCTION KEY

- **L1** Special Needs
- **L2** Basic
  - **ELL** English Language Learners
  - **LPR** Less Proficient Readers
- **L3** All Students
- **L4** Advanced Students

Economics online Visit www.PearsonSuccessNet.com for an interactive textbook with built-in activities on economic principles.

- ***The Wall Street Journal* Classroom Edition Video** presents a current topic related to globalization.
- **Yearly Update Worksheet** provides an annual update, including a new worksheet and lesson on this topic.
- **On the Go** resources can be downloaded so students and teachers can connect with economics anytime, anywhere.

ECONOMICS ONLINE

DIGITAL TEACHER TOOLS

The online lesson planner is designed to help teachers plan, teach, and assess. Teachers have the ability to use or customize existing Pearson lesson plans. Online lecture notes support the print lesson by providing an array of accessible activities and summaries of key concepts.

Two interactivities in this lesson are:

- **How the Economy Works** presents an activity in which students follow the story of a family living through their country's economic development.
- **Visual Glossary** Different effects of globalization around the world are illustrated.

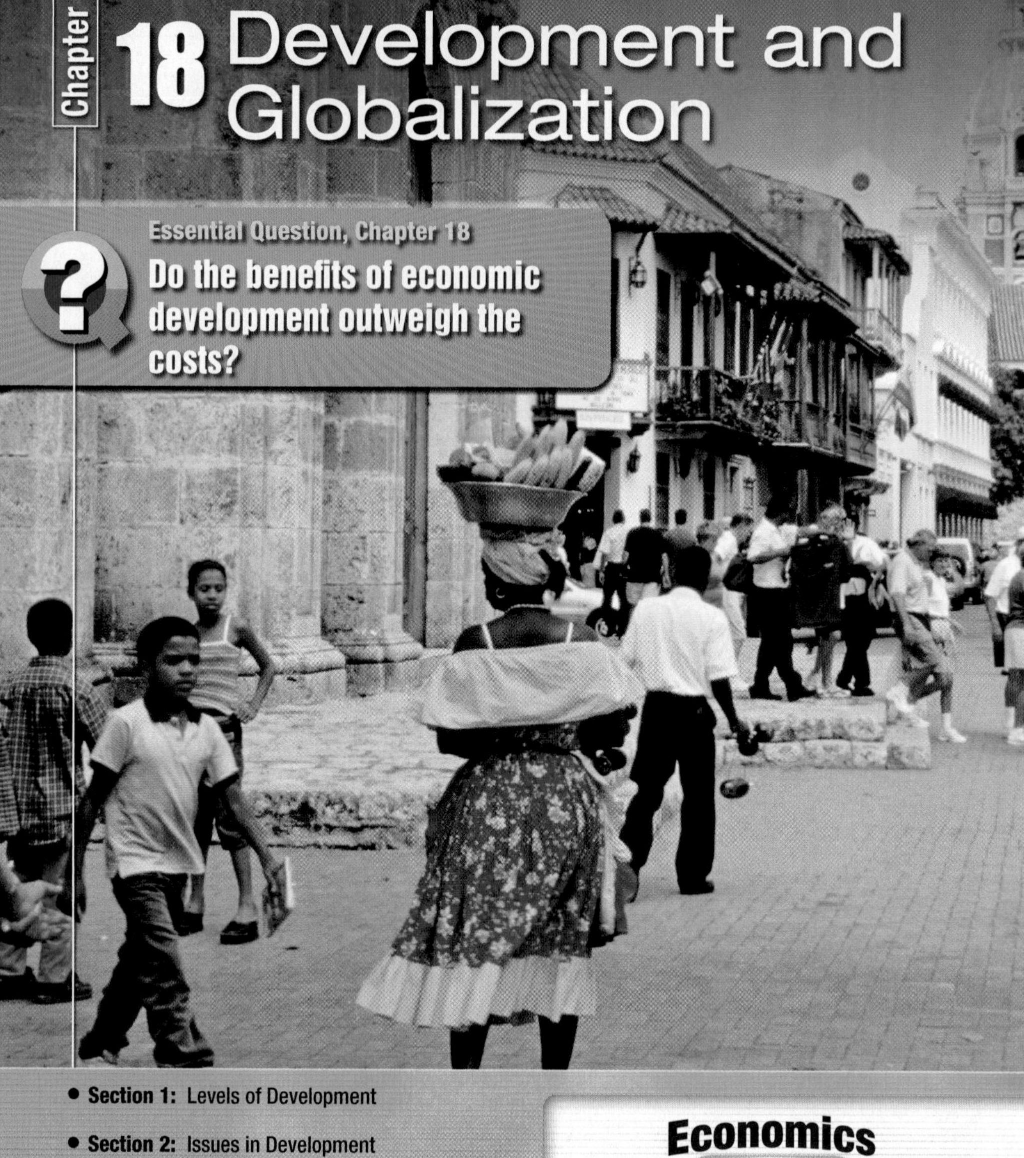

Chapter 18 Development and Globalization

Essential Question, Chapter 18

Do the benefits of economic development outweigh the costs?

- **Section 1:** Levels of Development
- **Section 2:** Issues in Development
- **Section 3:** Economies in Transition
- **Section 4:** Challenges of Globalization

Economics on the go

To study anywhere, anytime, download these online resources at ***PearsonSuccessNet.com*** ▶

Block Scheduling

BLOCK 1 Teach Sections 1 and 2 lessons, omitting the Extend options and using the Simulation Activity to explore issues in development.

BLOCK 2 Teach Sections 3 and 4 lessons, with special emphasis on the impact of globalization on the U.S. economy and American businesses and workers.

Pressed for Time

Group work Form four groups, assigning one group to each section. Have the groups create a study guide and quiz on the main ideas of the section. Have the groups copy their materials for the rest of the class. After students read the study guide for the sections unfamiliar to them and ask questions of the groups that created the study guides, have them take the quiz.

SECTION 1 Levels of Development

OBJECTIVES

1. **Understand** what is meant by developed nations and less developed countries.
2. **Identify** the tools used to measure levels of development.
3. **Describe** the characteristics of developed nations and less developed countries.
4. **Understand** how levels of development are ranked.

ECONOMIC DICTIONARY

As you read the section, look for the definitions of these **Key Terms:**

- development
- developed nation
- less developed country
- newly industrialized country
- per capita GDP
- industrialization
- literacy rate
- life expectancy
- infant mortality rate
- subsistence agriculture

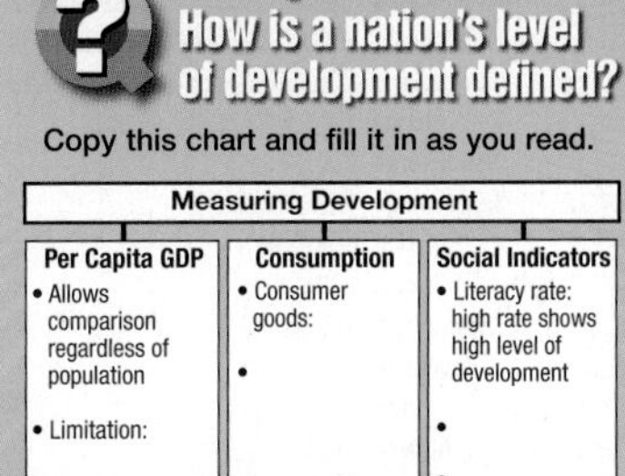

Guiding Question
How is a nation's level of development defined?

Copy this chart and fill it in as you read.

Measuring Development		
Per Capita GDP	**Consumption**	**Social Indicators**
• Allows comparison regardless of population • Limitation:	• Consumer goods: •	• Literacy rate: high rate shows high level of development • •

▶ Economics and You

Have you ever given money for world famine relief? Or taken part in a fundraising drive to build a school in a foreign country? Each year, Americans of all ages donate money and time to such efforts. And the need is very real. Some three billion people—about half the world's population—live in extreme poverty.

Principles in Action There are vast differences between prosperous nations—such as the United States or Canada—and poorer nations like Ethiopia or El Salvador. In this section, you will examine what some of these differences are and why they exist.

Levels of Development

Economists divide the world's nations into different categories according to their level of development. **Development** is the process by which a nation improves the economic, political, and social well-being of its people. It is important to remember that development refers to a nation's material well-being. It is not a judgment of the worth of a nation or its people. The level of development does not indicate cultural superiority or inferiority. It simply indicates how well a nation is able to feed, clothe, and shelter its people.

Nations with a relatively high average of material well-being are called **developed nations.** The United States, Canada, Japan, Australia, New Zealand, and the nations of Western Europe fall into this category.

development the process by which a nation improves the economic, political, and social well-being of its people

developed nation a nation with a relatively high average level of material well-being

Visual Glossary online

Go to the Visual Glossary Online for an interactive review of **globalization**.

Action Graph online

Go to Action Graph Online for animated versions of key charts and graphs.

How the Economy Works online

Go to How the Economy Works Online for an interactive lesson on **the stages of economic development.**

Guiding Question

How is a nation's level of development defined?

Get Started

Measuring Development		
Per Capita GDP	**Consumption**	**Social Indicators**
• Allows comparison regardless of population size • Limitation: doesn't account for income distribution	• Consumer goods: High availability shows high level of development • Means people can meet basic needs and enjoy nonessential items	• Literacy rate: high rate shows high development • Life expectancy: long lives shows high level of development • Infant mortality: low rate shows high level development

LESSON GOALS

Students will:

- Know the Key Terms.
- Identify characteristics of developed and developing nations.
- Analyze how per capita GDP and income distribution are used to measure development by completing a worksheet.
- Contrast nations by level of development.
- Make inferences about agriculture in LDCs using data on workforce distribution.

BEFORE CLASS

Have students complete the graphic organizer in the Section Opener as they read the text. As an alternate activity, have students complete the Guided Reading and Review worksheet (Unit 7 All-in-One, p. 53).

L1 L2 ELL LPR Differentiate Have students complete the Guided Reading and Review worksheet (Unit 7 All-in-One, p. 54).

Focus on the Basics

Students need to come away with the following understandings:

FACTS: • Economists define three general levels of development. • Economists use both economic and social statistics to measure development. • Nations judged to be developed nations share certain characteristics. • LDCs share certain characteristics as well.

GENERALIZATION: Development is a dynamic process, and a nation may move from one level of development to another.

CLASSROOM HINTS

SIMILAR ECONOMIES, DIFFERENT HISTORIES

Remind students that countries grouped under the same development category, such as LDC or NIC, are often very different. The categories are meant to be broad. When thinking about development, it is important to remember that no two countries are the same. Important historical, cultural, geographic, and economic differences exist between countries. For example, the United States and Germany are both considered developed countries, but there are many important differences between the two.

BELLRINGER

Draw a chart on the board with two rows and two columns. Label the top of each column with these heads: Developed Nation, Less Developed Nation. Ask students to use their notebooks to speculate on the characteristics each type of nation would have.

Teach

Economics online To present this topic using digital resources, use the lecture notes on www.PearsonSuccessNet.com.

L1 L2 ELL LPR Differentiate To help students who are struggling readers, assign the Vocabulary worksheet (Unit 7 All-in-One, p. 52).

DISCUSS

Call on students to offer their answers to the Bellringer activity. Ask **Why would economists compare nations' development?** *(to judge how well off a nation's people are; to predict what roles they might play in the world economy)*

Distribute the "Measuring Development" worksheet (Unit 7 All-in-One, p. 55). After students have answered the questions, discuss per capita GDP and income distribution. As a class, decide which measure is most useful for measuring development.

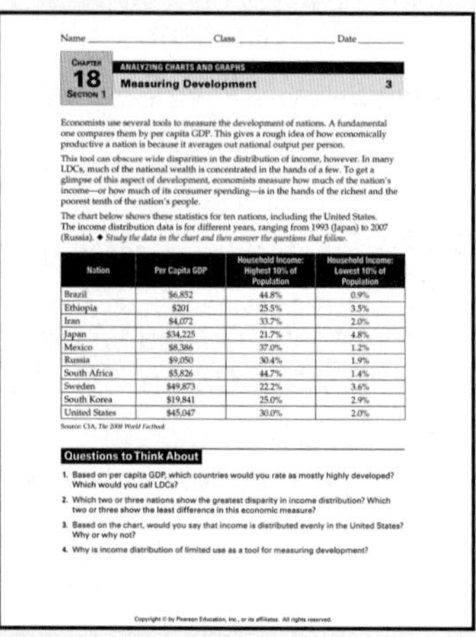

Name ________ Class ________ Date ________

CHAPTER 18 SECTION 1 ANALYZING CHARTS AND GRAPHS

Measuring Development 3

Economists use several tools to measure the development of nations. A fundamental one compares them by per capita GDP. This gives a rough idea of how economically productive a nation is because it averages out national output per person.

This tool can obscure wide disparities in the distribution of income, however. In many LDCs, much of the national wealth is concentrated in the hands of a few. To get a glimpse of this aspect of development, economists measure how much of the nation's income—or how much of its consumer spending—is in the hands of the richest and the poorest tenth of the nation's people.

The chart below shows these statistics for ten nations, including the United States. The income distribution data is for different years, ranging from 1993 (Japan) to 2007 (Russia). ◆ *Study the data in the chart and then answer the questions that follow.*

Nation	Per Capita GDP	Household Income: Highest 10% of Population	Household Income: Lowest 10% of Population
Brazil	$6,852	44.8%	0.9%
Ethiopia	$201	25.5%	3.5%
Iran	$4,072	33.7%	2.0%
Japan	$34,225	21.7%	4.8%
Mexico	$8,386	37.0%	1.2%
Russia	$9,050	30.4%	1.9%
South Africa	$5,826	44.7%	1.4%
Sweden	$49,873	22.2%	3.6%
South Korea	$19,841	25.0%	2.9%
United States	$45,047	30.0%	2.0%

Source: CIA, *The 2008 World Factbook*

Questions to Think About

1. Based on per capita GDP, which countries would you rate as mostly highly developed? Which would you call LDCs?
2. Which two or three nations show the greatest disparity in income distribution? Which two or three show the least difference in this economic measure?
3. Based on the chart, would you say that income is distributed evenly in the United States? Why or why not?
4. Why is income distribution of limited use as a tool for measuring development?

L1 L2 Differentiate Distribute the "Measuring Development" worksheet (Unit 7 All-in-One, p. 56) and have students complete it to use different measures of development.

Answers

Graph Skills 1. about 20 times larger 2. New Zealand's economy is much more productive relative to its population because its per capita GDP is much higher.

Checkpoint Not yet a developed nation, NICs have recently made great progress in developing their economies, and their people are generally better off than those in LDCs.

Figure 18.1 Per Capita GDP of Selected Nations, 2005

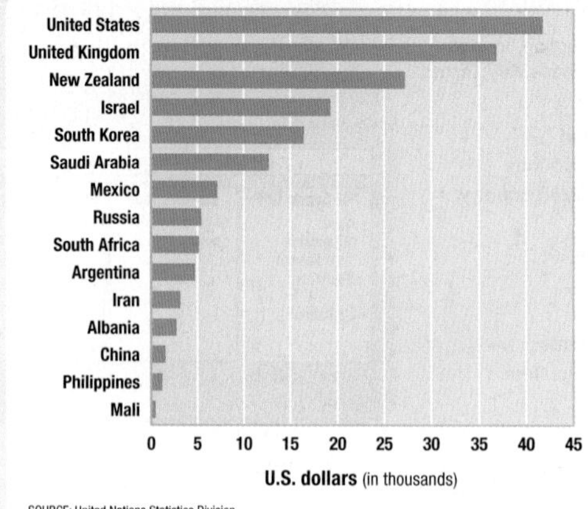

SOURCE: United Nations Statistics Division

GRAPH SKILLS

Per capita GDP is calculated by dividing a nation's gross national product by its population.

1. In 2005, how much larger was the per capita GDP of the United States than that of Albania?
2. Iran has a much larger population than New Zealand. What does this graph suggest about the economies of the two nations?

Most nations, however, have relatively low levels of material well-being. These **less developed countries** (LDCs) include the world's poorest countries, such as Bangladesh, Nepal, Albania, and nations of Central and Southern Africa.

One group of LDCs has made great progress toward developing their economies. These **newly industrialized countries** (NICs) include Mexico, Brazil, several countries in Eastern Europe, Saudi Arabia, and former republics of the Soviet Union. Some NICs are rich in resources, especially oil. Saudi Arabia, for example, has made a great deal of money from selling oil and oil products. Others have turned to manufacturing. Although the NICs have pulled ahead of the poorer LDCs, they have yet to achieve the high standard of living of developed nations.

less developed country a nation with a relatively low level of material well-being

newly industrialized country a less developed country that has made great progress toward developing its economy

per capita GDP a nation's gross domestic product divided by its population

✔ **CHECKPOINT** ***How do NICs differ from both developed nations and LDCs?***

Measuring Development

Economists use many different factors to measure a nation's level of development. They include production of goods and services, energy consumption, distribution of the workforce, availability of consumer goods, and social indicators.

Per Capita GDP

As you read in Chapter 12, gross domestic product (GDP) is the total value of all final goods and services produced within an economy in a year. GDP alone, however, is not adequate to compare the living standards of nations. Instead, economists use **per capita GDP,** a nation's GDP divided by its population. As **Figure 18.1** shows, per capita GDP can vary widely from nation to nation.

Why is per capita GDP considered to be a more accurate measure of development than GDP by itself? Look at two nations, Japan and India. Both have high GDPs—about $4.22 trillion for Japan and about $2.98 trillion for India. Yet Japan enjoys a high standard of living, while India is relatively poor.

The reason for this discrepancy is population size. Japan's $4.22 trillion is shared by fewer than 127.7 million people. Thus, its per capita GDP is around $33,100. India's $2.98 trillion is shared by about 1.1 billion people, so its per capita GDP is only around $2,659. These figures indicate that the average person in Japan is better off, in material terms, than the average person in India.

Of course, per capita GDP does not take into account distribution of income. Within every nation, some people are wealthier than most, while others are poorer than most. In many LDCs, the gap between rich and poor is especially wide.

The World Bank, an international economic organization that studies development, uses a similar measure called per capita gross national income (GNI). Using this yardstick, the World Bank classifies nations as *high income, middle income,* and *low income.* (See **Figure 18.2.**)

Energy Consumption

Energy consumption is another good way to measure development. The amount of energy that a nation consumes is closely

Differentiated Resources

- **L1 L2 Vocabulary worksheet** (Unit 7 All-in-One, p. 52)
- **L1 L2 Guided Reading and Review** (Unit 7 All-in-One, p. 54)
- **L1 L2 Measuring Development** (Unit 7 All-in-One, p. 56)

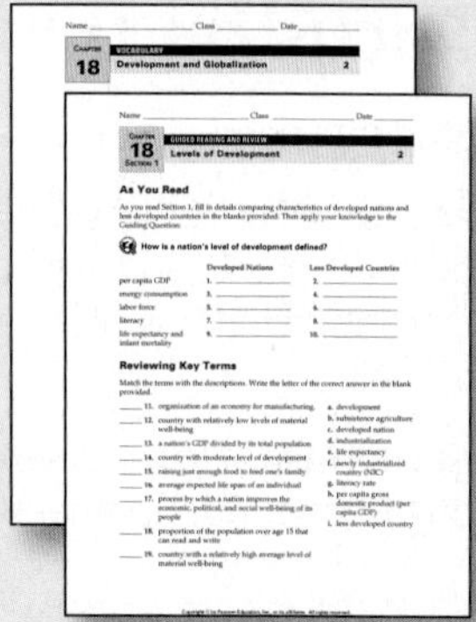

linked to its level of industrialization. **Industrialization** is the organization of an economy for the purpose of manufacture. Because industrial processes generally require large amounts of energy, high levels of energy use tend to indicate high levels of industrial activity.

Conversely, a low level of energy use tends to indicate that a nation has a low level of industrial activity. Most of the people are farmers working with simple tools and few machines.

Labor Force

Another sign of low development is if a large share of the population works in agriculture. Why is that the case?

If most people are raising food just for themselves, few are available to work in industry. As a result, there is little opportunity for workers to specialize. But, as you saw in Chapter 2, specialization makes an economy more efficient. If a nation cannot produce specialized goods to sell, it is unable to generate cash income.

Consumer Goods

The quantity of consumer goods a nation produces per capita also indicates its level of development. Availability of a large number of consumer goods indicates that people have enough money to meet their basic needs and still have enough left over to buy nonessential goods. Thus, economists measure how many people in a country own products such as computers, automobiles, washing machines, or telephones.

Social Indicators

Three social indicators also measure a nation's level of development. The first is **literacy rate,** the proportion of the population over age 15 that can read and write. In general, a high percentage of people attending school suggests a high level of development. An educated population has the potential to be more productive and to use or produce advanced technology.

Another indicator is **life expectancy,** the average expected life span of an individual.

industrialization the organization of an economy for the purpose of manufacture

literacy rate the proportion of a nation's population over age 15 that can read and write

life expectancy the average expected life span of an individual

Figure 18.2 Levels of Development

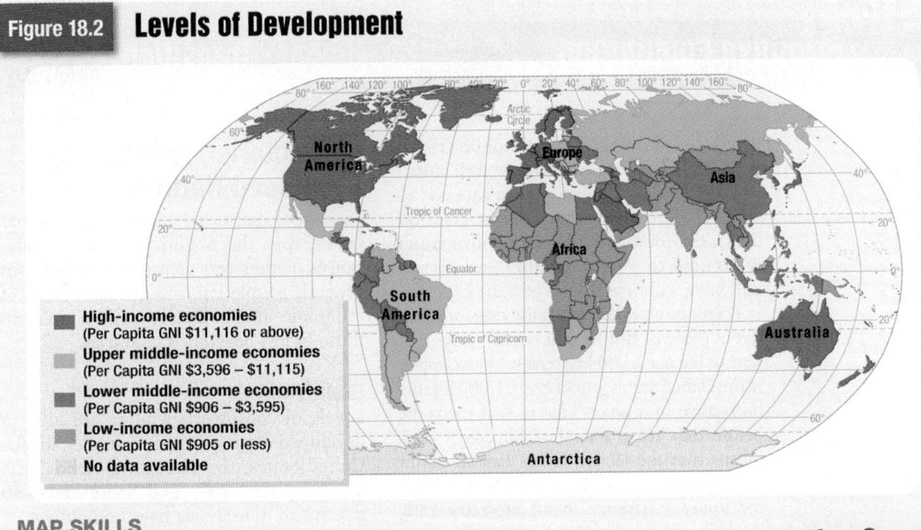

MAP SKILLS

Although income is only one measure of development, it gives a good indication of a nation's standard of living.

1. What is the average income level of the United States? Australia?
2. Based on this map, make one generalization about the relationship between geographic location and level of development.

Action Graph online

For an animated version of this map, visit PearsonSuccessNet.com

EVALUATE A MEASURE OF DEVELOPMENT

Display the "Workforce Distribution and Development" transparency (Color Transparencies, 18.a). Explain that the graph shows the distribution of the workforce in the three main sectors of the economy for eight nations. Ask **Based on the map in Figure 18.2, which high-income economies appear in the graph?** *(Australia, France, United States)* **How would you describe the distribution of the workforce in these countries?** *(Agricultural sector is small—less than 4 percent; industry is around 20 to 26 percent; service sector is large at about 70 to 79 percent.)*

Then ask **Which lower middle-income economies appear?** *(China, Colombia, Egypt)* How would you describe the workforce in these countries? *(Agriculture is a larger share, from about 11 to 14 percent; industry is about 35 to 50 percent; service sector is 40 to 50+ percent.)*

Finally, ask **Which low-income economies appear?** *(Nigeria, Sudan)* How would you describe the workforce in these economies? (In *Nigeria agriculture is about 18 percent, industry is about 53 percent. In Sudan, about 32–35 percent is in each sector.)*

As a class, discuss why workforce distribution is a predictor of economic development.

L1 L2 Differentiate To assist students in locating the countries, point to their locations on a wall map.

Action Graph online Have students review the Action Graph animation for a step-by-step look at levels of development.

L4 Differentiate Have students compare the level of industry in all eight economies and write a paragraph explaining why economists use the term *developed economy rather than industrialized economy.*

Virtual Economics

L3 Differentiate

Predicting Wealth Use the following lesson from the NCEE **Virtual Economics *CD-ROM*** to explore the relationship between economic growth and market economies. Click on Browse Economics Lessons, specify grades 9–12, and use the key word *wealthy.*

In this activity, students will work in small groups to examine data and predict whether a nation is rich or poor.

LESSON TITLE	WHY ARE SOME NATIONS WEALTHY?
Type of Activity	Using statistics
Complexity	Moderate
Time	45 minutes
NCEE Standards	15

Answers

Map Skills 1. $11,116 or above; the same
2. Possible answer: The wealthiest countries tend to be in Europe and North America, plus a few others. The poorest countries tend to be in Asia, Africa, and Latin America. Some students might note that many countries south of the Equator seem to have a lower level of development than northern countries.

CONTRAST NATIONS BY LEVELS OF DEVELOPMENT

Copy the following figures for five countries onto the board:

	Percent Urban	Infant Mortality (per 1,000 births)	Motor Vehicles (per 1,000 people)
United States	79%	6.6	787
China	45%	23.0	24
Guatemala	47%	34.0	107
Kenya	19%	77.0	18
Norway	67%	3.1	465

Ask **Based on what you have read, which kind of economy does the United States have?** *(developed)* **Which nation is closest to the United States in these three measures?** *(Norway)* **Based on this data, what generalizations can you make about social traits of developed nations?** *(They have a high degree of urbanization and low infant mortality.)* **What does the high level of car ownership reveal? Why?** *(high levels of wealth and consumption because cars are costly)*

How would you describe the less developed countries? *(half or less of the population living in urban areas, much higher levels of infant mortality, and much lower levels of consumption, suggesting fewer economic resources for families)*

L1 L2 Differentiate Call on volunteers to sketch the data as circle graphs (for percent urban) and bar graphs (other measures) to show the differences.

L4 Differentiate Remind students of the discussion of per capita GNP earlier in the section. Ask them to explain the similarities between that statistic and the three measures you have written on the board. *(These three measures also show data per a set number of people [100 or 1,000], which allows comparison from one country to another.)*

Answer

Checkpoint High levels of energy use tend to indicate high levels of industrial activity, and industrialization is linked to development

How the Economy Works

What are the stages of economic development?

All over the world, economic development commonly follows a pattern. The change may be rapid or it may take generations. The number of people who benefit also varies from place to place.

1 Society has a traditional economy, with no formal economic organization or monetary system. Economic decisions are based on tradition.

2 People adopt new living patterns and economic activities, often as the result of outside intervention. Industries are introduced. Cultural traditions begin to crumble as people begin to find work in new industries.

Primitive Equilibrium

Transition

It indicates how well an economic system supports life. People who are well nourished and housed and have access to medical care live longer. A population that lacks food and adequate housing and is exposed to poor sanitation and disease will have a shorter life expectancy.

A country's **infant mortality rate** indicates the number of deaths that occur in the first year of life per 1,000 live births. For example, in the United States, out of every 1,000 infants born alive in a given year, 6.4 of them die before they reach their first birthdays. This means that the United States has an infant mortality rate of 6.4. Generally speaking, the lower a nation's infant mortality rate, the higher its level of development. (See page 479 of the World Economy Databank to compare infant mortality and other measures among nations.)

infant mortality rate the number of deaths that occur in the first year of life per 1,000 live births

CHECKPOINT *How is energy use related to development?*

Characteristics of Developed Nations

Developed nations have high per capita GDPs, and the majority of the population is neither very rich nor very poor. In general, people enjoy a greater degree of economic and political freedom than do those in less developed countries.

Quality of Life

Levels of consumer spending are high in developed nations. For example, in the United States, the average household has 2.8 television sets, and more than 60 percent of households have computers.

The populations of developed nations are generally healthy, with low infant mortality rates and high life expectancy. Literacy rates are high as well. People tend to receive schooling well into their teens, and many go on to college.

Background Note

Quality of Life The concept of standard of living focuses strictly on the material aspects of life. It is a measure of material well being based on income or consumption. Quality of life—which addresses a person's total feeling of well being—includes social indicators, such as those indicating health, and broader aspects of societal conditions, including the state of the environment in which a person lives, his or her safety and level of freedom, and the security of the nation in which he or she lives.

How the Economy Works online

For an animated, interactive version of this feature, visit PearsonSuccessNet.com

3 New industries grow and profits are reinvested. As the economy expands, the society enters the international market. The traditional economic system continues to decline.

4 Economy is focused on consumer goods and public services. Basic human needs are met easily, but some people get left behind.

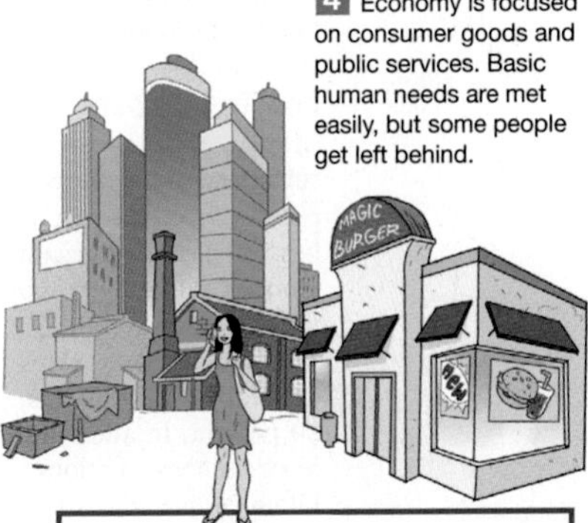

Check Your Understanding

1. What impact does development have on cultural traditions?
2. Why do you think economists use the word *equilibrium*, or balance, to describe the traditional economy?

Takeoff and Semidevelopment → Highly Developed

High Productivity

In most developed nations, agricultural output is high, but relatively few people work on farms. In the United States, for example, a single farmer can feed 80 people. Agriculture has largely become a high-tech big business:

> "New technologies are making the profession of farming more efficient, less risky, and less labor-intensive.... [Big farmers] are automating the entire farming process using GPS technology, genetically modified crops, automated irrigation systems, specialized fertilizers."
>
> — Bob Baddeley, "Farm Technology: Applying High Tech for High Yields"

Since only a small portion of the labor force is needed in agriculture, more people are available to work in industry and services. Widespread use of technology increases the productivity of this workforce.

Urbanization and Infrastructure

Developed nations tend to be urban rather than rural. Most of their populations live in cities and towns and have done so for many years. Major cities such as New York, London, and Tokyo are centers of finance and trade.

Hand-in-hand with urbanization goes a solid infrastructure. Power plants enhance a nation's capacity to produce goods. Transportation and communication systems allow easier transfer of products, services, people, and ideas. Schools increase a nation's literacy rate and productive capacity. Banks allow for secure transfer of financial assets.

CHECKPOINT ***Why is agricultural productivity high in developed nations?***

CHAPTER 18 SECTION 1 485

MAKE INFERENCES

Have a volunteer read the paragraph and quote on page 485 in the student text about agriculture in developed nations. Then display the "Workforce Distribution and Development" transparency (Color Transparencies, 18.a) a second time. Direct students' attention to the data on employment in the agricultural sector. Ask them to describe how they think the work life of an agricultural worker in China or Nigeria would be different from the work life of an agricultural worker on an American farm. Why is it likely the American farmer produces more? *(Workers in countries where agriculture is more labor intensive probably do more work by hand. The work is more physically difficult. Workers in high-tech farming use more machinery. They require different skills.)*

EXTEND

Using the "How the Economy Works" feature, have students identify the factors that might help or hinder further economic development at each stage.

L4 Differentiate Have students write a brief description of the characteristics of NICs, using the same features used in describing developed countries and LDCs.

GUIDING QUESTION WRAP UP

Have students return to the section Guiding Question. Review the completed graphic organizer and clarify any misunderstandings. Have a wrap up discussion about levels of development.

Assess and Remediate

L2 L3 Collect the "Measuring Development" worksheets and assess student understanding of measuring the economic development of nations.

L3 Assign the Section 1 Assessment questions; identify student misconceptions.

L3 Give Section Quiz A (Unit 7 All-in-One, p. 57).

L2 Give Section Quiz B (Unit 7 All-in-One, p. 58).

(Assess and Remediate continued on p. 486)

Background Note

Urbanization While developed nations are highly urbanized, LDCs are becoming increasingly urbanized as well. As a result, the Population Reference Bureau estimates that in 2008, for the first time in history, the majority of the world's people lived in urban areas. This fact is more remarkable considering that in 1950, less than a third of the world's people lived in cities. In that year, less than 20 percent of the populations of China, India, and Nigeria lived in cities. By 2008, China and Nigeria had an urbanization rate of nearly 80 percent and India was nearly 60 percent.

Answers

How the Economy Works 1. causes them to decline 2. because they change very slowly

Checkpoint The use of advanced irrigation techniques, fertilizers, pesticides, seed varieties, and heavy machinery all combine to make farmers very productive in developed nations.

Have students complete the Self-Test Online and continue their work in the **Essential Questions Journal**.

REMEDIATION AND SUGGESTIONS

Use the chart below to help students who are struggling with content.

WEAKNESS	REMEDIATION
Identifying key terms (Questions 3, 4, 5, 6, 7)	Have students use the interactive Economic Dictionary Online.
Understanding tools to measure development (Questions 1, 5, 6, 8, 9, 11)	Reteach by having students work in pairs to create flashcards defining each measure.
Contrasting different levels of development (Questions 2, 3, 4, 9, 10)	Have students use the chart of measures of development in the Quick Study Guide on page 509 to review.

Answer

Checkpoint Subsistence-level agriculture and underemployment do not provide families with enough income to buy these goods.

subsistence agriculture level of farming in which a person raises only enough food to feed his or her family

Characteristics of Less Developed Countries

Less developed countries generally have low per capita GDPs. Low per capita energy consumption is an indicator of their low level of industrialization.

Low Productivity

Many people in LDCs engage in **subsistence agriculture,** raising only enough food to feed themselves and their families. Subsistence agriculture requires heavy labor, leaving fewer workers available for industry or services.

Unemployment rates are high in less developed countries, often around 20 percent. In addition, much of the labor force in these nations is underemployed. Often people who are underemployed have work, but not enough to support themselves or their families because they work less than full time.

Quality of Life

Even if an LDC could produce consumer goods—which most do not—most of the population would be unable to buy them. Subsistence-level agriculture and underemployment do not provide families with enough income to buy these goods. Consumer goods that are produced are often shipped out of the country and sold in more developed nations.

A less developed country has trouble educating its populace. Resources for schools are limited. In addition, children are often needed to work on the family farm, limiting the amount of time they can spend in school. As a result, literacy rates in LDCs are very low. In Nepal, for example, only about 49 percent of the people over 15 years old can read and write. Compare this figure with the United States, where the literacy rate is nearly 100 percent.

In the world's poorest countries, housing and diet are of poor quality. Along with limited access to healthcare, these factors lead to high infant mortality rates and short life expectancy.

There are additional characteristics common to most LDCs. In the next section, you will read about some of the difficult issues challenging less developed countries.

CHECKPOINT ***Why do most people in LDCs have few consumer goods?***

SECTION 1 ASSESSMENT

Essential Questions Journal To continue to build a response to the Essential Question, go to your **Essential Questions Journal.**

Guiding Question

1. Use your completed chart to answer this question: How is a nation's level of development defined?
2. **Extension** What are some benefits of living in a developed nation?

Key Terms and Main Ideas

3. What are the characteristics of **developed nations?**
4. What is the difference between **less developed countries** and **newly industrialized countries?**
5. Why is **per capita GDP** a good tool to measure different countries' relative development?
6. Why are **life expectancy** and **infant mortality** considered to be good measures of a nation's level of development?
7. How is **subsistence agriculture** related to development?

Critical Thinking

8. **Analyze** Under what conditions might per capita GDP be an imperfect tool for comparing how well off people in different nations are?
9. **Connect** Explain how literacy, human capital, and economic development are interrelated.
10. **Apply** Explain why each of the following would be an important tool to enhance a country's rate of development: **(a)** a new airport, **(b)** high-speed Internet access, **(c)** an early childhood vaccination program, **(d)** opening an agricultural college.

Math Skills

11. Using the information in the table below, calculate per capita GDP of these nations. In which nations would you predict is the population most well-off? Explain.

Visit PearsonSuccessNet.com for additional math help.

Nation	Total GDP	Population
Taiwan	$690.1 billion	22.86 million
Turkey	$667.7 billion	71.16 million
Netherlands	$638.9 billion	16.57 million
Poland	$624.6 billion	38.52 million
Saudi Arabia	$572.2 billion	27.6 million

Assessment Answers

1. Possible answer: Development is defined based on various economic and social indicators.
2. Possible answer: It gives people access to a wide array of goods and services.
3. high level of material well-being; high per capita GDP; high energy consumption; small percentage of the labor force in agriculture; many consumer goods available; high literacy rates; long life expectancy; low infant mortality
4. LDCs have low levels of material well-being; they are poor. NICs have pulled ahead of the other LDCs but not yet reached the prosperity of developed countries.
5. averages GDP across whole population
6. A healthier population shows higher development.
7. Possible answer: Countries with subsistence agriculture have low productivity and low levels-of development.
8. Per capita GDP could be misleading if a nation's income is concentrated in the hands of only a few people.
9. Human capital grows as the literacy rate rises because educated people can work more efficiently, promoting economic growth.
10. Possible answers: (a) improves transportation, promotes trade (b) improves communication (c) lowers infant mortality (d) promotes human capital growth, improves agricultural productivity
11. Taiwan—$30,188; Turkey—$9,383; Netherlands—$38,558; Poland—$16,215; Saudi Arabia—$20,732. Netherlands should be the most well off, because they have the highest per capita GDP.

SECTION 2 Issues in Development

OBJECTIVES

1. **Identify** the causes and effects of rapid population growth.
2. **Analyze** how political factors and debt are obstacles to development.
3. **Summarize** the role investment and foreign aid plays in development.
4. **Describe** the functions of various international economic institutions.

ECONOMIC DICTIONARY

As you read the section, look for the definitions of these **Key Terms:**

- population growth rate
- malnutrition
- internal financing
- foreign investment
- foreign direct investment
- foreign portfolio investment
- debt rescheduling
- stabilization program
- nongovernmental organization

Guiding Question
What factors harm or help development?

Copy this chart and fill it in as you read.

Factors Affecting Development	
Factor	**Effect**
Population growth	High rate of population growth makes development more difficult
Physical capital	
Human capital	• Education and training • •
Political factors	
Economic factors	Large loans can lead to spiraling debt

Economics and You Even in a developed nation like ours, there are people who can't read or don't eat a healthy diet. But imagine that you never even had a *chance* to go to school. Imagine that a severe shortage of food reduced your chances of living to adulthood. For many people your age, such conditions are a grim reality.

Principles in Action Illiteracy and poor nutrition are just two of the factors that hinder development. In this section, you will see what LDCs and the world community are doing to combat these conditions and encourage economic growth.

population growth rate a measure of how rapidly a country's population increases in a given year

Rapid Population Growth

As long ago as 1798, the English economist Thomas Malthus predicted that rapid population growth would become a serious problem:

> "The power of population is indefinitely greater than the power in the earth to produce subsistence for man. . . . The food therefore which before supported seven millions, must now be divided among seven millions and a half or eight millions. The poor consequently must live much worse, and many of them be reduced to severe distress."
>
> — Thomas Malthus, *Essay on Population*

Thanks to modern technology, the earth now produces more food than Malthus could have imagined. Still, rapid population growth remains one of the most pressing issues facing many less developed countries. The already poor economies of many LDCs have trouble meeting the needs of their rapidly growing populations.

Measuring Population Growth

The **population growth rate** is a measure of how rapidly a country's population increases in a given year. It is expressed as a percentage of the population figure at the start of the year. The population growth rate takes into account the number of babies born, the number of people who died, and the number of people who migrated to or from a country.

▲ This picture shows a street scene in Cairo, Egypt. Cairo is one of the most densely populated cities in the world and the population is growing rapidly. ***What challenges might a fast-growing population pose for a country?***

 **Guiding Question**

What factors harm or help development?

Get Started

Factors Affecting Development	
Factor	**Effect**
Population growth	A high rate of population growth makes development more difficult.
Physical capital	Lack of physical capital hinders industrial growth.
Human capital	• Education and training: needed for people to develop skills, adapt to technology • Health: needed to prevent spread of disease • Nutrition: needed to promote health
Political factors	• Corruption benefits few, not the mass of people. • Civil wars, social unrest hinder development.
Economic factors	Large loans can lead to spiraling debt.

LESSON GOALS

Students will:

- Know the Key Terms.
- Demonstrate understanding of the impact of population growth rates.
- Compare the likelihood that different factors of production would promote development.
- Debate issues of development in LDCs.

BEFORE CLASS

Have students complete the graphic organizer in the Section Opener as they read the text. As an alternate activity, have students complete the Guided Reading and Review worksheet (Unit 7 All-in-One, p. 59).

L1 L2 ELL LPR Differentiate Have students complete the Guided Reading and Review worksheet (Unit 7 All-in-One, p. 60).

Answer

Caption Possible answers: need to educate children, feed all people, find jobs for more workers

CLASSROOM HINTS

OBSTACLES TO DEVELOPMENT

Explain to students that many of the poorest nations in the world face a combination of obstacles. Development is difficult in these countries, because their problems are interconnected and complex, and foreign aid or other development assistance alone cannot solve them. Policies that work well in one country do not always work in another. Foreign aid can help a country develop, but the greatest progress usually comes from positive internal changes made by the country itself, for example when citizens gain greater social and economic freedom.

Focus on the Basics

Students need to come away with the following understandings:

FACTS: • Rapid population growth has slowed development in some countries. • Limited resources and capital prevent development. • Poor and unfair policies, unrest, and civil wars have slowed development in some countries. • Rising debt has slowed development in some countries.

GENERALIZATION: Solutions to promote development must be complex to address many different factors.

BELLRINGER

Divide the class into three groups, each representing a country with a population of sixty million people. Assign each country an annual population growth rate: 4.0, 2.0, and 1.0 percents. Have each country determine what its population would be at the end of ten years. Remind students to use the new population for each year as they calculate. (Assume no deaths take place in those years.)

Teach

Economics online To present this topic using digital resources, use the lecture notes on www.PearsonSuccessNet.com.

ANALYZE POPULATION GROWTH

Call on each group to offer their answers to the Bellringer. Compare the populations of the countries at the end of ten years. Ask students to imagine the impact of the difference in population growth rate. Discuss the factors affecting population growth rates and the impact these growth rates might have on each nation's economy.

Action Graph online Direct students' attention to Figure 18.3. Have them review the Action Graph animation for a look at population growth.

Distribute the "Impact of Population Growth" worksheet (Unit 7 All-in-One, p. 61). Have students compare population growth.

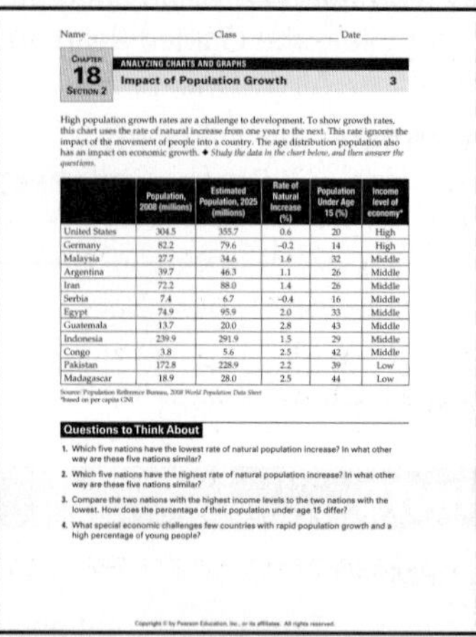

Name ______________ Class ______________ Date ________

CHAPTER 18 SECTION 2

ANALYZING CHARTS AND GRAPHS

Impact of Population Growth 3

High population growth rates are a challenge to development. To show growth rates, this chart uses the rate of natural increase from one year to the next. This rate ignores the impact of the movement of people into a country. The age distribution population also has an impact on economic growth. ◆ *Study the data in the chart below, and then answer the questions.*

	Population, 2008 (millions)	Estimated Population, 2025 (millions)	Rate of Natural Increase (%)	Population Under Age 15 (%)	Income level of economy*
United States	304.5	355.7	0.6	20	High
Germany	82.2	79.6	-0.2	14	High
Malaysia	27.7	34.6	1.6	32	Middle
Argentina	39.7	46.3	1.1	26	Middle
Iran	72.2	88.0	1.4	26	Middle
Serbia	7.4	6.7	-0.4	16	Middle
Egypt	74.9	95.9	2.0	33	Middle
Guatemala	13.7	20.0	2.8	43	Middle
Indonesia	239.9	291.9	1.5	29	Middle
Congo	3.8	5.6	2.5	42	Middle
Pakistan	172.8	228.9	2.2	39	Low
Madagascar	18.9	28.0	2.5	44	Low

Source: Population Reference Bureau, 2008 World Population Data Sheet
*based on per capita GNI

Questions to Think About

1. Which five nations have the lowest rate of natural population increase? In what other way are these five nations similar?
2. Which five nations have the highest rate of natural population increase? In what other way are these five nations similar?
3. Compare the two nations with the highest income levels to the two nations with the lowest. How does the percentage of their population under age 15 differ?
4. What special economic challenges few countries with rapid population growth and a high percentage of young people?

L2 Differentiate Distribute the "Impact of Population Growth" worksheet (Unit 7 All-in-One, p. 62).

Answers

Graph Skills 1. Guatemala and Chad 2. that of a low-income economy

Checkpoint because they have to expand their economies and social services just to keep up

Figure 18.3 Population of Selected Nations

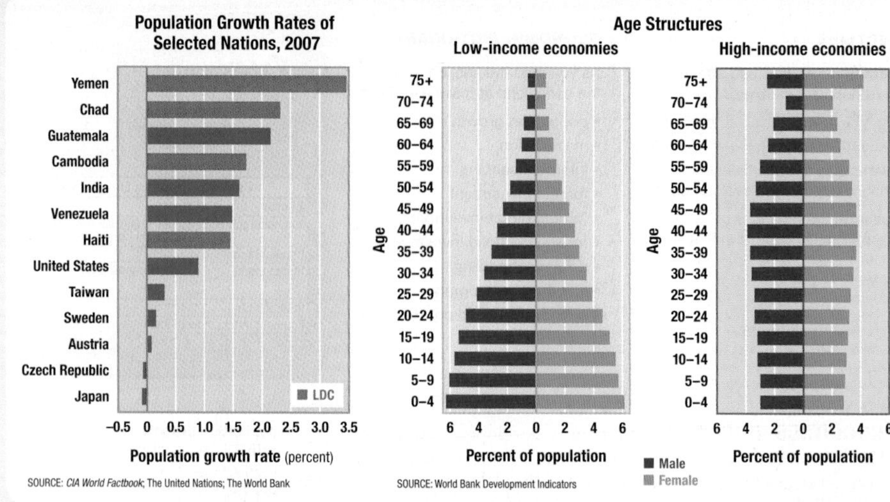

GRAPH SKILLS

The graph on the left shows rates of population growth for selected nations. The graphs in the middle and on the right show how age distribution is related to national income.

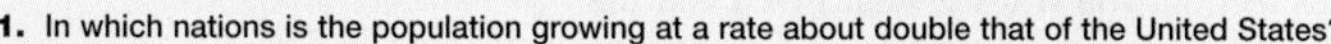

1. In which nations is the population growing at a rate about double that of the United States?
2. Based on these graphs, what shape would you expect Guatemala's age structure to have?

Action Graph online For an animated version of this graph, visit PearsonSuccessNet.com

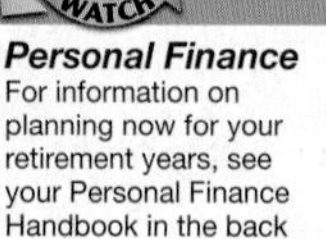

Personal Finance For information on planning now for your retirement years, see your Personal Finance Handbook in the back of the book or visit PearsonSuccessNet.com

Compare the growth rates shown in **Figure 18.3.** Average population growth of less developed countries is estimated to be around 1.8 percent. This may sound low to you, but at this rate the population of LDCs will increase by nearly two-thirds from 2007 to 2050. That is more than 20 times the population growth of developed nations during the same period.

Causes of Rapid Population Growth

Rapid population growth has several causes. Many LDCs are experiencing increased life expectancy. While people are living longer, birth rates have not significantly decreased. When births far outpace deaths, the population grows.

Age structure also contributes to rapid population growth. In many LDCs, a high proportion of the population is of child-bearing age (See **Figure 18.3.**). As these younger adults have children, the population continues to grow. In developed nations, a larger segment of the population is older, so population increases at a much slower rate.

Challenge of Population Growth

As its population grows, a country must expand employment opportunities, health-care, education, and infrastructure—just to maintain its existing standard of living. To actually improve the lives of its people, a nation has to generate a higher per capita GDP. Economic output must grow faster than the population grows.

In a less developed country with a high population growth rate, such accelerated economic growth is a daunting task. A primary reason is that these LDCs lack various factors of production.

CHECKPOINT ***Why is rapid population growth a problem for LDCs?***

Differentiated Resources

L1 L2 Guided Reading and Review (Unit 7 All-in-One, p. 60)

L2 Impact of Population Growth (Unit 7 All-in-One, p. 62)

L1 L2 Conducting Research skills worksheet (Unit 7 All-in-One, p. 64)

L3 How Will You Help? (Simulation Activities, Chapter 18)

Limited Resources and Capital

In parts of Africa, Asia, and Latin America, physical geography is a serious obstacle to development. Natural resources are not evenly distributed throughout the world. Some nations lack mineral resources or fertile farmland. Harsh temperatures, uncertain rainfall, and vulnerability to natural disasters such as floods or earthquakes also contribute to the economic problems of some LDCs.

The problem is not always lack of resources. Rather, less developed countries often lack the means to use their resources efficiently. Technology can help LDCs develop the resources they do have. Technology, however, is costly and requires much capital. The formation of capital is another important obstacle to development.

Physical Capital

The low productivity typical of LDCs is due in part to lack of physical capital. Without capital, industry cannot grow and farm output remains low. Also, subsistence agriculture does not give farmers the opportunity to save. As a result, they do not have the cash to purchase capital that would make their farmwork more productive or to pay for goods and services that would improve their lives.

Education and Training

Lack of human capital also hinders development. To be able to move beyond mere subsistence, a nation needs an educated workforce. Education and training allow people to develop new skills and adapt to new technologies and processes. As you read in Section 1, however, many less developed countries have low literacy rates. **Figure 18.4** compares figures for education and literacy of the United States and several less developed countries.

Two factors combine to lower literacy rates in these countries. First, only three out of four children in LDCs who begin primary school are still in school four years later. Many children are forced to leave school because they are needed at home to work on family farms.

Figure 18.4 Education and Literacy

Country	Primary School Enrollment Rate (percentage)		Literacy Rate (percentage)	
	Female	Male	Female	Male
United States	90	94	99	99
Peru	97	97	82.1	93.5
Indonesia	93	95	86.8	94
Nigeria	57	64	60.6	75.7
Yemen	63	87	30	70.5
Chad	46	68	39.3	56
Niger	32	46	15.1	42.9

SOURCE: *CIA World Factbook*, United Nations Children Fund

CHART SKILLS

Education and literacy rates vary from country to country. These rates can also vary between men and women in the same country.

1. What percentage of male children attend school in Nigeria? In which nation can the smallest percentage of the population read and write?
2. Based on these charts, which two nations show the greatest inequality in education between men and women? What impact might this have?

Virtual Economics

L3 Differentiate

Exploring Human Capital Use the following lesson from the NCEE **Virtual Economics *CD-ROM*** to examine the relationship between investment in human capital and income. Click on Browse Economics Lessons, specify grades 9–12, and use the key words *learn more.*

In this activity, students will take part in a simulation that illustrates how education is related to standard of living.

LESSON TITLE	LEARN MORE, EARN MORE
Type of Activity	Simulation
Complexity	High
Time	100 minutes
NCEE Standards	13

PERSONAL FINANCE ACTIVITY

Discuss with students how the needs of a society differ when the population is young versus when it is older. You may want to use the Personal Finance lesson on retirement planning on pages PF20–PF21, and the activity worksheets (Personal Finance All-in-One, pp. 59–60), to highlight the differences in needs between developed countries and LDCs.

COMPARE AND CONTRAST

Ask students to restate the factors of production. *(land, labor, capital)* Call on them to give examples of each factor. *(Possible answers: land—soil for growing food, mineral resources, timber; labor—people to do work; capital—money, equipment, human skills)*

Ask **Would having natural resources be likely to promote development? Why?** *(Having resources can help a nation but will not necessarily promote development if the resources are difficult to obtain or transport.)*

Ask **Would having abundant labor be likely to promote development? Why?** *(Having abundant labor does not necessarily encourage development because the labor might be expended in labor-intensive ways of doing work, which can be inefficient.)*

Ask **Would having abundant capital be likely to promote development? Why?** *(Capital includes technology and human skills, both of which make workers more productive, so having large amounts of capital would promote development.)* Ask **Why does an economy require all three factors of production to be successful?** *(If an economy is missing any of the three factors the other two will be underutilized.)*

L1 L2 Differentiate To explain how capital promotes development, break the process into steps: (1) Investing capital in technology or people's skills makes workers more efficient. (2) Efficiency leads to higher productivity. (3) Increased productivity fuels economic growth. (4) Growth generates income, which workers use to raise their standard of living and to invest, buying more capital goods. (5) Increased consumption and investment produces more growth. (6) Increased use of technology and the wider availability of consumer goods are features of a developed economy.

(lesson continued on p. 491)

Answers

Graph Skills 1. 64%; Niger 2. Yemen and Niger; Possible answer: The lack of education for females would tend to slow economic growth because the country would not be taking advantage of the potential of half the population.

Teach Case Study

SUMMARIZE AND EXPLAIN

Call on the students to explain why is it important to control diseases in the developing world. Ask **What does Africa have to gain by controlling the spread of malaria?** *(The fewer people, especially children, killed by a preventable disease means more people will be alive to enter the workforce. More workers can lead to increased production and sustainable development, which can lead to a stronger economy.)*

RESEARCH

Have the students use the Internet to research which diseases the United States is trying to combat in the developing world *(the case study cites AIDS and malaria)* and how it is helping *(cited in case study: money for new drugs, clinics, medical equipment, shipping systems, bed nets)*

L1 L2 Differentiate Ask the students to explain why the United States was able to stop the spread of malaria, but it is still a problem in developing countries. *(The United States had the financial resources to eradicate malaria thanks to better water drainage systems, insecticides, and medical treatment.)*

Economics online *All print resources are available on the Teacher's Resource Library CD-ROM and online at* www.PearsonSuccessNet.com.

Answer

Applying Economic Principles a stronger workforce, manufacturing jobs; by increasing trade and opening new markets

Case STUDY THE WALL STREET JOURNAL. CLASSROOM EDITION

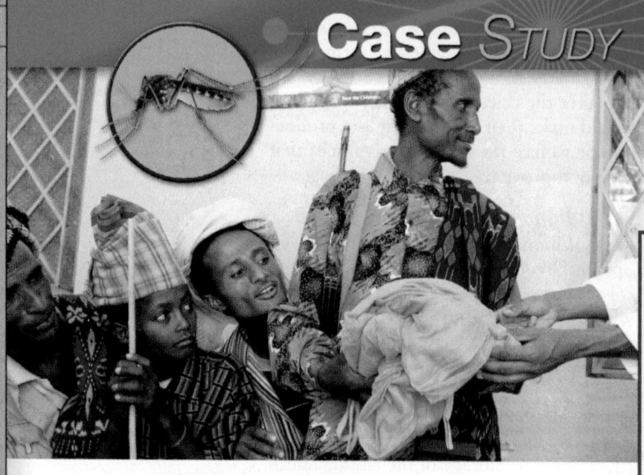

Economic Antidote

OBSTACLES TO DEVELOPMENT

Some experts say tackling malaria is key to broader gains for Africa.

By John D. McKinnon
The Wall Street Journal

President Bush's $18 billion campaign against AIDS in the developing world is spreading not only new antiviral drugs, but a wide range of improvements, such as new clinics, medical equipment and shipping systems. But the less noticed fight against malaria is having an impact that experts say holds equal significance for Africa in the long run.

While the fight against AIDS is aimed at limiting the damage from an epic social disaster, experts say the prospect of beating back malaria raised the possibility of rapid, permanent gains for Africa's society and economy. The gains come not just from improved productivity because the disease is less widespread, but from more fundamental changes.

As children—who are particularly vulnerable—stop dying of the disease, Africans likely will be induced to have smaller families. That, in turn, will allow more investment by families in children's education and nutrition, among other things, and eventually a stronger work force.

"There's huge evidence that, if you get malaria under control, you not only save more than one millions lives a year, but you change everything else," says Jeffrey Sachs, an expert in sustainable development and head of the Earth Institute at Columbia University. He believes that new investments in combating malaria—including Mr. Bush's initiative—are bringing the world close to being able to virtually end malaria deaths by 2012, including in Africa, which has some of the highest infection rates. "It's very exciting," he says.

The White House sought to highlight the broader economic benefits from Mr. Bush's malaria campaign at a recent event in Arusha, Tanzania. At a ramshackle rural hospital, surrounded by young women in vivid orange, green, purple and yellow dresses, Mr. Bush said malaria leaves "families devastated and economies crippled."

By contrast, the new efforts to combat malaria through insecticide-laced bed nets and other measures already are generating good manufacturing jobs, he noted. "So as this campaign protects women and children from malaria, it also ... boosts local economies," he said.

Millions of the nets have been distributed at reduced prices, and have helped lower new infection rates significantly. Mr. Bush announced a new phase of the U.S.-led effort in which 5.2 million more nets will be handed out free, enough so that every child in the country between 1 and 5 years old can be protected.

Applying Economic Principles
Identify two economic benefits to Africans from malaria reduction. How might the United States also benefit from leading the fight against malaria?

Video News Update Online Powered by *The Wall Street Journal* Classroom Edition
For a new case study, go to the online resources at **PearsonSuccessNet.com**

Second, in many LDCs, the literacy rate for women lags far behind that for men. Many women in these countries begin raising children at an early age. Those who do work have limited job opportunities and earn low wages. In addition, some cultures devalue women. Due to all these factors, a large part of a country's population lacks the training needed to be highly productive.

Nutrition and Health

Poor nutrition and health also impede the development of human capital. Many people in less developed countries suffer from **malnutrition,** or consistently inadequate nutrition. (A worldwide increase in food prices in the early 2000s aggravated the situation.) Malnutrition lowers the energy of adults and makes them more vulnerable to disease. Both results can reduce worker productivity. Malnutrition also slows the physical and mental development of children, hurting their chances of being productive workers once they become adults.

In many LDCs, poor sanitation leads to the spread of disease. In addition, many poorer countries have high rates of infection by HIV, the virus that causes AIDS. This epidemic removes large numbers of workers from the workforces of these countries. In addition, caring for these people and their families puts a strain on the resources of many LDCs. Money that could be spent on schools or infrastructure has to be devoted to healthcare or providing for orphaned children.

***CHECKPOINT** How do education and training contribute to development?*

Political Obstacles

Political factors may also limit or even reverse a nation's development. Many LDCs are former colonies of European powers. Colonies had to supply the ruling powers with resources and to rely on them for manufactured goods. This dependency prevented the development of industry.

In the decades after World War II, these colonies won independence. Many then turned to central planning, rather than free enterprise, as the way to modernize their economies quickly. These nations made some gains at first, but in the long run, central planning hindered their economic growth. Many are now making the transition to free enterprise systems.

Government corruption has also held back development in many LDCs. Some leaders have funneled huge sums of money into private accounts, allowing them to live luxurious lives while large numbers of their people remain poor.

Civil war and social unrest plague many countries, such as El Salvador, Rwanda, and Cambodia. Years of fighting may leave millions dead and millions more as refugees. Loss of workers, as well as damage to resources and infrastructure, can throw a nation's economy in chaos.

Finally, economic policies in many LDCs have favored small minorities. In some countries, policies benefit city dwellers and not the rural majority. In some, leaders favor only one ethnic group—typically their own. In extreme cases, governments practice policies of genocide—or the attempted extermination of an entire ethnic or religious group.

***CHECKPOINT** What political factors have hindered development?*

Financing Development

Building an infrastructure, providing services, and creating technology and industry all require large sums of money. A developing country can acquire these funds through a variety of means. These include internal financing, foreign investment, borrowing, and foreign aid. However, many of these solutions—especially borrowing—create problems of their own.

Internal Financing

In many ways, the most favorable source of development funds is internal financing. **Internal financing** is capital derived from the savings of the country's own citizens. As you read in Chapter 11, when savers deposit money in banks or other financial institutions, some of the money is used to make loans to firms. Firms invest in physical and human capital so they can expand, creating new jobs. Job growth enables workers to improve their standard of living. They buy more goods and services, which encourages

Simulation *Activity*

How Will You Help?
You may be asked to take part in a role-playing game about financing development in a poor nation.

malnutrition
consistently inadequate nutrition

internal financing
capital derived from the savings of a country's citizens

Background Note

HIV Rates The rate of HIV infection is extremely high in some regions. In Sub-Saharan Africa, as much as 5 percent of the population between the ages of 15 and 49 has HIV. This is the highest percentage for a region in the world. In Asia, Europe, Latin America, North America, and Oceania, rates are 0.6 percent or lower. One positive sign is that HIV infection rates declined from 2001 to 2007 in most regions of the world, including Sub-Saharan Africa. The only exceptions were Europe, where rates rose from 0.3 to 0.5 percent, and Oceania, where the increase was from 0.2 to 0.4 percent.

L3 Differentiate For alternative or additional practice with issues in development, have students use the "How Will You Help?" activity (Simulation Activities, Chapter 18). Acting as members of a national student organization that provides aid to a village in a Less Developed Country, students will decide how to apportion funds they have collected.

ANALYZE

Tell students that good nutrition may not simply be a matter of the availability of food. A study in several countries looked at stunted growth—a sign of malnutrition—in young children in several poor countries. Give students these results, which show percentages of growth-stunted children of women with different levels of education.

	Secondary Education or Higher	No Education
Cambodia	19%	39%
Colombia	8%	28%
Egypt	17%	23%
Haiti	10%	30%
India	22%	57%
Madagascar	36%	47%
Nigeria	29%	47%
Senegal	5%	17%

Ask **What do these statistics suggest?** *(A mother's level of education seems strongly related to the nutrition of her children.)* **Do the statistics prove that lack of education for mothers is the *cause* of malnutrition in children?** *(Not necessarily. The fact that they are related does not mean that one causes the other. They may both be effects of a single cause.)* **What approach do you think would be better for solving the problem of malnutrition—giving food aid or educating women? Why?** *(Possible answer: Giving food is a better solution to solve the short-term effects. Educating women might be a more effective long-term solution, especially since increasing the nation's human capital would help improve the nation's overall level of development.)*

Answers

Checkpoint Education and training let people develop new skills and adapt to new technologies.

Checkpoint The use of central planning, government corruption, civil wars or social unrest, and policies that favor a minority all have made it difficult for many LDCs to grow economically.

DEBATE

Point out that there are several controversial issues related to the question of developing the economies of LDCs. They include the following:

- Whether developed countries have an obligation to provide aid to LDCs to help their economies grow.
- Whether developed countries should forgive the debt of heavily indebted LDCs.
- Whether LDCs should be compelled to make changes in their economic systems—such as cutting government services—in order to qualify for debt rescheduling.

Have the class form six groups, assigning two groups to each topic, one on one side of the controversy and the other taking the opposite position. Give the groups a chance to meet and develop arguments for their position. After they have done so, stage a debate in which the two sides present their arguments to the rest of the class. After both sides have finished their presentations, give each a chance to respond to its opponents' arguments. Then call on students who listened to the debate to identify arguments they found convincing and to explain why.

Follow the same procedure for all three debate topics.

L1 L2 Differentiate Encourage students to take notes on the debate by recording arguments under the headings "For" and "Against." After completing the debate, call on students to choose one of the controversies and write a paragraph explaining their position on the issue.

L4 Differentiate After the debate, call on students to take the role of the leader of an LDC. Challenge them to write a speech the leader could deliver at a world economic conference on one of these controversies.

foreign investment capital that originates in other countries

foreign direct investment the establishment of a business by investors from another country

foreign portfolio investment purchases made in a country's financial markets by investors from another country

businesses to expand further. As a result, the entire economy grows.

In most LDCs, though, large segments of the population do not have enough money to save. The wealthy few often keep their money in foreign banks or invest in foreign firms because these investments are safer. As a result, most poor countries have little capital available from internal financing. In order to fund development, they must turn to foreign sources.

Foreign Investment

Capital that originates in other countries is called **foreign investment.** There are two types of foreign investment: direct investment and portfolio investment.

Foreign direct investment occurs when investors establish a business in another country. For example, multinational corporations often build factories or other facilities in an LDC. Multinationals make this investment to take advantage of natural resources available in the less developed country or to tap into the large and cheap labor force.

As you have seen, multinationals are controversial. Some economists say that the people of the LDC who work for the foreign corporation are better off than they would be doing other work. Their wages give them cash they can use to buy goods, which can help stimulate their country's economy. Critics say that multinationals exploit workers by paying them less than they would pay workers in developed nations. Critics also charge that multinationals can hurt a nation's economic growth by taking profits out of the country.

Instead of building businesses, foreign investors can make purchases in another country's financial markets. This is known as **foreign portfolio investment.** For example, an American investor might buy shares in a mutual fund. The mutual fund then buys stock in a foreign company. That company can use the funds to build another plant or to pay for research and development. Still, portfolio investment does present some problems. Since the investors live in another country, some or all of the company's profits may be drained away from the LDC.

Each year, the government-owned Bank of Namibia holds a symposium, or meeting, to discuss issues related to the nation's economic development. ▼

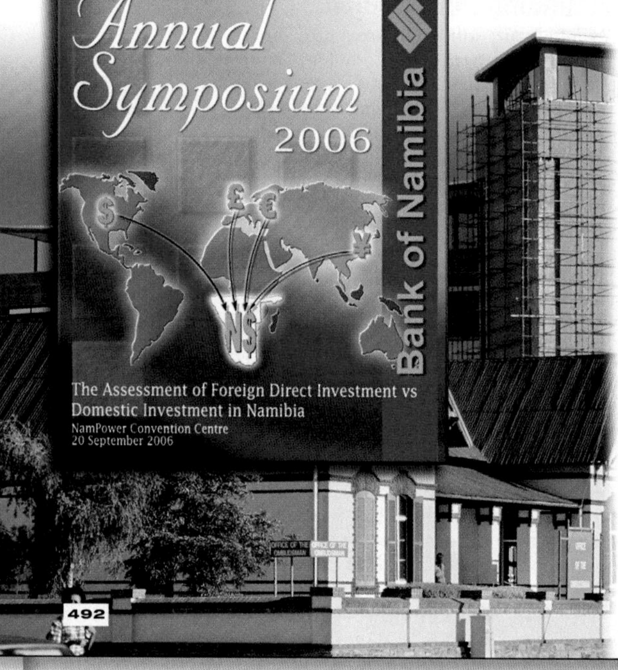

Borrowing and Debt

In the 1970s and 1980s, many less developed countries acquired loans from foreign governments and private banks to finance development. Some of that money was misspent because of inexperience or political corruption.

Changes in the world economy also caused problems for the LDCs. As oil prices rose, they borrowed more money to buy needed fuel. Also, many of the loans were issued in—and had to be repaid in—U.S. dollars. When the value of the dollar increased in the 1980s, many LDCs found it impossible to repay their loans. Once again, many were forced to borrow even more funds. As a result, the foreign debt in some countries grew to be greater than their annual GDP. As you will see, the world financial community has sought ways to relieve this severe debt crunch.

Foreign Aid

Sometimes, rather than making loans to developing nations, foreign governments give money and other forms of aid. For instance, many developed nations provide cash payments for building schools,

Background Note

Foreign Debt Developed economies also borrow money, and, in fact, 21 of the 25 countries with the highest levels of foreign debt are developed nations. The exceptions are China (20th), Russia (21st), Turkey (23rd), and Brazil (24th), all of which have large and growing economies. The United States leads the list, with $12.25 trillion in external debt. The United Kingdom, with $10.45 trillion in debt, is the only nation even close. Many LDCs, while they have far lower total amounts of external debt, have high levels of debt as a percentage of their gross national incomes.

sanitation systems, roads, and other infrastructure. These foreign aid grants do not need to be repaid. **Figure 18.5** shows the top recipients of U.S. foreign aid.

Foreign aid can be motivated by humanitarian concerns. At the same time, developed nations have military, political, economic, and cultural reasons to extend aid to LDCs. In the years following World War II, for instance, American officials gave aid to countries in Africa, Asia, and Latin America to try to block the influence of the Soviet Union in those areas. In the early 2000s, the United States provided money to Iraq and Afghanistan. American leaders hoped to fight international terrorism by building stable democracies in those countries.

CHECKPOINT ***Why is internal financing difficult for less developed countries?***

Figure 18.5 U.S. Foreign Aid, 2006

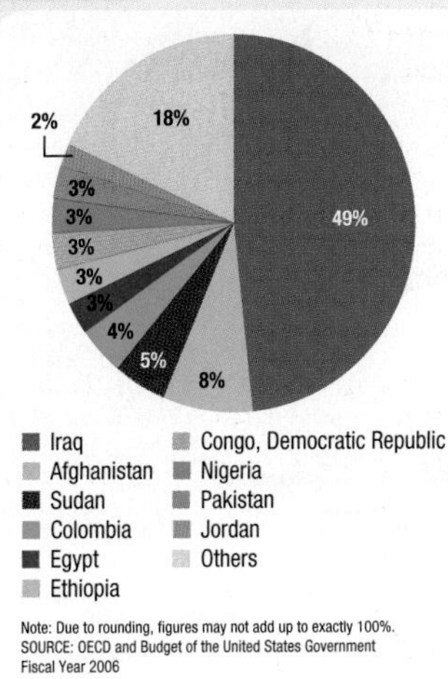

GRAPH SKILLS

This pie graph shows the ten countries that received the most foreign aid from the United States in 2006.

1. Identify the amount of foreign aid each of these countries received: Iraq, Colombia, Congo.
2. Why might it benefit the United States to provide aid to Afghanistan?

Note: Due to rounding, figures may not add up to exactly 100%.
SOURCE: OECD and Budget of the United States Government Fiscal Year 2006

International Institutions

Several international economic organizations promote development. The most prominent institutions are the World Bank, the United Nations Development Program, and the International Monetary Fund. In addition, privately run aid groups give economic help and advice in some less developed countries.

World Bank

The largest provider of development assistance is the World Bank, founded in 1944. The World Bank raises money on world financial markets and also accepts contributions from the wealthier member nations. The World Bank uses these funds to offer loans and other resources to more than 100 less developed countries. The World Bank also coordinates with other organizations to promote development throughout the world and provides advice to LDCs on how to build their economies.

United Nations Development Program

The United Nations Development Program (UNDP) is dedicated to the elimination of poverty. The UNDP is one of the world's largest sources of grant funding for economic and social development. It devotes 90 percent of its resources to 166 low-income nations, where 90 percent of the world's poorest people live. The UNDP is funded by voluntary contributions made by United Nations member states and agencies.

International Monetary Fund

As you learned in Chapter 17, the International Monetary Fund was founded in 1946 to stabilize international exchange rates. Today, the IMF has expanded its role in the world economy. It promotes development by offering policy advice and technical assistance to LDCs. It also intervenes when LDCs need help in financing their international transactions.

If a country has trouble repaying a debt, the IMF may arrange a rescheduling plan. **Debt rescheduling** is an agreement between a lending nation and a debtor nation. The lending nation lengthens the time of debt repayment and forgives, or dismisses, part of the loan. In return, the LDC agrees to accept a **stabilization program,** changing its economic policies to meet IMF goals.

A typical stabilization program involves providing incentives that will lead to higher export earnings and to fewer imports. By increasing exports, the LDC earns more foreign money to pay off its debt.

debt rescheduling an agreement between a lending nation and a debtor nation that lengthens the time of debt repayment and forgives part of the loan

stabilization program an agreement between a debtor nation and the International Monetary Fund in which the nation agrees to change its economic policy to match IMF goals

EXTEND

Distribute the "Conducting Research" skill worksheet (Unit 7 All-in-One, p. 63). Give students time to carry out online research into one World Bank and one IMF program. When they have completed the worksheet, discuss their conclusions as a class. Ask **What benefits and drawbacks do you see in the programs of these institutions?** As an alternate activity have students create their own WebQuest based on the worksheet information. See below.

Tell students to review the lesson in the Writing Skills Handbook on page S-2. Remind them to use the steps of the lesson to complete the activity.

L1 L2 Differentiate Give students the "Conducting Research" skill worksheet (Unit 7 All-in-One, p. 64) to carry out a research project on World Bank and IMF programs.

GUIDING QUESTION WRAP UP

Have students return to the section Guiding Question. Review the completed graphic organizer and clarify any misunderstandings. Have a wrap up discussion about factors that harm or help development.

Assess and Remediate

L2 L3 Collect the "Impact of Population Growth" worksheets and assess student understanding of population growth rates and age distribution.

L3 L2 Collect the "Conducting Research" skill worksheets and assess student ability to conduct research.

L3 Assign the Section 2 Assessment questions; identify student misconceptions.

L3 Give Section Quiz A (Unit 7 All-in-One, p. 65).

L2 Give Section Quiz B (Unit 7 All-in-One, p. 66).

(Assess and Remediate continued on p. 494)

Answers

Checkpoint Internal financing is difficult in less developed countries because poor people have no savings and those with wealth invest outside the country.

Graph Skills 1. Iraq: 49%; Colombia: 4%; Congo: 3% 2. Possible answer: Promoting economic growth there will help the fight against terrorists trying to gain power in that country.

Have students complete the Self-Test Online and continue their work in the **Essential Questions Journal**.

REMEDIATION AND SUGGESTIONS

Use the chart below to help students who are struggling with content.

WEAKNESS	REMEDIATION
Identifying key terms (Questions 3, 5, 6)	Have students use the interactive Economic Dictionary Online.
Obstacles to development (Questions 1, 3, 4, 7, 8)	Have students use their graphic organizers to review the content.
Promoting development (Questions 2, 5, 8, 9, 10)	Tell students to use a graphic organizer to list the pros and cons of different steps to promote development.

Answer

Checkpoint because they can have a negative impact on the poor in the short term

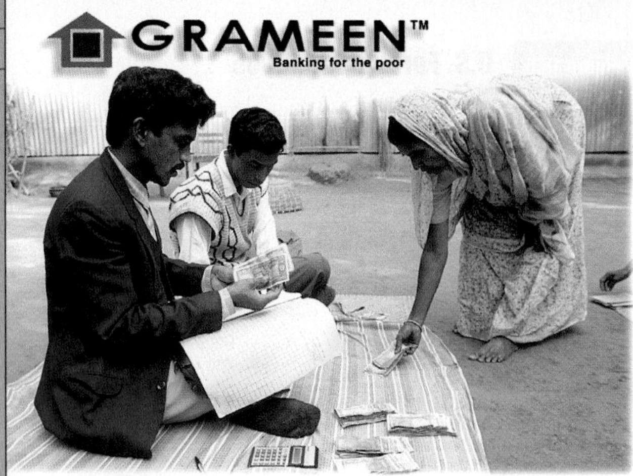

▲ Founded in Bangladesh, the Grameen Bank pioneered microlending, the practice of making very small loans to people like this village woman.

Stabilization programs are controversial because they can have a negative impact on the poor in the short term. They often require the LDC to lift wage and price controls. As wages drop and prices rise, the poor suffer. Stabilization may also force a government to cut spending on health, food, and education. Negative experiences in East Asia and Argentina have led some critics to question whether IMF policies are the most effective way to repair a troubled economy.

nongovernmental organization an independent group that raises money and uses it to fund aid and development programs

Nongovernmental Organizations

Some private aid groups also work to help the LDCs build their economies. **Nongovernmental organizations** (NGOs) are independent groups that raise money to fund aid and development programs. Examples are the Red Cross, CARE, and the World Wildlife Fund.

Some NGOs focus on providing food or medical help when natural disasters or wars cause problems. For instance, Oxfam International provides food to poor countries when they face extreme needs. Others try to promote development. For example, Heifer International gives animals to families in less developed countries. Families use these animals to produce and sell products such as wool, milk, or honey.

In 1976, Muhammad Yunus of Bangladesh founded the Grameen Bank. Since then, the bank has extended its operations to nearly every continent. The bank makes small loans—often, as little as a few dollars—to poor people. Many of the borrowers are women in rural villages. They use the loans to start their own businesses and lift their families out of poverty.

CHECKPOINT ***Why are stabilization programs controversial?***

SECTION 2 ASSESSMENT

Essential Questions Journal To continue to build a response to the Essential Question, go to your **Essential Questions Journal.**

Guiding Question

1. Use your completed chart to answer this question: What factors harm or help development?
2. **Extension** If you were given $100 to donate to a group that promoted development, what kind of group would you choose? Why?

Key Terms and Main Ideas

3. What factors contribute to a high **population growth rate?**
4. Why are literacy rates relatively low in less developed countries?
5. Why do many less developed countries need to rely on **foreign investment** rather than **internal financing?**
6. How do less developed countries benefit from **debt rescheduling?**

Critical Thinking

7. **Take a Position (a)** What prediction did Malthus make about population growth? **(b)** Do you agree that such results are inevitable? Explain.
8. **Prioritize** Suppose you were the head of a less developed country. Which obstacle to development would you tackle first? Why?
9. **Make a Decision** Do you think it would be more beneficial for a country to take a loan to fund new development or to invite in foreign investors? Explain your choice.

Quick Write

10. Suppose you are an economist with World Bank, International Monetary Fund, or United Nations Development Program. Write a memo to the president of the group explaining why the organization should take steps to combat corruption in less developed countries.

Assessment Answers

1. harm: high population growth, low rates of schooling, poor health and nutrition, corruption, spiraling debt; help: improving education, health, and government
2. Possible answers: a group that promotes education, because investment in human capital has great benefits; a group that provides health services, because the threat of malnutrition and disease is the most immediate problem
3. growing life expectancy, high birth rates, high percentage of people of childbearing age
4. Many children are forced to leave school to help the family economically. Often, women face restrictions on their education.
5. Internal financing is not available because people have little or no savings, so they must turn to foreign investors.
6. A nation's loans are either forgiven, or the payment period is stretched out.
7. (a) Population growth will outstrip the food supply, causing problems. (b) Possible answer: No. New technology makes it possible to produce more food. However, population growth is still a concern.
8. Possible answer: education first, to increase human capital and allow for more productive economic pursuits
9. Possible answer: Students might prefer the loan, if the interest rate and repayment terms would be reasonable, because once the loan is paid off, the benefits of the investment would remain in the country.
10. Possible answer: Students might propose such steps as giving money incrementally, with the threat of withholding future payments, or reducing them, if evidence of corruption surfaces, and instituting strict accounting measures to make it possible to track the flow of money.

OBJECTIVES

1. **Identify** the characteristics of economic transition.
2. **Describe** the political and economic changes that have taken place in Russia since the fall of communism.
3. **Analyze** the reasons for rapid economic growth in China and India.
4. **Summarize** the economic challenges facing Africa and Latin America.

ECONOMIC DICTIONARY

As you read the section, look for the definitions of these **Key Terms:**

- privatization
- special economic zone

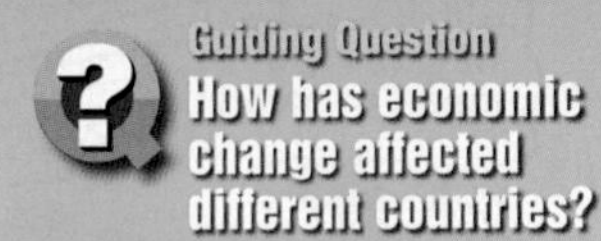

Copy this chart and fill it in as you read.

Russia	China	Brazil	Mexico
• Yeltsin: rapid switch to market • • •	• • • •	• Natural resources: iron, timber, land and climate • • •	• • • •

Economics and You

Change is always challenging. Suppose that suddenly no American could attend high school without paying tuition. It is easy to imagine the hardships this might cause. But if somebody gave you a million dollars, you might face different sorts of problems. Would you be tempted to spend the money on the wrong things? What new demands might friends and family make of you?

The same is true of nations. Economic change—even change for the better—always brings new challenges.

privatization the sale or transfer of government-owned businesses to individuals

Principles in Action Today, many countries are undergoing economic transition. Some are enjoying rapid growth, while others are changing their entire economic systems. In this section, you will look at the changing economies of Russia, China, India, and the countries of Africa and Latin America. In addition, the Economics & You feature shows some ways that economic change around the world may affect you.

Toward a Market Economy

For many nations, economic transition has meant moving from central planning to a market-based economy. As you saw in Chapter 2, in a command economy, the government owns and controls the factors of production. By contrast, in a market-based economy, the factors of production are owned and controlled by individuals. One of the first steps, then, in moving to a market economy is to sell or transfer government-owned businesses to individuals. This process is called **privatization.**

Privatization

A government can privatize businesses in several ways. It could simply sell the business to one owner. It could also sell shares to investors. A third alternative is to give every citizen a voucher that can be used to purchase shares in whatever businesses they wish, once those businesses are privatized.

Privatization can be a painful process. Only profitable enterprises will survive in a free market. No one will want to buy unprofitable ones, so many people will lose their jobs. Other job opportunities will eventually

▲ In China, transition from strict communism to free market practices has given rise to a new generation of entrepreneurs, such as this store owner.

Guiding Question

How has economic change affected different countries?

Get Started

Russia	China	Brazil	Mexico
• Yeltsin: rapid switch to market • Problems: high prices, wealth concentration, corruption • Crisis: 1998—debt high, low confidence • New policies: tight controls, high oil prices, new laws	• Deng: special economic zones • Later leaders: continue policies • Results: high growth, consumer goods in cities • Problems: rural areas lag, concerns about crime and pollution	• Natural resources: iron, timber, land, and climate • Industry: Increased manufacturing ability • Energy: developed ethanol industry	• Natural resources: oil, silver, land, and climate • Industry: increased manufacturing ability • Tourism: developed tourism industry

LESSON GOALS

Students will:

- Know the Key Terms.
- Explore results of economic changes in several countries and make generalizations about them.
- Compare results in several countries by using case studies in the "Economies in Transition" worksheet.
- Identify and evaluate possible solutions to the problem of rural poverty.

BEFORE CLASS

Students should read the section for homework before coming to class.

Have students complete the graphic organizer in the Section Opener as they read the text. As an alternate activity, have students complete the Guided Reading and Review worksheet (Unit 7 All-in-One, p. 67).

L1 L2 ELL LPR Differentiate Have students complete the Guided Reading and Review worksheet (Unit 7 All-in-One, p. 68).

Focus on the Basics

Students need to come away with the following understandings:

FACTS: • Many nations in recent decades have moved from centrally planned to market economies. • The transition in Russia has been difficult. • China and India have enjoyed some success in making this change. • Many nations in Africa and Latin America still face challenges.

GENERALIZATION: The transition to a market economy is not an easy change.

CLASSROOM HINTS

DEVELOPMENT TAKES TIME

In the United States, many people take prosperity and the existence of a large middle class for granted. The transition to a market economy leads to greater prosperity, but it can also make people less economically secure, especially at the beginning. This can make people reluctant to change, as people in Russia were. Also, it takes a long time for the benefits of economic prosperity to spread to the majority of a nation's citizens. Both India and China have growing middle classes, but they are much smaller as a proportion of the population than the middle class in the United States.

BELLRINGER

Write the phrases "New neighborhood," "New school," and "New job" on the board. Have students describe some of the opportunities and some of the difficulties people face when dealing with one of these changes. Tell them to share their ideas with a partner.

Teach

Economics online To present this topic using digital resources, use the lecture notes on www.PearsonSuccessNet.com.

DISCUSS

Call on pairs of students to offer their responses to the Bellringer activity, soliciting the ideas of two volunteers for each of the three topics. Use the exercise to launch a discussion of the opportunities and difficulties faced by the people of a nation when they experience an economic transition.

To help students understand the difficulty of making the transition, have them discuss the hypothetical situation about high school in the Economics and You text on page 495. Ask students how requiring students to pay tuition for high school might affect the percentage of students attending high school, the lives of teens in the future, and attitudes toward school.

Guide students to see that such a fundamental change has profound implications for people's attitudes and behavior. Similarly, the change from a command system to a market system requires citizens to completely shift their way of thinking and acting.

▲ This cartoon outlines some of the problems that Russia and other communist countries faced as they made the transition to free market economics. ***According to the cartoon, what economic problems did Russia face before and after the transition? Explain why each of these problems occurred.***

appear as the economy grows. However, the initial transition can be difficult for workers accustomed to jobs guaranteed by the government.

Another concern is corruption. Government leaders might make it easier for their own friends and associates to gain control of businesses. The result is an unfair distribution of ownership.

Protecting Property Rights

Moving to a market economy also requires changes in the legal system. Centrally planned economies have no need to protect private property rights. A free market economy, however, cannot function without such protections. As a result, the government must create new laws that ensure a person's right to own and transfer property. Such a basic overhaul of the legal system takes time.

Citizen Attitudes

In a planned economy, workers grow used to security. Many have guaranteed jobs where their only concern is to meet government quotas. In the free market, such guarantees do not exist. Incentives, not quotas, motivate people's labor. As a result, workers in a transitioning economy need to learn a new work ethic.

Not surprisingly, people accustomed to central planning often worry about how change will affect them. They might resist the shift to the free market out of fear and uncertainty.

CHECKPOINT ***Identify three challenges in moving to a free market economy.***

Transition in Russia

Russia has faced all of the challenges described above. It was once part of the Soviet Union, the world's most powerful communist nation. But in 1991, Soviet communism—and the Soviet Union itself—collapsed. Russia and the other former Soviet republics began the difficult transition to a free market economy.

Fall of Communism

Under communism, government planners directed the Soviet economy. The nation became an industrial giant and a military superpower. Still, as you saw in Chapter 2, the Soviet people faced frequent shortages of consumer goods, and the goods they did get were often low quality.

In the late 1980s, a new Soviet leader named Mikhail Gorbachev began a series of dramatic political and economic changes to revive the country's stagnant economy. Gorbachev did not want to overturn the communist economic and political system. Rather, he hoped to incorporate the use of markets and incentives into the existing structure of communism.

The transition to free market economics created problems, however. Economic reform produced some initial hardships. People lost secure government jobs, benefits, and pensions. Many people, especially the elderly, were hurt financially. Some Russians did begin to make the new system work for them, starting their own businesses and prospering. Still, unrest grew.

At the same time, some officials and army officers feared that the central government was becoming weak. In 1991,

Answers

Caption Before the transition, Russians faced shortages of basic goods due to the inefficiency of their centrally planned economy. After the transitions, people lost jobs because the free market system did not guarantee employment for everyone, as the Soviet system had.

Checkpoint privatization, the creation of new legal systems, and the development of a strong work ethic

Differentiated Resources

- **L1 L2 Guided Reading and Review** (Unit 7 All-in-One, p. 68)
- **L1 L2 Economies in Transition** (Unit 7 All-in-One, p. 71)
- **L4 Analyzing India** (Unit 7 All-in-One, p. 72)

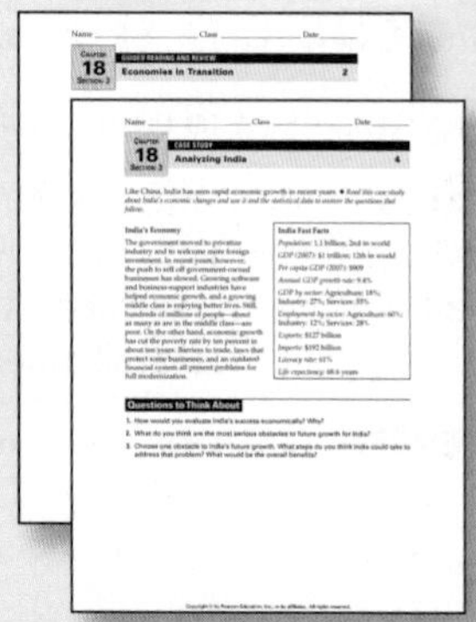

they tried to restore old-style communism. The attempt backfired. One by one, the 15 Soviet republics declared their independence. The largest of the new nations was the Russian Republic.

A Painful Transition

Russia's new president, Boris Yeltsin, promised rapid progress towards a market economy. Despite improvements, hardships continued. When Yeltsin lifted price controls in 1992, prices tripled. People on fixed incomes, such as retirees living on government pensions, could not afford to buy basics like food and clothing.

In the new Russia, wealth tended to become concentrated in cities such as Moscow. The uneven distribution of income led many to call for additional change. It also led to extensive corruption and widespread organized crime.

Billions of dollars in financial aid flooded into the country from the World Bank, the IMF, and independent investors. However, due to mismanagement and corruption, these funds were not used efficiently. By 1998, the Russian economy was in a shambles. Debt was high, investor confidence was low, and the nation was in the midst of an economic crisis.

Russia in a New Century

Tight controls from the central government, combined with rising prices for Russian oil, allowed Russian leaders to stem the crisis. By 2007, according to the IMF, Russia had the world's seventh largest national economy, and much of the nation's foreign debt had been repaid. Economic growth has fed growing consumer demand. New laws protect investments, encouraging foreign investors to supply capital to launch new businesses.

Still, problems persist. Russia's economy relies too much on the export of natural resources. If the prices of these goods drop, export income will fall. In recent years, Russian leaders have restored government control over many aspects of the economy. The transition to a market economy is far from complete.

CHECKPOINT ***How did communism end in the Soviet Union?***

Growth in Asia

Asia, the world's largest continent, is home to more than 4 billion people—over 60 percent of the world's total population. These people provide a huge workforce and a huge market for goods and services. In recent decades, Asia has become one of the most dynamic players in the global economy. Nations such as Singapore, South Korea, and Taiwan have incomes comparable to highly developed nations in the rest of the world.

As you can see from **Figure 18.6**, China is a major exporter of goods and a key trading partner of the United States. India, too, has experienced rapid economic growth. How did these two nations, once among the world's poorest, advance so far, so rapidly?

China

In 1949, after a long civil war, communists led by Mao Zedong took power in China. They quickly put in place communist policies, giving the government ownership of all land, resources, and enterprises. Government planners made all key decisions about the economy.

After Mao died in 1976, Deng Xiaoping became China's new leader. Deng soon began using the tools of the free market

Figure 18.6 Chinese Exports, 1995–2006

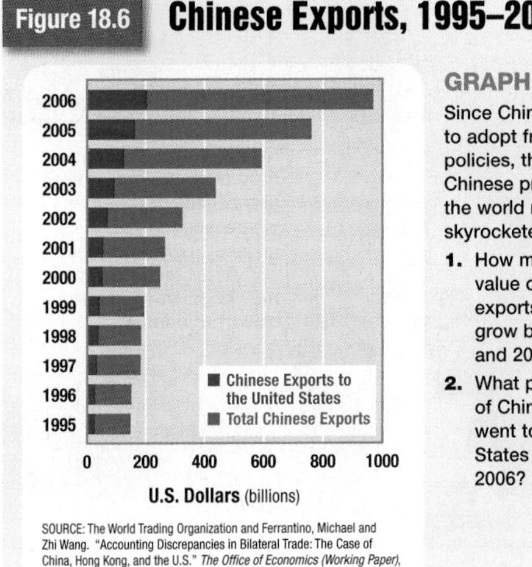

SOURCE: The World Trading Organization and Ferrantino, Michael and Zhi Wang. "Accounting Discrepancies in Bilateral Trade: The Case of China, Hong Kong, and the U.S." *The Office of Economics (Working Paper)*, The U.S. International Trade Commission, April 2007.

GRAPH SKILLS

Since China began to adopt free market policies, the export of Chinese products to the world market has skyrocketed.

1. How much did the value of Chinese exports to the world grow between 1995 and 2006?
2. What percentage of China's exports went to the United States in 2000? In 2006?

SUMMARIZE AND GENERALIZE

To help students explore economies in transition, use the Jigsaw strategy. Divide the class into numbered groups, assigning all number 1s to Russia, 2s to China, 3s to India, 4s to Africa, and 5s to Latin America. Give each group a chance to meet and prepare an oral presentation about the prior economic conditions and the successes and difficulties encountered by the country or region they were assigned. Students assigned to sub-Saharan Africa or Latin America could have the option of choosing a particular country in their region.

After the groups have completed their work, form new groups with at least one student from each of the original groups. Have the students take turns giving a summary of their original group's presentation to the others.

Once the students have completed their presentations, have each of the new groups develop two generalizations about the transition process. Finally, call on the groups to share their generalizations with the rest of the class. Discuss the groups' ideas as a class.

L1 L2 Differentiate Students use a flowchart graphic organizer to list the steps in transition of each country and to clarify the results of each step.

L2 ELL Differentiate If the classroom includes English language learners, pair them with English proficient students in the numbered groups, and then in the reformed groups. Have the pairs work closely together to record and present their summaries. If necessary, adjust the number of groups and assign one or more groups more countries or regions than in the assignment described above.

Virtual Economics

L3 Differentiate

Comparing Paths to Development
Use the following lesson from the NCEE **Virtual Economics *CD-ROM*** to compare the ways three countries reformed their command economies. Click on Browse Economics Lessons, specify grades 9–12, and use the key words *different paths.*

In this activity, students will work in small groups to study case studies of economic reform in Poland, China, and Russia.

LESSON TITLE	DIFFERENT PATHS TO REFORM: CASE STUDIES OF POLAND, CHINA, AND RUSSIA
Type of Activity	Case studies
Complexity	Moderate
Time	50 minutes
NCEE Standards	3

Answers

Checkpoint The failed attempt to return to old-style communism after Gorbachev's economic policies created many problems prompted the 15 Soviet republics to declare their independence.

Graph Skills 1. They increased by about five times. 2. Less than 20 percent in 2000; slightly more than 20 percent in 2006.

COMPARE AND CONTRAST

To help students explore the course of economic transition in several economies, distribute the "Economies in Transition" worksheet (Unit 7 All-in-One, p. 69). Students will use the worksheet to compare economic performance in Chile, China, Iraq, Kenya, Romania, Russia, and Vietnam.

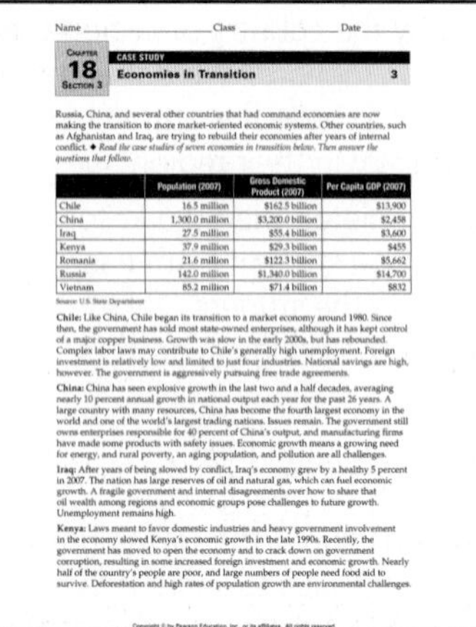

Name ______________ Class ______________ Date ________

CHAPTER 18 SECTION 3

CASE STUDY

Economies in Transition 3

Russia, China, and several other countries that had command economies are now making the transition to more market-oriented economic systems. Other countries, such as Afghanistan and Iraq, are trying to rebuild their economies after years of internal conflict. ♦ *Read the case studies of seven economies in transition below. Then answer the questions that follow.*

	Population (2007)	Gross Domestic Product (2007)	Per Capita GDP (2007)
Chile	16.5 million	$162.5 billion	$13,900
China	1,300.0 million	$3,200.0 billion	$2,458
Iraq	27.5 million	$55.4 billion	$3,600
Kenya	37.9 million	$29.3 billion	$455
Romania	21.6 million	$122.3 billion	$5,662
Russia	142.0 million	$1,340.0 billion	$14,700
Vietnam	85.2 million	$71.4 billion	$832

Source: U.S. State Department

Chile: Like China, Chile began its transition to a market economy around 1980. Since then, the government has sold most state-owned enterprises, although it has kept control of a major copper business. Growth was slow in the early 2000s, but has rebounded. Complex labor laws may contribute to Chile's generally high unemployment. Foreign investment is relatively low and limited to just four industries. National savings are high, however. The government is aggressively pursuing free trade agreements.

China: China has seen explosive growth in the last two and a half decades, averaging nearly 10 percent annual growth in national output each year for the past 26 years. A large country with many resources, China has become the fourth largest economy in the world and one of the world's largest trading nations. Issues remain. The government still owns enterprises responsible for 40 percent of China's output, and manufacturing firms have made some products with safety issues. Economic growth means a growing need for energy, and rural poverty, an aging population, and pollution are all challenges.

Iraq: After years of being slowed by conflict, Iraq's economy grew by a healthy 5 percent in 2007. The nation has large reserves of oil and natural gas, which can fuel economic growth. A fragile government and internal disagreements over how to share that oil wealth among regions and economic groups pose challenges to future growth. Unemployment remains high.

Kenya: Laws meant to favor domestic industries and heavy government involvement in the economy slowed Kenya's economic growth in the late 1990s. Recently, the government has moved to open the economy and to crack down on government corruption, resulting in some increased foreign investment and economic growth. Nearly half of the country's people are poor, and large numbers of people need food aid to survive. Deforestation and high rates of population growth are environmental challenges.

L1 L2 Differentiate Distribute the "Economies in Transition" worksheet (Unit 7 All-in-One, p. 71). Have students evaluate the relative success of the economies covered in the worksheet.

Discuss students' responses to the case histories as a class. Using the Idea Wave strategy, call on students to identify which of the seven economies they think will have the most economic success in the future and to explain why. Challenge them to give reasons for their responses. Give students two minutes to write. Then call on them to give their answers aloud. If they repeat the same reasons for a particular country, ask students to explain what issues might slow development in another country.

L1 L2 Differentiate Within the Idea Wave activity, encourage students to take notes on other students' responses.

L4 Differentiate Distribute the "Analyze India" worksheet (Unit 7 All-in-One, p. 72) so that students can explore economic changes in India, which is also undergoing transition.

special economic zones designated regions that operate under different economic laws from the rest of the country in order to attract foreign investment and promote exports

to increase productivity. He gave farmers and factory managers more freedom to make decisions about what to produce and how much to charge for it. He also rewarded farmers, managers, and workers who increased output. With such incentives, production increased.

Deng also set up four free market centers along China's east coast. Foreign businesses could operate, and local governments were allowed to offer tax incentives to foreign investors in these **special economic zones.** Chinese businesses could operate freely as well, with managers making most of their own investment and production decisions. This approach proved so successful that China now has hundreds of these zones.

Economics & YOU

Economic Growth in Asia

Since the 1970s, Chinese manufacturing and foreign trade have skyrocketed. ***Many of the clothes you buy today were imported from China.***

MADE IN CHINA

India

Many American companies have outsourced customer service jobs to countries where labor costs are cheaper. ***When you call for computer tech help, you may be speaking to an operator in India.***

USA

▲ Economic development in other countries can affect you. ***What products do you use that came from other countries?***

Deng's successors have continued his policies. The economic changes have led to huge economic growth. Where the country once lagged far behind most nations of Europe and North America, China now has the world's second most productive economy, after the United States. Chinese cities are now full of people who enjoy access to a wide variety of consumer goods.

Still, development has brought its share of problems. Rapid urban growth has led to increases in crime and pollution. The poor complain that the government is abandoning its promise to provide jobs and healthcare for all the nation's people. In addition, growth has not reached all parts of the country. Poverty and unemployment plague rural areas.

Finally, economic development has not meant political liberty. Chinese citizens still do not enjoy many political rights. The government tightly controls the press and stifles dissent.

India

India is the world's second most populous nation, after China. A former British colony, India struggled economically after winning independence. In the 1990s, though, India's government began to invite foreign investment and promote other free market practices.

New policies encouraged Indian companies to expand. One area of significant growth was in high-technology industries. Many software companies opened new facilities in India, where educated workers could offer technical support to computer users around the world. Manufacturing grew as well.

Economic growth helped promote the emergence of a much larger middle class. One business executive noted the significance of this development:

> **"When half the population in a society is middle class, its politics will change... its poor will be fewer — and society will have greater means to look after them."**
>
> Gurcharan Das, "India's Growing Middle Class"

India's middle class provides a growing market for consumer goods. While India had no shopping malls before 1999, it

Background Note

Bangalore The city of Bangalore, in south central India, has become the heart of that country's software and computer support industries, which are a dynamic part of India's growing economy. This industry grew for several reasons. India's educational system produced a high number of software engineers. These workers were fluent in English and—because of India's relatively low cost of living—were willing to work for lower wages than those in other areas. The growth of satellite networks made instantaneous communication between India and North America possible.

Answer

Economics & You Possible answers: clothing, running shoes, electronics

Innovators

Wangari Muta Maathai

"I always felt that our work was not simply about planting trees," said Wangari Maathai, the first African woman to win the Nobel Peace Prize. "It was about inspiring people to take charge of their environment, the system that governed them, their lives and their future." As a biology teacher at the University of Nairobi, she became the first woman associate professor in 1977. That year she began her second career, as an environmental activist. Maathai founded the Green Belt Movement (GBM). Her goal was to promote economic development while, at the same time, preserving her nation's forest and soil resources for future generations. Maathai believed that, without its forest, Kenya could eventually become a desert wasteland. The GBM also created jobs by hiring thousands of poor women to plant trees in rural Kenya.

From the outset, the Green Belt Movement faced strong opposition from the oppressive Kenyan government, which wanted to sell off the forests to foreign developers. Police disrupted peaceful demonstrations. Maathai herself was teargassed and severely beaten. "But I have an elephant's skin. And somebody must raise their voice."

After years of confrontation the environmentalists prevailed. GBM has now planted over 30 million trees and provided jobs for 80,000 people. Elected to Kenya's Parliament in 2002, Wangari Maathai continues to search for ways to improve living standards for both current and future generations.

Critical Thinking: ***What arguments might an economist make for and against the actions of the Green Belt Movement?***

Fast Facts

Wangari Muta Maathai
Born: April 1, 1940, in Nyeri, Kenya
Education: Ph.D., Veterinary Medicine, University of Nairobi
Claim to Fame: Founder of Green Belt Movement

now has more than a hundred. As the middle class seeks more (and more expensive) goods, local and foreign producers compete to meet that demand.

Still, as with China, India's growth is not complete. Some 60 percent of the labor force farms, but they furnish only about 18 percent of the nation's production. The result is a growing gap between the richest and poorest citizens. In fact, this is true of virtually all nations with developing economies. Urban dwellers with education and skills benefit the most from growth. Uneducated people in poor rural areas struggle with poverty and continue to rely on subsistence farming.

CHECKPOINT ***What free-market reforms did Deng Xiaoping introduce in China?***

Challenges in Africa and Latin America

Like Asia, Africa and Latin America are home to many poor countries. Some nations in these two regions have seen great economic growth in recent years. Others continue to struggle.

Persistent Poverty in Africa

Some North African nations have built productive economies. This success is mainly due to large reserves of oil.

South of the Sahara, however, most nations face the obstacles common to all LDCs, which you read about in Section 2. Economies are largely based on subsistence farming. Low literacy rates, inadequate health and nutrition, high rates of HIV infection, and mounting debt hinder development efforts. Some nations are also plagued by years of civil war or ethnic conflict. Only two African nations south of the Sahara have sizable economies—South Africa and Nigeria.

Nigeria benefits from large reserves of oil. Yet overdependence on oil has slowed growth in other areas. Nigeria also suffers from widespread political corruption and ethnic conflict. In 2007, new leaders took power in Nigeria. They promised to take steps to improve the economy and standards of living.

In the 1990s, South Africa shifted from longtime rule by the white minority to black majority rule. Problems in the

BRAINSTORM

Direct students' attention to the closing sentences of the discussion of the transition in India on page 499, which focuses on the problem of lingering rural poverty. Have students consider why a nation cannot reach its full potential when a large segment of the population remains in poverty. Have them consider what problems a disparity between an upwardly mobile urban population and a still-impoverished rural population will have on the development of a politically and economically strong nation. Point out that India is not the only developing country facing this problem.

EXTEND

Have students choose one of the countries profiled in the chapter other than China and India. Instruct them to list five steps that they suggest the country take to manage the transition to a market economy. Tell them to list the steps in order of priority and explain why they recommend that particular sequence.

L1 L2 LPR Differentiate Tell students to choose one of the countries profiled in the section and identify at least two problems it has had making the transition to a market economy. For each problem, they should identify a possible solution.

GUIDING QUESTION WRAP UP

Have students return to the section Guiding Question. Review the completed graphic organizer and clarify any misunderstandings. Have a wrap up discussion about how economic change has affected different countries.

Assess and Remediate

L2 L3 Collect the "Economies in Transition" worksheet and assess student understanding of the transition to a market-oriented economy.

L3 Assign the Section 3 Assessment questions; identify student misconceptions.

L3 Give Section Quiz A (Unit 7 All-in-One, p. 73).

L2 Give Section Quiz B (Unit 7 All-in-One, p. 74).

(Assess and Remediate continued on p. 500)

Answers

Critical Thinking Possible answers: Argument for: Trees can hold the soil, which can help keep the soil productive and support agriculture, so the action makes sense. Argument against: Trees are only a potential resource if they are harvested; if left to stand, they do not make an economic contribution.

Checkpoint giving farmers and factory managers more freedom to make decisions; creating special economic zones

Have students complete the Self-Test Online and continue their work in the **Essential Questions Journal**.

REMEDIATION AND SUGGESTIONS

Use the chart below to help students who are struggling with content.

WEAKNESS	REMEDIATION
Identifying key terms (Questions 3, 6)	Have students use the interactive Economic Dictionary Online.
Process of transition (Questions 1, 2, 3, 4, 8)	Have students make a step-by-step chart of the process of transition and potential pitfalls.
Progress toward transition in specific countries (Questions 5, 6, 7, 9, 10, 11)	Reteach the sections *Transitions in Russia, Growth in Asia,* and *Challenges in Africa and Latin America.*

Answers

Caption Possible answer: Tourists bring foreign currency into the country.

Checkpoint Brazil and Mexico

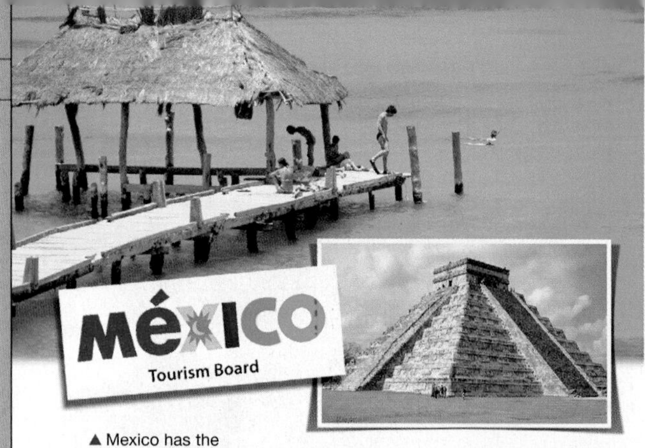

▲ Mexico has the eighth largest tourism industry in the world. The government-sponsored Tourism Board promotes such attractions as Mexico's exotic beach resorts (left) and its ancient Mayan ruins (right). ***Why would it be especially profitable for a developing nation to attract tourists from overseas?***

transition, along with high rates of HIV infection, slowed economic growth. Unemployment remains high, and poverty remains a problem. Still, South Africa has one of the 25 most productive economies in the world. It benefits from a rich array of natural resources and a strong manufacturing base.

Different Paths in Latin America

In Latin America, the two biggest success stories are Brazil and Mexico. Both countries have abundant resources. Both have also taken steps to make their economies more diverse.

Brazil exports iron ore and timber and its land and climate are highly suitable for growing coffee and soybeans.

The discovery of large offshore oil reserves in late 2007 promised to turn Brazil into a major oil-exporting power. Brazil has become a major manufacturing power, producing everything from vehicles to shoes. It has also adapted its sugar industry to produce ethanol. Brazil has also built cars that can run on either gasoline or ethanol. More than 40 percent of the fuel that powers Brazilian cars comes from ethanol derived from sugar cane.

Mexico has reserves of oil and silver and produces rich crops of cotton and coffee. Like Brazil, Mexico has diversified its economy by promoting its tourism industry and building factories.

By diversifying their economies, Mexico and Brazil have freed 80 percent or more of their labor forces from farm work. Employment in manufacturing and service industries have helped these two economies grow.

Venezuela also has large reserves of oil. Its leadership has turned in a different direction, though. President Hugo Chávez has shifted the economy away from the market system to socialism. Chávez has promised to use money derived from the sale of oil and gas to eliminate poverty and improve health and education. These advances have yet to be seen, however.

✔ **CHECKPOINT** ***Which countries in Latin America have built the strongest economies?***

Essential Questions Journal To continue to build a response to the Essential Question, go to your **Essential Questions Journal.**

SECTION 3 ASSESSMENT

Guiding Question

1. Use your completed chart to answer this question: How has economic change affected different countries?
2. **Extension** Imagine that you lived in a country switching to a market economy. What kind of business venture would you launch to succeed in the new economy?

Key Terms and Main Ideas

3. What is **privatization?**
4. Why do governments switching to a market economy need new laws?
5. How did Russia's economy change after 1991?
6. What was the purpose of China's **special economic zones?**
7. What economic challenges do many nations in Africa face?

Critical Thinking

8. **Identify Alternatives** Suggest two steps that a nation could take to ease the transition from a command economy to a free market economy.
9. **Predict** China has been criticized for stifling dissent and other violations of human rights. Do you think that will affect its trade relationships with other nations? Why or why not?
10. **Compare** Pick two countries discussed in this section. How were their economic transitions and challenges similar or different?

Math Skills

11. The table below shows changes in per capita income in urban and rural areas in China. **(a)** Which area enjoys the highest income? **(b)** Which area shows the greatest percentage of increase? **(c)** What economic problems does this chart reveal? ***Visit PearsonSuccessNet.com for additional math help.***

Per Capita Disposable Income (in Chinese currency)

	2003	2005	2007
Urban Areas	8,472.2	10,493.0	13,786.0
Rural Areas	2,622.2	3,254.9	4,140.0

Assessment Answers

1. Possible answer: Russia and Eastern European countries have struggled with change; China and India have enjoyed success, though they still have problems. Mexico and Brazil have done better than other countries in Latin America by diversifying their economies.
2. Possible answer: stores selling newly available consumer goods
3. the transfer of government-owned businesses to the private sector
4. to protect private property rights, which did not exist under the planned economy
5. Communism collapsed and Russia began a transition to a market economy, which continues today.
6. to promote economic growth by allowing local governments to attract foreign investors and by letting managers of Chinese businesses make most decisions
7. Economies rely on subsistence farming; countries have low literacy rates, poor health and nutrition, high rates of HIV infection, and high debt; some countries have had civil wars or ethnic conflict.
8. Possible answer: Give everyone in the country shares in new businesses, so they would be interested in seeing them succeed; invest in education.
9. Possible answer: No. Since other countries need the goods China produces, disagreements over human rights will not halt its trade.
10. Possible answer: Natural resources helped fuel economic growth in Russia, but were not as important a factor in China.
11. (a) urban (b) Urban income rose more, about 62 percent to about 58 percent. (c) Urban income is about three times higher, showing that cities have benefited more from growth.

Challenges of Globalization

OBJECTIVES

1. **Define** globalization and identify factors that promoted its spread.
2. **Explain** four problems linked to globalization.
3. **Describe** three challenges that globalization creates.
4. **Identify** the characteristics needed for American workers and companies to succeed in the future.

ECONOMIC DICTIONARY

As you read the section, look for the definitions of these **Key Terms:**

- globalization
- offshoring
- remittances
- "brain drain"
- sustainable development
- deforestation

Guiding Question

What are the effects of globalization?

Copy this concept web and fill it in as you read.

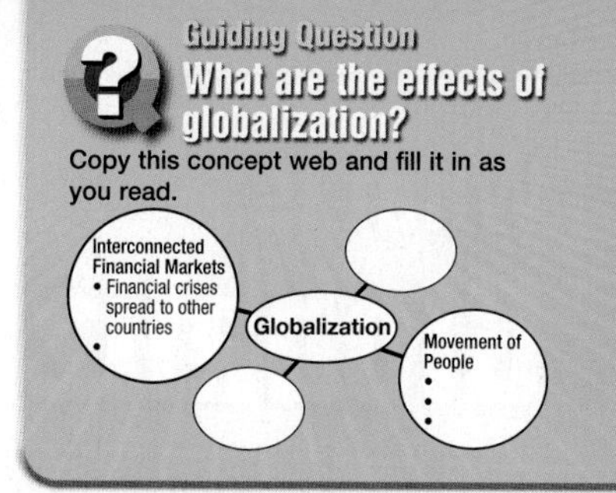

Economics and You By now, you have seen many examples of how the world's economies are interconnected. You pick up the telephone to get tech support for your computer, and the call is answered in India. You eat a banana that was grown in Costa Rica and fill your car with gas made from petroleum that originally came out of the ground in Saudi Arabia. The value of the dollar goes down, and the cost of a vacation goes up. The list goes on and on.

globalization the increasingly tight interconnection of producers, consumers, and financial systems around the world

Principles in Action The economies of the world's nations are interconnected in deep and complex ways—and they will remain interconnected. The global economy creates new issues that business managers, workers, and government leaders must take into account. In this section, you will look at many of these issues, from impact on the environment to increased competition for American businesses.

Causes of Globalization

The increasingly tight interconnection of producers, consumers, and financial systems around the world is known as **globalization.** Such connections are not a new phenomenon. In the Middle Ages, the Asian spice trade connected Europe, Asia, and Africa. The voyages of Columbus led to the colonization of the Americas by European sea powers and to the development of the African slave trade. The Age of Imperialism that began in the late 1800s forged even closer links between the economies of Europe and the United States and those of Africa and Asia.

Still, globalization today is taking place at a much faster pace than in the past. Several factors contribute to the ever-tightening links between economies around the world. They include the development of faster methods of communication and transportation, the

Globalization began long ago. This 14th century map shows a caravan on the Silk Road, a trade route linking the economies of China and Southwest Asia. ***Why do you think the pace of globalization has gotten faster?*** ▼

Focus on the Basics

Students need to come away with the following understandings:

FACTS: • The economies of the world have become more closely interconnected. • Globalization has caused some problems. • Developed and developing countries and LDCs all face challenges rising from global market competition.

GENERALIZATION: Preparing for economic success in the future means being ready for worldwide competition.

Guiding Question

What are the effects of globalization?

Get Started

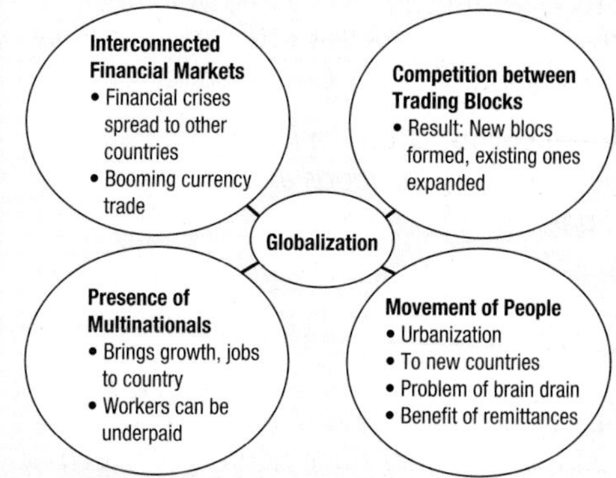

LESSON GOALS

Students will:

- Know the Key Terms.
- Discuss aspects of globalization.
- Debate the issue of investment in LDCs by multinational corporations.
- Show understanding of the effect of job relocation and offshoring on employment.
- Discuss the debate over pursuing developmental or environmental goals.

BEFORE CLASS

Have students complete the graphic organizer in the Section Opener as they read the text. As an alternate activity, have students complete the Guided Reading and Review worksheet (Unit 7 All-in-One, p. 75).

L1 L2 ELL LPR Differentiate Have students complete the Guided Reading and Review worksheet (Unit 7 All-in-One, p. 76).

Answer

Caption Modern transportation, communication

CLASSROOM HINTS

GLOBALIZATION IS NOT NEW

Though globalization has accelerated in recent decades, it is not a new or even recent phenomenon. Nations all over the world have been trading with each other for hundreds of years. In some regions, far longer than that. The volume and speed of trade have increased, but the basic reasons for trading are the same. Nations trade for mutual advantage, and to meet their domestic needs.

Teach Visual Glossary

REVIEW KEY TERMS

Pair students and have them write the definitions of the key terms related to the understanding of globalization.

free market economy – *an economic system in which decisions on the three key economic questions are based on voluntary exchange in markets*

multinational corporation – *a large corporation that produces and sells its goods and services in more than one country*

interdependence – *the shared need of countries for resources, goods, services, labor, and knowledge supplied by other countries*

free trade – *the lowering or elimination of protective tariffs and other trade barriers between two or more nations*

foreign exchange market – *system of financial institutions that facilitate the buying and selling of foreign currencies*

MAKE CHARTS

Form students into groups. Tell each group to draw a graphic organizer with three columns, which they should label "Aspect of Globalization," "Contribution to Globalization," and "Challenge Created." Have the group members write the six elements of globalization in rows underneath the first column heading. Then have them fill out the rest of the chart with details about those six elements.

L1 L2 Differentiate Have each group focus on two of the elements of globalization. Then have them share their findings with the class.

Economics online *All print resources are available on the Teacher's Resource Library CD-ROM and online at* www.PearsonSuccessNet.com.

Answers

Graphic Caption Possible answers: Spread of free market economies means more nations are interested in trade; rapid transportation and communication make it easier to move goods and information around.

Cartoon Possible answer: Globalization is a powerful force that poses risks for everyone involved in it. A financial problem in one nation can quickly spread to others.

Reviewing Key Terms
To understand *globalization*, review these terms:

free market economy, *p. 30*
multinational corporation, *p. 207*
interdependence, *p. 452*
free trade, *p. 458*
foreign exchange market, *p. 465*

What is Globalization?

◀ **globalization** the increasingly tight interconnection of producers, consumers, and financial systems around the world

Globalization

Rapid Transportation and Communication

Spread of Free Market Economies

Interconnected Financial Markets

Foreign Exchange Markets

Multinational Corporations

Free Trade Agreements

Globalization is not just one thing. It is a combination of many different elements that make the economies of the world increasingly interdependent. ***Choose two of the elements above and explain how each contributes to globalization.***

◀ Increasing interdependence carries risks as well as opportunities. ***What point is this cartoon making about globalization?***

"GLOBALISATION RISKY? HOW D'YOU MEAN?"

Visual Glossary online
To expand your understanding of this and other key economic terms, visit **PearsonSuccessNet.com**

widespread adoption of free-market economic principles, and the growth of international trade agreements.

Rapid Transportation and Communication

What do the domestication of the camel, the invention of the compass, and the creation of the Internet have in common? All these innovations allowed greater movement of products, people, and ideas. Today, as in the past, globalization depends on breaking through barriers of time and space.

In the past, camels and ships made it possible to trade across vast deserts and oceans. Today, jet airplanes allow producers to sell goods in distant markets that would have been impossible to reach quickly in the past. For example, flower growers in the Netherlands or Colombia can send fresh flowers for sale in the United States.

Today's communications revolution has also sped the pace of globalization. Thanks to satellite communications, customers and suppliers on opposite sides of the world can talk quickly and clearly. Computers give people greater access to information about the availability and price of products in distant countries. Investors in one country can get up-to-date information and use it to buy stocks on financial markets anywhere.

Expansion of the Free Market

As you read in Section 3, many nations have moved away from central planning to pursue free-market policies. As a result, the proportion of the world that practices free market economics has more than tripled. At the same time, the fall of communism in the Soviet Union and Eastern Europe allowed nations that had once been locked out of world trade to enter the global marketplace. The opening of new markets has created new global economic ties.

The new free market economies are more open to foreign investment. In 1975, the value of foreign investment worldwide totaled only about $23 billion. By 1997, the total had grown to nearly $640 billion.

Trading Blocs

In Chapter 17, you saw that many nations have signed regional trade agreements. The creation of trading blocs has changed the nature of competition in the global market.

The United States is the world's most productive single economy, with output far exceeding that of any single nation in Europe. However, the *combined* output of the 27 nations that make up the European Union is competitive with that of the United States. People, goods, and services can flow freely among members of the EU, making it almost like a single economy.

Concern about competition from the EU was one of the factors that spurred the United States, Canada, and Mexico to sign the North American Free Trade Agreement. By making it easier to trade with some partners, countries hope to prevent companies from making deals with those in other trading blocs.

Trading blocs do not remain fixed. The EU has repeatedly expanded to include more nations. It is also working to forge trade tries with other regions. Similarly, members of NAFTA are engaged in talks to extend free trade to more of Latin America. All of this activity has added to the tighter globalization of the world economy.

CHECKPOINT ***How have modern communications contributed to globalization?***

FUTURE WATCH

Personal Finance For information on dealing with the increasing threat of Internet crime, see your Personal Finance Handbook in the back of the book or visit **PearsonSuccessNet.com**

Issues in Globalization

"Arguing against globalization," said former UN Secretary General Kofi Annan, "is like arguing against the laws of gravity." While globalization is a fact of modern economic life, it has also created challenges.

Interconnected Financial Markets

In 2007, many American financial firms lost money—or went out of business—as a result of making too many risky home mortgage loans. Worried that the crisis would cause a downturn in the economy, investors sold stocks. Heavy losses on the New York Stock Exchange raised concerns among investors elsewhere in the world. They, in turn, sold stocks on European and Asian exchanges.

BELLRINGER

Write the following question on the board: "What does the word *globalization* mean to you?" Ask students to list at least three words or ideas that come to mind.

Teach

Economics online To present this topic using digital resources, use the lecture notes on www.PearsonSuccessNet.com.

DISCUSS

Call on students to share some of their responses to the Bellringer question. On the board, write the headings "Positive" and "Negative." Ask students to suggest items to add under each heading. If students do not come up with the following on their own, prompt them to consider whether each statement represents a benefit or drawback of globalization.

- Less expensive goods and services
- Possibility of losing jobs
- Greater variety of goods and services
- Access to goods and services anywhere in the world
- Possibility of companies going out of business if they cannot compete effectively
- Possibility of raising world living standards
- Possibility of loss of local cultures

Call on volunteers to explain their reasoning. Invite other students to comment for or against the previous speaker's opinion, giving reasons for their own position.

L1 L2 Differentiate Go over each element of the diagram on the Visual Glossary to help students understand globalization.

L4 Differentiate Challenge students to choose one statement about globalization that they think is a drawback and to write an essay identifying positive features of that aspect of globalization.

PERSONAL FINANCE ACTIVITY

To help students make safe choices, you may want to use the Personal Finance Handbook lessons on identity theft and shopping online on pages PF36–PF37 and PF38–PF39, along with the activity worksheets (Personal Finance All-in-One, pp. 93–94, 96–97).

Differentiated Resources

L1 L2 Guided Reading and Review (Unit 7 All-in-One, p. 76)

L1 L2 Land Use, Urbanization, and Development (Unit 7 All-in-One, p. 78)

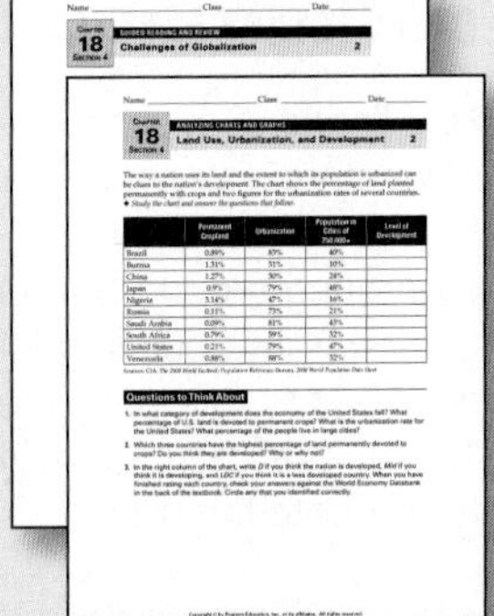

Answer

Checkpoint Satellites allow customers far from each other to converse quickly and clearly. Computers can move information quickly anywhere in the world.

DEBATE

Review the discussion of multinational corporations on pages 504–505. Use the Opinion Line strategy (p. T28) to give students the opportunity to debate the issue. Pose the question: "Should LDCs encourage multinational corporations to invest in their economies?" Along one wall of the room, post three labels reading "Yes," "No," and "Under some conditions." Invite students to stand in the area that represents their opinion.

Give a few individuals in each group a chance to state the reasons for their position. After they have done so, give students a minute or two to revise their original positions and move to a new area if they wish. Call on students who changed their minds to explain what arguments they found most persuasive.

L1 L2 Differentiate Encourage students to take notes on the multinationals issue by recording arguments under the headings "For" and "Against." After the Opinion Line exercise, call on students to write a paragraph stating and explaining their final position on the issue.

L4 Differentiate After the debate on multinationals, call on students to take the role of the CEO of a multinational corporation wishing to establish a manufacturing plant in an LDC. Challenge them to write a speech that they could deliver to the LDC's leaders explaining why the country should welcome the company. Remind them that they need to address possible objections to the company's presence.

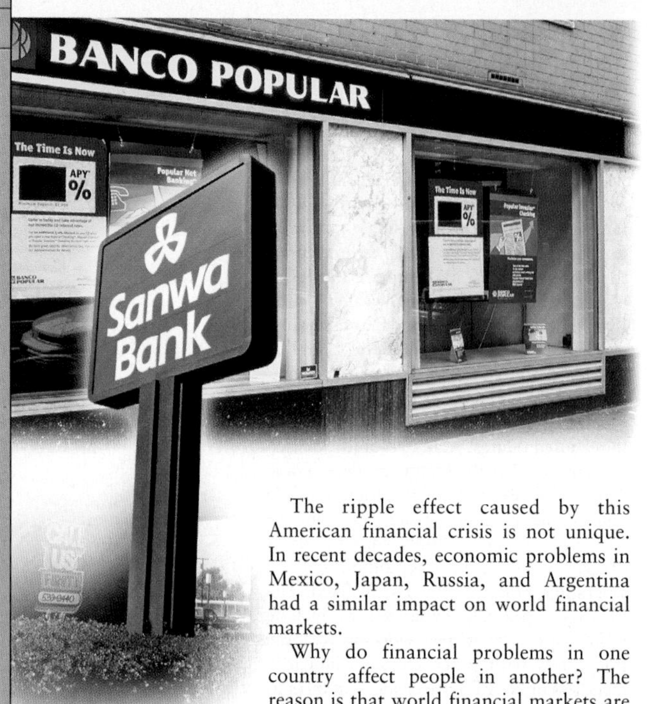

▲ Banks are among the most influential multinational corporations. Institutions like the Sanwa Bank of Japan and the Puerto Rico–based Banco Popular have branches in dozens of countries.

The ripple effect caused by this American financial crisis is not unique. In recent decades, economic problems in Mexico, Japan, Russia, and Argentina had a similar impact on world financial markets.

Why do financial problems in one country affect people in another? The reason is that world financial markets are closely connected. Investors around the world watch the values of stocks in many different markets. They move quickly to buy the stock of promising companies in whatever country they find them—and sell just as quickly at any sign of trouble.

Another reason for the widespread impact of these financial crises is the booming trade in currencies. As you read in Chapter 17, most of the world now follows a flexible exchange-rate system. The values of various national currencies go up or down every day. Investors holding money in a particular currency sell it off if the value of that currency declines. As sales of a country's currency mount, its economy will suffer.

These effects do not just hurt investors who risk their money in the hope of making profits. They have an impact on ordinary people as well. Banks buy assets in other countries. If the value of those assets falls, the banks have less capital available to make loans to people in their own countries.

Multinational Corporations

As you read in Section 2, the expansion of multinational corporations has sparked controversy. Some economists argue that these companies have a beneficial impact on the countries where they set up operations. For example, multinationals have been credited with much of the development of Eastern Europe after the fall of communism:

> **"[Multinationals] brought countless benefits. These include … improving the environment; rescuing collapsing factories and rotting company towns; establishing new industries; laying new telecommunications networks; stabilizing banking systems … and facing down corrupt vested interests in governments that in too many cases had plundered their own countries."**
>
> —Paul Lewis, "Harnessing the Power of the Multinationals"

Multinationals have the capital to introduce technology to developing countries, offer jobs, train the labor force, and provide the opportunity for related services and industries to develop.

Critics, however, claim that multinationals do little to aid less developed countries. Some point out that most of the profits go, not to the host LDC, but to the foreign owners of the corporation. Others say that multinationals create far fewer job opportunities than they claim. Many of the industries are highly mechanized, allowing high productivity with little labor. Thus, they provide few jobs relative to the massive size of the labor pool and may even drive traditional craftworkers out of business.

Another area of controversy is wages. Generally, wages in less developed countries are very low compared to wages in industrialized nations. Supporters argue that the lower wages are justified since the cost of living in LDCs is also relatively low. In addition, many of the people employed by multinationals might not have jobs at all otherwise. Critics argue that multinationals benefit unfairly from the low wages. Also, many LDCs do not require companies to provide the same high standard of working conditions that industrialized countries require.

Background Note

Fair Trade One response to the criticisms of multinationals is the fair trade movement. Fair trade is based on the principles of helping LDCs develop while paying fair wages in the context of the local economy: building safe, healthy workplaces; promoting growth that does not threaten the environment; respecting cultural traditions and building long-term relationships with suppliers. Many corporations now do business following these principles. The fair trade movement had its origins in the 1940s. The International Fair Trade Association is a global network of groups working to promote fair trade.

Job Loss

Much of the debate over multinationals and globalization focuses on its impact on less developed countries. However, people in developed nations are equally concerned about a related issue—job loss.

In the global economy, companies may move parts of their operations to other countries. This practice is known as **offshoring.** Offshoring may involve a single process, as when an American bank hires a call center in India or Kenya to handle its telemarketing. Or it can be total, as when a multinational manufacturer closes a plant in the United States to build one in another country. In either case, the result is job loss. As you learned in Chapter 13, movement of jobs overseas is one of the key causes of structural unemployment.

CHECKPOINT ***What problems can result from interconnected financial markets?***

Population Shifts

People have always moved from place to place in hopes of building a better life. Globalization and development have accelerated these population shifts.

Rural to Urban

Much of this migration takes place within a nation's borders. In many less developed countries, cities offer more job opportunities than rural areas. As a result, large numbers of people in villages are streaming into cities. In 1950, less than 20 percent of the people in Africa and Asia lived in cities. By 2005, nearly 40 percent did. Today, thirteen of the world's twenty largest cities are located in less developed countries. Each of them has more than 10 million people.

Rapid urbanization has caused several problems. Cities have grown so fast that they cannot provide enough housing, schools, and sanitation for all of the people. Poverty, crime, and disease are widespread.

Country to Country

Each year, millions of workers leave less developed countries in the hopes of finding jobs in developed nations. This migration has an economic impact on both the source country and the destination country.

Most immigrants come legally, with proper visas and proof of work. While their labor contributes to a country's GNP, they may face resentment from native-born workers who view the newcomers as competition for jobs. Other people come without legal authorization. Illegal immigration raises security concerns and puts a strain on public resources.

Migration also affects the source country. Once they find work, many immigrants send regular cash payments to their families back home. These **remittances** provide an important source of income. The World Bank estimated that, in 2006 alone, the value of remittances to LDCs totaled $250 billion.

offshoring the movement of parts of a company's operations to another country

remittances cash payments sent by workers who have migrated to a new country to family members in their home country

FUTURE WATCH Global Impact

Immigrants On the Move
As in the past, immigrants continue to come to the United States from all over the world. However, illegal immigration has become a major political issue. It raises concerns about national security and the distribution of scarce resources. ***What economic incentives might lead people to immigrate?***

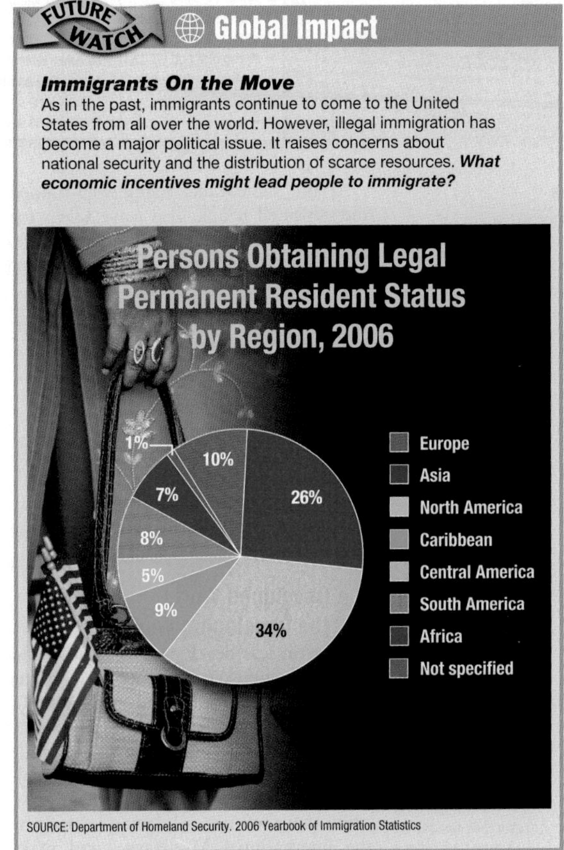

SOURCE: Department of Homeland Security, 2006 Yearbook of Immigration Statistics

COMPARE

To explore the issue of offshoring, display the "Job Losses and Relocation" transparency (Color Transparencies, 18.b). The transparency shows two sets of data—a chart and a map.

Direct students' attention to the chart first. Explain that the chart shows percentages of jobs lost because a business relocated them either within the United States or outside the country. That last figure is percentage of jobs that were lost due to offshoring.

Ask **How does the percentage of jobs lost due to relocation within the United States compare to the number of jobs lost due to offshoring?** *(The number of jobs lost due to offshoring is smaller in each quarter.)* Discuss with students what jobs or industries they think are most likely to be affected by offshoring. Ask them which areas of the country would feel the impact most.

Then direct students' attention to the map. It shows which regions of the United States lost which share of jobs due to relocation and layoffs. Emphasize that this includes both movement of the jobs within the United States and offshoring to another country. Ask them which region was hardest hit and which suffered the fewest job losses. *(The South was hardest hit in each quarter. The Northeast had the smallest share of job losses from offshoring.)* Invite students to speculate on what regional economic conditions might account for these differences.

L4 Differentiate Have students look up data for the most recent four quarters and prepare similar charts and maps. Then have them write a paragraph comparing those results to the ones on the transparency to explain why the situation did or did not change.

Background Note

Migration The Migration Policy Institute compiled these figures for the countries with the most international migrants in a recent year:

United States: 38.35 million
Russia: 12.08 million
Germany: 10.14 million
France: 6.47 million
Saudi Arabia: 6.36 million
Canada: 6.11 million
India: 5.7 million
United Kingdom: 5.41 million
Spain: 4.79 million
Australia: 4.1 million

Answers

Checkpoint Possible answer: Financial problems in one country can have an effect on others.

Future Watch Possible answer: People might leave their home country in the hope of finding work or a better standard of living in another country.

EVALUATE ALTERNATIVES

Remind students that the effects of development on the environment have caused tension, especially between developed nations and LDCs. Ask **Do scientists in developed nations have the right to tell people in LDCs how to use their environment?**

If students respond that they do, challenge them with two other questions:

- **Do people in LDCs have a greater responsibility to improve the lives of their children or to protect the environment?**
- **Do people in LDCs have a right to tell people in developed nations how to use their environment?**

If students respond that scientists do *not* have that right, challenge them with two other questions:

- **Don't experts have a responsibility to point out when problems arise?**
- **Can the environment be improved if all the world's peoples are not sharing in the effort to fix it?**

CREATE A PROFILE

Have students use the Career Link worksheet to record their research for the activity (Unit 7 All-in-One, p. 88).

Answer

Checkpoint Possible answers: The shift to cities can strain the ability to produce jobs, housing, schools, and health services; educated people who leave the country cause a loss of human capital.

FUTURE WATCH

CAREER CENTER
PHYSICAL SCIENCES

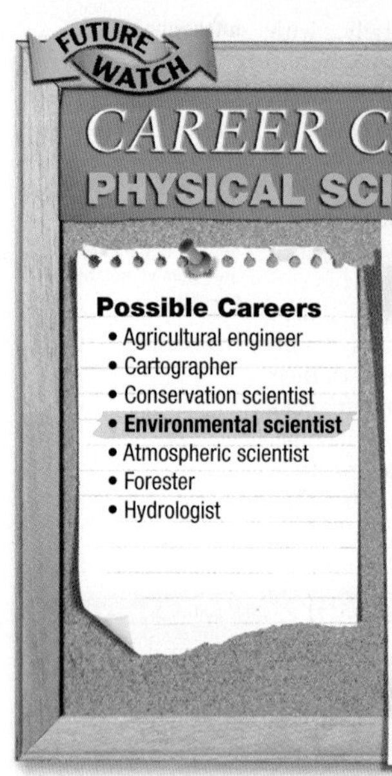

Possible Careers
- Agricultural engineer
- Cartographer
- Conservation scientist
- **Environmental scientist**
- Atmospheric scientist
- Forester
- Hydrologist

Profile: Environmental Scientist

Duties:
- conduct research to identify or eliminate sources of pollutants or hazards
- analyze observations of air, food, water, soil, and other sources
- make recommendations on how best to clean and preserve the environment

Education:
- master's degree in a natural science

Skills:
- computer skills
- excellent interpersonal skills
- strong oral and written communication skills
- physical stamina

Median Annual Salary:
- $58,380 (2007)

Future prospects:
- Job growth for environmental scientists will be strongest at private-sector consulting firms.
- Demand will be spurred largely by rules, which will oblige companies and organizations to comply with complex environmental laws and regulations.

Career Link *Activity*
Choose another career in the physical sciences from the list of possible careers. Create a profile for that career similar to the one for Environmental Scientist.

At the same time, many well-trained and educated people also leave LDCs for well-paying jobs in developed nations. This **"brain drain"** may hurt development by siphoning off vital human capital.

"brain drain" migration of the best-educated people of less developed countries to developed nations

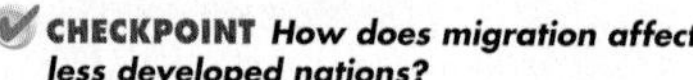

CHECKPOINT ***How does migration affect less developed nations?***

Challenges Ahead

Globalization is creating new opportunities, but also new challenges, for the world's economies. Many of these challenges have become sources of tension between the developed world and the developing world.

The Developed World and the Developing World

Leaders in less developed countries—and even newly industrialized countries—argue that international trade and financial policies favor the wealthier nations. They charge that the trade rules set by the World Trade Organization give preference to developed nations at their expense. They also claim that the financial demands made by the International Monetary Fund make lives more difficult for poor people in their countries.

In an effort to give emerging economies a greater voice, about two dozen countries have formed an organization called the Group of 20. The G-20 includes financial ministers from growing nations such as China, India, Brazil, and Mexico, as well as representatives of the United States and the EU. The G-20 has discussed such issues as promoting growth and how to combat the financing of terrorist operations.

Environmental Protection Versus Development

The environment can be another source of tension. Environmental scientists—mostly based in developed nations—worry that rapid development can cause environmental damage. They seek to promote **sustainable development,** that is, the goal of meeting current development needs without using up the resources needed by future generations.

sustainable development the goal of meeting current development needs without using up resources needed by future generations

On the other hand, leaders in many less developed nations see an urgent need to exploit their resources *now*. They view combating poverty and creating modern economies as a higher priority than protecting the environment. Developed nations, they argue, were able to use resources such as oil without restriction. LDCs now seek the same opportunity.

One major issue is **deforestation,** or large-scale destruction of forests. Many developing nations are cutting down forests at a rapid rate. Cleared land is used for farming and industry, while timber sales fund other projects that create jobs. Environmentalists warn that deforestation contributes to global warming and destroys rare animal and plant species. To such concerns, the president of Brazil replied:

> **"There are meddlers who have no political authority, who emit carbon dioxide like nobody else, who destroy everything they have, and who put forth opinions about what we should do.... We can't allow people to dictate rules to us about what we should do in the Amazon."**
>
> —Luiz Inacio Lula da Silva, quoted in *Terra Daily*, June 5, 2008

Competition for Resources

A related challenge is competition for scarce resources. In some regions, it is increasingly difficult to find enough clean, healthy water to meet the needs of a growing population.

In China, for example, rapid population and economic growth has led to serious contamination of an already uncertain water supply. Some experts warn that reserves of oil and gas are dwindling as well. They fear that, unless new sources of these fuels—or different sources of energy—are found, the world's economies may grind to a halt.

Even if resources do not run out, the cost of scarce water and fuel causes problems. In 2008, world oil prices skyrocketed. Even in developed nations, this inflation strained the financial resources of businesses and consumers. In less developed countries, the impact was even more severe. The world oil crunch became yet another challenge to the struggle of LDCs to build their economies.

✔ CHECKPOINT ***How can environmental protection conflict with economic development?***

The United States in the World Economy

Globalization poses challenges even for the world's most successful economy—our own. For the United States to compete in global markets, American workers must be ready to meet changes in the workplace. And American companies must continue their long tradition of innovation.

Adapting to a Changing Workplace

Information now drives the economy of the United States and the world. Workers need to gain the skills that are necessary to access, understand, and use all sorts of information. Getting as much education as possible is a good first step.

The need for education does not end when people find jobs. Workers must constantly keep up-to-date with new technology so that they can remain productive in their current jobs. Others must learn completely new skills when they find that their existing jobs no longer pay a good wage—or when jobs are lost due to offshoring.

As you read in Chapter 13, some companies provide the retraining that their workers need. When that is not the case, though, workers must take responsibility to learn needed skills. If they fail to do so, they risk being left behind as work moves in a new direction.

deforestation the large-scale destruction of forests

Staying competitive in a global marketplace is one of the main economic challenges facing Americans now and in the future. ***Why might this little boy be afraid to 'come out and play'? What might happen if he doesn't?*** ▼

"Can Billy come out and compete in the global economy?"

EXTEND

Distribute the "Land Use, Urbanization, and Development" worksheet (Unit 7 All-in-One, p. 77). Have students explore the connection between land use and economic development and make predictions about the level of economic development based on land use and urbanization patterns.

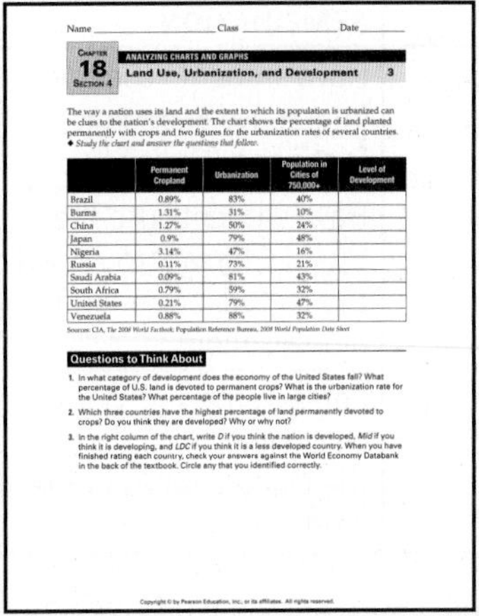

Name ______ Class ______ Date ______

CHAPTER 18 SECTION 4

ANALYZING CHARTS AND GRAPHS

Land Use, Urbanization, and Development 3

The way a nation uses its land and the extent to which its population is urbanized can be clues to the nation's development. The chart shows the percentage of land planted permanently with crops and two figures for the urbanization rates of several countries.
◆ *Study the chart and answer the questions that follow.*

	Permanent Cropland	Urbanization	Population in Cities of 750,000+	Level of Development
Brazil	0.89%	83%	40%	
Burma	1.31%	31%	10%	
China	1.27%	50%	24%	
Japan	0.9%	79%	48%	
Nigeria	3.14%	47%	16%	
Russia	0.11%	73%	21%	
Saudi Arabia	0.09%	81%	43%	
South Africa	0.79%	59%	32%	
United States	0.21%	79%	47%	
Venezuela	0.88%	88%	32%	

Sources: CIA, *The 2008 World Factbook*; Population Reference Bureau, *2008 World Population Data Sheet*

Questions to Think About

1. In what category of development does the economy of the United States fall? What percentage of U.S. land is devoted to permanent crops? What is the urbanization rate for the United States? What percentage of the people live in large cities?
2. Which three countries have the highest percentage of land permanently devoted to crops? Do you think they are developed? Why or why not?
3. In the right column of the chart, write *D* if you think the nation is developed, *Mid* if you think it is developing, and *LDC* if you think it is a less developed country. When you have finished rating each country, check your answers against the World Economy Databank in the back of the textbook. Circle any that you identified correctly.

L1 L2 Differentiate Distribute the "Land Use, Urbanization, and Development" worksheet (Unit 7 All-in-One, p. 78) to give students a vehicle for thinking about the connection between land use and development.

GUIDING QUESTION WRAP UP

Have students return to the section Guiding Question. Review the completed graphic organizer and clarify any misunderstandings. Have a wrap up discussion about the effects of globalization.

Assess and Remediate

L2 L3 Collect the "Land Use, Urbanization, and Development" worksheets and assess student understanding of urbanization's relationship to development.

L3 Assign the Section 4 Assessment questions; identify student misconceptions.

L3 Give Section Quiz A (Unit 7 All-in-One, p. 79).

L2 Give Section Quiz B (Unit 7 All-in-One, p. 80).

(Assess and Remediate continued on p. 508)

Answers

Checkpoint Possible answer: Protecting the environment might mean not fully using resources, or it could result in more costs to install environmentally friendly technology.

Caption Possible answers: The global economy is highly competitive, which can make the idea of coming out to "play" scary. However, if the little boy does not compete, he risks being left behind.

Virtual Economics

L4 Differentiate

Analyzing the WTO Use the following lesson from the NCEE **Virtual Economics *CD-ROM*** to analyze six international institutions, especially the WTO. Click on Browse Economics Lessons, specify grades 9–12, and use the key word *wto.*

In this activity, students will participate in a game to evaluate their comprehension of the international institutions.

LESSON TITLE	**"HEY, HEY! HO, HO! WHY DO WE NEED THE WTO?"**
Type of Activity	Simulation
Complexity	High
Time	100 minutes
NCEE Standards	5, 6, 10, 15, 16

Have students complete the Self-Test Online and continue their work in the **Essential Questions Journal**.

REMEDIATION AND SUGGESTIONS

Use the chart below to help students who are struggling with content.

WEAKNESS	REMEDIATION
Identifying key terms (Questions 4, 5, 6)	Have students use the interactive Economic Dictionary Online.
Causes of globalization (Questions 3, 7)	Have students use the Visual Glossary to review the factors promoting globalization.
Effects of globalization (Questions 1, 2, 4, 5, 6, 8, 9, 10)	Reteach the sections on challenges ahead and the United States in the world economy.

Answer

Checkpoint by learning how to understand and use information and to work closely and smoothly with people of different backgrounds

Another feature of the changing American workplace is greater diversity. The population of the United States has changed. As a result of population shifts, a growing percentage of American workers are foreign-born. There are more Asian Americans and Latinos than in the past. To be productive, American workers must be prepared to work closely with people of different backgrounds.

The Pressure to Compete

Globalization has made economic competition more intense. Consumers in developing nations are demanding a greater variety of products and services. As you read, the growth of India's middle class has led to a boom in shopping malls. In Africa, the number of people who own cellular phones rose from only 2 million in 1998 to over 60 million by 2004. At the same time, more countries are competing to meet this growing demand.

Competition affects business relationships as well. One business might have a long relationship with a local supplier. Yet, if a different supplier can offer lower prices or better service, they will make a deal with that supplier—even when that supplier is located on the other side of the world.

For all these reasons, American companies need to stay competitive. Business managers face constant pressure to cut costs and increase profits. They must insure high productivity to avoid wasting money and work. They need to be constantly on the lookout for better ways to respond to customer needs. Only by staying competitive can American companies thrive.

The Pressure to Innovate

As in the past, growing competition spurs innovation. The companies that develop new products or processes can quickly gain a large share of the world market. For example, in 1996, two young American entrepreneurs began work on the Internet search engine company that became Google. Ten years later, the company had worldwide sales of $10.6 billion.

Still, introducing a new innovation and enjoying its success is not the end of the story. Any new product or service can quickly be replaced by a newer one, developed by another entrepreneur hungry to succeed.

Writer Thomas Friedman, who has studied globalization, says that the new economic world is like a sprint that competitors must run over and over again. Anyone who wins one race cannot guarantee winning a later one. The only solution is to go back to the starting line and—with new innovations to help—run as fast as possible, again and again.

CHECKPOINT ***How can American workers help companies stay competitive?***

SECTION 4 ASSESSMENT

Essential Questions Journal To continue to build a response to the Essential Question, go to your **Essential Questions Journal.**

Guiding Question

1. Use your completed concept web to answer this question: What are the effects of globalization?
2. **Extension** How can you prepare yourself for the global economy?

Key Terms and Main Ideas

3. How did the spread of market economies help promote globalization?
4. Why are many Americans concerned about **offshoring?**
5. How does increased migration lead to **"brain drain"?**
6. Why is **deforestation** controversial?

Critical Thinking

7. **Connect (a)** What role has communications technology played in globalization? **(b)** How might communications be related to changing consumer demands around the world?
8. **Recommend** Suppose you were the finance minister of a nation with a growing economy. Explain why you think trade in the nation's currency should be discouraged or encouraged.
9. **Take a Position** Do you think immigration should be encouraged or more restricted? Explain.

Quick Write

10. Thomas Friedman said globalization means that businesses must constantly innovate to succeed in the global economy. Write an outline and opening paragraph for a newspaper column that discusses the following questions: What can business leaders do to make sure their companies innovate constantly? How can governments help in this effort?

Assessment Answers

1. Possible answers: risk of financial problems in one part of the world spilling over into others; increased competition between nations for goods and resources; greater movement of people and jobs; conflict between developed and less developed nations over environmental issues and the role of multinationals
2. Possible answers: getting higher education or job training; learning innovative skills; learning a foreign language
3. Countries opened their markets, promoted trade, and became more open to foreign investment.
4. because many may become unemployed as their jobs go overseas
5. Educated people are leaving LDCs to find more opportunities in developed countries.
6. Environmental scientists say cutting down forests harms the environment. Leaders in LDCs argue that they have a right to cut down forests to improve their economies.
7. Possible answer: (a) Businesses can hear from customers around the world. (b) Communications can promote trade by making consumers all over the world aware of a wide range of goods and services.
8. Possible answer: Discouraging currency trading would probably freeze trade and foreign investment in the nation, which would be bad for its economy.
9. Possible answers: Encouraged: discouraging immigration means losing the talent and ideas that immigrants bring. Discouraged: Newcomers may compete for jobs and strain public resources.
10. Possible answer: Students might mention investment in R&D, recruitment of workers with innovative thinking, opening the company to worker suggestions for new practices, and frequent experimentation with new products and processes.

QUICK STUDY GUIDE

Chapter 18: Development and Globalization

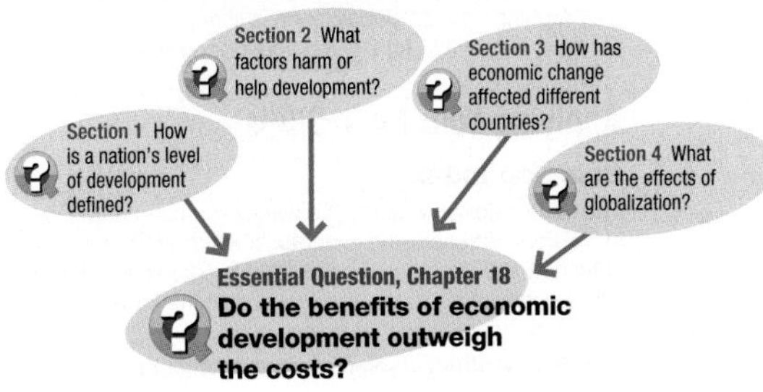

Section 1 How is a nation's level of development defined?
Section 2 What factors harm or help development?
Section 3 How has economic change affected different countries?
Section 4 What are the effects of globalization?
Essential Question, Chapter 18
Do the benefits of economic development outweigh the costs?

Measures of Development

Measure	Developed Countries	Less Developed Countries
Per capita GDP	High	Low
Population growth rate	Low	High
Literacy	High	Low
Life expectancy	High	Low
Infant mortality	Low	High
Labor force	Large percentage manufacturing, services	Large percentage subsistence agriculture
Settlement	Urban	Rural
Energy consumption	High	Low
Consumer goods	Plentiful	Scarce

Economic Dictionary

development, *p. 481*
developed nation, *p. 481*
less developed country, *p. 482*
newly industrialized country, *p. 482*
per capita GDP, *p. 482*
industrialization, *p. 483*
literacy rate, *p. 483*
life expectancy, *p. 483*
infant mortality rate, *p. 484*
subsistence agriculture, *p. 486*
population growth rate, *p. 487*
malnutrition, *p. 491*
internal financing, *p. 491*
foreign investment, *p. 492*
foreign direct investment, *p. 492*
foreign portfolio investment, *p. 492*
debt rescheduling, *p. 493*
stabilization program, *p. 493*
nongovernmental organization, *p. 494*
privatization, *p. 495*
special economic zone, *p. 498*
globalization, *p. 501*
offshoring, *p. 505*
remittances, *p. 505*
"brain drain", *p. 506*
sustainable development, *p. 506*
deforestation, *p. 507*

Economics on the go

Study anytime, anywhere. Download these files today.

Economic Dictionary online	Audio Review online	Action Graph online	Visual Glossary online	How the Economy Works online
Vocabulary Support in English and Spanish	Audio Study Guide in English and Spanish	Animated Charts and Graphs	Animated feature	Animated feature

Download to your computer or mobile device at PearsonSuccessNet.com

ASSIGN THE ESSENTIAL QUESTIONS JOURNAL

After students have finished studying the chapter, they should return to the chapter's essential question in the Essential Questions Journal and complete the activity.

Tell students to go back to the chapter opener and look at the image. Using the information they have gained from studying the chapter, ask **How does this illustrate the main ideas of the chapter?** *(Possible response: The photograph shows life in a country that might be an LDC with a strong tourist industry, showing the connection between wealthier and poorer nations in the global economy.)*

STUDY TIPS

To help students prepare for college, teach them active reading. Suggest that they begin each section by reviewing the list of terms, illustrations, features, and subheadings. Based on that review, they should develop a list of questions that they think the section will help them answer. As they read, they should look for those answers. While reading, they should also develop new questions and seek the answers to them in the material that follows.

Economics on the go Have students download the digital resources available at Economics on the Go for review and remediation.

Assessment at a Glance

TESTS AND QUIZZES

Section Assessments

Section Quizzes A and B, **Unit 7 All-in-One**

Self-Test Online

Chapter Assessments

Chapter Tests A and B, **Unit 7 All-in-One**

Economic Detective, **Unit 7 All-in-One**

Document-Based Assessment, p. 511

Exam*View*

AYP Monitoring Assessments

PERFORMANCE ASSESSMENT

Teacher's Edition, pp. 482, 488, 493, 498, 506, 507

Simulation Activities, Chapter 18

Virtual Economics, pp. 483, 489, 497, 507

Essential Questions Journal, Chapter 18

Assessment Rubrics

Chapter Assessment

1. (a) poor education, shorter life expectancy, and high infant mortality rates (b) Investing in schools will improve education; better health services and nutrition will increase life expectancy and reduce infant mortality. (c) Possible answer: Improving education and developing more high-paying jobs would help reverse the other trends.
2. (a) Though the wages the MNCs pay are higher than wages in the LDC, investment in the LDC helps promote economic growth there. (b) environmental damage, profits drained out of the country, low wages and poor working conditions (c) Possible answer: LDCs are better off with the investments of MNCs. They create jobs and link the country to the global trade network.
3. (a) Russia is the world's seventh-largest economy, much of its foreign debt has been repaid, and foreign investors were encouraged to invest. (b) China has become the world's second largest economy, with a wide array of consumer goods available in cities. (c) Possible answer: China, because it has grown more and its growth is founded on industrial expansion
4. (a) encouraging economic growth without using up resources needed by future generations (b) Possible answer: Use part of the forests but continue to plant trees to preserve resources.
5. Possible answers: (a) expanded trade, power of multinationals, interconnected financial markets, widespread availability of goods, movement of people (b) Globalization is here to stay. (c) Students should state an opinion and support it with reasons.
6. (a) $505 (b) $55 (c) $285 (d) $95
7. Wages in Brazil are 12 percent of wages in Germany.
8. Australia, Canada, Japan, France, and Germany because they have relatively high wages
9. Possible answers: Brazil, Mexico, Hong Kong, Taiwan, Poland, Portugal; Factors: education of workforce; investment required; infrastructure; shipping, energy costs; tax policies; environmental regulations; political stability.
10. Organize students into ten groups, and assign each group a different country. Give the groups time to research and brainstorm. Check their worksheets before they modify the activity.
11. Discuss the various groups' suggestions as a class. Guide the class to comment on the strengths and drawbacks of each proposal.

CHAPTER 18 ASSESSMENT

Self-Test online To test your understanding of key terms and main ideas, visit **PearsonSuccessNet.com**

Key Terms and Main Ideas

To make sure you understand the key terms and main ideas of this chapter, review the Checkpoint and Section Assessment questions and look at the Quick Study Guide on the preceding page.

Critical Thinking

1. **Analyze (a)** List three conditions that help determine the quality of life in a less developed country. **(b)** Identify one program or policy that could help change each of these three conditions. **(c)** Which of these conditions do you think it is most important to change in order to promote faster development? Why?
2. **Take a Position (a)** What arguments are given in favor of multinational investing in LDCs? **(b)** What arguments are given against such investment? **(c)** Which side do you agree with and why?
3. **Compare (a)** What success has Russia had in establishing a free market economy? **(b)** What success has China had? **(c)** Which nation do you think has been more successful? Why?
4. **Make a Decision (a)** What do environmentalists mean when they talk about sustainable development? **(b)** Suppose you were the leader of a developing nation. Would you favor clearing more forestland in order to provide immediate jobs and income or preserving the resources of the forest for future generations? Give reasons for your choice.

5. **Evaluate (a)** Describe three characteristics of globalization. **(b)** Explain the meaning of the following statement: "Arguing against globalization is like arguing against the laws of gravity." **(c)** Do you agree or disagree? Explain.

Applying Your Math Skills

Using an Index

The table below compares the wages for manufacturing jobs in different nations using an index in which U.S. wages are valued at 100. Numbers above 100 indicate higher wages; those below show lower wages. Look at the index and answer the questions that follow.

Visit PearsonSuccessNet.com for additional math help.

Index of Manufacturing Wages

Country	Value	Country	Value
Australia	105	South Korea	57
Brazil	17	Taiwan	27
Canada	101	France	104
Mexico	11	Germany	140
Hong Kong	24	Poland	19
Japan	92	Portugal	31

6. For every $500 a U.S. manufacturing worker earns, how much would a worker in the following countries earn: **(a)** Canada, **(b)** Mexico, **(c)** South Korea, **(d)** Poland?
7. Express the difference between manufacturing wages in Germany and Brazil as a percentage.
8. Based on this index, which of the nations shown would you say had the most highly developed economies? Why?
9. If you were the head of a multinational company trying to determine where to locate a new factory, in which of these countries would you consider building a factory? What factors besides wages would you consider?

Essential Question Activity

Essential Questions Journal To respond to the chapter Essential Question, go to your **Essential Questions Journal.**

10. Complete the activity to answer the Essential Question **Do the benefits of economic development outweigh the costs?** For this activity, the class will be divided into ten groups. Each group will take the part of a panel of officials at the International Monetary Fund investigating economic conditions in a different LDC. Use the library or Internet resources to find basic social, economic, and political information about your country. Using the worksheet in your Essential Questions Journal or the electronic worksheet available at **PearsonSuccessNet.com,** gather the following information:
    (a) What are current social and economic conditions in the nation?
    (b) What resources or economic advantages does the nation have?
    (c) What economic problems does the nation face?
    (d) What is the nation's political system, and how stable is it?
11. **Modify** Based on the information that was gathered, members of each group should meet to create a development plan for the nation they are studying. The development plan should address the following issues:
    (a) What new or existing goods or services should be produced and sold? Why?
    (b) How should the nation obtain needed development funds?
    (c) What social or political changes will be needed for this program to succeed?
    (d) What social and economic benefits will result from this investment?
    (e) What potential negative effects might result from this development program? How can they be prevented?
    Each group will present its conclusions to the rest of the class.

WebQuest online The Economics WebQuest challenges students to use 21st century skills to answer the Essential Question.

THE ESSENTIAL
VIDEO
By Students For Students
For videos on Essential Questions, go to PearsonSuccessNet.com

Remind students to continue to develop an Essential Questions video. Guidelines and a production binder are available at www.PearsonSuccessNet.com.

Does movement of jobs overseas hurt or help the U.S. economy?

Some U.S. companies are sending jobs overseas, a process called *outsourcing* or *offshoring*. Economists say these decisions make sense: the companies save money, and keep higher-paying jobs at home. Workers say that these decisions are hurting American workers and the nation's economy.

Document A

Document B

"Concerns about a massive loss of jobs due to offshoring do not seem justified. Companies have found outsourcing abroad profitable primarily for jobs that can be routinized and sharply defined.... For the foreseeable future, however, most high-value work will require creative interaction among employees, interaction which is facilitated by physical proximity and personal contact. Moreover, in many fields, closeness to customers and knowledge of local conditions are also of great importance. These observations suggest that, for some considerable time, outsourcing abroad will be uneconomical for many types of jobs, particularly high-value jobs."

—Ben Bernanke, Chairman of the Federal Reserve, May 2007

Document C

Professional and business services: "Employment is projected to grow 2.1 percent annually, slowing from the 2.7-percent rate experienced from 1996 to 2006, mainly due to productivity gains and offshore outsourcing."

Computer systems design and related services: "Employment is projected to increase by 489,400 jobs ... by 2016. This represents an average annual growth rate of 3.3 percent, which is less robust than the rate experienced during the previous decade, largely due to productivity increases and offshore outsourcing."

Software publishing: "Relative to the previous decade, slower employment growth is expected as the industry matures and cost pressures lead to further outsourcing of routine tasks offshore."

—Bureau of Labor Statistics, Nov. 2007

ANALYZING DOCUMENTS

Use your knowledge of economic systems and Documents A, B, and C to answer questions 1–3.

1. **The picketers in Document A are most likely to be**
   A. managers of multinational corporations.
   B. consumers.
   C. stock investors.
   D. workers.

2. **According to Document B, outsourcing would be least likely to affect**
   A. computer programmers.
   B. factory workers.
   C. healthcare workers.
   D. telephone support staff.

3. **Document C predicts that slow job growth is not due just to outsourcing but also to**
   A. decline in manufacturing.
   B. declining consumer demand.
   C. lack of innovation.
   D. increases in productivity.

WRITING ABOUT ECONOMICS

Whether outsourcing is hurting American workers and the U.S. economy is a hotly debated issue. Use the documents on this page and resources on the Web site below to answer the question: ***Does movement of jobs overseas hurt or help the U.S. economy?*** Use the sources to support your opinion.

In Partnership

THE WALL STREET JOURNAL. CLASSROOM EDITION

To read more about isssues related to this topic, visit **PearsonSuccessNet.com**

Document-Based Assessment

ANALYZING DOCUMENTS

1. D
2. C
3. D

WRITING ABOUT ECONOMICS

Possible answer: *Advantages of outsourcing:* This step allows companies to remain competitive; high-quality, high-wage jobs remain; outsourcing helps lower the cost of goods. *Disadvantages of outsourcing:* This action costs Americans jobs, replacing high-wage jobs with low-paying service jobs and leading to lower tax revenues and declining communities.

Student essay should demonstrate an understanding of the issues involved in the outsourcing activity. Use the following as guidelines to assess the essay.

L2 Differentiate Students use all documents on the page to support their thesis.

L3 Differentiate Students use the documents on this page and additional information available online at www.PearsonSuccessNet.com to support their answer.

L4 Differentiate Students incorporate information provided in the textbook and online at www.PearsonSuccessNet.com[end and include additional research to support their opinion.

Go Online to www.PearsonSuccessNet.com for a student rubric and extra documents.

Economics online *All print resources are available on the Teacher's Resource Library CD-ROM and online at* www.PearsonSuccessNet.com.

 **Essential Question**

How might scarcity divide our world or bring it together?

BELLRINGER

Ask students to read the paragraph under the Essential Question. Then have volunteers suggest examples of how scarcity could divide our world or bring it together.

EXPLAIN

Before you read aloud the second excerpt by Jacques Diouf, you may want to explain that the UN Food and Agriculture Organization (FAO) works to defeat hunger worldwide. The FAO provides a neutral way for nations to discuss agreements and policies. It also helps less developed countries modernize their food industries and provide nutrition for their citizens.

DISCUSS

Have students review the quotations on the page. Ask students to explain the impact of scarcity on the global economy. **Why are developing countries highly dependent on environmental resources?** *(They do not have the resources for an industrial economy, so exploiting natural resources is the quickest way to build their economies.)* **Why is it important for the world to join together to address the scarcity of clean water?** *(A lack of clean water puts financial resources and the health of nations' citizens at risk.)*

L2 Differentiate Pair students to read the articles and summarize the main thesis. Ask them to give any supporting details or arguments to the thesis.

ANALYZE A CARTOON

Have students silently examine the cartoon. Have them work in small groups to discuss what issue the cartoonist is trying to convey. Have small groups work together to create their own humorous cartoon about an economic issue. Invite volunteers to share their cartoons with the class.

BULLETIN BOARD ACTIVITY

Have students revisit the Unit Essential Question articles that they have posted as they have studied the chapters. Have them discuss the relevance of the articles to the question and whether their opinions have changed since they first read the article.

EXTEND

Have students complete their work on the Essential Questions Video and present their work to the class.

L4 Differentiate Have students find one circumstance where nations either worked together or disagreed over scarce water. Ask them to explain how the nations dealt with the situation.

Unit 7 Challenge

Essential Question, Unit 7

How might scarcity divide our world or bring it together?

THE ESSENTIAL
VIDEO
By Students For Students
For videos on Essential Questions, go to PearsonSuccessNet.com

In the global economy of the future, will scarcity lead to further interdependence—or will it lead to conflict? Look at the opinions below, keeping in mind the Essential Question: How might scarcity divide our world or bring it together?

"Preliminary research indicates that scarcities of critical environmental resources—especially of cropland, freshwater, and forests—contribute to violence in many parts of the world. These environmental scarcities usually do not cause wars among countries, but they can generate severe social stresses within countries, helping to stimulate . . . ethnic clashes, and urban unrest. Such civil violence particularly affects developing societies because they are, in general, highly dependent on environmental resources and less able to buffer themselves from the social crises that environmental scarcities cause."

—Thomas F. Homer-Dixon, *Environment, Scarcity, and Violence*

"The potential exists to provide an adequate and sustainable supply of quality water for all, today and in the future. But there is no room for complacency. It is our common responsibility to take the challenge of today's global water crisis and address it in all of its aspects and dimensions."

—Jacques Diouf, UN Food and Agriculture Organization Director-General, March 2007

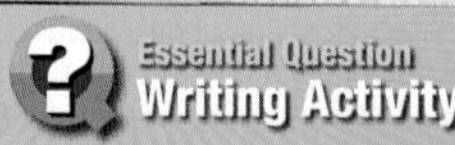
Essential Question
Writing Activity

Consider the different views of economics expressed in the sources on this page and what you have learned about the global economy. ***Then write a well-constructed essay expressing your view of the impact of scarcity on the world economy.***

Writing Guidelines

- Address all aspects of the Essential Question Writing Activity.
- Support the theme with relevant facts, examples, and details.
- Use a logical and clear plan of organization.
- Introduce the theme by establishing a framework that is beyond a simple restatement of the question and conclude with a summation of the theme.

For help in writing a Persuasive Essay, refer to the *Writer's Handbook* in the Reference section, page S-5.

Essential Questions Journal

To respond to the unit Essential Question, go to your **Essential Questions Journal.**

Essential Question Writing Activity

Before students begin the writing activity, remind them to skim through the unit chapters to read the headings on each page. Have them read through any notes they took and review their chapter assessments and chapter projects.

Students should write a two-paragraph article. Paragraph one should outline how scarcity could divide the world. Paragraph two should explain how scarcity could bring the world together.

L2 Differentiate Students should write a paragraph that explains how scarcity impacts the world economy, providing detailed examples.

L4 Differentiate Students should write a three-paragraph article that provides relevant examples of how scarcity impacts the world economy.

Before students begin work, distribute the Writing Assessment rubric, available at the Online Teacher Center at PearsonSuccessNet.com.

Personal Finance Handbook

REFERENCE SECTION

Personal Finance Handbook

The Personal Finance Handbook can be taught as a separate unit of study or can be integrated into the study of the principles of economics. Each Student Edition chapter includes a suggested point of use for specific Personal Finance topics.

A lesson plan for each topic is in the Teacher's Edition, with additional background notes and suggestions for differentiated instruction. There is a Web Quest activity online for each topic that will expand the lesson and connect it to the students' lives. Questions in the Exam*View* Test Bank enable you to integrate Personal Finance assessment into chapter or unit tests or to create a specific test for Personal Finance.

Teacher Resources are available on the Online Teacher Center at PearsonSuccessNet.com and the Teacher's Resource Library CD-ROM.

Your Fiscal Fitness: An Introduction

Get Started

LESSON GOALS

Students will:

- Become familiar with basic financial terms by comparing fiscal fitness to physical fitness.
- Practice making financial choices by outlining what students might choose to do with $100.
- Contrast the results of various personal financial decisions by completing a decision tree.

DIFFERENTIATED INSTRUCTION KEY

L1 Special Needs
L2 Basic
ELL English Language Learners
LPR Less Proficient Readers
L3 All Students
L4 Advanced Students

Teach

BRAINSTORM

Review with students how staying fiscally fit is similar to staying physically fit through exercise and eating well. Point out the similarities between working at a job and playing sports: in each case, effort brings reward. Ask **What are two similarities between saving for the future and working out?** *(Possible responses: Both require discipline; both need to be done consistently; both can be done in a way that best suits an individual.)*

L1 L2 ELL LPR Differentiate To help students who are struggling readers, preteach vocabulary words such as *fiscal*, *discipline*, and *gratification*.

L4 Differentiate Ask students to find an article about U.S. saving habits. Have them read the article and summarize it for the class.

L3 Differentiate To assess students' understanding of personal finance assign the Self-Test (Personal Finance All-in-One, p. 28).

Your Fiscal Fitness: An Introduction

No pain, no gain. It applies as much to fiscal fitness as it does to physical fitness.

Think Long-term

If you start investing $40 a week at a 5 percent rate of return, in 20 years you will have accumulated $17,800. If you get a higher return, say 7 percent, then by the time you retire in 45 years, you would have $163,688.

"Whoa! Slow down! 20 years? Retirement? I'm still living at home! I don't even own my first car yet! Who do you think you are—my parents?"

If that's your reaction, you're not alone. A great many high school students do not think much about their financial future. They also don't like to get stern lectures from Mom or Dad—whether it's about financial planning or about those 5,000 extra text messages that appeared on last month's cellphone bill.

But let's face it: free room and board doesn't last forever. And often, it comes to an end soon after you get handed a diploma. At some point in the not too distant future, the bills in the mail will be yours.

The fact is that responsible financial citizens were not born that way. Even your parents had to learn how to comparison shop, avoid impulse buying, and put money aside that they would much rather spend on fun. Chances are they made mistakes along the way. And they wish you could avoid all the same pitfalls.

Take a Checkup

Start by taking a good look at your own money habits. Are you a big spender? Moderate saver? Do you save anything at all? The answer is pretty easy to figure out. If you have an unexpected windfall, a bigger than expected birthday check, or an opportunity to earn overtime money, what do you do with the money? Save it all? Save half? Look to see what you can buy now?

You don't have time to waste. Mess up your credit rating now and you could be paying the price until you're in your thirties. You might find yourself living at home after college and beyond. (And which sounds cooler to you—writing a check for your own apartment, or paying rent for the same bedroom you had in the sixth grade?)

GO FIGURE

$269,040

The estimated cost of raising a child born in 2007 through age 17.

SOURCE: United States Department of Agriculture. "Expenditures on Children by Families, 2007"

Skip the Fats, Go for the Protein!

It comes down to fiscal fitness. Developing a solid, fiscal muscle also involves training or budgeting, short and long-term goal setting, and most of all patience. Personal finance, like athletics, requires discipline.

ON TRACK TO FINANCIAL CITIZENSHIP

Discipline is one of the qualities that defines a winner. If you want to come out on top, learn the rules of good financial citizenship and put them into action.

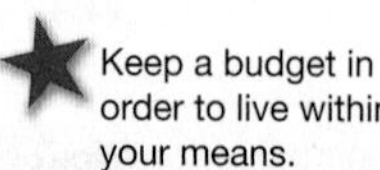

Keep a budget in order to live within your means.

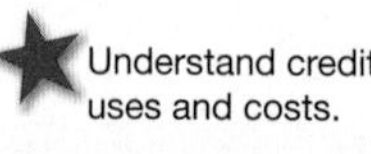

Understand credit uses and costs.

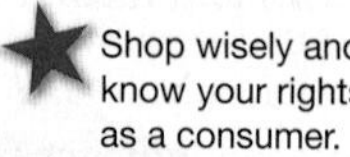

Shop wisely and know your rights as a consumer.

Background Note

Is It Free? In his book *Predictably Irrational: The Hidden Forces That Shape Our Decisions* (HarperCollins Publishers, 2008), MIT behavioral economist Daniel Ariely describes his studies of consumers' buying decisions. In one experiment, each person received three Hershey's Kisses. They were then offered a choice: trade one kiss (about 1/6 ounce each) for a one-ounce Snickers bar, or trade two kisses for a two-ounce bar. In this case, 93 percent chose to swap two kisses for the larger bar. However, when the offer changed so that the one-ounce bar was free and the two-ounce bar "cost" one kiss, 70 percent of consumers chose the small bar. They ended up with just under 1.5 ounces of chocolate. If instead they had traded one kiss for the larger bar, their chocolate would have totaled more than two ounces. Ariely calls this "the power of zero," and contends that the word *free* leads people to make irrational choices.

Preparing for a long race often involves delayed gratification. An athlete will sacrifice fast-food because it's bad for his health, but healthy eating will pay off in the long run. The same is true of investing in your future. It may mean putting off purchases today for financial security sometime later on.

That's easy to say but hard to do, especially if you want to keep up with your peers. You and your dollars are the target of marketers and advertisers. According to a national survey, teenagers are rabid consumers of high-tech products. About 75 percent of U.S. teenagers own a cellphone, 60 percent have an MP3 player, and 43 percent have a car.

Savvy Savers Today's teens spend more than previous generations of teens. This 2007 survey, however, shows that many teens do understand the importance of saving and have begun to develop good saving habits.

What percentage of your income, from a job or your allowance, do you save?

Response	Percentage
I save at least 75% of my income every month.	15.6
I save 25–75% of my income every month.	51.4
I save less than 25% of my income every month.	21.9
I do not save any of my income.	11.2

Note: 1,512 teens between the ages of 13 and 18 were surveyed
SOURCE: Junior Achievement Personal Finance 2007: Executive Summary

The Long Race

The spirit is willing but the flesh is weak. The impulse to get what we want now is far stronger than the motivation to save for something that is months or even years down the road. You may have to trick yourself into saving by promising yourself a reward when you have met certain goals.

Obstacles

What could slow down your progress? One outstanding speed bump is credit card abuse. You don't want to join the ranks of those who struggle to pay their credit card balance in full every month. They let matters slide—failing to balance their checkbooks, check their credit card statements, or keep an eye on bank fees and interest rates. You want to develop the fiscal awareness that will keep you out of trouble.

Grow Your Money

Despite the difficulty of thinking long-term, 65 percent of teens actually admit that they want to learn how to grow their money. This is good news. Even better, 84 percent of teens have savings, with an average amount of $1,044. Fueling those savings is their attitude that the future is now. Savings could translate into a car and college in the short run and a secure life and retirement in the years to come. With the right attitude, you're ready for basic training.

In no time at all, the following words will be part of your conversation. *Budgeting*—how to spend your income in such a way that there's something left over to invest. *Compounding*—how saving a little now can translate into big money later on in life. *Investing*—why the stock market can be both friend and foe. (Over the last 50 years or more, the stock market has averaged a higher return than bank accounts or bonds.)

Ready, set, grow.

RESPONSIBLE CITIZEN

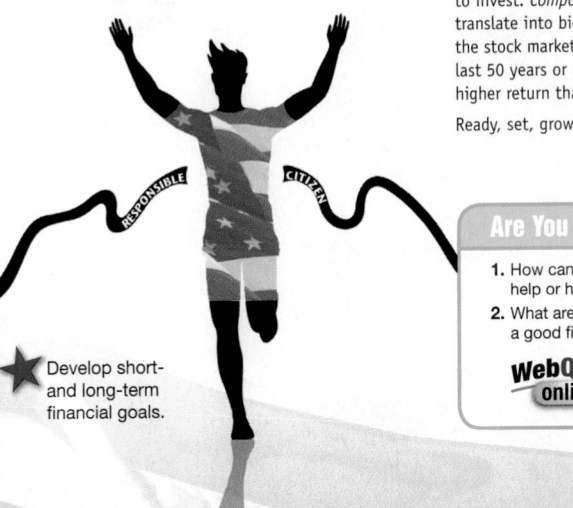

★ Develop short- and long-term financial goals.

Are You Ready?

1. How can your own spending habits help or hinder you?
2. What are some key steps to staying on a good financial track?

WebQuest online To learn more about this topic, visit PearsonSuccessNet.com

COMPARE

Have students look at the chart about saving on page PF3. Ask students to consider in which category they consider themselves to be.

Have students suppose that they have been given $100. They must decide what they will do with the money. Have students write down how they would apportion the money. Emphasize that there is no right or wrong answer to the question.

Then have volunteers describe their decisions. Ask **When you spent the money, what did you give up?** Remind students that what they had to give up is a trade-off.

DISTRIBUTE ACTIVITY WORKSHEET

Distribute the "It's Your Choice" worksheet (Personal Finance All-in-One, pp. 30–31). Discuss how to go about setting up a decision-making grid in order to assess different modes of transportation to school. Have students complete the grid on the worksheet and answer the questions. Have them discuss their choices in pairs or small groups.

L2 Differentiate Have students work in pairs or small groups to complete the worksheet.

After students have completed the worksheet, ask them to give examples of trade-offs that they had to make when they made each choice.

EXTEND

Ask students to choose two goals they would consider to be long-term. Have them determine a time frame for each item. For example, they might want to have a car in six months; they might want to have money saved for college in a year. Have students work individually or with a partner to list possible short-term goals that could lead toward their long-term goals.

Assess and Remediate

L3 Collect the "It's Your Choice" worksheets and assess student understanding of the considerations involved in making decisions.

L3 Collect the Self-Test and use the results to guide your instruction.

Answers

Are You Ready? 1. Student responses should indicate that they have thought about their habits, such as how they spend their allowance or earnings, whether they save money, and so on. 2. Key steps might include not buying on credit, not borrowing money, not making impulse purchases.

Get Started

LESSON GOALS

Students will:

- Understand the reasons for a budget.
- Explain how a budget can help them achieve financial goals.
- Learn how they spend money by keeping a spending journal.
- Differentiate between wants and needs by completing a chart, and identify changes they could make in their personal spending behavior.

DIFFERENTIATED INSTRUCTION KEY

- **L1** Special Needs
- **L2** Basic
  - **ELL** English Language Learners
  - **LPR** Less Proficient Readers
- **L3** All Students
- **L4** Advanced Students

Teach

ANALYZE A CARTOON

Display the "Fixed Income" transparency (Color Transparencies, p. PF.a) and ask students to state the problem characterized in the cartoon. Ask **Is this a realistic picture of the problem people who make a budget face? Why?** *(Yes. People often spend more than they earn.)*

DISCUSS

Tell students that most millionaires have budgets. Help them conclude that one reason millionaires have money is because they pay attention to how they spend it. Then ask **How many of you know how much money you spent on beverages last week? How many of you know how much money you'll spend on gas next week?**

Discuss how knowing the answers to these questions is a step toward financial security.

ROLE-PLAY

Ask four volunteers to imagine they are renting an apartment together. After paying rent and utilities, they have $100 left. Have them role-play a conversation about spending the money on needs or wants. Assign two students to each position. Discuss why it can be a difficult decision.

L2 Differentiate Draw a T-chart with columns for *wants* and *needs*. Have students add examples.

Wise Choices for Your Money

Learning how to live within your means will help you make the most of what you have and to plan for a more secure future.

Budgeting 101

A **budget** is simply a plan for spending and saving. The word may conjure up images of driving a junk car or eating canned spaghetti every night. But the reality can be just the opposite. In fact, most millionaires use a budget to manage their money. And most of them started early.

Spending Awareness

Surveys show that almost one half of Americans between the ages of 13 and 18 know how to budget their money. That's the good news. The bad news is more than half don't. Which group do you fall into? Take this quick quiz:

1. How much money did you spend on beverages—from coffee or water to energy drinks—last week?
2. How much money will you spend on gas next week?
3. How long will it take you to save up for the most expensive thing you'd like to buy?

If you could answer these questions without much trouble, you've already taken the first steps to good money management. If you didn't have a clue, maybe it's time to think about making a budget.

Good Habits Start Early

Now here's another question. Did you ever ask for money to spend on concert tickets—or a piece of jewelry, or a ski trip—only to hear *"You don't need it, and we can't afford it"*? Odds are you didn't think of it as an economics lesson. But according to surveys, students who learned about money management at home scored higher than those who learned about it only in school.

A Balancing Act

Budgeting is a balancing act between income and expenses. It also means weighing your needs against your wants.

Income and Expenses

To begin creating a budget, follow these steps.

1. Make a list of your earnings per month from all sources. Add these up to calculate your expected monthly income.
2. For one month, keep a record of everything you spend, from chewing gum to car payments. Collect receipts or write everything in a notebook. Make sure you don't leave anything out. (And that includes savings!)
3. At the end of the month, organize your spending into categories such as food, entertainment, and car payments. Total the amount in each category.
4. On a sheet of paper, list your income and expenses.

If your total expenses are less than your total income, you're doing fine. If not, you need to take a hard look at where your money is going.

GO FIGURE

$948,611

The amount you might earn over 40 years if you skip paying $5 a day for a latte and muffin.*

SOURCE: www.finishrich.com
*Assumes $150 per month invested at a rate of 10 percent annual return

PF4

Background Note

Millionaires Next Door In a book called *The Millionaire Next Door,* Thomas Stanley and William Danko describe the millionaires who may live next door or down the street. They're ordinary people who share these seven characteristics:

1. They live on less than they make and invest the rest to build financial security.
2. They have a specific plan for building their wealth.
3. They think financial independence is more important than showy spending.
4. Their parents didn't hand them everything; they learned to be financially responsible as children and teens.
5. Their own adult children are financially independent and secure.
6. They look for opportunities, assess them, and take advantage of them.
7. They chose their occupations wisely.

Needs and Wants

Right now, many of your basic needs are probably part of the household budget. Still, some of your personal funds may be going toward needs such as car insurance, lunches, or college savings. The rest goes toward buying things you want. So, if you are looking to cut down expenses, you should focus first on the wants.

Consider the example of Michelle, a high school senior. She works 20 hours a week at a department store, where she earns $10.00 an hour. Her net income—that is, her take-home pay after taxes—is $150. Her monthly necessities include $40 for her cellphone bill, $60 on average for gas, and $65 a month on car insurance. Michelle has already set aside $300 for her prom and hopes to have $500 by the time prom rolls around. To stay within her budget, she gives up her daily soda habit, saving almost $30 a month. She and her friends also decide to rent movies rather than go out. This trade-off will allow them to rent a limousine to go to their prom.

1. Keep a spending journal for one week: Include every latte, vending-machine snack and music download.
2. Identify needs: bills, car payment, etc.
3. Downsize or eliminate impulse buys such as coffee and soda.
4. Make saving a priority and a habit.
5. Add to your savings weekly, even if just a small amount.
6. Identify a long-term want and start saving for it. (You'll be surprised how fast those fast-food outings diminish when you set your mind on something.)
7. Prioritize and pay down any outstanding debt–including that $5 you owe your sister.
8. Use cash for daily spending.
9. During vacations or the summer, pick up some extra hours at work.
10. Live within your means. Spend less than you make.

What's in Your Budget? This budget shows the typical spending for a single earner, living alone. Budgets change according to lifestyle and income. What doesn't change is the need to save and pay for essentials, such as housing and food.

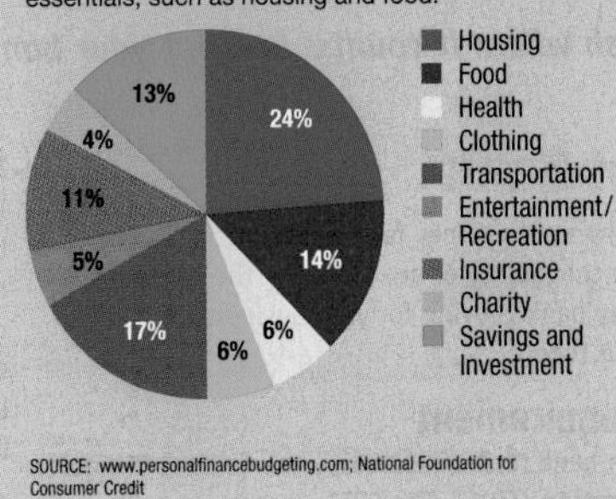

SOURCE: www.personalfinancebudgeting.com; National Foundation for Consumer Credit

Michelle has planned for a long-term goal and budgeted correctly. She has drawn a fine line between needs and wants.

If you find you have a difficult time staying within your budget, enlist a friend or family member to review your expenditures each week to help keep on track. Try not to rationalize impulse buys. Consider them your sworn budget enemies!

Long-Term Rewards

Err on the side of thrift and responsibility. Live within your means and try to save a set percentage of your income. Some budget counselors suggest alotting 80 percent for needs, 10 percent for wants, and 10 percent for savings. Do that and you might find yourself with a tidy savings within a few short years.

Spend without a plan and you might end up like many Americans: deep in debt. In fact, U.S. consumer debt topped an estimated $2.2 trillion dollars in 2005, or $7,400 per American. In 2008, studies showed that one in seven American families was dealing with a debt collector. Learning to budget now may spare you from being part of this grim statistic later.

Are You Ready?

1. What are the steps for creating a budget?
2. Why are people with a budget more likely to be financially secure than those who don't have a budget?

To learn more about this topic, visit **PearsonSuccessNet.com**

CREATE A BUDGET

Distribute the "My Spending Journal" worksheet (Personal Finance All-in-One, pp. 32–33). Tell students to use the worksheet to find out where their money goes by recording every expenditure for one week.

Call students' attention to the pie chart on page PF5. Ask them to compare their own spending to that of the typical young person living alone.

Distribute the "My Monthly Budget" worksheet (Personal Finance All-in-One, p. 34). Tell students to create a monthly budget. Explain that they should use their "My Spending Journal" worksheet as a basis, but some monthly expenses will not show up. Discuss fixed and variable expenses. Give these examples: car insurance (fixed), gas (variable). Have students give other examples. Tell them to include both types in their budgets.

DISTRIBUTE ACTIVITY WORKSHEET

Tell students that the people who most often achieve their goals do more than just decide they want something. They make a specific, detailed plan, and then they work with the plan. Distribute the worksheet called "The Trouble with Budgets" (Personal Finance All-in-One, pp. 35–36). When students finish, guide them in listing the main ideas and important details. Invite volunteers to share their thoughts.

EXTEND

Refer students to the Go Figure feature. Challenge each student to suggest one item they could give up that could amount to a substantial savings.

L4 Differentiate Have students calculate the amount of their savings over a period of 40 years. Ask them to share their results with the class.

Assess and Remediate

L3 Collect worksheets and assess student understanding of spending journals and budgeting.

L3 Give students the Budgeting Quiz (Personal Finance All-in-One, p. 37).

Answers

Are You Ready? 1. list monthly earnings, record monthly spending, organize into categories and total the amounts, list income and expenses. 2. They know how much they have to spend, and they can live within their means.

Checking Up on Checking Accounts

Get Started

LESSON GOALS

Students will:

- Understand checking by completing a sample check and balancing a register.
- Evaluate types of checking accounts and checking services by comparing features.
- Explain why it's important to reconcile a checking/debit account.

DIFFERENTIATED INSTRUCTION KEY

- **L1** Special Needs
- **L2** Basic
  - **ELL** English Language Learners
  - **LPR** Less Proficient Readers
- **L3** All Students
- **L4** Advanced Students

Teach

ANALYZE

Ask for a show of hands to answer these questions: **How many of you have checking accounts? How many of your accounts are insured by FDIC?** Point out that a checking account is one of the foundations for personal finance, so understanding it and using it correctly is essential.

Refer students to the check on page PF6 and stress that all checks have these basic components. Discuss each element. Then review the four keys to avoiding problems with checks.

L2 Differentiate Draw a blank check on the board. Have students direct you in writing a check to the Retread Bicycle Shop for $74.62 to pay for a bike tune-up and repairs. After completing it, erase the entries and have students take turns completing it.

Checking Up on Checking Accounts

Park your cash where it counts, and put your bank to work for you.

The Right Bank

Banks are everywhere. Often they face each other at busy intersections in a community or are tucked in the corner of a supermarket. Every bank is vying for your business. How do you choose among them?

The Basic Requirement

You want to use a bank that is insured by the **Federal Deposit Insurance Corporation** (FDIC). The FDIC protects your money and the interest it has earned—up to the insurance limit—in the event that your bank fails. For an account held by a single individual, the limit was raised to $250,000 in 2008. Banks are generally considered to be financially sound, but failures do occur.

Endless Variety

It may be impossible for you to believe, but not so very long ago even the biggest cities offered only ten different television stations. That was it for choices. The services offered by banks have grown in a similar way to the expansion of TV entertainment options. Although banks may look very similar, their services are not one-size-fits all. The bank that is most convenient for you may not have the services that best meet your needs. First, you have to figure out what you want and then figure out where to get it.

GO FIGURE

The number of checks forged annually in the United States, with losses totaling more than $10 billion.

SOURCE: Ernst & Young

How to Write a Check

All bank checks have the same basic layout and require the same information. To avoid problems with checks:

1. Write clearly.
2. Do not cross out or write over a mistake.
3. Tear a check with errors into small pieces, and write "Void" next to the check number in your check register.
4. NEVER write a check for more than your account balance.

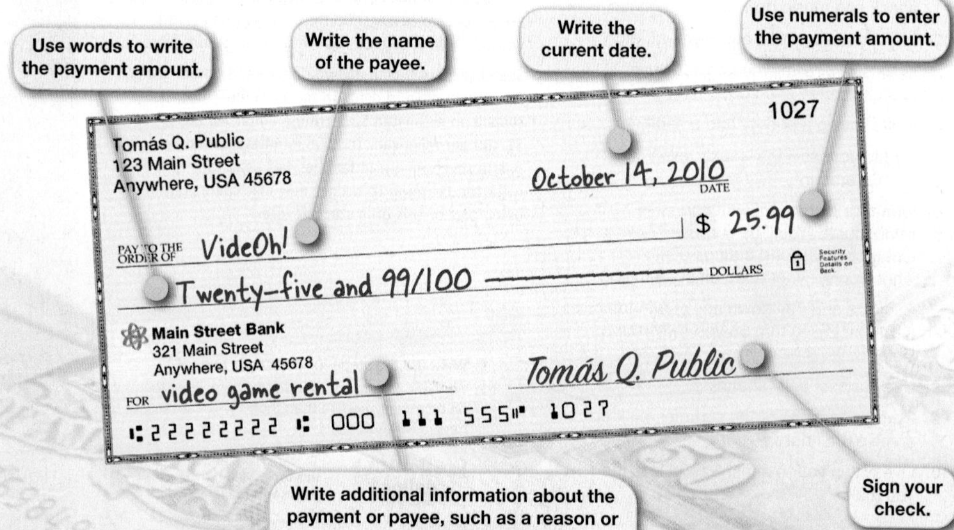

PF6

Background Note

Fighting Check Forgery Banks face two primary threats to checks: forgeries and counterfeiting. Forgeries are authentic checks with forged signatures. Banks are obligated to compare signatures on checks against the checking account owners' signatures. Doing this manually is impossible due to the vast numbers of checks processed daily, so banks rely on automatic systems. Current image analysis and pattern recognition technology give systems a 99 percent accuracy rate. Counterfeit checks are reproductions of authentic checks. To counter this threat, banks use check-stock verification software that analyzes the entire check—check number, payee, dollar amount, date, dollar sign, memo, payor block, and payor bank field. The placement of each check element and the distance between items is measured to identify copies or imitations of checks.

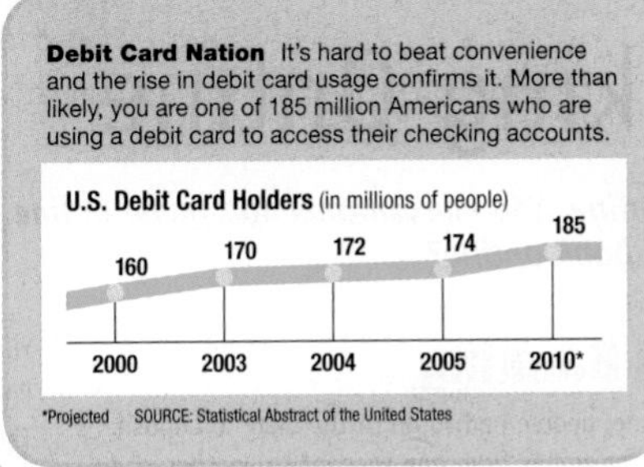
Debit Card Nation It's hard to beat convenience and the rise in debit card usage confirms it. More than likely, you are one of 185 million Americans who are using a debit card to access their checking accounts.

The Right Services

One universal need is convenient and safe access to your money. Checking accounts and debit cards have made both readily available.

Checking Accounts

To open a checking account you will need identification, such as a birth certificate or a driver's license and a Social Security number. You will also need money to deposit.

Which checking account meets your needs?

Basic checking: Best bet for customers who use a checking account to pay some bills and use a debit card for some daily expenses.
Drawback: Monthly maintenance fees may apply unless you retain a minimum balance or enroll in direct deposit. Some banks may limit the number of checks you can write each month and charge you a per item fee if you exceed the limit.

Free checking: The operative word here is "free," meaning a no-strings attached account with no monthly service charges or per-item fees, regardless of the balance or activity.
Drawback: These are harder to find and the "free" part may be an introductory offer that expires in six months or a year.

Checking with overdraft protection: In effect, if you write checks for more than the balance of your deposits, the bank will honor the check by lending you the money you need, up to a preset limit.
Drawback: This service comes with hefty fees.

The Debit Card

Most banks offer you a debit card with a checking account. With a credit card logo, it has the look and feel of a credit card, but there is a major difference. The money you spend is deducted from your checking account balance. Debit cards are also used to withdraw money from ATMs, giving you access to your money 24/7. If you use an ATM from a bank other than your own, you will likely be charged a fee. You could pay $2 to get access to your own $20. Convenience comes with a price.

Direct Deposit

Banks and employers encourage people to take advantage of direct deposit. A win-win for you and the environment, the paperless transaction enlists your employer to deposit your paycheck directly into your bank account. An employer may ask for your social security number, a voided check containing your bank's routing number, and your account number. Direct deposit saves you a trip to the bank and protects you from lost or stolen funds.

Keeping Track

When you open a checking account, you will receive a checkbook that includes sequentially numbered checks and a check register, or a booklet in which you'll record your account transactions. Every time you write a check, make a deposit, or use an ATM, you should take a few seconds to write it down. It is also important to hold onto your ATM receipts. They are the only proof that you withdrew $40, not $400.

Each month the bank will send you a statement of the activity on your account. It lists deposits, withdrawals, ATM transactions, interest paid, and fees charged. You will get a photocopy of any checks that were cashed during that month. Check your statement as soon as it arrives, comparing the transactions on the bank statement to your own records to make sure they agree.

By taking a little time to be a good record keeper, you will make life a lot easier and protect yourself from mistakes and fraud.

For more banking tips, check out fdic.gov

Are You Ready?

1. How should you choose a checking account?
2. What are some of the fees that banks place on checking accounts?

To learn more about this topic, visit **PearsonSuccessNet.com**

Checking

EVALUATE

Review the kinds of checking accounts with students. Ask **What are the main drawbacks of basic checking?** *(maintenance fees, minimum balances, limits on numbers of checks written)* **Why might you want overdraft protection?** *(to protect against having checks returned and bills unpaid if the amount of the checks exceeds your balance)*

DISTRIBUTE ACTIVITY WORKSHEET

Distribute the "Checks and Balancing" worksheet (Personal Finance All-in-One, pp. 38–39). Direct students to the second page of the worksheet. Explain the purpose of each column and how balances are figured following each transaction. Have students complete the worksheet.

ANALYZE GRAPH

Draw students' attention to the Debit Card Nation graph. Ask **What intervals of time are shown on the graph?** *(3 years; 1 year, twice; 5 years)* **About how many debit card holders were there in 2008?** *(about 180 million)* Ask students to explain their preferred method of payment: cash, check, or debit card.

EXTEND

Point out to students that debit cards can get them in trouble if they don't watch their checking account balances carefully. Distribute the "Debit? Yes. Debt? No." worksheet (Personal Finance All-in-One, p. 40). After students read the article, discuss the Questions to Think About.

L4 Have students research checking accounts at a local bank. Ask students to identify banks to visit; try to have as many banks represented as possible. Tell them to gather information about checking accounts offered and any fees. Have students share their findings in class.

Assess and Remediate

L3 Collect the "Checks and Balancing" and the "Debit? Yes. Debt? No." worksheets and assess student understanding of how to write checks and balance their checking/debit accounts.

L3 Give students the Checking Up on Checking Accounts Quiz (Personal Finance All-in-One, p. 41).

Answers

Are You Ready? 1. First figure out what check services you want and then find a bank that offers those services. 2. They may charge a monthly maintenance fee for checks written beyond a certain number. They may charge for overdraft protection.

Banking Online

Get Started

LESSON GOALS

Students will:

- Describe the benefits of online banking by completing a worksheet.
- Assess the risks of online banking by analyzing a cartoon.
- Compare traditional and online banking, and describe the services that financial institutions offer for online account management.

DIFFERENTIATED INSTRUCTION KEY

L1 Special Needs
L2 Basic
  ELL English Language Learners
  LPR Less Proficient Readers
L3 All Students
L4 Advanced Students

Teach

CONNECT

Display the "Dear Computer User" transparency (Color Transparencies, p. PF.b). Ask **Who is the "Trustworthy Person" in the cartoon?** *(someone trying to deceive the user and steal his money)* Ask students if they have ever experienced phishing. Explain that *phishing* is a criminal attempt to get sensitive information by pretending to be a trustworthy source.

COMPARE

Ask **What are the benefits of online banking?** *(access accounts, pay bills, transfer funds, view canceled checks, 24/7)* Ask students to compare the benefits of online and traditional banking.

ANALYZE A CHART

Discuss the Online Revolution chart with students. Ask **Why do you think using direct deposit and ATM cards are more prevalent than computer banking?** *(Possible answers: Some people are not comfortable with or may not own a computer; some banks do not offer computer banking.)*

Banking Online

You shop online. You chat online. You game online. So why not bank online?

Modern Banking

Once upon a time, people had to go to the bank to deposit money, to transfer money from one account to another, or to withdraw money from an account. They had to write a check or use cash to pay bills. This has become ancient history. The online bank is growing fast in popularity. An online bank can be a virtual extension of a brick-and-mortar bank or can exist solely in cyberspace. As long as a bank is insured by the FDIC, deposits are safe up to $250,000.

Online Benefits

As one of today's online banking customers, you can access your accounts, pay your bills, and transfer funds from one account to another twenty-four hours a day. Internet banks also offer the environmentally friendly option to stop paper records, allowing you to access your statements, canceled checks, and notices online only. You can even arrange **automatic bill payment**. Although you receive a bill in the mail or in your e-mail, the amount you owe is automatically deducted from your bank account on a predetermined date. You save time, postage, and the possibility of missing a payment and incurring late fees.

There can be other financial advantages to using online banks. Internet bank fees can be as much as 80 percent less than those charged by traditional banks. They may also offer checking, savings, or money market and CD accounts that yield higher interest rates than those offered by traditional banks.

A major benefit to the consumer is the ability to find these good deals by comparison shopping online. In the wise words of Benjamin Franklin, "A penny saved is a penny earned." By getting in the habit of looking for the lowest interest rates on loans and the highest interest rates on savings, the wise consumer will slowly pull ahead of the pack. Add a little compound interest into the mix and the pace of progress will pick up.

GO FIGURE

67.9 million

The number of U.S. households that banked online in 2008, up from 27.3 million in 2002.

SOURCE: "2008 Consumer Banking and Bill Payment" survey by FiServ

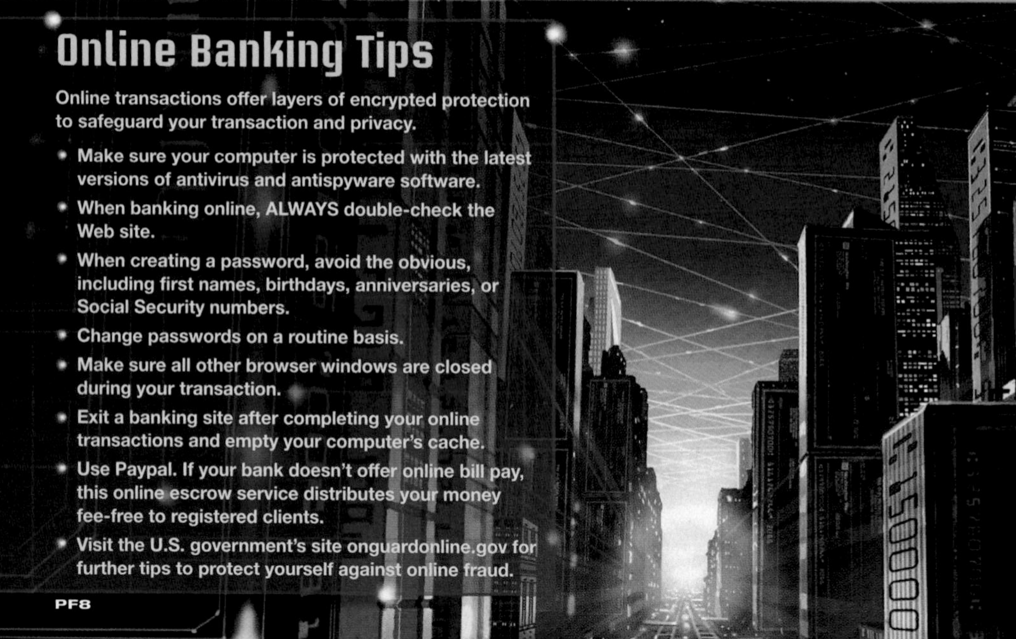

Online Banking Tips

Online transactions offer layers of encrypted protection to safeguard your transaction and privacy.

- **Make sure your computer is protected with the latest versions of antivirus and antispyware software.**
- **When banking online, ALWAYS double-check the Web site.**
- **When creating a password, avoid the obvious, including first names, birthdays, anniversaries, or Social Security numbers.**
- **Change passwords on a routine basis.**
- **Make sure all other browser windows are closed during your transaction.**
- **Exit a banking site after completing your online transactions and empty your computer's cache.**
- **Use Paypal. If your bank doesn't offer online bill pay, this online escrow service distributes your money fee-free to registered clients.**
- **Visit the U.S. government's site onguardonline.gov for further tips to protect yourself against online fraud.**

PF8

Background Note

Security of Online Banking Most people who hesitate to use online banking cite security as their number one concern. Studies show, however, that people are at a greater risk of ID theft or fraud when using conventional banking. The reason is simple: people lose checkbooks and bank statements and they throw away sensitive paper documents that can be found and used by criminals to access bank accounts. Online banking eliminates much of this risk because most transactions are entirely electronic and banks, knowing that people are concerned about security, are especially careful to ensure the highest levels of online safety. Although statistics vary, one study indicates that 68 percent of fraud and ID theft happen to people offline compared with 11.6 percent online.

Be Responsible

Even though you may choose to bank online, every month you will get a statement in the mail from your financial institution. It is your responsibility to check this against your online transactions and report any discrepancies to your bank. Laws regulating an **Electronic Funds Transfer** (EFT), a system for transferring money from one bank to another, protect you in the case of fraud. You, however, have to do your part. In order to be protected by the law, you must report any errors in transactions within 60 days of the receipt of your bank statement. No matter how careful banks are not to make errors, no one is perfect.

If you use automatic bill pay, it is your responsibility to have sufficient funds in the account to cover the transaction. Some procedures of online banking are still affected by the business hours of the bank. If you are transferring funds to cover your bills, the money may not show up in your account unless you have made the transfer the previous day before a specific cutoff time. A deposit made at 1 A.M. may not show up on your account until the next business day. Plan your transactions accordingly, particularly if you wait until the last moment to pay your bills.

Gone Phishing

Phishing is a scam in which a fraudulent web site is used to gain personal and financial data to commit fraud. There are several steps you can take to protect yourself.

- Online banking transactions should be done through the bank's Web site only.
- Never respond to e-mails from your "alleged" bank that request sensitive personal or financial information.
- If you suspect fraud, contact your bank by phone to determine if it's a legitimate communication from the bank. If not, alert them to the scam.

If you think you can't be fooled, think again. Phishing techniques can be highly elaborate. Many even set up mirror Web pages intended to look like your financial institution's Web site to earn your trust.

Traditional Banking

In the balance, why would anyone still use a brick-and-mortar bank? There are a number of reasons that make some consumers reluctant to drop traditional banking altogether.

Online Revolution In 1995, Wells Fargo became the first financial institution to offer online statements. By 2012, it is estimated that 82 million Americans will be banking online. This chart shows trends in some methods of e-banking.

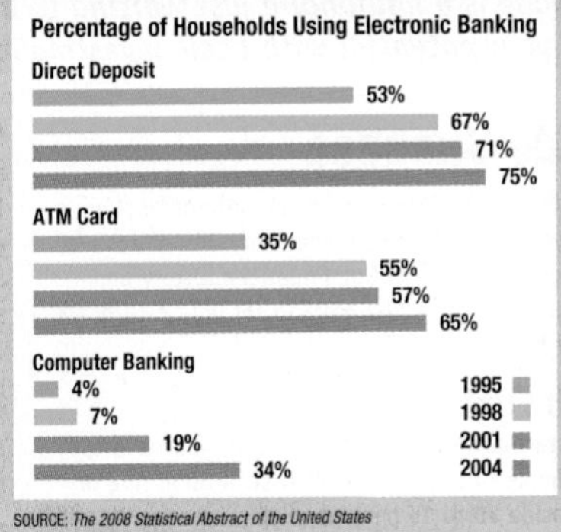

SOURCE: *The 2008 Statistical Abstract of the United States*

Convenience Factor

While Internet-only banks receive high marks for convenience, they also can be inconvenient.

- To fund an account, you will have to mail in a check, arrange for direct deposit or make a transfer from another bank. This is not a problem, of course, with banks that also operate a physical branch.
- Not having the option of being able to speak with someone face-to-face is another inconvenience. Some customers prefer to interact with people who know them personally. Making a phone call or communicating by e-mail is not to everyone's liking.
- Another drawback is the difficulty of finding fee-free ATMs, although online banks often have ATM networks for their customers to use at minimal cost.
- Lack of paper checks is a fourth issue. Instead, Internet-only banks offer a bill-pay service. But payments have to be scheduled ahead of time and take several days to process. As a result, you have to keep close tabs on your account to ensure that you have money to cover the payments.

Are You Ready?

1. What are the advantages of online banking?
2. How can you protect yourself against phishing scams?

To learn more about this topic, visit **PearsonSuccessNet.com**

Checking

DISTRIBUTE ACTIVITY WORKSHEET

Explain that although online banking is different than traditional banking, both use many of the same methods for managing accounts. Distribute the "Keeping Track Online" worksheet (Personal Finance All-in-One, pp. 42–43). Explain that the first page shows an online bank statement. These statements show the most recent activity, which makes it easier to see the current status of a bank account than traditional bank statements that arrive once a month. Tell students that the second worksheet page shows how an online bill pay page is set up. Have students complete the worksheets on their own.

L2 Differentiate Pair students to complete the worksheets and provide assistance as needed.

EXTEND

Have students work in pairs or small groups to list several local banks where they might open an account. Then have students work independently and visit the Internet home page of a bank. Have them make a chart to compare their findings on such issues as fees, ease of navigating the site, and services offered.

L4 Differentiate Tell students that many banks have online tutorials or demonstrations of online banking. Have students locate and view some of these. Tell them to report back to class on five new things they learned about online banking.

Assess and Remediate

L3 Collect "Keeping Track Online" worksheets and assess student understanding of how to use online banking.

L3 Give students the Banking Online Quiz (Personal Finance All-in-One, p. 44).

Answers

Are You Ready? 1. You can access your accounts, pay bills, transfer funds, access bank statements, view canceled checks, and arrange automatic bill pay 24 hours a day, 7 days a week from your personal computer. 2. Only conduct online banking through the bank's official Web site. Never respond to e-mails that ask for sensitive information. If you suspect fraud, contact the bank to verify the communication.

Investing with Dollars and $ense

Get Started

LESSON GOALS

Students will:

- Understand the rate of return on an investment by calculating the amount of interest earned at various rates.
- Analyze a variety of investment vehicles, including bonds, stocks, and mutual funds according to their risk and return profiles.
- Identify different investment strategies, including dollar cost averaging.
- Evaluate different ways to reach a financial objective by completing a worksheet.

DIFFERENTIATED INSTRUCTION KEY

L1 Special Needs
L2 Basic
  ELL English Language Learners
  LPR Less Proficient Readers
L3 All Students
L4 Advanced Students

Teach

CALCULATING INTEREST

Direct students' attention to the definition of interest in the third paragraph on this page. Demonstrate how to calculate interest by using the example of 5 percent interest paid on $100 deposited. *(Multiply $100 by 0.05 to find the amount of interest, which is $5.).* Then have students practice the skill by calculating the amount of interest in the following situations:

2.1% on $50 *($1.05)*
2.5% on $50 *($1.25)*
3% on $50 *($1.50)*
3.4% on $50 *($1.70)*

Ask volunteers to make a generalization about interest rates based on these examples. *(The higher the interest rate, the more the principal earns in interest.)*

L1 L2 **ELL LPR Differentiate** To reinforce understanding of the relationship between principal and interest have students explain how they calculated the interest payments.

Investing With Dollars and $ense

Inside, everyone is a millionaire just waiting to happen. You can tap your potential with basic investments.

Self-Made Success

Look in the mirror and the face of a future millionaire may be staring back at you. More than 80 percent of millionaires are self-made, first-generation rich. But forget the lottery and other get-rich-quick schemes. You have to set your own goals and work toward them.

Pay Yourself First

In order to get started on your road to wealth, you have to remember one simple rule: Pay yourself first. A good rule of thumb is to set aside 10 to 15 percent of your income. We will talk later about how to achieve this goal, but for the time being, accept the fact. The lifestyle you choose to live now will determine the lifestyle you will be able to have in the future.

Get Help From Interest

Let's assume that you have made the decision to save. The positive news is that your savings will work for you. Banks pay you interest for using your money. Interest rates are expressed as percentages and indicate how much money an account will earn on funds deposited for a full year. Interest is compounded when it is added to your principal and you earn interest on both amounts. In effect, compound interest is interest on interest.

Most first-generation millionaires acquire their wealth over a lifetime. Their road to riches has more to do with budgeting, compound interest, and careful investing than with salary and inheritances.

Basic Investing

Putting money in a savings account is very safe. The only danger to money in a savings account is that the rate of inflation will be greater than the interest rate. Over time, the money in your savings account could lose value—it will buy less and less. But you will never lose your principal, the amount of money you put in the account.

Investing money is not the same as "saving" money. Investors take more risk—even possibly losing money—in the hopes of getting a higher return on their money.

GO FIGURE

2/3

The ratio of millionaires who are self-employed.

SOURCE: "The Millionaire Next Door" by Thomas Stanley and William Danko

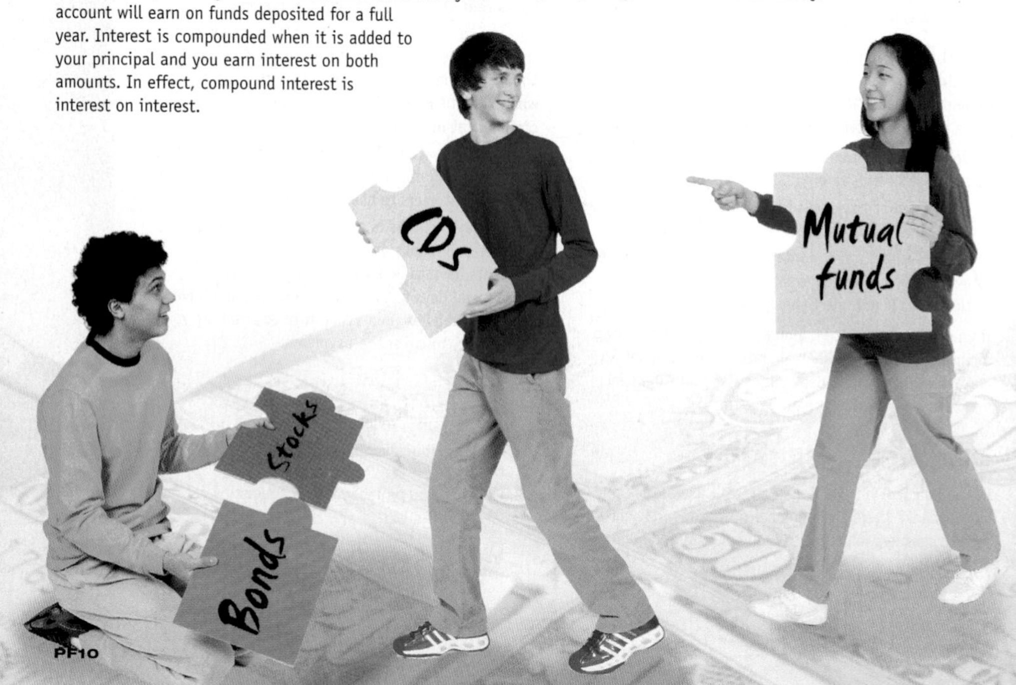

Investing your money can give your dollars a greater opportunity to grow. Bonds, stocks, and mutual funds are among the many investment choices that you have. Of course, with the possibility of greater growth comes the possibility of greater loss. If you invest in a corporate bond, stock, or mutual fund, you stand the risk of losing some or all of the money you invested. This risk is offset by the possibility of greater gain, allowing your money to grow at a faster rate than the rate of inflation.

The Name Is Bond

A **bond** is an IOU issued by a corporation or by some level of government. When you buy a bond, you are lending money in return for a guaranteed payout at some later date. The safest bonds to buy are government-issued bonds because it is unlikely that a government will go bankrupt. You can get U.S. government bonds through your bank, and they can be bought in small denominations. Many corporate bonds carry a low-to-moderate risk to investors and take anywhere from 5 to 30 years to mature.

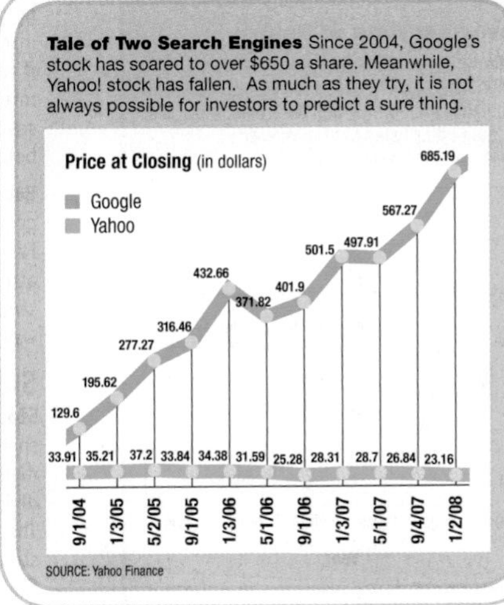

Tale of Two Search Engines Since 2004, Google's stock has soared to over $650 a share. Meanwhile, Yahoo! stock has fallen. As much as they try, it is not always possible for investors to predict a sure thing.

The value of some bonds varies. For example, if you buy a bond when interest rates are 6 percent but you want to sell it before it matures, then the bond's value will be affected by current interest rates. If rates have

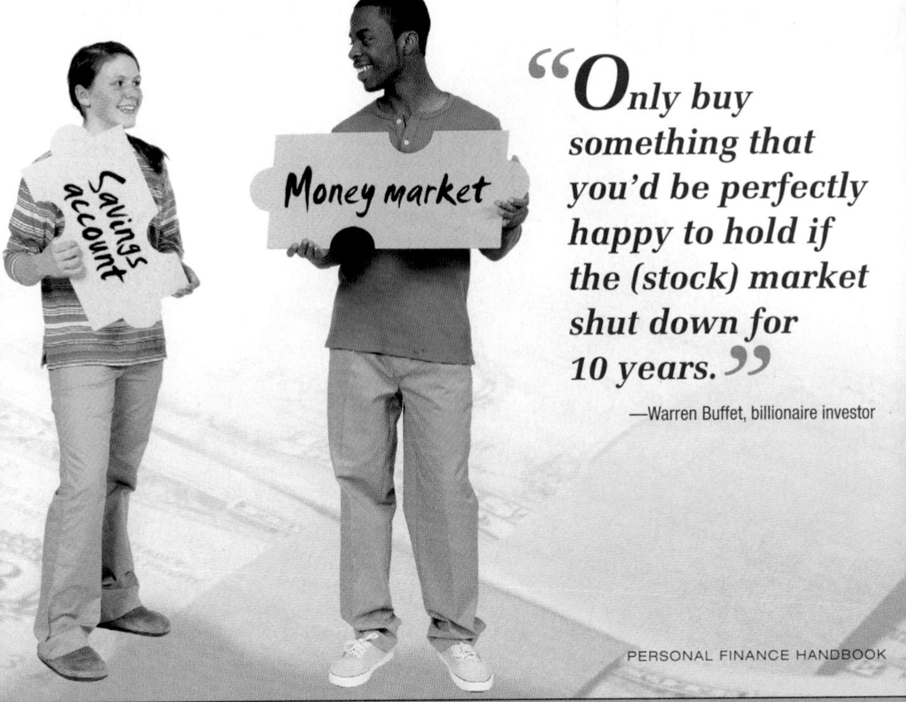

"Only buy something that you'd be perfectly happy to hold if the (stock) market shut down for 10 years."

—Warren Buffet, billionaire investor

Investments

COMPARE

Have students look at the Tale of Two Search Engines graph on this page. Discuss with students how, in hindsight, it might be possible to analyze why Google soared and Yahoo did not.

MAKE ANALOGIES

Explain the question of bond prices with an analogy to tickets to a sporting event. Tell students to assume that they are holding a $10 ticket to a college football game. Ask **How much is the ticket worth?** *($10)*

Tell them now to assume that one of the players on the university's team has the chance to set a school record for touchdowns in that game. Ask **What do you think the ticket would be worth now? Why?** *(It will be worth more than $10 because demand for the ticket will be higher, since the player might set a new record.)* Explain that this is similar to the situation a bondholder faces when interest rates for new bonds are *lower* than the interest rate on the bond the investor holds. The investor's bond now has more value relative to current bonds, so that bond—if he or she sells it—would be worth more than its stated value.

Then tell students to suppose that the star player became injured at practice during the week and was not going to play in the game. Ask **What would the ticket be worth in that situation?** *(It will be worth less than $10 because demand would not be as great.)* Explain that this situation is similar to what happens if current bonds pay *more* in interest than the bond an investor holds. If the investor wants to sell that bond he or she will have to offer it for *less* than the stated value because the lower interest rate makes it less desirable.

L4 Differentiate Point out that investors do not consider all bonds to be equally attractive. Have students compare and contrast ratings of government and corporate bonds. Ask **How do bonds get higher ratings? Why are the ratings important to an investor?** Have students present their findings from the point of view of an investor or a banker.

Background Note

All About Bonds Investors consider these factors with bonds:

- **Par Value** The amount to be paid to the bondholder at maturity. It is also called the face value of principal.
- **Coupon Rate** The interest rate that a bond issuer will pay to a bondholder. The higher the interest rate, the more desirable the bond—and sometimes the more risky.
- **Maturity** This refers to the date at which the entity that issued the bond is obliged to pay the principal back to the bondholder.
- **Yield** A bond's yield is determined two ways. Annual yield is simply the interest rate that the bond pays. Yield to maturity takes into account two factors—annual yield and the sum the bondholder will receive if he or she holds the bond until it matures.

ANALYZE

Direct students' attention to the chart showing the five-year rate of return on different types of investments. Ask **Which type of investment shows the greatest potential reward? Why?** *(stocks; because the rate of return reaches the highest—near 30 percent in 2003)* **Which shows the greatest risk? Why?** *(stocks; because it is the only type of investment that shows losses)* **How do 10-year bonds and Treasury bills compare to each other?** *(Based on these years, Treasury bills generally pay less than 10-year bonds but sometimes the rates are much closer.)* Ask **Which type of investment would you prefer? Why?** *(Students' responses should take into account the variations in risk as well as the differences in reward.)*

Next, direct students' attention to the risk pyramid at the bottom of the page. Discuss whether they think the categories of risk make sense based on the information in the bar graph. Call on volunteers to suggest where on the graph the highest risk investments from the pyramid—penny stocks, art and collectibles, and commodities—might appear.

Five-Year Rate of Return

The rate of return (profit and loss) on investments changes over time. Historically, stocks have provided investors with the greatest potential for profit. But data also show that they're riskier than other types of investments.

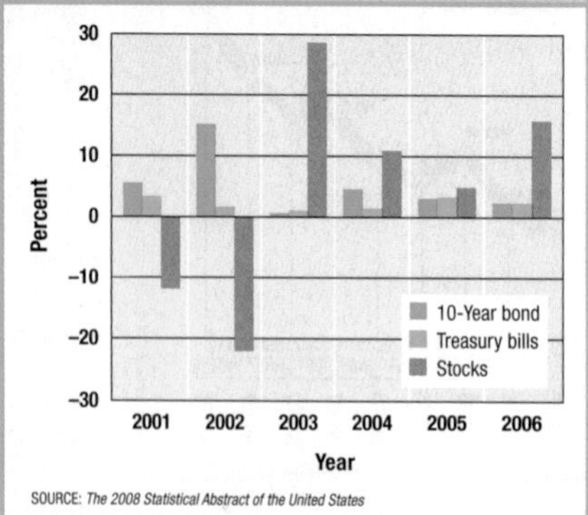

SOURCE: *The 2008 Statistical Abstract of the United States*

gone up since you bought the bond, then you will have to discount the price to sell it. Why else would anyone want it, if they could get a higher rate of interest elsewhere? But, if interest rates have gone down, then that 6 percent rate will seem much more inviting. In this case, you could sell the bond for more than you paid for it.

Because the value of bonds is relatively stable, they are a good investment for people who cannot tolerate much risk. Families saving to send children to college may find bonds attractive because they generally earn higher interest than a savings account, and aren't likely to fall sharply in value the way stocks can.

Stock Up

Stocks represent ownership in a public company. If you buy shares in a corporation, you become a part owner. You will make money if the price of the stock goes up and if you receive dividends, which are a portion of the profits paid to the owners. There are two kinds of stock, preferred stock and common stock. Preferred stock holders get a set dividend and are paid from the corporate profits before the common stock holders.

THE RISK PYRAMID

"Risk" means the danger that an investment will disappoint you. A pyramid is sometimes used to demonstrate the riskiness of various investments. At the top are very risky investments like futures in precious metals. At the bottom, and least risky, are savings accounts, money market funds, and short-term CDs.

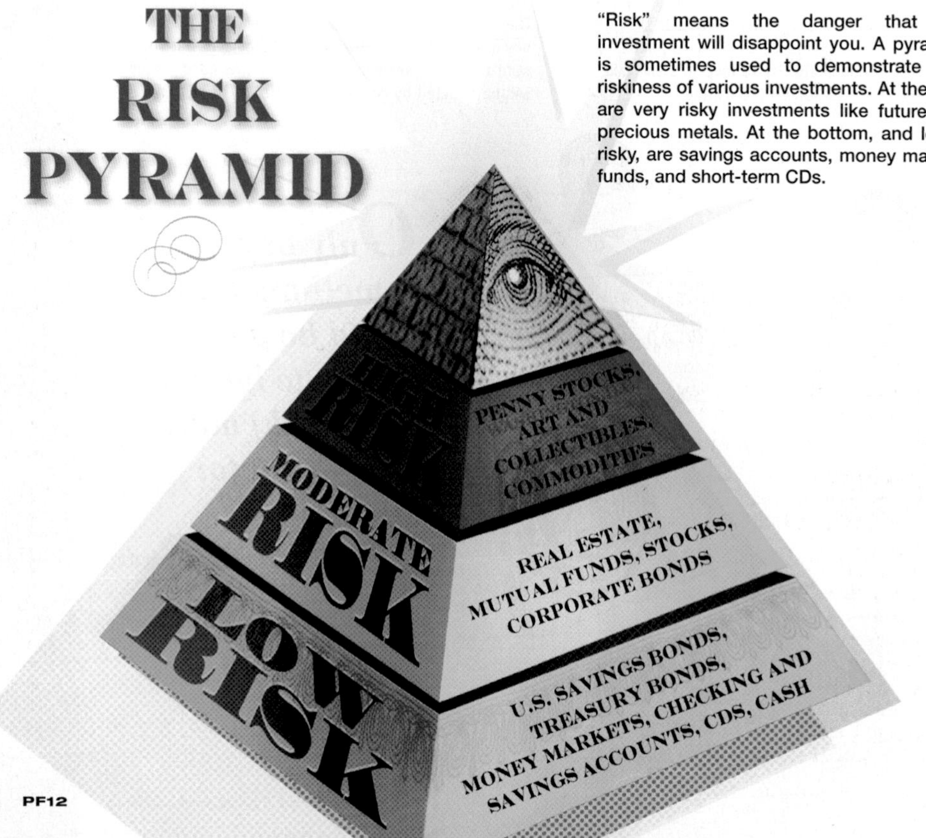

PF12

Background Note

Stock Tips Investing in stocks is risky—and offers potential rewards. Investment advisors give several tips to stock buyers:

- Have an investment plan—and stick to it.
- Do not use money that should be set aside for other purposes, such as emergency savings.
- Take the time to get informed, and check on the quality of the advice you get from professional advisors.
- Do not follow tips from unqualified people.
- Avoid being too emotional about highs and lows in the market or about individual stocks.
- Do not buy low-priced stocks because you assume they will go up in value.

Stocks are generally a riskier investment than bonds. Historically, however, stocks have rewarded their owners with higher returns than bonds or savings accounts.

What About Mutual Funds?

A mutual fund is an investment in a company that buys and sells stocks and bonds in other companies. By combining your money with that of other investors, the managers of the mutual fund can buy a wide variety of stocks and bonds. When you buy a mutual fund, you are buying a part ownership of the stocks or bonds owned by the investment company. The biggest advantage of investing in this way is that you instantly have a diversified portfolio. Your risk is spread out.

Three kinds of mutual funds have three levels of risk.

- Money market funds, which are not the same as money market accounts, are short-term, low-risk investments. The money you invest is used to make short-term loans to businesses or governments.
- Bond funds are investments in bonds. Though riskier than money market funds, they have a higher potential return.
- Stock funds are made up of a variety of stocks. Over the long term, they have provided higher returns than either market funds or bond funds.

Mutual fund companies are required by law to register reports and statements with the SEC. You can check up on them through the SECs database at www.sec.gov/edgar. Morningstar and Standard and Poors are two companies that rate mutual funds, stocks, bonds, and other investments.

Investment Strategy

Many first-time investors think that the way to make money is to buy low and sell high. But, trying to time the stock market has proven elusive to even the most savvy investor. When all is said and done, it's best to use common sense. Dollar cost averaging is one simple investment strategy that rewards the patient investor.

Dollar Cost Averaging

Dollar cost averaging is the strategy of investing on a regular schedule over a period of time. In this way, you capture both the lower and higher prices as prices rise and fall. In the long run, you hope to get a better average price for the purchase or sale of stocks and mutual funds. People use dollar cost averaging because they know they can't predict the market. It is especially useful for common stocks, which can be very volatile—that is, the price can swing far above and below the average price. Dollar cost averaging is an attempt to hedge against the ups and downs of the stock market. It does not guarantee gains or eliminate all possible losses, but it improves your odds of coming out ahead.

The Case for Dollar Cost Averaging

Let's say that you put $500 a month into a mutual fund for five months. The price of a share has gone from $10 to $10. You own 308.3 shares, worth $3,083. You invested only $2,500 (five times $500). You made $583 because the average price per share was $8.40.

Month	Price per Share	Shares You Buy
January	$10	50
February	8	62.5
March	6	83.3
April	8	62.5
May	10	50
TOTAL		308.3

Other Options

The risk and payout on investments covers a range from the most secure to the really, really risky. Junk bonds didn't get their name because they were a secure place to park money. Some people invest in collectibles—fine art, baseball cards, Civil War memorabilia. If the market remains strong, people who can part with what they have bought stand to make a lot of money. But, if no one is interested in your stamp collection, you may end up using it for postage.

What you choose depends on the risk you are willing to accept. You also need to consider the length of your investments and any tax burdens the investment may carry. If your scheme is to count on "sure things" or use tips from the cousin of your neighbor's son-in-law, you are likely to be very disappointed.

The Final Word

The federal government encourages investment. Even though the government taxes interest and dividends at the same rate as earned income, the profits from the sale of stocks or property are capital gains. In recent years, the taxes on capital gains have been lower than the tax rate on the interest from bonds and savings accounts. As an added bonus, interest earned on U.S. government bonds is exempt from state and local taxes. What it comes down to in the end is that informed decisions and careful planning are your best strategies for successful investment.

Are You Ready?

1. What is the difference between saving and investing money?
2. How can dollar cost averaging protect your investments?

To learn more about this topic, visit PearsonSuccessNet.com

Investments

SHOW TRANSPARENCY

Display the transparency "Many Happy Returns" (Color Transparencies, p. PF.c). Explain that the graph shows the one-year returns and five-year returns on five different categories of mutual funds. Explain that the data is from the period from late 2007 to late 2008, when the stock market fell very sharply.

Ask **How does the performance of stock funds compare to that of bond funds?** *(They perform much worse.)* **What does that say about the relative risk of these kinds of investments?** *(The returns show that stocks are much riskier and more volatile than bonds.)*

ANALYZE CHART

Ask students how to determine the average price paid for stock over the five months shown in the chart on page PF13. *(Add the prices over the five months and divide by 5.)* Ask **How much is your stock worth in May?** *($3,083)*

DISTRIBUTE ACTIVITY WORKSHEET

Distribute the "Informed Investing" worksheet (Personal Finance All-in-One, pp. 45–46). Use it as a vehicle for assessing students' understanding of the basics of savings and investing.

L2 Differentiate Sketch a bar chart on the board to illustrate the differences in the four amounts a person must invest to produce the $1 million. The varying sizes of the bars should dramatize the differences for visual learners.

Assess and Remediate

L3 Collect the "Informed Investing" worksheets and assess student understanding of savings and investing basics.

L3 Give students the Investing with Dollars and Sense Quiz (Personal Finance All-in-One, p. 47).

Answers

Are You Ready? 1. Money placed in a savings account earns interest and is safe. Money invested in bonds, stocks, or mutual funds can earn much more than money in a savings account, but it is at greater risk, and even the principal—the amount invested—can be lost. 2. Dollar cost averaging protects investments by allowing investors to limit the damage caused by increases and decreases in the stock market.

Building Your Portfolio

Get Started

LESSON GOALS

Students will:

- Assess their own attitudes toward risk and investing by completing a survey.
- Explain the rationale behind diversifying an investment portfolio and choosing an investment strategy appropriate for achieving one's objectives at various life stages.
- Analyze risks and rewards of six common investment vehicles by completing a worksheet.
- Evaluate investment advice.

DIFFERENTIATED INSTRUCTION KEY

L1 Special Needs
L2 Basic
ELL English Language Learners
LPR Less Proficient Readers
L3 All Students
L4 Advanced Students

Teach

ASSESS ATTITUDES

To introduce the topic, distribute the "Attitude Inventory" form (Personal Finance All-in-One, p. 50). Have students complete the inventory to assess their attitudes toward saving and investing. Tell students to hold on to the sheet to use again later.

EXPLAIN

Ask students if they have ever heard the phrase "Don't put all your eggs in one basket." Call on a volunteer to explain the phrase. Ask **How does this phrase relate to diversifying?** *(Possible answer: The saying explains the rationale for diversifying, which aims to prevent investors from putting too much money at risk in the same kind of investment.)*

L1 L2 ELL LPR Differentiate Make sure students understand the meaning of the word *diverse*, meaning "varied." Explain that *diversify* means "to make diverse." In the case of investments, this means to vary the amount of risk you take in your investments.

Building Your Portfolio

An 'investment portfolio' may seem currently out of your realm, but learning about them can't come a moment too soon.

Your Assets

An investment **portfolio** is made up of different investment assets. These include the basics: stocks, bonds, mutual funds, CDs, and a 401(k). A healthy portfolio depends on a variety of factors. No two are alike because every investment plan is designed according to individual needs and goals.

Diversify

As you have learned, all investments carry different levels of risk. Stocks, for example, carry much more risk of losing value than, say, a money market account. To protect your investment you need to diversify. In the uncertain world of financial markets, a properly diversified investment portfolio is better equipped to survive the ups and downs of stock prices. If your portfolio consisted only of stocks in companies that made gumballs, its value could take a nose dive if stores stopped ordering gumballs. If your portfolio was properly diversified, only the investments tied to gumball makers would suffer.

Life Stages

Investing should be seen as a lifelong process, and your investment portfolio should change over time. The way it changes will depend on your income and needs. For example, you probably won't need an investment to supplement the money you make from a full-time job, if you're 22 years old and single. By the time you're 40, however, you might already be married with children. In this case, you might need income

GO FIGURE

2 million

The number of young investors in the U.S., between grades 8 and 12, who actively trade stocks and bonds.

SOURCE: www.doughnet.com

Portfolios: Where do you stand?

No government agency provides a standard model for how you should invest your money. Experience suggests a good strategy is focused on a mix of assets that includes stocks, bonds, and cash. The allocations should change as a person ages. This is one widely accepted model of such allocations.*

Cash
Bonds
Stocks

Age 20: 86%, 9%, 5%
Age 35: 72%, 17%, 11%
Age 50: 43%, 35%, 22%
Age 75: 58%, 25%, 17%

*Based on the Iowa Public Employees' Retirement System calculator (www.ipers.org)

PF14

Background Note

Stocks and Bonds, Bulls and Bears Generally speaking, the stock and bond markets move in opposite directions. When stocks are rising in value, bonds are less attractive to investors. A falling stock market makes bonds more appealing, as investors prefer their typically more reliable returns. Wall Street followers have two colorful words for rising and falling stock markets. A strong market, when stocks in general grow in value, is a *bull* market. Falling values signal a *bear* market.

from investments to help pay for a child's first year at college. Those income-producing investments probably will be more conservative because your needs have changed. Generally speaking, the younger you are the greater risk you can tolerate.

Investments can lose a significant amount of their value over the short-term. Over the long-term, however, those same investments could well recover their initial value and, even, gain much value. That is why it would be unwise for a 75-year-old investor to have the same aggressive investments as a 20-year-old.

Lisa's Story

With a new promotion under her belt, Lisa at age 25 decided she was ready to invest. Already participating in her company's 401(k), Lisa wanted to take her own investments to the next level: A professionally managed portfolio outside of her company.

Choose a Guru

Lisa wanted to manage her assets on her own. Who should she choose? Financial planner? Financial consultant? Financial Broker? If Lisa's main goal is to get financial advice, she might seek out the Certified Financial Planner (CFP).

Background Check

Lisa can perform a background check on her CFP through the CFP Board of Standards Web site. Financial planners and consultants are required by law to act in the best interest of the client, whereas brokers and brokerage firms make commissions off their sales. The Central Registration Depository (CRD) database provides background data on brokers. The Financial Industry Regulatory Authority's Broker Check Web site www.finra.org provides information from the CRD.

Commissions and Fees

When Lisa narrows down her list, she will find out if the advisers operate on commission, hourly fees, or a percentage of assets or some combination. She will ask for a complete breakdown of the fee structures. A reputable adviser or broker will give her information on their fees as well as documents outlining the risks of each investment.

How Much Risk?

Since Lisa is just starting out, her financial planner is likely to steer her toward stocks and bonds. Lisa is conservative and wants to limit her risk, sticking to CDs and bonds. But since Lisa is young and single, she should consider taking a higher level of risk for aggressive growth. She knows that she also needs to keep some money available for an emergency. Life happens, and she could face an unexpected expense.

Rule of 72

Thanks to the **Rule of 72,** Lisa easily can calculate how long it will take to double her investment at any given interest rate of return. The Rule of 72 is a mathematical shortcut in which an investor can divide the number "72" by the expected rate of return to estimate the number of years it will take for an investment to double in value. This assumes that the interest is compounded every year. For example, if Lisa invests $500 into an account that earns a 6 percent return, it will take 12 years for that account value to become $1,000, because 72 divided by 6 equals 12. Her account value will double, even if she doesn't invest another penny in it. If Lisa has an investment that earns 10 percent interest, then it will take 7.2 years to double.

Mind Your Business Managing people's money typically requires training in finance. It is one of the fields contributing to the popularity of majors in business at U.S. colleges. In 2005, twenty-two percent of all bachelor's degrees were in business.

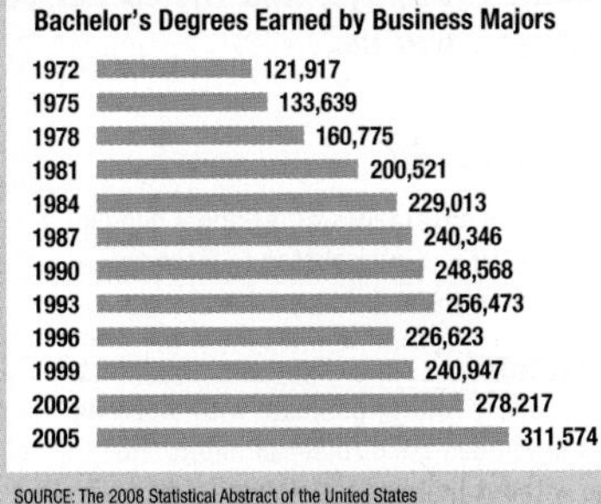

SOURCE: The 2008 Statistical Abstract of the United States

Are You Ready?

1. Estimate how much of Lisa's portfolio should consist of stocks.
2. Use the Rule of 72 to find how long it will take for $1,500 to double at 4 percent interest.

To learn more about this topic, visit PearsonSuccessNet.com

DISTRIBUTE ACTIVITY WORKSHEET

Remind students that each investment vehicle has a different level of risk. Distribute the "Assessing Risk and Reward" worksheet (Personal Finance All-in-One, pp. 48–49). Have students use the worksheet to analyze the relative risks and rewards of six common investment vehicles.

After students have completed the worksheet, ask them to discuss which of these vehicles they think would be most appropriate for the four people at different life stages shown in the figure on page PF14. Remind students that the figure shows diversified portfolios, so they need to identify a variety of investments for someone at each life stage.

ADVISE

Draw students' attention to the Mind Your Business chart on page PF15. Ask students to consider whether they might have an interest in managing other people's money. Have students work in pairs to evaluate each other's investment strategies for the people at different life stages.

REASSESS ATTITUDES

After students have discussed the topic and finished the worksheet, have them reassess their attitudes toward saving and investing using the "Attitude Inventory" form. Call on a few volunteers to identify any statements that they see in a very different way and to explain why. Discuss how students can apply what they have learned from study of this topic to their own lives.

EXTEND

Give students the "Good Advice?" worksheet (Personal Finance All-in-One, p. 51). Have them read the various pieces of investment advice and comment on the two quotations they find most and least useful.

Assess and Remediate

L3 Collect the "Assessing Risk and Reward" and "Good Advice?" worksheets and assess student understanding of investment risk.

L3 Give students the Building Your Portfolio Quiz (Personal Finance All-in-One, p. 52).

Answers

Are You Ready? 1. Possible answer: Given Lisa's age and single status, about 86 percent of her portfolio should be stocks. 2. At 4 percent interest, savings of $1,500 would take 18 years to double.

Saving for the Long Haul

Get Started

LESSON GOALS

Students will:

- Identify savings strategies, including various ways of "paying yourself first."
- Calculate how much of their weekly spending they could turn into savings.
- Calculate how many weeks they would need in order to save toward a specific short- or long-term goal.
- Compare the terms and conditions of different savings accounts by completing a worksheet.

DIFFERENTIATED INSTRUCTION KEY

L1 Special Needs
L2 Basic
ELL English Language Learners
LPR Less Proficient Readers
L3 All Students
L4 Advanced Students

Teach

EVALUATE SPENDING

Distribute the "Pay Yourself First" worksheet (Personal Finance All-in-One, pp. 53–54).

Tell students to use the chart to track their spending for a week. Tell them that they should evaluate each expense to determine if it was a necessity, such as transportation to school or to a job, or discretionary, such as a snack. Remind them that some expenses could be both. They might have to spend some money to buy a meal, but they should consider whether they could have spent less. Instruct them to enter all the discretionary spending amounts in the fourth column. At the end of the week, they should total the money in that column to determine how much of the week's spending they could have devoted to savings.

L4 **Differentiate** Encourage students to calculate how much money they would have at the end of the year if they saved the same amount every week and it earned 2 percent interest.

Saving for the Long Haul

Saving is one habit that pays. And the earlier you start, the bigger the payoff will be.

Pay Yourself First

You already know about the advantages of making a budget. Spending less than you earn is a critical step to financial freedom. But it's only the beginning.

A Hole in the Budget

Meet Ricky. Ricky is a recent college graduate with a decent entry-level job. He's developed good financial habits. He got through college without building up a huge credit card debt. He budgets carefully—so much for rent, so much for food, so much for car insurance. Only after he has paid all his necessary expenses does Ricky use what's leftover to pay for the things he enjoys, such as a weekend trip or a new jacket. This may seem like a good plan—*UNTIL*

- he decides to buy a house.
- he starts a family.
- he loses his job.
- he gets hit with a long-term illness.
- he retires.

Ricky's habit of living within his budget month to month does not allow for life changes and emergencies. On his list of people to pay, Ricky has left someone out. He has forgotten to pay himself.

Get in the Habit

What does it mean to pay yourself first? It simply means to make personal savings a regular part of your budget, just like rent and food. Everyone has the potential to save, even if it means sacrificing a few immediate wants. You'd be surprised where the savings can come from. Cut out the daily $2.00 for soft drinks at the vending machine, and you've just saved $14 a week. Multiply that by 52, and you've pocketed a tidy sum in just one year.

Saving is a habit and takes discipline. You can get into the habit of saving money every month by taking a percentage of your monthly income and then paying yourself first. For example, you can have your employer automatically deposit a certain amount into your savings account. But don't touch

GO FIGURE

$140.6 trillion

The 2008 value of the $24 worth of trinkets that colonists paid to the Manhattoes tribe for Manhattan in 1626, with 8 percent interest compounded annually.

TALE OF TWO SAVERS

The age you start saving can make a big difference in the amount you have at retirement. In the case of the two savers shown here, the difference is more than $1 million! Both savers start with $200 and put way $200 a month. Both earn 8 percent interest compounded annually. Saver 1 starts at age 18. Saver 2 starts at age 36.

PF16

it! People who have trouble saving manage their money in reverse. They spend first, and then save what is left. But what if there's nothing left? Then there's nothing left to save. Saving doesn't mean you don't get to spend your money. It means you get to spend it later.

Why Save?

Not many young people think about saving for retirement. ("Retirement? I haven't even started working!") Yet, when it comes to saving, time is money. There are at least three big benefits to thinking *now* about the day you finally stop working. The biggest benefit is compound interest.

The Magic of Compound Interest

The earlier you start saving, the faster your money will grow. The reason: compound interest. **Compound interest** is interest you earn, not only on the money you put into an account, but also on all the interest you have previously built up. Today's interest earnings will start earning interest tomorrow. The more you save today, the more interest you will gain tomorrow. And that savings will add up at a faster rate. For every year that you put off saving, you could lose thousands of dollars in the long haul.

Save Yourselves Economists warned years ago that Americans faced financial burdens not seen by previous generations. Data show that the decline in savings accounts is a national trend.

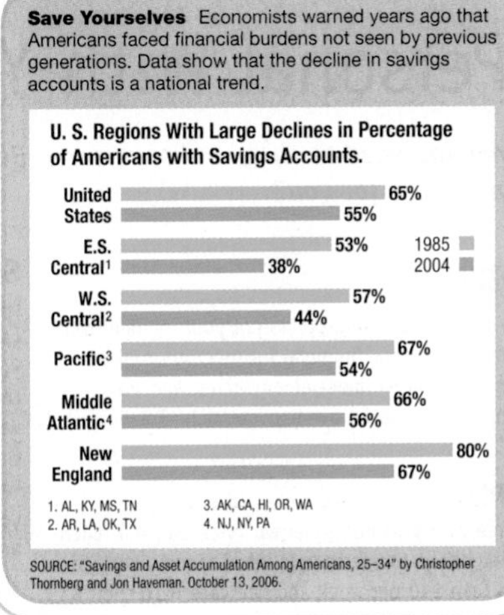

SOURCE: "Savings and Asset Accumulation Among Americans, 25–34" by Christopher Thornberg and Jon Haveman. October 13, 2006.

Other Benefits

There are also big tax benefits when you stash money away for retirement. If you put funds into an **Individual Retirement Account** (IRA), the money may escape taxation until you retire—or at least until you reach age 59 1/2. That cuts your tax bill NOW. Even better, when you withdraw your money from a special IRA (called a Roth IRA), the money you make—the appreciation—may not be taxed at all.

Finally, putting money away now allows you to have a cushion in case of emergencies. There are even circumstances in which—despite the government's restrictions—you can dip into a retirement fund to pay for other expenses. For example, you can access some retirement accounts to buy your first house or to cover high medical expenses.

Whether your dream is a comfortable retirement, a nice home, or foreign travel, you're going to need a savings plan to make it come true. As you'll see, there are many options to choose from. But it all starts with developing the saving habit—with paying yourself first.

Are You Ready?

1. What are the reasons teens should save?
2. What are three things you can sacrifice in order to save money?

WebQuest online To learn more about this topic, visit **PearsonSuccessNet.com**

Background Note

Compounding Period The period at which interest is compounded affects the interest earned, just as the interest rate does. Suppose an investor left $500 for one year in a savings account that earned 2.5 percent interest. Here's the amount of interest earned at different compounding rates:

Daily: $12.66
Monthly: $12.64
Quarterly: $12.62
Annually: $12.50

ANALYZE A CHART

Have students look at the chart on this page that shows a decline in savings accounts. Ask students why they think this decline may have taken place during a time when the economy was growing. *(Possible response: people were spending instead of saving.)*

CALCULATE

Tell students to identify a goal for savings. Their target might be a digital camera, a new computer to use in college, or a new outfit they can wear to their high-school graduation. Have them use online or print resources to find the price of their goal. Then have them figure out how many weeks it would take them to save for that item if they put aside $5 each week. Encourage students to begin saving toward their goal. Then ask students to identify a long-term goal (retirement, buying a house) and encourage them to put part of their savings aside to reach these goals.

UNDERSTANDING COMPOUND INTEREST

Have students complete the second page of the "Pay Yourself First" worksheet. Ask students to explain how compound interest can increase their savings and help them reach their long-term goals.

L1 L2 ELL Differentiate Before having students complete the worksheets, preteach the meanings of the terms *compound* and *interest* on their own. Then help students put together the concept of compound interest.

L4 Differentiate Invite students to develop a "Students' Guide to Savings" that makes basic information about savings understandable to middle-school students.

Assess and Remediate

L3 Collect the "Pay Yourself First" worksheet and assess student understanding of different types of accounts.

L3 Give students the Saving for the Long Haul Quiz (Personal Finance All-in-One, p. 55).

Answers

Are You Ready? 1. to take advantage of compound interest, to benefit from tax advantages, and to have a cushion for emergencies 2. Possible answers: unnecessary snacks, entertainment expenses, unneeded clothing, impulse purchases, and so on

Get Personal With Your Savings Plan

Get Started

LESSON GOALS

Students will:

- Assess the advantages and disadvantages of different savings plans and determine which are best in certain situations by completing a worksheet.
- Understand the benefits and drawbacks of CDs.
- Search for the best interest rates for different savings accounts.
- Practice saving by collecting change for a week.
- Brainstorm ideas for generating savings.

DIFFERENTIATED INSTRUCTION KEY

L1 Special Needs
L2 Basic
ELL English Language Learners
LPR Less Proficient Readers
L3 All Students
L4 Advanced Students

Teach

DISTRIBUTE ACTIVITY WORKSHEET

Distribute the "Saving on Your Terms" worksheet (Personal Finance All-in-One, pp. 56–57). After students have completed the worksheet, have them discuss the different savings plans. Call on volunteers to explain which account they think is best and why. Encourage them to think about different specific purposes for saving when they respond.

DISCUSS

After completing the worksheets, use the Opinion Line strategy (p. T28) to have students show whether they agree or disagree with using CDs as a savings plan. Ask volunteers to explain why they think CDs are desirable or not. Students are likely to mention the fixed term and the withdrawal penalty. Point out that some banks offer CDs for as short a time as one month and ask if that consideration changes their mind. Ask **Under what circumstances would even a short-term CD be undesirable despite a higher interest rate than other savings plan?** *(Possible answer: If the saver absolutely needed complete access to the money at all times.)* Give students an opportunity to move to a different spot on the opinion line if they have changed their minds.

Get Personal With Your Savings Plan

You know why you need to save, and save early. But which savings plan is right for you?

Three Savers

Okay, so you've decided to take a portion of your income every week and put it towards your financial future. Your goal is to achieve financial freedom, meet emergencies, and have a comfortable retirement—maybe even to 'get rich.' But not all paths are equal.

Different "Plans"

Let's look at three young adults: Amanda, Tyler, and A.J. Each of them is making about the same amount of money. Each of them decides to take $10 per week and dedicate it to their financial future.

Amanda takes her $10 and puts it in a shoebox under her bed.

Tyler takes his $10 and puts it in a simple savings account paying 3.6 percent interest.

A.J. takes his $10 and invests in lottery tickets in the hopes of winning a million dollars.

Different Results

Each of the three keeps this up regularly for 20 years. Each of them would say, "I'm paying myself first." But see how different the results are:

- Amanda has paid herself a total of $10,400. She now has $10,400.
- Tyler has paid himself a total of $10,400. He now has $15,392.
- A.J. has paid himself a total of $10,400. He now has $0.

The fact is, the odds of winning a state lottery are something like one in 18 million. So what sounds better to you? A 100 percent chance of increasing your savings by nearly $5,000 … or a 99.99999995 percent chance of losing it all? That's a no-brainer. Tyler's savings account is also clearly more profitable than Amanda's shoebox. But even the savings account may not be the best option of all.

Park Your Savings

In making a personal savings plan, the first question you have to ask yourself is: How much can I save? You've seen how putting aside even a small amount can build up as long as you do it regularly. The amount you save per week should be one that you can reasonably commit to for a year. The key to success is that you must do this even if you cannot afford it. Then, pay your other bills as usual.

Savings Account

Usually, saving starts with setting up a basic savings account carrying no monthly fee. But when choosing a place to park your savings, *shop around*. Make sure the bank is FDIC insured. Some banks will charge you excessive fees just for the privilege of having your money. Web sites such as bankrate.com show you what interest different banks are currently paying for checking accounts.

GO FIGURE

39%

The percentage of Americans who say they have enough money to cover 3 months of living expenses.

SOURCE: "Most Americans Fail the Emergency Test", www.bankrate.com

CDs

Once you start making more money, think about moving some cash into a **certificate of deposit**, or CD. Like a savings account, a CD is insured and therefore very low-risk. But CDs generally offer higher interest than a savings account. The catch is, once you put your money in, you can't take it out for a fixed period of time. Depending on the length of the CD, you would have to part company with your money for as little as three months or as long as five years. There are penalty fees for early withdrawal.

As with savings accounts, you can compare CD rates online. You might even opt for an online bank that offers even higher interest rates than traditional brick and mortar banks. Here are the details for one available CD:

Initial Deposit: $1,000
Length of CD: 1 year, 6 months (18 months)
Interest Rate: 4% compounded daily
Annual Percentage Yield (APY): 4.081%
Ending Balance: $1,061.83

Money Markets

What if you want higher yield than a regular savings account without tying up your money? You might open a **money market account.** This is a type of savings account with a high yield that allows you to write checks as long as you maintain a high balance in the account.

So which is the best plan? It all depends on how much you can afford to put aside, and whether high yield is more important to you than easy access to your money. Your early savings plan may involve a combination of options. As you get nearer to retirement, your options change and multiply.

Background Note

Finders Keepers Why not just hide your money in a place only you know about? You can withdraw it whenever you want to, and there is no risk, right? In a court case in Oregon, $122,000 belonging to the previous owners of a house was left hidden in the basement ceiling when their house was sold. The owners had died, and those selling the house did not know the money was there. The court ruled that the money rightfully belonged to the new owner rather than to the previous owners' estate. The contents of the house were sold with the house, the court said. Of course, everyone lost out on the interest the money could have earned, more than $200,000 over 20 years at 5 percent interest.

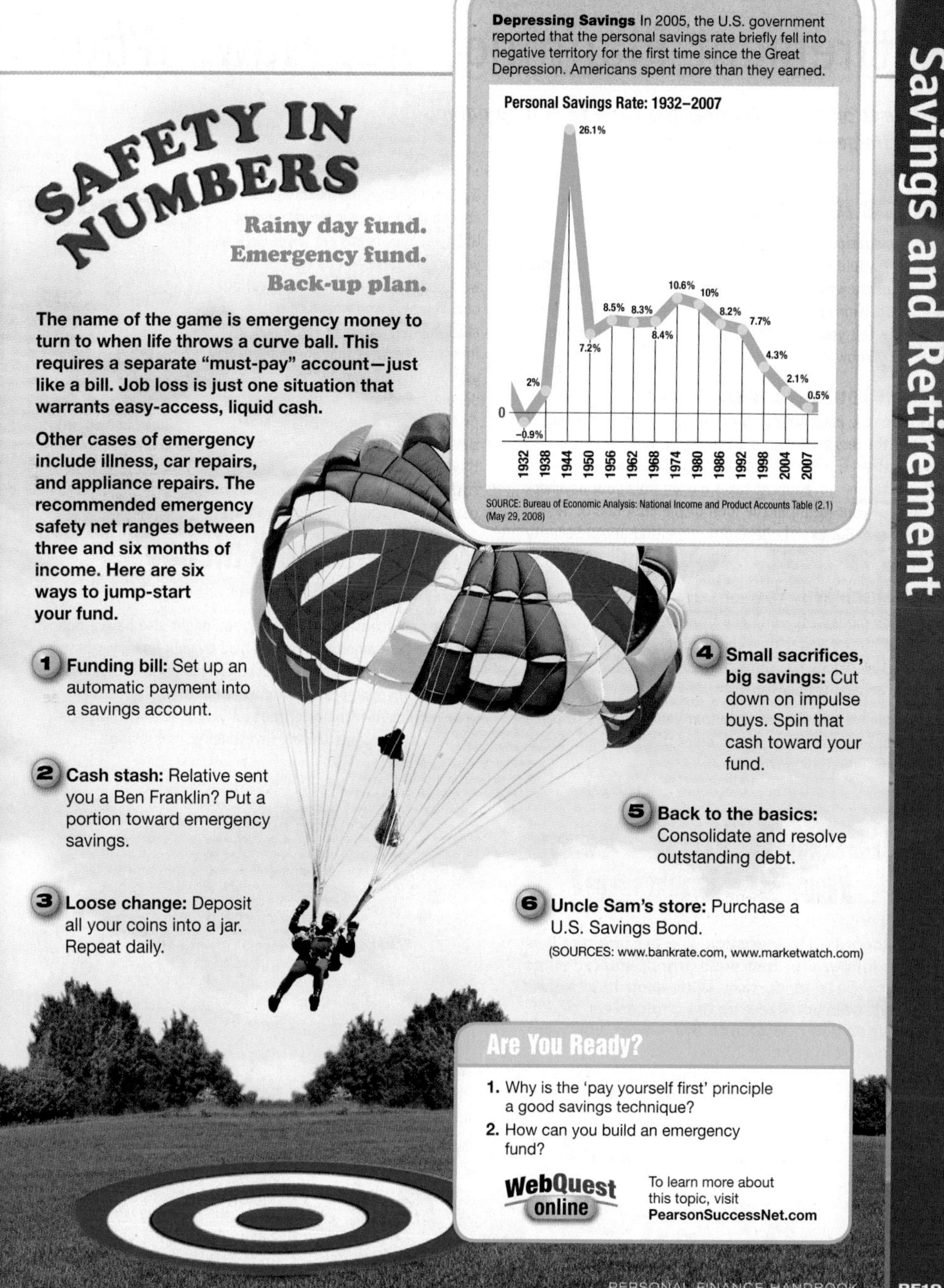

SAFETY IN NUMBERS

Rainy day fund.
Emergency fund.
Back-up plan.

The name of the game is emergency money to turn to when life throws a curve ball. This requires a separate "must-pay" account—just like a bill. Job loss is just one situation that warrants easy-access, liquid cash.

Other cases of emergency include illness, car repairs, and appliance repairs. The recommended emergency safety net ranges between three and six months of income. Here are six ways to jump-start your fund.

1. **Funding bill:** Set up an automatic payment into a savings account.
2. **Cash stash:** Relative sent you a Ben Franklin? Put a portion toward emergency savings.
3. **Loose change:** Deposit all your coins into a jar. Repeat daily.
4. **Small sacrifices, big savings:** Cut down on impulse buys. Spin that cash toward your fund.
5. **Back to the basics:** Consolidate and resolve outstanding debt.
6. **Uncle Sam's store:** Purchase a U.S. Savings Bond.

(SOURCES: www.bankrate.com, www.marketwatch.com)

Depressing Savings In 2005, the U.S. government reported that the personal savings rate briefly fell into negative territory for the first time since the Great Depression. Americans spent more than they earned.

SOURCE: Bureau of Economic Analysis: National Income and Product Accounts Table (2.1) (May 29, 2008)

Are You Ready?

1. Why is the 'pay yourself first' principle a good savings technique?
2. How can you build an emergency fund?

WebQuest online — To learn more about this topic, visit **PearsonSuccessNet.com**

Savings and Retirement

PERSONAL FINANCE HANDBOOK PF19

ANALYZE A GRAPH

Have students examine the Depressing Savings graph on page PF19. Ask **What was the highest personal savings rate after the spike in 1944?** *(10.6 percent in 1974)* Ask students to consider how much money they would be able to save if they committed to saving 10 percent of their income. Have students think about what percentage of their income they could realistically save every month.

FIND RATES

If computers are accessible in class, divide the class into thirds and assign each third one type of savings plan: savings accounts, money market accounts, and CDs. Challenge students in each group to search online for the best rates for their type of account.

PRACTICE SAVING

Encourage students to empty their pockets and purses of coins at home at the end of each day, placing them in a jar. Instruct them to count the change at the end of a week. Suggest that they store these funds until they have enough to open a savings account—and then to do so!

BRAINSTORM

Call on students to suggest other ways of finding money to put into savings. Have the class vote on the top ten savings tips.

Explain to students that one great way to save is to have money deducted from a paycheck before you receive the check. This method enforces saving on a regular basis. Have students fill in the Authorization for Payroll Deduction form (Personal Finance All-in-One, p. 58).

Assess and Remediate

L3 Collect the "Saving on Your Terms" worksheets and assess student understanding of the suitability of different accounts to different savings needs.

L3 Give students the Get Personal with Your Savings Plan Quiz (Personal Finance All-in-One, p. 59).

Answers

Are You Ready? 1. Possible answer: Paying yourself first is a good savings technique because it ensures that some money is saved. If you cover expenses first, before saving, you may well spend all your money without saving anything. 2. Possible answers: by setting up an automatic payment to a savings account, using money received as a gift, saving loose change, cutting impulse buying, removing debt, and buying a savings bond

Retirement Planning: Me? Now? *Why?*

Get Started

LESSON GOALS

Students will:

- Explain the benefits of beginning to save for retirement when you are young.
- Analyze a Social Security benefits statement.
- Compare the features of different retirement plans, such as Social Security, personal investment, and employer plans by completing a worksheet.
- Analyze graphs and charts to draw conclusions about income needed in retirement.

DIFFERENTIATED INSTRUCTION KEY

L1 Special Needs
L2 Basic
ELL English Language Learners
LPR Less Proficient Readers
L3 All Students
L4 Advanced Students

Teach

ANALYZE

Remind students of the benefit gained from beginning to save for retirement early in life. Direct their attention back to the illustration on pages PF16–17. Point out that the difference in the two retirement accounts is more than $1 million. Ask **If that $1 million earned 5 percent a year in yield, how much income would it generate each year?** *($50,000)* **If a person could live on that income alone, how much of the principal would remain untouched?** *(all of it)* **How would the retiree benefit from that fact?** *(Possible answers: If the principal remained untouched, it would continue producing the same level of income. The principal would also be available to cover any emergencies that might arise.)*

ANALYZE A GRAPH

Draw students' attention to the Retiring Nations graph on page PF21. Ask students to brainstorm about the factors that a person might consider when deciding at what age to retire. *(Students should consider such things as amount of money saved, availability of work, type of work, cultural values)*

Retirement Planning: Me? Now? *Why?*

Believe it or not, it is never too early to start planning for retirement. Here's why.

Retire in Style

Prom, graduation, car, college. With so much on your mind now, why would you even think about retirement? The answer is simple. You will have to live later with the consequences of your decisions now. Most people on the brink of retirement today will tell you that they wished they had known then what they know now.

Wait at Your Own Risk

It is never too early to plan for retirement. The longer you wait to save, the less time your money has to work for you. If you have a job now, you're already putting some money away for retirement. The government takes money from your paycheck to save for your future in the form of the FICA tax, or Social Security tax. But experts generally agree that Social Security payments alone will not fund a comfortable retirement.

How Much Will You Need?

How much money will you need in retirement? That depends on mountains of variables—your health, your lifestyle, where you live. Everybody has different needs. Let's look at some current, general estimates.

Many financial advisers estimate that you will need 70 percent of your pre-retirement income in order to retire comfortably. By comfortably they mean you will be able to keep up your pre-retirement lifestyle. Your needs are lower because you do not have to buy clothes for work, pay for commuting, and eating out. You also won't have to put as much money into your retirement investments. It is time for them to pay you. No one is average, however. Some people spend more money when they first retire because they have more time for travel and entertainment. As they age, they travel less, and those costs go down. But, in many cases the cost of healthcare goes up.

GO FIGURE

The amount that 1 in 3 U.S. workers born in 1990 will have in a 401(k) plan at retirement.

SOURCE: U.S. Government Accountability Office report, November 29, 2007

Where Does the Money Come From?

The first source is Social Security. You might also have a defined pension, a set amount of money paid by your employer based on your wages and length of employment. Defined pensions, however, are disappearing in private industry. The rest of your retirement income depends on you: a 401(k), Individual Retirement Accounts (IRAs), investments, and savings.

Launch Your Plans for Retirement

According to statistics, you are going to live a longer life than your grandparents. What you have to do now is develop habits that will help you live with the choices you make. When you ride off into the sunset, you want to do it in style.

Background Note

Where to Retire People nearing retirement age have to consider not just *when* they retire, but *where*. Each person has his or her own considerations—the location of family, the types of activities they most enjoy—but the cost of living is one factor that most people have to look at. Many magazines publish lists of the most affordable places to retire, and they include towns not just in the sunny states of Florida and Arizona, but also in Idaho, Colorado, Texas, Louisiana, North Carolina, and Maine. It's not clear where the Baby Boomers are headed. The Census Bureau shows that the states with the highest percent of households that have retirement income are West Virginia (23.7%), Delaware (23.1%), and Hawaii (22%). The states with the largest percentage of people aged 65 years or older are Florida, West Virginia, and Pennsylvania.

Social Security

Each year the Social Security Administration sets the minimum amount of earnings you need to have to be entitled to Social Security benefits. You can begin to collect reduced benefits at age 62 and full benefits at age 67 for people born after 1959. As the population ages, the point will come when Social Security will pay out more in benefits than it collects each year in payroll taxes. There is a lively debate in progress about how long Social Security will last and what it will provide in the future. The message here is that you have to prepare to take care of yourself.

401(k)

This leads us to the 401(k). You want to pay attention to this retirement plan. The law allows you to set aside a portion of your pay before taxes are withheld. Rent, credit cards, and student loans may limit what you can contribute to your 401(k), but the returns are worth the sacrifice. Some employers match every dollar you save up to three percent of your salary. Others may choose to contribute 50 cents per dollar you save, up to six percent of your salary. Either way, you get an immediate return on your money and you don't pay taxes on any of it until you withdraw it years later.

Employers have come to realize that many people do not have a clue how to invest the money in their 401(k) accounts. More and more employers are providing sources of investment advice to their employees to help them make the most of their money.

Other Accounts

The federal government also encourages you to save for retirement by providing special tax advantages for other retirement accounts.

- You can open up a traditional Individual Retirement Account (IRA) at a bank and contribute $4,000 per year. Depending on your income, this money may be tax deductible. You have to be ready to leave this money alone. Tapping an IRA prior to age 59 1/2 will cost you dual penalties. You will forfeit 10 percent of your interest, plus pay taxes on what you have withdrawn as though it were added income. The 10 percent penalty is waived if the money is used for higher education or first-time home ownership.
- In a **ROTH IRA,** contributions are taxed prior to investing but withdrawals after age 59 1/2 are tax free, meaning you never pay taxes on the interest or dividends that have accumulated over the years. Roth IRA money may be withdrawn for first-time homeowners or higher education on the condition that the account has been open for 5 years. Early withdrawals will be subject to the 10 percent penalty.

Federal regulations regarding these kinds of accounts are subject to change by Congress. In recent years, the Congress has raised the savings limits to encourage people to save more for retirement.

Retiring Nations Although the average age of retirement among American workers has risen in the past decade, it's still about four years less than in Japan. As people live longer, the retirement age is likely to rise even more.

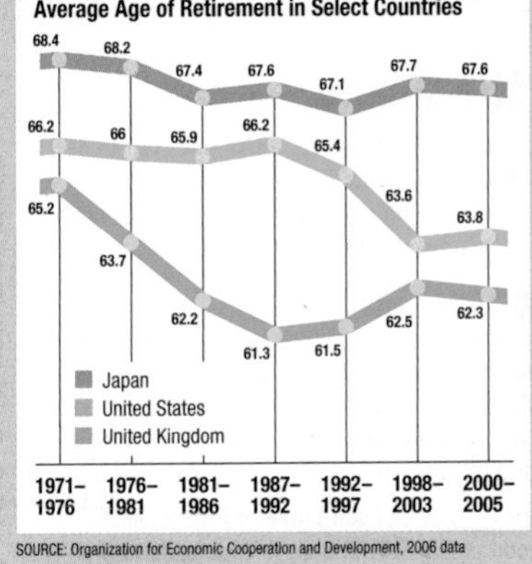

Are You Ready?

1. What factors influence how much you will need to retire?
2. Describe two ways you can save for retirement.

To learn more about this topic, visit **PearsonSuccessNet.com**

Savings and Retirement

Secure Retirement

DISPLAY TRANSPARENCY

Display the transparency "Social Security Statement" (Color Transparencies, p. PF.d). Explain that the Social Security Administration sends such statements to workers each year once they have worked long enough to be eligible for Social Security benefits (which typically takes about ten years of full-time work). Ask **How do the benefits change if the worker delays retirement from age 62 to age 67?** *(The benefits increase by $458.)* **How else would the worker benefit by working those additional five years?** *(The worker could make additional contributions to another retirement plan in those five years, increasing the retirement income available.)* **Suppose the worker who receives this statement currently needs $4,000 a month to live. How can that worker maintain the same standard of living?** *(He or she will have to earn about $2,500 a month more from other retirement plans if he or she retires at 67.)*

DISTRIBUTE ACTIVITY WORKSHEET

Distribute the "Your Nest Egg" worksheet (Personal Finance All-in-One, pp. 60–61) to explore the differences between Social Security and other retirement plans. After students have completed the worksheet, have the class discuss their answers to the last question. Call on respondents to give reasons for their conclusions.

EXTEND

Give students the "How Much Will You Need to Retire?" worksheet (Personal Finance All-in-One, p. 62). Give them time to study the graphs and chart about pensions. Then have them present their findings to the class.

Assess and Remediate

L3 Collect the "Your Nest Egg" and "How Much Will You Need to Retire?" worksheets and assess student understanding of retirement plans.

L3 Give students the Retirement Planning: Me? Now? *Why?* Quiz (Personal Finance All-in-One, p. 63).

Answers

Are You Ready? 1. your health, your lifestyle, and where you will live 2. Possible answers: through any savings account, with a 401(k), with an IRA or ROTH IRA

Fundamentals of Good Credit

Get Started

LESSON GOALS

Students will:

- Apply the three C's to a credit granting situation.
- Analyze changes in the percentage of income that households have to pay on debt.
- Explain the factors that influence a credit score.
- Examine the impact of different consumer actions on credit score by analyzing a chart.

DIFFERENTIATED INSTRUCTION KEY

L1 Special Needs
L2 Basic
  ELL English Language Learners
  LPR Less Proficient Readers
L3 All Students
L4 Advanced Students

Teach

MAKE DECISIONS

Tell students to put themselves in the position of a loan officer at a bank. Three customers come to the bank asking to borrow $15,000 over five years to buy a new car. Monthly payments would be $275. Customer 1 has no credit history. Customer 2 has had two store cards for a year. Customer 3 has paid off a car loan and has had a credit card for two years. Write the following additional information on the board:

	Current Savings	Current Debts	Monthly Income	Rent
#1	$200	$0	$2,000	$700
#2	$1,000	$500	$3,000	$500
#3	$2,000	$1,000	$4,000	$1,000

Have the class discuss how creditworthy they think each applicant is, giving reasons for their evaluations. After discussing all three applicants, have the class vote on whether to approve the loan for each applicant. Explain that in evaluating these applicants, they were taking into account the "three C's." Call on volunteers to explain how they weighted each of those factors in making their decision in this hypothetical case.

Fundamentals of Good Credit

Are you credit worthy? It matters more than you think.

Making the Grade

Congratulations! You got great grades. You're one step closer to the college of your choice and maybe even lower car insurance costs—all for being responsible. Believe it or not, your credit history will have a similar impact.

Establishing Your Credit

As a first-time borrower, you may find it tough to get a credit card or a car loan on your own. Without a credit history to check, lenders often will require a co-signer to guarantee that the loan will be repaid if you fail to repay. This person could be your parent or another relative with a good credit history.

The rest is up to you. How can you prove to future lenders that you are a good credit risk? The most important step is simple: Pay your bills on time. Every late or missed payment will end up on your credit report.

Your Credit Report

Your **credit report** is your financial report card. In addition to your payment history, it includes the details of your bank and credit card accounts. Lenders can see how much debt you are already carrying. They can also see if you have had any bankruptcies or judgments against you, or if you owe back taxes.

National credit reporting agencies create a **FICO score** based on your credit history. The score falls in a range from about 300 to 900. Usually, a score of at least 700 gives you access to reasonable credit. (The chart on the next page shows how your credit score is calculated.) For a fee, you can find out your credit score at MyFico.com.

GO FIGURE

$1,585

The average credit card debt of a U.S. college freshman.

SOURCE: 2005 Sallie Mae report "Undergraduate Students and Credit Cards"

ADVENTURES IN CREDIT
Whether or not you are judged to be a good credit risk depends on the three C's.
Good Credit
CAPACITY
Your expenses, your job, and how long you have had it
CHARACTER
Financial history and payment record
CAPITAL
What assets you have to back up a loan, like a savings account, property, investments

A bad credit report can sink more than a loan. It also affects your chances of getting insurance, an apartment, a mortgage—even a job. Like lenders, many landlords and employers check credit histories. They see on-time bill paying as an indication of whether you will be a responsible tenant or worker. The **Fair Credit Reporting Act** sets the terms by which credit information about you can be gathered and used.

Protecting Your Credit

Suppose there are mistakes in your credit report or you have made poor credit choices. What can you do?

Check It Out

Free credit reports are available once per year from each of the three national credit-reporting agencies: Experian, Transunion, and Equifax. To get a free credit report go online: www.annualcreditreport.com; call (877) 322-8228; or mail: Annual Credit Report Request Service, P.O. Box 105281, Atlanta, GA, 30348. A credit report is not the same as a credit score.

You should review credit reports from all three agencies to check for errors and possible fraud. In some states, consumers who suspect fraud can place a security freeze on their credit file. This action prevents any new accounts from being opened in your name.

If you find an error in your credit report, send a separate letter to each agency where the mistake is found as soon as possible. Include a copy of the credit report with the misinformation highlighted. The credit reporting agency is required by law to investigate with the creditor in question. It should remove from your credit report any mistakes a creditor admits. The **Fair Credit Billing Act** requires creditors to correct errors without lowering your credit rating.

How Do You Score? The chart below shows the factors that affect your credit score. Paying your bills on time has the greatest influence. Knowing the factors that affect credit should help you understand how you can improve your score.

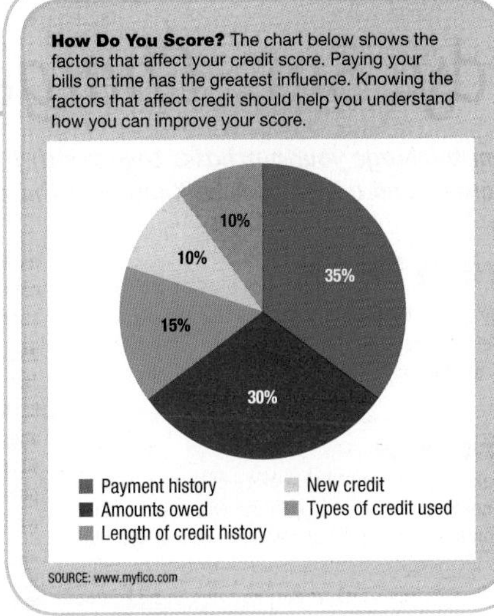

SOURCE: www.myfico.com

Clean It Up

No matter how careful you might be with your finances, circumstances my get the better of you. The loss of a job or a medical emergency could leave you in a world of financial difficulty. Here are some steps to take if you have trouble paying your bills on time.

Reassess your needs and wants. Be prepared to make hard choices.

- Stop using credit until you are out of trouble.
- Contact your lenders to negotiate a different payment schedule or interest rate.
- Contact nonprofit credit counseling organizations who, for a small fee, can provide debt-management assistance and intervene with card issuers. Make sure the service is affiliated with a third party such as the Association of Independent Consumer Credit Counseling Agencies or National Foundation of Credit Counseling.

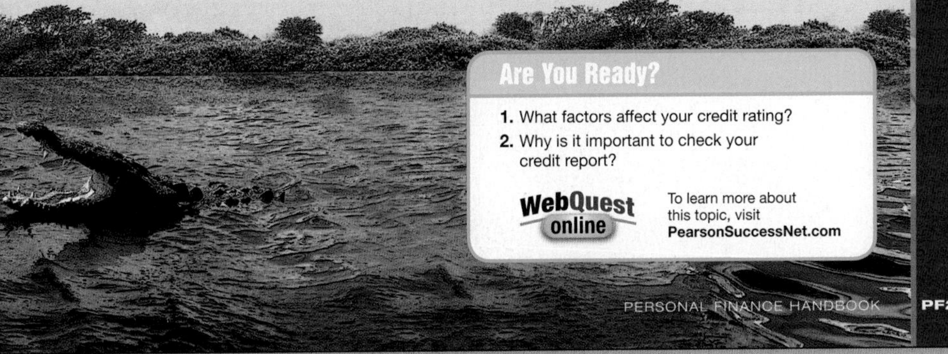

Are You Ready?

1. What factors affect your credit rating?
2. Why is it important to check your credit report?

WebQuest online — To learn more about this topic, visit **PearsonSuccessNet.com**

Credit and Debt

WEIGHT THE FACTORS

Direct students' attention to the How Do You Score pie chart. Ask them to weight the factors in their decision about the loan approval according to the weights shown in the pie chart. Ask **Did your evaluation change?**

DISPLAY TRANSPARENCY

Display the transparency, "Growing Household Debt" (Color Transparencies, p. PF.e). Explain that *disposable income* is income after taxes; it is the income that households have for spending on all their needs and wants. Ask students **What trend does the data show?** *(The percentage has gone up from just over 10 percent in 1980 to just over 14 percent in 2008.)* Ask **What does that trend suggest about household borrowing? Why?** *(Since more of households' income is used to pay debts, the amount of money they borrowed probably was increasing.)* **What will happen to household finances if the trend continues?** *(Households will have less and less money available for spending other than paying back debt.)* **How can households prevent that problem from developing?** *(Possible answers: pay off existing debt to eliminate it; hold down future spending)*

DISTRIBUTE ACTIVITY WORKSHEET

Distribute the "Keep Track of Your Score" worksheet (Personal Finance All-in-One, pp. 64–65) and the "Credit Report" form (Personal Finance All-in-One, p. 66). Have students answer the questions on the first page of the worksheet and then use the credit report form to answer the second page.

L2 ELL Differentiate Pair English language learners with English proficient students to complete the worksheet.

After students have completed the worksheet, discuss what they learned about credit scores and the wise use of credit. Call on volunteers to identify their idea of the fundamentals of good credit.

Background Note

Credit Reports and Credit Scores The three chief credit-reporting agencies are required by law to issue free credit reports to each consumer once a year. When consumers access the Web sites, the agencies offer many other fee-based services—including the consumer's credit score. Consumers may choose to exercise this option, but the law requiring that the agencies provide credit reports at no charge does not apply to these additional services. It applies only to the basic credit report. Consumers who wish to see their credit score will have to pay for that privilege.

Assess and Remediate

L3 Collect "Keep Track of Your Score" worksheets and assess student understanding of the importance of establishing and maintaining a good credit score.

L3 Give students the Fundamentals of Good Credit Quiz (Personal Finance All-in-One, p. 67).

Answers

Are You Ready? 1. Five factors (in order from most to least important): payment history; amounts owed; length of credit history; new credit; types of credit used 2. to check for errors and possible fraud

Ready. Set. *Charge?*

Get Started

LESSON GOALS

Students will:

- Discuss whether teens under age 18 should be allowed to have their own credit cards and how they should use family cards.
- Explain what factors consumers should consider in evaluating credit cards and compare the terms and conditions of different cards.
- Complete a credit card application form for practice.
- Understand debt cost to consumers by analyzing a repayment schedule and steps to take to manage excessive debt.

DIFFERENTIATED INSTRUCTION KEY

L1 Special Needs
L2 Basic
ELL English Language Learners
LPR Less Proficient Readers
L3 All Students
L4 Advanced Students

Teach

DEBATE

Ask **Why are teens under age 18 prevented from having their own credit cards?** *(Possible answer: They are minors.)* Have students debate whether they think this prohibition is fair or advisable. Call on both dissenters and supporters to give reasons for their positions.

Tell students to take the role of parents who allow a teenager to use a family credit card. Ask **Can teens learn anything by using a family credit card? How?** *(Possible answer: They can learn how to use credit carefully and, if they are required to pay for their own charges, how to manage the account.)* **What possible problems might arise from such use?** *(Possible answers: Teens might charge too much out of inexperience. Teens might not inform their parents of purchases, leading to unpleasant surprises.)* Call on the class to develop a set of rules that they, as parents, would want to set for teens to use a family credit card.

Ready. Set. *Charge?*

The freedom to charge your purchases comes with fine print, finance charges, and a host of fees. Know your limits.

The Lure of Credit

"Buy now—pay later." Those four words sum up the attraction of **credit**, or deferred payment. Credit comes in many forms, from car loans to mortgages—and most popular of all, the credit card.

Credit Convenience

Credit cards make buying easy. With a piece of plastic, you can walk into nearly any store and walk out with merchandise. As for buying online, it would be almost unthinkable without credit cards.

No wonder credit card use by Americans has skyrocketed. And no wonder the companies that issue credit cards enjoy tremendous profits.

Teens and Credit

Americans under 18 are prohibited from having their own credit cards. Still, about one third of all high school students use cards linked to the account of a parent or relative. And when you turn 18, the flood really begins! Expect a ton of mail from credit card companies eager to issue you your first card. Some may even offer you freebies, such as T-shirts or sports gear, just for filling out an application.

Why do they want your business? The answer is simple: *teens spend*. Each year, consumers between the ages of 12 and 19 spend well over $100 billion of their own and their parents money. Credit card companies want to tap into this spending power.

GO FIGURE

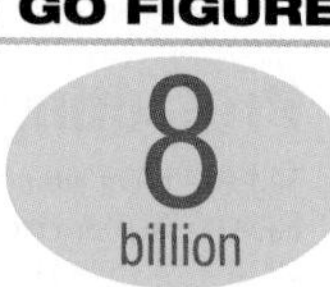

The number of credit card solicitations that American households received in their mailboxes in 2006.

SOURCE: Mintel comperemedia

Credit Traps and Tips

So there you are, card in hand and a world of things to buy. Unless you learn how to use credit responsibly, you could find yourself in a deep hole. You won't be there alone. It is estimated a majority of Americans between the ages of 18 and 24 spend nearly 30 percent of their monthly income on debt repayment.

PF24

Background Note

Opting Out Consumers do not *have* to receive unsolicited offers of credit. Federal law allows consumers to opt out of such offers by calling a phone number or registering online. Searching online using the terms "opt out" and "credit offers" will provide up-to-date information on the numbers and URLs to use. Consumers can block all unsolicited telemarketing calls—not just credit offers—by registering their phone numbers on the federal government's "Do Not Call" list. Using the name of the list as an online search tool will provide the phone number to call.

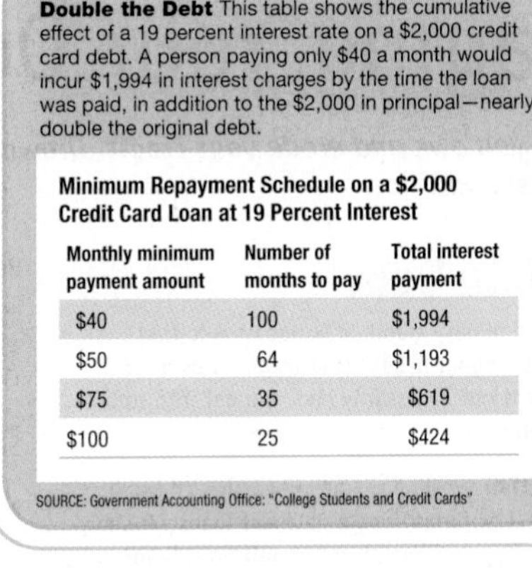

Double the Debt This table shows the cumulative effect of a 19 percent interest rate on a $2,000 credit card debt. A person paying only $40 a month would incur $1,994 in interest charges by the time the loan was paid, in addition to the $2,000 in principal—nearly double the original debt.

Minimum Repayment Schedule on a $2,000 Credit Card Loan at 19 Percent Interest

Monthly minimum payment amount	Number of months to pay	Total interest payment
$40	100	$1,994
$50	64	$1,193
$75	35	$619
$100	25	$424

SOURCE: Government Accounting Office: "College Students and Credit Cards"

Avoid Those Charges

Ideally, you'll want to pay off your credit card balance in full every month. True, you are *required* to make only a small minimum payment. But look at the table on the right. For every dollar you don't pay this month, you'll pay interest next month. Worse, first-time cardholders without an established credit rating are often subject to a higher-than-normal **annual percentage rate** (APR).

What if you pay late or miss a payment entirely? You'll be subject to a late penalty. The finance charges, which include the APR and any related fees, can quickly add up to more than your initial purchase.

Suppose a credit card company requires a $10 minimum payment on a $290 outfit. If your payment is late by even one day, you'll get hit with a late fee and more than likely a significantly higher APR. And if your balance goes over the credit limit set by the issuer, there's a charge for that, too. Suddenly, the $290 "bargain" can turn into a $600 headache.

The Cost of Cash

Fees mount up even faster if you use your credit card to get cash. A cash advance carries an up-front fee of 2 percent to 4 percent, plus a higher interest rate than the regular card. And the charges start the second the ATM coughs out the cash.

Read the Fine Print

The importance of reading the fine print of a credit card's terms of agreement should not be lost on any cardholder. The **Truth in Lending Act** requires banks to provide complete information on the APR, fees, and surcharges. This information is usually located on the back of a credit card application and monthly statements. Still, banks can change these terms, raising rates and fees when they feel it is necessary. You can opt out of the changes, which will close the account. You can then pay off the balance under the old terms. The time it takes to review these terms could save you headaches and money.

Credit or Debit?

The surest way to avoid the debt trap is to keep credit card use to a minimum. For lower-cost purchases, you are better off using a debit card, a check, or cash. A **debit card** offers the same convenience as a credit card. But because the money comes straight out of your bank account, there is no interest rate and no risk of going over your limit. The danger of debit cards is that they are so easy to use, you may lose track of your spending.

For online purchases, however, it's wisest to use a credit card. It offers greater security.

Are You Ready?

1. Give three examples of bank fees.
2. What is the difference between a debit card and a credit card?

WebQuest online To learn more about this topic, visit **PearsonSuccessNet.com**

Credit and Debt

DISTRIBUTE ACTIVITY WORKSHEET

Distribute the worksheet, "The Best Card for You" (Personal Finance All-in-One, pp. 68–69). Have students complete the activity to learn more about different factors they should consider in evaluating credit cards and to compare the terms and conditions of different cards.

L2 LPR Differentiate Make sure that students understand how APR and finance charges are related. Clarify that finance charges are the interest added to a credit card balance that is not paid in full. The APR is simply the *rate* that determines how much the added finance charge will be.

Distribute the "Credit Card Application" form (Personal Finance All-in-One, p. 70). Have students fill out the form using fictional information—not their own name, address, income, and so on. After students have completed the form, discuss their reactions to it as a class. Ask **Did you find the form easy or difficult to follow? Were you surprised by any of the information that was requested?**

ANALYZE

Direct students' attention to the chart on the page. Ask **How much interest would the person pay in the first month, on the full amount of $2,000?** *($2,000 at 19% interest equals $380)* **How much interest would the person pay in the last month?** *($100 at 19% interest equals $19)* **How does this information affect your decisions about the repayment schedule?** *(Possible answer: I should try to pay as much as possible monthly to reduce my total debt.)*

L3 Differentiate Have visual learners translate the information in the chart into a bar graph to better see the different cost to a consumer of paying the various amounts.

EXTEND

Distribute the "Making Peace with Your Plastic" worksheet (Personal Finance All-in-One, pp. 71–72). Have students complete the activity to learn more about effective ways of managing credit cards.

Assess and Remediate

L3 Collect the worksheets—"The Best Card for You" and "Making Peace with Your Plastic"—and assess student understanding of the terms of credit cards.

L3 Give students the Ready. Set. *Charge?* Quiz (Personal Finance All-in-One, p. 73).

Answers

Are You Ready? 1. *any three:* late penalties, finance charges, charges for going over the credit limit, cash advance fees 2. A debit card is convenient, like a credit card, but withdraws money from the cardholder's account rather than borrowing money.

Managing Your Debts

Get Started

LESSON GOALS

Students will:

- Discuss the impact of growing household debt and develop a list of suggestions for using credit wisely.
- Explore strategies for getting out of debt and discuss their effectiveness.
- Determine the impact of different debt reduction strategies.
- Describe the purpose of bankruptcy and the effects it can have on one's future.

> **DIFFERENTIATED INSTRUCTION KEY**
>
> **L1** Special Needs
>
> **L2** Basic
>
> **ELL** English Language Learners
>
> **LPR** Less Proficient Readers
>
> **L3** All Students
>
> **L4** Advanced Students

Teach

DISCUSS

Direct students' attention to the "Go Figure" fact on the page. Ask **How does this level of spending affect the financial condition of households?** *(It results in ever-growing debt.)* **What kinds of problems can that cause?** *(Possible answers: financial problems, such as the loss of possessions if payments cannot be maintained; interpersonal problems due to growing financial pressure and tension; health problems if healthcare is ignored)* Challenge students to develop a five- or six-point list of suggestions for using credit wisely to avoid these problems.

L4 **Differentiate** Have students write and design a brochure that can be used to educate other teens on developing a good credit history and using credit wisely.

DISTRIBUTE ACTIVITY WORKSHEET

Distribute the "Bills, Bills, Bills" worksheet (Personal Finance All-in-One, pp. 74–75). Have students complete the worksheet to explore strategies for getting out of debt. After students have completed the worksheet, discuss the strategies as a class. Call on volunteers to explain how effective they think the strategies are and why.

Managing Your Debts

Ignore what you owe and erode your credit. Drowning in debt is as bad as it sounds.

Getting Into Debt

With today's world of easy credit, it is not hard to find yourself in debt over your head. Using credit cards or borrowing money is not necessarily bad. You get into trouble when you go overboard.

Types of Loans

Loans come in several forms. Single-payment loans are short-term loans paid off in one lump sum. **Installment loans,** such as home mortgages or auto loans, are repaid at regularly scheduled intervals. Each payment is divided between principal, or the amount borrowed, and interest. (The earlier you are in the life of the loan, the higher the proportion of each payment goes toward interest.) A third kind of debt is revolving credit, where the amount borrowed and paid changes each month. The best example is a credit card.

How Much Is too Much?

Carrying some debt is not a problem—almost everybody does it. But you need to stay within safe limits. A general rule is that your debt payments, including a mortgage, should not be more than 36 percent of your gross income (income before taxes and deductions). You can estimate your own debt-to-income ratio by dividing the amount of money that you owe by the amount of money that you earn. If the result is higher than 36 percent, you probably owe too much money.

Here are some warning signs:

- ▶ Inability to make minimum payments
- ▶ Relying on credit cards out of necessity and not convenience
- ▶ Borrowing from one credit card in order to pay another
- ▶ Tapping retirement savings or other investments to pay loans

Getting Out

One reason people take on too much debt is that they want stuff NOW and ignore the fact that credit is a promise to pay later. They don't adequately plan for the fact that the repayment of principal and interest begins to eat into money needed for necessities.

Caught in the Debt Spiral

Take Andy. His entry-level job had an entry-level salary. The debt he ran up in college soared as he depended more and more on "plastic" to cover the basics. Paying just the minimum spared his credit temporarily, but he was racking up high finance charges. Once he started missing payments, creditors began calling. Now what?

> **GO FIGURE**
>
> **$1.22**
>
> **The amount American consumers spent for every dollar they earned in 2004.**
>
> SOURCE: "The Basics: How Does Your Debt Compare?" by Kim Khan

Background Note

An Option to Using Credit The credit crunch of 2008 made it difficult for some consumers to obtain credit. Others hesitated to borrow, concerned about their future situation in a time of economic uncertainty. This slowdown in consumer spending came when the holiday season approached, alarming retailers who rely on consumer spending at that time to generate most of the year's profits. Several responded by bringing back an old method that had gone out of style with the expansion of credit—installment buying, commonly called layaway. With installment buying, consumers put some money down on an item they desire, which the retailer sets aside for them. The consumer then makes regular weekly or monthly payments. When the good is completely paid for—with no interest but possibly a low one-time fee—the consumer owns it and can take it home.

Credit Counseling

Andy hated to admit it, but he needed help. He tried credit counseling. A credit counseling agency will negotiate on your behalf with the creditors, trying to get you an extension of time and lower interest rates. For a small service fee, it will take over your monthly payments. Andy checked with the National Foundation for Credit Counseling and the Association of Independent Consumer Credit Counseling Agencies to find a reputable agency. He now writes one check per month to the agency, instead of three to his creditors.

Other Options

If you find yourself in Andy's shoes, there are other options to consider—with caution. You could swallow your pride and ask a relative or friend for a loan. If you go this route, though, make sure that you have a written repayment plan and offer to pay interest.

You could also try taking out a loan from a credit union. Credit unions usually offer more lenient credit terms than banks. You may, however, need a co-signer.

Bankruptcy: The Last Resort

Bankruptcy is truly your last option. Common reasons for bankruptcy are large hospital and medical bills, uninsured losses, or high credit card bills. Some of these are unavoidable, but many people get into serious debt because of poor decisions and lack of foresight. Once you declare bankruptcy it will be harder for you to obtain credit. Nearly every credit application asks: *Have you ever declared bankruptcy?* So take this step only with the help of a lawyer who specializes in bankruptcy and can explain the options and consequences.

Credit Slips Over the past three decades, the number of Americans who filed for bankruptcy has risen over 300 percent. The 2005 law that changed the rules for bankruptcy appeared to have little effect on the number of Americans who sought protection from their creditors. New cases in 2006 were down only slightly from 2004.

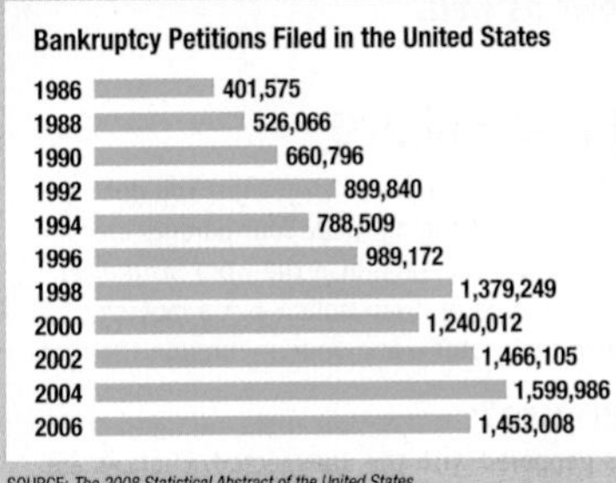

One option is known as Chapter 7, or liquidation. You give up your assets in exchange for your debts. The cash value of your assets is paid to the creditors. To reduce fraud and make it harder to declare bankruptcy, the federal government passed the Bankruptcy Abuse Prevention and **Consumer Protection Act** of 2005. Debtors must prove that their income is below their state's median income and complete financial counseling and financial management education. Also, the government randomly audits debtors to check up on the accuracy of the bankruptcy documents.

A second option is known as Chapter 13, or debt adjustment, which involves temporarily suspending foreclosures and collection actions while you draft and execute a plan to repay some or all of the debts in three to five years. The amount to be repaid depends on how much you have versus how much you owe. Any form of bankruptcy will make it far more difficult to rebuild a secure financial future.

> *"If you think nobody cares if you're alive, try missing a couple of car payments."*
>
> —Earl Wilson, author and newspaper columnist

Are You Ready?

1. Give several reasons why some people get into trouble with debt.
2. Why is bankruptcy a last resort?

WebQuest online — To learn more about this topic, visit PearsonSuccessNet.com

Credit and Debt

CALCULATE

Direct students' attention to the steps taken by a credit counseling agency. Ask **How would extending the time over which loans are due help a consumer?** *(Possible answer: If the loan is repaid over a longer time and the interest rate is reduced, payments will probably be smaller and thus more manageable.)* **How would lowering interest rates help?** *(Lower interest rates mean more of the payment going to reduce the principal.)*

To demonstrate this effect, write the following chart on the board:

Principal	Interest Rate	Monthly Payments (24)	Total Payments
$2,500	21.9%	$129.57	$3,109.68
$2,500	12.9%	$118.74	$2,849.76

Have students calculate the difference between the two total payments. *($259.92)*

DISCUSS

Tell students to think about whether they would want to buy a new car or a home in the future. Ask **What impact would declaring bankruptcy have on achieving those goals? Why?** *(Declaring bankruptcy would make both difficult or at least delay them because declaring bankruptcy makes it difficult to develop the credit history needed to make these purchases.)* **What is the best solution to this problem?** *(Possible answer: avoiding credit problems in the first place)*

ANALYZE CHART

Have students look at the Credit Slips chart at the top of page PF27. Ask **Why do people declare bankruptcy?** Have students look back at the chart on page PF19, Depressing Savings. Ask them to compare the two charts and describe any similarities they see. *(The percent Americans saved went down steadily from 1986 to 2007. The number of bankruptcy petitions more than tripled during that period.)*

Assess and Remediate

L3 Collect the "Bills, Bills, Bills" worksheets and assess student understanding of how to avoid and manage debt.

L3 Give students the Managing Your Debts Quiz (Personal Finance All-in-One, p. 76).

Answers

Are You Ready? 1. Possible answers: buying more goods than they can afford; making only minimum payments; not planning for repayment of loans 2. because it is harder to obtain credit in the future

Insurance Basics, Part I

Get Started

LESSON GOALS

Students will:

- Compare the cost of car insurance for two different vehicles by completing a worksheet.
- Analyze the insurance needs of people in different life situations.
- Discuss living wills and power of attorney.
- Discuss the purpose of a last will and testament.

DIFFERENTIATED INSTRUCTION KEY

L1 Special Needs
L2 Basic
ELL English Language Learners
LPR Less Proficient Readers
L3 All Students
L4 Advanced Students

Teach

DISTRIBUTE ACTIVITY WORKSHEET

Distribute the "Buying Car Insurance" worksheet (Personal Finance All-in-One, pp. 77–78) so students can explore the cost of car insurance.

L3 Differentiate Have students choose hypothetical drivers of different ages. Then have them collect the data on car insurance rates for all the age groups for each type of car. They should show their findings on a bar graph that divides the drivers into age clusters, such as 18–24, 25–34, and so on. Have them give a short presentation to the class. Discuss possible reasons for the different rates.

ANALYZE NEEDS

Direct students' attention to the "Kid Care" chart on page PF29. How might uninsured children receive medical care? *(through government programs)* Give students the following situations. Have them discuss which of the four main types of insurance each individual might need:

- A college student who lives on campus most of the year but is at home during the summer. The student drives only during school vacations. *(car—yes; health—no [should be covered by parent's policy or school policy]; property—yes; life—no)*
- A single father of two who rents and uses public transportation to get to and from work. *(car—no; health—yes; property—yes; life—yes)*

Insurance Basics, Part I

As you grow older and acquire more assets, your need for insurance grows as well.

Insuring the Future

You just got ticketed for sailing past a stop sign. You got distracted while you were changing a CD. Your parents are using the word *grounded* a lot—and also the word *insurance*. Sure, they have you covered on their policy, but a moving violation could raise their rates—and yours—through the roof.

What Is Insurance?

The road of life is peppered with the unexpected. Chances are you'll hit a few bumps along the way. Insurance is part of a **risk management plan** that will protect you against financial losses. Basically, insurance is a bet between you and your insurer. You are betting that something bad will happen to you, such as illness or a car accident. The company is betting against it.

Types of Insurance

There are four basic types of insurance coverage most adults should have. Your age, family situation, and income are some major factors to consider when deciding the type and amount of coverage you should get.

- Auto: Protects you and other drivers in case of an accident that results in damage and injury. It also protects you in case of theft, vandalism, and natural disasters. Most states require you to have your own auto insurance or to be listed as a driver on someone else's policy.
- Health: Protects you in case of illness or injury. It also covers the cost of routine medical and preventive care, prescriptions, and in some cases dental care. Even if you're healthy, having health insurance is a very good idea.
- Property: Protects your home or apartment in case of damage or loss of your belongings due to water, fire, or wind. It can cover your liability if someone is injured in your home and sues you for damages. Most policies do not, however, protect you against flood damage. You need to buy that coverage separately.
- Life: Pays a set amount to your **beneficiary** in case of your death. The beneficiary is the person or entity, such as a charity, that you name as the recipient of the death benefit of your life insurance policy. The two most common types of life insurance are *term*, or temporary, insurance and *whole life* insurance. Rates for term insurance increase over time. The only way to collect from a term policy is to die during the term. Whole life insurance remains in effect for one's entire lifetime at a set rate. It builds cash value. The insured can borrow against the policy.

What It Costs

The payment you make to an insurance company is called a premium. The cost of insurance is high, and getting higher. So does it pay to buy it? Absolutely. You may never have an accident and file a claim. But if you do, the amount you collect could be many times what you paid in premiums. Even a brief stay in a hospital, for example, can run up a bill of hundreds of thousands of dollars.

Besides, in many cases, insurance is not optional. You can't even register a car without proof of auto insurance. Nor can you get a mortgage without homeowner coverage.

GO FIGURE

1/8

The ratio of Americans who used Medicaid coverage in 2005.

SOURCE: Pew Research Center

Deductibles

Insurance companies spread out their risk by collecting premiums from a lot of customers. They also reduce their costs by requiring co-pays and deductibles. A **deductible** is an amount you have to pay before your coverage kicks in. For example, if your car insurance policy has a $1,000 deductible, and you have an accident, you'll have to pay the first $1,000 in damages. The company pays the rest. The higher the deductible, the lower the premium.

Co-pays

If you have a **co-pay**, you are responsible for a small portion of the total cost of a service covered by your insurance policy. Every time you go to a doctor, you might have to pay a relatively small amount of the bill and your insurance company pays the rest. Generally, you can keep co-pays to a minimum if your medical provider—a doctor, hospital, or specialist—is part of your insurance company's healthcare network.

Changing Needs

As you get older, acquire more possessions, and expand your family, you have more to replace and more to protect.

Coreen at 18–25

Coreen is three months into her first full-time job. Finally eligible for employee health benefits, she lets her parents know that they can remove her from their policy. She also

Background Note

Beneficiaries Life insurance policies and wills are two documents that require that a beneficiary be named. That person or organization will receive the money from a life insurance policy or the money or property left to them in someone's will. Life insurance usually requires a contingent beneficiary, who will receive the money if the primary beneficiary has died. If the contingent beneficiary is dead, the life insurance benefit becomes part of the deceased person's estate, or property. A will specifies how someone's estate will be distributed. If someone dies without a will, what happens to the estate? It depends on the laws of the state the person lived in. In some cases, the state may take some or all of the estate of "intestate decedents," those who die without a will.

finds an apartment and gets rental insurance to protect her possessions from damage or theft. With no dependents, Coreen leads a relatively carefree existence. She can probably get by with basic auto, rental and health coverage—for now.

Karen and Bill at 25–54

Coreen's sister Karen and her husband Bill have purchased their first home. They are also expecting their second child. With a new home, children, and two cars, their insurance needs are due for a tune-up.

Kid Care It is estimated that more than 9 million children in the U.S. are not covered by health insurance. According to a 2008 study*, researchers found that uninsured children with serious illnesses are far more likely to have their care delayed or to receive no care. Some programs such as Medicaid and State Children's Health Insurance Program provide aid to about 3.6 million children. The table below shows some background on children without insurance.

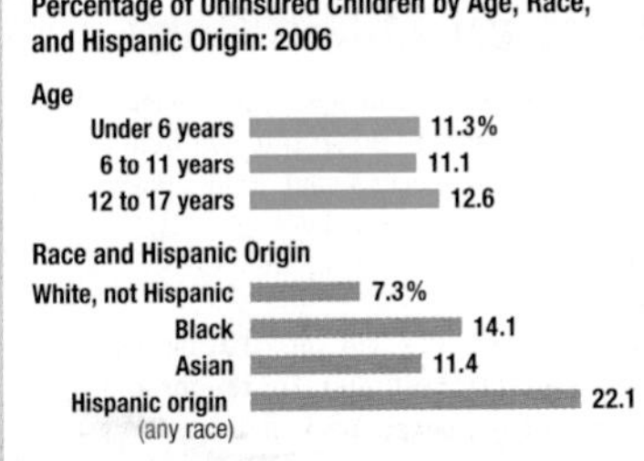

* 2008 report by Robert Wood Johnson Foundation

SOURCE: U.S. Census Bureau, Current Population Survey, 2007 Annual Social and Economic Supplement

Karen and Bill now need a medical policy that covers more checkups for the children. They also can't risk having to pay for a new car if they have an accident. With lives and assets to protect, this young family will focus on adding collision insurance to their auto policy and purchasing home, mortgage, and life insurance coverage.

Alex and Isabel, over 54

Coreen's parents, Isabel and Alex, decide to revisit their insurance needs as well. Free of dependents, they are less concerned about term or whole life insurance coverage. They are far more concerned about the cost of long-term healthcare. Once again, insurance needs change according to age and life circumstances. Because Alex and Isabel are in their 50s, they can expect to pay more for their coverage, perhaps as much as hundreds of dollars a month. Their problem will be trying to find the right coverage at an affordable price. To find the best rates, they will want to get group coverage through an employer or a large organization.

Are You Ready?

1. Why is it important to have insurance?
2. Describe the insurance needs of people at different stages of life.

WebQuest online To learn more about this topic, visit **PearsonSuccessNet.com**

Risk Management

DISCUSS

Distribute the "Last Will and Testament" form (Personal Finance All-in-One, p. 79).

Explain that states have laws that give people certain rights in terms of giving advance directions about the medical care they will receive if they are hospitalized but are not conscious. One provision is a "living will," which stipulates what kind of life-saving care a person accepts and excludes. Another allows the individual to give another person, typically a close family member, power of attorney to direct such care.

Ask students **Why might someone want to give such a direction?** *(Possible answer: to be able to have some control over end-of-life treatment when he or she is not conscious)*

DISCUSS

Explain that adults often write wills to stipulate how property should be divided after their death. Give students copies of the "Last Will and Testament" form (Personal Finance All-in-One, p. 79). Give students time to read the form. Ask **Why is such a document important to people?** *(Possible answer: They wish to determine how a surviving spouse is taken care of or how children divide their property.)*

Assess and Remediate

L3 Collect the "Buying Car Insurance" worksheets and assess student understanding of how to evaluate policies.

L3 Give students the Insurance Basics, Part I Quiz (Personal Finance All-in-One, p. 80).

Answers

Are You Ready? 1. Insurance coverage protects insured people from the risk of financial damage. 2. Possible answer: Children are generally covered by the parent's or guardian's insurance for health and do not need auto, life, or property insurance. Teens must be added to car insurance policies when they begin to drive. Young adults need to obtain health and property insurance when they begin living independently. Adults generally add life insurance when they have children. Older adults sometimes eliminate their life insurance and buy long-term care insurance. While the need for different types of insurance changes throughout life, so does the value of insurance within each type depending on the person's circumstances.

Insurance Basics, Part II

Get Started

LESSON GOALS

Students will:

- Make a decision based on the risk presented by three people applying for insurance.
- Demonstrate understanding of terms of health insurance and compare health plans by completing a worksheet.
- Discuss whether healthcare should be available to uninsured people.
- Work in groups to present ways to slow the growth of healthcare and insurance costs and vote on the most convincing solutions.

DIFFERENTIATED INSTRUCTION KEY

L1 Special Needs
L2 Basic
ELL English Language Learners
LPR Less Proficient Readers
L3 All Students
L4 Advanced Students

Teach

DISCUSS

Have students note the climbing claims as shown in the chart on page PF31. Then, give students the following descriptions of drivers:

- A: No accidents in 20 years
- B: Three accidents in 20 years
- C: Three speeding tickets in 20 years

Tell students to assign premiums to these drivers. Have them vote on which they would charge the most, which the least, and which an amount in between. Tally the votes. The class probably will vote to give A the lowest premium, B the highest, and C a premium in between. Explain that in doing so, they were acting like any insurance company by trying to minimize its risk.

L3 **Differentiate** Have students work in groups to develop lists of ways that consumers can limit risk in terms of car, health, property, and life insurance.

DISTRIBUTE ACTIVITY WORKSHEET

Distribute the "Choosing a Health Insurance Plan" worksheet (Personal Finance All-in-One, pp. 81–82). Have students complete the worksheet to learn health insurance terms and to compare two plans.

Insurance Basics, Part II

People who don't get insurance are betting that nothing bad will ever happen to them. Are you willing to take that gamble?

Insurance Is an Investment

You wind up in the hospital for an emergency appendectomy. Your house is robbed. An uninsured driver hits you from behind. You get to pick up the pieces – and, unless you're insured, the bill.

It's All About Risk

Insurance is all about avoiding risk. For you, that means paying now to avoid a gigantic cost later. For the insurance company, it means identifying people who are likely to cost them a bundle.

Insurers set rates based on **risk factors,** hard statistics that predict whether someone is likely to be a bad risk. Do you plan to become a pilot or take up mountain climbing? That will make you a higher risk than a lawyer who spends leisure time doing crossword puzzles. A smoker must pay higher health insurance premiums than a nonsmoker. In the worst case, a risky lifestyle may make you uninsurable.

Who's Got You Covered?

Right now, insurance costs are probably not your concern. Most teens are covered for pretty much everything—life, health, property—by a parent or guardian. However, some teens must foot their own auto insurance bill. And that's expensive. Statistically, new drivers are high-risk. But if you want wheels, you have no choice.

Health Insurance

No matter how healthy your lifestyle is, you are going to face illness or accident. A bout of pneumonia or a broken leg may cost hundreds, even thousands. Even with health insurance, you'll have to pay something. But it's better than paying it all.

Employer Plans

Most kids are covered under parents' health insurance for as long as they're in school—at least up to age 23. Once you enter the working world, it's up to you. If you work for a company that offers health insurance, you can usually choose from a variety of group plans. Some cover you from day one. More often, there is a waiting period. Your share of the premium is deducted from your paycheck each pay period. The higher the deductible, the lower the premium.

GO FIGURE

$1,896

The average auto insurance premium in the U.S. in 2007. Louisiana had the nation's highest average at $2,740. Wisconsin had the lowest with $1,335.

SOURCE: "Most Expensive States for Car Insurance", Insurance.com

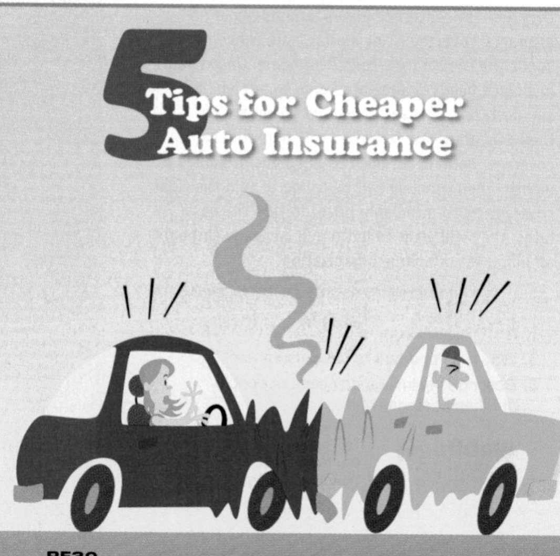

5 Tips for Cheaper Auto Insurance

Searching for ways to cut down on the cost of insuring a car doesn't mean you have to skimp on coverage. Even with the best of companies, there are steps you can take that will help lower your bill.

1. Increase your deductible. If you have to file a claim, can you afford to pay a higher deductible? The higher your deductible, the lower your premium.
2. Buy safely. Some cars cost more to insure because they are a favorite target for thieves. Find out which makes and models these are before you buy.
3. Drive carefully. Don't think insurance companies won't notice speeding tickets or accidents. Unsafe driving makes for a big risk and a big bill.
4. Go back to school. Most, if not all, insurers offer discounts for completing a defensive driving course.
5. Install safety and anti-theft devices in your car. These will lower your risk profile.

The least expensive health insurance plan is generally a **Health Maintenance Organization** (HMO). An HMO allows you to pick a primary care physician, to whom you pay a co-pay. If you need to see a specialist, your primary doctor will refer you to an in-network doctor. This is a doctor who has agreed to accept the payment level paid by the insurance company.

The Uninsured

Not a full-time student or employee? You are on your own unless you can get private health insurance, which is usually much more expensive than a group policy. Some insurance companies raise premiums or deny coverage for pre-existing conditions. If you are denied coverage, you may be eligible for assistance through Medicaid for low-income or disabled persons.

Cut Your Costs

The rising number of claims, plus increasing cases of fraud, have caused insurance premiums to skyrocket. But there are a number of steps you can take to get the best coverage for your buck.

1. **Comparison shop.** Compare the rates of different companies. Check with the local Better Business Bureau. And don't forget word of mouth. For example, if you're shopping for auto insurance, talk to people with similar driving records. Don't just ask about premium costs. Ask about customer service as well. Low price is no bargain if an insurer takes forever to service your claim.
2. **Make yourself a better risk.** If you smoke—or collect speeding tickets like they were trading cards—it's going to cost you. But insurers also reward behavior that lowers risk. A healthy lifestyle and a good driving record can keep costs in check. And while good grades won't reduce health or life insurance premiums, they might get you a discount on car insurance.
3. **Cover yourself.** You and your insurer may not always see eye to eye on a claim. It's up to you to provide evidence of loss. Take pictures of that busted headlamp. And keep receipts. That way, you'll be more likely to be covered for everything you've paid.
4. **Know your policy.** Being smart about insurance involves keeping your policy updated. Talk to your insurer to make sure you have the coverage you need. Review your coverage before filing a claim. You'll avoid nasty surprises that way.

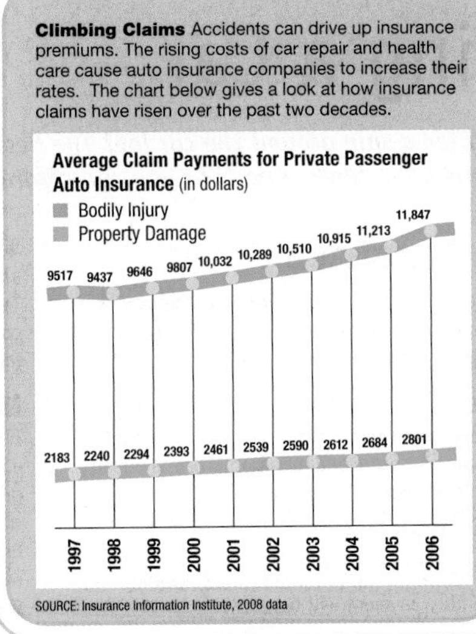

Climbing Claims Accidents can drive up insurance premiums. The rising costs of car repair and health care cause auto insurance companies to increase their rates. The chart below gives a look at how insurance claims have risen over the past two decades.

Should I Use an Agent?

Nowadays, you can often buy insurance online. Still, it might pay for you to use a licensed agent. It all depends on your needs.

There are two kinds of insurance agents: captive and independent. Captive agents represent a single insurance company. Independent agents offer policies from many different companies. Both types of agents must be licensed by the state in which they sell.

For most purposes, buying directly with a company or its agents works out just fine. But if you are difficult to insure—for example, if you have a bad driving record—an independent agent might be the way to go. With access to many different companies, the independent agent can help you find a company that can meet your special needs.

A good agent also helps you through the process of filing a claim and acts on your behalf in dealing with the provider. Many insurance agents are also certified to help you with other kinds of financial planning.

Are You Ready?

1. Why is insurance an investment?
2. What are some ways you can reduce the cost of insurance?

To learn more about this topic, visit **PearsonSuccessNet.com**

Risk Management

DISCUSS

Display the "What About the Uninsured?" transparency (Color Transparencies, p. PF.f). Explain that the sign shown in the transparency is one that appears in emergency rooms throughout the country. Using the Opinion Line strategy (p. T28), have the class discuss whether they agree that all people should have the right to emergency medical care. Challenge students to discuss not only the rights to such care but the responsibilities that each person—insured or uninsured—has to reducing his or her own risk of needing emergency care.

EXTEND

Debate over healthcare in the United States involves issues of access, efficiency, quality, and sustainability. Give students the worksheet, "The Healthcare Debate" (Personal Finance All-in-One, p. 83). Divide the class into groups and give each group time to research one aspect of healthcare, such as the price of medicines or procedures; the cost of insurance; the issue of the uninsured; medical malpractice and law suits; or state proposals for reform. Then have the groups meet to develop specific ideas that they think will address some of the problems in healthcare. Finally, call on each group to present their suggestions to the rest of the class. After each group presentation, allow some time for questions and answers from other students. When all the groups have made their presentations, have the class vote on the ideas that they think would be most effective.

Assess and Remediate

L3 Collect the "Choosing a Health Insurance Plan" and "The Healthcare Debate" worksheets and assess student understanding of health insurance.

L3 Give students the Insurance Basics, Part II Quiz (Personal Finance All-in-One, p. 84).

Background Note

Chronic Healthcare Problems An effective way of reducing the cost of health insurance—and of healthcare in general—is to teach people how to prevent chronic healthcare problems. When people develop chronic diseases, such as diabetes, learning to manage it can prevent the need for expensive care and treatment—and lower health insurance premiums.

Type 2 diabetes accounts for about 90 percent of all diabetes cases. It used to be called "adult-onset" diabetes, but its frequency among children seems to be increasing. The statistics for children are not solid, but the number of new cases among adults has almost tripled over the last 25 years, according to the Centers for Disease Control. The biggest risk factor for developing this type of diabetes is being overweight. Over that same period, the rate of obesity in children aged 12 to 19 has increased from 5 to 17.4 percent.

Answers

Are You Ready? 1. Possible answer: Insurance is an investment in that the insured pays a sum of money up front for protection against higher costs that arise later. 2. You can reduce the cost of insurance by comparison shopping, making yourself a better risk, taking steps to verify your claims, and knowing the details of your policy.

Buying a Car

Get Started

LESSON GOALS

Students will:

- Estimate the cost of car ownership and use comparison shopping to evaluate options by completing a worksheet.
- Practice negotiating car prices.
- Understand ways to limit risks when buying a car.
- Fill out an application for a car loan.

DIFFERENTIATED INSTRUCTION KEY

L1 Special Needs
L2 Basic
 ELL English Language Learners
 LPR Less Proficient Readers
L3 All Students
L4 Advanced Students

Teach

CONNECT

Ask **How many of you own a car?** Call on students to tell about their car-buying experiences. Ask them to tell how they decided on the type of car they wanted and picked out the specific car they bought. Who helped them negotiate the deal? Ask **Are you satisfied with your purchase? What was the hardest part of buying the car?**

EVALUATE CHOICES

Call students' attention to the list of issues to consider when calculating the costs of ownership. Emphasize that they need to be aware of the cost of car ownership before going to the car dealership, but that the costs will vary depending upon the model and condition of the car they buy. Distribute the "Guide to Buying a Car" worksheet (Personal Finance All-in-One, pp. 85–86). Tell students that this worksheet will help them decide on the type of car that would meet their needs. They may *want* a certain kind of car, but this worksheet will help them systematically evaluate alternatives.

Discuss the categories of cars listed under item 5 to make sure students understand these different types of cars. Call on students to explain anti-lock brakes and the other options. Have students name and describe other options they want.

Buying a Car

Ready to go for a spin around the car lot? The best car is the one that suits your needs, and that you can afford.

A Major Purchase

Like most young people, your first major purchase may be a car. You need to do your homework, and spend some time and effort to get a good deal.

The Costs of Ownership

Step one is to determine what kind of car you can afford to buy and adequately insure and maintain. There are many money issues to consider:

- how much you can put down
- how much you need to borrow
- what your monthly payment will be
- how much your insurance premiums will be
- how much car maintenance will cost
- what gasoline, parking, and tolls will do to your budget

Since you have no credit history, you may have to search around for a bank or credit union that will lend you money. To get a vehicle loan, a bank may require you to have a co-signer, a person who is responsible for paying the loan if you default.

New or Used

If you are going to buy a new car, you want to determine the invoice price of the model you want, and then get at least five competitive bids from dealers. Request bids in writing and then try to negotiate. Will the dealer closest to you match the price of the dealer who is less conveniently located? You can use Web sites such as cars.com, yahoo!autos, and myride.com

GO FIGURE

$800–$2,400

The average range of annual repair costs in the first 5 years of car ownership in the U.S.

SOURCE: new-cars.com

ON THE ROAD

You've done your car shopping and driven your ride off the dealer's lot. Now what? Do you know how to change a flat? Do you have an emergency tow-truck number handy? Many service stations and dealership service centers will stick a note on the windshield letting you know when the next servicing is due. Likewise, the state will remind you when you need to renew your registration. Keep your insurance card in the car, and file your car title and insurance policy in a safe place!

POINTS TO REMEMBER

- ✓ Follow the maintenance schedule for your vehicle in the Owner's Manual. Don't skimp on oil changes.
- ✓ Wash your car regularly and wax it once in a while to keep the car body shiny and free from corrosion.
- ✓ Treat minor problems early before they become big, expensive problems later.
- ✓ Use only original parts for repairs.

PF32

Background Note

Vehicle History Buying a used car can be a gamble: it's easy for unscrupulous sellers to cover-up problems. Sometimes these problems can be severe. A vehicle may have been stolen, wrecked, or abandoned for days in a flood. Damaged cars may have been repaired or repainted, disguising the damage so it is not immediately visible. Buyers can improve their odds of buying a reliable car that doesn't have undisclosed problems. A good mechanic can spot many hidden problems. For a fee, car history research companies do research on the car using its vehicle identification number (VIN). The report provides detailed information, including the car's title history, odometer readings, accident history, number of owners, service records, emissions inspection results, and whether it was ever used as a taxi or rental car.

as online resources for researching and getting bids.

If you're buying used, get a history of the **Vehicle Identification Number** (VIN) and have a mechanic inspect the car. That way you can determine how well the car has been cared for. There are also online sites that deal with buying used cars. They offer reviews of online used car classifieds, how to buy a used car from dealers or private sellers, how to negotiate with tough sellers, scams to avoid, and a list of questions for you to print out to ask the seller.

New automobiles **depreciate,** or lose value, quickly. A new car loses half its value in the first three years. But buying a new car can make sense if you plan to keep the car for a long time. You have to carry collision insurance if you have a car loan. Used cars are less expensive to buy and insure, but maintenance costs will likely be higher. Budget accordingly.

Leasing

Leasing is primarily used by businesses or by those who don't plan on driving many miles. If you go over the mileage allowed for the term of the **auto lease,** generally 12,000 miles per year, you have to pay a substantial fee for each additional mile. If you have a long drive to college or a job, the commute could eat up the mileage limit in no time.

It's Your Money

You might want to consider taking a more experienced person along with you when you buy your first car. It pays to have an ally.

Dealing With Dealers

In many cases, salespeople hold the upper hand when it comes to negotiating car prices. You can take a few steps, however, to level the buying field and avoid being pressured into spending more money than you want or can afford.

- Be prepared. Know what you want, and get bids based on the invoice price.
- Don't be talked into unnecessary options.
- Don't ever discuss trade-in until after you've settled on a sale price. A dealer might want to consider the trade-in vehicle as a reduction in the sticker price. In fact, any trade-in should have nothing to do with the price of the new car.

License to Ride Fewer American 16-year-olds are driving now than in 1998. Some possible reasons for the decline are tougher drivers license laws, the students' choice to spend more social time online instead of on the road, and the drop in the number of high schools offering driver's education courses.

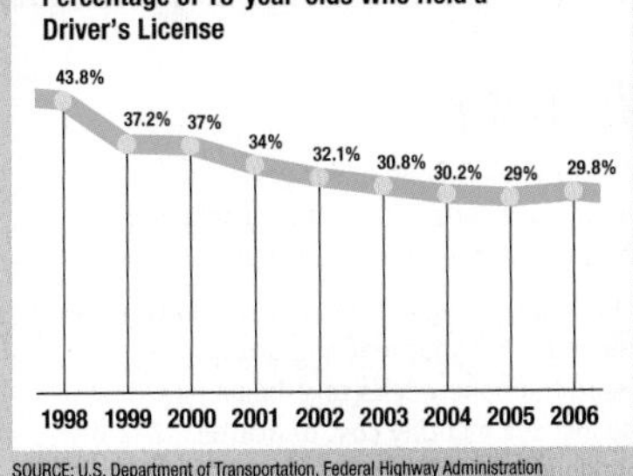

SOURCE: U.S. Department of Transportation, Federal Highway Administration

- Don't be pushed into a quick decision, no matter what one-day specials are dangled before you.
- Get the sale offers in writing. If a dealer is not willing to put all agreements in writing, walk away.

Warranties

Dealers are required by federal law to post a Buyer's Guide on the used cars they offer for sale. This guide must specify whether the vehicle is being sold "as is" or with a **warranty,** and what percentage of the repair costs the dealer will pay. Most new and some used cars come with a manufacturer's warranty that covers certain repairs for a set period of time or up to a certain mileage limit. Extended warranties increase the amount of time or mileage that repairs will be covered. No warranty covers basic maintenance, like oil changes or new tires.

If you do happen to buy a car and the next day the engine falls out, you're protected by federal and state "lemon laws." First, however, you should go back to the dealer if you think you've bought a lemon. If you cannot reach an agreement, check the law to see what recourse you have.

Are You Ready?

1. How should you prepare to buy a car?
2. What are some negotiation strategies you can use when buying a car?

To learn more about this topic, visit **PearsonSuccessNet.com**

Consumer Smarts

ANALYZE A GRAPH

Call students' attention to the graph on page PF33. Have students discuss at what age they think driver's licenses should be issued.

L4 Have students research accident statistics for drivers at ages 16 and 18 and report to the class.

ROLE PLAY

Ask students what steps they can take to prepare for talking with car salespeople. Ask why they should know how much they can afford and what options they want before walking into a new car dealership. Have students role-play a negotiation.

DISTRIBUTE FORM

Point out that most people borrow money to make a car purchase. Tell students to complete the "Application for a Car Loan" form (Personal Finance All-in-One, p. 87).

L2 **Differentiate** Review and explain the categories of information called for on the form. Make sure students understand what information to provide for the make, model, and VIN.

EXTEND

Explain that state governments set minimal levels for car insurance coverage. Tell students to do research to learn what their state requires. Have them discuss in groups what these different requirements mean. Then have them briefly report their findings to the class.

Assess and Remediate

L3 Collect the "Guide to Buying a Car" worksheets and assess student understanding of how to choose a car.

L3 Give the Buying a Car Quiz (Personal Finance All-in-One, p. 88).

Answers

Are You Ready? 1. Learn the invoice price of the car before you go to a dealership. 2. Don't be talked into unnecessary options. Don't discuss any trade-in until you've settled the purchase price. Don't make quick decisions. Get sale offers in writing.

Renting an Apartment

Get Started

LESSON GOALS

Students will:

- Evaluate the costs of renting an apartment by completing a worksheet.
- Discuss ways to protect oneself when renting by analyzing a cartoon.
- Understand the rights and responsibilities of renting an apartment by filling out a residential lease agreement.

DIFFERENTIATED INSTRUCTION KEY

L1 Special Needs
L2 Basic
  ELL English Language Learners
  LPR Less Proficient Readers
L3 All Students
L4 Advanced Students

Teach

CONNECT

Ask **What will be the benefits of having your own apartment?** List students' responses on the board. Then distribute the "Renting an Apartment" worksheet (Personal Finance All-in-One, pp. 89–90) and explain that enjoying their own apartment comes at a price. Have them complete the worksheet as a way to begin deciding what kind of apartment they can afford.

Point out the renter's insurance in the first chart. Ask **What is the purpose of renter's insurance?** *(It will insure them against loss of personal property in the apartment in case of burglary, fire, or other causes.)* Point to the chart for item 3 and ask **What is a security deposit?** *(It protects the property owners against damage a tenant may do to the property beyond normal use.)* Emphasize that they should get this deposit back after they move out if they have not damaged the property.

Direct students to the Comparing Apartments chart on page 90 of the worksheet. Explain the items on the chart to be sure students understand what each of these is and the choices they will need to consider.

L2 **Differentiate** Organize students into groups of three to complete the apartment comparison chart on page 90. Have each student find details about one apartment. They can then combine their results on one chart.

Renting an Apartment

Home is more than a place to hang your hat. Think twice and act once before unlocking the door to independent living.

Can I Afford It?

You've dreamed of this day of living under your roof and by your own rules. Independence. Rent. Bills. Cooking and cleaning. Yes, life is full of both ups and downs.

The first reality check is figuring out what you can afford. A general rule of thumb is that your rent and utility payments should not cost more than one week's take-home pay. How can you figure the average monthly cost of utilities? Ask the landlord or the previous tenant.

You will have to plan ahead. Many landlords require that you pay the first and last month's rent up front. In addition, you may have to pay a **security deposit**. This money is set aside for repairs of any damage you may do to the apartment beyond normal wear and tear.

KEY QUESTIONS

Finding the right apartment can be hard. Before you sign a lease, be sure you get the answers to these questions.

- How long is the term of the lease?
- When is the rent due?
- What are the penalties for paying late?
- Are utilities included in the rent?
- Are there working smoke detectors?
- Is parking available?
- Is the neighborhood safe?
- Is there public transportation nearby?
- Are there laundry facilities?
- Are pets allowed?
- How much advance notice is required before moving?
- What happens if you break the lease?
- How are repairs handled?
- Can you make cosmetic changes such as painting or hanging pictures?

Finding the Right Place

Finding the right apartment takes more than a little time, effort, and money. The federal government has stepped in to level the playing field. The **Federal Fair Housing Act of 1968** makes it illegal for a landlord to discriminate against a potential tenant because of that person's race, sex, national origin, or religion.

GO FIGURE

4

The number of students that legally can live in a rental unit in Boston.

SOURCE: City of Boston Rental Housing Resource Center

You can make the rental process easier by defining your needs and wants. Usually to rent an apartment you have to make a commitment of at least six months. So while the cheap one-bedroom with high ceilings and walk-in closets may seem like a steal, the fact that it's near the firehouse could make it a case of home, sleepless home.

Online Web sites are a good place to begin your apartment hunting. You can also look for apartments in the real estate section of a local newspaper. And if you're hiring a realtor to search on your behalf, keep in mind that they will charge you a fee based on the rental price. So do your homework, and check out the Key Questions list on this page for important factors you'll want to consider before making your decision. What if the ideal apartment is beyond your means? That might be the time to consider getting a roommate to share the cost.

Background Note

Renter's Insurance Some people think renter's insurance isn't necessary because the property owner has insurance, but the owner's insurance covers only structural damage to the building, not damage to the tenants' possessions. People may also think they don't own much of value, but they probably own more than they realize. If they add up the replacement cost for their possessions, most people are surprised at what it would cost to replace the things they own. Renter's insurance is relatively inexpensive, and it covers most of the things in their possession. Plus, it covers property when it is stolen or destroyed while in the renter's car or while the renter is traveling. Policies by different carriers are flexible, but most will even cover injuries suffered by visitors to the renter's apartment.

Consumer Smarts

Roommates

Can two live more cheaply than one? More often than not, a two-bedroom apartment in many locales is not much more expensive than a one-bedroom place. Plus, you can split the utilities and rent. The sources for finding a roommate are the same as those for finding an apartment—Web sites like roommates.com, newspaper classifieds, and word of mouth. You want someone who has a compatible lifestyle and who can pay their share of the bills on time. Your search for the right roommate is just as important as your search for the right place to live.

Furnishings

If you have decided to rent an unfurnished apartment, you will need to be resourceful to avoid major expenses. After you have tapped family and friends, yard sales and thrift shops are potential gold mines. An unfurnished apartment is not only empty, it will probably also be bare, right down to the windows and shower—not to mention the cupboards.

Protect Yourself

Learn from others' mistakes. Many apartment complex Web sites are chock-full of comments posted by current or previous tenants. You might even ask a passerby in the parking lot. To protect yourself from being charged for pre-existing conditions, assess and photograph any existing damage before you sign a lease.

The Lease

You, as **tenant** or "lessee," and the property owner, as "landlord" or "**lessor,**" enter into a contract called the lease or rental agreement. Here are some tips to make it a positive experience.

- Be prepared with the documents you will need to provide. These items include proof of income and identity, letters of reference, and a check for any required deposit.
- Get the lease in writing! Never take an apartment on the basis of a handshake with the landlord.
- If you don't understand something, don't sign the lease!

Costs of Living Geography is one factor that will have a major impact on your living expenses. If you live in cities like New York, Boston, or Los Angeles, expenses will be much higher than those in smaller cities or rural areas.

Living Expenses in Select U.S. Metropolitan Areas (monthly, per household)

Metro area	Electricity	Food and beverages	Transportation
Los Angeles, CA	$261	$211	$183
Miami, FL	150	211	190
Chicago, IL	133	200	176
New York, NY	168	211	190
Boston, MA	202	213	176
Houston, TX	185	186	167

SOURCE: Bureau of Labor Statistics (Consumer Price Index), 2007 data

Renter's Insurance

Even if you furnish with hand-me-downs or thrift-store treasures, be sure to consider renter's insurance. Maybe your roommate comes fully loaded with a flat-screen television. Should it disappear, you'd be left footing the bill. The benefits can far outweigh the costs.

Rights and Responsibilities

This is your money and your home, and you have rights. For example, you have the right to privacy. A landlord or maintenance worker is prohibited from entering your apartment without your permission. Renter's rights and responsibilities vary according to location, but most states provide a tenant-landlord bill of rights. Check with your local housing or consumer affairs office for specific information.

Tenants also have responsibilities, such as paying the rent on time and keeping the apartment clean. There may also be quiet hours, a policy imposed on most apartment dwellers. As always, a tenant's rights come with certain responsibilities.

Are You Ready?

1. What are some potential pitfalls in searching for an apartment?
2. What are four things you should do before signing a lease?

To learn more about this topic, visit PearsonSuccessNet.com

DISCUSS CHART

Have students reflect on the chart on page PF35. Ask them to brainstorm other costs that might vary by location, and therefore affect rents. *(insurance rates, heating and cooling, state and local taxes)*

ANALYZE

Display the "Just Paperwork" transparency (Color Transparencies, p. PF.g) and ask students to explain the humor. Then tell students that the cartoon brings up the point that signing a lease, like many other transactions, is a legal agreement in which all parties try to protect themselves from liability or loss. Warn students to be prepared for seemingly unnecessary paperwork when they lease an apartment.

Distribute the "Residential Lease Agreement" form (Personal Finance All-in-One, p. 91) and point out that most leases have a statement of tenant responsibilities and guidelines written in "legalese," similar to the language shown in the form.

L2 Differentiate Review the lease agreement with students. Read each paragraph and help students paraphrase the meaning. Circulate as students complete the worksheet to assist as needed.

EXTEND

Explain that every state and some cities have slightly different laws regarding the rights of renters. Have students research these rights in their community and state. During follow-up discussion, have students give examples of how those rights are applied.

L4 Differentiate Have students form two teams and debate the laws governing tenant rights. Have one team represent the point of view of renters and one the point of view of property owners.

Assess and Remediate

L3 Collect the "Renting an Apartment" worksheets and assess student understanding of how to choose and rent an apartment.

L3 Give the Renting an Apartment Quiz (Personal Finance All-in-One, p. 92).

Answers

Are You Ready? 1. Possible responses: the length of the lease, a bad location, property owners who do not maintain the apartment, noisy neighbors, a fee if a realtor conducts the search on your behalf. 2. Check comments by current or previous tenants on Web sites; assess and photograph any existing damage to the apartment; get the lease in writing; don't sign if you don't understand something.

Get Started

LESSON GOALS

Students will:

- Summarize the costs of identity theft.
- Investigate a variety of types of online scams and other consumer fraud.
- Describe ways to reduce the risk of identity theft and how to restore personal security.

DIFFERENTIATED INSTRUCTION KEY

- **L1** Special Needs
- **L2** Basic
  - **ELL** English Language Learners
  - **LPR** Less Proficient Readers
- **L3** All Students
- **L4** Advanced Students

Teach

DEFINE

Ask **What is identity theft?** Help students understand that identity theft is the stealing of someone's personal information, such as personal identification numbers (PINs), bank account numbers, and Social Security numbers, and using them to access the person's assets. Guide a discussion of ways in which identity thieves can obtain personal information.

Point to the "Go Figure" box and explain that the financial cost of identity theft is only part of the cost to victims. Discuss the personal costs—the victims' loss of reputation and the work and time it takes for them to clear their record.

Distribute "The Identity Theft Report" worksheet (Personal Finance All-in-One, p. 95). Discuss the information presented in the graphs. After students think about and write answers to the questions, have them discuss their answers in class.

L2 Differentiate Discuss each of the charts and ensure that students understand that the bars break down each range of costs into subcategories: new accounts, existing accounts, and existing credit cards. Help students read the bars.

Identity Theft

Keep your personal information personal. Learn how to protect yourself, before somebody else shows up as you.

A Growing Crime

An estimated 9 million Americans have their identities stolen every year. Chances are you know someone who has been victimized. You may be a victim yourself—without even knowing it.

It Can Happen Anywhere

Question: What do going to the beach ... taking out the garbage ... and answering your e-mail have in common?

Answer: *They can all leave you vulnerable to identity theft.*

A thief can raid your wallet while you're splashing in the water. A dumpster diver can retrieve old bank statements. Or an innocent-looking e-mail could be a phishing scam to get your personal info. Most people don't realize they've been victimized until it's too late. You might not find out until you're denied a student loan because you've missed several car payments—and you don't even own a car.

The Cost of Theft

Once they have your ID, thieves can use it to commit a wide variety of fraud, such as obtaining credit cards or even a mortgage in your name. Worse, if the crook who stole your identity gets arrested for *any* crime, you could get stuck with a criminal record.

In too many cases, the burden of proof is on the victim. According to the Identity Theft Resource Center, it can take 600 hours to repair the damage. Some victims need up to 10 years to fully clear their records. If your identity is stolen, you could face higher insurance costs, credit card fees, and interest rates for loans—or may even have trouble finding a job.

GO FIGURE

$500

The median loss due to I.D. theft per U.S. consumer.

SOURCE: "Top 5 consumer complaints," CNN Money, February 7, 2007

To download or not to download

After you go through all the trouble of protecting your stuff, did you ever think you might be taking somebody else's stuff illegally?

That's what you're doing if you download software from the Internet or make unauthorized copies of music or movies. It's like cheating on a test. You're taking someone else's hard work without permission.

Just like ID theft, "software piracy" has far-reaching consequences for teens, for teachers and parents, and for software creators and manufacturers. Some of the issues are:

1. Getting files or software secondhand exposes a computer's data and hard drive to viruses and worms that can cause damage.
2. When software is stolen, companies must adjust their budgets to make up those losses, which means software creators may lose their jobs, affecting the families those jobs support.
3. It's very easy to get caught. Internet search engines make it easy for teachers to find the source of plagiarized passages in seconds.

PF36

Background Note

Losing Your Identity Thieves use many techniques to steal identities. At least 60 percent of the time, they don't use computers. Techniques include these:

- shoulder surfing, where a thief stands next to you in a checkout line and memorizes your name, address, phone number, PIN, and other essential information
- skimming, that is, using a data collection device called a skimmer that attaches to ATMs or similar processors and steals account numbers and PINs
- stealing mail from mailboxes to collect bank and credit card statements
- business theft, which includes breaking into businesses and stealing customers' records, which may include personal information
- authorized access theft, in which employees appropriate private information about customers from their employers' files.

Prime Target: You

So should you be worried? Well, of the more than 255,000 **identity theft** complaints filed with the U.S. Federal Trade Commission in 2005, about 5 percent were against those under age 18—up from 3 percent in 2003. So congratulations: you are part of the fastest-growing target group for identity thieves.

Why Me?

Why are young people so vulnerable? One reason is that most teens have not established credit records that can be monitored. In addition, studies show that teens—

- are less likely than adults to check their credit card records.
- are more likely than adults to frequent the Internet and provide personal information.
- take greater risks relative to older age groups.
- often have an "it can't happen to me" attitude.

Finally, many Americans do not use their Social Security number until around the age of 15, when they apply for driver permits or first jobs. As a result, identity thefts against them may go unnoticed for years. There have even been cases of babies being the victims of identity theft!

At College

Over half of all personal information security breaches take place at universities, experts say. Part of the reason may be that nearly half of all college students have had their grades posted by using a Social Security number. It's within your rights to tell a college administrator not to post or otherwise give out your personal information.

Lower Your Risk

Although there is no foolproof way to safeguard your identity, there are a number of common-sense steps you can take to protect yourself against fraud. Here are some tips.

Be alert online. Think twice before sharing personal information. Social networking sites like Facebook.com and MySpace.com not only post your favorite music and relationship status, but also your addresses, cellphone numbers, and previous employers. All of this information could be used to create a credit account or take out a loan in your name.

Identity Crisis In 2007 the Federal Trade Commission received more than 800,000 complaints of identity theft, making it the agency's most widely reported consumer crime. Nearly one third of all victims fall in the 18–29 age bracket. One reason for this trend could be that younger people tend to spend more time on the Internet, where identity thieves thrive on credit and banking scams.

SOURCE: "Consumer Fraud and Identity Theft Complaint Data, January–December 2006," the Federal Trade Commission, February 2007.

Use passwords. Always use a password to protect your cellphone, laptop, and PDA. Do not store personal information on these electronic devices. Create passwords that contain upper- and lowercase letters, numbers, and special characters such as !, $, &.

Check your credit. Check your credit report with a major credit agency like Equifax, Experian, and TransUnion at least once a year. You are entitled to one free report yearly. You can find them online at www.annualcreditreport.com.

Check and shred your statements. Always check your bank and credit card statements for anything unusual. Then make sure to dispose of those documents containing personal information using a paper shredder. Simply tearing up documents isn't enough to keep thieves from easily reassembling those statements.

Watch your mailbox. If you're too young to have a credit card, or don't have one already, you should be suspicious of any unsolicited credit-card offers in the mail addressed to you. For more information on identity theft and what you can do to protect yourself, check out the government's Web site www.ftc.gov/bcp/edu/microsites/idtheft.

Are You Ready?

1. Why are young people especially vulnerable to identity theft?
2. What are some steps you can take to protect yourself?

WebQuest online To learn more about this topic, visit **PearsonSuccessNet.com**

DISCUSS

Call students' attention to the Identity Crisis chart on page PF37. Ask **Why are young people so vulnerable to identity theft?** *(Compared with adults, they are less likely to check their credit card records and more likely to share personal information on the Internet. They take greater risks and may have an "it can't happen to me" attitude.)* Have students discuss these generalities and give examples of times when they may have put their identities at risk. Ask students to describe ways they can reduce their risk of identity theft.

Distribute the "Avoiding Identity Theft" worksheet (Personal Finance All-in-One, pp. 93–94). Ask students to complete the first page on their own, and then discuss their answers. Have students read page 94. Ask them to explain each step and tell why it is important.

L2 Differentiate Read the first scenario on page 93 of the worksheet aloud to students and ask them what they would do if they received this phone call. Would they give out the information? Help students analyze the situation and identify the clues that should alert them to a risk of identity theft.

EXTEND

The federal government offers practical tips to prevent Internet fraud and protect personal information.

Tell students to visit the Web site www.onguardonline.gov. Have them write a review of the site, identifying five points of new information they have learned. Have them decide whether they would recommend the site to others and explain why or why not.

Assess and Remediate

L3 Collect the "Avoiding Identity Theft" and "The Identity Theft Report" worksheets and assess student understanding of identity theft and ways to reduce their risk.

L3 Give the Identity Theft Quiz (Personal Finance All-in-One, p. 96).

Answers

Are You Ready? 1. Compared with adults, they are less likely to check their credit card records and more likely to share personal information on the Internet. They are willing to take greater risks and have an "it can't happen to me" attitude. 2. Be alert online, use passwords, check your credit at least once a year, check bank and credit card statements for anything unusual, shred documents that have personal information, and beware of unsolicited credit-card offers that come in the mail.

Shopping Online: Be Safe, Not Sorry

Get Started

LESSON GOALS

Students will:

- Understand the factors that go into making good online buying choices.
- Investigate how online shopping sites advise customers to conduct online buying.
- Describe your options if you are a victim of online shopping fraud by completing a worksheet.

DIFFERENTIATED INSTRUCTION KEY

L1 Special Needs
L2 Basic
ELL English Language Learners
LPR Less Proficient Readers
L3 All Students
L4 Advanced Students

Teach

CONNECT

Ask **Has anyone ever bought merchandise online?** After a show of hands, ask volunteers to tell how satisfied they were with the experience. Discuss the use of reviews as a way of choosing products and also of choosing merchants. Have students talk about their experiences. Have they written reviews of products or services?

Ask students to name their favorite online retailers, and list their answers on the board. Have them help you identify those retailers that have physical stores somewhere. Ask **Why do people generally have more confidence in these retailers?** *(They believe these retailers are more invested in their businesses and less likely to put them at risk by providing poor service or practicing fraud.)* Ask **How did you decide whether the online-only retailers listed on the board were reliable?** *(Possible answers: through recommendations of friends, by reading online reviews.)*

Call students' attention to the Virtual Sales chart on page PF39. Ask **Why might someone choose to buy the products shown in the chart online?** *(Possible answers: They are often small, so shipping costs are not prohibitive; people go looking for particular brands and labels they know; there is no issue with proper fit or color; comparison shopping is easy.)*

Shopping Online: Be Safe, Not Sorry

It's hard to put a price tag on convenience. But by taking a little care, you can get your money's worth.

Buying Online

Online shopping may already be a regular part of your life. You don't have to drive anywhere, stand in line, or haul the stuff home. A few clicks will do it all. And you can shop 24/7.

It's Easy to Be Smart

If you have ever gone from store to store looking for a hard-to-find item, you will appreciate the ease of shopping online. Who has the item in stock? Who has the lowest price? Free shipping? Quickest delivery? You can get the answers to all of these questions with the click of your mouse. For starters, you can check price comparison sites such as bizrate.com, mysimon.com or pricegrabber.com.

Read the Reviews

All right, so you can't try on shoes or a shirt online. Online buyers trade that advantage for online customer reviews. A recent study of online buyers shows that 9 out of 10 Americans read reviews posted by other customers online before they make a purchase. You can access detailed customer-driven product reviews for almost any product. Love the product, you can let the world know. Hate it, you can warn others as well.

E-Buyer Be Aware

Along with its unique benefits, online shopping includes some unique challenges. How do you really know if the online retailer you're dealing with is reputable and your information will be secure? For the most part, you have a higher degree of confidence if there is a brick-and-mortar backup to the online stores. Major retailers devote a lot of resources to ensuring that their customers have a satisfying and secure online shopping experience.

That does not mean that you should not deal with online-only vendors. See the Five Online Shopping Tips below for advice on making sure the sites you use are secure and reputable.

GO FIGURE

6%

The amount of all merchandise sold online that gets returned.

SOURCE: University of Nevada Center for Logistics Management

Five Online Shopping Tips

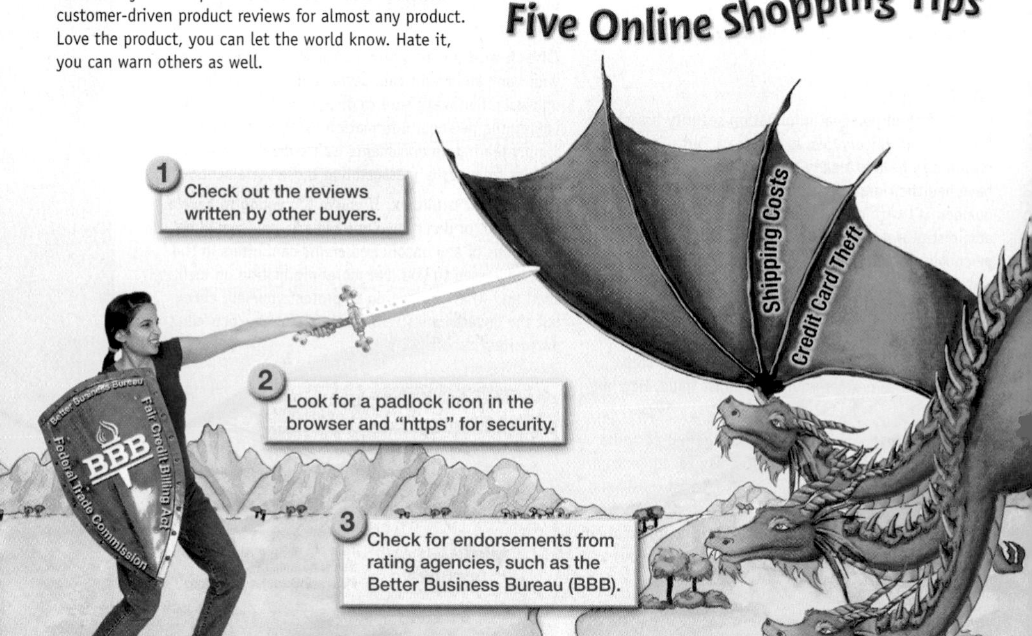

Background Note

Online Shopping Trends As of 2007, online shopping represented about 5 percent of all retail sales, or about $175 billion, which represented an increase of 21 percent over 2006. However, studies indicate that the growth in online shopping is slowing. Predictions suggest that by 2012, annual increases in online shopping will be just 11 percent—a healthy increase, but evidence of a maturing market that fewer new shoppers are entering. Analysts offer several reasons for the trend. For one thing, brick-and-mortar stores are working harder to attract shoppers, while online stores remain dull and uninteresting. People sometimes shop to escape boredom and to relax. Online shopping doesn't fill that need. Shoppers usually shop online to find an item they want or need, but unlike in-store shopping, they seldom do much browsing.

Bidding Online

Comfortable online? The biggest and best deals often exist beyond the big stores. Two of the most-widely used alternatives are the relatively free classified and message boards and auction sites. These offer shopping alternatives that come with a different set of rules tailored for the online marketplace.

Local appeal can be a major advantage. Online classifieds provide access to backyard buyers and sellers at relatively no cost. Your next entertainment center might very well be three towns or three blocks away.

In its attempt to keep you scam- and worry-free, these services encourage buyers to deal locally with folks you can meet in person. The site also includes detailed safety guidelines.

On Internet auctions, buyers can quickly and easily comparison shop for just about anything, from used cars and leather bomber jackets to concert tickets and, even, private jets. In this auction format, shoppers can engage in competitive bidding wars.

4 Steer clear of sellers who offer low prices only to squeeze you on shipping costs.

5 Use a credit card as it offers the best safeguard against fraud, but never e-mail a credit card number, bank account information, password, or PIN number.

Unsecured Sites

Identity Theft

Virtual Sales In 2007, Americans bought over $20 billion worth of music and video products on the Internet, making them the most popular online purchase. By 2011, however, it is projected that consumer electronics sales will far outpace other products sold online.

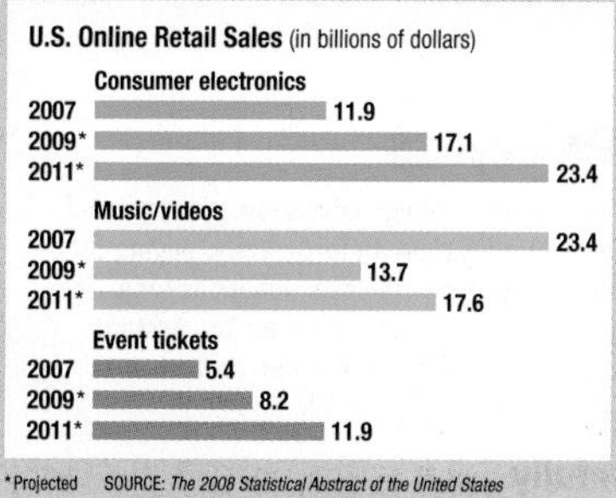

*Projected SOURCE: *The 2008 Statistical Abstract of the United States*

So how are buyers and sellers protected? Buyers rate the reliability and service provided by sellers and eBay makes these ratings available to you. However, if you win a bid and do not go through with the purchase, you are stuck with a negative rating for the rest of your eBay life. There are also services that make it possible for you to pay an individual seller using your credit card.

Fighting Fraud

There is a new charge on your credit card bill! But where is the merchandise? You never got it, or even worse, you never ordered it. Many credit card companies will investigate suspected cases of fraud on your behalf, limiting your liability to $50. Also, the Fair Credit Billing Act allows you to withhold payment if you believe that someone has stolen your card number.

You also have the option of filing complaints with the Federal Trade Commission (FTC) at www.ftc.gov. The FTC offers you advice on how to protect against fraud, identity theft, and questionable business practices. The site guides you step-by-step through the process of filing a consumer complaint.

Are You Ready?

1. What are the advantages of shopping online?
2. What are two possible pitfalls?

WebQuest online To learn more about this topic, visit **PearsonSuccessNet.com**

DISCUSS

Ask students who have bought merchandise through online classifieds or an online auction to describe their experiences. Draw a T-chart on the board and help students compare the two kinds of sites. Ask students how these sites are different from other online retailers.

Point out that online shoppers sometimes have misunderstandings about what they are buying and sometimes businesses may not provide the service or product they promise. Discuss how students can decide if they are victims of fraud or are just experiencing a misunderstanding. Ask students what they can do if they decide they are victims of fraud.

Distribute the "Virtual Customer Service" worksheet (Personal Finance All-in-One, pp. 97–98). Have students read the passage on their own. Then discuss it point by point with the class. Divide students into pairs to complete the worksheet assignment. Call on pairs to perform their role-play for the class.

L2 Differentiate Organize these students into small groups to plan the activity. Tell them to work together to write a script before they do the role-play.

EXTEND

Divide students into two groups and have each group visit a popular online shopping or auction site. Tell them to investigate whether these sites provide safe-shopping guidelines. Guide a class discussion of students' findings.

Assess and Remediate

L3 Collect the "Virtual Customer Service" worksheets and assess student understanding of how to effectively complain to an online retailer.

L3 Give the Shopping Online Quiz (Personal Finance All-in-One, p. 99).

Answers

Are You Ready? 1. You can find out which retailer has an item in stock, which has the best prices, and which provides free and rapid shipping. 2. Retailers may not ship the product ordered or honor returns.

Paying for College

Get Started

LESSON GOALS

Students will:

- Understand the real costs of college by completing a worksheet.
- Describe options for obtaining financial aid and the characteristics of each.
- Examine issues regarding repayment of college loans.

DIFFERENTIATED INSTRUCTION KEY

L1 Special Needs
L2 Basic
ELL English Language Learners
LPR Less Proficient Readers
L3 All Students
L4 Advanced Students

Teach

ANALYZE

Ask **What colleges are you interested in? Why?** Call on several students and write their college choices on the board. Summarize their responses. Continue with the other questions: **Does location matter? How much debt can you tolerate?** Encourage volunteers to respond. Then ask students if they would reconsider any of their college choices based on their answers to the questions.

Distribute the "How Much Does It Cost?" worksheet (Personal Finance All-in-One, pp. 100–101). Review the bills with students. Discuss some of the charges listed. Ask students if the costs of college surprise them. Have students write answers to the questions on their own. Then discuss some of the answers in class.

L2 **Differentiate** Organize these students into small groups to discuss and write answers to the questions.

ANALYZE A GRAPH

Call students' attention to the graph on page PF41, Sticker Shock. Ask **What might have caused the steep rise in the costs of college?** *(Possible answers: Most jobs now require a college degree; the growth of colleges may not have kept up with population growth; demand has outpaced supply.)*

Emphasize to students that although college costs are high, they should not assume they will have to pay all of the costs. Review the Financial Aid Tips with students. Define terms such as *grants* and *scholarships* to ensure student understanding.

Paying for College

Learning how to pay for college is an education in itself.

Almost Priceless

It's hard to put a price on a college education. The personal and career rewards last a lifetime. Unfortunately, paying off the costs of a four-year degree can seem almost as long. The hard facts about paying for college are these: In constant dollars, the average cost of **tuition** at public and private universities nearly doubled between 1990 and 2005.

Choose Carefully

If rapidly rising costs continue, in 2014 a four-year public education will cost over $125,000 (in constant dollars) for incoming freshman. The cost at a private university will be almost twice that amount. For most students, those are pretty scary numbers. Here are a few questions to consider:

- **What school do you want to attend, and why?** Examine your goals. Look for the educational resources you need at less-expensive public schools. Private schools generally are more costly, but can be more generous with their financial aid offers.
- **Does location matter?** Tuition costs vary considerably from region to region.
- **How much debt can you tolerate?** If your career goal is to be a freelance artist rather than a brain surgeon, you might want to choose the less-expensive college to cut down on your post-graduation debt.

GO FIGURE

9/10

The fraction of Americans who believe that access to higher education is a basic right.

SOURCE: Public Agenda 2007 report

Financial Aid Basics

The thought of paying for college might send you into panic mode. But there is help. It comes in three forms: (a) grants and scholarships; (b) work-study programs; and (c) loans. The idea is to reduce the amount you're going to owe by applying for as many sources of aid as possible.

FINANCIAL AID TIPS

Apply early: There is a limited amount of aid available, so make sure you get your fair share.

Seek free money: Grants and scholarships need not be repaid. Search for local and government sources of financial aid.

Limit your debt: Finance just what you need.

Use the Web: Several sites have calculators that allow you to estimate your expected family contribution, the amount of your aid awards, and the amount of your loan payments. The College Board has one as well as a search tool for scholarships. The Sallie Mae (www.salliemae.com) site includes a listing of major private lenders.

PF40

Background Note

Ivy League or State University The question is continually brought up: Does the cost of an education at an expensive, prestigious university pay for itself over a lifetime, or is a lower-cost education at a quality public institution just as good? Two studies were conducted to answer this question, and they yielded two different answers. Princeton economist Alan Krueger and Andrew Mellon Foundation researcher Stacy Berg Dale concluded that bright students who chose less expensive schools earned about the same over their careers as bright students who attended elite schools. On the other hand, Cornell economist Ronald Ehrenberg and two Rand Corporation researchers came to opposite conclusions: earnings were substantially more for graduates of elite universities, and the earnings differential seemed to be increasing. The debate goes on.

And if you're like most students, you will qualify for some type of assistance. The biggest financial aid error is not to apply at all. Many colleges are substituting loans for grants and some are experimenting by waiving tuition for certain income levels altogether.

Types of Lenders

Financial aid comes in many packages and, regardless of income, you can qualify for some type of government loan. You might need to supplement it with a loan from your school or a commercial loan.

Federal Government

When it comes to government aid, the Department of Education offers three basic loans: Direct Loans and Stafford Loans for parents or students, as well as the Parent Loan for Undergraduate Students (PLUS).

For those in financial need, there is the Federal Perkins Loan. These loans have a fixed interest rate and are made available through the college. Students who go on to take teaching jobs in certain areas or who volunteer in the Americorps, Peace Corps, or VISTA programs may be eligible to have their federal loans partially repaid or even canceled.

Private Sources

If money from government loans does not cover all your college expenses, private lending sources could fill the gap. Compared to government loans, regular commercial loans typically have higher interest rates, fees, and credit requirements. Trade organizations and educational institutions also offer lending aid. Check with your guidance counselor to find out more information.

Other Sources

All kinds of students can qualify for financial aid that does not have to be repaid. You need not be valedictorian or an all-state basketball star.

Grants

A no-strings attached grant is a no-brainer to consider when applying for financial aid. Available from the federal government, state governments and higher education institutions, grants are usually awarded according to financial need and tuition rates.

Don't forget FAFSA, also known as, the Free Application for Federal Student Aid available at www.fafsa.ed.gov. All students should complete the FAFSA, even if they believe they will not qualify for aid. There is always a chance that family circumstances will change. You need to complete this form if you want to be considered for federal aid, such as the Pell Grant and Supplemental Educational Opportunity Grant. These grants are given to students with "exceptional financial need." Find out more by checking out the U.S. Department of Education Web sites, www.federalstudentaid.ed.gov, www.students.gov, your state education agency, or your high school guidance office.

Scholarships and Work Study

Besides aid from the school itself, there are scholarships available from local community and civic groups. Check with local organizations such as the Kiwanis and Lions Clubs. Some companies also offer scholarships to children of their employees. Work-study programs are a win-win situation for the student, college, and community. This type of aid allows students to earn money to offset their educational expenses.

Sticker Shock In recent years, the cost of attending a U.S. four-year-college has risen at twice the inflation rate. A 2007 study*, however, finds that the benefits outweigh the short-term cost. Over a lifetime, a college education increases a worker's earning potential by about $800,000.

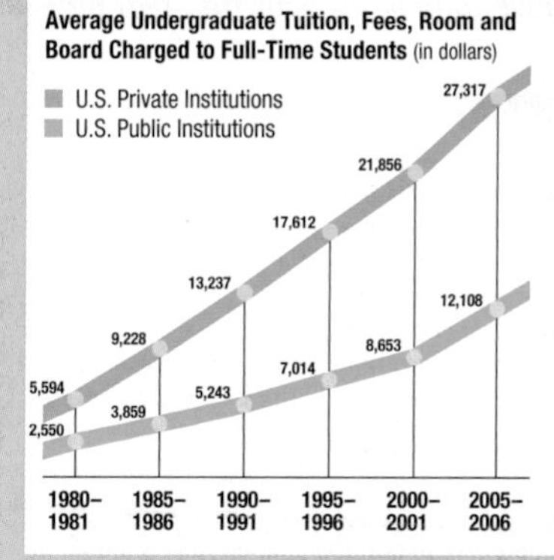

*Report by the College Board, "Education Pays" SOURCE: Digest of Education Statistics

Are You Ready?

1. Why is it important to complete the FAFSA form?
2. What is the advantage of seeking a federal loan instead of one from a private lender?

To learn more about this topic, visit **PearsonSuccessNet.com**

After High School

DISCUSS

Discuss the sources of financial aid. Ask **What kinds of government loans are available?** *(Direct Loans, Stafford Loans, Parent Loan for Undergraduate Students, Federal Perkins Loan)* Write these names on the board. Ask students to describe private loans. Ask them what the advantage of government loans is over private loans.

Call on students to explain grants. Add Pell Grants, and Supplemental Education Opportunity Grant to your list on the board.

EXTEND

Have students do research on trends in the repayment of college loans. American Student Assistance (www.amsa.com) is one source of information. Ask them to find out why it is important to be careful how much money you borrow. Ask **When does repayment begin? What happens if you are late with payments or default on the loan?** Have students report their findings on student loan delinquency.

Assess and Remediate

L3 Collect the "How Much Does It Cost?" worksheets and assess student understanding of the cost of a college education.

L3 Give the Paying for College Quiz (Personal Finance All-in-One, p. 102).

Answers

Are You Ready? 1. There is always a chance that family circumstances might change. You must complete the form to be considered for certain types of federal aid. 2. Federal loans usually have lower interest rates, fees, and credit requirements.

Getting a Job

Get Started

LESSON GOALS

Students will:

- Understand what to include in a resumé by completing a resumé worksheet.
- Describe how to prepare for and follow up after a job interview.
- Determine appropriate dress for an interview by analyzing a transparency.

DIFFERENTIATED INSTRUCTION KEY

- **L1** Special Needs
- **L2** Basic
  - **ELL** English Language Learners
  - **LPR** Less Proficient Readers
- **L3** All Students
- **L4** Advanced Students

Teach

ANALYZE

Ask **Who has applied for a job?** Call on volunteers to describe how they learned about the job. **Did you have an interview? What kinds of questions did the interviewer ask?** Encourage descriptions of students' experiences.

Point out that when they begin searching for a full-time job after high school or college, the process will become more formal and more will be expected of them. They will have to be prepared and will probably need a resumé.

Distribute the "What's in a Resumé?" worksheet (Personal Finance All-in-One, pp. 103–104). Read through the parts of a resumé with students and discuss the kinds of information they would provide in each. Then have students complete the worksheet on their own.

L2 Differentiate Circulate as students work. Pay particular attention to their efforts in writing an objective statement. Provide assistance as needed.

DISCUSS

Refer students to "Where to Look" and discuss the different places to find job information. Have them share what they know about these sources. Ask if they have used any of these when hunting for jobs. Ask students where else they can look for job leads.

Getting a Job

Engineer? Store manager? Teacher? Whatever you want to be, you'll soon have to look for your first real job—and then get it.

Be Prepared!

You may already have had your first job—after school, weekends, or summers. But for most of us, finding a full-time, long-term job doesn't come until after we graduate from high school or college.

Your Resumé

The first step is to prepare a **resumé,** a written summary of your educational and work experience. Think of it as an advertisement to market yourself to an employer.

You might be thinking, "That's fine if I have a lot of experience to list. But this is my first real job." True, but that doesn't mean you don't have qualities that employers are interested in. For example, suppose you worked the same job every summer for three years running. That shows that somebody liked you enough to keep hiring you back. Your service in school clubs or volunteer organizations could indicate qualities such as leadership, planning abilities, and a strong work ethic. Academic honors can count for a lot, too.

Organize your resumé in a neat, readable fashion—no fancy type. And have plenty of copies on hand. (For more tips, see the resumé-writing worksheet available online.)

References

Some employers may ask for references. If you've been applying for colleges, you know the drill. Pick people—other than family—who can tell potential employers about your character and work ethic: a former boss, a colleague from an internship, a professor or advisor. Be ready with names, home or business addresses, e-mail addresses, and phone numbers.

GO FIGURE

3-5

The average number of careers a U.S. worker will have in a lifetime.

SOURCE: Careers in Transition, LLC

Where to Look

There are plenty of good sources of job information out there. Any or all of these can help you land the right job.

The Internet More and more companies are using sites like monster.com and careerbuilder.com to advertise for help.

Newspapers Maybe you don't read the newspaper so much. But a lot of employers do. Find out what day your local newspaper publishes want ads.

Employment Agencies For a fee, the agency can help you connect with a company looking for someone with your skills.

Job/Career Centers High schools and colleges offer career counseling. In addition to helping you find a job, counselors can appraise your resumé at no cost and give you interviewing tips.

Job Fairs Companies get a chance to meet recent graduates—you get a chance to meet possible employers.

PF42

Background Note

Social Networking for Jobs Job recruiters say the best approach to job hunting is to search in as many places as possible, not just on Internet job sites and in help wanted classifieds. Networking is and always has been a strong source of job leads, and now, with Internet social networking Web sites, it's even more powerful. Sites such as LinkedIn, Plaxo, and Facebook can connect job hunters with people who know about job openings at their workplace and what qualities their employers are looking for. Even employers visit these sites to find people for job openings. People using these sites to find jobs, however, should first make a comprehensive review of all information they may have posted about themselves and remove anything that is remotely negative. Creating the right first impression is as important online as it is during the interview.

Paid in Full? Not all benefit packages are created equal. For instance, rising medical costs in recent years have forced many private companies to scale back, or even drop, health coverage. The chart below shows that the types of benefits private companies offer can vary greatly.

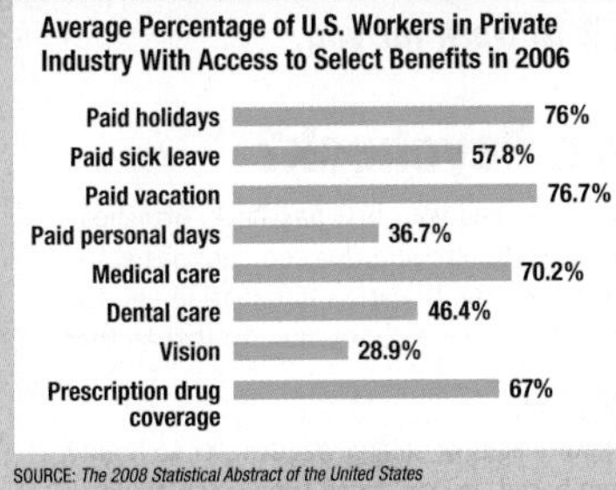

Know Where to Look

So you're ready to look for a job. Where should you start? Some common sources of job information are listed on the previous page. Make a list of places that seem most promising. And try to find out something about a company before you apply there. It's all just part of being prepared.

The Interview

That very first job interview can be an exciting but nerve-wracking experience. But you can prepare for it. Hold a mock interview with family members or friends. Have them ask you possible questions and then critique your responses and your delivery.

Make a Good Impression

The minute you step into a potential employer's office, you are being judged. Don't blow it before you open your mouth. Posture, eye contact, and a firm handshake go a long way to making a positive impression.

> "You never get a second chance to make a *first* impression."
>
> —Maxim attributed to 20th century Dutch author William Triesthof

Believe it or not, dressing wrong can be a deal-breaker. What works on the beach or in a dance club won't cut it in the office. Even a company that allows "casual" dress on the job doesn't want to see you in tank tops, cutoffs, or flip-flops. Be safe. Think conservative and professional. Yes, that may mean a suit or a dress. Let them tell you that you don't have to dress that way—after you get the job.

Turn Off That Cellphone

The person interviewing you may have to interrupt to take a phone call. But you do not get the same privilege. Before you step in that office, make sure your cellphone is switched off. Nothing will ruin a good interview faster than a ringing cellphone.

Ask the Right Questions

Where do you see yourself in five years? Why did you choose your particular college major? Why are you the best candidate for this position? Expect to be peppered with questions. But be equally as prepared to ask them. Questions like these show you're interested in the job:

- What are the company's goals for the next year or so?
- How does this job fit in with the company's goals?
- Describe a typical day here in this department.

Steer clear of questions about pay, benefits, hours, and vacation time. All that will be covered if you are asked back for a second interview.

After the Interview

Follow up with a handwritten or e-mailed thank you note. This reaffirms your interest and makes a lasting impression. If you're rejected, try not to get discouraged. It's part of the interview process. And remember: rejection can work either way. You're under no obligation to accept the first offer that comes along. Factor in benefits, commuting costs, work environment, and the possibility of career advancement. Look for the best fit for you.

Are You Ready?

1. How should you dress for an interview?
2. What are important things about yourself you should highlight during an interview?

To learn more about this topic, visit PearsonSuccessNet.com

ANALYZE A CHART

Have students look at the Paid in Full? chart on page PF43. Ask **Why are benefits often considered an addition to the pay for a job?** *(Possible answer: Benefits consist of things an employee would likely have to pay for if the company did not.)*

DISPLAY TRANSPARENCY

Display the "Dress for Success" transparency (Transparencies, p. PF.h). Tell students that there are three job openings: a bank has an opening for a bank teller; a greenhouse and plant nursery has an opening for a sales clerk; and an architectural firm has an opening for an administrative assistant. Ask students which person in the transparency is dressed appropriately for an interview for each job. Ask **Which person is not dressed appropriately for a job interview? Why?** Explore students' answers and help them form a judgment on proper dress for an interview.

BRAINSTORM

Discuss the purpose and types of questions they might ask during a job interview. Using the jobs discussed with the transparency, have students brainstorm questions they might ask if interviewed for each position. Critique their suggestions.

EXTEND

Distribute the "Prepare for the Interview" worksheet (Personal Finance All-in-One, p. 105). Have students complete the worksheet on their own. Then have students practice interviewing each other.

Assess and Remediate

L3 Collect the "What's in a Resumé?" and "Prepare for the Interview" worksheets and assess student understanding of the job application process.

L3 Give the Getting a Job Quiz (Personal Finance All-in-One, p. 106).

Answers

Are You Ready? 1. You should dress in a professional, conservative fashion. If in doubt, err on the side of overdressing. 2. Possible response: work experience, service in school clubs or volunteer organizations, skills, and work ethic.

Understanding Your Paycheck

Get Started

LESSON GOALS

Students will:

- Practice reading a paycheck to understand terms such as *gross pay, net pay, FICA,* and *Medicare*.
- Understand how to assess deductions and estimate their tax obligation by completing a worksheet and filling out a W-4 form.
- Analyze an earnings statement.

DIFFERENTIATED INSTRUCTION KEY

L1 Special Needs
L2 Basic
ELL English Language Learners
LPR Less Proficient Readers
L3 All Students
L4 Advanced Students

Teach

DISCUSS

Ask **Who has received a paycheck? Were you shocked when you first saw the difference between what you thought you had earned and what you were paid?** Allow student responses, and then discuss the difference between gross pay and net pay. Have students give examples of payroll withholdings. Define and discuss each type.

L2 Differentiate Clarify the difference between *wages* and *salary*. Provide examples of jobs that pay wages and jobs that pay salaries.

Have students discuss the jobs listed in the Pay Check chart on page PF44. Ask students to describe the type of training needed for some of these jobs.

Point out that most of the large withholdings are state and federal taxes. When students take a job, their employer will ask them to complete a W-4 form. Discuss the purpose of the W-4. Then distribute the "How Much Will You Owe?" worksheet (Personal Finance All-in-One, pp. 107–108). Explain that the IRS provides this form to help taxpayers estimate their earnings and deductions in order to make the W-4 forms as accurate as possible. Have students complete the worksheet on their own.

Distribute the W-4 form. Instruct students to use the information they gathered on the worksheets to complete the form.

Understanding Your Paycheck

Your pay stub is an important tool in managing your personal finances. Put it to work for you.

What's in a Paycheck?

You've got your first job—and your first paycheck. Attached to your check is a pay stub, also known as an earnings statement, which includes your identification information and the pay period you worked. But there's a lot more to it than that.

Salary and Wages

It all begins with your wages or salary. Wages refer to hourly pay, and can change based on how much time you worked. Salary is monthly or yearly pay, which is not dependent on the number of hours worked.

Your pay stub shows your **gross pay,** the total amount of income you earned during the pay period. If you are paid hourly, it should be equal to the number of hours you worked times your hourly wage. (It will also show if you worked overtime at a higher rate.) If you are on an annual salary, it's your salary divided by the number of pay periods in the year.

Withholdings

You will immediately notice that your **net pay**—the amount the check is made out for—is far less than your gross pay. Where did the rest of the money go?

Your stub lists all your **payroll withholdings,** the earnings that come out of your check before you get it. Some of these withholdings are voluntary. For example, if you join a company medical or insurance plan, your share of these benefits comes out of your check. Other withholdings, however, go in taxes to the state and federal government.

Federal and State Deductions

Most workers have federal and state taxes deducted from their earnings. Your employer is also required to pay the federal government a certain percentage your earnings.

Social Security and Medicare

Social Security (FICA) and Medicare taxes are based on a percentage of your earnings. FICA stands for Federal Insurance Contributions Act. It is a U.S. payroll tax on employees and employers to fund programs that provide benefits for retirees, the disabled, and children of deceased workers. Medicare provides hospital insurance benefits.

The W-4 Form

Federal and state taxes are deducted based on an estimate of how much you will owe in yearly taxes. Most workers are required to fill out the W-4 form when they start a new job. It includes guidelines to help you do the calculations needed to estimate how much will be withheld from each paycheck. The W-4 gives you the option of taking certain personal allowances that will lower the amount of tax withheld from your income. For example, you may take an exemption for yourself and your spouse. You also can take an exemption for anyone who is dependent on your income, such as a child. Young people who are not married and have no children will generally claim a single exemption. The IRS offers an online withholding calculator (www.irs.gov/individuals) to help you avoid having too much or too little income tax withheld from your pay.

GO FIGURE

9 million

The number of trees that would be saved if all U.S. households switched to electronic records, including using direct deposit for payment instead of paper paychecks.

SOURCE: PayItGreen Alliance

Pay Check Level of education, skill and supply and demand are major factors that determine a worker's entry-level pay. Typically, college graduates with technical, medical, or business degrees will command higher salaries.

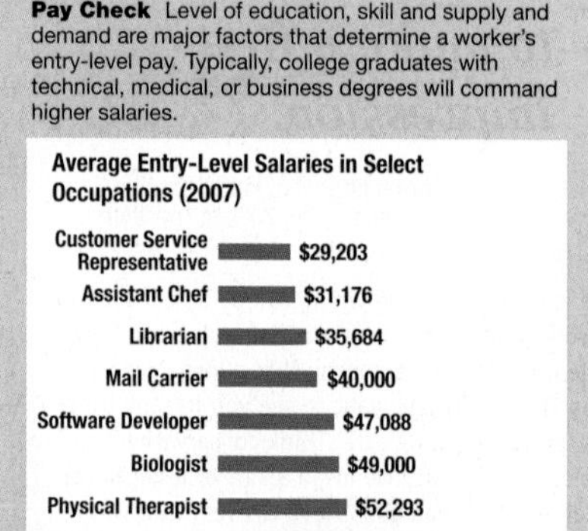

PF44

Background Note

Total Compensation When employees look at their earnings statement, they often do not realize that while they lose a large portion of their earnings to taxes and to pay for other benefits, their employers are kicking in another large amount to pay for workers' benefits. The wages and salaries a business pays to each employee represent just 70 percent of the total cost of paying that employee. The other 30 percent goes to paying for benefits. Among the benefits employers pay for employees are paid leave (7%), insurance (8.4%), retirement and savings (4.4%), and Social Security and Medicare (5.7%). To look at it another way, the average worker earned $19.85 per hour in June 2008. That worker cost the employer a total of $28.49, with $8.64 going toward benefits.

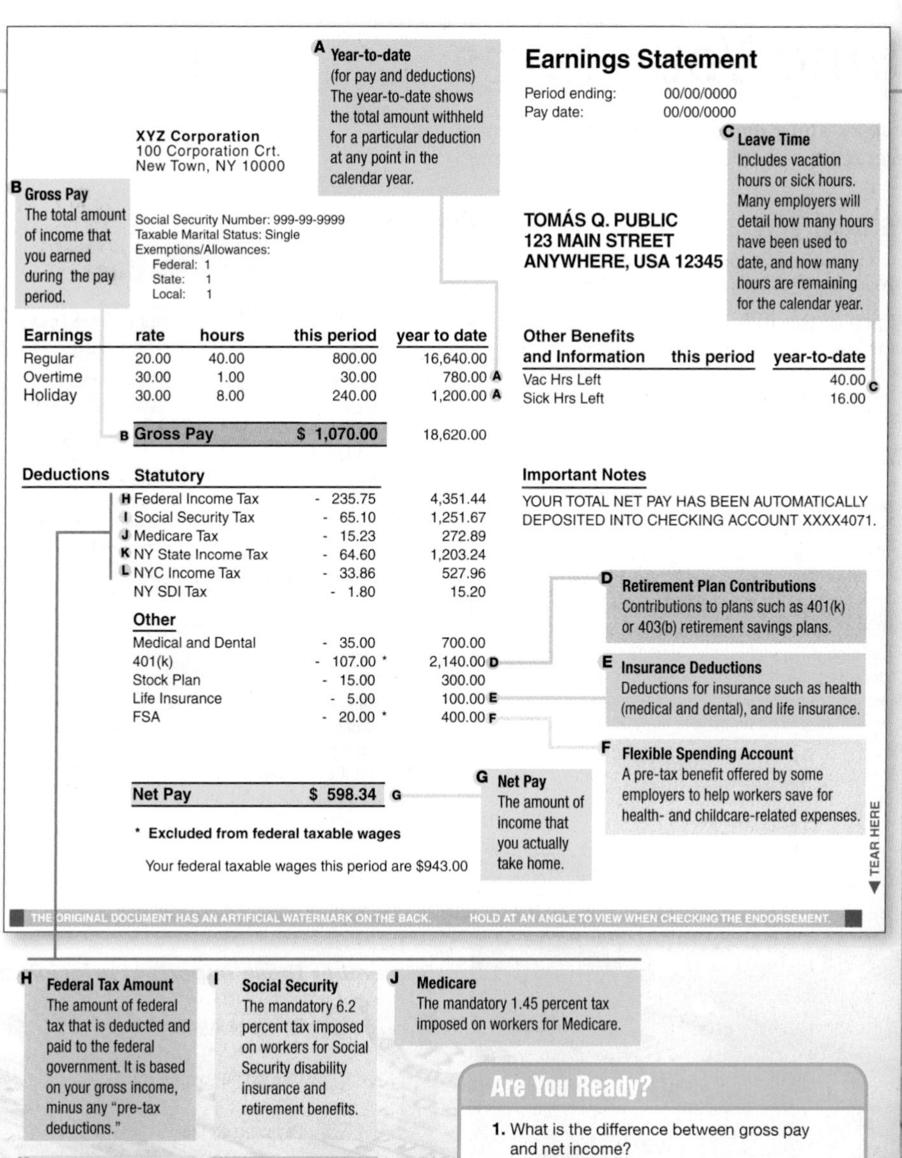

Earnings Statement

Period ending: 00/00/0000
Pay date: 00/00/0000

XYZ Corporation
100 Corporation Crt.
New Town, NY 10000

Social Security Number: 999-99-9999
Taxable Marital Status: Single
Exemptions/Allowances:
Federal: 1
State: 1
Local: 1

TOMÁS Q. PUBLIC
123 MAIN STREET
ANYWHERE, USA 12345

A Year-to-date (for pay and deductions) The year-to-date shows the total amount withheld for a particular deduction at any point in the calendar year.

B Gross Pay The total amount of income that you earned during the pay period.

C Leave Time Includes vacation hours or sick hours. Many employers will detail how many hours have been used to date, and how many hours are remaining for the calendar year.

Earnings	rate	hours	this period	year to date
Regular	20.00	40.00	800.00	16,640.00
Overtime	30.00	1.00	30.00	780.00 A
Holiday	30.00	8.00	240.00	1,200.00 A
B **Gross Pay**			**$ 1,070.00**	18,620.00

Other Benefits and Information	this period	year-to-date
Vac Hrs Left		40.00 C
Sick Hrs Left		16.00

Deductions		this period	year to date
Statutory			
H	Federal Income Tax	- 235.75	4,351.44
I	Social Security Tax	- 65.10	1,251.67
J	Medicare Tax	- 15.23	272.89
K	NY State Income Tax	- 64.60	1,203.24
L	NYC Income Tax	- 33.86	527.96
	NY SDI Tax	- 1.80	15.20
Other			
	Medical and Dental	- 35.00	700.00
	401(k)	- 107.00 *	2,140.00 D
	Stock Plan	- 15.00	300.00
	Life Insurance	- 5.00	100.00 E
	FSA	- 20.00 *	400.00 F
	Net Pay	**$ 598.34** G	

* Excluded from federal taxable wages

Your federal taxable wages this period are $943.00

Important Notes

YOUR TOTAL NET PAY HAS BEEN AUTOMATICALLY DEPOSITED INTO CHECKING ACCOUNT XXXX4071.

D Retirement Plan Contributions Contributions to plans such as 401(k) or 403(b) retirement savings plans.

E Insurance Deductions Deductions for insurance such as health (medical and dental), and life insurance.

F Flexible Spending Account A pre-tax benefit offered by some employers to help workers save for health- and childcare-related expenses.

G Net Pay The amount of income that you actually take home.

TEAR HERE

THE ORIGINAL DOCUMENT HAS AN ARTIFICIAL WATERMARK ON THE BACK. HOLD AT AN ANGLE TO VIEW WHEN CHECKING THE ENDORSEMENT.

H Federal Tax Amount The amount of federal tax that is deducted and paid to the federal government. It is based on your gross income, minus any "pre-tax deductions."

I Social Security The mandatory 6.2 percent tax imposed on workers for Social Security disability insurance and retirement benefits.

J Medicare The mandatory 1.45 percent tax imposed on workers for Medicare.

K State Tax Amount The amount of tax paid to the state government.

L Local Tax Amount The local tax is sometimes applied to residents of certain cities, counties or school districts.

Are You Ready?

1. What is the difference between gross pay and net income?
2. What would be the year-to-date Medicare tax withholding for a worker whose gross pay was $9,845?

WebQuest online To learn more about this topic, visit **PearsonSuccessNet.com**

ANALYZE

Call students' attention to the Earnings Statement and help them read and analyze the information it gives. Ask **What was Tomás's gross pay for the period?** *($1,070)* **How much overtime did he work?** *(1 hour)* **How much money did he make by working on holidays so far this year?** *($1,200)* Continue to ask students to find data in the earnings statement.

Discuss the different entries, such as 401(k) and retirement accounts and the flexible spending account. Ensure that students understand these different types of benefits.

Point out that Tomás had a gross income of $1,070.00, but took home only $598.34. Guide a discussion of the value that Tomás gets from the money that has gone toward benefits.

EXTEND

Give students a hypothetical salary and have them create their paycheck. Have them calculate what will be deducted and how much will be taken out for various items. What is their net pay?

L4 Differentiate Ask **Why are taxes automatically deducted from your pay?** Have students research the history of income tax in the United States. Ask them to answer the following questions: **When did it begin? Why does the government withhold taxes?**

Assess and Remediate

L3 Collect the "How Much Will You Owe?" worksheets and assess student understanding of how to determine how much to have withheld from their paychecks.

L3 Give the Understanding Your Paycheck Quiz (Personal Finance All-in-One, p. 110).

Answers

Are You Ready? 1. Gross pay is the total amount of income earned; net income is the amount a worker's check is made out for—it's the gross pay, minus taxes and the costs of benefits. 2. $142.75

Paying Your Taxes

Get Started

LESSON GOALS

Students will:

- Describe the different kinds of state and federal taxes.
- Describe the W-2 form and Forms 1040 and 1040EZ.
- Learn where to get help filing taxes.

DIFFERENTIATED INSTRUCTION KEY

L1 Special Needs
L2 Basic
ELL English Language Learners
LPR Less Proficient Readers
L3 All Students
L4 Advanced Students

Teach

DISCUSS

Quote Benjamin Franklin's famous adage: "In this world nothing can be said to be certain, except death and taxes." Ask students if they think this is an accurate description of how taxes fit into our lives. Then ask students to name benefits we derive from taxes. List the benefits on the board. Encourage students to compare the value of these benefits with the burden that taxes impose.

L2 Differentiate Explain the term *progressive tax* to students by comparing it with a *flat tax,* where everyone pays the same percentage of their income. Ask students why the United States has chosen to use a progressive tax.

COMPARE

List the different kinds of taxes on the board: income tax, sales tax, property tax, inheritance tax. Call on students to define each term. Then have students look at the State Tax Bites chart on page PF47. Have them discuss the differences between paying a sales tax and income tax to a state.

DISPLAY TRANSPARENCY

Display "The Tax Code" transparency (Transparencies, p. PF.I). Ask **What does this cartoon say about our tax laws?** Follow up by having students tell why they think the tax code is so complicated. Discuss how Congress continually revises tax laws and adds new ones to refine our tax laws to meet the needs of the people.

Paying Your Taxes

Your country, state, and community want a share of your paycheck. It's a cost of being a responsible citizen.

Taxes and You

Welcome to the workforce! You have joined the ranks of taxpayers. But why do you have to pay taxes anyhow?

Your Share of the Bill

Governments have expenses. They have to pay salaries for thousands of employees and provide services for millions of citizens. The biggest source of government revenue is taxes. And you are required by law to pay your share.

Don't Mess With the IRS

Among taxes, the federal income tax is top dog. The Internal Revenue Service (IRS), an agency within the Treasury Department, applies federal income tax laws passed by Congress. The agency generates tax forms and collects taxes. The IRS will notice if you don't pay what you owe and impose hefty financial penalties for any misdeeds.

The federal income tax is a progressive tax, so people with the highest income have the highest tax rates. The system also includes hundreds of tax breaks for people with special financial burdens, such as people paying for college or starting a business, as well as rewards for actions like making a donation to charity.

Other Taxes

Most state governments collect income tax, too. In addition, states and local communities levy other kinds of taxes, such as sales tax and property tax. Sales taxes vary from state to state, but they generally involve paying a fixed percentage on most items you buy. Essentials of life—such as food and medicine—are generally exempt from sales tax. Property taxes are based on the value of privately owned homes and land.

Taxes are also collected on income you didn't work for. If Aunt Bessie leaves you money in her will, you have to pay an inheritance tax. If you buy stock and you make a lot of money when you sell it, that's also taxed.

GO FIGURE

$1.236 trillion

Gross collections from individual U.S. taxpayers in 2006.

SOURCE: Internal Revenue Service

Forms, Forms, Forms

Sometime during the 'tax season', which runs from January to April 15, you need to fill out and file the appropriate tax forms. Filing is the only way to get a refund, or return of excess taxes paid. But whether you've got a refund coming or not, it's against the law not to file an income tax return.

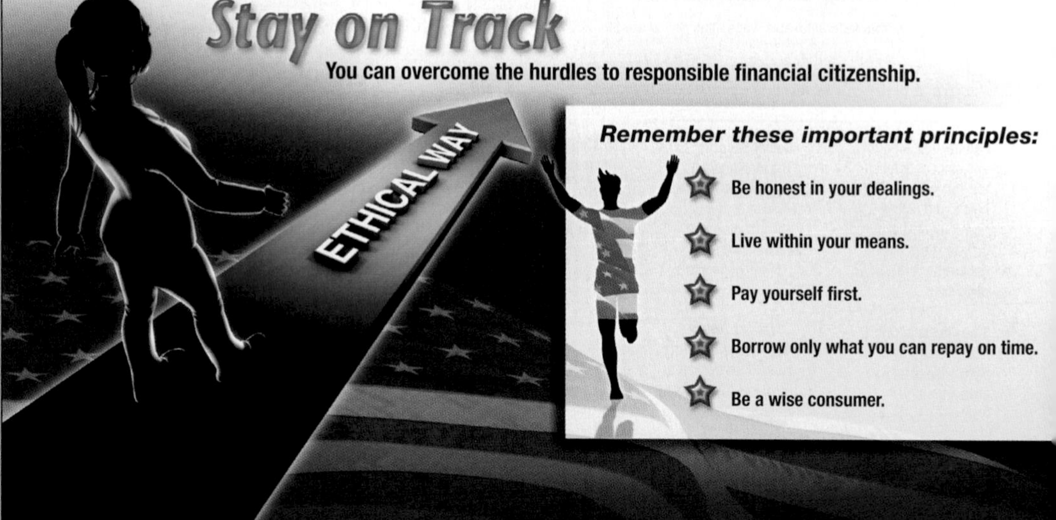

Stay on Track
You can overcome the hurdles to responsible financial citizenship.
ETHICAL WAY
Remember these important principles:
Be honest in your dealings.
Live within your means.
Pay yourself first.
Borrow only what you can repay on time.
Be a wise consumer.

Background Note

Income Tax History For much of its history, the United States did not have an income tax. It relied on excise taxes on specific goods and tariffs to raise needed revenue. When the Civil War began, the government turned to income taxes for the first time. The taxes were progressive: people earning up to $10,000 a year paid 3 percent; those earning more than that paid 5 percent. The income tax was repealed after the war when government costs returned to normal. Income taxes were tried again in 1894, but they were declared unconstitutional a year later. It was not until passage of the Sixteenth Amendment in 1913 that income taxes became a fact of life. Congress imposed a tax of between 1 percent and 7 percent, the highest rate for those earning more than $500,000. Form 1040 was introduced at the same time. Both the form and income taxes have been with us ever since.

The W-2

The most common federal tax form is the W-2, which reports wages paid to employees and taxes withheld from them. The form also reports FICA taxes to the Social Security Administration. Employers must complete and send out a W-2 to every employee by January 31. Save these documents! Your W-2's must be attached to your tax return when you file.

1040 and Beyond

When you file your income tax return, which is due by April 15, you'll use Form 1040, the Individual Income Tax Return. By filling it out properly, you will learn if you owe more money to the government or if the government owes you money.

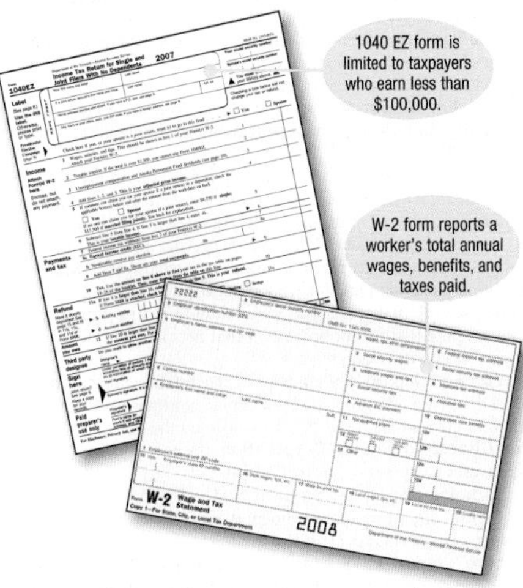

1040 EZ form is limited to taxpayers who earn less than $100,000.
W-2 form reports a worker's total annual wages, benefits, and taxes paid.

To make life easier, the government introduced the Form 1040EZ, which is the simplest tax form. Its use is limited to taxpayers with taxable income below $100,000 who take the standard deduction instead of itemizing deductions, that is, listing them separately. Many unmarried people with no children also qualify to use this form.

If you have income other than wages, salaries, and tips, Form 1099 comes into play. It's a statement you receive from payers of interest income, such as banks and savings institutions, that summarizes your interest income for the year.

State Tax Bites Americans pay federal taxes no matter where they live. State taxes are another matter. Some states, like Florida and Texas, do not impose an income tax. But they assess a sales tax. Alaska residents, who pay no sales or income tax, have the least per capita tax rates in the nation.

State Sales Tax Rate: Highs and Lows

Highest Tax Rate	
California	7.25%
Lowest Tax Rate	
Colorado	2.9%
No Sales Tax	
Alaska	New Hampshire
Delaware	Oregon
Montana	

SOURCE: State Sales Tax Rates, January 1, 2008 www.taxadmin.org

Don't Guess—Get Help!

You want to make sure you get all the tax deductions that the IRS allows. Each form has step-by-step instructions, but they might not answer all your questions. Here are some other places to get advice:

- The IRS has a user-friendly Web site, with lots of information. It can be found at www.irs.gov.
- Call the IRS at (800) 829-1040. You can talk to a tax specialist, or even schedule an appointment for help at IRS service centers. But don't delay. The closer you get to April 15, the harder it may be to get timely help.
- Tax-preparation services and tax accountants will prepare your tax return for you for a fee. Some will file your return for you.

If you prepare your return on paper, you must send it to the IRS Service Center listed in the instruction booklet and at the IRS Web site. There are ways you can prepare and "e-file" your return online. Filing in this way will get you a faster tax refund. But you usually will have to pay a fee, especially if you use a tax preparation firm.

Are You Ready?

1. Describe the role of a W-2 form when filing your taxes.
2. Why do governments collect taxes?

WebQuest online

To learn more about this topic, visit **PearsonSuccessNet.com**

Taxes and Income

ANALYZE

Explain that the government has tried to address the problem of a complicated tax code by creating streamlined forms that fit what many people require. Distribute the "Tax Time" worksheet (Personal Finance All-in-One, pp. 111–112) and Form 1040EZ Form (Personal Finance All-in-One, p. 113). Read through the instructions and discuss the W-2 Form with students. Then have students study the second page of the worksheet and complete the 1040EZ Form on their own.

L2 Differentiate Work with students as a group and take them step-by-step through the process of completing the 1040EZ Form.

DISCUSS

When students have completed their 1040EZ Form, discuss what they've learned. Ask **How much of your income has gone toward taxes?** *($878)* Ask students how they would feel if their taxes were increased by 10 percent. How would this affect what they have to spend and save?

Point out that taxpayers have a responsibility to pay the taxes they owe on their income. Explain that they also have the responsibility to themselves to pay only what they owe. They should look for and use any deductions that they are entitled to. Distribute the "Taxes and Income" worksheet (Personal Finance All-in-One, p. 114). When students complete the worksheet, discuss their answers and review the deductions and common mistakes.

EXTEND

Have students go to www.irs.gov and learn about "e-file." Ask **What do you have to do to use e-file? What does it cost? Can anyone do it?** Have students share their findings in class discussion.

Assess and Remediate

L3 Collect the "Tax Time" and "Taxes and Income" worksheets and assess student understanding of how to complete a 1040EZ Form.

L3 Give the Paying Your Taxes Quiz (Personal Finance All-in-One, p. 115).

Answers

Are You Ready? 1. The W-2 form reports wages paid to the employee and the amount of taxes withheld. It's the basic information you need to file your taxes. 2. Governments collect taxes to pay for the operation of the government and the services provided to the public.

Glossary

annual percentage rate a finance charge, or the cost of credit, expressed as an annual rate
tasa de porcentaje anual cargo financiero, o costo del crédito, expresado como tasa anual

annual percentage yield the annual rate of return on an investment, which must be disclosed by law and which varies by the frequency of compounding
rentabilidad porcentual anual tasa de interés anual de una inversión que, según la ley, se debe dar a conocer, y que varía por la frecuencia del compuesto

auto lease a method of financing a car by essentially renting it for a predetermined period of time
arrendamiento de vehículo método de financiamiento de un auto que consiste en alquilarlo por un período preestablecido de tiempo

automatic bill pay an automatic deduction from your bank account on a predetermined date
pago automático de facturas deducción automática de fondos de una cuenta bancaria en una fecha determinada

---

bankruptcy a state of being legally released from the obligation to repay some or all debt in exchange for the forced loss of certain assets
bancarrota condición que consiste en liberarse legalmente de la obligación de pagar parte de una deuda, o la deuda completa, a cambio de la pérdida forzosa de ciertos bienes

beneficiary a person or organization named to receive assets after an individual's death
beneficiario persona u organización designada a recibir bienes tras la muerte de un individuo

---

certificate of deposit a savings certificate entitling the bearer to receive interest
certificado de depósito certificado de ahorros que autoriza al poseedor a recibir intereses

compound interest accumulated interest added back to the principal, so that interest is earned on interest
interés compuesto interés acumulado agregado al capital, de modo que se ganan intereses sobre el interés

consumer protection act an act designed to reduce fraud and make it harder to declare bankruptcy
acto de protección al consumidor ley designada para disminuir el fraude y dificultar el proceso de declaración de bancarrota

co-pay a small portion of the total cost of a service covered by your insurance that you are required to pay
copago porción pequeña, que una persona debe pagar, del costo total de un servicio cubierto por el seguro

credit an agreement to provide goods, services, or money for future payments with interest by a specific date or according to a specific schedule
crédito acuerdo por medio del cual se proveen bienes, servicios o dinero a cambio de pagos con interés, en una fecha específica futura o según un cronograma de pago específico

credit report a detailed report of an individual's credit history prepared by a credit bureau and used by a lender to determine a loan applicant's creditworthiness
informe de crédito reporte detallado preparado por la agencia de información crediticia y usado por un prestamista para determinar la solvencia de una persona que solicita un préstamo

---

deductible an amount you have to pay before your insurance benefits can be applied
deducible cantidad que se debe pagar antes de beneficiarse de la cobertura del seguro

depreciate to decrease in value
depreciar disminuir en valor

dollar cost averaging a method of investing a fixed amount in the same type of investment at regular intervals, regardless of price
promediación de costos método que consiste en realizar regularmente la misma inversión con una cantidad fija de dinero, independientemente del precio

---

electronic funds transfer the shifting of money from one financial institution account to another without the physical movement of cash
transferencia electrónica de fondos paso de dinero de una cuenta en una institución financiera a otra cuenta, sin necesidad de movilizar dinero en efectivo

---

Fair Credit Billing Act a federal law that addresses billing problems by requiring that consumers send a written error notice within 60 days of receiving the first bill containing the error, and preventing creditors from damaging a consumer's credit rating during a pending dispute
Ley de Facturación Justa de Crédito ley federal que trata los problemas de facturización al requerir a los consumidores que notifiquen por escrito sobre cualquier error de una factura, durante los 60 días después de recibir la factura errónea, y que evita que los acreedores afecten negativamente el crédito del consumidor mientras se resuelve el problema

Fair Credit Reporting Act a federal law that covers the reporting of debt repayment information, requiring the removal of certain information after seven or ten years, and giving consumers the right to know what is in their credit report, to dispute inaccurate information, and to add a brief statement explaining accurate negative information
Ley de Informe Justo de Crédito ley federal que cubre el reporte de información sobre la cancelación de deudas, exige la eliminación de cierta información después de siete o diez años y le otorga al consumidor el derecho de acceder a su informe de crédito, cuestionar información errónea y agregar una declaración breve que explique información negativa correcta

Fair Housing Act makes it illegal for a landlord to discriminate against a potential tenant because of that person's race, sex, national origin or religion
Acta de Equidad en la Vivienda ley que establece que es ilegal que el dueño de una propiedad discrimine contra un posible inquilino por su raza, sexo, país de origen o religión

Federal Deposit Insurance Corporation the government agency that insures customer deposits if a bank fails
Corporación Federal de Seguros de los Depósitos Bancarios organismo gubernamental que asegura los depósitos de los clientes si un banco falla

FICO score a type of credit score that makes up a substantial portion of the credit report that lenders use to assess an applicant's credit risk and whether to extend a loan
puntaje FICO tipo de puntaje de crédito que representa una porción considerable del informe de crédito que los prestamistas usan para evaluar el riesgo crediticio de un solicitante y si se le debe hacer un préstamo

---

gross pay wages or salary before deductions for taxes and other purposes
ingreso neto salario antes de incurrir en deducciones fiscales o de otro tipo

---

Health Maintenance Organization (HMO) least expensive insurance plan that allows you to pick a primary care physician, that will refer you to in-network doctors
Organización para el Mantenimiento de la Salud (OMS) tipo de seguro médico menos costoso que le permite al beneficiario escoger un doctor que lo remite a otros doctores dentro de una red

PF48

identity theft the crime of using another person's name, credit or debit card number, Social Security number, or another piece of personal information to commit fraud
robo de identidad crimen que consiste en usar el nombre de otra persona, su número de tarjeta de crédito o débito, su número del seguro social o cualquier otra información personal con fines fraudulentos

Individual Retirement Account An investment account that provides certain tax advantages to people who set aside money for retirement.
Cuenta Personal de Jubilación Cuenta de inversión que les otorga ciertas ventajas tributarias a quienes ahorran dinero para su jubilación

installment loans loans, divided between principal and interest, that are repaid at regularly scheduled intervals
préstamos a plazo préstamos, divididos entre capital e interés, que se pagan en intervalos regulares establecidos

lessor landlord
arrendador dueño de un local o lugar que se ha alquilado

money market account a savings account that offers a competitive rate of interest in exchange for larger-than-normal deposits
cuenta de alto rendimiento cuenta de ahorros que ofrece una tasa de interés competitiva a cambio de recibir depósitos de grandes sumas

net pay an individual's income after deductions, credits and taxes are factored into gross income
salario neto ingreso de un individuo después de calcular las deducciones, los créditos y los impuestos que se deben considerar del ingreso bruto

payroll withholding any tax that is taken directly out of an individual's wages or other income before he or she receives the funds
retención en nómina cualquier impuesto que se retiene del pago de un individuo o de otro ingreso antes de que él o ella reciba los fondos

phishing an Internet scam used to gain personal and financial data to commit fraud
phishing delito cometido a través de Internet que consiste en adquirir información personal y financiera para fines fraudulentos

resumé a document summarizing an individual's employment experience, education, and other information a potential employer needs to know
currículo documento donde se resume la experiencia profesional, la educación y otra información de un individuo que un empleador puede necesitar

risk factors statistics that predict whether someone is likely to be a bad risk
factores de riesgo estadísticas que predicen la probabilidad de que alguien sea un riesgo

risk management plan the process of calculating risk and devising methods to minimize or manage loss
plan de manejo de riesgos proceso que calcula el riesgo y crea métodos para minimizar o manejar pérdidas

risk pyramid a portfolio strategy that allocates assets according to the relative safety and soundness of investments
pirámide de riesgo estrategia del portafolio que asigna activos de acuerdo a lo seguro y aconsejable que sean las inversiones

Roth IRA an individual retirement plan that bears many similarities to the traditional IRA, but contributions are not tax deductible and qualified distributions are tax free
IRA Roth plan de jubilación personal que tiene bastantes similitudes con una cuenta personal de jubilación, IRA (por sus siglas en inglés), pero sus contribuciones no son deducibles de impuestos y ciertas distribuciones que califican son libres de impuestos

Rule of 72 a method of finding the number of years required to double your money at a given interest rate, divide 72 by the compound return
Regla de 72 fórmula para calcular el número de años necesarios para duplicar una suma de dinero a cierta tasa de interés; dividir 72 por el rendimiento compuesto

security deposit money given to the landlord by the tenant to cover any damage to the apartment
depósito de seguridad dinero que un arrendador le entrega a un inquilino para cubrir cualquier daño que se le cause a una propiedad

Social Security a federal government program that provides retirement, survivor's, and disability benefits, funded by a tax on income, which appears on worker's pay stubs as a deduction labeled FICA (for Federal Insurance Contributions Act)
seguro social programa del gobierno federal que proporciona a los ciudadanos beneficios en caso de jubilación, muerte o incapacitación; se acumula mediante la deducción de impuestos al ingreso y aparece identificado en los talones de pago de los trabajadores como Ley Federal de la Contribucíon al Seguro Social (FICA, por sus siglas en inglés)

tenant someone that pays rent to use or occupy land, a building, or other property owned by another
inquilino persona que paga un alquiler para usar u ocupar un terreno, un edificio o cualquier propiedad que le pertenece a otra persona

Truth in Lending Act a federal law that requires financial institutions to disclose specific information about the terms and cost of credit, including the finance charge and the annual percentage rate (APR)
Ley de Divulgación de los Términos Totales de Crédito ley federal que requiere que las instituciones financieras proporcionen información específica sobre los términos y costos del crédito, incluyendo el cargo financiero y la tasa de porcentaje anual

tuition the charge for instruction, especially at a college or private school
matrícula cargo por la educación, especialmente en una universidad o una escuela privada

Vehicle Identification Number a unique serial number used by the automotive industry to identify individual motor vehicles
Número de Identificación del Vehículo serial único que usa la industria automotriz para identificar cada vehículo

warranty a written guarantee from a manufacturer or distributor that specifies the conditions under which the product can be returned, replaced, or repaired
garantía documento de un fabricante o distribuidor que especifica las condiciones en las cuales un producto se puede devolver, reemplazar o reparar

PF49

Expository Writing

Get Started

LESSON GOALS

Students will:

- Write an expository essay using prewriting, drafting, revising, and publishing and presenting.
- Understand that expository writing explains ideas or information in detail.
- Identify the most useful strategies for writing expository essays.

Teach

INTRODUCE

Point out that the primary purpose of expository writing is to inform or explain something to a reader. Also called "explanatory writing," it is the type of writing students use most often in school. Narrative writing, on the other hand, seeks to entertain, persuade, or convey insights by telling a story.

ACTIVATE PRIOR KNOWLEDGE

Ask students to recall school assignments in which they had to explain a process; compare and contrast products, ideas, or policies; identify causes and effects; or describe a problem and solution. Point out that expository writing is a skill required by workers in a variety of jobs; for example, many jobs in business and finance require analysts to write reports that compare and contrast products, companies, and proposals. Government policymakers and analysts routinely write reports that explain cause and effect, define problems, and recommend solutions.

PRACTICE PREWRITING

Divide students into groups and lead them through the grab-bag strategy for choosing a topic to compare and contrast. Ask each group to share ideas for research topics with the class, including both the problems and solutions that they came up with. Have each student choose one of the topics from their group grab bag. Then help them create a graphic organizer such as a Venn diagram or a two-column chart to compare and contrast their ideas.

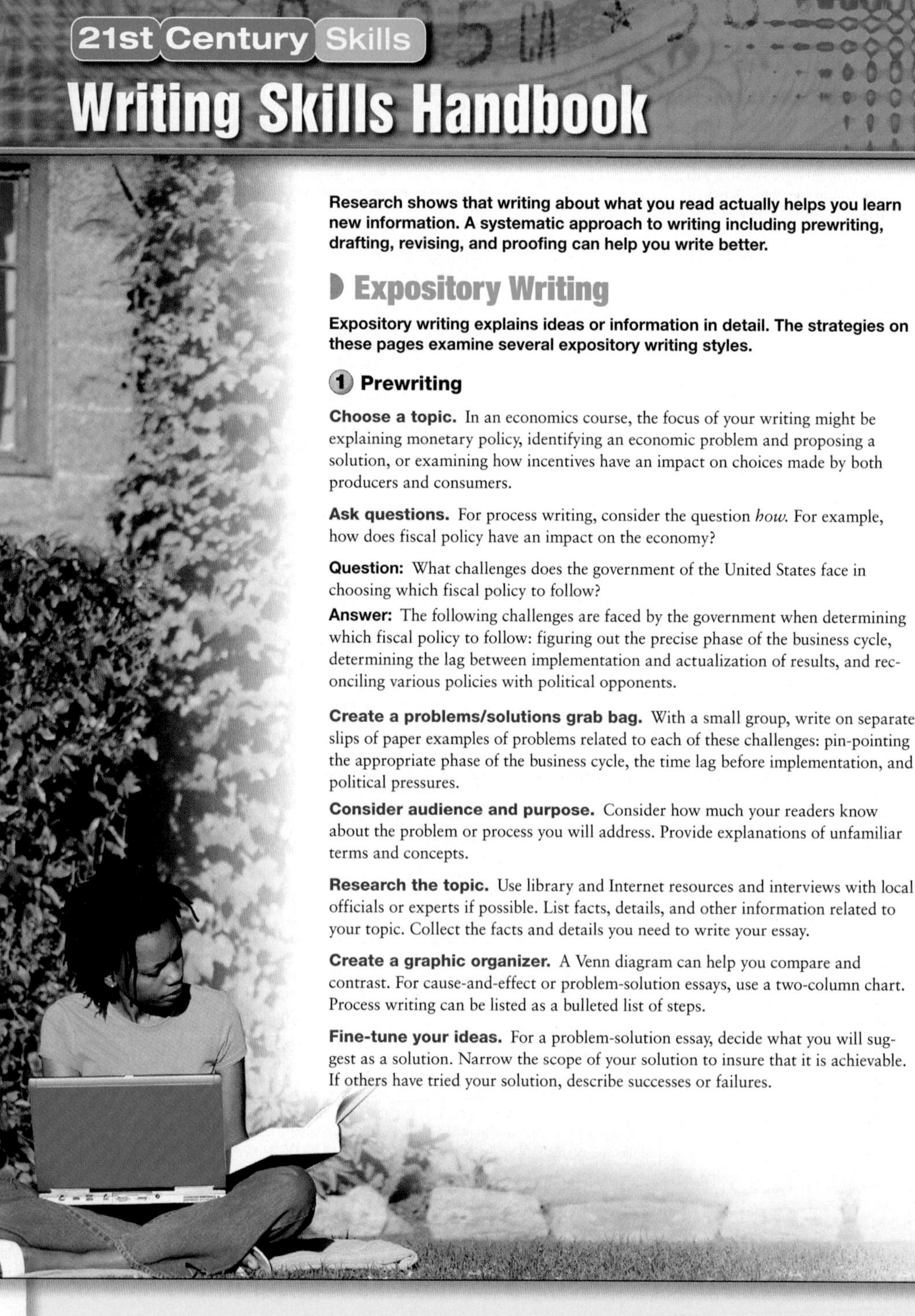

21st Century Skills

Writing Skills Handbook

Research shows that writing about what you read actually helps you learn new information. A systematic approach to writing including prewriting, drafting, revising, and proofing can help you write better.

Expository Writing

Expository writing explains ideas or information in detail. The strategies on these pages examine several expository writing styles.

1 Prewriting

Choose a topic. In an economics course, the focus of your writing might be explaining monetary policy, identifying an economic problem and proposing a solution, or examining how incentives have an impact on choices made by both producers and consumers.

Ask questions. For process writing, consider the question *how.* For example, how does fiscal policy have an impact on the economy?

Question: What challenges does the government of the United States face in choosing which fiscal policy to follow?

Answer: The following challenges are faced by the government when determining which fiscal policy to follow: figuring out the precise phase of the business cycle, determining the lag between implementation and actualization of results, and reconciling various policies with political opponents.

Create a problems/solutions grab bag. With a small group, write on separate slips of paper examples of problems related to each of these challenges: pin-pointing the appropriate phase of the business cycle, the time lag before implementation, and political pressures.

Consider audience and purpose. Consider how much your readers know about the problem or process you will address. Provide explanations of unfamiliar terms and concepts.

Research the topic. Use library and Internet resources and interviews with local officials or experts if possible. List facts, details, and other information related to your topic. Collect the facts and details you need to write your essay.

Create a graphic organizer. A Venn diagram can help you compare and contrast. For cause-and-effect or problem-solution essays, use a two-column chart. Process writing can be listed as a bulleted list of steps.

Fine-tune your ideas. For a problem-solution essay, decide what you will suggest as a solution. Narrow the scope of your solution to insure that it is achievable. If others have tried your solution, describe successes or failures.

2 Drafting

Match structure to purpose. Typically, problem-solution essays benefit from block organization, which presents the entire problem and proposes a solution. Put process and cause-and-effect essays in sequence order and organize compare/contrast essays by subject or by point.

Give background. To discuss fiscal policy, the economy, or trade, first orient the reader to its context. Choose the important facts but don't overwhelm the reader with details. If you need to, return to prewriting to narrow your topic further.

Elaborate for interest and emphasis. Give details about each point in your essay. Add facts that make the link between the reasons for decisions made and their consequences so that a cause-and-effect relationship is clear.

Identify the topic to orient readers. → Fiscal policy is an important tool used by the government to stabilize the economy. In order to avoid a recession, either supply-side or demand-side policies are adopted at different times.

Chronological order walks readers through the cause-and-effect sequence. → Economist John Maynard Keynes believed that in order to stabilize the economy, the government needed to engage in both approaches. By purchasing goods, the government set in motion an economic chain of events that causes economic growth. In order to provide goods to the government, firms naturally increase output. To increase output, firms have to hire more workers. These workers spend money in other areas of the market. Keynes also believed that the government, in order to control growth and prevent inflation, had to raise taxes.

Elaboration supports the relationship you are highlighting. → By purchasing large quantities of steel, the government increases demand for this product. Steel mills hire new workers in order to meet this demand. As steelworkers begin to spend their salaries, this increases demand in other sectors of the market.

Connection to today tells readers why this matters to them. → Today debates over the role of the government in the market are, in part, a debate over how best to implement fiscal policy.

3 Revising

Add transition words. Make cause-and-effect relationships clear with words such as *because, as a result,* and *so.* To compare or contrast policies and processes, use linking words, such as *similarly, both, equally,* or *in contrast, instead,* and *yet.* Use words such as *first, second, next,* and *finally* to help readers follow steps in a process. Look at the examples below. The revised version more clearly shows the order followed by supply-side economics.

First Draft	Revised
Although Keynesian economics was employed for a number of decades in the twentieth century, President Reagan followed a supply-side policy during the 1980s.	When President Reagan assumed office, he adopted a supply-side economic policy. A supply-side economist first studies the current tax rate. Secondly, the economist determines what the appropriate rate should be and advises that tax cuts be made to that level. These tax cuts allow businesses to hire more workers. As a result of more people working, the government's revenue increases.

DISCUSS DRAFTING

Review the drafting steps with students. Invite several volunteers to tell the class the topics they have chosen. Write the topics on the board and ask students to suggest structures for organizing and presenting the information. Clarify for students the difference between a compare and contrast essay organized by subject and by point. For example, a report on deregulation organized by subject might be structured as a comparison of the airline industry as it was before and after deregulation. An essay on deregulation organized by point might introduce a category, or point, such as effects on consumers of regulated and deregulated industries, comparing and contrasting the two forms of operation based on their costs to consumers. Emphasize that all expository essays should begin with a clear statement of purpose.

EXAMINE STRUCTURE

Model the steps in drafting an expository essay by working through the passage in the text on fiscal policy. Have students explain how this passage is structured. To give students additional practice in identifying different ways of organizing expository essays, bring examples of expository writing such as newspaper and newsmagazine editorials and op/ed pieces, computer or software instruction manuals, home remodeling magazines, or online sources. Display materials and have students take turns identifying the structure of each document.

Challenge students to use each transition word in the text in a sentence. Ask **What transition words or phrases in the text can you use in your own essay?** *(in order to, by, today)* Have them compare the first draft and revised passage in the text. Ask students to explain why the revised version is more effective than the original.

REVIEW

As a final step in the revision process, students should end with a concluding paragraph that restates the problem and summarizes the options for solving it, summarizes how subjects are alike or different, or briefly restates the causes of an event and how they are related to the outcome.

Assess and Remediate

Have students write an expository essay. Essays might focus on topics such as Social Security or another current economic issue facing government. Ask them to use one of the prewriting steps to choose the type of essay that fits their topic.

Have students review the Writing Rubric on page S-9 and suggest ways of revising it to create an expository essay rubric.

Research Writing

Get Started

LESSON GOALS

Students will:

- Write a research paper using prewriting, drafting, revising, publishing and presenting.
- Demonstrate understanding of research writing by gathering information and tying it together with a unifying idea.
- Evaluate Internet sources.

Teach

INTRODUCE

Point out that research writing is based heavily on information from outside sources. Research writing is often required in job settings as well as in schools. In private businesses and government offices, workers write research papers on a wide variety of topics.

DISCUSS PREWRITING

Point out that choosing a topic requires not only identifying a subject of interest, but also making sure that accurate, verifiable sources of information are available. For example, many Web sites and blogs do not have fact checkers or credentialed reviewers.

Have students search for topics using an online library catalog. Then divide students into groups to brainstorm topics. Encourage students to choose topics that are of interest to them as writers. Remind students that they can use sources such as magazines, Web sites, and newspapers to get ideas.

Remember purpose. Shape your draft so that it answers the question or thesis with which you began. Try to anticipate opposing arguments and respond to them. For a process essay, be sure to include all steps, and don't assume readers will make the connections. Always tell readers why they should care about your topic.

Review organization. Confirm that your ideas flow in a logical order. Write and number main points on your draft. Reorganize these points until you are satisfied that the order clearly strengthens your essay.

Revise sentences and words. Vary sentence length to include both short and long sentences. Then scan for vague words, such as *good*. Replace them with specific and vibrant words, such as *effective*.

Peer Review. Ask a peer to read your draft. Is it clear? Can he or she follow your ideas? Revise areas of confusion.

4 Publishing and Presenting

Create an economics manual. Contribute your writing to a class manual on economics.

Research Writing

In a research paper, you gather information about a subject from several different sources. Then, you tie this information together with a single unifying idea and present it to your readers.

1 Prewriting

Choose a topic. Often a teacher will assign your research topic. You may have flexibility in choosing your focus or you may have the opportunity to completely define your topic.

- **Catalog scan.** Using an online or electronic library catalog, search for topics that interest you. When a title looks promising, find the book on the shelves. Because libraries group research materials by subject, you should find other books on similar subjects nearby that may help you decide on your final topic.
- **Notes review.** Review your class notes. Jot down topics that you found interesting. You might find a starting point for research into oligopolies from a lecture on competition.
- **Brainstorm topics with a group.** As a group, list categories of issues that interest group members. Within each category, take turns adding subtopics.

Analyze the audience. Your research and your paper should be strongly influenced by the audience. How much will readers know about this topic and how much will you have to teach them?

Gather details. Collect the facts and details you need to write your paper. Use a variety of resources such as nonfiction books or journal articles, newspapers, news magazines, and publications by government agencies or advocacy groups on issues that interest you.

Organize evidence and ideas. Use notecards or create a computer file on your topic to record information. Start by writing down a possible thesis statement. Then begin reading and taking notes. Write a heading at the top of each notecard to group it under a subtopic. Note a number or title to identify the information source. In the examples below, the number 3 is used. Use the same number for an additional source card or notation containing the bibliographic information you will need.

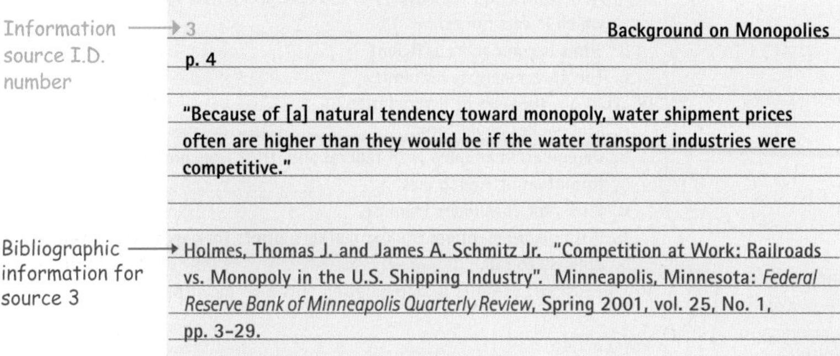

Information source I.D. number → 3 | Background on Monopolies

p. 4

"Because of [a] natural tendency toward monopoly, water shipment prices often are higher than they would be if the water transport industries were competitive."

Bibliographic information for source 3 → Holmes, Thomas J. and James A. Schmitz Jr. "Competition at Work: Railroads vs. Monopoly in the U.S. Shipping Industry". Minneapolis, Minnesota: *Federal Reserve Bank of Minneapolis Quarterly Review*, Spring 2001, vol. 25, No. 1, pp. 3–29.

2 Drafting

Fine-tune your thesis. Review your notes to find relationships between ideas. Shape a thesis that is supported by the majority of your information, then check that it is specific enough to address thoroughly in the time and space allotted.

Plan your organization. Depending on your topic and purpose, you can use various methods to organize your research paper. If you are discussing two items, one approach would be to compare and contrast them. If you are focusing on a complex event or a process, you could use a chronological organization.

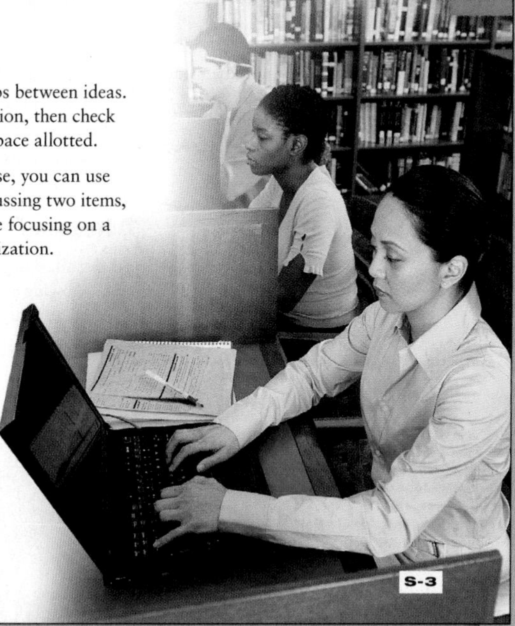

EVALUATE SOURCES

Direct students' attention to the sample note cards in the text. Ask them to identify each piece of information on the cards. Point out that the researcher has identified sources by numbering the cards. Strongly encourage students to document facts as they write. Searching through a stack of index cards to find one piece of information or missing citation can be very time-consuming. Correct documentation of sources saves time and reduces errors.

DISCUSS DRAFTING

Explain that research papers often begin with a thesis statement, usually in the introductory paragraph. The thesis statement clearly states the purpose of the report and provides the reader with a preview of what will be discussed in the paper. For example, a thesis statement for a research paper on women in the workforce might be: "Although there has been a steady increase of women in the labor force over the last 50 years, women are still earning less income than their male counterparts. Despite immense progress in the movement for equal rights for women, their role in the workplace remains beneath the glass ceiling."

OUTLINE

Review the sample outline in the text. Have students read the Introduction and paraphrase the thesis statement. Ask students what kinds of facts or statistics the writer might use to support this thesis. Discuss each step in the outline, pointing out how the information is organized. Explain that each paragraph of a student's research paper should link to an outline entry. Note that the Introduction puts the topic in context and conveys the thesis statement, while the Conclusion recaps key points. Emphasize that students will make a stronger case for their thesis if they draw on several sources of information rather than relying on a single source.

DISCUSS REVISING

Throughout the revision process, students should check their outlines against their paper to make sure that all statements are supported by evidence. Review the sample first draft and discuss the revision. Note that the revised version provides more information on who benefits from deregulation and makes the case for deregulation easier to understand. Stress the importance of documenting each fact. If a fact cannot be documented, it should not be included.

PRESENT

Give students a list of topics to be discussed at the conference. You may want to have all presenters with similar topics present their research papers on the same day. Encourage students to think of questions to ask the presenters. Presenters should anticipate questions and prepare answers. If possible, provide access to computers so that students can create accompanying visuals for their presentations.

Assess and Remediate

Have students choose a topic for a research paper. Once they have selected a general topic, have them create a word web of possible subtopics and then list possible sources for researching them.

Have students review the Writing Rubric on page S-9 and suggest ways of revising it to create a research writing rubric.

Make an outline. Create an outline in which you identify each topic and subtopic in a single phrase. Turn these phrases into sentences and then into the topic sentences of your draft paragraphs. Address a subtopic of your main topic in each body paragraph. Support all your statements with the facts and details you gathered.

An outline helps you structure your information.

Each body paragraph looks at a part of the whole topic.

The introduction puts the topic in context. The entire paragraph conveys the thesis.

The conclusion recaps key points and leaves readers with a final statement to remember.

Monopolies and Deregulation
Outline

I. Introduction
II. What is regulation and what is deregulation?
III. What are the benefits of deregulation?
- A. New firms enter an industry and create greater competition, which lowers prices.
- B. Firms become more efficient.
- C. The government saves money.

IV. What are the risks of deregulation?
- A. Monopolies could form.
- B. Deregulation coupled with federal anti-trust laws prevents the formation of monopolies.
- C. Prices for consumers increase.
- D. With government controlling markets, prices for consumers are unlikely to fall.

V. Conclusions: Benefits of deregulation outweigh incentives.

Introduction
In the late nineteenth and early twentieth centuries, the government began to regulate various industries. Toward the end of the twentieth century, the government reversed course. It realized that competition, absent of government regulation, lowers prices for customers.

Conclusion
When a government regulates an industry, it stifles growth and creates inefficiencies that lead to high prices.

3 Revising

Add detail. Mark points where more details would strengthen your statements. In the following example, notice the added details in the revised version. When adding facts, verify accuracy.

Make the connection for readers. Help readers find their way through your ideas. First, check that your body paragraphs and the information within them flow in a logical sequence. If they do not, revise to correct this. Then add transition words to link ideas and paragraphs.

First Draft	Revised
When governments deregulate industries, new companies can enter the field. These new companies have innovative ideas that increase efficiency and lower prices.	In 1978, President Carter deregulated the airline industry. New airlines emerged. This change forced larger airlines into competition, resulting in lower prices for consumers.

Give credit. Check that you have used your own words or given proper credit to other sources with parenthetical notes, which include the author's last name and the relevant page number from the source. For example, you could site the notecard here as (Holmes and Schmitz 4).

4 Publishing and Presenting

Plan a conference. Gather a group of classmates and present your research projects.

Persuasive Essay

Persuasive writing supports an opinion or position. This writing style often takes the form of position papers, editorials, blogs, and Op-Ed pieces. Persuasive essays often argue for or against economic positions such as free trade.

1 Prewriting

Choose a topic. Choose a topic that provokes an argument and has at least two sides. Use these ideas as a guide.

Round-table discussion. Talk with classmates about issues you have studied recently. Outline pro and con positions about these issues.

Textbook flip. Scan the table of contents or flip through the pages of your textbook.

Make connections. Look at blogs, editorials, or Op-Ed pieces in current newspapers. Develop a position on an issue of importance today.

Narrow your topic.

Cover part of the topic. If you find too many pros and cons for a straightforward argument, choose part of the topic.

Use looping. Write for five minutes on the general topic. Circle the most important idea. Then write for five minutes on that idea. Continue looping until the topic is manageable.

Consider your audience. Choose arguments that will appeal to the audience you are writing for and that are likely to persuade them to agree with your views.

Gather evidence. Collect evidence that will help you support your position convincingly.

Persuasive Essay

Get Started

LESSON GOALS

Students will:

- Write a persuasive essay using prewriting, drafting, revising, and publishing and presenting.
- Understand that a persuasive essay supports an opinion or position.
- Clearly state a position and answer opposing arguments.

Teach

INTRODUCE

Read aloud or display an editorial from a current newspaper or magazine. Have students identify arguments and counter-arguments. Point out that the purpose of a persuasive essay is to convince other people to share your point of view. To be convincing, a writer must support their arguments with reliable evidence.

DISCUSS PREWRITING

Review all suggestions for choosing a topic: round-table discussion, textbook flip, and making connections. Divide students into small groups and assign each group one of the prewriting strategies. Have each group share its list of topics with the class. Encourage students to pick topics that matter to them, and that people disagree about. Examples include welfare, income taxes, deregulation, free trade, government spending, and outsourcing.

ANALYZE AND DISCUSS

Direct students' attention to the graphic organizer in the text about whether the United States should participate in free trade. Ask students to paraphrase the writer's position and supporting arguments. Have the class brainstorm arguments for opposing positions, using the chart's right column as a starting point.

Remind students that in a persuasive essay, the thesis is a position statement. Have a volunteer read aloud the sample thesis statement in the text. Point out that it clearly takes a position on the free trade issue and states the writer's strongest supporting argument. Readers then know what to expect from the essay and can assess whether its other arguments support the thesis.

PROVIDE A CONTEXT

Students should not assume that all readers will be familiar with their issue. Emphasize the importance of providing context. In the introductory paragraph, the writer should briefly cover the "who, what, when, where, and why" of the issue. Throughout the essay, students should use their research to provide specific evidence, such as quotes or supporting details. An argument supported by facts and careful reasoning is effective because it appeals to readers' intelligence rather than to their emotions.

ANSWER COUNTERARGUMENTS

Writers should anticipate the arguments that might be made by those who disagree with their positions and include responses to these arguments in the essay. A review of the pros and cons listed on the graphic organizers students created in the prewriting activity will help them identify the counterarguments that need to be addressed.

REVISING

Throughout the revision process, encourage students to check for areas where logic is faulty or arguments are not clear. Students should also add transition words to help guide readers through their argument and clarify ideas.

PRESENT

Have several students deliver their essays as speeches. Emphasize that a persuasive speech should be delivered with feeling, but never involve anger, shouting, or use of inappropriate language.

Assess and Remediate

Have students write persuasive essays about topics that matter to them. Have them discuss their positions with a partner. One partner can state his or her position and the other can try to refute it. Then they should switch roles.

Have students suggest ways of revising the Writing Rubric on page S-9 to create a persuasive writing rubric.

Identify pros and cons. Use a graphic organizer like the one below to list points on both sides of the issue.

Interview. Speak to people who have first-hand knowledge of your issue.

Research. Investigate the subject to get your facts straight. Read articles about the topic.

The United States Should Participate in Free Trade

Pro	Con
• Citizens will pay less for some goods and services. • Free access to foreign markets could mean greater profits for exports. • Government imposed monopolies or oligopolies are unable to form. • The free movement of capital and labor.	• Increased competition could hurt domestic industries. • Potential exploitation of workers. • Increased job insecurity.

2 Drafting

State your thesis. Clearly state your position, as in this example:

Because of its many resources and greater comparative advantage in producing goods and services, the United States should participate in free trade.

Acknowledge opposition. State and refute opposing arguments. Use facts and details. Include quotations, statistics, or comparisons to build your case. Include the comments and opinions of community members or officials who were interviewed.

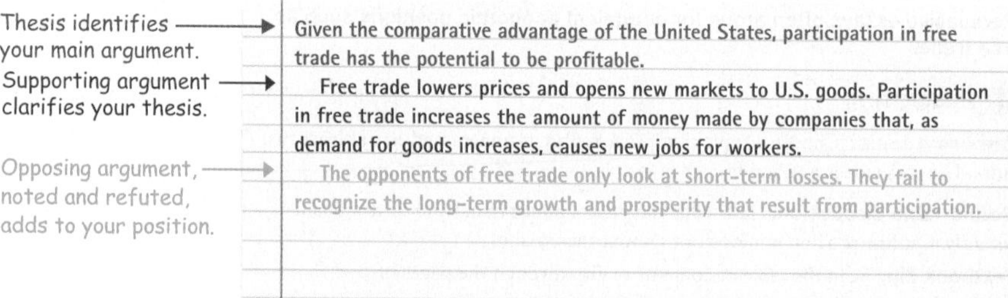

Thesis identifies your main argument.
Supporting argument clarifies your thesis.
Opposing argument, noted and refuted, adds to your position.
Given the comparative advantage of the United States, participation in free trade has the potential to be profitable.
Free trade lowers prices and opens new markets to U.S. goods. Participation in free trade increases the amount of money made by companies that, as demand for goods increases, causes new jobs for workers.
The opponents of free trade only look at short-term losses. They fail to recognize the long-term growth and prosperity that result from participation.

Write a conclusion. Your conclusion should restate the thesis and close with a strong, compelling argument or a brief summary of the three strongest arguments.

3 Revising

Add information. Extra details can generate interest in your topic. For example, add a quotation from a news article that describes the positive impact that NAFTA has had on the U.S. beef industry.

Review arguments. Make sure your arguments are logically sound and clearly developed. Evidence is the best way to support your points.

Use transition words. Guide readers through your ideas using the following words:

- To show contrast: *however, although, despite*
- To point out a reason: *since, because, if*
- To signal conclusion: *therefore, consequently, so, then*

4 Publishing

Persuasive Speech. In addition to position papers, editorials, blogs, and Op-Ed pieces, persuasive essays are also delivered orally. How effective were your efforts to persuade? Report your results and evaluate the effectiveness.

Writing for Assessment

Assessment writing differs from all other writing that you do. You have many fewer choices as a writer and you almost always face a time limit.

1 Prewriting

Choose a topic. Short-answer questions seldom offer a topic choice. For extended response, however, you may have a choice of more than one question.

Examine the question. To choose a question you can answer effectively, analyze what each question is asking. Use key words such as those listed in the chart below to help you choose topics and respond to short-answer questions in which the topic is given. Notice in the examples below that the key words are underlined:

> **Short Answer Question:** Why do governments impose taxes?
>
> **Extended Response Question:** How have taxes been used by governments? Give examples to support your conclusion.

Measure your time. Your goal is to show that you've mastered the material. To stay focused on this goal, divide your time: one-quarter on pre-writing; half on drafting; one-quarter on revising. For short-answer questions, determine how much of the overall test time you can spend on each question. Don't spend more than that.

Key Words	What You Need In an Answer
Explain	• Give a clear, complete account of how something works, or what the causes or effects are of a particular decision or policy.
Compare/Contrast	• Show how two or more things are alike and different.
Define	• Give examples to explain meaning.
Argue, Convince, Support, Persuade	• Take a position on an issue and present strong reasons to support your side of the issue.
Summarize	• Provide the most important elements of a subject.
Evaluate/Judge	• Assign a value or explain an opinion.
Interpret	• Support a thesis with examples from the text.

Writing for Assessment

Get Started

LESSON GOALS

Students will:

- Write for assessment using prewriting, drafting, revising, publishing and presenting.
- Identify the features that distinguish assessment writing.
- Identify strategies for time management and successfully completing writing assessments.

Teach

ACTIVATE PRIOR KNOWLEDGE

Ask students to name in-class assignments or different kinds of exams or tests they have completed in recent years. Have them identify assessments that included a writing component. Point out that many job applications and college exams require students to write for assessment.

DISCUSS PREWRITING

Point out that many strategies exist for improving scores. Extended response items sometimes provide several questions to choose from. Emphasize that students should select questions about their areas of greatest knowledge.

Review with students the chart of Key Words in the text. This chart will help them identify the structures associated with different types of test questions and topics. Ask students to suggest the appropriate organization for each question type shown.

Remind students that tests require time management. Caution them to be aware of the total time available to finish the test, how many questions they must answer, and how much time they can spend on each question.

DISCUSS DRAFTING

Explain to students that a good way to prepare to answer short response questions is to identify which facts and details are required. Ask **How can using a graphic organizer help you plan an extended response answer?** *(by organizing information into sub-topics)*

Emphasize the importance of restating the question at the beginning of the essay. This helps the writer focus and shows understanding of the question. Have students link the opening sentence of the sample response in the text to the question about taxes on page S-7.

REVISING

Have students read the First Draft and Revised examples. Ask them to list the words and phrases added to the revised version and explain how each change improves the passage. Point out that revising can be a critical step and students should not omit it. Emphasize that correct use of grammar, spelling, and mechanics are an essential part of the scoring. Remind students to make sure all questions have been answered before turning in an assessment.

Assess and Remediate

Give students a choice of three sample assessment questions for a practice test. The questions should be on topics students have discussed in class. Before beginning the practice test, ask students to read the Writing Rubric on page S-9. Announce how much time students will have to write their essays and write the start time for the test on the board. Give students a five-minute warning before completion time. During the test, circulate to make sure students are staying on task and monitoring their time appropriately. If students are spending too much time on planning, give them a discreet reminder to move on to the next step. If students appear stuck, refer them back to the prewriting steps and urge them to either choose a different question or repeat their analysis of the question they have chosen.

After students have handed in their essays, have the class reflect on their experience. Ask students how they chose their topic and how they decided what structure to use. Then invite volunteers to explain how they managed their time, any problems they encountered, and how much time they spent on each step in the writing process.

Gather information. Identify and organize the information you need to write your answer. For short-answer questions, this usually involves identifying exactly which facts and details are required.

Use a graphic organizer. For extended responses, divide your topic into sub-topics that fit the type of question. Jot down facts and details for each.

2 Drafting

Governments need the ability to impose taxes in order to raise revenue. Governments that have been able to raise taxes successfully are able to pay for services for its citizens.

Choose an organization that fits the question. With short-answer questions, write one to three complete sentences. Extended responses require more elaborate organization. For an extended response on the use of taxes, describe how taxes have been used in a number of ways. For compare/contrast, present similarities first, then differences.

Open and close strongly. Start your answer by restating the question or using its language to state your position. This helps you focus and shows the instructor that you understand the question. Finish with a conclusion that restates your position. For short answers, include some language from the question in your response.

Support your ideas. Each paragraph should directly or indirectly support your main idea. Choose facts that build a cohesive argument.

3 Revising

Examine word choice. Replace general words with specific words. Add transitions where these improve clarity.

First Draft	Revised
Taxes play an important role in fiscal policy, international trade, and collecting revenue.	Taxes play a multi-faceted role in the American economy. In addition to being a valuable source of revenue for all levels of government, taxes figure prominently in international trade and in the application of fiscal policy.

Check organization. Make sure your introduction includes a main idea and briefly defines each subtopic. Review each paragraph for a single main idea. Check that your conclusion summarizes the information you've presented.

4 Publishing and Presenting

Edit and proof. Check spelling, grammar, and mechanics. Make sure that tenses match, that subjects agree with verbs, and that sentences are not too long. Finally, confirm that you have responded to all the questions you were asked to answer.

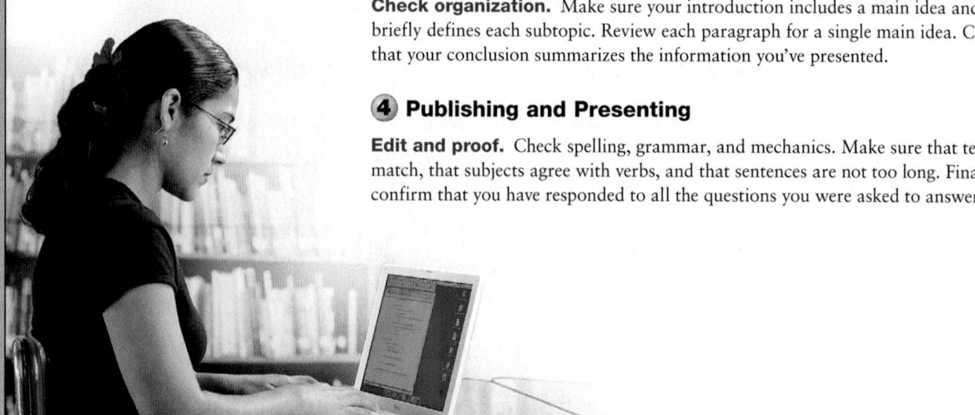

Writing Rubric

Use this chart, or rubric, to evaluate your writing.

SAT	
SCORE OF 6 An essay in this category is outstanding, demonstrating **clear and consistent mastery,** although it may have a few minor errors. A typical essay: • effectively and insightfully develops a point of view on the issue and demonstrates outstanding critical thinking, using clearly appropriate examples, reasons, and other evidence to support its position • is well organized and clearly focused, demonstrating clear coherence and smooth progression of ideas • exhibits skillful use of language, using a varied, accurate, and appropriate vocabulary • demonstrates meaningful variety in sentence structure • is free of most errors in grammar, usage, and mechanics	**SCORE OF 5** An essay in this category is **effective,** demonstrating **reasonably consistent mastery,** although it will have occasional errors or lapses in quality. A typical essay: • effectively develops a point of view on the issue and demonstrates strong critical thinking, generally using appropriate examples, reasons, and other evidence to support its position • is well organized and focused, demonstrating coherence and progression of ideas • exhibits facility in the use of language, using appropriate vocabulary • demonstrates variety in sentence structure • is generally free of most errors in grammar, usage, and mechanics
SCORE OF 4 An essay in this category is **competent,** demonstrating **adequate mastery,** although it will have lapses in quality. A typical essay: • demonstrates variety in sentence structure • develops a point of view on the issue and demonstrates competent critical thinking, using adequate examples, reasons, and other evidence to support its position • is generally organized and focused, demonstrating some coherence and progression of ideas, exhibits adequate but inconsistent facility in the use of language, using generally appropriate vocabulary • demonstrates some variety in sentence structure • has some errors in grammar, usage, and mechanics	**SCORE OF 3** An essay in this category is **inadequate,** but demonstrates **developing mastery,** and is marked by one or more of the following weaknesses: • develops a point of view on the issue, demonstrating some critical thinking, but may do so inconsistently or use inadequate examples, reasons, or other evidence to support its position • is limited in its organization or focus, but may demonstrate some lapses in coherence or progression of ideas • displays developing facility in the use of language, but sometimes uses weak vocabulary or inappropriate word choice • lacks variety or demonstrates problems in sentence structure • contains an accumulation of errors in grammar, usage, and mechanics
SCORE OF 2 An essay in this category is **seriously limited,** demonstrating little mastery, and is flawed by **one or more** of the following weaknesses: • develops a point of view on the issue that is vague or seriously limited, demonstrating weak critical thinking, providing inappropriate or insufficient examples, reasons, or other evidence to support its position • is poorly organized and/or focused, or demonstrates serious problems with coherence or progression of ideas • displays very little facility in the use of language, using very limited vocabulary or incorrect word choice • demonstrates frequent problems in sentence structure • contains errors in grammar, usage, and mechanics so serious that meaning is somewhat obscured	**SCORE OF 1** An essay in this category is **fundamentally lacking,** demonstrating **very little or no mastery,** and is severely flawed by one or more of the following weaknesses: • develops no viable point of view on the issue, or provides little or no evidence to support its position • is disorganized or unfocused, resulting in a disjointed or incoherent essay • displays fundamental errors in vocabulary • demonstrates severe flaws in sentence structure • contains pervasive errors in grammar, usage, or mechanics that persistently interfere with meaning **SCORE OF 0** Essays not written on the essay assignment will receive a score of zero.

Writing Rubric

Get Started

LESSON GOAL

Students will:

- Analyze how the SAT writing assessment is scored by examining its writing rubric.

Teach

INTRODUCE

Poll the class to see how many students are familiar with the SAT. Explain that an important part of this exam involves essay writing. Explain that the Writing Rubric on this page shows students how graders score the essays on the SAT writing exam. Ask volunteers to name the five criteria used to rate these essays. Then ask them to explain in their own words the characteristics of a strong essay and identify the evaluation criteria on the rubric that they think reflect their own greatest strengths or weaknesses.

Assess and Remediate

Ask each student to choose the best essay they have written so far. Pair each student with a partner with similar writing skills. Ask pairs to exchange essays and evaluate each other's work using the rubric. Have them explain their assessments to their partners, starting with strengths. Then ask pairs to brainstorm how they can make their essays stronger and to write self-evaluations of their essay writing skills. Collect students' essays and self-evaluations. Meet with students to go over good points and areas for improvement.

Analyze Primary and Secondary Sources

Get Started

LESSON GOAL

Students will:

- Distinguish between primary and secondary sources by examining two sources about the OPEC oil embargo.

Teach

ACTIVATE PRIOR KNOWLEDGE

Have students read the steps in analyzing primary and secondary sources and share any questions they have. Ask them to recall major national events that have occurred during their lifetimes, or stories family members have told them about past events. Ask students how these accounts might differ from secondary sources.

DISCUSS

After students read both sources in the text, point out the primary source was written at the time of the embargo, and the secondary source was written much later. Ask **According to the author of the secondary source, did the oil embargo cause the shortages described in the primary source?** *(No. The author of the secondary source argues that the shortages were a result of U.S. policy.)* **What can you infer from the title of the secondary source about the writer's opinion of U.S. energy policy?** *(It is negative.)* **What examples does the writer of the primary source give to show the impact of shortages?** *(closed stations, shorter hours of operation, purchase limits, long lines, price increases)*

Assess and Remediate

Have students answer the Practice and Apply the Skill questions. Discuss their responses as a class. Have students bring examples of a primary and a secondary source to class. Have them write three questions about each source and exchange sources and questions with a partner.

Answers

1. Primary source observes events at the time, secondary source article interprets events later on. 2. Reporter's purpose is to observe, describe events; secondary source writer's purpose is to present an opinion. 3. The 1970s gas shortage was caused by energy policies, not the embargo.

21st Century Skills

Social Studies Skills Handbook

Analyze Primary and Secondary Sources

A primary source is information produced during or soon after an event, by a participant or observer. These include letters, photographs, memos, and legal documents. A secondary source provides an analysis or interpretation of an event based on primary sources.

Identify the document. Determine when, where, why, and by whom the document was written to decide if the document is a primary or a secondary source.

Find the main idea. A main idea is the most important point in a paragraph or section of text. After identifying the main idea, identify supporting details.

Evaluate the document for point of view and bias. Primary sources convey a strong sense of an event, but are limited to a single frame of reference or bias.

In 1973 Saudi Arabia and several other members of OPEC began an oil embargo, refusing to sell oil to the United States. ▼

Primary Source

The gasoline shortage was acutely felt in Chicago last week with drivers waiting sometimes several hours alongside a pump. Several hundred stations, their January allotments depleted, were closed. Many others had…curtailed their hours of operation. The Root Brothers service station…was typical. Cars were lined up for blocks, police had to direct traffic and the limit a customer could purchase was set at $5.00….According to Platt's Oilgram Service…the average price a year ago for a gallon of gasoline in the Midwest was 40.9 cents for regular. The range of regular gasoline now runs from 47.9 cents a gallon to 55.9 [cents a gallon]."

—William Farrell, "Oil is a National Problem, But Seriousness Varies," *The New York Times*, February 3, 1974

Read the excerpt below from the 2003 article "Still Holding Customers over a Barrel." ▼

Secondary Source

The Arab embargo has become a symbol of the…chaos and economic troubles endured by the West during the oil shocks of the 1970s….The [long lines] and shortages in America that are now linked in the popular imagination with that period had little to do with the Arab Embargo. Jerry Taylor of the Cato Institute argues, correctly, that the shortages were due chiefly to the…energy policies…adopted by America…In 1971 for example, the Nixon administration imposed price controls…that prevented oil companies from passing on the full cost of imported oil to consumers. That led…to the companies making decisions to reduce their imports…Congress made the situation worse in September 1973 by trying to allocate oil to…different parts of the country through bureaucratic fiat….These measures led…to the panic and hoarding…"

—*The Economist*, October 23, 2003

PRACTICE AND APPLY THE SKILL

Use the excerpts above to answer the following questions.

1. What makes one newspaper article a primary source and another article a secondary source?
2. What is the primary source reporter's purpose?
3. What is the main idea of the secondary source?

Compare Viewpoints

Economists often disagree on economic policies or recommend different responses to the same problem. Comparing viewpoints will help you understand issues and form your own opinions. The excerpts below provide different views on globalization and offshoring, the practice of sending some of a corporation, manufacturing, service operations, or jobs overseas.

Identify the authors. Determine when and where each person was speaking. Identify the intended audience for each speech and the purpose of each.

Determine the author's frame of reference. Consider how each speaker's attitudes, beliefs, frame of reference, values, social, economic, or political concerns and affiliations as well as past experiences might affect his or her viewpoint.

Determine the author's bias. Bias may be revealed in the use of emotionally charged words or strong, faulty logic, or exaggerated claims. Identify which statements are facts and which are opinions that represent the speaker's viewpoint.

Compare and contrast. Determine how the viewpoints are different and consider factors that might have contributed to differing positions on this issue.

Diana Farrell, director of McKinsey Global Institute, the economics research division of a global consulting firm for multinational businesses. ▼

"[F]ears of job losses caused by offshoring are greatly exaggerated. New research...shows that the United States will likely lose to offshoring no more than 300,000 jobs each year....Savings from offshoring allow companies to invest in next-generation technologies, creating jobs at home as well as abroad. ...Protectionism may save a few jobs...but it will stifle innovation and job creation in the longer term. Rather than trying to stop globalization, the goal must be to let it happen, while easing the transition for workers who lose out."

—Diana Farrell in *Economists' Voice*, www.bepress.com, March 2006

Richard Trumka, secretary-treasurer of the AFL-CIO, a federation of labor unions representing over 10 million U.S. workers. ▼

"Over the past three years, the U.S. has lost 2.6 million manufacturing jobs....[T]he vast majority...due to offshoring and outsourcing....Everyone talks about retraining, but the problem is that these days, if you're out of work, there's not a job in the area you're trained in and not a job in the area you're retrained in.... Retraining is not the magic solution because there isn't an industry that is safe from the trend anymore that provides the solid jobs needed by the American middle class."

—Richard Trumka, participating in a *Wall Street Journal* Online roundtable on outsourcing, 2004

PRACTICE AND APPLY THE SKILL

Use the excerpts above to answer the following questions.

1. How do you think each person's frame of reference is influenced by his or her viewpoint?
2. How does Farrell's statement that "fears" of job losses are "greatly exaggerated" reflect her point of view?
3. How do the views of Farrell and Trumka about job losses differ?

Compare Viewpoints

Get Started

LESSON GOAL

Students will:

- Identify the steps to compare viewpoints by examining two sources about globalization and offshoring.

Teach

COMPARE AND CONTRAST

Have students read the steps of comparing viewpoints and share any questions they have. Ask a student to read aloud each of the quotes. Ask **What is the main idea of the first passage?** *(Offshoring is good for the economy.)* **What is the main idea of the second passage?** *(Offshoring causes permanent U.S. job losses.)* Have class members identify the statements that are facts, and the statements that are opinions. Then ask students to identify one fact or argument from each quote that supports the speaker's point of view.

RESEARCH

Have students find two differing opinions on the same economic policy topic. Have students use the steps in comparing viewpoints to write a brief comparison of the two opinions.

Assess and Remediate

Have students answer the Practice and Apply the Skill questions. Discuss their responses as a class.

Answers

1. Farrell's viewpoint is probably influenced by the fact that multinationals benefit from offshoring. Trumka's is probably influenced by the fact that unionized U.S. workers are hurt by offshoring.
2. It shows that she believes that globalization and offshoring do not have as many consequences as others believe they have.
3. Farrell claims offshoring will not cost many jobs and will eventually increase them; Trumka claims offshoring has cut lots of jobs and leaves no industry safe from further cuts.

Drawing Inferences and Conclusions

Get Started

LESSON GOALS

Students will:

- Make inferences about Americans' lack of response to rising gas prices by analyzing a news article.
- Draw conclusions about alternatives to driving cars by analyzing a news article.

Teach

SUMMARIZE AND EXPLAIN

Have students read the steps of drawing inferences and conclusions and share any questions they have. Have students write a sentence that summarizes the main idea of the article and give three examples of facts or opinions that support that idea.

Have students explain how they or their parents get to work and how long it takes them. Do they live in suburbs and drive into a city to work? Do they use public transportation? Ask if they can recall a time when their or their parents' driving habits changed. Then ask students what inferences or conclusions they can draw from their peers' experiences.

Assess and Remediate

Have students answer the Practice and Apply the Skill questions. Discuss their responses as a class. Have students bring to class a newspaper article or editorial on a local economic problem or issue that makes inferences or draws conclusions about how this problem might be solved. Have students use the steps in the lesson to analyze the article. Have several students explain to the class what inferences and conclusions they drew from the article.

Answers

1. Americans will change their driving habits only if gas prices increase dramatically, and stay high for an extended period of time.
2. Possible answer: Demand for gasoline is inelastic.
3. It would have a major impact on the cost of commuting; it might force Americans to buy smaller cars, move closer to their jobs, or carpool to work.

Drawing Inferences and Conclusions

When people "read between the lines," they are drawing inferences. They have formed their conclusions not from what is stated directly, but from what is suggested by other facts.

Summarize information. Confirm your understanding of the text by identifying the main idea of the passage. To find information in a passage that is suggested but unstated, you have to understand the content of the passage.

Apply other facts or prior knowledge. Consider what you know about the topic. Use this prior knowledge to evaluate the information. A combination of what you already know and what you learn from reading the passage may help you draw inferences.

Decide if the information suggests an unstated fact or conclusion. Integrate or combine what you learned from the text and your own knowledge to draw inferences and conclusions about the topic.

Read the excerpt from "The Grip of Gas" by University of Chicago economics professor Austan Goolsbee. ▼

"In repeated studies of consumer purchases... drivers in the United States consistently rank as the least sensitive to changes in gas prices....The... estimates, based on a [2002] study...predict that if prices rose from $3 per gallon to $4 per gallon and stayed there for a year...purchases of gasoline... would fall only about 5 percent.

Why don't we ratchet down more when fuel prices go up? The rule of thumb in economics is that people react to price increases only when they can turn to substitutes. Raise the price of Ford trucks and sales go down because you can buy your truck from Chrysler or GM or Toyota instead. Raise the price of gasoline and what are the alternatives?...

Gasoline purchases are, in fact, the kind of buying affected least by price changes because they are so closely tied up with other things we already own...In the last two decades when gasoline was cheap, Americans switched from cars to minivans and SUVs, seriously reducing their gas mileage. Also, many moved farther from their places of work...As jobs moved...into suburbs, car-pooling became more difficult and public transportation often unavailable....In Europe and Japan, people drive less when the cost of gas goes up because they still can. On average, they live closer to their jobs. About 20% of Europeans walk or ride their bike to work.

...The only hope of changing America's driving habits is a hefty price increase that lasts. ...Higher commuting costs...could induce you to buy a smaller car, move closer to work, find a car pool...few people change their behavior when gas prices spike temporarily.... moral exhortation doesn't change people's behavior. Prices do..."

—Austan Goolsbee, *Slate Magazine*, September 27, 2005

PRACTICE AND APPLY THE SKILL

Use the magazine article to answer the following questions.

1. What is the main idea or key point made by this article?
2. Based on this article, what can you infer about the demand for gasoline in the United States?
3. Based on this article, what conclusions can you draw about the impact of a gas tax that would substantially raise the price of gas? How will American driving habits be affected?

Analyze Political Cartoons

Political cartoons express the cartoonist's opinion on a recent issue or current event. Often the artist's purpose is to influence the opinion of the reader about political leaders, current events, or economic or political issues. To achieve this goal, cartoonists use humor or exaggeration. When analyzing a political cartoon, be sure to examine all words, images, and labels to help you fully understand the artist's intent. Use the following steps to analyze the cartoon below.

Identify the symbols in the cartoon. Decide what each image or symbol represents. Examine the title and any labels or words in the cartoon. Cartoonists often use caricatures, or images of people that exaggerate a physical feature.

Analyze the meaning of the cartoon. Consider how the cartoonist uses the images and symbols in the cartoon to express his or her opinions about people or events.

Draw conclusions about the cartoonist's intent. Identify the opinion or statement the cartoonist is making through this cartoon.

PRACTICE AND APPLY THE SKILL

Use the cartoon to answer the following questions.

1. What do the bulls in the cartoon represent?
2. What does the flower symbolize?
3. What does the title of the cartoon suggest about the cartoonist's view of the economic situation?

21st Century Skills SOCIAL STUDIES SKILLS HANDBOOK

Analyze Political Cartoons

Get Started

LESSON GOAL

Students will:

- Use steps to analyze a political cartoon.

Teach

DISCUSS

Have students read the steps in the process of analyzing political cartoons and share any questions they have. Make sure students understand that the items written on the bulls—insurance, housing prices, gasoline, and so on—are daily living costs. Remind students that most people pay living costs with wages they earn.

ANALYZE

Ask students to write a sentence that explains the issue the cartoon addresses and the opinion the cartoonist is expressing on it. Have students identify the symbols the cartoonist has used. Ask **What does the fact that the bulls are stampeding represent?** *(Increasing costs of living are increasing fast.)* **Why did the cartoonist use two symbols that vary so widely from each other?** *(to show contrast and indicate a problem)* Conclude by asking students to identify the advantages and limitations of political cartoons as a way of expressing opinions.

CREATE

Discuss with the class other concerns or opinions people have about costs of living today. Then divide students into groups and ask each group to create a political cartoon on some aspect of the economy.

Assess and Remediate

Have students answer the Practice and Apply the Skill questions. Discuss their responses as a class. To give students additional practice with this skill, have students find a political cartoon and analyze it for the class.

Answers

1. rising costs of living
2. the small wages of an average person
3. Cost of living is "stampeding"—that is, trampling and destroying—wages

Understanding Cause and Effect

Get Started

LESSON GOAL

Students will:

- Show understanding of cause and effect by analyzing relationships between events.

Teach

BRAINSTORM

Have students read the steps of understanding cause and effect and share any questions they have. Then write the following events on the board: *school wins top state academic ranking, funding for school athletic programs cut, reductions in parking spaces in student parking lot, enrollment triples,* and *price of fuel for school activity buses goes up sharply.* Have class members identify the effects these events might have on students.

IDENTIFY CAUSES AND EFFECTS

Tell students to read the article. Make a list on the board of the causes and effects of the downward spiral of the economy, without showing which is which. Have students take turns identifying which items are causes and which are effects. Remind them that some may be both. Ask **Which effects are likely to be long term? Why?** *(election, because term is four years.)* Then have students make predictions about what effect raising the minimum wage might have on the economy.

Assess and Remediate

Have students answer the Practice and Apply the Skill questions. Discuss their responses as a class. Ask students to choose one of the economic issues discussed in the article and create a graphic organizer identifying possible further effects.

Answers

1. causes: falling housing prices, limited ability to borrow; effects: limited ability to borrow, limited ability to spend
2. Cause: if consumer spending slows, businesses cut costs, which slows hiring and lowers wages; effect: fewer jobs, lower wages lessen people's ability to spend.
3. Possible answer: multiple causes: falling housing prices, slowdown in consumer and business spending, banks' unwillingness to lend

Understanding Cause and Effect

Recognizing cause and effect means examining how one event or action brings about others. One challenge economists face is finding and defining relationships between events.

Identify the central event. Determine the core event or issue that is the subject of the article.

Identify the two parts of a cause-effect relationship. A cause is an event or an action that brings about an effect. Words such as *because, due to,* and *on account of* signal causes. Words such as *so, thus, therefore,* and *as a result* signal effects.

Decide if an event has more than one cause or effect. Most events have multiple causes and many have more than one effect.

Identify events that are both causes and effects. Causes and effects can form a chain of events. An effect may in turn become the cause of another effect. For example, a sharp decline in new home sales can result in reduced profits for building supply and furniture stores. This in turn may lead to layoffs of workers in factories that produces the goods sold in these stores.

Read the excerpt below from "No Quick Fix on the Downturn." ▼

> In the view of many analysts, the economy is now in a downward spiral, with each piece of negative news setting off the next. Falling housing prices have eroded the ability of homeowners to borrow against their property, threatening their ability to spend freely. Concerns about tightening consumer spending have prompted businesses to slow hiring, limiting wage increases and in turn applying the brakes anew to consumer spending....
>
> ...Nouriel Roubini, an economist at...New York University...envisions foreclosures accelerating this year, and banks counting fresh losses. That could make them less able to lend and further slow economic activity....Federal Reserve chairman, Ben S. Bernanke, zeroed in on the nervousness of bankers as a prime factor slowing the economy.... "Developments have prompted banks to become protective of their liquidity [available funds] and thus to become less willing to provide funding to other market participants."
>
> A recession could pack enormous political consequences. Over the last century, the economy has been in a recession four times in the early part of a presidential election year, according to the National Bureau of Economic Research. In each of those years—1920, 1932, 1960 and 1980—the party of the incumbent president lost the election."
>
> —Peter Goodman and Floyd Norris, *The New York Times,* January 13, 2008

PRACTICE AND APPLY THE SKILL

Use the news article to answer the following questions.

1. Identify the causes and effects in the following statement from the article: "Falling housing prices have eroded the ability of homeowners to borrow against their property, threatening their ability to spend freely."
2. How was the slowdown in consumer spending both a cause and an effect of the economic slowdown?
3. Did the downturn in the economy have a single cause or multiple causes? Explain your answer.

Problem Solving

One difference between successful and unsuccessful business is the ability to solve problems.

Identify the problem. Begin by clearly identifying what the problem is. Write a statement or question that summarizes the problem you are trying to solve.

Gather information and identify options. Collect factual information and data. Consider the causes of the problem and brainstorm strategies for addressing it. Most problems have multiple solutions. Identify as many options as possible.

Consider advantages and disadvantages of each option. Analyze each option by predicting benefits, drawbacks, and possible consequences.

Choose, implement, and evaluate a solution. Pick the option with the greatest benefits and fewest drawbacks. Once a strategy is in place, look at the results. Decide if the solution works.

Read the excerpt below which looks at how a popular shoe manufacturer prepared to meet its supply and demand requirements as its business boomed. ▼

> "From tots walking with their mothers in the mall to the president of the United States captured on camera wearing a pair of black Crocs…the rubbery boat shoe…fueled a business success story….
>
> Crocs now is the country's second-largest footwear manufacturer…."It was the perfect storm: They had the right product, people wanted it, and they were able to produce it in increasing quantities and broaden their focus…" [says Reed Anderson, senior research analyst at D.A. Davidson & Co.].
>
> [CEO Ron Snyder] says Crocs' ascent has proved manageable because the company laid the groundwork to handle it before it arrived in full force. "Since the beginning, we've always assumed we're a larger company, so we made decisions as a larger company, investing in an infrastructure that was more than we needed at the time," Snyder says.
>
> "Most of the footwear industry works off pre-orders," Snyder says. "If a particular product isn't selling well, you'll still be building it for late in the season….We take early season orders, then we build more of whatever is popular. Say we have a model that's selling out in our early season," he says. "We'll be making more of that immediately in our local facilities, and we'll get it to the market in a few weeks. If it continues to go, we'll have another larger shipment from China in six or eight weeks."…Snyder says…"We told our retailers we're going to do our best…to meet demand."
>
> —by Eric Peterson, *Coloradobiz Magazine*, February 2008

PRACTICE AND APPLY THE SKILL

Use the article to answer the following questions.

1. What three conditions led to Crocs success?
2. What problem could have limited their success?
3. What were the advantages of the option Snyder chose for solving this problem?

2l1st Century Skills SOCIAL STUDIES SKILLS HANDBOOK

Problem Solving

Get Started

LESSON GOAL

Students will:

- Show understanding of problem solving by examining an article.

Teach

ACTIVATE PRIOR KNOWLEDGE

Have students read the steps of problem solving and share any questions they have. Ask students to think about a problem they have faced or helped solve at school or in a workplace. Have students recall the problem, the options considered, the steps taken to resolve it, and the solution. Invite volunteers to share their examples with the class.

DISCUSS

Have students read the article. Ask **What does the Crocs company make?** *(footwear)* **What problem did Crocs face because of its success?** *(difficulty in meeting high demand for its products)* Point out that the problem Crocs had is one that many new businesses face. Ask **What did Crocs do and how did it solve the problem?** *(built more of popular items at local facilities; by getting the products to market faster)* **What did Crocs do to anticipate the problem?** *(invested in infrastructure)*

L1 **L2** Remind students that to meet high demand for a good or service, businesses must rapidly increase the supply. Explain that increasing supply quickly can be difficult for new businesses, because they do not yet have the infrastructure required to do so. Clarify the meaning of the word *infrastructure* if necessary.

Assess and Remediate

Have students answer the Practice and Apply the Skill questions. Discuss their responses as a class.

Answers

1. good product; people wanted it; able to produce it in increasing quantities 2. lack of ability to produce enough to meet demand 3. able to meet the high demand, did not waste capital by producing items with no demand.

Decision Making

Get Started

LESSON GOAL

Students will:

- Show understanding of decision making by examining the decision-making process used by a tea producer.

Teach

ACTIVATE PRIOR KNOWLEDGE

Have students read the steps in the decision making process and share any questions they have. Ask students to identify an important decision they have made and write down the process they used. Students might think about such events as choosing jobs, scheduling classes, or making a major purchase. Have students read the excerpt and compare the process they used with the steps outlined in the text.

ANALYZE

Ask **What kind of business did Seth Goldman start and what was his company called?** *(bottled tea business; Honest Tea)* **What challenge did Honest Tea face because of the crowded market for bottled tea?** *(standing out among similar products)* Divide students into groups. Ask each group to create a graphic organizer based on the article, showing the goal, the decisions to be made, options, and the final decisions. After completing the organizers, ask students to share their opinions about whether the decisions made were good ones, and why.

L4 Ask students what other options they might have considered in the same situation. Have them write a paragraph explaining their decisions.

Assess and Remediate

Have students answer the Practice and Apply the Skill questions. Discuss their responses as a class. Ask groups of students to pick a new product and research how production and marketing decisions were made, and list the steps of the decision-making process.

Answers

1. He felt there was a market for a less sweet beverage. 2. having a positive social and environmental impact 3. organic sources, health benefits; fair trade tea, labor practices

Decision Making

Decision making in your daily life and in the economy both require a similar approach.

Identify the problem and gather information. Figure out what decision has to be made. What are you trying to accomplish? Decide what information you need to make an informed decision. Apply what you know and what you can learn about the subject. Look at what others have done.

List and assess alternatives. List and review all possible alternatives. Choose the options with fewest drawbacks or costs and greatest number of benefits.

Identify possible consequences and make decisions. Consider various possible outcomes and predict consequences of each option.

Below is an excerpt from an article on Honest Tea, a beverage company started in 1998 by Seth Goldman and Barry Nabeloff. ▼

"For Seth Goldman starting a business was a lot like brewing tea it all came down to the right blend of ingredients. Goldman took the plunge into the bottled tea business...convinced there was an opportunity in the crowded but fast-growing market for a "less sweet" beverage....But the sweetness profile was not the only thing that set Honest Tea apart. It was the approach Goldman took to business," he said..."I knew that what we were going to do would somehow have a social and environmental impact...."

Their challenge...was finding a way to stand out in a market full of bottled teas. Taste was one obvious way to be distinctive, but it was the second element -- applying the approach known as sustainability -- that led to a host of decisions about the product itself.

The program soon evolved on a number of fronts, involving choices about ingredients, packaging and partnerships that expanded the aim of its social and environmental mission. As Goldman learned more about the business, his first aim was to shift the ingredients to organic sources to avoid toxic pesticides and synthetic fertilizers..."Tea... undergoes no rinsing once it is picked," he said. Whatever pesticide residues are present on the leaf are not washed off until hot water is poured over the dried leaves in a pot or cup of brewed tea."

Organics were the more expensive way to go, Goldman concedes, but the company shaved costs in other areas. It eschewed [avoided] a distinctive shaped glass bottle and went with a cheaper, more generic look...

Another key pillar of the business has been pursuing "fair trade," buying tea from one estate in India, that is certified for its fair labor practices...

[This] adds another dimension to the business by creating a distinct marketing presence...That distinction might be invaluable in a shelf crowded with competitors..."

—by Samuel Fromartz, Reuters News Service, November 15, 2004

PRACTICE AND APPLY THE SKILL

Use the article to answer the following questions.

1. Why did Seth Goldman decide to go into the bottled tea business?
2. What goal drove Goldman's decisions about ingredients, packaging, and partnerships?
3. What costs and benefits did Goldman consider in deciding on the ingredients?

Note Taking and Active Listening

Note taking and active listening are skills that can increase your ability to remember and understand a speech or a lecture.

Identify the main ideas. Once the main idea of the overall topic has been identified, it becomes easier to identify and record key points related to the speaker's topic.

Take notes selectively. Do not write down every word you hear. Instead summarize key points and the examples or details that support these points.

Practice active listening. Active listening is a key component of the communication process. It requires engaged participation. Think about what you hear and see. Don't let your mind wander.

Listen for transitions, repetition, and emphasis. Listen for the words or phrases that indicate key points or transition from one point to the next. Statements that are frequently repeated may suggest that these are the main points.

Here is an excerpt from a speech entitled "Education and Economic Competitiveness" by Federal Reserve Board Chairman Ben Bernanke: ▼

"...The demand for more-educated workers has been increasing rapidly, partly because of the...widespread use of computers and other...information and communication technologies in the workplace...At the start of the 1980s, 22 percent of young adults aged 25 to 29 held a college degree or more; by last year, that fraction had moved up to 28.5 percent. Nevertheless, the supply of educated workers has not kept pace with demand...

The educational challenges our society faces should be considered in the context of three broad trends: the retirement of the baby-boom generation, the...advance of the technological frontier, and the ongoing globalization of economic activity.

As the baby boomers...leave the workforce, their places will be taken by the smaller cohort of workers born in the mid-to-late 1960s and early 1970s. As a result, the U.S. workforce...will increase more slowly...imply[ing] slower growth of potential output...

Continuing advances in technology also put a premium on education...

Ongoing globalization...will also lead to continuing changes in the...U.S. economy...The world economy is benefiting from...the rising productivity of countries abroad that are...expanding...the educational attainment of their workforces....Our ability to reap the benefits of globalization will depend on the flexibility of our labor force to adapt to changes in job opportunities, in part by investing in...education and training....

If we are to successfully navigate such challenges as the retirement of the baby-boom generation, advancing technology, and increasing globalization, we must work...to maintain the quality of our educational system..."

—Ben S. Bernanke, in a speech to the U.S. Chamber Education and Workforce Summit, Washington, D.C., September 24, 2007

PRACTICE AND APPLY THE SKILL

Use the speech to answer the following questions.

1. What are the key points made in the first paragraph?
2. What sentence tells the audience that the speaker will talk about three topics he thinks are important to his main idea?
3. What is the purpose of the final paragraph of this speech?

Note Taking and Active Listening

Get Started

LESSON GOALS

Students will:

- Practice note taking by taking notes on a speech.
- Practice active listening and note taking by taking notes on class presentations.

Teach

ACTIVATE PRIOR KNOWLEDGE

Have students read the steps of note taking and active listening and share any questions they have. Ask **What do people mean when they say someone is a "good listener"?** *(They pay careful attention when listening.)* Point out that "good listeners" are active listeners. *Active listening* means focusing on what someone is saying and listening in a way that fits the situation. That might mean listening empathetically, appreciatively, or critically.

DISCUSS

Divide students into small groups. Ask each group to choose a current economic topic or issue. Have each group present a short oral report on its topic. Each group can write its own report, or read aloud a newspaper editorial or excerpt from a speech. Remind students that many speakers begin by summarizing the key points they will make and conclude by summarizing the points they have covered. As each group gives its presentation, have the class take notes. After each speech, ask one or two students to share their notes with the class.

Assess and Remediate

Have students answer the Practice and Apply the Skill questions. Discuss their responses as a class. Give students additional practice by showing a segment from a newscast or documentary on an economic topic. Have students take notes and share the key points and supporting details with the class.

Answers

1. Demand for more-educated workers is rising because of advances in technology; the supply has not kept up with demand 2. second paragraph, which mentions "three broad trends" 3. to emphasize that a quality educational system must be maintained to meet future challenges topic. Have students take notes and share the key points and supporting details with the class.

Think Creatively and Innovate

Get Started

LESSON GOALS

Students will:

- Show understanding of innovation by giving an example.
- Think creatively about and suggest ideas for an innovation on a product.

Teach

BRAINSTORM

Have students read the steps of thinking creatively and innovating and share any questions they have. Explain that an innovation is an idea for improving upon an existing product or process. For example, hybrid cars are an innovation on traditional car engines. Ask students for other examples.

Tell students to read the excerpt for an example of an innovator who designed better running shoes. Then have groups of students brainstorm their own idea for improving a product. Encourage them to think of products they use daily, such as computers, cars, bicycles, clothing, cellphones, and backpacks.

Have each group make a presentation explaining its proposed innovation, why it is an improvement, and how it is useful.

Assess and Remediate

Have students answer the Practice and Apply the Skill questions. Discuss their responses as a class. Have students research innovative partnerships between the Environmental Protection Agency and businesses, and how these partnerships can cut energy costs while helping the environment.

Answers

1. that he could make a better running shoe sole by using a waffle design
2. coaching track-and-field, competitive nature, interest in physiology
3. It allowed him to regularly observe the movement of runners; it gave him testers for his products.

Think Creatively and Innovate

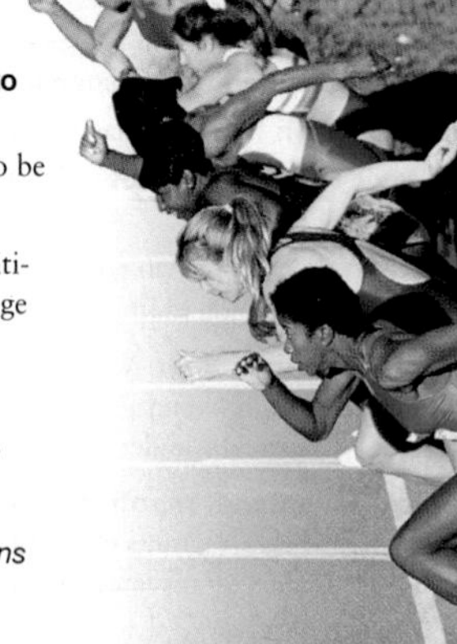

An innovation is a new idea that improves upon an existing product or process. Innovators think creatively and take risks to turn their ideas into realities.

Identify what it is that needs improving. Define and clarify what needs to be changed or improved. Consider the goal to be achieved.

Brainstorm as many ideas as possible. If working with a group, don't criticize the ideas of others and don't hesitate to suggest ideas that might seem strange or impractical. Innovation often results from an unexpected insight.

Understand the factors involved. Consider the skills, tools, or methods needed to realize the goal. Identify such factors as costs, materials, competition, consumer behavior, and potential suppliers and markets for product.

Read the excerpt below from "Nike Co-founder Bill Bowerman: His Innovations for Runners Helped Build an Empire." ▼

> Track coach Bill Bowerman was eating breakfast one morning in 1971 when his wife, Barbara, opened the waffle iron to pour another serving. He constantly looked for ways to help his athletes improve. Then it hit him. If he mixed synthetic rubber, poured it into the back of the waffle iron and let it cool, he could make a better sole for a running shoe.
>
> It took some grunting and wrenching with pliers to get the rubber off, wrote Bowerman…But when he finally did, he'd come up with the first lightweight outsole, the Waffle sole, which revolutionized the running shoe. Today, every athletic shoemaker uses a waffle sole or some variation on everything from running to hiking shoes.
>
> Bowerman…the head track-and-field coach at the University of Oregon in Eugene from 1948 to 1972, was hugely competitive and at the same time fascinated with physiology. In studying the dynamics of running, he saw that the shoes runners used were cumbersome. In the late 1950s, he devised a shoe with a heel wedge…One problem: He couldn't find a company to make it….He decided to make the shoes himself. Bowerman tested his designs on his team members, including Phil Knight…After that, Bowerman would sit in his garage and tinker with the shoe designs, which his team members gladly wore…
>
> In 1964, he and Knight teamed up to found Blue Ribbon Sports Inc. In 1972, the duo started the Nike brand…That year, four of the top seven finishers in the Olympic marathon wore Nikes. The company name was changed to Nike Inc. in 1980.
>
> "Bowerman had a laser focus to solve a problem with an athlete and then move on," said Geoff Hollister, [Nike] marketing manager….Knight, a marketing wiz, was expert at taking Bowerman's solution and making it available to the masses. Bowerman's actions were "all driven by helping us perform better…" Hollister said. This drive led Bowerman to experiment and innovate… Bowerman led by example. He taught his young men and the team at Nike to accept when they were beaten and then pick themselves up again so they could work harder for a better day. He had an insatiable curiosity and a mind that perceived gaps in the progress of human inventions…"
>
> —by William O'Neil in his 2003 book *Business Leaders & Success*

PRACTICE AND APPLY THE SKILL

Use the excerpt to answer the following questions.

1. What insight led Bowerman to his innovation?
2. What personal experiences and interests helped Bowerman to think creatively about the problem that concerned him?
3. How did Bowerman's position as a coach help him assess the effectiveness of his product?

Give an Effective Presentation

One key to an effective presentation is to combine text, video, audio, and graphics in a multimedia presentation.

Define your topic. In choosing a topic, consider the amount of time you have for the presentation and the complexity of the subject.

Find out what types of media are available for the presentation. Do you have a computer and the software to create a podcast, a PowerPoint presentation, a slide show, a video, audio clips of speeches, or animated graphics?

Make a storyboard or blueprint for the presentation. Create a storyboard by brainstorming ideas. Identify the medium that will work best for each part of the presentation.

Practice your presentation. A trial run gives presenters a chance to check the time allotted for each segment of the presentation, identify technical problems, and make sure that all participants know their roles.

Below is a storyboard for a presentation to aid urban planners in choosing among roadbuilding and other options for alleviating traffic congestion. ▼

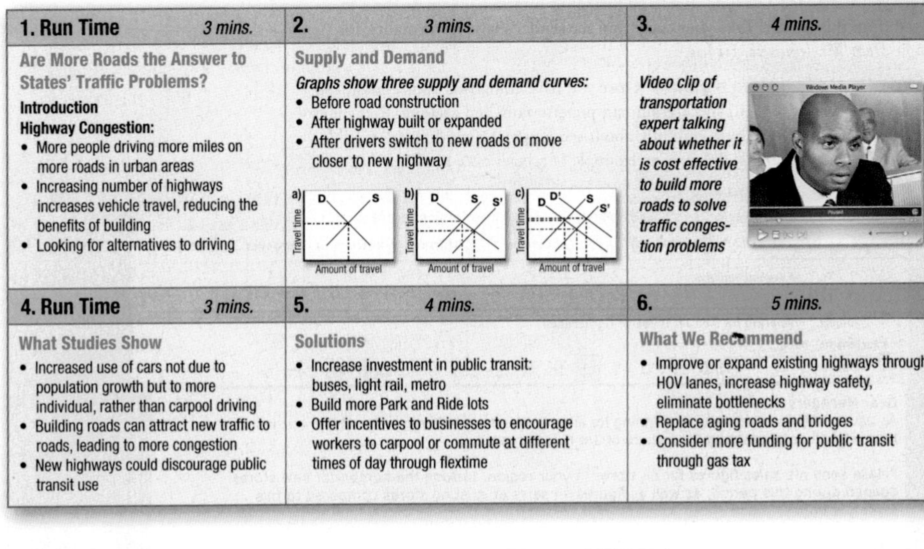

1. Run Time 3 mins.
Are More Roads the Answer to States' Traffic Problems?
Introduction
Highway Congestion:
• More people driving more miles on more roads in urban areas
• Increasing number of highways increases vehicle travel, reducing the benefits of building
• Looking for alternatives to driving
2. 3 mins.
Supply and Demand
Graphs show three supply and demand curves:
• Before road construction
• After highway built or expanded
• After drivers switch to new roads or move closer to new highway
a) b) c)
D S S' D'
Travel time
Amount of travel
3. 4 mins.
Video clip of transportation expert talking about whether it is cost effective to build more roads to solve traffic congestion problems
4. Run Time 3 mins.
What Studies Show
• Increased use of cars not due to population growth but to more individual, rather than carpool driving
• Building roads can attract new traffic to roads, leading to more congestion
• New highways could discourage public transit use
5. 4 mins.
Solutions
• Increase investment in public transit: buses, light rail, metro
• Build more Park and Ride lots
• Offer incentives to businesses to encourage workers to carpool or commute at different times of day through flextime
6. 5 mins.
What We Recommend
• Improve or expand existing highways through HOV lanes, increase highway safety, eliminate bottlenecks
• Replace aging roads and bridges
• Consider more funding for public transit through gas tax

PRACTICE AND APPLY THE SKILL

Use the storyboard to answer the following questions.

1. What issue does the presentation address?
2. How did the presenters narrow or focus the presentation of their topic?
3. How were participants encouraged to stay within the time limits in their presentations?

Give an Effective Presentation

Get Started

LESSON GOALS

Students will:

- Learn how to give an effective presentation by examining a storyboard.
- Create a multimedia presentation.

Teach

ACTIVATE PRIOR KNOWLEDGE

Have students read the steps for giving a multimedia presentation and review the types of media available to them. Ask students to describe a multimedia presentation they have seen. Have students read the storyboard in the text. Assess how familiar they are with the technologies discussed.

BRAINSTORM AND PRESENT

Have students divide into groups. Ask each group to brainstorm a list of current topics of concern to them. Groups might think of current local, state, or national issues or a school event or fundraising activity they would like to promote. Tell the class how much time groups will have for their presentations. Point out that topics should be narrow enough to be covered in the time allotted.

Ask each group to prepare a short presentation on their topic by creating a storyboard similar to the one in the text. Point out that visual and sound effects add interest. Photos, audio and video clips, or maps can also be used. Remind students that the technology is a tool for communicating information rather than an end in itself. Students should decide which technology is best for communicating their ideas.

Assess and Remediate

Have students answer the Practice and Apply the Skill questions. Discuss their responses as a class.

Answers

1. whether traffic problems can be solved by building more roads
2. by using specific examples and charts
3. run-time for each segment noted on storyboard and time limits identified during run-through

Digital Literacy

Get Started

LESSON GOALS

Students will:

- Distinguish between personal and business e-mails and learn how to write a business e-mail.
- Learn how the Internet is used for collaborative research projects.
- Find and evaluate a blog entry.

Teach

ACTIVATE PRIOR KNOWLEDGE

Have students read the steps of using the Internet to create business e-mail, engage in collaborative research, and read blogs. Have students suggest reasons why digital literacy is becoming an increasingly essential 21st century skill. Ask students how they use the Internet and list responses on the board.

WRITE A BUSINESS EMAIL

Have students read the example e-mail in the text. Tell them to write a business e-mail to apply for a part-time job, request information from a university library, ask local businesses for donations to a charity, or request information about college scholarships. Have students exchange e-mails with a partner and analyze the language and tone of each other's e-mails.

Digital Literacy

The Internet is a valuable research tool that provides links to millions of sources of information created by corporations, small businesses, government organizations, and individuals all over the world. E-mails, wikis, and blogs all provide ways for Internet users to share information and express opinions.

Writing an E-mail

Identify the purpose of the e-mail in the subject line. Indicate the topic of the e-mail in the subject line. A busy person is more likely to open the e-mail promptly if the subject of the e-mail is stated.

Focus on why you are writing. Include the subject of your e-mail in the first sentence. Make sure the message states why you are writing and what you expect to receive in terms of information or action from the recipient. Keep e-mails short and to the point.

Respect your reader. If you are responding to or following up on an e-mail that is more than a few days old, remind the recipient of why you are writing. Identify yourself clearly if the person is someone you don't know. If you are uncertain about whether your language and tone should be formal or informal, examine the e-mail received from this sender. Take your cues from the sender's level of formality, for example *Dear Mr. Jones* vs. *Hi Joe*.

Proofread e-mails before sending. Once you have composed your e-mail, use spell checker or other tools to check grammar, punctuation, and spelling. Remember that e-mail is not private. Think carefully about sending messages that you would not want shared with others. Below is an example of a business e-mail.

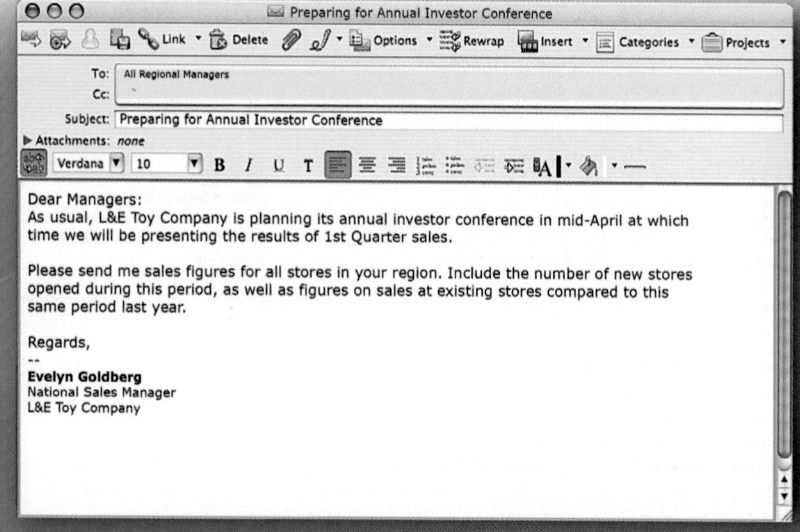

Understanding and Evaluating Wikis

A **wiki** is a Web site that allows users to easily create, edit, and link Web pages to create an online document. One of the most visited wikis is the online encyclopedia **Wikipedia.** Anyone can add or change the articles they find on this Web site. While many Internet users are enthusiastic about sites like Wikipedia, critics question their accuracy. Today corporations and government agencies are creating their own internal wikis. These wikis are almost always password-protected sites only for employees. These wikis allow staff to brainstorm, share knowledge, and update project information.

Identify the sources of the information on the Web site. Look for information on the Web site that tells you who provided this information or presented the data. Consider whether the writer is an expert or has special knowledge of this topic that would make his or her opinion especially worthwhile.

Determine when the article was written. Look for a date that shows when the article was written or last updated. Does the entry reflect changing events or provide current information on this topic?

Verify information by checking other sources. Do not rely on a single source. Compare the information on the wiki with official sources such as government Web sites, medical or legal Web sites sponsored by respected professional organizations, or reliable encyclopedias. Be skeptical and do further research if your sources disagree.

Reading and Assessing Blogs

Blogs are online journals. The word blog is short for weblog. Most blogs are short posts or entries expressing a single author's opinions. Blogs can be found on everything from politics, finance, economics, and legal issues to health and sports. Most bloggers add a new entry daily or weekly. Most blogs are interactive, providing a space where readers can comment on the opinions or information expressed.

Identify the writer. Look for information upfront that gives the name of the author and his or her business or professional affiliation.

Assess the sources the blogger links to. Evaluate the credibility and accuracy of the sources the blogger recommends to readers. Does the blog link to reputable sources?

Identify the writer's bias. Most bloggers do express a point of view. Consider the arguments and evidence the writer presents in support of these opinions. Are positions presented in a balanced way that acknowledges other points of view or is the language clearly one-sided? Scan reader comments to determine whether the blog allows comments by readers with opposing points of view or with different opinions.

PRACTICE AND APPLY THE SKILL

Use the information above to answer these questions.

1. How might the language in a business e-mail be different from the language in a personal e-mail sent to friends?
2. What makes wikis useful for projects that require input from many other people?
3. What are the advantages and drawbacks of online encyclopedias like Wikipedia?

DEBATE

Have students debate the accuracy of user-created content Web sites. Create two three-member teams to debate the following statement: *Information obtained from public wikis and blogs is not a reliable source of information for research reports.* As they debate, remind students that the accuracy of information depends on its source, whether the information is on a wiki, in a blog, or in a printed book.

DISCUSS

Explain that the term *blog* is short for weblog. Point out that blogs are usually an expression of the opinions of a particular person or group of people. Ask **What do you need to consider when reading a blog?** *(the author's bias)* **What should a reader check to assess whether information on a blog is accurate?** *(sources cited, links to sources)* Ask students to find a blog entry they agree or disagree with. Have them write a response to the entry they chose. Ask them to identify the writer, assess the writer's sources, and identify the writer's bias in their response. Have several students read their blog entries and responses to the class. Monitor entries for appropriateness and post them on the bulletin board.

L4 Have students write a blog entry on an economic topic of their choice. They should identify themselves, include reliable sources, and present a consistent point of view in their entry.

Assess and Remediate

Have students answer the Practice and Apply the Skill questions. Discuss their responses as a class.

Answers

1. Business e-mail is formal and concise. Personal e-mail is informal or casual in language and tone.
2. Wikis allow multiple users to share, update, and access information from diverse sources collaboratively. This allows them to cooperate more easily in problem-solving and decision-making.
3. Advantages: easy to find information on a variety of subjects; easy to change inaccurate or outdated information. Drawbacks: not guaranteed to be accurate.

Math Skills Online

VISUAL LEARNING ANIMATION

Economic information is often transmitted through diagrams. Having a basic knowledge of graphs makes understanding economics easier. This animated feature provides a step-by-step guide that will help students with the principles needed to comprehend the graphs used in this textbook.

MATHEMATICS TUTORIALS

Some economic principles require students to have a basic understanding of certain mathematical elements. These video-like tutorials provide instruction on some of the more frequently used math skills that are related to economics.

INTERACTIVE MATH ACTIVITIES

Throughout the textbook, a number of mathematical skills related to economics are explained. By asking students questions and providing them with correct answers, the Interactive Math Activities measure whether or not students truly understand the relationship between mathematics and economics.

MATH LAB

Math Lab provides students with tools that explain the practical application of mathematical skills. This demonstrates how mathematics can be used in everyday personal finance situations. In this lab, students will follow a step-by-step guide for balancing a checkbook.

Math Skills Online

Economics and mathematics are related in many ways.
Economists use mathematics to analyze data and to test and communicate their theories. Your ability to understand economics will depend to some extent on your ability to use and understand mathematics.

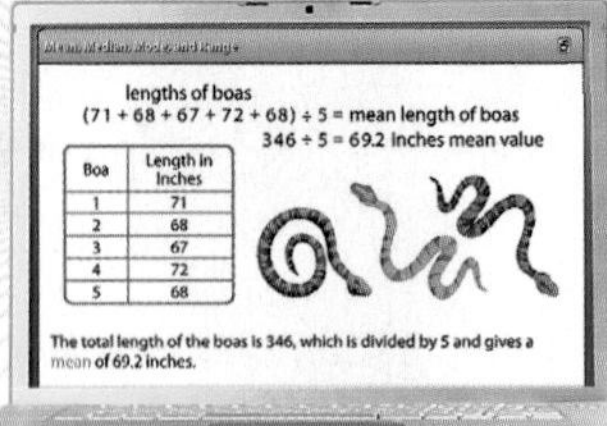

Visual Learning Animations

- Reading and Making Graphs
- Circle Graphs
- Misleading Graphs
- Mean, Median, Mode, and Range
- Line Plots
- Stem and Leaf Plots
- Effects of Outliers
- Appropriate Use of Statistical Measures

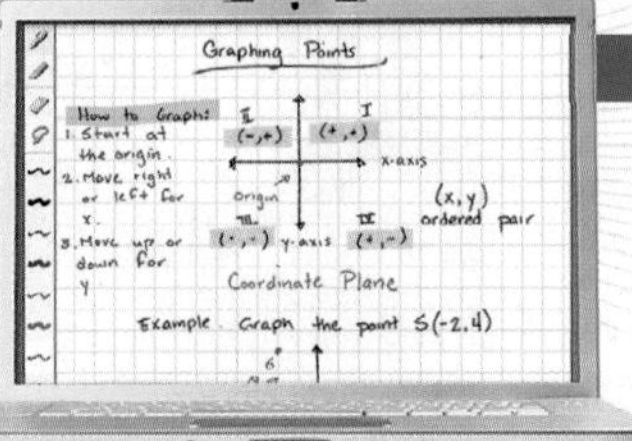

Mathematics Tutorials

- Making a Histogram
- Finding Slope Using Rise/Run
- Graphing Points on the Coordinate Plane
- Finding the Percent of a Number
- Finding Part of a Whole
- Finding Percent Using a Proportion
- Finding Simple Interest
- Finding Compound Interest

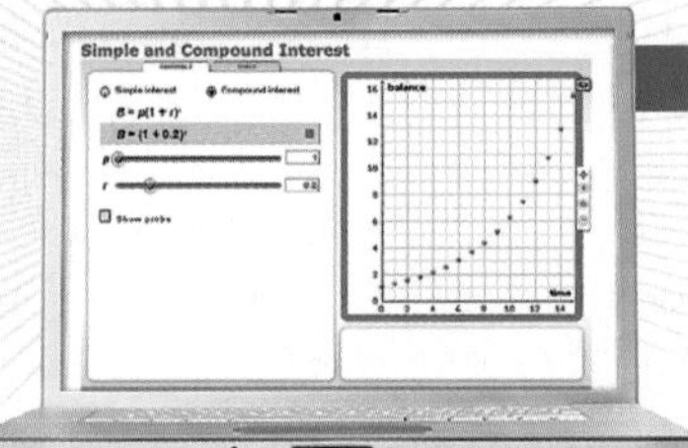

Interactive Math Activities

- Histograms
- Exploring Slope
- Points in the Coordinate Plane
- Percents and Proportions
- Simple and Compound Interest

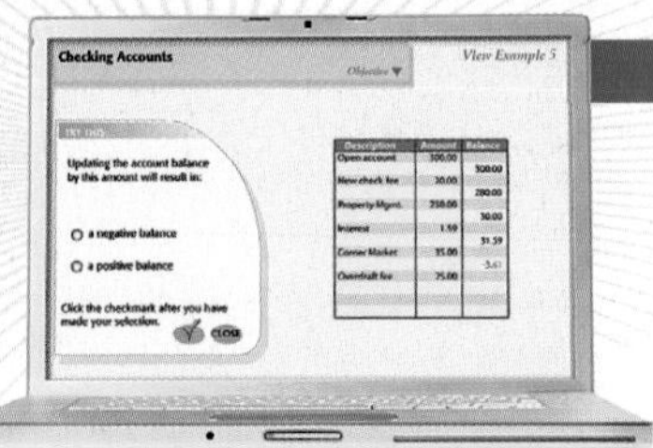

Math Lab

- Using Addition and Subtraction to Balance a Checking Account

You can access help with mathematics at point of use in your Online Student Edition or review these skills at any time.

English and Spanish Glossary

A

absolute advantage the ability to produce more of a given product using a given amount of resources (p. 449)
ventaja absoluta capacidad para producir más de cierto producto usando una cantidad determinada de recursos

aggregate demand the amount of goods and services in the economy that will be purchased at all possible price levels (p. 314)
demanda agregada cantidad de bienes y servicios que serán comprados a todos los niveles de precio posibles

aggregate supply the total amount of goods and services in the economy available at all possible price levels (p. 313)
oferta agregada cantidad total de bienes y servicios disponibles a todos los niveles de precio posibles

antitrust laws laws that encourage competition in the marketplace (p. 181)
leyes antimonopolio leyes que promueven la competencia en el mercado

appreciation an increase in the value of a currency (p. 464)
apreciación incremento del valor de una moneda

appropriations bill a bill that authorizes a specific amount of spending by the government (p. 394)
ley de presupuesto ley que autoriza una cantidad específica de gasto para el gobierno

arbitration a settlement technique in which a neutral third party listens to both sides and then imposes a decision that is legally binding for both company and the union (p. 242)
arbitraje tipo de acuerdo en el que un tercer grupo neutral escucha a ambos lados e impone una decisión con vínculo legal entre la compañía y el sindicato

articles of partnership a partnership agreement that spells out each partner's rights and responsibilities (p. 197)
estatutos de asociación acuerdo de una sociedad que determina los derechos y responsabilidades de cada socio

assets the money and other valuables belonging to an individual or business (p. 198)
activos dinero y otros valores pertenecientes a un individuo o una empresa

authoritarian describing a form of government that limits individual freedoms and requires strict obedience from its citizens (p. 36)
autoritario tipo de gobierno que limita la libertad de los individuos y requiere obediencia estricta de sus ciudadanos

automatic stabilizer a tool of fiscal policy that increases or decreases automatically depending on changes in GDP and personal income (p. 404)
estabilizador económico herramienta fiscal que se incrementa o disminuye dependiendo de cambios en el PIB y los ingresos personales

average cost total cost divided by the quantity produced (p. 121)
costo total promedio costo que surge al dividir el costo total por la cantidad producida

B

balance of payments the value of all monetary transactions between a country's economy and the rest of the world (p. 469)
balanza de pagos valor de todas las transacciones monetarias entre la economía de un país y la del resto del mundo

balance of trade the relationship between the value of a country's exports and the value of its imports (p. 468)
balanza comercial relación entre el valor de las exportaciones de un país y el valor de sus importaciones

balanced budget a budget in which revenue and spending are equal (p. 382)
presupuesto equilibrado presupuesto en el que los ingresos y los gastos son equitativos

bank an institution for receiving, keeping, and lending money (p. 256)
banco institución que recibe, mantiene y presta dinero

bank holding company a company that owns more than one bank (p. 426)
compañía tenedora de bancos compañía dueña de más de un banco

bank run a widespread panic in which many people try to redeem their paper money at the same time (p. 258)
pánico bancario situación de pánico general en la cual muchas personas retiran su dinero del banco simultáneamente

barrier to entry any factor that makes it difficult for a new firm to enter a market (p. 160)
barrera comercial cualquier factor que dificulta la entrada de una nueva entidad al mercado

barter the direct exchange of one set of goods or services for another (p. 249)
trueque intercambio directo de bienes o servicios

bear market a steady drop or stagnation in the stock market over a period of time (p. 296)
mercado bajista caída constante o estancamiento de la bolsa de inversiones por un período de tiempo

black market a market in which goods are sold illegally, without regard for government controls on price or quantity (p. 153)
mercado negro mercado en el que se venden bienes ilegalmente, sin considerar los controles gubernamentales sobre precio y cantidad

block grants federal funds given to the states in lump sums (p. 356)
subvención de bloque fondos federales otorgados a los estados en cantidades fijas

blue-collar worker someone who performs manual labor, often in a manufacturing job, and who earns an hourly wage (p. 238)
obrero persona que realiza trabajo manual, a menudo en el área industrial, y que recibe un salario por hora

bond a formal contract issued by a corporation or other entity that includes a promise to repay borrowed money with interest at fixed intervals (p. 205)

bono contrato formal expedido por una corporación u otra entidad que estipula pagar un préstamo con intereses a intervalos fijos

"brain drain" migration of the best-educated people of less developed countries to developed nations (p. 506)
fuga de cerebros emigración de individuos con alta capacitación de países menos desarrollados a naciones más desarrolladas

brokerage firm a business that specializes in trading stocks (p. 293)
firma de corretaje empresa de corredores de bolsa

budget an estimate of future revenue and expenses (p. 381)
presupuesto estimación de ingresos y gastos a futuro

budget deficit a situation in which budget expenditures exceed revenues (p. 408)
déficit presupuestario situación en la cual los gastos son mayores que los ingresos

budget surplus a situation in which budget revenues exceed expenditures (p. 408)
superávit presupuestario situación en la cual los ingresos son mayores que los gastos

bull market a steady rise in the stock market over a period of time (p. 296)
mercado alcista incremento constante en la bolsa de valores durante un período de tiempo

business association a group organized to promote the collective business interests of an area or group of similar businesses (p. 212)
asociación de empresas grupo que promueve los intereses colectivos de un área o grupo de empresas similares

business cycle a period of macroeconomic expansion, or growth, followed by one of contraction, or decline (pp. 57, 315)
ciclo económico período de expansión o crecimiento macroeconómico, seguido por una contracción o declive

business franchise a semi-independent business that pays fees to a parent company in return for the exclusive right to sell a certain product or service in a given area (p. 200)
franquicia negocio que paga honorarios a una empresa matriz a cambio del derecho exclusivo de venta de cierto producto o servicio en un área específica

business license authorization to operate a business issued by a local government (p. 193)
licencia comercial autorización emitida por un gobierno local para operar un negocio

business organization the ownership structure of a company or firm (p. 191)
negocio estructura propietaria de una compañía o entidad

C

call option a contract for buying stock at a particular price until a specified future date (p. 295)
opción de compra contrato que permite la compra de acciones a un precio estipulado hasta una fecha determinada

capital any human-made resource that is used to produce other goods and services (p. 6)
capital cualquier recurso fabricado por el hombre que se usa para producir otros bienes y servicios

capital budget a budget for spending on major investments (p. 381)
presupuesto de capital presupuesto destinado para inversiones de gran importancia

capital deepening the process of increasing the amount of capital per worker (p. 324)
desarrollo de capital proceso en el cual se incrementa la cantidad de capital por trabajador

capital gain the difference between the selling price and purchase price that results in a financial gain for the seller (p. 293)
plusvalía diferencia entre el precio de venta y el precio de compra que resulta en una ganancia financiera para el vendedor

capital loss the difference between the selling price and purchase price that results in a financial loss for the seller (p. 293)
minusvalía diferencia entre el precio de venta y el precio de compra que resulta en una pérdida financiera para el vendedor

capital market a market in which money is lent for periods longer than a year (p. 290)
mercado de capitales mercado en el cual se hacen préstamos por períodos de más de un año

cartel a formal organization of producers that agree to coordinate prices and production (p. 179)
cartel organización de productores que acuerdan la coordinación de precios y producción

cash transfers direct payments of money by the government to poor, disabled, and retired people (p. 69)
pensión pagos de dinero hechos directamente por el gobierno a los infortunados, incapacitados y jubilados

central bank a bank that can lend to other banks in times of need (p. 260)
banco central banco que puede hacer préstamos a otros bancos en momentos de necesidad

centrally planned economy an economic system in which the government makes all decisions on the three key economic questions (p. 35)
economía centralizada sistema económico en el cual el gobierno toma todas las decisiones sobre las tres preguntas económicas clave

certificate of incorporation a license to form a corporation issued by a state government (p. 205)
documento de constitución licencia expedida por el gobierno estatal, que permite formar una corporación

ceteris paribus a Latin phrase that means "all other things held constant" (p. 91)
ceteris paribus frase en latín que significa "lo demás permanece constante"

check clearing the process by which banks record whose account gives up money and whose account receives money when a customer writes a check (p. 426)
compensación de cheques proceso en el cual un banco lleva un registro de las cuentas que ceden dinero y las cuentas que reciben dinero cuando un cliente emite un cheque

classical economics a school of thought based on the idea that free markets regulate themselves (p. 399)
economía clásica corriente de pensamiento basada en la idea de que los mercados libres se regulan solos

closely held corporation a type of corporation that issues stock to only a few people, who are often family members (p. 203)
sociedad cerrada tipo de empresa que expide acciones a pocas personas, quienes por lo general son familiares

collective bargaining the process in which union and company management meet to negotiate a new labor contract (p. 240)
convenio colectivo de trabajo proceso en el cual la administración del sindicato y de la compañía se reúnen con el fin de negociar un contrato de trabajo

collusion an illegal agreement among firms to divide the market, set prices, or limit production (p. 179)
colusión acuerdo ilegal entre entidades con el fin de dividir el mercado, ajustar precios o restringir la producción

command economy another name for a centrally planned economy (p. 35)
economía controlada otro nombre para la economía centralizada

commodity a product such as petroleum or milk that is considered the same no matter who produces or sells it (p. 160)
bien de consumo producto, tal como el petróleo o la leche, que se considera igual independientemente de quién lo produzca o lo venda

commodity money objects that have value in and of themselves and that are also used as money (p. 254)
mercancía objetos que tienen valor por sí mismos y que también se usan como dinero

communism a political system in which the government owns and controls all resources and means of production and makes all economic decisions (p. 36)
comunismo sistema político en el cual el gobierno posee y controla todos los recursos y medios de producción y toma todas las decisiones económicas

comparative advantage the ability to produce a product most efficiently given all the other products that could be produced (p. 449)
ventaja comparativa habilidad para producir cierto producto de la manera más eficiente considerando todos los otros productos que se podrían producir

competition the struggle among producers for the dollars of consumers (p. 33)
competencia lucha entre productores por el dinero de los consumidores

complements two goods that are bought and used together (p. 96)
bienes complementarios dos bienes que se compran y se usan conjuntamente

conglomerate a business combination merging more than three businesses that produce unrelated products or services (p. 207)
conglomerado combinación de negocios donde se unen más de tres negocios que producen productos o servicios no relacionados entre sí

consumer cooperative a retail outlet owned and operated by consumers that sells merchandise to members at reduced prices (p. 209)
cooperativa de consumidores agrupación operada por consumidores que ofrece bienes y servicios para sus socios a precios reducidos

Consumer Price Index a price index determined by measuring the price of a standard group of goods meant to represent the "market basket" of a typical urban consumer (p. 343)
índice de precios al consumidor índice de precios determinado al medir el precio de un grupo de bienes estándar que representa la "canasta familiar" del consumidor urbano común

consumer sovereignty the power of consumers to decide what gets produced (p. 34)
soberanía del consumidor poder del consumidor para decidir qué se produce

contingent employment a temporary and part-time job (p. 221)
trabajo a destajo trabajo temporal a tiempo parcial

contraction a period of economic decline marked by falling real GDP (p. 316)
recesión período de declive económico caracterizado por el descenso del PIB

contractionary policy a fiscal policy used to reduce economic growth, often through decreased spending or higher taxes (p. 395)
política de contracción política fiscal que reduce el crecimiento económico, usualmente por medio de la disminución de gastos o de impuestos más altos

cooperative a business organization owned and operated by a group of individuals for their shared benefit (p. 208)
cooperativa organización comercial que pertenece y es operada por un grupo de individuos para un beneficio común

copyright a government document that grants an author exclusive rights to publish and sell creative works (p. 61)
derechos de autor documento gubernamental que garantiza los derechos exclusivos a un autor para publicar y vender sus obras

core inflation rate the rate of inflation excluding the effects of food and energy prices (p. 345)
tasa de inflación subyacente tasa de inflación que excluye los efectos del precio de la comida y la energía

corporate bond a bond issued by a corporation to help raise money for expansion (p. 288)
bonos corporativos bono expedido por una corporación para ayudar a recaudar dinero para su expansión

corporate income tax a tax based on a company's profits (p. 366)
impuesto sobre sociedades impuesto que se basa en las ganancias de la compañía

corporation a legal entity, owned by individual stockholders, each of whom has limited liability for the firm's debts (p. 202)
corporación entidad legal que pertenece a los accionistas, los cuales tienen responsabilidad limitada ante las deudas de la firma

cost/benefit analysis a decision-making process in which you compare what you will sacrifice and gain by a specific action (p. 11)
análisis del costo/beneficio proceso de toma de decisiones en el cual se compara el costo y la ganancia de una operación en particular

coupon rate the interest rate that a bond issuer will pay to the bondholder (p. 284)
cupón de interés tasa de interés que un emisor de bonos paga al titular del bono

credit card a card entitling its owner to buy goods and services based on the owner's promise to pay for those goods and services (p. 268)
tarjeta de crédito tarjeta que autoriza a su titular a comprar bienes y servicios partiendo de su promesa de pagar por esos bienes y servicios

creditor a person or institution to whom money is owed (p. 272)
acreedor persona o institución a la cual se le debe dinero

crowding-out effect the loss of funds for private investment caused by government borrowing (p. 411)
efecto expulsión pérdida de fondos destinados para inversiones privadas a causa de la deuda pública

currency coins and paper bills used as money (p. 252)
moneda monedas y billetes que se usan como dinero

cyclical unemployment unemployment that rises during economic downturns and falls when the economy improves (p. 338)
desempleo cíclico desempleo que incrementa al empeorar la economía y disminuye al mejorar la economía

D

debit card a card used to withdraw money from a bank account (p. 271)
tarjeta de débito tarjeta que se usa para retirar dinero de una cuenta bancaria

debt rescheduling an agreement between a lending nation and a debtor nation that lengthens the time of debt payment and forgives part of the loan (p. 493)
renegociación de deudas acuerdo entre la nación acreedora y la nación deudora que extiende el plazo de pago y perdona parte del préstamo

default to fail to pay back a loan (p. 268)
mora situación que consiste en suspender el pago de una deuda

deflation a sustained drop in the price level (p. 348)
deflación descenso general de precios

deforestation the large-scale destruction of forests (p. 507)
deforestación destrucción forestal masiva

demand the desire to own something and the ability to pay for it (p. 85)
demanda deseo de poseer algo y la capacidad para pagar por ello

demand curve a graphic representation of a demand schedule (p. 89)
curva de demanda representación gráfica de la tabla de demanda

demand deposit money in a checking account that can be paid "on demand," or at any time (p. 264)
depósito a la vista dinero en una cuenta corriente que se paga "a petición" o en cualquier momento

demand schedule a table that lists the quantity of a good a person will buy at various prices in the market (p. 88)
tabla de demanda tabla que representa la cantidad de bienes que un consumidor está dispuesto a adquirir a diferentes precios en el mercado

demand-side economics a school of thought based on the idea that demand for goods drives the economy (p. 400)
economía de demanda corriente de pensamiento basada en la noción de que la demanda de bienes dirige la economía

demographics the statistical characteristics of populations and population segments, especially when used to identify consumer markets (p. 94)
demografía estudio estadístico de la población humana y sus segmentos, especialmente relacionados con el mercado de consumo

depreciation 1. the loss of the value of capital equipment that results from normal wear and tear (p. 312) 2. a decrease in the value of currency (p. 465)
depreciación 1. reducción del valor de los bienes de capital de equipo como resultado del uso 2. reducción en el valor de una moneda

depression a recession that is especially long and severe (p. 316)
depresión recesión económica que se caracteriza por ser larga y grave

deregulation the removal of government controls over a market (p. 183)
desregulación supresión del control del gobierno sobre la actividad económica

derived demand a type of demand that is set by the demand for another good or service (p. 226)
demanda derivada demanda que depende de la demanda de otro bien o servicio

developed nation a nation with a relatively high average level of material well-being (p. 481)
país desarrollado país con un bienestar económico relativamente alto

development the process by which a nation improves the economic, political, and social well-being of its people (p. 481)
desarrollo proceso mediante el cual una nación mejora la situación económica, política y social de su población

differentiation making a product different from other, similar products (p. 175)
diferenciación hacer que un producto se distinga de otros productos similares

diminishing marginal returns a level of production at which the marginal product of labor decreases as the number of workers increases (p. 117)
rendimiento marginal decreciente nivel de producción en el cual el producto laboral marginal disminuye al incrementar el número de trabajadores

discount rate the interest rate that the Federal Reserve charges commercial banks for loans (p. 427)
tasa de descuento interés que cobra la Reserva Federal sobre los préstamos a los bancos comerciales

discouraged worker someone who wants a job but has given up looking (p. 341)
trabajador desanimado persona que quiere conseguir un trabajo pero ha desistido de la búsqueda

discretionary spending spending about which Congress is free to make choices (p. 375)
gastos discrecionales gastos sobre los cuales el Congreso es libre de tomar decisiones

disequilibrium any price or quantity not at equilibrium; when quantity supplied is not equal to quantity demanded in a market (p. 134)
desequilibrio estado de desigualdad económica; desigualdad entre la cantidad de oferta y la cantidad de demanda

diversification the strategy of spreading out investments to reduce risk (p. 280)
diversificación estrategia en la que se distribuyen las inversiones para reducir el riesgo

dividend the portion of corporate profits paid out to stockholders (p. 205)
dividendo porción de los beneficios corporativos que les pagan a los accionistas

durable goods those goods that last for a relatively long time, such as refrigerators, cars, and DVD players (p. 309)
bienes duraderos bienes de consumo cuya durabilidad es relativamente larga, por ejemplo refrigeradores, automóbiles y reproductores de DVD

E

easy money policy a monetary policy that increases the money supply (p. 436)
política de dinero fácil política monetaria que incrementa la disponibilidad de dinero

economic growth a steady, long-term increase in real GDP (p. 315)
crecimiento económico aumento constante a largo plazo del PIB

economic system the structure of methods and principles that a society uses to produce and distribute goods and services (p. 23)
sistema económico estructura de métodos y principios que una sociedad usa para producir y distribuir bienes y servicios

economic transition a period of change in which a nation moves from one economic system to another (p. 43)
transición económica período de cambio en el cual una nación pasa de un sistema económico a otro

economics the study of how people seek to satisfy their needs and wants by making choices (p. 4)
economía rama del saber que estudia cómo las personas buscan satisfacer sus necesidades y deseos al tomar decisiones

economies of scale factors that cause a producer's average cost per unit to fall as output rises (p. 165)
economías de escala factores que hacen que el costo promedio por unidad de un producto disminuya cuando la producción aumenta

efficiency the use of resources in such a way as to maximize the output of goods and services (p. 15)
eficiencia uso de los recursos de manera que se alcance el máximo de producción de bienes y servicios

elastic describes demand that is very sensitive to a change in price (p. 97)
elasticidad describe la demanda que es muy susceptible a los cambios de precio

elasticity of demand a measure of how consumers respond to price changes (p. 97)
elasticidad de la demanda medida de cómo responden los consumidores a los cambios de precio

elasticity of supply a measure of the way quantity supplied reacts to a change in price (p. 113)
elasticidad de la oferta medida de la forma en que la cantidad ofrecida responde a un cambio de precio

embargo a ban on trade with a particular country (p. 456)
embargo prohibición de comerciar con un país determinado

eminent domain the right of a government to take private property for public use (p. 52)
dominio eminente (expropiación) derecho de un gobierno de tomar la propiedad privada de alguien para darle un uso público

enterprise zone area where businesses can locate free of certain local, state, and federal taxes and restrictions (p. 355)
zona franca área en la que se pueden establecer negocios libres de ciertos impuestos y restricciones municipales, estatales y federales

entitlement social welfare program that people are "entitled to" benefit from if they meet certain eligibility requirements (p. 376)
derecho consuetudinario programa de beneficencia social al que las personas tienen "derecho" si cumplen con ciertos requisitos

entrepreneur a person who decides how to combine resources to create goods and services (p. 5)
empresario persona que decide cómo combinar recursos para crear bienes y servicios

equilibrium the point at which the demand for a product or service is equal to the supply of that product or service (p. 134)

equilibrio punto en el cual la demanda de un producto o servicio es igual a su oferta

equilibrium wage the wage rate, or price of labor services, that is set when the supply of workers meets the demand for workers in the labor market (p. 227)
salario de equilibrio tasa salarial, o precio de la mano de obra, que se establece cuando la disponibilidad de trabajadores cubre la demanda de trabajadores en el mercado laboral

estate tax a tax on the total value of the money and property of a person who has died (p. 373)
impuesto de sucesión impuesto sobre el valor total del dinero y las propiedades que deja una persona fallecida

excess reserves bank reserves greater than the amount required by the Federal Reserve (p. 431)
exceso de reservas reservas bancarias que sobrepasan la cantidad que la Reserva Federal necesita

exchange rate the value of a nation's currency in relation to a foreign currency (p. 463)
tasa de cambio valor de la moneda de una nación en relación con una moneda extranjera

excise tax a tax on the production or sale of a good (p. 124)
impuesto sobre artículos de uso y consumo impuesto sobre la producción o venta de un bien

expansion a period of economic growth as measured by a rise in real GDP (p. 315)
expansión período de crecimiento económico determinado por un aumento del PIB real

expansionary policy a fiscal policy used to encourage economic growth, often through increased spending or tax cuts (p. 395)
política de expansión política fiscal que se usa para estimular el crecimiento económico a través de un aumento del gasto o de una reducción de impuestos

export a good or service sent to another country for sale (p. 449)
exportaciones bien o servicio que se envía a otro país para la venta

externality an economic side effect of a good or service that generates benefits or costs to someone other than the person deciding how much to produce or consume (p. 65)
externalidad efecto económico de un bien o servicio que le genera beneficios o costos a alguien distinto a quien decide cuánto producir o consumir

F

factor market the arena of exchange in which firms purchase the factors of production from households (p. 31)
mercado de factores área de intercambio en la cual hay compañías que compran los factores de producción de las economías domésticas

factor payment the income people receive in return for supplying factors of production (p. 25)
pago a los factores ingreso que reciben las personas a cambio de proveer factores de producción

factors of production the resources that are used to make goods and services (p. 5)
factores de producción recursos que se usan para generar bienes y servicios

fad a product that is popular for a short period of time (p. 145)
moda pasajera producto que es popular por un período breve de tiempo

featherbedding the practice of negotiating labor contracts that keep unnecessary workers on the company's payroll (p. 233)
sinecura contratación retribuida de empleados innecesarios

federal budget a written document estimating the federal government's revenue and authorizing its spending for the coming year (p. 392)
presupuesto federal documento escrito donde se estima el ingreso del gobierno federal y por medio del cual se autorizan los gastos del año siguiente

federal funds rate the interest rate that banks charge each other for loans (p. 427)
tasa de los fondos federales tasa que se cobran entre sí los bancos por el préstamo de sus reservas

fiat money objects that have value because the government has decreed that they are an acceptable means to pay debts (p. 255)
dinero fiat objetos que tienen valor sólo porque el gobierno ha decretado que son medios aceptables para pagar deudas

financial asset a claim on the property or income of a borrower (p. 278)
activo financiero derecho que tiene una entidad sobre la propiedad o los ingresos de un prestatario

financial intermediary an institution that helps channel funds from savers to borrowers (p. 279)
intermediario financiero institución que ayuda a canalizar los fondos de los ahorristas a los prestatarios

financial system the network of structures and mechanisms that allow the transfer of money between savers and borrowers (p. 278)
sistema financiero red de estructuras y mecanismos que permiten la transferencia de dinero entre ahorristas y prestatarios

firm an organization that uses resources to produce a product or service, which it then sells (p. 31)
empresa organización que usa recursos para crear un producto o servicio, que después vende

fiscal policy the use of government spending and revenue collection to influence the economy (p. 392)
política fiscal uso de los gastos y del ingreso del gobierno para causar una reacción en la economía

fiscal year any 12-month period used for budgeting purposes (p. 392)
año fiscal período de doce meses con fines presupuestarios

fixed cost a cost that does not change, no matter how much of a good is produced (p. 118)
costo fijo costo que no cambia, independientemente de la cantidad que se produzca de un bien

fixed exchange-rate system a system in which governments try to keep the values of their currencies constant against one another (p. 467)
sistema de tasa cambiaria fija sistema en el cual el gobierno trata de mantener constante el valor de su moneda con respecto a otra moneda

fixed income income that does not increase even when prices go up (p. 347)
ingreso fijo ingreso que no aumentan aunque los precios suban

flexible exchange-rate system a system in which the exchange rate is determined by supply and demand (p. 467)
sistema de tasa cambiaria flexible sistema en el cual la tasa de cambio depende de la oferta y la demanda

food stamp program government program that helps low-income people buy food (p. 351)
programa de cupones para alimentos cupones que el gobierno distribuye y que se pueden cambiar por alimentos

foreclosure the seizure of property from borrowers who are unable to repay their loans (p. 263)
embargo acción que consiste en tomar la propiedad de prestatarios que no pueden pagar sus préstamos

foreign direct investment the establishment of a business by investors from another country (p. 492)
inversión directa extranjera establecimiento de un negocio de inversionistas de otro país

foreign exchange market system of financial institutions that facilitate the buying and selling of foreign currencies (p. 465)
mercado de divisas sistema de instituciones financieras que facilitan la compra y venta de monedas extranjeras

foreign investment capital that originates in other countries (p. 492)
inversión extranjera capital generado en otros países

foreign portfolio investment purchases made in a country's financial markets by investors from another country (p. 492)
cartera de inversión extranjera compras que los inversionistas de un país hacen en mercados financieros de otro país

fractional reserve banking a banking system that keeps only a fraction of funds on hand and lends out the remainder (p. 267)
sistema de reserva fraccionaria sistema bancario en el cual el banco mantiene solamente una fracción de los fondos en reserva y presta el resto de los fondos

franchise a contract that gives a single firm the right to sell its goods within an exclusive market (p. 167)
franquicia contrato que le otorga a una firma el derecho de vender sus bienes dentro de un mercado exclusivo

free contract the principle that people may decide what agreements they want to enter into (p. 51)
principio de libre contrato principio que establece que las personas pueden decidir qué acuerdos quieren hacer

free enterprise system an economic system characterized by private or corporate ownership of capital goods (p. 43)
sistema de libre empresa sistema económico en el cual los bienes capitales les pertenecen a compañías privadas o corporaciones

free market economy an economic system in which decisions on the three key economic questions are based on voluntary exchange in markets (p. 30)
economía de libre mercado sistema económico en el cual las decisiones relacionadas con las tres preguntas económicas clave se basan en el intercambio voluntario en el mercado

free rider someone who would not be willing to pay for a certain good or service but who would get the benefits of it anyway if it were provided as a public good (p. 64)
polizón persona que no está dispuesta a pagar por un bien o servicio determinado, pero quien se beneficiaría de él de todos modos si se le ofreciera como beneficio público

free trade the lowering or elimination of protective tariffs and other trade barriers between two or more nations (p. 458)
libre comercio disminución o eliminación de las tarifas y otras barreras comerciales entre dos o más naciones

free trade zone a region where a group of countries agrees to reduce or eliminate trade barriers (p. 460)
zona de libre comercio región en la que un grupo de países acuerda reducir o eliminar las barreras comerciales

frictional unemployment type of unemployment that occurs when people take time to find a job (p. 335)
desempleo friccional tipo de desempleo que ocurre cuando a las personas les toma tiempo encontrar empleo

fringe benefits payments to employees other than wages or salary (p. 195)
beneficio adicional pago que los empleados reciben además de su sueldo o salario

full employment the level of employment reached when there is no cyclical unemployment (p. 340)
pleno empleo nivel de empleo alcanzado cuando no hay desempleo cíclico

futures contracts to buy or sell commodities at a particular date in the future at a price specified today (p. 295)
contrato de futuros contratos que establece la compra o venta de bienes o valores en el futuro a un precio establecido con anticipación

G

general partnership a type of partnership in which all partners share equally in both responsibility and liability (p. 196)
sociedad colectiva tipo de sociedad en la cual todos los socios asumen la misma cantidad de responsabilidades y obligaciones

gift tax a tax on the money or property that one living person gives to another (p. 373)
impuesto sobre donaciones impuesto sobre el dinero o la propiedad que una persona viva le da a otra

glass ceiling an unofficial barrier that sometimes prevents some women and minorities from advancing to the top rank of organizations dominated by white men (p. 231)
techo de cristal barrera no oficial que les impide a algunas mujeres y minorías avanzar a la cima de organizaciones dominadas por hombres blancos

globalization the increasingly tight interconnection of producers, consumers, and financial systems around the world (pp. 337, 501)
globalización interconexión, cada vez más fuerte, entre productores, consumidores y sistemas financieros a nivel mundial

gold standard a monetary system in which paper money and coins had the value of a certain amount of gold (p. 259)
patrón oro sistema monetario en el cual el papel moneda y las monedas tienen el mismo valor de una cantidad de oro determinada

goods the physical objects that someone produces (p. 3)
bienes objetos físicos que alguien produce

government monopoly a monopoly created by the government (p. 167)
monopolio gubernamental monopolio creado por el gobierno

grant a financial award given by a government agency to a private individual or group in order to carry out a specific task (p. 72)
subvención cantidad de dinero que otorga una organización gubernamental a una organización o grupo privados con el fin de utilizarlo en una actividad específica

greenback a paper currency issued during the Civil War (p. 259)
greenback dinero creado durante la Guerra Civil estadounidense

gross domestic product the dollar value of all final goods and services produced within a country's borders in a given year (pp. 57, 309)
producto interno bruto valor en dólares de todos los bienes y servicios producidos en un país, en un año específico

gross national product the annual income earned by a nation's firms and citizens (p. 312)
producto nacional bruto ingreso anual que obtienen las compañías y los habitantes de una nación

guest workers members of the labor force from another country who are allowed to live and work in the United States only temporarily (p. 222)
trabajadores invitados miembros de la fuerza laboral que vienen de otro país y tienen permiso para vivir y trabajar en Estados Unidos temporalmente

"guns or butter" a phrase expressing the idea that a country that decides to produce more military goods ("guns") has fewer resources to produce consumer goods ("butter") and vice versa (p. 9)
"pan o armas" frase que expresa la idea de que un país que decide producir más objetos militares (armas) tiene menos recursos para producir bienes de consumo (pan) y viceversa

H

hedge fund a private investment organization that employs risky strategies to try to make huge profits for investors (p. 279)
fondo de inversión libre organización privada inversionista que emplea estrategias riesgosas para intentar obtener grandes ganancias para los inversionistas

horizontal merger the combination of two or more firms competing in the same market with the same good or service (p. 206)
fusión horizontal combinación de dos o más empresas que compiten en el mismo mercado y ofrecen el mismo bien o servicio

household a person or group of people living in a single residence (p. 31)
unidad familiar persona o grupo de personas que viven bajo el mismo techo

human capital the knowledge and skills a worker gains through education and experience (p. 6)
capital humano conocimientos y destrezas que un trabajador obtiene a través de la educación y la experiencia

hyperinflation inflation that is out of control (p. 345)
hiperinflación inflación descontrolada

I

imperfect competition a market structure that fails to meet the conditions of perfect competition (p. 160)
competencia imperfecta estructura del mercado que no cumple con las condiciones de la competencia perfecta

import a good or service brought in from another country for sale (p. 449)
importaciones bienes o servicios que se traen de otro país para la venta

import quota a set limit on the amount of a good that can be imported (p. 456)
cuota de importación límite establecido de la cantidad de un bien que se puede importar

incentive the hope of reward or fear of penalty that encourages a person to behave in a certain way (p. 33)
incentivo esperanza de obtener una recompensa o temor de recibir un castigo que anima a una persona a comportarse de cierta manera

incidence of a tax the final burden of a tax (p. 367)
incidencia fiscal peso final de un impuesto

income distribution the way in which a nation's total income is distributed among its population (p. 351)
distribución de ingresos forma en que se distribuye el ingreso total de una nación entre la población

income effect the change in consumption that results when a price increase causes real income to decline (p. 87)
efecto ingreso cambio en el consumo que ocurre cuando el aumento de un precio hace que el ingreso real disminuya

increasing marginal returns a level of production in which the marginal product of labor increases as the number of workers increases (p. 117)
aumento del ingreso marginal nivel de producción en el cual la productividad marginal aumenta a medida que el número de trabajadores aumenta

individual income tax a tax based on a person's earnings (p. 366)
impuesto sobre la renta individual impuesto que se basa en los ingresos de una persona

industrialization the organization of an economy for the purpose of manufacturing goods (p. 483)
industrialización organización de una economía con el propósito de fabricar bienes

inelastic describes demand that is not very sensitive to price changes (p. 97)
demanda inelástica demanda que es poco sensible a las variaciones de precio

infant industry an industry in the early stages of development (p. 458)
industria en período de arranque industria en etapa temprana de desarrollo

infant mortality rate the number of deaths that occur in the first year of life per 1,000 births (p. 484)
tasa de mortalidad infantil número de muertes que ocurren en el primer año de vida por cada 1000 nacimientos

inferior good a good that consumers demand less of when their incomes increase (p. 94)
bien inferior bien cuya demanda disminuye a medida que el ingreso de los consumidores aumenta

inflation a general increase in prices across an economy (p. 342)
inflación aumento general de los precios en una economía

inflation rate the percentage rate of change in price level over time (p. 343)
tasa de inflación porcentaje de cambio en los precios al transcurrir el tiempo

inflation-indexed bond a bond that protects the investor against inflation by its linkage to an index of inflation (p. 288)
bonos indexados por inflación bono que protege al inversionista de la inflación porque se ajusta de acuerdo con un índice de inflación

infrastructure the basic facilities that are necessary for a society to function and grow (p. 63)
infraestructura instalaciones básicas que una sociedad necesita para funcionar y desarrollarse

in-kind benefits goods and services provided for free or at greatly reduced prices (p. 70)
beneficios en especies bienes y servicios que se ofrecen de forma gratuita o a un precio considerablemente bajo

innovation the process of bringing new methods, products, or ideas into use (p. 27)
innovación proceso que consiste en usar nuevos métodos, productos o ideas

inside lag the time it takes to implement monetary policy (p. 437)
demora interna tiempo que toma implementar una política monetaria

interdependence the shared need of countries for resources, goods, services, labor, and knowledge supplied by other countries (p. 452)
interdependencia necesidad que comparten los países de obtener recursos, bienes, servicios, mano de obra y conocimiento provenientes de otros países

interest the price paid for the use of borrowed money (p. 268)
interés precio que se paga por el uso de dinero prestado

interest group a private organization that tries to persuade public officials to act in ways that benefit its members (p. 52)
grupo de presión organización privada que intenta persuadir a miembros de la administración pública de que actúen de una manera que beneficie a los miembros del grupo

intermediate goods products used in the production of final goods (p. 309)
bienes intermedios productos usados en la producción de bienes finales

internal financing capital derived from the savings of a country's citizens (p. 491)
financiamiento interno capital derivado de los ahorros de los ciudadanos de un país

inventory the quantity of goods that a firm has on hand (p. 143)
inventario cantidad de bienes que una empresa tiene a su disposición

investment the act of redirecting resources from being consumed today so that they may create benefits in the future; the use of assets to earn income or profit (p. 277)
inversión acto de redirigir recursos del presente para que puedan generar más beneficios en el futuro; uso de los bienes para obtener ingresos o ganancias

invisible hand a term coined by Adam Smith to describe the self-regulating nature of the marketplace (p. 33)
mano invisible expresión acuñada por Adam Smith para describir la naturaleza autorregulatoria del mercado

junk bond a bond with high risk and potentially high yield (p. 289)
bono basura bono que representa un gran riesgo y que podría tener un alto rendimiento

K

Keynesian economics a school of thought that uses demand-side theory as the basis for encouraging government action to help the economy (p. 401)
Economía keinesiana escuela que usa la teoría de la demanda como base para provocar acciones gubernamentales que ayuden la economía

L

labor the effort people devote to tasks for which they are paid (p. 5)
trabajo esfuerzo dedicado a tareas por las que se recibe compensación económica

labor force all nonmilitary people who are employed or unemployed (p. 217)

mano de obra toda persona empleada o subempleada que no pertenece a las fuerzas armadas

labor union an organization of workers that tries to improve working conditions, wages, and benefits for its members (p. 233)
sindicato organización de trabajadores que busca mejorar las condiciones de trabajo, los salarios y los beneficios laborales de sus miembros

laissez faire the doctrine that government generally should not intervene in the marketplace (p. 39)
liberalismo doctrina que rechaza la intervención del gobierno en el mercado

land all natural resources used to produce goods and services (p. 5)
terreno todo recurso natural que se utiliza para producir bienes y servicios

law of comparative advantage the principle that a nation is better off when it produces goods and services for which it has a comparative advantage (p. 450)
ley (principio) de la ventaja comparativa principio que reconoce la ventaja que disfruta un país cuando puede producir un bien o servicio a menor costo que otro país

law of demand consumers will buy more of a good when its price is lower and less when its price is higher (p. 85)
ley de la demanda los consumidores compran más de un bien cuando su precio es bajo y menos cuando su precio es alto

law of increasing costs an economic principle which states that as production shifts from making one good or service to another, more resources are needed to increase production of the second good or service (p. 17)
ley de los costos crecientes principio económico según el cual al producirse un producto o bien adicional, éste requerirá cantidades cada vez mayores de recursos para aumentar su producción

law of supply producers offer more of a good as its price increases and less as its price falls (p. 109)
ley de la oferta los fabricantes proveen más de un bien cuando su precio sube y menos cuando su precio baja

leading indicators a set of key economic variables that economists use to predict future trends in a business cycle (p. 320)
indicadores principales conjunto de variables económicas clave que los economistas utilizan para predecir las futuras tendencias del ciclo económico

learning effect the theory that education increases efficiency of production and thus results in higher wages (p. 220)
efecto aprendizaje teoría que sostiene que la educación incrementa la productividad y por consiguiente genera mayores sueldos

legal equality the principle that everyone has the same legal rights (p. 51)
igualdad legal principio según el cual todas las personas tienen los mismos derechos legales

less developed country a nation with a relatively low level of material well-being (p. 482)
país en vías de desarrollo nación con un bajo nivel de bienestar material

liability the legal obligation to pay debts (p. 194)
responsabilidad obligación legal de pagar deudas

license a government-issued right to operate a business (p. 168)
licencia permiso que el gobierno otorga a empresas para que puedan operar

life expectancy the average expected life span of an individual (p. 483)
expectativa de vida promedio de vida anticipado de una persona

limited liability corporation a type of business with limited liability for the owners, with the advantage of not paying corporate income tax (p. 205)
corporación de responsabilidad limitada compañía que tiene propietarios con responsabilidad limitada y no paga el impuesto sobre sociedades

limited liability partnership a type of partnership in which all partners are limited partners (p. 197)
sociedad de responsabilidad limitada sociedad en la que la responsabilidad de los socios está limitada al capital aportado

limited partnership a type of partnership in which only one partner is required to be a general partner (p. 197)
sociedad limitada tipo de sociedad que solamente requiere un socio general

liquidity the ability to be used as, or directly converted into, cash (p. 264)
liquidez capacidad para utilizar el dinero o para convertir algo en dinero fácilmente

literacy rate the proportion of a nation's population over age 15 that can read and write (p. 483)
índice de alfabetización proporción de la población mayor de 15 años de un país que sabe leer y escribir

Lorenz Curve the curve that illustrates income distribution (p. 353)
Curva de Lorenz curva que ilustra la distribución de los ingresos

M

macroeconomics the study of economic behavior and decisions in a nation's whole economy (p. 56)
Macroeconomía estudio del comportamiento y la toma de decisiones de toda la economía nacional

malnutrition consistently inadequate nutrition (p. 491)
desnutrición nutrición inadecuada continua

mandatory spending spending that Congress is required by existing law to do (p. 375)
gasto obligatorio gasto que el Congreso debe realizar de acuerdo con leyes preexistentes

marginal benefit the extra benefit of adding one unit (p. 11)
beneficio marginal beneficio adicional que surge al añadirse una unidad

marginal cost the cost of producing one more unit of a good (pp. 11, 119)

costo marginal costo que resulta al producirse una unidad adicional de un producto

marginal product of labor the change in output from hiring one additional unit of labor (p. 116)

producto marginal del trabajo producción adicional que se obtiene con una unidad adicional de trabajo

marginal revenue the additional income from selling one more unit of a good; sometimes equal to price (p. 120)

ingreso marginal ingreso recibido al vender una unidad más de producto; en algunos casos similar al precio

market any arrangement that allows buyers and sellers to exchange things (p. 29)

mercado cualquier arreglo que les permite a compradores y vendedores intercambiar cosas

market basket a representative collection of goods and services (p. 343)

canasta de mercado conjunto representativo de bienes y servicios

market demand schedule a table that lists the quantity of a good all consumers in a market will buy at each different price (p. 88)

tabla de demanda tabla que muestra la cantidad de un producto determinado que los consumidores de un mercado estarían dispuestos a comprar a diferentes precios

market failure a situation in which the free market, operating on its own, does not distribute resources efficiently (p. 65)

falla del mercado situación en la que el mercado, operando de forma autónoma, asigna recursos ineficientemente

market power the ability of a company to control prices and total market output (p. 171)

poder de mercado capacidad de una empresa para influir en los precios y la producción del mercado

market supply curve a graph of the quantity supplied of a good by all suppliers at various prices (p. 113)

curva de oferta gráfico que ilustra la cantidad de un producto que las empresas proveerán a diferentes precios

market supply schedule a chart that lists how much of a good all suppliers will offer at various prices (p. 112)

tabla de oferta tabla que muestra la cantidad de un producto determinado que las empresas proveerán a diferentes precios

maturity the time at which payment to a bondholder is due (p. 284)

vencimiento día en que se cumple el plazo dado para el pago de una deuda u obligación

mediation a settlement technique in which a neutral person, the mediator, meets with each side to find a solution that both sides will accept (p. 242)

mediación proceso de resolución en el que una persona neutral, el mediador, se reúne con las partes en conflicto para hallar una solución mutuamente aceptable

medium of exchange anything that is used to determine value during the exchange of goods and services (p. 249)

medio de intercambio estructura que se utiliza para asignar valor a algo durante un intercambio de bienes y servicios

member bank a bank that belongs to the Federal Reserve System (p. 260)

banco miembro banco que pertenece al Sistema de la Reserva Federal

merger when two or more companies join to form a single firm (p. 182)

fusión proceso mediante el cual dos o más compañías se unen para formar una sola

microeconomics the study of economic behavior and decision-making in small units, such as households and firms (p. 56)

microeconomía estudio del comportamiento económico de unidades individuales de decisión tales como familias y empresas

minimum wage a minimum price that an employer can pay a worker for an hour of labor (p. 139)

salario mínimo cantidad mínima que un empleador puede pagar a un empleado por la hora de trabajo

mixed economy a market-based economic system in which the government is involved to some extent (p. 40)

economía mixta sistema económico de mercado en el que el gobierno tiene cierto grado de intervención

monetarism the belief that the money supply is the most important factor in macroeconomic performance (p. 435)

monetarismo doctrina que sostiene que el control del dinero en circulación es el factor más importante en el comportamiento macroeconómico de la economía

monetary policy the actions that the Federal Reserve System takes to influence the level of real GDP and the rate of inflation in the economy (p. 419)

política monetaria medidas que el Sistema de la Reserva Federal utiliza para conseguir la estabilidad del PIB real y de la tasa de inflación de la economía

money anything that serves as a medium of exchange, a unit of account, and a store of value (p. 249)

dinero todo lo que sirve como medio de cambio, unidad de cuenta y depósito de valor

money creation the process by which money enters into circulation (p. 429)

emisión de dinero proceso que pone en circulación billetes y monedas

money market a market in which money is lent for periods of one year or less (p. 290)

mercado monetario o de dinero mercado que ofrece créditos por períodos de un año o menos

money market mutual fund a fund that pools money from small savers to purchase short-term government and corporate securities (p. 265)

fondos mutuales fondo que reúne el dinero de pequeños ahorristas para comprar instrumentos de crédito a corto plazo emitidos por el gobierno o el sector privado

money multiplier formula formula (initial cash deposit × 1 ÷ RRR) used to determine how much new money can be created with each demand deposit and added to the money supply (p. 430)

fórmula del multiplicador monetario fórmula (depósito a la vista inicial × 1 ÷ tasa de encaje legal) que se utiliza para calcular la cantidad de dinero que cada depósito a la vista puede añadir a la oferta de dinero

money supply all the money available in the United States economy (p. 264)
oferta monetaria todo el dinero disponible en la economía de los Estados Unidos

monopolistic competition a market structure in which many companies sell products that are similar but not identical (p. 174)
competencia monopolística situación de mercado en la que muchas empresas venden bienes que son similares, pero no idénticos

monopoly a market in which a single seller dominates (p. 164)
monopolio situación de mercado en la que un solo vendedor controla la oferta

mortgage a specific type of loan that is used to buy real estate (p. 268)
hipoteca tipo de préstamo que se utiliza para comprar bienes inmuebles

multinational corporation a large corporation that produces and sells its goods and services in more than one country (p. 207)
compañía multinacional gran empresa que produce y vende sus bienes y servicios en más de un país

multiplier effect the idea that every one dollar change in fiscal policy creates a change greater than one dollar in the national income (p. 401)
efecto multiplicador concepto según el cual por cada dólar de cambio en una política fiscal, se producirá un cambio aún mayor en el ingreso nacional

municipal bond a bond issued by a state or local government or a municipality to finance a public project (p. 288)
bono público bono emitido por un estado, gobierno local o municipio para financiar obras públicas

mutual fund an organization that pools the savings of many individuals and invests this money in a variety of stocks, bonds, and other financial assets (p. 279)
fondo de inversión organización que reúne los ahorros de múltiples individuos e invierte el dinero en una cartera de acciones, bonos y otros activos financieros

N

national bank a bank chartered by the federal government (p. 257)
banco nacional banco regulado por el gobierno federal

national debt the total amount of money the federal government owes to bondholders (p. 410)
deuda nacional cantidad total de dinero que el gobierno federal debe a sus acreedores

national income accounting a system economists use to collect and organize macroeconomic statistics on production, income, investment, and savings (p. 307)
contabilidad nacional sistema que los economistas utilizan para recopilar y organizar estadísticas macroeconómicas sobre producción, ingresos, inversión y ahorros

natural monopoly a market that runs most efficiently when one large firm supplies all of the output (p. 166)
monopolio natural mercado que funciona más eficientemente cuando una sola empresa produce un bien o servicio

need something essential for survival (p. 3)
necesidad algo considerado esencial para sobrevivir

net worth total assets minus total liabilities (p. 427)
patrimonio neto bienes que posee una persona al deducirse sus deudas

newly industrialized country a less developed country that has made great progress toward developing its economy (p. 482)
país recientemente industrializado país no completamente industrializado que ha logrado grandes avances en el desarrollo de su economía

nominal GDP GDP measured in current prices (p. 310)
PBI nominal producto interno bruto medido en precios actuales

nondurable goods those goods that last a short period of time, such as food, light bulbs, and sneakers (p. 309)
bienes perecederos bienes que duran un corto período de tiempo como comida, bombillas y zapatos deportivos

nongovernmental organization an independent group that raises money and uses it to fund aid and development programs (p. 494)
organización no gubernamental grupo independiente que recauda dinero para financiar programas de ayuda y desarrollo

nonprice competition a way to attract customers through style, service, or location, but not a lower price (p. 175)
competencia sin precios estrategia para atraer consumidores enfocándose en el estilo, el servicio o la ubicación de un bien, sin tener que bajar su precio

nonprofit organization an institution that functions much like a business, but does not operate for the purpose of general profit (p. 209)
organización sin fines de lucro institución que funciona como una empresa, pero no opera con el propósito de generar ganancias

normal good a good that consumers demand more of when their incomes increase (p. 92)
bien normal bien que el consumidor demanda más cuando sus ingresos aumentan

O

obsolescence situation in which older products and processes become out-of-date (p. 59)
obsolescencia situación que ocurre cuando productos o procesos antiguos caen en desuso

offshoring the movement of some of a company's operations to another country (pp. 219, 505)

deslocalización traslado de las plantas productivas de una empresa a otro país

oligopoly a market structure in which a few large firms dominate a market (p. 177)
oligopolio estructura en la cual el mercado está dominado por unas pocas grandes empresas

open market operations the buying and selling of government securities in order to alter the supply of money (p. 433)
operaciones de mercado abierto compra y venta de valores del Estado para controlar la cantidad de dinero en circulación

open opportunity the principle that anyone can compete in the marketplace (p. 51)
oportunidad abierta principio que sostiene que cualquier persona puede competir en el mercado

operating budget a budget for day-to-day spending needs (p. 381)
presupuesto de operación presupuesto para los gastos diarios

operating cost the cost of operating a facility, such as a factory or a store (p. 122)
costo de operación costo de operar instalaciones como fábricas y tiendas

opportunity cost the most desirable alternative given up as the result of a decision (p. 9)
costo de oportunidad mejor alternativa que se desechó al tomarse una decisión

options contracts that give investors the right to buy or sell stock and other financial assets at a particular price until a specified future date (p. 295)
opciones contratos que le dan al inversionista el derecho de comprar o vender acciones u otros activos financieros a un determinado precio y dentro de un cierto período de tiempo

outside lag the time it takes for monetary policy to have an effect (p. 438)
demora externa cantidad de tiempo que demora en surtir efecto una política monetaria

outsourcing the practice of contracting with another company to do a specific job that would otherwise be done by a company's own workers (p. 219)
subcontratación práctica que consiste en contratar a otra compañía para realizar una tarea específica que los trabajadores de la compañía original podrían haber hecho

P

par value a bond's stated value, to be paid to the bondholder at maturity (p. 285)
valor nominal valor original de un bono u obligación que debe pagarse a su vencimiento

partnership a business organization owned by two or more persons who agree on a specific division of responsibilities and profits (p. 196)
sociedad dos o más personas organizadas para un fin comercial y con una división específica de responsabilidades y ganancias

patent a license that gives the inventor of a new product the exclusive right to sell it for a specific period of time (pp. 61, 167)
patente licencia que otorga al inventor de un nuevo producto el derecho exclusivo de venderlo por un determinado período de tiempo

patriotism love of one's country (p. 52)
patriotismo amor por el país propio

peak the height of an economic expansion, when real GDP stops rising (p. 315)
punto máximo máxima expansión económica, cuando el PIB cesa de crecer

per capita GDP a nation's gross domestic product divided by its population (p. 482)
PIB per cápita producto interno bruto de un país dividido entre su población

perfect competition a market structure in which a large number of firms all produce the same product and no single seller controls supply or price (p. 159)
competencia perfecta mercado en el que numerosas empresas producen el mismo producto y ninguna controla la oferta o el precio

personal exemption a set amount that taxpayers may subtract from their gross income for themselves, their spouse, and any dependents (p. 372)
deducción personal cantidad fija que el contribuyente puede deducir de su ingreso bruto a cuenta de sí mismo, su cónyuge y otros dependientes

personal property movable possessions or assets (p. 384)
propiedad personal activos o bienes muebles

physical capital the human-made objects used to create other goods and services (p. 6)
capital físico objetos construidos que se utilizan para crear bienes y servicios

population growth rate a measure of how rapidly a country's population increases in a given year (p. 487)
tasa de crecimiento de la población medida de cuán rápido crece la población de un país en un año

portfolio a collection of financial assets (p. 282)
portafolio conjunto de activos financieros

poverty rate the percentage of people who live in households with income below the official poverty line (p. 350)
tasa de pobreza porcentaje de personas que viven en hogares con un ingreso por debajo de la línea de pobreza

poverty threshold an income level below that which is needed to support families or households (pp. 68, 349)
nivel de pobreza ingreso por debajo del nivel necesario para mantener a una familia o un hogar

predatory pricing selling a product below cost for a short period of time to drive competitors out of the market (p. 180)
precios depredatorios vender un producto por debajo de su costo por un corto período de tiempo para sacar a los competidores del mercado

price ceiling a maximum price that can legally be charged for a good or service (p. 137)
precio tope precio máximo que un vendedor puede cobrar legalmente por un bien o servicio

price discrimination the division of consumers into groups based on how much they will pay for a good (p. 171)
discriminación de precios práctica que consiste en dividir a los consumidores en grupos según la cantidad que están dispuestos a pagar por un bien

price fixing an agreement among firms to charge one price for the same good (p. 179)
fijación de precios acuerdo entre compañías para cobrar un determinado precio por el mismo bien

price floor a minimum price for a good or service (p. 139)
precio mínimo límite inferior al que puede llegar el precio de un bien o servicio

price index a measurement that shows how the average price of a standard group of goods changes over time (p. 343)
índice de precios medida que muestra el cambio del precio promedio de un grupo de bienes estándar durante un tiempo determinado

price level the average of all prices in an economy (p. 313)
nivel de precios promedio de los precios en una economía

price war a series of competitive price cuts that lowers the market price below the cost of production (p. 179)
guerra de precios serie de cortes de precio competitivos que reduce el precio de mercado por debajo de su costo de producción

primary market a market for selling financial assets that can be redeemed only by the original holder (p. 290)
mercado primario mercado para vender activos financieros que sólo pueden ser cobrados por el propietario original

prime rate the rate of interest that banks charge on short-term loans to their best customers (p. 433)
tipo de interés preferencial tipo de interés que un banco aplica a los préstamos de corto plazo de sus mejores clientes

principal the amount of money borrowed (p. 268)
capital cantidad de dinero prestado

private property property that is owned by individuals or companies, not by the government or the people as a whole (p. 40)
propiedad privada propiedad que le pertenece a individuos o a compañías, no al gobierno o al público en general

private property rights the principle that people have the right to control their possessions and use them as they wish (p. 51)
derechos de propiedad privada principio según el cual una persona tiene el derecho de controlar y usar sus pertenencias como quiera

private sector the part of the economy that involves the transactions of individuals and businesses (p. 63)
sector privado parte de la economía que tiene que ver con los negocios de individuos y de compañías

privatization the process of selling businesses or services operated by the government to individual investors, and then allowing them to compete in the marketplace (pp. 43, 495)
privatización proceso de venta de compañías o servicios operados por el gobierno a inversionistas individuales para que compitan en el mercado

producer cooperative an agricultural marketing cooperative that helps members sell their products (p. 209)
cooperativa de productores cooperativa agraria que ayuda a sus miembros a vender sus productos

product market the arena of exchange in which households purchase goods and services from firms (p. 31)
mercado de productos lugar de intercambio comercial en el que una familia compra bienes y servicios de empresas

production possibilities curve a graph that shows alternative ways to use an economy's productive resources (p. 13)
curva de posibilidades de producción gráfico que muestra distintas maneras de utilizar los recursos de producción en una economía

production possibilities frontier a line on a production possibilities curve that shows the maximum possible output an economy can produce (p. 14)
frontera de posibilidades de producción línea en una curva de posibilidad de producción que indica el límite máximo de lo que puede producir una economía

productive capacity the maximum output that an economy can sustain over a period of time without increasing inflation (p. 400)
capacidad de producción volumen máximo de producción que una economía puede sostener por un período de tiempo sin que aumente la inflación

productivity of labor the quantity of output produced by a unit of labor (p. 226)
productividad cantidad de rendimiento que genera una unidad de trabajo

professional labor work that requires advanced skills and education (p. 229)
trabajo profesional trabajo que requiere habilidades y estudios avanzados

professional organization a nonprofit organization that works to improve the image, working conditions, and skill levels of people in particular occupations (p. 211)
organización profesional organización sin fines de lucro que busca mejorar la imagen, las condiciones de trabajo y la competencia técnica de individuos que ejercen una determinada profesión

profit the amount of money a business receives in excess of its expenses (p. 25)
ganancias cantidad de dinero que una compañía recibe al deducirse sus gastos

profit motive the incentive that drives individuals and business owners to improve their material well-being (p. 51)
motivación de ganancia incentivo que conlleva al individuo o compañía a mejorar su bienestar material

progressive tax a tax for which the percentage of income paid in taxes increases as income increases (p. 364)
impuesto progresivo impuesto cuyo porcentaje aumenta al aumentar el ingreso del contribuyente

property tax a tax based on real estate and other property (p. 366)
impuesto sobre la propiedad impuesto basado en bienes inmuebles y otros tipos de propiedad

proportional tax a tax for which the percentage of income paid in taxes remains the same at all income levels (p. 364)
impuesto proporcional impuesto cuyo porcentaje permanece constante en cualquier nivel de ingreso

prospectus an investment report that provides information to potential investors (p. 282)
prospecto documento que provee información pertinente a posibles inversionistas

protectionism the use of trade barriers to shield domestic industries from foreign competition (p. 457)
proteccionismo uso de barreras comerciales para proteger las industrias domésticas de los competidores extranjeros

public disclosure laws laws requiring companies to provide information about their products or services (p. 54)
ley de divulgación pública ley que exige que una compañía provea información acerca de sus productos o servicios

public good a shared good or service for which it would be inefficient or impractical to make consumers pay individually and to exclude those who did not pay (p. 62)
bien público bien que satisface una necesidad pública o colectiva por lo que resulta ineficiente hacer pagar a los consumidores individualmente

public interest the concerns of society as a whole (p. 53)
interés público preocupaciones de la sociedad en conjunto

public sector the part of the economy that involves the transactions of the government (p. 63)
sector público parte de la economía que tiene que ver con los negocios del gobierno

publicly held corporation a type of corporation that sells stock on the open market (p. 203)
compañía pública corporación que vende acciones en el mercado abierto

purchasing power the ability to purchase goods and services (p. 342)
poder adquisitivo capacidad para comprar bienes y servicios

put option a contract for selling stock at a particular price until a specified future date (p. 295)
opción de venta contrato para vender acciones a un determinado precio durante un período de tiempo preestablecido

Q

quantity supplied the amount that a supplier is willing and able to supply at a specific price (p. 109)
cantidad ofrecida cantidad que un proveedor está dispuesto a ofrecer por un precio específico

quantity theory the theory that too much money in the economy causes inflation (p. 346)
teoría de la cantidad teoría que establece que la presencia de mucho dinero en la economía causa inflación

R

rationing a system of allocating scarce goods and services using criteria other than price (p. 151)
racionamiento sistema de distribución de los bienes y servicios escasos usando un criterio que no se basa en el precio

real GDP GDP expressed in constant, or unchanging, prices (p. 310)
PIB real PIB expresado a precios constantes o invariables

real GDP per capital real GDP divided by the total population of a country (p. 323)
PIB real per cápita PIB real dividido por la población total de un país

real property land and any permanent structures on the land to which a person has legal title (p. 384)
inmueble terreno y cualquier estructura permanente en el terreno que le pertenece a una persona según un título legal

recession a prolonged economic contraction (p. 316)
recesión contracción económica prolongada

referendum a proposed law submitted directly to the public (p. 58)
referendo propuesta de ley que se somete directamente al público

regressive tax a tax for which the percentage of income paid in taxes decreases as income increases (p. 366)
impuesto regresivo impuesto para el cual el porcentaje de ingresos que se paga disminuye a medida que el ingreso aumenta

regulation government intervention in a market that affects the production of a good (p. 125)
regulación intervención del gobierno en un mercado que afecta la producción de un bien

remittances cash payments sent by workers who have migrated to a new country to family members in their home country (p. 505)
remesas pagos en efectivo que les envían los trabajadores inmigrantes a sus familiares en sus países de origen

rent control a price ceiling placed on apartment rent (p. 137)
control de renta precio tope del alquiler de apartamentos

representative money objects that have value because the holder can exchange them for something else of value (p. 254)
dinero representativo objetos que tienen valor porque su dueño lo puede cambiar por otros objetos de valor

required reserve ratio the fraction of deposits that banks are required to keep in reserve (p. 430)
tasa de encaje fracción de los depósitos que los bancos tienen que guardar en reserva

reserve requirements the amount of reserves that banks are required to keep on hand (p. 421)
encaje cantidad de reservas que los bancos deben mantener disponibles

reserves deposits that a bank keeps readily available as opposed to lending them out (p. 421)
reservas depósitos que un banco tiene disponible, en vez de prestarlos

return the money an investor receives above and beyond the sum of money initially invested (p. 282)
rendimiento dinero que un inversionista recibe por encima de la suma de dinero original que invirtió

revenue the income received by a government from taxes and other nontax sources (p. 364)
ingreso dinero recibido por un gobierno que proviene de los impuestos y otras fuentes que no son fiscales

right-to-work law a measure that bans mandatory union membership (p. 238)
ley de derecho al trabajo medida que establece que no es obligatorio ser miembro de un sindicato

royalties the share of earnings given by a franchisee as payment to the franchiser (p. 201)
regalías ganancias compartidas que otorga el dueño de una franquicia como pago a quien otorga la concesión

S

safety net a set of government programs that protect people who face unfavorable economic conditions (p. 26)
programas de ayuda social grupo de programas del gobierno que protegen a las personas con dificultades económicas

sales tax a tax based on goods or services that are sold (p. 366)
impuesto a las ventas impuesto sobre los bienes y servicios que se venden

sanctions actions a nation or group of nations takes in order to punish or put pressure on another nation (p. 456)
sanciones acciones que una nación o un grupo de naciones toma para castigar o presionar a otra nación

saving income not used for consumption (p. 325)
ahorro ingreso que no se consume

savings bond a low-denomination bond issued by the United States government (p. 287)
bono de ahorro bono de baja denominación ofrecido por el gobierno de los Estados Unidos

savings rate the proportion of disposable income that is saved (p. 325)
tasa de ahorro proporción de los ingresos disponibles que se ahorran

scarcity the principle that limited amounts of goods and services are available to meet unlimited wants (p. 4)
escacez situación en la que existe una cantidad limitada de bienes y servicios disponibles para satisfacer deseos ilimitados

screening effect the theory that the completion of college indicates to employers that a job applicant is intelligent and hard working (p. 221)
efecto de selección teoría de que completar estudios universitarios indica que un candidato a un empleo es inteligente y trabaja duro

search costs the financial and opportunity costs that consumers pay when searching for a good or service (p. 146)
costo de búsqueda costos financieros y de oportunidad que los consumidores pagan mientras buscan un bien o servicio

seasonal unemployment type of unemployment that occurs as a result of harvest schedules, vacations, or when industries make seasonal shifts in their production schedule (p. 338)
desempleo estacional tipo de desempleo que ocurre durante las cosechas, las vacaciones o cuando las industrias establecen turnos durante ciertos períodos especiales de su calendario de producción

secondary market a market for reselling financial assets (p. 290)
mercado secundario mercado en el que se revenden bienes financieros

self-interest an individual's own personal gain (p. 33)
interés personal beneficio de una persona

semi-skilled labor work that requires minimal specialized skills and education (p. 229)
trabajo semicalificado trabajo que requiere destrezas especializadas y educación mínimas

service cooperative a type of cooperative that provides a service rather than a good (p. 209)
cooperativa de servicios tipo de cooperativa que ofrece un servicio en vez de un bien

services the actions or activities that one person performs for another (p. 3)
servicios acciones o actividades que una persona ejecuta para otra persona

share a portion of stock (p. 291)
acción porción del capital de una empresa

shortage a situation in which consumers want more of a good or service than producers are willing to make available at a particular price (pp. 4, 134)
escasez situación en la que los consumidores quieren un bien o servicio en una cantidad mayor a la que los productores están dispuestos a producir a un precio determinado

skilled labor work that requires specialized skills and training (p. 229)
trabajo calificado trabajo que requiere destrezas y capacitación profesional especializadas

socialism a range of economic and political systems based on the belief that wealth should be evenly distributed throughout society (p. 36)
socialismo serie de sistemas económicos y políticos que se basan en la creencia de que la riqueza de una sociedad debe ser distribuida en partes iguales entre sus miembros

sole proprietorship a business owned and managed by a single individual (p. 191)
empresa unipersonal negocio que le pertenece y es administrado por un solo individuo

special economic zone designated regions that operate under different economic laws from the rest of the country, in order to attract foreign investment and promote exports (p. 498)

zona económica especial región designada en un país donde se promueve la inversión extranjera, los negocios toman la mayoría de sus decisiones y se permite el funcionamiento de compañías extranjeras

specialization the concentration of the productive efforts of individuals and businesses on a limited number of activities (p. 30)
especialización concentración del esfuerzo productivo de las personas y los negocios en un número limitado de actividades

specie coined money, usually gold or silver, used to back paper money (p. 254)
metálico dinero en monedas, generalmente de oro o plata, que se usa para respaldar el papel moneda

speculation the practice of making high-risk investments with borrowed money in hopes of getting a big return (p. 298)
especulación práctica que consiste en hacer inversiones de alto riesgo con dinero prestado, con la esperanza de obtener una ganancia alta

stabilization program an agreement between a debtor nation and the International Monetary Fund in which the nation agrees to change its economic policy to match IMF goals (p. 493)
programa de estabilización acuerdo entre una nación deudora y el Fondo Monetario Internacional mediante el cual la nación se compromente a cambiar su política económica para cumplir con los objetivos del FMI

stagflation a decline in real GDP combined with a rise in the price level (p. 316)
estanflación disminución del PIB real combinado con un aumento de precios

standard of living level of economic prosperity (p. 27)
nivel de vida nivel de prosperidad económica

start-up costs the expenses a new business must pay before it can begin to produce and sell goods (p. 162)
costos de inicio gastos que un negocio nuevo debe hacer antes de que comience a producir y vender bienes

stock a certificate of ownership in a corporation (p. 202)
acción certificado de propiedad de parte de una corporación

stock exchange a market for buying and selling stock (p. 294)
bolsa de valores mercado en el cual se compran y venden acciones

stock split the division of each single share of a company's stock into more than one share (p. 293)
desdoble división de cada acción de una compañía en más de una acción

stockbroker a person who links buyers and sellers of stock (p. 293)
corredor de bolsa persona que conecta a compradores y vendedores de la bolsa

store of value something that keeps its value if it is stored rather than spent (p. 251)
mantenimiento del valor algo que mantiene su valor si se guarda, no cuando se gasta

strike an organized work stoppage intended to force an employer to address union demands (p. 237)
huelga suspensión organizada del trabajo, que se ejecuta para obligar a un empleador a cumplir con las peticiones de un sindicato

structural unemployment type of unemployment that occurs when workers' skills do not match those needed for the jobs available (p. 336)
desempleo estructural tipo de desempleo que ocurre cuando las destrezas de los trabajadores no cubren las necesidades de los empleos disponibles

subsidy a government payment that supports a business or market (p. 124)
subsidio pago del gobierno que apoya un negocio o mercado

subsistence agriculture level of farming in which a person raises only enough food to feed his or her family (p. 486)
agricultura de subsistencia tipo de agricultura en el que una persona sólo cosecha lo necesario para mantenerse a sí misma y a su familia

substitutes goods that are used in place of one another (p. 96)
sustitutos bienes que se usan para remplazar otros bienes

substitution effect when consumers react to an increase in a good's price by consuming less of that good and more of a substitute good (p. 87)
efecto de sustitución reacción de los consumidores ante el aumento del precio de un bien, que consiste en disminuir el consumo de un producto y aumentar el consumo de un sustituto

supply the amount of goods available (p. 109)
oferta cantidad disponible de bienes

supply curve a graph of the quantity supplied of a good at various prices (p. 113)
curva de la oferta gráfica que representa la cantidad ofrecida de un bien a varios precios

supply schedule a chart that lists how much of a good a supplier will offer at various prices (p. 112)
tabla de la demanda tabla que muestra la cantidad de un bien que un proveedor ofrecerá a diferentes precios

supply shock a sudden shortage of a good (p. 151)
shock de la oferta escasez repentina de un bien

supply-side economics a school of thought based on the idea that the supply of goods drives the economy (p. 404)
economía por el lado de la oferta escuela de pensamiento que se basa en la idea de que la oferta de bienes mueve la economía

surplus when quantity supplied is more than quantity demanded (p. 136)
superávit condición en la que la oferta es mayor que la demanda

sustainable development goal of meeting current development needs without using up resources needed by future generations (p. 506)
desarrollo sostenible objetivo que consiste en cubrir las necesidades de desarrollo actuales sin gastar todos los recursos que necesitarán las generaciones futuras

T

tariff a tax on imported goods (pp. 374, 455)
arancel impuesto que se aplica a las importaciones

tax a required payment to a local, state, or national government (p. 364)
impuesto tributo o pago hecho al gobierno local, estatal o nacional

tax assessor an official who determines the value of property (p. 385)
tasador especialista que determina el valor de una propiedad

tax base the income, property, good, or service that is subject to a tax (p. 366)
base imponible ingreso, propiedad, bien o servicio bajo obligación tributaria

tax credit a variable amount that taxpayers may subtract from the total amount of their income tax (p. 372)
crédito fiscal cantidad variable que los contribuyentes pueden restar del total de su deuda tributaria

tax deduction a variable amount that taxpayers may subtract from their gross income (p. 372)
deducción fiscal cantidad variable que los contribuyentes pueden restar de su ingreso bruto

tax exempt not subject to taxes (p. 383)
libre de impuestos exento de impuestos

tax incentive the use of taxation to discourage or encourage certain types of behavior (p. 374)
incentivo fiscal régimen tributario que tiene como objetivo estimular o no fomentar ciertas actividades económicas

tax return a form used to file income taxes (p. 370)
declaración de impuestos formulario en el cual se reporta un impuesto, como la declaración de impuestos sobre la renta

taxable income the earnings on which tax must be paid; total income minus exemptions and deductions (p. 372)
ingreso imponible entradas sobre las cuales se pagan impuestos; ingreso total menos exenciones y deducciones

technological progress an increase in efficiency gained by producing more output without using more inputs (p. 327)
progreso tecnológico incremento en la eficiencia al producir más usando menos recursos

thinking at the margin the process of deciding how much more or less to do (p. 11)
pensar al margen decidir si se debe hacer o usar una cantidad mayor de algún recurso

tight money policy a monetary policy that reduces the money supply (p. 436)
política monetaria restrictiva política monetaria que reduce la oferta de dinero

total cost the sum of fixed costs plus variable costs (p. 119)
costo total suma de costos fijos y costos variables

total revenue the total amount of money a company receives by selling goods or services (p. 103)
ingreso total cantidad total de dinero que recibe una compañía al vender bienes y servicios

trade association nonprofit organizations that promote the interests of particular industries (p. 212)
asociación mercantil organizaciones sin fines de lucro que promueven los intereses de ciertas industrias en particular

trade barrier a means of preventing a foreign product or service from freely entering a nation's territory (p. 455)
barreras comerciales medida preventiva que reduce el flujo de bienes importados a un país

trade deficit situation in which a nation imports more goods and services than it exports (p. 468)
déficit comercial situación en la cual las importaciones de bienes y servicios de un país son más altas que sus exportaciones

trade surplus situation in which a nation exports more goods and services than it imports (p. 468)
superávit comercial situación en la cual las exportaciones de bienes y servicios de un país son más altas que las importaciones

trade war a cycle of escalating trade barriers (p. 457)
guerra comercial ciclo en el cual las barreras comerciales escalan

trade-off the alternatives that we give up when we choose one course of action over another (p. 8)
compensación acto de entregar un beneficio para obtener otro beneficio mayor

traditional economy an economic system that relies on habit, custom, or ritual to decide the three key economic questions (p. 28)
economía tradicional sistema económico que depende de hábitos, costumbres o rituales para decidir las tres preguntas económicas clave

Treasury bill a government bond with a maturity date of 26 weeks or less (p. 409)
Bono del Tesoro documento emitido por el Estado con un vencimiento a 26 semanas o menos

Treasury bond a government bond that is issued in terms of 30 years (p. 409)
Bono del Estado documento emitido por el Estado con un vencimiento a 30 años

Treasury note a government bond with a term of from 2 to 10 years (p. 409)
Pagarés del Tesoro documento emitido por el Estado con un vencimiento de 2 a 10 años

trough the lowest point of an economic contraction, when real GDP stops falling (p. 316)
punto mínimo punto más bajo en una contracción económica, cuando el PIB real deja de descender

trust an illegal grouping of companies that discourages competition, similar to a cartel (p. 181)
trust alianza sin fundamentación legal entre compañías para evitar la competencia

U

underemployed working at a job for which one is overqualified or working part-time when full-time work is desired (p. 340)
subempleado estar calificado en exceso para un trabajo o trabajar a tiempo parcial cuando se desea trabajar a tiempo completo

underutilization the use of fewer resources than an economy is capable of using (p. 15)
subutilización capacidad no utilizada de los recursos que una economía posee

unemployment rate the percentage of a nation's labor force that is unemployed (p. 339)
tasa de desempleo porcentaje de la población nacional sin empleo

Uniform Partnership Act a uniform law establishing rules for partnerships, which partnerships must follow if they have no partnership agreement (p. 198)
Ley de Estandarización de Sociedades de Personas ley que establece las reglas que los socios deben seguir si no existe un contrato de asociación

unit of account a means for comparing the values of goods and services (p. 251)
unidad de cuenta medida para comparar los valores de bienes y servicios

unitary elastic describes demand whose elasticity is exactly equal to one (p. 98)
elasticidad unitaria relación de demanda con un coeficiente igual a uno

unskilled labor work that requires no specialized skills, education, or training (p. 229)
trabajo no especializado trabajo que no requiere habilidades, estudios o entrenamiento especializados

V

variable a factor that can change (p. 112)
variable factor que puede cambiar

variable cost a cost that rises or falls depending on the quantity produced (p. 118)
costo variable costo que aumenta o disminuye cuando la cantidad producida incrementa o disminuye

vertical merger two or more firms involved in different stages of producing the same good or service (p. 206)
fusión vertical agrupación de dos o más compañías involucradas en distintas fases de la producción de un bien o servicio

voluntary exchange the principle that people may decide what, when, and how they want to buy and sell (p. 51)
intercambio voluntario principio según el cual toda persona puede decidir cómo, cuándo y qué vender

W

wage-price spiral the process by which rising wages cause higher prices, and higher prices cause higher wages (p. 347)
espiral salarios-precios aumento de los precios, producido por el aumento de los salarios, que resulta en una nueva demanda de aumento de los salarios

want something that people desire but that is not necessary for survival (p. 3)
deseo algo que una persona quiere, pero que no es necesario para sobrevivir

welfare government aid to the poor (p. 69)
asistencia social ayuda que el gobierno presta a los pobres

white-collar worker someone who works in a professional or clerical job and who usually earns a weekly salary (p. 239)
empleado de oficina persona que desempeña un trabajo de tipo profesional o administrativo y que generalmente gana un salario semanal

withholding taking tax payments out of an employee's pay before he or she receives it (p. 370)
retención porcentaje que se descuenta del salario de un empleado a cuenta del pago de impuestos

work ethic a commitment to the value of work (p. 61)
ética profesional respeto al valor del trabajo

workfare a program requiring work in exchange for temporary government assistance (p. 356)
workfare programa ofrecido por el gobierno mediante el cual las personas deben trabajar para poder recibir asistencia social temporal

Y

yield the annual rate of return on a bond if the bond is held to maturity (p. 285)
rendimiento tasa anual de rendimiento que da un bono u obligación a su vencimiento

Z

zoning laws laws in a city or town that designate certain areas, or zones, for residential and business use (p. 193)
reglamentos de zonificación leyes que designan ciertas áreas o zonas de una ciudad para uso residencial o comercial

R-19

Note: Entries with a page number followed by a *(c)* denote reference to a chart on that page; those followed by a *(p)* denote a photo; those followed by an *(m)* denote a map; those followed by a *(g)* denote a graph.

A

B

C

INDEX

D

E

F

INDEX

INDEX

INDEX

INDEX

Q

R

S

INDEX

T

INDEX

Y

Z

Acknowledgments

Staff Credits

The people who made up the ***Prentice Hall Economics*** team—representing Bilingual Editorial, Design, Editorial, Editorial Services, Marketing, and Publishing Services—are listed below. Boldface type denotes the core team members.

Scott Baker, **Lynn Burke,** Jennifer Ciccone, Michael DiMaria, **Anne Falzone, Diane Grossman,** Judie Grudin, Tom Guarino, Monduane Harris, **Brian Heyward, Michael Hornbostel,** Paul Hughes, Judie Jozokos, **John Kingston, Kate Koch, Ann Lurie, Marian Manners, Constance McCarty, Michael McLaughlin,** Angelina Mendez, Claudi Mimó, **Xavier Niz, Roger Ochoa, Linda Punskovsky, Maureen Raymond, Jennifer Ribnicky,** Charlene Rimsa, Amanda Seldera, Melissa Shustyk, **Rose Sievers, Frank Tangredi,** Kristen Van Etten, Ana Sofia Villaveces, **Rachel Winter**

Art/Map Credits

Art: Keithley and Associates (all charts/graphs except where noted) Jennifer Ribnicky: 70–71, S-1, S-3–S-9. John Kingston: S-19–S-20.

Illustrations: Asaf Hanuka/Gerald & Cullen Rapp: 3, 23, 49, 85, 109, 133, 155, 159, 191, 217, 249, 277, 307, 335, 363, 391, 419, 447, and 481 plus all *How the Economy Works* feature's art. Marcelo Baez/Shannon Associates: all *Economics & You* feature's art. Funnel Inc.: 32, 50, 204, 308, 364, 393, 421, 459. Doug Holgate/Shannon Associates: 228 and 292. **Personal Finance Illustrations:** Dale Rutter PF 8; Spork PF 12; John Sledd PF 16–17; Shane Rebenschied PF 22–23; Christopher Short PF 24; Nick Dimitriadis PF 26–27; Sean Kane PF 29; Mitch Mortimer PF 42; Ernest Albanese PF 45; John Sledd PF 46.

Infographics: Leslie Carlson/Martha Productions Inc. with additional design by John Kingston: 06, 52, 178, 200, 222, 271, 321, 366, 457, 505.

Maps: GeoNova.

Photo Credits

Every effort has been made to credit all vendors. Any omissions brought to our attention will be corrected in subsequent printings.

Cover and End Paper images: Speakers: © Christopher Gould/Getty Images; **Hi-rise construction:** © Luis Castaneda Inc./The Image Bank/Getty Images; **Central Park:** © Mitchell Funk/Getty Images; **Traffic:** © Kim Steele/Getty Images; **House construction:** © Lester Lefkowitz/The Image Bank/Getty Images; **Basketball, Cows, Satellite Dish, Piggy Bank, Wood, Pulley, Grass, U.S. Capitol, Water Cooler, Condiments, Conveyor Belt, Dog/cat:** Getty Images; **Stock Board:** © Mark Segal/Getty Images; **Tractor:** Hemera; **Wind Turbines:** © Spike Mafford/Getty Images; **Recycle Bin:** © ThinkStock/SuperStock; **Tomato & Diploma/Books:** Jupiter Royalty Free; **ATM, Sneakers, Coins, Game Controller:** Pearson Curriculum Group

Title page: istockphoto.com/KATIV; bkarn, Jan Halaska/Photo Researchers, Inc.

ii, Dynamic Graphics; **iii & v,** istockphoto.com/Emrah Turudu; **vi t,** Riley & Riley Photography, Inc./Picturesque, Inc/Jupiter Images – Workbookstock; **vi b,** istockphoto.com/Erick Nguyen; **vii tm,** © Joseph Sohm/Visions of America/Corbis; **vii tl,** istockphoto.com/Emrah Turudu; **vii tr,** Gary D. Gold/Creative Eye/MIRA.com; **viii t,** istockphoto.com/Emrah Turudu; **viii tm,** David Bishop/Phototake; **viii tr,** Riley & Riley Photography, Inc./Picturesque, Inc/Jupiter Images – Workbookstock; **ix tm,** © Joseph Sohm/Visions of America/Corbis; **ix tr,** Gary D. Gold/Creative Eye/MIRA.com; **ix tl,** Riley & Riley Photography, Inc./Picturesque, Inc/Jupiter Images – Workbookstock; **x tm,** © Joseph Sohm/Visions of America/Corbis; **x tl,** istockphoto.com/Emrah Turudu; **x tr,** Gary D. Gold/Creative Eye/MIRA.com; **xi tm,** © Joseph Sohm/Visions of America/Corbis; **xi tl,** istockphoto.com/Emrah Turudu; **xi tr,** Gary D. Gold/Creative Eye/MIRA.com; **xii tm,** © Joseph Sohm/Visions of America/Corbis; **xii tl,** istockphoto.com/Emrah Turudu; **xii tr,** Gary D. Gold/Creative Eye/MIRA.com; **xii b,** istockphoto.com/joaquin ayllon; **xiii tm,** © Joseph Sohm/Visions of America/Corbis; **xiii tl,** istockphoto.com/Emrah Turudu; **xiii tr,** Gary D. Gold/Creative Eye/MIRA.com; **xiii b,** istockphoto.com/joaquin ayllon; **xiv tm,** © Joseph Sohm/Visions of America/Corbis; **xiv tl,** istockphoto.com/Emrah Turudu; **xiv tr,** Gary D. Gold/Creative Eye/MIRA.com; **xiv b,** istockphoto.com/joaquin ayllon; **xv tl,** Gary D. Gold/Creative Eye/MIRA.com; **xv tm,** Jan Halaska/Photo Researchers, Inc.; **xv tr,** istockphoto.com/Christine Balderas; **xv mr,** istockphoto.com/Jim Jurica; **xv br,** David Bishop/Phototake; **xvi,** Riley & Riley Photography, Inc./Picturesque, Inc/Jupiter Images – Workbookstock; **xx t,** New York, 2002 Photo by Martin Rowe, Lantern Books; **xx m,** Darren McCollester/Stringer/Getty Images; **xxiii,** © Danny Kerr; **xxiv r,** Shutterstock, Inc.; **xxiv l,** Rui Vale de Sousa/Shutterstock, Inc.; **xxviii-xxxii,** Dynamic Graphics

Photo Credits

01, istockphoto.com/Kativ; **02 t,** Bill Aron/PhotoEdit, Inc.; **02 b,** istockphoto.com/joaquin ayllon; **03 b,** istockphoto.com/joaquin ayllon; **03,** © Joe Sohm/The Image Works; **04,** Scott Olson/Getty Images; **06 bkgrnd,** istockphoto.com/yhloon; **06,** Eric Gevaert/1stockphoto.com; **10 b,** www.CartoonStock.com; **10 t,** istockphoto.com/stocksnapper; **14,** FRANK & ERNEST: © Thaves/Dist. by Newspaper Enterprise Association, Inc.; **15,** AP/Wide World; **16,** © Richard Cummins/SuperStock; **18,** www.CartoonBank.com; **20,** istockphoto.com/Mark Evans; **22,** © David H. Wells/Corbis; **25 t,** AP/Wide World Photos; **28,** © Gail Mooney-Kelly/Alamy; **29 tr,** AP/Wide World Photos; **29 l,** © Najlah Feanny/Corbis; **30 l,** Edward Lallo, Courtesy of Mary Kay Cosmetics, Inc.; **30 r,** Pearson; **32 b,** www.CartoonStock.com; **33 t,** Corbis/Bettmann; **33 b,** The Granger Collection, New York; **34,** www.CartoonStock.com; **36,** Jeremy Nicholl/Woodfin Camp & Associates, Inc.; **37,** The Granger Collection, New York; **39,** © Barbara Davidson/Dallas Morning News/Corbis; **42,** © Jack Sullivan/Alamy; **44,** Pearson Education; **46,** istockphoto.com/edfuentesg; **47,** © Fritz Hoffmann/Corbis; **48,** Tony Freeman/PhotoEdit, Inc.; **50 tr,** © Plain and Simple Books; **50 tl,** Pearson; **50 tm,** istockphoto.com/Andy Dean; **50 rm,** istockphoto.com/Simon McConico; **50 bl,** istockphoto.com/David H. Lewis; **50 br,** Superstudio/Getty Images, Inc.; **50 bm,** © Todd Gipstein/Corbis; **52,** istockphoto.com/Jan Rysavy; **53 r,** Seth Wenig/Reuters/Corbis; **53 tl,** AP/Wide World Photos; **55,** www.CartoonStock.com; **56 r,** © Tom & Dee Ann McCarthy/Corbis; **56 l,** RICHARD NOWITZ/NGS Image Collection/National Geographic Society; **57,** istockphoto/ictor; **58 l,** © David Butow/Corbis SABA; **58 tr,** David Young-Wolff; **58 m,** Jeff Greenberg/PhotoEdit, Inc.; **58 br,** Tony Freeman/PhotoEdit, Inc.; **59,** Tony Bee/Photolibrary.com; **60,** © David Young-Wolff/PhotoEdit, Inc.; **60 r,** © Entrepreneur, Summser 2008; **61,** AP/Wide World Photos; **62,** istockphoto.com/Ben Russell; **63,** AP/Wide World Photos; **66,** istockphoto.com/Yan-chun Tung; **67,** EPA; **68,** Time & Life Pictures/Getty Images; **70 l,** © Corbis; **70 r,** © Bettmann/Corbis; **71 tl,** Jose Luis Pelaez, Inc/Blend Images/Getty Images, Inc.; **71 bl,** Pearson Education Curriculum Group; **71 tr,** Brooks Kraft/Corbis; **71 br,** AP/Wide World Photos; **72 t,** © Dennis MacDonald/PhotoEdit, Inc.; **72 b,** © Mark Richards/PhotoEdit, Inc.; **74,** Shutterstock, Inc.; **75 bl,** Gary Brookins/Richmond Times Dispatch; **82 m,** www.CartoonStock.com; **82 tr,** Linda McCarthy; **82 br,** David Bishop/Phototake; **82 bl,** Jan Halaska/Photo Researchers, Inc.; **83,** ©Joe Sohm/The Image Works; **84,** © Max Whittaker/Corbis; **86 tl,** Topeka Capital-Journal, David Eulitt AP/Wide World Photos; **86 b,** Spencer Grant/PhotoEdit, Inc.; **89,** Time & Life Pictures/Getty Images; **91,** © MARC SEROTA/Reuters/Corbis; **93,** © Bill Stormont/Corbis; **94 t,** A. Ramey/PhotoEdit, Inc.; **95 bl,** Tony Freeman/PhotoEdit, Inc.; **95 b,** AP/Wide World Photos; **95 tl,** First Vintage Books, 1985; **96,** © J. A. Kraulis/Masterfile; **99,** Brian Duffy/Des Moines Register; **102,** Andy Crawford and Steve Gorton © Dorling Kindersley; **106,** istockphoto.com/Pamela Moore; **107,** www.CartoonStock.com; **108,** Scott Olson/Getty Images; **110 t,** © Edward Rozzo/Corbis; **110 b,** © Joel W. Rogers/Corbis; **111,** www.CartoonStock.com; **115,** © Catherine Karnow/Corbis; **116,** Jeff Greenberg/PhotoEdit, Inc.; **122,** Bill Pugliano/Getty Images; **123 r,** Chris Jones/Corbis; **123 l,** istockphoto.com/Andrew Manley; **126 bkgrnd,** © ML Sinibaldi/Corbis; **126 m2,** Mehau Kulyk/Photo Researchers, Inc.; **126 m4,** © Mark E. Gibson/Corbis; **126 m3,** © Kevin Fleming/Corbis; **126 m1,** istockphoto.com/David Freund; **126 tr,** © Firefly Productions/Corbis; **127 l,** © Ray Stubblebine/Reuters/Corbis; **127 r,** © Peter Foley/epa/Corbis; **130,** Vivian Moos/Corbis; **132,** © Lauren Zeid/eStock Photo; **132 b,** istockphoto.com/joaquin ayllon; **133 b,** istockphoto.com/joaquin ayllon; **135 b,** www.CartoonStock.com; **137,** © courtesy of City Harvest <http://www.cityharvest.org/>; Photo by Danny Bright; **140,** Nick Anderson/Cartoonist Group; **141,** Robert Brenner/PhotoEdit, Inc.; **142,** AP/Wide World Photos; **146 t,** © Kim Kulish/Corbis; **146 tl,** Getty Images, Inc.; **149,** T. Kruesselmann/Corbis Zefa Collection; **150,** © Scott Barrow, Inc./SuperStock; **150 t,** Dynamic Graphics; **152 l,** The Granger Collection, New York; **152 r,** AP/Wide World Photos; **156,** Jean-Paul Ferrero/Minden Pictures; **157 bl,** Mike Davies, the Journal News/TMS; **158,** Nigel Kinrade/Sports Illustrated; **161 b,** www.CartoonStock.com; **163 l,** Copyright ©GEMMA GIANNINI/Grant Heilman Photography—All rights reserved.; **163 r,** © Digital Vision/Alamy; **164,** istockphoto.com/Tomas Bercic; **167 l,** The Granger Collection, New York; **167 r,** © 1998 Applewood Books; **169,** Terrell Lloyd/NFL/Getty Images; **172 m,** © 2006 Royalty-Free/Corbis; **172 r,** Chip Henderson; **172 l,** © Peter Titmuss/Alamy; **173 t,** © Tom Grill/Corbis; **173,** Robert Harbison; **174,** istockphoto.com/Soren Pilman; **178,** istockphoto.com/Andrew Penner; **180,** The Granger Collection, New York; **181 t,** © Corbis; **181 b,** istockphoto.com/Jeremy Swinborne; **186,** istockphoto.com/Monika Adamczyk; **187,** © Copyright 2006 Eric Allie/Cagle Cartoons. All rights reserved.; **188 m,** FRANK & ERNEST: © Thaves/Dist. by Newspaper Enterprise Association, Inc.; **188 tr,** Linda McCarthy; **188 br,** David Bishop/Phototake; **188 bl,** Jan Halaska/Photo Researchers, Inc.; **189,** © Masterfile; **190,** Jeff Greenberg/PhotoEdit, Inc.; **192,** Connie Coleman/Getty Images; **193,** © Kevin Dodge/Masterfile; **195,** www.CartoonBank.com; **197,** Tony Freeman/PhotoEdit, Inc.; **200 1,** Alan Schein/Corbis; **200 2,** istockphoto.com/Eric Gevaert; **200 3,** Dragan Trifunovic/Shutterstock; **200 4,** istockphoto.com; **203,** Pepsi-Cola North America; **204 r,** www.CartoonStock.com; **205 m,** AP/Wide World Photos; **205 mr,** SolarCity; **205,** © 3M. Photo by Pearson; **209 t,** © Steven Dahlman/SuperStock; **209 b,** "Mike Mergen/The New York Times/Redux"; **210,** Zhu Jianguo/ChinaFotoPress/Getty Images; **211,** Darren McCollester/Stringer/Getty Images; **212,** Atlantic Features Syndicate/Mark Parisi; **214,** Kathryn Bell/Shutterstock, Inc.; **216,** NASA/JPL/UA/Lockheed Martin; **218,** istockphoto.com/stockcam; **220,** istockphoto.com/Skip ODonnell; **222,** © Nikhil Gangavane/Dreamstime.com; **223,** AP/Wide World Photos; **224,** Rob Marmion/Shutterstock, Inc.; **227,** © James Leynse/Corbis; **228 tr,** istockphoto.com/malcolm romain; **231,** www.cartoonstock.com; **234 tl,** © James L. Amos/Corbis; **234 t,** © Gideon Mendel/Corbis; **236 t,** The Granger Collection, New York; **236 b,** Photo by Time Life Pictures/Time Magazine, © Time Inc./Time Life Pictures/Getty Images; **236 bm,** AP/Wide World Photos; **236 tm,** Underwood & Underwood/Corbis; **237 r,** AP/Wide World Photos; **237 tl,** © Bettmann/Corbis; **242,** © Marmaduke St. John/Alamy; **244,** AP/Wide World Photos; **246 m,** © The New Yorker Collection 1970 Alan Dunn from cartoonbank.com. All rights reserved.; **246 tr,** Linda McCarthy; **246 br,** David Bishop/Phototake; **246 bl,** Jan Halaska/Photo Researchers, Inc.; **247,** Spencer Platt/Getty Images; **248,** Tetra Images/Getty Images; **250 b,** Kate Warren/© Dorling Kindersley; **252,** © Bob Daemmrich/PhotoEdit, Inc.; **253 l,** JoAnn Frederick/Mira.com; **253 tr,** U.S. Treasury Dept.; **253 br,** Pearson; **254 t,** That's Life © Mike Twohy. All rights reserved. Used with permission of Mike Twohy and the Cartoonist Group; **256,** Pearson Education Curriculum Group; **257,** The Granger Collection, New York; **258,** The Granger Collection, New York; **260 r,** © Bettmann/Corbis; **260 tl,** Stephen Chernin/Getty Images; **262,** Spencer Grant/PhotoEdit, Inc.; **268,** © Ed Bock/Corbis; **269,** Ian Mckinnell/Getty Images; **271,** LEE JAE-WON/Reuters/Corbis; **272 r,** Marc Schlossman/Getty Images; **272 ml,** Pearson; **272 bl,** istockphoto.com/Jesus Jauregui; **272 tl,** Pearson; **274,** The Granger Collection, New York; **276,** AP/Wide World Photos; **278,** © Artiga Photo/Corbis; **281 b,** istockphoto.com/Ravi Tahilramani; **281 t,** © Alan Schein/zefa/Corbis; **282,** www.CartoonBank.com; **284,** © Images.com/Corbis; **291,** White Packert/Getty Images, Inc.; **292,** © Rosandich-Rothco Cartoons; **297,** © Justin Lane/epa/Corbis; **298,** AP/Wide World Photos; **299 tr,** © Bettmann/Corbis; **299 tl,** © Corbis; **299,** © Bettmann/Corbis; **303,** www.CartoonStock.com; **304 m,** Mike Peters/

Acknowledgments

Cartoonist Group; **304 tr,** Linda McCarthy; **304 br,** David Bishop/Phototake; **304 bl,** Jan Halaska/Photo Researchers, Inc.; **305,** © C. Devan/zefa/Corbis; **306 t,** © age fotostock/SuperStock; **308,** istockphoto.com/bluestocking; **317 rb,** FRANK & ERNEST: © Thaves/Dist. by Newspaper Enterprise Association, Inc.; **320,** © Bettmann/Corbis; **327 t,** Digital Vision; **328 b,** AP/Wide World Photos; **328 t,** Jeff Greenberg/Omni; **329,** © George B. Diebold/Corbis; **332,** istockphoto.com/Kutberk; **334,** Getty Images, Inc.; **338 bl,** © Bob Sacha/Corbis; **340,** © 2008 The Howroyd Group; **342 bl,** istockphoto.com/YinYang; **344 b,** Adam Zyglis, The Buffalo News/Cagle Cartooons. All rights reserved.; **344 t,** istockphoto.com/pertusinas; **349,** © Jeff Greenberg/The Image Works; **352,** Toby Herr of Project Match; **354 b,** Scott Olson/Getty Images, Inc.; **354 tl,** AP/Wide World Photos; **355,** Spencer Grant/PhotoEdit, Inc.; **358,** shutterstock, Inc.; **360 m,** www.CartoonStock.com; **360 tr,** Linda McCarthy; **360 br,** David Bishop/Phototake; **360 bl,** Jan Halaska/Photo Researchers, Inc.; **361,** © Rudy Sulgan/Corbis; **362,** © age fotostock/SuperStock; **365,** Born Loser: © Newspaper Enterprise Association, Inc.; **367,** Everett Kennedy Brown/epa/Corbis; **368,** Tony Mathews/Shutterstock, Inc.; **371 l,** Robert Brenner/PhotoEdit, Inc.; **371 r,** Acclaim Images; **372,** AP/Wide World Photos; **373,** www.CartoonStock.com; **374,** AP/Wide World Photos; **376,** © Bettmann/Corbis; **377,** Mark Richards/PhotoEdit, Inc.; **380,** Rothco Cartoons; **383,** © Construction Photography/Corbis; **385,** istockphoto.com/Slobo Mitic; **386,** Alan Schein/Corbis; **388,** Jozsef Szasz-Fabian/Shutterstock, Inc.; **389,** www.CartoonBank.com; **390,** JIM WATSON/AFP/Getty Images; **392 bl,** istockphoto.com/DHuss; **393 b,** Mike Peters/King Features Syndicate; **394,** Gary Connor/PhotoEdit, Inc.; **399,** © Minnesota Historical Society/Corbis; **400,** © Hulton-Deutsch Collection/Corbis; **401 t,** © David J. & Janice L. Frent Collection/Corbis; **401,** © Underwood & Underwood/Corbis; **402,** © George Mattei/Photo Researchers, Inc.; **406 r,** © Barnabas Bosshart/Corbis; **406 l,** Houghton Mifflin Company © 1998; **411,** istockphoto.com; **414,** © James Leynse/Corbis; **416,** Bill Ellzey/National Geographic Image Collection; **418,** Jeff Greenberg/Omni-Photo Communications, Inc.; **420 b,** Daryl Cagle, MSNBC.com Cartoons. All rights reserved.; **424 b,** AFP/Getty Images; **424 t,** UPI Photo/Monika Graff/Newscom; **425,** istockphoto.com/igor vorobyov; **429,** © Lew Long/Corbis; **432,** Gabe Palmer/Corbis; **435,** © Jeff Greenberg/PhotoEdit, Inc.; **436 b,** © Roger Ressmeyer/Corbis; **436 t,** Harcourt Brace & Company © 1980; **442,** © Antar Dayal/Illustration Works/Corbis; **443,** www.CartoonStock.com; **444 m,** King Features Syndicate; **444 tr,** Linda McCarthy; **444 br,** David Bishop/Phototake; **444 bl,** Jan Halaska/Photo Researchers, Inc.; **445,** © Michael Newman/PhotoEdit, Inc.; **446,** © George Ostertag/SuperStock; **449,** Pearson Education/PH School Division; **452,** AP/Wide World Photos; **452 l,** www.brandsoftheworld.com; **453,** Kim Kulish/Corbis; **456,** Todd Plitt; **457,** Jason Stitt/Shutterstock; **459 b,** Engleman/Rothco Cartoons; **460,** Lisa Knouse Braiman/Business Week; **462,** © Ryan Pyle/Corbis; **464,** Kaj R. Svensson/Photo Researchers, Inc.; **466,** AP/Wide World Photos; **467,** Stephen Chernin/Getty Images; **468 bkgrnd,** © Michael Newman/PhotoEdit, Inc.; **468,** Image Source White/Alamy; **472,** Alex Segre/Alamy; **474,** Billy E. Barnes/PhotoEdit, Inc.; **476 t,** istockphoto.com/Scott Leigh; **476,** © Bill Stormont/Corbis; **480,** © Cindy Miller Hopkins—All rights reserved.; **487,** Felix Heyder/Newscom; **489,** Owen Franken/Corbis; **490,** © Louise Gubb/Corbis; **490 inset,** Kim Taylor/nol/Minden Pictures; **492 b,** © Louise Gubb/Corbis SABA; **494 t,** Newscom; **494 b,** Gil Moti/Peter Arnold, Inc.; **495,** Newscom; **496,** Rothco; **499 b,** New York, 2002 Photo by Martin Rowe, Lantern Books; **499 t,** Lantern Books © 2006; **500 bl,** Mexico Tourism Board; **500,** Mexico Tourism Board; **500 br,** salamanderman/Shutterstock, Inc.; **501,** Bildarchiv Preussischer Kulturbesitz/Art Resource, NY; **502 b,** Nick Baker/www.cartoonstock.com; **502 tl,** Newscom; **502 tm,** NATALIE BEHRING/KRT/Newscom; **502 tr,** AP/Wide World Photos; **502 bl,** AFP/Getty Images; **502 bm,** Lisa Knouse Braiman/Business Week; **502 br2,** www.brandsoftheworld.com/; **502 br3,** www.brandsoftheworld.com/; **502 br1,** www.brandsoftheworld.com/; **504 t,** © Rudi Von Briel/PhotoEdit, Inc.; **504 b,** © Tony Freeman/PhotoEdit, Inc.; **505,** Stefan Zaklin/epa/Corbis; **506,** © Annie Griffiths Belt/Corbis; **507,** www.CartoonStock.com; **510,** Courtesy of MODIS Science Team, Goddard Space Flight Center, NASA and NOAA.; **511,** www.alliancelbm.org/offshorenews.htm; **512 m,** © Arcadio Esquivel/Cagle Cartooons. All Rights Reserved.; **512 tr,** Linda McCarthy; **512 br,** David Bishop/Phototake; **512 bl,** Jan Halaska/Photo Researchers, Inc.; **PF1 br,** David Bishop/Phototake; **tl,** Gary D. Gold/Creative Eye/MIRA.com; **tm,** Jan Halaska/Photo Researchers, Inc.; **tr,** istockphoto.com/Christine Balderas; **mr,** istockphoto.com/Jim Jurica; **br,** David Bishop/Phototake; **PF2-3 bkgrnd,** istockphoto.com/Sheri Bigelow; **PF2 l,** Sylwia Nowik/Shutterstock, Inc.; **PF2 r,** istockphoto.com/Brandon Laufenberg; **PF3,** istockphoto.com; **PF4 bkgrnd,** istockphoto.com/Mark Stay **PF4 l,** Pearson Education Curriculum Group; **PF4-5 bkgrnd,** Jan Halaska/Photo Researchers, Inc.; **PF4 tl,** Pearson Education Curriculum Group; **PF4 tr,** istockphoto.com/Kelly Cline; **PF4 br,** istockphoto.com/Filonmar; **PF4 m1,** Pearson Education Curriculum Group; **PF4 m2,** istockphoto.com/Mat Barrand; **PF4 m3,** istockphoto.com/Amanda Rohde; **PF4 b,** istockphoto.com/Marie-France Bélanger; **PF6,** istockphoto.com/Carl Hebert; **PF6-7 bkgrnd,** Jan Halaska/Photo Researchers, Inc.; **PF8-9 bkgrnd,** Jan Halaska/Photo Researchers, Inc.; **PF10-11 bkgrnd,** Jan Halaska/Photo Researchers, Inc.; **PF10,** Pearson Education Curriculum Group(4); **PF14-15 bkgrnd,** Jan Halaska/Photo Researchers, Inc.; **PF14,** Pearson Education Curriculum Group (4); **PF16-17 bkgrnd,** Yurok/Shutterstock, Inc.; **PF16 b,** ©Ron Chapple studios/Dreamtime.com; **PF18 bkgrnd,** Jan Halaska/Photo Researchers, Inc. **PF19,** M Werner H. Muller/Peter Arnold, Inc.; **PF19 t,** istockphoto.com/Nadezda Firsova; **PF19 b,** istockphoto.com/KMITU; **PF20 tm,** Pearson Education Curriculum Group; **PF20 b,** istockphoto.com/Brett Lamb; **PF22-23 tr,** ©2007 Photos.com; **PF22-23 m,** istockphoto.com/Alexander Hafemann; **PF22-23 b,** istockphoto.com/Karim Hesham; **PF22 ml,** Pearson Education Curriculum Group; **PF22 tl,** istockphoto.com/Alexander Hafemann; **PF22 br,** istockphoto.com/Tan Kian Khoon; **PF22 bl,** istockphoto.com/Patriek Vandenbussche; **PF23 b,** istockphoto.com/Paul Woodson; **PF24-25,** Angelo Cavalli/Getty Images; **PF25,** Pearson Education Curriculum Group; **PF30,** istockphoto.com/Mark Stay; **PF32 bkgrnd,** istockphoto.com/egdigital; **PF32 br,** © Comstock Select/Corbis; **PF32 bl,** Pearson Education Curriculum Group; **PF34 l,** istockphoto.com/Bluestocking; **PF34 r,** © Scott Tysick/Masterfile; **PF34 bl,** Tom McGhee/Jupiter Images; **PF34 m,** ©Geri Engberg/The Image Works; **PF36,** Pearson Education Curriculum Group; **PF38-39,** istockphoto.com/Martina Orlich; **PF38 l,** Pearson Education Curriculum Group; **PF40,** © Masterfile; **PF46 l,** Pearson Education Curriculum Group; **PF40-41 bkgrnd,** Jan Halaska/Photo Researchers, Inc.; **PF42-43 bkgrnd,** Jan Halaska/Photo Researchers, Inc.; **PF42 l,** Pearson Education Curriculum Group; **PF44-45 bkgrnd,** Jan Halaska/Photo Researchers, Inc.; **PF46-47 bkgrnd,** istockphoto.com/Sheri Bigelow; **PF46,** istockphoto.com; **S0-S21** Dynamic Graphics; **S-0** Neil Overy/Getty Images,Inc; **S-3** Jupiter Images; **S-4** © Michael Newman/PhotoEdit; **S-7 L.** Clarke/CORBIS; **S-8** © Michael Newman/PhotoEdit; **S-11,** AP/Wide World Photos; **S-12,** © moodboard/Corbis; **S-13,** © 2006 Jeff Parker, Florida Today, and PoliticalCartoons.com; **S-15,** Tony Robinson/SHUTTERSTOCK, INC.; **S-17,** Arlene Jean Gee; **S-18,** William Sallaz/Duomo/Corbis; **S-19,** © Masterfile; **S-21 t,** AP/Wide World Photos

Repeating border images: Keyboard:istockphoto.com/Joaquin Ayll; Dollar bill pyramid: Dynamic Graphics

Grateful acknowledgment is made to the following for copyrighted material:
"Top 10 Reasons to Support Development in ANWR" from *http://www.anwr.org/topten.htm.* Copyright © 2005 Arctic Power. Used by permission of ANWR.

"The Grip of Gas: Why You'll Pay Through the Nose to Keep Driving" by Austan Goolsbee from *http://www.slate.com/id/2126981/.* Used by permission of Austan Goolsbee.

"Children Now Statement in Response to FCC Commissioner Adelstein's Speech on Children's Media" from *www.childrennow.org/newsroom/press_releases/pr_080611.html.* Copyright © 2007 Children Now. Used by permission.

"Washington, We Have a Problem: Proposed NASA Missions Mean Tax Dollars Lost in Space" from *http://www.cagw.org/site/News2?JServSessionIdr011=ixvnb701l1.app27a&page=NewsArticle&id=7821.* Copyright © by Citizens Against Government Waste. Used by permission.

"New Yorkers Walk as Transit Strike Ruled Illegal" from *http://www.cnn.com/2005/US/12/20/nyc.* transit/index.html. Copyright © 2007 Cable News Network. Used by permission.

"If the Foam Shoe Fits" by Eric Peterson from *Colorado Biz Magazine.* Copyright © WiesnerMedia, LLC.

"The High Road and the Low Road" by Dan Swinney from *http://www.transformationcentral.org/ussf2007/ussfvideoclips8.html.* Used by permission of Dan Swinney.

"OPEC Still Holding Customers Over a Barrel" from *The Economists, October 23rd 2003.* Copyright © 2008 The Economists Newspaper Limited.

"U.S. Offshoring: Small Steps to Make it Win Win" by Diana Farrell from *The Economists' Voice, March 2006.* Copyright © The Berkeley Electronic Press.

"Myths vs Realties for the United States National Debt" by Elizabeth Dunne Schmitt from *http://www.oswego.edu/-edunne/debtmyths.html.* Used by permission of Elizabeth Dunne Schmitt.

"Tea EO Aims for Sustainable Brew" by Samuel Fromartz from *http://www.planetark.com/avantgo/dailynewsstory.cfm?newsid=28144.* Copyright © 2008 Reuters News Service. Used by permission.

"Business Leaders and Success: 55 Top Business Leaders and How They Achieved Greatness" by William O'Neil and Investor's Business Daily. Copyright © The McGraw-Hill Companies.

"Dude, Where's My Summer Job" by Kristen Lopez Eastlick from *The Examiner, June 9, 2008.* Copyright © Kristen Lopez Eastlick. Used by permission. The Employment Policies Institute is a nonprofit research organization dedicated to studying public policy issues surrounding employment growth.

"Against Universal Coverage" from *http://article.nationalreview.com/?q=ZWFkZDBlNjk3YjFhMDE1MWVlODc5NGM4MmQ4MmRhMTM=.* Copyright © 2007 by The National Review Online. Used by permission.

"No Quick Fix to Downturn" by Peter S. Goodman and Floyd Norris from *The New York Times, January 13, 2008.* Copyright © 2008 The New York Times Company.

"Oil is a National Problem, but Seriousness Varies" by Robert A. Wright and Martin Waldron from *The New York Times, February 3, 1974.* Copyright © The New York Times Company.

"Second Thoughts on Free Trade" by Charles Schumer and Paul Craig Roberts from *The New York Times, January 6, 2004.* Copyright © The New York Times Company.

"Single-Payer National Health Insurance" from *http://www.pnhp.org/facts/single_payer_resources.php.* Copyright © 2008 Physicians for a National Health Program. Used by permission.

"Wall Street Journal Online Roundtable on Outsourcing" by Richard Trumka from *www.wsjclassroom edition.com/archive/04apr/04apr_related_roundtable.htm.* Copyright © 2005 Dow Jones & Company, Inc.

Note: Every effort has been made to locate the copyright owner of material reproduced on this component. Omissions brought to our attention will be corrected in subsequent editions.